The Hebrew Bible
Volume 1C

Textual History of the Bible

General Editor

Armin Lange

Volume Editors for Volume 1

Armin Lange and Emanuel Tov

For more information please visit the Brill website *brill.com/thb* or for the online edition *brill.com/thbo*

The Hebrew Bible

Volume 1C
Writings

Edited by

Armin Lange
Emanuel Tov

Area Editors

Alessandro Maria Bruni (Georgian Translations, Old Church Slavonic Traditions)
Ignacio Carbajosa Pérez (Syriac Translations [Peshitta, Syro-Hexapla, Jacob of Edessa, Syro-Lucianic])
Claude Cox (Armenian Translations)
Sidnie White Crawford (Samaritan Pentateuch)
Steve Delamarter (Ethiopic Translations)
Beate Ego (Targumim)
Frank Feder (Coptic Translations)
Peter J. Gentry (Pre-Hexaplaric, Post-Hexaplaric Translations and the Hexapla)
Michael Graves (Vulgate)
Armin Lange (Ancient Hebrew/Aramaic Texts)
Meira Polliack (Arabic Translations)
Michael Segal (The Biblical Text as Attested in Ancient Literature)
Pablo Antonio Torijano Morales (Vetus Latina)
Emanuel Tov (Septuagint)
Julio Trebolle Barrera (Vetus Latina)

BRILL

LEIDEN | BOSTON

Originally published in hardback in 2017.

 THB logo design: Lika Tov, Jerusalem

Cover design: Celine van Hoek Leiden, the Netherlands.

The Library of Congress has cataloged the hardcover edition as follows:

Names: Lange, Armin, 1961- editor.
Title: The Hebrew Bible / edited by Armin Lange, Emanuel Tov.
Description: Leiden ; Boston : Brill, 2016- | Series: Textual history of the Bible, ISSN 2468-3027 | Includes bibliographical references and index. Contents: Vol. 1C Writings.
Identifiers: LCCN 2016013903 | ISBN 9789004337114 (v. 1C : hardback : alk. paper)
Subjects: LCSH: Bible. Old Testament–Criticism, Textual.
Classification: LCC BS1136 .H43 2016 | DDC 221.6/7–dc23 LC record available at https://lccn.loc.gov/2016013903

Typeface for the Latin, Greek, and Cyrillic scripts: "Brill". See and download: brill.com/brill-typeface.

ISSN 2468-3027
ISBN 978-90-04-73612-2 (paperback, 2025)
e-ISSN 2452-4107 (THB online)
ISBN 978-90-04-33711-4 (hardback)

Copyright 2017 by Koninklijke Brill NV, Leiden, The Netherlands.
Koninklijke Brill NV incorporates the imprints Brill, Brill Hes & De Graaf, Brill Nijhoff, Brill Rodopi and Hotei Publishing.
All rights reserved. No part of this publication may be reproduced, translated, stored in a retrieval system, or transmitted in any form or by any means, electronic, mechanical, photocopying, recording or otherwise, without prior written permission from the publisher.
Authorization to photocopy items for internal or personal use is granted by Koninklijke Brill NV provided that the appropriate fees are paid directly to The Copyright Clearance Center, 222 Rosewood Drive, Suite 910, Danvers, MA 01923, USA. Fees are subject to change.

This book is printed on acid-free paper and produced in a sustainable manner.

Contents of THB Volume 1

VOLUME 1A

Preface
Introduction to the Textual History of the Bible
Introduction to Textual History of the Bible, Vol. 1: The Hebrew Bible

1   Overview Articles

VOLUME 1B

2   **Pentateuch**
3–5   **Former Prophets**
      3   Joshua
      4   Judges
      5   Samuel–Kings
6–9   **Latter Prophets**
      6   Isaiah
      7   Jeremiah
      8   Ezekiel
      9   Minor Prophets

VOLUME 1C

10–20   **Ketuvim (Writings)**
      10   Psalms
      11   Job
      12   Proverbs
      13–17   Five Scrolls
           13   Ruth
           14   Canticles
           15   Qohelet
           16   Lamentations
           17   Esther
      18   Daniel
      19   Ezra–Nehemiah
      20   1–2 Chronicles
21   **The Biblical Text as Attested in Ancient Literature**

Addenda et corrigenda to volumes 1A and 1B

Contents of THB Volume 1C

	Area Editors	XIV
	Authors	XV
	Notes to the Reader / Abbreviations	XVI
	Collective Bibliography	XXI

10–20 *Ketuvim (Writings)*

10 *Psalms*

10.1	Textual History of Psalms (Brent A. Strawn)	5
10.2	**Ancient Hebrew Texts**	24
10.2.1	Ancient Manuscript Evidence (Armin Lange)	24
10.2.2	(Proto-)Masoretic Texts and Ancient Texts Close to MT (Brent A. Strawn)	42
10.2.3	Other Texts (Brent A. Strawn)	61
10.3	**Primary Translations**	82
10.3.1	Septuagint (Jannes Smith)	82
10.3.2	Pre-Hexaplaric Greek Translations (John D. Meade)	88
10.3.3	Targum (David Stec)	88
10.3.4	Peshitta (Ignacio Carbajosa)	93
10.3.5	Hexaplaric Greek Translations (John D. Meade)	98
10.3.6	Post-Hexaplaric Greek Translations (Matthew M. Dickie)	103
10.3.7	Vulgate (Justin Rogers)	104
10.3.8	Arabic Translations (Ilana Sasson)	110
10.4	**Secondary Translations**	115
10.4.1	Vetus Latina (José Manuel Cañas Reíllo)	115
10.4.2	Coptic Translations (P. Nagel)	119
10.4.3	Ethiopic Translation(s) (Steve Delamarter)	122
10.4.4	Late Syriac Translations (Robert Hiebert)	125
10.4.5	Armenian Translations (Claude Cox)	130
10.4.6	Georgian Translations (Bernard Outtier)	132
10.4.7	Old Church Slavonic Translations (Alessandro Maria Bruni)	135
10.4.8	Arabic Translations (Juan Pedro Monferrer Sala)	143

11 *Job*

11.1	Textual History of Job (R. Althann)	151
11.2	**Ancient and Late Ancient Hebrew Texts**	156
11.2.1	Ancient and Late Ancient Manuscript Evidence (Armin Lange)	156
11.2.2	Masoretic Texts and Ancient Texts Close to MT (Brent A. Strawn)	158

		11.2.3	Other Texts (Brent A. Strawn)	169
11.3	**Primary Translations**			175
		11.3.1	Septuagint (Claude Cox)	175
		11.3.2	Pre-Hexaplaric Greek Translations (John D. Meade)	181
		11.3.3	Targum and Qumran Aramaic Versions (David Shepherd)	181
		11.3.4	Peshitta (Ignacio Carbajosa)	187
		11.3.5	Hexaplaric Greek Translations (John D. Meade)	190
		11.3.6	Post-Hexaplaric Greek Translations (Matthew M. Dickie)	196
		11.3.7	Vulgate (Soenksen, Jason)	198
		11.3.8	Arabic Translations (Ilana Sasson)	202
11.4	**Secondary Translations**			207
		11.4.1	Vetus Latina (Jean-Claude Haelewyck)	207
		11.4.2	Coptic Translations (Frank Feder)	209
		11.4.3	Ethiopic Translation(s) (Curt Niccum)	211
		11.4.4	Job, Proverbs, Canticles, and Qohelet in Late Syriac Translations (Peter J. Gentry)	213
		11.4.5	Armenian Translations (Claude Cox)	224
		11.4.6	Georgian Translations (Alessandro Maria Bruni)	227
		11.4.7	Old Church Slavonic Translations (Alessandro Maria Bruni)	228
		11.4.8	Arabic Translations (Miriam Lindgren Hjälm)	236
12	*Proverbs*			
12.1	**Textual History of Proverbs (Cook, Johann)**			243
12.2	**Ancient Hebrew Texts**			248
		12.2.1	Ancient Manuscript Evidence (Armin Lange)	248
		12.2.2	Texts and Ancient Texts Close to MT (Cook, Johann)	250
12.3	**Primary Translations**			253
		12.3.1	Septuagint (Forti, Tova)	253
		12.3.2	Pre-Hexaplaric Greek Translations (John D. Meade)	259
		12.3.3	Targum (Díez Merino, Luis)	259
		12.3.4	Peshitta (Ignacio Carbajosa)	263
		12.3.5	Hexaplaric Greek Translations (John D. Meade)	267
		12.3.6	Post-Hexaplaric Greek Translations (Matthew M. Dickie)	270
		12.3.7	Vulgate (Justin Rogers)	271
		12.3.8	Arabic Translations (Ilana Sasson)	275
12.4	**Secondary Translations**			280
		12.4.1	Vetus Latina (José Manuel Cañas Reíllo)	280
		12.4.2	Coptic Translations (Frank Feder)	283
		12.4.3	Ethiopic Translation(s) (Curt Niccum)	285
		12.4.4	Late Syriac Translations (Peter J. Gentry)	287
		12.4.5	Armenian Translations (Claude Cox)	287

CONTENTS OF THB VOLUME 1C IX

	12.4.6	Georgian Translations (Alessandro Maria Bruni)	289
	12.4.7	Old Church Slavonic Translations (Alessandro Maria Bruni)	291
	12.4.8	Arabic Translations (Miriam Lindgren Hjälm)	295

13–17 *Five Scrolls*

13 *Ruth*

13.1 **Textual History of Ruth (Melanie Köhlmoos)** 303

13.2 **Ancient Hebrew Texts** 306
 13.2.1 Ancient Manuscript Evidence (Armin Lange) 306
 13.2.2 Masoretic Texts and Ancient Texts Close to MT (Veronika Bachmann) 307
 13.2.3 Other Texts (Armin Lange) 315

14 *Canticles*

14.1 **Textual History of Canticles (Bénédicte Lemmelijn)** 321

14.2 **Ancient Hebrew Texts** 327
 14.2.1 Ancient Manuscript Evidence (Armin Lange) 327
 14.2.2 Masoretic Texts and Ancient Texts Close to MT (Armin Lange) 329
 14.2.3 Other Texts (Armin Lange) 332

15 *Qohelet*

15.1 **Textual History of Qohelet (Michael V. Fox)** 339

15.2 **Ancient Hebrew Texts (Armin Lange)** 345
 15.2.1 Ancient Manuscript Evidence (Armin Lange) 345
 15.2.2 Masoretic Texts and Ancient Texts Close to MT (Armin Lange) 346
 15.2.3 Other Texts (Armin Lange) 350

16 *Lamentations*

16.1 **Textual History of Lamentations (Gideon Kotzé)** 357

16.2 **Ancient Hebrew Texts** 361
 16.2.1 Ancient Manuscript Evidence (Armin Lange) 361
 16.2.2 Masoretic Texts and Ancient Texts Close to MT (Rolf Schäfer) 362
 16.2.3 Other Texts (Rolf Schäfer) 367

17 *Esther*

17.1 **Textual History of Esther (Kristin De Troyer)** 377

17.2	**Ancient Hebrew Texts**	385
	17.2.1 Ancient Manuscript Evidence (Armin Lange)	385
	17.2.2 Masoretic Texts and Ancient Texts Close to MT (Veronika Bachmann)	385

13–17.1	**Primary Translations**	389
	13–17.1.1 Septuagint	389
	13–17.1.1.1 Ruth (Cécile Dogniez)	389
	13–17.1.1.2 Canticles (Cécile Dogniez)	391
	13–17.1.1.3 Qohelet (Cécile Dogniez)	392
	13–17.1.1.4 Lamentations (Cécile Dogniez)	394
	13–17.1.1.5 Esther (Kristin De Troyer)	396
	13–17.1.2 Pre-Hexaplaric Greek Translations	402
	13–17.1.2.1 Lamentations (John D. Meade)	402
	13–17.1.2.2 Ruth (John D. Meade)	402
	13–17.1.2.3 Qoheleth (Peter J. Gentry)	402
	13–17.1.2.4 Canticles (John D. Meade)	402
	13–17.1.2.5 Esther (Peter J. Gentry)	402
	13–17.1.3 Targumim (Christian Brady)	402
	13–17.1.4 Peshitta	409
	13–17.1.4.1 Ruth (Michael G. Wechsler)	409
	13–17.1.4.2 Canticles (Ignacio Carbajosa)	413
	13–17.1.4.3 Qoheleth (Maya Goldberg)	415
	13–17.1.4.4 Lamentations (Claudio Balzaretti)	418
	13–17.1.4.5 Esther (Michael G. Wechsler)	419
	13–17.1.5 Hexapla	424
	13–17.1.5.1 Lamentations (John D. Meade)	424
	13–17.1.5.2 Ruth (McClurg, Andrew)	425
	13–17.1.5.3 Qoheleth (Peter J. Gentry)	425
	13–17.1.5.4 Canticles (John D. Meade)	433
	13–17.1.5.5 Esther (McClurg, Andrew)	437
	13–17.1.6 Post-Hexaplaric Greek Translations (Matthew M. Dickie)	439
	13–17.1.7 Vulgate (Vincent Skemp)	441
	13–17.1.8 Arabic Translations (Ilana Sasson)	446

13–17.2	**Secondary Translations**	452
	13–17.2.1 Vetus Latina	452
	13–17.2.1.1 Ruth (Bonifatia Gesche)	452
	13–17.2.1.2 Canticles (José Manuel Cañas Reíllo)	454
	13–17.2.1.3 Ecclesiastes (José Manuel Cañas Reíllo)	456
	13–17.2.1.4 Lamentations (José Manuel Cañas Reíllo)	457
	13–17.2.1.5 Esther (Jean-Claude Haelewyck)	459
	13–17.2.2 Coptic Translations (Alin Suciu)	461
	13–17.2.3 Ethiopic Translation(s)	466
	13–17.2.3.1 Ruth (Meley Mulugetta)	466
	13–17.2.3.2 Canticles (Steve Delamarter, Ralph Lee, Curt Niccum & Melaku Terefe)	467

	13–17.2.3.3 Qoheleth (Curt Niccum)	470
	13–17.2.3.4 Lamentations (Curt Niccum)	472
	13–17.2.3.5 Esther (Veronika Bachmann)	474
13–17.2.4	Late Syriac Translations	475
	13–17.2.4.1 Ruth (Michael G. Wechsler)	475
	13–17.2.4.2 Canticles (Peter J. Gentry)	477
	13–17.2.4.3 Qoheleth (Peter J. Gentry)	477
	13–17.2.4.4 Lamentations (Claudio Balzaretti)	477
	13–17.2.4.5 Esther (Michael G. Wechsler)	478
13–17.2.5	Armenian Translations	478
	13–17.2.5.1 Ruth (Peter Cowe)	478
	13–17.2.5.2 Canticles (Peter Cowe)	480
	13–17.2.5.3 Qohelet (Peter Cowe)	484
	13–17.2.5.4 Lamentations (Peter Cowe)	486
	13–17.2.5.5 Esther (Peter Cowe)	489
13–17.2.6	Georgian Translations (Alessandro Maria Bruni)	490
13–17.2.7	Old Church Slavonic Translations (Alessandro Maria Bruni)	497
13–17.2.8	Arabic Translations (Ronny Vollandt & Miriam Lindgren Hjälm)	506

13–17.3 **Medieval Text of MT (Elvira Martín-Contreras)** ... 512

18 *Daniel*

18.1 Textual History of Daniel (Daniel Olariu) ... 517

18.2 Ancient Hebrew-Aramaic Texts ... 528
18.2.1 Ancient Manuscript Evidence (Armin Lange) ... 528
18.2.2 Masoretic Texts and Ancient Texts Close to MT (Michael Segal) ... 532
18.2.3 Other Texts (Michael Segal) ... 537

18.3 Primary Translations ... 542
18.3.1 Septuagint (D. Amara) ... 542
18.3.2 Other Greek Versions Prior to the Hexapla (Jason T. Parry) ... 554
18.3.3 Peshitta (Richard A. Taylor) ... 558
18.3.4 Hexapla (Jason T. Parry) ... 561
18.3.5 Post-Hexaplaric Greek Translations (Jason T. Parry) ... 565
18.3.6 Vulgate (Michael Graves) ... 568
18.3.7 Arabic Translations (Miriam Lindgren Hjälm) ... 571

18.4 Secondary Translations ... 575
18.4.1 Vetus Latina (José Manuel Cañas Reíllo) ... 575
18.4.2 Coptic Translations (Sofía Torallas Tovar) ... 579
18.4.3 Ethiopic Translation(s) (Curt Niccum) ... 582
18.4.4 Late Syriac Translations (Richard A. Taylor) ... 584
18.4.5 Armenian Translations (Peter Cowe) ... 586
18.4.6 Georgian Translations (Alessandro Maria Bruni) ... 589

	18.4.7 Old Church Slavonic Translations (Alessandro Maria Bruni)	591
	18.4.8 Arabic Translations (Miriam Lindgren Hjälm)	595

19 *Ezra–Nehemiah*

19.1 Textual History of Ezra–Nehemiah (Lisbeth Fried) ... 603

19.2 Ancient Hebrew-Aramaic Texts ... 610
- 19.2.1 Ancient Manuscript Evidence (Armin Lange) ... 610
- 19.2.2 Masoretic Texts and Ancient Texts Close to MT (David Marcus) ... 611

19.3 Primary Translations ... 615
- 19.3.1 Septuagint (Zipora Talshir) ... 615
- 19.3.2 Other Greek Versions Prior to the Hexapla (Jason T. Parry) ... 620
- 19.3.3 Peshitta (Claudio Balzaretti) ... 623
- 19.3.4 Hexapla (Jason T. Parry) ... 626
- 19.3.5 Post-Hexaplaric Greek Translations (Matthew M. Dickie) ... 629
- 19.3.6 Vulgate (Edmon L. Gallagher) ... 630
- 19.3.7 Arabic Translations (Meira Polliack, Meirav Nadler-Akirav & Yair Zoran) ... 634

19.4 Secondary Translations ... 638
- 19.4.1 Vetus Latina (Bonifatia Gesche) ... 638
- 19.4.2 Coptic Translations (Frank Feder) ... 639
- 19.4.3 Ethiopic Translation(s) (Curt Niccum) ... 640
- 19.4.4 Late Syriac Translations (Claudio Balzaretti) ... 643
- 19.4.5 Armenian Translations (Peter Cowe) ... 645
- 19.4.6 Georgian Translations (Alessandro Maria Bruni) ... 648
- 19.4.7 Old Church Slavonic Translations (Alessandro Maria Bruni) ... 651
- 19.4.8 Arabic Translations (Ronny Vollandt) ... 653

20 *1–2 Chronicles*

20.1 Textual History of Chronicles (Andrés Piquer Otero) ... 659

20.2 Ancient Hebrew Texts ... 665
- 20.2.1 Ancient Manuscript Evidence (Armin Lange) ... 665
- 20.2.2 (Proto-)Masoretic Texts and Ancient Texts Close to MT (Mika Pajunen) ... 665

20.3 Primary Translations ... 670
- 20.3.1 Septuagint (Gary N. Knoppers) ... 670
- 20.3.2 Pre-Hexaplaric Greek Translations (John D. Meade) ... 676
- 20.3.3 Targum (Leeor Gottlieb) ... 676
- 20.3.4 Peshitta (David Phillips) ... 681
- 20.3.5 Hexaplaric Greek Translations (John D. Meade) ... 684
- 20.3.6 Post-Hexaplaric Greek Translations (Matthew M. Dickie) ... 687
- 20.3.7 Vulgate (Edmon L. Gallagher) ... 688
- 20.3.8 Arabic Translations (Polliack, Meira) ... 692

20.4	**Secondary Translations**	693
	20.4.1 Vetus Latina (José Manuel Cañas Reíllo)	693
	20.4.2 Coptic Translations (Frank Feder)	695
	20.4.3 Ethiopic Translation(s) (Steve Delamarter)	696
	20.4.4 Late Syriac Translations (David Phillips)	699
	20.4.5 Armenian Translations (Peter Cowe)	701
	20.4.6 Georgian Translations (Alessandro Maria Bruni)	704
	20.4.7 Old Church Slavonic Translations (Alessandro Maria Bruni)	708
	20.4.8 Arabic Translations (Miriam Lindgren Hjälm)	710
10–20.1	Ketuvim: The Medieval text of MT (Elvira Martín-Contreras)	714
21	*The Biblical Text as Attested in Ancient Literature*	
21.1	**Apocrypha and Pseudepigrapha (Michael Segal)**	721
	21.1.1 Jubilees (Michael Segal)	721
	21.1.2 Pseudo-Philo (Howard Jacobson)	724
21.2	**Qumran Literature**	726
	21.2.1 Exegetical Compositions (Alex P. Jassen)	726
	21.2.2 Rewritten Bible/Parabiblical texts (Molly Zahn)	731
21.3	**Josephus (Paul Spilsbury)**	737
21.4	**Philo (James R. Royse)**	741
21.5	**New Testament (Peter Rodgers)**	747
21.6	**Rabbinic Literature (Assaf Rosen-Zvi)**	751
21.7	**Greek Church Fathers (Reinhart Ceulemans)**	755
21.8	**Latin Church Fathers (Michael Graves)**	759
21.9	**Syriac Church Fathers (Yifat Monnickendam)**	764
21.10	**Coptic Church Fathers (Anne Boud'hors)**	768
	Addenda & Corrigenda to Volumes 1A and 1B	771

Area Editors

Alessandro Maria Bruni (Ca' Foscari University of Venice): Georgian and Old Church Slavonic Translations

Ignacio Carbajosa Pérez (Universidad Eclesiástica San Dámaso): Syriac Translations (Peshitta, Syro-Lucianic Translation, Syro-Hexapla, Jacob of Edessa)

Claude Cox (McMaster Divinity College): Armenian Translations

Sidnie White Crawford (University of Nebraska-Lincoln): Samaritan Pentateuch

Steve Delamarter (George Fox Evangelical Seminary): Ethiopic Translations

Beate Ego (Ruhr-Universität Bochum): Targumim

Frank Feder (Akademie der Wissenschaften zu Göttingen): Coptic

Peter J. Gentry (Southern Baptist Theological Seminary): Pre-Hexaplaric Translations, Hexapla, Post-Hexaplaric Translations

Michael Graves (Wheaton College): Vulgate

Armin Lange (University of Vienna): Hebrew/Aramaic Texts

Meira Polliack (Tel Aviv University): Arabic Translations

Michael Segal (Hebrew University of Jerusalem): The Biblical Text as Attested in Ancient Literature

Emanuel Tov (Hebrew University of Jerusalem): Greek Texts

Julio Trebolle Barrerra and Pablo Antonio Torijano Morales (Universidad Complutense, Madrid): Vetus Latina

Authors

Althann, Robert
Amara, Dalia
Ausloos, Hans
Bachmann, Veronika
Balzaretti, Claudio
Bosson, Nathalie
Boud'hors, Anne
Brady, Christian
Brown, Jeremy
Bruni, Alessandro Maria
Cañas Reíllo, José Manuel
Carbajosa, Ignacio
Ceulemans, Reinhart
Cook, Johann
Cowe, Peter
Cox, Claude
Crawford, Sidnie White
De Troyer, Kristin
Delamarter, Steve
Dickie, Matthew M.
Díez Merino, Luis
Dogniez, Cécile
Dorman, Anke
Ego, Beate
Everson, David
Feder, Frank
Finsterbusch, Karin
Fischer, Georg
Flint, Peter
Forti, Tova
Fox, Michael V.
Fresch, Christopher J.
Fried, Lisbeth
Fuller, Russell T.
Gallagher, Edmon L.
Gentry, Peter J.
Gesche, Bonifatia
Glenny, W. Edward
Goldberg, Maya
Gottlieb, Leeor
Graves, Michael
Haelewyck, Jean-Claude
Heide, Martin

Hendel, Ronald
Hiebert, Robert
Hugo, Philippe
Jacobson, Howard
Jassen, Alex P.
Jastram, Nathan
Joosten, Jan
Kartveit, Magnar
Knibb, Michael A.
Knoppers, Gary N.
Köhlmoos, Melanie
Kooij, Arie van der
Kotzé, Gideon
Kraus, Matthew
Kreuzer, Siegfried
Lange, Armin
Lee, Ralph
Lemmelijn, Bénédicte
Lier, Gudrun Elisabeth
Lindgren Hjälm, Miriam
Lund, Jerome A.
Lust, Johan
Marcus, David A.
Martín Contreras, Elvira
McClurg, Andrew
Meade, John D.
Meer, Michaël van der
Meiser, Martin
Metso, Sarianna
Monferrer Sala, Juan Pedro
Monnickendam, Yifat
Morrison, Craig
Müller-Kessler, Christa
Mulugetta, Meley
Nadler-Akirav, Meirav
Nagel, Peter
Niccum, Curt
Olariu, Daniel
Outtier, Bernard
Pajunen, Mika
Parry, Jason T.
Perkins, Larry J.
Phillips, David

Piquer Otero, Andrés
Polliack, Meira
Prather, James
Rodgers, Peter R.
Rogers, Justin M.
Rösel, Martin
Rosen-Zvi, Assaf
Royse, James R.
Ryan, Stephen D.
Salvesen, Alison G.
Sasson, Ilana
Schäfer, Rolf
Schenker, Adrian
Segal, Michael
Shepherd, David
Shinan, Avigdor
Sigismund, Marcus
Skemp, Vincent T.M.
Smelik, Willem
Smith, Jannes
Soenksen, Jason
Spilsbury, Paul
Stec, David M.
Strawn, Brent A.
Suciu, Alin
Swinney, J. Kipp
Tal, Abraham
Talshir, Zipora
Taylor, Richard A.
Terefe, Melaku
Tooman, William A.
Torallas Tovar, Sofía
Torijano Morales, Pablo
Tov, Emanuel
Trebolle Barrera, Julio
Ulrich, Eugene C.
Vollandt, Ronny
Wechsler, Michael G.
Weis, Richard D.
Zahn, Molly
Zewi, Tamar
Zipor, Moshe A.
Zoran, Yair

Notes to the Reader / Abbreviations

In its stylesheet, THB follows the first edition of *The SBL Handbook of Style: For Ancient Near Eastern, Biblical, and Early Christian Studies* (eds. P.H. Alexander et al.; Peabody: Hendrickson Publishers, 1999). Publications that are quoted often in the articles of THB 1 are collected in a → Collective Bibliography. When quoted, they are indicated with an asterisk and a short title; thus, Lieberman, **Hellenism* refers to S. Lieberman, *Hellenism in Jewish Palestine: Studies in the Literary Transmission, Beliefs and Manners of Palestine in the I Century B.C.E.–IV Century C.E.* (2nd ed.; New York: Jewish Theological Seminary, 1962). Biblical books, deuterocanonical books, and textual witnesses are abbreviated and quoted as follows:

1 Abbreviations

Hebrew Bible

Gen	Genesis
Exod	Exodus
Lev	Leviticus
Num	Numbers
Deut	Deuteronomy
Josh	Joshua
Judg	Judges
Ruth	Ruth
1–2 Sam	1–2 Samuel
1–2 Kgdms	1–2 Kingdoms (LXX)
1–2 Kgs	1–2 Kings
3–4 Kgdms	3–4 Kingdoms (LXX)
Isa	Isaiah
Jer	Jeremiah
Ezek	Ezekiel
MinP	Minor Prophets/Dodekapropheton
Hos	Hosea
Joel	Joel
Amos	Amos
Obad	Obadiah
Jonah	Jonah
Mic	Micah
Nah	Nahum
Hab	Habakkuk
Zeph	Zephaniah
Hag	Haggai
Zech	Zechariah
Mal	Malachi
Ps/Pss	Psalm(s)

Job	Job
Prov	Proverbs
Ruth	Ruth
Cant	Canticles/Song of Songs
Qoh	Qohelet/Ecclesiastes
Lam	Lamentations
Esth	Esther
Dan	Daniel
Ezra	Ezra
Neh	Nehemiah
1–2 Chron	1–2 Chronicles

Deuterocanonical Scriptures

Add Dan	Additions to Daniel
Pr Azar	Prayer of Azariah
Bel	Bel and the Dragon
Sg Three	Song of the Three Young Men
Sus	Susanna
Add Esth	Additions to Esther
Bar	Baruch
2–4 Bar	2–4 Baruch
1–3 En	1–3 Enoch
Ep Jer	Epistle/Letter of Jeremiah
3 Ezra	3 Ezra (1 Esdras)
4–6 Ezra	4–6 Ezra
Jdt	Judith
Jub	Jubilees
1–4 Macc	1–4 Maccabees
Odes Sol	Odes of Solomon
Pss Sol	Psalms of Solomon
Pss 151–155	Psalms 151–155
Ps 151, etc.	Psalm 151, etc.
Sir	Sirach/Ben Sira/Ecclesiasticus
Tob	Tobit
Wis	Wisdom of Solomon

New Testament

Matt	Matthew
Mark	Mark
Luke	Luke
John	John
Acts	Acts
Rom	Romans
1–2 Cor	1–2 Corinthians

Gal	Galatians
Eph	Ephesians
Phil	Philippians
Col	Colossians
1–2 Thess	1–2 Thessalonians
1–2 Tim	1–2 Timothy
Titus	Titus
Phlm	Philemon
Heb	Hebrews
Jas	James
1–2 Pet	1–2 Peter
1–3 John	1–3 John
Jude	Jude
Rev	Revelation

Textual Witnesses

Manuscripts are indicated by numbers and characters in superscript. Versions of biblical books are identified as follows MT-Ezek, LXX-Ezek, VL-Ezek, V-Ezek, Arm-Ezek, LXX-MinP, etc. The Dead Sea Scrolls are abbreviated according to Tov, *Revised Lists.

anon	anonymous
Aq	Aquila
Arab	Arabic Translation
Arm	Armenian
Arm 1	Armenian Translation 1
Arm 2	Revision of Armenian Translation 1
Cop	Coptic
Cop^{Akh}	Coptic: Akhmimic
Cop^{Boh}	Coptic: Bohairic
Cop^{Sa}	Coptic: Sahidic
Cop^{Fa}	Coptic: Fayyumic
Cop^{Mes}	Coptic: Mesokemic
Cop^{palBoh}	Coptic: paleo-Bohairic
	Manuscript numbers of Coptic manuscripts are given in superscript according to Schüssler, *Biblia Coptica*, e.g., Cop$^{Sa\ 10}$
CPA	Christian Palestinian Aramaic
Eth	Ethiopic
	Designations and numbers of Ethiopic manuscripts are given in superscript as detailed in →, e.g., Eth$^{Ber\ Or\ Fl\ 3067}$. The abbreviations EMIP and EMML refer to the Ethiopic Manuscript Imaging Project and to the *Catalogue of Ethiopian Manuscripts* respectively.
Georg	Georgian
	Designations and numbers of Georgian manuscripts are given in superscript as detailed in →, e.g., Georg^Y.
Hex	Hexapla
kaige-Th	*kaige*-Theodotion
LXX	Septuagint

	Designations of Greek manuscripts and recensions are quoted in superscript following the abbreviation LXX according to the system of the *Septuaginta Unternehmen*, in particular Rahlfs–Fraenkel, **Verzeichnis*. E.g., LXX^A, LXX^{967}, LXX^O.
ms	manuscript
mss	manuscripts
MasF	Masorah Finalis
MasM	Masorah Magna
MasP	Masorah Parva
MT	Masoretic Text
MT+	MT group: MT together with T, (S), V, *kaige*-Th, Aq, Sym
MT^A	MT, Codex Aleppo
MT^B	British Library, Oriental Ms. 4445
MT^{Bl}	British Library Add. 15251
MT^C	Cairo Codex of the Prophets
MT^{C3}	Cairo Pentateuch Codex (Ms Gottheil 18).[1]
MT^{DeRossi}	Masoretic manuscript according to De Rossi, *1784–1788. Manuscript numbers are indicated in superscript, e.g., MT^{DeRossi12}
MT^{Kenn}	Masoretic manuscript according to Kennicott, *1776–1780. Manuscript numbers are indicated in superscript, e.g., MT^{Kenn12}
MT^L	Codex Leningradensis, Codex EBP. I B 19a of the National Library of Russia in St. Petersburg
MT^{L10}	Codex EBP. II B 10 of the National Library of Russia in St. Petersburg
MT^{L17}	Codex EBP. II B 17 of the National Library of Russia in St. Petersburg
MT^{L34}	Codex EBP. II B 34 of the National Library of Russia in St. Petersburg
MT^{L94}	Codex EBP. II B 94 of the National Library of Russia in St. Petersburg
MT^{M1}	Codex M1 in the Complutensian Library of Madrid
MT^{ms}	a single Masoretic manuscript
MT^{mss}	several Masoretic manuscripts
MT^N	Codex New York (E.N. Adler 246 = JTS 232)
MT^P	Codex Babylonicus Petropolitanus
MT^R	Codex Reuchlinianus 3; Badische Landesbibliothek. Karlsruhe
MT^{S1}	Manuscript Sassoon 1053
MT^{S5}	Codex ms Heb 5702 in the National Library of Israel, also named Damascus Pentateuch. Formerly part of the Sassoon Collection (ms 507)
MT^V	Manuscript Vatican ebr. 448
MT^Y	Codex Cambridge University Add. Ms. 1753
OG	Old Greek
OTPh	Philoxenian translation of the Old Testament
proto-MT	proto-Masoretic text
S	Peshitta
	Manuscript designations are given in superscript following the siglum S according to the *List of Old Testament Peshiṭta Manuscripts (Preliminary Issue)* (ed. Peshiṭta Institute, Leiden University; Leiden: Brill, 1961), e.g., S^{7a1}.

---

1 R. Gottheil, "Some Hebrew Manuscripts in Cairo," *JQR* 17 (1905): 608–55 (631–34); J.S. Penkower, "A Tenth-Century Pentateuchal MS from Jerusalem (MS C3), Corrected by Mishael Ben Uzziel," *Tarbiz* 58 (1988): 49–74 (Hebr. with Eng. summary).

semi-MT	semi-Masoretic text
SP	Samaritan Pentateuch
OSC	Old Church Slavonic
Syh	Syro-Hexapla
Syl	Syro-Lucianic
Sym	Symmachus
Th	Theodotion
T	Targum(im)
T^{Frag}	Fragment Targum
T$^{Frag(P)}$	Fragment Targum, Manuscript Paris
T$^{Frag(V)}$	Fragment Targum, Manuscript Venice
T^{Gen}	Targum Fragments from the Genizah
T^{J}	Targum Jonathan
T^{N}	Targum Neofiti
T^{Ps-J}	Targum Pseudo-Jonathan
T^{O}	Targum Onqelos
V	Vulgate
VL	Vetus Latina
	Designations and numbers of Old Latin manuscripts are given in superscript following the abbreviation VL according to Gryson, *Altlateinische Handschriften* 1–2; Gryson, *Répertoire general*, e.g., VL^{109}.
Vrs	Versions

Other Abbreviations

All other abbreviations of ancient literature as well as scholarly journals, book series, and reference works are according to the first edition of *The SBL Handbook of Style: For Ancient Near Eastern, Biblical, and Early Christian Studies* (eds. P.H. Alexander et al.; Peabody: Hendrickson Publishers, 1999). In addition, *THB* uses the following abbreviation:

TAD	B. Porten and A. Yardeni, *Textbook of Aramaic Documents from Ancient Egypt: Newly Copied, Edited and Translated into Hebrew and English* (4 vols. Winona Lake: Eisenbrauns, 1986–1999).

2 Further Information

In all articles, the Hebrew and Aramaic text is quoted with vocalization only when it is taken from MT or when required by the context. Accents are only indicated when necessary for the analysis.

The articles on the biblical Dead Sea Scrolls are updated summaries of Lange, *Handbuch*, except for → 6.2.1 (Isaiah) and → 9.2.1 (Minor Prophets).

Cross references to articles within the same *THB* volume are indicated with Arabic numerals. Thus, in *THB* 1, the cross reference → 6.3 refers the reader to the entry on the Septuagint of Isaiah. In *THB* 2, a cross-reference to the same article would appear as → 1.6.3.

Collective Bibliography

*Accordance
: Accordance computer program.

Aejmelaeus, *Trail
: A. Aejmelaeus, *On the Trail of the Septuagint Translators: Collected Essays* (rev. and expanded ed.; SBET 50; Leuven: Peeters, 2007).

Albrektson, *Text
: B. Albrektson, *Text, Translation, Theology: Selected Essays on the Hebrew Bible* (SOTSMS; Farnham: Ashgate, 2010).

Albright, *"New Light"
: W.F. Albright, "New Light on the Early Recensions of the Hebrew Bible," *BASOR* 140 (1955): 27–33.

Andersen–Forbes, *Spelling
: F.I. Andersen and A.D. Forbes, *Spelling in the Hebrew Bible* (BibOr 41; Rome: Biblical Institute Press, 1986).

Ap-Thomas, *Primer
: D.R. Ap-Thomas, *A Primer of Old Testament Text Criticism* (2nd ed.; FBBS 14; Philadelphia: Fortress Press, 1966).

Barr, *Literalism
: J. Barr, *The Typology of Literalism in Ancient Biblical Translations* (MSU 15; Göttingen: Vandenhoeck & Ruprecht, 1979).

Barr, *Variable Spellings
: J. Barr, *The Variable Spellings of the Hebrew Bible* (The Schweich Lectures of the British Academy; Oxford: Oxford University Press, 1989).

Barthélemy, *Devanciers
: D. Barthélemy, *Les devanciers d'Aquila* (VTSup 10; Leiden: Brill, 1963).

Barthélemy, *Études
: D. Barthélemy, *Études d'histoire du texte de l'Ancien Testament* (OBO 21; Fribourg: Éditions Universitaires, 1978).

Barthélemy, *Interim Report
: D. Barthélemy et al., *Preliminary and Interim Report on the Hebrew Old Testament Text Project* (5 vols.; New York: United Bible Societies, 1974; 2nd ed. 1979–1980).

Barthélemy, *Critique textuelle 1982
: D. Barthélemy, *Critique textuelle de l'Ancien Testament*, Vol. 1: *Josué–Esther* (OBO 50.1; Göttingen: Vandenhoeck & Ruprecht, 1982).

Barthélemy, *Critique textuelle 1986
: D. Barthélemy, *Critique textuelle de l'Ancien Testament*, Vol. 2: *Isaïe, Jérémie, Lamentations* (OBO 50.2; Göttingen: Vandenhoeck & Ruprecht, 1986).

Barthélemy, *Critique textuelle 1992
: D. Barthélemy, *Critique textuelle de l'Ancien Testament*, Vol. 3: *Ézéchiel, Daniel et les 12 Prophètes* (OBO 50.3; Göttingen: Vandenhoeck & Ruprecht, 1992).

Barthélemy, *Critique textuelle 2005
: D. Barthélemy, *Critique textuelle de l'Ancien Testament*, Vol. 4: *Psaumes* (OBO 50.4; Göttingen: Vandenhoeck & Ruprecht, 2005).

Barthélemy, *Studies
: D. Barthélemy, *Studies in the Text of the Old Testament: An Introduction to the Hebrew Old Testament Text Project* (Textual Criticism and the Translator 3; Winona Lake: Eisenbrauns, 2012).

Bassano, *Beluy Kidan
: F. da Bassano, *Beluy Kidan* (4 vols.; Asmarā: ba-Māḥtama Ferānčeskān, 1915–1918).

*BDSS
: J.H. Charlesworth (ed.), *The Bible and the Dead Sea Scrolls: The Second Princeton Symposium on Judaism and Christian Origins* (3 vols.; Waco: Baylor University Press, 2006).

Ben-Hayyim, *LOT
: Z. Ben-Hayyim, *The Literary and Oral Tradition of Hebrew and Aramaic amongst the Samaritans* (5 vols.; Jerusalem: Bialik Institute, 1957–1977) [Hebr.].

Ben-Hayyim, *Grammar of Samaritan Hebrew
: Z. Ben-Hayyim, *A Grammar of Samaritan Hebrew: Based on the Recitation of the Law in Comparison with the Tiberian and Other Jewish Traditions* (Jerusalem: Magnes Press, 2000).

Benoit et al., *"Editing"
: P. Benoit et al., "Editing the Manuscript Fragments from Qumran," *BA* 19 (1956): 75–96.

Benoit et al., *"Travail"
: P. Benoit et al., "Le travail d'edition des fragments manuscrits de Qumrân," *RB* 63 (1956): 49–67.

*BH
: *Biblia Hebraica* (ed. R. Kittel; Leipzig: Hinrichs, 1905–1906. 2nd ed. 1909–1913. 3rd ed.; eds. R. Kittel and P. Kahle; Stuttgart: Württembergische Bibelanstalt, 1929–1937).

*BHQ
: *Biblia Hebraica Quinta* (eds. A. Schenker et al.; Stuttgart: Deutsche Bibelgesellschaft, 2004–): Part 5: *Deuteronomium* (ed. C. McCarthy, 2007); Part 7: *Judges* (ed. N. Fernández Marcos, 2011); Part 13: *The*

Twelve Minor Prophets (ed. A. Gelston, 2010); Part 17: *Proverbs* (ed. J. de Waard, 2008); Part 18: *General Introduction and Megilloth* (ed. P.B. Dirksen et al., 2004); Part 20: *Ezra and Nehemiah* (ed. D. Marcus, 2006).

*BHS
Biblia Hebraica Stuttgartensia (eds. W. Rudolph and K. Elliger; Stuttgart: Deutsche Bibelgesellschaft, 1967–1977).

*Bible d'Alexandrie
La Bible d'Alexandrie (Paris: Cerf, 1986–).

*BibleWorks
BibleWorks computer program.

*Biblia Coptica
See Schüssler, *Biblia Coptica.

*Biblia Qumranica
Biblia Qumranica, Vol. 3B: Minor Prophets (eds. B. Ego et al.; Leiden: Brill, 2004).

*Biblia Sacra Arabica
Biblia Sacra Arabica: Sacrae Congregationis De Propaganda Fide Iussu Edita: Ad usum Ecclesiarum Orientalium: Additis e regione Bibliis Latinis Vulgatis: al-Kitāb al-muqaddas bi-'l-lisān al-'arabī (eds. S. Risius, F. Guadagnoli, and A. Ecchellenis; Rome: Sacrae Congregatio de Propaganda Fide, 1671–1673).

Bickerman, *"Septuagint"
E. Bickerman, "The Septuagint as a Translation," in *Studies in Jewish and Christian History* 1 (AGJU 9; Leiden: Brill, 1976), 167–200 (published first in *PAAJR* 28 [1959]: 1–39).

Bickerman, *"Notes"
E. Bickerman, "Notes on the Greek Book of Esther," *Studies in Jewish and Christian History: A New Edition in English including The God of the Maccabees*, Vol. 1 (AGJU 9; Leiden: Brill, 1976), 246–74.

Blau, *Studien
L. Blau, *Studien zum althebräischen Buchwesen und zur biblischen Literatur- und Textgeschichte* (Strasbourg i.E.: Adolf Alkalay, 1902).

Blau, *Grammar
J. Blau, *A Grammar of Christian Arabic: Based Mainly on South-Palestinian Texts from the First Millennium* (3 vols.; Louvain: Secrétariat Du Corpus SCO, 1966–1967).

Bogaert, *"Septante"
P.-M. Bogaert, "Septante et versions grecques," *DBSup* 12:536–692.

*Border Line
On the Border Line: Textual Meets Literary Criticism: Proceedings of a Conference in Honor of Alexander Rofé on the Occasion of his Seventieth Birthday (eds. Z. Talshir and D. Amara; Beer-Sheva Studies by the Department of Bible and Ancient Near East 18; Beer Sheva: Ben-Gurion University of the Negev Press, 2005) [Hebr.].

Brekelmans, *Questions
Questions disputées d'Ancien Testament: Méthode et théologie (ed. C. Brekelmans; rev. ed.; BETL 33; Leuven: Peeters, 1989).

*Brennpunkt, Vol. 1
Im Brennpunkt: Die Septuaginta, Vol. 1: Studien zur Entstehung und Bedeutung der griechischen Bibel (eds. H.-J. Fabry and U. Offerhaus; BWANT 153; Stuttgart: Kohlhammer, 2001).

*Brennpunkt, Vol. 2
Im Brennpunkt: Die Septuaginta, Vol. 2: Studien zur Entstehung und Bedeutung der Griechischen Bibel (eds. S. Kreuzer and J.P. Lesch; BWANT 161; Stuttgart: Kohlhammer, 2004).

*Brennpunkt, Vol. 3
Im Brennpunkt: Die Septuaginta, Vol. 3: Studien zur Theologie, Anthropologie, Ekklesiologie, Eschatologie und Liturgie der Griechischen Bibel (eds. H.-J. Fabry and D. Böhler; BWANT 174; Stuttgart: Kohlhammer, 2007).

Brock, *"Phenomenon"
S.P. Brock, "The Phenomenon of the Septuagint," *OTS* 17 (1972): 11–36.

Brock, *Bibliography
S.P. Brock et al., *A Classified Bibliography of the Septuagint* (Leiden: Brill, 1973).

Brock, *"Aspects"
S.P. Brock, "Aspects of Translation Technique in Antiquity," *GRBS* 20 (1979): 69–87.

Brooke–McLean, *The Old Testament in Greek
A.E. Brooke and N. McLean, *The Old Testament in Greek according to the Text of Codex Vaticanus: Supplemented from Other Uncial Manuscripts: With a Critical Apparatus Containing the Variants of the Chief Ancient Authorities of the Text of the Septuagint*, Vol. 1: *The Octateuch* (4 parts; Cambridge: Cambridge University Press, 1906–1917).

Brooke–McLean–Thackeray, *The Old Testament in Greek
A.E. Brooke, N. McLean, and H.St.J. Thackeray, *The Old Testament in Greek according to the Text of Codex Vaticanus: Supplemented from Other Uncial Manuscripts: With a Critical Apparatus Containing the Variants of the Chief Ancient Authorities of the Text of the Septuagint*, Vol. 2: *The Later Historical Books* (4 parts; Cambridge: Cambridge University Press, 1906–1935).

*CAL
: The Comprehensive Aramaic Lexicon (Bar-Ilan Project, Miqra'ot Gedoloth). Online: http://cal1.cn.huc.edu.

Cappellus, *Critica Sacra
: L. Cappellus, *Critica Sacra sive de variis quae in sacris Veteris Testamenti libris occurrunt lectionibus libri sex* (Paris: Cramoisy, 1650; repr. Halle: Hendel, 1775–[1786]).

Carr, *Formation
: D.M. Carr, *The Formation of the Bible: A New Reconstruction* (New York: Oxford University Press, 2011).

*Catalogue of Ethiopian Manuscripts
: *A Catalogue of Ethiopian Manuscripts: Microfilmed for the Ethiopian Manuscript Microfilm Library, Addis Ababa, and for the Hill Monastic Manuscript Microfilm Library, Collegeville* (eds. F.W. Macomber and G. Haile; 10 vols.; Collegeville: Monastic Microfilm Library St. John's Abbey, 1979–1993).

*CATSS
: *Computer-Assisted Tools for Septuagint Studies* (directed by R.A. Kraft and E. Tov; Philadelphia and Jerusalem, 1999. http://ccat.sas.upenn.edu/rak/catss.html).

Ciasca, *Fragmenta Copto-Sahidica
: A. Ciasca, *Sacrorum Bibliorum Fragmenta Copto-Sahidica Musei Borgiani* (2 vols.; Rome: Typis Eiusdem S. Congregationis, 1885–1889).

Ciasca, *Sacrorum Bibliorum fragmenta I
: See Ciasca, *Fragmenta Copto-Sahidica.

Ciasca, *Sacrorum Bibliorum fragmenta II
: See Ciasca, *Fragmenta Copto-Sahidica.

Clines, *Dictionary
: D.J.A. Clines, *The Dictionary of Classical Hebrew* (9 vols.; Sheffield: Sheffield Academic Press and Sheffield Phoenix Press, 1993–2016).

Cohen, *"Masoretic Text"
: M. Cohen, "The 'Masoretic Text' and the Extent of Its Influence on the Transmission of the Biblical Text in the Middle Ages," in *Studies in Bible and Exegesis 2: Presented to Yehuda Elitzur* (ed. U. Simon; Ramat Gan: Bar-Ilan University Press, 1986), 2.229–56 [Hebr.].

Cohen, *Miqra'ot Gedolot "Haketer"
: M. Cohen (ed.), *Miqra'ot Gedolot "Haketer": A Revised and Augmented Scientific Edition of 'Miqra'ot Gedolot' Based on the Aleppo Codex and Early Medieval mss* (8 vols.; Ramat Gan: Bar-Ilan University Press, 1992–2007) [Hebr.].

Cohen, *"Introduction"
: M. Cohen, *Miqra'ot Gedolot "Haketer": Joshua–Judges* (1992) 16*–99* (Introduction to the *Miqra'ot Gedolot "Haketer"* edition) [Hebr.].

*Complutensian Polyglot
: *Biblia Sacra Polyglotta, complectentia Vetus Testamentum ...* (6 vols.; eds. A. de Lebrixa et al.; Madrid: Complutenti Universitate, 1514–1517).

Cowe, *"The Bible in Armenian"
: S.P. Cowe, "The Bible in Armenian," in *The New Cambridge History of the Bible*, Vol. 2: *From 600–1450* (eds. R. Marsden and E.A. Matter; Cambridge: Cambridge University Press, 2012), 143–61.

Cowley, *Ethiopian Biblical Interpretation
: R.W. Cowley, *Ethiopian Biblical Interpretation: A Study in Exegetical Tradition and Hermeneutics* (University of Cambridge Oriental Publications 38; Cambridge: Cambridge University Press, 1988).

Cross, *"Development"
: F.M. Cross, "The Development of Jewish Scripts," in *The Bible and the Ancient Near East: Essays in Honor of William Foxwell Albright* (ed. G.E. Wright; Garden City: Doubleday, 1961), 133–202.

Cross, *"History"
: F.M. Cross, "The History of the Biblical Text in Light of the Discoveries in the Judaean Desert," *HTR* 57 (1964): 281–99 (repr. in Cross–Talmon, *QHBT, 177–95).

Cross, *"Evolution"
: F.M. Cross, "The Evolution of a Theory of Local Texts," in Cross–Talmon, *QHBT, 306–20.

Cross, *ALQ1,2,3
: F.M. Cross, *The Ancient Library of Qumrân and Modern Biblical Studies* (1st ed.; London: Duckworth, 1958); *The Ancient Library of Qumran and Modern Biblical Studies* (2nd ed.; Grand Rapids: Baker, 1961); *The Ancient Library of Qumran* (3rd ed.; Sheffield: Sheffield Academic Press, 1995).

Cross, *"Fixation"
: F.M. Cross, "The Fixation of the Text and Canon of the Hebrew Bible," in F.M. Cross, *From Epic to Canaan: History and Literature in Ancient Israel* (Baltimore: The Johns Hopkins University Press, 1998), 205–18.

Cross *"Paleography"
: F.M. Cross, "Palaeography and the Dead Sea Scrolls," in Flint–VanderKam, *DSS, 1.379–402; pls. 8–14.

Cross–Talmon, *QHBT
: *Qumran and the History of the Biblical Text* (eds. F.M. Cross and S. Talmon; Cambridge: Harvard University Press, 1975).

Crown, *The Samaritans
: *The Samaritans* (ed. A.D. Crown; Tübingen: Mohr Siebeck, 1989).

Crown, *Samaritan Scribes*
A.D. Crown, *Samaritan Scribes and Manuscripts* (TSAJ 80; Tübingen: Mohr Siebeck, 2001).

Daniel, *Vocabulaire du Cult*
S. Daniel, *Recherches sur le vocabulaire du culte dans la Septante* (Paris: Libraire C. Klincksieck, 1966).

Debel, *"Variant Literary Editions"*
H. Debel, "Greek 'Variant Literary Editions' to the Hebrew Bible?" *JSJ* 41 (2010): 161–69.

Delitzsch, *Lese- und Schreibfehler*
F. Delitzsch, *Die Lese- und Schreibfehler im Alten Testament nebst den dem Schrifttexte einverleibten Randnoten klassifiziert* (Berlin: Vereinigung Wissenschaftlicher Verleger, 1920).

Díez Merino, *Biblia babilónica*
L. Díez Merino, *La Biblia babilónica* (Madrid: Consejo Superior de Investigaciones Cientificas, 1975).

Dillmann, *Biblia*
A. Dillmann, *Biblia Veteris Testamenti Aethiopica* (2 vols.; Leipzig: F.C.G. Vogel, 1853–1861).

DJD
Discoveries in the Judaean Desert (of Jordan) (40 vols.; Oxford: Clarendon Press, 1955–2010).

DJD I
D. Barthélemy and J.T. Milik, *Qumran Cave 1* (DJD I; Oxford: Clarendon Press, 1955).

DJD II
P. Benoit, J.T. Milik, and R. de Vaux, *Les grottes de Murabbaʿât* (DJD II; Oxford: Clarendon Press, 1961).

DJD III
M. Baillet et al., *Les 'petites grottes' de Qumrân* (DJD III; Oxford: Clarendon Press, 1962).

DJD IV
J.A. Sanders, *The Psalms Scroll of Qumrân Cave 11 (11QPsa)* (DJD IV; Oxford: Clarendon Press, 1965).

DJD V
J.M. Allegro, *Qumran Cave 4.I* (with the collaboration of A.A. Anderson; DJD V; Oxford: Clarendon Press, 1968).

DJD VI
R. de Vaux and J.T. Milik, *Qumrân grotte 4.II: I. Archéologie, II. Tefillin, Mezuzot et Targums (4Q128–4Q157)* (DJD VI; Oxford: Clarendon Press, 1977).

DJD VII
M. Baillet, *Qumrân grotte 4.III (4Q482–4Q520)* (DJD VII; Oxford: Clarendon Press, 1982).

DJD VIII
E. Tov with the collaboration of R.A. Kraft, *The Greek Minor Prophets Scroll from Naḥal Ḥever (8ḤevXIIgr) (The Seiyal Collection I)* (DJD VIII; Oxford: Clarendon Press, 1990).

DJD IX
P.W. Skehan, E. Ulrich, and J.E. Sanderson, *Qumran Cave 4.IV: Palaeo-Hebrew and Greek Biblical Manuscripts* (DJD IX; Oxford: Clarendon Press, 1992).

DJD XI
E. Eshel et al., in consultation with J. VanderKam and M. Brady, *Qumran Cave 4.VI: Poetical and Liturgical Texts*, Part 1 (DJD XI; Oxford: Clarendon Press, 1998).

DJD XII
E. Ulrich et al., *Qumran Cave 4.VII: Genesis to Numbers* (DJD XII; Oxford: Clarendon Press, 1994).

DJD XIII
H. Attridge et al., *Qumran Cave 4.VIII: Parabiblical Texts*, Part 1 (DJD XIII; Oxford: Clarendon Press, 1994).

DJD XIV
E. Ulrich et al., *Qumran Cave 4.IX: Deuteronomy, Joshua, Judges, Kings* (DJD XIV; Oxford: Clarendon Press, 1995).

DJD XV
E. Ulrich et al., *Qumran Cave 4.X: The Prophets* (DJD XV; Oxford: Clarendon Press, 1997).

DJD XVI
E. Ulrich et al., *Qumran Cave 4.XI: Psalms to Chronicles* (DJD XVI; Oxford: Clarendon Press, 2000).

DJD XVII
F.M. Cross et al., *Qumran Cave 4.XII: 1–2 Samuel* (DJD XVII; Oxford: Clarendon Press, 2005).

DJD XXIII
F. García Martínez, E.J.C. Tigchelaar, and A.S. van der Woude, *Qumran Cave 11.II: 11Q2–18, 11Q20–30* (DJD XXIII; Oxford: Clarendon Press, 1998).

DJD XXVIII
M. Bernstein et al., *Qumran Cave 4.XXVIII: Miscellanea*, Part 2 (DJD XXVIII; Oxford: Clarendon Press, 2001).

DJD XXX
D. Dimant, *Qumran Cave 4.XXI: Parabiblical Texts*, Part 4: *Pseudo-Prophetic Texts* (DJD XXX; Oxford: Clarendon Press, 2001).

DJD XXXII
E. Ulrich and P.W. Flint, *Qumran Cave 1.II*, Parts 1–2: *The Isaiah Scrolls* (2 vols; DJD XXXII; Oxford: Clarendon Press, 2010).

DJD XXXVI
S. Pfann, P. Alexander, et al., *Qumran Cave 4.XXVI: Cryptic Texts and Miscellanea*, Part 1 (DJD XXXVI; Oxford: Clarendon Press, 2000).

*DJD XXXVIII
J. Charlesworth et al., in consultation with J. VanderKam and M. Brady, *Miscellaneous Texts from the Judaean Desert* (DJD XXXVIII; Oxford: Clarendon Press, 2000).

*DJD XXXIX
E. Tov et al., *The Texts from the Judaean Desert: Indices and an Introduction to the Discoveries in the Judaean Desert Series* (DJD XXXIX; Oxford: Clarendon Press, 2002).

Dogniez, *Bibliography
C. Dogniez, *Bibliography of the Septuagint = Bibliographie de la Septante 1970–1993* (VTSup 60; Leiden: Brill, 1995).

Dorival–Harl–Munnich, *Septante
G. Dorival, M. Harl, and O. Munnich, *La Bible grecque des Septante: Du judaïsme hellénistique au christianisme ancien* (Paris: Cerf, 1988).

Driver, *Introduction
S.R. Driver, *An Introduction to the Literature of the Old Testament* (8th ed.; Edinburgh: T & T Clark, 1898; repr. New York: Meridian Books, 1956).

Driver, *Samuel
S.R. Driver, *Notes on the Hebrew Text and the Topography of the Books of Samuel: With an Introduction on Hebrew Palaeography and the Ancient Versions* (2nd ed.; Oxford: Clarendon, 1913).

*DSI
De Septuaginta Investigationes

*DSSB
M. Abegg, P. Flint, and E. Ulrich, *The Dead Sea Scrolls Bible* (Edinburgh: T & T Clark, 1999).

*EAE
Encyclopaedia Aethiopica (ed. S. Uhlig; Wiesbaden: Harrassowitz, 2003–).

*EBR
Encyclopedia of the Bible and its Reception (eds. D.C. Allison et al.; Berlin: De Gruyter, 2009–).

Eichhorn, *Einleitung
J.G. Eichhorn, *Einleitung in das Alte Testament* (3 vols.; Göttingen: Carl Eduard Rosenbusch, ⁴1823).

*EDSS 1–2
Encyclopedia of the Dead Sea Scrolls (eds. L.H. Schiffman and J.C. VanderKam; New York: Oxford University Press, 2000).

Feder, *Biblia Sahidica
F. Feder, *Biblia Sahidica: Ieremias, Lamentationes (Threni), epistula Ieremiae et Baruch: Die koptisch-sahidische Textgestalt der Bücher Jeremias, Lamentationes, Epistula Jeremiae und Baruch als Übersetzung der Septuaginta* (TUGAL 147; Berlin: De Gruyter, 2002).

Fernandez Marcos, *Introduction
N. Fernandez Marcos, *The Septuagint in Context: Introduction to the Greek Version of the Bible* (Leiden: Brill, 2000).

Field, *Hexapla
F. Field, *Origenis Hexaplorum quae supersunt sive veterum interpretum graecorum in totum Vetus Testamentum fragmenta* (Oxford: Clarendon Press, 1875).

Fischer, *Text
A.A. Fischer, *Der Text des Alten Testaments: Neubearbeitung der Einführung in die Biblia Hebraica von Ernst Würthwein* (Stuttgart: Deutsche Bibelgesellschaft, 2009).

Fischer, *Vulgata
Biblia Sacra iuxta vulgatam versionem (eds. B. Fischer et al.; 2nd ed.; Stuttgart: Deutsche Bibelgesellschaft, 1975).

Fishbane, *Biblical Interpretation
M. Fishbane, *Biblical Interpretation in Ancient Israel* (Oxford: Clarendon Press, 1985).

Flesher–Chilton, *The Targums
P.V.M. Flesher and B. Chilton, *The Targums: A Critical Introduction* (Waco: Baylor University Press, 2011).

Flint–VanderKam, *DSS
The Dead Sea Scrolls after Fifty Years: A Comprehensive Assessment (2 vols.; eds. P.W. Flint and J.C. VanderKam; Leiden: Brill, 1998–1999).

Fraenkel, *Studien zur Septuaginta
Studien zur Septuaginta: Robert Hanhart zu Ehren (eds. D. Fraenkel et al.; MSU 20; Göttingen: Vandenhoeck & Ruprecht, 1990).

Frankel, *Vorstudien
Z. Frankel, *Vorstudien zu der Septuaginta* (Leipzig: Vogel, 1841; repr. Westmead: Gregg, 1972).

Frankel, *Einfluss
Z. Frankel, *Über den Einfluss der palästinischen Exegese auf die alexandrinische Hermeneutik* (Leipzig: J.A. Barth, 1851).

Geiger, *Urschrift
A. Geiger, *Urschrift und Übersetzungen der Bibel in ihrer Abhängigkeit von der innern Entwickelung des Judentums* (2nd ed.; Breslau: Heinauer, 1857; repr. Frankfurt a.M.: Madda, 1928).

Gentry, *"Text"
P.J. Gentry, "The Text of the Old Testament," *JETS* 52 (2009): 19–45.

Gesenius, *Pent. Sam.
F.H.W. Gesenius, *De Pentateuchi Samaritani origine*

indole et auctoritate commentatio philologico-critica (Halle: Bibliotheca Rengeriana, 1815).

Ginsburg, **Massorah*
C.D. Ginsburg, *The Massorah Compiled from Manuscripts: Alphabetically and Lexically Arranged* (4 vols.; London: Brög, 1880–1905; repr. Jerusalem: Makor, 1971).

Ginsburg, **Introduction*
C.D. Ginsburg, *Introduction to the Massoretico-Critical Edition of the Hebrew Bible* (London: Trinitarian Bible Society, 1897; repr. New York: Ktav, 1966).

Glassius, **Philologia*
Salomonis Glassii Philologia Sacra his temporibus accomodata post primum volume Dathii opera in lucem emissum sunc continuata et in novi plane operis formam redacta, Vol. 2.1: *Critica Sacra* (ed. G.L. Bauer; Leipzig: Sumptibus Weygandianis, 1795).

*Gleanings
Gleanings from the Caves: Dead Sea Scrolls and Artifacts from the Schøyen Collection (ed. T. Elgvin; Library of Second Temple Studies; London: T & T Clark, forthcoming).

Gordis, **Biblical Text*
R. Gordis, *The Biblical Text in the Making: A Study of the Kethib–Qere* (Philadelphia: Dropsie College for Hebrew and Cognate Learning, 1937; repr. New York: Ktav, 1971).

Goshen-Gottstein, **"History"*
M.H. Goshen-Gottstein, "The History of the Bible-Text and Comparative Semitics," *VT* 7 (1957): 195–201.

Goshen-Gottstein, **Sample Edition*
M.H. Goshen-Gottstein, *The Book of Isaiah: Sample Edition with Introduction* (Jerusalem: Magnes Press, 1965).

Goshen-Gottstein, **"Biblical Manuscripts"*
M.H. Goshen-Gottstein, "Hebrew Biblical Manuscripts: Their History and Their Place in the HUBP Edition," *Bib* 48 (1967): 243–90.

Goshen-Gottstein, **HUB, Isaiah*
M.H. Goshen-Gottstein, *The Hebrew University Bible: The Book of Isaiah* (Jerusalem: Magnes Press, 1995).

Goshen-Gottstein–Talmon, **HUB, Ezekiel*
M.H. Goshen-Gottstein and S. Talmon, *The Hebrew University Bible: The Book of Ezekiel* (Jerusalem: Magnes Press, 2004).

Graf, **GCAL 1*
G. Graf, *Geschichte der christlichen Arabischen Literatur*, Vol. 1: *Die Übersetzungen* (Studi e Testi 118; Vatican City: Bibliotheca Apostolica Vaticana, 1944).

Greenberg, **"Stabilization"*
M. Greenberg, "The Stabilization of the Text of the Hebrew Bible Reviewed in the Light of the Biblical Materials from the Judean Desert," *JAOS* 76 (1956): 157–67.

Griffith, **The Bible in Arabic*
S.H. Griffith, *The Bible in Arabic: The Scriptures of the "People of the Book" in the Language of Islam* (Princeton: Princeton University Press, 2013).

Gryson, **Altlateinische Handschriften 1*
R. Gryson, *Altlateinische Handschriften/Manuscrits vieux latins: Répertoire descriptif*, Part 1: *Mss 1–275 (d'après un manuscrit inachevé de Hermann Josef Frede †)* (VL 1.2a; Freiburg i.B.: Herder, 1999).

Gryson, **Altlateinische Handschriften 2*
R. Gryson, *Altlateinische Handschriften/Manuscrits vieux latins: Répertoire descriptif*, part 2: *Mss 300–485 (Manuscrits du psautier)* (VL 1.2b; Freiburg i.B.: Herder, 2004).

Gryson, **Répertoire général*
R. Gryson, *Répertoire général des auteurs ecclésiastiques latins de l'antiquité et du haut moyen-âge* (2 vols.; 5th ed.; VL 1.1–2; Freiburg i.B.: Herder, 2007).

Gryson (ed.), **Vetus Latina Database*
See **Vetus Latina Database*

Habermann, **Ketav*
A.M. Habermann, *Ketav, Lashon Wa-Sefer: Reflections on Books, Dead Sea Scrolls, Language and Folklore* (Jerusalem: R. Mas, 1973) [Hebr.].

Hall, **Companion*
F.W. Hall, *A Companion to Classical Texts* (Oxford: Clarendon Press, 1913; repr. Chicago: Argonaut, 1970).

*HALOT
L. Koehler and W. Baumgartner, *The Hebrew and Aramaic Lexicon of the Old Testament* (trans. M.E.J. Richardson et al.; Leiden: Brill, 1994–2000; based on earlier German editions: 1953; 2nd ed. 1958; 3rd ed. 1967–1996).

Harl–Dorival–Munnich, **Bible grecque*
M. Harl, G. Dorival, and O. Munnich, *La Bible grecque des Septante: Du judaïsme hellénistique au christianisme ancien* (Paris: Cerf, 1988).

Hatch–Redpath, **Concordance*
E. Hatch and H.A. Redpath, *A Concordance to the Septuagint and the Other Greek Versions of the Old Testament* (Oxford: Clarendon Press, 1897–1906; repr. Graz: Akademische Druck- u. Verlagsanstalt, 1954; repr. eds. R.A. Kraft and E. Tov; 2nd ed.; Grand Rapids: Baker, 1998).

Haupt, *Critical Edition
: A Critical Edition of the Hebrew Text, Printed in Colors, Exhibiting the Composite Structure of the Book (ed. P. Haupt; Leipzig: Hinrichs et al., 1893–1904, incomplete).

Haupt, *Polychrome Bible
: The Polychrome Bible: The Sacred Books of the Old and New Testaments: A New English Translation, Printed in Colors, Exhibiting the Composite Structure of the Book (ed. P. Haupt; London: Clark et al., 1897–1899, incomplete).

*HBCE
: The Hebrew Bible: A Critical Edition (ed. R.S. Hendel; Atlanta: SBL, 2015–).

Hendel, *Genesis 1–11
: R.S. Hendel, The Text of Genesis 1–11: Textual Studies and Critical Edition (New York: Oxford University Press, 1998).

Hendel, *"Prologue"
: R.S. Hendel, "The Oxford Hebrew Bible; Prologue to a New Critical Edition," VT 58 (2008): 324–51.

*HOTTP
: Hebrew Old Testament Text Project. See Barthélemy, Interim Report

Houbigant, *Notae criticae
: A.F. Houbigant, Notae criticae in universos Veteris Testamenti libros: cum Hebraice, tum Graece scriptos (2 vols.; Frankfurt: Varrentrapp Filium & Wenner, 1777).

*HUB
: The Hebrew University Bible (Jerusalem: Magnes Press, 1995–); The Book of Isaiah (ed. M. Goshen-Gottstein, 1995); The Book of Jeremiah (eds. C. Rabin, S. Talmon, and E. Tov, 1997); The Book of Ezekiel (eds. M.H. Goshen-Gottstein and S. Talmon, 2004).

Jastrow, *Dictionary
: M. Jastrow, A Dictionary of the Targumim, the Talmud Babli and Yerushalmi, and the Midrashic Literature (2nd ed.; New York: Pardes, 1903).

*JB
: The Jerusalem Bible (Garden City: Doubleday, 1970).

Jellicoe, *SMS
: S. Jellicoe, The Septuagint and Modern Study (Oxford: Clarendon Press, 1968).

Jepsen, *"Aufgaben"
: A. Jepsen, "Von den Aufgaben der alttestamentlichen Textkritik," in Congress Volume: Bonn 1962 (eds. G.W. Anderson et al.; VTSup 9; Leiden: Brill, 1962), 332–41.

Kahle, *"Untersuchungen"
: P. Kahle, "Untersuchungen zur Geschichte des Pentateuchtextes," TSK 88 (1915): 399–439 (repr. in P. Kahle, Opera Minora [Leiden: Brill, 1956], 3–37).

Kahle, *Cairo Geniza
: P. Kahle, The Cairo Geniza (2nd ed.; Oxford: Blackwell, 1959).

Karrer–Kraus, *Septuaginta 2008
: Die Septuaginta: Texte, Kontexte, Lebenswelten: Internationale Fachtagung veranstaltet von Septuaginta Deutsch (LXX.D), Wuppertal 20.–23. Juli 2006 (eds. M. Karrer and W. Kraus; WUNT 219; Tübingen: Mohr Siebeck, 2008).

Karrer–Kraus, *Septuaginta 2010
: Die Septuaginta: Texte, Theologien, Einflüsse: 2. Internationale Fachtagung veranstaltet von Septuaginta Deutsch (LXX.D), Wuppertal 23.–27.7.2008 (eds. W. Kraus and M. Karrer; WUNT 252; Tübingen: Mohr Siebeck, 2010).

Kennicott, *Dissertation
: B. Kennicott, The State of the Printed Text of the Old Testament Considered: A Dissertation in Two Parts (Oxford: The Theatre, 1753–1759; = idem, Dissertatio secunda super ratione textus hebraici Veteris Testamenti [trans. G.A. Teller; Leipzig: Dyck, 1765]).

Kennicott, *1776–1780
: B. Kennicott, Vetus Testamentum hebraicum, cum variis lectionibus (2 vols.; Oxford: Clarendon Press, 1776–1780).

Kennicott, *Dissertatio generalis
: B. Kennicott, Appendix to Vol. 2 of Kennicott, *1776–1780: Dissertatio generalis in Vetus Testamentum Hebraicum, cum variis lectionibus ex codicibus manuscriptis et impressis. Also published separately (Brunovici: Orphanotrophei, 1783).

*KJV
: King James Version (London: Robert Barker, 1611).

Klein, *Textual Criticism
: R.W. Klein, Textual Criticism of the Old Testament: The Septuagint after Qumran (GBS Old Testament Series 4; Philadelphia: Fortress Press, 1974).

Knibb, *Translating the Bible
: M. Knibb, Translating the Bible: The Ethiopic Version of the Old Testament (Oxford: Oxford University Press, 1999).

Koenig, *"L' activité herméneutique"
: J. Koenig, "L' activité herméneutique des scribes dans la transmission du texte de l' Ancien Testament," RHR 161 (1962): 141–74; 162 (1962): 1–43.

Koenig, *L' herméneutique analogique
: J. Koenig, L' herméneutique analogique du judaïsme

antique d'après les témoins textuels d'Isaïe (VTSup 33; Leiden: Brill, 1982).

Kraft, **Septuagintal Lexicography*
Septuagintal Lexicography (ed. R.A. Kraft; SBLSCS 1; Missoula: SBL, 1972).

Kraus–Kreuzer, **Septuaginta 2014*
Die Septuaginta: Text, Wirkung, Rezeption: 4. Internationale Fachtagung veranstaltet von Septuaginta Deutsch (LXX.D), Wuppertal 19.–22. Juli 2012 (eds. W. Kraus and S. Kreuzer; WUNT 325; Tübingen: Mohr Siebeck, 2014).

Kreuzer–Meiser–Sigismund, **Septuaginta 2012*
Die Septuaginta: Entstehung, Sprache, Geschichte: 3. Internationale Fachtagung veranstaltet von Septuaginta Deutsch (LXX.D), Wuppertal 22.–25. Juli 2010 (eds. S. Kreuzer, M. Meiser, and M. Sigismund; WUNT 286; Tübingen: Mohr Siebeck 2012).

Kutscher, **Language*
E.Y. Kutscher, *The Language and Linguistic Background of the Isaiah Scroll (1 Q Isa)* (STDJ 6; Leiden: Brill, 1974).

de Lagarde, **Anmerkungen*
P. de Lagarde, *Anmerkungen zur griechischen Übersetzung der Proverbien* (Leipzig: Brockhaus, 1863).

Lamsa, **Holy Bible*
G.M. Lamsa, *The Holy Bible from Ancient Eastern Manuscripts Containing the Old and New Testaments: Translated from the Peshitta: The Authorized Bible of the Church of the East* (Nashville: Holman Bible Publishers, 1957).

Lange, **Handbuch*
A. Lange, *Handbuch der Textfunde vom Toten Meer*, Vol. 1: *Die Handschriften biblischer Bücher von Qumran und den anderen Fundorten* (Tübingen: Mohr Siebeck, 2009).

Lange et al., **From Qumran to Aleppo*
From Qumran to Aleppo: A Discussion with Emanuel Tov about the Textual History of Jewish Scriptures in Honor of his 65th Birthday (eds. A. Lange et al.; FRLANT 230; Göttingen: Vandenhoeck & Ruprecht, 2009).

Leaney, **"Greek Manuscripts"*
R.C. Leaney, "Greek Manuscripts from the Judaean Desert," in *Studies in New Testament Language and Text: Essays in Honour of George D. Kilpatrick on the Occasion of His Sixty-Fifth Birthday* (ed. J.K. Elliott; NTSup 44; Leiden: Brill, 1976), 283–300.

Le Jay, **Biblia*
G.M. Le Jay, *Biblia: 1. Hebraica, 2. Samaritana, 3. Chaldaica, 4. Græca, 5. Syriaca, 6. Latina, 7. Arabica: quibus textus originales totius scripturae, quorum pars in editione Complutensi, deinde in Antverpiensi regiis sumptibus extat, nunc integri, ex mauscripti toto fere orbe quaesitis exemplaribus, exhibentur* (Paris: Vitré, 1645).

Levita, **Massoreth Ha-Massoreth*
E. Levita, *Massoreth Ha-Massoreth* (Venice: D. Bomberg, 1538; repr. ed. C.D. Ginsburg; London: Longmans, Green, Reader & Dyer, 1867; repr. New York: Ktav, 1968).

Lieberman, **Hellenism*
S. Lieberman, *Hellenism in Jewish Palestine: Studies in the Literary Transmission, Beliefs and Manners of Palestine in the I Century B.C.E.–IV Century C.E.* (2nd ed.; New York: Jewish Theological Seminary, 1962).

*Logos
Logos computer program

Loveless and Loveless, **Dead Sea Scrolls and the Bible*
G. Loveless and S. Loveless, *Dead Sea Scrolls and the Bible: Ancient Artifacts, Timeless Treasures* (Fort Worth: Seminary Hill Press, 2012).

Lust, **Lexicon of the Septuagint*
Greek-English Lexicon of the Septuagint (eds. J. Lust et al.; rev. ed.; Stuttgart: Deutsche Bibelgesellschaft, 2003).

Maas, **Textual Criticism*
P. Maas, *Textual Criticism* (trans. B. Flower; Oxford: Clarendon Press, 1958 = "Textkritik," in A. Gercke and E. Norden, *Einleitung in die Altertumswissenschaft*, Vol. 1.2 [3rd ed.; Leipzig: Teubner, 1957]).

*Madrid Qumran Congress
The Madrid Qumran Congress: Proceedings of the International Congress on the Dead Sea Scrolls: Madrid, 18–21 March, 1991 (eds. J. Trebolle Barrera and L. Vegas Montaner; 2 vols.; STDJ 11.1–2; Leiden: Brill, 1992).

*Manchester Symposium
Septuagint, Scrolls and Cognate Writings: Papers Presented to the International Symposium on the Septuagint and Its Relations to the Dead Sea Scrolls and Other Writings, Manchester, 1990 (eds. G.J. Brooke and B. Lindars; SBLSCS 33; Atlanta: Scholars Press, 1992).

Margolis, **"Scope"*
M.L. Margolis, "The Scope and Methodology of Biblical Philology," *JQR* 1 (1910–1911): 5–41.

Martin, **Scribal Character*
M. Martin, *The Scribal Character of the Dead Sea Scrolls* (2 vols.; Bibliothèque du Muséon 44–45; Louvain: Publications Universitaires, 1958).

*Masada I–VIII
Masada: The Yigael Yadin Excavations 1963–1965: Final

Reports (8 vols.; Jerusalem: Israel Exploration Society, 1989–2007).

Maspero, *"Fragments de la version thébaine de l' Ancien Testament"
G. Maspero, "Fragments de la version thébaine de l' Ancien Testament," *Mémoires publiés par les membres de la Mission archéologique française au Caire* 6.1 (1892): 1–150; 6.3 (1892): 161–296.

McCarter, *Textual Criticism
P.K. McCarter, *Textual Criticism: Recovering the Text of the Hebrew Bible* (GBS Old Testament Series 11; Philadelphia: Fortress Press, 1986).

McCarthy, *Tiqqune Sopherim
C. McCarthy, *The Tiqqune Sopherim and Other Theological Corrections in the Masoretic Text of the Old Testament* (OBO 36; Göttingen: Vandenhoeck & Ruprecht, 1981).

*Mélanges Barthélemy
Mélanges Dominique Barthélemy: Études bibliques offertes à l'occasion de son 60e anniversaire (eds. P. Casetti et al.; OBO 38; Göttingen: Vandenhoeck & Ruprecht, 1981).

*Mikra
Mikra computer program, Bar-Ilan University.

Milik, *Ten Years
J.T. Milik, *Ten Years of Discovery in the Wilderness of Judaea* (SBT 26; London: SCM Press, 1959).

Morinus, *Exerc.
J. Morinus, *Exercitationum biblicarum de hebraei graecique textus sinceritate libri duo* (2nd ed.; Paris: G. Meturas, 1660).

Mulder, *Mikra
Mikra: Text, Translation, Reading and Interpretation of the Hebrew Bible in Ancient Judaism and Early Christianity (ed. M.J. Mulder; CRINT 2.1; Assen: Van Gorcum, 1988).

*NEB
The New English Bible with the Apocrypha (Oxford: Oxford University Press, 1970).

*NETS
A New English Translation of the Septuagint and the Other Greek Translations Traditionally Included Under That Title (eds. A. Pietersma and B.G. Wright; Oxford: Clarendon Press, 2007).

*NIV
Holy Bible: New International Version (Grand Rapids: Zondervan, 1984).

*NJPS
Tanakh—The Holy Scriptures: The New JPS Translation According to the Traditional Hebrew Text (Philadelphia: Jewish Publication Society, 1988; 2nd ed. 1999).

*NRSV
The Holy Bible Containing the Old and New Testaments with the Apocryphal/Deuterocanonical Books: New Revised Standard Version (Glasgow: Collins, 1989).

Nyberg, *"Problem"
H.S. Nyberg, "Das textkritische Problem des Alten Testaments am Hoseabuche demonstriert," *ZAW* 52 (1934): 241–54.

Oesch, *Petucha
J.M. Oesch, *Petucha und Setuma: Untersuchungen zu einer überlieferten Gliederung im hebräischen Text des Alten Testaments* (OBO 27; Göttingen: Vandenhoeck & Ruprecht, 1979).

*Okhlah we-Okhlah
Sefer Oklah we-Oklah (ed. F. Díaz Esteban; Madrid: Consejo Superior de Investigaciones Cientificas, 1975).

Olofsson, *Essays
S. Olofsson, *Translation Technique and Theological Exegesis: Collected Essays on the Septuagint Version* (ConBOT 57; Winona Lake: Eisenbrauns, 2009).

*OTP
J.H. Charlesworth, *The Old Testament Pseudepigrapha* (2 vols.; New York: Doubleday, 1983–1985).

Pérez Castro, *Profetas de el Cairo
F. Pérez Castro, *El codice de profetas de el Cairo* (9 vols.; Madrid: Consejo Superior de Investigaciones Cientificas, 1979–1992).

Perles, *Analekten
F. Perles, *Analekten zur Textkritik des Alten Testaments*, Vol. 1 (Munich: Ackermann, 1895); Vol. 2 (Leipzig: Engel, 1922).

*PEUDSS
B.Z. Wacholder and M. Abegg, *A Preliminary Edition of the Unpublished Dead Sea Scrolls: The Hebrew and Aramaic Texts from Cave Four* (4 vols.; Washington: Biblical Archaeology Society, 1991–1996).

Prijs, *Jüdische Tradition
L. Prijs, *Jüdische Tradition in der Septuaginta* (Leiden: Brill, 1948; repr. Hildesheim: Olms, 1987).

*PTSDSSP
The Princeton Theological Seminary Dead Sea Scrolls Project (ed. J.H. Charlesworth; Tübingen: Mohr Siebeck, 1991–).

Qimron, *DSS
E. Qimron, *The Hebrew of the Dead Sea Scrolls* (HSS 29; Atlanta: Scholars Press, 1986).

Rabin–Talmov–Tov, *HUB, Jeremiah*
C. Rabin, S. Talmon, and E. Tov, *The Hebrew University Bible: The Book of Jeremiah* (Jerusalem: Magnes Press, 1997).

Rahlfs, *Septuaginta*
A. Rahlfs (ed.), *Septuaginta: Id est Vetus Testamentum graece iuxta LXX interpretes* (Stuttgart: Württembergischer Bibelanstalt, 1935).

Rahlfs–Fraenkel, *Verzeichnis*
A. Rahlfs and D. Fraenkel, *Verzeichnis der griechischen Handschriften des Alten Testaments: Die Überlieferung bis zum VIII. Jahrhundert* (Septuaginta Vetus Testamentum Graecum Supplement I.1; Göttingen: Vandenhoeck & Ruprecht, 2004).

Rahlfs–Hanhart, *Septuaginta*
A. Rahlfs and R. Hanhart (eds.), *Septuaginta: Id est Vetus Testamentum graece iuxta LXX interpretes* (2nd ed.; Stuttgart: Deutsche Bibelgesellschaft, 2006).

*RB1
F. Pratensis (ed.), *Biblia Rabbinica Miqra'ot Gedolot* (Venice: Daniel Bomberg, 1516–1517).

*RB2
J. ben Hayyim ben Isaac ibn Adonija et al., *Biblia Rabbinica Miqra'ot Gedolot* (4 vols.; 2nd ed.; Venice: Daniel Bomberg, 1524–1525).

*REB
The Revised English Bible with the Apocrypha (Oxford: Oxford University Press, 1989).

Reynolds–Wilson, *Scribes and Scholars*
L.D. Reynolds and N.G. Wilson, *Scribes and Scholars: A Guide to the Transmission of Greek and Latin Literature* (3rd ed.; Oxford: Clarendon Press, 1991).

Roberts, *OTTV*
B.J. Roberts, *The Old Testament Text and Versions: The Hebrew Text in Transmission and the History of the Ancient Versions* (Cardiff: University of Wales Press, 1951).

Rofé, *"Historical Significance"*
A. Rofé, "The Historical Significance of Secondary Readings," in *Quest for Context and Meaning: Studies in Biblical Intertextuality in Honor of James A. Sanders* (eds. C.A. Evans and S. Talmon; Biblical Interpretation Series 28; Leiden: Brill, 1997), 393–402.

Rofé, *Deuteronomy*
A. Rofé, *Deuteronomy: Issues and Interpretation* (OTS; London: T & T Clark, 2002).

De Rossi, *1784–1788*
J.B. De Rossi, *Variae lectiones Veteris Testamenti* (5 vols.; Parma: Regio, 1784–1788; repr. Amsterdam: Philo, 1969).

*RSV
The Bible Containing the Old and New Testaments: Revised Standard Version (2nd ed.; New York: Collins, 1971).

Sabatier, *Bibliorum*
P. Sabatier (ed.), *Bibliorum sacrorum latinae versions antiquae seu vetus Italica, et caeterae quaecunque in codicibus Ms. et antquorum libris reperiri potuerunt: Quae cum Vulgata Latina et cum Textu Graeco comparantur: Accedunt praefationes, observations, ac notae indexque novus advulagatam e regione editam idemque locupletissimus: Opera et studio* (3 vols.; Reims: Florentain, 1743–1749).

Sadaqa, *Jewish and Samaritan Version*
A. and R. Sadaqa, *Jewish and Samaritan Version of the Pentateuch: With Particular Stress on the Differences between Both Texts* (Tel Aviv: R. Mass, 1961–1965).

Salvesen, *Hexapla*
Origen's Hexapla and Fragments: Papers Presented at the Rich Seminar on the Hexapla, Oxford Centre for Hebrew and Jewish Studies, 25th July–3rd August 1994 (ed. A. Salvesen; TSAJ 58; Tübingen: Mohr Siebeck, 1998).

Sanderson, *Exodus Scroll*
J.E. Sanderson, *An Exodus Scroll from Qumran: 4QpaleoExod^m and the Samaritan Tradition* (HSS 30; Atlanta: Scholars Press, 1986).

Schenker, *Septante*
A. Schenker, *Septante et texte Massorétique dans l'histoire la plus ancienne du texte de 1 Rois 2–14* (CahRB 48; Paris: Gabalda, 2000).

Schenker, *Earliest Text*
The Earliest Text of the Hebrew Bible: The Relationship between the Masoretic Text and the Hebrew Base of the Septuagint Reconsidered (ed. A. Schenker; SBLSCS 52; Atlanta: Scholars Press, 2003).

Schenker, *"General Introduction"*
A. Schenker et al., "General Introduction," in *BHQ 18: General Introduction and Megilloth*, vii–xxxvi.

Schenker, *"Ursprung"*
A. Schenker, "Der Ursprung des massoretischen Textes im Licht der literarischen Varianten im Bibeltext," *Textus* 23 (2007): 51–67.

Schiffman, Tov, and VanderKam, *Fifty Years*
The Dead Sea Scrolls Fifty Years after their Discovery: Proceedings of the Jerusalem Congress, July 10–25, 1997 (eds. L.H. Schiffman, E. Tov, and J.C. VanderKam; Jerusalem: Israel Exploration Society, 2000).

Schorch, *Euphemismen*
S. Schorch, *Euphemismen in der Hebräischen Bibel*

(Orientalia Biblica et Christiana 12; Wiesbaden: Harrassowitz, 2000).

Schorch, *Vokale
S. Schorch, *Die Vokale des Gesetzes: Die samaritanische Lesetradition als Textzeugin der Tora*, Vol. 1: *Das Buch Genesis* (BZAW 339; Berlin: De Gruyter, 2004).

Schüssler, *Biblia Coptica
K. Schüssler, *Biblia Coptica: Die koptischen Bibeltexte: Das Sahidische Alte und Neue Testament: Vollständiges Verzeichnis mit Standorten*, Vol. 1.1–4 (Wiesbaden: Harrassowitz, 1995–2000, sa 1–120); Vol. 2.1–2 (Wiesbaden: Harrassowitz, 2012–2015, sa 121–260).

*Scrolls and Cognate Writings
See *Manchester Symposium

*Septuaginta Deutsch
M. Karrer and W. Kraus (eds.), *Septuaginta Deutsch: Das griechische Alte Testament in deutscher Übersetzung* (Stuttgart: Deutsche Bibelgesellschaft, 2009).

*Septuaginta Deutsch, Erläuterungen
Septuaginta Deutsch: Erläuterungen und Kommentare zum griechischen Alten Testament (eds. M. Karrer and W. Kraus; Stuttgart: Deutsche Bibelgesellschaft, 2011).

*SESB
Stuttgart Electronic Study Bible computer program.

Sirat, *Papyrus
C. Sirat, *Les papyrus en caractères hébraïques trouvés en Egypte* (with contributions by M. Beit-Arié et al.; calligraphy and illustrations by A. Yardeni; Paris: Centre national de recherche scientifique, 1985).

Skehan, *"Qumran Manuscripts"
P.W. Skehan, "The Qumran Manuscripts and Textual Criticism," in *Volume du Congrès International pour l'étude de l'Ancien Testament, Strabourg 1956* (eds. G.W. Anderson et al.; VTSup 4; Leiden: Brill, 1957), 148–60.

Skehan, *"Qumran, Littérature de Qumran"
P.W. Skehan, "Qumran, Littérature de Qumran, A. Textes bibliques," *DBSup* 9: 805–22.

Sperber, *Bible in Aramaic
A. Sperber, *The Bible in Aramaic Based on Old Manuscripts and Printed Texts* (4 vols.; Leiden: Brill, 1959–1968).

Sperber, *Grammar
A. Sperber, *A Historical Grammar of Biblical Hebrew: A Presentation of Problems with Suggestions to Their Solution* (Leiden: Brill, 1966).

Stipp, *"Textkritik"
H.J. Stipp, "Das Verhältnis von Textkritik und Literarkritik in neueren alttestamentlichen Veröffentlichungen," *BZ* 34 (1990): 16–37.

Strugnell, *"Notes en marge"
J. Strugnell, "Notes en marge du volume V des Discoveries in the Judaean Desert of Jordan," *RevQ* 7 (1969–1971): 163–276.

Sundberg, *Old Testament
A. Sundberg, *The Old Testament of the Early Church* (HTS 20; Cambridge: Harvard University Press, 1964).

Swete, *Introduction
H.B. Swete, *An Introduction to the Old Testament in Greek* (2nd ed.; Cambridge: Cambridge University Press, 1914).

Tal, *Shekhem
A. Tal, *The Samaritan Pentateuch: Edited According to MS 6 (C) of the Shekhem Synagogue* (Texts and Studies in the Hebrew Language and Related Subjects 8; Tel Aviv: Tel Aviv University, 1994).

Tal–Florentin, *Samaritan Version
A. Tal and M. Florentin, *The Pentateuch: The Samaritan Version and the Masoretic Version* (Tel Aviv: Haim Rubin Tel Aviv University Press, 2010).

Talmon, *"Old Testament Text"
S. Talmon, "The Old Testament Text," in *The Cambridge History of the Bible*, Vol. 1: *From the Beginnings to Jerome* (eds. R.P. Ackroyd and C.F. Evans; Cambridge: Cambridge University Press, 1970), 159–99; repr. in Cross–Talmon, *QHBT* (1975): 1–41.

Talmon, *Qumran
S. Talmon, *The World of Qumran from Within: Collected Studies* (Jerusalem: Magnes Press, 1989).

Talmon, *Masada VI
S. Talmon and Y. Yadin, *Masada VI: The Yigael Yadin Excavations 1963–1965, Final Reports, Hebrew Fragments from Masada* (Jerusalem: Israel Exploration Society, 1999).

Talmon, *Text
S. Talmon, *Text and Canon of the Hebrew Bible: Collected Studies* (Winona Lake: Eisenbrauns, 2010).

Talmon, *"New Outlook"
S. Talmon, "The Textual Study of the Bible: A New Outlook," in idem, *Text, 19–84.

Talmon, *"Synonymous Readings"
S. Talmon, "Synonymous Readings in the Masoretic Text," in idem, *Text, 171–216.

Talmon, *"Double Readings"
S. Talmon, "Double Readings in the Masoretic Text," in idem, *Text, 217–67.

Talmon, *"Ancient Versions"
S. Talmon, "Textual Criticism: The Ancient Versions," in idem, *Text, 383–418.

Thackeray, *Grammar
  H.St.J. Thackeray, *A Grammar of the Old Testament in Greek according to the Septuagint* (Cambridge: Cambridge University Press, 1909).
Thackeray, *The Septuagint and Jewish Worship
  H.St.J. Thackeray, *The Septuagint and Jewish Worship* (Schweich Lectures 1920; London: Milford, 1921).
*The Bible as Book
  The Bible as Book: The Hebrew Bible and the Judaean Desert Discoveries (eds. E.D. Herbert and E. Tov; London: British Library, 2002).
*Theory and Practice
  Theory and Practice of Translation: Nobel Symposium 39, Stockholm 1976 (ed. L. Grähs et al.; Bern: P. Lang, 1978).
Tigay, *Models
  Empirical Models for Biblical Criticism (ed. J.H. Tigay; Philadelphia: University of Philadelphia Press, 1985).
Van der Toorn, *Scribal Culture
  K. van der Toorn, *Scribal Culture and the Making of the Hebrew Bible* (Cambridge: Harvard University Press, 2007).
Tov, *Jeremiah–Baruch
  E. Tov, *The Septuagint Translation of Jeremiah and Baruch: A Discussion of an Early Revision of Jeremiah 29–52 and Baruch 1:1–3:8* (HSM 8; Missoula: Scholars Press, 1976).
Tov, *"Socio-Religious Background"
  E. Tov, "The Socio-Religious Background of the Paleo-Hebrew Biblical Texts Found at Qumran," in *Geschichte–Tradition–Reflexion: Festschrift für Martin Hengel zum 70. Geburtstag* (eds. H. Cancik et al.; 3 vols.; Tübingen: Mohr Siebeck, 1996), 1.353–74.
Tov, *TCU
  E. Tov, *The Text-Critical Use of the Septuagint in Biblical Research* (2nd ed.; Jerusalem Biblical Studies 8; Jerusalem: Simor, 1997).
Tov, *Greek-Hebrew Bible
  E. Tov, *The Greek and Hebrew Bible: Collected Essays on the Septuagint* (VTSup 72; Leiden: Brill, 1999).
Tov, *"Septuagint Translators"
  E. Tov, "Did the Septuagint Translators Always Understand Their Hebrew Text?" in idem, *Greek-Hebrew Bible*, 203–18.
Tov, *"Synthese"
  E. Tov, "Die biblischen Handscriften aus der Wüste Juda—Eine neue Synthese," in *Die Textfunde vom Toten Meer und der Text der Hebräischen Bibel* (eds. U. Dahmen, A. Lange, and H. Lichtenberger; Neukirchen-Vluyn: Neukirchener Verlag, 2000), 1–34.

Tov, *$TCHB^{1,2}$
  E. Tov, *Textual Criticism of the Hebrew Bible* (Minneapolis: Fortress Press, 1992. 2nd revised ed.; Minneapolis: Fortress Press, 2001).
Tov, *"Biblical Texts"
  E. Tov, "The Biblical Texts from the Judaean Desert: An Overview and Analysis of the Published Texts," in *The Bible as Book: The Hebrew Bible and the Judaean Desert Discoveries* (eds. E.D. Herbert and E. Tov; London: British Library, 2002), 139–66.
Tov, *"List"
  E. Tov, "List of the Texts from the Judaean Desert," *DJD XXXIX, 27–114.
Tov, *"Place of Masoretic Text"
  E. Tov, "The Place of the Masoretic Text in Modern Text Editions of the Hebrew Bible: The Relevance of Canon," in *The Canon Debate* (eds. L. McDonald and J.A. Sanders; Peabody: Hendrickson, 2002), 234–51.
Tov, *Scribal Practices
  E. Tov, *Scribal Practices and Approaches Reflected in the Texts Found in the Judean Desert* (STDJ 54; Leiden: Brill, 2004).
Tov, *HB, GB, and Qumran
  E. Tov, *Hebrew Bible, Greek Bible, and Qumran: Collected Essays* (TSAJ 121; Tübingen: Mohr Siebeck, 2008).
Tov, *"Coincidental Textual Nature"
  E. Tov, "The Coincidental Textual Nature of the Collections of Ancient Scriptures," in *Congress Volume Ljubljana 2007* (ed. A. Lemaire; VTSup 133; Leiden: Brill, 2010), 153–69.
Tov, *Revised Lists
  E. Tov, *Revised Lists of the Texts from the Judaean Desert* (Leiden: Brill, 2010).
Tov, *TCHB
  E. Tov, *Textual Criticism of the Hebrew Bible* (revised and expanded 3rd ed.; Minneapolis: Fortress Press, 2012).
Tov, *Collected Writings 3
  E. Tov, *Textual Criticism of the Hebrew Bible, Qumran, Septuagint: Collected Writings*, Vol. 3 (VTSup 167; Leiden: Brill, 2015).
Tov, *"Source Criticism"
  E. Tov, "The Source of Source Criticism: The Relevance of Non-Masoretic Textual Witnesses," in *Text—Textgeschichte—Textwirkung: Festschrift zum 65. Geburtstag von Siegfried Kreuzer* (eds. T. Wagner et al.; AOAT 419; Münster: Ugarit-Verlag, 2015), 283–301.
Trebolle Barrera, *Jewish Bible
  J. Trebolle Barrera, *The Jewish Bible and the Christian

Bible: An Introduction to the History of the Bible (trans. W.G.E. Watson; Leiden: Brill, 1998).

Turner, **Greek Manuscripts*
E.G. Turner, *Greek Manuscripts of the Ancient World* (rev. and enlarged by P.J. Parsons; 2nd ed.; Institute of Classical Studies Bulletin Supplement 46; London: University of London, 1987).

Ullendorff, **Ethiopia and the Bible*
E. Ullendorff, *Ethiopia and the Bible: The Schweich Lectures of the British Academy, 1967* (Oxford: Oxford University Press, 1967).

Ulrich, **DSS*
E. Ulrich, *The Dead Sea Scrolls and the Origins of the Bible* (Grand Rapids/Leiden: Eerdmans/Brill, 1999).

Ulrich, **BQS*
E. Ulrich, *The Biblical Qumran Scrolls: Transcriptions and Textual Variants* (VTSup 134; Leiden: Brill, 2010).

Ulrich, **DSSDCB*
E. Ulrich, *The Dead Sea Scrolls and the Developmental Composition of the Bible* (VTSup 169; Leiden: Brill, 2015).

Van Seters, **Edited Bible*
J. Van Seters, *The Edited Bible: The Curious History of the "Editor" in Biblical Criticism* (Winona Lake: Eisenbrauns, 2006).

Veltri, **Eine Torah*
G. Veltri, *Eine Tora für den König Talmai: Untersuchungen zum Übersetzungsverständnis in der jüdisch-hellenistischen und rabbinischen Literatur* (TSAJ 41; Tübingen: Mohr Siebeck, 1994).

Veltri, **Gegenwart*
G. Veltri, *Gegenwart der Tradition: Studien zur jüdischen Literatur und Kulturgeschichte* (JSJSup 69; Leiden: Brill, 2002).

*Vetus Latina Database
R. Gryson (ed.), *Vetus Latina Database: Bible Versions of the Latin Fathers: The Comprehensive Patristic Records of the Vetus Latina Institut in Beuron* (CD-ROM; Turnhout, Brepols Publishers, 2002).

Walters, **Text*
P. Walters, *The Text of the Septuagint: Its Corruptions and Their Emendation* (Cambridge: Cambridge University Press, 1973).

Walton, **Polyglotta*
B. Walton, *Biblia Sacra Polyglotta complectentia textus originales, Hebraicum, cum Pentateucho Samaritano, Chaldaicum, Graecum, versionumque antiquarum, Samaritanae, Graecae LXXII Interpretum, Chaldaicae, Syriacae, Arabicae, Aethiopicae, Persicae, Vulg. Lat. etc.* (London: Roycroft, 1653–1657; repr. Graz: Akademische Druck und Verlagsanstalt, 1965).

Walton, **Prolegomena*
B. Walton, *Briani Waltoni in Biblia Polyglotta Prolegomena* (Leipzig: Weygand, 1777).

Weber and Gryson, **Vulgata*
Biblia Sacra iuxta vulgatam versionem (eds. R. Weber and R. Gryson; 5th ed.; Stuttgart: Deutsche Bibelgesellschaft, 2007).

Weil, **Massorah Gedolah ... Léningrad*
G.E. Weil, *Massorah Gedolah manuscrit B.19a de Léningrad*, Vol. 1 (Rome: Pontificium Institutum Biblicum, 1971).

Wellhausen, **Bücher Samuelis*
J. Wellhausen, *Der Text der Bücher Samuelis* (Göttingen: Vandenhoeck & Ruprecht, 1871).

Van der Woude, **"Pluriformity and Uniformity"*
A.S. van der Woude, "Pluriformity and Uniformity: Reflections on the Transmission of the Text of the Old Testament," in *Sacred History and Sacred Texts in Early Judaism: A Symposium in Honour of A.S. van der Woude* (eds. J.N. Brenner and F. García Martínez; CBET 5; Kampen: Kok Pharos, 1992), 151–69.

Würthwein, **Text*
E. Würthwein, *Der Text des Alten Testaments: Eine Einführung in die Biblia Hebraica* (5th ed.; Stuttgart: Deutsche Bibelgesellschaft, 1988).

Würthwein, **Text (English)*
E. Würthwein, *The Text of the Old Testament: An Introduction to the Biblia Hebraica* (trans. E.F. Rhodes; 2nd ed.; Grand Rapids: Eerdmans, 1995).

Yardeni, **Hebrew Script*
A. Yardeni, *The Book of the Hebrew Script: History, Paleography, Script Styles, Calligraphy and Design* (Jerusalem: Carta: 1997).

Yeivin, **Introduction*
I. Yeivin, *Introduction to the Tiberian Masorah* (trans. and ed. E.J. Revell; SBLMasS 5; Missoula: Scholars Press, 1980).

Yeivin, **Masorah*
I. Yeivin, *The Biblical Masorah* (Studies in Language 3; Jerusalem: Academy of the Hebrew Language, 2003) [Hebr.].

Young, **"Stabilization"*
I. Young, "The Stabilization of the Biblical Text in the Light of Qumran and Masada: A Challenge for Conventional Qumran Chronology?" *DSD* 9 (2002): 364–90.

Zohrapian, **Scriptures*
H. Zohrapian (ed.), *Astuatsashunch' Matean ew Nor Ktakaranats'* (Scriptures of the Old and New Testa-

ments; Venice, 1805; repr., with introduction by C. Cox [Classical Armenian Text Reprint Series; Delmar: Caravan Books, 1984]).

10–20
Ketuvim (Writings)

∴

10

Psalms

∴

10.1 Textual History of Psalms

The importance of the book of Psalms can hardly be overstated. To cite what is perhaps the most obvious proof of the signal import of Psalms, it can be noted that it is often the case that more copies of this composition exist than for any other book of the Bible, and this is as true for the earliest Hebrew copies of the Psalms recovered from Qumran (→ 10.2.1; → 10.2.2; → 10.2.3) as it is for much later versions. So, for example, more manuscript evidence survives for LXX-Ps than for any other Septuagintal book, with copies of Psalms outpacing its nearest competitor (Genesis) by a ratio of as many as 10 to 1 (→ 10.3.1.2). Or, in the Ethiopian tradition, it has been estimated that more than twenty-five percent of all Christian books copied in Ethiopic are Psalters (→ 10.4.3.2). The proliferation of copies, which is to say, *texts*, is indubitably what facilitated the proliferation of variants and thus *text types*, making Psalms, especially in particular text traditions (versions), easily the most complex of books in textual criticism of the Hebrew Bible.[1]

The importance of Psalms lies in the book's liturgical significance, its popularity, and, correlatively, its widespread use. These factors left their mark on the book in terms of textual variants,[2] but they are also manifested in other ways,[3] one of which is that Psalms is often transmitted as a self-standing composition. Numerous such editions (Psalters) exist, and they present the book of Psalms alone and apart from being included with other compositions to form a larger copy of the Bible (e.g., → 10.4.3.2).[4] No other single book of the Bible is treated in this way as extensively as Psalms.

There are still other indicators pointing to the book's prominence. So, according to both the New Testament and the important Qumran sectarian composition, *Miqṣat Maʿaśe ha-Torah* (4QMMT), "the Psalms" (Luke 24:44: ψαλμοῖς) or "David" (4QMMT C 10: דויד), the likely surrogate for the same,[5] is found listed alongside the (apparently canonical) rubrics "the Law of Moses" (τῷ νόμῳ Μωϋσέως) or "the Book of Moses" (בספר מושה) and "the Prophets" (τοῖς προφήταις) or "the book[s of the Pr]ophets" (ובספר]י הנ[ביאים]). In these instances, "Psalms/David" may stand for a larger collection (or sub-collection) of books from the Ketuvim, but, quite apart from that determination (which is far from certain),[6] the point is simply that it is Psalms, and/or its patron, David (the putative author of so many of the individual psalms), that is mentioned alongside the law and the prophets, not, say, Proverbs or Solomon or some other. At Qumran proper, Psalms is the only book outside certain prophetic texts (Isaiah, Hosea, Micah, Nahum, Habakkuk, Zephaniah) to

---

[1] E.g., → 10.4.1 and → 10.3.4.1, → 10.4.4.8, respectively, for multiple editions of Psalms in Latin and Syriac, with some Latin manuscripts including two or more Psalters at the same time. In the case of the Latin Psalms, note that Jerome made no less than three translations of the book (→ 10.1.1.2 and → 10.1.1.4 below, and, further, → 10.3.7.1, → 10.4.1.3): The "Roman Psalter" (ca. 384 C.E.); the "Gallican Psalter" (ca. 388 C.E.), which was ratified at the Council of Trent (1545–1563 C.E.) as the Vulgate Psalter; and the "Hebrew Psalter" (ca. 392 C.E.).

[2] E.g., → 10.4.5.1 on memory variants in Arm-Psalms. Note the possibility of composition from memory and memory variants in excerpted Psalm manuscripts (→ 10.2.3.6) and → 10.4.3.2 for memorization of the Psalter in Ethiopian Christianity. Liturgical use could also function to standardize or stabilize the text, as in the case of the Psalter in Byzantium; → 10.3.6.1; also → 10.2.3.7; and see N. Fernández Marcos, "Some Reflections on the Antiochian Text of the Septuagint," in Fraenkel, *Studien zur Septuaginta*, 219–29 (221).

[3] E.g., → 10.4.8 for rubrics and marginal notes written in the trilingual Psalter BL Harley MS 5786; and → 10.4.3.2 for elaborate paratextual elements in Ethiopian Orthodox Psalters that include, *inter alia*, section headings in Psalm 118 (= ET 119) that explain the spiritual meaning of the Hebrew letters.

[4] The latter situation, too, is often found. When it does, the order of the books in the Ketuvim can vary. Psalms follows Ruth in the Ketuvim according to *b. Bat.* 14b, but in some manuscripts (e.g., MT^L), it follows Chronicles, while in still others it heads the Ketuvim (see Swete, *Introduction*, 200; Ginsburg, *Introduction*, 6–8). The order of the uncial Greek manuscripts varies widely, as does the placement of Psalms in patristic and synodical lists in both the eastern and western tradition (see Swete, *Introduction*, 201–14).

[5] "David" is frequently found as a metonym for the Psalms across the textual tradition. E.g., → 10.4.4.2, → 10.4.6.1.

[6] See the important cautions of Ulrich, *DSSDCB*, 300–304.

be the subject of continuous commentary, and no less than three such Pesher-manuscripts are attested: 1QpPs (1Q16), 4QpPsᵃ (4Q171), and 4QpPsᵇ (4Q173).[7] Similarly, the use of red ink at Qumran is restricted in biblical scrolls to Numbers (4QNumᵇ) and Psalms (2QPs [2Q14]).[8] While the red ink by itself does not suffice to identify the entire book as special, it is nevertheless noteworthy that its use is limited among biblical manuscripts to these two compositions. The special ink probably served some sort of liturgical function in 2QPs, perhaps to draw "the attention of the reader or reciter to the first four verses of Psalm 103,"[9] which comprise the words written in red.

There can be little doubt that the liturgical use of Psalms is what has produced some of the more intriguing aspects of its textual history, including the sheer number of copies of the composition that are extant but also other curiosities that include, *inter alia*, 1) interpolations of some psalms into other psalms,[10] a phenomenon that might have been facilitated by overlap between similar and memorized texts;[11] 2) the transmission of a set of "Odes" (ΩΔΑΙ/ᾠδαί) in the Greek manuscript tradition, though obviously these were not part of the original translation (→ 10.3.1.5), since, among other things, they include texts from the New Testament (Luke 1:46–55, 68–79; 2:29–32);[12] and 3) the transmission of manuscripts that include only one or a select number of psalms (excerpted texts; → 10.2.1.5; → 10.2.3.6, and see further below).

The various articles collected in *THB* cover in detail the full range of the text-critical data for the Psalms across the various languages and traditions. The purpose of this article is to provide a brief overview of and entrée into that material (→ 10.1.1) and then to offer a few remarks on some factors that are of special significance if not unique to the Psalms, above all their arrangement (→ 10.1.2), with special attention paid

---

[7] See Ulrich, *DSSDCB*, 288. His conclusion, made in part on the basis of comparison with other base texts for the pesharim – namely, that Psalms was accorded scriptural status "because it was viewed as a prophetic book rather than a wisdom book" (ibid.) – is not a necessary one, nor are the texts he adduces (11QPsᵃ 27:11; 1 Macc 7:17; and Acts 2:29–31) definitive (or, perhaps better, determinative) on this point. In fact, the history of interpretation shows that Psalms has often been understood in ways more akin to wisdom and/or legal instruction – not to mention its obvious content as liturgical poetry – than prophecy per se. E.g., → 10.3.8 on Saadia Gaon's (882–942 C.E.) first introduction to his Arabic translation of the Psalms, and compare the Karaite reception of the Psalms as the basis for daily prayer. See further U. Simon, *Four Approaches to the Book of Psalms: From Saadiah Gaon to Abraham Ibn Ezra* (trans. L.J. Schramm; Albany: State University of New York, 1991). For the texts of the Psalm pesharim, see *PTSDSSP* 6B, 6–33.

[8] In 4QNumᵇ, red ink is used at the beginning of ten sections, whether the first verse or the first line, before writing the rest of the section or verse in black ink (see *DJD* XII: 210–11). In 2QPs, the first two lines of Psalm 103 are written in red ink. Red ink is also used in 4QDᵉ (4Q270) 3 i 19 and 4Q181d. In each case, with the possible exception of the last mentioned, the use of red ink is apparently to mark new units or headings and/or to draw attention to the material so inscribed. For discussion, see Tov, *Scribal Practices*, 54, 148–49.

[9] Flint, *Dead Sea Psalms Scrolls*, 32; further, pp. 31–32 and nn. 18–21.

[10] E.g., LXX-Ps 13:3³⁻¹⁰, which is comprised of LXX-Pss 5:10; 139:4; 9:28; LXX-Isa 59:7–8; and LXX-Ps 35:2, and which is quoted in Rom 3:13–18. See Rahlfs, *Psalmi cum Odis*, 30–32, 95–96; Swete, *Introduction*, 251; Limburg, "Psalms," 5:524. This specific passage, along with several others, has been omitted in *NETS*, which judges it to be secondary.

[11] Beyond memory variants like those found in Arm-Ps (→ 10.4.5.1), see → 10.1.1 below on doublets/parallel texts. The phenomenon of "twin psalms" (e.g., Pss 103/104; 105/106; 111/112; and 135/136) is not unrelated (see Witte, "The Psalter," 531).

[12] The specific list of Odes, not to mention their individual contents and delimitation, varies in the main uncial manuscripts. See Swete, *Introduction*, 253–55. Rahlfs, *Psalmi cum Odis*, 341–65, includes the following fourteen (or fifteen) compositions: 1) Exod 15:1–19 (Song of the Sea); 2) Deut 32:1–43 (Song of Moses); 3) 1 Kgdms 2:1–10 (Prayer of Hannah); 4) Hab 3:2–19 (Prayer of Habakkuk); 5) Isa 26:9–20 (Prayer of Isaiah); 6) Jonah 2:3–10 (Prayer of Jonah); 7) Dan 3:26–45 (Prayer of Azariah); 8) Dan 3:52–88 (Song of the Three Hebrew Children); 9a–b) Luke 1:46–55, 68–79 (Prayer of Mary and Prayer of Zechariah); 10) Isa 5:1–9 (Song of Isaiah); 11) Isa 38:10–20 (Prayer of Hezekiah); 12) Prayer of Manasseh; 13) Luke 2:29–32 (Prayer of Simeon); and 14) Morning Hymn/*Gloria in Excelsis*. Odes are also found in various liturgical Psalters in other languages, for example, Christian Arabic versions (→ 10.4.8), which have ten Odes, or Georg-Ps which has nine (→ 10.4.6.3). Ethiopic Psalters typically include fifteen biblical canticles, the Song of Songs, and two Maryan works: Praises of Mary and Gate of Light (→ 10.4.3.2).

to matters of numbering/sequencing (→ 10.1.2.1), titles/superscriptions (→ 10.1.2.2), and stichometry (→ 10.1.2.3).

10.1.1 Survey of the Textual History of Psalms

The earliest origins of the psalms as compositions, if not also their collection – even if only in preliminary form(s) – lies antecedent to the extant textual witnesses (but see further → 10.1.2). This situation has not kept scholars from speculating about such matters, sometimes quite apart from the extant manuscript data (→ 10.1.2.1 below). However, not all such speculation is unwarranted. So, for example, one notes the existence of doublets or parallel texts between different psalms or, occasionally, between a psalm and a non-psalmic text (→ 10.2.2.1.1):

Ps 14:1b–7	= Ps 53:2–7
Ps 18:3–51	= 2 Sam 22:2–51
Ps 40:14–18	= Ps 70:2–6
Ps 57:8–12 + 60:7–14	= Ps 108:2–14
Pss 105:1–15 + 96:1–13 + 106:1, 47–48	= 1 Chr 16:8–36a

Doublets like these would probably not exist, Weiser rightly notes, "if all the psalms had been grouped together all at once and by the same compiler."[13] The existence of psalm doublets, coupled with the fact that there are often significant differences between the parallel texts, is already enough to raise the issue of textual development, quite apart from (and even well before) the recovery of the many varying Psalms texts from the Judean Desert.[14] From another side, questions of textual development and text typology are also raised by research on LXX-Ps and its relationship to other Septuagintal texts, which has suggested that the origins of the Greek translation of Psalms lie in the second, if not the third century B.C.E. (→ 10.1.1.2). Whatever the case, a watershed moment in the study of the textual history of Psalms came with the discovery of the Psalms manuscripts from Qumran and its environs.

10.1.1.1 Hebrew Texts

The texts recovered from various sites around the Dead Sea are our earliest Hebrew manuscripts of Psalms. All told, there as many as forty-two possible Psalms manuscripts from these sites (→ 10.2.1).[15] The data from these scrolls, while rich, are not entirely straightforward, and their interpretation has been the subject of debate.[16] Text-typological classification is complicated in the case of Psalms more generally given the nature of its constituent compositions (the individual psalms themselves)

---

[13] A. Weiser, *The Psalms: A Commentary* (trans. H. Hartwell; OTL; Philadelphia: Westminster, 1962), 99.

[14] See, e.g., the work of F.M. Cross and D.N. Freedman, *Studies in Ancient Yahwistic Poetry* (2nd ed.; Grand Rapids: Eerdmans, 1997), though "even here criticism has its limits," according to Kraus (*Psalms 1–59*, 15). Ulrich ("The Dead Sea Scrolls and Their Implications for an Edition of the Septuagint Psalter," 336) points out that the variants in Psalm 18 with MT-2 Sam 22 and 4QSam^a "show … the rich textual pluriformity of the Hebrew Psalms in antiquity." See further Schmuttermayr, *Psalm 18 und 2 Samuel 22*.

[15] This formulation indicates the uncertain nature of some of these manuscripts, due to their poor preservation, as actual copies of Psalms or a part of Psalms as opposed to, say, a quotation of a psalm within another, non-psalmic composition. Quotations comprise another textual witness to Psalms in antiquity, as do the pesharim mentioned above (→ 10.2.1; → 21.2.1).

[16] Not every psalm known from later tradition is found in these manuscripts. The following psalms are not attested in the biblical manuscripts: Psalms 3–4; 20–21; 32; 41; 46(?); 55; 57–58; 61; 64–65; 70; 72–75; 79–80; 87; 90; 108(?); 110–11; 117 (Flint, "Unrolling," 242). Flint thinks these compositions were probably once present but have simply been lost due to damage (ibid.), though not all would agree (see Brütsch, *Israels Psalmen*). The psalms that are missing from the Psalms manuscripts are sometimes quoted or alluded to elsewhere in the Dead Sea Scrolls, which indicates that they were known in some form. The only psalms that are not quoted or alluded to are Psalms 3–4; 10; 14; 19; 23; 28–29; 36; 38–39; 45; 47; 49–50; 53; 55; 58; 59–62; 66–67; 70–72; 74–75; 80–81; 83–85; 87; 93; 95; 99; 100–01; 108; 110–12; 114–15; 117; 120; 124–27; 129–30; 133–36; 138; 142; 147; and 149. See A. Lange and M. Weigold, *Biblical Quotations and Allusions in Second Temple Jewish Literature* (Journal of Ancient Judaism Supplements 5; Göttingen: Vandenhoeck & Ruprecht, 2011), 163–78. Collating these two lists leaves only Psalms 3–4; 46(?); 55; 58; 61; 70; 72; 74–75; 80; 87; 108(?); 110–11; and 117 without representation, citation, or allusion among the manuscripts from the Judean Desert.

as brief religious poems that often seem to bear no obvious relationship to their adjoining psalms, a situation that lends each psalm something of a self-standing or isolated character. This situation may have been what led to the phenomenon of alternative psalm sequencing, which is well attested in many of the Psalms manuscripts from Qumran (→ 10.2.2–3), but which perdures very late into the Masoretic tradition in a related, but slightly different way as alternative psalm numbering or psalm division (→ 10.1.2.1; further → 10.2.2.1.3). Whatever the case, among the Dead Sea Scrolls, text type is most obviously assessed by differences that manuscripts manifest in terms of psalm sequencing, which is quite common, and by the rarer and occasional presence of additional, non-(proto-)MT content (→ 10.2.1; → 10.2.3.1).

Both of these characteristics were abundantly evident in 11QPs[a] (11Q5), the great Psalms scroll from Qumran Cave 11, which was first published by J.A. Sanders in 1965 (*DJD* IV). 11QPs[a] did not contain the entire book of Psalms as we now know it in MT-Ps, though where, exactly, this scroll began its collection is a matter of some debate.[17] Whatever the case, 11QPs[a] preserves a sequence of psalms that diverges in major ways from that known in MT-Ps and includes no less than ten compositions that are not found in MT-Ps or, for that matter, in most other versions of the Psalter (underlined):[18]

> Psalms 101 → 102 → 103 → ... → 109 → ... → 118 → 104 → 147 → 105 → 146 → 148 → ... → 121 → 122 → 123 → 124 → 125 → 126 → 127 → 128 → 129 → 130 → 131 → 132 → 119 → 135 → 136 + 118:1 → vv. 15–16 → vv. 8–9 → x_1 → v. 29 → x_2 (≈ Catena?) → 145 → 154 → Plea for Deliverance → 139 → 137 → 138 → Sir 51:13–30 → Apostrophe to Zion → 93 → 141 → 133 → 144 → 155 → 142 → 143 → 149 → 150 → Hymn to the Creator → 2 Sam 23:[1–]7 → David's Compositions → 140 → 134 → 151A → 151B.

---

[17] The first psalm extant in 11QPs[a] is 101, but it has been posited that the scroll may have begun with Psalm 90 or Psalm 100 (→ 10.2.1.2.1; → 10.2.3.2.1.1).

[18] In the listing that follows, → signifies "immediately followed by."

Some of the non-(proto-)MT content is attested elsewhere, just not in Psalms: most obviously Sir 51:13–30 and 2 Sam 23:1–7. Psalm 151 is also found in LXX-Ps and S-Ps, while Psalms 154–155 are also preserved in certain manuscripts of S-Ps (→ 10.1.1.2–3; further → 10.2.3.2.1.1).[19]

Sanders' several publications on 11QPs[a] opened the question on the precise nature of 11QPs[a]: Was it a "true, Scriptural Psalter" – a copy, that is, of the book of Psalms but in a different version, even (to use Ulrich's later terminology) a variant literary edition – or did it look the way it did because it was a secondary liturgical collection produced for some religious purpose? Subsequent debate was lively with several scholars such as Talmon, Goshen-Gottstein, and Haran disagreeing with Sanders.[20] Many of Sanders' notions were furthered in the important Yale dissertation-turned-monograph by Wilson, who deserves credit for first drawing on the Cave 4 Psalms manuscripts that were available at that time.[21] This line of research came to fruition following the full publication of the Cave 4 finds (*DJD* XVI) in the research of Flint, who codified what he calls the "Qumran Psalms Hypothesis."[22] According to Flint, the evidence from Qumran argues *against* an early stabilization of the Psalter, at least in the form we now have it. Flint believes that the extant manuscript data reveal that Psalms 1–89 were stabilized prior to the Qumran texts but that Psalms continued to manifest considerable fluidity in Books IV–V of the Psalter (Psalms 90–

---

[19] Contrast MasPs[b], which clearly ends its presentation with Psalm 150 (→ 10.2.1.1.2; → 10.2.2.1.2). Some of the non-(proto-)MT material is found in other texts as well, e.g., 4QPs[f], which contains the Apostrophe to Zion, and 11QPs[b], which contains the Plea for Deliverance.

[20] Talmon, "Pisqah Be'emṣa' Pasuq and 11QPs[a]"; Goshen-Gottstein, "The Psalms Scroll (11QPs[a])"; and Haran, "11QPs[a] and the Canonical Book of Psalms." See further B.A. Strawn, "David as One of the Perfect of (the) Way: On the Provenience of *David's Compositions* (and *11QPs[a]* as a Whole?)," *RevQ* 24 (2010): 607–27; and → 10.2.3.

[21] Wilson, *Editing of the Hebrew Psalter*. Note his other works in the bibliography below and also → 10.2.3.

[22] See especially Flint, *The Dead Sea Psalms Scrolls*, but also his several other publications listed in the bibliography and in → 10.2.1–10.2.3.

150) well into the first century C.E.[23] In his opinion, the book of Psalms was stabilized only gradually in a two- or three-stage process.[24]

Many, but not all, scholars have found Flint's conclusions compelling.[25] It seems irrefutable that at least three but perhaps more non-proto-MT collections of Psalms existed at Qumran (→ 10.2.3.2–5). But then again the data are, at least in some instances, equivocal due partly to the state of preservation that often limits our full knowledge of the size, extent, and contents of a scroll, and partly because of the nature of the individual psalms themselves, which are by their very nature (see above) amendable to different sequencing, especially (or so it would seem) for liturgical purposes. That this is a real possibility, not simply a theoretical one, is aptly demonstrated by the phenomenon of excerpted or partial Psalms manuscripts (→ 10.2.1.5; → 10.2.3.6). At least four Psalms manuscripts from Qumran have been classified as such: 4QPs^g, 4QPs^h, and 5QPs appear to have contained only Psalm 119, while 4QPs^l, which begins with Psalm 104 and so contains at least that psalm, may have included other compositions as well in what would be an excerpted collection. The excerpted Psalms manuscripts establish that scribes *could* and *did* feel free to excerpt or abbreviate texts for some purpose(s), which, again, in the case of Psalms, was probably a liturgical and/or a devotional one.[26] The phenomenon of excerption together with the nature of the psalms as brief religious poetry combines to suggest that any number of alternative psalm sequences could similarly have been for some liturgical/devotional reason and thus be a matter of text function and editorial production and *not* (at least not necessarily) a matter of text type or composition/transmission (→ 10.2.2.1.2; → 10.2.2.5; → 10.2.3). Stated differently, the two most important criteria for text-typological classification in Psalms manuscripts – namely, psalm sequence and the inclusion of non-(proto-)MT-Ps content – are not foolproof. These criteria may not and apparently did not always obtain, as proven by the existence of the excerpted texts (→ 10.2.3.6). To reiterate the point once more: At least some Psalms manuscripts may look the way they do because of *text function* and not necessarily *text affiliation* (→ 10.2.3.7).[27]

With that important caveat duly entered, it remains the case that the Dead Sea texts are "our earliest extant witness to the scriptural text of the psalms."[28] While Flint may overstate things somewhat in his oft-repeated claim that "no manuscript from Qumran *unambiguously* supports the arrangement found in Books IV–V of the MT-150 Psalter,"[29] he is certainly right in noting the many

---

[23] See Flint, *Dead Sea Psalms Scrolls*, passim. See also → 10.2.2.1.2, → 10.2.3, → 10.2.3.2.4 for further discussion.

[24] See especially *Dead Sea Psalms Scrolls*; also, briefly, Flint, "Unrolling," 237–38. For more discussion, → 10.2.3.2.4.

[25] See n. 20 above for the debate that raged over the nature of 11QPs^a and that continues, in one way or the other, to the present day, though it must now be conducted with reference to the Cave 4 Psalms manuscripts. On 11QPs^a, see recently Ulrich, *DSSDCB*, 194–99; Strawn, "David as One of the Perfect of (the) Way," 607–27; and A.C. Witt, "David, the 'Ruler of the Sons of His Covenant' (מושל בבני בריתו): The Expansion of Psalm 151 in 11QPs^a," *Journal for the Evangelical Study of the Old Testament* 3 (2014): 77–97. See further → 10.2.3. The most extensive critical response to Flint is found in Dahmen, *Psalmen- und Psalter-Rezeption*.

[26] On excerpted manuscripts more generally, see E. Tov, "Excerpted and Abbreviated Biblical Texts from Qumran," *RevQ* 16 (1995): 581–600 (reprinted in Tov, *HB, GB, and Qumran*, 27–41); B.A. Strawn, "Excerpted Manuscripts at Qumran: Their Significance for the Textual History of the Hebrew Bible and the Socio-Religious History of the Qumran Community and its Literature," in *The Bible and the Dead Sea Scrolls: The Princeton Symposium on the Dead Sea Scrolls* (3 vols.; ed. J.H. Charlesworth; Waco: Baylor University Press, 2006), 2.107–67; and B.A. Strawn, "Excerpted 'Non-Biblical' Scrolls at Qumran? Background, Analogies, Function," in *Qumran Studies: New Approaches, New Questions* (eds. M.T. Davis and B.A. Strawn; Grand Rapids: Eerdmans, 2007), 65–123.

[27] Still further, any particular assemblage of psalmic content is, by itself, unable to determine if that collection is "scriptural" or "secondary" (→ 10.2.2.1). Various sequencing does demonstrate the functional utility and thus authority of that particular organization of psalms, if not also Psalms as a whole, throughout the history of its textual transmission and reception (cf. → 10.2.2.5).

[28] Flint, "Unrolling," 229.

[29] Flint, *Dead Sea Psalms Scrolls*, 239 (his emphasis); see also ibid., 157–58; Flint, "Psalms and Psalters," 243; Flint, "Dead Sea Psalms Scrolls," 16–17.

divergences that will simply not permit any simplistic assumption of an early stabilization of the Psalter as a whole.[30] 11QPs[a] is, in a word, not alone. It has several other "friends" that together comprise just one of the non-proto-MT collections found among the Dead Sea Scrolls.[31] That said, it is equally true that there is *no* non-Qumran evidence for the "11QPs[a] Psalter" or any of the other non-(proto-)MT collections attested amongst the scrolls (→ 10.2.2.1.2). Indeed, no less than four manuscripts clearly seem to support (proto-)MT (→ 10.2.1; → 10.2.2.4): 4QPs[c] (4Q85); 5/6ḤevPs (5/6Ḥev1b), MasPs[a] (1039–1160, Mas1e) and MasPs[b] (1103–1742, Mas1f), and two others may reasonably be added to this listing (→ 10.2.2.1.2; → 10.2.3.2.3): 11QPs[c] (11Q7) and 11QPs[d] (11Q8).[32] These manuscripts demonstrate that the (proto-)MT tradition of Psalms is attested at least by the late first century C.E. at Qumran *but also outside of it*, something that cannot be said for the non-proto-MT collections (→ 10.2.1; → 10.2.2.1.2; → 10.2.2.4). So, while it is possible that the pluriformity of Psalms at Qumran is indicative of wider tendencies in Judaism at this time, it is also possible that the Qumran evidence is *not* so indicative, especially given the fact that three of the (proto-)MT texts come from non-Qumran sites (Naḥal Ḥever and Masada), which may suggest that the specifically Qumranic texts are, instead, a local phenomenon.[33] It is to be hoped that further manuscript discoveries will help to decide the issue definitively. Whatever the case, it is clear that the book of Psalms was of great importance at Qumran, and it is equally clear that alternative psalmic sequences, whether attested in scrolls that were (truly) "scriptural" or (merely) "liturgical,"[34] are well attested. If these particular manuscripts are not alternative versions of Psalms, or variant literary editions of the Psalter, they are nevertheless popular psalm collections with multiple attestations, "hymnals" of sorts, as it were.

Through one process or another – or several! – that is (are) now unknown, what is known today as MT-Ps was eventually codified. If the Qumran data are both definitive and representative, we may say only that the (proto-)MT texts that are found there (or that may be present there, notwithstanding Flint's important cautions) and elsewhere somehow became the norm. The stabilization of the individual compositions themselves must have been taking place still earlier, at least in some cases, given the general scholarly assessment that text-critical differences within specific psalms are often quite limited.[35] However, that general judgment should not be overstated: While many scholars deem the versional evidence to be based on Hebrew texts quite similar to (proto-)MT, at least in consonantal form (see further below), this does not mean there are no text-critical divergences, some of which are extensive, and some of which may indeed go back to alternative Hebrew formulations (see further below). Whatever the case, the Hebrew textual tradition – at least in terms of sequencing of specific psalm content – must have been settled at some point *after* the evidence from Qumran, where pluriformity is the norm, but *before* the medieval manuscripts of the tenth to the fifteenth centuries

---

[30] Contrast, e.g., Witte, "The Psalter," 543: "Around 100 B.C.E., the qualitative, if not yet the quantitative 'canonicity' ... of the Psalter was established."

[31] See → 10.2.3.2, → 10.2.3.2.3 for the fact that this first non-(proto-)MT collection is attested in as many as five manuscripts from three different caves (11QPs[a], 11QPs[b], and 4QPs[e]; perhaps also 1QPs[b] and 4QPs[n]), may have undergone subsequent literary development (→ 10.2.3.2.1.3 on 4QPs[e]), and/or may have produced an excerpted manuscript (→ 10.2.3.2.1.4 on 4QPs[n]). Non-Proto-MT Collection 3 may also reflect slight literary development (→ 10.2.3.4).

[32] For an alternative perspective on MasPs[a] and MasPs[b], see E. Ulrich, "Two Perspectives on Two Pentateuchal Manuscripts from Masada," in *Emanuel: Studies in Hebrew Bible, Septuagint, and Dead Sea Scrolls in Honor of Emanuel Tov* (eds. S.M. Paul et al.; VTSup 94; Brill: Leiden, 2003), 453–64. Whatever the case, the paleographical dates of Non-Proto-MT Collection 1 (→ 10.2.3.2) are *not* demonstrably earlier than the (proto-)MT texts from the Dead Sea.

[33] Cf. Strawn, "Excerpted Manuscripts at Qumran," 134–47 on a theory of "hyper-local" texts.

[34] → 10.2.2.1; → 10.2.3.7; and see Yarchin, "Psalms Collections," for comments that resist the dichotomy "scriptural" vs. "liturgical."

[35] E.g., → 10.2.1; → 10.2.2; Lange, *Handbuch*, 423–35; Lange, "Collecting," 301–02; Flint, "Unrolling," 247.

C.E. that demonstrate that the (proto-)MT text type carried the day (→ 10.2.2.4).[36] The latter judgment does not hold true, however, on one notable point: that of psalm numbering, division, or arrangement, a matter that remains in flux until the sixteenth century C.E. (→ 10.1.2.1 below; further → 10.2.2.1.3; → 10.2.2.4).

10.1.1.2 Greek Texts

Numbering/arrangement is an obvious point of difference between MT-Ps and the Greek Psalms insofar as LXX-Ps (→ 10.3.1) ends with Psalm 151, a text that is not included in MT, although, as already noted, it is found in 11QPsᵃ (→ 10.2.1.2.1; → 10.2.3.2) and in S-Ps (→ 10.3.4). Even in the Greek tradition, various manuscripts designate Psalm 151 as supernumerary by either the explicit tag ἔξωθεν or ἐκτὸς τοῦ ἀριθμοῦ ("outside the number [i.e., of the Psalms]") or by other means,[37] and so, not surprisingly, this psalm is excluded from Jerome's *iuxta Hebraeos* translation (PsH; → 10.3.7), though it is included in his Gallican Psalter (PsG), which is indebted to LXX (→ 10.1.1.4; → 10.3.7; → 10.4.1). Beyond Psalm 151, the Septuagint also combines and/or divides several psalms differently than does MT-Ps (→ 10.2.2.1.3; cf. also → 10.4.1.2):

MT	LXX
1–8	1–8
9–10	9
11–113	10–112
114–115	113
116:1–9	114
116:10–19	115
117–146	116–145
147:1–11	146
147:12–20	147
148–150	148–150
∅	151

This alternative numeration may strike one as odd, but in fact it is quite common and was found also in the Masoretic tradition well into the sixteenth century (see further → 10.1.2.1 below; also → 10.2.2.1.3). Indeed, this latter situation suggests that it is imprecise to designate the left column in the preceding chart as MT (unless it appears in scare quotes as 'MT') since there is a considerable amount of variation in the Masoretic tradition until the First and Second Rabbinic Bibles (RB1 1517 C.E., RB2 1525 C.E.; → 10.1.2.1 below).

The date of the Greek translation of Psalms is unknown, but, on the basis of literary allusions and borrowed translations, it postdates the one of the Pentateuch, and is placed by many in the second half of the second century[38] if not still earlier, in the early second or even late third century B.C.E.[39] Any or all of these dates might be challenged, if, for instance, there proves to be more than one translator, though several scholars favor just one.[40] An early date for the translation might perhaps

---

[36] Another possibility, also raised below (→ 10.1.1.2), is that the Hebrew tradition that carried the day at a later stage is one that already existed at some point in the pre-Christian period, perhaps even in the Judean Desert sites (and texts). This model posits a *selection* of some sort from a pre-existing text tradition (not yet finalized or definitive, to be sure) rather than the *imposition* or *creation* of a new text tradition.

[37] See Swete, *Introduction*, 252–53 and further there on precursors of (or construction of) Psalm 151 in (from) previous biblical texts. Swete's statement that "there is no evidence that it ever existed in Hebrew," is obviously incorrect in light of 11QPsᵃ (he wrote before its discovery), though he immediately comments that "[w]hether it had a Hebrew or a Greek original, it was probably added to the Greek Psalter after the translation of the fifth book was complete" (ibid., 253). See Segal, "The Literary Development of Psalm 151," for an argument that the Greek, not Hebrew, form is original.

[38] So Swete, *Introduction*, 25.

[39] → 10.3.1.1; Williams, "Towards a Date for the Old Greek Psalter," 248–76; Aitken, "Psalms," 321. Both Schaper (*Eschatology*; "Septuaginta Psalter") and van der Kooij ("On the Place of Origin of the Old Greek of Psalms") have argued for Hasmonean traces, which would have obvious bearing on the date, if not also the place, of the translation. See Aitken, "Psalms," 321, 329.

[40] See Aitken, "Psalms," 325.

be challenged on the basis of the pluriformity of the Hebrew texts described above since the Hebrew text seemed to be fluid in many ways into at least the first century C.E. Alternatively, the translation of Psalms into Greek might challenge any overly extreme understanding of the extent or significance of the fluidity or pluriformity of the Hebrew (cf. → 10.3.1.1–2): at any rate, the Greek translation had to be made from *some* Hebrew text and many deem that *Vorlage* to be relatively close to consonantal MT (see immediately below). The location of the translation is unknown and debated by scholars, though the general opinion favors an Egyptian provenience.[41]

The evidence provided by LXX-Ps is also debated by scholars. Some believe that the plethora of Septuagintal manuscripts that have survived allow for a recovery of OG-Ps with others thinking that at best only traces of the Old Greek remain, which would mean that what we have in LXX-Ps manuscripts is ultimately a recension that has been brought into conformity with (proto-)MT.[42] If this latter perspective proves correct, it would mean that OG-Ps was based on a Hebrew text that was both older than and perhaps significantly different from (proto-)MT. Other scholars, however, are not convinced by this option. They deem the Old Greek recoverable, at least to some degree, and do not think that the pluriformity of the Hebrew text at, say, Qumran, necessarily means that agreement between MT-Ps and LXX-Ps is at best or only somehow secondary. Assuming for the sake of argument that some version of the "Qumran Psalms Hypothesis" is correct (→ 10.1.1.1), Greek-Ps must have been translated from some Hebrew base text, which raises the following questions: Which one(s)? And is that *Vorlage*(*n*) similar to any currently known Hebrew edition(s) of Psalms? Moreover, even if Flint et al. are correct about the fluidity of Psalms in Hebrew more generally in early Judaism, it remains the case that the Hebrew text and order (and, later, the numbering) eventually stabilized, and one possible model for such stabilization is selection from a pre-existing text tradition (replete, to be sure, with variation and subsequent modification), and not merely or only a model that posits the creation or imposition of a new tradition.

Translation technique is obviously an important consideration at this point, with some scholars arguing that LXX-Ps is quite formal, even interlinear,[43] marked by a high degree of lexical equivalence (where specific Hebrew terms are translated consistently with certain Greek terms) and other factors that seem more characteristic of a true translation rather than for a secondary revision.[44] The source-oriented nature of the translation technique and the extensive use of translation equivalents makes LXX-Ps an extremely valuable source

---

[41] → 10.3.1.1; also Aitken, "Psalms," 323–24.

[42] So Ulrich, "The Dead Sea Scrolls and Their Implications for an Edition of the Septuagint Psalter," 323–62.

[43] For a definition of the interlinear paradigm, cf. A. Pietersma and B.G. Wright, "To the Reader of NETS," in *NETS, xiv: "While it is obvious that the so-called Septuagint *in time* achieved its independence from its Semitic parent, and that it *at some stage* in its reception history sheds its subservience to its source, it is equally true that it was, at its stage of production, a Greek *translation* of a Hebrew (or Aramaic) *original*. That is to say, the Greek had a dependent and subservient *linguistic* relationship to its Semitic parent ... [F]or the vast majority of books the linguistic relationship of the Greek to its Semitic parent can best be conceptualized as a Greek interlinear translation of a Hebrew original within a Hebrew-Greek diglot. Be it noted immediately, however, that the terms 'interlinear' and 'diglot' are intended to be nothing more than (or less than) visual aids to help the reader conceptualize the linguistic relationship that is deemed to exist between the Hebrew original and the Greek translation ... NETS is presupposing a Greek translation which aimed at bringing the Greek reader to the Hebrew original rather than bringing the Hebrew original to the Greek reader. Consequently, the Greek's subservience to the Hebrew may be seen as indicative of its aim" (their emphases). See further C. Boyd-Taylor, *Reading between the Lines: The Interlinear Paradigm for Septuagint Studies* (BTS 8; Leuven: Peeters, 2011), and, for LXX-Ps specifically, see Joosten, "The Impact of the Septuagint Pentateuch on the Greek Psalms"; and, more critically, Gauthier, "Examining the 'Pluses' in the Greek Psalter." Note also Pietersma, "Exegesis in the Septuagint: Possibilities and Limits (The Psalter as a Case in Point)."

[44] That is to say that factors such as these could argue against Ulrich's view of LXX-Ps as a secondary recension (a revised translation of an earlier translation), and thus not the presumed original translation of Psalms in Old Greek, perhaps based on a different Hebrew *Vorlage*. See further → 10.3.1.2–3; cf. Aitken, "Psalms," 320, 325.

for the textual criticism of MT-Ps, especially as it appears that the parent text was close to consonantal MT.[45] Differences between LXX-Ps and MT-Ps must be taken quite seriously, therefore,[46] though one must always factor into consideration translation technique as well as matters such as alternative vocalization of the consonantal text, different word or verse divisions, and so forth, and this listing does not yet mention the occasional interpretive translation.[47] Unfortunately, analysis of the full range of the Greek evidence is somewhat limited since LXX-Ps does not yet exist in a fully critical edition (→ 10.3.1.4). Regardless, on a number of rather obvious points, LXX-Ps preserves significant variants that either improve upon MT (e.g., the preservation of the *nun*-stich in LXX-Ps 144 [= ET 145]:13b) and/or add to it as is the case with the inclusion of different superscriptions/titles (see below) or the inclusion of Psalm 151. The presence of Psalm 151, in particular, has often figured in larger developmental and composition-critical analyses of the textual history of Psalms, especially since it is also found in 11QPs[a] and S-Ps (see above and also → 10.1.1.3 below).

The work of the Greek revisers, Theodotion, Aquila, and Symmachus, is also of great worth (→ 10.3.5.3). The first two are marked by a rather formal equivalence technique, often translating each word in the source with a Greek equivalent and in the same word order of the source. Symmachus is less formal and more sense-based, though here too an attempt is made frequently to preserve the word order of the source text. Even so, Symmachus is freer than Theodotion and Aquila insofar as he incorporates some haggadic elements into the translation (→ 10.3.5.3).

10.1.1.3 Syriac and Aramaic Versions

It appears that S-Ps (→ 10.3.4) was translated from a Hebrew text that predated both V-Ps (→ 10.3.7) and T-Ps (→ 10.3.3), since these latter stand closer to MT as evidenced by, for example, loss of the *nun*-stich in Psalm 145 (v. 13).[48] LXX, LXX[mss], 11QPs[a], and S-Ps all contain the missing stich: נאמן אלוהים בדבריו וחסיד בכול מעשיו "God is trustworthy in all his words, and faithful in all his deeds."

The textual tradition of the Peshitta generally speaking is Christian (→ 1.3.4), but the specific identity of the translators is not entirely certain (→ 10.3.4.1), with some scholars arguing that the translators were Jewish converts who embraced Christianity.[49] This theory has the advantage of explaining data that appear to reflect a Jewish origin (above all, favoring a Hebrew parent text) as well as the data that reflect a Christian context and influence. It remains possible, of course, that the latter aspects are traces of a Christian reviser(s) and so not necessarily the work of the original translator (→ 10.3.4.4).

Despite S-Ps's dependence on a Hebrew *Vorlage*, a point of debate remains the extent of LXX (→ 10.3.1) influence on S-Ps. Earlier scholarship believed that S-Ps was extensively related to, if not dependent upon, the Greek, but more recent work has argued for direct translation from a Hebrew text, though it may be that the translation followed LXX at some points and, at others went its own way.[50] Several scholars have argued that Greek readings entered the tradition in the course of S-Ps's transmission, which would mean they have little or nothing to do with the original translation.[51] Whatever the case, S-Ps is fairly free in translation approach and frequently accommodates to its context, harmonizes, and/or assimilates (→ 10.3.4.5). This free approach means that S-Ps can only be used cautiously as a witness to its Hebrew *Vorlage*, despite the fact that it seems to be based on such a parent text (see above and → 10.3.4.6). That is, differences from MT-Ps need not mean that the *Vorlage* of S-Ps was different, but may stem from

---

[45] → 10.3.1.4; Aitken, "Psalms," 327.
[46] Cf., e.g., Kraus, *Psalms 1–59*, 15 on LXX deserving "strong recognition in the process of reconstructing the hypothetical original text."
[47] See Aitken, "Psalms," 325.
[48] → 10.3.4.1. For Psalms in the Syro-Hexapla, → 10.1.1.4, → 10.4.4.
[49] → 10.3.4.4; see further, Weitzman, *The Syriac Version*.
[50] → 10.3.4.3; Weitzman, "The Peshitta Psalter."
[51] → 10.3.4.3; see Lund, "The Influence of the Septuagint on the Psalter"; Carbajosa, *The Character of the Syriac Version of Psalms*.

translation technique or reflect the translator's exegesis. A different situation may obtain in those cases where S-Ps agrees with LXX-Ps or other ancient versions against MT-Ps (→ 10.2.2).[52]

A famous aspect of S-Ps is the presence of several additional non-MT psalms, specifically, the inclusion of Psalms 151–155 in some manuscripts of S-Ps. However, the significance of these compositions should not be overestimated. Psalm 151, for instance, does not appear in Peshitta manuscripts prior to the tenth century C.E. It appears to enter the tradition through the Syro-Hexaplaric (Syh) version (→ 10.4.4).[53] Indeed, all five "Syriac Apocryphal Psalms" are found in only one twelfth century biblical manuscript (S[12t4]), and, after that, only in later manuscripts of the fourteenth century and beyond.[54] The history of the five apocryphal psalms is, therefore, ultimately just "a short footnote" in the story of Psalms in Syriac.[55]

T-Ps (→ 10.3.3) is hard to date and the first extant work to quote extensively from it comes from 1102 C.E. (→ 10.3.3.2). A reference to Rome and Constantinople in T-Ps 108:11 would suggest a *terminus ad quem* of 476 C.E., but that may hold true only for the translation of that particular psalm, since it is probable that T-Ps contains material from more than one period (→ 10.3.3.2). If that is the case, it becomes possible that portions of T-Ps could well pre-date the fifth century C.E., though it seems just as likely that T-Ps is a product of the fifth century C.E. or thereafter, and, again, the date(s) of the translation(s) may not be uniform if pieces come from different periods.[56]

Scholars deem T-Ps to be a fairly literal translation from a text similar to MT that was expanded subsequently in various ways (→ 10.3.3.6).[57] Not surprisingly, there are also paraphrastic and expansionistic segments in the translation that draw from midrashic and haggadic traditions (see, e.g., T-Ps 18; T-Ps 68; → 10.3.3.4).[58] Another notable feature of T-Ps is the double translation of particular verses (e.g., T-Pss 76:11; 77:11; 78:64; 88:3; 110:1) that preserve two different renderings: one literal and one free/paraphrastic, or where both are rather free (→ 10.3.3.4). While it is possible that some readings in T-Ps could reflect a different Hebrew *Vorlage*, most of these instances may be explained by mechanical errors such as graphic confusion or metathesis (cf. → 10.3.3.6). Instances where T-Ps agrees with LXX-Ps and S-Ps against MT-Ps are a different matter, though even some of these may be the result of different vocalizations or, again, graphic confusion (→ 10.3.3.6). So, while in a few instances T-Ps may suggest that it was at these points translated from a *Vorlage* that is different from MT, these instances are truly few in number[59] and even here a different *Vorlage* is by no means certain or the only possible explanation. Indeed, it is probably more reasonable to posit alternative reasons for these renderings than to imagine an entirely different *Vorlage* (cf. → 10.3.3.6).

10.1.1.4 Other Versions

Apart from S-Ps (→ 10.3.4), which appears to be translated directly from a Hebrew text – though not without some degree of Greek influence (see above) – other versions of Psalms are largely daughter translations of the Greek.[60] This holds true, obviously, for the Syro-Hexapla (→ 10.4.4), the Syriac translation of the fifth column of Origen's Hexapla (→ 10.3.5), but is also true for Cop-Ps (→ 10.4.2) and Georg-Ps (→ 10.4.6), both of which follow the LXX-Ps numbering system and thus include Psalm 151 (→ 10.4.2.1 and → 10.4.6.3, respectively). While dependent on LXX-Ps (→ 10.3.1), later versions of Psalms sometimes bear evidence of

---

[52] → 10.3.4.6; see further, Carbajosa, *The Character of the Syriac Version of Psalms*.

[53] → 10.3.4.6; cf. van Rooy, "The Psalms in Early Syriac Tradition," 548–49.

[54] → 12.3.4.6; see van Rooy, "The Psalms in Early Syriac Tradition," 549.

[55] van Rooy, "The Psalms in Early Syriac Tradition," 549.

[56] → 10.3.3.2; see Edwards, *Exegesis in the Targum of the Psalms*.

[57] Stec, "The Aramaic Psalter."

[58] See further Edwards, "The Targum of Psalms."

[59] Edwards, *Exegesis in the Targum of the Psalms*, lists only two.

[60] See, e.g., the essays collected in Aejmelaeus and Quast (eds.), *Der Septuaginta-Psalter und seine Tochterübersetzungen*.

being related to other traditions as well, especially s-Ps. So, for example, both LXX-Ps and s-Ps appear to underlie Arabic psalters (→ 10.4.8) and Arm-Ps (→ 10.4.5.2).[61] To be sure, each of the daughter translations have their own textual histories, some of which can be complex and elaborate. Four examples illustrate the point: 1) The text of Georg-Ps is quite fluid into the tenth century C.E. (→ 10.4.6.3); 2) Arm-Ps gives evidence of memory variants from pre-existing Syriac translations of Psalms, despite the dependence of Arm-Ps on the Greek (→ 10.4.5.1); 3) Given its importance in Ethiopic Christianity (see above), the Psalter in Eth-Ps has a rich textual and reception history beyond its dependence on LXX-Ps (→ 10.4.3.4); 4) Finally, the later, daughter translations are frequently marked by religious tendencies. So, as one example among many, Cop-Ps has a Christianizing plus in Ps 95:10: "the Lord reigns *from the tree*" (ἀπὸ τοῦ ξύλου).[62]

A notable exception that stands outside of direct genetic dependence from the Greek is Jerome's late fourth-century *iuxta Hebraeos* translation (PsH; → 10.3.7), the third version of the Psalter produced by this early Christian father. In it, he sought to return to the original Hebrew and so PsH does not include Psalm 151, though the Greek tradition of numbering the other 150 psalms prevails in PsH.[63] Even in PsH, there is evidence that Jerome utilized previous translations, including LXX/Old Latin (→ 10.4.1), and PsH also shows influence from Aquila and Symmachus, and perhaps also Theodotion (→ 10.3.5), though the last listed is not as clear (→ 10.3.7.3.1–2). Generally speaking, PsH is more literal than his earlier Gallican Psalter (PsG), even as PsH also manifests greater concern than PsG for good Latin style (→ 10.3.7.4.3). Not surprisingly, PsH eliminates additions from LXX-Ps that are preserved in PsG, with Psalm 151 being the most obvious of these. PsH generally reflects the consonantal text of MT (→ 10.3.7.5.1–2) and usually follows the vocalization reflected therein as well (→ 10.3.7.5.3).

10.1.2 Arrangement of the Psalms

The arrangement of the psalms may be examined in two primary ways: The first way is the sequencing of the individual psalmic compositions, which is one of the more fascinating issues in the textual history of Psalms (→ 10.1.2.1; → 10.2.1). A somewhat independent, but not unrelated, matter that can be treated as a corollary to psalm sequencing is the issue of psalm titles/superscriptions (→ 10.1.2.2) The second matter of arrangement concerns how the psalms are presented in manuscripts, whether stichometrically, as lined poetry, or not (→ 10.1.2.2).

10.1.2.1 Psalm Sequencing

Alternative sequencing has been mentioned several times in the preceding discussion, not only in the case of the Dead Sea manuscripts, which often present psalms in drastically different orders (→ 10.1.1.1; → 10.2.1; see further → 10.2.3), but also in the case of LXX-Ps (→ 10.3.1), which divides and/or combines compositions to achieve a different presentation than MT-Ps (→ 10.1.1.2; see further → 10.2.2.1.3), and this is not yet to mention those texts and traditions (e.g., 11QPs^a, LXX-Ps, and s-Ps) that contain additional, non-(proto-)MT-Ps content. The various orderings of MT's 150 psalms attested at Qumran are, to this point at least, not attested outside that site and, even if they were more widely distributed at one time, these alternative sequences have not survived and were replaced by the ordering now familiar in MT-Ps. That process must have taken place at some point prior to the medieval Hebrew manuscripts that attest to a rather stable text. What had not stabilized by the medieval period, however, was the matter of specific psalmic delimitation – namely, what text belongs to which psalm – and, as a result, the question of how many individual psalms belong to the Psalter. Indeed, the earliest extant Hebrew manuscript that numbers the individual psalms, MT^L (ca. 1008/1009 C.E.) contains only 149 (= קמ״ט)

---

[61] See also Cox, "The Armenian Version and the Text of the Old Greek Psalter."

[62] → 10.4.2.2, see further Ralhfs, *Psalmi cum Odis*, 30–32.

[63] → 10.4.1.2; see Bogaert, "Le psautier latin des origines au XIIe siècle"; Salmon, *Les "Tituli Psalmorum" des Manuscrits latins*.

psalms, not 150, since it combines Psalms 114 and 115 and numbers them as a single composition (קיד = 114).

Yarchin has authored several studies on the numeration of psalms in the MT tradition, examining several hundred Hebrew manuscripts, texts from the Cairo Genizah, and relevant editions from the incunabula (→ 10.2.2.1.3; for medieval Masoretic manuscripts, see → 10–20.1). Yarchin's work shows a high degree of fluidity in numbering the psalms – a fluidity that endures until the Rabbinic Bible in its first (*RB1; 1517 C.E.) and especially in its second (*RB2; 1525 C.E.) editions. It is only at this point in the sixteenth century that the tradition becomes fixed with regard to psalmic numbering. That is to say that, while the text type of the individual psalms and their order is stable in these manuscripts (granting the expected range of microvariant variation), the way in which the compositions are "counted" – that is, combined or divided – varies widely with some manuscripts yielding collections that contain only 143 psalms, with others having 154, with still others having far more (→ 10.2.2.1.3). Ginsburg, for example, has collated manuscripts that number as many as 170 psalms, with Sanders mentioning "ancient Psalters with up to 200 psalms."[64] These high counts are, again, not produced by the addition of new psalmic compositions but by dividing or (re)combining those psalms that are already present and sequenced in MT-Ps. So, for example, the highest counts are created by, among other things, giving each individual acrostic stanza of Psalm 119 its own number. However these variations are achieved, the main takeaways from Yarchin's work are three: 1) "MT-150" is something of a misnomer, since 2) the MT-Ps tradition frequently includes more or less than 150 compositions, a situation that remains fluid until 3) the First and Second Rabbinic Bibles, after which point it is appropriate to speak of a *textus receptus* configuration of 150 psalms (Yarchin's "TR-150") as now known and represented in, for example, the *Biblia Hebraica* series, though ironically not evident in the base text of that series, MT[L] itself. In Yarchin's words, "TR-150 may have been the Hebrew psalter-configuration scribes *copied* most, [but] it is not the psalter that people *used* the most" because "TR-150 was never the single authoritative shape for *sefer tehillim* until the modern era of printed editions, ushered in by the sixteenth-century Rabbinic Bibles."[65]

Similar fluidity exists in other versions of the Psalms, though not to the same degree,[66] except for the somewhat related but ultimately rather different issue of variant sequences found in the Qumran Psalms scrolls. Whatever the case, data like these should have significant impact on discussions of the composition and present shape of the book of Psalms, especially in its "TR-150" form but also for any and all of its putative Ur-forms (cf. → 10.2.2.5). The scholarly discussion of the "shape and shaping" of the Psalms – or of the book's compositional logic – is a vibrant one but one that often proceeds without sufficient engagement with the full range of the text-critical data.[67] To be sure, the "Qumran Psalms Hypothesis," and especially the work of Wilson, has laid great emphasis on 11QPs[a] and its potential impact on the development of Books IV–V of the Psalter (Psalms 90–150), but divergent ar-

---

[64] Ginsburg, *Introduction*, 725 (see also ibid., 777) and Sanders, "The Modern History of the Qumran Psalms Scroll," 401, respectively.

[65] Yarchin, "Authoritative Shape," 363 (his emphases). For additional discussion, see → 10.2.2.1.3.

[66] See the various psalm combinations listed in → 10.2.2.1.3 and, for evidence from Qumran, note the following two manuscripts: 1) 4QPs[o] (→ 10.2.1.6.1), which may treat Psalms 114 and 115 as one psalm (so also MT[L], MT[mss], LXX, Theodotion, S and Jerome) and which may have divided Ps 116:1–9 from Ps 116:10 ff. (as also LXX, Jerome); and 2) 4QPs[a] (→ 10.2.1.4.1.1), which may have divided each of Psalms 36 and 56 into two different compositions and which apparently treated Psalms 38 → 71 as a single composition (→ 10.2.3.4.1).

[67] See, e.g., Witte, "The Psalter," 535, summarizing the extensive work done especially by Hossfeld and Zenger, *Die Psalmen I*; Hossfeld and Zenger, *Psalms 2*; Hossfeld and Zenger, *Psalms 3*. See further, McCann (ed.), *The Shape and Shaping of the Psalter*; deClaissé-Walford (ed.), *The Shape and Shaping of the Book of Psalms*; and → 10.2.2.5. As one example, when Hossfeld and Zenger (*Psalms 2*, 4) speak of the "addition of the superscription 'Of David' or 'Of David, when he ...'" to their hypothetical early form of *Psalms 52–68, they cite no empirical support for such additions.

rangement/sequencing in other textual traditions beyond 11QPsª and beyond Qumran, and/or that is attested in Books I–III (Psalms 1–89) is often completely ignored (→ 10.2.3.7).[68] This is unfortunate because Lange has demonstrated that resequencing seems to be a characteristic element of the textual transmission of poetic texts in ancient times.[69] Such resequencing or "reshaping," according to Yarchin, is probably "for ritual reading purposes."[70] This is to say that the occasion of reading or, put differently, the function of the manuscript, directly impacts the shape and reshaping of the macro-structure of the Psalms (→ 10.2.2.1).

A final point that deserves to be underscored, especially as it leads directly to the next topic to be discussed, is that these matters of arrangement bear directly and profoundly on the interpretation of the psalms. Are Psalms 114 and 115 two distinct psalms or one? Is Psalm 116 one psalm or two? Proper delimitation is crucial in interpreting a poem lest one end up interpreting not one integral composition but one-and-a-half or even two (or more!). Numbering of the psalms in the Hebrew tradition is sometimes associated with Karaite influence but, regardless, it should be obvious that numbering or other delineating devices plays an important role for liturgical and study purposes. Numbering or, more generally, delimitation is necessary at least in part to disambiguate among highly similar even formulaic compositions (or expressions), which is precisely the situation one encounters in religio-liturgical poetry like the psalms.

10.1.2.2 Psalm Titles/Superscriptions

A factor in proper delimitation is the presence or absence of superscriptions or titles in the psalms. The absence of these markers makes delimitation far more difficult.[71] The presence of titles is widespread throughout many of the psalms though the meaning of many of the terms found therein (e.g., מִזְמוֹר/*mizmôr* "praise song (?)"; מִכְתָּם/*miktām* (uncertain meaning); etc., even לְדָוִד/*lĕdāwid*, "of/for/by/concerning David") remains elusive.[72] These superscriptions differ widely in the versional evidence of Psalms. Most scholars believe the titles found in MT-Ps are secondary additions of one sort or another and thus not integral to the compositions themselves.[73] This opinion is bolstered by the fact that the versions often have altogether different titles.[74] This tendency is most pronounced in S-Ps (→ 10.3.4), which attests to a large number of differences in the superscriptions, most of which reflect late and Christianized departures from the Hebrew text.[75] Kraus may go too far in regarding the titles, even in MT-Ps, as "untrustworthy distortions,"[76] but it is nevertheless clear that the superscriptions simply did not enjoy the same authority as the words of the individual psalm compositions themselves, and so later tradents felt free to alter

---

[68] The data that are used are also sometimes overread. So, e.g., Wilson's conclusion that 11QPsª was organized by principles similar to those underlying Books IV and V of MT-Ps does not prove much about 11QPsª and certainly does not support Flint's view "that the Great Psalms Scroll contains the latter part of an edition of the Book of Psalms and is part of a true Davidic Psalter" (Flint, "Unrolling," 236). Also the existence of 4QPsª or other manuscripts that attest to the first part of the Psalter once again does not necessarily support "the view that 11QPsª bears witness to a Psalter that was stabilized over time in two distinct stages" (Flint, "Unrolling," 236).

[69] Lange, "Collecting."

[70] Yarchin, "Psalms Collections," 784.

[71] Prinsloo, "Unit Delimitation," 251.

[72] See Kraus, *Psalms 1–59*, 21–32 for a detailed discussion of no less than twenty-five titles.

[73] Kraus, *Psalms 1–59*, 31–32; Aitken, "Psalms," 327; Pietersma, "David in the Greek Psalter"; Dorival, "Autour des titres des Psaumes"; see also Flint, *Dead Sea Psalms Scrolls*, 117; and further, 146–48, 222–26, where he attempts to tie the use of superscriptions to stabilization.

[74] See the previous note and further, e.g.: 1) for LXX-Ps, Swete, **Introduction*, 250–51; Driver, **Introduction*, 348–55; and **NETS*, 545: "there is reason to believe that the superscriptions grew in a piecemeal, atomistic fashion"; 2) for Georg-Ps, → 10.4.6.2 and M. Shanidze, "The Old Georgian Psalter and the Titles of the Psalms," in *Textual Research on the Psalms and Gospels: Papers from the Tbilisi Colloquium on the Editing and History of Biblical Manuscripts* (eds. C.-B. Amphoux, J.K. Elliott, with B. Outtier; Leiden: Brill, 2012), 19–41; and 3) → 10.4.3.5 for Eth-Ps, which attests to two different sets of titles, an older and a newer (see also Schneider, "Les titres" and Pederson, *Traditional Ethiopian Exegesis*, 19–29).

[75] → 10.3.4.2; see van Rooy, "The Psalms in Early Syriac Tradition." One of the key figures is Theodore of Mopsuestia.

[76] Kraus, *Psalms 1–59*, 31.

them. Therefore, the versional evidence for the titles has as much to do with the reception history of Psalms as it does the putative original form of the psalms (and/or their titles) themselves. And this judgment holds true for MT-Ps (→ 10.2.2) as much as it does for LXX-Ps (→ 10.3.1) or S-Ps.[77] To be sure, there can be little doubt that the freedom enjoyed by the versions vis-à-vis the superscriptions, coupled with the important role that titles may play as unit markers, contributed to the various alternative combinations/divisions and arrangements/sequences that are evident in the textual history of Psalms.

10.1.2.3 Stichometry

The nature of the psalms as *poetry* occasioned several conundrums in the textual history of the book, though, insofar as many other Old Testament compositions are poetic, several of these problems are not limited to Psalms. So, for example, one signal poetic aspect, namely, parallelism – the way two or three (rarely more) lines relate to each other in Hebrew poetry – occasionally caused problems in the versions since it forced translators to decide what equivalent (or non-equivalent) words they would employ to mimic (or not mimic) the phenomenon (→ 10.3.7.4.3 on Jerome).

While parallelism is an important marker of Hebrew poetry it is certainly not the only one. Hebrew poetry, as all poetry, depends on the line,[78] but what is fascinating is that the manuscripts do not always represent the psalms in stichometric fashion.[79] Indeed, running or prose format is by far the standard presentation.[80] Special (poetic) formatting of some sort is found in the following fifteen psalm texts from the Judean Desert (→ 10.2.1): 1QPs^a (only Psalm 119 in this scroll is so written, the others are in prose/running format), 4QPs^b, 4QPs^c, 4QPs^d (parts of Psalm 104 are so written; other parts of the psalm and other psalms in the scroll are written in prose/running format), 4QPs^g, 4QPs^h, 4QPs^l, 4QPs^w, 5QPs, 8QPs, 11QPs^a (Psalm 119 only), 11QPs^b (Psalm 119 only), 5/6ḤevPs, MasPs^a, and MasPs^b. No less than twenty-three Psalm texts from these sites are presented in prose/running format: 1QPs^a (all psalms but Psalm 119), 1QPs^b, 1QPs^c, 3QPs, 4QPs^a, 4QPs^d (col. iii 5 onwards), 4QPs^e, 4QPs^f, 4QPs^j, 4QPs^k, 4QPs^m, 4QPs^n, 4QPs^o, 4QPs^p, 4QPs^q, 4QPs^r, 4QPs^s, 4QPs^u, 6QpapPs(?), 11QPs^a (all psalms except Psalm 119), 11QPs^b (all psalms except Psalm 119), 11QPs^c, and 11QPs^d.[81] The significance of these mixed data (note that several scrolls manifest both types of formatting)[82] is not entirely clear. The mixed presentation obviously proves that "the tradition of stichographic writing was not fixed [and/]or that different traditions were in vogue during different periods."[83] But, beyond that, does stichometric presentation recognize the poetic nature of the composition[84] and/or signal liturgical function, with running format indicating otherwise? If so, that judgment cannot be a totalizing one since some manuscripts present certain psalms in stichometric format with others

---

[77] Cf. Kraus, *Psalms 1–59*, 31–32: "Historical-critical research since the end of the 18th century has discovered more and more that the instructions above the psalms do not provide an adequate introduction for understanding the songs ... What, for instance, have Psalms 32; 45; 78; and 89 in common, all of which have the title משכיל? Basically, nothing."

[78] See F.W. Dobbs-Allsopp, *On Biblical Poetry* (Oxford: Oxford University Press, 2015), 29–42; and J.B. Couey, *Reading the Poetry of First Isaiah: The Most Perfect Model of the Prophetic Poetry* (Oxford: Oxford University Press, 2015), 21–54.

[79] For stichometry in the Hebrew, Greek, and Latin Psalters, see also Barthélemy, *Critique textuelle 2005*, xli–xliv; Dobbs-Allsopp, *On Biblical Poetry*, 32–38.

[80] Dobbs-Allsopp, *On Biblical Poetry*, 36: "[O]n all current evidence, it appears that poetic texts (verse) from the biblical period, like their prosaic counterparts, were written normatively in a running format."

[81] See Tov, *Scribal Practices*, 168–69; Dobbs-Allsopp, *On Biblical Poetry*, 29–34; Dobbs-Allsopp, "Space, Line, and the Written Biblical Poem in Texts from the Judean Desert," in *Puzzling Out the Past: Studies in Northwest Semitic Languages and Literatures in Honor of Bruce Zuckerman* (eds. M.J. Lundberg, S. Fine, and W.T. Pitard; CHANE 55; Leiden: Brill, 2012), 19–61; and Flint, "Psalms and Psalters," 235. Note also the stichometric presentation of Psalm 122 in 4Q522.

[82] Tov, *Scribal Practices*, 167: "All biblical units for which special stichographic arrangements are preserved among the Qumran texts, have also been preserved in Qumran copies which do not display any special arrangement."

[83] Tov, *Scribal Practices*, 167.

[84] Tov, *Scribal Practices*, 167.

presenting the same psalms in running formats. Conversely, does prose formatting mean that the scribes did not always deem poetic compositions to be poetic? Or is it simply that poetic compositions need not be stichometrically presented because the innate aspects of poetry that reveal it to be such (i.e., specific markers of verse) are present in the text regardless of how it is written?[85] For his part, and perhaps not surprisingly, Flint takes the different formats of the Psalms scrolls as proof that there was more than one type of Psalter at Qumran and that these had varying liturgical functions.[86] On the other side of the debate, Talmon thinks that the special formatting in a manuscript such as MasPs[b] – formatting that is "even more accentuated in the columnar structure of MT" – strengthens the idea that a scroll like 11QPs[a] "is a copy of an extra-biblical compilation of songs which the Qumran covenanters used in their prayer service, rather than a copy of the biblical book of Psalms."[87] But, again, the evidence of varied formatting seems to preclude a definitive conclusion per Talmon, even as it may have little to do with text or Psalter type per Flint.

10.1.3 Conclusion

Much more would need to be said to provide even a minimally adequate overview of the rich, vast, and deep textual history of Psalms. Even so, as noted above and in other entries on Psalms in *THB*, most scholars believe that the individual psalms are relatively stable in text-critical perspective and this point, coupled with the scholarly observation that the versions seem, in the main, dependent on a text that is similar to consonantal MT-Ps means that there is less textual variation in Psalms than in many other texts from the Hebrew Bible. It also means that what is now preserved in MT-Ps more broadly (→ 10.2.2) is text-critically stable and thus useful as a good starting point for subsequent textual analysis.[88] However, this judgment should be immediately qualified in several ways. First and foremost, it should not be overstated and must not in any way minimize the complexity of the manuscript finds from the Judean Desert. It is those finds – and the pluriformity of Psalms texts reflected therein – far more than the versional evidence proper, that comprise one of the more vexed questions in the textual history of Psalms. Furthermore, one should also not underestimate the fluidity that obtains and endures in the matter of psalm arrangement, division, and numbering, not only between LXX-Ps (→ 10.3.1) and MT-Ps, but even within the Hebrew tradition itself well into the sixteenth century CE.

Briggs and Briggs, writing in the early twentieth century, were surely correct, then, when they stated that the prevalence of variants – and, we might add now with knowledge unavailable to them at that time, of both micro- and macro-varieties – "make[s] it evident that even 𝔥 [MT-Ps] ... is as truly an *interpretation* of an older text [of Psalms] as 𝔊 and other ancient Vrss."[89] And so it is the case, they continue, that "[t]he text of the Psalter is one thing, the text of the original Pss. is another thing."[90] The full range of the textual evidence may be of assistance here and there toward recovering or reconstructing "the original Psalms," or, perhaps it may afford us access to early (earlier) forms of the various Psalters in different versions (Hebrew, Old Greek, Old Latin, etc.). But the work of textual

---

[85] See Dobbs-Allsopp, *On Biblical Poetry*, 36: "written poetic texts are readable as 'verse' even in the absence of ... spatial cues ... [T]he poetic line has rhythmic, sonic, and even syntactic structure such that its shape is ultimately apprehensible no matter the matter of presentation." Cf. Tov, *Scribal Practices*, 172 on MasPs[b] ii 22–24 (Ps 83:9–11) where "the stichographic arrangement ... [actually] goes against the meaning of the stichs themselves."

[86] See, e.g., Flint, "Unrolling," 244.

[87] Talmon, "Fragments of a Psalms Scroll from Masada, MPs[b]," 324. Cf. Tov, *Scribal Practices*, 170 on the naturalness of the assumption "that the texts which do *not* reflect such a [special poetic] layout, especially the Psalms scrolls, are not Scripture in the regular sense of the word." Tov himself does not support this assumption (see Tov, *Scribal Practices*, 170; cf. p. 168 on 11QPs[a] proper).

[88] Cf. P.K. McCarter, *Textual Criticism: Recovering the Text of the Hebrew Bible* (GBS; Philadelphia: Fortress, 1986), 92, who states that MT-Ps is in "fair condition," a judgment that is probably too cautious.

[89] Briggs and Briggs, *Psalms*, 1.liii (emphasis added).

[90] Briggs and Briggs, *Psalms*, 1.xxxiv.

criticism is not (or *should not* be) only about the "earliest" or "original" text form(s). The textual history of the book of Psalms provides far more data to interpret than just those pertaining to early forms or stages of its text. That textual history also begins to expose us to the lengthy life, history, and reception of Psalms from earliest times up to the present day.[91]

Aejmelaeus, A., "Characterizing Criteria for the Characterization of the Septuagint Translators: Experimenting on the Greek Psalter," in *The Old Greek Psalter: Studies in Honour of Albert Pietersma* (eds. R.J.V. Hiebert, C.E. Cox, and P.J. Gentry; JSOTSup 332; Sheffield: Sheffield Academic Press, 2001), 54–73.

Aejmelaeus, A. and U. Quast (eds.), *Der Septuaginta-Psalter und seine Tochterübersetzungen: Symposium in Göttingen 1997* (MSU 24; Göttingen: Vandenhoeck & Ruprecht, 2000).

Aitken, J.K., "Psalms," in *The T & T Clark Companion to the Septuagint* (ed. J.K. Aitken; London: Bloomsbury, 2015), 320–34.

Amphous, C.-B., J.K. Elliott, and B. Outtier, *Textual Research on the Psalms and Gospels: Papers from the Tbilisi Colloquium on the Editing and History of Biblical Manuscripts* (NovTSup 142; Leiden: Brill, 2012).

Auwers, J.-M., *La composition littéraire du Psautier: Un état de la question* (CahRB 46; Paris: Gabalda, 2000).

Barnes, W.E. (ed.), *The Peshitta Psalter According to the West Syrian Text: Edited with an Apparatus Criticus* (Cambridge: Cambridge University Press, 1904).

Barthélemy, **Critique textuelle 2005*.

Barthélemy, *Interim Report, Vol. 3: *Poetical Books*, 163–442.

---

[91] For some of this history, see S. Gillingham, *Psalms Through the Centuries*, Vol. 1 (London: Wiley-Blackwell, 2008); S. Gillingham, *A Journey of Two Psalms: The Reception of Psalms 1 and 2 in Jewish and Christian Tradition* (Oxford: Oxford University Press, 2013); S. Gillingham (ed.), *Jewish and Christian Approaches to the Psalms: Conflict and Convergence* (Oxford: Oxford University Press, 2013); W.L. Holladay, *The Psalms through Three Thousand Years: Prayerbook of a Cloud of Witnesses* (Minneapolis: Fortress, 1993); H.W. Attridge and M.E. Fassler (eds.), *Psalms in Community: Jewish and Christian Textual, Liturgical, and Artistic Traditions* (SBLSymS 25; Atlanta: SBL, 2003); S. Moyise and M.J.J. Menken (eds.), *The Psalms in the New Testament* (London: T & T Clark International, 2004); and E. Werner, *The Sacred Bridge: Liturgical Parallels in Synagogue and Early Church* (New York: Schocken, 1970), 128–66.

Bernstein, M., "A Jewish Reading of Psalms: Some Observations on the Method of the Aramaic Targums," in *The Book of Psalms: Composition and Reception* (eds. P.W. Flint and P.D. Miller; VTSup 99; Leiden: Brill, 2005), 476–504.

Bogaert, P.M., "Le psautier latin des origines au XIIe siècle," in *Der Septuaginta-Psalter und seine Tochterübersetzungen: Symposium in Göttingen 1997* (eds. A. Aejmelaeus and U. Quast; MSU 24; Göttingen: Vandenhoeck & Ruprecht, 2000), 51–81.

Briggs, C.A. and E.G. Briggs, *A Critical and Exegetical Commentary on the Book of Psalms* (2 vols.; ICC; Edinburgh: T & T Clark, 1906–1907).

Brütsch, M., *Israels Psalmen in Qumran: Ein textarchäologischer Beitrag zur Entstehung des Psalters* (BWANT 193; Stuttgart: Kohlhammer, 2010).

Caloz, M., *Étude sur la LXX origénienne du psautier: les relations entre les leçons des psaumes du manuscrit Coislin 44, les Fragments des Hexaples et le texte du psautier Gallican* (OBO 19; Göttingen: Vandenhoeck & Ruprecht, 1978).

Capelle, P., *Le texte du psautier latin en Afrique* (CLB 4; Rome: 1913).

Carbajosa, I., "11QPs[a] and the Hebrew Vorlage of the Peshitta Psalter," *Aramaic Studies* 2 (2004): 3–24.

Carbajosa, I., *The Character of the Syriac Version of Psalms: A Study of Psalms 90–150 in the Peshitta* (Monographs of the Peshitta Institute Leiden 17; Leiden: Brill, 2008).

Cox, C., "The Armenian Version and the Text of the Old Greek Psalter," in *Der Septuaginta-Psalter und seine Tochterübersetzungen: Symposium in Göttingen 1997* (eds. A. Aejmelaeus and U. Quast; MSU 24; Göttingen: Vandenhoeck & Ruprecht, 2000), 174–247.

Dahmen, U., *Psalmen- und Psalter-Rezeption im Frühjudentum: Rekonstruktion, Textbestand, Struktur und Pragmatik der Psalmenrolle 11QPs[a] aus Qumran* (STDJ 47; Leiden: Brill, 2003).

deClaissé-Walford, N.L. (ed.), *The Shape and Shaping of the Book of Psalms: The Current State of Scholarship* (SBLAIL 20; Atlanta: SBL, 2014).

De Rossi, *1784–1788, 4:1–88, 238–40; 5:95–11.

Díez Merino, L., *Targum de Salmos: Edición Príncipe del Ms. Villa-Amil n. 5 de Alfonso de Zamora* (Bibliotheca Hispana Biblica 6; Madrid: Consejo Superior de Investigaciones Científicas, Instituto "Francisco Suárez," 1982).

*DJD IV.

Dorival, G., "Autour des titres des Psaumes," *RSR* 73 (1999): 165–76.

Edwards, T.M., "The Targum of Psalms," in *Interpreting the Psalms: Issues and Approaches* (eds. P.S. Johnston and D.G. Firth; Downers Grove: IVP Academic, 2005), 279–94.

Edwards, T., *Exegesis in the Targum of the Psalms: The Old, the New, and the Rewritten* (Gorgias Dissertations 28; Piscataway: Gorgias Press, 2007).

Field, *Hexapla*, 2.83–305.

Flint, P.W., *The Dead Sea Psalms Scrolls and the Book of Psalms* (STDJ 17; Leiden: Brill, 1997).

Flint, P.W., "Variant Readings of the Dead Sea Psalms Scrolls against the Massoretic Text and the Septuagint Psalter," in *Der Septuaginta-Psalter und seine Tochterübersetzungen: Symposium in Göttingen 1997* (eds. A. Aejmelaeus and U. Quast; MSU 24; Göttingen: Vandenhoeck & Ruprecht, 2000), 337–66.

Flint, P.W., "Psalms and Psalters in the Dead Sea Scrolls," in *The Bible and the Dead Sea Scrolls: The Princeton Symposium on the Dead Sea Scrolls* (3 vols.; ed. J.H. Charlesworth; Waco: Baylor University Press, 2006), 1.233–72.

Flint, P.W., "Unrolling the Dead Sea Psalms Scrolls," in *The Oxford Handbook of the Psalms* (ed. W.P. Brown; Oxford: Oxford University Press, 2014), 229–50.

Flint, P.W. and P.D. Miller (eds.), *The Book of Psalms: Composition and Reception* (VTSup 99; Leiden: Brill, 2005).

Gauthier, R.X., "Examining the 'Pluses' in the Greek Psalter: A Study of the Septuagint Translation *qua* Communication," in *Septuagint and Reception: Essays Prepared for the Association for the Study of the Septuagint in South Africa* (ed. J. Cook; VTSup 127; Leiden: Brill, 2009), 45–76.

Gentry, P.J., "The Greek Psalter and the καίγε Tradition: Methodological Questions," in *The Old Greek Psalter: Studies in Honour of Albert Pietersma* (eds. R.J.V. Hiebert, C.E. Cox, and P.J. Gentry; JSOTSup 332; Sheffield: Sheffield Academic Press, 2001), 74–97.

Goins, S., "Jerome's Psalters," in *The Oxford Handbook of the Psalms* (ed. W.P. Brown; Oxford: Oxford University Press, 2014), 185–98.

Goshen-Gottstein, M.H., "The Psalms Scroll (11QPs^a): A Problem of Canon and Text," *Textus* 5 (1966): 22–33.

Haran, M., "11QPs^a and the Canonical Book of Psalms," in *Minḥah le-Naḥum: Biblical and Other Studies Presented to Nahum M. Sarna in Honour of His 70th Birthday* (eds. M.Z. Brettler and M.A. Fishbane; JSOTSup 154; Sheffield: JSOT Press, 1993), 193–201.

Hiebert, R.J.V., *The "Syrohexaplaric" Psalter* (SBLSCS 27; Atlanta: Scholars Press, 1989).

Hiebert, R.J.V., "The 'Syrohexaplaric' Psalter: Its Text and Textual History," in *Der Septuaginta-Psalter und seine Tochterübersetzungen: Symposium in Göttingen 1997* (eds. A. Aejmelaeus and U. Quast; MSU 24; Göttingen: Vandenhoeck & Ruprecht, 2000), 123–46.

Hiebert, R.J.V., "Syriac Biblical Textual History and the Greek Psalter," in *The Old Greek Psalter: Studies in Honour of Albert Pietersma* (eds. R.J.V. Hiebert, C.E. Cox, and P.J. Gentry; JSOTSup 332; Sheffield: Sheffield Academic Press, 2001), 178–204.

Hiebert, R.J.V., "The Place of the Syriac Versions in the Textual History of the Psalter," in *The Book of Psalms: Composition and Reception* (eds. P.W. Flint and P.D. Miller; VTSup 99; Leiden: Brill, 2005), 505–36.

Hiebert, R.J.V., C.E. Cox, and P.J. Gentry (eds.), *The Old Greek Psalter: Studies in Honour of Albert Pietersma* (JSOTSup 332; Sheffield: Sheffield Academic Press, 2001).

Hossfeld, F.-L. and E. Zenger, *Die Psalmen I: Psalm 1–50* (NEchtB; Würzburg: Echter, 1993).

Hossfeld, F.-L. and E. Zenger, *Psalms 2: A Commentary on Psalms 51–100* (trans. L.M. Maloney; Herm; Minneapolis: Fortress, 2005).

Hossfeld, F.-L. and E. Zenger, *Psalms 3: A Commentary on Psalms 101–150* (trans. L.M. Maloney; Herm; Minneapolis: Fortress, 2011).

Jain, E., *Psalmen oder Psalter? Materielle Rekonstruktion und inhaltliche Undersuchung der Psalmenhandschriften aus der Wüste Juda* (STDJ 109; Leiden: Brill, 2014).

Joosten, J., "The Impact of the Septuagint Pentateuch on the Greek Psalms," in J. Joosten, *Collected Studies on the Septuagint: From Language to Interpretation and Beyond* (FAT 83; Tübingen: Mohr Siebeck, 2012), 147–55.

Kennicott, *1776–1780, 2:307–437 (online at: http://aleph.nli.org.il/nnl/dig/books/bk002093934.html).

Kharanauli, A., "Einführung in die georgische Psalterübersetzung," in *Der Septuaginta-Psalter und seine Tochterübersetzungen: Symposium in Göttingen 1997* (eds. A. Aejmelaeus and U. Quast; MSU 24; Göttingen: Vandenhoeck & Ruprecht, 2000), 248–308.

Knibb, M.A., "The Ethiopic Translation of the Psalms," in *Der Septuaginta-Psalter und seine Tochterübersetzungen: Symposium in Göttingen 1997* (eds. A. Aejmelaeus and U. Quast; MSU 24; Göttingen: Vandenhoeck & Ruprecht, 2000), 107–22.

van der Kooij, A., "On the Place of Origin of the Old Greek of Psalms," *VT* 33 (1983): 67–74.

Kraus, H.-J., *Psalms 1–59: A Commentary* (trans. H.C. Oswald; CC; Minneapolis: Augsburg, 1988).

de Lagarde, P., *Psalterium, Job, Proverbia arabice* (Göttingen: Kaestner, 1876).

Lange, A., "Collecting Psalms in Light of the Dead Sea Scrolls," in *A Teacher for All Generations: Essays in Honor of James C. VanderKam* (2 vols.; eds. E.F. Mason et al.; JSJSup 153; Leiden: Brill, 2012), 1.297–308.

Limburg, J., "Psalms, Book of," *ABD* 5:522–36.

Lund, J.A., "The Influence of the Septuagint on the Peshitta: A Re-evaluation of Criteria in Light of Comparative Study of the Versions in Genesis and Psalms" (PhD diss., The Hebrew University of Jerusalem, 1988).

Marks, J.H., *Der textkritische Wert des Psalterium Hieronymi iuxta Hebraeos* (Winterthur: P.G. Keller, 1956).

McCann, J.C. (ed.), *The Shape and Shaping of the Psalter* (JSOTSup 159; Sheffield: Sheffield Academic Press, 1993).

Mozley, F.W., *The Psalter of the Church: The Septuagint Psalms Compared with the Hebrew: With Various Notes* (Cambridge: Cambridge University Press, 1905).

Pedersen, K.S., *Traditional Ethiopian Exegesis of the Book of Psalms* (Aethiopistische Forschungen 36; Wiesbaden: Harrassowitz, 1995).

Perry, S.G.F. and E. Nestle, *Psalterium Tetraglottum* (London: Williams and Norgate, 1879).

Pietersma, A., "David in the Greek Psalter," *VT* 30 (1980): 213–26.

Pietersma, A., "The Present State of the Critical Text of the Greek Psalter," in *Der Septuaginta-Psalter und seine Tochterübersetzungen: Symposium in Göttingen 1997* (eds. A. Aejmelaeus and U. Quast; MSU 24; Göttingen: Vandenhoeck & Ruprecht, 2000), 12–32.

Pietersma, A., "The Place of Origin of the Old Greek Psalter," in *The World of the Aramaeans: Biblical Studies in Honor of Paul-Eugène Dion* (3 vols.; eds. P.M.M. Daviau, J.W. Wevers, and M. Weigl; JSOTSup 324; Sheffield: Sheffield Academic Press, 2001), 1.252–74.

Pietersma, A., "Septuagintal Exegesis and the Superscriptions of the Greek Psalter," in *The Book of Psalms: Composition and Reception* (eds. P.W. Flint and P.D. Miller; VTSup 99; Leiden: Brill, 2005), 443–75.

Pietersma, A., "Exegesis in the Septuagint: Possibilities and Limits (The Psalter as a Case in Point)," in *Septuagint Research: Issues and Challenges in the Study of the Greek Jewish Scriptures* (eds. W. Kraus and R.G. Wooden; SBLSCS 53; Atlanta: SBL, 2006), 33–45.

Prinsloo, G.T.M., "Unit Delimitation in the Egyptian Hallel (Psalms 113–118): An Evaluation of Different Traditions," in *Unit Delimitation in Biblical Hebrew and Northwest Semitic Literature* (eds. M.C.A. Korpel and J.M. Oesch; Pericope 4; Assen: Van Gorcum, 2003), 232–63.

Rahlfs, A., *Septuaginta-Studien I–III* (2nd ed.; Göttingen: Vandenhoeck & Ruprecht, 1965), 105–360.

Rahlfs, A., *Psalmi cum Odis* (2nd ed.; Septuaginta Vetus Testamentum Graecum 10; Göttingen: Vandenhoeck & Ruprecht, 1967).

van Rooy, H.F., *Studies on the Syriac Apocryphal Psalms* (JSSSup 7; Oxford: Oxford University Press, 1999).

van Rooy, H.F., "The Psalms in Early Syriac Tradition," in *The Book of Psalms: Composition and Reception* (eds. P.W. Flint and P.D. Miller; VTSup 99; Leiden: Brill, 2005), 537–50.

Salmon, P., *Les "Tituli Psalmorum" des Manuscrits latins* (Collectanea Biblica Latina 12; Vatican City: Libreria Vaticana, 1959).

Sanders, J.A., *The Dead Sea Psalms Scroll* (Ithaca: Cornell University Press, 1967).

Sanders, J.A., "The Modern History of the Qumran Psalms Scroll and Canonical Criticism," in *Emanuel: Studies in Hebrew Bible, Septuagint, and Dead Sea Scrolls in Honor of Emanuel Tov* (eds. S.M. Paul et al.; VTSup 94; Brill: Leiden, 2003), 393–411.

Schaper, J., *Eschatology in the Greek Psalter* (WUNT 2.76; Tübingen: Mohr Siebeck, 1995).

Schaper, J., "The Septuagint Psalter," in *The Oxford Handbook of the Psalms* (ed. W.P. Brown; Oxford: Oxford University Press, 2014), 173–84.

Schmuttermayr, G., *Psalm 18 und 2 Samuel 22: Studien zu einem Doppeltext: Probleme der Textkritik und Übersetzung und das Psalterium Pianum* (SANT 25; Munich: Kösel-Verlag, 1971).

Schneider, R., "Les titres des psaumes en éthiopien," in *Mélanges Marcel Cohen* (ed. D. Cohen; The Hague: Mouton, 1970), 424–28.

Segal, M., "The Literary Development of Psalm 151: A New Look at the Septuagint Version," *Textus* 21 (2002): 139–58.

Skehan, P.W., E. Ulrich, and P.W. Flint, "Psalms," *DJD* XVI: 7–167.

Stec, D.M., *The Targum of Psalms: Translated, with a Critical Introduction, Apparatus, and Notes* (ArBib 16; Collegeville: The Liturgical Press, 2004).

Stec, D.M., "The Aramaic Psalter," in *The Oxford Handbook of the Psalms* (ed. W.P. Brown; Oxford: Oxford University Press, 2014), 161–72.

Talmon, S., "Pisqah Be'emṣaʿ Pasuq and 11QPsª," *Textus* 5 (1966): 11–21.

Talmon, S., "Fragments of a Psalms Scroll from Masada, MPsᵇ (Masada 1103–1742)," in *Minḥah le-Naḥum: Biblical and Other Studies Presented to Nahum M. Sarna in Honour of his 70th Birthday* (eds. M. Brettler and M. Fishbane; JSOTSup 154; Sheffield: Sheffield Academic Press, 1993), 318–27.

Talmon, S., "Fragments of a Psalms Scroll: MasPsª Ps 81:2b–85:6a (1039–160; Mas1e; final photo 5255)," *DSD* 3 (1996): 296–314.

Ulrich, E., "The Dead Sea Scrolls and Their Implications for an Edition of the Septuagint Psalter," in *Der Septuaginta-Psalter und seine Tochterübersetzungen: Symposium in Göttingen 1997* (eds. A. Aejmelaeus and U. Quast; MSU 24; Göttingen: Vandenhoeck & Ruprecht, 2000), 323–36.

Ulrich, *BQS, 627–726.

Ulrich, *DSSDCB.

Weitzman, M.P., "The Origin of the Peshitta Psalter," in *Interpreting the Hebrew Bible: Essays in Honour of E.I.J. Rosenthal* (eds. J.A. Emerton and S.C. Reif; Cambridge: Cambridge University Press, 1982), 277–98.

Weitzman, M.P., "The Peshitta Psalter and its Hebrew Vorlage," *VT* 35 (1985): 341–54.

Weitzman, M.P., *The Syriac Version of the Old Testament: An Introduction* (University of Cambridge Oriental Publications 56; Cambridge: Cambridge University Press, 1999).

Williams, T.F., "Towards a Date for the Old Greek Psalter," in *The Old Greek Psalter: Studies in Honour of Albert Pietersma* (eds. R.J.V. Hiebert, C.E. Cox, and P.J. Gentry; JSOTSup 332; Sheffield: Sheffield Academic Press, 2001), 248–76.

Wilson, G.H., "The Qumran Psalms Manuscripts and the Consecutive Arrangement of Psalms in the Hebrew Psalter," *CBQ* 45 (1983): 377–88.

Wilson, G.H., *The Editing of the Hebrew Psalter* (SBLDS 76; Chico: Scholars Press, 1985).

Wilson, G.H., "The Qumran Psalms Scroll Reconsidered: Analysis of the Debate," *CBQ* 47 (1985): 624–42.

Wilson, G.H., "The Qumran *Psalms Scroll* (11QPsª) and the Canonical Psalter: Comparison of Editorial Shaping," *CBQ* 59 (1997): 448–64.

Witte, M., "The Psalter," in *T & T Clark Handbook of the Old Testament: An Introduction to the Literature, Religion, and History of the Old Testament* (eds. J.C. Gertz et al.; London: T & T Clark International, 2012), 527–49.

Yarchin, W., "The Psalter and the Modern Bible in the Making," *The Folio* 29.2 (Fall 2012): 1, 3–4, 8.

Yarchin, W., "Is There an Authoritative Shape for the Hebrew Book of Psalms?" *RB* 122 (2015): 355–70.

Yarchin, W., "Were the Psalms Collections at Qumran True Psalters?" *JBL* 134 (2015): 775–89.

Yarchin, W., "Why Were the Psalms the First Bible Chapters to be Numbered?" (forthcoming paper presented at the 21st Congress of the International Organization for the Study of the Old Testament in Munich, Germany, August 2013).

Yeivin, I., "The Division into Sections in the Psalms," *Textus* 7 (1969): 76–102.

Brent A. Strawn

10.2 Ancient Hebrew Texts

10.2.1 Ancient Manuscript Evidence

Between fourteen and thirty-six manuscripts from antiquity of various psalms collections as well as four excerpted psalms scrolls from the different sites around the Dead Sea have been published. The way in which I understand the evidence of these manuscripts has been influenced significantly by the work of Flint, who developed his views following the publication of his PhD thesis[1] in many articles and other publications on the Psalms.[2]

Unlike many other biblical books, the main textual difference between the ancient Psalms manuscripts does not pertain to their wording but to the sequence and repertoire of the psalms they include.[3] Manuscripts in which only parts of one psalm are preserved are thus difficult to classify. The list below identifies seven different psalms collections to which fourteen of the biblical Dead Sea scrolls as well as MT-Pss belong. Several of them are attested by more than one manuscript.

1. MT-Pss (for the psalm sequence of MT-Pss, the reader is referred to its critical Editions)
   MasPs^a
   MasPs^b
   5/6ḤevPs
   4QPs^c
2. 11QPs^a (… Psalms 101–103 → … → 109 → … → 118 → 104 → 147 → 105 → 146 → 148 → … → 121–132 → 119 → 135 → 136 + 118:1, 15, 16, 8, 9, X, 29? → 145 → 154 → Plea for Deliverance → Psalms 139 → 137–138 → Sir 51:13–30 → Apostrophe to Zion → Psalms 93 → 141 → 133 → 144 → 155 → 142–143 → 149–150 → Hymn to the Creator → 2 Sam 23,[1–]7 → David's Compositions → Psalms 140 → 134 → 151A → 151B …)
   11QPs^b (Psalms 77 → 78; 119; 118:1, 15–16; Plea for Deliverance; Apostrophe to Zion; Psalms 141 → 133 → 144)
   4QPs^e (Psalms 76 → 77,1; 78; 81; 86; 88; 89; 103 → 109; 114; 115 → 116; 118 → 104;105 → 146; 120; 125 → 126; 129 → 130)
3. 4QPs^a (Psalms 5 → 6; 25; 31 → 33; 34 → 35 → 36; 38 → 71; 47; 53 → 54; 56; 62 → 63; 66 → 67; 69)
   4QPs^q (Psalms 31 → 33[→ 34 →]35)
4. 4QPs^b (Psalms 91[→]92[→]93[→]94; 96; 98; 99[→]100; 102 → 103[→]112; 113; 115; 116; [117 →]118)
5. 4QPs^d (Psalms 106 → 147 → 104)
6. 4QPs^f (Psalms 22; 107; 109 → Apostrophe to Zion; Eschatological Hymn[→]Apostrophe to Judah)
7. 4QPs^k (Ps 135[→]99)

Although some of the additional psalms of LXX-Pss and S-Pss are included in a few of the above psalms collections, no Hebrew Psalms manuscript from Qumran or elsewhere attests to the psalm sequence and repertoire of these collections. In contrast to the psalm sequences and repertoires of the various psalms collections among the Dead Sea Scrolls, the text of the individual songs remains – with exceptions – relatively stable.

The up to seven different psalms collections among the Dead Sea Scrolls demonstrate that the proto-Masoretic collection of psalms as preserved in MT-Pss was just one psalms collection among several. In antiquity, this situation also existed for other collections of songs such as the *Hodayot* from Qumran[4] and thus should not be viewed as characteristic merely of Psalms.

Beyond psalms collections, in the Second Temple period, Psalm 119 and perhaps also other psalms were transmitted individually. Four such excerpted

---

[1] Flint, *The Dead Sea Psalms Scrolls and the Book of Psalms*.
[2] See esp. Flint, "The Book of Psalms in the Light of the Dead Sea Scrolls"; Flint, "Psalms and Psalters in the Dead Sea Scrolls"; Flint, "Five Surprises."
[3] Cf. A. Lange, "Die Endgestalt des protomasoretischen Psalters und die Toraweisheit: Zur Bedeutung der nichtessenischen Weisheitstexte aus Qumran für die Auslegung des protomasoretischen Psalters," in *Der Psalter in Judentum und Christentum* (ed. E. Zenger; Herders Biblische Studien 18; Freiburg: Herder, 1998), 101–36, esp. 109–11; Lange, **Handbuch*, 416–20, 435; Lange, "Collecting Psalms."

[4] Cf. Lange, "Collecting Psalms."

Psalms manuscripts can still be identified (4QPs^g, 4QPs^h, 4QPs^l, 5QPs). In some cases, whole psalms were quoted in non-biblical manuscripts.[5]

As the major textual difference between these manuscripts is their repertoire and psalm sequence, it is more difficult than for other biblical books to determine the text-typological affiliation of individual psalms manuscripts. As a rule of thumb, with a reasonable degree of certainty, psalms manuscripts can only be affiliated with the different psalms collections when the sequence of several psalms is preserved in a given manuscript. For this reason, eleven Psalms scrolls among the Dead Sea Scrolls can no longer be classified because characteristic psalms sequences are not preserved in them (1QPs^a, 1QPs^b, 2QPs, 4QPs^j, 4QPs^m, 4QPs^o, 4QPs^r, 4QPs^s, 8QPs, 11QPs^c, 11QPs^d). Of six Psalms scrolls, only parts of one psalm are preserved (1QPs^c, 4QPs^p, 4QPs^w, 4QPs^x, 11QPs^e?, manuscript Schøyen 5233/2) and another five manuscripts attest to only a few psalm verses at best (3QPs, 4QPs^t, 4QPs^u, 4QPs^v, 6QpapPs?). As non-biblical texts can quote up to one psalm, it remains uncertain for both groups if they attest to Psalms manuscripts or to quotations from psalms in non-biblical manuscripts. For this reason, I will describe the ancient Psalms manuscripts for which their text-typological affiliation can no longer be determined in several lists at the end of this entry. For more detailed descriptions, the reader is referred to my *Handbuch*.[6]

In addition to the published Psalms scrolls from the various sites around the Dead Sea, the Green Collection includes a manuscript with remnants of Ps 11:1–4 (DSS F.Ps1)[7] and Southwestern Baptist Theological Seminary owns a manuscript attesting to parts of Ps 22:4, 6–9, 11–13 (DSS F.165 = DSS F.Ps1).[8] According to Flint, both fragments were penned in a Herodian hand.[9] The two unpublished Psalms fragments raise the number of Psalms manuscripts among the Dead Sea Scrolls to a maximum of forty-two manuscripts.

The up to forty-two possible Psalms manuscripts among the Dead Sea Scrolls are not the only textual witnesses to the Psalms in antiquity. A running text of one or more psalms is also quoted by various pesharim (1QpPs, 4QpPs^a, 4QpPs^b, 4QMidrEschat^a, ^b; cf. → 21.2.1).

10.2.1.1 Manuscripts Affiliated with MT-Pss

The only manuscript that attests to the proto-Masoretic psalms collection beyond a shadow of doubt is MasPs^b. Statistical evidence could also identify MasPs^a, 5/6ḤevPs, and 4QPs^c as further copies of the proto-Masoretic psalms collection among the Dead Sea Scrolls.

10.2.1.1.1 MasPs^a (Mas1e; 1030–1160)

The two surviving fragments of MasPs^a derive from three consecutive columns of this scroll. The manuscript preserves 279 complete and partial words from Pss 81:2–17; 82;1–8; 83:1–18; 84:1–13; 85:1–6. The paleographic classification of MasPs^a is debated. Before the *editio princeps*, Yadin suggested a late Herodian bookhand from the first half of the first century C.E.[10] or from the time twenty to thirty years before the fall of Masada (74 C.E.).[11] Nebe argues for a late Herodian bookhand from the year 20–50 C.E.[12] Talmon describes the hand of MasPs^a in his *editio princeps* as an early Herodian bookhand from the end of the first century B.C.E.[13] The script of MasPs^a combines early with late characteristics of the Herodian bookhand. A date at the end of the first century B.C.E. or the beginning of the first century C.E. therefore seems most likely. Of the two cor-

---

[5] Cf., e.g., Psalm 122 in 4Q522 22–25.

[6] Lange, *Handbuch*, 374–406.

[7] I am indebted to David Trobisch and Emanuel Tov for this information.

[8] I am indebted to Sidnie White Crawford for this information. For the Psalms fragment of the Southwestern Baptist Theological Seminary, see also Loveless and Loveless, *Dead Sea Scrolls and the Bible*, 90.

[9] Flint, "Unrolling," 239.

[10] Y. Yadin, "The Excavation of Masada – 1963/64: Preliminary Report," *IEJ* 15 (1965): 1–120 (103).

[11] Y. Yadin, *Masada: Herod's Fortress and the Zealots' Last Stand* (New York: Random House, 1966), 172.

[12] Nebe, "Masada-Psalmen-Handschrift," 93–94.

[13] Talmon, "Fragments of a Psalms Scroll–MasPs^a," 305; Talmon, "Hebrew Fragments," 79.

rections in Ps 83:9 and 11, only the correction in Ps 83:11 can be assigned with certainty to the original scribe.[14]

The orthography of MasPs[a] closely resembles MT-Pss. MasPs[a] reads only twice more fully and once more defective than MT-Pss. As no variant psalm sequence is preserved for Psalms 81–85 in any extant textual witness, the classification of MasPs[a] can be based only on variant statistics. In 279 complete and partial words, only five smaller non-aligned readings occur. Otherwise, MasPs[a] reads twelve times with MT (→ 10.2.2) against LXX (→ 10.3.1).[15] Based on statistical evidence, MasPs[a] should therefore be classified as a proto-Masoretic text.[16]

10.2.1.1.2 MasPs[b] (Mas1f; 1103–1742)

Two fragments are extant from two consecutive columns of MasPs[b]. They attest to twenty-nine complete and partial words from Ps 147:18–19 and Ps 150:1–6. Psalm 150 is followed by uninscribed leather and the remains of a seam with which a handlesheet was attached to this scroll. Hence, there can be no doubt that MasPs[b] ended with Psalm 150.[17] This is all the more probable as the measurements[18] of MasPs[b] would provide enough space for the whole contents of the proto-Masoretic psalms collection. MasPs[b] is written in a late Hasmonean or early Herodian bookhand from the years 50–1 B.C.E.[19] In its orthography, the manuscript is close to MT. It reads only twice more defective and only once fuller than MT.[20] As no known psalms collection other than MT-Pss ends with Psalm 150 and because MasPs[b] ends with this psalm, there can be no doubt that MasPs[b] attests to the proto-Masoretic psalms collection (→ 10.2.2) although only little text of it survives. This conclusion is underlined by the fact that no textual variants toward MT-Pss are extant in the preserved text.[21]

10.2.1.1.3 5/6ḤevPs (5/6Ḥev1b)

Fourteen fragments of 5/6ḤevPs survive from antiquity. The text of frg. 14 can no longer be identified. Frgs. 1–13 come from eleven columns (cols. III–IX; XI–XII; XV–XVI) of the original scroll[22] and preserve 623 complete and partial words from Pss 7:13–18; 8:1, 4–10; 9:12–21; 10:1–6, 8–10, 18; 11:1–5; 12:6–9; 13:1–3; 14:2–4; 15:1–5; 16:1; 18:6–13, 17–36, 38–43; 22:4–9, 15–21; 23:2–6; 24:1–2; 25:4–7; 29:1–2; 30:3; 31:2–22. A material reconstruction by Annette Steudel demonstrates that the undamaged scroll of 5/6ḤevPs could have provided enough space for all 150 psalms of the proto-Masoretic psalms collection but does not exclude a much smaller manuscript that included only Psalms 1–41.[23] The paleographic date of 5/6ḤevPs is debated. Yardeni mentions one or more "Herodian bookhand(s)" from the first century C.E.[24] while Flint classifies the script of 5/6ḤevPs as a late Herodian bookhand from the years 50–68 C.E.[25]

The orthography of 5/6ḤevPs is conservative but even more defective than MT-Pss.[26] The text-

---

[14] Cf. Talmon, "Fragments of a Psalms Scroll–MasPs[a]," 312; Talmon, "Hebrew Fragments," 88–89.

[15] For a list of variants, see Talmon, "Fragments of a Psalms Scroll–MasPs[a]," 309–13; Talmon, "Hebrew Fragments," 86–89.

[16] Thus also Yadin, "Excavation," 104; Yadin, *Masada*, 172; Y. Yadin, "Masada," EAEHL 3:793–816, 812; Nebe, "Masada-Psalmen-Handschrift," 92; Talmon, "Fragments of a Psalms Scroll–MasPs[a]," 309; Talmon, "Hebrew Fragments," 86; Lange, *Handbuch*, 404.

[17] Cf. Talmon, "Fragments of a Psalms Scroll from Masada: MPs[b]," 321; Talmon, "Hebrew Fragments," 91–92.

[18] Cf. Talmon, "Fragments of a Psalms Scroll from Masada: MPs[b]," 322; Talmon, "Hebrew Fragments," 92.

[19] Cf. Talmon, "Fragments of a Psalms Scroll from Masada: MPs[b]," 322; Talmon, "Hebrew Fragments," 92.

[20] Cf. Talmon, "Fragments of a Psalms Scroll from Masada: MPs[b]," 323; Talmon, "Hebrew Fragments," 92.

[21] Cf. Talmon, "Fragments of a Psalms Scroll from Masada: MPs[b]," 323; Talmon, "Hebrew Fragments," 93–94; "Masada," 3:811–12; Flint, *Dead Sea Psalms Scrolls*, 157; Ulrich, "Two Perspectives," 463; Lange, *Handbuch*, 405.

[22] Cf. Flint, "5/6ḤevPsalms," 141–42; Flint, "Preliminary Edition of 5/6ḤevPsalms," 19–20.

[23] See the report on Steudel's work in Flint, "5/6Ḥev-Psalms," 142.

[24] See the report on Yardeni's work in J.C. Greenfield, "The Texts from Naḥal Ṣe'elim (Wadi Seiyal)," in *Madrid QumranCongress*, 2.661–65, 663.

[25] Flint, "5/6ḤevPsalms," 143; Flint, "Preliminary Edition of 5/6ḤevPsalms," 20; cf. already Yadin, "Expedition D," 40.

[26] Cf. Flint, "5/6ḤevPsalms," 144; Flint, "Preliminary Edition of 5/6ḤevPsalms," 20.

typological classification of 5/6ḤevPs needs to rely on statistical evidence. In 623 identifiable complete and partial words, 5/6ḤevPs attest to only three textual variants toward MT-Pss (→ 10.2.2). Thus, Flint describes the text of 5/6ḤevPs as follows: "5/6ḤevPsalms contains very few variant readings against 𝔐ᴸ as in *BHS*; most of the listed variants are against 𝔐ᵐˢˢ. (a) The most important variant is at Ps 15:3 (col. VII 3), for which the scroll contains only two or three cola found in 𝔐; v 3a (לא רגל על לשנו) is not present in 5/6ḤevPsalms. (b) It appears that the Davidic superscription for Psalm 15 was lacking, since verse 1 proper begins on the first line of col. VII. (c) As for the textually troubled acrostic psalm now found in Ps 9–10 in 𝔐 (combined as Psalm 9 in 𝔊), 5/6ḤevPsalms presents the textual form, also in two psalms, that occurs in 𝔐. (d) The form of Psalm 18, much of which is preserved in cols. VIII and IX, is close to that found in 𝔐, and not the form in 2 Samuel 22."[27] In its preserved consonantal text, 5/6ḤevPs is thus very close to MT-Pss. Although no evidence is preserved from 5/6ḤevPs after Psalm 31, that could attest to the characteristic psalms sequence of MT-Pss; the very close agreement of 5/6ḤevPs with MT-Pss argues for the classification of its text as proto-Masoretic.[28]

10.2.1.1.4 4QPsᶜ (4Q85)

Of the twenty-six surviving fragments of 4QPsᶜ, only the text of frgs. 1–17 can be identified. They attest to ca. 320 complete and partial words from Pss 16:7–10; 17:1?; 18:1–14, 16–18, 32–36, 39–41; 27:12–14; 28:1–5; 35:27–28; 37:18–19; 42:5; 44:8–9?; 45:8–11; 49:1–17; 50:14–23; 51:1–5; 52:5–11; 53:1. Frgs. 13–17 derive from three consecutive columns of the original scroll and attest to remains of Pss 49:1–53:1. A material reconstruction of 4QPsᶜ by Hartmut Stegemann shows that all extant fragments were part of the beginning of the original scroll and that 4QPsᶜ was long enough to include MT-Pss or a similarly extensive collection of psalms.[29] 4QPsᶜ is written in a carefully executed late Herodian script from the years 50–68 C.E. The two corrections in Pss 28:1 and 51:4 were inserted by the original scribe of the scroll.[30]

In its orthography, 4QPsᶜ resembles MT but is even more defective.[31] As the characteristic differences in psalm sequence do not occur in Psalms 16–53, the textual classification of 4QPsᶜ relies on statistical evidence only. In 320 complete and partial words, 4QPsᶜ reads only nine times against MT (→ 10.2.2). The text of 4QPsᶜ can thus be classified on statistical grounds as semi-Masoretic.[32] However, it cannot be ruled out that later parts of 4QPsᶜ could have included additional psalms or followed a different psalms sequence than MT. As 4QPsᶜ is not as close to MT as 5/6ḤevPs, it can only the speculated that 4QPsᶜ might be in the tradition of the Masoretic psalms collection based on the statistical evidence mentioned above.[33]

10.2.1.2 The 11QPsᵃ Psalms Collection
10.2.1.2.1 11QPsᵃ (11Q5)

11QPsᵃ is the largest preserved Psalms manuscript from antiquity. Twenty-eight columns and six further fragments (A–F) are extant.[34] 11QPsᵃ still attests to the whole text or parts of Pss 101:1–8; 102:1–2, 18–29; 103:1; 109:21–31; 118:25–29; 104:1–6, 21–35; 147:1–2, 3?, 18–20; 105:1–11, 24–45; 146:9?–10; 148:1–12; 121:1–8; 122:1–9; 123:1–2; 124:7–8; 125:1–5; 126:1–6; 127:1; 128:4–6; 129:1–8; 130:1–8; 131:1; 132:8–18; 119:1–6, 15–28, 37–49, 59–73, 82–96, 105–20, 128–42, 150–

---

[27] Flint, "5/6ḤevPsalms," 144; Flint, "Preliminary Edition of 5/6ḤevPsalms," 21; cf. already Yadin, "Expedition D," 40.

[28] Cf. Lange, *Handbuch*, 406.

[29] See the report in Skehan, Ulrich, and Flint, "Psalms," 49.

[30] For the paleography of 4QPsᶜ and its scribal corrections, see Skehan, Ulrich, and Flint, "Preliminary Edition," 344; Skehan, Ulrich, and Flint, "Psalms," 50.

[31] Skehan, Ulrich, and Flint, "Preliminary Edition," 344; Skehan, Ulrich, and Flint, "Psalms," 50.

[32] Cf. Skehan, Ulrich, and Flint, "Preliminary Edition," 345; Skehan, Ulrich, and Flint, "Psalms," 50.

[33] Cf. Lange, *Handbuch*, 380.

[34] When Sanders published his *editio princeps* of 11QPsᵃ in *DJD* IV, frg. E was still unknown. Frg. F was identified much later by García Martínez, Tigchelaar, and van der Woude and hence is also lacking in the *editio princeps* of 11QPsᵃ. For editions of frgs. E–F, see Yadin, "Another Fragment," *passim*; Sanders, *Dead Sea Psalms Scroll*, 155–65; García Martínez, Tigchelaar, and van der Woude, *DJD* XXIII, 29–36.

64, 171–76; 135:1–9, 17–21; 136:1–16, 26b?; 118:1, 15–16, 8–9?, 29?; 145:1–7, 13–21?; 154:5–37; Plea for Deliverance; Ps 139:8–24; 137:1, 9; 138:1–8; Sir 51:13–19aα, 20aα, 19b, 30; Apostrophe to Zion; Ps 93:1–3; 141:5–10; 133:1–3; 144:1–7, 15; 155:1–33; 142:4–8; 143:1–8; 149:7–9; 150:1–6; Hymn to the Creator; 2 Sam 23:7; David's Compositions; 140:1–5; 134:1–3; 151A and B (vv. 6–7). The different psalms repertoire and sequence leave no doubt that 11QPs^a attests to a psalms collection (→ 10.2.3.2) that is different from both MT-Pss (→ 10.2.2) and LXX-Pss (→ 10.3.1). However, it is debated whether this psalms collection began originally with Psalm 90,[35] Psalm 100,[36] or Psalm 101.[37] A calculation by Stegemann shows that "the 11Q Psalms^a scroll was originally *much* longer than the preserved 37 columns."[38] Two further manuscripts, 4QPs^e and 11QPs^b, which attest to the 11QPs^a psalms collection, also confirm not only Stegemann's reconstruction but exceeds it by including parts of Psalms 76; 77; 78; 81; 88; and 89.[39] The 11QPs^a psalms collection therefore also included a significant number of psalms from Psalms 1–100.[40]

11QPs^a is written in a Herodian bookhand from the first half of the first century C.E.[41] The supralinear corrections and erasures were all inserted by the original scribe of the scroll.[42] A second scribe added the Tetragrammaton in paleo-Hebrew characters into empty spaces left blank by the first scribe of the scroll.[43]

The orthography of 11QPs^a is baroque and displays both the plene spellings and long suffixes and affixes of the baroque orthography.[44]

Scholars debate the text-typological classification of 11QPs^a extensively. The text-typological character of the 11QPs^a psalms collection, its relationship with MT-Pss, as well as the questions of its canonical authority are discussed in → 10.2.3.2. Here I will only ask how 11QPs^a aligns with other textual witnesses of Psalms; the psalms repertoire and sequence of 11QPs^a are decisive. It includes several psalms that are not part of MT-Pss but are sometimes known from elsewhere: S-Ps 154 (11QPs^a XVIII); Plea for Deliverance (11QPs^a XIX); Sir 51:13–30 (11QPs^a XXI:11–XXII:1); Apostrophe to Zion (11QPs^a XXII:1–15); P-Ps 155 (11QPs^a XXIV:3–17); Hymn to the Creator (11QPs^a XXVI:9–15); 2 Sam 23:7 (11QPs^a XXVII:1); David's Compositions (11QPs^a XXVII:2–11); LXX-Pss 151A and B (11QPs^a XXVIII:3–14). The psalms sequence of 11QPs^a is radically different from both MT-Pss and LXX-Pss:

Psalms 101–103 → … → 109 → … → 118 → 104 → 147 → 105 → 146 → 148 → … → 121–32 → 119 → 135 → 136 + 118:1, 15, 16, 8, 9, x, 29? → 145 → 154 → Plea for Deliverance → Psalms 139 → 137–38 → Sir 51:13–30 → Apostrophe to Zion → Psalms 93 → 141 → 133 → 144 → 155 → 142 → 143 → 149–150 → Hymn to the Creator → 2 Sam 23:[1–]7 → David's Compositions → Psalms 140 → 134 → 151A → 151 B. A further characteristic of 11QPs^a is the double occurrence of at least parts of Psalm 118. Frg. E i 1–5 attests to Ps 118:25–29 without significant variants to MT-Pss. Ps 118:1, 15, 16, 8, 9, x, 29? follows Ps 136:26 directly and without any structural divider in 11QPs^a XVI:1–6. The scribe of 11QPs^a therefore regarded Psalm 136 and Ps 118:1, 15, 16, 8, 9, x, 29? as one psalm.[45]

---

[35] Thus, e.g., H. Stegemann, "Methods for the Reconstruction of Scrolls from Scattered Fragments," in *Archaeology and History in the Dead Sea Scrolls: The New York Conference in Memory of Yigael Yadin* (ed. L.H. Schiffman; JSPSup 8; Sheffield: Sheffield Academic Press, 1990), 189–220 (213 n. 55).

[36] B.Z. Wacholder, "David's Eschatological Psalter 11Q Psalms^a", *HUCA* 59 (1988): 23–72 (42–43).

[37] P.W. Skehan, "Qumran and Old Testament Criticism," in *Qumrân: Sa piété, sa théologie et son milieu* (ed. M. Delcor; BETL 46; Paris: Duculot, 1978), 163–82 (169–70); Dahmen, *Psalmen- und Psalter-Rezeption*, 25–38.

[38] Stegemann, "Methods," 212 n. 55.

[39] → 10.2.1.2.2 and → 10.2.1.2.3.

[40] Cf. Flint, *Dead Sea Psalms Scrolls*, 160–64; Flint, "11QPs^a-Psalter," 182–83, 186; Flint, "Five Surprises," 192–94; Flint, "11QPs^b and the 11QPs^a-Psalter," 164–66; Skehan, Ulrich, and Flint, "Psalms," 74, 76. For a detailed discussion of this problem and the various suggestions made in scholarly literature, see Lange, *Handbuch, 395–98.

[41] Thus Sanders, *DJD IV, 6–9; cf. Yadin, "Another Fragment," 2–3.

[42] Cf. Sanders, *DJD IV, 13–14.

[43] A. Wolters, "The Tetragrammaton in the Psalms Scroll," *Textus* 18 (1995): 87–99.

[44] Cf. Sanders, *DJD IV, 9–13; Yadin, "Another Fragment," 3–4; Dahmen, *Psalmen- und Psalter-Rezeption*, 27.

[45] Flint and Alvarez, "The Oldest of All Psalms Scrolls," 144.

11QPs^b and 4QPs^e preserve parallels to the psalms sequence and repertoire of 11QPs^a and should therefore be regarded as further copies of the 11QPs^a psalms collection.[46] 11QPs^b knows the psalms sequence Psalms 141 → 133 → 144 and includes parts of the Plea for Deliverance and the Apostrophe to Zion. Furthermore, 11QPs^b includes the characteristic combination of Ps 118:1 and 15–16. 4QPs^e attests to the psalms sequence Psalms 118 → 104 → … → 105 → 146?

In addition to these macro-variants, 11QPs^a reads in 3,418 complete and partial words eight times with and 335 times against MT, fifty-five times with and 251 times against LXX, as well as 280 times non-aligned. Furthermore, 11QPs^a reads eight times with and fifty times against the other Psalms manuscripts from the Dead Sea area.[47] On the whole, the manuscript should therefore be regarded as a witness to a non-aligned psalms collection that is also attested in 11QPs^b, 4QPs^e, and maybe 4QPs^n.

10.2.1.2.2 11QPs^b (11Q6)

Nine fragments survive of 11QPs^b deriving from six or seven columns of the original scroll. Frgs. 1–8 preserve remnants of Pss 77:18–21; 78:1; 119:163–64; 118:1, 15–16; Plea for Deliverance (par. 11QPs^a XIX:1–9, 12–15); Apostrophe to Zion 4–5 (par. 11QPs^a XXII:4–5);[48] Pss 141:10; 133:1–3; 144:1–2. The manuscript is written in a Herodian script from the beginning of the first century C.E., "showing mainly formal, but also semi-formal features."[49] In contrast to 11QPs^a, 11QPs^b does not write the Tetragrammaton in paleo-Hebrew characters but in square script and, unlike 11QPs^a, it is committed in its orthography to the conservative approach of MT-Pss.[50]

For the text-typological classification of 11QPs^b, both its psalms repertoire and sequence are decisive. Like 11QPs^a, 11QPs^b attests to the sequence Psalms 141 → 133 → 144[51] and includes the non-Masoretic psalms Plea to Deliverance and Apostrophe to Zion. Furthermore, the combination of Ps 118:1, and 15–16 in 11QPs^b 3 resembles the compilation of various verses from psalms in 11QPs^a XVI.[52] In addition to these macro-variants, 11QPs^b reads in fifty-six complete and partial words of biblical psalms text once with and four times against MT (→ 10.2.2), never with and five times against LXX (→ 10.3.1), three times with and once against 11QPs^a, and once non-aligned. In the forty-six complete and partial words that are preserved from non-biblical psalms, 11QPs^b attests to only one non-orthographic variant towards 11QPs^a. 11QPs^b thus needs to be regarded as another textual witness to the 11QPs^a psalms collection.[53] As with 4QPs^e, 11QPs^b demonstrates that the 11QPs^a psalms collection (→ 10.2.3.2) also included psalms from Psalms 1–89 and did not begin only with Psalm 90 or 101.[54]

10.2.1.2.3 4QPs^e (4Q87)

Of the forty-four surviving fragments of 4QPs^e, only the text of frgs. 1–26 can still be identified. These fragments attest to ca. 220 complete and partial words from Pss 76:10–12; 77:1; 78:6–7, 31–33; 81:2–3; 86:10–11; 88:1–5; 89:44–48, 50–53; 103:22?; 109:1?,

---

[46] → 10.2.1.2.2 and → 10.2.1.2.3.

[47] These statistics were compiled for my *Handbuch* by Jared Anderson based on lists published in Flint, *Dead Sea Psalms Scrolls*, 65–80, as well as in Sanders, *DJD* IV and García Martínez, Tigchelaar, and van der Woude, *DJD* XXIII, 29–36. For a discussion of the more important variants, see Sanders, *Dead Sea Psalms Scroll*, 15–20.

[48] The verse count of Apostrophe to Zion is according to Sanders, *DJD* IV, 86–87. For the Plea for Deliverance, Sanders does not provide a verse count.

[49] García Martínez, Tigchelaar, and van der Woude, *DJD* XXIII, 38; cf. van der Ploeg, "Fragments d'un manuscrit de Psaumes de Qumran," 409; García Martínez and Tigchelaar, "Preliminary Edition," 75.

[50] Cf. García Martínez, Tigchelaar, and van der Woude, *DJD* XXIII, 38–39.

[51] Cf. García Martínez, Tigchelaar, and van der Woude, *Qumran Cave 11 II*, 38, 45.

[52] Cf. van der Ploeg, "Fragments d'un manuscrit de Psaumes de Qumran," 412; García Martínez, Tigchelaar, and van der Woude, *DJD* XXIII, 38, 42.

[53] Cf. van der Ploeg, "Fragments d'un manuscrit de Psaumes de Qumran," 408, 412; Flint, *Dead Sea Psalms Scrolls*, 159–60; Flint, "11QPs^a-Psalter," 177–78; Flint, "Five Surprises," 191–92; Flint, "11QPs^b and the 11QPs^a-Psalter," 163–66; García Martínez and Tigchelaar, "Preliminary Edition," 75–76; García Martínez, Tigchelaar, and van der Woude, *DJD* XXIII, 38; Lange, *Handbuch*, 400–01.

[54] See → 10.2.1.2.3 and → 10.2.1.2.1.

8?, 13; 114:5; 115:15–18; 116:1–4; 118:29; 104:1–3, 20–22; 105:1–3, 23–25, 36–45; 146:1?; 125:2–5; 126:1–5; 129:8; 130:1–3, 6. For frgs. 27–44, it remains uncertain whether or not they belonged to 4QPs^e.[55] 4QPs^e is written in a late Herodian script from the middle of the first century C.E.[56] All supralinear corrections occur in frg. 1 and were all inserted by the original scribe of the scroll: "it appears that the scribe first copied a text in which the superscriptions to Ps 126 and 130 and other elements were not present, and later inserted these headings and made other changes with the purpose of conforming to another Hebrew text similar to consonantal M."[57] Against Skehan, Ulrich, and Flint, it needs to be emphasized that in 4QPs^e 26 i–ii, except for two cases, the supralinear corrections to Psalms 125–26 and 129–30 read not only with MT-Pss but also with the text of 11QPs^a. The many corrections of frgs. 26 as well as the different numbers of lines per column show that 4QPs^e was copied carelessly.[58]

The orthography of 4QPs^e is characterized by the lavish use of plene spellings but does not attest the characteristic morphology of the baroque orthography.[59] The text-typological classification of 4QPs^e relies on its sequence of psalms, which can only be reconstructed in some cases. The transition from one psalm to another is normally marked with a *vacat* at the end of a line and an empty line. The only exception to this rule is the transition from Psalm 125 to Psalm 126. In this case, Ps 125:5 and Ps 126:1 are separated only by a small *vacat* in the middle of the line in frg. 26 i 6; the heading for Ps 126:1 (שיר המעלות "A Song of Ascents") is written above that *vacat*. It seems possible that the parent text of 4QPs^e regarded Psalms 125–126 as one song and that the scribe of 4QPs^e wanted to adjust his parent text to either MT-Pss (→ 10.2.2) or to the psalms collection of 11QPs^a (→ 10.2.3.2), but nevertheless wanted to inform his reader about the different text in his *Vorlage*.[60] The material reconstruction of 4QPs^e demonstrates further that Psalm 88 began in the second half of the line in frg. 5 1.[61] 4QPs^e read either a different text for Psalm 88 or merged this psalm with the one that preceded it in the scroll, which is no longer extant due to damage. Except for such unclear cases, the below comparison of psalms sequences show that 4QPs^e attests to the same psalms collection as that in 11QPs^a and 11QPs^b.[62]

4QPs^e	Psalms 118 → 104 … 105 → 146(?)
11QPs^a	Psalms 118 → 104 → 147 → 105 → 146 → 148
4QPs^d	Psalms 106(?) → 147 → 104
MT	Psalms 104 → 105 … 118 … 146 → 147
LXX	Psalms 103 → 104 … 117 … 145 → 146 → 147[63]

In addition to these macro-variants, 4QPs^e reads five times with and twelve times against MT, five times with and twelve times against LXX (→ 10.3.1), four times with 11QPs^a, and twelve times non-aligned. In the case of Psalms 125–126 and 130, the scribe of 4QPs^e corrected his parent text toward another psalms text. In these six corrections, 4QPs^e reads four times with MT and LXX, three times with 11QPs^a, and twice non-aligned. The existing textual differences between 4QPs^e and 11QPs^a do not point to two different psalms collections attested by the two manuscripts respectively.[64] They demonstrate

---

[55] Skehan, Ulrich, and Flint, "Psalms," 73, 84.

[56] Skehan, Ulrich, and Flint, "Psalms," 74; Flint, "11QPs^a-Psalter," 178, 185.

[57] Skehan, Ulrich, and Flint, "Psalms," 74.

[58] Cf. Dahmen, *Psalmen- und Psalter-Rezeption*, 52–53.

[59] Cf. Flint, "11QPs^a-Psalter," 185; Skehan, Ulrich, and Flint, "Psalms," 74–75.

[60] Cf. Lange, *Handbuch*, 382.

[61] Cf. Skehan, Ulrich, and Flint, "Psalms," 78.

[62] Cf. Flint, *Dead Sea Psalms Scrolls*, 160–64; Flint, "11QPs^a-Psalter," 182–83, 186; Flint, "Five Surprises," 189–91, Flint, "11QPs^b and the 11QPs^a-Psalter," 162; Skehan, Ulrich, and Flint, "Psalms," 74, 76; Lange, *Handbuch*, 382–83. Against Dahmen, *Psalmen- und Psalter-Rezeption*, 52–59.

[63] The counting of the psalms differs between MT and LXX because the two versions sometimes group two psalms together or split one psalm into two. In the table below, LXX-Ps 103 equals MT-Ps 104 etc. MT-Ps 147 is split into two psalms in LXX-Ps: LXX-Ps 146 = MT-Ps 147:1–11 and LXX-Ps 147 = MT-Ps 147:12–20.

[64] Against Dahmen, *Psalmen- und Psalter-Rezeption*, 52–59, who rejects the affiliation of 4QPs^e with the 11QPs^a Psalms collection. Dahmen's arguments are based on his material reconstruction, according to which 11QPs^a would have begun

instead that the 11QPsa psalms collection was subject to textual change in its transmission.

Of special interest for the reconstruction of the 11QPsa psalms collection is the fact that 4QPse attests to Psalms 114–116 and 118. This confirms Skehan's hypothesis that the 11QPsa psalms collection included originally the Pesach Hallel (Psalms 113–118).[65] Furthermore, the inclusion of Psalms 76, 77, 78, 81, 88, and 89 leaves no doubt that the 11QPsa psalms collection did not begin only with Psalm 90 or Psalm 101.[66]

10.2.1.2.5 4QPsⁿ (4Q95)

Three columns of the original scroll of 4QPsⁿ survive, attesting to twenty-five complete and partial words from Pss 135:6–8, 11–12 and 136:23–24.[67] The manuscript was executed in an early Herodian bookhand from the end of the first century C.E.[68] In the extant text, the orthography of 4QPsⁿ is somewhat fuller than that of MT.[69] The small amount of preserved text makes the text-typological classification of 4QPsⁿ difficult. "On frg. 3 Psalm 135:11–12 is directly followed by 136:23–24, which constitutes a major difference from both the 𝔐 Psalter and 11QPsa where 136:1 follows 135:21."[70] "The transition between the two psalms took place in two ways: by introducing after 135:12a and after 135:12b the characteristic refrain found in Psalm 136, and by the colon from 135:12b leading in to the similar colon in 136:22a ... This transition shifts the focus from a survey of God's saving deeds in Israel's history in the third person (135:8–12) to a more personal account that includes the first person ... The resultant text comprises a new Psalm."[71] The preserved text represents a new psalm, which forms a coherent whole and presumably comprised Pss 135:1–12 + 136:23–26. "But since the refrain suddenly appears from v 12 onwards, it seems that the compiler fashioned the new Psalm by combining material from Psalms 135 and 136."[72] Furthermore, 4QPsⁿ attests against MT (→ 10.2.2) and LXX (→ 10.3.1) to the same addition to Ps 135:6 that appears in 4QPsᵏ and 11QPsa.[73] Due to the small amount of preserved text, it remains uncertain whether 4QPsⁿ is the remnant of a psalms collection or represents an excerpted text. As 4QPsⁿ creates a new psalm out of Psalms 135–136 with 11QPsa, but against MT and LXX, and reads in a substantial variant with 11QPsa, it can be speculated that 4QPsⁿ is either another copy of the 11QPsa psalms collection (→ 10.2.3.2) or an excerpt of this psalms collection.[74] Given the small amount of text preserved, there is even a possibility that 4QPsⁿ represents what is left of an employment of the combined Psalms 135–36 in another literary composition.[75]

10.2.1.3 The 4QPsᶠ Psalms Collection (4Q88)

This psalms collection (→ 10.2.3.3) is only preserved in the manuscript 4QPsᶠ. Of the thirteen fragments of 4QPsᶠ, only the text of frg. 13 remains unidentified. Frgs. 3–12 can still be at-

---

with Psalm 101. However, Dahmen's material reconstruction of 11QPsa is based on wrong premises (see Lange, *Handbuch, 397). Dahmen argues furthermore that 4QPse disagrees with 11QPsa in some readings and claims that some of the transitions between individual psalms that Flint would need for his arguments are tentative. But Dahmen demonstrated himself that the scribe of 4QPse produced his scroll carelessly and made many mistakes. If this is the case, textual differences between 4QPse and 11QPsa originate in mistakes made by the scribe of 4QPse and do not argue against the classification of 4QPse as another witness to the 11QPsa Psalms collection.

[65] P.W. Skehan, "A Liturgical Complex in 11QPsa," *CBQ* 37 (1975): 343–47.

[66] Flint, "11QPsa-Psalter," 193. See above, → 10.2.1.2.1.

[67] Dahmen, "New Identifications," 484, wants to identify frgs. 2–3 1–3 as remnants of Ps 136:20–22. However, for this identification he needs to adjust the wording of Ps 136:20–23 to the text of Ps 135:11–12. Dahmen's identification is therefore not convincing.

[68] Cf. Flint, Skehan, and Ulrich, "Three Psalms," 42; Skehan, Ulrich, and Flint, "Psalms," 135.

[69] Cf. Flint, Skehan, and Ulrich, "Three Psalms," 42; Skehan, Ulrich, and Flint, "Psalms," 135.

[70] Skehan, Ulrich, and Flint, "Psalms," 135.

[71] Skehan, Ulrich, and Flint, "Psalms," 135.

[72] Skehan, Ulrich, and Flint, "Psalms," 137.

[73] לעשות יעש[ה אין כיה אין ביהוה ואין שיעשה כמלך אלהים "to do what he doe[s; there is no one like the L., there is no one like the Lord, and there is no one who acts like the king of the gods." Cf. Flint, Skehan, and Ulrich, "Three Psalms," 42–43. The *lacunae* are reconstructed guided by 4QPsᵏ and 11QPsa.

[74] Cf. Dahmen, "New Identifications," 484–85.

[75] For the various possible classifications of 4QPsⁿ, see Lange, *Handbuch, 388–89.

tributed to nine columns of the original scroll, which are counted by the *editio princeps* as cols. I–IV and VI–X.[76] Frgs. 1–12 preserve 161 complete and partial words from Pss 22:14–17; 107:2–5, 8–16, 18–19, 22–30, 35b–42; 109:4–6, 24–28. In addition, the fragments of 4QPs[f] preserve 145 complete and partial words of three non-canonical psalms: Apostrophe to Zion 1–2, 11–18 (cf. 11QPs[a] XXII:1–10); Eschatological Hymn; and Apostrophe to Judah. Eschatological Hymn and Apostrophe to Judah are only attested in 4QPs[f]. 4QPs[f] is written in a late Hasmonean semi-cursive hand from around the year 50 B.C.E. The two supralinear corrections in Ps 107:27 and Apostrophe to Judah 6 were inserted by the original scribe of the scroll.[77]

4QPs[f] employs a plene orthography that is incoherent in its use of *waw* as a *mater lectionis*. The manuscript also attests to several occurrences of כה- for the suffix of the second person masculine singular meaning "your."[78]

In 161 complete and partial words of biblical text, 4QPs[f] reads thirty-three times against MT and only once with MT[mss], thirty-two times against and once with LXX as well as twice with LXX[mss], three times against 11QPs[a], once against 5/6ḤevPs, and thirty-three times non-aligned. Three different types of variants exist in the preserved text of 4QPs[f]. 4QPs[f] attests to a shorter text than MT and LXX in Ps 109:26–27 (26a and 27a are missing).[79] In Ps 107:9ba, 30bc*a, the manuscript disagrees with MT and LXX in the sequence of *stichoi*.[80] 4QPs[f] attests to extensive differences from MT and LXX in the wording of individual psalms. In addition to these three types of variants, 4QPs[f] includes three psalms that became part of neither the proto-Masoretic nor the Old Greek psalms collections (Apostrophe to Zion, Eschatological Hymn, Apostrophe to Judah). Two of these psalms (Eschatological Hymn, Apostrophe to Judah[81]) are also not known from 11QPs[a]. In Apostrophe to Zion, 4QPs[f] reads in 52 complete and partial words nine times against the original scribe of 11QPs[a] and once with and once against corrections in 11QPs[a]. In its preserved sections, 4QPs[f] differs with neither MT nor LXX in the sequence of its psalms but disagrees instead with 11QPs[a]:

4QPs[f]	Psalm 109 → Apostrophe to Zion → Eschatological Hymn → Apostrophe to Judah
11QPs[a]	Psalms 139 → 137 → 138 → Sir 51:13–20 → Apostrophe to Zion → Psalm 93

On the whole, 4QPs[f] includes more Aramaisms than any other textual witness to the Psalms. For the Apostrophe to Zion, 4QPs[f] preserves an earlier version of this song than that in 11QPs[a]: "Comparison of the *Apostrophe to Zion* preserved in 4QPs[f] against the form found in 11QPs[a] shows that 4QPs[f] is earlier with respect to both its script and stage of textual transmission. Moreover, 4QPs[f] was strongly influenced by the spoken Aramaic of its author, whereas 11QPs[a] reflects a more literary Hebrew."[82] Taking all textual differences together, the conclusion is unavoidable that 4QPs[f] attests to yet another psalms collection that differs from MT-Pss (→ 10.2.2), LXX-Pss (→ 10.3.1), as well as the 11QPs[a] psalms collection (→ 10.2.3.2).[83]

---

[76] Skehan, Ulrich, and Flint, "Psalms," 85–86.

[77] For the paleography and scribal corrections of 4QPs[f], see Starky, "Psaumes," 354–55; Skehan, Ulrich, and Flint, "Psalms," 86; Skehan, Ulrich, and Flint, "Scroll," 269–70.

[78] For the orthography of 4QPs[f], see Skehan, Ulrich, and Flint, "Psalms," 86–87; Skehan, Ulrich, and Flint, "Scroll," 270.

[79] The reconstruction of 4QPs[f] also makes it likely that Ps 107:21 was missing in 4QPs[f] (cf. Skehan, Ulrich, and Flint, "Psalms," 86, 92; Skehan, Ulrich, and Flint, "Scroll," 273), and that 4QPs[f] included an additional *stichos* in Ps 107:30 (cf. Skehan, Ulrich, and Flint, "Psalms," 87, 94).

[80] Cf. Skehan, Ulrich, and Flint, "Psalms," 87, 92, 94.

[81] H. Eshel and J. Strugnell think that these two compositions represent one and not two psalms ("Alphabetical Acrostics in Pre-Tannaitic Hebrew," *CBQ* 62 [2000]: 441–58 [446–49]).

[82] Skehan, Ulrich, and Flint, "Psalms," 88.

[83] Cf. Jain and Steudel, "manuscrits psalmique," 538 n. 53. For the text-typological classification of 4QPs[f], see Lange, *Handbuch*, 384–85.

10.2.1.4 Possible Further Psalms Collections

Five further Qumran manuscripts could attest to additional psalms collections although their poor state of preservation does not allow for definite conclusions.

10.2.1.4.1 4QPsᵃ and 4QPsᑫ

In their psalm sequence and also in the delimitation of individual psalms, 4QPsᵃ and 4QPsᑫ disagree with MT-Pss (→ 10.2.2). 4QPsᵃ begins a new psalm after Pss 36:5 and 56:5 respectively.[84] Furthermore, 4QPsᵃ attests to transitions from Psalm 5 to Psalm 6, Psalm 31 to Psalm 33, and Psalm 38 to Psalm 71. A transition from Psalm 31 to Psalm 33 can also be found in 4QPsᑫ. As this psalms sequence is not attested in any other textual witness to Psalms, 4QPsᵃ and 4QPsᑫ are most likely the only two remaining manuscripts of yet another psalms collection (→ 10.2.3.4).[85]

10.2.1.4.1.1 4QPsᵃ (4Q83)

Twenty-four fragments of 4QPsᵃ are extant. The text of frgs. 1–20 can still be identified and includes ca. 420 complete and partial words from Pss 5:9–13; 6:1–4; 25:8, 10, 12, 15; 31:23–24; 33:2, 4–6, 8, 10, 12; 34:21–22; 35:2, 13–18, 20, 26–27; 36:1, 3, 5–7, 9; 38:2, 4, 6, 8–10, 12, 16–23; 71:1–14; 47:2; 53:2, 4–5, 27; 54:2–3, 5–6; 56:4; 62:13; 63:2, 4; 66:16, 18–20; 67:1–2, 4–8; 69:1–19. A material reconstruction of 4QPsᵃ by Stegemann[86] makes it likely that this manuscript attested once to a complete psalms collection and that 4QPsᵃ also included the now missing Psalms 64–65 and 68.[87] The manuscript is written in a semi-formal hand from the middle of the second century B.C.E.[88] Therefore, 4QPsᵃ is, with the possible exception of 4QPsˣ, the earliest known Psalms manuscript.

The orthography of 4QPsᵃ is committed to the baroque system, as demonstrated by plene spellings such as לוא "not" and the affixes כה- "your" and תה- "you."[89] In its psalms repertoire and sequence as well as in its delimitation of individual psalms, 4QPsᵃ disagrees with MT. 4QPsᵃ reads a *vacat* after Pss 36:5 and 56:6, indicating the end of a psalm.[90] In its psalms sequence, 4QPsᵃ differs from MT in the following way: Psalm 5 → 6 … Psalm 31 → Psalm 33 … Psalm 38 → 71. As no delimiter separates Ps 38:23 and Ps 71:1, 4QPsᵃ most likely regarded both songs as one psalm.[91] Furthermore, 4QPsᵃ did not include Psalms 64–65 and 68.[92] In addition to these macro-variants, 4QPsᵃ reads three times with and seventy times against MT (→ 10.2.2), eight times with and sixty-one times against LXX (→ 10.3.1), as well as sixty-four times non-aligned. As the psalms sequence Psalm 31 → Psalm 33 is also attested by 4QPsᑫ, the manuscripts 4QPsᵃ and 4QPsᑫ attest most likely to the same non-aligned psalms collection (→ 10.2.3.4).[93] The non-aligned character of 4QPsᵃ is also underlined by the above statistics.

10.2.1.4.1.2 4QPsᑫ (4Q98)

Of 4QPsᑫ, only one fragment with remains of two columns survives with 111 complete and partial words from Pss 31:24–25; 33:1–18; and 35:4–20. J. Starky and the Musée Bible et Terre Sainte regarded 4QPsᑫ as a fragment of 5/6ḤevPs[94] but there can be no doubt that this fragment derives

---

[84] Wilson, *Editing*, 131; Ulrich, "Oldest Psalms Manuscript," 75, 80, 84–85; Skehan, Ulrich, and Flint, "Psalms," 10, 12, 18; Jain and Steudel, "manuscrits psalmique," 538 n. 53.

[85] Cf. Lange, *Handbuch, 377–78 and 391.

[86] See the reports by Ulrich, "Oldest Psalms Manuscript," 73, and by Skehan, Ulrich, and Flint, "Psalms," 7–8.

[87] Ulrich, "Oldest Psalms Manuscript," 72–73; Skehan, Ulrich, and Flint, "Psalms," 8.

[88] See Skehan, *"Qumran, Littérature de Qumran," 814; Ulrich, "Oldest Psalms Manuscript," 73; cf. Cross, *ALQ³, 122.

[89] For the orthography of 4QPsᵃ, see Ulrich, "Oldest Psalms Manuscript," 73–75; Flint and Alvarez, "The Oldest of All Psalms Scrolls," 147–48; Skehan, Ulrich, and Flint, "Psalms," 8–9.

[90] Wilson, *Editing*, 131; Ulrich, "Oldest Psalms Manuscript," 75, 80, 84–85; Skehan, Ulrich, and Flint, "Psalms," 10, 14, 18; Jain and Steudel, "manuscrits psalmique," 538 n. 53.

[91] Cf. Ulrich, "Oldest Psalms Manuscript," 75, 81–82; Skehan, Ulrich, and Flint, "Psalms," 10, 15–16.

[92] See above, → 10.2.1.4.1.1.

[93] Cf. Lange, *Handbuch, 377–78.

[94] Cf. J. Briend, "Le musée Bible et Terre Sainte," *MdB* 86 (1994): 44–45 (45).

from Qumran's Cave 4.[95] Although only a small amount of text is preserved, a calculation of the original length of the scroll shows that 4QPs^q could have contained a full-fledged psalms collection.[96] 4QPs^q was executed in a Herodian semi-cursive hand from the end of the first century B.C.E. or the beginning of the first century C.E.[97]

The orthography of 4QPs^q is sometimes fuller and sometimes more defective than that of MT but none of the special morphological features of the baroque orthographic system appear in the preserved text.[98]

The text-typological classification of 4QPs^q is difficult. With 4QPs^a but against MT (→ 10.2.2) and LXX (→ 10.3.1), 4QPs^q attests to the psalm sequence Psalm 31 → Psalm 33. That 4QPs^q has a large *vacat* of almost a whole line after Ps 33:12 suggests that this manuscripts regarded Ps 33:1–12 and Ps 33:13–22 as two separate psalms.[99] Furthermore, 4QPs^q includes, against MT and 4QPs^a, an additional heading (לדויד שיר מזמור "of David, a song of psalm"; cf. LXX τῷ Δαυιδ "of David") in Ps 33:1. In addition, 4QPs^q reads a longer text than MT after Ps 33:7, which according to the reconstruction of Skehan, Ulrich, and Flint[100] is also found in 4QPs^a: נצבו כמו נוד[שם המים "there [stands] the water[like]a wineskin."[101] In addition to these macro-variants, 4QPs^q goes five times with and nine times against MT, twice with and twelve times against LXX, and reads eight times non-aligned. The manuscript also includes five readings against MT^mss and one against 4QPs^a. The divergent psalms sequence as well as the long texts mentioned above and eight non-aligned readings argue for a non-aligned text that is close to 4QPs^a. The agreement in psalm sequence makes it likely that 4QPs^q attests to the same non-aligned psalms collection as does 4QPs^a (→ 10.2.3.4).[102]

10.2.1.4.2 4QPs^b (4Q84)

There are thirty-seven surviving fragments of 4QPs^b. Only the text of frgs. 1–34 can still be identified. They preserve ca. 490 complete and partial words from Pss 91:5–8, 12–15; 92:4–8, 13–15; 93:5; 94:1–4, 7–9, 10–14, 17–18, 21–22; 96:2; 98:4–5; 99:5–6; 100:1–2; 102:5?, 10–29; 103:1–6, 9–14, 20–21; 112:4–5; 113:1; 115:2–3; 116:17–19; 118:1–3, 5–10, 12, 18–20, 23–26, 29. The preserved text derives from twenty-six columns of the original scroll, which are counted by the *editio princeps* as cols. I–VIII, X, XIII, XV–XVI, XIX–XXVII, XXIX, XXXIII–XXXVI. This enumeration does not suggest that 4QPs^b began with Psalm 91.[103] The relatively short column height of seventeen lines or 14 cm[104] makes it physically impossible that 4QPs^b included the whole proto-Masoretic psalms collection. Its high-quality thin leather[105] as well as the careful work of its scribe imply that 4QPs^b was a luxury copy. The manuscript was written in a late Herodian bookhand from the middle of the first century C.E.[106] The three supralinear corrections in Pss 102:16; 103:2, 3 were inserted by the original scribe who also overwrote text in Ps 91:14.[107]

In its orthography, 4QPs^b is conservative but even more defective than MT-Pss.[108] The psalm sequence in 4QPs^b disagrees at least once with MT-Pss (→ 10.2.2): 4QPs^b has Psalms 102 → 103 → 112 → 113. Overall, thirty-three cases of textual variation can be found in the text of 4QPs^b, of which only three concern more than three words of text. 4QPs^b

---

[95] Cf. Milik, "Deux documents," 245; Skehan, Ulrich, and Flint, "Psalms," 145.

[96] Cf. Jain and Steudel, "manuscrits psalmique," 538 nn. 52–53.

[97] Skehan, Ulrich, and Flint, "Psalms," 146.

[98] Cf. Milik, "Deux documents," 246, and Skehan, Ulrich, and Flint, "Psalms," 146.

[99] Cf. Skehan, Ulrich, and Flint, "Psalms," 146.

[100] Skehan, Ulrich, and Flint, "Psalms," 12.

[101] Reconstruction according to Ps 78:13; cf. Skehan, Ulrich, and Flint, "Psalms," 147.

[102] Cf. Jain and Steudel, "manuscrits psalmique," 538 n. 53; Lange, *Handbuch*, 390–91.

[103] Skehan, Ulrich, and Flint, "Psalms," 23–24.

[104] For the measurements, see Skehan, Ulrich, and Flint, "Psalms," 23.

[105] Cf. Skehan, "Qumran Manuscripts," 154; Skehan, Ulrich, and Flint, "Psalms," 23.

[106] Thus Skehan, "Qumran Manuscripts," 153; Skehan, Ulrich, and Flint, "Psalms," 24; cf. Skehan, "Psalm Manuscript," 313.

[107] Skehan, Ulrich, and Flint, "Psalms," 25–26.

[108] Cf. Skehan, Ulrich, and Flint, "Psalms," 24. For a list of orthographic variants, see op. cit., 26.

reads thirteen times with and twenty times against MT, nine times with and twenty-four times against LXX, once with and eight times against 11QPsᵃ, as well as nineteen times non-aligned. In addition, five readings against MT cannot be translated into a non-Semitic language. Next to the divergent psalm sequence, the most significant variant reading of 4QPsᵇ is the lack of Ps 118:11. In Psalm 91, 4QPsᵇ aligns with MT and LXX (→ 10.3.1) against 11QapocrPsalms but reads twice with MT against LXX and 11QapocrPsalms. Due to its divergent psalm sequence and its high number of non-aligned readings, 4QPsᵇ needs to be characterized as a non-aligned text. The manuscript attests either to an independent psalms collection (→ 10.2.3.5)[109] that was shorter than MT-Pss or represents an excerpted Psalms manuscript with a non-aligned text. The former is more likely due to the great care with which the scribe copied this manuscript and the high quality of its leather.

10.2.1.4.3 4QPsᵈ (4Q86)

Fourteen fragments survive from five consecutive columns of 4QPsᵈ. The fourteen fragments of 4QPsᵈ attest to 139 complete and partial words from Pss 106:48?; 147:1–4, 13–17, 20; 104:1–5, 8–11, 14–15, 22–25, 33–35. The measurements of 4QPsᵈ (nineteen lines per column, height of the scroll = 16 cm) demonstrate that this manuscript could not have included all 150 songs of MT-Pss (→ 10.2.2).[110] In 4QPsᵈ, the text of Psalms 106, 147, and 104 would have filled eight columns.[111] However, it remains uncertain whether 4QPsᵈ included further psalms or represents an excerpted Psalms manuscript that contained only Psalms 106, 147, and 104. 4QPsᵈ was copied in a carefully executed late Hasmonean bookhand from the middle of the first century B.C.E.[112] In col. II:13, the original scribe of the scroll added Ps 104:2b in a supralinear correction.[113]

In its orthography, 4QPsᵈ is close to MT.[114] The text-typological classification of 4QPsᵈ is difficult. In col. I:5, the ה[לוּיה]]י[אמן "Amen, Halleluja" is followed by a *vacat* and Ps 147:1. As ה[לוּיה]]י[אמן only appears at the end of a psalm in Ps 106:48, 4QPsᵈ attests in cols. I and II to the psalms sequence Psalms 106 → 147 → 104.[115] This psalm sequence goes against both MT (Psalms 104 → 105 → 106 … 146 → 147 → 148) and 11QPsᵃ (Psalms 118 → 104 → 147 → 105). There are three further macro-variants: Ps 104:34a is missing in 4QPsᵈ against MT, LXX, and 11QPsᵃ; 4QPsᵈ and MT lack the heading of Psalm 104 that is attested in 11QPsᵃ and 4QPsᵉ; and 4QPsᵈ attests with 11QPsᵃ but against MT and LXX to the same long text in Ps 147:1. Overall, 4QPsᵈ reads eight times with and nineteen times against MT, nine times with and seventeen times against LXX (→ 10.3.1), twice with and ten times against 11QPsᵃ, once with and five times against 4QPsˡ, and fourteen times non-aligned. The psalms text of 4QPsᵈ is best characterized as non-aligned.[116] However, it remains uncertain whether 4QPsᵈ once contained a small psalms collection (→ 10.2.3.5) that is otherwise unknown[117] or whether it represents what is left of an excerpted Psalms manuscript.

10.2.1.4.4 4QPsᵏ (4Q92)

4QPsᵏ is extant in two fragments from two consecutive columns of the original scroll and preserves twenty-seven complete and partial words from Pss 135:6–16 and 99:1–5. In 4QPsᵏ, Psalm 99 is placed after Psalm 135. The material reconstruction of 4QPsᵏ makes it likely that another psalm stood between Psalm 135 and Psalm 99 in this manuscript, which would result in the sequence

---

[109] Thus Jain and Steudel, "manuscrits psalmique," 538 n. 53. Against Skehan, "Qumran Manuscripts," 154, who characterized 4QPsᵇ in an early publication as "quite close to the Masora."

[110] Cf. Flint, "Preliminary Edition of 4QPsᵈ," 94; Skehan, Ulrich, and Flint, "Psalms," 63.

[111] Flint, "Preliminary Edition of 4QPsᵈ," 94; Skehan, Ulrich, and Flint, "Psalms," 63.

[112] For the paleography of 4QPsᵈ, see Flint, "Preliminary Edition," 95; Skehan, Ulrich, and Flint, "Psalms," 63.

[113] Skehan, Ulrich, and Flint, "Psalms," 68.

[114] Cf. Flint, "Preliminary Edition of 4QPsᵈ," 95–96; Skehan, Ulrich, and Flint, "Psalms," 64–65.

[115] Cf. Skehan, Ulrich, and Flint, "Psalms," 64.

[116] Cf. Flint, "Preliminary Edition of 4QPsᵈ," 95–96; Skehan, Ulrich, and Flint, "Psalms," 65; Lange, *Handbuch*, 381.

[117] Thus Jain and Steudel, "manuscrits psalmique," 538 n. 53.

Psalm 135 → Psalm ? → Psalm 99. 4QPs^k was written in an early Herodian bookhand with some Hasmonean paleographic elements. The manuscript should therefore be dated to the second half of the first century B.C.E.[118] "Only two orthographic differences from other scrolls or the received text are preserved: at 135:7 מאצרתיו (מאוצרותיו 4QPs^n 𝔐) and 99:5 רממו (רוממו 𝔐). The scroll may have a longer text at 135:6 in agreement with 4QPs^n and 11QPs^a against 𝔐 and 𝔊."[119] Regardless of the long text shared with 4QPs^n, 4QPs^k does not agree with the characteristic psalm sequence of 4QPs^n (Ps 135:12 → 136:23; → 10.2.1.2.5). As the psalm sequence Psalm 135 → Psalm ? → Psalm 99 can only be found in 4QPs^k, although Psalms 99 and 135 are also attested in 4QPs^b,n,v and 11QPs^a, it can be speculated with due caution that 4QPs^k attests to an independent psalms collection (→ 10.2.3.5). This conclusion remains speculative as the twenty-seven preserved complete and partial words of 4QPs^k are insufficient for text-typological classification. In addition to the more substantial variants discussed above, 4QPs^k reads twice non-aligned, once with MT^mss and LXX (→ 10.3.1) against MT (→ 10.2.2), and once with LXX^mss against MT and LXX.

10.2.1.5 Excerpted Psalms Manuscripts

The size of the manuscripts discussed in 10.2.1.5 show that they only included Psalm 119 (4QPs^g; 4QPs^h; 5QPs) or Psalm 104 plus at most a few more psalms (4QPs^l). The characteristic psalm sequences of the various psalm collections from which these manuscripts excerpted their psalms therefore cannot be identified and their textual character remains difficult if not impossible to determine. The exception to this rule is the excerpted Psalms manuscript 4QPs^n that was discussed above (→ 10.2.1.2.5).

10.2.1.5.1 4QPs^g (4Q89)

The six surviving fragments of 4QPs^g derive from five columns of the original scroll (cols. VI–VII and XI–XIII). Approximately seventy complete and partial words from Ps 119:37–46, 49–50, 73–74, 81–83, 89–92 are extant. Each column was eight lines or 5.3 cm high. A material reconstruction by Hartmut Stegemann[120] demonstrates that the original scroll was twenty-five columns long and, like 4QPs^h and 5QPs, included only the text of Psalm 119. 4QPs^g is therefore beyond doubt an excerpted Psalms manuscript (→ 10.2.3.6).[121] 4QPs^g was written in a late Herodian bookhand from ca. 50 C.E.[122] The sole supralinear correction was inserted by the original scribe of the scroll.[123] The orthography of 4QPs^g is conservative but somewhat fuller than that of MT.[124] Due to the small amount of preserved text, the text-typological classification of 4QPs^g is not possible. In what survives, 4QPs^g reads four times non-aligned, ten times with MT (→ 10.2.2), eight times with LXX (→ 10.3.1), but fourteen times against 11QPs^a.

10.2.1.5.2 4QPs^h (4Q90)

The two surviving fragments of 4QPs^h attest to thirty-seven complete and partial words from Ps 119:10–21. The material reconstruction of this manuscript shows that, like 4QPs^g and 5QPs, 4QPs^h included only the text of Psalm 119. 4QPs^h is thus an excerpted Psalms manuscript (→ 10.2.3.6).[125]

The scribe of 4QPs^h employed a Herodian bookhand.[126] In its orthography, 4QPs^h follows a conservative approach using more vowel letters than MT but less than 11QPs^a.[127] The small amount of

---

[118] Cf. Lange, *Handbuch, 387; contra Skehan, Ulrich, and Flint, "Psalms," 123.

[119] Skehan, Ulrich, and Flint, "Psalms," 123.

[120] See the report in Skehan, Ulrich, and Flint, "Psalms," 107–08. Cf. also Skehan, Ulrich, and Flint, "Two Manuscripts," 478–79; Jain and Steudel, "manuscrits psalmique," 538 n. 50.

[121] Cf. Brooke, "Psalms," 8; Swanson, "Qumran and the Psalms," 252.

[122] Cf. Skehan, Ulrich, and Flint, "Two Manuscripts," 478; Skehan, Ulrich, and Flint, "Psalms," 108.

[123] Cf. Skehan, Ulrich, and Flint, "Psalms," 109.

[124] Cf. Skehan, Ulrich, and Flint, "Psalms," 109.

[125] For 4QPs^h as an excerpted manuscript and for the material reconstruction of 4QPs^h, cf. Skehan, Ulrich, and Flint, "Psalms," 112–13; Skehan, Ulrich, and Flint, "Two Manuscripts," 482–83. Cf. Jain and Steudel, "manuscrits psalmique," 538 n. 50; Brooke, "Psalms," 8; Swanson, "Qumran and the Psalms," 252.

[126] Cf. Skehan, Ulrich, and Flint, "Psalms," 114.

[127] Cf. Skehan, Ulrich, and Flint, "Two Manuscripts," 482; Skehan, Ulrich, and Flint, "Psalms," 114.

preserved text prohibits a text-typological classification. 4QPs^h reads twice with MT (→ 10.2.2) and three times against MT, twice with and three times against LXX (→ 10.3.1), three times with and once against 11QPs^a, once non-aligned, twice with MT^ms(s) and twice against MT^mss, as well as once against LXX^ms. One further reading against MT and 11QPs^a cannot be translated into a non-Semitic language.

10.2.1.5.3 4QPs^l (4Q93)

There is one extant fragment of 4QPs^l preserving twenty-three complete and partial words from Ps 104:3–5, 11–12 from two columns of the original scroll. The wide right-hand column margin of col. I, demonstrates that 4QPs^l began with Psalm 104. The short height of both page (15.4 cm) and column (fifteen lines) demonstrates that 4QPs^l cannot have included a complete Psalms collection (→ 10.2.3.6).[128] How many psalms 4QPs^l contained originally remains uncertain.[129] The scroll was copied in an early Herodian bookhand from the second half of the first century B.C.E.[130] Too little text survives for orthographic and text-typological classifications. 4QPs^l reads once with and five times against MT (→ 10.2.2), once with and five times against LXX (→ 10.3.1), once with and three times against 4QPs^d, once against 11QPs^a, and four times non-aligned.

10.2.1.5.4 5QPs (5Q5)

Four fragments from two columns survive of 5QPs, attesting to forty-one complete and partial words from Ps 119:99–101, 104, 113–20, 138–42. The short column height of sixteen or seventeen lines[131] demonstrates that 5QPs did not include a complete Psalms collection but was an excerpted manuscript limited to Psalm 119.[132] The manuscript was executed in a Herodian bookhand from the first century C.E.[133] The orthography of 5QPs agrees in every detail with MT-Pss. The small amount of preserved text prohibits a text-typological classification. 5QPs reads four times with MT (→ 10.2.2) against LXX (→ 10.3.1).

10.2.1.6 Unclassifiable Psalms Manuscripts[134]

The remainder of the Psalms manuscripts from the various sites around the Dead Sea are addressed here in list form as too little of them is preserved to allow for proper classification.

10.2.1.6.1 Manuscripts of Which Insufficient Text Is Preserved To Classify Them by Way of Psalms Sequence

1QPs^a (1Q10): Twenty-two fragments; frgs. 1–11 preserve fifty-eight complete and partial words from Pss 86:5–6, 8; 92:12–14; 94:16; 95:11; 96:1–2; 119:31–34, 43–48, 77–79; early Herodian bookhand from 30–1 B.C.E.; conservative orthography; reads three times non-aligned, once with MT^Ketiv against MT^Qere and LXX.

1QPs^b (1Q11): Six fragments with twenty complete and partial words from Pss 126:6; 127:1–5; and 128:5; might have preserved only Psalms 120–130;[135] Herodian bookhand from 20–50 C.E.;[136] conservative orthography?; reads once with LXX against MT, and once non-aligned.

2QPs (2Q14): Two fragments with twenty-three complete and partial words from Pss 103:2, 4, 6,

---

[128] Cf. Flint, Skehan, and Ulrich, "Three Psalms," 37; Skehan, Ulrich, and Flint, "Psalms," 127. The text of Psalm 104 alone would have required six columns.

[129] Against Swanson, "Qumran and the Psalms," 252–53, who regards 4QPs^l as an excerpted manuscript that included only Psalm 104.

[130] Cf. Flint, Skehan, and Ulrich, "Three Psalms," 38; Skehan, Ulrich, and Flint, "Psalms," 127.

[131] For the column height of 5QPs, cf. Skehan, Ulrich, and Flint, "Psalms," 107–08.

[132] For the material reconstruction of this manuscript, see also Jain and Steudel, "manuscrits psalmique," 538.

[133] Milik, "Psaume 119," 174.

[134] For the paleographic, orthographic, and textual data listed below, see Lange, *Handbuch, 374–406, and the literature discussed there. If orthographic and textual characterizations are not mentioned, the amount of preserved text does not allow for such classifications.

[135] Cf. Jain and Steudel, "manuscrits psalmique," 538.

[136] Cf. E. Ulrich, "Identification of a Scribe Active at Qumran: 1QPs^b – 4QIsa^c – 11QM," *Meghillot* 5–6 (2007): *201–*10 (*208). Ulrich argues in this article that 1QPs^b was copied by the same scribe who produced 4QIsa^c and 11QM.

8–11; 104:6, 8–9, 11; early Herodian bookhand from 30–1 B.C.E.; conservative orthography?; one non-aligned reading.

4QPs^j (4Q91): Nine fragments; frgs. 1–8 preserve twenty-eight complete and partial words from Pss 48:1–9; 49:6?, 9–12, 15, 17; 51:2–6; late Herodian bookhand; baroque orthography.

4QPs^m (4Q94): Nine fragments with forty-two complete and partial words from Pss 93:3–5; 95:3–7; 97:6–9; 98:4–8; early Herodian bookhand from 30–1 B.C.E.; the manuscript reads four times with MT and LXX against MT^mss, once with MT against LXX, and once against MT, the latter cannot be translated to a non-Semitic language; close to MT?

4QPs^o (4Q96): Two fragments with twenty-one complete and partial words from Pss 114:7; 115:1–2, 4; 116:3, 5, 7–10; early Herodian bookhand from the late first century B.C.E.; baroque orthography?; three non-aligned readings, one reading with LXX against MT, and one reading with MT^mss and T against MT, which cannot be translated to a non-Semitic language; 4QPs^o includes significant variants against MT-Pss: "Despite so few preserved words, 4QPs^o preserves several variant readings. In frg. 1 Psalms 114 and 115 most likely form a single Psalm, as in the Leningrad Codex and other 𝔐 manuscripts, followed by 𝔊 θ' 𝔖 Hier. In frg. 2 the aligment of text on lines 4–5 shows that a long interval followed Ps 116:9, indicating that vv. 10 onwards most likely consitute a new Psalm as in 𝔊 Hier."[137]

4QPs^r (4Q98a): Four fragments with twenty-six complete and partial words from Pss 26:7–27:1; 30:9–13; late Herodian bookhand from the first century C.E.; the manuscript reads two times non-aligned, once with MT^2mss and T against MT and LXX, and includes one reading against MT which cannot be translated into a non-Semitic language.

4QPs^s (4Q98b): One fragment with eighteen complete and partial words from Pss 5:8–6:1; late Herodian bookhand.

8QPs (8Q2): Fourteen fragments; frgs. 1–13 include ca. thirty-five complete and partial words from Pss 17:5–9, 14; 18:6–13; Herodian bookhand from the first century C.E.; no orthographic variants toward MT; two readings with MT against LXX.

11QPs^c (11Q7): Twelve fragments with 189 complete and partial words from Pss 2:1–8; 9:3–8; 11:1–4; 12:5–9; 13:2–3, 5–6; 14:1–6; 17:9–15; 18:1–12, 15–17?; 19:4–5, 7–8; 25:2–3, 5–7; early Herodian semi-formal bookhand with features of a developed Herodian bookhand from the first half of the first century B.C.E.; baroque orthography; the manuscript reads four times with and twenty times against MT, three times with and twelve times against LXX, as well as nineteen times non-aligned; probably a non-aligned text depending on MT-Pss.

11QPs^d (11Q8): This is the best-preserved unclassifiable Psalms manuscript, and therefore needs to be described in more detail. Of the seventeen preserved fragments, frgs. 1–15 attest to remnants of Pss 9:3, 5–6; 18:26–29,[138] 39–40, 42; 36:13; 37:1–4, 5?; 39:13–14; 40:1; 43:1–3; 45:6–8; 59:5–6, 8; 68:1, 3–5, 14, 16–18; 78:5–12; 81:4–9; 86:11–14; 115:16–18; 116:1. For frgs. 16–17, it remains uncertain if they attest to remnants of Pss 78:36–37 and 60:9. García Martínez, Tigchelaar, and van der Woude propose further that three (partial) words from a piece of marl preserve a remnant of the text of Ps 6:2–4 from 11QPs^d in mirror writing.[139] There can be no doubt that due to humidity a portion of the ink of a scroll adhered to this piece of marl. However, Es-

---

[137] Skehan, Ulrich, and Flint, "Psalms," 139.

[138] For the attribution of frg. 3 to 11QPs^d and possible problems with this attribution, see E. Tigchelaar, "Notes on the Three Qumran-Type Yadin Fragments Leading to a Discussion of Identification, Attribution, Provenance, and Names," *DSD* 19 (2012): 198–214 (199–202).

[139] Cf. García Martínez, Tigchelaar, and van der Woude, *DJD XXIII, 62–63. Today, only a photograph of the marl object in question exists (PAM 44.012 and plate 7 of *DJD XXIII).

hel[140] points to paleographic differences between the marl mirror writing and 11QPs[d]. He argues furthermore that insufficient humidity could have entered cave 11 in order to create such a mirror writing. The Bedouin who sold the mirror writing in question most likely found it in another cave; hence, it does not belong to 11QPs[d].

The scribe of 11QPs[d] employed a script that is described as a "developed to late formal Herodian" hand.[141] The orthography of the manuscript is incoherent but fuller than that of MT-Pss and employs at least some baroque features such as כה- instead of ך- for the suffix of the second person singular masculine.[142]

As only very few transitions between two psalms[143] are preserved in 11QPs[d] and because none of these transitions is characteristic for known psalms collections from the Second Temple period, the text-typological classification of 11QPs[d] is difficult. In 113 complete and partial words, 11QPs[d] reads seven times with and five times against MT, never with but eleven times against LXX, as well as five times non-aligned. In frg. 5 (Pss 36:13; 37:1–4), frg. 13 (Ps 81:4–9), and frg. 14 (Ps 86:11–14), the reconstructed line lengths do not agree with the texts of either MT or LXX. This difference in line length could imply a non-aligned text for these verses in 11QPs[d], but frg. 12 demonstrates that the scribe was able to write lines of the very different lengths.[144] Although the preserved text of 11QPs[d] is statistically close to MT-Pss, it remains uncertain whether this scroll attested to the proto-Masoretic Psalms collection or another psalms collection.[145]

10.2.1.6.2 Manuscripts of Which Only Parts of One Psalm Are Preserved

1QPs[c] (1Q12): Nine fragments; frgs. 1–7 preserve twenty complete and partial words from Ps 44:3–5, 7, 9, 23–25; late Herodian formal hand from the first century C.E.; baroque orthography; reads once with MT against LXX.

4QPs[p] (4Q97): Two fragments with seventeen complete and partial words from Ps 143:2–4, 6–8; Herodian bookhand.

4QPs[w] (4Q98f): Two fragments with thirteen complete and partial words from Ps 112:1–9; middle or late Hasmonean semi-cursive hand from 50–30 B.C.E.

4QPs[x] (4Q98g): One fragment with thirty-two complete and partial words from Ps 89:20–22, 26, 23, 27–28, 31; semi-cursive hand from 175–125 B.C.E.; inconsistent orthography with archaic and Aramaic traits; eleven non-aligned readings; different verse sequence from MT; Ps 89:24–25, 27b, 29–30 are lacking; non-aligned text form of Psalm 89.[146]

11QPs[e]? (11Q9): Remnants of six words from Ps 50:3, 5, 7; early or middle Herodian hand from the end of the first century B.C.E. or the beginning of the first century C.E.

Manuscript Schøyen 5233/2:[147] Eight complete and partial words from Ps 9:10, 12–13; according

---

[140] H. Eshel, "A Note on 11QPsalm[d] Fragment 1," *RevQ* 23 (2007–2008): 529–31.

[141] Talmon, "Unidentified Hebrew Fragments," 114; cf. also García Martínez and Tigchelaar, "Preliminary Edition," 93; García Martínez, Tigchelaar, and van der Woude, *DJD* XXIII, 64.

[142] Cf. García Martínez and Tigchelaar, "Preliminary Edition," 93–94; García Martínez, Tigchelaar, and van der Woude, *DJD* XXIII, 65.

[143] Only the transitions between Psalms 36 and 37 (frg. 5), Psalms 39 and 40 (frg. 6), and Psalms 115 and 116 (frg. 15) survive in 11QPs[d]. As only one character of Ps 36:13 is extant and only one word survives of Ps 40:1, the transitions between Psalms 36 and 37 and between Psalms 39 and 40 remain uncertain.

[144] Cf. García Martínez and Tigchelaar, "Preliminary Edition," 94; García Martínez, Tigchelaar, and van der Woude; *DJD* XXIII, 65, 68, 73–74.

[145] Cf. Lange, *Handbuch*, 402–03.

[146] Pajunen, "Collective Interpretation," has recently argued that 4QPs[x] is the remnant of a handlesheet on which "an abbreviated collective interpretation of the oracle to David and his descendants in Psalm 89:20–38" was noted. In this case, all readings against MT in 4QPs[x] would be secondary.

[147] I am obliged to Torleif Elgvin who provided me with a preprint copy of his edition of manuscript Schøyen 5233/2 ("MS 5233/2"). All information about this manuscript given below is based on Elgvin's edition.

to Langlois, Herodian hand from the second half or most likely the third quarter of the first century B.C.E.;[148] it is significant that Ps 9:10 is followed directly by Ps 9:12; non-aligned text of Psalm 9?

10.2.1.6.3 Manuscripts for Which It Is Uncertain If They Preserve a Psalms Manuscript or a Quotation from a Psalm

3QPs (3Q2): Remnants of six words from Ps 2:6–7; Herodian bookhand from the first century C.E.

4QPs^t (4Q98c): Remnants of six words from Ps 88:15–17; late Herodian hand from 50–68 C.E.

4QPs^u (4Q98d): Remnants of three words from Ps 42:5; late Herodian hand from ca. 50 C.E.

4QPs^v (4Q98e): Remnants of two words from Ps 99:1; early Herodian hand from the end of the first century B.C.E.

6QpapPs? (6Q5): Remnants of three words from Ps 78:36–37; Herodian bookhand from the first century C.E.

Baillet, M., "14. Psautier," *DJD III.1: 69–71.
Baillet, M., "2. Psaume 2," *DJD III.1: 94.
Baillet, M., "5. Psaume 78(?)," *DJD III.1: 112.
Baillet, M., "2. Psautier," *DJD III.1: 148–49.
Barthélemy, D., "10. Psautier (premier exemplaire)," *DJD I: 69–70.
Barthélemy, D., "11. Psautier (second exemplaire)," *DJD I: 71.
Barthélemy, D., "12. Psaume 44," *DJD I: 71–72.
Brooke, G.J., "The Psalms in Early Jewish Literature in the Light of the Dead Sea Scrolls," in *The Psalms in the New Testament* (eds. S. Moyise and M.J.J. Menken; The New Testament and the Scriptures of Israel; London: T & T Clark, 2004), 5–24.
Dahmen, U., "New Identifications and Re-Groupings of Psalms Fragments from Qumran Cave I and IV," *RevQ* 20 (2001–2002): 479–85.
Dahmen, U., *Psalmen- und Psalter-Rezeption im Frühjudentum: Rekonstruktion, Textbestand, Struktur und Pragmatik der Psalmenrolle 11QPs^a aus Qumran* (STDJ 49; Leiden: Brill, 2003).
Elgvin, T., "MS 5233/2: 4Q(?)Ps (Ps. 9.10, 12–13)," in *Gleanings*, forthcoming.
Eshel, E. and H. Eshel, "A Preliminary Report on Seven New Fragments from Qumran," *Meghillot* 5–6 (2007): 271–78 [Hebr.].
Fitzmyer, J.A., "98f. 4QPs^w," *DJD XVI: 161–62.
Flint, P.W., *The Dead Sea Psalms Scrolls and the Book of Psalms* (STDJ 17; Leiden: Brill, 1997).
Flint, P.W., "The '11QPs^a-Psalter' in the Dead Sea Scrolls: Including the Preliminary Edition of 4QPs^e," in *The Quest for Context and Meaning: Studies in Biblical Intertextuality in Honor of James A. Sanders* (eds. C.A. Evans and S. Talmon; BibInt 28; Leiden: Brill, 1997), 173–96.
Flint, P.W., "The Book of Psalms in the Light of the Dead Sea Scrolls," *VT* 48 (1998): 453–72.
Flint, P.W., "A Preliminary Edition of 4QPs^d (4Q86)," in *The Provo International Conference on the Dead Sea Scrolls: Technological Innovations, New Texts, and Reformulated Issues* (eds. D.W. Parry and E. Ulrich; STDJ 30; Leiden: Brill, 1999), 93–105.
Flint, P.W., "1b. 5/6ḤevPsalms," *DJD XXXVIII: 141–66.
Flint, P.W., "The Preliminary Edition of 5/6ḤevPsalms," *JJS* 51 (2000): 19–41.
Flint, P.W., "Psalms and Psalters in the Dead Sea Scrolls," in *The Bible and the Dead Sea Scrolls: The Princeton Symposium on the Dead Sea Scrolls* (3 vols.; ed. J.H. Charlesworth; Waco: Baylor University Press, 2006), 1:233–72.
Flint, P.W., "Five Surprises in the Qumran Psalms Scrolls," in *Flores Florentino: Dead Sea Scrolls and Other Early Jewish Studies in Honour of Florentino García Martínez* (eds. A. Hilhorst, É. Puech, and E. Tigchelaar; JSJSup 122; Leiden: Brill, 2007), 183–95.
Flint, P.W., "11QPs^b and the 11QPs^a-Psalter," in *Diachronic and Synchronic: Reading the Psalms in the Real Time: Proceedings of the Baylor Symposium on the Book of Psalms* (eds. J.S. Burnett, W.H. Bellinger, and W.D. Tucker; Library of Hebrew Bible/Old Testament Studies 488; New York: T & T Clark International, 2007), 157–66.
Flint, P.W., "The Dead Sea Psalms Scrolls: Psalms Manuscripts, Editions, and the *Oxford Hebrew Bible*," in *Jewish and Christian Approaches to the Psalms: Conflict and Convergence* (ed. S. Gillingham; Oxford: Oxford University Press, 2013), 11–34.
Flint, P.W., "Unrolling the Dead Sea Psalms Scrolls," in

---

[148] See M. Langlois, "Palaeographical Analysis of the Dead Sea Scrolls," in *Gleanings*, forthcoming.

10.2.1 ANCIENT MANUSCRIPT EVIDENCE

The Oxford Handbook of the Psalms (ed. W.P. Brown; Oxford: Oxford University Press, 2014), 229–50.

Flint, P.W. and A.A. Alvarez, "The Oldest of All Psalms Scrolls: The Text and Translation of 4QPs^a," in *The Scrolls and the Scriptures: Qumran after Fifty Years* (eds. S.E. Porter and C.A. Evans; JSPSup 26; Sheffield: Sheffield Academic Press, 1997), 142–69.

Flint, P.W., P.W. Skehan, and E. Ulrich, "Three Psalms of Praise from Qumran: The Preliminary Editions of 4QPs^l and 4QPs^n," *JNSL* 24/2 (1998): 35–44.

García Martínez, F. and E.J.C. Tigchelaar, "Psalms Manuscripts from Qumran Cave 11: A Preliminary Edition," *RevQ* 17 (1996): 73–107.

García Martínez, F., E.J.C. Tigchelaar, and A.S. van der Woude, *DJD XXIII: 29–78, 181–205.

Jain, E. and A. Steudel, "Le manuscrits psalmique de la Mer Morte et la réception du Psautier à Qumran," *RevScRel* 77 (2003): 529–43.

Lange, A., *Handbuch, 373–450.

Lange, A., "Collecting Psalms in Light of the Dead Sea Scrolls," in *A Teacher for All Generations: Essays in Honor of James C. VanderKam* (2 vols.; eds. E.F. Mason et al.; JSJSup153; Leiden: Brill, 2012), 1:297–309.

Milik, J.T., "Deux documents inédits du Désert de Juda," *Bib* 38 (1957): 245–68.

Milik, J.T., "5. Psaume 119," *DJD III.1: 174.

Milik, J.T., "Fragment d'une source du Psautier (4Q Ps 89) et fragments des Jubilées, du Document de Damas, d'un phylactère dans la grotte 4 de Qumran," *RB* 73 (1966): 94–106.

Nebe, G.W., "Die Masada-Psalmen-Handschrift M1039–160 nach einem jüngst veröffentlichten Photo mit Text von *Psalm 81,2–85,6*," *RevQ* 14 (1989–1990): 89–97.

Pajunen, M.S., "4QPs^x: A Collective Interpretation of Psalm 89:20–38," *JBL* 133 (2014): 479–95.

van der Ploeg, J.P.M., "Fragments d'un manuscrit de Psaumes de Qumran (11QPs^b)," *RB* 74 (1967): 408–12 with plate xviii.

van der Ploeg, J.P.M., "Fragments d' un psautier de Qumrân," in *Symbolae Biblicae et Mesopotamicae Francisco Mario Theodoro de Liagre Böhl dedicatae* (eds. M.A. Beek et al.; Leiden: Brill, 1973), 308–09.

van der Ploeg, J.P.M., "Fragments de Psaumes de Qumrân," in *Intertestamental Essays in Honor of Józef Tadeusz Milik* (ed. Z.J. Kapera; Krakow: Enigma Press, 1992), 233–37.

Sanders, J.A., *DJD IV.

Sanders, J.A., *The Dead Sea Psalms Scroll* (Ithaca: Cornell University Press, 1967).

Skehan, P.W., "The Qumran Manuscripts and Textual Criticism," in *Volume du congrès: Strasbourg 1956* (ed. P.A.H. de Boer; VTS 4; Leiden: Brill, 1957), 148–60, esp. 153–55.

Skehan, P.W., "A Psalm Manuscript from Qumran (4Q Ps^b)," *CBQ* 26 (1964): 313–22.

Skehan, P.W., E. Ulrich, and P.W. Flint, "Psalms," *DJD XVI: 7–167.

Skehan, P.W., E. Ulrich, and P.W. Flint, "The Preliminary Edition of *4QPs^c (4Q85)*," *RevQ* 18 (1997): 343–57.

Skehan, P.W., E. Ulrich, and P.W. Flint, "A Scroll Containing 'Biblical' and 'Apocryphal' Psalms: A Preliminary Edition of 4QPs^f (4Q88)," *CBQ* 60 (1998): 267–82.

Skehan, P.W., E. Ulrich, and P.W. Flint, "Two Manuscripts of Ps 119 from Qumran Cave 4," *RevQ* 16 (1993–1995): 477–86.

Starky, J., "Psaumes apocryphes de la grotte 4 de Qumrân (4QPs^f VII–X)," *RB* 73 (1966): 353–71.

Swanson, D.D., "Qumran and the Psalms," in *Interpreting the Psalms: Issues and Approaches* (eds. P.S. Johnston and D.G. Firth; Downers Grove: InterVarsity Press, 2005), 247–61.

Talmon, S., "Fragments of a Psalms Scroll from Masada: MPs^b (Masada 1103–1742)," in *Minḥah le-Naḥum: Biblical and Other Studies Presented to Nahum M. Sarna in Honour of His 70th Birthday* (eds. M. Brettler and M. Fishbane; JSOTSup 154; Sheffield: Sheffield Academic Press, 1993), 318–27.

Talmon, S., "Fragments of a Psalms Scroll–MasPs^a Ps 81:2b–85:6a (1039–160; Mas1e; final photo 5255)," *DSD* 3 (1996): 296–314.

Talmon, S., "Unidentified Hebrew Fragments from Y. Yadin's *Nachlass*," *Tarbiz* 66 (1997): 113–21, viii [Hebr.].

Talmon, S., "Hebrew Fragments from Masada," in S. Talmon and Y. Yadin, *Masada VI: The Yigael Yadin Excavations 1963–1965: Final Reports* (Jerusalem: Israel Exploration Society, 1999), 1–149, esp. 76–97.

Ulrich, E., "The Oldest Psalms Manuscript: 4QPs^a (4Q83)," in *The Provo International Conference on the Dead Sea Scrolls: Technological Innovations, New Texts, and Reformulated Issues* (eds. D.W. Parry and E. Ulrich; STDJ 30; Leiden: Brill, 1999), 72–92.

Ulrich, E., "Two Perspectives on Two Pentateuchal Manuscripts from Masada," in *Emanuel: Studies in the Hebrew Bible, Septuagint, and Dead Sea Scrolls in Honor of Emanuel Tov* (eds. S. Paul et al.; VTS 94; Leiden: Brill, 2003), 453–64.

Ulrich, E., *BQS, 627–726.

Wilson, G.H., "The Qumran Psalms Manuscripts and the

Consecutive Arrangement of Psalms in the Hebrew Psalter," *CBQ* 45 (1983): 377–88.

Wilson, G.H., *The Editing of the Hebrew Psalter* (SBLDS 76, Chico: Scholars Press, 1985).

Wilson, G.H., "The Qumran Psalm Scroll (11QPsᵃ) and the Canonical Psalter," *CBQ* 59 (1997): 448–64.

Wilson, G.H., "The Structure of the Psalter," in *Interpreting the Psalms: Issues and Approaches* (eds. P.S. Johnston and D.G. Firth; Downers Grove: InterVarsity Press, 2005), 229–46.

Yadin, Y., "Expedition D," *IEJ* 11 (1961): 36–52, esp. 40 with plate 20.D.

Yadin, Y., "Another Fragment (E) of the Psalms Scroll from Qumran Cave 11 (11QPsᵃ)," *Textus* 5 (1966): 1–10.

Armin Lange

10.2.2 (Proto-)Masoretic Texts and Ancient Texts Close to MT

Locating the earliest witness to the (proto-)MT text of Psalms is a matter of considerable debate in the wake of the Dead Sea Scrolls discoveries. The earliest finds from the Judean Desert and the first scholarly assessments thereof suggested that these manuscripts were largely if not entirely (proto-)Masoretic.[1] The picture became considerably less clear, however, with the publication of 11QPsᵃ by Sanders in *DJD* IV (1965)[2] and the full publication of the Cave 4 Psalms manuscripts in *DJD* XIV (2000) coupled with the extended analysis thereof in the dissertation-turned-monograph by Flint.[3] Prior to Flint's work – and the equally ground-breaking work of Wilson[4] – Sanders had been rather alone in suggesting that 11QPsᵃ was an alternative, but legitimate version of the Psalter at Qumran.[5] Armed with the full repertoire of Psalms manuscripts, Flint reinvigorated Sanders' "Qumran Psalms Hypothesis," arguing that the vast majority of the Dead Sea evidence indicates that only the first eighty-nine psalms (Books I–III of the Psalter) had been stabilized, with the rest (Psalms 90–150; Books IV–V) still in flux well into the first century C.E.[6]

Further discussion of the manuscript evidence and its assessment vis-à-vis possible or probable non-MT alignment may be found in → 10.2.1 and → 10.2.3. This debate must be mentioned briefly here as well, however, because, following Flint's research, the pendulum seems to have swung in the other direction entirely. So, according to Flint, while some manuscripts appear to support (proto-)MT, this impression may be misleading since even non-MT Psalms manuscripts occasionally corroborate (in ways both small and large) what is now found in MT. What this means – to use a formulation Flint is fond of – is that "no manuscript from Qumran *unambiguously* supports the arrangement found in Books IV–V of the MT-150 Psalter."[7]

Flint's text-critical analysis of the Dead Sea Psalms manuscripts is unparalleled, but his assessment may be overly confident regarding the extent of the purported non-(proto-)MT data (and its meaning/significance), on the one hand, and, on the other hand, overly skeptical about those data that do, *prima facie*, seem to align with (proto-)MT.[8] One of the main problems in making definitive judgments about such matters (in either direction) is the poor state of the preserved manuscripts; in many cases, there is simply not enough extant material to permit firm de-

---

[1] See, e.g., *DJD* III, 94 on 3QPs (3Q2); *DJD* III, 148 on 8QPs (8Q2). See Flint, "Unrolling," 231–39, for five phases in the history of scholarship on the Psalms scrolls (see also → 10.2.3.1).

[2] See also Sanders, *Dead Sea Psalms Scroll*.

[3] Flint, *Dead Sea Psalms Scrolls*. See also Flint, "The Book of Psalms"; Flint, "Psalms and Psalters"; Flint, "Five Surprises"; Flint, "11QPsᵇ"; Flint, "11QPsᵃ-Psalter"; Flint, "Dead Sea Psalms Scrolls"; and Flint, "Unrolling."

[4] Wilson, *Editing of the Hebrew Psalter*.

[5] See, e.g., Flint, "Unrolling," 232–33. Tov, *TCHB*, 321 deems the *contra* Sanders opinion "preferable." For further discussion, see → 10.2.3.2.4.

[6] See → 10.1; → 10.2.2; → 10.2.3.2.4; Flint, *Dead Sea Psalms Scrolls*, 141; and throughout Flint's several studies (see n. 3 above). Note that only five manuscripts preserve material from *both* Psalms 1–89 and 90–150: 1QPsᵃ, 4QPsᵉ, 4QPsᶠ, 11QPsᵇ, 11QPsᵈ.

[7] Flint, *Dead Sea Psalms Scrolls*, 239 (his emphasis); see also Flint, *Dead Sea Psalms Scrolls*, 157–58; Flint, "Psalms and Psalters," 243; Flint, "Dead Sea Psalms Scrolls," 16–17; and further below (→ 10.2.2.1.3) on "MT-150."

[8] See → 10.2.3, and, for recent (re)assessments of the evidence, Dahmen, *Psalmen- und Psalter-Rezeption*; and Jain, *Psalmen oder Psalter*.

cisions as to text type (see → 10.2.1; → 10.2.3). So, for example, are manuscripts that contain text from only one psalm best understood as excerpted or abbreviated manuscripts, whatever that mean might for their text-typological classification (see → 10.2.1.5; → 10.2.3.6); or, in those cases where the preserved text is even more minimal, might such texts simply be citations of a psalm (whether in whole or in part) in another, originally *non*-psalmic manuscript (see → 10.2.1.6, esp. → 10.2.1.6.2–3; also → 10.2.3.6)?

These kinds of questions – some of which simply cannot be answered with the data presently at hand – are taken up in various ways and to varying degrees elsewhere (→ 10.1; → 10.2.1; → 10.2.3). Even so, → 10.2.3 proceeds under the assumption that there are no less than three non-proto-MT collections of the Psalms at Qumran, attested in as many as eight different manuscripts (*Collection 1:* 11QPs^a, 11QPs^b, 4QPs^e, 4QPsⁿ, and 1QPs^b; *Collection 2:* 4QPs^f; *Collection 3:* 4QPs^a and 4QPs^q). The present article operates with another working assumption, namely (and contrary to Flint's more cautious approach), that the following manuscripts are best understood as belonging to the proto-MT text type if there is no obvious reason to consider otherwise: MasPs^a, MasPs^b, 5/6ḤevPs, and 4QPs^c (see → 10.2.2.1.2 below; further → 10.2.1; → 10.2.1.1). The nature of this approach as *assumptive* must be heavily underscored, given two important caveats: 1) the possibility that some (or many) of the unclassifiable psalms manuscripts (see → 10.2.1.6) could belong to the proto-MT family (but just as possibly to other textual families); and 2) that certain issues germane if not unique to the Psalms problematize text-critical analysis.

These latter issues are several, but the following three are paramount, with each one greatly complicating text-typological classification of the Psalms manuscripts, specifically, and the textual criticism of the Psalms, more generally.

– The *nature of the psalms as brief religious poems* (i.e., short liturgical compositions) that seldom relate obviously to each other in the same way that two sections of a continuous narrative composition do, thus lending to each individual psalm something of an isolated character.[9]

This issue leads directly to the second issue:

– The fact that *text-critical differences within psalms are often limited* across various witnesses, which means: a) that individual compositions are typically quite stable, many showing little disturbance, others far more;[10] and b) that text type is most obviously assessed by differences in psalm sequencing across witnesses coupled with the presence (or absence) of additional/non-(proto-)MT psalmic content (see → 10.2.1; → 10.2.3.1).[11]

And, finally, related to both of the preceding:

– The *question of the order/sequence of MT-Pss*, including the determination of when that order was established and how it may or may not be used in text-typological classification and text-critical analysis.

Each of these issues is addressed in what follows.

---

[9] Cf. Pajunen, "Perspectives," 139–63; and note that at Qumran, individual psalms could be transmitted by themselves as excerpts (see → 10.2.3.6).

[10] See, similarly (*inter alia*), Lange, **Handbuch*, 423–35; Lange, "Collecting," 301–02; Flint, "Unrolling," 247; deClaissé-Walford, Jacobson, and Tanner, *Psalms*, 3–4; and P. Kyle McCarter, *Textual Criticism: Recovering the Text of the Hebrew Bible* (GBS; Philadelphia: Fortress, 1986), 92, who states that MT-Pss is in "fair condition."

[11] Only six manuscripts contain additional content: 4QPs^f, 4QApocr. Psalm and Prayer, 4QProphecy of Joshua, 11QPs^a, 11QPs^b, 11QapocrPs. Three of these are not Psalms manuscripts proper (4QApocr. Psalm and Prayer, 4QProphecy of Joshua, 11QapocrPs), containing significant amounts of non-psalmic material or belonging to a different genre altogether (e.g., 4QProphecy of Joshua is a rewritten Bible text). Even so, these three do contain Psalms 154 (a non-MT-Pss composition), 122, and 91, respectively.

10.2.2.1 History of Research

Differences between (proto-)MT-Pss and LXX-Pss (→ 10.3.1) have been known for centuries, if not millennia, if only given the different sequencing of the two text-forms and the inclusion of Psalm 151 in the latter, though that composition is already recognized as being "outside the number" (ἔξωθεν τοῦ ἀριθμοῦ) by its superscription (see → 10.2.2.1.3). Equally well known were the differences in superscriptions between these two text types and yet still other forms of the superscriptions elsewhere in the textual history of Psalms.[12] This does not yet mention differences in the psalm-texts proper in the other major versions beyond LXX. As a result of such divergence, modern scholarship has vacillated in its estimation of the Hebrew text and/or its favoring of this or some other version. Prior to the late nineteenth and early- to mid-twentieth centuries, scholars concerned primarily with the Hebrew text of Psalms favored the form known in MT-Pss,[13] but after that time scholars not infrequently favored the Greek, looking askance at MT-Pss.[14] Doubt about the state of MT was prompted, in part, by the recognition of doublets or parallel texts in the Psalter as well as comparative work facilitated, especially, by the Ugaritic texts (→ 10.2.2.1.1). Following the discoveries at Ugarit, the next watershed in Psalms scholarship was the publication of the Dead Sea Scrolls, which afforded unique insight on the earliest history of the text and its stabilization, at least as that could be assessed from the earliest preserved manuscripts (→ 10.2.2.1.2; → 10.2.3). Finally, recent research on the medieval manuscripts has cast significant light on the end(s) of that textual history, namely, when the book of Psalms was finally stabilized in the form now familiar in MT-Pss.

10.2.2.1.1 Doublets/Parallel Texts and Comparative Poetics

The necessity of text-critical work on Psalms is obvious already from the existence of parallel passages within the psalms and occasionally outside the Psalter proper. Note the following equivalences:

Ps 14:1b–7	=	Ps 53:2–7
Ps 18:3–51	=	2 Sam 22:2–51
Ps 40:14–18	=	Ps 70:2–6
Pss 57:8–12 + 60:7–14	=	Ps 108:2–14
Pss 105:1–15 + 96:1–13 + 106:1, 47–48	=	1 Chr 16:8–36a

These doublets might be used in "outlining the history of development" within the Psalter.[15] Why such parallel texts exist, however, is debated,[16] though Weiser seems correct when he states that the "phenomenon ... would hardly have been possible if all the psalms had been grouped together all at once and by the same compiler."[17] The existence of doublets within (and without) the Psalms, that is, suggests multiple authorial and editorial hands, just as it does in the case of similar passages in the Pentateuch.[18] The Psalmic doublets are, furthermore, characterized by textual divergence to greater or lesser degrees (see the apparatus in *BHS*).

---

[12] See, e.g., Flint, *Dead Sea Psalms Scrolls*, 117–34; also → 10.1.2.2; → 10.3.4; → 10.4.4.

[13] See, e.g., W.M.L. de Wette, *Die Psalmen* (3rd ed.; Heidelberg: J.C.B. Mohr, 1829); F. Delitzsch, *Biblical Commentary on the Psalms* (3 vols.; 2nd ed.; trans. F. Bolton; Edinburgh: T & T Clark, 1884).

[14] See, e.g., Duhm, *Psalmen*; and T.K. Cheyne, *The Book of Psalms* (2 vols.; London: Kegan Paul, Trench, Trübner, 1904), viii–xi, lxviii–lxix.

[15] Witte, "Psalter," 543. The same may be true for the reception of some psalms in others, e.g., the use of Psalm 29 in Psalm 96, or Psalm 115 in Psalm 135 (see Witte, "Psalter," 544 n. 22).

[16] See, *inter alia*, Schmuttermayr, *Psalm 18 und 2 Samuel 22*; Hossfeld–Zenger, *Psalms 2*, 36–39, 68, 75, 103; Hossfeld–Zenger, *Psalms 3*, 114–16; Goldingay, *Psalms*, 1.211, 253; 2.150; 3.264; C.C. Torrey, "The Archaeology of Psalms 14 and 53," *JBL* 46 (1927): 186–92.

[17] Weiser, *Psalms*, 99.

[18] See R. Müller, J. Pakkala, and B. ter Haar Romeny, "Evidence of Psalm Composition: Psalm 108 as a Secondary Compilation of Other Psalm Texts," in Müller, Pakkala, and ter Haar Romeny, *Evidence of Editing: Growth and Change of Texts in the Hebrew Bible* (SBLRBS 75; Atlanta: SBL, 2014), 159–77. Their own opinion of the composition-critical relationship between Psalms 57, 60, and 108 may be contrasted with, e.g., Briggs and Briggs, *Psalms*, 1.xxxiv.

According to Kraus, it was "the numerous divergences and variations of these double texts" that first led scholars to recognize "how unreliable the Hebrew text tradition is in the area of the Psalms."[19] It is not always clear where (or when) such "unreliability" entered the tradition, however. Terrien, for instance, notes that textual divergence between doublets "may ... be due not to copyists' errors but to oral transmission in the prewritten stages."[20] If this is the case, then one must account for text forms that lie prior to, for example, Psalm 18 and 2 Samuel 22.[21] Furthermore, the extant textual witnesses do not always help in deciding which doublet is superior (if one is).[22] Finally, in the case of psalms that seem to be quite literally constructed from other psalms, the issue may not be text-critical so much as redaction- or composition-critical.

Whatever the case, prior to the first discoveries in the Judean Desert, text-critical research on the Psalms – at all points, not just in the case of doublets – relied heavily on the versional evidence, especially the Greek and Latin translations (see → 10.3.1; → 10.3.5; → 10.3.6; → 10.3.7; → 10.4.1). Scholarly opinion waxed and waned as to the trustworthiness of MT, with some favoring the versions (especially LXX-Pss) as a matter of course and adopting highly critical stances toward MT.[23]

After the discovery of the Ugaritic materials (1929), the study of MT-Pss became dominated by comparative approaches. In the work of Albright, continued by his students Cross and Freedman, MT-Pss was often emended so as to reconstruct its putative early or "original" form, even if such correction was not always supported by the versions, and even if this work was predicated, as it often was, on certain presumptions regarding diachronic developments in Northwest Semitic prosody, especially parallelism.[24] The most extreme form of "pan-Ugariticism" in the Psalms is typically located in Dahood's three-volume commentary in the Anchor Bible series.[25] Here one finds numerous creative suggestions about MT-Pss, even in places where MT seems perfectly acceptable and not in need of extensive alteration or novel interpretation. Less extreme approaches to the relationship between the comparative evidence and the textual criticism of the Psalms may be found[26] and, though Ugaritic does not enjoy the status it once did, it remains clear that it has left an indelible mark on the study of the Psalter and its poetics.[27]

---

[19] Kraus, *Psalms 1–59*, 13–14.

[20] Terrien, *Psalms*, 25; cf. Briggs and Briggs, *Psalms*, 1.xxiv. Another possibility could be copying or composing from memory; see, e.g., the discussion of 11QPs^a XVI at → 10.2.3.2.1.1; and the possible blending of Psalms 135 and 136 in 4QPs^n (see → 10.2.3.2.1.4). See, more generally, Carr, *Formation*.

[21] So, e.g., Goldingay, *Psalms*, 1.253. See, further, Cross and Freedman, *Studies*.

[22] Cf. Kraus, *Psalms 1–59*, 15, speaking of Cross and Freedman's work (*Studies*) remarks: "But even here criticism has its limits." Flint, "5/6HevPsalms," 144, has noted that the text form in this case favors MT-Pss not the 2 Samuel 22 version.

[23] See Kraus, *Psalms 1–59*, 13–14, on what he deems the extremely skeptical approach of Duhm (*Psalmen*) and Gunkel (*Psalmen*). Kraus cautions against "strong assaults on the transmitted text," and rejects "the preference on principle of Gk, for instance, over against MT, and ... a premature resort to the old translations" (*Psalms 1–59*, 14–15; cf. Briggs and Briggs, *Psalms*, 1.xxv).

---

[24] See, e.g., W.F. Albright, "A Catalogue of Early Hebrew Lyric Poems (Psalm LXVIII)," *HUCA* 23 (1950–1951): 1–39; and esp. Cross and Freedman, *Studies*. For one critical assessment, see D.W. Goodwin, *Text-Restoration Methods in Contemporary U.S.A. Biblical Scholarship* (Naples: Istituto Orientale di Napoli, 1969).

[25] M. Dahood, *Psalms I–III: Introduction, Translation, and Notes* (3 vols.; AB 16–17A; New York: Doubleday, 1966–1970). Note also Dahood's extensive work on "Ugaritic-Hebrew Parallel Pairs" in *Ras Shamra Parallels: The Texts from Ugarit and the Hebrew Bible* (3 vols.; eds. L.R. Fisher and S. Rummel; AnOr 49–51; Rome: Pontifical Biblical Institute, 1972–1981), 1.71–382; 2.1–33, 34–39; 3.1–177, 178–206.

[26] E.g., O. Loretz, *Die Psalmen II: Beitrag der Ugarit-Texte zum Verständnis von Kolometrie und Textologie der Psalmen: Psalm 90–150* (AOAT 207; Neukirchen-Vluyn: Neukirchener Verlag, 1979); B.A. Strawn, "*kwšrwt* in Psalm 68:7, Again: A (Small) Test Case in Relating Ugarit to the Hebrew Bible," *UF* 41 (2009): 631–48.

[27] E.g., O. Loretz and I. Kottsieper, *Colometry in Ugaritic and Biblical Poetry: Introduction, Illustrations and Topical Bibliography* (Altenberge: CIS-Verlag, 1987).

10.2.2.1.2 (Proto-)MT Psalms among the Dead Sea Scrolls

With the discovery of the Dead Sea Scrolls, and especially the "surprises" afforded by 11QPs^a and other non-MT-aligned manuscripts from Cave 4,[28] the text of Psalms was investigated afresh and anew, particularly by Sanders, Wilson, and Flint. The work of these three scholars – but especially the last – refuted all postulations of an early stabilization of the Psalter, at least in the form we now have it.[29] According to Flint, the manuscript evidence supports a fairly early stabilization of Psalms 1–89 (prior to the Qumran manuscripts), but shows considerable flux in Books IV–V, which persisted well into the first century C.E.[30] This has profound ramifications for scholarship concerned with the growth and final shape of the Psalter (see → 10.1.2.1; → 10.2.2.1.3; → 10.2.2.5 below).

Despite the important work of Sanders, Wilson, and Flint, the picture afforded by 11QPs^a and other non-MT-aligned manuscripts is not entirely clear, and so the "Qumran Psalms Hypothesis" remains hypothetical – not yet axiomatic – for at least two reasons:

1) The first is the nature of the psalms *qua* compositions, which was already mentioned above. Many if not most psalms, at least *prima facie* (or at the time of initial composition), seem to have little or no obvious relationship with psalms that precede or follow them.[31] This means they can quite easily be (and have been) placed in more than one acceptable sequence. Indeed, given their nature as (originally) independent, short, liturgical compositions, any arrangement that involves more than one psalm is virtually by definition and almost entirely an *editorial or production* matter, not always or necessarily an *authorial or transmissional* one. This leads directly to the second reason, but it should be noted first that an important index of the liturgical nature and use of the psalms – and their popularity as such if not *because* of such – is the sheer number of manuscripts preserved of the Psalter, which typically outnumbers other texts by a fair margin.[32] The Psalter seems to have been (re)used and (re)copied more than any other biblical composition; a reflex of this popularity is the proliferation of variants at both micro- (specific words) and macro- (psalm sequences) levels.

2) In light of the first point, it is possible – if not, in fact, quite likely – that any number of psalms manuscripts could be editorial selections made for liturgical use rather than copies of the book of Psalms (in whole or in part). That is to say that at least some non-aligned texts – more specifically, non-MT texts (as determined by alternative sequencing) – may look the way they do (again, in terms of sequencing) due to their nature as psalm collections or editions, designed for some specific use, rather than because they were intended to be copies of "the book of Psalms."[33] This reasonable possibility is in part what has divided scholars in the "Great 11QPs^a Debate,"[34] though it must be immediately chastened by the fact that, barring early and pristine witness to a stable text form, one simply cannot presume that manuscript differences are derivations therefrom since they may just as likely be constituent elements in the growth and development of the Psalms (see → 10.2.3.7).[35] This

---

[28] Sanders, "Cave 11 Surprises"; Flint, "Five Surprises"; Wilson, *Editing of the Hebrew Psalter*.

[29] Cf., e.g., Briggs and Briggs, *Psalms*, 1.lxxxix: "*the present Psalter was finally edited and arranged … in the middle of the second century B.C.*" (their emphasis).

[30] Flint, *Dead Sea Psalms Scrolls*, 7, 9, 89; and *passim* in his corpus (see n. 3 above and the bibliography).

[31] This is a debatable claim in light of work on the shape and shaping of the Psalter, for which see → 10.1.2.1 and → 10.2.2.5 (below).

[32] This is true not only for Psalms manuscripts at Qumran (see → 10.2.1), but also for other manuscript evidence, e.g., the Greek (see Briggs and Briggs, *Psalms*, 1.xxv–xxix) and Ethiopic (→ 10.4.3).

[33] If this is even a meaningful concept, in light of the manuscript evidence. Flint, of course, would say it is not. Note also Pajunen, "Perspectives."

[34] See Strawn, "David," esp. 607–10.

[35] Wilson, "Consecutive Arrangement," 385: "We should be careful not to allow ourselves to be persuaded by our own knowledge of the subsequent shape of the canonical Psalter to presume that the presence of … supportive readings

latter option, too, is entirely possible, if not in fact highly likely, because the Dead Sea Psalms scrolls, in all their pluriformity, remain "our earliest extant witness to the scriptural text of the psalms."[36] But even this possibility must be chastened, at least somewhat, by the fact that there is some evidence supporting (proto-)MT. At least four manuscripts deserve consideration:

- MasPs[a] (1039–1160; Mas1e; → 10.2.1.1.1) contains Pss 81:2b–85:6a. According to the editor, it "corresponds for all intents and purposes to MT."[37] It agrees twelve times with MT against LXX and contains only five small non-aligned readings.[38]
- MasPs[b] (1103–1742; Mas1f; → 10.2.1.1.2) contains portions of Ps 147:18–19 and all of Ps 150:1–6. The manuscript clearly ended with Psalm 150, which is important in terms of aligning this text with MT-Pss (see → 10.2.2.1.3 below).[39] Beyond this important factor, the editor indicates that MasPs[b] is "identical with MT save for some small orthographic differences."[40] Further, it reads with MT against 11QPs[a] twice, which underscores "the close textual affinity of the Masada scroll with MT and concomitantly its divergence from the practically contemporaneous Psalms scroll [11QPs[a]]."[41]
- 5/6ḤevPs (5/6Ḥev1b; → 10.2.1.1.3) is orthographically more defective than MT, but the vast majority of variant readings in this manuscript align with MT[L] (against MT[mss]) and thus this scroll is best classified as (proto-)MT.[42] Even so, it does have some notable features vis-à-vis MT: the probable lack of the superscription in Psalm 15, the minus of the first colon of Ps 15:3a (לֹא רָגַל עַל לְשֹׁנוֹ "he does not slander with his tongue"; via homoioteleuton with *waw* on בִּלְבָבוֹ "in his heart" in v. 2b, or homoioarkton with לֹא "not" in v. 3b?).[43]
- 4QPs[c] (4Q85; → 10.2.1.1.4) is orthographically more defective than MT, but, out of 320 complete and partial words, only contains nine readings against MT. Lange deems it "semi-Masoretic."[44]

It is noteworthy that three of these four manuscripts were recovered from sites *other* than Qumran. Their significance for the state of Psalms at Qumran, then, may be small. Even so, if nothing else, the presence of (proto-)MT texts *outside* Qumran chastens Flint's claim that the "11QPs[a]-Psalter" was widely known and used (perhaps predominantly) in early Jewish circles beyond Qumran.[45] In point of fact, there is *no* non-Qumran evidence for the 11QPs[a]-Psalter. Further, it should be recalled that it is possible that some of the other manuscripts from Qumran may also belong to the (proto-)MT group. Indeed, it seems reasonable to add 11QPs[c] (11Q7; → 10.2.1.6.1) and 11QPs[d]

---

necessarily signifies the existence of the fixed, authoritative canonical Psalter." Cf. Swanson, "Qumran," 261.

36 Flint, "Unrolling," 229; similarly Flint, "11QPs[a]-Psalter," 176. See also Wilson, "Consecutive Arrangement," 377, 385. Cf. E. Ulrich, "Qumran and the Canon of the Old Testament," in *The Biblical Canons* (eds. J.-M. Auwers and H.J. de Jonge; BETL 163; Leuven: Leuven University Press, 2003), 57–80, 62: the scrolls "are the oldest, the best, and the most authentic evidence we have for the shape of the Scriptures at the time of the beginning of Christianity and rabbinic Judaism … The Qumran scriptural scrolls should now become the standard criteria for understanding and judging the Jewish Scriptures in late Second Temple Palestinian Judaism."

37 Talmon, "Hebrew Fragments," 86; see also 89.

38 See Talmon, "MasPs[a]," 309–13; Talmon, "Hebrew Fragments," 86; Lange, *Handbuch*, 404; Flint, *Dead Sea Psalms Scrolls*, 44. For the variant statistics, see → 10.2.1.1.1.

39 Talmon, "MPs[b]," 321; Talmon, "Hebrew Fragments," 91–92; Flint, *Dead Sea Psalms Scrolls*, 45.

40 Talmon, "Hebrew," 93.

41 Talmon, "Hebrew," 94. See also → 10.2.1.1.2.

42 Of fifty-seven variants, only five are against MT (at least one of which might be orthographic). See → 10.2.1.1.3; Lange, *Handbuch*, 406; Flint, "5/6ḤevPsalms," 144; Flint, *Dead Sea Psalms Scrolls*, 43–44.

43 See further Flint, "5/6ḤevPsalms," 144.

44 → 10.2.1.1.4; cf. Lange, *Handbuch*, 380. Skehan, Ulrich, and Flint are much stronger in their assessment, deeming 4QPs[c] "a representative of the edition of the Psalter that is also preserved in the Masoretic Text" ("Psalms," 50).

45 See, e.g., Flint, *Dead Sea Psalms Scrolls*, 198–201; Flint, "Book of Psalms," 459, 469–71; Flint, "Psalms and Psalters," 249–51; Flint, "11QPs[a]-Psalter," 174–75. Note his more nuanced presentation in Flint, "Unrolling," 240. See further → 10.2.1.2; → 10.2.3.2.4.

(11Q8; → 10.2.1.6.1), at least, to the four (proto-)MT manuscripts listed above, though scholars admittedly differ as to the classification of both scrolls, even disagreeing about whether such classification may be attempted (especially in the case of 11QPs^d).[46] If these manuscripts do belong to the (proto-)MT family, this would add to the overall strength of that text type, especially at Qumran proper.[47]

Be that as it may, the particular issues besetting the textual criticism of Psalms noted above continue to make text-typological classifications of many of these manuscripts extremely difficult. Apart from MasPs^b, which clearly ends with Psalm 150, thereby securing its alignment with MT-Pss (see → 10.2.2.1.3), many of the other manuscripts that may belong to proto-MT do not witness to (alternative) sequencing or (additional) content that would help to secure their text typology. The presence of the latter would obviously remove them from MT alignment, but, again, very few manuscripts contain non-MT psalmic content.[48] The former characteristic, too, is not definitive, since these manuscripts preserve portions of the Psalter that do not manifest alternative sequences, and because even the non-MT collections frequently have MT-like sequences for certain psalms (especially for Books I–III).[49] This situation is what leads Flint to speak of the paucity of unambiguous data supporting "MT-150."[50]

The paucity of extant text also complicates analysis or at least cautions against hard-and-fast decisions. So, e.g., Ulrich has stated that, from one perspective, "the Masada remains may be described as close to the (proto-)MT," but, seen from another perspective, the Masada evidence preserves "only a very limited amount of useful evidence for the history of the biblical text" because most of the compositions found there have "little or no practical overlap with the ... books found in variant editions at Qumran and in the SP and LXX."[51] Of course, this does not hold true for MasPs^a and MasPs^b since they preserve proto-MT-Pss forms and the book of Psalms is a parade example of what Ulrich calls a variant literary edition.[52] But Ulrich is not quite convinced, thinking that the case for the Masada Psalms being proto-MT is "less strong than the edition suggests."[53] Ulrich's argument at this point, however, seems overly fine, especially since the differences he notes between MasPs^b and MT-Pss are truly slight and almost entirely orthographic. He concludes that MasPs^b might be "categorized, *with regard to text*, as not especially closely related to the proto-MT within the text family, but, *with regard to edition*, as sharing the same general text tradition as the proto-MT (in contrast to that of 11QPs^a and the LXX)."[54] For the sake of the argument being made here, Ulrich's observation that the edition (text type) reflected at Masada is aligned with proto-MT as opposed to 11QPs^a suffices.

10.2.2.1.3 Sequence of (Proto-)MT Psalms

Despite the great attention that has been paid to psalm sequencing in the Dead Sea Scrolls for text-typological classification, it turns out that even this matter is not a straightforward one. Happily, a few things are certain, such as that MT-Pss ends with

---

[46] See → 10.2.1.6.1; Lange, *Handbuch*, 402–03; Flint, *Dead Sea Psalms Scrolls*, 42; *DJD* XXIII, 52, 65. Note also the revision of 4QPs^e frg. 26 i–ii, which may be toward proto-MT (→ 10.2.3.2.1.3), and that the text of Psalm 122 in 4QProphecy of Joshua is also "closer to that of 𝔐 than to the text of 11QPs^a" (É. Puech, "522. Ps 122 in '4QProphecy of Joshua'," *DJD* XVI, 169–70 [169]).

[47] Viz., six manuscripts from three locations (Naḥal Ḥever, Masada, Qumran) including two different caves (4 and 11) at Qumran. Cf. Non-Proto-MT Collection 1 (→ 10.2.3.2), which contains, *at most*, five manuscripts (11QPs^a, 11QPs^b, 4QPs^e, 4QPs^n, 1QPs^b), all of which come from one site, but from three different caves.

[48] See n. 11 above.

[49] A possible exception might be 11QPs^d, though the identification of frgs. 16–17 is uncertain, as is their placement *vis-à-vis* the rest of the scroll.

[50] Cf. Wilson, "Consecutive Arrangement," 385: "one is

left without a single example from a fully supportive MS in opposition to any of these instances of conflict ... It is quite feasible that supportive readings represent one *possible* arrangement of the psalms at a time prior to the final fixation of the Psalter-text" (his emphasis).

[51] Ulrich, "Two Perspectives," 462.

[52] Ulrich, *DSS*, 34–50, 99–120.

[53] Ulrich, "Two Perspectives," 463.

[54] Ulrich, "Two Perspectives," 463.

Psalm 150. The fact that MasPs[b] does the same is sufficient evidence alone that it should be aligned with the proto-MT family since other text types do not end with Psalm 150. LXX-Pss' conclusion with Psalm 151 (→ 10.3.1) is well known (even if the superscription indicates that it is ἔξωθεν τοῦ ἀριθμοῦ "outside the number"), as is the inclusion of still other psalms in the Syriac tradition (→ 10.3.4; → 10.4.4).[55] These alternative end-points are why Flint has used "MT-150" as shorthand to describe the proto-MT tradition as opposed to 11QPs[a], which ends with Psalm 151, and which is, as a result (in his judgment), decidedly *not* (proto-)MT. Of course, text types differ not only at the end-point of the Psalter but also at various points within it. Here again, the difference with regard to what compositions comprise which psalms in MT-Pss vs. LXX-Pss is well known (→ 10.3.1):

MT	LXX
1–8	1–8
9–10	9
11–113	10–112
114–115	113
116:1–9	114
116:10–19	115
117–146	116–145
147:1–11	146
147:12–20	147
148–150	148–150
	151

What is somewhat less well known or discussed, however, is that this fluidity in order and division of the psalms evident from LXX-Pss is also found within the MT-Pss text type itself.[56] As it happens, "MT-150" is not as straightforward as such nomenclature might suggest. The manuscript evidence is divided, that is, on whether both MT-Pss and earlier semi- and proto-Masoretic psalms manuscripts are comprised of 150 compositions or more or less than that. The final enumeration of Psalms into "MT-150," that is, is not as obvious – or as early – as is sometimes thought. Not all of the psalms are attested in the Judean Desert finds, after all,[57] and differentiation between individual compositions is not always clearly made;[58] the individual psalms themselves are not numbered, in any event, so as to produce 150.[59] This curious situation endures, as MT[L] (perhaps also MT[A] though numbering is not found there) contains only 149 (= קמ״ט) psalms, not 150, since it treats Psalms 114 + 115 as a single composition (קי״ד = 114).[60] This is not the case, of course, in *BHS, which numbers Psalms 114 and 115 inde-

---

[55] But see → 10.3.4.6 for the possibility that Psalms 151; 154; and 155 do not belong to the manuscript tradition of the Peshitta at all.

[56] What follows is heavily indebted to Yarchin, "Authoritative Shape"; Yarchin, "Psalms Collections"; Yarchin, "First Bible Chapters"; as well as Yarchin, "The Psalter and the Modern Bible." I am grateful to Prof. Yarchin for making his work, some unpublished, available to me. For a brief summary of Yarchin, see deClaissé-Walford, Jacobson, and Tanner, *Psalms*, 3–4. See also M. Dukan, "Le livre des Psaumes dans la tradition juive," *REJ* 163 (2004): 87–109; and J.-M. Auwers, "La numérotation des Psaumes dans la tradition hébraïque: une enquête dans le fonds hébreu de la Bibliothèque Nationale," *RB* 109 (2002): 343–70.

[57] 123 psalms of 150 are found there, 124 psalms if one counts the citation of Psalm 1 in 4QMidrEschat[a] (4Q174) III:14 (olim 4QFlor 1–2 i 21). See Flint, "Unrolling," 239. For a full listing of citations of the Psalms, see A. Lange and M. Weigold, *Biblical Quotations and Allusions in Second Temple Jewish Literature* (Journal of Ancient Judaism Supplements 5; Göttingen: Vandenhoeck & Ruprecht, 2011), 163–78.

[58] See Tov, *Scribal Practices*, 163–64.

[59] Yarchin, "First Bible Chapters," identifies MT[L] as the first datable appearance of numbers applied to chapters in a manuscript of the Hebrew Bible, particularly the Psalms, and argues that "numbering the psalms in Hebrew manuscripts first took place in the tenth and eleventh centuries as a result of the interest Karaites had in scripture according to the codex format and to systematic numerical referencing" (forthcoming). Numbering chapters was a much earlier phenomenon in Christian circles (see Ginsburg, *Introduction*, 25–31; Yarchin, "First Bible Chapters"). Ginsburg, *Introduction*, 107, traces the first instance of the use of Arabic numbers for verses in Psalms to 1563 C.E.

[60] Note that 4QPs[o] (→ 10.2.1.6.1) may also have considered Psalms 114–115 to be one psalm, as do some MT manuscripts, LXX, Theodotion, the Peshitta, and Jerome. 4QPs[o] may also have considered Ps 116:1–9 to be a separate psalm from Ps 116:10–19, as do LXX and Jerome.

pendently, in Arabic numeration, even though the base text does not, so as to culminate in Psalm 150 (in Arabic numeration) at the end of the book.

Yarchin has devoted extensive attention to the numeration of psalms in MT-Pss, examining over 400 medieval Hebrew manuscripts, 200 manuscripts from the Cairo Genizah, and all the relevant incunabula (for the medieval Masoretic manuscripts, see → 10–20.1). His work has demonstrated a high degree of fluidity in numbering the psalms, a fluidity that persists, in the main, until the Rabbinic Bible in the first (*RB1; 1517) and especially the second edition (*RB2; 1525), after which point the order that is now standard becomes fixed.[61] To be clear, the text type in the manuscripts Yarchin has examined is resolutely MT, with the expected range of micro-variant variation therein,[62] but within that overall (perhaps one might say macrostructural) stability, there is a great deal of (internal) variation in the way compositions are combined or divided so as to produce Psalters that run anywhere from 143 to 154 psalms.[63] Higher counts are also attested.[64] "In all," Yarchin writes, "at least 152 different psalm-configurations are attested in the pre-modern manuscript evidence."[65]

Again, these different psalm-counts – whether higher or lower than 150 – are not achieved by adding new compositions *à la* LXX (→ 10.3.1), the Peshitta (→ 10.3.4), or 11QPs^a (→ 10.2.1.2; → 10.2.3.2), or leaving some out, respectively, but by renumbering/rearranging the psalms that are already present and sequenced in MT-Pss. So, e.g., manuscript Or. 4227 combines Psalms 42 + 43 and 53 + 54, divides Psalm 118 into two psalms (vv. 1–25 and vv. 26–29), and numbers separately each acrostic stanza of Psalm 119 to yield a Psalter of 170 psalms.[66] Even those Psalms manuscripts that share the same totals often diverge in how those are achieved. Of the 123 manuscripts that contain 149 psalms, no less than twenty-five different configurations are attested. In fact, only eighty-four of the manuscripts Yarchin has catalogued witness to 150 psalms in the now-familiar order that Yarchin calls the *textus receptus* (TR) configuration, and that he deems to have been definitively established in the Second Rabbinic Bible (*RB2) in 1525. The TR configuration is the most frequently attested order, but the percentage of manuscripts that attest to it is far from overwhelming (21 %). Moreover, even these eighty-four manuscripts do not correspond in every detail. Thirty-three of the eighty-four (39 %) represent configurations that differ in some fashion from the TR configuration.[67]

The divergence of the manuscript evidence on psalm enumeration is so great that Yarchin concludes that "there is no identifiable quantitative configuration of *sēper təhillîm* by virtue of which we can assert that that particular configuration is authoritative or standard."[68] Still further, "there seems never to have been a single-psalter configuration taken up by the majority of Jews during the manuscript era."[69] The same might be said for the book of Psalms in other languages (cf., e.g., → 10.4.3). Whatever the case, to make the point even more clearly, the matter can be put as follows: "while TR-150 may have been the Hebrew psalter-configuration scribes *copied* most, it is not the psalter that people *used* the most."[70] So, Yarchin concludes, "TR-150 was never the single authoritative shape for *sēper təhillîm* until the modern era of printed editions, ushered in by the sixteenth-century Rabbinic Bibles."[71]

---

[61] See the works listed in n. 56. Before Yarchin, see Ginsburg, *Introduction*.

[62] See the works of Kennicott and de Rossi, discussed below (→ 10.2.2.2).

[63] Yarchin, "Authoritative," offers evidence for psalters of 143, 144, 145, 146, 147, 148, 149, 150, 151, 152, 153, and 154 psalms. For the 147-psalm possibility, see Barthélemy, *Critique textuelle 2005*, xxxiii–xxxix. Among other things, this total may be intended to accord with the age of Jacob in Gen 47:28 (see *y. Šabb.* fol. 15c; Yarchin, "Authoritative Shape," 357–58 n. 10; Ginsburg, *Introduction*, 547, 777).

[64] See below. Sanders, "Modern History," 401, mentions "later ancient Psalters with up to 200 psalms."

[65] Yarchin, "Psalms Collections," 782.

[66] See Ginsburg, *Introduction*, 725–26. See Ginsburg, *Introduction*, 536–37 on Add. 9399, which has 159 psalms.

[67] See Yarchin, "Authoritative Shape," 362–63.

[68] Yarchin, "Authoritative Shape," 360.

[69] Yarchin, "Authoritative Shape," 363.

[70] Yarchin, "Authoritative Shape," 363.

[71] Yarchin, "Authoritative Shape," 363; Yarchin, "Psalms Col-

10.2.2 (PROTO-)MASORETIC TEXTS AND ANCIENT TEXTS CLOSE TO MT

What this means is that even "MT-150" is something of a moving target, because different manuscripts have (significantly) less or (significantly) more than 150 discrete psalms (though all manuscripts in the MT-Pss tradition end with the composition presently numbered 150 in TR-Pss). And, again, even those manuscripts that have 150 discrete psalms often differ as to how they achieve this total. A few examples of the compositions that are frequently combined or divided are as follows:[72]

- Psalm 1 + 2
- Psalm 9 + 10
- Ps 33:1–12
- Ps 33:13–18
- Psalm 42 + 43
- Psalm 70 + 71
- Psalm 90 + 91
- Psalm 92 + 93
- Psalm 93 + 94
- Psalm 94 + 95
- Psalm 95 + 96
- Psalm 96 + 97
- Psalm 98 + 99
- Psalm 114 + 115
- Psalm 114 + 115:1–11
- Ps 115:12–18
- Psalm 116 + 117 + 118:1–4
- Psalm 117 + 118:1–4
- Ps 118:5–29

Some of these combinations and divisions are well known, especially where they are also found in LXX-Pss (→ 10.3.1) or posited in biblical scholarship, whether on the basis of manuscript/versional evidence or not.[73]

Another conclusion that can be made from the fluidity of psalm numeration is that "TR-150," no less than other arrangements, is the creation of editors of the Hebrew Bible more than it is an obvious or invariable trait of the Masoretic tradition proper. Indeed, "the current ubiquity of the 150-psalm TR psalter resulted from a 'modern Masoretic' move to standardize the total sign-system of the Masoretic Text (and not just of the Hebrew Bible)."[74] This has bearing on current discussions of the shape of MT-Pss, a point taken up below (→ 10.2.2.5), but it is also not without significance for non-proto-MT collections, if sequencing is indeed a matter of text-typology.

Two final remarks: 1) Lange has argued persuasively that resequencing may be a characteristic of textual transmission of poetic texts in antiquity, as evidenced by the Psalms manuscripts, on the one hand, and the *Hodayot* manuscripts, on the other.[75] Such resequencing clearly perdured for centuries, even if later resequencing was conducted within a (relatively) fixed order of compositions (as in the medieval Psalms manuscripts) as opposed to operating across compositions (as, e.g., in 11QPsa). 2) Yarchin believes that the reshaping of psalmic delimitations so as to produce (new) discrete textual units was "for ritual reading purposes." While the content of Psalms was fixed, he continues, the configuration of the content "varied depending – at least in some cases – on *ritual uses for which a given psalter manuscript was produced.*"[76] So, "[w]hen we ask how many psalms – that is, how many פרקים – are in *sēper təhillîm*, the answer depends on the occasion of reading from the psalms that is in view" because a community's use of Psalms "continually shaped and re-shaped its macro-compositional contours."[77]

---

lections," 779: "although among the *ancient manuscripts* the sequence and quantity of semantic content may have become fixed and stable by the second century CE ... the *configuration and quantity of discrete compositions* comprising that semantic content remained fluid among the *medieval manuscripts*" (his emphases).

[72] In addition to Yarchin's works, see Briggs and Briggs, *Psalms*, 1.xlviii–xlix.

[73] Cf., e.g., the famous variant in manuscript Bezae (fifth century C.E.) at Acts 13:33, which cites Ps 2:7 as being from "the first psalm." For another example, see manuscript Madrid,

---

Complutense University Library HB MSS 1, one of the model texts for the Complutensian Polyglot, which counts Psalms 1 + 2 as a single psalm (Yarchin, "Authoritative Shape," forthcoming).

[74] Yarchin, "Authoritative Shape," forthcoming.

[75] Lange, "Collecting."

[76] Yarchin, "Psalms Collections," forthcoming (my emphasis). Note that later Psalters were often produced separately precisely for liturgical use (Briggs and Briggs, *Psalms*, 1.xxviii).

[77] Yarchin, "Psalms Collections," forthcoming.

What this means, of course, is that (all?) (re)sequencing is the product of, or at least suggests, intentional use, purpose, or function no less than does a text form like abbreviation or exerption (→ 10.2.3.6; → 10.2.3.7).[78] If this is correct, there are significant ramifications for non-MT-aligned manuscripts at Qumran (→ 10.2.3). On the one hand, the ubiquity of text use and its impact on text form in various manuscripts of the Psalms (including manuscripts in other languages beyond Hebrew) raises the serious question of what, if anything, would count as a "bona fide *sefer tehillim*" manuscript or a "copy" of the Psalter.[79] On the other hand, if the "final form" of the book of Psalms is in perpetual flux (until 1525 C.E.!), all bets are off in saying any one form is established or definitive, with all others derivative or "secondary."[80] Said differently, despite the importance of sequence to text-typological classification, the particular assemblage of psalmic material is, on its own, insufficient to determine "scriptural" vs. "secondary" status "because we cannot point to a stable, standard configuration of the material even in the MT tradition."[81] To ask if a manuscript is a "true psalter," then, or a "secondary collection" on the basis of configuration alone "is to frame the question in a manner incommensurate with the evidence."[82]

10.2.2.2 Manuscripts and Editions

Beyond the Qumran fragments discussed above (see also → 10.1; → 10.2.1; → 10.2.3), the most important Hebrew manuscripts are the Aleppo Codex (MT^A, ca. 925 C.E.) and Codex Leningradensis (MT^L; codex EPB I B 19a of the National Library of Russia in St. Petersburg, from 1008/1009 C.E.) though neither is perfect (→ 10–20.1).[83] Unfortunately, MT^A is not complete (it lacks Pss 15:1–25:2) and is not yet available in a critical edition.[84] At the time of writing, two critical editions of MT^L-Pss are available in the BH series with a third in process.[85] The first, by F. Buhl, is found in *BH³ (1930), and remains useful as its apparatus is occasionally more extensive than that found in the second edition, which is by H. Bardtke (*BHS, 1969). The edition of Psalms in *BHQ is being prepared by G.R. Norton. The *BHQ edition will be superior to *BH³ and *BHS in terms of apparatus, presentation of the Masorah, and commentary on both. *HUB will publish a major critical edition of MT^A, though a date for that has not been announced. An eclectic edition, replete with commentary, will be published by P.W. Flint in *HBCE.

Prior to these modern editions, the most important text of Psalms is found in the Rabbinic Bible, especially the second edition of 1525 (RB2). The importance of this edition for the establishment of "TR-150" is discussed above (→ 10.2.2.1.3). Collections of medieval Masoretic variants may be found in the works of Kennicott (*1776–1780, 2.307–437; online at: http://aleph.nli.org.il/nnl/dig/books/bk002093934.html) and de Rossi (*1784–1798, 4.1–88, 238–40; 5.95–11).

For comparative purposes, the great multilingual Bibles of the sixteenth and seventeenth centuries are useful, especially the Complutensian Polyglot (1514–1517; vol. 3),[86] the so-called Psalterium octuplex (1516),[87] the Antwerp Royal

---

[78] Cf. Briggs and Briggs, *Psalms*, 1.l: "Thus the editors of the various Psalters did exactly what the editors of prayerbooks, liturgies, and hymn-books have always done. They had greater interest in editing the Pss. for public worship than in preserving their original literary form and meaning." Cf. Briggs and Briggs, *Psalms*, 1.lxxxviii.

[79] Cf. Yarchin, "Psalms Collections," 784.

[80] See Yarchin, "Psalms Collections," and → 10.2.3.7.

[81] Yarchin, "Psalms Collections," 789.

[82] Yarchin, "Psalms Collections," 789.

[83] See, respectively, *The Jerusalem Crown: The Bible of the Hebrew University of Jerusalem* (Jerusalem: Ben Zvi, 2000), [13]–[23]; and A. Dotan, *Biblia Hebraica Leningradensia: Prepared according to the Vocalization, Accents, and Masora of Aaron ben Moses ben Asher in the Leningrad Codex* (Leiden: Brill, 2001), 1229–37.

[84] See M. Goshen-Gottstein (ed.), *The Aleppo Codex* (Jerusalem: Magnes, 1976); several pages are badly faded. For a text edition, see *The Jerusalem Crown*.

[85] In addition to the BH series, see also Dotan, *Biblia Hebraica Leningradensia*.

[86] *Complutensian Polyglot*.

[87] G. Agostino, *Psalterium Hebreum, Grecum, Arabicum et Chaldeum cum tribus Latinis interpretationibus et glossis* (Genoa: Petrus Paulus Porrus, 1516).

Polyglot (1569–1573; vol. 3.288–538),[88] the Paris Polyglot (1645; vol. 3 and vol. 8),[89] and the London Polyglot[90] (1655–1657; vol. 3.88–319).[91]

10.2.2.3 The Nature and Text-Critical Character of (Proto-)MT-Pss

Much has been said in the preceding sections that bears directly on the nature and text-critical character of (proto-)MT-Pss. Beyond the macrovariants of sequence and repertoire, there are, quite literally, thousands of micro-variants, far too many to discuss or catalogue here.[92] It must suffice to make some general remarks (some obvious) about (proto-)MT-Pss in list-like fashion, and comment on a few selected examples:

1) First, "[t]he Hebrew text presumed by ancient versions ... is often in conflict with the MT,"[93] which means that the versions, especially the rather literal LXX (→ 10.3.1),[94] are of great significance for the analysis of MT-Pss.
2) Scholars have long catalogued mistakes and errors in MT-Pss, frequently but not exclusively on the basis of the versions.[95] These include letter exchanges/confusion, transpositions (of letters, words, or clauses), misdivision of words or sentences, haplography, dittography, and various other (unintentional) errors of copying.[96] Occasionally, the manuscripts provide clear evidence of such deficiencies in MT-Pss or at least certain exemplars, like MT^L. For example:

   a) In MT^L-Ps 145, the *nun*-stich is missing from its acrostic structure, which should appear after v. 13 but before v. 14. The missing line is present in 11QPs^a (also MT^{ms}, LXX, LXX^{mss}, S): נאמן אלוהים בדבריו וחסיד בכול מעשיו "God is trustworthy in all his words, and faithful in all his deeds." Some similarity to v. 17 may have led to the loss of the line.[97] The reading of MT^L, at least, is mutilated in this case. Even without manuscript evidence like that existing for Psalm 145, irregularities like these in the acrostic psalms (missing or disordered letters/lines) indicate that significant errors of various types have entered the proto-MT tradition, even in compositions that have, as it were, built-in safeguards protecting their contents and structure.[98]
   b) Misdivision may be found in Pss 44:5; 75:2; 77:7.
   c) Two errors of punctuation can be observed in Pss 42:4; 77:7.
   d) Graphic errors may be traced in Pss 28:8; 35:15; 36:2; 38:20; 41:3; 59:4, 10; 72:5; 74:6; 77:3; 104:17; 119:119; 139:16; 141:7.
   e) The following texts witness to errors in vocalization: Pss 16:2; 17:14; 60:6; 72:17; 110:3 (4×).

3) Frequently, scholars have posited (intentional) changes of various types: glosses, supplements, explanations, and the like,[99] again, far too many to catalogue here, though one famous instance might be the scholarly controversy over the so-called "Elohistic Psalter."[100]

---

[88] B.A. Montano, *Biblia Polyglotta: hebraice, chaldaice, graece, et latine* (8 vols.; Antwerp: Platin, 1569–1573).

[89] Le Jay, **Biblia*.

[90] Walton, **Polyglotta*.

[91] Pursuant to → 10.2.2.1.3 note, for example, that the Paris Polyglot, vol. 8 (Syriac, Arabic, and Latin) combines Psalms 114 + 115 into one (psalm "CXIV") but retains independent numbering for each. Only the London Polyglot includes Psalm 151.

[92] While there are many *cruxes interpretationis* throughout the Psalms, few rise to the level of fame enjoyed by MT-Ps 22:17 (see below). For a presentation of variants among the Dead Sea Psalms scrolls, see Ulrich, **BQS*, 627–726; and Flint, *Dead Sea Psalms Scrolls*, 50–116. See also Barthélemy, **Critique textuelle 2005*, *passim*, on which much of the following depends.

[93] Terrien, *Psalms*, 25.

[94] Pietersma, "Psalms," 543: LXX-Pss is "heavily circumscribed by linguistic interlinearity." Cf. Briggs and Briggs, *Psalms*, 1.xxv.

[95] Note that Psalms is the most frequently cited book in the index to Delitzsch, *Die Lese- und Schreibfehler*.

[96] See Briggs and Briggs, *Psalms*, 1:xxii, li–lii for a listing; cf. Kraus, *Psalms 1–59*, 14, who thinks "[a] complete confusion of the verse sequence is observable in Psalm 87."

[97] See Haran, "11QPs^a and the Canonical Book of Psalms," 195 and n. 3 for the loss of an entire psalm (Psalm 47) in British Library ms 9399 due to homoioteleuton and homoioarkton.

[98] Briggs and Briggs, *Psalms*, 1.l–lii; cf. Terrien, *Psalms*, 25.

[99] See Briggs and Briggs, *Psalms*, 1.l–li for a partial listing.

[100] See, among many others, Briggs and Briggs, *Psalms*, 1.lxix; F.-L. Hossfeld and E. Zenger, "The So-Called Elohistic

4) Closely related to the preceding, if not examples of the same, are those instances that seem to reflect secondary readings of one sort or another. Though it is not always possible to characterize the nature of these readings, the following examples might be mentioned:

a) The reading of Ps 76:5, מֵהַרְרֵי טָרֶף "more than mountains of prey" has led some to posit a case of *modernization*, with MT updating a reading of עד "eternal," which is also reflected in LXX (ὀρέων αἰωνίων),[101] but this is not certain.[102]

b) Some deem the reading יְשׁוּעוֹת פָּנָיו אֱלֹהַי "the salvation of his face. My God" at the end of Ps 42:6 and the start of 42:7 to be a *deliberate transference* of waw from its original position on the third word (as a conjunction) to the second (as a pronominal suffix), since this is not reflected in MT[mss], LXX, and the Peshitta, which instead represent יְשׁוּעֹת פָּנַי וֵאלֹהָי (perhaps to be read as singular construct, יְשׁוּעַת, or a complex plural) "my saving presence and my God" as in Pss 42:12; 43:5.[103] While this could be a mechanical error (mistaken separation of lines or word division), it is possible that the *waw* has been intentionally moved to make the divine name into a vocative in light of the 2nd masc. sg. suffixed form אֶזְכָּרְךָ "I remember you" in v. 7.

c) A case of *facilitating syntax* may be found in MT[K] of Ps 10:10 where MT[Q] (so also LXX, S, and T) reads a verbal form, יִדְכֶּה "he is crushed," but the *Ketiv* reads ודכה, probably to be vocalized as וְדָכָה "and the crushed

(one)," supported by Aquila, Symmachus, and Jerome's Psalter (Hebr).

d) MT-Pss contains a number of passages where the text has been *assimilated* to either the immediate context (e.g., MT[Q]-Ps 11:1; 17:11 [2×, once in MT[K] and once in MT[Q]]; MT[K]-Ps 100:3); to the near-context (e.g., Ps 59:11: [MT[Q]: חַסְדִּי] אֱלֹהֵי חַסְדּוֹ "God of his [MT[Q]: my] steadfast love," which is twice assimilated to Ps 59:18 אֱלֹהֵי חַסְדִּי; contrast LXX-Ps 58:11: ὁ θεός μου τὸ ἔλεος αὐτοῦ "my God, his mercy ..."); to a parallel psalm text (MT[Q]-Ps 60:7 assimilates to Ps 108:8); to similar forms found elsewhere in the Psalter (Ps 65:2's דֻּמִיָּה [defective] "silence" to the plene form, דוּמִיָּה in Pss 22:3; 39:3; and 62:2); or even to a text that is not identical but that employs similar language (Ps 72:7's יִפְרַח בְּיָמָיו צַדִּיק "let the righteous one flourish in his days" [LXX's δικαιοσύνη "righteousness" reflects צֶדֶק, as do MT[mss], S, and Jerome's Psalter (Hebr)] is assimilated to Ps 92:13: צַדִּיק כַּתָּמָר יִפְרָח "the righteous will flourish like a palm tree").

e) Ps 106:20 traditionally instances one of the corrections of the scribes (*tiqqunê sopherim*), which would represent an instance of *theological revision*: for וַיָּמִירוּ אֶת־כְּבוֹדוֹ "and they exchanged *his* glory" (MT[L]: כְּבוֹדָם "their glory") read כבדי "*my* glory." Another example of theological revision by means of vocalization may be found in Ps 42:3 where MT, LXX, and the Vulgate reflect וְאֵרָאֶה פְּנֵי אֱלֹהִים "I will *appear* before God," while MT[mss], the Targum, and Peshitta reflect וְאֶרְאֶה פְּנֵי אֱלֹהִים "I will *see* the face of God." A further example of possible theological revision is Ps 68:5: לָרֹכֵב בָּעֲרָבוֹת "for the Rider through the deserts," which scholars have long related to the Ugaritic formula *rkb 'rpt* (/*rākibu 'arapāti*/) "the Rider of the clouds," an epithet used of Baal. The interchange between *b*/*p* is well attested, of course, but it is not impossible that MT here is "a deliberate distortion" of the preexisting (pagan) formulation.[104] This point may

---

Psalter: A New Solution for an Old Problem," in *A God So Near: Essays on Old Testament Theology in Honor of Patrick D. Miller* (eds. B.A. Strawn and N.R. Bowen; Winona Lake: Eisenbrauns, 2003), 35–51.

[101] See Briggs and Briggs, *Psalms*, 2.166; Barthélemy, *Critique textuelle 2005*, 557–59.

[102] Cf. B.A. Strawn, *What Is Stronger than a Lion? Leonine Image and Metaphor in the Hebrew Bible and the Ancient Near East* (OBO 212; Göttingen: Vandenhoeck & Ruprecht, 2005), 338.

[103] Barthélemy, *Critique textuelle 2005*, 252–56; Briggs and Briggs, *Psalms*, 1.369, 373.

[104] J. Day, "Baal (Deity)," *ABD* 1:549.

gain further support by the somewhat unusual phrase that follows immediately, בְּיָהּ שְׁמוֹ "in (?) YAH is his name," especially if the בְּ here is to be understood as a "*beth* of identity," clarifying that the preceding epithet applies, in fact, to YHWH, not to Baal.[105] The famous crux at Ps 22:17 may be a final example. MT reads (apparently unintelligibly): כָּאֲרִי יָדַי וְרַגְלָי "like a lion [?] my hands and my feet." Most other versions differ, to greater or lesser degrees, with LXX, the Peshitta, and Aquila, for example, reflecting a verb "to dig."[106] It is possible that the latter are exegetical, but given the importance of this verse in certain later Christological interpretations of Psalm 22, could MT be secondary, some sort of intentional revision away from a text that was related by some Christians to Christ's passion? While not impossible, this seems unlikely in the face of 5/6ḤevPs XI:12, which appears to read כארו "dug > pierced" (with MT^mss, LXX, S, Aq) though some would deem that a graphic error.[107]

f) The reading in Ps 8:2: אֲשֶׁר תְּנָה "which/because give!" is *corrupt* in some way as the 2nd masc. sg. imperative form makes no sense in context. The smoother readings in LXX (ὅτι ἐπήρθη "because [your majesty] is exalted"), Symmachus, the Peshitta, Targum, and Jerome's Psalter (Hebr.) may all be exegetically motivated. It seems at the very least that a word-initial נ has been lost somehow such that the original reading was something like אֲשֶׁר נָתַתָּה "because you set [your majesty]" (*Qal* 2nd masc. sg. with plene ending) or אֲשֶׁר נִתַּן "because [your majesty] is set" (*Niphal* 3rd masc. sg. with the ה on תנה in MT a ditto-graphy from the next word) or even a form of the infinitive or imperative ("O set [your majesty]").[108]

5) There are a host of *paratextual elements* that are part of the tradition of MT-Pss, especially via the Masorah proper. These include *Ketiv/Qere* readings,[109] the use of inverted *nun*s at Ps 107:21–26, 40; a suspended letter (ע) in Ps 80:14; and extraordinary points (for cancellation) at Ps 27:13.[110]

As with any other book of the Hebrew Bible, all such readings like the ones discussed above for MT-Pss must be taken up on a case-by-case basis. The sheer number of small micro-variants, coupled with the need to assess them individually – not to mention the size and extent of the Psalter as a whole – makes an overall characterization of MT-Pss quite difficult. This important point granted, it is nevertheless clear that all such elements "make it evident that even 𝕳 ... is as truly an interpretation of an older text as 𝕲 and other ancient Vrss."[111] Even so, it seems that the text of MT-Pss can be characterized generally as being in "fair" condition,[112] if not far better than that, as demonstrated by: 1) the relative stability of the individual psalms themselves, as attested in the Dead Sea Scrolls;[113] 2) the observation that in some instances revisions for theological consideration (cf. 11QPs^a at Ps 142:5) or additions for the facilitation of style (e.g., Pss 31:20; 34:21) were evidently avoided, indicating that such changes were not leveled through the entire book but, when present, remain mostly at the level of the

---

[105] See B.T. Arnold and B.A. Strawn, "*b^eyāh š^emô* in Psalm 68,5: A Hebrew Gloss to an Ugaritic Epithet?" *ZAW* 115 (2003): 428–32.

[106] For discussion with bibliography of earlier literature, see B.A. Strawn, "Psalm 22:17b: More Guessing," *JBL* 119 (2000): 439–51, and Barthélemy, *Critique textuelle 2005*, 127–32.

[107] See Barthélemy, *Critique textuelle 2005*, 127, which grants the present reading a rating of {B}. Note that, of the great polyglots, only the Complutensian reads כארו.

[108] See Barthélemy, *Critique textuelle 2005*, 21–23; Briggs and Briggs, *Psalms*, 1.62, 65.

[109] See Terrien, *Psalms*, 25; Briggs and Briggs, *Psalms*, 1.xxiii–iv (who mention a total of seventy). See further Barthélemy, *Critique textuelle 2005* on Pss 10:10; 11:1; 17:11; 41:3; 59:11; 74:6; 100:3; and 139:16, some of which are mentioned above.

[110] See, generally, Tov, *TCHB*, 47–62.

[111] Briggs and Briggs, *Psalms*, 1.liii; similarly 1.xxxiii.

[112] McCarter, *Textual Criticism*, 92.

[113] So, Terrien, *Psalms*, 25, who states that "[t]he fragments from Qumran suggest that the consonantal text deserves the scholarly respect it had largely lost at the end of the nineteenth century."

individual psalm; and 3) the fact that the fairly literal LXX-Pss apparently depended on a parent text that was quite close to consonantal MT (→ 10.3.1.4). It nevertheless remains the case that "[t]he text of the Psalter is one thing, the text of the original Pss. is another thing."[114]

A final comment that should be made is that the commentary literature is of mixed utility when it comes to much of the text of MT[L], let alone the textual history of (proto-)MT-Pss or of the Psalms more broadly. Fewer and fewer modern commentaries include treatments of the Hebrew text and versions in their introductions, let alone offer extended engagement with the text-critical evidence for each individual psalm.[115] One must return to older commentaries for more fulsome treatments, though these works are now often quite dated, especially in the light of the manuscript evidence recovered from the Dead Sea area. It is precisely this latter evidence – its extent and significance (and, now, availability post-publication) – that signals that the exact opposite should be the case: more, not less, consideration of the early Hebrew evidence, proto-MT or otherwise, should mark Psalms scholarship in the future.[116] One example of the possible interaction of the proto-MT manuscript evidence and modern Psalms scholarship is discussed in → 10.2.2.5.

10.2.2.4 Date and Milieu

While it is true that "[t]he exact process by which the Book of Psalms came into existence is lost to the pages of history,"[117] that is not the whole truth. Something can still be said about the date and milieu of proto-MT-Pss that casts light on this process, even if much remains elusive and uncertain. The earliest attestation and final stabilization, at the very least, are relatively clear.

1) The dates of the proto-MT manuscripts from the Dead Sea region fall near the turn of the eras (→ 10.1.1.1; → 10.2.1.1):

MasPs[a]	end of first century B.C.E./beginning of first century C.E.
MasPs[b]	50–1 B.C.E.
4QPs[c]	50–68 C.E.
5/6Ḥev/Ps	50–68 C.E.

One of the earliest Psalms manuscripts from Qumran, 4QPs[w] (125–75 B.C.E.), contains no variants from MT, though since so little text is preserved, certain affiliation is not permitted. In any event, the dates for the (most certain) proto-MT manuscripts from the Judean Desert are not demonstrably earlier, nor later, than those supporting Non-Proto-MT Collection 1 (see → 10.2.3.2.3). Either way, the proto-MT tradition of Psalms is attested at least by the late first century C.E. and its origins must, therefore, be earlier, though how much earlier one can only speculate.[118] Of course, by the time this text type is first attested, it is attested alongside other Hebrew text types, at least at Qumran. However, the fact that, at present, there is *no* non-Qumran Hebrew manuscript evidence for non-proto-MT-Pss (see above and → 10.2.3.2.4; → 10.2.3.7) indicates that the proto-MT-Pss text type was known at Qumran and also outside of it (at least at Naḥal Ḥever and Masada), and perhaps predominantly so, though the meagerness of the non-Qumran finds must always and constantly be kept in mind. Of course, a

---

[114] Briggs and Briggs, *Psalms*, 1.xxxiv.

[115] Even multivolume commentaries can lack introductory material devoted to the versions (e.g., Goldingay; Hossfeld and Zenger); those that do include such material are often fairly short (Terrien, *Psalms*, 25–26; deClaissé-Walford, Jacobson, and Tanner, *Psalms*, 2–9, cf. 24). Extended treatments are rare (Kraus, *Psalms 1–59*; Briggs and Briggs, *Psalms*).

[116] The Hebrew Old Testament Text Project produced a preliminary treatment of hundreds of debated passages in the Psalms: D. Barthélemy et al., *Interim Report*, Vol. 3: *Poetical Books*, 163–442. This work often takes the scrolls data into account, though it does not have the benefit of the full publication of the Cave 4 texts. Barthélemy died before completing the final report, but it was edited and published by Ryan and Schenker in 2005: Barthélemy, *Critique textuelle 2005*. See also Barthélemy, *Studies*.

[117] N. deClaissé-Walford, *Reading from the Beginning: The Shaping of the Hebrew Psalter* (Macon: Mercer University Press, 1997), 32.

[118] See → 10.2.3.2.3 and → 10.2.3.6 for a discussion of 4QPs[x] and its possible bearing on this question.

plethora of non-MT readings (microvariants, that is) have also left traces in the versions.

2) If Flint is right, the last two books of the Psalter were still in flux in the first century C.E. At some point thereafter – when, exactly, we cannot say, though it has to be prior to the medieval manuscripts of the tenth to fifteenth centuries – the proto-MT text type won the day in terms of psalmic *content*. The niceties of psalmic configuration (number and division of compositions), however, remained fluid into the sixteenth century. The 150-psalm sequence now found in modern editions of the Hebrew Bible (Yarchin's "TR-150") was apparently the result of Daniel Bomberg's Rabbinic Bibles, especially the first and second editions published in Venice in 1517 (*RB1) and 1525 (*RB2), respectively. In this light, the final stabilization of MT-Pss did not reach its final stage in the late first century C.E., let alone earlier, as previous scholars have often maintained.[119] Rather, the fluidity of the Hebrew psalm collection effectively came to an end only in the sixteenth century C.E. with the arrival of TR in the "publication and subsequent universal printed reproduction of the *sēper təhillîm* found in Bomberg's Second Rabbinic Bible."[120]

10.2.2.5 Relevance for Exegesis and Literary Analysis

Beyond the obvious pertinence variant readings have for establishing a critical text of a biblical passage and thus its proper exegesis, the primary relevance of the preceding discussion bears on the scholarly investigation of the "shape and shaping" of the Psalms/Psalter. This type of analysis traces back to the canonical approach of Childs,[121] which was subsequently taken up by his student, Wilson.[122] Most work on the shape and shaping of the Psalms/Psalter depends directly on Wilson.[123] Unfortunately, unlike Wilson's own work, which was ground-breaking for its careful consideration of 11QPs[a] and, to the extent that it was available (only in preliminary form), some of the Cave 4 Psalms data – making the latter, in particular, available to a broader scholarly public for the first time – most recent work does not incorporate the latest developments subsequent to the publication of Wilson's monograph in 1985.[124]

The general thrust of shape and shaping research is to investigate the compositional logic of the Psalter.[125] The contribution of the manuscript evidence to this discussion is to ask: "*Which Psalter?*" because different Psalters have *different orders* and thus *different compositional logics*. The different psalm sequences ("Psalters") in the Dead Sea Scrolls are well documented, but "MT-150" is also remarkably fluid prior to the establishment of "TR-150."

The relevance of the manuscript data – both antique and medieval – has profound ramifications, then, on shape and shaping discussions. Four points deserve mention:

1. First, the fluidity of the manuscript evidence seriously chastens suppositions regarding early fixation of the Psalms/Psalter (if not also some of its subcollections),[126] as well as all composi-

---

[119] E.g., Briggs and Briggs, *Psalms*, 1.lxxxviii, who state that already in the middle of the second century, "*shortly before its translation into Greek*, [the Psalter] *was divided into five books, after the division of the pentateuch, and was numbered as 150 psalms*" (their emphasis). Similarly, Briggs and Briggs, *Psalms*, 1.lxxxix.

[120] Yarchin, "Psalms Collections," 787.

[121] B.S. Childs, *Introduction to the Old Testament as Scripture* (Philadelphia: Fortress, 1979), 504–25.

[122] Wilson, *Editing of the Hebrew Psalter*; see also, among other publications, Wilson, "Consecutive Arrangement"; Wilson, "Comparison of Editorial Shaping"; and Wilson, "Analysis of the Debate."

[123] See deClaissé-Walford (ed.), *Shape and Shaping*; also McCann (ed.), *Shape and Shaping*.

[124] E.g., Hossfeld–Zenger, *Psalms 3*, has Dahmen, *Psalmen- und Psalter-Rezeption*, in the bibliography but nothing from Flint. In Hossfeld–Zenger, *Psalms 2*, neither scholar is represented.

[125] Cf. deClaissé-Walford, *Reading from the Beginning*, 35: "While we cannot know the precise historical processes behind the formation of the Psalter, we can study its hermeneutical logic." Cf. Hossfeld–Zenger, *Psalms 2*, who speak of psalm collection "according to a definite plan revealing liturgically and/or theologically relevant compositional arcs" (1).

[126] Cf., e.g., Hossfeld–Zenger, who speak of the "so-called final redaction of the Psalter between 200 and 150 B.C.E."

tional theories depending upon or constructed therefrom, many of which are simply without support from, if not directly controverted by, the manuscript evidence.[127] Indeed, the manuscript evidence is so fluid, even within MT-Pss (up to 1525 C.E. and the establishment of TR-150) that reading the "final form" of the Psalms as a "book" might be seen as not only anachronistic but downright mistaken.[128]

2. Alternatively, and more positively, the diversity of such approaches might be identified as exercises in reader-response criticism, which is to say that such studies do not traffic in "the" compositional logic of "The Psalter" (again, *which one*?) but showcase, rather, the ability of readers to construct meaning(s) on the basis of prearranged materials. One of the hallmarks of the manuscript evidence, after all – in Hebrew and so many other versions – is the liturgical utility of the Psalms that has lent itself to, or, rather, resulted in the fluidity of the manuscript evidence in the first place.[129]

3. Such considerations do not obviate investigations of shape and shaping altogether so much as relocate them and require greater precision from them. Scholars should not talk about the shape and shaping of "the Psalter" generally without immediately specifying *which Psalter* they are investigating. Most discussions seem to proceed as if they are discussing the shape and shaping of MT-150 when in all actuality they are discussing TR-150 not MT-150 (which is fluid), and not even MT^L, which contains only 149 psalms.[130] Once the text base is identified, questions of compositional logic (shape and shaping) are altogether appropriate, but not only for how such logic might be *read out* of the form of the text base but how such logic might actually *have produced* this particular text/manuscript-form (i.e., for liturgical use). It is certainly correct, at any rate, that every (new) psalm sequence creates (new) meaning for each psalm therein, a meaning that is more than the meaning of the individual psalm taken by itself. It remains possible, then, and necessary to "consider both faces of a psalm: each psalm is a text in itself with an individual profile, and at the same time it is open to the context in which it stands within the book of Psalms,"[131] – though *which* book of Psalms, not *the* book of Psalms, is precisely what must be specified in light of the manuscript evidence.

4. Finally, in light of the multiple shapes in which Psalms has come down to us, future studies of shape and shaping should be conducted in comparative modes, such that a study of, say, TR-150 would not be conducted without some awareness of at least one (ideally more) alternative "shape" known from the manuscript tradition. Such comparisons would ideally go beyond the differences in Books IV–V, especially as revealed in the Dead Sea Scrolls evidence,[132] and consider alternative sequences in Books I–III as well. There is still much work to be done on the conjunction and division of various psalms throughout the manuscript evidence.[133]

(*Psalm 2*, 1); and state "We can *imagine* this [final] redaction taking place between 200 and 150 B.C.E., in the context of the struggle against the Seleucids, but it could have been completed as early as the third century" (*Psalm 3*, 7; my emphasis).

[127] See, e.g., Witte, "Psalter," 543; Hossfeld–Zenger, *Psalmen 1–50*, 5–16; Hossfeld–Zenger, *Psalms 2*, 1–7; and Hossfeld–Zenger, *Psalms 3*, 1–7. As one specific example, when they speak of the "addition of the superscription 'Of David' or 'Of David, when he …' " to Psalms 52–68*, they cite no manuscript support.

[128] See Pajunen, "Perspectives"; Whybray, *Reading*; Yarchin, "Psalms Collections."

[129] Cf. Yarchin, "Psalms Collections," 789: "The medieval manuscript evidence clearly shows that, *precisely as Jewish scripture*, sēper təhillîm has functioned as an assemblage of liturgical pieces and that the configuration of those pieces has varied depending on the liturgical practices of those who used it for worship" (his emphasis).

---

[130] See above and note Hossfeld–Zenger, *Psalms 3*, 186–212, which treats Psalm 114 and Psalm 115 independently in contrast to MT^L.

[131] Hossfeld and Zenger, *Psalms 2*, 7.

[132] See Wilson, "Comparison of Editorial Shaping."

[133] E.g., the sequence Psalms 31 → 33 in 4QPs^a and 4QPs^q, or the sequence Psalm 38 → 71 in 4QPs^a. See →10.2.3.7; and Prinsloo, "Unit Delimitation."

Barthélemy, *Studies.
Barthélemy, *Critique textuelle 2005.
Barthélemy, *Interim Report, Vol. 3: Poetical Books, 163–442.
Briggs, C.A. and E.G. Briggs, A Critical and Exegetical Commentary on the Book of Psalms (2 vols.; ICC; Edinburgh: T & T Clark, 1906–1907).
Brueggemann, W., "Bounded by Obedience and Praise: The Psalms as Canon," JSOT 50 (1991): 63–92.
Carr, D.M., The Formation of the Hebrew Bible: A New Reconstruction (Oxford: Oxford University Press, 2011).
Childs, B.S., Introduction to the Old Testament as Scripture (Philadelphia: Fortress, 1979), 504–25.
Cross, F.M. and D.N. Freedman, Studies in Ancient Yahwistic Poetry (2nd ed.; Grand Rapids: Eerdmans, 1997).
Dahmen, U., Psalmen- und Psalter-Rezeption im Frühjudentum: Rekonstruktion, Textbestand, Struktur und Pragmatik der Psalmenrolle 11QPs^a aus Qumran (STDJ 47; Leiden: Brill, 2003).
deClaissé-Walford, N., Reading from the Beginning: The Shaping of the Hebrew Psalter (Macon: Mercer University Press, 1997).
deClaissé-Walford, N. (ed.), The Shape and Shaping of the Book of Psalms: The Current State of Scholarship (Ancient Israel and Its Literature 20; Atlanta: SBL, 2014).
deClaissé-Walford, N., R.A. Jacobson, and B.L. Tanner, The Book of Psalms (NICOT; Grand Rapids: Eerdmans, 2014).
Delitzsch, F., Die Lese- und Schreibfehler im Alten Testament (Berlin: Vereinigung wissenschaftlicher Verleger, 1920).
Duhm, B., Die Psalmen (2nd ed.; KHC 14; Tübingen: Siebeck, 1922).
Field, *Hexapla, 2.83–305.
Flint, P.W., The Dead Sea Psalms Scrolls and the Book of Psalms (STDJ 17; Leiden: Brill, 1997).
Flint, P.W., "The '11QPs^a-Psalter' in the Dead Sea Scrolls: Including the Preliminary Edition of 4QPs^e," in The Quest for Context and Meaning: Studies in Biblical Intertextuality in Honor of James A. Sanders (eds. C.A. Evans and S. Talmon; BibInt 28; Leiden: Brill, 1997), 173–96.
Flint, P.W., "The Book of Psalms in the Light of the Dead Sea Scrolls," VT 48 (1998): 453–72.
Flint, P.W., "1b. 5/6ḤevPsalms," *DJD XXXVIII (2000): 141–66.
Flint, P.W., "Psalms and Psalters in the Dead Sea Scrolls," in The Bible and the Dead Sea Scrolls: The Princeton Symposium on the Dead Sea Scrolls (3 vols.; ed. J.H. Charlesworth; Waco: Baylor University Press, 2006), 1.233–72.
Flint, P.W., "Five Surprises in the Qumran Psalms Scrolls," in Flores Florentino: Dead Sea Scrolls and Other Early Jewish Studies in Honour of Florentino García Martínez (eds. A. Hilhorst, É. Puech, and E. Tigchelaar; JSJSup 122; Leiden: Brill, 2007), 183–95.
Flint, P.W., "11QPs^b and the 11QPs^a-Psalter," in Diachronic and Synchronic: Reading the Psalms in the Real Time: Proceedings of the Baylor Symposium on the Book of Psalms (eds. J.S. Burnett, W.H. Bellinger, and W.D. Tucker; Library of Hebrew Bible/Old Testament Studies 488; New York: T & T Clark International, 2007), 157–66.
Flint, P.W., "The Dead Sea Psalms Scrolls: Psalms Manuscripts, Editions, and the Oxford Hebrew Bible," in Jewish and Christian Approaches to the Psalms: Conflict and Convergence (ed. S. Gillingham; Oxford: Oxford University Press, 2013), 11–34.
Flint, P.W., "The Contribution of Gerald Wilson toward Understanding the Book of Psalms in Light of the Psalms Scrolls," in The Shape and Shaping of the Book of Psalms: The Current State of Scholarship (ed. N. deClaissé-Walford; Ancient Israel and its Literature 20; Atlanta: SBL, 2014), 209–30.
Flint, P.W., "Unrolling the Dead Sea Psalms Scrolls," in The Oxford Handbook of the Psalms (ed. W.P. Brown; Oxford: Oxford University Press, 2014), 229–50.
García Martínez, F., E.J.C. Tigchelaar, and A.S. van der Woude, *DJD XXIII (1998): 29–78, 181–205.
Ginsburg, *Introduction.
Goldingay, J., Psalms (3 vols.; Baker Commentary on the Old Testament Wisdom and Psalms; Grand Rapids: Baker Academic, 2006–2011).
Gunkel, H., Die Psalmen (5th ed.; Göttingen: Vandenhoeck & Ruprecht, 1968).
Haran, M., "11QPs^a and the Canonical Book of Psalms," in Minhah le-Nahum: Biblical and Other Studies Presented to Nahum M. Sarna in Honour of His 70th Birthday (eds. M.Z. Brettler and M.A. Fishbane; JSOTSup 154; Sheffield: JSOT Press, 1993), 193–201.
Holladay, W.L., The Psalms through Three Thousand Years: Prayerbook of a Cloud of Witnesses (Minneapolis: Fortress, 1993).
Hossfeld, F.-L. and E. Zenger, Die Psalmen I: Psalm 1–50 (NEchtB; Würzburg: Echter, 1993).
Hossfeld, F.-L. and E. Zenger, Psalms 2: A Commentary on Psalms 51–100 (trans. L.M. Maloney; Herm; Minneapolis: Fortress, 2005).
Hossfeld, F.-L. and E. Zenger, Psalms 3: A Commentary

on *Psalms 101–150* (trans. L.M. Maloney; Herm; Minneapolis: Fortress, 2011).

Jain, E., *Psalmen oder Psalter? Materielle Rekonstruktion und inhaltliche Untersuchung der Psalmenhandschriften aus der Wüste Juda* (STDJ 109; Leiden: Brill, 2014).

Kraus, H.-J., *Psalms 1–59: A Commentary* (trans. H.C. Oswald; CC; Minneapolis: Augsburg, 1988).

Lange, **Handbuch*, 373–450.

Lange, A., "Collecting Psalms in Light of the Dead Sea Scrolls," in *A Teacher for All Generations: Essays in Honor of James C. VanderKam* (2 vols.; eds. E.F. Mason et al.; JSJSup 153; Leiden: Brill, 2012), 1.297–308.

McCann, J.C. (ed.), *The Shape and Shaping of the Psalter* (JSOTSup 159; Sheffield: JSOT Press, 1993).

Ouellette, J., "Variations Qumrâniennes du Livre des Psaumes," *RevQ* 7 (1969–1971): 105–23.

Pajunen, M.S., "Perspectives on the Existence of a Particular Authoritative Book of Psalms in the Late Second Temple Period," *JSOT* 39 (2014): 139–63.

Pietersma, A., "Psalms," in **NETS*, 542–620.

Prinsloo, G.T.M., "Unit Delimitation in the Egyptian Hallel (Psalms 113–118): An Evaluation of Different Traditions," in *Unit Delimitation in Biblical Hebrew and Northwest Semitic Literature* (eds. M.C.A. Korpel and J.M. Oesch; Pericope 4; Assen: Van Gorcum, 2003), 232–63.

Sanders, **DJD* IV.

Sanders, J.A., *The Dead Sea Psalms Scroll* (Ithaca: Cornell University Press, 1967).

Sanders, J.A., "Cave 11 Surprises and the Question of Canon," *McCQ* 21 (1968): 1–15 (repr. in *New Directions in Biblical Archaeology* [eds. D.N. Freedman and J.C. Greenfield; Garden City: Doubleday, 1969], 101–16).

Sanders, J.A., "The Modern History of the Qumran Psalms Scroll and Canonical Criticism," in *Emanuel: Studies in Hebrew Bible, Septuagint, and Dead Sea Scrolls in Honor of Emanuel Tov* (eds. S.M. Paul et al.; VTSup 94; Brill: Leiden, 2003), 393–411.

Schmuttermayr, G., *Psalm 18 und 2 Samuel 22: Studien zu einem Doppeltext: Probleme der Textkritik und Übersetzung und das Psalterium Pianum* (SANT 25; Munich: Kösel-Verlag, 1971).

Skehan, P.W., E. Ulrich, and P.W. Flint, "Psalms," **DJD* XVI: 7–167.

Strawn, B.A., "David as One of the 'Perfect of (the) Way': On the Provenience of *David's Compositions* (and 11QPs^a as a Whole?)," *RevQ* 24 (2010): 607–27.

Swanson, D.D., "Qumran and the Psalms," in *Interpreting the Psalms: Issues and Approaches* (eds. P.S. Johnston and D.G. Firth; Downers Grove: InterVarsity Press, 2005), 247–61.

Talmon, S., "Fragments of a Psalms Scroll from Masada, MPs^b (Masada 1103–1742)," in *Minhah le-Nahum: Biblical and Other Studies Presented to Nahum M. Sarna in Honour of his 70th Birthday* (eds. M. Brettler and M. Fishbane; JSOTSup 154; Sheffield: Sheffield Academic Press, 1993), 318–27.

Talmon, S., "Fragments of a Psalms Scroll: MasPs^a Ps 81:2b–85:6a (1039–160; Mas1e; final photo 5255)," *DSD* 3 (1996): 296–314.

Talmon, S., "Hebrew Fragments from Masada," in Talmon, **Masada VI*, 76–97.

Terrien, S., *The Psalms: Strophic Structure and Theological Commentary* (Grand Rapids: Eerdmans, 2003).

Tov, **Scribal Practices*.

Tov, **TCHB*.

Ulrich, **DSS*.

Ulrich, E., "Two Perspectives on Two Pentateuchal Manuscripts from Masada," in *Emanuel: Studies in Hebrew Bible, Septuagint, and Dead Sea Scrolls in Honor of Emanuel Tov* (eds. S.M. Paul et al.; VTSup 94; Brill: Leiden, 2003), 453–64.

Ulrich, **BQS*, 627–726.

Weiser, A., *The Psalms: A Commentary* (trans. H. Hartwell; OTL; Philadelphia: Westminster, 1962).

Wellhausen, J., *The Book of Psalms* (The Polychrome Bible; London: James Clark & Co., 1898).

Whybray, N., *Reading the Psalms as a Book* (JSOTSup 222; Sheffield: Sheffield Academic Press, 1996).

Wilson, G.H., "The Qumran Psalms Manuscripts and the Consecutive Arrangement of Psalms in the Hebrew Psalter," *CBQ* 45 (1983): 377–88.

Wilson, G.H., *The Editing of the Hebrew Psalter* (SBLDS 76; Chico: Scholars Press, 1985).

Wilson, G.H., "The Qumran Psalms Scroll Reconsidered: Analysis of the Debate," *CBQ* 47 (1985): 624–42

Wilson, G.H., "The Qumran *Psalms Scroll* (11QPs^a) and the Canonical Psalter: Comparison of Editorial Shaping," *CBQ* 59 (1997): 448–64.

Witte, M., "The Psalter," in J.C. Gertz et al., *T & T Clark Handbook of the Old Testament: An Introduction to the Literature, Religion, and History of the Old Testament* (London: T & T Clark International, 2012), 527–49.

Yarchin, W., "The Psalter and the Modern Bible in the Making," *The Folio* 29.2 (2012): 1, 3–4, 8.

Yarchin, W., "Is There an Authoritative Shape for the Hebrew Book of Psalms?" *RB* 122 (2015): 355–70.

Yarchin, W., "Were the Psalms Collections at Qumran True Psalters?" *JBL* 134 (2015): 775–89.

Yarchin, W., "Why Were the Psalms the First Bible Chapters to be Numbered?" (forthcoming paper presented at the 21st Congress of the International Organization for the Study of the Old Testament in Munich, Germany, August 2013).

Brent A. Strawn

10.2.3 Other Texts

The manuscript evidence from Qumran that exists for the Psalms is described in detail in → 10.2.1.[1] That section, building off of the work of several scholars, but especially the extensive corpus of Flint,[2] delineated no less than seven possible collections of psalms among these manuscripts, only one of which was MT or proto-MT (see → 10.2.2). Beyond the proto-MT collection, three collections are particularly significant given their multiple attestation in more than one scroll and/or by the inclusion of unusual content: the 11QPs^a Psalms Collection (→ 10.2.1.2); the 4QPs^f Psalms Collection (→ 10.2.1.3); and the 4QPs^a and 4QPs^q Psalms Collection (→ 10.2.1.4.1).[3]

Alongside the four collections mentioned thus far, → 10.2.1 notes the possible existence of three more groupings (nos. 5–7), though since these are attested by only a single manuscript, it cannot be certain that they reflect a "collection" properly so-called, especially in light of an eighth collection or grouping comprised of those psalms manuscripts that seem to be excerpted texts (4QPs^g, 4QPs^h, 4QPs^l, 5QPs; see → 10.2.1.5; → 10.2.3.6). These eight groupings do not yet include the ten psalms manuscripts that cannot be classified because they do not contain enough preserved text to make a judgment on the matter (viz., 1QPs^a, 1QPs^b [but see → 10.2.3.2.1.5], 2QPs, 4QPs^j, 4QPs^m, 4QPs^o, 4QPs^r, 4QPs^s, 8QPs, 11QPs^d: a *ninth* grouping of sorts, for which, see → 10.2.1.6.1), nor the six manuscripts that only preserve one psalm (viz., 1QPs^c, 4QPs^p, 4QPs^w, 4QPs^x, 11QPs^e [?], ms Schøyen 5233/2; → 10.2.1.6.2: a *tenth* grouping),[4] nor the five manuscripts that may contain only a quotation of a psalm (3QPs, 4QPs^t, 4QPs^u, 4QPs^v, 6QpapPs; → 10.2.1.6.3: an *eleventh* grouping).[5]

Given the uncertain classification of several of these eleven groupings (particularly nos. 5–11), the present entry focuses on nos. 2–4, as these three are the most likely to represent a text other than that of proto-MT.[6] After a brief history of research (→ 10.2.3.1), the next sections cover the following:

– the *Non-Proto-MT Collection 1* (→ 10.2.3.2);
– the *Non-Proto-MT Collection 2* (→ 10.2.3.3); and
– the *Non-Proto-MT Collection 3* (→ 10.2.3.4).

Three important caveats should be made: 1) These sections initially proceed as if these three collections are *indeed* non-proto-MT; but 2) this assumption is *not* a necessary one: it is possible that one

---

[1] For the bibliographical details of their editions, see → 10.2.1.

[2] Flint, *The Dead Sea Psalms Scrolls*; Flint, "The Book of Psalms"; Flint, "Psalms and Psalters"; Flint, "Five Surprises"; Flint, "11QPs^b"; Flint, "11QPs^a-Psalter"; Flint, "Dead Sea Psalms Scrolls"; and Flint, "Unrolling."

[3] For the language of "Psalms collection(s)" rather than "Psalter(s)" see Lange, *Handbuch*, 415–16. Flint prefers "Psalter," given his belief that these collections are authoritative and scriptural (see further below → 10.2.3.2.4; → 10.2.3.6).

[4] Actually, this should probably be eight texts if, along with ms Schøyen 5233/2, one includes the manuscripts that have been recently acquired by the Southwestern Baptist Theological Seminary (containing portions of Ps 22:4–13) and by the Green Collection (containing portions of Ps 11:1–4; see Wolfe et al., "Psalm 11:1–4"). Flint, "Unrolling," 239 designates these three manuscripts XQPs A, B, and C, respectively. It is possible that these manuscripts, too, could be excerpted texts. See → 10.2.1.5; → 10.2.2; → 10.2.3.6.

[5] As noted in → 10.2.1, non-biblical manuscripts could quote not only select sections or verses of a psalm, but even an entire psalm composition (see, e.g., 4Q522 22–25, which includes all of Psalm 122) so that in the case of groupings nos. 8–11 it is unclear if the manuscripts in question are actually from a Psalms manuscript properly so-called or from a manuscript that simply cited the psalm in full or in part. The Psalms pesharim (1QpPs, 4QpPs^a, 4QpPs^b) should not be forgotten in this connection. See on these texts, Lange, *Handbuch*, 407; M.P. Horgan in *PTSDSSP 6b (2002): 6–33.

[6] For more on the significance of psalms collections that seem to be at odds with proto-MT, see → 10.1.1.1; → 10.1.2.1; → 10.2.1; → 10.2.2.

or all of these could be secondary liturgical collections that, as a result, may be less significant for the *textual history* of the composition of the psalms even while remaining crucial for the *reception history* of the psalms.[7] Of course reception history is, in the end, very much a part of textual history – even inextricably so[8] – therefore this distinction, while important, may be overly precise or ultimately pragmatically moot. 3) Finally, various manuscripts from nos. 5–11 may well belong to these three non-proto-MT collections, or, conversely, may have lent support to the proto-MT collection or still yet some other collection(s) (cf. → 10.2.3.5). Unfortunately, we simply can no longer know for sure given the present state of preservation.[9] This final caveat duly entered, it is nevertheless important to note that grouping no. 8, that of the excerpted or abbreviated manuscripts of psalms, has something important to say about the possible use, function, and text-form of at least some manuscripts from the Dead Sea. For this reason, they are discussed in → 10.2.3.6.

10.2.3.1 History of Research

Much from the history of research on the textual history of Psalms may be gleaned from the various articles collected in the present volume.[10] Flint has recently categorized the history of research on the Hebrew texts from the Dead Sea and their bearing on the textual history of the psalms into five phrases:

Phase I: Cave I and the Minor Caves (1947–1962)
Phase II: The Great Psalms Scroll from Cave 11 (1965–1985)
Phase III: Psalms Scrolls (or Texts Incorporating Psalms) from Cave 4 (1965–2000)
Phase IV: Additional Psalms Scrolls from Cave 11 and Psalms Scrolls from Other Sites in the Judean Desert (1998–2000)
Phase V: Psalms Scrolls "Discovered" (Since 2000).[11]

There is overlap between some of these stages, as is clear from the dates, but the stages are nevertheless distinguishable and marked by certain trends. So, for example, given the nature of the manuscript finds dating to Phase I, scholars active at this time were largely unaware of major variations in these manuscripts from MT, and so it seemed that, for the scribes of these texts, "the Book of Psalms was very much like the collection of 150 psalms found in the Masoretic Text."[12] This situation began to change with the publication of 11QPs[a] by Sanders in 1965 (*DJD* IV),[13] and the publication of the full lot of Cave 4 psalms manuscripts by Skehan, Ulrich, and Flint in 2000 (*DJD* XVI).[14] Sanders' work on the former, and (especially) Flint's work on the latter, has led to what Flint has dubbed "The Qumran Psalms Hypothesis," discussed in greater detail below (→ 10.2.3.2.4; cf. → 10.1; → 10.2.2).

As has been noted on more than one occasion (→ 10.2.1), the main textual differences between the ancient Psalms manuscripts concerns less their wording than their *sequence* (which psalms

---

[7] See, e.g., Dahmen, *Psalmen- und Psalter-Rezeption*; cf. further → 10.1; → 10.2.2; → 10.2.3.6.

[8] See B.W. Breed, *Nomadic Text: A Theory of Biblical Reception History* (Bloomington: University of Indiana Press, 2013), 4.

[9] Cf. Flint, "Unrolling," 240; Flint, "Psalms and Psalters," 244–45.

[10] For the Hebrew texts, see esp. → 10.1; → 10.2.1; → 10.2.2; and, most extensively, the works of Flint and Lange. For Flint, see n. 2 above; for Lange, see his "Die Endgestalt des protomasoretischen Psalters und die Toraweisheit: Zur Bedeutung der nichtessenischen Weisheitstexte aus Qumran für die Auslegung des protomasoretischen Psalters," in *Der Psalter in Judentum und Christentum* (ed. E. Zenger; Herder's Biblical Studies 18; Freiburg: Herder, 1998), 101–36; Lange, **Handbuch*, 416–20, 435; Lange, "Collecting Psalms."

[11] Flint, "Unrolling," 231–39.

[12] Flint, "Unrolling," 231. It should be noted that this stage demonstrates, despite the additional information that came to light in subsequent stages, that it is indeed possible to understand many of the Psalms scrolls as (closely) related to proto-MT.

[13] Note also the "Cornell Edition": Sanders, *Dead Sea Psalms Scroll*. For an autobiographical account of his work on the Psalms material, especially 11QPs[a], see Sanders, "Modern History." Other important works by Sanders include "*Variorum*"; "Cave 11 Surprises"; and "Qumran Psalms Scroll."

[14] The edition of 4QPs[w] in **DJD* XVI is by J.A. Fitzmyer; also included is Psalm 122 in 4Q522 by É. Puech ("522. Ps 122 in '4QProphecy of Joshua,'" **DJD* XVI: 169–70).

appear in which order) and, correlatively, their *content* (which psalms, especially of the "non-canonical" variety does a manuscript include, if any).[15] Scholars agree that, despite the hundreds of microvariants that exist across these manuscripts, the wording of the individual psalms compositions themselves remains relatively stable and this complicates text-typological classification.[16] To put the situation differently, textual affiliation among these manuscripts is best determined by means of the macrovariants of psalm sequence and "non-canonical" content as opposed to the microvariants of individual readings.[17] The following discussion focuses on the macrovariants of sequence and content (see further → 10.2.1; → 10.2.2), not only because they are most important for text-typology, but also because, with forty-five psalms manuscripts attested – the largest number among biblical compositions found in the Judean Desert – there are simply too many microvariants to categorize here.[18] Even so, the poor state of preservation means that much is uncertain and unknowable about sequence and content for many of these manuscripts (esp. groupings nos. 5–11 described above).

10.2.3.2 Non-Proto-MT Collection 1

The first non-proto-MT collection (→ 10.2.1.2) is attested in 11QPs^a, 11QPs^b, and 4QPs^e, and perhaps also 4QPs^n and 1QPs^b.

10.2.3.2.1 Manuscripts Attesting to the Collection: Sequence and Contents
10.2.3.2.1.1 11QPs^a

Since 11QPs^a is the largest preserved psalms manuscript, it often lends its name to this collection: either the "11QPs^a-Psalter" (Flint) or "11QPs^a-Psalms-Collection" (Lange; cf. → 10.2.1.2). For the sequence of psalms in 11QPs^a that differs markedly from both MT and LXX, see → 10.2.1.2.1; → 10.2.3.2.2. Notable is that amidst this *different sequence* is also *different content*, namely, the inclusion of the following ten compositions:

1. Psalm 154 (coming between Psalm 145 and Plea for Deliverance, in that order);
2. Plea for Deliverance (coming between Psalms 154 and 139);
3. Sir 51:13–30 (coming between Psalm 138 and Apostrophe to Zion);
4. Apostrophe to Zion (coming between Sir 51:13–30 and Psalm 93);
5. Psalm 155 (coming between Psalm 144 and Psalm 142);
6. Hymn to the Creator (coming between Psalm 150 and 2 Sam 23:[1–]7);
7. 2 Sam 23:[1–]7 (coming between Hymn to the Creator and David's Compositions);
8. David's Compositions (coming between 2 Sam 23:[1–]7 and Psalm 140);
9. Psalm 151A (coming between Psalms 134 and 151B); and
10. Psalm 151B (coming after Psalm 151A).

It is equally fascinating that Psalm 118 is evidently utilized in different parts of the scroll. So, in frg. e i 1–5, Ps 118:25–29 precedes Psalm 104 (which follows on line 6 after a *vacat*), but Ps 118:1, 15–16, 8, 9, and 29 (in that order)[19] are found much later (col. XVI) following Ps 136:26 but coming before Ps 145:1–7 (after a *vacat*). It is not entirely clear if the scribe of 11QPs^a deemed Psalm 136

---

[15] That is, text from compositions traditionally classified as "apocryphal" along with still other texts like David's compositions. These additional compositions are found in only six manuscripts, three from Cave 4 (4QPs^f, 4Q448, 4Q522; the latter two are not Psalms manuscripts proper but contain Psalm 154 and Psalm 122, respectively) and three from Cave 11 (11QPs^a, 11QPs^b, 11QapocrPs; the latter is not a Psalms manuscript proper, but contains Psalm 91).

[16] See → 10.2.1; Lange, *Handbuch*, 423–35; Lange, "Collecting," 301–02; Flint, "Unrolling," 247.

[17] For the language of "macro-" and "microvariants," see Flint, *Dead Sea Psalms Scrolls*, 153–55; Flint, "Psalms and Psalters," 236.

[18] For statistics on each manuscript, see → 10.2.1. For presentation of the variants, see Flint, *Dead Sea Psalms Scrolls*, 50–116; and Ulrich, *BQS*, 627–726.

[19] Sanders, *DJD* IV, 37 is uncertain about Ps 118:1; note also that there is text between v. 9 and v. 29 (here designated x$_1$); the same is true for text after v. 29 and prior to Psalm 145 (here designated x$_2$).

+ Ps 118:1, 15–16, 8, 9, [x₁], and 29 [x₂]²⁰ to be one psalm (see → 10.2.1.2.1) or if the material from Psalm 118 in col. XVI is a catena of sorts (one summoned or composed from memory?),²¹ which may not bear on the text-form of Psalm 136 (or 118) proper. If the latter is the case, the situation would perhaps be analogous to several of the other additional compositions included in 11QPsᵃ (that is, a "non-psalmic" addition)²² and not entirely unlike (though far longer than) the doxologies that were added to the end of the different books within the Psalter (e.g., Pss 41:14; 72:18–19, 20; 89:53; 106:48) and also utilized in various Psalms manuscripts.²³ Against this consideration is the fact that there is no *vacat* between the end of Psalm 136 and this material from Psalm 118⁺, though there is such a *vacat* after the Psalm 118⁺ material before Psalm 145 (i.e., the spacing suggests that the Psalm 118⁺ material goes with the Psalm 136 material, and that the Psalms 136 + 118⁺ complex is separate from the Psalm 145 composition). In favor of it, perhaps, is that the x₁ and x₂ material in Psalm 118⁺ cannot be located there,²⁴ and the fact that x₂, in particular, is identical to the doxology in Book 4 of MT-Pss: הַלְלוּ־יָהּ, "praise the LORD" (11QPsᵃ XVI:6; Ps 106:48b). Whatever the case, it is more than apparent that 11QPsᵃ attests to a very different collection than that found in MT-Pss (→ 10.2.2) and LXX-Pss (→ 10.3.1).

It is uncertain where 11QPsᵃ originally began, with viable options including Psalms 90, 100, or 101,²⁵ but it clearly runs through Psalm 151B, though it does not include all of the Psalms known in the MT-Pss 101–150 complex and definitely not in the order known there. Reconstruction of 11QPsᵃ suggests that it was longer than what is presently preserved;²⁶ moreover, since 4QPsᵉ and 11QPsᵇ also appear to belong to this same non-proto-MT collection and preserve material from earlier in the book of Psalms as it is now known, it is possible, if not likely, that this first non-proto-MT collection included materials from the first half or two-thirds of the psalms, not just from Psalms 101–150⁺.²⁷

10.2.3.2.1.2 11QPsᵇ

11QPsᵇ contains material from Ps 77:18–78:1 (frg. 1),²⁸ appears to witness to the same transition of Ps 118:1 → vv. 15–16 (frg. 3) known in 11QPsᵃ (but note that Psalms 136 and 145 are not extant in 11QPsᵇ), contains the Plea for Deliverance (frgs. 4–5) and Apostrophe to Zion (frg. 6), and also knows of the sequence Psalms 141 → 133 → 144 (frg. 7a–e). So, according to the editors, "[t]he extant fragments indicate that 11QPsᵇ and 11QPsᵃ ... represent two copies of the same composition."²⁹ They continue: "[D]ifferences between the two copies of this Qumran Psalter are minimal," though they do note a defective orthographic preference in

---

[20] See previous note.

[21] Cf. Sanders, *Dead Sea Psalms Scroll*, 20 on the scribe "having copied off the lines at this point in the scroll either from memory or from dictation." Note also the plus at Ps 146:1–4, which may be taken from Ps 33:8 and/or Ps 145:10–12 (Sanders, *Dead Sea Psalms Scroll*, 19).

[22] Cf. Flint, *Dead Sea Psalms Scrolls*, 40 n. 75, 188 for scholars entertaining such a position.

[23] See Flint, *Dead Sea Psalms Scrolls*, 117–34, 146–48; cf. Wilson, *Editing*, 139–97.

[24] Of course, one might argue that 11QPsᵃ preserves here an early or alternative text form of Psalm 136 and/or Psalm 118. See, e.g., Flint, *Dead Sea Psalms Scrolls*, 191; Chyutin, "Redaction."

[25] The first extant text on the scroll is from Ps 101:1–8 (frgs.

a–c i; Sanders, *Dead Sea Psalms Scroll*, 28; Flint, *Dead Sea Scrolls*, 190).

[26] See → 10.2.1.2.1 and H. Stegemann, "Methods for the Reconstruction of Scrolls from Scattered Fragments," in *Archaeology and History in the Dead Sea Scrolls: The New York Conference in Memory of Yigael Yadin* (ed. L.H. Schiffman; JSPSup 8; Sheffield: Sheffield Academic Press, 1990), 189–220 (213 n. 55).

[27] See, among others, Flint, *Dead Sea Psalms Scrolls*, 160–64; Flint, "11QPsᵃ-Psalter," 182–83, 186; Flint, "Five Surprises," 192–95; Flint, "11QPsᵇ," 164–66; Skehan, Ulrich, and Flint, *DJD XVI, 74, 76; also, Lange, *Handbuch*, 395–98. Cf. → 10.2.3.4.2.

[28] This fragment was previously assigned to 11QPsᶜ, in which case it would undermine the attestation of Psalms 77–78 in this first non-proto-MT collection, at least from this scroll (but see on 4QPsᵉ below). While the reassignment may be debated, the arguments of the editors on the basis of the paleographic differences between 11QPsᵇ 1 and 11QPsᶜ appear sound, especially with regard to the writing of ל, מ, and א (see García Martínez, Tigchelaar, and van der Woude, *DJD XXIII, 51).

[29] García Martínez, Tigchelaar, and van der Woude, *DJD XXIII, 38.

11QPsᵇ and the fact that this scroll writes the divine name in square script, not in paleo-Hebrew script as does 11QPsᵃ.³⁰

10.2.3.2.1.3 4QPsᵉ

Although it must be partially reconstructed, 4QPsᵉ seems to have "a distinctive arrangement found also in 11QPsᵃ": Psalms 118 → 104 [→ 147 →] 105 → 146 (?), though Psalm 147 must be entirely reconstructed and the identification of Ps 146:1 is not completely certain.³¹ If correct, this sequencing would make 4QPsᵉ another witness to the first non-proto-MT collection.³² It would also make 4QPsᵉ "the only exemplar of the 11QPsᵃ-Psalter from Cave 4."³³ It is intriguing, however, that in six supralinear corrections to Psalms 125–26 and 130 (frg. 26 i–ii) – all made by the original scribe – 4QPsᵉ was revised toward a consonantal text quite similar to MT (→ 10.2.2) and LXX (→ 10.3.1).³⁴ Why corrections like these would be limited to just this one part of the manuscript is unclear, but in point of fact four of the six corrections also agree with 11QPsᵃ.³⁵ This leaves one correction that is not extant in 11QPsᵃ and so unable to be verified, and another that is clearly against 11QPsᵃ (Ps 125:5). So, despite some curiosities, it seems unlikely that 4QPsᵉ is from an altogether different psalm collection than that represented by 11QPsᵃ.³⁶ Instead, the data from 4QPsᵉ may show that this first non-proto-MT collection was subject to textual change (→ 10.2.1.2.3), perhaps even change *toward* proto-MT in some instances, sections, or compositions. Finally, 4QPsᵉ contains material that comes before what is extant in 11QPsᵇ, namely, Ps 76:10–12 and 77:1. It also contains material from Psalms 78, 81, 88, 89, and 114–116. This rounds out information about this collection not found in the other two manuscripts, and shows that the collection included psalms from the first half of the book of Psalms as well as from the Pesach-Hallel complex (Psalms 113–118).

10.2.3.2.1.4 4QPsⁿ

It is possible that 4QPsⁿ could represent "(at least in part) a *Psalms* composition identical and parallel to that represented by 11QPsᵃ,"³⁷ particularly given the variant at Ps 135:6 (which also agrees with 4QPsᵏ at this point against both MT and LXX).³⁸ According to the editors, frg. 3 moves directly from Ps 135:11–12 → 136:23–24, which differs from both 11QPsᵃ and MT. If accurate, "[t]he resultant text comprises a new Psalm"; however, they also note that "[i]dentification of some verses is complex due to the paucity of extant text and similar terminology found in Psalms 135 and 136."³⁹ Even so, if they are correct, "the compiler fashioned the new Psalm by combining material from Psalms 135 and 136," and "succeeded in blending material from Psalms 135 with that of 136 at points where the separate psalms contain very similar readings."⁴⁰ They believe that "[t]he composition found in 4QPsⁿ intensifies the focus on God's saving deeds in Israel's history and renders it more personal by including first person objects."⁴¹ Dahmen has argued that all of frgs. 2–3 come from Ps 136:19–24 so there is in fact no transition from Ps 135:12 → 136:23. This may be possible but is not without its problems (particularly the *lamed* on לְנַחֲלָה "for a heritage" in MT-Ps 136:21: contrast נַחֲלָה "as a heritage" in MT-Ps 135:12

---

³⁰ García Martínez, Tigchelaar, and van der Woude, *DJD* XXIII, 38. Note also 11QPsᵇ 8, the identification and placement of which is uncertain. If it does come from Psalm 109, and if it does rightly follow frg. 7, 11QPsᵇ would reflect a different order than that found in 11QPsᵃ. However, it may not come from Psalm 109 (see García Martínez, Tigchelaar, and van der Woude, *DJD* XXIII, 46–47).

³¹ Flint, "Unrolling," 236.

³² See Skehan, Ulrich, and Flint, *DJD* XVI, 81; and Flint, "11QPsᵃ-Psalter," 178–83. In Flint, "Five Surprises," 189–91, 194, and Flint, "11QPsᵇ," 162, 165, he is much more cautious about the support 4QPsᵉ offers for the 11QPsᵃ collection, evidently due to the work of Dahmen, *Psalmen- und Psalter-Rezeption*, esp. 52–59.

³³ Flint, "Unrolling," 236. But see → 10.2.3.2.1.4 on 4QPsⁿ.

³⁴ Skehan, Ulrich, and Flint, *DJD* XVI, 74.

³⁵ See Skehan, Ulrich, and Flint, *DJD* XVI, 84; cf. → 10.2.1.2.3.

³⁶ But see Dahmen, *Psalmen- und Psalter-Rezeption*, 52–59, 231, etc., who disputes the connection.

³⁷ Dahmen, "New Identifications," 485; cf. Dahmen, *Psalmen- und Psalter-Rezeption*, 231.

³⁸ See Skehan, Ulrich, and Flint, *DJD* XVI, 124, 136.

³⁹ Skehan, Ulrich, and Flint, *DJD* XVI, 135–36.

⁴⁰ Skehan, Ulrich, and Flint, *DJD* XVI, 137.

⁴¹ Skehan, Ulrich, and Flint, *DJD* XVI, 137; Flint, Skehan, and Ulrich, "Three Psalms of Praise," 42.

but so also in MT^mss of Ps 136:21!). So, again, it is possible that 4QPs^n is part of this first non-proto-MT collection, but the very limited extant remains means that it is possible that it could be an excerpted manuscript from this collection or some sort of (re)use of Psalms 135–136 in a completely different kind of composition.[42]

10.2.3.2.1.5 1QPs^b

Finally, Dahmen has posited that 1QPs^b "could contain the remnants of a *Psalms* scroll (or at least a group of Psalms, esp. the מעלות-Psalms) which is (at least textually) identical and parallel to the *Psalms* manuscript represented by 11QPs^a."[43] He reaches this conclusion primarily on the basis of the shared variant between 1QPs^b and 11QPs^a at Ps 126:6 with LXX and Jerome but against MT.[44] But, since this is the only complete word on this particular fragment of 1QPs^b, there is precious little data on which to base an opinion.

10.2.3.2.2 Remarks on Text-Critical Character

11QPs^a is by far the most extensive and well-preserved manuscript in this first non-proto-MT collection. Its macrovariants in terms of order/sequence and content are easily seen in the following chart (cf. → 10.2.1.2.1):

101 → 102 → 103 → … → 109 → … → 118 → 104 → 147 → 105 → 146 → 148 → … → 121 → 122 → 123 → 124 → 125 → 126 → 127 → 128 → 129 → 130 → 131 → 132 → 119 → 135 → 136 + 118:1 → vv. 15–16 → vv. 8–9 → x_1 → v. 29 → x_2 (≈ Catena?) → 145 → 154 → Plea for Deliverance → 139 → 137 → 138 → Sir 51:13–30 → Apostrophe to Zion → 93 → 141 → 133 → 144 → 155 → 142 → 143 → 149 → 150 → Hymn to the Creator → 2 Sam 23:[1–]7 → David's Compositions → 140 → 134 → 151A → 151B.

Beyond these, 11QPs^a reads only eight times with but 335 times against MT; fifty-five times with but 251 times against LXX; and 280 times non-aligned (→ 10.2.1.2.1). It clearly represents a non-aligned textual witness; interestingly, 11QPs^a reads only eight times with and fifty times against other psalms manuscripts from the Dead Sea, indicating a certain independence at Qumran as well.

Sanders has ably discussed the most intriguing of the microvariants in 11QPs^a.[45] These include the addition of a refrain, וברוך שמו לעולם ועד "and blessed be his name forever and ever" to every verse in Psalm 145, "like a chorus."[46] This addition is found only here. In the scroll, this composition is called "a prayer" (תפלה) of/for/by David as opposed to a praise song (תהלה) of/for/by David. This psalm is an acrostic poem, and, in MT^L, is missing the *nun*-verse, but that verse is attested in 11QPs^a (so also MT^ms, LXX, LXX^mss), and so is restored now in most modern translations in large part because of 11QPs^a. Another fascinating variant is found at the end of Psalm 145, though unfortunately it is broken. After Ps 145:21, the scroll has זאת לזכרון "this is for a memorial …" Sanders deems this subscription "to have been of the same order as the many superscriptions to the biblical psalms, that is, sort of program notes, to those who could make sense of them, indicating the cultic use of the psalm in temple services in antiquity … A 'memorial' would have been a special use of the psalm."[47] Perhaps so, and perhaps nothing further can be said, but it should be underscored that this is *additional* material found only in this scroll, and, if it is a subscription, represents *non-* or *extra-*biblical content. Although Sanders rightly warns against "[t]he tendency to find the peculiar ideas and beliefs of the Qumran sect in the variants and in the apocryphal compositions in the scroll,"[48] it is equally to be emphasized that the presence of such elements – if and when they are there – should not be *under*estimated.[49] This is just such a case.

---

[42] Cf. → 10.2.1.2.5; Lange, *Handbuch*, 388–89. There is an unparalleled plus, regardless, in frg. 3 line 2: נו]לל[.

[43] Dahmen, "New Identifications," 481; Dahmen, *Psalmen- und Psalter-Rezeption*, 231.

[44] See Dahmen, "New Identifications"; further Sanders, *DJD* IV, 25; and *DJD* I, 71; cf. → 10.2.1.6.1.

[45] Sanders, *Dead Sea Psalms Scroll*, 15–21.

[46] Sanders, *Dead Sea Psalms Scroll*, 16. Goshen-Gottstein, "Psalms Scroll," 29, takes this as proof that 11QPs^a is a liturgical collection.

[47] Sanders, *Dead Sea Psalms Scroll*, 16.

[48] Sanders, *Dead Sea Psalms Scroll*, 18.

[49] See → 10.2.3.2.4 and n. 69 below. Note also Sanders, *Dead Sea Psalms Scroll*, 19, where he speaks of the pluses in Ps 135:2

11QPs[b] supports part of the 11QPs[a]-sequence (underlined below) and its content (dotted):

77 → 78; 119:163–164; 118:1 → 15–16 (≈ Catena?); Plea for Deliverance; Apostrophe to Zion; 141 → 133 → 144; 109:3–4 (?)

It reads only once with, but four times against MT, never with and five times against LXX, and once non-aligned. It reads three times with but only once against 11QPs[a]. In contrast to the latter, 11QPs[b] writes the Tetragrammaton in square script. Although the two manuscripts should not be simplistically equated, 11QPs[b]'s distinctive smaller sequence, 118:1 → vv. 15–16 (≈ Catena?), and distinctive larger sequence, 141 → 133 → 144, are found only here and in 11QPs[a], suggesting a close connection between the two.

Although it contains no "non-canonical" contents, the reconstructed (N.B.!) order of 4QPs[e] also supports the 11QPs[a] sequence (underlined):

76 → 77; 115 → 116; 118 → 104 [→ 147 →] 105 → 146 (?); 125 → 126 [→ 127 → 128] → 129 → 130.

As noted above, 4QPs[e] contains several supralinear corrections (from the original scribe) that appear to conform the manuscript "to another Hebrew text similar to consonantal 𝔐,"[50] but these corrections also agree (except for two cases) with the text of 11QPs[a] (→ 10.2.1.2.3). The manuscript was copied carelessly.[51] It is possible that the parent text of 4QPs[e] considered Psalms 125–126 to be one song (→ 10.2.1.2.3), especially as the original text (*sans* supralinear correction) lacks the superscription found in Ps 126:1; however, the text seems to contain a short *vacat*, so the combination of Psalms 125–126 is somewhat unclear. A small *vacat* may also have existed prior to Psalm 88, which probably began in the second half of the line (frg. 5 line 1), so that 4QPs[e] may not have read a different text for Psalm 88 or merged it with the psalm that once preceded it (cf. → 10.2.1.2.3). Whatever the case, this scroll reads five times with and twelve times against MT and LXX, four times with 11QPs[a], and twelve times non-aligned.

It is hard to be certain about 4QPs[n], especially given the state of frgs. 2–3 and whether they attest to the sequence Ps 135:11–12 → Ps 136:23–24 (see above). If they do, this is against 11QPs[a], but in Ps 135:6, 4QPs[n] agrees in a substantial variant with 11QPs[a] (also 4QPs[k]). If frgs. 2–3 belong only to Psalm 136, the alternative sequence from 11QPs[a] disappears and the manuscript shifts closer to the 11QPs[a]-type. As for 1QPs[b], it reads once with LXX against MT and once non-aligned. It may have only contained Psalms 120–134[52] in which case, if it is part of the first non-proto-MT collection, it would fit in amidst that sequence in 11QPs[a], a sequence that is admittedly identical to that found in MT.

If all of these manuscripts are indeed witnesses to a significant non-proto-MT collection, then something like the following might reflect the sequence of this collection (though not in every manuscript and with a few differences as noted previously):[53]

76 → 77 → 78...101 → 102 → 103 → ... → 109...115 → 116...118 → 104 → 147 → 105 → 146 → 148 → ... → 121 → 122 → 123 → 124 → 125 → 126 → 127 → 128 → 129 → 130 → 131 → 132 → 119 → 135 → 136 + 118:1 → vv. 15–16 → vv. 8–9 → x₁ → v. 29 → x₂ (≈ Catena?) → 145 → 154 → Plea for Deliverance → 139 → 137 → 138 → Sir 51:13–30 → Apostrophe to Zion → 93 → 141 → 133 → 144 → 155 → 142 → 143 → 149 → 150 → Hymn to the Creator → 2 Sam 23:[1–]7 → David's Compositions → 140 → 134 → 151A → 151B.

10.2.3.2.3 Date and Milieu

The paleographical dates for the manuscripts attesting to this first non-proto-MT collection cluster in the latter part of the community's existence:

(against MT and LXX) as "a kind of homily directed at those who in Jerusalem are not quite praising and exalting the Lord as they should."

50 Skehan, Ulrich, and Flint, *DJD* XVI, 74.
51 Dahmen, *Psalmen- und Psalter-Rezeption*, 52–53.

52 Cf. Jain and Steudel, "Le manuscrites psalmique," 538.
53 The underline indicates attestation of the text in question by two manuscripts. For a full reconstruction of 11QPs[a], see Flint, *Dead Sea Psalms Scrolls*, 190.

4QPsⁿ	30–1 B.C.E.
11QPsᵇ	30–1 B.C.E.
11QPsᵃ	1–68 C.E.
1QPsᵇ	20–50 C.E.
4QPsᵉ	30–68 C.E.[54]

However, this later dating should not be taken as automatic proof of the secondary status of the collection. The earliest psalms scrolls are 4QPsᵃ and 4QPsˣ – both dating to the mid-second century B.C.E. – and 4QPsʷ, dating to between 125 and 75 B.C.E.[55] The latter manifests no variants from MT, but is very fragmentary, containing only Ps 112:1–9, so little can be said about its affiliation. 4QPsᵃ and 4QPsˣ, on the other hand, are quite different than MT.[56] Then, too, the scrolls that appear to support proto-MT are also from later periods (→ 10.2.2.1.2; → 10.2.2.4):[57]

MasPsᵃ	end of first century B.C.E./ beginning of first century C.E.
MasPsᵇ	50–1 B.C.E.
4QPsᶜ	50–68 C.E.
5/6ḤevPs	50–68 C.E.[58]

---

[54] For the dates, see, conveniently, B. Webster, "J. Chronological Index of the Texts from the Judaean Desert," *DJD* XXXIX (2002): 351–446, 371–75; Flint, "Unrolling," 241; see also → 10.2.1; cf. Jain, *Psalmen oder Psalter*, 305.

[55] See → 10.2.1.4.1.1; → 10.2.1.6.2; Webster, "Index," 371–72; cf. Flint, "Unrolling," 241; → 10.2.1.6.2 puts 4QPsʷ in 50–30 B.C.E. J.P.M. van der Ploeg dated 4QPsˣ to the second half of the first century B.C.E. ("Le sense et un problème textuelle du Ps LXXXIX," in *Mélanges bibliques et orientaux en l'honneur de M. Henri Cazelles* [eds. A. Caquot and M. Delcor; AOAT 212; Neukirchen: Neukirchen-Vluyn, 1981], 471–81 [475]).

[56] Cf. Flint, "A Form"; → 10.2.1.6.2 deems it a non-aligned text of Psalm 89, but see further below (→ 10.2.3.6).

[57] Cf. Wilson, "Consecutive Arrangement," 387–88.

[58] For more on these scrolls, see → 10.2.2. For the dates, see → 10.2.1.1.1–4; Webster, "Index," 438; Flint, "Unrolling," 241.

This is to say that one cannot argue, at least not on the basis of the paleography alone,[59] that Non-Proto-MT Collection 1 is secondarily derived from a secure, pre-existing, and well-attested proto-MT collection. Even so, Wilson is not quite correct when he writes that "[c]onflicting MSS occupy the earliest position and totally supportive MSS only appear much later," nor when he asserts that "there is *no* fully supportive MS dated prior to the first half of the first century A.D."[60] What is clear, regardless, is that this first non-proto-MT collection does belong primarily to the later stages of the community's existence. If it is a "true scriptural Psalter,"[61] this collection suggests that the book of Psalms – especially the latter two-thirds of it as known in MT/LXX – was in flux as late as the first century C.E. (see → 10.2.3.2.4). But, even if it is only or somehow a secondary liturgical collection, this psalms collection can be recognized as rather popular at Qumran, especially as it appears to be attested in as many as five manuscripts from three different caves (Caves 1, 4, and 11). It may even have been a collection that underwent subsequent literary development or that was excerpted. Further comments on the date and milieu of this collection are made in the next section on relevance for exegesis and literary analysis (→ 10.2.3.2.4; see also → 10.2.3.6). The role of David's Compositions in 11QPsᵃ (xxvii 2–11), and the possibly sectarian provenience of that text, is also particularly important for the debate on 11QPsᵃ and, correlatively, this first non-proto-MT collection.

---

[59] Despite the confirmation of paleographical analysis provided by AMS-C14 dating (see conveniently J.C. VanderKam, *The Dead Sea Scrolls Today* [2nd ed.; Grand Rapids: Eerdmans, 2010], 33–39; J. VanderKam and P. Flint, *The Meaning of the Dead Sea Scrolls: Their Significance for Understanding the Bible, Judaism, Jesus, and Christianity* [San Francisco: HarperSanFrancisco, 2002], 22–32), the temporal range offered by various scholars – not to mention altogether different estimation of dates (cf. n. 55 above) – should be kept in mind.

[60] Wilson, "Consecutive Arrangement," 387.

[61] This language is Flint's (e.g., "Psalms and Psalters," 240; *Dead Sea Psalms Scrolls*, 202; "11QPsᵇ," 161); he uses it in contrast to "secondary liturgical collection." For discussion, see → 10.2.3.6 below.

10.2.3.2.4 Relevance for Exegesis and Literary Analysis

This first non-proto-MT collection is quite important insofar as it attests to a non-aligned psalms collection represented by no less than three but perhaps as many as five manuscripts at Qumran. At least three items should be mentioned in connection to its significance for exegesis and literary analysis of the psalms:

1) The fact that so much of what is extant from this first non-proto-MT collection concerns the last third of the Psalter has been used by scholars such as Sanders, Wilson, and Flint to argue that the book of Psalms was gradually stabilized, from front to back, with Books I–III (Psalms 1–89) largely in place *prior* to the Qumran community but with Books IV–V (Psalms 90–150) still in a great deal of flux.[62]

2) This theory of gradual stabilization has been developed further by Flint into what he calls "The Qumran Psalms Hypothesis," which holds that this first non-proto-MT collection represents (in Ulrich's terms) a "variant literary edition"[63] of the book of Psalms and that the Psalter did not gradually stabilize so much as grow through two distinct editions:[64]

> *Edition I:* An early edition of the Psalter that was mostly stabilized, beginning with Psalms 1 or 2 and ending with Psalm 89 or 92 (the cutoff point is not certain).
>
> *Edition IIa:* The 11QPs^a Psalter, consisting of Edition I plus Psalms 101–151 as found in the Great Psalms Scroll and including at least Psalm 93.
>
> *Edition IIb:* The MT-150 Psalter, comprising Edition I plus Psalms 90–150 as found in MT.[65]

This might be presented stemmatically as:

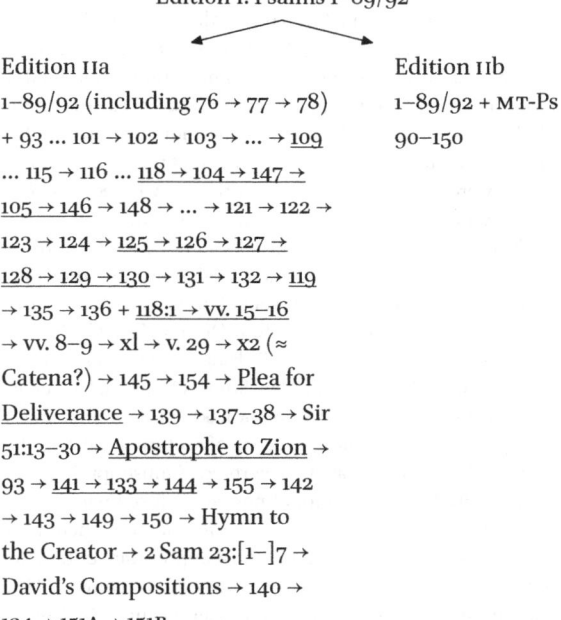

or as:

Flint has gone farther than all others in arguing that Edition IIa was widely known in various Jewish groups of the Second Temple period, especially those who kept to a solar calendar.[66] This seems unwarranted, however, since we have *no* non-Qumranic evidence for the "11QPs^a-Psalter," and what little evidence exists outside of Qumran – at Masada and Naḥal Ḥever – appears to sup-

---

[62] In Swanson's phrase: "They [the Scrolls] show us the very process of creation at the midpoint of its development" ("Qumran," 261).

[63] See, e.g., Ulrich, *DSS*, 34–50, 99–120.

[64] Interestingly, only five manuscripts contain psalms from both Psalms 1–89 and Psalms 90–150: 1QPs^a, 4QPs^e, 4QPs^f, 11QPs^b, and 11QPs^d.

[65] Flint, "Unrolling," 240.

[66] Flint, *Dead Sea Psalms Scrolls*, 198–201; Flint, "Book of Psalms," 459, 469–71; Flint, "Psalms and Psalters," 249–51; Flint, "11QPs^a-Psalter," 174–75. The qualification in Flint, "Unrolling," 240, is better: "at least among the *Yahad* or Essene movement." Cf. VanderKam, *Dead Sea Scrolls*, 176: "We cannot determine whether other groups in Judaism at the time had variant Psalters because we have no evidence for their views on the matter"; see also Wilson, *Editing*, 89.

port MT.⁶⁷ Then, too, several aspects of 11QPsᵃ give the impression that they are the result of sectarian concerns, interpretation, exegesis, or redaction.⁶⁸ Once again, Sanders rightly cautions against overstating matters in this regard, but his own analysis of several 11QPsᵃ variants suggests as much.⁶⁹ More recently, Strawn has argued that David's Compositions is a sectarian text, and, given its important place and role in the 11QPsᵃ sequence, that may indicate that the latter, too, is a sectarian compilation (as a whole).⁷⁰ Similarly, Witt has argued that Psalm 151 in 11QPsᵃ contains a sectarian phrase unattested in LXX (ומושל בבני בריתו "and ruler over the sons of his covenant") so that 11QPsᵃ reflects a "community-specific" collection, one authored or revised by the community.⁷¹ Dahmen has argued this point most fully.⁷² The kind of work suggested by these latter studies vis-à-vis Flint's extensive cor-

---

⁶⁷ See → 10.2.2; Strawn, "Review of Flint," 148; Talmon, "Review of Flint," 545–47. This has bearing on the question of the provenience of 11QPsᵃ (and the first non-proto-MT collection). Flint believes it is pre-Qumranic (e.g., "Psalms and Psalters," 250) with Sanders believing it was brought into the community from elsewhere (see his remarks in *Dead Sea Psalms Scroll*, 134; Sanders, "Review of Flint," *DSD* 6 [1999]: 84–89; cf. Flint, *Dead Sea Psalms Scrolls*, 199–200), but both positions are far from certain. Just because some of the compositions contained in 11QPsᵃ are pre-Qumranic does not mean that this is true for the whole composition/collection. Furthermore, it appears that *all* of the manuscripts representing the first non-proto-MT collection were copied at Qumran. Contrary to what Flint asserts ("Psalms and Psalters," 251), this is no minor point.

⁶⁸ *Contra* Flint, "Psalms and Psalters," 250, who offers as an example of such a variant, "references to the Righteous Teacher." Cf. Ulrich, "Absence"; but see C.A. Newsom, "'Sectually Explicit' Literature from Qumran," in *The Hebrew Bible and Its Interpreters* (eds. B. Halpern, W.H. Propp, and D.N. Feedman; Biblical and Judaic Studies from the University of California, San Diego 1; Winona Lake: Eisenbrauns, 1990), 167–87, for a broader understanding of sectarian use. See also Strawn, "David"; and Strawn, "Excerpted Manuscripts," 142–45. Additionally, "sectarian" should not be confused with "exclusively" sectarian (*contra* Sanders, "*Variorum*," 89). There is, of course, a large discussion on the most appropriate criteria for identifying "sectarian" texts. See, *inter alia*, D. Dimant, "The Qumran Manuscripts: Content and Significance," in *Time to Prepare the Way in the Wilderness: Papers on the Qumran Scrolls by Fellows of the Institute for Advanced Studies of the Hebrew University, Jerusalem, 1989–1990* (eds. D. Dimant and L.H. Schiffman; STDJ 16; Leiden: Brill, 1995), 23–58; D. Dimant, "Between Sectarian and Non-Sectarian: The Case of the *Apocryphon of Joshua*," in *Reworking the Bible: Apocryphal and Related Texts at Qumran* (eds. E.G. Chazon, D. Dimant, and R.A. Clements; STDJ 58; Brill: Leiden, 2005), 105–34; both reprinted with additional pertinent essays in D. Dimant, *History, Ideology and Biblical Interpretation in the Dead Sea Scrolls* (FAT 90; Tübingen: Siebeck, 2014), esp. 1–151, 171–83; C. Hempel, "Kriterien zur Bestimmung 'essenischer Verfasserschaft' von Qumrantexten," in *Qumran kontrovers: Beiträge zu den Textfunden vom Toten Meer* (eds. J. Frey and H. Stegemann; Paderborn: Bonifatius, 2003), 71–85; A. Lange, "Kriterien essenischer Texte," in *Qumran kontrovers: Beiträge zu den Textfunden vom Toten Meer* (eds. J. Frey and H. Stegemann; Paderborn: Bonifatius, 2003), 59–69; R. Nam, "How to Rewrite Torah: The Case for Proto-Sectarian Ideology in the *Reworked Pentateuch* (4QRP)," *RevQ* 23 (2007): 153–67; H.W.M. Rietz, "Identifying Compositions and Traditions in the Qumran Community: The *Songs of the Sabbath Sacrifice* as a Test Case," in *Qumran Studies: New Approaches, New Questions* (eds. M.T. Davis and B.A. Strawn; Grand Rapids: Eerdmans, 2007), 29–52.

⁶⁹ See Sanders' remarks in *Dead Sea Psalms Scroll*, 19–20, cited in nn. 21 and 49 above. Perhaps to be included here is the heavy emphasis on David found in 11QPsᵃ. See Strawn, "David"; Dahmen, *Psalmen- und Psalter-Rezeption*, 317; Leuenberg, "Aufbau und Pragmatik"; and Wacholder, "David's Eschatological Psalter."

⁷⁰ Strawn, "David." Of course this would not mean that every composition contained in 11QPsᵃ is sectarian, which is clearly not the case (e.g., 2 Samuel 23; Psalms 151; 154; 155; Sirach 51), only that its overall text form is. Note also R. Beckwith, *Calendar and Chronology, Jewish and Christian: Biblical, Intertestamental and Patristic Studies* (AGJU 33; Leiden: Brill, 1996), 141–66, who argues that David's Compositions indicates that 11QPsᵃ had knowledge of a 150-Psalm Psalter. Cf. Brooke, "Psalms," 10; Jain, *Psalmen oder Psalter*, 284. An important detail that should not be neglected at this point is that David's Compositions uses the Tetragrammaton, and writes it in paleo-Hebrew script (11QPsᵃ xxvii 4). Some would take this as evidence against a sectarian provenience for the composition, but see Tov, *Scribal Practices*, 218–21, 238–46 for a full presentation of the data that shows at least some use of the Tetragrammaton (including paleo-Hebrew instances) in sectarian texts and in non-quotation contexts (ibid., esp. 242). The practice of writing the divine name(s) seems varied enough (ibid., 240–41, 243–44) to prove insufficient as the only criterion in determining provenience (see further the literature in n. 68 above). So, e.g., 11QPsᵃ and 11QPsᵇ, both of which belong to the first non-proto-MT collection, treat the Tetragrammaton differently, with the former using paleo-Hebrew, the latter employing square script in an overlapping passage (11QPsᵃ XXIII:10 par 11QPsᵇ 7 5; cf. 4QShirShabbᵍ 1 2 and MasShirShab i 6–7).

⁷¹ Witt, "David."

⁷² Dahmen, *Psalmen- und Psalter-Rezeption*. More recently, see Leuenberg, "Aufbau und Pragmatik"; and also Jain, *Psalmen oder Psalter*.

pus of work is somewhat reminiscent of the debate between Sanders and others on the nature of 11QPs[a], not long after it was published, concerning whether it was a "scriptural" Psalter or a secondary liturgical collection.[73]

3) Regardless of its relationship to the textual history of the book of Psalms – that is, even if it proves somehow secondary – this first non-proto-MT collection is remarkably significant in what it says about the reception, use, and practice of the psalms.[74] At the very least, it shows that it was possible (for whatever purpose[s] need not detain us at present) to arrange the psalms in orders that differ radically from what ended up in the MT and LXX traditions. It was also possible, at least occasionally, to have manuscripts that contained the "biblical" psalms alongside other psalms that did not end up in MT (→ 10.2.2) and LXX (→ 10.3.1). Further, this first non-proto-MT collection seems to have been quite popular, attested in as many as five manuscripts from three different caves. It is even possible that one of these manuscripts, 4QPs[n], is an excerpted text from this collection, with another, 4QPs[e], perhaps representing literary development. All of these factors – the existence of multiple exemplars, spread across different caves, possible ex-

cerption if not also subsequent literary development – indicate not only that the psalmic content but *this particular collection* was authoritative, at least functionally, in the community (see → 10.2.3.6 below).

10.2.3.3 Non-Proto-MT Collection 2: The 4QPs[f] Psalms Collection
10.2.3.3.1 Contents and Character
This second non-proto-MT collection is found in only one manuscript, 4QPs[f] (→ 10.2.1.3). It contains fragments of Psalm 22 and then, in consecutive columns, material from Psalms 107 [→ 108 (reconstructed) →] 109, so that in terms of its extant text, 4QPs[f] manifests no large-scale differences from MT/LXX (→ 10.2.2; → 10.3.1) in terms of psalmic sequence. As noted in → 10.2.1.3, however, 4QPs[f] reads only once with and thirty-three times against MT (once with MT[mss]), once with and thirty-two times against LXX (twice with LXX[mss]), and thirty-three times non-aligned, clear proof that it is a non-aligned witness. Variants from MT/LXX include: 1) a shorter text in both Ps 109:26–27 (4QPs[f] lacks vv. 26a and 27a) and 2) Ps 107:21 (reconstructed); 3) a longer text in Ps 107:30c (reconstructed; but cf. VL); and 4) a different sequence for Ps 107:9ba and 30bc*a.[75]

Beyond these differences, there is a large difference in content insofar as 4QPs[f] contains three "non-canonical" compositions: Apostrophe to Zion, Eschatological Hymn, and Apostrophe to Judah. The latter two are only found in this manuscript, and, while Apostrophe to Zion is also found in 11QPs[a], the 4QPs[f] version reads nine times against the original scribe of 11QPs[a] and only once with (but also once against) 11QPs[a corr] in this particular composition. According to the editors, 4QPs[f] contains a different and earlier version of the work.[76] 4QPs[f] also locates the Apostrophe to Zion (directly after Psalm 109) differently than 11QPs[a] (where it follows Sirach 51). These factors, coupled with the fact that the shorter text of 4QPs[f] at Ps 109:26–27 is also against 11QPs[a], indicates that

---

[73] For Sanders, see *Dead Sea Psalms Scroll*; Sanders, "Variorum," Sanders, "Cave 11 Surprises"; Sanders, "Qumran Psalms Scroll"; Sanders, "Modern History." On the other side of the debate, see Talmon, "Pisqah"; Talmon, "Qumran"; Skehan, "Liturgical Complex"; Goshen-Gottstein, "The Psalms Scroll"; Haran, "11QPs[a]"; and Wacholder, "David's Eschatological Psalter." For discussion, see Flint, "Psalms and Psalters," 245–46; Strawn, "David"; Strawn, "Excerpted Manuscripts," 153–57; Lange, *Handbuch*, 425–30; Wilson, "Reconsidered"; Wilson, *Editing*, 63–92. See further below → 10.2.3.6 on the "canonical" or "authoritative" status of 11QPs[a].

[74] On the matter more generally, see H.A. Attridge and M.E. Fassler (eds.), *Psalms in Community: Jewish and Christian Textual, Liturgical, and Artistic Traditions* (SBLSymS 25; Atlanta: SBL, 2003); S. Gillingham, *Psalms Through the Centuries* (Malden: Wiley-Blackwell, 2012); Gillingham, *A Journey of Two Psalms: The Reception of Psalms 1 and 2 in Jewish and Christian Traditions* (Oxford: Oxford University Press, 2013); Gillingham (ed.), *Jewish and Christian Approaches to the Psalms: Conflict and Convergence* (Oxford: Oxford University Press, 2013).

[75] See Skehan, Ulrich, and Flint, *DJD* XVI: 86–87.
[76] Skehan, Ulrich, and Flint, *DJD* XVI, 88.

4QPsf is not a part of the first non-proto-MT collection, but represents a different collection altogether.⁷⁷

10.2.3.3.2 Date and Relevance

Insofar as this second collection is represented by only one manuscript, the term "collection" may not be entirely apt. Be that as it may, 4QPsf is dated to ca. 50 B.C.E. (→ 10.2.1.3), which places it on the earlier side of the chronological window represented of the first non-proto-MT collection. If 11QPsa is to be dated to 1–68 C.E., 4QPsf is at least half a century earlier, which might explain its different (and earlier?) text form for Apostrophe to Zion.

The relevance of 4QPsf for the exegesis and literary analysis of the psalms is fourfold: 1) it attests to an additional non-aligned text-type, distinct from MT and LXX; 2) it may be representative of a larger text-type or collection of psalms/psalm texts, but at the very least represents a text-type (if not collection) that is different than the first non-proto-MT collection; 3) it contains material from early in the book of Psalms (Psalm 22) as well as from its latter third (Psalms 107–109); and 4) it contains "non-canonical" material like 11QPsa, but also two new compositions known only here. The last-mentioned item can be understood in more than one way. Insofar as 11QPsa also preserves Apostrophe to Zion, and if that scroll is deemed a "true, scriptural Psalter," then 4QPsf, too, might be considered likewise, its "non-biblical" content notwithstanding. Alternatively, the inclusion of still other compositions unknown from other manuscripts may suggest not simply that 4QPsf is different than 11QPsa but that it is an alternative psalm collection in general and perhaps a secondary one at that, representing a new composition, not a copy of the book of Psalms proper. If so, the presence of Apostrophe to Zion in 11QPsa might be understood analogously: as an additional marker that it, too, is a secondary collection, not a copy of the book of Psalms.

10.2.3.4 Non-Proto-MT Collection 3: The 4QPsa and 4QPsq Psalms Collection

10.2.3.4.1 Contents and Character

The third non-proto-MT collection is attested in two manuscripts, 4QPsa and 4QPsq, though the state of preservation precludes certainty on a number of fronts. Still, insofar as both represent a transition from Psalm 31 to Psalm 33 (against MT and LXX), and this sequencing is not found in any other scrolls, it is possible that 4QPsa and 4QPsq are two exemplars of a third non-proto-MT Psalms collection (cf. → 10.2.1.4.1).

Beyond the sequence of Psalms 31 → 33, 4QPsa also attests to the sequence Psalms 38 → 71, which is not found elsewhere. 4QPsa may have divided Psalm 36 into two compositions (Pss 36:1–5; 36:6–9) and did the same with Psalm 56, deeming each of these compositions to be two, not one, but this is not certain.⁷⁸ It seems far more certain that 4QPsa treats Psalms 38 → 71 as one composition since Ps 71:1 follows Ps 38:23 on the same line with "virtually no interval."⁷⁹ 4QPsa reads three times with, but seventy times against MT, eight times with and sixty-one times against LXX, and sixty-four times non-aligned (for the variant statistics, see → 10.2.1.4.1.1).

4QPsq is the only other Psalms manuscript to preserve the sequence Psalms 31 → 33, which connects it to 4QPsa against MT and LXX (→ 10.2.2; → 10.3.1). Beyond this macrovariant, there is a large *vacat* after Ps 33:12, which may indicate that 4QPsq deemed Psalm 33 to be two distinct compositions: Ps 33:1–12 and Ps 33:13–22.⁸⁰ In only one instance (Ps 35:15), 4QPsq *may* read against 4QPsa, but this is not clear and the difference may be simply orthographic.⁸¹ A significant difference from both MT

---

⁷⁷ Cf. Flint, "Five Surprises," 188.

⁷⁸ See Skehan, Ulrich, and Flint, *DJD* XVI, 10, 14, 18; cf. → 10.2.1.4.1.1. In the first case, the *vacat* separating the two parts (or psalms?) of Psalm 36 is entirely reconstructed. Even if it were present, perhaps the *vacat* functioned only to indicate some sort of internal interval or even a bit of leather that was avoided for some reason.

⁷⁹ Skehan, Ulrich, and Flint, *DJD* XVI: 15; see ibid., 15–16 for possible reasons for this conjunction.

⁸⁰ Skehan, Ulrich, and Flint, *DJD* XVI: 146.

⁸¹ Skehan, Ulrich, and Flint, *DJD* XVI: 13, 149; cf. Ulrich, *BQS*, 639.

(and perhaps also 4QPsᵃ though it is not extant at this point) is that 4QPsᵠ has a superscription before Psalm 33: לדויד שיר מזמור "to/for/by David, a song, a psalm" (cf. LXX: τῷ Δαυιδ "to/for/by David"; cf. MTᵐˢˢ). On the other hand, the editors think that 4QPsᵠ had a longer text than MT at Ps 33:7, a reading that might also have stood in the now-lost section of 4QPsᵃ.[82] 4QPsᵠ reads five times with but nine times against MT, twice with but twelve times against LXX, and eight times non-aligned.

10.2.3.4.2 Date and Relevance
4QPsᵃ may be the earliest of all Psalms manuscripts, dating to the middle of the second century B.C.E.[83] 4QPsᵠ comes from a century or so later, and dates to the late first century B.C.E. or the beginning of the first century C.E. Assuming the two manuscripts do indeed belong together as exemplars of a third non-proto-MT collection, the difference in their dating witnesses to an older collection than the second non-proto-MT collection, and a longer timespan than the first, but alongside this antiquity and longevity, this third collection also seems relatively stable.

The relevance of this third collection is not unlike what was specified for the first two *mutatis mutandis*: 1) it attests to a non-aligned text-type; 2) one that is attested in more than one manuscript and thus properly a "collection"; 3) it contains material not preserved in the other two non-proto-MT collections, especially a number of compositions from the first two books of the Psalter (Psalm 5 is the first attested, Psalm 69 is the last; both in 4QPsᵃ). In point of fact, there is no overlap between this third collection and the first non-proto-MT collection, which means that this third collection could conceivably represent the earlier half of the first collection, though this cannot be known for certain. Additional significance is found in the observation that: 4) some compositions that are presently unified in MT-Pss and LXX-Pss may have been divided up in this third collection (Psalms 36 and 56), and still others that are delineated as two psalms in MT- and LXX-Pss may have been considered one (Psalms 38 + 71). If so, such fluidity in the delineation of at least some psalmic compositions is no doubt part of the larger phenomenon of multiple numeration schemata for the Psalms (see → 10.1.2.1; → 10.2.2.1.3). Finally, the very slight differences that the later manuscript 4QPsᵠ manifests from the earlier 4QPsᵃ – once again, assuming they belong to the same collection – could be evidence of (very slight) literary development, particularly in the addition of the superscription in Ps 33:1 in 4QPsᵠ (probably absent in 4QPsᵃ).

10.2.3.5 Other Possible Non-Proto-MT Collections (?)
As noted above (→ 10.2.3; see further → 10.2.1), other Psalms manuscripts, too, might reflect additional non-proto-MT collections. Unfortunately, these others are not attested in more than one manuscript. However, insofar as the second non-proto-MT "collection" was only found in 4QPsᶠ (→ 10.2.3.3), perhaps these other manuscripts, too, represent "collections" and could be treated as such. 4QPsᶠ is rather unique, however, in manifesting significant additional "non-biblical" content that distinguished it from both proto-MT and the first non-proto-MT collection; this justified its separate treatment. Even so, it cannot be ruled out that other manuscripts, too, may reflect additional non-proto-MT collections. Note, for example, the following:

– 4QPsᵇ attests to the sequence Psalms 102 → 103 → 112 → 113, against both MT and LXX and (probably) 11QPsᵃ. It reads mostly against MT, LXX, and 11QPsᵃ, and has nineteen non-aligned readings (see → 10.2.1.4.2).
– 4QPsᵈ appears to attest to the sequence Psalms 106 → 147 → 104, against MT, LXX, 11QPsᵃ, and 4QPsᵉ. In Psalm 104, 4QPsᵈ lacks the superscription (also absent in MT) that is attested in LXX, 11QPsᵃ, and 4QPsᵉ (reconstructed); it is also missing Ps 104:34a, against MT, LXX, and 11QPsᵃ. It reads eight times with but nineteen

---
[82] Skehan, Ulrich, and Flint, *DJD* XVI: 147.
[83] See → 10.2.3.2.3 above; also → 10.2.1.4.1; Ulrich, "Oldest Psalms Manuscript"; Flint and Alvarez, "Oldest of All the Psalms Scrolls." The only older text may be 4QPsˣ.

times against MT, nine times with but seventeen times against LXX, twice with but ten times against 11QPs^a, once with and five times against 4QPs^l, and has fourteen non-aligned readings (see → 10.2.1.4.3). Hence it "preserves a mixed type of text that cannot be easily categorized."[84]

– Material reconstruction of 4QPs^k suggests that Psalm 135 preceded Psalm 99, with some composition coming between these two, so this manuscript preserves a sequence against both MT and LXX: Psalms 135 → ? → 99.[85] It may also have read a longer text at Ps 135:6 with 4QPs^n and 11QPs^a against MT and LXX, though this is not certain.[86] It contains two non-aligned readings (see → 10.2.1.4.4).

Each of these three manuscripts is best deemed non-aligned, but their precise nature as (representatives of) other non-proto-MT collections is unclear and may be seriously doubted due to the last grouping of Psalms manuscripts to be considered, namely, the excerpted texts.

10.2.3.6 Excerpted or Abbreviated Psalms Manuscripts

Scholars agree that at least four psalms manuscripts could not have contained entire Psalters and so represent excerpted or abbreviated manuscripts (→ 10.2.1.5).[87] Three of these four (4QPs^g, 4QPs^h, and 5QPs) contained only Psalm 119. The fourth, 4QPs^l, began with Psalm 104 and may have included others.[88]

The earliest of these manuscripts seems to be 4QPs^l (second half of first century B.C.E.), followed by 4QPs^h (ca. 30 B.C.E.–70 C.E.), 4QPs^g (ca. 50 C.E.),

---

[84] Flint, "4QPs^d," 96.

[85] This is also against 4QPs^n's sequence Ps 135:12 → 136:23, if that is, in fact, the correct reading; see above → 10.2.3.2.1.4 and → 10.2.1.2.5.

[86] Skehan, Ulrich, and Flint, *DJD XVI: 123–24.

[87] See → 10.2.1.5; further Tov, "Excerpted and Abbreviated"; Strawn, "Excerpted Manuscripts"; and Strawn, "Excerpted 'Non-Biblical' Scrolls," all with bibliography.

[88] Skehan, Ulrich, and Flint, *DJD XVI, 127; Swanson, "Qumran," 252–53; cf. → 10.2.1.5.3. See above (→ 10.2.3.2.1.4) for the possibility that 4QPs^n is an excerpted text, perhaps one from Non-Proto-MT Collection 1.

and 5QPs (first century C.E.). Insofar as they preserve only one biblical psalm, the macrovariant issues of *sequence* and *content* are not applicable. Indeed, given their excerpted/abbreviated status, it is unclear what kind of larger text-type or text collection (proto-MT or non-proto-MT?) they were taken from. Further complicating text-typological classification is the fact that in each case very little text is preserved. Even so, the following statistics are noteworthy:

– 4QPs^g reads ten times with MT, eight times with LXX, fourteen times against 11QPs^a, and four times non-aligned (→ 10.2.1.5.1);
– 4QPs^h reads twice with and three times against MT, twice with and three times against LXX, three times with and once against 11QPs^a, and once non-aligned (→ 10.2.1.5.2);
– 4QPs^l reads once with and five times against MT, once with and five times against LXX, once with and three times against 4QPs^d, once against 11QPs^a, and four times non-aligned (→ 10.2.1.5.3); and
– 5QPs reads four times with MT against LXX (→ 10.2.1.5.4).

While full certainty is not to be had, these statistics nevertheless suggest that 4QPs^g and 5QPs stand somewhat closer to the text-type of proto-MT, with 4QPs^h and 4QPs^l less so. One should not assume, however, that this means 4QPs^g and 5QPs were excerpted from a proto-MT collection or that 4QPs^h and 4QPs^l were excerpted from a non-proto-MT collection.[89] The reason one cannot make such assumptions is the paucity of the extant remains. If, for instance, Psalm 104 was followed by something else in 4QPs^l, say Psalm 147, we would have occasion to affiliate it with Non-Proto-MT Collection 1. Still further, if such were the case, 4QPs^l would not only support that collection and text-type, its excerption from such a collection would

---

[89] If one were forced to pick from the three non-proto-MT collections delineated above, the first would be the obvious choice as the only one to contain Psalms 104 and 119 (at least now, in extant text).

10.2.3 OTHER TEXTS

also say something about the authoritative status of that collection (cf. → 10.2.3.2.1.4 on 4QPs^n). This hypothetical scenario, were it true, would be quite significant, but in point of fact the text-typology of excerpted and abbreviated manuscripts is typically hard to define, with some tending toward a slightly expansionistic and harmonizing style (cf., e.g., 4QDeut^{j,k,l,n} with SP) with others representing a "free approach" and manifesting "an independent textual nature."[90] This may obviate the quest for textual affiliation, especially if some of the excerpted manuscripts were quoted from memory,[91] which could be taken as further evidence that these texts were for personal use.[92]

Many questions remain unanswered about the excerpted texts but the existence of such manuscripts along with some of their characteristics suggests that several additional psalms manuscripts may also be excerpts.[93] So, beyond 4QPs^g, 4QPs^h, 4QPs^l, and 5QPs, it is possible that 4QPs^b, 4QPs^n, and 4QPs^x might be excerpts.[94] 4QPs^n was mentioned earlier as possibly belonging to Non-Proto-MT Collection 1, with 4QPs^b as possibly representative of yet another non-proto-MT collection. If these texts are excerpts from non-proto-MT collections, they would testify that such collections were sufficiently well known and/or authoritative to excerpt therefrom.[95] However, the excerpted status of these manuscripts (assuming this for the moment, for sake of argument) actually *complicates* their text-typological classification; more specifically, it may undercut the significance of their text form. Excerpted texts can, if they so desire, not only *selectively abbreviate* their base texts (cf. the *mezuzot*), they can also *rearrange* their base texts *in alternative order* (see 2QExod^b; 4QExod^d; 4QDeut^j; 4QDeut^n), and can even include material from *different base texts* (4QDeut^j; cf. 4QTest, 4QTanḥ, as well as the *tefillin*).

What this means, of course, is that the two most important criteria for text-typological classification in the Psalms manuscripts – namely, *sequence* and *content* – may not, need not, and often do not obtain in the case of excerpted texts. This raises the possibility, moreover, that a number of the non-proto-MT texts could be excerpts; if so (and as such) they would not reflect non-proto-MT-type collections (or text traditions) but simply non-aligned excerpts. This is, in fact, Tov's opinion: beyond 4QPs^g, 4QPs^h, and 5QPs, he posits that 11QPs^a, 11QPs^b, 4QPs^a, 4QPs^b, 4QPs^d, 4QPs^e, 4QPs^f, 4QPs^k, 4QPs^n, and 4QPs^q are all possibly excerpted or abbreviated.[96] If some or all of these manuscripts may be so identified, they would represent "only small liturgical collections."[97] In such instances, the matters of an excerpted manuscript's text form (sequence and content) may be less significant for is text-typology – though the microvari-

---

[90] Tov, "Excerpted and Abbreviated," 600; see further Strawn, "Excerpted Manuscripts," 118–20.

[91] Cf. Strawn, "Excerpted Manuscripts," 119–20; J.A. Duncan, "Excerpted Texts of Deuteronomy at Qumran," *RevQ* 19 (1997): 60–61. Cf. the possible blending of Psalms 135 and 136 in 4QPs^n, which may have been produced by misremembering highly similar texts.

[92] See Tov, "Excerpted and Abbreviated," 600 and also *passim* on the size of these kinds of scrolls. A related issue is whether they were made with great care (e.g., 4QPs^b, 4QPs^g) or, conversely, sloppily executed (e.g., 4QPs^e). See further Strawn, "Excerpted Manuscripts," 119–20, 148–57, 160–67; Brooke, "Psalms," 7–8.

[93] See Tov, "Excerpted and Abbreviated"; Strawn, "Excerpted Manuscripts"; Brooke, "Psalms," 5–10.

[94] See Tov, "Excerpted and Abbreviated"; Strawn, "Excerpted Manuscripts," esp. 163. For 4QPs^x, note the sloppy writing and the otherwise unattested order of Ps 89:20–22, 26, 23, 27–28, and 31. Skehan, "Gleanings," 439, deemed this manuscript a "practice page written from memory" and thus "secondary to the canonical Psalm." See now M. Pajunen, "4QPs^x: A Collective Interpretation of Psalm 89:20–38," *JBL* 133.3 (2014): 494 for the possibility that 4QPs^x is "an abbreviated collective interpretation" of Ps 89:20–38, "a later interpretation" of the psalm, and thus "mostly secondary to the MT version."

[95] This would not necessarily mean that the parent text was "biblical," as it appears that scribes at Qumran could excerpt or abbreviate "non-biblical" compositions just as they did "biblical" ones. See Strawn, "Excerpted 'Non-Biblical' Scrolls"; cf. Lange, "Collecting," 306.

[96] Tov, "Excerpted and Abbreviated," 594–95; cf. Strawn, "Excerpted Manuscripts," 153–57, 164 n. 215.

[97] Flint, "Five Surprises," 189, speaking of 4QPs^g, 4QPs^h, 5QPs, and 4QPs^b, which "may have ended with Psalm 118." See further Flint, *Dead Sea Psalms Scrolls*, 32, 34–35; Flint, "Psalms and Psalters," 244–45; Flint, "Book of Psalms," 463.

ants might still be significant[98] – even while that text form would bear directly on the manuscript's utility and function.[99] So, to provide a specific example, 4QPs[g], 4QPs[h], 4QPs[l], and 5QPs may contain important variants that should be assessed in the study of Psalm 119, but they are, at best, copies of that psalm only; they are not full Psalters proper. And, since they are not full Psalters proper, the significance of their text form (if not also some of their microvariants?) is of little to no consequence for the book of Psalms as such.[100]

10.2.3.7 Conclusion

Several points should be made in conclusion:

1) There is significant evidence among the ancient Hebrew manuscripts of the Psalms for "other" texts that cannot be aligned simplistically with proto-MT (or LXX; → 10.2.2; → 10.3.1).

2) This evidence can be interpreted in more than one way; at least two main options could be considered.[101] The *first* is that "these manuscripts attest to diversity concerning the shape of the Psalter, not to uniformity in accordance with the MT-150 Psalter."[102] The diversity and non-uniformity is obvious (point 1 above) but how it pertains to "the shape of the Psalter," especially "the MT-150 Psalter" is still open to debate. According to Flint and others, the Psalms evidence, especially Non-Proto-MT Collection 1, is sufficient to establish a variant literary edition (or editions) of the Psalms,[103] and for the growth and (gradual) stabilization of the Psalter in at least two stages.[104] While this is possible, the existence of a genre of excerpted manuscripts leaves open the possibility that some or all of these alternative psalms collections may be somehow "secondary" and not intended as copies of the (entire) book of Psalms but as functional copies intended and used for some specific purpose or set of purposes: personal, devotional, liturgical, or all of the above. The nature of the Psalms, their style, religious content, short length, and so forth, means they are especially likely to have been used in such ways.[105] Assessing these "other" texts as secondary in some way, developed for liturgical purposes or the like, is the *second* possible way the evidence can be read. Once again, certain characteristics of the first non-proto-MT collection might support its interpretation as a secondary if not sectarian product.[106]

---

[98] Cf. Tov, *TCHB, 320: these texts are "not Scripture scrolls in the regular sense of the word" so "their major deviations from M+, G* should not be taken into consideration in the textual-literary analysis, while small differences remain relevant for the text-critical analysis." See further, Tov, "Excerpted and Abbreviated"; Strawn, "Excerpted Manuscripts."

[99] See Strawn, "Excerpted Manuscripts"; also Brooke, "Psalms," 7–8. According to Tov, excerpted texts were "probably meant for personal use" (*TCHB, 321; cf. Tov, "Excerpted and Abbreviated").

[100] Lange, "Collecting," has noted that resequencing may be a particular characteristic of textual transmission of poetic texts in antiquity, especially as the situation encountered in the Psalms scrolls is replicated in no small way in the *Hodayot* manuscripts (stability of individual compositions coupled with fluidity of order).

[101] Cf. Ulrich, "Two Perspectives"; and → 10.2.2.

[102] Flint, "Unrolling," 239–40.

[103] Flint, "Unrolling," 240; Flint, "Psalms and Psalters," 244–45. Note also E. Ulrich, "The Old Testament Text and Its Transmission," in *The New Cambridge History of the Bible*, Vol. 1: *From the Beginnings to 600* (eds. J.C. Paget and J. Schaper; Cambridge: Cambridge University Press, 2013), 83–104 (92), who argues that "variant editions for half or more of the twenty-four books of the Hebrew Bible existed in Jewish circles at the birth of Christianity and rabbinic Judaism."

[104] So Flint, *Dead Sea Psalms Scrolls*; cf. Wilson, *Editing*; Wilson, "Consecutive Arrangement," 386–87. Brooke, "Psalms," 9–12 stresses the possible existence of more than Flint's three editions and goes on to discuss the evidence from 4Q380, 4Q381, and 4Q448. Note also his comment: "Tobit's allusions to the psalms are almost entirely from the first three books of the psalter which were stabilized relatively early" (23).

[105] Cf. E.M. Schuller, "Prayer, Hymnic, and Liturgical Texts from Qumran," in *The Community of the Renewed Covenant: The Notre Dame Symposium on the Dead Sea Scrolls* (eds. E. Ulrich and J. VanderKam; Notre Dame: University of Notre Dame Press, 1994), 153–71 (165): "all psalters are, to some extent, liturgical collections." Cf. Swanson, "Qumran," 254: "Interpretation of a psalm cannot be divorced from the purpose of its setting." Note also Sanders, "Surprises," 294; Wilson, *Editing*, 90; Lange, "Collecting," 307.

[106] See → 10.2.3.2.4 and n. 69 above, to which one might add still other considerations such as matters of stichometry (see Flint, "Unrolling," 244), the tendencies of certain variants (e.g., the "more personal" nature of 4QPs[n]'s rendering of Psalms 135 + 136 [Skehan, Ulrich, and Flint, *DJD XVI, 137]; or

In many ways, it seems impossible to resolve this impasse.[107] To be sure (and above all else), one must avoid anachronistic assumptions, including and especially the assumption that proto-MT was established and stable long before Qumran and therefore everything found (later) at the Dead Sea that deviates from that is automatically derivative.[108] Calling a psalms collection "secondary" implies a "primary" collection and in point of fact the Dead Sea Psalms scrolls remain "our earliest extant witnesses to the scriptural text of the psalms,"[109] and the very earliest of these manuscripts do not align easily with proto-MT. These early, divergent data are significant evidence in favor of diversity, not uniformity, in the textual history of the Psalms. And yet, the genre of excerpted manuscripts, several of which are definitely found among the Psalms scrolls, coupled with the likely utility of these texts, is also significant evidence – even if there is no *pre*-Qumran evidence for the proto-MT Psalms – making it likely that at least some of the Psalms manuscripts look the way they do because of text-*function* not text-*affiliation*.[110]

Here again, things seem to be at an impasse, with the issue undecidable.[111] But perhaps one need not resolve the issue in either direction for at least two reasons: first, because text function is one measure of a composition's authority, so that, "secondary" or not, these manuscripts are of great importance (see further below); and, second, because in the textual history of the Psalms, "secondary" collections – excerpted Psalters or prayer books and the like – have often preserved excellent text-types.[112]

3) As impressive as the work of Sanders, Wilson, and Flint has been, their (non-identical) theories of the growth and (gradual) stabilization of the Psalter leave some questions unanswered. Note, for example, Wilson: "The impression gained from this analysis is of a certain looseness of psalms-arrangement which continued until ca. A.D. 50, and apparently died out soon after."[113] Or consider Sanders: "[t]he focus of the later tradents in the proto-Masoretic period shifted to textual accuracy."[114] But what might explain the demise of psalmic pluriformity and the shift to textual uniformity? Put in Flint's terms, whence comes Edition IIb? Was it simply created after Edition IIa or concurrently with it (or even Edition I)? Here, too, is an unanswerable question – one related to the history of (proto-)MT writ large – but it must be underscored that there is *no* non-Qumranic evidence for the non-proto-MT collections described above. Although all arguments *ex silentio* are problematic,

---

the non-aligned reading in 1QPs[b] at Ps 128:3, which Dahmen deems an interpretation "analogous to the tendencies of clarification and explanation in other textual variants of 11QPs[a]" ["New Identifications," 481]), or (again) the Davidic interest of the scroll, which Sanders takes as proof "that the scribe who compiled and copied the scroll believed in the Davidic authorship of what he was writing" (*Dead Sea Psalms Scroll*, 18; cf. Brooke, "Psalms," 10). Quant, "Rewriting Scripture," has suggested that changes in base text, new literary setting, and/or new narrative voice are marks that a text is a new composition, not a copy (even a variant literary edition) of a previous work.

107 Cf. Brooke, "Psalms," 6–8.

108 As, e.g., in Briggs and Briggs, 2:lxxxix. Note the cautions of Sanders, "Modern History," 404; Flint, "Psalms and Psalters," 243, 248–49; M.S. Pajunen, "Perspectives on the Existence of a Particular Authoritative Book of Psalms in the Late Second Temple Period," *JSOT* 39 (2014): 139–63; Brütsch, *Israels Psalmen*; Lange, **Handbuch*, 425–30.

109 Flint, "Unrolling," 229; similarly, Flint "11QPs[a]-Psalter," 176; Wilson, "Consecutive Arrangement," 377, and esp. 385.

110 Strawn, "Excerpted Manuscripts," 158: "functionality can dictate form." For this reason, I find Wilson's remarks unreasonably skeptical: "while evidence of conflict with the canonical arrangement is always clear and certain, supportive evidence from fragmentary MSS must be viewed with some qualification" (Wilson, "Consecutive Arrangement," 388). Contrast Flint's recent statement ("Unrolling," 240) that some manu-

scripts are not "editions of the Book of Psalms but rather arrangements of material from Edition IIa or Edition IIb and other poems," including as "most prominent" of these 4QPs[b], 4QPs[d], 4QPs[k], 4QPs[n], and 11QapocrPs. Elsewhere, Flint adds 4QPs[f] to this list ("Dead Sea Psalms Scrolls," 18)!

111 Note Flint, "Psalms and Psalters," 248: "the Judean data in general allow for both possibilities: that 11QPs[a] ... belongs to an edition of the book of Psalms, or that it is a collection drawn from a Psalter that had previously been finalized."

112 See → 10.1 and note, e.g., M. Noth's study of the five Syriac Psalms that were preserved in a Syrian bishop's Book of Discipline ("Die fünf syrisch überlieferten apokryphen Psalmen," *ZAW* 48 [1930]: 1–23; cf. Sanders, "Modern History," 400).

113 Wilson, "Consecutive Arrangement," 387, similarly 388.

114 Sanders, "Modern History," 407–08.

perhaps this is proof that these collections were only known there, at Qumran. Further, while Flint frequently asserts that there is no "unambiguous" evidence supporting the MT-150 Psalter at Qumran,[115] perhaps (read backwards) that evidence is less ambiguous than it would seem, and thus proof that the non-proto-MT collections are "secondary" or "liturgical."[116] The MT-150 collection must, in any event, come into existence at some point (even if only later) and emerge from somewhere. Perhaps its form and subsequent dominance is not the result of a slow and gradual development – or at least not only that – but (also) rather a survival (if not selection) and correlate pairing away of other possible text forms for various reasons and/or (as) the result of various processes and developments.[117]

4) In my judgment, the binary opposition of 11QPs[a] (and, as a result, Non-Proto-MT Collection 1) as a "true scriptural Psalter" or a "secondary liturgical collection" is, in some ways at least, a false dichotomy. If by "true" and "scriptural," one means "authoritative," there can be no doubt that Non-Proto-MT Collection 1 (and perhaps also Non-Proto-MT Collection 3) satisfies the criteria.[118] We seem to have multiple exemplars of this collection – at least three but as many as five from two or three caves – not all of which stem from the same time period. If 4QPs[n] is not simply a copy but an excerpt from this collection, it provides still further occasion to deem the collection authoritative *in terms of function*: it was used by and useful to the community.[119] This kind of functionality is one measure of "authority," even if it is, for whatever reason, not deemed coterminous with the definition of "canonical" as "a copy of a 'biblical' book."[120] This is to say that authoritative function does not necessarily relate to canonical status. So also the reverse: even if the non-proto-MT collections are not "canonical," they may still have been popular and authoritative.[121] To return, by way of example, to the Psalms manuscripts that excerpt Psalm 119, while they may not attest to the "authority" of the book of Psalms as a whole, or provide evidence of its "canonical" shape, at the very least they demonstrate that "Psalm 119 by itself was of considerable interest to some people."[122] To use a modern example, the Anglican Book of Common Prayer or a Christian hymnal of some sort may contain an entire Psalter or significant selections therefrom; these may even be a religious adherent's *primary* point of access to the psalms but they are not, per se, copies of the book of Psalms, neither are they Bibles properly so-called.[123]

---

[115] E.g., Flint, "Psalms and Psalters," 243; Flint, "Dead Sea Psalms Scrolls," 16–17.

[116] E.g., the sequence from Psalms 125–130 in 4QPs[e] is also found in 11QPs[a], but that does not mean that this sequence is non-proto-MT (cf. Flint, "Dead Sea Psalms Scrolls," 16–17); it could, rather, indicate that 4QPs[e] and 11QPs[a] witness to the proto-MT ordering, but with pluses and rearrangements.

[117] Cf. Talmon, "Old Testament Text"; Tov, *TCHB*, 174–90. This would offer a different model than the three found in Wilson, "Reconsidered," 641; and Wilson, *Editing*, 91–92.

[118] See, e.g., Flint, "Scriptures"; and VanderKam, *Dead Sea Scrolls*, 175, 186–95. Cf. also Wilson, *Editing*, 88–90; Wilson, "Reconsidered," 638–40.

[119] See Lange, *Handbuch*, 436–39 for possible citations or allusions to 11QPs[a] in other documents at Qumran.

[120] For more on function and functional authority, see Strawn, "Excerpted Manuscripts"; Strawn, "Excerpted 'Non-Biblical' Scrolls"; and Strawn, "Authority: Textual, Traditional, or Functional? A Response to C.D. Elledge," in *Jewish and Christian Scriptures: The Function of "Canonical" and "Non-Canonical" Religious Texts* (eds. J.H. Charlesworth and L.M. McDonald; Jewish and Christian Texts in Context and Related Studies 7; New York: T & T Clark, 2010), 104–12. See also Brooke, "Psalms," 8–9.

[121] Cf. Lange, *Handbuch*, 415–16.

[122] Brooke, "Psalms," 8.

[123] Against Wilson's categorization of Skehan's take on 11QPs[a] as "nothing more than ... [a] 'library edition'" (*Editing*, 92; cf. Skehan, "Qumran," 168–69), the point is that even a library edition can be very important. While it seems true that scholars on the "secondary collection" side of the debate have assumed too readily the pre-existence, stability, and dominance of the MT-150 Psalter, it also seems that Flint assumes such presumptions to be necessary to the "secondary collection" argument, which, of course, they are not (see Strawn, "Excerpted Manuscripts," 156 n. 196). Note also the important points on authority in Wilson, *Editing*, 89–90; Wilson, "Reconsidered," 639–40.

5) While much will remain uncertain, there is still work to be done, particularly on how these other non-proto MT texts (and text collections) relate to the present MT-Psalter. Both Flint and Wilson have done extensive work on this, to be sure, but mostly in terms of the growth and (gradual) stabilization of the Psalter, and with particular focus on Books IV and V. In the end, it is unclear that the similarities identified by Wilson in the structuring of 11QPs^a and MT prove much – especially with regard to the provenance or pertinence of 11QPs^a to the textual history of the Psalms[124] – but, regardless, the entire range of the non-proto-MT evidence has yet to be fully considered. The dominant theories of the Psalter's shape and shaping often take Wilson as their starting point,[125] but, unlike Wilson, many proceed completely innocent of the alternative evidence outside of Books IV and V and beyond 11QPs^a.[126] But theories of smaller units, the relationship of particular psalms one to another, and so forth, should reckon seriously with the evidence from the Dead Sea, especially with regard to the combination of psalm compositions, the division of psalms into distinct units, excerption and collection of individual psalms or groups thereof, and unusual junctures that exist between various psalms and why those might be present.[127] If nothing else, the various Psalms collections from the Dead Sea offer primary evidence of how the psalms were received and read in antiquity.[128]

Briggs, C.A. and E.G. Briggs, *A Critical and Exegetical Commentary on the Book of Psalms* (2 vols.; ICC; Edinburgh: T & T Clark, 1906–1907).

Brooke, G.J., "The Psalms in Early Jewish Literature in the Light of the Dead Sea Scrolls," in *The Psalms in the New Testament* (eds. S. Moyise and M.J.J. Menken; The New Testament and the Scriptures of Israel; London: T & T Clark, 2004), 5–24.

Brütsch, M., *Israels Psalmen in Qumran: Ein textarchäologischer Beitrag zur Entstehung des Psalters* (BWANT 193; Stuttgart: Kohlhammer, 2010).

Chyutin, M., "The Redaction of the Qumranic and the Traditional Book of Psalms as a Calendar," *RevQ* 16 (1994): 367–95.

Dahmen, U., "New Identifications and Re-Groupings of Psalms Fragments from Qumran Cave I and IV," *RevQ* 20 (2001–2002): 479–85.

Dahmen, U., *Psalmen- und Psalter-Rezeption im Frühjudentum: Rekonstruktion, Textbestand, Struktur und Pragmatik der Psalmenrolle 11QPs^a aus Qumran* (STDJ 47; Leiden: Brill, 2003).

Dahmen, U., "Die Psalter-Versionen aus den Qumranfunden: Ein Gespräch mit P.W. Flint," in *Qumran kontrovers: Beiträge zu den Textfunden vom Toten Meer* (eds. M. Becker and A. Maurer; Paderborn: Bonifatius, 2003), 127–46.

*DJD IV.

*DJD XVI, 7–167.

*DJD XXIII, 29–78, 181–205.

Fabry, H.-J., "Der Psalter in Qumran," in *Der Psalter in Judentum und Christentum* (ed. E. Zenger; Herder's Biblical Studies 18; Freiburg: Herder, 1998), 137–63.

Flint, P.W., *The Dead Sea Psalms Scrolls and the Book of Psalms* (STDJ 17; Leiden: Brill, 1997).

Flint, P.W., "A Form of Psalm 89 (4Q236 = 4QPs89)," in *PTSDSSP 4a (1997): 40–45.

Flint, P.W., "The '11QPs^a-Psalter' in the Dead Sea Scrolls: Including the Preliminary Edition of 4QPs^e," in *The Quest for Context and Meaning: Studies in Biblical Intertextuality in Honor of James A. Sanders* (eds.

---

[124] *Contra* Flint, "Unrolling," 236. Similar structuring devices or organizational principles show only that – similarity – and need not bear directly on text-affiliation or disaffiliation, and certainly not on scriptural status (*contra* Flint, "Psalms and Psalters," 246–47), even if similarities remain helpful comparatively. Indeed, a major point of Wilson's work was that the two versions of Books IV and V attested in 11QPs^a and MT had quite different connotations (e.g., Wilson, "Qumran Psalms Scroll," 463–64; Wilson, "Structure," 243–44).

[125] See, e.g., N.L. deClaissé-Walford (ed.), *The Shape and Shaping of the Book of Psalms: The Current State of Scholarship* (Ancient Israel and Its Literature 20; Atlanta: SBL, 2014).

[126] See the work of Hossfeld and Zenger discussed in → 10.1.2 and → 10.2.2.

[127] E.g., what if 1QPs^b preserved only the Songs of Ascent? Or why would Psalm 32 be omitted from the sequence Psalms 31 → 33 (4QPs^a, 4QPs^q)? Or what explains the sequence Psalms 38 → 71 (4QPs^a)? For the latter, cf. Skehan, Ulrich, and Flint, *DJD XVI: 15–16; Ulrich, "Oldest," 75.

[128] See Dahmen, *Psalmen- und Psalter-Rezeption*; cf. N. Whybray, *Reading the Psalms as a Book* (JSOTSup 222; Sheffield: Sheffield Academic Press, 1996); Brütsch, *Israels Psalmen*, 222.

C.A. Evans and S. Talmon; *BibInt* 28; Leiden: Brill, 1997), 173–96.

Flint, P.W., "The Book of Psalms in the Light of the Dead Sea Scrolls," *VT* 48 (1998): 453–72.

Flint, P.W., "A Preliminary Edition of 4QPs^d (4Q86)," in *The Provo International Conference on the Dead Sea Scrolls: Technological Innovations, New Texts, and Reformulated Issues* (eds. D.W. Parry and E. Ulrich; STDJ 30; Leiden: Brill, 1999), 93–105.

Flint, P.W., "1b. 5/6ḤevPsalms," *DJD* XXXVIII (2000): 141–66.

Flint, P.W., "The Preliminary Edition of 5/6ḤevPsalms," *JJS* 51 (2000): 19–41.

Flint, P.W., "Scriptures in the Dead Sea Scrolls: The Evidence from Qumran," in *Emanuel: Studies in Hebrew Bible, Septuagint, and Dead Sea Scrolls in Honor of Emanuel Tov* (eds. S.M. Paul et al.; VTSup 94; Brill: Leiden, 2003), 269–304.

Flint, P.W., "Psalms and Psalters in the Dead Sea Scrolls," in *The Bible and the Dead Sea Scrolls: The Princeton Symposium on the Dead Sea Scrolls* (3 vols.; ed. J.H. Charlesworth; Waco: Baylor University Press, 2006), 1.233–72.

Flint, P.W., "Five Surprises in the Qumran Psalms Scrolls," in *Flores Florentino: Dead Sea Scrolls and Other Early Jewish Studies in Honour of Florentino García Martínez* (eds. A. Hilhorst, É. Puech, and E. Tigchelaar; JSJSup 122; Leiden: Brill, 2007), 183–95.

Flint, P.W., "11QPs^b and the 11QPs^a-Psalter," in *Diachronic and Synchronic: Reading the Psalms in the Real Time: Proceedings of the Baylor Symposium on the Book of Psalms* (eds. J.S. Burnett, W.H. Bellinger, and W.D. Tucker; Library of Hebrew Bible/Old Testament Studies 488; New York: T & T Clark International, 2007), 157–66.

Flint, P.W., "The Dead Sea Psalms Scrolls: Psalms Manuscripts, Editions, and the *Oxford Hebrew Bible*," in *Jewish and Christian Approaches to the Psalms: Conflict and Convergence* (ed. S. Gillingham; Oxford: Oxford University Press, 2013), 11–34.

Flint, P.W., "Unrolling the Dead Sea Psalms Scrolls," in *The Oxford Handbook of the Psalms* (ed. W.P. Brown; Oxford: Oxford University Press, 2014), 229–50.

Flint, P.W. and A.E. Alvarez, "The Oldest of All the Psalms Scrolls: The Text and Translation of 4QPs^a," in *The Scrolls and the Scriptures: Qumran after Fifty Years* (eds. S.E. Porter and C.A. Evans; JSPSup 26; Sheffield: Sheffield Academic Press, 1997), 142–69.

Flint, P.W., P.W. Skehan, and E. Ulrich, "Three Psalms of Praise from Qumran: The Preliminary Editions of 4QPs^l and 4QPs^n," *JNSL* 24 (1998): 35–44.

Goshen-Gottstein, M.H., "The Psalms Scroll (11QPs^a): A Problem of Canon and Text," *Textus* 5 (1966): 22–33.

Haran, M., "11QPs^a and the Canonical Book of Psalms," in *Minḥah le-Naḥum: Biblical and Other Studies Presented to Nahum M. Sarna in Honour of His 70th Birthday* (eds. M.Z. Brettler and M.A. Fishbane; JSOTSup 154; Sheffield: JSOT Press, 1993), 193–201.

Jain, E., *Psalmen oder Psalter? Materielle Rekonstruktion und inhaltliche Undersuchung der Psalmenhandschriften aus der Wüste Juda* (STDJ 109; Leiden: Brill, 2014).

Jain, E. and A. Steudel, "Le manuscrits psalmique de la Mer Morte et la réception du Psautier à Qumrân," *RevScRel* 77 (2003): 529–43.

Lange, *Handbuch*, 373–450.

Lange, A., "Collecting Psalms in Light of the Dead Sea Scrolls," in *A Teacher for All Generations: Essays in Honor of James C. VanderKam* (2 vols.; eds. E.F. Mason et al.; JSJSup 153; Leiden: Brill, 2012), 1.297–308.

Leuenberg, M., "Aufbau und Pragmatik des 11QPs^a-Psalters: Der historisierte Dichter und Beter David als Vorbild und Identifikationsfigur: 11QPs^a als eschatologisches Lese- und Meditationsbuch des qumranischen יחד," *RevQ* 22 (2005): 165–211.

Quant, J.F., "Rewriting Scripture Inside and Out: A Typology of Rewriting in Variant Editions and Rewritten Scripture" (PhD diss., Emory University, 2014).

Sanders, J.A., "*Variorum* in the Psalms Scroll (11QPs^a)," *HTR* 59 (1966): 83–94.

Sanders, J.A., *The Dead Sea Psalms Scroll* (Ithaca: Cornell University Press, 1967).

Sanders, J.A., "Cave 11 Surprises and the Question of Canon," *McCQ* 21 (1968): 1–15, repr. in *New Directions in Biblical Archaeology* (eds. D.N. Freedman and J.C. Greenfield; Garden City: Doubleday, 1969), 101–16.

Sanders, J.A., "The Qumran Psalms Scroll (11QPs^a) Reviewed," in *On Language, Culture, and Religion: In Honor of Eugene A. Nida* (eds. M. Black and W.A. Smalley; The Hague: Mouton, 1974), 79–99.

Sanders, J.A., "The Modern History of the Qumran Psalms Scroll and Canonical Criticism," in *Emanuel: Studies in Hebrew Bible, Septuagint, and Dead Sea Scrolls in Honor of Emanuel Tov* (eds. S.M. Paul et al.; VTSup 94; Brill: Leiden, 2003), 393–411.

Skehan, P.W., "A Liturgical Complex in 11QPs^a," *CBQ* 35 (1973): 195–205.

Skehan, P.W., "Qumran and Old Testament Criticism,"

in *Qumrân: Sa pieté, sa théologie et son milieu* (ed. M. Delcor; BETL 46; Paris: Duculot, 1978), 163–82.

Skehan, P.W., "Gleanings from Psalm Texts from Qumrân," in *Mélanges bibliques et orientaux en l' honneur de M. Henri Cazelles* (eds. A. Caquot and M. Delcor; AOAT 212; Neukirchen: Neukirchen-Vluyn, 1981), 439–52.

Strawn, B.A., "Review of Peter W. Flint, *The Dead Sea Psalms Scrolls and the Book of Psalms*," *Koinonia* 11 (1999): 145–49.

Strawn, B.A., "Excerpted Manuscripts at Qumran: Their Significance for the Textual History of the Hebrew Bible and the Socio-Religious History of the Qumran Community and its Literature," in *The Bible and the Dead Sea Scrolls: The Princeton Symposium on the Dead Sea Scrolls* (3 vols.; ed. J.H. Charlesworth; Waco: Baylor University Press, 2006), 2.107–67.

Strawn, B.A., "Excerpted 'Non-Biblical' Scrolls at Qumran? Background, Analogies, Function," in *Qumran Studies: New Approaches, New Questions* (eds. M.T. Davis and B.A. Strawn; Grand Rapids: Eerdmans, 2007), 65–123.

Strawn, B.A., "David as One of the 'Perfect of (the) Way': On the Provenience of *David's Compositions* (and *11QPs*ᵃ as a Whole?)," *RevQ* 24 (2010): 607–27.

Swanson, D.D., "Qumran and the Psalms," in *Interpreting the Psalms: Issues and Approaches* (eds. P.S. Johnston and D.G. Firth; Downers Grove: InterVarsity Press, 2005), 247–61.

Talmon, S., "Pisqah Beʾemṣaʿ Pasuq and 11QPsᵃ," *Textus* 5 (1966): 11–21.

Talmon, S., "The Old Testament Text," in Cross–Talmon, *QHBT, 1–41.

Talmon, S., "Review of Flint, *The Dead Sea Psalms Scrolls and the Book of Psalms*," *JBL* 119 (1999): 545–47.

Tov, *TCHB.

Tov, E., "Excerpted and Abbreviated Biblical Texts from Qumran," *RevQ* 16 (1995): 581–600; reprinted in Tov, *HB, GB, and Qumran, 27–41.

Ulrich, *BQS, 627–726.

Ulrich, E., "The Oldest Psalms Manuscript: 4QPsᵃ (4Q83)," in *The Provo International Conference on the Dead Sea Scrolls: Technological Innovations, New Texts, and Reformulated Issues* (eds. D.W. Parry and E. Ulrich; STDJ 30; Leiden: Brill, 1999), 72–92.

Ulrich, E., "The Absence of 'Sectarian Variants' in the Jewish Scriptural Scrolls Found at Qumran," in *The Bible as Book: The Hebrew Bible and the Judaean Desert Discoveries* (London: The British Museum, 2002), 179–95.

Ulrich, E., "Two Perspectives on Two Pentateuchal Manuscripts from Masada," in *Emanuel: Studies in Hebrew Bible, Septuagint, and Dead Sea Scrolls in Honor of Emanuel Tov* (eds. S.M. Paul et al.; VTSup 94; Brill: Leiden, 2003), 453–64.

Wacholder, B.Z., "David's Eschatological Psalter: 11QPsalmsᵃ," *HUCA* 59 (1988): 23–72.

Wilson, G.H., "The Qumran Psalms Manuscripts and the Consecutive Arrangement of Psalms in the Hebrew Psalter," *CBQ* 45 (1983): 377–88.

Wilson, G.H., *The Editing of the Hebrew Psalter* (SBLDS 76; Chico: Scholars Press, 1985).

Wilson, G.H., "The Qumran Psalms Scroll Reconsidered: Analysis of the Debate," *CBQ* 47 (1985): 624–42.

Wilson, G.H., "The Qumran *Psalms Scroll* (11QPsᵃ) and the Canonical Psalter: Comparison of Editorial Shaping," *CBQ* 59 (1997): 448–64.

Wilson, G.H., "The Structure of the Psalter," in *Interpreting the Psalms: Issues and Approaches* (eds. P.S. Johnston and D.G. Firth; Downers Grove: InterVarsity Press, 2005), 229–46.

Witt, A.C., "David, the 'Ruler of the Sons of His Covenant' (מושל בבני בריתו): The Expansion of Psalm 151 in 11QPsᵃ," *Journal for the Evangelical Study of the Old Testament* 3 (2014): 77–97.

Wolfe, L.M. et al., "Psalm 11:1–4 (Inv. MOTB.SCR.000121)," in *Dead Sea Scrolls Fragments in the Museum Collection* (eds. E. Tov, K. Davis, and R. Duke; Publications of Museum of the Bible 1; Leiden: Brill, 2016), 190–99.

Brent A. Strawn

10.3 Primary Translations

10.3.1 Septuagint

10.3.1.1 Background

Precisely when Psalms was translated into Greek is unknown, though borrowed translation equivalents and literary allusions confirm the traditional view that it postdates the Pentateuch.[1] Swete dated the translation to "the second half of the second century" B.C.E. at the latest.[2] To posit a single date presupposes that the translation is the product of a single effort and that the Hebrew text of the book was fixed by that time.

A variety of data supports the unity of the Greek Psalter, such as the consistency of its Hebrew-Greek equivalents (particularly those unique to the Psalter), the distribution of particular etymological renderings or "isolates" (e.g. εἰς τὸ τέλος "regarding completion" for למנצח "for the director" and παραπικραίνω "embitter" for מרה "rebel"), and the ubiquity of translation-technical "quirks," such as a differentiation between ἀκούω "hear" and εἰσακούω "hearken" for שמע "hear" (depending on context), and between accusative and dative case for objects of ἐλπίζω ἐπί "hope in" (depending on word order).[3] Thackeray, Soffer, Munnich, and Williams made similar observations to affirm the unity of LXX-Ps.[4]

Many scholars have argued on the basis of the Qumran scrolls – particularly 11QPsª (→ 10.2.1.2.1; → 10.2.3.2) – that the Hebrew text of Psalms was not fixed before the first century C.E., but Williams has indicated that such arguments have not taken the evidence from the Greek Psalter into serious consideration, and that allusions to LXX-Ps in Old Greek Isaiah (→ 6.3), Proverbs (→ 12.3.1), and 1 Maccabees (→ 11.10), as well as in Philo (→ 21.4), push the date of that translation back into the second, and possibly the late third century B.C.E. Munnich, Olofsson, and Schaper likewise favor a second-century date.[5]

As for its provenance, LXX-Ps was traditionally thought to have been produced in Egypt. Venetz favored Palestine, however, on the basis of supposed links to the so-called *kaige* recension (which he associated with rabbinic exegesis), and particularly on the strength of Jerome's remark that βάρις with the meaning "fortress" rather than "boat" (as in LXX-Ps 44:9; 47:4, 14; cf. 121:7) was characteristic of the Greek spoken in Palestine.[6] Greenspoon noted, however, that the validity of the link between the *kaige* tradition and rabbinic exegesis has been contested, while Pietersma questioned Venetz's use of the Jerome citation and rehearsed the evidence supporting the traditional position.[7] Van der Kooij, Schaper, and Rüsen-Weinhold have defended a Palestinian provenance, but in Tov's view "there are no convincing arguments in favor of a Palestinian origin of this book." Currently the odds are in favor of Pietersma's position that the cumulative weight of the evidence points to Egypt.[8]

---

[1] Smith, *Translated Hallelujahs*, 284; J. Joosten, "The Impact of the Septuagint Pentateuch on the Greek Psalms," in *XIII Congress of the International Organization for Septuagint and Cognate Studies, Ljubljana 2007* (ed. M.K.H. Peters; SBLSCS 55; Atlanta: SBL, 2008), 197–205.

[2] Swete, *Introduction*, 25.

[3] Smith, *Translated Hallelujahs*, 31.

[4] H.St.J. Thackeray, "The Bisection of Books in Primitive Septuagint MSS.," *JTS* 8 (1907–1908): 88–98 (92); Thackeray, *Grammar*, 68, 69; A. Soffer, "The Treatment of Anthropomorphisms and Anthropopathisms in the Septuagint Psalms," *HUCA* 38 (1957): 85–107 (106–07); Munnich, "Indices d' une Septante originelle," *Bib* 63 (1982): 406–16 (407); T.F. Williams, "Towards a Date for the Old Greek Psalter," in Hiebert, Cox, and Gentry, *The Old Greek Psalter*, 248–76 (255, 260).

[5] O. Munnich, "La Septante des Psaumes et le groupe *kaige*," *VT* 33 (1983): 75–89; S. Olofsson, *The LXX Version: A Guide to the Translation Technique of the Septuagint* (ConBOT 30; Stockholm: Almqvist & Wiksell, 1990), 43; G. Dorival in Dorival-Harl-Munnich, *Septante*, 97; Schaper, *Eschatology*, 45.

[6] H.-J. Venetz, *Die Quinta des Psalteriums: Ein Beitrag zur Septuaginta- und Hexaplaforschung* (Hildesheim: Gerstenberg, 1974), 80–84.

[7] L.J. Greenspoon, "Recensions, Revision, Rabbinics: Dominique Barthélemy and Early Developments in the Greek Traditions," *Textus* 15 (1990): 153–67; Pietersma, "Place of Origin," 254–57.

[8] A. van der Kooij, "On the Place of Origin of the Old

10.3.1.2 Original Form, Editions, Tools

Far more manuscript evidence survives for LXX-Ps than for any other book of the Septuagint collection: according to Pietersma, there are "roughly ten times" as many manuscripts as for Genesis, the next most-attested book. Notwithstanding the sheer volume of textual evidence, there is good reason to believe that the Old Greek may be recovered from the wealth of data. Some scholars, however, hold a different view. According to Venetz, Ulrich, and Rüsen-Weinhold,[9] the totality of the Greek evidence at best attests to an early recension of the Old Greek translation.

To begin with Venetz, this scholar followed a suggestion of his teacher, Barthélemy, and argued that the Psalter's use of καί γάρ "for indeed" for גם "indeed" and κύριος τῶν δυνάμεων "Lord of hosts" for יהוה צבאות "Yhwh of hosts" linked it to the *kaige*-Th recension.[10] This view has not gained credence, however. Munnich has shown that the link between καί γάρ "for indeed" and *kaige*-Th, as well as their connection to rabbinic exegesis, is tenuous at best. In addition, Munnich has argued that LXX-Ps predates the *kaige*-Th tradition and that any similarity between them is largely due to the fact that Hebrew-Greek equations present in the former were radicalized in the latter.[11] While Olofsson entertained the possibility that the surviving manuscript evidence points to a revision belonging to the *kaige*-Th tradition and that the Old Greek has been lost completely, in the end he opted for the more likely alternative that "the traits identical with the characteristics of the καίγε group reflect the vocabulary of the original translator of Psalms."[12] Finally, Gentry concluded that without a full-blown analysis of the translation technique of the Psalter one can go no further than to say that the latter "may represent an early stage" of the *kaige*-Th tradition.[13]

Analyzing LXX-Ps from a different angle, Ulrich and Rüsen-Weinhold believe that the preserved manuscripts do not attest to the Old Greek of that book. Ulrich noted that MT is not the only possible candidate for the *Vorlage* of the Greek Psalter. Given that the Qumran material (particularly 11QPs^a) differs from MT-Ps in order and content, he suggested an alternative explanation for the considerable agreement between LXX-Ps and the consonantal text of MT, namely, "that the textual tradition attested in the extant Greek Mss is a recensional text, secondarily brought into conformity with the proto-MT, while the OG of the Psalter has simply been lost."[14] Rüsen-Weinhold, for his part, has argued that the main manuscript evidence of LXX-Ps is a revision towards (proto-)MT, while the older Greek version was a translation of a Hebrew text form older than (proto-)MT, typified by 4QPs^x (which lacks verses said to reflect later messianic aspirations for the house of David; → 10.2.1.6.2).[15] 4QPs^x has been dated to 175–125 B.C.E., which then provides Rüsen-Weinhold with a *terminus a quo* for proto-MT and hence for the subsequent revision of the Greek translation exemplified by the so-called "Hauptüberlieferung" (main tradition) of LXX-Ps.

However, Ulrich's and Rüsen-Weinhold's hypotheses, while intriguing, remain unverified. Rüsen-Weinhold assumes, but fails to prove, that the

---

Greek of Psalms," *VT* 33 (1983): 67–74; Schaper, *Eschatology*, 34–39; U. Rüsen-Weinhold, "Der Septuaginta-Psalter in seinen verschiedenen Textformen zur Zeit des Neuen Testaments," in Zenger, *Der Septuaginta-Psalter*, 1–87 (82); E. Tov, "Reflections on the Septuagint with Special Attention Paid to the Post-Pentateuchal Translations," in Karrer–Kraus, *Septuaginta 2010*, 3–22 (11); Pietersma, "Place of Origin," 252–74.

[9] See notes 10–15.
[10] Venetz, *Die Quinta des Psalteriums*, 80–84.
[11] O. Munnich, "Contribution à l'étude de la première révision de la Septante," *ANRW* 2.20.1: 192–220.
[12] S. Olofsson, "The Kaige Group and the Septuagint Book of Psalms," in *IX Congress of the International Organization for Septuagint and Cognate Studies: Cambridge, 1995* (ed. B.A. Taylor; SBLSCS 45; Atlanta: Scholars Press, 1997), 189–230 (204).
[13] P.J. Gentry, "The Greek Psalter and the καίγε Tradition: Methodological Questions," in Hiebert, Cox, and Gentry, *The Old Greek Psalter*, 74–97 (87).
[14] E. Ulrich, "The Dead Sea Scrolls and Their Implications for an Edition of the Septuagint Psalter," in *Der Septuaginta-Psalter und seine Tochterübersetzungen: Symposium in Göttingen 1997* (eds. A. Aejmelaeus and U. Quast; MSU 24; Göttingen: Vandenhoeck & Ruprecht, 2000), 323–36 (334).
[15] U. Rüsen-Weinhold, "Der Septuaginta-Psalter in seinen verschiedenen Textformen zur Zeit des Neuen Testaments," in Zenger, *Der Septuaginta-Psalter*, 61–87.

text of 4QPs^x predates proto-MT (→ 10.2.2). Further, apart from the question whether Qumran offers sufficient evidence to allow one to speak of a pluriform Hebrew text for the book of Psalms, MT remains one of the candidates for the *Vorlage*. That is to say, the existence of several Hebrew text forms does not of itself imply that the agreement between MT-Ps and LXX-Ps is secondary. Moreover, the view that the manuscript tradition attests to a revision of a translation that has been lost does not sufficiently account for features of the Greek Psalter that are characteristic of a translation rather than a revision, such as its use of: 1) diverse Greek renderings for the same Hebrew expression; 2) "favorite" words to translate a variety of Hebrew expressions; and 3) what Flashar called *Verlegenheitsübersetzungen* (renderings that suggest that the translator struggled to understand the meaning of the source text).[16]

Finally, both Rüsen-Weinhold and Ulrich appeal to the analogy of Daniel, for which most manuscripts attest a revised version rather than the Old Greek translation, and propose that the same could be true of Psalms.[17] The sheer number of manuscripts for the Psalter, however, makes it unlikely that Old Greek could have disappeared altogether. More importantly, for the analogy to have value, it must be supported by textual-linguistic evidence for revisionary activity. In the absence of such evidence, the common assumption that the close correspondence between LXX-Ps and MT-Ps reflects the relationship between target and source texts is a far simpler solution than one that involves two phantoms, the original Greek text (Old Greek) and its *Vorlage*, and that effectively relegates all of the Greek manuscript evidence to secondary status.[18]

If one proceeds from the premise that Old Greek is in large part recoverable from the manuscript evidence, then one needs a critical edition, no small endeavor. Rahlfs' groundwork for such an edition in his 1907 volume, *Der Text des Septuaginta-Psalters*, allowed him to produce an edition far superior to those of Swete and others.[19] To be sure, as Rahlfs himself admitted in the preface, his edition was not fully critical since it did not incorporate all of the textual evidence for Greek Psalms.[20] Pietersma summarizes Rahlfs' evidence as follows: "The total number of witnesses cited for the Psalms on Rahlfs' own authority is 59 Greek mss and 5 daughter versions (Bo Ga La Sa Sy). All but six of the mss (A B R S 1219 55) are in very fragmentary condition, some containing as little as a single verse each. Of Apostolic/Patristic evidence, he tells us, he has fully collated only Augustine (notably his *Enarrationes in Psalmos*), Hesychius of Jerusalem (his commentary on the Psalms), Jerome (with special focus on the letter to Sunnia and Fretela), and Theodoret, though he cites from time to time an additional 15, often from the best available editions but sometimes from manuscript ... this textual information is then bolstered by the undigested mass of manuscripts cited on the authority of Holmes-Parsons."[21]

Rather than starting from a fresh study of the texts, Rahlfs adopted and refined a model for textual affiliation previously developed by Baethgen to classify the witnesses.[22] The model was essentially "bi-polar": Rahlfs arranged the witnesses around two poles on the basis of 129 test passages in Psalms.[23] On the one side, Rahlfs placed Vaticanus (LXX^B), to which he related the oldest Greek manuscripts as well as the daughter versions, grouped under three types: Lower Egyptian, Upper Egyptian, and Western texts. On the other side, he placed the so-called "Vulgar text," based on the majority of manuscripts previ-

---

[16] Flashar, "Exegetische Studien," 94; Smith, *Translated Hallelujahs*, 4–5.

[17] Ulrich, "Dead Sea Scrolls," 333, 336; Rüsen-Weinhold, "Der Septuaginta-Psalter," 83.

[18] Smith, *Translated Hallelujahs*, 4.

[19] Hedley, "Göttingen Investigation," 66. A. Rahlfs, *Septuaginta-Studien 2: Der Text des Septuaginta-Psalters: Nebst einem Anhang: Griechische Psalterfragmente aus Oberägypten nach Abschriften von W.E. Crum* (Göttingen: Vandenhoeck & Ruprecht, 1907).

[20] Rahlfs, *Psalmi cum Odis*, 5.

[21] Pietersma, "Present State," 22.

[22] F. Baethgen, "Der textkritische Wert der alten Übersetzungen zu den Psalmen," *Jahrbücher für protestantische Theologie* 8 (1882): 405–59, 593–667 (407–8).

[23] Pietersma, "Present State," 14, 15.

ously collated by Holmes and Parsons,[24] to which he related the younger Greek witnesses, divided among the Hexaplaric (→ 10.3.5) and Lucianic recensions (→ 10.3.6). A sixth group Rahlfs characterized as "Mischtexte und nicht sicher einzureihende Texte."[25] He then outlined the four principles by which he determined the original reading: 1) where the three old text types agreed, he adopted their reading; 2) where they disagreed, he adopted the reading that matched MT (→ 10.2.2); 3) where the old text types disagreed with MT, and the younger ones agreed with MT, he adopted the old reading, assuming the younger to be a Hebraizing correction; 4) when in doubt, he adopted the reading of LXX^B and LXX^S.[26]

As Hedley noted, the model tended to prejudice the edition against the Lucianic witnesses, which, while younger, also have "an ancient element which is not preserved elsewhere."[27] Further, Pietersma has criticized the model for failing to account for the fact that original readings are meaningless for determining manuscript affiliation, and has urged that the evidence be classified anew, based on "an exhaustive analysis of translation technique."[28]

A number of ancient manuscripts of the Greek Psalter have come to light since Rahlfs published his edition, most notably Papyrus Bodmer XXIV (usually cited as LXX^{2110}), which "in a half dozen instances" "has uniquely (or virtually so) preserved the OG text," in Pietersma's view, not to mention that, in a number of instances, readings that Rahlfs adopted on very slim attestation have since been confirmed from newly discovered witnesses, while items that Rahlfs retained between square brackets out of respect for tradition are demonstrably secondary.[29] The recent publication of the oldest witness of LXX-Ps discovered to date, namely Oxyrhynchus Papyrus 5101 (LXX^{2227}) of the first/second century C.E., underscores the need for a new, fully critical edition.[30]

Such an edition has long been in progress at the Septuaginta Unternehmen in Göttingen, but will still take at least twenty years to produce, according to a recent projection: according to plan, the manuscript collations will be finished in 2015 and assigned to a team of editors under the supervision of an editor-in-chief, who will publish both a printed and online edition.[31]

An important reference tool for the study of the Greek Psalter is its translation in *NETS, which reflects the current state of text-critical research by incorporating some 152 departures from Rahlfs' *Psalmi cum Odis* (indicated in footnotes). Further, *NETS has omitted eight items that Rahlfs had placed in square brackets to indicate his considered opinion that these were not Old Greek despite their considerable manuscript support (Pss 13:3$^{3-10}$ [= Rom 3:13–18]; 17:20$^{3-4}$; 24:14^2; 70:21^3; 118:104^3; 134:17$^{2-5}$; 146:8^4).[32] *NETS has also bracketed a further twelve items (located in Rahlfs' edition at Pss 7:12^{1b}; 26:1^{1b}; 47:1^{1b}; 65:1^{1b}; 67:5^3; 72:28^4; 93:1^{1b}; 95:1^1; 96:1^{1b}; 113:11^2; 133:1^4; 135:16$^{3-4}$; 148:5^2) whose originality Pietersma considers to be "suspect."[33] Another worthwhile resource, particularly for discussions of individual variants *vis-à-vis* MT, is Barthélemy, *Critique textuelle 2005*.

10.3.1.3 Translation Character and Translation Technique

Scholars agree that LXX-Ps is a translation of the formal equivalence kind, but they describe its character variously and account for it in differ-

---

[24] R. Holmes and J. Parsons (eds.), *Vetus Testamentum Graecum cum Variis Lectionibus* (Oxford: Clarendon Press, 1798–1820).
[25] Rahlfs, *Psalmi cum Odis*, 6.
[26] Rahlfs, *Psalmi cum Odis*, 71–72.
[27] Hedley, "Göttingen Investigation," 69.
[28] Pietersma, "Present State," 17–21, 24.
[29] Pietersma, "Present State," 26–27.

[30] D. Colomo and W.B. Henry, "5101. LXX, Psalms xxvi 9–14, xliv 4–8, xlvii 13–15, xlviii 6–21, xlix 2–16, lxiii 6–lxiv 5," in *The Oxyrhynchus Papyri*, Vol. 77 (ed. A. Benaissa; Graeco-Roman Memoirs 98; London: Egypt Exploration Society, 2011), 1–11; J. Smith, "The Text-Critical Significance of Oxyrhynchus Papyrus 5101 (Ra 2227) for the Old Greek Psalter," *Journal of Septuagint and Cognate Studies* 45 (2012): 5–22.
[31] Private communication from Christian Schäfer, Septuaginta-Unternehmen der Akademie der Wissenschaften, dated June 24, 2013.
[32] Rahlfs, *Psalmi cum Odis*, 8.
[33] Pietersma, "To the Reader of Psalms," 542.

ent ways (→ 1.3.1.1.9). This variety illustrates the different approaches that scholars have taken to the Greek translation over time and highlights the need for a theoretical framework that helpfully describes the relationship of a translation to its parent text. Thackeray, for instance, placed the Greek Psalter in the category of "indifferent Greek," between the "good κοίνη Greek" of the Pentateuch (→ 2.4.1), part of Joshua (→ 3.3), Isaiah (→ 6.3.1), and 1 Maccabees (→ 11.10.1.2) on the one hand, and the "literal or unintelligent versions" of Judges (LXX^B-text; → 4.3), Ruth (→ 13–17.1.1.1), parts of Kingdoms (→ 5.4; → 5.5), Jeremiah 29–51 (→ 7.3), Canticles (→ 13–17.1.1.2), and Lamentations (→ 13–17.1.1.4) on the other.[34] He called it "the most careful piece of work in the Greek collection of writings," but did not present data to support this characterization.[35] For Thackeray, the quality of its Greek style was a reflection of the translator's capability.

For Flashar, on the other hand, it was a function of how the translator approached the task of translating. He concluded that the Psalms translator had a deficient knowledge of the Hebrew language, and that the obscure, unintelligible, and un-Greek facets of the translation are the result of a propensity to preserve the syntax and constructions of the *Vorlage* and of a mechanical deployment of standard equivalents (such as ἐκκλησία for קָהָל [both meaning "assembly"] and συναγωγή "gathering" for עֵדָה "congregation"; ἔλεος "mercy" for חֶסֶד "steadfast love"; θέλω "will" for חפץ "desire"; ἐξομολογέω "acknowledge" for ידה *Hiphil* "give thanks"), though abandoning such equivalents where the same Hebrew word occurred more than once in close succession or where he had already used the Greek equivalent for a different Hebrew word in the immediate context.[36] In short, the translator typically operated in a fairly mechanical fashion.

More recently, Gzella has returned to a characterization of LXX-Ps in terms of its Greek style. He typifies LXX-Ps as a translation closely oriented to the Hebrew text; yet the great deal of interpretative activity that he detects in such psalms as Pss 15; 16; and 89 shifts the translation to a middle position between fully free, often simply paraphrasing versions such as the book of Proverbs (→ 12.3.1) on the one hand, and slavishly literal renderings such as Ecclesiastes (→ 13–17.1.1.3) on the other.[37] Gzella goes so far as to call the translator an "author" and a "theological thinker," though such labels suggest a degree of independence from the source text that the translation does not display.[38]

Austermann has offered the most detailed recent description of the Psalter translation, in which he dispenses with the popular labels "literal" versus "free," preferring Aejmelaeus' categories of quantitative and qualitative aspects. On the quantitative side, he finds the Greek Psalter to be source-oriented, containing much usage that is unusual and grammatically barely possible, with occasional evidence of an interest in correct Greek,[39] while on the qualitative side the translator shows a pronounced tendency to use equivalents that suit the context.[40]

Finally, for Pietersma, the character of LXX-Ps does not reflect the translator's facility in Greek but the "interlinear" relationship of the translation to its source text. He describes the translation as "isomorphic" at both the lexical and grammatical levels, with a relatively high number of many-to-one Hebrew-Greek equations (resulting in semantic leveling of the Greek vis-à-vis the Hebrew). Particular favorites include ἀντιλήμπτωρ "supporter," ἀδικία "injustice," ἀνομία "lawlessness" (and other "law-related" words), βοηθός "helper," δόξα "glory," ἐλπίζω "hope," σαλεύω "shake," σώζω "save," and ταπεινόω "humble." By contrast, the translation has relatively few one-to-many Hebrew-Greek equations (displaying contextual differentiation), and only occasional "literary sparks."[41] In short, while

---

[34] Thackeray, *Grammar*, 13.
[35] Thackeray, *Grammar*, 15.
[36] Flashar, "Exegetische Studien zum Septuagintapsalter," 103, 114, 161, 183.
[37] H. Gzella, *Lebenszeit und Ewigkeit: Studien zur Eschatologie und Anthropologie des Septuaginta-Psalters* (BBB 134; Berlin: Philo, 2002), 28.
[38] Gzella, *Lebenszeit und Ewigkeit*, 5, 26–27.
[39] Austermann, *Von der Tora zum Nomos*, 102.
[40] Austermann, *Von der Tora zum Nomos*, 69–90, 103.
[41] Pietersma, "To the Reader of Psalms," 542–43.

most of his Greek is "intelligible ... if not idiomatic," the Greek translator "all too often" had "an isomorphic approach with a primary focus on representing the source text, not infrequently at the expense of coherent sense."[42]

A marked improvement in more recent attempts to describe the translation character of the Greek Psalter has been the shift away from conclusions about the translator's proficiency or mindset to a description of the text in terms of the strategies by which it was derived from its source. In that respect, Septuagint scholarship has benefited from the discipline of translation studies. Applying Toury's descriptive categories, for example, one may characterize LXX-Ps as a text in which the translator preserved Hebrew word order and tended to: 1) maintain standard equivalents; 2) account for all morphemes of the source text; and 3) maintain its syntactic categories, with the result that its Greek is characterized by linguistic interference, both negative (deviations from normal, codified practices of the target system) and positive (a greater likelihood of selecting features that do exist and are used in any case).[43]

10.3.1.4 Text-Critical Value

Its translation from a parent text close to (consonantal) MT (→ 10.2.2), the source-orientedness of its translation technique, and the relative consistency of its translation equivalents combine to make LXX-Ps a valuable version for text-critical study of MT-Ps, provided that one bears two considerations in mind. The first is to take translation technique into account at every instance. One should not assume that differences between the Greek and the Hebrew are due to a different *Vorlage*; it is possible, for instance, that the translator read the same consonants as MT but different vowels (e.g. verbal וְעֻזּוֹ "and be strengthened" instead of nominal וְעֻזּוֹ "and his strength" in Ps 104[105]:4; *qal* וַיָּבֹא "and he came" instead of *Hiphil* וַיָּבֵא "and he brought" in Ps 104[105]:40), a different word division (e.g. the participle עֹלִים "going up" for the prepositional phrase עַל יָם "at the sea" in Ps 105[106]:7), or even a different verse division (e.g. in Psalm 26[27] where MT begins v. 13 at לוּלֵא "if not" but the translator evidently read לוֹ "to itself" at the end of v. 12). Differences may also be due to interpretive moves on the part of the translator. The second consideration is to treat its text as *sub iudice* pending the publication of a fully critical edition. For example, while Rahlfs reads καταπίεται "it will devour" (uncontested) at 57:10, Bodmer Papyrus XXIV (LXX[2110]) now provides the variant καταιγιεῖται "it will bestorm," which is not only a better semantic match for its Hebrew counterpart ערש "sweep away" but also correlates with the translator's choice of the noun καταιγίς "storm" for the same Hebrew root in Pss 49:3, 54:9, 82:16, 106:25, 29, and 148:8. With these two caveats in mind, there are nevertheless instances in which LXX-Ps preserves important variants *vis-à-vis* MT, such as כרו "they dug" for כארי "like a lion" in Ps 21(22):17, קברם "their grave" for קרבם "their midst" in Ps 48(49):12, ויאריך "and he will endure" for ייראוך "may they fear you" in Ps 71(72):5, גרשו "may they be driven" for דרשו "may they seek" in Ps 108(109):10, and the inclusion of the *nun*-stich in Ps 144(145):13b, to mention only a few.

10.3.1.5 Literary-Critical Value

Several features of the Greek translation make it of literary-critical value for the Hebrew Psalter. Firstly, concomitant with the translator's choice of διάψαλμα "interlude on strings" for סלה "Selah," one never finds the Greek word at the end of a psalm, where one would hardly expect to find an "interlude on strings" (*NETS). Secondly, whereas in the Masoretic evidence the phrase הללו יה "Praise Yah!" often "floats" between the end of one psalm and the beginning of the next, the Greek translator consistently employed ἁλληλουϊα "Hallelujah" to mark it as a superscription.[44] Thirdly, while the sequence of psalms is the same in the Greek and Masoretic

---

[42] Pietersma, "To the Reader of Psalms," 544.

[43] G. Toury, *Descriptive Translation Studies and Beyond* (Benjamins Translation Library 4; Amsterdam: Benjamins, 1995); Smith, *Translated Hallelujahs*, 24, 282–83.

[44] On the use of ἁλληλουϊα in LXX-Ps, see Smith, *Translated Hallelujahs*, 37–50.

Psalters (→ 10.2.2), their division of psalms is not. LXX combines Psalms 9 and 10 (Psalm 9), which affects the numbering of subsequent psalms. It further combines MT-Ps 114 and 115 (LXX-Ps 113), but divides MT-Ps 116:1–9 and 116:10–19 (LXX-Ps 114 and 115 respectively) and MT-Ps 147:1–11 and 147:12–20 (LXX-Ps 146 and 147) with the cumulative result that the Greek book has the same number of psalms as the Hebrew. True, the Greek adds Psalm 151 but labels it as "outside the number." This heading notwithstanding, its inclusion in virtually the entire manuscript tradition makes Psalm 151 part of the distinct literary profile of the Greek book. Finally, it should be noted that while Rahlfs' edition (*Psalmi cum Odis*) adds the Odes to the Psalter in keeping with most of the Greek evidence, these were of course not part of the original translation and are therefore a pseudo-literary feature of the book.

Austermann, F., *Von der Tora zum Nomos: Untersuchungen zur Übersetzungsweise und Interpretation im Septuaginta-Psalter* (MSU 27; Göttingen: Vandenhoeck & Ruprecht, 2003).

Flashar, M., "Exegetische Studien zum Septuagintapsalter," *ZAW* 32 (1912): 81–116, 161–89, 241–68.

Hedley, P.L., "The Göttingen Investigation and Edition of the Septuagint," *HTR* 26 (1933): 57–72.

Hiebert, R.J.V., C.E. Cox, and P.J. Gentry (eds.), *The Old Greek Psalter: Studies in Honour of Albert Pietersma* (JSOTSup 332; Sheffield: Sheffield Academic Press, 2001).

Pietersma, A., "On the Place of Origin of the Old Greek Psalter," in *The World of the Aramaeans: Biblical Studies in Honour of Paul-Eugène Dion* (eds. P.M.M. Daviau, J.W. Wevers, and M. Weigl; 3 vols.; JSOTSup 324; Sheffield: Sheffield Academic Press, 2001), 1.252–74.

Pietersma, A., "The Present State of the Critical Text of the Greek Psalter," in *Der Septuaginta Psalter und seine Tochterübersetzungen: Symposium in Göttingen 1997* (eds. A. Aejmelaeus and U. Quast; MSU 24; Göttingen: Vandenhoeck & Ruprecht, 2000), 12–32.

Pietersma, A., "To the Reader of Psalms," in *NETS, 542–47.

Rahlfs, A., *Psalmi cum Odis* (Septuaginta Vetus Testamentum Graecum 10; Göttingen: Vandenhoeck & Ruprecht, 1931).

Schaper, J., *Eschatology in the Greek Psalter* (WUNT 2.76; Tübingen: Mohr, 1995).

Smith, J., *Translated Hallelujahs: A Linguistic and Exegetical Commentary on Select Septuagint Psalms* (CBET 56; Leuven: Peeters, 2011).

Zenger, E. (ed.), *Der Septuaginta-Psalter: Sprachliche und theologische Aspekte* (Herders Biblische Studien 32; Freiburg i.B.: Herder, 2001).

Jannes Smith

10.3.2 Pre-Hexaplaric Greek Translations

See → 10.3.5 Hexaplaric Greek Translations (Psalms > Primary Translations).

10.3.3 Targum

10.3.3.1 Manuscripts, Printed Editions, and Translations

The most comprehensive list of manuscript sources for the Targum of Psalms is provided by Smelik in a paper published on the internet, in which he gives details of nineteen complete manuscripts:[1] Paris, Bibliothèque Nationale manuscripts Héb. 17, 114, 110; Berlin, Staatsbibliothek Preussischer Kulturbesitz manuscript Or. Fol. 4; Nuremberg, Stadtbibliothek Cod. Solger 6.2; Vatican, Biblioteca Apostolica Cod. Urbinati-Vaticano 1; Florence, Biblioteca Mediceo-Laurenziana Plut. III.1; Rome, Biblioteca Angelica Cod. Or. 72; Parma, Biblioteca Palatina manuscripts 3095, 3231, 3232, 3189; Genoa, Biblioteca Civica Berio manuscript B.H. VII; Wrocław, Biblioteka Uniwersytecka manuscript M.1106; Madrid, Biblioteca Complutense manuscript 5 (116-Z-40); Madrid, Biblioteca de el Escorial manuscript G 1–5; Salamanca, Biblioteca de la Universitaria manuscript M-2; London, Jew's College Library manuscript H.116; Cambridge, University Library manuscript Ee. 5.9. Smelik also lists a further nine manuscripts that are damaged, incomplete, or fragmentary.

No complete critical edition of the Targum of Psalms is yet available. A partial critical edition,

---

[1] Smelik, *Extant Manuscripts of the Targum to Psalms*.

covering books 1 and 2 of the Psalter, with the text given in transliteration, was produced by Emanuel White in his (unpublished) doctoral dissertation of 1988.[2] White, largely following Wilcox,[3] classifies the manuscripts used by him into three groups: 1) Sephardi manuscripts: Complutense, London, Paris 110, Escorial, Salamanca; 2) Ashkenazi manuscripts: Cambridge, Paris 17, 114, Parma 3095, 3231, 3232, Wrocław, Vatican, Berlin, Rome, Florence; 3) Nuremberg, which occupies a place between groups one and two. The First and Second Rabbinic Bibles printed by Daniel Bomberg in Venice in 1517 and 1525 (*RB¹ and *RB²) probably used the Nuremberg manuscript as the basis for their text of the Targum of Psalms, and most printed editions since then, including de Lagarde's *Hagiographa Chaldaica*, have reproduced essentially the same text. The Sephardi textual tradition was first represented in print by the Antwerp Polyglot or *Biblia Regia* of 1569–1572,[4] and more recently Díez Merino has published a transcription of the Madrid Complutense manuscript 5 (Villa-Amil n. 5).[5]

A study of the Targum of Psalms published by Edwards in 2007,[6] based upon a selection of fifteen psalms (Pss 1; 2; 24; 45; 48; 68; 80; 81; 82; 92; 93; 94; 110; 118, 137), reproduces the text of the Wrocław manuscript for each and has an apparatus showing variants from manuscripts belonging to each of the text types.

The first English translation of the Targum of Psalms was published on the internet in 2001 by Cook,[7] who translated the text of de Lagarde and also noted variants from Díez Merino's edition of the Complutensian manuscript. An English translation by Stec then appeared in printed form in The Aramaic Bible series in 2004, based on Paris manuscript Héb. 17, and with an apparatus giving variants from four other manuscripts and the printed editions.[8] Edwards gives an English translation of each of the psalms used in his study.[9]

10.3.3.2 Date

The date of the Targum of Psalms is difficult to determine with any confidence. It does not seem to have been widely known, or at least widely used, until a relatively late date. There is just one oblique reference in the Babylonian Talmud to an Aramaic translation of at least part of the Psalter: *b. Meg.* 21b states that, "During the Hallel and the Megillah, even ten people can read simultaneously and ten can translate simultaneously." But there is some doubt about the presence of the word "Hallel" in the text, with at least one manuscript and some early commentators omitting it.[10] The first medieval work to quote extensively from the Targum of Psalms is the *Arukh* of Rabbi Nathan ben Jehiel of Rome, completed in 1102.[11] Within the Targum of Psalms itself, the only clear historical reference with any bearing upon dating is the mention of Rome and Constantinople at Ps 108:11, which would suggest a *terminus a quo* of early in the fourth century C.E., and a *terminus ad quem* of 476 C.E. when the Western Roman Empire came to an end. But it is possible and even likely that the Targum of Psalms as a whole contains material from more than one period, in which case Ps 108:11 would be of only limited relevance to establishing its date. Edwards concludes that the earliest datable tradition in the Targum of Psalms comes from dependence on Aquila (Ps 92:15), and can thus be dated to the early second century C.E., whereas the majority of its exegetical traditions are close to Amoraic traditions, which would suggest that any date before the fifth century C.E. for the "original" Targum of Psalms is very unlikely.[12]

---

[2] White, "A Critical Edition of the Targum of Psalms."
[3] Wilcox, "The Aramaic Targum to Psalms."
[4] *Biblia Sacra Hebraice, Chaldaice, Graece et Latina* ... (ed. B. Arias Montano; Antwerp: Christophorus Plantinus, 1569–1572).
[5] Díez Merino, *Targum de Salmos*.
[6] Edwards, *Exegesis in the Targum of the Psalms*.
[7] Cook, *Targum Psalms*.

[8] Stec, *The Targum of Psalms*.
[9] Edwards, *Exegesis in the Targum of the Psalms*.
[10] White, *A Critical Edition of the Targum of Psalms*, 12–13.
[11] White, *A Critical Edition of the Targum of Psalms*, 14–17.
[12] Edwards, *Exegesis in the Targum of The Psalms*, 221; cf. 28–34.

10.3.3.3 Language

The language of the Targum of Psalms is probably to be understood as a dialect of Palestinian Aramaic, as can be seen from its use of such forms as ארום rather than ארי as an equivalent for the Hebrew particle כי "for," and חמי rather than חזי for the verb "to see" (though חזי is occasionally found), and also the preference for the third masculine singular suffix with plural nouns as והי- rather than וי- (though both forms are found). Its dialect is similar to that of the other Targumim to the Hagiographa, especially the Targum of Job, and also to that of Targum Pseudo-Jonathan to the Pentateuch (→ 2.4.3.4.1). In a detailed study of the language of the Targum of Psalms, Dan concludes that despite the classical Western character of its Aramaic, "the eastern component is not foreign to it, and is not entirely due to late copyists."[13] He points out that it even has some vocabulary known from Syriac, such as מטול "on account of" and יומנא "today." The vocabulary of the Targum of Psalms also includes several loan words from Greek.[14]

10.3.3.4 Character

The Targum of Psalms is made up for the most part of a fairly literal base translation (of a text essentially similar to MT [→ 10.2.2]) into which several expansions have been inserted. Where changes are made to the original, these are mainly stylized and follow certain well-established conventions representing the translation method of the Targumist (→ 10.3.3.5). Nevertheless, there are also occasionally passages of a rather different character, which provide an expansive and paraphrastic rendering, making use of various midrashic and haggadic traditions. For examples of this latter type of passage, see especially T-Ps 18 and 68.

Within the expansions and paraphrastic translations of the biblical text, the following themes stand out: the law and instruction (Pss 34:5; 40:8; 42:7; 44:4; 46:7; 49:16; 68:9; 84:7; 94:10; 102:5; 110:1; 144:12), prophecy and prophets (Pss 14:1; 18:1; 49:17; 68:34; 74:9; 90:12; 107:23, 33; 110:7), prayer (Pss 4:5; 46:5; 50:16; 72:5; 132:6; 140:14), the temple (Pss 24:7; 45:13; 68:16; 80:11), priests (Pss 23:5; 45:14; 51:9; 134:2), angels (Pss 57:4; 68:11, 18; 78:25; 89:8; 91:5; 96:1; 137:7–8), demons (Pss 91:5, 6, 10; 121:6), reward and punishment, righteousness and merit (Pss 21:10; 49:10; 50:3; 55:24; 58:2; 63:4; 68:23; 84:10; 92:10; 110:4; 119:56), and exile (Pss 18:28; 23:4; 69:3, 15; 88:7; 102:24).[15] The Targum of Psalms also frequently brings in persons and events from biblical history, including the Garden of Eden (Pss 50:10; 90:17), Noah and the generation of the flood (Ps 29:10), the patriarchs (Ps 18:26–27), the overthrow of Sodom (Ps 107:34), the exodus (Ps 42:8), Pharaoh and his army (Ps 68:7), Moses and Aaron (Ps 68:12, 26), the receiving of the law on Mt Sinai (Ps 42:7), Saul (Ps 7:1), Goliath (Ps 9:6), Doeg and Ahithophel (Ps 55:16), Sennacherib (Ps 83:9), Hezekiah (Ps 107:17), and Zedekiah (Ps 107:10).

Many of the exegetical traditions in the midrashic and haggadic material of the Targum of Psalms have parallels in *Midrash Tehillim* (e.g. Pss 50:2; 68:7; 84:8; 90:2; 110:1; 137:4). But it is difficult to draw any firm conclusions about the relationship between the two, since the date and redaction history of both is very uncertain. Churgin was of the opinion that in most cases they draw upon a third source.[16] After looking at interpretations unique to the Targum of Psalms and *Midrash Tehillim* in the fifteen psalms that he studies, Edwards concludes that there is "no evidence that these two texts are related in any specific way, beyond being based on the same biblical book from which they both derive their name."[17]

A feature that the Targum of Psalms shares with the Targum of Job (→ 11.3.3.1) is the use of multiple translation. Some verses are given two translations, one mainly literal and the other free or paraphrastic, or both paraphrastic. In the Targum of Psalms, however, this is found on a smaller scale than in the Targum of Job. In the printed editions

---

[13] Dan, *The Targum of Psalms*, xxi.

[14] More than forty such words are listed in Stec, *The Targum of Psalms*, 20–21.

[15] For more details of the treatment of these themes in the Targum of Psalms, see Stec, *The Targum of Psalms*, 4–9.

[16] Churgin, *Targum of the Hagiographa*, 31–34.

[17] Edwards, *Exegesis in the Targum of The Psalms*, 168.

that follow Bomberg, the Targum of Job has forty-two verses with a double translation, and four with a triple translation, whereas the Targum of Psalms has only five verses with a double translation (Pss 76:11; 77:11; 78:64; 88:3; 110:1), and none with a triple translation. The manuscripts of the Targum of Psalms have just a few more verses with a double translation, and many individual words and phrases are also given an alternative translation, usually in the margin.[18]

10.3.3.5 Aspects of Translation Method

1) Use of reverential devices, largely in a stereotypical way.

   a) מימרא *Memra* "word" is used mainly in order to keep a proper distance between God and humans, e.g., "*the Memra of* the LORD derides them," for MT "the LORD derides them" (Ps 2:4); "Blessed are all who trust in *his Memra*," for MT "Blessed are all who take refuge in *him*" (Ps 2:12).

   b) שכינה *Shekinah* "presence" is used for sayings concerned with the presence of God, e.g., "*The Shekinah of* the LORD is in her midst," for MT "*God* is in her midst" (Ps 46:6); "Mount Zion, in which *your Shekinah* dwelt," for "Mount Zion, in which *you* dwelt" (Ps 74:2). The frequent MT expression הִסְתִּיר פָּנָיו "hide his face" is rendered סליק שכינתיה "remove his *Shekinah*" (22:25).

   c) איקרא "glory" is particularly associated with theophany, e.g., "his glory was revealed," for MT "he came down" (Ps 18:10). There are also such phrases as "throne of glory" (Ps 89:8), "clouds of glory" (Ps 68:14), and "*Shekinah* of glory" (Ps 115:16).

   d) Distance between God and humans is also maintained by the insertion of various nouns before "God" or "the Lord": דחלא "fear" (Ps 9:18), שמא "name" (Ps 103:2), אולפנא "instruction" (Ps 105:4).

2) Inconsistent treatment of anthropomorphisms. Often these are removed by substitution: *Shekinah* for MT "face" (Ps 22:25), *Memra* for "eyes" (Ps 18:25), יקר "glory" for "eyes" (Ps 31:23), מחת "stroke" for "hand" (Ps 32:4), תושבחתא "praise" for "mouth" (Ps 138:4). Sometimes they are softened by the insertion of words, e.g. סבר "brightness of" (Ps 11:7) or זיו "splendor of" (Ps 13:2) inserted before "face," מחת, "stroke of" inserted before "hand" (Ps 21:9). But frequently anthropomorphisms are simply retained. Thus, we find references to God's face (Ps 10:11), mouth (Ps 33:6), eyes (Ps 5:6), ears (Ps 10:17), hand (Ps 10:12), and fingers (Ps 8:4).

3) Explanation of what is unclear in MT (→ 10.2.2). Thus MT "this" is explained as "this *instruction*" (Ps 49:2), MT "these" as "these *miracles*" (Ps 42:5), MT "they band together" as "*the wicked* gather together" (Ps 94:21), MT "he remembers them" as "he remembers *the righteous*" (Ps 9:13), and MT "your devout ones" as "*the Levites*, your devout ones" (Ps 132:9).

4) Alternative derivation of words. The Targum of Psalms sometimes apparently derives Hebrew words from a root different from (but often superficially similar to) the generally accepted one. MT-Ps 5:9 שׁוֹרְרָי is usually taken to be the noun שורר "watcher," i.e. enemy, from the √ שור "behold," but the Targum of Psalms תושבחתי "my praise" apparently derives it from the √ שיר "sing." MT-Ps 35:15 וְלֹא־דָמּוּ "and they did not cease" (from the verb דמם) is translated ולא מפקין דמא "and they were not drawing blood," as though it was a denominative verb from דם "blood." MT-Ps 124:4 נַחְלָה is apparently the noun נחל "torrent" with *he locale*, but the Targum of Psalms מרעית "sickness" apparently takes it to be the *niphal* participle of חלה "be sick," used as a noun (cf. Isa 17:11). Sometimes, if a Hebrew word has a homonym, the Targum of Psalms translates not according to the generally accepted meaning in context, but according to the meaning of the homonym. Thus at MT-Ps 116:10 עָנִיתִי is normally understood to be from ענה III "be afflicted," but the Targum of Psalms translates שבחית as though it was from ענה IV "sing."

---

[18] On the origin of multiple translation, see D.M. Stec, *The Text of the Targum of Job: An Introduction and Critical Edition* (*AGJU* 20; Leiden: Brill, 1994), 86–94.

10.3.3.6 Relationship to MT and the Versions

When one disregards differences between the Targum of Psalms and MT (→ 10.2.2) that can be attributed to the methods of translation described above, and when one sets aside the more paraphrastic sections of the Targum of Psalms, one is left with what for the most part appears to be a fairly literal translation of a Hebrew text that does not differ greatly from MT. Nevertheless, some differences do remain, which could be evidence for a different *Vorlage*. Sometimes we find readings in the Targum of Psalms (or some manuscripts of it) that agree with textual variants of the manuscript tradition of MT. At Ps 54:5, *BHS reads זָרִים "strangers," but most manuscripts of the Targum of Psalms read זידנין "the arrogant," which suggests a Hebrew original of זדים (as read by some manuscripts of MT), though Complutense manuscript 5 of the Targum of Psalms reads נוכראין "strangers" (with זידנין as an alternative translation in the margin). At Ps 62:11, *BHS and most manuscripts of MT read תֶּהְבָּלוּ "act vainly," but some manuscripts read תבהלו "hasten"; most manuscripts of the Targum of Psalms read תיתבהלון "hasten," but Complutense manuscript 5 and Paris Héb. 110 read תתהבלון "act vainly."

Many of the deviations of the Targum of Psalms from MT have the support of other ancient versions, particularly LXX (→ 10.3.1) and the Peshitta (→ 10.3.4). Some of these involve nothing more than a different vocalization of the same consonantal text: At Ps 50:18, MT reads וַתִּרֶץ "and you were pleased" (√רצה), but the Targum of Psalms (+ LXX, Peshitta) suggests a vocalization of וַתָּרָץ "and you ran" (√רוץ). At Ps 78:60, MT reads *piel* שִׁכֵּן "he caused to dwell," but the Targum of Psalms (+ LXX, Peshitta) suggests a vocalization of *qal* שָׁכַן "it dwelt." At Ps 52:7, MT reads יַחְתְּךָ "he will snatch you away" (√חתה), but the Targum of Psalms (+ Aquila) suggests a vocalization of יְחִתְּךָ "he will shatter you" (√חתת). Other deviations involve consonants that may be easily confused: At Ps 18:46, for MT יִבֹּלוּ "they will wither" the Targum of Psalms (+ Peshitta) reads יסופון "they will perish," which suggests a Hebrew original of יכלו. At 56:7, for MT יָגוּרוּ "they stir up strife," the Targum of Psalms (+ Jerome) reads יכנשון "they gather together," which suggests a Hebrew original of יגדו. Various other readings also suggest an original with a different consonantal text: At Ps 38:3, for MT וַתִּנְחַת "and it has gone down," the Targum of Psalms (+ Peshitta) reads ושרת "and it rests," which suggests a Hebrew original of ותנח. At Ps 52:9, for MT בְּהַוָּתוֹ "in his wickedness," the Targum of Psalms (+ Peshitta) reads בממוניה "in his wealth," which suggests a Hebrew original of בהונו. At Ps 138:3, for MT תַּרְהִבֵנִי "you made me arrogant," the Targum of Psalms (and the LXX) reads אסגיתני "you made me great," which suggests a Hebrew original of תרבני.

The above examples suggest that at times the Targum of Psalms may have been based on a *Vorlage* different from what is witnessed by MT, and that its *Vorlage* had some features in common with that underlying some of the other ancient versions. Wilhelm Bacher in his article of 1872[19] was of the opinion that the Targum of Psalms often shares the same *Vorlage* with LXX (→ 10.3.1) and Peshitta (→ 10.3.4), and he took this as evidence of an early date for the Targum of Psalms. But modern scholarship is rather more cautious about drawing such conclusions. After a detailed examination of several examples from his fifteen psalms, Edwards concludes that only two suggest the possible use of a *Vorlage* different from that represented by MT (→ 10.2.2), and even in those cases the proof is far from conclusive.[20] Moreover, he stresses the essential independence of the Targum of Psalms as a translation *vis-à-vis* the other versions, and suggests that on numerous occasions similarity in translation or interpretation can be attributed to the Hebrew text (→ 10.2.2) itself or to a similarity in exegetical technique, which independently produced similar results.[21]

10.3.3.7 Internal Consistency

It will be seen from the above survey that the Targum of Psalms is a diverse work in many respects: it contains exegetical traditions from more than one

---

[19] Bacher, "Das Targum zu den Psalmen."
[20] Edwards, *Exegesis in the Targum of the Psalms*, 39.
[21] Edwards, *Exegesis in the Targum of the Psalms*, 53.

period; its language, while predominantly Western, embraces a wide variety of elements; and its style of translation varies between (mainly) literal and paraphrastic, and shows inconsistency in its treatment of anthropomorphisms.

Bacher, W., "Das Targum zu den Psalmen," *MGWJ* 21 (1872): 408–16, 463–73.
Churgin, P., *Targum of the Hagiographa* (New York: Horeb, 1945) [Hebr.].
Cook, E.M., *Targum Psalms: An English Translation*. Online: 2001, http://targum.info/targumic-texts/targumim-of-the-psalms.
Dan, B., "The Targum of Psalms: A Morphological Description" (PhD diss., The Hebrew University of Jerusalem, 2008).
Díez Merino, L., *Targum de Salmos: Edición Príncipe del Ms. Villa-Amil n. 5 de Alfonso de Zamora* (Bibliotheca Hispana Biblica 6; Madrid: Consejo Superior de Investigaciones Científicas, Instituto "Francisco Suárez," 1982).
Edwards, T., *Exegesis in the Targum of the Psalms: The Old, the New, and the Rewritten* (Gorgias Dissertations 28; Biblical Studies 1; Piscataway: Gorgias Press, 2007).
de Lagarde, P., *Hagiographa Chaldaica* (Leipzig: B.G. Teubner, 1873; repr.: Osnabrück: O. Zeller, 1967).
Smelik, W.F., *Extant Manuscripts of the Targum to Psalms: An Eclectic List*. Online: 2003, http://eprints.ucl.ac.uk/1373.
Stec, D.M., *The Targum of Psalms: Translated, with a Critical Introduction, Apparatus, and Notes* (ArBib 16; Collegeville: The Liturgical Press, 2004).
White, E., "A Critical Edition of the Targum of Psalms: A Computer Generated Text of Books I and II" (unpubl. PhD diss., McGill University, Montreal, 1988).
Wilcox, M., "The Aramaic Targum to Psalms," in *Proceedings of the Ninth World Congress of Jewish Studies, Jerusalem, August 4–12, 1985*, Division A: *The Period of the Bible* (ed. M. Goshen-Gottstein; Jerusalem: World Union of Jewish Studies, 1986), 143–50.

David Stec

10.3.4 Peshitta

10.3.4.1 Textual Tradition of S-Ps

The book of Psalms in the Peshitta was translated from a proto-Masoretic, unvocalized Hebrew text that was in circulation around the second century C.E. (→ 10.2.2), prior to the Vulgate (→ 10.3.7) and Targum translations (→ 10.3.3), since the *Vorlagen* of these versions attest to a text that is already much closer to MT (as demonstrated by Ps 145:13, an acrostic psalm in which both the Latin and Aramaic versions reflect a Hebrew text resembling that of MT that has already lost the stich that began with the letter *nun*, which S-Ps, LXX [→ 10.3.1], and 11QPsª [→ 10.2.1.2; → 10.2.3.2] preserve).

Aside from the problem of the identity of the translators (Jewish? Christian?), the whole textual tradition of S-Ps that has come down to us is Christian. The liturgical use of this book has, to a great extent, conditioned the characteristics of the textual transmission of S-Ps. To the abundance of manuscripts, we must add the wealth of variants that complicate the "reconstruction" of the "original translation" of this book.

At the end of the nineteenth century, Rahlfs[1] considered that the division of Peshitta manuscripts into two traditions, with substantial doctrinal differences, made it impossible to reconstruct the text prior to the schism. Almost a century later, Dirksen called into question what had become a dogma that never had been grounded in textual study. On the basis of recent studies on the textual transmission of the various books of the Peshitta, he concluded that the schism between the Eastern and Western Churches "has been of no consequence for the transmission of the text of the O.T. Peshitta."[2] Based on the studies of Koster,[3] Dirksen proposed recognizing a more real division: the one between the oldest manuscripts (prior to the ninth century C.E.), which were probably the most faithful witnesses to the "original" translation, and those more recent (subsequent to the ninth century C.E.), into which a great number of secondary variants had probably been introduced. However, Dirksen considers that the book of Psalms is an exception to his conclusions. Dirksen thinks that in the case of S-Ps it is possible to

---

[1] Rahlfs, "Beiträge zur Textkritik der Peshitta," 161–210.
[2] Dirksen, "East and West," 468–84 (478).
[3] Koster, *The Peshitta of Exodus*.

continue to maintain the radical division between Eastern and Western manuscripts.

In 2008, Carbajosa[4] demonstrated that the radical division between manuscripts that was held by Rahlfs and supported, with qualifications, by Barnes cannot be held for the book of Psalms. Carbajosa analyzed the list of eighty-four cases of "Nestorian" readings presented by Barnes in his edition of S-Ps, which are supposed to constitute the textual support for the theory of the radical division between manuscripts proposed by Rahlfs. In his study, Carbajosa concludes that none of the eighty-four readings can be characterized, from a "confessional" point of view, as "Nestorian." That is, the differences between Western and Eastern manuscripts cannot be attributed to confessional arguments that have found their way into the textual tradition. Rather, Carbajosa has shown that in a good number of the cases on Barnes' list it is possible to determine which reading is original and which is secondary.

Thus, it is possible to consider the "dogma" of the radical division between manuscripts for doctrinal reasons to be unjustified and to have been superseded, which condemned us to skepticism regarding the possibility of getting closer to the original version of S-Ps. The proper exercise of internal textual criticism, supported by the study of the characteristics of the manuscripts (and not just the distinction between older and more recent manuscripts) can allow us to confidently draw closer to the original version of S-Ps.

10.3.4.2 Critical Edition

Since the invention of the printing press, S-Ps has gone through many printings, both alone (as the Psalter) and in the whole Bible.

In 1980, a critical edition of S-Ps was published as part of the Peshitta Institute.[5] This is a diplomatic edition that reproduces manuscript S^{7a1} as its main text (= manuscript B21 Inferiore, Biblioteca Ambrosiana, Milan), from the sixth–seventh centuries C.E. The new wealth of this edition is found in the critical apparatus which presents variants of manuscripts prior to the thirteenth century. This edition does not include the Syriac titles of the psalms, usually late (and Christian) additions to the Hebrew text.

10.3.4.3 Manuscripts of the Peshitta Psalms

The choice of manuscript S^{7a1} as the base text is a good one, considering that in the Psalms, too, the oldest manuscripts, dated prior to the ninth century C.E., preserve the text that is closest to the original Syriac translation. In this case, manuscripts $S^{6t1, 7a1, 8a1, 8t1}$ are the best witnesses to the stage closest to the original version. Aside from these manuscripts, it is necessary to say a word about a completely novel manuscript, S^{9a1}, and about the collection of late manuscripts that attest to the progressive influence that the Greek LXX (→ 1.3.1.1) has had on the textual transmission of the Peshitta (→ 1.3.4.9).

Manuscript S^{9a1} (Or. Ms 58, Biblioteca Medicea-Laurenziana, Florence, ninth century C.E.) contains 240 unique variants in the book of Psalms, more than any other manuscript. What makes these variants noteworthy is that in most cases (considering only the significant variants) they are readings that agree with the Hebrew text (MT; → 1.2.2) against the rest of the Peshitta tradition (→ 1.3.4). Two explanations have been offered for these coincidences: some authors consider that S^{9a1} attests to a revision of the original text of the Peshitta to bring it closer to the Hebrew text (→ 10.2.2),[6] while other scholars consider that this manuscript preserves original readings that the rest of the tradition has lost.[7] In fact, the first of these hypotheses, that of revision, has little likelihood of being true. In the first place, no reports have come down to us of a cultural context in the Christian environment in which the manuscript transmission of the Peshitta took place and for

---

[4] Carbajosa, "The Division between Western and Eastern Manuscripts in the Peshitta Psalter," 145–74.

[5] Walter, Vogel, and Ebied (eds.), *The Book of Psalms*.

[6] Barnes, *An Apparatus Criticus to Chronicles*.

[7] Diettrich, *Ein Apparatus criticus zur Pešitto zum Propheten Jesaia*; Weitzman, "The Originality of Unique Readings in Peshitta MS 9a1," 225–58; Walter, Vogel, and Ebied, *The Book of Psalms*.

which it would be possible to conceive a revision bringing s-Ps closer to the "Hebrew original." Moreover, in a revision we would expect to find more systematic work, which is not found in s9a1. In fact, one of the characteristics of this manuscript is that, together with its exclusive agreements with MT, we find deviations from that Hebrew text when the rest of the textual tradition, or a part of it, agrees with MT. The hypothesis that s9a1 uniquely preserves some original readings seems the most likely one. This is the hypothesis that Carbajosa supports for the book of Psalms.[8]

In the manuscript tradition of s-Ps we find a series of manuscripts characterized by their agreements with the Greek version of LXX (→ 10.3.1), against the readings of the oldest manuscripts. The question of the possible influence of LXX on the Peshitta has dominated a good part of the research on the Syriac version since the end of the nineteenth century (→ 1.3.4.9). With regard to the Psalter, the dominant thesis at the dawn of this research was that the Syriac translator had worked under the influence of the Greek version.[9] Vogel, on the basis of a textual study of the Psalter, was the first to attenuate the importance of Greek influence, dismissing a systematic use of LXX in the translation, and locating the contact in the process of textual transmission.[10] Weitzman, however, believed that a s-Ps free of the influence of LXX never existed, although in his opinion the translator, who was working from the Hebrew text, sometimes followed the choices of LXX and sometimes showed himself independent.[11]

Lund[12] and Carbajosa have argued strongly for the absence of the influence of LXX on the original translation of s-Ps. Carbajosa[13] has shown that Greek readings entered the manuscripts of s-Ps during the process of its textual transmission, in the wake of the growing prestige of LXX and of the Greek language and literature in general, in both the Western and Eastern Syriac Churches. In a group of manuscripts, s[10t1, 12t2, 12t5, 12t7], this influence is particularly visible.

10.3.4.4 Identity of the Translator(s)

With regard to the book of Psalms, Weitzman[14] considers that the Syriac translation is the work of a Jewish community that had given up rabbinic Judaism (in which it had translated the Pentateuch into Syriac) and had embraced Christianity. In this way, it would be possible to explain some theological features peculiar to s-Ps that do not agree with rabbinic Judaism, as well as the readings that, in his opinion, reflect the influence of LXX (the version used by Christians; → 10.3.1) on the translator. The hypothesis of a Judeo-Christian origin attempts in fact to explain both the data that point toward a Jewish origin and those (few) that hint at a Christian context.

In his monograph on s-Ps, Carbajosa concludes that "most of the traits of a theological or exegetical character that have been identified are quite ambiguous with regard to the matter of the identity of the author."[15] However, there are two terms in the Syriac translation of the Psalms that seem to betray a Christian origin, the nouns ܥܕܬܐ and ܟܢܘܫܬܐ (both meaning "assembly"). In fact, Carbajosa says that

> the Syriac version shows a clear interest in avoiding the use of ܥܕܬܐ in a "negative" context, regardless of the terms that MT uses [normally קהל or עדה]. Instead, it uses the noun ܟܢܘܫܬܐ. This translation policy seems to imply a Christian background, which is interested in preserving the noun ܥܕܬܐ, applied since the beginning of Syriac

---

[8] Carbajosa, *The Character*, 376–78.

[9] Baethgen, "Der textkritische Werth der alten Übersetzungen zu den Psalmen," 405–59, 593–667; Oppenheim, *Die syrische Übersetzung des fünften Buches der Psalmen*; Berg, *The Influence of the Septuagint upon the Pešittâ Psalter*; Barnes, "On the Influence of the Septuagint on the Peshitta," 186–97.

[10] Vogel, "Studien zum Peschitta-Psalter," 32–56, 198–231, 336–63, 481–502.

[11] Weitzman, "The Peshitta Psalter and its Hebrew Vorlage," 341–54.

[12] Lund, "The Influence of the Septuagint on the Peshitta."

[13] Carbajosa, "The Syriac Old Testament Tradition," 109–30.

[14] Weitzman, "The Origin of the Peshitta Psalter," 277–98; Weitzman, "From Judaism to Christianity: The Syriac Version of the Hebrew Bible," 147–73; Weitzman, *The Syriac Version of the Old Testament*.

[15] Carbajosa, *The Character*, 155.

Christian literature to the Church, to the detriment of the other noun, ܟܢܘܫܬܐ, with which the same literature identified the synagogue of the Jews. The combined use of ܥܡܐ with the plural ܥܡ̈ܡܐ (ܥܡܐ ܕܥܡ̈ܡܐ, *Church of the gentiles*, according to the Syriac literature referred to), deviating from MT, seems to support the Christian origin of these readings. It is still an open question whether this translation policy should be attributed to the translator or to a later Christian reviser. If it is attributed to the translator, he would very likely be a Christian of Jewish origin, which would explain his familiarity with the Jewish interpretive traditions identified in P-Ps.[16]

10.3.4.5 Translation Technique

One of the most characteristic traits of S-Ps is the clarity of its translation. It is a version whose final result is readable and fully comprehensible, more concerned with the reader than with fidelity to each of the details of the text.

Three phenomena characteristic of S-Ps illustrate the (free) character of this translation: accommodation to the context, harmonization, and assimilation. Accommodation to the context is a very frequent device by which the Syriac version clearly deviates from its Hebrew base text and accommodates the translation to the immediate context, following a certain logic or overcoming a certain difficulty. Harmonization and assimilation are two very similar devices by which some details of the source text are modified, bringing them closer to other details of one or several similar texts in the same psalm, another psalm, or other books of the Bible. This is one of the most striking phenomena of S-Ps, given the freedom with which the Hebrew base text is modified. In these cases, it is not always easy to know whether the device is conscious or unconscious, nor is it simple to determine whether the harmonization or assimilation should be attributed to the Syriac translator (or a later copyist) or whether it was already found in its Hebrew *Vorlage*.

10.3.4.6 The Hebrew *Vorlage* of the Peshitta Psalms

In the textual criticism of the Psalms, the Peshitta "should be used with caution, bearing in mind the freedom with which it deals with the original text, and knowing that this is a version more concerned with ultimate clarity than with the exact reproduction of each of the elements of its source text ..." In many cases (especially those that are included under the categories of accommodation to the context, harmonization, and assimilation), "the reading of P-Ps clearly departs from MT without any need to consider the hypothesis of a Hebrew *Vorlage* different from MT as the origin of the Syriac *lectio*"[17] (→ 10.2.2).

Nevertheless, in numerous cases the testimony of S-Ps, together with LXX (→ 10.3.1) or other ancient versions or together with the Qumran manuscripts (→ 10.2.1), preserves readings that go back to a Hebrew *Vorlage* different from MT. In addition, in some cases, together with other versions or alone, S-Ps is a witness to an alternative vocalization to that of MT. The cases in which S-Ps may be alone in preserving Hebrew readings that are alternatives to those of MT are more unusual.

Attention should be paid to the extra-Masoretic S-Ps–LXX–Targum (→ 10.3.3) agreements, which normally go back to a Hebrew *Vorlage* different from MT. Carbajosa has, in addition, underlined the importance of extra-Masoretic S-Ps–Targum agreements as a source of possible Hebrew readings that differ from MT, especially when the Aramaic version preserves two alternative readings of the same Hebrew term, one of which coincides with S-Ps.[18]

Special attention is merited by the agreements between S-Ps and some Qumran manuscripts that so far have not been taken into account. However, it is necessary to avoid hasty conclusions about the relationship between the Hebrew textual families found at Qumran and the Hebrew *Vorlage* of the Peshitta.

---

[16] Carbajosa, *The Character*, 176.

[17] Carbajosa, *The Character*, 389.
[18] Carbajosa, *The Character*, 389.

The fact that Qumran scroll 11QPs^a (→ 10.2.1.2; → 10.2.3.2) shares some common readings with s-Ps is what led Flint to suggest that "[t]he relationship between scrolls such as 11QPs^a and the Syriac Psalter may be profitably explored, since many readings and even entire compositions (e.g. Psalms 151, 154, 155) are common to both."[19] Carbajosa[20] has explored this question by comparing the variants of 11QPs^a with respect to MT, with the Syriac translation in Pss 120–134 (a substantial portion of the forty canonical psalms which, in part or in whole, are contained in this manuscript). He concludes:

> In the Psalms studied, the Hebrew *Vorlage* of P does not follow the textual tradition attested in 11QPs^a. On the contrary, this study reveals a close relationship between the Hebrew *Vorlage* of P and the textual tradition of MT, not only because of the numerous cases in which both agree in contrast with 11QPs^a, but also because of those cases in which P can be derived (by means of translation techniques) from a text like MT despite the apparent contradiction between the two.[21]

Flint's suggestion also referred to the apocryphal psalms (Psalms 151; 154; and 155) contained in 11QPs^a, which might hypothetically be found in the manuscript tradition of the Peshitta. However, it cannot be said that Psalms 151; 154; and 155 belong to the manuscript tradition of the Peshitta. The first of these psalms, which also appears in LXX (→ 10.3.1), is not present in any of the Peshitta manuscripts prior to the tenth century. In later manuscripts, it seems clear that Psalm 151 arrives via the Syro-Hexaplaric version (→ 10.4.4) and because of the important role of LXX. In the same way, Psalms 154 and 155 only appear in a manuscript of the twelfth century of the Peshitta Psalter (s^12t4). Apart from this biblical manuscript, these apocryphal psalms appear, with different numeration, in manuscripts from the fourteenth century and later as filler material between the first and second part of a theological work of Eliah of al-Anbār, a tenth-century Nestorian bishop.

10.3.4.7 Auxiliary Tools

Among the auxiliary tools for the study of s-Ps, Sprenger's concordance should be highlighted since it has the advantage, unlike the other volumes in the same collection, of indicating the Hebrew equivalents of each Syriac lemma.[22] However, it must be used with caution since it contains numerous errors.

While the English translation of s-Ps to be carried out in the Bible of Edessa project has not yet appeared in 2016, the English translation published in the mid-nineteenth century by Oliver is useful.[23] This translation attempts to follow the King James Version whenever the Syriac does not depart from the Hebrew. In the places where s-Ps does depart from MT (→ 10.2.2), the author gives a literal translation, adding a note in which he calls attention to the variant and, in many cases, attempts to give an explanation of it.

Baethgen, F., *Untersuchungen über die Psalmen nach der Peshitta* (Kiel: Schwers'sche Buchhandlung, 1878).

Baethgen, F., "Der textkritische Werth der alten Übersetzungen zu den Psalmen," *Jahrbücher für protestantische Theologie* 8 (1882): 405–59, 593–667.

Barnes, W.E., *An Apparatus Criticus to Chronicles in the Peshitta Version: With a Discussion of the Value of the Codex Ambrosianus* (Cambridge: Cambridge University Press, 1897).

Barnes, W.E., "On the Influence of the Septuagint on the Peshitta," *JTS* 2 (1901): 186–97.

Barnes, W.E. (ed.), *The Peshitta Psalter according to the West Syrian Text: Edited with an Apparatus Criticus* (Cambridge: Cambridge University Press, 1904).

Berg, J.F., *The Influence of the Septuagint upon the Pešittâ Psalter* (New York: W. Drugulin, 1895).

Carbajosa, I., "11QPs^a and the Hebrew Vorlage of the Peshitta Psalter," *Aramaic Studies* 2 (2004): 3–24.

Carbajosa, I., "The Syriac Old Testament Tradition: Moving from Jerusalem to Athens," in *Eastern Crossroads:*

---

[19] Flint, *The Dead Sea Psalms Scrolls and the Book of Psalms*, 241.
[20] Carbajosa, "11QPs^a and the Hebrew Vorlage," 3–24.
[21] Carbajosa, "11QPs^a and the Hebrew Vorlage," 24.

[22] Sprenger, *Konkordanz zum Syrischen Psalter*.
[23] Oliver, *A Translation of the Syriac Peshito Version of the Psalms of David with Notes Critical and Explanatory*.

Essays on Medieval Christian Legacy (ed. J.P. Monferrer Sala; Gorgias Eastern Christian Studies 1; Piscataway: Gorgias Press, 2007), 109–30.

Carbajosa, I., *The Character of the Syriac Version of Psalms: A Study of Psalms 90–150 in the Peshitta* (Monographs of the Peshitta Institute Leiden 17; Leiden: Brill, 2008).

Carbajosa, I., "The Division between Western and Eastern Manuscripts in the Peshitta Psalter: An Insurmountable Obstacle for a Critical Edition?" *Aramaic Studies* 6 (2008): 145–74.

Diettrich, G., *Ein Apparatus criticus zur Pešitto zum Propheten Jesaia* (BZAW 8; Giessen: De Gruyter, 1905).

Dirksen, P.B., "East and West, Old and Young, in the Text Tradition of the Old Testament Peshitta," *VT* 35 (1985): 468–84.

Eriksson, J.-E., "The Hymns of David Interpreted in Syriac: A Study of Translation Technique in the First Book of Psalms (Ps 1–41) in the Pešitta" (PhD diss., University of Uppsala, 1989).

Flint, P.W., *The Dead Sea Psalms Scrolls and the Book of Psalms* (STDJ 17; Leiden: Brill, 1997).

Koster, M.D., *The Peshitta of Exodus: The Development of its Text in the Course of Fifteen Centuries* (SSN 19; Assen: Van Gorcum, 1977).

Lund, J.A., "The Influence of the Septuagint on the Peshitta: A Re-evaluation of Criteria in Light of Comparative Study of the Versions in Genesis and Psalms" (PhD diss., The Hebrew University of Jerusalem, 1988).

Oliver, A., *A Translation of the Syriac Peshito Version of the Psalms of David with Notes Critical and Explanatory* (New York: James Pott, 1867).

Oppenheim, B., *Die syrische Übersetzung des fünften Buches der Psalmen (Psalm 107–150) und ihr Verhältnis zu dem massoretischen Texte und den älteren Übersetzungen, namentlich den LXX, Trg.* (Leipzig: W. Drugulin, 1891).

Rahlfs, A., "Beiträge zur Textkritik der Peshitta," *ZAW* 9 (1889): 161–210.

Rahlfs, A., *Septuaginta-Studien. II: Der Text des Septuaginta-Psalters* (2nd ed.; Göttingen: Vandenhoeck & Ruprecht, 1965).

Rowlands, E.R., "A Critical Study of the Peshitta Text of Psalms, Books III and IV (Pss. 73–106) in Relation to the Massoretic Text and the Septuagint Version" (PhD diss., Bangor University, 1939).

Sprenger, N., *Konkordanz zum Syrischen Psalter* (Göttinger Orientforschungen: Syriaca 10.8; Wiesbaden: Harrassowitz, 1976).

Vogel, A., "Studien zum Peschitta-Psalter besonders im Hinblick auf sein Verhältnis zu Septuagint," *Bib* 32 (1951): 32–56, 198–231, 336–63, 481–502.

Walter, D.M., A. Vogel, and R.Y. Ebied (eds.), *The Book of Psalms* (The Old Testament in Syriac according to the Peshitta Version 2.3; Leiden: Brill, 1980).

Weitzman, M.P., "A Statistical Approach to Textual Criticism with Special Reference to the Peshitta of the Old Testament" (PhD diss., University of London, 1973).

Weitzman, M.P., "The Origin of the Peshitta Psalter," in *Interpreting the Hebrew Bible: Essays in Honour of E.I.J. Rosenthal* (eds. J.A. Emerton and S.C. Reif; Cambridge: Cambridge University Press, 1982), 277–98.

Weitzman, M.P., "The Peshitta Psalter and its Hebrew Vorlage," *VT* 35 (1985): 341–54.

Weitzman, M.P., "The Originality of Unique Readings in Peshitta MS 9a1," in *The Peshitta: Its Early Text and History. Papers Read at the Peshitta Symposium Held at Leiden 30–31 August 1985* (eds. P.B. Dirksen and M.J. Mulder; Monographs of the Peshitta Institute Leiden 4; Leiden: Brill, 1988), 225–58.

Weitzman, M.P., "From Judaism to Christianity: The Syriac Version of the Hebrew Bible," in *The Jews among the Pagans and Christians: In the Roman Empire* (eds. J. Lieu, J. North, and T. Rajak; London: Routledge, 1992), 147–73.

Weitzman, M.P., *The Syriac Version of the Old Testament: An Introduction* (University of Cambridge Oriental Publications 56; Cambridge: Cambridge University Press, 1999).

Ignacio Carbajosa

10.3.5 Hexaplaric Greek Translations

10.3.5.1 Background

LXX-Pss (→ 10.3.1) exhibits a literal translation technique applied to a text similar to proto-MT (→ 10.2.2).[1] The revisions of Theodotion and Aquila developed the literalness of this version, while Symmachus revised the version according to proto-MT in readable Greek.[2]

---

[1] For an excellent discussion of the original form of LXX-Pss, cf. → 10.3.1.2.

[2] → 1.3.1.2.

10.3.5.2 Sources, Editions, and Auxiliary Tools

Since the publication of Field's edition, new evidence has expanded the collection of Hexaplaric fragments.[3] In addition to the sources cited in Fernandez Marcos, there has been significant work done on the Palestinian Catena of Psalms.[4] This catena is most relevant for a collection of Hexaplaric fragments, since it contains the relevant Greek church fathers: Origen, Eusebius, Theodoret, Didymus, Apollinaris, Athanasius, Chrysostom, and Hesychius. Of the six manuscripts identified as containing the Palestinian Catena of Psalms, Field incorporated only two (LXX[1133] and LXX[1175]). Subsequent research has shown that these manuscripts are not only low on the manuscript stemma but they also descend from the same putative *Vorlage*. Harl and Dorival identified two manuscripts as the principal witnesses to the catena (LXX[1675] [Pss 83:4–150] and LXX[1756] [Psalms 78–150]).[5] These two scholars prepared the materials of Psalm 118 and Curti edited the materials for the Psalms of Ascent (Psalms 119–33) and has also provided long sections of these manuscripts in his work on Eusebius' commentary of the Psalms, which contained Hexaplaric fragments. These manuscripts need to be collated completely both for patristic exegetical fragments and Hexaplaric fragments.

There is no critical edition of the Hexaplaric fragments of the Psalter, and Rahlfs' critical edition of LXX-Pss[6] does not contain a second apparatus, which in subsequent editions is a repository for the Hexaplaric fragments. The most recent collection of the Hexaplaric fragments of the Psalter is Field's work published in 1875.[7] Therefore, as of 2015, a new edition of the Hexaplaric fragments of the Psalter in conjunction with the ongoing work of establishing the critical edition of the Greek Psalter is a clear *desideratum*. For auxiliary tools related to the Hexapla, see the bibliography.

10.3.5.3 Translation Character and Technique
10.3.5.3.1 Theodotion

Theodotion employs a formal translation technique where he seeks to render each word of his Hebrew source in the same word order of the source. Ps 87(86 LXX):5–6a provides a good example:

MT-Pss וּלֲצִיּוֹן יֵאָמַר אִישׁ וְאִישׁ יֻלַּד־בָּהּ וְהוּא יְכוֹנְנֶהָ עֶלְיוֹן: יְהוָה יִסְפֹּר בִּכְתוֹב עַמִּים
And of Zion it shall be said, "This one and that one were born in it"; for the Most High himself will establish it. The Lord records, as he registers the peoples (*NRSV*)

LXX-Pss Μήτηρ Σιών, ἐρεῖ ἄνθρωπος, καὶ ἄνθρωπος ἐγενήθη ἐν αὐτῇ, καὶ αὐτὸς ἐθεμελίωσεν αὐτὴν ὁ ὕψιστος. κύριος διηγήσεται ἐν γραφῇ λαῶν
With regard to Sion [note Rahlfs has "Mother Sion"], surely no person will say, "And a person was born in it?" And himself founded it – the Most High! The Lord will recount, in a list of peoples (*NETS*)

Th-Pss καὶ τῇ Ζιών ῥηθήσεται, ἀνὴρ καὶ ἀνὴρ ἐγεννήθη ἐν αὐτῇ, καὶ αὐτὸς ἡτοίμασεν αὐτὴν ὁ ὕψιστος. κύριος διηγήσεται ἐν γραφῇ λαῶν.
And to Zion it will be said, "Each one will be born in it"; and the Most High himself founded it. The Lord will recount in a list of peoples.

This fragment illustrates that Theodotion revised LXX according to the Hebrew. For וּלֲצִיּוֹן "and of Zion," LXX-Pss has μήτηρ Σιών "Mother Sion," which Theodotion revised to καὶ τῇ Ζιών "and to Zion," which is in closer alignment with the Hebrew. For the יֵאָמַר *Niphal* "it shall be said," LXX-Pss has an active verb, ἐρεῖ "will say," while Theodotion has the passive ῥηθήσεται "it will be said," agreeing with the vocalization of MT. For אִישׁ וְאִישׁ "this one and that one," LXX-Pss has ἄνθρωπος, καὶ ἄνθρωπος "person, and person," reading ἄνθρωπος[1] "person" with the active verb in the first line and ἄνθρωπος[2] "person" with ἐγενήθη "was born" in the second line. LXX-Pss uses ἀνθρώπος for אִישׁ (both meaning

---

[3] Field, *Hexapla*. For the evidence relevant to the Hexapla of Psalms that has appeared since Field, *Hexapla*, see Fernandez Marcos, *Introduction*, 113–15. Cf. also Schenker, *Psalmen in den Hexapla*, which appeared after the work by Fernandez Marcos and analyzed the Hexaplaric notes in Ott. Gr. 398 (= LXX[264]).

[4] Curti, *La catena palestinese*; Curti, *Eusebiana I*; Dorival, "L'apport des chaines exégétiques grecques"; Harl and Dorival, *La chaîne palestinienne*.

[5] Rahlfs, *Verzeichnis*, 129, 218.

[6] Rahlfs, *Psalmi cum Odis*.

[7] Field, *Hexapla*.

"person") in many places (e.g., Pss 4:2; 21:6; 30:20; 33:12; 36:7). By contrast, Theodotion understood the construction as a distributive and rendered it with ἀνὴρ καὶ ἀνήρ "each one." The rendering of אִישׁ with ἀνήρ (both meaning "person"), even when used for the distributive, is a trait of the καίγε group, which Theodotion used elsewhere (cf. Th-Job 41:9a).[8] Aquila also has ἀνὴρ καὶ ἀνήρ "each one." Symmachus has καθ' ἕκαστον "each one," ἄνθρωπος "person" indicating that he read the Hebrew as a distributive and also revised the Greek since he includes ἄνθρωπος[2] "person" as the subject of the following verb. In this instance, Theodotion contrasts with LXX-Pss. Theodotion is closer to the καίγε group and Aquila than to LXX-Pss.

10.3.5.3.2 Aquila

The Aquila materials indicate that he employed a formal equivalence translation technique, which attempted to render each Hebrew element with a Greek equivalent isomorphically. On the word level, Aquila's version is very literal and demonstrates the concordance principle of translation, even employing equivalents to maintain etymological connections between Hebrew and Greek. However, when Aquila's syntax and Greek vocabulary are considered, his version furnishes more appropriate and even ingenious renderings of the Hebrew source.[9]

Ps 89(88 LXX):8 provides a good example:

MT-Pss אֵל נַעֲרָץ בְּסוֹד־קְדֹשִׁים רַבָּה וְנוֹרָא עַל־כָּל־סְבִיבָיו
a God feared in the council of the holy ones, great and awesome above all that are around him? (*NRSV)

LXX-Pss ὁ θεὸς ἐνδοξαζόμενος ἐν βουλῇ ἁγίων, μέγας καὶ φοβερὸς ἐπὶ πάντας τοὺς περικύκλῳ αὐτοῦ
God is glorified in a council of holy ones, great and awesome to all that are around him. (*NETS)

Aq-Pss ἰσχυρὸς κατισχυρευόμενος ἐν ἀπορρήτῳ ἁγίων, πλῆθος καὶ ἐπίφοβος ἐπὶ πάντας κύκλῳ αὐτοῦ.
a Powerful One is strengthing himself in a secret of holy ones, great and terrible to all that are around him.

Aquila provides a quantitative rendering of the Hebrew. The equivalent ἰσχυρός "Powerful One" for אֵל "God" is a characteristic of Aquila's version (cf. Pss 21:2; 35:7; 80:10; 81:1; 84:9) and is one of the precursor equivalences present in the καίγε tradition and perfected by Aquila.[10] Theodotion and the καίγε group used this same equivalent usually with the article (e.g., ὁ ἰσχυρός "the Powerful One"; cf. Th-Job 22:13a, 33:29a), but Aquila employed it as a proper noun usually without the definite article.[11] LXX-Pss in this verse uses ὁ θεός "the God" and Symmachus used the vocative θεέ "O God."

10.3.5.3.3 Symmachus

Symmachus produced a revision of LXX (→ 10.3.1) that was faithful to the sense of the Hebrew (→ 10.2.2) in readable Greek.[12]

Ps 87(86 LXX):5–6a provides a good example of Symmachus:

MT-Pss וּלְצִיּוֹן יֵאָמַר אִישׁ וְאִישׁ יֻלַּד־בָּהּ וְהוּא יְכוֹנְנֶהָ עֶלְיוֹן יְהוָה יִסְפֹּר בִּכְתוֹב עַמִּים זֶה יֻלַּד־שָׁם
And of Zion it shall be said, "This one and that one were born in it"; for the Most High himself will establish it. The Lord records, as he registers the peoples, "This one was born there." (*NRSV)

LXX-Pss Μήτηρ Σιών, ἐρεῖ ἄνθρωπος, καὶ ἄνθρωπος ἐγενήθη ἐν αὐτῇ, καὶ αὐτὸς ἐθεμελίωσεν αὐτὴν ὁ ὕψιστος. κύριος διηγήσεται ἐν γραφῇ λαῶν καὶ ἀρχόντων τούτων τῶν γεγενημένων ἐν αὐτῇ
With regard to Sion [note Rahlfs has "Mother Sion"], surely no person will say, "And a person was born in it?" And himself founded it – the Most High! The Lord will recount, in a list of peoples and rulers, those that were born in it. (*NETS)

Sym-Pss περί τε Σιὼν λεχθήσεται καθ' ἕκαστον, ἄνθρωπος οὗτος ἐτέχθη ἐκεῖ, αὐτὸς δὲ ἥδρασεν αὐτὴν ὁ ὕψιστος. κύριος ἀριθμήσει γράφων λαούς, οὗτος ἐτέχθη ἐκεῖ
And concerning Sion it will be said singly, 'this man was born there.' And he established it, the Most High. The Lord will count, writing the peoples, 'this one was born there'.

---

[8] → 1.3.1.2.2.2.
[9] Hyvärinen, *Die Übersetzung von Aquila*, 111–12.
[10] → 1.3.1.2.2.3.2.1.
[11] → 1.3.1.2.2.3.2.1.
[12] → 1.3.1.2.5; cf. Salvesen, *Symmachus*, 198.

Symmachus provides a functional equivalence translation of this verse, which follows the Hebrew word order. Symmachus rendered יֵאָמֵר *Niphal* "it will be said" with a middle-passive verb λεχθήσεται "it will be said," while LXX-Pss has the active ἐρεῖ "he will say." As noted above, Symmachus renders the Hebrew distributive אִישׁ וְאִישׁ "each one" with an idiomatic Greek expression (καθ' ἕκαστον "singly") in contrast to Theodotion and Aquila. Symmachus adds the demonstrative pronoun οὗτος "this," which is not represented in the Hebrew. Perhaps Symmachus made recourse to the last part of the verse in Hebrew, which has זֶה "this," for his rendering here. LXX-Pss does not have the demonstrative pronoun. Another difference between Symmachus and LXX-Pss is the rendering of בָּהּ "in it." Symmachus uses ἐκεῖ "there," while LXX-Pss has ἐν αὐτῇ "in it." Symmachus renders *waw* "and" with δέ "now" where both Theodotion and LXX-Pss have καί "and." This example illustrates Symmachus' reaction to the καίγε tradition and its ultra-literal principles and his desire for a more readable Greek translation.

10.3.5.4 Inner-Translational Features

The provisional nature of Field and the work done on the Palestinian Catena by Curti, Harl, and Dorival provide warrant for a few comments regarding Hexapla criticism of the Psalms.

First, some of the fragments from the Palestinian Catena are new or provide significant variants to already known fragments. In Ps 93:15, LXX[1675] contains the following note and attribution in a comment attributed to Theodoret: Σαφέστερον δὲ Σύμμαχος· καὶ ἀκολουθήσουσιν [= אַחַר "after"; also in Sym-Ps 77:71] αὐτῇ πάντες οἱ εὐθεῖς τῇ καρδίᾳ· ὁ δὲ Ἀκύλας καὶ Θεοδοτίων· καὶ ὀπίσω αὐτοῦ [= אַחֲרָיו "after it/him"] πάντες οἱ εὐθεῖς τῇ καρδίᾳ "But more clearly Symmachus: And all the straight in heart will follow it; but Aquila and Theodotion: and after it / him are all the straight in heart."[13] The Symmachus fragment is new to the corpus of Hexaplaric fragments, since Field did not use or have access to LXX[1675]. Concerning the fragment of Aquila and Theodotion, Field had αὐτῆς "it" instead of αὐτοῦ "it." He listed this variant in a footnote, but it is probably the original text since: 1) it agrees with the Hebrew pronoun in gender; 2) αὐτῆς "it" probably arose due to secondary influence from the Bible text; and 3) αὐτοῦ "him/it" now appears in the best textual witness to the Palestinian Catena.

Second, the Palestinian Catena also confirms retroversions of fragments known only from the Syro-Hexapla. In Ps 121:4, Field lists his retroversion of the Syro-Hexapla for Symmachus: ἐκκλησία τῷ Ἰσραήλ "assembly in Israel." The catena preserves the same reading in Greek in a comment attributed to Eusebius.[14] The reading is now based on a surer foundation from the Greek catena.

Third, Ps 131:18b provides a final example of the significance of this catena for a critical edition of the Hexaplaric fragments. Field listed Aq ἀφόρισμα αὐτοῦ "his distinction" Syh and Sym ὁ ἁγιασμὸς αὐτοῦ "his holiness" Syh Nobil. The catena provides the following: Aq καὶ ἐπ' αὐτὸν ἀνθήσει ἀφόρισμα αὐτοῦ "and upon him his distinction will shine" and Sym αὐτῷ δ' ἐπανθήσει ὁ ἁγιασμὸς αὐτοῦ "but for him his holiness will be bright." Field had two words retroverted from the Syro-Hexapla for both Aquila and Symmachus. The Palestinian Catena confirmed the retroversions of Field and preserved the entire line for both revisers in an exegetical fragment attributed to Eusebius.[15]

These fragments and more like them will need to be included in the Hexapla Institute's future critical edition of the Hexaplaric fragments of Psalms.

10.3.5.5 Text-Critical Value for the Hebrew Text

Sometimes the versions of the Three reflect variant Hebrew readings. An example of this phenomenon comes at Ps 9:21. Here are the relevant texts of the Three from Field:

---

[13] Curti, *Eusebiana I*, 45.

[14] Curti, *La catena palestinese*, 55.

[15] Curti, *La catena palestinese*, 195.

MT	שִׁיתָה יְהוָה מוֹרָה לָהֶם	
	Put them in fear, O Lord (*NRSV)	
LXX	κατάστησον, κύριε, νομοθέτην ἐπ' αὐτούς	= מוֹרֶה
	Set a lawgiver over them, O Lord	= lawgiver
Th	κατάστησον, κύριε, φόβον αὐτοῖς	= מוֹרָא
	Set fear for them, O Lord	= fear
Aq	θοῦ, κύριε, φόβημα, αὐτοῖς	= מוֹרָא
	Place fear for them, O Lord	= fear
Sym	τάξον, κύριε, νόμον αὐτοῖς	= מוֹרָה
	Assign a law/instruction for them, O Lord	= law/ instruction

The word in Codex Leningradensis and the Aleppo Codex is II מוֹרָה, which is otherwise unattested in the Hebrew Bible. It is sometimes suggested that this word ought to be read as מוֹרָא "fear," which is actually attested in Kennicott manuscripts 239, 266 and de Rossi manuscripts 31, 39, 196, 231, 277, and 828.[16] The cause of the variant could be attributed to א/ה confusion.[17] The -מ prefix combined with the -ָה suffix could mark a noun from III ירה "to teach, instruct," which could then indicate a form parallel with תּוֹרָה "instruction, teaching." Therefore, the noun probably means "instruction" and this appears to be how Symmachus (νόμον) understood it, since he renders words of the ירא group most often with words of the φοβ group in Greek.[18] LXX-Pss read the consonants of MT but probably understood the form as מוֹרֶה, the Hiphil participle from III ירה, meaning "teacher, lawgiver." Theodotion and Aquila read מוֹרָא "fear." The versions of Aquila and Theodotion are significant because they attest to the early reading "fear," which appeared later in some of the Hebrew manuscript tradition. Symmachus, however, confirms that the consonantal text of Leningrad and Aleppo should be read "instruction."

---

[16] For example, see HALOT, II מוֹרָה.
[17] An alternative view is that the Greek versions could be employing a biliteral exegesis of the יר type (yrʾ / yrh). For biliteral exegesis in the Septuagint, cf. Tov, *HB, GB, and Qumran, 378–97.
[18] Busto Saiz, La traducción de Símaco, 661, 674.

Busto Saiz, J.R., *La traducción de Símaco en el Libro de los Salmos* (Textos y Estudios "Cardenal Cisneros" 22; Madrid: Consejo Superior de Investigaciones Científicas, 1978).

Caloz, M., *Étude sur la LXX origénienne du psautier: les relations entre les leçons des psaumes du manuscrit Coislin 44, les fragments des Hexaples et le texte du psautier Gallican* (OBO 16; Göttingen: Vandenhoeck & Ruprecht, 1978).

Curti, C., *Eusebiana I: Commentarii in Psalmos* (Catania: Centro di studi sull'antico cristianesimo, Università di Catania, 1989).

Curti, C., *La catena palestinese sui Salmi graduali: introduzione, edizione critica, traduzione note di commento e indici* (Catania: Centro di studi sull'antico cristianesimo, Università di Catania, 2003).

Dorival, G., "L' apport des chaines exégétiques grecques à une réédition des Hexaples d' Origène (Psaume 118)," in *Revue d' histoire des textes* 4 (1974): 45–74.

Fernández Marcos, *Introduction.

Field, *Hexapla.

Gentry, P.J., *The Asterisked Materials in the Greek Job* (SBLSCS 38; Atlanta: Scholars Press, 1995).

Gentry, P.J., "The Greek Psalter and the καίγε Tradition: Methodological Questions," in *The Old Greek Psalter: Studies in Honor of Albert Pietersma* (eds. R.J.V. Hiebert, C.E. Cox, and P.J. Gentry; JSOTSup 332; Sheffield: Sheffield Academic Press, 2001), 74–97.

Harl, M. and G. Dorival, *La chaîne palestinienne sur le psaume 118 (Origène, Eusèbe, Didyme, Apollinaire, Athanase, Théodoret)* (Paris: Cerf, 1972).

Hyvärinen, K., *Die Übersetzung von Aquila* (ConBOT 10; Uppsala: G.W.K. Gleerup, 1977).

*NETS.

Pietersma, A., "The Present State of the Critical Text of the Greek Psalter," in *Der Septuaginta-Psalter und seine Tochterübersetzungen: Symposium in Göttingen 1997* (eds. A. Aejmelaeus and U. Quast; MSU 24; Vandenhoeck & Ruprecht, 2000), 12–32.

Rahlfs, A., *Verzeichnis der griechischen Handschriften des Alten Testaments für das Septuaginta-Unternehmen* (Berlin: Weidmann, 1914).

Rahlfs, A., *Psalmi cum Odis* (3rd ed.; Septuaginta Vetus Testamentum Graecum 10; Göttingen: Vandenhoeck & Ruprecht, 1979).

Reider, J. and N. Turner, *An Index to Aquila: Greek-Hebrew, Hebrew-Greek, Latin-Hebrew* (Leiden: Brill, 1966).

Salvesen, A., *Symmachus in the Pentateuch* (JSS Mono

graph 15; Manchester: Victoria University of Manchester, 1991).

Schenker, A., *Hexaplarische Psalmenbruchstücke: Die hexaplarischen Psalmenfragmente der Handschriften Vaticanus graecus 752 und Canonicianus graecus 62* (OBO 8; Göttingen: Vandenhoeck & Ruprecht, 1975).

Schenker, A., *Psalmen in den Hexapla: Erste kritische und vollständige Ausgabe der hexaplarischen Fragmente auf dem Rande der Handschrift Ottobonianus Graecus 398 zu den PS 24–32* (Vatican City: Vatican Library, 1982).

John D. Meade

10.3.6 Post-Hexaplaric Greek Translations

10.3.6.1 Background

The only post-Hexaplaric recension known to us is that of Lucian. In Jerome's letter to Sunnias and Fretela, he attributes the "common" (κοινή) version of the Psalter to Lucian.[1] Jerome corrects the notion that Lucian's revision was the most reliable text (i.e., LXX). Lucian's text is distinct from Origen's text (→ 10.3.5), which was the source text for Jerome's Latin translation of the Psalter (→ 10.3.7; → 10.4.1). The widespread use of Lucian's recension of the Psalter is noted by Fernández Marcos, who suggests that the text was standardized through liturgy alongside Lucian's revision of the New Testament. The resultant text became the official version of the Psalter in Byzantium.[2] The extent of Lucianic improvements in LXX-Pss has been questioned by Perkins, whose study of LXX-Pss 72–82 demonstrates "little affinity between the 'Lucianic' characteristics or tendencies which appeared in Reigns and the characteristics and tendencies of the L group in the Psalter."[3]

10.3.6.2 Original Form, Editions, Auxiliary Tools

Although a critical edition of the Psalter exists,[4] it does not incorporate relatively new witnesses such as Bodmer papyrus 2110 and other significant witnesses. Nonetheless, it is the best reference for Lucianic readings. Rahlfs notes that there are more than one hundred manuscripts in the edition of Holmes and Parsons of the Septuagint[5] that preserve the text of L.[6] Hence, their edition of LXX-Pss (→ 10.3.1) is indispensable. The ubiquity of the witnesses lends credibility to Jerome's comment about how widely the text had circulated. In addition to the many Greek manuscripts that preserve the recension, Theodoret, Chrysostom, the correctors of Codices Vaticanus and Sinaiticus, and the Syro-Hexapla (→ 10.4.4) preserve Lucianic variants. Papyri LXX^{1046} and LXX^{2040} also evince the LXX^L text. Ancillary studies, such as Pietersma's analysis of the textual affiliations of Chester Beatty Papyrus XIII (LXX^{2149}), improves the textual picture of all Greek witnesses of the Psalter, including the LXX^L group, which preserves thirty-four sub-singular agreements with papyrus LXX^{2149}.[7]

10.3.6.3 Translation Character and Technique

The characteristics of the Lucianic Psalter follow patterns found elsewhere in the recension.[8] The LXX^L text of the Psalter regularly employs εἶπον for εἶπαν "they said". The preference for second aorist forms and other Atticisms in Lucianic witnesses has been questioned by Perkins. He suggests that medieval copyists may have introduced variants from Classical Greek grammar or that Hellenistic forms were not always employed during the late Hellenistic period so that Attic forms may be

---

[1] B. Metzger, *The Text of the New Testament: Its Transmission, Corruption, and Restoration* (3rd ed.; Oxford: Oxford University Press, 1992), 274.

[2] N. Fernández Marcos, "Some Reflections on the Text of the Antiochian Septuagint," in *Studien zur Septuaginta – Robert Hanhart zu Ehren* (eds. D. Fraenkel, U. Quast, and J.W. Wevers; MSU 20; Göttingen: Vandenhoeck and Ruprecht, 1990), 219–30 (221).

[3] Perkins, "The So-called 'L' Text of Psalms 72–82," 60.

[4] A. Rahlfs (ed.), *Psalmi cum Odis* (3rd ed.; Septuaginta Vetus Testamentum Graecum 10; Göttingen: Vandenhoeck & Ruprecht, 1979).

[5] A.R. Holmes and J. Parsons, *Vetus Testamentum Graecum cum Variis Lectionibus* (Oxford: Clarendon Press, 1732).

[6] Rahlfs, *Psalmi cum Odis*, 61.

[7] This unpublished data was given to me by Peter Gentry.

[8] The characteristics of the Lucianic recension are fairly uniform, though they vary in degree of distribution. For a list of characteristics, see Ziegler, "Hat Lukian den griechischen Sirach rezensiert?"

original to the translation.[9] Nonetheless, the manuscripts evince Attic forms. There is variation of words with and without epenthetic μ (e.g., ἀναλήμψεται and ἀναλήψεται "he will take up"). Hence, Hellenistic forms exist alongside Classical ones.

10.3.6.4 Text-Critical Value

Rahlfs notes that agreements with the Syro-Hexapla (→ 10.4.4) are substantial enough to warrant special attention. This fact is evinced by his text groupings (LXX$^{L'}$ = LXX^{L} + Syh). Likewise, he notes that the Syro-Hexapla commonly preserves doublets, a feature found in LXX^{L}, especially in the books of Kingdoms (→ 3–5.1.6).[10] Pietersma found no evidence for a proto-Lucianic text.[11] Hence, the recension is likely the work of the historical Lucian. The "brilliance of style" in Chrysostom's commentary on the Psalter clouds the picture. For this reason, many readings cannot be attributed to Lucian with certainty. This situation is compounded by the fact that Chrysostom used texts from different textual traditions.[12] Hence, *contaminatio* abounds. Nonetheless, the LXX^{L} text of LXX-Pss is valuable for Byzantine studies wherever the recension can be reconstructed with confidence.

Cimosa, M., "John Chrysostom and the Septuagint (Job and Psalms)," in *XII Congress of the IOSCS: Leiden, 2004* (ed. M.K.H. Peters; SBLSCS 54; Leiden: Brill, 2006), 117–30.
Perkins, L.J., "The So-called 'L' Text of Psalms 72–82," *BIOSCS* 11 (1978): 44–63.
Pietersma, A., "Proto-Lucian and the Greek Psalter," *VT* 27 (1977): 66–72.
Rahlfs, *Septuaginta.
Ziegler, J., "Hat Lukian den griechischen Sirach rezensiert?" *Bib* 40 (1959): 210–29.

Matthew M. Dickie

10.3.7 Vulgate

10.3.7.1 Background

Jerome is associated with no less than three Psalters during his early academic career (see also → 1.3.5). The "Roman Psalter" is a revision completed in Rome in approximately 384 C.E. The work was merely a cursory emendation according to the LXX (→ 10.3.1), as Jerome himself states.[1] After settling in Bethlehem, Jerome undertook a more thorough revision of the Psalter according to Origen's Hexapla (→ 1.3.1.2; → 10.3.5) in ca. 388 C.E.[2] This "Gallican Psalter" (so called because of its early widespread use in Gaul) became dominant following the liturgical reforms of Alcuin, and ultimately was ratified at the Council of Trent as the "Vulgate" Psalter (hereafter v-PsG). In this work, Jerome included the obelus and the asterisk to mark textual divergences between LXX and the Hebrew text (→ 10.2.2).[3]

After publishing the translation of Samuel and Kings, *iuxta Hebraeos* "according to the Hebrews," Jerome yet again turned to the Psalter, releasing a fresh translation from the Hebrew in ca. 392 C.E.[4] This "Hebrew Psalter" (hereafter PsH) was widely reproduced throughout the Latin West until the time of Alcuin, after which it enjoyed only regional popularity (→ 1.3.5.2; → 1.3.5.3; → 1.3.5.4). The Gallican and the Hebrew Psalters are conveniently

---

[9] Perkins, "The So-called 'L' Text of Psalms 72–82," 46.
[10] Rahlfs, *Psalmi cum Odis*, 67.
[11] Pietersma, "Proto-Lucian and the Greek Psalter," 66–72.
[12] Cimosa, "John Chrysostom and the Septuagint (Job and Psalms)," 127.

---

[1] *PsG Prol.* Scholars have questioned whether the transmitted Roman Psalter is the version made by Jerome. De Bruyne has been the strongest opponent of its authenticity ("Le problème du Psautier Romain," 101–26), while Allgeier attempted to demonstrate the authenticity of the work ("Die erste Psalmenübersetzung des Hieronymus," 447–82). See the discussion in Estin, *Les Psautiers de Jérôme*, 26–28.
[2] Jerome seems to have been motivated to revise the Psalter again because his previous edition had fallen victim to textual corruption (see *PsG Prol.*). On the Psalter in general, see Jerome, *Epist.* 106 (to Sunnia and Fretela) where he discusses 178 passages from the Psalms.
[3] The textual symbols are not generally preserved in the Vulgate manuscript tradition.
[4] Jerome claims an apologetic motive in producing the translation (*PsH Prol.*; cf. *Epist.* 112.20 to Augustine, and *Epist.* 106.12).

10.3.7.2 Translation Character

The "Hebrew" Psalter was one of the earliest of Jerome's translations, *iuxta Hebraeos*. As such, the translation is closer to the Hebrew (→ 10.2.2) than later translations of other biblical books. While there are several examples of literalisms that would have seemed harsh to Latin readers of the time, e.g., מִדָּמִים/*de sanguinibus* "from blood" (Ps 50:16 [MT-Ps 51:16]), the translation as a whole is idiomatic. The "Hebrew" Psalter is not slavishly literal.

10.3.7.3 Translation Sources

10.3.7.3.1 Use of LXX

Jerome had already received a solid foundation in Hebrew before he began the *iuxta Hebraeos* translation project. But in translating the Psalms he clearly utilized previous translations, including LXX/VL (→ 10.3.1; → 10.4.1). In very few cases, Jerome agrees with LXX/VL as opposed to the Hebrew and the Hexaplaric versions (→ 1.3.1.2; → 10.3.5). An example may be seen in הַאֻמְנָם אֵלֶם צֶדֶק תְּדַבֵּרוּן "Is it truly in silence that you speak righteousness?" (Ps 57:2 [MT-Ps 58:2]), which Aquila translated as οὐκ ἀληθῶς ἀλαλίᾳ δικαιοσύνην ἐλάλησαν "Not truly in silence did they speak righteousness," and Symmachus rendered as ἆρα ἀληθῶς, φῦλον, δίκαια λαλεῖτε "Do you truly, o people, speak righteous things?" By contrast, LXX has εἰ ἀληθῶς ἄρα δικαιοσύνην λαλεῖτε, which v-PsG and PsH (identical here) follow closely: *si vere utique iustitiam loquimini* "So then do you truly speak righteousness?" Another example of Jerome's agreement with LXX/VL is עֲצַבֵּיהֶם "their idols" (Ps 113:12 [MT-Ps 115:4]), for which LXX has τὰ εἴδωλα τῶν ἐθνῶν "the idols of the nations," represented in v-PsG by *simulacra gentium* "images of the nations" and in PsH by *idola gentium* "idols of the nations."[6]

10.3.7.3.2 Use of Aquila, Symmachus, and Theodotion

Jerome often reflects the renderings of the Hexaplaric versions (→ 1.3.5.10; → 10.3.5). PsH especially shows the influence of Aquila, even on incidental points, e.g., שֵׁבֶט "rod, staff" (Ps 44:7 [MT-Ps 45:7]) is rendered *virga* "staff" in v-PsG (= ῥάβδος in LXX), but *sceptrum* "sceptre" in imitation of Aquila in PsH (= Aquila's σκῆπτρον); and מִיַּד רְשָׁעִים "from the hand of wicked ones" (Ps 96:10 [MT-Ps 97:10]), for which v-PsG has *de manu peccatoris* "from the hand of the sinner" (cf. LXX: ἐκ χειρὸς ἁμαρτωλῶν), is translated based on Aquila in PsH, *de manu impiorum* "from the hand of impious ones" (= Aquila: ἐκ χειρὸς ἀσεβῶν). Jerome also follows Aquila in transliterating Hebrew words that lack a precise equivalent in Latin, e.g., לִוְיָתָן "Leviathan" (Ps 103:26 [MT-Ps 104:26]) becomes *Leviathan* in PsH (= Aquila: Λευιαθάν), as opposed to *draco* "dragon" in v-PsG (= LXX: δράκων); and כִּנֹּרוֹתֵינוּ "our lyres" (Ps 136:2 [MT-Ps 137:2]) is translated *citharas nostras* "our citharas" in PsH (= Aquila: κιθάρας ἡμῶν), and not *organa nostra* "our instruments" as in v-PsG (= LXX: τὰ ὄργανα ἡμῶν) (see also Ps 149:3).

While Aquila certainly provided assistance for the translation of PsH, Symmachus (→ 10.3.5) was also utilized, especially when Symmachus' rendering was closer to the meaning of the Hebrew than Aquila and/or LXX. For example, כִּי רֶגַע בְּאַפּוֹ "because a moment in his anger" (Ps 29:6 [MT-Ps 30:6]) is translated in PsH *quoniam ad momentum est ira eius* "because for a moment is his anger" in agreement with Symmachus (ὅτι ἐπ' ὀλιγοστὸν ἡ ὀργὴ αὐτοῦ), as opposed to Aquila, ὅτι ἀθροισμὸς ἐν τῷ θυμῷ αὐτοῦ "because a gathering in his anger" and LXX, ὅτι ὀργὴ ἐν τῷ θυμῷ αὐτοῦ "because wrath is in his anger" (LXX is followed by v-PsG: *quoniam ira in indignatione eius* "because wrath is in his anger"). As another illustration of Jerome's utilization of Symmachus: יָדַעְתָּ בְּצָרוֹת נַפְשִׁי "you have known [in] the distresses of my soul" (Ps 30:8 [MT-Ps 31:8]) becomes in PsH *cognovisti tribulationes animae meae* "you have known the tribulations of my soul" (= Symmachus: ἔγνως τὰς θλίψεις τῆς ψυχῆς μου), whereas Aquila has ἔγνως ἐν θλίψει ψυχήν μου "you have known my soul in tribulation."

---

[5] Weber and Gryson, *Vulgata*; Weber also edited the Roman Psalter (*Le Psautier Romain*).

[6] Jerome informs us in *Epist.* 34.2 that Aquila had rendered the expression *elaborationes eorum* "with painstaking efforts" proving that our MT of the verse was known to Aquila and perhaps also to Jerome.

Jerome's usage of Theodotion (→ 10.3.5) in PsH is more difficult to detect. There are, however, examples, e.g., בְּכֶתֶם אוֹפִיר "in the gold of Ophir" (Ps 44:10 [MT-Ps 45:10]), which is rendered *in diademate aureo* "in a golden diadem" in PsH (= Theodotion: ἐν διαδήματι χρυσῷ), with the other versions translating differently;[7] and also כְּמוֹ ... נֵפֶל אֵשֶׁת בַּל־חָזוּ שָׁמֶשׁ "like ... the miscarriage of a woman, they do not see the sun" (Ps 57:9 [MT-Ps 58:9]), which is translated following Theodotion in PsH *quasi ... abortivum mulieris quod non vidit solem* "Like ... the premature birth of a woman which does not see the sun" (= Theodotion, ὡς ... ἔκτρωμα γυναικὸς οὐκ εἶδεν ἥλιον), against Aquila (ὁμοίως ... ἔκτρωμα γυναικὸς οὐ μὴ ὁραματισθῶσιν ἥλιον "similarly ... the premature birth of a woman, let them not behold the sun") and Symmachus (ὥσπερεὶ ... ἔκτρωμα γυναικὸς ἵνα μὴ ἴδωσιν ἥλιον "just as ... the premature birth of a woman, that they may not see the sun").

Although, in translating PsH, Jerome did not have the benefit of the Hebraic learning he would acquire over the next several decades, the translation is generally faithful to the Hebrew. PsH makes clear that Jerome used the resources available to him in order to understand difficult passages and sometimes to check his own previous renderings. Jerome made thorough use of the Hexaplaric versions (→ 10.3.5), especially Aquila. Nevertheless, he does not follow Aquila in every case, and he is perfectly capable of making his own judgments about the Hebrew text.

10.3.7.4 Translation Technique
10.3.7.4.1 Stereotyping and Semantic Leveling

While stereotyping is not a general feature of Jerome's Psalms, there are some stereotyped renderings, especially for poetical terminology. The mysterious term סֶלָה "Selah" is rendered consistently in V-PsG as *diapsalma* "musical interlude," which is a transliteration taken from LXX. But in PsH, Jerome follows Aquila (ἀεί) and Jewish tradition by translating *semper* "always."[8] Another mysterious term found in the superscriptions is לַמְנַצֵּחַ "for the director," translated in LXX as εἰς τὸ τέλος "unto the end" and hence in V-PsG as *in finem* "to the end." In PsH, however, Jerome follows Aquila (τῷ νικοποιῷ "for the victory maker"), Symmachus (ἐπινίκιος "victorious") and Theodotion (εἰς τὸ νῖκος "for the victory") by translating *victori* "for the victor" or *pro victoria* "on behalf of the victory." Jerome's Psalters also provide examples of semantic leveling. Various Hebrew words referring to poverty are rendered by the Latin *pauper* "poor," even in the same verse, e.g., אֶבְיוֹן ... עֲנִיִּים "poor ... afflicted" (Ps 9:19). In general, אֶבְיוֹן "poor," דַּל "weak," and עָנִי "afflicted" are all rendered by *pauper* "poor," e.g., Pss 40:2 (MT-Ps 41:2); 68:30 (MT-Ps 69:30); 112:7 (MT-Ps 113:7). Jerome can also render different Hebrew verbs for judgment by the Latin *iudicare* "judge," e.g., יְהוָה יָדִין עַמִּים שָׁפְטֵנִי יְהוָה "The Lord adjudicates among the peoples. Judge me, Lord!" (Ps 7:9), *Dominus iudicabit* [V-PsG: *iudicat*] *populos, iudica me Domine* "The Lord will judge [judges] the peoples. Judge me, Lord!" (PsH = LXX: Κύριος κρινεῖ λαούς κρῖνόν με Κύριε). Similarly, different words for man/mankind can be rendered as *homo* "human/person": מָה־אֱנוֹשׁ ... וּבֶן־אָדָם "What is a man ... and the son of human" (Ps 8:5), which is translated *quid est homo ... vel* [V-PsG: *aut*] *filius hominis* "What is a human ... or else [or] the son of a human" (= LXX τί ἐστιν ἄνθρωπος ... ἢ υἱὸς ἀνθρώπου).[9]

---

[7] Jerome states in *Epist.* 65.15: *Ubi ego posui: in diademate aureo, Symmachus transtulit: in auro primo, Aquila, quinta et sexta: in tinctura vel in auro Ophir* "Where I put, 'in a golden diadem,' Symmachus translated 'in first gold,' and Aquila, Quinta, and Sexta put 'in dye (or "in gold") of Ophir'." Although Jerome borrows his rendering from Theodotion, he does not acknowledge his debt (*ego posui* "I put").

[8] Jerome is aware of the mysteries surrounding this Hebrew term (see *Epist.* 28). His rendering in PsH represents the Jewish opinion of the time, as evidenced by the rendering of Aquila and by the Targumic לעלמין "forever" or תדירא "perpetually."

[9] At Ps 89:3 (MT-Ps 90:3), Jerome prefers transliteration in PsH, rendering בְּנֵי־אָדָם "sons of a human" as *filii Adam* "sons of Adam," but in V-PsG he translates *filii hominum* "sons of humans." Kedar-Kopfstein believes that perhaps this rendering is influenced by Jerome's doctrine of original sin ("The Vulgate as a Translation," 85).

10.3.7.4.2 Hebrew Idioms

Although Jerome has concern for Latinity (see below → 10.3.7.4.4), he also allows a number of Hebrew idioms to stand in each of his translations of the Psalms, e.g., בְּלֵב וָלֵב "with heart and a heart" (i.e., "double-minded"; Ps 11:3 [MT-Ps 12:3]) is rendered *in corde et corde* "with heart and a heart" (v-PsG and PsH); and לְכוּ וְנַכְחִידֵם מִגּוֹי "Come, and let us efface them from (being) a nation" (Ps 82:5 [MT-Ps 83:5]) becomes *venite et conteramus eos de gente* "Come and let us rub them out from (being) a nation" (PsH), and *venite et disperdamus eos de gente* "Come and let us ruin them, from (being) a nation" (v-PsG). Some Hebrew idioms had already been established by VL (→ 10.4.1) and thus did not present any particular scandal for readers familiar with the Latin Bible. As in VL, the Hebrew construct state is rendered by the qualitative genitive where a simple adjective would be more in line with standard Latin usage, e.g., בִּנְאוֹת דֶּשֶׁא "in pastures of grass" (Ps 22:2 [MT-Ps 23:2]) is translated *in pascuis herbarum* "in pastures of grass" (PsH), and *in loco pascuae* "in a place of pasture" (v-PsG); and שֵׁבֶט מִישֹׁר שֵׁבֶט מַלְכוּתֶךָ "a staff of uprightness is the staff of your rule" (Ps 44:7 [MT-Ps 45:7]) is rendered *sceptrum aequitatis sceptrum regni tui* "a sceptre of equity is the sceptre of your rule" (PsH), and *virga directionis virga regni tui* "a rod of correcting is the rod of your rule" (v-PsG). Hebrew distributive clauses also presented a problem for Jerome. For example, אִישׁ וְאִישׁ "a man and a man" (i.e., "each one"; Ps 86:5 [MT-Ps 87:5]) becomes *homo et homo* "a person and a person" (v-PsG), and *vir et vir* "a man and a man" (PsH).

A specific example of the problem posed by Hebrew idiom is Jerome's translation of אִם "if." Normally, אִם introduces a conditional or concessive statement, as the Latin *si* "if," but in oaths it functions as a negative. v-PsG follows LXX by stereotyping *si* (= LXX: εἰ) for אִם. So נִשְׁבַּעְתִּי בְאַפִּי אִם־יְבֹאוּן אֶל־מְנוּחָתִי "I swore in my anger, if they will enter my rest" (i.e., "they will not enter my rest"; Ps 94:11 [MT-Ps 95:11]) is translated by Jerome in v-PsG as *iuravi in ira mea si intrabunt in requiem meam* "I swore by my anger, if they will enter into my rest" (= LXX: ὤμοσα ἐν τῇ ὀργῇ μου εἰ εἰσελεύσονται εἰς τὴν κατάπαυσίν μου), but he translates in PsH *iuravi in furore meo ut non introirent in requiem meam* "I swore in my fury that they shall not enter into my rest." However, Jerome is inconsistent. In Ps 131:2–3 (MT-Ps 132:2–3), נִשְׁבַּע ... אִם־אָבֹא בְּאֹהֶל בֵּיתִי אִם־אֶעֱלֶה עַל־עֶרֶשׂ יְצוּעָי "He swore ... if I will go into the tent of my house or go up upon the couch of my bed" (i.e., "I will not go ... or go up ..."), PsH translates literally as *iuravit ... si intravero in tabernaculum domus meae si adsedero super lectum straminis mei* "He swore ... if I shall enter into the tent of my house, if I shall go up upon the couch of my straw." Such translations were potentially confusing for Latin readers.

10.3.7.4.3 Attention to Context

In poetry, parallelism offers a unique conundrum for the translator. Different Hebrew words with similar meaning are used in close proximity. When Latin does not have equivalent vocabulary, Jerome usually follows the course of previous translations. Jerome can provide paraphrastic renderings, e.g., for the poetic triplet שִׁמְעָה ... הַקְשִׁיבָה ... הַאֲזִינָה "Hear ... attend to ... give ear to" (Ps 16:1 [MT-Ps 17:1]), he renders *audi* [v-PsG: *exaudi*] ... *intende* ... *auribus percipe* "Hear ... attend to ... grasp with the ears" (= LXX: εἰσάκουσαν ... πρόσχες ... ἐνώτισαι); similarly פָּז ... זָהָב "gold ... refined gold" (Ps 18:11 [MT-Ps 19:11]) becomes *aurum ... lapidem pretiosum* "gold ... precious stone" (= LXX: χρυσίον ... λίθον τίμιον). Sometimes, Jerome is content simply to use imprecise equivalents, as with his treatment of צוּר "rock," for which he varies his renderings depending on the context. As a general rule, PsH provides a less interpretive rendering of צוּר than v-PsG, e.g., in reference to God, in Ps 17:32 (MT-Ps 18:32) v-PsG has *Deus* "God," where PsH renders *fortis* "strong"; likewise in Ps 70:3 (MT-Ps 71:3) v-PsG gives *Deus* "God," but PsH has *robustus* "firm." The equivalents *fortis*/*fortitudo* "strong/strength" (e.g., Pss 17:3 [MT-Ps 18:3]; 77:35 [MT-Ps 78:35]) or *robustus* (Ps 70:3 [MT-Ps 71:3]) are very common, but Jerome also translates צוּר with the Graecized term *petra* "rock" (Pss 77:20 [MT-Ps 78:20]; 104:41 [MT-Ps 105:41] = LXX: πέτρα).

Jerome also regularly shows regard for the context in his handling of prepositions. For example, in at least a few instances Jerome renders the Hebrew preposition בְּ (typically "in") by the Latin *de* "from, concerning" (Pss 17:14 [MT-Ps 18:14]; 77:27 [MT-Ps 78:26]), following LXX.[10] He can do the same with עַל (typically "upon"; *ab* "from, by": Ps 21:10 [MT-Ps 22:10], and *de* "from, concerning": Ps 80:6 [MT-Ps 81:6]), depending on the context.

10.3.7.4.4 Style

PsH reflects a greater concern for proper Latin style than does V-PsG. In PsH, Jerome cleans up certain stylistic problems in V-PsG. One example is the Hebrew object pronoun, which is sometimes used in V-PsG when Greek and Latin would normally omit it, e.g., קַיִץ וָחֹרֶף אַתָּה יְצַרְתָּם "summer and winter, you formed them" (Ps 73:17 [MT-Ps 74:17]), which is rendered in V-PsG as *aestatem et ver tu plasmasti ea* "summer and spring, you formed them" (= LXX: θέρος καὶ ἔαρ σὺ ἔπλασας αὐτά), but in PsH is translated *aestatem et hiemem tu plasmasti* "summer and winter you formed." Also, one sees greater preference for variation in rendering the Hebrew cognate accusative in PsH, e.g., וְיִזְבְּחוּ זִבְחֵי תוֹדָה "and let them sacrifice the sacrifices of thankgiving" (Ps 106:22 [MT-Ps 107:22]), rendered as *et sacrificent sacrificium laudis* "and let them sacrifice the sacrifice of praise" in V-PsG, but changed to *et immolent hostias gratiarum* "and let them offer the sacrificial victims of thanks" in PsH. In both Psalters, the Hebrew cognate accusative can be transferred into Latin by putting the noun into the ablative case, e.g., פָּחֲדוּ פָחַד "they feared a fear" (Ps 13:5 [MT-Ps 14:5]) is translated in PsH as *timebunt formidine* "they will be afraid with dread," and in V-PsG as *trepidaverunt timore* "they trembled with fear." When Latin style allows, the Hebrew cognate accusative can be rendered more literally, e.g., שִׁירוּ לַיהוָה שִׁיר (Ps 97:1 [MT-Ps 98:1]), *cantate Domino canticum* "Sing to the Lord a song" (V-PsG and PsH).

The comparative construction טוֹב ... מִן, literally, "good ... from" (i.e., "better than") is often rendered *bonum ... quam* "good ... than" in V-PsG, but is translated *melius ... quam* "better than" in PsH (e.g., Ps 117:8–9 [MT-Ps 118:8–9]). In general, though, the comparative is translated by the rather Hebraic construction of the comparative adjective/adverb plus *a* with the ablative case (e.g., Ps 8:6; 92:4 [MT-Ps 93:4]). The repetition of nouns in Hebrew is often rendered as a distributive clause in Latin, e.g., יוֹם יוֹם "day (by) day" (Ps 60:9 [MT-Ps 61:9]) becomes *de die in diem* "from day to day" in V-PsG, and is translated even more idiomatically in PsH, *per singulos dies* "throughout all days." Jerome's use of the verb *habere* illustrates his increased interest in Latin style in PsH, e.g., הַבֹּטְחִים עַל־חֵילָם "those trusting upon their strength" (Ps 48:7 [MT-Ps 49:7]) is rendered *qui confidunt in virtute sua* "They who trust in their own strength" in V-PsG, but in PsH becomes *qui fiduciam habent in fortitudine sua* "they who have confidence in their own might." Interrogatives are a special area of interest. In PsH, Jerome generally renders the Hebrew לָמָה, literally, "For what?" (i.e., "Why?") as *quare* "Why?" (Pss 2:1; 21:2 [MT-Ps 22:2]). Only once does he render with the more Septuagintal *ut quid* "For what?" (Ps 73:1 [MT-Ps 74:1]).

Certain Hebrew verb forms such as the *Hiphil* and *Hophal* have no straightforward equivalent in Latin, although one way to imitate the Hebrew is to use an auxiliary verb. In general the verbs *dare* "to give" and *facere* "to do" bear this responsibility. V-PsG makes regular use of these auxiliary verbs, but they are avoided whenever possible in PsH. For example, אַשְׂכִּילְךָ "I will cause you to understand" (i.e., "I will instruct you"; Ps 31:8 [MT-Ps 32:8]) is rendered as *intellectum tibi dabo* "I will give understanding to you" in V-PsG, but as *doceam te* "I will teach you" in PsH (see also Ps 118:169 [MT-Ps 119:169]). So also הוֹשִׁיעָה "Save!" (Ps 27:9 [MT-Ps 28:9]) is translated *salvam fac* "Make safe!" in V-PsG, but *salva* "Save!" in PsH. But Jerome is not always consistent, e.g., וַיַּצֶּב־מַיִם "and he made the waters to stand" (Ps 77:13 [MT-Ps 78:13]) is translated in V-PsG as *statuit aquas* "and he set up the waters," whereas in PsH it becomes *et stare fecit aquas* "and he made the waters to stand."

Jerome exhibits variation in rendering Hebrew constructions even in the same context, e.g.,

---

[10] This is actually the older meaning of the preposition, as the Ugaritic language attests (see D.G. Pardee, "The Preposition in Ugaritic (Part 2)," *UF* 8 [1976]: 215–322 [282]).

עִם־חָסִיד תִּתְחַסָּד עִם־גְּבַר תָּמִים תִּתַּמָּם "with the faithful you show yourself faithful, with the man of blamelessness you show yourself blameless," in which תִּתְחַסָּד "you show yourself faithful" is translated in PsH as *sanctus eris* "you will be pure," but תִּתַּמָּם "you show yourself blameless" is rendered *innocenter ages* "you will act blamelessly" (Ps 17:26 [MT-Ps 18:26]). By comparison, v-PsG renders the two matching Hebrew verbs with matching constructions in Latin: *sanctus eris* "you will be pure" and *innocens eris* "you will be innocent."

10.3.7.4.5 Transliterations

The transliterations of PsH reflect a desire to represent the Hebrew text more exactly than previous versions. The Hebrew שָׂטָן "satan, adversary" is rendered *diabulus* "devil" in v-PsG (= LXX), but is transliterated *Satan* in PsH (Ps 108:6 [MT-Ps 109:6]). The term מָן "manna" is transliterated *man* in PsH so as to better reflect the Hebrew consonants, in contrast to *manna* in v-PsG (Ps 77:24 [MT-Ps 78:24]). Also significant is the term הַלְלוּ־יָהּ "hallelujah, praise the Lord" as a superscription (e.g., Pss 104:1 [MT-Ps 104:35]; 105:1 [MT-Ps 105:45]). Jerome translates the verb הלל "praise" with a form of *laudare* "praise" when it occurs in the text of a Psalm (e.g., Pss 21:24 [MT-Ps 22:24]; 43:9 [MT-Ps 44:9]), but he prefers to transliterate when it is used as a superscription, following LXX (→ 10.3.1). Jerome can also alternate between transliteration and translation. For example, in Ps 47:8 (MT-Ps 48:8), the Hebrew תַּרְשִׁישׁ "Tarshish" is transliterated *Tharsis* in v-PsG, but it is translated *mare* "sea" in PsH. In Ps 71:10 (MT-Ps 72:10), however, the transliteration *Tharsis* is found in both v-PsG and PsH.

10.3.7.5 Text-Critical Value
10.3.7.5.1 Confusion of Consonants

PsH normally reflects the consonantal reading of MT (→ 1.3.5.11; → 10.2.2). It is possible for LXX (→ 10.3.1) and v-PsG to agree with MT when PsH does not. For example, כְּצִדְקֶךָ "according to your righteousness" (Ps 34:24 [MT-Ps 35:24]) is the reading of MT and is reflected in LXX and v-PsG, but in PsH Jerome apparently read כצדקתי "according to my righteousness."[11] In general, however, PsH is a witness to a text nearly equivalent to consonantal MT. This is proven by the cases in which PsH "corrects" LXX's apparent confusion of Hebrew consonants, e.g., Ps 27:7 (MT-Ps 28:7) where LXX and v-PsG apparently read ומלבי "from my heart" (= ἐκ θελήματός μου/*ex voluntate mea* "from my will") for MT's וּמִשִּׁירִי "from my song" (= PsH: *in cantico meo* "with my song"); Ps 29:8 (MT-Ps 30:8) where לְהַרְרִי "to my mountain" was apparently read by LXX and v-PsG as להדרי (LXX: τῷ κάλλει μου; v-PsG: *decori meo* "to my beauty"), whereas PsH translates to match MT (= PsH: *monti meo* "to my mountain");[12] Ps 48:12 (MT-Ps 49:12) where MT's קִרְבָּם "within them" (= PsH: *interiora sua*) was read as קברם "their grave" (= LXX, v-PsG);[13] and Ps 71:5 (MT-Ps 72:5) where LXX and v-PsG apparently read ויאריך (= καὶ συμπαραμενεῖ/*et permanebit* "and he shall continue") instead of MT's יִירָאוּךָ (= PsH: *timebunt te* "they shall fear you").

10.3.7.5.2 Omissions and Additions

Most of the additions of LXX (→ 10.3.1) are retained in v-PsG, but are absent in PsH, e.g., the addition of κύριε "Lord" in Ps 5:11; οἱ ζῶντες "the living" in Ps 113:26 (MT-Ps 115:18); and the expansive superscription in Ps 146:1 (MT-Ps 147:1), Ἀλληλουια Ἀγγαιου καὶ Ζαχαριου "Hallelujah, of Haggai and Zechariah," which is absent from PsH and MT. Omissions in LXX are also generally lacking in v-PsG, but PsH follows consonantal MT (→ 10.2.2). For example, אֵלֵינוּ "toward us" (Ps 39:6 [MT-Ps 40:6]) is not represented in LXX/v-PsG, but in PsH it is rendered *pro nobis* "for us." Also הַוּוֹת בְּקִרְבָּהּ "disaster is in its midst" (Ps 54:12 [MT-Ps 55:12]) is not represented in LXX/v-PsG, but in PsH it is translated *insidiae in vitalibus eius* "treachery is in his vital parts." There are excep-

---

[11] Some Hebrew manuscripts have כְּצִדְקָתִי "according to your righteousness," which could explain the misunderstanding.

[12] Jerome makes the same mistake himself in Ps 109:3 (MT-Ps 110:3) where he reads בְּהַדְרֵי־קֹדֶשׁ "in the beauties of holiness" as בהררי־קדש "in the mountains of holiness" (PsH: *in montibus sanctis* "in holy mountains"). In this case, LXX and v-PsG reflect consonantal MT.

[13] The Targum also reads קברם "their grave" here.

tions, e.g., both v-PsG and PsH translate וּבְשֵׁם יְהוָה אֶקְרָא "and on the name of the Lord I call" in Ps 115:8 (MT-Ps 116:17), where LXX omits the entire phrase. In general, however, PsH faithfully represents the consonantal text of MT.

10.3.7.5.3 Vocalization and *Ketiv/Qere*

Jerome typically follows the vocalization reflected in MT (→ 10.2.2). But there are many examples of variant vocalizations, especially when Jerome had precedents in previous translations (→ 10.3.5), e.g., the perfect יָדְעוּ "they know" is read as an imperfect יֵדְעוּ/*cognoscent* "they will know" as in Symmachus (Ps 13:4 [MT-Ps 14:4]); the imperative גֹּל "roll!" (i.e., "commit yourself") is read as a perfect גַּל/*confugit* "took refuge" as in LXX (Ps 21:9 [MT-Ps 22:9]); and the perfects הִבִּיטוּ "they looked" and וְנָהָרוּ "and they were radiant" are read as imperatives הַבִּיטוּ/*respicite* "look!" and וְנַהֲרוּ/*et confluite* "and come together!" as in Aquila (Ps 33:6 [MT-Ps 34:6]). Jerome sometimes rejects the judgment of his predecessors, e.g., at Ps 48:14 (MT-Ps 49:14) where LXX and v-PsG read יִרְצוּ "they are pleased with" as being from the root רצה but PsH assumes it is from רוץ "run" (PsH: *current*). As it turns out, LXX (→ 10.3.1) here matches MT.

Jerome often matches either the *Ketiv* or the *Qere* (→ 10–20.1) in agreement with the previous reading of LXX. Examples of the *Qere* rather than *Ketiv* include: דְּרָכָיו "his ways" (*Ketiv* = דַּרְכּוֹ "his way"; Ps 9:26 [MT-Ps 10:5]), which is translated *viae eius* "his ways"; and וַעֲנֵנִי "and hear me!" (*Ketiv*: וַעֲנֵנוּ "and hear us"; Ps 59:7 [MT-Ps 60:7]), which is rendered *et exaudi me* "and hear me!" Instances of the *Ketiv* rather than *Qere* include: סְבָבוּנִי "they have surrounded me" (*Qere*: סְבָבוּנוּ "they have surrounded us"; Ps 16:11 [MT-Ps 17:11]), which Jerome rendered *circumdederunt me* "they have surrounded me"; and וְלֹא "and not" (*Qere*: וְלוֹ "and to him"; Ps 138:16 [MT-Ps 139:16]), translated by Jerome as *et nemo* "and no one" in v-PsG and *et non est* "and there is not" in PsH. Jerome, however, can break with the judgment of LXX, e.g., Ps 99:3 (MT-Ps 100:3), where *ipsius* "his" (PsH) follows the *Qere* וְלוֹ "and to him" (*Ketiv*: וְלֹא "and not") against LXX and v-PsG; and Ps 144:6 (MT-Ps 145:6), where *et magnitudines tuas* "and your magnitudes" follows the *Ketiv* וּגְדוּלֹתֶיךָ "and your great deeds" (*Qere*: וּגְדֻלָּתְךָ "and your greatness") against LXX and v-PsG.

Allgeier, A., "Der Brief an Sunnia und Fretela und seine Bedeutung für die Textherstellung der Vulgata," *Bib* 11 (1930): 86–107.

Allgeier, A., "Die erste Psalmenübersetzung des Hieronymus und das Psalterium Romanum," *Bib* 12 (1931): 447–82.

Allgeier, A., *Die Psalmen der Vulgata* (Paderborn: F. Schöningh, 1940).

Barthélemy, **Critique textuelle 2005*.

de Bruyne, D., "La lettre de Jérôme à Sunnia et Fretela sur le Psautier," *ZNW* 28 (1929): 1–13.

de Bruyne, D., "Le problème du Psautier Romain," *RBén* 42 (1930): 101–26.

Estin, C., *Les Psautiers de Jérôme à la lumière des traductions juives antérieures* (Rome: San Girolamo, 1984).

Kedar-Kopfstein, B., "The Vulgate as a Translation: Some Semantic and Syntactical Aspects of Jerome's Version of the Hebrew Bible" (PhD diss., Hebrew University of Jerusalem, 1968).

Marks, J., *Der textkritische Wert des Psalterium Hieronymi iuxta Hebraeos* (Winterthur: P.G. Keller, 1956).

Weber, R., *Le Psautier Romain et les autres anciens Psautiers Latin* (Rome: Abbaye Saint-Jérôme, 1953).

Justin Rogers

10.3.8 Arabic Translations

10.3.8.1 Saadia's Translation

Very[1] few translations of the book of Psalms into Judeo-Arabic have been identified. Among those that were identified, no pre-Saadian translations, namely, early and often popular Jewish versions dating from the ninth century C.E., have been found as yet. The most widespread translation by Saadia (Gaon) b. Joseph al-Fayyumi (882–942 C.E.) is that of the Pentateuch (known as the *tafsīr*; → 2.4.9.1.2). This translation is believed to have disseminated standardized Judeo-Arabic orthography, which reflected the spelling system of Clas-

---

[1] The writing of this article was supported by the Israel Science Foundation, grant no. 410/10.

sical Arabic (→ 1.3.6).² The main features of Saadia's spelling system include using *matres lectionis* to indicate long vowels according to Arabic spelling, and the representation of phonemes according to their cognates instead of following phonetic similarities. Regarding the Pentateuch and several other books he translated, Saadia's versions are less literal than early Jewish translations and Karaite versions, and they are oriented towards the Arabic target language in their syntax and style.³ Other features of his translation include a tendency to succinctness, theological alterations, shortening and expanding the text for stylistic purposes, and avoidance of repetitions. In some instances, his rendition echoes the Aramaic Targum Onqelos (→ 2.4.3.3), especially with regard to his avoidance of anthropomorphism. Saadia's intention was to produce a translation that remains faithful to the literal sense of the biblical text, yet takes into account the rules of the Arabic target language. Nonetheless, the rationalistic theology of his time was occasionally at odds with this goal. The end result was an interpretive translation of the Pentateuch that he called *tafsīr*.⁴

Extant manuscripts of Saadia's translation of Psalms include Saadia's commentary, which follows the translation of a verse or cluster of verses, and his extensive introduction to this book. Saadia's Arabic title of his work on Psalms is *Kitāb al-Tasābīḥ* "The Book of Praise." A unique feature of Saadia's work on Psalms is the existence of three separate introductions. In light of these introductions, Yoseph Qafiḥ suggests that the work was prepared in three stages.⁵ At first, Saadia wrote a translation of the entire book that he prefaced with a short introduction. In this introduction, Saadia suggests that the purpose of the book of Psalms is to discipline people in the obedience of the Lord. At a later stage, perhaps as a response to a request by his students, Saadia wrote a commentary, in which he explains, among other things, the rationale behind his translation. He prefaced this commentary with an even shorter and separate introduction, in which he briefly states the reason for writing the commentary. Later, Saadia wrote a third introduction that was much more detailed and expansive than the previous two. A major aspect of the last introduction is the polemical arguments concerning the purpose of the book of Psalms. It seems that Saadia's third introduction was written as a polemic against the Karaite approach and use of the book of Psalms. A modern scholarly edition of Saadia's translation and commentary on the book of Psalms was published by Qafiḥ.⁶

10.3.8.2 Karaite Translations

Karaite Judaism, which emerged in the ninth century C.E., was motivated by the rejection of Jewish oral law and rabbinic authority, and an ethos of return to Scripture. Hence the Karaites inaugurated a translation enterprise of their own. Most Karaite translations were written in the tenth and eleventh centuries, the golden age of Karaite literary activity. Karaites used the same orthographical standards as Saadia. However, their translation system is different, and seems to be more akin to the literal characteristics of the pre-Saadian Jewish translation tradition (→ 1.3.6).⁷

Salmon ben Yeruḥam, another Karaite exegete and contemporary of Saadia, also appears to have translated the Bible into Judeo-Arabic, with an added commentary. Unfortunately, not all of Salmon's work survived. However, his translation and commentary on Psalms is extant. Eleven manuscripts attributed to Salmon's work on Psalms are listed in the catalogue of the Institute of Microfilmed Hebrew Manuscripts. Ten of them are housed in the Russian National Library in St. Petersburg and one is housed in the Oxford Bodleian Library. In the introduction to his work on Psalms, Salmon engages in polemics with Saadia concerning the purpose of Psalms. While Saadia insists that the Psalms were intended for recitation as prayers

---

² Polliack, "Cairo Genizah"; Polliack, "Types."
³ Polliack, "Cairo Genizah"; Polliack, *Karaite*.
⁴ See Polliack, *Karaite*; Polliack, "Concept"; Polliack, "Cairo Genizah"; Sasson, "Arabic"; Steiner, *Biblical Translation*.
⁵ Qafiḥ, *Psalms with the Translation and Commentary*.
⁶ Qafiḥ, *Psalms with the Translation and Commentary*.
⁷ Polliack, *Karaite*.

only at the time of the temple and only by the Levites while accompanied by their musical instruments, Salmon argues that some of the Psalms were David's prayers, which he recited before the building of the temple. Salmon's argument aims to justify the Karaites' acceptance of the book of Psalms as the basis for the daily prayer.[8] Parts of Salmon's work on Psalms were published in scholarly editions by Shunary (1982–1983)[9] and Vajda (1979).[10]

The Karaite Yefet ben ʿElī, Saadia's younger contemporary, translated and commented on the entire Bible in Judeo-Arabic, a translation that has survived in numerous manuscript sources (→ 1.3.6). Yefet, whose family originated from Baṣra, Iraq, lived and wrote in Jerusalem. His translation and a complementary commentary appear to have been meant to be studied together. An attestation to the popularity and dissemination of Yefet's translation and commentary on the book of Psalms is the list of sixty-eight manuscripts of his work on Psalms in the catalogue of the Institute of Microfilmed Hebrew Manuscripts at the Israel National Library. Like Saadia and Salmon, Yefet prefaced his work on each book of the Bible with an introduction, in which he specified the nature of the book and his goals as a translator and exegete. In his introduction to the book of Psalms, Yefet divides the Psalms into twelve different categories that represent the different stages in the history of the people as portrayed in the Bible. He then identifies several categories within the Psalms such as psalms of thanksgiving, psalms of song, psalms of petition, and psalms of praise. Modern scholarly editions of Yefet's work on Psalms were published by Bargès (1846), Hofmann (1880), Marwick (1956), Qafiḥ (1966), Alobaidi (1996), and Eissler (2002).[11]

10.3.8.3 Other Rabbanite and Karaite Translations

Several scores of anonymous translation fragments of the Psalms have been identified in the Cairo Genizah Arabic and Judeo-Arabic collections.[12] It is possible that more exist but have not yet been identified. Usually, these Genizah fragments represent ad hoc translations, sometimes in popular style and sometimes more akin to Saadia's translation methodology.[13]

A translation of the Psalms is also attested in the sixteenth-century *sharḥ* by the Rabbanite commentator Rabbi Issāchār ben-Sūsān ha-Maʿarāvī, who was born in the city of Fez in Morocco and moved to Safed at a young age. Ben-Sūsān proclaimed the necessity of updating Saadia's Bible version in the comprehensible Arabic of his time (→ 1.3.6; → 3–5.1.8; → 6–9.1.8).

David Sklare of the Israel National Library has graciously shared the following as-yet unpublished information: Tanḥum ben Yosef Ha-Yerushalmi, the fourteenth-century grammarian and exegete, included a commentary and perhaps also translation of Psalms in his book *Kitāb al-Bayyān*. Sklare also relays that the undated manuscript SP RNL EVR ARAB I 3675 has the beginning of a summary commentary including a translation by Ali ibn Sulayman, the twelfth-century Karaite exegete. Ali writes that he based his epitome on the commentary of Abu Saʿid David ibn Boaz al-Daʾudi (David ben Boaz ha-Nasi) and the commentary of Abu al-Tayyib al-Tinnisi. There is no further information about the last two commentaries; however, it is possible that they too included translations. In addition, Sklare points to SP RNL EVR ARAB I 1430, an anonymous manuscript dated to the thirteenth century, possibly Rabbanite, containing a

---

[8] Shunary, "Salmon."

[9] Shunary, "Salmon ben Yeruham's Commentary on the Book of Psalms."

[10] Vajda, "Le Psaume VIII commenté par Salmōn b. Yerūḥīm."

[11] Alobaidi, *Le commentaire des Psaumes par le qaraïte Salmon ben Yeruham*; Bargès, *Rabbi Yapheth ben Heli Bassorensis Karaïtae in Librum Psalmorum commentarii arabici*; Eissler, *Königspsalmen und karäische Messiaserwartung*; Hofmann, *Der XXII. Psalm in das Arabische übersetzt und erklärt*;

Marwick, *The Arabic Commentary of Salmon ben Yeruham the Karaite on the Book of Psalms*; Qafiḥ, *Psalms with the Translation and Commentary of Rabbi Saadia ben Joseph Fayyumi*. For a detailed discussion of Yefet's commentary on Psalms, see Simon, *Four Approaches*.

[12] See indices in Baker and Polliack, *Catalogue*; Shivtiel and Niessen, *Catalogue*.

[13] See the indices in Baker and Polliack, *Catalogue*; Shivtiel and Niessen, *Catalogue*.

commentary on Psalms written in Spanish-style script. This manuscript includes a translation into Judeo-Arabic. One other anonymous Rabbanite commentary on Psalms, in which the author quotes from a number of authorities such as Saadia and early Spanish commentators and grammarians, appears in several copies. One of the larger manuscripts of this commentary is SP RNL EVR ARAB I 1409, dated to the fourteenth century. This one includes a translation of the text into Judeo-Arabic.

Alobaidi, J. (ed. and trans.), *Le commentaire des Psaumes par le qaraïte Salmon ben Yeruham: Psaumes 1–10; Introduction, édition, traduction* (Bern: P. Lang, 1996).

Baker, C.F. and M. Polliack, *Arabic and Judaeo-Arabic Manuscripts in The Cambridge Genizah Collections: Arabic Old Series (T-S Ar.1a-54)* (Cambridge: Cambridge University Press, 2001).

Bargès, J.J.L. (ed. and trans.), *Rabbi Yapheth ben Heli Bassorensis Karaïtae in Librum Psalmorum commentarii arabici e duplici codice* MSS. *Bibliothecae Regiae Parisiensis* (Paris: Didot, 1846).

Bargès, J.J.L. (ed. and trans.), *Excerpta ex R. Yapheth ben Heli commentariis in Psalmos Davidis regis et prophetae* (Paris: Lutetle Parisiorum, 1846).

Ben-Shammai, H., "Editions and Versions in Yefet b. Ali's Bible Commentary," *Alei Sefer* 2 (1976): 17–32 [Hebr.].

Blau, J., "Saadya Gaon's Pentateuch Translation and the Stabilization of Medieval Judaeo-Arabic Culture," in *The Interpretation of the Bible: The International Symposium in Slovenia* (ed. J. Krašovec; JSOTSup 289; Sheffield: Sheffield Academic Press, 1998), 393–98.

Brody, R., *Rav Se'adya Gaon* (Jerusalem: The Zalman Shazar Center, 2006) [Hebr.].

Eissler, F., *Königspsalmen und karäische Messiaserwartung: Jefet ben Elis Auslegung von Ps 2.72.89.110.132 im Vergleich von Saadia Gaons Deutung* (Texts and Studies in Medieval and Early Judaism 17; Tübingen: Mohr Siebeck, 2002).

Goldstein, M., "The Beginning of the Transition from *Derash* to *Peshaṭ* as Exemplified in Yefet ben 'Eli's Comment on Psa. 44:24," in *Exegesis and Grammar in Medieval Karaite Texts* (ed. G. Khan; Oxford: Oxford University Press, 2001), 41–64.

Hofmann, T. (ed. and trans.), *Der XXII. Psalm in das Arabische übersetzt und erklärt von R. Jepheth ben Eli ha-Baçri* (Tübingen: L.F. Fues, 1880).

Khan, G., "The Orthography of Karaite Hebrew Bible Manuscripts in Arabic Transcription," *JSS* 38 (1993): 49–70.

Mann, J., *Texts and Studies in Jewish History and Literature*, Vol. 2 (New York: Ktav Publishing House, 1972).

Marwick, L. (ed.), *The Arabic Commentary of Salmon ben Yeruham the Karaite on the Book of Psalms Chapters 42–72* (Philadelphia: Dropsie College for Hebrew and Cognate Learning, 1956).

Polliack, M., *The Karaite Tradition of Arabic Bible Translation: A Linguistic and Exegetical Study of Karaite Translations of the Pentateuch from the Tenth and Eleventh Centuries C.E.* (Études sur le judaïsme médiéval 17; Leiden: Brill, 1997).

Polliack, M., "Arabic Bible Translations in the Cairo Genizah Collections," in *Jewish Studies in a New Europe* (eds. U. Haxen et al; Copenhagen: C.A. Reitzel, 1998), 595–620.

Polliack, M., "Se'adyā Gaon's Concept of Biblical Translation in Light of the Karaite Concept," in *Heritage and Innovation in Medieval Judaeo-Arabic Culture* (eds. J. Blau and D. Doron; Ramat-Gan: Bar-Ilan University Press, 2000), 191–201 [Hebr.].

Polliack, M., "Types of Arabic Bible Translations in the Cairo Geniza Based on the Catalogue of TS Arabic," *Te'uda* 15 (1999): 109–25 [Hebr.].

Qafiḥ, Y. (ed.), *Psalms with the Translation and Commentary of Rabbi Saadia ben Joseph Fayyumi of Blessed Memory* (New York: American Academy for Jewish Research, 1966). [Hebr.].

Sasson, I., "Arabic," in *EncJud* (²2007), 3:603–06.

Schenker, A., "Auf dem Weg zu einer Kritischen Ausgabe von Jafet ben Elis Kommentar zu den Psalmen," *BEK* 2 (1989): 29–38.

Shivtiel, A. and F. Niessen, *Arabic and Judaeo-Arabic Manuscripts in the Cambridge Genizah Collections: Taylor-Schechter New Series* (Cambridge: Cambridge University Press, 2006).

Shunary, J., "Salmon ben Yeruham's Commentary on the Book of Psalms," *JQR*, n.s., 73 (1982–1983): 155–75.

Simon, U., *Four Approaches to the Book of Psalms: From Saadiah Gaon to Abraham Ibn Ezra* (trans. L.J. Schramm; Albany: State University of New York Press, 1991).

Sixdenier, G.-D., "Le Psaume 2 dans 4QFlorilegium et dans Jephet ben Ali *In Psalmos*: essai de comparaison de leurs de leurs exégèses et méthodes," in *Études sémitiques et samaritaines offertes à Jean Margain* (eds. C.-B. Amphoux et al; Lausanne: Éditions du Zèbre, 1998), 51–257.

Sklare, D., "Unknown Karaite Works in the Firkovitch

Collection," in *Judaeo-Arabic Manuscripts in the Firkovitch Collections: The Works of Yusuf al-Basir: A Sample Catalogue: Texts and Studies* (eds. D. Sklare and H. Ben-Shammai; Jerusalem: Ben-Zvi Institute, 1997), 127–39.

Sklare, D., "A Guide to Collections of Karaite Manuscripts," in *Karaite Judaism: A Guide to Its History and Literary Sources* (ed. M. Polliack; Leiden: Brill, 2003), 893–924.

Steiner, R.C., *A Biblical Translation in the Making: The Evolution and Impact of Saadia Gaon's Tafsīr* (Cambridge: Harvard University Press, 2010).

Stroumsa, S., "'What is Man?:' Psalm 8:4–5 in Jewish, Christian and Muslim Exegesis in Arabic," *Hen* 14 (1992): 283–90.

Tobi, Y., "On the Antiquity of the Judeo-Arabic Biblical Translations and a New Piece of an Ancient Judeo-Arabic Translation to the Pentateuch," in *Ben 'ever la-'arav*, Vol. 2 (ed. Y. Tobi; Tel Aviv: Afikim, 2001), 17–60 [Hebr.].

Vajda, G., "Le Psaume VIII commenté par Salmōn b. Yerūḥīm," in *Essays on the Occasion of the Seventieth Anniversary of the Dropsie University (1909–1979)* (eds. A.I. Katsh and L. Nemoy; Philadelphia: Dropsie University, 1979), 441–48.

Walfish, B.D. and M. Kizilov, *Bibliographia Karaitica: An Annotated Bibliography of Karaites and Karaism* (Études sur le judaïsme médiéval 43; Leiden: Brill, 2011).

Zawanowska, M., "Review of Scholarly Research on Yefet and His Works," *REJ* (forthcoming).

Zucker, M., *Rav Saadya Gaon's Translation of the Torah* (New York: Philipp Feldheim, 1959).

Ilana Sasson

10.4 Secondary Translations

10.4.1 Vetus Latina

10.4.1.1 Evidence

No other book of the Old Testament in the Latin tradition has such a wealth of evidence and such a complex textual history as Psalms. Its central importance to Christian liturgy has been decisive for the preservation of ancient texts (VL) that have survived alongside regional Psalters, such as the Roman (Ro), the Ambrosian or Milanese (Mi), and the Mozarabic (Moz), as well as the Hexaplaric revision (Ga = Gallican) and Jerome's *iuxta hebraeos* translation (He; → 10.3.7). For VL-Ps, many manuscripts have preserved the complete book, sometimes as part of liturgical texts (manuscripts VL[31 32 109 111 136 189 263 300–453] in Gryson's catalogue[1]). The list includes VL texts of Ro, Ga, Moz, Mi; they have VL as their basis and can be grouped as follows according to Bogaert's classification:[2]

1) Hexaplaric psalter or *Gallican* (= Ga): manuscripts VL[309 322 357 366 367 386–92 420 422–29 430–43 446–51 466 471–76], Alcuin's Bibles (Φ), Italian Atlantic Bibles, Bibles of Paris (thirteenth century). This psalter is the Psalter of the Vulgate text in Gutenberg's Bible and in the Sixto-Clementina edition.

2) *Roman Psalter*: manuscripts VL[307 308 343–45 347–50 354–56 358–61 363–65 368–71 384 393–95 398 399 444 465 468]; manuscripts from England (from the eighth century C.E. onwards) and late Italian manuscripts (eleventh and twelfth centuries).

3) *Milanese Psalter*: manuscripts VL[400–07]; attested in Ambrose of Milan's quotations.

4) *Mozarabic Psalter*: manuscripts VL[109 189 312 410–14 416–19 452 457 479–84]; two text types can be distinguished: moz^x (First Bible of Alcalá, VL[109]) and moz^c (Bible of Cava, VL[189 312 410–14 416–19 452 457 479–84]).

5) Italian Psalter in Africa (text from north Italy used by Augustine of Hippo): manuscripts VL[300] (= Verona, Biblioteca Capitolare I[1]; sixth–seventh century C.E. [WE³ α]); VL[304] (= Sankt Gallen, Stifstbibliothek 12, palimpsest, eighth century [WE β]); VL[460] (= Sinai, Saint Catherine, slavon 5).

6) VL psalters, Gallican or Italian (related to Ro), which can be classified as follows:

   a. Psalters of Lyonese Gaul: manuscripts VL[301] (= *Psalterium Augiense 1*: Karlsruhe, Badische Landesbibliothek, Aug CCLIII; palimpsest, sixth century C.E. [WE κ]); VL[303] (= Paris, Bibliothèque Nationale, lat. 1197, sixth century [WE γ]); VL[325] (= Saint Petersburg, Rossijskaja Nacionalnaja Biblioteka F. v. I 5, second half of eighth century [WE δ]); VL[326] (= Chartres, Bibl. Municipale 22 [30]; triple Psalter [He, Ga, VL] with canticles; tenth century); VL[341] (= Greco-Latin Psalter,[4] which is related to manuscripts VL[303 325]: Cues an der Mosel, Bibl. des St. Nikolaus-Hospital 10 [ninth–tenth century C.E.])

   b. Psalters of Narbonense Gaul: manuscripts VL[302] (= *Psalterium Augiense 1*: Karlsruhe, Badische Landesbibliothek, Aug CCLIII; palimpsest, sixth century C.E. [WE κ]) and VL[333] (= Greco-Latin Psalter: Paris, Bibliothèque Nationale, Coislin 186; seventh century C.E. [WE ε])

   c. Saint Zenon of Verona's Psalter: manuscript VL[306] (= Vatican, Biblioteca Apostolica Vaticana, Vatic. lat. 5359; palimpsest, ca. 700 C.E. [WE ζ])

   d. Fragments of Nonantola: manuscripts VL[444] (= Rome, Bibl. Nazionale Centrale Sess. 77

---

[1] Gryson, *Altlateinische Handschriften 1*; Gryson, *Altlateinische Handschriften 2*.

[2] Bogaert, "Le psautier latin," 58–64. Jerome's *iuxta hebraeos* translation is excluded from this list. Bogaert's list is extended with the list of references of VL manuscripts in Gryson, *Altlateinische Handschriften 2*.

[3] The abbreviation WE identicates the sigla the following manuscripts have in the edition of Weber, *Le Psautier Romain*.

[4] Not included in Bogaert's classification; cf. Gryson, *Altlateinische Handschriften 2*, 99.

[2107] fol. 113, sixth century C.E. [Ro?[5]]) and VL[396] (= Vatican, Biblioteca Apostolica Vaticana, Palat. lat 187, fol. 1–7; eighth century C.E. [WE π])

e. Fragments of Sankt Gall, Zurich and Vienna: manuscript VL[305] (= Sankt Gallen, Stiftsbibliothek 1395 (III); Vienna, Österreichische Nationalbibliothek lat 587, fol: a b; Zurich, Zentralbibliothek C. 184 frg. 3, 5, 19; ca. 700 [WE σ])

f. Lyonese Psalter: manuscript VL[421] (= Lyon, Bibl. de la Ville 425 [351]; Paris, Bibliothèque Nationale, nouv. acq. lat. 1585; ca. 500). The text is a mixture of VL and Ga.

7) Amelli's *Psalter*, or Casinense: VL[136] (= Monte Cassino, Archivio della Badia 557A; twelfth century). It preserves an ancient text related to the quotations in both Tertullian and Cyprian.[6]

Many of these Psalters have been transmitted in Vulgate manuscripts (→ 10.3.7). The V-Ps was mostly Ga. There are often two or more Psalters in one Vulgate codex, with several possible combinations including Jerome's translation from the Hebrew. The Vulgate manuscript tradition is not unanimous:[7] Ro in Ψ^{DF} and Cassinese manuscripts (Π); Ga in Φ^{RGVP}Ψ^{B}Ω^{SM}; Moz in X (= *moz^x*, VL[109]), while He is present in the Amiatinus (A) and in most Spanish and Teodulphian Vulgate manuscripts (Λ^{L}Σ^{T}EΘ^{HAMG}H). Manuscripts CΩ^M have two psalters: the first has the Moz (VL[189]) copied after Job with He at the end of the volume, the second one has He and Ga.

To the wealth of the manuscript tradition, it must be added that the Psalter is quoted by all Latin Christian writers (→ 21.8) beginning with Tertullian and features prominently in Christian liturgy. Therefore, the indirect transmission of Psalms is the richest and most complex in the entire Latin Bible. There are currently no studies about Latin Psalms quotations. The principal one is that developed by Capelle[8] for the textual history of the African Psalter based on quotations of Tertullian, Cyprian of Carthage, the Pseudo-Augustinian *Liber de Divinis Scripturis*, Donatists, and Augustine's circles.

10.4.1.2 Editions

The importance of Psalms for church and Christian liturgy explains why from a very ancient period it has been the most published book of the Latin Old Testament, both as part of Vulgate editions, and in quintuple, quadruple, triple, and double Psalters that collected the different known textual traditions. For the history of Jerome's two translations (→ 10.3.7) from sixteenth century onwards, Allgeier's study[9] is essential. Allgeier reviews Jacobus Faber Stapulensis' quintuplex Psalter (1509), the first Mi editions after the Council of Trent, the Sixto-Clementina edition, the 1593 edition of the Ro text and Sabatier's edition of 1743.[10] The latter is especially important for the history of the textual criticism of VL-Ps. Sabatier edited three texts, the *Vulgata hodierna* (Ga), He, and *Versio antiqua* (VL) according to *Psalterium Sangermanensis* (VL[303]). Sabatier edited Psalm 151 as a part of the *Antiqua Version* according to the same manuscript and other witnesses (VL[322 329] and manuscript Paris, Bibliothèque Nationale, lat. 102). Psalm 151 poses a particular editorial and textual problem:[11] It is not part of He and is present only in a part of the Latin manuscript tradition. When Psalm 151 is present, as in Alcuinian manuscripts, it is always accompanied by the following annotation: *hic psalmus in hebraeis codicibus non habetur sed ne a septuaginta quidem interpretibus editus est est idcirco repudiandus* "this psalm is not included in Hebrew codices but it was edited assuredly by the seventy translators, on that account it is to be rejected."

In the nineteenth and twentieth centuries, there were reports of many discoveries of new VL-Ps

---

[5] See Gryson, *Altlateinische Handschriften 2*, 272.
[6] Amelli, *Liber Psalmorum*.
[7] Cf. Quentin, *Liber Psalmorum*, vii–viii.
[8] Capelle, *Le texte du Psautier*.
[9] Allgeier, *Die altlateinischen Psalterien*.
[10] Sabatier, *Bibliorum*, 2:9–288.
[11] Bogaert, "Le psautier latin," 57–58.

manuscripts.[12] The 1950s were decisive for the textual criticism of Latin Psalters as critical editions were published: in 1953, Ro by Weber[13] and Ga by Quentin,[14] He by de Sainte-Marie in 1954,[15] Moz by Ayuso Marazuela in 1957,[16] and in 1959 the volume devoted to the *Tituli Psalmorum* by Salmon.[17] In 1961, Ziegler made a detailed analysis of the Latin psalters.[18] Shortly afterwards, a new critical edition of the Psalter was published by Ayuso Marazuela (1962).[19] He edited five types of Latin texts (Ga, Moz, Ro, that of Hispanic writers, and He) and in the sixth column incorporates a LXX text. In 1954, the Latin Sinai Psalter was discovered (VL^{460}).[20] Between 1954 and 2001, many studies on this manuscript and partial editions were published and in 1978 a facsimile edition of it appeared.[21] Gryson and Thibaut edited the Latin Sinai Psalter in 2010 providing next to its text an apparatus containing readings of VL^{300} (WE α; Verona) and VL^{304} (WE β; St. Gallen).[22]

10.4.1.3 Text

The oldest translations of Psalms from Greek into Latin were made in Africa in the second century C.E. None of them is completely preserved (see above). As proved by Capelle,[23] the starting point for the study of the history of the Psalter text are quotations from Tertullian and Cyprian. Many features of their quoted text survive in later stages of the transmission, as shown by authors such as Ambrose, Augustine, Jerome, and the regional Psalters (VL, Ro, Mi, Ga, and Moz). Capelle placed Cyprian's text of Psalms in the field of popular Latin with African textual features.[24] Table 1 below illustrates this phenomenon.[25]

The ancient Latin Psalms texts were revised successively.[26] The Donatists' Psalms are a witness to this development. In Europe, Novatian quotes a text that differs considerably in vocabulary from African texts, such as the one quoted by Cyprian. In the fourth century C.E., in Augustine's times, ancient African texts were revised according to versions coming from Italy that were more literary and of a higher quality. In the fifth century, Jerome (→ 10.3.7) produced his recension of a VL version of Psalms based on a Hexaplaric text (→ 10.3.5), and this text began to spread very quickly. Latin texts of psalms spread rapidly throughout Italy, Gaul, Spain, and England. Ambrose's quotations (→ 21.8) attest a revised text in northern Italy. It is in Italy, as well, that Ro is found, which faithfully preserves original features of ancient texts, and where Mi is used in the Ambrosian liturgy although it is less widespread in manuscript tradition. Ro predominated also in England following the eighth century C.E. Moz was used in Spain. It is related to African texts and Ro. In Gaul, two types of Psalters are found: a primitive text is preserved in central regions, while in the south we find a text type highly contaminated by Moz.

Jerome (→ 10.3.7) twice revised the text of Psalms. He notes in his *Preface* to Ga that he had made a quick revision of the text in Rome (384 C.E.?). Scholars have failed to identfy this revision. He revised the Latin according to Origen's Hexaplaric text (→ 10.3.5) between the years 389 and 392/398 C.E. in Bethlehem. That recension was named Ga. Jerome also produced a new translation *iuxta hebraeos* (He) based on Hexaplaric material (Aquila and, especially, Symmachus). Ga was introduced as the Psalms text by Alcuin in his edition of the Vulgate, and because of this it spread throughout Gaul. For this reason, this Psalter received the name of *Gallican Psalter*. It eventually became the

---

[12] Remarks taken from Bogaert, "Le psautier latin," 51–52.
[13] Weber, *Le Psautier Romain*.
[14] Quentin, *Liber Psalmorum*.
[15] De Sainte-Marie, *Sancti Hieronymi Psalterium*.
[16] Ayuso Marazuela, *Psalterium visigothicum*.
[17] Salmon, *Les "Tituli Psalmorum" des Manuscrits latins*.
[18] Ziegler, "Altlateinische Psalterien."
[19] Ayuso Marazuela, *El Salterio*.
[20] History of research and bibliography in Gryson and Thibaut, *Le psautier latin du Sinaï*, 7–10, 14–16.
[21] Altbauer, *Psalterium latinum Hierosolymitanum*.
[22] Gryson and Thibaut, *Le psautier latin du Sinaï*.
[23] Capelle, *Le texte du Psautier*.

[24] Capelle, *Le texte du Psautier*.
[25] Greek readings are taken from Rahlfs, *Psalmi cum odis*. Latin readings are taken from Capelle, *Le texte du Psautier*, 7.
[26] For following observations: Estin, "Le traductions du Psautier," 67–88; Bogaert, "Le psautier latin," *passim*.

TABLE 1   *African lexical features in VL texts*

	LXX-Ps[27]	Tertullian	Cyprian	Ambrose	Augustine	Other VL Texts
Ps 2:1[28]	ἐφρύαξαν "they did grow insolent"	*tumultuatae sunt* "they did brawl"	*tumultuatae sunt*	*tumultuatae sunt*		*fremuerunt* "they repined"
Ps 2:3	ἀπορρίψωμεν "let us cast"	*abiciamus* "let us cast"	*abiciamus*		*abiciamus*	*proiciamus* "let us throw out"
Ps 2:7	γεγέννηκα "I have begotten"	*generaui* "I have begotten"	*generaui*			*genui* "I have begotten"
Cf. Ps 109 (110):3	ἐξεγέννησα "I brought forth"	*generaui* "I have begotten"	*generaui*			*genui* "I have begotten"
Ps 18:7 (19:6)	ἔξοδος "starting point"	*profectio* "departure"	*profectio*			*egressio* "starting point"
Ps 32(33):6	τῷ λόγῳ "by the word"	*sermone* "by the speech"	*sermone*		*sermone*	*uerbo* "by the word"
Ps 33:20 (34:19)	θλίψεις "afflictions"	*pressurae* "oppressions"	*pressurae*			*tribulations* "troubles"
Ps 44:3 (45:2)	ἐξεχύθη "was poured"	*effusa est,* "was poured"	*effusa est*	*effusa est*		*diffusa est* "was poured out"
Ps 44:7 (45:6)	θρόνος, "throne"	*thronus,* "throne"	*thronus*			*sedem* "seat"
Cf. Ps 131 (132):11	θρόνον "throne"	*thronum* "throne"	*thronum* (cf. Jerome)			*sedem,* "seat"
Ps 81 (82):6	υἱοὶ ὑψίστου "sons of the Most High"	*filii altissimi* "sons of the Most High"	*filii altissimi*		*filii altissimi*	*filii excelsi* "sons of the exalted"

Psalter in the Vulgate rather than He, and so it is found in Atlantic Italian Bibles and in the Paris Bibles. Ga is also the text of Psalms in Gutenberg's Bible and in the Sixto-Clementina edition.

10.4.1.4 *Vorlage*

For his edition of the Greek text of Psalms, Rahlfs collated some Latin witnesses as representative for the Latin Psalters: VL330 (manuscript Vatican Regin. 11) for the Ga text ("Ga" in Rahlfs), and two manuscripts for VL (VL300 [La^R in Rahlfs] and VL303 [La^G in Rahlfs]). Both manuscripts are indirect witnesses for the Greek "Western text," along with the Psalms quotations of Tertullian and Cyprian. In the Greek transmission, the most important evidence for this text type is the Greek text in the bilingual Greek-Latin Verona Psalter (= VL300). Ga (and He) are indirect witnesses for Origen's Hexaplaric text (→ 10.3.5).[29] Capelle had already referred to the importance of the Verona manuscript for Greek and Latin textual criticism: its Greek text contains ancient Western readings, and its Latin text is very closely related to Augustine's Psalter.[30] Bogaert has demonstrated the great importance of the Latin Psalter evidence for Greek textual criticism.[31] The richness and antiquity of some of these Latin texts, such as the Psalms quotations of Tertullian, Cyprian, and Augustine's *Enarrationes in Psalmos* (→ 21.8), provide access to ancient textual stages of LXX-Ps (→ 10.3.1).

Allgeier, A., *Die altlateinischen Psalterien: Prolegomena zu einer Textgeschichte der hieronymianischen Psalmenübersetzungen* (Freiburg i.B.: Herder, 1928).

---

[27] English translations of LXX are according to *NETS.
[28] Psalms are numbered according to LXX. MT numbering is given in parenthesis.
[29] Rahlfs, *Psalmi cum Odis*, 52–60.
[30] Capelle, *Le texte du Psautier*, 85.
[31] Bogaert, "Le psautier latin," 78–81.

Allgeier, A., *Bruchstücke eines altlateinisches Psalters aus St. Gallen* (SHAW, Philos.-hist. Klasse 1928/1929, 2. Abhandlung; Heidelberg: Winter, 1929).

Altbauer, M., *Psalterium latinum Hierosolymitanum: Eine frühmittelalterliche lateinische Handschrift*: Sin. Ms. n° 5 (Vienna: Böhlau, 1978).

Amelli, A.M., *Liber Psalmorum iuxta antiquissimam latinam versionem nunc primum ex Casinensi Cod. 557* (Collectanea Biblica Latina 1; Rome: Pustet, 1912).

Ammasari, A., *Il salterio latino di Pietro* (3 vols.; Rome: Città nuova edizioni, 1987).

Ayuso Marazuela, T., *Psalterium visigothicum* (Biblia Polyglotta Matritensis 7.21; Madrid: Editorial Catolica, 1957).

Ayuso Marazuela, T., *El Salterio* (3 vols.; La Vetus Latina Hispana 5; Madrid: C.S.I.C., 1962).

Bogaert, P.M., "Le psautier latin des origines au XIIe siècle: Essai d'histoire," in *Der Septuaginta-Psalter und seine Tochterübersetzungen: Symposium in Göttingen 1997* (eds. A. Aejmelaeus and U. Quast; MSU 24; Göttingen: Vandenhoeck & Ruprecht, 2000), 51–81.

Capelle, P., *Le texte du Psautier latin en Afrique* (Collectanea Biblica Latina 4; Rome: Pustet, 1913).

Estin, C., "Le traductions du Psautier," in *Le monde latin antique et la Bible* (eds. J. Fontaine and C. Pietri; Bible de Tous les Temps 2; Paris: Ed. Beauchesne, 1985), 67–88.

Fischer, B., *Verzeichnis und Sigel für Handschriften und Kirchenschriftsteller* (VL 1; Freiburg i.B.: Herder, 1949).

Gryson, *Altlateinische Handschriften 1*.

Gryson, *Altlateinische Handschriften 2*.

Gryson, R. and A. Thibaut, *Le psautier latin du Sinaï* (VL: Aus der Geschichte der altlateinischen Bibel 39; Freiburg i.B.: Herder, 2010).

Quentin, E. (ed.), *Liber Psalmorum ex recensione sancti Hieronymi* (Biblia Sacra iuxta latinam Vulgatam versionem 10; Rome: Libreria Editrice Vaticana, 1953).

Rahlfs, A., *Psalmi cum odis* (Septuaginta Vetus Testamentum Graece 10; Göttingen: Vandenhoeck & Ruprecht, 1931).

Sabatier, *Bibliorum*.

de Sainte-Marie, H., *Sancti Hieronymi Psalterium iuxta Hebraeos* (Collectanea Biblica Latina 11; Vatican City: Libreria Vaticana, 1954).

Salmon, P., *Les "Tituli Psalmorum" des Manuscrits latins* (Collectanea Biblica Latina 12; Vatican City: Libreria Vaticana, 1959).

Weber, R., *Le Psautier Romain et les autres anciens psautiers latins* (Collectanea Biblica Latina 10; Rome: Abbaye Saint-Jérôme, 1953).

Ziegler, J., "Altlateinische Psalterien: Neue Ausgaben und Beiträge," *BZ* NF 5 (1961): 94–115 (reprinted in J. Ziegler, *Sylloge* [MSU 10; Göttingen: Vandenhoeck & Ruprecht, 1971], 565–86).

José Manuel Cañas Reíllo

10.4.2 Coptic Translations

10.4.2.1 Background and Text Transmission

The Coptic Psalter is a translation of the Greek Septuagint Psalter (→ 10.3.1) and not of MT-Ps (→ 10.2.2). The numbering of the Coptic Psalms follows LXX.[1] All Coptic versions, like LXX, include the "apocryphal" Psalm 151. The Psalter was the most used and widespread book of the bible in the Coptic churches and monasteries,[2] and is attested in four dialects of Coptic: Sahidic, Bohairic, Middle Egyptian (Mesokemic), and Fayyumic, although in a quite different manner. In the form of complete books (codices) it has been transmitted in Sahidic, Bohairic, and Middle Egyptian, whereas only fragments are preserved in Fayyumic. In addition, some tiny fragments from Psalm 46 survived in the Akhmimic dialect,[3] and a quotation of Ps 3:2–9 in Akhmimic is saved in the famous *Epistula Apostolorum*.[4] Clearly, there was no complete Akhmimic version of the Psalms.

---

[1] For differences in numbering between LXX and Cop within Psalms 113–117, see H. Quecke, "Zur sahidischen Psalmenzählung," in *Nubia et Oriens Christianus: Festschrift für C. Detlef G. Müller zum 60. Geburtstag* (eds. P.O. Scholz and R. Stempel; Bibliotheca Nubica 1; Cologne: Dinter, 1987), 205–09.

[2] Cf. S.G. Richter, "Verwendung von Psalmen im koptischen Christentum," in *Ritual und Poesie: Formen und Orte religiöser Dichtung im Alten Orient, im Judentum und im Christentum* (ed. E. Zenger; Herders Biblische Studien 36; Freiburg im Breisgau: Herder, 2003), 283–92.

[3] W.E. Crum, "Un psaume en dialecte d'Akhmim," in *Mélanges Maspero*, Vol. 2: *Orient grec, romain et byzantin* (Mémoires publiés par les membres de l'Institut français d'archéologie orientale du Caire 67; Cairo: Impr. de l'Institut Français d'Archéologie Orientale, 1934), 73–76.

[4] C. Schmidt, *Gespräche Jesu mit seinen Jüngern nach der Auferstehung: Ein katholisch-apostolisches Sendschreiben des 2. Jahrhunderts* (TUGAL 43; Leipzig: J.C. Hinrichs, 1919), 8*–9* [xii.10–xiii.8]; the quotation is, with some slight variants, a transposition from the Sahidic Psalter.

The "material" transmission of the Coptic Psalter took place, according to Horn,[5] in four main forms:

- Group A – text manuscripts: codices of the complete Psalter or single leaves/fragments from dispersed codices
- Group B – Psalm texts in the service of the Coptic Church (*ritualia*): pericopes in lectionaries and *horologia*
- Group C – quotations and allusions in Coptic literature (*quotations*): patristic-ecclesiastical literature, Coptic gnostic literature, above all the *Pistis Sophia*, and the New Testament[6]
- Group D – casual texts (*occasionalia*), for private reading, exercises, or as magical means (especially as amulets)

The main groups A and B are accompanied by Greek-Coptic (mostly Greek-Sahidic) bilingual texts.[7]

The Psalter belongs to the earliest translations of the Bible into Coptic. Already newcomers ("novices") to the Pachomian monasteries[8] were obliged to recite the Our Father and a number of psalms.[9] The members of monastic communities had to memorize continually the New Testament and the Psalter.[10]

10.4.2.2 Translation Character and Text-Critical Value

The Sahidic version is of particular importance for the textual history of the Greek Psalter (→ 10.3.1). According to Rahlfs, the Sahidic translation renders its Greek *Vorlage*, by and large, in a very literal manner.[11] Besides its translation technique, Cop^{Sa}-Ps is an important witness of the Upper Egyptian recension of the Greek Psalter[12] and supports the Upper Egyptian Greek manuscripts LXX^U, P. Lips inv. 2013, and P. Bodmer XXIV.[13]

An archaic feature of the Coptic Psalter (both Cop^{Sa}-Ps and Cop^{Boh}-Ps, but not Cop^{Mes}-Ps) in Ps 95:10 ὁ κύριος ἐβασίλευσεν is the addition ἀπὸ τοῦ ξύλου[14] "the Lord reigns *from the tree*."[15]

The Bohairic Psalter is a representative of the Lower Egyptian recension, in Greek (→ 10.3.1) mainly attested by the uncial codices LXX^B ("Codex Vaticanus," Vat. gr. 1209; fourth century) and LXX^S ("Codex Sinaiticus," *olim* Leningrad/St. Petersburg, Public Library, manuscript Graec. 259, *nunc* (major part) London, British Library Add. 43725; fourth

---

[5] J. Horn, "Die koptische (sahidische) Überlieferung des alttestamentlichen Psalmenbuches: Versuch einer Gruppierung der Textzeugen für die Herstellung des Textes," in *Der Septuaginta-Psalter und seine Tochterübersetzungen: Symposium in Göttingen 1997* (eds. A. Aejmelaeus and U. Quast; MSU 24; Göttingen: Vandenhoeck & Ruprecht, 2000), 97–106 (with some subdivisions within the main groups).

[6] The Coptic gnostic texts and the New Testament are not mentioned as sources in Horn, "Die koptische (sahidische) Überlieferung," 103. The psalm text in the *Pistis Sophia* has been evaluated by Rahlfs, *Berliner Handschrift*, 7. For the psalm quotations in the Coptic versions of the Gospels, see the thorough study by P. Luisier, *Les citations vétéro-testamentaires dans les versions coptes des Évangiles: Receuil et analyse critique* (Cahiers d'Orientalisme 22; Geneva: Patrick Cramer, 1998), 117–48. G. Emmenegger, *Der Text des koptischen Psalters aus al-Mudil* (TUGAL 159; Berlin: De Gruyter, 2007), 226–52, investigates by detailed comparison the psalm quotations in the Middle Egyptian versions of the Gospels and Acts.

[7] Cf. P. Nagel, "Griechisch-Koptische Bilinguen des Alten Testaments," in *Graeco-Coptica: Griechen und Kopten im byzantinischen Ägypten* (ed. P. Nagel; Martin-Luther-Universität Halle-Wittenberg Wissenschaftliche Beiträge 1984/48; Halle: Martin-Luther-Universität, 1984), 231–57.

[8] The foundation of Pachomius' monastic community at Tabennese in Upper Egypt took place in 323–324 C.E.

[9] See the monastic rules in A. Boon, *Pachomiana latina* (Bibliothèque de la Revue d'histoire ecclésiastique 7; Louvain: Bureaux de la Revue, 1932), 25 (no. 49): *quantos potuerit discere* "as much as one could learn."

[10] Boon, *Pachomiana latina*, 50 (no. 140), 16 (no. 13), 46 (no. 122).

[11] A. Rahlfs, *Septuaginta-Studien*, Vol. 2: *Der Text des Septuaginta-Psalters* (Göttingen: Vandenhoeck & Ruprecht, 1907), 143.

[12] On this recension, cf. Rahlfs, *Septuaginta*, 28–32 (§ 4).

[13] R. Kasser and M. Testuz, *Papyrus Bodmer XXIV: Psaumes XVIII–CVIII* (Cologny: Bibliotheca Bodmeriana, 1967); manuscripts U and 2013 have been re-edited by Emmenegger, *Text des koptischen Psalters*, 259–327 (U), and 328–70 (2013).

[14] On the attestation of this additional variant, cf. Rahlfs, *Psalmi cum Odis*, 247, critical apparatus to Ps 95:10.

[15] For further Christian additions, cf. Rahlfs, *Psalmi cum Odis*, 30–32 (§ 4.4). Of special interest is the addition in Ps 50:9 "Purge me with *hyssop*" ※ ἀπὸ τοῦ αἵματος τοῦ ξύλου ※ ("from the blood of the tree"), supported by P. Bodmer XXIV, Cop^{Sa}-Ps, and Cop^{Me}-Ps.

century C.E.).[16] From the perspective of the textual history of LXX, the Bohairic version is less "interesting" than its (older) Sahidic sister.

The scarcely attested Fayyumic Psalter belongs to the Lower Egyptian type, but its translation seems to be independent from Cop^{Boh}-Ps.[17]

The "bipartite" division into Upper Egyptian and Lower Egyptian types was challenged by P. Bodmer XXIV (Greek) and a recently discovered Coptic Psalm codex in the Middle Egyptian dialect,[18] both unknown to Rahlfs. These texts exhibit typical Upper Egyptian readings (around 50%) and also agree with other text families, and, in addition, show some otherwise unknown peculiarities.[19] In view of the "mixed" textual character of the Middle Egyptian Psalter (also termed "Mudil-Psalter"), only with hesitation can it be regarded as a representative of a supposed "Middle Egyptian" recension of the Coptic Psalter.[20]

For further investigation of the Coptic translations of the Psalms we need most urgently critical editions of the Psalter in the main Sahidic and Bohairic dialects. As for the Sahidic Psalter, an *editio minor*, based on a selection of the best-preserved manuscripts,[21] seems to be preferable to an *editio maior*, which would include all available fragments (and quotations), since this task could hardly be completed in our generation.

Boud'hors, A., *Catalogue des Fragments Coptes de la Bibliothèque Nationale et Universitaire de Strasbourg*,

---

[16] For the Lower Egyptian recension, cf. Rahlfs, *Psalmi cum Odis*, 26–28 (§ 3).

[17] Cf. Richter, "Psalter, Psalmen und Hymnen," 2.

[18] Edited by Gabra, *Der Psalter im oxyrhynchitischen Dialekt*.

[19] According to the thorough evaluation and conclusions by Emmenegger, *Text des koptischen Psalters*, 255.

[20] The estimation of Nagel, "Der sahidische Psalter," 92–93, and N. Bosson and A. Boud'hors, "Le psaume 21 (22): Son attestation dans les diverses dialects coptes," in *David, Jésus et la reine Esther: Recherches sur le Psaume 21 (22 TM)* (ed. G. Dorival; Collection de la Revue des études juives 25; Paris: Peeters, 2002), 43–100 (esp. 96) that the "Mudil-Psalter" is a witness of a Middle Egyptian recension needs further qualification. As it stands, the "Mudil-Psalter" is an *unicum* in the textual history of the Coptic Psalter.

[21] For some proposals for such manuscripts, see Nagel, "Der sahidische Psalter," 94.

Vol. 1: *Fragments bibliques* (CSCO 571 Subsidia 99; Leuven: Peeters, 1998), 65–75.

Boud'hors, A. and C. Nakano, "Vestiges bibliques en copte fayoumique au Musée du Louvre," *Journal of Coptic Studies* 5 (2003): 17–53 (pls. 1–12).

Budge, E.A.W., *The Earliest Known Coptic Psalter: The Text in the Dialect of Upper Egypt: Edited from the Unique Papyrus Codex Oriental 5000 in the British Museum* (London: Kegan Paul, 1898).

Burmester, O.H.E. and E. Devaud, *Psalterii versio memphitica e recognitione Pauli de Lagarde: Réédition avec le texte copte en caractères coptes* (Louvain: Imprimerie J.-B. Istas, 1925).

Ciasca, *Fragmenta Copto-Sahidica*, 2.69–151.

Elanskaya, A.I., "A Fayyumic Text of Psalm 118:50–52.62–67.74–77 (The ms. I.1.b 637 of the Pushkin Museum of Fine Arts)," *BSAC* 30 (1991): 25–28 (reprinted in A.I. Elanskaya, *The Literary Coptic Manuscripts in the A.S. Pushkin State Fine Arts Museum in Moscow* [VCSup 18; Leiden: Brill, 1994], 414–17, pls. clv–clvi).

Gabra, G., *Der Psalter im Oxyrhynchitischen (Mesokemischen / Mittelägyptischen) Dialekt* (Abhandlungen des Deutschen Archäologischen Instituts Kairo: Koptische Reihe 4; Heidelberg: Heidelberger Orientverlag, 1995).

de Lagarde, P., *Psalterii Versio Memphitica* (Göttingen: Akad. Druckerei, 1875).

Nagel, P., "Der sahidische Psalter: Seine Erschließung und Erforschung neunzig Jahre nach Alfred Rahlfs," in *Der Septuaginta-Psalter und seine Tochterübersetzungen: Symposium in Göttingen 1997* (eds. A. Aejmelaeus and U. Quast; MSU 24; Göttingen: Vandenhoeck & Ruprecht, 2000), 82–96.

Quecke, H., "Ein faijumisches Fragment aus Ps 90 (91) (pHeid. Kopt. 184)," in *Festschrift Elmar Edel, 12. März 1979* (eds. M. Görg and E. Pusch; Ägypten und Altes Testament 1; Bamberg: Görg, 1979), 332–37.

Quecke, H., "Ein faijumisches Psalterfragment (Ps 16,4 ff.)," in *Studies Presented to Hans Jakob Polotsky* (ed. D.W. Young; East Gloucester: Pirtle and Polson, 1981), 300–313.

Rahlfs, A., *Die Berliner Handschrift des sahidischen Psalters* (Berlin: Weidmann, 1901).

Rahlfs, A. (ed.), *Psalmi cum Odis* (3rd ed.; Septuaginta Vetus Testamentum Graecum 10; Göttingen: Vandenhoeck & Ruprecht, 1979).

Richter, T.S., "Psalter, Psalmen und Hymnen in koptischer Überlieferung" (unpublished paper presented at the University of Leipzig, Ägyptologisches Institut, 2008).

Schüssler, *Biblia Coptica* 1.4, 152–55 (general index).

Till, W., "Wiener Faijumica," *Mus* 49 (1936): 169–217 (179–80).

Worrell, W.H., *The Coptic Manuscripts in the Freer Collection* (University of Michigan Studies, Humanistic Series 10: New York: Macmillan, 1923).

Peter Nagel

10.4.3 Ethiopic Translation(s)

10.4.3.1 Background and Inscriptional Evidence[1]

One imagines that the liturgical use of "The Psalms of David" (መዝሙር ዘዳዊት) made it one of the first to be translated into Ethiopic shortly after Christianity came to the old Axumite Kingdom sometime in the fourth century C.E. (→ 1.4.3.1). Indeed, there is hard evidence for a translation of the Psalms by the sixth century C.E. Three Old Ethiopic inscriptions from this time contain quotations from the Psalms of David. RIÉth 195, frg. 1 contains Ps 67(68):2 and frgs. 2–3 contain Pss 65(66)16–17; 19(20):8–9.[2] The quotations are fragmentary and the text in Ps 65(66):16 varies slightly from πάντες οἱ φοβούμενοι τὸν θεόν "all you who fear God" (*NETS*) but "correspond exactly to that in the older manuscripts as represented by Vat Etio 4 and BL Add 18,994."[3] Likewise, RIÉth 192 contains quotations of Pss 17(18):48; 117(118):10; 34(35):1b–2; 34(35):4b–5; 17(18):38a + 40–41a; 117(118):15b–16a. Again, though they contain five minor variations from the later manuscripts, "the text of the psalm passages in the inscription agrees with that of the text of the manuscripts"[4] that have survived to this day, mostly from the fourteenth century and later.

10.4.3.2 Distinctives and Centrality of the Ethiopian Psalter

Eth-Ps is far and away the most important book in Ethiopian Christian book culture generally, let alone in terms of being the book of the Ethiopic Old Testament with the most impact on its culture. Judging by the surviving collections, perhaps more than twenty-five percent of all Ethiopian Christian books ever copied are Psalters. Its mastery was, and still is, one of the primary goals of the traditional educational system of the Ethiopian Orthodox Church. It is a book that lived not only in the hands of the faithful, but in their memories as well. The earliest reports that came to Europe about Christian Ethiopia included assertions that the memorization of the Psalter was common throughout the Christian population.[5] The Ethiopians received the text of the Psalms from a Greek *Vorlage* (→ 10.3.1; more below), but produced a Psalter that reflected their own identity and tastes. In the first place, the content of the Psalter always included not only the Psalms of David but also four other works, the fifteen *Biblical Canticles*, Canticles, and two Maryan works, the *Praises of Mary* (ውዳሴ ማርያም) and the *Gate of Light* (አንቀጸ ብርሃን). Knibb cites the two examples in which biblical manuscripts (in the narrow sense) contained the Psalms, "Ber Or Qu 986 and a manuscript in the Church of Zion in Axum" (Eth[Davies Axum 3]) to which we can add only one other, Eth[BL Or 493]. Normally, the Psalms always circulated as part of the Psalter and always with these other works. Whereas with the other books of the Ethiopic Old Testament one can speak about their proximity to one another in the biblical manuscripts, Eth-Ps never traveled with the books other than those in the Psalter, all of which appear to have been treated with an equal devotion, and quite out of proportion to any of the other books in the Old Testament. The same point can be established by attention to the demographics of collections of manuscripts within churches. It would be a rare church indeed that possessed a single copy of another book of the Old Testament, and every church would have had several copies of

---

[1] Psalms are counted according to LXX-Ps in this article. The numbers of MT-Ps are given in parenthesis.

[2] RIÉth is an established abbreviation in Ethiopic studies referring to *Recueil des inscriptions de l'Éthiopie des périodes pré-axoumite et axoumite* (eds. E. Bernand, A.J. Drewes, and R. Schneider; 3 vols.; Paris: Éditions de Boccard and Académie des inscriptions et belles lettres, 1991–2000).

[3] Knibb, "Ethiopic Translation," 110.

[4] Knibb, "Ethiopic Translation," 111.

[5] Ludolf, *Psalterium Davidis Aethiopice*, 1.

10.4.3 ETHIOPIC TRANSLATION(S)

the Psalter. This raises interesting questions regarding functional canonicity.

One will find further indications of the role of the Ethiopian Orthodox Psalter as a means of expression of group identity, by taking note of the unique scribal practices developed by the Ethiopians not only for script and language, but also for page layout, line length, marking the midpoint of Eth-Ps, columetric layout of rubricated letters in the 150th Psalm and in the tenth Biblical Canticle, section headings in Ps 118(119) (= Eth-Ps 119) that specify the spiritual meanings of the Hebrew letters, rubrication for the divine name and the name of Mary, the layout and abbreviations in the antiphonal Psalm 135(136), etc. All of these elements were considered essential features of an approved Ethiopian Psalter as the representatives of the British and Foreign Bible Society were to discover when they brought printed copies of the Psalms to Ethiopia in 1815.[6]

A major study is under way with regard to the textual history of Eth-Ps. Led by Albert ten Kate, Marc Malevez, and Steve Delamarter, the study is based on transcriptions of substantial samples of the Psalms from more than forty-five manuscripts representing the full sweep of the extant manuscript tradition.[7]

10.4.3.3 Early Printed Editions of the Ethiopian Psalter (→ 1.4.3.4)

The earliest edition of Eth-Ps published in Europe was by Potken in 1513,[8] but it was the one produced by Ludolf in 1701[9] that became the standard work on which all subsequent European editions have been based, including that of the British and Foreign Bible Society.

---

[6] D.L. Appleyard et al., *Letters from Ethiopian Rulers: Early and Mid-Nineteenth Century* (Oxford: Oxford University Press, 1985). See, in particular, letter 6 from Emperor Takla Giyorgis in 1817, in which he complains about the failure of the Bible Society to produce Psalters according to the specifications of traditional Ethiopian book culture.

[7] Results will be published in the series Ethiopic Manuscripts, Texts, and Studies (Eugene: Pickwick, forthcoming).

[8] Potken, *Psalmi et Cantica*.

[9] Ludolf, *Psalterium Davidis Aethiopice*.

10.4.3.4 Textual Affiliation of the Ethiopic Psalms

The early dissertation by Dorn (1825)[10] compared the Ethiopic text with LXX (→ 10.3.1) as represented by Vaticanus and Alexandrinus and concluded, "Our version is rendered just as if from the Greek exemplars Vaticanus and Alexandrinus, in support the Hebrew text is sometimes summoned."[11]

In his study of the Greek traditions of the Psalter,[12] Rahlfs identified 129 passages that provided characteristic variations between witnesses. He included the Ethiopic in these collations and concluded that, after the Bohairic (→ 10.4.2), the Ethiopic showed greatest affinity with the text of Vaticanus (LXX^B) of any of the witnesses. Rahlfs considered two readings to be particularly telling in this regard: In Ps 58(59):16, Eth-Ps agrees with LXX$^{B'' 55}$ in not reading the μη "not" of ἐὰν δὲ μὴ χορτασθῶσιν "but if they do not get their fill" (*NETS*). In Ps 118(119):59, Eth-Ps lacks with LXX^B and against LXX$^{S' A'}$ the preposition κατά "according" before τὰς ὁδούς σου "your ways." And again, in Ps 89(90):17, Eth-Ps lacks in agreement with LXX$^{B' R'' 55}$ the added stich καὶ τὸ εργον τῶν χειρῶν ημῶν κατευθυνον "and prosper upon us the work of our hands" (*NETS*) of LXX$^{S L' A'}$.

However, Knibb shows that the relationships are even more complex, underscoring examples in Rahlfs' list where the Ethiopic aligns with LXX^A (Ps 24[25]:14 and 26[27]:6), where it aligns with Lucianic readings (Ps 10[11]:3; 24[25]:2; 33[34]:5; 36[37]:23; 41[42]:11; → 10.3.6), and where the Ethiopic aligns with LXX^A readings where both the Ethiopic and LXX^B agree against Lucianic readings (Ps 7:10–11, 9:33[10:12]; 9:36[10:15]; 13[14]:1; 13[14]:3–10; 13[14]:6; 19[20]:8; 20[21]:3; 20[21]:10; 21[22]:26). He concludes that "in light of the above it would appear that although the Ethiopic translation be-

---

[10] Dorn, *De Psalterio*.

[11] "Versio nostra concinnata est aeque ex exemplari Graecorum Vaticano atque Alexandrino, in auxilium vocato nonnumquam textu Hebraeo." Cited in Knibb, "Ethiopic Translation," 113.

[12] Rahlfs, *Der Text des Septuaginta-Psalters*.

longs with the B-text, it was influenced by a manuscript belonging to the A-text such as 55 or 1219."[13]

In all of these analyses of textual affiliation, however, the only form of the Ethiopic under consideration has been the Old Ethiopic. Western scholarship has been singularly uninterested in the exploration of the further textual history of the Ethiopic Psalter beyond the witness of the Old Ethiopic to some form of the Greek text. A study of the subsequent textual history within Ethiopia is greatly needed to establish if and how the developments that took place in other books of the Ethiopic Old Testament were replicated in the Psalter.

10.4.3.5 Old and New Psalm Titles

The titles of Eth-Ps provide an instructive case study regarding new developments beyond the Old Ethiopic. Schneider drew attention to two sets of Psalm titles in the Ethiopic manuscripts, one form in the older manuscripts, and another form in more recent manuscripts.[14] With access to the considerable collections in Jerusalem, Pedersen carried out a more detailed study,[15] confirming what Schneider knew, namely that the old set of titles followed the LXX (→ 10.3.1) titles fairly closely. But she went a step further and showed how the new set of titles were indebted to the system of headings produced by Theodore of Mopsuestia in the fifth century C.E., and which were apparently taken up by the scholars of Gondar after the sixteenth century. Further, this new system of titles is the one employed in the *andemta* commentaries that come to written form in the late seventeenth and early eighteenth centuries. A study of fifty-four Psalters demonstrates a dramatic and precise division between those containing the old titles that follow LXX and those that possess the new titles. The change occurred in the early to mid-sixteenth century and may correspond to the appearance in Ethiopia of a translation of the commentary of Ibn at-Tayyib, one recension of which was produced in Egypt

and reflected more Miaphysite views. A sixteenth-century Ethiopic manuscript of the Gospel commentary appears to follow this recension.[16]

The convergence of these two lines of evidence – new ideas about the text finding expression in the *Andemta* alongside a new system of titles in the biblical text itself – corresponds to the sorts of patterns observed elsewhere in the Ethiopic Old Testament, particularly by Lee and Rodas in the book of Genesis.[17] These provide another example of the kind of developments taking place during the epoch of the revised Ethiopic text.

10.4.3.6 Character of the Old Ethiopic Translation (→ 1.4.3.7.3)

Knibb characterizes the translation technique of the Old Ethiopic Psalms as literal in character, owing in part to the line-by-line approach taken by the translator. But, particularly in places where the translator did not understand his Greek *Vorlage* (→ 10.3.1), this could also result in renderings that were completely free. In places, the translation seems aimed at producing a smoother text. This was accomplished through "the addition of odd words or phrases, simplification of the text, simplification of vocabulary, imprecision in translation, or free translation."[18]

Bassano, *Beluy Kidan*.
Devens, M., *A Concordance to Psalms in the Ethiopic Version* (Äthiopistische Forschungen 59; Wiesbaden: Harrassowitz, 2001).
Dorn, J.A.B., *De Psalterio Aethiopico Commentatio* (Leipzig: Breitkopf & Haertel, 1825).
Faultless, J., "The Two Recensions of the Prologue to John in Ibn al-Tayyib's Commentary on the Gospels," in *Christians at the Heart of Islamic Rule: Church Life and Scholarship in 'Abbasid Iraq* (ed. D.R. Thomas; The History of Christian-Muslim Relations 1; Leiden: Brill, 2003), 177–98.

---

[13] Knibb, "Ethiopic Translation," 117–19 (119).
[14] Schneider, "Les titres."
[15] Pedersen, *Traditional Ethiopian Exegesis*, 19–29.

[16] Faultless, "The Two Recensions."
[17] In the 2012 annual SBL meeting, Ralph Lee reported on his work with Merigeta Rodas Tadesa Ababa on "Textual Variations as Recorded in the Ethiopian Andəmta Biblical Commentaries."
[18] Knibb, "Ethiopic Translation," 121.

Knibb, M.A., "The Ethiopic Translation of the Psalms," in *Der Septuaginta-Psalter und seine Tochterübersetzungen: Symposium in Göttingen 1997* (eds. A. Aejmelaeus and U. Quast; MSU 24; Göttingen: Vandenhoeck & Ruprecht, 2000), 107–22.

Ludolf, J., *Psalterium Davidis Aethiopice et Latine* (Frankfurt a.M.: Zunner & Helwig, 1701).

Pedersen, K.S., *Traditional Ethiopian Exegesis of the Book of Psalms* (Äthiopistische Forschungen 36; Wiesbaden: Harrassowitz, 1995).

Potken, J. (ed.), *Psalmi et Cantica: Psalterium et canticum canticorum et alia cantica biblica aethiopice et syllabarium seu de legende ratione* (Rome: Silber, 1513).

Rahlfs, A., *Septuaginta-Studien 2: Der Text des Septuaginta-Psalters: Nebst einem Anhang: Griechische Psalterfragmente aus Oberägypten nach Abschriften von W.E. Crum* (Göttingen: Vandenhoeck & Ruprecht, 1907).

Rahlfs, A. (ed.), *Psalmi cum Odis* (Septuaginta Vetus Testamentum Graecum 10; Göttingen: Vandenhoeck & Ruprecht, 1931).

Schneider, R., "Les titres des psaumes en éthiopien," in *Mélanges Marcel Cohen* (ed. D. Cohen, The Hague: Mouton, 1970), 424–28.

Steve Delamarter

10.4.4 Late Syriac Translations

10.4.4.1 Background

Tracing the history of Syriac translations of Psalms subsequent to the appearance of the Peshitta (S) in perhaps the second half of the second century or the first part of the third century C.E. involves an investigation of both textual and literary evidence. A key aspect of that history has to do with the impact of the Greek versions of the Hebrew Scriptures on Syriac biblical texts. Although there are traces of LXX (→ 1.3.1.1) influence on the Peshitta (→ 1.3.4), this Syriac "Vulgate" is based on the Hebrew Bible (→ 1.2.2). During the course of the five centuries or so after the translation of the Peshitta, a growing conviction on the part of important figures in the constellation of Syriac luminaries regarding the authoritativeness of "the version of the seventy" resulted in the production of Syriac versions that were closely aligned with ܝܘܢܝܐ "the Greek."[1]

---

[1] Hiebert, "Syriac Versions," 509.

10.4.4.2 Philoxenian Version

Perhaps the first such Graecized version was completed in 508 C.E. and attributed to Philoxenus, the Monophysite bishop of Mabbug in the ecclesiastical province of Euphratesia.[2] The earliest-known literary reference to it is by the sixth-century C.E. Mesopotamian monk, Moses of Aghel, in an introduction to his translation into Syriac of Cyril of Alexandria's *Glaphyra*. Moses mentions "the version of the New (Testament) and of David" that a certain chorepiscopus ("rural bishop") named Polycarp prepared for Philoxenus.[3] The reference to a version "of David" is, however, somewhat perplexing. If Moses is referring to the Psalter, one might expect the usual Syriac term for Psalms (ܡܙܡܘܪܐ), though admittedly the name David can be used as a metonym for the Psalter. But the unusual placement of "and of David" has led to the suggestion that it is a later gloss and not attributable to Moses at all:[4] ܟܕ ܡܛܝܬ ܕܝܢ ܠܡܦܩܢܐ ܕܚܕܬܐ ܕܥܒܕ܂ ܘܕܕܘܝܕ܂ ܦܘܠܘܩܪܦܘܣ "When one encounters the version of the New that made – and of David – Polycarp ..." Nevertheless, whether it is to Moses or some later glossator that the reference to the version of David may be attributed, there is clearly a Syriac ecclesiastical tradition regarding a Philoxenian version of the Psalter. The thirteenth-century monk, Eli of Qartamin, also asserts that the Philoxenian version included both testaments of the Christian Bible.[5] Thomas of Harkel, who in the early seventh century C.E. produced a version of the Syriac New Testament that he said was a revision of the one made "in the days of ... Philoxenus," does not mention a Philoxenian Old Testament, but he knows about

---

[2] Venables, "Philoxenus (4) (Xenaias)," 392; Gwynn, "Polycarpus (5)," 431–34. The sixth-century C.E. Nestorian Catholicus (or Patriarch) Mar Aba I is said to have translated the Old Testament from Greek to Syriac (Assemani, *Bibliotheca Orientalis*, 3.1, 75). Textual evidence for such a translation is, however, lacking (Vööbus, *The Hexapla and the Syro-Hexapla*, 48).

[3] Guidi, "Mosè di Aghel e Simone Abbate," 404.

[4] Lebon, "La version philoxénienne," 413–15; Delekat, "Die syrolukianische Übersetzung," 23, n. 11.

[5] De Halleux, *Éli de Qartamīn*; A. Mingana, "New Documents on Philoxenus of Hierapolis, and on the Philoxenian Version of the Bible," *The Expositor* 8/19 (1920): 150–53.

the textual work that was carried out under the auspices of the renowned bishop of Mabbug.⁶

In addition to the preceding literary evidence, there is also textual evidence that points to the existence of at least portions of a Philoxenian Old Testament. One such example exists in the form of a variant reading to the Syro-Hexapla (Syh; → 6–9.2.4.3) of Isa 9:6(5)b–7(6)a that is attributed to Philoxenus in a marginal scholion: "From another tradition that was translated into Syriac by the care of the holy Philoxenus, bishop of Mabbug."⁷ To be sure, the variant itself exhibits evidence of having been revised in accordance with post-Philoxenian translation technique. Yet there is reason to believe that the text upon which the reading is based was an excerpt from an authentic Philoxenian version of Isaiah.⁸ Another possible witness to that version is the so-called Syro-Lucianic (Syl; → 1.4.4) text contained in a fragmentary British Museum manuscript.⁹ What makes the linkage between this anonymous text and Philoxenus a plausible one is that some of his quotations of Isaiah are virtually identical to the Syro-Lucianic text in situations in which that involves divergence from the Peshitta in the direction of significant agreement with the "Lucianic" or Byzantine textual tradition of LXX.¹⁰ Furthermore, even when Philoxenus' citations of Isaiah do not overlap with the extant portions of the Syro-Lucianic text, there is significant stylistic comparability between them in terms of general linguistic characteristics.

With the case made for the likely existence of a Philoxenian version of Isaiah, the question remains as to whether there is textual evidence for a Philoxenian Psalter as Moses of Aghel seems to suggest. As it turns out, there is some that is indirect or circumstantial in nature, though uncovering it requires careful analysis of a version that made its appearance a little more than a century after that attributed to Philoxenus.

10.4.4.3 Paul of Tella's Version

In the second decade of the seventh century C.E., Paul, the Jacobite bishop of Tella in Mesopotamia (→ 1.4.5.2), along with the above-mentioned Thomas of Harkel and other clerics from the patriarchate of Syrian Antioch, fled to the Antonian monastery outside of Alexandria, Egypt to escape the invasion of Khosrau II and his Persian forces. While in Egypt, Paul supervised the production of the Syro-Hexapla (→ 1.4.5), a version of the Old Testament that is characterized by isomorphic fidelity to the Greek.¹¹

The Syro-Hexapla is regarded to be the Syriac rendering of specifically the fifth column of a work known as the Hexapla (Hex; → 1.3.1.2) that was compiled by the third-century C.E. scholar, Origen. This column contained the version of LXX (→ 1.3.1.1) that he undertook to bring into closer conformity with the Hebrew text of his day, by marking with an obelus the Greek words or phrases that had no counterpart in the Hebrew (→ 1.2.2), and by supplying what was lacking in comparison to the Hebrew from one of "the three" – Aquila, Symmachus, or Theodotion (→ 1.3.1.2) – which appeared in three other columns of the Hexapla, additions that he marked with an asterisk.¹² Paul of Tella's version of the Old Testament is indeed a key witness to the Hexaplaric recension, everywhere, that is, except in the Psalter. As Rahlfs has demonstrated in his edition of the LXX Psalter, the so-called Syro-Hexapla of Psalms contains a text that agrees primarily with his LXX^L group (→ 10.3.6), which he associates with the Lucianic recension.¹³

---

⁶ This evidence is found in the colophons of the Harklean New Testament. Gospels: White, *Sacrorum Evangeliorum*, 561–62; Acts and Catholic Epistles: White, *Actuum Apostolorum et Epistolarum*, 274–75; Corpus Paulinum: Wright and Cook, *A Catalogue of the Syriac Manuscripts*, 1.11; Apocalypse: Vööbus, *The Apocalypse*, 35*, 52–62.

⁷ Ceriani, *Codex Syro-Hexaplaris*, folio 176ʳ.

⁸ Jenkins, *Old Testament Quotations*, 178–86.

⁹ MS Br. Mus. Add. 17106, published by Ceriani (*Esaiae fragmenta syriaca*, 1–40). The extant portions of Isaiah are 28:3–17, 42:17–49:18, and 66:11–23.

¹⁰ Jenkins, "Some Quotations from Isaiah," 21–24. See also De Halleux, *Philoxène de Mabbog: Commentaire*, 90; Hiebert, *The "Syrohexaplaric" Psalter*, 250–51, 300–301 n. 27.

¹¹ Gwynn, "Paulus (48) Tellensis," 266–69; Vööbus, *The Hexapla and the Syro-Hexapla*, 42; Zuntz, *Ancestry*, 8.

¹² Hiebert, *The "Syrohexaplaric" Psalter*, 1–2.

¹³ Rahlfs, *Psalmi cum Odis*, 60–70.

10.4.4 LATE SYRIAC TRANSLATIONS

This is not to say that there is no indication of Hexaplaric activity in Paul of Tella's Psalter. A number of obelized and asterisked readings furnish evidence that, at some point in the textual history, Origen's recension exerted a certain degree of influence. Furthermore, in the margins of some of the existing manuscripts, hundreds of non-LXX readings attributed to Aquila, Symmachus, Theodotion, Quinta, and Sexta are recorded.[14] Nonetheless, Paul's Psalter text itself is not essentially Hexaplaric.

It is noteworthy that Paul departed from his usual *modus operandi* and employed a Greek text that was different than the Hexapla. Given the fact that there are very few extant witnesses to the Hexaplaric recension for Psalms, one wonders if he took this course of action because a Greek Hexaplaric exemplar may not have been readily available. The best and only complete witness to this textual tradition is, in fact, not a Greek one but Jerome's Gallican Psalter (→ 10.3.7.1). Apart from this Latin translation and Jerome's quotations of the Psalter in his *Letter to Sunnia and Fretela*, Rahlfs had available to him when he prepared his edition of LXX-Ps only two fragmentary Hexaplaric Greek texts, LXX[1098] and LXX[2005]. Furthermore, it is possible that Paul of Tella did not translate the Psalter afresh from the Greek. Instead, he may have revised an existing Syriac version of Psalms that was of a Byzantine rather than a Hexaplaric type, perhaps one like Syl-Isa mentioned above.[15] There is textual evidence to suggest that this could have been the case.

10.4.4.4 Textual Affinities between SyrPs and the *Philoxeniana*

Textual evidence that points to the possible existence of a Philoxenian Psalter is discernible in the text tradition attested by the majority of the witnesses collated for my edition of the so-called Syro-Hexapla of Psalms (SyrPs).[16] Among the stylistic features that SyrPs shares with *Philoxeniana*, such as the Syl-Isa text and Philoxenus' quotations of Isaiah, are the marked preference for the interrogative pronoun ܐܝܠܝܢ in rendering the article that accompanies a Greek plural participle, and for the direct attachment of a pronominal suffix to a substantive as the counterpart to a Greek substantive plus possessive pronoun. In the Syro-Hexapla (→ 1.4.5) elsewhere in the Old Testament and in the Harklean New Testament, however, the preference is for the demonstrative pronouns ܗܢܘܢ and ܗܠܝܢ in the first case, and for the substantive plus independent possessive pronoun ܕܝܠ with accompanying suffix in the second. The following examples are representative:

- Ps 24:3: οἱ ἀνομοῦντες "those who are lawless" – ܐܝܠܝܢ ܕܡܥܘܠܝܢ (SyrPs) "those who do wrong"
- Isa 45:20: οἱ σῳζόμενοι "those who are being saved" – ܐܝܠܝܢ ܕܡܬܦܪܩܝܢ (Syl) "those who are being redeemed"; ܗܢܘܢ ܕܡܬܦܪܩܝܢ (Syh) "those who are being saved"
- Ps 24:2: οἱ ἐχθροί μου "my enemies" – ܒܥܠܕܒܒܝ̈ (SyrPs) "my enemies"
- Isa 43:5: τὸ σπέρμα σου "your offspring" – ܙܪܥܟ (Syl) "your offspring"; ܙܪܥܐ ܕܝܠܟ (Syh) "your offspring"

10.4.4.5 Textual Distinctions between SyrPs and the *Philoxeniana*

Because SyrPs also exhibits features that are characteristic of the Syro-Hexapla and the Harklean version but not of the Philoxenian version, it is unlikely that SyrPs constitutes an unrevised Philoxenian Psalter. This would parallel the situation that obtains in regard to the alternative reading in Syh-Isa 9 mentioned above, a reading that appears to be a revision of Philoxenian Isaiah (→ 6–9.2.4.2) in accordance with the translation technique of Paul of Tella (→ 1.4.5.2; → 10.4.4.3). Representative examples of Syro-Hexaplaric and Harklean features in SyrPs but not in the *Philoxeniana* include ܗܘܝܘ ܗܘ ܗܘ, ܠܗܘܢ "himself," "themselves" etc. for the

---

[14] Field, *Hexapla*, 2.87–305; Hiebert, *The "Syrohexaplaric" Psalter*, 261–73.
[15] Hiebert, "Syriac Biblical Textual History," 185–86.
[16] SyrPs consists of manuscripts that I have designated *a,*

b, c, d, e, f, g, h₁. For a description of each, see Hiebert, *The "Syrohexaplaric" Psalter*, 5–12.

Greek third person reflexive pronoun ἑαυτοῦ "of himself" etc. (Phil.: ܢܦܫܐ "oneself" with appropriate suffix); the uncontracted negative ܠܐ ܐܝܬ "there is not/no" (Phil.: the contracted negative ܠܝܬ "there is not/no"); the periphrastic construction ܠܐ ܢܡܘܣܘܬܐ "unlawfulness" for ἀνομία "lawlessness" (Phil.: ܥܘܠܐ "iniquity"); and ܫܝܢܐ "peace" for εἰρήνη "peace" (Phil.: ܫܠܡܐ "peace, welfare").

10.4.4.6 A Possible Harklean Psalter

Another text tradition that is part of the textual history of the so-called SyrPs and that I have designated SyrPsᵃ is found in the initial portions of two manuscripts.[17] This tradition is characterized by even greater servility to the Greek than is the case with SyrPs. Thus, for example, SyrPsᵃ is almost totally consistent in the use of the independent possessive pronoun with a substantive, whereas in SyrPs, although the ܕܝܠ form is fairly common, the overall preference is for a suffix that is attached directly to a noun (e.g., Ps 24:2: οἱ ἐχθροί μου – ܒܥܠܕܒܒܐ ܕܝܠܝ [SyrPsᵃ]; ܒܥܠܕܒܒܝ [SyrPs] all meaning "my enemies"). Furthermore, SyrPsᵃ exhibits periphrastic constructions to render Greek compound words in places where SyrPs does not adopt that strategy (e.g., Ps 9:26[25], 31[30]: κατακυριεύω "exercise dominion" – ܗܘܐ ܡܪܐ [SyrPsᵃ] "be lord"; ܫܠܛ/Ethpaal "rule" [SyrPs]; Ps 11:4[3]: μεγαλορρήμων "boastful" – ܪܘܪܒ ܡ̈ܠܐ [SyrPsᵃ] "magnify words"; ܡܬܪܘܪܒܢܐ [SyrPs] "boastful"). SyrPsᵃ also distinguishes itself from SyrPs in that it normally has the demonstrative ܗܢܘܢ as the counterpart to the article accompanying a Greek plural participle, while SyrPs prefers the interrogative pronoun ܐܝܠܝܢ (e.g., Ps 24:3: οἱ ἀνομοῦντες "those who are lawless" – ܗܢܘܢ ܕܡܥܘܠܝܢ "those who do wrong" [SyrPsᵃ]; ܐܝܠܝܢ ܕܡܥܘܠܝܢ "those who do wrong" [SyrPs]).

I have previously suggested the possibility that SyrPsᵃ might be attributable to Thomas of Harkel, Paul of Tella's (→ 1.4.5.2; → 10.4.4.3) companion at the monastery outside of Alexandria, based on Moses of Aghel's reference to a Philoxenian version of the New Testament "and of David" and on the fact that Thomas is known to have revised the Philoxenian version.[18] Furthermore, Scher reports that manuscript *h*, one of the witnesses to the SyrPsᵃ text, contains "la version héracléenne."[19] In the final analysis, however, it must be admitted that a linkage between SyrPsᵃ and Thomas cannot be confirmed.

10.4.4.7 Jacob of Edessa's Version

While the textual traditions associated with the so-called Syro-Hexaplaric Psalter exhibit a high degree of conformity to the Greek text upon which they were based, the recension of the Old Testament that was produced by Jacob of Edessa (→ 1.4.6) in the early eighth century C.E. and that has survived in fragments and citations (→ 21.9) of certain books including Psalms represents a blending of readings from the Peshitta and Syro-Hexapla (→ 10.3.4).[20] A representative example is found in Ps 9:9(8):

- MT תֵּבֵל בְּצֶדֶק "the world with righteousness"
- S ܐܪܥܐ ܒܩܘܫܬܐ "the earth with truth" (ܐܪܥܐ "the earth") pr ܠ "*l*" in manuscripts S$^{9t3\ 12a1\ 12t2.5}$)[21]
- LXX τὴν οἰκουμένην ἐν δικαιοσύνῃ "the world with righteousness"
- SyrPs ܠܡܥܡܪܬܐ ܒܙܕܝܩܘܬܐ "the habitable world with righteousness"
- SyrPsᵃ "the inhabited world with righteousness" (*h** transposes ܠܡܬܥܡܪܢܝܬܐ "the inhabited world" and the preceding word ܢܕܘܢ "he will judge")[22]

---

[17] The text of SyrPsᵃ is contained only in the first part of manuscripts *h* and *j*. For a description of each, see Hiebert, *The "Syrohexaplaric" Psalter*, 11–12.

[18] Hiebert, *The "Syrohexaplaric" Psalter*, 248–50, 259–60.

[19] Scher, "Notice sur les manuscrits syriaques," 332.

[20] Baars, "Ein neugefundenes Bruchstück," 551–54; van Rompay, "Development of Biblical Interpretation," 560–62; Hiebert, "Syriac Versions," 515–16, 530–32.

[21] Peshiṭta Institute, ed., *Book of Psalms*, ad loc. The above sigla designate the following witnesses: 9t3 = London, British Library, Add. 17,109; 12a1 = Cambridge University Library oo 1.1,2; 12t2 = London, British Library, Add. 14,674; 12t5 = Vatican Library, Borg. sir. 23. The → points to manuscripts younger than the twelfth century and not belonging to a family.

[22] *h** signifies the original reading in ms Baghdad, Libr. of

- Jacob ܐܠܐܪܥܐ ܒܙܕܝܩܘܬܐ "the earth with righteousness"[23]

10.4.4.8 Conclusion

It appears that Jacob of Edessa's recension of the Old Testament was the last of the prominent Syriac versions to be produced, though the Peshitta (→ 10.3.4) remained the most popular. The versions of Paul of Tella and Jacob of Edessa did, however, continue to be copied, cited by scholars, and even used in some lectionaries. The trend toward the increasingly isomorphic rendering of the Greek Scriptures (including the Psalter) into Syriac in the sixth and seventh centuries C.E. was not conducive to the production of elegant translations, but that kind of approach did give rise to versions that are useful for the task of textual criticism in the identification of the text types upon which those versions are based.

Assemani, G.S., *Bibliotheca Orientalis Clementino-Vaticana* (3 vols.; Rome: Typis sacrae congregationis de propaganda fide, 1719–1728).

Baars, W., "Ein neugefundenes Bruchstück aus der syrischen Bibelrevision des Jakob von Edessa," *VT* 18 (1968): 548–54.

Baars, W., *New Syro-Hexaplaric Texts: Edited, Commented upon, and Compared with the Septuagint* (Leiden: Brill, 1968).

Ball, C.J., "Jacobus (24) Edessenus," *DCB* 3:332–35.

Brock, S.P., "Syriac Versions," *ABD* 6:794–99.

Brock, S.P., "The Resolution of the Philoxenian/Harclean Problem," in *New Testament Textual Criticism – Its Significance for Exegesis: Essays in Honour of Bruce M. Metzger* (eds. E.J. Epp and G.D. Fee; Oxford: Clarendon Press, 1981), 325–43.

Ceriani, A., *Esaiae fragmenta syriaca versionis anonymae et recensionis Jacobi Edesseni* (Monumenta sacra et profana 5.1; Milan: Bibliotheca Ambrosiana, 1868).

Ceriani, A., *Codex Syro-Hexaplaris Ambrosianus photolithographice editus* (Monumenta sacra et profana 7; Milan: Bibliotheca Ambrosiana, 1874).

Delekat, L., "Die syrolukianische Übersetzung des Buches Jesaja und das Postulat einer alttestamentlichen Vetus Syra," *ZAW* 69 (1957): 21–54.

Field, **Hexapla*.

Guidi, I., "Mosè di Aghel e Simone Abbate," *Rendiconti della R. Accademia dei Lincei* 4.2 (1886): 397–416, 545–57.

Gwynn, J., "Paulus (48) Tellensis," *DCB* 4:266–71.

Gwynn, J., "Polycarpus (5)," *DCB* 4:431–34.

Gwynn, J., "Thomas (17) Harklensis," *DCB* 4:1014–21.

Gwynn, J., *Remnants of the Later Syriac Versions of the Bible* (London: Williams and Norgate, 1909).

de Halleux, A., *Élī de Qartamīn: Mēmrā sur S. Mār Philoxène de Mabbog* (CSCO Syr. 101; Louvain: Secrétariat du Corpus SCO, 1963).

de Halleux, A., *Philoxène de Mabbog: Sa vie, ses écrits, sa théologie* (Louvain: Imprimerie orientaliste, 1963).

de Halleux, A., *Philoxène de Mabbog: Commentaire du prologue johannique (Ms. Br. Mus. Add. 14,534)* (CSCO Syr. 165; Louvain: Secrétariat du Corpus SCO, 1977).

Hiebert, R.J.V., *The "Syrohexaplaric" Psalter* (SBLSCS 27; Atlanta: Scholars Press, 1989).

Hiebert, R.J.V., "The 'Syrohexaplaric' Psalter: Its Text and Textual History," in *Der Septuaginta-Psalter und seine Tochterübersetzungen: Symposium in Göttingen 1997* (eds. A. Aejmelaeus and U. Quast; MSU 24; Göttingen: Vandenhoeck & Ruprecht, 2000), 123–46.

Hiebert, R.J.V., "Syriac Biblical Textual History and the Greek Psalter," in *The Old Greek Psalter: Studies in Honour of Albert Pietersma* (eds. R.J.V. Hiebert, C.E. Cox, and P.J. Gentry; JSOTSup 332; Sheffield: Sheffield Academic Press, 2001), 178–204.

Hiebert, R.J.V., "The Place of the Syriac Versions in the Textual History of the Psalter," in *The Book of Psalms: Composition and Reception* (eds. P.W. Flint and P.D. Miller; VTSup 99; Leiden: Brill, 2005), 505–36.

Jenkins, R.G., "Some Quotations from Isaiah in the Philoxenian Version," *Abr-Nahrain* 20 (1981–1982): 20–36.

Jenkins, R.G., *The Old Testament Quotations of Philoxenus of Mabbug* (CSCO Subsidia 84; Louvain: Peeters, 1989).

de Lagarde, P., *Bibliothecae Syriacae ... quae ad philologiam sacram pertinent* (Göttingen: Horstmann, 1892).

Lebon, J., "La version philoxénienne de la Bible," *RHE* 12 (1911, repr. 1967): 413–36.

Peshiṭta Institute (ed.), *The Book of Psalms* (The Old Testament in Syriac according to the Peshiṭta Version 2.3: Leiden: Brill, 1980).

Rahlfs, A. (ed.), *Psalmi cum Odis* (Septuaginta: Vetus

---

the Chald. Patr., 1112, also known as Diarbakir Cod. 2, which I have designated as *h*.

[23] Rücker, *Die syrische Jakobosanaphora*, 18 line 2.

Testamentum Graecum 10; Göttingen: Vandenhoeck & Ruprecht, 1931).

van Rompay, L., "Development of Biblical Interpretation in the Syrian Churches of the Middle Ages," in *Hebrew Bible/Old Testament: The History of Its Interpretation*, Vol. 1: *From the Beginnings to the Middle Ages (Until 1300)*: Part 2: *The Middle Ages* (ed. M. Sæbø; Göttingen: Vandenhoeck & Ruprecht, 2000), 559–77.

Rücker, A. (ed.), *Die syrische Jakobosanaphora nach der Rezension des Ja'qôb(h) von Edessa* (eds. P.K. Mohlberg and A. Rücker; Liturgiegeschichtliche Quellen 4; Münster: Verlag der Aschendorffschen Verlagsbuchhandlung, 1923).

Scher, A., "Notice sur les manuscrits syriaques et arabes conservés à l'archevêché chaldéen de Diarbékir," *JA* 10 (1907): 331–62, 385–431.

Venables, E., "Philoxenus (4) (Xenaias)," *DCB* 4:391–93.

Vööbus, A., "New Data for the Solution of the Problem concerning the Philoxenian Version," *Spiritus et Veritas: Carolo Kundzins dedicant collegae amici discipuli* (ed. J. Grinbergs; Eutin: Andr. Ozolins, 1953), 169–86.

Vööbus, A., *History of the School of Nisibis* (CSCO Subsidia 26; Louvain: Secrétariat du Corpus SCO, 1965).

Vööbus, A., *The Hexapla and the Syro-Hexapla* (Papers of the Estonian Theological Society in Exile 22; Stockholm: ETSE, 1971).

Vööbus, A., *The Apocalypse in the Harklean Version* (CSCO Subsidia 56; Louvain: Secrétariat du Corpus SCO, 1978).

White, J. (ed.), *Sacrorum Evangeliorum versio syriaca Philoxeniana* (Oxford: Clarendon Press, 1778).

White, J. (ed.), *Actuum Apostolorum et Epistolarum tam Catholicarum quam Paulinarum: Versio syriaca Philoxeniana* (2 vols.; Oxford: Clarendon Press, 1799–1803).

Wright, W. and S.A. Cook, *A Catalogue of the Syriac Manuscripts Preserved in the Library of the University of Cambridge* (2 vols.; Cambridge: Cambridge University Press, 1901).

Zuntz, G., *The Ancestry of the Harklean New Testament* (The British Academy Supplemental Papers 7; London: Oxford University Press, 1945).

Robert J.V. Hiebert

10.4.5 Armenian Translations

10.4.5.1 Nature of the Evidence

The textual analysis of Arm-Ps is rendered complex by the use of the Psalms in Syriac (→ 10.3.4) for liturgical purposes in Armenia before their translation into Armenian in the early fifth century C.E.[1] This means that it was easy for scribes to introduce readings known by memory from liturgical texts into the early manuscript tradition. The large number of manuscripts of Arm-Ps has discouraged the preparation of a critical edition. However, the nature of the Psalter, its popularity, and people's love for its contents have meant that there have been numerous printed editions, apart from Zohrapian's edition of 1805.[2]

Rahlfs' Edition of LXX-Ps

Rahlfs did not collate the Armenian and other subversions (Ethiopic, Palestinian, Arabic) because, he says, they are less important than Greek witnesses (→ 10.3.1) for the purposes of textual criticism and were not available in reliable editions.[3] It turns out that Zohrapian's base manuscript for collation is an excellent witness to Arm-Ps (see below). Rahlfs could not have known that in the 1920s.

10.4.5.2 Textual Character of Arm-Ps: Baumstark and Ter-Petrosyan

In the 1920s, Baumstark[4] published a series of articles in which he argued that Arm-Ps derives from a Peshitta-based translation (→ 10.3.4) that was edited on the basis of a form of LXX-Ps (→ 10.3.1) and, further, that this Greek text was not Hexaplaric (→ 10.3.5). Baumstark used Rahlfs' delineation of the text groups in LXX-Ps and argued that Armenian agreements are strongest with the Western text.[5] Some fifty years later, the Syriacist Ter-Petrosyan[6] contributed a useful study on this same issue. He provides a list of readings shared uniquely by Arm-Ps and the Peshitta and suggests, much like Baumstark, that an earlier Peshitta-based translation was revised to a Greek text, specifically a Lu-

---

[1] Mathews, "Syriac," citing the fifth century C.E. historian, Ghazar of P'arp, 20–21.
[2] Anassian, cols. 382–454; Zohrapian, *Scriptures.
[3] Rahlfs, *Psalmi*, 16–17, n. 3.
[4] Baumstark, "Der armenische Psaltertext."
[5] See Cox, "Text of the Old Greek Psalter," 179–80.
[6] Ter-Petrosyan, "The Armenian Translation of Psalms."

10.4.5 ARMENIAN TRANSLATIONS

cianic Greek text (→ 10.3.6).[7] It appears from these analyses that Arm-Ps is a composite text.

10.4.5.3 More Recent Studies

Two more recent studies by Cox collate Arm-Ps 10–20 and "The Songs of Zion" (Psalm 46; 48; 76; 84; 87; 122; 132; 137) against Rahlfs' edition. In the former case,[8] the text and apparatus of Zohrapian's edition was expanded with the addition of Armenian manuscripts Jerusalem 1925 and (Yerevan) Matenadaran 1500, two manuscripts that are regarded as the Vaticanus and Sinaiticus of the Armenian biblical text tradition. Several important conclusions are arrived at: for Arm-Ps, the text of Zohrapian's edition[9] offers as pure a form of text as manuscripts J1925 and M1500: it is an excellent text form; Zohrapian's text and apparatus preserve Arm 1 readings (on Arm 1, see → 1.3.7); there are Peshitta-based translations in Arm-Ps and these deserve examination, though some agreements with the Hebrew may derive from Hexaplaric readings in the LXX^L-type text; in terms of Rahlfs' delineation, Arm-Ps shows significant agreements with his LXX^R-type text, i.e., his "Western" text.[10] Zohrapian's text and apparatus, together with J1925 M1500, will serve well as representative of Arm-Ps in a new Göttingen edition of Psalms.

The study of the "Songs of Zion" compares the text and apparatus of Zohrapian's edition with the Greek of Rahlfs' edition and the Leiden Peshitta edition of Psalms.[11] The translation of Arm-Ps is "quite literal, but not slavish." It usually follows the word order of LXX; particles like ὅτι "that/because" and δή "now/already/truly/exactly" are disregarded; circumstantial participles are rendered by relative clauses; personal pronouns are freely added; the tenses of verbs often differ from those of the Greek. Textually, there are occasional striking agreements with the Peshitta (→ 10.3.4).[12] Three types of agreement are decisive: first, transpositions (an entire line is transposed at Ps 75:8); second, shared readings, on which compare Ps 86:5:

> LXX: "Mother Zion, a person will say" (NETS^{mg})
> Peshitta: "and to Zion it was said"
> Arm-Ps: "and to Zion it is said, 'Mother'" ("Mother" is conflated from the Greek).

Third, variation in number (singular, plural) in Arm-Ps is likely attributable to Syriac manuscripts that poorly preserved the *seyame*, the marker of plurality.[13] Cumulatively, these characteristics of Arm-Ps point to a textual relationship with the Peshitta (→ 10.3.4).

10.4.5.4 Assessment of Arm-Ps

The Armenian translation of Psalms is of interest textually to both Syriac (→ 10.3.4) and LXX (→ 10.3.1) scholars: to the former for the preservation of early readings that date to a time when the textual tradition of the Syriac was still fluid, and to the latter for access to an early witness of the Greek text. The textual situation is complex and awaits a suitable successor to Zohrapian's edition[14] as well as a new, critical edition of the Greek. Then a proper assessment of the textual affiliations of Arm-Ps can be made and a clearer understanding of its textual history will emerge.

Baumstark, A., "Der armenische Psaltertext: Sein Verhältnis zum syrischen der Peschitta und seine Bedeutung für die LXX Forschung," *OrChr* 22 (1922–1924): 180–213; 23 (1926): 158–69, 319–33; 24 (1927): 146–59.

Cox, C., "The Armenian Version and the Text of the Old Greek Psalter," in *Der Septuaginta-Psalter und seine Tochterübersetzungen (Symposium in Göttingen 1997)* (eds. A. Aejmelaeus and U. Quast; MSU 24; Göttingen: Vandenhoeck & Ruprecht, 2000), 174–247.

Cox, C., "The 'Songs of Zion' in Armenian," in *The Armenians in Jerusalem and the Holy Land* (eds. M.E. Stone, R.R. Ervine, and N. Stone; Hebrew University Armenian Studies 4; Leuven: Peeters, 2002), 33–59.

---

[7] Summary in Cox, "Text of the Old Greek Psalter," 180–81.
[8] Cox, "The Armenian Version and the Text of the Old Greek Psalter."
[9] Zohrapian, *Scriptures*.
[10] On these text types, see → 10.3.1.
[11] Cox, "The 'Songs of Zion' in Armenian."
[12] Cox, "The 'Songs of Zion' in Armenian," 45.
[13] Cox, "The 'Songs of Zion' in Armenian," 47–49.
[14] Zohrapian, *Scriptures*.

Mathews, E.G., "Syriac into Armenian: The Translations and Their Translators," *Journal of the Canadian Society of Syriac Studies* 10 (2010): 20–44.

Peshiṭta Institute Leiden (ed.), *The Book of Psalms* (The Old Testament in Syriac according to the Peshiṭta Version 2.3; Leiden: Brill, 1980).

Rahlfs, A. (ed.), *Psalmi cum Odis* (Septuaginta Vetus Testamentum Graecum 10; Göttingen: Vandenhoeck & Ruprecht, 1931; 2nd ed. 1967).

Ter-Petrosyan, L., "*Saghmosneri Hayerēn Tʻargmanutʻiwně ew nra Nakhorinakě*" ("The Armenian Translation of Psalms and its Parent Text"), *Etchmiatsin* (1975): 1, 41–51; 4, 31–45; 6, 58–64; 9, 49–57.

Claude Cox

10.4.6 Georgian Translations

10.4.6.1 Background

The Psalms are as essential to Christian liturgy as they are to their Jewish counterpart; therefore, they must have been translated into Georgian at a very early stage. A good critical edition of the two ancient versions of Georg-Ps was published in 1960 by Šaniʒe,[1] who recently produced also a very rich concordance of them, including variants of every manuscript.[2] The text of the lectionary is not included; unfortunately it is poorly documented only by *incipit* and *desinit*.

The Georgian name of the book ვსალმუნნი is probably a transcription of the Greek (book of) ψαλμῶν "of Psalms." This fact is already an indication of the *Vorlage* of the Georgian translation. We also find დავითი "the (book of) David" (in the *Life of Grigol Xancteli*, 951) and, in colophons, the plural form დავითნი "the (books of) David."

10.4.6.2 Date, Versions, Editions, Inner-Translational Features

There are several Georgian translations of Psalms. The first (= Georg-Ps 1) was created no later than the fifth century C.E. and is today available in two redactions (hereafter: Georg-Ps 1a and Georg-Ps 1b). The second (= Georg-Ps 2) was prepared at Mount Athos in the eleventh century by George the Agiorite (Giorgi Mtacʻmideli, † 1065); this text is the result of a revision of Georg-Ps 1 towards Greek models.[3] A third liturgical translation (= Georg-Ps 3), of which only a few sections are extant, is to be found in the Old Georgian lectionary. It was based on a Greek model from Jerusalem, where it was also most likely produced in the fifth century C.E.[4]

10.4.6.2.1 Georg-Ps 1

We may find evidence for the existence of Georg-Ps 1 in the Typikon of St. Sabbas (beginning of the second half of the fifth century C.E.), as well as in the *Martyrdom of Holy Shushanik* (ca. 480). One of the testimonies of Georg-Ps 1, the Psalter of Mtskheta (Tbilisi, National Centre of Manuscripts, A-38; hereafter: Georg^{Aa}), was probably copied in 974 C.E. but no later than the first decade of the eleventh century (the exact date is a *questio vexata*). In the first half of the eleventh century, this earliest textual stratum was revised according to the Armenian translation (→ 10.4.5).[5]

10.4.6.2.2 Georg-Ps 2

More than 300 manuscripts of the revised, now Vulgate, edition of Georg-Ps (= Georg-Ps 2) have survived. They are all copied as liturgical books and not as a part of a complete Bible. The only exception is the Bible of Mtskheta, intended for the publication of the first printed Bible in Georgian (Tbilisi, National Centre of Manuscripts, A-51 = Georg^s). In this source, the text is that of George the Agiorite, but there are variants in the titles of the Psalms.

According to Eprem Mcire (eleventh century), George the Agiorite corrected the earliest translation of the Psalms twice: the first revision, being still too close to the Old Georgian translation, had to be revised again. George's base texts were Georg-

---

[1] Šaniʒe, *Psalmunis ʒveli kartuli redakciebi*.
[2] Šaniʒe, *Kartuli psalmunis simponia*.
[3] In Šaniʒe's edition, the two redactions of the earliest translation (Georg-Ps 1a and Georg-Ps 1b) are marked respectively with the sigla Ⴀ and Ⴁ, while the second version (Georg-Ps 2) is indicated with the abbreviation Ⴂ; see Šaniʒe, *Psalmunis ʒveli kartuli redakcieʻbi*, 013–025.
[4] Renoux, "Quelques psaumes," 57–70.
[5] Čeliʒe, "Cʻminda cʻerilis kartulad targmna-redaktʻirebis ʒiritadi etʻapʻebi," 327–46.

Ps 1 and a number of Byzantine manuscripts of the Psalms, among which were commentaries on the book. There are nearly no variants in Georg-Ps 2.

For a previous revision of Georg-Ps, also made based on Greek sources, there is no extant evidence; it is only known that it was prepared by Euthymius the Agiorite (Eptwme Mtac'mideli, † 1028) at the turn of the tenth and eleventh centuries.

10.4.6.2.3 Textual Harmonization

In the testimonies of Georg-Ps 1, textual variety in the titles and text of the Psalms points to textual freedom and fluidity. It seems also likely that single manuscripts underwent individual revisions according to new or different Greek texts (→ 10.3.1). For instance, in Ps 103:20, Georg[Aa] (Georg-Ps 1a) reads მჴეცნი ველისანი "the beasts of the field" (τὰ θηρία τοῦ ἀγροῦ), but Georg[Ba, Cc, Da, Ea, Fa] (Georg-Ps 1b) have მჴეცნი მაღნარისანი "the beasts of the forests" (τὰ θηρία τοῦ δρυμοῦ). As found in Greek manuscripts, Georg-Ps 1a harmonizes Ps 103:20 with the same expression in v. 11.[6] There are many examples of this kind of "automatic formulary" in Georg-Ps 1a.

Further cases of variants in Georgian that reflect known Greek readings include the following: Ps 55:14: Georg[Aa, Ba, Cc, Da] (Georg-Ps 1b) read სოფელსა "in the world" (ἐν χώρᾳ), while Georg[Ea] (Georg-Ps 1b) features ნათელსა "in the light" (ἐν φωτί);[7] Ps 82:14: Georg[Aa, Ba, Da] (Georg-Ps 1a) read ქარსა "the wind" (ἀνέμου), while Georg[Cc, Ea, Fa] (Georg-Ps 1b) have ცეცხლსა "the fire" (πυρός).[8]

10.4.6.3 Text-Critical Value, Translation Character

The commonly held opinion within Western biblical studies was that the first version of Georg-Ps (Georg-Ps 1) was translated from Armenian (→ 10.4.5) into Georgian, the Armenian being in turn translated from the Syriac (→ 10.3.4; → 10.4.4); therefore, Georg-Ps was considered as being of no use for the study of LXX-Ps (→ 10.3.1). Accordingly, Šanize thought that the text of manuscript Georg[Aa] (Georg-Ps 1a) with its Armenianisms was a representative of this first translation.[9] However, a new examination undertaken by Čelize proved that this source originated in the same text as the other testimonies of the old translation (Georg-Ps 1b), but had been corrected in accordance with the Armenian version in the first half of the eleventh century.[10]

For a direct dependence of Georg-Ps on LXX-Ps (→ 10.3.1) also argues that the former has the same numeration and division of the Psalms as the latter, whereas the Syriac (→ 10.3.4) follows MT-Ps (→ 10.2.2) in its numeration and division of Psalms. As in LXX, the 151 Psalms are followed in Georg-Ps by nine odes used in the liturgy.

Text-critical details underline the dependency of Georg-Ps on LXX-Ps. Some errors point to the misreading of a Greek model: Ps 15(16):7 ἔτι "moreover" > ὅτι/რამეთუ "since/because." The genitive of Τάνις "Tanis," Τάνεως has been retained in Ps 77:12 and 43: ტანეოს-[ს]ა and this can be explained by neither the Syriac ܕܨܥܢ "of Saʿan(?)" nor by the Armenian Սայանու "of Tayan."

Moreover, as in many other books of the Bible, one finds in Georg-Ps examples of calques of double preverbs or double prepositions in one word, a phenomenon that is found in neither Syriac nor Armenian: In Ps 1:3, თანა-წარ-სადინელსა "streams" renders δι-εξ-όδους "channels" and in Ps 93(94):16 თანა-წარ-მომიდგეს "will stand with me" translates συμ-παρα-στήσεται "will stand beside."

Nevertheless, some rare agreements between the Syriac, Armenian, and Georgian against the Greek as we know it today need to be explained: In Ps 32(33):17, the Greek has οὐ σωθήσεται "he will not be saved" whereas the Syriac (Peshitta: ܠܐ ܢܦܠܛ ܠܪܟܒܗ) and Armenian (ոչ ապրեցուցանէ զհեծեալն) read "he will not save his rider" and the Georgian text attests to "he will not save the rider" (ვერ განარინოს მჴედარი). In Ps 44:3 (45:2), the Greek reads ὡραῖος "you are fair" but

---

[6] See Rahlfs, *Psalmi*, 258–59.
[7] See Rahlfs, *Psalmi*, 172 and 283 (Ps 114:9).
[8] See Rahlfs, *Psalmi*, 225.

[9] Šanize, *Psalmunta c'ignis zveli kartuli targmanebi*, 159.
[10] Čelize, "C'minda c'erilis kartulad targmna-redakt'irebis ziritadi et'ap'ebi," 327–46.

the Syriac (ܚܙܘܬܐ), Armenian (տեսանելով), and Georgian (ხილვად) translations add "to see" to the Greek text. In Ps 73:15, the Greek understood the Hebrew as a toponym, Ηθαμ "Etham," and not as an adjective, as did the Syriac (ܚܣܝܢܐ), Armenian (սաստիկս), and Georgian სასტიკნი "mighty."

The textual affiliation of the above list seems to be contradicted by the situation in Ps 16(17):14. MT reads יִשְׂבְּעוּ בָנִים "the sons are satisfied" while LXX has ἐχορτάσθησαν υἱῶν "they were satisfied with sons" (LXX^A; LXX^B, Cop^Sa have υιεων "pigs"). The Armenian (յագեցան կերակրովք) and Georgian (განძღეს ჭამადითა) read "they were satisfied with food." However, Ghazar Pharpeci (end of fifth century C.E.) knows an Armenian variant that reads "pigs" as does a Georgian commentator on the Psalms. This play on υἱῶν/υιεων "sons/pigs" implies that the Armenian did not translate here the Syriac ܒܢܝܐ "sons" but the Greek.[11]

We also have some rare agreements between the Armenian and Georgian against the Greek and Syriac, despite the fact that latter is supposed to be the base text of the Armenian (→ 10.4.5). An example can be found in Ps 17:35(18:34) where Georg-Ps reads მტკიცე (= Arm հաստ) "solid" against χαλκοῦν "of bronze" in the Greek and the Syriac ܕܢܚܫܐ. Ps 129:8 provides another example: LXX reads ἀνομία "lawlessness" (= MT and Syriac ܥܘܠܐ) but Armenian (նեղութեանց) and Georgian (ჭირთა) have "afflictions."

For the first Georgian translation of Psalms, it seems possible that when the translator had to render a rare word or a hapax legomenon, he looked at an Armenian translation (→ 10.4.5). Examples of this phenomenon include the translation of κιθάρα as "benediction" (კურთხევად), which was guided by the Armenian word աւրհնութիւն (Pss 42:4; 56:8; 70:22; 91:3; 97:5); the rendering κύμβαλον as ჴმითა "voice," guided by the Armenian words բան "words" and բարբառ "voice" in Ps 150:5 (twice).

The first Georgian translation of Psalms (Georg-Ps 1) was "ad sensum," but the revision by George the Agiorite (Georg-Ps 2) was intended to give a very precise rendering of the Greek in Georgian. Nevertheless, the older translation, though not literal, has sometimes been kept unchanged. Examples can be found in Ps 77:12, 43 as well as in Ps 131:4.

The text of Georg-Ps was still fluid in the tenth century. Sometimes every translation and manuscript is choosing its own way as illustrated in the example of Ps 59:5(60:3): Syriac: ܚܡܪܐ ܕܚܠܐ "turbid wine"; Greek: οἶνον κατανύξεως "wine of compunction"; Armenian: գինի լմարութեան "wine of madness"; Georg-Ps 1: ღვნო მწუხარებისა "wine of sadness"; Georg-Ps 2: ღვნო გულისხმის-ყოფისა "wine of understanding"; Georg-Ps 3: ღვნო ლმობიერებისა "wine of suffering."

Georg-Ps also includes some doublets, i.e., two words to translate one, a phenomenon found also in Syriac and Armenian (although scarcely in Bible translations). Ps 117(118):27 provides an example: ἑορτήν "feast" is translated as დღესასწაული სიხარულისა "a feast of joy." In my opinion, this is a general literary device that goes back to Iranian influence.

It can be concluded that the story of the text of Georg-Ps is not at all a simple one. The best researcher on the topic, Kharanauli, concludes in her thorough investigation that the text of Georg-Ps was translated from a Lucianic Greek model (→ 10.3.6), but that it agrees now and then with some other old translations, e.g., with the Old Latin (→ 10.4.1).[12]

Amphoux, C.B. and J.K. Elliott with B. Outtier (eds.), *Textual Research on the Psalms and Gospels/Recherches textuelles sur les psaumes et les évangiles: Papers from the Tbilisi Colloquium on the Editing and History of Biblical Manuscripts/Actes du Colloque de Tbilisi, 19–20 septembre 2007* (NovTSup 142; Leiden: Brill, 2012).

Čelize, E., "C'minda c'erilis kartulad targmna-redakt'irebis ʒiritadi et'ap'ebi (mcxeturi davitnisa da adišis otxtavis magalit'ze)," in *Krist'ianobis 20 sauk'une*

---

[11] Mouradian, "Importance des citations bibliques," 171–79.

[12] Kharanauli, "Einführung in die georgische Psalterübersetzung," 307–08.

sakartveloši (ed. R. Gordeziani; Tbilisi: Logosi, 2004), 327–46.

Čeliʒe, E. (ed.), *Psalmunni: axali šesc'orebuli gamocema* (Tbilisi: Axali ivironi, 2006).

Davitni (psalmunebi) (Tbilisi: Vaxt'angis st'amba, 1709).

Dočanašvili, E. (ed.), *Mcxeturi xelnac'eri (t'obis, ivditis, esteris, iobis c'ignebi, psalmuni, igavta c'igni)* (Tbilisi: Mecniereba, 1983).

Kharanauli, A., "Einführung in die georgische Psalterübersetzung," in *Der Septuaginta-Psalter und seine Tochterübersetzungen: Symposium in Göttingen 1997* (eds. A. Aejmelaeus and U. Quast; MSU 24; Göttingen: Vandenhoeck & Ruprecht, 2000), 248–308.

Mouradian, P., "Importance des citations bibliques rencontrées dans les documents littéraires et épigraphiques médiévaux arméniens," in *Armenia and the Bible: Papers Presented to the International Symposium Held at Heidelberg, July 16–19, 1990* (ed. C. Burchard; Armenian Texts and Studies 12; Atlanta: Scholars Press, 1993), 171–79.

Outtier, B., "Une énigme enfin résolue? Le modèle de la traduction géorgienne de la Bible," in *Poïkiloï Karpoï (Récoltes diverses): Exégèses païennes, juives et chrétiennes: Études réunies en hommage à Gilles Dorival* (eds. M. Loubet and D. Pralon; Aix-en-Provence: Presses universitaires de Provence, 2015), 35–40.

Rahlfs, A., *Psalmi cum Odis* (Septuaginta Vetus Testamentum Graecum 10; Göttingen: Vandenhoeck & Ruprecht, 1931).

Renoux, C., "Quelques psaumes dans les documents liturgiques anciens géorgiens et arméniens," in *Textual Research on the Psalms and Gospels/Recherches textuelles sur les psaumes et les évangiles: Papers from the Tbilisi Colloquium on the Editing and History of Biblical Manuscripts/Actes du Colloque de Tbilisi, 19–20 septembre 2007* (NovTSup 142; Leiden: Brill, 2012), 57–70.

Šaniʒe, M. (ed.), *Psalmunis ʒveli kartuli redakciebi X–XIII sauk'uneta xelnac'erebis mixedvit*, Vol. 1: *T'ekst'i* (Ʒveli kartuli enis ʒeglebi 11; Tbilisi: Sakartvelos ssr mecnierebata ak'ademiis gamomcemloba, 1960).

Šaniʒe, M., *Psalmunta c'ignis ʒveli kartuli targmanebi* (Tbilisi: Mecniereba, 1979).

Šaniʒe, M., *Kartuli psalmunis simponia: masalebi adreuli versiebisatvis da giorgi mtac'midliseuli redakciis simponia* (Tbilisi: Nek'eri, 2010).

Šaniʒe, M., "The Old Georgian Psalter and the Titles of the Psalms," in *Textual Research on the Psalms and Gospels/Recherches textuelles sur les psaumes et les évangiles: Papers from the Tbilisi Colloquium on the Editing and History of Biblical Manuscripts/Actes du Colloque de Tbilisi, 19–20 septembre 2007* (NovTSup 142; Leiden: Brill, 2012), 19–41.

Bernard Outtier

10.4.7 Old Church Slavonic Translations

The Psalms were first translated into the Old Church Slavonic language (= OCS) during the Cyrillo-Methodian period (863–885 C.E.). The earliest version of this book, along with that of the Byzantine Prophetologium, lies at the very core of the tradition of the Old Church Slavonic Scriptures (→ 1.4.10.3).[1]

10.4.7.1 Oldest Corpus

The primary textual stratum of OCS-Ps has come down to us in medieval sources written both in Glagolitic and Old Cyrillic alphabets. Moreover, a parchment codex, presumably dating from the fourteenth century, is also preserved (*Vat.slav.* 8),[2] in which OCS-Pss are copied in a very peculiar graphic system consisting of abbreviated Cyrillic letters.[3]

Manuscript evidence of OCS-Ps is very abundant and variegated in redactional, structural, liturgical,[4] and linguistic terms. This is the inevitable result of the wide branching out of the texts over several centuries and across the different regions of the Slavic world (→ 1.4.10.3).

As of mid-2016, critical editions based on systematic *recensio* and genealogical analysis unfortunately are not available. Besides numerous diplomatic transcriptions or photographic reproductions of single sources,[5] collated editions were pro-

---

[1] For the lack of any evidence of the existence among Slavs of portions of the Bible translated even prior to the Cyrillo-Methodian mission to Moravia, see Thomson, "The Slavonic Translation," 633–37; Cooper, "The Bible in Slavonic," 179–83.

[2] De Nunzio, "O slavjanskoj rukopisi," 141–47.

[3] Speranskij, *Tajnopis'*, 82–87.

[4] For liturgical types, see Thomson, "The Slavonic Translation," 797–98; Alekseev, "Tekstologija," 223, 35–36, MacRobert, "The Linguistic Peculiarities."

[5] Severjanov, *Sinajskaja psaltyr'*; Bolonski; Altbauer, *Sinajski Psaltir*; Altbauer and Lunt, *An Early Slavonic Psalter*; Kievskaja;

duced on the basis of a limited number of testimonies.[6]

10.4.7.1.1 Manuscript Evidence

Recent archeological excavations in Russia have brought to light a set of three waxed wooden tablets written in Cyrillic that can be dated to between the late tenth and early eleventh centuries. The new finds from Novgorod, which contain Psalms 67:4–6; 75; and 76, represent at the same time the oldest testimony of OCS-Ps and the earliest extant Slavonic book.[7]

Complete or almost complete witnesses of OCS-Ps have come down to us dating presumably at the earliest from the second half of the eleventh century. A number of Glagolitic and Cyrillic parchment codices can be dated paleographically to this epoch. This earliest documentary legacy consists of the Glagolitic "Psalterium Sinaiticum" (*Sin.slav* 38 + 2/N)[8] and the "Psalterium Demetrii" (*Sin.slav.* 3/N),[9] and of the Cyrillic "Byčkov" (St. Petersburg, National Library of Russia, Q. п. I. 73 + *Sin. slav.* 6),[10] "Eugenius" (St. Petersburg, National Library of Russia, *Pogod.* 9 + Library of the Academy of Sciences, 4.5.7/Keppen, 19),[11] and "Čudov" Psalters (Moscow, State Historical Museum, *Čud.* 7).[12] Following the loss of Evseev's inventory of the Old Church Slavonic biblical manuscripts (→ 1.4.10.2.1), apparently no attempt has been made to compile a comprehensive register of the existing East and South Slavic sources of OCS-Ps.[13]

10.4.7.1.2 Redactions

The oldest tradition of OCS-Ps was judged to have split into three or, most likely, two redactions, each of which can be proven to have existed since at least the eleventh century.[14] Scholars maintain almost unanimously that the earliest textual stratum (OCS-Ps 1) is to be found in the abovementioned Glagolitic testimonies from Sinai, in a number of Croat Glagolitic sources starting from the fourteenth century,[15] as well as in several East[16] and South Slavic Cyrillic codices.[17] The second redaction (OCS-Ps 2)[18] is preserved in East and South Slavic Cyrillic testimonies only. The East Slavic group includes eleventh-century Cyrillic witnesses, such as the abovementioned Novgorod tablets,[19] as well as the "Byčkov"[20] and "Čudov" Psalters.[21]

Manuscripts of both redactions are usually flanked by Old Church Slavonic translations of exegetical commentaries, which were added to OCS-Ps presumably during the Old Bulgarian period (reign of Symeon I the Great, 893–927 C.E.).[22] They are the translation of Theodoret of Cyrrhus'

Mareš et al., *Psalterii Sinaitici*; Miklas et al., *Psalterium Demetrii*.

[6] See Jagić, *Psalterium Bononiense*; *Čudovskaja*; Vajs, *Psalterium*. On the Salzburg edition (*Die Methodbibel*), see the critical remarks in Thomson, "The Slavonic Translation," 829.

[7] Zaliznjak, "Problemy"; Zaliznjak and Janin, "Novgorodskij," 3–25; Sobolev, "Novgorodskaja"; Stančev, "Po povodu"; Alekseev, "O Novgorodskich."

[8] Severjanov, *Sinajskaja psaltyr'*; Altbauer, *Sinajski Psaltir*; Mareš et al., *Psalterii Sinaitici*.

[9] Miklas et al., *Psalterium Demetrii*; MacRobert, "The Place."

[10] Altbauer and Lunt, *An Early Slavonic Psalter*.

[11] Kolesov, "Evgenievskaja."

[12] *Čudovskaja Psaltyr'*; Pogorelov, *Slovar'*; Lépissier, *Les commentaires*.

[13] A number of codices are listed in MacRobert, "The Textual Tradition," 935–38.

[14] Pogorelov, *Psaltyri*; MacRobert, "The Textual Tradition"; MacRobert, "On the Problems."

[15] Vajs, *Psalterium*, ix–xi, 1–191. Thomson, "The Slavonic Translation," 809.

[16] Particularly noteworthy among the oldest copies, besides the abovementioned "Eugenius" Psalter, are the twelfth-century "Tolstoj" Psalter (St. Petersburg, National Library of Russia, F.п.I.23) and the "Kiev" Psalter (St. Petersburg, National Library of Russia, OLDP F 6, year 1397; facsimile: *Kievskaja*).

[17] As for the South Slavic sources, mention should be made here of at least the "Psalterium Bononiense" (Bologna, University Library, № 299, thirteenth century: Ščepkin, *Bolonskaja*) and of the "Pogodin" Psalter (St. Petersburg, National Library of Russia, *Pogod.* No. 8, early thirteenth century). For a synoptic edition of both codices, see *Psalterium Bononiense*. Several other testimonies are listed in MacRobert, "The Textual Tradition," 935–38; and MacRobert, "The Place," 89–90.

[18] Manuscripts currently grouped into this text type were previously divided into two different classes. See Pogorelov, *Psaltyri*, vi–liv.

[19] Zaliznjak and Janin, "Novgorodskij"; Alekseev, "O Novgorodskich."

[20] On the linguistic features of this codex and on the problem of the origin of the so-called "Russian redaction," see Krivko, *Očerki*, 9–107.

[21] *Čudovskaja Psaltyr'*; Pogorelov, *Slovar'*; Lépissier, *Les commentaires*.

[22] Šivarov, "Drevni"; Alekseev, "Tekstologija," 35–36, 160.

commentaries (CPG 6202)[23] and that of the *Commentarius brevis* of Hesychius of Jerusalem (CPG 6553).[24]

10.4.7.2 Other Text Types Originated up to the Late Fourteenth Century

The third redaction (OCS-Ps 3), which is usually called the "Athonite,"[25] has come down to us both in South and East Slavic codices.[26] A fourth recension (OCS-Ps 4) is to be found in the fourteenth-century Bulgarian "Norov" Psalter,[27] while a fifth one (OCS-Ps 5), widely known as the "Cyprianic,"[28] survives in a number of East Slavic manuscripts starting from the late fourteenth century, although it was based on South Slavic models.[29] OCS-Ps 5 was subsequently included in the late fifteenth-century Gennadian Bible (→ 1.4.10.2.4.3),[30] and thence into the printed Ostrog Bible of 1581 (→ 1.4.10.3.4).[31] Several codices containing translations of OCS-Ps dating from the Middle Slavic period are provided with translations of Byzantine catenae of different types.[32]

10.4.7.3 Translations and Revisions in Sixteenth- and Seventeenth-Century Russia

In the first half of the sixteenth century, OCS-Ps was revised or retranslated in Russia as a consequence of several editorial enterprises (→ 1.4.10.3.3.2).[33] By 1522, Maksim Grek (Maximus Triboles, ca. 1470–1555) translated a Byzantine catena, while in 1552 he prepared a new version of Psalms from LXX (→ 10.3.1).[34] In 1535, Demetrius Gerasimov (ca. 1465–1536) rendered into Slavonic the commentary on the Psalms composed in Latin by Bruno of Würzburg (1005–1045).[35] This work along with other earlier translations of Psalms was included in the Great Menologia (*Velikie minei čet'i*), compiled at the initiative of Archibishop Macarius of Novgorod (1526–1542; metropolitan of Russia in 1542–1563).[36] A further revision of OCS-Ps based on LXX was undertaken by Epiphanius Slavinetsky (died 1675) and printed in the 1663 Moscow Bible (→ 1.4.10.3.4).[37]

10.4.7.4 Translation of Psalms in the Vilnius Codex

A translation of Psalms was undertaken in the second half of the fifteenth century. This text is based on the Old Church Slavonic text and the Vulgate (→ 10.3.7) and is to be found in a sixteenth-century manuscript (Vilnius, Lithuanian Academy of Sciences, f. 19, no. 262), which also contains Ruthenian vernacular translations from MT-Prov (→ 12.4.7; → 12.2.2), MT-Job (→ 11.4.7; → 11.2.2), MT-Five Scrolls (→ 13–17.2.7; → 13.2.2; → 14.2.2; → 15.2.2; → 16.2.2; → 17.2.2), and MT-Dan (→ 18.4.7; → 18.2.2). The question of its authorship remains open.[38]

---

[23] *Čudovskaja Psaltyr'*; Pogorelov, *Slovar'*; Lépissier, *Les commentaires*.

[24] Jagić, *Psalterium Bononiense*; Jagić, *Supplementum*; Bolonski; Kolesov, "Evgenievskaja." On the authorship of the Greek original, see Rondeau, *Les Commentaires*, 142–43. On the earliest Old Church Slavonic catenae and their redactions, see Karačorova, "Novonajdennaja," 55–56.

[25] Češko, "Ob Afonskoj."

[26] For manuscripts and further bibliography, see MacRobert, "The Textual Tradition," 923; MacRobert, "The Place," 9; MacRobert, "Translation," 254–84; Thomson, "The Slavonic Translation," 815; Alekseev, "Tekstologija," 187.

[27] For an edition, see Češko et al., *Norovskaja*.

[28] It was revised by Metropolitan Cyprian of Kiev (1375–1406). In some studies, the order of OCS-Ps 4 and OCS-Ps 5 is reversed (see, e.g.: MacRobert, "The Textual Tradition," 924.) However, as pointed out by Thomson, the text of the "Norov" Psalter influenced the Cyprianic redaction (Thomson, "The Slavonic Translation," 820 n. 1016).

[29] MacRobert, "The Textual Tradition," 924.

[30] Thomson, "The Slavonic Translation," 823, 825; Tomelleri, "Psaltir'."

[31] *Ostrožskaja biblija*; MacRobert, "The Textual Tradition," 924.

[32] MacRobert, "The Compilatory"; Karačorova, "Novonajdennaja." On the translation of Nicetas of Heraclea's commentary, see Thomson, "The Slavonic Translation," 801; Alekseev, "Tekstologija," 36, n. 3.

[33] On Francis Skorina's (1490–1541/51) Ruthenian editions, not discussed in *THB* (→ 1.4.10), see Thomson, "The Slavonic Translation," 826–28.

[34] On the textual history of Maksim's work on Psalms, see Kovtun, Sinicyna, and Fonkič, "Maksim Grek," 99–127; Sinicyna, *Prepodobnyj Maksim Grek*, 37, 151–70.

[35] Tomelleri, "O nekotoryx sintaksičeskich osobennostjach."

[36] Iosif, *Podrobnoe*, 423–30.

[37] *Biblija*, 1663.

[38] Taube, "The Vilnius 262 Psalter"; Temčin, "Scharija," 290.

10.4.7.5 Parent Text

This manuscript tradition may be seen generally as an indirect witness to LXX-Ps (→ 10.3.1), although the assessment of the parent text of the earliest textual stratum of OCS-Ps poses serious challenges for research. Scholarly contributions to the debate surrounding the identification of the sources of OCS-Ps 1 have hitherto been based exclusively on Rahlfs' edition[39] and on far too narrow a range of evidence. Moreover, the need for comparative analysis with other secondary versions was not even raised in previous studies.[40] A preliminary attempt to elucidate this last aspect has been undertaken for *THB*.

10.4.7.5.1 Lucianic and Western Readings in OCS-Ps 1

OCS-Ps 1 shows a clear textual affinity with LXX^L (→ 10.3.6),[41] although it frequently deviates from its basic tradition.[42] As several scholars have pointed out, OCS-Ps 1 shares a number of readings with testimonies of VL (→ 10.4.1.1). Parallels have been detected in VL^{300} (Italian Psalter in Africa), VL^{330} (Hexaplaric Psalter or Gallican), and in VL^{303} (*Psalterium Sangermanensis*).[43] Moreover, some of these common variants are not found in LXX^L, while others have not yet been traced in the Greek tradition. In a few cases, sporadic influence of Jerome's *iuxta hebraeos* (→ 10.3.7.1) has also been assumed.[44]

These features have been explained as: *a*) the result of the use by the translator of both Byzantine and Latin sources or of a bilingual codex such as VL^{300}; *b*) the consequence of a revision of the original version based on LXX^L towards a highly conflated Latin text. Both options are equally possible and can be explained well in light of the ties of the Cyrillo-Methodian tradition with the Western world.[45]

Despite these valuable remarks, the textological basis of OCS-Ps still remains uncertain given the lack of a comprehensive comparative study of Old Church Slavonic and Greek manuscript evidence. Much work needs to be done before definitive conclusions can be drawn. In the writer's view, an additional promising line of research would be to focus on a systematic collation of OCS-Ps 1 with other secondary versions of Eastern origin (→ 10.4). Such an opportunity seems not to have been explored at all.

10.4.7.5.2 Towards a More Comprehensive Approach: A Preliminary Comparison with Georg-Ps

A preliminary collation of OCS-Ps 1 with Georg-Ps 1 and 2 (→ 10.4.6), undertaken for the present entry, has offered encouraging results. It emerged that the Caucasian tradition offers equivalents to some readings of OCS-Ps 1 that apparently have no counterpart in Greek. In this regard, the following data have a probative value.

a) Ps 18:9 τὰ δικαιώματα Κυρίου εὐθέα, εὐφραίνοντα **καρδίαν** ἡ ἐντολὴ Κυρίου τηλαυγής, φωτίζουσα ὀφθαλμούς[46] "the statutes of the Lord are upright, making glad the **heart**; the commandment of the Lord is radiant, enlightening the eyes";[47] VL^{460}: *Iustitia domini recta letificantis* **corda** ["hearts"], *preceptum domini lucidum inluminans oculos*;[48] OCS-Ps 1: оправъданъѣ гнѣ права веселѧшта **срьдьца** ["hearts"] ҳаповѣди гнѣ иҳдалече просвѣштѫшти очи;[49] Georg-Ps 1a: სიმართლენი უფლისანი წრფელ არიან და ახარებენ გულთა ["hearts"], მცნებანი უფლისანი მარწყინვალე არიან და

---

[39] Rahlfs, *Psalmi cum Odis*.
[40] See, e.g., Aejmelaeus and Quast (eds.), *Der Septuaginta-Psalter*.
[41] Vajs, "Které recenze."
[42] Laurenčík, "Nelukianovská."
[43] Lépissier, "La traduction"; Pantelić, "Zapadne"; Ziffer, "Appunti." In later redactions, these readings were corrected progressively towards Greek sources in order to bring them into conformity with LXX (MacRobert, "The Greek," 7–10).
[44] Thomson, "The Slavonic Translation," 806–07.

[45] Lépissier, "La traduction"; Thomson, "The Slavonic Translation," 806–07; Ziffer, "Appunti," 195.
[46] Rahlfs, *Psalmi cum Odis*, 106.
[47] *NETS, 555.
[48] Gryson and Thibaut, *Le psautier latin du Sinaï*, 39.
[49] Severjanov, *Sinajskaja psaltyr'*, 22.

10.4.7 OLD CHURCH SLAVONIC TRANSLATIONS

განანათლებენ თუალთა;⁵⁰ Georg-Ps 2: სიმართლენი უფლისანი წრფელ არიან და ახარებენ გულთა ["hearts"], მცნებაჲ უფლისაჲ ბრწყინვალე არს, განმანათლებელ თუალთა.⁵¹

b) Ps 26:12 μὴ παραδῷς με εἰς ψυχὰς θλιβόντων με, ὅτι ἐπανέστησάν μοι μάρτυρες ἄδικοι, καὶ ἐψεύσατο ἡ ἀδικία ἑαυτῇ⁵² "Do not give me up to **the souls** of people that afflict me, because unjust witnesses rose against me and injustice lied to itself";⁵³ VL⁴⁶⁰: *ne tradideris me in animas* ["souls"] *persequentibus me, quoniam insurrexerunt in me testes iniqui et mentita est iniquitas sibi;*⁵⁴ OCS-Ps 1: не прѣдаждъ мене въ рѫцѣ ["hands"] сътѫжаѭштіихъ мнѣ· ѣко въсташѩ на мѩ съвѣдѣтелі неправедьні ихъже· не съвѣдѣхъ· и солга неправдѣ себѣ;⁵⁵ Georg-Ps 1a: ნუ მიმცემ მე ჴელთა ["hands"] მაჭირებელთა ჩემთასა, რამეთუ აღდგეს ჩემ ზედა მოწამენი სიცრუვისანი და ტყუოდეს უშჯულოებითა მათითა;⁵⁶ Georg-Ps 2: ნუ მიმცემ მე სულთა ["souls"] მაჭირვებელთა ჩემთასა, რამეთუ აღდგეს ჩემ ზედა მოწამენი ცრუნი და უტყუვა სიცრუემან თავსა თჳსსა.⁵⁷

c) Ps 32:18 ἰδοὺ οἱ ὀφθαλμοὶ Κυρίου ἐπὶ τοὺς φοβουμένους αὐτὸν τοὺς ἐλπίζοντας ἐπὶ τὸ ἔλεος αὐτοῦ⁵⁸ "Look, the eyes of the Lord are on those who fear him, those who hope in his mercy";⁵⁹ VL⁴⁶⁰: *Ecce oculi domini super timentes eum et* ["and"] *in eos qui sperant in misericordia eius;*⁶⁰ OCS-Ps 1: се очі гні на боѩщиихъ сѩ его: и ["and"] на оупъваѭщиѩ на милость его;⁶¹ Georg-Ps 2: აჰა ესერა თუალნი უფლისანი მოშიშთა მისთა ზედა და ["and"] რომელნი ესვენ წყალობასა მისსა.⁶²

d) Ps 48:18 ὅτι οὐκ ἐν τῷ ἀποθνήσκειν αὐτὸν λήψεται τὰ πάντα, οὐδὲ συγκαταβήσεται αὐτῷ ἡ δόξα αὐτοῦ⁶³ "Because, when he dies, he will take nothing, nor will his glory go down **to him**";⁶⁴ VL⁴⁶⁰: *Quoniam non dum morietur accipiet omnia neque simul descendat cum eo* ["with him"] *gloria domus eius;*⁶⁵ OCS-Ps 1: иже оуміраѩі не оставітъ лі въсего: ниже сънідетъ **съ німъ** ["with him"] слава домоу его;⁶⁶ Georg-Ps 1a: რამეთუ არა სიკუდილსა მისსა წარიღოს მან ყოველი, არცალა შთაჰყვეს დიდებაჲ სახლისა მისისაჲ მის თანა ["with him"];⁶⁷ Georg-Ps 2: რამეთუ არა სიკუდილსა მისსა წარიღოს მან ყოველი, არცა შთაჰყვეს დიდებაჲ მისი მის თანა ["with him"].⁶⁸

e) Ps 73:15 σὺ διέρρηξας πηγὰς καὶ χειμάρρους, σὺ ἐξήρανας ποταμοὺς Ἠθάμ⁶⁹ "it was you who broke through springs and wadis; it was you who dried up streams of **Etham**";⁷⁰ VL⁴⁶⁰: *Tu disripuisti fontes et torrentes, tu siccasti flubibus ethan;*⁷¹ OCS-Ps 1: ты растръже істочьнікы и потокы· ты ісѫчи **рѣкы наводьненыѩ** ["flooding rivers"];⁷² Georg-Ps 1a: შენ გამოადინენ წყარონი და მდინარენი, შენ განაჴმენ მდინარენი სასტიკნი ["strong rivers"].⁷³ See also Arm-Ps (→ 10.4.5): Դու բղխեցուցեր զաղբերս եւ զկուակս, դու ցամաքեցուցեր զգետս սաստիկս ["strong rivers"].⁷⁴

f) Ps 82:5 εἶπαν δεῦτε καὶ ἐξολοθρεύσωμεν αὐτοὺς ἐξ ἔθνους, καὶ οὐ μὴ μνησθῇ τὸ ὄνομα Ἰσραὴλ ἔτι⁷⁵ "They said, 'Come, and let us destroy them **from**

---

⁵⁰ Šaniʒe, *Psalmunis ʒveli kartuli redakciebi*, 41.
⁵¹ Šaniʒe, *Psalmunis ʒveli kartuli redakciebi*, 41.
⁵² Rahlfs, *Psalmi cum Odis*, 119.
⁵³ *NETS*, 559.
⁵⁴ Gryson and Thibaut, *Le psautier latin du Sinaï*, 48.
⁵⁵ Severjanov, *Sinajskaja psaltyr'*, 32.
⁵⁶ Šaniʒe, *Psalmunis ʒveli kartuli redakciebi*, 62.
⁵⁷ Šaniʒe, *Psalmunis ʒveli kartuli redakciebi*, 62.
⁵⁸ *Psalmi cum Odis*, 128.
⁵⁹ *NETS*, 562.
⁶⁰ Gryson and Thibaut, *Le psautier latin du Sinaï*, 54.
⁶¹ Severjanov, *Sinajskaja psaltyr'*, 40.
⁶² Šaniʒe, *Psalmunis ʒveli kartuli redakciebi*, 77.
⁶³ Rahlfs, *Psalmi cum Odis*, 160.
⁶⁴ *NETS* translation: "with him" (*NETS*, 571).
⁶⁵ Gryson and Thibaut, *Le psautier latin du Sinaï*, 73.
⁶⁶ Severjanov, *Sinajskaja psaltyr'*, 62.
⁶⁷ Šaniʒe, *Psalmunis ʒveli kartuli redakciebi*, 124.
⁶⁸ Šaniʒe, *Psalmunis ʒveli kartuli redakciebi*, 124.
⁶⁹ Rahlfs, *Psalmi cum Odis*, 206.
⁷⁰ *NETS*, 584.
⁷¹ Gryson and Thibaut, *Le psautier latin du Sinaï*, 100–101.
⁷² Severjanov, *Sinajskaja psaltyr'*, 94.
⁷³ Šaniʒe, *Psalmunis ʒveli kartuli redakciebi*, 193.
⁷⁴ Baumstark, "Der armenische Psaltertext," II, 168.
⁷⁵ Rahlfs, *Psalmi cum Odis*, 224.

being a nation, and the name of Israel shall be remembered no more'";⁷⁶ VL⁴⁶⁰: *Dixerunt: benite* [sic!] *diperdamus eos **ex gentibus** ["from the nations"] et non sit in memoria nomen israel amplius*;⁷⁷ OCS-Ps 1: рѣшѩ прїдѣте і потрѣбімъ ѩ отъ ѩҙыкъ ["*from the nations*"] і не помѣнетъ сѩ імѩ їйлиево къ томоу.⁷⁸ Georg-Ps 1a: და თქუეს: მოვედით და მოვსრნეთ იგინი თესლთაგან ["*from the nations*"], და არღარა მოიჴსენოს სახელი ისრაელისაჲ.⁷⁹

g) Ps 118:47 καὶ ἐμελέτων ἐν ταῖς ἐντολαῖς σου, ἃς ἠγάπησα **σφόδρα**⁸⁰ "And I would meditate on your commandments, which I loved **very much**";⁸¹ OCS-Ps 1: ї поѹчаахъ сѩ въ ҙаповѣдехъ твоїхъ: ѩже въҙлюбихъ [omits "*very much*"];⁸² Georg-Ps 1a: ვზრახევდ მცნებათა შენთა, რომელნიცა შევიყუარენ [omits "*very much*"];⁸³ Georg-Ps 2: და ვიწურთიდ მცნებათა შენთა, რომელნიცა შევიყუარენ ფრიად ["*very much*"].⁸⁴

h) Ps 143:6 ἄστραψον **ἀστραπὴν** καὶ σκορπιεῖς αὐτούς, ἐξαπόστειλον τὰ βέλη σου καὶ συνταράξεις αὐτούς⁸⁵ "Flash a **lightning flash**, and you will scatter them";⁸⁶ OCS-Ps 1: блъсни млънїѫ **твоѭ** ["*your lightning flash*"] и раждениши ѩ: посли стрѣлъї твоѩ и смѩтеши ѩ;⁸⁷ Georg-Ps 1a: გამოაბრწყინე ელვანი შენნი ["*your lightning flashes*"] და შეაძრწუნენ იგინი.⁸⁸

10.4.7.5.3 Text-Critical Value of OCS-Ps 1

The highlighted concordances between OCS-Ps 1 and Georg-Ps (→ 10.4.6) have important implications for a more precise assessment of the text-critical value of OCS-Ps for biblical scholarship.

---

⁷⁶ *NETS*, 589.
⁷⁷ Gryson and Thibaut, *Le psautier latin du Sinaï*, 112.
⁷⁸ Severjanov, *Sinajskaja psaltyr'*, 111.
⁷⁹ Šaniʒe, *Psalmunis ʒveli kartuli redakciebi*, 223.
⁸⁰ Rahlfs, *Psalmi cum Odis*, 291–92.
⁸¹ *NETS*, 607.
⁸² Severjanov, *Sinajskaja psaltyr'*, 157.
⁸³ Šaniʒe, *Psalmunis ʒveli kartuli redakciebi*, 334.
⁸⁴ Šaniʒe, *Psalmunis ʒveli kartuli redakciebi*, 334.
⁸⁵ Rahlfs, *Psalmi cum Odis*, 330.
⁸⁶ *NETS*, 617.
⁸⁷ Jagić, *Psalterium Bononiense*, 674.
⁸⁸ Šaniʒe, *Psalmunis ʒveli kartuli redakciebi*, 394.

Since the Caucasian text was certainly not influenced by Latin models (→ 10.4.6), the existing textual affinity between OCS-Ps 1 and Georg-Ps can only be explained by postulating independent derivations of the shared readings from a common, still unidentified or lost, Greek source. This outcome entails a change in our approach towards the issue as to why OCS-Ps 1 at times deviates from LXX (→ 10.3.1) and agrees with VL (→ 10.4.1).

Alongside the traditional widespread hypothesis about the Western influence on OCS-Ps 1 (→ 10.4.7.5.1), a new one can therefore be proposed. OCS-Ps could not derive from a conflation of textual variants taken from different traditions (Greek and Latin). Instead, it could indeed have been a translation of an untraced Byzantine source. The latter was purportedly similar typologically to those used not only by the translators of VL, but also those of Georg-Ps (→ 10.4.6). This assumption may also be corroborated indirectly by the recent detection of a number of textual agreements among Georgian, LXX^L (→ 10.3.6), and VL witnesses.⁸⁹

Consequently, OCS-Ps 1 would represent an additional indirect testimony of both the Greek "Western" and Hexaplaric readings (→ 10.3.5) and accordingly should be placed next to VL and the Psalms quotations of the Latin fathers (→ 10.4.1.4; → 21.8). If this conjecture were true, it would mean advances in the field of comparative textual criticism. By cross-checking data from secondary translations, researchers could gain access to fresh material for their investigations into the textual history of LXX-Ps during late antiquity. Future research should aim to clarify this issue by preparing critical editions of OCS-Ps 1 and detecting further cases of textual agreement with Georg-Ps.

10.4.7.5.4 Text-Critical Value of OCS-Ps 2 and Later Versions

The text-critical value of OCS-Ps 2 lies in the vast and still unexplored Hexaplaric material found in the manuscripts of the catena type. The Old Church Slavonic version of Theodoret of Cyrrhus'

---

⁸⁹ Kharanauli, "Einführung," 307–08.

commentaries (CPG 6202)[90] preserves several readings from the Three (→10.3.5) that still await a thorough collation with the Greek evidence.[91] Similar investigations should be undertaken for codices containing translations of Byzantine commentaries dating from the Middle Slavic period (→10.4.7.2).

Aejmelaeus, A. and U. Quast (eds.), *Der Septuaginta-Psalter und seine Tochterübersetzungen: Symposium in Göttingen 1997* (MSU 24; Göttingen: Vandenhoeck & Ruprecht, 2000).

Alekseev, A.A., *Tekstologija slavjanskoj Biblii* (Bausteine zur slavischen Philologie und Kulturgeschichte Neue Folge, Reihe A: Slavistische Forschungen 24; Cologne: Böhlau Verlag, 1999).

Alekseev, A.A., "O Novgorodskich voščenych doščečkach načala XI v.," *Russkij jazyk v naučnom osveščenii* 2 (2004): 203–08 [reprinted in: A.A. Alekseev, *Očerki i ètjudy po istorii literaturnogo jazyka v Rossii* (St. Petersburg: Peterburgskoe linvističeskoe obščestvo, 2013), 83–89.]

Altbauer, M. (ed.), *Sinajski Psaltir: Glagolski rakopis od XI vek* (Skopje: Makedonska akademija na naukite, 1971).

Altbauer, M. with collaboration of H.G. Lunt (eds.), *An Early Slavonic Psalter from Rus'*, Vol. 1: *Photoreproduction* (Cambridge: Harvard Ukrainian Research Institute, 1978).

Baumstark, A., "Der armenische Psaltertext: sein Verhältnis zum syrischen der Peschitta und seine Bedeutung für die LXX Forschung," *OrChr* 22 (1922–1924): 180–213; 23 (1926): 158–69, 319–33; 24 (1927): 146–59.

Biblija, sireč' knigi vetchago i novago zavěta, po jayzku slavensku (Moscow: Pečatnyj dvor, 1663).

Bolonski psaltir: bălgarski knižoven pametnik ot XIII vek (Psalterium bononiense) (ed. I. Dujčev; Sofia: Bălgarska Akad. na Naukite, 1968).

Busto Saiz, J.R., *La traducción de Símaco en el Libro de los Salmos* (Textos y Estudios "Cardenal Cisneros" 22; Madrid: Consejo Superior de Investigaciones Científicas, 1978).

Češko, E.V., "Ob Afonskoj redakcii slavjanskogo perevoda Psaltyri v ee otnošenii k drugim redakcijam," in *Jazyk i pismennost' srednebolgarskogo perioda* (ed. E.I. Demina; Moscow: Nauka, 1982), 60–92.

Češko, E.V. et al. (eds.), *Norovskaja psaltyr': Srednebolgarskaja rukopis' XIV veka, v dvuch častjach* (Sofia: Izdat. Bolgarskoj Akad. Nauk., 1989).

Cooper, H.R., "The Bible in Slavonic," in *The New Cambridge History of the Bible*, Vol. 2: *From 600 to 1450* (eds. R. Marsden and E.A. Matter; Cambridge: Cambridge University Press, 2012), 179–97.

Čudovskaja Psaltyr' XI veka, otryvok Tolkovanija Feodorita Kirrskago na Psaltyr' v drevne-bolgarskom perevode (ed. V. Pogorelov; St. Petersburg: Izd. otděl. russkogo jazyka i slov. Imperat. Akad. nauk, 1910).

Dunkov, D. (ed.), *Die Methodbibel*, Vol. 3: *Die Psalmen* (Die slawischen Sprachen 37; Salzburg: Institut für Slawistik der Universität Salzburg, 1994).

Field, **Hexapla*, Vol. 2.

Fraenkel, D., "Hexapla-Probleme im Psalter," in *Der Septuaginta-Psalter und seine Tochterübersetzungen: Symposium in Göttingen 1997* (eds. A. Aejmelaeus and U. Quast; MSU 24; Göttingen: Vandenhoeck & Ruprecht, 2000), 309–22.

Iosif (Archimandrit), *Podrobnoe oglavlenie Velikich Čet'ich Minej vserossijskogo mitropolita Makarija, chranjaščichsja v Moskovskoj patriaršej (nyne Synodal'noj) biblioteke* (Moscow: Sinodal'naja tipografija, 1892).

Jagić, V. (ed.), *Psalterium Bononiense: interpretationem Veterem Slavicam cum aliis codicibus collatam, adnotationibus ornatam, appendicibus auctam adiutus Academieae Scientiarum Vindobonensis liberalitate* (Vienna: Gerold, 1907).

Jagić, V. (ed.), *Supplementum Psalterii Bononiensis: incerti auctoris explanatio Psalmorum Graeca* (Vienna: Adolphus Holzhausen, 1917).

Karačorova, I., "Kăm văprosa za Kirilo-Metodievija starobălgarski prevod na Psaltira," in *Kirilo-Metodievski studii*, Vol. 6 (Sofia: Bălgarska Akad. na Naukite, 1989), 130–245.

Karačorova, I., "Novonajdennaja katena k Psaltyri v dvuch rukopisjach Chilandarskogo monastyrja," *Palaeobulgarica* 39.1 (2015): 55–71.

Kharanauli, A., "Einführung in die georgische Psalterübersetzung," in *Der Septuaginta-Psalter und seine Tochterübersetzungen: Symposium in Göttingen 1997* (eds. A. Aejmelaeus and U. Quast; MSU 24; Göttingen: Vandenhoeck & Ruprecht, 2000), 248–308.

Kievskaja Psaltir' 1397 goda (Moscow: Iskusstvo, 1978).

Kolesov, V.V., "Evgenievskaja Psaltir'," *Acta Universitatis Szegediensis de Attila József Nominatae: Dissertationes Slavicae: Sectio Linguistica* 8 (1972): 58–69.

---

[90] *Čudovskaja Psaltyr'*; Pogorelov, *Slovar'*; Lépissier, *Les commentaires*.
[91] Field, **Hexapla*, Vol. 2; Schenker, *Hexaplarische*; and Schenker, *Psalmen*; Busto Saiz, *La traducción*; Fraenkel, "Hexapla-Probleme."

Kovtun, L.S., N.V. Sinicyna, and B.L. Fonkič, "Maksim Grek i slavjanskaja Psaltyr' (složenie norm literaturnogo jazyka v perevodčeskoj praktike XVI v.)," in *Vostočnoslavjanskie jazyki: istočniki dlja ich izučenija* (eds. L.P. Žukovskaja and N.I. Tarabasova; Moscow: Nauka, 1973), 99–127.

Krivko, R.N., *Očerki jazyka drevnich cerkovnoslavjanskich rukopisej* (Moscow: Indrik, 2015).

Laurenčík, J., "Nelukianovská čtení v Sinajském žaltáři," in *Slovanské studie: sbírka statí, věnovaných prelátu univ. prof. dr. Josefu Vajsovi k uctění jeho životního díla* (eds. J. Kurz, M. Marko, and J. Vašica; Prague: Vyšehrad, 1948), 66–83.

Lépissier, J., "La traduction vieux-slave du Psautier," *Revue des études slaves* 43 (1964): 59–72.

Lépissier, J., *Les commentaires des psaumes de Théodoret (version slave)*, Vol. 1: *Étude linguistique et philologique* (Paris: Institut d' études slaves, 1968).

Gryson, R. and A. Thibaut (eds.), *Le psautier latin du Sinaï* (VL 39; Freiburg im Breisgau: Herder, 2010).

MacRobert, C.M., "The Greek Textological Basis of the Early Redactions of the Church Slavonic Psalter," *Palaeobulgarica* 14.2 (1990): 7–15.

MacRobert, C.M., "Translation is Interpretation: Lexical Variation in the Translation of the Psalter from Greek into Church Slavonic up to the 15th Century," *Zeitschrift für slavische Philologie* 53.2 (1993): 254–84.

MacRobert, C.M., "The Textual Tradition of the Church Slavonic Psalter up to the Fifteenth Century," in *The Interpretation of the Bible: The International Symposium in Slovenia* (ed. J. Krašovec; JSOTSup 289; Sheffield: Sheffield Academic Press, 1998), 921–42.

MacRobert, C.M., "On the Problems of Identifying a Preslav Redaction of the Psalter," in *Studia in honorem professoris Angelinae Minčeva* (eds. M. Dimitrova, P. Petkov, and I. Hristova; Acta palaeoslavica 2; Sofia: Heron Press, 2005), 39–46.

MacRobert, C.M., "The Compilatory Church Slavonic Catena on the Psalms in Three East Slavonic Manuscripts of the Fifteenth and Sixteenth Centuries," in *CyrilloMethodiana 2005 ad honorem Zdeňka Ribarova et Ludmila Pacnerová* (eds. E. Bláhová and E. Šlaufová; Slavia 74.2–3; Prague: Slovanský ústav AV ČR, Euroslavica, 2005), 213–38.

MacRobert, C.M., "The Linguistic Peculiarities and Textological Importance of the Novgorod Antiphonal Psalters," *Slověne* 2.2 (2013): 31–51.

MacRobert, C.M., "The Place of Dimitri's Psalter (MS Sinai 3N) in the Early Transmission of the Church Slavonic Psalter," in *The Bible in Slavic Tradition* (eds. A. Kulik et al.; Studia Judaeoslavica 9; Leiden: Brill, 2016), 89–106.

Mareš, F.V. et al. (eds.), *Psalterii Sinaitici pars nova (monasterii s. Catharinae codex slav. 2/N)* (Vienna: Österreichische Akademie der Wissenschaften, 1997).

Miklas, H. et al. (eds.), *Psalterium Demetrii Sinaitici (monasterii s. Catharinae codex slav. 3/N) adiectis foliis medicinalibus*, Vol. 1 (Vienna: Holzhausen, 2012).

De Nunzio, U., "O slavjanskoj rukopisi Vatikanskoj biblioteki No. VII," *Žurnal Ministerstva narodnogo prosveščenija* 11 (1892): 141–47.

Ostrožskaja biblija: Fototipičeskoe pereizdanie teksta s izdanija 1581 g. (Moscow: Slovo-Art, 1988).

Pantelić, M., "Zapadne varijante u staroslovenskim psaltirima," in *Simpozium 1100-godišnina od smrtta na Kiril Solunski*, Vol. 2 (ed. H. Polenakovik; Skopje: Maked. Akad. na Nauk. i Umetn., 1970), 291–99.

Pogorelov, V., *Psaltyri* (Biblioteka Moskovskoj Sinodal'noj Tipografii 1.3; Moscow: Sinodal'naja tipografija, 1901).

Pogorelov, V., *Slovar' k tolkovanijam Feodorita Kirrskago na Psaltyr' v drevne-bolgarskom perevode* (Warsaw: Tipografija Varšavskogo učebnogo okruga, 1910).

Rahlfs, A. (ed.), *Psalmi cum Odis* (Septuaginta Vetus Testamentum Graecum 10; Göttingen: Vandenhoeck & Ruprecht, 1931; 3rd ed. 1979).

Rondeau, M.-J., *Les Commentaires patristiques du Psautier (IIIe–Ve siècles)*, Vol. I: *Les travaux des Pères grecs et latins sur le Psautier. Recherches et bilan* (OrChrAn 219; Rome: Pontificio Istituto Orientale, 1982).

Schenker, A., *Hexaplarische Psalmenbruchstücke: Die hexaplarischen Psalmenfragmente der Handschriften Vaticanus graecus 752 und Canonicianus graecus 62* (OBO 8; Göttingen: Vandenhoeck & Ruprecht, 1975).

Schenker, A., *Psalmen in den Hexapla: Erste kritische und vollständige Ausgabe der hexaplarischen Fragmente auf dem Rande der Handschrift Ottobonianus Graecus 398 zu den PS 24–32* (Studi e testi 295; Vatican City: Vatican Library, 1982).

Severjanov, S.N. (ed.), *Sinajskaja psaltyr': glagoličeskij pamjatnik XI veka* (St. Petersburg: Rossijskaja Gosudarstvennaja Akademičeskaja Tipografija, 1922).

Sinicyna, N.V. (ed.), *Prepodobnyj Maksim Grek: Sočinenija*, Vol. 1 (Moscow: Indrik, 2008.)

Sobolev, A.N., "Novgorodskaja psaltyr' XI veka i ee antigraf," *Voprosy jazykoznanija* 3 (2003): 113–42.

Speranskij, M.N., *Tajnopis' v jugo-slavjanskich i russkich pamjatnikach pis'ma* (Leningrad: Izd. Akademii Nauk SSSR, 1929).

Stančev, K., "Po povodu Novgorodskoj psaltyri na voske, najdennoj v 2000 godu," *Russica Romana* 11 (2004): 185–98.

Taube, M., "The Vilnius 262 Psalter: A Jewish Translation?" in *Judaeo-Slavica et Russica: Festschrift Professor Ilya Serman* (eds. W. Moskovich et al.; Jews and Slavs 14; Jerusalem: Gešarim, 2004), 27–38.

Temčin, S.J., "Scharija i Skorina: ob istočnikach Vilenskogo Vetchozavetnogo svoda (F 19–262)," *Senoji Lietuvos Literatūra* 21 (2006): 289–316.

Thomson, F.J., "The Slavonic Translation of the Old Testament," in *The Interpretation of the Bible: The International Symposium in Slovenia* (ed. J. Krašovec; JSOTSup 289; Sheffield: Sheffield Academic Press, 1998), 605–920.

Thomson, F.J., *A Brief Survey of the History of the Church Slavonic Bible from its Cyrillomethodian Origins until its Final Form in the Elizabethan Bible of 1751* (Slavica Gandensia 33.2; Ghent: University of Ghent, 2006).

Tomelleri, V., "Psaltir' Gennadievskoj Biblii 1499 g. (K izučeniju rukopisnoj tradicii v Novgorode)," in *Sub Rosa: In Honorem Lenae Szilárd* (eds. D. Atanaszova-Szokolova, A. Han, and A. Hollós; Budapest: ELTE BTK Irodalomtudományi Doktori Iskola, 2005), 578–84.

Tomelleri, V.S., "O nekotoryx sintaksičeskich osobennostjach Tolkovoj Psaltiri Brunona (1535): Datel'nyj samostojatel'nyj, infinitivnye i pričastnye konstrukcii, gerundij i gerundiv," in *Lingvističeskoe istočnikovedenie i istorija russkogo jazyka (2012–2013)* (eds. A.M. Moldovan and E.A. Mishina; Moscow: Drevlechranilišče, 2013), 196–225.

Vajs, J., *Psalterium palaeoslovenicum croato-glagoliticum*, Vol. 1: *Textus, annotationes, tabulae* (Prague: Sumptibus Academiae palaeoslavicae Veglensis, 1916).

Vajs, J., "Které recenze byla řecká předloha staroslověnského překladu žaltáře," *Byzantinoslavica* 8 (1939–1946): 55–88.

Zaliznjak, A.A., "Problemy izučenija Novgorodskogo kodeksa XI veka, najdennogo v 2000 g.," in *Slavjanskoe jazykoznanie: XIII Meždunarodnyj s"ezd slavistov, Ljubljana, 2003 g. Doklady Rossijskoj delegacii* (Moscow: Indrik, 2003), 190–212.

Zaliznjak, A.A. and V.L. Janin, "Novgorodskij kodeks pervoj četverti XI v. – drevnejšaja kniga Rusi," *Voprosy jazykoznanija* 5 (2001): 3–25.

Ziffer, G., "Appunti sul Salterio Sinaitico," *Incontri linguistici* 21 (1998): 189–95.

Šaniʒe, M. (ed.), *Psalmunis ʒveli kartuli redakciebi X–XIII sauk'uneta xelnac'erebis mixedvit*, Vol. 1: *T'ekst'i* (3veli kartuli enis ʒeglebi 11; Tbilisi: Sakartvelos ssr mecnierebata ak'ademiis gamomcemloba, 1960).

Ščepkin, V.N., *Bolonskaja psaltyr'* (St. Petersburg: Tip. Imp. akademii nauk, 1906).

Šivarov, N., "Drevni iztočni komentarii na Psaltira i starobalgarskite im prevodi," *Godišnik na Duchovnata akademija* 28.54 (1978–1979): 6–81.

Alessandro Maria Bruni

10.4.8 Arabic Translations

Some scholars have claimed that pre-Islamic translations of Arabic texts of the Bible (especially the Gospels and the Psalms) were available to Christian Arabs, and that these Arabic versions were subsequently borrowed, copied, and transmitted by the monks of St. Sabas and St. Catherine in Palestine. However, these early Arabic translations were made in Palestine by Palestinian Christian translators from the eighth century C.E. onwards. In the eighth and ninth centuries C.E., bilingual Psalters (Greek-Arabic) were used by the Melkites in their liturgy in the Judean Desert monasteries.[1]

Unfortunately, important early Palestinian translations have not survived. This is the case of the version of the book of Psalms included in Codex Vaticano Arabo 13, dated in the ninth century C.E. A leaf in Greek uncials at the end of the codex says that it contained an Arabic translation of the Psalms together with the four Gospels, Acts, and all the Epistles, although only Paul's Epistles and large portions of the Gospels remain today. If it had survived, this version would be of great interest for determining the exegetical techniques and origins of the translation of the book of Psalms by Christian Arab translators.[2]

The earliest surviving translation of the Psalms in Christian Arabic is a bilingual parchment fragment from Damascus. The fragment, discovered by Violet in the *Qubbat al-Khaznah* of the *Masjid al-Umawwiyyīn*, contains twenty-three verses (Ps

---

[1] Baumstark, "Problem"; Shahîd, *Byzantium*, 435–43; cf. the introduction to Blau, *Grammar.

[2] Monferrer Sala, "Una traducción árabe con 'pseudoescolio exegético anónimo,'" 67–74.

78:20–31, 51–61) in Greek according to the Septuagint (= Psalm 77; → 10.3.1) together with an Arabic translation written in Greek uncials.[3] This version, most probably of Syrian provenance according to paleographical and linguistic considerations, is dated to the late seventh or early eighth century C.E., and exhibits a linguistic register that represents the birth certificate of Nabaṭī Arabic, the immediate forerunner of Neo-Arabic.[4] However, Macdonald has suggested that this fragment could be dated some time before the sixth century AD.[5]

Another interesting bilingual (Greek-Arabic) translation of the book of Psalms is preserved in the Zurich Public Library (Or. Ms 94). Although Baumstark proposed that the Arabic version could be traced to pre-Islamic times (even as early as the fifth century C.E.) based on the archaic form of the Arabic text,[6] this translation exhibits a text of ninth- or tenth-century C.E. southern Palestine.[7]

In the eighth and ninth centuries C.E., Arabic versions of Psalms circulated in the libraries of the Palestinian desert monasteries for liturgical use, as evidenced by three surviving bilingual Psalters from Sinai.[8] Also of great interest is a set of fragments of a trilingual Psalter (Greek-Syriac-Arabic) from the *lavra* of Mār Sābā, which is currently preserved in St. Petersburg Library. The manuscript is dated to the ninth century C.E. Forty verses from Pss 70:7–16; 73:4–14; 77:28–38; 79:9–16 survive.[9] An almost-complete Arabic manuscript of the tenth century containing a Psalter (Psalms 1 and 2 as well as the beginning of Psalm 3 are missing) with an appendix of the biblical canticles is preserved in the Bryn Mawr College Library (Pennsylvania) under the signature manuscript BV 47.

One of the most important Christian Arabic versions is undoubtedly that of the Melkite ʿAbdallāh ibn al-Faḍl al-Anṭākī (d. ca. 1050), perhaps one of the most prolific Christian Arab translators. The text, which became by far the most influential among the Christian Arabs, contains an Arabic translation of the Psalms that circulated widely in Melkite circles, and even in the Coptic Church, made from the Greek text of the Septuagint (→ 10.3.1) according to the recension of the Melkite Church (*al-nuskhah al-yūnāniyyah al-latī istakhrajnā minhā hadhihi l-tafāsīr* "the Greek copy from which we have drawn these commentaries"). Ibn al-Faḍl also acknowledges having used various Greek texts of the Psalms, among them the versions of Theodotion, Aquila, and Symmachus that were preserved thanks in part to Origen's *Hexapla* (→ 10.3.5): ... *Thāwudhūtiyūs wa-Akīlās wa-Simmākhus wa-Thawudhūrīṭūs wa-ghayrihim min al-Abāʾ al-ajillāʾ al-qiddīsīn qad tarjamnā minhā mā ihtamalathu ḥawāshī hadhihi l-nuskha* "Theodotion, Aquila, Symmachus, Theodoretus and other illustrious holy Fathers from whom we have translated what the glosses of this copy gather." The liturgical Psalter containing the 150 Psalms is divided into twenty *kathisma* (together with their rubrics) of three stanzas each. They are followed by ten biblical canticles introduced in the *orthros* office.[10] Ibn al-Faḍl also composed an interlinear commentary (*tafsīr*) to the Psalms. Ibn al-Faḍl's translation was transmitted in numerous manuscripts. In fact, it is included in the famous manuscript Vat. Ar. 468.

Ibn al-Faḍl's text knew numerous editions that are divided into several groups, the most important of which are the editions of Aleppo 1706 and 1709. A second group comprises the revision of the Aleppo recension edited in 1735 by the Melkite deacon ʿAbdallāh Ẓākhir in the printing press of the Monastery of al-Shuwayr, with subsequent reprints between 1739 and 1899. Al-Shuwayr's recension was the base text for the Orthodox editions of

---

[3] Violet, "Ein zweisprachiges Psalmfragment"; Kahle, *Die arabischen Bibelübersetzungen*; Haddad, "La phonétique de l' arabe chrétien vers 700"; Blau, *Handbook*, 68–71.

[4] Corriente, "The Psalter Fragment."

[5] Macdonald, "Literacy in an Oral Environment," 96–99.

[6] Baumstark, "Der älteste erhaltene griechisch-arabische Text von Psalm 110 (109)."

[7] J. Blau, "Sind uns Reste arabischer Bibelübersetzungen aus vorislamischer Zeit erhalten geblieben?" *Mus* 86 (1973): 67–72.

[8] Griffith, *The Bible in Arabic*, 146.

[9] Pigulevskaya, "Greco-Siro-Arabskaia Rukopis IXV."

[10] Nasrallah, *Histoire*; Monferrer Sala, "En torno a dos manuscritos árabes bíblicos inéditos."

Beirut and Jerusalem, and also for three different groups of editions: the Jesuit edition in Beirut from 1855 onwards, the Franciscan editions in Jerusalem (1866, 1870, 1888), and the Aleppo edition in 1864 used in the Maronite schools. Likewise, the Protestants used Ibn al-Faḍl's translation in the edition prepared for the "Society for Promoting Christian Knowledge" (London, 1725).[11]

A trilingual Psalter in Greek, Latin, and Arabic in three parallel columns (British Library Harley manuscript 5786) was reproduced in Sicily in the Norman kingdom of Roger II (1130–1154). The Greek translation is that of LXX (→ 10.3.1), the Latin corresponds to the Latin Vulgate (→ 10.3.7), whereas the Arabic version was translated from a Greek text by a deacon of the Melkite Church in Antioch. The rubrics and marginal notes written in Arabic alongside the Greek column inform us that this Psalter had a liturgical use.[12]

One of the best-known translations of the Psalms in the Copto-Arabic tradition comes from the Wādī al-Naṭrūn libraries. Known as the Barberini Psalter, it contains five versions in Coptic (→ 10.4.2), Ethiopic (→ 10.4.3), Armenian (→ 10.4.5), Syriac (→ 10.3.4; → 10.4.4), and Arabic and is dated to the thirteenth or fourteenth century. The manuscript became the property of the Monastery of St. Macarius in 1635 and was finally given to Cardinal Barberini and kept in the Vatican Library.[13]

In the sixteenth and seventeenth centuries, several Arabic editions of the Psalter were prepared from both Greek (→ 10.3.1) and Syriac Vorlagen (→ 10.3.4; → 10.4.4). The most important of these editions is that of Giustiniani, bishop of Nebbio, who prepared the first polyglot edition of the Psalms in Hebrew, Greek, Latin, Arabic, and Aramaic in 1516.[14] The Arabic version included in this *Psalterium Hebreum, Grecum, Arabicu(m) et Chaldeu(m) cu(m) tribus latinis i(n)terp(re)tat(i)o(n)ibus et glossi* was translated from LXX according to the Syro-Lucianic version (→ 10.4.4.2). The Polyglots (except the Complutense Polyglot, which did not incorporate an Arabic column) included Giustiniani's text. An earlier polyglot edition of the Psalter was promised by Aldus Manuzio in the preface to the Greek edition of Psalms of around 1497, although this edition never saw the light and only some specimens remain.[15]

For their part, Maronites Gabriel Sionita and Victorinus Scialac Accurensis edited the *Liber Psalmorum Davidis et Prophetae* in Arabic together with a Latin translation in Rome in 1614 (repr. 1619; an edition of the Psalter in Arabic only was also printed in 1614).[16] The Paris Polyglot (1645),[17] the Arabic text being translated from Greek, was edited with no accuracy.[18]

Raphael al-Ṭūkhī (1703–1787), a young Coptic convert to Catholicism who worked intensively in the Vatican Library on the transcription of codices, also prepared a Coptic Bohairic-Arabic Psalter in Rome in 1744 (reprinted in 1749): *Kitāb zubūr Dāwud* [*Psalterium coptico-arabicum*]. The text, prepared for ecclesiastical use, was full of grammatical and lexicographical errors. Of course, this was not the only edition of the book of Psalms, nor even the first, but al-Ṭūkhī's text launched in turn a series of editions of the book of Psalms during the nineteenth century,[19] such as those of de Lagarde[20] and Labīb.[21]

The oldest biblical text translated into Arabic in al-Andalus was composed after the alleged martyrdoms of Cordoba in the ninth century C.E. The translation is dated to the second half of the ninth century C.E., specifically in the year 889 C.E. if the data of the colophon of one of the two extant manuscripts is correct. The text is a versified Arabic version of the book of Psalms prepared by Ḥafṣ b. Al-

---

[11] *Arabic Psalter* (London: Society for Promoting Christian Knowledge, 1725); cf. Vollandt, "Che portono al ritorno," 409.

[12] Griffith, *The Bible in Arabic*, 149.

[13] Evelyn-White and Hauser, *The Monasteries of the Wadi'n Natrûn*, 1.xxxvii–xxxviii n. 14.

[14] Giustiniani, *Psalterium*; Monferrer Sala, "Dos impresos italianos del siglo XVI de la BPC."

[15] Cf. Renouard, *Annales*.

[16] Scialac and Sionita, *Liber Psalmorum Davidi*.

[17] Le Jay, *Biblia.

[18] Graf, *GCAL 1, 121–24.

[19] Graf, *GCAL 1, 119–21.

[20] De Lagarde, *Psalterium, Job, Proverbia*.

[21] Macarius, Archbishop of Siut, and C. Labīb (eds.), *Pčōm nte ni Psalmos*.

bar al-Qūṭī[22] that has survived in two manuscripts from the thirteenth and fourteenth centuries.[23] The translation was commissioned by Valens, who was the bishop of Cordoba at that time.[24] This version is not only of interest due to the translation but also due to a fascinating introduction in verse (*urjūzah*, i.e., rhyming couplets in the *rajaz* meter), which fails to mention the dramatic events that supposedly had just taken place in Cordoba in the form of martyrdoms. Certain features of the Arabic translation are also of interest, providing linguistic elements that are typical of Eastern Christian traditions, as well as a variety of sources that suggest the participation of an Eastern Christian author in preparing or correcting the final version of this translation of the book of Psalms.

In the introduction to his Arabic translation of Psalms, consisting of 143 verses in the *rajaz* meter, Ḥafṣ explains the reason for his translation, i.e., the existence of an earlier prose translation that was used by the Andalusi Christians that contained numerous errors. Ḥafṣ' explanation for his use of the *rajaz* internal rhyme meter is interesting. He states that he made that choice because it resembled to some extent the Iambic pentameter used by the Christians. Therefore, it seems clear that this was an example of the "reversed acculturation" experienced by the Andalusi Arabized Christians, namely the use of Arabic to preserve their Christian Latin legacy as a form of *imitatio* of the schemes of the superior language of the Christians of al-Andalus, that is, the Latin language in opposition to the Arabic language.[25]

Arabic Psalter (London: Society for Promoting Christian Knowledge, 1725).

Baumstark, A., "Das Problem eines vorislamischen christlich-kirchlichen Schrifttums in arabischer Sprache," *Islamica* 4 (1929–1931): 562–75.

Baumstark, A., "Der älteste erhaltene griechisch-arabische Text von Psalm 110 (109)," *OrChr* 31 (1934): 55–66.

Blau, **Grammar*.

Blau, J., *A Handbook of Early Middle Arabic* (The Max Schloessinger Memorial Series Monographs 6; Jerusalem: The Hebrew University of Jerusalem, 2002).

Corriente, F., "The Psalter Fragment from the Umayyad Mosque of Damascus: A Birth Certificate of Nabaṭī Arabic," in *Eastern Crossroads: Essays on Medieval Christian Legacy* (ed. J.P. Monferrer Sala; Gorgias Eastern Christian Studies 1; Piscataway: Gorgias Press, 2007), 303–20.

Evelyn-White, H.G. and W. Hauser, *The Monasteries of the Wadi'n Natrûn* (3 vols.; New York: Metropolitan Museum of Art, 1926–1933).

Giustiniani, A., *Psalterium Hebreum, Grecum, Arabicu(m) et Chaldeu(m) cu(m) tribus latinis i(n)terp(re)tat(i)o(n)ibus et glossi* (Genoa: Petrus Paulus Porrus, 1516).

Goussen, H., *Die christlich-arabische Literatur der Mozaraber* (Beiträge zur christlich-arabischen Literaturgeschichte 4; Leipzig: Harrassowitz, 1909).

Graf, **GCAL* 1, 114–26.

Griffith, S.H., *The Bible in Arabic: The Scriptures of the 'People of the Book' in the Language of Islam* (Princeton: Princeton University Press, 2013).

Haddad, R., "La phonétique de l'arabe chrétien vers 700," in *La Syrie de Byzance a l'Islam: VIIe–VIIIe siecles: actes du colloque international, Lyon, Maison de l'Orient Méditerranéen, Paris, Institut du Monde Arabe, 11–15 septembre 1990* (eds. P. Canivet and J.-P. Rey-Coquais; Damascus: Institut Français d'Etudes Arabes, 1992), 159–64.

Kahle, P., *Die arabischen Bibelübersetzungen*: *Texte mit Glossar und Literaturübersicht* (Leipzig: Hinrichs, 1904).

de Lagarde, P., *Psalterium, Job, Proverbia: Arabice* (Göttingen: W.F. Kaestner, 1876).

Macarius, Archbishop of Siut, and C. Labīb (eds.), *Pčōm nte ni Psalmos nte Dauid Piprophētēsouoh piouro Nem nihōdē Kitāb zabūr Dā'ūd al-Nabī wa-al-malik ma'a al-tasābīḥ* (the Psalms, followed by a series of biblical canticles and prayers, in the Coptic version accompanied by an Arabic translation) (revised and corrected by the Hegoumenos 'Abd al-Masīḥ Ṣalīb; Cairo: no publisher given, 1897).

Mcdonald, M.C.A., "Literacy in an Oral Environment," in *Writing and Ancient Near Eastern Society. Papers in Honour of Alan R. Millard* (ed. P. Bienkowski, Ch. Mee

---

[22] Monferrer Sala, "Ibn Albar al-Qūṭī (Ḥafṣ b. Albar al-Qūṭī)," 1.433–35; Monferrer Sala, "Ibn Albar al-Qūṭī (Ḥafṣ b. Albar al-Qūṭī)," 2.87–89.

[23] Urvoy, *Le Psautier Mozarabe de Hafs le Goth*.

[24] Goussen, *Die christlich-arabische Literatur der Mozaraber*.

[25] Monferrer Sala, "Salmo 11 en versión árabe versificada."

and E. Slater, New York–London: T & T Clark, 2006), 45–114.

Monferrer Sala, J.P., "En torno a dos manuscritos árabes bíblicos inéditos," *Philologia Hispalense* 14 (2000): 334–38.

Monferrer Sala, J.P., "Salmo 11 en versión árabe versificada: Unas notas en torno a las fuentes del Psalterio de Ḥafṣ b. Albar al-Qūṭī," *Miscelánea de Estudios Árabes y Hebraicos* 492 (2000): 303–19.

Monferrer Sala, J.P., "Una traducción árabe con 'pseudoescolio exegético anónimo': Una nota de crítica textual interna a propósito del ms. sabaítico *Vaticano arabo 13*," *Boletín de la Asociación Española de Orientalistas* 37 (2001): 67–82.

Monferrer Sala, J.P., "Dos impresos italianos del siglo XVI de la BPC: Una *editio princeps* bilingüe arabelatina de los Evangelios y un *octaplum* del Salterio," *Alfinge* 13 (2001): 92–96.

Monferrer Sala, J.P., "Ibn Albar al-Qūṭī (Ḥafṣ b. Albar al-Qūṭī)," in *Diccionario Enciclopédico de al-Andalus: Diccionario de autores y obras andalusíes* (eds. J. Lirola Delgado and J.M. Puerta Vílchez; 2 vols.; Granada: Junta de Andalucía-Fundación El Legado Andalusí, 2002), 1.433–35.

Monferrer Sala, J.P., "Ibn Albar al-Qūṭī (Ḥafṣ b. Albar al-Qūṭī)," in *Enciclopedia de la cultura andalusí: Biblioteca de al-Andalus* (ed. J. Lirola Delgado; 7 vols.; Almería: Fundación Ibn Tufayl de Estudios Árabes, 2009), 2.87–89.

Nasrallah, J., *Histoire du mouvement littéraire dans l'église melchite du Ve au XXe siècle: Contribution à l'étude de la littérature arabe chrétienne*, Vol. 3.1: *Reconquête byzantine: 969–1250* (Louvain: Peeters, 1983), 217–18.

Pigulevskaya, N.V., "Greco-siro-arabskaia rukopis IX v.," *Palestinskii Sbornik* 1 (63) (1954): 59–90.

Renouard, A.A., *Annales de l'imprimerie des Alde: Ou histoire des trois Manuce et de leurs éditions* (3rd ed.; New Castle: Oak Knoll Books, 1991 [reprint of Paris: Renouard, 1834]).

Scialac, V. and G. Sionita, *Liber Psalmorum Davidi regis et prophetae: Ex Arabico idiomate in Latinum translatus* (Rome: Typographia Sauariana, 1614).

Shahîd, I., *Byzantium and the Arabs in the Fourth Century* (Washington: Dumbarton Oaks Research Library and Collection, 1984).

Urvoy, M.-T., *Le Psautier Mozarabe de Hafs le Goth* (Toulouse: Presses Universitaires du Mirai, 1994).

Violet, B., "Ein zweisprachiges Psalmfragment aus Damaskus," *OLZ* 4 (1901): 384–403, 425–41, 475–88.

Vollandt, R., "Che portono al ritorno quì una Bibbia Arabica integra: A History of the *Biblia Sacra Arabica* (1671–73)," in *Graeco-Latina et Orientalia: Studia in honorem Angeli Urbani heptagenarii* (eds. S.K. Samir and J.P. Monferrer Sala; Córdoba: CNERU, 2013), 401–18.

Juan Pedro Monferrer Sala

11
Job

∴

11.1 Textual History of Job

11.1.1 Name and Position

The book takes its name from the principal character around whom the narrative revolves: Job. In this respect, it is like several other books of the Old Testament: Joshua, Samuel, Jonah, Ruth, Esther, Daniel, Ezra, and Nehemiah. In the Hebrew canon (→ 1.1.2.1), Job is placed among the Ketuvim, the Writings, between Psalms and Proverbs. In the Babylonian Talmud, the oldest witness of the Jewish tradition, we already find the juxtaposition of these three books. Thus, we read in the Babylonian Talmud, *b. B. Bat.* 14b, "The order of the Ketuvim is: Ruth and the book of Psalms and Job and Proverbs ..." These three books are given a special accentuation by the Masoretes. The precise order varies, though Psalms always precedes.[1] This fluctuation in the sequence is connected with the question of the book's reputed date. Ruth, set in the period of the Judges, would precede Psalms, many of which are attributed to King David. Proverbs, connected to King Solomon, would follow Psalms. On the other hand, for Job no clear date can be found. In the Greek Bibles (→ 1.1.2.2), the position of Job varies considerably. For example, it comes between Canticles and the Wisdom of Solomon in Codex Vaticanus, at the end of the Old Testament in Sinaiticus, after the Wisdom of Solomon and Sirach, and between Psalms and Proverbs in Alexandrinus.[2] This variation in order is connected with the "Alexandrian desire to arrange the books according to their literary character or contents, or their supposed authorship."[3] Here again, the book of Job, while certainly poetic and treating wisdom, does not have an obvious position.

The variations in the place of Job in the canon are, however, connected with the question of the date of the book. The Babylonian Talmud offers a number of possibilities. One is that the author of the book is Moses, another is that the author is one of the patriarchs. The period of the spies (Numbers 13) is proposed, but it is also proposed that Job was among those who returned from the Babylonian exile. Job may even have been a typological figure who never existed.[4] The ancient church historian Eusebius of Caesarea in his *Praeparatio Evangelica* draws on the pagan author Alexander Polyhistor who refers to a work of Aristeas, *On the Jews*, according to which Job, identified with Jobab (Gen 36:33–34), was a "son" (descendant) of Esau by his wife Bassara.[5] The identification of Job with Jobab is in fact found in the epilogue to the book of Job, which is an addition of LXX (→ 11.3.1), not found in MT (→ 11.2.2). Since Alexander Polyhistor lived ca. 105–30 B.C.E., Aristeas would have flourished before the middle of the first century B.C.E.

11.1.2 Ancient Versions: LXX

While the exact nature of the relationship between Aristeas and LXX is unclear, it is certain that the Greek text of Job (→ 11.3.1) existed by about 100 B.C.E. (→ 11.3.1.1.1).[6] On the strength of cultural and religious links with its Hellenistic environment and in view of translation techniques, a date around 150 B.C.E. has been proposed.[7] This Greek text differed considerably from MT (→ 11.2.2), especially in its shortness.[8] It has been estimated that 389 stichs were not present.[9] This number is, in fact, approximate because there are different ways of computing the missing material. Furthermore, the translator does not always translate stich by

---

[1] Cf. Ginsburg, *Introduction*, 6–8.
[2] See Swete, *Introduction*, 201–02.
[3] Swete, *Introduction*, 218. For a different view, see → 1.1.2.2.
[4] *B. B. Bat.* 15a.
[5] *Praep. ev.* 9.25:1–4. See PG 21,728.
[6] Cf. C.R. Holladay, "Aristeas," in *Fragments from Hellenistic Jewish authors*, Vol. 1 (SBLTT 20; Atlanta: SBL, 1983), 261–75.
[7] See M. Cimosa, "La data probabile della traduzione greca (LXX) del libro di Giobbe," *Sacra Doctrina* 51.6 (2006): 17–35.
[8] Ziegler, *Iob*. See 11.3.1.3, cf. also → 11.2.2.
[9] Cf. Ziegler, *Iob*, 150–51; Gentry, *Asterisked Materials*.

stich, and frequently renders his text quite freely.[10] LXX was later revised due at least in part to the numerous differences between the Hebrew and Greek texts. Theodotion (around the turn of the era?)[11] revised the text towards the Hebrew, dependent perhaps on an already existing Greek translation (→ 11.3.1.1.3).[12] Aquila (ca. 100 C.E.) translated the Hebrew very literally. Symmachus (ca. 150 C.E.) translated faithfully but in good Greek. In the third century, Origen tried to recover the Greek text based on the Hebrew (→ 11.3.1.1.3). In his Hexapla, he organized the text in six columns, including the versions of Aquila, Theodotion (in part), and Symmachus (→ 11.3.5). Origen also used three other versions known as Quinta, Sexta, and Septima, although none is complete. Quinta and Sexta contained Job. The Hexapla of Origen is lost but numerous manuscripts preserve portions of it and these have been edited by Field.[13] There are also translations of it, in particular the Syro-Hexapla (made in 616–617 C.E. in Alexandria by Paul, bishop of Tella; → 11.4.4), the Latin translation by Jerome (→ 11.3.7), and the Armenian translation (→ 11.4.5).[14] The Syro-Hexapla and Jerome retained Origen's diacritical signs, the asterisk that marked additions to the Greek text (usually taken from Theodotion) and the obelus where the Greek showed an addition to the Hebrew. In this way, the reader could distinguish between LXX and the additions with which Origen tried to fill the lacunae in the Greek text. Another witness to the Old Greek text is the Coptic Sahidic translation (→ 11.4.2), which omits Origen's additions (it lacks only Job 39:10–40:13a). According to Ziegler, this translation may not have preceded the Hexapla since it probably simply omitted stichs marked with an asterisk (but see → 11.4.2).[15] The Bohairic translation is complete and includes stichs marked with an asterisk. It is closer to the text of LXX than is the Sahidic version (→ 11.4.2).[16] The Fayyumic translation survives in only one fragment containing Job 32:7–10 (→ 11.4.2.1). The Ethiopic version is a very free translation of the Greek (Cf. → 11.4.3).[17]

11.1.3 Ancient Versions: Peshitta

The Peshitta or Syriac translation is made from the Hebrew (→ 11.3.4). Printed texts of the Peshitta are found in the Parisian Polyglot of 1645[18] and in the London Polyglot of 1657, which reproduced the text of the Parisian Polyglot.[19] An edition that took account of the most important manuscripts was still lacking. Then Gösta Rignell edited the text based on manuscript B.21 Inferiore of the Ambrosian Library in Milan, a sixth or seventh century C.E. manuscript, and the oldest known of the Syriac manuscripts, the Codex Ambrosianus. He also made use of other manuscripts. This edition was published by the Peshitta Institute in Leiden.[20] A matter for discussion is whether Jews or Christians were responsible for the translation. Rignell hypothesized that Jews with a good knowledge of Hebrew and less proficiency in Syriac translated individual words, producing a kind of glossary. Later, Christians with a good knowlege of Syriac but less proficiency in Hebrew used this glossary to make a translation that often fails to reproduce the Hebrew syntax. A feature of the text is frequent double translation. Rignell also offers a translation into English with commentary (→ 11.3.4).[21]

---

[10] Cf. Fernández Marcos, "The Septuagint Reading of the Book of Job," 254–55; Gorea, *Job*, 226–28.

[11] P.J. Gentry, "The Place of Theodotion-Job in the Textual History of the Septuagint," in *Origen's Hexapla and Fragments* (ed. A. Salvesen; TSAJ 58; Tübingen: Mohr Siebeck 1998), 199–230.

[12] Cf. Barthélemy, *Devanciers*.

[13] Field, *Hexapla*.

[14] On Jerome's first translation of Job, cf. P.-M. Bogaert, "Job latin chez les pères et dans les bibles," 75–82; on the Armenian translation, cf. Cox, *Armenian Job*.

[15] See Ziegler, *Iob*, 42–45.

[16] Ziegler, *Iob*, 45–47.

[17] Ziegler, *Iob*, 48–50.

[18] Le Jay, *Biblia*.

[19] Walton, *Polyglotta*.

[20] Rignell, *Job*.

[21] Rignell, *The Peshitta to the Book of Job*.

11.1.4 Ancient Versions: Targumim

The Targum or Aramaic translation of Job (→ 11.3.3.1) is presented in various critical editions. The first printed edition was edited by Felix Pratensis and printed by Daniel Bomberg in 1517 (*RB1). This text has been "reproduced, with only a few changes, in every printed edition (except the Antwerp Polyglot) published since."[22] The Antwerp Polyglot, edited by Benito Arias Montano and printed in Antwerp between 1569 and 1572, may have used manuscript 116-Z-40 of the Library of the Complutensian University of Madrid and manuscript M-2 of the Library of the University of Salamanca.[23] Arias Montanto also used the printed editions of Bomberg.[24] The Targum of Job is also found in the *Biblia Rabbinica* edited by Johannes Buxtorf, published in Basle in 1618–1619 "and is essentially a revision of that found in the editions of Bomberg."[25] De Lagarde produced an unpointed edition of the Targumim to the Hagiographa under the title *Hagiographa Chaldaice* (1873).[26] De Lagarde based it on Daniel Bomberg's 1517 edition of the *Biblia Rabbinica* (*RB1). Stec points out that the text of the Targum of Job "found in the manuscripts presently known is rather different from that found in the printed editions."[27] Weiss in his study made use of five manuscripts as well as the printed editions, but he abandoned the plan to produce a critical edition.[28] Fernández Vallina did attempt a critical edition in his 1980 doctoral thesis.[29] He used as his base text manuscript Cambridge, University Library Ee.5.9 and collated a further seven manuscripts and two printed editions.[30] He did not, however, use all manuscripts known to contain the Targum of Job. Díez Merino transcribed manuscript Madrid, Biblioteca de la Universidad Complutense 116-Z-40 in 1984.[31] Stec has produced a new critical edition of the Targum of Job based on Codex Urbinas I of the Vatican Library.[32] At the same time, he consulted all known manuscripts of the Targum of Job and the edition presents variant readings (→ 11.3.3.1).

In 1956, bedouin found remains of a number of manuscripts in a cave at Qumran. Among these was a Targum of the book of Job, later edited by two Dutch scholars.[33] The editors were of the opinion that it was probably translated around 100 B.C.E. The Targum is a simple translation, lacking long paraphrases and expansions. The Hebrew text it renders is close to MT (→ 11.2.2). Sometimes in matters of detail it follows LXX (→ 11.3.1), which points to a common exegetical tradition (→ 11.3.3.2).

11.1.5 Ancient Hebrew Texts

Also found at Qumran were fragments of the Hebrew text of the book of Job (→ 11.2.1; → 11.2.3). 4QJob[a] contains elements of Job 31–37 (though not of Job 34). The hand is Hasmonean and it is dated to the early or mid-first century B.C.E.[34] 4QJob[b] contains fragments from Job 8; 9; 13; and 31. Only a few words are preserved and these follow MT. The editors date it to the first century B.C.E.[35] Of 2QJob a fragment containing Job 33:28–30 is extant. Its text is close to MT. The script is Herodian.[36] Fragments of 4QpaleoJob[c] attesting to parts of Job 13–14 survive. It is dated between 225 and 150 B.C.E. and is noteworthy for a very conservative orthography, using no internal *matres lectionis* (→ 11.2.1).[37]

---

[22] Stec, *The Text of the Targum of Job*, 6.
[23] Stec, *Text*, 7–8.
[24] Stec, *Text*, 11.
[25] Stec, *Text*, 16.
[26] P. de Lagarde (ed.), *Hagiographa Chaldaice* (Leipzig: Teubner, 1873); see Stec, *Text*, 39.
[27] Stec, *Text*, 2.
[28] R. Weiss, *The Aramaic Targum of Job* (Tel Aviv: Chaim Rosenberg School for Jewish Studies, 1979) [Hebr.]; see Stec, *Text*, 2.
[29] F.J. Fernández Vallina, "El Targum de Job: edición crítica" (PhD diss., Universidad Complutense de Madrid, 1980).
[30] See Stec, *Text*, 2.

[31] L. Díez Merino (ed.), *Targum de Job: edición principe del MS. Villa-Amil n. 5 de Alfonso de Zamora* (Bibliotheca Hispanica Biblica 8; Madrid: Consejo Superior de Investigaciones Científicas, Inst. Francisco Suárez, 1984).
[32] Stec, *Text*, 103.
[33] Van der Ploeg and van der Woude, *Le Targum de Job*.
[34] Ulrich and Metso, "4QJob[a]."
[35] Ulrich and Metso, "4QJob[b]."
[36] Baillet, "2QJob."
[37] Skehan, Ulrich, and Sanderson, "4QpaleoJob[c]."

11.1.6 Secondary Translations

Arabic translations have been made from the Greek and Peshitta versions (→ 11.4.8),[38] while Saadia Gaon (ob. 942) translated directly from the Hebrew (→ 11.3.8.1).[39]

There are no direct witnesses to the text of VL or Old Latin translation of the book of Job from the Greek (→ 11.4.1). What remains are quotations in the Fathers of the church and ancient commentaries (→ 21.8). Sabatier collected this scattered evidence of the Bible used and commented on by the church fathers.[40] Jerome's (→ 11.1.7) translation of the Hexaplaric edition of LXX (→ 11.1.3) included the book of Job, but he also translated Job directly from the Hebrew, using the translations of Aquila and especially of Symmachus (→ 11.1.5). This second translation, known as "iuxta Hebraeos," is the text found in the Vulgate, a term employed for the Latin Bible only from the sixteenth century.[41]

11.1.7 Text-Critical Value

The Hebrew text of the book of Job presents a challenge to the reader. There are the *hapax legomena*, estimated as numbering 145 by Ullendorff.[42] Then there is the Hebrew poetic style that often does not permit easy comprehension of the syntax. Connected with this is the question of the corruption of the text. Dhorme lists fairly numerous errors under different headings: transpositions, wrong separation of words, omissions, additions, and more.[43] Driver and Gray also view many passages as containing errors in the Hebrew text.[44] G. Fohrer assumes over three hundred errors.[45] Pope, in similar fashion, finds much need for emendation, relying heavily on the evidence of other Northwest Semitic literature, in particular Ugaritic.[46] In view of the comparatively small body of biblical Hebrew, the search for a wider literary context is clearly desirable. It does not necessarily follow that this requires more emendation of the received text; in fact, in this regard, a more conservative position is discernible. Thus Habel writes, "The *translation* offered in this commentary is conservative, avoiding emendation or paraphrase wherever possible."[47] Fokkelman offers a translation of the Hebrew text that limits itself to some thirty emendations.[48] This different perspective on the text is connected to a new emphasis on its literary characteristics. Both Habel and Fokkelman attach much importance to viewing the book as a work of poetry, with all the implications for rich and varied meaning that this implies. The ancient versions attest traditions of exegesis that need to be considered carefully by the commentator. At the same time, the purely literary dimension of the text is most important for it can frequently illuminate the apparently refractory syntax of the poetry. If the ancient versions had difficulties understanding their *Vorlage*, the Masoretes themselves were not always sure how to deal with the text. There are, for example, differences between the Babylonian and Palestinian schools.[49] The modern commentator has access to a variety of tools: the witness of the ancient versions themselves, the growing body of ancient Semitic – particularly Northwest Semitic – literature and relevant philological studies, and modern literary theory. With these helps, the Hebrew text of Job will hopefully become increasingly comprehensible.

Baillet, M., "15. 2QJob," *DJD III: 71.
Barthélemy, *Devanciers.
Bogaert, P.-M., "Job latin chez les pères et dans les Bibles: d'une version courte à des versions longues sur le grec et sur l'hébreu," *RBén* 122 (2012): 48–99, 366–93.

---

[38] Ziegler, *Iob*, 54.
[39] Cf. Dhorme, *Livre de Job*, clxxv.
[40] Sabatier, *Bibliorum.
[41] Cf. Bogaert, "Job latin," 82–99.
[42] Ullendorff, "Is Biblical Hebrew a Language?" 15.
[43] Dhorme, *Livre de Job*, cliv–clvi.
[44] Driver and Gray, *Job*.
[45] Fohrer, *Hiob*, 55.

[46] Pope, *Job*, xlvii.
[47] Habel, *Book of Job*, 21.
[48] Fokkelman, *The Book of Job in Form*, 23.
[49] Dhorme, *Livre de Job*, cliv.

Ceriani, A., *Codex Syro-Hexaplaris Ambrosianus photolithographice editus* (Monumenta sacra et profana 7; Milan: Bibliotheca Ambrosiana, 1874).

Cimosa, M., "La data probabile della traduzione greca (LXX) del Libro di Giobbe," *Sacra Doctrina* 51.6 (2006): 17–35.

Clines, D.J.A., *Job* (WBC 17–18B; Nashville: Nelson, 1989–2011).

Cohen, H., *Biblical Hapax Legomena in the Light of Akkadian and Ugaritic* (SBLDS 37; Missoula: Scholars Press, 1978).

Cox, C.E., *Armenian Job: Reconstructed Greek Text, Critical Edition of the Armenian with English Translation* (Hebrew University Armenian Studies 8; Leuven: Peeters, 2006).

Cox, C.E., "The Nature of Lucian's Revision of the Text of Greek Job," in *Scripture in Transition: Essays on Septuagint, Hebrew Bible, and Dead Sea Scrolls in Honour of Raija Sollamo* (eds. J. Jokiranta and A. Voitila; JSJSup 126; Leiden: Brill, 2008), 423–42.

De Troyer, K., "The Seventy-Two and Their Many Grandchildren: A Review of Septuagint Studies from 1997 Onward," *Currents in Biblical Research* 11 (2012): 8–64.

Dhorme, P., *Le Livre de Job* (2nd ed.; Paris: Gabalda, 1926).

Driver, S.R. and G.B. Gray, *A Critical and Exegetical Commentary on the Book of Job: Together with a New Translation* (ICC; Edinburgh: Clark, 1921; repr. 1986).

Fernández Marcos, N., "The Septuagint Reading of the Book of Job," in *The Book of Job* (ed. W.A.M. Beuken; BETL 114; Leuven: Peeters, 1994), 251–66.

Field, **Hexapla*.

Fohrer, G., *Das Buch Hiob* (KAT 16; Gütersloh: Mohn, 1963).

Fokkelman, J., *The Book of Job in Form: A Literary Translation with Commentary* (SSN 58; Leiden: Brill, 2012).

Gentry, P.J., "The Place of Theodotion-Job in the Textual History of the Septuagint," in *Origen's Hexapla and Fragments: Papers Presented at the Rich Seminar on the Hexapla, Oxford Centre for Hebrew and Jewish Studies, 25th July–3rd August 1994* (ed. A. Salvesen; TSAJ 58; Tübingen: Mohr Siebeck, 1998), 199–230.

Gentry, P.J., *The Asterisked Materials in the Greek Job* (SBLSCS 38; Atlanta: SBL, 1995).

Ginsburg, **Introduction*.

Gorea, M., *Job repensé ou trahi?: omissions et raccourcis de la Septante* (EBib 56; Paris: Gabalda, 2007).

Habel, N., *The Book of Job: A Commentary* (OTL; Philadelphia: Westminster, 1985).

Holladay, C.R., "Aristeas," in *Fragments from Hellenistic Jewish authors*, Vol. 1 (SBLTT 20; Atlanta: SBL, 1983).

van der Ploeg, J. and A. van der Woude (eds.), *Le Targum de Job de la Grotte XI de Qumrân* (Leiden: Brill, 1971).

Pope, M., *Job: Introduction, Translation, and Notes* (3rd ed.; AB 15; New York: Doubleday, 1974).

Rignell, L.G., *Job* (The Old Testament in Syriac according to the Peshitta Version 2.1a; Leiden: Brill, 1982).

Rignell, L.G., *The Peshitta to the Book of Job Critically Investigated with Introduction, Translation, Commentary and Summary* (ed. K.-E. Rignell; Kristianstad: Monitor, 1994).

Sabatier, **Bibliorum*.

Skehan, P., E. Ulrich, and J.E. Sanderson, "101. 4Qpaleo-Job^c," **DJD* IX: 155–57.

Stec, D., *The Text of the Targum of Job: An Introduction and Critical Edition* (AGJU 20; Leiden: Brill, 1994).

Swete, **Introduction*.

Ullendorff, E., "Is Biblical Hebrew a Language?" in *Is Biblical Hebrew a Language? Studies in Semitic Languages and Civilizations* (Wiesbaden: Harrassowitz, 1977), 3–17.

Ulrich, E. and S. Metso, "99. 4QJob^a," **DJD* XVI: 171–78.

Ulrich, E. and S. Metso, "100. 4QJob^b," **DJD* XVI: 179–80.

Walton, **Polyglotta*.

Witte, M., "The Greek Book of Job," in *Das Buch Hiob und seine Interpretationen: Beiträge zum Hiob-Symposium auf dem Monte Verità vom 14.–19. August 2005* (eds. T. Krüger et al.; ATANT 88; Zürich: Theologischer Verlag, 2007), 33–54.

Ziegler, J. (ed.), *Iob* (Septuaginta Vetus Testamentum Graecum 11.4; Göttingen: Vandenhoeck & Ruprecht, 1982).

R. Althann

11.2 Ancient and Late Ancient Hebrew Texts

11.2.1 Ancient and Late Ancient Manuscript Evidence

In addition to two manuscripts attesting to Aramaic translations of Job (→ 11.3.3.2; 4QtgJob and 11QtgJob), four Hebrew Job manuscripts from Qumran survive from antiquity. While insufficient text is extant of 2QJob, 4QJob[b], 4QpaleoJob[c], and 4QJob[d] for text-typological classification, 4QJob[a] attests to a non-aligned text of Job. Job is among the few texts for which also a late ancient manuscript might be preserved, i.e., Antinoopolis 49–50. Its text is proto-Masoretic in character but its paleographic date remains debated. The only other books for which late ancient or early medieval manuscript evidence is or might be extant are Genesis (→ 2.2.1.11.1), Exodus (→ 2.2.1.11.2; → 2.2.1.11.3; → 2.2.1.11.4), and 1–2 Kings (→ 5.3.1.12).

11.2.1.1 2QJob (2Q15)

Of 2QJob, only one fragment with remnants of five words from Job 33:28–30 is extant. The manuscript was executed in a Herodian hand.[1] The small amount of extant text makes further paleographic conclusions impossible. For the same reason, neither are orthographic and text-typological classifications of 2QJob possible.[2] The preserved text of 2QJob does not attest to textual differences from MT-Job. As Job 33:28 and Job 33:29–30 are somewhat loosely connected in the line of argument in Job 33, it seems more likely to me that 2QJob represents a remnant of an ancient Job scroll and not a Job quotation in another literary context.

11.2.1.2 4QJob[a] (4Q99)

4QJob[a] represents the best-preserved ancient Hebrew Job manuscript. Its twenty-two extant fragments[3] attest to remnants of Job 31:14–19; 32:3–4; 33:10–11, 24–26, 28–30; 35:16; 36:7–11, 13–27, 32–33; 37:1–5, 14–15. The manuscript is written stichometrically. The height of the original text block can be reconstructed as ca. 10 cm or sixteen lines.[4] This small height poses the question as to whether 4QJob[a] originally contained the whole book of Job. Due to the lack of information about the thickness of the leather of this scroll, no reliable conclusions are possible regarding how much text 4QJob[a] could have included originally. 4QJob[a] is written in a Hasmonean book hand from the first half or the middle of the first century B.C.E.[5] The supralinear correction in frg. 16 ii 11 (= Job 37:2) and the erasure in frg. 15 16 (= Job 36:24) are *prima manu*.[6] 4QJob[a] mostly follows the orthographic system of MT-Job, but on six occasions the scroll has fuller readings than MT. In addition, on three occasions 4QJob[a] employs, against its normal habits, baroque spellings characteristic of the so-called Qumran orthography:[7] וֹאליהוא "and Elihu" in Job (32:4; but cf. אֱלִיהוּא in MT-Job 32:2, 5–6); יטכה "turn you" in Job 36:18; and פעלתה "you have done" in Job 36:23. The text of 4QJob[a] was characterized as being close to MT (→ 11.2.2),[8] but the variant statistics advise against such a classification. In 190 fully or partly preserved words, 4QJob[a] reads once with and fourteen times against MT,[9] five times with and seven

---

[1] Cf. Baillet, "Job," 71.

[2] Against Baillet, "Job," 71: "un texte de type massorétique." For a different view → 11.2.2.

[3] Frg. 23 belongs to another manuscript (cf. Ulrich and Metso, "Job," 171, 178).

[4] Cf. Ulrich and Metso, "Job," 171, 175; Ulrich and Metso, "Edition," 29, 34.

[5] Cf. Ulrich and Metso, "Job," 171; Ulrich and Metso, "Edition," 30.

[6] Cf. Ulrich and Metso, "Job," 172, 175–77; Ulrich and Metso, "Edition," 34–36. The erasure in frg. 15 16 (= Job 36:24) corrects a reading with MT towards LXX.

[7] For the orthography of 4QJob[a], see Ulrich and Metso, "Job," 171–72; Ulrich and Metso, "Edition," 30.

[8] Cf. G.W. Nebe, "Qumranica I: Zu unveröffentlichten Handschriften aus Höhle 4 von Qumran," ZAW 106 (1994): 307–22, esp. 308; Tov, *"Synthese," 27.

[9] In three cases, the textual differences between 4QJob[a] and MT-Job cannot be rendered into Greek. Although Ulrich and Metso ("Job," sub loc.; "Edition," sub loc.) do not indicate LXX readings for the variant readings of 4QJob[a] in Job 33:11; 36:32, 33; 37:1, 14, they are included in the above count as non-aligned

times against LXX (→ 11.3.1), as well as six times non-aligned.[10] Therefore, 4QJob[a] should be classified as attesting to a non-aligned text of the book of Job.[11]

11.2.1.3 4QJob[b] (4Q100)

Of 4QJob[b], only six frgs. with remnants of twenty-two words from Job 8:15–17; 9:27; 13:4; 14:4–6; 31:20–21 are extant. It remains uncertain whether several fragments belong to 4QJob[a] or 4QJob[b].[12] Frg. 1 of 4QJob[b] was written stichometrically,[13] while the reconstruction of Ulrich and Metso suggests that frg. 4 was not.[14] Paleographically, 4QJob[b] is attributed to a late Hasmonean or early Herodian hand from the middle of the latter part of the first century B.C.E.[15] The extant text of 4QJob[b] attests only to two orthographic variants towards MT (Job 8:15: יחזק instead of יַחֲזִיק "seizes hold"; Job 14:5: חוֹדְשָׁיו] instead of חֳדָשָׁיו "their months"). There is insufficient preserved text for the assigning of orthographic and text-typological classifications.

11.2.1.4 4QpaleoJob[c] (4Q101)

4QpaleoJob[c] is the only Qumran biblical manuscript written in a paleo-Hebrew script that contains text from a book outside of the Torah. Its three extant fragments are heavily damaged and attest to thirty-two complete and partial words from Job 13:18–20, 23–27; 14:13–18. The manuscript was written stichometrically with one stich per line.[16] As 4QpaleoJob[c] is dated paleographically to 225–150 B.C.E.,[17] the manuscript is one of the earliest witnesses of the stichometrical arrangement of a Hebrew text. "The manuscript displays a very conservative orthography, using no internal *matres lectionis* except possibly in ימ[וֹת (14:14, which may reflect the radical), and in ידיך (14:15, which may reflect the historical spelling of the diphthong, *yadayk*). In contrast, for the few words preserved, 𝔐 uses *waw* 6 times to indicate long *o* or long *u*."[18] A text-typological classification of 4QpaleoJob[c] is not possible because insufficient text is preserved.[19] The single extant variant reading towards MT-Job (→ 11.2.2) goes with LXX-Job (→ 11.3.1).

11.2.1.5 4QJob[d] (4Q101a)

Based on plate PAM 43.662, this small fragment was recently identified by Puech as another Job manuscript from Qumran Cave 4.[20] It attests to six words and partial words out of Job 15:16–18. Puech counts the manuscript as 4Q101a or 4QJob[d]. It is written in a Hasmonean hand from the first half of the first century B.C.E.[21] In the extant text, no variants toward MT occur but insufficient text survives for orthographic and text-typological classification. The *waw* of ואספרה "I will declare" (Job 15:17) is written in paleo-Hebrew and detached from the word by a blank letter-space. Although only very little text survives of 4QJob[d], it is unlikely that the fragment attests to a quotation of Job in a non-biblical text. As the verses Job 15:16–18 belong to two paragraphs and Job is rarely quoted in Jewish literature from the Second Temple period, the fragment preserves more likely the remains of a Job manuscript.

11.2.1.6 Antinoopolis 49–50

Although counted as two papyri, already McHardy proposed that Antinoopolis 49 and 50 are two fragments of the same manuscript based on their resemblance.[22] No proper text-critical edition of this

---

(the variant readings in Job 33:11 and 36:32, 33; 37:1) or going with LXX against MT (the variant reading in Job 37:14).

[10] For a discussion of the individual variants, see below, → 11.2.3.
[11] Similar recently Seow, "Text Critical Notes."
[12] Thus Ulrich and Metso, "Job," 179.
[13] Cf. Ulrich and Metso, "Job," 179.
[14] Against Ulrich and Metso, "Job," 179. For the reconstruction of frg. 4 by Ulrich and Metso, see "Job," 180.
[15] See Ulrich and Metso, "Job," 179.
[16] Cf. Ulrich, "Paleo-Hebrew Biblical Manuscripts," 121; Skehan, Ulrich, and Sanderson, "4QpaleoJob[c]," 155.
[17] McLean, "Development," 47–57; cf. Ulrich, "Paleo-Hebrew Biblical Manuscripts," 121; Skehan, Ulrich, and Sanderson, "4QpaleoJob[c]," 155.

[18] Skehan, Ulrich, and Sanderson, "4QpaleoJob[c]," 155; cf. Ulrich, "Paleo-Hebrew Biblical Manuscripts," 122.
[19] For a different view, see → 11.2.2.
[20] Puech, "quatrième manuscript."
[21] Puech, "quatrième manuscript," 432.
[22] See McHardy, "Appendix," 105.

manuscript exists,²³ nor are photographs or facsimilies available. Based on Ada Yardeni's drawings,²⁴ it is sometimes difficult to decide which text is preserved and which text is reconstructed. Until the publication of a proper edition with photographs, the below information needs to remain somewhat speculative. In Antinoopolis 49, I count fifty-one words and partial words out of Job 20:24–21:14 and twenty words and partial words out of Job 1:19–2:4 in Antinoopolis 50. The text is unvocalized and without Masoretic annotations. The paleographic date is set by McHardy²⁵ to between the third and sixth centuries C.E. For Antinoopolis 47–48 (→ 5.3.1.12), Birnbaum²⁶ and Yardeni²⁷ propose the fifth century and the eighth century C.E. respectively. Probably because Job 1:19–2:4 belongs to the narrative framework of Job, its text is not arranged stichometrically. The stichometric arrangement of Job 20:24–21:14 displays differences to both MT^L and MT^A. Neither orthographic nor textual variants toward the text of MT^L are preserved in the extant text. The only exception is that Antinoopolis 49 reads in Job 21:10 the *plene* spelling יגעיל "he fails" instead of the more defective יִגְעִל in MT^L and MT^A. The reconstructed text of Job 1:19–2:4 in Yardeni's drawing displays several disagreements with the consonantal text of MT.²⁸ Until a proper critical edition of Antinoopolis 49–50 is published, the manuscript should be characterized with due caution as proto-Masoretic given its almost complete textual and orthographic agreement with MT^L and MT^A (→ 11.2.2).

Baillet, M., "15. Job," *DJD III.1: 71.
Lange, *Handbuch*, 451–66.
McHardy, W.D., "Appendix (Nos. 47–50)," in *The Antinoopolis Papyri Part 1: Edited with Translations and Notes* (ed. C.H. Roberts; London: Egypt Exploration Society, 1950), 105–06.
McLean, M.D., "The Use and Development of Palaeo-Hebrew in the Hellenistic and Roman Periods" (PhD diss.; Harvard University, 1982), 47–57.
Puech, É., "Un quatrième manuscrit du livre de Job dans la grotte 4 de Qumrân (4Q101ª–4QJobᵈ)," *RevQ* 26 (2013–2014): 430–33.
Seow, C.L., "Text Critical Notes on 4QJobª," in *DSD* 22 (2015): 189–201.
Skehan, P.W., E. Ulrich, and J.E. Sanderson, "101. 4Qpaleo-Jobᶜ," *DJD* IX: 155–57.
Ulrich, E., "The Paleo-Hebrew Biblical Manuscripts from Qumran Cave 4," in *Time to Prepare the Way in the Wilderness: Papers on the Qumran Scrolls by Fellows of the Institute for Advanced Studies of The Hebrew University, Jerusalem, 1989–1990* (eds. D. Dimant and L.H. Schiffman; STDJ 16; Leiden: Brill, 1995), 103–29, esp. 121–22.
Ulrich, *BQS*, 727–29.
Ulrich, E. and S. Metso, "Job," *DJD* XVI: 171–80.
Ulrich, E. and S. Metso, "A Preliminary Edition of 4QJobª," in *Antikes Judentum und frühes Christentum: Festschrift für Hartmut Stegemann zum 65. Geburtstag* (eds. B. Kollmann, W. Reinbold, and A. Steudel; BZNW 97; Berlin: De Gruyter, 1999), 29–38.

Armin Lange

11.2.2 Masoretic Texts and Ancient Texts Close to MT

MT-Job is the only complete Hebrew text of Job or witness to the (proto-)MT of the book. The manuscripts from Qumran (→ 11.2.1) are either: 1) incomplete; and/or 2) Targumim (4QtgJob [4Q157]; 11QtgJob [11Q10]; see → 11.3.3.2). The latter are obviously at some remove from (proto-)MT, if only due to their nature as Aramaic *translations*, but it

---

²³ McHardy, "Appendix," 105–06 does not go beyond a brief description of the scroll.

²⁴ The drawings are published in Sirat, *Papyrus*, 33.

²⁵ McHardy, "Appendix," 105.

²⁶ Birnbaum, *Hebrew Scripts*, 1.223–25; cf. M. Dukan, *La Bible hébraïque: Les codices copiés en Orient et dans la zone séfarade avant 1280* (Bibliologia 22; Turnhout: Brepols, 2006), 13.

²⁷ Yardeni, *Book of Hebrew Script*, 85 fig. 103; cf. J. Olszowy-Schlanger, "On the Hebrew Script of the Greek-Hebrew Palimpsests from the Cairo Genizah," in *The Jewish-Greek Tradition in Antiquity and the Byzantine Empire* (eds. J.K. Aitken and J. Carleton Paget; Cambridge: Cambridge University Press, 2014), 279–99 (295).

²⁸ In Job 1:21, the reconstructed text of Antinoopolis 50 reads אני "I" instead of MT's אִמִּי "my mother" and in Job 2:2 the reconstructed text of Antinoopolis 50 misses MT's לְבַלְּעוֹ "to destroy him." Furthermore, the reconstructed text of Antinoopolis 50 displays two orthographic variants towards MT in Job 1:22 (א[יב] instead of אִיּוֹב "Job") and Job 2:1 (ויבא instead of וַיָּבוֹא "and he came"). Without a published photograph and a proper critical edition, these reconstructed variants cannot be judged with any degree of certainty.

is possible that one or more of the former, insofar as they do not preserve major differences from MT-Job, could be witnesses to such a text.¹ This is perhaps especially true of 2QJob (2Q15);² unfortunately, it only preserves one complete word and parts of four others from Job 33:28–30, so it remains possible that the text here is little more than a citation of Job in a scroll about something else.³ 4QJobᵇ (4Q100) could also witness to a (proto-)MT text, as it preserves only two orthographic variants from MT (Job 8:15; 14:5), but here, too, there is very little text preserved, complicating a thorough assessment (see → 11.2.1.3). Furthermore, this manuscript or some of its six fragments may belong to 4QJobᵃ (4Q99), which is best understood as non-aligned (see discussion at → 11.2.1.2; → 11.2.3.3). Finally, 4QpaleoJobᶜ (4Q101) is noteworthy for its use of paleo-Hebrew script⁴ and its almost complete avoidance of internal *matres lectionis* (see → 11.2.1.4 and below). But here again, there is very little text to go on and the one variant that is extant (at Job 14:14) reads with the Old Greek (→ 11.3.1). Compounding the difficulties is that there is no material overlap among the Cave 2 and Cave 4 manuscripts. So, for several reasons – above all the state of the material remains – text-typological classifications for 2QJob, 4QJobᵇ, and 4QpaleoJobᶜ cannot be made and their relationship to the (proto-)MT text of Job cannot be ascertained with confidence. Discussion of the (proto-)MT of Job must then proceed via different routes and with reference to non-Hebrew translations and traditions (on which see further → 11.2.1; → 11.3–4).

11.2.2.1 History of Research

Virtually all scholars agree that MT-Job is notoriously difficult, "textually the most vexed"⁵ or "one of the most obscure"⁶ in the Old Testament, "far and away the most difficult in the Bible."⁷ In this light, the question becomes how best to address these difficulties. Prior to the discovery of the Qumran texts (and even thereafter, given the paucity of the Dead Sea Scrolls data), the majority of text-critical work on Job was devoted to assessing the utility of the ancient versions, particularly LXX, vis-à-vis MT. This is especially true of the commentary literature, which tends to discuss individual and isolated variants somewhat intermittently.⁸ Given the importance of the Greek evidence, it deserves brief discussion here (see also → 11.1; → 11.3.1)

The Old Greek (OG; → 11.3.1) is famously one-sixth shorter than MT, a difference of some 400 lines.⁹ The discrepancy was known already in Origen's time (cf. his *Letter to Julius Africanus*, 3–4; ANF 4.386–87), who supplemented the Old Greek with Theodotion's version (→ 11.3.5.3.1), marking the additions with an asterisk (※) at the start and a metobelus (✓) at the end.¹⁰ This composite Greek version is called the Ecclesiastical Text (sometimes "LXX-Job") and was used in subsequent daughter translations. A shorter text resembling Old Greek is attested in the Sahidic Coptic version (mid-third century C.E.; → 11.4.2),¹¹ which may be pre-

---

¹ For convenient presentation of the Cave 2 and Cave 4 texts, see Ulrich, *BQS, 727–29.

² So Baillet, "15. Job," 71: "un texte de type massorétique."

³ See → 11.2.1.1; Lange, *Handbuch, 451.

⁴ 4Q101 and 4QpaleoparaJosh (4Q123) are the only non-Pentateuchal scrolls at Qumran to be written this way, though a few unidentified paleo-Hebrew texts are extant (see *DJD XXXIX, 214).

⁵ Pope, *Job*, xliii.

⁶ Hartley, *Book of Job*, 3.

⁷ Seow, *Job 1–21*, 20.

⁸ Important text-critical treatments of Job from the seventeenth through early-twentieth centuries include: Cappellus, *Critica sacra (1650); Houbigant, *Notae criticae (1777); Beer, *Der Text des Buches Hiob* (1897); Driver and Gray, *Book of Job* (1921), and Dhorme, *A Commentary on the Book of Job* (1984 [French original: 1926]).

⁹ See Seow, *Job 1–21*, 6; Pope, *Job*, xliii; Cox, "Iob," 667–68. Slightly larger figures are also found. See, e.g., Driver and Gray, *Book of Job*, 1.lxxiv n. 1 (on Klostermann); and Dhorme, *A Commentary on the Book of Job*, cc, who provides an extensive listing of the lacunae in Old Greek (ccii).

¹⁰ Origen also marked those places in the Old Greek that were longer than the Hebrew text, in this case with an obelus (÷) in front and a metobelus (✓); at the end. Seow rightly observes that the textual criticism of Job can be said to begin with Origen, even "if only in a rudimentary fashion" (*Job 1–21*, 2).

¹¹ For other witness to the Old Greek, see Seow, *Job 1–21*, 8–9; Cox, "Iob," 668.

TABLE 1   *Differences between Old Greek and* MT

Sections of Job	Lines Absent from Old Greek	Approximate Percentage of Total Number of Lines in MT
Prologue	1	
First Cycle of Speeches		
Job 3–6	0	
Job 7–11	6	
Job 12–14	17–23	4 %
Second Cycle of Speeches (Job 15–21)	59	16 %
Third Cycle of Speeches (Job 22–31)	124	25 %
Elihu (Job 32–37)	114	35 %
Yahweh Speeches (Job 38:1–42:26)	43	16 %
Epilogue	3	

Hexaplaric though the point is debated.[12] (For further discussion on these matters, see → 11.3.1–2; → 11.3.5–6; → 11.4.2.) Driver and Gray tallied the differences between Old Greek and MT as shown in Table 1.[13]

While some early scholars posited that the shorter Greek text was original, with MT later and expansionistic[14] – perhaps because the Greek translation was done at a point before Hebrew Job was finalized[15] – this position is now seen as erroneous for several reasons. One is that the Greek translation is "rather free, even paraphrastic ... something of an epitome of the longer and often difficult original";[16] it is thus more likely that the shorter Old Greek text is "to be attributed to the time of translation,"[17] and so does not reflect a shorter Hebrew *Vorlage*. Additional proof of this point may be found in the fact that the Qumran manuscripts, where extant, preserve some portions missing from Old Greek.

Second, it is telling that the amount of abbreviation increases as one moves through Job.[18] This increased rate of omission may be due to the wearying of the translator,[19] though Seow has recently speculated that it could also be due to the translator's concerns over wearying *the reader*.[20] The result, regardless, is a simplified version of Job that eliminates much redundancy. Seow goes so far as to call the Old Greek "a more 'reader friendly' version";[21] others might call it "vulgar."[22] Whatever the case, it appears that the shorter Old Greek text was

---

[12] See, e.g., Dhome, *A Commentary on the book of Job*, cci–ccii, ccix–ccx, who deems it a post-Hexaplaric redaction.

[13] Driver and Gray, *Book of Job*, 1.lxxv; repeated and epitomized in others, e.g., Hartley, *Book of Job*, 4; Dhorme, *A Commentary on the Book of Job*, ccii–cciii; Cox, "Iob," 667; Seow, *Job 1–21*, 7.

[14] Famously E. Hatch, *Essays in Biblical Greek* (Oxford: Clarendon Press, 1889), 215–45. See further Dhorme, *A Commentary on the Book of Job*, cciii for others who followed a similar line of argument.

[15] See Hartley, *Book of Job*, 4; but he deems "intentional abridgement" more likely. Cf. Gray, *Job*, 76 (on analogy with 4QSam^b).

[16] Cox, "Iob," 667, who also writes "OG Iob stands as a clear foil to the interlinear paradigm of translation," deeming it "one of a kind in the Septuagint corpus ... among the least literal." Similar statements on the nature of the Greek translation can be found in Driver and Gray, *Book of Job*, 1.xxxi; Pope, *Job*, xliv; Seow, *Job 1–21*, 6; and Dhorme, *A Commentary on the Book of Job*, cxci–cxcii, cxcvi–ccvi. Contrast Hartley, *Book of Job*, 3, who deems it "essentially a faithful translation."

[17] Cox, "Iob," 667.

[18] Cox, "Iob," 667.

[19] Dhorme, *A Commentary on the Book of Job*, cciii.

[20] Seow, *Job 1–21*, 7.

[21] Seow, *Job 1–21*, 7.

[22] See Tov, *TCHB*, 172–73, 184 for discussion of this term and its meaning(s), which includes scribes adopting a "free approach" to the text at hand and/or manuscripts that "facilitated reading."

likely produced from a Hebrew *Vorlage* that was altogether similar in length to MT-Job. The reduction in Old Greek was due to the obscurity of the Hebrew parent text and the "tediously long and repetitive" nature of the book.[23]

Third, the Old Greek also has some additions, two rather large and famous ones that border on the midrashic (Job 2:9a–d and 42:17aa–ea).[24] Other qualities of the Old Greek translation[25] support Pope's conclusion that "more often recourse to the Greek complicates rather than clarifies a problem."[26] For reasons like these – and unmentioned thus far have been many small interpretive omissions[27] and the Greek cast of the translation[28] – the Old Greek is no longer privileged in textual assessments of Job. Even so, the Old Greek does preserve some genuine variants that occasionally prove superior to MT.[29]

Beyond the Old Greek's bearing on (proto-)MT-Job, the discovery of the Qumran Aramaic Job Targumim (→ 11.3.3.2), especially 11Q10 (mid-first century C.E.),[30] created significant scholarly interest. Commentaries published around the time of 11QtgJob's publication in 1971 were eager to draw on it.[31] Most now agree that, in the main, 11QtgJob supports MT[32] – in contrast to the later rabbinic Job Targumim (→ 11.3.3.1)[33] – and so scholarly discussion has waned because the differences preserved by 11QtgJob are not overwhelming. The support that this manuscript offers to the structure of MT-Job, particularly in the ordering of Job 24–27, is quite important, however. This early witness to the text also evidences "[t]he incompletion or disruption of the third cycle of speeches,"[34] showing that MT-Job 24–27 is not corrupt at this point, or, if it is, the corruption is a *very early* one (see → 11.2.2.5 below).

The ending of 11QtgJob is also significant since the manuscript appears to break off at Job 42:11. Some scholars – Gray, for example – have thought this "probably indicates that the Book of Job as the [Qumran] targumist knew it … ended at 42.11, [with] the rest being a later midrashic expansion like 'the Syriac book' to which LXX refers … [thus] indicating a certain fluidity of the Job tradition at this point."[35] In the official DJD edition, however, García Martínez reads traces of Job 42:12, though he admits that the line in question is "no longer visible."[36] It remains possible, then, that 11QtgJob once contained more text, perhaps even all of what is now found in MT-Job.[37]

The question of the end point aside, 11QtgJob contains some notable differences from MT-Job. A large variation is found at Job 42:3, where 11QtgJob reads Job 40:5 instead. 11QtgJob also has a different ordering of lines in Job 37:16–18: vv. 16a > 17a > 16b > 18, with v. 17b omitted.[38]

With the Old Greek and Qumran evidence of mixed and minimal utility, scholars have been

---

[23] See Seow, *Job 1–21*, 6–7; and Cox, "Iob," 667, who adds a further reason: perhaps Job did not have the same level of authority and so was more easily subject to abbreviation.

[24] See Cox, "Iob," 667–68, 671, 696; Dhorme, *A Commentary on the Book of Job*, cxcviii.

[25] On which, see Cox, "Iob," 668; and, extensively, Dhorme, *A Commentary on the Book of Job*, cxcvi–cxcix.

[26] Pope, *Job*, xliii.

[27] See Dhorme, *A Commentary on the Book of Job*, cxcviii–cxcix.

[28] Dhorme, *A Commentary on the Book of Job*, cxci: "*ad usum Graecorum*" (further, cxcvi–cxcvii); Hartley, *Book of Job*, 4; Gray, *Job*, 76.

[29] See Seow, *Job 1–21*, 6; cf. → 11.3.1.

[30] Some scholars are wont to date the translation/tradition much earlier, perhaps as old as the latter half of the second century (see Gray, *Job*, 79; van der Ploeg and van der Woude, *Le Targum de Job*, 2–4). Note *b. Šabb.* 115a; *t. Šabb.* 13:2 on the existence of a Job Targum prior to the mid-first century C.E.

[31] See Pope, *Job*; Anderson, *Job*. A more recent and extensive discussion is found in Gray, *Job*, 80–87.

[32] Pope, *Job*, xlvi; similarly Hartley, *Book of Job*, 4–5; Seow, *Job 1–21*, 13. 11QtgJob corroborates Old Greek at several points, e.g., Job 17:6; 18:2, 19:13, 15; 22:3. See Seow, *Job 1–21*, 13, 768, 779, 816–17; García Martínez, "11QtargumJob," 91, 93, 99.

[33] See Seow, *Job 1–21*, 14–15; Dhorme, *A Commentary on the Book of Job*, ccxviii–ccxix; and, most extensively, Stec, *The Text of the Targum of Job*.

[34] Pope, *Job*, xlvi; *pace* Pope, however, 11QtgJob is not the earliest witness.

[35] Gray, *Job*, 87.

[36] García Martínez, "11QtargumJob," 170.

[37] Cf. Seow, *Job 1–21*, 13.

[38] García Martínez, "11QtargumJob," 146; Hartley, *Book of Job*, 5.

forced to make recourse to other resources to understand the (proto-)MT of Job. There are at least two large issues that have garnered significant attention: 1) First, the large number of *hapax legomena* in MT-Job, or words and forms that are uniquely Joban, even if they occur more than once in the book. Insofar as the versions, too, evidently often did not know what these words meant, standard text-critical analysis is often of little help. Hence, this first issue has frequently been passed along to those working in comparative philology (but see further → 11.2.2.3 below).³⁹ 2) The second item is the conservative orthography found in MT-Job. This was first treated by Freedman in 1969 and, more recently, by Seow.⁴⁰ Freedman used the conservative orthography of MT-Job to argue that the book was of northern, pre-exilic provenience, and that the *Urtext* of Job was similarly conservative. Seow has furthered Freedman's work while also disputing his conclusions. Seow notes, first, that the phenomenon of conservative orthography is far more extensive than Freedman recognized, leaving traces in the manuscript tradition and the versional evidence (note, e.g., 4QpaleoJobᶜ, which is even more conservative than MT). In the case of those readings that reflect defective spellings, Seow argues that "the conservative form is superior because those without *matres* account for the variants more readily than MT,"⁴¹ in a clear appeal to the rule that the reading that explains all other readings is to be preferred. Seow challenges Freedman, however, in noting that the orthography does *not* require an early date; neither does it indicate northern provenience. Instead, Seow deems this textual characteristic a literary device (see → 11.2.2.4 below).

Beyond the two large matters of rare terminology and defective orthography, scholars have varied on specific details. Dhorme, for example, catalogued a number of what he deemed to be errors in MT, most of which he thought were accidental.⁴² Despite his listing (see further → 11.2.2.3 below), he preferred MT-Job over the versional evidence, even while granting that the latter might occasionally improve upon MT. Similar dispositions have been adopted by most modern commentators, even if they differ from Dhorme on the niceties of his list, the nature of such details as "errors," and/or the utility or non-utility of the versions.⁴³ Also like Dhorme, many scholars have believed that sometimes "conjecture alone can enlighten us as to the original state of a notoriously corrupt passage."⁴⁴ So it is that the same conclusion is found in the earlier work of Driver and Gray who stated that there were many places "in which neither 𝔉 nor any text to which the versions point can be regarded as original: in these cases the original must be regained, if at all, by conjecture."⁴⁵ Here, too, not all would agree, but these scholarly tendencies – including the tendency for textual critics to disagree amongst themselves – indicate that the textual criticism of Job will remain a lively topic for years to come.

11.2.2.2 Manuscripts and Editions

Beyond the Qumran fragments discussed above (see → 11.2.1; cf. also → 11.1; → 11.2.3), the most important Hebrew manuscripts are the Aleppo Codex (MTᴬ, ca. 925 C.E.) and Codex Leningradensis (MTᴸ; Codex EPB I B 19a of the National Library of Russia in St. Petersburg, from 1008/1009 C.E.). According to Seow, MTᴬ has superior readings in a few instances

---

³⁹ See → 11.2.2.3 below, and, more generally (*inter alia*), Grabbe, *Comparative Philology*; also H.R. (Chaim) Cohen, *Biblical Hapax Legomena in the Light of Akkadian and Ugaritic* (SBLDS 37; Missoula: Scholars Press, 1978); and F.E. Greenspahn, *Hapax Legomena in Biblical Hebrew: A Study of the Phenomenon and Its Treatment Since Antiquity with Special Reference to Verbal Forms* (SBLDS 74; Chico: Scholars Press, 1984).

⁴⁰ Freedman, "Orthographic Peculiarities in the Book of Job," *35–*44; Seow, "Orthography, Textual Criticism, and the Poetry of Job," 63–85; Seow, *Job 1–21*, 17–20. See also Barr, "Hebrew Orthography and the Book of Job," 1–33.

⁴¹ Seow, *Job 1–21*, 20.

⁴² Dhorme, *A Commentary on the Book of Job*, cxcii–cxcv.

⁴³ The work of Seow, for example, is quite different than that of Dhorme. For yet another interpretation, see Tur-Sinai, *Book of Job*, esp. viii–xxx, xl–li.

⁴⁴ Dhorme, *A Commentary on the Book of Job*, cxcii; cf. also Pope, *Job*, xlvii.

⁴⁵ Driver and Gray, *Book of Job*, 1.lxxvi.

where MT^L is deficient.⁴⁶ Unfortunately, MT^A-Job is not yet available in a full critical edition, and a few of the pages in the facsimile edition are heavily faded.⁴⁷

Prior to modern editions of these two great codices, the standard scholarly text of Job was found in the Second Rabbinic Bible (1525; *RB2).⁴⁸ Collections of medieval Masoretic variants may be found in the works by Kennicott (*1776–1780, 2.478–524; online at: http://aleph.nli.org.il/nnl/dig/books/bk002093934.html) and De Rossi (*1784–1798, 4.105–38; 5.118–26), and these remain valuable, especially on matters of orthography (see → 11.2.2.1; → 11.2.2.3). But, while the differences are "extensive," they are – outside of orthographic matters, at any rate – mostly "of relatively minor significance ... seldom of themselves help to recover the original text."⁴⁹ Differences between Western and Eastern Masoretic traditions, the Ben Asher and Ben Naphtali families, and *Ketiv-Qere* variants can be found in Baer and Delitzsch.⁵⁰

For comparative purposes, the great multilingual Bibles of the sixteenth and seventeenth centuries are useful, especially the Complutensian Polyglot (1514–1517), the Antwerp Royal Polyglot (1569–1572), the Paris Polyglot (1645), and the London Polyglot (1655–1657).⁵¹

At the time of writing, two editions of MT-Job are available in the *BH series with a third in process. All are diplomatic in nature and based on MT^L. The first, by Beer in *BH³*,⁵² remains useful given his earlier text-critical work on Job.⁵³ The second is by Gerleman (in *BHS) and is quite selective in its apparatus.⁵⁴ The edition of Job in *BHQ is being prepared by R. Althann and is certain to be a vast improvement over both *BH³ and *BHS in terms of apparatus, presentation of the Masorah, and brief commentary on both. A critical, eclectic edition – also with commentary – will be published in *HBCE.

11.2.2.3 Nature and Text-Critical Character of (Proto-)MT-Job

After an extended discussion, Dhorme concluded that the Old Greek along with the "Greek versions ... of Aquila, of Symmachus, and of Theodotion, the Vulgate or Latin version, and the Syriac version, the Peshitta, and also the Aramaic interpretation of the Targum ... are based on a text which is perceptibly the same as the Massoretic text"⁵⁵ (→ 11.3.1; → 11.3.5; → 11.3.7; → 11.3.4; → 11.3.3.1). He is not alone in such a judgment, which ultimately posits that MT-Job "remains our primary source for the Book of Job,"⁵⁶ at least as a whole. Even so (and once again), virtually all commentators are agreed that MT-Job is tremendously difficult.⁵⁷ The versions themselves "testify to the fact that many passages were unintelligible even to the earliest translators,"⁵⁸ beyond the rather obvious and important fact that translation of the Hebrew text was, in fact, required.⁵⁹ So, again, in the case of the Old Greek, to cite but one example, the translation reflects "a particular approach to the Hebrew text, one that goes to considerable lengths

---

⁴⁶ See Seow, *Job 1–21*, 4, who lists, *inter alia*, Job 1:21; 4:9; 7:21; 8:1; 22:21.

⁴⁷ M. Goshen-Gottstein (ed.), *The Aleppo Codex* (Jerusalem: Magnes Press, 1976). For a text edition of MT^A, see *The Jerusalem Crown: The Bible of the Hebrew University of Jerusalem* (Jerusalem: Ben Zvi, 2000).

⁴⁸ Note also C.D. Ginsburg's edition of MT^B, with variants from manuscripts and editions prior to 1525: *The Old Testament, Diligently Revised According to the Masorah and the Early Editions with Various Readings* (4 vols.; London: British Foreign Society, 1926), 3.443–566.

⁴⁹ Gray, *Job*, 76.

⁵⁰ Baer and Delitzsch, *Liber Iobi*; see also Dhorme, *A Commentary on the Book of Job*, cxcii.

⁵¹ *Biblia Sacra Polyglotta, complectentia Vetus Testamentum* ... (Madrid: Complutenti Universitate, 1514–1517); *Biblia Sacra Hebraice, Chaldaice, Graece et Latina* ... (ed. B. Arias Montano; Antwerp: Christophorus Plantinus, 1569–1572); Le Jay, *Biblia*; Walton, *Polyglotta*.

⁵² G. Beer, *Iob et Proverbia* (*BH³ 12; 1932).

⁵³ Beer, *Der Text des Buches Hiob*.

⁵⁴ G. Gerleman, "Iob," in G. Gerleman and J. Fichtner, *Iob et Proverbia* (*BHS 12; 1974), 1227–74.

⁵⁵ Dhorme, *A Commentary on the Book of Job*, cxcii. Some have posited that the Peshitta (→ 11.3.4) may come from a Hebrew text that differed from MT-Job (Seow, *Job 1–21*, 16).

⁵⁶ Pope, *Job*, xlvii.

⁵⁷ Pope, *Job*, xliii adds that if all the difficult parts were omitted, the size the book "would be greatly reduced."

⁵⁸ Hartley, *Book of Job*, 3.

⁵⁹ Cf. Seow, *Job 1–21*, 14.

to make a certain sense of it, even to the extent of changing and rearranging letters of words to do so."⁶⁰

As noted above, two textual characteristics of MT-Job have occasioned considerable difficulty in the history of the text and its interpretation. The first is the specific language used in MT-Job, as it is "full of rare vocabulary and archaic verbal forms."⁶¹ Indeed, according to some scholars, there are no less than 170 *hapax legomena* in the book.⁶² The second issue is the conservative orthography, since MT-Job is sparing in its use of internal *matres lectionis*.

1) Regarding rare terms and difficult forms, textual criticism proper may have little to offer. There were no doubt reasons that the author(s) and/or editor(s) employed the rare vocabulary and morphology. If nothing else, such language indicates that Job is an "immensely learned and cosmopolitan book."⁶³ Another reason for this language may be literary design, i.e., that the author(s) and/or the characters are "straining the limits of human vocabulary"⁶⁴ in their attempt to discuss one of the most vexed problems in theology and philosophy: suffering and the problem of evil (theodicy). The difficult language found in MT-Job may be the result, then, of authorial skill or literary design, if not in fact both. The same judgment may hold true for the pronounced use of (putative) loanwords in MT-Job or terminology that some scholars deem reflective of Aramaic or Arabic influence.⁶⁵ All of that could be less a matter of translation or language-contact⁶⁶ so much as another literary device (i.e., affectations that belong to a larger literary conceit), lending an exotic air or foreign flavor to the book. Indeed, Seow has argued that the language used is not archaic but *archaizing*, the function of which is to add an ancient feeling to the book though the composition itself stems from the Persian period (see → 11.2.2.4).⁶⁷ While textual criticism cannot definitively adjudicate such interpretive matters,⁶⁸ it can at least underscore how the complexity of the Hebrew of Job (whatever its origin or *raison d'etre*) caused significant problems for the versions.

2) The conservative orthography in MT-Job might be treated in similar fashion. On the one hand, it is clear that MT-Job abounds in such conservative spelling, especially in contracted dipthongs without *matres lectionis* (e.g., תֵמָן/*tēmān* "south wind" rather than the expected form תֵימָן/*têman* in Job 9:9; or אֵתָן/*ʾētān* "constant" rather than אֵיתָן/*ʾêtān* in Job 33:19 [cf. Job 12:19]).⁶⁹ MT-Job is not alone in this regard. 4QpaleoJobᶜ is also quite conservative, lacking internal *matres* in all but two cases.⁷⁰ Seow speaks of "literally hundreds of Hebrew variants without internal vowel markers" in the manuscript tradition.⁷¹ Note, for example, יוֹמוֹ (MTᴸ) vs. יֹמוֹ (MTᵐˢ) in Job 1:4 ("his day"); or לְמוֹעֲדֵי (MTᴸ) vs. לְמֹעֲדֵי (4 MTᵐˢˢ) in Job 12:5 ("for the one who slips"). Seow goes still further, arguing that the versions themselves often reflect defective spellings in their *Vorlagen*.⁷² So, for example, MT-Job 19:18 has עֲוִילִים "young lads" though the *Vorlage(n)* of (some of?) the versions apparently read a defective form – either עֹולִים, which was apparently read as *ʿawwālîm* "wicked ones" by 11QtgJob (רשעין "wicked"), s

---

⁶⁰ Cox, "Iob," 668.
⁶¹ Newsom, "The Book of Job," 4.326.
⁶² See Seow, *Job 1–21*, 20–21; Andersen, *Job*, 56.
⁶³ Newsom, "The Book of Job," 4.326.
⁶⁴ Seow, *Job 1–21*, 21.
⁶⁵ See Seow, *Job 1–21*, 21–24.
⁶⁶ Tur-Sinai, for example, believed that the "extant form" of Job was "mainly a translation from an Aramaic original" (*Book of Job*, xxx–xxxxi).
⁶⁷ See Seow, *Job 1–21*, 24; see also 20, 39–45.
⁶⁸ So, e.g., in contrast to Seow (see previous note), Anderson, *Job*, 57, who also admits that "the antique flavor could be cultivated (archaizing)" – which would explain "why such effects are not consistently secured" – but who also goes on to note that "the same impression would be given if an old text were only partly modernized in transmission."
⁶⁹ See Freedman, "Orthographic Peculiarities in the Book of Job," who tallied forty-two forms like this. See further Seow, *Job 1–21*, 17–20; and Barr, "Hebrew Orthography and the Book of Job," 1–33.
⁷⁰ See Seow, *Job 1–21*, 18; Ulrich, *BQS*, 727–28.
⁷¹ Seow, *Job 1–21*, 18–19.
⁷² Seow, *Job 1–21*, 19–20.

('wl' "the wicked"); or עולם (doubly defective!) by Old Greek (τὸν αἰῶνα "forever"). In cases like these, Seow not only suggests that the more conservative form is superior (see above), but also rightly asserts that "the presence of the *matres* is as much an interpretation as the introduction of vowel points."[73]

If the original version of Job was extremely conservative orthographically (cf. 4QpaleoJob^c) – perhaps even entirely defectively written – several possible considerations follow. One might be the date and provenience of the original composition; another would be how the putative original spelling bears on MT-Job, since, as orthographically conservative as it is, it does have fuller spellings, at least at times, than 4QpaleoJob^c, MT^{mss}, and the versions. If such fuller readings are part of the history of interpretation or reception, as Seow asserts, what does this say about the (later) date and nature of MT-Job?

The matter of date and provenience have been touched on above (→ 11.2.2.2) and I will return to them further below (→ 11.2.2.4). Before doing so, two further comments should be made on this matter of orthography and how it bears on the textual criticism of Job. *First*, defectively written forms are a good bit more ambiguous than plene spellings. On the one hand, this explains their varied reception, interpretation, and translation in the versions. On the other hand, it is possible that such defective forms are an intentional poetic device, allowing "for rich wordplays in many passages."[74] The addition of *matres lectionis* (not to mention vowel points and other paratextual elements) significantly affects – typically in a reductive way – the interpretation of a spare, unvocalized, and defectively written text.[75] The *second* comment to be made is that the not unreasonable supposition of a hyper-conservative textual archetype raises the issue of subsequent orthographic revision in MT-Job.

While it is impossible "to prove that the orthographic conservatism" in 4QpaleoJob^c "reflects the autograph," it is nevertheless worth noting that MT-Job has the longer form in six instances vis-à-vis that manuscript: Job 13:24 (לְאוֹיֵב vs. ל[איב "as an enemy"), 26 (עֲוֹנוֹת vs. עונת "iniquities"), 26 (נְעוּרָי vs. נערי "my youth"), 27 (אָרְחוֹתָי vs. ארחתי "my paths"); 14:16 (תִּסְפּוֹר vs. תספר "you number"), 17 (בִּצְרוֹר vs. ב[צרר "in a bag"). This is a significant statistic given the small amount of text preserved in 4QpaleoJob^c. Then again, there are the occasional readings in the versions that also appear to reflect more conservative *Vorlagen* than what is presently found in MT-Job (see above). These data combine to suggest that MT-Job was revised, even if only slightly, toward a fuller orthographic system. When such a revision may have taken place is debatable (see → 11.2.2.4); it is enough here to note that the evidence suggesting such a revision indicates that: a) MT-Job, despite its status as the best overall witness to the book as a whole, is still at considerable remove from the archetype; and b) what is found in MT-Job is already and inevitably an *interpretation* of what we presently call "the book of Job."[76]

Once one moves outside of these more concrete, if not empirical, data concerning low-frequency terms and differently spelled forms, far less certainty obtains. Dhorme's list of accidental errors in MT, for instance,[77] would not be greeted with acclaim by all scholars, some of whom would deem at least some of these "errors" to not be erroneous at all, with others finding occasional traces of intentionality in such "errors," and, finally, with still

---

[73] Seow, *Job 1–21*, 20.

[74] Seow, "Orthography, Textual Criticism, and the Poetry of Job," 74. See further pp. 74–85.

[75] For examples, see Seow, "Orthography, Textual Criticism, and the Poetry of Job," *passim*; and Pope, *Job*, xliv–xlv (on Job 13:15; but contrast Seow, *Job 1–21*, 659–60). Cox, "Iob," 668 believes that the Hebrew available to the Old Greek translator was unvocalized and perhaps also lacking word divisions.

[76] For a sophisticated treatment of text, interpretation, and reception, see B.W. Breed, *Nomadic Text: A Theory of Biblical Reception and History* (Indiana Series in Biblical Literature; Bloomington: Indiana University Press, 2014), esp. 15–74.

[77] See Dhorme, *A Commentary on the Book of Job*, cxcii–cxcv, which includes transposition of passages, verses, or words; misdivision of words or clauses (cf. 4QpaleoJob^c at Job 14:14); omissions via haplography or parablepsis; additions via dittography or glosses; changes of consonants perhaps due to mishearing; and mistakes in vocalization. Even with this listing, Dhorme deems the results to be "not alarming" when the sheer size of MT-Job is considered (cxcv–cxcvi).

others adding or subtracting to the list, if not offering their own lists instead.[78]

In sum, MT-Job remains the best witness to the book of Job as a whole, though it, no less than any other book in the Hebrew Bible, has suffered its share of scribal interventions. While scholars will continue to debate the nature and extent of such interventions, the two most obvious are the introduction of *matres lectionis* (see above) and the two famous instances where tradition holds that the scribes have corrected the text (*tiqqunê sopherim*), namely, Job 7:20: וָאֶהְיֶה עָלַי לְמַשָּׂא "I will be a burden for *myself* (OG: ἐπὶ σοὶ 'for *you*' [i.e., God])"; and Job 32:3: וַיַּרְשִׁיעוּ אֶת־אִיּוֹב "they had declared Job to be wrong" (rather than וירשיעו האלהים "they had declared *God* to be wrong").[79] The latter could be taken as proof that MT-Job has undergone a *theological revision* of some sort, but the precise nature and significance of the *tiqqunê sopherim* continue to be debated.[80] Interestingly enough, the two instances of ברך "to bless" in Job 1:5 and 2:9 are not listed as official scribal corrections though most scholars posit some sort of theological intervention at these points as well (where קלל "to curse," would seem more suitable). The Hebrew tradition is unanimous in supporting the reading of MT-Job in both instances. The versions, when they differ, may contain true variants but are probably simply interpretive, taking ברך in these instances to be euphemistic. Most modern studies and translations do the same.[81]

11.2.2.4 Date and Milieu

Linguistic analysis of MT-Job has suggested that the prose tale may be Late Biblical Hebrew and thus no earlier than the sixth century B.C.E.[82] On the opposite end, 4QpaleoJob[c], which dates to 225–150 B.C.E.,[83] provides a *terminus ante quem*.[84] On the basis of other considerations, especially external evidence, Seow believes "the book is most at home between the very late sixth and the first half of the fifth century and in Yehud."[85] A host of other possible dates may be found in the secondary literature.

Whatever the case, the range offered above is the date and milieu of the *book* of Job, especially its time of composition. What of the *text* of (proto-)MT-Job? As noted above, MT-Job, despite its conservative orthography, may have been revised on this matter so as to have fuller forms. Dating such a revision would be useful information for the dating of the text-type, but it is a difficult endeavor to say the least. It would most likely have occurred sometime after the still more conservative 4QpaleoJob[c], if not also after the date of those versions (or at least readings) that reflect defective forms.[86] It is virtually impossible to say more, however, since 4QJob[a] (100–50 B.C.E.) is *fuller* than MT-Job in six (possibly seven) instances, shorter than MT twice (see → 11.2.1.2; → 11.2.3.3.2); and because 4QJob[b] (middle or latter part of first century B.C.E.) is equivocal: preserving one fuller (Job 14:5) and one shorter (Job 8:15) reading than MT-Job (see → 11.2.1.3; → 11.2.3.2). Moreover, it is highly unlikely that MT-Job was revised subsequent to all of the versions wherein there is evidence of conservative orthographic *Vorlagen*. In some instances, that is,

---

[78] See further the commentary literature, especially Driver and Gray, *Book of Job*; Seow, *Job 1–21*; and Tur-Sinai, *Book of Job*. Note that Gray, *Job*, 89 considers errors in transmission in the Old Hebrew script (!) as well as in the later square script.

[79] See Dhorme, *A Commentary on the Book of Job*, cxciii; 110, 473–74; Seow, *Job 1–21*, 510–11; contrast Tur-Sinai, *Book of Job*, 457 (on Job 32:3). See further Ginsburg, **Introduction*, 347–63, esp. 360–61; McCarthy, **Tiqqune Sopherim*; and Tov, **TCHB*[3], 59–61.

[80] Tov, **TCHB*[3], 60–61. Dhorme, *A Commentary on the Book of Job*, cxciii, suggests a scribal suggestion (*sbr*) at Job 9:24.

[81] See Seow, *Job 1–21*, 270–71, 305; Tov, **TCHB*[3], 251; cf. also Barthélemy, **Interim Report*, 3.2–4.

[82] See Hurvitz, "The Date of the Prose-Tale of Job Linguistically Reconsidered," *HTR* 67 (1974): 17–34; Seow, *Job 1–21*, 26, 40; cf. Young, "Is the Prose Tale of Job in Late Biblical Hebrew?" 606–29.

[83] Skehan, Ulrich, and Sanderson, "101. 4QpaleoJob[c]," 155.

[84] Seow, *Job 1–21*, 40.

[85] Seow, *Job 1–21*, 45; cf. also p. 44.

[86] See Seow, *Job 1–21*, 19–20; Seow, "Orthography, Textual Criticism, and the Poetry of Job," 66–67, who includes readings from the Vulgate, Symmachus, Old Greek, Peshitta, Aquila, Theodotion, Targum, 11QtgJob, 4QJob[a], 4QJob[b], and some Hebrew manuscripts.

conservative orthography may be rather idiosyncratic or circumstantial and not a direct reflection of (or on) the original archetype. Still further, it is likely that many of these manuscripts come from parallel (not directly dependent) lines of transmission.[87]

Even so (and once again), whenever internal *matres lectionis* were added – for example, to 2QJob, 4QJob[a], 4QJob[b], and especially MT-Job – such introduction is "part of the book's history of interpretation."[88] Moreover, as I noted above, even if MT-Job is close to the orthography of the archetype, this is not determinative for an early dating of this text-type or even of the composition as such. So, against Freedman's understanding of Job's provenience and date in light of MT-Job's orthography (see → 11.2.2.1), Seow has argued that the conservative spelling, no less than the rare terminology, is a literary device designed "to lend credibility to the fiction of the foreignness of the book's setting."[89] This is possible but hardly certain; what is clear, regardless, is that textual criticism cannot decide a hermeneutical issue like this one.

11.2.2.5 Relevance for Exegesis and Literary Analysis

The relevance of (proto-)MT-Job for exegesis and literary analysis may be summarized in four points:

- First, despite the problems found in MT-Job and the occasional merits of the versional evidence, MT-Job remains the best witness to the book of Job as a whole and so is fundamental for all study and analysis of the composition.
- Second, the conservative orthography of (proto-)MT-Job, which may be (somewhat) reflective of the archetype at this point, is important not only because it has generated numerous variants in the textual history of the book, but also because it gives rise to numerous wordplays that can and should be considered in exegetical work and assessment of the poet's craft in Job (→ 11.2.2.3).
- Finally, the integrity of MT-Job is supported by the extant textual witnesses (→ 11.2.2.1).[90] This has direct and significant bearing on many composition-critical theories of the book. Among the debated points in such theories are the following: 1) the original independence of the prose framework and poetic middle; 2) the "disordered" nature of the third cycle of speeches; and 3) whether the Elihu speeches are original to the book. The textual witnesses support the current structure of Job as *always* containing *both* the prose frame and poetic speeches (no. 1) and as *always* attesting to the third cycle in its present state (no. 2). Further, both 4QJob[a] and 4QJob[b] "provide evidence that the Elihu speeches ... which many scholars consider ... secondary ... were part of the book by the turn of the era"[91] (no. 3). So, "[i]f there had been different configurations of the book than what is extant, they have not been preserved."[92]
- The last two points might be profitably correlated. The conservative orthography of MT-Job runs throughout the book, "corroborating the view that a single composer was at work" across its various parts/sections.[93]

In these ways, the text-critical data should chasten overly excited theories regarding the redaction and/or composition history of Job.

Andersen, F.I., *Job: An Introduction and Commentary* (TOTC; Leicester: Inter-Varsity Press, 1976).

Arias Montano (ed.), *Biblia Sacra Hebraice, Chaldaice, Graece et Latina* ... (Antwerp: Christophorus Plantinus, 1569–1572).

---

[87] That is, the orthographic revision of MT-Job was not necessarily directly dependent on, say, 4QpaleoJob[c], or any other of the presently extant witnesses.

[88] Seow, *Job 1–21*, 18.

[89] Seow, *Job 1–21*, 18.

[90] An exception would be if 11QtgJob does, in fact, end at Job 42:11. But see → 11.2.2.1 above.

[91] Newsom, "Job, Book of," 1:412; similarly Seow, *Job 1–21*, 5.

[92] Seow, *Job 1–21*, 27.

[93] Seow, *Job 1–21*, 27.

Baer, S. and F. Delitzsch (eds.), *Liber Iobi* (Leipzig: Tauchnitz, 1875).

Baillet, M., "15. Job," *DJD* III.1: 71.

Barr, J., "Hebrew Orthography and the Book of Job," *JSS* 30 (1985): 1–33.

Barthélemy, *Interim Report*, 3.1–162.

Beer, G., *Der Text des Buches Hiob* (Marburg: N.G. Elwertsche Verlagsbuchhandlung, 1897).

Cappellus, *Critica sacra*.

Clines, D.J.A., *Job* (3 vols.; WBC 17–18B; Dallas: Word Books, 1989–2011), esp. 3.1334–44 (bibliography on philology, textual criticism, and ancient versions).

Cox, C.E., "Iob," in *NETS*, 667–96.

De Rossi, *1784–1798, 4:105–38; 5:118–26.

Dhorme, E., *A Commentary on the Book of Job* (trans. H. Knight; Nashville: Thomas Nelson, 1984) (French original: *Le Livre de Job* [Paris: Gabalda, 1926]).

Driver, S.R. and G.B. Gray, *A Critical and Exegetical Commentary on the Book of Job, together with a New Translation* (2 vols.; ICC; New York: Charles Scribner's Sons, 1921).

Freedman, D.N., "Orthographic Peculiarities in the Book of Job," *ErIsr* 9 (1969): *35–*44.

García Martínez, F., "10. 11QtargumJob," *DJD* XXIII: 79–180.

Gentry, P.J., *The Asterisked Materials in the Greek Job* (SBLSCS 38; Atlanta: Scholars Press, 1995).

Grabbe, L.L., *Comparative Philology and the Text of Job: A Study in Methodology* (SBLDS 34; Missoula: Scholars Press, 1977).

Gray, J., *The Book of Job* (ed. D.J.A. Clines; Sheffield: Sheffield Phoenix Press, 2010).

Hartley, J., *The Book of Job* (NICOT; Grand Rapids: Eerdmans, 1988).

Heater, H., *A Septuagint Translation Technique in the Book of Job* (CBQMS 11; Washington: Catholic Biblical Association of America, 1982).

Houbigant, *Notae criticae*, 2.155–218.

Hurvitz, A., "The Date of the Prose-Tale of Job Linguistically Reconsidered," *HTR* 67 (1974): 17–34.

Kennicott, *1776–1780, 2:478–524.

Kutz, K.V., "The Old Greek of Job: A Study in Early Biblical Exegesis" (PhD diss.; University of Wisconsin – Madison, 1997).

Lange, *Handbuch*, 451–66.

Le Jay, *Biblia*.

Milik, J.T., "Targum de Job," *DJD* VI: 90.

Morrow, F.J., "11Q Targum Job and the Massoretic Text," *RevQ* 8 (1973): 253–56.

Nebe, G.W., "Qumranica I: Zu unveröffentlichten Handschriften aus Höhle 4 von Qumran," *ZAW* 106 (1994): 307–22.

Newsom, C.A., "Job, Book of," in *EDSS* 1:412–13.

Newsom, C.A., "The Book of Job: Introduction, Commentary, and Reflections," in *NIB* 4 (1996): 317–637.

van der Ploeg, J.P.M. and A.S. van der Woude, *Le Targum de Job de la Grotte XI de Qumrân* (Leiden: Brill, 1971).

Pope, M.H., *Job: Introduction, Translation, and Notes* (3rd ed.; AB 15; Garden City: Doubleday, 1980).

Seow, C.L., "Orthography, Textual Criticism, and the Poetry of Job," *JBL* 130 (2011): 63–85.

Seow, C.L., *Job 1–21: Interpretation and Commentary* (Illuminations; Grand Rapid: Eerdmans, 2013).

Shepherd, D., *Targum and Translation: A Reconsideration of the Qumran Aramaic Version of Job* (SSN 45; Assen: Van Gorcum, 2004).

Skehan, P.W., E. Ulrich, and J.E. Sanderson, "101. 4QpaleoJob^c," *DJD* IX: 155–57.

Sokoloff, M., *The Targum to Job from Qumran Cave XI* (Ramat-Gan: Bar-Ilan University, 1974).

Stec, D., *The Text of the Targum of Job* (AGJU 20; Leiden: Brill, 1994).

Strawn, B.A., "Problems and Poetics in the Text History of Job," in *The Text of the Hebrew Bible and Its Editions: Studies in Celebration of the Fifth Centennial of the Complutensian Polyglot* (eds. A. Piquer Otero and P.A. Torijano; THBS 1; Leiden: Brill, 2016), 449–80.

Tov, *"Synthese."

Tur-Sinai, N.H., *The Book of Job: A New Commentary* (rev. ed.; Jerusalem: Kiryath Sepher, 1967).

Ulrich, *BQS*, 727–31.

Ulrich, E. and S. Metso, "A Preliminary Edition of 4QJob^a," in *Antikes Judentum und frühes Christentum: Festschrift für Hartmut Stegemann zum 65. Geburtstag* (eds. B. Kollmann, W. Reinbold, and A. Steudel; BZNW 97; Berlin: De Gruyter, 1999), 29–38.

Ulrich, E. and S. Metso, "99. 4QJob^a," *DJD* XVI: 171–78.

Ulrich, E. and S. Metso, "100. 4QJob^b," *DJD* XVI: 179–80.

Walton, *Polyglotta*.

Young, I., "Is the Prose Tale of Job in Late Biblical Hebrew?" *VT* 59 (2009): 606–29.

Ziegler, J. (ed.), *Iob* (Septuaginta Vetus Testamentum Graecum 11.4; Göttingen: Vandenhoeck & Ruprecht, 1982).

Brent A. Strawn

11.2.3 Other Texts

Under the category of other "ancient Hebrew-Aramaic texts" of Job (see also → 11.3.3.2), further discussion of two manuscripts of Job from Qumran Cave 4 (4Q99–100 = 4QJob^{a,b}) is in order (→ 11.2.1.2–3).

11.2.3.1 History of Research

Prior to *DJD* XVI, and apart from the short study of 4QJob^a and 4QJob^b by Nebe (1994) and the brief remark of Tov on 4QJob^a (2000),[1] the only extensive study of either of these manuscripts was a preliminary edition of 4QJob^a by Ulrich and Metso.[2] Subsequent to *DJD* XVI, there has been an almost total lack of further research, no doubt due to the highly fragmentary state of both manuscripts. A notable exception is found in Lange's *Handbuch*, which treats both 4QJob^a and 4QJob^b and which makes a brief case for 4QJob^a being a non-aligned text.[3] Among recent commentators, only Seow discusses 4QJob^a and 4QJob^b (as well as 2QJob and 4QpaleoJob^c; see → 11.2.1). Seow summarizes: "Notwithstanding a few variants, these manuscript fragments essentially corroborate MT, although there is still not enough evidence to align them with that tradition (as opposed to other Vrss)."[4] This judgment is generally true, but requires further specificity since a non-aligned text, by definition, does not corroborate MT; several of the variants reflect significant divergence from MT; and 2QJob and 4QpaleoJob^c are probably best considered proto-Masoretic (→ 11.2.2).[5]

11.2.3.2 Text of 4QJob^b (4Q100)

It is possible that the entirety of 4QJob^b, or at least some of its six extant fragments, belong to 4QJob^a.[6] While this would add further to the material evidence of 4QJob^a, the point cannot be determined conclusively. Its contribution, regardless, is limited to two orthographic variants (see → 11.2.1.3).

11.2.3.3 Text of 4QJob^a (4Q99)
11.2.3.3.1 Manuscript Evidence

The material remains of 4QJob^a have already been discussed in → 11.2.1.2, but, for purposes of text-typological classification, two material details should be highlighted here. The first is the fact that three very small fragments (frgs. 20–22) cannot be clearly identified with specific passages from Job, and a fourth (frg. 23) may not belong to 4QJob^a at all.[7] The second detail is that the manuscript seems to have been ca. 10 cm in height with 16 lines per column.[8] It is unclear, then, if 4QJob^a could have contained the entire book of Job.[9] If not, 4QJob^a would have to be some sort of excerpted or abbreviated manuscript of the book of Job.[10] The physical remains cannot prove (nor disprove) this possibility, but if 4QJob^a was an excerpted or abbreviated manuscript it might explain the presence of frgs. 20–22, if these do not, in fact, contain material from

---

[1] Nebe, "Qumranica I," 307–08; Tov, *"Synthese," 27.

[2] Ulrich and Metso, "A Preliminary Edition," 29–38. Since these scholars were also responsible for the *DJD* edition, the two studies are virtually identical.

[3] Lange, *Handbuch*, 452–53. See also Seow, "Notes."

[4] Seow, *Job 1–21*, 5; further Seow, "Notes."

[5] For a different view, see → 11.2.1.1 and → 11.2.1.4.

[6] See Ulrich and Metso, "4QJob^b," 179 (cf. also → 11.2.1.3; Lange, *Handbuch*, 453). Specifically, Ulrich and Metso note that 4QJob^b frgs. 5–6 might fit at the bottom left of 4QJob^a frg. 1 ("4QJob^b," 179).

[7] On frg. 23, see Ulrich and Metso, "4QJob^a," 178, who disassociate the fragment on the basis of its paleography and the word ענפים "branches" in line 1. That word does not appear in Job, nor anywhere else in the Hebrew Bible in the plural absolute. Although it is possible that the third letter is *bet* (hence, ענבים "grapes"), that word, too, is never found in Job. Frg. 23 is not included in Ulrich and Metso, "Preliminary Edition." Seow, "Notes," wonders if frg. 20 may reflect Job 37:13.

[8] Ulrich and Metso, "4QJob^a," 171; Ulrich and Metso, "Preliminary Edition," 29.

[9] Cf. → 11.2.1.2; and Lange, *Handbuch*, 452.

[10] For studies, see E. Tov, "Excerpted and Abbreviated Biblical Texts from Qumran," *RevQ* 16 (1995): 581–600; and B.A. Strawn, "Excerpted Manuscripts at Qumran: Their Significance for the Textual History of the Hebrew Bible and the Socio-Religious History of the Qumran Community and its Literature," in *The Bible and the Dead Sea Scrolls*, Vol. 2: *The Dead Sea Scrolls and the Qumran Community* (ed. J.H. Charlesworth; Waco: Baylor University Press, 2006), 107–67; B.A. Strawn, "Excerpted 'Non-Biblical' Scrolls at Qumran? Background, Analogies, Function," in *Qumran Studies: New Approaches, New Questions* (eds. M.T. Davis and B.A. Strawn; Grand Rapids: Eerdmans, 2007), 65–123.

Job, as well as the presence of frg. 23, if it really does belong to the same manuscript.[11]

11.2.3.3.2 Orthography

Orthographically (→ 1.2.2.4.1.2), 4QJob\u1d43 mostly follows the system known also in MT-Job, but is fuller than MT in six (possibly seven)[12] instances,[13] shorter than MT in two instances.[14] The latter are especially noteworthy since the text of MT-Job is orthographically conservative when it comes to *matres lectiones*.[15] So, while these orthographic differences are not of great text-critical significance, they nevertheless do not permit a simple classification of 4QJob\u1d43 with MT-Job (→ 11.2.2).

11.2.3.3.3 Text-Critical Character

Early assessments characterized 4QJob\u1d43 as close to MT-Job (→ 11.2.2),[16] but the matter is not so easily decided, partly due to the state of preservation.[17] The differences that are preserved, or partly preserved, in 4QJob\u1d43 are categorized below as to whether the reading in question is uncertain, ambiguous, or a clear and significant variant. The last category requires clarification: readings in the first two categories may also be significant, but various factors preclude them from being deemed certain or clear; hence, they should not be relied on overmuch in text-typological classifications.

11.2.3.3.3.1 Uncertain Readings

At Job 33:11, it is uncertain whether 4QJob\u1d43 3 2 read a suffix-conjugation (שמר "watched"; so also Old Greek: ἐφύλαξεν "watched") as opposed to MT's prefix-conjugation (יִשְׁמֹר "watches").[18] If it did, 4QJob\u1d43 may be the *lectio difficilior* with MT-Job the result of grammatical harmonizing. But 4QJob\u1d43 could be missing the *yod* due to haplography from רגלי "my feet" (now lost in the lacuna).[19] In Job 33:25, the first two extant letters of 4QJob\u1d43 4–5 2 are not clear but "cannot form *šin*, and thus the text differs from רטפש" in MT-Job.[20] Other readings are also unclear due to the state of the manuscript and the resulting uncertainties for its reconstruction.[21]

11.2.3.3.3.2 Ambiguous Readings

Even what is (mostly) legible is not always decisive. So, for example, at Job 31:15, 4QJob\u1d43 1 2 reads with MT הלא "were not" against Old Greek (πότερον οὐχ ὡς "were not as"; 11QtgJob: ארו "if"), but the next two words are transposed from their order in MT.[22]

---

[11] In some cases, excerpted manuscripts contain additional material from other texts. See, e.g., 4QTanḥ, and the discussion in Strawn, "Excerpted 'Non-Biblical' Scrolls." See also at Job 36:32 below (→ 11.2.3.3.3.3).

[12] If Job 36:33: רעיו (4QJob\u1d43 16 ii 9) vs. רֵעוֹ "its roar" (MT) is considered orthographic rather than a variant. The editors are unsure (Ulrich and Metso, "4QJob\u1d43," 172, 177; Ulrich and Metso, "Edition," 30, 37). See → 11.2.3.3.3.3 below.

[13] Job 32:4: ואליהוא (4QJob\u1d43 2 2) vs. וֶאֱלִיהוּ "and Elihu" (MT); Job 36:18: יטכה (4QJob\u1d43 7 ii + 12–16 i 9) vs. יְסִיתְךָ "turn you aside" (MT); Job 36:23: פעלתה (4QJob\u1d43 7 ii + 12–16 i 15) vs. פָּעָלְתָּ "you have done" (MT); Job 36:26: ולוא (4QJob\u1d43 17–18 line 2) vs. וְלֹא "and not" (MT); Job 36:26: ניד]ע (4QJob\u1d43 17–18 line 2) vs. נֵדָע "we know" (MT); and Job 37:14: [עמו]ד (4QJob\u1d43 19 line 1) vs. עֲמֹד "stand" (MT). Note that three of these (Job 32:4; 36:18; 36:23) reflect the baroque orthographic system prominent at Qumran.

[14] At Job 33:26: ל[אנ]ש (4QJob\u1d43 4–5 line 4) vs. לֶאֱנוֹשׁ "for a man" (MT); Job 36:11: בנעמים (4QJob\u1d43 7 i + 8–11 line 16) vs. בַּנְּעִימִים "with delight" (MT).

[15] For the importance of orthography for the textual criticism of Job, see Seow, "Orthography"; and Seow, *Job 1–21*, 17–20, with literature. Seow notes that, beyond text-critical matters in *sensu stricto*, conservative orthography often produces multiple readings of a word and thereby can greatly affect translation and exegesis. Cf. → 11.2.2 and → 11.3.1.

[16] Nebe, "Qumranica I," 308; Tov, *"*Synthese," 27.

[17] Abegg, Flint, and Ulrich, **DSSB*, 590.

[18] See Ulrich and Metso, "4QJob\u1d43," 173: "some trace of the *yod* should be visible if it were originally there." Ulrich and Metso, "Preliminary Edition," 32.

[19] Cf. the similar issue in Job 36:23, discussed below (→ 11.2.3.3.3.2).

[20] Ulrich and Metso, "4QJob\u1d43," 174; Ulrich and Metso, "Preliminary Edition," 32. Similarly, the letters in line 4 of the same fragment "may or may not have formed צדקתו" as in MT (Ulrich and Metso, "4QJob\u1d43," 174; Ulrich and Metso, "Preliminary Edition," 32).

[21] E.g., the reconstructed text at 4QJob\u1d43 7 ii + 12–16 i 6 (Job 36:16), which suggests either a different reading from MT, confused lineation in 4QJob\u1d43, or an incorrect material reconstruction (see Ulrich and Metso, "4QJob\u1d43," 175–76; Ulrich and Metso, "Preliminary Edition," 34; Abegg, Flint, Ulrich, **DSSB*, 592). Another example: in Job 36:22, 4QJob\u1d43 7 ii + 12–16 i 13 may preserve הנה against MT's הֶן "look."

[22] On transpositions in MT, see Dhorme, *A Commentary on*

At Job 33:26, 4QJob^a 4–5 3 reads אל אל rather than MT's אֶל־אֱלוֹהַּ "to God/Eloah" (cf. OG: πρὸς κύριον "to the Lord"). The former construction is not infrequent in Job (Job 5:8; 8:5; 13:3; 15:13, 25; 16:11; 34:23, 31; 38:41), indeed, it is more frequent than the latter (Job 10:2; 16:20; 22:26; 33:26). 4QJob^a could be a case of harmonization, perhaps influenced by memory, but it is not impossible that it is a case of paraplepsis with the following word (וַיִּרְצֵהוּ "and he is accepted by him"). The variant in Job 36:7, where 4QJob^a seems to read בכסא "on a throne" with LXX (εἰς θρόνον sub ※) against MT (לַכִּסֵּא "for the throne") may be a case of linguistic smoothing, but it is not of great diagnostic import. Even in Job 36:23, where 4QJob^a 7 ii + 12–16 i 15 clearly preserves יאמר "will say" rather than MT's אָמַר "said" (cf. OG: εἶπας) and where 4QJob^a could be taken as the *lectio difficilior* with MT-Job harmonizing, it remains possible that 4QJob^a is the result of dittography from the preceding מי "who" (cf. discussion of Job 33:11 above, → 11.2.3.3.3.1). The sense, in any case, is not significantly altered and either change could be taken as stylistic. A similar situation obtains at Job 36:27, where 4QJob^a 17–18 3 reads וזקו "and they will filter" with LXX (καὶ ἐπιχυθήσονται sub ※ "and they will be poured out"), against MT (יָזֹקּוּ "they filter"). Even if the reading of initial *waw* is correct – and the photograph seems clear on this point – the sense is not much altered, though, here, too, 4QJob^a would represent the more difficult reading with MT-Job harmonizing with the earlier prefix-conjugation. But perhaps this is a case of י/ו graphic confusion. Finally, at Job 37:2, 4QJob^a has a supralinear correction (*prima manu*) that seems to produce the reading ובגה "and in a rumbling (?)" as opposed to וְהֶגֶה "and a rumbling" in MT, LXX (καὶ μελέτη sub ※, "and a discourse"). But the sense is not clear; if the letter is ב (as seems likely from the plates),[23] the reading probably reflects a phonological loss of ה (ובגה > ובהגה) due to weakening of the gutturals at Qumran.[24] The meaning is unaffected though the inclusion of ב reflects a harmonizing move (see → 11.2.3.3.3.3).

11.2.3.3.3.3 Clear and Significant Variants

The clearest and most significant variants are as follows:

1) At Job 36:24, 4QJob^a 7 ii + 12–16 i 16 originally read תשגיא (2nd masc. sg. prefix-conjugation, "you will magnify") with MT, but the (same) scribe seems to have subsequently erased ת, yielding the adjective שגיא "great" in a correction away from MT and toward Old Greek (μεγάλα "great"). The resulting reading is smoother,[25] given the masc. sg. imperative earlier in the line (זְכֹר "remember"), but for that reason may be suspect. Indeed, it could be an anticipation of שַׂגִּיא "great" in Job 36:26.[26]

2) At Job 36:32, 4QJob^a 16 ii 8 reads]אם [, which is completely unparalleled in MT, where the correlative word should be כַּפַּיִם "palms" (cf. LXX: χειρῶν sub ※, "hands").[27] The meaning of 4QJob^a cannot be recovered, but it is clearly at odds with MT-Job and LXX.

3) At Job 36:33, 4QJob^a 16 ii 9 reads רעיו for MT's רֵעוֹ "its roar." As noted above (→ 11.2.3.3.2, note 12), the editors are not clear if the difference is orthographic or a true variant, and do not make a decision.[28] The verse is complicated with the Versions understanding רעו as "his friend" (so LXX: φίλον αὐτοῦ sub ※), but most commentators relate the word to the storm imagery of the surrounding context.[29] It is difficult to discern what, if any, special meaning obtains in 4QJob^a's reading. It is best not to speculate, but the (large) vari-

---

the Book of Job, cxciii–cxciv. Seow, "Notes," finds the transposition semantically meaningful.

[23] Nebe, "Qumranica I," 308 read ונגה erroneously.

[24] Ulrich and Metso, "4QJob^a," 177; Ulrich and Metso, "Preliminary Edition," 36, citing Qimron, *DSS*, § 200.11.

[25] Ulrich and Metso, "4QJob^a," 172 think it may be preferable, as does Seow, "Notes."

[26] Elsewhere in Job only at Job 37:23.

[27] Ulrich and Metso, "4QJob^a," 176–77; Ulrich and Metso, "Preliminary Edition," 36–37.

[28] Ulrich and Metso, "4QJob^a," 172, 177; Ulrich and Metso, "Preliminary Edition," 30, 36–37.

[29] See Dhorme, *A Commentary on the Book of Job*, 557–58, for discussion. Cf. Exod 32:17.

ant in the immediately preceding line (Job 36:32, see no. 2 above), not to mention the variants that follow in Job 37:1–2 (see nos. 4–7 below), probably indicate that 4QJob[a] diverged from MT-Job here as well.[30]

4) At Job 37:1, 4QJob[a] 16 ii 10 negates the verb (לא יחרד "does not tremble"), against MT, LXX (sub ※).[31] The sense is drastically changed in 4QJob[a], with the verb now negated and the subject of the verb uncertain (see nos. 3 and 5).

5) The following word in 4QJob[a] (Job 37:1) is broken, but probably reflects לא against MT (לבי "my heart") and LXX (ἡ καρδία μου sub ※, "my heart")[32] and so negates the following verb (see no. 6 next).

6) In Job 37:1, 4QJob[a] 16 ii 10 reads יתר [against MT (וְיִתֵּר "and leaps"), LXX (καὶ ἀπερρύη sub ※, "and dropped"). Two differences are apparent: i) the *waw* is missing, which accords with variant no. 5; and ii) the word in 4QJob[a] has an additional letter, perhaps *he* or *waw*.[33] The latter would pluralize the verb, which would then be in conflict with the 3rd masc. sg. יחרד "trembles" earlier in the line (unless the subject shifts to a plural in the following word now lost in the break [MT: מִמְּקוֹמוֹ "out of its place"]; but cf. no. 7 next).

7) At Job 37:2, 4QJob[a] reads שמע שמע "listen, listen" with LXX (ἄκουε ἀκοήν sub ※, "hear a report") against שִׁמְעוּ שָׁמוֹעַ "listen closely" in MT.[34] The second word could be purely an orthographic difference, but the first reflects a different grammatical number (singular rather than plural). It is hard to determine the nature of this change, but MT may be harmonistic with Job 13:17; 21:2.

8) The supralinear correction at Job 37:2 discussed above (→ 11.2.3.3.3.2) represents a harmonizing addition by reduplicating the preposition before the object of the verbal action.[35]

9) At Job 37:5, 4QJob[a] reads על for אֵל "God" in MT, LXX (ὁ ἰσχυρός sub ※, "the strong one"). על may represent a shortened form of the divine name עֶלְיוֹן "Highest/Most High" (or its synonym).[36] Note MT-Hos 11:7 (וְאֶל־עַל "to the Most High") and MT-2 Sam 23:1 (עָל "Most High"). In the latter instance, 4QSam[a] reads אל "God" for MT's עָל "Most High."

10) At Job 37:14, 4QJob[a] agrees with Old Greek in lacking the conjunction read by MT (וְהִתְבּוֹנֵן "and consider"). The difference is small, but MT may reflect linguistic updating.

These ten variants are significant, and, while it is difficult to categorize several of them (are nos. 2–7 corruptions or interpretive?) or even fully determine their meaning (mostly, again, due to poor preservation), it is sufficiently clear that 4QJob[a] is not easily aligned with MT-Job. 4QJob[a] represents a smoother and harmonizing text in two instances (Job 36:24 and 37:2 supralinear, respectively), but in four or five instances represents a drastically different text (Job 36:32; 37:1o1; 37:1o3; 37:2, and perhaps 37:1o2; perhaps the same holds true also for Job 36:33). To this, we might add Job 33:11 (perhaps; if so with OG), 36:23o1, and 36:27, where 4QJob[a] is more difficult than MT-Job, which may be harmonizing

---

[30] Given the lack of a verbal subject in Job 37:1 (see nos. 4–6 below), the subject might need to be found in Job 36:33. The number of לא יחרד "does not tremble" in Job 37:1, might mean that רעיו, regardless of its difficulties (see Dhorme, *A Commentary on the Book of Job*, 557–58), should be taken as a singular.

[31] For LXX, see Dhorme, *A Commentary on the Book of Job*, 559.

[32] See Ulrich and Metso, "4QJob[a]," 177; Ulrich and Metso, "Preliminary Edition," 36, who note that the traces could fit לבי "my heart" but also לא "not" or לה "for her/it." Material considerations incline them toward לא. To this, one might add the negated לא יחרד "does not tremble" earlier in the line. Seow, "Notes," favors the reconstruction [ל]ב "he[art]."

[33] Ulrich and Metso, "4QJob[a]," 177; Ulrich and Metso, "Preliminary Edition," 36.

[34] Cf. Dhorme, *A Commentary on the Book of Job*, 559, on the Greek evidence.

[35] Cf. Ulrich and Metso, "4QJob[a]," 177; Ulrich and Metso, "Preliminary Edition," 36.

[36] See B. Schmidt, "Al," and E. Elnes and P.D. Miller, "Elyon," in *Dictionary of Deities and Demons in the Bible* (eds. K. van der Toorn, B. Becking, and P.W. van der Horst; Leiden: Brill, ²1999), 14–17 and 293–99, respectively.

with the surrounding context. To be sure, in some places, 4QJob[a] reads with MT: Job 31:15 (against OG); 33:11 (perhaps; if so against OG); 36:11 (with LXX συντελέσουσιν sub ※, "they will complete"; against MT[mss] and Sym);[37] and *36:24 (originally, prior to the correction). It is also clear that 4QJob[a] is not always in agreement with LXX or Old Greek.[38] Considered as a whole, then, it is correct to say, with Lange (→ 11.2.1.2), that 4QJob[a] (and perhaps 4QJob[b], see → 11.2.3.2) is an independent, non-aligned witness with a certain proximity to MT.[39]

11.2.3.3.3.4 Date and Milieu

It is impossible to be certain about the date and milieu of 4QJob[a]. The only secure information is the date of the manuscript itself; the paleography puts it in the first half or middle of the first century B.C.E. (→ 11.2.1.2). That period, then, is the *terminus ante quem* for the text-type. The clustering of so many of the independent variants in the Elihu speeches could be taken as indicating that 4QJob[a] (at least in this unit) is earlier than the Versional evidence, or, alternatively, that it is an idiosyncratic interpretation of this material, perhaps limited to Qumran (see further → 11.2.3.3.5).

11.2.3.3.5 Relevance for Exegesis and Literary Analysis

4QJob[a] is relevant to both the exegesis and literary analysis of the book of Job. With regard to literary analysis, 4QJob[a] (so also 2QJob, which preserves Job 33:28–30) provides "evidence that the Elihu speeches (*Job* 32–37), which many scholars consider to be a secondary part of the composition, were part of the book by the turn of the era."[40] If the Elihu speeches are secondary, that is, their addition to Job would have to precede the date of 4QJob[a]. Exegetically, the significance of 4QJob[a] lies primarily in the unusual readings that cluster in the Elihu speeches and especially in Job 36–37; some of these readings may be superior to those found in MT (→ 11.2.2). Finally, the intriguing possibility that 4QJob[a] may not have contained the entire book of Job makes it of possible interest, not only for the study of the excerpted and abbreviated manuscript genre at Qumran, but also for what it would mean for its text-critical significance if it were, in fact, one of these kinds of manuscripts.[41]

11.2.3.4 Medieval Hebrew Non-Aligned Texts?

Von Mutius has recently argued that a citation of Job 38:35 in the medieval *Midrash Ha-Gadol* reflects a non-Masoretic version of the book.[42] The citation contains a plus (וישבו) also found in the Vulgate (*et reventia*) "and they shall return," but lacking in MT. While it is possible that such a reading reflects the ongoing life of non-(MT)-aligned Hebrew texts in the Middle Ages, especially in the light of other readings Von Mutius has gathered,[43] the uniqueness of this reading, combined with: 1) its relative insignificance in terms of meaning, let alone text-typology; and 2) its easy explanation as a smoothing addition,[44] counsels against any widescale conclusions.

Dhorme, E., *A Commentary on the Book of Job* (trans. H. Knight; Nashville: Thomas Nelson, 1984) (French original: *Le Livre de Job* [Paris: Gabalda, 1926]).
Lange, *Handbuch*, 451–53.
Nebe, G.W., "Qumranica I: Zu unveröffentlichten Handschriften aus Höhle 4 von Qumran," *ZAW* 106 (1994): 307–22.
Newsom, C.A., "Job, Book of," in *EDSS* 1:412–13.
Seow, C.L., "Orthography, Textual Criticism, and the Poetry of Job," *JBL* 130 (2011): 63–85.

---

[37] Ulrich and Metso, "4QJob[a]," 175; cf. Ulrich and Metso, "Preliminary Edition," 34; Dhorme, *A Commentary on the Book of Job*, 542.

[38] See → 11.2.1.2 for additional statistics.

[39] Lange, *Handbuch*, 452. See also Seow, *Job 1–21*, and Seow, "Notes."

[40] Newsom, "Job," 412.

[41] See Strawn, "Excerpted Manuscripts at Qumran."

[42] H.-G. von Mutius, "Drei nichtmasoretische Textzitate aus dem Midrasch ha-Gadol zu den Büchern Ijob (38,35), Sprüche (29,12), und Kohelet (3,14)," *BN* 149 (2011): 59–64.

[43] In addition to the previous note, see H.-G. von Mutius, *Nichtmasoretische Bibelzitate im Midrasch Ha-Gadol (13./14. Jahrhundert)* (Judentum und Umwelt 80; Frankfurt a.M.: Peter Lang, 2010).

[44] Alternatively, MT could be explained as a corruption. The addition of וישבו "and they shall return" seems to add unduly to the poetic lines, however, leading to imbalance.

Seow, C.L., *Job 1–21: Interpretation and Commentary* (Illuminations; Grand Rapids: Eerdmans, 2013).

Seow, C.L., "Text Critical Notes on 4QJob^a," *DSD* 22 (2015): 189–201.

Tov, *"Synthese."

Ulrich, *_BQS_, 727–31.

Ulrich, E. and S. Metso, "A Preliminary Edition of 4QJob^a," in *Antikes Judentum und frühes Christentum: Festschrift für Hartmut Stegemann zum 65. Geburtstag* (eds. B. Kollmann, W. Reinbold, and A. Steudel; BZNW 97; Berlin: W. de Gruyter, 1999), 29–38 (with two plates).

Ulrich, E. and S. Metso, "99. 4QJob^a," *_DJD_ XVI (2000): 171–78.

Ulrich, E. and S. Metso, "100. 4QJob^b," *_DJD_ XVI (2000): 179–80.

Brent A. Strawn

11.3 Primary Translations

11.3.1 Septuagint

11.3.1.1 Textual History
11.3.1.1.1 Provenance and Date

No provenance has been suggested for LXX-Job other than Alexandria, where much of the LXX corpus was translated (→ 1.3.1.1). According to the *Letter of Aristeas*, the Torah was rendered into Greek during the reign of Ptolemy II Philadelphus (ca. 285–246 B.C.E.). The remainder of the corpus was translated later, and the first attestation of LXX-Job is its use in Aristeas' *On the Jews*, a text excerpted by Alexander Polyhistor. That Aristeas is using LXX-Job is clear from the titles "king" and "tyrant" in the identification of the three friends. Since Polyhistor wrote around the middle of the first century B.C.E., Aristeas is to be dated to the first half of that same century. LXX-Job must belong somewhat earlier, probably the end of the second century B.C.E.[1]

11.3.1.1.2 Earliest Witnesses

The earliest textual witnesses to LXX-Job are fragmentary papyri that, taken together, preserve a handful of verses. They are listed below in chronological order through the first four centuries C.E. with their Rahlfs' (Göttingen) numbers, dates, and contents:

857	P. Oxy. L 3522	First C.E.	Job 42:11–12
974	P. Berlin Nr. 11778	ca. 220 C.E.	Job 33:23–24; 34:10c–15b
854	P. Chester Beatty XVIII	Third C.E.	Job 9:2, 12–13
955	Florenz, Bib. Laur., PSI 1163	Fourth C.E.	Job 1:19–2:1; 2:6–9b[2]

For the fourth century C.E., the great uncial manuscripts Vaticanus (LXX^B) and Sinaiticus (LXX^S) are extant and, for the fifth century C.E., manuscript Alexandrinus (LXX^A). A few later fragmentary papyri exist, belonging to the sixth and seventh centuries C.E.[3] The majority of the Greek manuscripts are medieval minuscules, dating mostly from the ninth to the fourteenth centuries. For the early period, we also have the Greek commentaries of Julian the Arian, Didymus of Alexandria, John Chrysostom, and Olympiodorus, though such commentaries are often preserved only in late manuscripts and lack critical editions. Finally, the sub-versions derive from Greek witnesses of an early date. Especially important are the Old Latin (→ 11.4.1), Sahidic (→ 11.4.2), Syro-Hexapla (→ 11.4.4), and Armenian translations (→ 11.4.5).

11.3.1.1.3 Origen's Hexapla and the Emergence of the "Ecclesiastical Text"

The most immediately noticeable characteristic of LXX-Job is the brevity of its text vis-à-vis MT; → 11.3.1.3. LXX-Job is about one-sixth shorter than MT. For example, Job 28, "the Wisdom poem," is shorter by one-half: LXX consists of vv. 1–3a, 4b, 9b–13, 20–21a, 22b–26a, 27b–28.

The first major development in the text history of LXX-Job took place at the hands of Origen, who addressed the issue of the shorter text. It was a "major" development because of its profound effect on the textual tradition.

In the third century C.E., Origen compared the LXX text with the Hebrew text of his day in a multicolumned book called "the Hexapla" that presented the texts word by word and phrase by phrase in the parallel columns (→ 1.3.1.2.7). Where LXX was shorter than the Hebrew, Origen added the words (or verses) that were lacking based on

---

[1] See Cox, "Historical, Social and Literary Context," 106.

[2] Data for nos. 955 and 974 are drawn from Ziegler, *Iob*: 14; nos. 854 and 857 do not appear in Ziegler, *Iob*. On 854, which consists of only a few words, see A. Pietersma, "New Greek Fragments of Biblical Manuscripts in the Chester Beatty Library," *BASP* 24 (1987): 45–47, 54–55; for 857, see *The Oxyrhynchus Papyri*, vol. L (ed. A.K. Bowman et al.; London: British Academy, 1983), 1–3.

[3] Ziegler, *Iob*, 14.

the translation associated with Theodotion's name. He marked what he added with critical signs, an asterisk (※) at the beginning and a metobelus (✓) at the end. Where the LXX text was longer than the Hebrew, Origen marked it with an obelus (÷) and metobelus. In the case of Job, hundreds of lines were added to make the Greek equal in length to the Hebrew source text as it existed in Origen's day. So popular did Origen's work become that it permeated the entire extant Greek text tradition of Job with the exception of the Sahidic sub-version, by and large, which preserves the pre-Origenic short text. All other witnesses attest the mixed text, called "the ecclesiastical text" because it was a Christian endeavor that produced, disseminated, and preserved it.

For example, Origen added vv. 3b–4a, 5–9a, 14–19, 21b–22a, 26b–27a to Job 28 so that the Greek text corresponded *in length* to the Hebrew. The Syro-Hexapla (→ 11.4.4) is the major witness for the Hexaplaric text.

11.3.1.1.4 The Lucianic Recension

The text of LXX-Job entered its third stage of development with its revision at the hands of Lucian (→ 11.3.6), who was born in Syria around the time that Origen died (d. 254 C.E.; → 1.3.1.2.7). The text of Job that Lucian revised was the Hexaplaric text prepared by Origen (→ 11.3.5), with its hundreds of added lines. That he used this form of text is clear from the fact that his revisional work extends across the Hexaplaric additions. Lucian's revision, unlike that of Origen, did not seek to bring LXX-Job closer to the Hebrew; rather it sought to improve the translation in terms of clarity and Greek style. In its own way, Lucian's revision was equal to Origen's in its thoroughgoing application and widespread influence.

A sample analysis of Lucian's revision in Job 3–11 produced the following changes to the text: 1) addition of possessive pronouns, articles, conjunctions, prepositions, words, and phrases (sometimes drawn from elsewhere in LXX-Job); 2) change of conjunction, tense of verbs, the mood of verbs, gender, number, person, case, word order; rewriting of phrases; 3) replacement of a word with a synonym,

replacement of δέ "but" with καί "and," and of γάρ "for" with δέ; replacement of Hellenistic with Attic forms (e.g., εἶπα by εἶπον "I said"); replacement of a simple with a compound verb (e.g., ἐπέρχομαι for ἔρχομαι "come") and vice versa.[4] The result is a type of text that has been subjected to many changes, some made, it appears, simply for the sake of change.

The Lucianic type of text is the fullest representative of the Greek text of Job. Like Origen's Hexaplaric text, this text became popular; for example, when Armenian translators in the early fifth century C.E. rendered LXX-Job into Armenian, they used the Lucianic revision, the manuscript having come either directly from Syria or from Constantinople after the Council of Ephesus (431 C.E.; → 11.4.5).

11.3.1.2 Editions

The edition of Ziegler (*Iob*) with its critically established eclectic text supercedes all earlier editions of LXX-Job. These include the polyglots, from the Sixtina (1587) onwards, which, like the editions that followed (Holmes–Parsons [1798–1827], Swete [1887–1891], and the provisional edition of Rahlfs, *Septuaginta*), print the text of Vaticanus (LXX^B).[5] Ziegler too gives pride of place to manuscript LXX^B – codex Sinaiticus (LXX^S) is a sister manuscript in Job – for it preserves a pre-Lucianic, pre-Hexaplaric type of text and occasionally stands almost alone in attesting the original reading. The strength of Ziegler's edition lies not only in its text but also in its extensive apparatus, which presents the evidence of the development of the text along the lines sketched above.

Unfortunately, Ziegler's edition prints as text the ecclesiastical text, that is, it includes amidst the text of LXX-Job the Theodotionic additions

---

[4] For details, see Cox, "Lucian," 429–39.

[5] *Vetus Testamentum iuxta Septuaginta ex auctoritate Sixti V. Pont. Max.* (Rome: Francesco Zanetti, 1587); R. Holmes and J. Parsons, *Vetus Testamentum Graecum cum variis lectionibus* (5 vols.; Oxford: Clarendon Press, 1798–1827); H.B. Swete, The Old Testament in Greek according to the Septuagint (3 vols.; Cambridge: Cambridge University Press, 1887–1891); Rahlfs, *Septuaginta*. For details, see Würthwein, *Text*, 75–78.

placed by Origen. The latter translation is marked by asterisks and metobeli in Ziegler, *Iob*, but the two translations are punctuated as if they were one running text unit and appear in the same typeface. Further, the versification treats the two translations as one text. This type of presentation confuses the user, a confusion that appears to have begun with the editor himself.[6]

Therefore, the first task in the study of LXX-Job is to separate the Old Greek from Theodotion. Gentry and Pietersma, followed by Cox, have made small adjustments to Ziegler's demarcation.[7] Even established scholars can occasionally be caught confusing the two.[8]

11.3.1.3 Translation Technique

LXX-Job is a remarkable translation in several respects: the translator has abbreviated MT by some 390 lines; made additions to MT (→ 11.2.2);[9] practiced a form of intertextual sourcing, where parts of verses are inserted from elsewhere in LXX-Job or from the LXX version of other books; replaced lines of text with his own thoughts unrelated to the Hebrew source text; and, finally, often paraphrased and interpreted the Hebrew.[10]

Gray's oft-cited calculation notes that the abbreviation of the text of Job increases from chapter to chapter: little abbreviation through Job 1–13; 4 percent in Job 12–14; 16 percent in Job 15–21; 25 percent in Job 22–31; 35 percent in Job 32–37, the Elihu speeches; then less, only 16 percent in Job 38–42, the speeches of the Deity.[11] The translator has edited the text. The desire to make the text less repetitive is clear in the drastic shortening of the Elihu speeches, but that is not the sole reason for shortening the text as the Deity's speeches are also abbreviated.

In the past, it was occasionally argued that LXX-Job is witness to an equally short Hebrew parent text or that MT represents an expansion of such a shorter text,[12] but, on the basis of an examination of the translator's general approach to the Hebrew where MT and LXX can be compared, it is virtually certain that the translator is responsible for the abbreviation.[13]

In the course of producing the Greek text, the translator borrowed from other passages in Job and from other books in the LXX corpus. Such translations can sometimes be called "associative translations," or, to use the terminology of Heater, "anaphoric translations."[14] The following examples draw on LXX-Job and on other LXX texts:

---

[6] So Pietersma, "Review of Ziegler, *Iob*," with examples.

[7] Gentry, *Asterisked Materials*, Appendix D; Pietersma, "Review," 310–11; Cox, "Old Greek Job," 667.

[8] Dhorme, *Job*, (1926), 534 and Gray, *Job*, 268 (35:10: ὁ ποιήσας με is Th, not LXX); Gordis, 1978, 412 and Clines, *Job 21–37*, 810 (36:5: "LXX [= Th.]" and "on the basis of LXX" [no: Th], respectively); Gordis, *Job*, 420 (36:28: "LXX, derived from Th., …"), 423 (36:32), 428 (36:32); John Gray, *Job*, 415 (34:1, second note: *ʾokel* is Th, not LXX); and Scott Noegel's claim that LXX tries to preserve polysemy at 20:23–24 is vitiated by the failure to identify 20:23a as Theodotion ("Janus Parallelism in Job and its Literary Signficance," *JBL* 115 [1996]: 317–19).

[9] However, the major pluses, Job 2:9a–d; 42:17aα; and 42:17bα–eδ, do not belong to the translator but to an early stage in the transmission of the text.

[10] See in detail 11.2.2.1.

[11] G.B. Gray in Driver and Gray, *A Critical and Exegetical Commentary*, lxxv.

[12] E. Hatch, "On Origen's Revision of the LXX Text of Job," in *Essays in Biblical Greek* (Oxford: Clarendon Press, 1889), 215–45, argued that MT is an expansion of a shorter original Job represented by LXX. His problematic study is only of antiquarian interest for, among other things, it predated the proper demarcation of LXX from Theodotion. As a result, Hatch is found treating Theodotion's text as part of the witness to the old, original shorter Hebrew text. But a decade or so later Swete, *Introduction*, 256, says "recent critics" support the view that the shorter text is the work of the translator. By 1926, "no critic" accepted Hatch's hypothesis (Dhorme, *Job*: cciii); more recently, Clines (*Job* [1989–2011]) does not even cite Hatch's name in his bibliography. Nevertheless, Hatch's suggestion was bound to be made at some point in the early days of the scholarly study of the relationship between the shorter LXX and the longer MT texts of Job.

[13] For a discussion of these issues, see Cox, "Does a Shorter Hebrew Parent Text Underlie Old Greek Job?"

[14] Heater, *Translation Technique*, 6. Cf. B.O.G. Kvam, " 'Come, Let the Two of Us Go Out into the Field': The Targum Supplement to Genesis 4:8a – A Text-Immanent Reading?" in *Targum and Scripture: Studies in Aramaic Translations and Interpretation in Memory of Ernest G. Clarke* (ed. P.V.M. Flesher; Studies in the Aramaic Interpretation of Scripture 2; Leiden: Brill, 2002), 97–103 (99, n. 5), citing M.L. Klein, "Associative and Complementary Translation in the Targums," *ErIsr* 16 (1982): 134*–40*.

1) Job 7:2a (ὥσπερ θεράπων) + δεδοικὼς τὸν κύριον αὐτοῦ "(like an attendant) who fears his master" = Job 3:19b

2) Job 11:10b τίς ἐρεῖ αὐτῷ Τί ἐποίησας "who will say to him, 'What did you do?'" = Job 9:12b

3) Job 11:12b βροτὸς γεννητὸς γυναικός "a mortal, born of a woman" = Job 14:1a

4) Job 3:16a ὥσπερ ἔκτρωμα ἐκπορευόμενον ἐκ μήτρός μητρός "like a premature birth that comes from a mother's womb" = ὡσεὶ ἔκτρωμα ἐκπορευόμενον ἐκ μήτρας μητρός (may be translated identically) (Num 12:12a)

5) Job 4:21a ἐνεφύσησεν γὰρ αὐτοῖς καὶ ἐξηράνθησαν "he breathed on them and they withered" = ἔπνευσεν ἐπ' αὐτοὺς καὶ ἐξηράνθησαν "he blew upon them, and they withered" (Isa 40:24)

6) Job 13:9b προστεθήσεσθε αὐτῷ "you will join yourselves to him" = προστεθήσεσθε αὐτῷ (Deut 13:4)[15]

The translator makes additions to the text that have been created *ad hoc*. For example, at 19:4cd (an exegetical plus that draws on 15:3), the translator has Job admit that he was wrong:

λαλῆσαι ῥῆμα ὃ οὐκ ἔδει,
τὰ δὲ ῥήματά μου πλανᾶται καὶ οὐκ ἐπὶ καιροῦ

to have spoken a word that was not fitting, and my words err and are inappropriate.

In other instances, the translator replaces parts of verses: for example, Job 24:14a; 31:35b, 37; 32:17 (reduced to one line); 34:19c, 23b. Thus, the translator omits all of MT-Job 34:23 and replaces it with one line that summarizes v. 21 and at the same time serves to introduce the liturgical passage that follows in vv. 24–27. The single line appears as v. 23b in the ecclesiastical text: ὁ γὰρ κύριος πάντας ἐφορᾷ "For the Lord observes all people."

The translator often paraphrases the text of the speeches, constructing lines out of a few words of the source text and passing over other words and phrases for apparently no reason; however, these aspects of the translation are surely part of an overall approach to the text, as in Job 6:7:

MT מאנה לנגוע נפשי המה כדוי לחמי
*NRSV My appetite refuses to touch them;
they are like food that is loathsome to me.[16]
NJPS I refuse to touch them;
They are like food when I am sick.

LXX οὐ δύναται γὰρ παύσασθαί μου ἡ ψυχή·
βρόμον γὰρ ὁρῶ τὰ σῖτά μου ὥσπερ ὀσμὴν λέοντος.
*NETS So my life cannot cease,
for I loathe my food like the smell of a lion.

This verse forms a conclusion to the complaint begun in Job 6:5. English translations often add "them" as an object for לנגוע "to touch," in which case the referent appears to be the foods of v. 6.

The LXX translator adds γάρ, used as a confirmatory adv., "so." נפשי (interpreted as "my appetite" in *NRSV) is rendered literally with μου ἡ ψυχή "my life," and οὐ δύναται γὰρ παύσασθαι "is not able to cease" is loosely related to מאנה "(my life) refuses." The second line is joined to the first with the addition of γάρ, used now as a causative, "for." As it stands, MT-Job 6:7b reads literally, "they (are) as illness, my food." The translator paraphrases המה כדוי "they (are) as illness" with βρόμον ὁρῶ "I see something stinking," glossed in *NETS as "I loathe"; τὰ σῖτά μου "my food," an accusative of respect, renders לחמי literally. To "I loathe my food," the translator adds the striking simile ὥσπερ ὀσμὴν λέοντος "like the smell of a lion." Job says that his life cannot end as long as he is able to feel repulsion: it attests he is still alive.

Not much can be concluded from the examination of a single verse, but several elements of the translator's style are evident: the addition of particles (γάρ, twice); passing over words (לנגוע "to

---

[15] Items 1–5 are drawn from Heater, *Translation Technique*, who, in turn, is dependent upon Beer, *Hiob* and/or Dhorme, *Job* for nos. 1–3 and 5; no. 4, according to Heater, was also noted independently by T. Muraoka, "Literary Device in the Septuagint," *Textus* 8 (1973): 29–30.

[16] Meaning of Hebrew uncertain.

touch"; המה "they") to ferret out a translation suitable for the context; the loose relation to the source text (οὐ δύναται ... παύσασθαι "cannot cease" for מאנה "refuses"); continuation of the same person, 1st sg., from Job 6:7a through v. 7b (3rd pl. in Hebrew); use of a finite verb (ὁρῶ "I see") in what was a verbless clause in the parent text (v. 7b); the addition of a memorable simile ("like the smell of a lion"). The result is that the LXX translation bears little resemblance to its source text.

LXX-Job often cannot be retroverted into Hebrew because retroversions depend on a certain literalness in the translated text (→ 1.3.1.1.11). In turn, this means that LXX-Job is equally as often not useful for the textual criticism of the Hebrew Job (→ 11.2.2). The days are past when LXX-Job functioned as a mine for (retroverted) readings with which to emend the Hebrew.

The translator's approach to the Hebrew text and the freedom with which it is handled indicate that there was often no established, authoritative understanding of the Hebrew, or, if there was, the translator was disinclined to follow it. However, there are occasional agreements with 11QtgJob and T-Job that indicate a similar interpretation of the Hebrew.

11.3.1.4 History of Research

Important contributions to the study of LXX-Job in the modern period include, after Ziegler's edition, those of Beer, Dhorme, Gerleman, Orlinsky, Heater, and Gorea (see → Bibliography). For English readers, the translation of LXX-Job in *NETS also marks a milestone.

In chronological sequence, Beer sums up the work of nineteenth-century scholars and provides innumerable suggestive retroversions of LXX-Job into Hebrew. Dhorme incorporates the work of Beer and adds to it in his magisterial commentary, filled with text-critical observations. Gerleman brought to the fore the character of LXX-Job as Greek literature. Orlinsky's articles contributed to an understanding of translation technique and confronted assertions that over-emphasized the anti-anthropomorphic *tendenz* of the translator. Heater studies in detail an aspect of the translation technique in LXX-Job, the incorporation of pieces of text from elsewhere, as noted above (→ 11.3.1.3). Gorea examines the abbreviation of LXX-Job by analyzing the character of the pieces of text passed over. Mention should also be made of the contribution of Joosten,[17] who observed that meanings of Hebrew words in *late* Hebrew serve to explain some LXX renderings in LXX-Job and elsewhere in the LXX.

Among commentaries, aside from Dhorme, none is better than that of Clines in the attention given to LXX-Job in its text-critical notes. Gordis' work is also often helpful and, while Fohrer's comments on LXX-Job are not frequent, they are reliable. The commentary of Driver and Gray is less helpful than Dhorme, and the recent commentary of John Gray fails to live up to the statement on the cover of the book – "rich in text-critical detail" – with respect to its attention to LXX-Job (→ 1.3.1.1.12).

11.3.1.5 Relevance for Exegesis

LXX-Job contributes to our understanding of the book of Job as it was read by one prodigious, insightful scholar in the Alexandrian Jewish community in the late second century B.C.E. For example, the translation contains a well-developed vocabulary related to wrongdoing. Generally, the numerous Hebrew words for wrong are reduced to ἀδικία "injustice," ἀνομία "lawlessness," ἀσέβεια "impiety," and their cognates: the ἀδικία word group renders eleven different Hebrew words; the ἀνομία word group renders five. The translator of LXX-Job employs ἀσέβεια for רשע "wickedness," as in the Psalms (→ 10.3.1) and Wisdom literature (→ 12.3.1; → 13–17.1.1.3; → II.4.2; → 11.15.2): wrongdoing is understood in religious terms, as impiety. The use of ἀσέβεια with respect to Job corresponds to its use in the wider Greek world, where Aristotle and Socrates were both accused of ἀσέβεια.[18] Lawlessness, in the context of Hellenistic Judaism, comprises offenses committed against the law of Moses, whereas in Greek society it had a more

---

[17] Joosten, "Aramaising Renderings."
[18] For details, see Cox, "Old Greek Job."

general meaning that included the contravention of customs and mores. The translator of LXX-Job makes it clear that the wrong of which Job is being accused was lawlessness (Job 34:27). Notable for its sociological implications, LXX-Job adds to the circle of words for wrongdoers the word δυνάστης "ruler," chosen to render רשע "wicked" (Job 9:23) and עריץ "ruthless" (Job 6:23; 15:20; 27:13): the powerful are counted among the unjust, lawless, and impious.[19]

Beer, G., *Der Text des Buches Hiob* (Marburg: N.G. Elwertsche Verlagsbuchhandlung, 1897).

Clines, D.J.A., *Job 1–20* (WBC 17; Waco: Word Books, 1989).

Clines, D.J.A., *Job 21–37* (WBC 18A; Nashville: Thomas Nelson, 2006).

Clines, D.J.A., *Job 38–42* (WBC 18B; Nashville: Thomas Nelson, 2011).

Cox, C., "Vocabulary for Wrongdoing and Forgiveness in the Greek Translations of Job," *Textus* 15 (1990): 119–30.

Cox, C., "The Historical, Social and Literary Context of Old Greek Job," in *XII Congress of the International Organization for Septuagint and Cognate Studies, Leiden 2004* (ed. M.K.H. Peters; SBLSCS 54; Atlanta: SBL, 2006), 105–16.

Cox, C., "Iob, Translation and Introduction," in *NETS, 667–96.

Cox, C., "The Nature of Lucian's Revision of the Text of Greek Job," in *Scripture in Transition: Essays on Septuagint, Hebrew Bible, and Dead Sea Scrolls in Honour of Raija Sollamo* (eds. A. Voitila and J. Jokiranta; JSJSup 126; Leiden: Brill, 2008), 423–42.

Cox, C., "Does a Shorter Hebrew Parent Text Underlie Old Greek Job?" in *In the Footsteps of Sherlock Holmes: Studies in the Biblical Text in Honour of Anneli Aejmelaeus* (eds. T.M. Law, K. De Troyer, and M. Liljeström; CBET 72; Leuven: Peeters, 2014), 451–62.

Cox, C., "Job," in *T & T Clark Companion to the Septuagint* (ed. James K. Aitken; London: Bloomsbury T & T Clark, 2015), 385–400.

Dhorme, É., *A Commentary on the Book of Job* (trans. H. Knight; 2nd ed.; Nashville: Nelson, 1984 [1st ed. 1967; French original: Le livre de Job (Paris: Gabalda, 1926)]).

Driver, S.R. and G.B. Gray, *A Critical and Exegetical Commentary on the Book of Job* (ICC; Edinburgh: T & T Clark, 1921).

Fernández Marcos, N., "The Septuagint Reading of the Book of Job," in *The Book of Job* (ed. W.A.M. Beuken; BETL 114; Leuven: University Press/Peeters, 1994), 251–66.

Fohrer, G., *Das Buch Hiob* (KAT 16; Gütersloh: Gerd Mohn, 1963).

Gentry, P., *The Asterisked Materials in the Greek Job* (SBLSCS 38; Atlanta: Scholars Press, 1995).

Gerleman, G., *Studies in the Septuagint*, Vol. 1: *Book of Job* (LUÅ 1.43.2; Lund: C.W.K. Gleerup, 1946).

Gordis, R., *The Book of Job: Commentary, New Translation and Special Studies* (Moreshet Series 2; New York: Jewish Theological Seminary of America, 1978).

Gorea, M., *Job repensé ou trahi? Omissions et raccourcis de la Septante* (EBib 56; Paris: J. Gabalda, 2007).

Gray, J., *The Book of Job* (ed. D.J.A. Clines; The Text of the Hebrew Bible 1; Sheffield: Sheffield Phoenix Press, 2010).

Heater, H., *A Septuagint Translation Technique in the Book of Job* (CBQMS 11; Washington: Catholic Biblical Association of America, 1982).

Joosten, J., "On Aramaising Renderings in the Septuagint," in *Hamlet on a Hill: Semitic and Greek Studies Presented to Professor T. Muraoka on the Occasion of his Sixty-Fifth Birthday* (eds. M.F.J. Baasten and W.T. van Peursen; OLA 118; Leuven: Peeters, 2003), 587–600.

Kepper, M. and M. Witte, "Job: Das Buch Ijob/Hiob," in *Septuaginta Deutsch, Erläuterungen*, 2.2041–2126.

Konkel, A., "The Elihu Speeches in the Greek Translation of Job," in *"Translation Is Required": The Septuagint in Retrospect and Prospect* (ed. R.J.V. Hiebert; SBLSCS 56; Atlanta: SBL, 2010), 135–57.

Kutz, K., *The Old Greek of Job: A Study of Early Biblical Exegesis* (unpub. PhD diss., University of Wisconsin-Madison, 1997).

Kutz, K., "Characterization in the Old Greek of Job," in *Seeking out the Wisdom of the Ancients: Essays Offered to Honor of Michael V. Fox on the Occasion of his Sixty-Fifth Birthday* (eds. R.L. Troxel, K.G. Friebel, and D.R. Magary; Winona Lake: Eisenbrauns, 2005), 345–55.

Orlinsky, H., "Studies in the Septuagint of the Book of Job," *HUCA* 28 (1957): 53–74; 29 (1958): 229–71; 30 (1959): 153–67; 32 (1961): 239–68; 33 (1962): 119–51; 35 (1964): 57–78; 36 (1965): 37–47.

Pietersma, A., "Review of J. Ziegler, Iob, Septuaginta: Vetus Testamentum Graecum 11/4," *JBL* 104 (1985): 305–11.

---

[19] See Cox, "Vocabulary," 124–25.

Ziegler, J., *Iob* (Septuaginta Vetus Testamentum Graecum 11.4; Göttingen: Vandenhoeck & Ruprecht, 1982).

Claude Cox

11.3.2 Pre-Hexaplaric Greek Translations

See → 11.3.5 Hexaplaric Greek Translations (Job > Primary Translations).

11.3.3 Targum and Qumran Aramaic Versions

11.3.3.1 Targum
11.3.3.1 Targum Job
11.3.3.1.1 Background, Date, Milieu and Purpose of Targum Job

In addition to its inclusion of passages attesting an apparently early usage of "Memra" (→ 11.3.3.1.3), Targum Job contains a variety of exegetic traditions and usages that may be found in the New Testament, pseudepigraphical texts,[1] and indeed the ancient versions.[2] Moreover, already in the late nineteenth century, Bacher had pointed out links between traditions found in Targum Job and the Tannaitic traditions of the Mishnah.[3] Yet, as is often the case, internal evidence for a firm *terminus a quo* is elusive. There is little reason to associate Targum Job with rabbinic mention of a "Targum" of Job that was proscribed during the first century C.E., even if, as seems likely this translation was in Aramaic.[4] Indeed, while the addition of "Ishmael" (→ 11.3.3.1.3) might be taken as an indirect cipher (via Esau) for Rome, Bacher associates it rather more plausibly with Islam and sees it as evidence for the Targum's emergence after the conquest.[5] It is thus with some justification that Epstein[6] warns against drawing any such conclusions from the interpolation of names drawn (→ 11.3.3.1.3) from Judaism's historiographical traditions. While Targum Job certainly contains early traditions, the linguistic profile of Late Jewish Literary Aramaic (→ 11.3.3.1.3) suggests that Targum Job is not likely to have emerged much before the midrashim and the talmudic and gaonic traditions with which it and other Targumim of the Writings have most in common.[7] Indeed, the only certainty is that Targum Job must have emerged by the time of Saadia Gaon (882–942 C.E.) who cites it extensively.[8] Because Job was not used liturgically (as were for instance, the Pentateuch, Prophets, and even the Megillot), its Targum seems likely to have been produced as a compendium of authoritative translations and interpretations of the notoriously difficult Hebrew text of Job.

11.3.3.1.2 Textual Witnesses, Editions, and Translations

The textual witnesses to the Targum of Job are found in a diversity of manuscripts and printed editions that have begun to be explored only in recent years. Building on initial efforts by Weiss,[9] and Fernández Vallina,[10] Stec has produced a comprehensive critical edition of the text of the Targum of Job that includes the known manuscripts and principal printed editions.[11] The current stemmatological position is essentially a refinement of the early findings of Weiss, who arranged the manuscripts at his disposal into general divisions that correspond to the four groupings arrived at subsequently by Fernández Vallina. The first and largest of Stec's groups includes manuscript Vat., Bib. Apostol. Urbinas I, which serves as the base text for his critical edition. A second group that includes various manuscripts and the Antwerp Polyglot (1570)[12] appears to reflect a Sephardi tradition from northern Spain and

---

[1] For examples see Mangan, *Targum of Job*, 6.
[2] See Mangan, *Targum of Job*, 7 for examples of parallels with Peshitta (→ 11.3.4), Vulgate (→ 11.3.7), and to a lesser extent the Greek versions (→ 11.3.1; → 11.3.5; → 11.3.6).
[3] W. Bacher, "Das Targum zu Hiob," *MGWJ* 20 (1871): 213–23.
[4] *T. Šabb.* 13:2; cf. *b. Šabb.* 115a; *y. Šabb.* 16:1.
[5] Bacher, "Targum zu Hiob," 222.
[6] See n. 23.

[7] See P.V.M. Flesher and B. Chilton, *The Targums: A Critical Introduction* (Waco: Baylor University Press, 2011), 235–37.
[8] For references to Targum Job in early medieval texts, see Mangan, *Targum of Job*, 8.
[9] Weiss, *Aramaic Targum*.
[10] F.J. Fernández Vallina, *El Targum de Job* (Madrid: Editorial de la Universidad Complutense de Madrid, 1982).
[11] Stec, *The Text of the Targum*.
[12] *Biblia Sacra Hebraice, Chaldaice, Graece et Latina* ... (ed. B. Arias Montano; Antwerp: Christophorus Plantinus, 1569–1572).

Africa, while the third group may or may not belong to a Sephardi tradition, but has been shown subsequently to include manuscript Nürnberg, Stadtbibliothek Nürnberg, a witness that was clearly used in producing the first Rabbinic Bible (*RB1).[13] A fourth group includes two manuscripts, Paris, Bib. Nat. Heb. 17 and Parma, Bib. Palatina 3231. In addition to the expected variations arising from differing orthographic traditions and typical scribal activities, the textual traditions of Targum Job include, to varying degrees, alternative translations of whole verses under such rubrics as לשון/תרגם אחר "another version/edition" (e.g., Job 36:33, which includes both rubrics).[14] This phenomenon seems likely to reflect copyists' incorporation of variant translation traditions found by them in the margins of the manuscripts they were copying.[15] While Mangan's English translation of the Targum of Job is based on Vallina's critical edition (base text: manuscript Camb. Univ. Lib Or. Ee. 5.9), her comments and annotations refer to the manuscript traditions and, along with her introduction, offer a wealth of useful information.[16]

11.3.3.1.3 Language, Translation Character, and Technique

The presence of Greek, Latin, and even Persian loan words in the Aramaic of Targum Job and the latter's varied points of contact with other Aramaic dialects was already known and documented by Weiss,[17] but the subsequent clarification of the Targum's linguistic affinity to other Targumim of the Writings and Targum Pseudo-Jonathan has led to the classification of its language as Late Jewish Literary Aramaic (LJLA), which is itself a mixture of elements from various dialects.[18] Given the comparatively large number of texts written in LJLA and the liturgical use of the Targumim of the Megillot in which it is found, it is not inconceivable that LJLA was once a living dialect.[19] It seems more likely, however, that its curious linguistic admixture reflects not a living spoken language, but an artificial and specifically literary blend of languages of the sort seen by Scholem in the Zohar.[20]

Unlike some other Targumim to the Writings, such as Targum Esther (Sheni) and Targum Song of Songs (→ 13–17.1.3), Targum Job essentially conforms to the unusual translational approach characteristic of the Targumim.[21] Thus, on one hand, Targum Job insists on offering an equivalent for each Hebrew element in the order in which it appears in the source text, even at the expense of expected Aramaic idiom.[22] While linguistic/stylistic accommodation to the demands of Aramaic is thus comparatively limited, substitutional modifications of number (e.g. Job 5:5) and determination etc.,[23] are accompanied by the Targum's interpolation of particles, prepositions,[24] words, phrases,

---

[13] D. Shepherd, "Before Bomberg: The case of the Targum of Job in the Rabbinic Bible and the Solger Codex," *Bib* 79 (1998): 360–79.

[14] For further discussion and a fuller listing, see Mangan, *Targum of Job*, 10–11.

[15] Weiss, *Aramaic Targum*, xvii and Mangan, *Targum of Job*, 10–11. This practice is also found in Targumim Qohelet and Psalms and appears analogous to the midrashic rubric, *debar aher*.

[16] Mangan, *Targum of Job*.

[17] Weiss, *Aramaic Targum*, 75–95.

---

[18] E. Cook, "Rewriting the Bible: The Text and the Language of the Pseudo-Jonathan Targum" (unpubl. PhD diss., University of California at Los Angeles, 1986). Indeed, Targum Job shares more linguistic features with Pseudo-Jonathan than do any of its fellow Targumim to the Writings (cf. p. 276).

[19] P.V.M. Flesher, "The Literary Legacy of the Priests? The Pentateuchal Targums of Israel in their Social and Linguistic Context," in *The Ancient Synagogue from Its Origins until 200 C.E.: Papers Presented at an International Conference at Lund University, October 14–17 2001* (eds. B. Olsson and M. Zetterholm; Stockholm: Almqvist & Wiksell, 2003), 467–508.

[20] Cook, "Rewriting the Bible," 278.

[21] For a recent and accessible discussion of the translational character of Targum, see Flesher and Chilton, *The Targums*, chs. 1–2.

[22] For discussion of Targum Job's representation of the Hebrew text, see D. Shepherd, *Targum and Translation: A Reconsideration of the Qumran Aramaic Version of Job* (Assen: Van Gorcum, 2004).

[23] See E.L. Epstein, "A Critical Analysis of Chapters 1–26 of the Targum to the Book of Job" (PhD diss., University of Chicago, 1944), 104.

[24] See H.M. Szpek, "On the Influence of the Targum on the Peshitta to Job," in *Targum Studies*, Vol. 2: *Targum and Peshitta*

and whole sentences without formal correspondence in the Hebrew text. While greater study of Targum Job's translational consistency is required, such substitutions and interpolations, integrated seamlessly into Targum Job's Aramaic rendering of the Hebrew, reflect not only an accommodation of the Hebrew to the Aramaic idiom, but also the Targum's variable approach to rendering poetic aspects of the Hebrew of Job. Thus, while the parallelism of the Hebrew poetry is largely reproduced,[25] the Targum's addition of דרא דטובענא "the generation of the flood" in its rendering of Job 4:8 disrupts the poetic sequence of the Hebrew and identical Hebrew words in a single verse are regularly rendered with different Aramaic ones (e.g., Job 8:3; 27:13).[26] Yet, such variable translation sits alongside consistent renderings in other cases, including Aramaic חזור חזור "around, around" for Hebrew סָבִיב "all around" (e.g. Job 1:10; 18:11; 19:10).

In many cases, substitutions and interpolations arise from Targum Job's explication of the often-difficult text of Job in light of traditions gleaned from elsewhere in the Hebrew Scriptures and the ancient Jewish traditions that received them. Thus, in view of the association of Job with the period of the patriarchs, it is not surprising that Targum Job supplies references especially to Abraham, but also to Isaac and Jacob (see, e.g., Job 3:19; 4:7; 5:17; 15:10; 30:19).[27] Less positively, the generation of the flood is invoked repeatedly as a cipher for wickedness (Job 4:8; 6:17; 22:16, 17 [though Noah is mentioned]; 24:2)[28] while Jacob's daughter Dinah is associated with Job's recalcitrant wife (Job 2:9; cf. also *b. B. Bat.* 15a), and Esau (Job 4:10), Ishmael (Job 4:10, 11; 12:6), and Lot (Job 4:11; 14:18) are mentioned in association with waywardness. Exemplars of ungodliness from beyond the patriarchal narratives are also introduced, including Balaam (Job 5:21), Sihon and Og (Job 5:22), as well as the Canaanites (Job 5:23), and the eponymous Edom (Job 4:10), and Amalek (Job 5:20) etc. Unsurprisingly, Pharaoh and the Egyptians are also cited unfavourably (Job 5:12; 7:12). Targum Job's interest in angelic beings – first visible in Job 1:6 where "sons of God (בני האלהים)" is changed to "sons of angels (בני מלאכיא)" – leads to the introduction of Michael, Gabriel (both Job 25:2 [variant]), and Sammael (Job 28:7) as well as unnamed others both at birth (Job 3:3) and death (Job 18:13; 28:22).

Whereas the Hebrew of Job refers largely to Sheol, Targum Job introduces the notion of the world/life to come (e.g. Job 5:4; 15:21), referencing the prospect of resurrection (e.g. Job 11:17; 14:14) as well as gehenna, with its fuller association of punitive judgement (e.g. Job 2:11; 3:17; 5:4, 7; 15:21; 17:6; 20:26; 28:5; 38:17, 23). So, too, Targum Job's interest in the ultimate fate of the righteous and the wicked encourages an eschatological elaboration of a decisive judgment to come (see Job 1:6, 21; 10:16). Yet, unlike the Hebrew of Job, the Targum insists that one's fate in such a time of judgment depends on one's faithful keeping and study of Torah (אוריתא "law"; cf. Job 3:17; 5:7; 11:8; 22:22; 24:13; 30:4; 36:33; 37:21).[29]

Along with Targum Job's reverence for Torah, it sometimes appears reticent to represent God anthropomorphically, with מחת "blow" being added to (Job 1:11; 2:5; 12:9) or replacing the divine יָד "hand" (Job 19:21; 30:24) and שכינה "Shekinah" substituted for the divine פנה "face" (Job 13:24). Nevertheless, such a practice is far from consistent, with the divine "lips" (Job 11:5), "nostrils" (Job 4:9), "heart" (Job 36:5), and even "hand" sometimes retained in Targum Job's translation. Indeed, while the divine נְשָׁמָה "breath" is replaced with Aramaic מימר "Memra" (e.g. Job 4:9; 32:8; 33:4; 37:10), the extensive use of the latter in Targum Job may reflect an evolutionary development, with its initial pronominal usage for humans (e.g. Job 7:8; 19:18) being eventually extended to include God himself (e.g. Job 1:10, 11 etc.) before being used as a divine ti-

---

(ed. P.V.M. Flesher; South Florida Studies in the History of Judaism 165; Atlanta: Scholars Press, 1998), 142–58 (152–53).

[25] Epstein, "A Critical Analysis," 96.

[26] See Mangan, *Targum of Job*, 14 for other examples of Targum Job's treatment of poetic aspects of the Hebrew text.

[27] For further discussion and parallels in the rabbinic literature, see Mangan, *Targum of Job*, ad loc.

[28] As noted by Flesher and Chilton, *The Targums*, 255.

[29] For the significance of Torah in Targum Job, see Flesher and Chilton, *The Targums*, 257–58.

tle (e.g. Job 1:21; 2:9) and eventually replacing some anthropomorphic terms in relation to the deity (as indicated above).[30]

11.3.3.1.4 Value as a Witness to the Hebrew Text
While Targum Job may on occasion aid in the recovery of a forgotten nuance of the Hebrew text (e.g. Job 4:14),[31] only rarely does it appear to bear witness to a Hebrew *Vorlage* at variance with MT (e.g. Job 31:18).[32] While Targum Job typically follows the *Qere*, there are instances when the *Ketiv* is reflected instead (e.g. Job 6:23; 19:29; 41:4).[33]

Mangan, C., *The Targum of Job* (ArBib 15; Collegeville: The Liturgical Press, 1991).
Stec, D., *The Text of the Targum of Job: An Introduction and Critical Edition* (AGJU 20; Leiden: Brill, 1996).
Weiss, R., *The Aramaic Targum of Job* (Tel Aviv: Tel Aviv University Press, 1979) [Hebr. and Eng.].

David Shepherd

11.3.3.2 Qumran Aramaic Versions of Job
11.3.3.2.1 Background
Following their discovery, and the publication of their *editiones principes*, initial research focused on the Qumran Aramaic versions' presumed witness to the underlying Hebrew texts of Job. Subsequent study has compared these Aramaic translations to other ancient versions of Job, with attention increasingly focused on their relationship to other Aramaic versions.[1] Given the date, provenance, and distinctive character of the Qumran Aramaic versions of Job vis-à-vis the Targumim (see below), it seems likely that they circulated independently from the latter and, on the basis of datable manuscripts, may have done so considerably earlier. Such a conclusion invites speculation that 11Q10 (in scholarly literature often referred to as 11QtgJob) and 4Q157 (in scholarly literature often referred to as 4QtgJob)[2] are to be identified with certain "translations of Job" remembered by a rabbinic baraita (*t. Šabb.* 13:2; cf. *b. Šabb.* 115a; *y. Šabb.* 16:1) in which both Rabban Gamaliel and his grandson of the same name gave orders to remove one or more translations of Job from circulation. While the reasons for this removal remain unstated, it is not impossible that these translations of Job were rejected by successive generations of rabbis who objected to Aramaic translations which, like those found at Qumran, lacked not only the Targum's interpretive interpolations but also its highly literal representation of the Hebrew text (→ 11.3.3.1).

11.3.3.2.2 Original Form, Date, and Milieu
While the fragments of 4Q157 preserve an Aramaic version of only a few verses of Job chs. 3–5, 11Q10 preserves a translation of much of the dialogues of Job 17:14–36:3 on a collection of over thirty leather fragments, and the better part of Job 37:10–42:11 on a single roll.[3] Given their respective provenances in Caves 4 and 11 and differences of orthography, 4Q157 and 11Q10 likely reflect two different Aramaic versions of Job,[4] though the orthography of 4Q157 is similar to that found in the Aramaic version of Leviticus found in the same cave (4Q156).[5] While there is too little preserved of 4Q157 to allow it to be dated with certainty, the form of Aramaic into which the Hebrew of Job has been rendered in 11Q10 (see below) suggests it may have been produced as early as the third century B.C.E., although paleographic analysis and a selection of later linguistic traits may indicate an origin nearer to the

---

[30] R. Weiss, "The Translation of Anthropomorphic Expressions in Targum Job," *Tarbiz* 44 (1974): 54–71 [Hebr.].
[31] See L.L. Grabbe, *Comparative Philology and the Text of Job: A Study in Methodology* (SBLDS 34; Missoula: Scholars Press, 1977).
[32] Weiss, *Aramaic Targum*, 104–06.
[33] Weiss, *Aramaic Targum*, xii. To these instances, Mangan, *Targum of Job*, 14 adds Job 5:5 and 33:28.
[1] For a fuller discussion of the history of research relating to the Aramaic versions of Job, see Shepherd, *Targum and Translation*, 1–16.

[2] The use of the terms 4QJob ar and 11QJob ar rather than 4QtgJob and 11QtgJob reflect the increasing scholarly recognition of the ways in which these versions are different in character from later rabbinic Targumim.
[3] For a fuller discussion of the physical remains of 11Q10 and 4Q157, see respectively: *DJD* XXIII, 79–86 and *DJD* VI, 90.
[4] R.I. Vasholz, "4 Q Targum Job versus 11 Q Targum Job," *RevQ* 11 (1982): 109.
[5] For discussion of the likely date of 4Q157, see *DJD* VI, 90.

turn of the era, at which time the extant manuscript appears to have been copied in a Herodian hand.⁶ Apart from furnishing a likely *terminus ad quem* of 70 C.E., the Qumran provenance of the fragments may well point toward a Palestinian origin, though few have been persuaded by arguments for a specifically sectarian association.⁷

11.3.3.2.3 Selected Editions

- *DJD VI, 90, pl. xxviii [*editio princeps*].
- *DJD XXIII.
- Van der Ploeg and van der Woude, *Le Targum de Job de la Grotte XI de Qumrân*.
- Sokoloff, *The Targum to Job from Qumran Cave 11*.

11.3.3.2.4 Language, Translation Character, and Technique

The original editors suggested on the basis of stylistic and grammatical considerations that the Aramaic language of 11Q10 belongs to the late second century B.C.E., a conclusion supported by the subsequent study of Sokoloff.⁸ While other studies have suggested both earlier and later dates for the language,⁹ what may be said with reasonable confidence about the language is that: 1) it should be classified as Qumran Aramaic and/or Standard Jewish Literary Aramaic; 2) it appears somewhat earlier than that which appears in 1QapGen ar, with which it, however, shares many features; and 3) its inclusion of various grammatical and morphological features typically found in texts that are earlier and later and from Western and Eastern provenances reflects a phase of Aramaic that is in transition from Official/Imperial Aramaic to the later dialects.¹⁰ Thus, by way of illustration, the use of the preposition קדם "before" in 11Q10 (e.g. Job 42:1 [col. 11Q10 XXXVII:3]) is much more sporadic and of a different sort than the more widespread and evolved distribution found in the Targumim.¹¹ Likewise, while 11Q10 appears to employ the locution מאמר "word" as a substitute for Heb. פה "mouth" (Job 39:27 [11Q10 XXXIII:8], perhaps also Job 36:32) this reflects an early stage in the development of this usage that would blossom in the later Targumim.¹²

While the bulk of the Aramaic translator's divergences relate to the extraction of an idiomatic and intelligible Aramaic from the notoriously difficult Hebrew of Job, the Aramaic translator's exegetical interests may be seen in, for example, his demythologizing preference for "the morning stars" of Job 38:7 to חדא "shine" (Aram.) rather than "sing" (Heb. רן) and for "all the angels (Aram. מלאכי) of God" rather than "all the sons (בני) of God" to shout for joy. That the Targum and Peshitta versions of this same verse offer comparable adjustments at this point, however, suggests a shared exegetical aversion within the Aramaic tradition.

That such common exegetical cause is so rare, however, reflects the modest quantity and limited character of 11Q10's interpretation (akin to s-Job [→ 11.3.4] and LXX-Job [→ 11.3.1]) as opposed to those typically found in the targumic tradition

---

⁶ On the dating of 11Q10, see the discussion in Shepherd, *Targum and Translation*, 3–6.

⁷ As presented particularly by Tuinstra, *Hermeneutische Aspecten*.

⁸ Sokoloff, *The Targum to Job*, 9.

⁹ Kaufman, "The Job Targum from Qumran," 327, sees 11Q10 as belonging to the first century B.C.E., while R.I. Vasholz, "A Philological Comparison of the Qumran Job Targum and its Implications for the Dating of Daniel" (unpubl. PhD diss., Stellenbosch University, 1976) sees more affinities between 11Q10 and the older Aramaic texts and therefore dates it earlier (late third/early second century B.C.E.).

¹⁰ For a recent discussion of the Aramaic of Qumran (including 11Q10), see the linguistic/philological essays and appended discussions collected in K. Berthelot and D. Stökl Ben Ezra (eds.), *Aramaica Qumranica: Proceedings of the Conference on the Aramaic Texts from Qumran at Aix en Provence 30 June–2 July 2008* (STDJ 94; Leiden: Brill, 2010).

¹¹ See J. Joosten, "L' araméen de Qumran entre l' araméen d' empire et les Targumim: L' emploi de la préposition 'devant' pour exprimer le respect dû au roi et à Dieu," in *Aramaica Qumranica: Proceedings of the Conference on the Aramaic Texts from Qumran at Aix en Provence 30 June–2 July 2008* (eds. K. Berthelot and D. Stökl Ben Ezra; STDJ 94; Leiden: Brill, 2010), 83–96.

¹² See W.E. Aufrecht, "Aramaic Studies and the Book of Job," *Studies in Religion Supplements* 16 (1985): 63–65 who offers a cogent argument for seeing *Memra* "word" as being used initially as a simple equivalent of Hebrew פה "mouth" (whether human or divine), before eventually being restricted in the Palestinian Targum tradition to rendering God's פה.

(→ 1.3.3). More specifically, whereas Targum Job regularly interpolates within its Aramaic translation characters (e.g. Abraham, Isaac, Jacob) of the sacred history and the concerns of Jewish tradition (e.g. Torah, gehenna, etc.) (→ 11.3.3.1.3), 11Q10 displays none of this nor even a targumic willingness to significantly supplement its translation with amplifications of any great significance.[13] Moreover, 11Q10's willingness to omit and transpose elements of its Hebrew source text in its Aramaic translation suggests that, in terms of translation approach, the latter's primary affinity lies with the Peshitta of Job, which manifests similar tendencies, rather than the Targum of Job, with its scrupulous and sequential reproduction of each element of the Hebrew.[14] While the translational consistency of 11Q10 awaits substantive analysis, preliminary suggestions indicate that this version is more likely to render the same Hebrew word with a variety of different Aramaic words than is for instance the Targum of Job, which displays comparatively greater consistency.[15] As the Cave 4 and Cave 11 fragments do not translate the same portion of the Hebrew text of Job, synoptic comparison is not possible. However, the supplying of the Aramaic consecutive conjunction (where it is not attested in MT [→ 11.2.2]) on two occasions in 4Q157's meager fragments finds a clear correspondence in 11Q10, where the same conjunction is regularly supplied unprompted by the Hebrew and in identical circumstances.[16] Such a practice thus offers a marked contrast to the practice of the later Targumim, which are typically scrupulous in their reproduction of the minutiae of their Hebrew source.

11.3.3.2.5 Text-Critical Value

While, in general, scholars have concluded that 11Q10 seems to reflect a MT-type *Vorlage* (→ 11.2.2),[17] various commentators have suggested the reading of variants in 11Q10's *Vorlage* at different junctures.[18] So, for example, in Job 29:7, the similarity of 11Q10's ב[צפרין "in the morning/s" to LXX ὄρθριος "dawn" suggests to some that their shared *Vorlage* contained שחר "dawn" rather than MT's שַׁעַר "gate,"[19] with the confusion of the laryngeals being the root of the problem.[20] That MT's שַׁעַר "gate" is, however, also rendered with its Aramaic equivalent in 11Q10 (תרעי) here suggests the translator's willingness to offer double translations, as is common in other ancient versions.[21] So, too, the absence of Job 21:23 from both LXX-Job (→ 11.3.1) and 11Q10 may suggest this verse was missing from their respective *Vorlagen*;[22] this also may be the case in 11Q10's omission of a translation of Job 42:3 and the appearance of Job 40:5 in its place. Nevertheless, it is impossible to be entirely certain whether the final verses found in the Hebrew (Job 42:12–17) and perhaps even the longer epilogue contained in LXX-Job (and attributed by it to a "Syrian" tradition) were omitted by 11Q10, missing from its *Vorlage*, or subsequently perished due to the elements.[23] Moreover, the similarity between the adjustments seen in the

---

[13] For an example of the differences of approach between the Aramaic versions of Job, see S. Gold, "Making Sense of Job 37.13: Translation Strategies in 11Q10, Peshitta and the Rabbinic Targum," in *Biblical Hebrew, Biblical Texts: Essays in Memory of Michael P. Weitzman* (eds. A. Rapoport and G. Greenberg; JSOTSup 333; Sheffield: Sheffield Academic Press, 2001), 282–302.

[14] Shepherd, *Targum and Translation*.

[15] See Shepherd, *Targum and Translation*, 59.

[16] Shepherd, "Targum and Taxonomy," 189–206.

---

[17] Sokoloff, *The Targum to Job*, 6.

[18] The witness of 11Q10 to a non-MT *Vorlage* is of particular interest to F. Morrow, "11Q Targum Job and the Massoretic Text," *RevQ* 8 (1973): 253–56; H. Ringgren, "Some Observations on the Qumran Targum of Job," *ASTI* 11 (1978): 117–26; B. Jongeling, "The Job Targum from Qumran Cave XI," *FO* 15 (1975): 181–86.

[19] See van der Ploeg and van der Woude, *Le Targum*, 38 and *DJD* XXIII, 115.

[20] See Sokoloff, *The Targum to Job*, 121; Tuinstra, *Hermeneutische Aspecten*, 77.

[21] For early discussion of this phenomenon in Hebrew and the versions, see S. Talmon, "Double Readings in the Massoretic Text," *Textus* 1 (1960): 144–84 (also published in Talmon, *"Double Readings")*.

[22] As suggested by B.E. Zuckerman, "The Process of Translation in 11QtgJob: A Preliminary Study" (unpubl. PhD diss., Yale University, 1980), 194.

[23] For discussion of the relationship between 11Q10, LXX, and MT, see Gray, "The Massoretic Text of the Book of Job."

Qumran and Syriac translations (→ 11.3.4) would seem to suggest that the linguistic-stylistic constraints of Aramaic, rather than shared vernacular in the *Vorlage*, offer the most straightforward explanation for most of 11Q10's divergences from MT.[24]

Beyer, K., *Die aramäischen Texte vom Toten Meer samt den Inschriften aus Palästina, dem Testament Levis aus der Kairoer Genisa, der Fastenrolle und den alten talmudischen Zitaten: Aramaistische Einleitung, Text, Übersetzung, Deutung, Grammatik, Wörterbuch, deutsch-aramäische Wortliste, Register*, Vol. 1 (Göttingen: Vandenhoeck & Ruprecht, 1984), 280–98.

Beyer, K., *Die aramäischen Texte vom Toten Meer samt den Inschriften aus Palästina, dem Testament Levis aus der Kairoer Genisa, der Fastenrolle und den alten talmudischen Zitaten: Aramaistische Einleitung, Text, Übersetzung, Deutung, Grammatik, Wörterbuch, deutsch-aramäische Wortliste, Register*, Supplement Vol. (Göttingen: Vandenhoeck & Ruprecht, 1994), 133.

Beyer, K., *Die aramäischen Texte vom Toten Meer samt den Inschriften aus Palästina, dem Testament Levis aus der Kairoer Genisa, der Fastenrolle und den alten talmudischen Zitaten: Aramaistische Einleitung, Text, Übersetzung, Deutung, Grammatik, Wörterbuch, deutsch-aramäische Wortliste, Register*, Vol. 2 (Göttingen: Vandenhoeck & Ruprecht, 2004), 171–72.

*DJD VI, 90, pl. xxviii [editio princeps].

*DJD XXIII.

Fitzmyer, J.A., "The Targum of Job from Qumran Cave XI," *CBQ* 36 (1974): 503–24.

Fitzmyer, J.A. and D.J. Harrington, "A Manual of Palestinian Aramaic Texts," *BibOr* 34 (1978): 10–47.

Gray, J., "The Massoretic Text of the Book of Job, the Targum and the Septuagint Version in the Light of the Qumran Targum," *ZAW* 86 (1974): 331–50.

Jongeling, B., C.J. Labuschagne, and A.S. van der Woude, *Aramaic Texts from Qumran: With Translations and Annotations* (SSS 4; Leiden: Brill, 1976), 1–73.

Kaufman, S.A., "The Job Targum from Qumran," *JAOS* 93 (1973): 317–27.

van der Ploeg, J.P.M. and A.S. van der Woude, *Le Targum de Job de la Grotte XI de Qumrân* (Leiden: Brill, 1971) [*editio princeps*].

Reed, S.A. and B.E. Zuckerman, "A Fragment of an Unstudied Column of 11QtgJob: A Preliminary Report," *The Comprehensive Aramaic Lexicon Newsletter* 10 (1993): 1–7.

Shepherd, D.J., *Targum and Translation: A Reconsideration of the Qumran Aramaic Version of Job* (SSN 45; Assen: Van Gorcum, 2004).

Shepherd, D.J., "What's in a name? Targum and Taxonomy in Cave 4 at Qumran," *JSP* 17.3 (2008): 189–206.

Sokoloff, M., *The Targum to Job from Qumran Cave II* (Bar Ilan Studies in Near Eastern Languages and Culture; Ramat-Gan: Bar Ilan University, 1974).

Tuinstra, E.W., "Hermeneutische Aspecten van de Targum van Job uit Grot XI" (PhD diss., University of Groningen, 1970).

York, A.D., "A Philological and Textual Analysis of the Qumran Job Targum (11QtgJob)" (unpubl. PhD diss., Cornell University, 1973).

David Shepherd

11.3.4 Peshitta

11.3.4.1 Manuscripts of s-Job

s-Job has come down to us through the witness of major manuscripts. The two oldest, s^{6h8} and s^{6h20}, are from the sixth century C.E. and contain only the book of Job. The book is also preserved in the two oldest "complete" Bibles, s^{7a1} and s^{8a1}. In addition, it has come to us through manuscripts that bring together an original collection of books, the so-called Beth Mawtebhe (Book of Sessions): Joshua, Judges, 1–2 Samuel, 1–2 Kings (→ 3–5.1.4), Proverbs (→ 12.3.4), Ecclesiastes (→ 13–17.1.4.3), Ruth (→ 13–17.1.4.1), Song of Songs (→ 13–17.1.4.2), Sirach (→ 11.4.4), and Job (s$^{9c1, 10c1, 10c4, 11c1}$). The book of Job is not preserved in s^{9a1}, which is so important for other books because of the uniqueness of its variants. It is preserved, however, in another important though more recent Bible: s^{12a1} (the "Buchanan Bible").

The text transmitted in these manuscripts is substantially the same, that is, we do not find different editions of the book of Job. The most notable characteristics of the translation, including the numerous "errors," are found even in the oldest manuscripts. The form that the whole textual tradition has transmitted precedes the Nestorian schism and

---

[24] Shepherd, *Targum and Translation*, 262–71.

is found in the oldest and in the most recent[1] Eastern and Western manuscripts.[2]

11.3.4.2 Critical Edition

The critical edition of s-Job is found in the project of the Peshitta Institute. It was published in 1982 by Rignell, following the criteria of the rest of the volumes: a diplomatic edition of manuscript s⁷ᵃ¹ and a critical apparatus that takes into account the manuscripts prior to the twelfth century.[3]

11.3.4.3 The Character of the Translation

The Syriac version of the book of Job was translated from an unvocalized Hebrew text very close to the consonantal base of MT (→ 11.2.2). In fact, many of the variants of s-Job with respect to MT can be explained as different vocalizations of the same consonantal term. For example, in Job 18:20, MT reads שַׁעַר "horror," while s-Job reads ܣܥܪܐ "hair," which corresponds to the Hebrew שֵׂעָר. In other cases, it can be seen that the translator had before him the same Hebrew term as MT, but he interpreted it as belonging to a different root. For example, in Job 33:27, MT reads יָשֹׁר, an imperfect form of the verb שׁור "to observe," while s-Job reads ܬܪܝܨܘܬܐ "rectitude," a sign that he has interpreted the Hebrew term as belonging to the root ישר "to be straight, upright." These kinds of interpretations, which are very numerous, point to a translator unfamiliar with the oral reading tradition that the Masoretes would later put into writing. In the opinion of some authors, this is a sign that the translator was Christian.

As has happened with other books of the Peshitta (→ 1.3.4), there has been a great deal of speculation about the influence of the Greek LXX version (→ 11.3.1) and the Aramaic Targum version (→ 11.3.3) on the Syriac translation.[4] The points in common with these versions have to do chiefly with making explicit what is implicit in the Hebrew text, which could be attributed to a shared technique of translation or interpretation. On the other hand, s-Job contains numerous readings that depart from MT and have no parallel in LXX or the Targum. If s-Job had utilized these versions as support for its translation, it would not be possible to understand the numerous exclusive errors of the Syriac version.[5] Rignell thinks that s-Job is independent of LXX but that prior knowledge of this version by the translator could have determined some choices.[6] He holds the same opinion concerning its relationship with the Targum: that it is impossible to see the sense of Baumann's thesis that s-Job is based on a Palestinian Targum. The main deviations of s-Job with regard to the Hebrew text can be explained as errors or particular interpretations with regard to a Hebrew *Vorlage* shared with MT that cannot be explained by the Aramaic translations of Job that have come down to us.[7]

As far as translation techniques are concerned, s-Job does not depart significantly from the rules and style that characterize other books of the Peshitta in matters of grammar, syntax, and semantics. Thus, for example, it tends to harmonize disagreements in gender, number, and tense that it finds in its Hebrew source, and to accommodate to the context those details that seem inconsistent with it. Likewise, it has a marked tendency to make explicit what is implicit in Hebrew, whether by the addition of pronouns or by semantic specification. Sometimes it resolves rhetorical questions by translating them with positive statements, or it interprets certain terms in its Hebrew original according to its own ideology.[8]

Nevertheless, both Rignell and Szpek identify in s-Job a series of characteristics that make it unique and that suggest, according to them, a complex process of translation in several stages, quite unique among the books of the Peshitta. Errors attributable to oral transmission together with typical visual errors (both based on the Hebrew), par-

---

[1] Rignell, *The Peshitta*, 363.
[2] Rignell, *The Peshitta*, 381.
[3] Rignell, *Job*.
[4] Mandl, *Die Peschitta zu Hiob*; Baumann, "Verwendbarkeit der Pesita zum Buche Hiob"; Dhorme, *A Commentary on the Book of Job*; Roberts, *OTTV*.

[5] Szpek, *Translation Technique*, 268–69.
[6] Rignell, *The Peshitta*, 379.
[7] Rignell, *The Peshitta*, 380–81.
[8] Szpek, *Translation Technique*, 263–66.

ticular attention to parallel passages both in the book of Job and in other biblical books, the presence of doublets, and readings shared with other versions that coexist with elements that indicate an absence of the influence of these versions all point to widely varying influences and to a development of this Syriac version in several stages.[9] To this, we can add the different translation choices for the same Hebrew word (lexical leveling) throughout the book, a factor that seems to indicate the existence of more than one translator.[10]

On the basis of this data, while attempting to explain it, Szpek and Rignell propose two different models for reconstructing the various stages that the Syriac translation of Job has undergone. Szpek[11] proposes five stages: 1) first translation(s) from an unvocalized Hebrew *Vorlage* close to MT (→ 11.2.2), which contained numerous glaring errors, with the possible influence of LXX (→ 11.3.1) and the Targum (→ 11.3.3); 2) several text types begin to circulate, which would explain the current doublets; 3) one of the text types gradually gains prominence, specifically the one that incorporates a considerable number of variant readings from other text types by means of double readings; 4) readings are created for liturgical lectionaries taken from the text; 5) the text continues to be copied, and in this process new variants enter due to familiarity with the liturgical reading of the same text or of parallel texts from Job or the rest of the Bible; in this final stage, neither the Hebrew text nor that of the versions are consulted any longer. This whole process is supposed to have been completed before the Nestorian schism and before the date of our oldest manuscripts (that attest to a single text type), that is, before the fifth century C.E.

Rignell,[12] for his part, goes into detail in his proposal. Jews are taken to be those responsible for a "provisional" translation from Hebrew into Syriac; these translators would be well versed in Hebrew but with little knowledge of Syriac. This explains why we find in the present text certain Hebrew roots that are translated with the same Syriac root, despite the fact that it has a different meaning (for example, in Job 6:9, the root דכא "crush," is translated with the Syriac root ܕܟܐ "cleanse, purify"). Rignell proposes that this provisional translation was made as an interlinear translation on a Hebrew manuscript (sometimes above the line of the Hebrew text and sometimes in the margin), which explains a certain negligence in the order of words and phrases. The fact that double readings exist in the present text can also be attributed to this stage. The same author was able to produce alternative translations from the Hebrew without being sure which was the correct equivalent, and to incorporate the divergent opinion of another person knowledgeable in the languages. In some cases, those alternative readings might not have been noted next to competing readings due to lack of space, which explains why, in the present text, some double readings are not located in the expected positions.

In Rignell's opinion, this provisional translation is not, strictly speaking, a continuous translation of the book of Job as we understand it today, but a word-for-word translation, like an interlinear translation, which would leave many prepositions, pronouns, and verb suffixes untranslated. This would explain many inaccuracies in this area in the present translation. At this same stage, the mistaken translations of the frequent *hapax legomena* that appear in the book of Job may have been produced. This should not be seen as contradicting the fact that those responsible for this provisional translation were Jews. Even the Masoretes (→ 10–20.1) found themselves in a quandary when interpreting or vocalizing a good number of *hapax legomena* in the Hebrew Bible.

The Syriac version of Job that we know today is assumed to be based on this provisional translation. Those responsible for today's version are believed to have been Syriac-speaking Christians. In the first place, this can be seen in their limited or defective knowledge of Hebrew, such that they did not have sufficient ability to check the received translation against the Hebrew original. Moreover,

---

[9] Szpek, *Translation Technique*, 269.
[10] Rignell, *The Peshitta*, 364–65.
[11] Szpek, *Translation Technique*, 269–70.
[12] Rignell, *The Peshitta*, 366–71.

this is made evident in certain "confessional" readings, such as Job 30:23: "I know that you will take me from death to the meeting house of all the living," instead of MT "I know that you will take me to death, to the meeting house of every living being" (cf. also Job 28:13 and 42:6). In many cases, those responsible for this final version had to adapt the words (that they found translated) to the context, or to the understanding they had of the context. A clear example appears in Job 29:19, where the Hebrew כבוד "glory" originally must have been translated correctly as ܐܝܩܪܐ. When redacting the final version, it was felt that a verb was missing in v. 19, so those responsible for this version had to exchange the noun ܐܝܩܪܐ "glory" for the verb form ܐܬܩܪܐ "I am called," which is the surprising present Syriac reading (without any variants among the Peshitta manuscripts).

11.3.4.4 The Use of S-Job in Textual Criticism of the Hebrew Bible

The peculiar characteristics of S-Job make it necessary to be especially prudent when using this version as a source for investigating the Hebrew text. However, with due prudence, S-Job can be a useful tool to deduce the meanings of certain Hebrew words and expressions in a book replete with *hapax legomena* and *cruces interpretorum*, on account of the close relationship between the two languages. If it is true that the first translation was prepared word for word and considered provisional, this could be the useful characteristic of this version. Even so, it is necessary to pay attention to the numerous unique readings that are erroneous.

It would be very risky to go beyond this limited use, especially when bearing in mind the different stages through which the Syriac translation seems to have passed, favoring a legible final text far from the difficulties of the Hebrew text that, moreover, was probably not consulted in the final stage.

11.3.4.5 Auxiliary Tools

At present, we have available a concordance of Syriac terms in S-Job and the rest of the books of the Beth Mawtebhe, edited by Strothmann, Zumpe, and Johannes, in six volumes in the Göttingen Orientforschungen series.[13]

Baumann, E., "Verwendbarkeit der Pesita zum Buche Hiob für die Textkritik," ZAW 18 (1898): 305–38; 19 (1899): 15–95, 287–309; 20 (1900): 177–307.

Dhorme, E., *A Commentary on the Book of Job* (New York: Thomas Nelson Publishers, 1926).

Mandl, A., *Die Peschitta zu Hiob: Nebst einem Anhang über ihr Verhältnis zu LXX und Targum* (Budapest: Propper, 1892).

Rignell, G., *Job* (The Old Testament in Syriac according to the Peshitta Version. 2.1a; Leiden: Brill, 1982).

Rignell, G., *The Peshitta to the Book of Job: Critically Investigated with Introduction, Translation, Commentary and Summary* (Kristianstad: MonitorFörlaget, 1994).

Roberts, *OTTV*.

Stenij, E., *De Syriaca libri Jobi interpretatione quae Peschita vocatur* (Helsinki: Frenckell, 1887).

Strothmann, W., M. Zumpe and K. Johannes, *Konkordanz zur syrischen Bibel: Die Mautbe* (Wiesbaden: Harrassowitz, 1995).

Szpek, H.M., *Translation Technique in the Peshitta to Job: A Model for Evaluating a Text with Documentation from the Peshitta to Job* (SBLDS 137; Atlanta: Scholars Press, 1992).

Szpek, H.M., "On the Influence of the Septuagint on the Peshitta," CBQ 60 (1998): 112–19.

Ignacio Carbajosa

11.3.5 Hexaplaric Greek Translations

11.3.5.1 Background

According to Cox, (O)ld (G)reek Job (→ 11.3.1) is a literary work of good quality, which avoids the usual Hebraisms found in much of LXX. Furthermore, the translator abbreviated his Hebrew source by one-sixth or some 390 lines. He also employed "intertextual sourcing," replaced lines of text with his own thoughts distinct from the Hebrew source, and finally, paraphrased and interpreted the Hebrew.[1]

The nature of the LXX-Job translation created an ideal situation for its revision according to the Hebrew text. Origen (→ 1.3.1.2) supplied the missing

---

[13] Strothmann, Zumpe, and Johannes, *Konkordanz zur syrischen Bibel: Die Mautbe*.

[1] → 11.3.1.3.

lines in LXX-Job with lines from Theodotion and marked them with an asterisk (※), in order to bring LXX into greater quantitative alignment with the Hebrew text.² He also marked lines not present in the Hebrew text with an obelus (÷; e.g., the longer ending of LXX-Job). The extant evidence of Theodotion (Th), Aquila (Aq), and Symmachus (Sym) indicates that they likewise revised LXX according to proto-MT (→ 11.2.2). In Job, there are no o′ attributions that would indicate readings of the work of Origen from the fifth column of the Hexapla.

11.3.5.2 Sources, Editions, and Auxiliary Tools

The primary sources for the Hexaplaric fragments of Job are the marginal notes in the Job catena (LXX$^{C, cI, cII}$), marginal notes in LXX$^{161-248}$ and LXX^{252}, the commentary by Olympiodorus, and the Syro-Hexapla (Syh; → 11.4.4). A few fragments come from the catenae fragments of the Job catena, Jerome, and other sources.³

Field published his work in 1875.⁴ Since that time, Ziegler prepared a critical edition for the Göttingen *Septuaginta*, which listed all of the known Hexaplaric fragments in its second apparatus.⁵ After Ziegler's work, Ursula and Dieter Hagedorn provided a four-volume critical edition of the oldest Greek catena of Job and published new and revised Hexaplaric fragments in the *Nachlese*.⁶ Finally, Woods and Meade edited the Hexaplaric materials in their doctoral dissertations.⁷ The following comments on the Hexaplaric Greek transla-

tions are based on these two dissertations. For auxiliary tools related to the Hexapla, see the bibliography.

11.3.5.3 Translation Character and Technique

Theodotion (→ 1.3.1.2) employed a formal equivalence translation technique, which he applied to the longer ending of Job. In this way, Theodotion transmitted a resignified text since he applied his technique to a text nearly identical to MT (→ 11.2.2) and also to the longer ending of LXX-Job (→ 11.3.1). Aquila (→ 1.3.1.2) applied a formal equivalence translation technique to a parent text mostly identical to MT. He did not revise lines not found in the Hebrew. Symmachus (→ 1.3.1.2) used a functional equivalence translation technique, which sometimes resulted in expansive and contextual renderings, even though these renderings often agreed with the word order of the Hebrew. In Job, Symmachus did not revise lines not present in MT. Therefore, Aquila and Symmachus are more alike than Theodotion and Aquila, and Theodotion is more similar to LXX-Job. The following data probably support the theory that Theodotion did his work before 70 C.E., while Aquila and Symmachus worked after 70 C.E. It is interesting to note that from 250 to 600 C.E., there is no evidence that Theodotion was used by the Jews.⁸

11.3.5.3.1 Theodotion

Since LXX-Job (→ 11.3.1) is shorter than its Hebrew *Vorlage*, Origen added the omitted lines, primarily, from the Theodotion version to his LXX text (→ 1.3.1.2). This move created an ecclesiastical text, LXX-Job mixed with Theodotion, and it has influenced the entire textual tradition with few exceptions.⁹ Although LXX-Job was corrupted, the move

---

² Some verses in Origen's ecclesiastical text contain double renderings, one from LXX-Job and the other from Theodotion. This approach caused Origen to omit certain lines that are present in the Hebrew (cf. 18:9b; 23:15). For all of the examples, see Gentry, *Asterisked Lines*, 517–30.

³ For a full description of the primary witnesses, see the editions of the Hexaplaric fragments of Job by Meade and Woods.

⁴ Field, *Hexapla*.

⁵ Ziegler, *Iob*.

⁶ Hagedorn and Hagedorn, *Die Älteren Griechischen Katenen zum Buch Hiob*, Vols. 1–4; Hagedorn and Hagedorn, *Nachlese*.

⁷ Meade, "A Critical Edition of the Hexaplaric Fragments of Job 22–42"; Woods, "A Critical Edition of the Hexaplaric Fragments of Job: Chapters 1–21."

⁸ R. Ceulemans, "Greek Christian Access to 'the Three,' 250–600 C.E.," in *Greek Scripture and the Rabbis* (eds. T.M. Law and A. Salvesen; CBET 66; Leuven: Peeters, 2012), 165–91 (185 n. 53).

⁹ The Sahidic version (→ 11.4.2) along with a few patristic witnesses (→ 21.8) to the Old Latin version omitted the lines from the text. Syh (→ 11.4.4), VL (→ 11.4.1), Arm (→ 11.4.5), and significant witnesses to the catena tradition preserved the asterisked lines, while the majority of witnesses have omitted the asterisks and thus the lines appear to be part of LXX-Job.

preserved some 390 lines of Job, which are attributed to Theodotion. In addition to these lines, there are 177 Theodotion fragments in marginal notes and catena excerpts.[10] These lines and fragments of Theodotion were analyzed by Peter Gentry in his doctoral dissertation. Gentry concluded, "The character of the materials belonging to θ′ reveals a literal and straightforward translation of a parent text for the most part identical with MT (consonantal text and vocalization). The translation follows the elements and segments of the language of the parent text and also the sequence in which these elements are presented."[11] In terms of contrasting the Theodotionic materials with Aquila, Gentry continues, "The translation does not show an attempt to represent the root system of Hebrew in equivalents such as we see in Aquila … but his [Theodotion] translation, unlike that of Aquila's, evinces no consistent determination to represent the formal and semantic relationships obtaining in Hebrew so closely that absurdities abound."[12] Therefore, Theodotion's technique can be contrasted with Aquila's.

A couple of examples of Theodotion's technique will be sufficient to demonstrate his approach. In Job 24:14b, the reading of Theodotion is: וּבַלַּיְלָה יְהִי כַגַּנָּב "and in the night he is like a thief"/Th ※ καὶ νυκτὸς ἔσται ὡς κλέπτης "and at night he will be like a thief" (*NETS). This line illustrates both literalism and sensitivity to the target language. Essentially, it is a quantitative rendering of the Hebrew text. However, Theodotion did not render ב "in" but instead used the temporal genitive νυκτός "at/during night" to render the temporal ב "in." Out of eighty-six occurrences where Theodotion rendered ב he used ἐν "in" sixty-eight times, but in twelve cases he varied his approach due to concerns of the target language.[13] In contrast, Aquila used ἐν "in" almost exclusively and where he did not, he used another preposition to preserve quantitative equivalence with the Hebrew source.[14]

In Job 24:15b, the reading of Theodotion is: לֵאמֹר לֹא־תְשׁוּרֵנִי עָיִן "saying, 'No eye will see me'"/Th ※ λέγων Οὐ προσνοήσει με ὀφθαλμός "saying, 'No eye will observe me'" (*NETS). Theodotion rendered his source word for word. However, he did not render the ל "to/for" of the frozen form לֵאמֹר "saying" (lit. "to say") but translated it with a Greek present participle as he does in Isa 16:14. All LXX translators rendered this form in the same way.[15] In contrast, Aquila used τῷ λέγειν "to say," a more isomorphic equivalent for לֵאמֹר "saying."[16]

One final observation concerning Theodotion is in order. Though LXX-Job is one-sixth shorter than its Hebrew *Vorlage*, it contains a longer ending of sixteen lines (Job 42:17aα–17eα in Ziegler's *Edition*). Ziegler's *Edition* lists two Theodotion fragments from these verses and Meade's critical edition of the Hexaplaric fragments of Job lists four:

Th μεθ' ἡμῶν ὅτι θεὸς ἀναστήσει "with us that God will raise"/LXX-Job μεθ' ὧν ὁ κύριος ἀνίστησιν "with whom the Lord will raise"
Th υἱὸς Ἰωσαφατ "son of Iosaphat"/LXX-Job Ἐλιφάς τῶν Ἡσαῦ υἱῶν "Eliphas of the sons of Esau"
Th υἱὸς Ἀμμών τοῦ Χοβόρ "son of Ammon of Chobor"/LXX-Job Βαλδάδ "Baldad"
Th ὁ Ἰεμιναίων "the [king] of the Ieminites"/LXX-Job ὁ Μιναίων "the [king] of the Minites"

The presence of Theodotion fragments in this longer ending of Job supports early commentary that suggests only Theodotion followed LXX, while Aquila and Symmachus followed the Hebrew text. The oldest Job catena has the following comment attributed to Olympiodorus: "μέχρι τοῦ *πρεσβύτερος καὶ πλήρης ἡμερῶν* Ἀκύλας καὶ Σύμμαχος ἐλθόντες συνεπέραναν τὸ βιβλίον ὡς δὴ τῷ Ἑβραϊκῷ ἀκολουθοῦντες. ὁ δὲ Θεοδοτίων συμπεραίνει τοῖς Ἑβδομήκοντα".[17]

---

[10] All numbers are taken from Meade, "A Critical Edition" and Woods, "A Critical Edition." These numbers include explicit and conjectured attributions. They do not include the many fragments with double and triple attributions.

[11] Gentry, *Asterisked Lines*, 494.

[12] Gentry, *Asterisked Lines*, 494.

[13] Gentry, *Asterisked Lines*, 317–22. Theodotion also used the simple dative six times.

[14] Hyvärinen, *Die Übersetzung von Aquila*, 48–49.

[15] Gentry, *Asterisked Lines*, 270.

[16] Hyvärinen, *Die Übersetzung von Aquila*, 31.

[17] Hagedorns, *Die Älteren Griechischen Katenen*, Vol. 3, 405. Translation: "Having come to 'old and full of days,' Aquilas and Symmachos finished the book since indeed they were

LXX²⁴⁸ contains the following scholion: "ἐντεῦθεν οὐ κεῖται ἐν τῷ Ἑβραϊκῷ ὡς Ἀκύλας καὶ Σύμμαχος· παρὰ Θεοδοτίωνϊ κεῖται".¹⁸ Lastly, Origen writes in his letter to Africanus: "οὐ κεῖται παρὰ τοῖς Ἑβραίοις· διόπερ οὐδὲ παρὰ τῷ Ἀκύλα· παρὰ δὲ τοῖς Ἑβδομήκοντα καὶ Θεοδοτίωνι τὰ ἰσοδυναμοῦντα ἀλλήλοις" "It is not among the Hebrews; therefore, it is not even in Aquilas. But the Seventy and Theodotion are equal to one another."¹⁹ These texts show that Aquila and Symmachus followed the Hebrew text, while Theodotion followed the longer ending of LXX. It is interesting to recall that the consensus places Theodotion around 180 C.E., i.e., at the end of the process of revision where he putatively stands as a reaction to both the extreme literalism of Aquila and the functional equivalence of Symmachus. On this view, the resignified version of Theodotion would appear at a time when the Jews were only transmitting the conservatively copied text and not resignified texts. The evidence of Aquila and Symmachus evinces that the Jews were not transmitting a resignified text after 70 C.E. A better inference from the evidence places Theodotion in a context similar to LXX, in which the Jews are transmitting the text through both repetition and resignification, i.e., before 70 C.E. The Theodotion version shows certain signs of transmitting the repeated text (e.g., conformity to proto-MT) and the resignified text (e.g., inclusion of the longer ending of LXX-Job, which was not in the Hebrew). The translation typology of Theodotion accords with this conclusion as well as a probable re-reading of the relevant patristic sources as Gentry has suggested.²⁰ The evidence of the Hexaplaric Greek translations of Job indicates that the Three should be placed in the following typological order, which also probably indicates a chronological order: Theodotion, Aquila, and Symmachus.

11.3.5.3.2 Aquila

There are 342 fragments uniquely attributed to Aquila (→ 1.3.1.2) in Job. The Aquila materials indicate that he employed a formal equivalence translation technique, which attempted to render each Hebrew element with a Greek equivalent segment by segment. On the word level, Aquila's version is very literal and demonstrates the concordance principle of translation, even employing equivalents to maintain etymological connections between Hebrew and Greek. However, when Aquila's syntax and Greek vocabulary are considered, his version furnishes more appropriate and even ingenious renderings of the Hebrew source.²¹

Job 33:13 is a good example of this technique:

MT-Job מַדּוּעַ אֵלָיו רִיבוֹתָ כִּי כָל־דְּבָרָיו לֹא־יַעֲנֶה
Why do you contend against him, saying, "He will answer none of his words?"
LXX-Job λέγεις δέ Διὰ τί τῆς δίκης μου οὐκ ἐπακήκοεν πᾶν ῥῆμα
But you say, "Why has he not heeded one word of my case?" (*NETS)
Aq τί οὖν πρὸς αὐτὸν ἐδικάσω; ὅτι πάντα τὰ ῥήματα αὐτοῦ οὐκ ἀποκρινεῖται.
Why then did you contend with him? For he answers none of his words.

Aquila provides a quantitative rendering of the Hebrew and in the case of מַדּוּעַ "why" he appears to treat it as a compound word by translating its segments in order to preserve his rendering of מָה with τί (both meaning "what"). LXX-Job (→ 11.3.1) uses διὰ τί "why" in this instance. By using τί οὖν "why than" for מַדּוּעַ "why," Aquila also reserves εἰς τί "why" (lit. "for what") for לָמָה "why" (lit. "for what").²²

In Job 26:5, there is the following fragment:

MT הָרְפָאִים יְחוֹלָלוּ מִתַּחַת מַיִם וְשֹׁכְנֵיהֶם
The shades below tremble, the waters and their inhabitants. (*NRSV)

---

following the Hebrew. But Theodotion extends as far as the Seventy."

¹⁸ Translation: "From here it is not in the Hebrew as Aquilas and Symmachos; it is in Theodotion."

¹⁹ De Lange, *Sur les Ecritures*, 528.

²⁰ → 1.3.1.2.4.

²¹ Hyvärinen, *Die Übersetzung von Aquila*, 111–12.

²² Reider, *Index*, 238. The other equivalents for מַדּוּעַ in Reider need to be revised. In Job 21:4b, διὰ τί in LXX²⁵² is from LXX-Job not Aquila. The same is probably true for Jer 37(30):6.

Th ⁕ μὴ γίγαντες μαιωθήσονται ὑποκάτωθεν ὕδατος καὶ τῶν γειτόνων αὐτοῦ;
will giants be brought forth beneath the water and its neighbors? (*NETS)
Aq μήτι Ῥαφαΐμ ὠδίνουσιν ἀποκάτωθεν ὑδάτων καὶ σκηνούντων αὐτά.
are the Raphaim in anguish from below the waters and those who inhabit them?

There is no Old Greek to be revised for this verse and Origen used Theodotion as his equivalent for the Hebrew. Both Aquila and Theodotion understood the initial הַ "the" as the interrogative particle הֲ. Characteristically, Aquila used the Greek interrogative particle μήτι for the Hebrew interrogative particle הֲ. Aquila also transliterates רְפָאִים "Rephaim" with Ῥαφαΐμ "Raphaim," a technique he used in Job 1:1a (Οὒς "Ous"); 1:6c (Σατάν "Satan"); 3:8b (Λευϊάθάν "Leviathan"); 40:25a (Λευϊάθάν "Leviathan"), 40:30b (Χαναναίων "Cananites"); 42:14a (Ἰεμιμα "Iemima"); and 42:14c (Καρναφφούκ "Karnaphphouk") in order to render proper names. In a few places where Theodotion employed transliteration (Job 37:12b [תַּחְבּוּלֹתָו "his guidance"/Th θεεβουλαθώ "theeboulatho"/Aq οἰακώσεσιν "directing"]; 39:6a [עֲרָבָה "Araba"/Th ἀραβά "Araba"/Aq ὁμαλήν "level ground"]; 39:13ab [נֶעֱלָסָה "flap wildly"/Th νεέλασα "neelasa"/Aq συναναπλέκεται "entwined together"]), Aquila translated the Hebrew and avoided transliteration. The use of ἀποκάτωθεν "from below" in the LXX corpus is found only here. The LXX translators and Theodotion often used ὑποκάτωθεν "underneath" for מִתַּחַת "from under," but Aquila perfected this approach by employing ἀπό for מִן (both meaning "from") in the compound preposition.

11.3.5.3.3 Symmachus

There are 599 Hexaplaric fragments uniquely attributed to Symmachus (→ 1.3.1.2) in Job. Symmachus produced a revision of LXX that was faithful to the sense of the Hebrew and readable in Greek.[23] These characteristics are also detected in Job.

Job 2:4bc provides a good example:

MT-Job עוֹר בְּעַד־עוֹר וְכֹל אֲשֶׁר לָאִישׁ יִתֵּן בְּעַד נַפְשׁוֹ
Skin for skin! All that people have they will give to save their lives. (*NRSV)
LXX-Job δέρμα ὑπὲρ δέρματος· ὅσα ὑπάρχει ἀνθρώπῳ, ὑπὲρ τῆς ψυχῆς αὐτοῦ ἐκτείσει
Skin for skin; whatever a person has he will use to pay for his life. (*NETS)
Sym χρῶτα ὑπὲρ χρωτός καὶ πάντα ὅσα ἔχει προήσεται ὑπὲρ τῆς ψυχῆς αὐτοῦ
Skin for skin, and whatever he has, he will give it up for the sake of his own life.

In this text, Symmachus renders the Hebrew quantitatively with one exception: לָאִישׁ "for a man"/ἔχει "he has." Here, Symmachus renders the sense of the *lamed* of possession and does not provide a literal equivalent for *lamed* such as LXX-Job's use of the dative case: ὅσα ὑπάρχει ἀνθρώπῳ lit. "all which is to a person." With this translation, Symmachus appears to be less literal than LXX-Job (→ 11.3.1), but the position of the verb is also interesting to note. Symmachus places προήσεται "he will give up" where יִתֵּן "he will give" appears in the Hebrew, while LXX-Job places ἐκτείσει "he will use to pay" at the end of the line. Thus, Symmachus demonstrates both functional and formal tendencies since he brings over the sense of the Hebrew into good Greek but also maintains the Hebrew word order.

Job 4:12a–c presents another case in which Symmachus produces a functional equivalent translation of the Hebrew and still accomplishes a revision of the Greek toward the Hebrew:

MT-Job וְאֵלַי דָּבָר יְגֻנָּב וַתִּקַּח אָזְנִי שֵׁמֶץ מֶנְהוּ
Now a word came stealing to me, my ear received the whisper of it. (*NRSV)
LXX-Job εἰ δέ τι ῥῆμα ἀληθινὸν ἐγεγόνει ἐν λόγοις σου, οὐθὲν ἄν σοι τούτων κακὸν ἀπήντησεν. πότερον οὐ δέξεταί μου τὸ οὖς ἐξαίσια παρ᾽ αὐτοῦ;
But if there had been anything truthful in your words, nothing bad in them would have met you. "Will my ear not receive remarkable things from him?" (*NETS)
Sym πρὸς ἐμὲ δὲ ἐλαλήθη λαθραίως ὡς ἐν κλοπῇ καὶ ἐδέξατο οὖς μου ψιθυρισμὸν παρ᾽ αὐτοῦ.

---

[23] → 1.3.1.2.5; cf. Salvesen, *Symmachus in the Pentateuch*, 198.

Now it was spoken to me secretly as by stealth and my ear received whisper of it.

Symmachus preserves the Hebrew word order, but he expands דָּבָר יְגֻנָּב to ἐλαλήθη λαθραίως ὡς ἐν κλοπῇ. The Hebrew might be rendered "a word will be brought secretly," and Symmachus rendered "it was spoken secretly as by stealth." Another problem with this verse is that LXX-Job contains an extra line (Job 4:12b: οὐθὲν ἄν σοι τούτων κακὸν ἀπήντησεν "nothing bad in them would have met you"; sub ÷ in the LXX° group, indicating that the line was not in the Hebrew), which Symmachus omitted from his revision. This omission demonstrates Symmachus' tendency to revise only the Hebrew text (→ 11.2.2) represented in LXX-Job 4:12ac. The edition by Ziegler presented this fragment as two separate fragments in his II Apparatus (i.e., 12a and 12c), which would raise the question of whether Symmachus had a revision for LXX-Job 4:12b that is now lost. The evidence presented above is from Woods' edition and LXX^{788} and LXX^{3005} confirm it. These witnesses preserve one continuous fragment for Symmachus at Job 4:12. Therefore, Symmachus' version only contains a revision for LXX-Job 4:12ac in accordance with the Hebrew text.

Symmachus' technique is seen again in Job 39:24:

MT-Job בְּרַעַשׁ וְרֹגֶז יְגַמֶּא־אָרֶץ וְלֹא־יַאֲמִין כִּי־קוֹל שׁוֹפָר
With fierceness and rage it swallows the ground; it cannot stand still at the sound of the trumpet. (*NRSV)
LXX-Job καὶ ὀργῇ ἀφανιεῖ τὴν γῆν καὶ οὐ μὴ πιστεύσῃ, ἕως ἄν σημάνῃ σάλπιγξ
and in rage it will stamp out the ground and will not steady itself until the trumpet sounds. (*NETS)
Sym ἐν σάλῳ καὶ ὀργῇ ὡς καταπίνων γῆν καὶ οὐ δειλωθήσεται ὑπὸ ἤχους σάλπιγγος
in restlessness and anger as one devouring the ground and he will not be freightened by the sound of the trumpet.

LXX-Job describes the horse as ὀργῇ "in anger." LXX-Job compressed בְּרַעַשׁ וְרֹגֶז "in a roar and anger" into one word ὀργῇ, while Symmachus preserves the complete phrase, ἐν σάλῳ καὶ ὀργῇ "in restlessness and anger." LXX-Job used a finite verb (ἀφανιεῖ

"stamp out") that equals the Hebrew (יְגַמֶּא "swallows"). Alternatively, Symmachus renders the Hebrew finite verb with ὡς καταπίνων, thus adding a word not in the Hebrew, but the sense of the Hebrew is well conveyed ("as one devouring earth"). Hebrew, גמא, is used in the Hebrew Bible only here in the *Piel* and once in the *Hiphil* (cf. Gen 24:17) where it means "to give to drink." The lexicon has "to swallow"[24] and Symmachus' lexical choice renders this meaning well. Symmachus' translation of the B line is dynamic: 1) אמן *Hiphil* means "to trust, believe," which LXX-Job renders with πιστεύω "to believe." Symmachus has δειλόομαι "to be afraid, to be frightened."[25] Symmachus arrived at this rendering through appeal to context. At Job 39:22, the text says, "He [the horse] laughs at *fear* [פַּחַד] and he is not dismayed." The Peshitta has a similar rendering in Job 39:24: ܘܠܐ ܕܚܠ ܡܢ ܩܠܐ ܕܫܝܦܘܪܐ. "and he was not afraid of the sound of the trumpet" and probably employed the same strategy independently; 2) Symmachus has ὑπό "by" for כִּי "for, because," where LXX-Job has rendered temporal כִּי "for, because" with ἕως ἄν "until." Symmachus' knowledge of the wider context, not the meanings of individual Hebrew words, determined his rendering of this verse.

11.3.5.4 Text-Critical Value for LXX-Job and the Hebrew Bible

At Job 28:11a, MT has חִבֵּשׁ "to dam up." Theodotion has ἐξηρεύνησεν "he searched out," which presupposes חִפֵּשׂ "to search" as his *Vorlage*. Theodotion uses this equivalent also in Ps 64:7. The change in sibilants is accounted for by the graphemic identity of the respective phonemes /ś/ and /š/. The interchange between ב and פ is explained by dialect interference in Northwest Semitic (e.g., *npš/nbš*). The Theodotion and LXX-Job (βάθη δὲ ποταμῶν ἀνεκάλυψεν "he uncovered the depths of rivers") ver-

---

[24] *HALOT*, s.v. גמא.

[25] Ziegler, *Iob* listed only the reading δηλωθήσεται "it will be clear," but the new edition of the Hexaplaric fragments of Job has δειλωθήσεται "it will be freightened," since it is the reading in LXX^{788}, the purest textual witness to the oldest Greek catena of Job (see Meade, "A Critical Edition").

sions probably preserve the original text, for the text describes man's search for or uncovering of the sources of the rivers. At the least, the Theodotion version provides a very important variant to MT (→ 11.2.2).

Busto Saiz, J.R., *La traducción de Símaco en el Libro de los Salmos* (Textos y Estudios "Cardenal Cisneros" 22; Madrid: Consejo Superior de Investigaciones Científicas, 1978).
Field, *Hexapla*.
Gentry, P.J., *The Asterisked Materials in the Greek Job* (SBLSCS 38; Atlanta: Scholars Press, 1995).
Hagedorn, U. and D. Hagedorn (eds.), *Nachlese zu den Fragmenten der jüngeren griechischen Übersetzer des Buches Hiob* (NAWG 1 Philologisch-Historische Klasse 10 [1991]; Göttingen: Vandenhoeck & Ruprecht, 1991).
Hagedorn, U. and D. Hagedorn (eds.), *Die Älteren Griechischen Katenen zum Buch Hiob*, Vol. 1: *Einleitung, Prologue und Epilogue, Fragmente zu Hiob 1,1–8,22* (PTS 40; Berlin: De Gruyter, 1994).
Hagedorn, U. and D. Hagedorn (eds.), *Die Älteren Griechischen Katenen zum Buch Hiob*, Vol. 2: *Fragmente zu Hiob 9,1–22,30* (PTS 48; Berlin: De Gruyter, 1997).
Hagedorn, U. and D. Hagedorn (eds.), *Die Älteren Griechischen Katenen zum Buch Hiob*, Vol. 3: *Fragmente zu Hiob 23,1–42,17* (PTS 53; Berlin: De Gruyter, 2000).
Hagedorn, U. and D. Hagedorn (eds.), *Die Älteren Griechischen Katenen zum Buch Hiob*, Vol. 4: Register, Nachträge und Anhänge (PTS 59; Berlin: De Gruyter, 2004).
Hyvärinen, K., *Die Übersetzung von Aquila* (ConBOT 10; Uppsala: G.W.K. Gleerup, 1977).
Meade, J.D., "A Critical Edition of the Hexaplaric Fragments of Job 22–42" (PhD diss., The Southern Baptist Theological Seminary, 2012).
Harl, M. and N.R.M. de Lange (eds.), *Origène, Philocalie 1–20 sur les Ecritures et La Lettre à Africanus sur l' histoire de Suzanne: Introduction, texte, traduction et notes* (SC 302; Paris: Cerf, 1983).
Reider, J. and N. Turner, *An Index to Aquila: Greek-Hebrew, Hebrew-Greek, Latin-Hebrew* (Leiden: Brill, 1966).
Salvesen, A., *Symmachus in the Pentateuch* (JSS Monograph 15; Manchester: Victoria University of Manchester, 1991).
Woods, N., "A Critical Edition of the Hexaplaric Fragments of Job: Chapters 1–21" (PhD diss., The Southern Baptist Theological Seminary, 2009).
Ziegler, J. (ed.), *Iob* (Septuaginta Vetus Testamentum Graecum 11.4; Göttingen: Vandenhoeck & Ruprecht, 1982).
Ziegler, J., *Beiträge zum griechischen Iob* (MSU 18; Göttingen: Vandenhoeck & Ruprecht, 1985).

John D. Meade

11.3.6 Post-Hexaplaric Greek Translations

11.3.6.1 Background

The only post-Hexaplaric recension known to us is that of Lucian (→ 1.3.1.2). The text of the Old Greek of Job (→ 11.3.1) is shorter than the Hebrew text. Greek Job also is dynamic in translation technique. These two characteristics – especially the latter one – pose significant problems for locating the Lucianic recension in the manuscript tradition, because the Lucianic recension is also known for the elimination of redundant clauses and numerous stylistic improvements. Ziegler noted that the Lucianic recension frequently agrees with Origen's text (→ 11.3.5), a fact that Cox has confirmed.[1] For this reason, it is possible to overcome the difficulties associated with the character of the Old Greek and Lucian's scribal habits, because Lucianic improvements have been applied to a text that sometimes is distinguishable from the Old Greek.

11.3.6.2 Original Form, Editions, Auxiliary Tools

Ziegler's edition in the Göttingen LXX[2] is indispensable for study of Lucianic readings. He identifies four Lucianic groups: the chief group LXX^L (LXX$^{A, V, 575, 637}$, the Job commentaries of the Arian Julian and John Chrysostom), the subgroup LXX^{lI} (LXX$^{46, 249, 631}$), the subgroup LXX^{lIII} (LXX$^{254, 754}$), and the subgroup LXX^{lIIII} (LXX$^{106, 130, 261}$). The Hexaplaric nature of the Lucianic recension in LXX-Job, most notably in the subgroup LXX^{lI}, demands that scholars consult Hexaplaric sources (→ 11.3.5)

---

[1] J. Ziegler, *Iob* (Septuaginta Vetus Testamentum Graecum 11.2, Göttingen: Vandenhoeck & Ruprecht, 1982), 120; Cox, "The Nature of Lucian's Revision of the Text of Greek Job," 423–44.
[2] Ziegler, *Iob*.

from the three Jewish revisers. In addition to Ziegler's second apparatus, the theses of Woods[3] and Meade[4] are helpful. Similarly, augmenting Ziegler's apparatus is the edition of Julian the Arian's Job commentary by Hagedorn and Hagedorn.[5] Variants in the commentary frequently agree with Codex LXX^A.[6]

11.3.6.3 Translation Character and Translation Technique

The character of the LXX^L text of Job is consistent with its features in other LXX books.[7] The following characteristics, drawn from Cox's analysis,[8] include various additions: articles (Job 5:10b ἀποστέλλοντα "sent" LXX/τον ἀποστέλλοντα "the one sent" LXX^L 613), conjunctions (Job 6:19b ἀτραπούς "paths" LXX/και ἀτραπούς "and paths" LXX^L'-575'), pronouns (Job 5:26a κατὰ καιρόν "according to the season" LXX/κατὰ καιρόν αὐτοῦ "according to its season" LXX^L'-575 Syhmg), and phrases (Job 5:17a ἐπὶ τῆς γῆς "upon the earth" LXX^L'). The text is fuller than the Old Greek (→ 11.3.1). In addition to various changes to verbal morphology, there are numerous substitutions: compound verbs for simplex forms (Job 5:26a ἐλεύσῃ "you shall come" LXX/ἀπελεύσῃ "you shall come" LXX^L'), Attic Greek for Hellenistic forms (Job 9:25b εἴδοσαν "they saw" LXX/εἶδον "they saw" LXX^L'-575), and synonyms (Job 10:10b ἐτύρωσας "did you curdle" LXX/ἐπήξας "did you make solid" LXX^L'-575).

Peculiar changes to the text include elimination of hyperbaton (Job 4:12b οὐθὲν ἄν σοι τούτων κακὸν ἀπήντησεν "nothing bad in them would have met you" [*NETS] LXX/οὐθὲν ἄν τούτων κακὸν ἀπήντησέν σοι "nothing bad in them would have met you" LXX^L'-A 575) and a preference for καί "and" instead of δέ "but" (Job 20:26a πᾶν δὲ σκότος "then utter darkness" LXX/καὶ πᾶν σκότος "and utter darkness" LXX^L). Although the former involves transpositions toward normative, but stylized, Hellenistic Greek, the latter is the preference of the recensionist. This conclusion is bolstered when it is recognized that Lucian likely used a Hexaplaric text (→ 11.3.5), a text where Origen allowed the more stylized δέ "but" to stand. Pluses, however, sometimes include the conjunction δέ "but" (Job 6:14a ἀπείπατο "has renounced" LXX/ἀπείπατο δε "but ... has announced" LXX^L 644c).

11.3.6.4 Inner-Translational Features

Elsewhere in LXX, the Lucianic recension is considered a full text.[9] The Lucianic recension of LXX-Job, like the Old Greek (→ 11.3.1), is shorter than the Hebrew text. Nonetheless, pluses in the subgroup LXX^II frequently agree with the Hebrew text (→ 11.2.2) and, not coincidentally, Hexaplaric sources (→ 11.3.5), especially marginal readings in the Syro-Hexapla (→ 11.4.4; e.g., Job 10:5 ἀνδρός "of man" LXX/ὡς ἡμέραι ἀνδρός "as the days of man" ΚΧΧ^II La[10] = MT Aq Th Syh^mg).[11] A typical feature of the Lucianic recension in other LXX books is alignment toward the Hebrew text via Hexaplaric readings.[12] Improvements to readings in asterisked lines (Theodotion) are not uncommon (Job 10:4b ※ ἤ καθὼς ὁρᾷ ἄνθρωπος βλέψῃ "will you see as a human sees" [βλέψεις "will you see" LXX^L; βλέπεις "do you see" LXX^II and the Job commentary of John Chrysostom]).[13] Cox, however, argues that the LXX^L text of LXX-Job is not characterized by fidelity to

---

[3] N. Woods, "A Critical Edition of the Hexaplaric Fragments of Job: Chapters 1–21" (PhD diss., The Southern Baptist Theological Seminary, 2009).

[4] J.D. Meade, "A Critical Edition of the Hexaplaric Fragments of Job 22–42" (PhD diss., The Southern Baptist Theological Seminary, 2012).

[5] Hagedorn and Hagedorn, Der Hiobkommentar des Arianers Julian.

[6] Ziegler, Iob, 93–94.

[7] For a list of general characteristics, see Ziegler, "Hat Lukian den griechischen Sirach rezensiert?"

[8] Cox, "The Nature of Lucian's Revision of the Text of Greek Job," 430–39.

[9] N. Fernández Marcos, "On Symmachus and Lucian in Ezekiel," in *Interpreting Translation: Studies on the LXX and Ezekiel in Honour of Johan Lust* (eds. F. García Martínez and M. Vervenne; BETL 213; Leuven: Peeters, 2005), 151–61 (160).

[10] The abbreviation La refers to Jeromes Latin translation of LXX-Job.

[11] Ziegler, *Iob*, 104.

[12] For example, see R. Hanhart, *Text und Textgeschichte des 2. Esrabuches* (MSU 25; Göttingen: Vandenhoeck & Ruprecht, 2003), 18.

[13] Curiously, the subgroup LXX^IIII omits the entire asterisked line.

the Hebrew text: "The kinds of changes that = MT reflected in these L readings are the same kinds of changes that Lucian made generally, where the result does not equal the Hebrew or invite comparison with the Hebrew."[14] The relationship of the LXX[L] text to the Hebrew text is complicated by the former's Hexaplaric base text.

11.3.6.5 Text-Critical Value

Theoretically, it is possible that the LXX[L] text of LXX-Job preserves Hexaplaric readings, because of the recension's employment of a Hexaplaric text (→ 10.3.5). Readings from the three Jewish revisors, hitherto unknown, may be buried in the variants of the recension's manuscript tradition. But discovering Hexaplaric readings in Lucian's work, especially in a layered recension like the Lucianic recension, is likely an impossible task. Agreements with the Old Latin (Gloss[15] and La) are difficult to assess (e.g., Job 5:1b ἀγγέλων ἁγίων LXX/ἁγίων ἀγγέλων La[γμ] LXX[L] Gloss, both meaning "of the holy angels"), because it is possible that early Latin sources were harmonized with Jerome's later translation. Nonetheless, in reliance upon the research of Dieu, Gailey notes the close relationship between LXX[A], a member of the chief group LXX[L], and Jerome's translation of Job from the Greek (→ 11.3.7).[16] Curiously, Gailey subsequently mentions that some agreements between Jerome's translation and LXX[A] evince Hexaplaric influence. Hence, Origenic influence is discernible, though the chronology needs intense scrutiny.

Cimosa, M., "John Chrysostom and the Septuagint (Job and Psalms)," in *XII Congress of the International Organization for Septuagint and Cognate Studies* (ed. M.K.H. Peters; SBLSCS 54; Leiden: Brill, 2006), 117–30.

Cox, C.E., "The Nature of Lucian's Revision of the Text of Greek Job," in *Scripture in Transition*: Essays on Septuagint, Hebrew Bible, and Dead Sea Scrolls in Honour of Raija Sollamo (eds. A. Voitila and J. Jokiranta; JSJSup 126; Leiden: 2008), 423–44.

Dieu, L., "Le Texte de Job du Codex Alexandrinus et ses principaux témoins," *Mus* 13 (1912): 223–74.

Hagedorn, D. and U. Hagedorn, *Der Hiobkommentar des Arianers Julian* (PTS 14; Berlin: De Gruyter, 1973).

Ziegler, J., "Hat Lukian den griechischen Sirach rezensiert?" *Bib* 40 (1959): 210–29.

Matthew M. Dickie

11.3.7 Vulgate

11.3.7.1 Background

V-Job was completed at least by 393 or 394 C.E., not long after Jerome began his translation *iuxta Hebraeos* in 391 C.E. (→ 1.3.5.2).[1] In his preface, Jerome acknowledges the difficulty of the Hebrew text, though V-Job reveals his ability as a translator even at an early stage in his translation project. V-Job contains the longer version of Job represented by MT (→ 11.2.2); prior to the production of V-Job, Jerome compiled a Hexaplaric version of the book, which marked omissions and additions in comparison with the Hebrew.[2] Jerome claims that his translation is a completely original work. But it is known that he makes use of Aquila, Symmachus, and Theodotion (→ 11.3.5) in his translation elsewhere (→ 1.3.1.2). V-Job also shows Jerome's reliance on these ancient versions.[3]

---

[14] Cox, "The Nature of Lucian's Revision of the Text of Greek Job," 441.

[15] The abbreviation Gloss refers to glosses in VL manuscripts.

[16] J.H. Gailey, *Jerome's Latin Version of Job from the Greek: Chapters 1–26* (Princeton: Committee on Publications, 1948), 9–10; Dieu, "Le Texte de Job du Codex Alexandrinus et ses principaux témoins," 223–74.

---

[1] *Epist.* 49.4; P. Jay, "La datation des premières traductions de l'Ancien Testament sur l'hébreu par saint Jérôme," *REAug* (1982): 208, n. 3.

[2] This text is found in PL 29:61–118.

[3] E. Schulz-Flügel, "The Latin Old Testament Tradition," in *Hebrew Bible/Old Testament: The History of Interpretation*, Vol. 1: *From the Beginnings to the Middle Ages (Until 1300)*, Part 1: *Antiquity* (ed. M. Sæbø; Göttingen: Vandenhoeck & Ruprecht, 1996), 642–62 (655). Some examples of Jerome's reliance upon the Greek versions of Job include the following: LXX (ἀγρὸν ... οὐκ αὐτῶν ὄντα/*agrum non suum* "a field not their own," Job 24:6; ἀκούσατε/*audite* "hear," Job 32:10); Symmachus (αὐτοὶ γεγόνασιν ἀποστάται φωτός/*ipsi fuerunt rebelles luminis* "they have become rebels (against) the light," Job 24:13; ὑψηλὰ καὶ ὑπερηρμένα "high and lifted up"/*excelsa et eminenta* "high and

11.3.7.2 Translation Character

According to Jerome, his translation is characterized by a mixed approach: "now words, now meanings, now both at the same time sound forth" (Prol. in Job).[4] v-Job shows some evidence of literalisms, but literalistic renderings are relatively rare in the book and limited to shorter phrases rather than more extended passages. The translation style is characterized by freedom and concern for variety and general readability in Latin.

11.3.7.3 Translation Technique

11.3.7.3.1 Literalisms

Literalisms are not frequent in v-Job. Literal translations occur with prepositional phrases, such as *a facie Domini* "from the face of the Lord" (Job 1:12; מֵעִם פְּנֵי יְהוָה), *super faciem* "upon the face" (Job 5:10; 24:18; עַל־פְּנֵי), and *in manu iniquitatis suae* "in the hand of their iniquity" (Job 8:4; בְּיַד־פִּשְׁעָם). Etymological renderings are found, e.g., *umbram mortis* "shadow of death" (Job 28:3; צַלְמָוֶת "deep darkness"). Jerome renders the euphemism for "curse" in Job 2:9, בָּרֵךְ "bless" with the same euphemism, *benedic*. The "evil" (הָרָעָה) that God brought upon Job is found also in v-Job in Job 42:11 (*malo* "evil"). The Hebrew idiom מִי־יִתֵּן "would that ..." is often expressed literally by the Latin *quis det* "who will grant" (Job 6:8; 19:23; 23:3; 31:31; but more idiomatic is *utinam Deus loqueretur* "I wish that God would speak," Job 11:5). As in LXX (→ 11.3.1), the infinitive absolute is sometimes translated as a participle from the same root as the main verb, בָּרוֹחַ יִבְרָח "he will certainly flee"/ *fugiens fugiet* "fleeing he will flee" (Job 27:22). Though not frequent, v-Job sometimes retains the syntax of the original, as with *casus pendens*: *anima eius quodcumque voluerit hoc facit* "his soul, whatever it desires, this it does" (Job 23:13).

11.3.7.3.2 Style

Although v-Job does not rise to the level of high style, Jerome nevertheless strives to produce a readable Latin text. Where the Hebrew text repeats the same word, Jerome often uses a different word in the second instance כִּי ... כִּי "that ... that"/ *quod ... quoniam* "that ... that" (Job 5:24–25), *si ... sic* "if ... thus" (Job 24:17); עוֹד ... עוֹד "no more ... any more," *ultra ... amplius* "any more ... any more" (Job 7:10), יְעַוֵּת ... יְעַוֵּת "he perverts ... he perverts," *subplantat ... subvertit* "pervert ... overthrow" (Job 8:3), תִּקְוָתִי ... תִּקְוָתִי "my hope ... my hope," *praestolatio ... patientiam* "expectation ... patience" (Job 17:15); מָה ... מָה "how ... how" *cuius ... cui*, "whose ... to whom" (Job 26:2–3).

Jerome transforms Hebrew paratactic syntax into a variety of subordinate clauses, such as a *cum* clause (Job 6:25; 24:22; 26:14; 27:19), an *ut* clause (Job 12:24; 15:13; 23:5), or an ablative absolute (Job 1:18; 2:12; 24:11; 30:14). Jerome also varies the parataxis by the use of a participle, רָצַץ עָזַב "he has crushed, he has forsaken," *confringens nudavit* "breaking, he has stripped" (Job 20:19). Occasionally, Jerome uses indirect discourse (*vidi eos ... perisse ... esse consumptos* "I have seen that they ... perish ... are consumed," Job 4:8–9; *quis me potest arguere esse mentitum* "who can prove that I have lied," Job 24:25). In order to render the Hebrew text into idiomatic Latin, Jerome sometimes adds words not represented in the Hebrew. These additions include inferential particles, such as *ergo* "therefore" (Job 5:17; 33:12; 35:16), *autem* "moreover" (Job 23:1; 24:1; 30:1), *enim* "for" (Job 23:11; 27:6; 31:2), and *igitur* "so" (Job 32:4; 32:16; 35:1).

Where MT contains a nominal clause, Jerome often inserts a verb (Job 8:16; 9:19; 13:4; 14:12; 18:17; 22:25; 25:2). A prepositional phrase (בְּרִבָם "in their dispute") may be turned into a subordinate clause, *cum disceptarent* "when they had a dispute" (Job 31:13). Even in verbal sentences, Jerome sometimes inserts another verb (Job 6:28; 12:3; 13:19; 24:9). The insertion of a relative clause also serves to present a more connected syntax (Job 1:14; 12:14; 18:21; 24:8; 27:2; 30:2) and relative clauses often translate Hebrew participles, לֹא עֹזֵר לָמוֹ "there is not one helping them," *non fuit qui ferret auxilium*

---

eminent," Job 28:18); Theodotion (ἐν αὐτῷ "in him"/ *contra eum* "against him," Job 19:28).

[4] On Jerome's statements about translation, see further H. Marti, *Übersetzer der Augustin-Zeit* (Munich: Wilhelm Fink, 1974), 73–76.

"there was not one who offered help" (Job 30:13); אֵין לְאִיּוֹב מוֹכִיחַ "there is not one reproving Job," *non est qui arguere possit Iob* "there is not one who is able to convict Job" (Job 32:12). Rather than conveying the asyndeton of the Hebrew text, Jerome usually adds a conjunction, *et* "and" (Job 13:10; 24:17), or even a word such as *quia* "that," introducing a subordinate clause (Job 30:23).

Jerome usually does not seek to render Hebrew idioms literally. An example of his idiomatic Latin translation includes the rendering of phrases like אַף כִּי "How much less"/*quanto magis* "How much less" (Job 25:6). Jerome translates the Hebrew oath formula into understandable Latin: אִם־תְּדַבֵּרְנָה "they will not speak"/*non loquentur* "they will not speak" (Job 27:4). The common Hebrew idiom indicating possession, יֵשׁ לְ- ("there is to"), is translated with the verb *habet* "has": כִּי יֵשׁ לַכֶּסֶף מוֹצָא "surely there is a source for silver," *habet argentum venarum suarum principia* "silver has beginnings of its veins" (Job 28:1).

Jerome sometimes changes the person of the verb for stylistic reasons (Job 4:2; 4:14; 5:13; 12:4; 13:7; 15:3, 9). By using second-person verbs to address God where MT has a third-person verb, Jerome makes clear that the speaker continues to address God (Job 30:24). Elsewhere, Jerome alters the number where the Hebrew has number disagreement in a line (Job 20:11; 21:30). Jerome regularly exercises freedom in translating Hebrew tenses. To render a series of verses beginning with participles, Jerome uses present indicatives, a present participle, and a relative clause: מוֹלִיד ... מֵסִיר ... שׁוֹפֵךְ ... מְגַלֶּה "leading ... depriving ... pouring out ... uncovering"/*ducit ... commutans ... effundit ... qui revelat* "he leads ... changing ... he pours ... who discovers" (Job 12:19–22). Two perfect-tense verbs are rendered with a participle and a perfect קָמוּ ... עָמָדוּ "they rose up ... they stood"/*adsurgentes ... stabant* "rising up, they stood" (Job 29:8). Elsewhere, Jerome gives the same tense in Latin, where the Hebrew has two different verb forms: יַגִּידוּ ... לֹא כִחֵדוּ "they have told ... they have not hidden," "they declare ... they did not hide," *confitentur ... non abscondunt* "they confess ... they do not hide" (Job 15:18; cf. Job 15:25); גָּדַר ... יָשִׂים "he has hedged ... he has set," *circumsepsit ... posuit* "he has hedged ... he has set" (Job 19:8). Jerome often omits Hebrew particles or other words when the Latin is best expressed without them, for example: הֲלֹא "[is] not?" (Job 4:6), הֵן "behold" (Job 8:19; 24:5), infinitive absolute (Job 13:10), אִם "if" (Job 11:13), and the preposition *bet* (Job 24:13).

11.3.7.3.3 Exegesis

In order to clarify the meaning of a text, Jerome sometimes adds words or phrases, such as a noun to specify an unnamed feminine subject, *plaga* "misfortune" (Job 4:5); a genitive noun to explain a noun, *plagae meae* "of my misfortune" (Job 23:2); a prepositional phrase, *sine causa* "without cause" (Job 5:6), *per ignem* "through fire" (Job 23:10), *ex ea* "from it" (Job 23:11); a relative clause to clarify a construct chain, אָהֳלֵי־שֹׁחַד "tents of bribery," *tabernacula eorum qui munera libenter accipiunt* "the tents of those who freely take bribes" (Job 15:34); a gerund to explain a noun, *locum in te latendi* "a place of hidng in you" (v-Job 16:19); an infinitive as object of the verb, אָמְאַס מִשְׁפָּט "I reject the cause," *contempsi subire iudicium* "I have disdained to enter upon the judgment" (Job 31:13). Even where the text is not difficult, Jerome may add a phrase to clarify: כִּי־יָקוּם אֵל "when God shall rise" is rendered *cum surrexerit ad iudicandum Deus* "when God shall rise to judge" (Job 31:14).

Some glosses are guided by theological understanding of the text. Jerome adds a participle and a noun to explain the source of humankind's impurity, טָהוֹר מִטָּמֵא "a clean (thing) from an unclean," *mundum de immundo conceptum semine* "a clean (person) conceived from an unclean seed" (Job 14:4). Jerome's translation of Job 19:27 bears little resemblance to the Hebrew text, but aims to highlight Job's faith in a redeemer: כָּלוּ כִלְיֹתַי בְּחֵקִי "my kidneys are consumed in my bosom," *reposita est haec spes mea in sinu meo* "this hope of mine has been placed in my bosom." On occasion, Jerome's translation defends the justice or holiness of God: while the Hebrew text says that there is "not one" (לֹא אֶחָד) who could make the impure pure, Jerome adds a rhetorical question, *nonne tu qui solus es* "Are not you the only one?" (Job 14:4); while MT

(→ 11.2.2) presents God as leaving injustice unpunished, וֶאֱלוֹהַּ לֹא־יָשִׂים תִּפְלָה "but God does not regard (it) as unseemliness," v-Job presents a God of justice, *Deus inultum abire non patitur* "God does not permit (it) to go unavenged" (Job 24:12).

11.3.7.4 Text-Critical Value
11.3.7.4.1 Omissions and Additions

Jerome's frequent insertion of words or phrases for stylistic reasons and his relatively free translation style make it difficult to determine where v-Job represents a true omission or addition. A possible addition may be found in Job 30:20, where v-Job contains a negative that is generally absent from MT (→ 11.2.2), וַתִּתְבֹּנֶן "you (merely) look," *non respicis* "you do not regard," though this reading is found in one Hebrew manuscript. A reading that may be considered an omission is Job 23:12, where v-Job reads without the conjunction, *non recessi* "I have not departed," whereas MT contains it: וְלֹא אָמִישׁ "and I will not depart."

11.3.7.4.2 Alternative Readings

On occasion, v-Job agrees with other Hebrew manuscripts against the Leningrad Codex (→ 11.2.2) and offers a plausible variant. Most of these examples have to do with suffixes or with prepositions. v-Job 17:10 has *vos omnes* "you all" where the Leningrad Codex has כֻּלָּם "all of them," but a few manuscripts have כֻּלְּכֶם "all of you"; v-Job 19:28 renders *contra eum*, "against him," where the Leningrad Codex has בִּי "against me," but many Hebrew manuscripts and the versions witness בּוֹ "against him." Where the Leningrad Codex has a final *nun*, בְּחַיָּין "life," Jerome reads a *waw* pronominal suffix agreeing with a few Hebrew manuscripts, *vitae suae* "his life" (Job 24:22). In some instances, v-Job suggests emendations not represented by Hebrew manuscripts: *in sinu meo* "in my bosom" (Job 23:12) suggests בְּחֵקִי rather than the reading of MT מֵחֻקִּי "more than my statute," though Job 11:8 may validate the legitimacy of MT-Job 23:12. Jerome's translation *voluntatem suam* "his will" seems to reflect the confusion of the *yod* of MT חֻקִּי "my statute" for a *waw* (Job 23:14). On at least one occasion, v-Job 36:7 agrees with a Qumran text over MT: v-Job has *in solio* "on the throne" where 4QJob[b] (→ 11.2.1.3; → 11.2.3.3) has בכסא "on the throne," but MT has לַכִּסֵּא "on the throne." Besides differences involving prepositions and suffixes, a few other differences can be found; for example, the rendering *de convallibus* "out of the valleys" in Job 30:5 where MT has גֵּו "midst" suggests that Jerome may have thought of the Hebrew word גיא, sometimes vocalized as גַּיְא "valley."

11.3.7.4.3 Vocalization and *Ketiv/Qere*

Because he is working with an unvocalized Hebrew text, Jerome sometimes understands a different vocalization of the consonants found in MT (→ 11.2.2). The form אתה is rendered as a verb, *incesseris* "you will proceed," rather than as the pronoun, "you" (Job 8:6). Jerome renders the noun צַמִּים "snare" in MT as if it were from the root צמא by giving the translation *sitis* "thirst" (Job 18:9). Jerome's translation of the same form, צמים, in Job 5:5 as *sitientes* "the thirsty" may point to the vocalization of the word as צָמֵים (a shortened form of צְמֵאִים) rather than the vocalization צַמִּים "trap" found in MT (Job 18:9). Jerome's rendering *considerate ... expectate* "consider ... wait" assumes that the forms הביטו and קוו are imperatives "look ... hope," rather than perfects as in MT (Job 6:19). The rendering *in proverbiam* "as a byword" for למשל reflects the vocalization לְמָשָׁל rather than the form לִמְשֹׁל "to deride" of MT (Job 17:6), and *iudicium meum* "my judgment" for משפטי represents the vocalization מִשְׁפָּטִי rather than the form מִשֹּׁפְטִי "from my judge" in MT (Job 23:7). Jerome translates the verb ינאקו as *Hiphil* (*fecerunt ... gemere* "they have made ... to groan"), though it is *Qal* (יִנְאָקוּ "they groan") in MT (Job 24:12). He translates a *waw* as a pronominal suffix rather than as a verbal suffix, חטאו *peccatum illius* "his sin," in contrast to the form חָטָאוּ "they have sinned" in MT (Job 24:19).

In instances where there is a *Ketiv/Qere* divergence, Jerome more often supports the *Qere*: במי/*aquis* "with water" (Job 9:30); ושית/"and put"/*dimitte ergo* "therefore, let me be" (Job 10:20); לו/*in ipso* "in him" (Job 13:15); חקיו/*terminos eius* "his limits" (Job 14:5); בקדשיו/"in his holy ones"/*inter sanctos eius* "among his saints" (Job 15:15); וידעיו "and ones knowing him"/*qui ... noverunt eum* "they who know him" (Job 24:1). Jerome appears to follow the *Ketiv* in Job 16:16 (v-Job 16:17), חמרמרה "is red," since v-Job has the singular *intumuit* "is swollen," but this similarity is due to the fact that, "face" (*facies*) is singular in Latin, but plural in Hebrew. In Job 30:11, v-Job reads *faretram suam* "his quiver," reflecting the *Ketiv* יתרו.

Clines, D.J.A., *Job 1–20* (WBC 17; Dallas: Word Books, 1989).
Clines, D.J.A., *Job 21–37* (WBC 18A; Nashville: Thomas Nelson, 2006).
Clines, D.J.A., *Job 38–42* (WBC 18B; Nashville: Thomas Nelson, 2012).
Dhorme, É., *A Commentary on the Book of Job* (trans. H. Knight; Nashville: Nelson, 1984; 2nd French ed.: Paris: Gabalda, 1926).
Driver, S.R. and G. Gray, *A Critical and Exegetical Commentary on the Book of Job* (ICC; Edinburgh: T & T Clark, 1921).

Jason Soenksen

11.3.8 Arabic Translations

11.3.8.1 Saadia Gaon's Translation

Relatively[1] few Judeo-Arabic translations of the book of Job are known to date. Among these, some fragments have been identified in the Cairo Genizah collections, containing anonymous, early, or popular Jewish versions (see further below, → 11.3.8.3). By the tenth century, the need for standardization of the Arabic translations of the Bible, especially the Pentateuch, became pressing to the Jews. The most widespread translation of Job was prepared by Saadia (Gaon) b. Joseph al-Fayyumi (882–942 C.E.), at least as attested in Cairo Genizah sources. Saadia, who was born in Fayyum, Egypt, moved to Palestine in his youth and eventually settled in Iraq and became the Gaon of Sura (see Polliack's introductory survey → 1.3.6; and cf. Sasson's surveys on Proverbs → 12.3.8 and Psalms → 10.3.8). In Job, as in the Pentateuch, Saadia's versions are less literal than the early or popular Jewish translations and Karaite versions, and they are more oriented towards the Arabic target language in their syntax and style.[2] Other features include a tendency to succinctness, theological alterations, shortening and expanding the text for stylistic purposes, and avoidance of repetitions. Saadia's intention was to produce a translation that remains faithful to the literal sense of the biblical text, yet takes into account the rules of the Arabic target language. Nonetheless, the rationalistic theology of his time was occasionally at odds with this goal. The end result was an interpretive translation, which in the case of the Pentateuch he called *tafsīr* (→ 1.3.6.3.1),[3] and in the case of Job he entitled *Kitāb al-Taʿdīl* "The Book of Theodicy." Extant manuscripts of Saadia's work on Job include his translation and commentary on the book and an extensive introduction, in which Saadia presents his doctrine on divine justice, just retribution, and the suffering of the righteous. In this, he sets out the wider interpretive framework for his translation and commentary on the book. Saadia maintains that God's grace is immeasurable, that it fills the entire universe, and that creation itself is proof of God's grace. Human suffering is caused not by a whimsical God, but rather it serves one of three purposes: The first is discipline and education, the second is punishment for transgression, and the third is the testing and examination of the righteous in order to reward them in the future, either in this world or the world to come. It is the third category to which Saadia classifies Job's suffering in this treatise *Iyov*.[4]

Saadia's translation and commentary is based on three assumptions: 1) the ultimate coherence of scripture; 2) the significance of every expression in the text; and 3) the veracity of the text.[5] Several principles characterize Saadia's translation and commentary. A literal translation is always preferred. Exceptions to this rule are only called for when a statement clashes with reason, when a phrase does not conform to the common use of

---

[1] The writing of this article was supported by the Israel Science Foundation, grant no. 410/10.

[2] Polliack, "Cairo Genizah"; Polliack, *Karaite*.
[3] Polliack, *Karaite*; Polliack, "Concept"; Polliack, "Cairo Genizah"; Sasson, "Arabic"; Steiner, *Biblical Translation*.
[4] Qafiḥ (ed.), *Iyov*.
[5] Goodman, "Interpretive."

biblical language, or when tradition instructs us otherwise. Only in these instances is it permitted to interpret the text by means of metaphor.[6] Saadia sees it as his mission to find a rational explanation for every word in the Bible. He thus finds an equivalent term in Arabic for all the *hapax legomena* and to all geographical locations as well as all fauna and flora. In Saadia's Islamic rationalistic intellectual milieu, there is no room for mystical or mythological translation or interpretation of Job. Behemoth and Leviathan are natural beings and Uz is identified as a location in Syria near Damascus.[7] In a similar vein, Saadia does not allow for demons, monsters, or demigods in his translation. God is the absolute creator and the problem of Job is every person's problem.

Saadia exhibits great sensitivity to the poetic structure of the book of Job. This is demonstrated by his careful attempt to keep the size of lines in the translation the same as in the original text wherever possible. Saadia skillfully utilizes Arabic syntax, crafting it according to the original Hebrew text. Whenever possible he preserves the chiastic relationship between lines. By adhering to the precise structure, Saadia enables the reader of his Arabic translation to appreciate the diction without compromise. Alliteration is a common device in biblical poetry. Saadia makes an effort to reflect this feature in his translation. Being a poet himself, Saadia pays close attention to sounds and therefore uses cognates whenever possible. One can almost feel a sense of competition between him and the Joban poet when he successfully comes up with five different Arabic synonyms for "lion" in Job 4:10–11. At the same time, Saadia's careful avoidance of anthropomorphism is demonstrated in his translation of Job. For example, the notion of God actively seeking Job in 7:21, "When You seek me, I shall be gone," is turned into the passive voice: "I will be sought for and will not be found." It is noteworthy here that even as Saadia is making a point of refraining from anthropomorphism, he skillfully achieves this goal by making a minimal change in vocalization that does not disrupt the poetic fabric. Furthermore, Saadia offers a glimpse into his thought process by adding a comment explaining why he chose the passive voice here. In his remark, he says that he replaced the (Masoretic) active voice with a passive Arabic construction because it is not possible to assume such an action by God (i.e. actively seeking a person). Saadia's upholding of reason reaches beyond his concern about God's corporality. Thus, human traits attributed metaphorically to inanimate objects or concepts are transformed in translation, losing their poetic (non-literal) sense: "Days" cannot possibly see, hence in Saadia's rendition of Job 9:25, "My days fly swifter than a runner; They flee without seeing good," it is not the days that "see no good" but rather "I (Job) did not see good in them (the days)." Furthermore, in an attempt to avoid poetic exaggeration Saadia adds a restrictive element and renders: "it is as if I did not see good in them." Saadia is usually very careful to preserve word pairs as they are, but is sometimes compelled by reason to alter them. For instance, in Job 12:8a, since earth is inanimate and cannot be spoken to, Saadia replaces "speak to the earth, it will teach you" with "converse with the wild animals of the earth." Adding "wild animals" to the translation is in fact "correcting" the poetics of the original Hebrew by providing a symmetrical parallel to "the fish of the sea" found in Job 12:8b. Similarly in Job 20:27, "Heaven will expose his iniquity; Earth will rise up against him," is translated into Arabic as "therefore will the folk of the heavens reveal his guilt, and the folk of the earth rise up against him." Thus "folk of the heavens" and "folk of the earth" are replacing "heavens" and "earth" in an attempt to avoid the personification of the inanimate heavens and earth.[8] Saadia's theology leaves no room for monsters, demons, and semigods. Hence Job 1:6, "One day the sons of God presented themselves before the Lord, and Satan came along with them," posits two problems for Saadia. The first is the concept of the sons of God and the second is Satan. Saadia

---

[6] Saadia, *Emunot*. An edition is provided by Qafiḥ (ed.), *Sefer HaNivḥar be-Emunot*.

[7] Goodman, "Interpretive."

[8] Rosenthal, "Exegesis."

translates sons of God as "the ones who worship God." He bases his translation on Exod 4:22 and Deut 32:5 in which Israel is referred to as the sons of God. As for Satan, Saadia translates it as "adversary." Saadia explains that Satan is in fact a human being. One of the texts upon which he bases his claim is 1 Kgs 11:14, in which Satan is an epithet for the enemy of King Solomon, Hadad the Edomite. Saadia explains that Satan cannot possibly be an angel because angels are devoid of any desire, be it good or bad, whereas Satan expresses an evil desire and therefore cannot be an angel.[9] It is possible to detect the influence of the Jewish Aramaic version (Targum [→ 11.3.3.1]) in Saadia's translation. For instance, in Job 11:18 "entrenched" is translated as "you establish a house of burial" in the Targum. Influenced by the Targum, Saadia renders it in Arabic: "and when you build a house." Similarly, in Job 22:8, "a man of (a strong) arm" is translated in the Targum as "a man of victory" and in Saadia's translation as "the man of overpowering arm." In these two examples, it is evident that Saadia does not prefer the Aramaic over the Hebrew but rather combines both to come up with his own version.[10] Modern scholarly editions of Saadia's translation and commentary on the book of Job were published by Derenbourg (1879) and Qafiḥ (1973).[11],[12] An English translation of the work was published by Goodman (1988).[13]

11.3.8.2 Karaite Translations

Karaite Bible translations were motivated by the rejection of rabbinical authority and Jewish oral law. Most Karaite translations were written in the tenth and eleventh centuries, the golden age of Karaite literary activity. Karaites used the same orthographical standards as Saadia, yet their translations draw upon what appear to be earlier, pre-Saadian Jewish traditions.[14]

Yefet ben ʿElī, the major Karaite translator and exegete and younger contemporary of Saadia, translated the entire Hebrew Bible into Judeo-Arabic during the second half of the tenth century, a translation that has survived in numerous manuscript sources (see → 1.3.6.3.2), alongside an extensive complementary commentary meant to be studied together with it. Nineteen manuscripts containing Yefet's translation and commentary on Job are listed in the catalogue of the Institute of Microfilmed Hebrew Manuscripts at the Israel National Library. Like Saadia, Yefet prefaced his work on each book of the Bible with an introduction in which he specified the nature of the book and his goals as a translator and exegete. Sharing with Saadia the Islamic rationalistic milieu of their time, Yefet discusses in his introduction to the book of Job aspects of divine justice, just retribution, and the suffering of the righteous. He too classifies Job's suffering as the suffering of love, the suffering of the righteous whom God loves, the suffering that is to be rewarded in the future or in the world to come. In addition to the discussion of theodicy, Yefet lists thirteen benefits of the book of Job, that is, its educational and religious contributions. Several of these benefits relate to the supplying of information in the book about non-Israelite monotheists who lived in antiquity and congregated regularly to discuss and spread monotheism in the world. Other topics Yefet mentions include rhetorical patterns and possible manners in which to conduct theological debates, Satan's *modus operandi*, and God's greatness. The last contribution Yefet mentions is that God established in the book of Job the gracious memory of a righteous, noble, and learned person for posterity, as a universal model for righteous human behavior. Modern scholarly editions of Yefet's translation and commentary on Job are only partial and include Ben-Shammai (1969) and Hussain (1986).[15] A full edition is now in the process of preparation by Arik Sadan.

---

[9] Saadia, *Version*. An edition is provided by Derenbourg (ed.), *Version arabe du livre de Job de Saadia Ben Iosef al-Fayyoumi*.

[10] Rosenthal, "Exegesis."

[11] Derenbourg (ed.), *Version arabe du livre de Job de Saadia Ben Iosef al-Fayyoumi*; Qafiḥ (ed.), *Iyov ʿim targum*.

[12] Derenbourg (ed.), *Version arabe du livre de Job de Saadia Ben Iosef al-Fayyoumi*; Qafiḥ (ed.), *Iyov ʿim targum*.

[13] Goodman, *The Book of Theodicy*.

[14] Polliack, *Karaite*.

[15] Ben-Shammai, "Editions and Versions in Yefet b. Ali's

11.3.8.3 Other Translations

Several scores of anonymous translation fragments of Job have been identified in the Cairo Genizah Arabic and Judeo-Arabic collections. It is possible that more exist and have not yet been identified. Usually, these Genizah fragments represent ad hoc translations, sometimes in popular style and sometimes more akin to Saadia's translation methodology.[16]

A translation of Job is also attested in the sixteenth-century *sharḥ* by the Rabbanite commentator Rabbi Issāchār ben-Sūsān ha-Ma'arāvī, who was born in the city of Fez in Morocco and moved to Safed at a young age. Ben-Sūsān proclaimed the necessity of updating Saadia's Bible version in the comprehensible Arabic of his time (→ 1.3.6; → 3–5.1.8; → 6–9.1.8).

According to David Sklare of the Israel National Library, who graciously shared the following as-yet unpublished information, Salmon ben Yeruḥam, the tenth-century Karaite exegete, wrote a commentary on Job, presumably accompanied by a translation. Salmon mentions his work on Job in his translations and commentaries on Lamentations and Ecclesiastes. No manuscript containing this work has been identified as yet. Sklare suggests that Tanḥum ben Yoseph ha-Yerushalmi, the fourteenth-century Rabbanite exegete and grammarian, included a commentary on Job in his work *Kitāb al-Bayyān*. In addition, Sklare relays that the undated manuscript SP RNL EVR ARAB I 3812 contains a translation and commentary on Job. At the beginning of the manuscript, there is a flyleaf written in a different hand than the rest of the document. It includes a statement that it is a summary epitome (*talkhīṣ*) by Aharon ben David HaCohen based on the works of Salmon ben Ruhaym (Salmon ben Yeruḥam), al-Sijilmāsi, Yehudah ben Quraysh, Abu Sa'id Levi ben al-Hasan al-Baṣri (Levi ben Yefet), and Abu Ya'qūb Yusuf ibn Nūḥ, and compared with the work of Saadia. Presumably the reference to Yehudah ben Quraysh and Levi ben Yefet points to their grammatical works. Al-Sijilmāsi is the unknown author of an unknown commentary on Job.

Baker, C.F. and M. Polliack, *Arabic and Judaeo-Arabic Manuscripts in the Cambridge Genizah Collections, Arabic Old Series (T-S Ar.1a-54)* (Cambridge: Cambridge University Press, 2001).

Ben-Shammai, H., "Perusho ha-arvi shel Yefet ben Eli le-Iyov 1–5" (MA thesis, Hebrew University of Jerusalem, 1969) [Hebr.].

Ben-Shammai, H., "Editions and Versions in Yefet b. Ali's Bible Commentary," *Alei Sefer* 2 (1976): 17–32 [Hebr.].

Blau, J., "Saadya Gaon's Pentateuch Translation and the Stabilization of Medieval Judaeo-Arabic Culture," in *The Interpretation of the Bible: The International Symposium in Slovenia* (ed. J. Krašovec; SJOTSup 289; Sheffield: Sheffield Academic Press, 1998), 393–98.

Brody, R., *Rav Se'adya Gaon* (Jerusalem: The Zalman Shazar Center, 2006) [Hebr.].

Derenbourg, J. (ed.), *Œuvres complètes de R. Saadia ben Iosef al-Fayyoûmî*, Vol. 5: *Version arabe du livre de Job de Saadia Ben Iosef al-Fayyoumi* (Paris: E. Leroux, 1879).

Goodman, L.E., *The Book of Theodicy: Translation and Commentary on the Book of Job by Saadiah Ben Joseph Al-Fayyūmī* (New Haven: Yale University Press, 1988).

Goodman, L.E., "Saadiah Gaon's Interpretive Technique in Translating the Book of Job," in *Translation of Scripture: Proceedings of a Conference at the Annenberg Research Institute, May 1989* (Philadelphia: Annenberg Research Institute, 1990), 47–76.

Hussain, H.A., "Yefet ben 'Eli's Commentary on the Hebrew Text of the Book of Job I–X," (PhD diss., St. Andrews University, 1986).

Khan, G., "The Orthography of Karaite Hebrew Bible Manuscripts in Arabic Transcription," *JSS* 38 (1993): 49–70.

Mann, J., *Texts and Studies in Jewish History and Literature*, Vol. 2 (New York: Ktav Publishing House, 1972).

Polliack, M., *The Karaite Tradition of Arabic Bible Translation: A Linguistic and Exegetical Study of Karaite Translations of the Pentateuch From the Tenth and Eleventh Centuries C.E.* (Études sur le Judaïsme médiéval 17; Leiden: Brill, 1997).

Polliack, M., "Arabic Bible Translations in the Cairo

Bible Commentary"; Hussain, "Yefet ben 'Eli's Commentary on the Hebrew Text of the Book of Job I–X."

[16] See the indices in Baker and Polliack, *Catalogue*; Shivtiel and Niessen, *Catalogue*.

Genizah Collections," in *Jewish Studies in a New Europe* (eds. U. Haxen et al; Copenhagen: C.A. Reitzel, 1998), 595–620.

Polliack, M., "Se'adyā Gaon's Concept of Biblical Translation in light of the Karaite Concept," in *Heritage and Innovation in Medieval Judaeo-Arabic Culture* (eds. J. Blau and D. Doron; Ramat-Gan: Bar-Ilan University Press, 2000), 191–201.

Polliack, M., "Types of Arabic Bible Translations in the Cairo Geniza Based on the Catalogue of TS Arabic," *Te'uda* 15 (1999): 109–25 [Hebr.].

Qafiḥ, Y. (ed.), *Sefer HaNivḥar be-Emunot u-ve-De'ot le-Rabbenu Saadiah Ben Yosef Fayyumi zs"l* (Jerusalem: Sura, 1970) [Hebr.].

Qafiḥ, Y. (ed.), *Iyov 'im targum u-ferush ha-gaon rabbenu Saadiah ben Yoseph Fayyumi zṣ"l* (ed. Jerusalem: Hava'ad le-hoṣa'at sifre rasa"g, 1973) [Hebr.].

Rosenthal, E.I.J., "Saadya's Exegesis of the Book of Job," in *Saadya Studies in Commemoration of the One Thousandth Anniversary of the Death of R. Saady Gaon* (ed. E.I.J. Rosenthal; Publications of the University of Manchester, 282; Manchester: University Press, 1943), 177–205.

Sasson, I., "Arabic," in *EncJud* 3 (^{2}2007):603–06.

Shivtiel, A. and F. Niessen, *Arabic and Judaeo-Arabic Manuscripts in the Cambridge Genizah Collections: Taylor-Schechter New Series* (Cambridge: Cambridge University Press, 2006).

Sklare, D., "Unknown Karaite Works in the Firkovitch Collection," in *Judaeo-Arabic Manuscripts in the Firkovitch Collections: The Works of Yusuf al-Basir: A Sample Catalogue: Texts and Studies* (eds. D. Sklare and H. Ben-Shammai; Jerusalem: Ben-Zvi Institute, 1997), 127–39.

Sklare, D., "A Guide to Collections of Karaite Manuscripts," in *Karaite Judaism: A Guide to Its History and Literary Sources* (ed. M. Polliack; HdO 1.73; Leiden: Brill, 2003), 893–924.

Steiner, R.C., *A Biblical Translation in the Making: The Evolution and Impact of Saadia Gaon's Tafsīr* (Cambridge: Harvard University Press, 2010).

Tobi, Y., "On the Antiquity of the Judeo-Arabic Biblical Translations and a New Piece of an Ancient Judeo-Arabic Translation to the Pentateuch," in *Ben 'ever la-'arav*, Vol. 2 (ed. Y. Tobi; Tel Aviv: Afikim, 2001), 17–60 [Hebr.].

Walfish, B.D. and M. Kizilov, *Bibliographia Karaitica: An Annotated Bibliography of Karaites and Karaism* (Études sur le judaïsme médiéval 43; Leiden: Brill, 2011).

Zawanowska, M., "Review of Scholarly Research on Yefet and His Works," *REJ* (forthcoming).

Zucker, M., *Rav Saadya Gaon's Translation of the Torah* (New York: Philipp Feldheim, 1959).

Ilana Sasson

11.4 Secondary Translations

11.4.1 Vetus Latina

As shown by Burkitt,[1] the book of Job passed through three stages in Greek (→ 11.3.1): 1) In its original form, it lacked about 400 lines that were intentionally omitted by the translator. This short form survives in the Sahidic version (→ 11.4.2) and in the Old Latin version (see below); 2) In a following stage, most of the *lacunae* were supplied from Theodotion (→ 11.3.5). This is the form found in most of the extant Greek manuscripts including LXX$^{S, B, A, C}$; 3) In the Hexapla, Origen accurately filled in the gaps, placing the *stichoi* borrowed from Theodotion under asterisks (→ 11.3.5). Each of these text types is represented in the Latin. It can be demonstrated as we keep going back in time.

1) Around the year 387 C.E., Jerome translated the Hexaplaric text using his diacritical signs.[2] His work had been preserved in three Latin manuscripts: VL^{132}, VL^{160} (until Job 38:16), and VL^{161}. The diacritical signs have not always been transmitted correctly (they are even absent in VL^{160}). This is the text that Sabatier had edited in 1743 on the basis of the Marmoutier manuscript now preserved in Tours (VL^{161}).[3] Augustine remains the most important witness to Jerome's Hexaplaric translation. He glosses over this text in his *Adnotationum in Iob liber* (ca. 400 C.E.) but he also cites it elsewhere. However, this is not the only form of Job cited by him; he also happens to cite from Jerome's translation based on the Hebrew (V-Job → 11.3.7). Quotations from Jerome's Hexaplaric translation text (→ 21.8) are also found in Orosius (*Liber apologeticum*, dated 415 C.E.), in John Cassian (*Collationes*, between 420 and 426 C.E.), in the *Commentarius in Iob* of the priest Philip († 455/456 C.E.), disciple of Jerome, in the *Instructiones* of Eucherius of Lyon († ca. 450 C.E.), in Fulgentius of Ruspe († 527 C.E.), and in the glosses in three Spanish Bibles (VL$^{162, 193, 194A}$). Liturgical (Lauds in the office of St. Stephen) and iconographical (Job represented as a king and identified with Jobab = Job 42:17a–e) representations of Job also happen to be based on this text type.

2) The non-Hieronymic version of the longer Greek text (LXX$^{S, B, A, C}$) is mostly represented by Ambrose's citations of Job.[4] There are abundant citations of Job (→ 21.8) in his *De interpellatione Iob et David* (ca. 387/389 C.E.). It is certain that he quotes from a longer text that included the *stichoi* under asterisks (Job 13:19b, 21a; 21:15ab, 23ab, 32ab; 26:6ab, 7–8, 11; 27:19b; 28:8ab, 14ab, 18b, 21b, 27a; 39:4abc). Against Burkitt,[5] who thought that Ambrose translated directly from the Greek text, Bogaert holds the opinion that he had at his disposal a complete Latin translation of the longer text.[6] Ziegler had noted an affinity between the text used by Ambrose and the marginal glosses in certain Spanish Bibles (VL$^{91, 92, 94, 95, 96}$) that he edited,[7] an affinity that had been observed already in the case of the Proverbs (→ 12.4.1).

3) The Old Latin text itself (VL), i.e., the Latin translation of the shorter original form of LXX-Job, does not survive in direct transmission; no manuscript has transmitted it and only the patristic quotations help to reconstruct it.[8] This fact is explained for the most part by the success of Jerome's two Latin translations of Job that rapidly supplanted the oldest Latin version. The book of Job as well as the book of Revelation, which is a similar case, show the sheer importance of patristic quotations for certain biblical books (→ 1.7.2; → 21.8). In the case of Job, the Old Latin citations bring the Sahidic ver-

---

[1] Burkitt, *Old Latin*, 8–9, 32–34.
[2] Bogaert, "Job," 75–82.
[3] Sabatier, **Bibliorum*, 1.826–910.
[4] Bogaert, "Job," 68–70.
[5] See n. 1.
[6] Bogaert, "Job."
[7] Ziegler, *Randnoten*.
[8] Bogaert, "Job," 59–68.

sion (→ 11.4.2) out of its isolation and prove that the Sahidic did not purely and simply refuse to translate the asterisked *stichoi*, a hypothesis in itself highly improbable. The Old Latin text remains unedited and its publication in the collection of the Vetus Latina Institute (Beuron) is not yet scheduled. Meanwhile, we are able to provide partial indications on the text transmitted by the patristic witnesses. The earliest Old Latin citations (the African text, siglum K in the edition of Beuron) appear in Book III of Cyprian's *Ad Quirinum* (ca. 250 C.E.). Although short in length, they are numerous enough and are able to show that they correspond to a Latin text translated from the shorter Greek text. One example demonstrates this clearly: Cyprian cites Job 29:12–13 and Job 29:12–16 in two different places and each time he omits the *stichos* 13a that is under asterisk. In the European continent in the following century (ca. 357/358 C.E.), the quotations from Lucifer of Cagliari (normally referred to with the siglum R in the Beuron edition) also attest to the VL text. The author is all the more interesting as he has the habit of citing long extracts from the biblical texts. He therefore works on an open-book basis. The citation of Job 23:17–24:18 is most convincing: there is a noted absence of Job 24:4a, 5c, 8a, and 14b–18a, which are the thirteen *stichoi* under asterisk. In the citation of Job 21:2–20, the asterisked *stichoi* 15ab and 19b are also omitted (but the existence of other omissions renders the problem more complex). The citations in Priscillian († 385/386 C.E.) are also long, in particular the extracts from Job 40 and 41. One also takes note of the absence of the asterisked verses (Job 40:26a; 41:8a, 9ab, 21a, 24b) in the quotations. However, Job 40:9ab is also missing in the quotations of Priscillian although it is not under asterisk; nevertheless, it could have been omitted in the shorter Greek text. Finally, Priscillian's quotations also include some additions (in Job 40:13b and 17b). However, it is in the *Liber de divinis scripturis* (Italy, early fifth century C.E.; falsely attributed to Augustine) in which the largest number of citations of Job appears. Their brevity does not always help in determining if a *stichos* is absent or not, but one should note the absence of the following asterisked *stichoi*: Job 22:24ab; 29:13a; 31:18ab, 23b, 24a, 27a, 35a. The citations of Job contain a large number of readings without correspondence in the Greek text (which may be suggestive of some adaptations in function of the context). The author of the *Consultationes Zacchaei christiani et Apollonii philosophi* (Gaul, ca. 408/410 C.E.) cites Job, but probably through the intermediary of Cyprian. Primasius († ca. 560 C.E.), in his *Commentary on the Apocalypse*, cites Job 11:5–6 while omitting 5b (under asterisk), but he is also familiar with v-Job (→ 11.3.7). Finally Gildas, in his *De excidio et conquestu Britanniae* (Wales, between 515 and 530 C.E., or possibly ca. 700 C.E.), as shown by Burkitt,[9] cites Job following a Latin version not containing the asterisked verses. In fact, he omits the following asterisked verses: Job 21:15ab, 19b; 24:4b, 5c; 24:14b–18a, as well as some non-asterisked ones (omission likely to be traced back to Gildas). The commentary on Job by Julian of Eclanum (ca. 418/419 C.E.), an anonymous commentary of Job,[10] as well as the *Moralia in Job* of Gregory the Great are based on the version produced by Jerome on the basis of the Hebrew (v-Job), but they testify in some places to certain Old Latin readings.[11] The prologue *Peritorum mos est* (at the beginning of the anonymous Job commentary) could have been composed to introduce a Latin translation (revision) of Job that is now lost and that originated from within a Pelagian milieu towards the beginning of the fifth century C.E.[12]

Bogaert, P.-M., "Job latin chez les Pères et dans les Bibles: D'une version courte à des versions longues sur le grec et sur l'hébreu," *RBén* 122 (2012): 48–99, 366–93.

---

[9] Burkitt, "Gildas," 209–10, 215.
[10] K.B. Steinhauser, H. Müller, and D. Weber (eds.), *Anonymi in Iob commentarius* (CSEL 96; Vienna: Verlag der Österreichischen Akademie der Wissenschaften, 2006).
[11] Ziegler, *Iob*, 23–32, and Bogaert, "Job," 74, 86–91.
[12] Bogaert, "Job," 71–74.

Burkitt, F.C., *The Old Latin and the Itala: With an Appendix Containing the Text of the St. Gallen Palimpsest of Jeremiah* (TS 4.3; Cambridge: Cambridge University Press, 1896).

Burkitt, F.C., "The Bible of Gildas," *RBén* 46 (1934): 206–15.

Vattioni, F., *Per il testo di Giobbe* (Suppl. 89 agli Annali 56; Naples: Istituto Universitario Orientale, 1996).

Ziegler, J., *Randnoten aus der Vetus Latina des Buches Iob in spanischen Vulgatabibeln* (Bayerische Akademie der Wissenschaften, Philos.-Hist. Kl. Sitzungsberiche 1980/2; Munich: Verlag der Bayerischen Akademie der Wissenschaften, 1980).

Ziegler, J., *Iob* (Septuaginta Vetus Testamentum Graecum 11.4; Göttingen: Vandenhoeck and Ruprecht, 1982).

Ziegler, J., *Beiträge zum griechischen Iob* (MSU 18; Göttingen: Vandenhoeck and Ruprecht, 1985).

Jean-Claude Haelewyck

11.4.2 Coptic Translations

11.4.2.1 Background

The Coptic version of the book of Job certainly dates back to the fourth century C.E. when the Wisdom and Poetical Books were translated in all probability in monastic cycles. The earliest witnesses of Cop-Job are very fragmentary papyrus and parchment manuscripts of mostly unknown provenance.[1]

The Sahidic dialect provides not only the oldest but also the greatest number of manuscripts. The bulk of the known Cop^{Sa}-Job witnesses came from the Monastery of St. Shenoute ("White Monastery"), which is one of our main sources for the Sahidic version of the Coptic Old Testament. Unfortunately, the leaves of the manuscripts are often dispersed over several collections around the world. The major part (seventy-eight leaves) of the most complete manuscript, Cop$^{Sa\ 27}$ (eighty-two of a total of 112 leaves preserved),[2] is kept in the Vatican Collection in Rome. The remaining leaves or fragments are kept in London, Paris, and Strasbourg. In this tenth-century codex, the book of Job followed Proverbs and Qohelet. Nevertheless, Cop^{Sa}-Job is completely preserved apart from Job 39:10–40:11, corresponding to a single leaf, which is missing. The Sahidic manuscripts date from the fourth to the fourteenth centuries.

The Bohairic version is likewise complete and has been transmitted in various manuscripts, but the oldest relevant witness thereof dates no earlier than the fourteenth century (manuscript John Rylands Library 417).[3] The whole (late) text transmission of Cop^{Boh}-Job seems to be based on this manuscript or on its *Vorlage*.[4] Typical for this manuscript tradition is also its connection to Proverbs (→ 12.4.2), but the text ends with Prov 14:26; the remainder of Proverbs is missing in all manuscripts. Despite its late transmission, it is very likely that the Bohairic translation of Job was made in a single process at a much earlier date, probably already in the fifth or sixth century C.E. The only indication for an early Bohairic translation of Job is a school text on papyrus in the University of Michigan Collection.[5] In addition to spelling exercises, it contains Job 1:1 and Rom 1:1–8, 13–15. The dating of the papyrus seems difficult but the fourth or fifth century C.E. might be conceivable. However, it is striking that this short Job text on papyrus is almost identical to the version that is nearly one thousand years later than the school exercise. Moreover, it has been observed that the (late) Bohairic texts display a certain similarity to the Greek *Codex Ephremi rescriptus* (LXX^c), which dates to the fifth century C.E.[6]

Only very few traces from the book of Job have survived in other dialects of Coptic. A Fayyumic version has been discovered in tiny fragments. One

---

[1] Schüssler, *Biblia Coptica* 1.4 (Cop$^{Sa\ 111,\ 117ex}$); Schüssler, *Biblia Coptica* 2.2 (Cop$^{Sa\ 193,\ 231}$); for the dating of the manuscripts in question, an earlier date is mostly preferable.

[2] Schüssler, *Biblia Coptica* 1.2, 33–36 (Cop$^{Sa\ 27}$).

[3] Wagner, "Coptic Book of Job," 8–9; W.E. Crum, *Catalogue of the Coptic Manuscripts in the Collection of the John Rylands Library Manchester* (Manchester: University Press, 1909), 189–90.

[4] Wagner, "Coptic Book of Job," 7.

[5] E.M. Husselman, "A Bohairic School Text on Papyrus," *JNES* 6 (1947): 129–51, esp. 149–50 regarding Job 1:1.

[6] Porcher, *Livre de Job*, 214; Wagner, *Coptic Book of Job*, 4.

fragment appears in the University of Michigan Collection, P. Mich inv. 3585c (Job 32:7–10).[7] Another fragment dated to the fourth or fifth century C.E., P. Mich inv. 5421 (Job 30:21b–25, 26, 28–30),[8] has been reassigned as displaying instead another dialect within the Bohairic group.[9] In the same way, a further fragment (traces of Job 30:8, 9, 17, 18; fifth century C.E.)[10] has been classified as Fayyumic[11] but belongs clearly to another dialect, most probably the Middle Egyptian or Mesokemic[12] dialect.

11.4.2.2 Extant Biblical Text, Text Editions, and Auxiliary Tools

There is no critical edition of Cop[Sa]-Job. Therefore one has to consult the publications of the single extant manuscripts and the standard reference catalogue *Biblia Coptica* by Schüssler.[13]

The Monastery of St. Shenoute ("White Monastery") near Sohag in Upper Egypt possessed a number of codices[14] that usually combined the Poetical and Wisdom books of the Old Testament in one or several volumes. The sequence of these books seems not to have been canonized as is the case also in the LXX manuscripts (→ 11.3.1).[15] Until a critical edition of Cop[Sa]-Job is available, the old edition of the Vatican manuscript Cop[Sa 27] by Ciasca is still usable since Ciasca also provided an apparatus with variant readings (including LXX) so far as they were known to him.[16] The readings from Cop[Sa]-Job in liturgical manuscripts (lectionaries), overwhelmingly stemming from the White Monastery,[17] contribute additional testimony.

Cop[Boh]-Job was edited by Tattam already in 1846.[18] However, it is not completely clear on which manuscripts Tattam's text is based.[19] Later, Porcher provided a new edition based on three important manuscripts and the edition of Tattam.[20] Both editions are not fully reliable. Nevertheless a modern edition, based on manuscript John Rylands Library 417, is a desideratum.

11.4.2.3 Translation Character and Text-Critical Value of Cop-Job for LXX-Job

It seems quite clear that the translations of Cop[Sa]-Job and Cop[Boh]-Job are independent of each other. At any rate, the translation of Cop[Boh]-Job must be more recent as it generally follows the longer version of LXX-Job (→ 11.3.1) according to Origen's Hexapla and includes the asterisked material of Theodotion (→ 11.3.5).[21] Cop[Sa]-Job, however, is considered the best witness for the pre-Hexaplaric or short version of LXX-Job (→ 11.3.1; → 11.3.2).[22]

---

[7] W.H. Worrell, *Coptic Texts in the University of Michigan Collection* (University of Michigan Studies Humanistic Series 46; Ann Arbor: University of Michigan Press, 1942), 11, no photograph and no edition available.

[8] G.M. Browne, *Michigan Coptic Texts* (PapyCast 7; Barcelona: Papyrologica Castroctaviana, 1979), 2–8; Ziegler, *Iob*, 47.

[9] R. Kasser and H. Satzinger, "L'Idiome du P.Mich. 5421," *WZKM* 74 (1982): 15–32.

[10] W.E. Crum and H.I. Bell, *Wadi Sarga: Coptic and Greek Texts from the Excavations Undertaken by the Byzantine Research Account* (Coptica 3; Copenhagen: Gydendalske Boghandel-Nordisk, 1922), 29–30; B. Layton, *Catalogue of Coptic Literary Manuscripts in the British Library Acquired since the Year 1906* (London: The British Library, 1987), 233 (inv. Or. 9035 [41]).

[11] Ziegler, *Iob*, 47; Layton, *Catalogue of Coptic Literary Manuscripts*, 233; Takla, "Introduction," 75 n. 14.

[12] H.-M. Schenke, "Mesokemic (or Middle Egyptian)," *The Coptic Encyclopedia* 8.162a–64b.

[13] For an initial overview, the list in Ziegler, *Iob*, 42–44, is still useful.

[14] Two codices are known today, Cop[Sa 27] (containing Proverbs, Qohelet, and Job), and Cop[Sa 30] (containing Job and Proverbs). Cf. Schüssler, *Biblia Coptica* 1.2, 33–36 and 39–42.

[15] Wagner, "Coptic Book of Job," 5–6; Feder, "Die koptischen Versionen des Proverbienbuches," 10.

[16] Ciasca, *Fragmenta Copto-Sahidica*, 2.1–68; the preface is in Latin. The edition of the same manuscript(s) by É. Amélineau, "The Sahidic Translation of the Book of Job," *Transactions of the Society of Biblical Archaeology* 9 (1893): 405–75, is not reliable.

[17] Schüssler, *Biblia Coptica* 1.4 (Cop[Sa 105L, 108L]); 2.1 (Cop[Sa 48L]); 2.2 (Cop[Sa 197L, 211L, 226lit]). For liturgical texts and their Old Testament readings in general, see U. Zanetti, "Leçons liturgiques du Monastère Blanc: Ancien Testament," *BSAC* 46 (2007): 205–30.

[18] Tattam, *Job the Just*.

[19] Wagner, "Coptic Book of Job," 6–14.

[20] Porcher, *Le Livre de Job*; Wagner, *Coptic Book of Job*, 14; Ziegler, *Iob*, 45–47.

[21] Wagner, "Coptic Book of Job," 3; Ziegler, *Iob*, 149.

[22] Bogaert, *"Septante,"* 626; Ziegler, *Iob*, 147–49.

Ciasca[23] and Dieu[24] have discussed the textual character of Cop^Sa-Job. Dieu confirmed Ciasca's observations that prove that some obvious exceptions to the rule are due to the process of text transmission and copying rather than being real variants from the Greek parent text. The only known witness of Cop^Sa-Job that displays a clear Hexaplaric influence is a Job pericope from a late (twelfth or thirteenth century) paper lectionary from the White Monastery (Job 29:21–25; 30:1–7),[25] but this Hexaplaric influence could be due to an adaptation to Cop^Boh-Job. Reconsidering Ciasca's assessment, Ziegler counts 379 asterisked verses omitted by Cop^Sa-Job.[26] However, a more detailed description and assessment of the text character of Cop^Sa-Job and Cop^Boh-Job will only be possible when based on a modern critical edition of all available manuscripts.

Dieu, L., "Nouveaux Fragments préhexaplaires du livre de Job en copte sahidique," *Mus* 13 (1912): 147–85.
Feder, F., "Die koptischen Versionen des Proverbienbuches," in *Christliches Ägypten in der spätantiken Zeit* (ed. D. Bumazhnov; Studien und Texte zu Antike und Christentum 79; Tübingen: Mohr Siebeck, 2013), 1–13.
Porcher, E., *Le livre de Job: Version copte bohaïrique* (PO 18.2; Paris: Firmin-Didot, 1924), 211–339.
Takla, H., "An Introduction to the Coptic Old Testament," *Coptica* 6 (2007): 1–115.
Tattam, H., *The Ancient Coptic Version of Job the Just* (London: William Straker, 1846).
Wagner, S., "The Coptic Book of Job and Leiden Or. 14.544: An Inquiry into its Textual History and its Place with the Book of Proverbs," *St. Shenouda Coptic Quarterly* 1.3 (2005): 3–23.
Ziegler, J. (ed.), *Job* (Septuaginta Vetus Testamentum Graecum 11.4; Göttingen: Vandenhoeck & Ruprecht, 1982).

Frank Feder

---

[23] Ciasca, *Fragmenta Copto-Sahidica*, 2.xxiii–xxxii; Ziegler, *Iob*, 147–48.
[24] Dieu, "Fragments préhexaplaires," 147–56.
[25] Schüssler, *Biblia Coptica* 2.2 (Cop^Sa 211L), 60–67; Dieu, "Fragments préhexaplaires," 149; Ziegler, *Iob*, 148.
[26] Ziegler, *Iob*, 148.

11.4.3 Ethiopic Translation(s)

11.4.3.1 Title and Place in the Manuscripts

When a title is provided, the book is invariably called ዘኢዮብ "'Iyōb," which is also the subscription in the oldest manuscripts. Eth-Job always circulates conjoined to one or more other biblical books. The earliest Ethiopic codices pair Job with Daniel (→ 18.4.3). Although this collocation continues into modern times, it becomes rare starting in the fifteenth century when scribes tend to place Job after *1 Enoch* (→ 11.5.1.2) and before the Solomonic corpus (→ 12.4.3; → 13–17.2.3.2; → 13–17.2.3.3; → 11.15.5).

11.4.3.2 Background

The sole "critical" edition of Eth-Job appeared in 1907 when Esteves Pereira produced a text and apparatus based on three manuscripts.[1] Numerous transcriptions and the "additions apocryphes" in Eth-Job 2:9 and 42:17 convinced him that the Old Ethiopic derived from the Greek. With regard to the evolution of the book in Ethiopia, he identified Arabic (→ 11.3.8; → 11.4.8) as the source of pluses found in one of the manuscripts he studied.[2]

Gerleman, working from Esteves Pereira's edition, documented how the translator of Job rejected strict formal equivalency for larger literary aims.[3] Subsequently, Ziegler further nuanced and buttressed the claims of Esteves Pereira and Gerleman.[4]

11.4.3.3 Translation Character

Both in concept and in detail, the translator of Eth-Job differs from others who rendered religious literature into Gəʿəz. First, as Gerleman has demonstrated, the translator treasured readability, and

---

[1] Esteves Pereira, "Job."
[2] Esteves Pereira, "Job," 573–74. Ziegler's citation of Esteves Pereira is misleading (*Iob*, 48–49), for Esteves Pereira did not envision the corrector consulting a Hebrew *Vorlage*. Immediately prior to the quoted portion, Esteves Pereira states specifically that the revision was "certainly an Arabic version which derives from a Masoretic text" ("sur une version arabe provenant d' un texte massorétique"; → 11.3.8).
[3] Gerleman, "Job," 64–72.
[4] Ziegler, *Iob*, 48–50.

he did so to the point of creatively crafting readings. One sees this especially in Th-Job (→ 11.3.5.3.1). For many of the added stichs, which typically contain rare vocabulary and difficult grammatical constructions, he relied on his own imagination to provide substitutions.[5] As a result, there are no large omissions resulting from a translator despairing of a solution, a phenomenon met regularly in other Ethiopic books of the Bible.[6] Second, the translator exhibits particular idiosyncrasies. For example, rather than represent ἄγγελος "angel/messenger" with the otherwise ubiquitous መልአክ "angel/messenger," he treats the Greek word as if it were an arthrous participle ("the one who announces" = ዘይኔኑ).

Job's extensive vocabulary challenged the translator, who had limited knowledge of Greek. When confronted with unknown words, the translator often guessed at their meaning based on presumed etymology, literary context, or both. Thus, the technical terms Πλειάδος and Ὠρίονος ("Pleiades" and "Orion" *NETS*) in Job 38:31 are respectively translated ለብዙኃን "the many," as if from πλεῖστος "most," and ሙሐዝ "water channel," as if from ῥέω "to flow." Completely unaware of the switch to astrological wonders, and thus expecting a continuation of the previous meteorological context, he guessed "winter" and "summer" for Μαζουρωθ and Ἕσπερον (*"Mazouroth"* and "evening star" *NETS*) respectively in Job 38:32.

In Eth-Job, one also encounters errors resulting from unfamiliarity with uncial manuscripts. Sometimes, the translator and perhaps the scribe of the Greek *Vorlage* (→ 11.4.3.4) incorrectly identified letters or divided words. For example, በልዳዶስ መስፍን አውኬኔዎን "*Bäldadōs* ruler of *ʾAwkēnēwōn*" results from the translator mistaking the article (ὁ) and first letter of Σαυχαίων "Sauchites" (*NETS*), the place of origin, as a nominative ending for Baldad's name (Job 42:17e).

11.4.3.4 Text-Critical Value

Several factors currently complicate text-critical investigation of Eth-Job. First, where renderings are quite free, the underlying Greek text is difficult or impossible to recover. Second, limited availability of published resources hampers current efforts. Several important Ethiopic manuscripts have recently come to light, including one at least 200 years older than Esteves Pereira's best witness. Any work without recourse to these new finds is deficient.

Despite these severe limitations, enough evidence exists to conclude that the Old Ethiopic derives from a Greek manuscript that had combined LXX (→ 11.3.1) with numerous Theodotionic readings (→ 11.3.5.3.1). There may also be minor Lucianic influence (→ 11.3.6), but Ziegler rightly concludes that most of the agreements are likely due to other causes.[7] More detailed conclusions may be possible, but they must await a new critical edition.

11.4.3.5 Subsequent History

Perhaps because of the Old Ethiopic version's readability, the Transitional Period (→ 1.4.3.7.4) hardly impacted the book of Job. Certainly scholars at that time were noting major differences with other versions, for in Eth[EMML 1768] marginal sigla mark variants from an unknown comparison text.

However, significant change waited until the revisers of the Standardized Text (→ 1.4.3.7.5) made corrections based on an Arabic version (→ 11.3.8; → 11.4.8). Even then, they still followed their traditional text closely. For example, unable to correlate the very free renditions of Job 38 with the readings of their Arabic manuscript, they inserted a new translation of v. 31 after v. 33. Likewise, because their Old Ethiopic exemplar had dropped the reference to camels in Job 42:12 through parablepsis, they reinserted the phrase, but at the end of the list of Job's possessions instead of in its proper place. The Textus Receptus follows this Standardized Text closely, with only limited expansions and conflations (→ 1.4.3.7.6).

---

[5] See the examples below from Job 38:31–32.
[6] See Gerleman, "Job," 64–72. The omission of Job 13:3–8 was probably accidental rather than due to linguistic difficulty.

[7] Ziegler, *Iob*, 48–49.

As with the book of Daniel, around the seventeeth century a new translation was made from the Arabic (→ 11.3.8; → 11.4.8), which fully conformed the book to MT (→ 11.2.2). It appears that the translator retained nothing from previous iterations of Ethiopic Job. It is true that Job 38:31 reads virtually the same as the Standardized Text, but this probably resulted from similar Arabic *Vorlagen*, for in this new translation Job 38:31 immediately follows v. 30 (instead of v. 33) and none of the surrounding verses remotely approximate those found in the Standardized Text.

Esteves Pereira, F.W. (ed.), "Le Livre de Job: Version Éthiopienne," *PO* 2 (1907): 565–688.
Gerleman, G., "The Ethiopic Translation of the Book of Job," in G. Gerleman, *Studies in the Septuagint I* (Lund: Gleerup, 1946), 64–72.
Ziegler, J. (ed.), *Iob* (Septuaginta Vetus Testamentum Graecum 11.4; Göttingen: Vandenhoeck & Ruprecht, 1982).

Curt Niccum

11.4.4 Job, Proverbs, Canticles, and Qohelet in Late Syriac Translations

11.4.4.1 Background

The books in the corpus of the Greek Old Testament were normally transmitted in blocks. For this reason Job, Proverbs, Qohelet, and Canticles are treated together, since they belong together as the "block of sapiental texts" in textual transmission. Sirach and Wisdom were frequently included in this block as well.

Our source of the Syro-Hexapla texts of Job, Proverbs, Qohelet, and Canticles is a single manuscript, Milan, Biblioteca Ambrosiana, C. 313. Inf., commonly known as Codex Syro-Hexaplaris. This manuscript is dated to the eighth century C.E. Understanding this source entails knowledge of: 1) copying procedures; 2) codicology of the manuscript; 3) geography; 4) history; and 5) the textual relations of the various witnesses and history of the textual transmission. Much crucial information is embedded in colophons at the end of each book. These indispensable sources are accordingly presented as follows:

Colophon to Job, Codex Syro-Hexaplaris, folio 52r[1]

ܫܠܡ ܟܬܒܐ ܕܐܝܘܒ ܙܕܝܩܐ.
ܐܝܟ ܡܫܠܡܢܘܬܐ ܕܫܒܥܝܢ܀
~~~~~~~~~~~~~~~~
ܐܬܢܣܒ ܐܝܘܒ ܡܢ ܬ̈ܪܒܥܐ
ܩ̈ܪܐ ܥܬܝܩܐ܀

Translation:

> The book of Job, the righteous, has been completed according to the version of the Seventy. Job was taken from the old Tetrapla.

Commentary:

Punctuation signs, as well as a decorative line, divide the text into two. The first statement identifies the source text of the translation as LXX (→ 11.3.1). The second statement notes more particularly that for this purpose the source text for Job was the old Tetrapla.

Colophon to Proverbs, Codex Syro-Hexaplaris, folio 66r

ܪ̇ܫܝܡ ܗܘܐ ܟܬܒܐ ܗܢܐ
ܕܡܢܗ ܐܬܦܫܩ ܠܣܘܪܝܐ ܟܬܒܐ
ܗܢܐ ܕܦ̈ܠܐܬܐ: ܟܬܪ ܫܘܠܡܐ
ܕܠܗܘܢ ܗܟܢܐ ܀ ܐܬܒ̈ܨܩܘܢ
ܘܐܬܦܫ̈ܩܘܢ ܦܠ̈ܐܬܐ. ܡܢ ܝ̈ܚܢܐ
ܫܬܝܬܐ ܕܐܬܗܫܡ ܘܐܬܬܟܒܘ
ܒܗ ܡܢ ܠܒܪ ܡܫܘܠܚ. ܒܐܝܕܐ
ܕܦܡܦܠܘܣ ܘܕܐܘܣܒܝܘܣ. ܕܒܗ
ܕ̈ܫܝܡܝܢ ܗܘܘ ܘܗܠܝܢ ܀ ܐܬܒ̈ܨܩܘܢ
ܡܢ ܫܬܝܬܝ ܦ̈ܬܐ ܕܐܘܪ ܠܝܫܘܥ
ܗܠܝܢ ܕܐܫܒܚܢ ܀ ܀ ܀
ܘܬܘܒ ܀ ܒܟܬܒܐ ܕܠܗ. ܦܡܦܠܘܣ
ܘܕܐܘܣܒܝܘܣ ܬܪ̈ܝܢ ܀

---

[1] Taken from A.M. Ceriani, *Codex Syro-Hexaplaris Ambrosianus: Photolithographice editus curante et adnotante* (Monumenta Sacra et profana ex codicibus praesertim bibliothecae Ambronsianae 7; Milan: Bibliotheca Ambrosiana, 1874). Cited according to the folio number in the facsimile by Ceriani; the manuscript has a different numbering system.
~~~~~~~~~~~~~~~~

Translation:

It was noted in the Greek book from which this book of Proverbs was translated into Syriac, after the end of them, as follows: The Proverbs were copied and collated from an accurate copy that was made in which scholia were written in the margins by the hand of Pamphilus and Eusebius, and in which were noted also these things: These things that we found were taken from the Hexapla Version of Origen. And again: in their own handwriting "Pamphilus and Eusebius corrected."

Commentary:

Four major punctuation signs, one repeated three times after text that does not fill out the line, divides this colophon into four sections. The first part indicates that the last three parts constitute a colophon or colophons in the Greek *Vorlage* of the Syriac translation. The second part mentions a colophon in the Greek *Vorlage* of the Syriac translation that describes how it was produced. It claims that the source text was physically similar with marginal notes and that these marginal notes or scholia were copied by no less than Pamphilus and Eusebius themselves. The third and fourth sections constitute the colophon in the source text from which the Greek *Vorlage* was copied and belong together as the word "and again" (ܘܬܘܒ) indicates. The third section employs the first person plural to indicate Pamphilus and Eusebius found the materials that they provided in the marginal notes in Origen's Hexapla. The fourth section declares that Pamphilus and Eusebius corrected the text produced in this way.

The final statement is difficult to interpret. In fact, much of the commentary on these colophons by previous scholars is sheer speculation. I suggest that this statement means that the source text for the *Vorlage* of the Greek copy used by the Syriac translators was produced by scribes under the supervision of Pamphilus and Eusebius. The correction process involved one person reading the source text aloud and the other making corrections in the target copy.

What is the evidence for the copying scenario that I have suggested? One of the best discussions of ancient book-making is the 1956 study by Skeat.[2] He draws attention to the colophon to Esther in Codex Sinaiticus,[3] which is worth citing here, as a basis for understanding the colophons in Codex Syro-Hexaplaris:

Ἀντεβλήθη πρὸς παλαιώτατον λίαν ἀντίγραφον δεδιορθωμένον χειρὶ τοῦ ἁγίου μάρτυρος Παμφίλου. Πρὸς δὲ τῷ τέλει τοῦ αὐτοῦ παλαιωτάτου βιβλίου ὅπερ ἀρχὴν μὲν εἶχεν ἀπὸ τῆς πρώτης τῶν βασιλείων· Εἰς δὲ τὴν Εσθηρ ἔληγεν. τοιαύτη τις ἐν πλάτει ἰδιόχειρος ὑποσημείωσις τοῦ αὐτοῦ μάρτυρος ὑπέχειτο ἔχουσα οὕτως:

Μετελήμφθη καὶ διορθώθη πρὸς τὰ ἑξαπλᾶ Ὠριγένους ὑπ' αὐτοῦ διορθωμένα. Ἀντωνῖνος ὁμολογητὴς ἀντέβαλε, Πάμφιλος διώρθωσα τὸ τεῦχος ἐν τῇ φυλακῇ διὰ τὴν τοῦ θεοῦ πολλὴν καὶ χάριν καὶ πλατυσμόν. [καὶ εἴγε μὴ βαρὺ εἰπεῖν, τούτῳ τῷ ἀντιγράφῳ παραπλήσιον εὑρεῖν ἀντίγραφον οὐ ῥᾴδιον.]

\>\>\>\>\>\>

διεφώνει δὲ τὸ αὐτὸ παλαιώτατον βιβλίον πρὸς τόδε τὸ τεῦχος εἰς τὰ κύρια ὀνόματα

\>\>\>\>\>\>

Translation:

Transcribed in transmission from a very old copy; corrected by the hand of the holy martyr Pamphilus. At the end of this same very old book, which began at First Kingdoms and ended at Esther, such a signature, broadly speaking, in the martyr's own hand is appended as follows:

Copied and corrected in relation to the Hexapla of Origen, as corrected by himself. Antoninus the confessor collated, and I, Pamphilus corrected the volume in prison, by the great and wide favour of God. [And if it not be presumptuous to say so, it would not be easy to find a copy equal to this copy.]

Now the old book disagrees with this volume in respect to certain proper names.

Commentary:

The note is divided into two by indentation. The first part is by a corrector or scribe of Codex Sinaiticus who tells us that he used an extremely old manuscript containing Kingdoms to Esther to

---

[2] T.C. Skeat, "The Use of Dictation in Ancient Book-Production," in *The Collected Biblical Writings of T.C. Skeat* (ed. J.K. Elliott; VTSup 113; Leiden: Brill, 2004), 3–32.

[3] Based on the manuscript, http://www.codex-sinaiticus.net/en/, accessed July, 2013.

correct Codex Sinaiticus. This ancient copy was corrected by Pamphilus. The corrector of Codex Sinaiticus cites the colophon in his source text to prove this.

The second part of the note is a copy of the actual colophon in the source text that was written in Pamphilus' own handwriting. It states that the source text was first copied from the Hexapla and then corrected against the Hexapla with Antoninus as collator and Pamphilus as corrector. Also noted is the fact that Pamphilus did the work in prison.

For a date, Skeat suggests 309 C.E. since Pamphilus was martyred the following year.[4] The sentence stating that the manuscript is the best copy ever may have been written by Pamphilus or perhaps by the scribe who corrected Codex Sinaiticus using his manuscript.

The explanation provided by Skeat for the process of correcting the manuscript is that a team of two was required: one person, i.e., Antoninus, read the source text aloud at dictation speed, while the other person, the corrector, entered corrections into the manuscript that had been newly copied.

Skeat's explanation has been confirmed in further research in an article published in 1986 by Petitmengin and Flusin.[5] They cite a letter written by the Patriarch Timothy I (727/8–823 C.E.) of Baghdad around 800 C.E.[6] The letter is addressed to one Sergius, concerning a project entailing making three copies of a Syro-Hexapla manuscript in approximately six months by a team of eight people. Six of the eight people were copyists, while two were lectors. These lectors not only read the source text for the copyists, but were also responsible for correcting the manuscripts with one reading the source text aloud while the other entered corrections into the text of the copy. It is an extremely interesting document since so little documented description of the practices involved in book-making are available. Although the date of the letter written by Timothy I is indeed late, we may be able to assume consistent practices in copying over the previous four hundred years as the situation seems exactly parallel to the work of Pamphilus and Eusebius.

Another interesting parallel is the number of people in the scribal team and the number of copies made. When Constantine commanded Eusebius to send him fifty copies of the Bible for use in churches (→ 1.1.2.2.6.7), Eusebius promptly responded ἐν πολυτελῶς ἠσκημένοις τεύχεσιν τρισσὰ καὶ τετρασσὰ διαπεμψάντων ἡμῶν "we sent (him) threes and fours in richly wrought bindings."[7] Scholars have debated greatly the phrase τρισσὰ καὶ τετρασσά "threes and fours": does it mean books laid out in three or four columns; books copied in quires with three or four bifolia per quire; or three or four copies at a time? Skeat argues cogently for the last meaning, especially since these words modify the participle διαπεμψάντων. He explains that the urgency of the matter and the risk of incurring the wrath of a capricious emperor motivated Eusebius to send the manuscripts off as soon as they were completed rather than wait until all were completed. It may be, however, that three or four codices were all that could be produced at one time, given the mechanics of the process and the operational size of Eusebius' scriptorium, however magnificent at the time. The main point of the magisterial study of Codex Sinaiticus by Milne and Skeat was to show that the manuscript was produced by three scribes, not four.[8] This fits well with

---

[4] Skeat, "The Use of Dictation in Ancient Book-Production," 18.

[5] P. Petitmengin and B. Flusin, "Le Livre Antique et la Dictée: Nouvelles Recherches," in *Mémorial André-Jean Festugière: Antiquité Païenne et Chrétienne* (eds. E. Lucchesi and H.D. Saffrey; Geneva: Cramer, 1984), 247–62.

[6] For the text in Syriac, see O. Braun, "Ein Brief des Katholikos Timotheos I. über biblische Studien des 9. Jahrhunderts," *OrChr* 1 (1901): 299–313.

[7] *Vita Const.* 4.37.1.

[8] See H.J.M. Milne and T.C. Skeat, *Scribes and Correctors of the Codex Sinaiticus* (London: British Museum, 1938). Cf. also D. Jongkind, *Scribal Habits of Codex Sinaiticus* (Texts and Studies 3.5; Piscataway: Gorgias, 2007). Parker argues for four scribes on the basis of a recent study (see D.C. Parker, *Codex Sinaiticus: The Story of the World's Oldest Bible* [Peabody: Hendrikson, 2010], 49, 63). It is an unpublished paper by A.C. Myshrall, "The Presence of a Fourth Scribe in Codex Sinaiticus?" (October, 2006) which Prof. Parker passed on to me. Nonetheless, one of the scribes could be more of a lector/supervisor as well as a minor copyist. Thus, the evidence

the data given in the letter by Timothy I who assembled a double scribal team with one lector and three scribes each.

Before further parallels are drawn, we turn now to the colophons for Qohelet and Canticles.

Colophon to Qohelet, Codex Syro-Hexaplaris, folio 70ʳ

[Syriac text]

Translation:

> It was noted in the Greek book from which this book of Qoheleth was translated into Syriac, after its end, as follows: In the same manner Qoheleth was taken from the very same manuscript in which also those that are similar to it afterwards were set together. Moreover, by the hand of the Holy Pamphilus are these (books). Pamphilus and Eusebius, we corrected [them].

Commentary:

This colophon is carefully divided into four parts by a major punctuation sign in Syriac (❖). This punctuation sign has been represented in the translation by a colon and three periods set in bold type. Although Mercati was well aware of the importance of the punctuation, his retroversion into Greek and that of Middeldorpf into Latin do not clearly mark it or show it, which is the key to grasping the four-part structure of the colophon. The first part indicates that the last three parts constitute a colophon or colophons in the Greek *Vorlage* of the Syriac translation. The second part describes further how the Greek *Vorlage* or parent text was copied. It affirms that the text of Qohelet was taken from exactly the same manuscript of the Hexaplaric text. It indicates that there was one codex that contained all the sapiental books. The verb rendered "set together" (ܣܝܼܡܚ) means that all the sapiental books were put together in a single codex, in accordance with the practice of textual transmission in which the Greek Old Testament was transmitted in blocks (or groups of books). Moreover, the adverbial phrase "in the same way" (ܒܗ ܒܕܡܘܬܐ) clearly shows that this colophon is grammatically and semantically dependent on that of Proverbs. The third and fourth sections constitute the colophon in the source text of the Greek *Vorlage* and belong together as the wording "and again" indicates. The third could mean that this text was produced by Pamphilus, i.e., by scribes under his supervision, or it could mean that Pamphilus was the one who put the sapiental books into a block, i.e., a single codex. The fourth declares that Pamphilus and Eusebius corrected the text produced in this way. This correction involved one person reading the source text aloud and the other making corrections in the target copy.

Colophon to Canticles, Codex Syro-Hexaplaris, folio 72ʳ

[Syriac text]

Translation:

> The Book of the Song of Songs according to the Version of the Seventy-Two is completed. It was translated into Syriac from the Greek Book in which was the following note:
> In the same way also Song was taken from the very same codex. In which were noted at the end also

---

for Codex Sinaiticus coincides well with the description in Letter 47 of Timothy I.

these things: taken from the Hexapla, from these things that we found, of Origen, according to the version of the rest (of the books). Moreover, by his own handwriting: Pamphilus and Eusebius, we corrected [them].

Commentary:
Once again, a punctuation sign denoting a major break divides the text into four distinct sections. The first section affirms that the text translated into Syriac is from LXX, here called the Version of the Seventy-Two, i.e., a name that is neither shortened nor abbreviated. It also affirms that the last three sections constitute a translation of a colophon, or better colophons, in the Greek *Vorlagen*. The second section describes how the Greek *Vorlage* was copied. Note again, that this sentence is semantically dependent on the colophons for both Qohelet and Proverbs as we can see from the adverbial phrase "in the same way" (ܒܙܢܐ ܗܟܢܐ). Thus, Canticles was taken in transmission from a Hexaplaric text just as Qohelet and Proverbs were. In addition, it was taken from the very same codex, i.e., a codex in which the sapiental books had been placed together. Finally, this Greek *Vorlage* had a colophon indicating its source.

Parts three and four go together as is indicated by the phrase "and again." The third part has the first person plural indicating that Pamphilus and Eusebius discovered materials in the Hexapla of Origen (→ 1.3.2) that they wished to insert as marginal notes or scholia. The phrase "according to the version of the rest of the books" is semantically dependent on the earlier colophons to Proverbs and Qohelet where the Hexapla is specified. The source text of the Greek *Vorlage* had its colophon in Pamphilus' and Eusebius' own handwriting stating that they had corrected the text. This seems to mean that Pamphilus and Eusebius had scribes copy the sapiental texts into a codex and they checked it by one person reading the text aloud and the other making corrections in the target copy. They also would have added the marginal notes.

From the colophons to Proverbs, Qohelet, and Canticles considered so far, the following observations are worth noting. First by comparing our colophons with those attested in Greek, we can easily see the equivalents in Greek since the Syriac translators were so committed to formal equivalence:

Syriac	Greek	English
ܐܬܢܣܒ	μετελήφθη	copied in transmission
ܐܬܦܚܡ	ἀντεβλήθη	collated
ܐܬܬܣܝܡܘ	παρετέθησαν	set together
ܬܪܨܘ	διωρθώσαντο	corrected
ܢܣܚܐ	ἀντίγραφον	copy

Second, the sapiental books were transmitted in a block, or single codex/roll. The evidence for this is supplied at the back of Rahlfs' *Verzeichnis* where he lists all the manuscripts in the blocks in which they were transmitted. This section is entitled "Übersicht über das handschriftliche Material für die einzelnen Teile des A.T."[9] In Rahlfs' section, there are seven blocks section as follows:

1. Octateuchus
2. Reg., Par., Esdr.
3. Est., Idt., Tob.
4. Mac. I–IV
5. Ps.Od.
6. Libri sapientiales (Prov. Eccl. Cant. Iob. Sap. Sir. Ps. Sal.)
7. XVI prophetae

So when scribes attempted to produce a *pandect* Bible, they had to assemble a group of seven codices or rolls, roughly speaking. The colophons present early evidence for this. The colophon to Esther in Codex Sinaiticus speaks of a book that contained Kingdoms through Esther, i.e., the Historical literature. Here, Esther was part of the second block and not part of the third with Judith and Tobit. The columns in Codex Sinaiticus support this. The Historical Books and Prophets before the Poetical Books are written in four columns

---

[9] A. Rahlfs, *Verzeichnis der griechischen Handschriften des Alten Testament* (MSU 2; Berlin: Weidmannsche Buchhandlung, 1914), 373–439.

as are the Gospels, which follow. Nonetheless, the Poetical Books are written in two columns. This is doubtless due to the fact that it was normal practice for scribes to follow the physical layout of the source text.

Third, attention to the full texts of the colophons reveals a genealogy of at least three generations of texts:

Syriac Translation
|
Greek *Vorlage* of Syriac
|
Vorlage of Text in Alexandria

Some scholars suggest that the colophons by Pamphilus and Eusebius were copied through several generations of manuscripts. So perhaps the Greek *Vorlage* of the Syro-Hexapla was a copy of a manuscript that had been copied from the original of Eusebius and Pamphilus and also copied the colophon. The matter is uncertain. The colophons in the Codex Marchalianus are actually *before* the book and not after. This is an example of a colophon being copied but did not belong originally to the source copy and shows the scribe's way of indicating a good tradition but not a source text actually produced by Eusebius. Here the colophons are at the end of each text. Nonetheless, if Paul of Tella (→ 1.4.5.2) and his team translated around 617 C.E. and the copy in Alexandria was made between 300 and 350 C.E. it would make the source manuscript over 250 years old at the time of translation.

11.4.4.2 Geography and History

A number of colophons give information about dates, people, and places. We have opportunity to consider only one, the Colophon to 3 Kingdoms in manuscript BM Add. 14437:

Translation:

This book (from which the present work was translated from Greek into Syriac) was copied from the Hexapla, i.e. from the Six Columns that was among the texts of the Six Columns that was among the books of Caesarea in Palestine and was compared to a manuscript in which was noted at the end as follows: I, Eusebius, corrected as accurately as possible. Translated, then, from the Greek Language into Syriac in the month Shebat of the 927th [year] according to the numbering of Alexander, Fourth Indiction at Enaton of Alexandria in the Holy Monastery of Antonine Monks.

Elsewhere, Paul of Tella (→ 1.4.5.2) is mentioned as a translator. Here we have a claim for the same three generations of manuscripts.[10] The Syro-Hexapla is a translation of copies of the Fifth Column of Origen's Hexapla (→ 1.3.1.2.7) into Syriac. As we can see from the manuscript, included in the margins of this scholarly translation are notes on the text including translations of selected readings from Theodotion, Aquila, and Symmachus. This translation was made by Paul, Bishop of Tella, in 617 C.E. at the Antonine Monastery at Enaton, a relay post on the coastal road 14 kilometres west of the city of Alexandria. Tella d'Mauzalath (between Edessa and Mardin) was the centre of a diocese of the Syrian Orthodox Church. Paul, Bishop of Tella, probably fled to Alexandria due to the Persian invasion led by Khusraw II Parwez Hormezd. Nonetheless, Barsoum in *The Scattered Pearls*[11] claims that Patriarch Athanasius I had invited Paul of Tella to come to the Antonian

---

[10] The evidence is conveniently gathered in R.J.V. Hiebert, "Syriac Biblical Textual History and the Greek Psalter," in *The Old Greek Psalter: Studies in Honour of Albert Pietersma* (eds. R.J.V. Hiebert, C.E. Cox, and P.J. Gentry; JSOTSup 332; Sheffield: Sheffield Academic Press, 2001), 179, n. 3.

[11] A.I. Barsoum, *The Scattered Pearls: A History of Syriac*

Monastery to do the translation. No doubt, once Paul was granted asylum there, they needed to give him a job.

There is an interesting colophon at the very end of Codex Syro-Hexaplaris:

Colophon to Milan, Bib. Ambr. C 313 Inf. (folio 193v)

ܐܝܬܘܗܝ ܟܬܒܐ ܗܢܐ ܠܕܝܪܐ ܡܫܒܚܬܐ
ܕܝܠܕܬ ܐܠܗܐ ܕܒܡܕܒܪܐ ܕܐܣܩܝܛܣ
ܘܡܬܩܪܝܐ ܗܝ ܕܝܪܐ ܕܣܘܪ̈ܝܝܐ
ܗܘ ܕܩܪܐ ܢܨܠܐ ܥܠ ܕܝܪܝܐ ܝܘܚܢܢ
ܡܢ ܥܘܡܪܐ ܕܡܪܝ ܓܒܪܐܝܠ

> This book belongs to the renowned monastery
> of the 'Mother of God' which is in the desert of Scete
> (Nitria) and is designated monastery of the Syrians.
> May he who reads pray for the monk Yohanan
> from the abode of Mar Gabriel.[12]

Codex Syro-Hexaplaris belonged to the Syrian monastery of the Nitrian Desert in Egypt known as Deir Al-Suryan and is written in a late-eighth or early-ninth-century C.E. hand (s. colophon, fol. 193v). This area, also known as the Desert of Scete (Wadi Al-Natrun), is some 80–90 kilometres south of Alexandria. While the precise role of the monk called Yohanan is unclear, what is clear is that the manuscript belonged to the Deir Al-Suryan Monastery, south of Alexandria. Consequently, this manuscript is not far from its source in both place and time.

11.4.4.3 Sources, Editions, and Auxiliary Tools

Editions:

H. Middeldorpf, *Codex Syriaco-Hexaplaris: liber quartus Regum e codice parisiensi, Jesaias, duodecim Prophetae minores, Proverbia, Jobus, Canticum threni, Ecclesiastes e codice mediolanensi* (Berlin: Enslin, 1835).

R. Ceulemans, "A Critical Edition of the Hexaplaric Fragments of the Book of Canticles, with Emphasis on their Reception in Greek Christian Exegesis," (PhD diss., Katholieke Universiteit Leuven, 2009).

Facsimile:

A. Ceriani, *Codex Syro-Hexaplaris Ambrosianus photolithographice editus* (Monumenta Sacra et Profana 7; Milan: Biblioteca Ambrosiana, 1874).

Concordance:

W. Strothmann, *Konkordanz des syrischen Koheletbuches nach der Peshitta und der Syrohexapla* (Göttinger Orientforschungen 1.4; Wiesbaden: Harrassowitz, 1973).

11.4.4.4 Translation Character and Technique

For Canticles and Proverbs, no critical edition exists yet in the Göttingen Septuaginta and apart from Ceulemans' work on Canticles, no serious study of the Syro-Hexapla focused particularly on these books has been published since the edition of Field.[13] For Job, there is the edition of J. Ziegler, and for Qohelet, the edition of P.J. Gentry, both in the Göttingen Septuaginta.[14] Hence, the approach here is to focus mainly on Qohelet and Job, and in broad strokes, paint a similar scenario for Canticles and Proverbs.

Beginning with Qohelet, Codex Syro-Hexaplaris offers many different kinds of materials, all relevant for Hexaplaric studies and for the text of the Old Testament. First is the text itself, which includes words marked by an asterisk in ten instances and also names the source in eight of them. Before the discovery of LXX[788], only one other witness (i.e., Codex Venetus) preserves any asterisks for Qohelet and does so twice, erroneously in both instances.

Literature and Sciences (trans. and ed. M. Moosa; Piscataway: Gorgias, 2011), 39, 313.

12 I acknowledge gratefully the assistance of Jerome Lund in reading this text.

13 Field, *Hexapla.

14 J. Ziegler, *Iob* (Septuaginta Vetus Testamentum Graecum 11.4; Göttingen: Vandenhoeck & Ruprecht, 1982); P.J. Gentry, Ecclesiastes (Septuaginta Vetus Testamentum Graecum; Göttingen: Vandenhoeck & Ruprecht, forthcoming).

Twice words are marked in the text of the Syro-Hexapla by an obelus, and four times by a cursive obelus or lemnisk. Second, there are marginal notes offering at least six different types of information: 1) a few notes offer textual variants; 2) many marginal notes offer readings from the later Jewish revisers, Aquila, Symmachus, and Theodotion; 3) fifteen notes offer words in Greek to clarify evidence when retroversions may be uncertain; 4) seven notes offer explanatory glosses; these are always distinguished from Hexaplaric notes by being circled; 5) longer scholia are found in the top and bottom margins, with appropriate indices to connect them to the text; and 6) eight of the longer scholia contain seven citations from the Qohelet *Commentary of Olympiodorus* and one from that of Evagrius.

These materials are not always easy to interpret and use. In the introduction to the third volume of *Critique Textuelle de l'Ancien Testament*,[15] Barthélemy summarises such difficulties in using the Syro-Hexapla succinctly as follows: 1) sometimes the translator misinterpreted his *Vorlage*; 2) the intentions of the Greek scholiast or his Syriac translator must be considered in order to accurately use the marginal notes; 3) sometimes the indices or the notes are misplaced in the Syro-Hexapla; 4) sometimes the sigla for the sources are confused in the margin of the Syro-Hexapla or perhaps were already confused in the margin of his *Vorlage*; and 5) the biblical text may not always faithfully represent the Hexaplaric text. These difficulties can be easily illustrated from the footnotes to Field's edition.[16] Some examples are given below.

As a general rule, the Syriac translation both for the version of LXX and for the texts of the revisers is characterised by extreme formal equivalence. Usually, the same equivalents in Syriac are employed for the same words in the Greek source text so that retroversion into Greek is not difficult. Even the syntax in Syriac closely follows that of the source text and the order of the words as well, so that one cannot only reconstruct the original in Greek but also differentiate easily between different constructions in Greek.

A few statistics will reveal the relative riches provided by the Syro-Hexapla in terms of Hexaplaric readings. For Qohelet, before the discovery of LXX[788], Hexaplaric readings in the margins of Greek manuscripts were found in only six sources, as follows:

Source	Number of Readings
161	318
248	328
252	208
336	1
411	3
539	85

Manuscripts LXX[161] and LXX[248] preserve the same textual tradition and seventy-five percent of their readings are also shared with manuscript LXX[252]. The readings in manuscript LXX[539] are all *sine nomine* and only one is unique. About a dozen more readings are found embedded in the different *catenae* traditions in Qohelet, few of them unique. A probable stemma for the Greek manuscripts in respect to the marginal readings is as follows:

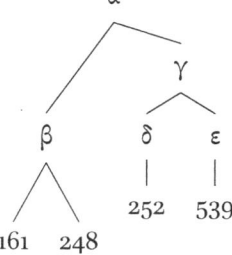

Jerome preserves about sixty-five readings in his commentary on Qohelet, approximately seventeen of them not shared by other sources.

---
[15] Barthélemy, *Critique textuelle 1992*, clxxii–clxxviii.
[16] Field, *Hexapla*.

11.4.4 JOB, PROVERBS, CANTICLES, AND QOHELET IN LATE SYRIAC TRANSLATIONS

TABLE 1 Qoh 12:13a

ἀκούεται "is heard"	ἄκου "hearing"	ἀκούετε "hear" (2nd pl.)	ἄκουε "hear" (2nd sg.)
LXX⁹⁹⁸; LXXᴼ = LXX^(V, 253); Jerome, Comm. Eccl.	LXX⁶³⁷	LXX⁴⁷⁵; Syh	Remaining manuscripts

TABLE 2 Qoh 3:19c

αὐτοῖς "for them"	τοῖς πᾶσιν αὐτοῖς "for all of them"	[Omitted]	αὐτοῖς πᾶσιν "for them all"
Remaining manuscripts	Corrector of LXXˢ; LXXᴼ + LXX^(411, 766); Arm; Jerome's Comm. Eccl.^(variant reading) 3:19e	Coptic Fayoumic version	Syh (text marked by obelus); Metrophanes (Lemma and Commentary III.20,8; x.8,96)

The Syro-Hexapla preserves a total of 250 marginal readings. The relationship of the marginal notes in the Syro-Hexapla to the other sources is of great interest and is charted as follows (the count is only proximate but gives data from which conclusions can be drawn):

Combination	Instances
161 248 252 539 Syh	39
161 248 252 Syh	16
161 248	14
252 Syh	8
TOTAL	77
v Syh	1
Syh = Sole Witness	103

Since the Syro-Hexapla preserves over a hundred readings not shared by other sources, its witness is extremely significant. When the Qohelet edition for the Göttingen Septuaginta was already finished in 2012, Reinhart Ceulemans discovered LXX⁷⁸⁸. This manuscript is extremely rich in Hexaplaric readings, having as much material alone for Qohelet as all of the texts collected by Field[17] put together. Thanks to Ceulemans' kindness, these materials will be included in the Göttingen edition, but analysis and relation to other sources must await his publication of them. The Syro-Hexapla provides the same sort of riches in Hexaplaric materials in Canticles, Proverbs, and Job.

11.4.4.5 Inner-Translational Features

Some of the issues in translation listed by Barthélemy can now be illustrated. First, sometimes the translator misinterpreted his *Vorlage*. Consider the problem in Qoh 12:13a (see Table 1).

Since the Hebrew text has נִשְׁמָע "has been heard," we are almost certain that ἀκούεται "is heard" represents the choice of the translator. The present indicative passive third person singular is easily confused as a present imperative active second person plural by etacism since the vowels were pronounced the same in the late Hellenistic and early Byzantine periods. It is possible that the *Vorlage* of the Syro-Hexapla had already the form ἀκού-

---

[17] Field, *Hexapla*.

TABLE 3   Qoh 7:7a

περιφέρει "it carries around"	πλανήσει "it leads astray"	θορυβήσει "it misleads"
LXX	Attributed by marginal notes In LXX²⁵² to Aq and Th In LXX¹⁶¹, ²⁴⁸ to Aq In Syh to Aq and erroneously to Sym instead of Th In LXX⁵³⁹ no attribution	Attributed by marginal notes In LXX¹⁶¹, ²⁴⁸, ²⁵² to Sym In Syh wrongly to Th In LXX⁵³⁹ no attribution

ετε "hear," but it is equally possible that the mistake was made by the translators of the Syro-Hexapla.

Sometimes, the indices or the notes are misplaced in the Syro-Hexapla. An example is Qoh 3:19 (see Table 2).

The text inherited by Origen had συνάντημα ἓν τοῖς πᾶσιν αὐτοῖς "one eventually is for all of them." The words τοῖς πᾶσιν "for all" constitute a conflation from 3:19e. Origen marked these words with an obelus since they were not in his Hebrew text. The Syro-Hexapla mistakenly marked the word αὐτοῖς instead of τοῖς πᾶσιν because, due to the word order in Syriac, αὐτοῖς precedes τοῖς πᾶσιν. Thus the scribe put the sign in the corresponding physical spot in his manuscript, but on the wrong word.

An example of confusion of sigla can be illustrated from Qoh 7:7a (see Table 3).

The Syro-Hexapla attributes πλανήσει "it leads astray" to Aquila and Symmachus and θορυβήσει "it misleads" to Theodotion, when the former should be attributed to Aquila and Theodotion and the latter to Symmachus. If a generation or two is involved in the sources in Greek, the placing of the notes in the margins can easily be shifted slightly and so confused by a later reader. In addition, early manuscripts employ a lunate *sigma*, which is easily confused with *alpha*, so that Aquila and Symmachus can be mixed up. An interesting way to demonstrate this is to compare mss LXX¹⁶¹ and LXX²⁴⁸, which come from exactly the same tradition. They also have an identical index system. Yet the placing of the indices and the marginal notes physically on the page differs slightly so that one does not always know whether the note refers to a particular word or to the entire line. Thus, some clarity regarding the marginal notes and what they refer to is lost in the generations of manuscripts that transmit them.

Furthermore, the intention of the original scholiast must be assessed. Perhaps the marginal note consists of two words, one assigned to Aquila and Theodotion and the other assigned to Symmachus. It could be intended that all three revisers have exactly the same text and differ only in one word in terms of lexical choice. Or there might be only one word in the margin and it has a different number so that the scholiast intends to show that, for example, Symmachus differs only in the grammatical number of one noun in the line. For differences between the three that are greater, the way the scholiast has both abbreviated and combined the data may make it difficult to discern precisely what each reviser had in his translation.

11.4.4.6 Text-Critical Value

For the critical edition of Qohelet in the Göttingen Septuaginta series, the Hexaplaric recension is attested by the following witnesses:

LXX^O = LXX$^{V\text{-}253\text{-}475\text{-}637}$ Jerome's *Comm. Eccl.*, Syh (LXX$^{S\ correction}$ LXX^{411})

The main members of the LXX^O group are LXX$^{V\text{-}253\text{-}475\text{-}637}$ as the hyphen indicates. The group is not always unified in attesting the reading of the Hexaplaric text (see discussion *infra*). Nonetheless, variants from LXX^O or a part thereof occur in approximately 320 instances (against the critical text).

The biblical text of Jerome's *Comm. Eccl.* is clearly related to the LXX^O group. There are sixty agreements with LXX^O, eighteen of which are singular agreements. The main problem is the extent to which Jerome's text really represents VL (→ 1.4.1) or the extent to which Jerome freely and spontaneously corrected his VL source text as he produced the lemma of his commentary.

Corrected readings in Codex Sinaiticus (LXX$^{\text{Sinaiticus correction}}$) agree with a member of the LXX^O group in approximately fifty cases and against the LXX^O group in eleven; approximately eight of these are singular agreements.

LXX^{411} is a late manuscript where the scribe used manuscripts from a variety of sources to correct his source text. Among these was the Hexaplaric group. There are over 180 readings where LXX^{411} agrees with LXX^O against the critical text; twenty-one of these are singular agreements.

The Syro-Hexapla also transmits a Hexaplaric text, but is a distant member of the group. The Syro-Hexapla agrees with at least one member of LXX^O in 107 instances, and in sixty-one of these instances, LXX^O is unified.

For the book of Job, the evidence for the Hexaplaric recension is given by Ziegler as follows: LXX^O = VL Syh; LXX$^{253-339}$ = LXX$^{253'}$; Armenian version. He notes that while LXX$^{253-339}$ are the main witnesses for the Hexaplaric recension in Wisdom, these do not transmit many readings from the LXX^O group in Job. Thus, we are in the difficult position of basing our knowledge of the Hexaplaric recension in Job on VL and the Syro-Hexapla. Both of these witnesses may not, in fact, be close to the original text of Origen's Fifth Column. Many scholars have noted that the lemma of the Syro-Hexapla is not a close witness of the actual text of the Fifth Column in various books.[18] It will be interesting to see how the evidence for the Syro-Hexapla in Proverbs and Canticles does or does not line up with the text of the LXX^O group.

11.4.4.7 Conclusion

We arrive at the following conundrum. The Syro-Hexapla claims to derive from the text of LXX in Origen's Hexapla (→ 1.3.1.2.7). Better and more than any other source, it preserves lines marked with the Aristarchian signs: asterisk, obelus, metobelus, and lemnisk. These signs appear to be used correctly for the most part. In the margins are readings from Theodotion, Aquila, and Symmachus. The Syro-Hexapla on the whole tends to preserve more of these readings than any other source. Nonetheless, the main text is not a very close witness of the Hexaplaric recension (→ 1.3.1.2.7) as far as we can tell from a study of relations in the textual tradition.

I propose the following solution: when we look at the Syro-Hexapla, we are looking at a recension derived and descended from the Tetrapla and not the Hexapla.[19] It seems that the Tetrapla was a text whose physical appearance was identical to that of the Syro-Hexapla, as the colophon to the Twelve Prophets actually states.

Eusebius states that Origen prepared the Tetrapla separately.[20] Once he had a good grasp on the relations between LXX and the Hebrew, he did not need the first two columns, nor did he even need the full text of the versions of the *recentiores*. The suffix -pla does not mean a text in columns, al-

---

[18] Most recently by T.M. Law, "La Version Syro-Hexaplaire et la Transmission Textuelle de la Bible Grècque," in *L'Ancien Testament en syriaque* (eds. F. Briquel Chatonnet and P. Le Moigne; Études syriaques 5; Paris: Geuthner, 2008), 101–20.

[19] This proposal is confirmed by the colophon to the Twelve Prophets in Codex Syro-Hexaplaris (→ 6–9.2.4), which says "the Twelve Prophets were taken in transmission from a copy that was like the version of the Tetrapla." See R.J.V. Hiebert, "Syriac Biblical Textual History and the Greek Psalter," in The Old Greek Psalter: Studies in Honour of Albert Pietersma (eds. R.J.V. Hiebert, C. Cox, and P.J. Gentry; JSOTSup 332; Sheffield: Sheffield Academic Press, 2001), 178–204. Hiebert provides an excellent list of colophons and notes the Tetrapla as the basis for the Syro-Hexapla in many books. Earlier, Jenkins, who pursued the same trail of evidence, concluded similarly: R.G. Jenkins, "Colophons of the Syrohexapla and the *Textgeschichte* of the Recensions of Origen," in *VII Congress of the IOSCS: Leuven 1989* (ed. C.E. Cox; SBLSCS 31; Atlanta: Scholars Press, 1991), 261–77; R.G. Jenkins, "Hexaplaric Marginalia and the Hexapla-Tetrapla Question," in *Origen's Hexapla and Fragments: Papers Presented at the Rich Seminar on the Hexapla, Oxford Centre for Hebrew and Jewish Studies, 25th July–3rd August 1994* (ed. A. Salvesen; TSAJ 58; Tübingen: Mohr Siebeck, 1998), 73–87.

[20] Eusebius, *Ecclesiastical History*, 6.16.

though this was true of the Hexapla. The Tetrapla was fourfold: it contained four Greek versions. By the way, the Syro-Hexapla is the only source that transmits the note ὁμοίως "the same one." This indicates that Aquila or Theodotion has the same text as that of LXX without copying it *verbatim*. In the Tetrapla, Origen had all the exegetical ammunition he needed to carry on debates or do exegesis.

Even if one does not accept this proposal concerning the Tetrapla, the following point is clear: the Greek *Vorlage* of the Syro-Hexapla was transmitted by Pamphilus and Eusebius and gradually altered to match the *vulgo* text. They are the originators of the Hexaplaric recension; perhaps even Origen made alterations to the base text of the Tetrapla in transferring his text of the Seventy from the Hexapla to Tetrapla.

Ceulemans, R., "Greek Christian Access to 'the Three', 250–600 CE," in *Greek Scripture and the Rabbis* (eds. T.M. Law and A. Salvesen; CBET 66; Leuven: Peeters, 2012), 165–91.

Ceulemans, R., "The ὁμοίως Notes in the Syro-Hexapla Version of the Song of Songs," *OCP* 79 (2013): 5–36.

Field, **Hexapla*.

Gentry, P.J., *The Asterisked Materials in the Greek Job* (SBLSCS 38; Atlanta: Scholars Press, 1995).

Liljeström, M., "Observations on the Mode of Translation in the Syrohexapla," in *Foundations for Syriac Lexicography V*: Colloquia of the International Syriac Language Project (eds. J. Loopstra and M. Sokoloff; Perspectives on Syriac Linguistics 7; Piscataway: Gorgias, 2013), 91–102.

Peter J. Gentry

11.4.5 Armenian Translations

11.4.5.1 Background

Arm-Job is a translation of the ecclesiastical text, i.e., it includes the Hexaplaric additions that Origen made to LXX with the use of Theodotion's translation (→ 1.3.1.2.7; → 11.3.5), as is immediately evident in the presence of asterisks and obeli in many Armenian manuscripts. Further, it reflects the work of Lucian, who made his revision of Job based on the Hexaplaric text (→ 11.3.6). The Armenian version is an early witness to the Lucianic text for Job (→ 11.3.6) and, as such, is of significance for the textual criticism of that book. Translated in the early fifth century C.E., Arm-Job is as early as Codex Alexandrinus – also a major Lucianic witness in Job – and the fragmentary manuscript Paris, Bibl. Nat., Gr. 9 (LXX^c). The great uncials Vaticanus and Sinaiticus are only a century earlier, as are a few papyri that attest only a few verses.

The challenge of the sub-versions, like the Armenian, is this: the manuscripts may be numerous but, apart from possible revisionary activity, they all derive from a single parent manuscript. That is, when all the work is done to reconstruct the parent text, that parent text is only one manuscript: the version has the weight of one manuscript out of all the Greek manuscripts that exist for that book, in this case Job. It is essential to reconstruct that one manuscript to assess the importance of the sub-version, no small task.

11.4.5.2 A Critical Edition of Arm-Job

Ziegler's edition of LXX-Job uses Zohrapian's edition (→ 1.4.7.3), whose base manuscript is a medieval manuscript, dated 1319. It was the best resource available for Arm-Job at that time but the text-critical value of Zohrapian's manuscript could not be assessed apart from a collation of the wider manuscript tradition. Now we know that Venice 1508, Zohrapian's base manuscript, not only contains a later, more developed type of text, but reflects secondary contact with a late Greek text through the first nineteen chapters of Job. Cox, *Armenian Job* is a critical edition that presents an eclectic text based upon nine manuscripts selected as representatives of the text groups that emerged from sample collations of 125 of the 138 extant manuscripts.

In *Armenian Job*, Cox uses manuscript Jerusalem 1925 as a base manuscript for collation, corrected through comparison with the LXX text tradition (→ 11.3.1) and other types of text in the Armenian tradition. Like Ziegler's edition of LXX, Cox attempts to reconstruct an Armenian text as close to the original as possible.

11.4.5.3 The Greek Parent Text of Arm-Job

Ziegler placed Arm-Job among the witnesses to the Hexaplaric recension,[1] but this requires correction. It is true that Arm-Job is Hexaplaric (→ 11.3.5), but it is Hexaplaric because Lucian's revision of Job (→ 11.3.6) was based on a Hexaplaric type of text. The parent text of Arm-Job was a Lucianic manuscript; indeed that manuscript can be placed with the witnesses of the main Lucianic group (LXX^L), so LXX$^{A-V(from\ 30:8)-575-637\ Arm}$.

The Greek parent manuscript of Arm-Job can be more closely defined in terms of its textual affiliations and character. Among the Lucianic witnesses just cited, Arm-Job shows a number of striking agreements with LXX^{637}.[2] Manuscript 637 is an eleventh-century minuscule. The agreements with Arm-Job indicate that the readings in this late Greek manuscript are as old at least as the parent manuscript of the early-fifth-century C.E. translation. That parent manuscript was an uncial manuscript and preserved the Hexaplaric signs. Therefore, it may have appeared much like the fifth-century C.E. Colberto-Sarravianus, a photograph of which Würthwein reproduces.[3] The manuscript was unaccented, so it was not always possible to distinguish between ἤ "or" and ἥ "really," or between οὐ, the negative particle, and οὗ, the genitive of the article. The continuous text of the Greek means that the translator had to decide where to divide the text. Sometimes the translator places final words or phrases at the end of the preceding verse in Ziegler's edition (Job 3:18a; 7:13b; 7:21d; 10:1a; 28:26a; 30:12c; 36:5b). Finally, the Greek parent text of Arm-Job attested the interpolation of Job 37:5b–7b at Job 36:28g–k.

Reconstruction of the Greek Parent Text

The reconstruction of the Greek parent text of Arm-Job has certain limitations placed upon it by the nature of the Armenian language: Armenian does not generally mark for gender and that is true for pronouns and demonstratives; it has numerous nouns that are morphologically plural, in which case it is not possible to determine whether its parent text had a singular or plural; Armenian has no future indicative form of the verb but, rather, expresses the future by means of the subjunctive mood so that, where the Greek tradition is divided between the future indicative and the subjunctive, one cannot say for certain what stood in the parent text. Though word order is flexible in Armenian, it nevertheless has a preferred word order so that a mechanical collation, as is sometimes true of Ziegler's work, can lead one astray with respect to what stood in the parent text.

With these caveats, it is possible to reconstruct the parent text of Arm-Job, as has been done in the edition entitled *Armenian Job*. This task is made immeasurably easier with access to Ziegler's critically established text and its apparatus, with its presentation of variant readings in the text tradition.

11.4.5.4 Character of the Translation into Armenian

The Armenian translation of Job is a sophisticated rendering of the ecclesiastical text (→ 11.4.5.1). It is neither a dynamic translation nor is it given to the literalism of Arm 2 (on Arm 2, see → 1.4.7.4). As such, Arm-Job represents the attempt to translate the Greek version into another language in the early fifth century C.E. and, at the same time, interpret it for a different audience. For the heavy collection of particles favoured by and typical of the LXX translator, i.e., οὐ μὴν δὲ ἀλλά "however/nonetheless,"[4] Arm-Job has no standard equivalent but employs ապա թէ ոչ ապէ "But now!" (Job 2:5a); բայց սակայն "but nevertheless" (Job 5:8a; 13:3a; 34:36a); սակայն "however" (Job 12:6a; 21:17a; 27:7a); and բայց արդ "but now" (Job 17:10a; 33:1a). LXX-Job is loaded with particles, especially δέ "but," which the translator often chooses to ignore.

The translator varies vocabulary. Such variety is no indication of a different parent text. For example, at Job 1:15c and 1:16c, LXX in both instances

---

[1] Ziegler, *Iob*, 64–66.
[2] Cox, *Armenian Job*, 398.
[3] Würthwein, *Text (English)*, 203.

[4] *NETS*.

reads σωθείς in the statement "When I alone *escaped*," but the Armenian reads ապրեալ "survived" at Job 1:15c and then մնացեալ "remained" at Job 1:16c. LXX also varies constructions, so at Job 1:17e and 1:19c, in the same refrain noted at Job 1:15c and 1:16c, we find the finite verb ἐσώθην "I alone *escaped*." At Job 1:17e and 1:19c, Arm-Job continues with the participial construction ապրեալ "survived."

The translator has a fondness for compound verbs, a verbal phrase consisting of a verb plus a noun or adjective to render a verb that is only one word in Greek. For example, at Job 4:8a, the articulated participle τοὺς ἀροτριῶντας "the plowers" is rendered զայնոսիկ որ ... արաւրադիր առնեն, perhaps literally "those who ... act as a ploughman," i.e, "those who plough." There are more than ninety instances of this construction that is characteristic of Arm 1.[5]

There are many finely nuanced translations in Arm-Job. Near the end of the book, God says to the three friends in Greek, καὶ εἰ μὴ δι᾿ αὐτόν, ἀπώλεσα ἂν ὑμᾶς "for if not for him, I would have destroyed you" (Job 42:8). In Armenian, this becomes: եւ եթէ ոչ վասն նորա էր, կորուսեալ էր իմ արդեաւք զձեզ "and if it was not for him, I would have made it my business to destroy you."

Rendering Theodotion's Translation into Armenian

The Greek translator of Job abbreviated the text by about one-sixth. That translation is LXX-Job or OG-Job (→ 11.3.1). In the Hexapla, Origen added the missing lines from a literalistic translation identified with the name of Theodotion (→ 11.3.5). As a result, the so-called ecclesiastical text is comprised of two entirely different types of translation.[6]

Theodotion's translation technique posed a special challenge for ancient translators and that is true of Arm-Job also. The translator levelled out the at-times incomprehensible Greek by providing an intelligible rendering. But how did the Arm-Job translator manage Theodotion's transliterations? At Job 37:12b, there is a transliteration that offers a fascinating example of the agility of the Armenian translator. The *NRSV* of this verse reads, "They (i.e., the clouds?) turn round and round by his guidance, to accomplish all that he commands them on the face of the inhabitable world." Theodotion translates Job 37:12b as follows: ἐν θεεβουλαθώ εἰς ἔργα αὐτῶν "by theebulatho to their works." The spelling of the transliteration of Arm-Job's parent text is *theebulathoth*. The Armenian translator provides an ingenious translation for this odd word, "odd" because it is Hebrew! For the Greek, we find in Armenian, ուր կամեցաւ` եդ զգործ նոցա "where he wished, he put their work." First, the translator saw that θεεβουλαθωθ contains the root βουλ- (see βούλομαι, "wish, want") and, continuing with the third person subject of v. 12a, offers կամեցաւ "he wished." The final -θ on θεεβουλαθωθ he takes with the following preposition εἰς to produce θείς, the masculine singular participle, nominative case, of the verb τίθημι "put, place." The translator renders θείς with the verb *dnem*, here in its aorist third singular form, *ed*. The result is, "where he wished, he put their work." This even makes sense and the rendering gives us a unique insight into how the translator works. The entire verse in Armenian reads, "And he will twist round the discs – where he wished, he put their work, and everything, whatsoever he commanded them."

11.4.5.5 Text-Critical Value of Arm-Job for LXX-Job

The text-critical importance of Arm-Job lies in its early date and its textual affiliation, i.e., it is an early representative of the Lucianic recension (→ 1.3.1.2; → 11.3.6). There are limitations to this usefulness, namely, that the Armenian translator departs from the syntax of the parent text and disregards the profusion of particles that characterise the Greek. Arm-Job is not an isomorphic translation.

An examination of the Armenian translation of Job reveals the surprises that a sub-version can

---

[5] See S.P. Cowe, "The Two Armenian Versions of Chronicles: Their Origin and Translation Technique," *Revue des Études Arméniennes* 22 (1990–1991): 53–96 (86).

[6] See further → 11.3.1.

hold for textual criticism, for an understanding of the development of the LXX text tradition, and for exegesis, once a critical edition of both it and its underlying Greek text are available, either in the text or in the apparatus of an edition like Ziegler's.

Readings from "The Three"
Armenian manuscripts of Job preserve nine readings from "the Three" (→ 11.3.5) in the margins, two of these, one Aquila's and the other Symmachus', uniquely (Job 3:23; 9:11).[7] Such readings are significant, but it seems to me that they were added in the medieval period and were not part of the parent text of Arm-Job (→ 1.4.7).[8]

Cox, C., *Armenian Job: Reconstructed Greek Text, Critical Edition of the Armenian with English Translation* (Hebrew University Armenian Series 8; Leuven: Peeters, 2006).
Cox, C., "Little Words are Important Too: The Use of Particles in the Armenian Translation of Job," in *The Armenian Bible: A Symposium Celebrating the 1600th Anniversary of the Discovery of the Armenian Alphabet and the Translation of the Bible into Armenian* (ed. B. Der Mugrdechian; Burbank: Western Diocese of the Armenian Church of North America, 2007), 17–37.
Cox, C., "Scribal Errors Corrected by the First Hand [in Armenian Job]," in *Between Paris and Fresno: Armenian Studies in Honor of Dickran Kouymjian* (ed. B. Der Mugrdechian; Costa Mesa Mazda Publishers, 2008), 219–39.
Cox, C., "The Use of *-s, -d, -n* Definite / Demonstrative Markers in Armenian Job," *Festschrift for Michael E. Stone* (eds. T. van Lint and S. La Porta; forthcoming).
Würthwein, *Text (English)*.
Ziegler, J. (ed.), *Iob* (Septuaginta Vetus Testamentum Graecum 11.4; Göttingen: Vandenhoeck & Ruprecht, 1982).

Claude Cox

11.4.6 Georgian Translations

11.4.6.1 Background

Georg-Job is preserved in Codices Georg⁰ (= Mount Athos, Library of the Iviron Monastery, geo. 1, year 978 C.E., in two volumes), Georg^D (National Centre of Manuscripts = NCM, H-855, seventeenth century), Georg^S (NCM, A–51, seventeenth or eighteenth century), and also in the so-called "Bakar Bible" (= Georg^B), i.e., the Moscow 1743 printed edition.[1] A full description of these sources is available in the first volume of the critical edition of the Old Georgian Octateuch.[2] Additional manuscript material is represented by the lectionary Georg^P (= Paris, Bibliothèque nationale de France, geo. 3, year 1040).[3]

A study of the manuscript tradition of Georg-Job has yet to be undertaken. Furthermore, none of the Georgian versions of Job has been collated with the Göttingen edition of LXX.[4]

11.4.6.2 Date, Versions, Editions

Georg-Job was translated from Greek (→ 11.3.1) between the fifth and the eighth centuries C.E. (= Georg-Job 1). This translation needs to placed within this time frame because it is included in the Oldest Georgian Lectionary. Georg-Job 1 is not completely preserved. As a consequence of the loss of two quaternions in manuscript Georg⁰, the book abruptly finishes with Job 30:26. Lectionary Georg^P contains only Job 1–7; 9–10; 12–14; 16–17; 19; 21; 25–31; 38–39. In Georg^D, the text ends with Job 32:7. A critical edition of this version has not been produced. Šaniʒe published the text of Codex Georg⁰[5] and Danelia that of Lectionary Georg^P.[6] An account of the textual features of Georg-Job 1 in manuscript Georg^D is at present not available.

In the late seventeenth century, Sulkhan Saba Orbeliani revised Georg-Job 1 and added the missing chapters. As a source, he used the Armenian

---

[7] C. Cox, *Aquila, Symmachus and Theodotion in Armenia* (SBLSCS 42; Atlanta: Scholars Press, 1996), 317–48.
[8] C. Cox, "Concerning a Cilician Revision of the Armenian Bible," in *De Septuaginta: Studies in Honour of John William Wevers on His Sixty-Fifth Birthday* (eds. Albert Pietersma and Claude Cox; Toronto: Benben, 1984), 209–21.

[1] *Biblia*.
[2] *C'igɴni*, 559–72, 607–19, 627–35.
[3] Tarchnischvili, *Le grand lectionnaire*.
[4] Ziegler, *Iob*.
[5] Šaniʒe, *C'igɴni* 1.2, 145–74.
[6] Danelia, *Kartuli lekcionaris p'arizuli xelnac'eri*, 186–216.

Bible printed in 1666. This second version (= Georg-Job 2) comprises the full text of the book.[7]

A new translation was made from the Old Church Slavonic Moscow Bible of 1663 (→ 11.4.7) during the early eighteenth century: this new version is to be found in Georg[B] (= Georg-Job 3).[8]

11.4.6.3 Translation Character, Translation Technique, and Inner-Translational Features

The analysis of Georg-Job 1 shows that typical Hexaplaric readings (→ 11.3.5) are preserved in manuscript Georg[O], but some have been omitted in the lectionary Georg[P] (Job 7:8ab; 9:24c; 10:4b; 21:15ab, 28–33c; 29:19–20; 38:26–27, 32). Traces of the Lucianic recension (→ 11.3.6) are not found in this version.

Georg-Job 2 is strongly influenced by the printed Armenian Bible (→ 11.4.5). Nevertheless, some exceptions are found. For instance, one may consider the case of Theodotion's reading ἐν θεεβουλαθὼ εἰς ἔργα αὐτῶν "by *theebulatho* to their works" (**NETS*) in Job 37:12b.[9] While the Armenian translates it as "where he wished, he put their work,"[10] the Georgian simply reiterates the transliteration ენთი ებულათოთ *enti ebulatot*.[11]

11.4.6.4 Text-Critical Value for the Primary Translation

The text-critical value of Georg-Job 1 lies in its date and its textual affiliation. As with the Armenian (→ 11.4.5), the Georgian seems to be an early representative of a Greek source text containing Origen's additions (→ 11.3.5), although it does not constitute early evidence of the Lucianic redaction (→ 11.4.6).

At present, two limitations exist in assessing the value of Georg-Job 1 for the study of the primary translation. The first is the lack of a critical edition of this secondary version. The second is that Ziegler did not take into consideration Šaniʒe's work in his monograph on LXX-Job (→ 11.3.1);[12] moreover,

a collation of the latter with Georg-Job 1 was not undertaken in the edition of lectionary Georg[P].[13] Consequently, in the years to come, the main task of research into Georg-Job 1 consists in addressing these two essential *desiderata*.

Biblia: Brʒanebita da c'arsagebelita sapasetata sakartvelos mepis bakar vaxt'angis ʒisata (Moscow: Bakaris st'amba, 1743).

C'ignni ʒuelisa aγtkumisani, Vol. 1: *Šesakmisaj, gamoslvataj* (eds. B. Gigineišvili and C. K'ik'viʒe; Tbilisi: Mecniereba, 1989).

Danelia, K., S. Čxenk'eli, and B. Šavišvili (eds.), *Kartuli lekcionaris p'arizuli xelnac'eri: ʒveli da axali aγtkmis sak'itxavebi*, Vol. 1: *Nac'ili I* (Tbilisi: Tbilisis universit'et'is gamomcemloba, 1987).

Dočanašvili, E. (ed.), *Mcxeturi xelnac'eri (t'obis, ivditis, esteris, iobis c'ignebi, psalmuni, igavta c'igni)* (Tbilisi: Mecniereba, 1983).

Melikišvili, N., *Bibliur c'ignta ʒveli kartuli targmanebi* (Tbilisi: Alilo, 2009).

Šaniʒe, A. (ed.), *C'ignni ʒuelisa aγtkumisani 978 c'lis xelnac'eris mixedvit*, Vol. 1.2: *Levit'eltaj, msaʒultaj, rutisi, iobisi, esaiajsi* (Tbilisi: Sak. ssr mecnierebata ak'ademiis gamomcemloba, 1948).

Tarchnischvili, M. (ed.), *Le grand lectionnaire de l'église de Jérusalem (Ve–VIIIe siècle)*, Vol. 1. (CSCO 188–89 Scriptores Iberici 9–10; Louvain: Secrétariat du Corpus SCO, 1959).

Ziegler, J., *Iob* (Septuaginta Vetus Testamentum Graecum 11.4; Göttingen: Vandenhoeck & Ruprecht, 1982).

Alessandro Maria Bruni

11.4.7 Old Church Slavonic Translations

11.4.7.1 Background

In the timespan between the ninth and the fifteenth centuries, the book of Job was rendered several times into Old Church Slavonic (OCS-Job). A broad manuscript tradition survives, which in the vast majority of cases preserves translations from LXX (→ 11.3.1); however, versions have also come down to us that were produced by taking the Vulgate (→ 11.3.7) or MT (→ 11.2.2) as a model. With a single exception, testimonies do not contain colophons or marginal notes that inform us about

---

[7] Dočanašvili, *Mcxeturi xelnac'eri*, 100–50.
[8] *Biblia*.
[9] See Tov, **Greek-Hebrew Bible*, 511.
[10] See → 11.4.5.
[11] Dočanašvili, *Mcxeturi xelnac'eri*, 28, 142.
[12] Ziegler, *Iob*.

[13] Danelia, *Kartuli lekcionaris p'arizuli xelnac'eri*, 186–216.

the date and place of origin of the different texts. Therefore, any attempt aimed at clarifying these issues can be based only on the analysis of the linguistical (morphological, lexical, orthographical) and palaeographical traits of the written sources.

The philological challenge in the study of OCS-Job is twofold. Firstly, critical editions of the Old Church Slavonic versions made from LXX have not yet been produced, with the inevitable result that the various reconstructions of their textual features remain approximate, if not completely uncertain. Secondly, these translations have not been collated, even on a single basis, with major reference works on Greek Job.[1] As already observed elsewhere in this volume (→ 2.5.7.4), the understanding of the Old Church Slavonic Bible suffers from a lack of interaction between paleoslavistics and contemporary philological investigations on LXX. Consequently, the relevance of this tradition for the textual criticism of the Scriptures still awaits a proper assessment. The purpose of the present article consists in paving the way to integrating OCS-Job into the framework of comparative research.

11.4.7.2 Earliest Textual Stratum: Cyrillo-Methodian Readings

The oldest Old Church Slavonic version of Job (hereafter: OCS-Job 1) should in all likehood be identified with a number of readings translated from LXX presumably during the Cyrillo-Methodian period (863–885 C.E.). They have come down to us both in Cyrillic and Croat Glagolitic traditions.[2]

11.4.7.2.1 Cyrillic Testimonies

The major Cyrillic source for OCS-Job 1 is the Old Church Slavonic Prophetologium, a collection of liturgical pericopes organized according to the liturgical year of the Byzantine Church,[3] which inclues Job 1:1–22; 2:1–10; 38:1–23; 42:1–5, 12–17. The earliest copy is the codex of the Russian State Library, Moscow, f. 87, no. M 1685 (*Grig.* 2), dating from the late twelfth or early thirteenth century. The remainder of the Prophetologium corpus points to the existence of two substrates as a consequence of a subsequent correction towards a different LXX text (→ 11.3.1).[4] Additional Cyrillic witnesses to OCS-Job 1a are the *Triodion*,[5] the *Uspenskij sbornik*, an East Slavic florilegium of the twelfth or thirteenth century,[6] and the so-called *Jewish Chronicle*, an extensive compilation consisting mostly of translations of Greek historical and literary works (Flavius Josephus, John Malalas, George Hamartolos, and pseudo-Callisthenes), biblical books (Octateuch, Tetrabasileon, excerpts from the Prophets and others), as well as several Old Russian annals.[7] Moreover, OCS-Job 1 was included in the full Old Church Slavonic translation of Job (→ 11.4.7.3).

11.4.7.2.2 Glagolitic Testimonies

The oldest and most significant Croatian Glagolitic testimonies of OCS-Job 1 are the codex kept at Vrbnik on Krk (Veglia), Župni ured (parish office) dating from 1391[8] and the Vienna manuscript, Österreichische Nationalbibliothek, *Slav.* 3 of the year 1396.[9] Unlike the Cyrillic Prophetologium, they do not contain Job 2:1–10; 38:1–23; 42:1–5, 12–17, but in turn they preserve some additional non-liturgical

---

[1] Field, *Hexapla*, Vol. 2; Ziegler, *Iob*; and Ziegler, *Beiträge*; Hagedorn, *Olympiodor*; Hagedorn und Hagedorn, *Die älteren griechischen Katenen*, vol. 1–3; Hagedorn und Hagedorn, "Nachlese."

[2] Afanas'eva, *K istorii teksta*; Afanas'eva and Švarc, "Drevnejšij slavjanskij perevod," 3–32; Alekseev, "Kirillo–Mefodievskoe perevodčeskoe nasledie," 131; Kostova, "Kăm văprosa za kirilometodievite," 61; Christova-Šomova, "Slavjanskie perevody," 128–29.

[3] For the use of the Scriptures in the Byzantine rite, see Alekseev, *Biblija v bogoslužernii*.

[4] Thomson, "The Slavonic Translation," 792. For editions, see Brandt, "Grigorovičev parimejnik"; Pechuška, *Staroslovanský překlad*, 240–46, 249–51; Afanas'eva and Švarc, "Drevnejšij slavjanskij perevod," 21–32; and Ribarova and Hauptova, *Grigorovičev Parimejnik*.

[5] Christova-Šomova, *Kniga Jov*, 12.

[6] *Uspenskij sbornik*, 160–64; Blagova, "Biblejskie citaty," 70–78.

[7] An extant manuscript of the *Jewish Chronicle* is Russian State Archive of Ancient Acts, Moscow, f. MGAMID 279/658, late fifteenth century, folios 42ᵛ–43ᵛ (see Istrin, *Aleksandrija*, 315–43).

[8] See Vajs, *Nejstarší*, lxix–lxxii.

[9] Birkfellner, *Glagolitische*, 57–61.

readings.[10] Accordingly, the earliest Croat Breviary includes in total Job 1:1–22; 2:11–13; 3:1–26; 4:1–9.[11]

11.4.7.3 First Complete OCS Translation of Job

The above-listed Cyrillo-Methodian pericopes were incorporated into the full translation (hereafter OCS-Job 2), which, in view of its linguistic features, may be deemed to have originated between the late ninth and early tenth centuries. Some scholars argue that it was carried out by Methodius shortly before his death (885 C.E.) based on the testimony of his hagiographic *Life*, according to which he translated from Greek into Slavonic the whole corpus of the Scriptures "with the exception of the Maccabees."[12] The analysis of the translation technique has been brought forward to support this assumption.[13] However, skepticism has been expressed concerning this attribution: according to a different view, OCS-Job 2 should be ascribed more confidently to an anonymous Bulgarian translator, who presumably revised a lost proto-Methodian text during the reign of Tsar Symeon (893–927 C.E.).[14] An even more categorical opinion was expressed by Thomson, who believes that a Methodian origin should be completely excluded.[15]

11.4.7.3.1 Manuscript Tradition of OCS-Job_2

OCS-Job 2 has come down to us in both East and South Slavic codices dating from no earlier than the late fourteenth century. A look at the typology of the surviving Cyrillic manuscripts reveals that OCS-Job 2 is usually transmitted separately from other books of the OCS Bible or, alternatively, in small collections.[16] It is included relatively rarely in larger corpora, such as in the sixteenth-century manuscript of the Russian State Library in Moscow, f. 256, no. 28 (folios 172ᵛ–226).

In this vast and varied tradition, several sub-redactions of the original translation, which differ from one another due to their linguistic and textual features, are preserved. Moreover, OCS-Job 2 still remains completely unpublished, even as a single testimony. These circumstances represent a major obstacle for the development of comparative research and consequently for a proper assessment of its relevance for LXX studies.

11.4.7.3.2 Text Types of OCS-Job 2

Among the surviving manuscripts of the complete translation of Job, three types of text may be detected. In almost all East Slavic testimonies, OCS-Job 2 is intermixed with the "catenae" of Olympiodorus of Alexandria,[17] which presumably were translated in eastern Bulgaria in the early tenth century (oldest testimony: State Historical Museum, Moscow, *Čud.* 6, year 1394 [*type 1*]). Only in rare cases does the East Slavic tradition preserve the biblical text without the commentaries (see Russian State Library, Moscow, f. 113, no. 605, sixteenth century [*type 2*]).[18] The lack of Olympiodorus' explanations is, on the contrary, a distinctive trait of the South Slavic corpus, in which only a few traces of this exegetical work may be found (major testimonies: National Library of Russia, St. Petersburg, F.I.461, late fourteenth century;[19] State Historical Museum, Moscow, *Ščuk.* 507, year 1475 [*type 3*]). *Type 1* is deemed to represent the ear-

---

[10] Zaradija-Kiš, "Hrvatsko-glagoljska i bugarska knjiga o Jobu," 122.

[11] For editions, see Pechuška, *Staroslovanský překlad*, 240–49; Vajs, *Liber Iob*, 68–74; Zaradija-Kiš, "Hrvatskoglagoljska knjiga," 427–35.

[12] See ch. 15 of the *Life of Methodius* (Angelov and Kodov, *Kliment Ochridski*, 191).

[13] Michajlov, *Opyt*, cccxxxvi; Kostova, "Kăm văprosa," 61–69; Nikolova, "Za naj-starija bălgarski srednovekoven răkopis," 118; Christova-Šomova, *Kniga Jov*, 11–12, 55, 107–08.

[14] Alekseev, *Tekstologija*, 158–59, 198; Alekseev, "Grammatičeskaja stat'ja," 374.

[15] Thomson, "The Slavonic Translation," 793–94.

[16] Several manuscripts written up to the year 1600 are listed in Mathiesen, "Handlist," 18–34.

[17] The original Greek text corresponds to No. 7453 in *Clavis patrum graecorum* (ed. M. Geerard et al.; Turnhout: Brepols, 1974–2003). For an edition, see Hagedorn, *Olympiodor*. On issues related to the authorship of the preface to the Old Church Slavonic translation of the commentaries, see Alekseev, "Grammatičeskaja stat'ja," 374–78; Christova-Šomova, "Grăckite versii na kniga Jov," 804; Thomson, "The Three Slavonic Translations", 166–72.

[18] Iosif, *Opis'*, 270.

[19] For this codex, see Nikolova, "Za naj-starija bălgarski srednovekoven răkopis," 110–18; Kostova, "Kăm văprosa," 61–69.

liest textual stratum of the translation, since the remaining two are judged to be the result of the extraction of OCS-Job 2 from Olympiodorus' "catenae." This assumption is based essentially on the fact that *type 3* has the same subdivision into 821 chapters that found in the collection with commentaries.[20]

Arguments adduced in support of such a conclusion cannot be said to be decisive. In addition to the evidence provided by the earliest Croat Breviary (→ 11.4.7.2.2), which shows no traces of a previous inclusion in a catena,[21] a few additional remarks may be offered when looking at the text's arrangement in *type 2*, which contrary to what has been claimed[22] does not indeed appear to derive from *type 1*. In the former, OCS-Job 2 is not subdivided into chapters but into dialogical sections: їѡвъ (Iovъ) "Job"; елифаӡъ (Elifazъ) "Eliphaz"; валдадъ (Valdadъ) "Bildad"; сафаръ (Safarъ) "Zophar" (f. 113, no. 605, folios 306ᵛ–307). A marginal numeration (1–4) can be found only at the very beginning of the translation, but it does not have any connection with the exegetical segmentation; instead, it refers to the four messengers mentioned in Job 1:14–18 (see Russian State Library, Moscow, f. 256, no. 28, folios 174ʳ⁻ᵛ). Moreover, in *type 2*, the insertion of the preface seems to be a later addition since it is attached as an appendix (see Russian State Library, Moscow, f. 113, no. 605, folios 306–345ᵛ).

In this regard, further aspects may also be considered, this time belonging to the translation's inner features. For instance, an examination of the lexicon in *types 2–3* reveals the occurrence of archaisms, such as the Cyrillo-Methodian rendering of the Greek τις "someone, a certain one" as етеръ (eterъ) and not its later equivalent, the Symeonic нѣкии (někii)[23] (see codices f. 113, no. 605, and F.I.461 respectively). Therefore, even a preliminary analysis based on both internal and external criteria shows clearly that the hypothesis of the derivation of *types 2–3* from *type 1* requires further investigation. Additional study is needed before reliable conclusions can be reached on this subject.

11.4.7.3.3 Gennadian Revision of OCS-Job 2 and the Text of the Printed Bibles

In the late fifteenth century, OCS-Job 2 was subject of a revision within the framework of the creation of the first complete corpus of the Old Church Slavonic Bible in Russia, promoted by Archbishop Gennadius of Novgorod (Gennadij Gonzov, ca. 1410–1505). The South Slavic text of OCS-Job 2 was corrected towards contemporary printed editions of the Vulgate (→ 11.3.7), among which, apparently, were those published by Anton Koberger (ca. 1440–1513) in 1487 (with commentaries by Nicholas of Lyra)[24] and Nikolaus Kessler (1450–post 1519) in 1487 or 1491.[25] This new redaction, besides entering the Gennadian Bible (State Historical Museum, Moscow, *Sin.* 915, year 1499)[26] and, subsequently, also the sixteenth-century Russian Macarian Menologium, where it is inserted in Job's commemoration (May 6th),[27] had moreover a separate circulation (see, e.g., manuscript Russian State Library, Moscow, f. 113, no. 10, sixteenth century). The only edition available today of the Gennadian revision of OCS-Job 2 is that based on the earliest testimonies of the Menologium.[28]

This renovated text underwent further amendments: the editors of the 1581 Ostrog Bible[29] re-

---

[20] Alekseev, *Tekstologija*, 31.
[21] In this regard, see Thomson, "The Slavonic Translation," 793; Pičchadze, "Perevody Biblii," 139–47.
[22] Alekseev, "Kirillo–Mefodievskoe perevodčeskoe nasledie," 129–30.
[23] For such a lexical opposition in the earliest Old Church Slavonic translations from Greek, see Pičchadze, "Slav. етеръ," 219–21.

[24] *Biblia, lat. / Cum postillis Nicolai <de Lyra> et expositionibus Guillelmi <Brito> in omnes prologos S. Hieronymi et additionibus Pauli Burgensis replicisque Matthiae Doering* (Nuremberg: Anton Koberger, 1487).
[25] *Biblia latina* (Basel: Nikolaus Kessler, 1487). See also Thomson, "The Slavonic Translation," 655–59; Thomson, *A Brief Survey*, 55–56.
[26] Gorskij and Nevostruev, *Opisanie*, 57–59; Alekseev, "Kirillo–Mefodievskoe perevodčeskoe nasledie," 129–30; Alekseev, *Tekstologija*, 196; Thomson, "The Slavonic Translation," 795.
[27] Iosif, *Podrobnoe oglavlenie*, 148.
[28] For an edition, see Weiher, Šmidt, and Škurko, *Die grossen Lesemenäen*, 511–42.
[29] *Ostrožskaja biblija*.

moved some passages of the catena that previously were not deleted by the redactors of the Gennadian Bible.[30] In the eighteenth century, this version was finally included in the Elizabethan Bible of 1751 with a few other changes based on LXX (→ 11.3.1).[31]

11.4.7.4 Other Translations

Besides the East and South Slavic manuscript corpus dating back to the ninth and tenth centuries, four additional Old Church Slavonic versions are also preserved that were undertaken from different sources. The first was made from the Vulgate (→ 11.3.7), presumably in the thirteenth century, and is known only in the Croat Glagolitic tradition (OCS-Job 3).[32] Two more (Cyrillic) are based on LXX (→ 11.3.1): they apparently originated independently from each other in the early fifteenth century. One was carried out on Mount Athos by a monk named Gabriel in 1412 (OCS-Job_4),[33] while the other was completed shortly afterwards by an anonymus translator of South Slavic, in all likelihood Serbian, origin (OCS-Job 5).[34] The last translation, also Cyrillic, which rendered MT (→ 11.2.2), was carried out in Ruthenia, probably in the late fifteenth century (OCS-Job_6).

11.4.7.4.1 OCS-Job_3

OCS-Job_3 is found in twelve copies of the Croat Glagolitic Breviary dating from the fourteenth to the sixteenth centuries. Only four, however, have preserved the text in its entirety. The main testimony is the codex Russian State Library, Moscow, f. 270, no. 51/1481 of the year 1442/1443,[35] which has been used as a base text for the collation in the 1997 critical edition.[36]

11.4.7.4.2 OCS-Job_4

OCS-Job_4 survives in two manuscripts of South Slavic origin. The first is kept currently at the State Historical Museum in Moscow (Sin. 202, year 1412) and was judged to be the author's autograph.[37] According to the colophon (folio 309), "… this book of the righteous and long-suffering Job was written and translated at the Great Lavra of Hilandar from a Greek model of the Monastery of Esphigmenou in the year 6920 [= 1412]" (напиcа се и прѣложи сїѧ кнїга праведнаго и мнѡгострадалнааго іѡва, при велицѣи лаврѣ хїландарсцѣи, ѿ извода грьчьскаго обитѣли єсфѵгмена. въ лѣто ѕ҃ ц҃ к҃). The second is kept at the Library of the Romanian Academy of Sciences in Bucharest (no. 96, year 1503).[38] This translation is currently unedited and, with the exception of a short description of both codices,[39] no account of its textual features has hitherto been published.

11.4.7.4.3 OCS-Job 5

OCS-Job_5 has come down to us in two testimonies stored at the Rila Monastery in Bulgaria, namely no. 1/4, late fifteenth century and no. 4/14, year 1456. A diplomatic edition of this version based on the second manuscript was produced by Christova-Šomova.[40]

11.4.7.4.4 OCS-Job_6

OCS-Job 6 has come down to us in a sixteenth-century testimony from the Lithuanian Academy of Sciences in Vilnius (f. 19, no. 262), which also contains a translation from MT of the Five Scrolls

---

[30] Christova-Šomova, *Kniga Jov*, 12.

[31] *Biblija*, 1751; Thomson, "The Slavonic Translation," 795–96.

[32] Zaradija-Kiš, *Knjiga*; Reinhart, "Review," 285.

[33] Trifunović, "Zapisi," 108–11.

[34] Christova-Šomova, "Slavjanskie perevody," 132; Reinhart, "Review," 290.

[35] On this codex and its linguistic features, see Zaradija-Kiš, "Jezična tradicija," 489–97.

[36] Zaradija-Kiš, *Knjiga*.

[37] Trifunović, "Zapisi," 108–11.

[38] Information provided about this codex by Christova-Šomova is quite contradictory. In two instances, she states that this manuscript preserves the same translation as Sin. 202 (Christova-Šomova, "Grăckite versii na kniga Jov," 802–03; Christova-Šomova, *Kniga Jov*, 17–20), while in a third she asserts that it contains a different translation (Christova-Šomova, "Slavjanskie perevody," 129–33). See Trifunović, "Zapisi," 108.

[39] Gorskij and Nevostruev, *Opisanie*, 53–59; Jacimirskij, *Slavjanskie*, 644–45; Christova-Šomova, *Kniga Jov*, 17–18; Thomson, "The Three Slavonic Translations", 157–59.

[40] Christova-Šomova, *Kniga Jov*, 166–301; Thomson, "The Three Slavonic Translations", 159–62.

11.4.7 OLD CHURCH SLAVONIC TRANSLATIONS

(→ 13–17.2.7) and of Daniel (→ 18.4.7). The peculiarity of this version consists in the linguistic register that, even if literary, is nevertheless markedly orientated towards the Ruthenian vernacular. Moreover, a number of Hebrew words are left untranslated and are merely given in Cyrillic transcription. This version was carried out by an author who had a good knowledge of the Jewish exegetical tradition.[41]

11.4.7.5 Parent Text and Text-Critical Value

The various existing Old Church Slavonic versions of Job made from LXX (→ 11.3.1) must be placed safely among the witnesses to the Hexaplaric recension, namely to the so-called "ecclesiastical text" (→ 11.3.1.1.3). The inclusion of many readings from Aquila, Symmachus, and Theodotion make OCS-Job an important source for studying the various Greek traditions once collected by Origen, especially in view of the new research undertaken on this subject in recent years (→ 11.3.5).[42]

11.4.7.5.1 OCS-Job 2

Given the lack of textual research and of a collation with the editions of Ziegler and Hagedorn,[43] it remains to be verified whether OCS-Job 2 was initially translated from a Byzantine model containing commentaries. As noted above, it cannot be ruled out that the "catenae" may have been added to an already existing translation of Job. The textual allegiancies of OCS-Job 2 with the various manuscript groups of LXX (→ 11.3.1; → 11.3.5; → 11.3.6) still need to be established. In this regard, a few remarks can be made on a sample basis, which in any case clearly indicate its reliance on the Hexaplaric recension (→ 11.3.5). For instance, one may consider Job 36:28c–f ὥραν ἔθετο κτήνεσιν, οἴδασι δὲ κοίτης τάξιν. ἐπὶ τούτοις πᾶσιν οὐκ ἐξίσταταί σου ἡ διάνοια οὐδὲ διαλλάσσεταί σου ἡ καρδία ἀπὸ σώματος "He appointed a time for cattle, and they know their schedule for rest. Is your mind not amazed at all these things, and does your heart not take leave of your body?" (*NETS), which Origenes marked by an obelus.[44] In OCS-Job 2, these four verses are placed after Job 37:5,[45] as found in a Byzantine tradition that differs from LXX^BS and LXX^O.[46] Furthermore, OCS-Job 2 also includes Theodotion's additions such as, for example, those in Job 3:23 οὗ ἡ ὁδὸς ἀπεκρύβη ἀπ'αὐτοῦ "whose way is hidden from him" and Job 37:17 ἀπὸ νότου "from south."[47]

11.4.7.5.2 OCS-Job_4

The vast majority of the commentaries found in OCS-Job_4 belongs to Olympiodorus' work,[48] although a number of other exegetes are also quoted such as Origen, Julian the Arian, Didymus of Alexandria, Olympiodorus, Chrysostomus, Polychronios, and others (→ 11.3.1.1.2).[49] In view of its composition, OCS-Job 4 was judged to have been translated from a Byzantine model very close to the catena compiled by Nicetas Heracleensis[50] (a revision of the γ-redaction according to Hagedorn and Hagedorn).[51] For the purposes of comparative textual criticism, the most importat feature of OCS-Job 4 consists probably in the large number of quotations from Aquila, Symmachus, and Theodotion (→ 11.3.5) that are found in the margins of the manuscripts, where their names are abbreviated respectively to ӓ ("A"), c̈ ("S"), and ӫ ("Th").[52] Unfortunately, these readings are unpub-

---

[41] Taube, "The Book of Job," 281–96; Alekseev, Tekstologija, 184; Temčin, "Scharija i Skorina," 301–07.

[42] Gentry, The Asterisked Materials; Meade, "A Critical Edition"; Woods, "A Critical Edition."

[43] Ziegler, Iob; Hagedorn and Hagedorn, Die älteren griechischen Katenen.

[44] Ziegler, Iob, 83–84, 379.

[45] Christova-Šomova, "Grăckite versii na kniga Jov," 806.

[46] Ziegler, Iob, 83–84, 379.

[47] Field, *Hexapla, 2.9, 68; Christova-Šomova, "Grăckite versii na kniga Jov," 808; Christova-Šomova, Kniga Jov, 164.

[48] Trifunović, "Zapisi," 108–11.

[49] Gorskij and Nevostruev, Opisanie, 53–59; Jacimirskij, Slavjanskie, 644–45; Christova-Šomova, Kniga Jov, 44–45.

[50] This claim was made by Gorskij and Nevostruev, Opisanie, 54. Greek original: Catena Græcorum patrum in beatum Iob.

[51] Hagedorn and Hagedorn, Die älteren griechischen Katenen, 1.134–35; Thomson, "The Three Slavonic Translations", 159–62.

[52] Gorskij and Nevostruev, Opisanie, 57; Jacimirskij, Slavjanskie, 644–45; Trifunović, "Zapisi," 108; Christova-Šomova, Kniga Jov, 19.

lished and still await a meticulous analysis that may shed light on their text-critical value for the primary version.

11.4.7.5.3 OCS-Job 5

The following remarks may be made regarding the identification of the Byzantine prototype of OCS-Job 5. Christova-Šomova's assertion that this version renders a "catena" belonging to the γ-redaction is documented properly in neither the edition of OCS-Job 5 nor in the many articles published in recent years on this translation.[53] Moreover, in contradiction to this statement, the edition is based inexplicably on only the text of the second Rila manuscript (→ 11.4.7.4.3), in which the exegetical scholia are almost entirely missing.[54] Whereas both testimonies were to be used for accomplishing this task, this choice appears to be methodologically inconsistent if it is true that the translation originally included the commentaries, whose textual relationship with the texts published by Hagedorn and Hagedorn[55] remains to be established.

As far as the analysis of the biblical text in OCS-Job 5 is concerned, Christova-Šomova's monograph does not provide reliable remarks on the subject of comparative textual criticism. Firstly, no complete collation with Ziegler's edition[56] is offered. Secondly, the claim that OCS-Job 5 contains a number of longer elements not found in LXX-Job requires correction. The alleged additions in Job 3:18; 4:12, 16; 5:13, 27; 35:2 are clearly the result of the insertion of phrases taken from Greek patristic commentaries and should therefore not be considered as untraced variants of LXX-Job.[57]

11.4.7.5.4 Conclusions

With regard to the issue of establishing the relevance of OCS-Job for the textual history of the Bible, the following general conclusions may now be drawn. For the most part, this tradition presents itself as a vast and virtually unexplored manuscript legacy, which deserves to be taken into full consideration by researchers of the Hexaplaric tradition of Job (OCS-Job 1m OCS-Job 2, OCS-Job 4, OCS-Job 5). Additionally, it may also offer significant material for studies focusing on the reception of the Vulgate (OCS-Job 3; → 11.3.7) and of MT (OCS-Job 6; → 11.2.2).

Afanas'eva, E.V., *K istorii teksta i jazyka drevnejšego slavjanskogo perevoda Knigi Iova: Avtoreferat dissertacii na soiskanie učenoj stepeni kandidata filologičeskich nauk* (Leningrad: Leningradskij Gosudarstvennyj Universitet, 1988).

Afanas'eva, E.V. and E.M. Švarc, "Drevnejšij slavjanskij perevod Knigi Iova (po pergamennym rukopisjam)," in *Istočnikovedenie literatury Drevney Rusi* (ed. D.S. Lichačev; Leningrad: Nauka, 1980), 7–32.

Alekseev, A., "Kirillo–Mefodievskoe perevodčeskoe nasledie i ego istoričeskie sud'by: perevody sv. Pisanija v slavjanskoj pis'mennosti," in *Istorija, kul'tura, ètnografija i fol'klor slavjanskich narodov: X Meždunarodnyj s"ezd slavistov: Sofija, sentjabr' 1988: Doklady sovetskoj delegacii* (ed. I.I. Kostjuško; Moscow: Nauka, 1988), 124–45.

Alekseev, A.A., *Tekstologija slavjanskoj Biblii* (Bausteine zur slavischen Philologie und Kulturgeschichte Reihe A: Slavistische Forschungen 24; St. Petersburg: Dmitrij Bulanin, 1999).

Alekseev, A.A., "Grammatičeskaja stat'ja patriarcha Fotija v slavjanskom perevode," *Trudy Otdela drevnerusskoj literatury* 55 (2004): 374–78.

Alekseev, A.A., *Biblija v bogosluženii: Vizantijsko-slavjanskij lekcionarij* (St. Petersburg: Nestor-Istorija, 2008).

St. Angelov, B. and C. Kodov (eds.), *Kliment Ochridski: Săbrani săčinenija*, Vol. 3: *Prostranni žitija na Kiril i Metodii* (Sofia: Izdatelstvo na Bălgarska Akademija na naukite, 1973).

Biblija: Sirěč' knigi svjaščennago pisanija vetchago i novago zavěta (St. Petersburg: Tipografija Aleksandro-Nevskogo monastyrja, 1751).

Birkfellner, G., *Glagolitische und kyrillische Handschriften in Österreich* (Schriften der Balkan-Kommission philologische Abteilung 23; Vienna: Verlag der Österreichischen Akademie der Wissenschaften, 1975).

---

[53] Christova-Šomova, *Kniga Jov*, 50–54; "Grăckite versii na kniga Jov," 802–05; "Dvata slavjanski prevoda," 3–26; "Slavjanskie perevody," 128–47.

[54] Christova-Šomova, *Kniga Jov*, 166–301.

[55] Hagedorn and Hagedorn, *Die älteren griechischen Katenen*.

[56] Ziegler, *Iob*.

[57] Christova-Šomova, "Grăckite versii na kniga Jov," 807–08; Christova-Šomova, *Kniga Jov*, 162–65.

11.4.7 OLD CHURCH SLAVONIC TRANSLATIONS

Blagova, È., "Biblejskie citaty v Uspenskom sbornike XII–XIII vv.," *Cyrillomethodianum* 6 (1982): 67–79.

Brandt, R., "Grigorovičev parimejnik: v sličenii s drugimi parimejnikami," *Čtenija v Imperatorskom Obščestve istorii i drevnostej rossijskich* 168 (1894): 1–90; 170 (1894): 91–178; 193 (1900): 179–290; 197 (1901): 291–308.

Catena Græcorum patrum in beatum Iob collectore Niceta Heracleæ metropolita ex duobus mss. bibliothecæ Bodleianæ codicibus: Græcè nunc primùm in lucem edita, et Latinè versa (ed. P. Iunius; London: Ex typographio regio, 1637).

Christova-Šomova, I., "Dvata slavjanski prevoda na katenata na Kniga Jov," *Palaeobulgarica* 30.2 (2006): 3–26.

Christova-Šomova, I., *Kniga Jov s tălkuvanija v slavjanski prevod: Po Vladislavovija prepis ot 1456 g., răkopis N° 4/14 ot sbirkata na Rilskija manastir* (Sofia: Izdatelska kăšta "Anubis," 2007).

Christova-Šomova, I., "Grăckite versii na kniga Jov i technite slavjanski prevodi," in *Problemi na Kirilo-Metodievoto delo i na bălgarskata kultura prez IX–X vek* (eds. B. Belčeva, E. Dogramadžieva, and S. Nikolova; Kirilo-Metodievski studii 17; Sofia: Bălgarska Akademija na naukite, 2007), 799–813.

Christova-Šomova, I., "Slavjanskie perevody knigi Iova," in *Svjaščennoe pisanie kak faktor jazykovogo i literaturnogo razvitija: Materiały Meždunarodnoj konferencii "Svjaščennoe pisanie kak faktor jazykovogo i literaturnogo razvitija v areale avraamičeskich religij": Sankt-Peterburg, 30 ijunja 2009 g.* (ed. E.N. Meščerskaja; St. Petersburg: Dmitrij Bulanin, 2011), 128–48.

Gentry, P.J., *The Asterisked Materials in the Greek Job* (SBLSCS 38; Atlanta: Scholars Press, 1995).

Gorskij, A. and K.I. Nevostruev, *Opisanie slavjanskich rukopisej Moskovskoj Sinodal'noj (Patriaršej) biblioteki*, Vol. 2: *Pisanija svjatych otcev*, Part 1: *Tolkovanie svjaščennogo pisanija* (Moscow: Sinodal'naja tipografija, 1857).

Hagedorn, U. (ed.), *Olympiodor, Diakon von Alexandria: Kommentar zu Hiob* (PTS 24; Berlin: De Gruyter, 1984).

Hagedorn, U. and D. Hagedorn, "Nachlese zu den Fragmenten der jüngeren griechischen Übersetzer des Buches Hiob," *Nachrichten der Akademie der Wissenschaften in Göttingen: Philologisch-Historische Klasse* 10 (1991): 377–411.

Hagedorn, U. and D. Hagedorn (eds.), *Die älteren griechischen Katenen zum Buch Hiob* (4 vols.; PTS 40, 48, 53, 59; Berlin: De Gruyter, 1994–2004).

Iosif (Ieromonach), "Opis' rukopisej perenesennych iz Biblioteki Iosifova monastyrja v Biblioteku Moskovskoj duchovnoj akademii," *Čtenija v Imperatorskom obščestve istorii i drevnostej rossijskich pri Moskovskom universitete* 1881 no. 3 (1882): 1–308.

Iosif (Archimandrit), *Podrobnoe oglavlenie Velikich Čet'ich Minej vserossijskogo mitropolita Makarija, chranjaščichsja v Moskovskoj patriaršej (nyne Synodal'noj) biblioteke* (Moscow: Sinodal'naja tipografija, 1892).

Istrin, V., *Aleksandrija russkich chronografov: Issledovanie i tekst* (Moscow: Universitetskaja tipografija, 1893).

Jacimirskij, A.I., *Slavjanskie i russkie rukopisi rumynskich bibliotek* (Sbornik Otdelenija russkogo jazyka i slovesnosti Imperatorskoj Akademii nauk 79; St. Petersburg: Tipografija Imperatorskoj Akademii nauk, 1905).

Kostova, K., "Kăm văprosa za kirilo-metodievite prevodačeski pochvati v Kniga Iov ot răkopis F.I. 461 na Ruskata Nacionalna Biblioteka v Sankt Peterburg," *Palaeobulgarica* 24.2 (2000): 61–69.

Kostova, K., "Kăm văprosa za prevoda na otkăsite ot kniga Jov v Simeonovija sbornik (po Svetoslavovija prepis ot 1073)," in *Ezik i istorija na bălgarskite srednovekovni tekstove: Sbornik v čest na Ekaterina Dogramadžieva* (ed. S. Nikolova; Kirilo-Metodievski studii 14; Sofia: Bălgarska Akademija na naukite, 2001), 91–96.

Mathiesen, R., "Handlist of Manuscripts Containing Church Slavonic Translations of the Old Testament," *Polata knigopisnaja* 7 (1983): 3–48.

Meade, J.D., "A Critical Edition of the Hexaplaric Fragments of Job 22–42" (PhD diss., The Southern Baptist Theological Seminary, 2012).

Michajlov, A.V., *Opyt izučenija teksta knigi Bytija proroka Moiseja v drevne-slavjanskom perevode*, Vol. 1: *Parimejnyj tekst* (Warsaw: Tipografija Varšavskogo učebnogo okruga, 1912).

Nikolova, S., "Za naj-starija bălgarski srednovekoven răkopis na Starija Zavet," *Starobălgarska literatura* 28–29 (1994): 110–18.

Ostrožskaja biblija: Fototipičeskoe pereizdanie teksta s izdanija 1581 g (Moscow: Slovo-Art, 1988).

Pechuška, F., *Staroslovanský překlad Knihy Job* (Prague: Knih. časopisu Katol. duchovenstva, 1935).

Pičchadze, A.A., "Perevody Biblii na drevnie jazyki: cerkovnoslavjanskij," *Pravoslavnaja ènciklopedija* 5:139–47.

Pičchadze, A.A., "Slav. етеръ: k voprosu o gruppirovke drevneslavjanskich pamjatnikov," *Scrinium: Journal of Patrology, Critical Hagiography and Ecclesiastical History* 7–8 (2011–2012): 219–36.

Reinhart, J., "review of I. Christova-Šomova, *Kniga Jov s tălkuvanija v slavjanski prevod*," *Slovo* 62 (2012): 285–91.

Ribarova, Z. and Z. Hauptova, *Grigorovičev Parimejnik* (2 vols.; Skopje: Makedonska Akademija na naukite i umetnostite, 1998–2014).

Taube, M., "The Book of Job in Vilnius 262," in *Judaeo-Bulgarica, Judaeo-Russica et Palaeoslavica* (eds. W. Moskovich and S. Nikolova; Jews and Slavs 15; Jerusalem: Hebrew University of Jerusalem, Center for Slavic Languages and Literatures, 2005): 281–96.

Temčin, S.J., "Scharija i Skorina: ob istočnikach Vilenskogo Vetchozavetnogo svoda (F 19–262)," *Senoji Lietuvos Literatūra* 21 (2006): 289–316.

Thomson, F.J., "The Slavonic Translation of the Old Testament," in *The Interpretation of the Bible: The International Symposium in Slovenia* (ed. J. Krašovec; JSOTSup 189; Sheffield: Sheffield Academic Press, 1998), 605–920.

Thomson, F.J., *A Brief Survey of the History of the Church Slavonic Bible from its Cyrillomethodian Origins until its Final Form in the Elizabethan Bible of 1751* (Slavica Gandensia 33.2; Ghent: Department of Slav and East European Studes of the University of Ghent, 2006).

Thompson, F.J., "The Three Slavonic Translations of the Greek Catena on Job. With an Appendix on the Author of the First Prologue to the First Translation: Polychronius or Photius?", in *The Bible in Slavic Tradition* (A. Kulik et al. (eds.); Studio Judaeoslavica 9; Leiden: Brill, 2016), 143–78.

Trifunović, Đ., "Zapisi inoka Gavriila, prevodioca tumačenja knjige o Jovu," in *Literaturoznanie i folkloristika: V čest na 70-godišninata na akad. P. Dinekov* (ed. A. Stojkov; Sofia: Izdat. na Bălg. Akad. na Naukite, 1983), 108–11.

Uspenskij sbornik XII–XIII vv. (ed. S.I. Kotkov; Moscow: Nauka, 1971).

Vajs, J. (ed.), *Liber Iob: Ex breviario Noviano II: transcriptum variis lectionibus aliorum codicum ornavit* (Veglae: Academia Palaeoslavica Veglensis, 1903).

Vajs, J., *Nejstarší Breviář hrvatsko-hlaholský* (*Prvý Breviář Vrbnický*) (Prague: Nákl. Král. České Společnosti Náuk, 1910).

Weiher, E., S.O. Šmidt, and A.I. Škurko (eds.), *Die grossen Lesemenäen des Metropoliten Makari: Uspenskij spisok*, Vol. 1: *1.–8. Mai* (Monumenta linguae slavicae dialecti veteris 51; Freiburg: Weiher Verlag, 2007).

Woods, N., "A Critical Edition of the Hexaplaric Fragments of Job: Chapters 1–21" (PhD diss., The Southern Baptist Theological Seminary, 2009).

Zaradija-Kiš, A., "Hrvatskoglagoljska knjiga o Jobu prema Septuaginti," *Kačić* 25 (1993): 427–35.

Zaradija-Kiš, A., *Knjiga o Jobu u hrvatskoglagoljskoj književnosti* (Zagreb: Hrvatsko filološko društvo, 1997).

Zaradija-Kiš, A., "Hrvatsko-glagoljska i bugarska knjiga o Jobu," in *Acta Palaeoslavica*, Vol. 1: *Dokladi predstaveni na Šestija meždunaroden kolokvium po starobălgaristika* (ed. M. Mladenova; Sofia: Heron Press, 2000), 119–31.

Zaradija-Kiš, A., "Jezična tradicija i leksičke posebnosti Knjige o Jobu u glagoljskom Moskovskom brevijaru," in *O kraljevstvu nebeskom novo i staro* (ed. M. Cifrak; Zagreb: Kršćanska sadašnjost, 2001), 489–97.

Ziegler, J. (ed.), *Iob* (Septuaginta Vetus Testamentum Graecum 11.4; Göttingen: Vandenhoeck & Ruprecht, 1982).

Ziegler, J., *Beiträge zum griechischen Iob* (MSU 18; Göttingen: Vandenhoeck & Ruprecht, 1985).

Alessandro Maria Bruni

11.4.8 Arabic Translations

11.4.8.1 Background

Several ninth-century C.E. translations of the book of Job have been identified among our earliest Christian Arabic texts. We may therefore surmise that the sufferings of Job intrigued Arabic-speaking Christians more than many other books in the Christian Old Testament. In contrast, based on the number of extant manuscripts, few new translations or reproductions of the early manuscripts appear to have been produced between the eleventh and sixteenth centuries.

11.4.8.2 Original Form, Editions, Tools

In his famous *GCAL, Graf records less than thirty manuscripts that contain the Arabic book of Job.[1] The first and perhaps most ancient version is

---

[1] Graf, *GCAL 1, 126–27. Unfortunately, this work is not free of errors. Most importantly, it is not always clear whether the reference is to a class mark or to a catalogue number. For converting catalogue numbers referring to the collections of the Coptic Orthodox Patriarchate and the Coptic Museum in Cairo to shelf marks, a helpful tool is: K. Khalil, *Tables de concordance des manuscrits arabes chrétiens du Caire et du Sinaï* (CSCO 482 Subsidia 75; Leuven: Peeters, 1986).

11.4.8 ARABIC TRANSLATIONS

partly contained in manuscript London, BL, Ar. 1475 (Add. 26116), which was taken to Europe by Constantin Tischendorf and dates on paleographic grounds approximately to the first half of the ninth century C.E.[2] Baudissin published these fragments and supplied them with a Latin translation in 1870.[3] More recently, several scholars have noted that the remainder of this version is contained in manuscript Sinai Ar. 1, located at the Monastery of St. Catherine in the Sinai Desert.[4]

The *Vorlage* of this version of Job is not evident. It appears to be translated principally from the Syro-Hexapla (→ 11.4.4), yet there appears to be an influence of the Peshiṭta (→ 11.3.4) and LXX (→ 11.3.1).[5] Monferrer Sala points out that the manuscript is written in a special *Kufic* hand (*cúfico en evolución*), which is characteristic primarily of texts from the lavra of *Mār Sābā* in the Judean Desert.[6] Among the orthographic peculiarities of the text are the frequent omission or misplacement of diacritics, the lack of /*hamza*/ in all positions, and the marking of /*qāf*/ either with two dots above or with one dot below the consonantal letter.[7] The language is generally identified as Classical Arabic but the translation contains a certain number of Middle Arabic traits.[8]

In his unpublished doctoral dissertation on early Job versions, Blackburn adds to the list yet another ancient translation composed by the Egyptian monk Ṭōmā al-Fusṭāṭī.[9] The translation is attested in manuscript Sinai Ar. 514 (folios 141ᵛ–160ʳ.), a volume of hagiographical works preserved in the Monastery of St. Catherine. Atiya discovered that this manuscript, which he refers to as Codex Arabicus, is a palimpsest consisting of no less than five layers: two in Syriac, one in Greek, and two in Arabic. He dates the upper Arabic layer, written in early Kufic or pre-Kufic archaic Naskh, to the late eighth or early ninth century C.E.[10] The Job version of this manuscript was published by 'Iyyād[11] and text samples from Job 1; 3; 11; 18; 22; 28; 32; 38 are transcribed and discussed, foremost from a theological perspective, by Blackburn.[12] According to the latter, this Egyptian version is translated principally from the Syro-Hexapla (→ 11.4.4) but in the prose sections the influence of the Peshiṭta (→ 11.3.4) is unmistakable. It appears to be influenced indirectly by the translation contained in manuscripts Sinai Ar. 1 and London, BL, Ar. 1475, whose grammar it occasionally corrects according to Classical Arabic. The translation still displays many Middle Arabic features, especially Egyptian lexical traits.[13]

The second version Graf refers to represents the translation of Job attributed to a certain Pethion (Fatyūn b. Ayyūb). We read on folio 173ʳ of manuscript London, BL, Or. 1326 (Ar. Suppl. 1):[14]

كتاب ايوب الصديق القديس الطاهر مما ترجمه من العبرانيه الي
العربيه فيتون بن ايوب الترجمان رحمة الله عليه

The book of Job the Righteous, Holy and Pure, according to what Pethion b. Ayyūb the translator translated from Hebrew to Arabic. May the mercy of God be upon him.

---

[2] London, BL, Ar. 1475 contains Job 1:8–13, 18; 6:26–28:1. See also H.L. Fleischer, "Zur Geschichte der arabischen Schrift," *ZDMG* 18 (1864): 288–91; H.L. Fleischer, *Kleinere Schriften* (3 vols.; Leipzig: S. Hirzel, 1888), 3.395–97, 399.

[3] Baudissin, *Translationis Antiquae Arabicae*.

[4] See Blau, *Grammar*, 1.31–32, and Monferrer Sala, "Liber Iob," 126–28.

[5] Baudissin, *Translationis*, 16–18; Monferrer Sala, "Liber Iob," 128–42; and Blackburn, "Job," 383, 397–98.

[6] Monferrer Sala, "Liber Iob," 128–42.

[7] Monferrer Sala, "Liber Iob," 122. See also B. Levin, *Die Griechisch-Arabische Evangelien-Übersetzung: Vat. Borg. Ar. 95 und Ber. orient. oct. 1108* (Uppsala: Almqvist & Wiksells Boktryckeri, 1938), 12–16.

[8] See relevant sections in Blau, *Grammar*, Vol. 1. Cf. also Blackburn, "Job," 379.

[9] Blackburn, "Job."

[10] A.S. Atiya, "Codex Arabicus," *Homage to A Bookman: Essays on Manuscripts, Books and Printing: Written for Hans P. Kraus on His 60th Birthday Oct. 12, 1967* (ed. H. Lehmann-Haupt; Berlin: Gebr. Mann Verlag, 1967), 75–85.

[11] B. 'Iyyād, *Sifr 'Ayyūb* (Cairo: Machad al-dirāsāt al-Qibṭiyya al-'anbā rū'īs, 1967).

[12] Blackburn, "Job."

[13] Blackburn, "Job," 379–80, 383, 387, 395–97.

[14] Job is found in this codex in folios 173ʳ and 183ᵛ. The same version is attested in manuscripts Copt. Orth. Patr., Bibl. 89 (Graf no. 232; Simaika 98); Bibl. 34 (Graf no. 246; Simaika 36). See Graf, *GCAL* 1, 126–27.

By "Hebrew" is clearly meant "Syriac." The diacritics on the name "Pethion" are missing and /tāʾ/ is more reminiscent of /qāf/ but the same name is found in other translations with slightly different spellings (→ 6–9.2.8). Vaccari[15] identified this Pethion as the ninth-century C.E. East Syriac monk from Mesopotamia regarding whom al-Nadīm states in the Fihrist: "There was also Pethiōn, who was the most accurate of the translators from the point of view of translation, also the best of them for style and diction."[16]

According to Blackburn, the prose section in Pethion's translation exhibits statistically a closer dependence on the Syro-Hexapla (→ 11.4.4) than on the Peshiṭta (→ 11.3.4; 50 % against 25 %) whereas in the poetic sections the influence from the Peshiṭta is more distinguished (4:5). As for translation technique, he states that the prose passages are relatively literal whereas the poetry sections are freer. For instance, in the poetic section, the translator introduces elements as a means to augment God's role and highlight his power and transcendence. Blackburn claims that the treatment of Classical Arabic is less adequate in the prose part yet the poetic section is characterized by its elevated style and inner coherence. There is a clear lexical affinity between Pethion's translation and Muslim literature. For example, al-razaq "divine beneficence" is used in Job 28:5a and al-jihād "struggle, holy war" in Job 38:23b.[17]

In *GCAL 1, Graf lists several manuscripts that contain translations of Job from a Syriac Vorlage (→ 11.3.4; → 11.4.4). To this group belongs the Arabic version that was published in the Paris Polyglot[18] according to manuscript Paris, BNF, Ar. 1.[19] This Polyglot version was reprinted by de Lagarde.[20]

Moreover, the Arabic version printed in the Propaganda Fide edition of the *Biblia Sacra Arabica, which according to Graf is based on manuscript Vatican, Ar. 468 (folios 381ᵛ–399ᵛ), is of Syriac provenance.[21] Additional manuscripts based on a Syriac Vorlage are Coptic Orthodox Patriarchate Bibl. 45 (Graf no. 222, folios 47ʳ–64ʳ), Bibl. 47 (Graf no. 225, folios 67ᵛ–102ʳ), Bibl. 49 (Graf no. 229, folios 44ʳ–65ᵛ), and Jerusalem, St. Anna 1 (folios 24ʳ–53ʳ) dated 1816.[22]

A few manuscripts appear to have been translated from a Coptic Vorlage (→ 11.4.2). De Lagarde edited and published a translation from a Coptic version, primarily according to manuscript Berlin, Staatsbibliothek, Or. Oblongus 447 (dated 1792).[23] The following Arabic texts of Job are also from a Coptic Vorlage: manuscripts Coptic Museum, Bibl. 70 (Graf no. 17, folios 57ʳ–184ʳ; dated 1794), Coptic Orthodox Patriarchate, Bibl. 6 (Graf no. 247, folios 240ᵛ–271ʳ; dated to the nineteenth century), and London, BL Ar. 794 (Add. 18, 997, folios 50–165).[24]

Graf further refers to a translation from LXX (→ 11.3.1) preserved in manuscript Copenhagen, Royal Library, Or. 76 (folios 4ᵛ–20ᵛ) containing Job 1:1–40:29.[25] He finally records a few manuscripts as being of unknown origin, the most ancient being the tenth-century manuscript in K. Hiersemann's

---

[15] A. Vaccari, "Le Versioni Arabe dei Profeti," Bib 3 (1922): 401–23 (413–16).

[16] The Fihrist of al-Nadīm: A Tenth-Century Survey of Muslim Culture, Vol. 1 (ed. and trans. B. Dodge; New York: Columbia University Press, 1979), 46.

[17] Blackburn, "Job," 380–82, 389–94, 398–99.

[18] Le Jay, *Biblia.

[19] In this connection, see Eichhorn, *Einleitung, 2.282–85.

[20] De Lagarde, Psalterium, Job, Proverbia, 247–99 (left-hand pages).

[21] This manuscript has been discussed by A. Vaccari in "Una Bibbia Araba: Per Il Primo Gesuita Venuto Al Libano," Mélanges de l'Université Saint-Joseph 10.4 (1925): 79–104; A. Vaccari, "La Storia d'Una Bibbia Araba," Bib 11 (1930): 350–55; and S. Euringer, "Zum Stammbaum der Arabischen Bibelhandschriften Vat. ar. 468 und 467," Zeitschrift für Semitistik und Verwandte Gebiete 7 (1929): 259–73.

[22] For further manuscripts, see Graf, *GCAL 1, 127.

[23] De Lagarde, Psalterium, Job, Proverbia (246–98; right hand side). Cf. also the prologue in P. de Lagarde, Psalterii versio memphitica: accedunt psalterii thebani fragmenta parhamiana, proverbiorum memphiticorum fragmenta berolinensia (Göttingen: W.F. Kaestner, 1875), v.

[24] For additional manuscripts and related works, see Graf, *GCAL 1, 127.

[25] For this manuscript and its completion, see B. Knutsson, Studies in the Text and Language of Three Syriac-Arabic Versions of the Book of Judicum with Special Reference to the Middle Arabic Elements: Introduction–Linguistic Notes–Texts (Leiden: Brill, 1974), 13 n. 11.

Catalogue 500, Nr. 16 (folios 65ʳ–94ᵛ). This manuscript has been identified as part of a larger codex whose various parts are disseminated among Western libraries.[26] Of unknown origin are also manuscripts Milan, Ambros. (de Hammer) Or. 88; Paris, BNF, Ar. 153 (folios 341ᵛ–362ʳ) dated to the seventeenth century; Šarfeh, Monastery Library, Ar. 1/9, 4; Coptic Orthodox Patriarchate Bibl. 55 (Graf no. 260, fols. 1ʳ–73ʳ, forty-two chapters, the beginning is missing) dated to the nineteenth century; and Dair Abū Maqār, Bibl. 12 (the Minor Prophets, Copt. and Arab.) dated 1804.[27] Finally, Mingana refers to a collection of biblical books containing the book of Job that are preserved in the catalogue of Mingana, Ar. Christ. 121 (Add. 199), dated to the tenth century.[28] Among the new findings in the Sinai collection, Meimaris lists an ancient Arabic Job version written on parchment (Membr. 18), seemingly translated from LXX (Ar. incipit: *mimā qussa min al-rūmiyya*).[29]

11.4.8.3 Text-Critical and Literary Value

Needless to say, thorough studies on the Arabic versions of Job with regard to translation technique, text type, and *Vorlage* are badly needed. When such studies have been accomplished, the early ninth-century C.E. manuscripts may be of some value for textual criticism of the Peshiṭta (→ 11.3.4) and the Syro-Hexapla (→ 11.4.4). In general, Christian Arabic Bible translations are to be primarily regarded as documents in their own right with the capacity to introduce us to the literary and intellectual ideals of the remote world of early Christian Arabic literature.

Atiya, A.S., *The Arabic Manuscripts of Mount Sinai: A Hand-List of the Arabic Manuscripts and Scrolls Microfilmed at the Library of the Monastery of St. Catherine, Mount Sinai* (Baltimore: John Hopkins Press, 1955).

Atiya, A.S., *Al-Fahāris al-Tahīliyya li-Makhṭūṭāt ṭūr Sīnā al-ʿarabiyya* (trans. J.N. Youssef; Alexandria: Munšaʿat al-Maʿārif, 1970).

von Baudissin, W.W.F., *Translationis Antiquae Arabicae libri Iobi quae supersunt* (Leipzig: Dörffling und Franke, 1870).

Blackburn, S.P., "The Early Arabic Versions of Job (First Millennium C.E.)" (PhD diss., University of St. Andrews, 1998).

Graf, *GCAL 1.

de Lagarde, P., *Psalterium, Job, Proverbia: Arabice* (Göttingen: W.F. Kaestner, 1876).

Meimaris, Y., *Katalogos tōn neōn aravikōn cheirographōn tēs Hieras Monēs Aikaterinēs tou Orous Sina Athens* (Athens: Ethnikon Hidryma Ereunōn, 1985) [Greek].

Monferrer Sala, J.P., "Liber Iob detractus apud Sin. Ar. 1. Notas en Torno a la Vorlage Siriaca de un Manuscrito Árabe Cristiano (s. IX)," *Collectanea Christiana Orientalia* 1 (2003): 119–42.

Walton, *Polyglotta, Vol. 3.

Miriam Lindgren Hjälm

---

[26] M. van Esbroeck, "Remembrement d'un Manuscrit Sinaitique Arabe 950," in *Actes Du Premier Congrès International D'Études Arabes Chrétiennes, Goslar, Septembre 1980* (ed. K. Samir; Rome: Pont. Institutum Studiorum Orientalium, 1982), 135–47.

[27] For additional manuscripts, see Graf, *GCAL 1, 128.

[28] A. Mingana, *Catalogue of the Mingana Collection of Manuscripts Now in the Possession of the Trustees of the Woodbrooke Settlement, Selly Oak, Birmingham*, Vol. 3: *Additional Christian Arabic and Syriac Manuscipts* (Cambridge: W. Heffer and Sons, Limited, 1939).

[29] Meimaris, *Katalogos*.

12
Proverbs

∴

12.1 Textual History of Proverbs

12.1.1 Extant Witnesses

The following Hebrew manuscripts are available for MT: the Leningrad Codex = Codex EBP. I B 19a of the National Library of Russia in St. Petersburg (MT^L); the Aleppo Codex (MT^A); Codex Cambridge University, Add. ms 1753 (MT^Y) → 12.2.2.2.[1]

Notable Qumran texts from Cave 4 are 4QProv^a (fragments from Prov 1:27–2:1), 4QProv^b (fragments from Prov 13:6–9; 14:5–10, 12–13; 14:31–15:8; and 15:19–31); → 12.2.1.[2]

Greek texts: LXX-Prov is an important textual witness. It differs drastically from MT and other textual witnesses (→ 12.1.3 and → 12.3.1) and may be consulted in Rahlfs–Hanhart, *Septuaginta*. R. Holmes and J. Parsons, *Vetus Testamentum graecum cum variis lectionibis*, Vol. 3 (Oxford: Clarendon Press, 1823) should be used cautiously.

Aramaic (Syriac) texts: S-Prov (→ 12.3.4), a significant textual witness, was probably translated by a Jewish convert to Christianity (→ 12.3.4.4).[3] There is also a close relationship between LXX-Prov and S-Prov (→ 12.3.4.5),[4] and Fox is of the opinion that the translator of the Peshitta drew on LXX more than any other Peshitta translator.[5] T-Prov (→ 12.3.3) is generally agreed to represent an Aramaic rendering of S-Prov (→ 12.3.4.6),[6] and should therefore not be considered an independent witness.

12.1.2 History of Research

Only those aspects that have a direct bearing upon the textual history of Proverbs are discussed here. According to Fox,[7] the book of Proverbs pursues a central theme, namely wisdom that not only concerns doing but also knowing. The Proverbs corpus consists of collections of instructions, sayings, and poems by anonymous Israelite/Judean sages.[8] The dating of this corpus is subject to scholarly discussion. Traditionally its authorship was ascribed to King Solomon (see Prov 1:1; 10:1; and 25:1). This could point to the time of the united monarchy.[9] Fox[10] disagrees; although he thinks that some of the material dates to the First Temple period, he argues that other material dates to the Second Temple period. He proposed new ideas on the nature of the corpus included in Proverbs 1–9, which he deems to be an instruction handbook for young people. He also takes it as an introduction to the other earlier collections, part of a final redaction that took place during the Persian or Hellenistic periods.[11] Of great importance in determining the social[12] setting of Proverbs is the question of whether it was used in the setting of a scribal school or of village life.[13] Westermann[14] argued that the majority of the proverbs were created by the "simple people" in the villages. Whybray[15] located the sayings as originating among the smallholding farmers. Hermisson[16] connected the setting of Wisdom

---

[1] De Waard, *Proverbs*, 5*.

[2] The Qumran manuscripts are published in P.W. Skehan and E. Ulrich, "Proverbs," *DJD* XVI: 181–86. See also de Waard, *Proverbs*, 5*-6*. For a detailed text-critical evaluation of these fragments, see also de Waard, "4QProv," 87–96.

[3] See M.P. Weitzman, "From Judaism to Christianity: The Syriac Version of the Hebrew Bible," in *The Jews Among the Pagans and Christians in the Roman Empire* (eds. J. Lieu, J. North, and T. Rajak; London: Routledge, 1992), 147–73; M.P. Weitzman, *The Syriac Version of the Old Testament: An Introduction* (University of Cambridge Oriental Publications 56; Cambridge: Cambridge University Press, 1999), 206–62; and Fox, "Peshitta of Proverbs."

[4] Fox, "LXX-Proverbs."

[5] Fox, "Peshitta of Proverbs" and Fox, "How the Peshitta of Proverbs Uses the Septuagint."

[6] Fox, "LXX-Proverbs," 95.

[7] Fox, *Proverbs*, 346.

[8] Perdue, *The Sword*, 85.

[9] Perdue, *The Sword*, 85.

[10] Fox, *Proverbs*, 11.

[11] Fox, *Proverbs*, 6.

[12] In Fox, *Proverbs*, 49; Fox quotes the views of scholars who disagree with him.

[13] Fox, *Proverbs*, 6.

[14] Westermann, *Wurzeln der Weisheit*, 75.

[15] Whybray, *Wealth and Poverty*, 75.

[16] Hermisson, *Studien*.

literature with schools at the royal court, so also Lemaire.[17] Lang[18] is also of the opinion that the origin of Proverbs is to be found in a school setting. However, it remains problematic that there is no clear evidence of schools in ancient Israel before the Hellenistic era, when Ben Sira refers to the בית המדרש ("in the house of instruction"; Sir 51:23). Perdue[19] is also sceptical, since there is no decisive textual or archaeological evidence. In the final analysis, he opts for the Ptolemaic period for the final redaction of Proverbs. McKane[20] also argues that a final Jahwistic redaction took place in the post-exilic period. This covered Proverbs 1–9 and 31. The application of the lexeme צוֹפִיָּה transcribing the Greek word σοφία "wisdom" in Prov 31:27 could be used as an argument for the Hellenistic (Ptolemaic?) period.[21] Another possible Greek loan word in Prov 7:16 is אֵטוּן "linen" from ὀθόνη "fine linen."[22]

12.1.3 Textual History

The books (sic!) of Proverbs have complicated textual and compositional histories. The role of LXX-Prov (→ 12.3.1) is significant in this regard. It differs rather drastically from MT (→ 12.2.2) and other textual witnesses, and are explained in different ways. There are primarily two schools of thinking: one group of scholars thinks that the Greek text represents a Hebrew parent text different from MT. Tov[23] is of the opinion that the translator used a recensionally different Hebrew text for his translation. Another group of scholars argues that the translator created the differences. Cook[24] takes as his point of departure the free translation technique of this book and demonstrates that in most cases the translator brought about the changes. In the same vein, Cook has argued that the text-critical value of this unit is rather limited,[25] since the Hebrew parent text upon which the LXX translation is based agrees to a great extent with MT.

Fox,[26] who has written extensively on the Wisdom books of the Hebrew Bible against their Near-Eastern background, has a nuanced view in this regard and differs from Cook in various respects. He, firstly, agrees with Tov that LXX-Prov is based on a recensionally differing parent text.[27] He also thinks that it is possible to utilize this rendering in order to reconstruct the Semitic *Vorlage*. Secondly, he agrees that in many verses LXX departs significantly from MT.[28] However, he prefers to define the translation technique followed by the translator as mimetic, rather than as free or interpretive, thus diminishing its text-critical value. He also demonstrates that LXX-Prov has a diversity of translation types and that it is an oversimplification to characterize the translation of the book as one unit and then to apply the assessment to individual elements. He, thus, holds the view that a significant percentage of the differences between MT and LXX-Prov arose in the Hebrew scribal tradition.[29]

The strong point of Fox's approach is his balance in evaluation. On the one hand, he employs nuanced philological insights to identify variant readings and, on the other hand, he has the openness to accept extensive interpretation.[30]

Fox has also demonstrated that the Peshitta version (→ 12.3.4) can be a significant textual witness for the book of Proverbs. Various scholars have evaluated S-Prov, but Fox[31] is the first to address this issue rather exhaustively. He demonstrates the intricate relationship between the Peshitta and LXX by discussing the following aspects: 1) S = MT; 2) S combines MT and LXX in various ways; and 3) S = LXX. He demonstrates that the Syriac translator had a good knowledge of Hebrew and Greek and

---

[17] Lemaire, *Les écoles*.
[18] Lang, *Wisdom*, 7–11.
[19] Perdue, *The Sword*, 88.
[20] McKane, *Proverbs*, 280.
[21] See Fox's evaluation of various scholarly views in this regard (*Proverbs*, 342–45).
[22] McKane, *Proverbs*, 8.
[23] Tov, "Recensional Differences."
[24] Cook, "The Greek of Proverbs," 609–17; Cook and van der Kooij, *Provenance*, 132–33.

[25] Cook, "Text-Critical Value."
[26] Fox, *Proverbs*, 361.
[27] Fox, "Editing Proverbs," 4.
[28] Fox, "LXX-Proverbs," 198.
[29] Fox, "LXX-Proverbs," 120.
[30] Fox, "LXX-Proverbs," 112.
[31] Fox, "Peshitta of Proverbs."

that he "negotiates flexibly and creatively between M and G."[32]

Fox argues lucidly and convincingly. His conclusion, that the Peshitta made use of LXX extensively, is a novel interpretation that applies only to the book of Proverbs. Goshen-Gottstein rejected the opinion that the Peshitta was fundamentally influenced by LXX, by stating that the Peshitta only occasionally looked into LXX.[33]

Depending on one's methodological stance, the difference between the Hebrew (MT) and LXX could be significant for the textual history of Proverbs.[34]

12.1.4 Relevance for Exegesis

The Proverbs corpus is relevant for exegesis, textual and literary criticism (see above). Since the Hebrew text (→ 12.2.2) of Proverbs has a complicated transmission history, the available textual witnesses (especially LXX [→ 12.3.1] and Peshitta [→ 12.3.4]) are important for the textual criticism. The differences between MT and LXX are relevant for literary criticism (→ 12.3.1.6): one group of scholars thinks that the Greek text represents a Hebrew parent text different from MT, while another one thinks that these differences are the work of the translator.

These differences have implications for the theology[35] and exegesis of Proverbs. According to Cook, the Greek translator of Proverbs had a rather systematic approach towards the parent text,[36] visible in the treatment of the "strange woman" (אִשָּׁה זָרָה)[37] in Proverbs 2; 5; 7; 8; and 9. Proverbs 2 can be divided into two main parts: the protasis, vv. 1–4, and the rest of the chapter that makes up the apodosis.[38] The Greek has a different division. Verses 1–12 refer to the good realm and vv. 13–22 describe the bad realm. Verses 11 and 17 contain related but contrasting concepts.

In the Greek, there is a clear contrast between the good and bad counsels, the latter being a metaphor for foreign wisdom, namely Hellenism.[39] This interpretation differs from MT and results from contextual factors. The same Hellenistic background influenced the treatment of the Law of Moses in LXX-Prov.

Accordingly, νόμος "law" in pluses to MT-Prov (Prov 9:10 and 13:15) in the phrase "to know the law is the sign of a sound mind" is part of the systematic application of exegetical perspectives by the translator. Scholars have different views on these additions. In connection with Prov 9:10, de Lagarde[40] rightly thinks that the addition is to be deemed original. Seeligmann,[41] on the contrary, takes the added stich in Prov 9:10 as a secondary addition (doublet).[42] The quotation from Ps 110:10 in Prov 1:7[43] has the literary and ideological function of indicating where the wise should find wisdom in order to solve interpretational questions.[44] The first stich in Prov 9:10 corresponds largely with Prov 1:7.

These additions should be interpreted contextually. It became necessary in the wake of a specific historical situation to stress the importance of the law of Moses. The translator thus warns the readers of the inherent "dangers" of foreign wisdom (the Hellenism of the day). One of these prominent dangers was the depreciation of the law of Moses.[45]

Of special significance is the way the law of Moses is depicted in Proverbs 28, which contains the highest number of occurrences of the word תּוֹרָה "law." Note v. 4: "but those who love the law *build a wall around themselves.*" In this verse, there seems to be no logical relationship between the

---

[32] Fox, "Peshitta of Proverbs".

[33] M.H. Goshen-Gottstein, *Text and Language in Bible and Qumran* (Jerusalem: Orient Publishing House, 1960), xii.

[34] Tov, *TCHB*, 304–05. See also d'Hamonville, *Les Proverbes*, 30–31.

[35] See Cook, "Towards the Formulation of a Theology of the Septuagint," 621–40.

[36] See Cook and van der Kooij, *Provenance*, 108–21.

[37] Cook, "אשה זרה (Prov 1–9 in the Septuagint)," 465.

[38] McKane, *Proverbs*, 188.

[39] Thus Hengel, *Judentum und Hellenismus*, 281.

[40] De Lagarde, *Anmerkungen*, 30.

[41] Cf. Seeligmann, "Voraussetzungen," 179.

[42] See Cook, "Intertextual Readings in the Septuagint," 117–34.

[43] See Cook, "Intertextual Relations between the Septuagint Versions of the Psalms and Proverbs," 218–28.

[44] Cf. Cook, *The Septuagint of Proverbs*, 262.

[45] Cf. Cook, "The Law of Moses," 457.

Greek and the Hebrew,[46] but it is, nevertheless, possible that גור "to struggle" was deliberately understood as גדר "wall" with the understanding that the law has a protective function towards the righteous. A similar point is made in *Letter of Aristeas* 139 and 143.[47] These traditions are markedly different from the view found in some later rabbinical writings – for example, the Mishnah – and in even later rabbinical writings such as ʾAbot 1.1, according to which the Torah must be protected.

Baumgartner, A.J., *Etude critique sur l'état du texte du livre des Proverbes d'après les principales traductions anciennes* (Leipzig: W. Drugulin, 1890).

Camp, C.V., *Wisdom and the Feminine in the Book of Proverbs* (Bible and Literature Series 1; Sheffield: Almond Press, 1985).

Cook, J., "The Septuagint as Contextual Bible Translation: Alexandria or Jerusalem as Context for Proverbs?" *JNSL* 19 (1993): 25–39.

Cook, J., "אִשָּׁה זָרָה (Prov 1–9 in the Septuagint) a Metaphor for Foreign Wisdom?" *ZAW* 106 (1994): 458–76.

Cook, J., *The Septuagint of Proverbs – Jewish and/or Hellenistic Proverbs? Concerning the Hellenistic Colouring of LXX Proverbs* (VTSup 69; Leiden: Brill, 1997).

Cook, J., "Intertextual Relations between the Septuagint Versions of the Psalms and Proverbs," in *The Old Greek Psalter: Studies in Honour of Albert Pietersma* (eds. R.J.V. Hiebert, C.E. Cox, and P.J. Gentry; JSOTSup 332; Sheffield, 2001), 218–28.

Cook, J., "The Greek of Proverbs – Evidence of a Recensionally Deviating Hebrew Text?" in *Emanuel: Studies in Hebrew Bible, Septuagint, and Dead Sea Scrolls in Honor of Emanuel Tov* (eds. S.M. Paul et al.; VTSup 94; Leiden: Brill, 2003), 605–18.

Cook, J., "The Text-Critical Value of the Septuagint of Proverbs," in *Seeking out the Wisdom of the Ancients: Essays in Honor of Michael V. Fox on the Occasion of his Sixty-Fifth Birthday* (eds. R.L. Troxel, K.G. Friebel, and D.R. Magary; Winona Lake: Eisenbrauns, 2005), 407–19.

Cook, J., "Intertextual Readings in the Septuagint," in *The New Testament Interpreted: Essays in Honour of Bernard C. Lategan* (eds. J.C. Thom, J. Punt, and C. Breytenbach, NovTSup 124; Leiden: Brill, 2006), 117–34.

Cook, J., "Towards the Formulation of a Theology of the Septuagint," in *Congress Volume Ljubljana 2007* (ed. A. Lemaire; VTSup 133; Leiden: Brill, 2010), 621–40.

Cook, J. and A. van der Kooij, *Law, Prophets, and Wisdom: On the Provenance of Translators and Their Books in the Septuagint Version* (CBET 68; Leuven: Peeters, 2012).

Eissfeldt, O., *Einleitung in das Alte Testament: Unter Einschluß der Apokryphen und Pseudepigraphen, sowie der apokryphen- und pseudepigraphenartigen Qumrān-Schriften: Entstehungsgeschichte des Alten Testaments* (2nd completely revised ed.; Tübingen: Mohr, 1956).

Fox, M.V., *Proverbs 1–9: A New Translation with Introduction and Commentary* (AB 18A; Doubleday: New York, 2000).

Fox, M.V., "LXX-Proverbs as a Text-Critical Resource," *Textus* 22 (2005): 95–128.

Fox, M.V., "Editing Proverbs: The Challenge of the Oxford Hebrew Bible," *JNSL* 32.1 (2006): 1–22.

Fox, M.V., "How the Peshitta of Proverbs Uses the Septuagint," *JNSL* 39.2 (2013): 37–56.

Fox, M.V., משלי *Proverbs: An Eclectic Edition with Introduction and Textual Commentary* (SBL Hebrew Bible: A Critical Edition 1; Atlanta: SBL Press, 2015).

d'Hamonville, D.-M., *Les Proverbes: Traduction du texte grec de la Septante, introduction et notes* (in collaboration with É. Dumouchet; *Bible d'Alexandrie* 17; Paris: Cerf, 2000).

Hengel, M., *Judentum und Hellenismus: Studien zu ihrer Begegnung unter besonderer Berücksichtigung Palästinas bis zur Mitte des 2.Jh.s v.Chr.* (WUNT 10; Tübingen: Mohr, 1973).

Hengel, M., "Judaism and Hellenism Revisited," in *Hellenism in the Land of Israel* (eds. J.J. Collins and G.E. Sterling; Christianity and Judaism in Antiquity 13; Notre Dame: University of Notre Dame Press, 2001), 7–29.

Hermisson, H.-J., *Studien zur israelitischen Spruchweisheit* (WMANT 28; Neukirchen-Vluyn: Neukirchener Verlag, 1968).

Hurvitz, A., "The Recent Debate on Late Hebrew: Solid Data, Expert's Opinions, and Inconclusive Arguments," *HS* 47 (2006): 191–210.

de Lagarde, P., *Anmerkungen zur griechischen Übersetzung der Proverbien* (Leipzig: F.A. Brockhaus, 1863).

Lang, B., *Wisdom and the Book of Proverbs: A Hebrew Goddess Redefined* (New York: Pilgrim, 1986).

---

[46] Cf. Cook, "The Law of Moses," 189.
[47] Cf. Cook, "The Law of Moses," 459.

Lemaire, A., *Les ecoles et la formation de la Bible dans l'ancien Israël* (OBO 39; Göttingen: Vandenhoeck & Ruprecht, 1981).

McKane, W., *Proverbs: A New Approach* (London: SCM Press, 1970).

Mezzacasa, G., *Il libro dei proverbi di Salomone: Studio critico sulle aggiunte greco-allesandrine* (Rome: Pontificum, 1913).

Perdue, L.G., *The Sword and the Stylus: An Introduction to Wisdom in the Age of Empires* (Grand Rapids: Eerdmans, 2008).

Seeligmann, I.L., "Voraussetzungen der Midraschexegese," in *Congress Volume Copenhagen* (VTSup 1; Leiden: Brill, 1953), 150–81.

Tov, E., "Recensional Differences between the Masoretic Text and the Septuagint of Proverbs," in *Of Scribes and Scrolls: Studies on the Hebrew Bible, Intertestamental Judaism, and Christian Origins Presented to John Strugnell* (eds. H.W. Attridge, J.J. Collins, and T.H. Tobin; Lanham: University Press of America, 1990), 43–56.

Tov, E., *Textual Criticism of the Hebrew Bible* (Minneapolis/Assen, Maastricht: Fortress Press/Van Gorcum, 1992.

de Waard, J., "4QProv and Textual Criticism," *Textus* 19 (1998): 87–96.

de Waard, J., **BHQ Part 17: Proverbs*.

Westermann, C., *Wurzeln der Weisheit: Die ältesten Sprüche Israels und anderer Völker* (Göttingen: Vandenhoeck & Ruprecht, 1990).

Whybray, R.N., *Wealth and Poverty in the Book of Proverbs* (JSOTSup 99; Sheffield: JSOT Press, 1990).

Wolters, A., "Ṣôpiyyâ (Prov 31:27) as Hymnic Participle and Play on *Sophia*," *JBL* 104 (1985): 577–87.

Johann Cook

12.2 Ancient Hebrew Texts

12.2.1 Ancient Manuscript Evidence

Three, four, or five ancient manuscripts are preserved of the book of Proverbs. All were found in the Qumran caves.

12.2.1.1 4QProv^a (4Q102)

Of 4QProv^a, two frgs. are extant that attest to forty-two partly or completely preserved words from Prov 1:27–2:1. In principal, such a small passage could also be a quotation from Proverbs in a nonbiblical book. However, as Prov 2:1 begins a new instruction, it is more likely that 4Q102 is a Proverbs manuscript than one that merely preserves a Proverbs quotation including parts of two different discourses from the book of Proverbs. The manuscript is written stichometrically with two bicola per line.[1] Skehan and Ulrich classify the manuscript paleographically as "transitional to the Herodian" period and date it to the second half of the first century B.C.E.[2] The orthography of the preserved text of 4QProv^a is identical to that of MT;[3] the small amount of extant text does not allow for a text-typological classification of this manuscript. With the exception of one variant reading in Prov 1:32,[4] the manuscript follows MT-Prov (→ 12.2.2).[5]

12.2.1.2 4QProv^b (4Q103)

The fourteen extant frgs. of 4QProv^b preserve remnants of Prov 13:6–9; 14:5–10, 12–13, 31–33; 15:1–8, 19–31. The manuscript is copied stichometrically. The *stichoi* are distributed inconsistently throughout the lines.[6] The script of 4QProv^b reflects a Herodian hand of the late first century B.C.E.[7] In its orthography, 4QProv^b agrees with MT with one exception. The sixty-eight extant words of 4QProv^b make a text-typological classification of this manuscript difficult. 4QProv^b reads three times with and twice against MT (→ 12.2.2), as well as twice with and three times against LXX (→ 12.3.1). 4QProv^b attest to two words from Prov 15:31. Because this verse is lacking in LXX-Prov, the variant is mentioned neither by Skehan and Ulrich ("Proverbs," 186) nor by Ulrich, *BQS, 734. It seems likely that 4QProv^b attests to a semi-Masoretic text.[8]

12.2.1.3 4QProv^c (4Q103a)

Puech[9] identified a fragment mentioned already by Skehan and Ulrich[10] as belonging together with 4QProv^b to a third Proverbs manuscript from Qumran cave 4. Six words with remnants of Prov 9:16 and 10:30–32 survive. The small amount of preserved text makes orthographic and text-typological classifications of 4QProv^c impossible. In its paleography, the manuscript resembles 4QProv^b.

---

[1] For the stichometrical arrangement of 4QProv^a, cf. Puech, "Proverbi," 170, and Skehan and Ulrich, "Proverbs," 181.

[2] Skehan and Ulrich, "Proverbs," 181; cf. de Waard, "4QProv," 88.

[3] Skehan and Ulrich, "Proverbs," 181.

[4] Due to character confusion and metathesis, 4QProv^a reads מושכת "belt" instead of the מְשׁוּבַת "apostasy" in MT-Prov (cf. Skehan and Ulrich, "Proverbs," 182).

[5] For the closeness of 4QProv^a to MT-Prov, cf. Puech, "Proverbi," 173, 189; Jastram, "Proverbs," 702; Tov, *"Synthese," 27. Cf. also, without distinction between 4QProv^a and 4QProv^b, P.W. Skehan, "Qumran and Old Testament Criticism," in *Qumrân: sa piété, sa théologie et son milieu* (ed. M. Delcor; BETL 46; Paris: Duculot), 163–82, esp. 163.

[6] Cf. Skehan and Ulrich, "Proverbs," 183.

[7] Skehan and Ulrich, "Proverbs," 183; cf. de Waard, "4QProv," 88.

[8] Cf. R.J. Clifford, "Observations on the Text and Versions of Proverbs," in *Wisdom, You are My Sister: Studies in Honor of Roland E. Murphy, O. Carm., on the Occasion of His Eightieth Birthday* (ed. M.L. Barré; CBQMS 29; Washington: Catholic Biblical Association of America, 1997), 47–61, esp. 49; Puech, "Proverbi," 173, 189; de Waard, "4QProv," 96; Jastram, "Proverbs," 702; Tov, *"Synthese," 27. Cf. also, without distinction between 4QProv^a and 4QProv^b, Skehan, "Qumran and Old Testament Criticism," 163.

[9] Puech, "Identification," 121–23.

[10] Skehan and Ulrich, "Proverbs," 183.

12.2.1.4 6Q30 = 6QpapProv? (6QpapCursive Unclassified frgs.)

Eshel identified the eight preserved words of the cursive manuscript 6Q30[11] as parts of Prov 11:5–7, 10.[12] He emphasizes "it is significant that line 4 (scil. Prov 11:7) follows the MT, 'When a wicked man dies,' rather than the LXX, 'When a good man dies.' The omission of Prov 11:8–10a ... may be the result of a variant text or a scribal error ... Or it may be that the scribe is deliberately grouping together verses that deal with the death of the wicked."[13] Thus, 6Q30 represents either a fourth Proverbs manuscript from Qumran or it preserves remnants of a *testimonium* that might have been concerned with the death of the wicked and that contained at least two passages from Proverbs. It is not possible to reach conclusions with any degree of certainty in this matter or in the paleographic, orthographic, and text-typological classification of 6Q30.

12.2.1.5 MS Schøyen 4612/11[14]

Of this manuscript one small fragment is extant which attests to fifteen words and partial words out of Prov 4:22–5:1. Manuscript Schøyen 4612/11 includes remnants of several proverbs which are loosely connected thematically and at the end of this fragment a typical opening address of a sapiential didactic speech can be found. It is therefore unlikely that manuscript Schøyen 4612/11 attests to the remains of a Proverbs-quotation in a non-biblical manuscript. Elgvin expresses some doubt about the authenticity of manuscript Schøyen 4612/11 based on several observations:

> First, in a few instances strokes of ink appear to follow the contours of damage. The second *mem* in line 1 forms an odd ligature with the preceding letter along the edge of the damaged part of the surface. The third *mem* in line 2 is oversized, and the pen strokes neatly surround an abrasion. Second, there are possibly two places in line 2 where there are small traces of ink on the underlayer where the surface has flaked off (cf. the *taw* and the *ḥet*). Finally, along the bottom edge there is a very well preserved trace of ink where the surface is obviously worn (the first *kap* on line 3). In spite of these observations, there is insufficient evidence to make any firm judgments about the authenticity of the text.[15]

The paleographic date of manuscript Schøyen 4612/11 is set differently:[16] Ada Yardeni describes its script as a late Hasmonaean formal hand from the years 75–50 B.C.E. Michael Langlois characterizes the script of manuscript Schøyen 4612/11 as a late Hasmonaean semiformal book hand from the middle of the first century B.C.E. The remaining proverbs text is written not stichometrically but in prose format. The orthography of manuscript Schøyen 4612/11 is baroque. Not enough text survives for a texttypological classification. Should the manuscript be authentic, it remains uncertain at which of the sites around the Dead Sea it was found although its baroque orthography would point to a Qumran origin.

Baillet, M., "30. Fragments en cursive," *DJD III.1: 140.
Elgvin, T., "MS 4612/11 (4Q[?]Prov, Prov. 4.23–5.1)," in *Gleanings, forthcoming.
Eshel, H., "6Q30, a Cursive *Śîn*, and Proverbs 11," *JBL* 122 (2003): 544–46.
Jastram, N., "Proverbs, Book of," *EDSS 2:701–02.
Lange, *Handbuch, 467–71.
Puech, É., "Qumrân e libro dei Proverbi," in *Libro dei Proverbi: tradizione, redazione, teologia* (eds. G. Bellia and A. Passaro; Casale Monferrato: Piemme, 1999), 169–89.
Puech, É., "Identification de nouveaux manuscrits bibliques: Deutéronome et Proverbes dans les débris de la grotte 4," *RevQ* 20 (2001–2002): 121–27.
Skehan, P.W. and E. Ulrich, "Proverbs," *DJD XVI: 181–86.

---

[11] Baillet described the manuscript in his *editio princeps* only as "fragments en cursive" ("Fragments," 140).

[12] Eshel, "6Q30," 544–46.

[13] Eshel, "6Q30," 545.

[14] I am indebted to Torleif Elgvin who provided me with a preprint copy of his edition of manuscript Schøyen 4612/11 ("MS 4612/11"). The information given below about this manuscript depends on Elgvin's publication.

[15] Elgvin, "MS 4612/11," forthcoming.

[16] For the paleographic dates of Yardeni and Langlois, see Elgvin, "MS 4612/11," forthcoming and M. Langlois, "Palaeographical Analysis of the Dead Sea Scrolls," in *Gleanings, forthcoming.

Ulrich, E., *BQS, 732–34.
de Waard, J., "4QProv and Textual Criticism," *Textus* 19 (1998): 87–96.

Armin Lange

12.2.2 Texts and Ancient Texts Close to MT

12.2.2.1 Background

For some books of the Hebrew Bible (e.g. Isaiah and the Psalms) there are many texts and fragments available in the Dead Sea Scrolls, but for Proverbs only a few fragments are extant. However, there are a multitude of manuscripts that attest to Masoretic texts (→ 10–20.1; → 1.2.2.2.1). Three manuscripts are significant and have been collated for the *BHQ.[1] This first is MT^L, the Leningrad Codex, kept in the Russian National Library, St. Petersburg (manuscript EBP. I B 19a). The text of Proverbs has been well preserved on the whole. De Waard[2] does mention a small number of textual errors in MT^L. One example is the omission of the zero vowel indicator in the final *kap* in Prov 8:20 in MT^L, in contrast to MT^A and MT^Y. The second manuscript is MT^A, the Aleppo Codex, and the third is MT^Y, housed at the University of Cambridge (Add. Ms. 1753). According to de Waard,[3] the latter two manuscripts occasionally can be deciphered with difficulty, but show no lacunae, although, as is well known, MT^A has been partly destroyed. Other prominent Masoretic manuscripts include MT^{L17,L34,M1,S1}, and MT^{S5}. MT^{L17} (EBP. II B 17) and MT^{L34} (EBP. II B 34) are both stored in the Russian National Library, St. Petersburg. MT^{M1} is in the Complutensian Library in Madrid (M1). MT^{S1} (Sassoon 1053) and MT^{S5} (ms 24° 5702, Jewish National and University Library, Jerusalem) were part of the Sassoon collection.

MT-Prov is relatively free from scribal corruption in contrast to MT-1–2 Sam. Moreover, it is not harmonistic in character and I would argue that it is very close to the supposed *Urtext* of Proverbs (see my discussion of LXX-Prov under → 12.1; also → 12.3.1). I, for one, think that LXX-Prov is not based on deviating, recensional texts.[4] The main problem in this regard remains the lack of primary textual evidence. De Waard quotes a number of secondary readings in MT-Prov:[5] MT-Prov 1:10 reads אַל־תֹּבֵא "do not consent" in most MT manuscripts. MT^{Kenn494} has instead אל תבוא "do not go"; cf. MT^{Kenn573} תֵּבֹא.[6] In Prov 1:32, 4QProv^a reads for MT's מְשׁוּבַת "rebellion" the word מושבת "idleness." According to de Waard,[7] the MT reading could be the result of a metathesis. In Prov 11:23, MT^{DeRossi941} reads אבדה "destruction" for MT's עֶבְרָה "indignation."[8] In Prov 14:35, MT reads וְעֶבְרָתוֹ "his wrath," which in de Waard's[9] opinion seems to be read in 4QProv^b as ועבתו "his twisting." According to de Waard,[10] עבת was in fact the *Vorlage* for the LXX (→ 12.3.1) rendering. Proverbs 8 contains a crucial variant, MT reads אָמוֹן "artificer" for אֵמוּן[11] "faithfulness" in verse 30.

4QProv^b is fragmentary but, according to de Waard,[12] in at least five instances it supports MT (→ 12.2.1.2): Prov 13:6; 14:32; 15:2, 24, and 28. He also thinks that three other cases are probably related to MT, i.e. Prov 15:22, 26, and 31. In connection with ועבתו "his twisting" in Prov 14:35, there seems to be some relationship between 4QProv^b, LXX, and S (→ 12.3.4).

A number of editions of MT-Prov are available. *BHQ has been mentioned. The Oxford Hebrew Bible's version of Proverbs has been published in 2015.[13] Meanwhile, HUBP's version of Proverbs has not yet been completed as of 2016. Other useful editions are *BH and *BHS. The problems concerning the critical apparatus of the various *BH editions are well known. A significant improvement is found in the new *BHQ project where a commentary on the critical apparatus has been included.

---

[1] De Waard, *Proverbs*, 5.
[2] De Waard, *Proverbs*, 5.
[3] De Waard, *Proverbs*, 5.
[4] Cook, "The Greek of Proverbs."
[5] De Waard, *Proverbs*.
[6] De Waard, *Proverbs*, 31.
[7] De Waard, *Proverbs*, 31.
[8] De Waard, *Proverbs*, 41.
[9] De Waard, *Proverbs*, 45; de Waard, "4QProv," 93.
[10] De Waard, *Proverbs*, 45.
[11] De Waard, *Proverbs*, 37.
[12] De Waard, *Proverbs*, 6.
[13] Fox, M.V., 2015, משלי *Proverbs: An eclectic edition with introduction and textual commentary* (Atlanta, GA: SBL Press).

There are also other improvements, such as the notes on the MasP.

As far as the book of Proverbs is concerned, many *Ketiv-Qere* readings need to be evaluated. It is rather difficult to determine whether any scribal corruption took place in connection with individual cases. A *waw* is frequently confused for a *yod*. Examples include Prov 11:3 (*Ketiv* וְשַׁדָּם "and their destruction"; *Qere* ישדם "destroys them"); 12:14 (*Ketiv* יָשׁוּב "will return"; *Qere* ישיב "will cause to return"); 13:20 (*Ketiv* וְחֲכָם "and wise"; *Qere* יחכם "becomes wise"); 17:13 (*Ketiv* תָּמִישׁ "will depart"; *Qere* תמוש "will remove"); and 18:17 (*Ketiv* יָבֹא "will come"; *Qere* ובא "and came"). A clear case of a scribal error is the *reš* read as a *dalet* in Prov 19:19 (*Ketiv* גְּרָל "lot"; *Qere* גדל "big"). In Prov 21:29, *bet* and *kap* are interchanged (*Ketiv* יָכִין "establish"; *Qere* יבין "give thought"). Another example is found in Prov 20:21, where *he* and *ḥet* are confused (*Ketiv* מְבֹחֶלֶת "abhorrent"; *Qere* מבהלת "hastily"). Many cases involve grammatical categories such as plural instead of singular forms. Cases in point can be found in Prov 3:27, 28; and 30:10. In Prov 30:18, there is a grammatical inconsistency, feminine instead of masculine. In Prov 31:16, the *Qere* reading is accepted, since it refers to a feminine third-person form as in the first part of the strophe.

12.2.2.2 MT-Prov in Relation to LXX-Prov

The Septuagint differs dramatically from MT and other textual witnesses to Proverbs. Two approaches are taken to explain these differences. One group of scholars[14] thinks that the Greek text represents a different Hebrew parent text. Another group of scholars,[15] argues that the Greek translator(s) were responsible for the differences. This question is discussed in more detail below (→ 12.3.1).

12.2.2.3 Relevance for Exegesis

I argue above (→ 12.1) that MT-Prov and the book of Proverbs are one and the same. The distinction between these two corpora is hypothetical. By this,

---

[14] E.g. Tov, *TCHB*, 315.
[15] E.g. Cook, "The Greek of Proverbs."

I do not deny that there are variant readings in MT-Prov;[16] however, I am sceptical about retroverting the Greek to a supposedly more original Hebrew text in these cases.[17] I also think that MT-Prov is relatively free of secondary readings.

12.2.2.4 Provenance of MT-Prov

There seems to be consensus that the final form of the Hebrew collection came into existence in Judea in the postexilic, including the Hellenistic, period (for a more detailed argumentation, see → 12.1). This could either be the result of what McKane[18] calls a "Yahwistic reinterpretation" or a "recontextualization" as postulated by Camp.[19] It is also possible that this final redaction took place under Greek philosophical influence as might be indicated, for example, by the use of the Hebrew term צוֹפִיָּה "sofia" in Prov 31:27.

12.2.2.5 Relevance for Literary Analysis

Taking into account the complicated history of the origin of MT-Prov and its transmission history, it is to be expected that scholars would have made literary analyses of MT-Prov. The research by Tov[20] on the literary growth of Proverbs and its implications for the redactional history of the book is important here. The Septuagint is an important textual witness in this regard. Tov[21] is of the opinion that the translators used a recensionally different Hebrew text to translate. Cook[22] takes as point of departure the free translation technique of this unit and demonstrates that in most cases the translator brought about these changes.

Baumgartner, A.J., *Etude critique sur l'état du texte du livre des Proverbes d'après les principales traductions anciennes* (Leipzig: W. Drugulin, 1890).

---

[16] Cf. e.g. Fox, "LXX-Proverbs."
[17] See Cook, "The Text-Critical Value."
[18] McKane, *Proverbs*, 8.
[19] Camp, *Proverbs*, 21–27.
[20] Tov, *TCHB*, 315.
[21] Tov, "Recensional Differences."
[22] Cook, "The Greek of Proverbs," 609–17; and Cook and van der Kooij, *Provenance*, 132–33.

Camp, C.V., *Wisdom and the Feminine in the Book of Proverbs* (Bible and Literature Series 1; Sheffield: Almond Press, 1985).

Cook, J., "The Greek of Proverbs: Evidence of a Recensionally Deviating Hebrew Text?" in *Emanuel: Studies in Hebrew Bible, Septuagint, and Dead Sea Scrolls in Honor of Emanuel Tov* (eds. S.M. Paul et al.; VTSup 94; Leiden: Brill, 2003), 605–18.

Cook, J., "The Text-Critical Value of the Septuagint of Proverbs," in *Seeking out the Wisdom of the Ancients: Essays in Honor of Michael V. Fox on the Occasion of His Sixty-Fifth Birthday* (eds. R.L. Troxel, K.G. Friebel, and D.R. Magary; Winona Lake: Eisenbrauns, 2005), 407–19.

Cook, J. and A. van der Kooij, *Law, Prophets, and Wisdom: On the Provenance of Translators and their Books in the Septuagint Version* (CBET 68; Peeters: Leuven, 2012).

Dotan, A. (ed.), *Biblia Hebraica Leningradensia* (Peabody: Hendrickson, 2001).

Driver, G.R., "Problems in the Hebrew Text of Proverbs," *Bib* 32 (1951): 173–97.

Fox, M.V., משלי *Proverbs: An eclectic edition with introduction and textual commentary* (SBL Press: Atlanta, GA, 2015).

Fox, M.V., *Proverbs 1–9: A New Translation with Introduction and Commentary* (AB 18 A; New York: Doubleday, 2000).

Fox, M.V., "LXX-Proverbs as a Text-Critical Resource," *Textus* 22 (2005): 95–128.

McKane, W., *Proverbs: A New Approach* (London: SCM Press, 1970).

Tov, E., "Recensional Differences between the Masoretic Text and the Septuagint of Proverbs," in *Of Scribes and Scrolls, Studies on the Hebrew Bible, Intertestamental Judaism, and Christian Origins Presented to John Strugnell* (eds. H.W. Attridge, J.J. Collins, and T.H. Tobin; Lanham: University Press of America, 1990), 43–56.

Tov, E., "Textual Criticism (OT)," in *ABD* 6:393–412.

Tov, E., *Textual Criticism of the Hebrew Bible* (Minneapolis/Assen, Maastricht: Fortress Press/Van Gorcum, 1992.

de Waard, J., "4QProv and Textual Criticism," *Textus* 19 (1998): 87–96.

de Waard, J., משלי *Proverbs: Introduction and Commentaries on Proverbs* (*BHQ 17; Stuttgart: Deutsche Bibelgesellschaft, 2008).

Johann Cook

12.3 Primary Translations

12.3.1 Septuagint

12.3.1.1 Background

Although LXX-Prov is universally accepted as exhibiting signs of the Hellenizing process that occurred in the aftermath of Alexander the Great's (356–323 B.C.E.) expeditions throughout the ancient Near East, no consensus exists regarding either the precise time or place at which the text was produced. Cook maintains – on primarily ideological grounds – that the book was composed in Jerusalem, the translator being antagonistic to the spread of Hellenism.[1] Dick similarly views LXX-Prov as the product of a Greek-speaking Jewish school – presumably Judaean – advocating an early second-century B.C.E. date on the basis of the author's rejection of the belief in an afterlife that became prominent in the wake of the Maccabean martyrs.[2] Gerleman contends that the translator displays an intimate knowledge of Greek literary tradition – in particular Hellenistic Stoicism – while Mezzacasa attributes the provenance of the text to a Jewish colony in Egypt.[3] The attempt to date the translation on the basis of ideological views remains highly disputed. From a literary perspective, the association of the book with LXX-Job (→ 11.3.1) via parallels in style, diction, vocabulary, and favorite expressions, the fact of its apparent non-usage in the citations of Proverbs in the Hebrew text of Ben Sira (180 B.C.E.), and the *terminus ad quem* established by Philo's quotation of Prov-LXX (ca. 20 B.C.E.–45 C.E.) all suggest a date not later than the second century B.C.E.[4]

12.3.1.2 Original Form, Editions, Tools

In the absence of a critical edition of LXX-Prov, the best available text at present is Rahlfs' *Septuaginta*. Based on Codex Vaticanus (LXX^B), Alexandrinus (LXX^A), and Sinaiticus (LXX^S), this edition adduces variants from these manuscripts and the Syro-Hexapla.[5] The third volume of Holmes' and Parsons' critical edition constitutes an indispensable tool for the textual criticism of LXX-Prov in making different Greek manuscript readings available.[6] The Hexaplaric variants principally represent adjustments of the Old Greek to MT (→ 12.2.2).[7] Fritsch's comparison of the doublets in LXX-Prov with the Origenian signs in the fifth column of the Syro-Hexapla (→ 12.4.4) has challenged the widely held view that the Origenian signs have been scrupulously retained in the latter.[8] Auxiliary tools for the study of LXX-Prov are offered by modern translations and commentaries.[9]

12.3.1.3 Translation Character

A quantitative comparison between LXX-Prov and MT-Prov (→ 12.2.2) reveals that while the Greek text contains approximately forty-eight additional stichs, the Hebrew has only twenty-five.[10] LXX-

---

[1] Cook, "The Septuagint as Contextual Bible Translation," 32–37.

[2] Dick, "Ethics."

[3] Gerleman, *Studies*; Mezzacasa, *Il libro dei proverbi*, 44.

[4] Gerleman, *Studies*, 58–60; G.B. Caird, "Ben Sira and the Dating of the Septuagint," *Studia Evangelica VII: Papers Presented to the Fifth International Congress on Biblical Studies Held at Oxford* (ed. E.A. Livingstone; TU 126; Berlin: Akademie der Wissenschaften, 1982), 95–100; Dick, "Ethics," 21. Both LXX-Prov and LXX-Job are presumed to have been rendered into Greek after the translation of the Pentateuch but prior to the middle of the second century B.C.E.: see Gerleman, *Studies*, 59–60; S.P. Brock, "The Phenomenon of Biblical Translation in Antiquity," in *Studies in the Septuagint: Origins, Recensions, and Interpretations* (ed. S. Jellicoe; New York: Ktav, 1974), 541–71 (551); J.G. Gammie, "The Septuagint of Job: Its Poetic Style and Relationship to the Septuagint of Proverbs," *CBQ* 49 (1987): 14–31.

[5] Field, **Hexapla*.

[6] Holmes and Parsons, *Vetus Testamentum graecum*.

[7] See Mezzacasa, *Il libro dei proverbi*, 23–26, 98–100.

[8] Swete, **Introduction*, 112; Fritsch, "Hexaplaric Signs." For a critique of Fritsch's conclusions, see Jellicoe, **SMS*, 138–40.

[9] **CATSS*; **BibleWorks*; d' Hamonville, *Les Proverbes*; J. Cook, "Proverbs," in **NETS*, 627–41; M. Karrer and W. Kraus in **Septuaginta Deutsch, Erläuterungen*, 1.1450–2000; **BHQ*: de Waard, *Proverbs*; Fox, *Proverbs: An Eclectic Edition with Introduction and Textual Commentary*; McKane, *Proverbs*, 33–47; Fox, *Proverbs 1–9*, 367–423; Fox, *Proverbs 10–31*, 982–1068.

[10] See the **CATSS* database.

Prov diverges from MT both in the arrangement and wording of some of the proverbs. In the last third of the book – the "words of the wise" (Prov 22:17–24:22) – the Greek order differs significantly from MT, proceeding as follows (according to the MT verse numbering): Prov 30:1–14 ("The words of Agur," part one); Prov 24:23–34 ("These too are of the wise"); Prov 30:15–33 ("The words of Agur," part two); Prov 31:1–9 ("The words of Lemuel," part one); Prov 25:1–29:27 ("These too are proverbs of Solomon which the men of Hezekiah king of Judah copied"); Prov 31:10–31 ("The words of Lemuel" part two). In addition to the variant sequence after Prov 24:22, LXX also contains glosses and in a number of instances it is shorter than MT.[11] It is also characterized by the occurrence of double translations of verses (e.g., Prov 1:7; 2:21; 3:15), stichs (e.g., Prov 1:14c, 27d; 2:2c, 3c, 19c), phrases (e.g., Prov 2:18; 6:3, 10; 20:11), and words (e.g., Prov 3:10, 18, 23; 5:19; 11:30).[12] Several additions in LXX-Prov have direct counterparts in other books.[13]

12.3.1.4 Translation Technique and Inner-Translational Features

Much attention has been drawn to the "literal" vs. "free" distinction in the text-critical process of isolating deviations or equivalents.[14] The same approach is reflected in Aejmelaeus' characterization of LXX-Prov as a free translation whose aim is to deliver a faithful rendering of the original text and Fox's suggestion that "mimetic" should replace the ambiguous term "literal" in indicating a translation that attempts to "map the maximal number of linguistic features of the source onto the receptor text."[15]

LXX-Prov exhibits a free and even paraphrastic nature, frequently diverging significantly from the literal sense of MT (→ 12.2.2) and recasting Hebrew sentences by taking liberties with grammatical forms and syntax or attributing new meanings to Hebrew expressions.[16] With the exception of some essential terms,[17] recurrent Hebrew words are customarily translated by a variety of Greek equivalents.[18] This suggests that the translator was largely unconcerned with providing an idiomatic Greek rendering of the Hebrew.

The literary style and diction of the text and its familiarity with Greek poetical tradition and metrical arrangement is exemplified by the use of assonance, repetition of roots, rhymes, and anaphora.[19] The translator's predilection is evident in his accentuation of the correspondence between semantic or morphological components in sayings governed by parallelism.[20] Synonymous parallels in MT are

---

[11] Thus, e.g., LXX 3:16a, 22a; 4:27a–b; 6:8a–c, 11a; 7:1a; 8:21a; 9:12a–c, 18a–d; 10:4a; 12:11a, 13a; 13:9a, 13a; 17:6a; 19:7a–b; 22:9a, 14a; 24:22a–e; 25:10a; 27:20a, 21a; and 28:17a are all additional to MT, while MT 1:16; 4:7; 7:25b; 8:29a, 33; 11:4, 10b, 11a; 15:31; 16:1, 3, 4, 6; 18:23–24; 19:1–2; 20:14–19; 21:5, 18b; 22:6; 23:23 are lacking in LXX. There are also minor variations – such as LXX 8:32b, which appears after 8:34 – and several displacements in 15:27a–16:9 (LXX 15:27a = MT 16:6; LXX 15:28a = MT 16:7; LXX 15:29a–b = MT 16:8–9): see the table and excursus in Fox, *Proverbs: An Eclectic Edition with Introduction and Textual Commentary* following the comment on 15:27; Scoralick, "Salomos griechische Gewänder," 43–75.

[12] Fritsch, "Hexaplaric Signs," 170; Cook, *The Septuagint of Proverbs*, 13–16.

[13] E.g., LXX-Prov 1:7 prefixes a couplet taken from MT-Ps 111[110]:10. LXX-Prov 4:27a likewise partially corresponds to MT-Ps 1:6 and LXX-Prov 26:11a to Sir 4:21.

[14] Tov, *TCU, 50–66; Tov, "The Septuagint," 173. See, further, Thackeray, *Grammar, 13; Baumgartner, Étude critique, 247; Gerleman, Studies; d'Hamonville, Les Proverbes, 19. Aejmelaeus (*Trail, 84) classifies LXX-Prov amongst the freest translations, including the Pentateuch (Genesis and Exodus in particular), Joshua, OG-Esther, Job, Isaiah, and OG-Daniel.

[15] Fox, "LXX-Proverbs," 97 n. 9; Fox, "Translation and Mimesis," 207–21; Aejmelaeus, *Trail, 64.

[16] Cf. Prov 11:25; 13:23; 16:8; 18:8; 23:27.

[17] רשע "evildoer" is translated by ἀσεβής "impious" sixty-five out of seventy-three times; צדיק "righteous" by δίκαιος "righteous" fifty-seven out of sixty-three times; חכמה "wisdom" by σοφία "wisdom" thirty out of thirty-three times, אויל "fool" by ἄφρων "fool" ten out of thirteen times; עצל "lazy" by ὀκνηρός "lazy" eight out of twelve times.

[18] Thus, for example, the term תורה "law, instruction" is rendered by θεσμός "laid down and established, a law," λόγος "a law," νόμιμος "statute," νομοθέσμως "according to the law," τάξις "an arranging, order," and ἐννόμως "legal, lawful" in addition to νόμος "law."

[19] Thus, for example, in Prov 13:9 the MT synonyms אור "light" and נר "lamp" are represented by φῶς "light" at the beginning of both clauses: see Thackeray, "Poetry," 46–66; Gerleman, *Studies*, 15–17.

[20] Cf. Prov 5:16; 6:1; 10:10, 18; 11:7, 25, 30; 13:14; 14:17; 15:10; 16:21; 17:4, 14; 21:14, 26; 22:7; 26:20; 27:9.

also turned into antithetical forms by means of added elements (e.g., Prov 17:5, 21; 18:22a), with several difficult sayings (e.g., Prov 10:10; 11:7, 30; 27:9) being given an exegetical twist. Numerous modern scholars regard this use of contrast as a translational device that seeks to enhance parallelism.[21]

The blend of ethical and sapiential language in MT-Prov (→ 12.2.2) takes on a more principled tone in the Greek text, which frequently employs moralistic terms such as κακός "evil" (Prov 1:18, 28; 6:3, 11; 14:25; 18:3; 21:26), δίκαιος "righteous" (Prov 10:17; 12:25; 16:11; 20:8; 28:21, 28), and ἀσεβής "impious" for כסיל "fool" (Prov 1:22, 32; 3:35; 13:19), thereby identifying the "dolt" as a sinner rather than merely lacking intellectual keenness.[22] This tendency is also exemplified by the transformation of "wisdom statements" into clear-cut doctrinal expressions (→ 11.3.1.5). Thus, for example, MT-Prov 13:23 ("The tillage of the poor yields much food; but substance is swept away for lack of moderation"; NJPS) is rendered as: "The just will spend many years in wealth, but the unjust will perish suddenly" (*NETS).[23]

Septuagint scholars commonly regard several inserted couplets in LXX-Prov as inner-translational additions reflecting a Hellenistic imprint.[24] For instance, the praise of the diligent bee in Prov 6:8a–c may well have been introduced by a translator in Alexandria extolling industriousness, while the epigram in Prov 9:18a–d warning against close contact with a foreign culture appears to highlight the fact that Lady Folly's enticements are cultural as well as sexual.[25]

Some exegetical additions reflect a midrashic approach towards the text that resembles rabbinic hermeneutical methods. Thus, for example, the first line of LXX-Prov 18:22a – ὃς ἐκβάλλει γυναῖκα ἀγαθήν "He who drives out [מוציא] a good woman" – constitutes a word play on the root מצ״א "to find" (ὃς εὖρεν "he that has found") in Prov 18:22, the insertion of the notation ἀγαθήν "good" further ensuring that the reader understands that a *good* wife is intended. The fact that the Babylonian Talmud (*Yebam.* 63b; *Ber.* 8a; cf. *Midr. Shoher Tov* 151a–b) includes the epithet טובה "good" in its uses of this verse may, however, suggest that this word was inserted in some Hebrew manuscripts.[26]

12.3.1.5 Text-Critical Value

The study of translation technique in LXX-Prov is impaired by the lack of a critical edition, making it difficult to determine which "deviations" from MT (→ 12.2.2) should be identified as belonging to the Old Greek (→ 1.3.1.1.12). Although many scholars regard LXX-Prov as a paraphrase or free rendering on a par with 1 Esdras, Daniel, Esther, and Job (→ 12.3.1.4), even after the discovery of the Qumran texts (→ 12.2.1) it remains the most important full textual witness to the pre-MT text circulating during the second century B.C.E.[27] Prior to the mid-nineteenth century, scholars attributed the disparities between MT and LXX to variant readings (even

---

[21] Gerleman, *Studies*, 17–26; Cook, "Contrasting," 403–14; d'Hamonville, *Les Proverbes*, 71; Tauberschmidt, *Secondary Parallelism*, 43–61. *Contra* Tauberschmidt, see Fox ("Review of Tauberschmidt"; Fox, *Proverbs: A Critical Edition and Commentary*, § 3.1.8.8) who ascribes the contrastive manner of LXX to the Hebrew source text rather than to the translator, especially when supported by Theodotion and Aquila (e.g., Prov 14:33).

[22] Cf. Bertram, "Die religiöse Umdeutung," 153–67; Gerleman, *Studies*, 44–45; McKane, *Proverbs*, 45–47; Fritsch, "Hexaplaric Signs," 170; Forti, "Conceptual Stratification," 241–58.

[23] רָב־אֹכֶל נִיר רָאשִׁים וְיֵשׁ נִסְפֶּה בְּלֹא מִשְׁפָּט/δίκαιοι ποιήσουσιν ἐν πλούτῳ ἔτη πολλά, ἄδικοι δὲ ἀπολοῦνται συντόμως.

[24] Baumgartner, *Étude critique*; Gerleman, "The Septuagint Proverbs"; Gerleman, *Studies*; Cook, *The Septuagint of Proverbs*.

[25] Gerleman (*Studies*, 30–31) draws attention to the fact that the ant and bee appear together in Aristotle's *Historia animalium* (622b, 627a). See also de Lagarde, **Anmerkungen*, 22–23; Baumgartner, *Étude critique*, 68; Mezzacasa, *Il libro dei proverbi*, 127; Giese, "Strength through Wisdom," 404–11; Cook, *The Septuagint of Proverbs*, 166; d'Hamonville, *Les Proverbes*, 193; Fox, *Proverbs 1–9*, 397; T. Forti, "Bee's Honey: From Realia to Metaphor in Biblical Wisdom Literature," *VT* 56 (2006): 327–41. For Lady Folly, see Fox, *Proverbs: An Eclectic Edition with Introduction and Textual Commentary*.

[26] Forti, "Conceptual Stratification," 248–50; Fox, "LXX-Proverbs," 119–20; Weingreen, "Rabbinic-Type Commentary," 407–15.

[27] The extant fragments of 4QProverbs cover parts of forty-eight verses (see Ulrich, **BQS*, 732–34).

if unattested in Hebrew sources), treating LXX primarily as a tool for textual criticism. Jäger's reconstructions of the Hebrew source text suggest retroversions on the basis of an interchange of consonants,[28] metathesis, disparate vocalizations of the MT consonantal text,[29] orthography,[30] and Aramaic etymology.[31] As increasing emphasis is being placed of late on understanding the character of LXX, scholars have become more attentive to the translator's proclivities.[32] When the LXX text is regarded as reflecting the translator's exegetical approach, its divergences become less relevant for the textual analysis of the Hebrew text (→ 12.3.1.4).

12.3.1.6 Relevance for Literary Analysis

No consensus exists regarding the source of the sequence disparities between LXX and MT (→ 12.2.2) or the absence of personal names in the LXX section headings (שלמה "Solomon" [Prov 10:1]; אגור "Agur" [Prov 30:1]; למואל "Lemuel" [Prov 31:1]). Some scholars argue against assuming that the plethora of variations between LXX and MT derive from inner-translational factors, positing a different Hebrew *Vorlage* from that of MT.[33] Tov's assumption that the discrepancies already existed in various segments of Proverbs 24–31 in the *Vorlage* is unrelated either to the textual transmission of the Hebrew text (as suggested by de Lagarde) or to the disorderly status of the manuscript(s) from which the translation was made (as suggested by Baumgartner), deriving rather from the existence of different literary editions of the Hebrew text.[34] Cook, on the other hand, maintains that the order of LXX reflects the translator's Jewish Hellenistic ideological worldview and conservative hermeneutics, his text thus primarily representing an exegetical enterprise.[35] Fox alternatively contends that, despite the significant differences between LXX-Prov and MT-Prov and the translator's specific dogmas, the Greek translation primarily seeks to communicate faithfully the message of the Hebrew *Vorlage*.[36]

In the wake of Gerleman's study, which attributes many of the deviations from MT in matters of style and ideas to the translator's poetical creativity and Hellenistic cultural setting, recent scholars – such as Cook, Harl, and d' Hamonville[37] – have propounded that LXX-Prov is *sui generis*. The argument that the translation should be studied primarily as a religious document – the first exegetical commentary on the Hebrew text – rather than as a witness to a different Hebrew *Vorlage* also functions as a corrective to the classical studies by such scholars as de Lagarde, Baumgartner, and Mezzacasa.[38]

Although many of the LXX/MT divergences may be attributed to the translator's techniques, any textual evaluation of LXX-Prov must take into ac-

---

[28] Cf. the interchange between ד and ר in LXX-Prov 15:14: γνώσεται, "will know" (יד״ע) vs. MT (רע״ה), יִרְעֶה, "associate with").

[29] Barr, "Vocalization"; Barr, "Reading a Script"; Tov, *TCU*, 120–23; Talshir, "Greek Translations," 1179.

[30] Cf. κεπφωθείς, "simpletons" (פְּתָאִים) vs. MT פִּתְאֹם, "suddenly" in 7:22.

[31] The rendering of ד(א)ב in 17:12 as μέριμνα, "care" (reconstructed by Jäger as דאבה, "care") and as λύκος, "wolf" in 28:15 exemplifies a combined use of both tools: variant vocalization and Aramaic reading.

[32] Forti and Talshir, "Proverbs 7 in MT and LXX," 129–32. Jäger (*Observationes in Proverbium Salomonis versionem alexandrinam*) is frequently cited by de Lagarde (*Anmerkungen*) and Baumgartner (*Étude critique*).

[33] Cf. the addition in LXX-Prov 3:16a that appears to be based on an expanded Hebrew text of Isa 45:23: יָצָא מִפִּי צְדָקָה "from my mouth righteousness goes forth" and Prov 31:26 וְתוֹרַת חֶסֶד עַל-לְשׁוֹנָהּ "and the teaching of kindness is on her tongue": see Tov, "Recensional Differences," 49–50.

[34] De Lagarde, *Anmerkungen*, 51; Baumgartner, *Étude critique*, 149; Tov, "Recensional Differences," 53–56. Cf. Toy, *Proverbs*, xxxiii; Clifford, *Proverbs*, 28; Clifford, "Wisdom," 50–51; Cuppi, "Treatment of Personal Names," 28.

[35] Cook ("The Greek of Proverbs," 605–18) identifies the translator's exegetical approach on the basis of his frequent use of *hapax legomena*, neologisms, and the large number of words that appear exclusively in Proverbs (cf. Cook, *The Septuagint of Proverbs*; Cook, "Text-Critical Value," 408). Cf. Dick, "Ethics," 20–50; d' Hamonville, *Les Proverbes*, 28.

[36] Fox, *Proverbs 1–9*, 361; Fox, "LXX-Proverbs," 95–128.

[37] Cook, "The Septuagint as Contextual Bible Translation," 25–39; Cook, "אִשָּׁה זָרָה (Prov 1–9 in the Septuagint) a Metaphor for Foreign Wisdom?", 458–76 (esp. 459); Cook, "Text-Critical Value," 407–20; Harl, "La Bible d' Alexandrie dans les débats actuels sur la Septante," 7–24; d' Hamonville, *Les Proverbes*, 19.

[38] De Lagarde, *Anmerkungen*, 3–4; Baumgartner, *Étude critique*, 2–3, 11; Mezzacasa, *Il libro dei proverbi*, 1–14.

count the fact that, by its very nature, the aphoristic genre is protean and versatile. This recognition is crucial when evaluating its interpolations as expansions, corrections, and/or commentary, and when discussing the reliability of the textual transmission of the book. With proverbial sayings undergoing constant transformation in the course of oral and written transmission in Hebrew and Greek alike, some of the alterations may well represent literary elaboration rather than errors. Jewish exegetical traditions, dogmatic-type rabbinic ideas, and inner-translational additions that reflect the imprint of Hellenistic influence likewise complicate the retroversion of the Hebrew *Vorlage*. The compositional process of LXX-Prov has yet to be determined; many of the issues relating to whether the variants, additions, and omissions should be ascribed to a Hebrew or Greek scribe involved in the transmission of the text or to the Greek translator are still being disputed and thus remain firmly on the agenda of literary criticism.

Aejmelaeus, *Trail.
Barr, J., "Vocalization and the Analysis of Hebrew among the Ancient Translators," in *Hebräische Wortforschung: Festschrift zum 80. Geburtstag von Walter Baumgartner* (VTSup 16; Leiden: Brill, 1967), 1–11.
Barr, J., "Reading a Script without Vowels," in *Writing without Letters* (ed. W. Haas; Mont Follick Series 4; Manchester: Manchester University Press, 1976), 71–100.
Baumgartner, A.J., *Étude critique sur l'état du texte du livre des Proverbes d'après les principales traductions anciennes* (Leipzig: Drugulin, 1890).
Bertram, G., "Die religiöse Umdeutung altorientalischer Lebensweisheit in der griechischen Übersetzung des AT," *ZAW* 13 (1936): 153–67.
*BHQ.
*CATSS.
Clifford, R.J., "Observations on the Text and Versions of Proverbs," in *Wisdom You are My Sister: Studies in Honor of R.E. Murphy on the Occasion of his Eightieth Birthday* (ed. M.L. Barré; Washington: Catholic Biblical Association of America, 1997), 47–77.
Clifford, R.J., *Proverbs: A Commentary* (OTL; Louisville: Westminster/John Knox Press, 1999).
Cook, J., "The Dating of Septuagint Proverbs," *ETL* 69 (1993): 383–99.

Cook, J., "The Septuagint as Contextual Bible Translation: Alexandria or Jerusalem as Context for Proverbs?" *JNSL* 19 (1993): 25–39.
Cook, J., "אִשָּׁה זָרָה (Prov 1–9 in the Septuagint) a Metaphor for Foreign Wisdom?" *ZAW* 106 (1994): 458–76.
Cook, J., *The Septuagint of Proverbs: Jewish or Hellenistic Proverbs? Concerning the Hellenistic Colouring of LXX Proverbs* (VTSup 69; Leiden: Brill, 1997).
Cook, J., "Contrasting as a Translation Technique in the LXX of Proverbs," in *The Quest for Context and Meaning: Studies in Biblical Intertextuality in Honor of James A. Sanders* (eds. C.A. Evans and S. Talmon; Biblical Interpretation Series 28; Leiden: Brill, 1997), 403–14.
Cook, J., "Contextual Exegetical Interpretations in the Septuagint of Proverbs," *JNSL* 25 (1999): 119–52.
Cook, J., "The Law of Moses in Septuagint Proverbs," *VT* 49 (1999): 448–61.
Cook, J., "Textual Problems in the Septuagint Version of Proverbs," *JNSL* 26 (2000): 171–76.
Cook, J., "Ideology and Translation Technique: Two Sides of the Same Coin?" in *Helsinki Perspectives on the Translation Technique of the Septuagint* (eds. R. Sollamo and S. Sipilä; Publications of the Finnish Exegetical Society 82; Göttingen: Vandenhoeck & Ruprecht, 2001), 195–216.
Cook, J., "The Greek of Proverbs: Evidence of a Recensionally Deviating Hebrew Text?," in *Emanuel: Studies in the Hebrew Bible, Septuagint and Dead Sea Scrolls in Honor of Emanuel Tov* (eds. S.M. Paul et al.; VTSup 94; Leiden: Brill, 2003), 605–18.
Cook, J., "The Text-Critical Value of the Septuagint of Proverbs," in *Seeking Out the Wisdom of the Ancients: Essays Offered to Honor Michael V. Fox on the Occasion of His Sixty-Fifth Birthday* (eds. R.L. Troxel et al.; Winona Lake: Eisenbrauns, 2005), 407–20.
Cuppi, L., "The Treatment of Personal Names in the Book of Proverbs from the Septuagint to the Masoretic Text," in *Greek Scripture and the Rabbis* (eds. T.M. Law and A. Salvesen; CBET 66; Leuven: Peeters, 2012), 19–38.
Dick, M.B., "The Ethics of the Old Greek Book of Proverbs," *The Studia Philonica Annual: Studies in Hellenistic Judaism* (1990), 2:20–50.
Forti, T., *Animal Imagery in the Book of Proverbs* (VTSup 118; Leiden: Brill, 2008).
Forti, T., "Conceptual Stratification in LXX Prov 26,11: Toward Identifying the Tradents Behind the Aphorism," *ZAW* 119 (2007): 241–58.

Forti, T. and Z. Talshir, "Proverbs 7 MT and LXX: Form and Content," *Textus* 22 (2005): 129–67.

Fox, M.V., *Proverbs 1–9: A New Translation with Introduction and Commentary* (AB 18A; New York: Doubleday, 2000).

Fox, M.V., "Translation and Mimesis," in *Biblical Translation in Context* (ed. F.W. Knobloch; Bethesda: University Press of Maryland, 2002), 207–21.

Fox, M.V., "[Review of] Gerhard Tauberschmidt, *Secondary Parallelism: A Study of Translation Technique in the LXX*," RBL (2004). Online: http://www.bookreviews.org/pdf/4192_4111.pdf.

Fox, M.V., "LXX-Proverbs as a Text-Critical Resource," *Textus* 22 (2005): 95–128.

Fox, M.V., *Proverbs 10–31: A New Translation with Introduction and Commentary* (Anchor Yale Bible 18B; New Haven: Yale University Press, 2009).

Fox, M.V., *Proverbs* משלי: *An Eclectic Edition with Introduction and Textual Commentary* (*HBCE; Atlanta, GA: SBL Press, 2015).

Fritsch, C.T., "The Treatment of the Hexaplaric Signs in the Syro-Hexaplar of Proverbs," *JBL* 72 (1953): 169–81.

Gammie, J.G., "The Septuagint of Job: Its Poetic Style and Relationship to the Septuagint of Proverbs," *CBQ* 49 (1987): 14–31.

Gemser, B., *Sprüche Salomos* (HAT 16; Tübingen: Mohr, 1963).

Gerleman, G., "The Septuagint Proverbs as a Hellenistic Document," *OTS* 8 (1950): 15–27.

Gerleman, G., *Studies in the Septuagint III: Proverbs* (LUÅ 1.52.3; Lund: Gleerup, 1956).

Giese, R.L., "Qualifying Wealth in the Septuagint of Proverbs," *JBL* 111 (1992): 409–25.

Giese, R.L., "Strength through Wisdom and the Bee in LXX-Prov 6:8a–c," *Bib* 73 (1992): 404–11.

d'Hamonville, D.-M., *Les Proverbes: Traduction du texte grec de la Septante, introduction et notes* (in collaboration with É. Dumouchet; *Bible d'Alexandrie* 17; Paris: Cerf, 2000).

Harl, M., "La Bible d'Alexandrie dans les débats actuels sur la Septante," in *La double transmission du texte biblique: études d'histoire du texte offertes en hommage à Adrian Schenker* (eds. Y. Goldman and C. Uehlinger; OBO 179; Göttingen: Vandenhoeck & Ruprecht, 2001), 7–24.

Holmes, R. and J. Parsons, *Vetus Testamentum Graecum cum Variis Lectionibus*, Vol. 3 (Oxford: Clarendon Press, 1823).

Jäger, J.G., *Observationes in Proverbium Salomonis versionem alexandrinam* (Meldorf: Boie, 1788).

Jellicoe, *SMS.

Joosten, J., "The Aramaic Background of the Seventy: Language, Culture and History," *BIOSCS* 43 (2010): 53–72.

De Lagarde, *Anmerkungen.

Lust, *Lexicon of the Septuagint.

McKane, W., *Proverbs: A Commentary* (OTL; London: SCM, 1979).

Mezzacasa, G., *Il libro dei proverbi di Salomone: Studio critic sulle aggiunte Greco-alessandrine* (Rome: Pontifical Biblical Institute, 1913).

Muraoka, T., *Hebrew/Aramaic Index to the Septuagint* (Grand Rapids: Baker, 1998).

Murphy, R.E., *Proverbs* (WBC 22; Nashville: Thomas Nelson, 1998).

*NETS. Online: http://ccat.sas.upenn.edu/nets/edition/25-Proverbs.

Rofé, A., "The Valiant Woman, *gunē synetē*, and the Redaction of the Book of Proverbs," in *Vergegenwärtigung des Alten Testaments: Beiträge zur biblischen Hermeneutik: Festschrift für Rudolf Smend zum 70. Geburtstag* (eds. C. Bultmann, W. Dietrich, and C. Levin; Göttingen: Vandenhoeck & Ruprecht, 2002), 382–90.

Scoralick, R., "Salomos griechische Gewänder: Beobachtungen zur Septuagintafassung des Sprichwörterbuches," in *Rettendes Wissen: Studien zum Fortgang weisheitlichen Denkens im Frühjudentum und im frühen Christentum* (ed. K. Löning; AOAT 300; Münster: Ugarit-Verlag, 2002), 43–75.

Schultens, A., *Proverbia Salomonis: Versionem integram ad hebraeum fontem expressit atque commentarium* (Leiden: Luzac, 1748).

*Septuaginta Deutsch.

*Septuaginta Deutsch, Erläuterungen.

Swete, *Introduction.

Talshir, Z., "Greek Translations of the Hebrew Bible (Griechische Übersetzung der hebräischen Bibel)," in *Übersetzung – Translation – Traduction: Ein internationales Handbuch zur Übersetzungsforschung – An International Encyclopedia of Translation Studies – Encylopédie internationale de la recherche sur la traduction*, Vol. 3 (eds. H. Kittel et al.; Berlin: de Gruyter, 2004), 1177–82.

Tauberschmidt, G., *Secondary Parallelism: A Study of Translation Technique in LXX Proverbs* (Academia Biblica 15; Atlanta: SBL, 2004).

Thackeray, *Grammar.

Thackeray, H.St.J., "The Poetry of the Greek Book of Proverbs," *JTS* 13 (1912): 46–66.

Thackeray, *The Septuagint and Jewish Worship*.

Tov, *TCU*.

Tov, E., "The Septuagint," in *Mikra: Text, Translation, Reading and Interpretation of the Hebrew Bible in Ancient Judaism and Early Christianity* (eds. M.J. Mulder and H. Sysling; Assen/ Philadelphia: Van Gorcum/Fortress, 1988).

Tov, E., "Recensional Differences between the Masoretic Text and the Septuagint of Proverbs," in *Scribes and Scrolls: Studies on the Hebrew Bible, Intertestamental Judaism, and Christian Origins Presented to John Strugnell* (eds. H.W. Attridge et al.; Lanham: University Press of America, 1990), 43–56.

Tov, E., "Some Reflections on the Hebrew Texts from Which the Septuagint Was Translated," *JNSL* 19 (1993): 107–22.

Toy, C.H., *A Critical and Exegetical Commentary on the Book of Proverbs* (5th impr.; ICC; Edinburgh: T & T Clark, 1959; 1st ed. 1899).

Vogel, G.J.L., *Schultensii Versio Integra Proverbia Salomonis cum Commentariis* (Halle: Curt, 1769).

Weingreen, J., "Rabbinic-Type Commentary in the LXX Version of Proverbs," in *Proceedings of the Sixth World Congress of Jewish Studies*, Vol. 1 (ed. A. Shinan; Jerusalem: World Union of Jewish Studies, 1977), 407–15.

Tova Forti

12.3.2 Pre-Hexaplaric Greek Translations

See → 12.3.5 Hexaplaric Greek Translations (Proverbs > Primary Translations).

12.3.3 Targum

12.3.3.1 Nature, Date, and Milieu

Targum Proverbs, one of the extant Targumim to the hagiographa, did not enjoy official recognition. Like the rest of the hagiographa, it originates in a later period and its final redaction was written at a later time by an unknown author, even though it contains old material. Bacher considers the hagiographa to have originated in Palestine.[1] The fact that T-Prov was not used in the liturgy could explain why it was not accepted in the public synagogue service, even though it was studied in the school. T-Prov has a particular place among the Targumim because of its unique problems. Although T-Prov has been commonly grouped with T-Job and T-Pss, it differs from these Targumim in two significant ways: 1) it is rather literal and avoids midrashic interpretation even when such interpretation might reasonably be expected (T-Prov 8:22–24);[2] 2) in many verses, T-Prov is identical to S-Prov (→ 12.3.4), sometimes agreeing with the Peshitta against MT (→ 12.2.2; e.g., Prov 1:7; 4:26; 5:9; 7:22–25; 9:11; 12:19; → 12.3.4.6).

With regards to the language of T-Prov,[3] several opinions have been proposed; Maybaum,[4] for instance, regarded it as an Aramaic dialect, while for Nöldeke it was a *Mischsprache* in which Syriac and Aramaic forms are used alternatively.[5] It is clear that no spoken dialect is reflected in T-Prov. The many Syriacisms found in T-Prov may be interpreted as an Aramaic text depending on a Syriac source, or as an artificial language produced by a translator. Notwithstanding in medieval tradition, in the *'Arûk* of Rabbi Nathan, T-Prov is quoted as Yerushalmi. The Aramaic of T-Prov seems to reflect a mixed dialect, e.g., it has the 3rd masc. sg./pl. impf. of the verb with prefixed נ (as in Syriac and Babylonian Jewish Aramaic) and the prefixed י (as in the dialects of Targum Onqelos and the Palestinian Targumim); cf. T-Prov 9:11. In the absence of a full analysis of the textual tradition of T-Prov, there is no solid basis for a final verdict on the linguistic character of this translation.

T-Prov is almost entirely literal and does not exploit rabbinic traditions. Since none of the rabbinic exegesis of Proverbs contained in Midrash Proverbs is reflected in T-Prov, the translation could have been authored before the rabbinic period. Kaminka argued that the non-masoretic *Vorlage* indicates a very early date and that T-Prov predates

---

[1] Bacher, "Targum," 62.

[2] Cf. Komlosh, "The Manner of Interpretation," 72.

[3] See L. Díez Merino, *Targum de Proverbios: Edición Príncipe del Ms. Villa-Amil n. 5 de Alfonso de Zamora* (Bibliotheca Hispanica Biblica 11; Madrid: Consejo Superior de Investigaciones Científicas, Inst. Francisco Suarez, 1984), 167–68.

[4] Maybaum, "Über die Sprache des Targum," 70–81.

[5] Nöldeke, "Das Targum," 246–49.

Prov-LXX (at the latest, the third century B.C.E.; → 12.3.1).⁶ Those who suggest dependence on the Peshitta (see below) prefer a much later date, particularly Mangenot has it as late as the eighth to ninth century C.E.⁷ We proposed a date after the middle of the second century C.E.,⁸ if we admit Peshitta influence on T-Prov. While no firm conclusion can be reached on the date of T-Prov, its Aramaic language suggests a late period.

Segal explains T-Prov in this way:⁹ the Peshitta version of Proverbs is a Christian edition of T-Prov that comes from a complete translation of the Bible older than the Peshitta, produced by the Jews of Edessa and its surroundings, east of Mesopotamia. The existence of the Syriacisms in T-Prov might be explained by supposing that the known Targum, or its original text, was composed somewhere in the East, perhaps for use in the Jewish community of Nisibis or some other center in North Mesopotamia, where the local Aramaic dialect would have been close to classical Syriac. According to that scenario, during the time of its transmission, the Eastern Aramaic of T-Prov was modified quite heavily, but unsystematically, to make it conform to standard Targumic Aramaic.

12.3.3.2 Manuscripts and Editions
12.3.3.2.1 Manuscripts
T-Prov is extant in most of the manuscripts that contain T-Job and T-Pss:¹⁰ Parma, Biblioteca Palatina w. 32, De Rossi 31 and 32 (fourteenth century); Cambridge, Univ. Libr. Ee 5,9 (1347 C.E.); Paris, Bibliothèque Nationale n° 110 (1455–1456 C.E.); Madrid, Biblioteca Complutense, S. Bernardo 116-Z-40 (1517 C.E.); Salamanca, Biblioteca Universitaria ms 2 (1532 C.E.); Breslau, ms 1106 (1238 C.E.); London, Montefiore Library (Hirschfeld Catalogue, n. 7) (1486 C.E.). And in the Giant Bibles: 1) Solger 1–7 2° (1291 C.E.); 2) Vatican Library Urbinati Ebr 1 (1294 C.E.); 3) Vatican Library Barberini Or 161–164 (Kennicott 471) (1295–1297 C.E.); 4) Berlin, Staatsbibliothek Preussischer Kulturbesitz, ms Or. Fol. 1210–1211 (1343 C.E.); 5) Berlin, Staatsbibliothek Preussischer Kulturbesitz, ms Or. Fol. 1–4 (fourteenth century) [Erfurt 1]; 6) Genoa, Biblioteca Civica Berio (1348 C.E.); Paris, Bibliothèque Nationale, Hébr. 17–18 (fourteenth to fifteenth century).

12.3.3.2.2 Editions and Tools
The *editio princeps* of T-Prov was presented in the *Bible of Leiria* (printed 1492 by Don Samuel d' Ortas); *Biblia Rabbinica* (*RB1, 1517 [Felix Pratensis]; RB2, 1524–1525 [J. ben Hayyim]); this edition was reprinted in the *Miqra'ôt Gedolot*; the *Antwerp Polyglot* [Benito Arias Montano] (1567–1571);¹¹ *Paris Polyglot* (1628–1655) [Morin];¹² the *London Polyglot* (1654–1657);¹³ as well as by de Lagarde (1873 = *Biblia Rabbinica*, 1577),¹⁴ Melamed,¹⁵ and Díez Merino.¹⁶ No critical edition is available. The major editions are by de Lagarde and Díez Merino. The translation in the Aramaic Bible Series was provided by Healy.¹⁷

12.3.3.3 History of Research
The major stages in the history of research are:¹⁸

1) Pinkuss¹⁹ presented the first critical analysis of T-Prov, comparing the text with de Lagarde's edition (1873) in a synopsis and collating the Greek

---

⁶ Kaminka, "Septuaginta und Targum," 172–73.

⁷ E. Mangenot, "Targums," cols. 1995–2008 in vol. 5 of *DB* (ed. F.G. Vigouroux; Paris: Letouzey et Ané, 1912), col. 2006.

⁸ Díez Merino, *Targum de Proverbios*, 163–67.

⁹ M.Z. Segal, מבוא המקרא, Vol. 3: כתובים (4th ed.; Jerusalem: Kiryat Sepher, 1955).

¹⁰ Díez Merino, *Targum de Proverbios*, 137–41.

¹¹ *Biblia Sacra Hebraice, Chaldaice, Graece et Latina* ... (ed. B. Arias Montano; Antwerp: Christophorus Plantinus, 1569–1572).

¹² Le Jay, *Biblia.

¹³ Walton, *Polyglotta.

¹⁴ P. de Lagarde, *Hagiographa Chaldaice* (Leipzig: Teubner 1873).

¹⁵ Melamed, "The Targum on Proverbs."

¹⁶ L. Díez Merino, *Targum de Proverbios: Edición príncipe del Ms. Villa-Amil n. 5 de Alfonso de Zamora* (Bibliotheca Hispanica Biblica 11; Madrid: Consejo Superior de Investigaciones Científicas, Inst. Francisco Suarez, 1984), 173–201

¹⁷ J.F. Healey, *The Targum of Proverbs* (ArBib 15; Collegeville: Liturgical Press, 1991).

¹⁸ See also 12.3.4.

¹⁹ Pinkuss, "Die syrische Übersetzung," 65, 161–222.

(→ 12.3.1), Aramaic, and Syriac texts (→ 12.3.4) with the Antwerp Polyglot and manuscript 1106 of Breslau (1238) as perused by Levy (1881) in his dictionary.[20] Pinkuss concluded that T-Prov depended on the Peshitta, and that T-Prov and Peshitta often agree with the LXX text.

2) Kaminka[21] realized that the Targum and Peshitta of Proverbs are identical in approximately 300 of the 915 verses of Proverbs, and that the Targum includes many terms and forms that derived from the Syriac language. This Targum also agrees often with LXX while differing from MT. Kaminka quotes a long list of examples from LXX[22] that could indicate a dependence of Targum in the third or second century B.C.E., such as T-Prov 3:12; 8:23, 30; 10:2; 14:30; 15:6; 19:7; 23:4; 26:28.[23]

3) Kaminka's views concerning the interdependence of Peshitta–Targum are rejected by Pinḥos Churgin[24] and by Gerleman[25] quoting Prov 29:8 and 30:31.

4) Churgin[26] affirms that T-Prov was written long after LXX, whose interpretations it incorporated, and that the Targum was composed after the Peshitta.[27] In those instances where the Targum differs from the Peshitta, it would have followed MT (→ 12.2.2). At the same time, some interpretations of the Targum that differed from the Peshitta derived from a different *Vorlage*, namely a text in Aramaic characters prior to the Peshitta that has not been preserved, but in this hypothesis such a lost text could be the older one. This suggestion could explain the differences between T-Prov and the manuscripts of the Peshitta[28] (for further aspects of the history of research, see → 12.3.4.2; → 12.3.4.3).

12.3.3.4 Translation Character

Usually T-Prov is a literal translation, and one of its main features is its lack of haggadic and midrashic expansions, except for a few cases (Prov 24:14; 28:1).[29] However, we do find some interpretative elements and occasionally the *meturgeman* tries to integrate pious considerations that go beyond the literal meaning of the text. There is a tendency to avoid anthropomorphisms, but it is not systematic, and in some cases the Targumist even introduces new anthropomorphisms. Usually the names YHWH and *Elohim* are translated as אלהא "God," while sometimes YHWH is left in the Targum. Sometimes the Targum uses verbal prefixes within the text that cannot have coexisted within one dialect. Thus the 3rd person imperfect prefix in -י and -נ (Maybaum noted 149 cases[30] with -נ and 79 with -י); the spelling of the ending of the masculine plural emphatic-state noun with -י (-*ê*) against regular Aramaic -יָא; the use of -ל as accusative particle alongside ית "to"; גיר "because" appears frequently (e.g., Prov 29:19) instead of ארום "because"/ ארי "because," and דין "that" (e.g., Prov 17:16).

12.3.3.5 Text-Critical Value
12.3.3.5.1 Relation to the Hebrew Text

Rarely, the Targum reflects a *Vorlage* different from MT (→ 12.2.2; e.g., Prov 6:6), and generally it reflects the wording of MT (Prov 2:3, 11; 3:13, 18; 4:8; 5:11, 20; 9:13; 13:10, 16; 15:6; 17:11; 26:2; 27:8). There are instances where the Targum and Peshitta (→ 12.3.4) agree against MT (e.g., Prov 1:7, 13; 4:26; 5:9, 21; 7:22–23; 9:11; 12:19; 15:4, 28; 16:4, 25; 25:20; 29:18; 31:8). Frequently, the Targum disagrees with the Peshitta while closely following MT; Maybaum[31] lists eighty-two cases (e.g., Prov 1:7; 3:8; 4:1; 5:3, 13, etc.). The arguments for the Targum's dependence on the Syriac are strong, and for this reason the Targum is

---

[20] J. Levy, *Chaldäisches Wörterbuch über die Targumim und einen grossen Theil des rabbinischen Schriftthums* (3rd ed.; 2 vols.; Leipzig: Verlag von Gustav Engel, 1881).

[21] Kaminka, "Septuaginta und Targum," 171.

[22] Kaminka, "Septuaginta und Targum," 179–87.

[23] Concerning the relationship between LXX and T-Prov, see also Geiger, Geiger, *Nachgelassene Schriften*, and → 12.3.4.3.

[24] Churgin, *The Targum*, 73.

[25] G. Gerleman, *Studies in the Septuagint*, Vol. 3: *Proverbs* (LUÅ 1.52.3; Lund: Gleerup, 1956), 46–51.

[26] Churgin, *The Targum*, 63–86.

[27] Churgin, *The Targum*, 74.

[28] Churgin, *The Targum*, 83.

[29] Pinkuss, "Die syrische Übersetzung," 109.

[30] Maybaum, "Über die Sprache des Targum," 75.

[31] Maybaum, "Über die Sprache des Targum," 89.

rarely of independent text-critical value. The Targum may support a minor variant independently by using a synonym rather than a transliteration of the word used in the Syriac (cf. T-Prov 9:1). T-Prov transcribes the Syriac in many occasions making dialectical and orthographical adjustments and harmonizing the translation with a Hebrew text very close to MT.

12.3.3.5.2 Relation to the Peshitta

A particular affinity with the Peshitta (→ 12.3.4) was discovered long ago (→ 12.3.3.3). About one-third of its text,[32] possibly even half of the book, corresponds word for word with that version.[33]

1. Most scholars (e.g. Pinḥos Churgin; → 12.3.3) believe that T-Prov had the Peshitta version in front of him (see the older commentaries).[34]
2. On the other hand, Maybaum suggested that the Peshitta depended on the Targum.[35] Black believed that the Syrian church received its version of Proverbs from the Jewish synagogue, as it did in the case of the Pentateuch,[36] but he denied that the *meturgeman* depended on the Peshitta. The reverse would be more likely.

Díez Merino[37] reviewed the work of the scholars who remarked on a connection between the Peshitta and T-Prov.[38] According to him, it remains unclear which version of the Peshitta was related to T-Prov. There probably was an older Peshitta text than those that are known to us. Explanations of the Syriac influence have been suggested in several ways:

1. Luzzatto[39] (1890 and 1895) quoted 125 expressions from T-Prov that can only reflect the Syriac language, e.g., ואשליו "and they neglected" (Prov 1:30); אסלי "and they hated" (Prov 5:12); דיצין "they rejoice" (Prov 2:14); עמר "sheaf" (Prov 2:21); נגר "carry along" (Prov 3:2, 16); ועתא "departure" (Prov 4:24); נאורן "they shall be straight" (Prov 4:25).
2. Bacher[40] suggested that the *meturgeman* incorporated the Peshitta or a revised Syriac text into the Targum, or perhaps the final edition of the Targum derived from the same source as the Syriac version, based on a translation for Syriac-speaking Jews.

This relation has been explained in several directions:

1. T-Prov is a reworking of S-Prov, namely the significant agreement between Peshitta and Targum is evidence of the latter's influence on the former;
2. It could be that a Jewish scholar, wanting to create a Targum of Proverbs, adapted, rather inconsistently, a revision of a Christian Aramaic version;
3. S-Prov is derived from T-Prov, or both Peshitta and Targum draw on a common earlier Jewish source;
4. The influence between Targum and Peshitta implies that T-Prov, or the *Ur*-Targum that lies behind T-Prov and the Peshitta, is a relatively early work based on a non-Masoretic *Vorlage*. However, there are instances where Targum is independent of the Peshitta (e.g., Prov 4:6, 11; 6:12; 10:23; 11:4, 25; 12:26; 14:33; 22:11, 12; 23:2, 21; 29:25).

Bacher, W., "Targum," *JE* 12:62.
Black, M., *An Aramaic Approach to the Gospels and Acts* (3rd ed.; Oxford: Clarendon Press, 1967).
Churgin, P., *The Targum to Hagiographa* (New York: Horeb, 1945).

---

[32] Walker, "Targum," 682.
[33] Geiger, *Nachgelassene Schriften*, 112; Weingreen, "Rabbinic Type Commentary," 408.
[34] Dathe, *De ratione consensus versionis*; Nöldeke, "Das Targum," 246–49.
[35] Maybaum, "Über die Sprache des Targum," 66–93.
[36] Black, *An Aramaic Approach*, 25.
[37] Díez Merino, *Targum de Proverbios*, 19.
[38] Díez Merino, *Targum de Proverbios*, 19–31.

[39] S.D. Luzzatto, *Oheb Ger* (Cracow: Joseph Fisher, 1895; repr. Jerusalem: Makor, 1969).
[40] Bacher, "Targum," 62.

Dathe, J.A., *De ratione versionis Chaldaicae et Syriacae Proverbiorum Salomonis Prolusio* (Leipzig: Langenheim, 1764).

Le Déaut, R., "Targum," *DBSup* 13:141*–46*.

Flesher–Chilton, *The Targums*.

Geiger, A., *Nachgelassene Schriften*, Vol. 4 (Berlin: Louis Gerschel, 1876).

Kaminka, A., "Septuaginta und Targum zu Proverbia," *HUCA* 8–9 (1931–1932): 169–91.

Komlosh, Y., "The Manner of Interpretation of Targum Qohelet," *Sinai* 54 (1964): 169–79 [Hebr.].

Mangan, C., J.F. Healy, and P.S. Knobel, *The Targum of Job, Proverbs, and Qohelet: Translated, with a Critical Introduction, Apparatus, and Notes* (ArBib 15; Collegeville: Liturgical Press, 1991).

Maybaum, S., "Über die Sprache des Targum zu den Sprüchen und dessen Verhältnis zum Syrer," *Archiv für Wissenschaftliche Erforschung des Alten Testamentes* 2 (1870–1871): 66–93.

Melamed, E.Z., "The Targum on Proverbs," *Bar-Ilan Annual* 9 (1972): 18–91.

Nöldeke, T., "Das Targum zu den Sprüchen von der Peschitta abhängig," in *Archiv für Wissenschaftliche Erforschung des Alten Testamentes* 2 (1870–1871): 246–49.

Owens, R.J., Jr., "The Relationship between the Targum and Peshitta Texts of the Book of Proverbs," *Targum Studies* 2 (1998): 195–207.

Pinkuss, H., "Die syrische Übersetzung der Proverbien textkritisch und in ihrem Verhältnisse zu dem masoretischen Text, den LXX und dem Targum untersucht," *ZAW* 14 (1894): 65–141, 161–222.

Walker, T., "Targum," in *Dictionary of the Bible* (ed. J. Hastings; 5 vols.; Edinburgh: T & T Clark, 1898–1904), 5.682.

Weingreen, J., "Rabbinic-Type Commentary in the LXX Version of Proverbs," in *Proceedings of the Sixth World Congress of Jewish Studies, Held at the Hebrew University of Jerusalem, 13–19 August, 1973, Under the Auspices of the Israel Academy of Sciences and Humanities* (ed. A. Shinan; Jerusalem: World Union of Jewish Studies, 1977), 1:407–15.

Weitzman, M.P., "Peshitta, Septuagint and Targum," in *VI Symposium Syriacum* (ed. R. Lavenant; OrChrAn 247; Rome: Pontifical Biblical Institute, 1994), 51–84.

Luis Díez Merino

12.3.4 Peshitta

12.3.4.1 Manuscripts of S-Prov

The oldest manuscript of S-Prov is S^{6h16} (sixth century C.E.), and it contains only the book of Proverbs (although it has lost the first four chapters). According to di Lella, this manuscript probably preserves the early stage of the text,[1] together with the manuscripts of the seventh (S^{7a1} and S^{7h6}) and eighth (S^{8a1}) centuries C.E. A second stage consists of the manuscripts that bring together the collection of books known as *Beth Mawtebhe*, "Book of Sessions": Joshua, Judges, 1–2 Samuel, 1–2 Kings (→ 6–9.1.4), Proverbs, Ecclesiastes (→ 13–17.1.4.3), Ruth (→ 13–17.1.4.1), Song of Songs (→ 13–17.1.4.2), Sirach (→ 11.4.4), and Job (→ 11.3.4) ($S^{9c1, 10c1, 10c2, 11c1}$). Secondary variants are introduced at this second stage to constitute a text type that is described as a "standard and authoritative text of the Book of Proverbs."[2] The book of Proverbs is not preserved in S^{9a1}, which is so important for other books because of the uniqueness of its variants, although it is preserved in the "Buchanan Bible" (S^{12a1}).

12.3.4.2 Critical Edition

The critical edition of S-Prov was published in 1979 as part of the project of the Peshitta Institute of Leiden.[3] Its editor is di Lella, and the work is found in vol. 2.5 of the collection, which also includes the books of Sirach (→ 11.4.4), Ecclesiastes (→ 13–17.1.4.3), and Song of Songs (→ 13–17.1.4.2). It is a diplomatic edition of manuscript S^{7a1}, accompanied by a critical apparatus that takes into consideration manuscripts prior to the twelfth century.

The introduction to the critical edition presents a detailed study of all extant manuscripts of S-Prov, grouping them by families and proposing a certain comprehension of the textual history of the book.

---

[1] Di Lella, *The Old Testament in Syriac*, ix.
[2] Di Lella, *The Old Testament in Syriac*, xiii.
[3] Di Lella, *Proverbs*.

12.3.4.3 Character of the Translation

As is the case with most of the books of the Peshitta, s-Prov was the object of a careful study toward the end of the nineteenth century, in this case in a work by Pinkuss, in which the characteristics of the translation are analyzed.[4] To this study must be added other works carried out in the same era. These studies covered the whole book of Proverbs, paying special attention to the ancient versions;[5] concern themselves with the value of the Syriac version for textual criticism;[6] and dealt with the literary dependence between the Peshitta and the Targum in this book (→ 12.3.3).[7]

However, unlike other books of the Peshitta, Proverbs has not been the subject of an exhaustive study in recent decades that could benefit from more than a century of advances in the textual criticism of the Hebrew text and of the versions (including the critical editions of MT [→ 12.2.2], Qumran [→ 12.2.1], LXX [→ 12.3.1], and the Peshitta).[8] There are only specific studies on some aspects of the translation,[9] on a small part of the book,[10] or the relationship between the Peshitta and the Targum.[11]

s-Prov translates a Hebrew text that differs little from the pre-Masoretic type; the use that it may make of LXX is analyzed below. The translation is quite free, although always with the intention of clearly reproducing the text of the *Vorlage*. This freedom in the interest of greater clarity is seen when it adds or omits possessive pronouns, transposes the order of words, changes the number of nouns or the tense of verbs, translates an abstract noun with a concrete one, gives substitutes for inelegant words, or translates a question (especially a rhetorical one) with a statement or a negative or conditional proposition.[12]

12.3.4.4 Date of the Translation and Identity of the Translator(s)

Pinkuss considers it very difficult to say anything about the identity of the translators, that is, whether they were Jews or Christians, since there are few passages in the text that relate to dogma.[13] In fact, we should make an exception for what wisdom says about herself in Prov 8:22 (יהוה קנני ראשית דרכו "YHWH acquired/created me the beginning of his path"), which was the object of Christological disputes in the early centuries of the Christian era. In this case, the Peshitta translates using the verb ܒܪܐ "create" (= LXX ἔκτισέν) and produces a correct translation from which it is hard to draw any conclusions.

Joosten links the question of identity to the date of the translation. He considers that s-Prov was translated late, since it is not known by the earliest Syriac versions of the New Testament. Indeed, the Syriac versions of the New Testament tend to follow the Peshitta of the Old Testament (→ 1.3.4) in their Scripture quotations. This does not happen with Proverbs. The New Testament quotes Proverbs on five occasions, of which only once does the Syriac version of the New Testament follow s-Prov (Prov 11:31, quoted in 1 Pet 4:18). And it is precisely in this case, according to Joosten, that it can be proven that s-Prov borrows the translation from the Syriac version of 1 Peter. From this, Joosten deduces that the translator of this late version was Christian, which supports Weitzman's theory that the Jewish community that was responsible for the Syriac version moved from Judaism to Christianity during the translation process.[14] Other data that support a late dating relate to the vocabulary, such as the use of the form ܣܡܟܐ instead of the usual ܙܢܝܘܬܐ

---

[4] Pinkuss, "Die syr. Übersetzung," 65–141, 161–222.

[5] Baumgartner, *Étude critique sur l'état du texte du Livre des Proverbes*.

[6] Chajes, "Etwas über die Peshitta," 86–91.

[7] Maybaum, "Über die Sprache des Targum zu den Sprüchen und dessen Verhältniss zum Syrer," 66–93; Nöldeke, "Das Targum zu den Sprüchen von der Peschita abhängig," 246–49.

[8] See in great detail → 12.1.1 and the studies of Fox quoted there.

[9] Joosten, "Doublet Translations," 63–72.

[10] Cook, "Are the Syriac and Greek Versions," 117–32.

[11] Melamed, "The Targum on Proverbs," 18–91; Steyn, "External Influences in the Peshitta Version of Proverbs."

[12] Cf. the list of characteristics, with numerous examples, offered by Pinkuss, "Die syr. Übersetzung," 114–16.

[13] Pinkuss, "Die syr. Übersetzung," 119.

[14] Weitzman, "From Judaism to Christianity," 147–73; Weitzman, *Syriac Version*, 206–62.

of other books of the Peshitta to translate the Hebrew אהבה (all three words meaning "love"). Since s-Prov is quoted by Aphrahat (→ 21.9), Joosten concludes that it must have been translated toward the beginning of the third century C.E.[15]

12.3.4.5 Influence of LXX on s-Prov

The question of the influence of LXX (→ 12.3.1) on s-Prov has attracted a great deal of attention among scholars (→ 12.3.3). It is here that the lack of a systematic study is felt (one conducted using the means that we now have available) that could aid in discerning the degree of influence of the Greek version, and whether this influence affected the translator, or whether it came during the process of manuscript transmission (through revisers).

Pinkuss considers that the translator was directly influenced by LXX, and he used the Greek version (although not always literally) when the Hebrew text (→ 12.2.2) was difficult, which occurs frequently in Proverbs. Even so, he acknowledges that some current readings that betray the influence of LXX may have entered as late interpolations, as is the case with the double readings.[16]

Joosten supports Pinkuss' conclusions about the influence of LXX on the translator, although curiously he does so by studying the doublet translations that the latter considered late interpolations. In Joosten's opinion, "doublet translations do not indicate conflation of two originally distinct translations, nor extensive editing of an 'Old Syriac' version of Proverbs; rather, they are typical of the working method of the author ... who produced the version roughly as we know it today."[17] In addition to the double readings, Joosten bases his conclusions on other data such as the fact that s-Prov includes many of the additional verses of LXX, follows the erroneous and sometimes nonsensical interpretation of LXX, or contains some "syntactical grecisms" (such as ܡܢ ܐܝܟܐ ܕ in Prov 22:27, which corresponds to πόθεν in LXX [the Syriac and Greek words all meaning "whence, how, in what way"]).

Joosten concludes that the translator followed the Hebrew when it was clear, but used the Greek when he ran into difficulties. However, when he found two alternative readings that were worth preserving, instead of choosing one form to the exclusion of the other, he combined the two, forming a kind of "versional patchwork."[18]

Baumgartner and Cook, who wrote almost contemporaneously with Pinkuss and Joosten, respectively, came to the opposite conclusion: They believe that the influence of LXX is to be located in the transmission process. In Baumgartner's opinion, the Syriac translation followed the Hebrew text and only later, in an era dominated by a return to the Greek version, was a revision of the translation attempted, following the text of LXX.[19] For his part, Cook, on the basis of a study of the theme of the foreign woman ("Madame Folly") in Proverbs 1–9, greatly reduces the general impression of the influence of LXX on the Syriac version. In his opinion, there are few clear cases of influence, and those that do exist are concentrated in obscure passages in which the translator may have used the Greek version for specific points. The image of a foreign (Greek) wisdom that the Jews of Alexandria were to avoid, as it emerges from Proverbs 1–9 according to LXX, is not found to be reflected in s-Prov.[20] Thus, the double readings of s-Prov should be attributed to late interpolations that came into the Syriac version through LXX.

12.3.4.6 Relationship between s-Prov and T-Prov

As early as 1764, in an inaugural lesson addressed to the University of Leipzig, Dathe called attention to the extraordinary coincidences between the Aramaic versions of Proverbs, the Peshitta, and the Targum (→ 12.3.3). These coincidences necessarily point to literary dependence. In Dathe's opinion, it is the Targum that depends on the Peshitta.[21] Since then, many authors have turned their atten-

---

[15] Joosten, "Doublet Translations," 65–66.
[16] Pinkuss, "Die syr. Übersetzung," 103–06.
[17] Joosten, "Doublet Translations," 63.
[18] Joosten, "Doublet Translations," 64–65.
[19] Baumgartner, *Étude critique*, 266.
[20] Cook, "Are the Syriac and Greek Versions," 131–32.
[21] Dathe, *De Ratione consensus versionis Chadaicae et Syriacae Proverbiorum Salomonis*.

tion to this matter, both in the nineteenth century (Eichhorn, Bertholdt, Haevernick, Maybaum, Nöldeke, Baumgartner, and Pinkuss)[22] and recently (Melamed, Steyn).[23] Only Haevernick and Maybaum argue for the priority of the Targum. The remainder hold to the opinion that this version depends on the Peshitta (→ 12.3.3).

Of the 915 verses in Proverbs, 300 are practically identical in the two versions, a fact that strongly demands attention despite the obvious coincidences between the two dialects of the same language. But where it is really proven that we have literary dependence is in the places where the Peshitta differs from MT (→ 12.2.2). In the majority of the cases, the Targum agrees with the Syriac version, which is unusual in the rest of the books of the Peshitta. It is here that we see the direction of dependence: the Targum (which tends to follow faithfully a text similar to MT) depends on the Peshitta (cf. Prov 1:32 שלות "complacency"; Prov 6:7 קצין "chief").

Other clear examples of the direction of dependence are those cases in which the reading of the Targum proceeds from a misunderstanding of the meaning of the text of the Peshitta (cf. Prov 29:8, ܩܪܝܬܐ "city" read as ܟܕܒܘ "falsehood" and Prov 30:31 ܥܙܐ "flock" read as ܓܝܪܐ "adulterer"), and those grammatical irregularities of the Targum that are explained by dependence on the Peshitta (such as the use of גיר [ܓܝܪ, γάρ (all three words meaning "for, now, then")] instead of the usual Aramaic form of the Targum [ארי "for, now, then"] and the presence of the preformative *nun* in the third person masculine singular).

12.3.4.7 Use of s-Prov in Textual Criticism of the Hebrew Bible

In 1901, Chajes presented seventy-two cases in which s-Prov could aid in reconstructing a Hebrew text different from MT (→ 12.2.2).[24] Today, most of the cases could be explained on the basis of the translation technique of the Syriac version (or other characteristics of the version), without the need to resort to the hypothesis of a Hebrew *Vorlage* different from MT. For this precise reason, and to provide greater clarity when using s-Prov in the textual criticism of the Hebrew Bible, it would be desirable to carry out a complete and rigorous study of the Syriac version of this book. Without a study of this nature, we will be unable to know with certainty whether a Syriac reading can be traced back (by translation technique) to the Hebrew text we know, or corresponds to a different Hebrew *Vorlage*, or was subject to the influence of LXX (→ 12.3.1) at its origin, or whether we have a secondary reading that was introduced in the process of manuscript transmission.

12.3.4.8 Auxiliary Tools

We presently have a concordance of the Syriac terms of s-Prov and the rest of the *Beth Mawtebhe* books edited by Strothmann, Zumpe, and Johannes in six volumes in the series *Göttinger Orientforschungen*.[25]

Baumgartner, A.J., *Étude critique sur l'état du texte du Livre des Proverbes d'après les principales traductions anciennes* (Leipzig: W. Drugulin, 1890).

Chajes, H.P., "Etwas über die Peshitta zu den Proverbien," *JQR* 13 (1901): 86–91.

Cook, J., "Are the Syriac and Greek Versions of the אשה זרה (Prov 1 to 9) Identical (On the Relationship between the Peshitta and the Septuagint)?" *Textus* 17 (1994): 117–32.

Dathe, J.A., *De Ratione consensus versionis Chadaicae et Syriacae Proverbiorum Salomonis* (Leipzig: Rosenmüller, 1796).

---

[22] J.G. Eichhorn, *Einleitung in das Alte Testament* (Leipzig: Weidmann und Reich, 1780–1783); L. Bertholdt, *Historisch-kritische Einleitung in sämmtliche kanonische und apokryphische Schriften des alten und neuen Testaments* (Erlangen: Johann Jacob Palm, 1812); H.A.C. Haevernick, *Handbuch der historisch-kritischen Einleitung in das Alte Testament* (Frankfurt a.M.: Heyder & Zimmer, 1836); Maybaum, "Über die Sprache des Targum zu den Sprüchen und dessen Verhältniss zum Syrer"; Nöldeke, "Das Targum zu den Sprüchen von der Peschita abhängig"; Baumgartner, *Étude critique*; Pinkuss, "Die syr. Übersetzung."

[23] Melamed, "The Targum on Proverbs"; Steyn, "External Influences in the Peshitta Version of Proverbs."

[24] Chajes, "Etwas über die Peshitta," 86–91.

[25] Strothmann, Zumpe, and Johannes, *Konkordanz zur syrischen Bibel: Die Mautbe*.

Joosten, J., "Doublet Translations in Peshitta Proverbs," in *The Peshitta as a Translation: Papers Read at the II Peshitta Symposium Held at Leiden 19–21 August* (eds. P.B. Dirksen and A. van der Kooij; Monographs of the Peshitta Intitute Leiden 8; Leiden: Brill, 1995), 63–72.

di Lella, A.A., *Proverbs* (The Old Testament in Syriac according to the Peshitta Version 2.5; Leiden: Brill, 1979).

Maybaum, S., "Über die Sprache des Targum zu den Sprüchen und dessen Verhältniss zum Syrer," *Archiv für Wissenschaftliche Erforschung des Altes Testamentes* 2.1 (1871): 66–93.

Melamed, E.Z., "The Targum on Proverbs," *Bar-Ilan Annual* 9 (1972): 18–91 [Hebr.].

Nöldeke, T., "Das Targum zu den Sprüchen von der Peschita abhängig," *Archiv für Wissenschaftliche Erforschung des Altes Testamentes* 2.2 (1872): 246–49.

Pinkuss, H., "Die syr. Übersetzung der Proverbien textkritisch und ihrem Verhältnisse zu MT, LXX und dem Targum untersucht," *ZAW* 14 (1894): 65–141, 161–222.

Steyn, P.E., "External Influences in the Peshitta Version of Proverbs" (PhD diss., Stellenbosch University, 1992).

Strothmann, W., M. Zumpe, and K. Johannes, *Konkordanz zur syrischen Bibel: Die Mautbe* (Wiesbaden: Harrassowitz, 1995).

Weitzman, M.P., "From Judaism to Christianity: The Syriac Version of the Hebrew Bible," in *The Jews Among the Pagans and Christians in the Roman Empire* (eds. J. Lieu, J. North, and T. Rajak; London: Routledge, 1992), 147–73.

Weitzman, M.P., *The Syriac Version of the Old Testament: An Introduction* (University of Cambridge Oriental Publications 56; Cambridge: Cambridge University Press, 1999), 206–62.

Ignacio Carbajosa

12.3.5 Hexaplaric Greek Translations

12.3.5.1 Background

The text of LXX-Prov (→ 12.3.1) has pluses and minuses vis-à-vis MT (→ 12.2.2) and from Proverbs 24 to the end of the book the materials are arranged differently.[1] This textual situation allows for the work of the revisers to be seen clearly, since they revised the Greek text by bringing it into greater alignment with the Hebrew in many places.

12.3.5.2 Sources, Editions, and Auxiliary Tools

The readings of the Hexaplaric fragments of Proverbs are found in the following manuscripts used by Montfaucon[2] and subsequently by Field:[3] LXX$^{560, 561, 563, 571, 562}$. In some cases, Field added the marginal notes of LXX$^{161-248}$ and LXX^{252}. Field's greatest contribution was the inclusion of the marginal notes in the Syro-Hexapla (→ 11.4.4) and his Greek retroversions. Finally, there are many Hexaplaric fragments in the newly found catena manuscript LXX^{788}. Without having performed an exhaustive study of the materials as of 2015, it appears that LXX^{788} will yield new Hexaplaric fragments for Proverbs. For his edition of Proverbs, Field also cites "Nobil" for many Hexaplaric readings (forty-eight Hexaplaric fragments in Proverbs 1 alone). It is now clear that Petrus Morinus is responsible for the majority of these readings, while Flaminius Nobilius supplemented the core collection of Hexaplaric fragments with some new fragments of his own.[4] It appears that LXX^{248} was the source of both Morinus and Nobilius. Based on a preliminary study of chapter 1, "Nobil" in Proverbs equals LXX^{248}. Field either did not consult the manuscript in each case or he was simply content to transmit Nobil readings where he found no contradiction in the manuscript. In any case, LXX^{248} will need to be freshly collated for the future critical edition.

As of 2015, there is no critical edition of the Hexaplaric fragments of Proverbs or a Göttingen edition of Proverbs, which would contain the Hexaplaric readings in the second apparatus. For Proverbs, the reader is directed to the work by Field.[5] For the auxiliary tools that pertain to the study of the Hexaplaric materials, see the bibliography.

---

[1] → 12.3.1.3.

[2] B. de Montfaucon, *Hexaplorum Origenis quae supersunt: multis partibus auctiora* (2 vols.; Paris: Ludovicus Guerin, 1713).

[3] Field, *Hexapla*.

[4] T.M. Law, "A History of Research on Origen's *Hexapla*: From Masius to the *Hexapla Project*," *BIOSCS* 40 (2007): 34.

[5] Field, *Hexapla*.

12.3.5.3 Translation Character and Technique
12.3.5.3.1 Theodotion

Regarding the translation technique of Theodotion in Job, Gentry says, "The character of the materials belonging to θ' reveals a literal and straightforward translation of a parent text for the most part identical with MT (consonantal text and vocalization). The translation follows the elements and segments of the language of the parent text and also the sequence in which these elements are presented."[6] The fragments attributed to Theodotion (→ 1.3.1.2) in Proverbs conform to this summary. The reading in Prov 3:3 is as follows:

> MT-Prov כָּתְבֵם עַל־לוּחַ לִבֶּךָ "write them on the tablet of your heart"
> LXX-Prov καὶ εὑρήσεις χάριν "and you will find grace"
> Th γράψον αὐτὰς ἐπὶ πλακὸς καρδίας σου "write them on the tablet of your heart"

The reading in Prov 3:3 appears in the text of the Syro-Hexapla (→ 11.4.4) under an asterisk with an attribution to Theodotion. It is also in the margin of LXX[788], where it is attributed to Aquila and Theodotion (γράψον αὐτὰ ἐπὶ τὸ πλατ[ὸς] καρδ[ίας] σ[ου] "write them on the breadth of your heart"). This reading is in the Bible text of the LXX[o] group according to the edition by Rahlfs,[7] who also notes that it entered the Bible text of LXX[A] (γράψον δὲ αὐτὰς ἐπὶ τὸ πλατὸς καρδίας σου "but write them on the breadth of your heart"). The exact wording of the fragment is not at issue here. LXX-Prov (→ 12.3.1) contains an interpretive translation where no word in the Greek aligns with the meaning of a word in the Hebrew text (→ 12.2.2). LXX adds the conjunction καί "and," which has no equivalent in the source. In contrast, Theodotion provides an isomorphic rendering of the Hebrew.

12.3.5.3.2 Aquila

Aquila (→ 1.3.1.2) employed a formal equivalence translation technique, which attempted to render each Hebrew element with a Greek equivalent segment by segment. On the word level, Aquila's version is very formal and demonstrates the concordance principle of translation, even employing equivalents to maintain etymological connections between Hebrew and Greek. However, when Aquila's syntax and Greek vocabulary are considered, his version furnishes more appropriate and even ingenious renderings of the Hebrew source.[8] In Prov 1:3, the reading is as follows:

> MT-Prov לָקַחַת מוּסַר הַשְׂכֵּל "for gaining instruction in wise dealing" (*NRSV)
> LXX-Prov δέξασθαί τε στροφὰς λόγων "and to grasp subtlety of words" (*NETS)
> Aq τοῦ λαβεῖν παιδείαν ἐπιστήμης "to receive instruction of understanding"

LXX-Prov renders the Hebrew freely. It does not formally represent the preposition ל "to/for" attached to the infinitive and it adds the particle τέ "and" where there is no Hebrew equivalent. Furthermore, the phrase στροφὰς λόγων "subtlety of words" employs plural nouns in the place of the singular nouns of the Hebrew text. Aquila revises this rendering by bringing the Greek into closer quantitative alignment with the Hebrew text. He employs an isomorphic approach where each element of the source has a corresponding element in the translation. Thus, the preposition ל "to/for" is rendered by τοῦ "in order to" (lit. "of the"), and the τέ "and" of LXX has been omitted. In addition, the phrase παιδείαν ἐπιστήμης "instruction of understanding" uses singular nouns that correspond to the nouns in Hebrew.

12.3.5.3.3 Symmachus

Symmachus produced a revision of LXX (→ 12.3.1) that both conformed to the Hebrew text and was readable in Greek.[9] These characteristics are also detected in Proverbs. At Prov 1:32b, one observes Symmachus' fidelity to the Hebrew text:

> MT-Prov וְשַׁלְוַת כְּסִילִים תְּאַבְּדֵם "and the complacency of fools destroys them" (*NRSV)

---

[6] Gentry, *Asterisked Materials*, 494.
[7] Rahlfs, *Septuaginta*.

[8] Hyvärinen, *Die Übersetzung von Aquila*, 111–12.
[9] → 1.3.1.2.5; cf. Salvesen, *Symmachus*, 198.

LXX-Prov καὶ ἐξετασμὸς ἀσεβεῖς ὀλεῖ "and an inquiry will ruin the impious" (*NETS)
Sym καὶ εὐθηνία ἀφρόνων ἀπολεῖ αὐτούς "and prosperity of fools will destroy them"

LXX[248] has ἀνελεῖ "will destroy," but Field corrected it to ἀπολεῖ "will destroy," and LXX[788] confirms that ἀπολεῖ is the correct reading. LXX[248] has a double attribution to Aquila and Symmachus, while LXX[788] preserves only an attribution to Symmachus. In Job 20:5a, Symmachus uses εὐθηνία for רִנָּה "rejoicing" as well as in Isa 33:20 for שַׁאֲנָן "undisturbed." LXX-Prov (→ 12.3.1) interpreted "fools" as "impious," while Symmachus used ἀφρόνων "fools" for כְּסִילִים "fools." The Hebrew text (→ 12.2.2) has a construct phrase "security of fools," but LXX-Prov does not render its source in an isomorphic manner. Rather, "impious ones" becomes the direct object of the verb. The Hebrew text has the pronoun "them" for the direct object and Symmachus also renders this pronoun. Symmachus, therefore, provides both a revision of LXX-Prov and a rather readable Greek text.

12.3.5.4 Inner-Translational Features

As of 2015, the Bible text, the catenae, the marginal exegetical notes, and the Hexaplaric fragments of LXX[788] await full analysis for Proverbs. However, a few preliminary remarks should be made regarding the great significance of this manuscript for the future collection of the Hexaplaric fragments of Proverbs. The following comments compare the edition by Field[10] with LXX[788].

At Prov 1:4, Field lists Th συλλογισμόν "reasoning," which is in LXX[248]. LXX[788] confirms the attribution to Theodotion and also preserves the following more complete fragment: Th γνῶσιν καὶ συλλογισμόν "knowledge and reasoning," which equals the Hebrew דַּעַת וּמְזִמָּה "knowledge and prudence." The full fragment will be listed in the future collection of Hexaplaric fragments of Proverbs.

At Prov 1:9, Field has Aq ὅτι προσθήκη χάριτός εἰσι τῇ κεφαλῇ σου "for they are an auxilliary for your head." LXX[788] preserves the following three fragments with an index at LXX-Prov στέφανον "crown"/לִוְיַת "garland": Aq προσθήκην "auxilliary," Th συνελεύσεις "strongholds," Sym ὁμόνοιαν "concord." In this instance, LXX[248] probably has the correct reading of Aquila since the Hebrew nominal clause is usually rendered by the use of the nominative case in Greek. The readings in LXX[788] are in the accusative case since στέφανον "crown," the word they revised, was also in the accusative case. The readings of Theodotion and Symmachus have not been listed previously. Although Theodotion and Symmachus use these respective terms, there is no other evidence that they are used for the rare לִוְיַת "garland." Unless there is forthcoming contrary evidence, LXX[788] should be sufficient evidence for admitting these readings into the corpus of Hexaplaric fragments.

There is a new fragment at Prov 1:33b, which has no attribution:

MT-Prov וְשַׁאֲנַן מִפַּחַד רָעָה "and will live at ease, without dread of disaster" (*NRSV)
LXX-Prov καὶ ἡσυχάσει ἀφόβως ἀπὸ παντὸς κακοῦ "and will be at ease without fear of any evil" (*NETS)
⟨Sym⟩ καὶ εὐθυμήσει ἀπὸ πτοήσεως κακίας "and will delight apart from deadful evil"

The Greek fragment is not a comment on the text but rather another version of it. The translation equivalents suggest that the fragment should be attributed to Symmachus. Out of the whole LXX corpus, only Symmachus uses εὐθυμεῖν "to delight" (Prov 15:15 = טוֹב־לֵב "good heart") and the noun εὐθυμία "to rejoice" (Ps 42[43]:4 = גִּיל "to rejoice"; 50[51]:10 = שָׂשׂוֹן "rejoicing"). Aquila and Symmachus use πτόησις "excitement, dread" for פַּחַד "dread" (e.g., Sym-Lam 3:47; Aq-Cant 3:8). Κακία "evil" is used by the Three and therefore is not helpful for establishing the attribution. Therefore, this fragment should probably be attributed to Symmachus in angle brackets ⟨Sym⟩. It has not been listed in prior collections, even as a scholion, because it was probably not in any of the witnesses available to Field, but it and similar fragments will need to be included in the future collection of Hexaplaric materials.

---

[10] Field, *Hexapla*.

12.3.5.5 Text-Critical Value for the Hebrew Text

Normally, the Three (→ 1.3.1.2) confirm MT (→ 12.2.2). Prov 8:28b provides an example of a variant to MT. In Prov 8:28b, LXX[788] provides new evidence for the Three (οἱ λ′) not listed previously in Field. Here are the relevant texts:

> MT-Prov בַּעֲזוֹז עִינוֹת תְּהוֹם "when he established the fountains of the deep" (*NRSV)
> LXX-Prov καὶ ὡς ἀσφαλεῖς ἐτίθει πηγὰς τῆς ὑπ᾽ οὐρανόν "and when he made secure the springs of what is under heaven" (*NETS)
> Aq Sym Th ἐν τῷ κραταιοῦν αὐτὸν πηγὰς ἀβύσσου "when he strengthened springs of the abyss"

In order to place this new evidence in context, the apparatus of *BHQ should be cited in full: בַּעֲזוֹז | καὶ ὡς ἀσφαλεῖς ἐτίθει G (v) S T (via בְּעַזֵּז).[11] As de Waard notes, the problem in the text is בַּעֲזוֹז, a Qal infinitive from עזז "to be strong." The Hebrew may be translated "when the springs of the deep became strong/swelled." He also notes that the LXX reading καὶ ὡς ἀσφαλεῖς ἐτίθει "and when he made secure" is equal to בְּעַזֵּז, a Piel infinitive + 3rd masc. sg. + בְּ from עזז "to make strong." LXX has an interpretive rendering "and when he made the springs secure under heaven." Since the Three usually render their Hebrew text quantitatively, the evidence of this fragment probably confirms that there was a variant Hebrew text: בְּעַזֵּז "when he made strong." Therefore, the evidence of the Three needs to be added to apparatuses of future editions of the Hebrew Bible. Barthélemy[12] chose the text of MT with a B rating, because the committee perceived the variant to have arisen due to simplifying the text and even harmonization, perhaps with v. 28a, which has בְּאַמְּצוֹ "when he made firm," a Piel infinitive + 3rd masc. sg. + בְּ.[13] Whether the Three preserve the original text in this instance is not the present concern. Rather, this variant serves as an example for text critics interested in collecting all of the variants to MT, and it and similar readings need to be listed in the apparatus.

---

[11] De Waard (ed.), *BHQ 17, 16.
[12] Barthélemy, *Interim Report.
[13] Barthélemy, *Interim Report, Vol. 3, 466.

Busto Saiz, J.R., *La traducción de Símaco en el Libro de los Salmos* (Textos y Estudios "Cardenal Cisneros" 22; Madrid: Consejo Superior de Investigaciones Científicas, 1978).

Field, *Hexapla.

Gentry, P.J., *The Asterisked Materials in the Greek Job* (SBLSCS 38; Atlanta: Scholars Press, 1995).

Hyvärinen, K., *Die Übersetzung von Aquila* (ConBOT 10; Uppsala: G.W.K. Gleerup, 1977).

Reider, J. and N. Turner, *An Index to Aquila: Greek-Hebrew, Hebrew-Greek, Latin-Hebrew* (Leiden: Brill, 1966).

Salvesen, A., *Symmachus in the Pentateuch* (JSS Monograph 15; Manchester: Victoria University of Manchester, 1991).

John D. Meade

12.3.6 Post-Hexaplaric Greek Translations

The only post-Hexaplaric recension known to us is that of Lucian. There has been little research on the Lucianic recension of LXX-Prov (→ 12.3.1). In 2015, there is no critical edition of the book in the Göttingen LXX. Therefore, the edition by Holmes and Parsons[1] is the best recourse. In his analysis of Malachias Monachus' text of the Book of Wisdom (→ 11.15.2), Busto Saiz comments on several quotations from Proverbs that likely originate with the Lucianic recension of the book.[2] These quotations are supported by Codex Venetus, which may preserve Lucianic variants. The variants are as follows:[3]

- Prov 11:28 πλούτῳ "wealth" LXX/τῷ ἑαυτῷ πλούτῳ "his own wealth" Malachias 23/πλούτῳ ἑαυτῷ "his own wealth"
- Prov 17:17 δέ "but" LXX; omitted in Malachias 23
- Prov 18:19 τεθεμελιωμένον "firmly founded" LXX/ μεμοχλευμένον "wrenched" Malachias 23

---

[1] R. Holmes and J. Parsons (eds.), *Vetus Testamentum Graecum cum Variis Lectionibus* (Oxford: Clarendon Press, 1798–1820).

[2] Busto Saiz, "The Biblical Text of Malachias Monachus to the Book of Wisdom," 267.

[3] Codex 23 of Holmes–Parsons is designated v in Ralhfs and in the editions of the Göttingen LXX.

– Prov 30:2 ἁπάντων "of all" LXX/πάντων "of all" Malachias 23

The agreements lead Busto Saiz to suggest future avenues of research, namely the LXX^L text of Proverbs. The value of the Lucianic recension for textual criticism will remain unknown until the manuscripts are stratified and characterized. Locating the recension may be a difficult task because of the nature of the Old Greek, a text characterized by freedom of arrangement, syntax, and morphology.[4]

Busto Saiz, J.R., "The Biblical Text of Malachias Monachus to the Book of Wisdom," in *La Septuaginta en la Investigación Contemporánea: V Congreso de la IOSCS* (ed. N. Fernández Marcos; Madrid: Instituo Arias Montano, 1985), 257–70.

Ziegler, J., "Hat Lukian den griechischen Sirach rezensiert?" *Bib* 40 (1959): 210–29.

Matthew M. Dickie

12.3.7 Vulgate

12.3.7.1 Background

Jerome claims to have translated the books of Solomon over the course of three days,[1] most likely in the summer or autumn of 398 C.E. (→ 1.3.5.2).[2] By the time Jerome undertook his translation *iuxta Hebraeos* "according to the Hebrews" he had already completed a revision of the Solomonic books according to the Hexapla (→ 12.3.5).[3] The work was intended to be part of a wholesale revision of the VL Bible according to LXX (→ 1.4.1).[4] Unfortunately,

---

[4] J. Cook, "Proverbs: To the Reader," in *NETS, 621–24 (623). For a helpful study on Lucianic style in Wisdom literature, see Ziegler, "Hat Lukian den griechischen Sirach rezensiert?" 210–29.

[1] See *Prol. Sal.*

[2] See J.N.D. Kelly, *Jerome* (London: Duckworth, 1975), 236 and Tkacz, "Labor Tam Utilis," 42–72 (50).

[3] The preface to Jerome's Hexaplaric revision of the Solomonic books states that the obelus and asterisk were inserted to mark divergences from the Hebrew text (cf. some manuscripts of the Gallican Psalter).

[4] Despite Jerome's claims to the contrary (e.g., *Apol.* 2.24; *Epist.* 71.5; 106.2), it is doubtful that he ever completed his

of Jerome's revision of the books of Solomon, only the preface survives. From his earlier work, Jerome must have gained an awareness of the divergences between the Hebrew and LXX textual traditions of the book of Proverbs (→ 12.3.1). While Jerome found LXX (→ 12.3.1) useful, v-Prov follows a Hebrew text very similar to MT (→ 12.2.2).

12.3.7.2 Translation Character

v-Prov represents an idiomatic rendering of the Hebrew (→ 12.2.2). Jerome does not find it necessary to maintain consistency in the translation, but often introduces variety for the sake of Latin style. Especially where the Hebrew text is difficult, Jerome relies on the Hexaplaric versions (→ 12.3.5), but he does not follow them uncritically. v-Prov stands in support of Jerome's Hebrew competence, as he often makes sense of what earlier translations had misunderstood.

12.3.7.3 Translation Sources
12.3.7.3.1 Use of LXX

Jerome must have believed that the LXX textual tradition (→ 12.3.1) was corrupt (since it did not match the Hebrew), but he did not disregard its value as a linguistic resource. Especially when confronted with difficult Hebrew, Jerome can follow LXX. Examples include the following:

Prov 18:1
MT-Prov לְתַאֲוָה יְבַקֵּשׁ נִפְרָד בְּכָל־תּוּשִׁיָּה יִתְגַּלָּע
the one separating himself seeks his desire and contends against all wisdom
v-Prov *occasiones quaerit qui vult recedere ab amico omni tempore erit exprobrabilis* (= LXX-Prov προφάσεις ζητεῖ ἀνὴρ βουλόμενος χωρίζεσθαι ἀπὸ φίλων ἐν παντὶ δὲ καιρῷ ἐπονείδιστος ἔσται)
He who chooses to depart from a friend is seeking opportunities; he shall always be worthy of reproach[5]

---

revision of the Latin Bible according to LXX. He mentions specifically only his revisions of Job, Psalms, the books of Solomon and Chronicles (see the Vulgate prefaces to these books).

[5] De Waard regards this case as an LXX error of reading לתאנה (= προφάσεις [both meaning "occasion, pretense"]) for לתאוה "desire," which Jerome follows by rendering *occasiones* (*Proverbs*, 9*).

Prov 18:19

MT-Prov אָח נִפְשָׁע מִקִּרְיַת־עֹז
a brother wronged is more than a strong city
v-Prov *frater qui adiuvatur a fratre quasi civitas firma* (= ἀδελφὸς ὑπὸ ἀδελφοῦ βοηθούμενος ὡς πόλις ὀχυρά)
a brother who is helped by his brother is like a strong city

Prov 30:21

MT-Prov תַּחַת שָׁלוֹשׁ רָגְזָה אֶרֶץ וְתַחַת אַרְבַּע לֹא־תוּכַל שְׂאֵת
For three things the earth trembles, and for four it will not hold up
v-Prov *per tria movetur terra et quartum non potest sustinere* (= διὰ τριῶν σείεται ἡ γῆ τὸ δὲ τέταρτον οὐ δύναται φέρειν)
By three things the earth is disturbed, and the fourth it cannot bear

Occasionally, he deletes a Hebrew word following LXX (e.g., נַפְשׁוֹ "his soul" in Prov 13:4; לֶחֶם "bread" in Prov 25:21), but Jerome normally matches LXX when it diverges from MT only in number, e.g., בָּנִים שִׁמְעוּ־לִי "sons, hear me" (Prov 5:7), *fili audi me* "son, hear me" (= υἱέ ἄκουέ μου); טוֹב "good" (Prov 12:14), *bonis* "goods" (= ἀγαθῶν); נָכְרִיָּה "stranger" (Prov 27:13), *pro alienis* "for strangers" (= τὰ ἀλλότρια).

12.3.7.3.2 Use of Aquila, Symmachus, and Theodotion

Jerome was certainly influenced by the Hexaplaric versions (→ 1.3.1.2; → 12.3.5). v-Prov betrays the influence of Aquila, especially in the interpretation of difficult Hebrew terms, e.g., the phrase כִּי לִוְיַת חֵן הֵם לְרֹאשֶׁךָ "for they are a wreath of grace for your head" (Prov 1:9), *ut addatur gratia capiti tuo* "that grace may be added to your head" (= Aq ὅτι προσθήκη χάριτός εἰσι τῇ κεφαλῇ σου); לְיוֹם הַכֵּסֶא "until the day of the full moon" (Prov 7:20), *in die plenae lunae* "in the day of the full moon" (= Aq εἰς ἡμέραν πανσελήνου).

Gordon calculated that Jerome used Symmachus in v-Prov more than Aquila and Thedotion combined.[6] Although a number of Gordon's examples are dubious, it holds true that Jerome made regular use of Symmachus, e.g., בְּאֵין מוּסָר "without instruction" (Prov 5:23), *quia non habuit disciplinam* "because he did not receive instruction" (= Sym διὰ ἀπαιδευσίαν), but rendered likewise nowhere else in the book (cf. Prov 8:24; 11:14; 14:4; 15:22; 29:18); הֹוֹת "ruin" (Prov 19:13), *dolor* "sorrow" (= Sym ὀδύνη); מוֹקֵשׁ "snare" (Prov 22:25), *scandalum* "scandal" (= Sym σκάνδαλον), but so rendered nowhere else in v-Prov (cf. Prov 12:13; 18:7; 20:25; 29:6). Jerome's usage of Theodotion in v-Prov is difficult to detect because it stands so close to LXX. Still, we can locate two certain examples, e.g., בְּחֻקוֹ חוּג עַל־פְּנֵי תְהוֹם "when he inscribed a circle over the face of the deep" (Prov 8:27), *quando certa lege et gyro vallabat abyssos* "when with a certain law and circle he enclosed the depths" (= Th ἐν τῷ ἀκριβάζειν γῦρον ἐπὶ πρόσωπον ἀβύσσου);[7] רְפָאִים "the dead" (Prov 9:18), *gigantes* "giants" (= Th γίγαντες). There are several instances in which two or all of the Hexaplaric versions essentially agree and Jerome follows them, e.g., מֹלֵל בְּרַגְלָיו "uttering with his feet" (Prov 6:13), *terit pede* "he treads with the foot" (= Aq τρίβων; and Sym προτρίβων); גֹּאֲלָם "the one redeeming them" (Prov 23:11), understood in its technical sense as *propinquus ... eorum* "the one near them" (= Aq, Sym, and Th ἀγχιστεύς) rather than in the generic sense, as LXX has it (ὁ λυτρούμενος) "the one redeeming."

12.3.7.4 Translation Technique
12.3.7.4.1 Stereotyping

Jerome stereotypes some of the characteristic vocabulary of Proverbs. Various words for "wisdom" are stereotyped, e.g., חָכְמָה = *sapientia* "wisdom" (e.g., Prov 1:2; 29:3), מוּסָר = *disciplina* "instruction" (e.g., Prov 4:1; 24:32), בִּינָה/תְּבוּנָה "understanding" = *prudentia* "prudence" (e.g., Prov 8:1; 14:29), although contextual considerations sometimes alter a stereotyped rendering (e.g., Prov 23:12–13). The term עָצֵל "slouch," found thirteen times in Proverbs, is stereotyped as *piger* "sluggard" (e.g., Prov 6:9; 24:30). The term מָשָׁל "proverb" is always rendered in v-Prov by the Latin *parabola* "parable" (Prov 1:1; 10:1; 25:1), but in Jerome's other works the term *proverbia* is used as the title of the book (e.g., *Epist.*

---

[6] Gordon, "Rabbinic Exegesis," 384–416 (399).

[7] Jerome apparently read בְּחֻקוֹ חוּג "when he cut a horizon" as בחוק וחוג "with a law and a horizon."

30.1; 125.19). In addition, the notoriously difficult שְׁאוֹל "Sheol" is rendered *infernus* "hell" in each of its nine occurrences (e.g., Prov 5:5; 27:20).

12.3.7.4.2 Hebrew Idioms
v-Prov reflects greater variation in rendering Hebrew idioms than Jerome's earliest translations *iuxta Hebraeos* (e.g., the "Hebrew" Psalter).[8] He could be both slavish, e.g., יָד לְיָד (Prov 11:21; 16:5), rendered *manus in manu* "hand in hand," and loose, e.g., וְטוֹב־לֵב "a good heart" rendered *secura mens* "a secure mind" (Prov 15:15). The Hebrew construct state can be rendered variously, e.g., לְשׁוֹן שֶׁקֶר "a tongue of falsehood" for which we have both the adjectival *lingua mendax* "a lying tongue" (Prov 6:17) and the more literal *lingua mendacii* "a tongue of falsehood" (Prov 12:19); שִׂפְתֵי־שָׁקֶר "lips of falsehood" rendered *labia mendacia* "lying lips" (Prov 10:18), but שְׂפַת־אֱמֶת (Prov 12:19) rendered literally *labium veritatis* "the lip of truth." The same idiom can be translated literally, e.g., בְּיַד־לָשׁוֹן (Prov 18:21), *in manu linguae* "in the hand of the tongue" and non-literally, e.g., בְּיַד־כְּסִיל "by the hand of a fool" (Prov 26:6), *per nuntium stultum* "through a foolish messenger." In v-Prov, Jerome seems to have no set policy for rendering the Hebrew idioms he encounters.

12.3.7.4.3 Attention to Context
Context determines or alters several of Jerome's renderings, e.g., מַלְאָךְ "messenger, angel" is rendered two of three times by the non-technical substantive *nuntius* "messenger" (Prov 13:17; 16:14), but in Prov 17:11 is rendered *angelus* "angel," leaving the impression that the "wicked man" (רָע) can expect direct divine retribution. Jerome also can render the Hebrew more interpretively, and hence more clearly, on the basis of context, e.g., שֵׁם "name" (Prov 22:1), *nomen bonum* "good name" (= LXX ὄνομα καλόν). Jerome's Roman context shines through occasionally. Examples include the following:

Prov 26:8
MT-Prov כִּצְרוֹר אֶבֶן בְּמַרְגֵּמָה "like one binding a stone in a sling"
v-Prov *sicut qui mittit lapidem in acervum Mercurii* "as one who casts a stone into the heap of Mercury"[9]

Prov 31:23
MT-Prov עִם־זִקְנֵי־אָרֶץ "among the elders of the land"
cum senatoribus terrae "among the senators of the land"

12.3.7.4.4 Style
v-Prov reflects Jerome's concern for Latinity in a number of ways. He strives for diversity even when it does not exist in the Hebrew, e.g., חֹרְשֵׁי רָע ... חֹרְשֵׁי טוֹב "devisers of evil ... devisers of good" (Prov 14:22), *qui operantur malum ... praeparant bona* "they who work evil ... prepare good things"; קְנֹה־חָכְמָה ... וּקְנוֹת בִּינָה "to acquire wisdom ... and to acquire understanding" (Prov 16:16), *posside sapientiam ... et adquire prudentiam* "possess wisdom ... and purchase prudence"; נוֹדֵד ... נוֹדֶדֶת "wanders ... wanders" (Prov 27:8), *transmigrans ... qui relinquet* "wandering ... who leaves." Multiple Latin words are used to translate a single Hebrew word, e.g., שָׂנְאוּ "they hated" (Prov 1:29), *exosam habuerint* "they regarded as odious"; אַל־תִּגְזָל־דָּל "Do not rob the poor" (Prov 22:22), *non facias violentiam pauperi* "Do no violence to the poor," and a single Latin word can translate multiple Hebrew words, e.g., לַחֲסַר־לֵב "to the one lacking of sense" (Prov 15:21), *stulto* "to the fool." Jerome feels free to add words for the sake of Latinity, e.g., in metaphorical expressions, וְאִם־זַמּוֹתָ יָד לְפֶה "and if you have plotted evil, a hand to the mouth" (Prov 30:32), *si enim intellexisset ori inposuisset manum* "for if he had understood, he would have laid his hand upon his mouth," and especially the verb *esse* "to be" for which the Hebrew has no formal equivalent (e.g., Prov 21:9; 25:24). In at least one case Jerome adds the participle *dicentes* "saying" when there is no corresponding לֵאמֹר or the like (Prov 30:15).

---

[8] See Kedar-Kopfstein, "The Vulgate as a Translation," 284–85.

[9] This is apparently a rabbinic tradition that Jerome follows (see de Waard, *Proverbs*, 9*).

Sometimes Jerome adds *cum* clauses for the sake of Latin style when there is nothing in the Hebrew to suggest them (e.g., Prov 6:7; 20:14; 24:32). But *cum* clauses are most often used to render the temporal infinitive construct with בְּ (e.g., Prov 1:27; 4:12; 6:22; 16:7; 18:3; 23:16; 24:17; 25:8; 28:28), less often to render temporal כִּי (e.g., Prov 22:6; 23:22; 23:31), although *quando* "when" may also be used for either purpose (e.g., Prov 5:11; 23:1). The *Hiphil* stem of the Hebrew verb lacks a strict equivalent in Latin. So Jerome resorts to periphrastic renderings, e.g., the use of *facere* "to do," e.g., הַרְחֵק מֵעָלֶיהָ דַרְכֶּךָ "Distance your way from her" (Prov 5:8), *longe fac ab ea viam tuam* "Make your way far from her"; אֲמָרֶיהָ הֶחֱלִיקָה "she smoothes her words" (Prov 7:5), *verba sua dulcia facit* "she makes sweet her words"; וְיַצֵּב "and he will strengthen" (Prov 15:25), *et firmos facit* "and will strengthen." But sometimes Jerome becomes more creative, e.g., לֵץ תַּכֶּה "strike the scoffer" (Prov 19:25), rendered *pestilente flagellato* "by flogging the wicked man."

12.3.7.4.5 Literalisms and Transliterations

In v-Prov Jerome prefers not to transliterate. Of course the names of well-known figures such as David (Prov 1:1), Solomon (Prov 1:1; 10:1; 25:1), and Hezekiah (Prov 25:1) are transliterated. Even the name of Lemuel is transliterated (Prov 31:1). But the apparent name of Agur ben Jakeh is translated, דִּבְרֵי אָגוּר בִּן־יָקֶה "the words of Agur son of Jakeh" (Prov 30:1), *verba congregantis filii vomentis* "the words of the gatherer the son of vomiter." Other examples of transliterations are rare, e.g., שֵׁכָר (Prov 31:6), *siceram* "strong drink"; perhaps סָדִין (Prov 31:24), *sindon* "linen" (= LXX σινδών). Literalisms exist in v-Prov, but they are not dominant, e.g., מֹרֶה בְּאֶצְבְּעֹתָיו "shows with his fingers" (Prov 6:13), *digitio loquitur* "he speaks with the finger"; רָחוֹק יְהוָה מֵרְשָׁעִים (Prov 15:29), *longe est Dominus ab impiis* "Far is the Lord from the wicked"; אֶבֶן וָאָבֶן אֵיפָה וְאֵיפָה "stone and stone, ephah and ephah" = "diverse weights and measures" (Prov 20:10), *pondus et pondus, mensura et mensura* "weight and weight, measure and measure."

12.3.7.4.6 Unusual Renderings, but Not Variants

v-Prov furnishes examples of unusual renderings that are, nevertheless, based on the same text as MT. Sometimes Jerome divides Hebrew characters differently than MT, e.g., reading סרים רע/*qui fugiunt mala* "who flee from evil" rather than סוּר מֵרָע "to turn aside from evil" (Prov 13:19); reading אב אוי/*patri vae* "father, woe" rather than אֲבוֹי "alas!" (Prov 23:29). At other times, he tries to make sense of a difficult text, e.g., וְדֶרֶךְ נְתִיבָה "and a way, path" (Prov 12:28), *iter autem devium* "but the deviating way" (cf. Prov 8:2); שֵׁן רֹעָה "broken tooth" (Prov 25:19), *dens putridus* "rotten tooth." It is also possible that Jerome's Hebrew text featured contiguous variant readings, both of which he translates at times, e.g., Prov 26:17 where v-Prov translates both MT's מִתְעַבֵּר (= *inpatiens* "becoming angry") and the possible variant מִתְעָרֵב (= *commiscetur* "meddles"). On at least one occasion Jerome leaves us in total confusion. In Prov 22:6, he renders the imperative חֲנֹךְ "train up" with the baffling *proverbium est* "it is a proverb." It is doubtful that Jerome had a different Hebrew text here since v-Prov stands alone among all ancient versions in this rendering.

12.3.7.5 Text-Critical Value
12.3.7.5.1 Confusion of Consonants

v-Prov furnishes a number of examples of Jerome's confusion of Hebrew consonants. These could be mistakes or Jerome could be following an established principle of rabbinic exegesis.[10] Jerome confuses י and ו (e.g., Prov 3:35 probably reading מרום/*exaltatio* "promotion" for MT מֵרִים "lifting up") and occasionally final ן (e.g., Prov 17:2 reading בְּבֵן מֵבִישׁ "over a son who causes shame," as בני־מביש, *filiis stultis* "over foolish sons"). Jerome can also confuse ר and ד (e.g., Prov 13:20) and ח and ת (e.g., Prov 21:17). Cases of metathesis are relatively frequent, e.g., reading יובא, *ductus* "is led" for יָבוֹא "comes" (Prov 7:22); reading במקשי, *ad laqueos*

---

[10] For metathesis of consonants, e.g., *b. Yoma* 48a. Especially in the Greek translation of Proverbs, see J. de Waard, "Metathesis as a Translation Technique," in *Traducere Navem: Festschrift für Katharina Reiß zum 70. Geburtstag* (ed. J. Holz-Mänttäri and C. Nord; Tampere: University of Tampere Press, 1993), 249–60.

"upon the snares" for מְבַקְשֵׁי "seekers of" (Prov 21:6). But v-Prov does not reflect metathesis as often as LXX (→ 12.3.1).

12.3.7.5.2 Vocalization and *Ketiv/Qere*
In the majority of cases, v-Prov anticipates the vocalization of MT (→ 12.2.2). But there are examples of alternative vocalizations, e.g., Prov 10:4, where Jerome reads a finite verb (*operata est* "worked" = עָשָׂה) rather than a participle (MT עֹשֶׂה "who works"); Prov 12:16, where Jerome reads a *Hiphil* (*indicat* "makes known" = יוֹדִעַ) rather than a *Niphal* (MT יִוָּדַע "is known"); Prov 16:4, where Jerome reads an emphatic preposition (*propter semet ipsum* "for his own sake" = לְמַעֲנֵהוּ) instead of a possessive noun (MT לַמַּעֲנֵהוּ "for his answer"); Prov 24:15, where Jerome reads an abstract noun (*impietas* "wickedness" = רֶשַׁע) instead of the substantive adjective (MT רָשָׁע "wicked man").

v-Prov reflects a preference for the *Qere* over the *Ketiv*. No less than eighteen times, Jerome follows the *Qere*, e.g., Prov 3:34; 8:35; 31:4, usually matching the decisions of other ancient versions. At least three times, however, Jerome follows the *Ketiv* when all other versions follow the *Qere* (Prov 18:17; 20:30; 23:24).

Clifford, R.J., "Observations on the Text and Versions of Proverbs," in *Wisdom, You are My Sister: Studies in Honor of Roland E. Murphy, O.Carm., on the Occasion of his Eightieth Birthday* (ed. E.E. Barré; CBQMS 29; Washington: Catholic Biblical Association, 1997), 47–61.
Gordon, C.H., "Rabbinic Exegesis in the Vulgate of Proverbs," *JBL* 49 (1930): 384–416.
Kedar-Kopfstein, B., "The Vulgate as a Translation: Some Semantic and Syntactical Aspects of Jerome's Version of the Hebrew Bible" (PhD diss., Hebrew University of Jerusalem, 1968).
Tkacz, C.B., "Labor Tam Utilis," *VC* 50 (1996): 42–72.
Toy, C.H., *The Book of Proverbs* (New York: Scribner's, 1916).
de Waard, J., *BHQ*, Part 17: *Proverbs*.

Justin Rogers

12.3.8 Arabic Translations

12.3.8.1 A Pre-Saadian Translation
Very few translations of the book of Proverbs into Judeo-Arabic have been identified so far. The earliest fragment, T-S Ar. 53.8, which was identified by Blau,[1] consists of two small continuous leaves that include a Hebrew-scripted Arabic translation of Prov 16:24–17:26. Based on the fragment's Hebrew orthography in the phonetic representation of Arabic, Blau suggests that it was prepared before Saadia Gaon's translation, and therefore represents the oldest extant Judeo-Arabic Bible translation. The three major characteristics of the fragment's phonetic spelling system are: the use of Hebrew /d/ rather than /ṣ/ to represent the Arabic /ḍ/ẓ/; the inconsistent use of vowel letters to represent short and long vowels; and the spelling of the definite article according to phonetic criteria, omitting it altogether before sun letters. Blau suggests that the authors of this fragment were not familiar with standard Arabic orthography and therefore invented a Hebraized spelling system. As of the tenth century, the dissemination of Saadia Gaon's translations determined the standard Judeo-Arabic transcription conventions. The heterogeneous character of this fragment suggests that it is based on other earlier translations (→ 1.3.6).[2]

12.3.8.2 Saadia's Translation
Saadia (Gaon) b. Joseph al-Fayyumi (882–942 C.E.) prepared several Arabic translations of biblical books (see → 1.3.6), the most widespread of which was his version of the Pentateuch (known as the *tafsīr*). It seems to have disseminated standardized Judeo-Arabic orthography, which reflected a Classical Arabic spelling system (→ 1.3.6.1.6).[3] The main features of Saadia's spelling system include using *matres lectionis* to indicate long vowels according to Arabic spelling, and the representation of phonemes according to their cognates instead of following phonetic similarities. As with the Penta-

---

[1] Blau, "Fragment."
[2] Cf. Blau, "Fragment"; Sasson, "Arabic."
[3] See also Polliack, "Cairo Genizah"; Polliack, "Types."

teuch and several other books he translated, Saadia's versions are less literal than early Jewish translations and Karaite versions, and they are oriented towards the Arabic target language in their syntax and style.⁴ Other features of his translation include a tendency to succinctness, theological alterations, shortening and expanding the text for stylistic purposes, and avoidance of repetitions (→ 1.3.6).⁵

Extant manuscripts of Saadia's translation of Proverbs include Saadia's commentary on that book and an extensive introduction to his work. Saadia titles the book of Proverbs *Kitāb ṭalab al-ḥikma* "The Book of Pursuit of Wisdom." Saadia's introduction to his work on the book of Proverbs is divided into four sections: 1) the uniqueness of the human intellect compared with the animal world; 2) the characteristics of the process of learning; 3) twelve categories of sayings found in the book of Proverbs; 4) five conditions essential to the pursuit of wisdom.⁶

Modern scholarly editions of Saadia's translation and commentary on the book of Proverbs were published by Derenbourg (1893) and Qafiḥ (1976).⁷

12.3.8.3 Karaite Translations

Karaite Judaism, which emerged in the ninth century C.E., was motivated by the rejection of Jewish oral law and rabbinic authority, and an ethos of return to Scripture. Hence the Karaites inaugurated a translation enterprise of their own. Most Karaite translations were written in the tenth and eleventh centuries, the golden age of Karaite literary activity. Karaites used the same orthographical standards as Saadia. However, their translation system is different, and seems to be more akin to the literal characteristics of the pre-Saadian Jewish translation tradition (→ 1.3.6.1; → 1.3.6.2; → 1.3.6.3; → 1.3.6.4; → 1.3.6.5).⁸

Yefet ben ʿElī, Saadia's younger contemporary, translated the entire Bible into Judeo-Arabic, a translation that has survived in numerous manuscript sources (→ 1.3.6.1; → 1.3.6.2; → 1.3.6.3; → 1.3.6.4; → 1.3.6.5). Yefet, whose family originated in Baṣra, Iraq, lived and wrote in Jerusalem. His translation is accompanied by a commentary and the two components are meant to be studied together. Like Saadia, Yefet prefaced his work on each book of the Bible with an introduction in which he specified the nature of the book and his goals as a translator and exegete. In his introduction to the book of Proverbs, Yefet states that his intention is to produce an accurate translation and a concise commentary. His work is characterized by a threefold structure consisting of the biblical verse, a translation of the verse or cluster of verses into Judeo-Arabic, and a passage of commentary. Yefet's translation and commentary on Proverbs (as well as on Job and other books) has survived in Arabic and in Hebrew script. In the case of Proverbs, it appears that the earliest manuscripts, which are dated to the eleventh century, are written in Arabic script, and that the later manuscripts are written in Hebrew script.⁹ Nevertheless, it is also possible that the different scripts preserve different, essentially contemporaneous, Arabic renditions of the translation and commentary that Yefet intended for different audiences, and are not a linear development from early to late in the reception of his work.

Yefet's translation is characterized by an emphasis on accuracy. He laces linguistic studies and lexicographic discussions into his commentary in order to explain his translation and choice of vocabulary. In contrast to Saadia, Yefet's translation is characterized by the occasional rendering of two terms when translating a single word. In addition, translations of a few verses include insertions of small interpretive clauses into the translations. Yefet writes in Middle Arabic with great affinity to Classical Arabic but also with a certain number some degree of vernacular features.¹⁰ Thirty manuscripts

---

⁴ Polliack, "Cairo Genizah"; Polliack, *Karaite*.

⁵ Polliack, *Karaite*; Polliack, "Concept"; Polliack, "Cairo Genizah"; Sasson, "Arabic"; Steiner, *Biblical Translation*.

⁶ See Blau, "Saadya"; Polliack, "Arabic"; Ilan, "*Ălukā*," and Zucker, *Rav*.

⁷ Derenbourg (ed.), *Version arabe des Proverbes*; Qafiḥ (ed.), *Mishle ʿim targum*.

⁸ See Polliack, *Karaite*.

---

⁹ See Khan, "Orthography."

¹⁰ See Polliack, *Karaite*; Sasson, "Methods."

labeled as Yefet's work on Proverbs are listed in the catalogue of the Institute of Microfilmed Hebrew Manuscripts in the Israel National Library. Some of these manuscripts are single units in sets of two volumes. A study of the transmission history of Yefet's translation points to mostly minor alterations that were introduced by later copyists either for the purpose of updating the vocabulary or in order to refine the literality of the translation.[11]

A few sections of Yefet's translation of and commentary on Proverbs were published in modern scholarly publications. The earliest one is Auerbach's edition of Yefet's work on Proverbs 30, which was published in 1866.[12] The second edition was prepared by Günzig in 1898 and included the introduction and the first three chapters.[13] An edition of Proverbs 10–12 was prepared in an unpublished MA thesis by Hacohen in 1967.[14] In 2002 and 2003, Wechsler published the edition of Proverbs 31 in two parts.[15] A comprehensive edition of the entire work of Yefet on the book of Proverbs is pending publication in two volumes by Sasson.[16] In his commentary on Ecclesiastes, Salmon ben Yeruḥam, the tenth-century Karaite exegete, mentions his own commentary on Proverbs three times.[17] It is most likely that he designed his commentary on Proverbs in the same fashion as that on Ecclesiastes (→ 13–17.1.8.4.2), meaning that it included a translation of the biblical text into Judeo-Arabic. Unfortunately, Salmon's work on Proverbs has not been identified with certainty so far.

12.3.8.4 Other Rabbanite and Karaite Translations

Several scores of anonymous translation fragments of Proverbs have been identified in the Cairo Genizah Arabic and Judeo-Arabic collections.[18] It is possible that more exist and have yet to be identified. Usually, these Genizah fragments represent ad hoc translations, sometimes in popular style and sometimes more akin to Saadia's translation methodology.[19]

A translation of Proverbs is also attested in the sixteenth-century *sharḥ* by the Rabbanite commentator Rabbi Issāchār ben-Sūsān ha-Maʿarāvī, who was born in the city of Fez in Morocco and moved to Safed at a young age. Ben-Sūsān proclaimed the necessity of updating Saadia's Bible version in the comprehensible Arabic of his time (→ 1.3.6; → 3–5.1.8; → 6–9.1.8).

David Sklare of the Israel National Library has graciously shared the following as-yet unpublished information about other translations of Proverbs into Judeo-Arabic: Ibn al-Hiti, who wrote the chronicles of Karaite sages of the Middle Ages, mentions the eleventh-century sage Ali ben Abraham al-Tawil. Ibn al-Hiti states that al-Tawil, who lived in Ramle, wrote commentaries on the entire Bible. Manuscript SP RNL EVR I 1396, which contains 146 folios in square script, is believed to be a segment of this commentary on Proverbs. This manuscript includes a translation of the biblical text into Judeo-Arabic. In addition, Sklare points to a number of unidentified manuscripts in the Firkovitch collection that contain translations of Proverbs.

---

[11] See Ben-Shammai, "Editions."
[12] Auerbach, *Proverbiorum*.
[13] Günzig, *Proverbien*.
[14] Hacohen, "*Mishle*."
[15] Wechsler, "The Arabic Translation and Commentary of Yefet ben ʿEli on Proverbs 31:1–9,"; Wechsler, "The Arabic Translation and Commentary of Yefet ben ʿEli on Proverbs 31:10–31."
[16] Sasson, *Arabic*.
[17] Robinson, *Asceticism*.

Auerbach, Z. (ed. and trans.), *Iepheti ben Eli Karaitae in Proverbiorum Salomonis coput XXX commentarius, nunc primum arabice editus, in latinum conversus, adnotationibus illustratus* (Bonn: Typis Caroli Georgii, 1866).

Baker, C.F. and M. Polliack, *Arabic and Judaeo-Arabic Manuscripts in The Cambridge Genizah Collections,*

---

[18] See the indices in Baker and Polliack, *Catalogue*; Shivtiel and Niessen, *Catalogue*.
[19] See the indices in Baker and Polliack, *Catalogue*; Shivtiel and Niessen, *Catalogue*.

Arabic Old Series (T-S Ar.1a-54) (Cambridge: Cambridge University Press, 2001).

Ben-Shammai, H., "Editions and Versions in Yefet b. Ali's Bible Commentary," *Alei Sefer* 2 (1976): 17–32 [Hebr.].

Blau, J., "On a Fragment of the Oldest Judaeo-Arabic Bible Translation Extant," in *Genizah Research after Ninety Years: The Case of Judaeo-Arabic* (eds. J. Blau and S.C. Reif; Cambridge: Cambridge University Press, 1992), 31–39.

Blau, J., "Saadya Gaon's Pentateuch Translation and the Stabilization of Medieval Judaeo-Arabic Culture," in *The Interpretation of the Bible: The International Symposium in Slovenia* (ed. J. Krašovec; SJOTSup 289; Sheffield: Sheffield Academic Press, 1998), 393–98.

Brody, R., *Rav Seʿadya Gaon* (Jerusalem: The Zalman Shazar Center, 2006) [Hebr.].

Derenbourg, J. (ed.), *Œuvres complètes de R. Saadia ben Iosef al-Fayyoûmî*, Vol. 6: *Version arabe des Proverbes* (Paris: E. Leroux, 1893).

Günzig, I. (ed.), *Der Commentar des Karäers Jephet ben ʿAli Halêvi zu den Proverbien* (Krakow: Josef Fischer, 1898).

Hacohen, O., "Book of Proverbs (Chapters 10–12) in the Commentary of the Karaite Yefet ha-Levi" (MA thesis, Hebrew University of Jerusalem, 1967) [Hebr.].

Ilan, N., "*Ălukā* as 'Nothing' and Its Use in Polemics with the Karaites: A Study of Saadia's Commentary on Proverbs 30:10–17," in *Pesher Naḥum: Texts and Studies in Jewish History and Literature from Antiquity Through the Middle Ages Presented to Norman (Naḥum) Golb* (eds. J. Kraemer and M. Wechsler; Studies in Ancient Oriental Civilization 66; Chicago: The Oriental Institute of the University of Chicago, 2012), 1*–10* [Hebr.].

Khan, G., "The Orthography of Karaite Hebrew Bible Manuscripts in Arabic Transcription," *JSS* 38 (1993): 49–70.

Polliack, M., *The Karaite Tradition of Arabic Bible Translation: A Linguistic and Exegetical Study of Karaite Translations of the Pentateuch from the Tenth and Eleventh Centuries C.E.* (Études sur le judaïsme médiéval 17; Leiden: Brill, 1997).

Polliack, M., "Arabic Bible Translations in the Cairo Genizah Collections," in *Jewish Studies in a New Europe* (eds. U. Haxen et al.; Copenhagen: C.A. Reitzel, 1998), 595–620.

Polliack, M., "Types of Arabic Bible Translations in the Cairo Geniza Based on the Catalogue of TS Arabic," *Teʿuda* 15 (1999): 109–25 [Hebr.].

Polliack, M., "Seʿadyā Gaon's Concept of Biblical Translation in Light of the Karaite Concept," in *Heritage and Innovation in Medieval Judaeo-Arabic Culture* (eds. J. Blau and D. Doron; Ramat-Gan: Bar-Ilan University Press, 2000), 191–201 [Hebr.].

Qafiḥ, Y. (ed.), *Mishle ʿim targum u-ferush ha-gaon rabbenu Saadiah ben Yoseph Fayyumi zṣ"l* (ed.; Jerusalem: Havaʿad le-hoṣaʾat sifre rasa"g, 1976) [Hebr.].

Robinson, J.T., *Asceticism, Eschatology, Opposition to Philosophy: The Arabic Translation and Commentary of Salmon ben Yeroham on Qohelet (Ecclesiastes)* (Études sur le judaïsme médiéval 45; Leiden: Brill, 2012).

Sasson, I., "Arabic," in *EncJud* 3 (^{2}2007): 603–06.

Sasson, I., "Methods and Approach in Yefet Ben ʿElī Al-Baṣrī's Translation and Commentary on the Book of Proverbs" (PhD diss., Jewish Theological Seminary, 2010).

Sasson, I., *The Arabic Translation and Commentary of Yefet ben Eli on the Book of Proverbs* (eds. M. Polliack and M. Wechsler; Leiden: Brill, forthcoming).

Shivtiel, A. and F. Niessen, *Arabic and Judaeo-Arabic Manuscripts in the Cambridge Genizah Collections: Taylor-Schechter New Series* (Cambridge: Cambridge University Press, 2006).

Sklare, D., "Unknown Karaite Works in the Firkovitch Collection," in *Judaeo-Arabic Manuscripts in the Firkovitch Collections: The Works of Yusuf al-Basir: A Sample Catalogue: Texts and Studies* (eds. D. Sklare and H. Ben-Shammai; Jerusalem: Ben-Zvi Institute, 1997), 127–39.

Sklare, D., "A Guide to Collections of Karaite Manuscripts," in *Karaite Judaism: A Guide to Its History and Literary Sources* (ed. M. Polliack; HdO 1.73; Leiden: Brill, 2003), 893–924.

Steiner, R.C., *A Biblical Translation in the Making: The Evolution and Impact of Saadia Gaon's Tafsīr* (Cambridge: Harvard University Press, 2010).

Tobi, Y., "On the Antiquity of the Judeo-Arabic Biblical Translations and a New Piece of an Ancient Judeo-Arabic Translation to the Pentateuch," in *Ben ʿever la-ʿarav*, Vol. 2 (ed. Y. Tobi; Tel Aviv: Afikim, 2001), 17–60 [Hebr.].

Walfish, B.D. and M. Kizilov, *Bibliographia Karaitica: An Annotated Bibliography of Karaites and Karaism* (Leiden: Brill, 2011).

Wechsler, M.G., "The Arabic Translation and Commentary of Yefet ben ʿEli on Proverbs 31:1–9," *REJ* 161 (2002): 393–409.

Wechsler, M.G., "The Arabic Translation and Commentary of Yefet ben ʿEli on Proverbs 31:10–31," *JJS* 54 (2003): 283–310.

Zawanowska, M., "Review of Scholarly Research on Yefet and His Works," *REJ* (forthcoming).

Zucker, M., *Rav Saadya Gaon's Translation of the Torah* (New York: Philipp Feldheim, 1959).

Ilana Sasson

12.4 Secondary Translations

12.4.1 Vetus Latina

12.4.1.1 Evidence

VL-Prov is preserved very fragmentarily in seven manuscripts:[1] VL[32] = Wolfenbüttel, Herzog-August-Bibliothek, Weissenburg 76, lectionary palimpsest, sixth century C.E.; VL[94–95] = marginal glosses in Spanish Vulgate Bibles: VL[94] = El Escorial, Bibl. de San Lorenzo 54.V.35, lat. 4859 (incunable; the glosses were copied in 1577), VL[95] = Madrid, Academia de la Historia 2–3; twelfth century; VL[160] = St. Gallen, Stiftsbibliothek cod. 11; eighth century C.E.; VL[165] = Vienna, Nationalbibliothek cod. lat. 954; palimpsest, fifth or sixth century C.E. (Prov 2:1–4:23; 19:4–24, but vv. 7–27 are Vulgate) and Milan, Bibl. Ambrosiana S.P. II 97, palimpsest (Prov 18:9–19:4[7]); VL[166] = Saint Paul in Kärnten, Stiftsbibliothek cod. 25.2.36, palimpsest, sixth century C.E. (Prov 15:9–26; 16:29–17:12 with gaps); VL[167] = Verona, Bibl. Capitolare, cod. I (1), App. fol. 1–3, early sixth century C.E. (fol. 2: Prov 6:7–19). The manuscript evidence is completed by the indirect tradition. Proverbs has been quoted in Latin literature since an early date; it is found in Tertullian, Cyprian of Carthage, and most Christian authors, especially in Ambrose of Milan, Augustine of Hippo, and in works such as Pseudo-Augustine's *Liber de Divinis Scripturis*. Cyprian's quotations are the most important evidence.

12.4.1.2 Editions

VL-Prov was edited for the first time by Sabatier (1743).[2] His edition is based on quotations in the works of Cyprian, Jerome, Lucifer of Cagliari, Augustin, Ambrose, and others (→ 21.8). From the mid-nineteenth century, the progressive discovery of new manuscripts led to successive editions, such as those by Vogel (VL[165] in 1868), Berger (VL[160] in 1893), and Clark (VL[167] in 1906).[3] VL[94] was published in 1920 by Revilla,[4] but VL[95] has not yet been published, although it was used by Schildenberger in his monograph.[5] Dold's edition of VL[32] was published in 1937[6] followed by that of VL[166] a year later.[7] The most recent edition was prepared by Frede (VL[165] in 1996).[8] Currently, there is no critical edition of all witnesses of VL-Prov.

12.4.1.3 Text

Schildenberger's[9] conclusions on VL-Prov were confirmed in later studies. Schildenberger bases his study on Cyprian's quotations, which display a very literal translation from the Greek (→ 12.3.1) written in popular Latin. Cyprian's text has Greek loanwords (sometimes together with Tertullian), more so than in other Latin Proverbs texts.[10] Examples include those listed in Table 1. This fidelity to the Greek is also visible in the syntax, as listed in Table 2. However, the VL text of Cyprian is not a slavish translation, as proven by the examples in Table 3.

Cyprian's text provides the earliest stage of VL-Prov that can be reconstructed. This text is not the original Latin translation, but is close to it.

The manuscript tradition of VL-Prov has preserved many features of the Latin Proverbs text type quoted by Cyprian.[11] VL[165 166] preserve early

---

[1] For VL numbers, see Gryson, *Altlateinische Handschriften 1*, 55–56, 150–52, 245–46, 251–53.

[2] Sabatier, *Bibliorum*, 2.297–347.

[3] Vogel, *Beiträge*, 55–99; Berger, "Notice," 137–42; Clark, "Some Itala Fragments in Verona," 10.

[4] Revilla, "La Biblia de Valvanera," 191–210 (203–10).

[5] Schildenberger, *Die altlateinischen Texte*.

[6] Dold, *Das älteste Liturgiebuch*, 64–66.

[7] Dold, "Die altlateinischen Proverbientexte," *Bib* 19 (1938): 245–48.

[8] Frede, "Zuwuchs zur Handschrift 165," 15, 17.

[9] Schildenberger, *Die altlateinischen Texte*.

[10] All examples are quoted from Schildenberger, *Die altlateinischen*.

[11] Comments on manuscripts VL[165–167] are taken from Gryson, *Altlateinische Handschriften*, 55–56, 150–52, 245–46, 251–53.

TABLE 1   Greek Loanwords in Cyprian's Text

	LXX-Prov[12]	Cyprian	Other VL Texts
Book title	παροιμίαι "proverbs"	*paroemiae*	
Prov 14:25	μάρτυς "witness"	*martyr*	*testis* "witness"
Prov 15:27a	ἐλεημοσύναις "by acts of mercy"	*eleemosynis*	*per misericordiam* "by mercy"

TABLE 2   Fidelity of the Texts of Cyprian and Tertullian to the Greek

	LXX-Prov	Cyprian	Tertullian	Other VL-Texts
Prov 8:27	συμπαρήμην αὐτῷ "I was present with him" (*NETS)	*aderam illi* "I was present with him"	*aderam illi* "I was present with him"	*cum illo eram* "I was with him"
Prov 20:9	τίς παρρησιάσεται καθαρὸς εἶναι "who can declare confidently to be pure"	*quis gloriabitur mundus esse* "who can boast to be pure"		... *mundum se esse* "that he is pure"

European texts that faithfully maintain features of old African texts. VL[165] attests to a text that is very close to that quoted by Cyprian and VL[94 95] are close to VL[165], although they are not as faithful to the Old Latin text as VL[165 167]. The situation is illustrated by the examples from the praise of the bee in Prov 6:8a–c in VL[94 167], which is absent in MT (see Table 4; → 12.2.2).[13]

VL[167] transmits a type of European text from northern Italy that is closer to a text type from ancient Africa than the Proverbs quotations in Pseudo-Augustine's *Liber de Divinis Scripturis*. The text of VL[167] is also very close to VL[166], a manuscript that is also related to an African text type. Regarding VL[165] Frede concludes therefore in agreement with Schildenberger's hypothesis:[14] VL[165 94 95] and the *Quaestiones salamonis* are testimonies of an ancient African text. This text does not differ much from that quoted by Cyprian.

12.4.1.4   *Vorlage*

The most comprehensive study on the *Vorlage* of VL-Prov is that by Schildenberger. He argues that the quotations of Cyprian have as their *Vorlage* a Greek text that was in use in Syria at the time of Lucian of Antioch[15] and that the agreements with Origen's recension (LXX[O]; → 12.3.5) are due to pre-Hexaplaric readings.[16] Frede confirms Schildenberger's conclusions in his study on VL[165] and describes the *Vorlage* of VL-Prov as a proto-Lucianic LXX text (→ 12.3.6) from Antioch.[17]

---

[12] Translations according to *NETS.
[13] For the Greek text, I use the text Rahlfs, *Septuaginta*, and for VL[94] and VL[167] the editions of Revilla ("La Biblia de Valvanera") and Clark ("Some Itala Fragments in Verona").
[14] Frede, "Zuwuchs," 30; Schildenberger, *Die altlateinischen Texte*.
[15] Schildenberger, *Die altlateinischen Texte*, 53.
[16] Schildenberger, *Die altlateinischen Texte*, 129.
[17] Frede, "Zuwuchs," 30.

TABLE 3   Lexical Differences Between the Text of Cyprian and Other VL Texts

	LXX-Prov	Cyprian	Other VL Texts
Prov 8:27	θρόνον "throne" (*NETS)	sedem "seat"	thronum "throne"
Prov 11:26	ὁ τιμιουλκῶν σῖτον (LXX^V 252 [sub x] 161) "the one who raises the price of grain"	captans annonam "who seizes grain"	pretio grauans tricitum "he who ways down on the price of grain"
Prov 16:27	θησαυρίζει "treasures" (*NETS)	condit "stores"	thensaurizat "treasures"
Prov 25:22	ἄνθρακας πυρός "coals of fire" (*NETS)	carbones uiuos "living coals"	carbones ignis "coals of fire"

TABLE 4   Differences between VL[167] and VL[94]

	LXX-Prov	VL[167]	VL[94]
Prov 6:8a	ἢ πορεύθητι πρὸς τὴν μέλισσαν "or go to the bee"	aut uade ad apem "or go to the bee"	uel ad apetum uade "or to the bee go"
Prov 6:8a	καὶ μάθε "and learn"	et uide "and see"	et uide et disce "and see and learn"
Prov 6:8b	ποθεινή "she is desired"	grata "beloved"	appetibilis "desired"
Prov 6:8c	τῇ ῥώμῃ "physically"	uiribus "in strength"	robore "in strength"

Berger, S., "Notice sur quelques textes latins inédits de l'Ancien Testament," *Notices et extraits des manuscrits de la Bibliothèque Nationale et autres bibliothèques* 34.2 (1893): 137–42.

Clark, C.U., "Some Itala Fragments in Verona," *Transactions of the Connecticut Academy of Arts and Sciences* 15 (1909): 7–18.

Dold, A., *Das älteste Liturgiebuch der lateinischen Kirche: Ein altgallikanisches Lektionar des 5./6. Jhs. aus dem Wolfenbütteler Palimpsest–Codex Weissenburgensis 76* (Texte und Studien 1.26–28; Beuron: Kunstschule der Erzabtei, 1936).

Dold, A., "Die altlateinischen Proverbientexte im Codex 25.2.36 von St. Paul in Kärnten," *Bib* 19 (1938): 241–59.

Frede, H.J., "Zuwuchs zur Handschrift 165," in *Vetus Latina–Fragmente zum Alten Testament: Die pelagianische epistula ad quandam matronam christianam* (ed. H.J. Frede; VL 28; Freiburg i.B.: Herder, 1996), 9–34.

Gryson, *Altlateinische Handschriften 1*.

Revilla, M., "La Biblia de Valvanera," *La Ciudad de Dios* 120 (1920): 191–210, esp. 203–10.

Sabatier, *Bibliorum*.

Schildenberger, J., *Die altlateinischen Texte des Proverbien-Buches: Untersucht und textgeschichtlich eingegliedert* (Texte und Arbeiten 1.32–33; Beuron: Beuroner Kunstverlag, 1941).

Vogel, A., *Beiträge zur Herstellung der alten lateinischen*

Bibel-Übersetzung: Zwei handschriftliche Fragmente aus dem Buche des Ezechiel und aus den Sprüchwörtern Salomo's zum ersten Male herausgegeben (Vienna: Braumüller, 1868).

José Manuel Cañas Reíllo

12.4.2 Coptic Translations

12.4.2.1 Background

Proverbs, like the other sapiential and poetic books, was held in high esteem in the Coptic monasteries from the earliest period of Coptic Christianity. In the case of Proverbs and some other books, their translation can even be dated as early as the third century C.E.[1] The oldest witness of a Coptic translation of the book of Proverbs is P. Bodmer VI.[2] It is kept in the collection of the so-called Bodmer Papyri,[3] which belonged probably to a Pachomian monastery near Dishna in Upper Egypt.[4] This witness is outstanding in every respect. Its text (Prov 1:1–21:4 with some gaps) has been copied on parchment, most probably in the fourth century C.E. and includes corrections by a second hand. But its alphabet and language demonstrate that the scribal *Vorlage* from which Papyrus Bodmer VI was copied must have been a papyrus attesting to one of the earliest translations of a biblical book into Coptic.[5] The text of P. Bodmer VI is written in an alphabet as yet non-standardized,[6] using different types of signs for the Egyptian phonemes from those that were established in the fourth century C.E. and appear in the later standardized Coptic biblical texts. These signs are closer to their paleographic ancestors in the (pagan) demotic script and resemble those characters known from pagan magical texts dating to the second, third, and fourth centuries C.E. These magical texts are reckoned among the first attempts to write Egyptian using the Greek alphabet along with some additional signs borrowed from the demotic script.[7] This early form of the Coptic alphabet was dubbed Old Coptic and is sometimes also characterized by archaic language.[8] Not only the script, but also the language of P. Bodmer VI is unique and not comparable with the classic Sahidic dialect; therefore, the language of P. Bodmer VI has been classified as proto-Sahidic (or proto-Theban).[9]

The book of Proverbs in the Sahidic dialect is completely and extraordinarily well preserved. We possess a series of manuscripts from the fourth to the thirteenth centuries.[10] Among this manuscript testimony are passages of Proverbs in mostly late liturgical manuscripts.[11] The Monastery of St. Shenoute ("White Monastery") near Sohag in Upper Egypt alone possessed at least six codices containing Proverbs. These codices today are all in a lamentable and fragmentary condition. Usually they combine the poetic and sapiential books of the Old Testament in one or several subsequent volumes with varying book sequences.[12] The most complete witness is a sixth or seventh century C.E.

---

[1] Feder, "Die koptischen Versionen des Proverbienbuches," 1.

[2] Kasser, *Papyrus Bodmer VI*.

[3] R. Kasser, "Bodmer Papyri," *The Coptic Encyclopedia* (ed. A. Atiya; New York: Macmillan, 1991), 8:48b–53b.

[4] See most recently J.M. Robinson, *The Story of the Bodmer Papyri: From the First Monastery's Library in Upper Egypt to Geneva and Dublin* (Cambridge: James Clarke & Co., 2013).

[5] Feder, "Die koptischen Versionen des Proverbienbuches," 1–2; cf. also F. Feder, "Die koptische Übersetzung des Alten und Neuen Testamentes im 4. Jahrhundert," in *Stabilisierung und Profilierung der Koptischen Kirche im 4. Jahrhundert: Beiträge zur X. Internationalen Halleschen Koptologentagung 2006* (eds. J. Tubach and S.G. Vashalomidze; Hallesche Beiträge zur Orientwissenschaft 44; Halle: Martin-Luther-Universität Halle-Wittenberg, 2007), 65–93.

[6] Kasser, *Papyrus Bodmer VI*, xiii–xxiii.

[7] Cf. R. Kasser, "Protodialects Coptes à Systèmes Alphabétiques de Type Vieux-Copte," in *Coptic Studies on the Threshold of a New Millennium: Proceedings of the Seventh International Congress of Coptic Studies: Leiden, August 27–September 2, 2000* (2 vols.; eds. M. Immerzeel et al.; OLA 133; Leuven: Peeters, 2004), 1.77–123.

[8] H. Satzinger, "Old Coptic," *The Coptic Encyclopedia* 8:169b–75b.

[9] R. Kasser, "Dialect P (or Proto-Theban)," *The Coptic Encyclopedia* 8:82a–87b.

[10] See Feder, "Die koptischen Versionen des Proverbienbuches," 3–7, and Schüssler, *Biblia Coptica* 2.2 regarding Cop^{Sa} 200, 209, 212L, 218, 236.

[11] For Coptic liturgical texts and their Old Testament readings in general, see U. Zanetti, "Leçons liturgiques du Monastère Blanc: Ancien Testament," *BSAC* 46 (2007): 205–30.

[12] Cf. Feder, "Die koptischen Versionen des Proverbienbuches," 10; cf. Job (→ 11.4.2).

parchment manuscript kept in the Oriental Institute collection in Chicago (inv. 10485).[13]

The Bohairic version of the book of Proverbs is only preserved in very late manuscripts dated no earlier than the fourteenth century.[14] The whole manuscript tradition transmits the text of Proverbs only until Prov 14:26 but often in combination with Job (→ 11.4.2). But some liturgical manuscripts contain a few additional verses of Proverbs.

It is an extraordinary fortune that an entire papyrus codex, kept in the Staatsbibliothek Berlin (manuscript Berol. orient. oct. 987), preserves the complete text of an Akhmimic version of Proverbs. The papyrus can be dated to the late third or early fourth century C.E. and is therefore an outstanding witness to the translation of Proverbs into Coptic.[15]

12.4.2.2 Extant Biblical Text, Text Editions, and Auxiliary Tools

Although the many witnesses of Cop^{Sa}-Prov call for a critical edition, no attempt has been made to date in this direction. Kosack published in 1973 a synoptic text of Cop-Prov together with a modern Arabic version.[16] However, he did not select the witnesses of his edition based on text-critical considerations and it remains unclear on which *Vorlage* the Arabic translation is based. For example, for inexplicable reasons, Kosack replaced the Bohairic text where it is lacking with P. Bodmer VI. All in all, Kosack's text presentation was meant to provide a synopsis of *some* of the Coptic manuscripts for the Coptic Christians in Egypt and abroad. However, the result resembles a polyglot Bible of the sixteenth or seventeenth century rather than a modern edition. Although he did not intend to produce a critical edition,[17] Worrell's 1931 publication of the most complete Cop^{Sa}-Prov manuscript[18] is still useful since he tried to include all of the Sahidic manuscript tradition that was available to him (even biblical quotations in Coptic ecclesiastical literature; → 21.10). This publication remains useful today in contrast to the situation with many other books of the Cop^{Sa} Old Testament for which one has first to assemble individual leaves or fragments of manuscripts that are often dispersed all over the world. For the recently discovered witnesses to Cop^{Sa}-Prov, one has to refer to the *Biblia Coptica* catalogue by Schüssler.

For Cop^{Boh}-Prov, Burmester and Dévaud prepared an edition based on a fourteenth-century paper codex (manuscript 8, John Rylands Library, Manchester) with variant readings from a series of considerably later manuscripts.[19] Although the (late) Bohairic version of the Coptic Old Testament is frequently preserved in complete manuscripts, only a small number of them have been edited. In this respect, Cop-Prov is an unusual case.

12.4.2.3 Translation Character and Text-Critical Value of Cop-Prov for LXX-Prov

It is particularly regrettable, given the richness of the Coptic (manuscript) evidence for Proverbs, that there is neither a critical edition of Cop-Prov nor an *editio critica maior* of LXX-Prov (→ 12.3.1) available yet. However, the rich transmission of Cop^{Sa}-Prov displays a considerable degree of variation.[20] It has been observed that the early Greek papyrus LXX^{928} (third century C.E.), which attests to an early revision of LXX-Prov (→ 12.3.5) that adapts it to MT (→ 12.2.2), has a closer relationship with Cop^{Sa}-Prov.[21]

So far, it seems clear that Cop^{Boh}-Prov is independent from Cop^{Sa}-Prov and generally follows[22] the mainstream of the Greek majuscule manuscripts that constitute the text of Rahlfs (prelim-

---

[13] Worrell, *Proverbs of Solomon*; Schüssler, *Biblia Coptica* 1.2 regarding Cop^{Sa} 26.

[14] Burmester and Dévaud, *Proverbes de Salomon*; Feder, "Die koptischen Versionen des Proverbienbuches," 8–10.

[15] Böhlig, *Der achmimische Proverbientext*; Feder, "Die koptischen Versionen des Proverbienbuches," 8.

[16] Kosack, *Proverbia*. Presumably, Kosack planned further publications in the series *Vetus Testamentum Coptice* but no other volumes have appeared.

[17] Worrell, *Proverbs of Solomon*, xxix–xxx.

[18] Worrell, *Proverbs of Solomon*.

[19] Burmester and Dévaud, *Proverbes de Salomon*, v–x.

[20] Böhlig, *Untersuchungen*, 1–2.

[21] Bogaert, *"Septante,"* 622. Although Bogaert does not specify which Coptic version is concerned, it can only be Cop^{Sa}-Prov; cf. Böhlig, *Untersuchungen*, 52.

[22] Böhlig, *Untersuchungen*, 2.

inary) edition.²³ Böhlig pointed to a considerable variation within the Cop^Sa-Prov witnesses and, despite some unique features, a general dependence of Cop^Akh-Prov on Cop^Sa-Prov.²⁴ In his opinion, Cop^Akh-Prov was "translated" from a Sahidic model. Böhlig observed that in some witnesses of Cop^Sa-Prov a recension is visible that is based on a Greek *Vorlage* that in turn adapted the text of LXX-Prov (→ 12.3.1) to MT-Prov (→ 12.2.2), whereas other witnesses of Cop^Sa-Prov and Cop^Akh-Prov show frequently a shorter or different text.²⁵ Böhlig supposed not only a dependence of Cop^Akh-Prov on Cop^Sa-Prov but also wanted to observe an intentional recension at work in Cop^Akh-Prov and its Sahidic *Vorlage*, respectively. This recension "cleansed" its *Vorlage* of additions and changes and corrected it. However, when publishing a parchment leaf from the collection in the Berlin Egyptian Museum (Prov 19:16–20:4),²⁶ the present writer noticed that Cop^Akh-Prov and P. Bodmer VI, as the earliest witnesses of Cop-Prov, follow LXX-Prov (→ 12.3.1) more closely – at least in Prov 19:16–20:4 – than the considerably more recent Sahidic witnesses. This would mean, contrary to Böhlig's supposition, that the later Cop^Sa-Prov tradition (itself still being diverse) underwent a recension after Cop^Akh-Prov and P. Bodmer VI were translated/written in the later fourth century(?) C.E. The recension reworked its text according to a Greek *Vorlage* that adapted LXX-Prov closer to MT.

Unfortunately, the many interesting questions emerging here can only be answered when we possess a critical edition of Cop^Sa-Prov and the *editio critica maior* of LXX-Prov. The reconstruction of the textual history of Cop^Sa-Prov could offer clues to understanding the development of the variations in the textual history of LXX-Prov and,

---

23 Rahlfs-Hanhart, *Septuaginta*, 183–238.
24 Böhlig, *Untersuchungen*, 1–2, 50.
25 Böhlig, *Untersuchungen*, 50–70.
26 F. Feder, "Koptische Bibelfragmente der Berliner Papyrussammlung III: Ein Blatt eines Proverbien-Codex mit Prv 19,16(19)–20,4," in *Liber amicorum: Jürgen Horn zum Dank* (eds. A. Giewekemeyer, G. Moers, and K. Widmaier; Göttinger Miszellen Beihefte 5; Göttingen: Seminar für Ägyptologie und Koptologie, 2009), 25–34.

perhaps, to understanding the early history of LXX in general.

Böhlig, A., *Untersuchungen über die koptischen Proverbientexte* (Stuttgart: Kohlhammer, 1936).
Böhlig, A., *Der achmimische Proverbientext nach Ms. Berol. orient. oct. 987* (Studien zur Erforschung des christlichen Ägyptens 3; Munich: Robert Lerche, 1958).
Böhlig, A., *Proverbien-Kodex/The Book of Proverbs: Faksimile des Codex Ms. or. oct. 987 der Deutschen Staatsbibliothek zu Berlin* (Leipzig: Edition Leipzig, 1963).
Burmester, O.H.E. and E. Dévaud, *Les Proverbes de Salomon: Texte Bohairique* (Vienna: Adolf Holzhausen, 1930).
Cherix, P., *Lexique analytique du parchemin pBodmer VI: Version copte du Livre des Proverbes* (Instruments pour l'Étude des Langues de l'Orient Ancien 2; Lausanne: Éditions du Zèbre, 2000).
Feder, F., "Die koptischen Versionen des Proverbienbuches," in *Christliches Ägypten in der spätantiken Zeit* (ed. D. Bumazhnov; Studien und Texte zu Antike und Christentum 79; Tübingen: Mohr Siebeck, 2013), 1–13.
Kasser, R., *Papyrus Bodmer VI: Livre des Proverbes* (2 vols.; CSCO 194–195 Scriptores Coptici 27–28; Louvain: Secrétariat du CorpusSCO, 1960).
Kosack, W., *Proverbia Salomonis achmimisch, bohairisch und arabisch* (Vetus Testamentum Coptice 1; Bonn: Rudolf Habelt, 1973).
Worrell, W.H., *The Proverbs of Solomon in Sahidic Coptic according to the Chicago Manuscript* (OIP 12; Chicago: University of Chicago Press, 1931).

Frank Feder

12.4.3 Ethiopic Translation(s)

12.4.3.1 Title and Place in the Manuscripts

Without exception, Proverbs circulates as two volumes in Ethiopia; they are entitled respectively መሰያተ ሰሎሞን "Proverbs of Solomon" at Prov 1:1 and ዝዘተግሣጸ ሰሎሞን "These are the Instructions of Solomon" at Prov 25:1, except the latter reads ወዝንቱ ምስሌ ሰሎሞን "And These Are the Proverbs of Solomon" in a few manuscripts. These books always head the Solomonic corpus and are followed by Ecclesiastes (→ 13–17.2.3.3) and Wisdom of Solomon (→ 11.15.5), although not always in that order. In general, scribes place the collection after Job (→ 11.4.3) or Chronicles (→ 20.4.3).

12.4.3.2 Background

Eth-Prov, probably translated before the dawn of the fifth century C.E., is based on LXX (→ 12.3.1). In addition to the observations made below, the sequence of chapters (cf. Prov 30:15–31:9; 25:1–29:27; 31:10–31) and verses (cf. Prov 20:13, 20) confirm a Greek *Vorlage*.

Anyone interested in greater detail about Eth-Prov is at a distinct disadvantage. Pilkington's untimely death and copyright regulations currently limit access to his dissertation;[1] it must be viewed on site at the Bodleian Library. If comments made by his *Doktorvater*, E. Ullendorff, are indicative, its focus was perhaps more linguistic than text-critical.[2] Regardless, its general unavailability is lamentable.

12.4.3.3 Translation Character

The translator of Eth-Prov possessed greater skills in Greek than most of his contemporaries. He seems familiar with more difficult vocabulary (e.g., περιχαράκωσον "secure" Prov 4:8)[3] and rarely resorts to transliteration (cf. ስንዶና "*Səndōna*" = σινδόνας "linen garments" Prov 31:24).

Despite having greater facility in the language, the translator still made errors. Occasionally, he guessed when he encountered unknown words. Thus ኩነኔ "judgment" renders ἀκολάστοις "for the intemperate" in Prov 19:29 while እኩይ "evil" translates the adjective ἀκόλαστον "intemperate" in Prov 20:1. Also, thinking that ἄοκνος "diligent" was related to ὀκνηρός "troublesome," he supplied ኢኮንክ ሀከየ "you were not agitated" for ἄοκνος ἦς "you are diligent" in Prov 6:11a. Presumably, mental lapse best explains the choice of ይነሥሦ "he will investigate" for ζημιουμένου "when he is punished" (Prov 21:11) and መሀበኒ "he gave me" for (δ)εδίδαχέν με "has taught me" (Prov 30:3). The Greek exemplar, written in *scriptio continua*, posed challenges at times. The translator incorrectly divides words: ተሀይጸ ("*Tähäypä*") = τὸ ἧπαρ "the liver" (Prov 7:23) and ዘበ ሕግ "which is in the law" for ἐννόμως "legitimately" (Prov 31:25).

There is some evidence of minor corruption from an earlier period: at Prov 13:12, ፍኖት "path," for example, almost certainly evolved from an original ፍትወት "desire."

12.4.3.4 Text-Critical Value

Disadvantages with Eth-Prov continue with attempts to investigate the text-type of the Greek *Vorlage* (→ 12.3.1). The Göttingen *Septuaginta* volume has yet to appear, so one must rely on the more recent hand editions or Holmes and Parsons.[4] All observations are therefore preliminary.

Among the great uncials, Eth-Prov is closer to Codex Alexandrinus (LXX^A), but it almost never reproduces its unique readings (cf., e.g., the addition at Prov 20:1b). It rarely agrees with Sinaiticus (LXX^S), although there are interesting correspondences with readings supplied by "corrector a" (as also in Ecclesiastes; → 13–17.2.3.3). No unique readings of Vaticanus (LXX^B) surface in Eth-Prov.

However, when the Ethiopic preserves a text found in LXX^{B, S}, and two or three additional codices, LXX[252] consistently appears as a supporting witness. Indeed, Eth-Prov displays notably greater agreement with a number of minuscules. In addition to the strong relationship with LXX[252], the Ethiopic version is consanguineous with LXX[68, 248, 296]. This result is compatible with but slightly different from the textual affinities identified in Ecclesiastes (→ 13–17.2.3.3).

12.4.3.5 Subsequent History

The Old Ethiopic is preserved in a number of witnesses, and it is followed closely in the Transitional Text (→ 1.4.3.7.4). As with several of the other biblical books that differ significantly between the LXX (→ 12.3.1) and Masoretic versions (→ 12.2.2), Proverbs saw only light editing during the Transitional Period. Significant change arrived

---

[1] Pilkington, "Critical Edition."
[2] Ullendorff, "Hebrew, Aramaic, and Greek," 253–54.
[3] English translations from LXX-Prov are according to *NETS.

[4] R. Holmes and J. Parsons, *Vetus Testamentum Graecum cum variis lectionibus*, Vol. 3 (Oxford: Clarendon Press, 1823).

only with the authoritative effort to produce a Standardized Text (→ 1.4.3.7.5). Although the reviser employed a Hebrew manuscript (→ 12.2.2) in addition to the Arabic (→ 12.3.8; → 12.4.8) and perhaps Coptic (→ 12.4.2) versions, the foundation of the Transitional Text remained intact, including the sequence of LXX (→ 12.3.1). Because the reviser was not well versed in Hebrew, he sometimes interpolated unusual renditions. For example, at Prov 10:4, he vocalizes רֹאשׁ עֹשֶׂה כַף־רְמִיָּה "a negligent hand creates poverty" incorrectly: ወርእስ ግብር አልዐሎ እድ "and the chief activity raised the hand."[5] Eth-Prov was also thoroughly revised in the late sixteenth century towards MT (→ 12.2.2). Manuscripts Eth[BN Abb 35, EMIP 881] attest what may be the Academic Recension (→ 1.4.3.7.7). There are some later tendencies toward conflation (cf. Eth[EMIP 1128]), but the Textus Receptus (→ 1.4.3.7.6) actually reverts back to the Transitional Text.

Pilkington, H., "A Critical Edition of the Book of Proverbs in Ethiopic" (PhD diss., Oxford University, 1978).
Ullendorff, E., "Hebrew, Aramaic, and Greek: The Versions Underlying Ethiopic Translations of Bible and Intertestamental Literature," in *The Bible World: Essays in Honor of Cyrus H. Gordon* (eds. G. Rendsburg, et al.; New York: KTAV, 1980), 249–57.

Curt Niccum

12.4.4 Late Syriac Translations

See → 11.4.4 Job, Proverbs, Canticles, and Qohelet in Late Syriac Translations [Job > Secondary Translations].

12.4.5 Armenian Translations

12.4.5.1 Provenance and Date

The translation of Proverbs is of unique interest because, after the invention of the Armenian alphabet, it was the first book of the Bible to be translated into Armenian, in Samosata, Syria, ca. 406 C.E. Further, the translators' names at that time are known: Mashtots' and his students, Hovhan from Ekeghiats' and Hovsēp' from the house of Paghan. For details, see → 1.4.7.1. As for why Proverbs was so chosen, perhaps its form and content lent itself to teaching the alphabet to youths, which, Koriwn says, immediately followed the translation.[1]

12.4.5.2 Source Text of Arm-Prov

As is true of the Armenian biblical corpus generally (→ 1.4.7), the question of the language of the parent text of Arm-Prov – Greek or Syriac; Greek and Syriac? – remains challenging in the absence of a clear statement in the historical record and the lack of critical editions of OG-Prov (→ 12.3.1) and the Armenian. It is a crucial question because it involves the nature of the translation itself – that goes without saying – but it also determines the role that Arm-Prov may play in the textual criticism of Old Greek (→ 1.3.1.1; → 12.3.1) and Syriac (→ 1.3.4; → 12.3.4) text traditions. Further, if Arm-Prov is a witness to the Peshitta, that allegiance might prove significant for the text criticism of the Hebrew Bible.

Given the limitations just stated, I made for this entry a collation of the text and apparatus of Zohrapian's edition of Arm-Prov[2] against the provisional Greek text of Rahlfs[3] for Proverbs 2; 9; and 20. It can be concluded that the parent text of Arm-Prov was a Hexaplaric Greek text (→ 1.3.1.2.7; → 12.3.5): it attests the dislocations of the Old Greek (Prov 30:1–14 to a position following 24:22; Prov 30:15–31:9 to a position following 24:34) and the additions made to Proverbs in the Greek, i.e., there is no Hebrew (e.g., Prov 2:21ab [sub ÷

---

[5] Ullendorff, relying upon Pilkington's work, draws attention to this reading in "Hebrew, Aramaic, and Greek," 254.

[1] Conybeare, "Armenian Version," 120, suggested that Mashtots' source text was a manuscript that contained the second half of the Old Testament and began with Proverbs. Cowe carries this suggestion forward by noting that there are Greek manuscripts that fit this description. He adds that Peshitta (→ 1.3.4) manuscripts are not so arranged (*Daniel*, 436). For his part, Ter-Movsessian thinks a translation of Psalms (→ 10.4.5) already existed, so Mashtots' took up a copy of the next book, Proverbs (*Istoriia*, 21). Indeed, Proverbs follows Psalms in Greek manuscripts like LXX[B S] (but not LXX[A]) and synodical lists of the church. See Swete, *Introduction*, 201–14.
[2] Zohrapian, *Scriptures*.
[3] Rahlfs, *Septuaginta*.

in LXX⁰ ᵐˢˢ: Rahlfs' app.]; 9:12a–c; 19:18a–d; 11:16cd; 13:13a; 25:20a; 27:21a). That the parent text was Hexaplaric is clear from the presence of additions Origen made, and marked with asterisks preserved in some witnesses (e.g., Prov 4:5a [twice], 4.5b fin [see Rahlfs]; 20:14–19 sub asterisk in the Syro-Hexapla [see Ceriani's edition; → 12.3.4]) though not in Armenian manuscripts.

The question of Arm-Prov's parent text is complicated by the fact that s-Prov is, at a minimum, heavily indebted to the Old Greek (→ 12.3.4). In a series of verses where Fox compares the Greek and the Syriac against the Hebrew, Arm-Prov always agrees with the Greek against the Syriac (Prov 5:6; 6:16; 12:23; 13:2; 20:5; 22:15; 24:34; 28:21).[4] My study, though of an exploratory nature, unearthed no instance where Arm-Prov agreed with the Peshitta against the Greek. Therefore it seems most likely that the source text of Arm-Prov was Greek, not Syriac. This comports with the historical record that says Mashtots' sent students to the Greek school in Samosata and that it was there that, shortly later, he translated an unspecified text of Proverbs into Armenian. The Hexaplaric Arm-Prov (→ 12.3.5) that is preserved in the manuscript tradition is not necessarily identical to the translation Mashtots' made. If it is, the Hexaplaric parent text likely came directly from Caesarea to Syria, rather than from Constantinople after the Council of Ephesus (431 C.E.).[5]

12.4.5.3 Character of the Translation of Arm-Prov

Arm-Prov reveals itself to be a more than competent rendering of the Hexaplaric text of Greek Proverbs (→ 12.3.5). It generally follows the word order of the source text, but occasionally changes this for the sake of better style. There are no substantial differences between the text and apparatus of Zohrapian's edition[6] so that the textual tradition – at least as it is represented in Zohrapian – is unitary, not clearly divided between Arm 1 and Arm 2

---

[4] Fox, "How the Peshitta of Proverbs Uses the Septuagint," 41, 44–47.
[5] Cf. → 1.4.7.1 and Cox, "Introduction," xi, in Zohrapian, *Scriptures (1984 edition).
[6] Zohrapian, *Scriptures.

(see → 1.4.7.4 on the distinction; cf. Arm-Qoh, → 13–17.2.5). Arm-Prov reflects features of Arm 1, such as the rendering of participles by relative clauses and the frequent use of compound verbs (noun + verb) to represent Greek verbs, so that the translation belongs to the earlier rather than later stage of translation strategies.

12.4.5.4 Editions

There is no critical edition of the Armenian text so that we are dependent on the diplomatic edition of Zohrapian (1805).[7] This is a reliable resource, though the textual character of the base manuscript in Proverbs remains undetermined, as is also the case with the manuscripts only imprecisely identified in the apparatus.

12.4.5.5 Text-Critical Importance

Arm-Prov promises to be an important Hexaplaric witness (→ 12.3.5) in the textual tradition of OG-Prov (→ 12.3.1). Its date alone, early fifth century C.E., makes it a potentially significant text, and a brief study raised intriguing questions. A critical edition is a *deseridatum*. Further research should attempt to find evidence of any residual contact with the Peshitta (→ 1.3.4; → 12.3.4) or signs of Antiochene exegesis (→ 12.3.6).

Ceriani, A.M., *Codex Syro-hexaplaris Ambrosianus, photolithographice editus, curante et adnotante* (Monumenta sacra et profana 7; Milan: Bibliotheca Ambrosiana, 1874). Online: www.doaks.org/research/byzantine/resources/syriac/bible

Conybeare, F.C., "Armenian Version of the Old Testament," in *A Dictionary of the Bible* (4 vols.; ed. J. Hastings; New York: Scribner's, 1898–1904), 1.151–53 = repr. in *The Armenian Church: Heritage and Identity: Frederick Cornwallis Conybeare* (ed. N.V. Nersessian; New York: St. Vartan Press, 2001), 117–21.

Cowe, S.P., *The Armenian Version of Daniel* (Armenian Texts and Studies 9; Atlanta: Scholars Press, 1992).

Fox, M.V., "LXX-Proverbs as a Text-Critical Resource," *Textus* 22 (2005): 95–128.

Fox, M.V., "How the Peshitta of Proverbs Uses the Septuagint," *JNSL* 39 (2013): 37–52.

---

[7] Zohrapian, *Scriptures.

Rahlfs, *Septuaginta.
Swete, *Introduction.
Ter-Movsessian, M., *Istoriia Perevoda Biblii na Armianskii Yazyk* (*History of the Translation of the Bible into the Armenian Language*) (St. Petersburg: Pyshkinskaia Skoropechatnia, 1902).
Zohrapian, *Scriptures.

Claude Cox

12.4.6 Georgian Translations

12.4.6.1 Sources

Georg-Prov has come down to us in the following sources: palimpsest Georg^Pc (Tbilisi, National Centre of Manuscripts, H-999, fifth–sixth century C.E.), codices Georg^O (= Mount Athos, Library of the Iviron Monastery, geo. 1, 978 C.E., in two volumes), Georg^S (Tbilisi, National Centre of Manuscripts, A-51, seventeenth–eighteenth century), and also the so-called "Bakar Bible" (= Georg^B), the 1743 Moscow printed edition. A full description of these testimonies is to be found in the first volume of the critical edition of the Old Georgian Octateuch.[1] Additional manuscript evidence is provided by lectionaries Georg^P (= Paris, Bibliothèque nationale de France, geo. 3, 1040 C.E.), Georg^G1 (Tbilisi, National Centre of Manuscripts, H-1350, eleventh century) and Georg^G2 (Tbilisi, National Centre of Manuscripts, A-672, thirteenth–fourteenth century).[2]

Furthermore, some sections of the book are included in the Old Georgian version of the *Homilia in principium Proverbiorum* (= CPG 2856) of Basilius of Caesarea, translated in the late tenth century by Eptwme Mtac'mideli.[3]

12.4.6.2 Date, Redactions, Editions

Georg-Prov is available in three redactions. The first (= Georg-Prov 1) is contained in Georg^Pc,P,O, the second (= Georg-Prov 2) is to be found in Georg^S and the third (= Georg-Prov 3) is preserved in the 1743 printed edition, Georg^B.

Manuscript evidence of Georg-Prov 1 has come down to us since the earliest period of Georgian literature. Palimpsest Georg^Pc, dating from the fifth or sixth century C.E., contains Prov 9:1–4. The full text of Georg-Prov 1 is available in codex Georg^O, which presents archaic linguistic traits. Forty-two excerpts of Georg-Prov 1 are also to be found in the lectionary Georg^P, in which the translation is basically the same as in Georg^O, although it frequently features minuses.[4] The origin of Georg^P dates back to the fifth to the eighth centuries C.E.[5] A new version of the lectionary was undertaken by George the Athonite (Giorgi Mtac'mideli, ca. 1009–1065) in the eleventh century and is to be found in manuscripts Georg^G1 and Georg^G2. At times, it preserves the text of Georg^O and Georg^P; however, several sections have been retranslated from Greek (→ 12.3.1).[6]

The origin of Georg-Prov 2 dates from a considerably later period. It was created by the eminent Georgian philologist Sulkhan Saba Orbeliani (1658–1725) at the end of the seventeenth century. Codex Georg^O was not available to him; therefore, in preparing his work he took as a basis both the ancient and the middle-Georgian versions of the lectionary.[7] However, since the latter do not preserve the book in full, he had to produce a new translation for the missing sections of the text. The source he chose for this purpose was the printed Armenian Bible of 1666 (Oskan's edition; → 12.4.5).[8]

Georg-Prov 3 was carried out in the early eighteenth century. It represents a revision of Georg-Prov 1–2 based on the Slavonic Bible printed in Moscow in 1663 (→ 12.4.7). Textual agreement with the former two is frequent in the first half of the

---

[1] C'ignni, 559–72, 609–19, 627–35.
[2] Met'reveli, "Mcxetis bibliis," 108.
[3] Editions: Č'q'onia, "Ioane," 88–116; Kurcik'iʒe, *Basili*, 121–140 (electronic version: http://titus.uni-frankfurt.de/texte/etcg/cauc/ageo/bascaes/baskessc/baske.htm). List of manuscripts: Gabiʒašvili, *3veli kartuli*, 383–384.
[4] Met'reveli, "Mcxetis bibliis," 104.
[5] Tarchnischvili, *Le grand lectionnaire*.
[6] Met'reveli, "Mcxetis bibliis," 109.
[7] On Orbeliani's autographic notes in the margins of lectionary Georg^P, see Met'reveli, "Mcxetis bibliis," 102; Dočanašvili, *Mcxeturi xelnac'eri*, 31.
[8] Dočanašvili, *Mcxeturi xelnac'eri*, 32; Melikišvili, *Bibliur c'ignta targmanebi*, 143; Oskan, *Bible*.

book.[9] The text is accessible in the 1743 printed edition, Georg[B].[10]

The Georg-Prov 1 has been only partially edited (Georg[Pc]'s fragments and Georg[P]'s pericopes).[11] Georg-Prov 2 was published in 1983.[12]

12.4.6.3 Translation Character, Translation Technique, Inner-Translational Features

Over the centuries, Georg-Prov 1 was used as a base text for later versions. Consequently, in the various manuscripts, several sections of the book may be read in a very similar (at times identical) translation. Codices Georg[O, P, S] generally agree with each other, showing common readings that deviate from Georg[B]. However, Georg[S] often differs from the remaining testimonies due to the addition of a number of verses. Therefore, depending on the interdependence of the sources, three redactions for each single section of the book are available.

According to Gigineišvili, Georg-Prov 1 was presumably translated from LXX (→ 12.3.1).[13] In his opinion, the following features bear out this assumption. Firstly, Georg-Prov 1, unlike the two recent revisions, has the same minuses as attested in LXX, namely the omissions of Prov 8:33; 11:4; 15:31; 16:1; 16:3–4; 18:23–19:2.[14] Secondly, it preserves in full Prov 20:9–9c, 24:22–22e. Thirdly, after Prov 24:22e it presents the same arrangement of the sections found in LXX: Prov 30:1–14; 24:23–34; 30:15–33; 31:1–9; 25–29; 31:10–31.[15] These peculiarities distinguish Georg-Prov 1 not only from the remaining Georgian redactions, but also from the Armenian version (→ 12.4.5).[16]

Even if Georg-Prov 1 was translated from LXX, in several instances it features constructs that deviate from the Greek text. According to Gigineišvili, the differences between Georg-Prov 1 and LXX can be explained by the fact that the translator adopted a free translation technique, which takes account of the characteristics of the Georgian language.[17] For instance, in Prov 19:26, Georg-Prov 1 translates the Greek Ὁ ἀτιμάζων πατέρα καὶ ἀπωθούμενος μητέρα αὐτοῦ καταισχυνθήσεται καὶ ἐπονείδιστος ἔσται "he who disgraces his father and drives away his mother will be put to shame and will become rebuked" (*NETS) as რომელი შვილი შეურაცხ-ჰყოფდეს მამასა და განიშორებდეს დედასა თჳსსა, სარცხჳნელ და საყუედრელ იქმნეს "the son who scorns his father and rejects his mother will be shamed and will be blameworthy."

With regard to the textual relationship between the Georg-Prov 1 and the Armenian version, the following observations can here be offered. Unlike the latter (→ 12.4.5.2), the former does not include the Hexaplaric additions (→ 12.3.5) in Prov 4:4–7; 20:16–22,[18] as shown by the readings of Georg[P].[19]

Both Georg-Prov 2 and Georg-Prov 3 are the result of a simultaneous translation and revision process of the ancient textual stratum, Georg-Prov 1, in the form that is found in the lectionaries. Moreover, as already noted above, in both cases their authors have made extensive use of the seventeenth-century Armenian (→ 12.4.5) and OCS (→ 12.4.7) printed editions of the Bible.[20]

12.4.6.4 Text-Critical Value for the Primary Translation

At present, a detailed and definitive account of the textual relationship existing between Georg-Prov and LXX (→ 12.3.1), unfortunately, cannot be offered, since the translation has not yet been collated with Rahlfs' edition,[21] the Proverbs volume of the Göttingen Septuagint is lacking, and Georg-Prov 1 is still unpublished in its entirety. Nevertheless, although a full overview of the textual features

---

[9] Melikišvili, *Bibliur c'ignta targmanebi*, 142.

[10] See: *Biblija*, 1663; *Biblija*, 1743.

[11] The fragments contained in Georg[Pc] were published in 1956 (Molitor, *Monumenta iberica*). The text of Georg[P] is available in Danelia, Čxenk'eli, and Šavišvili, *Kartuli lekcionaris p'arizuli xelnac'eri*, 217–50.

[12] Edited in Dočanašvili, *Mcxeturi xelnac'eri*, 278–318.

[13] Gigineišvili, "Solomonis igavta," 55–56.

[14] See Tov, *Greek-Hebrew Bible*, 431.

[15] See Tov, *Greek-Hebrew Bible*, 429.

[16] Gigineišvili, "Solomonis igavta," 56–57.

[17] Gigineišvili, "Solomonis igavta," 57.

[18] Field, *Hexapla*, 2.317, 352.

[19] See Danelia, Čxenk'eli, and Šavišvili, *Kartuli lekcionaris p'arizuli xelnac'eri*, 222, 238.

[20] Gigineišvili, "Solomonis igavta," 58.

[21] Rahlfs, *Septuaginta*.

is missing, Georg-Prov 1 may be judged to be of text-critical value for its primary translation, especially if one takes into consideration its early origin and a number of textual dissimilarities with the Armenian version (→ 12.4.5). As shown above, this version is faithful to LXX in all instances in which the latter differs from MT (→ 12.2.2). Georg-Prov 1 shares with LXX not only minuses and pluses, but also the major differences in sequence between MT-Prov and LXX-Prov in Proverbs 24–31.

Therefore, even if at a so preliminary stage of research, it is possible to conclude that this manuscript tradition, still almost unexplored in terms of textual criticism, merits full consideration and, accordingly, should be included in future comparative studies on the textual history of LXX-Prov.

Biblia: brzanebita da c'arsagebelita sapasetata sakartvelos mepis bakar vaxt'angis zisata (Moscow: Bakaris st'amba, 1743).

Biblija, sirěč' knigi vetchago i novago zavěta, po jayzku slavensku (Moscow: Pečatnyj dvor, 1663).

C'ignni zuelisa aytkumisani, Vol. 1: *Šesakmisaj, gamoslvataj* (eds. B. Gigineišvili and C. K'ik'vize; Tbilisi: Mecniereba, 1989).

Č'q'onia, T., "Ioane P'et'ric'is 'ganmart'ebis' bolosit'q'vaobis axali c'q'aros šesc'avlisatvis," in *3veli kartuli mc'erlobis otxi 3egli: X–XII sauk'uneta xelnac'erebis mixedvit* (ed. I. Abulaze; Tbilisi: Mecniereba, 1965), 69–125.

Danelia, K., S. Čxenk'eli, and B. Šavišvili (eds.), *Kartuli lekcionaris p'arizuli xelnac'eri: zveli da axali aytkmis sak'itxavebi*, Vol. 1: *Nac'ili I* (Tbilisi: Tbilisis universit'et'is gamomcemloba, 1987).

Dočanašvili, E. (ed.), *Mcxeturi xelnac'eri (t'obis, ivditis, esteris, iobis c'ignebi, psalmuni, igavta c'igni)* (Tbilisi: Mecniereba, 1983).

Gabizašvili, E., *3veli kartuli mc'erlobis natargmni zeglebi: bibliograpia*, Vol. 3: *homilet'ik'a* (Tbilisi: Xelnac'erta erovnuli cent'ri, 2009).

Gigineišvili, B., "Solomonis igavta kartuli redakciebi," *Mravaltavi* 2 (1973): 51–60.

Kurcik'ize, C., *Basili k'esarielis sc'avlata eptvime atoneliseuli targmani* (Tbilisi: Mecniereba, 1983).

Kurcik'ize, C., *Kartuli biblia* (Tbilisi: Xelnac'erta erovnuli cent'ri, 2010).

Melikišvili, N., *Bibliur c'ignta zveli kartuli targmanebi* (Tbilisi: Alilo, 2009).

Met'reveli, E., "Mcxetis bibliis igavta c'ignis c'q'aroebis šesc'avlisatvis," *Mravaltavi* 7 (1980): 98–115.

Molitor, J., *Monumenta iberica antiquiora: Textus Chanmeti et Haemeti: Ex inscriptionibus s. bibliis et patribus* (CSCI Subsidia 10; Louvain: Durbecq, 1956).

Oskan Erevants'i (ed.), *Astuatsashunch' Hnots' ew Norots' Ktakaranats': Neren Parunakōgh* (Scriptures of the Old and New Testaments) (Amsterdam, 1666).

Tarchnischvili, M. (ed.), *Le grand lectionnaire de l'église de Jérusalem* (Ve–VIIIe siècle), Vol. 1. (CSCO 188–89; Scriptores Iberici 9–10; Louvain: Secrétariat du Corpus SCO, 1959).

Alessandro Maria Bruni

12.4.7 Old Church Slavonic Translations

12.4.7.1 Date, Versions, Manuscripts

It is generally assumed that the surviving Old Church Slavonic manuscript tradition of Proverbs contains texts that belong to the earliest corpus of the Slavic Scriptures. On the one hand, a number of readings are to be found in the OCS Prophetologium, a collection of liturgical pericopes translated from LXX-Prov presumably during the Cyrillo-Methodian period (863–885 C.E.).[1] On the other hand, a full OCS version of Proverbs (= OCS-Prov) has come down to us: it is believed to have been carried out by Methodius shortly before his death (885 C.E.).[2] Furthermore, quotations from Proverbs may be found in miscellaneous codices as well as in a number of OCS florilegia containing translations of Byzantine gnomologia.[3]

Up to the present day Slavicists have focused mainly on the study of the OCS translations of Proverbs that are preserved in the Prophetologium and in its derivative traditions, which are to be found in the Croat Glagolitic Breviary and Missal.

---

[1] The earliest copy of the OCS Prophetologium is the codex of the Russian State Library, Moscow, f. 87, no. M 1685 (*Grig. 2*), dating from the late twelfth or early thirteenth century. For general issues related to the liturgical use of the Scriptures, see Alekseev, *Biblija v bogosluženii*.

[2] See ch. 15 of the *Life of Methodius*: Angelov and Kodov, *Kliment Ochridski*, 191; Alekseev, *Tekstologija*, 155.

[3] See: Wątróbska, *The Izbornik*, 151–152; Thomson, "The Slavonic Translation," 831.

In contrast, the alleged Methodian full version of the book remains unpublished and no account of its textual features is currently available. Moreover, a collation with LXX (→ 12.3.1) has yet not been undertaken. Therefore, these circumstances limit the possibility of providing the reader with an appraisal of the text critical value of this tradition for Biblical Studies. This problem remains an open issue which calls for further investigation.

In addition to the vast and still unexplored manuscript legacy dating back to the ninth-tenth centuries C.E., an independent fifteenth-century Ruthenian translation of Proverbs also exists. It was undertaken from MT-Prov (→ 12.2.2) and is to be found in a sixteenth-century codex, kept at the Library of the Lithuanian Academy of Sciences in Vilnius (f. 19, no. 262).[4] This testimony further comprises a second version of only Prov 31:9–31, namely the "Praise of the Virtuous Woman," apparently undertaken (or revised) taking v-Prov as its basis (→ 12.3.7).[5]

12.4.7.2 The Prophetologium and the Croat Glagolitic Sources

The Prophetologium contains Prov 1:1–7:1; 8:1–30; 8:32–10:22; 10:31–11:12; 11:19–12:6; 12:8–13:9; 13:20–14:6; 14:15–15:4; 15:7–29a–b; 16:13, 17–33; 17:17–18:5; 19:16–25; 21:3–21; 21:23–22:4; 23:15–24:5; 29:2; 31:8–31.[6] The Croat Glagolitic Breviary[7] and Missal[8] basically include the same translation as the OCS Prophetologium. It was based on LXX-Prov (→ 12.3.1), but in some instances it was revised by using the Vulgate (→ 12.3.7).[9]

12.4.7.3 The Full OCS Version of Proverbs

The pericopes of Proverbs translated for the OCS Prophetologium were incorporated into the full version, as shown by the inclusion in the latter of a number of additions of liturgical origin. The subdivision of the text in the manuscripts of the complete translation seems to confirm this very impression, although further study is undoubtedly required.[10]

The earliest manuscript sources of the complete translation date back to the second half of the fourteenth century (National Library of Russia, St. Petersburg, F.I.461).[11] The exact number of testimonies has still to be determined, although several codices of the fifteenth to seventeenth centuries have already been listed in existing scholarly publications.[12] When taking into account their linguistic features, they may be divided into two categories: the East-Slavic[13] and South-Slavic sources.[14] As far as the typologies of manuscripts are concerned, they vary from small to larger collections of texts.[15]

---

[4] See: Taube, "The Book of Proverbs," 179–94.

[5] Altbauer, "Ze studiów," 181 (edition of Prov 31:10–31); Thomson, "The Slavonic Translation," 874–75; Temčin, "Scharija i Skorina," 290–93. The translation of the "Praise of the Virtuous Woman" found in a fragment from Mount Athos derives from the ancient OCS translation made from LXX (see Taube, "Praise," 546).

[6] Editions: Brandt, "Grigorovičev parimejnik"; Ribarova and Hauptova, *Grigorovičev Parimejnik*. See also Čermák, "Proverbia," 251–58; and Čermák, "Zu der neueren Erforschung," 333–47.

[7] The First Vrbnik Breviarium contains Prov 1:1–3:18 (Vajs, *Nejstarší Breviář*, 40–49), while the Vitus codex has a longer portion of text, i.e., Prov 1:1–15:3 (Thomson, "The Slavonic Translation," 833–35).

[8] *Vat. Borg. Illir.* 4, fourteenth century (Vajs, *Najstariji hrvatskoglagolski misal*); Schmidt-Deeg, *Das New Yorker Missale*, XIX (list of readings); Reinhart, "The Sapiential Collection," 81.

[9] Čermák, "Proverbia," 251–58; Alekseev, *Tekstologija*, 144; Thomson, *A Brief Survey*, 43.

[10] Čermák, "K nekotorym osobennostjam," 830–31.

[11] Nikolova, "Za naj-starija bălgarski srednovekoven răkopis," 110–18.

[12] Logačev, "Dokumenty," 224; Mathiesen, "Handlist," 59; Thomson, "The Slavonic Translation," 831–34; Taube, "Praise," 546.

[13] See, e.g., the following manuscripts: National Library of Russia, St. Petersburg, *Pogod.* 78 and 227; Library of the Russian Academy of Sciences, St. Petersburg, *Sobr.Srezn.* 24.4.28 ("*Suprasl'skij Sbornik Matfeja Desjatogo*"), 1507 C.E.; Russian State Library, Moscow, f. 310, no. 1, 1480 C.E. and f. 204, no. 189, fifteenth century.

[14] Besides the above mentioned codex F.I. 461, see also: State Historical Museum, Moscow, *Ščuk.* 507, 1475 C.E.; Library of the Romanian Academy, Bucharest, no. 171, fifteenth century.

[15] Mathiesen, "Handlist," 18–34; Mathiesen "Typology," 193–202.

In both East- and South-Slavic sources,[16] the translation presents an arrangement of verses that corresponds to that of LXX (→ 12.3.1):[17] Prov 22:17–24:22; 30:1–14; 24:23–34; 30:15–33; 31:1–9; 25–29; 31:10–31.[18]

According to an East-Slavic codex dating from the sixteenth century (Russian State Library, Moscow, f. 113, no. 605), this translation includes the Hexaplaric pluses in Prov 4:5,7 (fol. 211ᵛ) and 8:29 (215r/v), but omits those in Prov 8:33 (215ᵛ); 16:1,3 (223ᵛ); and 20:14–22 (folios 228r/v).[19] Moreover, this source features a number of additions after Prov 31:31 taken from the books of Proverbs and Wisdom (→ 11.15.9). They are: 1) Wis 5:15–6:3 (folios 241ᵛ–242); 2) Wis 3:1–9 (folios 242–242ᵛ); 3) Wis 4:7–20 (242ᵛ–243ᵛ); 4) Prov 10:31–32 (243ᵛ–244); 5) Prov 29:2–27 (244–245); 6) Wis 4:7–20 (245r/v).

12.4.7.3.1 The Problem of Attributing the Translation to Methodius

According to a number of scholars, the OCS-Prov, along with the earliest OCS versions of Ruth (→ 13–17.2.7), Qohelet (→ 13–17.2.7), Canticles (→ 13–17.2.7), and Ben Sira (→ 11.4.10), belongs undoubtedly to the Methodian corpus, generally characterized by a free rendering of the original. Furthermore, the inclusion of the Prophetologium sections in the full version without having undergone major alteration would suggest that the original Slavic translation of Proverbs needs to be ascribed to Methodius.[20]

This opinion was however challenged on the grounds that this translation contains several errors that reveal an inadequate command of Greek. Nevertheless, the archaic language and some grammatical features, such as the asigmatic aorist, indicate an early origin of the version, which may be attributed confidently to the late ninth century C.E.[21]

Concerning this issue, the following remarks may be added. Speculation on the matter of the translation's authorship is altogether premature, given the lack of adequate research on the topic of translation technique. Moreover, as long as the entire OCS tradition of Proverbs will not be subjected to an in-depth text-critical study, a major task so far completely neglected by scholars in the field, any conclusions in this regard will remain unproven.

12.4.7.3.2 The Late-Fifteenth-Century Gennadian Revision

The alleged Methodian complete translation of Proverbs was corrected towards the Vulgate (→ 12.3.7) in late-fifteenth-century Russia. This revision is to be found in the first full Slavic manuscript corpus of the Scriptures, which is known as the Gennadian Bible (State Historical Museum, Moscow, *Sin.* 915, 1499), in view of the fact that it was assembled under the patronage of Archbishop Gennadius of Novgorod (Gennadij Gonzov, ca. 1410–1505).

While copying OCS-Prov, the editors of the Gennadian Bible noted that after Prov 29:27 the text did not correspond to the Vulgate (→ 12.3.7). Having not realized that this section was already included in the ancient version after Prov 24:22, they retranslated Prov 30:1–14 from the Vulgate. Moreover, they did not correct a number of translation mistakes found in the earliest OCS translation of Proverbs.[22]

The Gennadian redaction was subsequently incorporated with minor amendments, made on the basis of LXX, in the printed Ostrog Bible of 1581, as well as in its derivative Moscow edition of 1663. Finally, it ended up with additional changes in the printed Elizabethan Bible of 1751.[23]

---

[16] In this regard, I have checked the following manuscripts: Russian State Library, Moscow, f. 113, no. 605, sixteenth century, folios 207–241ᵛ; and State Historical Museum, Moscow, *Sčuk.* 507, folios 199–218.

[17] Gorskij and Nevostruev, *Opisanie*, 66–67, 196.

[18] See Tov, *Greek-Hebrew Bible*, 429; Tov, *TCHB*, 304–05.

[19] See respectively Field, *Hexapla*, 2.317, 327, 343 and 352.

[20] Pičchadze, "Cerkovnoslavjanskij," 142; Alekseev, *Tekstologija*, 155–156.

[21] Thomson, "The Slavonic Translation," 832; Thomson, *A Brief Survey*, 37.

[22] Thomson, "The Slavonic Translation," 832.

[23] See respectively *Ostrožskaja biblija*; *Biblija* 1663; and *Biblija* 1751.

12.4.7.4 Text-Critical Value for the Primary Translation

The earliest version of OCS-Prov was undertaken from LXX (→ 12.3.1). However, a precise evaluation of its text-critical value for philological investigation into the latter is unfortunately not possible due to the absence of an edition and a comprehensive study of the entire East and South Slavic manuscript tradition. Furthermore, the translation has never been collated with Rahlfs' work[24] and the Proverbs volume of the Göttingen Septuagint has yet to be published. Firm conclusions about what minuses or pluses are to be found in OCS-Prov are therefore out of the question: on the basis of the preliminary analysis of the above mentioned Moscow codex N° 605 it was only possible to show that this translation is apparently little influenced by the Hexaplaric recension (→ 12.3.5). However, much work has still do be done before the Byzantine prototype of OCS-Prov can be safely identified. Clarifying this aspect, which has hitherto eluded the attention of Slavicists, must indeed be considered crucial when embarking on any future study of OCS-Prov.

The testimony of the Gennadian Bible and of the printed OCS Bibles (1581, 1663 and 1751) has limited relevance for the purposes of the present research, since they preserve contaminated readings that are furthermore influenced by systematic revisions made on the basis of the Vulgate (→ 12.3.7).

Alekseev, A.A., *Tekstologija slavjanskoj Biblii* (Bausteine zur slavischen Philologie und Kulturgeschichte Neue Folge A: Slavistische Forschungen 24; St. Petersburg: Dmitrij Bulanin, 1999).

Alekseev, A.A., *Biblija v bogosluženii: Vizantijsko-slavjanskij lekcionarij* (St. Petersburg: Nestor-Istorija, 2008).

Altbauer, M., "Ze studiów nad wschodniosłowiańskimi przekładami Biblii: o dwóch przekładach biblijnego akrostychu o zacnej niewieście," *Studia Filologii Polskiej i Słowiańskiej* 7 (1969): 179–90.

Angelov, B.S. and C. Kodov (eds.), *Kliment Ochridski: Săbrani săčinenija*, Vol. 3: *Prostranni žitija na Kiril i Metodii* (Sofia: Izdatelstvo na Bălgarska Akademija na naukite, 1973).

Biblija, sirěč' knigi vetchago i novago zavěta, po jayzku slavensku (Moscow: Pečatnyj dvor, 1663).

Biblija, sirěč' knigi svjaščennago pisanija vetchago i novago zavěta (St. Petersburg: Tipografija Aleksandro-Nevskogo monastyrja, 1751).

Brandt, R., "Grigoroviečev parimejnik: v sličenii s drugimi parimejnikami," *Čtenija v Imperatorskom Obščestve istorii i drevnostej rossijskich* 168 (1894): 1–90; 170 (1894): 91–178; 193 (1900): 179–290; 197 (1901): 291–308.

Čermák, V., "Proverbia v charvátskohlaholských breviářích a jejich neslovanské předlohy," *Slavia* 68 (1999): 251–58.

Čermák, V., "K nekotorym osobennostjam členenija slavjanskogo perevoda knigi Pritč v rukopisi F.I.461," in *Problemi na Kirilo-Metodievoto delo i na bălgarskata kultura prez IX–X vek* (ed. S. Nikolova; Kirilo-Metodievski studii 17; Sofia: Bălgarska Akademija na naukite, 2007), 827–31.

Čermák, V., "Zu der neueren Erforschung der Übersetzungen des slavischen Parömienbuchs," *Byzantinoslavica* 66 (2008): 333–47.

Gorskij, A. and K.I. Nevostruev, *Opisanie slavjanskich rukopisej Moskovskoj Sinodal'noj (Patriaršej) biblioteki*, Vol. 1: *Svjaščennoe pisanie* (Moscow: Sinodal'naja tipografija, 1855).

Logačev, K., "Dokumenty Biblejskoj komissii," *Bogoslovskie trudy* 13 (1975): 209–35.

Mathiesen, R., "The Typology of Cyrillic Manuscripts (East Slavic vs. South Slavic Old Testament Manuscripts)," in *American Contributions to the Ninth International Congress of Slavists, Kiev, September 1983*, Vol. 1: *Linguistics* (ed. M.S. Flier; Columbus: Slavica, 1983), 193–202.

Mathiesen, R., "Handlist of Manuscripts Containing Church Slavonic Translations of the Old Testament," *Polata knigopisnaja* 7 (1983): 3–48.

Nikolova, S., "Za naj-starija bălgarski srednovekoven răkopis na Starija Zavet," *Starobălgarska literatura* 28–29 (1994): 110–18.

Ostrožskaja biblija: Fototipičeskoe pereizdanie teksta s izdanija 1581 g. (Moscow: Slovo-Art, 1988).

Pičchadze, A.A., "Perevody Biblii na drevnie jazyki: cerkovnoslavjanskij," *Pravoslavnaja ènciklopedija*, Vol. 5: *Bessonov-Bonveč* (ed. Aleksij, Patriarch Moskovskij i Vseja Rusi II; Moscow: Cerkovno-Naučnyj Centr "Pravoslavnaja ènciklopedija," 2002): 139–47.

Reinhart, J.M., "The Sapiential Collection in the Croatian Glagolitic Missal," in *Proceedings of the Ninth World*

---

[24] Rahlfs, *Septuaginta*.

Congress of Jewish Studies, Jerusalem, August 4–12, 1985, Division D, Vol. 1 (Jerusalem: World Union of Jewish Studies, 1986), 77–84.

Ribarova, Z. and Z. Hauptova, *Grigorovičev Parimejnik*, Vol. 1: *Tekst so kritički aparat* (Skopje: Makedonska Akademija na naukite i umetnostite, 1998).

Ribarova, Z. and Z. Hauptova, *Grigorovičev Parimejnik*, Vol. 2: *Leksika* (Skopje: Makedonska Akademija na naukite i umetnostite, 2014).

Schmidt-Deeg, E.-M., *Das New Yorker Missale: Eine kroato-glagolitische Handschrift des frühen 15. Jahrhunderts: Kritische Edition* (Munich: Otto Sagner, 1994).

Taube, M., "The 'Praise of the Virtuous Woman' from Hilandar," *Slovo* 56–57 (2006–2007): 545–58.

Taube, M., "The Book of Proverbs in Vilnius 262," in *The Bible in Slavic Tradition* (A. Kulik et al. (eds.); Studia Judaeoslavica 9; Leiden: Brill, 2016), 179–94.

Temčin, S.J., "Scharija i Skorina: ob istočnikach Vilenskogo Vetchozavetnogo svoda (F 19–262)," *Senoji Lietuvos Literatūra* 21 (2006): 289–316.

Thomson, F.J., "The Slavonic Translation of the Old Testament," in *The Interpretation of the Bible: The International Symposium in Slovenia* (ed. J. Krašovec; JSOTSup 189; Sheffield: Sheffield Academic Press, 1998): 605–920.

Thomson, F.J., *A Brief Survey of the History of the Church Slavonic Bible from its Cyrillomethodian Origin until its Final Form in the Elizabethan Bible of 1751* (Gent: Slavica Gandensia, 33-2, 2006).

Vajs, J., *Nejstarší Breviář hrvatsko-hlaholský (Prvý Breviář Vrbnický)* (Praha: Nákl. Král. České Společnosti Náuk, 1910).

Vajs, J., *Najstariji hrvatskoglagolski misal: s bibliografskim opisima svih hrvatskoglagolskih misala* (Zagreb: Jugoslavenska akademija znanosti i umjetnosti, 1948).

Wątróbska, H., *The Izbornik of the XIIIth Century: Cod. Leningrad, GPB, Q.p.I.18. Text in Transcription* (Nijmegen: Polata knigopisnaja, 19–20, 1987).

Alessandro Maria Bruni

12.4.8 Arabic Translations

12.4.8.1 Background

By the turn of the tenth and eleventh centuries, at least two disparate versions of the Arabic book of Proverbs had appeared. One version represents a free translation from the Syriac Peshiṭta (→ 12.3.4) whose earliest text witness is dated to the year 1002 C.E. The second version appears to be translated from LXX (→ 12.3.1) and transmitted in liturgical collections. The earliest representative of the latter is attested in a manuscript dated to the tenth century. Another Greek-based version, of which the earliest surviving manuscript dates to the sixteenth century, was selected for the Polyglot editions (→ 1.4.11).

12.4.8.2 Text Types, Manuscripts, Tools

Modern scholarship on the Arabic Proverbs is still in its infantile stage and only a handful of scholarly works relate to this neglected book. Graf lists three groups of manuscripts as containing the Arabic Proverbs.[1] The first group represents a translation from LXX (→ 12.3.4) that is transmitted in several homogenous manuscripts. In this version, Proverbs is divided into two books: "Parables" (Arab. *'amṯāl*) containing Proverbs 1–24; 30; 31:1–9 and "Education" (Arab. *'ādāb*) comprising Proverbs 25–29; 31:10–31. This Arabic version, whose translator is as yet unknown to us, was selected for the Paris Polyglot edition[2] and printed according to manuscript Paris, BNF, Ar. 1 (fols. 397r–406v) dated to 1584/1585.[3] The same version was edited with minor modifications by de Lagarde and printed in 1876.[4] It is attested in a number of additional manuscripts, among these are manuscript Vatican, Ar. 468 (fols. I: 459v–475r; II: 475v–479r) dated to 1578/1579 and manuscript Borg., Syr. 28 (karš. fols. 1r–30r, chapter division according to the Vulgate) dated to 1581. The former manuscript is undoubtedly reminiscent of the Arabic translation of Proverbs published in *Biblia Sacra Arabica (the

---

[1] Graf, *GCAL* 1, 127–31. Unfortunately, this work is not free of errors. Most importantly, it is not always clear whether references are to class marks or to catalogue numbers. For converting catalogue numbers of manuscripts of the Coptic Orthodox Patriarchate and the Coptic Museum to class marks, a helpful tool is K. Samir, *Tables de concordance des manuscrits arabes chrétiens du Caire et du Sinaï* (CSCO 482 Subsidia 75; Leuven: Peeters, 1986).

[2] Le Jay, *Biblia*.

[3] For a reprint of this manuscript, see Walton, *Polyglotta*, 3.1652–57.

[4] Lagarde, *Psalterium, Job, Proverbia*.

Propaganda Fide edition) dated 1671–1673, though the latter was extensively altered upon printing.[5]

In the Sinai collection, we find another version of Proverbs that is not mentioned by Graf but likewise appears to be translated from LXX (→ 12.3.1). It is transmitted in the *Prophetologion*, i.e., collections of biblical lectionaries mostly from the Christian Old Testament that are read during the church year. The earliest witness thereof is contained in manuscript Sinai Ar. 588, an ancient parchment triple palimpsest dated to the tenth century. The same translation is attested in, for example, mss Sinai Ar. 595 (dated 1290) and Sinai Ar. 18 (dated 1350).[6]

The second group referred to by Graf is represented by a Syriac-based translation attributed to al-Ḥāriṯ ibn Sinān ibn Sinbāṭ from Ḥarrān who was active in the tenth century. The famous Coptic scholar Abū al-Barakāt Ibn Kabar (early fourteenth century) writes in ch. 6 of *Lamp of Darkness* that al-Ḥāriṯ translated Solomon's four books of Wisdom into Arabic, that is Proverbs, Ecclesiastes, Song of Solomon, and Wisdom of Solomon. This statement corresponds well with the introduction to Solomon's books provided in the sixteenth-century London manuscript BL, Or. 1326 (fol. 184 r), where we read:

نبتدي بعون الله وحسن توفيقه بنقل كتاب حكمة سليمان بن داود ملك اسرايل مما ترجمه الحرت بن سنان

We begin with the help of God and in the goodness of His favor to transmit the book of the Wisdom of Solomon, son of David, king of Israel, from that which al-Ḥāriṯ b. Sinān translated.

According to Graf, the attribution to al-Ḥāriṯ is given only in connection to the book of Wisdom of Solomon but the statement by Abū al-Barakāt and the translation character are indicative of the common authorship of all four books.

This version of Proverbs is commonly preceded by a prologue in which the translator treats various subjects, such as the use of acrostics in Greek, Syriac, and Hebrew, the content of Solomon's books of Wisdom with special attention given to the Proverbs, as well as the use of parables and riddles in the Bible. On occasion, the same prologue is attached to the Wisdom of Solomon.

The earliest witness of al-Ḥāriṯ's translation is preserved in manuscript Mingana Ar. Christ. 121 (Add. 199), which is dated to the tenth century on paleographical grounds.[7] This manuscript consists of only three leaves confined to the prologue. Fuller versions of al-Ḥāriṯ's translation are attested in manuscripts Florence, Pal. Med., Or. 78 (formerly 18) (fols. 31ᵛ–83ʳ); Paris, BNF, Ar. 50 (dated to the sixteenth century; fols. 60ᵛ–91ʳ); London, BL, Or. 1326 (Ar. Suppl. 1) (dated to 1585–1587 C.E.; fols. 190–99); and in many other manuscripts not predating the seventeenth century.[8]

Subsequent to a preliminary study by the current author, we may add two considerably older Sinai manuscripts to the above recension, namely Sinai Ar. 597, which contains the books of Daniel and Proverbs dated 1002, and Sinai Ar. 500 dated to the twelfth or thirteenth century.[9] The latter manuscript appears to be partly revised according to LXX (→ 12.3.1).

---

[5] The *Sacra Arabica* text is attested in a number of manuscripts now in the collections of the Coptic Orthodox Patriarchate and Coptic Museum in Cairo; see Graf, *CGAL* 1, 128–29. This version was adopted by American missionaries but revised according to MT (→ 12.2.2) and printed in 1834 in Malta; it is supplemented with a French translation and entitled ʾAmtāl Sulaimān al-ḥākim. For a discussion of Vatican, Ar. 468, see A. Vaccari, "La Storia d'Una Bibbia Araba," *Bib* 11 (1930): 350–55; A. Vaccari, "Una Bibbia Araba: Per Il Primo Gesuita Venuto Al Libano," *Mélanges de l'Université Saint-Joseph* 10.4 (1925): 79–104; and S. Euringer, "Zum Stammbaum der Arabischen Bibelhandschriften Vat. ar. 468 und 467," *Zeitschrift für Semitistik und Verwandte Gebiete* 7 (1929): 259–73.

[6] Atiya, *The Arabic Manuscripts*, 24 (no. 3).

[7] A. Mingana, *Catalogue of the Mingana Collection of Manuscripts Now in the Possession of the Trustees of the Woodbrooke Settlement, Selly Oak, Birmingham*, Vol. 3: *Additional Christian Arabic and Syriac Manuscripts* (Cambridge: W. Heffer and Sons, Limited, 1939).

[8] For additional manuscripts, see Graf, *GCAL* 1, 129–30.

[9] Atiya, *The Arabic Manuscripts*, 18, 24.

A comparison follows of the rendering of Prov 1:7 in manuscript Sinai Ar. 597 with that in manuscript London, BL, Or. 1326; the former is identical except for a change from first person plural "we know" to second person singular "you know":

[ولكن ينبغي ان تعلم /نعلم ان] اول الحكمة خشية الله فاما الاثمة فيزرون بالعلم والادب

[But it is necessary that you/we know that] the beginning of wisdom is the fear of God and as to the wicked, they despise learning and education.

This rendition diverges from the substantially longer version given in LXX (→ 12.3.1) and the Syro-Hexapla (→ 11.4.4) but corresponds well with the Peshiṭta (→ 12.3.4), which reads: "the beginning of wisdom is the fear of the Lord [but] the wicked despise knowledge and education." The Arabic text unit "But it is necessary that you know that" has no translation equivalent in any known *Vorlage* and is attested only in the manuscripts containing al-Ḥāriṯ's translation.

Graf finally lists a number of manuscripts whose origin is unknown. Among these we find manuscripts Leipzig, Univ. Or., 1057 (fols. 3ʳ–84ᵛ); the bilingual Coptic-Arabic London, BL, Copt. 724 (Ar. Suppl. 794 = Add. 18, 997) dated 1796 (fols. 2ʳ–49ᵛ); London, BL, Copt. 725; and St. Petersburg, Russian National Library, Or. 3 dated 1205 C.E. (pp. 17–45).

12.4.8.3 Translation Character and Translation Technique

Since virtually no research has been dedicated to the translation character and technique of Arab-Prov, we can only give preliminary remarks and relate these findings to the Arabic traditions of which we know more.[10]

Although a thorough study on text type and technique is highly desirable, we may conclude that the anonymous version printed in the Polyglots based on LXX (→ 12.3.4) appears to be relatively faithful to its *Vorlage*. Compare Prov 1:2–3 where the Arabic text carefully reflects LXX:

γνῶναι σοφίαν καὶ παιδείαν νοῆσαί τε λόγους φρονήσεως δέξασθαί τε στροφὰς λόγων νοῆσαί τε δικαιοσύνην ἀληθῆ καὶ κρίμα κατευθύνειν

To learn wisdom and discipline, to understand words of prudence and to grasp subtlety of words and to understand true righteousness and to direct judgment (*NETS)

اعرف حكمة وادبا تفهم اقوال الفطنة اقبل حجج الاقوال افهم العدل المحق والانصاف المثقف

Know wisdom and education and perceive words of understanding, receive words of argument, understand true justice and fair equity

The differences in translation character and techniques between the above version and the Syriac-based translation attributed to al-Ḥāriṯ is immediately observed. The translator of the latter did not hesitate to add textual units that had no equivalent in any known *Vorlage* as a means of enhancing the cohesiveness of the Arabic text. The following example is from Prov 1:2–3 (the underlined words are missing in all *Vorlagen* and were added by the Arabic translator):

ܠܡܕܥ ܚܟܡܬܐ ܘܡܪܕܘܬܐ ܘܠܡܣܬܟܠܘ ܡܠܐ ܕܒܘܝܢܐ P
ܘܡܩܒܠܘ [3] ܡܠܦܢܘܬܐ ܘܙܕܝܩܘܬܐ ܘܕܝܢܐ ܘܬܪܝܨܘܬܐ

to know wisdom and instruction and to perceive words of understanding; [3] to receive cultivation and fear and righteousness and judgement and guidance

[هذه امثال ...] كتبها لنتعلم بها الادب والحكمة ونعرف بها فهم الكلام [3] ويقبل بها المتعلمون الادب وخشية الله والبر والحكومة والعدل

[These proverbs ...] he wrote so that we may learn through them education and wisdom and through them comprehend the understanding of speech and through them the learned men receive education and fear of God and righteousness, and wisdom and justice.

---

[10] The Arabic samples presented here are extracted from M. Lindgren Hjälm, *Christian Arabic Versions of Daniel: A Comparative Study of Early MSS and Translation Techniques in MSS Sinai Ar. 1 and 2* (Leiden: Brill, 2016).

12.4.8.4 Text-Critical and Literary Value

The disparities in translation character and technique between al-Ḥāriṯ's Syriac-based translation and the LXX-based version included in the Polyglots conforms with what we know to be a common trend among many Arabic translations of the Christian Old Testament (→ 18.4.8).

Although the latter translation may be of value for the criticism of LXX (→ 12.3.1), al-Ḥāriṯ's version displays many free translation techniques that compromise its value for textual criticism. The Arabic translations are to be regarded primarily as documents in their own right. As such, they have the ability to initiate us into the literary and intellectual ideals of the remote world of early Christian Arabic literature.

Atiya, A.S., *The Arabic Manuscripts of Mount Sinai: A Hand-List of the Arabic Manuscripts and Scrolls Microfilmed at the Library of the Monastery of St. Catherine, Mount Sinai* (Baltimore: John Hopkins Press, 1955).

Atiya, A.S., *Al-Fahāris al-Tahīliyya li-Makhṭūṭāt ṭūr Sīnā al-ʿarabiyya* (trans. J.N. Youssef; Alexandria: Munšaʿat al-Maʿārif, 1970).

Graf, *GCAL 1.

de Lagarde, P., *Psalterium, Job, Proverbia: Arabice* (Göttingen: W.F. Kaestner, 1876).

Walton, *Polyglotta, Vol. 3.

Miriam Lindgren Hjälm

13–17
Five Scrolls

∴

13
Ruth

∴

13.1 Textual History of Ruth

13.1.1 Extant Witnesses

The oldest manuscripts of Ruth derive from the late Second Temple period are 2QRuth[a],[1] and 4QRuth[a],[2] both dated to the first century B.C.E. From the first century C.E., there are 2QRuth[b] (2Q17; Baillet, *DJD* III, 71–74) and 4QRuth[b] (4Q105; Ulrich and Murphy, *DJD* XVI, 187–89).[3] However, all Ruth manuscripts from Qumran are fragmentary (→ 13.2.1).

Manuscripts of the received MT (→ 13.2.2) date from the Middle Ages, e.g., the Aleppo Codex from 925 C.E. (MT[A]), the Leningrad Codex from 1008/1009 C.E. (MT[L]), and Cambridge Univ. Libr. Add. Ms. 1753 (MT[Y]; fifteenth-sixteenth century) (→ 13.2.2.1; → 10–20.1).

The oldest complete manuscript of LXX-Ruth is Codex Vaticanus (fourth century C.E.; → 13–17.1.1.1). From the Hexapla, six fragments have survived altogether (Field, *Hexapla*; → 2.4.6).

As to Latin witnesses, only one manuscript of VL contains Ruth: Madrid, Bibl. Univ. 31, fol. 80[v]–81[v][4] (→ 13–17.2.1.1).

The oldest extant Syriac witness is Codex Ambrosianus (approx. 600 C.E.; Milan, Ambrosian Library, B.21. Inf. 7.1). In many cases, the Peshitta version points to a *Vorlage* different from MT[5] (for a different view, see → 13–17.1.4.1.4). In contrast to this, the Targum (→ 13–17.1.3) represents MT. The oldest manuscript is Vat. Library, Man. Urbinas Ebr. 1, dated 1294 C.E.[6]

13.1.2 History of Research

Research into the text of Ruth is much in line with the general history of textual studies. Until the sixteenth century, the Greek and Latin texts provided the basis for the theological and philological study. From early on, Genesis through Ruth were treated as one biblical unit called the "Octateuch." Due to the importance of these books for biblical history and theology, there is a great number of Octateuch manuscripts, whose textual value for Ruth has not yet been systematically examined.[7]

Of central interest for textual studies in general, and for Ruth in particular, are Rahlfs' studies *Das Buch Ruth griechisch als Probe einer kritischen Handausgabe der Septuaginta* and *Studie über den griechischen Text des Buches Ruth*. Within Rahlfs' project of a reliable edition of LXX-Ruth and also a sound theory of textual history, Ruth served as the topic for a pilot study. The reason was pragmatic, due to the shortness and simplicity of the book. Rahlfs succeeded in drawing a model of textual families and textual history that served as a paradigm for LXX studies.[8] His LXX "Handausgabe"[9] serves as the basic text for most of the subsequent editions of the Hebrew (*BHQ*) and Greek texts.

13.1.3 Ancient Translations

13.1.3.1 LXX

The existing Greek version of Ruth (→ 13–17.1.1.1) bears some features characteristic of the so-called *kaige* recension (Ruth 1:5; 2:15, 16, 21; 3:12; 4:10, and 4:4; → 1.3.1.2). According to Barthélemy,[10] this points to Ruth's affiliation with this recension. In this case, the original Old Greek translation

---

[1] M. Baillet, "16. Ruth (premier exemplaire)," *DJD* III.1: 71–74.

[2] E. Ulrich and C.M. Murphy, "Ruth," *DJD* XVI: 187–94 (187–89).

[3] M. Baillet, "17. Ruth (second exemplaire)," *DJD* III.1: 74–75; Ulrich and Murphy, "Ruth," 191–94; for a recently found "small scroll," see T. Elgvin, "MS 5441 (4Q(?)Ruth, Ruth 2.1–2)," in *Gleanings*, forthcoming.

[4] Cantera Ortiz de Urbina, *Vetus Latina – Rut*.

[5] Gerleman, *Ruth*, 3–4.

[6] For a complete overview of witnesses, see de Waard, "Introductions: Ruth," 5*–7*.

[7] See Brandt, *Endgestalten des Kanons*, 174–77. An example can be found in Hill and Petruccione, *Theodoret of Cyrus: The Questions on the Octateuch*.

[8] For a full appreciation, see Jellicoe, *SMS*, 12–16.

[9] Rahlfs, *Septuaginta*.

[10] Barthélemy, *Critique textuelle 1982*, 69.

of Ruth has been lost. However, Bons states that while LXX-Ruth bears traits attributed to the *kaige* recension, it may not have been part of it.[11] It is possible that the now-existing LXX-Ruth had these characteristics right from the beginning. At any rate, the LXX readings point to a *Vorlage* not too different from MT and its predecessors.[12] Most differences can be ascribed to "[t]he desire of the translator to produce a receptor language text which could be well understood" (Ruth 1:15; 1:14; 4:7; 1:2; 4:16).[13]

13.1.3.2 Peshitta

A critical edition of S-Ruth (→ 13–17.1.4.1) is not available in 2015. The Peshitta may have used a Greek *Vorlage*, which may have been very similar to LXX. It often agrees with LXX against MT[14] (Ruth 1:5; 1:14; 1:15; 1:18; 2:13; 3:8; for a different view, see → 13–17.1.4.1.4). On the other hand, some Peshitta features point to a *Vorlage* different from LXX, and maybe reflecting not only a different Greek text but also a different Hebrew text that served as the basis. The Peshitta has some minuses (Ruth 1:6, 7, 12; 2:1, 6, 12, 16; 4:3, 16) and also some pluses compared to MT (Ruth 1:8, 10, 14, 18; 3:16).[15]

13.1.3.3 Latin Translations

Ruth was one of the last books translated by Jerome (ca. 405–406 C.E.). His *Vorlage* may have been slightly different from MT. Interestingly, he sometimes agrees with 4QRuth^a (Ruth 1:2) and 2QRuth^b (Ruth 3:14) against MT. Most of the Vulgate variants however, can be explained by reasons of translation technique, stylistic features, or theological reasons (see → 13–17.1.7).

The VL (→ 13–17.2.1.1) remarkably supports MT without aligning with any known Greek evidence.[16]

---

[11] See Bons, "Die Septuaginta-Version des Buches Ruth," 202–24.
[12] Harl–Dorival–Munnich, *Bible grecque*, 159–60.
[13] De Waard, *BHQ, 6*. For a detailed analysis, see C. Ziegert, "Das Buch Ruth in der Septuaginta als Modell einer integrativen Übersetzungstechnik," *Bib* 89 (2008): 221–51.
[14] See Gerleman, *Ruth*, 3.
[15] See Gerleman, *Ruth*, 4.
[16] De Waard, *BHQ, 6*.

In these cases – Ruth 2:14; 3:7; 4:8, 11 – VL is always in agreement with the Targum.[17] Although the Targum's underlying text seems to be MT, the VL variants make it possible that a slightly different Hebrew text existed.

13.1.4 Textual History

As in almost every biblical book, a textual history of Ruth prior to the earliest manuscripts remains conjectural. Following the current consensus, Ruth is a work of the late Persian period (fifth–fourth centuries B.C.E.).[18] The late insertion of Ruth 1:1a and 4:18–22 has been suggested. If they date from the second century B.C.E., as Zenger suggests,[19] these insertions cannot be proven from the Qumranic evidence as the Qumran fragments do not cover these verses. In the words of de Waard, "[s]ometimes, the Qumran evidence is so fragmentary that almost nothing can be concluded ... Where it can be deciphered, it frequently supports MT (Ruth 1:14; 2:14; 2:20; 3:7)."[20] Regarding the textual variation in Hebrew sources and the ancient translations, see above, → 13.1.1 and → 13.1.2.

By and large, the text of Ruth shows a remarkable stability right from its very beginning. Most variants in any of the witnesses are due to stylistic reasons, and seldom to theological or moral reasons. Whether once variant literary editions existed that were notably different from MT (→ 13.2.2), and, if so, how many and to what extent, is impossible to say. Nevertheless, the variations point to a living tradition of textual transmission, often improving the small book of Ruth or clarifying its stylistic features.

Baars, W., "Review: Vetus Latina – Rut: Estudio crítico de la versión latina prejeronimiana del libro de Rut," *VT* 18 (1968): 125–27.
Barthélemy, *Critique textuelle 1982*.
Berger, S., *Notice sur quelques textes latins inédits de l'Ancien Testament* (Paris: Impr. nationale, 1893).

---

[17] De Waard, *BHQ, 6*.
[18] For a discussion, see Köhlmoos, *Ruth*, xiv–xvi.
[19] Zenger, *Rut*, 52.
[20] De Waard, *BHQ, 5*.

Bons, E., "Die Septuaginta-Version des Buches Ruth," *BZ* 42 (1998): 202–24.

Brandt, P., *Endgestalten des Kanons: Das Arrangement der Schriften Israels in der jüdischen und christlichen Bibel* (BBB 131; Berlin: Philo, 2001).

Brooke–McLean, **The Old Testament in Greek*, Vol. 1.4 (1917).

Cantera Ortiz de Urbina, J., *Vetus Latina – Rut: Estudio crítico de la versión latina prejeronomiana de libro de Rut* (Textos y estudios del Seminario Filologico Cardenal Cisneros 4; Madrid: C.S.I.C., 1965).

*DJD III.

*DJD XVI.

Field, **Hexapla*.

Gerleman, G., *Ruth, Das Hohelied* (BKAT 18; Neukirchen-Vluyn: Neukirchener, 1965).

Harl–Dorival–Munnich, **Bible grecque*.

Hill, R.C. and J. Petruccione (transl.), *Theodoret of Cyrus: The Questions on the Octateuch: On Leviticus, Numbers, Deuteronomy, Joshua, Judges, and Ruth* (Washington: Catholic University of America Press, 2008).

Jellicoe, **SMS*.

Köhlmoos, M., *Ruth* (ATD 9.2; Göttingen: Vandenhoeck & Ruprecht, 2009).

Levine, É., *The Aramaic Version of Ruth* (AnBib 58; Rome: Pontifical Biblical Institute, 1973).

Rahlfs, A., *Das Buch Ruth griechisch als Probe einer kritischen Handausgabe der Septuaginta* (Stuttgart: Privileg. Württ. Bibelanstalt, 1923).

Rahlfs, A., *Studie über den griechischen Text des Buches Ruth* (MSU 3.2; Berlin: Wiedmannsche Buchhandlung, 1922).

de Waard, J., "Introductions: Ruth," in **BHQ* 18, *5–*7.

de Waard, J. and E.A. Nida, *A Translator's Handbook on the Book of Ruth* (2nd ed.; New York: United Bible Societies, 1992).

Zenger, E., *Rut* (ZBK; Zurich, 1986).

Melanie Köhlmoos

13.2 Ancient Hebrew Texts

13.2.1 Ancient Manuscript Evidence

Five Hebrew Ruth manuscripts are preserved from antiquity among the manuscripts from Qumran caves 2 and 4. Extensive damages make the text-typological classification for all five manuscripts difficult, if not impossible.

13.2.1.1 2QRuth[a] (2Q16)

The eight heavily damaged frgs. of 2QRuth[a] can be identified as cols. IX–XIII (frgs. 1–7) and XVI (frg. 8) of the original scroll. They attest to remnants of Ruth 2:13–3:8 and 4:3–4. Paleographically, 2QRuth[a] resembles the early Herodian formal hands of 1QpHab and 4QDeut[j] (4Q37) and thus can be dated to the last third of the first century B.C.E.[1] In its orthography, 2QRuth[a] resembles MT except for some more defective and more plene readings. In 152 extant words and remnants of words, 2QRuth[a] attests to three small non-aligned readings against MT (→ 13.2.2) and LXX (→ 13–17.1.1.1). 2QRuth[a] is thus rather close to the consonantal text of MT,[2] and can therefore be classified as proto-Masoretic.[3]

13.2.1.2 2QRuth[b] (2Q17)

Of 2QRuth[b], only two heavily damaged fragments survive. Only the text of frg. 1 can still be identified. It preserves twenty-six words and remnants of words from Ruth 3:13–18. Baillet compares 2QRuth[b] with 1QIsa[b] paleographically and dates it to the third quarter of the first century B.C.E.[4] With the exception of one more plene spelling, the orthography of 2QRuth[b] follows that of MT (→ 13.2.2). A text-typological classification is not possible because of the small amount of preserved text. That 2QRuth[b] reads twice non-aligned and once with one LXX manuscript (→ 13–17.1.1.1) could point to the non-aligned character of 2QRuth[b].[5]

13.2.1.3 4QRuth[a] (4Q104)

Of 4QRuth[a], only one fragment with remnants of Ruth 1:1–12 is preserved. The manuscript is written in the late Hasmonean hand of the middle of the first century B.C.E. The only extant supralinear correction is *prima manu*.[6] The manuscript follows the orthographic system of MT but attests to six orthographic variants.[7] In the seventy-eight preserved words and remnants of words, 4QRuth[a] reads three times with and twice against MT (→ 13.2.2), once with and three times against LXX (→ 13–17.1.1.1), as well as once with and once against 4QRuth[b]. The small amount of preserved text makes definite text-typological conclusions difficult. The evidence could point to a semi-Masoretic text.[8]

13.2.1.4 4QRuth[b] (4Q105)

The four extant fragments of 4QRuth[b] come from the first two columns of the original scroll. The thirty-two preserved words and remnants of words are from Ruth 1:6–11, 12–15. 4QRuth[b] was copied in a Herodian book hand from the end of the first century B.C.E. The only extant supralinear correction is *prima manu* (above frg. 4 line 3; Ruth 1:13).[9] As only thirty-two words and remnants of words are preserved in 4QRuth[b], reaching conclusions regarding its orthography and text type are

---

[1] For the material reconstruction of 2QRuth[a] and its paleography, see Baillet, "premier exemplaire," 72. Baillet still refers to 4QDeut[j] as 4QDeut[d].

[2] Cf. Campbell, *Ruth*, 40; Bons, "Septuaginta-Versionen," 205.

[3] This is all the more the case because 2QRuth[a] reads שמל[תיך "your [garm]ents" in Ruth 3:3 with three versions that stand in the Masoretic tradition (S, V, T) against שִׂמְלֹתַ֖יִךְ "your garment" in MT[L] (cf. LXX).

[4] Baillet, "second exemplaire," 74.

[5] Thus Baillet, "second exemplaire," 74: "manifeste une certaine indépendance"; cf. Campbell, *Ruth*, 40–41, and Bons, "Septuaginta-Versionen," 205.

[6] For the paleography of 4QRuth[a], see Ulrich and Murphy, "Ruth," 188.

[7] See Ulrich and Murphy, "Ruth," 188.

[8] Cf. G.W. Nebe, "Qumranica I: Zu unveröffentlichten Handschriften aus Höhle 4 von Qumran," *ZAW* 106 (1994): 307–22, esp. 309; Campbell, *Ruth*, 40; Ulrich and Murphy, "Ruth," 188.

[9] For the material reconstruction of the paleography of 4QRuth[b], cf. Ulrich and Murphy, "Ruth," 193.

difficult, if not impossible. In what is preserved, the manuscript employs the orthographic system known from MT but twice reads more plene than MT-Ruth. Textually, 4QRuth[b] reads twice with and five times against MT (→ 13.2.2), never with and five times against LXX (→ 13–17.1.1.1), and attests to five non-aligned readings. In two of the five non-aligned readings the textual differences cannot be rendered into Greek. The material reconstruction leaves no doubt that 4QRuth[b] has a shorter text than MT-Ruth and LXX-Ruth in Ruth 1:2–4.[10] In Ruth 1:14, 4QRuth[b] agrees with MT in lacking the long text of LXX-Ruth. Thus, 4QRuth[b] cannot be compared text-typologically with 2QRuth[a,b], 4QRuth[a], MT-Ruth, and LXX-Ruth.[11] Although the preserved text does not allow for a text-typological classification, 4QRuth[b] resembles a non-aligned text.

13.2.1.5 Manuscript Schøyen 5441[12]

Of this manuscript one small fragment is extant which attests to nine words out of Ruth 2:1–2. Manuscript Schøyen 5441 is most likely a biblical manuscript and less likely a Ruth quotation in a non-biblical text because Ruth 2:1–2 include narrative text and the beginning of direct speech by Ruth. Michael Langlois describes the script of manuscript Schøyen 5441 as a semiformal but hesitant late Herodian hand from the middle of the first century C.E.[13] For an orthographic or a texttypological classification of this manuscript, not enough text survives. It remains equally uncertain if the fragment was found in one of the Qumran caves or at one of the other sites around the Dead Sea.

---

[10] See Ulrich and Murphy, "Ruth," 191, 193–94; cf. also Campbell, *Ruth*, 41.

[11] Contra Ulrich and Murphy, "Ruth," 192. I cannot comprehend why Bons, "Septuaginta-Versionen," 206, claims that 4QRuth[b] attests only to minor differences from MT-Ruth.

[12] I am indebted to Torleif Elgvin who provided me with a preprint copy of his edition of manuscript Schøyen 5441 ("MS 5441"). The information given below about this manuscript depends on Elgvin's publication.

[13] M. Langlois, "Palaeographical Analysis of the Dead Sea Scrolls," in *Gleanings*, forthcoming.

Baillet, M., "16. Ruth (premier exemplaire)," *DJD III.1: 71–74.

Baillet, M., "17. Ruth (second exemplaire)," DJD III.1: 74–75.

Bons, E., "Die Septuaginta-Versionen des Buches Rut," BZ 42 (1998): 202–24, esp. 205–06.

Campbell, E.F., *Ruth: A New Translation with Introduction, Notes, and Commentary* (AB 7; Garden City: Doubleday, 1975), 40–41.

Elgvin, T., "MS 5441 (4Q(?)Ruth, Ruth 2.1–2)," in *Gleanings*, forthcoming.

Lange, *Handbuch*, 473–76.

Ulrich, *BQS*, 735–38.

Ulrich, E. and C.M. Murphy, "Ruth," *DJD XVI: 187–94.

Weiss, R., "Fragment of a Ruth Scroll among the Hidden Scrolls," *Sinai* 27 (1963): 165–66 [Hebr.].

Armin Lange

13.2.2 Masoretic Texts and Ancient Texts Close to MT

The Masoretic Text that is preserved in medieval manuscripts is the only witness attesting a complete Hebrew text of Ruth. As mentioned above (→ 13.2.1), the Hebrew book of Ruth is attested by fragments of four ancient manuscripts stemming from Qumran Caves 2 and 4 and one ancient Hebrew manuscript of uncertain origin: 2QRuth[a], 2QRuth[b], 4QRuth[a], 4QRuth[b], and manuscript Schøyen 5441. Only the proto-Masoretic manuscript 2QRuth[a] displays sufficient preserved text for text-typological classification. 2QRuth[b] and 4QRuth[b] exhibit non-aligned tendencies and 4QRuth[a] might be semi-Masoretic in character, while nothing can be said any longer about manuscript Schøyen 5441.

Given the general agreement that MT-Ruth is close, if not identical, to the original text of the book, only very little comprehensive text-critical investigation has been done on the consonantal text of MT-Ruth. It is symptomatic of the situation that in the text-critical introduction to his commentary on Ruth, Gerleman does not even mention MT-Ruth[1] and that in the most recent com-

---

[1] Gerleman, *Ruth*, 2–5.

mentary on Ruth, Schipper describes MT-Ruth as follows:[2]

> Overall, the evidence from the other ancient versions suggests that the text is much better preserved in Ruth MT[L] than in some other books in MT[L]. For example, unlike Samuel MT[L], Ruth MT[L] does not require much textual reconstruction. It has only a handful of spelling errors … also there is only one case of textual corruption …

That the Qumran manuscripts of Ruth are heavily damaged and provide few insights into the early Hebrew textual history of Ruth did not help the situation either. Therefore, manuscripts of Ruth from Qumran are seriously understudied, which has led to misleading generalizations, such as Quast's statement that there are no Qumran readings with LXX against MT (→ 13.2.3.1).[3]

Early works on the Hebrew text of Ruth are thus restricted to the discussion of individual variant readings. An example is Wright's eclectic text of Ruth with text-critical commentary.[4] With few exceptions, de Waard sides with MT in the apparatus of his text-critical edition of Ruth as well as in the text-critical commentary to this apparatus.[5] Recent examples of the study of individual readings include Martín Contreras' article on the form הָבִי in Ruth 3:15, which she interprets in light of rabbinic and Masoretic evidence as an imperative feminine singular in a masculine form of the root בוא in the *Hiphil*, meaning "bring."[6] A welcome exception to the focus on individual variant readings is a study by Martín Contreras that engages with details about the transmission of MT-Ruth in rabbinic times.[7]

13.2.2.1 Manuscripts and Editions

Beside the Qumran manuscripts 2QRuth[a] and 4QRuth[a] (discussed in → 13.2.1 and below in → 13.2.2.2), the three most important witnesses to the (proto-)Masoretic text of Ruth that cover the complete text are EBP. I B 19a (Codex Leningradensis; MT[L]), the Aleppo Codex (MT[A]), and Ass. Ms. 1753, a Yemenite manuscript from the Cambridge University Library (MT[Y]). These three medieval manuscripts concur in most aspects. For instance, all of them present only one *petuchah* (between Ruth 4:17 and 4:18).[8] The punctuation of וְאלקטה and בשבלים in Ruth 2:2 and of והלכת in Ruth 2:9 figures among their few disagreements: MT[L] offers וַאֲלַקֳטָה "and let me glean," בַּשִּׁבֳּלִים "among the ears of grain," and וְהָלַכְתְּ "and walk" against וַאֲלַקֳטָה "and let me glean," בַּשִּׁבֳּלִים "among the ears of grain," and וְהָלַכְתְּ "and walk" read by MT[A] and MT[Y].[9] In Ruth 3:14, MT[L] reads the *Qere* מַרְגְּלֹתָיו (*Ketiv*: מַרְגְּלֹתָו), whereas MT[A] and MT[Y] offer מַרְגְּלֹתָו (all meaning "his feet"). In the cases where the punctuation of MT[L] differs from that found in MT[A] and MT[Y], the readings of the latter are to be preferred (→ 10–20.1).

Both critical editions of MT-Ruth in *BHS and *BHQ are of a diplomatic nature and based on MT[L], in spite of MT[L]'s erroneous punctuation in several places. The *HUB edition of MT-Ruth based on MT[A] has not yet appeared. The same is true for *HBCE. By including the four Qumran manuscripts in its apparatus, the *BHQ edition by de Waard offers a more comprehensive discussion of the textual variants than the preceding *BHS edition by Robinson. Kennicott's edition (*1776–1780) and De Rossi's collection of variant readings (*1784–1788) still provide important information about the variants within the medieval MT manuscript tradition.

13.2.2.2 2QRuth[a] and 4QRuth[a]

The variant readings of the Qumran manuscripts 2QRuth[a] and 4QRuth[a] provide ancient evidence

---

[2] J. Schipper, *Ruth: A New Translation with Introduction and Commentary* (The Anchor Yale Bible; New Haven: Yale University Press, 2016), quoted according to www.books.google.com, no page number given.

[3] Quast, *Ruth*, 124.

[4] Wright, *The Book of Ruth in Hebrew*.

[5] De Waard, "Ruth."

[6] Martín Contreras, "Masoretic and Rabbinic Lights."

[7] Martín Contreras, "Text-preserving Observations in the Midrash Ruth Rabbah."

[8] Cf. de Waard, "Ruth," 5*.

[9] Cf., furthermore, Ruth 2:10 (וְאָנֹכִי in MT[L] against וְאָנֹכִי in MT[A] and MT[Y]; all meaning "and I"); 2:11 (אָבִיךְ in MT[L] against אָבִיךְ in MT[A] and MT[Y]; all meaning "your father"); 3:9 (אָתְּ in MT[L] against אַתְּ in MT[A] and MT[Y]; all meaning "you").

that illuminates the textual character of MT-Ruth and thus they need to be discussed first before we can turn to MT-Ruth.¹⁰

13.2.2.2.1 2QRuthᵃ – A Proto-Masoretic Text of Ruth

2QRuthᵃ is classified in → 13.2.1.1 as proto-Masoretic based on the observation that the 152 extant words of this fragment show only three small textual variant readings towards MT-Ruth. Beside these textual variants, two orthographic variants are of interest for the study of Ruth.

The three textual variants of 2QRuthᵃ are all secondary readings and go back to either scribal corruption (Ruth 2:23) or harmonizing and linguistic editing (Ruth 2:18 and 2:21):

– In Ruth 2:18, 2QRuthᵃ reads בשבעה "when she was satisfied" against MT's מִשָּׂבְעָהּ "after she was satisfied" (cf. LXX). Although not impossible, to construe a temporal subclause by pairing an infinitive with the preposition מִן "after" is rare. Therefore, 2QRuthᵃ replaces the preposition מִן "after" by way of linguistic editing with the preposition -בְּ "when" because the latter is paired far more often with an infinitive to express a temporal subclause. 2QRuthᵃ's בשבעה "when she was satisfied" is thus an editorial reading.¹¹
– In Ruth 2:21, 2QRuthᵃ writes לי instead of MT's אֵלַי (both meaning "to me") in harmonization with the two following occurrences of לי in the same verse. The reading can best be classified as a harmonizing editorial reading.
– In Ruth 2:23, 2QRuthᵃ contains a case of scribal corruption. The scribe originally wrote ללוט "to wrap," which would result in a senseless text. Recognizing the error, either the original scribe or a later copyist corrected it by adding a supralinear *qof*, resulting in the *Qal* infinitive form ללקוט. Because this *Qal* infinitive has the same meaning as MT's *Piel* infinitive לְלַקֵּט "to glean," the corrector did not erase the *waw*.

The two orthographic variants of 2QRuthᵃ are both concerned with the lack or addition of the masculine plural construct ending *ay/ey*, which is added to the feminine plural ending when suffixes are attached to feminine plural nouns. 2QRuthᵃ reads once in an original reading more defective (Ruth 2:22) and once in a secondary reading more plene than MT (Ruth 3:3).

– Reading נערותו against MT's נַעֲרוֹתָיו (both meaning "his young women"), 2QRuthᵃ preserves in Ruth 2:22 the original text of Ruth.¹² Below, it will be argued that MT-Ruth includes remnants of an early orthography that was even more defective than the conservative orthography of MT. As a typical feature, this early orthography neither inserted a *yod* between the feminine plural construct ending and a suffix (cf. Ruth 3:3, 14) nor between the masculine plural construct and a suffix (cf. Ruth 2:12, 20; 3:10?).¹³ A scribe adjusted this early defective form in Ruth 2:22 to adhere to the later rules of MT's conservative orthography and morphology either in antiquity and/or in medieval times.
– In Ruth 3:3, MT lacks the interspersed *yod* between the feminine plural construct noun and the suffix attached to it (שמלתך), while 2QRuthᵃ adds it (שמל[תיך). De Waard and Ulrich treat this case as a textual variant in which the witnesses would differ in a singular and plural number of the noun שִׂמְלָה, i.e., "your garment" (MT^Ketiv, LXX) vs. "your garments" (2QRuthᵃ, MT^Qere,Kenn 2,99,111,121,129,166,270,196,224,236,259, V, S, T).¹⁴ While medieval Masoretic scribes clearly

---

¹⁰ For the variants of 2QRuthᵇ and 4QRuthᵇ, → 13.2.3.
¹¹ For the category of the editorial readings and editorial texts, → 1.2.2.3 and see A. Lange, "4QXIIᵍ (4Q82) as an Editorial Text," (forthcoming in *Textus*).

¹² Against de Waard, "Ruth," 7, who presumes a graphical error.
¹³ See Barr, *Variable Spellings*, 131–37; cf. also Joüon, § 94g. S.L. Gogel, *A Grammar of Epigraphic Hebrew* (SBLRBS; Atlanta: Society of Biblical Literature, 1998) 154–62, lists examples of inscriptions without *yod*, providing evidence for the early character of this morphology.
¹⁴ De Waard, "Ruth," 7; Ulrich, *BQS*, 738.

agree with the positions of Ulrich and de Waard (see MT^Qere; MT^Kenn 2,99,111,121,129,166,270,196,224,236, 259 [שמלותיך]), a comparison with the lack of the plural marker *yod* in Ruth 2:12, 20, 22; 3:10(?), 14, allows us to understand the defective reading of MT as the remnant of an earlier more defective morphology. This interpretation is supported by LXX-Ruth, which understood שמלתך as a singular form (τὸν ἱματισμόν σου "your clothing") thus attesting to the antiquity of the reading שמלתך. Both forms thus mean "your garments."

The limited amount of preserved text makes a textual characterization of 2QRuth^a difficult. The manuscript suffered from a limited amount of scribal corruption and displays remnants of linguistic editing as compared to MT-Ruth, but still preserves one earlier orthographic reading.

13.2.2.2.2 4QRuth^a: A Possible Semi-Masoretic Text of Ruth

The fact that only seventy-eight words from Ruth 1:1–12 survive of 4QRuth^a makes difficult and speculative the text-typological classification of this manuscript that dates from the middle of the first century B.C.E. Variant statistics could point to a semi-Masoretic text (→ 13.2.1.3).[15]

Aside from the two textual variants in Ruth 1:2, 9 discussed below, two orthographic readings against MT are of interest in 4QRuth^a. The manuscript reads in Ruth 1:1, 2 בשדה מוא־ and שדה מואב, respectively.[16] In both cases, MT reads בִּשְׂדֵי מוֹאָב "in the fields of Moab" and שְׂדֵי־מוֹאָב "fields of Moab" respectively. At first glance, the two texts seem to disagree in the number of the construct noun שדה, i.e., singular or plural construct or "field of Moab" vs. "fields of Moab." MT^L-Ruth itself suggests that the situation is more complicated as it reads in some verses שָׂדֶה (Ruth 1:6; 2:6; 4:3) and in others שְׂדֵי (Ruth 1:1, 2, 6, 22). With the exception of Ruth 2:6, MT^A generally supports MT^L in its orthographic diversity. In Ruth 2:6, MT^A reads שְׂדֵי against the שָׂדֶה of MT^L. The different readings of MT^L and MT^A in Ruth 2:6 point to the textual diversity of the medieval Masoretic codices in reading either שָׂדֶה or שְׂדֵי in the various attestations of the lexeme in the book of Ruth. However, no medieval manuscript seems to be coherent in reading either one of the two forms.[17] The medieval textual diversity is best explained as secondary as harmonizations of the plural to the singular form and vice versa. However, this explanation does not apply to 4QRuth^a and the ancient proto-Masoretic text of Ruth. The solution to the problem can be found in Ruth 2:6, which uses both שָׂדֶה and שְׂדֵי in one verse.

וַתָּקָם הִיא וְכַלֹּתֶיהָ וַתָּשָׁב מִשְּׂדֵי מוֹאָב כִּי שָׁמְעָה בִּשְׂדֵה מוֹאָב
And she started to return with her daughters-in-law from the fields of Moab, because she had heard in the fields of Moab.

שָׂדֶה and שְׂדֵי clearly designate here the same location and thus must mean the same thing. Therefore, the two readings indicate an orthographic and not a textual difference. שָׂדֶה represents an earlier orthography in which final *he* could be used as a *mater lectionis* for *ē*.[18] This interpretation of the evidence is confirmed by Judg 9:7, which speaks of "all the fields of the inheritance of Israel" (בְּכָל־שְׂדֵה נַחֲלַת יִשְׂרָאֵל) and 2 Sam 9:7, which mentions "all the fields" of Saul (כָּל־שְׂדֵה שָׁאוּל). Both times, the particle כָּל "all" indicates the plural number of שָׂדֶה.

The two textual variants of 4QRuth^a can be found in Ruth 1:2, 9:

– In Ruth 1:2, 4QRuth^a reads וישבו שם "and they lived there" (cf. s) instead of MT's וַיִּהְיוּ־שָׁם "and they were there" (cf. LXX, T). MT is clearly the more difficult reading. 4QRuth^a should be understood as a harmonization with the וַיֵּשְׁבוּ שָׁם "and they lived there" in Ruth 1:4.[19]

---

[15] Cf. Nebe, "Qumranica I," 309; Campbell, *Ruth*, 40; Ulrich and Murphy, "Ruth," 188.

[16] For the interpretation of these two differences between 4QRuth^a and MT as orthographic variants, see also Ulrich and Murphy, "Ruth," 188, 192.

[17] De Rossi, *1784–1788, 3.234–36, 239, provides a good impression of the evidence.

[18] Cf. GKC § 9.6.

[19] Cf. de Waard, "Ruth,"4, 51*.

- In Ruth 1:9, 4QRuth[a] has קולם "their voice" against MT's קוֹלָן of the same meaning. 4QRuth[a] preserves here most likely an old feminine dual form.[20]

On the whole, the textual typology of 4QRuth[a] remains speculative and not enough variant readings are preserved for its textual characterization. Nevertheless, with three more original readings than MT and only one secondary harmonization, 4QRuth[a] demonstrates that the consonantal text of MT-Ruth includes a certain number of secondary readings (see below, → 13.2.2.3). Furthermore, the three more original readings all point to an early form of Hebrew of which remnants also can be found elsewhere in MT-Ruth.

13.2.2.3 Nature and Text-Critical Character of (proto-)MT-Ruth

Although many commentators tend to describe MT-Ruth as relatively unproblematic,[21] it is difficult to define (proto-)MT's nature and character clearly due to several factors. For instance, we find many *Ketiv/Qere* passages within MT in which the value of the *Ketiv* is debated in several cases. Furthermore, both Kennicott (*1776–1780) and De Rossi (*1784–1788) point to the fact that there are many minor disagreements within the MT tradition. These disagreements also raise the question of how to judge certain variant readings attested in the Qumran manuscripts (→ 13.2.1; → 13.2.2.2.1; → 13.2.2.2.2; → 13.2.3). The extent to which the Qumran manuscripts confirm MT-Ruth is not as clear as commonly stated, even though manuscript deterioration prohibits reaching certain conclusions.[22] Although the consonantal text of Ruth is of the highest textual quality, it does include a certain number of secondary readings. Furthermore, traces of an early orthography and morphology make it likely that the Hebrew text of Ruth as known today is the result of orthographic and linguistic editing. The characteristic features of the consonantal text of MT-Ruth thus pertain both to its orthography/morphology and its text.

13.2.2.3.1 Orthography and Morphology of (proto-)MT-Ruth

In general, the consonantal text of Ruth follows the conservative orthographic system of MT as described in → 1.2.2.4.1.2. Together with Canticles, Daniel, and Esther, Ruth is among those biblical books whose (proto-)Masoretic text barely includes traces of the baroque orthography typical of many of the biblical Qumran manuscripts (see Table 8 and Graph 2 in → 1.2.2.4.1.2).[23] Only three spellings in MT-Ruth adhere to the rules of baroque orthography:

- Ruth 2:8 reads the pausal form תַּעֲבוּרִי "pass over" in a non-pausal position.[24]
- MT-Ruth 2:8, 9 attest to two occurrences of the negation לוֹא spelled plene paired with the interrogative particle as הֲלוֹא "(have I) not?" The latter is not uncommon in many books of MT but nevertheless attests to the double *mater lectionis* characteristic of baroque orthography.

With these exceptions, (proto-)MT-Ruth shares no characteristics of the so-called Qumran orthography. On the contrary, MT-Ruth includes a remarkable number of spellings and morphological features that are even more defective than the conservative orthography of MT.[25] In five cases, MT-Ruth attests to shorter morphological forms that do not add a *yod* to indicate the plural number of a noun when a suffix is attached. Some of these cases were recognized as *Ketiv-Qere* readings by the Masoretes

---

[20] Thus Campbell, *Ruth*, 66 and de Waard, "Ruth," 51*.
[21] Cf. Sasson, *Ruth*, 8.
[22] Cf. Lange, *Handbuch, 475.

[23] Cf. also A. Lange, "The Question of the So-Called Qumran Orthography, the Severus Scroll, and the Masoretic Text," *Hebrew Bible and Ancient Israel* 3 (2014): 424–75 (440).
[24] Cf. Lange, "Question," 466. For pausal forms in non-pausal position as a characteristic of the Qumran orthography, see Tov, *Scribal Practices*, 254.
[25] Several of the examples mentioned below are discussed in Martín Contreras, "Text-preserving Observations in the Midrash Ruth Rabbah."

implying grammatical differences in number, while others were not.

- Ruth 2:12 פָּעֳלֵךְ "your deeds" (vocalized as a singular form by the Masoretes)
- Ruth 2:20 מִגֹּאֲלֵנוּ "among our redeemers" (vocalized as a singular form by the Masoretes)
- Ruth 3:3 *Ketiv* שמלתך *Qere* שִׂמְלֹתַיִךְ "your garments" (cf. 2QRuth^a; → 13.2.2.2.1)
- Ruth 3:9 כְּנָפֶךָ "garment" (lit. "edges, wings")
- Ruth 3:14 *Ketiv* מרגלתו *Qere* מַרְגְּלוֹתָיו "at his feet"
- A further example can be found in 2QRuth^a. This manuscript reads in Ruth 2:22 נערותו which is corrected by MT to נַעֲרוֹתָיו "his young women" (→ 13.2.2.2.1)

MT-Ruth spells the imperative feminine plural three times without the *he*-affix of MT's conservative orthography. In the *Ketiv-Qere* system, the Masoretes indicate the lacking affix regularly by the vowel sign *qameṣ* at the end of the word.

- Ruth 1:9 וּמְצֶאןָ "that you may find"
- Ruth 1:12 לֵכְןָ "go"[26]
- Ruth 1:20 קְרֶאןָ "call"

In two cases, MT-Ruth includes alternative forms or the inverted imperfect of the second person feminine singular (Ruth 3:3, 4).[27] Again, the Masoretes indicate these cases by way of *Ketiv* and *Qere*.

- Ruth 3:3 *Ketiv* וירדתי *Qere* וְיָרַדְתְּ "and go down"
- Ruth 3:4 *Ketiv* ושכבתי *Qere* וְשָׁכַבְתְּ "and lie down"

Other morphological idiosyncrasies of MT-Ruth include the following verbal and nominal morphological and orthographic features, again indicated by the Masoretes in their marginal notes. Some of these cases attest to longer and others to shorter forms than MT's conservative orthography.

- Ruth 1:6; 2:6; 4:3 spell the construct plural of the noun שָׂדֶה "field" not as שְׂדֵי but as שְׂדֵה "fields" (see above, → 13.2.2.2.2).
- Ruth 1:14 includes a defective spelling of the third person feminine plural inverted imperfect of the verb "to take (up)" נשׂא, i.e., וַתִּשֶּׂנָה instead of ותשאנה "and they took up."[28]
- In Ruth 3:14, MT has the form בטרום for בְּטֶרֶם "before."[29]
- Ruth 3:15 has the short form הָבִי, which Martín Contreras classifies as a feminine imperative singular in the *hiphil* of the root בוא which is executed in a very defective spelling as a masculine imperative singular in its form "bring" (הָבִיא; → 10–20.1).[30]
- Ruth 4:4: reads a cohortative form of the root ידע without a final *he*: ואדע instead of וְאֵדְעָה "and I may know."

In addition to the more archaic spellings discussed above, the Qumran manuscripts 2QRuth^a and 4QRuth^a demonstrate that the text of MT-Ruth also applied orthographic linguistic editing to eliminate such archaic features. That MT-Ruth mostly follows the conservative orthography of MT-Ruth should therefore be understood as the result of a process of orthographic revision that did not eliminate all cases of the earlier orthographic system. The remaining cases of archaic orthography were already adjusted to the conservative orthographic system in ancient Ruth manuscripts. After the standardization of MT, the Masoretes addressed these remaining cases of archaic orthography and morphology in their notes. Examples of such individual orthographic and morphological adjustments can be identified in MT-Ruth itself by way of comparison with Qumran manuscripts.

---

[26] Cf. de Waard, "Ruth," 51*–52*.

[27] Among the latest contributions on Ruth, this view holds; cf., for instance, Zevit, "Dating Ruth," 598 n. 38.

[28] See recently especially Martín Contreras, "Text-preserving Observations in the Midrash Ruth Rabbah," 314.

[29] De Waard, "Ruth," 8 classifies this reading as a graphic error.

[30] See Martín Contreras, "Masoretic and Rabbinic Lights."

- For Ruth 1:2, 9, 4QRuthᵃ provides evidence that MT-Ruth adjusted בשדה מואב and שדה מואב to בִּשְׂדֵי־מוֹאָב "in the fields of Moab" and שְׂדֵי־מוֹאָב "fields of Moab" respectively (→ 13.2.2.2.2).
- In Ruth 1:9, MT adjusted the old feminine dual form of 4QRuthᵃ (קולם) to קוֹלָן (both meaning "their voice"; → 13.2.2.2.2).
- In Ruth 2:22, the reading of 2QRuthᵃ (נערותו) helps in determining MT's נַעֲרוֹתָיו (both meaning "his young women") as a morphological adjustment to the conservative orthographic system (→ 13.2.2.2.1).

13.2.2.3.2 Textual Variants: Scribal Corruption in MT-Ruth's Editing

In addition to such orthographic and morphological revision, cases of accidental scribal corruption occur in MT-Ruth, many of which the Masoretes again addressed in their annotations. Examples include the following:

- In MT-Ruth 2:1, the *Ketiv* מידע represents a masculine singular participle in the *pual* meaning "acquaintance," whereas the *Qere* מוֹדָע "relative" makes more sense. The awkward *Ketiv* can be explained easily as the result of a *waw/yod* confusion, two characters that appear identical in the early Herodian formal script.
- In Ruth 3:5, 17, the word אֵלַי, "to me" is missing in MT. In Ruth 3:5, the short text is attested by MT*Ketiv*, LXX, and the Vulgate, while MT*Qere*, the Peshitta, and Targum support the longer text. In Ruth 3:17, MT*Ketiv* and the Vulgate lack the word, while it appears in MT*Qere*, LXX, the Peshitta, and Targum. In Ruth 3:5, the shorter text of MT*Ketiv* is the result of a homoioteleuton between the *yod* of תֹּאמְרִי "you tell" and the *yod* of אֵלַי "me." In Ruth 3:17, the shorter text of MT*Ketiv* was caused by a homoiarcton between אֵלַי "to me" and "not."
- In Ruth 3:12, the MT*Ketiv* reading כי אם "(but) rather, otherwise" is missing in LXX, V, and S. MT*Ketiv* is supported by the Targum. In their *Qere*, the Masoretes recommend not reading אם "if." The *Qere* is supported by MT*Kenn 4*. The support of the versions and the syntactic and semantic problems of the *Ketiv* argue in the case of כי אם "but rather" for "an accidental dittography of the preceding כי אם(נם)."³¹

- In Ruth 3:15, MT reads with LXX and the Targum וַיָּבֹא הָעִיר "he came into the city" although the beginning of v. 16 implies that Ruth and not Boaz should be the subject in this short sentence. Therefore, a large group of Masoretic manuscripts have וַתָּבֹא הָעִיר "and she came into the city."³² This reading is supported by LXXᴸ⁻⁵⁴' ³¹⁴ (καὶ Ρουθ εἰσῆλθεν εἰς τὴν πόλιν "and Ruth entered the city"), the Peshitta, and the Vulgate. While the MT reading seems to be the *lectio difficilior* and the MTᵐˢˢ reading could easily be an editorial adjustment, MT-Ruth attests to a *taw/yod* confusion in Ruth 4:4, which makes the case of scribal corruption for Ruth 3:15 more likely.
- In Ruth 3:15, 2QRuthᵇ preserves a more original text than MT and the versions. The שם "there" got lost in MT by way of a homoiarcton with the *shin* of the following שֵׁשׁ "six." The original text of Ruth 3:15 was thus וימד שם שש שערים "and he measured there six measures of barley" (→ 13.2.3.1).
- In Ruth 3:16, MT's incomprehensible reading מִי־אַתְּ "Who are you?" goes back to a character confusion between *yod* and *he* that could have happened easily during the paleo-Hebrew transmission of Ruth. 2QRuthᵇ preserves the original reading with מה את "How are you?" the more original text. (→ 13.2.3.1).
- In Ruth 4:4, MTᴬ·ᴸ read יִגְאַל "he will redeem," while a large number of other medieval Masoretic manuscripts have תִּגְאַל "you will redeem."³³ Because "he will redeem" yields no sense, this reading most likely originated in a rare confusion of *yod* and *taw*, which could oc-

---

³¹ De Waard, "Ruth," 54* (cf. p. 8); cf., e.g., Gerleman, *Ruth*, 30, and, Campbell, *Ruth*, 125, who want to delete only אם "if."
³² See, e.g., De Rossi, *1784–1788, 238.
³³ Cf. De Rossi, *1784–1788, 239, which illustrates the quantitatively strong manuscript evidence for תִּגְאַל "you will redeem" and the critical discussions of the case in Barthélemy, "Ruth," 134 and de Waard, "Ruth," 55*.

cur, for example, in a Herodian script in the case of a slightly damaged *taw* in a scribe's *Vorlage*.[34]
– In Ruth 4:5, the *Ketiv* קניתי "I acquired" could go back to a *he/yod* confusion in a paleo-Hebrew copy of Ruth, as it is also attested in Ruth 3:16 (see above). The correct reading in this case would be the *Qere* קָנִיתָה "you acquired"; interestingly enough, this morphological form is typical of the baroque orthography. However, a few scholars argue for the priority of the *Ketiv* קניתי "I acquired."[35] A compelling argument against the *Qere* reading would be that it mistakenly assumes that the institutions of land redemption and levirate marriage belong together. Since both prepositions (מֵאֵת "from" and מִיַּד "from the hand/authority") can be combined with the verb קנה "to buy, acquire," Zevit's second translation proposal could explain the text without the emendation of the *Qere*: "On the day of your acquiring the field from the hand/authority of Naomi and from Ruth the Moabitess, the wife of the dead, I acquired in order to raise up the name of the dead over his portion."[36]

13.2.2.3.3 The Textual Character of MT-Ruth and Its Relation to the Versions

The above observations show that MT-Ruth is the result of orthographic and linguistic editing and includes a limited number of scribal corruptions. The original text of Ruth was most likely written in an archaic and very defective orthography. Once the conservative orthographic system of MT became prominent, the orthography of MT-Ruth was adapted to it. The revision happened somewhat unsystematically as seen in the occurrence of two different morphologies for the same grammatical form in the same verse. An example are the two imperative feminine plural forms in Ruth 1:12:

שֹׁבְנָה בְנֹתַי לֵכְןָ כִּי זָקַנְתִּי מִהְיוֹת לְאִישׁ

Return, my daughters, go (home), because I am too old to have a man.

---

[34] Cf., e.g., de Waard, "Ruth," 9.
[35] Cf. Beattie, "Kethibh and Qere in Ruth IV 5"; Sasson, *Ruth*, 103, 119–36; Zevit, "Dating Ruth."
[36] Zevit, "Dating Ruth," 596.

The remnants of the earlier archaic morphology and orthography were corrected later on a case-by-case basis by individual scribes. In addition to these orthographic features, MT-Ruth includes a limited number of scribal corruptions. That some character confusions are more likely in a paleo-Hebrew alphabet could point to the old age of the textual ancestor of MT-Ruth.

The Qumran manuscripts (→ 13.2.1; → 13.2.3) do not preserve an earlier text than MT-Ruth, but do include original readings in their texts. The textual deviations of 2QRuth[b], 4QRuth[a], and 4QRuth[b] from MT make it likely that these texts branched off from the proto-Masoretic textual tradition to form possible semi-Masoretic (4QRuth[a]) and non-aligned texts (2QRuth[b], 4QRuth[b]).

The same is true for the versions. The LXX variants can generally be explained as modifications of the MT version (→ 13–17.1.1.1). Among them are additions with explicatory character (cf. Ruth 1:14) and omissions that free the text from possible unpleasantness (cf. Ruth 3:7).[37] Another example of this phenomenon is the Vulgate. Jerome's parent text for V-Ruth seems to have been close to MT-Ruth with slight disagreements, although most Vulgate variants result from translation technique as well as stylistic emendations and theological changes made by Jerome himself.

13.2.2.4 Date and Milieu

Given the many traces of an early orthography in MT-Ruth and the general absence of this orthography in the late Second Temple period, the orthographic revision of MT-Ruth occurred quite early. There is no remaining evidence to provide answers as to where and in what milieu this revision took place. It can no longer be determined when the later isolated orthographic and morphological adjustment took place as well as the insertion into the text of MT-Ruth of the cases of scribal corruption. The textual differences in medieval Masoretic manuscripts even allow for the possibil-

---

[37] For more examples and types of modifications, see, for instance, Bons, "Ruth," 701–02, but also Barthélemy, "Ruth," *passim*.

ity that some of these adjustments happened in (early) medieval times.

Baillet, M., "16. Ruth (premier exemplaire)," *DJD III.1: 71–74.
Barthélemy, D., "Ruth," in Barthélemy, *Critique textuelle 1982, 130–36.
Beattie, D.R.G., "Kethibh and Qere in Ruth IV 5," VT 21 (1971): 490–94.
Bons, E., "Ruth: Das Buch Rut," in *Septuaginta Deutsch, Erläuterungen, 1.701–13.
Campbell, E.F., Ruth: A New Translation with Introduction, Notes, and Commentary (AB 7; Garden City: Doubleday, 1975).
Gerleman, G., Ruth, Das Hohelied (BKAT 18; Neukirchen-Vluyn: Neukirchener Verlag, 1965).
Joüon, P., Ruth: Commentaire philologique et exégétique (2nd ed.; SubBi 9; Rome: Biblical Institute Press, 1986).
Lange, *Handbuch, 473–76.
Martín Contreras, E., "Masoretic and Rabbinic Lights on the Word הָבִי, Ruth 3:15 – יהב or בוא?," VT 59 (2009): 257–65.
Martín Contreras, E., "Text-preserving Observations in the Midrash Ruth Rabbah," JJS 62 (2011): 311–23.
Myers, J.M., The Linguistic and Literary Form of the Book of Ruth (Leiden: Brill, 1955).
Nebe, G.W., "Qumranica I: Zu unveröffentlichten Handschriften aus Höhle 4 von Qumran," ZAW 106 (1994): 307–22.
Quast, U., Ruth (2nd ed.; Septuaginta Vetus Testamentum 4.3; Göttingen: Vandenhoeck & Ruprecht, 2009).
Robinson, T.H., "Librum Ruth," in *BHS, 1320–25.
Sasson, J.M., Ruth: A New Translation with a Philological Commentary and a Formalist-Folklorist Interpretation (2nd ed.; The Biblical Seminar 10, Sheffield: Sheffield Academic Press, 1989).
Schipper, J., Ruth: A New Translation with Introduction and Commentary (The Anchor Yale Bible 7.4; New Haven: Yale University Press, 2016).
Ulrich, *BQS.
Ulrich, E. and C.M. Murphy, "Ruth," *DJD XVI: 187–94.
de Waard, J., "Ruth רות," in *BHQ 18, 3–10, 5*–7*, 51*–56*.
Wright, C.H.H., The Book of Ruth in Hebrew: With a Critically Revised Text, Various Readings, Including a New Collation of Twenty-Eight Hebrew Mss. (Most of Them not Previously Collated) and a Critical and Grammatical Commentary to Which Is Appended the Chaldee Targum with Various Readings, Grammatical Notes and a Chaldee Glossary (London: Williams and Norgate, 1864).

Zevit, Z., "Dating Ruth: Legal, Linguistic, and Historical Observations," ZAW 117 (2005): 574–600.

Veronika Bachmann
Armin Lange

13.2.3 Other Texts

As detailed in → 13.2.1, 2QRuth[b] (→ 13.2.1.1) and 4QRuth[b] (→ 13.2.1.4) are too damaged to allow for orthographic and text-typological classifications and neither do they allow for an overall textual characterization of the texts of Ruth to which they attest. Nevertheless, they include a number of non-aligned readings that warrant discussion.

13.2.3.1 2QRuth[b] (2Q17)

The twenty-six preserved words of 2QRuth[b] (→ 13.2.1.2) allow neither for a text-typological classification nor for a textual characterization. Nevertheless, this manuscript from the third quarter of the first century B.C.E. contains non-aligned and other readings that are important for the understanding of MT-Ruth. Therefore, scholars have observed repeatedly the non-aligned tendency of 2QRuth[b].[1]

– In Ruth 3:15, 2QRuth[b] preserves more original text than MT and the versions. MT reads in Ruth 3:15 with LXX, V, and T וַיָּמָד שֵׁשׁ־שְׂעֹרִים "and he measured six measures of barley." 2QRuth[b] attests to an additional שם "there" that got lost by way of homoiarcton with the *shin* of the following שֵׁשׁ "six." The original text of Ruth 3:15 was thus וימד שם שש שערים "and he measured there six measures of barley."
– In Ruth 3:16, MT's מִי־אַתְּ "Who are you?" is clearly the *lectio difficilior* as it does not result in a meaningful text. MT might go back to a scribal error in a paleo-Hebrew manuscript tradition as the characters *yod* and *he* can be confused in this alphabet. In this case, 2QRuth[b] would preserve with its reading מה את "How are you?" the more

---

[1] Thus Baillet, "Second exemplaire," 74: "manifeste une certaine indépendance"; cf. Campbell, *Ruth*, 40–41, and Bons, "Septuaginta-Versionen," 205.

original text. The LXX text tradition is split and seems to have been influenced by both Hebrew readings. The more original reading is confirmed by two LXX manuscripts (LXX¹⁰⁸ ³¹⁸: τι συ "What are you?"; LXX¹⁹' ³¹⁸ ⁵⁰⁹: τι σοι "What is for you?"; LXX⁵⁸: τι σοι εστιν; LXX⁶²⁸: εστι τι σοι [the latter three all meaning "What is for you?"]), while LXXᴬ⁺ read with MT and while LXXᴮ has τις αυτη "Who is she?"

- 2QRuthᵇ itself suffered from scribal corruption. In Ruth 3:14, 2QRuthᵇ lacks the word הָאִשָּׁה "the woman" (cf. V and S), resulting in "that she came to the threshing floor" as opposed to MT's (with T; cf. LXX²) כִּי־בָאָה הָאִשָּׁה הַגֹּרֶן "that the woman came to the threshing floor." When copying the text, a scribe erroneously omitted הָאִשָּׁה by way of homoiarcton, his eye skipping from the *he* of הָאִשָּׁה to the *he* of הַגֹּרֶן "threshing floor."

- Furthermore, 2QRuthᵇ attests in Ruth 3:14 to one editorial reading³ that aims at making linguistic adjustments. The reading concerns the morphology of the pronominal suffix of the third person singular masculine appended to a feminine plural noun. In a case of *Ketiv* and *Qere*, Ruth-MT reads מַרְגְּלֹתָו "his feet." The *Qere* would be מַרְגְּלֹתָיו also meaning "his feet." This reading is also attested in 2QRuthᵇ (מ]רג[לתיו), thirty-seven manuscripts in Kennicott's edition (*1776–1780), and seemingly LXX, V, S, and T. MT seems to lack the plural ending י־. But מַרְגְּלֹתָו should be understood as following an earlier morphological convention in which the suffix of the third person singular masculine could be construed without the preceding plural ending although a plural form was intended (→ 13.2.2.2.1; → 13.2.2.3.1).⁴ This earlier and more defective morphology

---

² LXX reads only γυνή "woman." The missing article was probably lost due to scribal error in its Hebrew *Vorlage* (see De Waard, "Ruth," 8).

³ For the category of the editorial readings and editorial texts, → 1.2.2.3 and see A. Lange, "4QXIIᵍ (4Q82) as an Editorial Text," (forthcoming in *Textus*).

⁴ See Barr, *Variable Spellings*, 131–37; cf. Joüon, § 94g. S.L. Gogel, *A Grammar of Epigraphic Hebrew* (SBLRBS; Atlanta: Society of Biblical Literature, 1998) 154–62, lists examples of inscriptions without *yod* that provide evidence for the early character of this morphology.

agrees well with the extremely defective orthography in MT-Ruth 1:12: שֹׁבְנָה בְנֹתַי לֵכְןָ "turn back my daughter, go your way" (→ 13.2.2.3.1). In 2QRuthᵇ, the earlier morphology was adjusted linguistically to the morphology of the late Second Temple period.

Given the disparate nature of the extant variant readings of 2QRuthᵇ, it is not even possible to speculate on its textual character. However, that the manuscript preserves two readings that are more original than those in MT points to the text-critical value of its lost text.

13.2.3.2 4QRuthᵇ (4Q105)

The thirty-two preserved words and remnants of words in 4QRuthᵇ (→ 13.2.1.3) attesting to Ruth 1:6–11, 12–15 are too damaged for textual characterization. However, a study of the extant variants reveals an editorial tendency in this manuscript that dates from the end of the first century B.C.E. The material reconstruction of 4QRuthᵇ shows that the manuscript had a shorter text than MT-Ruth and LXX-Ruth in Ruth 1:2–4,⁵ but 4QRuthᵇ agrees with MT in Ruth 1:14 in lacking the long text of LXX-Ruth. This constellation allows for the suspicion that 4QRuthᵇ preserves the remnants of a non-aligned text. Ulrich and Murphy speculate that the short text of 4QRuthᵇ in Ruth 1:2–4 resulted from parablepsis.⁶ In this case, 4QRuthᵇ would have developed out of (proto-)MT-Ruth. The secondary nature of the text of 4QRuthᵇ as compared to MT-Ruth becomes more likely due to four editorial readings⁷ in the scant remains of this manuscript.

- In Ruth 1:2, 4QRuthᵇ reads ש]ם האיש "the name of the man" against MT's וְשֵׁם הָאִישׁ "and the name of the man" (with 4QRuthᵃ and LXX), in order to avoid beginning a listing of three names with the copula "and."

---

⁵ See Ulrich and Murphy, "Ruth," 191, 193–94; cf. also Campbell, *Ruth*, 41.

⁶ Ulrich and Murphy, "Ruth," 193–94.

⁷ For the categorization of editorial readings and editorial texts, see → 1.2.2.3 and Lange, "4QXIIᵍ (4Q82)."

13.2.3 OTHER TEXTS

- In Ruth 1:12, MT-Ruth reads וְגַם יָלַדְתִּי בָנִים "and even bear sons." 4QRuth[b] adds, against MT, T, S, the word שֵׁנִית "second" and thus clarifies "and even] bear sons for a second time" (יָלַדְתִּי שֵׁנִית [בנים]). The editorial reading facilitates understanding in making clear that Naomi would have sons a second time after her deceased sons, the husbands of Ruth and her sister-in-law, died.
- In Ruth 1:15, 4QRuth[b] reads ל[עַ]מָּ[ה] ולא[להיה against MT's אֶל־עַמָּהּ וְאֶל־אֱלֹהֶיהָ. Both readings mean "to her people and to her gods" and differ only in using the preposition -לְ instead of the preposition אֶל. The editorial text of 4QRuth[b] changed the preposition אֶל to the preposition -לְ in harmonization with Ruth 1:8 and 1:10, in which Naomi asks each of her daughters-in-law to "go back to (-לְ) the house of her mother" (Ruth 1:8) but the daughters-in-law insist "we will return with you to (-לְ) your people" (Ruth 1:10).

Although there is insufficient text preserved in 4QRuth[b] for textual characterization, the remaining and reconstructed variants argue for a non-aligned text that developed out of MT-Ruth by way of an editorial reworking, which also had its share of scribal corruption. That 4QRuth[b] follows MT in Ruth 1:14 against the longer text of LXX could corroborate this hypothesis.

Baillet, M., "17. Ruth (second exemplaire)," *DJD III.1: 74–75.
Bons, E., "Die Septuaginta-Versionen des Buches Rut," BZ 42 (1998): 202–24, esp. 205–06.
Campbell, E.F., *Ruth: A New Translation with Introduction, Notes, and Commentary* (AB 7; Garden City: Doubleday, 1975), 40–41.
Ulrich, *BQS, 735–38.
Ulrich, E. and C.M. Murphy, "Ruth," *DJD XVI: 187–94.

Armin Lange

14
Canticles

14.1 Textual History of Canticles

The book of Canticles or Song of Songs, following the Hebrew title *Shir HaShirim*, has been transmitted in several textual forms.[1]

14.1.1 Hebrew Text

MT (→ 14.2.2) has been quite well preserved in three manuscripts (→ 10–20.1). The main one is the Codex Leningradensis (Codex EPB I B 19a of the National Library of Russia in St. Petersburg; MT^L), which offers the text of Canticles on fols. 423^r–425^r. Secondly, it is partly transmitted in the Aleppo Codex (MT^A; folios 587–88), which contains the text of Cant 1:1–3:11. The third can be found in the Cambridge University Library in Manuscript Add. 1753, pp. 98^v–100^v (MT^Y). Apart from very few cases in which textual corruption could be seen and emendations could be carefully proposed,[2] the main differences consist in varying *plene* or defective writing as well as in (minor) differences in vocalisation (for a slightly different view, → 14.2.2). MT has recently been re-edited, in light of all new textual discoveries, in *BHQ.[3]

In addition to MT, Hebrew fragments of Song of Songs have been found in four different Qumran scrolls (→ 14.2.1; → 14.2.3):[4] 1) 4QCant^a, in which remnants of two columns partially offer the text of Cant 3:7–4:6 and 6:11–7:7; 2) 4QCant^b, which presents the text of (a) Cant 2:9–3:2, (b) Cant 3:5,9–11; 4:1b–3,8–11a and (c) Cant 4:14–5,1; 3) 4QCant^c, which contains a few letters and one complete word of (probably) Cant 3:7–8; and 4) 6QCant with remains of two columns seemingly reflecting parts of Cant 1:1–7. These fragmentary texts can reveal a much more complicated textual history of Canticles than ever before presumed.[5]

First, these scrolls display a number of minor variants. 4QCant^a differs from MT in a few instances with respect to *plene* and defective writing, and does not show any clear mistakes. 4QCant^b has somewhat more cases of differing *plene* and defective writing when compared to MT, and, moreover, it reveals a number of textual errors.[6] This scroll also shows a number of very peculiar scribal markings that seem to fill the shorter lines, which Tov suggests are possibly letters of the paleo-Hebrew script or of the cryptic A script, or a combination of both, even including Greek characters.[7] In addition, this scroll is also unique in revealing Aramaic influence.[8] Finally, 6QCant also reveals three orthographic differences when compared to MT (once in Cant 1:5 and twice in Cant 1:6).

Next to these minor variants, however, some peculiar characteristics are more important to discuss when trying to understand the textual development of Canticles. Of specific relevance thereto is the fact that both 4QCant^a and 4QCant^b lack significant and respectively different sections of text when compared to MT. 4QCant^a seems to continue its text with Cant 6:11 right after Cant 4:7, thus missing a counterpart for MT-Cant 4:8–6:10 (→ 14.2.1.1; → 14.2.3.1).[9] 4QCant^b reveals two larger significant minuses when compared to MT, namely Cant 3:6–8 and 4:4–7, and the structure of the scroll moreover suggests that it ended after Cant 5:1 (→ 14.2.1.2; → 14.2.3.2).

---

[1] See especially the introduction to the edition of *BHQ of Canticles by Dirksen ("Canticles," 8*–13*) as well as the introduction to the text ("il testo") by Barbiero, *Cantico dei Cantici*, 20–25.

[2] See e.g. Barbiero, *Cantico dei Cantici*, 21: "My personal research urges me to confirm that MT reveals itself, in any way, as superior to conjecture" (trans. BL).

[3] Cf. Dirksen (ed.), "Canticles."

[4] See editions of 4QCant^a, 4QCant^b, and 4QCant^c by E. Tov in *DJD XVI; and of 6QCant^a by M. Baillet in *DJD III.

[5] See Nebe, *Qumranica I*, 307–22; Tov, "Three Manuscripts," 88–111; Tov, "Excerpted and Abbreviated Biblical Texts," 581–600; Flint, "The Book of Canticles," 96–104.

[6] See, e.g., the textual apparatus of *BHQ at the instances of Cant 2:13, 15; twice in Cant 3:1, and in Cant 4:8.

[7] Cf. Tov, "Canticles," 203; Flint, "The Book of Canticles," 103.

[8] Cf. Tov, "Canticles," 208–09; Flint, "The Book of Canticles," 97.

[9] Cf. Flint, "The Book of Canticles," 100: "about 30%."

In the search for a reason for the absence of these sections of text, several explanations have been suggested. On the one hand, Tov opines that both scrolls offer a text that underwent a deliberate abbreviation of Song of Songs as we know it. This could have been done to avoid repetition in two quite similar sections in which parts of the human body are praised for their beauty (Cant 4:4–7 and 4:8–6:10).[10] This procedure might have been prompted by a lack of space in the scroll,[11] or it could reflect a concern to diminish erotic imagery in the song that might have been controversial.[12] On the other hand, according to Ulrich, the text as we know it in MT is not necessarily the only, nor even the oldest version of the collection of love poems that we find in Song of Songs.[13] It is quite possible that within the process of the literary growth of this book, earlier and shorter collections of love songs existed and were transmitted. In this way, 4QCant^a and 4QCant^b could simply reflect (a) different text(s) than the one we know from MT. In Ulrich's terms, they might reflect "variant literary editions" of Song of Songs. Given the fact that Cant 5:1 definitely seems to function as the end of 4QCant^b, Flint also suggests that at least 4QCant^b could reflect a shorter edition.[14]

In any event, the textual situation of the Hebrew text of Canticles has become much more multi-faceted since the findings at Qumran. This pluriform evidence of the text becomes all the more significant given the fact that Song of Songs in its longer form has also been preserved in the Septuagint as well as in several ancient translations that will be discussed below.

14.1.2 Septuagint

In terms of content, presentation, and length, LXX-Cant (→ 13–17.1.1.2; → 13–17.1.5.4) hardly differs from the Hebrew text of MT (→ 14.2.2). When the Greek text in itself is studied, however, several issues arise.

In 2016, scholars need to use the Rahlfs–Hanhart, *Septuaginta*, since the eclectic edition of the text undertaken by the Göttingen Septuaginta Unternehmen is not yet available.[15] Basing ourselves on the extant text,[16] LXX-Cant does suggest that it would have reflected a text like MT. It offers a translation of its *Vorlage*, which, when compared to MT as our only factual entry to and point of comparison with a supposed possible *Vorlage*, has traditionally been characterised as rather (or very) "literal" or even "slavish."[17] This characterisation made scholars suggest that the Old Greek of Canticles would have been influenced by the so-called *kaige* recension (→ 1.3.1.2),[18] and that it would be very close to or even stemming from Theodotion[19] (→ 1.3.1.2.2). However, more recent research nuances this conclusion by demonstrating

---

[10] Tov, "Excerpted and Abbreviated Biblical Texts," 591–92; Tov, "Canticles," 203 and Flint, "The Book of Canticles," 100–01.

[11] Cf. Lange, "The Textual Plurality of Jewish Scriptures," 43–96, esp. 90.

[12] See, e.g., VanderKam and Flint, *The Meaning of the Dead Sea Scrolls*, 130; Flint, "The Book of Canticles," 101–02.

[13] See, e.g., E. Ulrich, "The Scrolls and the Study of the Hebrew Bible," in *The Dead Sea Scrolls at Fifty: Proceedings of the 1997 Society of Biblical Literature Qumran Section Meetings* (eds. R.A. Kugler and E.M. Schuller; SBLEJL 15; Atlanta: Scholars Press, 1999), 31–41, esp. 33; E. Ulrich, "The Qumran Biblical Scrolls: The Scriptures of Late Second Temple Judaism," in *The Dead Sea Scrolls in Their Historical Context* (ed. T.H. Lim; Edinburgh: T & T Clark, 2000), 67–87, esp. 78; E. Ulrich, "The Qumran Scrolls and the Biblical Text," in Schiffman, Tov, and VanderKam, *Fifty Years*, 51–59, esp. 58; and E. Ulrich, "Deuteronomistically Inspired Scribal Insertions into the Developing Biblical Texts: 4QJudg^a and 4QJer^a," in *Houses Full of All Good Things: Essays in Memory of Timo Veijola* (eds. J. Pakkala and M. Nissinen; SESJ 95; Helsinki: Finnish Exegetical Society, 2008), 489–506, esp. 505.

[14] Cf. Flint, "The Book of Canticles," 102.

[15] It is being prepared by E. Schulz-Flügel.

[16] The textual history of the Greek text (→ 13–17.1.1.2), however, is an issue in itself, reaching beyond the scope of this contribution.

[17] Cf. Gerleman, *Das Hohelied*, 77: "Eine fast sklavische Treue gegen den hebräischen Text scheint die griechische Übersetzung durchgehend zu prägen."

[18] Cf. Barthélemy, *Devanciers*, esp. 33, 49. See also Harl, "La version LXX du Cantique des Cantiques," esp. 120, partly following also the lead of E. Tov, "Transliterations of Hebrew Words in the Greek Versions: A Further Characteristic of the Kaige-Th. Revision?" in Tov, *Greek-Hebrew Bible*, 501–12 (=*Textus* 8 [1973]: 78–92).

[19] See also M. Harl, "La version LXX du Cantique des Cantiques," 119–20.

non-*kaige* features in the text and by more carefully stating that it could have been a "transitional stage on the way to consistent *kaige*-practice."[20] With Auwers, it can be concluded that "the eight chapters of the Greek Song of Songs do not reveal sufficient indications to settle the question on its origin within the *kaige*-group nor in Theodotion." Rather, he states, it is "sufficient to conclude that it has been redacted quite late, in the 1st century C.E., most probably in Palestine, and that it particularly reveals a serious emphasis on literalism which seems to forerun Aquila's working methods."[21]

However, based on more accurate research of the translation technique of this book from the specific perspective of "content and context related criteria,"[22] it has been demonstrated that the translator of Canticles indeed tried to be "faithful" to his original, but that he nevertheless made considerable effort in translating in a creative, idiomatic, and meaningful way (→ 13–17.1.1.2.3).[23] This conclusion strongly nuances its "literalness."[24]

Concrete illustrations of this creativeness in Canticles,[25] based on the study of specific content-related criteria, can be found in the way the translator dealt with the numerous *hapax legomena* found in MT,[26] as well as in the subtle and original manner that he offered equivalent Greek renderings of jargon-defined Hebrew vocabulary in presenting the many proper names of plants, herbs, and flowers, with or without a supplementary metaphorical meaning.[27] Against this background, the Greek text of Canticles may be said to be "literal" to its *Vorlage* in the sense that it is "faithful," but it is not as literal as has traditionally been stated. It thereby offers evidence of its own particular translation character and its own care for the text. In any case, it is a highly valuable, be it indirect, ancient witness to the text of Song of Songs.

---

[20] Cf. Treat, "Lost Keys," 357–60, 382–83.

[21] See Auwers, "Les Septante," 36–37.

[22] Research on the basis of content-related criteria was initiated by H. Ausloos and B. Lemmelijn at the Louvain Centre of Septuagint and Textual Criticism in 2008, and is being developed by their work as well as that conducted under their supervision by a number of doctoral and postdoctoral researchers (H. Debel, D. De Crom, E. Verbeke, V. Kabergs, M. Dhont, B. Beeckman, A. Lwamba, A. Khokhar). It has been applied so far with respect to the rendering of *hapax legomena*, jargon-defined vocabulary, aetiology, and wordplay (i.e. within the context of proper names and toponyms) and is currently being tested to stylistic features such as parallelism in Hebrew poetry. With respect to the methodology, see, e.g., H. Ausloos, B. Lemmelijn, and V. Kabergs, "The Study of Aetiological Wordplay as a Content-Related Criterion in the Characterisation of LXX Translation Technique," in Kreuzer–Meiser–Sigismund, *Septuaginta 2012*, 273–94; H. Ausloos and B. Lemmelijn, "Content Related Criteria in Characterising the LXX Translation Technique," in Karrer–Kraus, *Septuaginta 2010*, 357–76; B. Lemmelijn, *A Plague of Texts? A Text-Critical Study of the So-Called 'Plagues Narrative' in Exodus 7,14–11,10* (OTS 56; Leiden: Brill, 2009), 124–25.

[23] Cf. also De Crom, "The LXX Text of Canticles." This study approaches the text with a function-oriented, product-oriented and a process-oriented focus. See also De Crom, "On Articulation in LXX Canticles," 151–69.

[24] On the important difference in meaning between "faithfulness" and "literalness," see especially A. Aejmelaeus, "The Significance of Clause Connectors in the Syntactical and Translation-Technical Study of the Septuagint," in *Sixth Congress of the IOSCS, Jerusalem, 1986* (ed. C.E. Cox; SBLSCS 23; Atlanta: Scholars Press, 1987), 361–80 [=*Trail*, 49–64], 378: "A distinction should be made between literalness and faithfulness" as well as, also on 378: "Changing the structure of a clause or a phrase, and by so doing replacing an un-Greek expression by a genuine Greek one closely corresponding to the meaning of the original, is quite a different thing from being recklessly free and paying less attention to the correspondence with the original ... A good free rendering is a faithful rendering." See also I. Soisalon-Soininen, "Die Auslassung des Possessivpronomens im Griechischen Pentateuch," in I. Soisalon-Soininen, *Studien zur Septuaginta-Syntax: Zu seinem 70. Geburtstag am 4. Juni 1987* (eds. A. Aejmelaeus and R. Sollamo; AASF Series B 237; Helsinki: Suomalainen Tiedeakatemia, 1987), 86–103 (= *Studia Orientalia memoriae Jussi Aro dedicato* [StOR 55; Helsinki: Suomalainen Tiedeakatemia, 1984], 277–94), 88: "Sie haben den Text möglichst getreu wiedergeben wollen, nicht aber wortwörtlich." Reaching even further beyond the differences between literalness, freedom and faithfulness, Ausloos and Lemmelijn recently introduced a new nuancing category in this discussion, i.e. 'creativity'. Cf. H. Ausloos and B. Lemmelijn, "Faithful Creativity Torn Between Freedom and Literalness in the Septuagint's Translations," *JNSL* 40 (2014): 53–69.

[25] Cf. also H. Ausloos and B. Lemmelijn, "Canticles as Allegory?" 35–48.

[26] Cf. Ausloos and Lemmelijn, "Rendering Love," 43–61.

[27] Lemmelijn, "Flora in Cantico Canticorum," 27–51.

14.1.3 Latin Texts

The Song of Songs has also been preserved in two Latin versions.

VL (→ 1.4.1; → 13–17.2.1.2) has been preserved in various manuscripts and is reflected in ancient literary sources. In addition to the old edition of Canticles by Sabatier in 1743 (vol. 2) and 1749 (vol. 3),[28] new material has been discovered and explored.[29] A critical edition is being prepared by E. Schulz-Flügel, within the context of the Vetus Latina Institute in Beuron (Germany).[30] The text of Canticles in VL mainly reflects LXX and it is especially significant in cases of variants that support particular LXX readings that are not preserved in any other textual versions.

The Vulgate text (→ 13–17.1.7), translated from Hebrew by Hieronymus between 390 and 405 C.E.,[31] reflects a limited number of readings differing from MT (e.g. Cant 4:12 and 7:10). However, it is unclear whether in these cases the Vulgate used a *Vorlage* other than the one we know starting from the comparison with MT (→ 14.2.2), or whether the translator misunderstood the Hebrew, as seems to be the case in most instances. Stylistic variation could also be one of the causes of differences (→ 1.3.5). Some variants of the Vulgate present a unique reading (e.g. Cant 4:1; 8:11, 12), but more often they are shared with LXX (e.g. Cant 1:2), the Peshitta (e.g. Cant 3:8), or both (e.g. Cant 6:4).

14.1.4 Peshitta

The Syriac version of Canticles (→ 11.4.4; → 13–17.1.4.2), called the Peshitta (→ 1.3.4), has been edited in volume 2.5 of the Leiden Peshitta by DiLella, Emerton, and Lane.[32] Generally speaking, the Peshitta seems to be a faithful translation,[33] when compared to MT (→ 14.2.2).[34] Variants often have to do with harmonisations with parallel verses. The translator, however, has simultaneously tried to render the original into rather idiomatic Syriac. As a result, he sometimes deviates from the very strict or literalistic wording of the Hebrew. In some cases, and parallel to the Greek text (→ 13–17.1.1.2), the Syriac translator apparently did not understand his Hebrew *Vorlage*. In those cases, he attempted to be creative and produce an understandable and meaningful text. As already remarked above, Canticles contains a lot of *hapax legomena*, proper names, and jargon. In this respect, and like the Greek translator, the Peshitta translator did his very best to deal wisely and creatively with the difficulties with which he was confronted. Moreover, the LXX and Peshitta sometimes agree over and against MT. This observation could lead scholars to suppose a dependence of the Syriac translation upon the Greek. However, this idea has not been substantially demonstrated.[35] On the contrary, there also seem to be cases where the Syriac translator obviously had trouble with the Hebrew and yet translated differently from LXX (e.g. in Cant 4:1). See further → 11.4.4.

14.1.5 Targum

More a paraphrase than a translation (→ 1.3.3), T-Cant (→ 13–17.1.3) reinterprets the plain text in terms of the history of Israel from the exodus until the expectation of a new era. The lovers from Song of Songs are interpreted as God and Israel. Notwithstanding the fact that, in some cases,

---

[28] Sabatier, *Bibliorum*.

[29] Cf., e.g., De Bruyne, "Les anciennes versions latines du Cantique des Cantiques," 97–122 as well as Vaccari, *Cantici Canticorum vetus latina translatio*.

[30] Schulz-Flügel (ed.), *Canticum Canticorum*. See also already published: Schulz-Flügel, *Gregorius Eliberritanus*.

[31] See: *Biblia Sacra iuxta Latinam Vulgatam versionem* (Rome: Vatican Press, 1926), prepared by F.A. Gasquet et al. (eds.), *Libri Salomonis* (vol. 11; Rome, 1957). See also the more recent edition of R. Weber (ed.), *Biblia Sacra iuxta Vulgatam versionem* (Stuttgart: Deutsche Bibelgesellschaft, ⁴1994).

[32] DiLella, Emerton, and Lane (eds.), *Song of Songs*.

[33] Sometimes called more faithful than LXX. See Rudolph, *Das Hohe Lied*, 80–81 and Gerleman, *Das Hohelied*, 82–84. Cf. in this respect also Barbiero, *Cantico dei Cantici*, 24: "ancore più fedele di quella greca al testo ebraico."

[34] See Dirksen, "The Peshitta Text of Song of Songs," 181; Gerleman, *Das Hohelied*, 82; Salkind, *Die Peschitta zu Schir-Haschirim*; van Wyk, *The Peshitta of the Song of Songs*, 181–89.

[35] See also Garbiero's discussion in this respect, in his *Cantico dei Cantici*, 24.

14.1.6 Conclusion

The text of Canticles has come to us in a variety of textual witnesses. Nevertheless, most of them reveal a text quite close to the one found in MT (→ 14.2.2). Only the Qumran scrolls, and in particular 4QCant^a and 4QCant^b (→ 14.2.1; → 14.2.3). present significant differences in terms of length. Whether these textual witnesses can support the conclusion of abbreviation on the one hand or lengthening on the other, and of respective supposed originality or further evolution, is a question surrounded by principal doubt in terms of the mere possibility of claiming a definite point of comparison. When MT is considered as this point of comparison, answers can be formulated. However, when MT is realised to be a much later edition of some pre- or proto-Masoretic text that functioned within the multiplicity and pluriformity of texts in the era of the literary creation and simultaneous textual transmission, the answer to such questions becomes much less certain. Therefore, I would urge caution in terms of defining matters of (inter-)dependency,[36] and rather keep to a descriptive, objective approach of the factual multifacetedness of the extant textual witnesses.

Keeping in mind this textual plurality and pluriformity, and although it seems at first sight a technical aspect in our approach ot the Bible, it is also utterly important to deal with Biblical texts from that perspective in hermeneuteical terms. Indeed, being aware of the multifacetedness of the biblical texts implies not reading nor imposing them as 'abosute' text but instead being conscious of their grown character throughout the interpretation and actualising re-interpretation of humans, in search of meaning and cautiously trying to touch transcendence in their lives.

Ausloos, H. and B. Lemmelijn, "Canticles as Allegory? Textual Criticism and Literary Criticism in Dialogue," in *Florilegium Lovaniense: Studies in Septuagint and Textual Criticism in Honour of Florentino García Martínez* (eds. H. Ausloos, B. Lemmelijn, and M. Vervenne; BETL 224; Leuven: Peeters, 2008), 35–48.

Ausloos, H. and B. Lemmelijn, "Rendering Love: Hapax Legomena and the Characterisation of the Translation Technique of Song of Songs," in *Translating a Translation: The LXX and its Modern Translations in the Context of Early Judaism* (eds. H. Ausloos et al.; BETL 213; Leuven: Peeters, 2008), 43–61.

Ausloos, H. and B. Lemmelijn, "Praising God or Singing of Love? From Theological into Erotic Allegorisation in the Interpretation of Canticles," *AcT* 30 (2010): 1–18.

Auwers, J.M., "Les Septante, lecteurs du Cantique des Cantiques," *Graphè* 8 (1999): 33–47.

Barbiero, G., *Cantico dei Cantici: Nuova versione, introduzione e commenti* (I Libri Biblici Primo Testamento 24; Milan: Figlie di San Paolo, 2004).

De Bruyne, D., "Les anciennes versions latines du Cantique des Cantiques," *RBén* 38 (1962): 97–122.

Ceulemans, R., "A Critical Edition of the Hexaplaric Fragments of the Book of Canticles: With Emphasis on their Reception in Greek Christian Exegesis" (PhD diss., Katholieke Universiteit Leuven, 2009).

De Crom, D., "On Articulation in LXX Canticles," in *Florilegium Lovaniense: Studies in Septuagint and Textual Criticism in Honour of Florentino García Martínez* (eds. H. Ausloos, B. Lemmelijn, and M. Vervenne; BETL 224; Leuven: Peeters, 2008), 151–69.

De Crom, D., "The LXX Text of Canticles: A Descriptive Study in Hebrew-Greek Translation" (PhD diss., Katholieke Universiteit Leuven, 2009).

DiLella, A.A., J.A. Emerton, and D.J. Lane (eds.), "Song of Songs," in A.A. DiLella, J.A. Emerton, and D.J. Lane (eds.), *Proverbs, Wisdom of Solomon, Ecclesiastes, Song of Songs* (The Old Testament in Syriac according to the Peshitta Version 2.5; Leiden: Brill, 1979).

Dirksen, P.B. (ed.), "Canticles," in *BHQ 18.

Dirksen, P.B., "The Peshitta Text of Song of Songs," *Textus* 19 (1998): 171–81.

Dirksen, P.B., "Septuagint and Peshitta in the Apparatus to Canticles in Biblia Hebraica Quinta," in *Sôfer Mahir: Essays in Honour of Adrian Schenker Offered by the Editors of Biblia Hebraica Quinta* (eds. Y.A.P. Gold-

---

[36] More so than, e.g., Barbiero, *Cantico dei Cantici*, 21: "Le versione antiche si rivelano tutte dipendenti, talora in modo servile, dal testo ebraico," or certainly more prudent than the attempt to reconstruct a hypothetical original Hebrew text, as does Garbini, *Cantico dei Cantici*.

man, A. van der Kooij, and R.D. Weis; VTSup 110; Leiden: Brill, 2006), 15–32.

Flint, P.W., "The Book of Canticles (Song of Songs) in the Dead Sea Scrolls," in *Perspectives on the Song of Songs/Perspectiven der Hoheliedauslegung* (ed. A.C. Hagedorn; BZAW 346; Berlin: De Gruyter, 2005), 96–104.

Garbini, G., *Cantico dei Cantici: Testo, traduzione, note e commento* (Biblica 2; Brescia: Paideia, 1992).

Gerleman, G., *Ruth, Das Hohelied* (BKAT 18; Neukirchen-Vluyn, 1965).

Harl, M., "La version LXX du Cantique des Cantiques et le groupe Kaige-théodotion – quelques remarques lexicales," *Textus* 18 (1995): 101–20.

Lange, A., "The Textual Plurality of Jewish Scriptures in the Second Temple Period in Light of the Dead Sea Scrolls," in *Qumran and the Bible: Studying the Jewish and Christian Scriptures in Light of the Dead Sea Scrolls* (eds. N. and A. Lange; CBET 57; Leuven: Peeters, 2010), 43–96, esp. 65–66.

Lemmelijn, B., "Flora in Cantico Canticorum: Towards a More Precise Characterisation of Translation Technique in the LXX of Song of Songs," in *Scripture in Transition: Essays on Septuagint, Hebrew Bible and Dead Sea Scrolls in Honour of Raija Sollamo* (eds. A. Voitila and J. Jokiranta; JSJSup 126; Leiden: Brill, 2008), 27–51.

Nebe, G.W., "Qumranica I: Zu unveröffentlicheten Handschriften aus Höhle 4 von Qumran," *ZAW* 106 (1994): 307–22.

Rudolph, W., *Das Buch Ruth, das Hohe Lied, die Klagelieder* (KAT 17; Gütersloh: Gerd Mohn, 1962).

Salkind, J.M., *Die Peschitta zu Schir-Haschirim textkritisch und in ihrem Verhältnisse zu MT und LXX untersucht* (Leiden: Brill, 1905).

Schulz-Flügel, E. (ed.), *Canticum Canticorum* (VL 10.3; Freiburg: Herder, 1992–).

Schulz-Flügel, E., *Gregorius Eliberritanus: Epithalamium sive Explanation in Canticis Canticorum* (AGLB 26; Freiburg: Herder, 1994).

Tov, E., "Excerpted and Abbreviated Biblical Texts from Qumran," *RevQ* 16 (1995): 581–600.

Tov, E., "Three Manuscripts (Abbreviated Texts?) of Canticum from Qumran Cave 4," *JSS* 46 (1995): 88–111.

Tov, E., "Canticles," *DJD XVI: 195–219.

Treat, J.C., "Lost Keys: Text and Interpretation in Old Greek Song of Songs and Its Earliest Manuscript Witnesses" (PhD diss., University of Pennsylvania, 1996).

Vaccari, A., *Cantici Canticorum vetus latina translatio a S. Hieronymo ad graecum textum hexaplarem emendate* (Rome: Edizioni di Storia e Letteratura, 1959).

VanderKam, J.C. and P.W. Flint, *The Meaning of the Dead Sea Scrolls: Their Significance for Understanding the Bible, Judaism, Jesus, and Christianity* (San Francisco: Harper, 2002).

van Wyk, W.C., "The Peshitta of the Song of Songs," *Die ou-testamentiese werkgemeenskap in Suid-Afrika* 20–21 (1977–1978): 181–89.

Bénédicte Lemmelijn

14.2 Ancient Hebrew Texts

14.2.1 Ancient Manuscript Evidence

Four damaged manuscripts of Canticles survive from antiquity. All four manuscripts were found in Caves 4 and 6 at Qumran. Two scrolls attest to non-aligned texts of Canticles (4QCant[a] and 4QCant[b]) while the other two scrolls are too damaged for textual classification (4QCant[c] and 6QCant). 4QCant[c] could even represent a quotation from Canticles in a non-biblical text.

14.2.1.1 4QCant[a] (4Q106)

Of the six extant fragments of 4QCant[a], frgs. 1–5 were part of three consecutive columns of the original scroll. 4QCant[a] attests to remnants of Cant 3:4–5, 7–11; 4:1–7; 6:11?–12; 7:1–7. 4QCant[a] was penned in a tiny but early Herodian bookhand.[1] In its orthography, the manuscript is very close to MT-Cant. For the textual classification of 4QCant[a], it is essential to recognize that Cant 4:7 is followed directly by Cant 6:11 in 4QCant[a] 2 ii 1–3. As the missing text amounts to 30 percent of the book of Canticles, it is very unlikely that the omission of Cant 4:8–6:10 is due to a *homoioteleuton*.[2] The short text of 4QCant[a] represents either an earlier form of the book of Canticles than that in MT-Cant or results from an intentional omission. Nebe suggested a "Stichwortanschluß"[3] because of the use of לבונה "frankincense" in Cant 4:6 and לבנה "moon" in Cant 6:10 and because of the two occurrences of יפה "beautiful" in Cant 4:7 and 6:10. Tov points to the similar images that are used to describe similar body parts (neck as a tower in Cant 4:4 and 7:5; breasts as fawns and gazelles in Cant 4:5 and 7:4; the mention of pomegranates in Cant 4:3 and 6:11; the description of eyes in Cant 4:1 and 7:5). These parallels could have motivated the deletion of Cant 4:8–6:10.[4] Tov's arguments are supported by the parallel rhetoric in Cant 4:5a and Cant 7:4, such as the use of the noun מִגְדָּל "tower" in Cant 4:4 and 7:5. In addition to the deletion of Cant 4:8–6:10, 4QCant[a] reads in 108 complete and partial words twice with and eleven times against MT (→ 14.2.2), once with and twelve times against LXX (→ 13–17.1.1.2), as well as nine times non-aligned and five times against 4QCant[b]. Furthermore, 4QCant[a] attests to three readings against MT that cannot be translated into a non-Semitic language. In addition to the deletion of Cant 4:8–6:10, significant variant readings include the different text sequence in Cant 4:1, 2 and the substantial textual differences in Cant 3:11; 4:3, 5; 7:1. All things considered, 4QCant[a] needs to be classified as attesting to a non-aligned text of Canticles (→ 14.2.3.1).[5]

14.2.1.2 4QCant[b] (4Q107)

Three fragments survive of 4QCant[b] attesting to portions of Cant 2:9–17; 3:1–2, 5, 9–11; 4:1–3, 8–11, 14–16; 5:1. The three fragments derive from four columns of the original scroll.[6] The manuscript was written in an early Herodian bookhand from the end of the first century B.C.E.[7] In Cant 5:1, the final *mem* of דוד[י]ם "love" is written in a larger size. In light of a corresponding scribal sign in the lower column margin, Tov wonders whether the scroll ended at this point.[8] However, 4QJosh[a] attest to the same scribal practice in Josh 8:18 but the manuscript does not end there. The orthography of 4QCant[b] resembles that of MT but in-

---

[1] For the paleography and orthography of 4QCant[a], see Tov, "Three Manuscripts," 90–92; Tov, "Canticles," 199.

[2] Cf. Nebe, "Qumranica I," 310; Tov, "Three Manuscripts," 96–98; Tov, "Canticles," 203; Gault, "Fragments," 353–54.

[3] Nebe, "Qumranica I," 310.

[4] Tov, "Three Manuscripts," 89, 97; Tov, *"Biblical Texts," 591–92; Tov, "Canticles," 195–96. See Gault ("Fragments," 354–71) for an extensive discussion of various theories in English scholarly literature on what motivated the omission of Cant 4:8–6:10 in 4QCant[a].

[5] Cf. Tov, *"Biblical Texts," 599–600; Tov, *"Synthese," 27; Lange, *Handbuch*, 477–78.

[6] Cf. Tov, "Canticles," 207.

[7] Thus Ada Yardeni in a communication with E. Tov ("Three Manuscripts," 99; Tov "Canticles," 208).

[8] Tov, "Three Manuscripts," 109–10; Tov, "Canticles," 217.

cludes many Aramaizing spellings.⁹ In addition, there are five or six scribal errors.¹⁰ Tov describes the scroll, therefore, as follows: "The relatively large number of scribal errors and of Aramaic influence on the scribe of 4QCantᵇ make it into an imprecise copy. It further omits two large segments of text, Cant 3:6–8 and 4:4–7."¹¹ In the surviving 166 complete and partial words of 4QCantᵇ, twenty-one cases of textual variation occur. The manuscript reads four times with and seventeen times against MT (→ 14.2.2), never with and twenty-one times against LXX (→ 13–17.1.1.2), as well as seventeen times non-aligned. In addition, 4QCantᵇ reads six times against 4QCantᵃ. Furthermore, 4QCantᵇ attests to three readings against MT that cannot be translated into a non-Semitic language. It is most striking that Cant 3:6–8 and 4:4–7 are omitted.¹² In addition, MT has more text than 4QCantᵇ in Cant 2:17; 4:8 (*homoioteleuton*?) while 4QCantᵇ attests to additional text in Cant 2:12–13 and 4:11. The manuscript also attests to a different text sequence than MT in Cant 5:1. Remnants of letters are visible in the top margins of photograph PAM 40.604, representing either a superscription or a scribal annotation.¹³ The large number of scribal errors, the Aramaizing spellings, and scribal omission point to a careless scribe who abbreviated the text of Canticles intentionally.¹⁴ The omissions of 4QCantᵇ do not seem substantial enough to describe the manuscript as an abbreviated text.¹⁵ Those parts of the text of 4QCantᵇ that the scribe did not change intentionally or by way of scribal error align with MT-Cant. Although, statistically, 4QCantᵇ is best described as non-aligned,¹⁶ this observation shows that a non-aligned text could develop in the Second Temple period from a manuscript that was close to the consonantal text of MT (→ 14.2.3.2).

14.2.1.3 4QCantᶜ (4Q108)

Of 4Q108, only one small fragment of two lines is preserved with remnants of three words from Cant 3:7–8. In their paleography, the ten extant characters of this manuscript resemble 4QCantᵇ and should be described as a Herodian bookhand. As so little text of Canticles is preserved in 4Q108, it is equally possible that this manuscript preserves a quotation of Cant 3:7–8 in a non-biblical text.¹⁷ The single fragment of 4Q108 provides an insufficient amount of text for orthographic and textual classifications.

14.2.1.4 6QCant (6Q6)

One fragment with remains of two columns survives of 6QCant. Remnants of Cant 1:1–7 are extant. The manuscript was executed in a late Herodian bookhand from the middle of the first century C.E.¹⁸ Except for two plene spellings in Cant 1:6, 6QCant agrees in its orthography with MT. The textual classification of 6QCant must remain somewhat speculative because only forty complete and partial words are preserved. 6QCant reads five times against MT-Cant (→ 14.2.2) but goes once with V-Cant (Cant 1:3aα; → 13–17.1.7), and once with S-Cant (Cant 1:3aβ; → 13–17.1.4.2). The three remaining readings against MT-Cant are non-aligned.¹⁹

Baillet, M., "6. Cantique des Cantiques," *DJD III.1: 112–14.
Flint, P., "The Book of Canticles (Song of Songs) in the Dead Sea Scrolls," in *Perspectives on the Song of Songs – Perspektiven der Hohenliedauslegung* (ed. A.C. Hagedorn; BZAW 346; Berlin: De Gruyter, 2005), 96–104.

---

⁹ Cf. Tov, "Three Manuscripts," 99–100; Tov, "Canticles," 208.
¹⁰ For the scribal errors in 4QCantᵇ, see also A. Lange, "The Textual Plurality of Jewish Scriptures in the Second Temple Period in Light of the Dead Sea Scrolls," in *Qumran and the Bible: Studying the Jewish and Christian Scriptures in Light of the Dead Sea Scrolls* (eds. N. Dávid and A. Lange; CBET 57; Leuven: Peeters, 2010), 43–96 (65–66).
¹¹ Tov, "Three Manuscripts," 99; cf. Tov, "Canticles," 208.
¹² For the intentional deletion of these verses, see Tov, "Three Manuscripts," 89, 106–07; Gault, "Fragments," 353.
¹³ Thus Tov, "Three Manuscripts," 89, 100, 102; Tov, "Canticles," 210.
¹⁴ Against Flint, "Book of Canticles," 102.
¹⁵ Against Tov, *"Biblical Texts," 591–92; Tov, "Canticles," 195–96.

¹⁶ Cf. Lange, *Handbuch, 479.
¹⁷ Cf. Lange, *Handbuch, 479.
¹⁸ For the paleography, orthography, and text of 6QCant, see Baillet, "Cantique," 112–13.
¹⁹ Thus Tov, *"Synthese," 27; Lange, *Handbuch, 479; against Tov, "Three Manuscripts," 88.

Gault, B.P., "The Fragments of Canticles from Qumran: Implications and Limitations for Interpretation," *RevQ* 24 (2010): 351–71.

Lange, **Handbuch*, 375–81.

Nebe, G.W., "Qumranica I," *ZAW* 104 (1994): 307–22 (309–12).

Tov, E., "Canticles," **DJD* XVI: 195–219.

Tov, E., "Excerpted and Abbreviated Biblical Texts from Qumran," *RevQ* 16 (1993–1995): 581–600, esp. 591–92, 600.

Tov, E., "Three Manuscripts (Abbreviated Texts?) of Canticles from Qumran Cave 4," *JJS* 46 (1995): 88–111.

Ulrich, **BQS*, 739–45.

Armin Lange

14.2.2 Masoretic Texts and Ancient Texts Close to MT

The only complete Hebrew text of Canticles is MT-Cant. It is also the only textual witness to the (proto-)Masoretic text of Canticles. Of the four Canticles manuscripts from Qumran, 4QCant[a] and 4QCant[b] are non-aligned in character while 4QCant[c] and 6QCant are too damaged for text-typological classification (→ 14.2.1). The text of 4QCant[b] (→ 14.2.3.2) as well as the texts of the ancient versions all developed out of MT-Cant, while 4QCant[a] preserves an abbreviated version of a textual predecessor of MT-Cant (→ 14.2.3.1).

14.2.2.1 History of Research

The textual history of the Hebrew Canticles is rarely addressed in scholarship. Research focuses mainly on the ancient versions or discusses individual variant readings. Before the discovery of the Dead Sea Scrolls and even today, Ewald's dictum of 1867 influenced and influences most studies. Ewald[1] regarded MT-Cant as a well-preserved text that suffered from a very limited amount of textual corruption. Ewald's influence can even be traced to Dirksen's **BHQ* edition of Canticles: "The text of Canticles is well preserved. There are only a few cases where textual corruption is likely."[2] Thus, commentaries on Canticles emphasize the "good repair" of the Hebrew text of Canticles[3] or do not address the Hebrew textual history of Canticles at all.[4] Only a minority of scholars find a large amount of textual corruption in MT-Cant. An early example of this position is Graetz.[5]

14.2.2.2 Manuscripts and Editions

The most important manuscripts attesting to the (proto-)Masoretic text of Canticles are MT[L] (Russian National Library in St. Petersburg; EBP. I B 19a) and a Yemenite manuscript at the Cambridge University Library (Add. ms 1753: MT[Y]). In the Aleppo Codex (MT[A]), only Cant 1:1–3:11 is extant. For MT-Cant, two critical editions are currently available in the **BH* series. Superseding earlier editions in

---

[1] H. Ewald, *Die Dichter des Alten Bundes: Erklärt*, Part 2: *Die Salômonischen Schriften* (2nd ed.; Göttingen: Vandenhoeck & Ruprecht's Verlag, 1867), 355–56: "Da die sprache hier keineswegs überall so leicht ist und das mifsverständnifs dieses für die Späteren immer schwerer verständlichen buches früh genug anfing, so würde man eher manche verderbte oder doch weniger ursprüngliche lesart erwarten, und sieht sich desto angenehmer getäuscht. Wirklich findet sich abgesehen von der eben erläuterten überschrift kein einziger fremdartiger zusaz in unserm wortgefüge" (355).

[2] Dirksen, "Canticles," 8*.

[3] R.E. Murphy, *The Song of Songs: A Commentary on the Book of Canticles or the Song of Songs* (Hermeneia; Minneapolis: Fortress Press, 1990), 7; cf., e.g., Y. Zakovitch, *Das Hohelied* (HTKAT; Freiburg i.B.: Herder, 2004), 101–02.

[4] E.g., G. Gerleman, *Ruth, Das Hohelied* (BKAT 18; Neukirchen-Vluyn: Neukirchener Verlag des Erziehungsvereins, 1965); O. Keel, *The Song of Songs* (CC; Minneapolis: Fortress Press, 1994).

[5] Graetz, *Schir Ha-Schirim*: "Der Text zeigt an vielen Stellen verderbte Lesarten, und die ganze Fabel 'vom Raube der Sulamit für den Salomonischen Harem' beruht einzig und allein auf Textverderbniss. Man muss eigentlich umgekehrt urtheilen, als es Ewald gethan hat. Da das H.L. mehrere Jahrhunderte hindurch ohne kanonisches Ansehen war, es vielmehr für ein profanes Liebeslied gehalten und erst am Ende des ersten Jahrhunderts n. C. heilig gesprochen wurde, aber auch damals noch nicht allgemein dafür anerkannt war, so gliche es einem Wunder, wenn der Text sich unverdorben erhalten haben sollte ... Kurz das H.L. war durchaus vom dritten Jahrhundert v. C. bis Ende des ersten Jahrhunderts n. C. ohne masoretische Controlle. In der That zeigt sich in demselben eine ganze Reihe von Textverderbnissen, und auch bei wesentlichen Punkten, von denen das Verständnis des Ganzen abhängt" (pp. 100–01). Graetz provides on pp. 101–16 of his commentary a long list of scribal corruptions and textual emendations.

that series, both are diplomatic in nature and are based on MT^L. The edition by Horst in *BHS is selective in the number of variants recorded in its apparatus. The *BHQ edition by Dirksen is also not comprehensive but recognizes more variant readings and includes the Canticles manuscripts from Qumran. Its text-critical introduction and commentary make the *BHQ edition of Canticles an inestimable tool. For the variants of the medieval Masoretic manuscript tradition, the edition of Kennicott (*1776–1780, 2.525–33) and the variant list of De Rossi (*1784–1788, 3.226–33) remain indispensable.

14.2.2.3 Nature and Text-Critical Character of (Proto)-MT-Cant

The differences between MT^{A,L,Y} concern only details of vocalization and plene and defective spellings.[6] Unlike the other books of the Hebrew Bible, MT-Cant does not include any of the baroque spellings that are common in the so-called Qumran orthography.[7] This absence of baroque spellings implies that Canticles was transmitted during the Second Temple period by way of a limited number of manuscripts that did not undergo orthographic and textual standardization. Due to the small group of ancient copies by which Canticles was transmitted, MT-Cant suffered only from a limited amount of accidental and intentional scribal corruption. Examples for scribal errors include the following:

– In Cant 1:7, כְּעֹטְיָה "like one who is veiled" results from a metathesis of 'ayin and tet. The correct reading would be כטעיה "like a wandering woman" (cf. P, Sym, V, T);[8]
– In Cant 1:17, MT's untranslatable hapax legomenon רַחִיטֵנוּ results from a confusion of he and het. The correct reading is given in the Qere רהיטנו "our rafters" (cf. LXX, Sym, V, T);[9]

– In Cant 4:12, גַּל "heap of stones" yields no sense and needs to be emended to גן "garden" (cf. LXX, P, V);[10]
– In Cant 7:5, the MT reading בְּרֵכוֹת "pools" lost the preposition כְּ "like" by way of haplography due to the similarity of bet and kaph. The correct text was most likely כברכות "like pools" (cf. LXX, T, V);[11]
– In Cant 7:7, the incomprehensible בַּתַּעֲנוּגִים "in delights" developed by way of a haplography of the letter taw and a missing word divider out of בת תענוגים "daughter of delights" (cf. Aq, Sym).[12]

In addition to such scribal errors, a comparison with 4QCant^b (→ 14.2.1.2 and → 14.2.3.2) reveals several occurrences of linguistic harmonization in MT-Cant:

– In Cant 2:14, MT reads קוֹלֵךְ "your voice" for the שמעך "your sound" of 4QCant^b in harmonization with the second occurrence of קוֹלֵךְ in that verse;
– In Cant 4:8, MT changes the plural מן ראשי "from the peaks of" (4Cant^b) to the singular מֵרֹאשׁ "from the peak" in harmonization with the second occurrence of מֵרֹאשׁ in this verse;
– In Cant 4:10, MT changes the singular form שמנך "your oil" (4QCant^b) to the dual form שְׁמָנַיִךְ "your oils" in harmonization with the שִׂפְתוֹתַיִךְ "your lips" in Cant 4:11.[13]

Comparison with 4QCant^a (→ 14.2.1.1 and → 14.2.3.1) reveals further cases of linguistic editing that dissolve cases of asyndesis:[14]

– In Cant 3:11, MT adds a waw-copulativum to the ביום "on the day" of 4QCant^a resulting in וּבְיוֹם "and on the day." With its textual change, MT

---

[6] Dirksen, "Canticles," 8*.
[7] See A. Lange, "The Question of the So-Called Qumran Orthography, the Severus Scroll, and the Masoretic Text," Hebrew Bible and Ancient Israel 3 (2014): 424–75 (440–41).
[8] Graetz, Schir Ha-Schirim, 131; Hamp, "Textkritik," 198–99; Gerleman, Hohelied, 102; Dirksen, "Canticles," 58*.
[9] Dirksen, "Canticles," 58*.
[10] Graetz, Schir Ha-Schirim, 161; Hamp, "Textkritik," 204; Gerleman, Hohelied, 157; Dirksen, "Canticles," 61*.
[11] Gerleman, Hohelied, 194; Dirksen, "Canticles," 63*.
[12] Graetz, Schir Ha-Schirim, 197; Gerleman, Hohelied, 201; Dirksen, "Canticles," 63*.
[13] Cf. Tov, "Canticles," 216.
[14] Cf. Tov, "Canticles," 201, 202, 204.

14.2.2 MASORETIC TEXTS AND ANCIENT TEXTS CLOSE TO MT

avoids the tautology of two expressions being introduced with ביום "on the day";

- In Cant 4:6, MT changes the אל "to" in 4QCantª to וְאֶל "and to" to avoid the asyndesis in אל הר המו[ר] אל גבעת הלבונה "to the mountain of myr]rh, to the hill of the Lebanon";
- In Cant 7:7, MT adds a *waw-copulativum* to the מה "how" of 4QCantª resulting in the reading וּמַה "and how" to avoid the tautological expression מה יפית מה נעמת אהבה בת תענוגים "How beautiful, how sweet you are, love, daughter of delights";[15]
- In Cant 4:2, MT-Cant adds a relative particle (שֶׁעָלוּ "that have come up") to the עָלוּ "coming up" of 4QCantª, in order to avoid an asyndetic relative clause.

Comparison with 4QCantª also reveals linguistic actualization in MT-Cant:

- In Cant 4:3, 4QCantª preserves the *hapax legomenon* מזקנתך. The meaning of this word is uncertain but it indicates a part of the face, most likely the chin.[16] MT-Cant (cf. LXX) replaced the unusual term with רַקָּתֵךְ "your temple," because knowledge about the meaning of the *hapax legomenon* got lost. Examples for similar Hebrew-Hebrew translations include the following: In 1 Sam 20:34, MT-Sam renders the וַיִּפְחַז "and he shot up" of 4QSamᵇ as וַיָּקָם "and he got up."[17] In Hos 7:15, 4QXII⁶ replaces MT's זְרוֹעֹתָם "their arms" with אזרועותם "their arms." The same replacement of Hebrew זְרוֹעַ with the Aramaism אֶזְרוֹעַ can be observed in the quotation of Ps 37:17 in 4QpPsª (4Q171) 1–2 ii 24 as well as in various other biblical manuscripts from Qumran (Deut 5:15 in 4QPhyl J, 4QPhyl L, and XQPhyl 3; Deut 11:2 in 4QPhyl A, 4QPhyl K, and 8QPhyl; Isa 52:10 in 4QIsaᶜ; and Ps 136:12 in 11QPsª);[18]

- In Cant 4:4, MT-Cant replaces the תלוי בו "on it hang" of 4QCantª with תָּלוּי עָלָיו "upon it hang" (cf. LXX). The verb תלה "to hang" is normally combined with the preposition עַל to indicate the place upon which somebody or something is hung (2 Sam 4:12; Isa 22:24; Ezek 15:3; 27:11; Job 26:7; Esth 5:1; 7:9, 10), often together with the word עֵץ indicating "wood," a "tree," or a "gallows" on or upon which someone is hanged (Gen 40:19; Deut 21:22; Josh 8:29; 10:26; Esth 2:23; 6:4; 8:7; 9:13, 25; 4QpNah 3–4 i 7; 4QapocrJer Cᵃ 15 i 3; 11QTª LXIV:8, 9, 10, 12 par 4QTª 14 2, 3, 4). Only rarely is תלה "to hang" used with the preposition בְּ "in/on" (2 Sam 18:9 [4QSamª, LXX, T, S, V]; 18:10; Ezek 27:10, 11; Sir 7:18) as in 4QCantª in Cant 4:4 (→ 14.2.2.3). MT-Cant replaced בו "on it" with עָלָיו "upon it" to avoid a preposition that is unusual with תלה and to harmonize Cant 4:4 with other occurrences of the verb תלה "to hang."

On the whole, MT-Cant can be characterized as a good text that is relatively close to the supposed *Urtext* of Canticles but which suffered from a certain number of scribal errors and experienced a limited amount of linguistic and harmonizing editing. The few secondary readings are not enough to qualify MT-Cant as an editorial text. Whether it was "the memory of the musical rhythm to which the text was sung (or chanted) that served to preserve the text (scil. of Canticles) in its original form"[19] must remain speculation, as other texts that were musically performed, such as Psalms (→ 10.1; → 10.2.1; → 10.2.2; → 10.2.3), are not in as good a state of textual repair as is Canticles. In my opinion, it is more likely that only very few Canticles manuscripts existed during the Second Temple period. This narrow textual transmission allowed only for a limited amount of scribal corruption.

---

[15] For the reading בת תענוגים "daughter of delights," see the list of scribal errors in MT above.

[16] Cf. Tov, "Canticles," 202.

[17] See A. Lange, "Die Wurzel *phz* und ihre Konnotationen," *VT* 51 (2001): 497–510 (500–01).

[18] See A. Lange, "4QXII⁶ (4Q82) as an Editorial Text," *Text* (forthcoming).

[19] D.L. Christensen, "The Masoretic Accentual System and Repeated Metrical Refrains in Nahum, Song of Songs, and Deuteronomy," in *VIII International Congress of the International Organization for Masoretic Studies: Chicaco 1988* (ed. E.J. Revell; SBLMasS 6; Missoula: Scholars Press, 1990), 31–36 (33).

14.2.2.4 Date and Milieu

It remains uncertain when the textual corruption in MT-Cant occurred and who was responsible for it. It seems likely though that several scribes were involved. Given that 4QCant[a] (→ 14.2.1.1) and 4QCant[b] (→ 14.2.1.2) both date to the late first century B.C.E. and that the Canticles text of 4QCant[b] developed from MT-Cant, a date for the text of MT-Cant in the later part of the Second Temple period seems likely.

14.2.2.5 Relevance for Exegesis

As 4QCant[b] (→ 14.2.3) and the texts of the ancient versions all developed out of MT-Cant (→ 14.1), it can be speculated that the consonantal text of MT-Cant is close to the final redactional stage of Canticles. However, 4QCant[a] points to an earlier textual stage of Canticles that employed asyndesis more often as a stylistic device and used rare Hebrew expressions and unusual constructions.

Dirksen, P.B., "Canticles שיר השירים," in *BHQ, Part 18: General Introduction and Megilloth*, 8*–13*, 26*–28*, 38*–40*, 56*–64*, 11–24.

Graetz, H., *Schir Ha-Schirim שיר השירים oder das salomonische Hohelied: Übersetzt und erklärt* (Vienna: Wilhelm Braumüller, 1871).

Hamp, V., "Zur Textkritik am Hohenlied," *BZ* 1 (1957): 197–214.

Horst, F., "*Libros Cantici Canticorum et Ecclesiastes*," in *BHS, 1336–54.

Armin Lange

14.2.3 Other Texts

Of the four ancient Hebrew Canticles manuscripts found at Qumran (→ 14.2.1) only two do not align with MT-Cant (4QCant[a] and 4QCant[b]; → 14.2.2). 4QCant[b] developed out of MT-Cant, while 4QCant[a] is an abbreviated version of a forerunner of MT-Cant. 4QCant[c] and 6QCant are too badly damaged for text-typological and textual characterization.

14.2.3.1 Text of 4QCant[a] (4Q106)

The text of 4QCant[a] (→ 14.2.1.1) is difficult to characterize. Most if not all of the manuscript's secondary readings represent intentional changes introduced by a copyist. The most significant difference from MT-Cant (→ 14.2.2) and LXX-Cant (→ 13–17.1.1.2) is the omission of Cant 4:8–6:10 to avoid the graphic erotic language of this passage.[1] The extent of the omission was probably determined by parallels in language and motives. Nebe pointed to the use of לבונה "frankincense" in Cant 4:6 and לבנה "moon" in Cant 6:10 and to the two occurrences of יפה "beautiful" in Cant 4:7 and 6:10. Tov emphasized the similar images that are used to describe similar body parts (neck as a tower in Cant 4:4 and 7:5; breasts as fawns and gazelles in Cant 4:5 and 7:4; the mention of pomegranates in Cant 4:3 and 6:11; the description of eyes in Cant 4:1 and 7:5). Due to the omission of Cant 4:8–6:10, the text of 4QCant[a] should be characterized as abbreviated.

The other secondary readings of 4QCant[a] attest to linguistic editing and harmonization:

– In Cant 3:11, 4QCant[a] changes MT's singular phrase בְּנוֹת צִיּוֹן "daughters of Zion" in harmonization with Cant 3:10 to the more popular locution בנ[וֹת ירושלם "daug]hters of Jerusalem";[2]
– In Cant 4:2, 4QCant[a] replaces MT's אֵין "none" with the alternate form אינה which has the same meaning but conforms with rabbinic Hebrew;[3]
– In Cant 4:1 and 4:2, 4QCant[a] moves the comparative phrases כעדר] העזים "like a flock[of goats" and כְּעֵדֶר הַקְּצוּבוֹת "like a flock of shorn ones" to the beginning of a hemistich. In this way, 4QCant[a] harmonizes the word sequence of Cant 4:1–2 with the word sequence of Cant 4:3–4, where the comparative phrases כְּחוּט הַשָּׁנִי "like crimson thread," כְּפֶלַח הָרִמּוֹן "like a slice of

---

[1] For the intentional deletion of Cant 4:8–6:10, see Tov, "Three Manuscripts," 89, 106–07; Flint, "Canticles," 101; H. Ausloos and B. Lemmelijn, "Canticles as Allegory? Textual Criticism and Literary Criticism in Dialogue," in *Florilegium Lovaniense: Studies in Septuagint and Textual Criticism in Honour of Florentino García Martínez* (eds. H. Ausloos, B. Lemmelijn, and M. Vervenne; BETL 224; Leuven: Peeters, 2008), 35–48 (39–40); cf. also the extensive survey of the various explanations for the omission of Cant 3:6–8 and 4:4–7 in 4QCant[b] in Gault, "Fragments," 353–71. Cf. Tov, "Excerpted," 591.

[2] Tov, "Canticles," 201.

[3] Tov, "Canticles," 201.

pomegranate," and כְּמִגְדַּל דָּוִיד "like the tower of David" each introduce a hemistich;
- In Cant 4:5, 4QCantᵃ reads רעים "feeding ones" instead of MT's הָרוֹעִים "the feeding ones." The determinative -ה was deleted by 4QCantᵃ because the preceding participles of vv. 4–5 also lack such a determinative and because the nouns in v. 5 to which רעים relates are also construed as indeterminate.

In the surviving 108 complete and partial words of 4QCantᵃ, the surprising number of six original readings can be found. This unusually high number of original readings points to the high textual quality of 4QCantᵃ in those sections where it does not suffer from abbreviation.

- A recurring feature of 4QCantᵃ is that its text preserves asynetic readings (→ 14.2.2.3) that were dissolved in MT-Cant by the addition of a *waw-copulativum* (Cant 3:11: MT's וּבְיוֹם "and on the day" against בְּיוֹם "on the day" in 4QCantᵃ; Cant 4:6: MT's וְאֶל "and to" against אֶל "to" in 4QCantᵃ; Cant 7:7: MT's וּמַה "and how" against מַה "how" in 4QCantᵃ).⁴
- In Cant 4:3, 4QCantᵃ preserves the *hapax legomenon* מזקנתך whose meaning is uncertain but which could indicate the chin.⁵ MT-Cant (cf. LXX) replaced the unusual term with רַקָּתֵךְ "your temple" (→ 14.2.2.3).
- In Cant 4:4, MT-Cant replaces the בו "on it" of 4QCantᵃ with עָלָיו "upon it" (cf. LXX) because the verb תלה "to hang" with which בו is construed in 4QCantᵃ is normally combined with the preposition עַל "upon" (→ 14.2.2.3).

Disregarding the omission of Cant 4:8–6:10, more than half of the variant readings of 4QCantᵃ are of better quality than the corresponding MT text. Therefore, 4QCantᵃ goes back to a textual ancestor that was an earlier Canticles text than MT as argued by several original readings. This earlier Canticles text was abbreviated by the scribe of 4QCantᵃ or its parent text and also suffered some scribal corruption. MT-Cant developed out of this earlier Canticles text. Except for the large omission of Cant 4:8–6:10, the few secondary readings point to a small amount of linguistic editing and harmonization in 4QCantᵃ, which is reminiscent of editorial texts.⁶

14.2.3.2 4QCantᵇ (4Q107)

Although only 166 complete and partial words from Cant 2:9–17; 3:1–2, 5, 9–11; 4:1–3, 8–11, 14–16; and 5:1 are preserved of 4QCantᵇ (→ 14.2.1.2), the manuscript is characterized by a large amount of scribal corruption. Especially striking are thirteen Aramaisms.⁷ Apocopated *mi-* is e.g. constantly replaced by *min* in 4QCantᵇ:⁸ מן לבנון "from Lebanon" (twice in Cant 4:8); מן ראשי "from the peaks of" (Cant 4:8); מן הררי "from the mountains of" (Cant 4:8); מן יין "than wine" (Cant 4:10); מן כל "than any" (Cant 4:10); מן]דיו "from his good fortune" (Cant 4:16).⁹ Other Aramaisms include the use of הטללים "the shadows" (MT הַצְּלָלִים "the shadows") and הררי "mountains" in Cant 2:17, the two uses of Hebrew את "you" instead of אַתְּי "you" in Cant 4:8,¹⁰ the plural form בשמין "spices" in Cant 4:10, as well as אמנון "Omonon" instead of MT's אֲמָנָה "Amanah" in Cant 4:8. That the scribe of 4QCantᵃ can use Hebrew forms elsewhere in his manuscript and that his Aramaisms occur in only three parts of 4QCantᵇ, i.e., frgs. 1 12–23; 2 ii 7–13; and 3 12, argues against a systematic Aramaizing revision of Canticles in 4QCantᵇ. It seems more probable that the Aramaisms of 4QCantᵇ are unconscious adjustments of the Hebrew text by the scribe of 4QCantᵇ.¹¹ Such unconscious adjustments could have easily hap-

---

⁴ Cf. Tov, "Canticles," 201, 202, 204.

⁵ Cf. Tov, "Canticles," 202.

⁶ For the term "editorial," see A. Lange, "4QXIIᵍ (4Q82) as an Editorial Text," *Text* (forthcoming).

⁷ Cf. Tov, "Three Manuscripts," 99–100; Tov, "Canticles," 209; Young, "Notes," 122–27.

⁸ Tov, "Canticles," 209.

⁹ Contra Luzarraga, "El cilantro."

¹⁰ In the Masoretic punctuation "with you." The scribe "may have explained אתי as the Aramaic 2nd person fem. Pronoun, changed by him to the Hebrew את" (Tov, "Canticles," 216).

¹¹ Contra Young, "Notes," 127–30, who reckons with the possibility that 4QCantᵇ preserves an earlier linguistic form of Canticles.

pened when the scribe's attention slipped while copying a complicated Hebrew text like Canticles.

Other scribal errors in 4QCant[b] include:

- haplography (e.g., ש[ועלים "foxes" [cf. LXX, V] instead of שׁוּעָלִים שׁוּעָלִים "foxes, foxes" [MT] in Cant 2:15);[12]
- dittography (e.g., בלי[לות בלילות "at ni]ght, at night" instead of בַּלֵּילוֹת "at night" [MT] in Cant 3:1);
- homoioteleuton (e.g., מֵרֹאשׁ שְׂנִיר וְחֶרְמוֹן "from the peaks of Senir and Hermon" [MT-Cant 4:8 > 4QCant[b]]);[13]
- metathesis (e.g., התנאה instead of הַתְּאֵנָה "fig tree" [MT] in Cant 2:13; בשקתי instead of בִּקַּשְׁתִּי "I searched" [MT] in Cant 3:1);
- phonetic interchange of *resh* and *lamed* (Cant 2:14, המדלגה "the place of leaping" instead of MT's הַמַּדְרֵגָה "the steep pathway" in Cant 2:14);[14]
- erroneous additions (עת "time" in Cant 2:12 [crossed out by the scribe himself], an erroneous addition of a word in Cant 4:10 [deleted by way of *sigma* and *antisigma*? 4QCant[b] III:12], an added word might also be attested in a supralinear addition still visible on photograph PAM 40.604);[15]
- the reading of אבאי "let me come" instead תָּבוֹאִי "come" (MT) in Cant 4:8.

In addition to this long list of examples for accidental scribal corruption, the scribe of 4QCant[b] or its textual ancestor also introduced intentional changes into Canticles. These changes include both abbreviated and editorial readings:

- In Cant 2:12 and 2:13, 4QCant[b] inserts an additional הנה "behold" to emphasize how the lover alerts his beloved to the end of winter;
- 4QCant[b] omits Cant 3:6–8 and 4:4–7 because of their erotic content;[16]
- In Cant 4:3, 4QCant[b] changes the difficult plural form וּמִדְבָּרֵיךְ "and your mouths" (MT; cf. Targum) to the singular ומדברך "and your mouth";
- In Cant 4:3, 4QCant[b] adds a conjunction to an asyndectic phrase: ומבעד "and behind" instead of MT's מִבַּעַד "behind" (cf. LXX);
- 4QCant[b] inserted אחותי "my sister" into Cant 4:11 because of its similar occurrence in Cant 4:9, 10, 12; 5:1;[17]
- In Cant 4:16, 4QCant[b] did not understand the rare word מֶגֶד "choice produce" and changed the phrase וְיֹאכַל פְּרִי מְגָדָיו "and eat from the fruit of his choice produce" in MT to ויאכל מן ג]דיו "and eat from his good fortune" (Cant 4:16).[18]

In addition to these secondary readings, 4QCant[b] preserves in Cant 2:14 (שמעך "your sound" instead of MT's קוֹלֵךְ "your voice"), Cant 4:8 (מן ראשי "from the peaks of" instead of MT's מֵרֹאשׁ "from the peak"), and Cant 4:10 (שמנך "your oil" instead of MT's שְׁמָנַיִךְ "your oils") three original readings for which MT attests to harmonizations (→ 14.2.2.3).

On the whole, 4QCant[b] can be described as attesting to an abbreviated text that suffers from scribal corruption and includes a limited number of editorial readings. When all scribal errors and intentional alterations are removed from 4QCant[b], it becomes clear that its underlying *Vorlage* was close to the consonantal text of MT.[19] The large number of copyist errors in 4QCant[b] demonstrates how scribal carelessness can be responsible for

---

[12] Cf. Zakovitch, *Hohelied*, 159. The identification of the haplography in 4QCant[b] is based on the letter-count of frg. 1 10; cf. Tov, "Three Manuscripts," 99 and Tov, "Canticles," 212.

[13] Tov, "Canticles," 216.

[14] Tov, "Canticles," 212. This scribal error might have been inspired by the מְדַלֵּג עַל־הֶהָרִים "leaping over mountains" of Cant 2:8 (cf. Nebe, "Qumranica I," 311).

[15] Cf. Tov, "Three Manuscripts," 106; Tov, "Canticles," 215; Tov, *Scribal Practices*, 202.

[16] For the intentional deletion of these verses, see Tov, "Three Manuscripts," 89, 106–07; Flint, "Canticles," 101–02; Ausloos and Lemmelijn, "Fragments," 39–40; cf. also the extensive survey of the various explanations for the omission of Cant 3:6–8 and 4:4–7 in 4QCant[b] in Gault, "Fragments," 353–71.

[17] Cf. Tov, "Three Manuscripts," 108; "Canticles," 216. This insertion is reminiscent of the harmonizing editing, discussed below.

[18] Contra Luzarraga, "El cilantro."

[19] Cf. Lange, *Handbuch*, 478–79.

the unintended emergence of a new (non-aligned) Canticles text, that in terms of its text-typology is far removed from its semi- or proto-Masoretic base text.[20]

Flint, P., "The Book of Canticles (Song of Songs) in the Dead Sea Scrolls," in *Perspectives on the Song of Songs – Perspektiven der Hohenliedauslegung* (ed. A. Hagedorn; BZAW 346; Berlin: Walter de Gruyter, 2005), 96–104.

Gault, B.P., "The Fragments of Canticles from Qumran: Implications and Limitations for Interpretation," *RevQ* 24 (2009–2010): 351–71.

Lange, **Handbuch*, 477–81.

Lange, A., "The Textual Plurality of Jewish Scriptures in the Second Temple Period in Light of the Dead Sea Scrolls," in *Qumran and the Bible: Studying the Jewish and Christian Scriptures in Light of the Dead Sea Scrolls* (eds. N. and A. Lange; CBET 57; Leuven: Peeters, 2010), 43–96, esp. 65–66.

Luzarraga, J., "El cilantro in 4QCant^b," *EstBib* 60 (2002): 107–23.

Nebe, G.W., "Qumranica I," *ZAW* 104 (1994): 307–22, esp. 309–12.

Tov, E., "Three Manuscripts (Abbreviated Texts?) of Canticles from Qumran Cave 4," *JJS* 46 (1995): 88–111.

Tov, E., "Canticles," **DJD* XVI: 195–219.

Tov, E., "Excerpted and Abbreviated Biblical Texts from Qumran," *RevQ* 16 (1993–1995): 581–600, esp. 591–92, 600.

Ulrich, **BQS*, 739–45.

Young, I., "Notes on the Language of 4QCant^b," *JJS* 52 (2001): 122–31.

Armin Lange

---

[20] Cf. Lange, "The Textual Plurality of Jewish Scriptures," 65–66.

15
Qohelet

∵

15.1 Textual History of Qohelet

15.1.1 Earliest Developments

Text-critical research on the Hebrew text of Qohelet has largely been confined to the commentaries on the book and articles on specific verses. Euringer's 1890 study goes through the book proposing corrections.[1] It is difficult to see any notable developments in the modern ideas of the *text* of Qohelet, but opinions have changed with regard to the formation of the book in its earliest stages (see further → 15.2.2.1).

The authorial unity of the book of Qohelet, though assumed by traditional commentators, was strongly contested in the late nineteenth and twentieth centuries. Some scholars argued on literary grounds that several important stages in the book's development can be identified.

In 1893, Siegfried employed source-critical methodology to identify numerous layers: the original Qohelet, a Sadducee influenced by Epicureanism, a "Chakham" (sage), a "Chasid" (an orthodox pietist), four main glossators, two epilogists, some unidentifiable glossators, and two editors.[2] Siegfried's working principle was that each writer must be absolutely consistent and represent a distinct point of view.

No one seems to have accepted Siegfried's intricate theory, but it did provide a grid for some more moderate proposals. The influential commentary of Barton,[3] for example, affirmed the basic unity of the book, as assembled from Qohelet's words by an editor, but assigned third-person utterances, including the epilogue, to an editor or glossator. Further additions were by a Chasid glossator, who added pietistic sentiments, such as the affirmation of retribution (Qoh 2:26), and a Chakham, a sage who affirmed the value of wisdom. The components that Barton (pp. 43–46) identifies as secondary can be listed as typical of commentators of his era: By the Chasid: Qoh 2:26; 3:17; 7:18b–26b, 29; 8:2b, 3a, 5, 6a, 11–13; 11:9b; 12:1a, 13, 13–14; by the Chakham: Qoh 4:5; 5:3, 7a; 7:1a, 3, 5, 6–9, 11, 12, 19; 8:1; 9:17–18; 10:1–3, 8–14a, 15, 18, 19; editorial addition: "says Qohelet" in Qoh 1:2; 7:27; and Qoh 12:8, 11–12. Podechard used a similar model, discerning three main stages: the original book, additions by a Chasid, and additions by a Chakham.[4]

A more restrained analysis distinguishes some pietistic glosses, but without major revisions or additions. Crenshaw, for example, regards the following as secondary: Qoh 2:26a; 3:17a; 8:12–13; 11:9b; perhaps Qoh 5:18 and 7:26b, as well as Qoh 12:9–11, 12–14.[5]

The literary-critical attempt to restore the original text of Qohelet assumes that Qohelet was a consistently radical, pessimistic, and skeptical thinker, so that statements that do not fit this image must be assigned to other writers. The problem with all the theories of later additions is that the statements considered traditional and conservative use vocabulary and style typical of ones considered in line with Qohelet's spirit. They are, moreover, often intertwined with observations of life's inequities and absurdities. Moreover, the putative additions do not fulfill the purposes ascribed to their authors, for they do not neutralize the skeptical statements but simply contradict them. They are, moreover, sometimes located *before* the unorthodox opinions they are supposed to neutralize.[6] The fundamental problem with the source-critical assumption is that Qohelet is inconsistent throughout. He sees a

---

[1] Euringer, *Masorahtext des Koheleth*. Though outdated in many ways, this book is valuable as a compilation of information. Euringer assembles a wide variety of sources, including some that get little attention in the commentaries, including the secondary translations, namely the Syro-Hexapla, Coptic, and Old Latin. He also cites rabbinic sources and has an extensive appendix with rabbinic citations of Qohelet.

[2] Siegfried, *Prediger und Hoheslied*, 2–12.

[3] Barton, *The Book of Ecclesiastes*.

[4] Podechard, *L'Ecclésiaste*, 142–70, with a detailed survey of earlier research.

[5] Crenshaw, *Ecclesiastes*, 48.

[6] For fuller argumentation, see Fox, *A Time to Tear Down and a Time to Build Up: A Rereading of Ecclesiastes*.

world that is full of inconsistencies and contradiction, and these are what trouble him. His true consistency, in fact, lies in his insistence on observing both sides, positive and negative, of all that is valued in life, primarily work, pleasure, wisdom, justice, etc.

Most commentators regard the title (Qoh 1:1) and the epilogue (Qoh 12:9–14) as later additions to Qohelet's words. Many see two stages in the epilogue (Qoh 12:9–12 and 13–14). Among the commentators arguing for the essential unity of Qoh 1:2–12:8 are Gordis,[7] Hertzberg,[8] and Seow.[9]

There is no textual evidence for any of the literal-critical theories. LXX (→ 13–17.1.1.3) and the Peshiṭta (→ 13–17.1.4.3) include all of the 222 verses of MT-Qoh (and no more). 4QQoh[a] (which covers Qoh 5:13–17; 6:1, 3–8, 6:12–7:6, 7–10, 19–20; → 15.2.1.1) includes Qoh 7:1a, 3, 6, 9, 19, which various scholars consider secondary (→ 15.1.2.2).

Fox has gone further and argued that the third-person statements, as well as Qoh 7:27, are authorial and constitute a frame narrative in the voice of the author, who is relaying the words of a fictional sage, Qohelet. Several ancient Near Eastern wisdom books use a framing device of this sort.[10] Longman likewise regards the book as a unity, with Qohelet's words framed by the narrator's. He adduces the example of Akkadian fictional autobiographies.[11]

The book is, in the view of the present writer, basically a textual unity that has reached us in a form that is probably close to the original. This does not exclude the possibility of minor changes, including additions, in the Hebrew transmission. One likely gloss is Qoh 11:9b, in which a statement disrupts a series of imperatives.

15.1.2 Hebrew Texts

In the absence of evidence for a text form that differs significantly from MT (→ 15.2.2), we can at most retrieve some early variants from the Qumran fragments and the ancient translations, particularly LXX, and suggest conjectural emendations. All the variants for which there is textual evidence are minor.

The only Hebrew manuscripts earlier than the medieval Masoretic codices are two sets of fragments from Qumran (→ 15.1.2.2). These agree with MT except insofar as they introduce (or perhaps preserve, → 15.2.2.3) features of non-Masoretic orthography and morphology that are in line with some Qumran practices (for a different view, see → 15.2.1 and → 15.2.3). Both LXX (→ 13–17.1.1.3) and Peshitta (→ 13–17.1.4.3) reflect Hebrew source texts close to MT.

The following survey begins with the Hebrew sources, then looks at the ancient versions, and finally offers a selection of plausible conjectural variants.

15.1.2.1 *Qere-Ketiv*

Most of the *Qere-Ketiv* pairs in Qohelet pertain to orthographic and morphological differences. The *Qere* is usually preferable in terms of the syntax and context (Qoh 4:8, 17; 7:22; 10:10).[12] (We should recognize, however, that these unproblematic readings may be later than the more difficult text.) There are minor consonantal differences at Qoh 5:8 (K הִיא "is," Q הוּא "is" [Q preferable]); 5:10 (K רָאִית "seeing," Q רְאוּת "sight" [equal]); 6:10 (K שֶׁהִתְקִיף "one who is stronger," Q שֶׁתְּקִיף "one who is stronger" [Q preferable]); 9:4 (K יְבָחֵר "is chosen," Q יְחֻבַּר "is joined" [Q preferable]); 10:3 (K כְּשֶׁהַסָּכָל "when the fool," Q כְּשֶׁסָּכָל "when a fool" [equal]); 10:10 (K הַכְשֵׁיר

---

[7] Gordis, *Koheleth: The Man and his World*, 69–74. Gordis maintains the book's "integrity" by identifying many of the pietistic sentiments as unmarked quotations.

[8] H.W. Hertzberg, *Der Prediger* (KAT 17; Gütersloh: G. Mohn, 1963), 41. Hertzberg, 39–41, provides a good survey of the theories on the book's composition.

[9] C.L. Seow, *Ecclesiastes: A New Translation with Introduction and Commentary* (AB 18C; New York: Doubleday, 1997), 38–43.

[10] Fox, "Frame-Narrative and Composition in the Book of Qohelet," 83–106. A similar approach is taken by Longman, *The Book of Ecclesiastes*, who compares this text to Akkadian fictional autobiographies (pp. 18–20).

[11] Longman, *The Book of Ecclesiastes*.

[12] For an evaluation of these readings, see A. Schoors, "Kethibh-Qere in Ecclesiastes," in *Studia Paulo Naster Oblata* (OLA 13; Leuven: Peeters, 1982), 215–22.

"to make suitable," Q הַכְשֵׁר "to make suitable" [K preferable[13]]); 10:20 (K הַכְנָפַיִם "the winged [creature]," Q כְּנָפַיִם "a winged [creature]" [equal]); 12:6 (K יְרחַק "is distant," Q יֵרָתֵק "is severed" [Q preferable]). The alternative readings affect interpretation only in Qoh 9:4 and 12:6.

The *Qere* variants serve to cue readers on pronunciation while protecting the text proper – the *Ketiv* – from graphic "correction" by alerting copyists to readings that might seem natural but should not be incorporated in the text. Evidence that the *Qere* forms are not textual variants is the abbreviated form in which they are sometimes cited in the MasP. In Qoh 10:10b, for example, where the *Ketiv* is הַכְשִׁיר "making suitable," MasP has י יתיר "an extra *yod*." This is a statement about the spelling of the *Ketiv*, directed to scribes. It is not a cue to readers, nor is it a way of recording a variant text. To be sure, some *Qere* forms may have existed in manuscripts known to the Masoretes, but this does not mean that the MasP cited these to preserve them.[14] On the *Ketiv-Qere*, see → 1.5.4.2.

15.1.2.2 4QQoh[a] and 4QQoh[b]

The two sets of Qumran fragments, 4QQoh[a] (4Q109; → 15.2.3.1) and 4QQoh[b] (4Q110; → 15.2.3.2), are the only pre-medieval texts of Qohelet.[15] In 4QQoh[a], there are ninety-five words that are legible or can be restored with certainty as words appearing in MT. Among them are at least thirteen consonantal variants as well as seventeen orthographic ones, all in plene spellings. There is one morphological difference (ה]ואה] for הוא in 7:2), which introduces a form common in Qumran documents. In 4QQoh[b], of the twenty legible or securely reconstructible words, there are two orthographic variants, both providing a plene writing, and one morphological variant.

Table 1 lists the substantial variants in the two manuscripts, excluding orthographical and morphological details.[16]

In most of the above variants, the Qumran reading is secondary. (Not noted above are Qoh 6:8, 12; and 7:6, where 4QQoh[a] seems to differ from MT but is illegible.) In three cases, Qoh 7:5, 7, and 19, the Qumran reading seems earlier. The orthographical variants in Qumran are invariably later in character than the MT readings. In two cases, priority cannot be determined. The Qohelet scrolls show evidence of scribal modifications in the direction of simplification and updating in the first century of the book's existence.[17] Similar activity is visible in a few cases in MT (→ 15.2.2).

Although the variants of 4QQoh[a] are few in number and statistical conclusions cannot be drawn, the *density* of its variants is worthy of attention. Among the readable ninety-five words in this manuscript, thirteen are substantive variants, or 13.6 percent of the total, and seventeen are orthographical variants, or 17.8 percent of the total, together 31.57 percent. It is suggestive to compare 1QIsa[a] (→ 6.2.1.1; → 6.2.3), in which Ulrich and Flint count "well over 2600" textual variants.[18] This is 15 percent of the 17,000 words in MT-Isa, in a manuscript characterized by frequent modifications of spelling and wording, mostly for the sake of easier study and understanding. Since most of the non-Masoretic readings in 4QQoh[a] move from Masoretic readings toward greater simplification and clarification, we may tentatively categorize 4QQoh[a] as deriving from proto-MT (→ 15.2.2).[19]

---

[13] The correct vocalization is הַכָּשִׁיר "the skilled man" (as in Aramaic); hence "but the skilled man has the advantage of wisdom."

[14] Another example (of many) is in Prov 23:6, where the *Ketiv* is תִּתְאָו and the MasP has תִּתְאָיו (both meaning "desire"). This cannot possibly be intended as a textual variant.

[15] Published by Ulrich, "Qohelet."

[16] Based on Ulrich, "Qohelet," 222–26. English translations are guided by *DSSB.

[17] According to Ulrich ("Qohelet," 221), F.M. Cross dated this manuscript to 175–150 B.C.E. Most commentators date Qohelet itself to the mid-third century B.C.E. See Schoors, *Preacher*, 499–502.

[18] Ulrich and Flint, *DJD XXXII, Part 2, 89.

[19] For a slightly different view, see → 15.2.3.1.

TABLE 1   Qumran Variants

	MT	4QQoh^a	Explanation of Qumran Variant
5:14	כַּאֲשֶׁר (= LXX) "as"	כיא "because"	apparently an attempt to clarify the syntax of MT
5:15	וְגַם (= LXX) "and also"	גם "also" (MT^{Kenn80, 147, 180, 188})	equally valid
6:3	מִמֶּנּוּ הַנָּפֶל (= LXX) "[better] than he is a stillborn child"	הנפל ממנו "a stillborn child [is better] than he"	word-order inversion; equally valid
6:6	וְאִלּוּ (= LXX) "and though"	ואם לוא "and even if [לוא]"	the variant represents the constituents of ואלו even though ואם לוא does not have the required sense of "if"
6:8	כִּי מַה (= LXX) "for what"	כמה "how much"	a copyist error creating a contextually inferior reading
7:2	מִשְׁתֶּה (= LXX) "feasting"	ש[מ]חה "leasure"	adjusting to 7:4
7:2	סוֹף כָּל (= LXX) "end of all"	כול סוף "all the end"	word-order inversion; inferior
7:4a	בְּבֵית (= LXX) "in the house"	בית "house"	haplography
7:5	מֵאִישׁ שֹׁמֵעַ (= LXX) "than a man who hears"	מלשמוע, corr., "than to hear"	מלשמוע is superior to MT. The supralinear correction shows that the variant was present in the source manuscript.
7:7	וִיאַבֵּד (= LXX) "and destroys"	ויעוה "and perverts"	synonymous variants. MT may represent a simplification of the rare עוה.
7:19	תָּעֹז "strengthens"	תעזר "helps" (= LXX βοηθήσει)	synonymous variant.²⁰ תעזר represents a normalization of the rare ל-עזז.
7:19	אֲשֶׁר הָיוּ "who are"	ש[היו] "who are"	morphological updating to LBH
7:20	אֲשֶׁר יַעֲשֶׂה "that he does"	ש[יע]שה "that he does"	morphological updating to LBH
	MT	4QQoh^b	
1:14	שֶׁנַּעֲשׂוּ "that occur"	אשר נעשו "that occur"	MT updates the morphology to LBH.

15.1.3.1 Septuagint (→ 13–17.1.1.3)

The literalistic, mimetic character of LXX-Qoh justifies a fair degree of confidence in reconstructing its *Vorlage*, which was very likely close to MT (→ 15.2.2). A few likely variants are listed in → 13–17.1.1.3.4. The list could be expanded by, for example, variants in Qoh 2:25 (πάρεξ αὐτοῦ = ממנו, "except for him" = Peshitta and some MT manuscripts, for מִמֶּנִּי, "except for me"); 5:5 (τοῦ θεοῦ = האלהים, "God" for הַמַּלְאָךְ, "the messenger," a significant variant); 5:16 (καὶ πένθει = ואבל, "and

---

²⁰ On the interchangeability of these roots, see Brin, "The Roots עזר and עזז in the Bible."

mourning" wrongly, for יֹאכַל, "he eats"); and perhaps 5:19 (περισπᾷ αὐτόν = מענהו, "keeps him occupied" = Peshitta and Targum, for מַעֲנֶה, "answers"). There are also differences in implicit vocalization.

15.1.3.2 Peshiṭta (→ 13–17.1.4.3)

Kamenetzky's careful study of the Syriac translation of Qohelet shows its *Vorlage* to have been close to MT.[21] (Kamenetzky counts only forty-three minor variants in matters other than vocalization, and even some of these are doubtful.) According to Kamenetzky, the Peshitta often depends on LXX. Schloors argues that Peshita-LXX similarities are often better explained by factors other than dependence: shared variants, similar but independent interpretations, and a revision of the Peshiṭta toward LXX.[22]

15.1.3.3 Other Translations

V-Qoh (→ 13–17.1.7) was translated by Jerome in 398 C.E., who consulted LXX while translating the Hebrew. It does not reflect any consonantal variants to MT. T-Qoh (→ 13–17.1.3) is highly paraphrastic and expansive.[23] It is in the midrashic tradition and in fact dependent on some Tannaitic midrashim. It cannot serve as evidence for the textual history of this book.

15.1.4 Conjectures

Numerous details can be reasonably conjectured. Following is a sample of conjectures especially worthy of the exegete's attention. Frequently used in modern commentaries,[24] these conjectures are required by the context, and the mechanism of error is easily recognizable.

15.1.4.1 Consonantal Conjectures, with Implicit Vocalization

Qoh 2:24 מִשֶּׁיֹּאכַל "than to eat" (MT שֶׁיֹּאכַל "to eat"); 5:6 כְּרֹב "like a lot" (MT בְּרֹב "in a lot"); 5:16 וְחֳלִי "and sickness" (MT וְחָלְיוֹ "and his sickness"); 7:19 מֵעֹשֶׁר הַשַּׁלִּיטִים "more than the wealth of the magnates" (MT מֵעֲשָׂרָה שַׁלִּיטִים "than ten magnates"); 7:27 אָמַר הַקֹּהֶלֶת "said the Qohelet" (MT אָמְרָה קֹהֶלֶת "says [feminine] Qohelet"); 7:28a אִשָּׁה "a woman" (MT אֲשֶׁר "which"); 8:1 כֹּה חָכָם "so wise" (MT כְּהֶחָכָם "like the wise man"); 8:1b–2a יְשַׁנֵּאנּוּ "changes it" (MT יְשֻׁנֶּא אֲנִי "is changed. I"); 8:8 עֹשֶׁר "wealth" (MT רֶשַׁע "wickedness"); 8:10 קֶבֶר מוּבָאִים "being brought to the grave" (MT קְבָרִים וָבָאוּ "buried. And they came"); 10:1 זְבוּב יָמוּת "a fly dies" (MT זְבוּבֵי מָוֶת "flies of death"); 10:15 הַכְּסִיל מְיַגְּעֶנּוּ "the fool's [toil] exhausts him" (MT הַכְּסִילִים תְּיַגְּעֶנּוּ "the fools [toil], exhausts him" [ungrammatical]); 11:5 בַּעֲצָמִים "in the limbs" (MTmss) (MT כַּעֲצָמִים "like the limbs").

15.1.4.2 Vocalic Conjectures

Qoh 3:21 הַעֹלָה "whether rises" (MT הָעֹלָה "the rising one"); 3:21 הַיֹּרֶדֶת "whether goes down" (MT הַיֹּרֶדֶת "the one going down"); 8:10 וּמִמָּקוֹם "from a place" (MT וּמִמְּקוֹם "from a place of"); 10:10 הַכָּשִׁיר "the skilled man" (MT *Ketiv* הכשיר "making suitable"); 12:6 וְתָרֹץ "and it is smashed" (MT וְתָרָץ "and it races"); 12:10 וְכָתוּב "and wrote" (MT וְכָתֻב "and it was written").

15.1.5 Implications for Exegesis

All the witnesses are closely aligned to MT. The possibility that other textual forms with greater divergences in wording and quantity once existed cannot be disproved, but nothing in MT has the character of a later supplement, with the arguable (but uncertain) exception of the sentences that speak of Qohelet in the third person: Qoh 1:1, 2; 7:27; and 12:9–14, and perhaps Qoh 11:9b. Neither are such supplements reflected in the ancient versions and Hebrew manuscripts.

Qohelet is one of the few books in the Bible for which it is meaningful to speak of an *Urtext*, a textual form produced by a single author and from which all evidence ultimately derives (→ 1.1.1.2.4).

---

[21] Kamenetzky, "Die P'šita zu Kohelet," 181–239.
[22] Schoors, "The Peshiṭta of Koheleth," 345–57.
[23] For a translation and introduction, see Knobel, *The Targum of Qohelet*, and Levine, *The Aramaic Version of Qohelet*.
[24] For argumentation in support of these readings, see Fox, *A Time*, ad loc.

In support of this hypothesis is a literary argument for the book's unity. The book presents itself as the intellectual autobiography of a single person (not as a collection of proverbs) and shows considerable cohesion (even repetitiveness) in style and thought. The unmistakable tensions and contradictions within Qohelet's words are best explained as expressions of the writer's thoughts as he observes the strains and fissures in life itself. Indeed, Qohelet himself is aware of these contradictions and responds in frustration, calling them הבל "vanity/absurd."

Even apart from this hypothesis, MT is a solid basis for exegesis, while the other texts and translations provide little evidence for alternative textual traditions.

Barton, G.E., *A Critical and Exegetical Commentary on the Book of Ecclesiastes* (ICC; Edinburgh: T & T Clark, 1908; repr. 1971).
Brin, G., "The Roots עזר and עזז in the Bible," *Leš* 24 (1960): 8–14 [Hebr.].
Crenshaw, J.L., *Ecclesiastes: A Commentary* (OTL; Philadelphia: Westminster Press, 1987).
Euringer, S., *Masorahtext des Koheleth* (Leipzig: Commissionsverlag der J.C. Hinrichs'schen Buchhandlung, 1890).
Fox, M.V., "Frame-Narrative and Composition in the Book of Qohelet," *HUCA* 48 (1977): 83–106.
Fox, M.V., *A Time to Tear Down and a Time to Build Up: A Rereading of Ecclesiastes* (Grand Rapids: Eerdmans, 1999; repr. Wipf & Stock, 2010).
Gordis, R.A., *Koheleth: The Man and His World* (2nd ed.; New York: Ktav, 1968).
Kamenetzky, A.S., "Die P'šita zu Kohelet textkritisch und in ihrem Verhältnis zu dem massoretischen Text, der Septuaginta und den andern alten griechischen Versionen," *ZAW* 24 (1904): 181–239.
Knobel, P.S., *The Targum of Qohelet* (ArBib 15; Collegeville: Liturgical Press, 1991).
Levine, E., *The Aramaic Version of Qohelet* (New York: Genesis, 1978).
Longman III, T., *The Book of Ecclesiastes* (Grand Rapids: Eerdmans, 1998).
Podechard, E., *L'Ecclésiaste* (Paris: J. Gabalda, 1912).
Schoors, A., "The Peshiṭta of Koheleth and its Relation to the Septuagint," in *After Chalcedon: Studies in Theology and Church History: Offered to Professor Albert van Roey for his 70. Birthday* (eds. C. Laga; J.A. Munitz, and L. van Rompay, OLA 18: Leuven: Peeters, 1985), 215–22.
Schoors, A., *The Preacher Sought to Find Pleasing Words: A Study of the Language of Qoheleth* (OLA 41; Leuven: Peeters, 2004).
Siegfried, C.A., *Prediger und Hoheslied* (HAT 2.3.2; Göttingen: Vandenhoeck & Ruprecht, 1898).
Tov, *TCHB*.
Ulrich, "Qohelet," *DJD* XVI: 221–27.
Ulrich and Flint, *DJD* XXXII, Part 2.

Michael V. Fox

15.2 Ancient Hebrew Texts

15.2.1 Ancient Manuscript Evidence

The only complete witness to the Hebrew text of Qohelet from antiquity is the consonantal text of MT-Qoh (→ 15.2.2; for the most important medieval Qohelet manuscripts, see → 15.2.2.2). Two ancient fragmentary Qohelet manuscripts were found in the Qumran library, i.e. 4QQoh^a and 4QQoh^b.[1]

15.2.1.1 4QQoh^a (4Q109)

The seven extant fragments of 4QQoh^a (4Q109) can be attributed to three columns of the original scroll and preserve sections of Qoh 5:13–17; 6:1?, 3–8, 12; 7:1–10, 19–20. 4QQoh^a is among the earliest manuscripts from Qumran. It was copied in an archaic semi-cursive script dating to the years 175–150 B.C.E.[2] The manuscript contains two erasures (cols. II:19; III:1) and corrections *prima manu* in both the upper and lower margins of col. II as well as above line 19 of that col.

The orthography of 4QQoh^a is characterized by its extensive use of plene spellings, characteristic of the baroque orthography of many Dead Sea scrolls. Examples include כול "all" (I:7; II:4, 15), לוא "not" (II:2, 4, 5), כיא "because" (I:1), and ה[ואה "he" (col. II:15).[3] The morphological characteristics of the baroque orthography, such as the suffixes -כה and -המה, are not attested in 4QQoh^a because no forms typical of this morphology are extant in what is preserved of this scroll. An orthographic peculiarity of 4QQoh^a is the use of *he* instead of *'alep* in Qoh 6:4 (בה instead of בָּא "he came"; II:1). In its 124 preserved and/or partly reconstructed words, 4QQoh^a reads seventeen times against MT; sixteen of these readings against MT are non-aligned.[4] On one occasion, 4QQoh^a reads with LXX (→ 13–17.1.1.3) against MT. Due to its large number of non-aligned readings, 4QQoh^a is best described as attesting to a non-aligned text.[5]

15.2.1.2 4QQoh^b (4Q110)

Only two small fragments of 4QQoh^b (4Q110) are extant,[6] preserving remnants of Qoh 1:10–14, x. The manuscript was copied in a late Hasmonean or early Herodian book hand from the middle of the first century B.C.E. In two cases, the spellings in 4QQoh^b are more plene than in MT. 4QQoh^b 1–2 1 reads לעולמים instead of the לְעֹלָמִים "in the ages" in MT-Qoh 1:10, and 4QQoh^b 1–2 2 has לוא instead of the לֹא "not" in MT-Qoh 1:11.[7] Because only twenty-one words are preserved in 4QQoh^b, neither an orthogpraphic nor a text-typological classification of this manuscript are possible. Its two variant readings will be discussed in → 15.2.3.

Lange, *Handbuch*, 483–85.
Muilenburg, J., "A Qohelet Scroll from Qumran," *BASOR* 135 (1954): 20–28.
Nebe, G.W., "Qumranica I," *ZAW* 104 (1994): 307–22, esp. 312–13.
Puech, É., "Le livre de Qohélet à Qumrân," *HTh* 18 (2000): 109–14.

---

[1] For a more detailed description of 4QQoh^a and 4QQoh^b, see Lange, *Handbuch*, 483–85.

[2] Cf. Cross, *"Development,"* 137, 145; Ulrich, "Ezra and Qohelet," 143; Ulrich, "Qohelet," 221.

[3] Cf. Muilenburg, "Qohelet Scroll," 24; Schoors, *Preacher*, 32–33; Ulrich, "Ezra and Qohelet," 143; Ulrich, "Qohelet," 221–22.

[4] In two non-aligned readings (Qoh 7:19, 20), the variant readings of 4QQoh^a concern a textual difference that cannot be rendered into Greek. See below, → 15.2.3.1.1. In two further readings, 4QQoh^a reads with MT^{Kenn80,147,188} and MT^{Kenn104} against MT.

[5] Cf. Tov, *"Synthese,"* 27; contra M. Burrows, *More Light on the Dead Sea Scrolls* (New York: Viking Press, 1958), 143–44.

[6] É. Puech, "Un nouveau fragment du manuscrit b de l'*Ecclésiaste* (*4QQohélet*^b ou *4Q110*)," *RevQ* 19 (1999–2000): 617–21, wants to identify 4Q468l as another fragment of 4QQoh^b due to paleographic similarities. But Puech's identification is based on problematic transcriptions. 4Q468l most likely preserves a passage from a text that employed Qoh 1:8–9 in another context (cf. Lange, *Handbuch*, 485; for 4Q468l, see also D. Ernst and A. Lange, "468l. 4QFragment Mentioning Qoh 1:8–9," *DJD* XXXVI: 422).

[7] For the material description, paleography, and orthography of 4QQoh^b, cf. Ulrich, "Ezra and Qohelet," 148; Ulrich, "Qohelet," 227.

Puech, É., "Qohelet a Qumran," in *Il libro del Qohelet: Tradizione, redazione, teologia* (eds. G. Bellia and A. Passaro; Milan: Paoline, 2001), 144–70.

Schoors, A., *The Preacher Sought to Find Pleasing Words: A Study in the Language of Qoheleth* (OLA 41; Leuven: Peeters, 1992), 33–40.

Ulrich, E., "Ezra and Qohelet Manuscripts from Qumran (4QEzra and 4QQoh[a, b])," in *Priests, Prophets and Scribes: Essays on the Formation and Heritage of Second Temple Judaism in Honour of Joseph Blenkinsopp* (eds. E. Ulrich et al.; JSOTSup 149; Sheffield: Sheffield Academic Press, 1992), 139–57.

Ulrich, "Qohelet," *DJD* XVI: 221–27.

Ulrich, *BQS*, 746–48.

Armin Lange

15.2.2 Masoretic Texts and Ancient Texts Close to MT

The only complete Hebrew text of Qohelet is MT-Qoh. It is also the only textual witness to the (proto-)Masoretic text of Qohelet. The two Qumran manuscripts 4QQoh[a] and 4QQoh[b] attest only to small portions of the book and are non-aligned in character (→ 15.2.1; → 15.2.3). Because MT-Qoh and the known textual sources of the book – especially the early primary translations of Qohelet – are close to one another, there is general agreement that the Hebrew text of Qohelet did not suffer much during its transmission and is rather close to the supposed Hebrew original of the book.[1] Although the known textual transmission of Qohelet was very linear, the fact that, apart from 4QQoh[a] and 4QQoh[b], nothing is known about the textual history of Qohelet before the book was translated into Greek (→ 13–17.1.1.3) begs for caution with regard to the closeness of MT-Qoh to the *Urtext* of Qohelet.[2]

15.2.2.1 History of Research

The textual criticism of Qohelet has focused on the ancient versions and the Qumran manuscripts.[3] The discussion of the Hebrew text of Qohelet concerns either the two Qumran manuscripts or is restricted, with few exceptions, to the discussion of individual variant readings in commentaries.[4]

The early Mishnaic Hebrew of Qohelet[5] and its seeming lack of a coherent structure gave rise to two idiosyncratic speculations regarding the early textual history of the Hebrew text of Qohelet that are not based on the evidence of textual witnesses: 1) Bickell proposed, for example, that the textual structure of Qohelet as attested by both MT-Qoh and LXX-Qoh (→ 13–17.1.1.3) goes back to a confusion of pages in an ancient codex,[6] although the codex was not invented when both texts were produced;[7] 2) Burkitt,[8] Zimmermann,[9] Torrey,[10] and Ginsberg[11] argued that the Hebrew text of Qohelet was translated from an Aramaic original. Following Gordis' criticism of this theory,[12] it has no longer been regarded as valid because it presupposes a

---

[1] Cf., e.g., Salters, "Textual Criticism," 54.
[2] For a different view, see → 15.1.
[3] For a brief history of research, see also → 15.1.1.

[4] See, e.g., Bruno, *Prediger*, 208–17; Seow, *Ecclesiastes*, passim; and Goldman, "Qoheleth," 64*–112*. More recent studies on isolated readings include Mizrahi, "Qohelet 6:5b," passim; Goldman, "Le texte massorétique," passim; and H. Debel, "What about the Wicked? A Survey of the Textual and Interpretational Problems in Qoh 8,10a," in *Florilegium Lovaniense: Studies in the Septuagint and Textual Criticism in Honour of Florentino García Martínez* (ed. H. Ausloos; BETL 224; Leuven: Peeters, 2008), 133–50.
[5] For the early Mishnaic Hebrew of Qohelet, see, e.g., Schoors, *Preacher*, esp. 221–22.
[6] G. Bickell, *Der Prediger über den Wert des Daseins: Wiederherstellung des bisher zerstückelten Textes, Uebersetzung und Erklärung* (Innsbruck: Verlag der Wagner'schen Universitäts-Buchhandlung, 1884); G. Bickell, *Koheleth's Untersuchung über den Wert des Daseins: nach dem hergestellten Zusammenhange übersetzt* (Innsbruck: Verlag der Wagner'schen Universitäts-Buchhandlung, 1886).
[7] Cf. Euringer, *Masorahtext*, 19–29.
[8] F.C. Burkitt, "Is Ecclesiastes a Translation?" *JTS* 23 (1921–1922): 22–26.
[9] F. Zimmermann, "The Aramaic Provenance of Qohelet," *JQR* 36 (1945–1946): 17–45; F. Zimmermann, "The Question of Hebrew in Qohelet," *JQR* 40 (1949–1950): 79–102.
[10] C.C. Torrey, "The Question of the Original Language of Kohelet," *JQR* 39 (1948–1949): 151–60.
[11] H.L. Ginsberg, *Studies in Koheleth* (New York: Jewish Theological Seminary of America, 1950), 16–39.
[12] R. Gordis, "The Original Language of Qohelet," *JQR* 37 (1946–1947): 67–84; R. Gordis, "The Translation Theory of Qohelet Re-examined," *JQR* 40 (1949–1950): 103–16; R. Gordis, "Koheleth: Hebrew or Aramaic?" *JBL* 71 (1952): 93–109.

translator who completely misunderstood his base text, and because the Aramaisms in Qohelet do not go beyond those found in other contemporary Hebrew literature.[13]

Few studies that address the whole text of MT-Qoh have been published. Euringer[14] and Goldman[15] are restricted to the study of individual variant readings. That Euringer, in an appendix, discusses the rabbinic quotations of Qohelet text-critically makes his work particularly interesting.[16] Salters[17] does not deny that the textual quality of MT-Qoh exceeds that of the MT text of other books such as MT-1–2 Sam (→ 5.3.2). Nevertheless, Salters points to cases of scribal corruption in the transmission of MT-Qoh: "There are examples of dittography and haplography, there are signs that words could be wrongly divided, and evidence that letters/consonants have been mistaken for one another … Furthermore, while many of the differences between texts are the result of accidental errors, others may, for various reasons be deliberate."[18] The deliberate alterations, especially, go back to a time before Qohelet gained canonical status. In a specialized study, Schoors has demonstrated that the *Qere* readings in MT-Qoh are clearly of better quality than the *Ketiv* readings.[19] Subsequently, Mizrahi[20] and Goldman[21] have emphasized the interpretative nature of individual variant readings in MT-Qoh.

15.2.2.2 Manuscripts and Editions

In addition to the Qumran fragments discussed above (→ 15.2.1), the most important medieval Hebrew manuscripts (→ 1.2.2.1; → 1.5; → 10–20.1) are two manuscripts of the Russian National Library in St. Petersburg (EBP. I B 19a: MT^L [commonly known as Codex Leningradensis; EBP. II B 34: MT^L34]) and a Yemenite manuscript at the Cambridge University Library (Add. ms 1753: MT^Y). Qohelet is among the lost sections of the Aleppo Codex.

For MT-Qoh, two critical editions are currently available in the *BH series. Superseding earlier editions in that series, both are diplomatic in nature and are based on MT^L. The edition by Horst in *BHS is selective in the number of variants recorded in its apparatus. The *BHQ edition by Goldman is also not comprehensive but it represents a significant improvement with regard to its apparatus. Its text-critical introduction and commentary make it an inestimable tool.[22] For the variants of the medieval Masoretic manuscript tradition, the edition of Kennicott (*1776–1780, 2.549–61) and the variant lists of De Rossi (*1784–1788, 3.247–64) remain indispensable.

15.2.2.3 The Nature and Text-Critical Character of (Proto)-MT-Qoh

As in several other books of the Hebrew Bible, MT-Qoh attests to isolated cases of orthographic and morphological peculiarities that are close to the so-called Qumran orthography (→ 1.2.2.4.1.2). These isolated cases include the spelling of the 2nd per. masc. sg. suffix as כָה- instead of ךָ- (Qoh 2:1 אֲנַסְּכָה "I want to test you") and unusual plene spellings. In Qoh 5:10, what should be a *qames chatuf* is realized with a *cholem magnum*: אוֹכְלֶיהָ instead of אֹכְלֶיהָ "those who eat it." Another characteristic of this orthographic system is that לֹא "not" is regularly written as לוֹא. Although the spelling לוֹא does occur in the (proto-)Masoretic texts of other biblical books, it can be found in MT-Qoh only in Qoh 10:11 (בְּלוֹא "because no"). Otherwise, MT-Qoh consistently uses the spelling לֹא (Qoh 1:8, 11, 15; 2:10, 21, 23; 3:11; 4:3, 8, 12, 13, 16; 5:4, 9, 14,

---

[13] For a summary of the arguments, see J.R. Davila, "Qoheleth and Northern Hebrew," *Maarav* 5–6 (1990): 69–87, esp. 77–79.
[14] Euringer, *Masorahtext, passim.*
[15] Goldman, "Qoheleth," *passim.*
[16] Euringer, "Zusammenstellung aller Citate aus Koheleth in den Rabbinischen Schriften bis zum 7. Jahrhundert n.Chr.," in *Masorahtext* with separate page count.
[17] Salters, "Textual Criticism," *passim.*
[18] Salters, "Textual Criticism," 70.
[19] Schoors, "Ketibh-Qere in Ecclesiastes," 215–22; Schoors, *Preacher*, 33–40. For the *Qere* readings in Qohelet, see also → 15.1.2.1.
[20] Mizrahi, "Qohelet 6:5b," *passim.*
[21] Goldman, "Le texte massorétique," *passim.*

[22] Goldman, "Qoheleth," 13*–17*, 64*–112*.

19; 6:2, 3, 5, 6, 7, 10; 7:10, 17, 20, 21, 28; 8:5, 8, 13, 17; 9:11, 12, 15; 10:10, 14, 15, 17; 11:2, 4, 5; 12:1, 2, 6). Another unusual plene spelling is הַקּוֹהֶלֶת instead of הַקֹּהֶלֶת "the preacher" in Qoh 12:8. Otherwise, (הַ)קֹּהֶלֶת is consistently spelled defectively (cf. Qoh 1:1, 2, 12; 7:27, 12:9, 10). These isolated cases of variant spellings are surprising, as MT-Qoh is in its orthography relatively consistent,[23] the coherent spelling of לֹא "not" mentioned above being just one of many examples.

For me, the best explanation for such isolated forms of non-Masoretic orthography and morphology is that the text of MT-Qoh goes back to an orthographic revision (→ 1.2.2.4.1.2). This orthographic revision reworked a parent text that adhered at least to some extent to the baroque orthography, towards the conservative orthography and morphology so well known from MT. During this revision, isolated baroque spellings were overlooked.[24] Such a revision becomes all the more likely because 4QQoh[a] is a copy of Qohelet ascribed to the years 175–150 B.C.E. that employs the plene spellings and morphological forms of the Qumran orthography (→ 15.2.1.1). The orthographic system applied to the book by the *Urtext* of Qohelet can no longer be ascertained.

Although MT-Qoh is regarded as close to the *Urtext* of Qohelet[25], it is not free of secondary readings. The secondary readings of MT-Qoh attest to harmonizations, linguistic and stylistic corrections, as well as interpretative readings. On the whole, the intentional secondary readings of MT-Qoh can be described as editorial in nature (→ 1.2.2.3). While the number of intentional secondary readings in MT-Qoh will remain debated, their existence cannot be denied.

---

[23] A. Schoors, "The Use of Vowel Letters in Qoheleth," *UF* 20 (1988): 277–86; Schoors, *Preacher*, 22–33; C.L. Seow, "Linguistic Evidence and the Dating of Qohelet," *JBL* 115 (1996): 643–66, esp. 645.

[24] For other remnants of the baroque orthography in (proto-)Masoretic texts and the orthographic revision of MT, see A. Lange, "The Question of the So-Called Qumran Orthography, the Severus Scroll, and the Masoretic Text," *Hebrew Bible and Ancient Israel* 3 (2014): 424–75 and → 1.2.2.4.1.2.

[25] See n. 1.

- Examples of harmonizing readings can be found in Qoh 1:2 and 2:10. In Qoh 1:2, MT reads קֹהֶלֶת "preacher" but LXX-Qoh reads ὁ Ἐκκλησιαστής "the preacher." LXX-Qoh agrees well with the other two occurrences of the phrase in Qoh 7:27 and 12:8 (אָמַר הַקֹּהֶלֶת "the preacher says"; for Qoh 7:27, see below). In Qoh 1:2, MT has deleted the article of הַקֹּהֶלֶת in harmonization with the phrase דִּבְרֵי קֹהֶלֶת "words of a preacher" in Qoh 1:1.[26] In Qoh 2:10, LXX-Qoh reads ὅτι καρδία μου εὐφράνθη ἐν παντὶ μόχθῳ μου "because my heart found pleasure in all my toil" instead of the כִּי־לִבִּי שָׂמַח מִכָּל־עֲמָלִי "because my heart found pleasure from all my toil" in MT-Qoh. The *Vorlage* of LXX-Qoh read בכל instead of מכל. LXX-Qoh is supported in its reading by MT[Kenn225, 226, 348]. MT-Qoh adjusted בכל to מכל in harmonization with the מִכָּל־עֲמָלִי at the end of Qoh 2:10.[27]

- Examples of linguistic and stylistic corrections occur in Qoh 5:14; 6:4; 7:5, 7. In Qoh 5:14, MT-Qoh corrected an assertive כִּי "indeed" (cf. 4QQoh[a]) to כַּאֲשֶׁר "like." The conjunction כִּי produces a more difficult text and was smoothened by MT-Qoh.[28] In Qoh 6:4, 4QQoh[a] reads הלך "it went" instead of the יֵלֵךְ "it will go" in MT-Qoh. LXX-Qoh has πορεύεται "it goes," which renders the Hebrew participle הֹלֵךְ. Because 4QQoh[a] spells the word as הולך, the Qumran manuscript should be regarded as reading a perfect form,[29] which LXX-Qoh misinterpreted as a participle.[30] MT-Qoh subsequently changed the perfect to an imperfect in grammatical harmonization with

---

[26] Goldman, "Qoheleth," 65*; against Seow, *Ecclesiastes*, 102.

[27] Goldman, "Qoheleth," 72*; against Seow, *Ecclesiastes*, 132.

[28] Against G.W. Nebe, "Qumranica I," *ZAW* 104 (1994): 307–22, esp. 312, and Goldman, "Qoheleth," 85*, כִּי "indeed" does not preserve a textual plus at the beginning of Qoh 5:14 but is a variant reading of כַּאֲשֶׁר "like" (cf. J. Muilenburg, "A Qohelet Scroll from Qumran," *BASOR* 135 [1954]: 20–28, 27; E. Ulrich, "Ezra and Qohelet Manuscripts from Qumran [4QEzra and 4QQoh[a, b]]," in *Priests, Prophets and Scribes: Essays on the Formation and Heritage of Second Temple Judaism in Honour of Joseph Blenkinsopp* [eds. E. Ulrich et al.; JSOTSup 149; Sheffield: Sheffield Academic Press, 1992], 139–57, 144; Ulrich, "Qohelet," *DJD* XVI: 221–27, 223; Seow, *Ecclesiastes*, 207).

[29] Against Salters, "Textual Criticism," 56.

[30] Cf. Salters, "Textual Criticism," 56; Seow, *Ecclesiastes*, 212.

the imperfect form יְכֻסֶּה "will be covered" at the end of Qoh 6:4.[31] In Qoh 7:5, MT-Qoh reads the singular גַּעֲרַת "rebuke" while 4QQoh[a] has the plural גערות "rebukes." The plural form is unique in pre-rabbinic Hebrew[32] and MT-Qoh adjusted it to the more common singular form in harmonization with the singular number of the word שִׁיר "song" in Qoh 7:5b. In Qoh 7:7, MT-Qoh reads the word with וִיאַבֵּד "and destroys" (cf. LXX) but 4QQoh[a] attests to the reading וִיעַוֵּה "and perverts." The root עוה is unique in the book of Qohelet while forms of the root אבד occur five times (Qoh 3:6; 5:13; 7:15; 9:6, 18). Therefore, MT-Qoh and LXX-Qoh replaced וִיעַוֵּה with וִיאַבֵּד and καὶ ἀπόλλυσι "and it will destroy" respectively.[33]

– An interpretative variant can be found in Qoh 5:5. LXX-Qoh reads πρὸ προσώπου τοῦ θεοῦ "before God" (לִפְנֵי הָאֱלֹהִים) while MT-Qoh has לִפְנֵי הַמַּלְאָךְ "before the angel." MT-Qoh wants to avoid the impression of saying something negative about God and hence changes הָאֱלֹהִים to הַמַּלְאָךְ out of fear of irreverence.[34]

Next to such editorial changes, rare cases of unintentional scribal corruption occur in MT-Qoh, too. The reading אָמְרָה קֹהֶלֶת "she said a preacher" in Qoh 7:27 resulted from a misplaced space between the two words. The original reading was אמר הקהלת "the preacher said"; cf. LXX-Qoh εἶπεν ὁ Ἐκκλησιαστής.[35] Similar incorrect divisions of words can be found in Qoh 7:19; 8:1; and 10:1.[36] Other accidental secondary readings in MT-Qoh resulted from character confusion: מִמֶּנִּי "from me" in MT-Qoh 2:25 instead of מננו "from him" (cf. MT[Kenn147, 294, 488, 588, DeRossi592]; LXX; and S); מְצוֹדִים "nets" in MT-Qoh 9:14 instead of מצורים "fortifications" (cf. MT[DeRossi10]; LXX; and S).[37]

In addition to the reasons given at the beginning of this article, such secondary readings suggest that caution is needed in equating MT-Qoh with the *Urtext* of Qohelet. So far, no shared characteristic of the secondary readings in MT-Qoh has emerged that could point to a coherent textual layer. Therefore, for the time being, it seems unlikely that the secondary readings of MT-Qoh represent a separate literary edition of the book or a revision of its Hebrew text.

What can be observed with regard to the differences between MT-Qoh on the one hand and the ancient versions, including 4QQoh[a] and 4QQoh[b], on the other hand is also reflected in the medieval manuscripts. This is illustrated by the many disagreements among Masoretic manuscripts noted by Kennicott and De Rossi for Qohelet.[38] Sometimes these disagreements among the later Masoretic manuscripts have parallels among the ancient versions, as they present similar emendations for similar textual problems. An example is MT-Qoh 1:10: MT[Kenn17, DeRossi87, 386, 443] as well as LXX, V, and T read here the plural הָיוּ "were" instead of the singular הָיָה "was" in MT-Qoh.[39]

15.2.2.4 Date and Milieu

It remains uncertain when the orthographic revisions, textual harmonizations, and interpretative changes in MT-Qoh were applied and who was responsible for them. It is even impossible to decide whether the editorial, harmonizing, and interpretative readings described above were the work of a single scribe or were inserted by several scribes at different points in time. The latter seems more likely.

---

[31] Cf. M.V. Fox, *A Time to Tear Down and a Time to Build Up: A Rereading of Ecclesiastes* (Grand Rapids: Eerdmans, 1999), 243; Goldman, "Qoheleth," 87*; against Seow, *Ecclesiastes*, 212.

[32] Cf. Seow, *Ecclesiastes*, 236.

[33] Cf. Seow, *Ecclesiastes*, 238.

[34] A.H. McNeile, *An Introduction to Ecclesiastes: With Notes and Appendices* (Cambridge: Cambridge University Press, 1904), 68; Salters, "Textual Criticism," 67–68; Fox, *Time*, 232; Goldman, "Qoheleth," 83*; against Euringer, *Masorahtext*, 66–67, and Seow, *Ecclesiastes*, 196.

[35] Cf., e.g., Euringer, *Masorahtext*, 92; Salters, "Textual Criticism," 68; Seow, *Ecclesiastes*, 264.

[36] Cf. Salters, "Textual Criticism," 68.

[37] For these two examples of character confusion, see Euringer, *Masorahtext*, 54–55; Salters, "Textual Criticism," 65, 68; Seow, *Ecclesiastes*, 140–41, 309.

[38] Kennicott, *1776–1780, 2.549–61; De Rossi, *1784–1788, 3.247–64.

[39] Cf. Salters, "Textual Criticism," 62; Seow, *Ecclesiastes*, 110; Goldman, "Qoheleth," 66*.

That 4QQoh[a] employs the baroque orthography within the years 175–150 B.C.E. could argue for a *terminus post quem* in or after that time frame for the orthographic revision of MT-Qoh. However, the Qumran library leaves no doubt that manuscripts employing the orthographic system of MT coexisted in the late Second Temple period with those using baroque orthography. The evidence from other books of the Hebrew Bible makes it likely that the orthographic revision that led to the text of MT-Qoh was completed by the late first century B.C.E. (→ 1.2.2.4.2).[40]

15.2.2.5 Relevance for Exegesis and Literary Analysis

Due to the fact that there are few preserved textual differences between 4QQoh[a] and 4QQoh[b], MT-Qoh, and the ancient versions, and because the harmonizations in MT-Qoh are not concerned on the whole with the philosophy expressed by Qohelet, little can be said about the relevance of MT-Qoh for exegesis.[41] If 4QQoh[b] contained additional text between Qoh 1:14 and Qoh 1:15 (→ 15.2.1.1), then MT-Qoh might have erased some especially provocative statements.

Bruno, D.A., *Sprüche, Prediger, Klagelieder, Esther, Daniel: Eine rhythmische und textkritische Untersuchung* (Stockholm: Almqvist & Wiksell, 1958), 208–17.

Euringer, S., *Der Masorahtext des Koheleth kritisch untersucht* (Leipzig: J.C. Hindrich'sche Buchhandlung, 1890).

Goldman, Y.A.P., "Qoheleth קהלת," in *BHQ Part 18*, 25–53, 13*–17*, 64*–112*.

Goldman, Y.A.P., "Le texte massorétique de Qohélet, témoin d' un compromis théologique entre les 'disciples des sages' (Qoh 7,23–24; 8,1; 7,19)," in *Sôfer Mahîr: Essays in Honour of Adrian Schenker Offered by Editors of Biblia Hebraica Quinta* (eds. Y.A.P. Goldman et al.; VTSup 110; Leiden: Brill, 2006), 69–93.

Horst, F., *Libros Cantici Canticorum et Ecclesiastes*, *BHS, 1336–54.

Kennicott, *1776–1780, 2.549–61.

Mizrahi, N., "Qohelet 6:5b in Light of 4QQoh[a] ii 2 and Rabbinic Literature," *Textus* 21 (2002): 159–74.

De Rossi, *1784–1788, 3.247–64.

Salters, R.B., "Textual Criticism and Qoheleth," *JNSL* 23.1 (1997): 53–71.

Schoors, A., "Ketibh-Qere in Ecclesiastes," in *Studia Paulo Naster Oblata*, Vol. 2: *Orientalia Antiqua* (ed. J. Quaegebeur; OLA 13, Leuven: Peeters, 1982), 215–22.

Schoors, A., *The Preacher Sought to Find Pleasing Words: A Study in the Language of Qoheleth* (OLA 41; Leuven: Peeters, 1992), 33–40.

Seow, C.-L., *Ecclesiastes: A New Translation with Introduction and Commentary* (AB 18C; New York: Doubleday, 1997).

Armin Lange

15.2.3 Other Texts

Besides MT-Qoh (→ 15.2.2), only two further textual witnesses to the book of Qohelet are known in Hebrew, i.e. 4QQoh[a] (4Q109) and 4QQoh[b] (4Q110).[1] They will be discussed below.

15.2.3.1 4QQoh[a] (4Q109)

Although 4QQoh[a] was published already in 1954, the Qohelet text it attests to did not spark extensive discussion. Its text-typological classification as non-aligned is discussed above, → 15.2.1. In addition to this characterization, Muilenburg's hope that several variants "are strong enough to suggest that they preserve the original reading" needs to be mentioned.[2] Muilenburg and Dahood saw the reading כמה "how much" of 4QQoh[a] in Qoh 6:8 as support for Dahood's hypothesis that the author of the book of Qohelet lived in a Phoeni-

---

[40] See Lange, "Question."

[41] Goldman, "Le texte massorétique de Qohélet," wants to detect a theological revision in MT-Qoh 7:19, 23–24 and 8:1, which adjusts the thought of Qohelet towards the Torah-centered character of Judaism around the turn of the era. His arguments are based on a comparison of MT-Qoh and LXX-Qoh. While Goldman's arguments are interesting, it needs to be asked if LXX-Qoh (→ 13–17.1.1.3) could not represent an interpretative translation in Qoh 7:19, 23–24 and 8:1 that applied a specific theological reading to Qohelet. It also needs to be emphasized that the central role of the Torah in Judaism did not emerge around the turn of the era.

[1] For the descriptions of these manuscripts and their publications, → 15.2.1.

[2] Muilenburg, "Qohelet," 28.

cian city.[3] However, כמה most likely is the result of scribal error (see below, → 15.2.3.1.1). On the whole, Dahood's hypothesis that Qohelet has a Phoenician origin has been rightly criticized by Gordis, Schoors, and Seow, among others.[4] With the exception of this discussion, the discourse about 4QQoh[a] is restricted to the study of individual variants.

15.2.3.1.1 Nature and Text-Critical Character

In contrast to MT-Qoh (→ 15.2.2), 4QQoh[a] employs the baroque orthographic system prominent among the Dead Sea Scrolls. As MT-Qoh includes some plene spellings that are reminiscent of the baroque orthographic system and as 4QQoh[a] was produced already between 175–150 B.C.E. (→ 15.2.1.1), it could imply that the book of Qohelet was not written originally in the conservative orthographic system of MT.

The textual quality of 4QQoh[a] is mixed. Many readings are the result of scribal corruption, harmonization, and linguistic editing. However, surprisingly, the manuscript also preserves four original readings (for the secondary readings of MT-Qoh in the references below, see above → 15.2.2.3).[5]

- In Qoh 5:14, 4QQoh[a] reads an assertive כיא "indeed," which MT-Qoh corrected to כַּאֲשֶׁר "like" to achieve a smoother text.
- In Qoh 6:4, 4QQoh[a] reads the perfect form הלך "it went," which MT-Qoh harmonized with the imperfect form יְכֻסֶּה "will be covered" at the end of Qoh 6:4 to יֵלֵךְ "it will go."

- In Qoh 7:5, 4QQoh[a] has the unique plural form גערות "rebukes," which MT-Qoh corrected to the singular גַּעֲרַת "rebuke."
- In Qoh 7:7, 4QQoh[a] attests to the reading ויעוה "and perverts." As root עוה is unique in the book of Qohelet, MT-Qoh replaced the word with וִיאַבֵּד "and destroys"; cf. LXX (→ 13–17.1.1.3).

Three readings in 4QQoh[a] are the result of scribal corruption and it is uncertain if the scribe of 4QQoh[a] or another earlier copyist in the scribal tradition of 4QQoh[a] is responsible for them.

- In Qoh 6:8, a scribe overlooked a *yod* and read the words כִּי מָה "for what" of MT-Qoh as כמה "how much."[6]
- In Qoh 6:12, the words כַּצֵּל מִי אֲשֶׁר "like the shadow? For who" from MT-Qoh are lacking in 4QQoh[a]. The resulting text is meaningless. The most likely explanation is that the eye of the scribe while he wrote a medial *mem* in the word ויע[שׂם "and he made them" jumped from this *mem* to the *mem* of the word מִי "who." The words כַּצֵּל מִי אֲשֶׁר were thus omitted erroneously by way of paraplepsis.
- In Qoh 7:4, 4QQoh[a] reads the first בְּבֵית "in a house" of MT-Qoh as בית "a house." The reading בית is due to haplography.

The remaining majority of the variant readings in 4QQoh[a] result from linguistic correction and harmonization. 4QQoh[a] smoothens the text flow in several instances.

- It twice deletes a *waw copulativum* (גם "also" [cf. MT[Kenn80,147,188]] instead of וְגַם "and also" in MT-Qoh 5:15 and גם "also" instead of וְגַם "and also" in MT-Qoh 7:6).
- In Qoh 6:3, 4QQoh[a] moves the comparative phrase מִמֶּנּוּ "than he" into its correct position in the comparative clause (טוב הנפל ממנו "better is

---

[3] Muilenburg, "Qohelet," 25, 28, and M. Dahood, "Qohelet and Recent Discoveries," *Bib* 39 (1958): 302–18, esp. 306.

[4] R. Gordis, "Qohelet and Qumran – A Study of Style," *Bib* 41 (1960): 395–410; Schoors, *Preacher*, 19–33; C.L. Seow, "Linguistic Evidence and the Dating of Qohelet," *JBL* 115 (1996): 644–66.

[5] Against Muilenburg, "Qohelet," 26–27, 28, 4QQoh[a] does not indicate additional textual material between Qoh 7:6 and 7:7. At the beginning of col. III:1, the original scribe erased a few words of text (between 15 and 20 letter-spaces). Below the last line of col. II, he added the end of Qoh 7:6 most likely after erasing his scribal error in col. III:1. For a discussion of the meaning of the orthographic variant נוחת instead of נָחַת in MT-Qoh 6:5, see N. Mizrahi, "Qohelet 6:5b in Light of 4QQoh[a] II:2 and Rabbinic Literature," *Textus* 21 (2002): 159–74. Mizrahi understands נוחת as a masculine particle of the root נחת "to descend."

[6] Cf. Gordis, "Qoheleth and Qumran," 398; Schoors, *Preacher*, 29; contra Muilenburg, "Qohelet," 25, 28, and Dahood, "Qohelet," 306, who regard the reading of 4QQoh[a] as a Phoenician defective spelling.

the stillborn than he" instead of MT-Qoh's טוֹב מִמֶּנּוּ הַנָּפֶל "better than he is the stillborn").
- In Qoh 6:6, 4QQoh[a] replaces the Aramaic conjunction וְאִלּוּ "even if" of MT-Qoh with the Hebrew equivalent ואם לוא "though."
- In Qoh 7:2, 4QQoh[a] replaces מִשְׁתֶּה "feasting" (MT-Qoh) with ש[מחה "j]oy" (4QQoh[a]; MT[Kenn104]) in adjustment to Qoh 7:4.[7]
- In Qoh 7:2, 4QQoh[a] reads ה[וּ]אה כול סוֹף [האדם "[i]t is all the end [of humanity" instead of the הוא סוֹף כָּל־הָאָדָם "it is the end of all humankind" in MT-Qoh in order to clarify to what הוא "it" is referring.[8]
- In Qoh 7:5, 4QQoh[a] changes the מֵאִישׁ שֹׁמֵעַ "than a man who listens" of MT-Qoh to מ[לשׁמוֹע "than] to listen" (corrected *prima manu* from מ[למוֹע) in adjustment with the beginning of v. 5.[9]
- In Qoh 7:19, 4QQoh[a] replaces the abstruse תָּעֹז "strengthens" (MT-Qoh) with תעזר[10] "helps"; cf. LXX.[11]
- In Qoh 7:19 and 20, 4QQoh[a] substitutes the relative particle אֲשֶׁר in MT-Qoh with the relative particle שׁ-.[12]

15.2.3.1.2 Date and Milieu

Little can be said regarding when the text of 4QQoh[a] developed. The paleographic date of the manuscript sets a *terminus ante quem* before the middle of the second century B.C.E. The composition of the book of Qohelet in the third century B.C.E.[13] provides the *terminus post quem*.

15.2.3.1.3 Relevance for Exegesis and Literary Analysis

The variant readings of 4QQoh[a] are mainly of text-critical interest and have little impact on either the exegesis of the book of Qohelet or the study of its literary layers. Nevertheless, 4QQoh[a] is of immense importance for the dating of Qohelet. The scribal errors of 4QQoh[a] show that it cannot be the autograph of this book. The paleographic date of 4QQoh[a] between 175–150 B.C.E. therefore excludes settings in Maccabean or post-Maccabean times.[14]

15.2.3.2 4QQoh[b] (4Q110)

The small amount of preserved text of 4QQoh[b] prohibits general conclusions about the text of Qohelet to which it attests. The two extant variants are nevertheless of interest. That 4QQoh[b] reads in Qoh 1:14 אשר נעשו "that happens" (MT[Kenn95,200]) against the שֶׁנַּעֲשׂוּ "that happens" of MT-Qoh should be understood as a harmonization with כָּל־אֲשֶׁר נַעֲשָׂה "everything that happens" in Qoh 1:13. Of frg. 1 line 7, only the characters]גבוֹ[are preserved. They fit with no word in the immediate context of Qoh 1:14.[15] 4QQoh[b] most likely included additional text that was either deleted in MT-Qoh (→ 15.2.2) for being too heretical to be put into the mouth of Solomon or that was added later on by a scribe.[16]

15.2.3.3 Other Medieval Hebrew Texts?

Von Mutius has argued that some Qohelet quotations in the medieval *Midrash Ha-Gadol* employ a

---

[7] For the harmonization in Qoh 7:2, cf. Muilenburg, "Qohelet," 27; Seow, *Ecclesiastes*, 236. Salters, "Textual Criticism," 56, claims wrongly that 4QQoh[a] read משתה "feasting."

[8] Cf. Seow, *Ecclesiastes*, 236.

[9] Cf. Seow, *Ecclesiastes*, 236.

[10] Against Muilenburg, "Qohelet," 27; Ulrich, "Ezra and Qohelet," 147; Ulrich, "Qohelet," 225; and Salters, "Textual Criticism," 56, the edition of Kennicott (*1776–1780, 2.556) does not note the reading תעזר for Qoh 7:2. In his apparatus, Kennicott mentions only the orthographic variant תעוז (MT[Kenn17,19,57,77,99,109,136,150,152,155,223,260,384,680]).

[11] Cf. Salters, "Textual Criticism," 56; Seow, *Ecclesiastes*, 256.

[12] Cf. Goldman, "Qoheleth," 67*.

[13] For this date for Qohelet, see e.g. M.V. Fox, *Ecclesiastes* קהלת (The JPS Bible Commentary; Philadelphia: Jewish Publication Society, 2004), xiv.

[14] Cf. already Muilenburg, "Qohelet," 27 and, more recently, Puech, "Qohelet," 159. For the later date of 152–145 B.C.E. for Qohelet even after the publication of 4QQoh[a], see e.g. C.F. Whitley, *Kohelet: His Language and Thought* (BZAW 148; Berlin: Walter de Gruyter, 1979), 132–48.

[15] Cf. Ulrich, "Ezra and Qohelet," 148; Ulrich, "Qohelet," 227. Contra G.W. Nebe, "Qumranica I," *ZAW* 104 (1994): 307–22, esp. 313. Nebe suggests to read in line 7 הגברתי "I have shown myself mightier" as a variant reading to הגדלתי "I have magnified myself" in Qoh 1:16 and argues that Qoh 1:15 could have been lost due to parablepsis. The destroyed part of 4QQoh[b] could have accommodated at best 46 letter-spaces between תחת in line 6 and the characters גב in line 7. However, in Nebe's reconstruction, even without v. 15, a text of sixty-one letter-spaces would have needed to fit into a text gap of forty-six letter-spaces.

[16] Cf. Lange, *Handbuch, 484–85.

non-Masoretic text of Qohelet.[17] This observation could point to the development of one or more non-aligned texts of Qohelet in either late antiquity or the Middle Ages. The text-critical study of Qohelet quotations remains a desideratum, to which von Mutius' work points. However, the lack of a comprehensive study cautions against far-reaching conclusions.

Goldman, Y.A.P., "Qoheleth קהלת," in *BHQ 18, 25–53, 13*–17*, 64*–112*.

Mizrahi, N., "Qohelet 6:5b in Light of 4QQoh^a ii 2 and Rabbinic Literature," *Textus* 21 (2002): 159–74.

Muilenburg, J., "A Qohelet Scroll from Qumran," *BASOR* 135 (1954): 20–28.

Puech, É., "Le livre de Qohélet à Qumrân," *HTh* 18 (2000): 109–14.

Puech, É., "Qohelet a Qumran," in *Il libro del Qohelet: Tradizione, redazione, teologie* (eds. G. Bellia and A. Passaro; Milan: Paoline, 2001), 144–70.

Salters, R.B., "Textual Criticism and Qoheleth," *JNSL* 23.1 (1997): 53–71.

Schoors, A., *The Preacher Sought to Find Pleasing Words: A Study in the Language of Qoheleth* (OLA 41; Leuven: Peeters, 1992), 33–40.

Seow, C.-L., *Ecclesiastes: A New Translation with Introduction and Commentary* (AB 18C; New York: Doubleday), 1997.

Ulrich, E., "Ezra and Qohelet Manuscripts from Qumran (4QEzra and 4QQoh^{a, b})," in *Priests, Prophets and Scribes: Essays on the Formation and Heritage of Second Temple Judaism in Honour of Joseph Blenkinsopp* (eds. E. Ulrich et al.; JSOTSup 149; Sheffield: Sheffield Academic Press, 1992), 139–57.

Ulrich, E., "Qohelet," *DJD* XVI: 221–27.

Armin Lange

---

[17] H.-G. von Mutius, "Eine talmudische Textvariante zu Kohelet 5,9 und ihr Verhältnis zur LXX," *BN* 144 (2010): 87–93; H.-G. von Mutius, "Drei nichtmasoretische Textzitate aus dem Midrasch ha-Gadol zu den Büchern Ijob (38,35), Sprüche (29,12) und Kohelet (3,14)," *BN* 149 (2011): 59–64.

16

Lamentations

∴

16.1 Textual History of Lamentations

16.1.1 Extant Witnesses

16.1.1.1 Hebrew Witnesses

The main representatives of the Hebrew text of Lamentations include four fragmentary manuscripts from the Qumran caves (3QLam, 4QLam, 5QLam^a, and 5QLam^b; → 16.2.1) and medieval masoretic manuscripts (→ 10–20.1). The expositional midrash *Eichah Rabbah* and other rabbinic literature quote from and comment on passages in Lamentations (→ 21.6),[1] while only a few writings among the Dead Sea Scrolls make use of the Hebrew wording of the book (cf. 4Q179 and 4Q501). These instances are not *verbatim* quotations and it is debatable whether they allude to the meanings of these phrases as they are used in Lamentations.[2] The rabbinic writings and the Dead Sea Scrolls are, therefore, of limited value as witnesses to the text of Lamentations.

With regard to the Qumran manuscripts, their dates range from the first century B.C.E. to the first century C.E. The two small fragments of 3QLam contain single words from Lam 1:10–12 and Lam 3:53–62. Cave 5 yielded two fragmentary manuscripts. 5QLam^a preserves parts of Lam 4:5–8, 11–22, and 5:1–17, while the single fragment of 5QLam^b contains words from Lam 4:17–20. 4QLam is the largest Lamentations manuscript from Qumran. It exists in four fragments and presents portions of Lam 1:1–18 and a few words from Lam 2:5 (→ 16.2.1.2).

The eleventh-century manuscript, MT^L, is the chief representative of the complete MT wording of Lamentations. The book is, unfortunately, not preserved in MT^A.

16.1.1.2 Greek Witnesses

LXX-Lam (→ 13–17.1.1.4) was created by a member of the *kaige*-Th group of translators and revisers (→ 13–17.1.1.4.3) and exhibits an approach to translation whereby the translator endeavoured to follow the Hebrew *Vorlage* closely in the sequence of its words and the representation of its clause constituents. The translation is "literal," but not in a mechanical manner. In some instances, the translator attempted to make sense of the wording and content of his parent text and adapted the wording of his translation to his understanding or context. He even added a preamble before the translation of Lam 1:1 that connects LXX-Lam to the prophet Jeremiah (→ 13–17.1.1.4.4).[3] In other instances, the translator was content to reproduce the wording of the *Vorlage* to such an extent that he sacrificed the intelligibility of the Greek text. A date ranging from the middle of the first century B.C.E. to the middle of the first century C.E. has been suggested for the *kaige*-Th group (→ 1.3.1.2), including LXX-Lam. Although a more specific date for the creation of LXX-Lam has not been determined yet, scholars agree that its *Vorlage* was close but not identical to the consonantal base of MT (→ 13–17.1.1.4.4).[4]

---

[1] Cf. J. Kalman, "If Jeremiah Wrote It, It Must be OK: On the Attribution of Lamentations to Jeremiah in Early Rabbinic Texts," *AcT* (2009): 31–53.

[2] Quotations of Lamentations have been detected in 4Q282 (formerly 4Q241) frgs. h and i, but these fragments are so small that it is hardly possible to identify the individual words on them as quotations.

[3] It is debatable whether the preamble comes from the pen of the translator, since it has a Hebraic style. It might have been part of the parent text from which LXX-Lam was made. However, it is possible that the translator composed the preamble using a Hebraic style. Assan-Dhôte, **Lamentations*, 132, argues in favour of this possibility. The preamble could have been added only to the version of the Hebrew text that served as the parent text of LXX-Lam, but this is improbable in view of the fact that the *Vorlage* is very close to MT. Moreover, Assan-Dhôte, **Lamentations*, 132–33, draws attention to the similarity between the preamble in LXX-Lam and introductions of this type in other Greek translations (cf., e.g., LXX-Judg 1:1; LXX-Ruth 1:1; and 2 Kgdms 1:1). She suggests that the preamble could have been written by the translator of LXX-Lam in imitation of the other texts and that this would account for the "translational" character of its wording. On the preamble and the Greek translation of Lam 1:1, see also G.R. Kotzé, "Short Notes on the Value of the Septuagint and Vulgate for the Interpretation of Lamentations 1:1," *JNSL* 36.2 (2010): 77–93 (78–79, 83–87).

[4] Hirsch-Luipold and Maier, "Threnoi," 2831.

Individual readings from the Greek versions of Aquila and Symmachus, as well as readings that are not attributed to either are recorded in the margins of Greek and Syro-Hexapla codices (→ 13–17.1.5.1.3.2–3). A number of Symmachus readings can also be found in Origen's Lamentations commentary, while Theodoret of Cyrus cites passages from the version of "the Syrian" (ὁ σύρος) in his commentary (→ 21.7). There is only one example of a reading that is attributed to the version of "the Hebrew" (ὁ ἑβραῖος) in the available sources. This reading is found at Lam 4:3 in the Syro-Hexapla manuscript, Codex Ambrosianus (→ 13–17.2.4.4). A note in the margin of this manuscript refers to the equivalent ܬܢܝܢ (θανιν "ṯanin") for תנין "jackals" and credits "the Hebrew" version with this reading. The readings of Aquila, Symmachus, ὁ σύρος and ὁ ἑβραῖος largely agree with MT.

16.1.1.3 Other Versional Witnesses

S-Lam can be dated to the mid-second century C.E. and was based on a Hebrew parent text that was almost identical to proto-MT (→ 13–17.1.4.4).[5] Nevertheless, this Syriac translation includes minor additions (e.g., conjunctions, suffixes, etc.) and slight changes in wording when compared to MT (→ 16.2.2). The translator strove for clarity and intelligibility in his translation and not creativity and variation in his use of Syriac equivalents for Hebrew words.[6] There is hardly any evidence of influence from LXX-Lam (→ 13–17.1.1.4) and T-Lam (→ 13–17.1.3) on the Syriac translation.[7] It is, however, possible that the translator consulted a Greek manuscript in certain cases. For example, the Syriac equivalent for לאכזר "uncouth" in Lam 4:3, ܡܚܘܬܐ ܕܠܝܬ ܠܗ ܐܣܝܘܬܐ "a wound for which there is no cure," was in all probability inspired by the Greek reading εἰς ἀνίατον "incurable."[8]

V-Lam was made by Jerome in Bethlehem in the final decade of the fourth century (ca. 393 C.E.) (→ 13–17.1.7.1). According to Salters, it is a "stylish and readable" translation and it "usually agrees with the consonantal text of MT, although Jerome occasionally takes a different line regarding the vocalisation of the text" (→ 13–17.1.7.4.2).[9] There are instances where V-Lam presents a christological interpretation of a passage. Thus, the rendering of רוח אפינו משיח יהוה נלכד בשחיתותם "The Lord's anointed, the breath of our life, was taken in their pits" (*NRSV) with *spiritus oris nostri christus dominus captus est in peccatis nostris* "The breath of our mouth, Christ the Lord, is taken in our sins" (Douay-Rheims) at Lam 4:20 is an obvious example (→ 13–17.1.7.3.3).[10] It seems that Jerome depended on a Greek text and suggestions by a Jewish informant for his translation of certain phrases in Lamentations. V-Lam 1:8 presents an example where a Greek reading influenced the Latin translation. The Vulgate reading *propterea instabilis facta est* "therefore, she has been made unstable" is almost identical to the reading in LXX-Lam: διὰ τοῦτο εἰς σάλον ἐγένετο "therefore, she became unstable." Jerome might have been uncertain about the meaning of the difficult *hapax legomenon* לנידה "(morally) impure" in his *Vorlage* and translated it under the influence of εἰς σάλον "unstable" in a Greek text.[11] The translation equivalent of משבתה "her downfall" in V-Lam 1:7, *sabbata eius* "her sabbaths" was probably suggested to Jerome by one of his Jewish teachers. The connection of משבתה with the Sabbath can also be found in *Eichah Rabbah* 1:7 § 34 (→ 13–17.1.7.3.3).[12]

---

[5] H.F. van Rooy, "The Ancient Versions of Lamentations," *Scriptura* 110 (2012): 227–36 (229).

[6] Cf. Albrektson, *Studies*, 210–11.

[7] Albrektson, *Studies*, 212; Alexander, *Targum*, 48.

[8] M.P. Weitzman, *The Syriac Version of the Old Testament: An Introduction* (Cambridge: Cambridge University Press, 1999), 78.

[9] R.B. Salters, *A Critical and Exegetical Commentary on Lamentations* (ICC; London: T & T Clark, 2010), 26.

[10] On the christological interpretation in V-Lam 4:20, see the comments of W. Rudolph, "Der Text der Klagelieder," *ZAW* 56 (1938): 101–22 (120).

[11] G.R. Kotzé, "Lamentations 1:8a in the Wordings of the Masoretic Text and 4QLam," *Scriptura* 110 (2012): 190–207 (194).

[12] G.R. Kotzé, "A Text-Critical Analysis of Lamentations 1:7 in 4QLam and the Masoretic Text," *OTE* 24 (2011): 590–611 (604).

T-Lam (→ 13–17.1.3) was composed in the late fifth or early sixth century C.E. (→ 13–17.1.3.1.3 for a different view) in Galilee from a *Vorlage* that was not much different from MT (→ 16.2.2).[13] Its extant manuscripts bear witness to two recensions, a Western recension and a Yemenite recension. These recensions derive from a common ancestor.[14] The Western recension is longer and closer to this original text than its Yemenite counterpart. The latter abbreviated a text that was close to the Western recension in order to bring it into closer conformity with MT and to simplify its style.[15] The translation includes instances where the targumist rendered the Hebrew parent text literally with only very short additions (cf. e.g., Lam 3:1–3), instances where he translated literally and added a gloss (cf. Lam 5:5), and other instances where the translation takes the form of a paraphrase (cf. Lam 1:1–4).[16]

16.1.2 Textual Development

In text-critical work on Lamentations, MT (→ 16.2.2) is often treated as the central representative of the book's Hebrew text.[17] This influential role of MT-Lam can be attributed to two factors. The text of MT is in a good state of preservation and, with the exception of 4QLam, the Hebrew manuscripts from Qumran (→ 16.2.1; → 16.2.3) and the ancient translations have wordings that are very similar to MT.[18] Yet, MT cannot simply be equated with the original text of Lamentations.[19] Its wording contains scribal errors and secondary readings that came into being during the history of its transmission.[20] The ancient translations that were made from Hebrew *Vorlagen* different from MT are also valuable witnesses to the textual development of Lamentations. They are sources of original readings and shed light on how scribes created readings during the processes of translation and transmission.[21]

Concerning 4QLam (→ 16.2.3), there are many readings that differ from their counterparts in MT (→ 16.2.1.2).[22] Some of these readings are scribal errors, but the majority appear to be deliberate scribal changes.[23] One group of these changes forms a certain pattern. At Lam 1:7, 11, 12, and 13, a scribe made changes to the wording in order to ensure that the narrator remains the speaker in these verses.[24] Consequently, the complaints in the verses relate to him and his community. Conversely, in MT and the other textual witnesses, the complaints are about Jerusalem's circumstances and at Lam 1:12 the personified city becomes the speaker.

A few readings in 4QLam can, with varying measures of certainty, be interpreted as more original than the wording of MT. At Lam 1:7, 8, and 11, 4QLam contains readings that agree with LXX (→ 13–17.1.1.4) against MT, while at Lam 1:7, 9, 13, and 14, there are readings in the Qumran manuscript that agree with S-Lam (→ 13–17.1.4.4) against MT. Of these, the following readings are arguably original:

---

[13] Alexander, *Targum*, 87–90.
[14] Alexander, *Targum*, 5–11.
[15] Alexander, *Targum*, 6.
[16] Alexander, *Targum*, 39.
[17] Kotzé, *Qumran Manuscripts*, 13.
[18] Salters, *Lamentations*, 22.
[19] Salters, *Lamentations*, 22.
[20] Cf., e.g., Lam 1:7, 12, 13, 14; 2:9, 19; 3:22, 58; 4:18, 21; 5:5. This is a selection of passages from each of the five poems of the book where scholars have identified scribal errors and secondary readings in MT-Lam. For discussions of the problems in MT, suggested emendations, and additional literature, see Salters, *Lamentations*, 72–73, 75–77, 78–79, 140–41, 174–75, 224–25, 270, 327–28, 334–35, 347–48; Schäfer, **BHQ* 18, 114*, 116*, 117*–18*, 123*–24*, 127*, 135*; Barthélemy, **Critique textuelle 1986*, 864–914; and Rudolph, "Text," 102–04, 112, 115, 120–21.
[21] See the discussion of van Rooy, "Ancient Versions," 227–36.
[22] Kotzé, *Qumran Manuscripts*, 177.
[23] Kotzé, *Qumran Manuscripts*, 178.
[24] Kotzé, *Qumran Manuscripts*, 47–48, 68–70, 74–76, 85–86.

	4QLam	LXX	S
Lam 1:7	צריה "her enemies"	οἱ ἐχθροὶ αὐτῆς "her enemies"	ܐܠܘܨܝܗ̈ "her oppressors"
Lam 1:7	משבריה "her ruins"		ܬܒܪܗ "her ruin"
Lam 1:8	לנוד "wanderer"	εἰς σάλον "unstable"	
Lam 1:14	עולו "his yoke"		ܢܝܪ̈ܘܗܝ "his yokes"

4QLam evidently presents a different version of Lamentations 1 than the one in MT (→ 16.2.1.2; → 16.2.3).[25] This view is justified in light of the original and unique readings in 4QLam, as well as the fact that there are erroneous readings in MT that the Qumran manuscript does not share. From the perspective of text and interpretation history, 4QLam is, therefore, a very important textual representative of Lamentations.

Albrektson, B., *Studies in the Text and Theology of the Book of Lamentations: With a Critical Edition of the Peshitta Text* (Studia theologica Lundensia 21; Lund: Gleerup, 1963).
Alexander, P.S., *The Targum of Lamentations: Translated, with a Critical Introduction, Apparatus, and Notes* (ArBib 17b; Collegeville: Liturgical Press, 2007).
Assan-Dhôte, I. and J. Moatti-Fine, *Baruch, Lamentations, Lettre de Jérémie: Traduction du texte grec de la Septante, introduction et notes* (*Bible d'Alexandrie 25.2; Paris: Cerf, 2005).
Baillet, M., "3. Lamentations," *DJD III.1: 95.
Barthélemy, *Critique textuelle 1986.
Cross, F.M., "Lamentations," *DJD XVI: 229–37.
Hirsch-Luipold, R. and C.M. Maier, "Threnoi/Threni Seu Lamentationes/Die Klagelieder," in *Septuaginta Deutsch, Erläuterungen, 2827–41.
Kotzé, G.R., *The Qumran Manuscripts of Lamentations: A Text-Critical Study* (SSN 61; Leiden: Brill, 2013).
Milik, J.T., "Lamentations (Premier Exemplaire)," *DJD III.1: 174–77.
Milik, J.T., "Lamentations (Second Exemplaire)," *DJD III.1: 177–78.
Schäfer, R., "Lamentations," in *BHQ 18, 54–72, 113*–36*.
Tov, *Scribal Practices.
Ueberschaer, F., "Die Septuaginta der Klagelieder: Überlegungen zu Entstehung und Textgeschichte," in Kreuzer–Meiser–Sigismund, *Septuaginta 2012, 98–111.
Ziegler, J., *Ieremias, Baruch, Threni, Epistula Ieremiae* (3rd ed.; Septuaginta Vetus Testamentum Graecum 15; Göttingen: Vandenhoeck & Ruprecht, 2006).

Gideon Kotzé

---

[25] See Kotzé, *Qumran Manuscripts*, 179–80; H.F. van Rooy, "Klaagliedere by Qumran: 'n Tweede Redaksie?" *HvTSt* 68 (2012): 1–7; and Tov, *Scribal Practices, 335, who classifies 4QLam as a non-aligned text.

16.2 Ancient Hebrew Texts

16.2.1 Ancient Manuscript Evidence

The only four ancient Hebrew manuscripts of Lamentations that are extant were all found in the Qumran caves.[1]

16.2.1.1 3QLam (3Q3)

Only two small fragments of 3QLam are extant attesting to nine complete or partial words from Lam 1:10–12 and 3:53–62. The manuscript was executed in a Herodian formal hand.[2] The tetragrammaton is written in the paleo-Hebrew alphabet (3QLam 1 2 = Lam 1:11). Baillet's reconstruction of the text points to a stichometric arrangement of the two preserved acrostics, in which each line began with the next letter of the Hebrew alphabet.[3] The small amount of preserved text prohibits orthographic and text-typological classifications.[4]

16.2.1.2 4QLam (4Q111)

Four fragments of 4QLam are extant attesting to parts of Lam 1:1aβ–15, 16, 17, 18; 2:5.[5] Frgs. 1–3 belong to three consecutive columns in 4QLam. Cross' reconstruction shows that the first preserved column began with Lam 1:1aβ. Lam 1:1aα was either written with an indent in the last line of a preceding column or was copied as a heading on the upper part of the lost handle sheet of 4QLam. In the first case, another text would have preceded Lamentations in 4Q111 and this scroll might have contained several of the Five Scrolls.[6] The fact that 4QLam was written in a semi-vulgar script on a leather of low quality identifies the scroll as a low-budget manuscript.[7]

4QLam is executed in a vulgar semiformal Herodian script from the years 30–1 B.C.E.[8] In its orthography, 4QLam employs the baroque spellings of the so-called Qumran orthography.[9] In 193 extant words and remnants of words, 4QLam attests to forty-one textual differences from MT (→ 16.2.2) and LXX (→ 13–17.1.1.4). 4QLam reads once with and forty times against MT,[10] three times with and thirty-three times against LXX, and thirty-two times non-aligned. Therefore, 4QLam clearly attests to a non-aligned text.[11]

16.2.1.3 5QLam[a] (5Q6)

Of the fifty-seven small or very small fragments preserved from 5QLam[a], fourteen can no longer be identified.[12] The fragments whose text can still be identified belong to six different columns of the original scroll and attest to parts of Lam 4:5–

---

[1] T. Ilan recently suggested understanding 4Q179 as an alternative version of the book of Lamentations rather than a later literary composition influenced by it: "Gender and Lamentations: 4Q179 and the Canonization of the Book of Lamentations," *Lectio difficilior* (2008), [cited 27 September 2013]. Online: http://www.lectio.unibe.ch/08_2/pdf/Tal_Ilan_Gender_of_Lamentations.pdf; "Canonization and Gender in Qumran: 4Q179, 4Q184, 2Q18 and 11QPsalms[a]," in *The Dead Sea Scrolls and Contemporary Culture: Proceedings of the International Conference Held at the Israel Museum, Jerusalem (July 6–8, 2008)* (eds. A.D. Roitman, L.H. Schiffman, and S. Tzoref; STDJ 93; Leiden: Brill, 2011), 512–45, esp. 515–28. Although Ilan rightly points to the close parallels between Lamentations and the text attested by 4Q179, the latter is more likely to be understood as a rewritten version of Lamentations.

[2] For the description, reconstruction, and paleography of 3QLam, cf. Baillet, "Lamentations," 95.

[3] Cf. Baillet, "Lamentations," 95; Schäfer, "Der ursprüngliche Text," 242.

[4] Contra Schäfer, "Der ursprüngliche Text," 242, who speaks of a proto-Masoretic manuscript.

[5] For the description, reconstruction, and paleography of 4QLam, see Cross, "Studies," 133–34; Cross, "Lamentations," 229.

[6] Cf. Cross, "Lamentations," 229.

[7] Cf. Cross, "Lamentations," 229; Schäfer, "Der ursprüngliche Text," 243.

[8] See Cross, "Studies," 133; Cross, "Lamentations," 229.

[9] Cross, "Studies," 134; Cross, "Lamentations," 229.

[10] In five cases, the textual differences between 4QLam and MT cannot be reflected in a Greek translation.

[11] For this text-typological classification of 4QLam, cf. Hillers, *Lamentations*, 45–47; Tov, *"Synthese," 27; Schäfer, "Der Masoretische Text," 132–46; Schäfer, "Der ursprüngliche Text," 243–44; and the discussion of the individual variants of 4QLam in Cross, "Studies," 135–51 and Cross, "Lamentations," 229–30.

[12] For the description, reconstruction, and paleography of 5QLam[a], cf. Milik, "premier exemplaire," 174–77.

8, 11–16, 19–22; 5:1–13, 16–17. 5QLamᵃ was executed in a Herodian book hand from the middle of the first century C.E. The orthography of 5QLamᵃ is fuller than that of MT-Lam but does not display – with a few exceptions – the characteristic features of the so-called Qumran orthography.[13] In 141 words and remnants of words, 5QLamᵃ attests to twelve textual differences with MT (→ 16.2.2) and LXX (→ 13–17.1.1.4). The manuscript reads three times with and nine times against MT, never with and eleven times against LXX, as well as eight times non-aligned. Thus, the text of 5QLamᵃ can be classified as either semi-Masoretic or non-aligned. As most of the textual variants in 5QLamᵃ toward MT are rather small, a classification as semi-Masoretic seems to me to be more appropriate.[14]

16.2.1.4 5QLamᵇ (5Q7)

Only one small and heavily damaged fragment of 5QLamᵇ survives, attesting to six complete or partial words from Lam 4:17–20.[15] Paleographically, 5QLamᵇ resembles 5QLamᵃ but its script seems to be somewhat later than that of 5QLamᵃ. This observation would point to a paleographic date for 5QLamᵇ in the second quarter of the first century C.E. The small amount of preserved text does not suffice for orthographic and text-typological classifications.

Baillet, M., "3. Lamentations," *DJD III.1: 95.
Cross, F.M., "Studies in the Structure of Hebrew Verse: The Prosody of Lamentations 1:1–22," in *The Word of the Lord Shall Go Forth: Essays in Honor of David Noel Freedman in Celebration of his Sixtieth Birthday* (eds. C.L. Meyers and M. O'Connor; Winona Lake: Eisenbrauns, 1983), 129–55.
Cross, F.M., "Lamentations," *DJD XVI: 229–37.
Hillers, D.R., *Lamentations: A New Translation with Introduction and Commentary* (2nd revised ed.; AB 7A; New York: Doubleday, 1992), 39–48.

Lange, *Handbuch, 489–95.
Milik, J.T., "Lamentations (premier exemplaire)," *DJD III.1: 174–77.
Milik, J.T., "Lamentations (second exemplaire)," *DJD III.1: 177–78.
Nebe, G.W., "Qumranica I," ZAW 104 (1994): 307–22, esp. 313–15.
Schäfer, R., "Der Masoretische Text der Klagelieder und die Handschriften 3QLam, 4QLam und 5QLamᵃ·ᵇ aus Qumran," in *Die Textfunde vom Toten Meer und der Text der Hebräischen Bibel* (eds. U. Dahmen, A. Lange, and H. Lichtenberger; Neukirchen-Vluyn: Neukirchener, 2000), 127–47.
Schäfer, R., "Der ursprüngliche Text und die poetische Struktur des ersten Klageliedes (Klgl 1)," in *Sôfer Mahîr: Essays in Honour of Adrian Schenker Offered by Editors of Biblia Hebraica Quinta* (eds. Y.A.P. Goldman, A. van der Kooij, and R.D. Weis; VTSup 110; Leiden: Brill, 2006), 239–59, esp. 239–49, 259.
Ulrich, E., *BQS, 749–54.

Armin Lange

16.2.2 Masoretic Texts and Ancient Texts Close to MT

MT-Lam is the only available complete Hebrew text of Lamentations. The poetic lines, which are in general very regular throughout the five poems,[1] as well as the rigorous literary form of the alphabetic acrostics in Lamentations 1–4 contributed to the accurate transmission of the text. Thus MT-Lam is generally assumed to be "fairly well preserved."[2]

---

[13] For the orthography of 5QLamᵃ, see Milik, "premier exemplaire," 175.
[14] Cf. Lange, *Handbuch, 492.
[15] For a description and reconstruction of 5QLamᵇ, see Milik, "second exemplaire," 177.

[1] With good reason, Budde took Lamentations 1–4 (and among these especially Lamentations 3) as the starting point for his first description of the "Klageliedvers" (verse of the lamentation), i.e., the poetic form that was later called the *qinah* metre. Budde found throughout Lamentations 1–4 clear examples for this special type of verse with only very few irregularities that, in Budde's view, were mostly minor variations of the basic scheme and in some cases resulted from textual corruption. See Budde, "Klagelied," 5–8.
[2] Robinson, "Notes," 255, and in exactly the same words Berlin, *Lamentations*, 36; similarly Rudolph, *Klagelieder*, 189: "Der Text von Thr ist recht gut erhalten …"

16.2.2.1 History of Research

Apart from the discussion of text-critical details in commentaries[3] and a series of eclectic notes published in articles by Ehrlich,[4] Robinson,[5] and Driver,[6] there are three comprehensive text-critical studies on the text of Lamentations by Rudolph,[7] Albrektson,[8] and Gottlieb.[9] Rudolph (preparing his commentary on Lamentations for the KAT series) collected and discussed verse by verse the textual problems of MT-Lam and variant readings from the ancient versions, but without any general evaluation or conclusion. In contrast, Albrektson managed to evaluate the individual readings of MT, LXX (→ 13–17.1.1.4), and the Peshitta (→ 13–17.1.4.4) on the basis of a general characterization of these witnesses. In his thorough analyses of the textual variants, he most frequently concluded that MT is the superior reading. Albrektson's fundamental study aimed at a critical edition of S-Lam, which is also included in his book. Gottlieb understood[10] his own study as type of supplement to (and in a few cases a reconsideration of) Albrektson's work.

In addition to and also in competition with these text-critical studies, there are the approaches of Gordis,[11] McDaniel,[12] and Dahood[13] that seek to explain morphologically or lexically obscure passages of MT-Lam in the light of new Hebrew and Northwest Semitic linguistic material. McDaniel, in particular, found evidence of many archaic features in MT-Lam that in his view the ancient translators as well as the modern exegetes often failed to recognize.[14]

The Qumran manuscripts of Lamentations (→ 16.2.1), especially the 4QLam fragments published by Cross,[15] have aroused fresh debate recently on the relationship of 4QLam and MT and also the relation of either to the original Hebrew text. In his fundamental study on the Qumran manuscripts of Lamentations, Kotzé[16] has discussed these questions in great detail (→ 16.2.3).

16.2.2.2 Manuscripts and Editions

Lamentations is among the lost parts of the Aleppo Codex. Thus, the most important Hebrew manuscript of the complete Lamentations text remains the Leningrad Codex (MT^L = EBP. I B 19a of the Russian National Library in St. Petersburg). Two other important manuscripts are MT^{L34} (EBP. II B 34 of the Russian National Library in St. Petersburg), a "beautiful and carefully produced manuscript … probably written about 975"[17] that contains most of the writings, and MT^Y (Add. Ms. 1753 of the University Library in Cambridge), a manuscript "belonging to the fourteenth or fifteenth century," but at the same time "one of the most striking examples of Ben Asher's School in Yemen."[18] The oldest available Hebrew witnesses are the Qumran fragments described in → 16.2.1.

Three critical editions of MT-Lam have been published in the *BH series, each of them exhibiting the text of MT^L in a different degree of diplomatic presentation: The edition by Robinson in *BHS is even more selective with regard to the number of variants recorded in the apparatus than the previous edition by the same editor in *BH³, and both of them lack the evidence of the Qumran fragments. The edition of Schäfer in *BHQ is not comprehen-

---

[3] See, e.g., K. Budde, *Die Klagelieder* (KHCAT 17.3; Freiburg: J.C.B. Mohr [Paul Siebeck], 1898); Berges, *Klagelieder*; Berlin, *Lamentations: A Commentary*; Hillers, *Lamentations: A New Translation*; H.-J. Kraus, *Klagelieder* (*Threni*) (2nd ed.; BKAT 20; Neukirchen-Vluyn: Neukirchener Verlag, 1960); J. Renkema, *Lamentations* (Historical Commentary on the Old Testament; Leuven: Peeters, 1998); Koenen, *Klagelieder* (*Threni*).

[4] Ehrlich, *Randglossen*, 7.30–54.

[5] Robinson, "Notes," 255–59.

[6] Driver, "Notes," 308–09 and Driver, "Hebrew Notes," 134–46.

[7] Rudolph, "Text," 101–22.

[8] Albrektson, *Studies*.

[9] Gottlieb, *Study*.

[10] Gottlieb, *Study*, 4.

[11] Gordis, "Commentary," 267–86, and Gordis, "Commentary (Part Two)," 14–33.

[12] McDaniel, "Philological Studies I" and McDaniel, "Philological Studies II."

[13] Dahood, "New Readings."

[14] McDaniel, "Philological Studies II," 217.

[15] Cross, "Studies in the Structure of Hebrew Verse" and Cross, "4QLam," 220–37.

[16] Kotzé, *Qumran Manuscripts*.

[17] Yeivin, *Introduction*, 26.

[18] Yeivin, "Division," 80.

sive either, but records significantly more readings including of course all relevant evidence from the Qumran manuscripts, and adds commentary on the text-critical apparatus as well as on the Masorah. For the variant readings found in the medieval Masoretic manuscripts, the works of Kennicott (*1776–1780) and de Rossi (*1784–1788) are still authoritative.

16.2.2.3 Nature and Text-Critical Character of MT-Lam

Although MT-Lam is apparently a well-preserved text that contains a number of archaic linguistic features, it cannot simply be regarded as representing the original text of Lamentations. In at least two cases (Lam 1:7 and 2:19), the very unusual length of verses suggests that their wording in MT is the result of secondary expansion:

- In Lam 1:7,[19] the line כֹּל מַחֲמֻדֶיהָ אֲשֶׁר הָיוּ מִימֵי קֶדֶם "all her treasures which were there from days of old" is usually identified as an addition because of its materialistic content. Kaiser, by contrast, has argued[20] that the addition is found instead in the following line בִּנְפֹל עַמָּהּ בְּיַד־צָר וְאֵין עוֹזֵר לָהּ "when her people fell into the hand of the enemy and there was no helper for her" in an effort to moderate the materialistic view of the preceding line. The evidence of 4QLam, however, supports neither of these suggestions, but presents a significantly different and shorter text (→ 16.2.3.4).
- In Lam 2:19, the phrase הָעֲטוּפִים בְּרָעָב בְּרֹאשׁ כָּל־חוּצוֹת "who are fainting with hunger at the head of all streets" is generally[21] regarded as an addition explaining the situation of the little children mentioned previously.

Scholars in the nineteenth and twentieth centuries identified further "glosses" in Lam 1:12a (לוֹא אֲלֵיכֶם "it is nothing to you"[?]);[22] 2:15 (מָשׂוֹשׂ לְכָל־הָאָרֶץ "joy of all the earth");[23] 3:56 (לְשַׁוְעָתִי "to save me");[24] and 4:15 (אָמְרוּ "they said").[25] However, in recent times, such emendations *metri causa* have been widely rejected due to a better and less schematic idea about both parallelism and rhythm in biblical poetry. On the other hand, in Lam 1:12 there is indeed evidence from 4QLam (→ 16.2.3.4) that MT's reading בְּיוֹם חֲרוֹן אַפּוֹ "on the day of the fierceness of his anger" represents an expansive assimilation to the usual form of the expression, while the original text probably read בְּיוֹם חֲרוֹנוֹ "on the day of his fierceness." Altogether, signs of MT's expansive tendency in relation to the original text cannot be denied.

In three cases, there is evidence of textual corruption in MT-Lam:

- In Lam 1:8, the difficult reading לְנִידָה "[she became] unclean" emerged by scribal error from an original לנוד "[she became] a wandering one," as still preserved in 4QLam.[26]
- In Lam 1:13, the problematic reading וַיִּרְדֶּנָּה "and he dominated her/it" developed from an original יוֹרִדֶנָּה "he made her/it descend," which can be deduced from the readings attested in LXX (→ 13–17.1.1.4), 4QLam (→ 16.2.3), and the Peshitta (→ 13–17.1.4.4).[27]
- In Lam 1:17, the reading צִוָּה "he has commanded" comes possibly from an original צפה "he lies in ambush," which is still preserved in 4QLam,[28] but the change might perhaps result from theological consideration rather than from a graphical or phonological error.

---

[19] See *BH*³ and *BHS*.
[20] Kaiser, "Klagelieder," 125.
[21] See *BH*³ and *BHS*.
[22] Rudolph, "Klagelieder," 207; Kraus, *Klagelieder*, 23; cf. Hillers, *Lamentations*, 71.
[23] Rudolph, "Klagelieder," 220; Hillers, *Lamentations*, 100–01.
[24] Rudolph, "Klagelieder," 233; Kraus, *Klagelieder*, 53; cf. Hillers, *Lamentations*, 118.
[25] Rudolph, "Klagelieder," 249; Kraus, *Klagelieder*, 72; cf. Hillers, *Lamentations*, 143.
[26] Cross, "4QLam," 233; Kotzé, *Qumran Manuscripts*, 53–58; Koenen, *Klagelieder*, 8–9.
[27] Hillers, *Lamentations*, 72; Kotzé, *Qumran Manuscripts*, 82; slightly differently: Koenen, *Klagelieder*, 12.
[28] Cross, "Studies," 147; Kotzé, *Qumran Manuscripts*, 104. In contrast, Koenen (*Klagelieder*, 14) and Hillers (*Lamentations*, 75–76) retain MT.

In a few other instances, lexical and syntactical/stylistic difficulties in MT possibly indicate textual corruption, for example, נִשְׂקַד עַל "...?... a yoke" in Lam 1:14; עֵינִי עֵינִי יֹרְדָה מַּיִם "my eye, my eye, water is running down" in Lam 1:16; הֵבֵאתָ יוֹם־קָרָאתָ "you have brought on the day you have announced" in Lam 1:21; וַיַּחְמֹס כַּגַּן שֻׂכּוֹ "he has done violence to his booth as to a garden" in Lam 2:6; צָעַק לִבָּם אֶל־אֲדֹנָי חוֹמַת בַּת־צִיּוֹן "their heart cried out to the Lord, the wall of daughter Zion" in Lam 2:18; לֹא־תָמְנוּ "we are not finished" in Lam 3:22; מְדֻקָּרִים מִתְּנוּבֹת שָׂדָי "pierced from the fruits of the field" in Lam 4:9; and עַל צַוָּארֵנוּ נִרְדָּפְנוּ "upon our necks we are pursued" in Lam 5:5. However, without further textual evidence from ancient translations or from Qumran, any judgment on such cases is only tentative and the various emendations remain hypothetical. Therefore, it is not surprising that the number of cases considered in this respect differs a lot among authors: Rudolph assumed "*sinnstörende Textbeschädigungen*" in sixteen places,[29] while for Berlin there are only four "irregularities in lexical or syntactic usage."[30]

Further, it has to be mentioned that within Lamentations 1, as an alphabetical acrostic, the original sequence of vv. 16 (ע) and 17 (פ) is debatable, since 4QLam presents them in reverse order (ע–פ), which is also the case in Lamentations 2; 3; and 4 (→ 16.2.3.4).

The Masorah of the Leningrad Codex records in Lamentations twenty-one cases of *Ketiv/Qere*[31] and one case of "superfluous *waw*."[32] One of these *Qere* readings (כַּיְעֵנִים "like ostriches" in Lam 4:3) corrects an error in the consonantal text resulting from a wrong division of words (כי ענים "because there are eyes/fountains"), and another one prefers in Lam 4:12 an asyndetic syntax over the smoother *Ketiv* reading with conjunction; in both of these cases, LXX-Lam aligns with the *Qere*. In all other instances, however, it appears that the *Ketiv* represents a more difficult or archaic reading (in many cases confirmed by LXX-Lam) that the *Qere* tends to normalize and facilitate:

- In six places[33] the *Qere* adds a conjunction where the *Ketiv* features an asyndetic syntax.
- Seven times, the *Qere* applies normal orthography or a more common morphology in contrast to archaic or unusual forms of the *Ketiv*: מן בת "from the daughter [of Zion]" > מִבַּת (id.) Lam 1:6; שביתך "your captivity" > שְׁבוּתֵךְ "your turnaround/destiny/captivity" Lam 2:14; בליל "in the night" > בַּלַּיְלָה (id.) Lam 2:19; ותשיח "and she is musing" > וְתָשׁוֹחַ "and she bows down/is despondent" Lam 3:20; יושבתי "a dwelling one [f.]" > יוֹשֶׁבֶת (id.) Lam 4:21; הביט "Consider!" > הַבִּיטָה (id.) Lam 5:1; ונשוב "and we shall return" > וְנָשׁוּבָה (id.) Lam 5:21.
- Two Aramaic forms are normalized in the *Qere* (אריה "lion" > אֲרִי Lam 3:10, and תנין "jackals" > תַּנִּים Lam 4:3); whereas a third one (שׁוֹמֵמִין "are desolate" Lam 1:4) is noted as "unique," but remains unchanged.
- Two sg. forms, both confirmed by LXX, are changed into pl. in the *Qere* (חסדו "his mercy" > חֲסָדָיו "his mercies" Lam 3:32, and חטאו "his sin" > חֲטָאָיו "his sins" Lam 3:39), either as a harmonization with the context (cf. Lam 3:22) or perhaps as a result of theological consideration.
- In Lam 1:18, the *Qere* adds an article to the *Ketiv* (כל־עמים > כָּל־הָעַמִּים "all peoples") in order to adjust the expression to the usual form; LXX apparently confirms the reading without the article.
- In Lam 4:17, the 1st pl. suffix of the *Qere* עוֹדֵינוּ "we still are" is also confirmed by LXX (→ 13–17.1.1.4), the Vulgate (→ 13–17.1.7), and the Peshitta (→ 13–17.1.4.4). However, the 3rd fem. pl. suffix of the *Ketiv* עודינה "they still are" does agree with a fragmentary reading of 5QLam^b (→ 16.2.2.4). Therefore, in spite of the massive support for the *Qere* from the ancient versions, the *Ketiv* may still be

---

[29] Lam 1:14a, 20c, 21a,c; 2:4a, 6a, 7b, 18a; 3:22, 39, 51, 63; 4:3b, 6b, 9b; 5:5; Rudolph, "Klagelieder," 189.

[30] Lam 1:14; 2:6; 3:22; 4:9; Berlin, *Lamentations*, 36.

[31] Lam 1:6, 18; 2:2, 14, 19; 3:10, 20, 32, 39; 4:3a, 3b, 12, 16, 17, 21; 5:1, 3, 5, 7(*bis*), 21.

[32] Lam 1:11.

[33] Lam 2:2; 4:16; 5:3, 5, 7 (*bis*).

regarded as an old and presumably preferable reading that makes good sense in the context.[34]

Apparently, the *Qere* in Lamentations very often suggests a more comprehensible or smoother reading (in text-critical terms, a *lectio facilior*) and in many cases the *Ketiv* readings were later replaced entirely by these easier *Qere* readings, as demonstrated in the collations by Kennicott and de Rossi. The consonantal text of MT-Lam, however, still includes a variety of archaic orthographical and morphological features from which we may conclude that, on the whole, this text is not yet very far from the original text, even though there is evidence of sparse expansive elements (see above). There are also occasional examples of possible corruption (see above) and a few secondary readings (→ 16.2.1).

16.2.2.4 Traces of Proto-MT-Lam in the Fragments of 3QLam, 5QLam^a, and 5QLam^b

The textual tradition represented by MT is also reflected in three fragmentary copies of Lamentations found in Qumran Caves 3 and 5 (→ 16.2.1).

The remains of 3QLam exhibit only a small amount of highly fragmentary text, which is insufficient for assigning 3QLam to a specific text type (→ 16.2.1.1). There are, however, two additional significant aspects: 1) 3QLam was a high-quality manuscript; and 2) its text was apparently written verse by verse in a stichographic layout visualizing the poetic form of the alphabetic acrostic along the right edge of the column. The first aspect indicates that 3QLam – in contrast[35] to 4QLam (→ 16.2.3) – is likely a copy for liturgical or other official use, and the second is a feature that is still reflected centuries later in the Masoretic manuscripts, in which the verses in Lamentations 1; 2; and 4 or groups of verses in Lamentations 3 are all separated by *Setumot*. These additional aspects indicate that it is quite possible or even probable (although, in light of the small amount of extant text, not provable!) that 3QLam was a representative of the proto-Masoretic text.[36]

The fragmentary text preserved in 5QLam^a is close to MT but also exhibits examples of modernization and simplification: It uses more *matres lectionis* than MT, shows a tendency toward morphological facilitation, and includes a set of secondary readings. Therefore, its text can be characterized as semi-Masoretic (→ 16.2.1.3). The following are significant morphological and textual variants against MT:

– In Lam 4:14b, the phrase בל י[ו]כֹלו יבג[(a dot below the ב of יבג[probably indicates that this character is to be ignored[37] so that the reading virtually corresponds with MT's יִגְּעוּ) represents a syntactical simplification versus MT's בְּלֹא יוּכְלוּ יִגְּעוּ "what was unbearable for them (to touch), they touched." Instead of MT's complex relative clause, 5QLam^a simply says "they could not touch."[38] The same simplification is found in the Peshitta (→ 13–17.1.4.4) while LXX (→ 13–17.1.1.4) reflects MT.

– In Lam 4:15, the pl. טמאו "They are unclean!" is a stylistic facilitation against the sg. טָמֵא "Unclean!" of MT.

– The longer form הַבִּיטָה "consider" (masc. sg. *hiphil* impv. plus paragogic *he*) in Lam 5:1 corresponds with the *Qere* הַבִּיטָה of MT versus the *Ketiv* הביט. The *Ketiv* represents either an irregular *plene* writing of the usual impv. form הַבֵּט or virtually the same form as the *Qere*, but in an archaic orthography without *mater lectionis* for the final vowel. In either case, it can be regarded as the *lectio difficilior*. 5QLam^a as well as MT *Qere* removed the irregularity by assimilating the reading to a form that already appeared three times in Lamentations (Lam 1:11, 2:20, 3:63).[39]

---

[34] Berges, *Klagelieder*, 233; for an excellent summary of the entire discussion, see Kotzé, *Qumran Manuscripts*, 121–22.

[35] Cross, "4QLam," 229: "evidently not a public copy of Lamentations."

[36] This is also suggested by Baillet, "Lamentations," 95: "*un texte voisin du TM*."

[37] Milik, "Lamentations (Premier Exemplaire)," 175.

[38] See Albrektson, *Studies*, 187.

[39] Schäfer, "Lamentations," 134*; Kotzé, *Qumran Manuscripts*, 149–50.

– In 5:3, MT's כְּאַלְמָנוֹת "(are) like widows" has been expanded in 5QLam^a to לֹא בָנוֹת וְאלמנות "(have) no daughters and (are) like widows"; if the transcription is correct, the expansion would syntactically follow the model of 1 Chr 2:30, 32.

5QLam^b, the smallest among the Lamentations fragments, overlaps with 5QLam^a in Lam 4:20 (אפינו "our nostrils"), which proves that the fragments were part of two different copies. At the beginning of Lam 4:17, the fragmentary reading ינה[... appears to align with the *Ketiv* of MT עודינה "they [fem.] still are/continue" against the *Qere* עוֹדֵינוּ "we still are/continue" (→ 16.2.2.3). Although the fragment corresponds in all details with the consonantal text of MT, it is obvious that its eighteen extant characters do not provide sufficient evidence to assign it to any particular text type (→ 16.2.1.4).

Albrektson, B., *Studies in the Text and Theology of the Book of Lamentations with a Critical Edition of the Peshitta Text* (Studia Theologica Lundensia 21; Lund: C.W.K. Gleerup, 1963).

Baillet, M., "3. Lamentations," *DJD* III.1: 95.

Berges, U., *Klagelieder* (HTKAT; Freiburg i.B.: Herder, 2002).

Berlin, A., *Lamentations: A Commentary* (OTL; Louisville: Westminster John Knox Press, 2002).

Budde, K., "Das hebräische Klagelied," *ZAW* 2 (1882): 1–52.

Cross, F.M., "Studies in the Structure of Hebrew Verse: The Prosody of Lamentations 1:1–22," in *The Word of the Lord Shall Go Forth: Essays in Honor of David Noel Freedman in Celebration of His Sixtieth Birthday* (eds. C.L. Meyers and M. O'Connor; Winona Lake: Eisenbrauns, 1983), 129–55.

Cross, F.M., "111. 4QLam," *DJD* XVI: 229–37.

Dahood, M., "New Readings in Lamentations," *Bib* 59 (1978): 174–97.

Driver, G.R., "Notes on the Text of 'Lamentations'," *ZAW* 52 (1934): 308–09.

Driver, G.R., "Hebrew Notes on 'Song of Songs' and 'Lamentations'," in *Festschrift für Alfred Bertholet zum 80. Geburtstag* (eds. W. Baumgartner et al.; Tübingen: J.C.B. Mohr [Paul Siebeck], 1950), 134–46.

Ehrlich, A.B., *Randglossen zur hebräischen Bibel: Textkritisches Sprachliches und Sachliches* (7 vols.; Leipzig: J.C. Hinrichs 1908–1914; Reprint: Hildesheim: G. Olms, 1968).

Gordis, R., "A Commentary on the Text of Lamentations," in *The Seventy-Fifth Anniversary Volume of the Jewish Quarterly Review* (eds. A.A. Neuman and S. Zeitlin; Philadelphia: *JQR*, 1967), 267–86.

Gordis, R., "Commentary on the Text of Lamentations (Part Two)," *JQR* 58 (1967–1968): 14–33.

Gottlieb, H., *A Study on the Text of Lamentations* (Acta Jutlandica 48 Theology Series 12; Århus: Aarhus Universitet, 1978).

Hillers, D.R., *Lamentations: A New Translation with Introduction and Commentary* (rev. ed.; AB 7A; New York: Doubleday, 1992).

Kaiser, O., "Klagelieder," in O. Kaiser, H.-P. Müller, and J.A. Loader, *Das Hohelied, Klagelieder, Das Buch Ester* (rev. ed.; ATD 16/2; Göttingen: Vandenhoeck & Ruprecht, ⁴1992), 91–198.

Koenen, K., *Klagelieder (Threni)* (BKAT 20; Neukirchen-Vluyn: Neukirchener Verlagsgesellschaft, 2015).

Kotzé, G.R., *The Qumran Manuscripts of Lamentations: A Text-Critical Study* (SSN 61; Leiden: Brill, 2013).

McDaniel, T.F., "Philological Studies in Lamentations I," *Bib* 49 (1968): 27–53.

McDaniel, T.F., "Philological Studies in Lamentations II," *Bib* 49 (1968): 199–220.

Milik, J.T., "6. Lamentations (Premier Exemplaire)," *DJD* III.1: 174–77.

Milik, J.T., "7. Lamentations (Second Exemplaire)," *DJD* III.1, 177–78.

Robinson, T.H., "Notes on the Text of Lamentations," *ZAW* 51 (1933): 255–59.

Rudolph, W., "Die Klagelieder," in W. Rudolph, *Das Buch Ruth, Das Hohe Lied, Die Klagelieder* (KAT 17.1–3; Gütersloh: Gütersloher Verlagshaus Gerd Mohn, 1962), 187–263.

Rudolph, W., "Der Text der Klagelieder," *ZAW* 56 (1938): 101–22.

Schäfer, R., "Lamentations," *BHQ* 18, 54–72, and 17*–20*, 30*–34*, 43*–46*, 113*–36*.

Yeivin, I., "The Division into Sections in the Book of Psalms," *Textus* 7 (1969): 76–102.

Rolf Schäfer

16.2.3 Other Texts

The manuscript 4QLam (4Q111; → 16.2.1.2) preserves remains of a Lamentations text distinct from MT-Lam (→ 16.2.2). It was first published by Cross in

1983[1] and finally edited by the same author in *DJD* XI in 2000.[2] Kotzé, in his text-critical study of 2013, has discussed and evaluated anew the textual variants of 4QLam in great detail.[3]

The fragments of 4QLam contain extensive text from Lam 1:1–18. Verses 6–8 and 11–17 are almost completely legible and exhibit a textual tradition that differs significantly from the proto-Masoretic text[4] including (apart from the orthographical differences) the considerable number of forty-five (or forty-six)[5] textual variants to MT among 193 legible words (→ 16.2.1.2).

The textual quality of 4QLam is mixed: On the one hand, there are many scribal errors that indicate that the manuscript was written without much care.[6] On the other hand, 4QLam is the only extant witness for some valuable old readings that are as good as or even superior to the corresponding readings in MT-Lam (→ 16.2.3.4).

---

[1] Cross, "Studies."

[2] Cross, "4QLam."

[3] Kotzé, *Qumran Manuscripts*, 23–29, 36–120.

[4] In the words of Hillers, 4QLam is "not just an exemplar of the ... emerging Masoretic text" (Hillers, *Lamentations*, 42) and does "not line up with any particular known recension" (Hillers, *Lamentations*, 47). This opinion is shared by Lange who notes that 4QLam is "*als eigenständige Handschrift zu werten*" (*Handbuch*, 490), and Tov who counts the manuscript among the scrolls "often named 'independent' or non-aligned" (*Scribal Practices*, 332 and 335). Cross, however, takes the view that in spite of the amount of variation found in 4QLam "its textual tradition ... is not far separated from the Proto-Rabbinic text" ("4QLam," 230).

[5] The counting of forty-five variants is based on the comprehensive list compiled by Kotzé, "Lamentations 1:8a," 201–02. In contrast, Cross, "4QLam," 231–37, records forty-two variants. There are simple explanations for the different numbers: On the one hand, the delimitation of the lemma is sometimes different and, on the other hand, Cross has skipped two cases (בלי in 4QLam versus MT's בלא in v. 6, and ואין versus אין in v. 9) listed by Kotzé, and he has included two items of which the first (an allusion to Lam 1:1 in 4QapocrLam A) is not a variant in the strict sense, and the second (4QLam's על [most probably to be read as עַל] versus MT's עַל in v. 14a) is not recorded in Kotzé's list; if we add this latter case, there would be a total of forty-six variants. Kotzé, *Qumran Mansucripts*, 177 presents a revised version of the list that includes only forty-one variants, as the author has now dropped four readings that do not imply a different meaning but only exhibit a different morphology.

[6] Cross, "4QLam," 229.

16.2.3.1 Orthographic and Morphological Variants

The orthography is nineteen times plene in 4QLam versus defective forms in MT (→ 16.2.2).[7] In contrast to such examples of typical Qumran orthography,[8] there are also three examples of defective spelling as in MT where, in manuscripts like 4QLam, a plene spelling would be expected: בנפל "when falling" (frg. 2 line 3, cf. Lam 1:7); הכל "the entirety" (frg. 3 line 2, cf. Lam 1:12); and עברי "of passersby" (frg. 3 line 2, cf. Lam 1:12). The morphology in 4QLam differs from MT in three cases: היא[ה] versus הִיא "she" (4QLam 1 5 = Lam 1:3); בלי versus בְּלֹא "without" (4QLam 2 2 = Lam 1:6); and [פ]לאות versus פְּלָאִם "astonishingly" (4QLam 2 9 = Lam 1:9).

Three readings of 4QLam align with the *Qere* and with the Masorah parva of MT respectively: מבת "from the daughter [of Zion]" (4QLam 1 11 = Lam 1:6); מחמדיה "her treasures" (4QLam 3 1 = Lam 1:11; disregarding the different suffix, the relevant detail is the defective spelling, i.e., the absence of the *waw* in 4QLam in accordance with the MasP); and ירושלים "Jerusalem" (4QLam 2 5 = Lam 1:8) in accordance with the *Qere* perpetuum of MT.

16.2.3.2 Scribal Mistakes

Six readings obviously result from scribal mistakes probably committed by the scribe of 4QLam:

– In Lam 1:6, the corrupt 4QLam text לוא לוא מצא ומרעה "not not he did find and pasture" includes a dittography at the beginning followed by an incorrect word division. The correct reading is found in MT: לֹא־מָצְאוּ מִרְעֶה "they do not find pasture."

– In Lam 1:10–11, eight words are lacking in 4QLam, namely the last two words at the end of v. 10 and the subsequent six words from the beginning of v. 11; presumably the scribe has accidentally skipped one line in his *Vorlage*.

---

[7] See the lists in Cross, "4QLam," 229, and Schäfer, "Der Masoretische Text," 133.

[8] Tov, "Orthography," 53 (Table 1b); cf. Tov, *Scribal Practices*, 335.

16.2.3 OTHER TEXTS

- Four readings result from graphical errors: משבריה "her collapse" for מִשְׁבַּתֶהָ "her extermination" (confusion of ת and רי) in Lam 1:7; חשיבני "he made me think [?]" for הֱשִׁיבַנִי "he caused me to return" (confusion of ה and ח) in Lam 1:13; אבידי "my perished ones [?]" for אַבִּירַי "my strong ones" (confusion of ר and ד) in Lam 1:15; and לנדוח "to a banished one [?]" for לְנִדָּה "to an unclean one" (confusion of ה and ח) in Lam 1:17.

16.2.3.3 Expansions and Other Intentional or Unintentional Alterations

In Lam 1:17, the text of 4QLam includes an expansion, apparently composed of two different glosses:

- The words מכול אוהביה "from all her lovers" were added to the phrase אין מנחם לה "[there is no] one to comfort her" as an assimilation to Lam 1:2.
- The phrase צדיק אתה יהוה "in the right are you, Lord" is a variant of the first line of Lam 1:18. Perhaps it was originally a marginal reading that was at some time copied into the text.[9]

The scribe of 4QLam probably copied these glosses from his *Vorlage*, since the general character of his manuscript proves that he tended towards omissions and mistakes rather than towards adding interpreting comments or making systematic revisions.

Twice there is an additional conjunction in 4QLam:

- ואין "and there is no …" in Lam 1:9 represents a syntactic simplification compared with the asyndetic connection in MT.
- וד[ו]י "and fai[n]t" as the last word in Lam 1:13 is a secondary variant that changes the syntax and destroys the balance of the poetic line.

The suffix pronouns differ four times in 4QLam and MT:

- In Lam 1:8b, 4QLam omits the pronoun (by mistake?) reading הֹזִלוּ "they despised" instead of הִזִּילוּהָ "they despised her" in MT.
- In Lam 1:11, the reading מחמדיה "her treasures" in 4QLam appears to be an assimilation to the same form that occurred already in Lam 1:10. The addition of the 3rd per. fem. sg. suffix in נפשה "her life/soul" – although the sense is "appealing"[10] – is either due to a specific interpretation of the original text or a mistake.
- In Lam 1:16b, the 1st per. sg. suffix of נַפְשִׁי "my life/soul" is missing in 4QLam probably by mistake.

In three cases, the use of the masculine forms זולל "worthless"; שומם "desolate"; and וד[ו]י "and fai[n]t" in 4QLam against feminine forms in MT (זוֹלֵלָה Lam 1:11c; שֹׁמֵמָה and דָּוָה Lam 1:13c) indicates a shift of perspective. Obviously the first person speaking was in the textual tradition of 4QLam understood as the narrator or the author of the text and no longer as personified Zion.[11] Hillers has addressed this phenomenon as the "loss of the poetic perspective"[12] and therefore identified these variants in 4QLam as secondary readings.[13]

Five times, the synonyms אדני/יהוה "YHWH"/"Lord" (Lam 1:14c, 15c, 17b, 18a) and ציון/ירושלם "Jerusalem"/"Zion" (Lam 1:17c) are used complementarily in 4QLam and MT. In Lam 1:17a, the scribe of 4QLam averted a sixth case at the last minute: He had started to write "Jerusalem," but then crossed out the four characters ירוש and wrote ציון "Zion" in accordance with MT.

16.2.3.4 Textual Variants That Probably Predate Their Corresponding Readings in MT

Quite a number of variants in the 4QLam text preserve old readings that probably have survived from a stage of the textual transmission still closer to the original than MT. These need careful consideration and evaluation:

---

[9] Cross, "4QLam," 237.

[10] Cross, "4QLam," 235.
[11] Kotzé, *Qumran Manuscripts*, 70, 85.
[12] Hillers, *Lamentations*, 45.
[13] Likewise Cross, "4QLam," 235–36.

- In Lam 1:7, the text of 4QLam is significantly shorter than MT. At the beginning of the verse, the reading of 4QLam זכורה יהוה (emphatic masc. sg. impv. + tetragrammaton: "Remember, YHWH, ...") represents the *lectio difficilior*[14] while the variant of MT זָכְרָה יְרוּשָׁלַֽם (3rd fem. sg. pf. + Jerusalem: "Jerusalem remembers ...") is easily explained as an assimilation to the immediate context (בַּת־צִיּוֹן "daughter of Zion" in v. 6; יְרוּשָׁלַֽם "Jerusalem" in v. 8; and זָכְרָה "she remembers/considers" in v. 9), probably triggered by a misunderstanding of the verb form that was not far to seek especially if the emphatic masc. sg. impv. was written defectively as זכרה.

- Hillers, in contrast, has argued that the reading זכורה יהוה in 4QLam was the result of a secondary shift "to a stance of direct address to God."[15] Hillers and recently, in particular, Kotzé recognize in 4QLam intentional modifications observable in a group of variants, namely the direct address to God followed by the occurrence of a 1st per. pl. suffix in 1:7 (מכאובנו "*our* pain" instead of MT's מַחֲמַדֶּיהָ "*her* treasures"),[16] and three masc. sg. forms (זוֹלל, שׁוֹמם, and ו[י]רד in Lam 1:11 and 1:13) in place of the corresponding fem. sg. forms of MT (→ 16.2.3.3). Hillers and Kotzé assume that these variants reflect the use that a worshipping community made of Lamentations, and result from some kind of deliberate redaction characterized by a loss of the poetic perspective in favor of a liturgical appropriation that emphasizes the perspective of the narrator and his community.[17] However, while the shift of perspective is obvious for the masc. sg. forms in vv. 11 and 13 and for the 1st com. pl. suffix in v. 7, the assignment of the reading זכורה יהוה to the same deliberate intervention of a scribe remains debatable. The assumption of such an extensive alteration at the beginning of the verse raises the question regarding why the rest of the verse then remained unchanged and why we find no more 1st per. com. pl. suffixes there but again 3rd per. fem. sg. suffixes. However, if the reading זכורה יהוה, "Remember, YHWH, ..." was part of the original text, it is easily assumed that at some point a 1st per. pl. suffix was added accidentally to the subsequent grammatical object.

- In 4QLam, the object is simply כל מכאובנו [...], "[a]ll our pain" in the place of MT's expansive phrase יְמֵי עָנְיָהּ וּמְרוּדֶיהָ כֹּל מַחֲמֻדֶיהָ "in the days of her affliction and wandering all her precious things." Neither of the two represents the original text. The 1st per. pl. suffix in 4QLam corresponds with (and is most likely triggered by) the preceding זכורה יהוה "Remember, YHWH, ...," but it does not fit with the 3rd per. fem. sg. suffixes in the following lines. From this, we can infer that at an earlier stage the reading was מכואביה or מכאביה "her pain"[18] in line with the context. The MT reading appears to be conflate; כֹּל מַחֲמֻדֶיהָ, "all her treasures" as the object to a preceding "Jerusalem remembers" is difficult within the context and almost impossible as the object to זכרה יהוה "Remember, YHWH, ...," the presumed original text. The original text probably read מרודיה "her wandering"[19] or כל מרודיה "all her wandering." From the uncommon word מרודיה "her wandering" as the hypothetical departing point, both existing readings can be explained: on one side, the expansive reading of MT as a conflation under the influence of Lam 3:19 and,

---

[14] This applies, although "Remember, YHWH ..." is a frequent invocation of God (e.g. Lam 3:19; 5:1; Ps 132:1; 137:7), because the usual form of the invocation is זְכֹר while the emphatic form זכורה in 4QLam is unique.

[15] Hillers, *Lamentations*, 46.

[16] Hillers, *Lamentations*, 46 considers another example that 4QLam perhaps exhibits in 1:13 (ויורידנו, "and he brought *us* down" instead of MT's וַיִּרְדֶּנָּה, "and he dominated over her/it"), but the reading of the final letter as *waw* is uncertain. Kotzé, *Qumran Manuscripts*, 75 seeks confirmation for his thesis of a redaction that emphasizes the perspective of "the narrator and his community" and therefore he considers a possible third example of a 1st per. pl. suff. in v. 12; he suggests the reconstruction of אלינו instead of Cross' reading, אליכ[י], but in footnote 138 he admits that the disputed letter is to be identified as a *kaf* rather than a *nun*.

[17] Hillers, *Lamentations*, 43–47; Kotzé, *Qumran Manuscripts*, 45–48, and 116.

[18] Koenen, *Klagelieder*, 8 suggests מַכְאֹבֶיהָ as the original reading. However, this leaves the emergence of the expansive reading in MT unexplained.

[19] Cross, "4QLam," 233.

on the other side, מכאבנו > מכאביה* "her pain" "our pain" in 4QLam as a simplification that replaced the original מרודיה "her wandering."[20] Thus the original text of Lam 1:7a probably read: זכרה יהוה [כל] מרודיה אשר היו מימי קדם "Remember, YHWH, [all] her wandering that lasted from the days of old."

- At the end of Lam 1:7c, 4QLam omits לָהּ "for her" and in Lam 1:7d the reading of 4QLam צריה שחקו על [כו]ל משבריה "her enemies laughed at [a]ll her collapse" facilitates the syntax compared to MT. Cross and Kotzé regard the reading משבריה "her collapse" of 4QLam as earlier than מִשְׁבַּתֶּהָ "her extermination" of MT,[21] but the *hapax legomenon* of MT is clearly the *lectio difficilior*, and in view of various secondary readings in the same line it seems more likely that the graphical error (confusion of of ת and רי) is also on the part of 4QLam.
- In Lam 1:8, the reading חטוא "sinning" of 4QLam against חֵטְא "sin" of MT adds evidence to Ehrlich's proposal[22] that the infinitive absolute should be read rather than the noun. The variant לנוד, "[she became] a wandering one" of 4QLam is reflected also in LXX, the Vulgate, and the Targum. It probably represents the original reading from which MT's difficult and unique לְנִידָה "[she became] a ... ? ..." arose by dittography of the subsequent ה plus confusion of ו and י and assimilation to לְנִדָּה "[she became] something unclean" in v. 17.[23] Alternatively, it might perhaps be the oldest witness for the interpretation of נידה as the female form of the nominalized infinitive of נוד "to stagger"/"to stray."[24]
- In Lam 1:12, the reading הוגירני "he frightened me" of 4QLam might appear as the *lectio difficilior* and thus seems preferable to הוֹגָה "he afflicted" of MT, which perhaps arose as a reminiscence of יְהוָה הוֹגָה "YHWH afflicted her" in v. 5.[25] However, Kotzé has argued that the evidence of LXX, Peshitta and Targum points to the existence of a reading הוגני "he afflicted me" that "might well qualify as the earliest Hebrew reading,"[26] from which the readings of MT and 4QLam both developed. Further, at the end of the same verse, the short reading חרו[נו "his fierceness" of 4QLam is probably to be preferred over the assimilation to the usual expression חֲרוֹן אַפּוֹ "the fierceness of his anger" in MT.
- In Lam 1:13, the reading ויורידני, "and he brought me down" or perhaps ויורידנו, "and he brought us down" of 4QLam against MT's וַיִּרְדֶּנָּה "and he dominated her/it" (from the root רדה) confirms the reading of ירד *Hiphil* that is also presupposed in the translations of LXX and the Peshitta, and allows us to trace back the extant variants to יוֹרִדֶנָה or perhaps וַיֹּרִדֶנָה/וַיֹּרְדֶנָה "[and] he made her/it descend" as the original reading.[27]

---

[20] Kotzé, *Qumran Manuscripts*, 49 argues that the shapes of the letters of מרודיה "her wandering" and מכאובנו "our pain" were "graphically too dissimilar for them to have been mistakenly interchanged by a scribe." This is obviously true for the time when the text was transmitted in square script, but if we imagine מרודיה and a reconstructed מכאביה ("her pain" in place of מכאובנו "our pain" that is attested in 4QLam), both written in paleo-Hebrew script, there is indeed striking similarity. From the sixth century B.C.E. onwards, there are examples of *kaf* and *resh* in which the most significant difference between them is that the vertical line of the former bends to the left at the bottom while the vertical line of the latter is straight; the shapes of *waw* and *alef* are both composed of a diagonal line descending from top left to the right and crossed orthogonally by two parallel or acute-angled strokes; *bet* and *dalet* are composed of a diagonal line (with *bet* usually descending from top right to the left, and *dalet* descending from top left to the right) with a characteristic loop to the left affixed to the upper end. Further, if we take account of the first and the last two letters in both words being identical, it seems quite possible that at an early stage of the textual transmission the uncommon word מרודיה was read by mistake as מכאביה. If, *vice versa*, מַכְאָבֶיהָ is regarded as the original reading (Koenen, *Klagelieder*, 8), the emergence of the expansive reading in MT remains unexplained.

[21] Cross, "4QLam," 233; Kotzé, *Qumran Manuscripts*, 50–51.
[22] Ehrlich, *Randglossen*, 7.31.
[23] Cross, "4QLam," 233, and Kotzé, *Qumran Manuscripts*, 58, arrive at the same conclusion; see also Koenen, *Klagelieder*, 9; Kotzé, "Text-Critical Analysis," 74–77; Kotzé, "Lamentations 1:8a," 193–200.
[24] Gesenius, *Handwörterbuch*, 814; cf. Bauer and Leander, *Historische Grammatik*, § 61q.
[25] Cross, "Studies," 144; Cross, "4QLam," 235.
[26] Kotzé, *Qumran Manuscripts*, 80.
[27] Hillers, *Lamentations*, 72; Kotzé, *Qumran Manuscripts*, 82; hesitantly: Koenen, *Klagelieder*, 12 considering the perfect הוֹרִידָה to be a preferable alternative; based mainly on LXX and without knowledge of the 4QLam evidence: Ehrlich,

- In Lam 1:14, the meaning of נִשְׂקַד in MT is unknown while 4QLam's נקשרה "bound am I [fem.]"²⁸ seems clear. The meaning and the syntax of the following phrase differ in 4QLam and MT: על in 4QLam is very likely the preposition עַל "on," because in the same line the noun עֹל "yoke" appears as עול in the scribe's orthography. In MT, the two verbs יִשְׂתָּרְגוּ "they were entangled" and עָלוּ "they went up" both refer to פְּשָׁעַי "my transgressions" while in the corresponding reading from 4QLam וישתרג עולו "his yoke is intertwined," the two words are the beginning of a new phrase. The reading עולו "his yoke" of 4QLam is to be preferred,²⁹ because עֻלּוֹ "his yoke" makes much better sense in the context than MT's עָלוּ "they went up." For the rest, it is difficult to decide whether the variants of 4QLam facilitate MT or the almost incomprehensible MT represents a corrupt form of the 4QLam text.
- In Lam 1:16, the text אֲנִי בוֹכִיָּה עֵינִי עֵינִי יֹרְדָה מַּיִם "I am weeping, my eye, my eye, water is running down" in MT is probably corrupt. 4QLam preserves a very clear and shorter reading: בכו עיני ירדה דמעתי "my eyes are weeping, my tears are running down." At first sight, one is tempted to accept the 4QLam reading as the original text. However, the obvious conflict between the principles of *lectio brevior* and *lectio difficilior* cannot be resolved easily and therefore a final decision remains as difficult as in the previous case of Lam 1:14. Moreover, the present case is probably linked to the different sequence of vv. 16 and 17 in 4QLam (see below).
- In Lam 1:17, the reading צפה "he lies in ambush" of 4QLam is to be preferred over צִוָּה "he has commanded" of MT, because it not only "makes admirable sense"³⁰ but also solves the awkward syntax of MT.³¹ צפה, followed by the preposition לְ- in the context of evil intent is attested in Ps 37:32. The reading in MT is an effort to avoid the anthropomorphism and thus results from theological consideration rather than from a simple graphical or phonological error.
- The inversion of vv. 16 and 17 in 4QLam reflects an order of the alphabet with פ preceding ע. In the alphabetic acrostics of MT-Lam, the same sequence *pe-'ayin* occurs in Lam 2:16–17; 3:46–51, and 4:16–17 while the "modern" sequence *'ayin-pe* in Lam 1:16–17 represents the exception. Mere text-critical considerations cannot resolve the question of the original order,³² but the analysis of the poetic structure³³ suggests that the sequence *pe-'ayin* makes good sense also in Lamentations 1. The textual variation at the beginning of v. 16 (see above) is probably linked to the different sequence of vv. 16 and 17.³⁴

16.2.3.5 Relevance for Exegesis and Literary Analysis

4QLam remains an important textual witness for the Hebrew text of Lamentations, although the value of the individual variants cannot always be determined easily. Many of the variants appear to be either simple mistakes or secondary readings that can be characterized partly as facilitations, partly as interpretative expansions, and partly as a shift of perspective. Further discussion is needed regarding whether the number of secondary readings in 4QLam reflects intentional and perhaps even coherent scribal activity (Hillers, Kotzé) or may still be understood within the range of accidental scribal alterations (Cross, Schäfer, Koe-

---

Randglossen, 7.33; Rudolph, "Text," 103; Dahood, *New Readings*, 176–77.

²⁸ Cross, "4QLam," 236.
²⁹ Cross, "Studies," 146; Cross, "4QLam," 236.
³⁰ Cross, "4QLam," 236.
³¹ For this very reason, Koenen (*Klagelieder*, 14) regards צפה as the easier and thus secondary reading.

³² See Cross, "4QLam," 236–37.
³³ Schäfer, "Der ursprüngliche Text," 255–58.
³⁴ Kotzé (*Qumran Manuscripts*, 112–14) and Koenen (*Klagelieder*, 14) note that the sequence *pe–'ayin* changes the referent of עַל־אֵלֶּה "over these [things]" in v. 16 and renders the narrator the subject speaking and weeping. In Kotzé's interpretation, this is another important piece of evidence for his hypothesis that 4QLam consistently moves the focus of the poem to the perspective of the narrator and those whom he represents (*Qumran Manuscripts*, 119): "The reversed order of the verses [16 and 17], compared to the MT, together with scribal mistakes and sundry scribal changes, ensure that the content of these verses in the manuscript from Qumran looks very different from the version in the MT."

nen). However, it is recognized that in some cases the text of 4QLam gives access to old and superior readings that have survived due to the antiquity of the manuscript and in spite of its careless scribe.[35] Such readings are relevant for both exegesis and literary analysis and deserve careful consideration.

Bauer, H. and P. Leander, *Historische Grammatik der hebräischen Sprache des Alten Testaments* (Halle: M. Niemeyer, 1922; reprint: Hildesheim: G. Olms 1965).

Berlin, A., *Lamentations: A Commentary* (OTL; Louisville: Westminster John Knox Press, 2002).

Cross, F.M., "Studies in the Structure of Hebrew Verse: The Prosody of Lamentations 1:1–22," in *The Word of the Lord Shall Go Forth: Essays in Honor of David Noel Freedman in Celebration of His Sixtieth Birthday* (eds. C.L. Meyers and M. O'Connor; Winona Lake: Eisenbrauns, 1983), 129–55.

Cross, F.M., "111. 4QLam," *DJD* XI: 229–37.

Dahood, M., "New Readings in Lamentations," *Bib* 59 (1978): 174–97.

Ehrlich, A.B., *Randglossen zur hebräischen Bibel: Textkritisches Sprachliches und Sachliches* (7 vols.; Leipzig: J.C. Hinrichs, 1908–1914; reprint: Hildesheim: G. Olms, 1968).

Gesenius, W., *Hebräisches und Aramäisches Handwörterbuch über das Alte Testament* (eds. R. Meyer and H. Donner; 18th ed.; Berlin: Springer, 1987–2012).

Hillers, D.R., *Lamentations: A New Translation with Introduction and Commentary* (rev. ed.; AB 7A; New York: Doubleday, 1992).

Koenen, K., *Klagelieder (Threni)* (BKAT 20; Neukirchen-Vluyn: Neukirchener Verlagsgesellschaft, 2015).

Kotzé, G.R., "A Text-Critical Analysis of Lamentations 1:7 in 4QLam and the Masoretic Text," *OTE* 24 (2011): 590–611.

Kotzé, G.R., "Lamentations 1:8a in the Wordings of the Masoretic Text and 4QLam," *Scriptura* 110 (2012): 190–207.

Kotzé, G.R., *The Qumran Manuscripts of Lamentations: A Text-Critical Study* (SSN 61; Leiden: Brill, 2013).

Lange, *Handbuch, 489–95.

Rudolph, W., "Der Text der Klagelieder," *ZAW* 56 (1938): 101–22.

Schäfer, R., "Der Masoretische Text der Klagelieder und die Handschriften 3QLam, 4QLam und 5QLam^a.b aus Qumran," in *Die Textfunde vom Toten Meer und der Text der Hebräischen Bibel* (eds. U. Dahmen, A. Lange, and H. Lichtenberger; Neukirchen-Vluyn: Neukirchener, 2000), 127–47.

Schäfer, R., "Lamentations," *BHQ 18, 54–72, and 17*–20*, 30*–34*, 43*–46*, 113*–36*.

Schäfer, R., "Der ursprüngliche Text und die poetische Struktur des ersten Klageliedes (Klg 1): Textkritik und Strukturanalyse im Zwiegespräch," in *Sôfer Mahîr: Essays in Honor of Adrian Schenker Offered by Editors of Biblia Hebraica Quinta* (eds. Y.A.P. Goldman, A. van der Kooij, and R.D. Weis; VTSup 110; Leiden: Brill, 2006), 239–59.

Tov, E., "The Orthography and Language of the Hebrew Scrolls Found at Qumran and the Origin of These Scrolls," *Textus* 13 (1986): 31–57.

Tov, *Scribal Practices*.

Rolf Schäfer

---

[35] See Cross, "4QLam," 230. In an earlier comment on two subsequent scribal errors in v. 6 (לוֹא לוא מצא ומרעה instead of MT's לֹא־מָצְאוּ מִרְעֶה, i.e., a dittography followed by a wrong division of words), Cross ("Studies," 139) concluded that 4QLam was apparently written by "a sleepy scribe."

17
Esther

∴

17.1 Textual History of Esther

17.1.1 History of Research

Research on the book of Esther was primarily done on MT (→ 17.2.2). The publication in 1655 of a second Greek text, the so-called Lucianic Text, Alpha Text, or A Text,[1] however, led to a substantial change in scholarship, albeit at a much later time (→ 13–17.1.1.5).

With regard to the Hebrew text of the book of Esther, as early as 1793, Michaelis[2] questioned the originality of the last sections of the book of Esther, Esth 9:17–32 and 10:1–3, ascribing them to a different hand.[3] From Bertheau onwards, however, the interpolated verses were considered to be Esth 9:20–32 and Esther 10 was beyond critique. In contrast, Riehm (1980) and Kuenen (1861; German edition, 1890)[4] maintained the unity of the entire book of Esther. In defending the integrity of the book and the possibility of interpolations, commentators frequently appealed to the language of the Hebrew Esther scroll. Michaelis argued that the style of the Hebrew was different from Esth 9:17 to the end of the book, even that the Hebrew syntax was slightly different, with constructions that normally seldom appear and others that are absent from the Bible but appear in Syriac being used suddenly in this section of the text.[5] Bertheau focused his attention primarily on the content of the said verses in relation to the content of vv. 20–28. Kuenen, however, stated that the form and the content of these verses pointed to their originality.[6] In contrast to Kuenen, König (1893) defended the interpolation of Esth 9:20–32 both "sprachlich und sachlich," although he offers no further remarks on the "grammar" of the Hebrew book of Esther.[7] It was only in 1937 that research into the style of the Hebrew book of Esther became the object of scholarly attention. Striedl's fundamental study of the syntax and style of the book was primarily historical and comparative in nature,[8] locating the language of the book of Esther within the history of the Hebrew language, in line as it were with the suggestion proposed by Driver.[9] Striedl also outlined the formal-stylistic features of the book.[10] Gerleman[11] and Dommershausen[12] tended to follow Striedl, with attention gradually beginning to shift from style and syntax to narrative technique, upholding in most cases the unity of MT-Esth.[13]

---

[1] Ussher, *De Graeca*.

[2] Michaelis, *Deutsche Übersetzung des Alten Testaments*.

[3] Followed by Bertheau, *Die Bücher Esra, Nehemia und Esther*, 273–353; E. Riehm, *Einleitung in das Alte Testament*, Vol. 2 (Halle: Strien, 1890), 339–43; König, *Einleitung in das Alte Testament mit Einschluss der Apokryphen und der Pseudepigraphen Alten Testaments*; Paton, *A Critical and Exegetical Commentary on the Book of Esther*; Steuernagel, *Lehrbuch der Einleitung in das Alte Testament*, 433–39, 788–90; Pfeiffer, *Introduction to the Old Testament*, 732–47.

[4] Kuenen, *Historisch-kritisch onderzoek naar het ontstaan en de verzameling van de boeken des Ouden Verbonds*, 1.364–79.

[5] Michaelis, *Deutsche Übersetzung des Alten Testaments*, 125. See also Bertheau, *Die Bücher Esra, Nehemia und Esther*, 277.

[6] He continues and argues that if one were to omit these verses, then a lacuna would have emerged that would have been impossible for an author not to fill; cf. Kuenen, *Historisch-kritischen Einleitung in die Bücher des Alten Testaments*, Vol. 1, 201. In the Dutch version, we read: "Samengenomen wekken deze verschijnselen eene zeer sterke praesumptie voor de eenheid van auteur" (= Taken together, these phenomena evoke a rather strong presumption in support of unity of author); cf. Kuenen, *Historisch-kritisch onderzoek naar het ontstaan en de verzameling van de boeken des Ouden Verbonds*, Deel 1, 533.

[7] König, *Einleitung in das Alte Testament*, 289–90. The conclusion in MT continues to be the object of scholarly research: cf. Daube, "The Last Chapter of Esther," 139–47; Löwenstamm, "Esther 9:29–32: The Genesis of a Late Addition," 117–24 (= Moore [ed.], *Studies*, 227–34).

[8] Striedl, "Untersuchungen," 73–108.

[9] Driver, *Introduction to the Literature of the Old Testament*, 478–87.

[10] Striedl refers, among others, to the work of Schötz, "Das hebräische Buch Esther," 255–76, and to Gunkel, *Esther*. Cf. Striedl, "Untersuchungen," 86–87. This approach was taken further in the form-critical analysis by Dorothy; see below.

[11] Gerleman, *Studien zu Esther*; Gerleman, *Esther*.

[12] Dommershausen, *Die Estherrolle*; Dommershausen, *Esther*.

[13] Y.T. Radday, "Chiasm in Joshua, Judges, and Others,"

A similar discussion concerning the integrity of the book of Esther was likewise underway with respect to the Old Greek and the second Greek text. Langen (1860),[14] for example, observed that Hebraisms were avoided in the second Greek text. He proposed that there were also secondary portions to be found in the second Greek text, such as the letter of Mordecai following the edict in Addition E. Langen was not the first to take the presence or absence of Hebraisms into consideration. Herbst,[15] for example, followed by Scholz,[16] was first to offer a list. Jacob (1890) endeavoured to establish the stylistic features of LXX and the second Greek text of Esther.[17] He also offered comments on Esth 8:36, 38 of the second Greek text (as well as Esth 8:2, 5, 6) and concluded that most likely in all these cases a different form of the Old Greek lay at the basis of this text; this other text, however, was "cleaned" with the help of the *obeli* of Origen.[18] The presence or absence of Hebraisms was also a prominent question in the debate between De Rossi and Eichhorn, their presence being used as an argument in support of the existence of a Hebrew *Vorlage*, with De Rossi asserting that the Additions belonged to the original book of Esther, and Eichhorn defending the shorter Hebrew text and considering them to be real additions.[19]

In 1940, with the publication of the *Cambridge Old Testament in Greek* volume on Esther, Judith, and Tobit,[20] research into the book of Esther took a major turn. In this volume, not only the so-called Septuagint text of Esther was printed, but also the second Greek text (→ 13–17.1.1.5).[21] The existence of a second Greek text required an innovative hypothesis in which different aspects and issues of the textual history of the book of Esther were brought together, which was formulated by Torrey.[22] Not only did he point to a possible older story of the book

---

LB 3 (1973): 6–11; Gordis, "Religion, Wisdom and History in the Book of Esther," 359–88; Gordis, "Studies in the Esther Narrative," 43–58 (= Moore [ed.], *Studies*, 408–23); Berg, "After the Exile," 107–27; Berg, *The Book of Esther: Motifs, Themes, and Structure*; Loader, *Esther*; Fox, "The Structure of the Book of Esther"; Meinhold, "Die Gattung der Josephsgeschichte und des Estherbuches," 72–93 (= Moore [ed.], *Studies*, 284–305); Meinhold, "Zu Aufbau und Mitte des Estherbuches," 435–49; Sasson, "Esther," 335–42; Clines, *The Esther Scroll*; Clines, "Reading Esther from Left to Right," 31–52; Day, *Three Faces of a Queen*; Levenson, *Esther: A Commentary*; T.K. Beal, *Esther* (Berit Olam, Studies in Hebrew Narrative & Poetry; Collegeville: Liturgical Press, 1999); Wahl, *Das Buch Esther*.

[14] J. Langen, "Die beiden griechischen Texte des Buches Esther," *TQ* 42 (1860): 244–72.

[15] Herbst, *Die deuterokanonische Bücher*, 263–76.

[16] Scholz, *Einleitung in die Heiligen Schriften des Alten und Neues Testaments*, 514–50.

[17] In his section on translational character, Jacob concludes that the Old Greek is of little value for the reconstruction of the original text. See Jacob, "Das Buch Esther bei den LXX," 241–98, esp. 270.

[18] Jacob, "Das Buch Esther bei den LXX," 259.

[19] De Rossi, *Specimen variorum*, 128–30. Eichhorn, *Einleitung ins Alte Testament*, 689–704. The following scholars followed de Rossi's line: Herbst, *Die deuterokanonischen Bücher*, 263–76; Scholz, *Einleitung in die Heiligen Schriften des Alten und Neues Testaments*, 514–50; Neteler, *Die Bücher Esdras, Nehemias und Esther aus dem Urtext übersetzt und erklärt*, 137–91, 200–207; Cornely, *Historicae et criticae introductionis in v.T. libros sacros compendium*, 293–99; Dignant, *Esdras, Nehemias, Tobias, Judith, Esther*, 169–213; Condamin, "Notes critiques sur le texte biblique," 258–61; Jahn, *Das Buch Esther nach der Septuagint hergestellt, übersetzt und kritisch erklärt*; Seisenberger, *Die Bücher Ezra, Nehemia und Esther*, 218–302; Keulers, *Tobias, Judith, Esther*; Soubigou, *Esther traduit et commenté*; Bauer, *Entwurf einer historisch-kritischen Einleitung in die Schriften des alten Testaments*, 350–55; Jahn, *Einleitung in die gottlichen Bücher des alten Bunde*, 2.295–317, 4, 885–90; Bertholdt, *Historisch-kritische Einleitung*, 2413–71; Hervey, *Esther*, 583–87; Schultz, *Die Bücher Ezra, Nehemia und Esther*, 218–302; Jacob, "Das Buch Esther bei den LXX," 241–98; Fritzsche, *ΕΣΘΗΡ: Duplicem libri textum*; Fritzsche, *Zusätze zu den Esther*, 67–108; Fritzsche, *Libri Apocryphi Veteri Testamenti Graece*, xi–xii, 30–72; Ryssel, "Zusätze zum Buch Esther," 193–212; Streane, *The Book of Esther, with Introduction and Notes*; Paton, *A Critical and Exegetical Commentary on the Book of Esther*; Bigot, "Le livre d' Esther," 5:850–71; Gregg, *The Additions to Esther*, 665–84; Schötz, "Das hebräische Buch Esther," 255–76; Striedl, "Untersuchungen," 73–108; Stummer, *Tobit, Judith, Esther*; Barucq, *Judith–Esther*, 73–130; Bückers, *Die Bücher Esdras, Nehemias, Tobias, Judith und Esther*, 325–92; Aalders, *Het boek Esther*; Poulssen, *Esther uit de grondtekst vertaald en uitgelegd*. For the most recent exhaustive treatment and analysis of the Additions, see Kottsieper, "Zusätze zu Ester." For further discussion of the Additions, see → 11.6.

[20] Brooke–McLean–Thackeray, *The Old Testament in Greek*, Vol. 3.1: *Esther, Judith, Tobit*.

[21] For the difficulty surrounding the names of the second Greek text, see De Troyer in → 13–17.1.1.

[22] Torrey, "The Older Book of Esther," 1–40.

of Esther, with an (Aramaic) text that differed from the Hebrew MT (→ 17.2.2), he also questioned where precisely this older book started and ended and formulated his ideas of how the additions fit into this shorter book. The debates on unity, ending, and additions had thus come together! The view of Torrey, or at least his defence of an older shorter text of the book of Esther, was upheld by Moore, Cook, Clines, Fox, Jobes, Dorothy, Koßmann, and Kahana,[23] although these scholars differ somewhat on precisely which addition (or part thereof) belonged to the so-called shorter Hebrew text of Esther.[24]

The debate about the textual place and history of the second Greek text and its possible Hebrew *Vorlage* was initially stimulated by the two different Hebrew traditions of Jeremiah found among the Qumran texts.[25] Furthermore, a major role was played by the study of VL-Esth (→ 13–17.2.15), which seems to buttress the hypothesis of an older and shorter Hebrew text, although the Esther volume in the Vetus Latina Beuron series has yet to be published in 2015.[26] In this context, it is important to see that the oldest Georgian version of Esther (→ 13–17.2.6) is also derived from the second Greek text of Esther (→ 13–17.1.1.5). Next, the discovery of some fragments at Qumran that were said to represent an "Esther" text (but see → 17.2.1) also buttressed the idea that there might have been a different older and shorter book of Esther in Hebrew, albeit that the Qumran fragments are now considered to be more a Persian court tale than a witness to a shorter Hebrew book of Esther.[27]

17.1.2 Relation between the Textual Witnesses

It is generally accepted that OG-Esth is a translation of a text that was very similar to MT (→ 13–17.1.1.5.A.3). There are no witnesses to a Hebrew (or Greek) text among the Dead Sea Scrolls. MT (→ 17.2.2) was translated into Aramaic (*Targum rishon* and *Targum sheni*; the existence of a third Targum is still under discussion; → 13–17.1.3),[28] Syriac[29] (→ 13–17.1.4.5) and Latin (Vulgata; → 13–17.1.7).[30] Whereas the Old Greek was further translated Sahidic, Ethiopic, and Armenian (→ 13–17.2.2; → 13–17.2.3.5; → 13–17.2.5.5), it seems that the oldest Georgian version was based on the second Greek text of Esther, as it displays the same omissions and the same readings (→ 13–17.2.6). With regard to the Slavonic version (→ 13–17.2.7), it has been argued

---

[23] Moore, "A Greek Witness to a Different Hebrew Text of Esther," 351–58; Moore, *Esther: Introduction, Translation and Notes*; Moore, "On the Origins of the LXX Additions to the Book of Esther," 382–93; Cook, "The A Text of the Greek Versions of the Books of Esther," 369–76; Clines, *The Esther Scroll: The Story of the Story*; Fox, *The Redaction of the Books of Esther*; Fox, "The Alpha Text of the Greek Esther," 27–54; Jobes, *The Alpha-Text of Esther*; Dorothy, *The Books of Esther: Structure, Genre and Integrity*; Kossmann, *Die Esthernovelle*; Kahana, *Esther*.

[24] For a summary on the additions, see De Troyer, "The Letter of the King and the Letter of Mordecai," 175–207.

[25] Moore, "Greek Witness."

[26] VL has long played an important role in the study of the book of Esther. Since Motzo and Schildenberger, VL has been read side by side with the Alpha Text and the version of Josephus. The further study of the mutual relationship between the texts will only be possible, however, when the VL critical edition is ready. This edition is being prepared by J.C. Haelewyck (*Ester* [VL 7.3; Freiburg i.B.: Herder, 2003–2008]). For an analysis of the first two chapters of VL-Esth, see Haelewyck, "La version latine du livre d'Esther dans le 'Monacensis' 6239," (1991), 7–27 and (1993), 289–306. See also Haelewyck, "La version latine du livre d'Esther dans la première Bible d'Alcalá," 165–93. See also Motzo, "La storia del testo di Ester," 205–08; Motzo, "I testi greci di Ester," 223–31; Miller and Schildenberger, *Die Bücher Tobia, Judith und Esther übersetzt und erklärt*. See also Bogaert's discussion of Motzo's work on VL-Esth entitled, "Septante et Versions Grecques," 536–692, esp. 607–08.

[27] Milik, "Les modèles araméens du livre d'Esther," 321–99, 400–407. For a survey of the discussion and an alternative suggestion for labelling the fragments, see De Troyer, "Once More the So-Called Esther Fragments of Cave 4," 401–22.

[28] Beelen, *Chrestomathia rabbinica et chaldaica*, 15–26, 45–88; De Lagarde, *Hagiographa Chaldaica*; Sperber, *The Hagiographa*. For a survey of publications, cf. also Grossfeld, *The Two Targums of Esther*. For a discussion on the relationship between the first and the third Targum, cf. Kasher and Klein, "New Fragments of Targum to Esther from the Cairo Genizah," 89–124; T. Legrand, "Les Targums d'Esther: Essai de Comparaison des Targums I et III du livre d'Esther," *Sem* 37 (1987) 71–94.

[29] *Biblia Sacra iuxta versionem simplicem quae dicitur Pschitta*; Lee, *Vetus Testamentum syriace*. See also Walton, *Polyglotta*, vol. II.

[30] For the Vulgate, see *Biblia Sacra iuxta Vulgatam versionem*; for VL, see Sabatier, *Bibliorum*, I.791–825.

that the *Vorlage* of the Slavonic text is a mixture of the Old Greek and a Targum.[31] VL is often aligned with the second Greek text of Esther and occasionally with the text of Josephus (→ 13–17.1.1.5).[32] With regard to readings from the early Jewish revisers (→ 13–17.1.5.5), it has been accepted ever since Jacob that there are readings of Aquila[33] transmitted in Esth 1:1, 5; 6:18; 7:10; and 8:10 but that there are no readings of Symmachus and Theodotion.

How the second Greek text is related to a Hebrew text, MT, or to the Old Greek is still debated (→ 17.1.1). There is also no consensus yet on the name of this Greek text, which is related to its place in the textual history. In any event, the name "Lucianic text" is no longer used, as it is rather clear that the second Greek text has nothing to do with the Lucianic text or the Lucianic characteristics[34] of, for example, the books of Samuel and Kings.

17.1.3 Development of the Text

If one accepts that the second Greek text (→ 13–17.1.1.5.A) is a revision of the Old Greek text and not an independent translation of a unknown Hebrew text, then the history of the book of Esther can be summarised as follows. The Hebrew book of Esther was most likely finished by the late third or mid-second century B.C.E. Unfortunately, there are no manuscripts of Esther dating to before the Middle Ages (see → 17.2.2). There are, however, references to the Hebrew text of Esther at Qumran (see → 17.2.1), although no Hebrew or Greek text of Esther was ever found there.

The Hebrew text was then translated into Greek, to form the Old Greek text. The earliest witness to the Old Greek Text of Esther can be found in the third century C.E. manuscript known as P967 (LXX^{967}), which belongs to the famous Chester Beatty Biblical Papyri.[35] The translator, however, not only translated the book into Greek, he/she also added a series of Additions to the text (→ 13–17.1.1.5; → II.6); some (parts) of the Additions may have been in Hebrew (such as the Dream and the Interpretation of the Dream in Additions A and F and the Prayers in Addition C) and were translated by the translator into Greek, and others were most likely in Greek (the edicts in Additions B and E). The translator further adapted the translation to merge with the Additions, such as in Addition D and the text of the beginning of Esther 5; but also the summary of the edict in Esther 8 and the edict in Addition E (→ 17.1.1).

Subsequently, a reviser of the Old Greek text produced a second Greek text. In the latter text, these additions were taken over, with only very minor changes. This reviser also adapted the story of the Old Greek text to form a new story. There are traces of the second Greek text in VL (→ 13–17.2.1.5) and in the text of Josephus (→ 21.3). The further study of the Georgian Esther manuscripts (→ 13–17.2.6) may yield more details about the textual development of the second Greek text of Esther.

The Hebrew text of the book of Esther was also the basis for the translations into Aramaic (→ 13–17.1.3), Syriac (→ 13–17.1.4.5), Latin (→ 13–17.1.7), etc. (→ 17.1.2).

The debate about the second Greek text of Esther, however, continues: Is it a translation of a hitherto-unknown (shorter and older) Hebrew text, or is it a revised version of the Old Greek trans-

---

[31] See Lunt and Taube, "The Slavonic Book of Esther," 347–62.

[32] Josephus, *Jewish Antiquities*, Books IX–XI, 402–57. It should be noted here that Josephus contains neither Mordecai's letter from the second Greek text (Esth 7:34–38) nor Esther's request that the ten sons of Haman be hanged from (Esth 7:18–21); both passages only appear in the second Greek text.

[33] Cf. Jacob, "Das Buch Esther bei den LXX," 241–98, esp. 260–61. For Esth 1:6 and 8:15, see also Hanhart, *Esther*, 63.

[34] Whereas quotations from the church fathers (→ 21.7) were used in the process of identifying the second Greek text, it has now become clear that these quotations are equally unhelpful with respect to the identification of the second Greek text. In 1967, Moore proposed that neither Chrysostomus nor Theodoretus quoted from the second Greek text of Esther and he concluded accordingly that the second Greek text could not as such be the Lucianic text. Cf. Moore, "A Greek Witness to a Different Hebrew Text of Esther," 351–58, esp. 352 (= Moore [ed.], *Studies*, 521–28, esp. 522). Both Hanhart and De Troyer have argued similarly.

[35] See F.G. Kenyon, *The Chester Beatty Biblical Papyri*, Vol. 7: *Ezekiel, Daniel, Esther* (London: Walker, 1937; Plates: London, 1938).

lation, with maybe some recensional elements towards a Hebrew text? An answer to this question needs to explain why so much of the second Greek text is similar to OG-Esth, both in the core text and in the additions. VL and the (paraphrased) text of Josephus occasionally have readings in common with the second Greek text. According to Hanhart, these occasional congruencies point to the existence of material that was independent of the Old Greek and that was used by the second Greek text. With regard to the second Greek text, Hanhart specifies that "incorporation of other traditions is visible where the Lucianic text aligns, independently of the Old Greek, with MT either where the Lucianic text is on its own or where it aligns with the Hexaplaric text, or where the other old tradition, which is not exclusively dependent on the Old Greek, aligns with the Old Latin and/or Josephus or where the Lucianic text presumes another Hebrew text, ... maybe also where the Old Latin or Josephus align with the Lucianic text and against MT" (my translation).[36] It needs to be noted, however, that these congruencies are extremely rare.

Aalders, G.C., *Het boek Esther* (Korte verklaring van de Heilige Schrift; Kampen: Kok, 1966).

Barucq, A., *Judith-Esther* (La sainte Bible traduite en français sous la direction de l'école biblique de Jérusalem; Paris: Cerf, 1952; 2nd ed. 1959), 73–130.

Bauer, G.L., *Entwurf einer historisch-kritischen Einleitung in die Schriften des Alten Testaments* (Nürenberg: Monath- und Kuszler'sche Buchhandlung, 1801), 350–55.

Beelen, J.T., *Chrestomathia Rabbinica et Chaldaica: Cum notis grammaticis, historicis, theologicis, glossaris et lexico abbreviatarum, quae in Hebraeorum scriptis passim occurrunt*, Vol. 1: *Seclecta Rabbinica et Chaldaica complectens*, Part 2: *Selecta Chaldaica* (Leuven: Vanlinthout et Vandenzande, 1841), 15–26, 45–88.

Berg, S.B., *The Book of Esther: Motifs, Themes, and Structure* (SBLDS 44; Missoula: Scholars Press, 1979).

Berg, S.B., "After the Exile: God and History in the Books of the Chronicles and Esther," in *The Divine Helmsman: Studies on God's Control of Human Events Presented to Lou H. Silberman* (eds. J.L. Crensham and S. Sandmel; New York: Ktav, 1980), 107–27.

Bertheau, A., *Die Bücher Esra, Nehemia und Esther* (KHAT 17; Leipzig: Hirzel, 1862; 2nd ed. 1887), 273–353.

Bertholdt, L., *Historisch-kritische Einleitung in sämmtliche kanonische und apokryphische Schriften des Alten und Neuen Testaments*, Vol. 6 (Erlangen: Palm, 1819), 2413–71.

Biblia Sacra iuxta versionem simplicem quae dicitur Pschitta (Beirut: Typis Typographiae Catholica, 1951).

Biblia Sacra iuxta Vulgatam versionem (eds. B. Fischer, R. Weber, and R. Gryson; Stuttgart: Deutsche Bibelgesellschaft, 1969; 2nd ed. 1975).

Bigot, L., "Le livre d' Esther," *DTC* 5:850–71.

Bogaert, P.-M., "Septante et versions grecques," *DBSup* 68:536–692, esp. 607–08.

Brooke–McLean–Thackeray, *The Old Testament in Greek*, Part 3.1: *Esther, Judith, Tobit* (1940).

Bückers, H., *Die Bücher Esdras, Nehemias, Tobias, Judith und Esther* (Herder Bibelkommentar. Die Heilige Schrift für das Leben erklärt 4.2; Freiburg i.B.: Herder, 1953), 325–92.

Clines, D.J.A., *The Esther Scroll: The Story of the Story* (JSOTSup 30; Sheffield: Sheffield Academic Press, 1984).

Clines, D.J.A., "Reading Esther from Left to Right: Contemporary Strategies for Reading a Biblical Text," in *The Bible in Three Dimensions: Essays in Celebration of Forty Years of Biblical Studies in the University of Sheffield* (eds. D.J.A. Clines, S.E. Fowl, and S.E. Porter; JSOTSup, 87; Sheffield: Sheffield Academic Press, 1990), 31–52.

Condamin, A., "Notes critiques sur le texte biblique, 2: La disgrace d' Aman (Esth. VII, 8)," *RevBib* 7 (1898): 258–61.

Cook, H., "The A Text of the Greek Versions of the Books of Esther," in *ZAW* 81 (1969): 369–76.

Cornely, R., *Historicae et criticae introductionis in V.T. libros sacros compendium* (Paris: P. Lethielleux, 1889; 8th ed. 1914), 293–99.

Daube, D., "The Last Chapter of Esther," *JQR* 37 (1946–1947): 139–47.

Day, L., *Three Faces of a Queen: Characterization in the*

---

[36] Hanhart, *Esther*, 90–91: "Verarbeitung anderer Überlieferung liegt mit Sicherheit dort vor, wo der L-Text unabhängig vom oᶜ-Text mit M zusammengeht, sei es daß L allein steht oder nur mit O zusammengeht, sei es daß auch die übrige alte Überlieferung, die nicht allein und ausschließlich vom oᶜ-Text abhängig ist, die altlat. Überlieferung und Iosephus, hinzutritt, oder dort, wo im L-Text eine andere hebr. Vorlage vorausgesetzt werden muß, ... vielleicht auch dort, wo La oder Ios mit L zusammen gegen den M-Text stehen."

Books of Esther (JSOTSup 186; Sheffield: Sheffield Academic Press, 1995).

Dignant, O.E., *Esdras, Nehemias, Tobias, Judith, Esther* (Het Oud Testament 3; Bruges: Beyaert, 1897), 169–213.

Dommershausen, W., *Die Estherrolle: Still und Ziel einer alttestamentliches Schrift* (SBM 6; Stuttgart: Katholisches Bibelwerk, 1968).

Dommershausen, W., *Esther* (NEchtB; Würzburg: Echter Verlag, 1980).

Dorothy, C.V., *The Books of Esther: Structure, Genre and Integrity* (JSOTSup 187; Sheffield: Sheffield Academic Press, 1997).

Driver, S.R., *Introduction to the Literature of the Old Testament* (Edinburgh: T & T Clark, 1891; 9th ed. 1929).

Eichhorn, J.-G., *Einleitung ins Alte Testament*, Vol. 2 (Leipzig: Weidmann und Reich, 1781).

Fox, M.V., *The Redaction of the Books of Esther: On Reading Composite Texts* (SBLMS 40; Altanta: Scholars Press, 1991).

Fox, M.V., "The Alpha Text of the Greek Esther," *Textus* 15 (1990): 27–54.

Fox, M.V., "The Structure of the Book of Esther," in *Isaac Leo Seeligmann Volume: Essays on the Bible and the Ancient World* (eds. A. Rofé and Y. Zakovitch; Jerusalem: E. Rubinstein, 1983), 291–303.

Fritzsche, O.F., *ΕΣΘΗΡ: Duplicem libri textum ad optimos codices emendavit et cum selecta lectionis varietate edidit* (Zurich: Orel, 1848).

Fritzsche, O.F., *Zusätze zu dem Buche Esther* (KEH; Leipzig: Hirzel, 1851), 67–108.

Fritzsche, O.F., *Libri Apocryphi Veteris Testamenti Graece: Apocrypha testamenti veteris accedunt libri veteris Testamenti pseuepigraphi selecti* (Leipzig: Brockhaus, 1871).

Gerleman, S., *Studien zu Esther: Stoff–Struktur–Sinn* (BibS(N) 48; Neukirchen: Neukirchener Verlag, 1966).

Gerleman, S., *Esther* (BKAT 21; Neukirchen-Vluyn: Neukirchener Verlag, 1973).

Gordis, R., "Religion, Wisdom and History in the Book of Esther: A New Solution to an Ancient Crux," *JBL* 100 (1981): 359–88.

Gordis, R., "Studies in the Esther Narrative," *JBL* 95 (1976): 43–58 (= Moore [ed.], *Studies*, 408–23).

Gregg, J.A.F., "The Additions to Esther," in *The Apocrypha and Pseudepigrapha of the Old Testament*, Vol. 1 (ed. R.H. Charles; Oxford: Clarendon Press, 1913), 665–84.

Grossfeld, B., *The Two Targums of Esther: Translated, with Apparatus and Notes* (ArBib 18; Edinburgh: T & T Clark, 1991).

Gunkel, H., *Esther* (Religionsgeschichtliche Volksbücher 2.19–20; Tübingen: Mohr, 1916).

Haelewyck, J.-C., "La version latine du livre d'Esther dans le 'Monacensis' 6239," *RBén* 101 (1991): 7–27; 103 (1993): 289–306.

Haelewyck, J.-C., "La version latine du livre d'Esther dans la première Bible d'Alcalá: Avec un appendice sur les citations patristiques vielles latines," in *Lectures et relectures de la Bible: Festschrift P.-M. Bogaert* (eds. J.-M. Auwers and A. Wénin; BETL 144; Leuven: Peeters, 1999), 165–93.

Hanhart, R., *Esther* (2nd ed.; Septuaginta Vetus Testamentum Graecum 8.3; Göttingen: Vandenhoeck & Ruprecht, 1983).

Herbst, J.G., *Die deuterokanonische Bücher* (Historisch-kritische Einleitung in die Schriften des Alten Testaments 2; Freiburg: Herder, 1844), 263–76.

Hervey, A.C., "Esther," in *A Dictionary of the Bible* (ed. W. Smith; London: John Murray, 1863), 1:583–87.

Jacob, B., "Das Buch Esther bei den LXX," *ZAW* 10 (1890): 241–98.

Jahn, G., *Das Buch Esther nach der Septuagint hergestellt, übersetzt und kritisch erklärt* (Leipzig: Pfeiffer, 1901).

Jahn, J., *Einleitung in die göttlichen Bücher des alten Bundes*, Vol. 2 (2nd totally rev. ed.; Vienna: Wappler, 1803), 295–317, 885–90.

Jobes, K.H., *The Alpha-Text of Esther: Its Character and Relationship to the Masoretic Text* (SBLDS 153; Atlanta: Scholars Press, 1996).

Josephus, *Jewish Antiquities, Books IX–XI* (ed. and transl. R. Marcus; LCL; Cambridge: Harvard University Press, 1958), 402–57.

Kahana, H., *Esther: Juxtaposition of the Septuagint Translation with the Hebrew Text* (CBET 40; Louvain: Peeters, 2005).

Kasher, R. and M.L. Klein, "New Fragments of Targum to Esther from the Cairo Genizah," *HUCA* 61 (1990): 89–124.

Keulers, J., *Tobias, Judith, Esther* (2nd ed.; Het Oud Testament 3.5; Bruges: Beyaert, s.d., 1930).

König, E., *Einleitung in das Alte Testament mit Einschluss der Apokryphen und der Pseudepigraphen Alten Testaments* (Sammlung Theologischer Handbücher 2.1; Bonn: Weber, 1893).

Kossmann, R., *Die Esthernovelle: Vom Erzählten zur Erzählung* (VTSup 79; Leiden: Brill, 1999).

Kottsieper, I., "Zusätze zu Ester," in O.H. Steck, R.G. Kratz, and I. Kottsieper, *Das Buch Baruch, Der Brief des Jeremia, Zusätze zu Ester und Daniel* (ATD-Apokryphen 5; Göttingen: Vandenhoeck & Ruprecht, 1998), 109–207.

Kuenen, A., *Historisch-kritisch onderzoek naar het ontstaan en de verzameling van de boeken des Ouden Verbonds* (3 vols.; Leiden: Brill, 1861–1863), see 1.364–79 (German ed. *Historisch-kritische Einleitung in die Bücher des Alten Testaments* [3 vols., Leipzig: Schulze, 1887–1894]).

de Lagarde, P., *Hagiographa Chaldaica* (Leipzig: Tuebner, 1873; photomech. repro. Osnabrück: Zeller, 1967).

Lee, S., *Vetus Testamentum syriace* (London: British and Foreign Bible Society, 1823).

Levenson, J.D., *Esther: A Commentary* (OTL; Louisville: John Knox, 1997).

Loader, J.A., *Esther* (Prediking van het Oude Testament; Nijkerk: Callenbach, 1980).

Löwenstamm, S.E., "Esther 9:29–32: The Genesis of a Late Addition," *HUCA* 42 (1971): 117–24.

Lunt, H.G. and M. Taube, "The Slavonic Book of Esther: Translation from Hebrew or Evidence for a lost Greek Text?" *HTR* 87 (1994): 347–62.

Meinhold, A., "Die Gattung der Josephsgeschichte und des Estherbuches: Diasporanovelle 2," *ZAW* 88 (1976): 72–93 (= Moore [ed.], *Studies*, 284–305).

Meinhold, A., "Zu Aufbau und Mitte des Estherbuches," *VT* 33 (1983): 435–49.

Michaelis, J.D., *Deutsche Übersetzung des Alten Testaments mit Anmerkungen für Ungelehrte* (Göttingen: Vandenhoeck, 1773–1783).

Milik, J.T., "Les modèles araméens du livre d' Esther dans la Grotte 4 de Qumrân," in *Mémorial Jean Starcky: Textes et études Qumrâniens*, Vol. 2 (eds. É. Puech and F. García Martínez; *RevQ* 59/15; Paris: Gabalda, 1992), 321–99, 400–407.

Miller, A. and J. Schildenberger, *Die Bücher Tobia, Judith und Esther übersetzt und erklärt* (Die Heilige Schrift des Alten Testaments 4.3; Bonn: Hanstein, 1940).

Moore, C.A. (ed.), *Studies in the Book of Esther* (Library of Biblical Studies; New York: Ktav, 1982).

Moore, C.A., "On the Origins of the LXX Additions to the Book of Esther," *JBL* 92 (1973): 382–93.

Moore, C.A., *Esther: Introduction, Translation and Notes* (AB 7B; New York: Doubleday, 1971).

Moore, C.A., "A Greek Witness to a Different Hebrew Text of Esther," *ZAW* 79 (1967): 351–58.

Motzo, B., "La storia del testo di Ester," *Ricerche Religiose* 3 (1927): 205–08.

Motzo, B., "I testi greci di Ester," *StMSR* 6 (1930): 223–31.

Neteler, B., *Die Bücher Esdras, Nehemias und Esther aus dem Urtext übersetzt und erklärt* (Münster: Theissing, 1877), 137–91, 200–07.

Paton, L.B., *A Critical and Exegetical Commentary on the Book of Esther* (ICC; Edinburgh: T & T Clark, 1907).

Pfeiffer, R.H., *Introduction to the Old Testament* (New York: Harper, 1941), 732–47.

Poulssen, N., *Esther uit de grondtekst vertaald en uitgelegd* (Boeken van het Oude Testament 6; Roermond: J.J. Romen, 1971).

de Rossi, G.B., *Specimen variorum lectionum sacri textus et chaldaica Estheris additamentis cum latina versione ac notis* (Rome: Venantii Monaldnini, 1772).

Ryssel, V., "Zusätze zum Buch Esther," in *Die Apokryphen und Pseudepigraphen des Alten Testaments* (2 vols.; ed. E. Kautzsch; Tübingen: Mohr, 1900), 1.193–212.

Sabatier, **Bibliorum*, 791–825.

Sasson, J.A., "Esther," in *The Literary Guide to the Bible* (eds. R. Alter and F. Kermode; Cambridge: Cambridge University Press, 1987), 335–42.

Scholz, A., *Einleitung in die Heiligen Schriften des Alten und Neues Testaments* (Cologne: Boisserée, 1845), 514–50.

Schötz, D., "Das hebräische Buch Esther," *BZ* 21 (1933): 255–76.

Schultz, F.W., *Die Bücher Ezra, Nehemia und Esther* (Theologisch-homiletisches Bibelwerk des Alten Testaments 9; Leipzig, 1876), 218–302.

Seisenberger, M., *Die Bücher Esdras, Nehemias und Esther* (Kurzgefasster wissenschaftlicher Kommentar der Heiligen Schriften des Alten Testaments 1.4; Vienna: Mayer, 1901), 160–210.

Soubigou, L., *Esther traduit et commenté* (La sainte Bible; Paris: Cerf, 1948; 2nd ed. 1952).

Sperber, A., *The Hagiographa: Transition from Translation to Midrash* (The Bible in Aramaic 4A; Leiden: Brill, 1968).

Steuernagel, C., *Lehrbuch der Einleitung in das Alte Testament mit einem Anhang über die Apokryphen und Pseudepigraphen* (Tübingen: Mohr, 1912), 433–39, 788–90.

Streane, A.W., *The Book of Esther: With Introduction and Notes* (Cambridge Bible for Schools and Colleges; New York: Cambridge University Press, 1907).

Striedl, H., "Untersuchungen zur Syntax und Stilistik des hebräischen Buches Esther," *ZAW* 55 (1937): 73–108.

Stummer, F., *Tobit, Judith, Esther* (EB; Würzburg: Echter Verlag, 1950; 3rd ed. 1954).

Torrey, C.C., "The Older Book of Esther," *HTR* 37 (1944): 1–40.

De Troyer, K., "Once More the So-Called Esther Fragments of Cave 4," *RevQ* 19 (1999–2000): 401–22.

De Troyer, K., "The Letter of the King and the Letter of Mordecai: An analysis of MT & LXX 8.9–13 and AT 7.33–38," *Textus* 21 (2002): 175–207.

Ussher, J., *De Graeca Septuaginta interpretum versione syntagma cum libri Estherae editione origenica et vetere Graece altera, ex Arundelliana bibliotheca nunc primum in lucem producta* (London: J. Crook, 1655; Leipzig: Meyer, 1695).

Wahl, H.M., *Das Buch Esther: Übersetzung und Kommentar* (Berlin: Walter de Gruyter, 2009).

Walton, **Polyglotta*.

Kristin De Troyer

17.2 Ancient Hebrew Texts

17.2.1 Ancient Manuscript Evidence

There are no surviving manuscripts of the book of Esther from antiquity. Since the discovery of the Dead Sea Scrolls, scholars have stated that no copy of Esther was found at the various sites around the Dead Sea.[1] Although this is certainly true, several Essene texts from the Qumran library allude to the book of Esther.[2]

Esth 2:9, 17	1QS (1Q28) II:4
Esth 3:7	4QD^b (4Q267) 9 i 1
Esth 3:7	4QMen of People Who Err (4Q306) 1 2
Esth 3:14	1QSa (1Q28a) I:26–27
Esth 9:22	4QpHos^a (4Q166) II:16–17

These allusions leave little doubt that the Essenes knew the book of Esther. Most likely, one or more Esther manuscripts from Qumran are hidden among the many Qumran fragments that are too damaged to allow for identification and that are edited in *DJD* XXXIII.[3] Therefore, the lack of an extant Esther manuscript from the Qumran library should not be taken as an indication that the Essene movement rejected the book of Esther for theological or ritual reasons.[4]

Lange, *Handbuch*, 499–501.

Armin Lange

---

[1] Cf. e.g. early on Milik, *Ten Years*, 23.

[2] For the various allusions, see Lange, *Handbuch*, 499–501, as well as A. Lange and M. Weigold, *Biblical Quotations and Allusions in Second Temple Jewish Literature* (Journal of Ancient Judaism Supplements 5; Göttingen: Vandenhoeck & Ruprecht, 2011), 186.

[3] D.M. Pike and A.C. Skinner, *Qumran Cave 4.XXIII: Unidentified Fragments* (*DJD XXXIII; Oxford: Clarendon Press, 2001).

[4] Cf. recently Abegg, Flint, and Ulrich, *DSSB*, 630–31.

17.2.2 Masoretic Texts and Ancient Texts Close to MT

17.2.2.1 Manuscripts

Due to the fact that no Hebrew manuscript of Esther is preserved from antiquity,[1] the medieval MT witnesses (→ 10–20.1) form the basis for the text-critical discussion of the book's (proto-)MT text. The Aramaic Qumran fragments labeled 4Q550 and related to Esther by Milik[2] must be considered as textual witnesses of a lost court story different from that of Esther.[3] Although several fragments among the Hebrew Esther fragments from the Cairo Genizah are labeled as "standard Tiberian,"[4] their value is not clear due to their uncertain origin. Since Esther is among the lost sections of Codex Aleppo, the three most important medieval MT witnesses are EBP. I B 19a (Codex Leningradensis; MT^L), EBP. II B 34 (MT^{L34}) from the Russian National Library, and Add. Ms. 1753 from

---

[1] This fact, of course, does not necessarily imply that the Esther story was unknown at Qumran. For an outline of the proposed allusions to the story in other Qumran texts and for a presentation of the corresponding bibliographical data, see Lange, *Handbuch*, 498–502 (→ 17.2.1).

[2] J.T. Milik, "Les modèles araméens du livre d'Esther dans la grotte 4 de Qumrân," *RevQ* 15 (1991): 321–99.

[3] Cf., e.g., S.W. Crawford, "Has Esther Been Found at Qumran? 4QProto-Esther and the Esther Corpus," *RevQ* 17 (1996): 307–25; J.J. Collins and D.A. Green, "Tales from the Persian Court (4Q550a–e)," in *Antikes Judentum und frühes Christentum: Festschrift für Hartmut Stegemann zum 65. Geburtstag* (eds. B. Kollmann, W. Reinbold, and A. Steudel; BZNW 97; Berlin: De Gruyter, 1999), 39–50; K. De Troyer, "Once More, the So-Called Esther Fragments of Cave 4," *RevQ* 19 (2000): 401–22; Kossmann, *Esthernovelle*, 257–91; M.G. Wechsler, "Two Para-Biblical Novellae from Qumran Cave 4: A Reevaluation of 4Q550," *DSD* 7 (2000): 130–72 (Wechsler, however, still proposes understanding 4Q550^{a-c} as "4QAramaic Esther Prequel," pp. 163–64); J. Holgenhaven, "Fortaellinger fra det persiske hof (4Q550): En Qumran-udgave af Ester-historien?," *DTT* 67 (2004): 15–34.

[4] Cf. M.C. Davis (ed.), *Hebrew Bible Manuscripts in the Cambridge Genizah Collections* (4 vols.; Cambridge University Library Genizah Series 2; Cambridge: Cambridge University Press, 1978–2003), *passim*.

the Cambridge University Library (MT^Y). Whereas MT^L and MT^Y offer a complete version of Esther, MT^L34 contains two major lacunae (Esth 1:1–22 and 8:7–9:15).

17.2.2.2 History of Research

As stated above (→ 17.1), in the ongoing discussion about the textual history of Esther, scholarly opinion differs considerably on the relationship between MT-Esth and the proto-version of Esther. Whereas some scholars place MT quite close to it,[5] others assume a stronger link between proto-Esther and a proto- or pre-proto-version of the Greek A text (→ 13–17.1.1.5.B).[6] Concerning the relationship between MT and the Greek LXX version (→ 13–17.1.1.5.A.2–3), scholars generally agree that LXX depends on MT and represents a more recent, reworked, and extended version of it.[7] The present article focuses on MT-Esth as the only extant Hebrew witness of the book and does not regard the Alpha Text of Esther as a translation of a distinct Hebrew Esther version earlier than MT.

As most scholars regard MT-Esth as the most original witness among the various texts and versions of Esther, it is not surprising that the Hebrew text of Esther has been the subject of few studies since the *communis opinio* on the secondary nature of LXX-Esth was reached (→ 17.1.1; → 13–17.1.1.5.A). Most commentaries and text-critical studies restrict themselves to the discussion of individual variants but do not give an overall characterization of MT-Esth.

17.2.2.3 Editions

The critical editions in *BHS and *BHQ are both diplomatic in nature, using MT^L as their running text. *BHQ improves Esth 1:4; 5:14; 9:31 in both *BH³ and *BHS by rendering more carefully MT^L's use of the *maqqēp̄*.[8] None of the available editions is comprehensive. Due to their uncertain value, *BHQ no longer includes the fifteen references to the fragments from the Cairo Genizah offered by *BHS at Esth 2:3, 8, 13; 3:9; 4:1, 10, 11, 13, 14; 5:2; 7:9; 8:2, 9 (*bis*); 9:27.[9] As of 2016, the editions of Esther in both *HUB and *HBCE still await publication.

17.2.2.4 Nature and Text-Critical Character of MT-Esth

The differences among the manuscripts mentioned above are minor and mainly of orthographic nature. The division in *parašiyyôt* varies.[10]

Linguistically, the language of MT-Esth shows clear signs of Late Biblical Hebrew.[11] The manuscripts share a few orthographic peculiarities such as the consonantal spelling יְרוּשָׁלַיִם "Jerusalem" in Esth 2:6 instead of ירושלם, the *qere perpetuum*

---

[5] Cf. Hanhart, *Esther*, 96; Kottsieper, "Zusätze," 129; Tov, "Text," and the contributions of K. De Troyer as listed in the bibliographies of → 17.1 and → 13–17.1.1.5; see, e.g., De Troyer, "Letter."

[6] Cf. Moore, "Witness" and Clines, *Story*, which became influential for further contributions such as M.V. Fox, *The Redaction of the Books of Esther: On Reading Composite Texts* (SBLMS 40; Atlanta: Scholars Press, 1991); K.H. Jobes, *The Alpha-Text of Esther: Its Character and Relationship to the Masoretic Text* (SBLDS 153; Atlanta: Scholars Press, 1996); and Kossmann, *Esthernovelle*.

[7] See, e.g., Tov, "Translation" and Tov, "Books," who examines this issue closely.

[8] Cf. Sæbø, "Esther," *21.

[9] Cf. Sæbø, "Esther," 20*–21*.

[10] Cf. the table offered in Sæbø, "Esther," 21*. On the differing systems for dividing the biblical book into section units (in medieval manuscripts as well as in modern commentaries), see E. Tov, "The Chapter and Section Divisions in Esther," in *Textual Criticism and Dead Sea Scrolls: Studies in Honour of Julio Trebolle Barrera: Florilegium Complutense* (eds. A. Piquer Otero and P.A. Torijano Morales; JSJSup 157; Leiden: Brill, 2012), 343–60.

[11] Cf. H. Striedl, "Untersuchung zur Syntax und Stilistik des hebräischen Buches Esther," *ZAW* 14 (1937): 73–108; R.L. Bergey, "The Book of Esther – Its Place in the Linguistic Milieu of Post-Exilic Biblical Hebrew Prose: A Study in Late Biblical Hebrew" (PhD diss., Dropsie College, 1983); H.M. Wahl, "Die Sprache des hebräischen Esterbuches: Mit Anmerkungen zu seinem historischen und traditionsgeschichtlichen Referenzrahmen," *ZAH* (1999): 21–47. MT's frequent use of the passive voice seems to be a skillful stylistic device accentuating not only the court environment, where orders are given and received (cf. De Troyer and Wacker, "Esther," 1266, who consider speaking of a "passivum monarchicum"), but also hinting at a power beyond any earthly king or high courtier. Since the Greek versions mention God explicitly, this stylistic device became less important for them.

prevalent in other MT manuscripts.[12] The same spelling occurs in 1 Chr 3:5; 2 Chr 25:1; 32:9; and Jer 26:18.

Another unique spelling in MT-Esth is יְהוּדִיִּים "Judeans/Jews," a form occurring only in Esth 4:7; 8:1, 7, 13; 9:15, 18. It represents a variant spelling used in addition to the commonly used יְהוּדִים (cf. Esth 3:6, 10, 13; 4:3, 13, 14, 16; 6:13; 8:3, 5, 8, 9, 16, 17; 9:1, 2, 3, 5, 6, 10, 12, 13, 16, 19, 20, 22, 23, 24, 25, 27, 28, 30; 10:3). Further variant spellings can be observed related to personal names: In the case of the royal counselor Memuchan, the *Ketiv* form מומכן "Mumechan" occurs once (Esth 1:16). Otherwise, the form מְמוּכָן "Memuchan" is used (Esth 1:14, 21), i.e., the *Qere* of Esth 1:16. The king's name Ahasuerus is spelled twenty-four times in its *plene* form אֲחַשְׁוֵרוֹשׁ (occurring also in Dan 9:1 and Ezra 4:6), four times in the shorter form אֲחַשְׁוֵרֹשׁ (Esth 2:21; 3:12; 8:7, 10), and once in the double defective form אֲחַשְׁרֹשׁ (Esth 10:1). The unique infinitive form וּבִמְלוֹאת "and when were completed" in Esth 1:5 should be interpreted as the result of a metathesis of the consonants א and ו.[13]

The lack of ancient Hebrew textual witnesses makes it difficult if not impossible to explain the origin of the variants and to determine secondary readings. Unintentional scribal corruption – in particular, a haplography – may explain the *crux interpretum* in Esth 3:7 (וּמֵחֹדֶשׁ לְחֹדֶשׁ שְׁנֵים־עָשָׂר "and from month to month, twelve").[14] Further possible cases of scribal corruption include the accidental deletion of a determinative in Esth 2:14 (הַשֵּׁנִי "the second" instead of שֵׁנִי "a second"; cf. LXX τὸν δεύτερον, "the second").[15] A particular case of (intentional) scribal corruption can be found in Esth 8:5. MT^L, MT^L34, further Masoretic manuscripts, and LXX (τοὺς Ιουδαίους; cf. V) read אֶת־הַיְּהוּדִים "the Judeans/Jews" while MT^Y, thirty-five manuscripts in Kennicott, *1776–1780, forty-one manuscripts in De Rossi, *1784–1788, VL, S and both Esther Targumim attest to the reading אֵת כָּל הַיְּהוּדִים "all the Jews." The added כָּל "all" serves as an amplification.[16] The example demonstrates that Esther, as with many other books, experienced a limited amount of scribal corruption even after the creation of the proto-Masoretic standard text.

Thus, MT-Esth can be characterized on the whole as a text that is relatively close to the original text of Esther and suffered from a limited amount of scribal corruption.

17.2.2.5 Date and Milieu

The date and milieu of (proto-)MT-Esth remain difficult to determine. The generally accepted view that LXX-Esth depends on MT-Esth (→ 17.2.2.2) allows for the assumption of an earlier origin of (proto-)MT-Esth than the date given by LXX-Esth's colophon ("the fourth year of the reign of Ptolemeus and Cleopatra"). If the mentioned couple refers to Ptolemy XII and Cleopatra V, as most scholars propose, the colophon points to the year 78/77 B.C.E.[17] It cannot be determined when the scribal corruptions occurred in MT-Esth.

Apart from having a *terminus ante quem*, scholars disagree on whether (proto-)MT-Esth stems from late Persian or Hellenistic times.[18] Observations supporting the idea that LXX-Esth shows traits of a Jerusalem adaptation of MT might speak in favor of an Eastern Diaspora origin of (proto-)MT-Esth.[19]

---

[12] The name of the city appears only once in MT-Esth.

[13] Cf. the discussion of this form in Sæbø, "Esther," 137*.

[14] Cf. Sæbø, "Esther," 141*–42*, proposing the original reading וּמֵחֹדֶשׁ לְחֹדֶשׁ שְׁנֵים־עָשָׂר "and from month to month, to (unto) the twelfth month (that is Adar)" (translation and punctuation thus in Sæbø, "Esther," 142*).

[15] See Gerleman, *Esther*, 73.

[16] See Sæbø, "Esther," 90.

[17] The two other royal couples who could come into consideration are Ptolemy IX and Cleopatra III (reigned from 116–107 B.C.E.) and Ptolemy XIII and Cleopatra VII (reigned from 51–47 B.C.E.).

[18] Cf. the arguments *pro* and *contra* listed by B. Ego, "The Book of Esther: A Hellenistic Book," *Journal of Ancient Judaism* 1 (2010): 279–302. As the article's title suggests, Ego, in sum, opts for a Hellenistic origin.

[19] Cf. Kottsieper, "Zusätze," 121–31. For an opposing view, see Macchi, "Textes." According to Macchi, theological aspects allow for a conclusion that "le texte massorétique d'Esther revêtit la forme que nous lui connaissons en Palestine durant la période (pré)maccabéenne" (Macchi, "Textes," 80).

Clines, D.J.A., *The Esther Scroll: The Story of the Story* (JSOTSup 30; Sheffield: JSOT Press, 1984).

De Rossi, *1784–1788, 3.265–67.

De Troyer, K., *The End of the Alpha Text of Esther: Translation and Narrative Technique in MT 8:1–17, LXX 8:1–17, and AT 7:14–41* (SBLSCS 48; Atlanta: Society of Biblical Literature, 2000).

De Troyer, K., "The Letter of the King and the Letter of Mordecai," *Textus* 21 (2002): 175–207.

De Troyer, K. and M.-T. Wacker, "Esther: Das Buch Ester (LXX und A-Text)," in *Septuaginta Deutsch, Erläuterungen*, 1253–96.

Driver, G.R., "Problems and Solutions," *VT* 4 (1954): 225–45.

Gerleman, G., *Esther* (2nd ed.; BKAT 21; Neukirchen-Vluyn: Neukirchener Verlag, 2003).

Hanhart, R., *Esther* (2nd ed.; Septuaginta Vetus Testamentum Graecum 8.3; Göttingen: Vandenhoeck & Ruprecht, 1983).

Haupt, P., "Critical Notes on Esther," *AJSL* 24 (1908): 97–186.

Kennicott, *1776–1780, 2.562–72.

Kossmann, R., *Die Esthernovelle: Vom Erzählten zur Erzählung: Studien zur Traditions- und Redaktionsgeschichte des Estherbuches* (VTSup 79; Leiden: Brill, 2000).

Kottsieper, I., "Zusätze zu Ester," in O.H. Steck, R.G. Kratz, and I. Kottsieper, *Das Buch Baruch, Der Brief des Jeremia, Zusätze zu Ester und Daniel* (ATD-Apokryphen 5; Göttingen: Vandenhoeck & Ruprecht, 1998), 109–207.

Maass, F., "Librum Esther," *BHS, 1367–80.

Macchi, J.-D., "Les textes d'Esther et les tendances du Judaïsme entre les 3e et 1er siècles avant J.-Chr.," in *Un carrefour dans l'histoire de la Bible: Du texte à la théologie au IIe siècle avant J.-C.* (eds. I. Himbaza and A. Schenker; OBO 233; Göttingen: Vandenhoeck & Ruprecht, 2007), 75–92.

Moore, C.A., "A Greek Witness to a Different Hebrew Text of Esther," *ZAW* 79 (1967): 351–58.

Paton, L.B., *A Critical and Exegetical Commentary on the Book of Esther* (ICC; Edinburgh: T & T Clark, 1908), 5–13.

Rudolph, W., "Textkritisches zum Estherbuch," *VT* 4 (1954): 89–90.

Sæbø, M., "Esther אסתר," in *BHQ 18, 73–96, 20*–24*, 136*–50*.

Tov, E., "The 'Lucianic' Text of the Canonical and the Apocryphal Sections of Esther: A Rewritten Biblical Book," in Tov, *Greek-Hebrew Bible, 535–48.

Tov, E., "The LXX Translation of Esther: A Paraphrastic Translation of MT or a Free Translation of a Rewritten Version?" in *Empsychoi logoi: Religious Innovations in Antiquity: Studies in Honour of Pieter Willem van der Horst* (eds. A. Houtman, A. de Jong, and M.W. Misset-van de Weg; Ancient Judaism and Early Christianity 73; Leiden: Brill, 2008), 507–26.

Tov, E., "Three Strange Books of the LXX: 1 Kings, Esther, and Daniel Compared with Similar Rewritten Compositions from Qumran and Elsewhere," in Karrer-Kraus, *Septuaginta 2008, 369–93.

Veronika Bachmann

13–17.1 Primary Translations

13–17.1.1 Septuagint

13–17.1.1.1 Ruth
13–17.1.1.1.1 Background

The book of Ruth recounts the story of a young foreign woman from Moab who would become the ancestor of David, the second king of Israel. In the Hebrew Bible, the book of Ruth is included among the Writings (Ketuvim) and – detached from any historical context – forms part of the five liturgical scrolls or Megilloth (Ruth, Canticles, Qohelet, Lamentations, and Esther). In the Greek Bible, this historical novella is inserted between Judges (→ 4.3) and 1–4 Kingdoms (→ 5.4; → 5.5). Within the history of the people of Israel, it is indeed set in the period of the judges (Judg 1:1) and ends with the genealogy of David (Ruth 4:22).

13–17.1.1.1.2 Original Form

In 1922, the textual history of this Greek book was analyzed accurately by Rahlfs,[1] who grouped all the collated manuscripts into four families: those belonging to the Origenian (→ 13–17.1.5.2) and the Antiochene recensions (→ 13–17.1.6), the *Catenae* ("chains") group, and a recension that he called R. He regarded the pre-recensional Codex Vaticanus (LXX[B]) as a textual witness of the Old Greek that had been translated in Egypt during the second century B.C.E. According to Barthélemy,[2] LXX[B] was in reality the witness of a translation issued from the *kaige*-Th group, which he dated to the first century C.E. (→ 3–5.1.5.2.3); in Campbell's opinion,[3] for instance, the latter is more likely a revision. Thornhill[4] considered LXX[B] to be the most faithful representative of ancient LXX, but viewed R, which is closer to MT (→ 13.2.2), and not LXX[B] as the most accomplished form of the *kaige*-Th revision of LXX-Ruth. R would thus represent a late Palestinian or Eusebian edition of the Hexaplaric text.

The critical edition of LXX-Ruth published by Quast[5] in 2006 concurs with Rahlfs' assessment of LXX[B] as the most faithful textual witness of the Old Greek, R being a Hebraizing revision.

13–17.1.1.1.3 Translation Character, Translation Technique

Ruth belongs to those books of LXX that are viewed as literal and quasi incomprehensible translations. First of all, it displays a certain number of characteristics that are distinctive of the translators from the *kaige*-Th group, such as καί γε "and even" for גם "also" or וגם "and also" in Ruth 1:5; 2:15, 16, 21; 3:12; 4:10 and ἐγώ εἰμι "I am" for אנכי "I" in Ruth 2:10; 3:9, 12; 4:4. However, these distinguishing marks of *kaige* translation are less prominent than in other books, are not always pertinent, and, finally, are also found in the majority of the Greek manuscripts and especially in R.[6] Additionally, specific lexical choices are close to those of Theodotion, one of the notable members of the *kaige*-Th group, such as the rendering of שדי "Almighty" as ὁ ἱκανός "The Sufficient One" in Ruth 1:20 and the use of the terms ἀγχιστεία "right of inheritance" (*NETS*), ἀγχιστεύειν "to act as nearest of kin," and ἀγχιστεύς "next-of-kin" when making repeated reference to the right of the next of kin. As a general rule, the Greek translator frequently copies the Hebrew syntax (notably the parataxis) and gives literal renderings of the metaphors, as in the case of "talking to the heart" in Ruth 2:14 or of "uncovering the ear" in Ruth 4:4.

---

[1] Rahlfs, *Studie über den griechischen Text des Buches Ruth*.

[2] Barthélemy, **Devanciers*, 34, 158–59.

[3] E.F. Campbell, *Ruth: A New Translation with Introduction and Commentary* (AB 7; Garden City: Doubleday, 1975), 38–39.

[4] See R. Thornhill, "The Greek of the Book of Ruth: A Grouping of Manuscripts according to Origen's Hexapla," *VT* 3 (1953): 236–49. See also S.P. Cowe, "The Armenian Version of Ruth and its Textual Affinities," in *La Septuaginta en la investigacion contemporanea: V Congreso de la IOSCS* (ed. N. Fernández Marcos; Textos y Estudios "Cardenal Cisneros" de la Biblia Políglota Matritense 34; Madrid: Instituto de Filología, 1985), 183–97.

[5] Quast, *Ruth*.

[6] See Assan-Dhôte and Moatti-Fine, *Ruth*, 33–34.

Although very literal, the translation of the book of Ruth demonstrates flexibility and freedom with regard to the Hebrew original and attests to a contextual approach during the work of translation. It is, first of all, written in language that strives to correspond to the norms of Classical Greek, as evidenced, for example, by the frequent usage of the particle δέ "now, then" for the translation of Hebrew ו "and" and by the use of the subjunctive in Ruth 2:3 and 3:18. It also deviates from the Hebrew original in particular cases. This may involve terms that are better suited to the context, such as υἱός "son" instead of Masoretic "child" in Ruth 1:5, and the use of the verb ῥαβδίζειν "to beat with a rod" in Ruth 2:17, which is more compatible with the gleaned ears of corn than the simple Hebrew "beating." Other examples include: the elucidation of a metaphor in Ruth 3:11 and 4:10, where the Greek word φυλή "tribe" replaces the "gate," a term which, in Hebrew, synecdochically evokes the city; the omission of a phrase in Ruth 1:19 for the purpose of avoiding repetition; the suppression of certain references such as "tonight" in Ruth 1:12, "and he drank" in Ruth 3:7, as well as "and she lay down" in Ruth 3:7, all of which may be taken as euphemizations of the narrative.

However, the Greek translation also contains a few minor additions: the explicitation of the subject of a verb omitted by MT (→ 13.2.2), for instance in Ruth 1:15, 18; 2:19, 21; the explicitation of an implicit action in Ruth 1:14; the addition of the particle δέ "now, then" and the personal pronoun σύ "you" for the purpose of livening up the dialogue in Ruth 1:15–16; a number of additions meant to render a quite incomprehensible Hebrew text more intelligible, as in Ruth 2:7 and 3:18; and finally the addition of a negation, and even the series of "pluses" in Ruth 4.

Most of these discrepancies are certainly not suggestive of a Hebrew *Vorlage* that would differ from that of MT but constitute yet more translation techniques that were intended to elucidate a frequently difficult Hebrew text.[7]

13–17.1.1.1.4 Text-Critical Value

The Old Greek of the book of Ruth is based on a Hebrew text that is close to that of MT (→ 13.2.2). It follows the Hebrew word order and copies the syntax and, at times, even the metaphors. Moreover, even if certain discrepancies may rest on a *Vorlage* that differed from that of MT, as for example in the case of the name Abimelech in Ruth 1:2, the four Hebrew manuscripts of Ruth attested at Qumran (→ 13.2.1) generally support the readings of MT against LXX.[8]

13–17.1.1.1.5 Relevance for Exegesis

Certain characteristics of the Greek text of Ruth are probably the consequence of exegesis. For example, even if it should correspond to an underlying Hebrew text, the occurrence of the proper name Abimelech instead of the Masoretic Elimelech in Ruth 1:2 evokes the negative connotations attached to this person in Judges 9 in order to emphasize the culpability of Naomi's husband who fled his country, in contrast to the continued observance of the Law by Ruth. Further discrepancies from MT (→ 13.2.2), such as the systematic recourse to the legal vocabulary of the Greek right of the next of kin (ἀγχιστεία "right of inheritance"), the importance of the "tribe" in Ruth 4:9–10, and the status of the field given to Naomi in Ruth 4:3, evidently set Boaz and Ruth's marriage in the context of Greek inheritance laws. Finally, with every detail that differs from MT, LXX-Ruth paints an increasingly positive picture of Boaz as someone akin to God, and anticipates Ruth's change of social status.[9]

Assan-Dhôte, I. and J. Moatti-Fine, *Ruth: Traduction du texte grec de la Septante, introduction et notes* (*Bible d'Alexandrie* 8; Paris: Cerf, 2009).
Barthélemy, *Devanciers*.
Quast, U., *Ruth* (Septuaginta Vetus Testamentum Graecum 4.3; Göttingen: Vandenhoeck & Ruprecht, 2006).

---

[7] See J. de Waard, "Translation Techniques Used by the Greek Translators of Ruth," *Bib* 54 (1973): 499–515.

[8] See, e.g., Lange, *Handbuch*, 473–76; Assan-Dhôte and Moatti-Fine, *Ruth*, 34–35.

[9] See Assan-Dhôte and Moatti-Fine, *Ruth*, 43–52.

Rahlfs, A., *Studie über den griechischen Text des Buches Ruth* (MSU 3; Berlin: Wiedmannsche Buchhandlung, 1922).

Cécile Dogniez

13–17.1.1.2 Canticles

13–17.1.1.2.1 Background

Accepted into the canon of Jewish Scriptures at a late date owing to its allegorical interpretation, this secular love dialogue still attested in the popular Jewish feasts of the time was classified among those Hebrew books that defile the hands (→ 1.1.2.1.4), i.e. among the Megilloth.[1] In the Greek Bible, this book concludes the Solomonic trilogy, following Proverbs and Qohelet.

13–17.1.1.2.2 Original Form

It is generally agreed that the Greek translation of Canticles dates to the first century C.E., probably before that of Qohelet. According to Barthélemy,[2] it would presumably be linked to the *kaige*-Th recension group (→ 1.3.1.2). Due to the fact that it does not share all of the latter's characteristics, however, this hypothesis has been challenged (→ 1.3.1.2.3.6).[3] The Greek original is said to have been revised on the basis of a repeatedly modified Hebrew text, notably in Origen's Hexapla.[4] The Old Greek is preserved in the uncial manuscripts, of which some, such as Codex Alexandrinus and Codex Sinaiticus, contain a number of *didascaliae* that allow for the identification of the speakers.[5]

In anticipation of the critical Göttingen edition, Rahlfs manual edition of 1935 (*Septuaginta*) remains the only one available.

13–17.1.1.2.3 Translation Character, Translation Technique

Often considered to be servile and laborious, the Greek translation of Canticles exhibits only few characteristics of the *kaige* recension:[6] the equivalence of καί γε "and even" and גם "also" in Cant 1:16a; 8:1, but πρός "indeed" in Cant 1:16b and 7:14, and ἀνήρ "man," in the sense of "everyone" for איש "each," in Cant 3:8 and 8:11. It is related to Ruth (→ 13–17.1.1.1) and Ecclesiastes (→ 13–17.1.1.3) through the formal reproduction of the number and order of Hebrew words and through the stereotyped nature of its equivalences. It thus translates the Hebrew words mechanically and in strict consecutive order, while reproducing the Hebrew syntax in a crude manner, sometimes in disregard of the rules of Greek grammar (e.g. Cant 3:4) or even of readability (e.g. Cant 4:1; 5:6; 6:12). The preposition מן is systematically rendered as ἀπό (both meaning "from"), even when it has a comparative sense as in Cant 4:10b and 5:9b. The same Hebrew word is usually always translated in the same manner, with no variation whatsoever (e.g. אהב as ἀγαπάω [both meaning "to love"] or יפה as καλός [both meaning "beautiful"]). Doublets are reproduced in identical fashion (Cant 1:15 = 4:1ab; 2:6 = 8:3; 2:7 = 3:5; 2:17a = 4:6a; 3:1c = 5:6d) and certain words are simply transliterated (θαλπιωθ in Cant 4:4, αλωθ in Cant 4:14, θαρσις in Cant 5:14, and φαζ in Cant 5:11 but not in Cant 5:15 [= χρυσᾶς "golden"]),[7] whereas others appear in translation instead of the expected transliteration (e.g. τοῦ πεδίου "of the plain" for השרון *Šaron* in Cant 2:1; πίστεως "faithfulness" for אמנה *Amana* in Cant 4:8).

Primarily concerned with rendering the original as faithfully as possible, in accordance with a frequently interlinear approach, the Greek translator of Canticles may at times still demonstrate poetic skills when seeking equivalents for the translation of the numerous *hapax legomena* or rare words of the Hebrew language. Where this is the case,

---

[1] See e.g. D. Barthélemy, "Comment le Cantique des cantiques est-il devenu canonique?" in *Mélanges bibliques et orientaux en l'honneur de M. Mathias Delcor* (eds. A. Caquot, S. Légasse, and M. Tardieu; AOAT 215; Neukirchen-Vluyn: Neukirchener Verlag, 1985), 13–22.

[2] Barthélemy, *Devanciers*, 33–34, 47. Cf. also, e.g., M. Harl, "La version LXX du Cantique des cantiques et le groupe kaige-Théodotion: Quelques remarques lexicales," *Textus* 18 (1995): 101–20.

[3] Treat, "Lost Keys," 382–83.

[4] Cf. J.C. Treat, "Song of Songs," *NETS*, 657–66 (657).

[5] See the *Corollarium* at the end of the edition published by Rahlfs, *Septuaginta*.

[6] Treat, *NETS*, 659.

[7] For this characteristic feature of the *kaige* group, see E. Tov, "Transliterations of Hebrew Words in the Greek Versions of the Old Testament: A Further Characteristic of the *Kaige*-Theodotion Revision?" *Textus* 8 (1973): 78–92.

he no longer proves servile but creative and very free with regard to his source text, while at the same time displaying his good knowledge of Greek and respecting the metaphorical particularities of both languages, depending on the respective context.[8]

13–17.1.1.2.4 Text-Critical Value

LXX-Cant is a very literal translation and exhibits a Hebrew that is often identical to that of MT (→ 14.2.2). Accordingly, it contains only very few "pluses": a few isolated explicitations, which are not suggestive of a *Vorlage* that might differ from that of MT, as for instance ἐπὶ τὴν θύραν "on the door" in Cant 5:2, ὑδάτων "of water" in Cant 5:12c, or ἡ ἐρχομένη "she who comes" in Cant 7:1, or else, more frequently, various harmonizations in parallel passages, as in Cant 1:3 // 4:10; 2:9 // 2:17; 2:13 // 2:10; 3:1 // 5:6; 6:7 // 4:3; 6:11 // 7:13; 5:8 and 8:4 // 2:7 and 3:5; 8:2 // 3:4.

In Cant 2:15, the word ἀλώπεκας "foxes" makes its only appearance in LXX, whereas MT uses the word שׁעלים "foxes" twice. According to Tov, however, this Greek rendering is supported by 4QCant[b] (→ 14.2.1.2; → 14.2.3.2),[9] which would suggest that the Greek translator was looking at a Hebrew text that differed from MT.[10]

13–17.1.1.2.5 Relevance for Exegesis

As Canticles was translated into Greek at a time when it was being interpreted in an allegorical fashion in Pharisaic circles and probably also at Qumran, it has sometimes been assumed that the Greek translator had allegorized his text. Auwers[11] appears to have shown that this is not the case: the choice of the word ἀδελφιδός "brotherkin" rather than ἀγαπητός "beloved," for instance, is by no means indicative of an allegorical interpretation of the love of God for his people, while the etymology-based translation of certain Hebrew toponyms in Cant 4:8; 6:4; and 7:5 only betrays an ignorance of these geographical locations. Equally, the use of μαστοί "breasts" for the plural of Masoretic דודים (e.g. Cant 1:2, 4, 13) would not seem to reveal an intention to eroticize Canticles, all the more as the text itself probably already contains an allegorical interpretation.

Ausloos, H. and B. Lemmelijn, "Rendering Love: Hapax Legomena and the Characterisation of the Translation Technique of Song of Songs," in *Translating a Translation: The Septuagint and its Modern Translations in the Context of Early Judaism* (eds. H. Ausloos et al.; BETL 213; Leuven: Peeters, 2008), 43–61.

Auwers, J.M., "Le traducteur grec a-t-il allégorisé ou érotisé le Cantique des Cantiques?" in *XII Congress of the International Organization for Septuagint and Cognate Studies, Leiden, 2004* (ed. M.K.H. Peters; SBLSCS 54; Atlanta: Society of Biblical Literature, 2006), 161–68.

Lemmelijn, B., "Flora in Cantico Canticorum: Towards a More Precise Characterisation of Translation Technique in the LXX of Song of Songs," in *Scripture in Transition: Essays on Septuagint, Hebrew Bible and Dead Sea Scrolls in Honour of Raija Sollamo* (eds. A. Voitila and J. Jokiranta; JSJSup 126; Leiden: Brill, 2008), 27–51.

Treat, J.C., "Lost Keys: Text and Interpretation of Old Greek Song of Songs and its Earliest Manuscripts Witness" (PhD diss., University of Pennsylvania, 1996).

Cécile Dogniez

13–17.1.1.3 Qohelet

13–17.1.1.3.1 Background

Ἐκκλησιάστης "Ecclesiast" is derived from ἐκκλησία "assembly." This translation of the original Hebrew name Qohelet (Qoh 1:1), itself a word of uncertain origin, is thought to designate a member of the assembly or, more likely, the one who speaks publicly, and whom Jerome refers to as the *contionator*, i.e., the "preacher." Consisting of "sayings" (ῥήματα), this peculiar book expounds the teaching of the Ecclesiast, the result of a somewhat disillusioned wisdom. Long the subject of discussion, its inclusion in the Jewish canon (→ 1.1.2.1.4) took place at a late date. Qohelet was finally integrated into the Megilloth. In the Greek Bible, Ecclesiastes was in-

---

[8] On this subject, see Ausloos and Lemmelijn, "Rendering Love," 43–61; Lemmelijn, "Flora in Cantico Canticorum," 27–51.
[9] E. Tov, "Three Manuscripts (Abbreviated Texts?) of Canticles from Qumran Cave 4," *JJS* 46 (1995): 88–111 (100, 104).
[10] Cf. Tov, "Three Manuscripts," 41.
[11] Auwers, "Le traducteur grec a-t-il allégorisé," 161–68.

serted after Proverbs and before Canticles, while the other three of the Five Scrolls are placed elsewhere.

13–17.1.1.3.2 Original Form

Barthélemy[1] viewed the Greek translation of Ecclesiastes as the work of Aquila in the early second century C.E. Since then, however, the attribution of the Greek Ecclesiastes to Aquila has been challenged.[2] Scholars now prefer to speak of a school that predates Aquila and is linked to the *kaige*-Theodotion group, which is currently dated to the first century C.E. (→ 1.3.1.2.4). The problem of the Hexaplaric materials attributed to Aquila with regard to Qohelet remains a complex issue.[3]

13–17.1.1.3.3 Translation Character, Translation Technique

The Greek translation of Ecclesiastes, the last of all the books of the Septuagint to have been translated, is extremely literal and adopts a stereotyped rendering of the Hebrew vocabulary and syntax, so much so that entire passages are sometimes difficult to understand for a Greek speaker with no knowledge of Hebrew. Through its rigorous adherence to the original text, this translation technique introduces a certain degree of crudeness into the Greek. Thus, typical aspects of Aquila's technique such as the systematic rendering of the accusative particle את with the preposition σύν "with,"[4] the regular translation of the preposition ל "for" as ἐν "in,"[5] or the absence – out of respect for the Hebrew – of articles in the Greek of Qohelet[6] (even when the Greek language requires one) are all part of this formal correspondence between the Greek and the Hebrew (→ 1.3.1.2.4). The same holds true for the persistent rendering of גם "also" as καί γε "and even," one of the characteristic features of the *kaige* group.[7] The standardization of the vocabulary is also an aspect of this trend to literalness, as in the choice of σοφία for חכמה (both meaning "wisdom"), σοφός for חכם (both meaning "wise"), ἥλιος for שמש (both meaning "sun"), or ἀγαθός for טוב (both meaning "good"), or of rarer words such as ματαιότης "vanity" for הבל "absurd" or μόχθος for עמל, both meaning "toil." Instances of homophony are not uncommon and have, in the eyes of some, less to do with interpretation than with literalness.[8] However, the translator makes skillful use of the possibilities offered by the Greek language by creating rhetorical and poetic effects[9] and, for instance, by playing on verbal prefixes in order to convey the meaning of the diversity of Hebrew roots with the help of composite Greek verbs.[10] Furthermore, a particular type of philosophical or moral vocabulary pertaining, among other things, to "knowledge" (γνῶσις or ἐπιστήμη), "choice" (προαίρεσις), and "courage" (ἀνδρεία) doubtlessly lends this Jewish translation a Hellenistic flair that evokes both the Greek philosophical tradition and the historical reality of the times.[11]

---

[1] Barthélemy, *Devanciers*, 21–33.

[2] See Hyvärinen, *Die Übersetzung von Aquila*, 99; J. Jarick, "Aquila's Kohelet," *Textus* 15 (1990): 131–39; P. Gentry, "The Relationship of Aquila and Theodotion to the Old Greek of Ecclesiastes in the Marginal Notes of the Syro-Hexapla," *Aramaic Studies* 2 (2004): 63–84.

[3] See Barthélemy, *Devanciers*, 22–30; P. Gentry, "Hexaplaric Materials in Ecclesiastes and the Role of the Syro-Hexapla," *Aramaic Studies* 1 (2003): 5–28; P. Marshall, "A Critical Edition of the Hexaplaric Fragments of Ecclesiastes" (PhD diss., Southern Baptist Theological Seminary, 2007).

[4] See Barthélemy, *Devanciers*, 15–26; J. Ziegler, "Die Wiedergabe der nota accusativi 'et, 'aet- mit σύν," *ZAW* 100 (1988): 222–23.

[5] See, e.g., Vinel, *L'Ecclésiaste*, 51.

[6] On this point, see J. Ziegler, "Der Gebrauch des Artikels in der Septuaginta des Ecclesiastes," in *Studien zur Septuaginta: Robert Hanhart zu Ehren aus Anlaß seines 65. Geburtstages* (eds. D. Fraenkel, U. Quast, and W. Wevers; MSU 20; Göttingen: Vandenhoeck & Ruprecht 1990), 83–120.

[7] See, e.g., Barthélemy, *Devanciers*, 32–33; P.J. Gentry, "Ecclesiast," **NETS*, 648–56 (649).

[8] See Vinel, *L'Ecclésiaste*, 56–57.

[9] See J.K. Aitken, "Rhetoric and Poetry in Greek Ecclesiastes," *BIOSCS* 38 (2005): 55–77.

[10] See Vinel, *L'Ecclésiaste*, 59.

[11] See, e.g., G. Bertram, "Hebräischer und griechischer Qohelet: Ein Beitrag zur Theologie der hellenistischen Bibel," *ZAW* 64 (1952): 26–49; Vinel, *L'Ecclésiaste*, 81–83.

13–17.1.1.3.4 Text-Critical Value

In view of this extreme respect for the original text, which was probably very close to that of MT (→ 15.2.2), discrepancies between the Hebrew and the Greek are rare: examples include the addition of Ισραηλ "Israel" in Qoh 1:1, the repetition of οἶδεν "he knows" in Qoh 8:1a, or of καρδία "heart" in Qoh 9:1, the doublets in Qoh 2:15 and 7:22, or the divergences in Qoh 1:18 or 2:12c, which may be explained by alternative consonantal readings or vocalization (in Qoh 7:19, e.g., 4QQoh[a] [→ 15.2.1.1; → 15.2.3.1] is concordant with LXX). In certain cases, some have indeed suspected the existence of a different Hebrew substratum that was deliberately altered at a later date.[12] But in reality, as for instance in the case of הוללות "madness" in Qoh 1:17 (which corresponds to παραβολάς "derangements" in LXX),[13] there is no compelling reason to question the originality of MT.[14]

Barthélemy, *Devanciers.
Gentry, P., "Special Problems in the Septuagint Text History of Ecclesiastes," in *XIII Congress of International Organization for Septuagint and Cognate Studies: Ljubljana, 2007* (ed. M.K.H. Peters; SBLSCS 55; Atlanta: Scholars Press, 2008), 133–53.
Gentry, P., "Issues in the Text-History of LXX Ecclesiastes," in Karrer–Kraus, *Septuaginta 2010*, 201–22.
Hyvärinen, K., *Die Übersetzung von Aquila* (ConBOT 10; Lund: LiberLäromedel-Gleerup, 1977).
Jarick, J., *A Comprehensive Bilingual Concordance of the Hebrew and Greek Texts of Ecclesiastes* (SBLSCS 36; Atlanta: Scholars Press, 1993).
Vinel, F., *L'Ecclésiaste: traduction du texte grec de la Septante, introduction et notes* (*Bible d'Alexandrie* 18; Paris: Cerf, 2002).
Yi, Y.Y., "Translation Technique of the Greek Ecclesiastes" (PhD diss., Southern Baptist Theological Seminary, 2005).

Cécile Dogniez

13–17.1.1.4 Lamentations
13–17.1.1.4.1 Background

In LXX, Lamentations is attached to the prophetic book of Jeremiah (→ 7.3) along with Baruch (→ 11.2.1.2) and the Letter of Jeremiah (→ 11.2.4.2), whereas the Hebrew Bible includes it among the Writings (Ketuvim), as one of the five Megilloth read during the five major Jewish festivals. The preamble, which is found solely in the Greek text, is indeed explicit in assigning the authorship of this lamentation over the destruction of Jerusalem and the deportation of its inhabitants to Jeremiah.

13–17.1.1.4.2 Original Form, Editions

In MT (→ 16.2.2), the Lamentations appear in acrostic form. Most manuscripts of the Greek Bible, with the exception of those stemming from the Antiochene tradition, bear the names of the Hebrew letters transliterated in Greek letters at the beginning of each stanza. The editors Rahlfs[1] and Ziegler[2] did not reproduce these alphabetical markers, although they would appear to have been placed there by the translator himself, as postulated by Pietersma.[3]

Two groups may be distinguished within the manuscripts that preserve the Greek text of Lamentations: one is represented by codex LXX[B], upon which Ziegler based his edition;[4] according to Barthélemy,[5] this textual witness of the ancient LXX should be seen less as a revision and rather as a translation issuing from the *kaige* group, which

---

[12] See Y.A.P. Goldman, "Le texte massorétique de Qohelet: Témoin d'un compromis théologique entre les 'disciples des Sages' (Qo 7,23–24; 8, 1; 7, 19)," in *Sôfer Mahîr: Essays in Honour of Adrian Schenker Offered by Editors of Biblia Hebraica Quinta* (eds. Y.A.P. Goldman, A. van der Kooij, and R.D. Weis; VTSup 110; Leiden: Brill, 2006), 69–93.

[13] See Y.A.P. Goldman in the apparatus of the *BHQ 18*, 26.

[14] See J.D. Meade and P.J. Gentry, "Evaluating Evaluations: The Commentary of BHQ and the Problem of הוללות in Ecclesiastes 1:17," in *Sophia-Paideia: Sapienza e educatione (Sir 1,27): Miscellanea di studi offerti in onore del prof. Don Mario Cimosa* (eds. G. Bonney and R. Vicent; Rome: LAS, 2012), 197–217.

[1] Rahlfs, *Septuaginta.
[2] J. Ziegler, *Ieremias, Baruch, Threni, Epistula Ieremiae* (3rd ed.; Septuaginta Vetus Testamentum Graecum 15; Göttingen: Vandenhoeck & Ruprecht, 2006).
[3] Pietersma, "The Acrostic Poems."
[4] Ziegler, *Threni*.
[5] Barthélemy, *Devanciers*, 33–34, 158–60.

is closely linked to Theodotion, and realized in Palestine around the turn of the era (→ 1.3.1.2.3.3). The second group, or Antiochene recension (→ 13–17.1.6), presents itself both as an Atticizing stylistic revision and as a text exhibiting the strong influence of Jewish oral tradition;[6] it is a long text with verses that are not included in LXX[B] (Lam 3:22–24, 29), but which appear to be original.[7] Referring to Lamentations, Origen states that the translations of Aquila and Theodotion are missing and that the only ones available are those of Symmachus and LXX;[8] in reality, however, the translation of the *kaige*-Th group is actually the ancient LXX, though probably not the work of Theodotion,[9] in spite of certain lexical similarities.

13–17.1.1.4.3 Translation Character, Translation Technique

The Greek text of Lamentations is generally considered to be a very literal translation of the Hebrew, not only in terms of the order, number, and sequence of words but also with regard to the copying of the syntax, be it, e.g., in the translation of the article, the construct state, or the infinitive construct, or in the usage of certain Hebrew prepositions. However, it still appears advisable to adopt a nuanced view of this literality, which is not systematic.[10] The translator does not exhibit a mechanical approach to the translation that would prevent him from rendering the Hebrew meaning;[11] when confronted with a difficult Hebrew, as for instance in Lam 5:10 and 5:13, he gives his own interpretation.[12] In the same manner as Canticles and Ruth, the translation of Lamentations displays a certain number of features that are characteristic of the *kaige* group: those, but *not all* of those mentioned by Barthélemy,[13] e.g., the rendering of גם "also" as καί γε "and even" in Lam 1:8; 2:9; 3:8; 4:3, 15, 21, of נצב Hi. "to set" as στηλοῦν "to set up a pillar" in Lam 3:12, of אין as οὐχ ὑπάρχει (both meaning "[there] is no one") in Lam 1:2; 5:3 or as οὐχ ἔστιν "(there) is no one" in Lam 1:9, 17; 2:9; 4:4; 5:8, but also characteristics attested elsewhere in the *kaige*-Th revision, such as the rendering of רדף as διώκειν (both meaning "to pursue") in Lam 1:6; 4:19; 5:5 or as καταδιώκειν "to pursue" in Lam 1:3; 3:66, of עון "iniquity" as ἀνομία "lawlessness" in Lam 4:6, 22, or of חרב as ῥομφαία (both meaning "sword") in Lam 2:21; 4:9; 5:9.[14] Generally speaking, this literality certainly does not hinder the translator of Lamentations from using a certain degree of literary license for the sake of the poem's intelligibility. Accordingly, he does not hesitate to provide it with new metaphors and to bring it up to date, but also strives to accentuate its signs of hope.[15]

13–17.1.1.4.4 Text-Critical Value

Except for the preamble that precedes the first lamentation, which is found only in the Greek version and which does not necessarily point to the existence of an original substrate,[16] the Greek translation of Lamentations reflects a Hebrew text that is very close to that of the well-preserved MT

---

[6] Cf. I. Assan-Dhôte, "Le texte antiochien du livre des Lamentations: tradition écrite, traditions orales," in *Selon les Septante: Hommage à Marguerite Harl* (eds. G. Dorival and O. Munnich; Paris: Cerf, 1995), 187–206.

[7] Cf. Pietersma, "The Acrostic Poems," 195–99.

[8] Origen, *Fragmenta in Lamentationes*, in *Klageliederkommentar* (ed. E. Klostermann; GCS 6; Leipzig: J.C. Hinrichs'sche Buchhandlung, 1901).

[9] See K.J. Youngblood, "The Character and Significance of LXX Lamentations," in *Great Is Thy Faithfulness: Reading Lamentations as Sacred Scripture* (eds. R.A. Parry and H.A. Thomas; Eugene: Pickwick, 2011), 64–69; P. Gentry, "Old Greek and Later Revisers: Can We Always Distinguish Them?" in *Scripture and Transition: Essays on Septuagint, Hebrew Bible, and Dead Sea Scrolls in Honour of Raija Sollamo* (eds. A. Voitila and J. Jokiranta; Leiden: Brill, 2008), 301–28 (327).

[10] See Kotzé, "The Greek Translation of Lamentations."

[11] As assumed by B. Albrektson, *Studies in the Text and*

Theology of the Book of Lamentations with a Critical Edition of the Peshitta Text (Studia Theologica Lundensia 21; Lund: Gleerup, 1963), 208–09.

[12] See G. Kotzé, "Two Difficult Passages in the Hebrew Texts of Lamentations 5: Text-Critical Analyses of the Greek translation," in *Text-Critical and Hermeneutical Studies in the Septuagint* (eds. J. Cook and H.J. Stipp; VTSup 157; Leiden: Brill, 2012), 275–95.

[13] See Barthélemy, *Devanciers*, 33–34, 60, 67.

[14] For further examples, see Assan-Dhôte, *Lamentations*, 155–57.

[15] See, e.g., Assan-Dhôte, *Lamentations*, 159–79.

[16] See, e.g., Assan-Dhôte, *Lamentations*, 130–34.

(→ 16.2.2), as generally evidenced by the Qumran fragments.[17] It should nevertheless be noted that the LXX readings "he brought it down" in Lam 1:13 (where MT presents difficulties) and "my eye" in Lam 1:16 are also attested in 4QLam (→ 16.2.1.2; → 16.2.3).

Assan-Dhôte, I. and J. Moatti-Fine, *Baruch, Lamentations, Lettre de Jérémie: Traduction du texte grec de la Septante, introduction et notes* (*Bible d'Alexandrie* 25.2; Paris: Cerf, 2005).

Barthélemy, *Devanciers*.

Kotzé, G., "The Greek Translation of Lamentations: Towards a More Nuanced View of its 'Literal' Character," in *Septuagint and Reception: Essays Prepared for the Association for the Study of the Septuagint in South Africa* (ed. J. Cook; VTSup 127; Leiden: Brill, 2009), 77–95.

Pietersma, A., "The Acrostic Poems of Lamentations in Greek Translation," in *Proceedings of the VIIIth Congress of the International Organization for Septuagtint and Cognate Studies: Paris, 1992* (eds. L. Greenspoon and O. Munnich; SBLSCS 41; Atlanta: Scholar Press, 1995), 183–201.

Cécile Dogniez

13–17.1.1.5 Esther

There are two Greek texts of the book of Esther. The Old Greek appears in all but four manuscripts and is also known as the Septuagint text. The Greek text found in manuscripts LXX[19, 93, 108, 319] is the so-called Alpha Text (AT).

13–17.1.1.5.A Old Greek Text of Esther
13–17.1.1.5.A.1 Witnesses[1]

The Old Greek (LXX) text of Esther (OG-Esth) appears in four uncial manuscripts (Codex Alexandrinus [LXX^A], Codex Vaticanus [LXX^B], Codex Friderico-Augustanus [LXX^S], and Codex Venetus [LXX^V]), in thirty-two minuscules (many of which offer a complete text) that have been collated only partially, in four additional manuscripts that have not been collated,[2] and in Papyrus Chester Beatty IX + X (LXX[967]). LXX[967] is the eldest witness, stemming from the third century C.E. It is noteworthy that it confirms the Old Greek text and that is does not witness to the second Greek text of Esther. The differences between the text of Codex Vaticanus and Papyrus 967 are rare and minor. There are some omissions that are clearly due to a technical error (*homoioteleuton*), some small explicative additions (e.g. the addition of the word "month," after "Nisa" in Esth 3:13) and some repetitions of articles. Although there are some readings in LXX[967] that look like pre-hexaplaric corrections to MT (such as omissions of the article), these readings are so minimal that one cannot conclude that LXX[967] already witnesses to a pre-hexaplaric recensional activity.[3]

13–17.1.1.5.A.2 Colophon and Additions

OG-Esth is the only book in the Septuagint that has a colophon at its end. It states that the preceding authentic and translated letter about Purim was brought to Egypt in the fourth year of the reign of Ptolemy and Cleopatra. There is discussion regarding the exact date, but at least it gives a *terminus ante quem* for OG-Esth: 78/77 B.C.E.[4] OG-Esth is characterized by its six additions,[5] which are positioned by Jerome at the end.[6] In the critical edition of OG-Esth by Hanhart, the additions are placed in their appropriate places in the running text and labeled with capital letters (see Table 1).

---

[17] See *DJD* III, V.

[1] For a full description of the witnesses, as well as a description of their textual character, see Hanhart, *Esther*, 7–99. For a further description of the witnesses, see also Rahlfs–Fraenkel, *Verzeichnis*.

[2] Fragments of OG-Esth also appear in five additional manuscripts that were only partly collated and in four more non-collated manuscripts. See Hanhart, *Esther*, 14.

[3] See Hanhart, *Esther*, 58–60.

[4] See Bickerman, "Colophon"; Bickerman, "Notes." See also, and upholding the 78 B.C.E. date, C. Cavalier, "Le 'colophone' d'Esther," *RB* 110 (2003): 167–77.

[5] Or seven, see below.

[6] See Weber and Gryson, *Vulgata* ad Esth 10:3.

TABLE 1 Position and Contents of the Additions

Hanhart	Vulgate	Position with Respect to MT	Content
A	Esth 11:2–12; 12:1–8	before Esth 1:1	Mordecai's dream
B	Esth 13:1–7	after Esth 3:13, before Esth 3:14	Haman's decree
	Esth 15:1–3	after Esth 4:8, before Esth 4:9	Supplement to Mordecai's alarm[7]
C	Esth 13:8–18	after Esth 4:17, before Add. D	Mordecai's prayer
	Esth 14:1–19		Esther's prayer
D	Esth 15:4–19	after Add. C, "before"[8] Esth 5:1	Esther in audience
E	Esth 16:1–24	after Esth 8:12, before Esth 8:13	Decree of Esther and Mordecai
F	Esth 10:4–13	after Esth 10:3	Dream explained
	Esth 11:1		Colophon

The two major critical editions of OG-Esth are: the Cambridge[9] and Göttingen editions[10] as well as Rahlfs–Hanhart, *Septuaginta*. These editions differ in their method of numbering the text as well as labeling and numbering the additions. Due to the fact that the Alpha Text occasionally summarises, shortens, and reorganises the text and that Hanhart, the editor of the Alpha Text, attempted to keep both the parallel numbering up with OG-Esther as well as to keep the principled of having at least a phrase in a verse, the numbering system of the Old Greek and the Alpha Text often differ slightly. For this reason, the editor added in brackets the chapter and verse numbering and the addition labeling.

As there are different editions of OG-Esth and AT-Esth in which there are different numbering and labeling of verses and additions, Table 2 might help in locating a specific verse in one of the editions.

The presence of the additions in OG-Esth has required scholars to deal with the issue of the original form of that book. The two main possibilities were: 1) an initial short form, as represented by the Masoretic Hebrew text; or 2) a longer Hebrew form, as represented by the Old Greek text, which was later abbreviated to form MT. The former hypothesis was formulated by Eichhorn in 1795,[11] the latter by de Rossi in 1782.[12] With the discoveries of the Dead Sea Scrolls, the hypothesis that there could have been another Hebrew text of the book of Esther came into vogue,[13] while at an earlier stage Torrey, in response to the 1940 Cambridge publication of the book of Esther, formulated the opinion that AT-Esth was a translation of an Aramaic text that was different from the Hebrew text.[14] Subsequently, research of the late twentieth and the twenty-first centuries has included reflections on the original language of the additions: Additions B and E are considered to have been written in Greek; Additions A, or part thereof, and F in Hebrew; Additions C and D are still under discussion.[15] Moreover, the original language of the additions is taken

---

[7] In the Roman Catholic traditions, a section of text in Esth 4:8 is labeled as a separate addition (C); thus, the numbering of the additions beyond Esth 4:8 differs and runs up to G in some Catholic studies.

[8] LXX does not contain a translation of Esth 5:1, but rewrote the first two verses of Esther 5.

[9] Brooke–McLean–Thackeray, *The Old Testament in Greek*, Vol. 3.1 (1940).

[10] Hanhart, *Esther*.

[11] Eichhorn, *Einleitung*, 689–704.

[12] De Rossi, *Specimen*, 117–36, 137–61.

[13] See below → 13–17.1.1.5.B.4.

[14] Torrey, "Esther."

[15] For a survey of the research on the additions, see De Troyer, "Letter." Kottsieper, "Zusätze," 117–21 distinguishes between two sets of additions. The first series is Esth A:1–11, C, and F:1–10, which have a Semitic background and were edited in order to fit with the rest of the (Aramaic) story. The second series of additions (Esth A:12–17, B, D:1–12, and E) must have existed in

TABLE 2   The Different Number Systems of the Additions in the Editions

MT	LXX Hanhart	AT Cambridge	AT Hanhart	AT Clines[16]	LXX Rahlfs–Hanhart
	A: 1–17	I:1–17	A:1–18	A:1–18	1:1a–1s?
1:1–22	1:1–22	II:1–21	1:1–21	2:1–21	1:S–1:22
2:1–23	2:1–23	III:1–18	2:1–18	3:1–18	2:1–23
3:1–15	3:1–13	IV:1–13	3:1–13	4:1–13	3:1–13
	B:1–7	IV:14–18	3:14–18	B:14–18	3:13a–g
	3:14–15	IV:19	03:19	04:19	3:14–15
4:1–17	4:1–17	V:1–12a	4:1–12	5:1–12a	4:1–17
	C:1–30	V:12b–29	4:12b–29	C:12b–29	4:17a–z
	D:1–16	VI:1–12	5:1–12	6:1–12	5:1:1a–f
5:1–14	5:3–14	VI:13–24	5:13–24	6:13–24	5:2(2a+b)–14
6:1–14	6:1–14	VII:1–23a	6:1–23	7:1–23	6:1–14
7:1–10	7:1–10	VII:23b	7:1–13a	8:1–13a	7:1–10
		VIII:13a			
8:1–17	8:1–12	VIII:13b–21	7:13b–21	8:13b–21	8:1–12
	E:1–24	VIII:22–32	7:22–32	E:22–32	8:12a–x
	8:13–17	VIII:33–38 (//15)	7:33–41	8:33–41	8:13–17
9:1–32	9:1–31	VIII:42 (//9:3)–49	7:42–49	8:42–49	9:1–32
10:1–3	10:1–3	VIII:50–52	7:50–52	8:50–52	10:1–3
	F:1–11	VIII:53–59	7:53–59	8:53–59	10:3a–l

into consideration in the discussion of the original shape of the book of Esther. More precisely, the question has centered on which of these additions might have been part of this different Hebrew *Vorlage* (→ 1.3.1.1.12).

13–17.1.1.5.A.3 Character of OG-Esth

After analyzing the translation technique of sections of OG-Esth, scholars have suggested that it is, aside from its additions, a translation of MT-Esth.[17]

Studies of the semantics, syntax, and style of OG-Esth in comparison with MT indeed confirm that it is based on a Hebrew text as witnessed by MT (→ 17.2.2). The character of OG-Esth in comparison with MT can be summarized as follows: The translator of OG-Esth was a careful translator who attempted to stay rather close to the Hebrew text, but also opted to find appropriate renderings, to be consistent, and more economic. Moreover, the translator made explicit what could have been implicit in the Hebrew text. Finally, the translator added additions to the text, some of which might have existed independently of the story of the book of Esther. More specifically, the translation can be characterized as follows:[18] 1) Most often, OG-Esth

---

the Diaspora and were added to the Greek text of the book of Esther. Traces of the editorial work connecting the latter series of additions can be found in D:13–15.

[16] Clines, *Esther Scroll* includes his own translation and numbering system.

[17] The following studies have sections with either an MT-OG-Esth presumption or a study of the translation technique of a particular chapter: Bardtke, *Zusätze*; Barthélemy, *Critique textuelle 1982*; Candido, *Ester*; Clines, *Esther*; Day, *Esther*; De Troyer, *Alpha Text*; Dorothy, *Esther*; Fox, *Redaction*; Kahana, *Septuagint*; Kossmann, *Esthernovelle*; Kottsieper, "Zusätze";

Moore, "Greek Text"; Moore, *Esther*; Moore, *Daniel*; Moore (ed.), *Studies*.

[18] See De Troyer and Wacker, "Esther: Das Buch Ester," 593–618 and De Troyer and Wacker, "Esther: Das Buch Ester (LXX und A-Text)," 1265–66.

follows the sequence of the verses of MT. Three verses of MT are not in the Old Greek (Esth 4:6; 9:5; 9:30). Occasionally, elements of a sentence have been moved but always retained within the immediate context (see, e.g., Esth 3:6–7 and 3:10–12); 2) OG-Esth has used more syntactical subordination structure than MT, which often uses co-ordinated syntax; 3) Often, OG-Esth has condensed two Hebrew words into one, especially when MT uses two nouns or verbs that are thematically linked (see, e.g., Esth 2:7, 8, 11, 20; 3:2 (2×), 5, 8; 4:5; 5:10; 7:6; 8:3, 14, 15; 9:24; similarly in Esth 9:12; 10:3); 4) Whereas MT only twice uses the expression "the city of Susa" (Esth 3:15; 8:15), Old Greek uses "the city of Susa" additionally for the translation of "the fortress Susa"; 5) Hebrew expressions in which a body part is used ("eyes": Esth 1:17, 21; 2:4, 9; 3:6, etc.; "face": Esth 1:10, 14; 4:5; 7:6, 8; 9:2; "hand": Esth 2:21; 3:6, 9; 6:9 [slightly different in Esth 6:2; 8:3]; 9:2, 10, 15, 16; "heart": Esth 6:6; 7:5) are rendered with a verb; 6) Whereas in MT the passive form or 3rd non-personal form is used to indicate actions or discourses of the king,[19] in the Old Greek the king speaks often in the 1st per. sg. and is addressed in the 2nd per. sg. (→ 1.3.1.1.12).

13–17.1.1.5.B Alpha Text of Esther

13–17.1.1.5.B.1 Witnesses and Editions

Whereas manuscripts LXX[19, 93, 108, 319] are the main witnesses for AT-Esth, it also appears in the mixed manuscript LXX[392].[20] Moreover, there are numerous similarities between AT-Esth and Josephus (→ 21.3) and/or VL (→ 13–17.2.1.5).[21] Scholars who defend the existence of a different Hebrew *Vorlage* underlying AT-Esth point to these similarities as proof of the existence of such a Hebrew *Vorlage*. I am of the opinion that VL and Josephus both knew and worked with AT-Esth.

Besides the Ussher edition of the text, there is also the de Lagarde edition, the Cambridge edition, and the Göttingen edition,[22] in which AT-Esth is printed together with OG-Esth.

13–17.1.1.5.B.2 Name

The Alpha Text of Esther (AT-Esth) received its name as its text was written as the first text of Esther (hence, alpha) in manuscript LXX[93], on folios 131ᵃ–136ᵇ (while OG-Esth appears on 180a–187b), and in manuscript LXX[108], namely on folios 488ᵃ–496ᵇ (with OG-Esth appearing on 496b–506b). This name was taken up in the first printed edition of the text by Ussher.[23] In 1890, Jacob mislabeled the second Greek text as "b-Text," a term that led to confusion (with, e.g., the text of Codex Vaticanus, labeled often as B).[24] As three of the four manuscripts in which AT-Esth has been handed down were Lucianic (LXX[19, 93, 108]), AT-Esth was also labeled Lucianic.[25] Finally, as the Lucianic text of 1–4 Kingdoms (1–2 Samuel; 1–2 Kings) and 1–2 Chronicles has been renamed Antiochene Text (AT)[26], the abbreviation AT-Esth could also be in-

---

[19] M.-T. Wacker, in De Troyer and Wacker, "Esther: Das Buch Ester," 1266, has labeled this a "passivum monarchicum."

[20] Manuscript LXX[392] is a compilation of the Old Greek and Alpha Text of Esther.

[21] See Motzo, "La storia del testo di Ester," 205–08; Motzo, "I testi greci di Ester," 223–31; Schildenberger, *Esther*; Haelewyck, "Lucianique."

[22] See above for the Cambridge and Göttingen editions. See also Ussher, *De Graeca* and de Lagarde, *Librorum Veteris Testamenti*.

[23] Ussher, *De Graeca*.

[24] B. Jacob, "Das Buch Esther bei den LXX," ZAW 10 (1890): 241–98. For a description of the confusion, see De Troyer, *Alpha Text*, 7–9.

[25] For instance, in the critical edition by Hanhart, the text is labeled "Der L-Text" (see Hanhart, *Esther*, 87–95) and indicated with L in the edition (in opposition to the o' text = OG-Esth). However, Hanhart specifies that one can only use the label "Lucianic" in the context of Esther in as far as AT-Esth is a text that could have been one of the *Vorlagen* used in the Lucianic recension (p. 94). Also note that the fourth manuscript in which AT-Esth is found is manuscript LXX[319] (also known as Vatopedi 600 – not 513, as printed in Hanhart, *Esther*, 15). Note also that manuscript LXX[93] offers the Old Greek version in nine textual gaps in the Alpha Text version of the text, five of which are in the additions.

[26] N. Fernández Marcos and J.R. Busto Saiz, *El Texto antioqueno de la Biblia griega*, Vol. 1: *1–2 Samuel* (with the collaboration of M.V. Spottorno Díaz-Caro and S.P. Cowe; Textos y estudios "Cardenal Cisneros" 50; Madrid: CSIC, 1989); N. Fernández Marcos and J.R. Busto Saiz, *El Texto antioqueno de la Biblia griega*, Vol. 2: *1–2 Reyes* (with the collaboration of M.V. Spottorno Díaz-Caro; Textos y estudios "Cardenal Cisneros" 53; Madrid: CSIC, 1992); N. Fernández Marcos and J.R. Busto

terpreted as indicating an Antiochene text of Esther.[27] In order to avoid confusion (AT standing for Alpha Text, Antiochene Text, and also, in German, for Altes Testament), it would be good to label the Alpha Text of Esther always as "Esther a," as in the edition of de Lagarde and the Cambridge edition.[28]

13–17.1.1.5.B.3 Character of the Alpha Test

The Alpha Text (A-Text) of Esther is not Antiochene since it does not share the characteristics of that text:[29] whereas the Antiochene text simplifies sentences, AT-Esth does not do so; also, whereas there are text additions in the Antiochene text, the additions in AT-Esth are far larger and atypical of the Antiochene text; also, the textual shortening as visible in AT-Esth (e.g., in Esther 2 and 9) is not typical of the Antiochene text. Moreover, text-historically, the Alpha Text cannot be an Antiochene text,[30] as usually in the historical books the Antiochene text uses the Hexapla, while in this case AT-Esth is used in the Hexapla.

13–17.1.1.5.B.4 Additions and Their Role in the Different Hypotheses, Especially in the Alpha Text

The additions, albeit with minor variations, are also part of AT-Esth, at least as it appears in the manuscript tradition; there are no Alpha Text manuscripts without the additions.[31] There is discussion, however, about the literary growth of the book and how the additions fit into the literary history.[32]

There are two main hypotheses with regard to AT-Esth: 1) It was a translation of a hitherto-unknown Hebrew *Vorlage* ([Torrey], Moore,[33] Clines, Fox, Macchi, etc.);[34] or 2) It was a revision of OG-Esth (Hanhart, De Troyer).[35] A compromise position is offered by Tov: the Alpha Text is a revision of the Old Greek, but it also had access to a different Hebrew text.[36] In my opinion, in a very limited number of cases, the Alpha Text may have revised towards the Hebrew text, namely where {Josephus = VL = AT} = MT and ≠ OG. However, these very minor recensional corrections are not corrections towards a hitherto-unknown Hebrew *Vorlage*, but towards MT (→ 1.3.1.1.12).[37]

Moreover, as Josephus (→ 21.3) and VL (→ 13–17.2.1.5) have knowledge of the second Greek text,[38] AT-Esth must have been available during the latter half of the first century C.E. Also, although there is no Esther text among the Dead Sea Scrolls, according to some scholars MT-Esth (→ 17.2.2) is quoted in the Dead Sea Scrolls.[39] However, there is no evidence among these scrolls of an older Hebrew text such as the one that is presumed to lay behind AT-Esth.

Bardtke, H., *Zusätze zu Esther* (*JSHRZ* 1.1: Historische und legendarische Erzählungen, 1; Gütersloh: Gütersloher Verlag, 1973).

---

[33] Torrey, "The Older Book of Esther"; Moore, *The Additions*, 153–252; Moore, *Esther*; Moore, "A Greek Witness"; C.A. Moore, "On the Origins of the LXX Additions to the Book of Esther," *JBL* 92 (1973): 382–93; Moore, "Greek Text." Moore can be credited with changing the Torrey hypothesis of an Aramaic book of Esther behind AT-Esth 2:1–8:17 or 21 – Cambridge numbering – into a different Hebrew *Vorlage* of the Alpha Text.

[34] Clines, *The Esther Scroll*; Fox, *The Redaction of the Books of Esther*; Macchi, *Le livre d'Esther*.

[35] Hanhart, *Esther*; De Troyer, *The End of the Alpha Text of Esther*; De Troyer, "The Letter of the King."

[36] Tov, "Lucianic Text"; Tov, *TCHB*, 318.

[37] Hanhart cautiously points to the possibility that an older tradition was available to the Alpha Text translator ("Verarbeitung anderer Überlieferung") where variants in AT-Esth (in comparison with OG-Esth) agree with Josephus or VL and are different from MT. Thus: {Josephus or VL = AT} ≠ MT and ≠ OG. See Hanhart, *Esther*, 91.

[38] Hanhart, *Esther*, 90–91.

[39] See Talmon, "Esther"; De Troyer, "Cave 4"; Lange, *Handbuch*, 497–502. See also → 17.2.1.

Saiz, *El Texto antioqueno de la Bibla griega*, Vol. 3: *1–2 Crónicas* (with the collaboration of M.V. Spottorno Díaz-Caro and S.P. Cowe; Textos y estudios "Cardenal Cisneros" 60; Madrid: CSIC, 1996).

[27] See below, → 13–17.1.1.5.B.3.

[28] De Lagarde, *Librorum veteris testameni*, 504–40; also Brooke–McLean–Thackeray, **The Old Testament in Greek*, Vol. 3.1. A good abbreviation for the text could also be: aT Esther.

[29] Hanhart, *Esther*, 92–93.

[30] Hanhart, *Esther*, 93–95.

[31] Note, however, that the manuscripts of the Alpha Text do not have the colophon (mentioned in → 13–17.1.1.5.A.2) that is typical for OG-Esth.

[32] See the publications by Candido, Clines, De Troyer, Fox, Kahana, Jobes, Kossmann, and Kottsieper mentioned in the bibliography.

Barthélemy, *Critique textuelle 1982.
Bickerman, E.J., "The Colophon of the Greek Book of Esther," *JBL* 63 (1944): 339–62.
Bickerman, E.J., "Notes on the Greek Book of Esther," *PAAJR* 20 (1950): 101–33.
Brooke–McLean–Thackeray, *The Old Testament in Greek*. Vol. 3.1: *Esther, Judith, Tobit* (London: Cambridge University Press, 1940).
Candido, D., *I Testi del Libro di Ester: Il caso dell'Introitus: TM 1,1–22 – LXX A1–17; 1,1–22 – Ta A1–18; 1,1–21* (AnBib 160; Rome: Editrice Pontificio Istituto Biblico, 2005).
Cavalier, C., "Le 'colophone' d' Esther," *RB* 110 (2003): 167–77.
Clines, D.J.A., *The Esther Scroll: The Story of the Story* (JSOTSup 30; Sheffield: Sheffield Academic Press, 1984).
Day, L., *Three Faces of a Queen: Characterization in the Books of Esther* (JSOTSup 186; Sheffield: Sheffield Academic Press, 1995).
Dorothy, C.V., *The Books of Esther: Structure, Genre and Textual Integrity* (JSOTSup 187; Sheffield: Sheffield Academic Press, 1997).
Eichhorn, J.-G., *Einleitung ins Alte Testament*, Vol. 2 (Leipzig: Weidmanns, 1781).
Fox, M.V., *The Redaction of the Books of Esther: On Reading Composite Texts* (SBLMS 40; Atlanta: SBL, 1991).
Haelewyck, J.-C., "Le texte dit 'Lucianique' du livre d' Esther: Son entendue et sa coherence," *Mus* 98 (1985): 5–44.
Hanhart, R., *Esther* (2nd ed. Septuaginta Vetus Testamentum Graecum 8.3; Göttingen: Vandenhoeck & Ruprecht, 1983).
Kahana, H., *Esther: Juxtaposition of the Septuagint Translation with the Hebrew Text* (CBET 40; Louvain: Peeters, 2005).
Kossmann, R., *Die Esthernovelle: Vom Erzählten zur Erzählung* (VTSup 79; Leiden: Brill, 1999).
Kottsieper, I., "Zusätze zu Ester," in O.H. Steck, R.G. Kratz, and I. Kottsieper, *Das Buch Baruch, Der Brief des Jeremia, Zusätze zu Ester und Daniel* (ATD-Apokryphen 5; Göttingen: Vandenhoeck & Ruprecht, 1998), 109–207.
de Lagarde, P.A., *Librorum Veteris Testamenti Canonicorum*: Part 1: *Graece* (Göttingen: Dietrich, 1883).
Macchi, J.-D., *Le livre d' Esther* (Commentaire de l' Ancien Testament; Genève: Labor et Fides, 2016).
Moore, C.A., "The Greek Text of Esther" (PhD diss., Johns Hopkins University, 1965).
Moore, C.A., "A Greek Witness to a Different Hebrew Text of Esther," *ZAW* 79 (1967): 351–58.
Moore, C.A., *Esther: Introduction, Translation and Notes* (AB 7B; New York: Doubleday, 1971).
Moore, C.A., *Daniel, Esther, and Jeremiah: The Additions: A New Translation with Introduction and Commentary* (AB 44; Garden City: Doubleday, 1977).
Moore, C.A. (ed.), *Studies in the Book of Esther* (Library of Biblical Studies; New York: Ktav, 1982).
Motzo, B., "La storia del testo di Ester," *Ricerche Religiose* 3 (1927): 205–08.
Motzo, B., "I testi greci di Ester," *SMSR* 6 (1930): 223–31.
Rahlfs–Fraenkel, *Verzeichnis.
Rahlfs–Hanhart, *Septuaginta.
de Rossi, G.B., *Specimen variorum lectionum sacri textus et chaldaica Estheris additamentis cum latina versione ac notis*, Part 4: *De Estheris additamentis, eorumque fide, auctore, primigeniis variisque codicibus* (Rome: Venantii Monaldnini, 1782).
Schildenberger, J., *Das Buch Esther*, in J. Schildenberger and A. Miller, *Die Bücher Tobias, Judith und Esther übersetzt und erklärt* (HSAT 4.3; Bonn, 1940).
Talmon, S., "Was the Book of Esther Known at Qumran?" *DSD* 2 (1995): 249–67.
Torrey, C.C., "The Older Book of Esther," *HTR* 37 (1944): 1–4.
Tov, E., "The Lucianic Text of the Canonical and Apocryphal Sections of Esther: A Rewritten Biblical Book," *Textus* 10 (1982): 1–25.
Tov, *TCHB.
De Troyer, K., *The End of the Alpha Text of Esther: Translation and Narrative Technique in MT 8:1–17, LXX 8:1–17 and AT 7:14–41* (SBLSCS 48; Atlanta: SBL, 2000).
De Troyer, K., "Once More the So-Called Esther Fragments of Cave 4," *RevQ* 19 (1999–2000): 401–22.
De Troyer, K., "The Letter of the King and the Letter of Mordecai: An Analysis of MT & LXX 8.9–13 and AT 7.33–38," *Textus* 21 (2002): 175–207.
De Troyer, K. and M.-T. Wacker, "Esther: Das Buch Ester," in *Septuaginta Deutsch.
De Troyer, K. and M.-T. Wacker, "Esther: Das Buch Ester (LXX und A-Text)," in *Septuaginta Deutsch, Erläuterungen*, 1253–96.
Ussher, J., *De Graeca Septuaginta interpretum versione syntagma cum libri Estherae editione origenica et vetere Graece altera, ex Arundelliana bibliotheca nunc primum in lucem producta* (London: J. Crook, 1655; Leipzig: Meyer, 1695).

Kristin De Troyer

13–17.1.2 Pre-Hexaplaric Greek Translations

13–17.1.2.1 Lamentations
See → 13–17.1.5.1 Lamentations (Five Scrolls > Primary Translations > Hexapla).

13–17.1.2.2 Ruth
See → 2.4.6 Hexaplaric Translations and Hexapla of the Octateuch (Pentateuch > Primary Translations).

13–17.1.2.3 Qoheleth
See → 13–17.1.5.3 Qoheleth (Five Scrolls > Primary Translations > Hexapla).

13–17.1.2.4 Canticles
See → 13–17.1.5.4 Canticles (Five Scrolls > Primary Translations > Hexapla).

13–17.1.2.5 Esther
See → 13–17.1.5.5 Esther (Five Scrolls > Primary Translations > Hexapla).

13–17.1.3 Targumim

The Targumim of the Five Scrolls are much more expansive than most other Targumim (→ 1.3.3), often incorporating extensive haggadic additions. The effect is to provide a new theological framework in which the biblical text is to be understood. The Five Targumim share a number of similarities in this respect: they emphasize God's control over Israel's history, they call the audience to study the law and be obedient to rabbinic practices, and they look towards the coming messianic age.

13–17.1.3.1 Background
The Targumim of the Five Scrolls are each as distinct as the biblical texts upon which they are based. However, they are worth considering together not only due to canonical tradition, but also because they share certain traits and characteristics such as origins, translation technique, and exegetical methods.

13–17.1.3.1.1 Liturgical Origins
The Five Scrolls have been considered as a unit for centuries within Judaism, but the collection and ordering of the scrolls is relatively late. *b. Ber.* 57b lists four of the five scrolls as a group, but the Leningrad Codex (1008/1009 C.E.) is the first known listing of all five as a group within the Writings. By the time of the Rabbinic Bible (1525 C.E.), the scrolls are listed together and in the order of the festivals with which the texts are associated.[1] These facts, coupled with the presence of ancient midrashic collections based upon these texts, strongly suggest that by the Geonic period communities were beginning to use these texts within their festal liturgy. The Targumim of the Five Scrolls would have developed at the same time. The Mishnah already suggests that a translation (Targum) of Esther was read at Purim (*m. Meg.* 4:4),[2] and once the Five Scrolls became associated with their relevant festivals, it seems likely that Targumim of these texts would have developed as well, either for reading in the service or for personal study (→ 1.3.3.5.2). The relatively short length of each text means that, while the biblical text would have been read *in toto* during services, its Targum would have been read with it as well. Each Targum also exhibits certain characteristics that are associated with liturgical use; they all contain extensive exegetical expansions at the beginning of the work and an exegetical agenda that is carried through the entire work.[3]

For example, Targum Lamentations expands the poetically terse biblical text of Lam 1:1–4 into a prolonged *Heilsgeschichte*. T-Lam 1:1 reads:

---

[1] They are: Song of Songs – Passover; Ruth – Shavuot; Lamentations – Tisha B'Av; Qohelet – Sukkoth; and Esther – Purim. For a detailed discussion, see Stemberger, "Die Megillot als Festlesungen der jüdischen Liturgie."

[2] It is unlikely that the translation the Mishnah references is exactly either of the two versions of Targum Esther that are extant today.

[3] As Shinan has pointed out with respect to the Pentateuchal Targumim, where larger exegetical expansions are found at the beginning or end of *sederim*, it is indicative of synagogal use. See Shinan, *The Aggadah in the Aramaic Targums*.

> *Jeremiah the Prophet and High Priest said, "How was it decreed that Jerusalem and her people should be punished with banishment and that they should be mourned with 'ekah. Just as when Adam and Eve were punished and expelled from the Garden of Eden and the Master of the Universe mourned them with 'ekah?" The Attribute of Justice replied and said, "Because of the greatness of her rebellious sin that was within her, thus she will* dwell alone *as a man plagued with leprosy upon his skin who sits alone. And* the city that was full *of crowds and many* peoples *has been emptied of them, and* she has become like a widow. She who was great among the nations and a ruler over provinces *that* had brought her tribute *has become lowly again and gives head tax to them from thereafter."*[4]

This extensive expansion continues through all four opening verses and sets the exegetical tone that is carried through the rest of the work (Israel has sinned; thus God was just in destroying Jerusalem and the temple).[5] The other Targumim of the Five Scrolls exhibit similar traits.[6] Targum Song of Songs, Targum Ruth, and Targum Esther II all open with significant expansions, and, in each of these cases, they include a list of ten items; each list ends with an eschatological figure or element.[7] Finally, Targum Qohelet too opens with extensive additions that provide a prolegomena for the work as a whole. In this case, the concern was to demonstrate authorship (Solomon) and inspiration. T-Qoh 1:2 reads:

> *When Solomon King of Israel saw through the holy spirit that the kingdom of Rehoboam his son would be divided with Jeroboam the son of Nebat and that Jerusalem and the Temple would be destroyed and the people of the household of Israel would go into exile,* he said *to himself,* "Vanity of vanities *is this world.* Vanity of vanities of everything *for which I and David my father labored.* All of it is vanity."[8]

13–17.1.3.1.2 Exegetical Character

These brief examples also serve to highlight another common characteristic of the Targumim of the Five Scrolls: they are extremely expansive. This led Sperber famously to remark, "These texts are not Targum-texts but Midrash-texts in the disguise of Targum."[9] Sperber's remark should be taken as hyperbole, but it contains some truth in it. These texts remain true to Targum in that they retain the form and function of a Targum, translating each Hebrew word found in the biblical text with an Aramaic equivalent and in order. There are double translations (as is evident in T-Lam 1:1). However, they are as rare as in other Targumim, and the Targumim of the Five Scrolls essentially follow the same principles of other Targumim. At the same time, the Targumim of the Five Scrolls do contain a *lot* of additional material alongside the translation of the Hebrew text. Some specific exegetical characteristics will be considered in the section on "Translation Character and Technique" (→ 13–17.1.3.3).[10]

13–17.1.3.1.3 Date and Language

Determining the date and language of the Targumim of the Five Scrolls is complicated by their multi-layered character. While each text is a unity unto itself, each shows evidence of development, most likely over centuries. There is general consensus, however, that they are all, in their current form, quite late, dating from the seventh to eighth centuries C.E.

Targum Song of Songs most likely dates to the seventh or eighth century C.E.[11] Targum Ruth in its final form also likely dates to the seventh or eighth century C.E., but Levine suggests that there

---

[4] The text in italics represents material added to the underlying biblical text. Thus, the text in plain type is considered by the translator to be the Aramaic equivalent for the Hebrew *Vorlage*. All translations of Targumic texts are the author's unless otherwise noted.

[5] Brady, "Targum Lamentations 1:1–4: A Theological Prologue."

[6] Brady, "Targum Lamentations 1:1–4: A Theological Prologue."

[7] Brady, "The Use of 'Eschatological Lists' within the Targumim of the Megilloth."

[8] Knobel, *The Targum of Qohelet*, 20.

[9] Sperber, *The Hagiographa: Transition from Translation to Midrash*, viii.

[10] Any study of the Targumim of the Five Scrolls should also consult the seminal work: Churgin, *Targum Ketuvim*.

[11] Alexander, *The Targum of Canticles*, 55.

are early, perhaps even pre-Mishnaic, Halakhic traditions in Targum Ruth.[12] Similarly, although Targum Lamentations contains early interpretive traditions, the Targum Lamentations that exists in our earliest manuscripts is certainly no earlier than the sixth century C.E. and most likely dates to the eighth century C.E.[13] The date of Targum Qohelet is most likely seventh century C.E.[14] Esther has two Targumim. Dating them is as difficult as any of the other Targumim of the Five Scrolls, but both Targumim to Esther are also to be dated to approximately the seventh century C.E.[15]

Again, while there is little clarity or certainty about the language of these Targumim, there is consensus that there are linguistic layers. For all six Targumim of the Five Scrolls (including the two of Esther) there are two primary manuscript traditions: Western (European) and Eastern (Yemenite). In most cases, the Western manuscripts seem to preserve an older tradition, whereas the Yemenite manuscripts, where they diverge, often have a simpler form.[16] Targum Qohelet and Targum Esther I and II are very similar in both traditions.[17]

Keeping in mind the complexity of the textual witness and that there is still much debate about the development of Aramaic dialects in late antiquity, there is a tentative consensus among scholars. These texts all seem to have a sub-stratum of Palestinian Aramaic that has then been adapted over the years so that there is a pastiche of Aramaic features. Alexander remarks of Targum Song of Songs that the "most significant feature about the Aramaic ... is its mixed character."[18] Similarly, Beattie concludes that "the language of the Targum [of Ruth] is a mixture of Palestinian Aramaic and 'official' or Babylonian forms such as are characteristic of the Targum of Onqelos."[19] Steve Kaufman and *CAL, on the other hand, classify all the Targumim of the Five Scrolls as Late Jewish Literary Aramaic.[20]

13–17.1.3.2 Manuscripts, Editions, and Translations

The introductions to *The Aramaic Bible* volumes pertaining to the Five Scrolls generally offer excellent summaries of the relevant extant manuscripts and their critical study. As noted above, there are two primary textual traditions, Western and Eastern, and there are many surviving manuscripts for each Targum. It is worth noting that the oldest manuscript that contains all Five Scrolls (albeit only Targum Esther Sheni) that is cited in most works as Sassoon 282 is, in fact, now known as Valmadonna Number 1 and currently is in the private collection of the Valmadonna Trust Library in London. A colophon at the end of the manuscript dates the work to 1189, and it is in the Western tradition. Many scholars of the Targumim of the Five Scrolls have preferred Paris manuscript Bibliothèque Nationale, Héb. 110 as the basis for their translations and studies.[21]

The earliest printed edition of the Targumim of the Five Scrolls is the Bomberg Rabbinic Bible dating to 1517 and edited by Felix Pratensis (*RB1). This represents a Western textual tradition, and recent scholarship has provided ample evidence that the manuscript that this text is based upon

---

[12] Levine, *Aramaic Version of Ruth*, 13.

[13] Brady, "The Date, Provenance, and Sitz im Leben of Targum Lamentations," *passim*.

[14] Knobel, *The Targum of Qohelet*, 15.

[15] See Grossfeld, *The Two Targums of Esther*, 19–21 and Ego, *Targum Scheni zu Ester: Übersetzung, Kommentar und theologische Deutung*, 21–25.

[16] With respect to Targum Lamentations, for example, Alexander ("The Textual Traditions of Targum Lamentations," 10) notes, "Of the two recensions ... West. is the older and Yem. the younger, in that West. takes us further back into the tradition."

[17] Van der Heide (*The Yemenite Tradition of the Targum of Lamentations*, 21) notes that the Yemenite tradition of Targum Esther, for example, "does not make a distinction between Targum Rishon and Targum Sheni, but has a mixture of both."

[18] Alexander, *The Targum of Canticles*, 9.

[19] Beattie, *The Targum of Ruth*, 10.

[20] *Comprehensive Aramaic Lexicon* (http://cal1.cn.huc.edu/text_browse.html; last accessed July, 2016). See also Cook, "Qumran Aramaic and Aramaic Dialectology," 19 and Cook, "Aramaic Language and Literature," 184.

[21] See Knobel, *The Targum of Qohelet*; Alexander, *The Targum of Canticles*; and Alexander, *The Targum of Lamentations*.

is Codex Solger ms 1–7.2⁰ in the Stadtbibliothek Nuremberg.[22] Levine's *The Targum to the Five Megillot* presents a facsimile edition of the manuscript Codex Urbinati 1, a thirteenth-century Western manuscript in excellent condition.[23] A notable modern edition where caution should be taken is Sperber's *The Bible in Aramaic*, vol. 4A: *The Hagiographa*.[24] The texts presented are a mix of readings, and the result is "a highly unsatisfactory hybrid text."[25] Levine's editions also ought to be used with care. Like Sperber's work, there is a convenience in the amount of material covered, but Levine's transcriptions and apparatus are full of errors and misattribution of sources.[26]

13–17.1.3.2.1 Song of Songs

Alexander's study of Targum Song of Songs presented in *The Aramaic Bible Series* vol. 17a is the most comprehensive to date and includes an English translation based upon the Paris manuscript Bibliothèque Nationale, Héb. 110.[27] For an examination of the Yemenite tradition, see Melamed's treatment from 1920–1921, which provides a diplomatic text based upon manuscript British Library Or. 1302 with reference to five other manuscripts.[28] Treat offers an English translation based upon Melamed's work.[29]

13–17.1.3.2.2 Ruth

Targum Ruth has received extensive treatment by Beattie. In addition to his volume in *The Aramaic Bible*,[30] he has produced what he calls "a preliminary edition" of the text.[31] It is a diplomatic text with manuscript Valmadonna 1 as the base text and readings from "the Antwerp and Paris polyglots, the readings recorded by Wright for the Dresden manuscript, and the passages quoted by Nathan ben Yechiel in his talmudic dictionary called the 'Arukh, since these constitute the earliest citations of the Targum of Ruth." Another older but still useful study is Levey's ordination thesis from 1934.[32]

13–17.1.3.2.3 Lamentations

Alexander based his translation and commentary of Targum Lamentations on the same Paris manuscript as he used for Targum Song of Songs, Bibliothèque Nationale, Héb. 110.[33] Brady's exegetical study *The Rabbinic Targum of Lamentations: Vindicating God* includes a transcription and translation of Codex Urbinati 1. The Yemenite tradition received extensive treatment by van der Heide in 1981 and includes a transcription and translation of manuscript British Library Or. 1476.[34]

13–17.1.3.2.4 Qohelet

The translation and study of Targum Qohelet by Knobel in *The Aramaic Bible Series* is based upon an eclectic text, not only using multiple manuscripts, but also using manuscripts from both the Western and Yemenite traditions: "It is a maximum text which sometimes provides more than one version of a particular verse."[35] This decision was based upon exegetical concerns rather than linguistic

---

[22] See Houtman, "Targum Isaiah according to Felix Pratensis," *passim*.

[23] Levine, *The Targum to the Five Megillot: Codex Vatican Urbinati 1*.

[24] Sperber, *The Hagiographa: Transition from Translation to Midrash*.

[25] Alexander, *The Targum of Canticles*, 4. Sperber's edition of Targum Lamentations, for example, is a pointed text based upon the Yemenite text of British Library Or. 2375, but Sperber (*The Hagiographa: Transition from Translation to Midrash*, viii) notes that "no attempt has been made in this volume to offer the texts published here in a critical edition."

[26] See, for example, Alexander's comments in *The Targum of Lamentations*, 2.

[27] Alexander, *The Targum of Canticles*, 1.

[28] Melamed, "The Targum to Canticles."

[29] Treat, *The Aramaic Targum to Song of Songs*.

[30] Beattie, *The Targum of Ruth*.

[31] Beattie, "The Targum Ruth: A Preliminary Edition." See also Beattie, *Jewish Exegesis of the Book of Ruth*; Beattie, "Ancient Elements in the Targum to Ruth"; Beattie, "The Yemenite Tradition of Targum Ruth"; and Beattie, "The Textual Tradition of Targum Ruth."

[32] Levey, "The Targum to the Book of Ruth."

[33] Alexander, *The Targum of Lamentations*.

[34] Van der Heide, *The Yemenite Tradition of the Targum of Lamentations: Critical Text and Analysis of the Variant Readings*.

[35] Knobel, *The Targum of Qohelet*, 2–3.

or stemmatological interests. Additional studies worthy of reference are by Taradach and Ferrer[36] as well as Díez Merino.[37]

13–17.1.3.2.5 Esther

There exist two Targumim to Esther, referred to as Targum Rishon (I) and Targum Sheni (II).[38] As with many of our other Targumim, manuscript Bibliothèque Nationale, Héb. 110 is considered one of the best representatives of the Western text, in this case, of Targum Esther I. Codex Solger ms 1–7.2⁰ and manuscript Valmadonna 1 are the best representations of Targum Esther II,[39] with Valmadonna 1 being the oldest attestation of Targum Esther II. For modern translations with annotations, see the publications of Ego and Grossfeld.[40]

13–17.1.3.3 Translation Character and Technique

The Targumim of the Five Scrolls follow the usual Targumic pattern of providing a word-for-word representation of the Hebrew text into Aramaic with additional material added to provide explanation of a problematic passage or to ensure that the audience would receive what the *meturgeman* felt was the proper interpretation.[41] As noted above, the Targumim of the Five Scrolls are, however, among the most paraphrastic of any of the Targumim. The amount of additional material included at times makes it quite difficult to discern which Aramaic term corresponds to its Hebrew counterpart, and Targum Song of Songs and Targum Esther II are particularly difficult in this respect.[42]

The result is that the Targumim's usefulness for text-critical work is mitigated. While in most cases a one-to-one correspondence can be recovered, one cannot always be certain of such an identification.

13–17.1.3.4 Relevance for Exegesis

Very often the Aramaic term chosen to represent the Hebrew was selected in order to provide what the *meturgeman* considered the theological rather than the linguistic equivalent. This translation strategy is the result of the fact that each of these Targumim has a sustained exegetical agenda carried throughout the text, unlike most other Targumim, and this approach is possibly due to the relatively short length of their base texts and was desirable because of their liturgical use. In each Targum of the Five Scrolls the *meturgeman* transforms the text in order to respond to perceived theological problems in the text. At the same time, there are certain themes that are introduced in each of the Targumim: God's control over Israel's history, the importance of doing good deeds, the obedience to Torah and the study of Mishnah, and the expectation of the messianic age.

13–17.1.3.4.1 Song of Songs

Perhaps one of the most problematic of all biblical texts, the Targum of the Song of Songs exemplifies particularly the sustained interpretation we find in the Targumim of the Five Scrolls. Alexander notes that "the Targumist offers a strikingly coherent reading of Canticles that imposes on the book a consistent and well-reasoned interpretation from beginning to end."[43] Following the usual rabbinic interpretation, the *meturgeman* understood the "Beloved" as God and the "Bride" as Israel. What is unique about Targum Song of Songs is its vigorously sustained reading of Song of Songs such that every translational decision is subordinate to

---

[36] Taradach and Ferrer, *Un targum de Qohélet: Ms. M-2 de Salamanca, editio princeps: texte araméen, traduction et commentaire critique*.

[37] Díez Merino, *Targum de Qohelet: Edición príncipe del Ms. Villa-Amil n. 5 de Alfonso de Zamora*.

[38] For discussion of the so-called "Third Targum" of Esther, see Grossfeld, *The Two Targums of Esther*, 23–25.

[39] Ego, *Targum Scheni zu Ester: Übersetzung, Kommentar und theologische Deutung*, 8–9.

[40] Ego, "God as the Ruler of History;" Grossfeld, *The Two Targums of Esther*.

[41] See Alexander, "Jewish Aramaic translations of Hebrew Scriptures," 225–28. for a discussion of the various translation techniques in the Targumim (→ 1.3.3.6).

[42] This is what Alexander ("Jewish Aramaic Translations of Hebrew Scriptures," 234–37) calls "Type B Targum." Cf. T-Cant 5:10–16.

[43] Alexander, *The Targum of Canticles*, 13.

its reading of the poem as the history of the relationship between God and his people.⁴⁴

Targum Song of Songs opens simply with "The Song of Songs, which is Solomon's." The *meturgeman* sets the exegetical stage by presenting a list of Ten Songs, beginning with the first song of Adam and concluding with the final song to be "recited by the children of the exile when they depart from their exiles," and Isa 30:29 is cited. The passage in the Targum begins:

> Songs and praises which Solomon, the prophet, the king of Israel, recited in the holy spirit before the Sovereign of all the World, the Lord.
> Ten songs were recited in this world; this song is the most excellent of them all.
> The first song was recited by Adam when his sin was forgiven him and the Sabbath day came and protected him. He opened his mouth and said: "A psalm, a song for the Sabbath day" (Ps 92:1).

This sample exemplifies the very midrashic characteristic of Targum Song of Songs. While it is fairly straightforward which Aramaic terms represent the Hebrew text, the *meturgeman* has not only expanded or embellished the text, he has used known midrashic traditions to do so and cited other biblical texts, something that is characteristic of midrashim, but not usually of Targumim.⁴⁵ After this introduction, the *meturgeman* carries this motif throughout the rest of the Targum, rarely with quite the same expansive fervor, but always furthering his exegetical agenda in a very disciplined manner. Other key elements include identifying Solomon as the author and asserting his prophetic status, the time in the wilderness with the reception of the Torah (T-Cant 1:9–2:7), and Israel's return to obedience to the Law and the Mishnah (T-Cant 5:10: "My pleasure is to worship that God who, wrapped by day in a robe white as snow, engages in [the study of] the Twenty Four Books [comprising] the Torah, the words of the Prophets, and the Writings, and [who] by night engages in [the study of all the Six Orders of the Mishnah"⁴⁶).

13–17.1.3.4.2 Ruth

The book of Ruth presents the obvious question of how a non-Israelite, and a Moabite at that, can be David's forebear. Answering this question occupies most rabbinic commentary on this book, and the Targum addresses the point in several ways, most notably by making Ruth the paragon of all proselytes. Targum Ruth is the least paraphrastic of the Targumim of the Five Scrolls, but as with Targum Song of Songs, it opens with a list of ten items, in this case fasts, the final of which will signal the messianic age. Ruth's statement of loyalty to Naomi in Ruth 1:16–17 in the Targum becomes a dialogue wherein Ruth demonstrates her willingness to become a proselyte. This is considered Ruth's true worth (rather than her loyalty to Naomi), and Boaz commends her for it. Boaz himself declares that Ruth is able to enter into the congregation of the Lord saying, "It has surely been told to me concerning the word of the sages that when the Lord decreed concerning them he did not decree against any but the men. And it was told to me by prophecy that there will come forth from you kings and prophets" (T-Ruth 2:11). The Targum also brings out the fact that from Ruth will come not just David, but the Messiah (T-Ruth 3:15).

13–17.1.3.4.3 Lamentations

Targum Lamentations has to address not only the difficulty of the destruction of the temple, but the very text of Lamentations itself. The biblical author, while often accepting responsibility for God's punishment due to sin, also asserts that God was the active agent in bringing about her downfall. Targum Lamentations seeks to tame such a theology while still asserting God's sovereignty. Thus, the first four verses of the Targum open with a *Heilsgeschichte* describing Israel's history of rebellion in order to justify God's punishment of Jerusalem. As with all poetry, the *meturgeman* has rendered the text into prose. Some unique aspects of Targum Lamenta-

---

⁴⁴ Alexander presents this quite clearly; see Alexander, *The Targum of Canticles*, 15.

⁴⁵ See Brady, "The Use of 'Eschatological Lists' within the Targumim of the Megilloth," 497–504.

⁴⁶ Alexander, *The Targum of Canticles*, 155–56.

tions are the rendering of the poetic "daughter" of Zion/Israel/house of Judah as the כנשתא "the congregation"[47] and already gruesome passages like Lam 1:15 that are made even more graphic and disturbing through "dramatic heightening."[48] The effect is to increase the pathos of the description of the historic events while extending the experience to the present "congregation" that was receiving the Targum, all the while underscoring the justice of God's actions and encouraging the audience to return to the study of Torah and Mishnah (T-Lam 2:19).

13–17.1.3.4.4 Qohelet

Ecclesiastes, Qohelet, is a challenging biblical text as it seems to suggest that being wise or foolish, faithful or wicked, makes little difference; all die in the end (Qoh 2:14). The *meturgeman* identifies Solomon as the inspired author and transforms this wisdom text so that it becomes a treatise on the value of the study of Torah and obedience to rabbinic principles in the expectation of "the day when the King Messiah will come" (T-Qoh 7:24). The biblical phrase "The heart of the wise inclines to the right, but the heart of a fool to the left" becomes "The heart of the sage is to acquire the Torah which is given by the right hand of the Lord, and the heart of the fool is to acquire possession of gold and silver" (T-Qoh 10:2).[49]

13–17.1.3.4.5 Esther

Both Targumim of Esther address the most unique trait of the biblical book, the lack of any reference to God. While Targum Esther I is often described as displaying more "standard" Targumic features in contrast with Targum Esther II, which includes significant haggadic additions with the underlying Hebrew equivalents "dissolved" throughout the text, both Targumim expand extensively on the base Hebrew text.[50] In both Targumim, it is made clear that the Lord is the designer of events and behind the circumstances that lead to Esther's role in saving her people. Both also depict Mordecai and Esther as obedient and faithful to the Law, even in the face of persecution.[51]

Alexander, P.S., "The Textual Tradition of Targum Lamentations," *AbrN* 24 (1986): 1–26.

Alexander, P.S., "Jewish Aramaic Translations of Hebrew Scriptures," in Mulder, **Mikra*, 217–53.

Alexander, P.S., *The Targum of Canticles* (ArBib 17A; Collegeville: T & T Clark, 2001).

Alexander, P.S., *The Targum of Lamentations* (ArBib 17B; Collegeville: Liturgical Press, 2007).

Beattie, D.R.G., *Jewish Exegesis of the Book of Ruth* (JSOTSup 2; Sheffield: Sheffield University, 1977).

Beattie, D.R.G., "Ancient Elements in the Targum to Ruth," in *Proceedings of the Ninth World Congress of Jewish Studies, Jerusalem, August 4–12, 1985*, Division A: *The Period of the Bible* (ed. M. Goshen-Gottstein; Jerusalem: World Union of Jewish Studies, 1986), 159–65.

Beattie, D.R.G., "The Yemenite Tradition of Targum Ruth," *JJS* 41 (1990): 49–55.

Beattie, D.R.G., *The Targum of Ruth* (ArBib 19; Collegeville: Liturgical Press, 1994).

Beattie, D.R.G., "The Textual Tradition of Targum Ruth," in *The Aramaic Bible: Targums in Their Historical Context* (eds. D.R.G. Beattie and M.J. McNamara; JSOTSup 166; Sheffield: Sheffield Academic Press, 1994), 340–48.

Beattie, D.R.G., "The Targum Ruth: A Preliminary Edition," in *Targum and Scripture: Studies in Aramaic Translations and Interpretations in Memory of Ernest G. Clarke* (ed. P.V.M. Flesher; Studies in Aramaic Interpretation of Scripture 2; Leiden: Brill, 2002), 231–90.

Brady, C.M.M., "The Date, Provenance, and Sitz im Leben of Targum Lamentations," *Journal of the Aramaic Bible* 1 (1999): 5–29.

Brady, C.M.M., "Targum Lamentations 1:1–4: A Theological Prologue," in *Targum and Scripture: Studies in Aramaic Translation and Interpretation in Memory of Ernest G. Clarke* (ed. P.V.M. Flesher; Studies in the Aramaic Interpretation of Scripture 2; Leiden: Brill, 2002), 175–83.

---

[47] Brady, *The Rabbinic Targum of Lamentations: Vindicating God*, 82–87.

[48] Brady, *The Rabbinic Targum of Lamentations: Vindicating God*, 66–82.

[49] Knobel, *The Targum of Qohelet*, 46–48.

[50] Grossfeld, *The Two Targums of Esther*, 8.

[51] For a summation of the exegetical themes in Targum Esther II, see Ego, "God as the Ruler of History: Main Thematic Motifs of the Interpretation of Megillat Esther in Targum Sheni."

Brady, C.M.M., *The Rabbinic Targum of Lamentations: Vindicating God* (Studies in the Aramaic Interpretation of Scripture 3; Leiden: Brill, 2003).

Brady, C.M.M., "The Use of 'Eschatological Lists' within the Targumim of the Megilloth," *JSJ* 40 (2009): 493–509.

Churgin, P., *Targum Ketuvim* (New York: Ḥorev, 1945). Online: http://hdl.handle.net/2027/uc1.b3379249.

Comprehensive Aramaic Lexicon. Online: http://cal1.cn.huc.edu.

Cook, E.M., "Qumran Aramaic and Aramaic Dialectology," in *Studies in Qumran Aramaic* (ed. T. Muraoka; AbrNSup 3; Leuven: Peeters, 1992), 1–21.

Cook, E.M., "Aramaic Language and Literature," *OEANE* 1:178–84.

Díez Merino, L., *Targum de Qohelet: Edición príncipe del Ms. Villa-Amil n. 5 de Alfonso de Zamora* (Bibliotheca hispana biblica 13; Madrid: Consejo Superior de Investigaciones Científicas Instituto "Francisco Suárez," 1987).

Ego, B., *Targum Scheni zu Ester: Übersetzung, Kommentar und theologische Deutung* (TSAJ 54; Tübingen: J.C.B. Mohr [Paul Siebeck], 1996).

Ego, B., "God as the Ruler of History: Main Thematic Motifs of the Interpretation of Megillat Esther in Targum Sheni," *Journal for the Aramaic Bible* 2 (2000): 189.

Grossfeld, B., *The Two Targums of Esther* (ArBib 18; Collegeville: Liturgical Press, 1991).

van der Heide, A., *The Yemenite Tradition of the Targum of Lamentations: Critical Text and Analysis of the Variant Readings* (StPB 32; Leiden: E.J. Brill, 1981).

Houtman, A., "Targum Isaiah According to Felix Pratensis," *Journal for the Aramaic Bible* 1 (1999): 191–202.

Knobel, P.S., *The Targum of Qohelet* (ArBib 15; Collegeville: Liturgical Press, 1991).

Levey, S.H., "The Targum to the Book of Ruth: Its Linguistic and Exegetical Character: Together with a Discussion of the Date, a Study of the Sources, and an Idiomatic English Translation" (Ordination Thesis, Hebrew Union College, 1934).

Levine, É., *Aramaic Version of Ruth* (Rome: Biblical Institute Press, 1973).

Levine, É., *The Targum to the Five Megillot: Codex Vatican Urbinati I* (Jerusalem: Makor, 1977).

Melamed, R.H., "The Targum to Canticles according to Six Yemen Mss. Compared with the 'Textus Receptus' (Ed. de Lagarde)," *JQR* New Series 10 (1919–1920): 377–410; 11 (1920–1921): 1–20; and 12 (1921–1922): 57–118.

Shinan, A., *The Aggadah in the Aramaic Targums to the Pentateuch* (2 vols.; Jerusalem: Makor, 1979), 30–38 [Hebr. with Eng. abstract].

Sperber, A., *The Hagiographa: Transition from Translation to Midrash* (vol. 4A of Sperber, *Bible in Aramaic*, 1992).

Stemberger, G., "Die Megillot als Festlesungen der jüdischen Liturgie," in *Das Fest: Jenseits des Alltags* (eds. I. Baldermann et al.; Jahrbuch für biblische Theologie 18; Neukirchen-Vluyn: Neukirchner, 2003), 261–76.

Taradach, M. and J. Ferrer, *Un targum de Qohélet: Ms. M-2 de Salamanca, editio princeps: texte araméen, traduction et commentaire critique* (Geneva: Labor et Fides, 1998).

Treat, J.C., *The Aramaic Targum to Song of Songs.* Online: http://www.sas.upenn.edu/~jtreat/song/targum/.

Christian Brady

13–17.1.4 Peshitta

13–17.1.4.1 Ruth

13–17.1.4.1.1 Background

Translated by the end of the second century C.E., the original text of the Peshiṭta version of Ruth (s-Ruth) – as far as such can be retrieved – represents a generally faithful rendering of the Hebrew text as represented by MT (→ 13.2.2); relatively minor adjustments away from a strictly "literal" rendering are evident throughout, attesting a consistent overarching desire to produce a version of the book that is both conceptually and idiomatically comprehensible to the Syriac reader as well as in which any semantic difficulties in the Hebrew *Vorlage* are resolved. At several points, the translator(s) appear to have taken recourse to LXX (→ 13–17.1.1.1), and in at least two instances (*ad* Ruth 1:21 and 2:4; see below) their word choice may suggest Jewish exegetical influence.

13–17.1.4.1.2 Text and Editions

As of 2016, the book of Ruth has not yet appeared in the Peshiṭta Institute's *Vetus Testamentum Syriace* (Leiden: Brill, 1977–); it is expected to be published before too long, thus fulfilling the urgent *desideratum* for a critical edition of this first in the series of four books otherwise comprising the Syriac canonical subdivision known as "The Book of

Women."[1] The *editio princeps* of s-Ruth was published in Le Jay's "Paris Polyglot" of 1645,[2] based primarily on manuscript Paris, Bibliothèque nationale syr. 6 (Ancien fonds 1 = s[17a5]), a relatively late (seventeenth century) and textually unreliable West Syriac witness.[3] This initial edition of Ruth was subsequently reproduced without any significant improvement by Walton (1655),[4] Lee (1823),[5] and Hübsch (1866; in vocalized Hebrew transcription),[6] though Walton did take the significant, albeit small, first step towards a critical presentation of s-Ruth by including Herbert Thorndike's scanty collation of variant readings (accompanied by a few brief text-critical comments) drawn from two manuscripts furnished respectively by James Ussher and Edward Pococke.[7] The text of s-Ruth appeared again in the editions of Urmia (1852)[8] and Mosul (1887),[9] which were based generally (i.e., for the Bible overall) on more reliable East Syriac witnesses; yet because these manuscripts are unspecified, and the method of their editing clearly uncritical, the text-critical value of these editions is insignificant.[10] The two giant steps that have been taken so far towards the presentation of a critical edition of s-Ruth (aside from the preparatory work currently being undertaken by the Peshitta Institute) are: 1) Ceriani's publication in 1883 of the second volume of his photolithographic reproduction of ms B. 21 Inferiore of the Ambrosian Library (Milan),[11] containing the oldest complete witness to s-Ruth (on folios 213ʳ–214ʳ);[12] and 2) Diettrich's publication in 1902 of a collation of all the variant readings in Ruth attested in five manuscripts dating from the ninth to the twelfth centuries.[13] Additional, potentially significant testimony to the text of s-Ruth are the quotations in pre-modern Syriac literature (→ 21.9), first and foremost in exegetical works containing specific treatments of the book, such as the commentary of Ishoʻdad of Merv,[14] the *scholia* of Gregory (Abu 'l-Faraj) Barhe-

---

[1] I.e., Ruth, Susanna (→ 11.3.3), Esther (→ 13–17.1.4.5), and Judith (→ 11.9.4), the order generally attested in those manuscripts (originally) containing the complete Peshitta Old Testament as well as in the separate Book of Women represented by the important early manuscript London, British Library Add. 14,652 (Peshitta Institute no. 6f1; the other separate Book of Women represented by manuscript Add. 14,447 [s[10f1]] of the same library lacks Ruth, strangely); see the Peshitta Institute's *List of Old Testament Peshitta Manuscripts* (Leiden: Brill, 1961), *passim*, and the supplement in *VT* 18 (1968): 130–32; and Haelewyck, "Le canon de l' Ancien Testament," 147.

[2] Le Jay, *Biblia*. While almost all the books of the Peshitta included therein were prepared by the Maronite Gabriel Sionita, s-Ruth was prepared by the Maronite Abraham Ecchelensis (see Bloch, "The Printed Texts," 136, n. 4).

[3] See Bloch, "The Printed Texts," 137–38.

[4] This is the date given in the colophon of vol. 2 of Walton, *Polyglotta*, in which s-Ruth appeared, pp. 181–93.

[5] S. Lee (ed.), *Vetus Testamentum Syriace: Eos tantum libros sistens qui in canone hebraico habentur, ordine vero, quoad fieri potuit, apud Syros usitato dispositos* (London: British and Foreign Bible Society, 1823), 477–80.

[6] A. Hübsch, *Die fünf Megilloth nebst dem syrischen Thargum genannt "Peschito": Zum ersten Male in hebräischer Quadratschrift mit Interpunktation edirt, ferner mit einem … Kommentare zum Thargum, mit sprachlichen Erläuterungen, Nachweisungen der verschiedenen Lesarten, Vergleichung mit andern alten Versionen, Erklärungen vieler thalmudischer und midraschischer Wörter und Sätze u. s. w.* (Prague: Druck von Senders und Brandeis, 1866), 1a–9a [Hebr.].

[7] In Walton, *Polyglotta*, vol. 6 (dated 1657), 21–22. For a critique of this collation, however, see Bloch, "The Printed Texts," 138 and the additional literature there cited.

[8] ܟܬܒܐ ܩܕܝܫܐ ܗ̇ ܟܬܒܐ ܕܕܝܬܩܐ [Vetus Testamentum Syriace et Neosyriace], 325–30.

[9] *Biblia sacra juxta versionem simplicem quae dicitur Pschitta*, vol. 1, 358–63.

[10] See, e.g., the assessments of Bloch, "The Printed Texts," 140–42, and Haefeli, *Die Peschitta des Alten Testamentes*, 66–70.

[11] A.M. Ceriani, *Translatio Syra Pescitto Veteris Testamenti ex codice Ambrosiano sec. fere VI, photolithographice edita*, vol. 2, *Epistola Jeremiae–ad finem* (Monumenta sacra et profana 6; Milan: Impensis Bibliothecae Ambrosianae, 1883).

[12] One *possibly* earlier witness to the text of s-Ruth is contained in manuscript London, British Library Add. 14,652 (= s[6f1]), folios 8ʳ–24ᵛ, though the text of Ruth 4:11–22 is missing. Aside from these two, forty-seven additional manuscript witnesses to s-Ruth are enumerated in the Peshitta Institute's *List of Old Testament Peshitta Manuscripts*, 104–5, with eleven more manuscript witnesses being identified in subsequent "Communications of the Peshitta Institute" published in *Vetus Testamentum* (i.e., manuscripts s[8g1], [10c4], [14c2], [14h1], [15a3], [16a1], [17m1], [19a1–4]; see *VT* 18 [1968]: 142; 27 [1977]: 509; 31 [1981]: 358).

[13] Diettrich, "Die Massora der östlichen und westlichen Syrer." The five manuscripts are s[9m1], [10m3], [11m2], [11m5], [12m2].

[14] In van den Eynde (ed.), *Commentaire d'Išoʻdad de Merv sur l'Ancien Testament*, 224–33; C. van den Eynde (trans.), *Commentaire d'Išoʻdad de Merv sur l'Ancien Testament*, Vol. 3.2:

braeus,[15] the anonymous East Syrian commentary in manuscript Diyarb.-Mos. 13 of the Chaldean Patriarchate of Mosul,[16] and the anonymous East Syrian *scholia* (viz., glossary of difficult words) edited by Hoffmann.[17]

13–17.1.4.1.3 Translation Character[18]

s-Ruth has been considered paraphrastic by previous scholars,[19] yet this assessment, in our view, is not quite fair. Generally speaking, the Syriac text – as represented by manuscript s7a1 and the collation of Diettrich – represents a close and faithful rendering of the Hebrew text as attested by MT (→ 13.2.2). Any deviations from a strictly "literal" rendering do not, for the most part, introduce absolutely "extraneous" information, but rather reflect the consistently applied strictures of good Syriac idiom and style, as well as the desire to present the reader with a semantically precise and logical text in which any ambiguities or difficulties in the Hebrew *Vorlage* have been resolved.[20] Hence, in addition to more intuitive – and, indeed, grammatically requisite – adjustments, such as in the gender of verbs (e.g., *ad* Ruth 1:8: ܚܒܕܬܝܢ "you have dealt," fem. pl., over against MT עֲשִׂיתֶם, masc. pl.) and pronominal suffixes (e.g., *ad* Ruth 1:8: ܚܡܟܝܢ "with you," fem. pl., over against MT עִמָּכֶם, masc. pl.; Ruth 1:13: ܠܗܘܢ "for them," masc. pl., over against MT לָהֶן, fem. pl.), the Syriac text also exhibits one-to-one *specification* (i.e., adopting a more specific lexeme where such may be reasonably inferred from the semantic range of a more general Hebrew lexeme, as *ad* Ruth 3:3:[21] ܘܐܨܛܒܬܝ "and adorn yourself" over against MT וְשַׂמְתְּ "and put on"), minimal *expansion* (likewise for the sake of specification or explanation, as *ad* Ruth 1:8: ܥܡ ܬܪܝܢ ܒܢܝ ܕܡܝܬܘ "with my two sons who died" over against MT עִם־הַמֵּתִים "with the dead" [masc. pl.]), and *condensation* or *reductive substitution* (as *ad* Ruth 1:7: ܐܪܥܐ ܕܡܥܡܪܗܝܢ "the land of their sojourning" over against MT הַמָּקוֹם אֲשֶׁר הָיְתָה־שָׁמָּה "the place where she was," in the rendering of which s-Ruth also attests *specification* [i.e., "land" for "place"] and contextual one-to-one *substitution* [i.e., fem. pl. for fem. sg.]).

More substantive adjustments than the aforementioned are relatively few, and in almost every instance they reflect a desire to avoid ambiguity and/or maintain logical consistency with the perceived context, as in the *omission* in Ruth 2:13 of the negative particle (s-Ruth: "I shall be as one of your servants," over against the contextually inconsistent reading of וְאָנֹכִי לֹא אֶהְיֶה וכו׳ as "and I

Livres des sessions (CSCO 230/Syr. 97; Louvain: Peeters, 1963), 267–76.

[15] Assuming that his *scholia* on Ruth – which, being so far unedited, we have not personally examined – are introduced by biblical citations, in keeping with his practice when introducing *scholia* on other books. The one brief *scholium* on Ruth offered by Theodore bar Koni contains no biblical citation; see A. Scher (ed.), *Theodorus bar Kōnī: Liber scholiorum, pars prior* (CSCO 55/Syr. 2.65; Paris: E Typographeo Reipublicae, 1910), 359.

[16] See the description of van den Eynde (trans.), *Commentaire d'Išoʿdad de Merv*, xxxv–xxxvi.

[17] In G. Hoffmann, *Opuscula nestoriana* (Paris: Maisonneuve et soc., 1880), 85–122. The *scholia* on Ruth are on 99 (l. 22)–100 (l. 2), the citations being: ܚܒܬܟܝ "your sister-in-law" (Ruth 1:15 [*bis*]), ܚܒܬܗ ܕܫܟܝܚ "(who) has (not) removed his kindness" (Ruth 2:20), ܗܘ ܓܒܪܢ "he is our kinsman" (Ruth 3:2), and ܛܝܒܘܬܟܝ "your kindness" (Ruth 3:10). The published editions agree with all of these (though we have been unable to check the Paris Polyglot), with the exception of manuscript s7a1 *ad* Ruth 3:2, which has the clearly erroneous form ܓܒܪܢܐ. The anonymous Syriac chronicle edited by J.-B. Chabot (Chronicon ad annum Christi 1234 pertinent [CSCO 81 Syr. 36; Paris: Gabalda, 1920]) also contains the complete text of Ruth (on which see M.D. Koster, "Peshitta Institute Communications II: Second Supplement of the List of the Old Testament Peshitta Manuscripts," *VT* 12 [1962]: 237–40 [237–38]).

[18] All citations from the text of s-Ruth are from Ceriani's photolithographic edition of manuscript s7a1, unless otherwise indicated.

[19] See Haefeli, *Die Peschitta des Alten Testamentes*, 28, and the sources cited there.

[20] On this perspective of the translation technique in the Peshiṭta generally and the text of Ruth in particular, see Weitzman, *The Syriac Version of the Old Testament*, 15–62, and in particular the examples from Ruth on pp. 23, 28, 34, and 121 (from which several of our own following examples are derived).

[21] So, as in all the printed editions, whereas in manuscript s7a1: ܘܐܨܛܒܬܝ "and adorn yourself," from which the omission of the silent *yod* (ܝ) is not necessarily an error (see T. Noldeke, *Compendious Syriac Grammar* [trans. J.A. Chrichton; London: Williams & Norgate, 1904], § 50B).

shall *not* be,"[22] etc.), the *addition* in Ruth 3:15, 17 of "measures" (ܟܝܠܢ) and in Ruth 2:8 of the phrase "in a proverb" (ܒܡܬܠܐ),[23] and the *expansion-substitution* in Ruth 1:22 of the seemingly redundant phrase הַשָּׁבָה מִשְּׂדֵי מוֹאָב ("who returned from the countryside of Moab"; s-Ruth: "who consented wholeheartedly to return [ܠܡܗܦܟ] with her, and they came [ܐܬܝ] from the land of Moab"). Theological sensitivity also seems to have had some influence on the Syriac translator(s), as in the *substitution* at Ruth 1:15 of "the house of her people" (ܒܝܬ ܥܡܗ) for "her gods" (MT אֱלֹהֶיהָ) – apparently to avoid the notion that Orpah was still a pagan – and at Ruth 2:4 of "Peace be with you" (ܫܠܡܐ ܥܡܟܘܢ) for "The LORD be with you" (MT יְהוָה עִמָּכֶם), in all likelihood reflecting both contemporary aversion to the use of the divine name in casual greeting as well as the early rabbinic tradition identifying "Peace" as a valid substitute.[24] In at least two instances, moreover, the extant text of s-Ruth attests a *doublet*, i.e., *ad* Ruth 1:13 ("for it is very embittering to me on your account *and* it is more bitter for me than for you") and *ad* Ruth 4:4 ("I said, 'I will open your ears and say to you: "Make the purchase in the presence of these who are seated!"' *and* I have presented myself to speak and to make the purchase in the presence of these elders of my people who are seated"). Rather than representing *double renderings* by the translator(s), however, these doublets may well reflect scribal interpolation of alternative renderings either drawn from the margins of their Syriac exemplar(s) or as known to them from other sources.[25]

The translator(s) also appear to have taken sporadic recourse to LXX (→ 13–17.1.1.1), as, e.g., in the rendering of שַׁעַר "gate" by ܫܒܛܐ "tribe" (corresponding to φυλή in LXX) in Ruth 3:11 and 4:10[26] but not in Ruth 4:1 and 11 (rendered literally by s ܬܪܥܐ and LXX πύλη), and, *ad* Ruth 4:15, in the rendering ܕܡܕܝܢܬܟ "your city," where MT has שֵׂיבָתֵךְ "your old age," reasonably suggesting the misreading of LXX πολιάν as πόλιν.[27] A thorough assessment of LXX influence on s-Ruth must, nonetheless, await the publication of a proper critical edition of the latter (→ 1.3.4.9).

13–17.1.4.1.4 Text-Critical Value

The text of s-Ruth as represented by manuscript s7a1 and the collation of Diettrich offer no clear evidence of a consonantal Hebrew *Vorlage* that – notwithstanding non-semantic orthographic differences – was any different from that represented by MT (→ 13.2.2). Of the twelve *Ketiv-Qere* distinctions in MT-Ruth, s-Ruth supports seven (i.e., *ad* Ruth 3:3 [*bis*], 4, 5, 12,[28] 17; 4:5) and offers no evidence either way for the remaining five (i.e., *ad* Ruth 1:8; 2:1; 3:14; 4:4, 6). In no instance, however, can one infer *consonantal* sup-

---

[22] Such appears to be the illogical alternative as perceived by the translator(s) of s-Ruth; the Hebrew text can also be understood in the contextually consistent sense: "*though* I *am* not as one of your maidservants."

[23] Weitzman (*The Syriac Version*, 34–35) considers this an example of "faulty translation," yet it seems to us just as reasonable – if not more so – to view this as an instance wherein the translator(s) sought to resolve a Biblical Hebrew idiom that, if translated literally, would have made little or no sense to the Syriac reader.

[24] See *b. t. Šabb.* 10b and Maimonides' comment on *m. Ber.* 9:5. In this instance we take a decidedly contrary view to that of Weitzman ("From Judaism to Christianity," 159; *The Syriac Version*, 238), who cites *m. Ber.* 9:5 as proof that the Syriac translator(s) here adopted a rendering that was clearly "sectarian" and forbidden by the rabbis. Yet this is a far too narrow reading of the mishnaic passage, for at no point therein do the rabbis actually *forbid* the substitution of "Peace" for the divine name; the validity of this substitution is in fact borne out by, *inter alia*, the aforecited talmudic tradition and Maimonides' comment ad loc.

[25] See J. Perles, *Meletemata peschitthoniana* (Breslau: W. Friedrich, 1859), 10–11.

[26] In this instance ܫܒܛܐ "tribe" also appears to encompass the following *nomen rectum* מקום "place"; this broader substitution is also attested in several minor LXX witnesses (*contra* the majority rendering of מקום "place" by either λαοῦ "people" or τόπου "place"; see Brooke–McLean, *The Old Testament in Greek*, Part 4: *Joshua, Judges, Ruth* [1917], ad loc.).

[27] See Abramowski, "Eine spätsyrische Überlieferung des Buches Ruth," 14–17; Weitzman, "From Judaism to Christianity," 159; Weitzman, *The Syriac Version*, 71–72.

[28] With respect to this instance we are somewhat tentative; we have included it insofar as the text of v. 12a in s-Ruth reads affirmatively, which *may* correspond to the omission of אם, yet s-Ruth offers no clear equivalent of the preceding כי, and it may be that the translator(s) simply ignored the troublesome collocation כי אם "(but) rather" entirely.

port for the *Qere* in the Hebrew *Vorlage* of s-Ruth, since all of those readings that support the *Qere* are reasonably implied by either context (Ruth 3:3 [*bis*], 4, 12; 4:5) or normative idiom (Ruth 3:5, 17). At least one possible vocalization variant, on the other hand, is suggested by the rendering of שדי in Ruth 1:21 as ܡܢ ܕܡܣܦܩ ܠܟܘܠ "The One who is Sufficient" (= שַׁדַּי over against MT שַׁדַּי "The Almighty"), which may well have been influenced by the LXX rendering ὁ ἱκανός "the Sufficient One," if not also by the early rabbinic tradition regarding this divine title as attested in (*inter alia*) Gen. Rab. 46.3.[29]

Abramowski, R., "Eine spätsyrische Überlieferung des Buches Ruth," in *In piam memoriam Alexander von Bulmerincq: Gedenkschrift zum 5. Juni 1938, dem siebzigsten Geburtstage des am 29. März 1938 Entschlafenen, dargebracht von einem Kreise von Freunden und Kollegen* (Abhandlungen der Herder-Gesellschaft und des Herder-Instituts zu Riga 6.3; Riga: Ernst Plates, 1938), 7–19.

Bloch, J., "The Printed Texts of the Peshitta Old Testament," *AJSL* 37 (1921): 136–44.

Diettrich, G., "Die Massora der östlichen und westlichen Syrer in ihren Angaben zum Buche Ruth nach fünf Handschriften," *ZAW* 22 (1902): 193–201.

van den Eynde, C. (ed.), *Commentaire d'Išoʿdad de Merv sur l'Ancien Testament*, Vol. 3.1: *Livres des sessions* (CSCO 229/Scriptores syri 96; Louvain: Peeters, 1962).

Haefeli, L., *Die Peschitta des Alten Testamentes: Mit Rücksicht auf ihre textkritische Bearbeitung und Herausgabe* (ATA 11.1; Münster i. W.: Aschendorff, 1927).

Haelewyck, J.-C., "Le canon de l'Ancien Testament dans la tradition syriaque (manuscrits bibliques, listes canoniques, auteurs)," in *L'Ancien Testament en syriaque* (eds. F. Briquel Chatonnet and P. Le Moigne; Études syriaques 5; Paris: Geuthner, 2008), 141–71.

Janichs, G., *Animadversiones criticae in versionem syriacam Peschitthonianam librorum Koheleth et Ruth* (Leipzig: Sumptibus H. Skutsch, 1869).

Weitzman, M.P., "From Judaism to Christianity: The Syriac Version of the Hebrew Bible," in *The Jews among Pagans and Christians in the Roman Empire* (eds. J. Lieu, J. North, and T. Rajak; London: Routledge, 1992), 147–73.

Weitzman, M.P., *The Syriac Version of the Old Testament* (University of Cambridge Oriental Publications 56; Cambridge: Cambridge University Press, 1999).

Michael G. Wechsler

13–17.1.4.2 Canticles

13–17.1.4.2.1 Manuscripts of s-Cant

The oldest manuscript of s-Cant is manuscript s[6h17] (sixth century C.E.). This manuscript, together with the complete Bibles, s[7a1] and s[8a1], probably preserves the oldest stage of the text to which we can gain access. The majority text or *textus receptus*, which is later, is attested by a large number of manuscripts of the Nestorian tradition, the best representatives of which are manuscripts s[9c1, 9h1, 10c1, 11c1] (ninth through eleventh centuries C.E.). Many of these manuscripts bring together the collection of books known as *Beth Mawtebhe* "Book of Sessions" (*c* in the nomenclature of the *Peshitta Institute*): Joshua, Judges, 1–2 Samuel, 1–2 Kings (→ 3–5.1.4), Proverbs (→ 12.3.4), Qohelet (→ 13–17.1.4.3), Ruth (→ 13–17.1.4.1), Canticles, Sirach (→ 11.4.4), and Job (→ 11.3.4). s-Cant is not preserved in s[9a1], which is important for other books due to the uniqueness of its variants.

13–17.1.4.2.2 Critical Edition

The critical edition of s-Cant is found in Vol. 2.5 of the collection *The Old Testament in Syriac according to the Peshitta*,[1] published by the *Peshitta Institute*. Its editors are J.A. Emerton and D.J. Lane. It is a diplomatic edition of manuscript s[7a1], accompanied by a critical apparatus that takes into account the manuscripts prior to the twelfth century.

Dirksen has offered a series of *corrigenda et addenda* to the critical edition of s-Cant on the basis of a study of the Syriac manuscripts.[2] In addition, he presents seven variants that are found in the critical apparatus and which should be preferred to the main text of the edition: Cant 1:7 (ܘܐܝܟܐ "and where"); Cant 2:5 (ܣܡܟܘܢܝ "sustain me"); Cant 2:8 (ܐܬܐ "he comes"); Cant 2:15 (ܐܚܘܕܘ "catch"); Cant 5:4 (ܙܥܘ "are moved"); Cant

---

[29] Cf. Weitzman, *The Syriac Version*, 51, 70, 121.

[1] Emerton and Lane, *Canticles*.
[2] Dirksen, "The Peshitta Text of Song of Songs," 171–83.

5:12 (ܝܘܢܐ "doves"); Cant 8:2 (ܘܠܩܝܛܘܢܐ "and into the chamber").³ Some of these variants are readings of s⁷ᵃ¹ that were discarded by the editors as errors and that Dirksen considers original readings.

13–17.1.4.2.3 Character of the Translation

The Syriac translation of s-Cant was made directly from an unvocalized Hebrew text close to the proto-Masoretic family (→ 14.2.2), probably in the second half of the second century C.E. Some of the differences between s-Cant and MT (shared or not with LXX [→ 13–17.1.1.2]) can be attributed precisely to a different vocalization of the same Hebrew *Vorlage* (cf. Cant 4:10 [דדיך] "your beloved ones"]; 5:16 [וכלו] "all of it"]; 7:13 [דדי] "my love"]). What we have is a version that is quite faithful to its original, though not slavishly so (it does not reproduce the ambiguities or difficulties of the original, but rather clarifies them).⁴

In some cases, especially when the Hebrew is difficult, s-Cant translates according to the sense, sometimes by turning to the immediate context rather than to the translation options of other versions such as LXX (cf. Cant 6:12). However, there are cases in which freedom in translating turns into a desire to follow the Hebrew text literally. This is the case with the translation of the particle את that marks the direct object, which is translated by s-Cant in four cases with the Syriac particle of the same function as ܠ (Cant 2:7; 3:4, 5; 8:4). Usually the Syriac omits this particle in translation. A translation like this one only appears in fourteen other cases in the Bible, eleven of them in s-Qoh (→ 13–17.1.4.3), a very literal version. If it is borne in mind that over the course of time translations tend to become more literal, s-Cant could belong to the last group of books translated, as late as the end of the second century C.E. The fact that it uses some Greek loanwords supports this late dating.⁵

In other cases, s-Cant confuses the roots of some Hebrew words. Thus, in Cant 4:1, 3, and 6:7, it derives לצמתך "for your veil" from the root צמת "silence," and not from צמה "veil." In Cant 6:4, כתרצה "as Tirzah" has been derived from the verb רצה (= ܪܥܐ) "to take pleasure," and not from the place name *Tirṣah*. The same happens with a good number of proper names, which do not appear to have been understood by the translator (in Cant 2:1, "Sharon" is translated as "cypresses"). On occasion, the error may be attributable to an "inner-Syriac corruption" that came about early in the process of manuscript transmission. This seems to be the case with the reading ܐܡܪܝ "my lambs" in Cant 8:1, which in Hebrew is אמי "my mother."⁶ The original translation was probably ܐܡܝ "my mother," which erroneously became ܐܡܪܝ "my lamb" (s⁶ʰ¹⁷) and then ܐܡܪܝ "my lambs."

s-Cant frequently changes the Hebrew syntax in agreement with the structure of the Syriac language or in order to clarify a Hebrew formulation that could turn out to be ambiguous (cf. Cant 1:8; 2:11; 2:15; 5:12). As in other books of the Peshitta, s-Cant does not follow its Hebrew *Vorlage* in its use of the conjunctive *waw* "and." Lane points out that although the Syriac translation was unable to express all the poetry of the original, even so "it has its own rhythms and attractiveness. It is not leaden or pedestrian."⁷ In Cant 2:1; 2:13; 4:10; and 6:9, s-Cant uses resources such as "formula and repetition," that are not found in the original, in order to obtain a poetic effect.⁸ Van Wyk attributes this to the limited vocabulary of the Peshitta (repeating the same root),⁹ while Lane considers it a stylistic device.

13–17.1.4.2.4 Influence of LXX on s-Cant

A much-discussed question in research on the Peshitta (→ 1.3.4.9) is the possible influence of the LXX version (→ 13–17.1.1.2). However, unlike other books, researchers of s-Cant have not seen clear

---

³ Dirksen, "The Peshitta Text of Song of Songs," 181.
⁴ Bloch, "A Critical Examination of the Text of the Syriac Version of the Song of Songs," 103–39 (135).
⁵ Salvesen, "Pigs in the Camps," 260–73 (262).

⁶ Salvesen, "Pigs in the Camps," 263.
⁷ Lane, "The Curtains of Solomon," 73–84 (73).
⁸ Lane, "The Curtains of Solomon," 81–82.
⁹ Van Wyk, "The Peshitta of the Song of Songs," 181–89 (183).

signs of this influence.[10] Some speak of the sporadic use of the Greek version on the part of the translator, especially in places in which the Hebrew is difficult. Weitzmann thinks that the interpretation of צמתך "your veil" in Cant 4:1, 3 and 6:7, shared by LXX and s-Cant as "your silence," must be an instance of literary dependence of the Syriac version on the Greek.[11] However, van Wyk, Dirksen, and Salvesen think that the two versions arrived at the same translation independently.[12] Salvesen offers other examples in which readings common to LXX and s-Cant that depart from MT (→ 14.2.2) can be attributed to a stream of Jewish interpretation of the text that reached both translations independently.[13]

Bloch considers that the coincidence of readings between LXX and s-Cant "is due to later ages having corrupted the Peshitta by consciously adopting some of the translations of the LXX."[14] This hypothesis was verified by Lane in the first study that takes into account the different manuscripts of s-Cant. In it, he has shown the way many variants have been introduced into the manuscript tradition due to the influence of the Greek version of LXX, which enjoyed great prestige in the Syriac Church.[15]

13–17.1.4.2.5 Auxiliary Tools

We presently have a concordance of the Syriac terms of s-Cant and the rest of the *Beth Mawtebhe* books edited by Strothmann, Zumpe, and Johannes in six volumes in the series *Göttingen Orientforschungen*.

Bloch, J., "A Critical Examination of the Text of the Syriac Version of the Song of Songs," *AJSL* 38 (1921/1922): 103–39.

Dirksen, P.B., "The Peshitta Text of Song of Songs," *Textus* 19 (1998): 171–83.

Emerton, J.A., "The Printed Editions of the Song of Songs in the Peshitta Version," *VT* 17 (1967): 416–29.

Emerton, J.A. and D.J. Lane (eds.), *Canticles* (The Old Testament in Syriac according to the Peshitta Version 2.5; Leiden: Brill, 1979).

Euringer, S., "Die Bedeutung der Peschitto für die Textkritik des Hohenliedes," in *Vom Münchener Gelehrten-Kongresse: Biblische Vorträge* (ed. O. Bardenhewer; BibS[F] 6; Freiburg: Herder, 1901), 117–28.

Lane, D.J., "'The Curtains of Solomon': Some Notes on the 'Syriacing' of Šir-Haššîrîm," in *The Peshitta as a Translation: Papers Read at the II Peshitta Symposium, Held at Leiden, 19–21 August 1993* (eds. P.B. Dirksen and A. van der Kooij; Monographs of the Peshitta Institute Leiden 8; Leiden: Brill, 1995), 73–84.

Salkind, J.M., *Die Peschitta zu Schir-Haschirim textkritisch in ihrem Verhältnisse zu MT. und LXX. untersucht* (Leiden: Brill, 1905).

Salvesen, A., "Pigs in the Camps and the Breast of my Lambs: Song of Songs in the Syriac Tradition," in *Perspectives on the Song of Songs/Perspektiven der Hoheliedauslegung* (ed. A.C. Hagedorn; BZAW 346; Berlin: De Gruyter, 2005), 260–73.

Strothmann, W., M. Zumpe, and K. Johannes, *Konkordanz zur syrischen Bibel: Die Mautbe* (Wiesbaden: Harrassowitz, 1995).

van Wyk, W.C., "The Peshitta of the Song of Songs," *Ou Testamentiese Werkgemeenskap van Suid-Afrika* 20–21 (1977/1978): 181–89.

Ignacio Carbajosa

13–17.1.4.3 Qoheleth

13–17.1.4.3.1 Manuscripts of s-Qoh and Critical Edition

Very few Syriac biblical manuscripts include the text of Ecclesiastes (Qoheleth). The manuscript on which the Leiden Qoheleth edition is based,[1] known as manuscript s7a1 (Milan, Ambrosian Library, Ms B.21 Inferiore, fols. 142b–144b), is one of the oldest extant manuscripts that contain Qoheleth, together with manuscripts s7g2 (London, British Library, Add. Ms 14,443 fols. 72a–81b) and s8a1 (Paris, National Library, Syr. Ms 341, fols. 124a–

---

[10] Euringer, "Die Bedeutung der Peschitto für die Textkritik des Hohenliedes," 117–28 (126).

[11] M.P. Weitzman, *The Syriac Version of the Old Testament: An Introduction* (University of Cambridge Oriental Publications 56; Cambridge: Cambridge University Press, 1999), 76.

[12] Cf. van Wyk, "The Peshitta of the Song of Songs," 182; P.B. Dirksen, *BHQ 18*, 13*; Salvesen, "Pigs in the Camps," 261.

[13] Salvesen, "Pigs in the Camps," 262–63.

[14] Bloch, "A Critical Examination of the Text of the Syriac Version of the Song of Songs," 138.

[15] Lane, "The Curtains of Solomon," 76–80.

[1] D.J. Lane (ed.), *Qohelet* (The Old Testament in Syriac According to the Peshitta Version 2.5; Leiden: Brill, 1979).

126ᵃ).² Not intended as a critical edition, however, the Leiden edition must be consulted selectively with its apparatus.

13–17.1.4.3.2 Influence of LXX on s-Qoh

As shown by Weitzman, Salters, and Schoors, although significant influence of the LXX version (→ 13–17.1.1.3) can be detected in s-Qoh, a close reading proves this influence to be weaker than that of the Hebrew (→ 15.2.2), serving, for the most part, what appears to be perceived interpretative *desiderata*.³ Indeed, it is often the case that the text of s-Qoh is much more transparent and accessible than both MT and LXX (→ 1.3.4.9).

13–17.1.4.3.3 Translation Technique

Variations and deviations of s-Qoh from LXX (→ 13–17.1.1.3) and MT (→ 15.2.2) can be generally classified into three categories:⁴

1. Interpretative
2. Aramaic influence
3. Greek influence

Interpretative instances in s-Qoh are cases where the translator's choices are semantically, or lexically, divorced from both MT and LXX, yet attempt to convey a more unambiguous meaning that is inspired by the translator's understanding of the source. The most common example for this category is ܠܥܘܬܐ ܕܪܘܚܐ "vexation of the spirit," or "billowing of the wind," appearing for the first time in Qoh 1:14, which stands for רעות רוח "union with the wind,"⁵ "striving [or seeking] after the

---

² For a detailed discussion of the different manuscripts, see D.J. Lane, "'Lilies That Fester...': The Peshitta Text of Qoheleth," *VT* 29 (1979): 481–90.
³ Weitzman, *The Syriac Version of the Old Testament*, 69; Salters, "Observations on the Peshitta of Ecclesiastes," 388–97; Schoors, "The Peshitta of Kohelet," 347–57.
⁴ Comprehensive analysis and classification of the Peshitta version is offered by Weitzman, *The Syriac Version of the Old Testament*.
⁵ L. Köhler and W. Baumgartner et al., *The Hebrew and Aramaic Lexicon of the Old Testament* (Leiden: Brill, 1996), sub voce II רעה. Rashi also interprets רעות רוח as "union with the wind" (A.J. Rosenberg, *The Five Megilloth*, Vol. 2:

wind,"⁶ or "shepherding the wind,"⁷ and προαίρεσις πνεύματος "inclination of the spirit." Clearly in this case, whereas the Greek has a semantic relation to the Hebrew – and even more so if it relies on the occurrences of רעיון רוח "disposition [or thought] of the wind"⁸ – the Syriac version appears to be an interpretation relating the idea of internal strife, or anguish.⁹ This is also suggested by the fact that the same Syriac translation is given for רעיון רוח.¹⁰

The second category refers to instances where it appears that the Peshitta may have been based on the translator's knowledge of Aramaic, whereby he adjusted the meaning of certain Hebrew roots according to context.¹¹ A common instance is the occasional change from סכלות or שכלות "folly, foolishness" to ܣܘܟܠܬܐ "understanding, intelligence" instead of using the equivalent term ܣܟܠܘܬܐ. An interesting case can be seen in Qoh 2:3, in which the logical sequence in MT, especially in the context of the complete verse, may seem awkward if סכלות is to be understood as "foolishness": "... and my heart conducts itself with wisdom and to grasp onto foolishness¹² ..." The Peshitta translator may have been aware of the

---

Lamentations/Ecclesiastes: A New English Translation [New York: The Judaica Press, 1992], 10).
⁶ Köhler and Baumgartner, *The Hebrew and Aramaic Lexicon* (sub voce III רעה). Rashbam also interprets רעות as "will" or "desire": R.B. Salters and S. Japhet (eds.), *The Commentary of R. Samuel Ben Meir Rashbam on Qoheleth* (Jerusalem: Magnes Press, 1985), 99.
⁷ Köhler and Baumgartner, *The Hebrew and Aramaic Lexicon* (sub voce I רעה).
⁸ *Ibid.* (sub voce רעיון).
⁹ There are two other, though less plausible, possibilities for the choice in ܠܥܘܬܐ: an association of רעות with the feminine noun רעה "wickedness," or a derivation from the Aramaic root רעע "to shatter," "break."
¹⁰ M. Sokoloff, *A Dictionary of Jewish Babylonian Aramaic of the Talmudic and Geonic Periods* (Ramat-Gan: Bar Ilan University Press, 2002), sub voce רעיונא.
¹¹ Although there is no concrete evidence for a significant connection between s-Qoh and the Targum (→ 13–17.1.3). See, for example, P.V.M. Fletcher (ed.), *Targum Studies*, Vol. 2: *Targum and Peshitta* (South Florida Studies in the History of Judaism 165; Atlanta: Scholars Press, 1998).
¹² The Greek offers a third version, εὐφροσύνη "with merriment."

existence of the two contrasting meanings associated with the Aramaic root סכל¹³ – as with the Syriac root ܣܟܠ and the Hebrew roots סכל and שכל – namely, its relation to both "understanding" (or "seeing") and "foolishness," and therefore alternated between them according to his understanding of the text, with no intention of making deliberate corrections.

The third category exhibits instances where different degrees of Greek influence can be detected in s-Qoh, cases that often show consideration of, rather than dependence on, LXX. A common example can be found in the Syriac and Greek translations of Qoh 1:17, where the plural noun הוללת "foolishness," "blindness" is translated as ܡܬܠܐ and παραβολαῖς (both meaning "parables"). Indeed, the Syriac translator's knowledge of the correct Hebrew meaning of הוללות is apparent in Qoh 2:12, where he uses the noun ܡܣܬܟܠܘܬܐ "transgression, folly," while the Greek translator chose περιφορά "madness."¹⁴ What is further plausible is how the different thematic contexts of Qoh 1:17 and 2:12 influenced these changes in translation, but for lack of scope this discussion will have to be developed elsewhere. In other instances belonging to this category, the Peshitta translator alternates or even combines both his Hebrew and Greek sources. A good example of this case can be found in Qoh 2:15–16, where the Syriac translator opted for the inclusion of a supplementary clause from the Greek, yet followed the Hebrew throughout the rest of the passage at the expense of the former. The clause ܣܟܠܐ ܡܢ ܡܡܠܠܐ ܣܓܝ ܡܡܠܠ "because the fool speaks excessively [or from excess]" at the beginning of s-Qoh 2:16 is a translation of διότι ἄφρων ἐκ περισσεύματος λαλεῖ at the end of LXX-Qoh 2:15, a phrase that does not appear in MT.¹⁵ The different placements of the clause in the Syriac and Greek versions, however, indicate the former's original consideration of the Hebrew verse order, having adjoined the clause to the discussion about the "wise one" in Qoh 2:16, possibly in order to preserve a thematic balance between the two verses (→ 1.3.4.9).

Though these categories can usefully outline the general nature and peculiarities of s-Qoh, there are copious instances where two or more are applicable to a single verse, as has been shown in some of the representative examples above. Indeed, there is still a significant *desideratum* of research in the field of Ecclesiastes in general, and its Syriac version in particular. Nevertheless, and most importantly perhaps, through a careful consideration of the text by means of classification it is possible to better reassess the particular nature of the Syriac translation and identify the subtleties in the Syriac translator's consideration of MT and LXX.

Dirksen, P.B., "The Old Testament Peshitta," in Mulder, *Mikra*, 255–97.
Fletcher, P.V.M. (ed.), *Targum Studies*, Vol. 2: *Targum and Peshitta* (South Florida Studies in the History of Judaism 165; Atlanta: Scholars Press, 1998).
Lane, D.J. (ed.), *Qohelet* (The Old Testament in Syriac According to the Peshitta Version 2.5; Leiden: Brill, 1979).
Lane, D.J., " 'Lilies That Fester ...': The Peshitta Text of Qoheleth," *VT* 29 (1979): 481–90.
Rosenberg, A.J., *The Five Megilloth*, Vol. 2: *Lamentations/Ecclesiastes: A New English Translation* (New York: The Judaica Press, 1992).
Salters, R.B., "Observations on the Peshitta of Ecclesiastes," *OTE* 8 (1995): 388–97.
Salters, R.B. and S. Japhet (eds.), *The Commentary of R. Samuel Ben Meir Rashbam on Qoheleth* (Jerusalem: Magnes Press, 1985).
Schoors, A., "The Peshitta of Kohelet and its Relation to the Septuagint," in *After Chalcedon: Studies in Theology and Church History Offered to Professor Albert Van Roey for His Seventieth Birthday* (eds. C. Laga, J.A. Munitiz, and L. Van Rompay; OLA 18; Leuven: Peeters, 1985), 347–57.
van Rompay, L., "The Christian Syriac Tradition of Interpretation," in *Hebrew Bible/Old Testament: The History of Its Interpretation*, Vol. 1: *From the Beginnings*

---

¹³ Sokoloff, *A Dictionary of Jewish Babylonian Aramaic*, sub voce #1 סכל; adj. סכל.

¹⁴ The difference between the Syriac and Greek translations in Qoh 2:12 can possibly also be a doublet, that is, the Syriac translator's intentional choice of a close alternative to the Greek translation.

¹⁵ For the origin of this clause in LXX, see Schoors, "The Peshitta of Kohelet," 351.

to the Middle Ages (*Until 1300*), Part 1: *Antiquity* (ed. M. Sæbø; Göttingen: Vandenhoeck & Ruprecht, 1996), 612–19.

Weitzman, M.P., *The Syriac Version of the Old Testament: An Introduction* (University of Cambridge Oriental Publications 56; Cambridge: Cambridge University Press, 1999).

Maya Goldberg

13–17.1.4.4 Lamentations
Manuscripts of s-Lam

The text of the book of Lamentations has always been transmitted together with Jeremiah (→ 6–9.1.4), and accordingly the colophon at the end of s-Lam refers in fact to the authoring of the whole book by Jeremiah. Forty-four manuscripts are known, especially complete Bibles and collections of the Prophets. Besides, s-Lam is also present in the so-called "Masoretic manuscripts," that is, a Syriac collection of difficult words and phrases from Scripture.

Albrektson, *Studies*, demonstrated that it is not possible to distinguish Nestorian from Jacobite readings. He identified two groups of manuscripts, the three most ancient ($s^{6h14,\,7a1,\,9a1}$) and the most recent ones. In addition, manuscripts s^{12a1} and s^{16g6} present some peculiar readings, which assume a common ancestor.

The Syriac "Masoretic manuscripts" represent a textual tradition that is closely connected with the ancient manuscripts. Manuscript s^{9a1} holds a special position in that it includes many readings agreeing with MT (→ 16.2.2) against all the other manuscripts.

Weitzman[1] created a map of the manuscripts displaying textual dissimilarity. He remarks that the three stages of Koster[2] are also reflected in the history of s-Lam, while some Western manuscripts escaped the standardisation of the text of the Peshitta that took place in the ninth century C.E. Weitzman notices that the greatest degree of textual independence exists between s^{9a1} on the one hand and $s^{12a1,\,16g6}$ on the other (all Western manuscripts).

Critical Edition

The critical edition of s-Lam was published in 1963 in Albrektson's *Studies*. He made use of thirty manuscripts, eleven of which are the so-called Masoretic manuscripts, all prior to the seventeenth century.

Unlike the project of the Peshitta Institute of Leiden, this is an eclectic edition. The resulting text represents the Peshitta text of the sixth century C.E., which is close to manuscript s^{7a1}, differing in only thirteen details.

Character of the Translation

In 1895, Abelesz wrote that the Hebrew text from which the s-Lam translation was prepared generally reflects MT (→ 16.2.2).[3] The translation is clear and precise, without being servile. The independent translation is sensitive to poetic peculiarities. According to him, the translator had a good knowledge of the Hebrew language. He is certainly Jewish, and did not use the Targum (→ 13–17.1.3) or LXX (→ 13–17.1.1.4).

Albrektson (1963)[4] also shared some of these conclusions, distancing himself from the opinion that s-Lam was a fairly free translation. According to him, the translator's knowledge of Hebrew was inadequate. He has a poor vocabulary as he used the same Syriac word for two Hebrew synonyms in the same verse. He sometimes seems to guess at the meaning of rare words. Sometimes he analyzes Hebrew forms incorrectly or chooses a phonetically similar Syriac word with a different meaning. His exegetical additions give the translation an explanatory flavour (he joins words or clauses with ܘ "and" in almost every verse). When the translator meets a difficult passage, he endeavours to produce clear and plausible meaning.

According to Wernberg-Møller,[5] Albrektson's reasoning presumes that MT is superior to all the

---

[1] Weitzman, *The Syriac*, 314–15.
[2] Koster, "Review."
[3] Abelesz, *Die syrische Übersetzung*.
[4] Albrektson, *Studies*.
[5] Wernberg-Møller, "Review."

other texts. He notices that Albrektson's reluctance to acknowledge the existence of variant readings is to a large extent due to the fear that it might suggest preference for a Hebrew text superior to MT.

Date of the Translation and Identity of the Translator(s)

Observing the different ways in which the same Hebrew word is translated into Syriac, Weitzman[6] thinks that S-Lam and S-Job (→ 11.3.4) represent conservative translations. The fact that S-Job probably was influenced by S-Lam suggests that Lamentations was translated earlier, as an appendix to Jeremiah (→ 6–9.1.4).[7]

Alexander[8] accepts Weitzman's theory that the Peshitta derived from a Jewish version of the Hebrew Bible made in Edessa around 200 C.E. He even suggests that S-Lam was translated long before. The closer one brings S-Lam to 70 C.E. the easier it is to understand the *raison d'être* of such a translation. According to Alexander, this view is confirmed by the hypothesis of Bogaert,[9] according to whom the presence of the *Apocalypse Baruch*, 4 Ezra (→ 11.7.2.2), and of the sixth book of the Jewish War in manuscript S7a1 reflects a Judeo(-Christian) tradition of the commemoration of the fall of Jerusalem. Against this hypothesis, in this manuscript, 4 Ezra took the place of 1 Esdras (3 Ezra; → 11.7.1.3), and therefore probably the translation of 1 Esdras was not available to the scribe.[10]

Abelesz, A., *Die syrische Übersetzung der Klagelieder und ihr Verhältniss zu Targum und LXX* (Privigye: Verlag der Verfassers, 1895).

Albrektson, B., *Studies in the Text and Theology of the Books of Lamentations* (Studia Theologica Lundensia 21; Lund: C.W.K. Gleerup, 1963).

Alexander, P.S., "The Cultural History of the Ancient Bible Versions: The Case of Lamentations," in *Jewish Reception of Greek Bible Versions: Studies in Their Use in Late Antiquity and the Middle Ages* (eds. N. de Lange, J.G. Krivoruchko, and C. Boyd-Taylor; Texts and Studies in Medieval and Early Judaism 23; Tübingen: Mohr Siebeck, 2009), 78–102.

Bogaert, P., *Apocalypse de Baruch: Introduction, traduction du syriaque et commentaire*, Vol. 1 (SC 144; Paris: Cerf, 1969).

Koster, M.D., "Review: B. Albrektson, *Studies in the Text and Theology of the Books of Lamentations*," *Or* 24 (1967): 78–81.

Weitzman, M.P., *The Syriac Version of the Old Testament* (University of Cambridge Oriental Publications 56; Cambridge: Cambridge University Press, 1999).

Wernberg-Møller, P., "Review: B. Albrektson, *Studies in the Text and Theology of the Books of Lamentations*," *JSS* 10 (1965): 103–10.

Claudio Balzaretti

13–17.1.4.5 Esther

13–17.1.4.5.1 Background

Translated by the end of the second century C.E., the original text of the Peshiṭta version of Esther (S-Esth) – as far as such can be retrieved – represents a clear and close (though not slavish) rendering of the Hebrew text as represented by MT (→ 17.2.2). In only a handful of instances, after allowing for the possibility of scribal corruption in the Syriac transmission process, does the extant text of S-Esth reasonably imply a consonantal reading and/or vocalization of the Hebrew text that differs from that of MT (→ 13–17.1.4.5.4). Moreover, the possibility of Jewish influence on the translator(s) of S-Esth is suggested not only by the high degree of Hebrew proficiency to which the Syriac translation attests, but also by the possible incorporation, in at least one instance, of early Jewish (i.e., rabbinic) exegetical tradition (→ 13–17.1.4.5.5).

13–17.1.4.5.2 Text and Editions

As of 2016, the book of Esther has not yet appeared in the Peshiṭta Institute's *Vetus Testamentum Syriace* (Leiden: Brill, 1977–). The earlier European editions of Walton (1655)[1] and Lee

---

[6] Weitzman, *The Syriac*, 178–81.

[7] Cf. Jerome's *Prologus Galeatus* attesting to a Jewish sequence in which Lamentations was combined with Jeremiah (→ 1.1.2.1.3; → 1.1.2.2.6.4).

[8] Alexander, "The Cultural History," 91–92.

[9] Bogaert, *Apocalypse*.

[10] He was aware of the arrangement of the books according to LXX.

---

[1] This is the date given in the colophon of vol. 2 of Walton, *Polyglotta* (London), in which the *editio princeps* of S-Esth

(1823),[2] – the latter reproducing the text of the former[3] – are based on only a few late West Syriac witnesses,[4] though Walton did take the significant first step towards a critical presentation of s-Esth by including Herbert Thorndike's collation of variant readings (accompanied by a few brief text-critical comments) drawn from two manuscripts furnished respectively by James Ussher and Edward Pococke.[5] The text of s-Esth appeared again in the editions of Urmia (1852)[6] and Mosul (1887),[7] which editions were based generally (i.e., for the Bible overall) on more reliable, albeit unspecified, East Syriac witnesses; yet the text of Esther (like that of Chronicles, Ezra, and Nehemiah), being poorly transmitted in the East Syriac tradition, appears to have been based primarily on the text of Walton/Lee. There are, nonetheless, twenty-seven instances[8] in which the Urmia text of Esther differs from that of Walton/Lee, in eleven of which[9] the Urmia text agrees with manuscript s[7a1], one of the most authoritative witnesses; likewise, there are seventeen instances[10] in which the Mosul text differs from that of Urmia, in thirteen of which[11] the Mosul text agrees with manuscript s[7a1]. The text of Esther in this latter witness – i.e., manuscript B. 21 Inferiore of the Ambrosian Library (Milan), folios 215[v]–218[r] – was published by Ceriani in 1883[12] and, being the oldest complete witness to s-Esth,[13] will serve as the base text for the Peshiṭta Institute's forthcoming edition. A collation of all five of the preceding editions, accompanied by a careful analysis of their variant readings and text-critical relevance vis-à-vis LXX and MT, was published by Grünthal[14] in 1900 and remains a valuable analysis.

Mention should also be made of the edition of s-Esth (along with the other four *Megillōt*) published by Hübsch in 1866,[15] containing his transcription of the Syriac text (of Walton/Lee) into Hebrew characters and (Tiberian) vocalization accompanied by a textual commentary (in Hebrew) in which he explains difficult words, considers variant readings, compares the other ancient translations, and cites linguistic parallels from early rabbinic literature.

---

appeared at the end (albeit with separate pagination). s-Esth was not included in the Paris Polyglot published by Le Jay (*Biblia*; see Haefeli, *Die Peschitta*, 61).

[2] S. Lee (ed.), *Vetus Testamentum Syriace: Eos tantum libros sistens qui in canone hebraico habentur, ordine vero, quoad fieri potuit, apud Syros usitato dispositos* (London: British and Foreign Bible Society, 1823), 483–90.

[3] The one discrepancy between the texts of Walton and Lee noted by Grünthal (*Uebersetzung*, 6) is clearly the result of a misprint, i.e., *ad* Esth 8:3, where, instead of ܕܢܥܒܪ "that he remove" [= MT] as in Walton's edition, Lee has ܕܢܥܒܕ "that he do."

[4] For a brief assessment of Walton's edition, see J. Bloch, "The Printed Texts of the Peshitta Old Testament," *AJSL* 37 (1921): 136–44.

[5] In Walton, *Polyglotta*, vol. 6 (dated 1657), 39–40. For a critique of this collation, however, see Bloch, "The Printed Texts of the Peshitta," 138 and the additional literature cited there.

[6] ܟܬܒܐ ܩܕܝܫܐ ܗ̄ ܟܬܒ̈ܐ ܕܕܝܬܩܐ: ܥܬܝܩܬܐ ܘܚܕܬܐ ܕܡܢ [Vetus Testamentum Syriace et Neosyriace].

[7] *Biblia sacra juxta versionem simplicem quae dicitur Pschitta*, vol. 1, 694–706.

[8] I.e. (per the collation of Grünthal, *Uebersetzung*, 2–7), *ad* Esth 1:3, 4, 5, 8 (*bis*), 10, 17; 2:5, 6, 7, 9, 15 (*bis*), 17; 3:12; 4:3, 8, 14, 16; 5:2; 7:8; 8:1, 10, 11; 9:12, 23; 10:2.

[9] I.e. (per Grünthal, *Uebersetzung*), *ad* Esth 1:3, 4, 8, 10, 17; 2:5, 6, 7, 15 (*bis*), 17.

[10] I.e. (per Grünthal, *Uebersetzung*), *ad* Esth 1:3, 6, 9 (*bis*), 14 (five times), 15; 2:23; 3:9; 6:8, 14; 8:11; 9:26; 10:2.

[11] I.e. (per Grünthal, *Uebersetzung*), *ad* Esth 1:3, 9, 14 (four times); 2:23; 3:9; 6:8, 14; 8:11; 9:26; 10:2.

[12] A.M. Ceriani, *Translatio Syra Pescitto Veteris Testamenti ex codice Ambrosiano sec. fere VI, photolithographice edita*, Vol. 2: *Epistola Jeremiae–ad finem* (Monumenta sacra et profana 6; Milan: Impensis Bibliothecae Ambrosianae, 1883).

[13] One *possibly* earlier witness to the text of s-Esth is contained in manuscript British Library (London) Add. 14,652 (s[6fl]), folios 8[r]–24[v], though the text of Esth 1:1–12 is missing. Aside from these two, thirty-four additional manuscript witnesses to s-Esth are enumerated in the Peshiṭta Institute's *List of Old Testament Peshiṭta Manuscripts* (Leiden: Brill, 1961), 106, with six more manuscript witnesses being identified in subsequent "Communications of the Peshiṭta Institute" published in *Vetus Testamentum* (i.e., s[8fl], 15a3, 15/8gl, 16a1, 17m1, 19d5; see *VT* 18 [1968]: 142).

[14] Grünthal, *Die syrische Uebersetzung zum Buche Esther*.

[15] A. Hübsch, *Die fünf Megilloth nebst dem syrischen Thargum genannt "Peschito": Zum ersten Male in hebräischer Quadratschrift mit Interpunktation edirt, ferner mit einem ... Kommentare zum Thargum, mit sprachlichen Erläuterungen, Nachweisungen der verschiedenen Lesarten, Vergleichung mit andern alten Versionen, Erklärungen vieler thalmudischer und midraschischer Wörter und Sätze u. s. w.* (Prague: Druck von Senders und Brandeis, 1866), 58b–76b.

Finally, with respect to biblical citations in the works of pre-modern Syriac writers (→ 21.9) – a category of textual testimony that is so rich with respect to other books of the Bible – little is to be found that bears directly on the text of Esther (not surprisingly, given the unpopularity and inconsistent canonicity of the book of Esther in Eastern Christianity[16]). Indeed, the only direct citation from s-Esth is apparently supplied by the pen of the fourth-century C.E. church father Aphrahaṭ, who, in his homily 21, "On Persecution," sec. 20, cites the proclamation of Haman in Esth 6:11: "So shall it be done for the man in whose honor the king delights,"[17] the text of which is identical to that in all of the above-mentioned editions (including manuscript s7a1).[18]

13–17.1.4.5.3 Translation Character[19]

The text of s-Esth, as attested by the published editions, represents a clear and generally faithful – though not slavish – rendering of the Hebrew text as attested by MT (→ 17.2.2).[20] Departures from a strictly "literal" rendering are for the most part characterized by adjustment towards Syriac idiom, e.g., *ad* Esth 2:19: ܒܬܪܥܐ ܕܡܠܟܐ "in the gate of the king" for MT בְּשַׁעַר־הַמֶּלֶךְ (as opposed to the *status constructus* ܒܬܪܥ ܡܠܟܐ); *ad* Esth 4:8: ܘܕܬܒܥܐ ܡܢܗ "and that she make entreaty of him" for MT וּלְבַקֵּשׁ מִלְּפָנָיו "and to make entreaty before him" (as opposed to rendering מלפני by ܡܢ ܩܕܡ [as *ad* Esth 1:19], which is not normative with the verb ܒܥܐ "to make entreaty"); and *ad* Esth 9:27: ܒܟܠ ܫܢܐ "in every year" for MT בְּכָל־שָׁנָה וְשָׁנָה. On a few occasions, s-Esth does seem to adopt a slavish rendering – as, e.g., *ad* Esth 4:16, where it reproduces Hebrew אָצוּם as ܐܨܘܡ (both meaning "I will fast") rather than ܢܨܘܡ "we will fast," which would be syntactically normative – although in such instances the translator(s) of s-Esth may well have intended to preserve what they perceived to be an interpretively significant element of the Hebrew text, especially (as in the example cited) where the underlying Hebrew syntax is itself non-normative.[21]

Among the more substantive semantic differences in s-Esth are:

- *Additions*, such as *ad* Esth 3:7, in which s-Esth clarifies the elliptical syntax of Hebrew וּמֵחֹדֶשׁ לְחֹדֶשׁ שְׁנֵים־עָשָׂר "and from month to month twelve" by inserting ܒܝܪܚܐ "in the month" (and construing such as the beginning of the next clause), hence: ܘܡܢ ܝܪܚܐ ܠܝܪܚܐ. ܒܝܪܚܐ ܕܬܪܥܣܪ "and from month to month. In the twelfth month …"; and *ad* Esth 3:13, in which, after ܠܒܙܬܐ "to take as plunder" (for MT לָבוֹז "to plunder," with which the verse ends), s-

---

[16] Cf., in this regard, the telling statement of Saadia Gaon b. Joseph, writing in the first half of the tenth century, probably in Babylonia (from his Judeo-Arabic commentary on Esth 2:16–20): "Some of the ignorant among the Gentiles may occasionally censure us over Esther's getting into a predicament with King Ahasuerus – especially in view of how we extol her and have continued to hand down the record of her affair over the course of time, and even more so for our saying, 'and the king loved Esther' (v. 17)" (see M.G. Wechsler, "Saadia's Seven Guidelines for 'Conviviality in Exile,'" *Intellectual History of the Islamicate World* 1 [2013]: 203–33 [209, n. 29]). On the canonicity of Esther in Syriac tradition, see Haelewyck, "Le canon de l'Ancien Testament dans la tradition syriaque," *passim*.

[17] See I. Parisot (ed. and trans.), *Aphraatis sapientis persae Demonstrationes*, Vol. 1: *Demonstrationes I–XXII* (PS 1.1; Paris: Firmin-Didot et socii, 1894), 981, lines 6–8: ܗܟܢܐ ܢܬܥܒܕ ܠܓܒܪܐ ܕܡܠܟܐ ܨܒܐ ܒܐܝܩܪܗ.

[18] The single *scholium* on Esther offered by Theodore bar Koni constitutes a précis of the book and, as far as we can tell, contains no direct citation from the biblical text; see A. Scher (ed.), *Theodorus bar Kōnī: Liber scholiorum, pars prior* (CSCO 55/Syr. 2.65; Paris: E Typographeo Reipublicae, 1910), 366–67.

[19] All citations from the text of s-Esth are from Ceriani's photolithographic edition of manuscript s7a1, unless otherwise indicated.

[20] See the similar assessment of Grünthal, *Uebersetzung*, 14: "er [d.h., der Übersetzer] sich in den weitaus meisten Fällen von sklavischer Wörtlichkeit ferngehalten und im ganzen bestrebt gewesen, eine gute und lesbare Übersetzung zu liefern." Cf. also Haefeli, *Die Peschitta des Alten Testamentes*, 31–32.

[21] Grünthal's assertion (*Uebersetzung*, 14) that the text of s-Esth is occasionally "weak and colorless" ("Öfter ist die Übersetzung schwach und farblos") is, in any event, rather unfair seeing that in the examples he cites (Esth 2:11; 3:14; 4:16; 6:12) s-Esth represents a semantically faithful rendering of the Hebrew text; indeed, his assertion might be applied equally to the latter.

Esth adds (possibly by influence of v. 12, if not an early scribal error) ܒܚܕ ܝܘܡ ܒܝܪܚܐ ܕܐܕܪ ܒܬܠܬܥܣܪ ܒܗ ܐܬܟܬܒ "in one day, in the month of Adar. On the thirteenth [day] it was written, …"

- *Omissions*, such as *ad* Esth 1:6: בַּהַט (RSV: "porphyry");[22] *ad* Esth 2:2: בְּתוּלוֹת "virgins/virginal" (cf., by contrast, ܒܬܘܠܬܐ "virgins" in v. 3); *ad* Esth 3:8: בֵּין הָעַמִּים "among the peoples"; *ad* Esth 4:11: וְעַם־מְדִינוֹת הַמֶּלֶךְ "and the people of the king's provinces"; *ad* Esth 5:5: אֲשֶׁר־עָשָׂתָה אֶסְתֵּר "that Esther had prepared"; *ad* Esth 6:13: וּלְכָל־אֹהֲבָיו "and to all of his friends"; *ad* Esth 8:5: וְטוֹבָה אֲנִי בְּעֵינָיו "and [if] I be pleasing in his eyes"; and *ad* Esth 9:28: דּוֹר וָדוֹר "every generation."

- *Substitutions*, comprising, on the one hand, *lexical* substitutions, such as *ad* Esth 8:3, in which MT וַתֵּבְךְּ "and she wept" is rendered ܘܡܦܝܣܐ "and (she was) imploring";[23] *ad* Esth 8:9, in which, for the sake of contextualization, MT סִיוָן "Sivan" is rendered by the Syriac month name ܚܙܝܪܢ "Ḥaziran"; and *ad* Esth 9:26, in which MT הַפּוּר "the Pur" (i.e., lot) is rendered ܦܨܚܐ "Passover" (on which see → 13–17.1.4.5.5 below); and, on the other hand, *grammatical-syntactic* substitutions, such as *ad* Esth 6:8, in which MT וַאֲשֶׁר (conj. + relative pron.) – representing a long-standing grammatical-exegetical crux – is rendered in s-Esth by the temporal adverb ܟܕ

"when" (as if reading כַּאֲשֶׁר), hence: "when the royal crown was placed[24] on his (i.e., the king's) head."

The degree to which LXX and its various recensions may have influenced the text of s-Esth – both in its earliest retrievable form as well as in its successive stages of transmission – remains indeterminate in the absence of a critical edition. So far, no conclusive examples of such influence on s-Esth have been adduced from manuscript s[7a1],[25] which represents one of the earliest extant text forms, although Munnich[26] has remarked several instances wherein the text represented in the editions of Walton and Urmia appears to have been corrected towards LXX (→ 13–17.1.1.5) and/or the Lucianic recension (away from manuscript s[7a1]; → 13–17.1.6).

13–17.1.4.5.4 Text-Critical Value

The text of s-Esth represented by manuscript s[7a1] reflects a Hebrew *Vorlage* that, notwithstanding any orthographic differences, was essentially identical to the unvocalized text of Esther represented by MT (→ 17.2.2). At the same time, however, – after accounting for a certain degree of stylistic adjustment on the part of the Syriac translator(s) – there are several instances wherein manuscript s[7a1] suggests a reading of the Hebrew *Vorlage* that differs (semantically) from the text of MT, e.g.: *ad* Esth 1:8 and 4:16: ܒܢܡܘܣܐ/ܒܢܡܘܣܐ "by (the) law," suggesting בְּדָת/בַּדָּת over against MT כְּדָת "according to the law"; Esth 2:3: ܦܘܩܕܢܐ, "orders," suggesting פִּקּוּדִים over against MT פְּקִידִים "commissioners"; Esth 4:14: ܐܢܬ ܐܒܕ ܐܢܬ "you yourself will perish," suggesting תֹּאבְדִי over against MT תֹּאבֵדוּ "you

---

[22] It may be the case, however, that the translator(s) of s-Esth construed בַּהַט־וָשֵׁשׁ "porphyry and marble" as a practical hendiadys (not necessarily reflecting ignorance of the meaning of בַּהַט "porphyry," as suggested by Grünthal, *Die syrische Uebersetzung*, 23), which he thus sought to resolve by the single lexeme ܫܝܫܐ "marble." Indeed, on the medieval identification of בַּהַט "porphyry" and שֵׁשׁ "marble" in this verse as denoting two varieties of marble, see M.G. Wechsler, *Strangers in the Land* (Jerusalem: Magnes Press, 2010), 197–98 and the notes therein.

[23] However, as pointed out by Weitzman, *The Syriac Version of the Old Testament*, 275, s[10f1] has here ܘܒܟܝܐ "and (she was) weeping," which corresponds more precisely to the Hebrew verb and in all likelihood represents the original reading of s-Esth. This underscores the provisional nature of our present discussion concerning the character of s-Esth and its relevance for textual criticism.

[24] So, reading ܐܬܬܣܝܡ in place of the clearly erroneous (since they are all contextually nonsensical) readings in all of the aforecited published editions, viz.: ܐܬܬܣܝܡܬ ܬܣܝܡ "was placed, you will place" (Walton, Lee, and Urmia editions) and ܐܢܬ ܬܣܝܡ "you will place" (s[7a1]; Mosul edition). This corrected reading was already suggested by Thorndike in his *variae lectiones* published in Walton, *Polyglotta* (Vol. 6, 40) and reiterated by Grünthal, *Uebersetzung*, 11.

[25] *Pace* Grünthal, *Uebersetzung*, 19–20. See, however, the next section concerning the parallel readings *ad* Esth 4:8 and 8:7 remarked by Munnich.

[26] Munnich, "La Peshitta d'*Esther*," 82.

(pl.) will perish"; and Esth 9:27: ܒܙܒܢܗܘܢ "in their times," suggesting בְּזְמַנָּם over against MT וְכִזְמַנָּם "and according to their times."²⁷ Two Hebrew variants that are more substantive, which also appear to be supported by LXX, have been suggested by Munnich,²⁸ viz.: the omission, *ad* Esth 4:8, of כתב הדת "the writ of the decree" and, *ad* Esth 8:7, of ולמרדכי היהודי "and to Mordecai the Jew." Nonetheless, for all of these examples the possibility remains that we are dealing with evidence, not of Hebrew variants, but of idiomatic or stylistic adjustment, if not simply errors (e.g., the misreading of the similar letters כ/ב, ד/כ, and י/ו). In the absence of a critical edition of s-Esth, any more decisive conclusions must be held in abeyance.

13–17.1.4.5.5 Exegetical Value

s-Esth, being a primary translation, offers a significant early contribution to the exegesis – or at least the exegetical history – of the various semantic-exegetical cruxes attested in MT (→ 13–17.2.2). While adhering to a generally close method of rendering their Hebrew *Vorlage*, the translator(s) of s-Esth also consistently strive for clarity, and hence – regardless of the merit one assigns to their rendering – there is usually little doubt as to their intended meaning and underlying construal of the Hebrew text (see, e.g., the renderings in s-Esth of the semantic cruxes in Esth 3:7 and 6:8, discussed in → 13–17.1.4.5.3). In at least one instance, moreover, s-Esth may offer insight into the exegetical consciousness of the translator(s) and the community they represent, attesting the presence/influence of Jewish exegetical tradition thereon: *ad* Esth 9:26, where all of the published editions (including manuscript s⁷ᵃ¹) have ܦܨܚܐ "Passover" for MT הַפּוּר "the Pur," apparently alluding to the early rabbinic tradition linking Purim and Passover as "mirrored bookends" (occurring on the same day in the first and last months) commemorating God's deliverance of His people (see *t. y. Meg.* 1:5).²⁹

Grünthal, J., *Die syrische Uebersetzung zum Buche Esther* (Breslau: H. Fleischmann, 1900).

Haefeli, L., *Die Peschitta des Alten Testamentes: Mit Rücksicht auf ihre textkritische Bearbeitung und Herausgabe* (ATA 11.1; Münster i. W.: Aschendorff, 1927).

Haelewyck, J.-C., "Le canon de l'Ancien Testament dans la tradition syriaque (manuscrits bibliques, listes canoniques, auteurs)," in *L'Ancien Testament en syriaque* (eds. F. Briquel Chatonnet and P. Le Moigne; Études syriaques 5; Paris: Geuthner, 2008), 141–71.

Munnich, O., "La Peshitta d'*Esther*: ses relations textuelles avec le texte massorétique et la Septante," in *L'Ancien Testament en syriaque* (eds. F. Briquel Chatonnet and P. Le Moigne; Études syriaques 5; Paris: Geuthner, 2008), 75–90.

Wechsler, M.G., "The Purim-Passover Connection: A Reflection of Jewish Exegetical Tradition in the Peshitta Book of Esther," *JBL* 117 (1998): 321–35.

Weitzman, M.P., *The Syriac Version of the Old Testament* (University of Cambridge Oriental Publications 56; Cambridge: Cambridge University Press, 1999).

Michael G. Wechsler

---

²⁷ All of these examples are remarked by Grünthal (*Uebersetzung*, 13), who also cites the example of ܘܐܦ "and also" in Esth 7:8 as reflecting the reading וְגַם "and also" over against MT הֲגַם "will he even ...?" We have discounted this example, however, since the Syriac rendering is in this case certainly within the bounds of idiomatic and stylistic adjustment. The situation regarding names – which are especially prone to variation in translation – is particularly tenuous, especially so for those in s-Esth, most of which, being non-Semitic, are not only more opaque to begin with, but in many cases have clearly suffered from misreading and/or scribal corruption (e.g., ܐܪܡܬ "Armath" [Esth 1:14] for (ܐ)ܐܕܡܬ "Admath(a)"; ܕܠܚܡ "Dalkhon" [Esth 9:7] for ܕܠܦܡ "Dalphon"; ܐܕܪܝ "Adirai" [Esth 9:9] for ܐܪܕܝ "Aridai") vis-à-vis the etymologically more precise forms attested in MT (on which see, *inter alios*, A.R. Millard, "The Persian Names in Esther and the Reliability of the Hebrew Text," *JBL* 96 [1977]: 481–88). Neither can anything be adduced from manuscript s⁷ᵃ¹ one way or the other with respect to the twelve instances of *Qere/Ketiv* in MT-Esth.

²⁸ Munnich, "La Peshitta d'*Esther*," 76–77. Munnich posits seven additional instances of a Hebrew variant attested jointly by the Peshitta and LXX, yet none of them, in our opinion, falls "beyond a reasonable doubt" of representing idiomatic or stylistic adjustment (e.g., the idiomatic rendering of ובכל מדינה ומדינה ובכל עיר ועיר "and in every province and in every city" *ad* Esth 8:17 by ܒܟܠ מדינתא ובכל קוריא/κατὰ πόλιν καὶ χώραν; or the stylistic-clarifying addition of ܠܡܐܡܪ "saying"/καὶ εἶπον "and say" to the end of Esth 4:10).

²⁹ For a detailed discussion of this rendering, see Wechsler, "The Purim-Passover Connection."

13–17.1.5 Hexapla

13–17.1.5.1 Lamentations

13–17.1.5.1.1 Background

For the translation character of LXX-Lam (→ 13–17.1.1.4), Youngblood concluded that the translator rendered a source for the most part identical to MT, employing an isomorphic translation technique.[1] Youngblood confirmed what previous scholars suspected: LXX-Lam belongs to the καίγε group (→ 1.3.1.2) since it shares more characteristics with the members of this group than the other LXX books.[2] There are no Hexaplaric fragments attributed to Theodotion in Lamentations in the edition by Ziegler, and therefore it is an open question as to whether LXX-Lam is the work of Theodotion or not.[3]

13–17.1.5.1.2 Sources, Editions, and Auxiliary Tools

For Lamentations, the sources for the Hexaplaric fragments are the marginal notes in LXX$^{Q, 86}$, Syh, and the two catena manuscripts LXX$^{87, 91}$. There are Hexaplaric readings in the commentaries of Jerome, Theodoret of Cyrus, John Chrysostom, and Olympiodorus (→ 21.7; → 21.8). Hexaplaric fragments are also found in *Hom. Jer.* and the catena fragments of Origen. Finally, Hexaplaric readings are in the *Onomasticon* of Eusebius and various works of some church fathers.[4] The second apparatus in Ziegler's edition contains the most current collection of Hexaplaric fragments and will be the base for the following comments. For auxiliary tools, see the bibliography.

13–17.1.5.1.3 Translation Character and Technique

13–17.1.5.1.3.1 Theodotion

There are no fragments attributed to Theodotion by Ziegler in the second apparatus of his edition.

13–17.1.5.1.3.2 Aquila

Although there are many fragments attributed to Aquila (→ 1.3.1.2) for Lamentations, they have been transmitted in Syriac (Syh; → 13–17.2.4.4). Translation analysis of retroversions is circular, so one is not in a position to comment on Aquila's translation technique in Lamentations. There is one short Greek fragment from Origen at Lam 4:20:

> MT-Lam רוּחַ אַפֵּינוּ "the breath of our life (lit. our nostrils)" (*NRSV*)
> LXX-Lam Πνεῦμα προσώπου ἡμῶν "the breath of our face" (*NETS*)
> Aq πνεῦμα μυκτήρων ἡμῶν "the breath of our nostrils"

These equivalents are not unique to Aquila, though he does employ אַף "nose"/μυκτήρ "nostril" with some frequency (e.g., Gen 24:47). At Lam 2:(2), LXX^Q preserves ※ σύν "with" before πάντα "all, every," which corresponds to the object marker אֵת in the Hebrew text. Ziegler corrected the Symmachus attribution to Aquila. This example furnishes a contrast between LXX-Lam and Aquila, since the former does not render the object marker אֵת with σύν "with" in the rather isomorphic way of the latter.

13–17.1.5.1.3.3 Symmachus

There are many Symmachus (→ 1.3.2.1) fragments for Lamentations, though the majority have been transmitted in Syriac (Syh). A representative example of his technique is found at Lam 3:49:

> MT-Lam עֵינִי נִגְּרָה וְלֹא תִדְמֶה מֵאֵין הֲפֻגוֹת
> My eyes will flow without ceasing, without respite (*NRSV*)
> LXX-Lam Ὁ ὀφθαλμός μου κατεποντώθη, καὶ οὐ σιγήσομαι τοῦ μὴ εἶναι ἔκνηψιν
> My eye was exhausted, and I will not be silent so that there will be no calming down (*NETS*)
> Sym ὁ ὀφθαλμός μου ἐπέμεινε καὶ οὐκ ἐπαύσατο τοῦ μὴ εἶναι ἄνεσιν
> My eye endured and did not cease so that there will be no rest

In this fragment, Symmachus provides a quantitative version of the Hebrew text, in which he rendered each word of the source with a Greek word. LXX-Lam (→ 13–17.1.1.4) facilitates the 3rd fem. sg.

---

[1] Youngblood, "Translation Technique," 356–57.
[2] Youngblood, "Translation Technique," 358.
[3] → 13–17.1.1.4.3.
[4] Ziegler, *Ieremias, Baruch, Threni, Epistula Ieremiae*, 101–05.

verb תִּדְמֶה "it will cease" with a 1st sg. σιγήσομαι "I will be silent," while Symmachus retains the 3rd sg. with ἐπαύσατο "it will cease."

13–17.1.5.1.4 Text-Critical Value for the Hebrew Text

Sym-Lam reflects no variants, while in Lam 1:12 הוֹגָה "to inflict" reflects either a different reading (הגה "to proclaim") or an etymological understanding different from MT. LXX-Lam has ἐταπείνωσεν "he humbled," while Symmachus has ἀνεκάλεσε "he called." LXX-Lam (→ 13–17.1.1.4) read the verb as a *Hiphil* pf. 3rd masc. sg. from יגה "to torment" (cf. ταπεινόω "to humble" for יגה in Lam 1:5; 3:32, 33). All of the manuscripts contain a double translation with φθεγξαμενος εν εμοι "calling to me" appearing either before or after ταπειν. με "he humbled me" (LXX^O group), and this is an accidental secondary addition to the text that Ziegler has reconstructed. Φθέγγομαι "to call" is a translation of I הגה "to proclaim." Symmachus has used ἀνακαλεῖν "to call" to render a form from I הגה "to proclaim" instead of יגה "to torment." The *BHQ commentary on the problem has noted the variant of Symmachus correctly.⁵

Busto Saiz, J.R., *La traducción de Símaco en el Libro de los Salmos* (Textos y Estudios "Cardenal Cisneros" 22; Madrid: Consejo Superior de Investigaciones Científicas, 1978).
Ceulemans, R., "Greek Christian Access to 'The Three,' 250–600 CE," in *Greek Scripture and the Rabbis* (eds. T.M. Law and A. Salvesen; CBET 66; Leuven: Peeters, 2012), 165–91.
Field, *Hexapla*.
Gentry, P.J., *The Asterisked Materials in the Greek Job* (SBLSCS 38; Atlanta: Scholars Press, 1995).
Hyvärinen, K., *Die Übersetzung von Aquila* (ConBOT 10; Uppsala: G.W.K. Gleerup, 1977).
Reider, J. and N. Turner, *An Index to Aquila: Greek-Hebrew, Hebrew-Greek, Latin-Hebrew* (Leiden: Brill, 1966).
Salvesen, A., *Symmachus in the Pentateuch* (JSS Monograph 15; Manchester: Victoria University of Manchester, 1991).

⁵ R. Schäfer, "Commentaries on the Critical Apparatus: Lamentations," *BHQ 18, 113*–36* (117*).

Youngblood, K.J., "Translation Technique in the Greek Lamentations" (PhD diss., The Southern Baptist Theological Seminary, 2004).
Ziegler, J. (ed.), *Ieremias, Baruch, Threni, Epistula Ieremiae* (Septuaginta Vetus Testamentum Graecum 15; Göttingen: Vandenhoeck & Ruprecht, 1957; 2nd ed. 1976).

John D. Meade

13–17.1.5.2 Ruth
See → 2.4.6 Hexaplaric Greek Translations and Hexapla of the Octateuch (Pentateuch > Primary Translations).

13–17.1.5.3 Qoheleth
13–17.1.5.3.1 Background
The Greek translation of Qohelet incorporated into the body of texts loosely termed "Septuagint" is characterised by extreme formal equivalence (→ 13–17.1.1.3). It is debated, in fact, as to whether or not the translator was Aquila.[1] As one might presume, scholiasts who selected readings in variation from LXX supplied not only a fair number from Symmachus, whose renderings are more oriented to the demands of the target language, but also a number attributed to Aquila and Theodotion, whose translations are just about as wooden. Note that almost half of the marginal notes concerning Theodotion simply affirm that his text is the same as the text of the Fifth Column of the Hexapla (→ 1.3.1.2).

Hexaplaric materials for Ecclesiastes were collected, collated, and analysed afresh for the Second Apparatus of the Göttingen Ecclesiastes (forthcoming in 2017). A preliminary step was the study of Marshall for the Hexapla Project.[2] In 2013, an important manuscript was discovered by Reinhart Ceulemans, namely LXX⁷⁸⁸, which preserved as much in terms of text as all of the other sources together (approximately 213 [frequently longer] readings).

[1] Cf. Jarick, "Aquila's Koheleth," 131–39 and Gentry, "The Relationship of Aquila and Theodotion," 63–84.
[2] Marshall, "A Critical Edition of the Hexaplaric Fragments of Ecclesiastes."

13–17.1.5.3.2 Sources, Editions, and Auxiliary Tools

The hexaplaric materials are derived from three types of sources: 1) marginal notes in manuscripts transmitting the biblical text of Ecclesiastes; 2) citations from church fathers (→ 21.7) whose texts are available either in surviving commentaries and exegetical works or in various *catena* traditions that excerpted these commentaries and exegetical works; and 3) marginal notes of the Syro-Hexapla (→ 11.4.4).

13–17.1.5.3.2.1 Marginal Notes in Greek Bible Manuscripts

The following manuscripts are the main sources in Greek for readings of the Three Jewish Revisors and associated hexaplaric notes (→ 1.3.1.2). The arrangement follows the Rahlfs numbers and provides library numbers as given in the *Einleitung* of the Göttingen Edition:[3]

LXX[161]	Moscow, Russian State Archive for Ancient Documents, Fonds 1607, Inv. 1.7 (before Dresden, Sächsische Landesbibliothek, A. 170); fourteenth century
LXX[248]	Rome, Vatican Library, Vat. gr. 346; thirteenth century
LXX[252]	Florence, Bibliotheca Medicea Laurenziana, Plut. VIII 27; tenth century
LXX[336]	Athos, Ἰβήρων 555; fourteenth century
LXX[411]	Jerusalem, Patriarchate Library, Τάφου 370; XVI. Jh.
LXX[539]	Paris, Bibliothèque Nationale de France, Coisl. 193; eleventh century with excerpts from catenas.
LXX[788]	Tirnavos, Δημοτική Βιβλιοθήκη 25; tenth century (Catena).

Some characterisation and quantification of these sources is both necessary and useful. Most of the marginal readings are derived from LXX[161, 248, 252], and also LXX[539]. The number of readings that are preserved in each source is approximated in a chart:

Source	Number of Readings
LXX[161]	318
LXX[248]	328
LXX[252]	208
LXX[336]	1
LXX[411]	3
LXX[539]	85

Manuscripts LXX[161] and LXX[248] preserve approximately 318 and 328 readings respectively. These two manuscripts are closely related in their textual tradition. This is indicated not only by congruence in both the number and the text of the marginal notes, but is obvious from the system used in both manuscripts to index the marginal readings. Exactly the same indices and signs are used in both LXX[161] and LXX[248], although the format and pagination of the manuscripts are not the same. LXX[248] is approximately a century earlier and has more notes than LXX[161]. Since there is a tendency both in manuscripts with marginal notes and in *catena* manuscripts for the number of the readings to decrease as copying continues through the centuries, it appears that LXX[248] may be an earlier witness to this tradition. LXX[248] has approximately ten more readings than LXX[161]. Nonetheless, no major analysis has been conducted to this point that could prove the exact nature of the relationship between these two manuscripts.

---

[3] Translation to English A.L. The German text is as follows:
LXX[161] Moskau, Russisches Staatsarchiv für alte Dokumente, Fonds 1607, Inv. 1.7 (früher Dresden, Sächsische Landesbibliothek, A. 170); XIV. Jh.
LXX[248] Rom, Bibl. Vat., Vat. gr. 346; XIII. Jh.
LXX[252] Florenz, Bibl. Laur., Plut. VIII 27; X. Jh.
LXX[336] Athos, Ἰβήρων 555; XIV. Jh.
LXX[411] Jerusalem, Patr.-Bibl., Τάφου 370; XVI. Jh.
LXX[539] Paris, Bibl. Nat., Coisl. 193; XI. Jh. Eccl. mit Catenen Exzerpten.
LXX[788] Tirnavos, Δημοτική Βιβλιοθήκη 25; X. Jh. (Cat.).

Manuscript LXX^{252} preserves about 208 readings of the Three. Some 147 of these are in combination with LXX^{161} and LXX^{248} and a further five with LXX^{248} where LXX^{161} has no reading. In approximately twenty-four instances, LXX^{252} is the sole witness of the reading and in approximately sixteen further instances, it is joined by LXX^{539}, Jerome or Syh, i.e., to the exclusion of LXX^{161} and LXX^{248}. In the remaining sixty instances, LXX^{252} preserves a longer reading of which other witnesses such as LXX^{161} and LXX^{248}, for example, preserve only part.

	Combination	Instances
LXX^{252}	+ LXX^{539}	1
	+ Syh	9
	+ LXX^{539} Syh	3
	+ Jerome	2
	+ Jerome Syh	1

These rough statistics are sufficient to show that, in terms of genealogical relationship or textual tradition, LXX^{161} and LXX^{248} come from a common parent and that this parent and the parent of LXX^{252} probably have a common parent in turn:

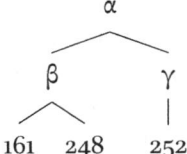

Manuscript LXX^{252} is dated to the tenth century while LXX^{161} and LXX^{248} are from the fourteenth and thirteenth centuries respectively. Thus LXX^{252}, in spite of copyist's errors, goes back independently to a parent related to the parent of LXX^{161} and LXX^{248}. As noted previously, there is a tendency to lose readings in the transmission through the centuries.

Manuscript LXX^{539} is an odd manuscript. It contains only excerpts of the biblical text of Ecclesiastes, followed by hexaplaric readings without attribution and these in turn are followed by scholia and excerpts from commentaries of the church fathers (→ 21.7). A chart indicates how the eighty-five readings preserved in LXX^{539} are correlated with other sources:

	Combination	Instances
LXX^{539}	+ LXX$^{161\ 248}$ etc.	75
	+ LXX^{252}	1
	+ LXX^{252} Syh	3
	+ Syh	4
	+ LXX° group	1
	= sole witness	1

Although a majority of readings preserved by LXX^{539} are also in common with LXX^{161} and LXX^{248}, some are in common only with LXX^{252} and a few only in common with the Syro-Hexapa. Once, LXX^{539} is the sole witness. To include LXX^{539}, perhaps the stemma could now be revised as follows:

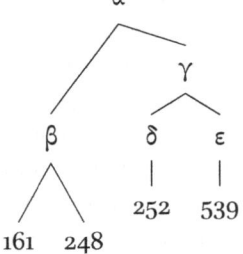

In about ten instances, LXX^{539} preserves only part of the text transmitted by LXX$^{161, 248}$, and other sources. Manuscript LXX^{539} may in fact represent the earliest form of the complicated and various *catena* traditions that have survived for Ecclesiastes.[4]

A long reading of twenty-one words attributed to Symmachus is preserved solely by manuscript

---

[4] Suggested by Detlef Fraenkel in conversation at the Septuaginta-Unternehmen in Göttingen, June 2008.

LXX[336] amidst scholia of Evagrius of Pontus on Ecclesiastes.[5]

Manuscript LXX[411] is dated to the sixteenth century and manuscripts after 1500 are not normally used in Göttingen editions. Nonetheless, this manuscript has readings in common with the LXX[o] group, witnessed by only three sources. It is thus an important witness in spite of its late provenance. In 2015, Felix Albrecht, a resident scholar of the Septuaginta-Unternehmen studied the marginal notes in LXX[411] and his search revealed one hexaplaric reading in the margins and two embedded in the biblical text, also witnessed by the members of the LXX[o] group.

Some five or so hexaplaric readings are actually embedded in the text of manuscripts in the LXX[o] group.

13–17.1.5.3.2.2 Patristic Sources

Of all the commentaries on Ecclesiastes by patristic writers (→ 21.7), only four survived in Greek and one in Latin. Three of these contain readings of the Three (→ 1.3.1.2) and, along with scholia from a fourth source, constitute the evidence found in commentaries and exegetical works. The sixth-century C.E. commentary on Ecclesiastes by Olympiodorus preserves six readings. A commentary attributed to Gregory Agrigentinus, but now recognised as written by Metaphranes of Smyrna (ninth–tenth century C.E.) preserves three readings. One reading of Symmachus is preserved in surviving scholia of the fourth-century C.E. Father Evagrius of Pontus. Of these ten readings, only three in Olympiodorus are unattested by other sources.

In Latin (→ 21.8), we have preserved a complete commentary on Ecclesiastes by Jerome. Jerome explicitly states in his *Comm. Ps.* and in *Comm. Tit.* that he went to Caesarea and used Origen's Hexapla there. He made extensive notes from the Hexapla, which he used both for his *Comm. Eccl.* and for the later translation in the Vulgate. Perhaps he even had copies of hexaplaric texts in his library in Bethlehem. His access to and direct use of Origen's Hexapla is evident in *Comm. Eccl.*, for he frequently cites one or more of the Jewish recensions in the course of his exegesis and explanation of the text and preserves for us some sixty-five readings in this way. A brief chart shows that the readings preserved by Jerome are independent of the Greek manuscript tradition. More than half of the readings are, of course, also preserved in Greek in the manuscripts just described. In some twelve cases, however, Jerome preserves a full text and the Greek manuscripts offer only a fragment of the same text. In four cases, the only other witness is the Syro-Hexapla (→ 11.4.4). In roughly seventeen cases, Jerome is the sole source, but in nine of these he actually provides the text in Greek and not in Latin. Thus, few readings remain that require retroversion from Latin. This is not as easy as creating retroversions from the Syro-Hexapla, given Jerome's method and style of translation (→ 1.3.5).

	Description of Witness	Instances
Jerome	part also in Greek manuscripts	12
	+ Syh	4
	= sole witness in Greek	9
	= sole witness in Latin	8

13–17.1.5.3.2.3 *Catena* Traditions

Another kind of patristic source are the *catena* manuscripts. Excerpts from the commentaries of the church fathers relating to the same stretch of biblical text were chained or linked together. These comments were either placed around the biblical text or between passages of the biblical text in a linear layout.

For Ecclesiastes, the *catena* traditions are complex and only a brief account of them can be given here. There are essentially four or five separate traditions: 1) an anonymous work commonly called the *Catena Trium Patrum*;[6] 2) the *Catena*

---

[5] P. Géhin, *Évagre le Pontique: Scholies à l'Ecclésiaste* (SC 397; Paris: Cerf, 1993), 29–30.

[6] S. Lucà (ed.), *Anonymus in Ecclesiasten Commentarius*,

Hauniensis;[7] 3) Olympiodorus *catena*;[8] 4) the Procopius *Catena*;[9] and 5) the Polychronius *Catena*. There are also manuscripts that show a mixture of these basic types. Fortunately, these have been analysed extensively by Labate, Leanza, and Lucá. The only major type not yet available in a critical edition is the Polychronius *Catena* and this has now been studied by Felix Albrecht at the Septuaginta-Unternehmen. Together, we have checked the following manuscripts as representative of the Polychronius *Catena*:

LXX[139]	Milan, Bibliotheca Ambrosiania, A 148 inf.; tenth–eleventh century (catena).
LXX[159]	Moscow, Russian State Archive for Ancient Documents, Fonds 1607, Inv. 1.22 (before Dresden, Sächsische Landesbibliothek, A. 107); eleventh–twelfth century (catena).[10]
LXX[522]	Cambridge, Trinity Coll., B. 7. 3; thirteenth century, Ecclesiastes with catena excerpts.
LXX[560]	Paris, Bibliothèque Nationale de France, Gr. 151; thirteenth century (catena).

The number of readings preserved in each of these major types of *catena* is tabulated as follows:

---

qui dicitur Catena Trium Patrum (CCSG 11; Turnhout: Brepols, 1983).

[7] A. Labate (ed.), *Catena Hauniensis in Ecclesiasten* (CCSG 24; Turnhout: Brepols, 1992).

[8] A. Labate, "Nuove catene esegetiche sull'Ecclesiaste," in Ἀντίδωρον: *Hulde aan Dr. Maurits Geerard bij de voltooiing van de Clavis Patrum Graecorum*, Vol. 1 (Wetteren: Cultura, 1984), 241–63.

[9] S. Leanza (ed.), *Procopii Gazaei Catena in Ecclesiasten, necnon Pseudochrysostomi Commentarius in Eundem Ecclesiasten* (CCSG 4; Turnhout: Brepols, 1978).

[10] For re-evaluation of the date of LXX[159] see P.J. Gentry and F. Albrecht, "The Amazing History of MS Rahlfs 159: Insights from Editing LXX Ecclesiastes," *Journal of Septuagint and Cognate Studies* 44 (2011): 31–50.

Catena Trium Patrum	2
Catena Hauniensis	14
Procopius *Catena*	0
Polychronius *Catena*	2

The Olympiodorus *catena* offers nothing that is not already in the extant commentary. The instances in the Polychronius *Catena* are also from the Commentary of Olympiodorus. Nonetheless, all the sources have been painstakingly searched for hexaplaric readings.

13–17.1.5.3.2.4 Syro-Hexapla

Our sole source for the Syro-Hexapla (→ 11.4.4) is the eighth-century C.E. Codex Ambrosianus in Milan, available in the facsimile by Ceriani. Elsewhere in description of this source, I have noted that it offers many different kinds of materials, all relevant for hexaplaric studies. First is the text itself, which includes words marked by an asterisk in ten instances and names the source in eight of them. Only one other witness (i.e., Codex Venetus) preserves any asterisks for Ecclesiastes and does so twice, erroneously in both instances. Twice words are marked in the text of the Syro-Hexapla by an obelus, and four times by an antisigma or lemnisk. Second, there are marginal notes offering at least six different types of information: 1) a few notes offer textual variants; 2) many marginal notes offer readings from the later Jewish revisers, Aquila, Symmachus, and Theodotion (→ 1.3.1.2); 3) fifteen notes offer words in Greek to clarify evidence when retroversions may be uncertain; 4) seven notes offer explanatory glosses (these are always distinguished from hexaplaric notes by being circled); 5) longer scholia are found in the top and bottom margins, with appropriate indices to connect them to the text; and 6) eight of the longer scholia contain seven citations from the Ecclesiastes commentary of Olympiodorus and one from Evagrius.

The Syro-Hexapla preserves a total of 250 marginal readings. The relationship of the marginal notes in the Syro-Hexapla to the other sources is of great interest and is charted as follows (the count is only proximate but gives data from which conclusions can be drawn):

Combination	Instances
LXX$^{161\ 248\ 252\ 539}$ Syh	39
LXX$^{161\ 248\ 252}$ Syh	16
LXX$^{161\ 248}$	14
LXX^{252} Syh	8
TOTAL	77
v Syh	1
Syh = sole witness	103

In some twenty-three instances, the Syro-Hexapla preserves a longer reading and other witnesses only part, and in perhaps thirty-five instances, the Syro-Hexapla preserves part of a longer reading preserved in other witnesses. These data corroborate the proposal I have advanced elsewhere[11] that the marginal notes come from a separate source than the text, a source similar to the *Catena* text traditions. Approximately 60 percent of the notes it transmits are also found in the archetype of the Greek witnesses while 40 percent are independent of this tradition. The fact that longer notes in the bottom and top margins cite from Evagrius and Olympiodorus, where they have readings of the Three, also demonstrates that those who produced the Syro-Hexapla gathered materials from several sources.

13–17.1.5.3.2.5 Comparison of Recent Research and Sources Used by Field

The sources scoured for the new Göttingen edition of Ecclesiastes as well as for the edition in the Hexapla Project may now be compared with the sources used in 1875 by Field for his *Origenis Hexaplorum quae supersunt*. First, Field lists the sources given in Montfaucon:

Codex Regius, num. 1890	= LXX^{560}
Codex Regius, num. 19902	= LXX^{562}
Codex Regius, num. 2435	= LXX^{561}
Codex Regius, num. 2436	= LXX^{563}
Hieronymi Commentarius in Ecclesiasten	
Notes from Drusius and "Roman" Edition	

Manuscripts LXX^{560} and LXX^{563} belong to the Polychronius *Catena*, LXX^{561} to the *Catena Trium Patrum*, and LXX^{562} is a manuscript of Olympiodorus' Commentary on Ecclesiastes. Montfaucon's sources for marginal notes in Greek manuscripts were slim.

Second, to Montfaucon's list of sources,[12] Field[13] adds manuscripts LXX$^{161, 248, 252}$ as collated and published in the edition of Holmes and Parsons.[14] The *Auctarium* of Field also gives "Mat" as another manuscript source. His source for "Mat" was the collation made by Spohn of marginal readings in LXX^{161} in 1785.[15] Spohn employed the siglum "Mat" because the manuscript was in the possession of Matthaei in Leipzig. In 1788, Matthaei sold this manuscript to the library in Dresden and was also the one who collated it along with LXX^{159} and LXX^{160} for the edition of Holmes and Parsons. Thus, Field mistakenly listed the evidence for LXX^{161} twice. Nonetheless, the evidence given by Field was a major step forward.

To the list of sources used by Field, we have added LXX$^{336, 411, 539}$ and a fresh search of the commentaries and *catenae*. Analysis of the commentary by Olympiodorus rests upon more than a

---

[11] Gentry, "Hexaplaric Materials in Ecclesiastes and the Rôle of the Syro-Hexapla."

[12] B. de Montfaucon, *Hexaplorum Origenis quae supersunt: multis partibus auctiora, quàm a Flaminio Nobilio et Joanne Drusio edita fuerint: ex manuscriptis et ex libris ed. eruit et notis illustravit* (2 vols.; Paris: Simart, 1713).

[13] Field, *Hexapla.

[14] R. Holmes and J. Parsons, *Vetus Testamentum Graecum cum variis lectionibus* (5 vols.; Oxford: Clarendon Press, 1798–1827).

[15] G.L. Spohn, *Der Prediger Salomo: Nebst einer Beylage, welche Varianten zu dem Prediger in den LXX. aus zweyen Manuskripten und dem Olympiodor enthält: Aus dem Hebräischen aufs neue übersetzt und mit kritischen Anmerkungen begleitet* (Leipzig: Breitkopf, 1785).

dozen manuscripts and of the Polychronius *Catena* on sixteen manuscripts, some three or four centuries older than those used previously. The fresh collations made by the Septuaginta-Unternehmen of LXX[161, 248, 252] have also revealed mistakes in the collations made for Holmes and Parsons. Finally, Field used the edition of Middeldorpf for the Syro-Hexapla[16] as the facsimile by Ceriani did not appear until one year before publication of his monumental work. The analysis of the Syro-Hexapla by myself and Marshall is based upon a better source, therefore, than the evidence given for the Syro-Hexapla in Field.

Although the body of hexaplaric materials for Ecclesiastes has grown both quantitatively (more than doubled since Field) and qualitatively as a result of extensive research, and indeed is fairly rich in relation to what remains for some books, we still have a limited amount of evidence for the work of the Three in Ecclesiastes.

13–17.1.5.3.3 Translation Character and Technique

For Qohelet, we have about 130 readings attested for Theodotion, 215 for Aquila, and 380 for Symmachus (→ 1.3.1.2). This is precisely what we would expect, since the original translation belongs to the *kaige* group of texts, but probably was not made by Theodotion himself (→ 1.3.1.2). Since the translation is most like Theodotion, there would be few readings from Theodotion that differ in a significant way, more from Aquila, and many more from Symmachus because his effort was to produce a translation more sensitive to the demands of the target language. In addition, approximately fifty readings are attributed to Aquila and Theodotion together, but only two to Theodotion and Symmachus and none to Aquila and Symmachus together. An example is given from each of the Jewish revisers.

13–17.1.5.3.3.1 Theodotion

Notes attributed to Theodotion for Qohelet indicate, in general, that the work of Theodotion is close to the Greek translation of Qohelet. In Qoh 5:10c, Old Greek renders כִּי אִם־רְאִית עֵינָיו (K = רָאִית, Q = רְאוֹת or רְאוֹת "looking" or "to see") "except to see with his eyes" by ὅτι ἀρχὴ τοῦ ὁρᾶν ὀφθαλμοῖς αὐτοῦ (construing אִם as אֵם; cf. Ezek 21:26) "because the beginning of seeing is with his eyes". A marginal reading attributed to Th in Syh reads ܐܠܐ ܐܢ ܠܡܚܙܐ ܒܥܝܢܘܗܝ = εἰ μὴ τοῦ ὁρᾶν ὀφθαλμοῖς αὐτοῦ "except to see with his eyes." What we see here is that Theodotion corrects the original translation to what is now the normal reading of the text. In fact, almost half of the notes attributed to Theodotion read θ′ ὁμοίως τοῖς ο′, telling us that Theodotion has the same text as that in the Fifth Column of the Hexapla.[17] This also confirms that the Old Greek belongs to the *kaige* group in character.

13–17.1.5.3.3.2 Aquila

As early as 1871, Grätz[18] proposed that the original translation of Qohelet was by Aquila. Most notable in the translation is the rendering of את + direct object by σύν + accusative in Greek (e.g. Qoh 2:17; 3:10, 11, 17bis and *passim*) [Direct object marker in Hebrew translated by preposition "with"].[19] How can we explain, then, the fact that there are even more readings attested for Aquila than Theodotion in the case of this book? Some have proposed that Aquila produced two versions. One was the original translation and the other a later revision, the source of the marginal notes attributed to Aquila. Others, like Barthélemy, denied the marginal notes attributed to Aquila as coming from him.[20] These proposals are not satisfactory since the character of the marginal notes better matches the system and translation technique of Aquila as Hyvärinen and

---

[16] Middeldorpf, *Codex Syriaco-Hexaplaris*.

[17] See Gentry, "Hexaplaric Materials in Ecclesiastes," 5–28.
[18] H. Grätz, Kohélet: *Der salomonische Prediger: Übersetzt und kritisch erläutert* (Leipzig: C.F. Winter, 1871), ad loc.
[19] Gentry, "Hexaplaric Materials in Ecclesiastes," 5–28.
[20] Barthélemy, *Devanciers*, 31–32.

Jarick have shown.[21] According to LXX[161, 248, 788], Aquila renders περασμός "crossing" (> "completing") in Qoh 4:8c instead by τέλος "end." This is characteristic since Aquila has a system whereby forms of the same root in Greek match forms of the same root in Hebrew, regardless of the part of speech.

13–17.1.5.3.3.3 Symmachus

In Qoh 1:9a, for מה־שהיה הוא שיהיה, Old Greek has τί τὸ γεγονός; αὐτὸ τὸ γενησόμενον, which Symmachus revises to τὸ προόν, αὐτό ἐστι τὸ ἐσόμενον (all meaning "what has happened, it is what will happen"; differences in style). One can immediately see the improvement according to the criteria of later Hellenistic Greek. Many of the readings for Symmachus are preserved only in Latin by Jerome (→ 1.3.5) who, as we know, had a preference for the text of Symmachus and made use of it as a tool in dealing with difficult passages in Hebrew and for his rendering in the Vulgate.

13–17.1.5.3.4 Text-Critical Value for the Hebrew Bible

The parent Hebrew text from which Qohelet was translated into Greek (→ 13–17.1.1.3) is extremely close to our present MT (→ 15.2.2); only a handful of instances constitute evidence for a different *Vorlage*. An example of the importance of the hexaplaric materials for Ecclesiastes is illustrated by the *crux criticorum* at Qoh 1:17. Until the discovery of manuscript LXX[788], all of our Greek witnesses attested παραβολάς "proverbs" where MT has הוֹלֵלוֹת "madness" (fem. sg., not pl). Already in 1937, Gordis[22] proposed that the original translation had παραφοράς "errors," now supported by LXX[788] and also adopted in the critical edition of the Göttingen Septuaginta as the original text. Yet the problem in the text in the Greek textual tradition is also matched by a problem in the Hebrew tradition. The editor of *BHQ proposed הוֹלֵלוּת "madness" (fem. sg.) as the preferred text in Hebrew[23] but Meade and Gentry have argued that proper analysis of both Greek and Hebrew traditions supports MT.[24]

Ceriani, A.M. (ed.), *Codex Syro-Hexaplaris Ambrosianus photolithographice editus* (Monumenta sacra et profana 7; Milan: Typis et impensis Bibliothecae Ambrosianae, 1874).

Gentry, P.J., "Hexaplaric Materials in Ecclesiastes and the Rôle of the Syro-Hexapla," *Aramaic Studies* 1 (2003): 5–28.

Gentry, P.J., "Propaedeutic to a Lexicon of the Three: The Priority of a New Critical Edition of Hexaplaric Fragments," *Aramaic Studies* 2 (2004): 145–74.

Gentry, P.J., "The Relationship of Aquila and Theodotion to the Old Greek of Ecclesiastes in the Marginal Notes of the Syro-Hexapla," *Aramaic Studies* 2 (2004): 63–84.

Gentry, P.J., "'The Role of the "Three" in the Text History of the Septuagint': II. Aspects of Interdependence of the Old Greek and the Three in Ecclesiastes," *Aramaic Studies* 4 (2006): 153–92.

Gentry, P.J. (ed.), *Ecclesiastes* (Septuaginta Vetus Testamentum Graecum; Göttingen: Vandenhoeck & Ruprecht, forthcoming).

Gentry, P.J. and F. Albrecht, "The Amazing History of MS Rahlfs 159 – Insights from Editing LXX Ecclesiastes," *Journal of Septuagint and Cognate Studies* 44 (2011): 31–50.

Hyvärinen, K., *Die Übersetzung von Aquila* (ConBOT 10; Lund: Gleerup, 1977).

Jarick, J., "Aquila's Koheleth," *Textus* 15 (1990): 131–39.

Marshall, P.S., "A Critical Edition of the Hexaplaric Fragments of Ecclesiastes" (PhD diss., The Southern Baptist Theological Seminary, 2007).

Meade, J.D. and P.J. Gentry, "Evaluating Evaluations: The Commentary of BHQ and the Problem of הוֹלֵלוֹת in Ecclesiastes 1:17," in *Sophia – Paideia: Sapienza e educazione (Sir 1,27): Miscellanea di Studi offerti in onore del prof. Don Mario Cimosa* (eds. G. Bonney and R. Vicent; Nuova Biblioteca di Scienze Religiose 34; Rome: Libreria Ateneo Salesiano, 2012), 197–217.

---

[21] Hyvärinen, *Die Übersetzung von Aquila*, 88–99 and Jarick, "Aquila's Koheleth," 131–39.

[22] R. Gordis, "Ecclesiastes 1:17: Its Text and Interpretation," *JBL* 56 (1937): 323–30.

[23] Y.A.P. Goldman, "Qohelet קהלת," in *BHQ 18, 25–53, 13*–17*, 28*–30*, 64*–112* (26, 68*–69*).

[24] For a full discussion, see Meade and Gentry, "Evaluating Evaluations."

Yi, Y.Y., "Translation Technique of the Greek Ecclesiastes" (PhD diss., The Southern Baptist Theological Seminary, 2005).

Peter J. Gentry

13–17.1.5.4 Canticles

13–17.1.5.4.1 Background

Before undertaking an analysis of the Hexaplaric versions of Canticles, it is first helpful to review the character of the translation of the LXX text.[1] Regarding the translation typology of LXX-Cant, De Crom situates it somewhere between Psalms and Ecclesiastes on the way to Aquila.[2] De Crom concludes that if one takes a "maximalist" approach towards the καίγε problem, then LXX-Cant is related to it. Therefore, in the case of LXX-Cant, the revisions of Theodotion, Aquila, and Symmachus (→ 1.3.1.2) were applied to a member of the καίγε group.[3]

There is no extant evidence of the pre-Hexaplaric Greek revisions of LXX-Cant outside of the evidence of Origen's Hexapla itself (→ 1.3.1.2). The versions of Aquila, Symmachus, Theodotion, Quinta, and Sexta are only attested in Christian sources that either directly or indirectly had contact with Origen's Hexapla. Thus, the evidence of the Hexaplaric Greek translations comes from the Hexapla.[4] In other words, the reception history of the Hexaplaric Greek versions is interrelated to the reception history of the Hexapla.

13–17.1.5.4.2 Sources, Editions, and Auxiliary Tools

The fragments of the Hexaplaric versions of Canticles are first preserved in the following Greek fathers (→ 21.7) directly or indirectly (i.e., through catena and translations): Origen of Alexandria, Apollinaris of Laodicea, Gregory of Nyssa, Nilus of Ancyra, Theodoret of Cyrrhus, and Catena of Ps.-Eusebius. The reader is directed to Ceulemans for the details.[5]

Second, Greek evidence exists in the four LXX manuscripts that contain Hexaplaric fragments in the margins: LXX[161, 248, 252, v]. The value of the first three was well known to Field, who included the Hexaplaric readings in the *Auctarium* to Canticles.[6] The last manuscript contains three Hexaplaric fragments. In addition to these, LXX[788], a catena manuscript, also preserves Hexaplaric fragments in the margins.

Third, there are fragments of the minor versions in the Latin father (→ 21.8), Ambrose of Milan, and perhaps traces in Jerome's Vulgate. Ceulemans' work surpasses Field's in this area, for he includes the fragments from Ambrose for the first time. From the extant evidence, it appears that Ambrose's citations of the minor versions are from Origen's commentary on Canticles. Furthermore, given the methodology of Ceulemans, the Vulgate can be used with great caution to discern the readings of the minor versions.[7]

Fourth, the Syro-Hexapla (→ 11.4.4) furnishes many marginal readings of the minor versions in Syriac, which Field had already utilized.

Before the completion of Ceulemans' dissertation, the only available edition of Canticles was the work of Field.[8] Ceulemans' dissertation will be the basis for the new critical edition of the Hexaplaric fragments of Canticles.

13–17.1.5.4.3 Translation Character and Technique

LXX-Cant (→ 13–17.1.1.2) was a member of the wider καίγε group and as such it was already a translation, which rendered the proto-MT (→ 14.2.2) with a formal equivalence translation technique. Therefore, Theodotion, Aquila, and Symmachus (→ 1.3.1.2) revised a text that agreed with their fundamental principle of revising LXX toward their Hebrew text. Theodotion shared the most agreement with LXX-

---

[1] See → 13–17.1.1.2, based on the earlier work of Treat, not that of De Crom.

[2] See → 1.3.1.2.3.6; cf. De Crom, "The LXX Text of Canticles," 623–24.

[3] For the characterization of the καίγε group see → 1.3.1.2.4.

[4] Ceulemans, "A Critical Edition," 39–40, 235 n. 808.

[5] Ceulemans, "A Critical Edition," 81–203.

[6] Field, *Hexapla*.

[7] Ceulemans, "A Critical Edition," 244–48.

[8] Field, *Hexapla*.

Cant since there are very few fragments attributed to him. However, Theodotion revised LXX-Cant in a sufficient number of places to show that he is not to be identified with LXX-Cant. From the short Aquila fragments we possess, he applied the principles of the καίγε group more consistently and thus his version exceeds LXX-Cant and Theodotion in terms of a quantitative or isomorphic approach to the source text. Symmachus represents a response to LXX-Cant, Theodotion, and Aquila, for he appears to reject many of the equivalents and the approaches of his predecessors. His approach still manifests a desire to render the Hebrew text, even preserving the Hebrew word order and syntax, but his renderings tend to be more free and interpretive than his predecessors.

13–17.1.5.4.3.1 Theodotion

There are seventeen Hexaplaric fragments attributed uniquely to Theodotion (→ 1.3.1.2) in Canticles and eight of these are ὁμοίως notes. That is, notes in Syh^mg-Cant that appear to indicate that Theodotion had the same text as Syh^txt-Cant or, in a few cases, may refer to a catena tradition.[9] The evidence indicates that Theodotion translated a Hebrew *Vorlage* that was nearly identical to MT (→ 14.2.2). From this minimal evidence, he employed a formal translation technique but was sensitive to the concerns of the target language.

A two-word fragment from Cant 1:6 demonstrates the sensitivity to context: שֶׁשְּׁזָפַתְנִי "because [the sun] has gazed on me" (*NRSV*)/LXX-Cant παρέβλεψέν με "[because the sun] has looked down on me" (*NETS*)/Th περιέφρυξέ με "[because the sun] scorched me." The Hebrew verb שׁזף "to catch sight," "to turn brown," is used three times in the Hebrew Bible (Cant 1:6; Job 20:9 and 28:7) and there are extant Theodotion readings for the Job references. In Job, Theodotion uses παραβλέπω "to look at" for שׁזף "to catch sight, to turn brown" because the subject in both places is עין "eye" and thus the meaning of the verb is "to look" or "to catch sight." That LXX-Cant also has παραβλέπω "to look at" for שׁזף "to catch sight, to turn brown" in Cant 1:6 indicates the tendency to translate שׁזף "to catch sight, to turn brown" with παραβλέπω "to look at" within the wider καίγε tradition. However, Theodotion altered his approach here and used περιφρύγω "to scorch, parch," since שמש "sun" is the subject. Aquila also chose a verb for "scorching, burning" (συγκαίω). Theodotion, therefore, shows more sensitivity to context than LXX-Cant. Theodotion and LXX-Cant were members of the καίγε tradition, but they are not identical in Canticles.[10]

In Cant 2:17, Theodotion renders עַל־הָרֵי בָתֶר "on the cleft mountains" with ἐπὶ τὰ ὄρη θυμιαμάτων "upon the mountains of perfumes." The Hebrew word, בָּתֶר, is a *hapax legomenon*. LXX-Cant renders it with ἐπὶ ὄρη κοιλωμάτων "upon mountains with torrents" probably after בתר "to cut" (cf. Gen 15:10). Theodotion probably translated the difficult word in Cant 2:17 by recourse to Cant 4:6 where the mountains are described as mountains of myrrh and the hills as hills of frankincense. Therefore, Theodotion probably translated the difficult phrase in Cant 2:17 according to the wider context.

In Cant 5:11, Theodotion renders כֶּתֶם פָּז "the finest gold" (*NRSV*) with ἐπίσημος ἐν χρυσίῳ "significant in gold." In Job 28:16, 19, Theodotion renders בְּכֶתֶם with χρυσίῳ (both meaning "in gold"), while in Job 28:17b he renders כְּלִי־פָז "fine gold" with σκεύη χρυσᾶ "gold vessel." In addition, he also translates זָהָב with χρυσίον (both meaning "gold") in Job 28:17a. Theodotion, therefore, prefers to translate these Hebrew terms for "gold" with the χρυσ-word group. LXX-Cant renders the phrase as χρυσίον καὶ φάζ "gold and phaz" (*NETS*). LXX-Cant (→ 13–17.1.1.2) employed a transliteration to avoid using χρυσ- words in succession. In Cant 5:11, Theodotion is faced with a difficult text. He does not render the first term according to his own equivalents, which would have perhaps yielded χρυσοῦν χρυσίον "golden gold," rather he interprets the sense of the

---

[9] All numbers are taken from Ceulemans, "A Critical Edition." These numbers include explicit and conjectured attributions. They do not include the fragments with multiple attributions. For the significance of the ὁμοίως notes, see Ceulemans, "A Critical Edition," 260–67; Ceulemans, "The ὁμοίως Notes," 28–36.

[10] → 1.3.1.2.

Hebrew, "significant in gold." It should be noted that the manuscript evidence for this fragment is not strong (LXX^161-248, 252), with only LXX^161-248 preserving the attribution. Still, the difficult Hebrew phrase may have caused the alteration in Theodotion's translation technique, which he employed in Job 28.

It is remarkable that there are precious few Theodotion fragments from Canticles in comparison with the fragments from Aquila and Symmachus. This fact may indicate that Theodotion's revision was already close to the original καίγε translation, and he only revised the text where it did not suit his principles. The few extant fragments stand as a contrast to LXX-Cant, showing that the versions were similar to one another but not identical in every place.

13–17.1.5.4.3.2 Aquila

There are eighty-two fragments uniquely attributed to Aquila (→ 1.3.1.2) in Canticles. The Aquila materials indicate that he employed a formal equivalence translation technique, which attempted to render each Hebrew element with a Greek equivalent segment by segment. On the word level, Aquila's version is most literal and demonstrates the concordance principle of translation, even employing equivalents to maintain etymological connections between Hebrew and Greek. However, when Aquila's syntax and Greek vocabulary are considered, his version furnishes more appropriate and even ingenious renderings of the Hebrew source.[11] The following examples exhibit Aquila's conservative translation technique and also his brilliance in refining former principles of revision.

In Cant 2:7, there is a longer Aquila fragment, which demonstrates his ultra-literal translation of MT:

> MT-Cant הִשְׁבַּעְתִּי אֶתְכֶם בְּנוֹת יְרוּשָׁלַָם בִּצְבָאוֹת אוֹ בְּאַיְלוֹת הַשָּׂדֶה
> I adjure you, O daughters of Jerusalem, by the gazelles or the wild does (*NRSV)

> LXX-Cant ὥρκισα ὑμᾶς, θυγατέρες Ἰερουσαλήμ, ἐν ταῖς δυνάμεσιν καὶ ἐν ταῖς ἰσχύσεσιν τοῦ ἀγροῦ
> I have adjured you, O daughters of Ierousalem, by the powers and by the forces of the field (*NETS)
> Αq ὥρκισα ὑμᾶς, θυγατέρες Ἰερουσαλήμ, ἐν δορκάσιν ἢ ἐν ἐλάφοις τῆς χώρας
> I adjured you, O daughters of Jerusalem, by the gazelles or by the does of the country

Aquila's rendering matches MT (→ 14.2.2) exactly. LXX-Cant (→ 13–17.1.1.2) contains definite articles before δυνάμεσιν "powers" and ἰσχύσεσιν "forces" respectively, while Aquila and the later MT vocalization do not.[12] Aquila renders אוֹ with the expected ἤ (both meaning "or"), while LXX-Cant has καί "and."[13] Aquila's rendering of צְבָאוֹת "hosts" accedes with modern lexicography, which also recognizes the root II "gazelle" and the feminine צְבִיָּה "female gazelle."[14] LXX-Cant used δύναμις "power" for צְבִיָּה "female gazelle," since he rendered צָבָא "host" with δύναμις "power" routinely. In the same way, LXX-Cant used ἰσχύς "strength, force" for אַיָּלָה "doe," perhaps thinking he was rendering a word from II אול "to be strong."[15] Aquila recognized the different root and translated it with ἔλαφος "doe."

The fragment in Cant 7:1 shows Aquila's tendency to translate proper nouns according to his concordance principle (i.e., words from one Greek root render words from one Hebrew root):

> MT-Cant שׁוּבִי שׁוּבִי הַשּׁוּלַמִּית "Return, return, O Shulammite" (*NRSV)
> LXX-Cant ἐπίστρεφε ἐπίστρεφε, ἡ Σουλαμῖτις "Return, return, O Soulamite" (*NETS)
> Αq ἐπίστρεφε ἐπίστρεφε, ἡ εἰρηνεύουσα "Return, return, O Peace Maker"

For the last word, LXX-Cant has the transliteration ἡ Σουλαμῖτις "the Soulamite," which renders the proper noun in the Hebrew text. Aquila has translated the term here and in Cant 6:12 with εἰρηνεύω

---

[11] Hyvärinen, *Die Übersetzung von Aquila*, 111–12.

[12] De Crom, "The LXX Text of Canticles," 246, notes that these articles may not be genuine since they are omitted in some textual witnesses.

[13] De Crom, "The LXX Text of Canticles," 246, shows that other LXX translators did the same (e.g., Lev 1:10, Job 38:31).

[14] See relevant entries in *HALOT*.

[15] De Crom, "The LXX Text of Canticles," 246.

"to make, keep peace" in accordance with his translation strategy for שלם "peace" (cf. Job 9:4).

Another fragment in Cant 7:1 shows Aquila's genius and his refinement of the καίγε tradition:

MT-Cant וְנֶחֱזֶה־בָּךְ "that we may look upon you" (*NRSV)
LXX-Cant καὶ ὀψόμεθα ἐν σοί "and we shall look upon you" (*NETS)
Aq καὶ ὁραματισθησόμεθα ἐν σοί "and we will look on you"

Aquila employs his unique equivalent ὁραματίζομαι "to look" for חזה "to see" (cf. ὁραματισμός for חָזוֹן [both meaning "vision"] in Job 33:15a).[16] Interestingly, LXX-Cant used ὀψόμεθα "we will look" for חזה "to see" here and in Cant 2:12 for ראה Niphal "to appear," showing that he tended toward semantic leveling. Theodotion also renders חזה (Job 34:32, 36:25a) and ראה (e.g., Job 23:9, 31:4a, 33:28b) with ὁράω [all meaning "to see"] showing agreement with the καίγε tradition. Aquila's distinct translation equivalents of ὁραματίζομαι for חזה (both meaning "to look") and ὁράω for ראה (both meaning "to see") are later refinements to the καίγε tradition. As a later member of the καίγε tradition, Aquila refined the earlier principles of revision and perfected them.[17]

13–17.1.5.4.3.3 Symmachus

There are 125 fragments uniquely attributed to Symmachus (→ 1.3.1.2) in LXX-Cant (→ 13–17.1.1.2). Symmachus produced a revision of LXX that was faithful to the sense of the Hebrew (→ 14.2.2). While not being constrained by a formal translation technique that rendered the source word for word, Symmachus does attempt to preserve the sense of the Hebrew in readable Greek.[18]

In Cant 7:6 (7:5 EV), Symmachus produced a version faithful to the Hebrew word order that was also readable in Greek:

MT-Cant וְדַלַּת רֹאשֵׁךְ כָּאַרְגָּמָן מֶלֶךְ אָסוּר בָּרְהָטִים
and your flowing locks are like purple; a king is held captive in the tresses (*NRSV)
LXX-Cant καὶ πλόκιον κεφαλῆς σου ὡς πορφύρα, βασιλεὺς δεδεμένος ἐν παραδρομαῖς
and the plaited hair of your head is like purple cloth; a king is bound by retinues (*NETS)
Sym καὶ ἡ διακόσμησις τῆς κεφαλῆς σου, ὡς πορφύρα βασιλικὴ περιδεδεμένη εἰλήμασι
and the adornment of your head is as royal purple being tied on with veils

Symmachus follows the word order of the Hebrew and he renders almost every Hebrew element with a Greek element. He renders the Hebrew-bound phrase וְדַלַּת רֹאשֵׁךְ "and your flowing locks" with a genitive construction in Greek: καὶ ἡ διακόσμησις τῆς κεφαλῆς σου "and the adornment of your head." He renders the ב "in" on the last word with the dative case in Greek thus not employing a Greek element for the Hebrew, while LXX-Cant used ἐν "by" for ב "in." Instead of using a genitive construction to render אַרְגָּמָן מֶלֶךְ "purple; a king," he employs an attributive adjective βασιλικὴ "royal" for the Hebrew noun מֶלֶךְ "king."

In Cant 8:1, Sym provided a version that followed the Hebrew closely though interpretively:

MT-Cant אֶמְצָאֲךָ בַחוּץ אֶשָּׁקְךָ גַּם לֹא־יָבוּזוּ לִי
If I met you outside, I would kiss you, and no one would despise me (*NRSV)
LXX-Cant εὑροῦσά σε ἔξω φιλήσω σε, καί γε οὐκ ἐξουδενώσουσίν μοι
If I found you outside, I would kiss you, and indeed no one would despise me (*NETS)
Sym ἵνα εὑροῦσά σε ἐν ἀγρῷ καταφιλήσω σε καὶ μηδεὶς ἐξευτελίζῃ με
so that having found you in a field I might kiss you and no one might disrespect me

He rendered the prefix forms אֶשָּׁקְךָ "I would kiss you" and יָבוּזוּ "no one would despise" as a purpose/result clause dependent on the previous line. The first verb remains a participle as in LXX-Cant (εὑροῦσα "having found"). Symmachus translates בַחוּץ "outside" quantitatively with a prepositional phrase ἐν ἀγρῷ "in a field" and yet also interpretively, since "outside" would most naturally be the

---

[16] Reider, *Index, 174.
[17] → 1.3.1.2.2.3.5.
[18] → 1.3.1.2.5; cf. Salvesen, Symmachus, 198.

"field." LXX used the adverb ἔξω "outside," an equivalent established in the wider LXX corpus (e.g., Gen 9:22; Exod 21:19; Isa 42:2; Job 31:32; Ps 30:12). LXX-Cant has καί γε "and indeed" for גם "also, indeed," which demonstrates affinity with the καίγε tradition, while Symmachus renders גם "indeed" with simple καί "and." This technique matches Symmachus' tendency in the Pentateuch to leave גם "indeed, also" untranslated or to render it with καί "and" (e.g., Exod 7:11) or some other equivalent.[19] This action appears to be a reaction to the καίγε group. Instead of the simple negated plural verb in MT, Symmachus translates the final verb with a negative indefinite pronominal adjective and a singular verb. LXX-Cant uses ἐξουδενοῦν "to despise" three times for בוז "to despise" (Cant 8:1; 8:7 bis). Aquila renders the roots בוז and בזה with ἐξουδενοῦν (all meaning "to despise") consistently.[20] The Psalter also used this Greek word to render בזה "to despise" (e.g., Ps 14:4) and מאס "to reject" (e.g., Ps 52:5), while Theodotion used ἐξουδενοῦν "to despise" for מאס "to reject" in Job 30:1. Interestingly, Symmachus rejects this equivalent and uses ἐξευτελίζειν "to disrespect" for בוז "to despise" in Canticles in the same three places and also in the Psalter (Ps 68:34; Ps 122:4) and the noun ἐξευτελισμός "disrespect" for בוז "to despise" (Ps 122:3).[21]

13–17.1.5.4.4 Text-Critical Value for the Hebrew Bible

Since the text history of LXX-Cant (→ 13–17.1.1.2) is still to be determined and therefore the relationship between revisions and Old Greek is still obfuscated, this section will focus on one example of text criticism of the Hebrew Bible. At Cant 7:7, Aquila's text preserves the original Hebrew text where MT (→ 14.2.2) probably preserves the variant. MT has בַּתַּעֲנוּגִים "in delights," while Aquila has θύγατερ τρυφῶν "daughter of pleasures," which is probably to be retroverted as בַּת תַּעֲנוּגִים "daughter of delights." Cant-LXX (ἐν τρυφαῖς σου "in your pleasures"), Symmachus (ἐν σπατάλαις "in luxuries"), and the Vulgate (in deliciis "in pleasures") agree with MT, while the Peshitta (ܒܪܬ ܕܗܢܝܐ "daughter of pleasures") agrees with Aquila. It appears that the text of MT resulted from haplography of ת, due to incorrect word division. Barthélemy chose the text of Aquila over MT with a C rating.[22] Even if Aquila's text is not chosen as the original text, this fragment still constitutes a significant textual variant to MT.

Busto Saiz, J.R., *La traducción de Símaco en el Libro de los Salmos* (Textos y Estudios "Cardenal Cisneros" 22; Madrid: Consejo Superior de Investigaciones Científicas, 1978).

Ceulemans, R., "A Critical Edition of the Hexaplaric Fragments of the Book of Canticles: With Emphasis on their Reception in Greek Christian Exegesis" (PhD diss., Katholieke Universiteit Leuven, 2009).

Ceulemans, R., "The ὁμοίως Notes in the Syro-Hexapla Version of the Song of Songs," *OCP* 79 (2013): 5–36.

De Crom, D., "The LXX Text of Canticles: A Descriptive Study in Hebrew-Greek Translation" (PhD diss., Katholieke Universiteit Leuven, 2009).

Field, *Hexapla.

Hyvärinen, K., *Die Übersetzung von Aquila* (ConBOT 10; Uppsala: G.W.K. Gleerup, 1977).

Reider, J. and N. Turner, *An Index to Aquila: Greek-Hebrew, Hebrew-Greek, Latin-Hebrew* (Leiden: Brill, 1966).

Salvesen, A., *Symmachus in the Pentateuch* (JSS Monograph 15; Manchester: Victoria University of Manchester, 1991).

Treat, J.C., "Aquila, Field and the Song of Songs," in *Origen's Hexapla and Fragments: Papers Presented at the Rich Seminar on the Hexapla, Oxford Centre for Hebrew and Jewish Studies, 25th–3rd August 1994* (ed. A. Salvesen; TSAJ 58; Tübingen, Mohr, 1998), 135–76.

John D. Meade

13–17.1.5.5 Esther
13–17.1.5.5.1 Background

The book of Esther has survived in two Greek versions (→ 13–17.1.1.5). Both Greek versions of Esther contain six additions labeled A–F (→ 11.6.2), at least five of which were probably originally composed in

---

[19] Salvesen, *Symmachus*, 242. Also, Symmachus does not use καίγε "and indeed" for גם "indeed, also" in the Psalter according to Busto Saiz, *La traducción de Símaco*, 210–11.

[20] Reider, *Index*, 87.

[21] Busto Saiz, *La traducción de Símaco*, 506.

[22] Barthélemy, *Interim Report*, Vol. 3, 612.

Greek,[1] and, in any case, have no counterpart in any known Hebrew text of Esther (→ 17.2.2).

Origen made "adjustments" throughout Greek Esther in line with his program of presenting the differences between LXX-Esth and his Hebrew text. However, very few of the Aristarchian signs have been preserved.

13–17.1.5.5.2 Sources, Editions, and Auxiliary Tools

Field published his large edition of available hexaplaric fragments in 1875.[2] Since then, and as of 2015, little if any additional hexaplaric material has surfaced for Esther.

13–17.1.5.5.2.1 Sources for Origen's Fifth Column

For LXX-Esth, an origenic group of manuscripts (→ 1.3.1.2) has been identified. These manuscripts are the main source of evidence for determining the contents of Origen's fifth column. Of these, however, only one contains any Aristarchian signs, and these are limited to asterisks.

13–17.1.5.5.2.2 Sources for Readings of the Three

Readings of the three translators (→ 1.3.1.2) for Esther are scant. We have evidence for one reading by Aquila from a midrash on Esther.[3]

13–17.1.5.5.3 Translation Character and Technique

13–17.1.5.5.3.1 Aquila

Of the Three translators (→ 1.3.1.2), we have evidence only for Aquila, and it is quite limited. At Esth 1:6, the Hebrew describes the decorations of the palace, and it uses the phrase חוּר כַּרְפַּס. The Hebrew is not well attested, but the phrase appears to mean something like "white fabric of linen." This is rendered by LXX-Esth as βυσσίνοις καὶ καρπασίνοις "fine linen and flax." A midrash on Esther mentions that here Aquila has ἀέρινον καρπάσινον "light gray fine flax."[4] This appears to have influenced Origen later in the book at Esth 8:15, where the Hebrew חוּר "white fabric" appears again. LXX-Esth has nothing corresponding to חוּר and the origenic texts add ἀέρινην (or a variant) to correspond with the Hebrew. The Vulgate has *aerinus* here, and so Aquila – or a Jewish tradition shared by Aquila – may have influenced the Vulgate as well, either directly, or indirectly via the Hexapla.

Aquila's possible influence on Origen may be seen in two other places. A well-attested example of Aquila's tendency to render quantitatively is his use of σύν "together, with" for the Hebrew אֶת, both when אֶת "with" is a preposition and when it is a direct object marker. In Esth 4:7, the Hebrew has וַיַּגֶּד־לוֹ מָרְדֳּכַי אֵת כָּל־אֲשֶׁר קָרָהוּ "And Mordecai related to him all that happened." LXX-Esth expresses this concisely as ὁ δὲ Μαρδοχαῖος ὑπέδειξεν αὐτῷ τὸ γεγονός "And Mordochaios showed him what [had] happened"; here, the phrase אֵת כָּל (direct object marker plus "all") is not rendered by the LXX translator. The origenic manuscripts add σύμπαν "with all," with the added preposition σύν "with" evidently accounting in an isomorphic way for the direct object marker. Origen may have used Aquila as his source for his addition. Another similar example can be seen at Esth 8:11, where the direct object marker אֵת appears again in the phrase אֵת כָּל (direct object marker plus "all"). This Hebrew phrase is part of a longer section that has no equivalent in LXX-Esth. Origen, as part of an asterisked addition, gives the rendering συμπᾶσαν "with all." The LXX-Esth (→ 13–17.1.1.5) translator nowhere displays a tendency to render אֶת by σύν (as for example, is the practice of the apparently *kaige*-influenced translator of LXX-Qoh [→ 13–17.1.1.3]). Thus, these origenic additions may give evidence of Aquila's influence.

13–17.1.5.5.3.2 Origen

Only a few Aristarchian signs are preserved in the surviving origenic texts. A total of six asterisks (※) occur, marking where Origen (→ 1.3.1.2.7) added Greek text corresponding to Hebrew (→ 17.2.2) for which LXX-Esth (→ 13–17.1.1.5) has no equivalent. The six locations are Esth 2:6, 7; 8:3, 11; 9:2, 4. No obeli have survived.

---

[1] Jobes, *NETS*, 424.
[2] Field, *Hexapla*.
[3] Wünsche, *Der Midrasch zum Buche Esther*, 21.
[4] Wünsche, *Der Midrasch zum Buche Esther*. See also Field, *Auctarium*, *Hexapla*, 5.

The number of unmarked origenic corrections towards the Hebrew, however, is much larger. Many of the additions and deletions that match the Hebrew originally may have been marked by asterisks and obeli that were later lost by copyists. A few examples of origenic additions that correct toward the Hebrew were given above, one under the asterisk (Esth 8:11) and one unmarked (Esth 4:7). Another example of an unmarked addition is found at Esth 8:16, where the final phrase in the Hebrew – וְשָׂשֹׂן וִיקָר "and jubilation and honor" – has no equivalent in LXX-Esth. Origen added καὶ ἀγαλλίαμα καὶ τιμή "and rejoicing and honor" to correspond to the Hebrew.

Occasionally, an origenic manuscript displays an omission that conforms to the Hebrew text, but omissions are much rarer than additions. For example, at Esth 5:3, for מַה־בַּקָּשָׁתֵךְ (a verbless clause that means "what [is] your request?"), LXX-Esth adds the explicit verb with the phrase σού ἐστιν τὸ ἀξίωμα. One origenic manuscript of three omits ἐστιν "is" and this matches the Hebrew. This example also illustrates another common correcting tendency of Origen: that of transposing the order of the Greek to match the Hebrew. Here, all three origenic manuscripts put the word σού "your" at the end of the phrase to match where the Hebrew pronominal suffix appears. Origen's fifth column for Esther contains many transpositions that conform to the Hebrew word order (e.g., at Esth 1:3, 5; 3:4, 12; 4:8, 11), but he did not mark transpositions with Aristarchian signs.

13–17.1.5.5.4 Text-Critical Value for LXX-Esth

Prior to Origen (→ 1.3.1.2.7), adjustments of the Greek text (→ 13–17.1.1.5) toward the Hebrew (→ 17.2.2) were already being made through the *kaige* tradition, and thus Origen's Greek *Vorlagen* may already have contained some of these changes. Nevertheless, understanding Origen's contributions is essential to unraveling the complicated text history of Greek Esther.

Field, *Hexapla.
Hanhart, R., *Esther* (Septuaginta Vetus Testamentum Graecum 8; Göttingen: Vandenhoeck & Ruprecht, 1983).
Hyvärinen, K., *Die Übersetzung von Aquila* (ConBOT 10; Uppsala: G.W.K. Gleerup, 1977).
Jobes, K., "Esther," *NETS*, 424–40.
Wünsche, A., *Der Midrasch zum Buche Esther* (Leipzig: Schulze, 1881).

Andrew McClurg

13–17.1.6 Post-Hexaplaric Greek Translations

13–17.1.6.1 Background

The only post-Hexaplaric recension known to us is that of Lucian (→ 1.3.1.2). The Five Scrolls, commonly called Megillot, consist of LXX-Ruth (→ 13–17.1.1.1), LXX-Lam (→ 13–17.1.1.4), LXX-Esth (→ 13–17.1.1.5), LXX-Cant (→ 13–17.1.1.2), and LXX-Eccl (→ 13–17.1.1.3). The analysis of Rahlfs is confirmed by Quast who demonstrates that there is lack of uniformity in the distribution of Lucianic manuscripts for the book of Ruth. Robert Hanhart does not attribute the LXX^L text of Esther to Lucian. For Ecclesiastes, the subsequent work of M.M. Dickie shows that the Lucianic recension is partially preserved.

13–17.1.6.2 Original Form, Editions, Auxiliary Tools

Critical editions exist for Ruth,[1] Lamentations,[2] and Esther.[3] In 2015, Canticles and Ecclesiastes are not yet published.[4] Ruth is uneven in the distribu-

---

[1] U. Quast, *Ruth* (Septuaginta Vetus Testamentum Graecum 4.3; Göttingen: Vandenhoeck & Ruprecht, 2006).

[2] J. Ziegler, *Ieremias, Baruch, Threni, Epistula Ieremiae* (Septuaginta Vetus Testamentum Graecum 15; Vandenhoeck & Ruprecht, 1957).

[3] R. Hanhart, *Esther* (Septuaginta Vetus Testamentum Graecum 8.3; Göttingen: Vandenhoeck & Ruprecht, 1966; 2nd ed. 1983).

[4] Fernández Marcos says, "We still lack critical editions of Proverbs, Qoheleth, and Song of Songs, and it would be quite interesting to know the text history of the latter two which had some difficulties in being accepted into the Hebrew canon, particularly if it is true that their translation originated in the circles of the Palestinian rabbinate in the 1st century A.D." (N. Fernández Marcos, "Some Reflections on the Antiochian Text of the Septuagint," in *Studien zur Septuaginta: Robert Hanhart zu Ehren aus Anlaß seines 65.*

tion of manuscripts. Manuscripts LXX[19, 108] – stellar witnesses to LXX[L] in Kingdoms – preserve the recension from Ruth 4:11. These manuscripts and LXX[54, 59, 75, 82, 93, 127, 315] form the chief group LXX[L]. Two subgroups, LXX[d] and LXX[t], preserve Lucianic readings.[5] Although Hanhart does not attribute the LXX[L] text in Esther to the historical Lucian, manuscripts LXX[19, 93, 108] preserve unique variants that Hanhart calls the LXX[L] text.[6] In Ecclesiastes, manuscripts LXX[106, 125, 130, 261, 545] preserve the recension. Manuscript LXX[443] – a congener of the group – and citations attributed to the Antiochian fathers (e.g., Chrysostom, Theodoret, Maximilian; → 21.7) also have Lucianic readings. The manuscripts of Ecclesiastes are more closely aligned with Wisdom (11) and Sirach than with the other books of the Five Scrolls, which preserve the recension in varying degrees in the well-known manuscripts boc$_2$e$_2$ (LXX[19, 82, 127, 93]).

13–17.1.6.3 Translation Character and Technique

The character of the variants in Lucianic manuscripts is similar to what has been found elsewhere in LXX.[7] In Ecclesiastes, the LXX[L] text consistently avoids Attic morphology even when Hexaplaric sources preserve Classical forms (Qoh 7:23 εἶπα LXX[L]/εἶπον LXX[o] "I said"), though there is a preference for ἄν to ἐάν in indefinite relative clauses (Qoh 1:10 ὅς "who" LXX/ὅς ἄν "whoever" LXX[L] 443). In Ruth, however, the second aorist is preferred as well as other Attic Greek forms (Ruth 4:11 εἴποσαν LXX/εἶπεν LXX[oI-15 54′] "said"; Ruth 1:8 ἔλεος LXX/ἔλεον LXX[L] "mercy"). The scholarly consensus is that the Lucianic recension is characterized as a full text with few omissions. In Ecclesiastes, the manuscripts contain as many omissions as they do pluses. This fact is not problematic for the consensus, because the omissions and additions serve a common purpose. For example, additions of the article commonly occur before nouns modified by a possessive genitive, especially in prepositional phrases (Qoh 3:18 καρδίᾳ μου LXX/τῇ καρδίᾳ μου LXX[L] "my heart"). Where the critical text preserves an article in similar syntactical environments, omissions of the article rarely occur in the LXX[L] text. In Ecclesiastes, doublets add clarity to texts that are difficult to understand (e.g., Qoh 5:9 καὶ τίς ἠγάπησεν ἐν πλήθει αὐτῶν γένημα "and who loved produce in a great quantity of them" (*NETS) LXX/καὶ τίς ἠγάπησεν ἐν πλήθει αὐτῶν γένημα καὶ τίς ἠγάπησεν δῶρα ἐν πλήθει οὐκ ἐλεύσεται "and he who loved produce in a great quantity of them and he who loved gifts in a great quantity will not come" LXX[L]/וּמִי־אֹהֵב בֶּהָמוֹן לֹא תְבוּאָה "nor the lover of wealth with gain" [*NRSV] MT). Most doublets are drawn from Hexaplaric sources (→ 13–17.1.6.4). The substitution of nouns for pronouns, which is a trait of the Lucianic recension, is absent from Ecclesiastes and present in Ruth (Ruth 3:15 αὐτῇ, "her" LXX/τῇ ρουθ, "Ruth" LXX[L]). Substitutions of synonyms are common (Ruth τὰ παιδάρια LXX/οἱ παῖδες LXX[L] "children"; Qoh 7:28 ἄνθρωπον LXX/ἄνδρα LXX[L] "man"). Substitution of verbs with similar meanings – especially verbs compounded with a preposition – is common (e.g., Ruth 1:21 ἀπέστρεψέν "turned back" LXX/ἐπέστρεψεν "turned about" LXX[L]). The books of the Five Scrolls are especially short, but the manuscripts preserve many Lucianic variants.

13–17.1.6.4 Inner-Translational Features

In Esther, Hanhart notes that LXX[392] is a mixed text characterized by many agreements with Hexaplaric readings (→ 13–17.1.1.5). Agreements between LXX[L] and LXX[o] are not uncommon in Ruth (e.g., Ruth 2:4 εἶπαν "they said" LXX/εἶπον "they said" LXX[L O] and Ruth 3:4 ὅπου "where" LXX/που "where" LXX[L O]). Influence from Hexaplaric sources is also notable in Ecclesiastes (e.g., Qoh 10:8 ἐν αὐτῷ ἐμπεσεῖται LXX/ἐμπεσεῖται ἐν αὐτῷ LXX[O L], both meaning "will fall into it"; → 13–17.1.5.3). Doublets in Ecclesiastes are created mostly from Hexaplaric sources

---

Geburtstages [eds. D. Fraenkel, U. Quast, J.W. Wevers; MSU 20; Göttingen: Vandenhoeck & Ruprecht, 1990], 219–30 [226]). Dickie's analysis shows that Lucian revised Ecclesiastes like other canonical books (Dickie, "An Analysis of the Lucianic Recension of the Greek Ecclesiastes"). For Ecclesiastes, see Gentry, *Ecclesiastes*.

[5] Quast, *Ruth*, 45.
[6] Hanhart, *Esther*, 15.
[7] See Ziegler, "Hat Lukian den griechischen Sirach rezensiert?" 210–29.

(e.g., Qoh 10:11 ἐν οὐ ψιθυρισμῷ "when there is no whispering" (*NETS*) LXX = MT/ἐν οὐ ψιθυρισμῷ ἀπούσης ἐπῳδῆς "when there is no whisper, when a spell is absent" LXX^L = Sym). Hence it is not uncommon to see at least two strata in the Five Scrolls: 1) Hexaplaric influence; and 2) later recensional activity attributed to the historical Lucian of Antioch or another recensionist. These strata hold especially for Ecclesiastes where there is no evidence for proto-Lucianic readings.

13–17.1.6.5 Text-Critical Value

In addition to clarifying what text of the Bible was widely used in Greek-speaking Syria, Lucianic manuscripts are an aid to discovering Hexaplaric readings (→ 13–17.1.5), because it is believed that Lucian used a Hexaplaric source as his base text or that the recension was brought into conformity with a Hexaplaric text at a date later than Lucian's life (e.g., Ruth 4:11 εἴποσαν LXX/εἶπεν LXX$^{oI–15\ 54'}$ [both meaning "said"]; Qoh 11:8 ἐάν "if" LXX/ἐάν γε "even if" LXX$^{O–V\ L}$; see above, → 13–17.1.6.4). The recension is not typically used in this way, because attributions are absent from the manuscripts. Hence, the recension is commonly used to gauge the influence of Hexaplaric sources on the establishing of popular texts.

Dickie, M.M., "An Analysis of the Lucianic Recension of the Greek Ecclesiastes" (PhD diss., The Southern Baptist Theological Seminary, 2013).

Fernández Marcos, N., "Theodoret's Biblical Text in the Octateuch," *BIOSCS* 11 (1978): 27–43.

Gentry, P.J. (ed.), *Ecclesiastes* (Septuaginta Vetus Testamentum Graecum; Göttingen: Vandenhoeck & Ruprecht, forthcoming).

Haelewyck, J.-C., "Le texte dit 'lucianique' du livre d'Esther: Son étendue et sa cohérence," *Mus* 98 (1985): 5–44.

Hautsch, E., *Der Lukiantext des Oktateuchs* (MSU 1; Berlin: Weidmannsche Buchhandlung, 1909), 518–43.

Rahlfs, A., *Studie über den griechischen Text des Buches Ruth* (MSU 3; Berlin: Weidmannsche Buchhandlung, 1922).

Ziegler, J., "Hat Lukian den griechischen Sirach rezensiert?" *Bib* 40 (1959): 210–29.

Matthew M. Dickie

13–17.1.7 Vulgate

13–17.1.7.1 Background

The Vulgate translations of the Five Scrolls were accomplished at three distinct phases. V-Lam was linked to the prophet Jeremiah and thus rendered with the prophetic corpus ca. 390–393, the earliest phase of Jerome's Hebrew translations. V-Qoh and V-Cant, among the Solomonic corpus, were translated ca. 398, the middle period. V-Ruth and V-Esth, produced ca. 405–406, were among his last translations (→ 1.3.5.2). V-Esth 1:1–10:3 is from Hebrew; V-Esth 10:4–16:24 is from the Greek supplements, a Hexaplaric form of the Old Greek (→ 13–17.1.1.5). Of the Five Scrolls, Jerome composed only a commentary on Ecclesiastes, ca. 388–389, a decade before his translation of this book. This commentary provides a window into his growth as a Hebrew scholar, as there are several instances in which renderings in the commentary based on LXX are altered in his later translation of the Hebrew.[1]

13–17.1.7.2 Translation Character

The translation styles of the Five Scrolls vary to some extent. The earliest translation, V-Lam, although it contains some pluses and is not always literal (e.g., the clause in Lam 4:7, *rubicundiores ebore antiquo* "more ruddy than the old ivory," renders עֶצֶם "bone" as *ebore* "ivory" and represents מִפְּנִינִים "than corals" as "old"), is nonetheless characterized by a more formal equivalency, *verbum e verbo* "word for word," than the last translations of Esther and Ruth, which tend to be freer renderings, *sensum e sensu* "sense for sense." Despite Jerome's claims in the preface to Esther of a literal translation *verbum e verbo*, his rendering of that book is often expansive, deviating from the extant Hebrew, including pluses without basis in any extant version (examples below). At times, the Vulgate demonstrates influence from the Hexaplaric translations (→ 1.3.1.2) and the Greek tradition generally (e.g., V-Esth 1:6 adds *pario* "from Paros" to describe the geographical origin of the marble, based on παρί-

---

[1] See Goodrich and Miller, *Commentary on Ecclesiastes*, 12–13.

νου in both the Old Greek and the Alpha-text of Esther; MT has no equivalent. And v-Qoh 6:5 *distantiam* "distance," derives from Symmachus' διαφορᾶς of the same meaning rather than from Hebrew נָחַת "rest"/LXX ἀνάπαυσας). And yet, Jerome often ignored the Greek versions' pluses (e.g., LXX-Ruth 4:8, καὶ ἔδωκεν αὐτῷ "and he gave (it) to him"). Also, the Vulgate follows MT-Esth 4:14 and 6:13 (6:22 Alpha-text) in not referring to God, in contrast to LXX. While it is difficult to know what to make of Jerome's claim in his preface *in libris Salomonis* "On the Books of Solomon" to have translated Canticles and Ecclesiastes in three days, his translation of Canticles is characterized by a strong effort to render the Hebrew poetry, sometimes in contrast to LXX. Nevertheless, neither v-Cant nor v-Qoh can be characterized as a word-for-word rendering of the Hebrew. This may be illustrated from Qoh 5:2, where the Vulgate, *et in multis sermonibus invenitur stultitia* "and in many words foolishness is found," recasts the Hebrew וְקוֹל כְּסִיל בְּרֹב דְּבָרִים "and a fool's voice (is) in a multitude of words," in contrast to LXX's imitation of the Hebrew, καὶ φωνὴ ἄφρονος ἐν πλήθει λόγων "and a fool's voice (is) in a multitude of words."

13–17.1.7.3 Translation Technique
13–17.1.7.3.1 Hebrew Idioms
Jerome handles Semitic idioms in a variety of ways in the Five Scrolls. He often did not imitate the Hebrew verb plus cognate noun (Qoh 5:3 תִּדֹּר נֶדֶר "you vow a vow," *vovisti* "you have vowed"). v-Cant 1:7, however, follows LXX in rendering the Hebrew idiom that employs *lamed* with the second-person pronoun, which is not idiomatic in Greek or Latin: אִם־לֹא תֵדְעִי לָךְ "if you do not know for yourself," *si ignoras te* "if you are unknowing yourself" (cf. LXX: ἐὰν μὴ γνῷς σεαυτήν). v-Esth 2:4b avoids a literal rendering of the common idiom בְּעֵינֵי "in the eyes of" (*placuit ... regi* "was pleasing to the king"), while earlier in the same verse and also in v-Esth 2:15 Jerome gives literal renderings of this idiom (*oculis regis* "in the eyes of the king"). v-Ruth 2:13 provides a literal translation of the idiom וְכִי דִבַּרְתָּ עַל־לֵב שִׁפְחָתֶךָ/*et locutus es ad cor ancillae tuae* "and you have spoken to the heart of your maidservant"

(contrast the freer renderings in Gen 50:21; 2 Sam 19:8). While he often omitted repetition found in MT (e.g., Cant 5:6 לְדוֹדִי וְדוֹדִי "to my beloved, but my beloved," *dilecto meo at ille* "to my beloved, but he"), at v-Cant 6:12(7:1) he retains the fourfold repetition of the imperative *revertere* "return."

The Hebrew infinitive construct is often rendered with *ut* plus the subjunctive: Ruth 2:15 *ut ... colligeret* "so that she might glean"; Esth 1:11 *ut introducerent* "that they should bring"; Esth 3:13 *ut occiderent* "that they should kill"; Esth 4:4 *ut ... induerent* "that they might clothe"; Esth 5:8 *ut det* "that he should grant"; Ruth 1:1 *ut peregrinaretur* "so that he might sojourn"; Lam 2:14 *ut ... provocarent* "so that they might provoke"; Lam 4:16 *ut respiciat* "that he may regard." Other times he uses a gerund: e.g., Qoh 3:2 *nascendi ... plantandi ... evellendi* "of being born ... of planting ... of plucking up."

Prepositions are sometimes added according to Latin idiom (e.g., Ruth 1:1 *cum uxore sua* "with his wife"; Ruth 1:3 *cum filiis* "with (her) sons"). Prepositions may also be omitted (e.g., the omission of מִן "than" in Qoh 2:13 *stultitiam*, "folly," and in Ruth 2:14 *comede panem* "eat of the bread"). At Ruth 1:15; Cant 2:9; 3:7; and Esth 7:9, the particle *en* replaces Hebrew הִנֵּה (LXX ἰδού; VL *ecce* [all meaning "behold"]). Jerome will at times add a relative pronoun to achieve a smoother Latin sentence (e.g., Lam 4:21 *quae*).

13–17.1.7.3.2 Attention to Context
Jerome will sometimes elaborate on a verse according to his understanding of the passage in context. The following are examples of such explanatory pluses: v-Qoh 5:10 adds *divitias* "the riches" to clarify what is only implied in the Hebrew and LXX. Similarly, v-Qoh 2:26 is unique in supplying *Deus* as the implied subject of the verb, "gives." In Qoh 2:8, the words שִׁדָּה וְשִׁדּוֹת, which are *hapax legomena*, probably refer to male and female cupbearers who were also prostitutes, whereas the Vulgate's translation, *scyphos et urceos in ministerio ad vina fundenda* "cups and vessels for pouring out wine in table service," avoids referring to prostitutes.

v-Esth 2:21 adds *qui ianitores erant* "who were porters" (absent in MT and Old Greek) to explain the previous clause. v-Esth 1:10 expands the phrase about the king being merry with wine: *et post nimiam potionem incalvisset* "and after very much drinking he was warm (with wine)." The plus at Esth 9:2 *magnitudinis eorum* "(fear) of their power" is added to כִּי־נָפַל פַּחְדָּם עַל־כָּל־הָעַמִּים "because fear of them fell on all the peoples," to clarify why the people were afraid of them, expanding the Hebrew third person suffix and improving the Latinity. In v-Qoh 2:3, *abstrahere a vino carnem meam* "to withdraw my flesh from wine," the prefix *abs* in *abstrahere* ("to withdraw") makes the statement negative, which *prima facie* seems to convey a meaning opposite to the enigmatic Hebrew clause, לִמְשׁוֹךְ בַּיַּיִן אֶת־בְּשָׂרִי "to draw my flesh through wine." However, a literal translation would have made little sense to a Latin audience and could have been taken to imply that imbibing wine enhances wisdom; in fact, if the Hebrew verse refers to an action that seems reasonable but which turns out to be unwise, then Jerome's rendering paradoxically captures the ultimate sense of the verse.[2]

Jerome occasionally assists his audience with an explanatory gloss, e.g., v-Ruth 1:14 adds *ac reversa* "and she returned" through the influence of LXX's plus, καὶ ἐπέστρεψεν εἰς τὸν λαὸν αὐτῆς "and she returned to her people" (VL: *et abiit* "and she went away"), which is absent from MT and 4QRuth[b]. v-Ruth 2:15, *spicas ex more* "ears (of corn), as (was her) custom" is a plus in which *spicas* ("ears of corn") fills out the sense and *ex more* ("as was her custom") is a contextual elaboration. v-Esth 3:12 adds *Nisan* to explain *mense primo* "in the first month"; and v- Ruth 1:20 adds *id est pulchram* "that is, beautiful" and *hoc est amaram* "that is, bitter" to elucidate Naomi's names.

Jerome sometimes inserts deferential language if the context is fitting, e.g., he adds *obsecro* "I beseech" in Esth 5:4 and 8:5 in deference to the king. At times, he will use an equivalent for the particle נָא "please" (Lam 1:18 *obsecro* "I beseech"; Lam 5:16 *vae* "woe"), although he often omits an equivalent (Ruth 2:2,7; Qoh 2:1; Cant 3:2; 7:9).

13–17.1.7.3.3 External Influences

Occasionally Vulgate renderings in the Five Scrolls are through outside influence from Roman classics, the New Testament, and Jerome's Jewish teachers. At Esth 9:4, the addition *per cunctorum ora volitabat* "and it flew about through the mouths of all" was inspired by Cicero's *Tusculan Disputations* 1,34, *volito vivos per ora virum* "I fly about alive through the mouths of men." The phrase *in peccatis nostris*[3] "in our sins" at v-Lam 4:20 is a Christological rendering that echoes 1 Cor 15:17.[4] Two instances of midrashic vocalization that parallel Vulgate renderings are as follows: first, v-Lam 5:13 *adulescentibus inpudice abusi sunt* "They abused the young men indecently" is likely indebted to the haggadic exegesis of *Lamentations Rabbati* 5:13 § 1, in which the reference to grinding in Lam 5:13, טְחוֹן "grinding mill," is taken as a euphemism for sexual intercourse;[5] second, Jerome reads the unpointed Hebrew of Lam 1:7, מִשְׁבַּתֶּהָ "her downfall," as *sabbata eius* "her sabbaths," which is a reading also found in *Lam. Rab.*[6]

---

[2] *Pace* Goodrich and Miller (*Commentary on Ecclesiastes*, 165), who surmise that a medieval copyist must have altered the verse. The manuscript evidence in the apparatus of H. Quentin (ed.), *Biblia sacra iuxta latinam vulgatam versionem ad codicum fidem iussu Pii PP. XI cura et studio monac.*, Vol: 11: *Libri Salomonis, id est Proverbia ecclesiastes canticum canticorum: ex interpretatione Sancti Hieronymi; cum praefationibus et variis capitulorum seriebus* (Rome: Typis Polyglottis Vaticanis, 1957) shows no significant variants. The other references to wine in Ecclesiastes (e.g., Qoh 2:4 planting vines; 9:7 enjoying wine; 10:19 wine with a feast) are understandable in context; the Vulgate translation need not imply complete abstinence and thus would cohere with Jerome's views on moderation (*Epist.* 69.9; 108.21).

[3] Adkin, "*Biblia Pagana*," 78–79.

[4] There are no variants to MT בִּשְׁחִיתוֹתָם "in their pits," and the Vulgate plus stands in contrast to the other ancient renderings.

[5] Cf. Job 31:10 where Jerome interprets the verb חטן "to grind" as a reference to sexual impropriety, *scortum sit alteri uxor mea* "Let my wife be a harlot to another." F. Stummer, "Spuren Jüdischer und Christlicher Einflüsse," *JPOS* 8 (1928) 35–48, here 39.

[6] Other v-Lam renderings with connections to *Lam. Rab.* include Lam 1:5b, 12b–c, 14.

13–17.1.7.3.4 Renderings Indebted to Jerome's Views on Women

There are instances in which Jerome deliberately adjusted his translation on account of his views about proper female roles and behavior. In v-Cant 1:3 (Cant 1:4), the king brought the young woman into his *cellaria* "storerooms" not "his bed chambers" (MT חֲדָרָיו/LXX τὸ ταμιεῖον αὐτοῦ "his chamber"),[7] a rendering that avoids having the young woman appear happy to enter the king's bed chamber. Jerome's interest in providing *exempla* in his letters and the *Vitae Patrum* extended to his translations of the books of Ruth and Esther. The rendering in v-Ruth 3:4 *pallium quo operitur* "the cloak with which he is covered" softens the Hebrew sexual metaphor out of concern to present Ruth engaging in proper conduct. This concern carries throughout the book, e.g., in v-Ruth 2:16 he adds *absque rubore* "without shame." The interpretive rendering at v-Esth 1:18, *hoc exemplo* "by this example," makes the behavior of wives in defying their husbands a negative example, an *exemplum aversionis*. The same noun as a plus occurs at v-Ruth 4:11 to emphasize Ruth's exemplary virtue (*exemplum virtutis* "an example of virtue"; cf. Ruth 3:11). Jerome's subtle deviations from the Hebrew craft Ruth as an *exemplum* by means of his translation up to the point when she remarries (Ruth 4:12–13),[8] whereas the rest of Ruth 4 is quite close to MT.[9]

13–17.1.7.3.5 Style

The following are examples of Jerome's desire to create variation and to improve readability: In v-Lam 4:15 סוּרוּ סוּרוּ "Depart, depart!" is translated *recedite abite* "Depart, go away!" v-Qoh 3:16–17 uses *inpietatem* "wickedness," *iniquitatem* "iniquity," and *impium* "wicked" for the Hebrew noun רשע. Whereas in v-Esth 1:21, כַּדָּבָר "as … said" is rendered *iuxta consultum* "according to the counsel," in v-Esth 5:8 it is recast as *aperiam voluntatem meam* "I will reveal my intention." In MT-Esth 3:2, the noun הַמֶּלֶךְ occurs three times, but in the Vulgate we find both *rex* and the rare *Imperator* "emperor." v-Cant 1:2(3) offers *unguentis* "ointments" and *oleum* "oil" as translations for שֶׁמֶן "oil." v-Cant 4:10 has *mammae* "breasts" and *ubera* "breasts" for the twofold דֹּדַיִךְ "your love." v-Lam 1:16 follows other ancient witnesses in not repeating עֵינִי "my eye." v-Ruth 1:8 uses one verb, *ite* "go" instead of two (לֵכְנָה שֹׁבְנָה "Go, return"), and Ruth 4:5 has *emeris* "you buy," and *debes accipere* "you must take" for the twofold קנה "to buy, redeem, acquire".

The following examples demonstrate ways in which Jerome sought to improve the Latinity of his translation. He uses syntactical subordination in place of Semitic parataxis, e.g., Ruth 2:15, *atque inde* "and thereupon"; Ruth 4:1, *ergo* "and so." For Hebrew וַיְהִי "and he was" in Esth 2:7, the parataxis is softened with a relative clause *qui fuit* "who was." In Esth 2:8, 3:4, and 5:2 וַיְהִי becomes *cumque* "and when." In order to clarify the flow of thought, Jerome often adds particles: *enim* "for" (Ruth 2:9); *autem* "moreover, yet" (Ruth 2:15; 3:1; Esth 1:7; 4:4; 5:1; Qoh 2:26; Lam 2:14); *vero* "but" (Qoh 1:4; Esth 10:1); *videlicet* "namely" (Ruth 1:5; Esth 1:4). V-Lam 1:9 renders the Hebrew plural noun פְּלָאִים "wonderous, terrible things" as an adverb, *vehementer* "violently," which assists the Latinity and is more accurate than LXX's literal plural noun ὑπέρογκα "difficult things."

Jerome's translations indicate he was aware of the variety of uses of the Hebrew conjunction כִּי "for, because, that." In contrast to the more literal LXX-Qoh, which normally uses ὅτι "because, that," the Vulgate often lacks an equivalent (Qoh 5:2; 6:8; and 7:7[8]), or varies the translation depending on meaning in context, e.g., Qoh 4:14 *quod* "that, which" (relative clause); Qoh 6:4 *enim* "for" (adverbial); Qoh 7:6(7) and Lam 1:10,18 *quia* "because" (causal).

---

[7] The usual Vulgate equivalent of חדר "chamber" is *cubiculum* (1 Kgs 20:30; 22:25; 2 Kgs 9:2). In v-Cant 3:4, *cubiculum* refers to the young woman's mother's bedroom.

[8] v-Ruth 1:12 recasts a hopeful expression of marriage by omitting an equivalent for the noun תקוה "hope"; Jerome chose not to use a common Latin expression for marriage, *esse cum aliquo* "to be with someone," in rendering מהיות לאיש "from being with a man"; Vulgate: *nec apta vinculo coniugali* "not to be fit for wedlock."

[9] For details on Jerome's renderings of these books, see V. Skemp, "Learning by Example: *Exempla* in Jerome's Translations and Revisions of Biblical Books," *VC* 65 (2011): 257–84, esp. 264–67, 276–78.

In sharp contrast to VL and LXX of Ruth, the Vulgate often substitutes a pronoun for a proper name if context indicates who is meant (e.g., Ruth 1:8, 11, 15, 16; 2:1, 4, 11, 16; 3:1, 5, 15; 4:1, 3, 9, 10). Conversely, if a pronoun or verb is ambiguous, an exact designation is inserted (e.g Ruth 1:18, 19; 3:11, 13, 16; 4:2).

Jerome will sometimes employ a collective singular where the Hebrew is plural. For instance, in v-Cant 4:13, the plural עִם־נְרָדִים "with nards" is rendered with a singular, *cum nardo* "with nard." Jerome often renders the dual "heavens" with the singular, e.g., Qoh 3:1 תַּחַת הַשָּׁמָיִם "under the heavens," *sub caelo* "under heaven" (so also LXX: ὑπὸ τὸν οὐρανόν "under the heaven").

13–17.1.7.3.6 Literalisms and Transliterations

Examples of literal renderings include: Ruth 1:17 כֹּה יַעֲשֶׂה יהוה לִי וְכֹה יֹסִיף "thus may the Lord do to me, and thus may he add," *haec mihi faciat Deus et haec addat* "these things may the Lord do to me, and these may he add"; Lam 1:13; 3:3, 14, 62 כָּל־הַיּוֹם/*tota die* "all the day"; Lam 2:19 נֹכַח פְּנֵי אֲדֹנָי/*ante conspectum Domini* "before the face of the Lord"; Ruth 2:10, 13 חֵן בְּעֵינֶיךָ/*gratiam ante oculos tuos* "favor in your eyes." Although the asyndetic construction of Cant 5:6 חָמַק עָבָר "he had withdrawn, was gone," forms a single action (so LXX: παρῆλθεν), the Vulgate follows Aquila and Symmachus in maintaining two verbs (adding parataxis): *declinaverat atque transierat* "he had turned aside, and was gone."

The following are examples of transliterations: Cant 4:8 אֲמָנָה/*Amana* (contrast LXX: πίστεως "of faithfulness"); Cant 4:13 פַּרְדֵּס/*paradisus* (LXX: παράδεισος "orchard"; but in Qoh 2:5 the Vulgate translates פַּרְדֵּס as *pomeria* "orchards"); Cant 6:12 עַמִּי־נָדִיב/*Aminadab* (agreeing with LXX).

Jerome often translates the *hiphil* with *facere* "to make" or *dare* "to give," e.g., Esth 2:17 וַיַּמְלִיכֶהָ/*fecitque eam regnare* "and he made her to rule"; Cant 8:13 הַשְׁמִיעִינִי/*fac me audire* "make me to hear." He sometimes mimics Hebrew constructions (e.g., Lam 1:2 בָּכוֹ תִבְכֶּה/*plorans ploravit* "Weeping, she has wept"), but may also render more freely (e.g., Qoh 4:17 וְקָרוֹב לִשְׁמֹעַ מִתֵּת "and coming near to hear [is better] than," *enim melior est oboedientia quam* "for obedience is better than").

13–17.1.7.4 Text-Critical Value

13–17.1.7.4.1 Consonantal Variants

Occasionally Jerome's Hebrew *Vorlage* may have been slightly different from MT (→ 13.2.2; → 14.2.2; → 15.2.2; → 16.2.2; → 17.2.2), but each instance must be weighed carefully. For the construct plural in Lam 3:58 רִיבֵי נַפְשִׁי "the causes of my soul," v-Lam has the singular, *causam animae meae* "the cause of my soul," which may reflect a *Vorlage* without the final *yod* (cf. Ps 43[42]:1, where the singular, *causam meam* "my cause" translates the masculine singular construct רִיבִי); or else the singular may be intended to capture the essence of the Hebrew phrase in a collective sense. In Lam 3:17, MT has the second person *Qal*, וַתִּזְנַח "you have rejected," while the Vulgate presupposes the third person *Niphal*, *et repulsa est* "(my soul) was rejected" (cf. LXX). Whereas both MT and 4QLam at Lam 1:12 read two words each with an *aleph*, לוֹא אֲלֵיכֶם (4QLam: לוא [אליכ]י) "(Is it) nothing unto you?," v-Lam 1:12, *o vos* "O you!" agrees with Symmachus in reading only one *aleph*. In Lam 1:13, MT attests וַיִּרְדֶּנָּה "and he prevailed against it," which appears to be from the stem רדה, whereas 4QLam 1:13 reads ויורידני "and it brought me down," from ירד. The Vulgate's *et erudivit me* "it instructed me," assumes a verb stem without a *dalet*, ויורני, perhaps partly through the influence of Symmachus, καὶ ἐπαίδευσέν με "it instructed me."

v-Ruth 1:2, *morabantur*, "they resided" agrees with 4QRuth[a] (וישבו) against MT (וַיִּהְיוּ) and LXX (καὶ ἦσαν), "and they were." v-Ruth 3:14 and 2QRuth[b] lack MT's הָאִשָּׁה "the woman." v-Cant 1:2(3) has *unguentis* "ointments," which agrees with 6QCant 1:3, שמנין "oils" in lacking the pronominal suffix of MT שְׁמָנֶיךָ "your oils."

13–17.1.7.4.2 Vocalization and *Ketiv/Qere*

The Vulgate of the Five Scrolls usually reflects the vocalization of MT (→ 10–20.1). The following are representative exceptions: v-Lam 1:9 *deposita est* "she is cast down" reads the *Qal* verb וַתֵּרֶד "she goes down," as if it were *hophal*, וַתּוּרַד, in agreement with Symmachus (καὶ κατήχθη). In Cant 4:8, the Vulgate *veni* "come" and LXX Δεῦρο presuppose a vocalization of the Hebrew as an imperative with final *he*, אֱתָה, whereas MT reads a preposition with first person suffix, אִתִּי "with me."

In cases where a distinction between *Ketiv* and *Qere* is clear from the translation, the Vulgate of the Five Scrolls agrees with the *Ketiv* much less often (3×: Esth 3:4; Lam 4:12; 5:5) than with the *Qere* (20×: Ruth 1:8; 3:3[2×], 4,14; Qoh 4:8, 17; 12:6; Esth 1:16; 9:27; Lam 2:2; 3:20, 25, 32, 39; 4:3, 16, 17; 5:3, 7[2×]).

Adkin, N., "*Biblia Pagana*: Classical Echoes in the Vulgate," *Aug* 40 (2008): 77–87.

Barthélemy, *Critique textuelle 1982.

Goodrich, R.J. and D. Miller, *St. Jerome: Commentary on Ecclesiastes: Translated, and Edited with Commentary* (ACW 66; New York: Newman, 2012).

Skemp, V., "Learning by Example: *Exempla* in Jerome's Translations and Revisions of Biblical Books," *VC* 65 (2011): 257–84.

Stummer, F., "Spuren Jüdischer und Christlicher Einflüsse auf die Übersetzung der Grossen Propheten durch Hieronymus," *JPOS* 8 (1928): 35–48.

Treat, J.C., "Aquila, Field, and the Song of Songs," in *Origen's Hexapla and Fragments: Papers Presented at the Rich Seminar on the Hexapla, Oxford Centre for Hebrew and Jewish Studies, 25th July–3rd August 1994* (ed. A. Salvesen; TSAJ 58; Tübingen: Mohr Siebeck, 1998), 135–75.

Vincent Skemp

13–17.1.8 Arabic Translations

13–17.1.8.1 Background

The most unstable textual history concerning the order of biblical books is associated with the collection of the Five Scrolls (*Megillot*).[1] The MT books of Song of Songs, Ruth, Lamentations, Ecclesiastes, and Esther (→ 13.2.2; → 14.2.2; → 15.2.2; → 16.2.2; → 17.2.2) are not grouped together in Qumran manuscripts and appear appended to certain books in the LXX versions and some Christian Bibles, where Ruth follows Judges and Lamentations follows Jeremiah (→ 1.3.1.1.4). In the medieval Leningrad Codex (→ 10–20.1), they are found grouped together in the following order: Ruth, Song of Songs, Ecclesiastes, Lamentations, and Esther. The practice of grouping these books together in codices emerges in the Middle Ages and appears to originate from the oral custom of reading out these five books in the synagogue on the Jewish festivals.

The two most common orders of the Five Scrolls in Jewish (Masoretic) medieval codices are based on either chronological or ritual principles, the latter based on the sequence of the holidays in which they are read out in synagogue worship. The order according to chronological considerations is based on the assumed historical period in which they were written. This order seems to be in agreement with the Palestinian tradition: Ruth, Song of Songs, Ecclesiastes, Lamentations, and Esther. The order based on the sequence of the Jewish holidays seems to be in agreement with the Babylonian tradition: Song of Songs – read on Passover; Ruth – read on *Shavu'ot* (Pentecost), Lamentations – read on Ninth of Av, Ecclesiastes – read on *Sukkot* (Feast of Booths), and Esther – read on *Purim*. In as much as ritual readings of these books take place throughout the year, it is not surprising to discover that they were translated, among other languages, into Judeo-Arabic. This entry is limited to the description of modern scholarly editions of medieval Judeo-Arabic translations of the Five Scrolls.

13–17.1.8.2 Ruth (Karaite Translations)

Karaite Judaism, which emerged in the ninth century C.E., was motivated by the rejection of Jewish oral law and rabbinic authority, and an ethos of return to Scripture. Hence, the Karaites inaugurated a translation enterprise of their own. Most Karaite translations were written in the tenth and eleventh centuries, the golden age of Karaite literary activity (→ 1.3.6).

The Karaite exegete of the tenth century, Yefet ben ʿElī, translated the entire Bible into Judeo-Arabic, a translation that has survived in numerous manuscript sources (→ 10.3.8; → 12.3.8). The Institute of Microfilmed Hebrew Manuscripts lists fourteen fragments of Yefet's translation and com-

---

[1] The writing of this article was supported by the Israel Science Foundation, grant No. 410/10.

mentary on Ruth, the oldest of which is dated to the eleventh century and written in Arabic characters. The first modern publication of Yefet's translation and commentary on Ruth was prepared by Schorstein in 1903.[2] Schorstein's edition includes the first two chapters of Ruth. It is based primarily on BL Or. 2554, which is written entirely in Arabic characters, including Hebrew verses and terms. Schorstein did not adhere to the script of the manuscript, rather he transcribed the Hebrew verses and terms into Hebrew characters. In addition, Schorstein further changed the Arabic orthography to conform to Classical Arabic.[3] Schorstein's edition was later translated into Hebrew by Markon, who mistakenly attributed it to Salmon b. Yerūḥam.[4] In 1952, Nemoy published a translation into English of Yefet's introduction and commentary on Ruth 1–2 as part of a collection of Karaite literature.[5] A study of Yefet's translation and commentary on Ruth, including the analysis of his translation techniques, was published as a PhD thesis by Blumfield in 2001.[6] Subsequently, in 2003, Butbul published a critical edition of Yefet's translation and commentary on Ruth including a translation into Hebrew. In an effort to reflect faithfully her sources, Butbul's edition combines both Hebrew and Arabic script.[7]

Tanḥum ben Yosef ha-Yerushalmi, a Rabbanite scholar who lived in Egypt in the thirteenth century, wrote a Judeo-Arabic commentary on Ruth. However, this commentary does not include a translation. A scholarly edition of this commentary was published by Michael Wechsler in 2010.[8]

13–17.1.8.3 Song of Songs (Karaite Translations)

The first scholar who edited and published parts of of Yefet ben 'Elī's translation and commentary on the Song of Songs was Paul Achilles Jung, the father of Carl Gustav Jung, the famous psychiatrist. Jung included in his unpublished dissertation the first chapter of Yefet's work on Song of Songs.[9] Subsequently, Bargès published Yefet's entire translation and commentary on Song of Songs with a translation into Latin. Bargès' edition presents Yefet's writing in Arabic script speckled with Hebrew-script insertions wherever Yefet cites Hebrew text. The edition is prefaced with an introduction, which includes information about Yefet, his life and work, and an update on the state of the field of Yefet's studies.[10] A study of Jung's work on Yefet's Song of Songs was published recently by Ryce-Menuhin.[11] A new edition of Yefet's translation and commentary on Song of Songs 1 that includes a translation into English was published lately by Alobaidi.[12] Yefet's approach to Song of Songs is manifested in his commentary, which is made up of a two-tier interpretation, one literal and the other allegorical. On the allegorical level, Yefet views the Song of Songs as a prophetic revelation in which the male-female relationship represents the relationship between God and the community of Israel, its leaders and nobles. In addition, Yefet suggests that there is a correlation between the Song of Songs and the thirty psalms that are titled *shir*. Frank has published several studies in which he uses Yefet's commentary on Song of Songs as a model of Karaite thought and exegesis. His work is replete with sample passages of Yefet's translation and commentary on Song of Songs accompanied by Frank's English translation.[13] Salmon b. Yerūḥam also translated and wrote a commentary on Song of Songs. Salmon's work on Song of Songs has not been published yet in a scholarly edition. However, a study of both Yefet and Salmon's work on Song of Songs was published by Frank in 2003.[14]

---

[2] Schorstein, *Commentar*.
[3] Butbul, "Ruth."
[4] Markon, "Ruth."
[5] Nemoy, *Anthology*.
[6] Blumfield, "Ruth."
[7] Butbul, "Ruth."
[8] Wechsler, *Strangers*.

[9] Jung, "Über des Karäers Jephet arabische Erklärung des Hohenliedes."
[10] Bargès, *Canticum*; Zawanowska, "Review."
[11] Ryce-Menuhin, *Jung*.
[12] Alobaidi, *Old*.
[13] Frank, "Song of Songs"; Frank, "Shoshanim"; Frank, *Search*.
[14] Frank, "Song of Songs."

13–17.1.8.4 Ecclesiastes
13–17.1.8.4.1 A Rabbanite Translation

An early Rabbanite Judeo-Arabic translation and commentary on Ecclesiastes was prepared by the Andalusian sage Isaac ben Judah Ibn Ghayyath (1038–1089) who lived in Lucena where he was the head of a Jewish academy. Ibn Ghayyath titled his work on Ecclesiastes *Kitāb al-Zuhd* "The Book of Asceticism." His translation reflects his approach to the book as a guide to ascetic living. His work betrays a great knowledge of philosophy and Greek sciences. He prefaces his work with a long introduction in which he includes a detailed study of the heavenly bodies, their positions and constellations. In addition to his emphasis on asceticism, his commentary includes long passages in which he further discusses the heavenly bodies and their movements. This work was included by Qafiḥ in his collection *Hamesh Megillot*[15] and translated into Hebrew. In his preface, Qafiḥ points out that the work is probably wrongly attributed to Saadia in Yemenite manuscript sources. Pines points out that this translation and commentary was identified as Ibn Ghayyath's by several scholars as early as the nineteenth century. He adds that the medieval Jewish proselyte who converted to Islam late in life, Hibatu Allah ʿAlī ibn Malkā Abū al-Barakāt al-Baghdādī (d. ca. 1164), cites passages from Ibn Ghayyath's commentary in his own work on Ecclesiastes. Abū al-Barakāt unambiguously mentions his source.[16] Abū al-Barakāt's Judeo-Arabic translation and commentary on Ecclesiastes has not yet been published.

13–17.1.8.4.2 Karaite Translations

The first modern edition of Yefet's translation and commentary on Qohelet 1–6 was prepared by Bland.[17] This edition includes an introduction on Yefet's methods and style, his sources, and mode of interpretation. It also includes a critical edition of Yefet's Judeo-Arabic translation and commentary on the first six chapters of Ecclesiastes followed by an English translation. Numerous passages of Yefet's work on Ecclesiastes coupled with translation into Hebrew were prepared by Ben-Shammai as part of his unpublished PhD dissertation.[18] Prior to that, a study of Yefet's commentary on Ecclesiastes was published by Vajda.[19] Currently, Robinson is working on a critical edition of the entire text of Yefet on Ecclesiastes including a translation into English.[20]

The medieval Karaite, Salmon ben Yerūḥam, also wrote a translation and commentary on Ecclesiastes. Robinson recently published a critical edition of Salmon's work. The introduction to this publication includes a discussion of the role of Ecclesiastes in Karaism, Salmon's methods and approaches, his sources, the ideology behind his commentary, and a description of the manuscripts used.[21]

13–17.1.8.5 Lamentations
13–17.1.8.5.1 A Rabbanite Translation

According to the online catalogue of the Institute of Microfilmed Hebrew Manuscripts, a few fragments of Saadia Gaon's translation and commentary on Lamentations have been identified. Based on some of these manuscripts, Qafiḥ published an edition of Saadia's translation of Lamentations in his collection *Five Megillot*.[22] The text is complemented with occasional comments that Qafiḥ refers to as "according to Saadia." He explains that these are a reworking of Saadia's comments by later copyists and commentators. Segments of Saadia's commentary on Lamentations found in the Cairo Genizah were published by Ratzaby.[23]

13–17.1.8.5.2 Karaite Translations

With regard to Yefet's work on Lamentations, Ben-Shammai, in his article in the *Encyclopaedia Judaica*, says "to date Lamentations is the only bib-

---

[15] Qafiḥ, *Hamesh*.
[16] Pines, "Four"; cf. Sáenz-Badillos, "Ibn Ghayyat".
[17] Bland, *Ecclesiastes*.
[18] Ben-Shammai, "Doctrines."
[19] Vajda, *Deux*.
[20] Robinson, *Qohelet*.
[21] Robinson, *Asceticism*.
[22] Qafiḥ, *Hamesh*.
[23] Ratzaby, "Selections"; Ratzaby, "Perakim."

lical book on which no trace of Japheth's commentary has been identified."[24] However, recently, three manuscripts have been listed by the Institute of Microfilmed Hebrew Manuscripts (Israel National Library) as Yefet's work on Lamentations. In addition, Frank mentions a fourth unidentified manuscript, RNL MS Yevr.-Arab. I. 3806, which he suggests includes Yefet's work on Lamentations.[25] Nevertheless, none of these manuscripts has been published in a scholarly edition as yet.

Salmon ben Yerūḥam also wrote a Judeo-Arabic translation and commentary on Lamentations. More than one hundred fragments of this work are listed in the catalogue of the Institute of Microfilmed Hebrew Manuscripts (Israel National Library). Modern scholarly publications of Salmon's work on Lamentations include Feuerstein's publication of the first chapter of Salmon's translation and commentary on Lamentations.[26] Much later, a critical edition of Salmon's work on Lamentations was completed by Abdul-Karim.[27] Lastly, Jessica Andruss is currently preparing a doctoral dissertation that will include the edition and translation of selected passages from Salmon's work on Lamentations. Her research entails primarily a study of Salmon's approach to theology and exegesis as reflected in his commentary.

13–17.1.8.6 Esther
13–17.1.8.6.1 A Rabbanite Translation
The earliest known translation of Esther into Judeo-Arabic is Saadia Gaon's. A modern critical edition of this translation, which does not include a commentary, was published in 1961 by Qafiḥ in his collection *Five Megillot*.[28] Recently, Wechsler published ten newly identified fragments of Saadia's commentary on Esther.[29] This publication does not include Saadia's translation of Esther. Wechsler included in this article a translation of these fragments into English. Often medieval commentators rename biblical books to reflect their own point of view concerning the essence of those books. In light of this tradition, Saadia titled his work on Esther *Kitāb al-īnās bi-'l-jalwa* "The Book of Conviviality in Exile."[30] Saadia's entire surviving commentary on Esther has been fully reconstructed and was published in 2015 by Wechsler.[31] For further details and background on Saadia's method and approach to translation, see, inter alia, → 10.3.8, → 11.3.8, or → 12.3.8.

13–17.1.8.6.2 Karaite Translations
Yefet's Arabic translation and commentary on Esther has survived in Hebrew script. It was edited and published in 2008 by Wechsler.[32] Interestingly, Yefet titled his work on Esther *Sharḥ megillat Ahashwerosh* "Commentary on the Scroll of Ahasuerus." The work includes an introduction in which Yefet outlines the events and transgressions that led to the exile. In his commentary on the first verse, he continues his introduction as he outlines the events that took place in exile and that led to the occurrences that are described in Esther. It is important to note that in his commentary, found at the end of chapter seven, Yefet suggests that the compiler (*mudawwin*) of Esther based his composition on the writings of Esther herself.[33] To wit, Yefet suggests that the book of Esther is based on the writings of the woman whose name comprises the title of the book.

No other translation of Esther into Judeo-Arabic has been published to date. Ten fragments of translation and commentary on Esther were identified as Salmon ben Yerūḥam's. However, they have not yet been published.[34] The commentary of Tanḥum ha-Yerushalmi on Esther was published by Wechsler together with his commentary on Ruth. However, Tanḥum did not include a translation into Judeo-Arabic.[35]

---

[24] Ben-Shammai, "Japheth."
[25] Frank, *Search*.
[26] Feuerstein, *Commentar*.
[27] Abdul-Karim, "Lamentations."
[28] Qafiḥ, *Hamesh*.
[29] Wechsler, "Ten."
[30] Wechsler, "Ten."
[31] Wechsler, *Conviviality*.
[32] Wechsler, *Esther*.
[33] Wechsler, *Esther*; Sasson, "Gender."
[34] Wechsler, *Esther*.
[35] Wechsler, *Strangers*.

Many of the sources mentioned in this entry that pertain to Yefet's work are listed in two recent publications of Zawanowska.[36] For other Karaite scholarship, see also Walfish's recent survey of Karaite bibliography.[37]

Abdul-Karim, M.A.-L., "Commentary of Salmon Ben Yeruham on Lamentations: A Critical Edition," (PhD diss., St. Andrews University, 1975).

Alobaidi, J., *Old Jewish Commentaries on the Song of Songs*, Vol. 1: *The Commentary of Yefet ben Eli* (Bible in History 9; Bern: Peter Lang, 2010).

Léandre Bargès, J.J. (ed.), *Rabbi Yapheth Abou Aly Ibn-Aly Bassorensis Karaitarum doctoris sapientissimi in Canticum Canticorum commentatium arabicum* (Paris: Ernestus Leroux, 1884).

Ben-Shammai, H., "The Doctrines of Religious Thought of Abû Yûsuf Ya'qûb a-Qirqisânî and Yefet ben 'Elî" (PhD diss., The Hebrew University of Jerusalem, 1977) [Hebr.].

Ben-Shammai, H., "Japheth Ben Eli Ha-Levi," *EncJud* 11:86–87.

Bland, R.M., "The Arabic Commentary of Yephet ben 'Ali on the Book of Ecclesiastes, Chapters 1–6" (PhD diss., University of California, 1966).

Blumfield, F., "The Commentary of Yefet ben 'Eli on the Book of Ruth: Studies in Translation and Exegetical Techniques" (PhD diss., University of London, 2001).

Butbul, S., "The Commentary of Yefet ben 'Eli the Karaite on the Book of Ruth," *Sefunot* 23 (2003): 459–571 [Hebr.].

Feuerstein, S., *Der Commentar des Karäers Salmon ben Jerucham zu den Klageliedern* (Krakow: J. Fischer, 1898).

Frank, D., "The Shoshanim of the Tenth-Century Jerusalem: Karaite Exegesis, Prayer and Communal Identity," in *The Jews of Medieval Islam: Community, Society, and Identity: Proceedings of an International Conference, Held by the Institute of Jewish Studies, University College London, 1992* (ed. D. Frank; Études sur le judaïsme médiéval 16; Leiden: Brill, 1995).

Frank, D., "Karaite Commentaries on the Song of Songs from Tenth-Century Jerusalem," in *With Reverence for the Word: Medieval Scriptural Exegesis in Judaism, Christianity, and Islam* (eds. J.D. McAuliffe et al.; Oxford: Oxford University Press, 2003), 51–69.

Frank, D., *Search Scripture Well: Karaite Exegetes and the Origins of the Jewish Bible Commentary in the Islamic East* (Études sur le judaïsme médiéval 29; Leiden: Brill, 2004).

Jung, P.A., "Über des Karäers Jephet arabische Erklärung des Hohenliedes" (PhD diss., Georg-August University Göttingen, 1866).

Markon, I.D., "The Commentary on the Scroll of Ruth by the Karaite Salmon ben Yerōḥam," in *Livre d' Hommage à la mémoire du Dr Samuel Poznański (1864–1921) offert par les amis et les compagnons du travail scientifique* (Warsaw: Comité de la Grande Synagogue, 1927), 78–96 [Hebr.].

Nemoy, L., *Karaite Anthology* (New Haven: Yale University Press, 1952).

Pines, S., "Four Extracts from Abu'l-Barakat Al-Baghdadi's Commentary on Ecclesiastes," *Tarbiz* 33 (1963): 198–213 [Hebr.].

Polliack, M., *The Karaite Tradition of Arabic Bible Translation: A Linguistic and Exegetical Study of Karaite Translations of the Pentateuch From the Tenth and Eleventh Centuries C.E.* (Études sur le Judaïsme médiéval 17; Leiden: Brill, 1997).

Ratzaby, Y., "Selections from Rav Sa'adiah's Commentary on *Lamentations*," *Bar-Ilan* 20–21 (1983): 349–81 [Hebr.].

Ratzaby, Y., "Perakim hadashim mi-perush R. Saadiah le-Ekha," *Sinai* 95 (1985): 1–23 [Hebr.].

Robinson, J.T., *Asceticism, Eschatology, Opposition to Philosophy: The Arabic Translation and Commentary of Salmon ben Yeroham on Qohelet (Ecclesiastes)* (Études sur le judaïsme médiéval 45; Leiden: Brill, 2012).

Robinson, J.T., *Establishing the Way of the Peshat: The Arabic Translation and Commentary of Yefet b. 'Eli on Qohelet (Ecclesiastes)* [provisional title] (Leiden: Brill, forthcoming).

Ryce-Menuhin, J., *Jung and Monotheism: Judaism, Christianity, and Islam* (London: Routledge, 1994).

Saadia, *Hamesh Megillot* (Jerusalem: Hotza'at ha-Aguda le-Hatzalat Ginze Teman, 1962) [Hebr.].

Sáenz-Badillos, A., "Ibn Ghayyat," *EncJud* 9:676–77.

Sarna, N.M. and S.D. Sperling, "The Canon," *EncJud* 3:574–86.

Sasson, I., "Gender Equality in Yefet Ben 'Eli's Commentary and Karaite Halakhah," *AJSR* 37 (2013): 51–74.

Schorstein, N. (ed.), *Der Commentar des Karäers Jephet ben 'Ali zum Buche Rûth: Zum ersten Male nach drei Mss. ediert: Mit Einleitung und Anmerkungen versehen* (Berlin: Itzkowski, 1903).

Vajda, G., *Deux commentaires karaïtes sur l'Ecclésiaste*

---

[36] Zawanowska, "Review"; Zawanowska, "Yefet Ben 'Elī."
[37] Walfish, *Bibliographia*.

(Études sur le judaïsme médiéval 4; Leiden: Brill, 1971).

Walfish, B.D. and M. Kizilov, *Bibliographia Karaitica: An Annotated Bibliography of Karaites and Karaism* (Études sur le judaïsme médiéval 43; Leiden: Brill, 2011).

Wechsler, M.G., *The Arabic Translation and Commentary of Yefet Ben 'Eli the Karaite on the Book of Esther* (Études sur le judaïsme médiéval 43 36; Leiden: Brill, 2008).

Wechsler, M.G., *Strangers in the Land: The Judaeo-Arabic Exegesis of Tanḥum ha-Yerushalmi on the Books of Ruth and Esther* (Jerusalem: Magnes Press, 2010) [Hebr.].

Wechsler, M.G., "Ten Newly Identified Fragments of Saadia's Commentary on Esther: Introduction and Translation," in *Pesher Naḥum: Texts and Studies in Jewish History and Literature from Antiquity through the Middle Ages Presented to Norman (Naḥum) Golb* (ed. J.L. Kraemer and M. Wechsler; Chicago: The Oriental Institute of the University of Chicago, 2012), 237–92, 17*–39*.

Wechsler, M.G., *The Book of Conviviality in Exile (Kitāb al-īnās bi-'l-jalwa). The Judaeo-Arabic Translation and Commentary of Saadia Gaon on the Book of Esther* (Leiden: Brill, 2015).

Zawanowska, M., "Yefet Ben 'Elī the Karaite and His Arabic Commentary on Genesis 12:1–7," *Jewish History Quarterly* 4/244 (2012): 530–66.

Zawanowska, M., "Review of Scholarly Research on Yefet and His Works," *REJ* (forthcoming).

Ilana Sasson

13–17.2 Secondary Translations

13–17.2.1 Vetus Latina

13–17.2.1.1 Ruth

The VL version of the book of Ruth is preserved in only a single manuscript, the so-called *Complutensis* or first Bible of Alcalá (VL[109]),[1] which was written in Spain as late as the tenth century. The book is preceded by a prologue, whose author is not named.[2] As the book of Ruth is not at the center of theological interest, quotations in the patristic literature are rare. The most extensive quotations are found in Claudius of Turin's commentary[3] from the ninth century C.E., who uses a version close to that of VL[109] as the underlying text but uses the Vulgate (→ 13–17.1.7) in his explanations. With this source, we remain in a late period and a well-defined area, as Claudius is also said to be from Spain. Early witnesses of VL-Ruth such as the author of Pseudo-Cyprian,[4] the Ambrosiaster,[5] Gregory of Elvira,[6] or Pseudo-Philo,[7] mention the text, but do not cite it. The only sources worth mentioning are Ambrosius' commentaries to Luke[8] and to Psalm 43.[9] However, it remains difficult to decide whether he had a VL text at hand or rather translated the text himself from a Greek *Vorlage* or revised it according to a Greek text. The book of Ruth is of little significance for the liturgy, although it was occasionally read.[10] Of some interest is the fact that the Council of Braga (561 C.E.) fixed the expression *dominus (sit) vobiscum* "the Lord be with you," which is taken from Ruth 2:4, as a liturgical formula.[11]

13–17.2.1.1.1 Editions, Auxiliary Tools

Sabatier[12] edited VL-Ruth mainly on the basis of Ambrosius' commentary to Luke because the *Complutensis* and Claudius' commentary were not yet known. Denk, who planned an edition of the VL text of the whole Bible, published the book of Ruth as a sample text.[13] Due to methodological deficiencies, this publication is strongly criticized among experts and cannot be taken as a critical edition.[14] Ortiz de Urbina[15] and Ayuso Marazuela[16] have edited the text with specific aims. Although both publications are valuable, for a critical edition that is based on all available sources one has to rely on the publication in the series of the Beuron Vetus Latina Institute.[17]

13–17.2.1.1.2 Translation Technique

The *Vorlage* of the VL text is a Greek version close to the R-recension of LXX (→ 2.4.6), a recension that is characterized by its frequent adjustments to the MT text (→ 13.2.2).[18] Although VL-Ruth generally represents an accurate translation of this Greek text, it provides us with a number of renderings that cannot be explained by the Greek *Vorlage*. In some places, it is closer to MT, either because

---

[1] See Gesche, *Ruth*, 9.
[2] Gesche, *Ruth*, 27–28.
[3] Douglas, "Commentary," 295–320.
[4] *Patrologia Latina Suplementum* 1, 83 to Ruth 3:12, 15, 17.
[5] A. Souter, *Pseudo-Augustini Quaestiones Veteris et Novi Testamenti CXXVII* (CSEL 50; Vienna, 1908), 431 to Ruth 1:22; 2:2; 4:5, 10.
[6] Schulz-Flügel, *Gregorius Eliberritanus*, 228 to Ruth 4:10, 13, 17, 22 and CCSL 69, 71 to Ruth 1:22; 2:2; 4:5, 10, 17, 21, 22.
[7] D.J. Harrington, *Les antiquités bibliques: Introduction et texte critique* (SC 229; Paris: Cerf), 370 to Ruth 1:14–16.
[8] CCSL 14.
[9] K. Schenkl, *Sancti Ambrosii Opera*, Vol. 4: *Expositio Evangelii secundum Lucam* (CSEL 32.4; Prague: 1902); M. Petschenig and M. Zelzer (eds.), *Sancti Ambrosi Opera*, Vol. 6: *Explanatio psalmorum XII* (CSEL 64; Vienna: Verlag der Österreichischen Akademie der Wissenschaften, 1999).

[10] See the Breviarium Gothicum (PL 86, 442B–446A) for the Mozarabic liturgy and Bogaert, "Eptaticus," 323–24 for the usage of the *libri mulierum* in the Bobbio Missal.
[11] Ramos-Lissón, "Le rôle de la Bible dans les Conciles Bracariens," 42.
[12] Sabatier, **Bibliorum*, 1.469–72.
[13] Denk, *Die altlateinische Bibel*.
[14] Compare the review by A. Jülicher, *TLZ* 42.2 (1917): 37–38.
[15] Ortiz de Urbina, *Rut*.
[16] Ayuso Marazuela, *El Octateuco*.
[17] Gesche, *Ruth*.
[18] U. Quast, *Ruth* (Septuaginta Vetus Testamentum Graecum 4.3; Göttingen: Vandenhoeck & Ruprecht, 2006), 86–87, 100.

of a slightly different *Vorlage* or because the Vulgate (→ 13–17.1.7) had influenced the translation. In addition, the direct influence of MT cannot be completely excluded. As an example, one can refer to personal names in the LXX text (→ 13–17.1.1.1), which are occasionally mentioned explicitly contrary to the Hebrew *Vorlage*, while the VL text leaves them out in accordance with MT (cf. Ruth 1:15; 2:14 [*bis*], 18, 19; 4:2, 3). The lack of Lucianic readings (→ 13–17.1.6) in this late text accords with the phenomenon in which the older a VL text is, the more Lucianic readings it contains.[19]

13–17.2.1.1.3 Inner-Translational Features

The quotations of the church fathers (→ 21.8) and manuscript VL[109] itself represent the same recension of the text with minor variants. The text of the *Complutensis* manuscript (VL[109]) offers some orthographic and grammatical features that are typical for late Latin in Spain,[20] such as monophthongization, the change from *-is* to *-es* in case endings, the confusion of word-final *d/t* and of the consonants *b/v* and *c/q*, the addition or omission of *h* and other minor orthographical peculiarities. The confusion of gender or number is a typical grammatical characteristic of the text of this manuscript.

13–17.2.1.1.4 Text-Critical Value

The text of VL-Ruth shows in some places that the dependencies among the different versions are not linear throughout. Ruth 2:7 can be taken as an example. The VL rendering *pausaret* "she rested" is based on the LXX (→ 13–17.1.1.1) rendering κατέπαυσεν "she rested," which misinterprets the Hebrew text (→ 13.2.2). Both VL and LXX falsely derive the שָׁבְתָה "she stayed" of MT-Ruth from the root שבת "to rest" instead of from the root ישב "to stay/remain/dwell," whereupon the rendering implies the vocalization שָׁבְתָה "she rested." In addition, the Vulgate (→ 13–17.1.7) text (*reversa est* "she did return") misinterpreted the Hebrew by deriving the word from the root שוב "to turn around/return." The following הַבַּיִת "the house" is rendered as ἐν τῷ ἀγρῷ "in the field" in LXX without any variants, while VL, probably depending on the Vulgate, translates with *domum* "home."

The text of the *Complutensis* manuscript (VL[109]) offers some more unusual words and *hapax legomena* and often renders difficult passages independently from other sources.[21]

Ayuso Marazuela, T., *La Vetus Latina Hispana: El Octateuco: Introducción general y edición crítica* (2 vols.; Textos y estudios del Seminario Filológico Cardenal Cisneros 6; Madrid: Consejo Superior de Investigaciones Científicas, 1967).

Bogaert, P.-M., "Eptaticus: Le nom des premiers livres de la Bible dans l'ancienne tradition chrétienne grecque et latine," in *Titres et articulations du texte dans les œuvres antiques: Actes du Colloque International de Chantilly 13–15 décembre 1994* (eds. J.-C. Fredouille et al.; Paris: Institut d'Études Augustiniennes, 1997), 313–37.

Denk, J., *Die altlateinische Bibel in ihrem Gesamtbestande vom 1–9. Jahrhundert* (Leipzig: Fock, 1914).

Douglas, I.M., "The Commentary on the Book of Ruth by Claudius of Turin," *SacEr* 22 (1974–1975): 295–320.

Fischer, B., "Lukian-Lesarten in der Vetus Latina der vier Königsbücher," in B. Fischer, *Beiträge zur Geschichte der lateinischen Bibeltexte* (VL 12; Freiburg i.B.: Herder, 1986), 9–17.

Gesche, B., *Ruth* (VL 4.5; Freiburg: Herder, 2005).

Ortiz de Urbina, J.C., *Vetus Latina – Rut: Estudio crítico de la Version Latina prejeronimiana del libro de Rut, segun el Mansucrito 31 de la Universidad de Madrid* (Textos y estudios del Seminario Filológico Cardenal Cisneros 4; Madrid: Seminario Filológico Cardenal Cisneros, 1965).

Rahlfs, A., *Studie über den griechischen Text des Buches Ruth* (MSU 3.2; Berlin: Weidmann).

Ramos-Lissón, D., "Le rôle de la Bible dans le Conciles Bracariens de vième siècle au Royaume Suève," *Annuarium Historiae Conciliorum* 18 (1986): 41–50.

Sabatier, *Bibliorum*, 1.469–72.

Schulz-Flügel, E., *Gregorius Eliberritanus: Epithalamium sive explanatio in canticis canticorum* (VL 26; Freiburg: Herder, 1994).

Bonifatia Gesche

---

[19] This has been shown for the books of Kingdoms (→ 3–5.2.1.2) by Fischer, "Lukian-Lesarten," 15.

[20] Ortiz de Urbina, *Rut*.

[21] For more examples, see the introduction to Gesche, *Ruth*, 14–26.

13–17.2.1.2 Canticles
13–17.2.1.2.1 Evidence

VL-Cant has been preserved completely in only two manuscripts:[1] VL[169] = Salzburg, Stiftsbibliothek, St. Peter a. IX. 16, late eighth century; and VL[170] = Graz, Universitätsbibliothek 167. Moreover, VL[160] (= St. Gallen, Stiftsbibliothek 11, second half of the eighth century C.E.) preserves a fragmentary text of Jerome's Hexaplaric recension with headwords of biblical text coming from the Latin translation of Philo of Carpasia's Greek commentary on Canticles (fifth century C.E.) made by Epiphanius in the sixth century C.E. (manuscript Vat lat. 5704). Several Vulgate manuscripts (→ 13–17.1.7) also preserve VL readings.[2] The most important examples for the indirect transmission of VL-Cant are excerpts from Gregory of Elvira (*Tractatus in Cantica Canticorum*, for Cant 1:1–3:4), Jerome, Ambrose of Milan, and others (→ 21.8). The commentaries on Canticles by Beda, Aponius, and Justus of Urgel are also relevant to VL textual criticism even though they are more related to the Vulgate.

13–17.2.1.2.2 Editions

Sabatier made the first edition of a VL text of Canticles.[3] The text is based mainly on quotations of Canticles in the works of Ambrose of Milan and, to a lesser extent, those of Jerome. Subsequently, research has focused on Gregory of Elvira's quotations as the main patristic testimony for the reconstruction of VL-Cant. In 1911, Wilmart published the VL text of Cant 1:1–3:4 from headwords in Gregorius' commentary.[4] In 1926, De Bruyne published the first critical edition of the complete text of Canticles according to VL on the basis of manuscripts VL[169] and VL[170], which he discovered in 1910 and 1913 respectively.[5] In 1992, the first issue of VL-Cant by Schulz-Flügel was published, containing also the introduction to her edition.[6] To date, no complete critical edition of VL-Cant is available. The importance of the testimony of Gregory of Elvira for VL-Cant justified the publication of a new critical edition of his commentary on Canticles in 1994, also by Schulz-Flügel.[7] In the introduction to this edition, she included a reconstruction of the biblical text of Cant 1:1–3:4 accompanied by an apparatus with readings from VL[169] and Ambrose.[8]

The study of the Hexaplaric recension that Jerome produced for Canticles (→ 13–17.1.7) proceeded parallel to the research and edition of VL-Cant. De Bruyne incorporated the text of the fragmentary manuscript VL[160] as an appendix to his edition. This manuscript, which testifies to Jerome's Hexaplaric recension, had been discovered by Berger in 1883.[9] The first edition of this text is based on VL[160], as well as on patristic quotations (→ 21.8) and headwords in manuscript Vat 5704.[10]

13–17.2.1.2.3 Text and *Vorlage*

One of the issues addressed by De Bruyne in his work on Canticles is what kind of text VL[169] contains: Jerome's Hexaplaric recension or VL-Cant (→ 13–17.1.7). He concludes that VL[169] is the best-preserved evidence for VL-Cant. Its text is closer to the original Greek (→ 13–17.1.1.2) than Gregory of Elvira's quotations.[11] In his opinion, VL[169] would not have been influenced by V-Cant (→ 13–17.1.7), except for some readings that may come from Jerome's Hexaplaric recension or even from V-Cant.[12] Both VL[169] and VL[170] would be independent; however, more recent studies suggest that VL[170] is dependent on VL[169].[13]

According to Schulz-Flügel,[14] all known Latin texts of Canticles can be considered variations of

---

[1] For the VL manuscripts and their numbers, see *Gryson, Altlateinische Handschriften 1*.

[2] De Bruyne, "Les anciennes versions latines," 115–18.

[3] Sabatier, *Bibliorum*, 2.375–88.

[4] Wilmart, "L' ancienne version latine," 15–18.

[5] De Bruyne, "Les anciennes," 98–104.

[6] Schulz-Flügel, *Canticum Canticorum*.

[7] Schulz-Flügel, *Gregorius*.

[8] Schulz-Flügel, *Gregorius*, 74–80.

[9] De Bruyne, "Les anciennes," 111–13.

[10] Vaccari, *Cantici canticorum*.

[11] De Bruyne, "Les anciennes," 105–07.

[12] De Bruyne, "Les anciennes," 98.

[13] Schulz-Flügel, *Canticum*, 22–24; Gryson, *Altlateinische Handschriften 1*, 257.

[14] Schulz-Flügel, *Canticum*, 14–16; cf. also Gryson, *Altlateinische Handschriften 1*, 255.

a single original text type; Jerome's Hexaplaric recension of VL-Cant would be an intermediate stage and V-Cant the last stage of the process. Schulz-Flügel distinguishes the following VL text types for Canticles: K: African text, attested in quotations of Cyprian and Tertullian; D: extended text in Italy, close to K, found in Gregory of Elvira's quotations, in manuscripts VL[169] [170], in early quotations by Ambrose, some quotations in Pseudo-Augustine's *Liber de divinis scripturis*, Rufinus, Jerome (→ 21.8), and in liturgical texts; M: readings in quotations by Ambrose and Paulinus of Nola; I: a revised text that influenced manuscripts VL[169] [170], as a prior stage to Jerome's Hexaplaric recension of VL-Cant (→ 13–17.1.7); O: development from I text, which is found in the headwords of Epiphanius Scholasticus' text and is supported by manuscript VL[160], Jerome's writings after 387 C.E., and some quotations by Augustine. Additionally, Schulz Flügel designates Jerome's translation *ex hebraica veritate* (V-Cant) as H, and as W the traces of O resulting from contamination.

Ambrose's quotations were the primary evidence in Sabatier's edition, with occasional quotations of Augustine and Jerome. However, Ambrose's quotations offer readings that can result from a direct translation of the Greek and not from the use of a pre-existing Latin text. Schulz-Flügel[15] and recently Ceulemans[16] have demonstrated the presence of Hexaplaric readings in Ambrose's quotations and their importance for textual criticism as a source for the text of Aq-Cant and Sym-Cant (→ 13–17.1.5.4).[17] Since De Bruyne, it has been accepted that Gregory of Elvira is the best ancient testimony of VL-Cant.[18]

Regarding Jerome's Hexaplaric recension of VL-Cant, De Bruyne characterized it as taking manuscript VL[160] and the Latin translation of Philo of Carpasia's commentary as its main basis: additions, glosses, and headings present in VL-Cant were removed, Hexaplaric additions were introduced, the Latin text was revised eliminating erroneous or inadequate VL translations, and stylistic changes were made.[19] This Hexaplaric text was widely cited, for example, by Jerome, Augustine, Eucherius of Lyon, etc.

Bazzana, G.B., "La 'Vetus Latina' del 'Cantico dei Cantici': Traduzione e interpretazione," in *Il Cantico dei Cantici nel medioevo: Atti del Convegno Internazionale dell'Università degli Studi di Milano et della Società Internazionale per lo Studio del Medioevo Latino (S.I.S.ME.L.), Gargnano sul Gardam, 22–24 maggio 2006* (ed. R.E. Guglielmetti; Millennio Medievale 76; Florence: Edizioni del Galluzzo, 2008), 91–108.

Berger, S., "Notice sur quelques textes latins inédits de l' Ancien Testament," *Notices et extraits des manuscrits de la Bibliothèque Nationale et autres bibliothèques* 34 (1895): 119–52.

De Bruyne, D., "Les anciennes versions latines du Cantique des Cantiques," *RBén* 38 (1926): 97–122.

Ceulemans, R., "The Latin Patristic Reception of the Book of Canticles in the *Hexapla*," *VC* 63 (2009): 369–89.

Gryson, *Altlateinische Handschriften 1*.

Sabatier, *Bibliorum*.

Schulz-Flügel, E., *Canticum Canticorum* (VL 10.3 fasc. 1; Freiburg i.B.: Herder, 1992).

Schulz-Flügel, E., "Interpretatio: Zur Wechselwirkung von Übersetzung und Auslegung im lateinischen Canticum canticorum," in *Philologia Sacra: Biblische und patristische Studien für Hermann J. Frede und Walter Thiele zu ihrem siebzigsten Geburtstag* (ed. R. Gryson; VL 24; Freiburg i.B.: Herder 1993), 131–49.

Schulz-Flügel, E., *Gregorius Eliberritanus: Epithalamium sive explanatio in Canticis Canticorum* (VL 28; Freiburg i.B.: Herder, 1994).

Vaccari, A., *Cantici canticorum translatio a S. Hieronymo ad Graecum textum hexaplarem emendata* (Rome: Edizioni di Storia e Letteratura, 1959).

Wilmart, A., "L' ancienne version latine du Cantique 1–3,4," *RBén* 28 (1911): 11–36.

José Manuel Cañas Reíllo

---

[15] Schulz-Flügel, *Canticum*, 71.
[16] Ceulemans, "Latin Patristic Reception," 369–89 (376).
[17] Ceulemans, "Latin Patristic Reception," 377–82.
[18] De Bruyne, "Les anciennes," 98.

[19] De Bruyne, "Les anciennes," 113–15.

13–17.2.1.3 Ecclesiastes

13–17.2.1.3.1 Evidence

VL-Qoh texts are preserved in manuscripts VL[94] (= VL marginal glosses in the v-Incunable 54.V.35, El Escorial, Bibl. de San Lorenzo, 1561 C.E.); VL[95] (= Madrid, Bibl. de la Academia de la Historia, *Aemilianensis* 2–3, thirteenth century); and VL[160] (= St. Gallen, Stiftsbibliothek, cod. 11, eighth century C.E.).[1] VL-Qoh is quoted in Jerome's *Commentarius in Ecclesiasten* (388 C.E.), and in other Latin texts such as Pseudo-Augustine's *Speculum* or *Liber de divinis scripturis* and Ambrose's *Expositio de Psalmo 118*.[2] Late evidence includes VL-Qoh excerpts in Ambrosius Autpertus and in Pseudo-Salonius' commentary, which is based mainly on Jerome.[3]

13–17.2.1.3.2 Editions

There is no edition that includes all the extant texts of VL-Qoh. In his edition of 1743, Sabatier published excerpts from Jerome's commentary on the text of VL-Qoh.[4] Fragments of VL[160] were published by Berger in 1895,[5] and glosses of VL[94] by Revilla in 1920,[6] but there is no edition of the VL[95] glosses. For Jerome's commentary, the critical edition of Adriaen can be used (1959).[7]

13–17.2.1.3.3 Text and *Vorlage*

The preserved evidence points to various stages in the textual history of VL-Qoh. VL-Qoh is thus another example of the textual plurality of VL, described in → 1.4.1.

1) Jerome's commentary on Qohelet and manuscript VL[160] share a common textual background and are sometimes supported by Ambrose's *Expositio de Psalmo 118*. Examples are Qoh 1:4, 6; and 7:3:[8] In Qoh 1:4, Jerome's *Commentarius in Ecclesiasten* and Ambrose's *Expositio de Psalmo 118* agree with VL[160] in reading *generatio uadit et generatio uenit* "a generation goes and a generation comes" for γενεὰ πορεύεται καὶ γενεὰ ἔρχεται "a generation goes, and a generation comes" (*NETS*) in LXX-Qoh (→ 13–17.1.1.3). And in Qoh 1:6, both Jerome and Ambrose share the reading *uadit ad austrum* "it goes to the south" with VL[160] for the πορεύεται πρὸς νότον "it goes to the south" (*NETS*) of LXX-Qoh. The situation is similar in Qoh 7:3 where Jerome's *Commentarius in Ecclesiasten* and VL[160] both have *melius* "better" for LXX-Qoh's ἀγαθόν "better" (*NETS*; lit. "good"), while Pseudo-Augustine's *Speculum* reads *optimum* "best."

2) Differences between Jerome's commentary on Qohelet, Ambrose's *Expositio de Psalmo 118*, and manuscript VL[160] point to another stage in the textual history of VL-Qoh. In Qoh 1:4, Jerome reads *in saeculo* "forever" for the εἰς τὸν αἰῶνα "forever" (*NETS*) of LXX and Ambrose has *in saeculum* "forever," while VL[160] and the Vulgate attest to *in aeternum* "for ever." Similarly, Jerome and Ambrose read in Qoh 4:10 *erigat* "he raises" for ἐγερεῖ "he will raise up" (*NETS*) of LXX-Qoh, while VL[160] has *eleuet* "he lifts up."

3) Another textual stage might be marked by VL[94] as the readings of this manuscript differ from the other witnesses to VL-Qoh but are sometimes supported by Ambrose's *Expositio de Psalmo 118*.

– Qoh 1:6 κυκλοῖ κυκλῶν "it circles going in circles" (*NETS*)] *g(i)rando g(i)rat* "going in circles it circles" VL[94] Ambrose, *g(i)rans g(i)rando* "circling going in circles" VL[160] Jerome

---

[1] Manuscripts are designated following Gryson, *Altlateinische Handschriften 1*.

[2] For quotations, I use the *Vetus Latina Database*. For abbreviations of authors and works, see Gryson, *Répertoire*.

[3] Edited in PL 53, 993–1012, and C. Curti, *Salonii episcopi Genavensis Comentarii in Parabolas Salomonis et in Ecclesiasten* (Catania: Centro di Studi sull'antico Cristianesimo, 1964), 89–152.

[4] Sabatier, *Bibliorum*, 2.353–73.

[5] Berger, "Notice," 139–40. Extant are Qoh 1:4–6, 9; 3:1–8; 4:10, 11; 7:3–6, 10, 14, 29; 8:2, 3; 9:4; 10:16, 20; 11:4.

[6] Revilla, *Fragmenta*, 35. Preserved are Qoh 1:6, 13, 15, 17; 2:2, 5, 8, 12, 18, 24; 3:15, 19.

[7] Adriaen, *S. Hieronymi*, 250–361.

[8] For the text of LXX-Qoh (→ 13–17.1.1.3), I use the edition by Rahlfs, *Septuaginta*, 2.238–60. For the text of VL-Qoh, I use the cited editions quoted in nn. 5 and 6.

- Qoh 1:6 πορεύεται "it goes" (2°)] omitted by VL⁹⁴ Ambrose, *uadit* "goes" VL¹⁶⁰ Jerome

4) The special character of VL⁹⁴ is underlined by the fact that in general the vocabulary of this manuscript is closer to the Greek than Jerome's commentary on Qohelet. Examples include the following:

- Qoh 1:13: *exquiro* "to seek out" (VL⁹⁴) for ἐκζητέω "to seek out" (*NETS*)] *inquiro* "to investigate" (Jerome)
- Qoh 1:13: *describo* "to describe" (VL⁹⁴) for κατασκέπτομαι "to examine" (*NETS*)] *considero* "to examine" (Jerome)
- Qoh 1:15: *quod deest* "what is lacking" (VL⁹⁴) for ὑστέρημα "what is lacking" (*NETS*)] *imminutio* "diminished" (Jerome)
- Qoh 2:2: *circunlatio* "madness" (VL⁹⁴) for περιφορά "madness" (*NETS*)] *amentia* "stupidity" (Jerome)
- Qoh 2:2: *oblectatio* "delighting" (VL⁹⁴) for εὐφροσύνη "enjoyment" (*NETS*)] *iucunditas* "pleasantness" (Jerome)
- Qoh 2:5: *uiridarium* "tree-garden" (VL⁹⁴) for παράδεισος "park" (*NETS*)] *pomarium* "orchard" (Jerome; V)

But regarding their Greek *Vorlage*, some differences are found also between VL⁹⁴ and Jerome. For example, VL⁹⁴ reads in Qoh 1:13 *coelo* "heaven" for the οὐρανόν "heaven" of LXX-Qoh (*NETS*), while Jerome has *sole* "sun" (cf. LXX^(s cor) ηλιον).

The picture is made even more complicated by the fact that some VL-Qoh readings are supported only by a part of the Greek manuscript tradition. For example, in Qoh 4:11, VL¹⁶⁰ reads *et etiam* "and now" with LXX^B (γε αν) while LXX-Qoh has καί "and."

Berger, S., "Notice sur quelques textes latins inédits de l'Ancien Testament," *Notices et extraits des manuscrits de la Bibliothèque Nationale et autres bibliothèques* 34 (1895): 119–52.
Gryson, *Altlateinische Handschriften*.
Gryson, *Répertoire général*.
Jerome, "Commentarius in Ecclesiasten," in *S. Hieronymi Presbyteri opera* (ed. M. Adriaen; CCSL 72.1.1; Turnhout: Brepols, 1959), 250–361.
Rahlfs, *Septuaginta*.
Revilla, M., *Fragmenta Biblica Scurialensia: La Biblia de Valvanera y el Códice Ovetense de los Evangelios* (El Escorial: Real Monasterio de El Escorial, 1920).
Sabatier, *Bibliorum*.

José Manuel Cañas Reíllo

13–17.2.1.4 Lamentations
13–17.2.1.4.1 Evidence

None of the textual witnesses preserves a complete VL-Lam text; only some fragmentary manuscripts have survived:[1] VL¹⁷⁷ (= *Codex rescriptus Wirceburgensis*: Univ. Bibl. M.P. th., Italy; fifth century C.E.; Lam 2:16–3:41 with gaps); VL²⁵¹ (= *Lectionarium Luxoviense*: Paris, BN lat 9427; ca. 700 C.E.; Lamentations 3); VL³³⁰ (= *Psalterium duplex* with canticles: Vatican, BAV, cod. Reg. lat. 11; Gaul; middle of the eighth century C.E.; Lam 5:11–22). VL-Lam 5:1–22 (*Canticum Ieremiae*) is transmitted as an individual song in Verecundus and in liturgical (Mozarabic) manuscripts.[2] Quotations from VL-Lam are found in Pseudo-Cyprian's *De paenitentia* and *De singularitate clericorum*, Pseudo-Augustine's *Speculum*, Ambrose's *Expositio de Psalmo 118*, in Casiodor, and other Latin Christian authors (→ 21.8).

13–17.2.1.4.2 Editions

At present, there is no comprehensive edition of the VL-Lam texts. We only have editions of some witnesses, such as VL³³⁰ by Sabatier (1743),[3] VL¹⁷⁷ by Ranke (1871),[4] and of some of the liturgical evidence, such as Salmon's work on VL²⁵¹.[5] For

---

[1] Manuscripts are designated following Gryson, *Altlateinische Handschriften 1*.

[2] For abbreviations of ancient writers, I use Gryson, *Répertoire général*. Quotations are taken from the Vetus Latina Database (Brepols).

[3] Sabatier, *Bibliorum*, 2.723–31 (*Threni id est, lamentationes Jeremiae prophetae*) and 2.732–33 (*Oratio Jeremiae Prophetae* = Lamentations 5).

[4] Ranke, *Par palimpsestorum*.

[5] Salmon, *Le lectionnaire*.

TABLE 1   Lexical Differences between the Texts of VL¹⁷⁷ and Ambrose

	LXX	VL¹⁷⁷	Ambrose
Lam 2:17	ἔξ "from"	*ex* "from"	*a* "from"
Lam 2:17	καθαιρέω "demolish"	*depono* "demolish"	*destruo* "destroy"
Lam 2:17	εὐφραίνω "make rejoice"	*iucunde accipio* "take pleasantly"	*laetifico* "make rejoice"
Lam 2:17	θλίβω "oppress"	*confligo* "fight"	*tribulo* "oppress"
Lam 2:18	βοάω "cry"	*clamo* "cry"	*exclamo* "cry out"
Lam 2:18	κατάγω "bring down"	*depono* "let drop"	*deduco* "eject"
Lam 2:18	χείμαρρος "wadi"	*chimarrus* "wadi"	*torrens* "rushing stream"
Lam 2:19	ἀνίστημι "arise"	*exsurgo* "rise"	*surgo* "rise"
Lam 2:19	ἀγαλλιάω "give a cry of joy"	*exalto* "exalt"	*expergisco* "awake"
Lam 2:19	φυλακή "watch"	*custodia* "watch"	*uigilia* "watch"
Lam 2:19	αἴρω "lift"	*tollo* "lift"	*extollo* "lift up"
Lam 2:19	ἔξοδος "exit"	*exitus* "exit"	*iter* "road"
Lam 2:20	ἐπιβλέπω "consider"	*inspicio* "consider"	*considero* "consider"

Verecundus' *Canticum Ieremiae*, Demeulenaere's edition should be used (1976).⁶

13–17.2.1.4.3 Text

The preserved textual witnesses reveal diversities, as shown in the following examples from VL¹⁷⁷ and Ambrose's *Expositio de Psalmo 118*:⁷ In Lam 2:18, for LXX-Lam μὴ δῷς ἔκνηψιν σεαυτῇ, μὴ σιωπήσαιτο θυγάτηρ, ὁ ὀφθαλμός σου, "Give yourself no calming down! May your eye not be silent, O daughter!" (*NETS), VL¹⁷⁷ reads *des in tristitiam et ipsam ne cessent filia oculi tui* "And you should give yourself into sadness! O daughter, your eyes should not rest," while Ambrose has *noli dare tibi requiem, non silenti pupilla oculi tui* "give yourself no respite, my your eyes, O orphan girl, not be silent ones!" Another example can be found in Lam 3:22. Although the earliest LXX manuscripts (→ 13–17.1.1.4) do not have this verse, it can be found in later Greek witnesses: τα ελεη κυριου οτι ουκ εξελ(ε)ιπεν με οτι ου συνετελεσθησαν οι οικτιρμοι αυτου⁸ "It is the mercies of the Lord, that he did not fail me, because his compassions are not exhausted." VL¹⁷⁷ renders this as *misericordia d(o)m(in)i non dereliquit me quoniam non est co(m)sumpta iustitia* "the mercy of the Lord did not abandon me because (his) justice is not exhausted" while Ambrose attests to the translation *misericordia Domini est, quod non defecimus, quia non sunt consummatae miserationes eius* "it is the mercy of the Lord, because we did not defect, because his compassions are not finished."

Differences between the texts of VL¹⁷⁷ and Ambrose's *Expositio de Psalmo 118* lie primarily in their lexical selections, with Ambrose's readings having some support from others witnesses. Examples include those listed in Table 1.

In addition to lexical differences there is also morphological diversity, which is illustrated by Lam 2:17 (see Table 2).

13–17.2.1.4.4 Vorlage

Differences regarding their Greek base texts (→ 13–17.1.1.4) are also evident in the preserved witnesses of VL-Lam. Thus, in Lam 2:17, Ambrose's *tribulantis* "the one oppressing" reflects the θλίβοντος of LXX-Lam while the *confligentium* "the ones fighting" of VL¹⁷⁷ goes with the θλιβόντων of LXX^(O L'-26 c'-91). Similarly, in Lam 2:18, the *muri Sion* of VL¹⁷⁷ reflects the

---

⁶ R. Demeulenaere, *Verecundi Iuncensis commentarii super cantica ecclesiastica: Carmen de satisfactione paenitentiae* (CCSL 93; Turnhout: Brepols, 1976), 67–82.

⁷ For LXX-Lam texts (→ 13–17.1.1.4), I use the edition by Ziegler, *Ieremias*, 467–94.

⁸ See the apparatus of Ziegler, *Ieremias*, 482.

TABLE 2   Morphological Differences between the Texts of VL¹⁷⁷ and Ambrose

LXX /*NETS	VL¹⁷⁷	Ambrose
ἐνεθυμήθη "he purposed"	cogitauerat "he had pondered"	cogitauit "he has pondered"
ἐνετείλατο "he commanded"	mandauerat "he had commanded"	mandauit "he has commanded"

τείχη Σιων "walls of Sion" of LXX-Lam, while Ambrose's *muri filiae Sion* goes with the τειχη θυγατρος Σιων "walls of daughter Sion" of LXXˢ* ᴼ⁻Qmg ᴸ'⁻⁵³⁸ c.

All of the VL-Lam texts display a close relationship to the Lucianic recension (LXXᴸ; → 13–17.1.6) and to a lesser extent to the Hexaplaric text (LXXᴼ → 13–17.1.5.1). Significant agreements can also be found with other ancient versions, such as the Armenian (→ 13–17.2.5.4), Arabic (→ 13–17.1.8; → 13–17.2.8.4), Ethiopic (→ 13–17.2.3.4), and, to a lesser extant, with the Coptic (→ 13–17.2.2). For example, VL¹⁷⁷ and Ambrose both know the text of Lam 3:22–24, which is omitted in LXX-Lam but present in LXXᴸ. The relationship of Verecundus with LXXᴸ is especially important.

Gryson, *Altlateinische Handschriften 1.
Gryson, *Répertoire général.
Quentin, H. (ed.), *Liber Hieremiae et Lamentationes* (Biblia Sacra iuxta latinam Vulgatam versionem ad codicum fidem 14; Rome: Typis Polyglottis Vaticanis, 1972).
Ranke, E., *Par palimpsestorum Wirceburgensium: antiquissimae veteris Testamenti versionis Latinae fragm.* (Vienna: Braumüller, 1871).
Sabatier, *Bibliorum.
Salmon, P., *Le lectionnaire de Luxeuil (Paris, ms. lat. 9427)* (Collectanea Biblica Latina 7; Rome: Abbaye Saint-Jérome, 1944).
Ziegler, J., *Ieremias, Baruch, Threni, Epistula Ieremiae* (4th ed.; Septuaginta Vetus Testamentum Graecum 15; Göttingen: Vandenhoeck & Ruprecht, 2013).

José Manuel Cañas Reíllo

13–17.2.1.5 Esther

The Vetus Latina of the book of Esther has come down to us through twenty manuscripts and a few patristic quotations (→ 21.8). No traces of the African text have been preserved. The oldest type of the European text (VLᴿ) has been transmitted by manuscripts VL¹⁵¹, ¹⁵⁵, ¹³⁰.[1] A first revision gave birth to the Italian text (VLᴵ) represented by VL¹²³ and its satellites (VL¹³⁵, ¹³⁶, ¹³⁷, ¹³⁸, ¹³⁹, ¹⁴⁰, ¹⁴¹, ¹⁴², ¹⁵⁴, ¹⁵⁹, ¹⁵⁹ᴮ, ¹⁵⁹ᶠ, ¹⁵⁹ᴳ) and by VL¹⁵². The text VLᴶ, the sole witness of which is VL¹⁴⁶, constitutes a further step in the development of the Old Latin tradition characterized by a partial alignment with the LXX text (→ 13–17.1.1.5). The last type of text (VLᶠ), which appears in VL¹⁰⁹, stems from an in-depth revision of the text. The author uses a style periodic in nature, and adds some narrative connective tissue while integrating elements of the text of LXXᴸ (→ 13–17.1.6). The agreements between the text types VLᴿ and VLᴵ certainly transmit the Old Latin text in its pure and unrevised form. The patristic quotations (→ 21.8) facilitate dating the text types: VLᶠ in Rome around 370 C.E.; VLᴿ and VLᴵ between 330 and 350 C.E.

Sabatier has edited Esther on the basis of manuscript VL¹⁵¹ (with variants from VL¹⁴² and VL¹⁵²).[2] Motzo brought out a more complete edition in 1926–1927.[3] However, the edition of Haelewyck[4] remains the most definitive.

The Latin translator happens to be a faithful witness to the Greek model (→ 13–17.1.1.5). The calque is sometimes of a servile nature, in particular when the Greek text is difficult (additions to Esther B and E; → 11.6.2). This leads to the creation of a Latin text that baffles the purists, but which provides a real opportunity for someone seeking to discover the wording of its Greek model. This Greek model is different from the forms hitherto attested.

---

[1] Manuscript numbers are given according to Gryson, *Altlateinische Handschriften 1*.
[2] Sabatier, *Bibliorum*, 1.796–825.
[3] Motzo, *Versione*.
[4] Haelewyck, *Hester*.

For the purpose of dating the Greek base text of VL-Esth, we have two types of arguments at our disposal: external criticism and literary criticism. Two external witnesses can be used here. Arm-Esth (→ 13–17.2.5.5) contains, within the prayer of Esther, a long addition (in Esth C:16)[5] which is absent from LXX (→ 11.6.7), but present in a slightly modified form in all Old Latin witnesses. The possibility of any direct contact between VL and the Armenian version is ruled out. The Armenian translator, who usually follows LXX, has drawn this addition from a Greek text that was also used by the Latin translator. The Armenian translation does not allow us to go back further in time since it dates to the first half of the fifth century C.E., but it brings VL out of its isolation. Oxyrhynchus Papyrus 4443,[6] on the other hand, takes us back quite a bit in time. This Greek papyrus, which contains Esth E:16–9:3, is dated sometime around 100 C.E. It is a witness to LXX, but it contains certain readings that are absent from the Greek but find a correspondence only in VL.[7] It indicates that by around 100 C.E. a contamination had already taken place between LXX and the Greek base text of VL. Therefore, this Greek base text was created prior to 100 C.E.

It is principally literary criticism of the different forms of the book that gives us the most valuable information about the antiquity of this Greek text of Esther, its place within the Greek tradition, and the origin of the additions A to F (→ 11.6.7). In their analyses of the Greek tradition, only four authors have taken the Greek base text of VL into account: Motzo, Schildenberger, Hanhart, and Haelewyck.

According to Motzo,[8] the tradition of Esther can be explained by a continuous process of contamination. The Hebrew original did not have Esther 9. For the use of the Hellenistic Jews of Egypt, Lysimachus made a Greek revision of the Hebrew (*rifacimento greco*) around 50 B.C.E., which is no longer extant. It contained the additions. After the victory of Judas Maccabeus over Nicanor (13 Adar, 161 B.C.E.), the story of the massacre was added and the commemorative date was changed from 14 to 13 Adar. Motzo postulates the existence of another literal Greek version (*versione greca*), faithful to the Hebrew, and therefore without the additions. But such additions would have been inserted later on the basis of the *rifacimento*. After their contamination, the *rifacimento* and the literal version came to be differentiated and gave birth to diverse forms towards the end of the first century of our era: LXX^L (Antioch → 13–17.1.6), LXX (Alexandria → 13–17.1.1.5), the Greek base text of the Old Latin (Western), and Flavius Josephus (→ 21.3). The Greek model of VL has much in common with LXX^L, LXX, and Flavius Josephus, but it has some material of its own since it has preserved abundant elements from the *rifacimento* and the literal version.

For Schildenberger,[9] the Hebrew text represents the original form of Esther. The Greek texts are only revisions. The Greek in its primitive form has been preserved in the Greek model of the Old Latin, which he calls La-GrIII. Schildenberger has shown that the *rifacimento greco* of Motzo is in fact La-GrIII and that its literal version is a mere illusion. The LXX text (→ 13–17.1.1.5) is the work of Lysimachus dating from around 50 B.C.E. (he dates the colophon to 48–47 B.C.E.). It is presented as a revision of La-GrIII. LXX^L (→ 13–17.1.6) is an abridged edition of his La-GrIII.

For Hanhart,[10] the Greek original is preserved principally in LXX (→ 13–17.1.1.5), which dates from the first half of the first century B.C.E. (he dates the colophon to 78–77). This original contained the additions right from the beginning. Hanhart rules out the hypothesis of a Greek translation that would have contained only the additions. Other Greek forms quickly appeared: LXX^L (→ 13–17.1.6), La-GrIII, and the model used by Flavius Josephus (→ 21.3). These forms are distinguished primarily by their agreement with LXX, but also secondarily by an independent return to the Hebrew.

---

[5] Latin translation in Hanhart, *Esther*, 34 and Haelewyck, *Hester*, 76.
[6] Luchner, "4443."
[7] Haelewyck, "Papyrus Oxyrhynque 4443."
[8] Motzo, *Storia*.
[9] Schildenberger, *Das Buch Esther*.
[10] Hanhart, *Esther*.

For Haelewyck,[11] the additions crept into the Greek tradition on the occasion of the first translation attested by the Greek model of VL (La-GrIII). His author remodelled the Hebrew in order to remove its vengeful side. He deleted the story of the massacre in Esther 9 and composed the additions in an irenic tone. LXX-Esth is a cumulative text that borrows from other texts while giving precedence to the Hebrew. This is how the contradictions can be explained. Hanhart's hypothesis, according to which LXX (→ 13–17.1.1.5) would have been the first draft of the Greek tradition from whence the other two forms, LXX^L (→ 13–17.1.6) and VL, would derive, can explain these texts as two texts seeking to eliminate the rough edges of LXX. But the hypothesis fails to explain where these rough edges come from in LXX. If one places the LXX text at the end of the Greek tradition, one is able to explain the narrative coherence in LXX^L and La-GrIII, and also the contradictions of the LXX text. If the colophon (Esth F:11) indeed dates around 78–77 B.C.E.,[12] the composition of the text of La-GrIII should be situated sometime between 120 and 100 B.C.E. at the latest.

Bickermann, E.J., "The Colophon of the Greek Book of Esther," *JBL* 63 (1944): 339–62.
Haelewyck, J.-C., "Le Papyrus Oxyrhynque 4443 et la *vetus latina* du livre d' Esther," *RBén* 109 (1999): 267–71.
Haelewyck, J.-C., *Hester* (VL 7.3; Freiburg i.B.: Herder, 2003–2008).
Haelewyck, J.-C., "The Relevance of the Old Latin Version for the Septuagint: With Special Emphasis on the Book of Esther," *JTS* 57 (2006): 439–73.
Hanhart, R., *Esther* (Septuaginta Vetus Testamentum Graecum 8.3; Göttingen: Vandenhoeck & Ruprecht, 1983).
Luchner, K., "4443. LXX, Esther E16–9.3," *The Oxyrhynchus Papyri* 65 (eds. M.W. Haslam et al.; London: Egypt Exploration Fund, 1998): 4–8.
Motzo, R.B., "La versione latina di Esther secondo i LXX," *Annali della Facoltà di Lettere della R. Università di Cagliari* 1–2 (1926–1927): 263–350 (reprint in R.B. Motzo and F. Parente, *Ricerche sulla letteratura e la storia giudaico-ellenistica* [Rome: Centro editoriale internazionale, 1977], 121–208).
Motzo, R.B., "La storia del testo di Ester," *Ricerche religiose* 3 (1927): 205–08.
Schildenberger, J., *Das Buch Esther übersetzt und erklärt* (HSAT 4.3; Bonn: Hanstein, 1940–1941).

Jean-Claude Haelewyck

13–17.2.2 Coptic Translations

13–17.2.2.1 Background

The scantiness of the sources frustrates any attempt to date precisely the Coptic translation of the books commonly designated as the Five Scrolls (FS). However, it is possible that the rendering into the Sahidic dialect dates to the fourth century C.E. at the latest. The fact that Canticles and Ecclesiastes are sometimes quoted by the fourth-century C.E. Pachomian authors who wrote Coptic suggests that some such hypothesis may not be inaccurate, at least as far as these two books are concerned.

With the exception of Esther, which has survived in only one manuscript, the Five Scrolls are relatively well attested in Coptic, notably in Sahidic, the main literary dialect of the Egyptian church in the first millennium. Although a complete set does not survive in one manuscript, many codices cluster together two or more of the Five Scrolls. Thus, as the Coptic tradition followed the LXX sets of books (→ 13–17.1.1), Canticles and Ecclesiastes were often included in codices containing sapiential texts, while Ruth and Esther are found in collections of Historical Books. Following the same pattern of the Greek LXX codices, Lamentations is usually transmitted together with other writings of the Jeremianic corpus. In a few cases, some of these five biblical books have survived in miscellanies that also include literary non-biblical texts.

There has been no attempt yet to systematically compare the Coptic versions of the Five Scrolls against the Greek parent text.

---

[11] Haelewyck, "Relevance."
[12] Bickermann, "Colophon."

13–17.2.2.2 Main Manuscript Witnesses and Their Editions

One of the most important Sahidic textual witnesses is Michigan MS 166 (Cop$^{Sa\ 90}$),[1] which contains three of the Five Scrolls: Ecclesiastes, Canticles, and Ruth. Cop$^{Sa\ 90}$ is a "pocket-book" unearthed together with four other similar small-sized manuscripts around the year 1924 near the pyramids of Giza.[2] The codices can be dated shortly before the year 600 C.E. on the basis of some coins discovered with them. The colophons of the manuscripts suggest that they were copied in the scriptorium of the Monastery of Apa Jeremias near Saqqara. Ecclesiastes, Canticles, and Ruth are preceded in Cop$^{Sa\ 90}$ by four literary texts: the *Epistle of Abgar* and the reply of Christ to the Edessan king, the *Epistle* of Paul of Tamma (Clavis Coptica 0248),[3] and an ascetic writing on the monastic cell by the same author (Clavis Coptica 0251). While Canticles and Ruth are virtually intact, the text of Ecclesiastes is heavily damaged. The three biblical books in Cop$^{Sa\ 90}$ were published by Shier in 1942.[4]

In 1911, Herbert Thompson edited the underlying writing of palimpsest London, British Library Add. 17183 (Cop$^{Sa\ 19}$),[5] which contains the Sahidic version of Ruth and Esther together with Joshua and Judges (→ 3–5.2.2), as well as Judith (→ 11.9.7).[6] The palimpsest's *scriptio superior* features a series of ascetic texts in Syriac.[7] The codex belongs to a hoard of Syriac manuscripts that came from the Monastery of the Virgin in Wadi el-Natrun, Lower Egypt. However, this provenance does not imply that the Sahidic manuscript used for the palimpsest originates from the same location. As no evidence has survived that Sahidic codices were produced in Wadi el-Natrun, it is possible that the manuscript was imported from Upper Egypt. Given that the Syriac text of Cop$^{Sa\ 19}$ is dated in the year 913 C.E., the underlying Sahidic text must necessarily be older. Although Thompson quoted various scholarly opinions according to which the Coptic handwriting can be dated to the seventh century C.E., he added correctly that we "lack evidence to enable us to fix these earlier literary hands with certainty."[8] All one can sensibly say is that the manuscript is highly "classicized" both in terms of language and paleography. These details probably date it prior to the period before the Arab conquest (641 C.E.) or shortly after it.

The papyrus codex British Library, Or. 5984 (Cop$^{Sa\ 75}$)[9] of unknown date and provenance preserves Canticles and Ecclesiastes fragmentarily.[10] This manuscript includes four other sapiential books: Job (→ 11.4.2), Proverbs (→ 12.4.2), Wisdom of Solomon (→ 11.15.6), and Sirach (→ 11.4.7). Ecclesiastes is the most heavily damaged text both in Cop$^{Sa\ 75}$ and Cop$^{Sa\ 90}$, but the complete text has survived in fragments of different dismembered codices from the White Monastery, situated near Sohag in Upper Egypt. For example, the Ecclesiastes text in White Monastery codex Cop$^{Sa\ 27}$[11] was collated by Shier to fill in the numerous lacunae in Cop$^{Sa\ 90}$.[12] Besides Ecclesiastes, the other surviving fragments of Cop$^{Sa\ 27}$ contain a small portion

---

[1] Schüssler, *Biblia Coptica* 1.4, 91–92.

[2] Three of these manuscripts are today in the Chester Beatty Collection in Dublin and two in Ann Arbor, Michigan.

[3] Clavis Coptica or Clavis Patrum Copticorum is a project developed by the *Corpus dei Manoscritti Copti Letterari* (Rome/Hamburg). The database is available online at http://www.cmcl.it (last accessed October, 2016).

[4] Shier, "Old Testament Texts," 44–68.

[5] Schüssler, *Biblia Coptica* 1.1, 97–98.

[6] Thompson, *A Coptic Palimpsest*.

[7] Described in W. Wright, *Catalogue of Syriac Manuscripts in the British Museum Acquired since the Year 1838*, Part 2 (London: British Museum, 1871), 812b–823b (= no. 812).

[8] Thompson, *A Coptic Palimpsest*, vi.

[9] Schüssler, *Biblia Coptica* 1.3, 71–73.

[10] Description in W.E. Crum, *Catalogue of the Coptic Manuscripts in the British Museum* (London: British Museum, 1905), 395a–396a (= no. 951); published in Thompson, *The Coptic (Sahidic) Version*, 37–60.

[11] Schüssler, *Biblia Coptica* 1.2, 33–36.

[12] Schüssler, *Biblia coptica*, 1.2, 33–36. Because Shier, "Old Testament Texts," did not have access to photographs of the fragments, it was not clear to her that all of them came from the same codex. Parts of this manuscript were published in Ciasca, *Fragmenta Copto-Sahidica*, 2.195–214, and W. Till, *Koptische Pergamente theologischen Inhalts*, Vol. 1 (Mitteilungen aus der Papyrussammlung der Nationalbibliothek in Wien [Papyrus Erzog Rainer], 2; Vienna: Druck und Verlag der österr. Staatsdruckerei, 1934), 11–12 (collation of the Vienna parchment fragment K 9176 against the text published by Ciasca).

of Proverbs (→ 12.4.2) and almost the entire book of Job (→ 11.4.2).

The complete Sahidic version of Lamentations is preserved in a parchment codex whose quires are held partly in the Bodmer Collection, Geneva, and partly in a private collection in England (Cop$^{Sa\,49}$).[13] Additionally, vestiges of at least six other Sahidic fragmentary manuscripts of Lamentations are extant. The directory of the fragments identified until now can be conveniently found in Feder's book on the Sahidic Jeremianic corpus.[14] Feder has also investigated the relationship of the Sahidic version of Lamentations with its Greek model and offered the most complete edition of the text.[15]

Lamentations also exists in a Bohairic version published by Tattam.[16]

13–17.2.2.3 Other Manuscript Witnesses

Beside the aforementioned codices, which are more or less well preserved, isolated portions of the Sahidic version of the Five Scrolls are known.

13–17.2.2.3.1 Ruth

A Sahidic papyrus fragment with Ruth 4:5–10 was edited with an English translation by Crum in 1913 (Cop$^{Sa\,76}$).[17] Till likewise published a codex leaf in Vienna containing Ruth 3:14–18, 4:1–3* (Cop$^{Sa\,184}$).[18] A fragment of Ruth 4:10–13, now at the Louvre Museum (call number E 10075), has also been published.[19] The Louvre fragment belonged to the White Monastery codex Cop$^{Sa\,22}$,[20] in which it is followed by Canticles and 4 Kings and preceded by Judges (→ 3–5.2.2).

The comparison of all available manuscripts of Ruth indicates that they belong to the same translation from Greek (→ 13–17.1.1).[21] However, the relationship between the Sahidic version of Ruth and its Greek model (→ 13–17.1.1.1) remains a desideratum for future research. Thompson subscribed to the view that the text is more akin to that of the Codex Gr. Vaticanus: "the Sahidic follows B as against A on an average twice for every time that it follows A against B, and it shows very few signs of any text independent of these two."[22] For his part, Oikawa documented the use of the conjunction "and" in Ruth.[23] Further research must also compare the Sahidic version against the multiple Arabic versions of Coptic provenance (→ 13–17.2.8.1).[24]

Additionally, Ruth 2:11–14 is transmitted in the Sahidic Holy Week lectionaries (Cop$^{Sa\,108L}$). The text, meant for liturgical reading, was edited by Ciasca and Amélineau in 1885 and 1886 respectively.[25] The two scholars published this portion of the text from a bilingual Copto-Arabic Holy Week lectionary, which is preserved in a late fourteenth-

---

[13] This codex contains the Jeremianic corpus. *Editio princeps* was done by Kasser, *Papyrus Bodmer XXII*. The leaves that are currently held by a British collector were formerly in the possession of the University of Mississippi, see J.M. Robinson, *The Story of the Bodmer Papyri: From the First Monastery's Library in Upper Egypt to Geneva and Dublin* (Cambridge: James Clarke & Co., 2013), 192.

[14] Feder, *Biblia Sahidica*, 27–39.

[15] Feder, *Biblia Sahidica*, 61–64, 198–216.

[16] H. Tattam, *Prophetae majores, in dialecto linguae Aegyptiacae Memphitica seu Coptica*, Vol. 1 (Oxford: Typographeo academico, 1852), 540–71 (Bohairic text and Latin translation on facing pages).

[17] W.E. Crum, *Theological Texts from Coptic Papyri* (Anecdota Oxoniensia Semitic Series, 12; Oxford: Clarendon Press, 1913), 1 (= no. 1); Schüssler, *Biblia coptica* I.3, 74.

[18] The call number of this fragment is K 67. Published in W. Till, "Saidische Fragmente des Alten Testamentes," *Mus* 59 (1937): 175–237 (190–92); Schüssler, *Biblia Coptica* 2.1, 143–44.

[19] A. Boud'hors, C. Nakano, and P. Werner, "Fragments coptes de l'Ancien Testament au Musée du Louvre," *Mus* 109 (1996): 17–58 (23–24) and pls. 3–4.

[20] On the codicological reconstruction of this codex, see Schüssler, *Biblia Coptica* 1.2, 11–16.

[21] The papyrus fragment published in Crum, *Theological Texts* is difficult to assess as it corresponds to a portion of the text that is lacking in Thompson's edition.

[22] Thompson, *A Coptic Palimpsest*, x.

[23] H. Oikawa, "A Notion of 'and' in the Coptic Translation of the Book of Ruth," in *Studies in Egyptology Presented to Miriam Lichtheim*, (2 vols., ed. S. Israelit-Groll; Jerusalem: Magnes Press, 1990), 2.730–50.

[24] On these versions, see Graf, *GCAL*, 1.110–13, and the important corrections in K. Samir, "Arabic Versions of the Old Testament: Ruth," *The Coptic Encyclopedia* (ed. A.S. Atiya; New York: Macmillan, 1991), 6.1835a–36a.

[25] Ciasca, *Fragmenta Copto-Sahidica*, 1.164; É. Amélineau, "Fragments de la version thébaine de l'Écriture (Ancien Testament)," *Recueil de travaux relatifs à la philologie et à l'archéologie égyptiennes et assyriennes* 8 (1886), 10–62, at 62.

or early fifteenth-century paper manuscript kept in the Vatican Library (Borg. copt. 109, cassetta 23, fasc. 99), originally from the White Monastery.²⁶ The same portion of Ruth is preserved in another Holy Week lectionary from the White Monastery.²⁷ The text of Ruth included in the lectionaries corresponds to the Sahidic version of the manuscript tradition.

13–17.2.2.3.2 Canticles

Fragments of two parchment codices from the White Monastery containing Canticles were published by Maspero.²⁸ Recently, an almost complete manuscript in the Bodmer Collection (P. Bodmer XL) was published by Kasser and Luisier (Cop$^{Sa\ 60}$).²⁹ Torallas Tovar has edited a bifolio of a miniature codex of unknown provenance, containing Cant 4:8–9, 8:2–4.³⁰ A small-format Sahidic paper codex from the White Monastery has Canticles followed by a selection of literary texts, including Severus of Antioch's sixtieth cathedral homily (on Elijah)³¹ (CPG 7035.60; Clavis Coptica 0594) and Gregory of Nyssa's fifteenth homily on Canticles (CPG 3158.15; Clavis Coptica 0896).³² Another fragmentary parchment manuscript from the same monastery preserves extensive portions from an unknown systematic commentary on this biblical book.³³ Due to the scarcity of ancient commentaries on Canticles, the publication of this still unknown Coptic text is imperative. Portions of Canticles are attested also in Sahidic lectionaries. Thus, Ciasca edited Cant 4:14, 15, 16 and 5:1, 2, 3 according to a Holy Week lectionary now in the Vatican Collection.³⁴

In the Bohairic dialect, only a small portion pertaining to Cant 4:14–5:10 is extant in the Holy Week lectionary.³⁵

13–17.2.2.3.3 Ecclesiastes

In 1991, Bosson published a palimpsest housed in the Coptic Museum in Cairo, whose underlying writing contains portions of Ecclesiastes (and Sirach [→ 11.4.7]) in Sahidic.³⁶ The *scriptio inferior* has tentatively been dated by Bosson to the fourth or fifth century C.E. The sheets of the codex were reused later to accommodate the text of the *Prayer of Shenoute*. A new fragment from a parchment manuscript of the same biblical book has surfaced recently in the collection of Trinity College, Dublin.³⁷ The fragment bears the inventory number 11062/7 and contains Qoh 1:9–11.

All the aforementioned Sahidic manuscripts of Ecclesiastes give the same version of the text. However, two fragmentary leaves from a papyrus manuscript of a different Sahidic translation were published by Lefort in 1938 and again in 1940.³⁸ The

---

²⁶ Description in G. Zoega, *Catalogus codicum copticorum manu scriptorium qui in Museo Borgiano Velitris adservantur* (Rome: Typis Sacrae Congregationis de Propaganda Fide, 1810), 189–92 (= no. 99); Schüssler, *Biblia Coptica* 1.4, 49–69.

²⁷ The fragment that preserves this portion of Ruth is Paris, BnF Copte 129¹⁹, folio 5, edited in G. Maspero, *Fragments de la version thébaine de l'Ancien Testament* (Mémoires publiés par les membres de la mission archéologique française au Caire 6.1; Paris: Leroux, 1892), 150–51.

²⁸ Maspero, *Fragments de la version thébaine*, 197–207.

²⁹ Kasser and Luisier, "P. Bodmer XL," 149–201 + pls. 29–43. This manuscripts lacks Cant 1:1–3; 3:1–4:1; and 8:12–14; Schüssler, *Biblia Coptica* 1.3, 28.

³⁰ The fragment is currently in the collection of the Montserrat Abbey near Barcelona; see S. Torallas Tovar, *Biblia Coptica Montserratensia: P. Monts. Roca II* (Orientalia Montserratensia 2; Barcelona: Publicaciones de l'Abadia de Montserrat, 2007), 55–58.

³¹ E. Lucchesi, "La version copte de l'homélie LX de Sévère d'Antioche," *Aeg* 84 (2004): 207–16.

³² This is codex MONB.CQ in the *Corpus dei Manoscritti Copti Letterari* database. The manuscript is dated to 1078. Cf. Crum, *Catalogue British Museum*, 76b (= no. 190). Gregory of Nyssa's homily was identified in T. Orlandi, *Elementi di lingua e letteratura copta* (Milan: Cisalpino, 1970), 121.

³³ The present author is preparing an edition of the fourteen leaves identified to date.

³⁴ Ciasca, *Sacrorum Bibliorum fragmenta II*, 215.

³⁵ O.H.E. Burmester, "The Bohairic Pericopae of Wisdom and Sirach (Introduction)," *Bib* 15 (1934): 451–65; O.H.E. Burmester, "The Bohairic Pericopae of Wisdom and Sirach (Text)," *Bib* 16 (1935): 25–57, 141–74.

³⁶ N. Bosson, "Un palimpseste du Musée Copte du Caire," *Mus* 104 (1991): 5–37.

³⁷ A. Suciu, "Coptic Biblical Fragments in the Possession of the Trinity College in Dublin," *ZPE* 183 (2012): 101–07 (106).

³⁸ L.-T. Lefort, "Coptica Lovaniensia (suite)," *Mus* 51 (1938): 1–32 (11–17) and pl. 2 (including a tentative retroversion in Greek); republished in L.-T. Lefort, *Les manuscrits coptes de l'Université de Louvain*, Vol. 1: *Textes Littéraires* (Louvain: Bibliothèque de l'Université, 1940), 59–65 and pl. 5.

fragments were housed in the Lefort Collection at the Catholic University in Louvain but, unfortunately, they were destroyed together with other ancient manuscripts in a fire that devastated the Louvain University library during Second World War bombings. The Louvain papyrus fragments featured Qoh 7:1–3, 8–12, 16–19, 26–27.

An early Fayyumic version of Ecclesiastes is extant in the Michigan codex P. Mich. 3520 and was published by Schenke and Kasser.[39] A comparably early Fayyumic version, joined by the Greek text, has survived in a papyrus codex in Hamburg (Hamb. Pap. bil. 1). The manuscript also features the *Acts of Paul* in Greek and Canticles and Lamentations in an early Fayyumic dialect.[40] The Fayyumic text of Lamentations in this bilingual Greco-Coptic manuscript has been studied by Feder and compared on the one hand with the Sahidic and Bohairic versions and on the other hand with the Greek text.[41]

According to Feder, the early Fayyumic version is not based on Sahidic, but represents an independent translation from Greek.

13–17.2.2.4 Translation Character and Text-Critical Value

Whereas for the time being, almost nothing can be said about the translation character and the Greek parental text of Ruth, Canticles, Ecclesiastes, and Esther, because of the lack of pertinent studies, this situation is much better for Lamentations in its Sahidic translation. Cop^{Sa}-Lam has been studied in the edition of the Sahidic translation of Jeremianic Corpus.[42] Cop^{Sa}-Lam is completely preserved and recorded in manuscripts from the fourth to the twelfth century.[43] Its transmission shows slightly more variations than Cop^{Sa}-Jer (→ 6–9.2.2.1.3), but the same conclusion can be drawn for its translation character and its text critical value as for Cop^{Sa}-Jer itself. The text of Cop^{Sa}-Lam remained almost unchanged from the fourth century until the end of the use of the Sahidic version (twelfth-thirteenth century). As Cop^{Sa}-Jer renders an early recension of OG-Jer (→ 7.3), so Cop^{Sa}-Lam is a witness to an early recension of OG-Lam (→ 13–17.1.1.4) adapting its text *partly* to MT (→ 16.2.2). A typical example for its textual character is the addition of Lam 3:22–24 which are absent in LXX.[44] Also Cop^{Boh}-Lam has the same features as Cop^{Boh}-Jer (→ 6–9.2.2.1.3).

Diebner, B.J., "Die biblischen Texte des Hamburger Papyrus bilinguis 1 (Cant., Lam. co., Eccl. gr. et co.) und ihr Verhältnis zum Text der Septuaginta, besonders des Kodex B (Vat. gr. 1209): Beobachtungen und methodische Bemerkungen," in *Acts of the Second International Congress of Coptic Studies, Roma, 22–26 September 1980* (eds. T. Orlandi and F. Wisse; Rome: C.I.M., 1985), 59–74.

Diebner, B.J. and R. Kasser, *Hamburger Papyrus bil. 1: Die alttestamentlichen Texte des Papyrus bilinguis 1 der Staats- und Universitätsbibliothek Hamburg: Canticum Canticorum (coptice), Lamentationes Ieremiae (coptice), Ecclesiastes (graece et coptice)* (Cahiers d' Orientalisme 18; Geneva: Patrick Cramer, 1989).

Kasser, R., *Papyrus Bodmer XXII et Mississippi Coptic Codex II: Jérémie XL,3–LII,34, Lamentations, Épitre de Jérémie, Baruch 1,1–V,5 en sahidique* (Cologny: Bibliotheca Bodmeriana, 1964).

Kasser, R. and P. Luisier, "P. Bodmer XL: 'Cantique des Cantiques' en copte saïdique," *Or* 81 (2012): 149–201 + pls. 29–43.

Schenke, H.-M. and R. Kasser, *Papyrus Michigan 3520 und 6868(a): Ecclesiastes, Erster Johannesbrief und Zweiter Petrusbrief im fayumischen Dialekt* (TUGAL 151; Berlin: Walter de Gruyter, 2003).

Shier, L.A., "Old Testament Texts on Vellum," in *Coptic Texts in the University of Michigan Collection* (ed. W. Worrell; Humanistic Series 46; Ann Arbor: University of Michigan Press, 1942), 23–167.

Thompson, H., *The Coptic (Sahidic) Version of Certain Books of the Old Testament from a Papyrus in the British Museum* (London: Henry Frowde, 1908).

---

[39] Schenke and Kasser, *Papyrus Michigan 3520 und 6868(a)*.
[40] Diebner and Kasser, *Hamburger Papyrus bil. 1*.
[41] F. Feder, "Die fajjumische Version der 'Klagelieder des Jeremias' (Lam) des Papyrus Bilinguis 1 Hamburg," in *Sprachen, Mythen, Mythizismen: Festschrift für Walter Beltz zum 65. Geburtstag am 25. April 2000* (Hallesche Beiträge zur Orientwissenschaft 32; Halle: Martin-Luther-Universität, 2001), 161–203.
[42] Feder, **Biblia Sahidica*.
[43] Feder, **Biblia Sahidica*, 61–64.

[44] Feder, **Biblia Sahidica*, 69–78.

Thompson, H., *A Coptic Palimpsest Containing Joshua, Judges, Ruth, Judith and Esther in the Sahidic Dialect* (London: Henry Frowde, 1911).

Alin Suciu

13–17.2.3 Ethiopic Translation(s)

13–17.2.3.1 Ruth

13–17.2.3.1.1 Title and Place in Manuscripts

Ruth (አርት ዘሩት "The *'orit* of Ruth") always occurs at the end of the Octateuch. Due to the size of that corpus, it often takes up an entire volume. For additional information about books with which it is collocated in larger codices, see the article on the Octateuch (→ 2.5.3).

13–17.2.3.1.2 Background

Nissel first published a version of Eth-Ruth in 1660.[1] The text remained generally untouched for two centuries until Dillmann published the final volume in his edition of the Octateuch in 1871.[2] Thanks to the recent availability of hitherto unknown texts, a new critical edition of Ethiopic Ruth is a *desideratum*. A team of scholars led by Daniel Assafa, Garry Jost, and Steve Delamarter are working on transcriptions of more than thirty manuscripts representing the full manuscript history.

13–17.2.3.1.3 Translation Character

Due to the small size of the book, precise assessments are impossible. However, Dillmann notes a number of parallels with Eth-Judg (→ 3–5.2.3.2) that may point to the same translator for both works. One may presume, then, that Eth-Ruth may be similarly characterized. As for Ruth specifically, Dillmann notes the struggles the translator had with his Greek exemplar (→ 13–17.1.1.1). At times, the original is nearly impossible to reconstruct (e.g., in Ruth 1:17) and, more frequently, individual words are misinterpreted (see, e.g., Ruth 3:10 and 4:1).[3]

13–17.2.3.1.4 Text-Critical Value

A preliminary study of Eth-Ruth reveals readings that closely follow LXX-Ruth (→ 13–17.1.1.1), a few instances of alignment with MT-Ruth (→ 13.2.2), and occasions where the scribal tradition has amended the text, resulting in readings unique to this version. Instances where the Ethiopic follows LXX (as opposed to MT) are apparent in Ruth 1:1; 2:7, 9, which are evidenced in the Old Ethiopic and later recensions (→ 1.4.3). The Old Ethiopic and its recensions even replicate the scribal errors of LXX, as in the omission in Ruth 4:7 due to homoioteleuton. The Old Ethiopic (Eth[EMML] 2098), which is closely related to Dillmann's manuscript F, and its various recensions also preserve readings attested among various Greek witnesses. Despite these early readings close to LXX, some later family groups appear to duplicate Hebrew readings, as in Ruth 1:5. There, the original has the noun ደቂቅ "son," while the majority of manuscripts demonstrate an intentional switch from ደቂቅ to ወሉድ "boy/young man." This practice seems to follow closely the Hebrew reading, which also abandons the use of בֵּן "son" (Ruth 1:1–3) in favor of יֶלֶד "boy/young man" (Ruth 1:5). This could present evidence of a later Ethiopic recension, possibly of the Standardized Text (see Eth[EMML 1163, 2388]). As has been noted by Campbell,[4] the switch from בֵּן "son" to יֶלֶד "boy/young man" in MT is intentional, with the desire to express the pain of the mother's loss; the use of the noun יֶלֶד is rarely used in MT to refer to a married man.

All Ethiopic manuscript family groups uniformly deviate both from LXX and MT in Ruth 1:13. The Ethiopic reads "the hand of God has abandoned me" implying loss of protection while MT and LXX imply aggression in reading "Because, the hand of God has *come against me*" (italics mine). Thus, the Ethiopic deflects blame from God. The same theological nicety is repeated in Ruth 1:20 ("Because I have become exceedingly bitter"), where all manuscripts of the Ethiopic make Naomi the source of her own woes. Neither LXX nor MT imply this at all, where the Lord is the cause

---

[1] Nissel, *Liber Ruth*.
[2] Dillmann, **Biblia*.
[3] Dillmann, **Biblia* ("Pars Posterior"), 216.

[4] E.F. Campbell, *Ruth: A New Translation with Introduction and Commentary* (AB 7; Garden City: Doubleday, 1975), ad. loc.

of her bitterness. These and other readings (cf. Ruth 1:21) make the Ethiopic text an important source for the reconstruction of LXX-Ruth (→ 13–17.1.1.1) while shedding light on the particularities of the scribal tradition and transmission of texts in Ethiopia.

13–17.2.3.1.5 Subsequent History

Current knowledge of the transmission history of Ethiopic Ruth is limited. Dillmann[5] identified two manuscript families that may be identified tentatively as the Old Ethiopic (Dillmann's manuscript F; → 1.4.3.7.3) and the Transitional Text (Dillmann's manuscripts C and G; → 1.4.3.7.4). As noted in → 1.4.3.7.5, the existence of a Standardized Text, which prevailed in the later history of Ethiopian transmission, is virtually certain but as of yet unestablished in the manuscripts. However, because Ruth did not circulate apart from the Octateuch, much of its history can be extrapolated cautiously from the more detailed studies of some of its other books.

Dillmann, *Biblia*, Vol. 1: *Octateuchus Aethiopicus*; Fasc. 3: *Joshua, Judices, et Ruth*.

Nissel, J.G., *Liber Ruth Aethiopice e vetusto manuscripto recens ex Oriente allato erutus et latinitate fideliter donatus* (Leiden: Typis et impensis Authoris, 1660).

Meley Mulugetta

13–17.2.3.2 Canticles

13–17.2.3.2.1 Title, Layout, and Placement in the Manuscripts

The Ethiopic Canticles, መኃልየ መኃልይ, has been transmitted in three types of manuscripts. The first is the Ethiopic Psalter, which invariably contains five works in the following order: the 151 Psalms of David (→ 10.4.3), the fifteen biblical Canticles, the book of Canticles in five sections, the Praises of Mary, and Gate of Light. The first three of these works are always laid out in one column, with one strophe on one line, while the last two works are always written in two columns. The second type of manuscript containing Eth-Cant is what we can rightfully call biblical manuscripts, i.e., they contain almost exclusively collections of books of the Ethiopic Old Testament. When Eth-Cant appears in these manuscripts, certain patterns prevail. Of all the books in the Ethiopic Old Testament, Eth-Cant is the most frequently appearing work, usually placed fourth in the collection of the four "Solomonic" works: Proverbs (→ 12.4.3), Wisdom of Solomon (→ 11.15.5), Qohelet (→ 13–17.2.3.3), and Canticles. Of the four, it is the most likely to appear in a location independent of the other three. Finally, Eth-Cant is transmitted, in whole, as part of the readings for Holy Saturday in the Lectionary for Passion Week (ግብረ ሕማማት, *Gäbrä Ḥəmamat*). Appearing as it does in all three types of manuscripts, Eth-Cant has the distinction of being the most copied of all the books in the Ethiopic Old Testament.

A recent study of thirty-two manuscripts[1] was able to show that Eth-Cant exists in three recensions: the common (short) version present in most Psalters, a medium-sized version with eighty-one strophes beyond the short version, and a long version with the eighty-one strophes of the medium-sized version and an additional forty-eight unique strophes as well as thirty-one single- and two-word phrases. The latter recension is found only in Eth-[EMML 2064], a fifteenth-century Psalter. The medium-sized recension is found not only in many Psalters, but also in at least three of the biblical manuscripts (Eth[EMIP 1128, EMIP 1134, EMIP 2007]), and in at least one manuscript of the Lectionary for Holy Week (Eth[EMIP 1290]). Further, the study showed that the government scriptoria of Menilek and Selassie showed a preference for the medium-sized recension.

The widespread distribution of Eth-Cant within classic Ethiopian Orthodox circles is apparently matched outside the core of Gəʿəz- and Amharic-speaking circles. Eth[Bruce 92] contains not only Can-

---

[5] Dillmann, *Biblia*.

[1] S. Delamarter, J. Jacobs, and T. Belachew, "The Single, Dual, and Triple Textual Histories of Ethiopic Old Testament Books: The Case of the Song of Songs," annual SBL meeting, San Diego, November, 2014.

ticles in Amharic, but also in Falâshâ, Gâfât, Dâmôt-Agaw, Tschîrâtachâ-Agaw, and in Gallanorum.

Similarly, in the West, Eth-Cant was among the first to be published in editions by Potken (1513),[2] Walton (ca. 1657),[3] Nissel (1656),[4] and Ludolf (1701).[5]

13–17.2.3.2.2 Gleave's Edition (→ 1.4.3.5)

Work on a critical edition of Eth-Cant was started by Gleave, who died before the project was ready for publication.[6] G.R. Driver stepped in and completed the job. By comparison with editions that had come before, Gleave's drew on a wealth of resources: five printed editions, twenty manuscripts, and twenty-three "service books" (Psalters). The initial conclusion of Gleave and Driver underscored the dependence of the Ethiopic manuscript tradition, generally, on a common Greek *Vorlage* (→ 13–17.1.1.2), though the editors remained uncertain about the specific family or type of Greek manuscript: "as the evidence from the comparison of the Ethiopic MSS with the Greek sources given above points to all the Ethiopic MSS having undergone approximately similar Greek influences and being derived from approximately similar Greek texts, it is possible to refer to these influences as the 'Greek source', … The Ethiopic affords no grounds for classifying the MSS as representing some one kind, some another, of Greek influence."[7]

There are certain challenges in reconstructing the critical principles on which manuscript evidence was read and organized by the editors. The first order of business was to gauge the proximity of each group to their supposed Greek *Vorlage*, as reflected in the Cambridge LXX and the readings in Field's Hexapla. Following this, they analyzed the Ethiopic as though it were a unique family of Greek manuscripts and categorized it accordingly. Viewed in this way, they concluded that "there is no one first-recension archetype from which all our existing mss are derived but that there were various more or less contemporary recensions made, using similar but not in every case identical Greek sources …"[8] This conclusion flows from a chart summarizing readings at Cant 1:9; 2:2, 6, 11, 17; 4:11; 5:4, 7, 8; 6:5, 13; 7:1, 5 in which the readings of various Ethiopic manuscripts have "isolated correspondences with the Greek source which are not found in the majority" of Ethiopian manuscripts. In the end, therefore, they conclude that "those mss nearest to the Greek source, as thus defined, are in general the mss whose date falls nearest to that which critical scholarship has, as we have seen, tended to ascribe to the first recension, viz. the thirteenth–fourteenth century."[9] Again, "the text given in this Edition is an attempted reconstruction, as far as possible with the materials available, of an average text of the first recension."[10] They hold out little expectation of being able to reconstruct the Old Ethiopic from the available manuscripts, at least until the Arabic (→ 13–17.1.8.3; → 13–17.2.8.3) versions are better known. Further, they take the level of variation among the available early manuscripts as an indication that "… it must not be assumed that a single unified text of the Ethiopic Bible, influenced throughout by the same Greek source, ever existed."[11] They do, however, make note of the family ARSTUV, a group of largely eighteenth-century manuscripts, "whose main characteristic is large-scale interpolations superimposed upon a text otherwise very largely indebted to early Ethiopic mss."[12]

Limitations of space do not allow us to go into the particulars, but we suspect that the early manuscripts in Gleave's study represent a combination of Old Ethiopic and Transitional Ethiopic texts (hence the confusion about their variations, → 1.4.3.7.3; → 1.4.3.7.4) and that the ARSTUV family presents witnesses to the medium-sized recension.

---

[2] Potken, *Psalmi et Cantica*.
[3] Walton, **Polyglotta*.
[4] Nissel, *Canticum Canticorum*.
[5] Ludolf, *Psalterium Davidis Aethiopice et Latine*.
[6] Gleave, *The Ethiopic Version of the Songs of Songs*.
[7] Gleave, *The Ethiopic Version of the Songs of Songs*, xviii.
[8] Gleave, *The Ethiopic Version of the Songs of Songs*, xxi–xxii.
[9] Gleave, *The Ethiopic Version of the Songs of Songs*, xix.
[10] Gleave, *The Ethiopic Version of the Songs of Songs*, xxv.
[11] Gleave, *The Ethiopic Version of the Songs of Songs*, xxiv.
[12] Gleave, *The Ethiopic Version of the Songs of Songs*, xxvi.

13–17.2.3.2.3 The So-Called "Hebraic Edition" of Eth-Cant

Gleave and Driver deny the existence of any revision of the Ethiopic based on direct access to Hebrew readings: "The theory, which, as we have seen, has been advanced from time to time, of a direct revision from the Hebrew can find no support in the Canticles; the two instances where only the Hebrew supports the reading of ms G, if not accidental (2:4; 8:5), may be due to Aquila or Symmachus, whose readings here are not preserved."[13] The argument from silence is not compelling, but the observation may be accurate.

There is, however, a version of Canticles that is referred to by modern Ethiopians themselves as the Hebraist or Hebraic edition. It has become clear that this edition is that which we have termed the medium-sized recension of Eth-Cant. Cowley provided a list of just under fifty interpolations that make up the variations of the Hebraic Edition.[14] We have identified many manuscripts that attest to this version (e.g., Eth[EMIP 28, 44, 87, 141, 145, 161, 176]) and we have noted some sort of relation that seems to exist between this form of the text and the government scriptorium in the late-nineteenth and early-twentieth centuries.[15]

The nature of this so-called Hebraic Version is not easy to characterize. Its features cannot be explained simply by recourse to MT-Cant (→ 14.2.2). Something akin to midrash is going on as the excerpts below from Cant 3:6–11 show. Pluses in the Hebraic version are shown in bold in the English translation.

- Gleave, Cant 3:6 – መኑ ይእቲ ዛቲ እንተ ተዐርግ እምገዳም፡ ከመ ሠርጋ ጢስ ዕጥነታ፡ ከርቤ ወስጌን እምኮሉ ጸበለ ኤፌንዮስ። "Who is she that is coming up from the meadow? Like a cloud of smoke is her perfume; myrrh and frankincense from all, like powder of Efenyos (a sweet-smelling perfume)."
- Eth[EMIP 176], Cant 3:6 – መኑ ይእቲ ዛዚ እንተ ተዓርግ እምገዳም። ከመ ደመና ዘጠፈረ ሰማይ። ወከመ ሠርዐ ጢስ ዕጥነታ። ፪ አጥባትኪ ይውኁዝ ሀሊብ። ከርቤ ወስሒን እምኮሉ ጸበለ ኢፈኔዎስ። "Who is she that is coming up from the meadow? **Like a cloud in the firmament of the sky**, and like a cloud of smoke is her perfume. **Your two breasts exude milk**, myrrh and frankincense from all, like powder of Efenyos."
- Gleave, Cant 3:8 – ኩሎሙ እኁዛን አስይፍት ወምሁራን ቀትል፤ ብእሲ ብእሲ ሰይፉ ዲበ መንቅዑቱ በድንጋጼ ሌሊት። "All of them girt with swords and skilled to slay, each man his sword upon his thigh in the terror of the night."
- Eth[EMIP 176], Cant 3:8 – ኩሎሙ እኁዛን አስይ[ፍ]ት ወምሁራን ቀትል ብእሲ ብእሲ ሰይፉ ዲበ መንቅዕቱ። ይትሜስሉ በድንጋጼ ሌሊት። "All of them girt with swords and skilled to slay, each man his sword upon his thigh **they resemble** the terror of the night."
- Gleave, Cant 3:10 – አዕማዲሁ ገብረ ዘብሩር፤ ምስግኩ ዘወርቅ፤ መንበሩ ዘሜላት፤ ውስጡ ንጹፍ በእብን ሰንፔር፤ አፈቅሮ እምአዋልደ ኢየሩሳሌም። "Its columns he made of silver; its base is of gold; its seat of purple; its inside is strewn with stone of sapphire, I love him more than the daughters of Jerusalem."
- Eth[EMIP 176], Cant 3:10 – አዕማዲሁ ገብረ ዘብሩር። ሰርዲኖስ ምስለ ተርሴለ። ኢዮጳሎግዮስ ዘምስለ ሶፌር። ምስግኩ ዘወርቅ። አቍላፊሁ ወአቍፋሊሁ ኢያሴሜር። መንበሩ ዘሜላት። ጎንብርቱ ዘቤረሊዘምስለ ኢያስጲድ በባሕርይ ክዱን። ውስጡ ንጹፍ በዕብን ሰንፔር። እፈቅሮ ፈድፋደ እምአዋለደ ኢሩሳሌም። "Its columns he made of silver; **Sardion with Tharseis (precious stones); 'Iyopalogiyos (with sapphire)**. Its base is of gold; **its embroidery and its guilding of 'Iyasemer;** its seat of purple. **Its middle is of Beryl with jasper with a pearl covering**. Its inside is strewn with stone of sapphire, I love him more than the daughters of Jerusalem."
- Gleave, Cant 3:11 – ፃአ ትርኣያ አዋልደ ጽዮን ለንጉሥ ሰሎሞን በአክሊል ዘአስተቀጸለቶ እሙ አመ ዕለተ መርዓዉ ወአመ ዕለተ ፍሥሓ ልቡ። "Go forth, that ye may see, daughters of Zion, King Solomon in the crown with which his mother crowned him on the day

---

[13] Gleave, *The Ethiopic Version of the Songs of Songs*, xxiv.
[14] Cowley, *Ethiopian Biblical Interpretation*, 97–101.
[15] V. Six et al., *Catalogue of the Ethiopic Manuscript Imaging Project*, Vol. 1: *Codices 1–105, Magic Scrolls 135–284*; Vol. 2: *Codices 106–200, Magic Scrolls 135–284* (Eugene: Pickwick, 2009 and 2011). The connection between the government scriptorium and this form of text is explored on p. xxxi of Vol. 2.

of his wedding and on the day of the gladness of his heart."
- Eth^EMIP 176, Cant 3:11 – ፃዕ ትርአያ አዋልደ ጽዮን። ለንጉሥ ሰሎሞን። በአክሊል ዘአስተቀጸለቶ እሙ። አመ ዕለተ ሕማሙ። ወአመ ዕለተ ስቅለቱ። ወአመ ዕለተ ሞቱ። አመ ዕለተ መርዓሁ ወአመ ዕለተ ፍሥሐ ልቡ። "Go forth, that ye may see, daughters of Zion, King Solomon in the crown with which his mother crowned him **on the day of his passion and the day of his crucifixion and on the day of his death and** on the day of his wedding and on the day of the gladness of his heart."

Though this edition carries the title "Hebraic Edition" among modern Ethiopians, it does not appear to be influenced by MT-Cant (→ 14.2.2). Cowley suggests "that the interpolated material may have originated as epexegetic glosses from the great Ethiopian scholar Abba Giyorgis of Gasəčča" and shows similarities to another work attributed to him, the *Harp of Praise*, አርጋኖነ ውዳሴ.[16]

Most recently, it has become clear that Eth^EMML 2064 preserves an even longer version of this recension, which calls for further investigation. Eth^EMML 2064 is much older than any previously identified member of the Hebraic edition of Eth-Cant. Further, it is clear that the form of the text carried in Eth^EMML 2064 stands behind the later medium-sized recension that survives in quantities of manuscripts from the eighteenth century and later.

Cowley, *Ethiopian Biblical Interpretation*.
Gleave, H.C., *The Ethiopic Version of the Songs of Songs: Critically Edited* (London: Taylor's Foreign Press, 1951).
Euringer, S., *Die Auffassung des Hohenliedes bei den Abessiniern: Ein historisch-exegetischer Versuch* (Leipzig: J.C. Hinrichs' Buchhandlung, 1900).
Euringer, S., "Schöpferische Exegese im äthiopischen Hohenliede," *Bib* 17 (1936): 327–44, 479–500; *Bib* 20 (1939): 27–37.
Euringer, S., "Ein Äthiopischer Scholienkommentar zum Hohenlied, herausgegeben und übersetzt," *Bib* 18 (1937): 257–76, 369–82.
Ludolf, H., *Psalterium Davidis Aethiopice et Latine* (Frankfurt a.M.: Zunner & Helwig, 1701).
Nissel, J.G., *Canticum Canticorum Schelomonis Aetiopice et Arabice cum Versione Latina* (Leiden: Typis Authoris, 1656).
Potken, J. (ed.), *Psalmi et Cantica: Psalterium et canticum canticorum et alia cantica biblica aethiopice et syllabarium seu de legende ratione* (Rome: Silber, 1513).
Treat, J.C., "Lost Keys: Text and Interpretation in Old Greek Song of Songs and its Earliest Manuscript Witnesses" (PhD diss., University of Pennsylvania, 1996).
Walton, *Polyglotta*.

Steve Delamarter
Melaku Terefe
Ralph Lee
Curt Niccum

13–17.2.3.3 Qoheleth

13–17.2.3.3.1 Title and Place in the Manuscripts

In the Ethiopic Bible, መክብብ ("Congregation" = Ἐκκλησιαστής) consistently circulates as part of the Solomonic corpus, which Proverbs (→ 12.4.3) heads. Ecclesiastes and Wisdom of Solomon (→ 11.15.5) typically take second and third position, but the Ethiopic manuscripts are divided as to the particular order. Sirach (→ 11.4.6) and/or Canticles (→ 13–17.2.3.2) may also circulate with this group, with the earlier manuscripts generally favoring Sirach and the later ones Canticles. The corpus most often follows historical works (usually 1–4 Kingdoms) and precedes the prophetical books.

13–17.2.3.3.2 Background

Ecclesiastes was translated from a Greek *Vorlage* (→ 13–17.1.1.2), presumably around the second half of the fourth century C.E. In 1931, Mercer published an edition of the Ethiopic version that included collations of twenty-four manuscripts.[1] Despite the scope of Mercer's study, unusual for the time period, knowledge of manuscripts and text-critical methodologies have since improved greatly.

---

[16] Cowley, *Ethiopian Biblical Interpretation*, 96.

[1] Mercer, *Ecclesiastes*.

13–17.2.3.3.3 Translation Character

The simpler vocabulary of Ecclesiastes allowed for a quality of translation that surpasses that found in many other biblical books. Although not having to struggle much with unfamiliar terminology, the translator still occasionally stumbled when deciphering the uncial Greek text written *scriptio continua*. As a result, he omits words (ὅτι "because" in Qoh 2:12), adds them (μου οὐ "my not" in Qoh 12:12), or misreads them (cf. ὅτι ὡς "because like" from ὅπως "indeed" in Qoh 7:22).

13–17.2.3.3.4 Text-Critical Value

Mercer implies in his introduction that the Ethiopic offers little of text-critical value. Throughout, though, he never defines the terms "translator," "editor," and "reviser," and he applies all three to each of the Ethiopic text types and to individual manuscripts. He further claims as "known fact" that the "translator" had access to one or more LXX manuscripts (→ 13–17.1.1.2), Hebrew manuscripts (both Masoretic [→ 15.2.2] and pre-Masoretic), and copies of the Syriac (→ 13–17.1.4.5; → 13–17.2.4.3), Coptic (→ 13–17.2.2.3.3), and Latin Vulgate versions (→ 13–17.1.7).[2] Disregarding the confusion produced by the terminological imprecision, this particular scenario is historically implausible for all but the most recent stage of Ethiopia's literary history.

It is certainly untrue for the period when Ecclesiastes was first translated, for the Old Ethiopic derives solely from a Greek text (→ 13–17.1.1.2), which the translator followed strictly. Of the eighteen passages Mercer lists where the translator "preferred" the Masoretic reading over LXX, only one might possibly depend upon the Hebrew (Qoh 1:15; → 15.2.2).[3] All other readings undoubtedly originated from the Greek. Mercer's erroneous conclusions stem from faulty philology (Qoh 1:1 and 5:18), incorrect assumptions about sentence divisions (Qoh 1:6 and 3:17, both of which follow LXX in Old Ethiopic manuscripts), transmission error (the Old Ethiopic reads ለኩሎሙ "to all of them" rather than ለክልኤሆሙ "to both of them" at Qoh 2:14), and erroneous definitions. Mercer further incorrectly assumes that any reading that diverges from his printed LXX must derive from the Hebrew or another version even though all of the substantial passages he musters agree word for word with known Greek witnesses (Qoh 2:6; 4:1, 4, 17; 6:6; 7:21[22]; 10:19; 12:5). The same mistakes occur with the supposed pre-Masoretic readings (Qoh 2:25; 3:1, 19; and 4:14) and apparent agreements with the Syriac and Vulgate (Qoh 1:5 and 2:12–13). Contrary to Mercer's conclusion, the Ethiopic faithfully reproduces a Greek text available in East Africa in the fourth century C.E.

Greater clarity about relationships with the Greek can be obtained once the Göttingen edition of Ecclesiastes appears. In the interim, one can note that Ethiopic Ecclesiastes shares some distinctive readings with Codex Venetus and a corrector of Codex Sinaiticus, for example. ἰσχύς οὐκ ἐστίν "strength is not" (Qoh 4:1) and ὑπὲρ τὸ δοῦναι ἀφρόνας θυσίαν "above the giving of fools is a sacrifice" (Qoh 4:17). Overall, the Ethiopic seems to exhibit a particular affinity with a group of minuscules that include LXX[155, 248, 296].[4]

13–17.2.3.3.5 Subsequent History

Mercer found that the manuscripts divided into three general groups: A, B, and C. These correspond roughly to the Old Ethiopic, the Transitional Text, and the Standardized Text respectively (→ 1.4.3.7.3–5) His only Old Ethiopic witness has since been supplemented by several more. The Transitional Text incorporates occasional corrections from the Arabic (→ 13–17.1.8.4; → 13–17.2.8.2); see, for example, ሰማይ "heaven" in Qoh 3:1; ወኢይማስን "and it will not corrupt" in Qoh 5:5; and ለነዳይ "the poor" in Qoh 6:8. From this text type, two separate revisions were made in the sixteenth century: the Standardized Text and the Academic Text. Revisers of

---

[2] Mercer, *Ecclesiastes*, 23–25.

[3] Mercer, *Ecclesiastes*, 60, draws attention to the active voice, but of greater significance is the choice of ረትዐ "to be right" for ἐπικοσμηθῆναι "to be set in order" in Qoh 1:15.

[4] Manuscript designations are from Holmes and Parsons, *Vetus Testamentum*.

both had access to Arabic and Hebrew resources (→ 15.2.2), but the Academic Recension (see Eth^(Ber Or Qu 283)) was more thorough. A distinct Textus Receptus does not appear. Manuscript Eth^(IES 77), which gives an "official" shape to the biblical text, preserves a Transitional Text closely akin to Eth^(BN 8) and Eth^(BN Abb 149).[5]

Holmes, R. and J. Parsons, *Vetus Testamentum Graecum cum variis lectionibus*, Vol. 3 (Oxford: Clarendon Press, 1823).
Mercer, S., *The Ethiopic Text of the Book of Ecclesiastes* (Oriental Research Series; London: Luzac and Co., 1931).

Curt Niccum

13–17.2.3.4 Lamentations
13–17.2.3.4.1 Title and Place in the Manuscripts

The earliest known title to Eth-Lam is ሰቆቃወ ኤርምያስ "Lamentation of Jeremiah," to which later codices append ነቢይ "the Prophet." In Ethiopian tradition, this book, except in a handful of manuscripts copied during the last 150 years, appears in a larger corpus of works attributed to Jeremiah. The core of this collection contains Jeremiah (→ 6–9.2.3.2), Baruch (→ 11.2.1.5), and Lamentations, and they almost always appear in that order. Occasionally, other books associated with Jeremiah (the Letter of Jeremiah [→ 11.2.4.5], the Prophecy of Jeremiah to Pashur (→ 11.2.5.2), the Wisdom of Jeremiah, and/or 3–4 Baruch [→ 11.2.3.3]) intervene, but scribes typically consign these works to the end of the collection.

When collocated with other prophetic works, the Jeremiah corpus appears most often with Ezekiel (→ 6–9.2.3.3; thirteen of nineteen manuscripts written before the nineteenth century). In the earlier manuscripts, Ezekiel precedes Jeremiah, but the order is permanently reversed starting in the fifteenth century. During the two subsequent centuries, scribes also began to place Isaiah (→ 6–9.2.3.1) and the Minor Prophets (→ 6–9.2.3.4) before Jeremiah. In the twentieth century, codices containing just Isaiah and the Jeremiah collection start to appear.

13–17.2.3.4.2 Background

LXX-Lam (→ 13–17.1.1.4) alone underlies the Ethiopic text of Lamentations, which was presumably translated near the end of the fourth century C.E. Knowledge of the earliest Ethiopic text comes primarily from Ziegler's comments and notes in his LXX edition,[1] for he consulted manuscript Eth^(Ber Or Fl 3067), which preserves the Old Ethiopic version (→ 1.4.3.4). Although, in 1893, Bachmann[2] published a critical text and apparatus based on four manuscripts, none of them contained the Old Ethiopic. Further, he corrected the base manuscripts' "faulty" passages, which actually attested the Old Ethiopic, with readings adopted from the later Standardized Text. Subsequent discoveries have confirmed the deficiencies of Bachmann's edition and established a firmer basis for investigating the Greek *Vorlage*. Rich material also exists for studying the more recent periods of Ethiopia's transmission history.

13–17.2.3.4.3 Translation Character

The translator labored to render the wording of the Greek exemplar strictly, but he found the vocabulary of LXX-Lam (→ 13–17.1.1.4) taxing, especially in Lamentations 3 where he omitted large sections of text. One must explain the omission of most of Lamentations 5 differently, however, for the wording appears easy enough. Since no clear theological or transcriptional catalysts present themselves, perhaps the section dropped out accidentally, either in the *Vorlage* or in a very early Ethiopian manuscript.

When not forced to omit material, the translator opted to render freely those passages that seemed inappropriate or incomprehensible. For example, in Lam 1:13, the translator substitutes ወአጋሎ "he scorched it" for κατήγαγεν "he brought down" (*NETS) to better match the context.[3] Other

---

[5] Mercer dates these to the sixteenth and seventeenth/eighteenth centuries, respectively.

[1] Ziegler, *Ieremias*, 467–94.
[2] Bachmann, *Die Klagelieder*.
[3] Because Bachmann, *Die Klagelieder*, 25–54, did not take

problems include incorrectly dividing words (e.g., ታሕተ መከየዱ "under his foot" for ὑποπόδιον "footstool" [*NETS] Lam 2:1) and parablepsis (e.g., ἐποίησας "you have acted" [*NETS] Lam 1:21), although this error may have already stood in the exemplar.

Of some interest is the inclusion of Hebrew letter names as division markers taken over from the Greek *Vorlage*. Although Ethiopic, a Semitic language, shares similar nomenclature, presumably making more native substitutions tempting, the translator adhered to the Greek. In later stages, the transliterations changed, but surprisingly not toward Ethiopian designations: The earliest manuscripts have ለብ ("Läb" = λαβδ) and ሳመኅ ("Samaḫ" = σαμχ) for *lamed* and *samech*, but the later manuscripts follow the Syriac spellings, ላሜድ ("Lamēd") and ሳምኬት ("Samkēt"), via the Arabic.

13–17.2.3.4.4 Text-Critical Value

Based on the limited evidence available, Bachmann argued that the translator consulted both Greek and Hebrew manuscripts (→ 16.2.2). With respect to the latter, the use in Lam 3:12b of መጠሪ "mark," a loanword presumably from the Hebrew, particularly impressed him.[4] Ziegler, having an Old Ethiopic manuscript available, correctly challenged this, for his manuscript did not contain that half of the verse.[5] Indeed, no Old Ethiopic manuscripts preserve the passage. *Contra* Bachmann, all of the evidence indicates that Eth-Lam derives solely from a Greek text (→ 13–17.1.1.4) closely aligned to codices Vaticanus (LXX[B]) and Sinaiticus (LXX[S]).

As expected, the textual character of Eth-Lam parallels that of Eth-Jer (→ 6–9.2.3.2). The Old Ethiopic shares a number of distinctive readings with Ziegler's "B-text." In Lamentations 2, one finds the following examples: omission of πάσας "all" (LXX[B S 106]; Lam 2:5); omission of κυρίου "of the Lord" (LXX[B S]; Lam 2:7); and replacement of ἐπί "upon" by εἰς "for" in Lam 2:10 (LXX[S]). Often, a reading the Ethiopic shares with LXX[B] and/or LXX[S] occurs also in Alexandrinus (LXX[A]) and LXX[106], with LXX[106] having a significantly higher rate of agreement. For example, in Lam 1:8, the Old Ethiopic reads ὀπίσω "back" (LXX[B S 106 130]) and omits ὅτι "because" (LXX[B A 106]). It also agrees with the addition of ὑπεναντίος "opponent" (*NETS) in Lam 2:4 (LXX[B S A 106']) and reads τὴν ἔξοδον "the exit" at Lam 2:21 (LXX[B A 106 130 538]).

As for the other groups identified by Ziegler, occasionally LXX[A] text readings appear and rarely a distinctive Hexaplaric (→ 13–17.1.5.1) passage (see Lam 2:21), but the Old Ethiopic is devoid of unambiguous Lucianic (→ 13–17.1.6) influence (cf. Lam 4:1) and displays none of the unique variants found in the LXX[Q]-text or Catena group.

13–17.2.3.4.5 Subsequent History

Lacking a critical edition, any reconstruction of the text's history must be considered tentative. Certainly Eth[EMML 2080, BN Abb 55, EMIP 1029, IES 722, Ber Or Fl 3067] preserve the Old Ethiopic (→ 1.4.3.7.3), although not without some corruptions within the Ethiopic tradition: በማኅበራ "in her assembly" for በማኅደራ "in her tabernacle" at Lam 2:4, for example. The two manuscripts underlying Bachmann's base text along with Eth[EMML 554, EMIP 1051, Cam 1570] represent the transitional text (→ 1.4.3.7.4), which Ziegler names "die vulgäre Rezension."[6] The presence of መጠሪ "mark" in Lam 3:12b in these witnesses is interesting if the word is indeed Hebrew. However, in all other instances corrections during the transition period originated from the Arabic. Presumably መጠሪ "mark" reflects an Arabic cognate instead, for the earliest known evidence of Ethiopians consulting a Hebrew manuscript is with the revision that produced the Standardized Text (→ 1.4.3.7.5). It is to this late-sixteenth century recension that most extant manuscripts belong.[7]

If an Academic Text for Lamentations exists (→ 1.4.3.7.7), Eth[Bruce 75] perhaps attests it. The word

---

these limitations and certain idiosyncrasies of the Ethiopic fully into account, his reconstruction of the Greek *Vorlage* is useless.

[4] Bachmann, *Die Klagelieder*, 39–40.

[5] Ziegler, *Ieremias*, 36, although still unnecessarily arguing for influence from the Academic Text, which is anachronistic, rather than the Arabic.

[6] Ziegler, *Ieremias*, 30.

[7] See Eth[EMML 562, 598, 827, 945, 1105].

order and rhythm of many alterations approximate MT, but many readings clearly derive from the Arabic (→ 13–17.1.8.5; → 13–17.2.8.5), which is itself a translation of the Peshitta (→ 13–17.1.4.4), and none necessitate a Hebrew *Vorlage*. (See in particular Lam 2:12 and 4:1 and the doublets at Lam 4:9.) Representatives of the Textus Receptus include Eth[EMML 348] and Eth[IES 77], with the latter placing Lam 3:65 before v. 66 rather than after in contrast to the other collated manuscripts (→ 1.4.3.7.6).

Bachmann, J. (ed.), *Die Klagelieder Ieremias in der aethiopischen Bibelübersetzung* (Halle: Max Niemeyer, 1893).
Schäfer, R., "Lamentations איכה," *BHQ 18*, 54–72, 17*–20*, 30–34*, *43–46, *113–36.
Ziegler, J. (ed.), *Ieremias, Baruch, Threni, Epistula Ieremiae* (Septuaginta Vetus Testamentum Graecum 15; Göttingen: Vandenhoeck & Ruprecht, 1957).

Curt Niccum

13–17.2.3.5 Esther

13–17.2.3.5.1 Place in the Manuscripts

A sample of twenty-nine manuscripts examined recently by S. Delamarter shows that Eth-Esth is not grouped together with the other *megillot* as in the Hebrew Bible. Instead it usually appears adjacent to the books of Tobit (→ 11.14.9) and Judith (→ 11.9.6), thereby following the LXX scribal tradition (→ 13–17.1.1.5). Only seven times was it copied in a manuscript without these two other books present. In the cases where these three books appear and are adjacent, the order of the books varies, but with a clear preference: In twelve cases, the order is Tobit, Judith, Esther.[1] Further, there was a clear tendency in the scribal tradition to locate Tobit, Judith, and Esther near the books of Esdras (once immediately preceding and eleven times following; → 19.4.3; → 11.7.1.5; → 11.7.2.4), the books of Maccabees (three times immediately following and three times preceding; → 11.10.1.5; → 11.10.2.5;

→ 11.10.5), and the book of Sirach (three times immediately preceding and four times following; → 11.4.6).

13–17.2.3.5.2 Background

Eth-Esth was edited by Esteves Pereira in 1911 (→ 1.4.3.4).[2] The edition lists sixteen manuscripts known at that time, the oldest of them stemming from the fifteenth or sixteenth century. Four of these manuscripts form the base of the edition, among them Eth[BN Abb 55], which is considered by the editor to be the most ancient and the version least corrected. As there is no edition based on more manuscripts, especially those recently catalogued and the many as yet uncatalogued, Hanhart and Haelewyck refer mainly to Esteves Pereira's edition when discussing the evidence of the Ethiopic version in their editions of LXX-Esth[3] (including the shorter so-called Alpha text; → 13–17.1.1.5) and VL-Esth[4] respectively (→ 13–17.2.1.5).

13–17.2.3.5.3 Translation Character

As for its literary profile, Eth-Esth includes the Esther Additions (→ 11.6.5) and renders quite literally the LXX-text of Esth (→ 13–17.1.1.5), which therefore can be considered as its parent text.[5] The following evidence suggests that Eth-Esth was translated directly from a Greek *Vorlage*: 1) The Greek case markers are conserved in several places;[6] 2) some passages render a word sequence difficult to follow in Ethiopic, which results from the translator's strategy of offering a word-by-word translation when confronted with a difficult Greek passage;[7] and 3) a few deviations from LXX-Esth can be understood best as misunderstandings of the LXX source text by the Ethiopic translator.[8]

---

[1] In three cases, the order is Tobit, Esther, Judith; in two cases it is Judith, Esther, Tobit; in two cases Judith, Tobit, Esther; and in one case Esther, Judith, and Tobit (information based on e-mail by S. Delamarter).

[2] F.M. Esteves Pereira, *Le livre d'Esther: Version éthiopienne* (PO 9.1; Paris: Firmin-Didot, 1911).

[3] Hanhart, *Esther*.

[4] Haelewyck, *Hester*.

[5] Esteves Pereira, *Esther*, 12.

[6] Esteves Pereira, *Esther*, 12–13.

[7] Cf. in particular the Ethiopic version of sections B and E rendering the royal edicts (see Hanhart, *Esther*, 31, for more details on this point).

[8] See Hanhart, *Esther*, 30, for examples of such misunderstandings in Eth-Esth 1:19; 2:7; and 3:15.

In spite of the generally faithful character of the Ethiopic translation, a certain tendency to improve the readability of the text by shortening or expanding it slightly or by modifying certain expressions is noticeable.⁹

13–17.2.3.5.4 Text-Critical Value

The rather minor disagreements among the Ethiopic manuscripts studied by Esteves Pereira are generally explained as reflecting efforts to revise Eth-Esth towards a later Greek text version. As a result, the view emerged that no particular Greek text form can be ascribed to the bulk of Eth-Esth manuscripts that represent such a later, corrected version.¹⁰ Whereas Esteves Pereira suggests the influence of Origen's (→ 13–17.1.5.5) and Hesychius' recensions (→ 1.3.2.1) on the Ethiopic version,¹¹ Haelewyck calls attention to possible links with the Greek source text of VL-Esth (→ 13–17.2.1.5).¹² Further studies are required for answering the question as to which extent Arabic sources influenced Eth-Est (cf.→ 1.5.4.8.1).

Almeida Filho, E.J., "El Vorlage de la Versión Ä del Libro de Ester," *Hermenêutica* 2 (2002): 99–110.
Esteves Pereira, F.M., *Le livre d'Esther: Version éthiopienne* (PO 9.1; Paris: Firmin-Didot, 1911).
Haelewyck, J.-C., *Hester* (VL 7.3; Freiburg i.B.: Herder, 2003), 75–76.
Hanhart, R., *Esther* (2nd ed.; Septuaginta Vetus Testamentum Graecum 8.3; Göttingen: Vandenhoeck & Ruprecht, 1983), 16, 29–32.

Veronika Bachmann

13–17.2.4 Late Syriac Translations

13–17.2.4.1 Ruth

13–17.2.4.1.1 Text

The complete Syro-Hexaplaric text of the book of Ruth is extant in a unique eighth-century C.E. manuscript,¹ i.e., Add. 17.103 of the British Library (London), containing both Judges (folios 4ʳ–61ᵛ) and Ruth (folios 62ᵛ–70ʳ), the text of which was edited by Rørdam in 1861,² and then again by de Lagarde in 1892.³ Undoubtedly, there are also citations from Syh-Ruth remaining to be found in pre-modern Syriac literature (→ 21.9), though we have found none in those exegetical works containing specific treatments of the book that have been published so far.⁴

---

⁹ See Hanhart, *Esther*, 29–30, for some examples (including a correction of Esteves Pereira's translation of Eth-Esth 1:19).
¹⁰ Hanhart, *Esther*, 32.
¹¹ Esteves Pereira, *Esther*, 13.
¹² Haelewyck, *Hester*, 76.

---

¹ See the description of W. Wright, *Catalogue of Syriac Manuscripts in the British Museum: Acquired Since the Year 1838*, Part 1 (London: Gilbert and Rivington, 1870), 32–33 (no. 52). A. Rahlfs (in *Bibliothecae syriacae*, 32ʰ) reasonably concludes that Syh-Ruth was not contained in the lost manuscript of Masius, seeing that the latter neither mentions it nor cites it in his *Peculium Syrorum*. De Lagarde's edition of the text is essentially identical to that of Rørdam, including almost all of the latter's suggested emendations; in several instances, however, de Lagarde offers his own minor emendations (e.g., *ad* 1:10: ܡܗܦܟܝܢ for ܡܗܦܟܝܢ "we are returning"; *ad* 2:16: ܬܟܣܘܢ for ܬܟܣܘܢ "[do not] rebuke").
² Rørdam, *Libri Judicum et Ruth*.
³ In his posthumously published *Bibliothecae syriacae*, 186–90.
⁴ I.e., in the commentary of Ishoʿdad of Merv (see C. van den Eynde [ed.], *Commentaire d'Išoʿdad de Merv sur l'Ancien Testament*, Part 3: *Livres des sessions* [CSCO 229/Syr. 96; Louvain: Peeters, 1962], 224–33; C. van den Eynde [trans.], *Commentaire d'Išoʿdad de Merv sur l'Ancien Testament*, Part 3: *Livres des sessions* [CSCO 230/Syr. 97; Louvain: Peeters, 1963], 267–76), the *scholia* of Theodore bar Koni (see A. Scher [ed.], *Theodorus bar Kōnī: Liber scholiorum*, Part 1 [CSCO 55/Syr. (ser. 2) 65; Paris: E Typographeo Reipublicae, 1910], 359; R. Hespel and R. Draguet [trans.], *Théodore bar Koni: Livre des scolies (recension de Séert)*, Part 1: *Mimrè I–V* [CSCO 431/Syr. 187; Louvain: Peeters, 1981], 298), and the anonymous East Syrian *scholia* (viz., glossary of difficult words) edited by G. Hoffmann in his *Opuscula nestoriana* (Paris: Maisonneuve et soc., 1880), 85–122 (the portion treating Ruth is on pp. 99–100). No citations from Syh-Ruth are to be found in Bar Hebraeus' *scholia* (so Baar, *New Syro-Hexaplaric Texts*, 24, n. 2). Still to be examined is the anonymous East Syrian commentary contained in manuscript Diyarb.-Mos. 13 of the Chaldean Patriarchate of Mosul (see the general description of C. van den Eynde, op. cit. [1963], xxxv–xxxvi). We would be surprised, moreover, if a citation or two from Syh-Ruth is not to be found lurking in a grammatical or lexicographical work.

13–17.2.4.1.2 Text-Critical Value

Notwithstanding the generally slavish nature of the Syro-Hexapla as a translation (one of the best over-all grammatical analyses of which is provided by Rørdam[5]), the significant grammatical-lexical differences between Syriac and Greek – and the limitations of the former in representing the latter – greatly vitiate the value of the Syro-Hexapla as a definitive witness to the underlying Greek text (→ 13–17.1.5).[6] Beyond this, additional caution must be exercised in ascertaining the text-critical value of Syh-Ruth considering: 1) that it is extant in only one (even if relatively early) manuscript;[7] 2) the possibility (given the dearth of evidence regarding the textual history of Syh-Ruth) of this one witness having been "contaminated" by (i.e., "corrected" per) s-Ruth (→ 13–17.1.4.1; as *ad* Ruth 4:1, in the [incorrectly] asterisked addition of ܕܡܕܝܢܬܐ "of the city"[8]); and 3) the possibility of a later Greek recension (e.g., the Lucianic [→ 13–17.1.6]) "contaminating" the Hexaplaric text form from which Syh-Ruth was translated, and so further clouding the value of the latter as a witness to the "original" text form of Origen's Hexapla (→ 13–17.1.5). This last possibility, in fact, has been shown to be a near-certainty in at least six instances drawn from what is generally one of the Syro-Hexapla's most important text-critical contributions, namely, its preservation (to a greater extent than in the extant Greek Hexaplaric witnesses) of Origen's asterisks and obeli. However, of the twenty-one asterisked passages in Syh-Ruth, seven clearly contradict Origen's practice of using such to mark his additions (per the Hebrew text) to LXX (→ 13–17.1.1.1), since none of them correspond to anything found in the extant Hebrew text (→ 13.2.2). Yet, rather than correcting these seven asterisks to obeli – as do Rørdam, de Lagarde, and (following the latter) Brooke and McLean[9] –, these Aristarchian signs should be ignored completely as erroneous post-Origenian additions,[10] since one (*ad* Ruth 4:1), for which there is no support in any Greek manuscript, was likely influenced by the Peshitta (see above and → 13–17.1.4.1), and the other six (*ad* Ruth 1:16, 21; 2:2; 4:1, 4, 13) are just as likely reflective of non-Origenian *Lucianic* readings that contaminated the Hexaplaric text form from which the Syro-Hexapla was eventually translated. In any event, in his recently published exemplary *editio maior* of LXX-Ruth, Quast addresses all the Syro-Hexaplaric evidence in a measured and thorough manner.[11]

Baars, W., *New Syro-Hexaplaric Texts: Edited, Commented upon and Compared with the Septuagint* (Leiden: Brill, 1968).

---

[5] Rørdam, *Libri Judicum et Ruth* (first part).

[6] In this respect, Brock's cautionary conclusion ("Limitations of Syriac," 98) regarding the Syriac versions of the New Testament may be just as well applied to the Syro-Hexapla, to wit: "where the Syriac at first sight appears formally to support a Greek variant, … closer examination, taking into account *over-all usage* in a particular version and book, will often indicate that formal identity can by no means be used as evidence that the Syriac supports the Greek variant in question." To cite a couple of examples from Syh-Ruth: *ad* 1:10, ܡܗܦܟܝܢܢ, "we are returning" (read ܡܗܦܟ) may reflect the basic reading ἐπιστρέφομεν, "we return" or the variant ἐπιστρέψωμεν, "we will return" (see Rørdam, *Libri Judicum et Ruth*, 188, n. ad loc.); *ad* 2:9, ܐܡܬܝ ܕ, "when" may reflect the extant Hexaplaric reading ὁπότε, "when" or the variant ὅτε, "when," supported by the Greek manuscripts of the so-called (see Quast's Göttingen LXX-Ruth critical edition) R-Recension (see ibid., 192, n. ad loc.; both of these options are covered by Quast's citation of the Syro-Hexapla under Lat. *quando*). See also the cautionary assessment of Thornhill, "The Greek Text," 238.

[7] Hence, for example, the possibility that the Syriac rendering, *ad* 1:1, of λιμὸς ἐν τῇ γῇ· καὶ ἐπορεύθη, "a famine in the land, and there went" (corresponding, as in the Peshitta, to ܟܦܢܐ ܒܐܪܥܐ. ܘܐܙܠ, "a famine in the land, and there went") was omitted by scribal error, though eminently reasonable (de Lagarde, following Rørdam, even includes the Syriac rendering as a bracketed emendation in his text [*Bibliothecae syriacae*, 186, line 29]), remains speculative at best.

[8] See Rørdam, *Libri Judicum et Ruth*, 197, note ad loc.; Thornhill, "The Greek Text," 237–38, 240; Quast, *Ruth*, 34 (The latter two following Rahlfs, *Studie*, 65).

[9] Rørdam (ed.), *Libri Judicum et Ruth secundum versionem Syriaco-hexaplarem*; Rahlfs (ed.), *Bibliothecae syriacae, a Paulo de Lagarde collectae*; Brooke–McLean, **The Old Testament in Greek*, Part 4: *Joshua, Judges, Ruth*.

[10] So Thornhill, "The Greek Text," 238 (building on the earlier conclusions of Rahlfs, *Studie*, 61–65). See also Quast, *Ruth*, 34–35.

[11] Quast (ed.), *Ruth*. See, aside from the *apparatus criticus* accompanying the edited text, his introductory analysis on pp. 24–44.

Brock, S.P., "The Syriac Versions: VII. Limitations of Syriac in Representing Greek," in *The Early Versions of the New Testament: Their Origin, Transmission, and Limitations* (ed. B.M. Metzger; Oxford: Clarendon Press, 1977), 83–98.

Brooke–McLean, **The Old Testament in Greek*, Part 4: *Joshua, Judges, Ruth* (1917).

Quast, U. (ed.), *Ruth* (Septuaginta Vetus Testamentum Graecum 4.3; Göttingen: Vandenhoeck & Ruprecht, 2006).

Rahlfs, A. (ed.), *Bibliothecae syriacae, a Paulo de Lagarde collectae, quae ad philologiam sacram pertinent* (Göttingen: Dietrichs, 1892).

Rahlfs, A., *Studie über den griechischen Text des Buches Ruth* (MSU 3.2; Berlin: Weidmannsche Buchhandlung, 1922).

Rørdam, T.S. (ed.), *Libri Judicum et Ruth secundum versionem Syriaco-hexaplarem ... praemittitur dissertatio de regulis grammaticism, quas secutus est Paulus tellensis in Veteri Testamento ex graeco syriace vertendo* (Copenhagen: O. Schwartz, 1861).

Thornhill, R., "The Greek Text of the Book of Ruth: A Grouping of Manuscripts according to Origen's Hexapla," *VT* 3 (1953): 236–49.

Michael G. Wechsler

13–17.2.4.2 Canticles
See → 11.4.4 Job, Proverbs, Canticles, and Qohelet in Late Syriac Translations [Job > Secondary Translations].

13–17.2.4.3 Qoheleth
See → 11.4.4 Job, Proverbs, Canticles, and Qohelet in Late Syriac Translations [Job > Secondary Translations].

13–17.2.4.4 Lamentations
The Syro-Hexaplaric version of the book of Lamentations is only preserved in manuscript C. 313 Inf. located in the Ambrosiana Library (Ceriani, *Codex*, folios 140ʳ–142ʳ) and dates back to the ninth century C.E. It is published in Ceriani's critical edition[1].

A previous edition was Middeldorpf's *Codex Syriaco-Hexaplaris* (pp. 371–82), not based on the original but on Matthias Norberg's copy, so various mistakes can be found in it. Both editions contain a comment on and comparison with the Greek text. The lessons of the Syriac version are also discussed by Field, **Hexapla*, and mentioned in the critical notes to Ziegler's edition of Jeremiah (siglum Syh). The Syriac text is considered a faithful translation of the Greek text.

A close connection has been established between our manuscript and the small LXX[88]. Both manuscripts have the same colophon: "the lamentations of the prophet Jeremiah; (the book) has been written in the *Hexapla*, to which it has also been committed." However, in Syriac it is preceded by "they are ended" (ܐܫܬܠܡܝ ܐܘܠܝܬܗ ܕܐܪܡܝܐ ܢܒܝܐ ܐܬܟܬܒ ܡܢ ܗܟܣܦܠܐ ܗܘ ܕܡܢ ܠܗ ܐܬܩܒܠ).

The manuscript presents two distinctive traits. First of all, it adds a sidenote to the preamble to LXX, containing the description of the occasion when Jeremiah pronounces the lament. The note says: "this is the proem to the lamentations according to LXX; it is not included in the remainders" (ܐܝܟ ܗܘ ܕܩܕܡ ܐܘܠܝܬܐ ܐܝܬܘܗܝ, ܗܢܐ ܕܐܘܠܝܬܐ ܕܠܐ ܣܝܡ ܠܗ ܗܘ ܕܐܪܝܟܐ), that is Aquila and Symmachus (→ 13–17.1.5.1). Besides, in contrast to the Greek manuscripts, the letters of the Hebrew alphabet, which indicate the beginning of the verses of the acrostic, are not transcribed as αλεφ etc. and used to divide the stanzas but are replaced by the corresponding Syriac signs (ܐ etc.).

Ceriani, A.M., *Fragmenta Latina evangelii S. Lucae, Parvae Genesis et Assumptionis Mosis: Baruch, Threni et Epistola Jeremiae versionis Syriacae Pauli Telensis cum notis et initio prolegomenon in integram ejusdem versionis editionem* (Monumenta sacra et profana opera Collegii doctorum bibliothecae Ambrosianae I.1; Milan: Bibliotheca Ambronsiana, 1861).

Ceriani, A.M., *Codex Syro-Exaplaris Ambrosianus photolithographice editus* (Monumenta sacra et profana opera Collegii doctorum bibliothecae Ambrosianae 7; Milan: Bibliotheca Ambronsiana, 1874).

Middeldorpf, H., *Codex Syriaco-Hexaplaris: Liber quartus Regum e codice parisiensi, Iesaias, Duodecim Prophetae Minores, Proverbia, Iobus, Canticum, Threni, Ecclesiastes e codice Mediolanensi* (Berlin: Enslin, 1835).

---

[1] Ceriani, *Fragmenta*, 16–62.

Ziegler, J., *Ieremias, Baruch, Threni, Epistula Ieremiae* (Septuaginta Vetus Testamentum Graecae 15; Göttingen: Vandenhoeck & Ruprecht, 1957).

Claudio Balzaretti

13–17.2.4.5 Esther

With the exception of forty single-word citations (in a couple of instances two words) in Andreas Masius' *Syrorum Peculium*,[1] the Syro-Hexaplaric text of Esther is, unfortunately, non-extant. The lost manuscript of Masius from which the citations were drawn, and which apparently contained the entire book of Esther, was proven by Rahlfs[2] to be closely related in character and age to the late-eighth-/early-ninth-century C.E. Milan manuscript (i.e., C. 313 Inf. of the Ambrosian Library, containing the Wisdom and Prophetic Books) published in its entirety by Ceriani.[3] Of these citations, only one (*ad* Esth 3:13: ܥܠܝܡܐ "young man," corresponding to the Hexaplaric addition of [ἀπὸ] νεανίσκου [κ.τ.λ.] "[from] young man [to elder, etc.]" after Ἰουδαίων "of the Judeans") is referenced by Hanhart in his critical apparatus to Esther in the Göttingen LXX, the other citations being reasonably deemed by him as inconclusive with respect to the precise Greek forms that they represent.[4]

Baars, W., *New Syro-Hexaplaric Texts: Edited, Commented upon and Compared with the Septuagint* (Leiden: Brill, 1968).
Hanhart, R. (ed.), *Esther* (2nd ed.; Septuaginta Vetus Testamentum Graecum 8.3; Göttingen: Vandenhoeck & Ruprecht, 1983).
de Lagarde, P., *Bibliothecae syriacae, a Paulo de Lagarde collectae, quae ad philologiam sacram pertinent* (ed. A. Rahlfs; Göttingen: Dietrich, 1892).

Michael G. Wechsler

13–17.2.5 Armenian Translations

13–17.2.5.1 Ruth

Extensive manuscript collations for a new edition of the Armenian version of Ruth significantly realize Rahlfs' expectations[1] of the translation's potential witness to the Old Greek obscured by the late secondary running text in Zohrapian's edition of 1805 and its limited apparatus.[2] The Greek text has been consulted according to Rahlfs' critical edition of 1922,[3] supplemented by the Cambridge Septuagint.[4] The version subsists in two strata, the original translation (Arm 1; → 1.4.7) from the early fifth century C.E. and a revision (Arm 2; → 1.4.7) effected about a generation later. Both textual levels derive primarily from Greek, though characterized by different text types and translation technique, as illustrated by the interchange between Boaz and Ruth at the threshing floor at Ruth 3:7. Whereas the revision reflects the Old Greek text's indirect reference to the young woman's appearance (ἡ δὲ ἦλθεν "but she came"; եւ նա եկն "and she came"), the original translation removes confusion by naming her (եւ եկն եւ Հռութ "and Ruth also came") in concert with the Lucianic text (και ηλθε ρουθ LXX^L "and Ruth came" → 13–17.1.6).

Additionally, the early stratum evinces an affiliation with the Peshitta (→ 13–17.1.4.1), as indicated at Ruth 2:19 where Naomi's question to her daughter-in-law is posed as ուր էիր "where were you?" in parallel with the Syriac formulation (ܐܝܟܐ ܗܘܝܬܝ "where were you?"), in contrast to the Old Greek ποῦ ἐποίησας "where did you work?," which is in agreement with MT (→ 13.2.2). The synthesis of the Peshitta to nuance the interpretation of the Greek parent text is well exemplified in determining who does what at Ruth 3:15. Since Semitic ver-

---

[1] A. Masius, *Syrorum Peculium, Hoc Est, Vocabula Apud Syros Scriptores Passim Usurpata: Targumistis Vero Aut Prorsus Incognita, Aut In Ipsorum Vocabulariis Adhuc Non Satis Explicata* (Antwerp: Plantin, 1572). Thirty-nine citations were identified and enumerated by A. Rahlfs in his supplement to de Lagarde's introduction in *Bibliothecae syriacae*, 32^e (published after the latter's death), and one was identified by Baars, *New Syro-Hexaplaric Texts*, 3, n. 5 (*pace* Hanhart, *Esther*, 62, n. 5).

[2] Rahlfs (ed.), *Bibliothecae syriacae*, 32^h–32^i.

[3] A.M. Ceriani, *Codex Syro-Hexaplaris Ambrosianus photolithographice editus* (Monumenta sacra et profana 7; Milan: Bibliotheca Ambrosiana, 1874).

[4] Hanhart, *Esther*, 62–63.

---

[1] Rahlfs, *Studie über den griechischen Text*, 139.

[2] Zohrapian, *Scriptures*.

[3] Rahlfs, *Das Buch Ruth griechisch*.

[4] Brooke–McLean, *The Old Testament in Greek*, Vol. 1.4: *Joshua, Judges, Ruth* (1917).

bal systems distinguish gender in the second and third persons, the Hebrew morpheme וַיָּבֹא "and he went" specifies that it is Boaz who leaves the threshing floor to enter the city. However, as Indo-European languages do not, the Old Greek equivalent καὶ ἦλθεν "and she *or* he went," followed by Arm 2 (եւ եմուտ), is ambiguous. In contrast, the Peshitta reading ܘܐܙܠܬ ܘܐܬܬ "and she went off and came" identifies Ruth as the agent. Perhaps influenced by this interpretive tradition, Lucianic witnesses (→ 13–17.1.6) resolve the Greek aporia by inserting Ruth as the subject. At the culmination of this exegetical process, Arm 1 reads եւ չոգաւ Հռութ եմուտ "and Ruth went off (and) entered."

In contrast, Arm 2 reflects the influence of the Hexaplaric and LXX^R text types (→ 1.3.1.2; → 2.4.6) that seem mostly mediated by the minuscule LXX^{58}, which – though Rahlfs classifies it in LXX^R subgroup 2b and it exhibits a mixed text – overall represents the single witness closest to Arm 2's complexion, and hence is destined to play a major role in reconstructing its earliest form.[5] Emblematic of Origenic associations is the plus tagged by an asterisk at Ruth 1:12 where Naomi is discounting the possibility of bearing another child. While the Old Greek merely rejects the possibility of being with, i.e., married to, a husband (τοῦ μὴ εἶναι ἀνδρί "[too old] for a husband"), the Hexaplaric addition λελαϊκομένην "made common" alludes more directly to the act of procreation. Since the verbal root relates to the people or lay community, the Armenian reviser coined the equivalent աշխարհականացեալ (lit. "laicized"), a *hapax legomenon*. Meanwhile, at Ruth 4:10, we observe the Armenian version bifurcate over the implications of continuing Abimelech's line. Arm 1 joins the critical text ἐκ τῆς φυλῆς λαοῦ αὐτοῦ "from the tribe of his people" in reading ի ցեղէ ժողովրդեան իւրոյ, while Arm 2 follows an LXX^R subgroup (λαοῦ] του τοπου "people] of the place") in rendering ի ցեղէ տեղւոյ իւրոյ "from the tribe of his place."

[5] See further, Cowe, "The Armenian Version of Ruth," 192–97.

13–17.2.5.1.1 Translation Technique

The Arm 1 translator valorizes the grammar and expression of the target language and sets the translation unit at the phrase length. This results in the frequent reformulation of the rather literal structure of the Old Greek text, categorized as a member of the *Kaige* (→ 1.3.1.2; → 13–17.1.1.1) group. Thus at Ruth 1:8, Arm 1 diverges from the Greek structuring of Naomi's injunction that her daughters-in-law return home ἑκάστη εἰς οἶκον "each to the house" in preference to Armenian idiom that does not substantivize the adjective յիւրաքանչիւր տուն "to each's house." As in other books, in addition to smoothening bald constructions by expressing pronoun subjects and objects and inserting nuancing particles, the translator seeks to heighten the moral standing of the main characters. Thus Boaz' command to his workmen at Ruth 2:9 is not only that they do not "touch" (ἄψασθαι) her, but that they do not even "come near" her (չմերձենալ). For her part, Ruth displays appropriate modesty in response in Ruth 2:10 by bowing "low" (խոնարհ).

As already remarked, Arm 2's penchant is to encode as much of the parent text's morphological and syntactic data as possible, replicating the latter word for word. Apart from its approximation to Greek roots that we noted, this policy is regularly applied to a close rendering of parts of speech, such as infinitives, as at Ruth 2:11 where the Old Greek refers to Abimelech's passing in the phrase μετὰ τὸ ἀποθανεῖν, lit. "after the dying." This is paralleled by Arm 2's յետ մեռանելոյ "after dying," in contrast to the more idiomatic Arm 1 rendering յետ մահուան, "after the death." The difference in practice is even more striking in handling participles, as at Ruth 1:22 where Arm 2 retains the Old Greek expression relating to Ruth's exodus from Moab, ἐπιστρέφουσα "returning," as դառցեալ "having gone," but Arm 1 articulates the activity in finite verbs, գնաց եւ ել "left and went out."

13–17.2.5.1.2 Translation Technique: Attention to Context

As one might expect from the foregoing, Arm 1 demonstrates a range of interpretive readings designed to attune the literal Old Greek reading to the unfolding narrative. This is well illustrated by Boaz' call to Ruth to join the workers in their repast at Ruth 2:14, where the Old Greek phrase ὥρα τοῦ φαγεῖν "hour of eating" is transformed into ժամ ճաշոյ "lunchtime." Similarly, at Ruth 3:17, whereas the Old Greek employs the bland adjective κενή "empty" to denote Boaz' counsel to Ruth about caring for her mother-in-law, the equivalent the Armenian translator preferred *in situ* is the compound ունայնամձեռն, "empty-handed," though the reviser reverted to the simple form.

13–17.2.5.1.3 Translation Technique: Literalisms and Transliterations

In keeping with a literalist approach, the reviser preserves many of the Hebraisms of the Old Greek, as in Ruth's statement at Ruth 2:2 where Arm 2 գտից շնորհս առաջի աչաց նորա mirrors the Greek εὕρω χάριν ἐν ὀφθαλμοῖς αὐτοῦ "I will find grace in his eyes." For its part, Arm 1 concludes more idiomatically with առաջի նորա, "before him."

13–17.2.5.1.4 Text Critical Value: Omissions and Additions

Among the few minuses the version witnesses is the non-representation of the introduction to Boaz' speech at Ruth 3:15 (καὶ εἶπεν αὐτῇ "and he said to her"), which is otiose in that the statement is actually the uninterrupted continuation of the preceding. Arm 1 features a larger number of small-scale additions, rounding out the scene painting, as at Ruth 3:13. There the translator provides an important spacial dimension to Boaz' instructions to Ruth – αὐλίσθητι τὴν νύκτα ... κοιμήθητι ἕως πρωί "spend the night ... lie down till morning" – in the formulation ագիր աստ զգիշերս ... ննջեա այդր մինչեւ ցառաւատ "pass the night here ... sleep where you are till morning."

13–17.2.5.1.5 Relevance for Exegesis

One of the most noteworthy readings the Armenian version exhibits is a singular plus at Ruth 2:1 containing an extrabiblical Targum-like tradition about Boaz granting Naomi a house of widowhood: եւ ետ Նոոմինայ տուն այրութեան բնակելոյ ի նմա "and he gave Noomi a house of widowhood for her to live in."

13–17.2.5.1.6 Text-Critical Value of Arm-Ruth for LXX-Ruth

Instances of primitive error remain, but the conscientious application to their task by both the initial translator and subsequent reviser is such that the complexion of their parent texts can usually be discerned with assurance. Arm 1 offers insights into the application of Antiochene exegetical practice (→ 1.3.1.2), while Arm 2 affords valuable testimony to the LXX^R text type (→ 1.3.1.2) several centuries earlier than extant Greek witnesses.

Barthélemy, *Devanciers.
Brooke–McLean, *The Old Testament in Greek*, Vol. 1.4: *Joshua, Judges, Ruth* (1917).
Cowe, S.P., "The Armenian Version of Ruth and its Textual Affinities," in *La Septuaginta en la investigacion contemporanea: v congreso de la IOSCS* (*Salamanca, 26 y 27 de agosto de 1983*) (ed. N. Fernández Marcos; Madrid: Consejo Superior de Investigaciones Científicas, 1985), 183–97.
Rahlfs, A., *Studie über den griechischen Text des Buches Ruth* (MSU 3.2; Berlin: Weidmansche Buchhandlung, 1922).
Rahlfs, A., *Das Buch Ruth griechisch: Als Probe einer kritischen Handausgabe der LXX* (Stuttgart: Priviligierte Württembergische Bibelanstalt, 1922).
Zohrapian, *Scriptures.

Peter Cowe

13–17.2.5.2 Canticles

13–17.2.5.2.1 Translation Character of Canticles

Oskean's study demonstrated that there are two strata to the Armenian version of this book, an original translation (Arm 1) followed by an in-depth revision (Arm 2),[1] each characterized by a distinctive parent text and translation technique. Oskean argued that Arm 1 is best preserved by manuscript 55 of the Vienna Mkhitarist collection, but subsequent research indicates that it is rather a prime witness to the revision, while the running text of Zohrapian's edition afforded by manuscript

---

[1] For Arm 1 and Arm 2, see → 1.4.7.

1508 of the Venice Mkhitarist collection actually provides a tolerable text of the initial translation, whose witness is improved by comparison with other codices.² Currently, a critical edition is in progress, whose present database includes most manuscripts to the end of the fourteenth century, as well as the recently published ninth-century C.E. palimpsest from Sinai, together with lemmata of the commentary by St. Grigor Narekacʻi composed in 977 C.E., which predates most of the manuscript evidence by about two centuries. That is the basis for the Armenian readings in this review: these were then correlated with Treat's study of the Greek tradition,³ which comprises a larger source pool than Rahlfs' compact edition.⁴

That both Armenian strata derive from Greek parent texts is underscored by Cant 1:6b where the Greek reading ὅτι παρέβλεψέν με ὁ ἥλιος – explaining the origin of the young woman's dark hue – is rendered զի խեթեւ հայեցաւ ընդ իս արեգակն "because the sun looked askance at me" by Arm 1 and զի անտես արար զիս արեգակն "because the sun overlooked me" by Arm 2, where the Peshitta (→ 13–17.1.4.2; → 1.3.4) reads "because the sun made me dark." Thus, the two layers appeal to different semantic levels of the Greek verb, the first stratum translating at the phrase unit and showcasing interpretation, the second focusing more on form; it matches the Greek construction with a direct object in the accusative case. That Arm 2 is a revision, not an independent undertaking, is suggested by a series of repeated formulae where the handling of the earlier instance is more invasive than later examples, implying a gradual decline in rigor. Compare the phrase ἀκούτισόν με τὴν φωνήν σου "let me hear your voice" at Cant 2:14d, idiomatically translated by Arm 1 as լսելի արա ինձ զբարբառ քո "make audible to me your speech." This is completely remodeled by the reviser to encode an equivalent of the Greek causative form, employing the rare verb լսուցանել in its rendering լուր ինձ զձայն քո "cause me to hear your voice," which also replaces the lexeme "speech" with a more stereotypical equivalent of "voice." In contrast, at Cant 8:13, Arm 2 is content to rearrange the identical Arm 1 phrase to match the Greek word order, along with the vocabulary change just mentioned, to produce the result զձայն քո լուելի արա ինձ "your voice make audible to me."

The Armenian version features a correction to the Masoretic standard (→ 14.2.2) at Cant 7:13 in agreement with LXX^V 253 Syh (+ ὅσα ἔδωκιν μοι ἡ μήτηρ μου "which my mother gave me"), which appears to derive from the Arm 2 stratum. The manuscripts of the version also manifest a unique addition of six verses with rubrics, either as a preface or appendix to the book, continuing the dialogue between the bride and bridegroom.⁵

13–17.2.5.2.2 Reconstruction of the Parent Texts of Arm-Cant

Certain instances of bifurcation within the Armenian tradition clearly indicate the divergent textual origins of the two strata where Arm 1 evinces affinities with the uncial LXX^B together with other pre-Hexaplaric witnesses, while Arm 2 is aligned with the uncial LXX^A and related minuscules, sometimes in the company of LXX^S, as illustrated by the following examples. Patristic witnesses have not been included.

- Cant 3:4c: αφηκα "did (not) let go" LXX^BSV 68 106 147 155 = Arm 1 թողի] αφησω "would (not) let go" LXX^A 161 248 252 253 = Arm 2 թողից
- Cant 4:8c Ερμων "Hermon" LXX^BV = Arm 1 Հերմոնի] Αερμων "Ahermon" LXX^SA 106 155 157 159 248 252 253 254 = Arm 2 Ահերմոնի
- Cant 5:11 φαζ "phaz" (Hebrew: "refined gold") LXX^B*A155 = Arm 1 բազեայ] κεφαζ "kephaz" LXX^S 147 168 157 161 248 25 Syh^mg = Arm 2 կեփազեայ

---

² The parallel finding in Ecclesiastes (→ 13–17.2.5.3) suggests that the part-Bible containing the Wisdom corpus in the transmission history behind the full Bible of manuscript Venice 1508 evinced much purer and earlier readings than those exhibited in other partial codices from which it was composed. Cowe, "A Typology of Armenian Biblical Manuscripts," 60–61.

³ Treat, "Lost Keys."

⁴ Rahlfs, *Septuaginta*.

⁵ Zohrapian, *Scriptures*, 463.

– Cant 7:2b(Zoh 1) Ναδαβ "Nadab" LXX^BSV 147 (Syh) = Arm 1 Նադաբայ] Αμιναδαβ "Aminadab" LXX^A 254 = Arm 2 Ամինադաբայ.

These data are confirmed by readings like the following at Cant 5:6e, which afford additional evidence for the divergent text types.

– ὑπήκουσεν μου "he answered me" LXX^BSV = Arm 1 ետ ինձ ձայն "he gave me voice," i.e., "replied to me"] επηκουσεν μου "he heard me" LXX^A = Arm 2 լուաւ ինձ

Here Arm 1 ետ ինձ ձայն "he replied to me" follows the printed text in Rahlfs' edition (ὑπήκουσεν μου), while Arm 2 լուաւ ինձ "he heard me" leans more towards the variant επηκουσεν μου. With some internal divergence, the Armenian version also reproduces the Sinaiticus rubric tradition, apportioning the lines to various speakers (bride, bridegroom, maidens, watchmen, etc.). The absence of rubrication from the Sinai palimpsest suggests that this aspect of the text derives from Arm 2.[6]

13–17.2.5.2.3 Cases of Readings Arising from Greek Variants

A number of Armenian renderings depend on Greek variants, either objective or so construed by the translator. At Cant 8:1, the Armenian second person singular form անգոսնեսցես "you will despise" parallels that of LXX^106 εξουδενωσεις "you will despise" against the majority of the Greek tradition ("they will despise"). In other cases, no exact model has been adduced. Thus, the verb բուրեն "exude," employed at Cant 5:13 of perfumes, presupposes not the lemma φύουσαι "breathing/producing" but a form of the graphically similar verb φυσάω. Meanwhile, the Arm 1 rendering զանուշահոտութիւն "like sweet fragrance" at Cant 6:4 seems to rest on the lexeme εὐωδία rather than the lemma εὐδοκία reflected by Arm 2 զհաճութիւն "goodwill." Similarly, at Cant 7:12(13), the Armenian reading նոճ "cypress" must derive from a variant κυπαρισσος "cypress" rather than the term κυπρισμός "blossom."

---
[6] Treat, "Lost Keys," 404–07, 439–514.

13–17.2.5.2.4 Translation Technique

As in other books, Arm 1 is characterized in Canticles by the idiomatic inclusion of personal pronouns, connectives, prepositions, etc., several of which are absent from the Greek text, in part because of the latter's predisposition to reflect the morphology of the underlying Hebrew (→ 14.2.2) in view of its affinity with the *kaige* tradition (→ 13–17.1.2.4). Focusing on the semantic content at the phrase level, it sometimes achieves this goal by brief explanatory additions. In contrast, it pays less attention to word order and the morphological structure of the Greek. One facet of this is fluidity in translation equivalents, e.g., ἀγαθός "good" is rendered by բարի "good" at Cant 1:2, but by ազնիւ "fine" at Cant 7:10.

Arm 2 exhibits the antithetical approach, as we have seen, of following Greek word order and stereotyping translation equivalents. Translating at the word level, it even seeks to articulate subcomponents of complex forms. A good example is afforded by the compound verb ἀναβήσομαι lit. "I will go up" (*NETS* "I will climb") at Cant 7:9, rendered by Arm 1 by the simple verb ելից "I will go up," where the reviser encapsulates the Greek preposition in the adverbial phrase (ելից) ի վեր "up," which however contributes relatively little semantically. Where no suitable equivalent exists, the reviser is prepared to create a neologism calqued on the Greek term, as at Cant 2:14. While Arm 1 renders the phrase ἐχόμενα τοῦ προτειχίσματος "near the outer wall" (*NETS*) by առ պատուարաւ պարսպին "next to the rampart of the wall," interpreting the compound term by a two-noun phrase, the reviser strives for greater precision in representation by inventing the term նախապարիսպ "outwork," which was to remain a *hapax legomenon* in Armenian literature.

Another facet of Greek style employed in much more restricted settings is the articulated participle. Normal Armenian translation practice tends to render this feature by a relative clause, as in the case of ὡς εὑρίσκουσα εἰρήνην "as one who finds peace" (*NETS*) at Cant 8:10b, where Arm 1 reads որ գտանիցէ "one who will find." Here, as at other points, Arm2 unidiomatically tries to replicate the form in իբրեւ գտեալ "as (one) finding."

Granted that one aspect of the Greek of Canticles is the predisposition to capture Hebraisms of its parent text, we find a number of these emerging in Arm 2's revision of the original translation, such as removing present tense forms of the copula. Hebrew achieves various nuances by tacking personal pronouns onto various verbs, especially in the context of motion. Both cases of this phenomenon (Cant 2:11 and 4:6) are manifest in the Greek and thereby pass into the text of Arm 2 through redrafting the original version. Thus, in the first instance, the phrase ἐπορεύθη ἑαυτῷ "it went on its own" appears as գնացեալ մեկնեցան "having gone they left" in Arm 1, which the reviser recast as գնաց ինքեամբ "went by itself." Similarly, in the second, the phrase πορεύσομαι ἑαυτῷ "I will go on my own" was rendered գնացից առանձին "I will go alone" in Arm 1, but transformed to գնացից ինձէն "I will go myself" by the reviser.

Perhaps the best example of Arm 2's realignment of word order to a Greek standard is offered by Cant 5:15c, εἶδος αὐτοῦ ὡς Λίβανος, ἐκλεκτὸς ὡς κέδροι "his appearance is like Lebanon, choice as cedars" (*NETS), where the two parallel phrases were integrated into one comprehensive expression by the original translator as տեսիլ նորա որպէս զընտիր եղեւնափայտից Լիբանանու "his look [is] like choice cedars of Lebanon," while Arm 2 reinstates the division of the line at the caesura in formulating տեսակ նորա իբրեւ Լիբանան ընտրեալ իբրեւ զմայրս "his appearance (is) like Lebanon, choice like cedars" with the variety in lexical selection we have already encountered.

13–17.2.5.2.4.1 Arm 1's Attention to Context

In contrast to Arm 2's stereotyping, Arm 1 nuances its choice of translation equivalents to reflect the contextual setting, as illustrated by the following three examples. In the phrase τῇ ἵππῳ μου ἐν ἅρμασιν Φαραω "to my mare among Pharao's chariots" at Cant 1:9(8), the youth is being likened to one of the horses pulling Pharaoh's chariot, which would imply qualities of breeding and skill. These overtones are conveyed by Arm 1's term երիվարացն "steeds," while Arm 2 valorizes its ordinary cousin, the generic ձիոյն "horse" in deference to the Greek form. The Greek reading ὡς χοροὶ τῶν παρεμβολῶν "she who comes like dances of armies" (*NETS) at Cant 7:1 reflects some of the uncertainty of the underlying Hebrew. As the situation appears military, Arm 1 seeks to soften the disconnect by rendering իբրեւ զգունդս բանակաց "like brigades of camps," while Arm 2 predictably returns us to our starting ground with իբրեւ զպարս բանակաց "like choruses of camps." Similarly, as the imagery at Cant 4:4 depicts King David's well-equipped arsenal, Arm 1 interprets the phrase πᾶσαι βολίδες τῶν δυνατῶν "all the mighty men's javelins" (*NETS) by ամենայն նետք սպառազինացն "all the darts of the well-armed," viewing the soldiers' might in this setting as residing in their weaponry, whereas Arm 2 reverts to a broader term to denote strength in its formulation ամենայն աշտեայք զօրաւորաց "all the javelins of the mighty," which also narrows the semantic range of Arm 1's term նետք – a word that can refer to a wide range of projectiles – by a more focused synonym.

13–17.2.5.2.4.2 Arm 1's Attention to Style

Arm 1's characteristic concern for narrative progression probably underlies its doublet translation of ἐν κώμαις "in the villages" at Cant 7:12 by ի շէնս եւ ի պարտէզս "in hamlets and gardens" in the context of the unfolding succession that sees going into the countryside, spending the night in a village, and visiting a vineyard early next morning. The reference to gardens thus provides a segway to the activities of Cant 7:13. As one might expect, Arm 2 mirrors the Greek in the phrase ի գեօղս "in villages," embodying a more stereotypical equivalent of the Greek term.

13–17.2.5.2.5 Text Critical Value of Arm-Cant for LXX-Cant

As the translation technique of each stratum is fairly predictable, it is relatively easy to reconstruct their parent texts. Consequently, each in its own way provides a valuable contribution to the evolution of the Greek text of the book and its early interpretation.

Ajamian, S., "Classical Armenian *editio minor* of Song of Songs" (ed. M.E. Stone), n.p. [cited July 6, 2015]. Online: http://micro5.mscc.huji.ac.il/~armenia (the text is based on ms Jerusalem 1925, with variants drawn from Matenadaran 1500 and Zohrapian's edition).
Cowe, S.P., "A Typology of Armenian Biblical Manuscripts," *Revue des Études Arméniennes* 18 (1984): 49–67.
Oskean, H., *Erg ergoci aṙaǰin ew erkrord t'argmanowt'iwnę: owsowmnasirowt'iwn ew bnagir* (*The First and Second Translation of Song of Songs*) (Vienna: Mxitarist Press, 1924).
Rahlfs, *Septuaginta.
Treat, J.C., "Lost Keys: Text and Interpretation in Old Greek Song of Songs and its Earliest Manuscript Witnesses" (PhD diss., University of Pennsylvania, 1996).
Zohrapian, *Scriptures.

Peter Cowe

13–17.2.5.3 Qohelet

13–17.2.5.3.1 Background: Editions

The Armenian text used for this entry is that of Zohrapian, in his diplomatic edition of 1805;[1] the Greek was collated according to Rahlfs' provisional edition.[2]

13–17.2.5.3.2 Translation Character

As in a number of books, a division into two strata – a translation at the beginning of the fifth century C.E. (Arm 1), and a revision that ensued about a generation later (Arm 2) – has been identified in Ecclesiastes. Arm-Qoh's dependence on a Greek source text (→ 13–17.1.1.3) and the two strata's derivation from different text types are well illustrated in the sage's counsel to the youth at Qoh 11:9. There, the imperative γνῶθι "know!" of Rahlfs' printed text is followed by the Arm 2 reading ծանիր "know!" whereas the reading of LXX^s* γνώσῃ "you will know" is reflected in Arm 1's equivalent, գիտասցես "you will know."[3]

Zohrapian's running text is largely Arm 1, with the regular support of an eighth- or ninth-century C.E. palimpsest from Sinai,[4] while Arm 2 can be partially reconstructed from the variants cited in his apparatus. Nevertheless, conflation between the strata in the early period of transmission occasionally results in alternation in the version's affiliation. Thus, at Qoh 8:17, Zohrapian's text affords the Arm 2 form զարարածն արարեալ "the work having been done," closely conforming to the number and morphology of the Greek τὸ ποίημα τὸ πεποιημένον "the work that is done" (*NETS*), in contrast to the Arm1 rendering, found in the apparatus, which is more respectful of Armenian idiom, զարարածս նորա որք արարեալ են "his works which have been done."

13–17.2.5.3.3 Reconstruction of the Parent Text of Arm-Qoh

On the basis of Gentry's alignment of the textual witnesses for the forthcoming edition of Ecclesiastes in the Göttingen LXX[5] (→ 13–17.1.1.3), Cox determined that Arm 1's primary affiliation is with the Catena group and, more particularly, with the subgroup LXX^cII, as illustrated by their agreement at Qoh 4:17. There, Arm 1 attests the addition of the imperative γινου "be!" adduced by LXX^cII and LXX^795 in reading լեր "be!" Similarly, at Qoh 5:8, it preserves the longer addition attested by LXX^cII 336' 339 και ισθι πιστος εν παντι· εστι(ν) βραχυ απο του ηρπασμενου "and be faithful in everything; it is shorter than the seized (object)" in reading եւ լիշիր դու հաւատարիմ յամենայնէ ի ծանր յափշտակելոյ անտի "and be you faithful from everything, from the heavy pillaged (object)."[6]

Since Zohrapian's method of citing variants in the apparatus is not systematic, the pool of read-

---

[1] Zohrapian, *Scriptures.
[2] Rahlfs, *Septuaginta.
[3] On Arm 1 and Arm 2, see → 1.4.7.
[4] For details, see Gippert, *The Armenian Layer*, iv–1 and iv–2.
[5] P.J. Gentry (ed.), *Ecclesiastes* (Septuaginta Vetus Testamentum Graecum; Göttingen: Vandenhoeck & Ruprecht, forthcoming).
[6] See Cox, "Armenian Ecclesiastes," 16–23.

ings from which to determine Arm 2's textual affinities is not very extensive, yet is sufficient for Cox to conclude that its parent text also shared an affiliation with the Catena group.[7]

13–17.2.5.3.4 Translation Technique

The Arm 1 translation unit was set at the phrase level and this allows for a series of interventions to signpost the narrative flow and to effect a more emphatic and nuanced rendering. These involve the addition of personal pronouns (e.g., "you" [Qoh 11:1]; "I" [Qoh 8:14]), and particles like իսկ "indeed" (Qoh 11:6), ինչ "a certain" (Qoh 2:10), and the copula (e.g., Qoh 11:8), which the Greek translator, striving for literalism, has frequently left aside. This approach also results in variation in translation equivalents, as illustrated by the treatment of the particle καί γε "indeed," characteristic of this type of Greek rendering. The words καί γε emerge in Arm 1 as նա եւ "also" (Qoh 5:15); սակայն եւ "but also" (Qoh 4:4); սակայն "but" (Qoh 7:15 [OG 14]); քանզի "because" (Qoh 3:13); զի "for" (Qoh 5:16); and այլ եւ "in addition" (Qoh 11:2).[8] In contrast, sometimes multiple Greek terms are rendered with a single Armenian lexeme, as in the case of ἄνεμος "wind" (Qoh 11:4) and πνεῦμα "spirit/wind" (Qoh 11:5), both rendered by հողմ "wind." Similarly, a penchant for concise, pungent expression leads the translator to excise verbiage, as at Qoh 7:28c, where the statement καὶ γυναῖκα ἐν πᾶσι τούτοις οὐχ εὗρον "and a woman among all these I did not find" is reduced to բայց կին՝ ամենեւին ոչ "but a woman – absolutely not."

Similarly, Greek participles tend to be represented in Arm 1 by finite verbs in full clauses, as in the case of τηρῶν "watching," rendered as որ խտրէ "the one who discerns" (Qoh 11:4), but may, sometimes, be represented by an infinitive, as in the case of βλέπων "looking," which became տեսանել "to see" (Qoh 8:16). Moreover, as early Armenian lacks compound verbs (prep. + verb), it reflects that category of verb by the use of the combination of a compound verbal adjective plus a simple verb.

---

[7] Cox, "Armenian Ecclesiastes," 23–27.

[8] For further details, see Cox, "Armenian Ecclesiastes," 10.

Thus, the particle παρεωραμένῳ "overlooked" is translated with the phrase անտես արարելոցն, lit. "having been made unseen" (Qoh 12:14).

The Arm 2 translation unit, as opposed to that of Arm 1, is set at the word level, which underlines the redactor's concern for encoding Greek morphological and syntactic information. Hence, the revision features a one-word imperative հեռացո "distance!" to render παράγαγε "divert!" instead of the three-word phrase selected in Arm 1 – ի բաց արա "take away" (Qoh 11:10). Likewise, where Arm 1 exhibits variation in employing synonyms for the same action in the parallel clauses ժամանեն ... հասանեն "they reach ... they arrive," Arm 2 reformulates this as հասանեն ... հասանեն "they overtake ... they overtake" to replicate φθάνει ... φθάνει, "it overtakes ... it overtakes" (Qoh 8:14).

13–17.2.5.3.4.1 Attention to Context

To evoke the aura of royal splendor the narrator of Ecclesiastes enjoyed in the person of Solomon, Arm-Qoh appeals to the conventions of the contemporary Armenian court in selecting գուսանս, "bards" to render ᾄδοντες "singers" (Qoh 2:8). He idiomatically establishes a correlation between the verbs անկցի ... կացցէ "it will fall ... it will stand" in contrast to the bland Greek formulation πεσεῖται ... ἔσται "it will fall ... it will be" (Qoh 11:10) and avoids replicating ἔστιν "there is" in favor of the more expressive գոյ "there exists" (Qoh 8:14). Perceiving the logical difficulty of a subject like ματαιότης "vanity" being the product of the verb πεποίηται "has been done," the translator reconstructs the phrase as ընդունայնութիւն որ եղեալ է "vanity that has occurred" (Qoh 8:14). Likewise he strives to be anatomically correct in alluding to the mysterious growth of the foetus in its mother's "womb," արգամն, rather than propagate the vaguer reference to the "belly" (γαστήρ) (Qoh 11:5).

13–17.2.5.3.4.2 Literalisms and Transliterations

In this sphere also, the two strata pursue different agendas: Arm 1 avoids Hebraisms retained in the Greek, whereas Arm 2 seeks to encode even these aspects of its parent text. Hence Arm 1 renders ἐπὶ πρόσωπον τοῦ ὕδατος "on the face of the water" as simply ի վերայ ջրոց "on the waters," but Arm 2 corrects this to the Greek structure in reading ի վերայ երեսաց ջրոց "on the face of the waters" (Qoh 11:1). Much more extreme is the Greek translator's extension of the function of the preposition σύν "with" to become a cipher for its Hebrew counterpart – outside the area of their semantic congruence – to represent the particle את when used as a direct object marker. This syntactical element of the Greek is not usually reflected by Arm 1, but is stereotypically rendered by Arm 2 as միանգամայն "together" (e.g., Qoh 1:14; 2:17; 8:15). However, for βλέπειν σὺν τὸν ἥλιον "to see the sun," the reviser adopted a different strategy: he selects the preposition ընդ – whose main semantic range intersects with σύν in denoting accompaniment – used with the instrumental case, to convey the sense of "under" (Qoh 11:7). The resulting Arm 2 phrase տեսանել ընդ արեգականբ "to see under the sun" not only represents σύν in a meaningful way, but thereby references one of the author's recurring themes (see Qoh 1:9, 13; 2:3, 11, 17, 18, 19, 20, 22, etc.).[9]

13–17.2.5.3.5 Text-Critical Value: Omissions and Additions

The version evinces a high degree of quantitative representation, so that minuses are infrequent (e.g., καί "and" [Qoh 11:8] and καί γε "indeed" [Qoh 2:14]). Pluses are also rare and justified, in fleshing out rather cryptic expressions in the Greek, as at Qoh 5:15. There, the relation of profit and loss at the heart of the phrase τίς περισσεία αὐτῷ, ᾗ μοχθεῖ εἰς ἄνεμον "what is his surplus, at which he toils for wind?" (*NETS*) is clarified by linking them to the expension of labor. Arm 1 rephrases the Greek as զի՞նչ օգուտ իցէ նմա ի վաստակոց անտի զոր չանայ նա հողմոյ "what benefit will there be to him from the labors which he strives (at) for wind?" This felicitous solution commends itself to the reviser also who leaves it largely intact.

13–17.2.5.3.6 Text-Critical Value of Arm-Qoh for LXX-Qoh

The relative consistency with which both the original translator and the later reviser approach their task assists us in defining their generally faithful witness to their source texts. The early-fifth-century C.E. date they represent provides valuable corroboration for the circulation of the Catena Group text type many centuries before its extant Greek manuscripts.

Cox, C.E., "Armenian Ecclesiastes: Arm 1 and Arm 2," *Revue des Études Arméniennes* 34 (2012): 9–28.
Gippert, J., *The Caucasian Albanian Palimpsests of Mt. Sinai*, Vol. 3: *The Armenian Layer* (eds. J. Gippert et al.; Monumenta Palaeographica Medii Aves Series Ibero-Caucasica 2.3; Turnhout: Brepols, 2010).
Rahlfs, **Septuaginta*.
Zohrapian, **Scriptures*.

Peter Cowe

13–17.2.5.4 Lamentations
13–17.2.5.4.1 Translation Character of Lamentations

The Armenian version was collated for Ziegler's edition[1] of the Greek text, but is unfortunately not well represented there. Certain of its readings are incorrectly reproduced in Latin translation (e.g., *respice* "look at …!" for *respexisti* "you looked at"; Lam 3:60); moreover, insufficient use was made of variants in Zohrapian's apparatus, which frequently preserve the version's original reading, a reading now obscured by secondary scribal error in the transmission history of his base manuscript (Venice 1508). Examples include the transformation of աջ "right hand" at Lam 2:3 to առաջ "front" by dittography, ունկն "ear" to անուն "name" in Lam 3:56, as well as cases of lacunae through homoioteleuton, graphic similarities, etc. The version is also cited much less than is warranted, as there are several unreported cases where an Armenian variant clearly originated from a divergent Greek reading (whether actual or so construed by the translator) as, for example, at Lam 3:43 where the

---

[9] For further details, see Cox, "Armenian Ecclesiastes," 10.

[1] Ziegler, *Ieremias*.

Armenian յայց եկեր "you came out to visit" clearly presupposes a form like ἐπεσκέψω that diverges from the mainstream ἐπεσκέπασας "you covered." The translator's familiarity with the latter verb is evinced by his correct rendering of the same Greek form by փակեցեր "you enfolded" in the following verse. The version's underrepresentation in the apparatus conveys the false impression of its greater affiliation with the Greek critical text, when in fact it has a significant number of deviations from it both in agreement with other witnesses and alone.

Similarly, Ziegler does not afford a separate discussion of the textual affinities of Arm-Lam, but inappropriately integrates the book (together with Baruch) into his analysis of Jeremiah.[2] Consequently, although his general remark on Armenian alignment with a text form that seeks to bring the Old Greek (→ 13–17.1.1.4) into greater conformity with a Masoretic standard (→ 16.2.2) applies to Lamentations, he does not develop the point, while his overall conclusions, emphasizing Hexaplaric connections (→ 1.3.1.2.7; → 13–17.1.5.1), as just mentioned, are more valid for Jeremiah than here.

One aspect of the Armenian version's alignment with MT is through agreements with the Lucianic text type (→ 1.3.1.2; → 13–17.1.6), which bear more weight than accorded by Ziegler, as in the case of misclassifications, e.g., at Lam 3:27 where the reading ի մանկութենէ "from youth" patently belongs with the Lucianic and Catena group. A second important parent text is the Peshitta (→ 1.3.4; → 13–17.1.4.4), with which the Armenian exhibits a range of singular agreements recorded in the apparatus (Lam 1:8, 3:28, 4:3, 4:14). Even more striking is the instance at Lam 3:1 where the Armenian follows the Peshitta in opening the verse with the phrase "the strong God looked on my poverty."[3] At Lam 3:56, the Armenian joins the Peshitta in paralleling the phrase "do not hide your ears from my pleas" with the contrasting formulation "but release me and save me." Other readings indicate that the Peshitta was not only a source of extra-Greek material, but was also to be consulted when the Greek was semantically challenging, as at Lam 3:63 where the aporia caused by the reading ἐγὼ ψαλμὸς αὐτῶν was resolved by appeal to the Syriac, "I pondered (some) of their thoughts." This suggests that the Armenian version derives from a hybrid parent text constituted by a Greek text with Lucianic affiliation together with the Peshitta. Moreover, Ziegler's apparatus reveals that the two text forms share a wide spectrum of readings with the Armenian, including the transposition of Lam 2:16 to a location following Lam 2:17 and that of Lam 3:46–48 to a location following Lam 3:51. The presence of several linguistic characteristics typifying the original translation (Arm 1) in those formulations, such as personal pronouns (e.g., in Lam 3:55) and the employment of the local adverb instead of the deictic suffix as a definition marker (ի խորհրդոց "against") suggest that this represents the first stratum and implies that the revision process, if it occurred, would have been relatively light.

13–17.2.5.4.2 Translation Technique

The Greek text (→ 13–17.1.1.4) presents difficulties for the translator because of its very literal cast, which has affinities to the *kaige* tradition. The lack of detailed research on reconstructing the Armenian version's parent text impedes analysis of its translation technique. For example, it appears to evince a preference in this book for plural forms over singular: some of these seem to depend on its sources, while other instances may be the result of interpretation. Overall, as already adumbrated, the version displays a fairly free handling of Greek morphology and word order and also appears to be informed by literary concerns.[4] Quite typical of Arm 1 is the formal representation of one Greek lexeme by two synonyms. A good example is provided in Lam 2:3 where the repetition of a form of the same verb հաւտաց եւ մաշեաց "wasted and wore down" conveys well the intensive nature of the corresponding Greek compound

---

[2] Ziegler, *Ieremias*, 38–40.

[3] Here I read the aorist form *hayec'aw* cited in the Zohrapean apparatus for the imperative *hayeac'* in the running text.

[4] In this connection, it is worth recalling that the Armenian version of the Letter of Jeremiah is also rather free, on which see Cowe, "Epistle of Jeremiah."

verb συνέκλασεν. In another case, the second component զղշեցին "they exclaimed" adds nuance to the rather bland opening ձայն ետուն "they gave voice," which literally reflects the Greek φωνὴν ἔδωκαν (Lam 2:7).

Another feature of Arm-Lam is the sustained focus on the psychological dimension of the situations described rather than on purely physical issues. A good illustration is the approach to the yoke that one must bear, at Lam 3:27. The addition of the adjective βαρύν "heavy," represented by the Lucianic text (→ 13–17.1.6) and other witnesses, seems the plausible matrix of the Armenian reading խոնարհութեան "of humility," a typical employment of the abstract noun in an adjectival sense, which places the emphasis on the yoke's impact on the bearer's state of mind rather than on his/her posture. Similarly, at Arm-Lam 3:55, a voice is depicted as calling upon God not from a physical but emotional distance, when we compare the Greek ἐκ λάκκου κατωτάτου "from the lowest cistern" with the rendering ի զրոյ տառապանաց "from the pit of tribulation." Even more emphatic is the contrast between the versions regarding the appeal for divine vengeance in Lam 3:64, where the formal Armenian equivalent of the Greek phrase κατὰ τὰ ἔργα τῶν χειρῶν αὐτῶν "the works of their hands" is հայեաց ի հպարտութիւն աչաց նոցա "look at the pride in their eyes."

13–17.2.5.4.3 Translation Technique: Attention to Context

Lamentations 2 relates how God in his wrath has overturned various manifestations of his cult. Thus v. 7 treats the temple, alluding to this in terms of the altar and holy place (v. 7a), followed by its towers (v. 7b), before finally identifying the location in v. 7c as the οἶκος κυρίου "house of the Lord."

To anchor the reference to walls and towers directly to the shrine and provide a parallel for the reference in v. 7c, the translator inserted the term տաճար "temple" at the end of v. 7b. In v. 8c, the author personifies the city's reaction to the devastation to resemble its inhabitants, stating τεῖχος ὁμοθυμαδὸν ἠσθένησεν "the wall became weak along with it" (*NETS). However, the translator seeks to clarify the reference as to how walls might become enervated, rendering the verb by the phrase դողացեալ կործանեցան "(the walls) having shaken, they collapsed."

13–17.2.5.4.4 Translation Technique: Style

The book richly manifests the tendency of Hebrew poetry to express itself in parallel phrases. So fully is the Armenian translator imbued with the principle that he sometimes recasts lines in order to create extra parallels on the basis of theme and variation or contrast. Hence, at Lam 2:9b–c, he forms the phrase ոչ գոյին օրէնք եւ մարգարէք "law and prophets did not exist," on the basis of which he continues with ոչ էին այնք որ տեսանէին տեսիլս "and there were none who used to see visions." At Lam 3:45, the translator actually produces a doublet translation of the single Greek phrase κάμψαι με καὶ ἀπωσθῆναι "to make me stoop and be rejected" (*NETS) in order to achieve parallelism, first through the simple verbs ընկեցեր մերժեցեր զմեզ "you cast down, rejected us," and then by the verbal phrase արհամարհեալս եւ անարգեալս արարեր զմեզ "you made us disdained and disrespected." Similarly, at Lam 3:66a, since a parallel already existed between the Greek verbs καταδιώξεις "you shall pursue" and ἐξαναλώσεις "(and) exterminate," but the modality by which the divine was to accomplish that was expressed merely as ἐν ὀργῇ "in anger," the translator added its close Armenian synonym սրտմտութեամբ քով "by your indignation" to enhance the symmetry.

13–17.2.5.4.5 Relevance for Exegesis

Perhaps the most notable item in this category is the Armenian witness to the variant χριστὸς κυριος with its metathesis Տէր Քրիստոս "Lord Christ," in contrast to the critical text χριστὸς κυρίου, "the Lord's anointed," at Lam 4:20. Whereas the latter is a royal title clearly referencing the king, the former interprets the formula as a Christological prophecy, as expatiated upon in Theodoret's commentary.[5] In this connection, it is significant that

---

[5] Schulze, *Theodoreti Cyrensis episcopi opera omnia*, col. 356.

the scribe of manuscript Venice 1508, which provided Zohrapian's running text, penned the phrase in red ink.

13–17.2.5.4.6 Text-Critical Value of Arm-Lam for LXX-Lam

Before the version's full potential can be determined, it is necessary to initiate expanded collations in order to retrieve more early readings and to clarify the interrelation between its Greek and Syriac parent texts. At this point, one of the remarkable facets of its witness to the Greek is its reading of the work as poetry and its attention to this feature in its rendering.

Cowe, S.P., "The Armenian Version of the Epistle of Jeremiah: Parent Text and Translation Technique," in *VII Congress of the International Organization for Septuagintal and Cognate Studies, Leuven 1989* (ed. C.E. Cox; SBLSCS 31; Atlanta: Scholars Press, 1991), 373–91.

Schulze, J.L., *Theodoreti Cyrensis episcopi opera omnia* (PG Latine Tantum 42; Paris: J.P. Migne, 1859).

Ziegler, J. (ed.), *Ieremias, Baruch, Threni, Epistula Ieremiae* (Septuaginta Vetus Testamentum Graecum 15; Göttingen: Vandenhoeck & Ruprecht, 1957).

Zohrapian, *Scriptures.

Peter Cowe

13–17.2.5.5 Esther

13–17.2.5.5.1 Translation Character of Esther

The Armenian version was collated for Hanhart's edition of the Greek, employing the Zohrapian edition of 1805, and supplemented by the readings of manuscript 55 (dated 1428) of the Vienna Mkhitarist collection, which were found to be in close agreement. The version was classified as a reliable rendering of a Greek parent text representing the LXX°' text (→ 13–17.1.6). Certain interpretative renderings seemed related to formulations in the distinct Alpha-text (→ 13–17.1.1.5.B), but no direct affinity can be established.

13–17.2.5.5.2 Translation Technique

The translation does not represent its parent text isomorphically, but reveals a few omissions and abbreviations as well as a set of minor grammatical additions (pronouns, prepositions, adverbs, etc.). Other readings expand on rather bald expressions in the Greek as, for example, at Esth 2:17 and 4:1 where the narratives treat the actions of crowning and casting of ashes as a sign of mourning. Whereas the first Armenian addition վերայ զլուխ նորա "on her head" is paralleled by MT (→ 17.2.2), the Alpha-text (→ 13–17.1.1.5.B), and the Peshitta (→ 13–17.1.4.5), it stands alone in the second, which describes Mordechai's reaction to Haman's scheme and where the Armenian translation specifies he sprinkled ashes *on his head*. The most striking addition the version adduces is a prayer treating Israelite history, which occurs after Esth C:16. Hanhart notes that a close parallel is attested in certain manuscripts of VL (→ 13–17.2.1.5), which seems to suggest they share a common Greek origin.[1]

Attention to Context

A number of the version's interpretative readings can be explained as closer harmonizations to the surrounding context. A good example is offered by Esth C:21 where the Greek phrase ἀνοῖξαι στόμα ἐθνῶν εἰς ἀρετὰς ματαίων "to open the mouth of the nations for the mighty deeds of vain things" is translated բանալ զբերանս ազգաց ի փառաւորել զոչինչ աստուածս իւրեանց "to open the nations' mouths to glorify their non-existent gods" (Zohrapian Esth 14:10). The appropriateness of the rendering is sustained by the previous two verses, which discuss the Persians' relation to their εἴδωλα "idols" and their desire to silence praise devoted to the Jewish God. A second is the detailed Armenian introduction of Artaxerxes' letter spelling Haman's demise at Esth E:1, where the Greek's succinct formula ὧν ἐστιν ἀντίγραφον τῆς ἐπιστολῆς "this is a copy of the letter" appears as եւ այս էր պատճէն հրովարտակին զոր կնքեալ էր մատանեաւ թագաւորին "and this was a copy of the edict that he had sealed with the king's ring" (Zohrapian Esth 8:12). While the Armenian employs the term "edict" to render a number of Greek

---

[1] Hanhart, *Esther*, 33–34.

words for letter or writing, reference to the document being sealed by the king's ring is already made at Esth 8:8 and 8:10.

13–17.2.5.5.3 Text-Critical Value of Arm-Esth for LXX-Esth

The Armenian version on the whole is a faithful though not slavish witness to its Greek parent text (→ 13–17.1.1.5).

Hanhart, R. (ed.), *Esther* (rev. ed.; Septuaginta Vetus Testamentum Graecum 8.3; Göttingen: Vandenhoeck & Ruprecht, 1983).
Zohrapian, *Scriptures*.

Peter Cowe

13–17.2.6 Georgian Translations

13–17.2.6.1 Sources, Origin, and Relevance of the Corpus

The Old Georgian translations of Ruth, Canticles, Qohelet, Lamentations, and Esther have come down to us in manuscripts dating from the late tenth up to the seventeenth centuries (→ 1.4.8.2). In the textual history of the corpus, three major phases may be distinguished (→ 1.4.8.3): the oldest (fifth to eighth centuries C.E.), the middle (eleventh and twelfth centuries), and the late periods (seventeenth and eighteenth centuries).

13–17.2.6.1.1 Evidence

Common sources for all books are codices Georg^O (Mount Athos, Library of the Iviron Monastery, geo. 1, 978 C.E., in two volumes) and Georg^S (Tbilisi, National Centre of Manuscripts, A-51, seventeenth or eighteenth century). The remaining major witnesses are: Georg^D (Tbilisi, National Centre of Manuscripts, H-855, seventeenth century), Georg^F (Tbilisi, National Centre of Manuscripts, A-646, sixteenth century), Georg^{Ga} (Tbilisi, National Centre of Manuscripts, Q-1152, twelfth or thirteenth century), Georg^{Gb} (Tbilisi, National Centre of Manuscripts, A-1108, twelfth century), Georg^I (Tbilisi, National Centre of Manuscripts, A-570, fifteenth century), Georg^{J2} (Jerusalem, Library of the Greek Patriarchate, geo. 11, eleventh century), Georg^{Ja} (Jerusalem, Library of the Greek Patriarchate, geo. 113, thirteenth century), Georg^P (Paris, Bibliothèque nationale de France, geo. 3, lectionary of the year 1040), Georg$^\pi$ (Tbilisi, National Centre of Manuscripts, A-61, thirteenth century), Georg^q (Tbilisi, National Centre of Manuscripts, Q-208b, tenth-century lectionary), Georg^Y (Vienna, Österreichische Nationalbibliothek, geo. 4, year 1160).[1] Further evidence for Georg-Cant is to be found in testimonies containing works of the church fathers (→ 13–17.2.6.3.2). Moreover, an additional witness for all texts is represented by Georg^B, the Moscow printed edition of the year 1743 ("Bakar Bible").

13–17.2.6.1.2 Date

Codices Georg^{O,J2,P,q} contain texts that can be traced back to the beginnings of Georgian literature, namely the fifth to seventh centuries C.E. (→ 1.4.8.4.1).[2] Georg$^{Ga,Gb,\pi}$ (and probably also Georg^Y) include Hellenophile versions of the Gelati School[3] dating to the end of the eleventh century (→ 1.4.8.4.2). Georg^{D,F,I,S} are heterogeneous from the point of view of the classes of translations that they preserve. In some cases, they comprise ancient versions, at times in an abridged redaction; in other instances, they transmit more recent texts dating to the middle or even to the late period of Old Georgian literature. Codex Georg^S contains redactions revised on the basis of the Armenian Bible printed in 1666 (→ 1.4.8.4.3).

13–17.2.6.1.3 Text-Critical Value

Even though much work remains to be done in the field of comparative textual criticism, this tradition can be shown to be of significant text-critical value for LXX studies. On the one hand, evidence of the reliance of the Georgian translations on Greek models can be collected. On the other hand, unique textual features can be detected against the background of other secondary versions. The most striking examples of this are the identification of the

---

[1] *C'ignni*, 1.557–639.
[2] Kurcik'iʒe, *Kartuli biblia*, 60; Melikišvili, *Targmanebi*, 28–37, 75–88, 99; Tarchnišvili, *Geschichte*, 324–25.
[3] See K'ek'eliʒe, Targmanebaj, lxviii, lxxxii–lxxxiii.

so-called Alpha-Text (AT) of Esther (→ 13–17.1.1.5) as the source of the earliest Georgian translation of Esther (→ 13–17.2.6.6.1), as well as the existence of a Georgian version of Josephus' text of Esther (→ 21.3). Therefore, even at this early stage of inquiry, this tradition shows its potentiality for biblical research and consequently merits full scholarly consideration.

13–17.2.6.2 Georg-Ruth

Georg-Ruth survives in two translations. The first (Georg-Ruth 1) is found in its entirety in Georg^{O,D,S,B} and partially also in lectionaries Georg^P and Georg^q (the latter includes only Ruth 1:1–4, 8–11, 14–17).[4] The second version (Georg-Ruth 2) is preserved in Georg^{Ga,Gb}. The synoptical edition of Georg-Ruth 1 and Georg-Ruth 2 is based on complete evidence[5] with the exception of lectionary Georg^P that was published separately.[6]

13–17.2.6.2.1 Georg-Ruth 1

The various testimonies of Georg-Ruth 1 greatly differ from one another in textual features. Georg^O has several minuses and a peculiar arrangement of the verses, which were judged to be the result of copy errors (scribal leaps and inversions).[7] Therefore, in the critical edition, Georg^O was largely emended on the basis of the remaining sources (Georg^{D,S,B}), despite the fact that their readings can hardly be thought of as belonging in every instance to the earliest textual stratum. Georg^D contains an abridged version of Georg-Ruth 1 that was considered to be the work of a later anonymous Georgian redactor.[8] Georg^B basically agrees with Georg^D, but contains several sections corrected towards the Slavonic Bible (→ 1.4.8.4.3) and contaminated with Georg-Ruth 2. Georg^s contains a revision carried out at the end of the seventeenth century based on the printed Armenian Bible.

13–17.2.6.2.2 Georg-Ruth 2

Georg-Ruth 2 represents a new independent Hellenophile translation, although its author undoubtedly made use of Georg-Ruth 1. Major textual discrepancies are not found between the two manuscripts containing this version (Georg^{Ga} and Georg^{Gb}).

13–17.2.6.2.3 Collations with LXX

As of mid-2016, no collation of Georg-Ruth with Quast's apparatus is available.[9] Georg-Ruth 1 was judged to reflect a model belonging to the LXX^A text type.[10] However, a closer look presents a more nuanced picture that points to the need for a reassessment of such a conclusion. A cursory survey of Georg-Ruth 1 seems to indicate agreements with the Hexaplaric and LXX^R text types (→ 13–17.1.1.5; → 13–17.1.5.5),[11] as well as with VL^{109}. The reliance on a Greek model seems to be indicated by deviations from the Armenian. In this regard, one should consider, for instance, Ruth 1:5 καὶ ἀπέθανον καί γε ἀμφότεροι "and both also died" (*NETS, 241); Arm եւ մեռան անդ երկոքին "and both died there"; Georg-Ruth 1 და მოყვდეს ორივე იგი ძენი მისნი "and both her sons died"; VL^{109} *ambo filii eius* "both of her sons." Future research should aim at clarifying precise textual allegiances with manuscript groups of LXX.

13–17.2.6.3 Georg-Cant

Two complete and three partial translations of Canticles are preserved in the Old Georgian language.

13–17.2.6.3.1 Georg-Cant: Complete Translations

The earliest complete version of Georg-Cant is to be found in Georg^{O,S,B} (Georg-Cant 1).[12] It was

---

[4] On Georg^q, see Outtier, "Nouveaux fragments," 31–34.

[5] For an edition, see *C'ignni*, 3.203–15. Other diplomatic editions are Šaniʒe, *C'ignni*, 133–44 (Georg^O); Dočanašvili, *Mcxeturi xelnac'eri*, 1981, 509–14 (Georg^s).

[6] Danelia, Čxenk'eli, and Šavišvili, *Kartuli lekcionaris p'arizuli xelnac'eri*, 134–41; Tarchnischvili, *Le grand lectionnaire*, nos. 353, 379, 450.

[7] *C'ignni*, 3.203–15.

[8] Melikišvili, *Targmanebi*, 118.

[9] Quast, *Ruth*.

[10] *C'ignni*, 3.203–15; Cindeliani, "Redakciebi," 21–30; Melikišvili, *Targmanebi*, 119.

[11] Rahlfs, *Studie*.

[12] See Dočanašvili, *Mcxeturi xelnac'eri*, 1985, 61–65.

printed twice according to Georg⁰,¹³ while once on the basis of Georgˢ.¹⁴ In the latter, the text is marked by the insertion of rubrics that indicate the groom and the bride (Canticles 1–5).¹⁵

The second complete translation is preserved in Georgʸ (Georg-Cant 2) and is accessible to scholars in Saržvelaʒe's edition.¹⁶ This version was carried out independently from Georg-Cant 1 and has the peculiarity of being written in iambic verses.¹⁷ Its reliance on LXX is shown by the misreading of Greek words, as well as by lexical borrowings.¹⁸

13–17.2.6.3.2 Georg-Cant: Partial Translations

The first partial translation (Georg-Cant 3) is included in the Georgian version of Hippolytus Romanus' commentary (CPG 1871).¹⁹ The text, which ends in Cant 3:8, is transmitted in the *Collection of Shatberdi* (*Šat'berdis k'rebuli*), a parchment codex of the years 973–976 C.E. (Tbilisi, National Centre of Manuscripts, S-1141: folios 162–176), as well as in a testimony of the twelfth or thirteen century (Jerusalem, Library of the Greek Patriarchate, geo. 44: folios 193ᵛ–207). Georg-Cant 3, which was rendered from Armenian, is accessible in three different editions.²⁰

The second partial translation (Georg-Cant 4), which is considered to be a revision of Georg-Cant 1,²¹ is to be found in the Georgian version of the commentaries of Gregory of Nyssa (CPG 3158), which were translated in the eleventh century by Giorgi Mtac'mideli (ca. 1009–1065) and are now preserved in a twelfth-century manuscript (Tbilisi, National Centre of Manuscripts, A-55: folios 73–165ᵛ). The text, which ends in Cant 6:8, was published by K'ik'naʒe in 1965 without the commentaries of Gregory of Nyssa.²²

The third selective version (Georg-Cant 5) is contained in an anonymous commentary copied in a codex of the late twelfth or early thirteenth century (Tbilisi, National Centre of Manuscripts, A-65, year 1188–1210: folios 412–19) and ends in Cant 8:7. A lithographic edition of Georg-Cant 5 was published by Šaniʒe.²³

13–17.2.6.3.3 Collations with LXX

Systematic collations between LXX (→ 13–17.1.1.2) and the Georgian traditions of Canticles still await production. Future research should aim at producing an assessment of the potential of this version for comparative textual criticism. A cursory survey of Georg-Cant 1 seems to indicate its reliance on LXX-Cant, from which Georg-Cant 2 certainly derives. Catena versions should be subjected to systematic examination against the background of the surviving Greek (→ 13–17.1.5.4)²⁴ and Old Church Slavonic (→ 13–17.2.7.2) Hexaplaric evidence.

13–17.2.6.4 Georg-Qoh

Georg-Qoh has come down to us in three versions.

13–17.2.6.4.1 Georg-Qoh 1

The oldest version (Georg-Qoh 1) is preserved in its entirety in Georg⁰, and partially in Georgᴶᵃ,ˢ. The translation is basically the same in all three codices. However, in Georgᴶᵃ,ˢ, the text is incomplete and in Georgˢ it was partially revised on the basis of the printed Armenian Bible of 1666. Consequently, codex Georg⁰ is the best source for analyzing the original textual features of Georg-Qoh 1.

Georg-Qoh 1 is based on LXX (→ 13–17.1.1.3), as proven by the translation of those passages of LXX, in which the Hebrew nota accusative אֶת was rendered with σύν "with" followed by an accusative to mark the direct object (→ 13–17.1.1.3; → 13–17.1.5.3.3.2). The Georgian obviously trans-

---

¹³ See, respectively, Cagareli, *Svedenija*, 17–56; Saržvelaʒe, "kebaj kebataj," 164–74.
¹⁴ Dočanašvili, *Mcxeturi xelnac'eri*, 1985, 61–68.
¹⁵ See Dočanašvili, *Mcxeturi xelnac'eri*, 1985, 61–65.
¹⁶ Saržvelaʒe, "Venaši," 75–85.
¹⁷ See Bruni, "Kebata-kebis," 244–46.
¹⁸ Saržvelaʒe, "Venaši," 78.
¹⁹ CPG = Geerard et al., *Clavis patrum graecorum*.
²⁰ Marr, *Ippolit*; Garitte, *Traités d'Hippolyte*, 32–70; Gigineišvili and Giunašvili, *K'rebuli*.
²¹ K'ik'naʒe, "Giorgi," 126–70; Dočanašvili, *Mcxeturi xelnac'eri*, 1985, 22.

²² G. K'ik'naʒe, "Giorgi," 126–70.
²³ Šaniʒe, *Targmanebaj*.
²⁴ See Field, **Hexapla*, 2.411–24; Treat, "Aquila"; Ceulemans, "A Critical Edition."

lated this construction *ad litteram*, resulting in the inevitable misapprehension of the sense. See, for instance, Qoh 3:17 და ვთქუ მე გულსა ჩემსა: მართლისა თანა და უღმრთოთა საჯოსმეა ღმერთმან, რამეთუ ჟამი არს ყოვლისა საქმისაჲ და ყოველთა ზედა ქმნულთაჲ/ εἶπα ἐγὼ ἐν καρδίᾳ μου σὺν τὸν δίκαιον καὶ σὺν τὸν ἀσεβῆ κρινεῖ ὁ θεός, ὅτι καιρὸς τῷ παντὶ πράγματι καὶ ἐπὶ παντὶ τῷ ποιήματι²⁵ "I said in my heart, God will judge the righteous and the impious, for there is a right time for every matter and for every work" (*NETS, 652).

13–17.2.6.4.2 Georg-Qoh 2

A second independent translation (Georg-Qoh 2) is inserted into the Georgian version of the commentaries on the book of Qohelet, composed by Mitrophanes of Smyrna (ca. second half of the ninth or early tenth century, *CPG* 7950; → 13–17.1.5.3.2.2).²⁶ This work was very likely translated from LXX in the late twelfth century by Ioane Č'imč'imeli, a representative of the literary school of Ioane P'et'ric'i;²⁷ today it is only preserved in the thirteenth-century manuscript Georg^π.²⁸

13–17.2.6.4.3 Georg-Qoh 3

A third translation (Georg-Qoh 3) is included in Georg^B. It basically represents a contamination of Georg-Qoh 1 and Georg-Qoh 2, besides displaying evidence of a further revision made most likely on the basis of the Old Church Slavonic printed Bible (→ 1.4.8.4.3).

13–17.2.6.4.4 Editions

In 1920, K'ek'elize published a synoptic text of Georg-Qoh 1 (based on Georg^o,s, which he printed in two separate columns up to Qoh 5:2 where the text of Georg^s ends),²⁹ Georg-Qoh 2, and Georg-Qoh 3.³⁰ In more recent times, Dočanašvili has re-edited Georg^s,³¹ while Saržvelaze re-edited Georg^o.³²

13–17.2.6.4.5 Collations with LXX

The Georgian witnesses are currently being collated for the apparatus of the forthcoming Göttingen edition of Ecclesiastes.³³ The reader is therefore directed to that edition for details (forthcoming in 2017; → 13–17.1.5.3.1).

13–17.2.6.5 Georg-Lam

Georg-Lam survives in two independent translations.

13–17.2.6.5.1 Georg-Lam 1

The earliest Georgian translation of Lamentations (Georg-Lam 1) can be reconstructed by overlapping the witness of Georg^o with Georg^J2 because of the several textual lacunae in the former.³⁴ The text is not divided into chapters but into eighty-eight verses numbered in succession and framed by the repetition of the four series of the Hebrew alphabet. A separate heading introduces Lamentations 5, which in Georg^o is entitled ლოცვაჲ-გოდებანი (προσευχή-θρῆνοι "prayer-lamentations") and as ლოცვა (προσευχή "prayer") in J2.³⁵ Georg-Lam 1 was published with a Latin translation in the *Patrologia Orientalis*.³⁶

13–17.2.6.5.2 Georg-Lam 2

The second version (Georg-Lam 2) is not transmitted in manuscript form. The Georgian Major Prophets (→ 6–9.2.6.1.4) and Lamentations were

---

²⁵ Rahlfs, *Septuaginta*, 244.

²⁶ In contrast to the Georgian tradition, in Greek manuscripts these commentaries are commonly ascribed to Gregory of Nyssa or Gregory of Agrigentum: Ettlinger and Noret, *Pseudo-Gregorii*; on the attribution to Mitrophanes, see van Deun, *La chasse*.

²⁷ See K'ek'elize, *Targmanebaj*, lxviii, lxxxii–lxxxiii; Tarchnišvili, *Geschichte*, 233–35; Melikišvili, *Targmanebi*, 149.

²⁸ Žordanija, *Opisanie*, 52–53; K'ek'elize, *Targmanebaj*, lxxv–lxxvii. For an edition, see K'ek'elize, *Targmanebaj*, 1–178.

²⁹ K'ek'elize, *Targmanebaj*, 202.

³⁰ K'ek'elize, *Targmanebaj*, 180–226.

³¹ Dočanašvili, *Mcxeturi xelnac'eri*, 1985, 44–49.

³² Saržvelaze, "Ek'lesiast'e," 145–63.

³³ See Gentry, "The Distinctive Aims," 92, 94.

³⁴ See Blake and Brière, *Critical Edition*, 666–85; Blake and Brière, *Apparatus*, 510–11.

³⁵ Kurcik'ize, "Godebaj," 31–40.

³⁶ Blake and Brière, *Critical Edition*, 666–85; Blake and Brière, *Apparatus*, 510–11.

first printed in Tbilisi in the early eighteenth century.[37] At that time, a set of printed folios was taken from this edition and sewn into manuscript Georg[s].[38] Moreover, a few decades later, the text was reprinted in Georg[B]. It was finally re-edited in the modern Georgian alphabet by Dočanašvili.[39] The arrangement of chapters is similar to that found in Georg-Lam 2.

13–17.2.6.5.3 Collations with LXX

Despite the availability of an edition with a Latin translation,[40] Ziegler did not include Georg-Lam 1 in the apparatus of his critical edition. Consequently, a collation with LXX (→ 13–17.1.1.4) and the remaining secondary versions is still lacking.[41]

13–17.2.6.6 Georg-Esth

Georg-Esth survives in three versions. The first (Georg-Esth 1) is to be found in Georg[O], the second (Georg-Esth 2) in Georg[D,F,I,S], while the third in Georg[B] (Georg-Esth 3).[42] Moreover, a Georgian translation of Josephus' Esther (→ 21.3) has also come down to us (Georg-Josephus).

13–17.2.6.6.1 Georg-Esth 1

Although a full collation of Georg-Esth 1 with LXX has not been produced yet, it can be stated safely that this translation is based on the Alpha-Text (AT) of Esther (→ 13–17.1.1.5). This is indicated not only by the omission in Georg-Esth 1 of Esth 1:15; 2:6, 10–15, 19–23; 4:3, 5–7; 8:5–12,[43] but also by a clear textual affinity that can be seen by analyzing even short portions of text. A number of examples are offered here:

---

[37] *Biblia: c'igni c'inasc'armet'q'velta*.
[38] Melikišvili, *Targmanebi*, 164.
[39] Dočanašvili, *Mcxeturi xelnac'eri*, 1985, 255–71.
[40] Blake and Brière, *Critical Edition*, 666–85; Blake and Brière, *Apparatus*, 510–11.
[41] Ziegler, *Threni*.
[42] An edition has been published recently: *Esteris c'ignis ʒveli kartuli versiebi*. This work remained inaccessible to the writer, who consequently is not aware if it includes all three versions and whether it is based on the entire manuscript evidence. Diplomatic edition of Georg[s]: Dočanašvili, *Mcxeturi xelnac'eri*, 1983, 79–99.
[43] See Tov, **Greek-Hebrew Bible*, 541, 545–46.

1. Esth A:1–3 ¹წელსა მეორესა მეფობასა ასუერ დიდისასა პირველსა მას დღესა თუესა ადარ და ნესასა (რომელ არს იგრიკად და ვარდობად) ჩუენებად იხილა მარდოქე – ქემან იარისმან, დისწულმან სემეისმან, რომელ იყო შვილი კესნი, ტომისაგან ბენიამენისი, ²კაცი იგი დიდ ²⁽³⁾ტყუეობასაცა, რომელ-იგი წარსტყუენა ნაბუქოდონოსორ მეფემან ბაბილონისამან იოვაკიმის თანა მეფისა ჰურიასტანელთაისა (GeorgO, fol. 495ᵛ)/¹"Ἔτους δευτέρου βασιλεύοντος Ἀσσυήρου τοῦ μεγάλου μιᾷ τοῦ μηνὸς Ἀδαρ Νισαν (ὅς ἐστι Δύστρος Ξανθικός) ἐνύπνιον εἶδε Μαρδοχαῖος ὁ τοῦ Ἰαείρου τοῦ Σεμεΐου τοῦ Κισαίου τῆς φυλῆς Βενιαμιν, ²ἄνθρωπος μέγας ²⁽³⁾τῆς αἰχμαλωσίας ἧς ᾐχμαλώτευσε Ναβουχοδονοσορ ὁ βασιλεὺς Βαβυλῶνος μετὰ Ἰεχονίου τοῦ βασιλέως τῆς Ἰουδαίας[44] "In the second year when Assyeros the Great was king, on the first day of the month of Adar Nisan (which is Dystros Xanthikos) Mardochaios the son of Iaeiros son of Semeias, son of Kisaios, of the tribe of Beniamin, saw a dream. ²He was a great man, ²⁽³⁾one of the exiles whom Nabouchodonosor, king of Babylon, took captive with Iechonias, the king of Judea" (**NETS*, 426).

2. Esth 1:1–3 ¹და იყო ამის სიტყუსა შემდგომად დღეთა ასუერ მეფისა დიდისათა, და დაემორჩილა მას ყოველი პინდოეთითგან ეთიოპედმდე ას ოცდა შუა საყარანო სოფლებისად. ²და განმტკიცნა ასურ საყდართა ზედა მეფობისა მისისათა, ³და ყო მეფემან სუმა შობისა მთავართა თანა ეზოისა მისისათა და შორის სპარსთა და უჟიკთა და არშაკთა და კარანები იგი სოფლებისად სხდა წინაშე პირსა მისსა (GeorgO, fol. 496ᵛ)/¹Καὶ ἐγένετο μετὰ τοὺς λόγους τούτους ἐν ἡμέραις Ἀσσυήρου τοῦ βασιλέως τοῦ μεγάλου, ὑπετάγησαν αὐτῷ ἀπὸ τῆς Ἰνδικῆς ἕως τῆς Αἰθιοπίας ἑκατὸν εἴκοσι ἑπτὰ χῶραι. ²ἐν τῷ καθῆσθαι Ἀσσυήρον ἐπὶ τοῦ θρόνου τῆς βασιλείας αὐτοῦ, 3 καὶ ἐποίησεν ὁ βασιλεὺς πότον τοῖς ³ἄρχουσι τῆς αὐλῆς Περσῶν καὶ Μήδων,

---

[44] Hanhart, *Esther*, 131–32.

καὶ οἱ ἄρχοντες τῶν χωρῶν κατὰ πρόσωπον αὐτοῦ⁴⁵ "Now it happened after these things in the days of Assyeros the great king, one hundred twenty-seven lands from India to Ethiopia were subjected to him. ²While Assyeros was sitting upon the throne of his kingdom, ³then the king gave a wine party for the rulers of the court of the Persians and Medes and the rulers of the lands before him" (*NETS*, 426).

3. Esth 3:19(15) და ესერა სუს შინა დაიდვა ეგეთივე ბრძანებაჲ (Georgᵒ, fol. 500)/Καὶ ἐν Σούσοις ἐξετέθη τὸ πρόσταγμα τοῦτο⁴⁶ "And in Susa this decree was posted" (*NETS*, 430).

4. Esth 4:1 მარდოქჱ ცნა ყოველი ესე საქმჱ, და თჳთ ქალაქიცა სუსს შეძრწუნდა საქმისა მისთჳს, და იყო ჰურიათა ტირილი დიდი და განმწარებაჲ ყოველსა ქუეყანასა. (Georgᵒ, fol. 500)/Ὁ δὲ Μαρδοχαῖος ἐπέγνω πάντα τὰ γεγονότα, καὶ ἡ πόλις Σοῦσα ἐταράσσετο ἐπὶ τοῖς γεγενημένοις, καὶ πᾶσι τοῖς Ἰουδαίοις ἦν πένθος μέγα καὶ πικρὸν ἐν πάσῃ πόλει⁴⁷ "Now Mardochaios learned everything that had happened, and the city of Susa was in turmoil because of the things that had taken place. For all the Judeans there was great and bitter sorrow in the whole city" (*NETS*, 430).

13–17.2.6.6.2 Georg-Esth 2

In Georg-Esth 2, the textual relationship between Georgᴰ,ᶠ,ᴵ,ˢ remains to be elucidated. It seems that in some sections Georgˢ deviates from Georgᴰ,ᶠ,ᴵ, forming a subredaction of this version.⁴⁸ The following feature in Georgˢ is noteworthy: as a consequence of the influence of the revision based on the printed Armenian text (Oskan's edition), the so-called Additions A–F to Esther (→ II.6; → II.6.8) are placed at the end of the book, where they constitute chapters 11–16.⁴⁹ In Esth 2:20, after რაათა ეშინოდეს ღმრთისა და ჰყოფდეს ბრძანებათა მისთა (φοβεῖσθαι τὸν θεὸν καὶ ποιεῖν τὰ προστάγματα αὐτοῦ "to fear God and to do his commandments"), all testimonies of Georg-Esth 2 present the addition რომელი-იგი მოსეს მიერ ამცნო ისრაჱლსა "[his commandments] that were announced to Israel by Moses," which seems to have no counterpart in LXX (→ 13–17.1.1.5).⁵⁰ In several other instances, this tradition deviates from LXX-Esth and exhibits signs of contamination with AT-Esth (see Esth 3:15–4:2).

13–17.2.6.6.3 Georg-Esth 3

Georg-Esth 3 is based on the Old Church Slavonic Bible of 1663,⁵¹ which reflects the OG text (→ 13–17.1.1.5) and includes the additions. Such a reliance is shown by phraseology, translation errors, rendering of proper names,⁵² and textual features (e.g., the omission of Esth 9:17–32; → 13–17.2.7.5.3).

13–17.2.6.6.4 Georg-Josephus

The existence of a Georgian version of Josephus' Esther (→ 21.3)⁵³ has on the whole escaped the attention of scholars. The text is included in the Georgian translation of his *Jewish Antiquities* that was undertaken in the twelfth and thirteenth centuries from a Greek model very similar to Codex Leidensis F 13.⁵⁴ Georg-Josephus has come down to us in five complete testimonies (and some other fragments), the earliest of which date to the thirteenth century.⁵⁵

13–17.2.6.6.5 Collations with LXX

Georg-Esth 1 represents a new indirect testimony of AT-Esth that in Greek has come down to us only in LXX¹⁹,⁹³,¹⁰⁸,³¹⁹ (→ 13–17.1.1.5.B). An urgent research task is to explore this translation carefully and to undertake a complete collation with Hanhart's apparatus in order to shed light on possible divergences or similarities with the surviving Greek evidence. A thorough analysis of this ver-

---

⁴⁵ Hanhart, *Esther*, 135–36.
⁴⁶ Hanhart, *Esther*, 156.
⁴⁷ Hanhart, *Esther*, 156–57.
⁴⁸ Dočanašvili, *Mcxeturi xelnac'eri*, 1983, 84–85; K'ik'naʒe, "Redakciebi," 21–22.
⁴⁹ Dočanašvili, *Mcxeturi xelnac'eri*, 1983, 92–99.

⁵⁰ K'ik'naʒe, "Redakciebi," 19–20; Melikišvili, *Targmanebi*, 139; Dočanašvili, *Mcxeturi xelnac'eri*, 1983, 79–99.
⁵¹ *Biblija*.
⁵² K'ik'naʒe, "Redakciebi," 22–23.
⁵³ Hanhart, *Esther*, 36–38.
⁵⁴ Melikišvili, "Ioseb," 29.
⁵⁵ For a critical edition, see N. Melikišvili, *Ioseb plaviosi*.

sion may be expected to bring fresh perspectives on unsolved problems and debated questions on the literary growth of AT-Esth (→ 13–17.1.1.5.B.3). Additional unexplored material for comparative research in the field of textual criticism is offered by Georg-Esth 2; its relationship with the Greek tradition remains unclear and it may perhaps, at least conjecturally, be of some relevance for studying the mixed type (LXX[392] → 13–17.1.1.5.B.1). Finally, Georg-Josephus also still awaits thorough scholarly analysis.

Biblia: brzanebita da c'arsagebelita sapasetata sakartvelos mepis bakar vaxt'angis zisata (Moscow: Bakaris st'amba, 1743).

Biblia: c'igni c'inasc'armet'q'velta da saxareba (Tbilisi: Vaxt'angis st'amba, 1709–1710).

Biblija: sirěč' knigi vetchago i novago zavěta, po jazyku slavensku (Moscow: Pečatnyj dvor, 1663).

Blagoveščenskij, M.D., *Kniga Plač: Opyt issledovanija isagogiko-èkzegetičeskogo* (Kiev: Tipografija S.A. Spilioti, 1899).

Blake, R.P. and C.M. Brière, *The Old Georgian Version of the Prophets: Critical Edition with a Latin Translation* (PO 29.4; Paris: Firmin-Didot, 1961).

Blake, R.P. and C.M. Brière, *The Old Georgian Version of the Prophets: Apparatus Criticus* (PO 30.3; Paris: Firmin-Didot, 1963).

Bruni, A.M., "Kebata-kebis zveli kartuli iambuk'uri targmani rogorc 'šesxmaj c'midisa γvtismšoblisaj' venis Georg. 4 xelnac'erši," *Logosi* 8 (2014): 240–52.

Cagareli, A., *Svedenija o pamjatnikach gruzinskoj pis'mennosti*, Vol. 1 (St. Petersburg: Tip. Imp. Akad. Nauk, 1886).

Ceulemans, R., "A Critical Edition of the Hexaplaric Fragments of the Book of Canticles: With Emphasis on Their Reception in Greek Christian Exegesis" (PhD diss., Katholieke Universiteit Leuven, 2009).

C'ignni zuelisa aγtkumisani, Vol. 1: *Šesakmisaj, gamoslvataj* (eds. B. Gigineišvili and C. K'ik'vize; Tbilisi: Mecniereba, 1989).

C'ignni zuelisa aγtkumisani, Vol. 2: *Levit'eltaj, ricxutaj, meorisa szulisaj* (eds. I. Abulaze et al.; Tbilisi: Mecniereba, 1990).

C'ignni zuelisa aγtkumisani, Vol. 3: *Iso navesi, msazultaj, rutisi* (eds. C. Kurcik'ize and U. Cindeliani; Tbilisi: Mecniereba, 1991).

Cindeliani, U., "Rutis c'ignis kartuli redakciebi," *Mravaltavi* 3 (1973): 21–30.

Danelia, K'., S. Čxenk'eli, and B. Šavišvili (eds.), *Kartuli lekcionaris p'arizuli xelnac'eri: zveli da axali aγtkmis sak'itxavebi*, Vol. 1: *Nac'ili I* (Tbilisi: Tbilisis universit'et'is gamomcemloba, 1987).

van Deun, P., "La chasse aux trésors: la découverte de plusieurs œuvres inconnues de Métrophane de Smyrne (IXe–Xe siècle)," *Byzantion* 78 (2008): 346–67.

Dočanašvili, E. (ed.), *Mcxeturi xelnac'eri (moses xutc'igneuli, iso nave, msazulta, ruti)* (Tbilisi: Mecniereba, 1981).

Dočanašvili, E. (ed.), *Mcxeturi xelnac'eri (t'obis, ivditis, esteris, iobis c'ignebi, psalmuni, igavta c'igni)* (Tbilisi: Mecniereba, 1983).

Dočanašvili, E. (ed.), *Mcxeturi xelnac'eri (ek'lesiast'e, sibrzne solomonisa, keba kebata solomonisa, c'inasc'armet'q'velta c'ignebi – esaia, ieremia, baruki, ezek'ieli)* (Tbilisi: Mecniereba, 1985).

Ettlinger, G.H. and J. Noret (eds.), *Pseudo-Gregorii seu Pseudo-Gregorii Nysseni Commentarius in Ecclesiasten* (CCSG 56; Turnhout: Brepols, 2007).

Garitte, G. (ed.), *Traités d'Hippolyte sur David et Goliath, sur le Cantique des cantiques et sur l'Antéchrist: Version géorgienne éditée et traduite* (CSCO 264 Scriptores Iberici 15–16; Louvain: Secrétariat du Corpus SCO, 1965).

Geerard, M. et al. (eds.), *Clavis patrum graecorum* (Turnhout: Brepols, 1974–2003).

Gentry, P.J., "The Distinctive Aims of the Göttingen Apparatus: Examples from Ecclesiastes – An Edition in Preparation," in *Die Göttinger Septuaginta: Ein editorisches Jahrhundertprojekt* (eds. R.G. Kratz and B. Neuschäfer; MSU 30; Berlin: De Gruyter, 2013), 73–106.

Gigineišvili, B. and E. Giunašvili (eds.), *Šat'berdis k'rebuli X sauk'unisa* (Tbilisi: Mecniereba, 1979).

Hanhart, R., *Esther* (2nd ed.; Septuaginta Vetus Testamentum Graecum 8.3; Göttingen: Vandenhoeck & Ruprecht, 1983).

K'ek'elize, K'., *Targmanebaj ek'lesiast'isaj mit'ropane zmwrnel mit'rop'olit'isaj* (Tbilisi: Saxalxo sakme, 1920).

K'ik'naze, G., "Giorgi mtac'midelis erti targmanis k'imeni da leksik'a," in *zveli kartuli mc'erlobis otxi zegli: X–XII sauk'uneta xelnac'erebis mixedvit* (ed. I. Abulaze; Tbilisi: Mecniereba, 1965), 126–70.

K'ik'naze, G., "Esteris c'ignis kartuli redakciebi," *Mravaltavi* 2 (1973): 14–24.

Kurcik'ize, C., "Godebaj ieremiajsis kartuli redakciebi," *Mravaltavi* 3 (1973): 31–40.

Kurcik'ize, C., *Kartuli biblia* (Tbilisi: Xelnac'erta erovnuli cent'ri, 2010).

Marr, N.J., *Ippolit: Tolkovanie Pesni pesnej: Gruzinskij tekst po rukopisi X v., perevod s armjanskogo* (Teksty i razyskanija po armjano-gruzinskoj filologii 3; St. Petersburg: Kiršbaum, 1901).

Melikišvili, N., "Ioseb plaviosis txzulebis *iudevelta siȝvelta* kartuli targmanis arsebuli nusxebi da mati bernȝnuli c'q'aro," *Mravaltavi* 11 (1985): 24–31.

Melikišvili, N. (ed.), *Ioseb plaviosi: motxrobani iudaebrivisa ȝuelsit'q'uaobisani* (2 vols.; Tbilisi: Mecniereba, 1987–1988).

Melikišvili, N., *Bibliur c'ignta ȝveli kartuli targmanebi* (Tbilisi: Alilo, 2009).

Mirot'aȝe, N. (ed.), *Esteris c'ignis ȝveli kartuli versiebi* (Tbilisi: Tbilisis universit'et'is gamomcemloba, 2014).

Outtier, B., "Nouveaux fragments onciaux du lectionnaire géorgien ancien," *Langues orientales anciennes: Philologie et linguistique* 4 (1993): 31–34.

Quast, U., *Ruth* (Septuaginta Vetus Testamentum Graecum 4.3; Göttingen: Vandenhoeck & Ruprecht, 2006).

Rahlfs, **Septuaginta*.

Rahlfs, A., *Studie über den griechischen Text des Buches Ruth* (MSU 3.2; Berlin: Weidmann, 1922).

Sarȝvelaȝe, Z., "Venaši daculi 'kebaj kebatajs' t'ekst'isatvis," *Mravaltavi* 10 (1983): 75–85.

Sarȝvelaȝe, Z. (ed.), "Ek'lesiast'e," in *Kartuli mc'erloba: ocdaat t'omad*, Vol. 1 (eds. A. Bakraȝe and R. Tvaraȝe; Tbilisi: Nak'aduli, 1987), 145–63.

Sarȝvelaȝe, Z. (ed.), "Kebaj kebataj," in *Kartuli mc'erloba: ocdaat t'omad*, Vol. 1 (eds. A. Bakraȝe and R. Tvaraȝe; Tbilisi: Nak'aduli, 1987), 164–74.

Tarchnišvili, M., *Geschichte der kirchlichen georgischen Literatur: Auf Grund des ersten Bandes der georgischen Literaturgeschichte von K. Kekelidze* (Studi e testi 185; Vatican City: Biblioteca Apostolica Vaticana, 1955).

Tarchnischvili, M. (ed.), *Le grand lectionnaire de l'église de Jérusalem (Ve–VIIIe siècle)*, Vol. 1. (CSCO 188–89 Scriptores Iberici 9–10; Louvain: Secrétariat du Corpus SCO, 1959).

Treat, J.C., "Aquila, Field and the Song of Songs," in Salvesen, **Hexapla*, 135–76.

Ziegler, J., *Ieremias, Baruch, Threni, Epistula Ieremiae* (3rd ed.; Septuaginta Vetus Testamentum Graecum 15; Göttingen: Vandenhoeck & Ruprecht, 2006).

Šaniȝe, A., *Targmanebaj kebisa kebatajsaj: p'aleograpiuli rveuli* (Tbilisi: Tbilisis universit'et'is st'udent'ta k'avširis gamocema, 1924).

Šaniȝe, A. (ed.), *C'ignni ȝuelisa aγtkumisani 978 c'lis xelnac'eris mixedvit*, Vol. 1.2: *Levit'eltaj, msaȝultaj, rutisi, iobisi, esaiajsi* (Tbilisi: Sak. ssr mecnierebata ak'ademiis gamomcemloba, 1948).

Žordanija, F.D., *Opisanie rukopisej Tiflisskogo Cerkovnogo muzeja Kartalino-Kachetinskogo duchovenstva*, Vol. 1 (Tbilisi: Gutenberg, 1903).

Alessandro Maria Bruni

13–17.2.7 Old Church Slavonic Translations

The Old Church Slavonic (OCS) versions of the books of Ruth, Canticles, Qohelet, Lamentations, and Esther survive in East and South Slavic codices dating from no earlier than the fourteenth century.[1] This corpus may be divided typologically into two categories of sources, the Croat Glagolitic breviaries and missals and the Cyrillic testimonies. Throughout the debates, attention was focused repeatedly on the question of whether OCS-Ruth (→ 13–17.2.7.1), OCS-Cant (→ 13–17.2.7.2), and OCS-Qoh (→ 13–17.2.7.3) should be ascribed to Methodius (815–885 C.E.)[2] or to translators working in the Old Bulgarian period (reign of Tsar Symeon, ca. 893–927 C.E.).[3] With the exception of the earliest Old Church Slavonic translations of Canticles (→ 13–17.2.7.2.1) and Qohelet (→ 13–17.2.7.3.1), and of the first Cyrillic version of Esther (→ 13–17.2.7.5.2), philological analysis of the witnesses has hitherto been undertaken on far too small a body of evidence. Moreover, systematic collations with the critical apparatus of the Göttingen editions currently available for LXX-Ruth[4] (→ 13–17.1.1.1), LXX-Lam[5] (→ 13–17.1.1.4), and LXX-Esth (→ 13–17.1.1.5)[6] still await production. The present entry aims at providing a preliminary assessment of the relevance of this vast manuscript legacy to biblical scholarship. Although much work remains to be done in the field of textual criticism, even at this early stage of inquiry it appears possible to glimpse some of the potential benefits that we may derive

---

[1] Mathiesen, "Handlist," 3–35.
[2] See the hagiographic account of the *Life of Methodius* (→ 1.4.10.3) in Angelov and Kodov, *Kliment Ochridski*, 191.
[3] For bibliography, see below in the respective subentries.
[4] Quast, *Ruth*.
[5] Ziegler, *Threni*.
[6] Hanhart, *Esther*.

from incorporating this tradition into LXX studies (→ 1.4.10.5).

13–17.2.7.1 OCS-Ruth

The book of Ruth was translated twice from LXX (→ 13–17.1.1.1) into Old Church Slavonic. The earliest version (OCS-Ruth 1) has come down to us in the Croat Glagolitic tradition, while the second (OCS-Ruth 2) appears in Cyrillic manuscripts.

13–17.2.7.1.1 OCS-Ruth 1

OCS-Ruth 1 is to be found in a Croat Glagolitic breviary dating from the late fourteenth century: Vienna, *Österreichische Nationalbibliothek, Slav.* 3, copied at Omišalj (Castelmuschio) on Krk (Veglia) in 1396. The extant text, which is accessible in several editions, lacks Ruth 4:7a–22 and has minuses in Ruth 1:6, 19, 20; 2:2, 11; and 4:4.[7]

By virtue of linguistic affinities with the OCS-Prophetologium (→ 1.4.10.3.1) and other Cyrillo-Methodian translations, OCS-Ruth 1 is numbered among the possible residues of the version of the entire Old Testament, allegedly undertaken by Methodius shortly before his death (→ 1.4.10.3).[8]

13–17.2.7.1.2 OCS-Ruth 2

OCS-Ruth 2 was probably penned in early tenth-century Bulgaria along with OCS-Pent (→ 2.5.7), OCS-Josh, OCS-Judg, and OCS-1–4 Kgdms (→ 3–5.2.7). It survives in two redactions, OCS-Ruth 2a and OCS-Ruth 2b, the latter being a revision of the former.[9] OCS-Ruth 2a has come down to us in East Slavic copies, while OCS-Ruth 2b in South Slavic manuscripts. In both cases, the earliest sources date back to the fourteenth century, but the types of collections differ from each other (East Slavic: → 1.4.10.2.4.1; South Slavic: → 1.4.10.2.4.2).[10]

OCS-Ruth 2a was published by Michajlov and Vajs,[11] while OCS-Ruth 2b was published by Savić.[12] An edition based on both East and South Slavic codices has been prepared by Dunkov.[13]

13–17.2.7.1.3 Relevance to LXX Studies

Both OCS-Ruth 1 and OCS-Ruth 2 were shown[14] to feature a number of textual affinities with LXX^R (→ 13–17.1.1.1).[15] However, additional research is needed in order to shed more light on this issue since critical editions of OCS-Ruth 2 based on entire manuscript evidence are not available and texts await collation with Quast's apparatus.[16]

13–17.2.7.2 OCS-Cant

Four translations of Canticles are preserved in the Old Church Slavonic language, three in Cyrillic and one in the Croat Glagolitic tradition.

13–17.2.7.2.1 OCS-Cant 1

The earliest translation (OCS-Cant 1) is contained in twenty-one East and South Slavic manuscripts dating from the fourteenth to the seventeenth centuries.[17] The pre-Symeonic origin of this version seems to be highly probable, although the attribution to Methodius[18] was judged to be anything

---

[7] Vajs, *Liber Ruth*, 11–16 (Glagolitic text); Vajs, *Kniha Rut*, 24–27 (Cyrillic transcription) with pls. i–vii (facsimile); Michajlov, "Drevne-slavjanskij perevod," 23–27.

[8] Thomson, "The Slavonic Translation," 751; Pičchadze, "Perevody Biblii," 139; Pičchadze, "K istorii," 21; Alekseev, *Tekstologija*, 155.

[9] Thomson, "The Slavonic Translation," 751–52.

[10] See Mathiesen, "The Typology," 198; Mathiesen, "Hand-list," 14–15. In the late fifteenth century, OCS-Ruth 2 was included in the "Gennadian Bible" (→ 1.4.10.2.4.3) and later in the Great Menologia (→ 1.4.10.2.4) of Archbishop Macarius of Novgorod (1482–1563). This redaction was subsequently subjected to a number of revisions and incorporated in the two major printed editions of the Scriptures, namely the 1581 Ostrog Bible and the 1751 Elizabethan Bible (→ 1.4.10.3.4). See Alekseev, *Tekstologija*, 41–42, 198; Dunkov, "Knigata Rut," 119–30; Thomson, "The Slavonic Translation," 752–53.

[11] Michajlov, "Drevne-slavjanskij perevod," 27–36; Vajs, *Kniha Rut*, 39–46.

[12] Savić, "Srpskoslovenska Knjiga," 31–37.

[13] Dunkov (ed.), *Die Methodbibel*, Vol. 1: *Das Buch Rut*. This work, based on nine manuscripts, was judged to be of dubious philological value; see Thomson, "The Slavonic Translation," 753–54. See also → 1.4.10.4.2.

[14] Vajs, *Kniha Rut*, 19–23; Alekseev, *Tekstologija*, 121–23.

[15] See Rahlfs, *Studie*, 104–10.

[16] Quast, *Ruth*.

[17] The earliest testimony is the South Slavic codex National Library of Russia, St. Petersburg, F.I. 416. See Alekseev, *Pesn'*, 15–16 (list of manuscripts), 24–30 (edition).

[18] Alekseev, "K opredeleniju," 229–31; Alekseev, "Kirillo–

but entirely reliable.[19] In 1983, Alekseev published a critical edition.[20] As for the Greek sources (→ 13–17.1.1.2) of OCS-Cant 1, fifteen cases of textual agreement have been claimed to occur with LXX[252], and nine each with LXX[161] and LXX[248].[21]

13–17.2.7.2.2 OCS-Cant 2

A second version (OCS-Cant 2) is to be found within an exegetical catena that comprises interpretations of Hippolytus Romanus (CPG 1871),[22] Gregory of Nyssa (CPG 3158), Philo of Carpasia (CPG 3810), and Pseudo-Procopius of Gaza (CPG 7431). The debate over its date and textual relationships with OCS-Cant 1 is ongoing. According to one view, OCS-Cant 2 is of East Slavic provenance and should be dated back to the mid-twelfth century,[23] while in the opinion of other scholars it was translated in Bulgaria in the tenth century by making use of OCS-Cant 1.[24]

OCS-Cant 2 has come down to us in twenty-three East Slavic testimonies from the thirteenth to the eighteenth centuries;[25] in seven additional East Slavic codices of the fifteenth and sixteenth centuries, two of which were copied from Bulgarian originals, OCS-Cant 2 is deprived of the commentaries.[26] As has been pointed out, OCS-Cant 2 omits Cant 1:16; 2:2; 3:5; 6:8; moreover, it has a number of minuses in Cant 1:3, 11; 2:9, 15; 3:6, 10–11; 4:1, 5–6, 8–12, 14; 5:1–2, 5, 9, 11, 17; 6:4–5, 10, 12; 7:1, 4, 12; 8:4, 6, 9, 11.[27] An edition based on six testimonies is available.[28]

In the late fifteenth century, OCS-Cant 2 was included in the Gennadian Bible (→ 1.4.10.2.4.3), while a conflated text of OCS-Cant 1 and 2 was inserted into the printed Ostrog Bible of 1581 (→ 1.4.10.3.4).[29]

13–17.2.7.2.3 OCS-Cant 3

A third version (OCS-Cant 3) is preserved in a number of Croat Glagolitic breviaries. OCS-Cant 3 lacks Cant 2:1–17; 4:5b–6a; furthermore, minuses are to be found in Cant 6:1 and 8:6.[30] Additional study is required in order to clarify the textual relationship of the translation to OCS-Cant 1 and OCS-Cant 2.[31] The parent text of OCS-Cant 3 still awaits assessment. The opinion has been expressed that it was based initially on OCS-Cant 1 and later revised by using the Vulgate (→ 13–17.1.7) as a model.[32] However, some readings in the Croat tradition (Cant 4:10 and 8:2) have been explained by assuming the influence of VL (→ 13–17.2.1.2).[33]

13–17.2.7.2.4 OCS-Cant 4

A fourth version made from LXX (OCS-Cant 4) is inserted into the Old Church Slavonic translation of Theodoret of Cyrrhus' *Explanatio in Canticum*

Mefodievskoe," 128; Alekseev, *Tekstologija*, 96–97; Alekseev, *Pesn'*, 40–42.

[19] Thomson, "The Slavonic Translation," 835–36. Moreover, conflicting results have been reached in the study of the translation technique of OCS-Cant 1. While Alekseev points to a literal and high-quality rendering of the LXX model (→ 13–17.1.1.2), Thomson speaks of a quite liberal translation method and underscores a number of errors that at times leave the meaning of the text unclear (Alekseev, "K opredeleniju," 241–45; Thomson, "The Slavonic Translation," 834–35; Thomson, *A Brief Survey*, 37, 50).

[20] Alekseev, "K opredeleniju," 251–55. Text in reconstructed Old Church Slavonic orthography: Alekseev, *Pesn'*, 24–30.

[21] However, these textual agreements are not quoted *in extenso*: Alekseev, "K opredeleniju," 245. According to Thomson, the translation is modeled on a "fairly eclectic" Greek recension that reflects LXX[R] (Thomson, "The Slavonic Translation," 835).

[22] The Old Church Slavonic version of this commentary is incomplete. See the Georgian tradition (→ 13–17.2.6.2.2).

[23] Alekseev, *Tekstologija*, 95–97; Alekseev, *Pesn'*, 16–19, 48–51.

[24] Lunt, "The OCS Song of Songs," 292–304; Thomson, "Made in Russia," 312.

[25] The earliest one is Moscow, Russian State Library, f. 205, N° 171, late thirteenth century. See Alekseev, *Pesn' pesnej*, 40–42.

[26] Alekseev, *Tekstologija*, 96–97.

[27] Thomson, "The Slavonic Translation," 836; Alekseev, *Pesn'*, 63–112 (edition).

[28] Alekseev, *Pesn'*, 63–122.

[29] Alekseev, *Pesn'*, 185–94.

[30] Alekseev, *Pesn'*, 31–34, 35–39 (edition in Cyrillic transcription); Hamm, "Starohrvatski prijevod," 195–230; Thomson, "The Slavonic Translation," 837.

[31] See Thomson, "The Slavonic Translation," 837–38; Thomson, *A Brief Survey*, 52.

[32] Alekseev, "K opredeleniju," 248.

[33] Thomson, "The Slavonic Translation," 837; Thomson, *A Brief Survey*, 51.

Canticorum (CPG 6203). It was undertaken by Constantine of Kostenets (c. 1380–post 1427) and is preserved in a few South Slavic manuscripts of the fifteenth to seventeenth centuries.³⁴ The source of the commentaries has been identified with a catena corresponding to Faulhaber's type B2.³⁵

13–17.2.7.2.5 Relevance to LXX Studies

The earliest textual stratum of OCS-Cant seems to share readings with LXX¹⁶¹,²⁴⁸,²⁵², which are known for containing Hexaplaric fragments in the margins (→ 13–17.1.5.4.2; → 13–17.1.5.3.2.1). However, in OCS-Cant 1, the Hexaplaric material (→ 13–17.1.5.4) appears to have been incorporated directly into the main text as shown, for instance, by the inclusion of Symmachus' reading κρατήσω τῶν βαΐων αὐτοῦ "I will take hold of its branches"³⁶ in OCS-Cant 7:8 имѫ сѧ za вѣтви ѥго "I will take hold of its branches."³⁷ Future research should aim at producing a thorough scholarly assessment of the potential of this version for comparative textual criticism. The translation should be subjected to systematic collation with the surviving Greek Hexaplaric evidence (→ 13–17.1.5.4).³⁸ The same conclusion applies to the later catena versions.

13–17.2.7.3 OCS-Qoh

The Old Church Slavonic tradition of Qohelet includes two complete versions, one Cyrillic (OCS-Qoh 1) and the other Croat Glagolitic (OCS-Qoh 2). Moreover, in East Slavic Cyrillic sources, a number of readings are also preserved that are flanked by exegetical commentaries (OCS-Qoh 3).

13–17.2.7.3.1 OCS-Qoh 1

OCS-Qoh 1 is to be found in thirty-three East Slavic Cyrillic testimonies dating from the fourteenth to the sixteenth centuries.³⁹ Consensus has not been reached among scholars regarding the date of the translation.⁴⁰

The reliance of OCS-Qoh 1 on a Greek model (→ 13–17.1.1.3) manifests itself clearly in a number of errors (many are due to itacism) and calque translation. As widely known, LXX renders the Hebrew nota accusative אֶת with σύν "with" followed by an accusative to mark the direct object, a feature typical of Aquila's technique (→ 13–17.1.1.3.3).⁴¹ In several instances, OCS-Qoh 1 translates this construction with the instrumental case governed by the preposition съ, "with." The use in OCS-Qoh 1 of the comitative complement results inevitably in a distortion of the meaning of several passages.⁴²

A critical edition of OCS-Qoh 1 was prepared by Osinkina on the basis of the Gennadian Bible (→ 1.4.10.2.4.3) with collations from twenty-five testimonies.⁴³ The critical apparatus includes only selected references to LXX readings according to the editions of Holmes and Parsons and of Rahlfs.⁴⁴ Six

---

³⁴ Dmitrova, "Prevod i tălkovanie," 213–32; Dmitrova, "The Short Version"; Dmitrova, "Biblical Quotations"; Dmitrova, *Tălkuvanija* (edition of the commentaries according to the Rila ms 2/24, late fifteenth century); Minčeva, "Za Venskija prepis," 3–22 (edition); Alekseev, *Tekstologija*, 37; Alekseev, *Pesn'*, 155–57 (manuscripts), 158–62 (edition).

³⁵ Dmitrova, *Tălkuvanija*; Faulhaber, *Hohelied-, Proverbien- und Prediger-Catenen*, 6–19, 64–65.

³⁶ Field, *Hexapla, 2.422.

³⁷ See Alekseev, "K opredeleniju," 245.

³⁸ See Field, *Hexapla, 2.411–24; Treat, "Aquila"; Ceulemans, "A Critical Edition."

³⁹ Mathiesen, "Handlist," 3–35; Osinkina, *The Textual History*, 14–27.

⁴⁰ Alekseev ascribes this version to Methodius (Alekseev, "Kirillo–Mefodievskoe perevodčeskoe nasledie," 128; Alekseev, *Tekstologija*, 155). Thomson strongly criticizes this view, claiming that the language of the translation is not as early as that of OCS-Prov (→ 12.4.7) and that the text is flawed with errors. Consequently, such a conclusion should be rejected outright (Thomson, *A Brief Survey*, 37; Thomson, "The Slavonic Translation," 844). Osinkina does not completely exclude the possibility of an Old Bulgarian origin of the earliest textual stratum. However, she thinks that a wider chronological framework stretching up to the beginning of the fifteenth century would be far more appropriate, taking into account present-day knowledge of the textual history of OCS-Qoh (Osinkina, *The Textual History*, 175, 210).

⁴¹ Ziegler, "Die Wiedergabe." On similarities between the work of Theodotion and LXX-Qoh (→ 13–17.1.5.3.3.1), see Yi, *Translation*.

⁴² Several examples may be found in Thomson, "The Slavonic Translation," 843.

⁴³ Osinkina, *The Textual History*, 29, 74 (stemma codicum), 92–93, 213–39.

⁴⁴ Holmes and Parsons, *Vetus Testamentum*; Rahlfs, *Septuaginta*.

cases of textual correspondence have been claimed to occur with LXX[B], five with LXX[A,V], and four with LXX[106,254]. Since clear textual allegiances on the basis of these agreements were not outlined, definitive conclusions on the parent text of OCS-Qoh 1 were not reached.[45]

13–17.2.7.3.2 OCS-Qoh 2

OCS-Qoh 2 is preserved in the earliest Croat Glagolitic Breviary. This text was shown to have been translated from the Vulgate (→ 13–17.1.7) in the twelfth or thirteenth century.[46] An edition was published by Vajs.[47]

13–17.2.7.3.3 OCS-Qoh 3

Partial translations of Qohelet flanked by exegetical commentaries, most of which derive from the catena of Olympiodorus of Alexandria (CPG 7454: → 13–17.1.5.3.2.2),[48] are to be found in a number of East Slavic sources dating to the thirteenth to sixteenth centuries (OCS-Qoh 3). Different text types are extant: a first one contains Qoh 2:14; 3:5; 4:6, 9; 5:5; 7:3–7, 16–23, 29; 10:7; 8:4, 8; 9:4; 10:1–8, 16–17; 11:2–4; 12:5; a second one comprises Qoh 1:6–7, 9–11; 2:14, 21, 24–26; 3:15–21; 4:4–6, 9–17; 5:2, 5, 9–10, 18–19; 6:7–9; 7:2–7, 9, 12–13, 15–23;[49] a third collection (*florilegia*) includes only a few quotations.[50]

The textual relationship of these readings to OCS-Qoh 1 still needs to be elucidated;[51] the date is controversial, ranging from the early tenth[52] to the thirteenth century.[53]

13–17.2.7.3.4 Relevance to LXX Studies

Although systematic collations with LXX (→ 13–17.1.1.3) have yet to be produced and the translation technique awaits careful study, it seems possible to argue that OCS-Qoh 1 reflects LXX-Qoh. For instance, in Qoh 5:10, OCS-Qoh 1 reads ꙗко начало видѣти очима его, which corresponds to the Old Greek ὅτι ἀρχὴ τοῦ ὁρᾶν ὀφθαλμοῖς αὐτοῦ "because the beginning of seeing is with his eyes" (see → 13–17.1.5.3.3.1). Moreover, OCS-Qoh 1 does not appear to include Hexaplaric readings. The same conclusion applies to the catena versions (OCS-Qoh 3), which seem not to preserve quotations from the Three (→ 13–17.1.5.3.2.2).[54]

13–17.2.7.4 OCS-Lam

OCS-Lam survives in two translations, one of which is full and the other partial. The first (OCS-Lam 1) has come down to us in the Cyrillic tradition, with the second (OCS-Lam 2) in the Croat Glagolitic Breviary.

13–17.2.7.4.1 OCS-Lam 1

OCS-Lam 1 is to be found in several East and South Slavic manuscripts containing a sylloge of the XVI Prophets,[55] which were translated during the Old Bulgarian period (→ 6–9.2.7). With minor amendments, this translation was incorporated

---

[45] Osinkina, *The Textual History*, 51–52.

[46] Vajs, *Liber Ecclesiastis*, v–vi; Osinkina, *The Textual History*, 176–208.

[47] Vajs, *Liber Ecclesiastis*, 1–25.

[48] Osinkina, *The Textual History*, 108–11. For an edition of the Greek text, see Boli, *Olympiodor*.

[49] For instance, see manuscripts St. Petersburg, National Library of Russia, *Pogod.* 1 and Moscow, Russian State Library, *Und.* 13, sixteenth century (some readings within this second codex are interpolated and do not belong to the earliest stratum of the catena; Thomson, "The Slavonic Translation," 844). For an edition, see Osinkina, *The Textual History*, 241–75. Other testimonies can be found in Alekseev, *Tekstologija*, 36–37; Osinkina, *The Textual History*, 156–74.

[50] Earliest codex: St. Petersburg, National Library of Russia, Q.п.I.18, thirteenth century. Edition: Wątróbska, *The Izbornik*, 152–53, 161, 174. Other sources: Osinkina, The Textual History, 105; Feder, "Meleckij sbornik."

[51] See Thomson, "The Slavonic Translation," 844 n. 1127; Osinkina, *The Textual History*, 209.

[52] For a tenth-century Bulgarian origin, see Thomson, "Made in Russia," 311; Feder, "Meleckij sbornik," 158–59.

[53] Alekseev proposed that this text was translated in Old Rus' in the twelfth or thirteenth century. To support his view, he has pointed out a number of linguistic traits as well as a quotation in an original Kievan work of the mid-twelfth century (Alekseev, "K istorii," 185–86).

[54] On the Hexaplaric tradition of Qohelet, see Marshall, "A Critical Edition," and esp. → 13–17.1.5.3.

[55] The earliest testimonies date from the mid-fourteenth century. See Mathiesen, "Handlist," 14, 18–33; Alekseev, *Tekstologija*, 133, 163–64.

into the late fifteenth-century Gennadian Bible (→ 1.4.10.2.4.3)[56] and in the sixteenth-century Russian Macarian Menologium (→ 1.4.10.2.4).[57] Subsequently, OCS-Lam 1 was included in the printed editions of 1581 (Ostrog Bible), 1663 (Moscow Bible), and, after a number of emendations based on LXX (→ 13–17.1.1.4),[58] also in the Elizabethan Bible of 1751.[59] Only a diplomatic edition of OCS-Lam 1 is currently available; it is based on the sixteenth-century Russian Macarian Menologium (→ 1.4.10.2.4).[60] Therefore, the entire manuscript tradition awaits exploration.

13–17.2.7.4.2 OCS-Lam 2

OCS-Lam 2 is to be found in early Croat Glagolitic breviaries that contain the following readings: Lam 1:1–22; 2:1–20; 3:1–20, 22–66; 4:1–9; 5:11–16.[61] This version was undertaken from the Vulgate (→ 13–17.1.7).[62]

13–17.2.7.4.3 Relevance to LXX Studies

A collation of OCS-Lam 1 with Ziegler's apparatus of LXX-Lam[63] is still lacking. As for the parent text, the claim has been made that OCS-Lam 1 follows LXX^L (→ 13–17.1.6) in view of the arrangement of the verses found in Lamentations 3 (Lam 3:1–45, 49–51, 46–48, 52–66).[64] However, the alternative sequence of LXX[65] is also attested by other Old Church Slavonic manuscripts such as Russian State Library, Moscow, f. 304/I, no. 89, late fifteenth century (folio 243).[66] Within the same chapter, the latter does not show reliance on LXX^L, which in Lam 3:51 reads οἱ ὀφθαλμοί μου ἐξέλιπον μετὰ τῆς ζωῆς μου ἐπὶ τὰς θυγατέρας τοῦ γένους μου "my eyes part with my life because of the daughters of my people."[67] Moreover, according to the Moscow codex, OCS-Lam 1 omits Lam 3:22–24, 29, which appear in Lucianic witnesses. In-depth research is therefore necessary before definitive conclusions can be reached and before the textual allegiances of OCS-Lam 1 with Greek manuscript groups can be established safely.

13–17.2.7.5 OCS-Esth

Four versions of Esther exist in the Old Church Slavonic language, one in Croat Glagolitic sources and the remaining in the East Slavic Cyrillic tradition.

13–17.2.7.5.1 OCS-Esth 1

A first translation (OCS-Esth 1) is preserved in the Croat Glagolitic Breviary and Missal.[68] This text is based on the Vulgate (→ 13–17.1.7).[69]

13–17.2.7.5.2 OCS-Esth 2

A second version (OCS-Esth 2) survives in thirty-one East Slavic testimonies dating from no earlier than the late fourteenth or early fifteenth century.[70] A critical edition based on the complete manuscript evidence is available, in which an analysis of the linguistic and translational features of the text is also given.[71] As for the origin of the translation, no definitive conclusions have been reached. Dates

---

[56] Alekseev, *Tekstologija*, 198.

[57] Iosif (Archimandrit), *Podrobnoe*, 134.

[58] For a list of these corrections, see Blagoveščenskij, *Kniga*, 267–93.

[59] *Ostrožskaja biblija*; *Biblija* 1663; and *Biblija* 1751; Blagoveščenskij, *Kniga*, 267–93; Thomson, "The Slavonic Translation," 711.

[60] See Weiher, Šmidt, and Škurko, *Die grossen Lesemenäen*, 17–18.

[61] For an edition, see Berčić, *Ulomci*, 46–51.

[62] Thomson, "The Slavonic Translation," 846.

[63] Ziegler, *Threni*.

[64] Thomson, "The Slavonic Translation," 857.

[65] Ziegler, *Threni*, 485.

[66] This source also includes the name of the Hebrew letter at the beginning of each stanza in ch. 1 (ff. 241r/v).

[67] Ziegler, *Threni*, 485.

[68] Vajs, *Liber Ecclesiastis*, iv–v; Vajs, *Nejstarší Breviář*, 34.

[69] This tradition has been studied recently by Badurina-Stipčević, *Hrvatskoglagoljska Knjiga*, 107–63, 203–05; Badurina-Stipčević, "The Old Testament Book," 5–39.

[70] For a list of witnesses, see Lunt and Taube, *The Slavonic Book*, 11–12. OCS-Esth is not included in the so-called *Jewish Chronicle* (→ 1.4.10.2.4.1). On the history of the study of this translation, see Thomson, "The Slavonic Translation," 787–88; Alekseev, *Tekstologija*, 180–81; Lunt and Taube, *The Slavonic Book*, 8–10.

[71] Lunt and Taube, *The Slavonic Book*, 24–53 (edition), 141–84 (linguistic analysis). This work replaced the previous edition by Meščerskij ("Izdanie").

ranging from the ninth to the fourteenth century and both an East and South Slavic provenance have been suggested.[72]

OCS-Esth 2 replicates MT-Esth. According to one view, this version was made directly from MT (→ 17.2.2).[73] According to a different opinion, it was undertaken by using a lost intermediate 167-verse Greek Esther that was available in the Greek-speaking Jewish communities of the Byzantine Empire.[74] As has been shown, in a number of instances, OCS-Esth 2 deviates slightly from the readings of MT (Esth 1:17; 3:5; 4:1) or presents contamination from MT and LXX (Esth 2:13 and 2:23; → 13–17.1.1.5).[75]

OCS-Esth 2 was included in the late fifteenth-century Gennadian Bible, in which the additions (→ 1.4.10.2.4.3) were translated from the Vulgate (→ 13–17.1.7) and appended at the end of the book.[76]

13–17.2.7.5.3 OCS-Esth 3

A third Slavic translation of Esther (OCS-Esth 3) dates to the sixteenth century and was judged to be the work of Maksim Grek (Maximus Triboles, ca. 1470–1555). It is based on the LXX$^{o'}$ text (→ 13–17.1.1.5) and includes the additions that are to be found at their appropriate places. The text is divided into thirty chapters and lacks Esth 9:17–31.[77]

13–17.2.7.5.4 OCS-Esth 4

A fourth translation (OCS-Esth 4) is to be found in the printed Ostrog Bible of 1581.[78] This text was formulated by collating OCS-Esth 3 (→ 13–17.2.7.5.3) with OCS-Esth 2 (→ 13–17.2.7.5.2) and the Vulgate (→ 13–17.1.7). The produced text was revised once again towards LXX (→ 13–17.1.1.5) by the editors of the 1751 Elizabethan Bible.[79]

13–17.2.7.5.5 Relevance to LXX Studies

The Old Church Slavonic translations on the whole are faithful witnesses to their respective parent texts, namely MT-Esth (→ 17.2.2), V-Esth (→ 13–17.1.7), and LXX$^{o'}$-Esth (→ 13–17.1.1). With regard to OCS-Esth 2, this conclusion remains valid regardless of whether it was translated directly from MT or from a putative Greek intermediate text.

13–17.2.7.6 Appendix: Ruthenian Versions from MT

Besides the abovementioned Old Church Slavonic translations of Ruth, Canticles, Qohelet, Lamentations, and Esther, additional material is available for research. One should consider first the vernacular-orientated translation of the Five Scrolls undertaken in Ruthenia from MT (→ 13.2.2;

---

[72] According to Lunt and Taube, no definitive answer can be given to this question (Lunt and Taube, *The Slavonic Book*, 245). In Veder's view, OCS-Esth 2 should be traced back to a Glagolitic source that was discovered and first read in Ruthenia in the mid-fourteenth century, after having been ignored for centuries given its minor liturgical importance (Veder, "Esther's Glagolitic Ancestry," 220–21). For linguistic arguments against the hypothesis of a South Slavic provenance, see Pičchadze, *Perevodčeskaja dejatel'nost'*, 45. In the opinion of Alekseev, OCS-Esth 2 originated in Galicia in the mid-thirteenth century and its translation was connected with that of Flavius Josephus' *Jewish War* (Alekseev, "Russko-evrejskie literaturnye svjazi," 172).

[73] See Meščerskij, "Izdanie"; Alekseev, "Ešče raz"; Alekseev, *Tekstologija*, 180–81. Lately, Alekseev has reiterated the possibility of a Hebrew *Vorlage* (Alekseev, "Russko-evrejskie literaturnye svjazi," 168) by referring to a number of presumed procedural shortcomings in previous studies that focused on the textual tradition of the book (he refers to Meščerskij, "Izdanie"; Lunt and Taube, *The Slavonic Book*; and Lysén, *Kniga Esfir'*). Furthermore, in his belief, OCS-Esth 2 was initially written in the Hebrew square script and only at a later stage transcribed into Cyrillic; see Alekseev, "Russko-evrejskie literaturnye svjazi," 172.

[74] A number of arguments have been adduced in support of the Greek origin (→ 13–17.1.1.5) of OCS-Esth 2. They include the rendering of proper names, syntactic constructions, as well as several misunderstandings of MT (→ 17.2.2) that can be explained by assuming the use of a Greek intermediate source. See Sobolevskij, *Perevodnaja literatura*, 433–36; Altbauer and Taube, "The Slavonic Book of Esther"; Lunt and Taube, *The Slavonic Book*, 245–48.

[75] Thomson, "The Slavonic Translation," 782–83; Lunt and Taube, *The Slavonic Book*, 88, 94, 98, 99, 105, 212.

[76] Thomson, "The Slavonic Translation," 788; Lunt and Taube, *The Slavonic Book*, 254–56.

[77] Taube and Olmsted, "Povest' o Esfiri," 101, 107, 112–13 (list of manuscripts).

[78] *Ostrožskaja biblija*, folios 260–64^v.

[79] Taube and Olmsted, "Povest' o Esfiri," 108–11; Thomson, "The Slavonic Translation," 789.

→ 14.2.2; → 15.2.2; → 16.2.2; → 17.2.2) in the second half of the fifteenth century.[80] A second independent (contemporary or perhaps slightly older) version of Canticles made from MT (→ 14.2.2) is included in the sixteenth-century manuscript Moscow, Russian State Library, *Muz.* 8222.[81]

Alekseev, A.A., "Pesn' pesnej po spisku XVI veka v perevode s drevneevrejskogo originala," *Palestinskij sbornik* 27 (1981): 63–79.

Alekseev, A.A., "K opredeleniju ob-ema literaturnogo nasledija Mefodija (četij perevod Pesni pesnej)," *Trudy Otdela drevnerusskoj literatury* 37 (1983): 229–55.

Alekseev, A.A., "Kirillo-Mefodievskoe perevodčeskoe nasledie i ego istoričeskie sud'by: perevody sv. Pisanija v slavjanskoj pis'mennosti," in *Istorija, kul'tura, ètnografija i fol'klor slavjanskich narodov: X Meždunarodnyj s"ezd slavistov: Sofija, sentjabr' 1988: Doklady sovetskoj delegacii* (ed. I.I. Kostjuško; Moscow: Nauka, 1988), 124–45.

Alekseev, A.A., "K istorii russkoj perevodčeskoj školy XII v.," *Trudy Otdela drevnerusskoj literatury* 41 (1988): 154–96.

Alekseev, A.A., *Tekstologija slavjanskoj Biblii* (Bausteine zur slavischen Philologie und Kulturgeschichte Neue Folge A Slavistische Forschungen 24; St. Petersburg: "Dmitrij Bulanin," 1999).

Alekseev, A.A., *Pesn' pesnej v drevnej slavjano-russkoj pis'mennosti* (St. Petersburg: "Dmitrij Bulanin," 2002).

Alekseev, A.A., "Ešče raz o knige Esfir'," *Russkij jazyk v naučnom osveščenii* 5.1 (2003): 185–214.

Alekseev, A.A., "Russko-evrejskie literaturnye svjazi Kievskoj èpochi: Rezul'taty i perspektivy issledovanija," in *Kenaanity: evrei v srednevekovom slavjanskom mire* (eds. V. Moskovič, A. Torpusman, and M. Členov; Jews and Slavs 24; Jerusalem: Gešarim, 2014), 166–82.

Altbauer, M., *The Five Biblical Scrolls in a Sixteenth-Century Jewish Translation into Belorussian (Vilnius codex 262)* (Jerusalem: The Israel Academy of Sciences and Humanities, 1992).

Altbauer, M. and M. Taube, "The Slavonic Book of Esther: When, Where, and from What Language Was It Translated?," *Harvard Ukrainian Studies* 8 (1984): 304–20.

Angelov, B.S. and C. Kodov (eds.), *Kliment Ochridski: Săbrani săčinenija*, Vol. 3: *Prostranni žitija na Kiril i Metodii* (Sofia: Izdatelstvo na Bălgarska Akademija na naukite, 1973).

Badurina-Stipčević, V., "The Old Testament Book of Esther in Croatian Glagolitic Vatican Illirico 5 Breviary from 14th century," *Palaeoslavica* 12.2 (2004): 5–39.

Badurina-Stipčević, V., "Hrvatskoglagoljska Knjiga o Esteri," in *Glagoljica i hrvatski glagolizam* (eds. M.-A. Dürrigl, M. Mihaljević, and F. Velčić; Zagreb: Staroslavenski institut, 2004), 157–66.

Badurina-Stipčević, V., *Hrvatskoglagoljska Knjiga o Esteri* (Biblioteka Hrvatska jezična baština 7; Zagreb: Matica hrvatska, 2012).

Berčić, I. (ed.), *Ulomci Svetoga Pisma obojega uvjeta staroslovenskim jezikom: Skupio iz rukopisah i tiskanih knjigah hrvatskoga razreda svećenik Ivan Berčić*, Vol. 3 (Prague: Sinovi Bogumila Haase, 1865).

Biblija, sirěč' knigi vetchago i novago zavěta, po jayzku slavensku (Moscow: Pečatnyj dvor, 1663).

Biblija, sirěč' knigi svjaščennago pisanija vetchago i novago zavěta (St. Petersburg: Tipografija Aleksandro-Nevskogo monastyrja, 1751).

Blagoveščenskij, M.D., *Kniga Plač: Opyt issledovanija isagogiko-ěkzegetičeskogo* (Kiev: Tipografija S.A. Spilioti, 1899).

Boli, T., "Olympiodor, Diakon von Alexandria, Kommentar zum Ekklesiastes: Eine kritische Edition" (PhD diss., Heidelberg University, 2004).

Ceulemans, R., "A Critical Edition of the Hexaplaric Fragments of the Book of Canticles: With Emphasis on Their Reception in Greek Christian Exegesis" (PhD diss., Katholieke Universiteit Leuven, 2009).

Dimitrova, M., "Prevod i tălkovanie: po material ot prevoda na tălkovanijata na Pesen na Pesnite v răkopis 2/24 ot Rilskija manastir," in *Problemi na Kirilo-Metodievoto delo i na bălgarskata kultura prez IX–X vek* (eds. B. Velčeva, E. Dogramadžieva, and

---

[80] It is to be found in the early sixteenth-century codex of the Library of the Lithuanian Academy of Sciences, Vilnius, f. 19, No. 262. See Altbauer, *The Five Biblical Scrolls*; Thomson, "The Slavonic Translation," 874–81; Alekseev, *Tekstologija*, 181–82; *Pesn'*, 149–54 (edition); "Russko-evrejskie literaturnye svjazi," 169; Temčin, "Scharija i Skorina," 289–312; Temčin, "Kirilličeskij rukopisnyj učebnik," 92.

[81] For editions, see Alekseev, "Pesn' pesnej po spisku XVI veka"; *Pesn'*, 144–48; Thomson, "The Slavonic Translation," 873–74. On the language, see Alekseev, "Russko-evrejskie literaturnye svjazi," 169. Moreover, two translations of Canticles from Czech into Ruthenian have also come down to us (Thomson, "The Slavonic Translation," 881–82; Alekseev, *Pesn'*, 163–84; Verkholantsev, "A Fifteenth-Century Ruthenian Translation," 195–226).

S. Nikolova; Kirilo-Metodievski studii 17; Sofia: Bălgarska Akademija na naukite, 2007), 213–32.

Dimitrova, M., *Tălkuvanija na Pesen na pesnite v răkopis 2/24 ot Rilskata sveta obitel* (Sofia: Cheron Pres, 2012).

Dimitrova, M., "The Short Version of Catena B2 with Commentaries on the Song of Songs in Manuscript 52 in Baltazar Bogišić's Collection in Cavtat (Croatia)," in *In honorem: Cătălina Velculescu la aniversară* (ed. E. Renhardt; Bucharest: Paideia, 2012), 111–20.

Dimitrova, M., "Biblical Quotations in the Late South Slavonic Translation of Catena B₂ with Commentaries on the Song of Songs," in *The Bible in Slavic Tradition* (eds. A. Kulik et al.; Studia Judaeoslavica 9; Leiden: Brill, 2016), 215–42.

Dunkov, D., "Knigata Rut v slavjanskata răkopisna tradicija i v Ostrožskata Biblija," in *Najstarsze druki cerkiewnosłowiańskie i ich stosunek do tradycji rękopiśmiennej: materiały z sesji* (eds. J. Rusek, W. Witkowski, and A. Naumow; Krakow: Instytut filologii słowiańskiej, 1993), 119–30.

Dunkov, D. (ed.), *Die Methodbibel*, Vol. 1: *Das Buch Rut* (Die slawischen Sprachen 34; Salzburg: Institut für Slawistik der Universität Salzburg, 1993).

Evseev, I.E., *Očerki po istorii slavjanskogo perevoda Biblii* (Petrograd: Tipografija Merkuševa, 1916).

Faulhaber, M., *Hohelied-, Proverbien- und Prediger-Catenen* (Theologische Studien der Leo-Gesellschaft 4; Vienna: Verlag von Mayer, 1902).

Feder, U., "Meleckij sbornik i istorija drevnebolgarskoj literatury," *Palaeobulgarica* 6.3 (1982): 154–65.

Hamm, J., "Starohrvatski prijevod Pjesme nad pjesmama," *Slovo* 6.8 (1957): 195–230.

Hanhart, R. (ed.), *Esther* (Septuaginta Vetus Testamentum Graecum 8.3; Göttingen: Vandenhoeck & Ruprecht, 1983).

Holmes, R. and J. Parsons (eds.), *Vetus Testamentum graecum cum variis lectionibus*, Vol. 3 (Oxford: Clarendon Press, 1823).

Iosif (Archimandrit), *Podrobnoe oglavlenie Velikich Čet'ich Minej vserossijskogo mitropolita Makarija, chranjaščichsja v Moskovskoj patriaršej (nyne Synodal'noj) biblioteke* (Moscow: Sinodal'naja tipografija, 1892).

Kulik, A., "O nesochranivšejsja grečeskoj knige Esfir'," *Slavianovedenie* 2 (1995): 76–80.

Lunt, H., "The OCS Song of Songs: One Translation or Two?," *Die Welt der Slaven* 30 (1985): 279–318.

Lunt, H.G. and M. Taube, "The Slavonic Book of Esther: Translation from Hebrew or Evidence for a Lost Greek Text?," *HTR* 87 (1994): 347–62.

Lunt, H.G. and M. Taube, *The Slavonic Book of Esther: Text, Lexicon, Linguistic Analysis, Problems of Translation* (Cambridge: Harvard University Press, 1998).

Lysén, I., *Kniga Esfir': K istorii pervogo slavjanskogo perevoda* (Studia Slavica Upsaliensia 41; Uppsala: Almqvist & Wiksell, 2001).

Marshall, P.S., "A Critical Edition of the Hexaplaric Fragments of Ecclesiastes" (PhD diss., The Southern Baptist Theological Seminary, 2007).

Mathiesen, R., "Handlist of Manuscripts Containing Church Slavonic Translations of the Old Testament," *Polata knigopisnaja* 7 (1983): 3–48.

Mathiesen, R., "The Typology of Cyrillic Manuscripts (East Slavic vs. South Slavic Old Testament Manuscripts)," in *American Contributions to the Ninth International Congress of Slavists, Kiev, September 1983*, Vol. 1: *Linguistics* (ed. M.S. Flier; Columbus: Slavica, 1983), 193–202.

Meščerskij, N.A., "Izdanie teksta drevnerusskogo perevoda Knigi Esfir'," *Acta Universitatis Szegediensis: Dissertationes Slavicae* 13 (1978): 131–64.

Michajlov, A.V., "Drevne-slavjanskij perevod knigi Ruf': Iz istorii perevoda Sv. Pisanija na drevne-slavjan. Jazyk," *Russkij filologičeskij vestnik* 60 (1908): 1–36.

Minčeva, A., "Za Venskija prepis na Pesen na pesnite (Cod.slav.14 na Avstrijskata nacional'na biblioteka)," *Palaeobulgarica* 13.2 (1989): 3–22.

Mostrova, T., "Starobălgarskijat prevod na knigata na prorok Ieremija po prepisi ot XIV–XVI vek," *Palaeobulgarica* 19.2 (1995): 9–26.

Mostrova, T., "Knigata na prorok Ieremija v bălgarski, srăbski i ruski prepisi ot XIV–XVI vek," *Palaeobulgarica* 32.2 (2008): 59–82.

Osinkina, L.V., "The Textual History of Ecclesiastes in Church Slavonic" (PhD diss.; University of Oxford, 2007).

Ostrožskaja biblija: Fototipičeskoe pereizdanie teksta s izdanija 1581 g. (Moscow: Slovo-Art, 1988).

Pičchadze, A.A., "K istorii čet'ego teksta slavjanskogo Vos'miknižija," *Trudy Otdela drevnerusskoj literatury* 49 (1996): 10–21.

Pičchadze, A.A., "Perevody Biblii na drevnie jazyki: cerkovnoslavjanskij," *Pravoslavnaja ènciklopedija* (ed. Aleksij, Patriarch Moskovskij i Vseja Rusi II; Moscow: Cerkovno-Naučnyj Centr "Pravoslavnaja ènciklopedija," 2002), 5:139–47.

Pičchadze, A.A., *Perevodčeskaja dejatel'nost' v domongol'skoj Rusi: lingvističeskij aspekt* (Moscow: Rukopisnye pamjatniki Drevnej Rusi, 2011).

Quast, U. (ed.), *Ruth* (Septuaginta Vetus Testamentum

Graecum 4.3; Göttingen: Vandenhoeck & Ruprecht, 2006).

Rahlfs, A., *Studie über den griechischen Text des Buches Ruth* (MSU 3.2; Berlin: Weidmannsche Buchhandlung, 1922).

Savić, V., "Srpskoslovenska Knjiga o Ruti prema rukopisu Pčinjske biblije," *Prilozi za književnost, jezik, istoriju i folklor* 77 (2011): 27–51.

Sobolevskij, A.I., *Perevodnaja literatura Moskovskoj Rusi XIV–XVII vv. Bibliografičeskie materialy* (St. Petersburg: Tipografija Imperatorskoj Akademii nauk, 1903).

Taube, M., "On Two Related Slavic Translations of the Song of Songs," *Slavica Hierosolymitana* 7 (1985): 203–10.

Taube, M. and H. Olmsted, "Povest' o Esfiri: The Ostroh Bible and Maksim Grek's Translation of the Book of Esther," *Harvard Ukrainian Studies* 11 (1987): 100–17.

Temčin, S.J., "Scharija i Skorina: ob istočnikach Vilenskogo Vetchozavetnogo svoda (F 19–262)," *Senoji Lietuvos Literatūra* 21 (2006): 289–316.

Temčin, S.J., "Kirilličeskij rukopisnyj učebnik drevneevrejskogo jazyka (XVI v.) i Vilenskij vetchozavetnyj svod," *Knygotyra* 57 (2011): 86–99.

Thomson, F.J., "Made in Russia: A Survey of the Translations Allegedly Made in Kievan Russia," in *Millennium Russiae Christianae: Tausend Jahre christliches Russland, 988–1988: Vorträge des Symposiums anlässlich der Tausendjahrfeier der Christianisierung Russlands in Münster vom 5. bis 9. Juni 1988* (ed. G. Birkfellner; Schriften des Komitees der Bundesrepublik Deutschland zur Förderung der Slawischen Studien 16; Cologne: Böhlau, 1993), 295–354.

Thomson, F.J., "The Slavonic Translation of the Old Testament," in *The Interpretation of the Bible: The International Symposium in Slovenia* (ed. J. Krašovec; JSOTSup 189; Sheffield: Sheffield Academic Press, 1998), 605–920.

Thomson, F.J., *A Brief Survey of the History of the Church Slavonic Bible from its Cyrillomethodian Origins until its Final Form in the Elizabethan Bible of 1751* (Slavica Gandensia 33.2; Ghent: Department of Slavonic and Eastern European Studies of Ghent University, 2006).

Treat, J.C., "Aquila, Field and the Song of Songs," in *Origen's Hexapla and Fragments: Papers Presented at the Rich Seminar on the Hexapla, Oxford Centre for Hebrew and Jewish Studies, 25th–3rd August 1994* (ed. A. Salvesen; TSAJ 58; Tübingen: Mohr, 1998), 135–76.

Vajs, J., *Liber Ecclesiastis* (Veglae: Academia palaeoslavica veglensis, 1905).

Vajs, J., *Liber Ruth* (Veglae: Academia palaeoslavica veglensis, 1905).

Vajs, J., *Nejstarší Breviář hrvatsko-hlaholský (Prvý Breviář Vrbnický)* (Prague: Nákl. Král. České Společnosti Náuk, 1910).

Vajs, J., *Kniha Rut v překladě staroslovanském* (Prague: "Politiky," 1926).

Veder, W., "Esther's Glagolitic Ancestry," *Ricerche Slavistiche* 8.54 (2010): 213–23.

Verkholantsev, J., "A Fifteenth-Century Ruthenian Translation of the Song of Songs from Czech," *Slavia* 72 (2003): 195–226.

Wątróbska, H., *The Izbornik of the XIIIth Century (Cod. Leningrad, GPB, Q.p.I.18): Text in Transcription* (Polata knigopisnaja 19–20; Zug: Interdocumentation Company, 1987).

Weiher, E., S.O. Šmidt, and A.I. Škurko (eds.), *Die grossen Lesemenäen des Metropoliten Makarij: Uspenskij spisok*, Vol. 1: *1.–8. Mai* (Monumenta linguae slavicae dialecti veteris LI; Freiburg i. Br.: Weiher Verlag, 2007).

Yi, Y.Y., "Translation Technique of the Greek Ecclesiastes" (PhD diss., The Southern Baptist Theological Seminary, 2005).

Ziegler, J. (ed.), *Ieremias, Baruch, Threni, Epistula Ieremiae* (2nd ed.; Septuaginta Vetus Testamentum Graecum 15; Göttingen: Vandenhoeck & Ruprecht, 1976).

Ziegler, J., "Die Wiedergabe der nota accusativi 'et, 'aet mit σύν," *ZAW* 100 (1988): 222–33.

Alessandro Maria Bruni

13–17.2.8 Arabic Translations

13–17.2.8.1 Ruth

The history of the Arabic book of Ruth has been mapped out more carefully than many other Arabic Bible translations. It is not represented by a large number of manuscripts and appears to have been translated into Arabic at a relatively late stage; the earliest extant manuscripts so far are dated to the thirteenth century.

The location of Ruth in the biblical corpus varies. It usually follows Judges or the books of Kings but is at times excluded from larger biblical collections.[1] A study confined to the Arabic version of Ruth as printed in the Polyglots was supplied

---

[1] Samir, "Old Testament."

by Rödiger (1829).² Graf aimed to record all extant manuscripts containing Ruth, though the list he presents is incomplete and partly erroneous.³

According to Samir,⁴ at least four different versions of Ruth circulated among the Copts prior to the nineteenth century (→ 13–17.2.2.3.1). The first appears to be of Syriac provenance (→ 13–17.1.4.1; → 13–17.2.4.1). Its earliest representative is attested in Vatican, BAV, Ar. 449 (folios 57ʳ–60ᵛ) composed in Egypt in 1335. The second version, he states, is likely translated from LXX (→ 13–17.1.1.1), perhaps via the Coptic Bible (→ 13–17.2.2). The earliest witness of this version is found in Paris BNF Ar. 23 (folios 132ʳ–134ʳ) made in Egypt in the fourteenth century. What Samir considered a third version, translated from the Peshitta, has its earliest witness in Vatican, BAV, Ar. 468 (folios 183ʳ–185ᵛ) dated 1578/1579. The manuscript served as the main basis for the *Biblia Sacra Arabica of the Congregation di Propaganda Fide (1671–1673). This work was copied in a number of manuscripts dated to the eighteenth and nineteenth centuries.⁵ With the exception of manuscripts Wādī Naṭrūn, Monastery of Anba Bishoy, Bibl. 2 (dated 1791); London, BL, India Office, Islamic 1280 (folios 281ᵛ–285ᵛ); and Paris, BNF, Ar. 2 (folios 381ʳ–383ᵛ), most of these manuscripts are now in the library of the Coptic Orthodox Patriarchate: Bibl. 31 (folios 193ᵛ–196ʳ, dated 1772); Bibl. 35 (folios 21ʳ–23ᵛ, dated 1779); Bibl. 41 (folios 189ᵛ–193ʳ); Bibl. 42 (folios 50ᵛ–53ᵛ); Bibl. 43 (folios 52ᵛ–55ᵛ, dated 1786), and Bibl. 48 (folios 210ᵛ–213ᵛ).⁶

However, Bengtsson argues for a Syriac origin of all the above manuscripts and claims that they represent a single version.⁷ He adds to the list of related copies manuscripts Cambridge, University Library, Add. 3044 (folios 188ᵛ–191ᵛ), dated 1355; and Coptic Orthodox Patriarchate, Bibl. 32 (folios 128ʳ–129ʳ) dated 1585. Though idiosyncratic in nature, these five manuscripts all exhibit the clear influence of LXX (→ 13–17.1.1.1) and contain readings unique to these manuscripts alone. A critical edition of the five manuscripts is included in his dissertation.⁸

Bengtsson discovered that the two Peshitta-based manuscripts (→ 13–17.1.4.1), i.e., manuscript St Peterburg, Institute of Oriental Manuscripts, D226 (folios 214ᵛ–216ʳ) dated 1235–1238 and manuscript Beirut, Bibliothèque Orientale, 419 (pp. 283–86) dated 1690 represent a second version of Ruth that differs from the previous tradition. The latter manuscript is substantially influenced by the *Biblia Sacra Arabica, the Vulgate (→ 13–17.1.7), and LXX (→ 13–17.1.1.1).⁹ Both translations appear to represent the old Peshitta text (s⁷ᵃ¹) with only minor influence the from later West and East Syriac recensions.¹⁰

The last version of Ruth is represented in al-Ṭūkhī's edition (1752).¹¹ Copies from this edition are attested in manuscripts Coptic Orthodox Patriarchate, Bibl. 36 (folios 50ᵛ–53ᵛ) dated to the nineteenth century and Coptic Orthodox Patriarchate, Bibl. 41 dated 1872. The relationship between this translation and the above-mentioned manuscripts is uncertain.¹²

---

² Rödiger, *De Origine et Indole Arabicae Librorum V.T. Historicorum*.

³ Graf, *GCAL 1, 110. Contrary to the information given by Graf, neither manuscript Paris, BNF, Ar. 1, used in the Paris Polyglot (G.M. Le Jay, *Biblia* [Paris: Antoine Vitré, 1629–1645]), the seventeenth-century manuscript Oxford, Bodl., 270, nor Oxford, Bodl., Hunt, 260 (Nicoll., Chr. Ar. 2 and 3) contain Ruth. At least two of the manuscripts enumerated among copies of the *Biblia Sacra Arabica are in fact copies of Ṭūkhī's edition (Al-Ṭūkhī, *Biblia Sacra in Lingua Arabica*). A number of additional manuscripts are attested; see Bengtsson, *Two Arabic Versions*, 32–36 and Samir, "Old Testament."

⁴ Samir, "Old Testament."

⁵ See Samir's article, "Old Testament."

⁶ Cf. Graf, *GCAL 1, 110; Bengtsson, *Two Arabic Versions*, 35–36.

⁷ Bengtsson, *Two Arabic Versions*. For a discussion of Bengtsson's work, see the review by M. Polliack in *VT* 48 (1998): 433–35.

⁸ Bengtsson, *Two Arabic Versions*, 12–13, 32–41, 59–84, 171–83, 197–204. Manuscript Sharfeh, Ar. 1/2.7, dated to the sixteenth century, is reported by Bengtsson as not available.

⁹ *Two Arabic Versions*, pp. 12–13, 32–59, 185–95.

¹⁰ Bengtsson, *Translation Techniques*, 15.

¹¹ Al-Ṭūkhī, *Biblia Sacra in Lingua Arabica*.

¹² Samir, "Old Testament"; Bengtsson, *Two Arabic Versions*, 36 n. 5.

Translation Character and Technique

In an additional work, Bengtsson treats the translation techniques of the two Peshiṭta-based translations (→ 13–17.1.4.1) he previously identified.[13] He states that the version attested in the five manuscripts mentioned above (designated by Bengtsson as Arab I) represent a free translation whereas the second group, contained in the two St. Petersburg and Beirut manuscripts (designated by Bengtsson as Arab III), is highly literal.[14]

The difference in translation technique is seen immediately. If the syntactic preferences of source and target language are at odds, the translation of Arab I adheres to the latter whereas Arab III to a great degree aims at imitating the structure of the source text. Compare the word order in Ruth 1:10, where the Peshiṭta reads "but with you we will go" (ܐܠܐ ܥܡܟܝ ܢܐܙܠ). Here, Arab III preserves the word order "but with you we will go" (بل معك ننطلق) while in Arab I the verb is placed in initial position as expected in Classical Arabic when no topicalization is intended: "but we will go with you" (ولكن ننطلق معك).

Bengtsson further demonstrates that various kinds of additions appear in Arab I whereas such deviations from the *Vorlage* are rare in Arab III. The technique of textual expansions may be resorted to in Arab I as a means of clarifying a rendering in the Syriac. For instance, in Ruth 1:1, the Syriac clause "and a man went from Bethlehem, Judah" (ܘܐܙܠ ܓܒܪܐ ܡܢ ܒܝܬ ܠܚܡ ܕܝܗܘܕܐ) is rendered faithfully in Arab III (وانطلق رجل من بيت لحم يهوذا) but as "and a man went out of Bethlehem, a village of Judah" (خرج رجل من بيت لحام قرية يهودا) in Arab I. Another kind of expansion attested in Arab I alone is the employment of "alternate renderings" (or "Parallelism"). This is a common feature of many Arabic Bible translations (→ 2.5.8) and designates the technique of reflecting one unit in the source text by two or more units in the target text. For example, in Ruth 1:8 the Syriac "and may the Lord have mercy upon you" (ܘܡܪܝܐ ܢܥܒܕ ܥܡܟܝܢ ܛܝܒܘܬܐ) is in Arab I rendered "and may the Lord have mercy upon you and be gracious to you" (والرب يرحمكما وينعم عليكما). Similarly, in Ruth 4:14 "and you shall call upon his name in Israel" (ܘܢܬܩܪܐ ܫܡܗ ܒܐܝܣܪܐܝܠ) is in Arab I rendered "that his name should be called upon and be mentioned among the Israelites" (يدعي اسمه ويذكر بين بني اسرايل).

Another salient feature of Arab I is the omission of a textual unit as a means to avoid repetition or what is perceived as pleonastic information. Thus, in Ruth 1:19 the Syriac reading "Bethlehem of Judah" (ܠܒܝܬ ܠܚܡ ܕܝܗܘܕܐ) is rendered in Arab I only "Bethlehem" (بيت لحام) since the geographical identification of Bethlehem was mapped out already in Ruth 1:1. One of many other examples can be found in Ruth 2:11 where the Syriac "your mother and your father" (ܐܡܟܝ ܘܐܒܘܟܝ) is abbreviated by Arab I to "your parents" (والديك). The latter example is related to the frequent replacement of a word or part of an expression as a way to simplify or clarify the text. Thus, in Ruth 3:13 the Syriac "as the Lord lives" (ܚܝ ܗܘ ܡܪܝܐ) is rendered as "I swear by the truth of the Lord" (حلفت بحق الرب) and in Ruth 1:20 "the Almighty" (ܐܠܫܕܝ) is rendered as "God of Promises" (الاه المواعيد).

13–17.2.8.2 Qohelet

13–17.2.8.2.1 A Translation from the Greek

For Qohelet, an Arabic version based on LXX (→ 13–17.1.1.3) is attested. Details on emergence and character are unknown. It is preserved in manuscripts Paris, BNF, Ar. 1 (folios 406ᵛ–409ᵛ; on the basis of this manuscript this version was included in the Paris and London Polyglots[15]); Tübingen, Universitätsbibliothek, Ar. 194 (folios 28ʳ–36ᵛ, dated 1566); Vatican, BAV, Ar. 468 (folios 479ᵛ–486ʳ); Borg. Syr. (folios 30ʳ–39ʳ, in Karshūnī, dated 1581); St. Petersburg, Institute of Oriental Manuscripts, D 226

---

[13] Bengtsson, *Translation Techniques*. See the reviews by W. Heinrich in *JAOS* 128 (2008): 565–67, and A. Shivtiel in *British Journal of Middle Eastern Studies* 35 (2008): 292–93.

[14] Bengtsson selected the markers Ar. I and Ar. III on the misleading assumption that the Historical Books were reproduced as comparatively cohesive units. Thus, his division of manuscripts follows the work of B. Knutsson, *Studies in the Text and Language of Three Syriac-Arabic Versions of the Book of Judicum with Special Reference to the Middle Arabic Elements: Introduction-Linguistic Notes-Texts* (Leiden: Brill, 1974).

[15] Le Jay, *Biblia*; Walton, *Polyglotta*.

(dated 1236–1238, Vol. 2, folios 24ᵛ–29ʳ); as well as Coptic Orthodox Patriarchate, Bibl. 34 (folios 403ᵛ–413ʳ); and Bibl. 83 (72ᵛ–85ᵛ).

13–17.2.8.2.2 Al-Ḥārith ibn Sinān's Translation from the Syriac

A translation of the book of Qohelet by the Melkite al-Ḥārith ibn Sinān (→ 2.5.8) is mentioned in Shams al-Riyāsa Abū al-Barakāt's (Copt, d. 1324) encyclopaedia.[16] He reports that al-Ḥārith translated all four sapiential books of Solomon: Proverbs (→ 12.4.8), Qohelet, Wisdom of Solomon (→ 11.15.10), and Canticles (→ 13–17.2.8.3.2). Indeed, this is well attested in the manuscripts. The four books are usually transmitted as a unit, being the medial section of what is called *bet mawthbē*, "the books of sessions" in the Syriac tradition, preceded by a preface in which al-Ḥārith deals with poetic traditions in Hebrew, Greek, and Syriac.[17] It appears that the translation was prepared on the basis of a Syriac *Vorlage* (→ 13–17.1.4.3; → 13–17.2.4.3). Several Arabic titles of the book can be found in the manuscripts, *al-jāmiʿ* "the gatherer," *qūhalath* "Qohelet" (< Syr. ܩܘܗܠܬ) or *hibāʾ al-ahabiyya* "vanity of vanities," based on the main motive of the book. Al-Ḥārith's version of Qohelet is found in the following manuscripts: Florence, BML, Or. 78 (formerly 18, folios 84ᵛ–105ᵛ); Vatican, BAV, Ar. 448 (folios 19ʳ–20ʳ); Paris, BNF, Ar. 50 (folios 91ʳ–100ᵛ) and Ar. 153 (folios 423ʳ–431ᵛ); London, BL, Or. 1326 (folios 200ʳ–203ᵛ); St. Petersburg, Russian National Library, Dorn 3 (dated 1205, folios 46ᵛ–64ᵛ); as well as Coptic Orthodox Patriarchate, Bibl. 75 (folios 196ʳ–210ᵛ, dated 1691), Bibl. 89 (folios 67ᵛ–72ʳ); Theol. 286 (folios 249ᵛ–282ᵛ, dated 1746); and Beirut, Bibliothèque Orientale, 419 (pp. 497–508, dated 1690).

13–17.2.8.2.3 Copies Based on the *Biblia Sacra Arabica* (1671–1673)

The book of Qohelet is also attested in not a few manuscript copies of the *Biblia Sacra Arabica* (→ 1.4.11): Paris, BNF, Ar. 2 (folios 82ᵛ–86ᵛ); London, BL, Or. 8745 (folios 190ᵛ–193ᵛ); Coptic Orthodox Patriarchate, Bibl. 45 (folios 121ʳ–126ʳ, dated 1759); Bibl. 49 (folios 87ᵛ–94ʳ, dated 1789); Bibl. 53 (folios 97ʳ–200ʳ); Bibl. 54 (folios 80ʳ–93ʳ, dated 1785); Bibl. 74 (folios 115ʳ–153ᵛ); Bibl. 76 (folios 130ᵛ–139ᵛ); Bibl. 78 (folios 24ᵛ–32ᵛ, dated 1871); Jerusalem, St. Anna, Ar. 1 (folios 79ʳ–88ʳ); and Birmingham, Mingana, Syr. 484 (folios 96ʳ–99ʳ, in Karshūnī).[18]

13–17.2.8.3 Canticles

Similar to Qohelet, the book of Canticles is extant in three versions.

13–17.2.8.3.1 A Translation from the Greek

This translation from the Greek (→ 13–17.1.1.2) was printed in the Paris and London Polyglots,[19] based on manuscript Paris, BNF, Ar. 1 (folios 410ᵛ–411ᵛ). Further copies are manuscripts Tübingen, Universitätsbibliothek, Ar. 194 (folios 36ᵛ–41ᵛ, dated 1566); Vatican, BAV, Ar. 468 (folios 486ᵛ–489ᵛ); and Borg. Syr. (folios 39ʳ–44ᵛ, in Karshūnī, dated 1581); St. Petersburg, Institute of Oriental Manuscripts, D 226 (dated 1236–1238, vol. 2, folios 29ᵛ–31ᵛ); and Coptic Orthodox Patriarchate, Bibl. 34 (folios 413ᵛ–417ᵛ) and Bibl. 83 (folios 86ʳ–92ᵛ).

13–17.2.8.3.2 Al-Ḥārith ibn Sinān's Translation from the Syriac

On al-Ḥārith's translation from the Syriac (→ 13–17.1.4.2; → 11.4.4), see above → 13–17.2.8.2.2. In the manuscripts, the book bears the titles *Nashīd al-anshād* "the Song of Songs," *Tartīl al-tarātīl* "the Chant of Chants," or *tasbīḥ al-tasābīḥ* "the Hymn of Hymns" (cf. Syr. ܬܫܒܚܬ ܬܫܒܚܬܐ "the Chant of Chants"). His version is found in manuscripts Florence, BML, Or. 78 (formerly 18, folios 106ᵛ–114ᵛ); Vatican, BAV, Ar. 448 (folios 21ʳ–28ʳ); Paris, BNF, Ar. 50 (folios 100ᵛ–105ᵛ), and Ar. 153 (folios 432ʳ–435ᵛ); London, BL, Or. 1326 (folios 204ʳ–205ʳ); Coptic Orthodox Patriarchate, Bibl. 89 (folios 72ᵛ–74ʳ) and Theol. 23 (folios 1ʳ–3ʳ); Beirut, Bibliothèque Orien-

---

[16] Khalil, *Miṣbāḥ al-ẓulma*, 236.
[17] See Albert, "Bet Mawtbe." For details on the preface, cf. Sadan, "In the Eyes of the Christian Writer."
[18] See Vollandt, "Che portono al ritorno."
[19] Le Jay, *Biblia*; Walton, *Polyglotta*.

tale, 419 (pp. 497–508, dated 1690); and possibly also Sbath 2570 (now lost).

13–17.2.8.3.3 Copies based on the *Biblia Sacra Arabica* (1671–1673)

As with the above books, there are a great many manuscript copies of the *Biblia Sacra Arabica* (1671–1673; → 1.4.11), e.g.: Paris, BNF, Ar. 2 (folios 86^v–88^r); Coptic Orthodox Patriarchate, Bibl. 45 (folios 126^v–128^r, dated 1759); Bibl. 49 (folios 94^v–97^v, dated 1789); Bibl. 53 (folios 97^r–200^r); Bibl. 54 (folios 93^r–99^v, dated 1785); Bibl. 74 (folios 115^r–153^v); Bibl. 76 (folios 139^v–143^v); and Bibl. 78 (folios 32^v–36^r, dated 1871); and Birmingham, Mingana, Syr. 484 (folios 99^r–110^v, in Karshūnī).

13–17.2.8.4 Lamentations

No thorough study on the Arabic book of Lamentations has been accomplished to date. The book does not appear to have been translated or copied extensively. It is attested in a meager number of manuscripts, commonly located with Baruch (→ II.2.1.10) and the Letter of Jeremiah (→ II.2.4.10). While awaiting a more exhaustive survey, we find Lamentations in manuscripts Paris, BNF, Ar. 1 (folios 76^r–79^r) dated 1584/1585; Manchester, John Rylands Library, Copt. 418 (folios 215^v–232^r, dated 1796); the bilingual Coptic-Arabic manuscript London, BL, Or. 1319 (folios 194^r–204^r, dated 1806); the bilingual Coptic-Arabic manuscript Coptic Orthodox Patriarchate, Bibl. 13 (folios 98^r–120^r, dated 1813); Bibl. 55 (folios 80^v–93^r, including the Prayer of Jeremiah), dated to the nineteenth century; and Sinai, Ar. 9 (folios 239^r–247^r, dated to the thirteenth century).

13–17.2.8.5 Esther

The book of Esther was binding in all oriental churches. An exception are those communities that adhered to the teachings of Theodore of Mopsuestia (mostly East Syriac), who refused to include it in the canon.[20] Some manuscripts of the Peshitta (→ 13–17.1.4.5), most notably the so-called Masoretic codices, dispense with the book.[21] Further, it is absent from the list of biblical books in the Arabic version of the Apostolic Canons, as well as in that of the East Syriac writers Abū al-Faraj b. al-Ṭayyib and Ishodad of Merv (mid-ninth century C.E.).[22] The disputed status of the book of Esther is reflected in the comparatively small number of extant manuscripts. No study on this version is available to date. Three different secondary Arabic translations can be identified in the manuscripts.

The first version is based on the Syriac (→ 13–17.1.4.5; → 13–17.2.4.5).[23] The following manuscripts can be allocated to this translation: Vatican, BAV, Ar. 468 (folios 375^r–381^r); London, BL, Or. 1326 (folios 63^v–67^v); Paris, BNF, Ar.1 (folios 219^r–221^v), Ar. 23 (folios 135^v–137^r), and Ar. 153 (folios 314^r–318^r); St. Petersburg, Institute of Oriental Manuscripts, D 226 (dated 1236–1238, vol. 2, folios 222^v–226^v); Coptic Orthodox Patriarchate, Bibl. 34 (folios 33^v–43^r); Bibl. 54 (folios 70^v–81^v); and Bibl. 185 (folios 36^r–39^r, copied 1788).

A somewhat freer translation from the Syriac (→ 13–17.1.4.5; → 13–17.2.4.5) is found in manuscripts Vatican, BAV, Ar. 448 (folios 159^r–167^v) and Coptic Orthodox Patriarchate, Bibl. 75 (folios 55^v–61^v, dated 1691).

Another group of manuscripts display the book of Esther in the version of the *Biblia Sacra Arabica* (1671–1673) of the Congregatio de Propaganda Fide, including, for instance, manuscripts Paris, BNF, Ar. 2 (folios 25^r–32^r); London, BL, Or. 8745 (folios 142^v–147^r); London India Office, Islamic 1280 (folios 570^r–586^v); Beirut, Bibliothèque Orientale, 419 (pp. 312–20); Coptic Orthodox Patriarchate, Bibl. 33 (folios 223^v–231^r); Bibl. 35 (folios 210^r–218^v); Bibl. 42 (folios 277^v–289^v), Bibl. 44 (folios 38^r–

---

[20] Cf. Dennefeld, *Der alttestamentliche Kanon*, 51–52.

[21] For details, see J.-C. Haelewyck, "Le canon de l' Ancien Testament dans la tradition syriaque (manuscrits bibliques, listes canoniques, auteurs)," in *L'ancien Testament en syriaque* (eds. F. Briquel Chatonnet and P. Le Moigne; Études syriaques 5; Paris: Geuthner, 2008), 141–71.

[22] Cf. Périer and Périer, "*127 canons des Apôtres,*" 690–91. On Abū al-Faraj b. al-Ṭayyib, see W. Hoenerbach and O. Spies (eds.), *Ibn at-Taiyib: Fiqh an-Nasrânîya: Das Recht der Christenheit* (4 vols; CSCO 161–162, 167–168; Louvain: L. Durbecq, 1956–1957), 2.2.7.

[23] See Graf, *GCAL* 1, 113.

46ᵛ); Bibl. 47 (folios 48ᵛ–67ʳ); Bibl. 49 (folios 33ʳ–43ᵛ); Jerusalem, St. Anna, Ar. 1 (folios 8ᵛ–23ᵛ); and Jerusalem Ar. 87 (pp. 30–50).

Al-Ṭūkhī, R., *Biblia Sacra in Lingua Arabica/Al-ʿahd al-qadīm wa-l-ḥadith* (Rome: apud Angelo Rutili, 1752).

Albert, M., "Les 'Bet Mawtbe' nestoriens," in *La formation des canons scripturaires* (ed. M. Tardieu; Paris: Cerf, 1993), 155–68.

Bengtsson, P.Å., *Two Arabic Versions of the Book of Ruth: Text Edition and Language Studies* (Studia Orientalia Lundensia 6; Lund: Lund University Press, 1995).

Bengtsson, P.Å., *Translation Techniques in Two Syro-Arabic Versions of Ruth* (Studia Orientalia Lundensia Nova Series 3; Lund: Almqvist & Wiksell International, 2003).

Dennefeld, L., *Der alttestamentliche Kanon der Antiochenischen Schule* (Freiburg i.B.: Herder, 1909).

Graf, *GCAL* 1.

Khalil, S. (ed.), *Abū al-Barakāt ibn al-Asʿad ibn Kubr: Miṣbāḥ al-ẓulma fī iḍāḥ al-khidma* (Cairo: Al-Ṭabʿa al-tijārīya al-ḥadītha, 1971) [Arab.].

Périer, J. and A. Périer (eds.), *Les "127 canons des Apôtres": Texte arabe en partie inédit, publié et traduit en français d' après les manuscrits de Paris, de Rome et de Londres* (PO 8.4; Turnhout: Brepols, 1912).

Rödiger, A., *De Origine et Indole Arabicae Librorum V.T. Historicorum: Interpretationis* (Halle: Kümmel, 1829).

Sadan, J., "In the Eyes of the Christian Writer al-Ḥāriṯ Ibn Sinān: Poetics and Eloquence as a Platform of Inter-Cultural Contacts and Contrasts," *Arabica* 56 (2009): 1–26.

Samir, K., "Old Testament, Arabic Versions of the," in *The Coptic Encyclopedia* (8 vols.; ed. A.Z. Atiya; New York: Macmillan, 1991), 6:1827–36.

Vollandt, R., "Che portono al ritorno quì una Bibbia Arabica integra: A History of the *Biblia Sacra Arabica* (1671–73)," in *Graeco-Latina et orientalia: Studia in honorem Angeli Urbani heptagenarii* (eds. J.P. Monferrer Sala and S.K. Samir; Beirut: CEDRAC, 2013), 401–18.

Ronny Vollandt
Miriam Lindgren Hjälm

13–17.3 Medieval Text of MT

13–17.3.1 Original Form and Editions[1]

Only two of the four manuscripts attributed to Ben Asher contain all or part of the five books that make up the Megilloth. The Leningrad Codex B19a (L) presents all the books; and the preserved section of the Aleppo Codex (A) only contains Ruth and Cant 1:1–3:11.

Diplomatic Editions: The five Megilloth have been published in the new edition of L, *BHQ (R. Althann [et al.], in *General Introduction and Megilloth*).

Even though A does not contain all the Megilloth, their reconstructed text is included in *Miqra'ot Gedolot "Haketer"* (Cohen, *The Five Scrolls*) based on the reconstruction by Penkower, *New Evidence*.

13–17.3.2 Text-Critical Character

The five Megilloth are short but contain numerous Masoretic notes and present important textual phenomena.

13–17.3.2.1 *Qere-Ketiv*[2]

Fifty-four cases of *Qere-Ketiv* are marked in L: 8 in Ruth, 4 in Canticles, 10 in Qoheleth, 21 in Lamentations, and 11 in Esther. Attention is drawn to the high number of cases, equaling those in the Pentateuch, despite their smaller size. The *Qere* is indicated by the abbreviated form, 'ק, except in Cant 2:13 where the complete form, קרי, is used. Moreover, in twenty-six cases, there is a sign resembling a final *nun* alongside the indication of *Qere*: 5 in Ruth, 1 in Canticles, 4 in Qoheleth, 15 in Lamentations, and 1 in Esther.[3]

This number is also quite high if one considers that throughout L there are sixty-nine cases of the sign resembling a final *nun*. Normally, the whole word is given in the *Qere*, but sometimes it only indicates the letter or letters that are affected (e.g. the MasP of שִׂמְלֹתֶךָ in Ruth 3:3: 'תיך ק; the MasP of הַיְּהוּדִיִּים in Esth 9:15: 'דים ק; etc.). Finally, five cases also have a MasM note listing the cases that share the same *Qere* reading.

In A, in the passages in common with L, there are nine cases of *Qere-Ketiv* (seven in Ruth and two in the three preserved chapters of Canticles), three less than in L. This phenomenon is marked mostly by the use of the shorter form, 'ק, except in Ruth 4:5 and Cant 2:13 where the full form, קרי, is used. The whole word is given in the *Qere* in all the cases. In Cant 1:17, there is also a MasM note that lists the cases that share the same *Qere* reading.

Qere we la Ketiv

A and L indicate in different ways the word that is not written in the text but should be read: אלי in Ruth 3:5 and 3:17.

In A, it is indicated in the biblical text with a *circellus* and an extra blank space. In A, in the MasP to Ruth 3:5, it is indicated as a simple *Qere*, קרי אלי, and in 3:17 with the formula קרי ולא כתב אלי.

In L, it is indicated in Ruth 3:5 with the vowels, accent, and the *circellus* without an extra blank space; in 3:17 it appears with the vowels and accent, but without a *circellus* or extra blank space. In the MasP note, the formula קרי ולא כת' אלי is used. There is also a MasM note for Ruth 3:5 that lists the total number of eleven cases and gives their *simanim*: Judg 20:13; 2 Sam 8:3; 16:23; 18:20; 2 Kgs 19:31; 19:37; Jer 31:38; 50:29; Ezek 9:11; Ruth 3:5; 3:17. In this manuscript, in the MasM note to Jer 50:29, just ten cases are listed (Martín Contreras 2012; → 1.5.4.2 and → 3–5.3.2.5).

Ketiv we la Qere

In Ruth 3:12, there is a case of the opposite phenomenon: אִם is written in the text but should not be read. In the text of A and L, the word is unvo-

---

[1] Cf. "medieval Masoretic Text," sections → 1.5.2–1.5.3, for more detailed information.

[2] The calculation of the *Qere-Ketiv* cases refers only to those indicated explicitly as such and not to cases of *yatir*.

[3] Cf. I. Himbaza, "Le *nûn* marginal et la petite massore," *Textus* 20 (2000): 173–91.

calized. In A, the MasP note indicates כת׳ ולא קרי and in L כת׳ ולא ק׳ together with the symbol resembling a final *nun*. In L, there is also a MasM note that lists the following passages: 2 Sam 15:21; 2 Kgs 5:18; Jer 38:16; 39:12; 51:3; Ezek 48:16. This list only gives six of the eight cases traditionally denoted as *Ketiv we la Qere* (→ 1.5.4.2).

13–17.3.2.2 *Sebirin*

In L, the MasP note to עַמִּי in Lam 3:14 reads: ג׳ סבר׳ עמים וקר׳ עמי, "three times עמים [the plural] is suggested but עמי [the singular] is read." The term *sebir* is intended to support the biblical text, as is apparent in this case, in which the written word is confirmed by the term וקר׳ (→ 1.5.4.3).

13–17.3.2.3 *Hillûfîm: Madinha'e-Ma'arbae*

In the Masorah of L, there are seven references to variants between Eastern and Western Masoretes: three in the MasP notes (Ruth 3:10; 4:17; Esth 8:7) and four cases in the MasM notes (Songs 5:2; Qoh 3:9; 8:2; Lam 5:21). In these four cases there is no *circellus* in the biblical text that indicates which word or expression is affected by the change, but the word is given in the MasM note (e.g., MasM to Qoh 3:9: מה יתרון העושה למערב׳ חס׳ ולמדנ׳ שלמ׳). The differences are related to the spelling of the words or to their full or defective writing, except in Lam 5:21 in which a whole word is changed (MasM: למערב׳ השיבנו יהוה כת׳ למדנח׳ אדני כת׳).

Except for Ruth 4:17 and Cant 5:2, the cases are included in the list of these variants in one of the appendices of the manuscript (466ʳ–468ᵛ).

13–17.3.3 Relevance for Exegesis

The case of הָבִי in Ruth 3:15 illustrates the benefits of using the Masorah in the textual criticism of the Hebrew Bible.[4] This word is usually interpreted as the 2nd per. fem. sg. impv. *Qal* of the root יהב, "give" but the information found in the MasP note in A questions this interpretation,[5] ל חס׳ לשון נקבה, "unique defective and in feminine form." The Masorah of other Masoretic manuscripts and some Masoretic works contain additional information that aids our understanding of this note. The MasP of the manuscript M1 of Complutense University (M1) to this word says: ח׳ חס׳ א׳, "eight [times written] lacking an *'alep*," implying that this word does not derive from the root יהב, but בוא. According to the MasM of M1 to Jer 19:15 and one list of Ginsburg's Masoretic compilation, the root בוא is written without the *'alep* in nine passages:[6] 1 Sam 25:8; 2 Sam 5:2; 1 Kgs 12:12; 21:21; 21:29; Jer 19:15; 39:16; Mic 1:15; Ruth 3:15. Both lists include the case of Ruth, which thus needs to be parsed as the 2nd per. masc. sg. impv. *hiphil* of the root בוא. The second part of the note in A, "in feminine form," should be understood in this way. The masculine form that appears in the biblical context where one would expect to find a feminine form is problematic from a grammatical point of view. For this reason, the MasP of A indicates that this word is understood as being feminine. This tradition of interpreting the word as feminine is also attested in other Masoretic notes. Therefore, the Masoretes' intention in this note was to ensure the correct interpretation of a word, the anomalies of which (defective in one of the root letters and its masculine instead of feminine form) could prevent the correct interpretation.

**BHQ, part 18.*
Cohen, **Mikra'ot Gedolot "Haketer."*
Martín Contreras, E., "The Phenomenon *Qere we la' ketib* in the Main Biblical Codices: New Data," *VT* 62 (2012): 77–87.
Penkower, J.S., *New Evidence for the Pentateuch Text in the Aleppo Codex* (Ramat Gan: Bar-Ilan University Press, 1992) [Hebr.].

Elvira Martín Contreras

---

[4] For a detailed explanation of this case, cf. E. Martín Contreras, "Masoretic and Rabbinic Lights on the Word הבי, Ruth 3:15: יהב or בוא?," *VT* 59 (2009): 257–65.

[5] The MasP note in L pertains only to the accent.
[6] Ginsburg, *Massorah, vol. I, list 66, p. 166.

18

Daniel

∴

18.1 Textual History of Daniel

18.1.1 Introduction

The book of Daniel is notorious for its plethora of textual difficulties that, to a greater or lesser extent, have bearings on tracing its textual history. The text has come to us in two languages (i.e., Hebrew [Dan 1:1–2:4a; 8:1–12:13] and Aramaic [Dan 2:4b–7:8]) and scholars have naturally disputed the precedence of either an Aramaic or Hebrew original.[1] However, the oldest witnesses to the MT text from Qumran scrolls (→ 18.2.1) evidences the shift in language both at Dan 2:4 and Dan 8:1 and might point to the bilingual skill of its author.

Furthermore, two divergent traditions are known regarding the placement of the book in the canon (→ 1.1.2.1; → 1.1.2.2). The first tradition is represented by MT (→ 18.2.2), which has included Daniel among the Writings. The second stems from LXX, which has maintained the book among the Prophets, where it is placed after Ezekiel. Whereas the former arrangement would suggest some shared affinities of Daniel with sapiential books, the latter – which accords well with traditions from Qumran and the New Testament[2] – would affirm its prophetical quality.

The book of Daniel is evidenced in textual witnesses in both Hebrew and ancient translations. The first category is represented by the findings from Qumran that evidence Daniel with eight Hebrew scrolls (→ 18.2.1). Generally speaking, "the Qumran discoveries provide powerful evidence of the antiquity of the textual tradition of the MT."[3] The second group of witnesses is represented by the ancient versions and includes translations/revisions in Greek (→ 18.3.1; → 18.3.2; → 18.3.4; → 18.3.5), Latin (→ 18.3.6; → 18.4.1), Syriac (→ 18.3.3; → 18.4.8), and Arabic (→ 18.4.8). Similar to Ezra–Nehemiah, with whom it also shares the bilingual feature, Daniel lacks for the Hebrew section an Aramaic Targum. Excepting Old Greek, these versions witness to a text more or less comparable to MT.[4]

Given the fact that most of the prominent disparities over against MT are evidenced by the Old Greek in Daniel 4–6[5] and since the relationship between the Greek versions – Old Greek (LXX-Dan)

---

[1] Wesselius has observed rightly that each model that attempts to solve the problem of bilingualism "describes a possible history of the text (...)." Cf. J.W. Wesselius, "The Writing of Daniel," in *The Book of Daniel: Composition and Reception* (eds. J.J. Collins and P.W. Flint; VTSup 83/2; Leiden: Brill, 2001), 291–310 (292). The adherents to an Aramaic-original view represent the most numerous group. Among them, see Charles, *The Book of Daniel*, xix–xxvi; H.L. Ginsberg, *Studies in Daniel* (Texts and Studies of the Jewish Theological Seminary of America 14; New York: Jewish Theological Seminary, 1948), 41–61; L.F. Hartman and A.A. Di Lella, *The Book of Daniel: A New Translation with Introduction and Commentary* (AB 23; Garden City: Doubleday, 1978), 14–15. The priority of a Hebrew original text was argued by A.F. von Gall, *Die Einheitlichkeit des Buches Daniel* (Giessen: Ricker, 1895), 122; A.A. Bevan, *A Short Commentary on the Book of Daniel* (Cambridge: Cambridge University Press, 1892), 27.

[2] 4QFlor refers to Daniel using a citation formula specific to other prophetical books: "The Book of Daniel the Prophet" (4QFlor 1–2 ii 3), "The Book of Isaiah the Prophet" (4QFlor 1–2 i 15), "The Book of Ezeckiel the Prophet" (4QFlor 1–2 i 16). Similarly, Matt 24:15 reads, "So when you see standing in the holy place 'the abomination that causes desolation,' spoken of through the prophet Daniel (...)" NIV.

[3] Collins, *Daniel*, 3.

[4] It goes without saying that by this statement we also acknowledge that often the versions reflect superior readings, e.g. Vulgate (→ 18.3.6.4.1).

[5] LXX-Daniel 4–6 diverge from MT in many ways. Besides smaller deviations such as pluses (e.g., Dan 4:9[12]; 6:4[3]) and minuses (e.g., Dan 4:17[20]; 5:2; 6:11[10]), which occur repeatedly over against MT, the Old Greek also displays long minuses (e.g., Dan 4:3–6[6–9]; 4:32[35]; 5:13–16, 18–22; 6:16[15]–17[16]), long pluses (e.g., Dan 4:37[34]; 5:0 [the brief abstract of Daniel 5]), differences in layout (the epistolary introduction that precedes Daniel 4 of MT [Dan 3:31–33] is reflected in LXX at the end of the story, cf. Dan 4:34[37b,c]), doublets (e.g., Dan 6:13[12a]; 4:14[17a]), and overall disparity in length (i.e., Daniel 4 is estimated as one-quarter longer than MT whereas Daniel 5 reflects a shorter version of the MT). Note also the intriguing absence in LXX of Daniel's qualification according to which he purportedly owns "the Spirit of the Holy God" (Dan 4:5–6, 15; 5:11, 14).

and Theodotion (Th-Dan) – to MT has raised many questions, we will proceed to survey the relevant scholarship in light of these issues (see further 18.2.2.3).[6]

18.1.2 History of Research

The textual studies of the book of Daniel in the twentieth century that advanced its investigation were prompted by three important findings:

1. The discovery of the Dead Sea Scrolls, among them the fragments of Daniel (→ 18.2.1; → 18.2.3)[7]. Of the biblical manuscripts discovered at Qumran, eight copies have been attributed to Daniel.[8] The number of copies as well as the length of the book compared with the number of fragments of other (lengthier) biblical books, ranks Daniel after the Pentateuch, Psalms, and Isaiah, which evidences its popularity within the sectarian group.[9]

2. A further boost for the textual scrutiny of Danielic literature came by way of the groundbreaking study of Barthélemy on the Greek scroll of the Minor Prophets discovered in Naḥal Ḥever.[10] The impact of Barthélemy's monograph, *Devanciers*, on LXX research has been described by Tov as "a book which in many ways has revolutionized scholarship."[11] Barthélemy's theory postulates the existence of a *kaige* group during the textual transmission process, as the name of his work implies, which could be considered the predecessor of Aquila's revision.[12]

---

[6] Though a relatively short book, Daniel presents numerous problems. As intimated earlier, the Greek text of Daniel has been transmitted in two versions: Old Greek and Theodotion. Furthermore, in contrast to MT, both Greek texts agree with each other in including additional poems and stories known to us as the Prayer of Azariah and the Song of the Three Young Men, Bel and the Dragon, and Susanna. This becomes even more intriguing since Th-Dan, which reflects a text close to MT, is assessed as a literal Greek translation (Cf. Jeansonne, *The Old Greek Translation of Daniel 7–12*, 131). As might be expected, this raises the question – with far-reaching implications – whether these Additions are indeed original. Di Lella contends that "The translators of OG-Dan and Th-Dan were consciously at work on a canonical text. These Greek forms with the Additions served as canonical Scripture for the several Greek-speaking Jewish and Christian communities that received (or revised) them. Being Scripture, OG-Dan and Th-Dan deserve the same respect and consideration as the MT." Cf. Di Lella, "The Textual History of Septuagint-Daniel and Theodotion-Daniel," in *The Book of Daniel: Composition and Reception* (eds. J.J. Collins and P.W. Flint; VTSup 83.2; Leiden: Brill, 2001), 604. See also C.A. Moore, *Daniel, Esther and Jeremiah: A New Translation with Introduction and Commentary* (AB 44; Garden City, New York: Doubleday & Company, Inc., 1977), 134. In a footnote to this analysis, notwithstanding their agreement in including the Additions, Th-Dan and LXX-Dan depart from each other in the layout of their chapters. Papyrus LXX[967], for instance, differs from LXX[88] and Syro-Hexapla and Th MSS by placing chapters 7 and 8 before chapters 5 and 6. Further, Papyrus LXX[967] in contrast with the other witnesses situates Susanna after Bel and the Dragon.

[7] This view was stressed by A.S. van der Woude, preface to *The Book of Daniel in the Light of New Findings* (Bibliotheca Ephemeridum Theologicarum Lovaniensium CVI; Leuven: University Press, 1993).

[8] Two scrolls were discovered in Cave 1 (1QDan[a] and 1QDan[b]) and published by Barthélemy in the *editio princeps*: D. Barthélemy, "71. Daniel (premier exemplaire)," *DJD* I: 150; D. Barthélemy, "72. Daniel (second exemplaire)," *DJD* I: 151–52. The five copies from Cave 4 (4QDan[a–e]) were published by E. Ulrich, "Daniel," *DJD* XVI: 239–77. One additional copy written on papyrus was discovered in Cave 6 (6QpapDan) and was published by M. Baillet, "7. Daniel," *DJD* III.1: 114–16. All biblical texts, including those of Daniel, were collected by Ulrich, *BQS*, 755–75.

[9] Statistically, the Book of Daniel ranks the same number of copies with Minor Prophets (8) and is followed by Jeremiah and Ezekiel (6 copies each) and Joshua, Judges, Samuel, Kings, Job and Proverbs (4 copies each). Cf. E. Ulrich, "Daniel, Book of: Hebrew and Aramaic Text," *EDSS* 1:171; "The Text of Daniel in the Qumran Scroolls," in *The Book of Daniel: Composition and Reception* (eds. J.J. Collins and P.W. Flint; VTSup 83/2; Leiden: Brill, 2001), 573. According to Flint, there are seventeen scrolls discovered at Qumran that are altogether relevant for the study of the Book of Daniel. See, P.W. Flint, "The Daniel Tradition at Qumran," in *The Book of Daniel: Composition and Reception* (eds. J.J. Collins and P.W. Flint; VTSup 83.2; Leiden: Brill, 2001; Leiden: Brill, 2001), 329–367.

[10] The first publication of the Greek scroll was prepared by Barthélemy, *Devanciers*. Excerpts from his previous study were republished in Barthélemy, *Études*, 66–90. The scroll in its entirety was published by E. Tov with the collaboration of R.A. Kraft and contribution of P.J. Parsons, in *DJD* VIII.

[11] Foreword to *DJD* VIII: ix.

[12] Barthélemy begins his analysis (cf. *Devanciers*) by presenting Aquila as having been influenced by the rabbinical hermeneutical principles of Rabbi Akiba.

18.1.2 HISTORY OF RESEARCH

Expressed differently, the *kaige* group displays intermediary revising techniques that turn the group into a link between Old Greek and the acute literalism of Aquila's revision.[13] Using the peculiar word equivalence καί γε "and also" for גַּם "also," at least as a criterion, Barthélemy has determined that a few Greek witnesses – among them also Th-Dan – belong to the *kaige* revision (→ 1.3.1.2).[14]

3. The discovery of papyrus LXX[967] in Aphroditopolis, Egypt in 1931 further advanced the study of Daniel.[15] Papyrus LXX[967] (→ 18.3.1) contains sections from the books of Ezekiel, Daniel, and Esther.[16] Until 1931, critical assessment of OG-Dan was based on two manuscripts only, namely, the Hexaplaric witnesses LXX[88] (Codex Chisianus)[17] and the Syro-Hexapla (→ 18.4.4)[18]. With the finding of papyrus LXX[967], it was now possible to access a time (ca. 200 C.E.) that antedates Origen's *magnum opus*, the Hexapla.[19] As a result of this discovery, scholars were in a better position to understand the transmission history of OG-Dan and consequently their appreciation for it grew.

As a result of these circumstances, three directions of analysis have predominated the text-critical

---

[13] D. Barthélemy, "Redécouverte d' un chaînon manquant de l' histoire de la Septante," *RB* 60 (1953): 18–29.

[14] In addition to Th-Dan and the Greek scroll of the Minor Prophets discovered in Naḥal Ḥever, the other LXX books and sections assigned by Barthélemy to the *kaige* group are: Lamentations, Song of Songs, Ruth, the sections βγ [2 Sam 11: 2–1 Kgs 2:11] and γδ [1 Kgs 22–2 Kgs], the extant Theodotionic fragments of Job and Jeremiah, the book of Judges as attested in LXX-manuscripts *i r u a2* and *B e f s z*, the column attributed to Theodotion in Origen's *Hexapla* and the Quinta of Psalms. Cf. Barthélemy, *Devanciers*, 47.

[15] Several facts and figures about papyrus LXX[967] are worth noting. Papyrus LXX[967] contains fifty-nine manuscript folios (118 pages) that have been preserved in five different locations: twenty-nine folios are now located in the Chester Beatty Library in Dublin, twenty-one folios are found in the Princeton University Library, two folios are kept in Barcelona at Santa Maria de Montserrat Abbey, and the remainder can be found in Cologne at the Cologne University Library and Madrid at Fundación Pastor de Estudios Clásicos. Each page of the codex is numbered and the number of lines per page varies between forty and forty-six. Two scribal hands have been detected: one copied both Daniel and Esther while the other reproduced the text of Ezekiel. In all, it took forty-six years to publish the whole of papyrus LXX[967]. See further S. Kreuzer, "Papyrus 967," in Karrer–Kraus, *Septuaginta 2008*, 64–82.

[16] The *editiones principes* of LXX[967] for the Book of Daniel have been prepared by W. Hamm, *Daniel 1–2: Der Septuaginta-Text des Buches Daniel, Kap. 1–2, nach dem Kölner Teil des Papyrus 967* (Papyrologische Texte und Abhandlungen 10; Bonn: Rudolf Habelt, 1969); W. Hamm, *Daniel 3–4: Der Septuaginta-Text des Buches Daniel, Kap. 3–4, nach dem Kölner Teil des Papyrus 967* (Papyrologische Texte und Abhandlungen 21; Bonn: Rudolf Habelt, 1977); F.G. Kenyon, *Daniel 3,72–6,18: The Chester Beatty Biblical Papyri: Description and Texts of Twelve Manuscripts on Papyrus of the Greek Bible, Fasc. 7: Ezekiel, Daniel, Esther* (2 vols.; London: E. Walker, 1938), text (vol. 1) + plates (vol. 2); A. Geißen, *Daniel 5–12; Susanna, Bel et Draco; Esther: Der Septuaginta-Text des Buches Daniel, Kap. 5–12, zusammen mit Susanna, Bel et Draco, sowie Esther Kap. 1,1a–2,15 nach dem Kölner Teil des Papyrus 967* (Papyrologische Texte und Abhandlungen 5; Bonn: Rudolf Habelt, 1968); R. Roca-Puig, *Daniel: dos semifolis del còdex 967: papir de Barcelona, Inv. n°. 42 i 43* (Barcelona: Grafos, 1974); R. Roca-Puig, "Daniel: Dos Semifogli del Codex 967," *Aeg* 56 (1976): 3–18. The *editiones principes* of LXX[967] for the book of Ezekiel were prepared by A.C. Johnson, H.S. Gehman, and E.H. Kase, *The John H. Scheide Biblical Papyri: Ezekiel* (Princeton University Studies in Papyrology 3; Princeton: Princeton University Press, 1938) and L.G. Jahn, *Der griechische Text des Buches Ezechiel, nach dem Kölner Teil des Papyrus 967* (Papyrologische Texte und Abhandlungen 15; Bonn: Rudolf Habelt, 1972).

[17] According to H.B. Swete (*The Old Testament in Greek* [3 vols.; Cambridge: University Press, 1894], 3.xii–xiii), LXX[88] belonged to Pope Alexander VII who was part of the Chigi family. Alexander entrusted the manuscript to the Vatican librarian Leo Allatius for publication. However, the publication was delayed approximately 100 years until after the death of Bianchini and Regibus who continued the work of Allatius (Montgomery, *Daniel*, 25–26). It was finally published by S. de Magistris, *Daniel secundum Septuaginta ex tetraplis Origenis nunc primum editus a singulari Chrisiano codice* (Rome: Typis Propagandae Fidei, 1772).

[18] Syro-Hexapla is a translation into Syriac of the fifth column included in Origen's *Hexapla* (→ 1.4.5) The translation was carried out from 615 to 617 C.E. and is attributed to Paul of Tella. Syro-Hexapla has been preserved in Codex Ambrosianus (ca. ninth century), which was published by A.M. Ceriani, *Codex syro-hexaplaris Ambrosianus photolithographice editus* (Monumenta sacra et profana 7; Milan: Bibliothecae Ambrosianae, 1874), folios 143ª–151ᵇ.

[19] Di Lella, "The Textual History of Septuagint-Daniel and Theodotion-Daniel," 590.

scholarship of the book of Daniel. The first area of research has continued to take advantage of the new findings from Qumran, focusing investigation not only on the biblical copies[20] but also on the extra-biblical scrolls that may have an impact on the interpretation of Daniel. As such, the Qumranic literature has proven profitable to those scholars who have endeavored to reconstruct stages in the tradition history of the book as well as the literary dependence of particular passages.[21]

The second area of analysis was inspired by the finding of the pre-Hexaplaric papyrus LXX^{967}. Due to its various discrepancies with MT in terms of content and layout,[22] OG-Dan as it is recorded in the three extant textual witnesses (LXX^{88} and LXX^{967} LXX and the Syro-Hexapla) inspired the studies of Ashley,[23] McCrystall, Jeansonne, Wenthe, Meadowcroft, and Amara as described below. Before McCrystall, only Bludau's study, which predates the discovery of papyrus LXX^{967}, addressed the relationship between MT (→ 18.2.2) and LXX-Dan (→ 18.3.1).[24] He suggested that the differences between MT and LXX-Dan should be attributed to the theological approach of the translator. The same view has been maintained in McCrystall's study, which alleges "a deliberate standpoint" on the part of the translator.[25] In response to Bludau and McCrystall, Jeansonne has argued convincingly that "the OG translator did not undertake the work with a particular agenda."[26] With the studies of Wenthe and Meadowcroft, the attention has shifted to the first part of Daniel. Wenthe had an interest in detecting the textual history behind Daniel 1–6 in light of Second Temple Judaism.[27] He concludes that while we have "a very uniform tradition in Daniel 1–3,"[28] OG-Dan in Daniel 4–6 has "frozen" an earlier form of the text during its transmission history.[29] Meadowcroft's analysis is unique in that it attempts to use the tools of narrative criticism to evaluate the textual differences between MT and LXX in Daniel 2–7.[30] Three types of results

---

[20] P.J. Lambach, "A Detailed Comparison of 4QDan^c and the Other Qumran Texts of Daniel with the Masoretic Text of Daniel" (PhD diss., Mid-America Baptist Seminary, 1997) represents a new study on the Daniel biblical scroll found at Qumran. Taking 4QDan^c (Dan 10:5–11:29) as his point of departure, Lambach describes its condition and analyzes its script, textual division, and transcription (ch. 2). After comparing the orthography and the other textual features (script, textual division, textual intervention, textual variation) of 4QDan^c with other Qumran copies of Daniel (ch. 3) and MT (ch. 4), Lambach concludes that 4QDan^c, 1QDan^a, 1QDan^b, and pap6QDan display the proto-MT tradition at Qumran (p. 190), that 4QDan^a could be categorized as a "proto-MT text with strong leanings towards LXX" (p. 190), and that 4QDan^b should be classified due to its editorial freedom as "a manuscript of the Qumran practice" (pp. 190–91). Furthermore, based on script, lack of final letters, and lack of paragraphing, Lambach dates 4QDan^c to 150–125 B.C.E. (p. 191). See also E. Ulrich, "Orthography and Text in 4QDan^a and 4QDan^b and in the Received Massoretic Text," in *Of Scribes and Scrolls: Studies on the Hebrew Bible, Intertestamental Judaism and Christian Origins Presented to John Strugnell* (eds. A. Attridge, J.J. Collins, and T.H. Tobin; Lanham: University Press of America, 1990), 29–42 and E. Ulrich, "The Text of Daniel in the Qumran Scrolls," in *The Book of Daniel: Composition and Reception* (eds. J.J. Collins and P.W. Flint; VTSup 83/2; Leiden: Brill, 2001), 573–85.

[21] M. Segal, "From Joseph to Daniel: The Literary Development of the Narrative in Daniel 2," *VT* 59 (2009): 123–49; R.E. Stokes, "The Throne Visions of Daniel 7, 1 'Enoch' 14, and the Qumran 'Book of Giants' (4Q530): An Analysis of Their Literary Relationship," *DSD* 15 (2008): 340–58.

[22] The next section will exhibit the textual problems related to the book of Daniel with an emphasis on the peculiarity of Daniel 4–6.

[23] Ashley's study is more in the nature of an exegetical enterprise of select passages in Daniel 1–4 and does not address textual questions. T.R. Ashley, "The Book of Daniel, Ch. 1–4: Text, Versions and the Problems of Exegesis" (PhD diss., University of St. Andrews, 1976).

[24] Bludau, *Die alexandrinische Übersetzung*.

[25] McCrystall, "Studies," 76.

[26] Jeansonne, *The Old Greek Translation of Daniel 7–12*, 133.

[27] Wenthe, "The Old Greek Translation of Daniel 1–6."

[28] Wenthe, "Daniel," 247.

[29] Wenthe, "Daniel," 248.

[30] Meadowcroft, *Aramaic Daniel and Greek Daniel*. This narrative criticism has been heralded by James Muilenburg in his presidential address at the SBL meeting in 1968 and further developed in the second half of the twentieth century by the referential works of R. Alter, *The Art of Biblical Narrative* (New York: Basic Books, 1981); R. Alter, *The Art of Biblical Poetry* (New York: Basic Books, 1985); R. Alter, *The World of Biblical Literature* (New York: Basic Books, 1992). Equally important are the studies of A. Berlin, *Poetics and Interpretation of Biblical Narrative* (Bible and Literature Series 9; Sheffield:

are advanced by Meadowcroft. First, from a literary perspective, the MT narrator is "covert" while the Old Greek appears to be "overt." Second, he contends that at a thematic level the symbolic and wisdom topics are differentiated in MT and Old Greek. Finally, his historical conclusions are similar to those of Wenthe's and concludes that the "Septuagint seems to take us closer to the *Ursprung* and further away from the putative Persian provenance of the Aramaic."[31]

Amara's study is structured as a full-scale analysis of OG-Dan.[32] This study not only covers the entire book (except the Additions; → 11.3.2), but also deals with the most important questions raised in the previous research. In terms of translation techniques, Amara differs from Wenthe's and Jeansonne's positive assessment of the Old Greek translator and maintains "The extremely non-literal nature of this translation turns it almost worthless for text-critical purposes, since one can never be certain whether a variant text actually goes back to a different *Vorlage* or originated from the hand of the translator."[33] Furthermore, she argues persuasively that Daniel 4–6 and the other sections of the book feature signs of a single translator.[34] She considers the text underlying OG-Dan to be secondary compared to MT including that of Daniel 4–6.[35] Furthermore, Amara contends that the OG-Dan translator is not accountable for the final form of the text, rather "his translation underwent redactional intervention by a Greek redactor whose main contribution is the more substantial additions to the book."[36]

The third area of investigation addresses Barthélemy's hypothesis about the nature of the relationship between Th-Dan and the supposed *kaige* group.[37] Two specific claims have been made in Barthélemy's groundbreaking research that have bearing on the textual studies of Daniel, namely, that Th-Dan should be more appropriately described as a revision, and that, in terms of affiliation, Th-Dan belongs to *kaige*.[38] The latter as-

---

The Almond Press, 1983), Y. Amit, *Reading Biblical Narratives: Literary Criticism and the Hebrew Bible* (Minneapolis: Fortress Press, 2001), and S. Bar-Efrat, *Narrative Art in the Bible* (trans. D. Shefer-Vanson; JSOTSup 70; Sheffield: Sheffield Academic Press, 1997).

[31] T.J. Meadowcroft, "A Literary Critical Comparison of the Masoretic Text and Septuagint Daniel 2–7," *TynBul* 45 (1994): 195–99. For the strengths and weaknesses of applying such an approach to textual problems, see the reviews of L.L. Grabbe, review of T.J. Meadowcroft, *Aramaic Daniel and Greek Daniel: A Literary Comparison*, *CBQ* 59 (1997): 128–29; R.A. Taylor, review of T.J. Meadowcroft, *Aramaic Daniel and Greek Daniel: A Literary Comparison*, *Biblioteca Sacra* 154 (1997): 501–02; B.A. Taylor, review of T.J. Meadowcroft, *Aramaic Daniel and Greek Daniel: A Literary Comparison*, *JBL* 117 (1998): 731–32; C.T.R. Hayward, review of T.J. Meadowcroft, *Aramaic Daniel and Greek Daniel: A Literary Comparison*, *VT* 51 (2001): 412–13.

[32] Amara, "The Old Greek Version of Daniel."
[33] Amara, "Old Greek," ii.
[34] Amara, "Old Greek," iii. Amara's view goes against of the opinion that has been advanced by Albertz and supported by McLay.
[35] Amara, "Old Greek," iv–v.
[36] Amara, "Old Greek," v–vi.
[37] Other biblical books investigated for their affiliation to the *kaige* group are: 1–2 Kings (J.D. Shenkel, *Chronology and Recensional Development in the Greek Text of Kings* [HSM 1; Cambridge: Harvard University Press, 1968]); Exodus (K.G. O'Connell, *The Theodotionic Revision of the Book of Exodus* [HSM 3; Cambridge: Harvard University Press, 1972]); Judges (W. Bodine, *The Greek Text of Judges* [HSM 23; Chico: Scholars Press, 1980]); Joshua (L.J. Greenspoon, *Textual Studies in the Book of Joshua* [HSM 28; Chico: Scholars Press, 1983]). Greenspoon's study is valuable not only because it attempts to trace *kaige* marks in LXX-Josh, but also because the monograph contains a comprehensive list of the alleged *kaige* features. The fact that these studies were written in the same university (Harvard) and under the guidance of the same mentor (Frank M. Cross) has prompted R.T. McLay to refer to them as the "Harvard school" (*The Use of the Septuagint in New Testament Research* [Grand Rapids: William B. Eerdmans Publishing Company, 2003], 9–14). See also the work of P.J. Gentry who has analyzed the asterisked fragments of Job in *The Asterisked Materials in the Greek Job* (SBLSCS 39; Atlanta: Scholars Press, 1995), and on the book of Psalms, see O. Munnich's analysis, "Étude lexicographique du Psautier des Septante" (PhD diss., Université de Paris-Sorbonne, 1982) and → 1.3.1.2.

[38] For further information about Barthélemy's hypothesis, see the discussion above. Critical assessment of the *kaige* theory and the problems that it involves can be found, among other works treated below, in Jellicoe, *SMS*, 83–94; McLay, *The Use of the Septuagint in New Testament Research*, 9–14; Fernandez Marcos, *Introduction*, 142–53.

sertion resulted in Schmitt's study that searches for an answer as to whether Th-Dan belongs to *kaige*.[39] To achieve his purpose, Schmitt first collated fragments ascribed to Theodotion from five biblical books (Proverbs, Job, Isaiah, Jeremiah, and Ezekiel).[40] In view of methodological considerations, he excluded the sections from 2 Kgs 11:2 to 3 Kgs 2:11 and the Minor Prophets Scroll since they were classified by Barthélemy as part of the *kaige* group. Subsequently, Schmitt engaged in a detailed comparison of translation techniques at the level of lexical choices[41] and syntactical features (agreement in number, the use of cases, syntax of prepositions, adjectives, verbs, the use of particles, the composition of words, and idiomatic Hebrew phrases)[42] between Th-Dan and the collated passages attributed to the historical Theodotion. In the last chapter of his study, after comparing the translation technique of the deuterocanonical sections extant only in the Greek witnesses (Susanna, Prayer of Azariah and the Song of the Three, and Bel and Draco),[43] Schmitt concluded that the Greek version of Daniel attributed to Theodotion (Th-Dan/"θ'"-Text) has no relation to the texts attributed by Barthélemy to the historical Theodotion.[44]

Since the implicit claim of Schmitt's study calls into question the affiliation of Th-Dan to the *kaige* group, it drew Barthélemy's critique,[45] which in turn prompted a response from Schmitt.[46] Schmitt's conclusion, however, was recently substantiated by McLay's study in which, after comparing ninety-seven features supposedly pertaining to the *kaige* group with Th-Dan, he concluded, "This examination of the *kaige* characteristics in Th vindicates the conclusion of A. Schmitt. The most that we can say that Th has in common with *kaige*-Theodotion is that they share a similar approach to translation, i.e. formal equivalence."[47]

Barthélemy's contention that Th-Dan should be classed as a revision of OG-Dan has been the main focus of McLay's and Obiajunwa's research and, secondarily, that of Amara. Before Barthélemy, given the number of citations from Th-Dan in works that predate the historical Theodotion, scholars postulated the existence of an Ur-/proto-Theodotion version.[48] Before McLay, Schmitt had referred to the Th-Dan version as a revision, though he disputed Barthélemy's claim regarding its affiliation to *kaige*.[49] Both Wenthe and Jeansonne expressed the same view.[50] Nevertheless, credit is due to McLay's challenge of this view, which mentions the absence of any systematic study that substantiated the theory of Th-Dan as a revision.

McLay's study, though conceived originally as a contribution to translation technique,[51] has proved

---

[39] Schmitt, *Theodotion*.

[40] For the complete list of the scriptural verses used by Schmitt, see *Theodotion*, 112.

[41] Schmitt, *Theodotion*, 26–61.

[42] Schmitt, *Theodotion*, 61–100.

[43] Schmitt, *Theodotion*, 100–12.

[44] Schmitt, *Theodotion*, 100–12.

[45] D. Barthélemy, "Notes critiques sur quelques points d'histoire du texte," in *Übersetzung und Deutung: Studien zu dem Alten Testament und seiner Umwelt Alexander Reinard Hulst gewidmet von Freunden und Kollegen* (Nijkerk: Uitgeverij G.F. Callenbach b.v., 1977), 9–23; repr. in **Études*, 289–303.

[46] Schmitt reiterated these conclusions twenty-five years later in his article, "Die griechischen Danieltexte ("θ'" und ο') und das Theodotionproblem," *BZ* 36 (1992): 1–29.

[47] McLay, *The OG and Th Versions of Daniel*, 239–40; see also T.R. McLay, "*Kaige* and the Septuagint Research," *Textus* 19 (1998): 127–39.

[48] L. Gwynn, "Theodotion," *Dictionary of Christian Biography* (eds. W. Smith and H. Wace; London: John Murrow, 1887), 4:970–79; Thackeray, **The Septuagint and Jewish Worship*; Swete, **Introduction* (rev. by R.R. Ottley; Peabody: Hendrickson, 1989), 42–49; Montgomery, *A Critical and Exegetical Commentary on the Book of Daniel*, 46–50.

[49] See the discussion above. Cf. Schmitt, *Theodotion*, 112, and Schmitt, "Die griechischen Danieltexte ("θ'" und ο') und das Theodotionproblem," 1–29.

[50] Jeansonne, *The Old Greek Translation of Daniel 7–12*, 56–57; Wenthe, "The Old Greek Translation of Daniel 1–6," 251–57. I agree, however, with McLay's criticism of Jeansonne's use of statistics without discussing the adequacy of the sample (cf. McLay, "Translation Technique," 33–34). By the same token, I concur with McLay in his criticism of Wenthe that he "does not evidence any careful analysis of the question [that Th-Dan is a revision]." McLay, "Translation Technique," 35–36 and n. 92.

[51] McLay states the objective of his dissertation at the outset: "The primary purpose of this thesis is to provide a descriptive analysis of the TT employed in the Old Greek (OG) and Theodotion (Th) versions of the Book of Daniel, which will also serve as a paradigm for others wishing to engage in similar

to be of benefit in the discussion of the relationship between OG-Dan and Th-Dan. To my knowledge, it was the first systematic study that was carried out in order to answer this question. As a consequence, his assessment of Th-Dan as a new translation (in contrast to the prevalent view) must no longer be ignored.[52]

Obiajunwa addressed the question of the relation between the two Greek versions by investigating first the "Semitic interference in θ-Dan by determining how it has rendered Semitic vocabulary, grammar, and syntax into Greek."[53] He then applied his results to test the claim that "θ-Dan came from a careful and generally consistent revision of the OG to correspond to MT or a text similar to MT."[54] Evaluating the data, Obiajunwa supports McLay's verdict and concludes that "θ-Dan is the work of a translator who worked for the most part independently of LXX-Dan."[55] Lastly, in her study of OG-Dan, Amara briefly analyzed the relation between LXX-Dan and Th-Dan.[56] After each possible alternative has been exemplified, she concludes that Th-Dan "is not really a revision but another translation which is dependent and influenced by the translation prior to it."[57]

As far as the special nature of Daniel 4–6 is concerned, several competing views have been advanced in critical scholarship in order to tackle the diverging materials in LXX-Dan in these chapters. The first view, which held the LXX translator accountable for the differences, is reflected in the recurring opinions expressed in scholarly publications in the nineteenth century.[58] Accordingly, scholars have viewed the differences mainly as midrashic, paraphrastic, and/or expansionistic interventions by the translator himself.[59]

At the turn of the twentieth century, a second trend in research was heralded by Bludau's influential study. In spite of the fact that in many instances he holds the LXX translator responsible for a midrashic and theological *Tendenz*,[60] Bludau deviated from the previous view by his positive appreciation of LXX as well as by his differentiation between Daniel 4–6 and the rest of the book.[61] Regarding these chapters, he suggested that LXX (→ 18.3.1) reflects a *Vorlage* much different from MT (→ 18.2.2) in a textual pattern that differed from the other chapters of the book.[62] This supposedly different *Vorlage* preoccupied scholars much in the twentieth century and different views were expressed regarding whether this text mirrors a superior text to MT-Dan or the

---

research" (McLay, "Translation Technique," 1). A comparison of his dissertation with its published form reveals the fact that significant portions of his original thesis were left out. The dissertation includes two additional chapters that are not included in its published form. The chapters omitted are those that tried to suggest a new model of translation techniques (see ch. 3 [pp. 101–22] and ch. 4 [pp. 123–73]). These chapters, however, are incorporated in McLay, *The Use of the Septuagint in New Testament Research*, 44–99.

[52] McLay, though he admits that after ten years of writing his dissertation it appears that "not much has changed regarding the evaluation of Th as a revision," has further substantiated his claim by producing other studies. Cf. T.R. McLay, "The Relationship between Greek Translations of Daniel 1–3," *BIOSCS* 37 (2004): 29–53; T.R. McLay, "The Old Greek Translation of Daniel IV–VI," 304–23.

[53] Obiajunwa, "Semitic Interference," iv.

[54] Obiajunwa, "Semitic Interference."

[55] Obiajunwa, "Semitic Interference," 237.

[56] Amara, "The Old Greek Version of Daniel," 13–25.

[57] Amara, "The Old Greek Version of Daniel," 25.

[58] Among others, see Bevan, *A Short Commentary on the Book of Daniel*, 45–46; G. Behrmann, *Das Buch Daniel* (HKAT: Die Prophetischen Bücher 3.3.2; Göttingen: Vandenhoeck & Ruprecht, 1894), xxviii–xxxviii. For a brief review of the nineteenth-century literature, see Bludau, *Die alexandrinische Übersetzung*, 29–33.

[59] This view is also partly implied by those who emphasize the translator as a interpreter who created readings that are valuable for the history of exegesis and reception of the text. Such an approach was accepted by F.F. Bruce in "The Earliest Old Testament Interpretation," *OTS* 17 (1972): 37–52; "The Oldest Greek Version of Daniel," *OTS* 20 (1977): 22–40; and "Prophetic Interpretation in the Septuagint," *BIOSCS* 12 (1979): 17–26.

[60] Bludau, *Die alexandrinische Übersetzung*, 27. See also Jeansonne's criticism of Bludau's view, Jeansonne, *The Old Greek Translation of Daniel 7–12*, 24–25.

[61] This view is reflected in the very structure of his study: separate analyses of Daniel 1–3; 7–12 and Daniel 4–6. Cf. Bludau, *Die alexandrinische Übersetzung*, 33–143 (Daniel 1–3; 7–12), 143–54 (Daniel 4–6).

[62] *Die alexandrinische Übersetzung*, 31–33, 143–154.

opposite. Thus, the priority of LXX's *Vorlage* has been argued by Riessler,[63] Jahn,[64] Charles,[65] Albertz,[66] Wills,[67] Munnich,[68] Lust,[69] and Meadowcroft,[70] whereas the preferential status of MT has been defended by Montgomery,[71] Grélot,[72] Satran,[73] and Amara.[74]

---

[63] In his work, Riessler argues against that LXX in Dan 2:4–7:28 reflects a "targumic paraphrase" or *Tendenz* in translation; he further contends that the LXX is rather based on a different *Vorlage* – most likely Hebrew – which has precedence over MT. Cf. *Das Buch Daniel*, 33, 44, 52.

[64] Similarly to Riessler, Jahn assumes an original, Hebrew underlying text older than MT, which he attempted to recover by retroverting LXX-Dan 1–12 into Hebrew. Cf. *Das Buch Daniel: Nach der Septuaginta hergestellt–übersetzt und kritisch erklärt*, iii–iv, vi.

[65] According to Charles the OG more closely resembled the original text – particularly in Dan 4–6. Implicitly he considers MT to be secondary. He asserts, "A long sustained and minute study of the text and versions has led him [Charles] to conclude that it is just in these chapters that the LXX makes its greatest contribution to the reconstruction of the original text, particularly in chapter iv." Charles, *The Book of Daniel*, xxx.

[66] Albertz's study focused particularly on Dan 4–6 and has come to the conclusion that these chapters constituted a separate collection of stories that were translated into Greek before being incorporated into the existing LXX-Dan. Consequently, the LXX translator of chapters 4–6 differs from the translator of the other Aramaic chapters (2–3, 7). Cf. *Der Gott des Daniel*. Albertz reiterates his view in a later article where he contends that the LXX in Dan 4–6 "represent an independent shape of the Daniel stories, which in my view is even older than the Aramaic, perhaps not in all details, but in their basic narrative plot." See R. Albertz, "The Social Setting of the Aramaic and Hebrew Book of Daniel," in *The Book of Daniel: Composition and Reception* (eds. J.J. Collins and P.W. Flint; VTSup 83.1; Leiden: Brill, 2001), 180.

[67] Wills, "Jew in the Court of the Foreign King," 12–87.

[68] Munnich's study on the the literary development of the book determined that LXX-Dan (particularly in LXX[967]) mirrors "a prior condition to the Masoretic text." See O. Munnich, "Texte massorétique et Septante dans le livre de Daniel," in Schenker, *Earliest Text*, 93–120 (120). See also, O. Munnich, "Les versions grecques de Daniel et leur substrats sémitiques," in *VIII Congress of the International Organization for Septuagint and Cognate Studies* (eds. L. Greenspoon and O. Munnich; SBLSCS 41; Atlanta: Scholars Press, 1995), 291–308.

[69] Against Albertz, Lust argued that the order of chapters in LXX[967] (Daniel 1–4; 7–8; 5–6; 9; 10–12) is preferable to their preserved arrangement in MT. He sees the differences between MT and LXX in Daniel 4 and 5 that "are connected with the heavily redacted composition of the Semitic text." In this article, Lust explains, "In the Vorlage of the MT the Aramaic materials, without the 'pluses' found in the LXX, were collected in a different order. In later stages of the transmission of the text, the LXX was progressively 'corrected' towards conformity with the MT. Notwithstanding these 'corrections' the differences proved too important, and the early Greek version was finally discarded and superseded by the so-called Theodotionic translation." Cf. L. Lust, "The Septuagint Version of Daniel 4–5," in *The Book of Daniel in the Light of New Findings* (ed. A.S. van der Woude; BETL 56; Leuven: University Press, 1993), 39–53 (52–563). Similarly, this view was presented in the work of his student P.S. David, "The Composition and Structure of the Book of Daniel: A Synchronic and Diachronic Reading" (PhD diss., Katholieke Universiteit Leuven, 1991).

[70] Cf. Meadowcroft, *Aramaic Daniel and Greek Daniel* in → 18.1.2.

[71] Montgomery agrees with Bludau that a distinction should be made between the special character of Dan 3–6 and the rest of the book. Cf. Montgomery, *Daniel*, 36. At variance with Bludau, however, he has posited that its Semitic *Vorlage* accounts for the divergent material of these chapters in OG. In this regard, Montgomery writes, "In the Notes the conclusion is reached that there is considerable evidence for translation from a Sem(itic) copy which is responsible for much of the additions, largely midrash, now in LXX" (Montgomery, *Daniel*, 37). Further, after discussing Daniel 4, he contends that "there is some evidence that the midrashic expansion took place in a semitic form of the text before translation" (248). After Daniel 6, however, Montgomery does not maintain his position and agrees with Bludau's assessment, namely, that we have here "a working-over than a translation" (Montgomery, *Daniel*, 280).

[72] A nuanced position has been advanced by Grélot. Not only has he pointed out that Th-Dan could be characterized in Daniel 4–6 as a "new version," but he describes the rest of the book in similar terms, as "a new translation entirely reworked." P. Grélot, "Les versions grecques de Daniel," *Bib* 47 (1966): 381–402 (394–95). He has elaborated on his view regarding a Semitic underlying text in Dan 4–6 in "La Septante de Daniel 4 et son substrat sémitique," *RB* 81 (1974): 5–23; "Le Chapitre 5 de Daniel dans la Septante," *Sem* 24 (1974): 45–66; and "Daniel VI dans la Septante," in Κατὰ τοὺς ὁ: *Selon les Septante: trente études sur la Bible grecque des Septante: en hommage à Marguerite Harl* (eds. G. Dorival and O. Munnich; Paris: Cerf, 1995), 103–18. Further, similarly to Montgomery's view, he attributes the variants between OG and Th to their underlying texts that may antedate the fixation of MT. In contrast to Charles, he maintains that a presumably older *Vorlage* is not an indication per se of its superiority over MT. See Grélot, "Les versions grecques de Daniel," 399.

[73] Satran, "Early Jewish and Christian Interpretation."

[74] See the review of Amara's study, "The Old Greek Version of Daniel" in → 18.1.2.

A third view that posits the existence of two parallel editions became apparent at the end of the twentieth century. In light of the Qumranic literature, which purportedly suggests a fluid textual milieu in the late Second Temple period, Ulrich,[75] Wenthe,[76] Henze,[77] and Tov,[78] have argued that the two texts in these chapters represent both original and secondary elements.

18.1.3 Textual History and Exegetical Relevance

In order to reconstruct the textual history of the book of Daniel, it is necessary to assess accurately the relationship between LXX-Dan (→ 18.3.1) and Th-Dan (→ 18.3.2) in general and, in the case of Daniel 4–6, in particular. However, little consensus regarding these relationships has been reached in the course of the textual research of Daniel. In Grabbe's words, "Barthélemy's thesis has been more repeated than examined."[79] Similarly, McLay,[80] Obiajunwa,[81] and most recently Amara[82] have called for a fresh examination. In response to this need, Olariu addressed the relationship between LXX-Dan and Th-Dan.[83] His results call into question the view of Th-Dan as an independent translation. He furthermore contends that it shows traces of revision.[84] As for Th-Dan's affiliation with the *kaige* group, the connections are too vague to affirm a definite relationship.[85] He believes that similar uncertainty characterizes the proposed link between Th-Dan and the historical Theodotion.[86]

The textual differences in Daniel 4–6 afford insight into the pre-final stages of the text. This could impact the way we evaluate literary and scribal patterns and practices operative at these early stages. The analysis of differences of this type should be conducted on a broad basis. It seems that LXX-Dan reflects the work of a single translator.[87] Moreover, the deviations in Daniel 4–6 affirm Jerome's claim that Th-Dan replaced LXX-Dan, based on the fact that "it differs widely from the original, and is rightly rejected."[88]

---

[75] Ulrich posits that both MT and LXX are secondary witnesses to the original tradition: "The conclusion to be drawn, but still to be demonstrated in detail, is that the Old Greek translator translated the entire book faithfully from his semitic Vorlage; he simply had a version of the book which contained a variant edition of the text of those three chapters. Furthermore, the variant editions found in the MT and in the Old Greek for Daniel 4–6 appear to be two different later editions of the story, both secondary, both expanding in different ways beyond a single form which lies behind both but which is no longer extant" (Ulrich, "The Canonical Process, Textual Criticism, and Later Stages in the Composition of the Bible," 285). This view was defended two years later in the PhD dissertation of his student Wenthe, "The Old Greek Translation of Daniel 1–6."

[76] Wenthe, "The Old Greek Translation of Daniel 1–6" (see the discussion in → 18.1.2).

[77] After he criticized both Wills and Satran for their "diametrically opposed" views, Henze claims that the relationship between the texts is better described as one of "double literary editions" or "duplicate narratives" (Henze, *The Madness of King Nebuchadnezzar*, 38–49 [38, 40]).

[78] Tov, "Three Strange Books of the LXX."

[79] L.L. Grabbe, "The Translation Technique of the Greek Minor Versions: Translations or Revisions?" in *Manchester Symposium*, 505–56 (506).

[80] McLay, "Translation Technique," 34, 35, 38–39; *The OG and Th Versions of Daniel*, 243.

[81] Obiajunwa, "Semitic Interference," 1–2.

[82] Amara, "The Old Greek Version of Daniel: The Translation, the Vorlage and the Redaction," 316–17.

[83] Cf. "The Quest for the Common Basis in the Greek Versions of the Book of Daniel" (M.A. thesis, The Hebrew University of Jerusalem, 2015). This thesis was carried out under the supervision of Emanuel Tov and Michael Segal.

[84] Pivotal in the discussion of Th-Dan as a revision is the issue relating to the common basis of the Greek versions. In my study quoted in the preceding note, I substantiated this common basis with more than eighty significant agreements shared by LXX-Dan and Th-Dan in Daniel 1–12 and with more than thirty significant agreements in the Additions.

[85] This view has been defended by McLay, *The OG and Th Versions of Daniel*, 216–40. By the same author, see also "*Kaige* and the Septuagint Research," *Textus* 19 (1998): 127–39.

[86] This conclusion is based on Schmitt's analysis, *Stammt der sogenannte "ϑ"-Text bei Daniel wirklich von Theodotion?*

[87] Both Albertz and McLay argued that LXX-Dan 4–6 reveal the hand of a different translator from the rest of the book. However, I agree with the results of Amara's thorough analysis, which point to the opposite (Albertz, *Der Gott des Daniel*; Amara, "The Old Greek Version of Daniel"; McLay, *The OG and Th Versions of Daniel*).

[88] Jerome comments once in the preface to his translation

Albertz, R., *Der Gott des Daniel: Untersuchungen zu Daniel 4–6 in der Septuagintafassung sowie zu Komposition und Theologie des aramäischen Danielbuches* (SBS 131; Stuttgart: Verlag Katholisches Bibelwerk, 1988).

Amara, D., "The Old Greek Version of Daniel: The Translation, the Vorlage and the Redaction" (PhD diss., Ben-Gurion University of the Negev, 2006) [Hebr.].

Barthélemy, *Devanciers*.

Bludau, A., *Die alexandrinische Übersetzung des Buches Daniel und ihr Verhältnis zum massorethischen Text* (BibS[F] II 2.3; Freiburg im Breisgau: Herder'sche Verlagshandlung, 1897).

Bogaert, P.-M., "Le témoignage de la Vetus Latina dans l'étude de la tradition des Septante Ézékiel et Daniel dans le Papyrus 967," *Bib* 59 (1978): 384–95.

Bogaert, P.-M., "Relecture et refonte historicisantes du Livre de Daniel attestées par la première version grecque (Papyrus 967)," in *Études sur le judaisme hellénistique* (eds. R. Kuntzmann and J. Schlosser; LD 119; Paris: Cerf, 1984), 197–224.

Braasch, B. "Die LXX-Übersetzung des Danielbuches: Eine Orientierungshilfe für das religiöse und politisch-gesellschaftliche Leben in der ptolemäischen Diaspora: Eine rezeptionsgeschichtliche Untersuchung von Dan 1–7" (PhD diss., Universität Hamburg, 2003).

Bruce, F.F., "The Earliest Old Testament Interpretation," in *The Witness of Tradition: Papers Read at the Joint British-Dutch Old Testamtent Conference Held at Woundschoten, 1970* (eds. M.A. Beek et al.; OtSt 17; Leiden: Brill, 1972), 37–52.

Bruce, F.F., "The Oldest Greek Version of Daniel," in *Instruction and Interpretation: Studies in Hebrew Language, Palestinian Archaeology and Biblical Exegesis* (eds. H.A. Brongers et al.; OtSt 20; Leiden: Brill, 1977), 22–40.

Bruce, F.F., "Prophetic Interpretation in the Septuagint," *BIOSCS* 12 (1979): 17–26.

Charles, R.H., *The Book of Daniel* (The Century Bible; Edinburgh: T.C. & E.C. Jack, 1921).

Charles, R.H., *A Critical and Exegetical Commentary on the Book of Daniel* (Oxford: Clarendon Press, 1929).

Collins, J.J., *Daniel: A Commentary on the Book of Daniel* (Hermeneia; Minneapolis: Fortress Press, 1993).

Collins, J.J. and P.W. Flint (eds.), *The Book of Daniel: Composition and Reception* (2 vols. VTSup 83; Leiden: Brill, 2001).

David, P.S., "The Composition and Structure of the Book of Daniel: A Synchronic and Diachronic Reading" (PhD diss., Katholieke Universiteit Leuven, 1991).

Delcor, M., "Un cas de traduction "Targumique" de la LXX à propos de la statue en or de Dan. III," *Textus* 7 (1969): 30–35.

Delcor, M., *Le Livre de Daniel* (SB; Paris: J. Gabalda, 1971).

Grélot, P., "Les versions grecques de Daniel," *Bib* 47 (1966): 381–402.

Grélot, P., "La Septante de Daniel 4 et son substrat semitique," *RB* 81 (1974): 5–23.

Grélot, P., "Le Chapitre 5 de Daniel dans la Septante," *Sem* 24 (1974): 45–66.

Grélot, P., "Daniel VI dans La Septante," in Κατὰ τοὺς ο': *Selon les Septante: Trente études sur la Bible grecque des Septante en hommage à Marguerite Harl* (eds. G. Dorival and O. Munnich; Paris: Cerf, 1995), 103–18.

Helms, D., *Konfliktfelder der Diaspora und die Löwengrube: Zur Eigenart der Erzählung von Daniel in der Löwengrube in der hebräischen Bibel und der Septuaginta* (BZAW 446; Berlin: De Gruyter, 2014).

Henze, M., *The Madness of King Nebuchadnezzar: The Ancient Near Eastern Origins and Early History of Interpretation of Daniel 4* (JSJSup 61; Leiden: Brill, 1999).

Henze, M., "The Narrative Frame of Daniel: A Literary Assessment," *JSJ* 32 (2001): 5–24.

Jahn, G., *Das Buch Daniel: Nach der Septuaginta hergestellt: Übersetzt und kritisch erklärt* (Leipzig: Verlag von Eduard Pfeiffer, 1904).

Jeansonne, P.S., *The Old Greek Translation of Daniel 7–12* (CBQMS 19; Washington: The Catholic Biblical Association of America, 1988).

Lust, L., "The Septuagint Version of Daniel 4–5," in *The Book of Daniel in the Light of New Findings* (ed.

---

of Daniel, *Patrologia Latina* 28, col. 1291 and once in his commentary on Dan 4:6, *Patrologia Latina* 25, col. 514. In his preface, Jerome writes: "The Septuagint version of Daniel the prophet is not read by the Churches of our Lord and Saviour. They use Theodotion's version, but how this came to pass I cannot tell. Whether it be that the Language is Chaldee, which differs in certain peculiarities from our speech, and the Seventy were unwilling to follow those deviations in a translation; or that the book was published in the name of the Seventy, by some one or other not familiar with Chaldee, or if there be some other reason, I know not; this one thing I can affirm – that it differs widely from the original, and is rightly rejected." Translation quoted from *The Principal Works of St. Jerome* (trans. W.H. Fremantle; NPNF 6; Grand Rapids: Eerdmans, 1979), 492. A similar view is presented by Schmitt, *Theodotion*, 1. By contrast, Bludau's judgment favors Dan 9:24–27 as the background for the decision (Bludau, *Die alexandrinische Übersetzung*, 24).

A.S. van der Woude; BETL 106; Leuven: University Press, 1993), 39–53.

McCrystall, A., "Studies in the Old Greek Translation of Daniel" (PhD diss., Oxford University, 1980).

McLay, T.R., "Translation Technique and Textual Studies in the Old Greek and Theodotion Versions of Daniel" (PhD diss., University of Durham, 1994).

McLay, T.R., *The OG and Th Versions of Daniel* (SBLSCS 43; Atlanta: Scholars Press, 1996).

McLay, T.R., "The Old Greek Translation of Daniel IV–VI and the Formation of the Book of Daniel," *VT* 55 (2005): 304–23.

Meadowcroft, T.J., *Aramaic Daniel and Greek Daniel: A Literary Comparison* (JSOTSup 198; Sheffield: Sheffield Academic Press, 1995).

Meadowcroft, T.J., "Point of View in Storytelling: An Experiment in Narrative Criticism in Daniel 4," *Did* 8.2 (1997): 30–42.

Meadowcroft, T.J., "Metaphor, Narrative, Interpretation, and Reader in Daniel 2–5," *Narrative* 8 (2000): 257–78.

Montgomery, J.A., *A Critical and Exegetical Commentary on the Book of Daniel* (ICC; Edinburgh: T & T Clark, 1964; 1st impr. 1927).

Munnich, O., "Les versions grecques de Daniel et leurs substrats sémitiques," in *VIII Congress of the International Organization for Septuagint and Cognate Studies* (eds. L. Greenspoon and O. Munnich; SBLSCS 41; Atlanta: Scholars Press, 1995), 291–308.

Munnich, O., "Texte Massorétique et Septante dans le livre de Daniel," in Schenker, *Earliest Text*, 93–120.

Obiajunwa, C.J., "Semitic Interference in Theodotion-Daniel" (PhD diss, Catholic University of America, 1999).

Olariu, D., "The Quest for the Common Basis in the Greek Versions of the Book of Daniel" (MA thesis, Hebrew University of Jerusalem, 2015).

Riessler, P., *Das Buch Daniel textkritische Untersuchung* (Stuttgart: Roth, 1899).

Satran, D., "Early Jewish and Christian Interpretation of the Fourth Chapter of the Book of Daniel" (PhD diss., Hebrew University of Jerusalem, 1985).

Schmitt, A., *Stammt der sogenannte "ϑ"-Text bei Daniel wirklich von Theodotion?* (MSU 9; Vandenhoeck & Ruprecht, 1966).

Tov, E., "Three Strange Books of the LXX: 1 Kings, Esther, and Daniel Compared With Similar Rewritten Compositions From Qumran and Elsewhere," in Karrer-Kraus, *Septuagint 2008*, 369–93 (repr. in Tov, *HB, GB and Qumran*, 283–309).

Ulrich, E., "The Canonical Process, Textual Criticism, and Later Stages in the Composition of the Bible," in *Sha'arei Talmon: Studies in the Bible, Qumran, and the Ancient Near East Presented to Shemaryahu Talmon* (eds. M. Fishbane and E. Tov; Winona Lake: Eisenbrauns, 1992), 267–91.

Ulrich, E., "The Parallel Editions of the Old Greek and Masoretic Text of Daniel 5," in *A Teacher for All Generations: Essays in Honor of James C. VanderKam* (eds. E.F. Mason eds.; 2 vols; JSJSup 153; Leiden: Brill, 2012), 1.201–17.

Wenthe, D.O., "The Old Greek Translation of Daniel 1–6" (PhD diss., University of Notre Dame, 1991).

Wills, L.M., "The Jew in the Court of the Foreign King: Ancient Jewish Court Legends" (PhD diss., Harvard University, 1987).

Daniel Olariu

18.2 Ancient Hebrew-Aramaic Texts

18.2.1 Ancient Manuscript Evidence

Eight ancient Hebrew/Aramaic manuscripts of the book of Daniel from the Qumran library have been published.[1] Of these manuscripts, the text of 1QDan[b] and 4QDan[d] is semi-Masoretic, while the text of 4QDan[a], 4QDan[b], and 4QDan[c] is non-aligned in character. 4QDan[a] and 4QDan[b] even stand in the same non-aligned textual tradition. Due to material damages, the text-typological classification of 1QDan[a], 4QDan[e], and 6QpapDan is impossible. 4QDan[e] most likely represents an excerpted Daniel text that included only Dan 9:4b–19. Three unpublished Daniel fragments from the Dead Sea scrolls are held in two collections: The Green Collection includes a small fragment with remnants of Dan 10:18–20 (Inv. MOTB.SCR.003170 = DSS F.Dan6)[2] and the Southwestern Baptist Theological Seminary owns two fragments that attest to Dan 6:22–24 and Dan 7:18–19 respectively (DSS F.166 = DSS F.Dan2; DSS F.167 = DSS F.Dan3).[3]

18.2.1.1 1QDan[a] (1Q71) with MS Schøyen 1926/4a

Only two fragments survive of 1QDan[a].[4] They include portions of two columns that attest to remnants of Dan 1:10–17; 2:2–6. The manuscript was written in a Herodian bookhand from the first half of the first century C.E., perhaps as late as the year 60 C.E.[5] With only two exceptions, 1QDan[a] goes in its orthography with MT-Dan.[6] In sixty-six (partly) preserved words, only four minor variant readings towards MT are extant.[7] The text of 1QDan[a] was therefore classified as proto-Masoretic,[8] but the small amount of preserved text does not allow for a certain text-typological classification. It is of importance for the study of the book of Daniel that 1QDan[a] 2 4–5 preserves, in the first half of the first century C.E., the transition from Hebrew to Aramaic in Dan 2:4 as known from MT (→ 18.2.2).

18.2.1.2 1QDan[b] (1Q72) with MS Schøyen 1926/4b

1QDan[b] survives in three fragments that were all part of the same column and attest to remnants of Dan 3:22–31. Two fragments were published by

---

[1] J.T. Milik ("Daniel et Susanne à Qumrân?" in *De la Tôrah au Messie: Mélanges Henri Cazelles* [eds. J. Doré, P. Grelot, and M. Carrez; Paris: Desclée, 1981], 337–59) and H.-J. Fabry ("Die Schriftfunde aus Qumran und ihre Bedeutung für den hebräischen Bibeltext," in *Qumran: Die Schriftrollen vom Toten Meer: Vorträge des St. Galler Qumran-Symposiums vom 2./3. Juli 1999* [eds. M. Fieger, K. Schmid, and P. Schwagmeier; NTOA 47; Göttingen: Vandenhoeck & Ruprecht, 2001], 112–28 [112]) understand the fragments of 4Q551 as attesting to remnants of the Aramaic parent text of the Susanna story among the additions to Daniel (Daniel 13). This identification is based on Milik's text reconstructions and on parallel idiomatic expressions and therefore was rightly criticized. 4Q551 attests most likely to a rewriting of Judges 19 (cf. G.W.E. Nickelsburg, "4Q551: A Vorlage to Susanna or a Text Related to Judges 19?" *JJS* 48 [1997]: 349–51). Lacerenza wants to understand a paleo-Hebrew fragment, which is in private ownership in Rome, as a fragment of a paleo-Hebrew Daniel scroll (G. Lacerenza, "Un nouveau fragment en écriture paleo-hébraïque," *RevQ* 19 [1999–2000]: 441–47; Tov, *Revised Lists*, 109, designates the fragment as XpaleoDan? [x8]). However, improved transcriptions by Puech show that Lacerenza's identification is faulty (É. Puech, "Note additionelle sur le fragment en paléo-hébreu," *RevQ* 19 [1999–2000]: 449–51).

[2] I am indebted to Emanuel Tov and David Trobisch for this information.

[3] I am obliged to Sidnie White Crawford for this information. For first photographs of the Southwestern Baptist Theological Seminary fragments, see Loveless and Loveless, *Dead Sea Scrolls and the Bible*, 91.

[4] The second fragment (MS Schøyen 1926/4a) is part of a "wad," i.e., a pile of several fragments glued together, which is now in the Schøyen Collection. I am obliged to Torleif Elgvin and Årstein Justnes who made a preprint copy of their reedition of 1QDan[a] available to me.

[5] Cf. Trever, "Completion," 333–34; Trever, "Latest," 278–83; Ulrich, "Text of Daniel," 574; Elgvin and Justnes, "1QDan[a]," forthcoming (between 50 and 60 C.E.).

[6] Cf. Barthélemy, "Premier exemplaire," 150; Ulrich, "Preliminary Edition of 4QDan[a]," 18.

[7] The numbers are based on the reedition of 1QDan[a] by Davis and Elgvin ("1QDan[a]," forthcoming), and differ therefore from the statistics given in Lange, *Handbuch*, 505.

[8] Cf. Tov, *"Synthese,"* 27, as well as Elgvin and Justnes, "1QDan[a]," forthcoming ("our text follows 𝔐 quite closely").

Barthélemy in *DJD* I.⁹ The third fragment was originally owned by John C. Trever and today is part of the Schøyen Collection (manuscript Schøyen 1926/4b).¹⁰ The paleography of 1QDanᵇ is debated. Trever¹¹ favors a paleographic date in the second half of the first century C.E. Ulrich thinks of a late Hasmonean semi-cursive hand from the beginning or middle of the first century B.C.E.¹² Davis and Elgvin date the manuscript to the second half of the first century B.C.E.¹³ and Flint speaks of a Hasmonean¹⁴ or Herodian¹⁵ date. In its orthography, the text of 1QDanᵇ is close to MT but reads sometimes more plene and sometimes more defective.¹⁶ Of interest is the Hebraism כול in Dan 3:29 instead of MT's Aramaic כָּל (both meaning "all"). Although only seventy-nine complete and partial words are preserved of 1QDanᵇ, the manuscript can be classified with some caution as semi-Masoretic. It attests only to two or three minor variants towards MT¹⁷ and does not know the Prayer of Azariah and the Song of the Three Young Men, which the two principal Greek versions of Daniel (→ 18.3.1; → 18.3.2, and → II.3.2) place between Dan 3:23 and 3:24 but are lacking in MT-Dan.¹⁸ It needs to be emphasized though that Davis and Elgvin propose several variant readings with LXX against MT in their reconstruction of 1QDanᵇ. Based on these reconstructed readings, they argue against the classification of 1QDanᵇ as an "𝔐-like text."¹⁹

18.2.1.3 4QDanᵃ (4Q112)

The twenty-one preserved fragments of 4QDanᵃ attest to remnants of Dan 1:16–20; 2:9–11, 19–49; 3:1–2; 4:29–30; 5:5–7, 12–14, 16–19; 7:5–7, 25–28; 8:1–5; 10:16–20; 11:13–16 coming from nine columns of the original scroll. The text of frgs. 18–21 can no longer be identified. 4QDanᵃ was written around the middle of the first century B.C.E. in an elegant bookhand from the late Hasmonean period or during the transition into the early Herodian period.²⁰ The three or four supralinear corrections and the one erasure in 4QDanᵃ are all *prima manu*.²¹ Of special interest for research on the book of Daniel is the change from Aramaic to Hebrew that takes place in 4QDanᵃ between Dan 7:28 and 8:1. The orthography of 4QDanᵃ is inconsistent but resembles that of MT-Dan.²² In ca. 580 complete and partial words, 4QDanᵃ reads never with and thirty-six times against MT, seventeen times with and nineteen times against Old Greek, nine times with and twenty-seven times against Theodotion, as well as nineteen times non-aligned. Twenty-four further readings against MT cannot be translated into Greek. Furthermore, Ulrich notes eight readings with and nine readings against LXX⁹⁶⁷.²³ Hence, 4QDanᵃ attests to a non-aligned text (→ 18.2.3.1) that is somewhat close to the Hebrew-Aramaic parent text of OG-Dan (→ 18.3.1).²⁴ A text-critical comparison of 4QDanᵃ and 4QDanᵇ demonstrates that the two manuscripts go back to the same parent text (→ 18.2.1.4).

18.2.1.4 4QDanᵇ (4Q113)

There are twenty surviving fragments of 4QDanᵇ. Frgs. 1–19 preserve remnants of Dan 5:10–12, 14–16, 19–22; 6:8–22, 27–29; 7:1–6, 11?, 26–28; 8:1–8, 13–16 coming from nine columns. The text of frg.

---

⁹ Barthélemy, "Second exemplaire," 151–52.

¹⁰ Cf. Davis and Elgvin, "1QDanᵇ," forthcoming; Lundberg and Zuckerman, "New Aramaic Fragments," 1–3. I am indebted to Kipp Davis and Torleif Elgvin for providing me with a preprint copy of their edition of 1QDanᵇ ("1QDanᵇ").

¹¹ Trever, "Completion," 334.

¹² Ulrich, "Text of Daniel," 574.

¹³ Davis and Elgvin, "1QDanᵇ," forthcoming.

¹⁴ Flint, "Daniel Tradition," 42 (1997).

¹⁵ Flint, "Daniel Tradition," 330 (2001).

¹⁶ For the orthography of 1QDanᵇ, see Davis and Elgvin, "1QDanᵇ," forthcoming; cf. Barthélemy, "Second exemplaire," 151.

¹⁷ The numbers are based on the reedition of 1QDanᵇ by Davis and Elgvin ("1QDanᵇ," forthcoming), and differ therefore from the statistics given in Lange, *Handbuch*, 506.

¹⁸ Cf. Barthélemy, "Second exemplaire," 151.

¹⁹ Davis and Elgvin, "1QDanᵇ," forthcoming.

²⁰ For the paleography of 4QDanᵃ, see Ulrich, "Preliminary Edition of 4QDanᵃ," 20–21; Ulrich, "Orthography," 31; Ulrich, "Daniel," 240–41.

²¹ Cf. Ulrich, "Preliminary Edition of 4QDanᵃ," 21; Ulrich, "Daniel," 241.

²² Cf. Ulrich, "Preliminary Edition of 4QDanᵃ," 20–21; Ulrich, "Orthography," 34–35; Ulrich, "Daniel," 241.

²³ Ulrich, "Daniel," 242–54.

²⁴ Cf. Tov, *"Synthese," 20, 27.

20 can no longer be identified. Paleographically, 4QDan^b is classified as a late Herodian bookhand from the years 20–50 C.E.[25] The two supralinear corrections in frgs. 7 i 14 (Dan 6:9) and 16 14 (Dan 8:7) are *prima manu*.[26] Beginning with Dan 8:1, 4QDan^b reads a Hebrew text, while what is preserved of Daniel 7 (Dan 7:1–6, 11?, 26–28) is written in Aramaic, thus confirming the change from Aramaic to Hebrew in MT-Dan 7:28–8:1. In 280 complete and partial words, 4QDan^b reads never with and fifteen times against MT, three times with and twelve times against Old Greek, twice with and thirteen times against Theodotion, three times with and twelve times against LXX[967], as well as twelve times non-aligned. One further reading against MT cannot be translated into Greek. The Daniel text of 4QDan^b can thus be described as non-aligned. A comparison of 4QDan^b with 4QDan^a in their overlapping text (Dan 8:1–5) shows that "when 4QDan^a and 4QDan^b overlap, they display agreement with each other (often accompanied by the OG against MT [and Theodotion]); neither ever clearly agrees with MT against the other."[27] Therefore, 4QDan^b stands most likely in the same textual tradition as 4QDan^a and it is even likely that 4QDan^b was copied from 4QDan^a.[28] In both Dan 8:1–5 and elsewhere, the orthography of 4QDan^b is fuller than that in 4QDan^a. Furthermore, 4QDan^b employs the morphological long forms of the baroque orthography. It is therefore likely that 4QDan^b or its parent text revised the orthography of 4QDan^a or its parent text.[29]

18.2.1.5 4QDan^c (4Q114)

The three surviving fragments of 4QDan^c attest to remnants of Dan 10:5–9, 11–16, 21; 11:1–2, 13–17, 25–29. The paleographic date of 4QDan^c is debated. Cross first suggested the late second century B.C.E.[30] but later revised the date to 100–50 B.C.E.[31] According to a communication with Ulrich, a comparison with the Wadi ed-Daliyeh papyri motivated Cross to re-date 4QDan^c once more to the late second century B.C.E., a date with which Ulrich is in agreement.[32] An even earlier date in the years 150–125 B.C.E. was suggested by Lambach but that seems problematic.[33] The two extant corrections in 4QDan^c III:14 (Dan 11:15) and IV:16 (Dan 11:27) are recognized by Ulrich as *prima manu*.[34] The orthography of 4QDan^c is as inconsistent as that of MT-Dan, but with one exception (נתתה instead of נָתַתָּ, "you gave" in MT-Dan 10:12) baroque suffix and affix forms are missing.[35] The text-typological classification of 4QDan^c is difficult,[36] because the passages of the book of Daniel in which the Greek texts read longer additions are not preserved in this manuscript.[37] In 206 identifiable complete and partial words, 4QDan^c reads once with and fifteen times against MT, five times with and eleven times against Old Greek, four times with and twelve times against Theodotion, five

---

[25] Thus Cross, *"Development," 139 line 6; Cross, *"Paleography," plate 10 line 6; Ulrich, "Preliminary Editions of 4QDan^b and 4QDan^c," 5; Ulrich, "Orthography," 31; Ulrich, "Daniel," 256.

[26] Cf. Ulrich, "Preliminary Editions of 4QDan^b and 4QDan^c," 6; Ulrich, "Daniel," 257.

[27] Ulrich, "Text of Daniel," 581.

[28] Thus Ulrich, "Orthography," 37–42; Ulrich, "Daniel, Book of," 172; Ulrich, "Text of Daniel," 581. For a different view, see → 18.2.3.2.

[29] Thus Ulrich, "Preliminary Editions of 4QDan^b and 4QDan^c," 5–6; Ulrich, "Orthography," 32–42; Ulrich, "Text of Daniel," 579–80; cf. Ulrich, "Daniel," 257.

[30] Cross, *ALQ², 43.

[31] Cross, *"Development," 149 line 2; cf. Cross, *"Paleography," plate 12 line 2.

[32] Cf. Ulrich, "Preliminary Edition of 4QDan^a," 17; Ulrich, "Preliminary Editions of 4QDan^b and 4QDan^c," 3, 18; Ulrich, "Daniel, Book of," 171; Ulrich, "Daniel," 270. For Cross' communication with Ulrich, see Ulrich, "Preliminary Editions of 4QDan^b and 4QDan^c," 18; Ulrich, "Daniel, Book of," 171; Ulrich, "Daniel," 270. For Cross' latest position, see now also Cross, *ALQ³, 43.

[33] Lambach, "Comparison," 16–21, 141–43, 187.

[34] Ulrich, "Preliminary Editions of 4QDan^b and 4QDan^c," 20; Ulrich, "Daniel," 271.

[35] Cf. Ulrich, "Preliminary Editions of 4QDan^b and 4QDan^c," 18, 20; Ulrich, "Daniel," 271; Lambach, "Comparison," 46–58.

[36] The detailed dissertation thesis of Lambach ("Comparison," *passim*) on the textual typology of 4QDan^c presupposes the priority of MT-Dan without providing reasoning for this axiomatic approach. It is therefore not very helpful in determining the textual character of 4QDan^c.

[37] Cf. Ulrich, "Text of Daniel," 583.

times with and seven times against LXX⁹⁶⁷, as well as seven times non-aligned. Two further readings in 4QDanᶜ against MT cannot be translated into Greek. 4QDanᶜ should therefore be classified as attesting to a non-aligned text (→ 18.2.3.3) that confirms Old Greek in some cases.

18.2.1.6 4QDanᵈ (4Q115)

Twelve fragments survive of 4QDanᵈ.³⁸ Frgs. 1–9 attest to remnants of Dan 3:8–10?, x–x, 23–25; 4:5–9, 12–16; 7:15–23. To reconstruct the original length of 4QDanᵈ is complicated; calculations by Pfann could hint to the fact that 4QDanᵈ was a collective manuscript that included not only the book of Daniel.³⁹ 4QDanᵈ was written in an early Herodian bookhand from the last quarter of the first century B.C.E.⁴⁰ In its orthography, 4QDanᵈ is close to both MT and 4QDanᵃ.⁴¹ For the text-typological classification of 4QDanᵈ, Dan 3:23–24 is key: "4QDanᵈ shares a shorter edition of Daniel with 4QDanᵃ,ᵇ,ᶜ and 𝔐 in contrast to longer forms preserved in o′ θ′. Dan 3:24 follows directly after 3:23 without the insertion of the Prayer of Azariah and the Song of the Three Youths."⁴² In 133 complete and partial words, 4QDanᵈ attests to six minor variants towards MT and can therefore be classified as semi-Masoretic (→ 18.2.2): "The text is relatively close to that of the Masoretic Text. Most of its textual variants (when compared with the Masoretic Text) are untranslatable and reflect differences in spelling of individual words … Those translatable variants which do exist are, in almost every case, mirrored by one or more of the versions."⁴³

18.2.1.7 4QDanᵉ (4Q116)

Seven fragments from two columns of the original scroll survive from 4QDanᵉ. They attest to sixteen (partly preserved) words from Dan 9:12–17. A material reconstruction based on the text of MT-Dan shows that the columns of 4QDanᵉ were nine lines or 6.1 cm high and that col. I was 10.5 cm wide. The characters of 4QDanᵉ are larger than normal among the Qumran manuscripts. To include the whole MT text of the book of Daniel, 4QDanᵉ would have needed 120 columns. As the diameter of a scroll cannot be wider than its height, it is unlikely that 4QDanᵉ was that long. Therefore, 4QDanᵉ attests most likely to an excerpt of the book of Daniel, and included probably only the prayer in Dan 9:4b–19.⁴⁴ The manuscript is written in an early Hasmonean semi-cursive hand from the beginning of the first century B.C.E.⁴⁵ That 4QDanᵉ employs the spelling באסתכה "on your fidelity" in Dan 9:13 could point to the use of baroque orthography.⁴⁶ The small amount of preserved text does not allow for a text-typological classification of 4QDanᵉ.

18.2.1.8 6QpapDan (6Q7)

Thirteen heavily damaged fragments are extant of 6QpapDan. Frgs. 1–8 attest to seventy-seven (partly preserved) words from Dan 8:16–17?, 20–21?; 10:8–16; 11:33–36, 38. The manuscript was written in a late Herodian bookhand with some cursive elements from the beginning or middle of the first century C.E.⁴⁷ In its orthography, 6QpapDan is conservative but reads sometimes more plene and sometimes more defective than MT.⁴⁸ 6QpapDan reads never with and four times against MT, twice with and twice against Old Greek, once with and three times against Theodotion, as well as twice non-aligned. One

---

³⁸ The fragments edited by Ulrich and Niccum in *DJD XVI as frgs. 13–16 do not belong to 4QDanᵈ but to another manuscript altogether (cf. Ulrich and Niccum, "4QDanᵈ," 286).

³⁹ Cf. Pfann, "4QDanielᵈ," 44–45, 60.

⁴⁰ Cf. Pfann, "4QDanielᵈ," 40–44, 60; Ulrich and Niccum, "4QDanᵈ," 279.

⁴¹ Cf. Pfann, "4QDanielᵈ," 53–54, 60; Ulrich and Niccum, "4QDanᵈ," 279.

⁴² Ulrich and Niccum, "4QDanᵈ," 279.

⁴³ Pfann, "4QDanielᵈ," 60. For the textual character of 4QDanᵈ, cf. also Pfann, "4QDanielᵈ," 53–60; Ulrich and Niccum, "4QDanᵈ," 279; Ulrich, "Daniel, Book of," 171–72.

⁴⁴ For the paleography of 4QDanᵉ, see Ulrich, "Daniel," 287; for the interpretation of 4QDanᵉ as an excerpt, see Ulrich, "Daniel," 287–88; Ulrich, "Daniel, Book of," 171; Tov, *"Synthese," 9, 27; and Flint, "Daniel Tradition," 331 (2001).

⁴⁵ For the orthography of 4QDanᵉ, see Ulrich, "Daniel," 287.

⁴⁶ Cf. Ulrich, "Daniel," 287.

⁴⁷ Cf. Baillet, "7. Daniel," 114; Ulrich, "Text of Daniel," 574.

⁴⁸ Cf. Baillet, "7. Daniel," 114.

further reading against MT cannot be translated into Greek. Insufficient text is preserved of 6QpapDan to allow for a text-typological classification.[49]

Baillet, M., "7. Daniel," *DJD III.1: 114–16.
Barthélemy, D., "71. Daniel (premier exemplaire)," *DJD I: 150.
Barthélemy, D., "72. Daniel (second exemplaire)," *DJD I: 151–52.
Davis, K. and T. Elgvin, "1QDan[b] (1Q72) with MS 1926/4b (Dan. 3.26–27)," in *Gleanings, forthcoming.
Elgvin, T. and Å. Justnes, "1QDan[a] (1Q71) with MS 1926/4a (Dan. 2.4–5)," in *Gleanings, forthcoming.
Flint, P.W., "The Daniel Tradition at Qumran," in Eschatology, Messianism, and the Dead Sea Scrolls (eds. C.A. Evans and P.W. Flint; Studies in the Dead Sea Scrolls and Related Literature; Grand Rapids: Eerdmans, 1997), 41–60.
Flint, P.W., "The Daniel Tradition at Qumran," in The Book of Daniel: Composition and Reception (2 vols.; VTSup 83/1–2; Leiden: Brill, 2001), 2:329–67, esp. 330–31 and 364–65.
Lambach, P.J., "A Detailed Comparison of 4QDan[c] and the Other Qumran Texts of Daniel with the Masoretic Text of Daniel" (PhD diss., Mid-America Baptist Theological Seminary, 1997).
Lange, *Handbuch, 505–21.
Lundberg, M. and B. Zuckerman, "New Aramaic Fragments from Qumran Cave One," The Comprehensive Aramaic Lexicon Newsletter 12 (1996): 1–5, esp. 1–3. (http://cal1.cn.huc.edu/newsletter/lundberg.html; accessed October 6, 2013).
Pfann, S., "4QDaniel[d]: A Preliminary Edition with Critical Notes," RevQ 17 (1996): 65–68.
Schøyen, M., "MS 1926/4: The Daniel B Dead Sea Scroll," http://schoyencollection.com/HebrewAramaic.html (last accessed October 6, 2013).
Trever, J.C., "Completion of the Publication of Some Fragments from Qumran Cave I," RevQ 5 (1964–1966): 323–44, esp. 329–34.
Trever, J.C., "1QDan[a]: The Latest of the Qumran Manuscripts," RevQ 7 (1969–1970): 277–86.
Ulrich, E., "Daniel Manuscripts from Qumran, part 1: A Preliminary Edition of 4QDan[a]," BASOR 268 (1987): 17–37.
Ulrich, E., "Daniel Manuscripts from Qumran, part 2: Preliminary Editions of 4QDan[b] and 4QDan[c]," BASOR 274 (1989): 3–26.
Ulrich, E., "Orthography and Text in 4QDan[a] and 4QDan[b] and in the Received Masoretic Text," in Of Scribes and Scrolls: Studies on the Hebrew Bible, Intertestamental Judaism, and Christian Origins Presented to John Strugnell on the Occasion of His Sixtieth Birthday (eds. H.W. Attridge, J.J. Collins, and T.H. Tobin; Lanham: University Press of America, 1990), 29–42 (reprint in Flint–VanderKam [eds.], *DSS, 148–62).
Ulrich, E., "Daniel," *DJD XVI: 239–77.
Ulrich, E., "Daniel, Book of: Hebrew and Aramaic Text," *EDSS, 1:170–74.
Ulrich, E., "The Text of Daniel in the Qumran Scrolls," in The Book of Daniel: Composition and Reception (eds. J.J. Collins and P.W. Flint; 2 vols.; VTSup 83; Leiden: Brill, 2001), 2.573–85.
Ulrich, E., *BQS, 755–75.
Ulrich, E. and C. Niccum, "115. 4QDan[d]," *DJD XVI: 279–88.

Armin Lange

18.2.2 Masoretic Texts and Ancient Texts Close to MT

MT-Dan is the only complete Hebrew-Aramaic text of Daniel.[1] MT-Dan starts with Hebrew (Dan 1:1–2:4a), changes to Aramaic (Dan 2:4b–7:28), and then returns to Hebrew until the end of the book (Daniel 8–12). This linguistic division is also present in all of the Qumran manuscripts of Daniel (→ 18.2.1), and the transitions between the languages are attested in 1QDan[a] 1 ii 3–4 (where the transition in Dan 2:4 is marked off by a *vacat*) and 4QDan[a] frg. 14 (where the transition between chs. 7 and 8 is marked by a blank line; in 4QDan[b] frgs. 15–19, the linguistic distinction between Daniel 7–8 is maintained but they are each located on different fragments). This early evidence[2] makes it almost

---

[49] Against Tov, *"Synthese," 20, 27, who describes 6QpapDan as non-aligned.

[1] The eight published Qumran biblical manuscripts (1QDan[a,b]; 4QDan[a–e]; 6QpapDan) together cover parts of the first eleven chapters, but only fragmentarily (→ 18.2.1). A quotation from 4Q174 (4QFlorilegium) contains an excerpt from Daniel 12, thus completing coverage of all the chapters in MT-Dan.

[2] 4QDan[c] (4Q114), which has been dated by Cross, *ALQ2, 43 (quoted by Ulrich, "Daniel Manuscripts," 20; Ulrich, "Daniel,"

certain that the bilingual text as found in MT-Dan reflects the original version of the book.³

MT-Dan consists of twelve chapters, divided evenly between stories (Daniel 1–6) and apocalyptic visions (Daniel 7–12). In contrast, OG-Dan (→ 18.3.1) and Th-Dan (→ 18.3.1, → 18.3.2 and esp. → 18.3.2.3.1) both preserve three Additions to the book, including two independent stories (Susanna, Bel and the Dragon) and an extensive poetic passage in Daniel 3 (Prayer of Azariah and the Song of the Three Youths), and these expanded versions comprise different literary editions than (proto)-MT-Dan. The Qumran Daniel manuscripts (see → 18.2.1) reflect the literary edition found in MT-Dan when positive evidence is preserved (see → 18.2.2.3; → 18.2.3).⁴ While exhibiting numerous variants vis-à-vis MT-Dan, the Qumran scrolls follow the general literary contours of MT-Dan and therefore attest to the antiquity of this edition.

18.2.2.1 History of Research

Textual criticism of Daniel has focused primarily on MT-Dan and OG-Dan (→ 18.3.1), with recourse to Th-Dan (→ 18.3.1; → 18.3.2) and the other ancient translations (S [→ 18.3.3] and V [→ 18.3.6])⁵ in reference to individual details.⁶ While individual readings of significance can be found in each of these textual versions, special attention has been paid to the relationship between MT-Dan and OG-Dan in Daniel 4–6, where there are major differences reflected between the two textual witnesses. These deviations are of such significance that they point to the existence of alternate literary editions of the chapters in question, and therefore do not necessarily allow for direct comparison of individual readings.⁷

Prior to the discovery and the publication of the Dead Sea scrolls, there was a general tendency among scholars to dismiss the value and quality of the text of MT-Dan as being of "secondary character."⁸ This assessment was also connected to

---

270) as the earliest of the Qumran Daniel scrolls, from the late second century B.C.E., preserves material from Daniel 10 and 11. Similarly 4QDan^e (4Q116), which has been dated based upon paleographical considerations "to the early Hasmonaean period, i.e. not far from the beginning of the first century BCE" (Ulrich, "Daniel," 287), preserves seven fragments from Dan 9:12–17. Since the apocalyptic section of Daniel (chs. 7–12) was composed in the second century, this early evidence is therefore invaluable for determining the original language(s) of the book.

³ Contra numerous scholars who posited that chapters Daniel 1 and 8–12 were translated from Aramaic into Hebrew; cf. (among many) Charles, *Daniel*, xxx–l (and the extensive review of scholarly approaches); Ginsberg, *Studies in Daniel*, 41–61; Hartman and Di Lella, *Daniel*, 14–15 and *passim*.

⁴ Contra Tov, *Scribal Practices*, 335 (Appendix 8); Lange, *Handbuch*, 505–21, who classify the Daniel scrolls from Qumran (specifically 4QDan^a–c, which preserve enough material to warrant an assessment) as "non-aligned" or "independent." However, the case of Daniel is typologically similar to Jeremiah in which the short and long editions of LXX and MT respectively are employed as the primary characteristic for determining the textual affiliations of the preserved Qumran scrolls.

⁵ There is no Jewish Aramaic Targum to Daniel, even for the Hebrew sections.

⁶ Among the critical commentaries that address textual issues in Daniel, see especially the commentaries of Montgomery (*Daniel*); Charles (*Daniel*); Hartman and Di Lella (*Daniel*); Goldingay (*Daniel*); and Collins (*Daniel*).

⁷ The issue has been discussed extensively in Daniel scholarship; see the summaries of Collins, *Daniel*, 5–7; Tov, "Three Strange Books"; Lange, *Handbuch*, 513–54; Segal, *Dreams*, ch. 4 (in reference to Daniel 4). Scholars have generally posited one of three possible explanations for the relationship between them: 1) the Vorlage of OG-Dan reflects an earlier edition from which MT-Dan later developed (Riessler, *Daniel*, 28–44; Jahn, *Daniel*, esp. 36–48; Charles, *Daniel*, lvi–lvii, 79–82, 103–06; Albertz, *Der Gott*, 19–76; Wills, *The Jew in the Court*, 87–121; Munnich, "Texte massorétique," 99–107); 2) MT-Dan reflects the earlier edition from which OG-Dan developed (Bludau, *Die alexandrinische Übersetzung*, 143–54; Montgomery, *Daniel*, 37–38, *passim* [esp. 247–48]; Satran, *Early Jewish and Christian Interpretation*, 62–94); or 3) parallel independent literary development of the two versions, from a hypothesized third version (Collins, *Daniel*, 220–21; Henze, *The Madness of King Nebuchadnezzar*, 38–49; Tov, "Three Strange Books"; Ulrich, "Parallel Editions").

⁸ See, e.g., the extensive list of supposedly secondary readings in MT-Dan provided by Charles, *Daniel*, lix–lxviii. Charles suggests that this putative textually problematic state is due to the pseudonymous attribution of Daniel, and Jewish apocalypses in general (pp. lix–lx), but this claim is unconvincing. Montgomery, *Daniel*, 11–12 is more generous than Charles in his assessment of MT-Dan, but still "the whole bk. exhibits an extraordinary amount of variation ... the problem of original text is peculiarly accentuated for this bk" (12). He suggests that there is greater variation in the Aramaic sections than in the

the issue of the bilingual text in MT-Dan, and the complex theories posited as to its origins. Following the publication of the scrolls, which demonstrated the antiquity of both the consonantal base of MT and its bilingual background, scholars have presented a more balanced, positive view of MT-Dan.[9]

18.2.2.2 Manuscripts and Editions

In addition to the Qumran fragments (see → 18.2.1; → 18.2.3), the most important textual witnesses of MT-Dan are the following medieval manuscripts: MT^L (Leningrad [St. Petersburg] Codex B19a; dated 1008/1009); MT^S1 (Codex Sassoon 1053; tenth century; Tiberian, accurate, although somewhat careless copying); MT^L94 (Leningrad II Firkovich 94; eleventh century, Tiberian, medium precision); MT^L34 (Leningrad II Firkovich 34; end of the tenth century, Tiberian, accurate); MT^B1 (British Museum Add. 15251 [Margoliouth catalog 61]; Sephardic, dated 1448; despite its late date, belongs to the early Tiberian school).[10] MT-Dan is unfortunately among the lost sections of the Aleppo Codex.

BH[3] (MT-Dan prepared by W. Baumgartner, 1937) and *BHS* (MT-Dan prepared by W. Baumgartner, 1976) are diplomatic editions based upon MT^L, with variants referenced from other textual witnesses (including non-Masoretic versions), while the edition of Dotan presents a precise transcription of MT^L without the Masoretic notes present in the original manuscript.[11] Variants from medieval Masoretic manuscripts of Daniel were collated by Kennicott,[12] De Rossi,[13] and Ginsburg.[14] However, many manuscripts have subsequently been discovered and identified, and therefore these earlier apparata are incomplete.

18.2.2.3 The Nature and Text-Critical Character of (Proto-)MT-Dan

The orthography of MT-Dan is not fully consistent and attests to some isolated peculiarities (→ 1.2.2.4.1.2). Note the following phenomena, some of which seemingly reflect early orthography while others are specifically late.[15] Significant defective orthographic forms (generally considered earlier than plene forms) in MT-Dan can be found in, e.g., Dan 11:38 וֶלֱאֱלֹהַּ, "god" (the only other instance of this spelling is Deut 32:17);[16] 9:25 מֹצָא, "issuance" (the only other instance of this defective spelling is Job 38:27);[17] and 11:8 יָבִא, "he will bring" for the third masculine singular *hiphil* imperfect (which appears also in Num 6:10; Ps 78:29; Cant 8:11; Qoh 12:14).[18] Another "early" sign is the use of the *mater lectionis he* for the third singular masculine possessive suffix ה- as in Dan 11:10 מָעֻזֹּה, "his stronghold." At the same time, one also finds late plene forms, perhaps most prominently Dan 11:30 קוֹדֶשׁ, "holiness" and 11:6 כּוֹחַ, "strength," the only instances of plene spellings of either of these

---

Hebrew because the former was the "Jewish vernacular" and unlike the Hebrew was not perceived as "divine."

[9] Cf. Ulrich, "Daniel Manuscripts"; Ulrich, "Daniel"; Collins, *Daniel*, 2–3.

[10] I thank Dr. Rafael Zer of the Hebrew University Bible Project for this information. Numerous early medieval manuscripts of Daniel were also preserved in the Cairo Genizah (images of these can be accessed through the website of the Friedberg Genizah Project: https://fgp.genizah.org), and they all reflect copies that belong to the MT tradition, with only minor differences between them. However, the Genizah biblical manuscripts as a whole need to be studied more extensively before definitive conclusions can be reached about their precise textual affiliations.

[11] Dotan, *Biblia Hebraica Leningradensia*.

[12] Kennicott, *1776–1780, 2.573–604.

[13] De Rossi, *1784–1788, 4.133–34.

[14] C.D. Ginsburg (ed.), *The Writings, Diligently Revised according to the Massorah and the Early Editions with the Various Readings from Mss. and the Ancient Versions* (2 vols.; London: British and Foreign Bible Society), 2.631–82.

[15] Barr, *Variable Spellings* has cautioned against the simplistic assumption of early and late orthography by demonstrating that the copyists of (proto-)MT were not fully consistent in their orthography, with variation from book to book (and often even in the same book), and not necessarily according to the date of composition. At the same time, certain orthographic phenomena do suggest a gradual expansion over time towards plene orthography, and thus I employ the terms "early" and "late" here.

[16] The inconsistent nature of the orthography in MT can be demonstrated by the presence of a plene form of this same word subsequently in this verse; cf. Barr, *Variable Spellings*, 34, 38.

[17] Barr, *Variable Spellings*, 87.

[18] Barr, *Variable Spellings*, 100–01, 199.

words throughout all of MT, but attested in post-biblical literature. The inconsistent orthography of MT-Dan is perhaps the result of an incomplete revision during the transmission process, in which most of the early forms were replaced, but not all. This explains the few instances of distinct defective spellings, while also allowing for the unique plene readings that became commonplace in postbiblical literature.[19]

The *Qere-Ketiv* notes in MT-Dan preserve a number of textual and linguistic variations. An example of a textual variant can be identified in Dan 8:11, where the *Qere* reading is הֻגַּה "was suspended" (perhaps reflected also in Th-Dan ἐρράχθη "was overthrown"[20]), while the consonants of the *Ketiv* are הרים. The *Ketiv* reading can either be a *hiphil* form of the same verb ("to lift up, raise"), or a noun meaning "mountains" (as attested, e.g., in OG-Dan). In any event, the existence of both the OG-Dan reading, which matches the consonants of the *Ketiv*, and Th-Dan, which corresponds to the *Qere*, demonstrates that they reflect two readings that were extant in antiquity.

Scholars have analyzed the variant grammatical forms in the *Qere-Ketiv* notes in the Aramaic passages. Morrow and Clarke suggested that the reading tradition reflected in the *Qere* notes was based upon a later stage of Aramaic dating to 200–600 C.E.[21] In contrast, Fassberg demonstrated that these morphological forms reflect a contemporaneous stage of Aramaic to the *Ketiv* forms, and therefore do not represent a linguistic updating performed by later scribes.[22]

The text of MT-Dan has presented exegetes with a number of difficulties, and some of these may best be explained as the result of scribal error. A well-known example is found in Dan 2:24, in which the words עַל עַל, "(he) entered into" (verb + preposition) are perhaps the result of dittography, since another verb, אזל "to go," appears later in the same verse. The reading with only one על is attested in 4QDan[a] (4Q112) (→ 18.2.3.1).[23] Dittography is the best explanation for the inconsistent use of the plural in the expression (משמם) שקוצים "appalling abomination(s)" (Dan 9:27), which was perhaps created due to the duplication of the *mem* (contrast Dan 11:31; 12:11). Other potentially secondary readings were created due to harmonization. Thus, for example, the description of the horn in Dan 8:9 as מצעירה "small" in contrast to Old Greek ἰσχυρόν "strong" can be traced to the description of the horn in Dan 7:8 as זעירה "small."

At the same time, while these difficulties often lead scholars to posit complex emendations to MT-Dan, upon closer examination they are frequently revealed to reflect the Hebrew of the Second Temple period or, alternatively, the somewhat enigmatic language of apocalyptic literature. Many of these exegetical cruxes can be solved using appropriate linguistic and philological methods. Thus, for example, Dan 8:11–13 has been described as "one of the most difficult passages in Daniel owing to the corruptions of the text,"[24] and various commentators have suggested multiple emendations to make sense of these verses. However, the recognition that the word צבא in v. 12, which is generally translated as "force" or "host," is in fact better understood as "set, appointed period of time" (cf. Isa 40:2; Job 7:1)[25] obviates the need for correcting the text.[26] This is not to suggest that MT-Dan is free from error

---

[19] For such an orthographic revision in almost all books of the Hebrew Bible, see A. Lange, "The Question of the So-Called Qumran Orthography, the Severus Scroll, and the Masoretic Text," *Hebrew Bible and Ancient Israel* 3 (2014): 424–75 and → 1.2.2.4.1.2.

[20] Although this variant might have originally translated (וְ)הֻשְׁלַךְ, it functions in Th-Dan as the equivalent of הורם.

[21] Morrow and Clarke, "The *Ketib/Qere*."

[22] Fassberg, "The Origin."

[23] Note that OG-Dan translates only one of the two verbs referring to going, which perhaps reflects the text with only one על as a preposition. Alternatively, OG-Dan might reflect the translator's reduction of the two verbs to one, in order to make better sense of the text.

[24] Charles, *Daniel*, 204.

[25] As already suggested by HaCohen and Kil, *Sefer Daniel*, 200*.

[26] The syntax of the string of words in MT-Dan 8:13bβ is somewhat difficult, but should probably be interpreted as a shorthand reference to all of the tribulations previously mentioned in the apocalypse. OG-Dan to this passage is most likely an attempt by the translator to smooth over these supposed difficulties.

or other secondary readings (see above). However, it is overall of high quality and precision.

Finally, as noted above, MT-Dan reflects a specific literary edition in Daniel 4–6,[27] different from OG-Dan (→ 18.3.1). Some passages in MT-Dan 4–6 reflect secondary additions that have been added to an earlier edition, and specific verses can be demonstrated to reflect later formulations of an earlier version, weaving the stories together more coherently. Thus, MT-Dan 4:3–6, absent in OG-Dan, recounts how the Babylonian king first called his wise men to interpret his dream, and only when they were unsuccessful did he turn to Daniel (note also the reformulation of Dan 4:15 vis-à-vis OG-Dan). This has the effect of bringing the story in Daniel 4 in line with those in Daniel 2 and 5. Similarly, in MT-Dan 5:18–22, also absent in OG-Dan, Daniel refers back to the incidents in Daniel 4 when addressing Belshazzar. These additions have the effect of integrating more fully the stories in Daniel.[28] At the same time, beyond the secondary additions one finds in MT-Dan, it appears that this textual witness preserves a literary stage closer to an earlier version of these chapters. Once these additions are recognized and omitted, the text of these chapters flows relatively logically and smoothly.[29] In contrast, OG-Dan 4–6 reflect a more thorough rewriting, including expansion and elaboration (often based on exegetical or harmonistic considerations), further removed from their putative original kernel (not identical to MT-Dan).[30]

18.2.2.4 Date and Milieu

One can identify differences in details between MT-Dan, the Qumran scrolls of Daniel (→ 18.2.1; → 18.2.3), and the other versions. At the same time, as noted above, the Qumran scrolls all reflect the same literary edition as MT-Dan when positive evidence is available. Amongst the Qumran scrolls, the earliest evidence for the proto-MT edition is found in 4QDan^c, which is dated to the late second century B.C.E. We can therefore conclude that this edition was already in existence by this date, and the medieval MT-Dan is a direct descendant of this edition. However, due to the differences between the Qumran scrolls and MT-Dan in details, the specific text of this literary edition was not yet established, and was still in a state of flux during the late Second Temple period, as is the case in a number of biblical books. The precise date of its textual stabilization is difficult to determine. The second half of the book (Daniel 7–12) exhibits less variety amongst the textual witnesses than the first half (Daniel 1–6), and in particular when comparing MT-Dan and OG-Dan. This seems doubly significant when one considers that the stories in the first half of the book are generally dated earlier than the apocalypses.[31] This perhaps suggests a complex process of textual transmission and development, or alternatively that textual stabilization occurred rather abruptly near the time of composition of the apocalypses.[32]

---

[27] See further → 18.1.

[28] This has been noted previously by many scholars; see the discussion in Segal, *Dreams*, ch. 4. Significantly, the secondary additions and reformulations are attested in the Qumran Daniel scrolls. MT-Dan 5:17, in which Daniel declines in advance any reward from the king, is also absent in OG-Dan and is probably also secondary in MT-Dan; note the contradiction with Dan 5:29. Verse 17 was possibly added to present Daniel in similar terms to Abraham as depicted in Gen 14:22–24.

[29] This claim refers to the broader contours of these chapters, and not to individual details, in which MT-Dan sometimes reflects a secondary text.

[30] This phenomenon of rewriting is typologically similar to the 4QReworked Pentateuch texts (4Q364–367). For a similar conclusion, see Tov, "Three Strange Books."

[31] Daniel 1 is perhaps an exception to this statement. However, overall it appears relatively safe to posit that the stories are in fact earlier. In any event, the greatest textual-literary variety is found in Daniel 4–6, and there is general consensus regarding the earlier date of these chapters.

[32] Despite the general trend of greater uniformity between the textual witnesses in the second half of Daniel, I have noted elsewhere that the quotation from Daniel in 4Q174 (4QFlorilegium), frgs. 1–3, col. ii, 3–4a, which appears to be a combination of Dan 11:32 and 12:10, perhaps reflects a secondary development in the history of the text of Daniel, typologically similar to the developments found in other texts generally referred to today as "reworked" or "rewritten"; cf. Segal, "Text of Daniel." This suggests that the text of the apocalyptic section also continued to develop, although this is attested only in indirect witnesses.

18.2.2.5 Relevance for Exegesis and Literary Analysis

MT-Dan is the only complete witness for the Hebrew-Aramaic version of the book, and coupled with its high quality, justifies beyond all doubt the important role that it plays in the exegesis of the book of Daniel. Moreover, the evidence that MT-Dan (when compared with OG-Dan) provides for the literary growth of Daniel 4–6 offers us a rare glimpse into the process of the literary development of the books of the Hebrew Bible.

Albertz, R., *Der Gott des Daniel: Untersuchungen zu Daniel 4–6 in der Septuagintafassung sowie zu Komposition und Theologie des aramäischen Danielbuches* (SBS 131; Stuttgart: Katholisches Bibelwerk, 1988).

Barr, *Variable Spellings.

Bludau, A., *Die alexandrinische Übersetzung des Buches Daniel und ihr Verhältnis zum massorethischen Text* (Freiburg: Herder'sche, 1897).

Charles, R.H., *A Critical and Exegetical Commentary on the Book of Daniel: With Introduction, Indexes, and a New English Translation* (Oxford: Clarendon Press, 1929).

Collins, J.J., *Daniel* (Hermeneia; Minneapolis: Fortress, 1993).

Cross, *ALQ².

Dotan, A., *Biblia Hebraica Leningradensia* (Peabody: Hendrickson, 2001).

Fassberg, S., "The Origin of the *Ketib/Qere* in the Aramaic Portions of Ezra and Daniel," VT 39 (1989): 1–12.

Ginsberg, H.L., *Studies in Daniel* (Texts and Studies of the Jewish Theological Seminary of America 14; New York: JTSA, 1948).

Goldingay, J.E., *Daniel* (WBC 30; Nashville: Thomas Nelson, 1989).

HaCohen, S. and Y. Kil, *Sefer Daniel* (Daat Mikra; Jerusalem: Mossad Harav Kook, 1994) [Hebr.].

Hartman, L.F. and A.A. Di Lella, *The Book of Daniel: A New Translation with Introduction and Commentary* (AB 23; New York: Doubleday, 1978).

Henze, M., *The Madness of King Nebuchadnezzar: The Ancient Near Eastern Origins and Early History of Interpretation of Daniel 4* (JSJSup 61; Leiden: Brill, 1999).

Jahn, G., *Das Buch Daniel nach der Septuaginta hergestellt* (Leipzig: Eduard Pfeiffer, 1904).

Lange, *Handbuch, 505–21.

Montgomery, J.A., *A Critical and Exegetical Commentary on the Book of Daniel* (ICC; Edinburgh: T & T Clark, 1927).

Morrow, W.S. and E.G. Clarke, "The *Ketib/Qere* in the Aramaic Portions of Ezra and Daniel," VT 36 (1986): 406–22.

Munnich, O., "Texte massorétique et Septante dans le livre de Daniel," in Schenker, *Earliest Text, 93–120.

Riessler, P., *Das Buch Daniel: Textkritische Untersuchung* (Stuttgart: J. Roth, 1899).

Satran, D., "Early Jewish and Christian Interpretation of the Fourth Chapter of the Book of Daniel" (PhD diss., Hebrew University of Jerusalem, 1985).

Segal, M., *Dreams, Riddles, and Visions: Textual, Intertextual and Exegetical Studies of the Book of Daniel* (BZAW; Berlin: De Gruyter, forthcoming).

Segal, M., "The Text of Daniel at Qumran," *Meghilloth* (forthcoming) [Hebr.].

Tov, *Scribal Practices.

Tov, E., "Three Strange Books of the LXX: 1 Kings, Esther, and Daniel Compared with Similar Rewritten Compositions from Qumran and Elsewhere," in Karrer–Kraus, *Septuaginta 2008, 369–93.

Ulrich, E.C., "Daniel Manuscripts from Qumran: Part 1: A Preliminary Edition of 4QDan^a," BASOR 268 (1987): 17–37.

Ulrich, E.C., "Daniel," *DJD XVI: 239–89.

Ulrich, E.C., "The Parallel Editions of the Old Greek and Masoretic Text of Daniel 5," in *A Teacher for All Generations: Essays in Honor of James C. VanderKam* (eds. E.F. Mason et al.; 2 vols.; JSJSup 153; Leiden: Brill, 2012), 1.201–17.

Wills, L.M., *The Jew in the Court of the Foreign King: Ancient Jewish Court Legends* (HDR 26; Minneapolis: Fortress, 1990).

Michael Segal

18.2.3 Other Texts

The Qumran manuscripts of Daniel (→ 18.2.1) provide the earliest evidence for the book in its original languages, Hebrew and Aramaic. Eight manuscripts have been published to date in the *DJD series: 1QDan^{a,b} (1Q71–72); 4QDan^{a-e} (4Q112–116); 6QpapDan (6Q7). The following three manuscripts are of significance for their textual relationship vis-à-vis the other versions.

18.2.3.1 4QDanᵃ (4Q112)

4QDanielᵃ, dated to the mid-first century B.C.E., preserves passages from all sections of Daniel.[1] This scroll offers complex evidence in terms of its affiliation with the other textual witnesses. Regarding minor textual details, the scroll preserves, for example, some unique or independent readings:

- Dan 2:31 חזוה "its appearance" instead of the graphically similar זיוה "its splendor" (all Versions);
- Dan 3:2 מכדנצר "Mechaᵈnezzar," although almost certainly a corruption of נבוכדנצר "Nebuchadnezzar" (4QDanᵃ also lacks the word מלכא, "king");[2]
- in Dan 2:24, the scroll reads only one על "to" instead of the dittography על על "went to" found in other versions.[3]

Other readings are shared with 4QDanᵇ (→ 18.2.3.2) when these two scrolls overlap: Dan 5:12 – the two additional words וּכְתָבָא יקרא "and read the writing" are found uniquely in these two scrolls;[4] or with 4QDanᵇ and OG-Dan, as in Dan 8:3 where all three share the additional adjective גדול "great" in reference to the ram. 4QDanᵃ shares a number of readings exclusively with OG-Dan, which suggests that there is also some degree of affinity between 4QDanᵃ and the *Vorlage* of OG-Dan. These include a longer text in Dan 1:20; 2:20: the divine epithet modified by רבא "great"; 2:23: [רא]ונהי "li[ght]" against all other versions וגבורתא "strength"; 2:28,[5] 40; 8:4: the additional direction ומזרחה "and to the east."[6] In Dan 2:30, the scroll has the additional word יתירא "more (than)" in agreement with the Peshitta. Thus, in reference to minor details, 4QDanᵃ can be classified as independent, with affinities to both 4QDanᵇ and OG-Dan.[7]

The textual background of these variants from MT-Dan (→ 18.2.2) can be evaluated with an attempt to determine the direction of development from "original"/"early" to "secondary." This evaluation is somewhat subjective, and although a definitive decision cannot be reached in every instance, it still allows for a general characterization of the textual witness in question. As suggested above, 4QDanᵃ preserves some original readings in contrast to MT (including Dan 2:24 and 5:12). At the same time, it has suffered from scribal corruption (Dan 3:2; perhaps also in Dan 2:31).[8] The text of 4QDanᵃ reflects small-scale harmonizations including Dan 2:20 (under the influence of 2:45); 2:23 (from 2:22); 2:28 (from 2:4; 3:5; 5:10; 6:7, 22); and 2:40 (from 2:35, 39). Small stylistic additions can be identified in Dan 2:30 and 8:3, while the addition of "and to the east" in Dan 8:4 reflects additional content, in order to indicate the idea that the ram will attack in all directions. The longer text of Dan 1:20 in both 4QDanᵃ and OG-Dan can be explained either as a *homoioteleuton* in MT-Dan,[9] or an expansion in the Qumran scroll.[10] In all of the instances above in which MT-Dan was determined to reflect a secondary reading in comparison to 4QDanᵃ, it was

---

[1] For a complete description of the contents and dating of 4Q112, see → 18.2.1.3.

[2] Note that Th-Dan lacks the complete phrase נבוכדנצר מלכא "King Nebuchadnezzar."

[3] OG-Dan similarly only reflects one verb in this verse, but might reflect reduction by the translator, cf. → 18.2.2, note 23. A similar reading is attested in some MT manuscripts.

[4] Some scholars have suggested that this is a secondary harmonization to the fuller expression "read the reading and tell its meaning" in Dan 5:7, 17 (Collins, *Daniel*, 3, 238 [second possibility]; Ulrich, "Daniel," 251). Others (including myself) have posited that the Qumran scrolls reflect the original text, while the other textual witnesses (MT, Th, S, V) reflect a secondary reading due to *homoioteleuton* (Collins, *Daniel*, 238 [first possibility]; M. Segal, "Rereading the Writing on the Wall [Daniel 5]," *ZAW* 125 [2013]: 161–76 [170–72]).

[5] For the arguments for this reconstruction of this reading, cf. Ulrich, "Daniel," 245.

[6] Charles, *Daniel*, 200 (offering both options) and Collins, *Daniel*, 325, 330 posit that this reading is original to the text of Daniel 8, but it seems to me more likely a secondary attempt to refer to all four directions. Note also the different location of this reading in the Hebrew and Greek evidence, which suggests that these are in fact independent attempts to complete the list of directions.

[7] Cf. Lange, *Handbuch*, 506. Tov, *Scribal Practices*, 335 (Appendix 8), classifies 4QDanᵃ as "independent," but does not refer to the web of affinities to other textual witnesses.

[8] Although this reading could also be categorized as harmonization to the same term in Dan 2:19, 28.

[9] So, e.g., Collins, *Daniel*, 128–29.

[10] Cf. a similar addition in OG-Dan 3:30.

concluded that this was due to scribal error. In contrast, 4QDanᵃ contains secondary readings that are the result of exegetical considerations, which lead to the conclusion that it is typologically later than (proto-)MT-Dan.¹¹

4QDanielᵃ reflects the same literary edition as MT-Dan (in contrast to the edition preserved in OG-Dan), where the remaining fragmentary evidence provides proof of such textual affiliation (cf. → 18.2.2).¹² OG-Dan (→ 18.3.1) lacks Dan 5:17–22 (according to the versification of MT-Dan), and scholars generally agree that they are secondary to this chapter.¹³ Verses 17–19 are partially preserved in 4QDanᵃ 12, demonstrating that the Qumran scroll preserves an MT-Dan edition of the book.¹⁴ The distinction between the textual affiliation based upon the individual variants versus the broader literary edition necessarily leads to a complex characterization of this scroll.

18.2.3.2 4QDanᵇ (4Q113)

4QDanielᵇ, dated to c. 20–50 C.E., preserves nineteen fragments of readable text spanning Daniel 5–8.¹⁵ This scroll offers somewhat limited evidence in terms of its affiliation with the other textual witnesses. Regarding minor textual details, the scroll preserves, for example, some unique or independent readings, such as Dan 6:15: לזבוּתה instead of MT לְשֵׁיזָבוּתֵהּ (= Vrs) "to save him," although this might simply be the result of scribal error; and the absence of the word יקום "arose" in Dan 6:20. Other readings are shared with 4QDanᵃ: 5:12; or with 4QDanᵃ and OG-Dan: 8:3 (for both, see above, → 18.2.3.1). The other variants found in this scroll vis-à-vis other witnesses are not significant enough to help determine its textual affiliations. Thus, in reference to individual textual details, 4QDanᵇ cannot be definitively aligned with any of the other textual witnesses of the book,¹⁶ other than its similarities to 4QDanᵃ in the passages in which they overlap. However, unlike 4QDanᵃ, 4QDanᵇ does not attest to significant shared readings with OG-Dan (other than the additional adjective גדול "great" in Dan 8:3 found in both scrolls and OG-Dan).¹⁷

The textual background of these variants from MT-Dan (→ 18.2.2) can be evaluated with an attempt to determine the direction of development from "original"/"early" to "secondary." This evaluation is somewhat subjective, and although a definitive decision cannot be reached in every instance, it still allows for a general characterization of the textual witness in question. As suggested above, 4QDanᵇ preserves an original reading in contrast to MT (Dan 5:12). At the same time, it has suffered from scribal corruption (Dan 6:15; perhaps also Dan

---

¹¹ If one disagrees regarding the evaluation of a specific reading, it still does not change the overall evaluation of 4QDanᵃ. If, for example, one considers MT-Dan 5:12 to be original (cf. above, note 4), then the reading preserved in 4QDanᵃ,ᵇ would be considered another example of harmonization.

¹² Cf. Ulrich, "Text of Daniel," 581–83; Segal, "Text of Daniel." Since 4QDanᵃ preserves only the beginning of Daniel 3, it is impossible to prove whether or not it included the addition to this chapter found in both Greek versions. Hence the claim about the literary edition reflected in this scroll should perhaps be qualified since it is possible that it follows the contours of the edition in Th-Dan. However, since there is no evidence whatsoever of the Additions to Daniel (→ 11.3) present in the Qumran manuscripts, it is preferable to refer to these scrolls as following the contours of MT-Dan (→ 18.2.2).

¹³ Verses 18–22 refer explicitly to Daniel 4, and were presumably added to solidify the connection between the stories in chs. 4 and 5. Verse 17 contradicts v. 29 and perhaps was added to the chapter in order to describe Daniel as similar to Abraham in Gen 14:22–23; see Collins, *Daniel*, 242, 249–50; Segal, "Text of Daniel."

¹⁴ The characterization of literary editions here is similar to the Qumran Cave 4 Jeremiah texts, which can be classified according to their respective correspondence to the two literary editions of the book.

¹⁵ For a complete description of the contents and dating of 4Q113, see → 18.2.1.4.

¹⁶ Tov, *Scribal Practices*, 335 (Appendix 8) has classified the scroll as "independent (?)."

¹⁷ Ulrich, "Orthography" has suggested that 4QDanᵇ was perhaps copied from 4QDanᵃ (albeit with orthographic differences); cf. also Tov, *Scribal Practices*, 29; Lange, *Handbuch*, 507–08, and above → 18.2.1.3–4. The minor amount of overlap between these two scrolls, however, prevents definitive conclusions about this issue. In addition, if the single unique shared reading in Dan 5:12 reflects the original reading of this verse (cf. above, n. 4), then this agreement is less significant for establishing a relationship between them. Furthermore, 4QDanᵇ does not exhibit the same special affinity to OG-Dan in the fragments where the former is extant.

6:20).[18] A small stylistic addition can be identified at 8:3 (shared with 4QDanᵃ and OG-Dan). Based upon this evidence alone, it is difficult to ascertain whether 4QDanᵇ is typologically earlier or later than (proto-)MT-Dan.[19]

4QDanielᵇ reflects the same literary edition as MT-Dan (in contrast to the edition preserved in OG-Dan), where the remaining fragmentary evidence provides proof of such textual affiliation (cf. above, → 18.2.2).[20] Frgs. 5–6 preserve Dan 5:19–22, which are absent from OG-Dan (cf. above, → 18.2.3.1). Similarly, the text of Daniel 6 that is preserved in frgs. 7–11 follows the contours of the text of MT-Dan, in contrast to the version in OG-Dan (→ 18.3.1). Taken together, these demonstrate that 4QDanᵇ preserves an MT-Dan edition of the book.[21] The distinction between the textual affiliations based upon the individual variants versus the literary editions necessarily leads to a complex characterization of this scroll.

18.2.3.3 4QDanᶜ (4Q114)

4QDanielᶜ, dated to the late second century B.C.E., preserves three fragments from Daniel 10–11. This is the earliest extant manuscript of Daniel, copied approximately only fifty years after the composition of the book as a whole.[22]

In reference to individual textual details, 4QDanᶜ cannot be definitively aligned with any of the other textual witnesses of the book,[23] and is therefore generally described by scholars as textually "independent."[24] Regarding minor textual details, the scroll preserves, for example, some unique or independent readings, e.g.: Dan 10:12 בעב[ו]רך "on your behalf" instead of the graphically similar בדבריך "because of your words" (= all Vrs, except LXX⁹⁶⁷ in which it is absent); or Dan 11:16 בעזו "in his power" instead of בידו "in his hand(s)" (= all Vrs). The difficulty in aligning 4QDanᶜ with other textual witnesses can be exemplified by two adjacent readings in Dan 11:1: the scroll reads דריוש המדי "Darius the Mede" in agreement with MT, Peshitta, and the Vulgate, in contrast to Κύρου τοῦ βασιλέως "Cyrus the king" in Old Greek and Theodotion. The next word, עמדתי "I stood" is in agreement with Theodotion and the Vulgate, in contrast to other readings in MT, the Peshitta, and Old Greek. Due to this complexity, 4QDanᶜ should be classified as independent, without any prominent textual affiliations.[25] Based upon the evidence alone, it is difficult to ascertain whether 4QDanᶜ is typologically earlier or later than (proto-)MT-Dan.

Charles, R.H., *A Critical and Exegetical Commentary on the Book of Daniel: With Introduction, Indexes, and a New English Translation* (Oxford: Clarendon Press, 1929).

Collins, J.J., *Daniel* (Hermeneia; Minneapolis: Fortress, 1993).

Lambach, P.J., "A Detailed Comparison of 4QDanᶜ and the Other Qumran Texts of Daniel with the Masoretic

---

[18] It is difficult to understand this sentence without the verb יקום. At the same time, it is unclear what would have caused this word to be omitted.

[19] If, for example, one considers MT Dan 5:12 to be original (cf. above, n. 4), then the reading preserved in 4QDanᵇ (and 4QDanᵃ) would be considered another example of harmonization, and together with the stylistic addition in Dan 8:3, point in the direction of a text typologically later than (proto-)MT-Dan.

[20] Cf. n. 12 above.

[21] Cf. n. 14 above.

[22] For a complete description of the contents and dating of 4Q114, see → 18.2.1.5.

[23] There are minor overlaps with 4QDanᵃ and 6QpapDan, but neither is significant enough to assess their respective relationships with 4QDanᶜ.

[24] Tov, *Scribal Practices*, 335 (appendix 8; although accompanied by question mark); Lange, *Handbuch*, 509 categorizes it as "non-aligned." Lambach, *Comparison*, provides a detailed analysis of all of the readings in 4QDanᶜ, comparing it with MT-Dan and the other Qumran manuscripts. He concludes that 4QDanᶜ (along with 1QDanᵃ, 1QDanᵇ, and pap6QDan) copied its *Vorlage* conservatively, having identified this *Vorlage* as a proto-MT version of Daniel (cf. Lambach, *Comparison*, 190). While this work is helpful in collecting the textual data, Lambach assumes that (proto-)MT-Dan reflects a putatively early stage in the textual history, which colors his analysis of the variant readings in the different scrolls and the textual character of each scroll.

[25] The surviving fragments of 4QDanᶜ only contain material from Daniel 10–12. Since these chapters are preserved in the same literary edition in all extant textual witnesses, and there are no large-scale differences in these fragments, there is no evidence in 4QDanᶜ for an alternate literary edition of the book of Daniel.

Text of Daniel" (PhD diss., Mid-America Baptist Theological Seminary, 1997).

Lange, *Handbuch*, 505–21.

Segal, M., "The Text of Daniel at Qumran," *Meghilloth*, forthcoming [Hebr.].

Ulrich, E., "Daniel Manuscripts from Qumran: Part 1: A Preliminary Edition of 4QDan^a," *BASOR* 268 (1987): 17–37.

Ulrich, E., "Daniel Manuscripts from Qumran: Part 2: Preliminary Editions of 4QDan^b and 4QDan^c," *BASOR* 274 (1989): 3–26.

Ulrich, E., "Orthography and Text in 4QDan^a and 4QDan^b and in the Received Masoretic Text," in *Of Scribes and Scrolls: Studies on the Hebrew Bible, Intertestamental Judaism, and Christian Origins Presented to John Strugnell on the Occasion of His Sixtieth Birthday* (eds. H.W. Attridge, J.J. Collins, and T.H. Tobin; Lanham: University Press of America, 1990), 29–42 (reprint in Ulrich, *DSS, 148–62).

Ulrich, E., "Daniel," *DJD XVI: 239–77.

Ulrich, E., "The Text of Daniel in the Qumran Scrolls," in *The Book of Daniel: Composition and Reception* (eds. J.J. Collins and P.W. Flint; 2 vols; VTSup 83; Leiden: Brill, 2001), 2.573–85.

Michael Segal

18.3 Primary Translations

18.3.1 Septuagint

18.3.1.1 Background

The book of Daniel has survived in two Greek translations that differ greatly one from the other: the older Old Greek Daniel (OG-Dan), and the subsequent so-called Theodotion version of Daniel (Th-Dan; → 18.3.2). At an early point in the transmission of the Septuagint, probably during the third century C.E., OG-Dan was rejected and, for reasons no longer known, it was replaced in church usage by Th-Dan, as is witnessed by Jerome in the prologue to his Daniel translation.[1] After offering several conjectures as to the cause of this replacement, Jerome finally declares that OG-Dan was rightly rejected because it differs greatly from the "original," by which he means the Textus Receptus of his time, proto-MT (→ 18.2.2). Indeed, OG-Dan deviates considerably from MT-Dan, especially in Daniel 4–6, while Th-Dan closely parallels the Hebrew and Aramaic found in MT.

The rejection of OG-Dan led to the unfortunate situation in which Th-Dan was transmitted as the authorized Septuagint version of Daniel in all known Septuagint manuscripts, while the transmission of OG-Dan was essentially discontinued. As a result, there remain today only three extant witnesses to OG-Dan, and only two of these are in Greek.

The three witnesses to OG-Dan are: 1) The Hexaplaric Codex Chisianus (the "Chigi" Manuscript, or LXX^{88} [87]). This cursive manuscript dates to the period between the ninth and eleventh centuries C.E., and was first published in 1772 by de Magistris.[2] It also contains Th-Dan;[3] 2) The Syro-Hexapla (Syh) version (this very slavish translation of OG-Dan into Syriac was made in 615–617 C.E. by Bishop Paul of Tella from the fifth column of Origen's Hexapla; it appears in folios 143^a–151^b of Codex Ambrosianus, → 18.4.4);000[4] and 3) Papyrus LXX^{967}. This pre-Hexaplaric text was discovered in Egypt in 1931 and has been dated to the second or third century C.E. It contains portions of Daniel, Ezekiel, and Esther. Sections of LXX^{967} are found in three different locations around the world and were published at different times.[5] Many significant differences can be identified between the text of papyrus LXX^{967} and LXX^{88}/Syh, the most interesting of which is the arrangement of the chapters: in LXX^{967}, Daniel 7–8 appear after Daniel 4 (→ 18.3.1.5; cf. also → 18.4.7).

Th-Dan is documented in all Septuagint manuscripts, including the uncials LXX$^{A, B, Q, V, \text{and } Z(VI)}$; papyri LXX^{921} and LXX^{925}; and thirty-one minuscule manuscripts.[6] Although all the chapters of Th-Dan have been affected to some extent or another by the Hexapla, LXX^B is considered to be relatively free of such influence.[7]

---

[1] Translated by K.P. Edgecomb: http://www.tertullian.org/fathers/jerome_preface_daniel.htm

[2] S. de Magistris, *Daniel secundum Septuaginta ex tetraplis Origenis nunc primum editus a singulari Chrisiano codice* (Rome: Typis Propagandae Fidei, 1772). Reprinted in Göttingen, 1773, 1774 (Michaelis); Utrecht, 1775 (Segaar); Milan, 1788 (Bugati); Leipzig, 1845 (Hahn), 1854 (Tischendorf); Rome, 1877 (Cozza). See Bludau, *Daniel*, 25–28; Swete, *Introduction*, 193; Montgomery, *Daniel*, 24–26.

[3] Swete, *The Old Testament in Greek*, xii.

[4] The part of Codex Ambrosianus that contains the Syro-Hexapla is from the ninth century C.E. and was published by A.M. Ceriani, *Codex Syro-Hexaplaris Ambrosianus photolithographice editus* (Monumenta sacra et profana 7; Milan: Bibliotheca Ambrosiana, 1874).

[5] The first publication was made in 1937 by K.G. Kenyon, *The Chester Beatty Biblical Papyri*, and contains OG-Dan 3:72–7:27. Kenyon also was the first to report on the discovery in the London newspaper *The Times* of November 19, 1931, and again in "The Chester Beatty Biblical Papyri," *Gn* 8 (1932): 46–49. The other portions were published by Geissen, *Daniel*, Hamm, *Daniel: Kap. 1–2* and *Daniel: Kap. 3–4*, and Roca-Puig, "Daniel."

[6] See J. Ziegler, *Susanna, Daniel, Bel et Draco* (Septuaginta Vetus Testamentum Graecum 16.2; Göttingen: Vandenhoeck & Ruprecht, 1954), 28–29.

[7] See Montgomery, "The Hexaplaric Strata."

Ziegler divides the Th-Dan manuscripts into four main groupings:[8] 1) LXX^B and its dependent cursives LXX$^{26, 46, 130, 239}$; along with LXX^A, its dependents LXX$^{106, 584}$; and LXX^Q, with its dependents LXX$^{230, 233, 541}$. LXX^B and LXX^Q are very close to each other, while LXX^A shows several variants. See, for example, Dan 4:30(33): Ναβουχοδονοσορ "Nabouchodonosor" + τον βασιλεα "the king" (LXX^A)[9]; and Dan 9:24: λαόν σου "your people" + ισραηλ "Israel" (LXX^A);[10] 2) The Hexaplaric group (→ 18.3.4), which includes the uncial LXX^V and the cursives LXX$^{62, 147}$. According to Montgomery, these texts represent the oldest form of Origen's recension;[11] 3) The Lucianic (LXX^L) group, consisting of manuscripts LXX$^{22, 36, 48, 51, 96, 231, 763}$ (= LXX^L), LXX$^{311, 538}$ (= LXX^{Li}), LXX$^{88, 449}$ (= LXX^{Lii}), and LXX$^{z(vi)}$; 4) The Catena group (LXX^c), which is further divided into a main group containing the three manuscripts LXX$^{87, 91, 490}$, while manuscripts LXX$^{49, 90, 405, 764}$ belong to a subgroup.

The older critical editions of the Septuagint (Holmes and Parsons,[12] Swete,[13] and Rahlfs[14]) present the Chigi manuscript for OG-Dan. In the edition of Holmes and Parsons, the Chigi text of both OG-Dan and Th-Dan is marked as manuscript 88. Th-Dan is placed first, based on codex LXX^B, followed by OG-Dan, based on de Magistris' edition. Swete uses Cozza-Luzi's edition[15] of OG-Dan (marked by Swete as manuscript 87), and codex LXX^B for Th-Dan. In Swete, OG-Dan is printed on the left-hand page, together with variants from Syh (→ 18.4.4) translated back into Greek, while Th-Dan is displayed on the right-hand page with variants from the other uncials. Rahlfs' eclectic edition reconstructs OG-Dan from Chigi (marked as manuscript 88) and Syh, placing it at the top of the page, with Th-Dan at the bottom. In the 1954 Göttingen edition by Ziegler,[16] the text of OG-Dan appears at the bottom of the page and Th-Dan at the top. This eclectic edition gives a text of OG-Dan based on the Chigi manuscript (LXX^{88}), Syh, and the Chester Beatty portion of papyrus LXX^{967} published by Kenyon. However, the other sections of the papyrus were not available to Ziegler at that time. Therefore, a new edition under the same title was published by Munnich in 1999,[17] in which OG-Dan is reconstructed by Munnich on the basis of LXX^{88}, Syh, and all extant parts of papyrus LXX^{967}, with considerable preference given to the readings of that papyrus.

18.3.1.2 Date

The generally accepted view is that OG-Dan was created sometime in the second half of the second century B.C.E., presumably in Alexandria.[18] Its existence is almost certainly reflected in 1 Maccabees, which in turn is dated to the late second century B.C.E.[19] Bludau[20] provides a list of the references to OG-Dan in 1 Maccabees (→ 11.10.1.2); a well-known example is 1 Macc 1:54: βδέλυγμα ἐρημώσεως "an abomination of desolation," an exact quotation of OG-Dan 11:31. Another illustration of the influence of OG-Dan can be seen in 1 Macc 1:9: ἐπλήθυναν κακὰ ἐν τῇ γῇ "they multiplied evils on earth," which clearly reflects OG-Dan 12:4: καὶ πλησθῇ ἡ γῆ ἀδικίας "and the earth is filled with injusice," against MT and Th-Dan: וְתִרְבֶּה הַדָּעַת "and the knowledge shall increase." The resemblance between OG-Dan and 1 Esdras, καὶ πληθυνθῇ ἡ γνῶσις "and the knowledge

---

[8] Ziegler, *Daniel*, 44 ff. See also Jellicoe, *SMS*, 302; Montgomery, "The Hexaplaric Strata," who displays a different method of grouping.

[9] In most cases, English translations of LXX are taken from or guided by *NETS* and English translations of the MT and the New Testament are from the *NRSV*.

[10] See more in Ziegler, *Daniel*, 46.

[11] Montgomery, "The Hexaplaric Strata"; Montgomery, *Daniel*, 51.

[12] *Vetus Testamentum Graecum cum variis lectionibus, edidit Robertus Holmes continuavit Jacobus Parsons*, Vol. 5 (Oxford: Clarendon Press, 1827).

[13] Swete, *The Old Testament in Greek*.

[14] Rahlfs, *Septuaginta*.

[15] G. Cozza-Luzzi, *Sacrorum Bibliorum vetustissima fragmenta graeca et latina*, Part 3 (Rome: Spithoever, 1877).

[16] Above, n. 6.

[17] J. Ziegler and O. Munnich, *Susanna, Daniel, Bel et Draco* (2nd ed.; Septuaginta Vetus Testamentum Graecum 16.2; Göttingen: Academia Scientiarum Gottingensis, 1999).

[18] Montgomery, *Daniel*, 38; Hartman and Di Lella, *Daniel*, 78; Collins, *Daniel*, 8–9; and many others.

[19] See Rappaport, *Maccabees*, 8.

[20] Bludau, *Alexandrinische Übersetzung*, 9 n. 1.

is increased," in terms of translation technique also indicates a similar date, and possibly even the same translator.[21]

Establishing the date of Th-Dan is more problematic. This translation is attributed to Theodotion, who is traditionally believed to have lived around 180 C.E.[22] However, both the New Testament and the book of Baruch (ca. 70 C.E.) provide evidence that a similar translation existed at an earlier date. While some citations in the New Testament correspond with OG-Dan,[23] others interestingly reflect Th-Dan.[24] For instance, Heb 11:33: ἔφραξαν στόματα λεόντων "shut the mouths of the lions" corresponds with Th-Dan 6:22(23). Muraoka notes Daniel 6:20 as the reference: ἐνέφραξε τὰ στόματα τῶν λεόντων "closed the mouths of the lions"; Rev 11:7: ποιήσει μετ' αὐτῶν πόλεμον "will make war with them" parallels Th-Dan 7:21: ἐποίει πόλεμον μετὰ τῶν …[25] "made war with the …" Therefore, most scholars assume that an older translation already existed in the first century, which was adapted by Theodotion. For example, Gwynn suggested that another Greek translation was circulating in the pre-Christian era alongside OG-Dan, and was known to the translator of the book of Baruch, to the authors of the New Testament, and to the earliest apostolic fathers. In Gwynn's view, this translation later became the basis for the Theodotion recension.[26] Montgomery spoke of "Ur-Theodotion," an oral Hellenistic translation, which was later adapted by the historical Theodotion in the early second century C.E.[27] On the other hand, Barthélemy argued for a Palestinian recension produced between 30 and 50 C.E., which he called "Proto-Theodotion" or *kaige*. His view was largely influenced by the discovery of the Greek translation of the twelve Minor Prophets found at Naḥal Ḥever.[28] A different proposal was offered by Ziegler, who denied the relation of Th-Dan to the historical Theodotion.[29] Schmitt built on Ziegler's research,[30] and made an extensive comparison of Th-Dan and Theodotion in the rest of the Old Testament. He arrived at the conclusion that Th-Dan does not belong to the same translational tradition as the Theodotion tradition in the rest of the Old Testament, and his analysis was accepted and strengthened by McLay[31] and Di Lella.[32]

Therefore, it is clear that the date of Th-Dan should be fixed at no later than the first half of the first century C.E. Other questions concerning the nature of Th-Dan and its relationship to OG-Dan will be discussed below; → 18.3.2 and → 18.3.5.

18.3.1.3 Form

The two Greek versions differ from MT-Dan (→ 18.2.2) in that they contain three deuterocanonical sections known as the "Additions to Daniel" (→ 11.3.2).[33] The first addition appears between Dan

---

[21] See Montgomery, *Daniel*, 38.

[22] We know practically nothing about the historical Theodotion. Irenaeus (202 C.E.), in his *Adversus Haereses* III.24, mentions him as a Jew who translated the Old Testament, and Epiphanius, bishop of Salamis at the end of the fourth century C.E., places him under Commodus (180–192 C.E.). See discussions by Gwynn, "Theodotion"; Bludau, *Daniel*, 16–25; Montgomery, *Daniel*, 46–50; Collins, *Daniel*, 10; Di Lella, "The Textual History."

[23] See Grelot, "Les Versions grecques."

[24] See the full list in the studies above, nn. 22–23.

[25] OG-Dan translates the same words as: πόλεμον συνιστάμενον πρὸς τοὺς … "preparing for war against …"

[26] Gwynn, "Theodotion."

[27] Montgomery, *Daniel*, 50.

[28] Barthélemy, *Devanciers*, 148. Barthélemy's assumption was accepted by Jellicoe, "Some Reflections," although he dates the recension to the second half of the first century B.C.E.

[29] Ziegler, *Daniel*, 28–29.

[30] Schmitt, *Stammt der sogenannte*; Schmitt, "Die griechischen Danieltexte."

[31] McLay, *OG and TH Version*, 222–27.

[32] Di Lella, "The Textual History"; Hartman and Di Lella, *Daniel*, 81–82.

[33] The Additions to Daniel also appear in all the ancient translations that are based on OG-Dan and Th-Dan. The question of the original language of the additions is still under discussion with most scholars tending toward Hebrew or Aramaic; see Delcor, *Daniel*, 100–106, 260–92; Schüpphaus, "Das Verhältniss"; Moore, *The Additions*; Koch, *Deuterokanonische Zusätze*; Collins, *Daniel*, 195–207, 405–39; Engel, *Susanna*; McLay, "Sousanna"; and McLay, "Bel and the Dragon" (for and electronic edition of the latter two publications, see http://ccat.sas.upenn.edu/nets/edition/). Joosten, "The Prayer of Azariah," tried to show that the addition in Daniel 3 was originally written in Greek.

3:23 and Dan 3:24 and is made up of three sections: the Prayer of Azariah; a prose section offering more details about the deliverance of Hananiah, Mishael, and Azariah (Shadrach, Meshach, and Abednego); and, finally, a hymn sung by these three men. The other two additions are the story of Susanna and that of Bel and the Dragon. The positions of these additions in the book are not fixed, differing in the various manuscripts. While both Th-Dan and OG-Dan contain all three additions, there remain considerable differences between these translations. The deviations between the two are relatively small in the addition to Daniel 3, very large in Susanna, while those found in Bel and the Dragon stand somewhere in the middle.[34]

In the canonical parts of the book, Th-Dan shows great affinity to MT-Dan, while in OG-Dan the situation differs among the various chapters. In Daniel 1–3 (excluding the additions) and Daniel 7–12, according to LXX[88]-Syh, OG-Dan runs quite parallel to MT/Theodotion, but in Daniel 4–6 the differences go beyond textual variants and seem more like independent accounts of the same events. Moreover, the nature of the differences varies greatly from one chapter to another. Daniel 4 in the Old Greek is much longer than MT/Theodotion and repeats many details. Daniel 5 is much shorter than MT/Theodotion, but contains two parallel Greek versions of the same account.[35] Daniel 6 is approximately the same length in the two versions, but the course of the account is different, and contains several pluses and minuses.

The survival of the book of Daniel in these different forms has raised numerous questions that are still under discussion: 1) Does papyrus LXX[967] reflect the original form of OG-Dan, both in terms of chapter order and in terms of textual variants? 2) What is the relationship between Th-Dan and OG-Dan? Is Th-Dan a recension of OG-Dan, a separate translation influenced by OG-Dan, or a completely independent translation? 3) Given that Daniel 4–6 differ so radically from MT/Theodotion, is it possible that we are dealing here with a different edition that was transmitted separately? If so, when were these chapters incorporated into the book of Daniel? Is the same translator responsible for these chapters and for the rest of the book, or were they translated by a different hand? 4) What is the nature of the Semitic *Vorlage* underlying OG-Dan, and is it older than MT/Theodotion?[36]

18.3.1.4 Old Greek: Relationship between Papyrus LXX[967] and Manuscript LXX[88]

The differences between these two texts are numerous, and many of them are rather significant. They also differ in the arrangement of the chapters. We now turn to the question as to which of these two manuscripts better reflects the original form of OG-Dan.

Some external criteria could point towards the priority of papyrus LXX[967]. Firstly, this papyrus is 600–900 years older than manuscript LXX[88], and therefore much closer to the time of the original translation since LXX[88] must have been copied several times prior to the ninth to eleventh centuries C.E. Secondly, LXX[88] is Hexaplaric (→ 18.3.4), while papyrus LXX[967] is pre-Hexaplaric. For these reasons, scholars show a preference for papyrus LXX[967] in most of the disagreements between the two manuscripts.[37] External criteria, however, do not provide enough weight to unequivocally ascertain the priority of either manuscript. Rather, each variant reading should be evaluated individually, and the text with the greatest number of preferable readings should be given priority.

In my PhD dissertation,[38] I systematically examined all the substantial variants between these two manuscripts in Daniel 1, and found no less then seventy percent preferable readings in LXX[88], while LXX[967] seemed to be secondary. Generally,

---

[34] See the bibliography in the previous note.
[35] See Amara, "The Third Version" [Hebr.].

[36] The assumption that the *Vorlage* of OG-Dan was Hebrew remains unsupported. See Charles, *Daniel*, xxx–xxxvii; Albertz, *Der Gott des Daniel*; Grelot, "La Septante de Daniel IV"; Grelot, "Le chapitre V"; Grelot, "Daniel VI."
[37] So Ziegler and Munnich, *Daniel*; Munnich, "Origene"; McLay, *OG and TH Versions*; McLay, "The Relationship."
[38] Amara, *The Old Greek Version*.

TABLE 1

	LXX⁹⁶⁷	LXX⁸⁸	Th-Dan	MT-Dan
Dan 1:3	καὶ εἶπεν ὁ βασιλεὺς Ασπανες "and the king told Aspanes" ἀγαγεῖν "to bring"	καὶ εἶπεν ὁ βασιλεὺς Αβιεσδρι "and the king told Abiesdri"[39] ἀγαγεῖν αὐτῷ "to bring him"[40]	καὶ εἶπεν ὁ βασιλεὺς Ασπανεζ "and the king told Aspanez" εἰσαγαγεῖν "to bring in"	וַיֹּאמֶר הַמֶּלֶךְ לְאַשְׁפְּנַז "the king commanded Ashpenaz" לְהָבִיא "to bring"
Dan 1:6	καὶ ἦσαν ἐκ τούτων ἀπὸ τῶν υἱῶν τῆς Ιουδαίας "and there were from these from the sons of Iouda"	καὶ ἦσαν ἐκ τοῦ γένους τῶν υἱῶν Ισραηλ τῶν ἀπὸ τῆς Ιουδαίας "and there were of the race of the sons of Israel who were from Judea"[41]	καὶ ἐγένετο ἐν αὐτοῖς ἐκ τῶν υἱῶν Ιουδα "and there were among them from the sons of Iouda"	וַיְהִי בָהֶם מִבְּנֵי יְהוּדָה "and among them were from the sons of Judah"
Dan 1:9	καὶ ἔδωκε κύριος τὸν Δανιηλ εἰς τιμήν ... "and the Lord gave Daniel to honor"	καὶ ἔδωκε κύριος τῷ Δανιηλ τιμήν ... "and the Lord gave Daniel honor"[42]	... τὸν Δανιηλ εἰς ... "... Daniel to ..."	וַיִּתֵּן הָאֱלֹהִים אֶת־דָּנִיֵּאל לְחֶסֶד ... "And God gave Daniel to (receive) favor"

the *lectio difficilior* was preferred, which in this case was the reading most remote from MT/Theodotion. Several examples for the priority of LXX⁸⁸ are presented in Table 1.

---

[39] The unique reading of LXX⁸⁸ cannot be attributed to a later scribe or to a scribal error either in the Semitic *Vorlage* or during the Greek transmission; the reading Αβιεσδρι is preferred because it is found in vv. 11 and 16 of LXX⁸⁸.

[40] There are no grounds for assuming that the pronoun was added by a later Greek scribe. Αὐτῷ probably goes back to the original translation and was omitted in accordance with the Hebrew text.

[41] In this case, LXX⁸⁸ contains a double translation that does not exist in papyrus LXX⁹⁶⁷; nevertheless, papyrus LXX⁹⁶⁷ seems secondary. The term γένος is typical of OG-Dan for defining ethnic relations; moreover, if papyrus LXX⁹⁶⁷ reflects the original text, the absence of ἐκ τούτων from LXX⁸⁸ cannot be explained. Therefore, it is more likely that the double translation was known to the Greek scribe and he adapted the text to the Hebrew original.

[42] OG-Dan is exegetical and biased; his aim is to present Daniel in a superior position, as reflected also by the other equivalents in the translation. This tendency is evident in

As to the arrangement of the book, it is most likely that the chapter order evidenced in LXX⁹⁶⁷ is secondary. In MT (→ 18.2.2), Th (→ 18.3.2), and LXX⁸⁸, the book is arranged in a very precise concentric structure,[43] and certainly, in terms of literary genre, Daniel 4–5 belong to the narrative section and Daniel 7–8 to the visions. It is also obvious that the chapter arrangement in papyrus LXX⁹⁶⁷ is intended to maintain a reasonable chronological framework (Daniel 1–4: Nebuchadnezzar; Daniel 7–8, 5: Belshazzar; Daniel 6, 9: Darius the Mede; Daniel 10–12: Cyrus of Persia). This avoids the problem created by the death of Belshazzar at the end of Daniel 5, since Daniel 7–8 report events that take place during his reign. On the other hand, some scholars argue for the priority of the chapter order found in papyrus LXX⁹⁶⁷, maintaining that Daniel

---

LXX⁸⁸, but papyrus LXX⁹⁶⁷ was adapted to the Hebrew original and Th-Dan.

[43] For the Aramaic section, see Langlet, "La Structure"; for

4 is more closely connected to Daniel in OG-Dan than in the MT-Dan, and the same pertains to the juxtaposition of Daniel 5–6 and 9.[44] However, this assumption does not stand up to closer scrutiny of the links between the chapters.[45] In any case, further study is required to determine whether LXX[967], although secondary, reflects the original arrangement of OG-Dan and LXX[88] restored the order according to MT, or if LXX[88] reflects the original order and a Greek editor rearranged the chapters in papyrus LXX[967] to settle the chronological difficulties.

18.3.1.5 Relationship between OG-Dan and Th-Dan

Regardless of the discussion of the historical Theodotion, there are three possibilities concerning the relationship of Th-Dan (→ 18.3.2) to OG-Dan, all of which have supporters and opponents: 1) Th-Dan is a recension of OG-Dan aimed at adapting the Greek version to MT (→ 18.2.2);[46] 2) Th-Dan is a completely new translation whose translator occasionally used OG-Dan;[47] and 3) Th-Dan is a new and independent translation, whose translator knew OG-Dan, but chose not to use it.[48]

The arguments for each of these positions are all based upon the degree of similarity and difference between the two translations in cases where their *Vorlage* is presumably identical. However, each scholar interprets the facts differently. For example, Jeansonne has found that Th-Dan follows OG-Dan in about sixty percent of the cases, and is therefore convinced that Th-Dan reworked OG-Dan.[49] McLay objected to this analysis, claiming that in most cases this similarity is based on stereotypical equivalents, and is to be expected.[50] In his view, in a significant minority of instances the similarity is not coincidental, and they actually show dependence in the opposite direction: the scribes of OG-Dan reworked Th-Dan.

A careful comparison of the two translations throughout the book reveals that when their *Vorlage* is presumably identical, Th-Dan often offers a different translation, mainly due to the relatively free translation of OG-Dan. In cases where they do resemble each other, there can be three possible causes: 1) both reflect an identical *Vorlage* different from that of MT-Dan; 2) Th-Dan follows OG-Dan; 3) Greek scribes amended OG-Dan according to Th-Dan. The following tables exemplify these possibilities:

1) Th-Dan gives an independent, literal translation where the Old Greek version is free (see Table 2).

2) Th-Dan relies on OG-Dan, mostly when the *Vorlage* was incomprehensible to the translators, but not always (see Table 3).

3) Th-Dan influenced OG-Dan during its transmission (see Table 4).

4) Th-Dan and OG-Dan reflect a common *Vorlage* that is different from MT, but present different translations (see Table 5).

The evidence shows that Th-Dan is neither a completely independent translation, nor merely a recension of OG-Dan. The later translator was familiar with OG-Dan and used it freely. On the other hand, during the transmission process, the influence of Th-Dan is clearly seen in the OG-Dan manuscripts.

18.3.1.6 Special Character of OG-Dan 4–6

Daniel 4–6 in OG-Dan differ radically from MT/Theodotion (→ 18.2.2; → 18.3.2). The most plausible and most commonly given explanation for this, since Bludau and Montgomery,[51] is that these

---

the entire book, see A. Rofé, *Introduction to the Literature of the Hebrew Bible* (Jerusalem Biblical Studies 9; Jerusalem: Simor, 2009).

[44] See, for instance, Grelot, "La Septante de Daniel IV"; Lust, "The Septuagint"; Munnich, "Texte Massorétique."

[45] See Albertz, *Der Gott des Daniel*, 78; Amara, "The Old Greek Version," 281–84.

[46] E.g., Jeansonne, "The Old Greek Translation"; Jobes, "Syntactic Analysis."

[47] E.g., Hartman and Di Lella, *Daniel*, 80; Di Lella, "The Textual History."

[48] So McLay, *OG and TH Versions*; McLay, "The Relationship."

[49] Jeansonne, *The Old Greek*.

[50] McLay, *The OG and TH versions*.

[51] Bludau, *Daniel*; Montgomery, *Daniel*.

TABLE 2

	MT	OG	Th
Dan 1:4	לַעֲמֹד בְּהֵיכַל הַמֶּלֶךְ וּלְלַמְּדָם סֵפֶר וּלְשׁוֹן כַּשְׂדִּים "to stand in the palace of the king, and they were to be taught the literature and language of the Chaldeans"	ὥστε εἶναι ἐν τῷ οἴκῳ τοῦ βασιλέως καὶ διδάξαι αὐτοὺς γράμματα καὶ **διάλεκτον Χαλδαικὴν** "to be in the king's house and to teach them letters and the Chaldean speech"	ἑστάναι ἐν τῷ οἴκῳ τοῦ βασιλέως καὶ διδάξαι αὐτοὺς γράμματα καὶ **γλῶσσαν Χαλδαίων**[52] "to stand in the king's house and to teach them the letters and language of the Chaldeans"
Dan 1:5	דְּבַר־יוֹם בְּיוֹמוֹ "a daily portion"	καθ' ἑκάστην ἡμέραν "every day"	τὸ τῆς ἡμέρας καθ' ἡμέραν "each day"

TABLE 3

	MT	OG	Th
Dan 1:5	מִפַּת־בַּג הַמֶּלֶךְ "from the king's table"	ἀπὸ τῆς βασιλικῆς τραπέζης "from the royal table"	ἀπὸ τῆς τραπέζης τοῦ βασιλέως "from the king's table"
Dan 6:11	כָּל־קֳבֵל דִּי־הֲוָא עָבֵד מִן־קַדְמַת דְּנָה "just as he had done previously"	καθὼς ἐποίει ἔμπροσθεν "just as he had been doing previously"	καθὼς ἦν ποιῶν ἔμπροσθεν "just as he was doing previously"
Dan 9:27	וְעַל כְּנַף שִׁקּוּצִים מְשֹׁמֵם "and in (their) corner shall be an abomination that desolates"	καὶ ἐπὶ τὸ ἱερὸν βδέλυγμα τῶν ἐρημώσεων "and in the temple there will be an abomination of desolations"	καὶ ἐπὶ τὸ ἱερὸν βδέλυγμα τῶν ἐρημώσεων[53] "and in the temple there will be an abomination of desolations"

chapters existed as an independent corpus that was transmitted separately from the rest of the book. This separate composition evolved into two different editions, one of which found its way into MT, while the other was adopted by Old Greek. However, were these chapters translated separately by an earlier translator and interpolated into the book in its Greek form,[54] or were they incorporated

---

[52] In this case, the Old Greek faithfully reflects its *Vorlage*, which is identical to MT and that of Theodotion, but the Old Greek translator chooses less common equivalents, such as διάλεκτον "speech" and Χαλδαικὴν "Chaldean," and translates more freely (ὥστε εἶναι "for the purpose of being").

[53] There can be almost no doubt that both translators had the same *Vorlage*, which was identical to MT, and neither understood it.

[54] So Albertz, *Der Gott des Daniel*, 164; McLay, *OG and TH Versions*; and McLay, "The Old Greek."

TABLE 4

	MT	OG-88	OG-967	Th
Dan 3:27	וְסָרְבָּלֵיהוֹן לָא שְׁנוֹ "their tunics were not harmed"	καὶ τὰ σαράβαρα[55] αὐτῶν "and their trousers"	=	καὶ τὰ σαράβαρα αὐτῶν "and their trousers"
Dan 5:5	בַּהּ־שַׁעֲתָה "immediately"	ἐν αὐτῇ τῇ ὥρᾳ ἐκείνῃ[56] "in that very same hour"	=	ἐν αὐτῇ τῇ ὥρᾳ "in that same hour"
Dan 8:13	וָאֶשְׁמְעָה אֶחָד־קָדוֹשׁ מְדַבֵּר וַיֹּאמֶר אֶחָד קָדוֹשׁ לַפַּלְמוֹנִי הַמְדַבֵּר "Then I heard a holy one speaking, and another holy one said to the one that spoke"	καὶ ἤκουον ἑτέρου ἁγίου λαλοῦντος καὶ εἶπεν ὁ ἕτερος τῷ φελμουνι τῷ λαλοῦντι ἕως τίνος ... "And I kept hearing another holy one speaking, and other one said to the Phelmouni who was speaking, 'How long ...' "	καὶ ἤκουον ἑτέρου ἁγίου λαλοῦντος καὶ εἶπεν ὁ ἕτερος ἕως τίνος ... "And I kept hearing another holy one speaking, and other one said ..., 'How long ...' "	καὶ ἤκουσα ἑνὸς ἁγίου λαλοῦντος καὶ εἶπεν εἷς ἅγιος τῷ φελμουνι τῷ λαλοῦντι ἕως πότε ... "And I heard one of the holy one speaking, and one holy one said to the Phelmouni who was speaking, 'How long ...' "

into the Semitic form of the book prior to its being translated?[57]

On the basis of the translation technique and the choice of equivalents, it is difficult to find any significant difference between the translation in Daniel 4–6 and that of the rest of the book. However, caution is required here for several reasons. Firstly, in order to evaluate the translation technique correctly, one should have a certain confidence concerning the *Vorlage*, which is certainly not the case for Daniel 4–6. Secondly, OG-Dan is a relatively free translation that attempts to preserve the quality of the target language.[58] Therefore, even in chapters that are close to MT/Theodotion, it is difficult to reconstruct its *Vorlage* (see Table 6).

In this case, there is little doubt that the *Vorlage* of Old Greek is similar to MT, but the translator chose not to repeat the long list that he translated in the previous verse. Additionally, we find in many cases that the translator assumes the role of interpreter in order to solve problems that were present in his *Vorlage*.[59] Thirdly, the extent of the freedom of the translator varies from chapter to chapter. His translation of Daniel 1–2 is the most free; he takes less liberty in Daniel 3 and 7; and in Daniel 8–12 he is struggling evidently with an

---

[55] The same term in v. 21 is translated by Old Greek as ὑποδήματα, but Theodotion has a transcription as in v. 27. See also McLay, "The Relationship."

[56] Here Old Greek has a double translation: ἐν τῇ ὥρᾳ ἐκείνῃ "in that hour" and ἐν αὐτῇ τῇ ὥρᾳ "in the same hour." One of them probably came from Theodotion.

[57] E.g., Ulrich, *DSS*, 71 and Munnich, "Texte Massorétique," who both advocate the priority of OG-Dan as presented in papyrus LXX[967].

[58] The translation technique of OG-Dan is very similar to that of 1 Esdras; see Talshir, *1 Esdras*.

[59] So much so that it is described as a "Greek Targum" by Bruce in "The Oldest Greek Version" and "The Earliest Old Testament."

TABLE 5

	MT	OG	Th
Dan 2:34	עַד דִּי הִתְגְּזֶרֶת אֶבֶן "until a stone was cut out"	ἕως ὅτου ἐτμήθη λίθος ἐξ ὄρους "until when a stone was cut from a mountain"	ἕως οὗ ἐτμήθη λίθος ἐξ ὄρους "until a stone was cut from a mountain"
Dan 3:28	וִיהַבוּ גֶשְׁמְהוֹן "and yielded up their bodies"	+ εἰς ἐμπυρισμόν "for burning"	+ εἰς πῦρ "to the fire"
Dan 6:13	בֵּאדַיִן קְרִבוּ וְאָמְרִין קֳדָם־מַלְכָּא עַל־אֱסָר מַלְכָּא "Then they approached the king and said concerning the interdict, 'O king!'"	τότε οὗτοι οἱ ἄνθρωποι ἐνέτυχον τῷ βασιλεῖ καὶ εἶπαν Δαρεῖε βασιλεῦ "then these men met with the king and said, 'O king Darius'"	καὶ προσελθόντες λέγουσιν τῷ βασιλεῖ βασιλεῦ "they approached the king and said, 'O king'"

incomprehensible *Vorlage*. Fourthly, the translator is not consistent in choosing equivalents. At times, he uses a Greek term for translating a certain Hebrew/Aramaic term in one chapter, and then chooses a different Greek term in another chapter (see Table 7).

With all due caution, the evidence seems to point to the work of one translator who translated both Daniel 4–6 and the rest of the canonical book. Nevertheless, there is some evidence that reveals the direction of the continuing development of Old Greek during its transmission process in Greek.

18.3.1.7 Development of OG-Dan

Many doublets in OG-Dan cannot be considered translations of Hebrew double readings, but double translations. The technique of a double translation may have been typical of this translation,[60] or it could have been introduced by Greek scribes during the transmission process. In the case of OG-Dan, the latter is more likely.[61] A Greek scribe or a Greek redactor of the translated book added glosses or alternative translations. The second element is always more literal than the original one

and closer to MT/Theodotion (→ 18.2.2; → 18.3.2), and in many cases it was placed before the original element. For example, the words ἀπέστη ἀπ' ἐμοῦ τὸ πρᾶγμα in Dan 2:8 are a "correction" deriving from Th-Dan, and are meant to replace the free version: καθάπερ οὖν προστέταχα οὕτως ἔσται "as I have commanded". In Dan 8:16, the words καὶ ἐκάλεσε καὶ εἶπεν Γαβριηλ συνέτισον ἐκεῖνον τὴν ὅρασιν "and it called and said, 'Gabriel, help this one understand the vision'" are a doublet, in which the original translation does not represent the Hebrew text due to a misreading of the name גבריאל "Gabriel" as הגבר אל "the man to …" The second element corrects it according to Th-Dan.[62]

However, the Greek translator and the Greek scribes are not the only hands that can be traced in OG-Dan. It seems that the translated book was revised by a Greek redactor who added several literary units to the translation. Such revisional activity is visible in internal difficulties in the Greek form of the book. For example, part of Dan 3:22 is repeated within the addition to Daniel 3, which causes the three youths to be thrown into the fire twice. There are also other contradictions between

---

[60] See n. 55.
[61] Amara, "The Old Greek Version."

[62] For more examples, see Amara, "The Old Greek Version," 243–77; McLay, "The Relationship."

18.3.1 SEPTUAGINT

TABLE 6

	MT	OG-LXX[88]	OG-LXX[967]
Dan 3:3	בֵּאדַיִן מִתְכַּנְּשִׁין אֲחַשְׁדַּרְפְּנַיָּא סִגְנַיָּא וּפַחֲוָתָא אֲדַרְגָּזְרַיָּא גְדָבְרַיָּא דְּתָבְרַיָּא תִּפְתָּיֵא וְכֹל שִׁלְטֹנֵי מְדִינָתָא לַחֲנֻכַּת צַלְמָא דִּי הֲקֵים נְבוּכַדְנֶצַּר מַלְכָּא וְקָאמִין (וְקָיְמִין) לָקֳבֵל צַלְמָא דִּי הֲקֵים נְבֻכַדְנֶצַּר "So the satraps, the prefects, and the governors, the counselors, the treasurers, the justices, the magistrates, and all the officials of the provinces, assembled for the dedication of the statue that King Nebuchadnezzar had set up. When they were standing before the statue that Nebuchadnezzar had set up ..."	καὶ ἔστησαν οἱ προγεγραμμένοι κατέναντι τῆς εἰκόνος "and the aforementioned stood in front of the image"	τότε συνήχθησαν οἱ προγεγραμμένοι καὶ ἔστησαν κατέναντι τῆς εἰκόνος "after that the aforementioned gathered and stood in front of the image"

the main story and the prose narrative in the addition.[63] Another example is the short version of Daniel 5, along with some of the doublets in Daniel 4, which certainly was the work of another Greek translator/redactor[64] who did not share the original translator's theological views.[65] For example, the Old Greek translator consistently refers to the "gods of the nations" as εἴδωλα "idols" or εἴδωλα χειροποίητα "handmade idols," but the doublet sections use the phrase οἱ θεοὶ τῶν ἐθνῶν "the gods of the nations." We may also attribute to this redactor the insertion of the three additions, the editing of the chronological titles in Old Greek, and possibly the chapter rearrangement reflected in papyrus LXX[967]. However, the extent of his work still requires further clarification.

18.3.1.8 *Vorlage* of the Old Greek: Its Value for Textual Criticism

Even if we ignore the problems in Daniel 4–6 and the development of the two separate editions of Daniel, the value of the Old Greek to the textual criticism of the book of Daniel would still be very limited. A thorough investigation of the Old Greek translator's translation technique indicates that he expands, shortens, paraphrases, and interprets his *Vorlage* without hesitation.[66] Even in cases of agreement between Theodotion (→ 18.3.2) and Old Greek against MT (→ 18.2.2), there is no certainty that this agreement is due to the *Vorlage* and not the result of mutual influence (as shown above, → 18.3.1.6). In a few instances, however, differences between OG-Dan and MT are supported by 4QDan[a] (→ 18.2.1.3; → 18.2.3.1), or are reflected in the different translation of Th-Dan (see Table 8).

In dozens of cases in which the *Vorlage* of Old Greek can be restored with a high degree of certainty, including in Daniel 4–6, it seems secondary when compared to MT. Only in a minority of cases, usually when Old Greek reflects a shorter text, can it be concluded that its *Vorlage* should be given priority over MT.

---

[63] The Old Greek translator would not have left these difficulties uncorrected. Thus also McLay, *OG and TH Versions*.
[64] Amara, "The Third Version."
[65] For Daniel 4, see also Wills, *The Jew*, 87–120.

[66] Amara, "The Old Greek Version." On the other hand, Jeansonne, *The Old Greek* and McLay, *OG and TH Versions* believe that the translator was faithful to his *Vorlage* in Daniel 1–3 and 7–12.

TABLE 7

Hebr./Aram.	Daniel 1 x2 Daniel 2; 4 x1 (without parallel)	Remainder of the book (Daniel 2; 3; 4; 6)		
מנה "to assign, to appoint"/השלט "to make rule"/הקים/ על- "to set upon"	ἀναδείκνυμι "to appoint"	καθίστημι "to put in charge"		
Aram. שלט "to rule"/שליט "official ruler"/שלטן "dominion"	Daniel 2 δυνάστης "ruler, official"/ κυριεύειν "to rule over, dominate"	Daniel 3–7 ἐξουσία "authority"		
Aram. פשרא "interpretation"	Daniel 2 σύγκρισις "interpretation"/κρίσις "interpretation"	Daniel 4 σύγκρισις "interpretation"	Daniel 5 σύγκρισις "interpretation"/σύγκριμα "interpretation"	Daniel 7 x1 κρίσις "interpretation"
Aram. חזה "to see"	Daniel 2–5 ὁράω "to see"	Daniel 7 θεωρέω "to see"		

Albertz, R., *Der Gott des Daniel: Untersuchungen zu Daniel 4–6 in der Septuagintafassungsowie zu Komposition und Theologie des aramäischen Danielbuches* (SBS 131; Stuttgart: Katholisches Bibelwerk, 1988).

Amara, D., "The Old Greek Version of the Book of Daniel: The Translation, the *Vorlage* and the Redaction" (PhD diss., Ben Gurion University, 2006) [Hebr.].

Amara, D., "The Third Version of the Story of Belshazzar's Banquet (Daniel 5)," *Textus* 23 (2007): xi–xli [Hebr.].

Barthélemy, **Devanciers*.

Bludau, A., *Die Alexandrinische Übersetzung des Buches Daniel und ihr Verhältniss zum massorethischen Text* (BibS[F] 2; Freiburg i.B.: Herder Verlagshandlung, 1897), 25–28.

Bruce, F.F., "The Earliest Old Testament Interpretation," OTS 17 (1972): 37–52.

Bruce, F.F., "The Oldest Greek Version of Daniel," OTS 20 (1977): 22–40.

Charles, R.H., *A Critical and Exegetical Commentary on the Book of Daniel* (Oxford: Clarendon Press, 1929).

Collins, J.J., *Daniel: A Commentary on the Book of Daniel* (Hermeneia; Minneapolis: Fortress, 1993).

Delcor, M., *Le livre de Daniel* (Paris: Gabalda et Cie, 1971).

Engel, H., *Die Susanna-Erzählung: Einleitug, Übersetzung und Kommentar zum Septuaginta-Text und zur Theodotion-Bearbeitung* (OBO 61; Göttingen: Vandenhoeck & Ruprecht, 1985).

Geissen, A., *Der Septuagintatext des Buches Daniel nach dem Kölner Teil des Papyrus 967: Kap. 5–12, zusammen mit Susanna, Bel et Draco, sowie Esther, Kap. I, 1a–2,15* (Papyrologische Texte und Abhandlungen 5; Bonn: Habelt, 1968).

Grelot, P., "Les Versions grecques de Daniel," *Bib* 47 (1966): 381–402.

Grelot, P., "La Septante de Daniel IV et son substrat sémitique," *RB* 81 (1974): 5–23.

Grelot, P., "Le chapitre V de Daniel dans la Septante," *Sem* 24 (1974): 45–66.

TABLE 8

	OG	Th	4QDan^a	MT
Dan 1:3	ἐκ τῶν υἱῶν τῶν μεγιστάνων τοῦ Ισραηλ "some of the sons of the nobles of Israel"	ἀπὸ τῶν υἱῶν τῆς αἰχμαλωσίας Ισραηλ "some of the sons of the captivity of Israel"		מִבְּנֵי יִשְׂרָאֵל "from the sons of Israel"
Dan 2:20	τοῦ κυρίου τοῦ μεγάλου "of the great Lord"	τοῦ θεοῦ "of God"	אלהא רבא "of the great God"	אֱלָהָא "of God"
Dan 2:40	καὶ σεισθήσεται πᾶσα ἡ γῆ "and the whole earth will be shaken"	καὶ δαμάσει "and overpower"	ותר[ע] כל ארעא "and it shall shatter all the earth"	וְתֵרֹעַ "and it shall shatter"
Dan 3:28	+ εἰς ἐμπυρισμόν "for burning"	+ εἰς πῦρ "to the fire"		וִיהַבוּ גֶשְׁמְהוֹן "and yielded up their bodies"

Grelot, P., "Daniel VI dans la Septante," in Κατὰ τοὺς ο': Selon les Septante: Trente études sur la Bible grecque des Septante en hommage à Marguerite Harl (eds. G. Dorival and O. Munnich; Paris: Cerf, 1995), 103–18.

Gwynn, J., "Theodotion," DCB 4:970–79.

Hamm, W., Der Septuaginta-Text des Buches Daniel: Kap. 1–2, nach dem Kölner Teil des Papyrus 967 (Papyrologische Texte und Abhandlungen 10; Bonn: Habelt, 1969).

Hamm, W., Der Septuaginta-Text des Buches Daniel: Kap. 3–4 nach dem Kölner Teil des Papyrus 967 (Papyrologische Texte und Abhandlungen 21; Bonn: Habelt, 1977).

Hartman, L.F. and A.A. Di Lella, The Book of Daniel: A New Translation with Notes and Commentary (AB 23; Garden City: Doubleday, 1978).

Jellicoe, *SMS.

Jellicoe, S., "Some Reflections on the ΚΑΙΓΕ Recension," VT 23 (1973): 15–24.

Jobes, K.H., "A Comparative Syntactic Analysis of the Greek Versions of Daniel: A Test Case for New Methodology," BIOSCS 28 (1995): 19–41.

Joosten, J., "The Prayer of Azariah (DanLXX 3): Sources and Origin," in Septuagint and Reception: Essays Prepared for the Association for the Study of the Septuagint in South Africa (ed. J. Cook; VTSup 127; Leiden: Brill, 2009), 5–16.

Kenyon, G., "The Chester Beatty Biblical Papyri," Gn 8 (1932): 46–49.

Kenyon, G., The Chester Beatty Biblical Papyri (London: E. Walker, 1937).

Koch, K., Deuterokanonische Zusätze zum Danielbild: Entstehung und Textgeschichte (2 vols.; AOAT 38.1–2; Neukirchen-Vluyn: Neukirchener Verlag, 1987).

Langlet, A., "La wtructure littéraire de Daniel 2–7," Bib 53 (1972): 169–90.

Di Lella, A.A., "The Textual History of Septuagint-Daniel and Theodotion-Daniel," in The Book of Daniel: Composition and Reception (eds. J.J. Collins and P.W. Flint; 2 vols.; VTSup 83; Leiden: Brill, 2001), 2.586–607.

Lust, J., "The Septuagint Version of Daniel 4–5," in The Book of Daniel in the Light of New Findings (ed. A.S. van der Woude; BETL 106; Leuven: Leuven University Press, 1993), 39–53.

McLay, R.T., The OG and TH Versions of Daniel (SBLSCS 43; Atlanta: Scholars Press, 1996).

McLay, R.T., "The Relationship between the Greek Translations of Daniel 1–3," *BIOSCS* 37 (2004): 29–54.

McLay, R.T., "The Old Greek Translation of Daniel IV–VI and the Formation of the Book of Daniel," *VT* 55 (2005): 304–23.

McLay, R.T., "Sousanna," in *NETS, 986–90.

McLay, R.T., "Bel and the Dragon," in *NETS, 1023–27.

Montgomery, J.A., "The Hexaplaric Strata in the Greek Texts of Daniel," *JBL* 44 (1925): 289–302.

Montgomery, J.A., *A Critical and Exegetical Commentary on the Book of Daniel* (ICC; Edinburgh: T & T Clark, 1927).

Moore, C.A., *Daniel, Esther and Jeremiah: The Additions: A New Translation with Introduction and Commentary* (AB 44; Garden City: Doubleday, 1977).

Munnich, O., "Origene, editeur de la Septante de Daniel," in *Studien zur Septuaginta – Robert Hanhart zu Ehren* (eds. D. Frankel, U. Quast, and J. Wevers; MSU 20; Göttingen: Vandenhoeck & Ruprecht, 1990), 187–218.

Munnich, O., "Texte Massorétique et Septante dans le Livre de Daniel," in Schenker, *Earliest Text, 93–120.

Jeansonne, S.P., *The Old Greek Translation of Daniel 7–12* (CBQMS 19; Washington: Catholic Biblical Association, 1988).

Rappaport, U., *The First Book of Maccabees: Introduction, Hebrew Translation, and Commentary* (Jerusalem: Yad Ben-Zvi Press, 2004) [Hebr.].

Roca-Puig, R., "Daniel: Dos semifolis del codex 967, Papir de Barcelona, Inv. no 42 i 43," *Aeg* 56 (1976): 3–18.

Schmitt, A., *Stammt der sogenannte θ′-Text bei Daniel wirklich von Theodotion?* (MSU 9; Göttingen, 1966).

Schmitt, A., "Die griechischen Danieltexte ("θ′" und o′) und das Theodotionproblem," *BZ* N.F. 36 (1992): 1–29.

Schüpphaus, J., "Das Verhältnis von LXX- und Theodotion-Text in den apokryphen Zusätzen zum Danielbuch," *ZAW* 83 (1971): 49–72.

Swete, H.B., *The Old Testament in Greek*, Vol. 3 (Cambridge: Cambridge University Press, 1894).

Swete, *Introduction.

Talshir, Z., "Double Translations in the Septuagint," in *VI Congress of the International Organization for Septuagint and Cognate Studies* (ed. C.E. Cox; SBLSCS 23; Atlanta: Scholars Press, 1986), 21–63.

Talshir, Z., *1 Esdras: From Origin to Translation* (SBLSCS 47; Atlanta: SBL, 1999).

Ulrich, *DSS.

Wills, L.M., *The Jew in the Court of the Foreign King: Ancient Jewish Court Legends* (HDR 26; Minneapolis: Fortress, 1990).

D. Amara

18.3.2 Other Greek Versions Prior to the Hexapla

18.3.2.1 Background

The versions of Aquila and Symmachus in the book of Daniel are known primarily through fragments that trace back to Origen's Hexapla (→ 1.3.1.2.7). The version attributed to Theodotion is completely extant, however, due to its unusual history. Around 240 C.E., Origen wrote a letter to Africanus in which he indicates that two Greek versions of Daniel, one according to the Seventy and the other according to Theodotion, were in circulation in the churches.[1] However, Jerome's commentary on Daniel, written ca. 407 C.E., reports that the churches had rejected the version of the Seventy in favor of the edition of Theodotion.[2] Consequently, most surviving witnesses to Greek Daniel attest to the latter. However, many scholars question the traditional attribution of this edition to Theodotion.[3] Nevertheless, the book of Daniel remains the only complete work for which a version traditionally attributed to Theodotion has been preserved.

18.3.2.2 Editions and Sources

The Göttingen Septuagint provides the most exhaustive account of the evidence for the Greek ver-

---

[1] Origen, *Ep. Afr.* 2(4) (PG 11:52a–b; SC 302:524–27).

[2] See Jerome's prologue and his comments on Dan 4:5 in *Expl. Dan.* (PL 25:493a, 514a; CCSL 75A:774, 811), which are discussed by Field, *Hexapla, 2.903–04. See also Jerome's prologue to Daniel in the Vulgate.

[3] In both the first (1954; pp. 28–29, 60–62) and second (1999; pp. 121–22, 153–55) editions of Daniel in the Göttingen Septuagint, Ziegler claims that the Th text of Daniel is not truly a Theodotion text primarily on the basis of minuses and pluses relative to MT, but Ziegler allows the possibility that Theodotion may have superficially edited the Th text. Schmitt argues in greater detail that differences between the Th text and Theodotion's translation in other books prove that the Th text has nothing to do with Theodotion (*Stammt der sogenannte "θ′"-Text*, 1–114; "Die griechischen Danieltexte," 1–29). Barthélemy criticizes Schmitt's approach as giving undue weight to special cases on the basis of unfounded assumptions ("Notes critiques," 297–301). McLay, however, claims that his analysis of the relationship between the Th text and the *kaige* tradition vindicates Schmitt's conclusion (*The OG and Th Versions*, 219–40).

sion traditionally attributed to Theodotion, which Joseph Ziegler designates as the "θ'" text with quotation marks in order to indicate his rejection of the attribution. The "θ'" text is critically reconstructed on the basis of a full Greek manuscript tradition, Greek commentaries by Hippolytus, Chrysostom, Polychronius of Apamea, and Theodoret of Cyrus, ancient translations including the Old Latin, Coptic, Syriac, Ethiopic, Arabic, and Armenian versions, and quotations in early Christian writers.[4] In the second edition of Daniel in the Göttingen Septuagint, Detlef Fraenkel presents additional fragmentary evidence from papyri, parchments, and inscriptions in an addendum, but Ziegler's "θ'" text remains unaltered.[5]

The Göttingen Septuagint also presents a Hexaplaric apparatus with the OG text, which provides the most complete list of fragments not only of Theodotion, but also of Aquila and Symmachus. The majority of these readings were published already in Field's edition of Hexaplaric fragments (1875), which remains valuable for its fuller descriptions of the evidence.[6] However, in the book of Daniel, the main text of Field's edition provides the established Th text of his day for each listed textual segment, regardless of whether Field actually collected a Theodotion fragment supporting that established Th text.[7] Consequently, the Theodotion readings collected by Field must be gleaned from his apparatus rather than his main text.

The most important Greek sources of fragments of Theodotion, Aquila, and Symmachus for the book of Daniel include Hexaplaric readings (→ 18.3.4) in the sixth-century uncial Codex Marchalianus (LXX^Q) and the tenth-century minuscule Codex Chisianus (LXX^88), citations in the Daniel commentaries of Theodoret and Polychronius, and citations by other writers such as Origen and Eusebius. Jerome's commentary on Daniel also provides excerpts from the three translators, usually rendered in Latin but occasionally given in Greek. The Syro-Hexapla (→ 18.4.4.1) provides the largest number of Hexaplaric readings, but these require back-translation from Syriac.[8] The Jerusalem Talmud attests one Aquila reading independently from the Hexaplaric tradition in Dan 5:5.[9]

18.3.2.3 Translation Character and Technique
18.3.2.3.1 Theodotion

Some aspects of the character of the version traditionally attributed to Theodotion (henceforth Th-Dan) are debated. Jeansonne concludes that Th-Dan represents a recension of OG-Dan, whereas McLay argues that Th-Dan represents an independent translation with very little influence from OG-Dan (→ 18.3.1).[10] Between these two extremes, Grelot characterizes Th-Dan as a "version" that retranslates the Hebrew-Aramaic without ignoring OG-Dan.[11] Barthélemy associates Th-Dan with the *kaige* group, whereas McLay concludes that Th-Dan has little to do with the *kaige* tradition beyond sharing a formal equivalence approach to translation.[12] In any case, it is clear that Th-Dan is more formally equivalent to MT (→ 18.2.2) than OG-Dan. However, Th-Dan departs from MT by incorporating revised forms of the Additions to Daniel (→ 11.3.2) found in OG-Dan.[13]

---

[4] Ziegler, *Susanna, Daniel, Bel et Draco*, 121–36.
[5] Ziegler, *Susanna, Daniel, Bel et Draco*, 170–214.
[6] Field, *Hexapla*, 2.901–36, Auct. 57–58.
[7] Field, *Hexapla*, 2.906.

[8] Ziegler, *Susanna, Daniel, Bel et Draco*, 160–61.
[9] Field, *Hexapla*, 1.xvii; 2.919. The Aquila reading from rabbinic tradition at Dan 8:13 represents a Hebrew "Targum" of Aquila rather than his Greek version. See Veltri, **Gegenwart*, 90–91; see also G. Veltri, *Libraries, Translations, and 'Canonic' Texts: The Septuagint, Aquila and Ben Sira in the Jewish and Christian Traditions* (JSJSup 109; Leiden: Brill, 2006), 184–85.
[10] Jeansonne, *The Old Greek*, 57; McLay, "It's a Question," 253; McLay, *The OG and Th Versions*, 242; McLay, "The Relationship," 52–53.
[11] Grelot, "Les versions grecques," 381, 394–95. Similarly Di Lella, who suggests that Th-Dan "translated the work anew with an eye, however, on OG-Dan," except in Daniel 4–6 where Th-Dan represents an independent translation due to the departure of OG-Dan from MT (Di Lella, "The Textual History," 596).
[12] Barthélemy, **Devanciers*, 44, 47, 67; Barthélemy, "Notes critiques," 301; McLay, *The OG and Th Versions*, 239–40, 243.
[13] The Additions to Daniel include Susanna, the Prayer of Azariah, and the Song of the Three Young Men (LXX-Dan 3:24–90), and Bel and the Dragon. Regarding the Additions to Daniel in Th-Dan, see especially Busto Saiz, "El texto Teodociónico," 41–55; Schüpphaus, "Das Verhältnis," 49–72.

18.3.2.3.2 Aquila

Aq-Dan is extant in fifty-five fragments attributed to Aquila in ancient sources, of which twenty-one are preserved in Greek.[14] The longest fragments are less than two verses in length. Jerome's commentary on Dan 1:3 shows that Daniel is among the books for which Aquila produced two distinct Greek editions, or at least revised his first edition with marginal corrections: Jerome reports that Aquila uses *electus* "chosen" in his first edition and *tyrannus* "ruler, prince" in his second edition to render the Hebrew word הַפַּרְתְּמִים "the nobles."[15] However, it is not possible to distinguish the two editions of Aq-Dan with certainty apart from this instance. Regarding the Additions to Daniel (→ 11.3.2), Origen's letter to Africanus specifically indicates that Aq-Dan omits the Prayer of Azariah and the Song of the Three Young Men (LXX-Dan 3:24–90).[16] Moreover, no fragment with a reliable attribution to Aquila is extant in any of the Additions.[17] On the whole, Aq-Dan reflects Aquila's well-known formal equivalence approach to translation.

18.3.2.3.3 Symmachus

Sym-Dan is extant in sixty-nine fragments attributed to Symmachus in ancient sources, of which eighteen are preserved in Greek.[18] The longest fragment is less than two verses in length. It is not clear whether Symmachus included all of the Additions to Daniel (→ 11.3.2), but two Symmachus fragments are extant from Susanna. The first fragment is found in the Hexaplaric witnesses to OG-Dan (LXX[88]-Syh; → 18.3.4), which attribute the text of Sus 1–5a jointly to Symmachus and Theodotion. The second fragment is found in Codex Marchalianus (LXX[Q]), which provides the version of Susanna attributed to Theodotion, but Symmachus is indicated above the word ἐπονηρεύσαντο "they acted wickedly" in the manuscript text of Sus 43 with the correction θ′ κατεμαρτύρησαν "they bore witness against" noted in the margin.[19] In any case, Sym-Dan generally reflects Symmachus' concern for producing a translation that takes into account the norms of the target language.

18.3.2.3.4 Comparison of Translation Styles

Th-Dan and Aq-Dan represent increasingly literal translation styles with less concern for the norms of the Greek language, whereas Sym-Dan represents an attempt to capture the meaning of the Hebrew-Aramaic text (→ 18.2.2) in clear Greek diction (→ 1.3.1.2.4 and → 1.3.1.2.5). The following quotations of the various versions of Dan 9:24a illustrate the different approaches to translation:

MT שָׁבֻעִים שִׁבְעִים נֶחְתַּךְ עַל־עַמְּךָ וְעַל־עִיר קָדְשֶׁךָ "seventy heptads were decided for your people and for your holy city"
OG ἑβδομήκοντα ἑβδομάδες ἐπὶ τὸν λαόν σου ἐκρίθησαν καὶ ἐπὶ τὴν πόλιν Σιων "seventy heptads for your people were decided and for the city, Zion"
Th ἑβδομήκοντα ἑβδομάδες συνετμήθησαν ἐπὶ τὸν λαόν σου καὶ ἐπὶ τὴν πόλιν τὴν ἁγίαν "seventy heptads were cut short for your people and for the holy city"
Aq …] ἐπὶ τὸν λαόν σου καὶ ἐπὶ πόλιν ἡγιασμένην σου "…] for your people and for your sanctified city"
Sym …] κατὰ τοῦ λαοῦ σου καὶ τῆς πόλεως τῆς ἁγίας σου "…] against your people and your holy city"

OG-Dan (→ 18.3.1) exhibits freedom to deviate from the Hebrew word order and to supply the name Σιων "Zion" for the city instead of rendering קָדְשֶׁךָ "your holy (city)." Th-Dan is similar to OG-Dan, but the translator adjusts the word order to match the Hebrew, chooses συνετμήθησαν "are cut short" as a

---

[14] Two of the fragments are jointly attributed to Aquila and LXX (Dan 1:3; 8:13), three to Aquila and Theodotion (Dan 3:21; 6:4; 8:13), and five to Aquila and Symmachus (Dan 1:4; 2:41; 9:26–27; 10:10; 11:1). My count excludes fragments attributed to οἱ λ′ or οἱ γ′.

[15] Jerome, *Expl. Dan.* 1 (PL 25:496a; CCSL 75A:778–79); see further Field, *Hexapla*, 1:xxiv–xxvii.

[16] Origen, *Ep. Afr.* 2(4) (PG 11:52a–b; SC 302:524–27).

[17] The double attribution of Sus 1–5a to σ′ θ′ in the Syro-Hexapla should probably be accepted as authentic instead of the triple attribution of the same text to α′ σ′ θ′ in ms 88.

[18] Two of the fragments are jointly attributed to Theodotion and Symmachus (Dan 3:27[94]; 10:6) and five to Aquila and Symmachus (Dan 1:4; 2:41; 9:26–27; 10:10; 11:1). My count excludes fragments attributed to οἱ λ′ or οἱ γ′.

[19] Ziegler's choice of the Symmachus reading for his "θ′" text of Sus 43 presumes that the earliest form of the "θ′" text of Sus 43 agreed with Symmachus' version of Susanna and that the Theodotion reading in LXX[Q(mg)] was drawn from a later form of the "θ′" text.

more apt lexical equivalent for נֶחְתַּךְ "is decided" (but also "is cut off" in Targumic Aramaic and Mishnaic Hebrew), and replaces OG's "Zion" with a proper rendering of קֹדֶשׁ except for the omission of the pronominal suffix. Aquila strives to represent the form of קָדְשֶׁךָ even more precisely by translating the pronominal suffix and by employing the stereotypical participle ἡγιασμένην "sanctified" instead of the adjective ἁγίαν "holy."[20] Finally, Symmachus shows greater concern for the norms of the target language by abandoning the stereotypical equivalency עַל/ἐπί "upon, for" in favor of the contextually appropriate κατά + genitive "against," and by rendering the repeated preposition עַל as a single preposition governing a compound object.[21]

18.3.2.4 Text-Critical Value for the Hebrew-Aramaic Text

The later Greek versions of Daniel (Theodotion, Aquila, Symmachus) generally corroborate MT (→ 18.2.2), although each attests occasional variants that must be evaluated on a case-by-case basis. The committee of the Hebrew Old Testament Text Project (HOTTP) examined sixty-nine textual problems in MT-Dan and chose MT as the reading most likely to be original in every case except one: in Dan 11:41, the Symmachus reading *et multa millia*/וְרִבּוֹת "and tens of thousands" given by Jerome is preferred over against MT וְרַבּוֹת "and many (lands)." Th-Dan supports the reading of MT in thirty-three of the sixty-nine cases. Th-Dan differs from MT in the majority of the remaining thirty-six cases in a way attributable to conscious changes by the translator that do not necessarily indicate a different Hebrew-Aramaic parent text than MT.[22]

An important difference between these Greek versions and MT that is not addressed by the HOTTP involves the length of time between the issuing of a word to rebuild Jerusalem and the coming of the anointed leader in Dan 9:25. The placement of the *ʾatnāḥ* in MT suggests that the Masoretes understood the period as "seven heptads" in length, whereas Th-Dan indicates "seven heptads and sixty-two heptads." Aq-Dan and Sym-Dan are not extant in Dan 9:25, but in Dan 9:26 they also both differ from MT by mentioning "the seven heptads and sixty-two [heptads]" as a unit. It is not clear whether these differences from MT result from a different Hebrew-Aramaic consonantal text or from intentional changes introduced by the translators. In any case, it seems certain that the Masoretic placement of the *ʾatnāḥ* in MT-Dan 9:25 reflects a different textual or exegetical tradition than that which is attested by these Greek versions.[23]

Barthélemy, *Critique textuelle 1992*.
Barthélemy, *Devanciers*.
Barthélemy, D., "Notes critiques sur quelques points d'histoire du texte," in *Übersetzung und Deutung: Studien zu dem Alten Testament und seiner Umwelt Alexander Reinard Hulst gewidmet von Freunden und Kollegen* (Nijkerk: Uitgeverij G.F. Callenbach b.v., 1977), 9–23 (= Barthélemy, *Études*, 289–303).
Busto Saiz, J.R., "El texto Teodociónico de Daniel y la traducción de Símaco," *Sefarad* 40.1 (1980): 41–55.
Busto Saiz, J.R., *La traducción de Símaco en el libro de los Salmos* (Textos y estudios "Cardenal Cisneros" 22; Madrid: C.S.I.C., 1978; repr., 1985).
Field, *Hexapla*.
Grelot, P., "Les versions grecques de Daniel," *Bib* 47 (1966): 381–402.
Hyvärinen, K., *Die Übersetzung von Aquila* (ConBOT 10; Lund: C.W.K. Gleerup, 1977).
Jeansonne, S.P., *The Old Greek Translation of Daniel 7–12* (CBQMS 19; Washington: The Catholic Biblical Association of America, 1988).
Di Lella, A.A., "The Textual History of Septuagint-Daniel and Theodotion-Daniel," in *The Book of Daniel: Composition and Reception* (2 vols.; eds. J.J. Collins and P.W. Flint; VTSup 83; Leiden: Brill, 2001), 2.586–607.

---

[20] Aquila tends to render the attributive genitive קֹדֶשׁ "holiness" with the participle ἡγιασμένος "sanctified" and the adjective קָדוֹשׁ "holy" with the adjective ἅγιος "holy," thereby distinguishing the two Hebrew constructions in his Greek translations. See Reider and Turner, *An Index to Aquila*, 3, 306. Cf. Hyvärinen, *Die Übersetzung von Aquila*, 60–61.

[21] On Symmachus' various renderings of עַל, see Busto Saiz, *La traducción de Símaco*, 195–200, 215.

[22] Barthélemy, *Critique textuelle 1992*, 435–96.

[23] Similarly R.T. Beckwith, "Daniel 9 and the Date of Messiah's Coming in Essene, Hellenistic, Pharisaic, Zealot and Early Christian Computation," *RevQ* 10 (1981): 521–22.

McLay, T., "It's a Question of Influence: The Theodotion and Old Greek Texts of Daniel," in Salvesen, *Hexapla*, 231–54.

McLay, T., *The OG and Th Versions of Daniel* (SBLSCS 43; Atlanta: Scholars Press, 1996).

McLay, T., "The Relationship between the Greek Translations of Daniel 1–3," *BIOSCS* 37 (2004): 29–53.

Reider, J. and N. Turner, *An Index to Aquila: Greek-Hebrew, Hebrew-Greek, Latin-Hebrew, with the Syriac and Armenian Evidence* (VTSup 12; Leiden: Brill, 1966).

Schmitt, A., *Stammt der sogenannte "θ'"-Text bei Daniel wirklich von Theodotion?* (MSU 9; Göttingen: Vandenhoeck & Ruprecht, 1966).

Schmitt, A., "Die griechischen Danieltexte ("θ'" und o') und das Theodotionproblem," *BZ* 36 (1992): 1–29.

Schüpphaus, J., "Das Verhältnis von LXX- und Theodotion-Text in den apokryphen Zusätzen zum Danielbuch," *ZAW* 83 (1971): 49–72.

Ziegler, J. (ed.), *Susanna, Daniel, Bel et Draco* (Septuaginta: Vetus Testamentum Graecum, Vol. 16/2; Göttingen: Vandenhoeck & Ruprecht, 1954; 2nd ed. 1999).

Jason T. Parry

18.3.3 Peshitta

18.3.3.1 Background

With the possible exception of the deuterocanonical books, the Peshitta of Daniel (s-Dan) was translated into Syriac from a Semitic *Vorlage* (→ 1.3.4). This *Vorlage* was presumably bilingual. In MT (→ 18.2.2), the language of Dan 2:4b–7:28 is Aramaic; the rest of the book is written in Hebrew. This bilingualism finds early support from the Qumran Daniel manuscripts (→ 18.2.1), the earliest of which (4QDan^c) likely dates to the early first century B.C.E. The Syriac translation of Daniel was made probably sometime in the second century C.E.,[1] although our earliest extant Syriac manuscript for Daniel (s^{6h10}) dates only to

---

[1] The date of the Syriac translation is not known for sure. Gelston favors a date for the Peshitta version in the mid- to late first century C.E. See A. Gelston, *The Peshiṭta of the Twelve Prophets* (Oxford: Clarendon, 1987), 193. Weitzman suggests a date of ca. 150 C.E. for most of the Peshitta Old Testament, with Ezra-Nehemiah and Chronicles dating to ca. 200 C.E. See Weitzman, *The Syriac Version of the Old Testament*, 248–62.

532 C.E.[2] s-Dan has an important role to play in the textual criticism of the Hebrew Bible, since it witnesses to the condition of this text in the early Christian period. Of the ancient versions of the Hebrew Bible, only LXX (→ 18.3.1) is older and arguably more important for text-critical purposes.

18.3.3.2 Manuscripts and Editions

All former editions of s-Dan have now been superseded by the Leiden edition. This edition is based primarily on manuscript s^{7a1}, but with some exceptions that are explained in the edition. The editors have taken into account for s-Dan all available ancient manuscripts and most later ones, as well as a number of Jacobite, Malkite, and Nestorian lectionaries. The critical apparatus of the Leiden edition provides users with a tool for evaluating the textual history of this version.

18.3.3.3 Translation Character

The Syriac translation of Daniel is fairly literal in style, belonging to what might be called *formal* rather than *dynamic* or *functional* correspondence. For the most part, the translator remained close to his *Vorlage*, departing from its linguistic structures only when the needs of Syriac readers dictated that he do so. The result is a translation that corresponds closely to its putative *Vorlage*, while at the same time achieving a readable and natural Syriac style. The translation does not strike the reader as artificial or wooden. On the contrary, ancient Syriac readers would have used this version apart from distraction caused by awkward or infelicitous renderings.

18.3.3.4 Translational Features

Several translational features of s-Dan are noteworthy. First, the word order and syntax of s-Dan frequently correspond to that of MT-Dan (→ 18.2.2). Not surprisingly, this is especially true with regard to the Aramaic portions of Daniel. Quite often, the Syriac translator was content to follow closely

---

[2] *The Old Testament in Syriac according to the Peshiṭta Version* Vol. 3.4: Dodekapropheton – Daniel-Bel-Draco (Leiden: Brill, 1980), iv.

the structure and patterns of his source text, even when other options might have been available to him. Second, lexical choices of s-Dan often show a preference for vocabulary that is cognate to that found in MT-Dan. The choice of words in s-Dan seems often to be influenced by the corresponding lexical items of the translator's Hebrew/Aramaic source text. In places where the source text uses Akkadian or Persian loanwords – as is especially the case with political, legal, and cultural terminology of the Babylonian or Persian periods – the translator tends to prefer native Syriac words rather than transliterations of foreign words that might be unfamiliar to Syriac readers.

There is a noticeable tendency in s-Dan to reverse the order of matched pairs of words. In a number of places where other external evidence has the word order "A and B," s-Dan has instead "B and A." Examples may be found in Dan 2:21, 35, 38, 40; 3:27; 4:19, 33; 5:23; 6:5, 8, 25; 7:14; 8:26; 9:7 [*v.l.*]; 9:16 [*v.l.*]; 10:9. It is not likely that such differences are due to textual variation found in the translator's *Vorlage*. Rather, it seems that the Syriac translator had a strange tendency to reverse the order of such pairs. Whether this was done inadvertently or deliberately is difficult to say. This tendency toward reversal of matched pairs, which occurs in certain other books of the Peshitta as well,[3] should be kept in mind lest the variation mistakenly be assigned text-critical value. It falls instead under the rubric of translation technique.

Early Syriac manuscripts of Daniel have a number of interpretive glosses in Daniel 7 and 8 that are important for the history of interpretation of this book.[4] Interpretive glosses dating no earlier than the tenth century appear in Daniel 11. The glosses of Daniel 7 and 8 identify Daniel's four unnamed kingdoms as Babylon, Media, Persia, and Greece. This interpretive scheme is elsewhere associated with the pagan philosopher Porphyry, whose views on this matter were adamantly rejected by Jerome. In his commentary on Daniel, Jerome insisted that Daniel's fourth kingdom was Rome rather than Greece.[5] Other Syriac manuscript glosses identify certain historical figures mentioned in Daniel (e.g., Alexander the Great, Darius, Antiochus Epiphanes). These glosses provide a unique and fascinating window into the reception history of s-Dan.

18.3.3.5 Origins

The community origins (whether Christian or Jewish) of s-Dan are not known. More or less opposite conclusions have been drawn from the available evidence, which is almost entirely of an internal nature. Wyngarden maintained that the Syriac translator of Daniel was most likely a Christian who made this translation for the use of Syriac-speaking Christians.[6] He based this conclusion largely on the Syriac renderings of two verses in particular: Dan 9:24 ("and the Messiah, [who is] the holy of holies") and Dan 9:27 ("Messiah shall be killed"). Wyngarden argued that in both of these cases the Syriac translation betrays a Christian rather than Jewish orientation. However, neither example is persuasive. In the first instance, Wyngarden assumes that "anointed one" (ܡܫܝܚܐ) necessarily refers to Christ (and not the temple); he asserts that attribution of holiness to this figure must be a Christian expression of divinity. But the context does not require such an interpretation. In the second instance, Wyngarden argues that the Syriac rendering "Messiah shall be killed" (ܡܫܝܚܐ ܠܡܘܬܐ) for the Hebrew expression "an anointed one will be cut off" (יִכָּרֵת מָשִׁיחַ) implies a Christian interpretation pointing to the death of Jesus. However, the verb כָּרַת "to cut off" often means "to kill" in the Hebrew Bible, and the expression "anointed one" does not require a Christological interpretation. In both of these cases, Wyngarden has lapsed into a *non sequitur*; his conclusions are not convincing.

---

[3] See, for example, Gelston, *Peshiṭta of the Twelve Prophets*, 71.

[4] Taylor, "Interpretive Glosses," 469–92.

[5] F. Glorie (ed.), *Jerôme, Commentariorum in Danielem* (CCSL 75A; Turnhout: Brepols, 1964); G.L. Archer Jr. (trans.), *Jerome's Commentary on Daniel* (Grand Rapids: Baker, 1958).

[6] Wyngarden, *The Syriac Version of the Book of Daniel*.

Kallarakkal reached conclusions somewhat opposite those of Wyngarden with regard to the religious identity of the Syriac translator of Daniel.[7] He argued that s-Dan was most probably the work of a Jewish translator living in Edessa during the first century B.C.E. He maintained that the author of Ur-Theodotion may have made use of the Syriac version since, according to him, s-Dan preceded the Greek version of Theodotion. However, Kallarakkal's examples cannot sustain the weight he places upon them. It is not convincing to claim, for example, that only a Jew would render "the land of beauty" (Dan 11:16) as "the land of Israel," or that only a non-Christian would use ܩܝܡܐ rather than ܕܝܬܩܐ for "covenant" (Dan 9:4; 11:28, 30, 32), or that attributing the end of the holy city to a flood (Dan 9:26) implies an understanding of the destruction of Jerusalem uninformed by the historical events of 70 C.E.

It seems best to leave unresolved the question of community origins for s-Dan. On the basis of evidence found in the biblical text, it is impossible to say with certainty whether the translator was of Jewish or Christian background. Likewise, whether the translation was originally intended to serve the needs of a Jewish or a Christian community is not entirely clear. Probability lies on the side of an intended Jewish audience, but not for the reasons that Kallarakkal supposed.

18.3.3.6 Text-Critical Value

s-Dan witnesses to a Hebrew/Aramaic *Vorlage* that was accepted by Syriac translators in the second century C.E. While there are many places where s-Dan has pluses, minuses, substitutions, and other types of variation from MT (→ 18.2.2), these are usually of a minor nature.[8] Unlike the Old Greek (→ 18.3.1), which for chronological consistency situates Daniel 7 and 8 between Daniel 4 and 5, s-Dan follows the order of presentation found in MT. Due to its general alignment with MT, s-Dan yields fewer textual variants than the Greek tradition, although its value as a textual witness should not be underestimated on this account. In some places, textual or translational features of the Greek versions of Daniel may have influenced s-Dan, although the extent of this influence is limited. s-Dan is important both as a text-critical tool for research in the Hebrew Bible and as a literary achievement in its own right.

Azzam, P.J., "Le Peshitta (A.T.) et le texte massorétique: Étude comparative," *ParOr* 26 (2001): 89–125.

Botha, P.J., "The Relevance of the Book of Daniel for Fourth-Century Christianity according to the Commentary Ascribed to Ephrem the Syrian," in *Die Geschichte der Daniel-Auslegung in Judentum, Christentum und Islam: Studien zur Kommentierung des Danielbuches in Literatur und Kunst* (eds. K. Bracht and D.S. du Toit; BZAW 371; Berlin: De Gruyter, 2007), 99–122.

Casey, M., "The Syrian Tradition," in *Son of Man: The Interpretation and Influence of Daniel 7* (London: SPCK, 1979), 51–70.

Casey, M., "The Fourth Kingdom in Cosmas Indicopleustes and the Syrian Tradition," *Rivista di storia e letteratura religiosa* 25 (1989): 38–403.

Casey, M., "Porphyry and Syrian Exegesis of the Book of Daniel," *ZAW* 81 (1990): 139–42.

Dirksen, P.B., "The Peshitta and Textual Criticism of the Old Testament," *VT* 42 (1992): 376–90.

Dirksen, P.B., "The Old Testament Peshitta," in Mulder, *Mikra, 255–97.

Dirksen, P.B. and M.J. Mulder (eds.), *The Peshiṭta: Its Early Text and History* (Monographs of the Peshitta Institute Leiden 4; Leiden: Brill, 1988).

Ferch, A.J., "Porphyry: An Heir to Christian Exegesis?" *ZAW* 73 (1982): 141–47.

Haefeli, L., *Die Peschitta des Alten Testamentes mit Rücksicht auf ihre textkritische Bearbeitung und Herausgabe* (ATA 11; Munich: Aschendorff, 1927).

Jenner, K.D., "Syriac Daniel," in *The Book of Daniel: Composition and Reception* (eds. J.J. Collins and P.W. Flint; 2 vols.; VTSup 83; Leiden: Brill, 2001), 2.608–37.

Kallarakkal, A.G., "The Peshitto Version of Daniel: A Comparison with the Massoretic Text, the Septuagint and Theodotion" (PhD diss., University of Hamburg, 1973).

van der Kooij, A., "The Four Kingdoms in Peshitta Daniel 7 in the Light of the Early History of Interpretation," in *The Peshitta: Its Use in Literature and Liturgy:*

---

[7] Kallarakkal, "The Peshitto Version of Daniel."
[8] For a full discussion of textual features of S-Dan, see Taylor, *The Peshiṭta of Daniel*.

Papers Read at the Third Peshitta Symposium (ed. B. ter Haar Romeny; Monographs of the Peshitta Institute Leiden 15; Leiden: Brill, 2006), 123–29.

Lund, J.A., "Telltale Signs of a Semitic Prototext for the Peshitta of Daniel," *Aramaic Studies* 7 (2009): 103–12.

McHardy, W.D., "The Peshitta Text of Daniel XI.4," *JTS* 49 (1948): 56–57.

Morrison, C.E., "The Reception of the Book of Daniel in Aphrahat's Fifth Demonstration, 'On Wars'," *Hugoye* 7 (2004): 1–24.

Mulder, M.J., "The Use of the Peshiṭta in Textual Criticism," in *La Septuaginta en la investigación contemporánea (V Congreso de la IOSCS)* (ed. N. Fernández Marcos; Textos y estudios "Cardenal Cisneros" 34; Madrid: Instituto "Arias Montano," 1985), 37–53.

Munnich, O., "La Peshitta de *Daniel* et ses relations textuelles avec la Septante," in *L'Ecrit et l'Esprit: Etudes d'histoire du texte et de théologie biblique en hommage à Adrian Schenker* (eds. D. Böhler, I. Himbaza, and P. Hugo; OBO 214; Göttingen: Vandenhoeck & Ruprecht, 2005), 229–47.

van Peursen, W., "Daniel's Four Kingdoms in the Syriac Tradition," in *Tradition and Innovation in Biblical Interpretation: Studies Presented to Professor Eep Talstra on the Occasion of His Sixty-Fifth Birthday* (eds. W.T. van Peursen and J.W. Dyk; SSN 57; Leiden: Brill, 2011), 189–207.

Rundgren, F., "On a Loan Translation in Daniel: Old Syriac *daxšā*," *Orientalia suecana* 40 (1991): 220–25.

Taylor, R.A., *The Peshiṭta of Daniel* (Monographs of the Peshitta Institute Leiden 7; Leiden: Brill, 1994).

Taylor, R.A., "The Peshiṭta of Daniel: Questions of Origin and Date," *OrChrAn* 247 (1994): 31–42.

Taylor, R.A., "The Book of Daniel in the Bible of Edessa," *Aramaic Studies* 5 (2007): 239–53.

Taylor, R.A., "The Interpretive Glosses in Syriac Manuscripts of Peshitta-Daniel," *ParOr* 36 (2011): 469–92.

Weitzman, M.P., "From Judaism to Christianity: The Syriac Version of the Hebrew Bible," in *The Jews among Pagans and Christians in the Roman Empire* (eds. J. Lieu, J. North, and T. Rajak; London: Routledge, 1992), 147–73.

Weitzman, M.P., "Lexical Clues to the Composition of the Old Testament Peshitta," in *Studia Aramaica: New Sources and New Approaches: Papers Delivered at the London Conference of the Institute of Jewish Studies, University College London, 26th–28th June 1991* (eds. M.J. Geller, J.C. Greenfield, and M.P. Weitzman; JSSSup 4; Oxford: Oxford University Press, 1995), 217–46.

Weitzman, M.P., *The Syriac Version of the Old Testament: An Introduction* (University of Cambridge Oriental Publications 56; Cambridge: Cambridge University Press, 1999).

Wilcox, M., "Some Recent Contributions to the Problem of Peshitta Origins," *AbrN* 1 (1961): 62–67.

Wyngarden, M.J., *The Syriac Version of the Book of Daniel* (Leipzig: W. Drugulin, 1923).

Richard A. Taylor

18.3.4 Hexapla

18.3.4.1 Background

Both OG-Dan and Th-Dan were in circulation in the churches of Origen's day.[1] Consequently, it is not surprising that evidence of the Hexaplaric recension (→ 1.3.1.2.7) exists for both versions. The extant asterisks and obeli in certain manuscripts mark passages where Origen's work on the text can be seen most clearly. Regarding the fragmentary preservation of the versions of Aquila and Symmachus through Hexaplaric readings, see → 18.3.2.

18.3.4.2 Editions and Sources

For OG-Dan, the tenth-century Greek Codex Chisianus (LXX⁸⁸) and the Syro-Hexapla (→ 18.4.4.1) are representatives of the Hexaplaric recension, but some pre- and post-Hexaplaric corrections also likely exist in LXX⁸⁸-Syh.[2] Both witnesses provide asterisks and obeli that are published in the first apparatus under the OG text in the Göttingen Septuagint.[3] Both witnesses contain colophons after Daniel 12 (but not after Susanna and not after Bel and the Dragon) that claim that their texts were produced from a copy made from the Tetrapla.[4]

For Th-Dan, Montgomery and Ziegler have identified the eighth-century C.E. uncial Codex Venetus (LXXᵛ) and two minuscules dating to the eleventh

---

[1] Origen, *Ep. Afr.* 2(4) (PG 11:52a–b; SC 302:524–27); see also → 18.3.2.1.

[2] Munnich, "Origène," 187–88, 195–98.

[3] Ziegler, *Susanna, Daniel, Bel et Draco*, 18. Olivier Munnich has made a comprehensive revision of the OG text and apparatus in the second edition of this work to account for new evidence since Ziegler's first edition.

[4] Ziegler, *Susanna, Daniel, Bel et Draco*, 394.

and twelfth centuries C.E. (LXX⁶², ¹⁴⁷) as the manuscript group that best corresponds to the character of the Hexaplaric recension.[5] Ziegler uses the siglum *O* to designate this group, but he does not consider it possible to attribute this recension to Origen with absolute certainty. He thinks that the insertion of the very smallest additions and particles in the LXX^O group probably indicates a later editor whose work was more meticulous than Origen's, so that the recension might be considered more accurately a Hexaplaric subgroup.[6] In any case, Munnich's study of the asterisked materials in OG-Dan confirms that Origen knew the form of Th-Dan (→ 18.3.2) represented by the LXX^O group.[7] Codex Venetus attests thirteen asterisked passages.[8]

Furthermore, manuscripts LXX⁸⁸ and LXX⁴⁴⁹, which show a strong Hexaplaric influence and are classified in the Lucianic subgroup LXX^lll, attest additional asterisked passages.[9] The Lucianic manuscripts LXX²², ⁴⁸, ⁹⁶, and ⁷⁶³ preserve one asterisk (Dan 3:3). Finally, Eusebius states that accurate manuscripts show an asterisked σου "your" following ἁγίαν "holy" in Dan 9:24 (*Dem. ev.* 8.2.383). All of these asterisked passages are published in the apparatus under the "θ′" text (= Th) in the Göttingen Septuagint. There are no known obeli for Th-Dan.[10]

18.3.4.3 Translation Character and Technique
18.3.4.3.1 Hexaplaric Recension of OG-Dan

There are a total of thirty-nine asterisked passages in the "canonical" sections of OG-Dan.[11] The source of the asterisked material is designated in only one case: The asterisked addition to OG-Dan 4:7 is attributed to Theodotion by Syh^txt. In thirty of the thirty-eight anonymous cases, however, the asterisked text corresponds to the form of Th-Dan (→ 18.2.3) represented by the LXX^O group.[12] In another seven cases, the asterisked material was probably adopted from Th-Dan, but minor alterations were made to the text by Origen or his successors.[13] In the final asterisked addition (Dan 11:41b–42), the text can be identified as Aquila's version with reasonable certainty.[14] Munnich suggests that Origen's switch to Aquila was motivated by a desire to reveal Matt 24:10 καὶ τότε σκανδαλισθήσονται πολλοί "and then many will be caused to stumble" as an allusion to Dan 11:41 by means of Aquila's rendering καὶ πολλαὶ σκανδαλισθήσονται (cf. Th-Dan καὶ πολλοὶ ἀσθενήσουσι "and many will be weak").[15] Nearly all of the asterisks in OG-Dan (→ 18.3.1) mark an addition that fills a gap in OG-Dan relative to MT (→ 18.2.2), but in a few cases the asterisks mark a substitution. Many gaps in OG-Dan were left unfilled, especially in sections of OG-Dan that depart from a straightforward translation of MT (e.g. OG-Dan 4–6).

There are a total of thirty-three obelized passages in the "canonical" parts of OG-Dan (→ 18.3.1).[16]

---

[5] Montgomery, "The Hexaplaric Strata," 294–99; Ziegler, *Susanna, Daniel, Bel et Draco*, 142–45.

[6] Ziegler, *Susanna, Daniel, Bel et Draco*, 144–45.

[7] Munnich, "Origène," 193, 216.

[8] Th-Dan 2:16; 3:22; 4:15; 5:10, 12; 6:3(4), 4(5), 20(21) (bis); 7:7, 10; 9:19; 11:36.

[9] Manuscript LXX⁸⁸ attests asterisks in Th-Dan 2:11, 35; 4:1; 5:6; 8:25, and manuscript LXX⁴⁴⁹ in Th-Dan 2:9, 16; 5:10; 7:7; 8:25.

[10] Ziegler, *Susanna, Daniel, Bel et Draco*, 145.

[11] Munnich, "Origène," 189; Ziegler, *Susanna, Daniel, Bel et Draco*, 30. Regarding the ten asterisked segments in the Additions to Daniel in chapter 3, see Munnich, "Origène," 203–05, and Ziegler, *Susanna, Daniel, Bel et Draco*, 33–36.

[12] In eighteen of the asterisked segments, the text corresponds to the earliest recoverable form of Th-Dan as reconstructed by Ziegler, but in all of these cases the relevant text is also attested in the LXX^O group (OG-Dan 1:2; 2:5, 15, 40a, 41; 3:6, 7b, 17, 18, 91[24]–92[25]; 7:15, 23; 8:7, 13; 9:24; 11:11 [bis], 29). Cf. Munnich, "Origène," 190–91, 198. In twelve of the asterisked segments, the text represents a revision of Th-Dan that is attested in the LXX^O group (OG-Dan 3:3b, 7a, 9, 10, 15, 19, 20, 98[31]–100[33]; 7:11; 8:2, 3, 5). See Munnich, "Origène," 192–93, 198–99.

[13] OG-Dan 2:40b; 3:3a, 21; 7:5, 9–10, 14; 11:9. In Dan 2:40b and 11:9, it is also plausible that Aquila is the source, but no Aquila fragments exist to provide confirmation. See Munnich, "Origène," 190, 194–203.

[14] The Aquila fragment α′ *et multae corruent* "Aquila many will be ruined" corresponds to ※ καὶ πολλαὶ σκανδαλισθήσονται "many will be offended" whereas the reading σ′ *et multa millia corruent* "Symmachus many thousands will be ruined" rules out Symmachus.

[15] Munnich, "Origène," 194.

[16] Cf. Munnich, "Origène," 189; Ziegler, *Susanna, Daniel, Bel et Draco*, 36–44. Munnich counts thirty-four obelized passages in the canonical sections of Daniel, but this total includes Dan 3:91a, which does not actually belong to the canonical part of Daniel since the translation of the Aramaic text does

In twenty-three of these cases, the obeli mark passages in OG-Dan that have no counterpart in MT (→ 18.2.2).[17] In another case, the obelus marks Old Greek text that is to be replaced by a more accurate rendering given in the adjacent asterisked addition (Dan 3:3).[18] In another case, Origen obelizes text that he probably considers to be the second member of a double rendering of MT (Dan 4:8).[19] Thus, most of the obeli are clearly used according to the principles of the Hexaplaric recension.

Surprisingly, however, eight of the thirty-three obelized segments contain text that corresponds to MT in whole or in part (Dan 2:18; 4:33; 6:28[29]; 9:24, 26, 27; 10:1; 11:30). None of these obelized segments represents the secondary member of a double rendering. In Dan 4:33, Origen probably obelized only the word ἐμοί "to me," which has no counterpart in MT, but a later scribe accidentally shifted the metobelus from ἐμοί to the following μοι (both meaning "to me").[20] For six of the other cases, Munnich proposes that the obelus takes on a secondary meaning that is precisely opposite its normal usage in the Hexaplaric tradition (Dan 6:28[29]; 9:24, 26, 27; 10:1; 11:30). Thus Origen obelized segments that have a counterpart in MT but not in Origen's best copies of OG-Dan.[21] Munnich's proposal finds some support in papyrus LXX[967] for the obelized text in Dan 6:28(29), but nevertheless seems problematic on the whole, because the intended meaning of any particular obelus in Hexaplaric manuscripts could then only be discerned by checking whether or not the Hebrew-Aramaic text, or perhaps Aquila's version, contains a counterpart to the obelized segment. The sign of the obelus would communicate nothing on its own about the relationship between the Hebrew and Greek texts.

I would suggest instead that these obeli are intended to be read together with corresponding marginal notes that are extant in Codex Chisianus or the Syro-Hexapla (→ 18.4.4.1) for four of the six cases (Dan 9:24, 26, 27; 10:1). The obeli indicate that OG-Dan does not render the Hebrew-Aramaic text as accurately as the translation provided in the margin. For example, the words τοῦ χριστοῦ "the anointed one" are probably obelized in Dan 9:26 to indicate that the corresponding word in Aquila's version in the margin of LXX[88]-Syh, namely ἡγουμένου "leader," provides a more accurate rendering of the Hebrew, which in this case is נָגִיד "leader." The obelus therefore functions according to its normal Hexaplaric usage, while the marginal reading functions like a complementary asterisked text, except that the marginal reading provides a longer sample of the passage than that which is obelized.

This explanation also accounts for the obelized segment καὶ τιμωρίαν ζητῆσαι in Dan 2:18, which was intended by the Old Greek translator in the sense "and to seek help," since it corresponds to MT וְרַחֲמִין לְמִבְעֵא "and to seek compassion." Later readers of OG-Dan were prone to misunderstand the Greek phrase in the more common, alternative sense "and to seek vengeance."[22] Therefore the segment is obelized in LXX[88]-Syh, and the Symmachus reading ὑπὲρ τοῦ ἐρωτῆσαι οἰκτιρμούς "for the sake of asking for compassion" in the margin of the Syro-Hexapla provides a more accurate and less ambiguous rendering of MT.

In any case, comparison of the Hexaplaric manuscripts (LXX[88]-Syh) to the pre-Hexaplaric pa-

---

not resume until Dan 3:91b (MT-Dan 3:24). Regarding the six obelized passages in the Additions to Daniel, see Munnich, "Origène," 206–07, 212, and Ziegler, *Susanna, Daniel, Bel et Draco*, 37, 41.

[17] OG-Dan 1:17, 20 (bis); 2:8, 9 (bis), 11, 38, 48; 3:1 (bis), 2 (bis), 15, 17, 95(28); 4:1; 6:3, 17; 7:8; 8:16; 12:6, 13. Cf. Munnich, "Origène," 206.

[18] In Dan 3:3, the first asterisked segment provides a long list of offices, which replaces the obelized οἱ προγεγραμμένοι "those appointed [as leaders]" (Ziegler, *Susanna, Daniel, Bel et Draco*, 30).

[19] Munnich, "Origène," 207–08.

[20] Ziegler, ed., *Susanna, Daniel, Bel et Draco*, 39; cf. Munnich, "Origène," 208–09.

[21] Munnich, "Origène," 209–12, 217; Ziegler, *Susanna, Daniel, Bel et Draco*, 36–42. Munnich assumes that Origen would have had conflicting copies of OG-Dan in these cases primarily on the basis of his observation that the obelized segments in question often occur in proximity to expansions of OG-Dan relative to MT. However, the expansionistic tendencies of the Old Greek translator make Munnich's assumption somewhat tenuous, since the expansions are not necessarily secondary.

[22] Munnich classifies this obelized segment as having no counterpart in MT ("Origène," 206). Perhaps he assumes this alternative sense of the phrase.

pyrus LXX⁹⁶⁷ demonstrates that Hexaplaric editing in OG-Dan was not necessarily limited to the changes marked by extant asterisks and obeli. The Hexaplaric recension introduces more than sixty transpositions in word order for the purpose of alignment to the Hebrew-Aramaic text.²³ There are also approximately one hundred additions, many of which originally may have been marked with an asterisk. Furthermore, there are thirty omissions common to both LXX⁸⁸ and Syh, but these may be pre- or post-Hexaplaric corrections since Origen would have merely obelized and not deleted such passages. Similarly, there are approximately fifty word variants that may be pre- or post-Hexaplaric corrections. In any case, the majority of these changes to OG-Dan represent attempts to bring the Greek text into greater alignment with MT.²⁴

18.3.4.3.2 Hexaplaric Recension of Th-Dan

There are a total of twenty-one asterisked passages in Th-Dan (→ 18.3.2) and all occur within the "canonical" sections. Two of these instances, however, should be attributed to the Lucianic recension since their readings do not occur in the manuscripts of the LXX⁰ group and since the insertions result in double renderings, which are contrary to the principles of the Hexaplaric recension (Dan 4:1; 8:25). The asterisked reading reported by Eusebius in Dan 9:24 is also not found in the LXX⁰ group (Dan 9:24).

All of the remaining eighteen asterisked passages are additions that fill gaps in Th-Dan relative to MT (→ 18.2.2), except for two instances in which the asterisked materials replace a pronoun in Th-Dan with a more accurate rendering of MT (Dan 6:3[4]; 7:10). All of the asterisked passages are anonymous. OG-Dan (→ 18.3.1) can be considered the source of the addition in only four instances (Dan 2:11; 7:7; 9:19; 11:36), so the editor probably resorted to the versions of Aquila and Symmachus in the majority of cases. Two instances indeed can be identified as Aquila's version on the basis of lexical equivalencies in related Aquila fragments (Dan 6:3[4]; 6:4[5]).²⁵ The fragmentary state of Aq-Dan and Sym-Dan makes further identifications difficult. In any case, the asterisked materials whose readings are attested in the LXX⁰ group of Th-Dan appear to be inserted in a manner consistent with the principles of the Hexaplaric recension, and therefore probably trace back to Origen.

The insertions marked with asterisks are not the only evidence of recensional activity in the LXX⁰ group. According to Ziegler, the minuscules LXX⁶²,¹⁴⁷ exhibit nearly ninety additions that bring the text into greater alignment with MT, including very small insertions like pronouns and particles. The rendering of the direct object marker אֶת with the preposition σύν "with" appears thirteen times among the insertions, so that the influence of Aquila's version can be recognized.²⁶ Such additions are the most common type of variants in the LXX⁰ group, but wording changes and transpositions also occur.²⁷

18.3.4.4 Text-Critical Value for the Hebrew-Aramaic Text

Readings attributable to the Hexaplaric recensions of OG-Dan (→ 18.3.1) and Th-Dan (→ 18.3.2) can be used as witnesses to the Hebrew-Aramaic text known to Origen, except in the case of the Additions to Daniel (→ 11.3.2). Variant readings within the asterisked materials should be evaluated in light of the translation technique of the relevant pre-Hexaplaric translator, when he can be identified. Furthermore, the text of the asterisked additions to OG-Dan and Th-Dan can be added to the corpus of pre-Hexaplaric witnesses (→ 18.3.2). On

---

²³ Ziegler, *Susanna, Daniel, Bel et Draco*, 44–45.
²⁴ Ziegler, *Susanna, Daniel, Bel et Draco*, 47–50.

²⁵ Specifically, the lexical equivalency סָרְכָא "high official"/συνεκτικός "chief" is unique to Aquila according to Jerome's commentary on MT-Dan 6:5 (cf. the Göttingen apparatus for OG-Dan 6:4), and therefore the asterisked material in Th-Dan 6:3(4) can be identified as Aquila. Similarly, the lexical equivalency שְׁחִיתָה "that which is corrupt"/ἀμπλάκημα "fault," which is known for Aquila in MT-Dan 6:5 (cf. the Göttingen apparatus for OG-Dan 6:4), suggests that Aquila is the source of the asterisked material in Th-Dan 6:4(5).
²⁶ Dan 8:4, 7 (bis), 15, 16, 19; 9:13; 10:7 (bis), 8, 11, 21; 12:7.
²⁷ Ziegler, *Susanna, Daniel, Bel et Draco*, 144.

the whole, the Hexaplaric recensions of OG-Dan and Th-Dan suggest that Origen's Hebrew-Aramaic text was close to MT.

Di Lella, A.A., "The Textual History of Septuagint-Daniel and Theodotion-Daniel," in *The Book of Daniel: Composition and Reception* (2 vols.; eds. J.J. Collins and P.W. Flint; VTSup 83; Leiden: Brill, 2001), 2.586–607.
Montgomery, J.A., "The Hexaplaric Strata in the Greek Texts of Daniel," *JBL* 44 (1925): 289–302.
Montgomery, J.A., *A Critical and Exegetical Commentary on the Book of Daniel* (ICC; Edinburgh: T & T Clark, 1927).
Munnich, O., "Origène, éditeur de la *Septante* de *Daniel*," in Fraenkel, *Studien zur Septuaginta*, 187–218.
Ziegler, J. (ed.), *Susanna, Daniel, Bel et Draco* (Septuaginta Vetus Testamentum Graecum 16.2; Göttingen: Vandenhoeck & Ruprecht, 1954; 2nd ed. 1999).

Jason T. Parry

18.3.5 Post-Hexaplaric Greek Translations

18.3.5.1 Background

The churches rejected OG-Dan sometime between 250 and 400 C.E. (→ 18.3.2.1), so the possibility of Lucianic and Hesychian recensions of OG-Dan (→ 1.3.1.2.7) cannot be excluded. Unfortunately, manuscript evidence is lacking. Limited post-Hexaplaric editing of OG-Dan can be detected, however, in certain types of corrections in the Hexaplaric witnesses LXX^{88}-Syh (→ 18.3.4).

For Th-Dan, Montgomery hypothesizes that the text form of the LXX^O group (LXX$^{V, 62, 147}$; see further → 18.3.4.2) became the basis of a subsequent revision (henceforth Or^c) carried out by Eusebius for Constantine. Or^c is represented by seven Greek manuscripts (LXX$^{A, Q, 393, 106, 35, 230, 42}$), the Arabic version (→ 18.4.8), and the Bohairic version (→ 18.4.2), according to Montgomery.[1] Gehman, who studied under Montgomery, concludes that LXX$^{Q, 230}$, the Bohairic version, and the Armenian version (→ 18.4.5) are members of a sub-

group within Or^c that represents an Egyptian text form and presumably the Hesychian recension.[2] Gehman suggests that Hesychius "adapted the Hexaplaric recension to a variant basal form of Theodotion [Daniel] in Egypt."[3] Gehman also notes some Hesychian influence in the Sahidic and Ethiopic versions.[4]

Ziegler, however, rejects Montgomery's identification of the Eusebian edition. According to Ziegler, the seven manuscripts of Or^c do not bear a uniform character, and the Hexaplaric influence seen in these manuscripts is also found in almost all other minuscules of Th-Dan.[5] Furthermore, Ziegler states that Gehman's assertion of an Egyptian or Hesychian provenance for the text form represented by LXX^Q cannot be proven.[6]

Consequently, the Lucianic recension of Th-Dan remains the only undisputed, definable post-Hexaplaric recension of Daniel and therefore is analyzed in the following sections.

18.3.5.2 Editions and Sources

The variants associated with the Lucianic recension of Th-Dan are presented in the apparatus of the Göttingen Septuagint. Ziegler identifies seven manuscripts as the best representatives of the Lucianic recension in Th-Dan (LXX^L = LXX$^{22, 36, 48, 51, 96, 231, 763}$).[7] He thus adds two manuscripts (LXX$^{96, 763}$) to the core group named some years earlier by Montgomery.[8] Ziegler also recognizes two Lucianic subgroups and one Lucianic uncial (LXX^{II} = LXX$^{311, 538}$; LXX^{III} = LXX$^{88, 449, 770}$; LXX^Z).[9] All of the manuscripts date from the tenth

---

[1] Montgomery, "The Hexaplaric Strata," 292–93, 297–99; Montgomery, *A Critical and Exegetical Commentary*, 51–53. Gehman concludes that the best representative of Or^c is the Arabic version ("The 'Polyglot' Arabic Text," 351).

[2] Gehman, "The Sahidic and the Bohairic Versions," 327; Gehman, "The Armenian Version," 89, 99.
[3] Gehman, "The Hesychian Influence," 330. Gehman echoes Montgomery here; cf. Montgomery, "The Hexaplaric Strata," 293.
[4] Gehman, "The Sahidic and the Bohairic Versions," 298–99; Gehman, "The Hesychian Influence," 330–31.
[5] Ziegler, *Susanna, Daniel, Bel et Draco*, 143.
[6] Ziegler, *Susanna, Daniel, Bel et Draco*, 132, 140.
[7] Ziegler, *Susanna, Daniel, Bel et Draco*, 146.
[8] Montgomery, "The Hexaplaric Strata," 291–92; Montgomery, *A Critical and Exegetical Commentary*, 53.
[9] Ziegler, *Susanna, Daniel, Bel et Draco*, 146–47.

TABLE 1   *The Lucianic Recension of Th-Dan 6:3(4) and Its Predecessors*

MT	אֱדַיִן דָּנִיֵּאל דְּנָה הֲוָא מִתְנַצַּח עַל־סָרְכַיָּא וַאֲחַשְׁדַּרְפְּנַיָּא כָּל־קֳבֵל דִּי רוּחַ יַתִּירָא בֵּהּ
	"Then this Daniel was distinguishing himself above the officials and satraps, because an extraordinary spirit was in him."
Th-Dan	καὶ ἦν Δανιηλ ὑπὲρ αὐτούς, ὅτι πνεῦμα περισσὸν ἐν αὐτῷ
	"And Daniel was above them, because an extraordinary spirit was in him."
Th-Dan (Origen)	καὶ Δανιηλ ※ ὑπὲρ τοὺς συνεκτικοὺς καὶ τοὺς σατράπας κατέναντι ✓ ὅτι πνεῦμα περισσὸν ἦν ἐν αὐτῷ
	"And Daniel was ※ above the cohesive ones and the satraps, before ✓ that (i.e., because) an extraordinary spirit was in him."
Th-Dan (Lucian)	καὶ ἦν Δανιηλ ὑπερνικῶν ὑπὲρ τοὺς τακτικοὺς καὶ τοὺς σατράπας κατέναντι ὅτι πνεῦμα περισσὸν ἦν ἐν αὐτῷ
	"And Daniel was prevailing over the tacticians and the satraps opposite him, because an extraordinary spirit was in him."

to the twelfth centuries C.E., except for the uncial LXX^z, which dates from the sixth century but preserves only Dan 3:2–15.[10]

These manuscripts can be identified as representatives of the text form in Constantinople and Antioch in the fourth and fifth centuries C.E. on the basis of frequent agreement with biblical quotations in the Daniel commentaries by John Chrysostom and Theodoret of Cyrus.[11] Jerome attributes the text form of the Septuagint in this region to Lucian.[12]

18.3.5.3 Translation Character and Technique

The Lucianic recension of Th-Dan appears to be dependent on the Hexaplaric recension at least in terms of Origen's additions to the text, yet Lucian sometimes makes adjustments in the lexical choices, style, and position of the addition.[13] Of the eighteen asterisked additions introduced by the Hexaplaric recension (→ 18.3.4.3.2), thirteen are also attested by the main LXX^L group, though sometimes with minor adjustments.[14] Another three of the asterisked additions are not attested by the LXX^L group, but are attested by the Lucianic subgroup LXX^III.[15] Thus, only two of the asterisked additions of the Hexaplaric recension are not found in the witnesses to the Lucianic recension.[16] At the same time, the Lucianic recension introduces three asterisked additions not found in the Hexaplaric recension, and two of these additions result in double renderings.[17]

In Table 1, a passage from Th-Dan 6:3(4) is shown in which asterisked material from the

---

[10] Ziegler, *Susanna, Daniel, Bel et Draco*, 121–22.

[11] Ziegler, *Susanna, Daniel, Bel et Draco*, 128–29, 147. Chrysostom's commentary is preserved fragmentarily in catena scholia that are collected in Migne, PG 56:191–246. The Greek text of Theodoret's commentary from Migne, PG 81:1255–1546 is published with an English translation in Hill, *Theodoret of Cyrus: Commentary on Daniel*.

[12] See Jerome's prologue to the book of Paralipomenon in the Vulgate.

[13] Ziegler, *Susanna, Daniel, Bel et Draco*, 145, 148.

[14] Th-Dan 2:9, 11, 16; 3:22; 4:15; 5:6, 10; 6:3(4), 20a(21a); 7:7, 10; 9:19; 11:36.

[15] Th-Dan 2:35; 3:3; 6:20b(21b). LXX^L attests an addition in Dan 3:3, but it deviates considerably from the Hexaplaric addition.

[16] Th-Dan 5:12; 6:4(5).

[17] Th-Dan 4:1; 8:25; 9:24; the double renderings are found in Dan 4:1 and 8:25.

Hexaplaric recension is adopted and modified according to the principles of the Lucianic recension. The earliest form of Th-Dan does not render every term of the Aramaic. Origen improves Th-Dan by replacing ὑπὲρ αὐτούς "above them" with an asterisked segment from Aquila's version that renders the words עַל־סָרְכַיָּא וַאֲחַשְׁדַּרְפְּנַיָּא כָּל־קֳבֵל "above the officials and satraps, because of."[18] Lucian retains Origen's insertion but changes the translation of סָרְכַיָּא "the officials" from Aquila's etymological rendering συνεκτικούς "cohesive ones" to τακτικούς "tacticians" in order to match the rendering used in the preceding verse of Th-Dan.[19] Lucian also inserts the participle ὑπερνικῶν "prevailing over," which corresponds to MT מִתְנַצַּח "distinguishing himself" in order to bring his version into alignment with MT and to improve clarity and style. The fact that Lucian does not also insert a rendering for דְּנָה "this" shows that clarity is more important to Lucian than strict quantitative equivalence to MT. The adverb κατέναντι "before, opposite" in Lucian's version originally comes from Aquila's literal rendering of כָּל־קֳבֵל, but Theodoret's commentary on Daniel understands κατέναντι in Lucian's version as follows: "Daniel was prevailing over the tacticians and satraps opposite (κατέναντι) him, because an extraordinary spirit was in him." Theodoret explains the term κατέναντι thus: "'opposite him,' that is to say, Daniel was set parallel to them, being compared to them and being examined next to them."[20] Theodoret's ignorance of the originally intended function of κατέναντι underscores the necessity of comparing Lucian's version to the Hexaplaric recension (→ 18.3.4) when evaluating readings in the Lucianic recension. Nevertheless, this example illustrates Lucian's intention to produce a version that often adopts Origen's additions to the text while making adjustments for the sake of clarity and style.

Ziegler collects a number of other examples of Lucian's editorial activity in Th-Dan, including additions, transpositions, word changes, and various other grammatical corrections similar to those found in the Prophetic Books. While many of Lucian's changes harmonize the Greek text to MT, the majority represent improvements in grammar and style.[21] In at least ten places, Lucian introduces an addition that results in a double rendering of MT, including the two asterisked additions mentioned above.[22]

18.3.5.4 Text-Critical Value for the Hebrew-Aramaic Text

The character of Lucian's version of Th-Dan should be taken into account when evaluating a particular Lucianic reading as a possible witness to the Hebrew-Aramaic text (→ 18.2.2). Some readings in the Lucianic witnesses originated with the Hexaplaric recension and should be evaluated accordingly (→ 18.3.4.4). Other readings in the Lucianic witnesses attest to Lucian's concern for improved clarity and style rather than a different Hebrew-Aramaic source. Moreover, Lucian's recension technique permits additions that result in a double rendering of MT. These possibilities should be considered before positing a different Hebrew-Aramaic text than MT for any particular Lucianic reading.

Gehman, H.S., "The 'Polyglot' Arabic Text of Daniel and Its Affinities," *JBL* 44 (1925): 327–52.
Gehman, H.S., "The Sahidic and the Bohairic Versions of the Book of Daniel," *JBL* 46 (1927): 279–330.
Gehman, H.S., "The Hesychian Influence in the Versions of Daniel," *JBL* 48 (1929): 329–32.

---

[18] For the identification of the asterisked material as Aquila, see → 18.3.4.3.2. Moreover, Origen's insertion of ※ κατέναντι ✓ before ὅτι in Th-Dan 4:15 shows that Origen (and possibly Aquila) considers κατέναντι ὅτι equivalent to the Aramaic idiom כָּל־קֳבֵל דִּי "because."

[19] Aquila's rendering is based on the semantic overlap between συνέχω "to hold together" and the Aramaic root סרך "to hold fast to."

[20] Author's translation. The Greek reads: "κατέναντι," τουτέστιν ἐκ παραλλήλου, τιθέμενος, συγκρινόμενος καὶ παρεξεταζόμενος. Migne's edition fails to punctuate κατέναντι as a quotation of biblical text (PG 81:1400a). Hill's translation attempts to make sense of Theodoret's comment while following Migne's punctuation (*Theodoret of Cyrus: Commentary on Daniel*, 159).

[21] Ziegler, *Susanna, Daniel, Bel et Draco*, 147–49.

[22] Th-Dan 4:1; 6:22(23); 7:23; 8:11, 25; 9:24; 11:10, 36, 40; 12:7; see Montgomery, *A Critical and Exegetical Commentary*, 54, and Ziegler, *Susanna, Daniel, Bel et Draco*, 148.

Gehman, H.S., "The Armenian Version of the Book of Daniel and its Affinities," *ZAW* 48 (1930): 82–99.

Hill, R.C., *Theodoret of Cyrus: Commentary on Daniel* (SBLWGRW 7; Atlanta: SBL, 2006).

Di Lella, A.A., "The Textual History of Septuagint-Daniel and Theodotion-Daniel," in *The Book of Daniel: Composition and Reception* (2 vols.; eds. J.J. Collins and P.W. Flint; VTSup 83; Leiden: Brill, 2001), 2.586–607.

Montgomery, J.A., "The Hexaplaric Strata in the Greek Texts of Daniel," *JBL* 44 (1925): 289–302.

Montgomery, J.A., *A Critical and Exegetical Commentary on the Book of Daniel* (ICC; Edinburgh: T & T Clark, 1927).

Ziegler, J. (ed.), *Susanna, Daniel, Bel et Draco* (Septuaginta Vetus Testamentum Graecum 16.2; Göttingen: Vandenhoeck & Ruprecht, 1954; 2nd ed. 1999).

Jason T. Parry

18.3.6 Vulgate

18.3.6.1 Background

v-Dan was completed at the latest by 393 C.E., shortly after Jerome began his *iuxta Hebraeos* translation project in 391 C.E. (→ 1.3.5.2).[1] As an early translation, v-Dan did not benefit from the Hebraic learning that Jerome acquired over the next twenty-five years through his translations and commentaries, nor did it reflect the exegetical work of Jerome's later *Commentary on Daniel* (completed in 407 C.E.). Still, v-Dan shows Jerome to be competent in understanding the Hebrew and usually capable of comprehending the Aramaic.

18.3.6.2 Translation Character

The translation is generally free in reworking the original into idiomatic Latin. Jerome shows no particular interest in maintaining consistency either in his lexical renderings or in his handling of syntactical structures; on the contrary, he often introduces variety for purely stylistic reasons. Especially where the text is difficult, Jerome frequently relies on the Hexaplaric versions, above all Theodotion (→ 18.3.1; → 18.3.2; → 1.3.1.2).[2] v-Dan represents an important linguistic interpretation of the Hebrew/Aramaic text and in a few places suggests a Hebrew/Aramaic *Vorlage* different from MT (→ 18.2.2).

18.3.6.3 Translation Technique
18.3.6.3.1 Hebrew/Aramaic Idioms

Jerome regularly recasts peculiar Hebrew/Aramaic idioms into Latin. Prepositions are handled strictly according to Latin usage, e.g., וַיָּצַר עָלֶיהָ "and he besieged against it," *et obsedit eam* "and he besieged it" (Dan 1:1); וּלְקֵץ "and to the end" *et post finem* "and after the end" (Dan 11:6). Prepositions are often added (e.g., *in visione mea* "in my vision," Dan 8:2) and sometimes omitted (e.g., וּמִמִּשְׁפָּטֶיךָ "and from your judgments"/*ac iudiciis* "and your judgments," Dan 9:5) following Latin idiom. Jerome renders לְ-plus-Inf. with *ut*-clauses (e.g., לְהוֹבָדָה "to destroy"/*ut perderet* "that he would destroy," Dan 2:24) over thirty-five times and occasionally uses gerundival clauses (e.g., Dan 2:14; 3:2). The Aramaic construction whereby active plural verbs express impersonal action are frequently rendered as passives by Jerome (e.g., אָמְרִין "saying"/*dicitur* "it is said," Dan 4:28).[3] Representative examples of idiomatic translation include: כֹּחַ בָּהֶם "strength was in them"/*possent* "they were able" (Dan 1:4; cf. 8:7); דְּבַר־יוֹם בְּיוֹמוֹ "the matter of a day in its day"/*annonam per singulos dies* "provision for each day" (Dan 1:5); וּבְרִיאֵי בָּשָׂר מִן "and fatness of flesh more"/*et corpulentiores* "and fatter" (Dan 1:15); וַאֲכַלוּ קַרְצֵיהוֹן דִּי יְהוּדָיֵא "and they ate the pieces of the Jews"/*accusaverunt Iudaeos* "they accused the Jews" (Dan 3:8; cf. 6:25); אַרְעָא מִנָּךְ "earthward from you"/*minus te* "inferior to you" (Dan 2:39); אֲשֶׁר־נִקְרָא שְׁמוֹ "whose name

---

[1] The completion of Daniel and the other prophets by 393 is indicated by comments in *Vir. Ill.* 134 and *Epist.* 49.4, and also by the biblical citations in Jerome's Minor Prophets commentaries written by this time; see C.B. Tkacz, "'Labor Tam Utilis': The Creation of the Vulgate," *VC* 50 (1996) 47.

[2] Jerome used Theodotion as his basis for translating the Song of the Three Youths, Susanna, and Bel and the Dragon, which he criticized as "apocryphal fables" (*apocryfas ... fabulas*) but included in his translation because of their widespread ecclesiastical usage and "so that the unlearned do not suppose that I have left out a great part of the book" (*ne videremus apud inperitos magnam partem voluminis detruncasse*) (*Dan. Prol.*). References to Theodotion in this entry refer to Theodotion-Daniel, which was the popular edition of Greek Daniel known to Jerome.

[3] Cf. F. Rosenthal, *A Grammar of Biblical Aramaic* (7th ed.; Wiesbaden: Harrassowitz, 2006) § 181.

is called"/*cognomento* "surnamed" (Dan 10:1); בַּעַל הַקְּרָנַיִם "possessor of two horns"/*cornutum* "horned" (8:6) and *habere cornua* "having horns" (Dan 8:20); בִּטְעֵם חַמְרָא "with the taste of the wine"/*iam temulentus* "now drunk" (Dan 5:2); and סְלִקוּ ... רַעְיוֹנָךְ "your thought ... arose"/*cogitare coepisti* "you began to think" (Dan 2:29). Often Jerome uses more than one Latin word to capture the sense of the original, e.g., הַתָּמִיד/*iuge sacrificium* "continual sacrifice" (Dan 8:11, 13; 11:31; 12:11); מְנַגֵּחַ/*cornibus ventilantem* "brandishing with horns" (Dan 8:4); וְנִפְלָאוֹת "wondrously"/*supra quam credi potest* "beyond what can be believed" (Dan 8:24); שַׁלְוָה "prosperity"/*copia rerum omnium* "abundance of all things" (Dan 8:25); מַרְגְּלֹתָיו "at his feet"/*quae deorsum usque ad pedes* "downward even to the feet" (Dan 10:6); לְיָבָא "to ascertain"/*diligenter discere* "diligently to learn" (Dan 7:19); וְיִשְׂתָּעֵר "shall whirl"/*quasi tempestas veniet* "shall come ... as a tempest" (Dan 11:40); וְיָצְרְפוּ "shall be refined"/*quasi ignis probabunter* "shall be tried as fire" (Dan 12:10).

18.3.6.3.2 Attention to Context

Jerome freely deviates from expected stereotyped renderings when the immediate context suggests a better translation. Thus, Jerome renders לֹא יַעַמְדוּ "they could not stand" in Dan 8:4 as *non poterant resistere* "they could not resist" (not employing עמד = *sto* "to stand"). Likewise, וְנִצְדַּק "shall be made right" in Dan 8:14 is translated with *mundabitur* "shall be cleansed" and not with some cognate of *iudico* "justify" as might be expected (here Jerome matches LXX and Theodotion). The practice of beginning speech with some version of "answered and said" is handled in a variety of contextually sensitive ways by Jerome (e.g., עָנֵה וְאָמַר Dan 3:14, 16, 24, 25, 28; 6:13, 17, 21). Jerome also uses a variety of expressions to translate כָּל קֳבֵל דִּי/דְּנָה "because of this, insofar as, although," e.g., כָּל קֳבֵל דִּי חֲזֵיתוֹן/*scientes* "knowing" (Dan 2:8); כָּל קֳבֵל דִּי/*sed* "but" (Dan 2:10), *quomodo* "in as much as" (Dan 2:40), *secundum quod* "according as" (Dan 2:45); כָּל קֳבֵל דְּנָה/*quo audito* "upon hearing this" (Dan 2:12), *post haec* "after this" (Dan 2:24). Often Jerome elaborates according to his understanding of the passage in context, e.g., וְאֵלֶּה "and these"/*hae autem solae* "and these only" (Dan

11:41); וְיִסְבַּר "he shall intend"/*et putabit quod possit* "and he shall think that he is able" (Dan 7:25); רֵאשׁ מִלִּין אֲמַר עָנֵה דָנִיֵּאל וְאָמַר "the sum of the matter he said. Daniel answered and said"/*brevi sermone conprehendit summatimque perstringens ait* "he comprised it in a few words: and relating the sum of it in short, he said" (Dan 7:1–2). Loose paraphrases are not uncommon in v-Dan (e.g., Dan 2:3, 5; 3:29; 4:16; 5:1; 6:9).

18.3.6.3.3 Style

Even when not necessary from a linguistic standpoint, Jerome commonly deviates from the surface structure of the original for the sake of style. One prominent motive behind such deviations is Jerome's desire to create diversity, e.g.: וַיָּשֶׂם ... וַיָּשֶׂם "he set ... he set"/*inposuit ... proposuit* "he gave ... he purposed" (Dan 1:7–8); חֲלוֹם חָלַמְתִּי "a dream I dreamed"/*vidi somnium* "I saw a dream" (Dan 2:3); קֳדָם ... קֳדָם ... קֳדָם "before ... before ... before"/*in conspectu ... ad ... coram* "in the presence ... to ... before" (Dan 2:24, 25, 27); הֲקֵים ... הֲקֵים ... הֲקֵים "set up ... set up ... set up"/*erexerat ... posuerat ... constituit* "erected ... set up ... established" (Dan 3:3, 5); כֹּחַ ... כֹּחַ "strength ... strength"/*fortitudo ... viribus* "power ... force" (Dan 8:24); פָּנַי ... וּפָנַי/*faciem ... vultusque* "face ... and face" (Dan 10:9); חֲזַק וַחֲזָק/*confortare et esto robustus* "take courage, and be strong" (Dan 10:19); וּמְשַׁל מִמְשָׁל "and he shall rule a rulership"/*dominabitur potestate* "shall rule with power" (Dan 11:3); וְיָבֹא ... וְיָבֹא "he shall come ... and shall come"/*veniet ... ingredietur* "he shall come ... and shall enter" (Dan 11:7). Jerome occasionally adds words to fill out the sentence (e.g., *universae* "of all," Dan 4:19; *suos* "their," Dan 5:4; *habebit* "he shall have," Dan 5:7; *putasne* "do you think," Dan 6:20; *quas videram* "which I had seen," Dan 7:7; *ecce* "behold," Dan 7:21, 9:21; *conplebitur* "it shall be fulfilled," Dan 8:17; *omnibus* "all," Dan 10:21),[4] and he frequently omits words for stylistic reasons (e.g.,

---

[4] The addition of *symphoniae* in 3:7 is a harmonization with 3:5,10,15. The addition of ἐξ ὄρους in the LXX and Theodotion in 2:34 is a harmonization with 2:45 (probably originating with LXX, since Theodotion at 2:45 has ἀπὸ ὄρους); this addition in 2:34 eventually made its way into copies of the Vulgate (*de monte*), including Codex Amiatinus.

וַיִּשֶׂם "and gave" [2nd], Dan 1:7; דָּנִיֵּאל "Daniel," Dan 2:17; מַלְכִין "kings" [2nd], Dan 2:21; וְכֵן "and thus," Dan 2:25; מַלְכָּא "O king," Dan 2:37; מַלְכָּא "O king" [1st], Dan 4:21; דִּי בֵית אֱלָהָא "of the house of God," Dan 5:3; אַנְתָּה "You," Dan 5:18; אֱלָהָא "God," Dan 5:21 [harmonized with Dan 4:22, 29]; הַשְׁכַּחְנָה "we find," Dan 6:6; תִנְיָנָה "a second one," Dan 7:5; וְחֶזְוֵהּ "and its appearance," Dan 7:20; בְּרֹאתִי "when I saw," Dan 8:2; וּרְאִיתִיו "and I saw it," Dan 8:7; אַרְצָה "to the earth," Dan 8:10; כִּי "indeed," Dan 9:14; אֲדֹנָי "O Lord" [1st], Dan 9:19; יְהוָה "the LORD," Dan 9:20; אֶת הַמַּרְאֶה "the vision" [2nd], Dan 10:7; אֶת קוֹל דְּבָרָיו "the sound of his words" [2nd], Dan 10:9; לוֹ בִלְתִּי "not his," Dan 11:18). Another important stylistic feature of v-Dan is the presence of syntactical subordination in the Latin where the original was paratactic; common forms of subordination introduced by Jerome include nominative participles (e.g., Dan 2:24; 3:6; 5:13), the ablative absolute (e.g., Dan 1:14; 2:13; 3:20; 5:29; 6:25), *cum*-clauses (e.g., Dan 1:19; 2:2; 8:27), and relative clauses (e.g., Dan 1:14; 2:2, 28; 4:2; 5:13; 6:18; 7:17, 20). Not infrequently, Jerome conveys the flow of logic by adding particles, such as *porro* "and so" (e.g., Dan 1:16; 2:32, 41; 6:4; 7:24) and *ergo* "therefore" (e.g., Dan 1:6; 2:38; 3:12; 4:15). Jerome's modest upgrades to the Latinity of v-Dan improve its readability as a Latin document but complicate modern attempts to reconstruct the underlying Hebrew/Aramaic text.

18.3.6.3.4 Literalisms and Transliterations

On occasion, v-Dan exhibits literalistic renderings, such as *condemnabitis caput meum regi* "you shall convict my head to the king" (Dan 1:10), *et brachia pugnantis expugnabuntur* "and the arms of the fighter shall be overcome" (Dan 11:22), *germen radicum eius id est arboris* "the stump of the roots of it, that is, of the tree" (Dan 4:23), and *in eo hoc est in Danihelo* "in him, that is, in Daniel" (Dan 5:12). In a few places, Jerome transliterates, as with "*Apedno*" in Dan 11:45 (Th: εφαδανω; Aq: αφαδανω),[5] "*Maozim*" in Dan 11:38, 39 (Th: μαωζιν in v. 38; καταφυγῶν in v. 39),[6] "*Malassar*" in Dan 1:11, 16 (Th: Αμελσαδ; LXX: Αβιεσδρι), and "*Ulai*" in Dan 8:16 (LXX: Ωλαμ; Th: Ουβαλ). It is not typical, however, for Jerome in v-Dan to deal with difficulties through literalism or transliteration.[7] When he does not seem to understand something, he is more likely to follow the context (e.g., הַרְגִּשׁוּ "rushed in"/*subripuerunt* "withdrew privately," ... *curiosius inquirentes* "prying inquisitively," ... *intellegentes regem* "perceiving the king," Dan 6:7, 12, 16), or one of the Hexaplaric versions (e.g., נֶחְתַּךְ "decreed"/*adbreviatae* "shortened," Dan 9:24; Th: συνετμήθησαν "cut short"; → 18.3.4).

18.3.6.3.5 Unusual Renderings, but Not Variants

Several unusual renderings that might be taken to reflect textual variants are best explained otherwise: in Dan 6:18, Jerome's *fieret* "would be done against" for תִשְׁנֵא "would change concerning" appears contextually driven; Jerome follows Theodotion (→ 18.3.1; → 18.3.2) in translating חָזוּת "conspicuous" simply with *cornua* "horns" in Dan 8:8, as it was difficult to know how חָזוּת could apply to horns;[8] Jerome's double rendering of הַדְרִי in Dan 4:33 (*decoremque perveni* "And I came to the

---

pronunciations of the Greek letter φ and the Hebrew letter פ (CC 75A, 934–35).

[6] MT מָעֻזִּים. In *Comm. Dan.* 11:37–39, Jerome gives Aquila on v. 38 as *fortitudinum* (= κραταιωμάτων), and on v. 39 he distinguishes between Theodotion as *praesidia* and Symmachus as *confugia* (CC 75A, 926–28). The transliteration μαωζειν was available in the Greek *onomastica* (P. de Lagarde, *Onomastica Sacra* (Göttingen, 1887) 183.36).

[7] Jerome found Theodotion to be a useful resource for transliterations in V-Daniel; cf. E. Tov, "Transliterations of Hebrew Words in the Greek Versions: A Further Characteristic of the KAIGE-TH Revision?" in *The Greek and Hebrew Bible: Collected Essays on the Septuagint* (Leiden: Brill, 1999), 501–12. Still, Jerome does not always follow Theodotion in transliterating difficult words (e.g., פרתמים in 1:3; עיר(ין) in 4:10,14,20; פלמוני in 8:13; בדין in 10:5, 12:6,7), and where he and Theodotion both transliterate, Jerome's transliterations appear to be corrections towards the Hebrew (note especially the corrections with respect to consonants in *Maozim* at 11:38,39 (final m), *Malassar* at 1:11,16 (final r), and *Ulai* at 8:16). Jerome's transliterations given here are capitalized (as in the editions), since he regarded them as proper nouns.

[8] Jerome gave *cornu insigne* for קרן חזות in 8:5, probably following the reading κέρας θεωρητόν found in certain Greek witnesses (and probably present in Jerome's copy of Theodotion).

---

[5] MT אַפַּדְנוֹ. In *Comm. Dan.* 11:44–45, Jerome transliterates both Theodotion and Aquila as *Apedno*; he also discusses the

glory") is best explained as Jerome combining his Hebrew text (הַדְרִי = *decoremque* "and the glory") with Theodotion (ἦλθον = *perveni* "I came"). There are numerous cases where v-Dan differs in grammatical number from MT (→ 18.2.2): two noteworthy examples are מַלְכֵי "kings"/*regem* "king" in Dan 10:13 (Aq and LXX = βασιλέως "king") and בְּתוֹרֹתָיו "in his laws"/*in lege eius* "in his law" in Dan 9:10 (LXX = τῷ νόμῳ σου "in your law"). Such differences in grammatical number reflect the translation process and generally should not be interpreted as indicating a Hebrew variant.

18.3.6.4 Text-Critical Value
18.3.6.4.1 Confusion of Consonants
The Hebrew text underlying v-Dan closely resembles MT (→ 18.2.1). v-Dan contains a few readings that might well reflect a consonantal text different from MT, e.g., *in his* "at these things" for בְּגוֹא נְדָנֶה "in the midst of the sheath" in Dan 7:15 (i.e., בגו דנה; cf. LXX); *faciet* "he shall make" for וְעָשֹׂה "and he will make" in Dan 11:17 (i.e., יעשה "he shall make"; = 4QDan^c, Th, LXX, one Masoretic manuscript); *nec stabit semen eius* "neither shall his seed stand" for וְלֹא יַעֲמֹד וּזְרֹעוֹ "and not shall he stand, and his arm" in Dan 11:6 (זַרְעוֹ for וּזְרֹעוֹ; = Th; two Masoretic manuscripts lack ו "and"); וְעַם "and the people"/*et consurgent* "and they shall rise up," Dan 11:15 (i.e., ורם; cf. Th and S). In other cases, the context and lack of supporting evidence suggest that the confusion of consonants occurred merely in Jerome's mind, e.g., פַּת בָּגוֹ "portion of his food"/*panem cum eo* "bread with him," Dan 11:26 (i.e., פת בו); בְּחֵמָא "with wrath"/*multitudine* "multitude," Dan 11:44 (perhaps הרבה); לְדִרְאוֹן "for abhorrence"/*ut videant* "so that they might see," Dan 12:2 (i.e., לראות).

18.3.6.4.2 Pluses and Minuses
There are a few cases of pluses and minuses in v-Dan worth considering as possible Hebrew variants. As for minuses: וּכְפַרְזְלָא דִּי מְרָעַע "and as iron that crushes" in Dan 2:40 is lacking in V, Th, and S; וְחָכְמָה כְּחָכְמַת אֱלָהִין "and wisdom like the wisdom of the gods" in Dan 5:11 and מְנֵא "MENE" (2nd) in Dan 5:25 are absent from V and Th; תַּקִּיפָה "strong" in Dan 2:40 and צָרָה "distress" in Dan 12:1 are lacking in V. As for pluses: *festinus* in Dan 4:15 is potentially significant (cf. בְּהִתְבְּהָלָה "with haste" in Dan 2:25; 6:20).

18.3.6.4.3 Vocalization and *Ketiv/Qere*
In the vast majority of cases, v-Dan presumes the same grammatical interpretation of the Hebrew text as reflected in the vocalization of MT. On rare occasions, v-Dan suggests an alternative vocalization, e.g., *cum* "with" for עַם "people" in Dan 9:26 suggests עִם (LXX, Th, one Masoretic manuscript match V; Aq matches MT). In cases where it is apparent from the translation, v-Dan agrees at least five times with the *Ketiv* (Dan 5:8; 8:11; 9:12; 11:18, 39) and five times with the *Qere* (Dan 5:23; 9:5; 11:10, 10, 12).

Barthélemy, **Critique textuelle 1992*, 435–96.
Collins, J.J., *Daniel* (Hermeneia; Minneapolis: Fortress, 1993).
Montgomery, J.A., *A Critical and Exegetical Commentary on the Book of Daniel* (ICC; Edinburgh: T & T Clark, 1927).

Michael Graves

18.3.7 Arabic Translations

18.3.7.1 Background
The book of Daniel was one of the most widely studied biblical books during the Middle Ages.[1] Thus, it is of no surprise that by the tenth and eleventh centuries, several Judeo-Arabic translations of the book of Daniel had appeared. Saadia Gaon b. Joseph al-Fayyūmī (882–942 C.E.) translated Daniel and supplied it with a commentary for the benefit of his community, as did his younger Karaite contemporaries, Salmon b. Yerūḥim and Yefet ben ʿElī (tenth century). No extant pre-Saadian Judeo-Arabic translation of Daniel has yet been identified although anonymous fragments ranging from the tenth century and beyond have survived in the Cairo Genizah Collections, which

---

[1] H. Ben-Shammai, "Saadia's Introduction to Daniel: Prophetic Calculation of the End of Days vs. Astrological and Magical Speculation," *Aleph* 4 (2004): 11–87.

have not been studied in depth.² Curiously enough, we may include a rare example of a Christian Arabic translation under the present heading.

18.3.7.2 Editions, Manuscripts, Tools

Saadia Gaon (882–942 C.E.) was born in the Fayyūm district in Egypt but moved to Palestine and finally to Iraq where he was appointed Gaon of the Sura Academy. It is not clear whether Saadia translated the entire Hebrew Bible or only parts of it into Arabic, yet from the books that have survived, which are also mentioned in medieval book-lists, it seems he was selective (see Polliack, → 1.3.6 and cf. → 3–5.1.8; → 6–9.1.8; → 19.3.7; → 20.3.8). One of Saadia's known and well-attested translations is his commentary on Daniel. The translation exhibits many non-literal tendencies and is generally referred to as his *tafsīr* "interpretation, explanation." Qafiḥ edited and published Saadia's translation and commentary in 1981.³ He based his edition primarily on manuscript Oxford, Bodl. 2486 (Opp. Add. fol., 64). The task of including additional manuscripts was undertaken by Alobaidi who published a new edition of Saadia's *tafsīr* in 2006.⁴ Nevertheless, Qafiḥ's edition still prevails.

One of Saadia's opponents was the Karaite scholar Yefet ben ʿElī (→ 1.3.6.3). Very little is known of Yefet's biography. It appears that his family originated from Baṣra and we know that he was active in Jerusalem in the second half of the tenth century. The Karaites rejected Jewish oral law and rabbinic authority, elevated a return to the Hebrew Bible as the source for Judaism, and called for an individual understanding of its message. Yefet translated the complete biblical corpus into Arabic and supplied it with a running commentary. His translation was referred to by the term *tarjama*. His biblical works have a threefold structure; they contain the biblical verse or part of it (incipit), a translation thereof into Judeo-Arabic, followed by a commentary in Judeo-Arabic. Some of Yefet's works have also survived in Arabic script.

Yefet's work on Daniel was edited, supplied with an English translation, and published by Margoliouth in 1889.⁵ Manuscripts in both Arabic and in Hebrew scripts were taken into account. Daniel was among Yefet's last compositions, and should be dated around 990–1010. Despite Yefet's disagreements with Saadia, the similarities between the two compositions are sometimes striking.⁶

We know further that the Karaite scholar Salmon ben Yerūḥim, active in the tenth century, translated and commented on Daniel. His works have not yet been published but are attested in manuscripts NLR Evr.-Arab. I 4002 and 4003 (JNUL microfilms nos. F 57618 and F 56985) (courtesy, Michael Wechsler). Yet another Jewish translation of Daniel was composed by Saadia Ben Levi Aznakūṭ, a learned man from Morocco who was active in the seventeenth century.⁷ His translation is attested in manuscript London, BL, Or., Harl 5505.

What appears to be a Christian Arabic translation of Daniel from MT (→ 18.2.2) is attested in manuscript Sinai Ar. 2 dated 939/40 C.E. A Syriac-based version of *Bel and the Dragon* is appended to the end of the Masoretic corpus.⁸

---

² Not all the Genizah fragments have been studied thoroughly. For identifications of Daniel, see the indices in C.F. Baker and M. Polliack, *Arabic and Judaeo-Arabic Manuscripts in the Cambridge Genizah Collections: Arabic Old Series* (T-S Ar.1a-54) (Cambridge: Cambridge University Press, 2001); A. Shivtiel and F. Niessen, *Arabic and Judaeo-Arabic Manuscripts in the Cambridge Genizah Collections: Taylor-Schechter New Series* (Cambridge: Cambridge University Press, 2006).

³ Qafiḥ, *Daniel*.

⁴ Alobaidi, *The Book of Daniel*. On occasion, Alobaidi's edition exhibits uncertain readings and mistakes; see Ben-Shammai's review of Alobaidi's work: "Le commentaire des Psaumes par le Qaraite Salmon ben Yeruham: Psaumes 1–10. Introduction, Edition, Traduction. Frankfurt a. M.: Peter Lang, 1996. Pp. 508," in *JQR, New Series*, 91 (2001): 438–46. The same critique is applicable to Alobaidi's edition of Saadia's translation and commentary on Daniel (courtesy, Michael Wechsler).

⁵ For additional studies related to Yefet's works, see M. Zawanowska, "Review of Scholarly Research on Yefet and his Works," *REJ* 173 (2014): 97–138.

⁶ Margoliouth, *A Commentary*, v–viii.

⁷ O. Löfgren, *Studien zu den arabischen Danielübersetzungen: mit besonderer Berücksichtigung der christlichen Texte: Nebst einem Beitrag zur Kritik des Peschittatextes* (Uppsala: Lundequistska Bokhandeln, 1936), 27–28, 31.

⁸ M. Lindgren and R. Vollandt, "An Early Copy of the

18.3.7.3 Translation Technique

Saadia Gaon is well known for his many non-literal translation techniques. He added material for the sake of textual clarification and even substituted elements in the original biblical narrative as a means of bringing the sacred text in line with extra-textual rabbinical sources or in order to avoid phrasings that may be contradicting of reason. For instance, in order to protect God's omnipresence, Saadia rendered the original clause "and I set my face unto the Lord God" in Dan 9:3 into "and I turned my attention toward God my Lord" (פקצדת אללה רבי), thus avoiding the idea that the godhead could to be spatially determined.

Similar features are characteristic also of the Targumim (→ 1.3.3) and result from the common notion that the biblical texts are "pregnant with meaning." Therefore, the many textual omissions and abbreviations we encounter in Saadia's translations are more notable. Though these features are not unknown in the history of Bible translation, Saadia pursued such techniques to a remarkable extent. Textual elements are omitted or substituted by pronouns in his translations for the sake of style or because they were regarded as void of meaning (pleonastic). Compare for instance, Dan 3:3, which in MT is rendered: "Then the satraps [...] were gathered together unto the dedication of *the image that Nebuchadnezzar the king had set up*; and they stood before *the image that Nebuchadnezzar had set up*." In order to avoid repetitive language, Saadia renders the repeated clause only once: "Then the military leaders [אלבטארקה ...] gathered together unto the inauguration [וכארה] of *the image that Nebuchadnezzar had set up* and stood before *it*." In a similar vein, a clause subject or object may be substituted by a pronoun as in Dan 2:47, where MT reads: "The king spoke unto Daniel, and said" abbreviated by Saadia into "then he said to him" (תם קאל לה).

Yefet ben ʿElī tackled the translation enterprise with a different set of techniques, partly in opposition to those employed by Saadia. His intention was not only to transmit *the message* of the sacred text into the Arabic tongue but also *its form*. Thus, Yefet's translation is highly imitative. He exploited the natural structural affinity between Semitic languages but if the syntactic preferences of source and target language were at odds, Yefet often preferred the former. Hence, as opposed to his commentaries that are written in idiomatic Arabic, Yefet's translations often appear literal and ungrammatical in Arabic.[9] The difference in translation character between Yefet and Saadia is seen immediately. Compare the translation of Dan 2:9 where in MT the verb follows its subject: ʿad dī ʿiddānā (s) yištanneʾ (v) "till the time *be changed*." As expected in Classical Arabic, Saadia reverts the order into verb-subject order: ʾin tataġayyaru (v) al-sāʿah (s) "if the hour changes." In contrast, Yefet preserves the word order: ḥattā alladī al-waqt (s) yataġayyaru (v) "till that the time *changes*."

Yefet's endeavor to reflect the structure of the source text in the target text is further detected in his frequent employment of cognates and similar roots. For instance, Yefet selected the Arabic cognate root ḥlm "dream" to represent the Hebrew ḥlm, with a similar meaning, in Dan 2:1, whereas Saadia employed the root rʾā "vision." In a similar vein, Yefet selected the homophone root ftḥ "opening" for the Aramaic fty "breadth" in Dan 3:1, while Saadia employed the semantic equivalent root ʿrḍ "breadth." In his aspiration to reflect every element in the source text, Yefet even invented words. Most notable is perhaps the rendition of the Hebrew particle of existence yēš "there is" into ʾis (ايس); a neologism in the Arabic language.

Another salient feature of Yefet's translation is the employment of "alternate renderings," i.e. the technique of reflecting one unit in the source text by two or more units in the target text. This technique, which was even further developed by later Karaite exegetes, results from the aspiration to

---

Pentateuch and the Book of Daniel in Arabic (MS Sinai–Arabic 2): Preliminary Observations on Codicology, Text types, and Translation Technique," *Intellectual History of the Islamicate World* 1 (2013): 43–68).

---

[9] Polliack, *The Karaite Tradition*, 39–45. See further relevant sections on Yefet's techniques in the same work.

reflect a wider semantic range of a word or clause in the source text.[10] Compare Dan 2:8: "I know of truth that you would gain (זְבִנִין) time," which is rendered "I know of truth that you would buy (مشترين) *or seek* (او بائعين) time." Likewise, Dan 2:15: "Wherefore is the decree so peremptory (מְהַחְצְפָה)" is rendered as "why is the decree so hasty (مسرعة), *or, it is said, impudent* (وقيل متقحة)" in Yefet's translation.

Just as with Saadia, Yefet would on occasion alter the original wording in order to avoid theologically improper readings. Such is Yefet's (and Saadia's) transformation in Dan 3:25 of "and the appearance of the fourth is like *a son of the gods* (דָּמֵה לְבַר־אֱלָהִין)" into "and the appearance of the fourth is like *that of the angels* (شابه للملائكة)."

The Christian Arabic translation preserved in manuscript Sinai Ar. 2 copied in 939/40 C.E. predates Yefet's translation and must be contemporary or even older than Saadia's work. Similarly to Saadia's translation, it exhibits many non-literal translation techniques. Reiterated information regarding clause subjects or objects is at times omitted or substituted by a pronoun if still inferable from the context. Complete phrases or clauses may be omitted, abbreviated, or rendered by paraphrastic varieties if repetitive in nature. Cohesive links such as temporal conjunctions are on occasion added in order to increase the logical coherence of the story. Elements are often added both in order to clarify the syntactic construction of the source text and to explain its content. Textual substitutions are common, such as in Dan 4:5 where MT's "Daniel [...] whose name was Belteshazzar, *according to the name of my god*" is rendered "Daniel [...] whose name was Belteshazzar, *the lord of the wise men*." In the same vein, the frequent phrase "the spirit of holy gods" in Daniel 5 is slightly adjusted and mostly rendered "the Holy Spirit of God" (*rūḥ al-ʾilāh al-muqadda/is*).

Just like Yefet, the translator of manuscript Sinai Ar. 2 often resorted to "alternate renderings." For instance, in Dan 1:14, the clause "So he hearkened (וַיִּשְׁמַע) unto them in this matter" is in manuscript Sinai Ar. 2 rendered *fa-ʾajābahum wa-qabila ra[ʾ]yahum* "and he answered them and accepted their opinion." In Dan 6:17, MT's "He will deliver you (יְשֵׁיזְבִנָּךְ)" is rendered *huwa yukhalliṣuka wa-yunjīka* "He is the one who will deliver you and save you."

Alobaidi, J. (ed. and transl.), *The Book of Daniel: The Commentary of R. Saadia Gaon: Edition and Translation* (La bible dans l'histoire 6; Bern: Peter Lang, 2006).

Hjälm, M.L., *Christian Arabic Versions of Daniel: A Comparative Study of Early MSS and Translation Techniques in MSS Sinai Ar. 1 and 2* (Leiden: Brill, 2016).

Margoliouth, D.S. (ed. and transl.), *A Commentary on the Book of Daniel by Yephet ibn Ali the Karaite* (Oxford: Clarendon Press, 1889).

Polliack, M., *The Karaite Tradition of Arabic Bible Translation: A Linguistic and Exegetical Study of Karaite Translations of the Pentateuch From the Tenth and Eleventh Centuries C.E.* (Études sur le Judaïsme médiéval 17; Leiden: Brill, 1997).

Qafiḥ, J. (ed.), *Daniel ʿim Targum u-firush Rabbenu Saʿadiah ben Yosef Fayyumi u-firush Rabbi Tanḥum ha-Yerushalmi* (Jerusalem: Makhon Mishnat ha-Rambam, 1981) [Hebr.].

Schlossberg, E., "Concepts and Methods in the Commentary of Saadia Gaon on the Book of Daniel" (PhD diss., Bar-Ilan University, 1988) [Hebr.].

Miriam Lindgren Hjälm

---

[10] M. Polliack, "Alternate Renderings and Additions in Yeshuʿah ben Yehudah's Arabic Translation of the Pentateuch," *JQR New Series* 84 (1993–1994): 209–25. For later additions of alternate renderings in Yefet's translations, see M. Wechsler, *The Arabic Translation and Commentary of Yefet Ben ʿEli the Karaite on the Book of Esther: Edition, Translation, and Introduction* (Études sur le judaïsme médiéval 36; Leiden: Brill, 2008).

18.4 Secondary Translations

18.4.1 Vetus Latina

18.4.1.1 Evidence

VL-Dan comprised the canonical text of Daniel and the additions Susanna (V-Dan 13), Prayer of Azariah, and Song of the Three Young Men (V-Dan 3:24–90), and Bel and the Dragon (V-Dan 14) (→ II.3.1; → II.3.4). The text has been preserved fragmentarily in various manuscripts:[1]

VL[175] Fragments of Darmstadt, Donaueschingen, Fulda, Sankt Paul im Lavantal (Kärnten), and Stuttgart (northern Italy, fifth century C.E.): Dan 2:18–33; 9:25–10, 11; 11:16–23, 35–39 in Darmstadt, Hessische Landes-und Hochschulbibliothek 895.

VL[176] Fragments of Sankt Gallen, Stiftsbibliothek 1398b; Zürich, Zentralbibliothek C 184 (390), Frgs. 23 and 24 (Sankt Gallen, ninth century C.E.): Dan 13:1–64 (Sus); 1:1–9; 3:36–60; 4:20–8:17; 8:21–9:2, 6–7, 15–16, 9:22–10:11, 16–21; 11:6–12:13; 14:1–42 (Bel).

VL[177] Würzburg, Universitätsbibliothek M. p. th. f. 64ª, palimpsest (Italy, fifth century C.E.): Dan 13:2–10 (Sus); 1:15–2:9; 3:15–50; 8:5–9:10; 10:3–11:6, 20–21, 23–25, 26–28, 31–33, 35–41.

VL[182] Verona, Biblioteca Capitolare II (2) fol. IV; Verona, BC XXVII (35) (early seventh century C.E.): Dan 1:1–2; 3:1–50, 91, 96 (with 51 in margin); only Dan 3:26–45 has a VL text.

VL[191] Fragments of Karlsruhe, Badische Landesbibliothek Aug CXXXII, fol. 101V–103R; palimpsest (ca. 850): Dan 3:1, 4, 5, 56, 57 ff.[2]

Sections of VL-Sg Three[3] have been transmitted as songs in liturgical collections, e.g., in VL[32] = Wolfenbüttel, Herzog August Bibliothek, Weissenburg 76, palimpsest, first half of the sixth century C.E.; VL[250] = Sedulius' Psalter: Paris, Bibl. de l'Arsenal 8407 (mid-eleventh century); VL[251] = Lectionary of Luxeuil: Paris, BN lat 9427, ca. 700, and others (VL[254, 255, 257, 300, 330], etc.). Manuscript VL[7] = *Sangermanensis* 15: Paris, BN lat 11553 (Saint Germain des Prés, ca. 810) had VL-Dan songs, now lost.

VL-Dan quotations in patristic writings (→ 21.8) are abundant and very important for their value for the VL text history and for the textual criticism of the two LXX-Dan text types (OG and Th; → 18.3.1).[4] There are remarkable quotations in Tertullian's *Aduersus iudaeos* 8, Cyprian of Carthage, Pseudo-Cyprian's *De Pascha computus* 13 and 15, Augustine's *Contra Faustum* and others.[5] Especially important are: Jerome's commentary on Daniel, Verecundus of Iunca for VL-Pr Azar, and Lucifer of Cagliari's *Pro sancto Athanasio* II,7 for VL-Sus 13:27–41.[6]

18.4.1.2 Editions

No comprehensive edition of all witnesses to VL-Dan is available. Existing editions are the following: Sabatier (1743)[7] used manuscripts VL[250] and VL[7] for the songs of VL-Dan 3, and patristic quotations for the rest of the text. Fleck (1837) published Pr Azar and Sg Three from VL[250].[8] Fragments of VL[175] and VL[177] were published by Ranke in 1860[9] and in 1871.[10] For VL[175, 176], and VL[32], there are the editions

---

[1] For VL manuscripts, see Gryson, *Altlateinische Handschriften 1*.

[2] This palimpsest is still undeciphered. It is only known that more text follows after Dan 3:57 but it remains uncertain for the time being how much (cf. Gryson, *Altlateinische Handschriften 1*, 312, and Bischoff, "Neue Materialien," 420).

[3] There are several possibilities: Dan 3:26–45; 3:51–90; 3:57–88a; or 3:64–88a.

[4] Texts edited by Ziegler, *Susanna*.

[5] For the text of the Daniel quotations, I use the *Vetus Latina Database*.

[6] Abbreviations used for ancient writers are those of Gryson, *Répertoire général*.

[7] Sabatier, *Bibliorum*, 2.855–88.

[8] Fleck, "XII. Fragmenta," 345–47.

[9] Ranke, *Fragmenta*, 2:48–51.

[10] E. Ranke, *Par palimpsestorum Wirceburgensium, an-*

TABLE 1   *Unity of VL-Dan Textual Tradition as Translation of Th-Dan*

	Th	VL
Dan 8:8	καὶ ὁ τράγος τῶν αἰγῶν ἐμεγαλύνθη ἕως σφόδρα, καὶ ἐν τῷ ἰσχῦσαι αὐτὸν συνετρίβη τὸ κέρας τὸ μέγα, καὶ ἀνέβη κέρατα τέσσαρα ὑποκάτω αὐτοῦ εἰς τοὺς τέσσαρας ἀνέμους τοῦ οὐρανοῦ	*et hircus caprarum magnificatus est uehementer et cum preualeret contritum est cornum maius et ascenderunt quattuor cornua subtus* (*suptus* VL[177]) *in* (*id* VL[177]) *cornum in quattuor uentos caeli* (VL[176 177])
Dan 8:8	And the male goat of the goats grew exceedingly great, and when it was strong, the great horn was crushed, and four horns came up under it toward the four winds of heaven. (*NETS)	And the male goat of the goats grew exceedingly great, and when it was strong, the great horn was crushed, and four horns came up under (it VL[177]) the horn toward the four winds of heaven.
Dan 13:20 (VL-Sus 20)	αἱ θύραι τοῦ παραδείσου κέκλεινται, καὶ οὐδεὶς θεωρεῖ ἡμᾶς, καὶ ἐν ἐπιθυμίᾳ σού ἐσμεν	*ostia paradisi* (*uiridarii* Lucifer) *clausa sunt et* (om. Lucifer) *nemo nos uidet et* (om. Lucifer) *in concupiscentia tui sumus* (VL[176] Lucifer).
Dan 13:20 (VL-Sus 20)	the orchard doors are shut, no one can see us, and we are in lust with you.	the orchard (treegarden Lucifer) doors are shut, and (om. Lucifer) no one can see us and (om. Lucifer) we are in lust with you.

and studies of Dold (1923/1940[11] and 1936[12]), for sections of VL[182] the edition of Carusi and Lindsay (1934) are available,[13] and for VL[191] see the edition of Bischoff (1941).[14]

18.4.1.3 Text

The extant VL-Dan manuscripts follow the sequence of Th-Dan (→ 18.3.1; → 18.3.2), that is, Susanna, Daniel (with Prayer of Azariah and Song of the Three Young Men in 3:24–90), Bel and the Dragon (→ 11.3.2). However, v-Dan has the order Daniel, Susanna, Bel and the Dragon (→ 18.3.6; → 11.3.4). In this sequence, v-Dan is supported by the Greek manuscript LXX[88] and the Syro-Hexapla. In general, the textual tradition of VL-Dan is unitary, as the examples in Table 1 illustrate.

The VL-Dan texts attest to a shared vocabulary in their rendition of Greek terms, as is illustrated by the examples in Table 2.

Sometimes, however, there are variations in the vocabulary: In Dan 8:9, VL[176] renders the νότος "south" of Theodotion as *auster* "south," while VL[177] has *notus* "south." Similary, in Dan 8:10, VL[176] renders the ἀστήρ "star" of Theodotion as *sidus* "star" while VL[177] has *aster* "star."

Often, the vocabulary of Lucifer of Cagliari differs from that of VL[176] as illustrated in Table 3.

Tertullian's VL text attests to many such differences from other VL witnesses, having many unique renderings for the vocabulary of Th-Dan.

---

tiquissimae Veteris Testamenti versionis Latinae fragmente e codd. rescriptis eruit (Vienna: Braumüller, 1871), 126–44.

[11] Dold, *Konstanzer*, 106–12 (VL[175]) and 250–64 (VL[176]); Dold, *Neue St. Galler*, 35, 36, 38, 41, 44–45, 47–48, 50, 52, 54–55, 57–58 (VL[176]).

[12] Dold, *Das älteste*, 8–9, 68.

[13] Carusi and Lindsay, *Monumenti*, 12–14 (Dan 1:1–2; 3:1–25, 46–51, 91–95).

[14] Bischoff, "Neue Materialen," 407–35.

18.4.1 VETUS LATINA

TABLE 2 Selection of Vocabulary

	Th	VL
Dan 1:8	ἀλισγέω "to defile"	*contamino* "to defile" VL[176] Augustine
Dan 2:19	ὅραμα "vision"	*uisum* "vision" VL[175]
Dan 8:11	ἀρχιστράτηγος "commander in chief"	*dux* "general" VL[176 177]
Dan 9:26	τὸ ἅγιον "the sanctuary"	*sanctum* "sanctuary" VL[175] Tertulian, Pseudo-Cyprian; but *sacrarium* "sanctuary" in Augustine
Dan 13:7, 28	λαός "the people"	*plebs* "people" VL[176] Lucifer
Dan 13:11	συγγίγνομαι "to be intimate"	*uiolo* "to violate" VL[176]
Dan 14:3	εἴδωλον "idol"	*simulacrum* "idol" VL[176]
Dan 14:3	μετρητής "measure"	*metreta* "measure" VL[176]
Dan 14:39	ἐσθίω "to eat"	*manduco* "to eat" VL[176 177]

TABLE 3 Lexical Differences between the Texts of Lucifer of Cagliari and VL[176]

	Th	Lucifer	VL[176]
Dan 13:15	παράδεισος "orchard"	*uiridarium* "treegarden"	*paradisus* "orchard"
Dan 13:28	ἔννοια "plot"	*mens* "plan"	*sensus* "understanding"
Dan 13:28	ἔρχομαι "to come"	*conuenio* "to come together"	*uenio* "to come"

TABLE 4 Lexical Differences between the Texts of Tertullian and VL[175]/Ps.-Cyprian

Th	Tertullian	VL[175] and Ps.-Cyprian
ἐκκόπτω "to cut off"	*concido* "perish"	*excido* "perish"
διαφθείρω "to destroy"	*extermino* "to burn"	*corrumpo* "to corrupt"

Two examples can be found in Dan 9:26 as shown in Table 4.

18.4.1.4 Vorlage

Some VL-Dan texts are related to a Greek *Vorlage* of an Old Greek type (→ 18.3.1), e.g., the quotations in Tertullian and Cyprian. Occasional readings with OG-Dan can also be found in other witnesses, such as in the *Consultationes Zacchaei et Apollonii* and in the writings of Hilarianus, and VL[176] goes in one reading with Old Greek (Dan 9:24). In his *Testimonia*, Cyprian's Daniel citations read sometimes with OG-Dan and sometimes with Th-Dan, though he quotes in particular the latter. Th-Dan (→ 18.3.1) provides the *Vorlage* for most of the VL-Dan tradition.[15] OG-Dan reads, e.g., in Dan 14:4 (LXX-Bel 5) οὐδένα σέβομαι ἐγὼ εἰ μὴ κύριον τὸν θεὸν τὸν κτίσαντα τὸν οὐρανὸν καὶ τὴν γῆν "I revere no one except the Lord God, who created heaven and earth" (*NETS). The Old Greek reading corresponds to the Daniel quotation in Cyprian (*Epistula* 58 and *Ad Fortunatum* XI, 80): *nihil colo ego nisi dominum deum meum qui condidit caelum et terram* "I worship no one

---

[15] See the introduction to the edition of Greek Daniel texts in Ziegler, *Susanna*, 98.

except the Lord, my God, who made heaven and earth." Th-Dan reads instead ὅτι οὐ σέβομαι εἴδωλα χειροποίητα, ἀλλὰ τὸν ζῶντα θεὸν τὸν κτίσαντα τὸν οὐρανὸν καὶ τὴν γῆν καὶ ἔχοντα πάσης σαρκὸς κυριείαν "because I do not revere idols made with hands, but the living God who created heaven and earth and has dominion over all flesh," which finds its equivalent in VL[176]: *quia non colo simulacra manu facta, sed uiuum d(eu)m qui creauit caelum et terram et habentem omnes carnis potestatem* "because I do not revere idols made with hands, but the living God who created heaven and earth and has dominion over all flesh." The affiliation of VL-Dan with Th-Dan is also illustrated by Dan 14:38 (LXX-Bel 39). The Old Greek reads καὶ ἔφαγε Δανιηλ "and Daniel ate" (*NETS*) but Theodotion has καὶ ἀναστὰς Δανιηλ ἔφαγεν "and having risen, Daniel ate" (*NETS*). Both VL[176] (*et surgit danihel et manducauit* "and Daniel rises and ate") and VL[177] (*et surrexit daniel et manducauit* "and Daniel rose and ate") go with the latter.

Although VL-Dan texts depend mostly on Th-Dan, sometimes their *Vorlage* is related to a Lucianic text (LXX^L; → 18.3.5). Tertullian's Daniel quotations display e.g., sometimes contacts with LXX^L as compared to other Latin witnesses that go with the majority text of Th-Dan. An example can be found in Dan 9:26 where Th-Dan reads with VL[175] and Pseudo-Cyprian ἐν κατακλυσμῷ "by a flood" (*NETS*), but LXX$^{L'-88}$ and Theodoretus prefix this with ὡς "as," which corresponds to Tertullian's *quomodo in cataclismo* "just as by a flood." In other cases, Tertullian does not support any Greek reading, e.g., in Dan 9:25, where he reads *innovabuntur* "they will be renewed" for Th-Dan's ἐκκενωθήσονται "they will be emptied out" (*NETS*) for which VL[175] has *exinanientur* "they will be emptied out" (cf. ...]nient[... in VL[176] and Pseudo-Cyprian).

Finally, some readings in VL-Dan do not affiliate with any part of the Greek Daniel texts (e.g., ἑξήκοντα "seventy" Th-Dan 9:25, 26 [cf. *septuaginta* "seventy" in VL[175]] and *sexaginta* "sixty" in Tertullian [= V]). Often, the Daniel quotations of Lucifer of Cagliari are the only ones among the VL-Dan texts that support good readings of Th-Dan (e.g., Dan 13:21, 28, 33, etc.), while other VL-Dan texts support LXX^L (e.g., Dan 13:33).

Bischoff, B., "Neue Materialen zum Bestand und zur Geschichte der altlateinischen Bibelübersetzungen," in *Miscellanea Giovanni Mercati* (6 vols.; Studi e Testi 121; Vatican City: Biblioteca Apostolica Vaticana, 1946), 1:407–35.

Burkitt, F.C., *The Old Latin and the Itala: With an Appendix Containing the Text of the St. Gallen Palimpsest of Jeremiah* (Cambridge: Cambridge University Press, 1896).

Carusi, E. and W.M. Lindsay, *Monumenti paleografici Veronesi* (2 vols.; Vatican City: Biblioteca Apostolica Vaticana, 1934), 12–14.

Dold, A., *Konstanzer altlateinische Propheten- und Evangelien Bruchstücke mit Glossen nebst zugehörigen Prophetentexten aus Zürich und St. Gallen* (Texte und Arbeiten 1.7–9; Beuron: Druck und Verlag der Kunstschule der Erzabtei Beuron, 1923).

Dold, A., *Das älteste Liturgiebuch der lateinischen Kirche* (Texte und Arbeiten 1.26–28; Beuron: Druck und Verlag der Kunstschule der Erzabtei Beuron, 1936).

Dold, A., *Neue St. Galler vorhieronymianische Propheten-Fragmente* (Texte und Arbeiten 1.31; Beuron: Druck und Verlag der Kunstschule der Erzabtei Beuron, 1940).

Fleck, F., "XII. Fragmenta Italae Vetustissimae Veteris Testamenti e Cod. Reg. Armamentarii Parisiensis," in *Anecdota maximam partem sacra in itineribus italicis et gallicis collecta* (Leipzig: Sumtibus Joannis Ambrosii Barth, 1837), 337–47.

Glorie, F. (ed.), *S. Hieronymi Presbyteri Commentariorum in Danielem Libri III <IV>* (CCSL 75A; Turnhout: Brepols, 1964).

Gryson, *Altlateinische Handschriften 1*.

Gryson, *Altlateinische Handschriften 2*.

Gryson, *Répertoire général*.

Ranke, E., *Fragmenta versionis Sacrarum Scripturarum latinae antehieronymianae e codice manuscripto* (Marburg: Koch & Sipmann, 1860).

Sabatier, *Bibliorum*.

Schneider, H., *Die altlateinischen biblischen Cantica* (Texte und Arbeiten 1.29–30; Beuron: Beuroner Kunstverlag, 1938).

Ziegler, J., *Susanna, Daniel, Bel et Draco* (Septuaginta Vetus Testamentum Graecum 16.2; Göttingen: Vandenhoeck & Ruprecht, 1954; rev. ed. O. Munnich, 1999).

José Manuel Cañas Reíllo

18.4.2 Coptic Translations

18.4.2.1 Background and Nature

The two main Coptic versions of Daniel are the Sahidic and Bohairic translations. The Sahidic Coptic versions, only preserved fragmentarily, were first studied by Gehman.[1] In this early work, based on the available fragments from Rome, Paris, London, and Berlin, Gehman established the dependence of the Sahidic version on Theodotion (→ 18.3.1; → 18.3.2), generally following LXX^B, with most frequent correspondences to LXX^Q and LXX^{230}, though not completely independent of Old Greek (→ 18.3.1)[2] and Hexaplaric influence (→ 18.3.4).[3] This is also true for the fragments of Cop^{Sa}-Dan, which were discovered subsequent to Gehman's work. In the few places where the fragments of Cop^{Sa}-Dan can be compared, the text seems to be quite uniform, with very few variants that can be characterized as orthographic. Examples for such comparisons include Cop^{Sa} 21 (Schüssler, *Biblia Coptica* 1.2, 6–10) with Cop^{Sa} 355 (in Dan 6:1–2),[4] and Cop^{Sa} 56 (Schüssler, *Biblia Coptica* 1.3, 24) with Cop^{Sa} 21 (in Dan 8:18–27).

The Bohairic version[5] is related instead to the Hexaplaric tradition (→ 18.3.4) and is preserved completely.

The Sahidic, Bohairic, Fayyumic, and Mesokemic versions of Cop-Dan will be discussed below. A complete and critical edition of their fragments is a desideratum as it would allow for a reconstruction of the Coptic textual history of Daniel and for an investigation of the dependence of the Coptic fragments on the Greek versions. The Additions to Daniel will be discussed in → II.3.6 and are only touched here tangentially.

18.4.2.2 The Sahidic Translation

As stated above, the text of Daniel was not preserved completely in Sahidic Coptic. It invariably follows the text of Theodotion (→ 18.3.1; → 18.3.2). The best-attested part are the additions to Daniel 3 (→ II.3.6), which were used profusely in liturgy. The *Biblia Coptica*[6] refers to a few codex fragments that probably contained originally the continuous text of Daniel. The earliest can perhaps be dated to the fifth century C.E.: Cop^{Sa} 353 is a fragment of a codex page featuring Dan 5:16–20.[7] The biblical manuscript Cop^{Sa} 56 is a sixth-century C.E. parchment codex that is only attested by a Yale fragment.[8] The fragment belongs to a single page that was reused as a magical text. Such a magical reuse was not uncommon for biblical manuscripts in the Coptic tradition. The fragment contains Dan 8:11–27; 9:1–13. Cop^{Sa} 355 is a small fragment from Milan containing Dan 5:21 and 6:2–4. This fragment is the only remnant of a sixth-century parchment C.E. codex. Two manuscripts of Cop^{Sa}-Dan are in Berlin.[9] Cop^{Sa} 326 is a folium from a sixth-century C.E. parchment codex attesting to Dan 4:10–12, 17–19. Cop^{Sa} 387 attests to Dan 11:36–12:1. Both codices probably originally included the complete text of the book of Daniel. Cop^{Sa} 21 is an eleventh-century parchment codex from the White Monastery (Dan 1:4–2:4; 5:30–6:11; 7:2–6, 7–10; 8:18–10:1; 10:13; 11:2), in which originally the complete text of Daniel followed the book of Judges (→ 3–5.2.2). Its fragments are scattered between

---

[1] Gehman, "The Sahidic and the Bohairic Versions," 279–330.

[2] Gehman, "The Sahidic and the Bohairic Versions," gives examples on pp. 287–88.

[3] Gehman, "The Sahidic and the Bohairic Versions," 289.

[4] S. Pernigotti, "I papiri copti dell'Università Cattolica di Milano: I," *Aeg* 65 (1985): 67–105, esp. 70–72.

[5] A. Schulte, *Die koptische Übersetzung der vier grossen Propheten* (Münster: Aschendorff, 1892), 76–90.

[6] See Schüssler, *Biblia Coptica*: all fragments mentioned here use the numbers assigned by him. All numbers above Cop^{Sa} 260 remain unpublished to date. For the unpublished manuscripts, see Schüssler, "Zum Stand der koptischen Bibeltexte," esp. 226–30, and the references to editions in the footnotes of the present article.

[7] A. Boud'hors, *Catalogue des Fragments Coptes de la Bibliothèque Nationale et Universitaire de Strasbourg*, Vol. 1: *Fragment biblique* (CSCO 571 Subsidia 99; Leuven: Peeters, 1998), 38–39.

[8] Schüssler, *Biblia Coptica*, 1.3, 24; cf. S. Emmel, "Coptic Biblical Texts in the Beinecke Library," *Journal of Coptic Studies* 1 (1990): 13–28, esp. 17–22.

[9] The Berlin manuscripts, BKU 1 165 and 1 166, are counted by Schüssler, *Biblia Coptica* as sa 326 and sa 387. For the two manuscripts, see also H. Leipoldt, *Ägyptische Urkunden aus den Königlichen Museen zu Berlin*, Vol. 2.1: *Koptische Urkunden* (Berlin: Weidmann, 1904), 133–34.

Paris, London, Rome, and Strasbourg. Two small fragments from the fifth and sixth centuries C.E., Cop^{Sa} 356 and Cop^{Sa} 388, follow the Theodotionic text of Daniel (→ 18.3.1; → 18.2.3). Cop^{Sa} 356 is a small fragment in Vienna,[10] containing Dan 5:6–10. Cop^{Sa} 388 is a fragment of a miniature codex in the John Rylands Library,[11] containing Dan 12:8–9. Finally, Cop^{Sa} 354 is a ninth-century C.E. parchment fragment that comes from the White Monastery[12] and contains Dan 3:36–53, 55–56. It cannot be excluded that this fragment could be part of a liturgical codex.

The other attestations of Cop^{Sa}-Dan come from liturgical manuscripts and attest mainly the Additions to Daniel 3 (→ II.3.6): The so-called Vienna "Odenhandschrift" from the Vienna Papyrus Collection (K 8706 or Cop$^{Sa\ 16lit}$)[13] is a bilingual papyrus codex from either the sixth[14] or seventh to eighth century C.E.[15] The papyrus contains in Sahidic Coptic both the Prayer of Azariah from Dan 3:26–45 and the ode of the three holy youths from Dan 3:52–54. The latter most likely originally comprised a longer text running until v. 90. The ode of the three holy youths appears also in Cop$^{Sa\ 54lit}$ (Schüssler, *Biblia Coptica* 1.3, 21–22), another liturgical parchment manuscript from the tenth or eleventh century of which only two folia are preserved.[16] They contain parts of Dan 3:52–70. Cop^{Sa} 163 is a papyrus codex from the sixth or seventh century C.E., today held in Paris.[17] It attests to Dan 3:54–55, 58–63, 69, 71–76, 79–81, and was also probably a liturgical codex.[18]

There are a number of lectionaries with pericopes from the book of Daniel. The earliest comes from the White Monastery: Cop$^{Sa\ 212L}$ dates from the eleventh century and attests to various parts of Daniel 3, 9, and 10.[19] Cop$^{Sa\ 837L}$ also comes from the White Monastery and can be dated between the eleventh and thirteenth centuries. It includes a fragment preserving Dan 7:9–15.[20] Finally, Cop$^{Sa\ 108L}$ is a bilingual lectionary (Coptic-Arabic) for the Holy Week that contains Dan 7:9–15 following Theodotion (→ 18.3.1).[21] Cop$^{Sa\ 108L}$ is a paper codex dated to the thirteenth century and is preserved in Rome.

18.4.2.3 The Bohairic Translation

According to Montgomery,[22] the Bohairic text of Daniel is Hexaplaric in nature (→ 18.3.2), though according to Gehman[23] it is very freely translated. As it seems, the translator understood the original perfectly but translated it in a flexible manner, following the sense rather than following the words literally. Cop^{Boh}-Dan was edited by Tattam[24] based on a seventeenth-century manuscript that he collated with two others. More recently, other fragments have appeared. One of them remains unedited (P.Bodmer XLIV), a codex written in classical Bohairic on parchment, to be dated to the tenth to twelfth centuries.[25] The abbreviation *P. Palau Rib.* 61–65 designates fragments of a twelfth-century parchment codex that contain

---

[10] W. Till, "Saidische Fragmente des Alten Testamentes," *Mus* 50 (1937): 175–237, esp. 236–37.

[11] W. Till, "Coptic Biblical Fragments in the John Rylands Library," *BJRL* 34 (1951–1952): 432–58, esp. 445–47.

[12] G. Maspero, *Fragments de la version thébaine de l'Ancien Testament* (Paris: Leroux, 1892), 269–70.

[13] W. Till and P. Sanz, *Eine griechisch-koptische Odenhandschrift: Papyrus Copt. Vindob. K 8706* (Monumenta biblica et ecclesiastica 5; Rome: Pontificium Institutum Biblicum, 1939); Schüssler, *Biblia Coptica* 1.1, 89–90.

[14] Thus Till and Sanz, *Eine griechisch-koptische Odenhandschrift.*

[15] Thus K. Aland, "Das Neue Testament auf Papyrus," in *Studien zur Überlieferung des Neuen Testaments und seines Textes* (ed. K. Aland; ANTF 2; Berlin: De Gruyter, 1967), 91–136, esp. 105, 122 for P^{42}.

[16] Schüssler, *Biblia Coptica* 1.3, 21–22.

[17] Schüssler, *Biblia Coptica* 2.1, 106.

[18] M. Pezin, "Coptica Sorbonica I (Ancien Testament)," *Langues orientales anciennes, philologie et linguistique* 2 (1989): 8–11.

[19] Schüssler, *Biblia Coptica* 2.2, 68–84.

[20] The manuscript is unfortunately unpublished and its fragments are scattered in different collections: Paris (BN copte 129^{19} 74.85.103.111; Louvre SN 500) and Vienna (K 9683, 9684, 9698, 9721).

[21] Schüssler, *Biblia Coptica* 1.4, 49–69; 4.4, 167.

[22] Montgomery, *Commentary*, 33.

[23] Gehman, "The Sahidic and the Bohairic Versions," 310.

[24] H. Tattam, *Prophetae maiores.*

[25] See A. Pietersma, "Bodmer Papyri," *ABD* 1.766–67.

parts of Daniel 11–14.[26] Cop[Boh]-Dan is also attested in Coptic lectionaries that present generally short passages from Daniel 3, 7, and 13.[27] There is even an attestation of the Bohairic text in a Sahidic liturgical codex, Cop[Sa 986lit]. Quecke states that the codex contains Dan 3:52 ff.[28]

18.4.2.4 The Fayyumic Translation

The Fayyumic version[29] has very few attestations. Two of them are preserved in Vienna. Cop[Fa 39] (K 3771+ K 3891),[30] a parchment fragment from a codex of the fifth or sixth century C.E., contains Sus 63 followed by Dan 1:2–4; 2:49; 3:1–3. Cop[Fa 40] (K 2582),[31] a fourth- or fifth-century C.E. parchment codex, contains Dan 3:79–85, 88–92 (probably liturgical). The other fragments of Cop[Fa]-Dan are preserved in Strasbourg: The papyrus fragments of Cop[Fa 32] (Coptes 591–592) come from two consecutive pages of a codex and were reused as filling material for a binding. They can be dated to the eighth or ninth century and comprise Dan 6:9–12, 13, 15(?), 17, 19–20. These three codices of Cop[Fa]–Dan all seem to follow Th-Dan (→ 18.3.1; → 18.3.2).

18.4.2.5 The Mesokemic and Akhmimic Translations

Remnants of the Mesokemic and Akhmimic versions of Daniel are sparse. Of the small unpublished fragment Cop[Mes 7], it is only known that it attests to some part of the book of Daniel.[32] The closest we get to an Akhmimic version of Daniel is Cop[Akh 5],[33] a bilingual miniature papyrus codex that contains Matt 11:25–30 in Greek followed by its translation in Akhmimic, and Dan 3:50–55 in Greek, but the expected Coptic text is lost.

18.4.2.6 Other Attestations

The use of the text of Daniel in amulets and school texts attests to the popularity of its Coptic versions: Cop[Sa 0109] (*P. Rainer Unterricht Kopt.* 214)[34] is an eighth-century C.E. school text written on an ostracon and contains Dan 1:8 in Sahidic. Magical texts include quotations of Cop-Dan. Generally, these quotations can be found in amulets and spells and refer to the companions of Daniel in the furnace. Examples include Berlin, ÄMP 11347,[35] a magical text on paper, dated to the eighth or ninth century C.E., manuscript Oxyrhynchus 39 5B 125A, also on paper, from the eleventh century,[36] and a Heidelberg ostracon (Kopt. 564).[37]

Gehman, H.S., "The Sahidic and the Bohairic Versions of the Book of Daniel," *JBL* 46 (1927): 279–330.

Montgomery, J.A., *A Critical and Exegetical Commentary on the Book of Daniel* (ICC 34; Edinburgh: T & T Clark, 1927).

Schüssler, K., "Zum Stand der koptischen Bibeltexte," in *Coptic Studies on the Threshold of a New Millennium: Proceedings of the Seventh International Congress of Coptic Studies, Leiden, 27 August–2 September 2000*

---

[26] B. Klakowicz, "A Bohairic Translation of the Last Books of Daniel (P. Palau Rib. inv. 61-inv. 65r)," *SPap* 17 (1978): 7–33.

[27] K.H.S. Burmester, "The Coptic-Greek-Arabic Holy Week Lectionary of Scetis," *BSAC* 16 (1961–1962): 83–137; K.H.S. Burmester, "The Bodleian Folio and Further Fragments of the Coptic-Greek-Arabic Holy Week Lectionary," *BSAC* 17 (1963): 35–56; K.H.S. Burmester, "Psalm-Fragments from the Monastery of Saint Macarius in Scetis," *Studia Orientalia Christiana Collectanea* 11 (1966): 389–512.

[28] Described in H. Quecke, "Die koptische Handschrift nr. 68 der Bibliothèque Nationale zu Paris," in *Untersuchungen zum koptischen Stundengebet* (Publications de l' Institut Orientaliste de Louvain 3; Louvain: Institut Orientaliste, 1970), 488–505.

[29] Schüssler's numbers for the dialectal fragments remain unpublished.

[30] W. Till, "Wiener Faijumica," *Mus* 49 (1936): 169–217, esp. 181–85.

[31] Till, "Wiener Faijumica," 185–87.

[32] Rome, manuscript Vat. Borgia copto 123.

[33] L. Amundsen, "Christian Papyri from the Oslo Collection," *Symbolae Osloenses* 24 (1945): 121–47, esp. 121–40.

[34] M. Hasitzka, *Neue Texte und Dokumentation zum Koptisch-Unterricht* (Mitteilungen aus der Papyrussammlung des Österreichischen Nationalbibliothek, Papyrus Erzherzog Rainer, NS 18; Vienna: Hollinek, 1990).

[35] W. Beltz, "Die koptischen Zauberpapiere und Zauberostraka der Papyrus-Sammlung der Staatlichen Museen zu Berlin," *APF* 31 (1985): 31–42; M. Meyer and R. Smith, *Ancient Christian Magic: Coptic Texts of Ritual Power* (Princeton: University Press, 1999), nr. 63, 117–19.

[36] Meyer and Smith, *Ancient Christian Magic*, nr. 51, 98–99; A. Alcock, "A Coptic Magical Text," *BASP* 19 (1982): 97–103.

[37] Meyer and Smith, *Ancient Christian Magic*, nr. 53, 100–101; H. Quecke, "Zwei koptische Amulette der Papyrussammlung der Universität Heidelberg," *Mus* 76 (1963): 247–65, esp. 255–65.

(2 vols.; eds. M. Immerzeel and J. van der Vliet; OLA 133; Leuven: Peeters, 2004), 1.221–35.

Tattam, H., *Prophetae maiores in dialecto linguae Aegyptiacae Memphitica seu Coptica* (2 vols.; Oxford: Typographeo Academico, 1852).

Sofía Torallas Tovar

18.4.3 Ethiopic Translation(s)

18.4.3.1 Title and Place in the Manuscripts

Eth-Dan includes all of the apocryphal additions known from Th-Dan (→ 18.3.1; → 18.3.2), with the entire corpus titled ዘዳንኤል "Daniel" or ዘዳንኤል ነቢይ "Daniel, the Prophet." As with Th-Dan, the heading ራእይ ፪ "Vision 2" (= ὅρασις β') marks the break between Susanna (→ 11.3.5) and Daniel instead of a separate title.

Although Eth-Dan circulated with Job in the earliest Ethiopic manuscripts, since the fourteenth century it has circulated with a wide variety of other texts with placement seemingly dependent upon whether Daniel was viewed as wisdom, prophecy, apocalypse, or history. There are no consistent patterns, but the book tends to appear more often with the Twelve (with an even split between having Daniel precede or follow; → 6–9.2.3.4) or with the Esdras material (→ 19.4.3; → 11.7.1.5; → 11.7.2.4).

18.4.3.2 Background

Eth-Dan was likely translated in the second half of the fourth century, but no later than 650 *if* ፋርስ "Fars" in Dan 1:4; 3:8, 48; 8:20; 10:1, 13, 20; and 11:2 is a contemporaneous reference to the Persians.[1] The translator worked from a Greek text, and the exemplar was undoubtedly Theodotionic (→ 18.3.2). In 1927, Löfgren produced an impressive critical text (→ 1.4.3.5), which he later supplemented with a collation of the Asmara Bible printed by the Catholic Mission.[2] Recent discoveries of significantly older manuscripts now require an update of his work.[3]

Apparently Daniel has remained popular since Axumite times, at least among the higher echelons of Ethiopian clerics. Moreover the "Songs of the Three Youths" (Dan 3:26–45, 52–56, and 57–88) were incorporated into the *Gəbrä Ḥəmamat* (the Passion Week liturgy) and the Biblical Canticles (Odes), which appear in every extant Ethiopian Psalter, the only "Scripture" generally known by the masses.

18.4.3.3 Translation Character

The translator had little facility in Greek. As a result, he omitted many passages that were indecipherable for him. For example, Daniel 11 lacks more than twenty verses in the Old Ethiopic. An exemplar written in *scriptio continua* presented additional challenges, for the struggling translator often misdivided words. Dan 3:46 illustrates some of the difficulties: First, καίοντες "the ones who heat" is read as καὶ ὄντες "and the ones who are." Second, difficult vocabulary is transliterated: ጴሳ ወስጢጲዮን ወቀሊሜጢዳ "*Ṗēsa* and *Səṭipiyōn* and *Qəlēmēṭida*" = πίσσαν καὶ στιππύον καὶ κληματίδα "pitch and tow and brushwood" (*NETS*). Even when reading accurately, though, the translator could misconstrue, for he takes ἔλεγον "they said" in Dan 7:5 wrongly as a first person singular instead of a third person plural verb.

Despite these deficiencies, the translator works hard to create meaningful renderings, often translating freely, occasionally paraphrasing loosely, in order to hold as closely as possible to the Greek original. Although full retroversion is impossible, in many cases, even with the freer renditions and the crude mistakes, the reading of the *Vorlage* can be determined.

18.4.3.4 Text-Critical Value

Ziegler argued that the Ethiopic version aligned with manuscripts related to LXX^B, although not standing very close to either LXX^B or LXX^{861}. On the other hand, there are a few distinctive readings shared with LXX^Q. For example, those two witnesses alone place ἐκ τῆς χειρός σου καὶ ἐκ before τῆς καμίνου "from your hand and from the furnace" in Dan 3:17 (እምእዴከ ወእምእቶን "from your hand and

---

[1] Thus Löfgren, *Daniel*, xlviii.
[2] Löfgren, *Daniel*, and Löfgren, "Bibelausgabe," 174–80.
[3] Ted Erho recently discovered that Eth$^{EMML\ 6977}$, which contains Job and Daniel, is the second oldest Ethiopic manuscript.

from the furnace"). Nevertheless, the Old Ethiopic displays much closer kinship with LXX[26, 46, 130, 239], and among these witnesses LXX[46, 130] especially stand out.[4] The order of Dan 3:66–73 is telling: LXX[46] and LXX[130] preserve the verse order 71, 66, 68–69, 72, 67, 70, 73, which the Ethiopic follows except for the transposition of vv. 66 and 71.[5] LXX[130], however, exhibits the highest degree of consanguinity throughout. Löfgren identified seven readings unique to LXX[130] and the Old Ethiopic and nine others that had additional support from just one or two other witnesses. For example, at Dan 5:15, the Ethiopic and LXX[130] alone read ἀναγνῶναι "to read" instead of ἀναγγεῖλαι "to tell."

The Old Ethiopic (→ 1.4.3.7.3) is an important witness to Theodotion's translation (→ 18.3.1; → 18.3.2). Ziegler concludes that "the purest form of the original text has not been transmitted by B alone but together with 26 46 130 239 La Sa Aeth (Arm) and Hippol."[6]

18.4.3.5 Subsequent History

Although the Old Ethiopic appears to preserve its Greek *Vorlage* faithfully, it was not immune from occasional incursions from external sources over the centuries. The most notable example is the interpolation of ዘይቀውም ውስተ መካን ቅዱስ ወዘያነብብ ለይለቡ "the one who stands in the holy place and let the one who reads understand" from Matt 24:15, found in all Ethiopic manuscripts. Since the Gospel had just quoted Dan 11:31, and exegetes assumed the citation formula, τὸ ῥηθὲν διὰ Δανιὴλ τοῦ προφήτου "that having been spoken of by the prophet Daniel," pointed to what followed, it made sense

that ἑστὸς ἐν τόπῳ ἁγίῳ, ὁ ἀναγινώσκων νοείτω "standing in the holy place, let the reader understand" must be a citation from the same general area.[7] Unable to determine precisely where this phrase had "dropped out," a scribe added it at the very end (Dan 11:35 in the Old Ethiopic).

All other Ethiopic versions descend from the Old Ethiopic, as the above example and other shared corruptions prove. Indeed, Daniel shares the same transmission history as most of the Gəʿəz Old Testament, but a few developments deserve special note. First, an Academic Text (→ 1.4.3.7.5) exists that attests interest in the Hebrew (→ 18.2.2). The editors began with an Old Ethiopic manuscript, to which they remained faithful, thus, for example, they retained the apocryphal additions. On the other hand, where the Ethiopic lacked clarity or exhibited significant omissions, as in ch. 11, they employed the Masoretic text (→ 18.3.7; → 18.4.8) for making improvements. Clearly, the reviser(s) lacked fluency in Hebrew and Aramaic, for some vocabulary was unfamiliar and they occasionally misread letters. Thus צִפֳּרִין "birds" was transliterated ጸፋሪዮን "Ṣəfariyōn" at Dan 4:30.[8] Also, mistaking a *kaf* for a *bet* resulted in ወነቤአ "and Nābeʾa" for וְנִכְאָה "and he will be checked" (Dan 11:30).[9] Second, around the seventeenth century at least two scholars translated independently an Arabic manuscript that contained both biblical text and commentary.[10] Interestingly, both of these new Arabic translations omitted *Susanna* and *Bel and the Dragon* yet kept the *Songs of the Three Youths* (→ 11.3), presumably because of the latter's liturgical importance.

The Hebraic readings, which Ullendorff found so remarkable in Eth-Dan, only appear in these later revisions from the Arabic and Hebrew.[11] There

---

[4] Ziegler (*Daniel*, xlix–l) provided independent confirmation of Löfgren's earlier observation.

[5] The only extant Greek witness with v. 71 following v. 66 is *Odes* in LXX[2147]. The fragment unfortunately breaks off in v. 71, prohibiting the identification of any additional parallels. See Fraenkel, "Nachtrag," 209. None of the *Odes* manuscripts examined by Rahlfs share the same order (*Psalmi cum Odi*, 357).

[6] "B nicht allein, sondern zusammen mit 26 46 130 239 La Sa Aeth (Arm) und Hippol. den ursprünglichen Text am reinsten überliefert." Ziegler and Munnich, *Daniel*, 139. This list must now also include LXX[861] and LXX[921]; see Fraenkel, "Nachtrag," 170–90 and 192–95.

[7] This perceived problem was handled differently in LXX[1010] and the Peshitta, which omit the phrase.

[8] The unexpected ending, -ዮን, conforms to endings frequently found with Greek toponyms, although dittography (reading the *yod* twice, but interpreting its second occurrence as a *waw*) is possible, cf. Löfgren, *Daniel*, 37.

[9] Löfgren, *Daniel*, 149.

[10] See Eth[Vienna 16] and Eth[EMIP 1074]. See also Sima, "kona yeqattel," 123–29.

[11] Ullendorff, "Ethiopic Translations," 254–56.

is no evidence prior to the late sixteenth century that Ethiopians consulted any Hebrew sources for the translation or revision of Daniel or any other biblical book.

Fraenkel, D., "Nachtrag zur 1. Auflage von 1954," in *Susanna, Daniel, Bel et Draco* (eds. J. Ziegler and O. Munnich; rev. ed.; Septuaginta Vetus Testamentum Graecum 16.2; Göttingen: Vandenhoeck & Ruprecht, 1999), 170–214.

Löfgren, O., *Die äthiopische Übersetzung des Propheten Daniel* (Paris: Paul Geuthner, 1927).

Löfgren, O., "Die äthiopische Bibelausgabe der katholischen Mission," *Le Monde Oriental* 23 (1929): 174–80.

Montgomery, J.A., *The Book of Daniel* (ICC; New York: Scribner's Sons, 1927).

Rahlfs, A. (ed.), *Psalmi cum Odis* (rev. ed.; Septuaginta Vetus Testamentum Graecum 10; Göttingen: Vandenhoeck & Ruprecht, 1967).

Sima, A., "*kona yegattel* in einer Wiener Handschrift des äthiopisches Danielbuches," *OrChr* 87 (2003): 123–29.

Ullendorff, E., "Hebrew, Aramaic, and Greek: The Versions Underlying Ethiopic Translations of Bible and Intertestamental Literature," in *The Bible World: Essays in Honor of Cyrus H. Gordon* (eds. G. Rendsburg et al.; New York: KTAV, 1980), 249–57.

Ziegler, J. (ed.), *Susanna, Daniel, Bel et Draco* (Septuaginta Vetus Testamentum Graecum 16.2; Göttingen: Vandenhoeck & Ruprecht, 1954).

Ziegler, J. and O. Munnich (eds.), *Susanna, Daniel, Bel et Draco* (rev. ed.; Septuaginta Vetus Testamentum Graecum 16.2; Göttingen: Vandenhoeck & Ruprecht, 1999).

Curt Niccum

18.4.4 Late Syriac Translations

Late Syriac versions of the book of Daniel are mainly limited to the Syro-Hexapla (→ 1.4.5) and the Syriac translation of Jacob of Edessa (→ 1.4.6).

18.4.4.1 Syro-Hexapla
18.4.4.1.1 Background

The fifth column of Origen's famed six-column Hexapla (→ 1.3.1.2) was an attempt to show how the Greek Old Testament text in use in the third century C.E. differed from the corresponding Hebrew text of that time. Using a system of text-critical marks (e.g., asterisks, obeli), Origen (185–254 C.E.) identified places where the accepted Greek text was different from the Hebrew text. Centuries later, in 616–617 C.E., Paul of Tella (→ 1.4.5.2), a Syrian Orthodox bishop living in Mesopotamia, completed a translation of Origen's fifth column into Syriac. This translation is known as the Syro-Hexapla (→ 1.4.5). Marginal notes in the Syro-Hexapla call attention to readings found in Greek versions other than Origen's fifth column.

18.4.4.1.2 Manuscripts, Editions, Tools

Toward the end of the nineteenth century (1874) Ceriani published a facsimile edition of the Ambrosian manuscript of the Syro-Hexapla. This edition is available electronically. In Ceriani's edition, the book of Daniel (including the deuterocanonical portions) is found on folios 143–51. At about the same time (1875), Field published all known readings of the Hexaplaric materials. In Field's edition, Daniel is found in vol. 2.903–36. Both of these works continue to be standard tools for research on the Syro-Hexapla.

18.4.4.1.3 Translation Character

A few examples of Syro-Hexaplaric readings in Daniel must suffice. In some places, the Syro-Hexapla has an explicative variant (e.g., ܠܒܒܠ "Babylon" [OG εἰς τὴν Βαβυλωνίαν "to Babylonia"] for MT אֶרֶץ־שִׁנְעָר "land of Shinar" in Dan 1:2; ܠܐܒܝܥܕܪܝ "Abiezar" [OG Αβιεσδρι "Abiesdri"] for MT לְאַשְׁפְּנַז "to Ashpenaz" in Dan 1:3; ܐܪܛܚܫܫܬ "Artaxerxes" [OG Ξέρξης "Xerxes"], with ܡܠܟܐ ܕܦܪܣܝܐ "king of the Persians" in the margin, for MT דָּרְיָוֶשׁ "Darius" in Dan 6.1). In other places, the Syro-Hexapla has an interpretive translation (e.g., ܪܒ ܡܗܝܡܢܘܗܝ ܕܡܠܟܐ "teacher of his eunuchs" [margin] for MT רַב סָרִיסָיו "chief of his eunuchs" in Dan 1:3; ܡܠܬܐ ܡܢܝ ܢܦܩܬ "the word from me has departed" [LXX[88] ὁ λόγος ἀπ' ἐμοῦ ἀπέστη "the word from me has departed"] for MT מִלְּתָא מִנִּי אַזְדָּא "the word from me is certain" in Dan 2:5; ܫܒܥ ܫܢܝܢ "seven years" [OG ἔτη ἑπτά "seven years"] for MT שִׁבְעָה עִדָּנִין "seven times" in Dan 4:29). Scribal metathesis occasionally causes distortion of meaning, as in ܘܐܬܝܗܒ ܠܗ ܠܫܢܐ "and language was given to it"

[OG καὶ γλῶσσα ἐδόθη αὐτῷ "and language was given to it"] for MT וְשָׁלְטָן יְהִיב לַהּ "and authority was given to it" in Dan 7:6.

18.4.4.1.4 Text-Critical Value
The Syro-Hexapla is valuable for text-critical research in part because of its retention of Origen's text-critical signs that identified disparities between the Hebrew and Greek texts. Unfortunately, many Greek manuscripts did not consistently retain these text-critical notations, which are actually the most valuable feature of the fifth column (→ 18.3.4).

18.4.4.2 Jacob of Edessa
18.4.4.2.1 Background
In addition to his scholarly contributions to philosophy, biblical exposition, liturgical and ecclesiastical compositions, grammatical treatises, and translations of Greek writers into Syriac, Jacob of Edessa (ca. 633 [640?]–708 C.E.) is remembered for his translation of the Old Testament into Syriac (→ 1.4.6).

18.4.4.2.2 Manuscripts, Editions, Tools
Five eighth-century C.E. manuscripts of Jacob's Old Testament translation survive. These manuscripts contain Jacob's Syriac translation for the following portions of the Old Testament: 1) the Pentateuch (Bibliothèque Nationale Syr. 26); 2) the books of Samuel and the beginning of 1 Kings (British Museum Add. Ms 14,429); 3) Isaiah (British Museum Add. Ms 14,441); 4) Ezekiel (Biblioteca Vaticana Sir. 5); 5) Daniel and Susanna (Bibliothèque Nationale Syr. 27). There is also a sixteenth-century fragment of Wisdom (Mardin, Syr. Orth. Bishopric, 2/47). The five early manuscripts may all be from the same exemplar.[1] MS Bibliothèque Nationale Syr. 27, containing Daniel and Susanna, is dated to 719 C.E., as is British Museum Add. Ms 14,429.[2]

18.4.4.2.3 Translation Character
Over the space of about ten years, Jacob worked on translating portions, if not all, of the Old Testament text. Although we do not know the order in which Jacob translated the Old Testament books, a colophon at the end of 1 Samuel dates the completion of that part of the translation to 704 or 705 C.E.[3] In addition to the Peshitta (→ 18.3.3), Jacob's sources included LXX (→ 18.3.1) and perhaps the Syro-Hexapla, which Paul of Tella had completed almost a century before (→ 1.4.5.2). Jacob's revision was an attempt to correct the Peshitta (→ 1.3.4) in light of the earlier Greek translations that differed in certain ways from the Peshitta. The result, according to Wright, was "a curious eclectic or patchwork text" that lacked methodological consistency.[4]

Saley, who has thoroughly investigated Jacob's Samuel text, concludes that Jacob's translation was mainly a revision of the Peshitta (→ 1.3.4) rather than the Syro-Hexapla (→ 1.4.5), making use of Greek texts that were Lucianic (→ 1.3.1.2) in terms of their textual alignment.[5] This conclusion seems to be accurate and serves to correct Goshen-Gottstein's notion that Jacob's translation was a revision of both the Peshitta and the Syro-Hexapla, with little influence from Lucianic Greek texts.[6] In some places, Jacob's Syriac text seems to be expansionistic and conflate, retaining distinctive elements of both the Peshitta and LXX (→ 1.3.1.1) rather than deciding in favor of a particular reading.[7]

18.4.4.2.4 Text-Critical Value
From what we can tell, Jacob's translation of the Old Testament received only a limited reception, even though he may have intended his translation

---

[1] So Saley, *Samuel Manuscript*, 5 n. 22.
[2] See Baars, "Bruchstück," 548 n. 2.
[3] See Salvesen, *Books of Samuel*. For the Syriac text of the colophon, see p. 90 (part 1); for an English translation, see p. 67 (part 2).
[4] Wright, Short History, 17. More than a century later, Romeny still regards this evaluation as an accurate appraisal. See Ter Haar Romeny, "Jacob of Edessa on Genesis," 147.
[5] Saley, "Textual Vorlagen," 124.
[6] On this observation, see ter Haar Romeny, "Jacob of Edessa on Genesis," 148.
[7] Salvesen, "Jacob of Edessa's Version of 1–2 Samuel," 144.

as a replacement for the Peshitta.[8] The Peshitta version of the Old Testament remained the version of choice among the Syriac-speaking communities.

Baars, W., "Ein neugefundenes Bruchstück aus der syrischen Bibelrevision des Jakob von Edessa," VT 18 (1968): 548–54.
Baars, W., *New Syro-Hexaplaric Texts: Edited, Commented upon and Compared with the Septuagint* (Leiden: Brill, 1968).
Baumstark, A., *Geschichte der syrischen Literatur: Mit Ausssschluß der christlich-palästinensischen Texte* (Bonn: A. Marcus and E. Webers, 1922; reprint, Berlin: Walter de Gruyter, 1968).
Ceriani, A.M., *Codex syro-hexaplaris ambrosianus* (Monumenta sacra et profana ex codicibus praesertim Bibliothecae Ambrosianae 7; Milan: Bibliotheca Ambrosiana, 1874).
Field, *Hexapla.
ter Haar Romeny, B., "The Peshitta and Its Rivals: On the Assessment of the Peshitta and Other Versions of the Old Testament in Syriac Exegetical Literature," *The Harp* 11–12 (1998–1999): 21–31.
ter Haar Romeny, B., "The Syriac Versions of the Old Testament," in *Nos sources: Arts et littérature syriaques* (Sources syriaques 1; Antélias: Centre d' Études et de Recherches Orientales, 2005), 75–105.
ter Haar Romeny, B., "Jacob of Edessa on Genesis: His Quotations of the Peshitta and His Revision of the Text," in *Jacob of Edessa and the Syriac Culture of His Day* (ed. B. ter Haar Romeny; Monographs of the Peshitta Institute Leiden 18; Leiden: Brill, 2008), 145–58.
Hatch, W.H.P., *An Album of Dated Syriac Manuscripts* (Boston: American Academy of Arts and Sciences, 1946; reprint, Piscataway: Gorgias Press, 2002), esp. 98–99.
Ibrahim, G.Y. and G.A. Kiraz (eds.), *Studies on Jacob of Edessa* (Gorgias Eastern Christian Studies 25; Piscataway: Gorgias Press, 2010).
Ortiz de Urbina, I., "Jacobus Edessae," in *Patrologia syriaca* (rev. ed.; Rome: Pont. Institutum Orientalium Studiorum, 1965), 177–83.
Saley, R.J., *The Samuel Manuscript of Jacob of Edessa: A Study of Its Underlying Textual Traditions* (Monographs of the Peshitta Institute Leiden 9; Leiden: Brill, 1998).

Saley, R.J., "The Textual Vorlagen for Jacob of Edessa's Revision of the Books of Samuel," in *Jacob of Edessa and the Syriac Culture of His Day* (ed. B. ter Haar Romeny; Monographs of the Peshitta Institute Leiden 18; Leiden: Brill, 2008), 113–25.
Salvesen, A., "The Purpose of Jacob of Edessa's Version of Samuel," *The Harp* 8–9 (1995–1996): 117–26.
Salvesen, A., "Jacob of Edessa and the Text of Scripture," in *The Use of Sacred Books in the Ancient World* (ed. L.V. Rutgers et al; CBET 22; Leuven: Peeters, 1998), 235–45.
Salvesen, A., *The Books of Samuel in the Syriac Version of Jacob of Edessa* (Monographs of the Peshitta Institute Leiden 10; Leiden: Brill, 1999).
Salvesen, A., "Did Jacob of Edessa Know Hebrew?" in *Biblical Hebrew, Biblical Texts: Essays in Memory of Michael P. Weitzman* (eds. A. Rapaport-Albert and G. Greenberg; JSOTSup 333; Sheffield: Sheffield Academic Press, 2001), 457–67.
Salvesen, A., "Jacob of Edessa's Life and Work: A Biographical Sketch," in *Jacob of Edessa and the Syriac Culture of His Day* (ed. B. ter Haar Romeny; Monographs of the Peshitta Institute Leiden 18; Leiden: Brill, 2008), 1–10.
Salvesen, A., "Jacob of Edessa's Version of 1–2 Samuel: Its Method and Text–Critical Value," in *Jacob of Edessa and the Syriac Culture of His Day* (ed. B. ter Haar Romeny; Monographs of the Peshitta Institute Leiden 18; Leiden: Brill, 2008), 127–44.
Wright, W., *A Short History of Syriac Literature* (1894; reprint, Amsterdam: Philo Press, 1966).
Ziegler, J. and O. Munnich (eds.), *Susanna, Daniel, Bel et Draco* (2nd ed.; Septuaginta Vetus Testamentum Graecum 16.2; Göttingen: Vandenhoeck & Ruprecht, 1999).

Richard A. Taylor

18.4.5 Armenian Translations

18.4.5.1 Nature; Background; Edition

Research has demonstrated that Arm-Dan comprises an initial translation based on both the Greek text of Theodotion (Th; → 18.3.2.3.1) and on the Peshitta (s; → 18.3.3); this translation was then revised on the basis of a Greek manuscript embodying a different textual complexion. Consequently, from the outset, Arm-Dan embraced the additions (→ II.3.1; → II.3.2) to the original form of

---
[8] So ter Haar Romeny, "The Syriac Versions of the Old Testament," 105.

the narrative encompassing Susanna, the Song of Azariah (Dan 3:26–45), Song of the Three Youths (Dan 3:52–90), and Bel and the Dragon. This information provided in this entry is based on my diplomatic edition, which presents a running text provided by manuscript M287 and the variants of fourteen further witnesses reflected in the apparatus, the latter selected to represent their diverse textual families as determined by soundings of all accessible extant codices. The theme of the man of God speaking truth to power that the book eloquently conveys (Daniel 1–6), together with its apocalyptic visions (Daniel 7–12), found deep resonance in Armenian culture, which assured the book's wide popularity and profound literary impact into the medieval period.[1]

18.4.5.2 Reconstruction of the Parent Texts of Arm-Dan

That Arm 1 is dependent on the Peshitta (→ 18.3.3) is underscored by its description of the invasion at Dan 11:39 where instead of "acting" against the fortresses according to Theodotion (= MT) (ποιήσει τοῖς ὀχυρώμασι "he will act against the fortresses"), the ruler "passes" into them (անցցէ յամուրսն "he passes into fortresses"), as depicted in the Syriac (ܢܥܘܠ ܠܚܣܢܐ "he will enter fortified places"). Even more striking is the stratum's representation of the Peshitta's Christological interpretation of the vision at Dan 9:26 that reads սպանցի աւծեալն "the anointed will be killed," in contrast to the Theodotion form (= MT) ἐξολεθρευθήσεται χρῖσμα "the unction will be destroyed." That the same early stratum is also dependent on Theodotion is suggested by its translation of the Hebrew transliteration preserved at Dan 11:45, εφαδανω (*ephadanō*) as յապարանսն "in the palace" (≠ S). The main profile of its Greek parent text is Lucianic (→ 18.3.5), as illustrated by several agreements, such as the plus at Dan 5:2 bestowing on Belshazzar his royal title: ο βασιλευς "the king" (LXX^L) = Բաղտասար արքայ "Baghtasar the king." Among its Lucianic affinities, it exhibits a particlar affiliation with the subgroup LXX$^{311-538}$ and with LXX^{410} with which it shares some singular agreements, such as the insertion of the superscription προσευχη δανιηλ = աղօթք Դանիէլի "Daniel's Prayer" at Dan 9:1. Its parent text also incorporated a high proportion of Old Greek readings, which Arm 1 mirrors.

Although Gehman[2] argued that Arm 2 represents a revision to an Origenic standard, the version actually evinces few Hexaplaric additions to Theodotion (→ 18.3.2.3.1). In contrast, its primary affinities are rather with the uncial LXX^B and its satellites, as at Dan 3:27 where its reading ճշմարտութիւն "truth" aligns with the nominal form ἀλήθεια "truth," attested by witnesses LXX$^{B-46'\,A\,V-62}$ Eth etc, rather than the adjective αληθιναι "true," represented by most of the other Greek witnesses. Arm 2 also attests a number of readings with Hippolytus' pre-Hexaplaric commentary, as in the description of the final judgment (Dan 12:2), where the phrase ի հողոյ "from the earth" has been construed with the action of rising, in agreement with LXX$^{231\,91\,26\,230'\,534\,594}$ et al. (εκ γης "from the earth") rather than with the verb of reposing ἐν γῆς χώματι "in a mound of earth," manifested by the other witnesses. Additionally, Arm 2 reveals clear affinities with LXX^{230}, as for example at Dan 4:20, where it reads the second person form տեսանէիր "you saw" in a singular agreement with LXX^{230} ειδες "you saw," over against the majority reading εἶδεν "he saw," in the sage's interpretation of Nebuchadnezzar's dream.

18.4.5.3 Translation Technique

Arm 1's translation unit is set at the phrase length and its approach valorizes Armenian idiom. Its rendering is also imbued with Antiochene exegetical principles (→ 1.3.1.2) such as explicating metaphors, as in rendering τῇ χειρί "the hand" with application to God by զաւրութեամբ "power" (Dan 4:32). Another related characteristic is the intertextual application of parallel passages in finessing the translation at various points, such as in the addition – to the description of idols at Dan 5:23, եւ ոչ գնան "and they do not go" – from Ps 113(MT 114):15

---

[1] Cowe, "The Reception of Daniel."

[2] Gehman, "The Armenian Version."

καὶ οὐ περιπατήσουσιν "and they will not walk," thus adding lack of ambulation to their other deficiencies.

In contrast, the Arm 2 translation unit focuses on the individual lexeme and the encoding of morphological and syntactical features of the source language. This relates to infinitives, as in the phrase μετὰ τὸ κρατῆσαι αὐτόν "after his becoming strong," rendered precisely by յետ զաւրանալոյ նորա (Dan 11:2). However, disparate usage requires a series of alternative strategies in rendering participles. Combinations of two may be rendered by participle and finite verb as at Dan 5:19, where the phrase τρέμοντες καὶ φοβούμενοι "shaking and fearing" appears as զարհուրեալ դողային "frightened, they were shaking." Articulated participles are usually translated as relative clauses, as at Dan 7:20, where the horn defined as τοῦ ἀναβάντος "the one coming up" is portrayed in Armenian as որ ելանէր "which was going up," while participles associated with the object of verbs of seeing or hearing are recast as subordinate clauses, as at Dan 8:4, where the phrase εἶδον τὸν κριὸν κερατίζοντα "I saw the ram charging" is translated տեսանէի զխոյն զի զգորէր "I saw that the ram was charging."

18.4.5.4 Translation Technique: Literalisms and Transliterations

The construct case construction in Hebrew that associates two nouns requires that adjectives qualifying the first noun follow the second. While Greek syntax permits such a formulation – as in πνεῦμα θεοῦ ἅγιον, lit. "spirit of God holy" (Dan 4:5) – this is alien to Armenian idiom, which necessitates locating noun and adjective together as in Arm 1 *in situ*, հոգի սուրբ Աստուծոյ "the holy spirit of God." Again, the retension of Semitic transliterations in the Greek is typical of Arm 2's isomorphic translation, as in the case of τῷ φελμουνι "to the Phelmouni" by փիլմունիս "(to) the P'ilmoni" (Dan 8:13), βαδδιν "baddin" by բադեան "badean" (= Hebrew for "linen"; Dan 10:5; 12:7), μαωζιν "Maozin" by մաուզիս "Mawozin" (proper name of a god; Dan 11:38).

18.4.5.5 Text-Critical Value: Omissions and Additions

As in other books, Arm 1 introduces a number of explanatory additions to express the pronoun subject or object, to smooth the sense flow – as with the addition արքայի "of the king" to define the dream being discussed (Dan 2:36) – and intensifying additions, as at Dan 4:22, where the generic expression τῆς βασιλείας τῶν ἀνθρώπων "the kingdom of humans" is individualized as ամենայն թագաւորութեան մարդկան "every kingdom of humankind." Arm 1 evinces very few minuses. Arm 2 also maintains a high degree of quantative representation. The few minuses it represents omit material patently redundant in context, such as the reference to the "king" (βασιλεῦ) at Dan 3:10, who has been explicitly referenced in the preceding verse, and the mention of viewing (καὶ εἶδον "and I saw") immediately after an allusion to the eyes (Dan 10:5).

18.4.5.6 Relevance for Exegesis

It is emblematic of Arm 1 to introduce a distinction between licit and illicit cultic paraphernalia, though this does not exist in MT and its Greek translations.

18.4.5.7 Text-Critical Value of Arm-Dan for LXX-Dan

Further investigation is required to define the parameters of Arm 1's employment of the Peshitta (→ 18.3.3) and the Lucianic text (→ 18.3.5) in the translation process. The stratum's agreements with VL (→ 18.4.1) illuminate the proto-Lucianic or pre-redactional phase of that text type, while it antedates by some centuries the minuscule evidence with which it shares affinities. Arm 2's largely isomorphic translation technique and agreements with LXX^B and satellites indicates it is also an important witness in this book. Nevertheless, the convolutions in the engagements between the assailant kings in Daniel 11 have created particular problems for the translator and redactor.[3]

---

[3] See Cowe, *The Armenian Version of Daniel*, 382–83.

Cowe, S.P., "Tendentious Translation and the Evangelical Imperative: Religious Polemic in the Early Armenian Church," *Revue des Études Arméniennes* 22 (1990–1991): 97–114.

Cowe, S.P., *The Armenian Version of Daniel* (University of Pennsylvania Armenian Texts and Studies 9: Atlanta: Scholars Press, 1992).

Cowe, S.P., "The Reception of Daniel in Medieval Armenian Society," in *The Armenian Apocalyptic Tradition: A Comparative Perspective* (eds. K. Bardakjian and S. La Porta; SVTP 25; Leiden: Brill, 2014), 81–125.

Gehman, H.S., "The Armenian Version of the Book of Daniel and Its Affinities," *ZAW* 48 (1930): 82–99.

Ziegler, J. (ed.), *Susanna, Daniel, Bel et Draco* (Septuaginta Vetus Testamentum Graecum 16.2; Göttingen: Vandenhoeck & Ruprecht, 1954).

Zohrapian, *Scriptures.

Peter Cowe

18.4.6 Georgian Translations

18.4.6.1 Background

Georg-Dan is preserved in Codices Georg^O (= Mount Athos, Library of the Iviron Monastery, geo. 1, 978 C.E., in two volumes), Georg^J2 (= Jerusalem, Library of the Greek Patriarchate, geo. 11, eleventh century), Georg^S (National Centre of Manuscripts, Tbilisi = NCM, A-51, late seventeenth–early eighteenth century), and also in the so-called "Bakar Bible," the 1743 Moscow printed edition (= Georg^B).[1] A full description of these sources is available in the first volume of the critical edition of the Old Georgian Octateuch.[2] Additional manuscript material is represented by the lectionary Georg^P (= Paris, Bibliothèque nationale de France, geo. 3, 1040 C.E.).

As with several other books of the Georgian Bible, there have been no studies to date of the manuscript tradition of Georg-Dan. A full collation with the Göttingen edition of LXX has yet to be undertaken.[3] Every precondition is in place today to advance the study of the material in question.

[1] *Biblia*.
[2] *C'ignni*, 559–72, 607–19, 627–35.
[3] Ziegler and Munnich, *Daniel*.

Each version of Georg-Dan is available in excellent scholarly editions.[4]

18.4.6.2 Date, Versions, Editions

The ancient translation (= Georg-Dan 1) is available in two redactions. Both date back to the early periods of Georgian literature, namely to the fifth–eighth centuries C.E. (→ 1.4.8.3). The first (= Georg-Dan 1a) is to be found in Georg^P. It contains Dan 1:1–21; 2:34–35; 3:1–89, 93–97; 7:2–28; 12:1–3. The text is published in the edition of the Paris codex of the Lectionary.[5]

The second redaction (= Georg-Dan 1b) is available in manuscripts Georg^O and Georg^J2. It preserves the full text of the book of Daniel. In 1961, Blake published the critical edition of this version, followed by a Latin translation.[6]

In the late seventeenth century, Sulkhan Saba Orbeliani produced a new version of the book (= Georg-Dan 2) that is contained in Georg^S and also partially in Georg^B.[7]

18.4.6.3 Textual Features

Although both redactions of Georg-Dan 1 have been published, their textual relationship has still to be investigated. Moreover, they have not yet been subjected to a comparative study, as principally shown by their exclusion from the critical apparatus of Ziegler and Munnich.[8] As a preliminary point, it is possible to observe the following.

At times, the text of Georg-Dan 1a deviates significantly from that of Dan 1b, while in other cases they are quite similar and differences reduce to mere lexical replacements. For example, in Dan 3:1, Georg-Dan 1a translates the Greek ὁ βασιλεὺς ἐποί-

[4] Danelia, Čxenk'eli, and Šavišvili, *Kartuli lekcionaris p'arizuli xelnac'eri*, 343–52; Blake and Brière, *Critical Edition*, 818–65; Blake and Brière, *Apparatus*, 510–11; Dočanašvili, *Mcxeturi xelnac'eri*, 3–38.
[5] Danelia, Čxenk'eli, and Šavišvili, *Kartuli lekcionaris p'arizuli xelnac'eri*, 343–52. See also Tarchnischvili, *Le grand lectionnaire*, n° 23 (Dan 3:1–97); n° 28 (Dan 2:34–35); n° 309 (Dan 12:1–3).
[6] Blake and Brière, *Critical Edition*, 818–65; Blake and Brière, *Apparatus*, 510–11.
[7] See Dočanašvili, *Mcxeturi xelnac'eri*, 262.
[8] Ziegler and Munnich (eds.), *Daniel*.

ησεν εἰκόνα χρυσῆν "the king made a golden image" as მეფემან ქმნა კერპი ერთი ოქროისაჲ "the king made an idol of gold," while Georg-Dan 1b renders it as მეფემან ქმნა ხატი ოქროისაჲ "the king made an image of gold." These features might suggest that a revision was undertaken. However, this issue requires further investigation that should be based on comparative analysis with LXX and the Armenian version (→ 18.4.5). In Georg-Dan 1a the use of proper names shows reliance on Greek: for instance, Ιωακιμ "Ioakim" is rendered as ომაკიმ "Ioak'im," while Georg-Dan 1b reads ომვაკიმ "Iovak'im" as found in Armenian (Յովակիմ).

Both redactions are representatives of Theodotion's version (→ 18.3.1). This affiliation clearly emerges in different parts of the book, especially in key sections, such as Daniel 4–6. For instance, Daniel 4 includes the typical pluses of Th-Dan/MT-Dan in vv. 14, 19, 23–25, 28, 30 as well as the minuses in vv. 20–22.

In Georg-Dan 1b, the typical Lucianic readings (→ 18.3.5) in Dan 2:23; 2:27; 6:13; 8:22 are not found and neither are the doublets in Dan 7:23; 8:25; 9:24; 11:10; 11:40; and 12:7. But the Lucianic reading მიუგეს და ჰრქუეს "[they] answered and said" (ἀποκριθέντες λέγουσιν, "[and] answering they said") is attested in Dan 3:91.

According to Dočanašvili, Georg-Dan 2 is based on LXX (Theodotion's version). However, the text was partially corrected according to the 1666 Armenian printed Bible.[9]

18.4.6.4 Text-Critical Value

The text-critical value of Georg-Dan 1a and Georg-Dan 1b lies in their date: they represent early witnesses to Theodotion's version (→ 18.3.1). However, this tradition still awaits the complete appraisal of Biblical scholars. Georg-Dan 1a has still to be analyzed in detail: at present no collation with the Göttingen edition of LXX is available. Future research should check whether this redaction was translated or revised by using a Greek source as a model.

Georg-Dan 1b has proven to be of great value for the study of the earliest stratum of the Armenian version (→ 18.4.5). Cowe has investigated the genealogical affinities between the two Caucasian translations.[10] He took into consideration agreements in the form of proper names, occurrence of Armenian cognates, dependence on the Armenian version's rendering of the Greek and the Syriac. He pointed out that Georg-Dan 1b betrays loan words and errors that may be explained by assuming reliance on an Armenian model. Furthermore, Georg-Dan 1b has yielded valuable information about the primitive aspect of the Armenian version and helped define its relationship with the Syriac (→ 18.3.3). Georg-Dan 1b preserves Syriac agreements, no trace of which can be found in Armenian manuscripts. However, Georg-Dan 1b was subject to a medieval revision, which therefore limits its capacity to reflect the Old Armenian version.

Biblia: brzanebita da c'arsagebelita sapasetata sakartvelos mepis bakar vaxt'angis zisata (Moscow: Bakaris st'amba, 1743).

Blake, R.P. and C.M. Brière, *The Old Georgian Version of the Prophets: Critical Edition with a Latin Translation* (PO 29.5; Paris: Firmin Didot, 1961).

Blake, R.P. and C.M. Brière, *The Old Georgian Version of the Prophets: Apparatus Criticus* (PO 30.3; Paris: Firmin Didot, 1963).

C'ignni zuelisa aγtkumisani, Vol. 1: *Šesakmisaj, gamoslvataj* (eds. B. Gigineišvili and C. K'ik'vize; Tbilisi: Mecniereba, 1989).

Cowe, S.P., *The Armenian Version of Daniel* (University of Pennsylvania Armenian Texts and Studies 9: Atlanta: Scholars Press, 1992).

Danelia, K., S. Čxenk'eli, and B. Šavišvili (eds.), *Kartuli lekcionaris p'arizuli xelnac'eri: zveli da axali aγtkmis sak'itxavebi, t'. 1: nac'ili I* (Tbilisi: Tbilisis universit'et'is gamomcemloba, 1987).

Dočanašvili, E. (ed.), *Mcxeturi xelnac'eri (danielis, mcire c'inasc'armet'q'velta da axali aγtkmis c'ignebi)* (Tbilisi: Mecniereba, 1986).

Melikišvili, N., *Bibliur c'ignta zveli kartuli targmanebi* (Tbilisi: Alilo, 2009).

---

[9] Dočanašvili, *Mcxeturi xelnac'eri*, 262.

[10] Cowe, *The Armenian Version*, 229–301.

Tarchnischvili, M. (ed.), *Le grand lectionnaire de l'église de Jérusalem (Ve–VIIIe siècle)*, Vol. 1 (CSCO 188–89; Scriptores Iberici 9–10; Louvain: Secrétariat du Corpus SCO, 1959).

Ziegler, J. and O. Munnich (eds.), *Susanna, Daniel, Bel et Draco* (Septuaginta Vetus Testamentum Graecum 16.2; Göttingen: Vandenhoeck & Ruprecht, 1999).

Alessandro Maria Bruni

18.4.7 Old Church Slavonic Translations

18.4.7.1 Background

OCS-Dan has a broad and extremely diverse manuscript legacy beginning in the twelfth century and stretching to at least the seventeenth century. More than one hundred manuscripts have been traced. They differ significantly from one another in terms of structure, typology, redactions, linguistic, and paleographic characteristics.[1] This is the inevitable outcome of a long, complex, and varied textual history that covers the entire period of Old Church Slavonic literature, starting from its very origins, namely the Cyrillomethodian (863–885 C.E.) and the Early Bulgarian (893–927 C.E.) periods, up to the publication of the printed Elizabethan Bible in 1751.[2]

The significance of OCS-Dan for the study of its Greek primary version (→ 18.3.1; → 18.3.2; → 18.3.4; → 18.3.5) appears to have been hitherto underestimated. A comprehensive reassessment of this manuscript material is now necessary. With the exception of the Old Church Slavonic translation of Hippolytus' *Commentarius in Danielem*, the importance of which is widely acknowledged among patrologists,[3] this tradition has neither been subjected to a thorough text-critical examination, nor to a systematic comparison with Greek sources, both with regard to external and internal criteria. Moreover, the Old Church Slavonic secondary versions of Daniel still await a meticulous collation with Ziegler's edition of LXX.[4]

In the present article, a number of preliminary observations are proposed. By highlighting various features not properly taken into consideration previously, an attempt is made to encourage fresh research into the textual history of OCS-Dan.

18.4.7.2 Versions, Sources, Dates, Editions

The Prophetologium presumably contains the oldest textual stratum of the book (= OCS-Dan 1), which is ascribed by scholars to the Cyrillomethodian phase. This tradition consists of fifty-three codices from the twelfth to the sixteenth centuries.[5] The earliest manuscripts preserve Dan 2:31–36, 44–45, and Dan 3:1–51, 57, while a number of East Slavic testimonies from the late-thirteenth century also include Dan 7:1–2, 9–10, 13–14; 10:1–21. However, this second group of readings in OCS-Dan 1 is considered to be the result of a later addition.[6]

A first full Old Church Slavonic translation of Daniel (= OCS-Dan 2) can be found in the so-called *Jewish Chronicle*, an extensive compilation consisting mostly of translations of Greek historical and literary works (Flavius Josephus, John Malalas, George Hamartolos, and pseudo-Callisthenes), biblical books (Octateuch [→ 2.5.7], Tetrabasileon, excerpts from the Prophets, and others), as well as several Old Russian annals.[7] According to the two surviving codices of the *Jewish Chronicle* (Russian State Archive of Ancient Acts, Moscow, f. MGAMID 279/658, late fifteenth century, folios 289–301ᵛ; Library of the Lithuanian Academy of Sciences, Vilnius, 109/147, early sixteenth century, folios 417–40), OCS-Dan 2 has three omissions: *i)* Dan 1:1–2; *ii)* Dan 9:5–19; and *iii)* Dan 12:6–13. In Evseev's opinion,[8] OCS-Dan 2 should be identi-

---

[1] See Evseev, *Kniga*, lii–lxx.

[2] For an introduction to the critical stages in the history of the Old Church Slavonic Bible, see Mathiesen, "Bible," 5–12; Alekseev, *Tekstologija*; Thomson, *A Brief Survey*; Cooper, "The Bible," 179–96. The Elizabethan Bible is published in *Biblija*.

[3] See Bonwetsch and Richard, *Hippolyt*.

[4] Ziegler and Munnich, *Susanna, Daniel, Bel et Draco*.

[5] Evseev, *Kniga*, lii–lix.

[6] For an edition, see Brandt, "Grigorovičev parimejnik," 56–58; Evseev, *Kniga*, xl–xli. See also Michajlov, *Opyt*, cccxiv; Thomson, "The Slavonic Translation," 847–48.

[7] For the content and description of the *Jewish Chronicle*, see Istrin, *Aleksandrija*, 315–43; Evseev, *Kniga*, lix–lx; Dobrjanskij, 246–55.

[8] Evseev, *Kniga*, xv–xxxii.

fied with the translation allegedly undertaken by Methodius shortly before his death (885 C.E.), to which reference is made in his biography.[9] According to Thomson, however, this ascription is based on *a priori* assumptions and is hence purely speculative: in his view, this version most likely originated in West Bulgaria (Macedonia) between the late-ninth and the early-tenth centuries.[10]

A second complete translation (= OCS-Dan 3) is attested in thirty-six East and South Slavic manuscripts dating from the fifteenth and sixteenth centuries, which contain a commented edition of the XVI Prophets. In these collections, however, the book of Daniel represents an exception, since no catena is attached to it.[11] In light of its linguistic features, the origins of OCS-Dan 3 are believed to be rooted in Eastern Bulgaria during the reign of Tsar Symeon (893–927 C.E.). A similar conclusion has been reached for the Old Church Slavonic translation of Hippolytus' *Commentarius in Danielem* (= OCS-Dan 4), whose manuscript attestation dates from the twelfth through the seventeenth centuries.[12]

A second fundamental stage in the Old Church Slavonic textual history of Daniel begins in the late fifteenth century in Russia. A revision of OCS-Dan 3, using the Vulgate as its model, was undertaken in Novgorod under the patronage of Archbishop Gennadius (Gennadij Gonzov, ca. 1410–1505). This new text (= OCS-Dan 5) was included in the 1499 "Gennadian-Bible," the first complete corpus of the Slavic Scriptures.[13] About a century later, this redaction, after having been revised yet again, although on this occasion taking LXX as its reference source, was printed in the 1581 Ostrog Bible.[14] This conflated version finally was incorporated into the Elizabethan Bible in 1751.[15]

Besides the Cyrillic tradition, OCS-Dan is attested also in the Croat Glagolitic breviary and missal. The former contains Daniel 1, 2, 3, 4, and 5:1–4 (*Vitus codex*), while the second (*Vat. Borg. Ill.* 4) attests to Dan 3:1–23 and 9:15–19.[16] According to Thomson, the Croat Glagolitic redaction is based on OCS-Dan 3.[17]

In addition to this material, an independent translation from MT-Dan (→ 18.2.2) was carried out in Ruthenia in the second half of the fifteenth century. It is today preserved in the early-sixteenth-century codex of the Library of the Lithuanian Academy of Sciences (Vilnius), folio 19 N. 262.[18]

Critical editions of the existing Old Church Slavonic versions of Daniel are at present not available. Texts have been hitherto edited on the basis of single testimonies. Today, the main body of reference still remains Evseev's monograph, in which he published the synoptic text of OCS-Dan 1, OCS-Dan 2, and OCS-Dan 3.[19]

18.4.7.3 Translational Features and Parent Text

OCS-Dan 2, OCS-Dan 3, and OCS-Dan 4 are believed to have been based on Greek sources, each belonging to a different redaction of Theodotion's version of Daniel (→ 18.3.1; → 18.3.2). In terms of translation technique, OCS-Dan 2 and OCS-Dan 3 appear to have been drawn up according to literal criteria; in contrast, OCS-Dan 4 is in all probability the result of a freer rendering of its original.[20]

---

[9] This attribution is based on the famous testimony of the *Life of Methodius*. See Angelov and Kodov, *Kliment Ochridski*, 191; cf. also Alekseev, *Tekstologija*.

[10] See Mathiesen, "Bible," 5–12; Thomson, "The Slavonic Translation," 855.

[11] For a list of manuscripts, see Evseev, *Kniga*, lx–lxvii; Mathiesen, "Handlist," 18–33.

[12] Evseev, *Kniga*, lxviii–lxix; Il'inskij, *Pogodinskie*; Thomson, "The Slavonic Translation," 865–66; Iliev, "The Slavonic Versions," 150–58; Iliev, "Ipolitovoto tălkuvanie"; Pljuchanova, "Kniga," 12.

[13] Gorskij-Nevostruev, *Opisanie*, 132; Romodanovskaja, "Gennadievskaja Biblija," 584; Curkan, *Slavjanskij perevod*, 208–09.

[14] *Ostrožskaja biblija*.

[15] Thomson, "The Slavonic Translation," 848.

[16] See Berčić, *Ulomci*, 61–76; Vajs, "Staroslověnský překlad," 117–21.

[17] Thomson, "The Slavonic Translation," 848 and Thomson, *A Brief Survey*, 43.

[18] Archipov, *Drevnerusskaja kniga*, 147–240; Temčin, "Scharija i Skorina," 290, 300.

[19] Evseev, *Kniga*, 1–41, 64–166.

[20] Ziegler and Munnich, *Susanna, Daniel, Bel et Draco*, 33; Thomson, "The Slavonic Translation," 866.

According to Evseev, OCS-Dan 2 reflects the Lucianic recension (→ 18.3.5), while OCS-Dan 3 is based on the Hesychian one (→ 18.3.5; → 1.3.1.2.7). In order to illustrate this textual divergence, he cites Dan 6:3–5, 14–15, 18; 7:1, 11; 8:1–2, 10, 11, 14.[21] In this regard, the following observations can be made here.

OCS-Dan 2 clearly depends on a Lucianic model in Dan 2:11; 3:91; 4:1; 7:23; 8:22, 25; 11:10, 40. In other cases, both versions either follow the Lucianic recension (for instance, in Dan 2:27; 9:24) or disagree with its readings (e.g., in Dan 2:23; 6:13). Furthermore, among the distinctive traits of OCS-Dan 3, two final pluses may be mentioned. The first occurs in Dan 4:26 and derives from the Old Greek text (μετὰ δωδεκάμηνον ἐπὶ τῷ ναῷ τῆς βασιλείας αὐτοῦ ἐν Βαβυλῶνι περιπατῶν + καὶ ἐπὶ τῶν τειχῶν τῆς πόλεως μετὰ πάσης τῆς δόξης αὐτοῦ περιεπάτει καὶ ἐπὶ τῶν πύργων αὐτῆς διεπορεύετο "After a twelvemonth, as he walked in his palace in Babylon" + "and [the king] was walking on the walls of the city in all his glory and going through its towers"; *NETS); the second is to be found in Dan 6:18 (καὶ ἀπῆλθεν ὁ βασιλεὺς εἰς τὸν οἶκον αὐτοῦ καὶ ἐκοιμήθη ἄδειπνος καὶ ἐδέσματα οὐκ εἰσήνεγκαν αὐτῷ καὶ ὁ ὕπνος ἀπέστη ἀπ᾽ αὐτοῦ + καὶ ἀπέκλεισεν ὁ θεὸς τὰ στόματα τῶν λεόντων καὶ οὐ παρηνώχλησαν τῷ Δανιηλ "And the king went into his house and slept without supper, and they brought no delicacies to him, and sleep fled from him" + "and God shut the mouths of the lions, and they did not bother Daniel"; *NETS).[22]

A fundamental characteristic of OCS-Dan 2 has thus far not been properly evaluated. In 1893, Istrin noted that in both codices of OCS-Dan 2 the translation has the following chapter sequence: Daniel 1–4; 7; 8; 5; 6; 9–12 and Bel and the Dragon (Susanna is omitted). A few years later, this sequence was judged by Evseev to be the result of a rearrangement of the text.[23] At the time, the importance of this feature for the study of the primary version could not be properly appreciated, since the famous Papyrus Chester Beatty 967 (LXX[967]) dating from the early third century C.E. was still unknown. This Greek source, discovered only in 1931, apart from being the earliest testimony of OG-Dan, attests to the same chapter order as found in the Old Church Slavonic codices dating back to the late-fifteenth through early-sixteenth centuries (→ 6–9.2.7.4). Even though many decades have passed, Slavicists have failed to recognize this remarkable structural coincidence. Consequently, Septuagint scholars remain unaware of the existence of such a unique witness to the textual history of Daniel.[24] The most fascinating aspect of this agreement is unquestionably that it is merely confined to the structure of the book and does not affect its internal features. In fact, while LXX[967] follows the Old Greek text, OCS-Dan 2 on the contrary reflects Th-Dan.

The implication is that the arrangement found in LXX[967] should no longer be considered a distinctive trait of the Old Greek version. Indeed, the OCS-Dan tradition attests firmly to the previous existence in Greek of a Lucianic redaction of Th-Dan with the very same chapter order. Since Th-Dan is believed to be an independent translation and not a revision of the Old Greek,[25] it may be assumed almost safely that the sequence Daniel 1–4; 7; 8; 5; 6; 9–12 belongs to an earlier literary edition of the book. The testimony of OCS-Dan 2 consequently enables us logically to suppose that at least in the Greek tradition two arrangements of Daniel were adopted for each of the two versions. This is shown by LXX[967] and codex *Vat.gr.* R VII 45 for the Old Greek version, and by OCS-Dan 2 and the rest of the Byzantine manuscript evidence in the case of the Th-Dan translation.

18.4.7.4 Text-Critical Value for the Primary Translation

The preliminary review of the OCS-Dan tradition, undertaken expressly for the preparation of the present article, permits the following conclusions

---

[21] Evseev, *Kniga*, lxxv.
[22] Evseev, *Kniga*, 76, 100; Ziegler and Munnich, *Susanna, Daniel, Bel et Draco*, 144, 162.
[23] Istrin, *Aleksandrija*, 335; Evseev, *Kniga*, xv.

[24] See MacLay, "The Old Greek Translation," 309; Munnich, "Texte Massorétique."
[25] MacLay, "The Old Greek Translation," 322.

to be reached. The importance of OCS-Dan for the textual criticism of the primary translation is not limited to the already well-known case of Hippolytus' *Commentarius in Danielem* (= OCS-Dan 4). The remainder of the Old Church Slavonic Cyrillic manuscript tradition, which dates back to Glagolitic models of the ninth through tenth centuries, unexpectedly offers highly significant new material for the purpose of investigating the early transmission of the primary version. OCS-Dan 2 represents an indirect testimony of a lost Greek literary edition of Th-Dan (→ 18.3.1; → 18.3.2) with exactly the same chapter arrangement as that found in the earliest available manuscript of OG-Dan (→ 18.3.1), i.e., LXX[967].

OCS-Dan 2 therefore provides scholars with a new and rare insight into the history of the Greek tradition of Daniel during Late Antiquity. This material, even if still unexplored in terms of textual criticism, due mainly to the lack of a collation with the Göttingen edition of Ziegler and Munnich, nevertheless merits the full attention of LXX scholars. This testimony will undoubtedly prove to be of fundamental importance in the existing debate surrounding the textual history of Daniel.[26]

Alekseev, A., "Kirillo–Mefodievskoe perevodčeskoe nasledie i ego istoričeskie sud'by: perevody sv. Pisanija v slavjanskoj pis'mennosti," in *Istorija, kul'tura, ètnografija i fol'klor slavjanskich narodov: X Meždunarodnyj s"ezd slavistov: Sofija, sentjabr' 1988: Doklady sovetskoj delegacii* (ed. I.I. Kostjuško; Moscow: Nauka, 1988), 124–45.

Alekseev, A.A., *Tekstologija slavjanskoj Biblii* (Bausteine zur slavischen Philologie und Kulturgeschichte A Slavistische Forschungen 24; St. Petersburg: Dmitrij Bulanin, 1999).

Angelov, B.St. and C. Kodov (eds.), *Kliment Ochridski: Săbrani săčinenija*, Vol. 3: *Prostranni žitija na Kiril i Metodii* (Sofia: Izdatelstvo na Bălgarska Akademija na naukite, 1973).

Archipov, A.A., *Drevnerusskaja kniga proroka Daniila v perevode s drevneevrejskogo (k istorii gebraizmov v drevnerusskom knižnom jazyke)* (3 vols.; Moscow: Institut russkogo jazyka AN SSSR, 1982).

---

[26] See Tov, *Greek-Hebrew Bible*, 283, 297–99, 305; Tov, *TCHB*, 319.

Berčić, I. (ed.), *Ulomci Svetoga Pisma obojega uvjeta staroslovenskim jezikom: Skupio iz rukopisah i tiskanih knjigah hrvatskoga razreda svećenik Ivan Berčić*, Vol. 3 (Prague: Sinovi Bogumila Haase, 1865).

Biblija, sirěč' knigi svjaščennago pisanija vetchago i novago zavěta (St. Petersburg: Tipografija Aleksandro-Nevskogo monastyrja, 1751).

Bonwetsch, G.N. and M. Richard, *Hippolyt: Werke*, Vol. 1.1: *Kommentar zu Daniel* (GCS N.F. 7; Berlin: Akademie Verlag, 2000).

Brandt, R., "Grigorovičev parimejnik: V sličenii s drugimi parimejnikami," *Čtenija v Imperatorskom Obščestve istorii i drevnostej rossijskich* 168 (1894): 1–90; 170 (1894): 91–178; 193 (1900): 179–290; 197 (1901): 291–308.

Cooper, H.R., "The Bible in Slavonic," in *The New Cambridge History of the Bible*, Vol. 2: *From 600 to 1450* (eds. R. Marsden and E.A. Matter; Cambridge: Cambridge University Press, 2012), 179–97.

Curkan, R., *Slavjanskij perevod Biblii: proischoždenie, istorija teksta i važnejšie izdanija* (St. Petersburg: Kolo-Letnij sad, 2001).

Dobrjanskij, F., *Opisanie rukopisej Vilenskoj Publičnoj Biblioteki: cerkovno-slavjanskich i russkich* (Vilna: Tipografija A.G. Syrkina, 1882).

Evseev, I.E., "Zametki po drevne-slavjanskomu perevodu Sv. Pisanija III: Sledy utračennogo pervonačal'nogo polnogo perevoda proročeskich knig na slavjanskij jazyk," *Izvestija Imperatorskoj Akademii nauk* X.4 (1899): 355–73.

Evseev, I.E., *Kniga proroka Daniila v drevne-slavjanskom perevode: Vvedenie i teksty* (Moscow: Tipografija G. Lissnera i D. Sobko, 1905).

Gorskij, A. and K.I. Nevostruev, *Opisanie slavjanskich rukopisej Moskovskoj Sinodal'noj (Patriaršej) biblioteki*, Vol. 1: *Svjaščennoe pisanie* (Moscow: Sinodal'naja tipografija, 1855).

Iliev, I., "Ipolitovoto tălkuvanie na Kniga na prorok Daniil v răkopis 741 ot Bukureštkija dăržaven Archiv," *Littera et Lingua* 3–4 (2013) [http://www.slav.uni-sofia.bg/naum/lilijournal/2013/3-4/ilievi].

Iliev, I.I., "The Slavonic Versions of Hippolytus of Rome's Commentaries on the Book of Prophet Daniel," *Scripta & e-Scripta* 13 (2014): 149–70.

Il'inskij, G.A., "Pogodinskie Kirillovsko-glagoličeskie listki," *Byzantinoslavica* 1 (1929): 86–118.

Istrin, V., *Aleksandrija russkich chronografov: Issledovanie i tekst* (Moscow: Universitetskaja tipografija, 1893).

MacLay, T., "The Old Greek Translation of Daniel IV–

vi and the Formation of the Book of Daniel," *VT* 55 (2005): 304–23.

Mathiesen, R., "Bible, Church Slavonic," *The Modern Encyclopedia of Russian and Soviet Literature* (ed. H.B. Weber; Sea Breeze: Academic International Press, 1979), 3:5–12.

Mathiesen, R., "Handlist of Manuscripts Containing Church Slavonic Translations of the Old Testament," *Polata knigopisnaja* 7 (1983): 3–48.

Michajlov, A.V., *Opyt izučenija teksta knigi Bytija proroka Moiseja v drevne-slavjanskom perevode*, Vol. 1: *Parimejnyj tekst* (Warsaw: Tipografija Varšavskogo učebnogo okruga, 1912).

Munnich, O., "Texte Massorétique et Septante dans le livre de Daniel," in Schenker, *Earliest Text*, 93–120.

Ostrožskaja biblija: Fototipičeskoe pereizdanie teksta s izdanija 1581 g (Moscow: Slovo-Art, 1988).

Pljuchanova, M., "Kniga proroka Danila v Ellinskom letopisce," in *Russica Romana* 10 (2003): 9–33.

Romodanovskaja, V.A., "Gennadievskaja Biblija," *Pravoslavnaja ènciklopedija* (Moscow: Cerkovno-naučnyj centr "Pravoslavnaja ènciklopedija," 2005), 10:584–88.

Temčin, S.J., "Scharija i Skorina: ob istočnikach Vilenskogo Vetchozavetnogo svoda (F 19–262)," *Senoji Lietuvos Literatūra* 21 (2006): 289–316.

Thomson, F.J., "The Slavonic Translation of the Old Testament," in *The Interpretation of the Bible: The International Symposium in Slovenia* (ed. J. Krašovec; JSOTSup 189; Sheffield: Sheffield Academic Press, 1998): 605–920.

Thomson, F.J., *A Brief Survey of the History of the Church Slavonic Bible from its Cyrillomethodian Origins until its Final Form in the Elizabethan Bible of 1751* (Slavica Gendensia 33.2; Ghent: Department of Slavonic Philology, 2006).

Vajs, J., *Nejstarší Breviář hrvatsko-hlaholský (Prvý Breviář Vrbnický)* (Prague: Nákl. Král. České Společnosti Náuk, 1910).

Vajs, J., "Staroslověnský překlad knihy proroka Daniele a jeho význam v dějinách slovanského překladu bible," *Časopis katolického duchovenstva* 56.61 (1915): 113–22.

Vajs, J., *Najstariji hrvatskoglagolski misal: s bibliografskim opisima svih hrvatskoglagolskih misala* (Zagreb: Jugoslavenska akademija znanosti i umjetnosti, 1948).

Ziegler, J. and O. Munnich (eds.), *Susanna, Daniel, Bel et Draco* (2nd ed.; Septuaginta Vetus Testamentum Graecum 16.2; Göttingen: Vandenhoeck & Ruprecht, 1999).

Alessandro Maria Bruni

18.4.8 Arabic Translations

18.4.8.1 Background

The book of Daniel was translated into Arabic no later than the early ninth century C.E. In the following centuries, several idiosyncratic or interrelated translations appeared. In addition to the corpus transmitted in MT (Daniel 1–12; → 18.2.2), most manuscripts further contain the Additions to Daniel (→ 11.3) as an integral part of Daniel 3 (i.e., the Prayer of Azariah and the Song of the Three Young Men) and Bel and the Dragon at the end of the book. Susanna is included in some versions while excluded in others.

18.4.8.2 Original Form, Editions, Tools

A thorough study of the history of the Arabic book of Daniel was initiated by Löfgren. In 1936, he published a study wherein he classified all manuscripts accessible to him and included text samples from Daniel 1 and 3 from almost a dozen different versions.[1] Another important study was accomplished by Gehman in 1925.[2] Gehman confined himself to a detailed study of the Arabic version that was printed in the Polyglots. Besides these two works, the Arabic Daniel has been mentioned only in passing.[3] A study on the earliest manuscripts contained in the Monastery of St. Catherine is being prepared by the current author.

Extant early manuscripts can be classified roughly into four groups based on *Vorlage* and intertextual relations. The first group represents the translation of al-ʿAlam al-Iskandarī who was active in Alexandria prior to the tenth century.[4] This translation is extant in a number of homogenous manuscripts, including Paris, BNF, Ar. 1 (1584–1585),

---

[1] Löfgren, *Studien*.
[2] Gehman, "The 'Polyglot' Arabic Text."
[3] Graf's account of Daniel in *GCAL* 1, 131–37 is essentially based on Löfgren's *Studien*. Vaccari only mentions Daniel in passing in his study on the Arabic versions of the Prophets in "Le Versioni" (1921 and 1922). A short account is provided by Wald in "Über die Arabische Übersetzung des Daniel in den Polyglotten."
[4] Vaccari, "Le Versioni" (1921): 408–12; Löfgren, *Studien*, 34–35; Graf, *GCAL* 1, 132–33.

which was selected for the Paris Polyglot (1645)[5] and reprinted with minor alterations in the London Polyglot (1657).[6] We know from the colophon in manuscript Vatican, Ar. 445 that al-'Alam used as his *Vorlage* an ancient parchment codex written in Greek uncials (Arab. *raqqa biqalam al-līṭon al-Rūmī*).[7] According to Gehman, al-'Alam's text is representative of the Origenian Constantinopolian recension (→ 18.3.5) and, in fact, constitutes one of our best witnesses thereof.[8] Löfgren classified all manuscripts known to him that contain al-'Alam's translation and called for a more detailed text-critical analysis, a task yet to be accomplished.[9]

Al-'Alam's version circulated widely in the Melkite (Greek Orthodox) community in Egypt. During the fourteenth century, if not before, it was adopted by the Coptic Church and revised slightly according to the Coptic tradition (→ 18.4.2). The earliest witness of the revised version is attested in the bilingual Coptic-Arabic manuscript London, BL, Or. 1314 (Crum 729, Rieu 2) dated 1373/1374.[10] The apocalyptic composition, The Fourteenth Vision of Daniel, has been added to the biblical corpus.

The second group is comprised of four heterogenous but interrelated manuscripts based on the Peshiṭta (→ 18.3.3). The most ancient manuscript is Sinai Ar. 1, written on parchment in the ninth century C.E. in an early Abbasid book hand. It was edited by Stapleton in an unpublished dissertation.[11] With the exception of manuscript Sinai Ar. 1,

the Song of the Three Young Men (→ 11.3.10) transmitted within this group represents not the biblical but the condensed liturgical version.[12]

The third group is likewise based on the Peshiṭta (→ 18.3.3). It is represented among others by manuscript Sinai Ar. 9 that is dated to the thirteenth century and by manuscript Berlin, Staatsbibliothek, Diez A fol. 41 (Ahlwardt 10173) dated 1325.[13]

The earliest representative of the fourth group is manuscript Sinai Ar. 539, commonly dated to the twelfth century. This version appears to have circulated in the Melkite (Greek Orthodox) community and has been reproduced in a number of manuscripts with only minor textual variants.[14] It is based on the Peshiṭta (→ 18.3.3) but elements from the Greek Bible (→ 18.3.1; → 18.3.2) have been incorporated, perhaps via the Coptic (→ 18.4.2). The author is unknown.[15] The biblical rendering of the Song of the Three Young Men has been supplanted by the shorter liturgical version. Susanna is transmitted as part of Daniel 1 and inserted there between vv. 2 and 3.

In addition to these four groups, there are other Arabic manuscripts of Daniel that attest to yet further Arabic versions of the book. Manuscript Sinai Ar. 2 is dated 939–940 C.E.; its Arabic text of Daniel is based on a Hebrew *Vorlage* of an MT

---

[5] Le Jay, *Biblia.

[6] Walton, *Polyglotta. See Gehman, "The 'Polyglot' Arabic Text," 332–33, and Löfgren, *Studien*, 89–92.

[7] A reproduction of the colophon is extant in Vaccari, "Le Versioni" (1921): 404.

[8] There is minor influence from other *Vorlagen*; see Gehman, "The 'Polyglot' Arabic Text," 331–33, 347–52.

[9] Manuscripts Vatican, Ar. 445; Paris, Ar. 1; Cairo Copt. Orth. Patr. 198 (Graf 243); London, BL, Or. 1326 (Rieu 1); Paris, BNF, Ar. 2; Rome, Casan. 2108. See Löfgren, *Studien*, 9–27, 34–41.

[10] Löfgren, *Studien*, 8, 24–27, 34–41; Vaccari, "Le Versioni" (1921): 407–08.

[11] Stapleton, "Edition." See also R. Steiner who compares some aspects of Saadia Gaon's translation of Daniel with that in Sinai Ar. 1 (*A Biblical Translation in the Making: The Evolution and Impact of Saadiah Gaon's Tafsīr* [Cambridge: Harvard University Press, 2010]).

[12] This liturgical version is attested in manuscripts Sinai Ar. 513 (tenth century), Sinai Ar. 597 (dated 1002), and Oxford, Bodl., Fraser 257 (eleventh century). For a partial reproduction of the Oxford manuscript, see Löfgren, *Studien*, 54–59.

[13] In manuscript Sinai Ar. 9, there is a gap between Dan 2:33 and Dan 11:13. For a partial reproduction of the Berlin manuscript, see Löfgren, *Studien*, 64–68.

[14] The same version is extant in manuscripts St. Petersburg, Institute of Oriental Manuscripts, D226, 1235/1238 C.E.; Milano, Ambr. 58 inf., dated 1226; Firenze, Med.-Laur., Or. 59 (Assemani XIII), dated 1334; London, BL, Or. 5918 (Ellis-Edwards S. 69), fourteenth century; Oxford, Bodl., Seld. Arch. A 67 (Uri Cod. Arab. Christ. VI), 1358/1458; Vatican, Ar. 468 (Mai S. 523), dated 1578; Rome, Casan. 169., ca. 1625 (in Karšuni script). See Löfgren, *Studien*, 9–27, 49–54, 59–64.

[15] Both Löfgren *Studien*, 49–51, and Vaccari, "Le Versioni" (1922): 413–16, are hesitant to assign this Daniel version to the famous Pethion from the ninth-century C.E., although at least Jeremiah and arguably all the Major Prophets transmitted in the same corpus are assigned to him (→ 6–9.2.8).

text type (→ 18.2.2). Yet another early version consists of the portions of Daniel that are included in the Prophetologion, i.e., collections of biblical lectionaries read during the church year, usually parts of Daniel 2 and 3. The oldest manuscript detected so far within this group is Sinai Ar. 588, an old Arabic-Syriac-Greek palimpsest whose Arabic section is dated to the tenth century. Other manuscripts belonging to this group are Sinai Ar. 11 dated 1116, Sinai Ar. 595 dated 1290, and Sinai Ar. 18 dated 1350. This group is seemingly translated from the Greek text (Theodotion; → 18.3.1; → 18.2.3). A different version of Daniel 3 is contained in the Coptic-Arabic *psalterium* issued by Raphael Tuki for the Coptic Catholic Church in 1744. Tuki most likely used manuscript Vatican, Ar. 406 dated 1334/1335 for this edition. Yet another version of Daniel 3 is represented by manuscripts Vatican, Ar. 9 dated 1583 and Vatican, Borg., Ar. 28 dated 1558.[16]

18.4.8.3 Translation Character and Translation Technique

The various groups exhibit disparate translation techniques.[17] Gehman maintains that textual deviations from the *Vorlage* in al-ʿAlam's translation as preserved in manuscript Paris BNF Ar. 1 are scarce. As a whole, the translation is literal yet not literalistic and written in idiomatic Arabic with the intention of explicating its content. An example of the latter trend is the translation of "the chief of the satraps" (ἄρχοντα σατραπῶν) in Dan 2:48 as "the commander in chief of the army" (رئيسا على عظماء الجيوش). In Dan 5:25, the enigmatic phrase "*Manē Thekel Phares*" (μανη θεκελ φαρες) is not transliterated but interpreted as "measured weighted divided" (مقيس موزون مقسوم). Personal names are often reflected in the native idiom thus "Nabouchodonosor" (Ναβουχοδονοσορ) is rendered "Buḫtanaṣṣar" (بختنصّر). Similarly, place names may be identified by contemporary locations as is the case in Dan 8:2 where "in the land of Eilam" (ἐν χώρᾳ Αιλαμ) is rendered "in the region of Al-Ahwāz" (في كورة الاهواز).[18]

The second group, represented by manuscript Sinai Ar. 1, is characterized by its free translation techniques. Most notable are the numerous textual additions and omissions. In the first case, the scribe aims at filling in semantic, syntactic, or cultural ellipses caused by the concise biblical narrative or by the remoteness of source and target culture; for example, in Dan 2:26, the Peshitta reads "and Daniel asked the king to give him time" (ܘܕܢܝܐܝܠ ܒܥܐ ܡܢ ܡܠܟܐ ܕܢܬܠ ܠܗ). The translator of Sinai Ar. 1 appears to consider Daniel's spontaneous entrance into the king's court problematic in terms of his own ideas of court etiquette and renders "and he asked of him that he would bring him before the king and when he entered to him he asked the king [...]" ([...] فرغب اليه ان يدخله على الملك فلما دخل عليه سال الملك). In Dan 5:5, the translator evades the possibility that it was a "a real human finger" (ܨܒܥܬܐ ܕܐܝܕܐ ܕܐܢܫܐ) that appeared on Belshazzar's wall by rendering a "likeness of human fingers" (شبه اصابع الانسان). Clauses linked by the conjunction *we* "and" in the Peshitta may be strung together by a temporal or causal linkage in the Arabic text with the intention of clarifying their structural interrelation.

Frequently, the translator omits material if repetitive in nature and the many verbatim repetitions so characteristic of the biblical narrative are partly or completely excluded. A proper name or metonym is often omitted or substituted by a suffixed pronoun if still inferable from the context. Frequently occurring words or phrases are generally not rendered consistently by a single equivalent but instead reflected by a variety of synonyms. Such omissions or lexical inconsistencies rarely hurt the story line but appear to be contextually or stylistically motivated as a means to avoid repetitive language.

There is a certain influence from Muslim literature in Sinai Ar. 1. For instance, in Dan 6:27, "for he is the living God and steadfast forever" (ܕܗܘܝܘ

---

[16] For the last two versions and more modern versions, see Löfgren, *Studien*, 25–26, 45–49 and Hjälm, L., *Christian Arabic Versions of Daniel*.

[17] Many of the Arabic samples presented here are extracted from Hjälm, L., *Christian Arabic Versions of Daniel*.

[18] Gehman, "The 'Polyglot' Arabic Text," 334–52.

ܐܠܗܐ ܚܝܐ ܘܩܝܡ ܠܥܠܡܝܢ) is rendered “for there is no god except the one who is living and eternal” (فانه لا اله الا الحى الدايم). Compare the latter phrasing with Sura 3:2 of the Qur’an: “there is no god except the one who is living and steadfast” (لَا إِلَٰهَ إِلَّا هُوَ الْحَيُّ الْقَيُّومُ).

The third group, represented by thirteenth-century manuscript Sinai Ar. 9, is written in stylish and idiomatic Arabic and displays yet another set of translation techniques. Most palpable is the frequent use of “alternate renderings” where one text unit in the source text is represented by two (or more) in the target text. For example, in Dan 2:19, the Peshiṭta reads “and Daniel blessed the God of heavens” (ܘܕܢܝܐܝܠ ܒܪܟ ܠܐܠܗܐ ܕܫܡܝܐ). This is rendered in Sinai Ar. 9 as “Then Daniel thanked the God of heaven and prayed” (فحمد دانيل اله السما وصلى). Similarly, in Dan 1:10, “he will see their faces being weaker [than the others]” (ܢܚܙܐ ܐܦ̈ܝܟܘܢ ܟܡܝܪ̈ܢ) is rendered as “he will see their faces being different [and] not similar to” (ينظر الى وجوهكم يتغير لا تشبه). Names of places are often translated by contemporary designations rather than transliterated so that the reader easily recognizes the current location of the biblical site. Thus, in Dan 1:2, “the land of Shin‘ar” (ܐܪܥܐ ܕܫܢܥܪ) is rendered as “the land of Iraq” (ارض العراق). Textual addition as a means of clarifying the context is common. An example appears in Dan 1:7 where “and the chief trustee gave them names” (ܘܣܡ ܠܗܘܢ ܪܒ ܡܗܝ̈ܡܢܐ ܫܡܗ̈ܐ) is translated as “and he who was responsible of the servants gave them names in Chaldean” (فسماهم القيم على الخدمة اسماهم بالكلدية). Textual omissions occur only rarely.

The fourth group, represented by twelfth-century manuscript Sinai Ar. 539, exhibits a set of techniques similar to those in group two, yet they are not carried out to the same extant. “Pleonastic” renderings of the kind “king” in “Nebuchadnezzar the king” or “golden” in “the golden image” are occasionally omitted. Reiterated information regarding clause subjects or objects is at times omitted or substituted by a pronoun if still inferable from the context. Cohesive links such as temporal conjunctions are on occasion added in order to improve the logical coherence of the story. For example, in Dan 2:13–14, compare the Peshiṭta and manuscript Sinai Ar. 539 and note the syntactic reconstructions and textual transpositions in the latter that serve to create a more fluent Arabic text: Peshiṭta reads “then Nebuchadnezzar [...] commanded to bring Shadrach, Meshach, and Abed Nego. And they brought them before the king. [14] Nebuchadnezzar answered” (ܗܝܕܝܢ ܢܒܘܟܕܢܨܪ [...] ܐܡܪ ܠܡܝܬܝܘ ܠܫܕܪܟ ܡܝܫܟ ܘܥܒܕܢܓܘ. ܘܐܝܬܝܘ ܐܢܘܢ ܩܕܡ ܡܠܟܐ [14] ܥܢܐ ܢܒܘܟܕܢܨܪ). Sinai Ar. 539 has “Then Buẖta Nāṣar [...] commanded to bring them to him and when they brought Šadrāẖ and Māšaẖ and Abda Nāġūn to the king [14] Buẖta Nāṣar answered” (حينيذ بخت ناصر [...] امر ان ياتون بهم اليه ولما اتوا بشذراخ وماشخ وعبد ناغون الى الملك [14] اجاب بخت ناصر).

The employment of cognate and similar roots appears relatively frequently provided that such structural affinity remains semantically sound. Expressions specific to the Syriac language are rendered in idiomatic Arabic. For example, compare literally the Peshiṭta and Sinai Ar. 539 in Dan 3:8: “and they ate the pieces of the Jews” (ܘܐܟܠܘ ܩܪ̈ܨܝܗܘܢ ܕܝܗܘ̈ܕܝܐ) rendered “and they conspired against the Jews” (فمحلوا باليهود).

18.4.8.4 Text-Critical and Literary Value

If all extant textual witnesses are studied carefully and compared, al-‘Alam’s faithful Arabic translation from a Greek uncial codex is valuable for the critical study of LXX (→ 18.3.1; → 18.3.2).

With few ambiguous exceptions, all Syriac-based manuscripts appear to represent the *textus receptus* of the Peshiṭta (→ 18.3.3). The text-critical value of these manuscripts is rather limited due to their free translation techniques. These translations are best regarded as documents in their own right that display an attempt by the Christian communities to bring the biblical narratives into the new linguistic paradigm of literary Arabic and in line with contemporary ideals.

Gehman, H.S., “The ‘Polyglot’ Arabic Text of Daniel and Its Affinities,” *JBL* 44 (1925): 327–52.
Graf, **CGAL* 1.
Hjälm L., M., *Christian Arabic Versions of Daniel: A Com-*

parative Study of Early MSS *and Translation Techniques in* MSS *Sinai Ar. 1 and 2* (Leiden: Brill, 2016).

Löfgren, O., *Studien zu den arabischen Danielübersetzungen: Mit besonderer Berücksichtigung der christlichen Texte: Nebst einem Beitrag zur Kritik des Peschittatextes* (Uppsala: A.B. Lundequistska Bokhandeln, 1936).

Stapleton, R., "An Edition of the Book of Daniel and Associated Apocrypha in Manuscript Sinai Arabic 1" (PhD diss., Brandeis University, 1989).

Vaccari, A., "Le Versioni Arabe dei Profeti," *Bib* 2 (1921): 401–23.

Vaccari, A., "Le Versioni Arabe dei Profeti," *Bib* 3 (1922): 401–24.

Wald, S.G., "Über die Arabische Übersetzung des Daniel in den Polyglotten," *Repertorium für Biblische und Morgenländische Litteratur* 14 (1784): 204–11.

Miriam Lindgren Hjälm

19
Ezra–Nehemiah

19.1 Textual History of Ezra–Nehemiah

19.1.1 Name and Original Form of the Book

19.1.1.1 Ezra-Nehemiah – One Book

Earliest evidence points to Ezra-Nehemiah's acceptance as one book, called Ezra.[1] LXX includes Ezra and Nehemiah as one book labeled Esdras β, or 2 Esdras (→ 19.3.1). This is dated by scholars to the second/first centuries B.C.E. (→ 19.3.1.2). The Talmud (*B. Bat.* 14b and 15a) counts them as a single book and, finally, the Masoretes total the number of verses of both Ezra-Nehemiah together (685), counting the middle of the text at Neh 3:32, not at the end of Ezra.

Although, according to earliest tradition, Ezra and Nehemiah formed one book called Ezra, scholars have questioned whether they were written originally as one book or as two. Several ancient authors mention Nehemiah but do not appear to know Ezra (i.e., Sir 49:12–13; 2 Macc 1:18, 20–36), and the apocryphal 1 Esdras knows Ezra but does not seem to know about Nehemiah. Further, Josephus' story of Ezra (*Ant.* XI:1–158) is based on 1 Esdras, and he does not begin his story of Nehemiah until he has narrated Ezra's death (*Ant.* XI:158).

However, the current story of Ezra-Nehemiah must be seen as one book. Ezra arrives in Jerusalem in order to teach statute and ordinance in Israel (Ezra 7:10). Yet the story of Ezra teaching the law to the assembled populace is not told until Nehemiah 8. Second, the book of Nehemiah begins: "The (following are the) words of Nehemiah son of Hacaliah: In the month of Chislev, in the twentieth year, while I was in Susa the capital, one of my brothers came (to me)" (Neh 1:1–2). The twentieth year refers to the twentieth year of the reign of a king, but we are not told which king. The reader does not need to be told this, since he is meant to assume that it is the same king, Artaxerxes, who was reigning in the previous four chapters, i.e., in Ezra 7–10.[2] Although the final product must be read as one book,[3] this final product combines the work of several independent authors and editors, which has now been completely intertwined.

19.1.1.2 Chronicles and Ezra-Nehemiah – Two Books

Many commentators, beginning with Zunz,[4] have concluded that Ezra-Nehemiah is a continuation of the books of Chronicles and was written by the same author. They emphasize that the last few verses of 2 Chronicles are duplicated in the first verses of Ezra. They also point to the fact that the Greek apocryphal book 1 Esdras (→ 11.7.1) contains all of 2 Chronicles 35–36 and continues directly on to the story of Ezra with no break and no repetition of the verses. Torrey[5] deviates from this view slightly in that he suggests that the Chronicler wrote Chronicles and continued with 1 Esdras, ending with Ezra's reading the law, and that he did not write Nehemiah. Others have maintained that Chronicles and Ezra-Nehemiah should be read as one book because of the many linguistic features (140!) that the two books share.[6] However, these similarities can be attributed to the nature of the language stratum – late Biblical Hebrew – and not to the identity of the author.[7] Japhet has shown, more importantly, that the linguistic forms that the Chronicler has rigidly altered in his sources

---

[1] This article reflects a segment in the Introduction to my study, *Ezra, A Commentary* (Sheffield: Sheffield Phoenix Press, 2015).

[2] Min, *The Levitical Authorship*, 25–26.

[3] *Pace* VanderKam, "Ezra-Nehemiah or Ezra and Nehemiah?"; Kraemer, "On the Relationship of the Books of Ezra and Nehemiah"; and Becking, "Ezra's Re-enactment of the Exile."

[4] E.g., Zunz, *Dibre Hajamim*; Batten, *The Books of Ezra and Nehemiah*; Rudolph, *Esra und Nehemia*; Freedman, "The Chronicler's Purpose"; Haran, "Explaining the Identical Lines"; Blenkinsopp, *Ezra-Nehemiah*; Talshir, *1 Esdras*, 22–36; D. Talshir, "A Reinvestigation."

[5] Torrey, *Ezra Studies*.

[6] E.g., Torrey, *Composition and Historical Value*; Driver, *Introduction*, 535–40; Curtis and Madsen, *Critical and Exegetical Commentary*, 27–36.

[7] Williamson, *Israel in the Books of Chronicles*, 37–59.

(i.e., in Samuel and Kings) remain unaffected in the Nehemiah memoir, thus demonstrating that the Chronicler could not have been the one who incorporated Nehemiah's memoir into the book of Ezra-Nehemiah.[8]

19.1.2 Ezra-Nehemiah's Composition and Transmission History

The key to understanding Ezra-Nehemiah's transmission history lies in the lists of returnees in Ezra 2 and Nehemiah 7.[9] Not only are these lists identical (except for errors of transmission), but they conclude with a similar narrative verse: a notice that when the seventh month arrived and the people Israel were settled in their towns, they gathered as one man in Jerusalem (Ezra 3:1 and Neh 7:72–8:1).[10] The intent of the narrative verse is to link the population as a whole (as one) to what follows, but Ezra 3 continues with an account of Zerubbabel and his kin and Jeshua and his fellow priests setting up the temple's sacrificial altar, whereas Nehemiah 8 continues its narrative with the story of Ezra reading the law to the gathered populace. Since only the story of the law-reading in Nehemiah 8 actually involves the entire population, the narrative linking verse must be original to Nehemiah 8 and not Ezra 3[11]. Therefore, there seems to have been at least two authors, an earlier one who compiled Ezra 7–Nehemiah 13 and a later one who added at least Ezra 1–6. The earlier author created his story from the Nehemiah memoir and from an early original version of Artaxerxes' letter to Ezra. The later author prefaced the story of Ezra-Nehemiah, which he received with an account of the return to Judah and the rebuilding and dedication of the temple.

19.1.3 Date

Determining the date of the final redaction of Ezra-Nehemiah comes down to one verse, Neh 12:22, and one name in the verse, "Yaddua." The verse lists the last four priests of the Persian Empire, up to "Darius the Persian," i.e., Darius III, as Eliyashib, Yoiada (Yehoiada), Yoḥanan (Yehoḥanan), and Yaddua. The list of priests in Neh 12:22 has been shown to be complete.[12] Ezra-Nehemiah therefore must have been finalized during the Hellenistic period, i.e., after the reign of Alexander, perhaps in the early Ptolemaic period. Constituent elements may be earlier.

19.1.4 Location in the Canon

In LXX (→ 13.1.1) and the Vulgate (→ 1.3.5), Ezra-Nehemiah immediately follows Chronicles, reflecting an early Babylonian talmudic tradition that the one is a continuation of the other (this order is followed in most Christian Bibles; → 1.1.2.2). In the Hebrew Bible (→ 1.1.2.1), however, they are not always placed together. The Aleppo and Leningrad Codices, for example, follow the Palestinian tradition in which Chronicles is placed first among the Writings with Ezra-Nehemiah placed last in that section and last in the Bible, in what David Noel Freedman (personal communication) called an "envelope construction." However, in the Babylonian Talmud's list of the order of the biblical books (*B. Bat.* 14b), the books are placed next to each other, with Ezra-Nehemiah preceding Chronicles, setting Chronicles as the last book in the Hebrew Bible. (This is the order followed in most Hebrew Bibles today). Placing Chronicles last allows the Hebrew Bible to end with Cyrus' command to go up to Jerusalem and rebuild the temple (2 Chr 36:23).

---

[8] Japhet, "Supposed Common Authorship."
[9] Williamson, "The Composition of Ezra i–vi"; Williamson, *Ezra, Nehemiah*, xxxiv–xxxv.
[10] Ezra 3:1: The seventh month came, and the people Israel were in the towns, then people gathered together as one to Jerusalem. Neh 7:72–8:1: The seventh month came and the people Israel were in their towns. Then all the people gathered as one to the square that is in front of the water gate.
[11] Fried, "Who Wrote Ezra-Nehemiah?"

[12] Fried, "A Silver Coin of Yoḥanan Hakkôhen"; VanderKam, *From Joshua to Caiaphas*, 44–99.

19.1.5 Witnesses to the Text

The primary text of Ezra-Nehemiah is MT (→ 19.2.2), defined as the agreement between three Tiberian manuscripts: the Leningrad Codex (MT^L; manuscript EPB, I B 19a of the Russian National Library, St. Petersburg, dated to 1008/1009 C.E.); a tenth-century manuscript, Sassoon 1053, of the National Library of Israel (MT^S1); and manuscript 1753 of the Cambridge University Library (MT^Y).[13] This last manuscript is Yemenite, but very close to the Leningrad Codex. In fact, all three manuscripts differ only slightly and only orthographically. Unfortunately, about one-third of Ezra-Nehemiah in the Sassoon manuscript is lost, and parts of the existing text are damaged and difficult to read.[14] All three manuscripts place Ezra-Nehemiah last, with Daniel preceding it. The resulting eclectic text of Ezra-Nehemiah is the text presented in *BHQ (→ 19.2.2), although the order of the books in these codices has been abandoned. The Masoretes record fifty-two *Ketiv-Qere* differences in Ezra-Nehemiah.

Among the fragments at Qumran were several of Ezra[15] and one of Nehemiah.[16] These are Ezra 4:2–6 (= 1 Esdr 5:66–70), Ezra 4:9–11 (no 1 Esdras parallel), Ezra 5:17–6:5 (= 1 Esdr 6:20–25), and Neh 3:14–15. Except for orthographic differences, the manuscripts found at Qumran and in the Judean Desert differ very little from one another or from the consonantal text of the Leningrad Codex (→ 19.2.1; → 19.2.2).

Other witnesses to the Hebrew text are two translations into Greek included in LXX (→ 19.3.1).[17] One, called Esdras β, or 2 Esdras, is a literal translation of the canonical Ezra-Nehemiah of MT.[18] 2 Esdras is so called because it is preceded in LXX by an apocryphal version of Ezra called Esdras α or 1 Esdras.[19] The basic texts of both these Greek versions are those prepared by Hanhart,[20] which primarily follow the text of ms Vaticanus. There are major differences between these two Greek versions of Ezra (MT-Ezra and 2 Esdras on the one hand, and 1 Esdras on the other). Ezra (and 2 Esdras) begin with the last two verses of Chronicles, whereas 1 Esdras begins with the entire last two chapters of those books. Secondly, the story of Zerubbabel's return to Judah and the chapters containing the correspondence with King Artaxerxes have exchanged positions in the two versions. Third, 1 Esdras contains a story of King Darius and his three bodyguards that is not present in MT-Ezra or 2 Esdras; and finally, MT-Ezra-Nehemiah (= 2 Esdras) contains the story of Nehemiah that is omitted from 1 Esdras. Both versions include the story of Ezra.[21]

In addition to the two Greek versions of Ezra, the Peshitta[22] (→ 19.3.3) is a translation into Syriac of MT that was maintained by the Syrian church (→ 1.3.4). Although its origin is not known, the original translation was likely completed in the first or second century C.E., essentially as a literal translation of the Hebrew. The earliest extant manuscripts are from the seventh and eighth centuries C.E.

The two Latin translations, VL (→ 19.4.1)[23] and the Vulgate (→ 19.3.6)[24] are extremely literal translations of the Hebrew.[25] The Latin editions refer to canonical Ezra as I Esdras, canonical Nehemiah as II Esdras, and the Greek 1 Esdras as III Esdras (→ II.7.1.4). The separation of Ezra and Nehemiah into two books is thus based on the Vulgate.

19.1.6 Relevance of the Textual Witnesses for Textual Criticism

Some of the textual differences among the versions may point to a better text or a better interpretation

---

[13] Marcus, *Ezra and Nehemiah*, 8*.
[14] Marcus, *Ezra and Nehemiah*, 8*.
[15] Ulrich, "117. 4QEzra."
[16] Charlesworth, "Announcing a Dead Sea Scrolls Fragment."
[17] Hanhart, *Esdrae Liber I*; Hanhart, *Esdrae Liber II*.
[18] Marcus, *Ezra and Nehemiah*, 9*.
[19] Talshir, *I Esdras*.

[20] Hanhart, *Esdrae I*; Hanhart, *Esdrae II*.
[21] For a discussion of the different views of the relative priority of MT-Ezra and 1 Esdras, see Fried, *Was 1 Esdras First?*
[22] Leiden Peshitta Project; *CAL on-line version.
[23] Recorded in the apparatus of Hanhart, *Esdrae Liber II*.
[24] Gasquet et al., *Biblia Sacra iuxta Latinam Vulgatam Versionem*.
[25] Marcus, *Ezra and Nehemiah*, 11*.

of MT (→ 19.2) at that location. Several improvements to Ezra can also be made based on the parallel text in Nehemiah. The name "Nahamani," for example, is included in the list of the leaders of the returnees in Neh 7:7 but is missing from the list at Ezra 2:2. This would provide a total of twelve names, which is considered complete, so this may indicate a better text here. However, the versions all have eleven names at Ezra 2:2 and twelve at Neh 7:7, so that if a name dropped out of Ezra 2 it was early in the transmission process.

Nehemiah may also have the better text at Neh 7:72 against MT-Ezra 3:1, so that the people Israel were in "their towns" and not "the towns."

Ezra 3:10 is a notable case where the versions help us understand a verse that has no parallel in Nehemiah. MT reads "the priests stationed" or "appointed" (וַיַּעֲמִידוּ), using a transitive verb but there is no object, so we may emend to יעמדו "the priests stood" (intransitive), with the versions. Rashi, not willing to emend the text, explains "the builders stationed the priests," which is not likely. More importantly, the Hebrew has usually been viewed as corrupt since it reads literally "they were dressed in their bugles" (מְלֻבָּשִׁים בַּחֲצֹצְרוֹת), so the *NRSV translates "priests *in their vestments* were stationed to praise the Lord with trumpets." Rashi translates by "the priests, elegantly attired, with their bugles." Ibn Ezra asserts that they were arrayed in their priestly vestments, even though they were prohibited from wearing them except during the sacrifices (*Klei HaMikdash* 8:12). However, LXX-Ezra (→ 19.3.1) enables us to solve the dispute. That text reads ἐστολισμένοι, which also carries the meaning "equipped," so we may translate "the priests stood equipped with their bugles." It may be that מלובש also carried the meaning "equipped" in the Second Temple period and that nothing has dropped out of the text. Thus there is no need to supply "their vestments" with the *NRSV or to concern ourselves with what these priests were wearing.

A more problematic case is Ezra 4:7 because the versions do not agree and MT is not clear. The Aramaic reads וּבִימֵי אַרְתַּחְשַׁשְׂתָּא כָּתַב בִּשְׁלָם מִתְרְדָת טָבְאֵל, and exegetes do not know whether to translate "in the days of Artaxerxes, Mithredates and Taba'el wrote in peace," or "in the days of Artaxerxes, Bishlam, Mithredates, and Taba'el wrote ..." LXX-Ezra and the Peshitta read "in peace," whereas 1 Esdras and the Vulgate supply a name (*Beslemos* and *Beselam*, respectively). Also problematic is Ezra 4:9 in which there is a list of either gentilics (according to LXX-Ezra and the Vulgate) or titles of Persian officials (1 Esdras and the Peshitta).

The versions are relied on most of all when interpreting Ezra 10:44, which is meaningless in the Hebrew. Translating literally it reads "All these (men) had taken foreign women, and there are among them women, and they put children." LXX-Ezra reads with the Vulgate and the Peshitta "All these had taken foreign women and had children from them," which is sensible. 1 Esdras reads "All these had married foreign women and had put them away with the children." Since this is the only version that actually states that a divorce occurred, this is the version that many commentators follow[26] but not all.[27]

As noted above (→ 19.1.1), in MT the book of Nehemiah follows immediately after Ezra on the same scroll. The only notice of a new beginning is the first half-verse: "The words of Nehemiah son of Hecaliah." Although this phrase is present in all the versions, it is surely a heading, a title added by a later editor. In fact, the Peshitta seems to read the book of Nehemiah as if that heading were not there. It adds the name "Ezra" to Neh 6:7, translating "you have set up prophets to prophesy over us in Jerusalem, saying 'behold, Ezra is king in Judah,'" clarifying that the "you" in MT is Ezra.[28] The Hebrew does not include a name, reading "You have set up prophets to proclaim concerning *yourself* in Jerusalem saying '(there is a) King in Judah.'" LXX-Ezra reads "You have set up prophets for yourself so that you may dwell in Jerusalem as king in Judah." The Vulgate is similar, reading, "You have set up prophets to proclaim about you in Jerusalem, saying 'there is a king in Judea.'" Only

---

[26] E.g., Rudolph, *Esra und Nehemiah*, 100; Blenkinsopp, *Ezra-Nehemiah*, 196.
[27] E.g., Williamson, *Ezra, Nehemiah*, 143.
[28] Balzaretti, *The Syriac Version*, 72–76.

the Peshitta supplies the name Ezra, indicating that at least to that translation, the "you" in this verse, and the "I" voice of the book of Nehemiah is Ezra, a continuation of the "I" from the previous chapters.[29] In this way of thinking, Ezra receives an official charge from the king in Ezra 7, and now serves as governor (Neh 5:14). If this is the implication of the addition of the name Ezra in the Peshitta, then the author of this translation understood the book of Nehemiah to actually be about Ezra.

The Dead Sea Scrolls (→ 19.2.1) can also be relevant for textual criticism. MT-Neh 3:14 reads "Malchiah son of Rechab, ruler of the district of Beth-haccherem, repaired the Dung Gate; he built it and set up its doors, its bolts, and its bars." Instead of "he built it," LXX reads "he and his sons set up its doors, etc." Charlesworth[30] notes that 4QNeh originally read "his sons" (ובניו), as in LXX, but it was corrected with a supralinear *nun* over the *yod* to conform to יבנונ "he built it" as in MT. Charlesworth suggests that a concern may have already existed by the first century C.E. (the probable date of this fragment) to make MT the dominant text type.

19.1.7 Relevance of the Textual Witnesses for Literary Criticism

Understanding the authors' arrangement of the chapters of Ezra-Nehemiah is key to understanding authorial (or editorial) intent, and a major difference between MT-Ezra-Nehemiah (→ 19.2.2) and 1 Esdras (→ 11.7.1) is the location of Ezra's law-reading.[31] In MT, Ezra arrives in Jerusalem in the seventh year of Artaxerxes with the express purpose of teaching the Torah in Israel (Ezra 7:10), but he is not shown doing so until thirteen years later and then only in the book of Nehemiah (Nehemiah 8). The author of Ezra-Nehemiah has used Ezra's Torah-reading to create a covenant renewal ceremony consisting of the Torah-reading (Nehemiah 8), a confessional prayer (Nehemiah 9), and an oath-signing (Nehemiah 10).[32] The author has sandwiched this ceremony between two lists of the legitimate population of Judah and Jerusalem (Nehemiah 7 and Nehemiah 11–12). He has prefaced his first population list (Nehemiah 7) with Nehemiah's account of his trip to Judah to rebuild the city wall, an account of the wall-building itself, and the portion of Nehemiah's memoir that ends with the comment that the wall is completed and the doors hung (Neh 7:5). He has followed the second population list in Nehemiah 11 and 12 with Nehemiah's description of the dedication of the wall, the ascent onto the wall, and the ceremonial celebration and the sacrificial feasting in the temple (Neh 12:27–44). The story of Nehemiah's wall-building (Nehemiah 1–6) is preceded by the mass divorce of the Judean population from their foreign wives (Ezra 9–10). The author/compiler of Ezra-Nehemiah has thus surrounded the Torah and the covenant-renewal ceremony firstly, and most closely, with the newly legitimated population of Judah, and secondly, and more distantly, with the creation, completion, and dedication of the city wall. The wall has become a fence, a *gādēr*, not only around the people, but around the Torah itself. Inside the dedicated wall is the rightful population of Judah, and in the center of that population is the Torah.

In spite of this careful construction of the events, the ending of the present book of Nehemiah threatens the effect of the Torah-reading[33]. The law reading of Nehemiah 8 is followed in Nehemiah 9 by a long confessional prayer, and then by the people's signing a written promise and an oath to keep the commandments (Nehemiah 10).[34] This is the so-called covenant-renewal ceremony.[35] The fact that the oath needed to be safeguarded by a curse (Neh 10:30 [Eng. trans.: 29]) emphasizes its fragility. This fragility is brought home in Nehemiah 13. Nehemiah had left Jerusalem to go to the king, re-

---

[29] Balzaretti, *The Syriac Version*, 72.
[30] Charlesworth, "Nehemiah."
[31] Fried, "Who Wrote Ezra-Nehemiah"; Fried, "Another Look at 1 Esdras."
[32] Duggan, *Covenant Renewal*.
[33] Fried, "Another Look at 1 Esdras."
[34] For the possible origin of Nehemiah 10, see Fried, "A Greek Religious Association."
[35] Duggan, *Covenant Renewal in Ezra-Nehemiah*.

turning now a few years later only to find that the promises made by the people in Nehemiah 10 were all for naught. The promise to bring the tithe to the Levites (Neh 10:37 [36]) was broken as soon as Nehemiah left the city (Neh 13:10). The promise to keep the Sabbath, and not to buy grain or produce on it (Neh. 10:32 [31]) was broken as soon as Nehemiah went away (Neh 13:15–16). In spite of the mass divorce of the Judeans (Ezra 10) and in spite of their promise never again to give their daughters to foreigners nor to take foreign daughters for their sons (Neh 10:31 [30]), Nehemiah returns after his short absence only to find that indeed Judeans had married the women of Ashdod, Ammon, and Moab (Neh 13:23, 24). The book of Nehemiah ends with only Nehemiah to guard the law from the people's backsliding (Neh 13:30).

1 Esdras presents an entirely different picture of the restoration period. In it, the mass divorce is followed immediately with the story of the law-reading and then, with the completion of the reading, the book ends. The purified people hear and understand the law and rejoice both because they have been inspired by it and because they have gathered together with their fellows. There is no story of backsliding and no possibility of it because the people have truly understood the law. The picture is one of extreme optimism and relief. Understanding the law has guaranteed its observance. In omitting the entire story of Nehemiah, and ending his story with the law-reading, the author of 1 Esdras emphasizes the power of the Torah alone to safeguard the people.

Balzaretti, C., *The Syriac Version of Ezra-Nehemiah: Manuscripts and Editions, Translation Technique and Its Use in Textual Criticism* (trans. M. Tait; BibOr 51; Rome: Pontifical Biblical Institute, 2013).

Batten, L.W., *A Critical and Exegetical Commentary on the Books of Ezra and Nehemiah* (ICC; Edinburgh: T & T Clark, 1913).

Becking, B., "Ezra's Re-Enactment of the Exile," in *Leading Captivity Captive: 'The Exile' as History and Ideology* (ed. L.L. Grabbe; JSOTSup 278; Sheffield: Sheffield Academic Press, 1998), 40–61.

Blenkinsopp, J., *Ezra-Nehemiah: A Commentary* (OTL; Philadelphia: Westminster Press, 1988).

Charlesworth, J., "Announcing a Dead Sea Scrolls Fragment of Nehemiah," in press; http://foundationjudaismchristianorigins.org/ftp/pages/dead-sea-scrolls/unpub/nehemiah.html.

Curtis, E.L. and A.A. Madsen, *A Critical and Exegetical Commentary on the Books of Chronicles* (ICC; Edinburgh: T & T Clark, 1910).

Driver, S.R., *An Introduction to the Literature of the Old Testament* (Edinburgh: T & T Clark, 1913).

Duggan, M.W., *The Covenant Renewal in Ezra-Nehemiah (Neh 7:72B–10:40): An Exegetical, Literary, and Theological Study* (SBLDS 164; Atlanta: SBL, 2001).

Freedman, D.N., "The Chronicler's Purpose," *CBQ* 23 (1961): 436–42.

Fried, L.S., "A Greek Religious Association in Second Temple Judah? A Comment on Nehemiah 10," *Transeu* 30 (2005): 75–93.

Fried, L.S., "A Silver Coin of Yohanan Hakkôhen," *Transeu* 26 (2003): 65–85, pls. ii–v.

Fried, L.S., "Another Look at 1 Esdras: The Law Triumphant," in *Making a Difference: Essays in Honor of Tamara Cohn Eskenazi* (eds. J.L. Wright, D. Clines, and K. Richards; Hebrew Bible Monographs 49; Sheffield: Sheffield Phoenix Press, 2012), 132–38.

Fried, L.S., *Was 1 Esdras First? An Investigation Into the Priority and Nature of 1 Esdras* (SBLAIL 7; Atlanta: Scholars Press, 2011).

Fried, L.S., "Who Wrote Ezra-Nehemiah and Why Did They?" in *Unity and Disunity in Ezra-Nehemiah: Redaction, Rhetoric, and Reader* (eds. M.J. Boda and P. Redditt; Hebrew Bible Monographs 17; Sheffield: Sheffield Phoenix Press, 2008), 75–97.

Gasquet, F.A. et al. (eds.), *Biblia Sacra iuxta Latinam Vulgatam Versionem* (18 vols.; Rome: Libreria Editrice Vaticana, 1926–1996).

Hanhart, R. (ed.), *Esdrae Liber I* (Septuaginta Vetus Testamentum Graecum 8.1; Göttingen: Vandenhoeck & Ruprecht, 1974).

Hanhart, R. (ed.), *Esdrae Liber II* (Septuaginta Vetus Testamentum Graecum 8.2; Göttingen: Vandenhoeck & Ruprecht, 1993).

Haran, M., "Explaining the Identical Lines at the End of Chronicles and the Beginning of Ezra," *BRev* 2 (1986): 18–20.

Japhet, S., "The Supposed Common Authorship of Chronicles and Ezra-Nehemiah Investigated Anew," *VT* 18 (1968): 330–71.

Kraemer, D., "On the Relationship of the Books of Ezra and Nehemiah," *JSOT* 59 (1993): 73–92.

Marcus, D., *Ezra and Nehemiah* (*BHQ 20; Stuttgart: Deutsche Bibelgesellschaft, 2006).

Min, K.-J., *The Levitical Authorship of Ezra-Nehemiah* (JSOTSup 409; London: T & T Clark, 2004).

Rudolph, W., *Esra und Nehemia samt 3. Esra* (HAT 1.20; Tübingen: Mohr, 1949).

Talshir, D., "A Reinvestigation of the Linguistic Relationship between Chronicles and Ezra-Nehemiah," *VT* 38 (1988): 165–93.

Talshir, Z., *1 Esdras: From Origin to Translation* (SBLSCS 47; Atlanta: SBL, 1999).

Torrey, C.C., *The Composition and Historical Value of Ezra-Nehemiah* (BZAW 2; Giessen: J. Ricker, 1896).

Torrey, C.C., *Ezra Studies* (Chicago: University of Chicago Press, 1910; repr. New York: Ktav, 1970).

Ulrich, E., "117. 4QEzra," in *DJD* XVI: 291–93.

VanderKam, J.C., "Ezra-Nehemiah or Ezra and Nehemiah?" in *Priests, Prophets and Scribes: Essays on the Formation and Heritage of Second Temple Judaism in Honour of Joseph Blenkinsopp* (eds. J.W. Wright, E. Ulrich, and R.P. Carroll; JSOTSup 149; Sheffield: Sheffield Academic Press, 1992), 55–75.

VanderKam, J.C., *From Joshua to Caiaphas: High Priests After the Exile* (Minneapolis: Fortress Press, 2004).

Williamson, H.G.M., "The Composition of Ezra i–vi," *JTS* NS 34 (1983): 1–30.

Williamson, H.G.M., *Ezra, Nehemiah* (WBC 16; Waco: Word Books, 1985).

Williamson, H.G.M., *Israel in the Books of Chronicles* (Cambridge: Cambridge University Press, 1977).

Yeivin, **Introduction*.

Zunz, L., "Dibre Hajamim oder die Bücher der Chronik," in *Die Gottesdienstliche Vorträge der Juden: Historisch Entwickelt* (Berlin: A. Asher, 1832), 13–36.

Lisbeth S. Fried

19.2 Ancient Hebrew-Aramaic Texts

19.2.1 Ancient Manuscript Evidence

Two manuscripts of the book of Ezra-Nehemiah from the Dead Sea Scrolls are published, one coming from the Qumran library and the other being of unknown origin and in private ownership (XNeh). A further fragment with remnants of Neh 2:13–16 is part of the Green collection (DSS F.Neh1).[1]

19.2.1.1 4QEzra (4Q117)

Of 4QEzra, three small and extensively damaged fragments were found at Qumran attesting to remnants of Ezra 4:2–6, 9–11; 5:17–6:5. Although no section of Nehemiah is preserved in 4QEzra, it is likely that the manuscript contained both books for two reasons: 1) Even medieval Masoretic manuscripts regard Ezra and Nehemiah as one book; 2) The earliest witness to the division of Ezra/Nehemiah into two books is Origen, according to Eusebius, *Hist. Eccl.* 6.25.2.

The manuscript was copied in a late Hasmonean book hand that already includes traces of the early Herodian book hand. The manuscript is hence dated paleographically to the middle of the first century B.C.E.[2] The orthography of 4QEzra resembles that of MT. The extensive textual damage to 4QEzra does not allow for a text-typological classification. In sixty-eight preserved or partly preserved words, 4QEzra reads three times with and three times against MT (→ 19.2.2), twice with and four times against LXX (→ 19.3.1), and is once non-aligned.[3] Reading in six cases against 3 Ezra (→ II.7.1), 4QEzra is in no way close to that book.[4]

19.2.1.2 XNeh (X25)

XNeh is a small fragment of a Nehemiah manuscript in private ownership.[5] A previous owner claimed that the fragment was found in Qumran cave 4. Thirteen words or parts of words are preserved from Neh 3:14–15. Although this small amount of text makes a paleographic analysis difficult, the manuscript was most likely written in a Herodian book hand.[6] However, due to the scanty extant remains, XNeh could also preserve a quotation of Neh 3:14–15 in a nonbiblical text, but the fact that Neh 3:14 and 3:15 describe two different building activities in Jerusalem argues against such a quotation. The mere thirteen preserved words prohibit a text-typological and orthographic analysis of XNeh.[7] The spelling כל "all" in line 2 is reminiscent though of the orthography of MT. XNeh reads twice with LXX (→ 19.3.1) against MT (→ 19.2.2),[8] twice with MT against LXX, and once non-aligned.[9]

---

[1] I am indebted to David Trobisch and Emanuel Tov for this information.

[2] Ulrich, "Ezra and Qohelet," 140; Ulrich, "4QEzra," 291.

[3] For the orthography and text of 4QEzra, cf. Ulrich, "Ezra and Qohelet," 140–42; Ulrich, "4QEzra," 291, and Pfann, "Aramaic Text," 129.

[4] Cf. Talshir, "Qumran Fragments," *passim*.

[5] James H. Charlesworth has posted a brief description of this fragments and two photographs at http://foundationjudaismchristianorigins.org/ftp/pages/dead-sea-scrolls/unpub/nehemiah.html (last accessed April 4th 2015). My remarks are based both on Charlesworth's work and the online photograph. For the description of XNeh, see also Lange, *Handbuch*, 523–24.

[6] Charlesworth, "Announcing," points to the first decade of the first century C.E.

[7] Against Charlesworth ("Announcing") who regards XNeh as proto-Masoretic: "Proto-Masoretic with a reading ('and his sons' = ובניו) preserved in the LXX but corrected by a supralinear consonant (= נ) over the Yod (and to replace it) to provide a reading more in line with the so-called MT ('he shall build' = יבננו). If the scribe is not merely influenced by the form in line two, he has edited his text to bring it in line with the MT. It is conceivable, that the scribe was influenced by the movement to make the MT the dominant text type. Most likely this procedure was already evident in the beginning of the first century CE."

[8] One of these readings derives from a supralinear correction that is most likely *prima manu*.

[9] Cf. Charlesworth, "Announcing."

Charlesworth, J.H., "Announcing a Dead Sea Scrolls Fragment of Nehemiah," http://foundationjudaismchristianorigins.org/ftp/pages/dead-sea-scrolls/unpub/nehemiah.html (last accessed April 9th 2015)

Lange, *Handbuch, 523–26.

Pfann, S., "The Aramaic Text and Language of Daniel and Ezra in the Light of some Manuscripts from Qumran," *Textus* 16 (1991): 127–37.

Talshir, Z., "The Qumran Fragments of the Book of Ezra (4QEzra)," *Meghillot* 1 (2003): 213–18 [Hebrew].

Ulrich, E., "117. 4QEzra," *DJD* XVI, 221–27.

Ulrich, E., *BQS, 776–77.

Ulrich, E., "Ezra and Qohelet Manuscripts from Qumran (4QEzra and 4QQoh[a,b])," in *Priests, Prophets and Scribes: Essays on the Formation and Heritage of Second Temple Judaism in Honour of Joseph Blenkinsopp* (ed. E. Ulrich et al.; JSOTSup 149; Sheffield: Sheffield Academic Press, 1992), 139–57.

Armin Lange

19.2.2 Masoretic Texts and Ancient Texts Close to MT

The Masoretes, following ancient Jewish tradition, considered the books of Ezra and Nehemiah as one book and referred to it as the book of Ezra. This was also the Greek tradition, and the same Greek name, Esdras, was given to both books. The division into separate books did not occur until the time of Origen (third century C.E.) and this division was transferred into the Vulgate, where the books are called 1 Esdras (Ezra) and 2 Esdras (Nehemiah). It was not until the fifteenth century that Hebrew manuscripts, and subsequently nearly all modern printed Hebrew editions, followed this practice of dividing the books.[1] However, there are good reasons (linguistic, literary, and thematic) for the argument that the two books were originally separate works, which were brought together by a later compiler, and are now to be read as a single unit.[2]

There are two traditions regarding the place of Ezra–Nehemiah in the Hebrew Bible. The more dominant Babylonian tradition, which is followed by all modern printed editions, places Ezra–Nehemiah immediately before Chronicles, the last book of the Writings. However, the Palestinian tradition, which is found in major Tiberian manuscripts places Chronicles first in the Writings (before Psalms), and places Ezra–Nehemiah last (cf. → 19.1.4). In the Protestant Old Testament (e.g., the *NRSV* version), Ezra–Nehemiah is placed among the Historical Books, after Chronicles and before Esther. In the Roman Catholic Old Testament (e.g., the *Douay-Rheims* version), the books are similarly placed after Chronicles but before Tobit, Judith, and Esther.

The language of Ezra–Nehemiah is late biblical Hebrew, and the text exhibits features that are characteristic of this later language. These include use of the *waw*-consecutive with the cohortative (e.g., וָאֶשְׁלְחָה "and I sent" Ezra 8:16; Neh 6:3), increased use of pronominal suffixes to the verb (e.g., וַיִּתְּנֵם "and he gave them" Ezra 1:7) and of הָיָה with the participle (e.g., הָיוּ אֹמְרִים "they were speaking" Neh 6:19), many Akkadian and Persian loan words (such as אִגֶּרֶת "letter" = Akk. *egirtu*; פַּרְדֵּס "garden" = Pers. *pairidaeza*) and many Aramaisms.[3] Parts of Ezra are written in Aramaic (Ezra 4:8–6:18; 7:11–26), and it has been suggested that originally the entire book of Ezra–Nehemiah was written in Aramaic and subsequently was translated.[4] In support of this theory is the fact that there is no extant Targum for Ezra–Nehemiah.

There are two major Greek witnesses to the Masoretic text of Ezra–Nehemiah. One is the Old Greek (→ 19.3.1), which is a very literal translation in which differences with MT for the most part concern minor grammatical matters such as variations in use of the ו-conjunction, singular and plural, and different suffixes. The Old Greek follows MT very closely except in Nehemiah 11 where, for vv. 16–35, it has a very much abbreviated text. The second major Greek witness to MT is that known as 1 Esdras

---

[1] Blenkinsopp, *Ezra-Nehemiah*, 38.
[2] Kraemer, "Relationship," 73–92.
[3] Naveh and Greenfield, "Hebrew and Aramaic in the Persian Period."
[4] Marcus, "Is the Book of Nehemiah a Translation from Aramaic?"

(→ 11.7.1.2), which unlike the Old Greek is not a simple translation of Ezra–Nehemiah. Rather it presents material paralleling parts of Chronicles–Ezra–Nehemiah. The relationship of 1 Esdras with these parallel parts of MT has been much debated (→ 19.3.1; → 19.1). One opinion, which is represented in the new critical edition of *BHQ*, where 1 Esdras is cited as a constant witness, is that 1 Esdras is a later revision of MT. Another opinion is that 1 Esdras reflects a Hebrew *Vorlage* earlier than MT.[5] 1 Esdras translates the entire book of Ezra and a small section of Nehemiah with two striking differences in order. The first is that MT-Ezra 4:6–24 is placed between chapters one and two, and the second is that the Ezra material from Nehemiah (7:72–8:13) is attached directly to Ezra 10.

19.2.2.1 Proto-Masoretic Evidence
19.2.2.1.1 Book of Ezra

Three fragments from the book of Ezra (4QEzra; → 19.2.1.1) were found in Cave 4 at Qumran and were published by Ulrich in 1992 and again in 2000.[6] The fragments contain parts of the text of Ezra 4:2–6; 9–11; and 5:17–6:5, and exhibit two orthographic and two grammatical variants from MT. The two orthographic variants, involving interchanges of א and ה, are at Ezra 4:10 where 4QEzra reads נהרא for MT's נַהֲרָה "the river," and at Ezra 6:2 where 4QEzra reads מדינתא for מְדִינְתָּה "the province." The two grammatical variants concerning singular and plural forms of verbs are at Ezra 6:1 where 4QEzra reads a singular ובקר "he searched" for וּבַקַּרוּ "they searched," and at Ezra 6:5 where 4QEzra reads a plural והיבלו "they brought" for וְהֵיבֵל "he brought." Apart from these minor variations, 4QEzra generally reflects MT and, where extant, agrees with it in those cases where other witnesses have different readings. For example, at Ezra 5:17, 4QEzra agrees with MT (and LXX and the Peshitta) against 1 Esdras and the Vulgate (both omit) in reading דָּךְ "this"; at Ezra 6:3, 4QEzra agrees with MT (and LXX) against

---

[5] Schenker, "Relation," 218–48; Böhler, "Relationship," 35–50.
[6] Ulrich, "Ezra and Qohelet Manuscripts from Qumran"; Ulrich, "4QEzra."

1 Esdras, the Vulgate, and the Peshitta (all omit) in reading בַּיְתָא "house"; and at Ezra 6:5, 4QEzra agrees with MT (and LXX, Vulgate, and Peshitta) against 1 Esdras (ἐκεῖ "there") in reading בְּבֵית אֱלָהָא "in the House of God."

19.2.2.1.2 Book of Nehemiah

A small fragment from the book of Nehemiah (XNeh; → 19.2.1.2) was also found in Cave 4 at Qumran, and was provisionally published by Charlesworth in 2008.[7] The fragment contains parts of Neh 3:14–15, and exhibits one major and two minor variants from MT. The major variation is at Neh 3:14 where the fragment, in agreement with LXX (καὶ υἱοὶ αὐτοῦ), has ובניו "and his sons" for MT's יִבְנֶנּוּ "he will rebuild it." It is noteworthy that in the fragment, a *nun* has been written on top of the *yod*, an indication that a second hand was endeavoring to bring the fragment in line with MT. The minor variations are firstly at Neh 3:15 where the fragment, in agreement with both the Vulgate (*Sellum*) and Peshitta, reads שלום "Shallum" for MT's שַׁלּוּן "Shallun," and secondly in the same verse, where it writes MT's defective form מַנְעֻלָיו plene as מנעוליו "its bolts." Apart from these minor variations, XNeh reflects MT and, where extant, agrees with it in those cases where other witnesses have different readings. Thus, at Neh 3:14, XNeh agrees with MT (and the Vulgate) reading a singular form וַיַּעֲמִיד "and he set up" against LXX and the Peshitta, which read the form as a plural. At Neh 3:15, XNeh agrees with MT (Vulgate and Peshitta) in reading מנעוליו "its bolts," whereas LXX omits this word.

19.2.2.2 Masoretic Text

The Masoretic text of Ezra–Nehemiah has been transmitted most reliably in manuscripts and printed editions. Very few errors have crept into the text, but some scribal errors have been preserved. These are cases such as at Ezra 2:25 where, instead of the familiar town קִרְיַת יְעָרִים "Kiriath-jearim," an otherwise unknown קִרְיַת עָרִים "Kiriath-arim" is written, and at Neh 9:17, the familiar phrase

---

[7] Charlesworth, "Announcing a Dead Sea Scrolls Fragment of Nehemiah."

19.2.2 MASORETIC TEXTS AND ANCIENT TEXTS CLOSE TO MT

וְרַב חֶסֶד "abounding in faithfulness" should have been read instead of MT's וְרַב וְחֶסֶד "and abounding and faithful." Similarly, at Ezra 10:32, an abnormal pointing of בְּנְמִן occurs for the common name בִּנְיָמִן "Benjamin," and an anomalous הָשְׁפוֹת occurs at Neh 3:13 instead of the correct form הָאַשְׁפּוֹת "the ashes." In Ezra 10:16, MT's reading לְדָרְיוֹשׁ "to Darius" makes no sense in the context, and appears to be a copyist error for לִדְרוֹשׁ "to examine," which is the underlying form that all the versions have used in their translations. Lastly, at Neh 7:67, a comparison with Ezra 2:65–66, and the partial support of LXX, shows that it is most likely that MT has suffered a textual dislocation involving the line beginning and ending with מָאתַיִם "two hundred." The scribe's eye wandered from the first מָאתַיִם to the second resulting in a homoioarcton, thus omitting seven words that include the listing for horses and mules.[8]

19.2.2.2.1 Tiberian Witnesses

The text of Ezra–Nehemiah has been preserved fully in the Leningrad Codex (M^L), and almost two-thirds of it is preserved in another early major Tiberian manuscript, Sassoon 1053 (MT^S1). Unfortunately, the book has not survived in the Aleppo Codex (MT^A). MT^L has been used as the base for the new critical edition of *BHQ, and the two Tiberian witnesses that have been collated with MT^L are MT^S1 and Cambridge ms Add. 1753 (MT^Y). The differences among the three Tiberian manuscripts are primarily orthographic such as:

- variation of consonants, e.g., Ezra 7:21, כָּהֲנָא "the priest" (MT^S1 and MT^Y)/כָּהֲנָה (MT^L)
- plene and defective writing, e.g., Ezra 10:32, בִּנְיָמִין "Benjamin" (MT^S1 and MT^Y)/בִּנְמִן (MT^L)
- variation of vowels, e.g., Ezra 6:8, תַעַבְדוּן "you shall do" (MT^Y)/תַּעַבְדוּן (MT^L).

At Neh 2:13, both MT^S1 and MT^Y read הַגַּיְא "valley" for הַגַּיְא (MT^L), and at Neh 1:6, MT^Y reads פְּתוּחוֹת "open" for the anomalous פְּתֻחוֹת in MT^S1 and MT^L. The only significant variant between the three Tiberian manuscripts is at Ezra 8:12, where MT^Y reads וְעֶשְׂרִים "and twenty" and MT^L reads וַעֲשָׂרָה "and ten."

There are fifty-two cases of *Ketiv* and *Qere* in Ezra–Nehemiah of MT^L and fourteen of *yattîr* (ו, א, and י), some of which *BHS takes as *Ketiv/Qere* cases. The *Ketiv* and *Qere* occurrences deal with the usual topics normally found for these notes such as different division of words, interchanges of consonants and vowels, metathesis of letters, and correction of errors. About a third of the cases involve proper names (e.g., זבוד/זַכּוּר "Zaccur/Zabbud" Ezra 8:14, and זבי/זַכַּי "Zaccai/Zabbai" Neh 3:20) and almost another third are purely orthographic (e.g., Ezra 5:15 אלה/אֵל "these" [Aramaic] and Neh 4:9 ונשוב/וַנָּשָׁב "we returned"). The most significant variants are those involving singulars and plurals (e.g., ויעל/וַיַּעֲלוּ "they/he went up" [Ezra 3:3] and ויעמיד/וְיַעֲמִידוּ "they/he set up" [Neh 3:13]), and cases such as ואוצאה/וָאֲצַוֶּה "I commanded/I brought out" (Ezra 8:17), עולם/עֵילָם "Elam/eternity" (Ezra 10:2), and ויאמר/וָאוֹמַר "I said/he said" (Neh 5:9; 7:3). Some cases of a *Qere* correcting an incorrect division of words are at Ezra 4:12 where the *Ketiv* ושורי אשכללו is corrected to וְשׁוּרַיָּא שַׁכְלִלוּ "they are completing the walls," and at Neh 2:13 where the *Ketiv* המפרוצים is corrected to הֵם פְּרוּצִים "they were breached." Some cases of a *Qere* correcting an error in the *Ketiv* are at Neh 1:9, where the *Ketiv* והבואתים is corrected by the *Qere* וַהֲבִיאוֹתִים "and I will bring them," and at Neh 4:7, where the *Ketiv* בצחחיים is corrected by the *Qere* to בַּצְּחִיחִים "bare rocks." Invariably, whenever a preference can be made between the *Ketiv* and the *Qere* it is for the reading of the *Qere* except at Ezra 4:9 where the *Ketiv* form דהוא "that is" is preferred over the *Qere* דֶּהָיֵא "Dehavites." The other manuscripts display a few differences in *Ketiv* and *Qere* forms from those in MT^L. Some forms taken as *yattîr* cases in MT^L are treated as *Ketiv/Qere* cases in MT^S1 and MT^Y. At Ezra 7:18, both עֲלָיִךְ "to you" and אַחֶיךָ "your brothers" are taken as *Ketiv/Qere* cases by MT^S1, but MT^Y and MT^L treats these forms as *yattîr* י. At Neh 9:17, both MT^S1 and MT^Y take וְחֶסֶד in the phrase וְרַב וְחֶסֶד "and abounding and faithful" as a *Ketiv/Qere* case whereas MT^L takes it as a *yattîr* ו.

---

[8] Barthélemy, *Critique textuelle 1992*, ccxxxiii–iv.

19.2.2.2.2 Masorah of MT^L

The MT^L text of Ezra–Nehemiah is embellished with a full Masorah parva (MasP), Masorah magna, and a very brief Masorah finalis. Of the hundreds of Masoretic notes in MT^L, there are over sixty cases where the Masoretic notes do not conform to the text of MT^L.[9] These notes mostly involve cases where the number of occurrences in the MasP does not correspond to the number of occurrences in MT^L. For example, at Ezra 1:4, the MasP note states that there are two occurrences of לְבֵית הָאֱלֹהִים "for the house of God" whereas MT^L actually has three occurrences of this lemma. Another type of difference is where the MasP states that a word is written plene whereas MT^L writes it defective, or the reverse. For example, at Neh 7:37, the MasP states that the form וְאֹנוֹ "and Ono" occurs defective. However, MT^L writes this lemma plene. At Neh 13:5, the MasP states that the form וְהַשֹּׁעֲרִים "and the gatekeepers" occurs plene, but MT^L writes this lemma defective. On one occasion (at Neh 12:44 on לָאוֹצָרוֹת "for the treasuries"), the MasP suggests a variant reading that turns out to be exactly the same as the form written in MT^L.

Barthélemy, *Critique textuelle 1992.
Blenkinsopp, J., *Ezra-Nehemiah* (OTL; Philadelphia: Westminster, 1988).
Böhler, D., "On the Relationship between Textual and Literary Criticism: The Two Recensions of the Book of Ezra-Neh (MT) and 1 Esdras (LXX)," in Schenker, *Earliest Text, 35–50.
Charlesworth, J.H., "Announcing a Dead Sea Scrolls Fragment of Nehemiah," http://www.ijco.org/?categoryId=28681 (accessed 04/23/2012).
Kraemer, D., "On the Relationship of the Books of Ezra and Nehemiah," *JSOT* 59 (1993): 73–92.
Lange, *Handbuch, 523–29.
Marcus, D., "Is the Book of Nehemiah a Translation from Aramaic?" in *Boundaries of the Ancient Near Eastern World: A Tribute to Cyrus H. Gordon* (eds. M. Lubetski et al; JSOTSup 273; Sheffield: Sheffield Academic Press, 1997), 103–10.
Marcus, D., *BHQ, Part 20: Ezra and Nehemiah (2006).
Naveh, J. and J.C. Greenfield, "Hebrew and Aramaic in the Persian Period," in *The Cambridge History of Judaism*, Vol. 1: *Introduction; The Persian Period* (eds. W.D. Davies and L. Finkelstein; Cambridge: Cambridge University Press, 1984), 115–29.
Schenker, A., "La Relation d'Esdras A* au texte massorétique d'Esdras-Néhémie," in *Tradition of the Text: Studies offered to Dominique Barthélemy in Celebration of his 70th Birthday* (eds. G.J. Norton and S. Pisano; OBO 109; Göttingen: Vandenhoeck & Ruprecht, 1991), 218–48.
Ulrich, E., "Ezra and Qohelet Manuscripts from Qumran (4QEzra and 4QQoh^{a,b})," in *Priests, Prophets and Scribes: Essays on the Formation and Heritage of Second Temple Judaism in Honour of Joseph Blenkinsopp* (ed. E. Ulrich et al.; JSOTSup 149; Sheffield: Sheffield Academic Press, 1992), 139–57.
Ulrich, E., "**117.** 4QEzra," *DJD* XVI (2000): 291–93.

David Marcus

---

[9] Marcus, *Ezra and Nehemiah*, 6*.

19.3 Primary Translations

19.3.1 Septuagint

The text of the book of Ezra–Nehemiah is fairly well preserved, as acknowledged by most commentators.[1] The book suffered from the customary textual mishaps characteristic of transmission processes, but on the whole it does not present a complicated process of textual transmission, in contradistinction to its rather complicated composition process. The ancient translations offer a moderate number of variants, some of which pave the way to the lost original text. As usually found, the most significant textual evidence is located in the Septuagint, in our case in both the apocryphal book of First Esdras (1 Esdras; → II.7.1.2), which contains an intriguing translation of 2 Chronicles 35–36; Ezra 1–10; and Nehemiah 8, and which in the straightforward literal Greek translation is labeled Second Esdras (2 Esdras). The Vulgate (→ 19.3.6) and Peshitta (→ 19.3.3), as in other books, offer their limited share of evidence, sometimes related to the Greek tradition. There is no Targum to this book. At Qumran, remnants of one scroll of Ezra survived (4QEzra, frgs. 1–3), whose affiliation with MT is clear.[2] This article focuses on 2 Esdras, its milieu, translation technique, and *Vorlage*, followed by a few remarks on the contribution of 1 Esdras and 4QEzra to the textual history of the book.

19.3.1.1 2 Esdras

2 Esdras comprises twenty-three chapters of the combined books of Ezra and Nehemiah and is placed in the LXX corpus (→ 1.3.1.1) at the close of the historical books. Besides its "external" testimony testifying that Ezra–Nehemiah was one continuous book, as perceived by the Masoretes, 2 Esdras makes no contribution whatsoever to the complicated literary-critical problems that characterize the composition process of this book.

19.3.1.2 Milieu of the Translator

Since the turn of the nineteenth century,[3] it has become customary to attribute 2 Esdras to Theodotion even though it is found within the canon of the "Septuagint" (just as Ecclesiastes is considered the work of Aquilas [→ 13–17.1.1.3]). It was said to be a revision, intended to bring the Old Greek closer to the established Hebrew/Aramaic text. It was also argued that the translation preserved in 1 Esdras (→ II.7.1.2) is in fact the Old Greek version of Ezra–Nehemiah, while 2 Esdras is a revision of it. At the same time, the attribution of this translation to Theodotion became increasingly doubtful; in fact, even Th-Dan was doubted to be Theodotion's work. On the other hand, a different scenario emerged for 2 Esdras – initiated by Barthélemy's *Devanciers* – that placed it in a different milieu, that of the *kaige*-Th group.

While the first mentioning of 2 Esdras is in Origen's writings, setting the *ante quem* date to the middle of the third century C.E., the fact that this translation was included in the Hexapla (→ 19.3.4; attested by the Syro-Hexapla [→ 19.4.4]) suggests that it had long been part of the established Greek tradition. Janz' thorough investigation of the language of 2 Esdras[4] places its linguistic usage and style close to the translations of books such as Ruth (→ 13–17.1.1.1), Canticles (→ 13–17.1.1.2), parts of Kingdoms (→ 5.4; → 5.5), and Th-Dan (→ 18.3.1; → 18.3.2). This affiliation would turn 2 Esdras into a member of the *kaige*-Th group, and would point to a much earlier date, the second/first century B.C.E. Janz offers all the relevant bibliographical references to the history of the problem, and presents ample relevant linguistic data for the assumption

---

[1] E.g., Bewer, *Ezra*, 1.
[2] For a different view, see → 19.2.1.1.

[3] H.H. Howorth, The True Septuagint Version of Chronicles-Ezra-Nehemiah, The Academy 44 (1893): 73–74; C.C. Torrey, *The Composition and Historical Value of Ezra-Nehemiah* (BZAW 2; Giessen: J. Ricker, 1896); C.C. Torrey, *Ezra Studies* (Chicago: University of Chicago Press, 1910; repr. New York: Ktav, 1970); Thackeray, *Grammar*, 13–14.
[4] Janz, *Deuxième Livre d'Esdras*.

that 2 Esdras is a marginal member of the *kaige*-Th group (→ 1.3.2.1).[5]

19.3.1.3 Translation Technique

The first feature that strikes the user of 2 Esdras is its utter literalism, at the expense of a decent target language. Thackeray divides the books of the Septuagint, from the point of view of style, into three groups. On the one side, he places the Pentateuch with its "fairly high level of style (for κοινή Greek), combined with faithfulness to the original, rarely degenerating into literalism," while at the other extreme stand the LXX[B] text of Judges and Ruth, parts of the books of Kingdoms (later described as the *kaige*-Th Recension, → 1.3.2.1), and 2 Esdras (as well as the Psalter), "in which we see the beginnings of the tendency towards pedantic literalism, which ended in the second century A.D. in the barbarous 'version' of Aquila."[6] It would seem that a detailed survey of the style of 2 Esdras is bound to place it within this "literal" group at the very end of the scale, quite close to a perfect literal translator. His strict literalism becomes immediately apparent; each and every Hebrew component finds its counterpart in the translation: every article, suffix, prefix, pronoun, and conjunction is presented in the same sequence as in MT. For example, in the following two verses, chosen at random, the first, Ezra 1:2, is as literal as can be:

כֹּה = οὕτως; אָמַר = εἶπεν; כֹּרֶשׁ = Κῦρος; מֶלֶךְ = βασιλεὺς; פָּרַס = Περσῶν; כֹּל = Πάσας; מַמְלְכוֹת = τὰς βασιλείας; הָ/אָרֶץ = τῆς γῆς; נָתַן = ἔδωκέν; לִ/י = μοι; יְהוָה = κύριος; אֱלֹהֵי = ὁ θεός; הַ/שָּׁמָיִם = τοῦ οὐρανοῦ; וְ/הוּא = καὶ αὐτός; פָּקַד = ἐπεσκέψατο; עָלַ/י = ἐπ᾿ ἐμὲ; לִ/בְנוֹת = τοῦ οἰκοδομῆσαι; לוֹ = αὐτῷ; בַיִת = οἶκον; בִּ/ירוּשָׁלִַם = ἐν Ιερουσαλημ; אֲשֶׁר = τῇ; בִּ/יהוּדָה = ἐν τῇ Ιουδαίᾳ.

"Thus says King Cyrus of Persia: The LORD, the God of heaven, has given me all the kingdoms of the earth, and he has charged me to build him a house at Jerusalem in Judah" (*NRSV*) = "Thus says Cyrus, the king of the Persians: the Lord, the God of heaven, has given me all the kingdoms of the earth, and he himself has visited upon me to build himself a house in Ierousalem, which is in Judea" (*NETS*).

The second verse, Ezra 9:11, has a few divergent components (marked in italics) that exemplify the minor degree of change exhibited by this translation:

אֲשֶׁר = ἃς; צִוִּיתָ = ἔδωκας ἡμῖν; בְּ/יַד = ἐν χειρὶ; עֲבָדֶי/ךָ = δούλων σου; הַ/נְּבִיאִים = τῶν προφητῶν; לֵ/אמֹר = λέγων; הָ/אָרֶץ = Ἡ γῆ; אֲשֶׁר אַתֶּם = εἰς ἥν; בָּאִים = εἰσπορεύεσθε; לְ/רִשְׁתָּ/הּ = κληρονομῆσαι αὐτήν; אֶרֶץ = γῆ; נִדָּה = μετακινουμένη; הִיא = ἐστὶν; בְּ/נִדַּת = ἐν μετακινήσει; עַמֵּי = λαῶν; הָ/אֲרָצוֹת = τῶν ἐθνῶν; בְּ/תוֹעֲבֹתֵי/הֶם = ἐν μακρύμμασιν αὐτῶν; אֲשֶׁר = ὧν; מִלְאוּ/הָ = ἔπλησαν αὐτὴν; מִ/פֶּה = ἀπὸ στόματος; אֶל = ἐπί; פֶּה = στόμα; בְּ/טֻמְאָתָ/ם = ἐν ἀκαθαρσίαις αὐτῶν.

"which you commanded by your servants the prophets, saying, The land that you are entering to possess is a land unclean with the pollutions of the peoples of the lands, with their abominations. They have filled it from end to end with their uncleanness" (*NRSV*) = "which *you gave us* by the hand of your slaves the prophets, saying, The land that you are entering to possess, it is a land undergoing change by the changing of the peoples of the nations, with their things put far away, who they have filled it from mouth *to* mouth with their impurities" (*NETS*)

While צִוִּיתָ "you commanded" = ἔδωκας ἡμῖν "you gave us" may well go back to a different *Vorlage* (נתת לנו), as may אֶל "to" = ἐπί (עַל "upon"), it is possible that the syntactic reformulation אֲשֶׁר אַתֶּם "that you" = εἰς ἥν "into that" is by the translator.

Only seldom do we encounter a case in which we would rather assume that the translator tries to make sense of a troubled text.

Such is the vague ending of the separation at the end of Ezra (10:44). MT reads וְיֵשׁ מֵהֶם נָשִׁים וַיָּשִׂימוּ בָנִים "among whom were some women who had borne children"; LXX reads instead καὶ ἐγέννησαν ἐξ αὐτῶν υἱούς "and had begotten sons of them"; given that the Hebrew text is awkward, it is not impossible that the Greek translator came to the rescue and offered a simple paraphrase. It may, however, also go back to a different *Vorlage* (either: וישימו מהם בנים, or a completely different text: וילידו מהם בנים). 1 Esd 9:36 offers a clear-cut ending: καὶ ἀπέλυσαν

---

[5] Janz, *Deuxième Livre d'Esdras*, 150–64.
[6] Thackeray, *Grammar*, 9.

αὐτὰς σὺν τέκνοις "and they put them away with their children." Adopting a text such as suggested in 1 Esdras would mean introducing the scenario of one book into another, whose design is different.

One facet of this literalness is the tendency to transliterate terms whose meaning was probably unknown to the translator: נְתִינִים "temple servants" (*passim* in Ezra–Nehemiah, 13 times); כְּפוֹרֵי "bowls" (Ezra 1:10); עַבְדֵי שְׁלֹמֹה "servants of Solomon" (Ezra 2:55); בְּשַׁעַר־הַגַּיְא לַיְלָה "by the valley gate at night" (Neh 2:13); וְאַדִּירֵיהֶם "but their nobles" (Neh 3:5); תַּנּוּרִים "ovens" (Neh 3:11); בֵּית הַגִּבֹּרִים "the house of the warriors" Neh (3:16); בֵּית אֶלְיָשִׁיב "the house of Eliashib" (Neh 3:20); הַכִּכָּר "the surrounding area" (Neh 3:22); הַמִּפְקָד "the Muster" (Neh 3:31); בִּירָה "citadel" (Neh 7:2).

The extreme literalness of this translator influences our judgment of the quality of his testimony regarding his *Vorlage*. While complete literalness does not exist, we have to consider any difference between the Greek and the Hebrew as a possible indication of a different *Vorlage*.

19.3.1.4 *Vorlage* of 2 Esdras

The *Vorlage* of 2 Esdras was very similar to MT (→ 19.2.2). The evidence does not allow for a different text form, let alone a different edition. 2 Esdras displays a shorter text in several lists. One major surprising discrepancy is found in Neh 11:15–35, where the text is substantially shorter (vv. 16, 20–21, 28–29, 32–35 are completely missing, together with large parts of vv. 15, 17–18, 23, 25–27, 30–31). Other lists in Nehemiah also hold shorter texts (Neh 3:7, possibly through *homoioarcton* ועל ידם/(ו)על ידו "and next to them/and next to him"; Neh 8:4 [only in LXX^B]; 8:7; 10:11 [LXX^B]; 12:3–7; and many names in Neh 12:14–42 [mainly in LXX^B]).

Besides the lists, there are a few other cases of a shorter text in 2 Esdras, e.g., 2 Esd 3:37b–38, in LXX^B. It would seem that such omissions originated in the scribe's negligence that is characteristic of LXX^B but is also detectable in LXX^A.[7]

Bewer warns against the tendency to correct MT, based on corrupted readings in the versions, especially in numbers and names.[8]

Rudolph mentions some twenty-five variants (some of which appear only in LXX^A or LXX^L) that may be considered as preserving older readings, compared with MT. Three examples follow, not necessarily unequivocal.[9]

1) MT-Ezra 6:4 reads: נִדְבָּכִין דִּי־אֶבֶן גְּלָל תְּלָתָא וְנִדְבָּךְ דִּי־אָע חֲדַת "three courses of great stones and a course of *new* timber"; the equivalent in 2 Esdras of the last word is εἷς probably reflecting חדא "one," which is more appropriate. Note that 1 Esdras has a doublet: καινοῦ ἑνός reflecting both חדת "new" and חדא "one."

2) In MT-Ezra 10:25, the name מַלְכִּיָּה "Malchija" occurs twice, while 2 Esdras has a different name for its second occurrence: Ασαβια "Hasabia," similarly 1 Esdras Ασιβιας "Hasabias," possibly reflecting חשביה "Hashabiah."

3) MT-Ezra 7:25 reads: מֶנִי שָׁפְטִין וְדַיָּנִין "appoint magistrates and judges." Rudolph[10] argues that שָׁפְטִין and דַּיָּנִין are tautological, and, besides, שפט "to judge" is not an Aramaic verb. He resorts to evidence in 2 Esdras, where κατάστησον γραμματεῖς καὶ κριτάς "appoint magistrates[11] and judges" seems to reflect a title of a different functionary, possibly ספרין "officials" (a meaning suggested by ספרי מדינתא "officials of the province" in Cowley 17:1, 6, 8).[12] We note, however, that while γραμματεῖς is the regular equivalent of סופר in 2 Esdras (and elsewhere), it also renders שטרים (throughout the Torah and in Joshua and Chronicles, where it renders both סופר "scribe" and שוטר "magistrate," and see 1 Chr 23:4 ושטרים/καὶ γραμματεῖς καὶ κριταί "magistrates and judges"). We tend to keep MT, tautological or not; the use of שפט "to judge" in Aramaic has

---

[7] On the whole, there is not enough evidence to substantiate the priority of either LXX^B or LXX^A; Bewer, *Ezra*, 5; Rudolph, *Esra und Nehemia*, xx.

[8] Bewer, *Ezra*, 3–4.
[9] Rudolph, *Esra und Nehemia*, xx.
[10] Rudolph, *Esra und Nehemia*, ad loc.
[11] Not "scribes" as in *NETS!
[12] A.E. Cowley, *Aramaic Papyri of the Fifth Century B.C.* (Oxford: Clarendon Press, 1923).

been explained as a Hebraism, but it is used elsewhere in Aramaic.[13]

On the whole, the variants are random and not too overwhelming. They do not add up to characterize this text in any way; therefore LXX-2 Esdras must be a representative of a text of the same type as MT (→ 19.2.2).

19.3.1.5 Evidence of 1 Esdras

In spite of its noncanonical status, 1 Esdras (→ II.7.1) is nevertheless a textual witness of the canonical books since it contains – in 1 Esdras 1–2 and 5–9 – a straightforward translation into Greek of 2 Chronicles 35–36; Ezra 1–10; and Nehemiah 8 immediately following Ezra. In terms of literary criticism, 1 Esdras is a later elaboration of a composition similar to the canonical books. Its secondary nature compared with the canonical book is visible first of all in the interpolation of the story of the three youths debating over ἕνα λόγον ὃς ὑπερισχύσει "one thing which will prove superior" (1 Esdras 3–4), which entailed changes in the course of events borrowed from the canonical book.

In terms of textual transmission, our survey of the Hebrew-Aramaic text underlying 1 Esdras[14] depicts the separate development of the two texts after they departed from one another. The discrepancy between them is not the result of a defined line of revision in one text or the other, but rather, it results from a fluid growth of both texts. Ulrich's comment that "the readings in 1 Esdras, when seen as a whole, demonstrate a consistent pattern which transcends the level of individual variants and constitutes an intentionally different form of the work"[15] is overstated since it applies only to a thin layer of variants, which are indeed part of the composition process that yielded 1 Esdras. At any rate, 1 Esdras is an important witness to the development of the text of Ezra–Nehemiah.

The translation technique in 1 Esdras is noteworthy.[16] It belongs at the very extreme end of nonliteral translations; were it not for the existence of the Hebrew text, 1 Esdras easily could have been mistaken for a work written in Greek, rather than a translation. Its vocabulary is quite similar to LXX-Dan (→ 18.3.1) and to other translations that Thackeray would classify as "paraphrases and free renderings."[17] However, in spite of the translator's concern for good Greek at the expense of an accurate rendering of his *Vorlage*, he is nevertheless faithful enough to his source to allow us recover his *Vorlage*, with the indispensable help of MT (→ 19.2.2).

19.3.1.6 Relationship between 1 Esdras and 2 Esdras

The two translations preserved for the same parts of the book in 1 and 2 Esdras are extremely different. Only seldom does there seem to be a real dependence between them. Hanhart summarizes the relationship between 1 Esdras and 2 Esdras as following: several similarities in equivalents and patterns of translation between the two texts suggest a slight dependence of the younger translation, 2 Esdras, on the older one, 1 Esdras. Basically, however, the two translations are so different from each other that similarities that occur only in part of the textual witnesses – mainly the Lucianic recension in 1 Esdras (→ II.7.1.2) and the (Hexaplaric-)Lucianic text in 2 Esdras (→ 19.3.4; → 19.3.5) – must belong to a secondary layer in the history of the text.[18] Moreover, quite a few of these similarities could be coincidental or go back to a *Vorlage* that differs from MT.[19] On the whole, the type of relationship between 1 Esdras and 2 Esdras resembles that between LXX-Dan (→ 18.3.1) and Th-Dan (→ 18.3.2).

19.3.1.7 Evidence of 4QEzra

Ezra–Nehemiah is attested at Qumran in one fragmentary scroll only, 4QEzra frag. 1–3 (→ 19.2.1.1). The prepublication by Ulrich discusses at length the

---

[13] Cowley, *Aramaic Papyri*, 104.
[14] Talshir, *I Esdras*, 111–79.
[15] Ulrich, "Ezra," 153.

[16] Talshir, *I Esdras*, 181–247.
[17] Thackeray, *Grammar*, 13.
[18] Hanhart, *Text und Textgeschichte*, 7.
[19] Hanhart, *Text und Textgeschichte*, 7–11.

problem of "variant editions of biblical books and passages."[20] However, 4QEzra offers no additional information regarding the relationship between 1 Esdras (→ 11.7.1), on the one hand, and the canonical books supported by 2 Esdras, on the other. The importance of 4QEzra is merely in its support of MT.[21] This support is true in more than one respect:

1. The more substantial text, 4QEzra frg. 3, runs parallel to Ezra 5:17–6:5 (1 Esd 6:20–25). It displays only some occasional readings that agree with MT-Ezra/2 Esdras, distinct from 1 Esdras.
2. Frag. 2 parallels Ezra 4:9–11 (1 Esd 2:15–16). MT is well known for its cluttered structure, which it shares with 2 Esdras, while 1 Esdras has a much shorter and articulate introduction to one official letter. The scroll attests to the literary design of MT.
3. We are very fortunate to have 4QEzra frg. 1 since it reflects the canonical arrangement of the book. Frag. 1 parallels Ezra 4:2–6 (1 Esd 5:66–70). While this fragment displays only a few lines in which only a handful of words are preserved, it covers exactly the juncture of materials (lines 5–6), which constitutes one of the main differences between the two redactions. The Qumran text agrees with the sequence of events in MT, awkward as it is, which proceeds directly from the interference of "the adversaries of Judah and Benjamin" in the time of Cyrus that caused the postponing of the work "until the reign of Darius" (Ezra 4:1–5; 4QEzra 1 1–5), to the complaint sent to Xerxes (Ezra 4:6; 4QEzra 1 6). 1 Esdras, on the other hand, not only forgoes Ezra 4:6 altogether, but does not share the same sequence of events: in 1 Esdras, the complaint to Artaxerxes is introduced immediately after Cyrus' edict, creating another puzzling sequence of events.

The Qumran text, then, corroborates the canonical text not only in random variants but also in its literary design and in the structure of Ezra-Nehemiah/2 Esdras versus 1 Esdras.

19.3.1.8 Tools

Hanhart prepared a meticulous critical edition of 2 Esdras in the Göttingen Septuagint series,[22] accompanied by a comprehensive volume on the text history.[23] While this is an eclectic edition, Hanhart is quite conservative, following mainly manuscript LXX^B, from time to time turning to other manuscripts, and rarely including a conjecture. Only seldom do we disagree with his decisions.

The critical edition of Ezra–Nehemiah within the *BHS was prepared by Rudolph in 1976 and within the *BHQ by Marcus in 2006.

The most helpful and methodologically sound text-critical commentaries on Ezra–Nehemiah are by Bewer (1922)[24] and Rudolph (1949),[25] and for 1 Esdras, the present writer's comprehensive commentary of 2001,[26] which includes a reconstruction of its *Vorlage* and constant reference to 2 Esdras. Many studies were dedicated to the relationship between the canonical books of Ezra–Nehemiah and 1 Esdras, without special reference to 2 Esdras since it mirrors the canonical books.

Bewer, J.A., *Der Text des Buches Ezra* (FRLANT 31; Göttingen: Vandenhoeck & Ruprecht, 1922).
Brooke–McLean–Thackeray, *The Old Testament in Greek*, Vol. 2.4: *1 Esdras, Ezra-Nehemiah* (Cambridge: Cambridge University Press, 1935).
Hanhart, R., *Esdrae liber II* (Septuaginta Vetus Testamentum Graecum 8.2; Göttingen: Vandenhoeck & Ruprecht, 1993).
Hanhart, R., *Text und Textgeschichte des 2. Esrabuches* (MSU 25; Göttingen: Vandenhoeck & Ruprecht, 2003).
Janz, T., *Deuxième Livre d'Esdras: Traduction du texte grec de la Septante: Introduction et notes* (*Bible d'Alexandrie 11.2; Paris: Cerf, 2010).
Rudolph, W., *Esra und Nehemia samt 3. Esra* (HAT 1.20; Tübingen: Mohr, 1949).

---

[20] Ulrich, "Ezra," 153–57.
[21] Talshir, "Synchronic Approaches."
[22] Hanhart, *Esdrae liber II*.
[23] Hanhart, *Text und Textgeschichte*.
[24] Bewer, *Der Text des Buches Ezra*.
[25] Rudolph, *Esra und Nehemia*.
[26] Talshir, *1 Esdras*.

Talshir, Z., *1 Esdras: From Origin to Translation* (ed. B. Taylor; SBLSCS 47; Atlanta: Scholars Press, 1999).

Talshir, Z., *First Esdras: A Text Critical Commentary* (Chs. 3–4 in collaboration with D. Talshir; SBLSCS 50; Atlanta: SBL, 2001).

Talshir, Z., "Synchronic Approaches with Diachronic Consequences in the Study of Parallel Redactions," in *Yahwism after the Exile: Perspectives on Israelite Religion in the Persian Era: Papers Read at the First Meeting of the European Association for Biblical Studies, Utrecht, 6–9 August 2000* (eds. R. Alberz and B. Becking; Studies in Theology and Religion 5; Utrecht: Van Gorcum, 2003), 199–218.

Thackeray, **Grammar*.

Ulrich, E., "Ezra and Qohelet Manuscripts from Qumran (4QEzra and 4QQoh[a,b])," in *Priests, Prophets and Scribes: Essays on the Formation and Heritage of Second Temple Judaism in Honour of Joseph Blenkinsopp* (ed. E. Ulrich et al.; JSOTSup 149; Sheffield: Sheffield Academic Press, 1992), 139–57.

Zipora Talshir

19.3.2 Other Greek Versions Prior to the Hexapla

19.3.2.1 Background

Evidence for the versions of Theodotion, Aquila, and Symmachus is scant for the book of Ezra–Nehemiah (→ 1.3.1.2.6). When Field published his edition of Hexaplaric fragments in 1875,[1] he knew of no readings explicitly attributed to any of these three. His edition instead lists over 550 anonymous variants and marginal readings gleaned primarily from several manuscripts (LXX[19, 93, 108]), which Field rightly associated with the Lucianic recension in 2 Esdras.[2] Field suggests that many of these readings probably originated with the three early translators and were incorporated anonymously into the Lucianic recension.[3] However, Field rarely assigns a specific translator to these readings.[4] Thus, the existence of the three translators in the book of Ezra–Nehemiah was assumed by Field, but explicit evidence was lacking at the time. In 1908, Charles C. Torrey concluded on the basis of transliterations that 2 Esdras is in fact Theodotion's version of Ezra–Nehemiah, but his argument has not found favor in subsequent scholarship.[5]

19.3.2.2 Editions, Sources, and Auxiliary Tools

Since the work of Field and Torrey, explicit evidence for the versions of Theodotion, Symmachus, and even Quinta has been found, but not yet for Aquila (as of 2015). In 1932, Rahlfs identified two instances in which Hexaplaric marginal notes have intruded into the text of 2 Esdras in Codex Sinaiticus.[6] In 2 Esd 13:15 (MT-Neh 3:15), Codex Sinaiticus reads και το τειχος κολυμβηθρα των θετουσιλωαμ' "and the wall at the pool of the *thetousiloam*" for MT וְאֵת חוֹמַת בְּרֵכַת הַשֶּׁלַח "and the wall of the pool of Shelah." Rahlfs argues that θετουσιλωαμ' represents an old Hexaplaric marginal note θ' ε' τοῦ Σιλωάμ (Th and Quinta: "of the Siloam") that has entered the text of Sinaiticus and has supplanted the original reading κωδίων "fleeces."[7] In 2 Esd 22:27 (MT-Neh 12:27), Codex Sinaiticus has a double translation of MT וּבְתוֹדוֹת "and with thanksgivings," namely εν θωλαθας · εν εξομολογησει "with *tholathas*, with praise." Rahlfs argues that the final sigma of θωλαθας was originally joined to the second rendering as a marginal Symmachus reading. Thus, an earlier manuscript must have read ἐν θωδαθά "with *thodatha*" in the main text with σ' ἐν ἐξομολογήσει "Sym: with praise" in the margin.

In 1935, two additional Symmachus readings were published in the third apparatus of the

---

[1] Field, **Hexapla*.
[2] Field, **Hexapla*, 1.lxxxvii.
[3] Field, **Hexapla*, 1.703.
[4] Field posits Symmachus as the possible translator in only six instances: MT-Neh 2:1; 4:2 (2 Esd 14:8); 5:18; 6:11; 9:1; 12:42.

[5] Torrey, "The Apparatus," 2.60–76; reprinted in Torrey, *Ezra Studies*, 66–82. For a list of studies refuting Torrey, see especially E. Tov, "Transliterations of Hebrew Words in the Greek Versions: A Further Characteristic of the *Kaige*-Th Revision?" in Tov, **Greek-Hebrew Bible*, 501–12 (502). See now also Hanhart, *Text und Textgeschichte des 2. Esrabuches*, 320–21.

[6] Rahlfs, "Curiosa im Codex Sinaiticus," 309–10; Hanhart, *Text und Textgeschichte des 2. Esrabuches*, 89–90, 142–43, 297–98.

[7] Rahlfs' explanation was anticipated already in 1898 by Klostermann ("Esra und Nehemia," 5:511), who identified the θε before τοῦ Σιλωάμ as denoting θε(οδοτιων). Rahlfs does not seem to be aware of Klostermann's prior observation.

TABLE 1 *Evidence for Other Greek Versions Prior to the Hexapla in Ezra–Nehemiah*

Verse	MT	2 Esdras (LXX)	Attributed reading	Manuscript
Neh 3:1 (2 Esd 13:1)	הַצֹּאן "the flock"	τὴν προβατικήν "pertaining to the sheep"	σ' τῶν βοσκημάτων "of those that are fed"	LXX[108]
Neh 3:15 (2 Esd 13:15)	הַשֶּׁלַח "the Shelah"	τῶν κῳδίων "of the fleeces"	θ' ε' τοῦ Σιλωάμ "of Siloam"	LXX[S]
Neh 3:31 (2 Esd 13:31)	וְהָרֹכְלִים "and the traders"	καὶ οἱ ῥοποπῶλαι "and the hucksters"	σ' οἱ ἔμποροι "the traders"	LXX[108(vid.)]
Neh 12:27 (2 Esd 22:27)	וּבְתוֹדוֹת "and with thanksgivings"	ἐν θωδαθά "with thodatha"	σ' ἐν ἐξομολογήσει "with praise"	LXX[S]

Larger Cambridge Septuagint[8] from the margins of a thirteenth-century manuscript normally associated with the Lucianic recension (LXX[108]). The reading τῶν βοσκημάτων for הַצֹּאן "the flock" in 2 Esd 13:1 (MT-Neh 3:1) and the reading οἱ ἔμποροι for הָרֹכְלִים "the traders" in 2 Esd 13:31 (MT-Neh 3:31) are attributed to Symmachus.[9]

The second apparatus of the Göttingen Septuagint includes the four attributed readings described above, but adds no others.[10] Auxiliary tools are listed in the bibliography.

19.3.2.3 Translation Character and Technique

The extant readings that are explicitly attributed to the early translators in ancient witnesses can be summarized as shown in Table 1.

These readings are reasonably consistent with the translation technique of each translator as known from their fragments in other books, as discussed in the following sections. For a general overview of these translators, see → 1.3.1.2.4 and → 1.3.1.2.5.

---

[8] Brooke–McLean–Thackeray, *1 Esdras, Ezra–Nehemiah*.

[9] Brooke–McLean–Thackeray, *1 Esdras, Ezra–Nehemiah*, 631, 634.

[10] Hanhart, *Esdrae liber II*, 153, 159, 164, 235.

19.3.2.3.1 Theodotion

There is only one other fragment attributed to Theodotion in which שלח is rendered as a place name for comparison to the rendering of MT הַשֶּׁלַח "the Shelah" as τοῦ Σιλωάμ "of the Siloam" attributed to Theodotion (and Quinta) in Neh 3:15. In Isa 8:6, the rendering Σιλωά "Siloa" is attributed to Theodotion (and Aquila and Symmachus) for MT הַשִּׁלֹחַ "the Shiloah" according to the uncial LXX[Q] ("Codex Marchalianus").[11] The difference in the Masoretic vocalization of השלח in Neh 3:15 and Isa 8:6 is not significant at this point, since the translator was working with consonantal texts and understood the referent as Siloam in both verses. At first glance, the Theodotion reading τοῦ Σιλωάμ "of the Siloam" in Neh 3:15 does not appear consistent with the Theodotion reading Σιλωά "Siloa" in Isa 8:6. Nevertheless, the question is whether the difference in spelling between Σιλωάμ in Neh 3:15 and Σιλωά in Isa 8:6 should raise doubts about the attribution of the former to Theodotion.

The available evidence suggests that the proper name "Siloam" did not have a standardized Greek spelling until the late second century C.E. The LXX translator of Isa 8:6 uses the indeclinable form

---

[11] J. Ziegler (ed.), *Isaias* (Septuaginta Vetus Testamentum Graecum 14; Göttingen: Vandenhoeck & Ruprecht, 1967), 150.

Σιλωάμ, which is likewise found in the New Testament (Luke 13:4; John 9:7, 11), a first-century C.E. Jewish apocryphal work (*Liv. Pro.* 1:2 [bis], 4), and Josephus (*J.W.* 5.505). Josephus also employs the spelling Σιλωᾶς as a first-declension masculine noun (as inferred from the form τοῦ Σιλωᾶ; see *J.W.* 2.340; 6.363) and the spelling Σιλωά as a first-declension feminine noun (as inferred from the forms τῆς Σιλωᾶς, τῇ Σιλωᾷ, τὴν Σιλωάν; see *J.W.* 5.140, 145, 252, 410; 6.401). The spelling Σιλωάμ (occasionally Σιλοάμ) appears to have become standard from the late second century C.E. onwards, probably due to the influence of LXX and the New Testament. The variation of the spelling in Josephus suggests that Theodotion, more or less a contemporary of Josephus, likewise could have chosen to spell the name of the water source as Σιλωά in his translation of Isa 8:6 and as Σιλωάμ in his translation of Neh 3:15 without recognizing the appended nasal as an inconsistency. This particular orthographical difference does not appear to be a reliable criterion for distinguishing between authors or translators belonging to the first or second centuries. Consequently, the attribution of the reading τοῦ Σιλωάμ to Theodotion in Neh 3:15 should probably be accepted as authentic despite the minor orthographical difference between Σιλωά in Isa 8:6 and Σιλωάμ in Neh 3:15.

19.3.2.3.2 Symmachus

The first Symmachus reading (τῶν βοσκημάτων "of those that are fed" for הַצֹּאן "the flock" in Neh 3:1) is consistent with Symmachus' typical rendering of צאן "flock" in other fragments. Symmachus most commonly renders צאן "flock" with the plural of βόσκημα "that which is fed."[12] In contrast, Theodotion most commonly renders צאן with πρό-

βατον "sheep," and Aquila usually employs ποίμνιον "flock."[13] The use of plural forms such as τῶν βοσκημάτων "those that are fed" to render singular collective nouns such as צאן is also a known tendency of Symmachus.[14]

The second Symmachus reading (οἱ ἔμποροι for הָרֹכְלִים in Neh 3:31; both meaning "the traders") is consistent with Symmachus' rendering of רֹכְלָיִךְ as ἔμποροί σου "your traders" in Ezek 27:24. Aquila also uses ἔμπορος "trader" (Ezek 17:4; 27:24), whereas Theodotion employs μετάβολος "dealer" (Ezek 17:4).

The third Symmachus reading (ἐν ἐξομολογήσει "with praise" for בְּתוֹדֹת "with thanksgivings" in Neh 12:27) is also consistent with Symmachus' most common rendering of תּוֹדָה "thanksgiving" in other fragments. Moreover, the available evidence suggests that Symmachus prefers to render תּוֹדָה with ἐξομολόγησις "praise" in contexts of giving thanks through verbal praise and song, and with αἴνεσις "praise" in contexts of giving thanks through sacrificial offerings.[15] The reading ἐν ἐξομολογήσει "with praise" in Neh 12:27 is consistent with this pattern, especially given the context of the dedication of the wall with songs and music. In contrast, Aquila consistently renders תּוֹדָה with εὐχαριστία (both meaning "thanksgiving"), and Theodotion employs δῶρον "gift" or "offering."[16] Symmachus' rendering of a plural form (תּוֹדֹת "thanksgivings") with a singular form (ἐξομολογήσει "praise") in Neh 12:27 is a

---

[12] According to the available evidence (excluding retroversions from the Syro-Hexapla), Symmachus renders צאן "flock" with the plural of βόσκημα "that which is fed" at least nine other times (Gen 30:38 [bis]; 30:41, 42; 37:14; Jer 13:20; 31[38]:12; Ps 44[43]:12; 49[48]:15), with the plural of ποίμνιον "flock" six times (Jer 50[27]:8; Ezek 34:8 [bis]; Ps 78[77]:52; 80[79]:2; Cant 1:8), with ποίμνη "flock" twice (Ps 79[78]:13; Ps 107[106]:41), with the plural of πρόβατον "sheep" once (Job 30:1), and with the plural of ποιμήν "shepherd" once (Jer 49:20 [29:21]).

[13] Theodotion renders צאן "flock" with πρόβατον "sheep" at least four times (Jer 12:3; Ezek 34:6; Ps 80[79]:2; Job 30:1). Aquila renders צאן with ποίμνιον "flock" at least seven times (Isa 7:21; 63:11; Zech 11:11; Ps 49[48]:15; 78[77]:52; 80[79]:2; 107[106]:41), with the plural of πρόβατον "sheep" twice (Jer 31[38]:12; Job 30:1), and with the plural of βόσκημα "that which is fed" once (Gen 37:14).

[14] Busto Saiz, *La traducción de Símaco*, 55–57.

[15] Symmachus renders תּוֹדָה "thanksgiving" with ἐξομολόγησις "praise" at least five other times (Ps 26[25]:7; 42[41]:5; 69[68]:31; 147[146]:7; Job 22:22), with αἴνεσις "praise" three times (Jer 17:26; Ps 50[49]:23; 56[55]:13), and with εὐλογία "praise" once (Ps 100[99]:1).

[16] Aquila renders תּוֹדָה "thanksgiving" with εὐχαριστία "thanksgiving" at least nine times (Lev 7:12[2]; Amos 4:5; Ps 26[25]:7; 42[41]:5; 50[49]:14; 69[68]:31; 100[99]:1; 107[106]:22; 147[146]:7), and with αἴνεσις "praise" once (Ps 50[49]:23). Theodotion uses the plural of δῶρον "gift" (Jer 33[40]:11).

practice found elsewhere in his fragments.¹⁷ He is also known for replacing transliterations found in LXX (such as ἐν θωδαθά "with *thodatha*") with translations of his own (such as ἐν ἐξομολογήσει "with praise").¹⁸

19.3.2.4 Text-Critical Value for the Hebrew Text

The four readings do not provide any significant variants from MT (→ 19.2.2). Theodotion's reading (τοῦ Σιλωάμ "of the Siloam") in Neh 3:15 does not necessarily indicate that Theodotion read the consonantal text as הַשִּׁלֹחַ "the Shiloah" (cf. Isa 8:6) over against the Masoretic pointing הַשֶּׁלַח "the Shelah," since Theodotion may have chosen to use a contemporary Greek place name for Siloam regardless of his vocalization of the Hebrew text. Symmachus' translation style accounts for the differences in grammatical number for the readings in Neh 3:1 and 12:27.

Brooke–McLean–Thackeray, *The Old Testament in Greek*, Vol. 2.4: *1 Esdras, Ezra–Nehemiah*.
Busto Saiz, J.R., *La traducción de Símaco en el libro de los Salmos* (Textos y estudios "Cardenal Cisneros" 22; Madrid: C.S.I.C., 1978; repr., 1985).
Field, *Hexapla*.
Hanhart, R. (ed.), *Esdrae liber II* (Septuaginta Vetus Testamentum Graecum 8.2; Göttingen: Vandenhoeck & Ruprecht, 1993).
Hanhart, R., *Text und Textgeschichte des 2. Esrabuches* (MSU 25; Göttingen: Vandenhoeck & Ruprecht, 2003).
Hatch–Redpath, *Concordance*.
Klostermann, A., "Esra und Nehemia," RE 5:500–23.
Muraoka, T., *A Greek ≈ Hebrew/Aramaic Two-way Index to the Septuagint* (Leuven: Peeters, 2010).
Rahlfs, A., "Curiosa im Codex Sinaiticus," ZAW 50 (1932): 309–10.
Reider, J. and N. Turner, *An Index to Aquila: Greek-Hebrew, Hebrew-Greek, Latin-Hebrew, with the Syriac and Armenian Evidence* (VTSup 12; Leiden: Brill, 1966).
Salvesen, A., *Symmachus in the Pentateuch* (JSS Monograph 15; Manchester: Victoria University of Manchester, 1991).
Torrey, C.C., "The Apparatus for the Textual Criticism of Chronicles–Ezra–Nehemiah," in *Old Testament and Semitic Studies in Memory of William Rainey Harper* (2 vols.; eds. R.F. Harper, F. Brown, and G.F. Moore; Chicago: University of Chicago Press, 1908), 2.53–111.
Torrey, C.C., *Ezra Studies* (Chicago: University of Chicago Press, 1910; repr., New York: Ktav, 1970).

Jason T. Parry

19.3.3 Peshitta

19.3.3.1 Manuscripts of S-Ezra–Neh

Ezra and Nehemiah are divided into two books by the Vulgate (→ 19.3.6) only, whilst in the Peshitta, just as in the other ancient traditions, there is only one book. The most ancient manuscripts go back to the seventh and eighth centuries C.E.: the two complete ancient Bibles, manuscripts S⁷ᵃ¹ and S⁸ᵃ¹, and a manuscript of 770 C.E. from the convent of Saint Mary Deipara, S⁸ʰ⁵. The book is also found in manuscript S¹²ᵃ¹ (the "Buchanan Bible"), which is almost illegible. It is found furthermore in more recent complete Bibles and in a group of six Nestorian manuscripts that contain the same group of books: 1–3 Maccabees (→ 11.10), 1–2 Chronicles (→ 20.3.4), Ezra–Nehemiah, Wisdom of Solomon (→ 11.15.3), Judith (→ 11.9.4), Esther (→ 13–17.1.4.5), Susanna (→ 11.3.3), Epistle of Jeremiah (→ 11.2.4.3), Epistle of Baruch, Baruch (→ 11.2.1.3).

The text transmitted by these manuscripts is substantially the same. The variants present in the three more ancient manuscripts cannot be explained as deriving from a unique archetype, but they assume a long transmission process. The recent manuscripts show a form of text very similar to that represented by manuscript S⁸ᵃ¹. In the three reconstructed development stages of the Peshitta, manuscript S⁸ʰ⁵ belongs to the oldest stage, manuscripts S⁷ᵃ¹ and S⁸ᵃ¹ to the second stage, and manuscript¹²ᵃ¹, the *textus receptus*, to the third.¹

---

¹⁷ Busto Saiz, *La traducción de Símaco*, 55.
¹⁸ Salvesen, *Symmachus in the Pentateuch*, 215–17.

¹ Koster, "Translation or Transmission?" 297–312 (312).

19.3.3.2 Critical Edition

The critical edition of s-Ezra and s-Neh was published in 2013 as part of the project of the Peshitta Institute of Leiden[2] in volume 4.4, which also includes 1–2 Maccabees. It is a diplomatic edition of manuscript s7a1, accompanied by a critical apparatus that takes into consideration manuscripts prior to the twelfth century. The text, prepared by M. Albert, was used in the critical apparatus of the *BHQ* in 2006. The introduction presents a detailed study of all extant manuscripts, grouped by families.

19.3.3.3 Character of the Translation

A first description of s-Ezra and s-Neh goes back to the end of the nineteenth century;[3] the deviations from MT (→ 19.2.2) are attributed to errors in the reading or to confusion in the interpretation of the Hebrew. In the first half of the twentieth century, four significant works can be found. The first is limited to the study of s-Ezra and is based on the assumption that the text we have today has been corrupted by copyists. Therefore, it is useless to search for variants amongst the manuscripts instead of focussing on the original Hebrew.[4] The second work is a collection of variants of six manuscripts of s-Ezra.[5] This is the work that today still constitutes the reference point for all those who cite manuscript s8h5 with regard to s-Ezra–Neh. The third is an analysis of the text of Nehemiah according to the variants of the five versions: LXX (→ 19.3.1), Vulgate (→ 19.3.6), Peshitta, Arabic (→ 19.3.7; → 19.4.8), and Ethiopic (→ 19.4.3).[6] The fourth work is limited to the study of s-Neh, but has remained unpublished.[7]

The conclusions of these works show that the Syriac translation is not based on LXX (→ 19.3.1) and is rather free. Apart from the omissions or additions that are often attributable to the copyists, the errors are often due to scarce knowledge of Hebrew or to the bad copy of the *Vorlage*. Scholars usually agree that the Peshitta is of little value for text-critical analysis. In this analysis, scholars base themselves on different sources such as s7a1 (Harris, "The Peshitta to Nehemiah") or Walton, *Polyglotta*. According to Rudolph, the two books were translated by two different persons.[8]

In 2013, the translation technique of Ezra–Nehemiah was studied with a focus on rhetorical and literary characteristics.[9] The unity of Ezra–Nehemiah was confirmed by the rendering of Neh 6:7:

MT: "there is a king in Judaea"
S: "behold Ezra has begun to reign in Judaea."

The addition of the name "Ezra" changed the sequence of events. In MT, the two protagonists act independently, first Ezra, later Nehemiah, while in the Peshitta the latter disappears. In the Peshitta, the first person narrator is Ezra, who subsequently becomes the protagonist of the so-called Memoirs of Nehemiah. This feature creates a narrative coherence because the narrator is always Ezra, as indicated by the title of the book.[10] As a consequence, all the chronological indications of MT always refer to Ezra's journeys. Ezra receives the assignment in the seventh year of Artaxerxes (Ezra 7:7), returns to Jerusalem in the twentieth year (Neh 2:1), and finally after the thirty-second year (Neh 13:6).

The Peshitta presents different translation equivalents in different parts of the book. For instance בני עבדי שלמה "sons of the servants of Solomon" are represented as "sons of Abar sons of Shalim" in Ezra 2:55 and as "sons of Abar and of Shalim" in Ezra 2:58, while in the parallel text, they are always "sons of the servants of Solomon" (Neh 7:57, 60). Likewise, התרשתא "the govenor," occurring five times, is translated in a variety of ways ("the chief of Israel," "the chiefs/elders of the priests").

Contradictions in MT are removed in the coherent story of the Peshitta by way of omissions and

---

[2] Albert and Nakano, "Ezra and Nehemiah."
[3] Klostermann, "Esra und Nehemia," 500–23 (504–07).
[4] Hawley, *Critical Examination*.
[5] Moss, "Peshitta Version of Ezra," 55–110.
[6] Gotthard, *Text des Buches Nehemia*.
[7] Harris, "The Peshitta to Nehemiah."

[8] Rudolph, *Esra und Nehemia*, xx–xxi.
[9] Balzaretti, *Syriac Version of Ezra–Nehemiah*.
[10] Balzaretti, "Esdra il coppiere," 475–97.

additions. For example, in MT three groups of people complain to Nehemiah (Neh 5:2–5), but in the Peshitta there is an additional one ("there were those who said," missing in MT-Neh 5:5), together with an actual complaint.

The Peshitta displays a tendency to harmonise the translation by using the same attribute on the recurrence of a name or by repeating a formula occurring elsewhere in the book. For example, Rehum appears three times as "Lord of Tegma," and that title is added in Ezra 4:23. Ezra is often accompanied by the epithet "scribe," which is added six more times.

S-Ezra–Neh preserves many of the parallelisms in MT and also creates new ones. On the other hand, sometimes, perhaps due to a tendency to variate, a parallelism present in MT is dismantled or replaced by another one.[11] In the case of identical passages, the Peshitta sometimes offers the same translation, and at other times not. Also, free allusions to other biblical passages are added in the Peshitta. Further, in the translation of a pair of terms *a* and *b*, one of the two is replaced by *c* appearing in other biblical passages together with one of the two terms of the pair.

The translation provides a clearer and more consistent presentation of the original Hebrew, though sacrificing some redundant expressions of the *Vorlage*, but with the aim of producing a well-ordered arrangement of the text by means of repetition.

19.3.3.4 Date of the Translation and Identity of the Translator(s)

Weitzman[12] maintains that Ezra–Nehemiah form a unit with 1–2 Chronicles (→ 10.3.4; to which Esther [→ 13–17.1.4.5] could also be added) on account of the elements they have in common. Basing himself on the supposition that these books are missing from the Nestorian canon and from the so-called Masoretic manuscripts (a collection of difficult words and phrases of Scripture) and were rejected by Theodore of Mopsuestia, he assigns the translation to around 200 C.E., that is, fifty years after the translation of most of the other books of the Peshitta. However, this *argumentum e silentio* is not sufficient proof to give a posterior date to the translation.[13] A number of clues seem to lead to the supposition that the translator probably was aware of the other books of the Peshitta, and that constitutes a fixed point for a relative chronology.

From the second half of the nineteenth century, it is customary to cite as proof of the Jewish origin of the Peshitta the translation of "evening sacrifice" with "ninth hour" in Ezra 9:4–5 on the basis of *b. Ber.* 26b,[14] but the same rendering could also be explained as Christian (Matt 20:5; 27:46; Mark 15:34; Luke 23:44; Acts 3:1; 10:30). Thus, the translator could have been aware of either a Targumic or a Christian tradition. Further, the rejection of musical instruments in the liturgy reflects a polemic against pagan practice that is found both in Judaism and in the early church. Likewise, in the translation of legislative regulations regarding the temple, omissions and changes create the impression of a greater interest in prayer and in free will in religious practice.

Further, some translation equivalents may indicate the historical and social context in which the translator lived. Thus, the nomenclature relating to the heads of the people shows a pre-eminence given to the role of the elders as opposed to the avoidance of naming the governor or any single head for the Jewish community.

In spite of all this, there remains an objection to the assumption of a Jewish origin: i.e., the use of ܟܘܡܪܐ to indicate "priests," reserved in the rabbinic literature for pagan priests.

Albert, M. and C. Nakano, "Ezra and Nehemiah," in *Ezra and Nehemiah – 1–2 Maccabees* (The Old Testament in Syriac according to the Peshitta Version 4.4; Leiden: Brill, 2013).

Balzaretti, C., *The Syriac Version of Ezra–Nehemiah: Manuscripts and Editions, Translation Technique and Its*

---

[11] Balzaretti, "Aspetti retorici," 109–25.
[12] Weitzman, *Syriac Version*, 169–86.
[13] Balzaretti, *Syriac Version of Ezra–Nehemiah*, 17–21.
[14] Perles, *Meletemata Peschitthoniana*, 16.

Use in Textual Criticism (BibOr 51; Rome: Gregorian & Biblical Press, 2013).

Balzaretti, C., "Aspetti retorici della versione siriaca di Esdra-Neemia," in *Studi del terzo convegno RBS: International Studies on Biblical & Semitic Rhetoric* (eds. R. Meynet and J. Oniszczuk; Retorica Biblica e Semitica 2; Rome: Gregorian & Biblical Press, 2013), 109–25.

Balzaretti, C., "Esdra il coppiere, ovvero la versione siriaca del libro di Esdra," *RivB* 62 (2014): 475–97.

Balzaretti, C., "Review of *The Old Testament in Syriac according to the Peshitta Version. 4,4: Ezra and Nehemiah – 1–2 Maccabees*" (Leiden: Brill, 2013), *OCP* 80 (2014): 538–42.

Gotthard, H., *Der Text des Buches Nehemia* (Wiesbaden: Otto Harrassowitz, 1958).

Harris, R.L., "The Peshitta to Nehemiah: A Textual-Critical Analysis" (PhD diss., Dropsie College, 1947).

Hawley, C.A., *A Critical Examination of the Peshitta Version of the Book of Ezra* (Contributions to Oriental History and Philology 7; New York: Columbia University Press, 1922).

Klostermann, A., "Esra und Nehemia," *RE* 5:500–23.

Koster, M.D., "'Translation or Transmission? That is the Question': The Use of the Leiden O.T. Peshitta Edition," in *"Basel und Bibel": Collected Communications to the XVIIth Congress of the International Organization for the Study of the Old Testament, Basel 2001* (eds. M. Augustin and H.M. Niemann; BEATAJ 51; Frankfurt a.M.: Peter Lang, 2004), 297–312.

Moss, C., "The Peshiṭta Version of Ezra," *Mus* 46 (1933): 55–110.

Perles, J., *Meletemata Peschitthoniana* (Breslau: W. Friedrich, 1859).

Rudolph, W., *Esra und Nehemia samt 3.Esra* (HAT 20; Tübingen: Mohr, 1949).

Weitzman, M.P., *The Syriac Version of the Old Testament* (University of Cambridge Oriental Publications 56 Cambridge: Cambridge University Press, 2005).

Claudio Balzaretti

19.3.4 Hexapla

19.3.4.1 Background

Origen lists two Greek books (1 and 2 Esdras) as corresponding to the single Hebrew book of Ezra–Nehemiah in his account of the Hebrew canon (→ 1.1.2.2.5.2), which raises the question of whether he included both Greek versions in the Hexapla (→ 1.3.1.2.7).[1] The presence of 1 Esdras in the Hexapla is possibly suggested by asterisked materials in Greek manuscripts and by a Syriac version of 1 Esdras from Paul of Tella (→ 19.4.4), which is usually considered Syro-Hexaplaric, but the value of these as witnesses to the Hexapla remains questionable. The presence of 2 Esdras in the Hexapla is confirmed by attributed Hexaplaric readings (→ 19.3.2), a marginal note in Codex Sinaiticus, Syro-Hexaplaric catena excerpts, and possibly by asterisked materials in Greek manuscripts.

19.3.4.2 Editions, Sources, and Auxiliary Tools

Field mentions the Syro-Hexaplaric version of 1 Esdras (→ 11.7.1.3) in the "Prolegomena" to his edition of Hexaplaric fragments, but he includes only 2 Esdras (→ 19.4.4) in the edition.[2] He reports asterisked material only in 2 Esd 17:72.[3] The Larger Cambridge Septuagint reports asterisked material twice in 1 Esdras (1:13; 8:40) and twice in 2 Esdras (4:14; 17:72).[4] The Göttingen Septuagint gives the fullest account by reporting asterisked material twice in 1 Esdras (1:13; 8:40) and three times in 2 Esdras (4:14; 17:72; 22:14–21).[5] These verses correspond to MT-2 Chr 35:14b, Ezra 8:14, 4:14, Neh 7:71, and Neh 12:14–21 respectively.

The sources of these asterisks include two tenth-century Greek minuscules associated with recension LXX^b (LXX$^{64, 243}$), and one tenth-century codex mixtus (LXX^{119}).[6] Two of the instances of asterisked material (2 Esd 17:72; 22:14–21) are attested

---

[1] Origen lists the biblical books known to his Greek audience alongside each book of the Hebrew canon. For Ezra-Nehemiah, he lists Ἔζρας α΄ β΄ ἐν ἑνί, Εζρα, ὅ ἐστιν 'βοηθός' (Eusebius, *Hist. eccl.* 6.25.2). 1 Esdras consists of a translation of selections from 2 Chronicles (35:1–36:23), Ezra (1:1–11; 4:7–24; 2:1–4:5; 5:1–10:44), and Nehemiah (7:72–8:13), and a story not attested in MT (1 Esd 3:1–5:6).

[2] Field, *Hexapla*, 1.lxviii.

[3] Field, *Hexapla*, 1.780.

[4] Brooke–McLean–Thackeray, *1 Esdras, Ezra–Nehemiah*, 558, 591, 611, 645.

[5] Hanhart, *Esdrae liber I*, 58, 124; Hanhart, *Esdrae liber II*, 93, 195, 232.

[6] Hanhart, *Esdrae liber I*, 8–11, 31; Hanhart, *Esdrae liber II*, 9–10, 30.

by seventh-century corrections to Codex Sinaiticus (LXX^S), some of which attest Hexaplaric variants.

According to a marginal note appended to the colophon of 2 Esdras by one of the Sinaiticus correctors, the manuscript "was collated with an extremely old copy corrected by the hand of the holy martyr Pamphilus, in which copy, at the end, a certain note in his own hand was given underneath, stating thus: 'It was acquired from and corrected to the Hexapla of Origen. Antoninus collated; I, Pamphilus, corrected.'"[7] The marginal note thus attests to a Hexaplaric recension of 2 Esdras, but the corrections to Sinaiticus are not all of Hexaplaric origin. Many of the corrections simply restore the Sinaiticus text to the original translation, and at least a few others are Lucianic (→ 19.3.5).[8] Unfortunately, the Sinaiticus text and corrections are extant only for 2 Esd 9:9–23:31 (MT-Ezra 9:9–Neh 13:31).

The Syro-Hexaplaric version of 1 Esdras is published as part of a volume of the Leiden Peshiṭta on account of its appearance in thirteen Peshiṭta manuscripts dating from the twelfth to mid-nineteenth centuries and one catena from the eighth or ninth century C.E.[9] This same catena is also the only source for the partially extant Syro-Hexaplaric version of 2 Esdras (London, British Museum, Add. 12, 168).[10] Asterisks are not preserved in these manuscripts, but they have value for assessing the Hexaplaric recension in 1 and 2 Esdras.

19.3.4.3 Translation Character and Technique
19.3.4.3.1 Hexaplaric Recension of 1 Esdras

For 1 Esdras, Hanhart characterizes the Syro-Hexaplaric version (→ 11.7.1.3) as having been "influenced" by the Lucianic recension (→ 11.7.1.2), and therefore he associates the Syriac translation with the Lucianic recension rather than treating it as a reliable witness to the Hexaplaric recension.[11] He maintains that no Hexaplaric recension has been handed down in 1 Esdras and that Hexaplaric and Lucianic recensional elements cannot be distinguished from one another.[12]

Analysis of the asterisked materials of 1 Esdras suggests that they are no exception. Genuine asterisked materials from the Hexaplaric tradition tend to correspond closely to MT, although minor differences can occur since Origen probably slavishly used the text of the later translators and since Theodotion's revision of an older text does not always correspond precisely to the Hebrew.[13] The Hexaplaric origin of the asterisked material in 1 Esd 1:13 is therefore questionable due to the two minuses relative to MT-2 Chr 35:14 (1° בְּנֵי אַהֲרֹן "descendants of Aaron" and הָעוֹלָה "the burnt offering"), the plus (ἀδελφοῖς αὐτῶν "for their brothers"), and the elsewhere-unattested rendering of לַיְלָה "night" with ἀωρία "a wrong time" or "midnight." The Hexaplaric origin of the asterisked material in 1 Esd 8:40 may likewise be questioned on the basis of the uncharacteristic rendering of the proper name וְזַכּוּר "and Zaccur" (Qere) in MT-Ezra 8:14 as ὁ τοῦ Ἰσταλκούρου "the son of Istalkouros" (Ἰστακούρου "of Istakouros" LXX^243), although in this case the difference could be due instead to textual corruption. The asterisked materials in 1 Esdras are therefore probably not Hexaplaric additions to LXX, but this assessment is necessarily tentative.

---

[7] Author's translation. The Greek reads: ἀντεβλήθη πρὸς παλαιώτατον λίαν ἀντίγραφον δεδιορθωμένον χειρὶ τοῦ ἁγίου μάρτυρος Παμφίλου, ὅπερ ἀντίγραφον πρὸς τῷ τέλει ὑποσημείωσίς τις ἰδιόχειρος αὐτοῦ ὑπέκειτο ἔχουσα οὕτως· Μετελήμφθη καὶ διορθώθη πρὸς τὰ ἑξαπλᾶ Ὠριγένους. Ἀντωνῖνος ἀντέβαλεν· Πάμφιλος διόρθωσα. See further Hanhart, *Esdrae liber II*, 8–9, 249; Hanhart, *Text und Textgeschichte des 2. Esrabuches*, 183.

[8] Hanhart, *Esdrae liber II*, 8, 30; Hanhart, *Text und Textgeschichte des 2. Esrabuches*, 16, 208–10, 215–18.

[9] Baars and Lebram, "1 (3) Esdras," ii–xii.

[10] Torrey, "Portions," 71–74; Gwynn, "Extracts," 19–25; 54–63; Torrey, *Ezra Studies*, 7–10; Hanhart, *Esdrae liber II*, 13–14. The Syro-Hexapla catena contains excerpts from 2 Esdras corresponding to MT-Neh 1:1–4; 2:1–8; 4:1–3, 10–16; 6:15–16; 8:1–9:3.

[11] Hanhart, *Text und Textgeschichte des 1. Esrabuches*, 19–20, 44; Hanhart, *Esdrae liber I*, 20, 32.

[12] Hanhart, *Text und Textgeschichte des 1. Esrabuches*, 20. Cf. Torrey, *Ezra Studies*, 96–99.

[13] Soisalon-Soininen, *Der Charakter der asterisierten Zusätze*, 42–45.

19.3.4.3.2 Hexaplaric Recension of 2 Esdras

For 2 Esdras, Hanhart provides a thorough analysis of the Hexaplaric recension as attested by the Sinaiticus corrections (LXX[s[c, mg]]) and the Syro-Hexapla (→ 19.4.4) on the basis of comparison to the more securely attested Lucianic recension (→ 19.3.5).[14] Many of the corrections found in the Hexaplaric witnesses are also attested in the Lucianic recension, with the main intention of both recensions being correction of the Greek text toward MT (→ 19.2.2).[15] In his edition, Hanhart treats the Hexaplaric witnesses (LXX[s[c, mg]] and Syh) primarily as co-witnesses to the Lucianic recension due to their similarity to the Lucianic recension and due to their special and fragmentary nature.[16] In his account of the text history, however, Hanhart identifies some of the readings in LXX[s(c, mg)] and the Syro-Hexapla as verifiably Hexaplaric (and not Lucianic) corrections to LXX, such as a number of instances in which the transcriptions of proper nouns were changed to represent Masoretic gemination by means of doubled consonants, e.g., the correction of original Ζαχχούρ "Zakchour" to Ζαχχούρ "Zachchour" (2 Esd 13:2) for זַכּוּר "Zaccur" (MT-Neh 3:2) as attested by LXX[s(c)].[17] On the other hand, he provides evidence that verifiably Lucianic (and not Hexaplaric) readings influenced the Hexaplaric witnesses at least in isolated cases, such as the Lucianic insertion of ἕως ἄκρου τοῦ οὐρανοῦ "to an end of the sky" from LXX-Deut 30:4 into 2 Esd 11:9 as attested by LXX[s(c)-L].[18]

Hanhart maintains that the asterisks in 2 Esd 17:72 and 22:14–21, although attested by LXX[s(c, mg)], do not identify additions to LXX from the Hexapla, but rather represent a secondary use of the Aristarchian signs in which the asterisks mark segments of text that correspond to lacunae elsewhere in the manuscript tradition. He interprets the asterisk in 2 Esd 4:14 as marking an addition to LXX that is handed down by the Lucianic recension and that may or may not have originated from the Hexapla.[19] It is difficult to confirm or refute Hanhart's assessment of the asterisked materials in 2 Esdras on the basis of translation technique, since the asterisked materials agree with MT reasonably well.

19.3.4.4 Text-Critical Value for the Hebrew-Aramaic Text

For 1 Esdras, it remains difficult to confirm any particular reading as originating from the Hexapla (→ II.7.1.2). For 2 Esdras, each reading found in the Hexaplaric witnesses (LXX[s(c, mg)] and Syh) or in the asterisked materials must be questioned in terms of whether it preserves the original LXX, the original Hexaplaric, the original Lucianic, or some other intermediate stage of the tradition. The truly Hexaplaric readings, as far as they can be distinguished, attest to a Hebrew-Aramaic parent text that stood very close to MT (→ 19.2.2).[20]

Baars, W. and J.C.H. Lebram (eds.), "1 (3) Esdras," in *Canticles or Odes; Prayer of Manasseh; Apocryphal Psalms; Psalms of Solomon; Tobit; 1 (3) Esdras* (The Old Testament in Syriac according to the Peshiṭta Version 4.6; Leiden: Brill, 1972), i–53.

Brooke–McLean–Thackeray, **The Old Testament in Greek*, Vol. 2.4: *1 Esdras, Ezra–Nehemiah*.

Field, *Hexapla.

Gwynn, J., "Extracts from the Syro-Hexaplar Version of the Septuagint," in *Remnants of the Later Syriac Versions of the Bible* (London: Williams and Norgate, 1909), i–78.

Hanhart, R. (ed.), *Esdrae liber I* (Septuaginta Vetus Testamentum Graecum 8.1; Göttingen: Vandenhoeck & Ruprecht, 1991).

Hanhart, R. (ed.), *Esdrae liber II* (Septuaginta Vetus Testamentum Graecum 8.2; Göttingen: Vandenhoeck & Ruprecht, 1993).

---

[14] Hanhart, *Text und Textgeschichte des 2. Esrabuches*, 16–18, 181–220, 296–98, 315–21.

[15] Hanhart, *Text und Textgeschichte des 2. Esrabuches*, 184–97, 319–20.

[16] Hanhart, *Esdrae liber II*, 30.

[17] Hanhart, *Text und Textgeschichte des 2. Esrabuches*, 209–15.

[18] Hanhart, *Text und Textgeschichte des 2. Esrabuches*, 216. See pp. 208, 215 for other examples.

[19] Hanhart, *Text und Textgeschichte des 2. Esrabuches*, 142, 190–91. Regarding the question of whether the doublets in the Hexaplaric witnesses resulted from previously asterisked additions, see pp. 206–08.

[20] For analysis of possible exceptions, see Hanhart, *Text und Textgeschichte des 2. Esrabuches*, 215–20.

Hanhart, R., *Text und Textgeschichte des 1. Esrabuches* (MSU 12; Göttingen: Vandenhoeck & Ruprecht, 1974).

Hanhart, R., *Text und Textgeschichte des 2. Esrabuches* (MSU 25; Göttingen: Vandenhoeck & Ruprecht, 2003).

Soisalon-Soininen, I., *Der Charakter der asterisierten Zusätze in der Septuaginta* (Suomalaisen Tiedeakatemian Toimituksia/AASF B.114; Helsinki: Suomalaisen Kirjallisuuden Kirjapaino Oy, 1959).

Torrey, C.C., "Portions of First Esdras and Nehemiah in the Syro-Hexaplar Version," *AJSL* 23.1 (1906): 65–74.

Torrey, C.C., *Ezra Studies* (Chicago: University of Chicago Press, 1910; repr., New York: Ktav, 1970).

Jason T. Parry

19.3.5 Post-Hexaplaric Greek Translations

19.3.5.1 Background

The only post-Hexaplaric recension known to us is that of Lucian. Robert Hanhart's research is the basis for the present description of the Lucianic recension of 2 Esdras. Hanhart's conclusions are both typical and unique. They are typical, because the LXX^L text frequently agrees with Hexaplaric witnesses. They are unique, because Hanhart does not distinguish between LXX^L and Hexaplaric sources (→ 19.3.4) as far as text groups are concerned.

19.3.5.2 Original Form, Editions, Auxiliary Tools

Two magisterial works by Hanhart are indispensable for study of the Lucianic text of 2 Esdras: the critical edition *Esdras II* of the Göttingen LXX and the volume *Text und Textgeschichte des 2. Esrabuches*. In addition to the two books, Hanhart's published essay on the LXX^L text and VL is helpful.[1] The L text of 2 Esdras is so closely related to the Hexaplaric text that Hanhart suggests that the two groups often agree (s^c-Syh-L′) such that he does not employ the sigla O.[2] The LXX^L group includes the following manuscripts: LXX$^{19, 93, 108, 121}$. The manuscripts consistently preserve the Lucianic recension in Kingdoms (→ 3–5.1.6.2) and the Latter Prophets (→ 6–9.1.6).

19.3.5.3 Translation Character and Technique

According to Hanhart, the general characteristics of 2 Esdras include alignments to a Hebrew *Vorlage*, stylistic improvements, and employment of Attic Greek forms (see also → 19.3.1). Otherwise, there are many variants that do not agree with the Hebrew text and cannot be explained as stylistic improvements (e.g., insertion of late Hellenistic word-forms and preservation of early corruptions of secondary importance).[3] Alignment of the Greek text to the Hebrew text is subordinate to the employment of stylistic Greek. Employment of the definite article evinces the recensionist's concern for proper Greek grammar more than other grammatical improvements. In places where the Hebrew text has a definite bound phrase with a definite bound member, the LXX^L text preserves an article on nouns in the genitive case and the *nomen regens*.[4] The LXX^L text commonly omits the article before the second noun in a compound phrase, a characteristic that is also consistent with proper Greek grammar.[5] Agreements with the Hebrew text with respect to the placement of the article are often coincidental.

In general, omissions are rarely in accord with the Hebrew text. Transpositions, however, frequently agree with the Hebrew text, though they are often stylistically motivated.[6]

Signature features[7] of the Lucianic recension are also preserved in the manuscripts: doublets (2 Esd 20:31 ἀπαίτησιν πάσης χειρός "and a claim of every hand" (*NETS) LXX/κρεὸς καὶ ἀπαίτησιν πάσης χειρός "flesh and claim of every hand" LXX^L), substitutions of case (2 Esd 6:4 δόμοι λίθινοι κραταιοί "courses of hard stones" (*NETS) LXX/δόμους λιθίνους κραταιοὺς "courses of hard stones" LXX^L), and substitutions of

---

[1] Hanhart, "Ursprünglicher Septuagintatext," 90–115.
[2] R. Hanhart, *Esdras II* (Septuaginta Vetus Testamentum Graecum VIII/2; Göttingen: Vandenhoeck & Ruprecht, 1993), 30.
[3] Hanhart, *Text und Textgeschichte des 2. Esrabuches*, 18.
[4] Hanhart, *Text und Textgeschichte des 2. Esrabuches*, 21.
[5] Hanhart, *Text und Textgeschichte des 2. Esrabuches*, 23–24.
[6] Hanhart, *Text und Textgeschichte des 2. Esrabuches*, 20.
[7] For a succinct description of the Lucianic recension, see Ziegler, "Hat Lukian den griechischen Sirach rezensiert?" 210–29.

synonyms (2 Esd 12:2 μετριάζων "unwell" LXX/ἀρρώστων "sickly" LXX^L).

19.3.5.4 Inner-Translational Features

Writing about the Lucianic recension in general, Fernández Marcos said: "Although it is not a new translation, it does present intriguing links to the Hebrew text. This can been [sic] seen, not only in the last level of the recension which incorporates Hexaplaric material ... but also in the traces of a pre-Hexaplaric approach to the Hebrew, which could situate it parallel to the Hebraisms detected in the *Vetus Latina*."[8] 2 Esdras evinces both levels of recensional activity. Hanhart's text grouping bears witness to the last (Hexaplaric) level. Agreements with the Old Latin (VL) show how the recension agrees with early sources and the Hebrew text (e.g., 2 Esd 16:11 οὐκ εἰσελεύσομαι LXX$^{s(c)-L}$ VL$^{123\ 125}$ *non introibo*/לֹא אָבוֹא MT, all meaning "I will not enter").[9] The aforementioned variant at 2 Esd 16:11 shows how difficult it is to differentiate the levels of the recension. The LXX^L text stands in agreement with the early Old Latin text (VL) and the later Hexaplaric text (LXX$^{s[c]}$), all of which agree with the Hebrew text but do not agree with LXX (the critical text). As Hanhart notes, it is difficult to declare what is "vorlukianisch, lukianisch, und nachlukianisch."[10]

19.3.5.5 Text-Critical Value

The *L* text is useful in textual criticism of the Hebrew Bible, because the recension preserves many variations from LXX toward the Hebrew text. Similarly, *L* often disagrees with other witnesses when it agrees with the Hebrew text.[11] In such cases, the recension is a witness to a Hebrew text that may not be the *Vorlage* of other ancient witnesses (e.g., LXX).

---

[8] Fernández Marcos, "The Antiochene Edition in the Text History of the Greek Bible," 60.

[9] For a discussion of how LXX^L relates to VL, see Hanhart, "Ursprünglicher Septuagintatext," 54.

[10] Hanhart, "Ursprünglicher Septuagintatext," 62.

[11] Hanhart, *Text und Textgeschichte des 2. Esrabuches*, 28.

Fernández Marcos, N., "The Antiochene Edition in the Text History of the Greek Bible," in *Der Antiochenische Text der Septuaginta in seiner Bezeugung und seiner Bedeutung* (eds. S. Kreuzer and M. Sigismund; De Septuaginta Investigationes 4; Vandenhoeck & Ruprecht, 2013), 57–73.

Hanhart, R., "Ursprünglicher Septuagintatext und lukianische Rezension des 2. Esrabuches im Verhältnis zur Textform der Vetus Latina," in *Philogia Sacra: Biblische und patristische Studien für Hermann J. Frede und Walter Thiele zu ihrem siebzigsten Geburtstag* (ed. R. Gryson; AGLB 24; Freiburg: Verlag Herder, 1993), 90–115.

Hanhart, R., *Esdrae liber II* (Septuaginta Vetus Testamentum Graecum 8.2; Göttingen: Vandenhoeck & Ruprecht, 1993).

Hanhart, R., *Text und Textgeschichte des 2. Esrabuches* (MSU 25; Göttingen: Vandenhoeck & Ruprecht, 2003).

Ziegler, J., "Hat Lukian den griechischen Sirach rezensiert?" *Bib* 40 (1959): 210–29.

Matthew M. Dickie

19.3.6 Vulgate

19.3.6.1 Background

Jerome produced V-Ezra–Neh in 394 or 395 C.E. (→ 1.3.5.2).[1] By this time, he had gained significant experience translating the Hebrew Bible, though about half of the work still lay ahead of him, along with most of the great commentaries on the prophets that he would publish in the coming years. As for the few Aramaic chapters of Ezra, Jerome had already published his translation of Daniel (→ 18.3.6), so he had at least some experience translating from this language. V-Ezra–Neh shows its translator to be usually competent at giving sensible Latin renderings for the Hebrew and Aramaic.

---

[1] See J.N.D. Kelly, *Jerome: His Life, Writings, and Controversies* (New York: Harper & Row, 1975), 190. P. Nautin gives no reason for dating V-Ezra–Neh to 400 C.E. ("Hieronymus," TRE 15:305–15 [310]), whereas the little evidence we have points to a date around or before 395 C.E. Jerome mentions in the preface to this translation that he would soon publish a work explaining that the apostles often quote Scripture according to the Hebrew text rather than LXX, a reference to *Epist.* 57, published in 395 C.E.

19.3.6.2 Translation Character

v-Ezra–Neh corresponds closely both textually and linguistically to MT (→ 19.2.2), so that one scholar has recently characterized it as "an extremely literal translation," perhaps a slight overstatement.[2] Jerome routinely imitates Semitic word order and typically maintains consistent translation equivalents throughout these books. Yet, he usually manages to produce clear (if inelegant) Latin that reflects closely its Semitic *Vorlage*, and he does not force his translation to represent each constituent of a Hebrew word if this would create awkward Latin.

19.3.6.3 Translation Technique
19.3.6.3.1 Hebrew/Aramaic Idioms

Jerome's treatment of Hebrew and Aramaic idioms varies throughout v-Ezra–Neh. Often he transforms them into appropriate corresponding Latin: יוֹם בְּיוֹם "day by day," *diebus singulis* "on each day" (Ezra 3:4); חֲלָק בַּעֲבַר נַהֲרָא לָא אִיתַי לָךְ "a share beyond the River will not be yours," *possessionem trans Fluvium non habebis* "you will not have a possession across the river" (Ezra 4:16); וּמְלַח דִּי־לָא כְתָב "and salt without prescript," *sal vero absque mensura* "and salt without measure" (Ezra 7:22); וְעַל־יָדוֹ "and by his hand," *et iuxta eum* "and next to him" (Neh 3:2); לְעֵינֵי "to his eyes," *coram* "before" (Neh 8:5); אִישׁ "(each) man," *unusquisque* "each one" (Neh 8:16). The infinitive construct with prefixed בְּ often becomes a *cum*-clause (e.g. Ezra 2:68). However, v-Ezra–Neh sometimes reproduces Hebrew idioms rather woodenly: וַיַּעֲבֵר־קוֹל/*et transduxit vocem* "and he made his voice to cross through" (Ezra 1:1; cf. 10:7; Neh 8:15); וְאַחַר הַדְּבָרִים הָאֵלֶּה/*post haec autem verba* "now after these things" (Ezra 7:1); וּבְבֹשֶׁת פָּנִים "and into shame of face," *et in confusionem vultus* "and into confusion of face" (Ezra 9:7); מִפֶּה אֶל־פֶּה/*ab ore usque ad os* "from mouth to mouth" (Ezra 9:11); בַּדָּבָר הַזֶּה/*in sermone isto* "in this word" (Ezra 10:13); מָה אֱלֹהַי נֹתֵן אֶל־לִבִּי "what my God was putting into my heart," *quid Deus dedisset in corde meo* "what God had put in my heart" (Neh 2:12). At one point, he misunderstands the idiomatic use of שׁוב to mean "again": הֲנָשׁוּב לְהָפֵר מִצְוֹתֶיךָ "Shall we again break your commandments?," *non converteremur et irrita faceremus mandata tua* "we should not turn away, nor break your commandments" (Ezra 9:14).[3]

19.3.6.3.2 Attention to Context

Frequently, Jerome deviates from the standard translation equivalents for particular words according to context: אֲבֹתֵיהֶם "their fathers," *familiarum* "families" (Ezra 8:1; cf. v. 29); וַיִּגַּע "and touched," *venerat* "had come" (Ezra 3:1); הַדָּבָר "the matter," *peccato* "the sin" (Ezra 10:9; cf. v. 14); רַע "bad," *quasi languidus* "as languishing away" (Neh 2:1); אֻכְּלוּ "are consumed," *conbustae sunt* "are burnt" (Neh 2:3) or *consumptas* "consumed" (Neh 2:13); הָיָה "was," *eminebat* "stood out" (Neh 8:5). This also applies to his handling of Aramaic: מִתְעֲבֵד "were done," *concitantur* "were stirred up" (Ezra 4:19); שִׂימוּ "set," *audite* "hear" (Ezra 4:21). He can be free with his prepositions: עַל "upon" can be *de* "concerning" (Neh 1:2), *pro* "for" (Neh 2:4), *ad* "to" (Neh 2:7), or *cum* "with" (Neh 2:8). Context also impacts Jerome's translations of verb tenses, as when pluperfect (*miserat* "had sent") renders the imperfect consecutive (Neh 2:9). Sometimes, Jerome resorts to a slightly expansive translation: מְלַח הֵיכְלָא מְלַחְנָא "salt of the palace we eat," *memores salis quod in palatio comedimus* "remembering the salt that we ate in the palace" (Ezra 4:14); מִן־בֵּית גִּנְזֵי מַלְכָּא "from the house of the treasuries of the king," *de thesauro et de fisco regis* "from the treasury and from the revenue of the king" (Ezra 7:20); וְעֻזּוֹ "and his strength," *et imperium eius et fortitudo eius* "and his power and his strength" (Ezra 8:22); לַאֲחַשְׁדַּרְפְּנֵי הַמֶּלֶךְ "to the satraps of the king," *satrapis qui erant de conspectu regis* "to the satraps who were in the king's presence" (Ezra 8:36)[4]; כנותיו "his colleagues," *qui erant in consilio eorum* "those who

---

[2] Marcus, *Ezra and Nehemiah*, 11*.

[3] Jerome seems to have taken the *non* "not" from the following הֲלוֹא "not?," which he does not translate in that location. For other instances of Jerome's having difficulty with the Semitic text, see below.

[4] This expansion may have been motivated by a desire not to have two occurrences of *regis* "of the king" with only one word separating them, in imitation of the Hebrew הַמֶּלֶךְ לַאֲחַשְׁדַּרְפְּנֵי הַמֶּלֶךְ "the king, to the satraps of the king."

were in their council" (Ezra 4:7; cf. v. 17). Jerome occasionally adds words to clarify the sense, e.g., *ad eos* "to them" (Neh 5:9). v-Ezra–Neh can also present a more periphrastic rendering: וְעַרְוַת מַלְכָּא לָא אֲרִיךְ־לַנָא לְמֶחֱזֵא "and it is not fitting for us to see the dishonor of the king," *et quia laesiones regis videre nefas ducimus* "and because we regard it as abominable to see injuries to the king" (Ezra 4:14); אֲנַחְנוּ בְּאַשְׁמָה גְדֹלָה "we (have been) in great guilt," *sed et nos ipsi peccavimus granditer* "and we ourselves also have sinned greatly" (Ezra 9:7); הוּא יְסַד הַמַּעֲלָה "he (had) a beginning of going up," *coepit ascendere* "he began to go up" (Ezra 7:9); דִּבְרֵי מִצְוֹת "the words of the commandments," *in sermonibus et praeceptis* "in the words and commandments" (Ezra 7:11); וְלָא־בַטִּלוּ הִמּוֹ עַד־טַעְמָא לְדָרְיָוֶשׁ יְהָךְ וֶאֱדַיִן יְתִיבוּן נִשְׁתְּוָנָא עַל־דְּנָה "and they did not stop them until a report could go to Darius, and then they could return a letter concerning this," *et non potuerunt inhibere eos placuitque ut res ad Darium referretur et tunc satisfacerent adversus accusationem illam* "and they could not hinder them. And it was agreed that the matter should be referred to Darius, and then they would give satisfaction against this accusation" (Ezra 5:5); הָאֵל "God," *fortis* "strong" (Neh 1:5); חֲבֹל חָבַלְנוּ לָךְ "we have done great corruption against you," *vanitati seducti sumus* "we have been seduced by vanity" (Neh 1:7); אֵין זֶה כִּי־אִם רֹעַ לֵב "this is nothing except a bad (sad) heart," *non est hoc frustra sed malum nescio quid in corde tuo est* "This is not something without cause, but an evil, I know not what, in your heart" (Neh 2:2).[5]

19.3.6.3.3 Style

v-Ezra–Neh typically exhibits a rather wooden style, imitative of its Semitic *Vorlage*. Jerome's Latin often reflects the paratactic style of the original and follows its word order (e.g. Neh 2:1), though occasionally he alters the word order for the sake of clarity: לַבְּהֵמָה לַעֲבֹר תַּחְתָּי "for the beast to pass through under me," *iumento cui sedebam ut transiret* "for the beast on which I was riding to pass through" (Neh 2:14). This imitative style is reflected in Jerome's rendering of וַיְהִי "and it came to pass,"
which almost always becomes *factum est* "and it was done" (12 of 15×).[6] But Jerome can also vary his translation style to produce a more pleasing result in Latin. The imperfect consecutive can become a participle (Ezra 4:2; Neh 2:15) or a gerundival clause (Ezra 6:20). Jerome can handle *waw* with some flexibility: *porro* "however" (Ezra 3:6); ablative absolute (Ezra 3:10); relative clause (Ezra 4:20); *ergo* "so then" (Ezra 8:1, 31); *itaque* "and so" (Ezra 8:16); omitted (Neh 4:7). Sometimes he uses an ablative absolute in place of a Semitic preposition (Ezra 6:14), infinitive (Ezra 10:1), or a כַּאֲשֶׁר-clause (Neh 4:6). The infinitive construct with *lamed* routinely becomes an *ut*-clause (e.g. Ezra 1:1; 4:21; Neh 4:2; 8:1), sometimes a gerundival clause (e.g., Ezra 1:5, following an *ut*-clause; 2:68), a gerund with preposition (Ezra 4:4), or a relative clause (Neh 2:10). A participle often becomes a relative clause (e.g. Ezra 2:1, 6:1; Neh 1:5). Sometimes adjectives stand for a Semitic genitive (Ezra 5:14; 6:5). Repetitions in the Semitic text might be preserved in Latin (Ezra 1:2–3; 4:3), or avoided by either omitting the repeated word (Ezra 3:3; Neh 4:7) or altering a translation (Ezra 6:22). Jerome might also create a repetition (Ezra 6:12). He occasionally omits words that he considers unnecessary (עֲלֵיהוֹן "unto them," Ezra 5:1). Jerome usually maintains standard translation equivalents in v-Ezra–Neh, though he might vary the translation if the word appears multiple times in a passage: e.g., שַׂר "leader, prince" usually becomes *princeps* "ruler" (27 of 28×) but becomes first *princeps* and then *dux* "leader" at Ezra 8:29. A few high-frequency words have no standard translation equivalent in v-Ezra–Neh: e.g., Aramaic טְעֵם "decree" becomes *sententia* "pronouncement" (Ezra 4:21), *iussum* "command" (Ezra 4:21), *consilium* "decision" (Ezra 5:3), *potestas* "authority" (Ezra 5:9), *edictum* "edict" (Ezra 5:13), *decretum* "decree" (Ezra 6:11, 12), or more periphrastically rendered (Ezra 4:19; 5:17; 6:1, 3, 8; 7:21).[7]

---

[5] For examples in Aramaic, see Ezra 4:22; 6:8.

[6] Cf. Ezra 4:4; Neh 1:1; 2:1; 3:33; 4:1, 6, 9, 10; 6:1, 16; 13:3, 19. The three other appearances of וַיְהִי are at Neh 1:4 (*cum*-clause); 3:38 (*provocatum est*); and 7:1 (omitted).

[7] Cf. also the varied translations of בַּיִת "house" (Ezra 1:2, 4; 2:68; etc.); גּוֹלָה "captivity" (Ezra 1:11; 2:1; 4:1; Neh 7:6).

19.3.6.3.4 Lexical Difficulties with Hebrew/Aramaic Words

Some expressions proved philologically difficult for Jerome. In such situations, he sometimes relied on the context to make sense of a word, especially when the Greek versions offered little help: כְּעֶנֶת "and now," which he takes to be some sort of greeting, alternating between *salus* "greeting" and *pax* "peace" (Ezra 4:10, 11, 17; 7:12);[8] הַגִּזְבָּר "the treasurer," *filii Gazabar* "the sons of Gazabar" (Ezra 1:8; LXX: Γαρβαρηνου "Gabarenou"); בצחיחים (*Qere*) "in the exposed (places)," *per circuitum* "round about" (Neh 4:7; LXX: ἐν τοῖς σκεπεινοῖς "in sheltered [places]"). Context probably leads him to understand הַצְּבָיִים "Hazzebaim" as a place name, rendering it *qui erant de Asebaim* "who were from Asebaim" (Ezra 2:57), or *qui erat ortus ex Sabaim* "who was born in Hazzebaim" (Neh 7:59). The puzzling use of גְּמִיר "perfect" at Ezra 7:12, often taken now as part of an abbreviated epistolary greeting, becomes a description of Ezra as *doctissimo* "the most learned" in Jerome's version.[9] At Ezra 7:5, he seems to follow both the context and LXX in rendering הַכֹּהֵן הָרֹאשׁ "the head priest" as *sacerdotis ab initio* "the priest from the beginning" (LXX: τοῦ ἱερέως τοῦ πρώτου). Jerome's rendering of לְנַצֵּחַ "to be in charge" (Ezra 3:8, 9) as first *ut urguerent* "so that they might urge forward" and then *ut instarent* "so that they might hasten" was perhaps influenced by LXX[L] (ἐπινικῶν in both verses).[10] His knowledge of Syriac may have led to his translation of נְוָלוּ "dunghill" with *publicetur* "be confiscated" (Ezra 6:11).[11] At one point, he seems to have interpreted כָּל־קֳבֵל "because" in accordance with Hebrew usage rather than Aramaic, rendering it *libere accipe* "take freely" (Ezra 7:17).[12] Jerome rarely resorts to transliteration to solve his problems, using this techinque only for cases of personal names or titles, often in conformity with LXX:[13] *Nathinnei* (Ezra 2:58, 70; 7:7), *Athersatha* (Ezra 2:63),[14] *Beelteem* (Ezra 4:8), *Apharsacei* (Ezra 5:6).

19.3.6.4 Text-Critical Value

19.3.6.4.1 Possible Hebrew Variants

V-Ezra–Neh evinces a text very similar to MT (→ 19.2.2; → 1.3.5.11). This increases the plausibility of identifying possible Hebrew variants in Jerome's *Vorlage*, of which there are a few minor examples. Jerome's Hebrew text for Ezra 2:59 apparently contained *waw*s instead of *aleph*s for MT's אַדָּן אִמֵּר "Addan, Immer" (*et Don et Mer* "and Don and Mer"; cf. Neh 7:61); the translation of Neh 12:44 (*in decore gratiarum actionis* "in honour of thanksgiving") implies the reading התודה "thanksgiving" rather than הַתּוֹרָה "the Torah" of MT, though, in the absence of additional textual evidence, the reading may have existed only in Jerome's mind. In several instances, v-Ezra–Neh agrees with a known Greek reading against MT: at Ezra 4:3 for MT's אֱלֹהֵי יִשְׂרָאֵל "the God of Israel" Jerome read אלהינו (*deo nostro* "our God"); at Ezra 7:8, Jerome and LXX read the plural ויבאו "and they came" rather than the singular

---

[8] The Old Greek omits the word at Ezra 4:10, 11, renders it καὶ φάσιν "and they say" at Ezra 4:17, and καὶ ἡ ἀπόκρισις "and the answer" at Ezra 7:12. In each place, we find καὶ νῦν "and now" in LXX[L]. See Janz, *Deuxième livre d'Esdras*, 226 (on 7:12). Jerome's translation is possibly related to the reading tradition represented in MT, where the term always appears at the end of a verse. The apparatus of Marcus, *Ezra and Nehemiah*, suggests that Jerome's rendering was based on cultural conventions.

[9] On the various suggestions for this word, among which something like Jerome's solution has been proposed in the modern period, see Williamson, *Ezra, Nehemiah*, 96. On the Greek rendering of the word (τετέλεσται λόγος "the word has been completed"), see Janz, *Deuxième livre d'Esdras*, 226.

[10] The Old Greek omits any equivalent for לְנַצֵּחַ "to be in charge" in both verses. Cf. the varied translations of this word in v-Chr: 1 Chr 15:21 (*epinikion* "victory song"); 23:4 (*electi sunt et distributi* "they were chosen and distributed"); 2 Chr 2:1, 17 (both have *praepositos* "supervising" for the participle מְנַצְּחִים "supervising"); 34:12 (*urguebant* "they were hastening"); 34:13 (periphrastic). In his translation of the Hebrew Psalter, Jerome always renders לַמְנַצֵּחַ "to the leader/choirmaster" in the superscriptions with either *victori* "for victory" or *pro victoria* "for victory."

[11] See Williamson, *Ezra, Nehemiah*, 72. On the LXX rendering (τὸ κατ' ἐμὲ ποιηθήσεται "made my possesion"), see Janz, *Deuxième livre d'Esdras*, 221.

[12] The phrase also appears several times in Daniel (e.g., Dan 2:12, 24; 3:7, 8, 22; 6:10), where Jerome managed to arrive more closely to the correct sense. Cf. Ezra 4:14; 7:14, where כָּל־קֳבֵל דִּי "because" appears.

[13] On transliterations in LXX-Ezra–Neh, see Janz, *Deuxième livre d'Esdras*, 100–06.

[14] See Janz, *Deuxième livre d'Esdras*, 111–12.

of MT;[15] at Ezra 8:25, Jerome seems to read the singular ההרים (*obtulerat* "he offered"; LXX: ὕψωσεν) rather than הֵרִימוּ "they offered" (= MT); at Ezra 10:16, Jerome reads לדרוש (*ut quaererent* "so that they might examine"; LXX: ἐκζητῆσαι) rather than the faulty לִדְרִיוֹשׁ of MT;[16] at Neh 2:18, Jerome perhaps reads ואמר (*et aio* "and I said"; LXX: καὶ εἶπα) rather than MT's וַיֹּאמְרוּ "and they said"; he translates Neh 3:20 as if his text reads ההרה (*in monte* "on the mount"; cf. LXX[L]) rather than הֶחֱרָה "earnestly" of MT.[17]

19.3.6.4.2 Vocalization and *Ketiv/Qere*

V-Ezra–Neh usually conforms to the vocalization of MT (→ 19.2.2), but not in every case. For instance, Jerome apparently read the consonants נתן in Neh 2:12 as a perfect (*dedisset* "had put"; cf. LXX: δίδωσιν) rather than the participle of MT. As for the *Ketiv/Qere*, *BHQ records fifty-two total instances for Ezra-Nehemiah, but in only thirty-one cases can a distinction be maintained in the Latin translation. V-Ezra–Neh follows the *Ketiv* in eight of these instances, and the *Qere* in the remaining twenty-three cases.[18]

Barthélemy, *Critique textuelle 1982.
Janz, T., *Deuxième Livre d'Esdras: Traduction du texte grec de la Septante: Introduction et notes* (*Bible d' Alexandrie 11.2; Paris: Cerf, 2010).
Marcus, D., *Ezra and Nehemiah* (*BHQ 20; Stuttgart: Deutsche Bibelgesellschaft, 2006).
Williamson, H.G.M., *Ezra, Nehemiah* (WBC 16; Waco: Word Books, 1985).

Edmon L. Gallagher

19.3.7 Arabic Translations

19.3.7.1 Medieval Rabbanite Translations

Little is known in 2015 about the Jewish Arabic translations of the three last books of the Hebrew Bible, Ezra–Nehemiah and Chronicles. Despite their importance to biblical history, these books do not have liturgical or synagogue functions, and so they seem to have received less attention in ancient rabbinic circles, Jewish schoolrooms, and other learned groups.[1] Another possibility is that they did draw interest at a particular time and were translated into Arabic among learned Rabbanite circles (no differently than among the Karaite circles mentioned below) but that, due to the change in such interest or the limited social circle involved in their study, these translations were lost or not copied sufficiently.[2] The Arabic versions of these books are attested sparingly in manuscript sources and are rarely referred to in medieval Jewish literature. Medieval Karaite Jewish thinkers, however, who related to all parts of the Hebrew Bible as equally important in the derivation of Jewish law, gave more attention to Ezra–Nehemiah and Chronicles, as we shall show below. The great medieval Rabbanite translator, Saadia Gaon (882–942 C.E.), does not appear to have composed Arabic versions of these books.[3] Two short manuscripts that include a translation and a commentary on the books of Ezra and Chronicles are nonetheless attributed to Saadia Gaon. The first is catalogued as Fustāt 2000 at the Institute of Microfilmed Hebrew Manuscripts at the National and University Library of Jerusalem [= IMHM]. The manuscript originates from Egypt and it contains two pages of a translation and a commentary on Chronicles 34. The second is British Library manuscript Add. 27298, dating from the twelfth–thirteenth centuries C.E. [IMHM 6088]. It includes parts of a translation of and commentary on the books of Daniel (→ 18.3.7), Ecclesiastes (→ 13–17.1.8), and Ezra. Although some features in the Ezra translation concur with the translation system of Saadia Gaon, it is unclear whether the Gaon himself composed it or whether it was copied alongside other works attributed to him by students or copyists, and is essentially the product of an anonymous translator who may have

---

[15] See Janz, *Deuxième livre d' Esdras*, 225.
[16] Cf. Marcus, *Ezra and Nehemiah*, 44*.
[17] See the discussion in Barthélemy, *Critique textuelle 1982, 552–53.
[18] V-Ezra–Neh reflects the *Ketiv* at Ezra 2:1; 8:14, 17; 10:43; Neh 2:13; 7:52; 11:17; 12:16.

[1] Ratzaby, "Selections," 350; Ratzaby, *Saadia's Translation*, 8.
[2] Blau and Hopkins, "Ancient Bible," 4.
[3] For further on his translation enterprise, see → 1.3.6.

been influenced by Saadia's versions.[4] In a surviving commentary on Chronicles attributed to one of Saadia's students, the commentator mentions Saadia's name six times, but does not mention that his teacher had written a commentary on Chronicles.[5] Further evidence may be gleaned from medieval book lists preserved in the Cairo Genizah that list many of Saadia's translation works, which were often collected or requested by private book owners or by vendors in the classical Genizah period (tenth to thirteenth centuries). None of these surviving lists attribute to him a translation and commentary on Nehemiah and Chronicles, yet one of them does list a *tafsīr daniel we-ʿezra le-rabbenu seʿadya* "a translation and commentary on Daniel and Ezra by our Rabbi Saadia."[6] Several scores of anonymous translation fragments of the three books have been identified in the Cairo Genizah Arabic and Judeo-Arabic collections.[7] It is possible that more exist and have not yet been identified. Usually, these Genizah fragments represent ad hoc translations, sometimes in popular style and sometimes more akin to Saadia's translation methodology.

Of a later period is the work of the Rabbanite commentator Rabbi Issāchār ben-Sūsān Hamaʿarāvī, who was born in Morocco and emigrated from Fez to Palestine, where he lived mostly in Safed. He composed an updated Arabic translation of the entire Hebrew Bible between 1570 and 1573, including the books of Ezra, Nehemiah, and Chronicles.[8] The translation of these three books is found in manuscript Susan 160 [IMHM 9269]. Rabbi ben-Sūsān was influenced by Saadia Gaon's versions but wished to adapt them to the needs of his time. He cites the first word of each verse (the *incipit*) and follows it with a Judeo-Arabic translation that is closer to the vernacular of his time, and then with a lengthier commentary. Such pre-modern Judeo-Arabic works are known by the generic Arabic terms *sharḥ/shuruḥ*, i.e., explanative (interpretation/s). After each chapter, ben-Sūsān added a *bayān*, i.e., a clarification of difficult Hebrew words and various discussions.[9]

19.3.7.2 Medieval Karaite Translations

Medieval Karaite sources preserve more tangible evidence concerning Jewish interest in rendering these three books into Arabic than the Rabbanite translations:[10]

The earliest source is a one-page translation of Chronicles attributed to the founder of the Karaite school of learning in Jerusalem in the early tenth century, Yūsuf ibn Nūḥ. It is preserved in manuscript Evr. Arab. I 2635 of the Firkovich Collections in the Russian National Library, St. Petersburg [IMHM 55741].[11] In addition, various manuscripts containing parts of Yefet ben ʿEli's translations of the books of Ezra, Nehemiah, and Chronicles (→ 20.3.8) are extant. This prolific commentator wrote a translation and commentary in Arabic on the entire Hebrew Bible during the second part of the tenth century. Yefet's entire translation and commentary on 1 Chronicles has survived in several manuscripts, while only parts of 2 Chronicles are extant. The most comprehensive manuscript is

---

[4] On the question whether Saadia translated the entire Hebrew Bible or only specific books or chapters, see Blau and Hopkins, "Ancient Bible," 4; Ratzaby, *Saadia's Translation*, 7; Ratzaby, "Seridīm," 169; Schlossberg, "The Spiritual Leadership," 222.

[5] See Kirchheim, *Ein Kommenator*.

[6] The title Ezra may include Nehemiah as well in Jewish sources. See Allony, *The Jewish Library*, 282. This specific Genizah fragment [TS MISC 36.134] contains a request to borrow books by a Bible scribe. The editors point out (see Allony, *The Jewish Library*, 282 n. 2) that this is the first time such a work is attributed to Saadia. In the appendix to the volume, there appear several other books entitled *tafsīr* in connection to Ezra and Chronicles (see Allony, *The Jewish Library*, 502–05) that are not attributed specifically to Saadia, and so they may reflect other translations and commentaries that were known at the time.

[7] See the indices in Baker and Polliack, *Arabic and Judaeo-Arabic Manuscripts* (2001); Shivtiel and Niessen, *Arabic and Judaeo-Arabic Manuscripts* (2006).

[8] For further on the pre-modern Judeo-Arabic Bible translations, see → 1.3.6.

[9] Doron, "From the Tafsir," 172–75; Doron, "On the Arabic Translation," 283–85; Doron, "Ben-Sūsān."

[10] For further on the Karaite translation enterprise, see → 1.3.6.

[11] On the Firkovich Collections and the Karaite school of learning in Jerusalem, see Goldstein, *Karaite Exegesis*, 1–14, and further references therein.

kept in the private collection of I. Elisha in Lausanne, Switzerland [IMHM 50817]. The manuscript was copied in Egypt and contains 233 pages, including the translation and commentary of 1 Chronicles and the five initial chapters of 2 Chronicles. It has many erasures, however, as well as additions and duplications of words or groups of words, and sometimes it neglects to translate verses.

A more reliable translation is preserved in the Russian National Library manuscript Evr. Arab. I 1395 [IMHM 55018]. It is much shorter, containing 129 pages, which include the translation and commentary on 1 Chronicles (except for 1 Chr 1:1–32) and 2 Chronicles 1; 2; and 4. In this manuscript, the pages are jumbled in order, torn, and difficult to decipher; its apparent continuation is found in manuscript Evr. Arab. I 4321 of the Russian National Library [IMHM 62628], which contains truncated sections of Yefet's work on 2 Chronicles 8–15. Other manuscripts containing a few chapters from Yefet's translation and commentary of various sections of Chronicles have also been preserved in the same collection.[12]

In addition, the translations and commentaries of Yefet ben 'Eli on the books of Ezra and Nehemiah are extant in various manuscript sources, none of which are complete.[13] Yefet's exegesis often draws on other works by Karaite scholars who preceded him or who belonged to the Jerusalem school during the ninth and tenth centuries C.E., such as Daniel al-Qūmisī, Salmon ben Yeruḥam, and David ben Boʿaz. It is likely that they also commented on verses from Ezra, Nehemiah, and Chronicles, and so sporadic translations from these books may be found in their vast exegetical and grammatical corpus. Nevertheless, no other independent and systematic Karaite translations and commentaries to these specific books have been uncovered so far. Mr. Yair Zoran is currently preparing an annotated critical edition and Hebrew translation of Yefet ben 'Eli's Arabic translation and Commentary on the Books of Ezra, Nehemiah and Chronicles.

Allony, N., "MeTargūm Rasag LiYehezkel," *Tarbiz* 16 (1945): 21–27 [Hebr.].

Allony, N., *The Jewish Library in the Middle Ages: Book Lists from the Cairo Genizah* (eds. M. Frenkel and H. Ben-Shammai; Jerusalem: Ben-Zvi Institute, 2006) [Hebr.].

Baker, C.F. and M. Polliack, *Arabic and Judaeo-Arabic Manuscripts in The Cambridge Genizah Collections, Arabic Old Series (T-S Ar.1a-54)* (Cambridge: Cambridge University Press, 2001).

Blau, J. and S. Hopkins, "Ancient Bible Translations to Judeo-Arabic," *Peʿamim* 83 (2000): 4–14 [Hebr.].

Doron, D., "On the Arabic Translation of the Torah by Issāchar ben-Sūsān Hammaʾarāvī," *Sefunot* 18 (1985): 279–98 [Hebr.].

Doron, D., "From the Tafsir of R. Saadia Gaon to the Translation of R. Mordechai Hai Dayyan of Tunis," *Sefunot* 20 (1991): 171–80 [Hebr.].

Doron, D., "Ben-Sūsān, Issachar ben Mordechai," in *Encyclopedia of Jews of the Islamic World* (ed. N. Stillman; Leiden: Brill, 2010), 1:394–95.

Goldstein, M., *Karaite Exegesis in Medieval Jerusalem: The Judeo-Arabic Pentateuch Commentary of Yūsuf ibn Nūḥ and Abū al-Faraj Harūn* (Texts and Studies in Medieval and Early Modern Judaism 26; Tübingen: Mohr Siebeck, 2011).

Kirchheim, R., *Ein Kommenator zur Chronik aus dem 10. Jahrhundert* (Frankfurt am Main: Brömer, 1874).

Ratzaby, Y., "Seridīm mi-targūm ʿaravī leneviʾīm rishonim mi-beyt midrasho shel Rasag," *Sinai* 25 (1949): 168–78 [Hebr.].

Ratzaby, Y., "Selections from Rav Saadia's Commentary on Lamentations," *Bar-Ilan* 20–21 (1983): 349–81 [Hebr.].

Ratzaby, Y. (ed.), *Saadia's Translation and Commentary on Isaiah: Collected, Edited with Translation and Notes by Yehuda Ratzaby* (Kiriat Ono, 1993) [Hebr.].

Schlossberg, E., "The Spiritual Leadership and Adminis-

---

[12] These are also held in the Russian National Library, including manuscript Evr. Arab. II 3345 (IMHM 62675), which contains Yefet's work on 1 Chr 4:21–11:25; manuscriptEvr. I 4050 (IMHM 57750), which consists of thirty-two pages and includes his work on 1 Chronicles 20–21; 27–29; manuscript Evr. I 4250 (IMHM 57480) has fourteen pages and includes parts of Yefet's work on 2 Chr 11:17–15:7. Mr. Yair Zoran is preparing a critical edition of Yefet's translation and commentary on Chronicles.

[13] For manuscripts that are not included in the Firkovich Collections of the Russian National Library, see Tamani, "Repertorio"; Tamani, "Prolegomeni"; Tamani, "La tradizione." For material from the Firkovich Collections, see the catalogue of the manuscript library of the National Library of Israel: http://aleph.nli.org.il/.

tration of Harav Saadia Gaon," *Amadot* 5 (2013): 213–42 [Hebr.].

Shivtiel, A. and F. Niessen, *Arabic and Judaeo-Arabic Manuscripts in the Cambridge Genizah Collections: Taylor-Schechter New Series* (Cambridge: Cambridge University Press, 2006).

Tamani, G., "Repertorio dei manoscritti ebraici Caraiti," *Hen* 1 (1979): 272–82.

Tamani, G., "La tradizione delle opere di Yefet b. Ali," *Bulletin d'études karaïtes* 1 (1983): 27–76.

Tamani, G., "Prolegomeni a un'edizione dei commenti biblici di Yefet b. Ali," *Bulletin d'études karaïtes* 2 (1989): 23–28.

Meira Polliack
Meirav Nadler-Akirav
Yair Zoran

19.4 Secondary Translations

19.4.1 Vetus Latina

VL-Ezra is known from a single manuscript (VL[123]) from the eleventh century that was written in northern Italy, which preserves the complete text of the book,[1] and from a fragmentary palimpsest (VL[125]) from St. Gallen, written in the second half of the eighth century, which contains passages from the second part of the book, Ezra 16:11–17:6 fin; 19:18–30.[2] Beside this, there are very sparse quotations in the works of the church fathers (→ 21.8) and some entries in a bible glossary, where the VL expressions are juxtaposed with the corresponding Vulgate forms.[3] Only with the careful examination of VL[123] by Bogaert[4] did it become clear that a VL version of Esdras A' (= 3 Esdras in the Vulgate and 1 Esdras in English Bibles; → II.7.1.4; → II.7.1.1) existed.[5] Manuscript VL[123] contains the translation of Esdras A' as the *liber primus hesdre* (folio 107 v), followed by *liber II*, the translation of Esdras B' (= Ezra–Nehemiah). The latter appears, like its Greek *Vorlage*, as a single book without any subdivision.[6]

Although the edition of the VL version has not yet appeared in the series of the Vetus Latina Institute, Hanhart quotes the Latin tradition extensively in the critical apparatus of his edition of LXX[7] and includes it in his comprehensive studies, thus making the text available for further study.

19.4.1.1 Translation Technique and Inner-Translational Features

The translation of the VL texts proves to be an accurate rendering of their Greek *Vorlagen* (→ 19.3.1; → II.7.1.2). A direct dependence on the Hebrew text does not exist, although in some cases the Greek text, which links VL to MT (→ 19.2.2), is not transmitted and so there seems to be a close connection between the two. It can be shown that within the VL recension the text of the earlier manuscript VL[125] represents an earlier stage in the transmission of the text.[8] VL[123] contains more Lucianic readings (→ 19.3.5) and has additional assimilations to MT. Both features point to a late text form. Doublets are important for the characterization of the VL text, even more so for VL[125] than for VL[123], and for its placement within the history of the text. The difference between the characteristics of the two VL versions can be demonstrated in Esd B 19:21 (= Neh 9:21), where two Lucianic manuscripts adapt MT against LXX and one of the texts also duplicates the passage: וְרַגְלֵיהֶם לֹא בָצֵקוּ "and their feet did not swell" is rendered in LXX as ὑποδήματα αὐτῶν οὐ διερράγησαν "their sandals did not tear" (*NETS*), which is corrected against MT in the Lucianic version as οἱ πόδες αὐτῶν οὐκ ἐτυλώθησαν "their feet were not made callous" and another manuscript contains both expressions. VL[125] translates both parts of the doublet, i.e., *calciamenta eorum non sunt disrupta et pedes eorum non intumuerunt* "their sandals are not torn and their feet are not swollen." The later manuscript VL[123] transmits only the second part of the doublet and thus follows MT.[9]

While the translators and revisers of the VL versions provide us with an accurate rendering of the Greek *Vorlagen*, in general they show little inter-

---

[1] Hanhart, *Esdrae liber II*, 12–13 with bibliography.
[2] Bischoff, "Neue Materialien," 417–19. For the manuscript, see St. Gallen, Stiftsbibliothek, Cod. Sang. 722, 259–62 (www.e-codices.unifr.ch).
[3] For this "*alia editio*," see Bischoff, "Neue Materialien," 407–36 and De Bruyne, "Fragments d' anciennes versions latines," 119–20.
[4] See Bogaert, *Arbeitsbericht*, 26–27 and Bogaert, "Les livres d' Esdras," 17–19.
[5] This problem is discussed in the careful study by Denter, *Stellung*, 90–103. He proposed that the first part of the translation of Esdras B' was replaced by the translation of Esdras A'.
[6] For this problem, see e.g. Bogaert, Numérotation, 11–13. In this context he also discusses the question of the ancient canon lists.
[7] Hanhart, *Esdrae liber II*.

[8] Hanhart, *Text und Textgeschichte*, 260. Following further studies concerning the relationship of these two text forms, Hanhart modifies the opinion (see p. 266, n. 3) that he presented in an earlier study, i.e., Hanhart, "Zur griechischen und altlateinischen Textgeschichte," 145–64.
[9] Hanhart, *Text*, 235–36.

est in maintaining consistency in their translation. This can be shown, for example, by comparing the diverse renderings of the expression גם(ו), "(and) also" in the different versions. Neither the Lucianic version nor the VL texts are consistent in their renderings. As already stated, the text of VL[123] adapts more MT readings than the Lucianic text.[10]

19.4.1.2 Reconstruction of the Parent Texts and Text-Critical Value

The VL text represented by VL[123] contains many elements of the Lucianic recension (→ 19.3.5), which in itself is characterized by its adaptations of MT (→ 19.2.2). But beyond that, the VL text is in general closer to MT than any of the Greek sources. Thus, one has to ask whether the VL text, although transmitted in a late manuscript, results from a *Vorlage* influenced by a proto-Lucianic text or whether it represents the last phase of harmonization to MT.[11] The analysis of the available sources suggests that the VL text of VL[123] is based on a lost late Greek *Vorlage* with extensive assimilations to MT.[12] There are neither signs that the Old Latin text of VL[123] might include elements that predate the (Hexaplaric-)Lucianic recension of the Greek text (→ 19.3.4; → 19.3.5), nor can one prove a direct dependence of VL[123] on MT.[13] The textual basis of the fragmentary manuscript VL[125] does not permit any definite conclusion about its placement within the textual history of VL. However, because of the preserved VL evidence, Hanhart still considers the existence of a more differentiated variation of Greek text forms in the early phase of VL's textual history than is transmitted in the Greek sources.[14] In consequence, the VL versions of the text are also of some importance for the reconstruction of the history of the Greek text of Esdras B.

---

[10] For the evaluation of this problem and the question regarding whether it is due to the translation technique or the recension technique, see Hanhart, "Ursprünglicher Septuagintatext," 105, n. 32.
[11] Hanhart, *Text*, 17.
[12] Hanhart, *Text*, 284–85.
[13] Hanhart, *Text*, 289–90.
[14] Hanhart, *Text*, 290.

Bischoff, B., "Neue Materialien zum Bestand und zur Geschichte der altlateinischen Bibelübersetzung," in *Miscellanea Giovanni Mercati* (6 vols.; Studi e testi 121; Vatican City: Biblioteca Apostolica Vaticana, 1946), 1.407–36.

Bogaert, P.-M., *Vetus Latina: 30. Arbeitsbericht der Stiftung: 19. Bericht des Instituts* (Beuron: Vetus Latina Institute, 1986).

Bogaert, P.-M., "Les livres d'Esdras et leur numérotation dans l'histoire du canon de la Bible latine," *RBén* 110 (2000): 5–26.

De Bruyne, D., "Fragments d'anciennes versions latines tirés d'un glossaire biblique," *Archivum Latinitatis medii aevi* 3 (1927): 113–20.

Denter, T., *Die Stellung der Bücher Esdras im Kanon des Alten Testamentes: Eine Kanongeschichtliche Untersuchung* (Marienstatt: Buch- und Kunsthandlung, 1963).

Hanhart, R., *Esdrae liber II* (Septuaginta Vetus Testamentum Graecum 8.2; Göttingen: Vandenhoeck & Ruprecht, 1993).

Hanhart, R., "Ursprünglicher Septuagintatext und lukianische Rezension des 2. Esrabuches im Verhältnis zur Textform der Vetus Latina," in *Philologia Sacra: Biblische und patristische Studien für Hermann J. Frede und Walter Thiele zu ihrem siebzigsten Geburtstag* (2 vols.; ed. R. Gryson; VL 24; Freiburg i.B.: Herder, 1993), 1.90–115.

Hanhart, R., "Zur griechischen und altlateinischen Textgeschichte des 1. und 2. Esrabuches in ihrem Verhältnis zueinander," in *Lectures et Relectures de la Bible: Festschrift P.-M. Bogaert* (eds. J.-M. Auwers and A. Wénin; BETL 144; Leuven: Peeters, 1999), 145–64.

Hanhart, R., *Text und Textgeschichte des 2. Esrabuches* (MSU 25; Göttingen: Vandenhoeck & Ruprecht, 2003).

Bonifatia Gesche

19.4.2 Coptic Translations

19.4.2.1 Background and Transmission

Due to the thorough archeological investigation of the necropolis in Western Thebes, we have three possible relatively early indications of the existence of the books of Ezra in Coptic. An ostracon (seventh or eighth century C.E.) containing the catalogue of the monastic library of the Monastery of St. Eliah[1] mentions ⲛⲉⲥⲇⲣⲁ "the (books of) Es-

---

[1] R.-G. Coquin, "Le Catalogue de la Bibliothèque du Cou-

dra." Another ostracon, from the same area and quite likely of the same date, was found in the far better known and properly excavated Monastery of Epiphanius.[2] It preserves a passage from the deuterocanonical book Esdras I (= 3 Ezra, → II.7.1), i.e., 3 Ezra 9:21–24.[3] As this passage comprises only names, it must remain open if the text on the ostracon is Greek or Coptic.

Particularly interesting is an as-yet unpublished papyrus fragment found in 1998 by an Australian team from Macquarie University, Sydney in the Theban tomb TT 233.[4] The fragment likewise presents a list of Old Testament books, probably from one of the nearby monasteries. The list, only part of which is extant, features the books of Isaiah, Jeremiah, Daniel, Esdra, Esdraz (sic?), and Judith. The relevant lines read:]ecapa· ū .[and]ecapaz [. Thus, Esdra and Esdraz (or only Esdra?) are listed. Unfortunately, the list breaks off exactly at the point where it would have specified to which Ezranic books it is referring.

However, the only Coptic textual witnesses we possess of an Ezranic text are from the deuterocanonical 4 Ezra (= 2 Esdras 3–14, → II.7.2.5). Suciu recently published a late Sahidic fragment of 4 Ezra and presented on this occasion all hitherto-known Coptic fragments of 4 Ezra.[5] Taking into account the book lists on ostraca, he considers also the possibility of a Coptic version of Ezra–Nehemiah. Since the Coptic versions normally follow the canon of LXX (→ 1.3.1.1), we can surmise that the fragmentary list from Thebes continued with Esdras I (deuterocanonical) and Esdras B (Ezra–Nehemiah).

As we have merely indications and not a single text fragment, it remains uncertain whether Ezra–Nehemiah was translated into Coptic or if the above-mentioned lists referred to versions of the deuterocanonical books of 3 and 4 Ezra.

Frank Feder

19.4.3 Ethiopic Translation(s)

19.4.3.1 Title and Place in the Manuscripts

The Ethiopians regard Ezra and Nehemiah as one book, which they traditionally call 3 Ezra (ዕዝራ ፫) in contrast to LXX ('Εσδρας β', "Second [Book of] Ezra"; → 19.3.1) and the Vulgate (1–2 *Esdrae*, "1–2 [book of] Ezra"; → 19.3.6). As a result, the beginning of Nehemiah lacks any distinguishing markers, but interestingly the biblical incipit itself is corrupt: ቃልሲንያ ወልደ ኬልያ "Qalsiniya son of Kēlya." Theological dialogue with Western forms of Christianity has introduced certain challenges. For example, the scribe of Eth^IES 77 provided the text with European chapter and verse divisions, which required renumbering Nehemiah, yet he refused to separate the two works. He also added a running title, which reads ዕዝራ "Ezra" for the first portion and thereafter switches to ዕዝራ ነህምያ "Ezra Nehemiah," the only other explicit nod to a different heritage.

Eth-1 Ezra (= 4 Esdras), Eth-2 Ezra (= 1 Esdras), and Eth-3 Ezra (= Ezra–Nehemiah) almost always circulate as a group. This corpus is rarely transmitted alone. Often, Tobit (→ II.14.9), Judith (→ II.9.6),

---

vent de Saint Élie 'du Rocher' (Ostracon IFA 13315)," *Bulletin de l'Institut Français d'Archéologie Orientale* 75 (1975): 207–39, esp. 209; J. Horn, "Die Präsenz des Alten Testamentes in der ägyptischen christlichen Frömmigkeit, aufgewiesen an zwei Werken der koptisch-sahidischen hagiographischen Literatur," in *Sprachen, Mythen, Mythizismen: Festschrift für Walter Beltz zum 65. Geburtstag* (eds. A. Drost-Abgarjan and J. Tubach; Hallesche Beiträge zur Orientwissenschaft 32; Halle: Martin-Luther-Universität Halle-Wittenberg, 2004), 355–82 (358–59).

[2] W.E. Crum, *The Monastery of Epiphanius at Thebes*, Part 2: *Coptic Ostraca and Papyri* (New York: Metropolitan Museum of Art, 1926), 119 (no. 581) and 300 (commentary; MMA, New York, Inv. Nr. 12.180.184).

[3] R. Hanhart (ed.), *Esdrae Liber I* (2nd ed.; Septuaginta Vetus Testamentum Graecum 8.1; Göttingen: Vandenhoeck & Ruprecht, 1991), 13 (ostracon 841).

[4] Personal communication from Malcolm Choat; cf. B. Ockinga and S. Binder, "The Macquarie Theban Tombs Project: 20 years in Dra Abu el Naga," *Ancient History: Resources for Teachers* 39.2 (2009): 205–47, esp. 243–44; cf. also H. Behlmer and M. Underwood, "Coptic Textual Finds from the Macquarie University Excavations at Dra Abu al-Naga (TT233)," in *Christianity and Monasticism in Upper Egypt*, Vol. 2: *Nag Hammadi-Esna* (eds. G. Gabra and H.N. Takla; Cairo: American University in Cairo Press, 2010), 7–19, esp. 17.

[5] A. Suciu, "On a Bilingual Copto-Arabic Manuscript of *4 Ezra* and the Reception of this Pseudoepigraphon in Coptic Literature," *JSP* 25.1 (2015): 3–22.

19.4.3 ETHIOPIC TRANSLATION(S)

and Esther (→ 13–17.2.3.5) follow. Manuscripts display greater variation concerning preceding material. Generally there is a preference for Chronicles (→ 20.4.3), one or more of the Major Prophets (→ 6–9.2.3.1; → 6–9.2.3.2; → 6–9.2.3.3), or the Twelve (in descending order; → 6–9.2.3.4).

19.4.3.2 Background

In 1919, Esteves Pereira[1] published an eclectic edition of Eth-3 Ezra based on two manuscripts (→ 1.4.3.5). From the numerous transliterations in the book, he concluded that the translator employed both a Lucianic Greek manuscript (→ 19.3.5) and a Masoretic Hebrew manuscript (→ 19.2.2). Both claims are certainly incorrect, for the manuscript Esteves Pereira favored (his manuscript A) was a late product of Arabic (→ 19.3.7; → 19.4.8) revision. Whereas, at Eth-3 Ezra 10:23, the Old Ethiopic transliterates Φαδαια καὶ Ἰοδομ "Phadaia and Iodom" (ፋዲሐ ወይሐዶም "Fadiḥä and Yəḥadōm"), Esteves Pereira opts for the reading of his manuscript A, ማልአከ ይሁዳ "ruler of Judah," the first word of which requires a misreading of an Arabic text and the second the Greek lemma (Ἰουδας) that lies behind the Arabic version (→ 19.3.7; → 19.4.8). In addition, Hanhart points to a number of doublets found in Esteves Pereira's manuscript A that: 1) are not from the Greek; and 2) expand a previously existing text akin to Esteves Pereira's manuscript B (= Old Ethiopic).[2] The Old Ethiopic unquestionably derives from a Greek source alone (→ 1.4.3.7.3).

19.4.3.3 Translation Character

The translator's knowledge of Greek was inadequate for the task. For example, the translator did not recognize the word γάζα "treasure" in Eth-3 Ezra 5:17; 6:1; and 17:20, so he transliterated it (a phenomenon found also in Acts).[3] Although far from fluent, the translator of Eth-3 Ezra felt comfortable providing paraphrases or making guesses based on the immediate context. Still, where the Greek wording matched his capabilities, he strictly adhered to what lay before him. Particularly illustrative are the long lists of names, which are handled well even if frequently misdivided. Despite the trouble recognizing individual names, the results are alphabetically correct: note in particular ፋሐድም አቤዱ ኒካሌም "Faḥēdəm, 'Äbēdu Nēkalēm" = Φααδμωαβ Ἐδενε Χαληλλ "Phadmoab, Edne, Chalel" (Eth-3 Ezra 10:30). Sometimes names are translated rather than transliterated (e.g., Φορος "Phoros"; Eth-3 Ezra 10:25). Rarely, metathesis occurs (ፋሐስ "Faḥēs," reading Φαης "Phaes" for Φαση "Phase" [*NETS] in Eth-3 Ezra 2:49). At times, the translator confused similar letters, although perhaps some of these errors originated in the exemplar. For example, the translator gives ሰሙይልኢ ምእት "Sämuyəl'i one hundred" for Σαμουι διακόσιοι "Samoui two hundred" (*NETS) at Eth-3 Ezra 21:17–18, which results from lambda/delta interchange, perhaps letter/numeral interchange, and incorrect word division (i.e., Σαμουιλι αʹ κοσιοι "Samouili one hundred").

19.4.3.4 Text-Critical Value

Lacking a decent critical edition complicates judgments about textual consanguinity, but a survey of Eth-3 Ezra 1–5; 10; 15; and 23 revealed numerous shared readings and often word-for-word agreements with Codex Vaticanus (LXX^B; → 19.3.1) and related minuscules, especially LXX55. For example, in the book's first three verses the Old Ethiopic lacks any reference to κύριος "Lord," reads Ἰουδα "in Judah" instead of Ἰουδαια "in Judea," and omits v. 3b. In Eth-3 Ezra 2, the names and numbers almost always correspond with LXX^B, including the two different spellings of Βερζελλαι "Berzellai" in v. 61. The three variations of Βααλταμ "Baaltam" in LXX^B are likewise paralleled in the Ethiopic (Eth-3 Ezra 4:8, 9, and 17). Of particular significance for understanding the textual background of Eth-3 Ezra is the highly abbreviated version of Eth-3 Ezra 21:15–35 shared with LXX^B and others. Hanhart observes, "As in 1 Esdr, the old uncials B A and V are ... along with those minuscules and secondary versions closely related to them – above all ms. 55 and the Ethiopic version as fellow witnesses of the B-

---

[1] Pereira, "Le Troisième Livre de 'Ezrâ."
[2] Hanhart, *Esdrae II*, 14–16.
[3] The translation in Eth-3 Ezra 7:21 is probably a guess based on the context. See also Acts 8:27.

text – representatives of an old text form relatively untouched by recensional activity."[4]

Intrigued by some of the later developments in Ethiopian transmission, Hanhart proposed that some of the Lucianic readings (→ 19.3.5) found in Esteves Pereira's manuscript A could prove to be valuable because, even though many of the variants betray Masoretic (→ 19.2.2) influence, some likely come from the Greek. Historically, this is improbable; later revisions from the Greek appear in no other Old Testament books, and almost always an Arabic version (→ 19.3.7; → 19.4.8) supplies the purportedly "Greek" readings.[5] Therefore, "the transmission of genuine Lucianic evidence" might be recoverable from the Arabic (→ 19.4.8), but certainly not from the Ethiopic.[6]

The literary relationship between Eth-2 Ezra (= 1 Esdras) and Eth-3 Ezra (= Ezra–Nehemiah) in the Ethiopic Bible has yet to be studied. Due to the conservative nature of transmission in the earlier periods it is possible that very little cross-pollination took place. On the other hand, of the identifiable changes from those periods, influence from parallels ranks very high. Usually such alterations derive from the immediate context, but the addition of Matt 24:15b at the end of Dan 11:35 (→ 18.4.3.5) reveals the extent to which supposed parallels could impact the text. However, in light of the translator's general fidelity to his *Vorlage* and Hanhart's assessment of the Old Ethiopic as a very strong witness to the text of LXX[B] in both books, any influence is likely to be minimal.[7]

---

[4] "Wie in Esdr 1 sind die alten Unzialen B A und V ... mitsamt den ihnen nahe stehenden Minuskeln und Sekundärübersetzungen – vor allem Hs. 55 und die äthiopische Übersetzung als Mitzeugen des B-Textes – die Vertreter einer alten, von rezensionellen Bearbeitungen noch relativ unberührten Textform." Hanhart, *Text*, 13. The kinship is closer than indicated here, because Hanhart relies on Esteves Pereira ("Le Troisième Livre de 'Ezrâ"), although not uncritically, and does not take into account the limitations inherent in Ethiopic for translating Greek.

[5] Hanhart's (*Esther*, 32) identification of a second Greek revision in Eth-Esth is mistaken (→ 13–17.2.3.5).

[6] Hanhart, *Esdrae II*, 17: "die Überlieferung genuin lukianischen Gutes."

[7] For Hanhart's judgments about 1 Ezra, see *Esdrae I*, 31.

19.4.3.5 Subsequent History

From partial collations of fourteen manuscripts it appears that Eth-3 Ezra may have a slightly different textual history than most of the other biblical books in Gəʿəz. Unexpectedly, a transitional period does not appear (→ 1.4.3.7.4). Presumably, the continued circulation of the Old Ethiopic into the twentieth century, which is rare for biblical materials, is a consequence of this (see Eth[UNES 2.18] and Eth[EMIP 1063] for examples).

Instead of capping a slow evolutionary process of textual alteration, the Standardized Text (→ 1.4.3.7.5) of Eth-3 Ezra just appears suddenly and then prevails among the later manuscripts. As expected, this Standardized Text reworks the Old Ethiopic using the Arabic (→ 19.3.7; → 19.4.8) and Hebrew versions (→ 19.2.2). The Arabic (→ 19.4.8), based on a Lucianic text (→ 19.3.5), necessitated quite a few changes. The Hebrew also resulted in considerable alterations, but the reviser did not know Hebrew as well as Arabic. As a result, some transliterations of Hebrew words appear (cf. ሐተሐላ "ḫätäḫēla" = הַתְּחִלָּה "prayer"; Eth-3 Ezra 21:17 [MT-Neh 11:17]).

This oddity also highlights the apparent absence of the seventeenth century Academic Text. Currently, the only other evidence for a recension based on MT (→ 19.2.2) is found in the Textus Receptus. Although clearly influenced by the Hebrew, the Textus Receptus is conflationary, incorporating not only Hebrew evidence, but readings and glosses from other traditions. See Eth-3 Ezra 21:14–17 in Eth[IES 77] for an example.

Esteves Pereira, F.W. (ed.), "Le Troisième Livre de 'Ezrâ (Esdras et Néhémie Canoniques) Version Éthiopienne," *PO* 13 (1919): 643–736.

Hanhart, R. (ed.), *Esther* (Septuaginta Vetus Testamentum Graecum 8.3; Göttingen: Vandenhoeck & Ruprecht, 1966).

Hanhart, R. (ed.), *Liber Esdrae I* (rev. ed.; Septuaginta Vetus Testamentum Graecum 8.1; Göttingen: Vandenhoeck & Ruprecht, 1991).

Hanhart, R. (ed.), *Liber Esdrae II* (Septuaginta Vetus Testamentum Graecum 8.2; Göttingen: Vandenhoeck & Ruprecht, 1993).

Hanhart, R., *Text und Textgeschichte des 2. Esrabuches* (MSU 25; Göttingen: Vandenhoeck & Ruprecht, 2003).

Curt Niccum

19.4.4 Late Syriac Translations

19.4.4.1 Manuscripts of Syh-Ezra–Neh

The only evidence as to the Syh-Ezra–Neh (LXX-Esd β → 19.3.1) is manuscript Add 12168 belonging to the British Library dating back to the eighth or ninth century C.E. The manuscript is classified by the editor of the catalogue as *Catena Patrum*; in fact, it contains only extracts of the biblical books with comments of the church fathers inserted (→ 21.9).[1] After the book of Chronicles, there is the "first book of Ezra according to the version of the Septuagint" then follows the second book ("again: from the second book of Ezra, from the words of Nehemiah the son of Chelqia"). At the end of the second book, the colophon says that "these were taken from the book of Ezra according to the version of the Septuagint." This expression means the Hexaplaric version (→ 19.3.4). In fact, a note reports at the end of the extracts from the book of Daniel that all these extracts come from the translation by Paul of Tella (→ 1.4.5.2).[2]

In the manuscript, however, there is no patristic comment on the two books of Ezra. Only some pericopes are recorded in order to give an exhaustive idea of the story contained in the two books. Only the section known as the book of Nehemiah is extant from the biblical book of Ezra–Nehemiah (1:1–4a; 2:1–8; 4:1–3, 10–16; 6:15–16; 7:72b–9:3).

19.4.4.2 Editions

The extracts from Nehemiah were published by Torrey, "Portions," and then by Gwynn, *Remnnants*. The comparison between the two transcriptions shows some differences. The text was also used in the Göttingen edition of the *Septuaginta*, and indicated with the abbreviation "Syh."[3]

---

[1] Wright, *Catalogue*, 904.
[2] F. 161b report in Wright, *Catalogue*, 907.
[3] Hanhart, *Esdrae liber II*, 13–14.

19.4.4.3 Character of the Translation

According to Gwynn, "The Daniel extracts are identified by comparison with Cod. Ambrosianus, as belonging to the Version of Paul; and there can be no doubt that the extracts from Chronicles and Esdras come from that Version likewise."[4] The text of the Syriac version of 1 Esdras preserved in this manuscript is, however, different from the tradition represented by the rest of the manuscripts.[5] According to the editors of the Syriac version of 1 Esdras, manuscript Add 12168 (siglum 9c) "nearly always provides a text closer to the underlying Greek than that in the remaining manuscripts."[6] Therefore, it is possible that the same could be said of the translation of Nehemiah preserved in the manuscript.

Wright thinks that the *Catena* was written before 651 C.E.,[7] i.e., not long after the version by Paul of Tella (→ 1.4.5.2). The first volume of the manuscript of the Syro-Hexapla, owned by Masius but now missing, also contained "Paralipomena, Ezram,"[8] therefore Gwynn and Torrey think that it deals only with LXX-1 Esd (3 Ezra, → II.7.1.1), perhaps with the additions of v-Neh (2 Esdrae; → 19.3.6). According to Gwynn, v-Ezra (1 Esdrae; → 19.3.6) was missing in the manuscript of the Syro-Hexapla whereas for Torrey it was easier to think that there were no verses from v-Ezra because the extracts from LXX-1 Esd (→ II.7.1.2) mainly coincide with the narrative of Ezra.[9] In fact, the compiler of this *Catena* "wanted to create a kind of Greek companion to the Peshitta."[10]

The version of Paul of Tella is so faithful to the Greek that Gwynn[11] was able to make a retroversion into Greek. Torrey recognises the characteristics of the version by Paul, but adds that "the character of the text is thus conflate, including both the Greek

---

[4] Gwynn, *Remnant*, xvii.
[5] Hanhart, *Esdrae liber I*, 16.
[6] Baars and Lebram, "1(3) Esdras," iv.
[7] Wright, *Catalogue*, 905–06.
[8] Masius, *Josuæ*, 6.
[9] Torrey, "Portions," 68–69.
[10] Ter Haar Romeny, "The Greek vs. the Peshitta," 307.
[11] Gwynn, *Remnant*, 54–63.

Version selected by Origen and also the *plus* of the Hebrew."[12]

The Syriac version almost always follows the so-called Lucianic recension (→ 19.3.5) indicated by Hanhart with the initials *L'* (manuscripts LXX[19,93,108,121]) and *L* (manuscripts LXX[19,93,108]). In the critical apparatus of the *Septuaginta* in the Göttingen edition, even the readings of the Syro-Hexapla are reported. In Neh 8:7, only the Syro-Hexapla has an addition after "Joshua and Banania" ܘܗܢܘܢ ܕܪܚܒܘܢܐ "and these (are son?) of Rehbona (?)." But the verse contains a series of proper names that might have been corrupted in the course of the transmission of the text (Καλλίτας "Kallitas" = ܩܡܦܛܘܣ "Qamptas (?)" misreading of the Greek as καμπτός "target"; Φαλαίας = ܦܝܢܚܣ "Phinehas"). Also in Neh 8:12 after "and to send portions," there is an addition by the Syro-Hexapla ܠܗܘܢ ܕܠܐ ܐܝܬ ܗܘܐ ܠܗܘܢ "to those who had none." This addition matches Neh 8:10, where the population was invited to "send portions to those who had none."

The tendency to match can also be seen in other verses. In MT-Neh 8:10–11, the population is invited twice not to complain "do not grieve" (וְאַל־תֵּעָצֵבוּ). In LXX-1 Esd 9:52–53, the same verb is repeated twice (μὴ λυπεῖσθε "do not grieve"); however, in LXX-Neh, there are two different verbs (μὴ διαπέσητε ... μὴ καταπίπτετε "do not faint ... do not despond"). Instead, the Syro-Hexapla uses the same verb twice, ܘܠܐ ܬܬܟܪܝܘܢ "do not dishearten." On one hand, LXX-Neh prefers variety, while on the other, the Syro-Hexapla reconstructs parallelisms. Another case of parallelism can be found in the translation of συνετίζοντες "who taught" (LXX-Neh 8:7, 9), which was translated initially as ܕܡܥܝܪܝܢ "who evoke attention"[13] and secondly as ܕܡܥܝܕܝܢ "who explain" (the diference between *d/r* is only a dot). The marginal reading reports even the first time ܕܡܣܟܠܝܢ "who instruct."

Regarding the rendering of proper names, the translator shows two tendencies. By avoiding a Syriac equivalent (example: *Chislev*, see below Neh 1:1) and by avoiding the transcription of Greek forms (Neh 2:1 ܐܪܬܚܫܫܬ "Artaxasta" versus ἀρταξέρξου "Artaxerxes" of the Lucianic recension).

Manuscript Add 12168 has also marginal variants. Some appear to come from S-Neh (→ 19.3.3), as in Neh 1:1, where the name of the month of Chislev, Χασελευ "Chaseleu," is ܐܟܣܠܘ "Achslow," but in the margin there is the reading ܟܢܘܢ "Canun," which is the current form in S-Neh. In Neh 1:3, "those remaining ... there in the country" (ἐν τῇ χώρᾳ/ܒܐܬܪܐ) have become "those remaining ... there in the town" (ܒܡܕܝܢܬܐ) in the margin; but in this case we do not know if it is an alternative reading that was taken from S-Neh or if it was only an addition, as in some Greek manuscripts (ἐν τῇ χώρᾳ ἐν τῇ πόλει "in the land, in the town" LXX[B',S,V]). In Neh 2:2, the king says to Nehemiah that he does not seem "disheartened" (ܟܡܝܪܐ) while in the margin there is the variant ܟܪܝܗܐ "ill," which corresponds to S-Neh. The Lucianic recension has ἀρρωστῶν "ill" and LXX-Neh has μετριάζων which means "to be moderate." There is, however, proof of the use of μετριαζω meaning "being ill,"[14] but it is difficult to decide which form goes back to the Lucianic *Vorlage*, whether the one in the text or that in the margin.[15] In Neh 4:16 ("each with her *boy*"), in the margin there is a variant ܛܠܝܐ "boy," which is found in S-Neh (ܛܠܝܗ "her boy") but perhaps a more genuine Syriac word was used rather than ܦܘܣܐ "youths," which is of clear Greek derivation.

In Neh 2:6, the marginal text attests a different reading of the Greek *Vorlage*; instead of "limits" (ὅρον/ܬܚܘܡܐ), there is "oaths" (ܡܘܡܬܐ), which assumes a Greek translation ὅρκον "oath" (not found in the manuscripts of LXX). In Neh 4:10, the marginal reading seems to be an interpretation of the text. "Half of *those who had violently shaken*" (ܕܢܦܨܐ, but in Greek with the passive form ἐκτετιναγμένων "who had shaken off") is understood as half "of the braves" (ܕܓܢܒܪܐ).

[12] Torrey, "Portions," 70–71.

[13] Torrey, "Portions," 73, transcribes here ܕܡܥܝܕܝܢ as "who are experts."

[14] Janz, *Deuxième*, 130–31.

[15] Hanhart, *Esdrae liber II*, 14.

Baars, W. and J.C.H. Lebram, "1(3) Esdras," in *Canticles or Odes, Prayer of Manasseh, Apocryphal Psalms, Psalms of Solomon, Tobit, 1(3) Esdras* (The Old Testament in Syriac according to the Peshitta Version 4.6; Leiden: Brill, 1972).

Gwynn, J., *Remnants of the Later Syriac Verions of the Bible*, Part 2: *Old Testament: Extracts from the Syro-Hexaplar Version of the Septuagint: Made in the Seventh Century by Paul of Tella: Genesis, Leviticus, 1 and 2 Chronicles, Nehemiah* (London: Williams and Norgate, 1909).

ter Haar Romeny, R.B., "The Greek vs. the Peshitta in a West Syrian Exegetical Collection," in *The Peshitta as a Translation: Papers Read at the II Peshitta Symposium Held at Leiden 19–21 August 1993* (eds. P.B. Dirksen and A. van der Kooij; Monographs of the Peshitta Institute Leiden 8; Leiden: Brill, 1995), 297–310.

Hanhart, R., *Esdrae liber I* (Septuaginta Vetus Testamentum Graecum 8.1; Göttingen: Vandenhoeck & Ruprecht, 1974).

Hanhart, R., *Esdrae liber II* (Septuaginta Vetus Testamentum Graecum 8.2; Göttingen: Vandenhoeck & Ruprecht, 1993).

Hanhart, R., *Text und Textgeschichte des 2. Esrabuches* (MSU 25; Göttingen: Vandenhoeck & Ruprecht, 2003).

Janz, T., *Deuxième livre d'Esdras* (*Bible d'Alexandrie 11.2; Paris: Cerf, 2010).

Masius, A., *Josuae imperatoris historia illustrata atque esplicata* (Antwerp: Christophorus Platinus, 1574).

Torrey, C.C., "Portions of First Esdras and Nehemiah in the Syro-Hexaplar Version," *AJSL* 23 (1906–1907): 65–74 (reprinted in C.C. Torrey, *Ezra Studies* [Chicago: Chicago Press, 1910], 1–10).

Wright, W., *Catalogue of Syriac Manuscripts in the British Museum: Acquired since the Year 1838* (parts 1–3; London: Longman, 1870–1872).

Claudio Balzaretti

19.4.5 Armenian Translations

19.4.5.1 Background

Although Ezra–Nehemiah were originally one, and have remained so in the Greek tradition, in the composite text of 2 Esdras from which the Armenian version derives, the latter, as witnessed in our extant biblical manuscripts, has been divided in transmission into the units of Second Ezra and Nehemiah. Granted its Greek origins, the Armenian lacks the following sections of the Hebrew of Nehemiah (Neh 3:37–38; 11:12–35; 12:2–9, 25, 29; → 19.2.2). The version has aroused relatively little scholarly interest apart from its inclusion in Hanhart's edition of the Greek,[1] with its collation based on the standard Zohrapian[2] edition, whose running text is provided by manuscript 1508 (dated 1319) of the Venice Mkhitarist collection. The latter's apparatus permits access to selected readings of seven other Old Testament manuscripts in the same collection, as well as comparisons with the first printed edition of the Armenian Bible, that of Oskan Erewancʻi,[3] whose base text was mainly provided by manuscript 180 of the Maštocʻ Matenadaran Institute of Ancient Manuscripts in Yerevan, Republic of Armenia, a manuscript commissioned by King Hetʻum II in 1295 from the accomplished scribe Stepʻanos Goynericʻancʻ.

19.4.5.2 Textual Character

The Armenian evinces no categoric affiliation with any of the major recensions in these books. Although it witnesses a number of agreements with the Lucianic text (→ 19.3.5) – especially additions and omissions in alignment with MT (→ 19.2.2) – these are neither as significant nor as frequent as to warrant classifying it as a representative of that text type.

19.4.5.3 Translation Technique

As the Greek version of the book (→ 19.3.1) is one of the most literal renderings in the Old Testament, following its Hebrew parent text (→ 19.2.2) so closely in word order and morphological structure that it has been likened to a modern "interlinear translation,"[4] often it not only ceases to preserve Greek idiom, but obscures the underlying sense. Consequently, all the daughter versions, to varying

---

[1] Hanhart, *Esdrae liber II*.
[2] Zohrapian, *Scriptures, 300–306 (Second Ezra) and 306–14 (Nehemiah).
[3] O. Erewancʻi, *Astowacašownčʻ Hnoy ew Norocʻ Ktakaranacʻ nerparownakōġ: Šarakargowtʻeamb naxneacʻn merocʻ ew čšmartasiracʻ tʻarmančacʻ* (Bible of the Old and New Testament) (Amsterdam: Holy Etchmiadzin and Holy Sargis Zoravar Press, 1666).
[4] Wooden, "Interlinearity," 119–44.

degrees, are compelled to engage the text creatively in order to reformulate its expression with a view to communicating its meaning to their constituencies. On the whole, the Armenian is very judicious in its approach, uniting overall fidelity to its prototype with interpretative flexibility.

Certain facets of the technique adopted closely resemble those typical of the original Armenian translation process referred to in historical sources (Arm 1; see → 1.4.7), rather than the more literal perspective pursued in the revision that occurred about a generation later (Arm 2; → 1.4.7). These features include "doublet" renderings of terms or phrases, which were a characteristic feature of early Armenian prose style.[5] Hence, at 2 Esd 3:1, the verb ἔφθασεν "arrived" is paralleled by the asyndetic combination ժամանեաց եհաս "arrived-reached." Other examples include the case of the vessels Nebuchadnezzar removed from the Jerusalem temple, which the Greek at 2 Esd 5:15 – and in the parallel passage at 1 Esd 6:18 – refers to as τὰ σκεύη, whereas the Armenian defines them as սպաս եւ զկահ "service and utensils," and the dilapidated state of the walls of Jerusalem after the Babylonian assault, described as καθῃρημένα "broken down" but enlarged in the Armenian as քակեալ եւ աւերեալ "demolished and ruined" (2 Esd 11:3).

19.4.5.3.1 Attention to Context
The translator's concern for the linguistic adequacy of his rendering moved him to elucidate uncertainties in his parent text. Thus he elaborated on the Lucanic (→ 19.3.5) variant διὰ τὸ θεμελιωθῆναι τὸν οἶκον "because the house had its foundation laid" of the original phrase ἐπὶ τῇ θεμελιώσει οἴκου κυρίου "for the foundation of the house of the Lord" at 2 Esd 3:11 to read վասն զի անկան հիմունք տանն Տեառն "because the foundations of the Lord's house were laid" as the cause of the people's jubilation. The complexity of reference in 2 Esd 11:9, first to the people directly, and then indirectly in the phrase ἐὰν ᾖ ἡ διασπορὰ ὑμῶν "if your dispersion," is smoothened by the translator's rendering

---

[5] Cowe, "The Bible in Armenian," 158.

եթէ իցէք զրուեալք "if you are scattered." In other cases, the Armenian translator expands on terse allusions by clarificatory additions, as in 2 Esd 23:26. There the Greek hints lightly at Solomon's religious syncretism through his marriage alliances in the phrase τοῦτον ἐξέκλιναν αἱ γυναῖκες αἱ ἀλλότριαι "foreign women ruined this man" (*NETS), whereas the Armenian removes any ambiguity attaching to the verb by glossing the equivalent խոտորեցուցին "turned aside" with the phrase եւ յանցուցին ի մեղս "and caused (him) to transgress in sin."

19.4.5.3.2 Handling of Transliterations
One facet of the literalness of the Greek version is the range of Hebrew terms it absorbs into its texture rather than translate them. A striking characteristic of the Armenian is the degree to which these are rendered rather than retained. Examples of this include the designation of Mithridates as Garbarenos, rendered գանձապետ "treasurer" by the Armenian (2 Esd 1:8; cf. 5:14 and 1 Esd 2:10); that of one of the temple vessels as χεφουρή "chephoure" (*NETS: "Heb = bowls") (1:10), rendered as skawaṙakkʻ "bowls"; and Susa as αβιρα "abira," rendered by the Armenian as ի մայր քաղաքացն "in the mother of cities, i.e., capital," followed by the transliteration at 2 Esd 11:1.

19.4.5.3.3 Unusual Renderings, but not Variants
Perhaps the most interesting case of this type of reading in the books occurs at 2 Esd 23:26, where we have an example of a growing text, in which Solomon is set up as an object lesson to illustrate how the great have fallen; in this context, over the issue of exogamy. The original Greek affirms that his like did not exist among many nations and then proceeds to highlight the affection in which he was held by God, and his status as ruler of the whole of Israel. The Lucianic text type (→ 19.3.5) embellishes this by the epithet "great," a feature upon which the Armenian version builds by evoking his stereotypical quality of wisdom, perhaps through an instance of intertextuality that draws on the formulation at 3 Kgdms 3:12. Finally, the version repeats these attributes at the end of the verse to reinforce the point, whereas the

Greek simply states τοῦτον "this man," i.e., Solomon, in the formulation զայսպիսի սիրելի Աստուծոյ եւ զիմաստուն եւ զմեծ թագաւոր "such a king beloved of God, wise, and great."

The subject matter of 2 Esdras deals with the treatment of the Jewish community by the Persian Empire, a topic that bore much relevance for an Armenian audience, since Armenia had frequently formed part of that empire and was again under Persian suzerainty at the time the Bible was translated into Armenian. Consequently, we observe instances of Armenian knowledge of Persian phenomena being exploited in these books. Thus, instead of following the Greek example of transliterating the Hebrew form of the capital at 2 Esd 11:1, the translator employed the traditional Armenian form Շաւշ "Šawš" which would be instantly familiar to readers. Similarly, in 2 Esd 4:23, after reproducing a corrupt version ("Arsasas") of the transliterated Hebrew form (Αρθασασθα) of the name of King Artaxerxes from his Greek parent text, the translator glossed this with the traditional Armenian form of the name, այսինքն է Արտաշիսի "that is, of *Artašēs*."

We encounter another aspect of Armenian involvement in the text in its treatment of cultic matters. A fairly consistent distinction between licit and illicit cults has been noted in various sections of the Armenian Bible, which seems to suggest a high degree of intentionality on the part of the translation team to impact the current interreligious ambience in Armenia through the powerful authority of scripture.[6] Consequently, a different coding is employed to mark off acceptable Judeo-Christian places of worship from pagan shrines. In the course of 1–2 Esdras, Nebuchadnezzar's pillage of the vessels of the Jerusalem temple and their removal to a site in Babylon is referred to on four occasions. The lack of consistency in the Greek lexicon in these instances clearly contrasts with Armenian practice. At 1 Esd 2:7, the Babylonian site is termed εἰδωλεῖον "idol temple," while at 1 Esd 6:17 it is referred to as ναός "shrine," the same term applied to the Jerusalem temple in the following verse. Similarly, at 2 Esd 1:7, Nebuchadnezzar placed the vessels ἐν οἴκῳ θεοῦ αὐτοῦ "in the house of his god," while at 2 Esd 5:14 the Jerusalem temple is referred to as ὁ οἶκος τοῦ θεοῦ "the house of God" and the Babylonian site as ναὸς τοῦ βασιλέως "the shrine of the king." Only in 1 Esd 2:9 do we note a demarcation between the two cults. In the contrast, at 1 Esd 2:9 (Zohrapian 2:10) the Armenian reads տուն կռոցն իւրոց "house of his idols" the same terminology that is used at 1 Esd 6:17 (Zohrapian 6:18), whereas the Jerusalem temple there is distinguished by the form տաճար "temple." Similarly, at 2 Esd 1:7, Nebuchadnezzar placed the vessels ի տուն աստուածոցն իւրոց "in the house of his gods," the same terminology used for the Babylonian site in 2 Esd 5:14, whereas the Jerusalem temple in that verse appears as տուն Տեառն "house of the Lord." Thus, the translator has introduced a clear distinction between monotheistic and polytheistic shrines into the text.

19.4.5.4 Significance of the Variants Cited in Zohrapian's Apparatus

Though the Zohrapian edition[7] does not correspond to modern requirements either in the comprehensiveness of the witnesses included or the consistency of their citation, it remains useful for the narrow "borehole" it affords the reader into the Armenian tradition. While many of these readings reflect secondary inner-Armenian corruptions – which are compounded in these books by the plethora of foreign names and numbers, always a second matrix of scribal error – several are of value in reconstructing the original state of the version. This relates particularly to the variants from the Hetʻum Bible employed in Oskan's edition. Thus, at 2 Esd 4:17, the latter corrects the form Կամսայի "Kamsaji" in the running text to Սամսայի "Samsaji," which parallels the Greek. Similarly, at 2 Esd 3:6 it reconstitutes the original reading յառաջնում աւուր "on the first day" where the noun had dropped out of Zohrapian's base manuscript by scribal omission.

---

[6] Cowe, "Tendentious Translation."

[7] Zohrapian, *Scriptures.

19.4.5.5 Relevance for Exegesis

As mentioned above, the terseness and, on occasion, the obscurity of the Greek text constrained translators to reformulate its expression. Some of these passages seem to rest on exegetical traditions, such as the following case. The rather abstruse reference to the Levites' songs of praise as ἐπὶ χειρὸς Δαυίδ at Ezra 3:10 is rightly interpreted by the Armenian translator as որպէս եւ կարգեաց Դաւիթ "as David also had ordained."

19.4.5.6 Text-Critical Value of Arm 2-Ezra–Neh for LXX-2 Esdras

The Armenian version emerges as a fairly faithful rendering of its Greek parent text, while evincing a profile at the opposite end of the spectrum from the Greek translator of 2 Esdras, valorizing linguistic adequacy over representation of word order and morphology. The effect of the Zohrapian[8] apparatus on reconstructing the original form of the version underlines the importance of expanding the collation pool to maximize our access to good early readings.

Cowe, S.P., "Tendentious Translation and the Evangelical Imperative: Religious Polemic in the Early Armenian Church," *Revue des Études Arméniennes* 22 (1990–1991): 97–114.
Cowe, S.P., "The Bible in Armenian," in *The New Cambridge History of the Bible*, Vol. 2: *From 600 to 1450* (eds. R. Marsden and E.A. Matter; Cambridge: Cambridge University Press, 2012): 143–61.
Hanhart, R. (ed.), *Esdrae liber II* (Septuaginta Vetus Testamentum Graecum 8.2; Göttingen: Vandenhoeck & Ruprecht, 1982).
Wooden, R.G., "Interlinearity in 2 Esdras: A Test Case," in *Septuagint Research: Issues and Challenges in the Study of the Greek Jewish Scriptures* (eds. W. Kraus and R.G. Wooden; SBLSCS 53: Atlanta: SBL, 2006), 119–44.
Zohrapian, Y., *Scripture*.

Peter Cowe

---

[8] Zohrapian, *Scriptures*.

19.4.6 Georgian Translations

19.4.6.1 Background

The Georgian translations of 2 Ezra 1–10 (= Georg-Ezra) and 2 Ezra 11–23 (= Georg-Neh) came down to us in codices Georg^O (= Mount Athos, Library of the Iviron Monastery, geo. 1, 978 C.E., in two volumes), Georg^J2 (= Jerusalem, Library of the Greek Patriarchate, geo. 11, eleventh century), Georg^D (Tbilisi, National Centre of Manuscripts H-855, seventeenth century), Georg^F (= Tbilisi, National Centre of Manuscripts A-646, sixteenth century), Georg^I (= Tbilisi, National Centre of Manuscripts A-570, fifteenth century), Georg^S (= Tbilisi, National Centre of Manuscripts A-51, seventeenth or eighteenth century), and also in the so-called "Bakar Bible" (= Georg^B), the 1743 Moscow printed edition. A full description of these sources is available in the first volume of the critical edition of the Old Georgian Octateuch.[1]

Unlike the Georgian versions of 3 Ezra (1 Esdras; → II.7.1.7) and 4 Ezra (*Apocalypse of Ezra*; → II.7.2.7), which have been published[2] and subjected to extensive study,[3] Georg-Ezra and Georg-Neh did not attract scholarly attention. At present, only a brief account of Georg-Neh is available, given in 1971 by Goguaʒe[4] (the results obtained were recently summarized by Melikishvili[5]). The ancient translations of Georg-Ezra and Georg-Neh remain unpublished and the text has still to be collated with the Göttingen edition of LXX.[6] Therefore, it does not seem possible at present to give a comprehensive survey of the tradition covering in

---

[1] C'ignni, 559–80, 597–619, 627–35.
[2] Kurcik'iʒe, ʒveli aγtkmis ap'ok'ripebis kartuli versiebi, 13–109 and 320–414; Dočanašvili, Mcxeturi xelnac'eri, 23–32 and 400–427; Gippert, Sarjveladze, Kajaia, The Old Georgian Palimpsest.
[3] See Blake, "The Georgian Version," 299–375; Blake, "The Georgian Text," 57–105; Birdsall, "Palimpsest Fragments," 97–105; Kurcik'iʒe, "Ezras III c'ignis redakciebi"; Kurcik'iʒe, "Ezras ap'ok'alipsisis kartuli redakciebi," 93–109; Kurcik'iʒe, ʒveli aγtkmis ap'ok'ripuli, 32–116, 270–343; Kharanauli, "Ein Chanmeti-Fragment," 181–216; Melikišvili, Targmanebi, 130–33, 176–80.
[4] Goguaʒe, "Neemias c'ignis ʒveli kartuli redakciebi," 79–92.
[5] Melikišvili, Targmanebi, 128–33.
[6] Hanhart, Esdrae liber II.

detail aspects related to the character, features, and text-critical value of these versions.

19.4.6.2 Date, Versions, Editions
19.4.6.2.1 Georg-Ezra

Georg-Ezra is available in two translations. The first (= Georg-Ezra 1) can be divided into three redactions. Georg-Ezra 1a is to be found in manuscript Georg^O, Georg-Ezra 1b in Codices Georg^{J2,D,F,I}, and Georg-Ezra 1c in Georg^S. This version presumably dates back to the earliest period of Georgian literature (fifth to eighth centuries C.E.), although the original text appears to have been modified in later editorial interventions. In Codex Georg^S especially, textual strata can be found that undoubtedly originate in the editorial work undertaken by Sulkhan Saba Orbeliani in the late seventeenth century. Georg-Ezra 1a and 1b are still unpublished, while the text of Georg-Ezra 1c is accessible in Dočanašvili's edition.[7]

A second translation (= Georg-Ezra 2) was carried out in the early eighteenth century taking as its basis the 1663 printed Old Church Slavonic Bible; it is preserved in Georg^B.[8]

19.4.6.2.2 Georg-Neh

As in the previous case, the ancient version of Georg-Neh is available in three redactions. The first (= Georg-Neh 1a) is preserved in Georg^O, the second in Georg^{J2,D,F,I} (= Georg-Neh 1b), and the third in Georg^S (= Georg-Neh 1c). Over the centuries, the ancient translation, presumably dating to the fifth to eighth centuries C.E., has been corrected repeatedly and contaminated by different sources.[9] Here, as well, the more systematic revision may be attributed to Sulkhan Saba Orbeliani. Georg-Neh 1a and 1b are unpublished. Georg-Neh 1c is available in Dočanašvili's edition.[10]

The 1743 Moscow printed edition, Georg^B, contains a new translation of this book (= Georg-Neh 2). It dates to the early eighteenth century and was carried out on the basis of the Old Church Slavonic Bible, printed in Moscow in 1663.[11]

19.4.6.3 Translation Character, Translation Technique, Inner-Translational Features
19.4.6.3.1 Georg-Ezra

In manuscript Georg^O, the text of Georg-Ezra 1a is incomplete: it preserves only Ezra 1; 2:1–68; and 3:1–5. Moreover, it presents a final addition: after Ezra 3:5, several verses belonging to 1 Esdras (3 Ezra) are repeated (from 3 Ezra 8:91 to 9:22). As noted by Blake, this chaotic arrangement derived from the archetype of manuscript Georg^O, because the quaternion signatures show no gap.[12] This feature is not to be found in Codices Georg^{J2,D,F,I,S}. Georg-Ezra 1c has readings that show reliance on the 1666 printed Armenian Bible (→ 19.4.5).[13]

19.4.6.3.2 Georg-Neh

Georg-Neh 1a stands out for having several minuses. Manuscript Georg^O omits the sequence from Neh 4(14):8 to 5(15):19. An unusual arrangement is to be found in Nehemiah 7: Neh 7(17):6–60 are omitted and sections from Georg-Ezra 1 are repeated in their place (Ezra 2:1–21 and Ezra 1:21–59).

Georg-Neh 1b and 1c basically represent subsequent revisions of the ancient translation. It should be noted, however, that manuscripts Georg ^{J2,D,F,I,S} are very heterogeneous and their relation to Georg^O changes in each single case. For instance, Nehemiah 13(23) is omitted in Georg^{D,F,I}, but appears in Georg^S in a new translation that completely differs from that available in Georg^O and Georg^{J2}.[14] Differences can be explained by the fact that Sulkhan Saba made extensive use of the 1666 printed Armenian Bible as a model (→ 19.4.5).[15]

---

[7] Dočanašvili, *Mcxeturi xelnac'eri*, 355–73.
[8] *Biblia*.
[9] Goguaӡe, "Neemias c'ignis ӡveli kartuli redakciebi," 79–92; Melikišvili, *Targmanebi*, 129.
[10] Dočanašvili, *Mcxeturi xelnac'eri*, 374–98.

[11] Melikišvili, *Targmanebi*, 128–29.
[12] Blake, "The Athos Codex," 44.
[13] Dočanašvili, *Mcxeturi xelnac'eri*, 26–32.
[14] Goguaӡe, "Neemias c'ignis ӡveli kartuli redakciebi," 84–85; Melikišvili, *Targmanebi*, 128–29.
[15] Dočanašvili, *Mcxeturi xelnac'eri*, 26–32.

19.4.6.4 Text-Critical Value for the Primary Translation

Establishing the *Vorlage* of the earliest redactions of Georg-Ezra 1 and Georg-Neh 1 still remains an unanswered question. According to Goguaʒe, neither the Armenian version (→ 19.4.5) nor LXX can be deemed to be the source of Georg-Neh 1, since in a number of instances the latter differs from them both.[16] However, this claim appears to be too categorical; in fact, a more flexible approach permits the following comments to be made.

On the one hand, the rendering of proper names clearly betrays reliance on the Armenian version as shown, e.g., by the translation of Ἀρταξέρξης "Artaxerxes" as არტაშე "Artaše," reflecting the Armenian Արտաշէս "Artašēš"; see → 19.4.5.3.3. On the other hand, cases of agreement with the Armenian translation against LXX can also be found. In Neh 1:1, Georg-Neh 1 reads და იყო, თუესა მას ქასლევსა, წელსა მას მეოცესა არტაშუსს მეფისასა, მე ვიყავ შუშს დედაქალაქთა მათ აბირაღსა "And it happened in the month of Chaseleu, in the twentieth year of the king Artaxerxes, and I was in the capital Sousan Habira," which corresponds perfectly to the Armenian Եւ եղեւ, յամսեանն Քասղեւ, յամի քսաներորդի Արտաշիսի արքայի, ես էի ի Շաւշ ի մայր քաղաքացն Աբիրայ "And it happened in the month of Chaseleu, in the twentieth year of the king Artaxerxes, and I was in the capital Sousan Habira"; see → 19.4.5.3.2. In this occurence, both translations deviate from LXX, which has καὶ ἐγένετο ἐν μηνὶ Χασεληυ ἔτους εἰκοστοῦ καὶ ἐγὼ ἤμην ἐν Σουσὰν ἀβιρά[17] "And it happened in the month of Chaseleu, in the twentieth year, and I was in Sousan Habira" (*NETS*, 414).

Despite the fact that these remarks are of a limited and preliminary nature, it seems possible to assume that the relationship between Georg-Neh and Arm-Neh may be comparable to that existing between Georg-Dan 1b and the earliest stratum of the Armenian version. In that case (→ 18.4.6.4), the Georgian translation has yielded valuable information about the primitive aspect of the Armenian version (→ 18.4.5) and helped define its relationship with the Syriac (→ 18.3.3). Future research work should aim at verifying whether a typologically similar textual dependence may be established between these secondary versions.

On the basis of the results achieved in the analysis of the manuscript tradition of Georg-Ezra and Georg-Neh, two general conclusions can be drawn with regard to the problem of establishing their parent text. As far as the ancient versions are concerned, such an assessment is currently not possible, given the lack of specific studies and critical editions of the translations. On the contrary, in the case of the translations contained in Georg[B], their source text can be safely identified with the 1663 printed version of the Old Church Slavonic Bible.[18]

Biblia: brʒanebita da c'arsagebelita sapasetata sakartvelos mepis bakar vaxt'angis ʒisata (Moscow: Bakaris st'amba, 1743).

Birdsall, J.N., "Palimpsest Fragments of a Khanmeti Georgian Version of 1 Esdras," *Mus* 85 (1972): 97–105.

Blake, R.P., "The Georgian Version of Fourth Esdras from the Jerusalem Manuscript," *HTR* 19 (1926): 299–375.

Blake, R.P., "The Georgian Text of Fourth Esdras from the Athos Manuscript," *HTR* 22 (1929): 57–105.

Blake, R.P., "The Athos Codex of the Georgian Old Testament," *HTR* 22 (1929): 33–56.

C'ignni ʒuelisa aγtkumisani, Vol. 1: *Šesakmisaj, gamoslvataj* (eds. B. Gigineišvili and C. K'ik'viʒe; Tbilisi: Mecniereba, 1989).

Dočanašvili, E. (ed.), *Mcxeturi xelnac'eri (mepeta I, II, III, IV, nešt'a I, II, ezras I, II, III c'ignebi)* (Tbilisi: Mecniereba, 1982).

Gippert, J., "The Application of Multispectral Imaging in the Study of Caucasian Palimpsests," *Bulletin of the Georgian National Academy of Sciences* 175 (2007): 168–79.

Gippert, J., Z. Sarjveladze, and L. Kajaia (eds.), *The Old Georgian Palimpsest: Codex Vindoboniensis georgicus*

---

[16] In this regard, he quotes, for instance, the Georgian and Armenian translations of Neh 2:4; 3:4; see Goguaʒe, "Neemias c'ignis ʒveli kartuli redakciebi," 88–89.

[17] Hanhart, *Esdrae liber II*, 144.

[18] Goguaʒe, "Neemias c'ignis ʒveli kartuli redakciebi," 89–91; Melikišvili, *Targmanebi*, 129.

2 (Monumenta palaeographica Medii Aevi Series Ibero-Caucasica 1; Turnhout: Brepols, 2007).

Goguaӡe, N., "Neemias c'ignis ӡveli kartuli redakciebi," *Mravaltavi* 1 (1971): 79–92.

Hanhart, R. (ed.), *Esdrae liber II* (Septuaginta Vetus Testamentum Graecum 8.2; Göttingen: Vandenhoeck & Ruprecht, 1993).

Kharanauli, A., "Ein Chanmeti-Fragment der georgischen Übersetzung von Esra I," *Mus* 116 (2003): 181–216.

Kurcik'iӡe, C., "Ezras III c'ignis redakciebi," in *Sakartvelos mecnierebata ak'ademiis K'. K'ek'eliӡis saxelobis xelnac'erta inst'it'ut'is VIII samecniero sesia: Tezisebi* (Tbilisi: Mecniereba, 1969), 11.

Kurcik'iӡe, C. (ed.), *Ӡveli aγtkmis ap'ok'ripebis kartuli versiebi (X–XVIII ss. xelnac'erta mixedvit): c'igni I* (Tbilisi: Mecniereba, 1970).

Kurcik'iӡe, C., "Ezras ap'ok'alipsisis kartuli redakciebi," *Mravaltavi* 1 (1971): 93–109.

Kurcik'iӡe, C., *Ӡveli aγtkmis ap'ok'ripuli (arak'anonik'uri) c'ignebis kartuli versiebi: c'igni II* (Tbilisi: Mecniereba, 1973).

Melikišvili, N., *Bibliur c'ignta ӡveli kartuli targmanebi* (Tbilisi: Alilo, 2009).

Alessandro Maria Bruni

19.4.7 Old Church Slavonic Translations

19.4.7.1 Absence of a Complete Medieval Translation

According to hagiographic accounts, shortly before his death in 885 C.E., Methodius translated the entire corpus of the Scriptures "with the exception of the Maccabees" from Greek into Slavonic.[1] However, in the case of Ezra–Nehemiah, as well as in several other instances (e.g. → 20.4.7), this literary testimony cannot be verified on the basis of textual evidence and the existence of such an early version of these books cannot be proved. On the one hand, the surviving Cyrillic manuscripts of the OCS Bible apparently do not preserve even traces of a textual stratum that may be dated back to the Cyrillo-Methodian period. On the other hand, the material provided by the Croat Glagolitic sources is too meager in order to reach trustworthy conclusions on this matter, since the Missal contains only fragments of Neh 8:1–10 and none of Ezra.

19.4.7.2 The Late Fifteenth-Century Gennadian Translation

The only fully preserved OCS translation of Ezra–Nehemiah is that produced in Russia in the last decade of the fifteenth century (= OCS-Ezra and OCS-Neh). It was undertaken in Novgorod under the patronage of Archbishop Gennadius (Gennadij Gonzov, ca. 1410–1505).

The prelate created a team with the purpose of preparing the first complete corpus of the OCS Bible.[2] In the vast majority of cases, Gennadius' assistants had access to earlier versions rooted in South Slavonic traditions, most of which were produced by the late tenth century. However, for Ezra–Nehemiah, 1–2 Chronicles (→ 20.4.7), as well as for some deuterocanonical Scriptures (1–2 Maccabees [→ 11.10.1.7; → 11.10.2.8], Judith [→ 11.9.10], Tobit [→ 11.14.13]), previous translations were apparently not available.[3] Therefore, new versions were produced with the aim of filling this void. As widely maintained, the sources used for accomplishing this task were late fifteenth-century editions of the Vulgate (→ 19.3.6), among which are those printed by A. Koberger (ca. 1440–1513) in 1487 (with commentaries by Nicholas of Lyra) and by N. Kessler (1450–post-1519) in 1487 or 1491.[4]

A large amount of work is believed to have been carried out by a certain Benjamin, a "Slav by birth but a Latin by faith."[5] Most scholars presume he was a Croatian or Czech monk, possibly a Dominican,[6] in view of several South and West

---

[1] See ch. 15 of the *Life of Methodius*: Angelov and Kodov, *Kliment Ochridski*, 191.

[2] Evseev, *Gennadievskaja Biblia*; Romodanovskaja, "Gennadievskaja Biblija," 584–85.

[3] These deuterocanonical books are also partially (1–2 Maccabees, Tobit) or fully (Judith) contained in the Croat Glagolitic breviaries and missals. See Vajs, *Nejstarši breviář*; Vajs, *Najstariji hrvatskoglagolski missal*; Thomson, "The Slavonic Translation," 768–71; Alekseev, *Tekstologija*, 141, 198.

[4] Thomson, "The Slavonic Translation," 655–59; Thomson, *A Brief Survey*, 55–56.

[5] Thomson, "The Slavonic Translation," 656.

[6] Sobolevskij, *Perevodnaja literatura*, 254–59; Sedel'nikov, "K izučeniju 'Slova kratka,'" 205–25; Lur'e, "Veniamin," 133–35.

Slavic traits in the language of his translations.[7] It has also been argued that he was connected with the Emmaus Monastery of the Glagolitic rite at Prague, but Thomson demonstrated the complete groundlessness of this view.[8]

On the basis of the scarce information contained in a late fifteenth-century manuscript (Russian State Library, Moscow, f. 256, No. 93),[9] it may be concluded logiously that Benjamin arrived in Novgorod in 1490 or 1491, where in 1493 he translated 1–2 Maccabees (→ II.10.1.7; → II.10.2.8).[10] It remains a matter of speculation whether or not he was the author of OCS-Ezra and OCS-Neh. The sources do not preserve any kind of information that sheds light on this question.

19.4.7.3 Manuscripts, Editions

The Croat Glagolitic readings from Neh 8:1–10 are available in Berčić's edition.[11] Contrary to the widely held belief that this version was translated from the Vulgate (→ 19.3.6), Jagić maintained it derived from LXX (→ 19.3.1).[12]

The Gennadian OCS-Ezra and OCS-Neh are unedited and still need to be thoroughly investigated. These versions are currently preserved in a number of East Slavic manuscripts starting from the late fifteenth century, which are thus contemporary to the translation.[13] The earliest preserved codex was written shortly after 1493 C.E. (Russian State Library, Moscow, f. 113, No. 11).[14] A second fragmentary source, consisting of only sixteen folios, dates from around the same time (National Library of Russia, St. Petersburg, NSRK Q 645).

OCS-Ezra and OCS-Neh are also contained in the oldest available testimony of the full "Gennadian Bible," copied in 1499 (State Historical Museum, Moscow, Sin. 915). In a few other cases, OCS-Ezra and OCS-Neh are included in smaller collections that typically also incorporate deuterocanonical books.[15]

Issues related to the translation method adopted in OCS-Ezra and OCS-Neh still await a more meticulous study. In general, the Novgorodian versions made from the Vulgate were undertaken with a quite literal approach.[16]

In 1581, OCS-Ezra and OCS-Neh became part of the printed Ostrog Bible. Its compilers largely revised the Gennadian text towards LXX.[17]

19.4.7.4 Parent Text

OCS-Ezra and OCS-Neh do not offer relevant material for the text-critical study of their primary version, since they appear to be based on the above-mentioned late fifteenth-century printed editions of the Vulgate (→ 19.3.6). Although a complete collation with the latter still has to be carried out, the analysis of both major and minor textual features of OCS-Ezra and OCS-Neh corroborates such dependence. These are, for instance, the translation of Hieronymus' preface, several calques from Latin, as well as words transcribed into Cyrillic without being rendered in Slavonic (corresponding translations are at times to be found in the margins of the manuscript folios).[18] Furthermore, the use of the Vulgate as a model is also confirmed by a number of translation errors and misunderstandings of the original Latin text.[19]

---

[7] Freidhof, *Vergleichende sprachliche Studien*, 145–50; Foster, "Croatian Language Elements," 557–67.

[8] Thomson, "The Slavonic Translation," 655–57.

[9] Vostokov, *Opisanie*, 164.

[10] For 1–2 Maccabees, see the colophon of the sixteenth-century manuscript: National Library of Russia, St. Petersburg, *Pog.* 84, folio 360ᵛ (Alekseev, *Tekstologija*, 197).

[11] Berčić, *Ulomci*, 99–100.

[12] Jagić, *Entstehungsgeschichte*, 465.

[13] For a list and description, see Romodanovskaja, "Rasprostranenie," 6–28.

[14] This manuscript was apparently copied in Novgorod for the Joseph-Volokolamsk Monastery (Romodanovskaja, "Gennadievskaja Biblija," 584–85).

[15] See Mathiesen, "Handlist," 18 no. 7; 19 no. 17; 21 no. 41.

[16] Romodanovskaja, "Zametki," 236.

[17] Gorskij and Nevostruev, *Opisanie*, 52; Alekseev, *Tekstologija*, 205–06.

[18] Romodanovskaja, "Gennadievskaja Biblija," 584–85.

[19] Gorskij and Nevostruev, *Opisanie*, 43, 47, 49.

Alekseev, A.A., *Tekstologija slavjanskoj Biblii* (Bausteine zur slavischen Philologie und Kulturgeschichte Neue Folge A Slavistische Forschungen 24; St. Petersburg: Dmitrij Bulanin, 1999).

Angelov, B.S. and C. Kodov (eds.), *Kliment Ochridski:*

Săbrani săčinenija, Vol. 3: *Prostranni žitija na Kiril i Metodii* (Sofia: Izdatelstvo na Bălgarska Akademija na naukite, 1973).

Berčić, I. (ed.), *Ulomci Svetoga Pisma obojega uvjeta staroslovenskim jezikom: Skupio iz rukopisah i tiskanih knjigah hrvatskoga razreda svećenik Ivan Berčić*, Vol. 1 (Prague: Sinovi Bogumila Haase, 1871).

Evseev, I.E., *Gennadievskaja Biblia 1499 g.* (Moscow: Sinodal'naja Tipografia, 1914).

Foster, P., "Croatian Language Elements in the Russian Church Slavonic Translations of Maccabees in the Gennadij Bible," in *Prvi Hrvatski slavistički kongres: Zbornik radova*, Vol. 1 (ed. S. Damjanović; Zagreb: Hrvatsko filološko društvo, 1997), 557–67.

Freidhof, G., *Vergleichende sprachliche Studien zur Gennadius-Bibel (1499) und Ostroger Bibel (1580/1581): Die Bücher Paralipomenon, Esra, Tobias, Judith, Sapientia und Makkabäer* (Frankfurt a.M.: Athenäum Verlag, 1972).

Gorskij, A. and K.I. Nevostruev, *Opisanie slavjanskich rukopisej Moskovskoj Sinodal'noj (Patriaršej) biblioteki*, Vol. 1: *Svjaščennoe pisanie* (Moscow: Sinodal'naja tipografija, 1855).

Jagić, V., *Entstehungsgeschichte der kirchenslavischen Sprache* (Berlin: Weidmann, 1913).

Lur'e, J.S., "Veniamin, monach-dominikanec," in *Slovar' knižnikov i knižnosti Drevnej Rusi*, Vol. 2: *Vtoraja polovina XIV–XVI v*, Part 1: *A–K* (ed. D.S. Lichačev; Leningrad: Nauka, 1988), 133–35.

Mathiesen, R., "Handlist of Manuscripts Containing Church Slavonic Translations of the Old Testament," *Polata knigopisnaja* 7 (1983): 3–48.

Pičchadze, A.A., "Perevody Biblii na drevnie jazyki: cerkovnoslavjanskij," *Pravoslavnaja ènciklopedija*, Vol. 5: *Bessonov-Bonveč* (ed. Aleksij, Patriarch Moskovskij i Vseja Rusi II; Moscow: Cerkovno-Naučnyj Centr "Pravoslavnaja ènciklopedija," 2002): 139–47.

Romodanovskaja, V.A., "Rasprostranenie perevedennych s latyni častej Gennadievskoj biblii, I: Rukopisi XV-pervoj treti XVI veka," in *Istočniki po russkoj istorii i literature: Srednevekov'e i Novoe vremja* (ed. N.N. Pokrovskij; *Archeografija i istočnikovedenie Sibiri* 19; Novosibirsk: Izdatel'stvo SO RAN, 2000), 6–28.

Romodanovskaja, V.A., "Zametki o perevode "latinskich" knig Gennadievskoj biblii 1499g.: biblejskij tekst i ènciklopedičeskie glossy," *Trudy Otdela drevnerusskoj literatury* 56 (2004): 235–50.

Romodanovskaja, V.A., "Gennadievskaja Biblija," *Pravoslavnaja ènciklopedija*, Vol. 10: *Vtorozakonie-Georgij* (ed. Aleksij, Patriarch Moskovskij i Vseja Rusi II; Moscow: Cerkovno-Naučnyj Centr "Pravoslavnaja ènciklopedija," 2005): 584–88.

Sedel'nikov, A.D., "K izučeniju 'Slova kratka' i dejatel'nosti dominikanca Veniamina," *Izvestija Otdelenija russkogo jazyka i slovesnosti Akademii nauk SSSR* 30 (1925–1926): 205–25.

Sobolevskij, A.I., *Perevodnaja literatura Moskovskoj Rusi XIV–XVII vv. Bibliografičeskie materialy* (St. Petersburg: Tipografija Imperatorskoj Akademii nauk, 1903).

Thomson, F.J., "The Slavonic Translation of the Old Testament," in *The Interpretation of the Bible: The International Symposium in Slovenia* (ed. J. Krašovec; JSOTSup 189; Sheffield: Sheffield Academic Press, 1998), 605–920.

Thomson, F.J., *A Brief Survey of the History of the Church Slavonic Bible from its Cyrillomethodian Origins until its Final Form in the Elizabethan Bible of 1751* (Slavica Gandensia 33.2; Ghent: Department of Slav and East European Studes of the University of Ghent, 2006).

Vajs, J., *Nejstarší Breviář hrvatsko-hlaholský (Prvý Breviář Vrbnický)* (Praha: Nákl. Král. České Společnosti Náuk, 1910).

Vajs, J., *Najstariji hrvatskoglagolski misal: s bibliografskim opisima svih hrvatskoglagolskih misala* (Zagreb: Jugoslavenska akademija znanosti i umjetnosti, 1948).

Vostokov, A.C., *Opisanie russkich i slovenskich rukopisej Rumjancevskogo muzeuma* (St. Petersburg: Tipografija Imperatorskoj Akademii nauk, 1842).

Alessandro Maria Bruni

19.4.8 Arabic Translations

Similar to other traditions, the books of Ezra and Nehemiah in Arabic were regarded as one book. In the list of authorised books of the Bible, the Coptic scholar al-Ṣafī ibn al-'Assāl (d. ca. 1265), following the Coptic recension of the Apostolical Canons, clearly states in his Nomocanon that "there are two books to the book of Ezra, the Scribe," Arab. *kitābāni li-'Azrā al-kātib*.[1] The encyclopaedia by the Copt Shams al-Riyāsa Abū al-Barakāt, also known as Ibn Kabr (d. 1324), reiterates this information.[2]

---

[1] For the Coptic version of the Apostolic Constitution, cf. Tattam, *The Apostolical Constitutions*, 210. The passage in al-Ṣafī's Nomocanon is found in 'Awaḍ, *al-Majmū' aṣ-ṣafawī*, 11.

[2] Khalil, *Miṣbāḥ al-ẓulma*, 210 and 220.

Among the Syriac churches they were similarly considered a single unit. Hence, Arabic manuscripts usually feature the two books as one entity, without interruption. Most commonly they bear the title "The Second Book of Ezra," which depending on their tradition (see below) is preceded by either 4 Ezra (→ II.7.2) or Esdras A′ (3 Esdras in the Vulgate; → II.7.1).

However, not all Arabic-speaking churches included the book of Ezra and Nehemiah in their canon. At least for the Syriac churches, in particular the Church of the East, there is ample evidence that it was first deuterocanonical and was incorporated only at a later stage.[3] In early manuscripts of the Peshitta (→ 19.3.3), the book is not featured among the historical books, as in Hebrew or Greek codicies, but found in the final section that groups together deuterocanonical books.[4] Eastern Syriac exegetes, including Theodore bar Koni (eighth century C.E.), Ishoʿ Bar Nun (d. 828 C.E.), and Ishoʿdad of Merv (mid-ninth century C.E.) do not accommodate the book in their commentaries, and neither did it have a place in lectionaries. It is equally absent in the list of biblical books found in Ibn al-Nadīm's *Fihrist*, which was communicated to him via the intermediation of an East-Syriac monk named Yūnis.[5] A similar list is also found in manuscript Berlin, Staatsbibliothek, Sprenger 30, containing a chronicle in Arabic by an anonymous Iraqī author.[6] Again, the book is missing in the list. For this reason, the book of Ezra and Nehemiah was not very widespread in Arabic. The historical narratives in general appear not to have attracted a wide appeal for translations. Three distinct versions are attested. The first two are medieval while the last is early modern and based on an early-modern printing.

19.4.8.1 A Version of Syriac Provenance

In the first group of manuscripts, the book of Ezra and Nehemiah is preceded by the book of 4 Ezra.[7] It includes manuscript Oxford, Bodl. Lib., 251 (folios 58ᵛ–105ʳ, dated 1335); Vatican, BAV, Ar. 3 (folios 30ʳ–42ᵛ); Coptic Orthodox Patriarchate, Bibl. 75 (folios 29ʳ–55ʳ, dated 1690), Bibl. 185 (folios 20ᵛ–35ᵛ, dated 1788), Theol. 286 (folios 322ʳ–354ʳ); and Paris, BNF, Ar. 1 (folios 206ᵛ–209ᵛ, dated 1785–1786). With the exception of the Parisian copy, the placement of the book is identical to some early manuscripts of the Peshitta (→ 19.3.3) such as, for example, Codex Ambrosianus (see above). Not much is known of the provenance of this version but, in light of the above, it has to be sought for within the West- or East-Syriac church. The manuscripts open with the formula: "This is the second book of ʿAzrā, which contains the account of the return of the children of Israel from the captivity of Babylon, the construction of the Temple, and the renewal of Jerusalem."

This version of Nehemiah was printed in the Paris[8] and London[9] Polyglots based on manuscript Paris, BNF, Ar. 1. Scholars disagree on the *Vorlage* of this book. According to Rödiger,[10] the translation was prepared by a Jew in the vicinity of Damascus, using MT (→ 19.2.2), and was used between the tenth and thirteenth centuries. On closer observation, however, it becomes clear that the Peshiṭta (→ 19.3.3) served as the source text for the translation, as is also the case for the book of Ezra.[11]

19.4.8.2 A Version of Melkite and Coptic Provenance

In the second group of manuscripts, the book of Ezra and Nehemiah follows the book of Esdras A′.[12] The translation is from LXX (→ 19.3.1). The manuscripts are of Melkite and Coptic prove-

---

[3] For details, the reader is referred to Wright, *A Short History*, 3–4; Rost, "Zur Geschichte des Kanons bei den Nestorianern"; Haelewyck, "Le Canon de l' Ancien Testament," and Albert, "Les 'Bet Mawtbe' nestoriens." It is likely that the Syriac churches followed Theodore of Mopsuestia in this respect; cf. Dennefeld, *Der alttestamentliche Kanon*, 49–52.
[4] Haelewyck, "Le Canon de l' Ancien Testament," 147.
[5] Ramaḍān, *al-Fihrist*, 37–40.
[6] See Rothstein, "Der Kanon der biblischen Bücher."

[7] On this text, see Drint, *The Mount Sinai Arabic Version*.
[8] Le Jay, *Biblia*, Vol. 8.
[9] Walton, *Polyglotta*.
[10] Rödiger, *De Origine et Indole*.
[11] Cf. Rudolph, *Esra und Nehemia*, xxi; Gotthard, *Der Text des Buches Nehemia*, 24–25.
[12] On the Arabic version of Esdras A′, cf. Monferrer Sala, *Scripta arabica orientalia*.

nance. Attested are manuscripts Vatican, BAV, Ar. 468 (folios 335ʳ–351ᵛ, dated 1578–1579); St. Petersburg, Institute of Oriental Manuscripts, D 226 (dated prior to MS Vatican, which is a direct copy of it., vol. 2, folios 168ᵛ–174ᵛ and 227ᵛ–232ᵛ); Coptic Orthodox Patriarchate, Bibl. 34 (folios 20ᵛ–32ᵛ) and Bibl. 86 (folios 257ʳ–267ᵛ, dated 1741); Paris, BNF, Ar. 1 (folios 202ʳ–206ʳ, dated 1785–1786). As a further particularity, they only feature Nehemiah up to Neh 2:13. The Parisian copy supplemented the truncated text of Nehemiah with the version of Syriac provenance (→ 19.4.8.1).

19.4.8.3 Manuscript Copies of the *Biblia Sacra Arabica* (1671–1673)

Originally printed by the *Congregatio de Propaganda Fide*, the *Biblia Sacra Arabica* is extant in many manuscript copies. Although the printing was based chiefly on manuscript Vatican, BAV, Ar. 468, it exhibits a strong revision towards the text of the Vulgate (→ 19.3.7).[13] For the book of Ezra and/or Nehemiah, cf. manuscripts Paris, BNF, Ar. 2 (folios 1ᵛ–13ʳ); London, BL, Or. 8745 (folios 130ʳ–138ᵛ); Birmingham, Mingana, Syr. 484 (folios 4ʳ–23ʳ, in *Karshūnī*); Aleppo, Syriac Orthodox Archdiocese, manuscript 1 (folios 22ᵛ–275ᵛ, in *Karshūnī*); Mardin, Church of the Forty Martyrs, manuscript 5 (Nehemiah is incomplete, folios 3ʳ–22ᵛ); Jounieh, Lebanese Maronite Missionary Order, manuscript 486 (folios 3ᵛ–23ʳ); Coptic Orthodox Patriarchate, Bibl. 31 (folios 335ᵛ–352ᵛ), Bibl. 33 (folios 202ʳ–223ʳ, dated 1873), Bibl. 35 (folios 173ʳ–191ᵛ, dated 1779), Bibl. 36 (folios 196ᵛ–221ᵛ), Bibl. 42 (folios 233ʳ–256ʳ, dated 1782), Bibl. 45 (folios 1ᵛ–20ᵛ, dated 1759), Bibl. 47 (only Ezra, folios 2ʳ–16ʳ, dated 1693), Bibl. 49 (folios 1ʳ–24ᵛ), Bibl. 53 (folios 312ᵛ–344ʳ, dated 1781), Bibl. 74 (folios 1ʳ–21ᵛ, dated 1758), and Bibl. 76 (folios 1ʳ–30ᵛ); and Jerusalem, St Anne, Ar. 87 (pp. 82–89, dated 1799).

Albert, M., "Les 'Bet Mawtbe' nestoriens," in *La formation des canons scripturaires* (ed. M. Tardieu; Patrimoines. Religions du livre; Paris: Cerf, 1993), 155–68.

'Awaḍ, J.F. (ed.), *al-Majmūʿ aṣ-ṣafawī: kitāb al-qawānīn al-kanāʾisīya li-kanīsa al-aqbāṭ al-urṯūduksīyajamaʿahu aṣ-Ṣafī Abī-ʾl-Faḍāʾil Ibn-ʿAssāl* (Cairo: Maṭbaʿat at-Taufīq, 1908).

Dennefeld, L., *Der alttestamentliche Kanon der Antiochenischen Schule* (Freiburg i.B.: Herder, 1909).

Drint, A., *The Mount Sinai Arabic Version of IV Ezra* (CSCO Scriptores Arabici 48–49; Louvain: Secrétariat du Corpus SCO, 1997).

Gotthard, H., *Der Text des Buches Nehemia* (Riga: Plates, 1932).

Haelewyck, J.-C., "Le Canon de l'Ancien Testament das la Tradition Syriaque (manuscrits bibliques, listes qanoniques, auteurs)," in *L'Ancien Testament en Syriaque* (eds. F. Briquel-Chatonnet and P. Le Moigne; Études syriaques 5; Paris: Geuthner, 2008), 141–71.

Jacob, A., *Septuagintastudien zu Ezra* (Breslau: H. Fleischmann, 1912).

Khalil, S. (ed.), *Abū al-Barakāt ibn al-Asʿad ibn Kubr: Miṣbāḥ al-ẓulma fī iḍāḥ al-khidma* (Cairo: al-Ṭabʿa al-tijārīya al-ḥadītha, 1971).

Monferrer Sala, J.P., *Scripta arabica orientalia: Dos studios de la literatura árabe cristiana* (Granada: Athos Pérgamos, 1999).

Ramaḍān, I. (ed.), *Muḥammad ibn Isḥāq ibn al-Nadīm: al-Fihrist* (Beirut: Dār al-Maʿrifa, 1994).

Rödiger, E., *De Origine et Indole Arabicae Librorum V. T. Historicorum Interpretationis Libri Duo* (Halle: Kümmel, 1829).

Rost, L., "Zur Geschichte des Kanons bei den Nestorianern," *ZNW* 27 (1927): 103–06.

Rothstein, J.W., "Der Kanon der biblischen Bücher bei den babylonischen Nestorianern im 9./10. Jhdt.," *ZDMG* 58 (1904): 634–63.

Rudolph, W., *Esra und Nehemia, samt 3. Esra* (HAT 20; Tübingen: J.C.B. Mohr [Paul Siebeck], 1949).

Tattam, H. (ed.), *The Apostolical Constitutions or Canons of the Apostles in Coptic* (London: Oriental Translation Fund of Great Britain and Ireland, 1848).

Vollandt, R., "Che portono al ritorno quì una Bibbia Arabica integra: A History of the Biblia Sacra Arabica (1671–73)," in *Græco-latina et orientalia: Studia in honorem Angeli Urbani Sexagenarii* (eds. J.P. Monferrer Sala and S. Khalil; Beirut: CEDRAC, forthcoming).

Wright, W., *A Short History of Syriac Literature* (London: A. and C. Black, 1894).

Ronny Vollandt

---

[13] See Vollandt, "Che Portono al ritorno."

20

1–2 Chronicles

20.1 Textual History of Chronicles

20.1.1 Extant Witnesses

The books of 1–2 Chronicles (דברי הימים) constitute the last two books in the Ketuvim, the third major division of the Hebrew Bible. Medieval codices do attest some variation in the position of 1–2 Chronicles, as some Spanish manuscripts place the books as the first works in the Writings, as is also the case in the Leningradensis (MT^L) and Aleppo Codices (MT^A). This location could make Chronicles an introduction to Psalms, given the emphasis placed by Chronicles on correct worship. The final position, which is the standard choice in printed editions and the one attested in the majority of manuscripts, could reflect Babylonian practice, as this order is described by *b. B. Bat.* 14b.[1] The division of Chronicles into two books is not present as such in any Hebrew source, but it is found earlier in LXX, and its appearance in medieval codices of MT became standard in the fifteenth century C.E. (→ 20.2.2).[2]

Besides MT, a Hebrew text of Chronicles has apparently been preserved in a tiny Qumran fragment (4Q118, which consists of five very damaged lines with text from 2 Chr 28:27–29:3[3]), but its ascription to Chronicles is contested (→ 20.2.1).[4] Given the extremely fragmentary and damaged state of the Qumran evidence, MT remains the most complete source for the Hebrew text of Chronicles.

The Greek version of LXX (→ 20.3.1) has preserved two translations of Chronicles material. These are: 1) a complete translation of 1–2 Chronicles (known in Greek as 1–2 Paralipomena), placed among the historical books in LXX; 2) the Greek version of 2 Chronicles 35–36 contained in the Deuterocanonical book of 1 Esdras (→ 19.3.1; → II.7.1.2). They constitute two different translations with their own particular features of form and style (→ 20.1.3). Chronicles is found in the several daughter versions of LXX, either fragmentarily (Old Latin [→ 20.4.1],[5] Syro-Hexapla [→ 20.4.4],[6] Coptic [→ 20.4.2][7]) or in its full text (Ethiopic [→ 20.4.3], Armenian [→ 20.4.5], Georgian [→ 20.4.6]). Some manuscripts of the Peshitta text also include 1 Esdras (→ II.7.1.3) and therefore a Syriac version of the 1 Esdras Greek text of 2 Chronicles 35–36. The following versions are close to MT: the Peshitta (where 1–2 Chronicles follow 1–2 Kings 20.3.4); a late Targum of Chronicles (→ 20.3.3);[8] Jerome's Vulgate (→ 20.3.7), and the Hexapla (→ 20.3.5).

20.1.2 History of Research

Since its early days, research of the Hebrew and Greek text of Chronicles involved distinct lines of study focusing on the relationship between 1–2 Chronicles, on the one hand, and Ezra-Nehemiah

---

[1] See Klein, "Chronicles, Book of 1–2," 992; Japhet, *I and II Chronicles*, 1–2. This placement should not be taken, according to some authors (e.g. Curtis and Madsen, *Books of Chronicles*, as a sign of late acceptance into the Hebrew canon; see T. Willi, *Die Chronik als Auslegung* [FRLANT 106; Göttingen: Vanderhoeck & Ruprecht, 1972], 179).

[2] See Japhet, *I and II Chronicles*, 2.

[3] Trebolle Barrera, "4QChr," 295–297.

[4] See Brooke, "The Books of Chronicles and the Scrolls from Qumran"; cf. also Lange, **Handbuch*, 527–29.

[5] See the inventory of surviving fragments in Fischer, *Verzeichnis*; Gryson, **Altlateinische Handschriften 1*. Materials from Chronicles are catalogued together with surviving evidence from Samuel-Kings under numbers 115–122.

[6] Beyond the classical works of Field, **Hexapla*, 670–757, and Gwynn, *Remnants of the later Syriac Versions of the Bible*, 5–18, see more recently Baars (ed.), *New Syro-Hexaplaric Texts*.

[7] Although the complete Septuagint text of the Old Testament was translated into Sahidic, remaining evidence from the books of Chronicles is scarce. Surviving texts in the Bohairic dialect come in their entirety from liturgical citations. See P. Nagel, "Old Testament, Coptic Translations of," in A.S. Atiya, *The Coptic Encyclopedia*, Vol. 6 (New York: McMillan, 1991), 1836a–1940a.

[8] For information on the Targum of Chronicles and of its context of writing and manuscript transmission along the other Targumim to the Writings, see P.M. Flesher and B. Chilton, *The Targums. A Critical Introduction* (Studies in the Aramaic Interpretation of Scripture 12; Leiden: 2011), 229–263, esp. 256–259. For the text, see R. Le Déaut and J. Robert, *Targum des Chroniques* (Rome: Pontificio Istituto Biblico, 1971).

and the Deuterocanonical book 1 Esdras on the other. This has led to different suggestions regarding the figure known as the "Chronicler" and the existence of a "Chronicler's History" in the Bible.[9] This is rather innovative from a textual point of view, as it leads to conceiving, in the history of academia, of an authored book in the biblical canon. In turn, the analysis of the composition process of Chronicles has far-reaching implications for other books of the Bible, as Chronicles exhibits a considerable volume of parallel passages with other biblical books,[10] in particular with Samuel-Kings (as a large portion of the books deals with the history of the united monarchy and later of the kingdom of Judah), a fact that has led some scholars to posit the theory of Chronicles being a rewriting of the Deuteronomistic History (more precisely, Samuel-Kings) under a particular ideological-theological setting.[11] Although these considerations surpass the realm of history of the text and enter into the related disciplines of literary and source criticism, the study of the text of Chronicles is heavily conditioned by the amount of parallel materials, a fact that has led over the centuries of transmission and copying of the text to cases of harmonization and change of the original text to conform with its parallels (→ 5.1; → 5.2). Nevertheless, the study of these parallels and their textual relationship with Samuel-Kings in its different textual forms (MT [→ 5.3.2], the *Vorlage* of the LXX translation [→ 5.4; → 5.5], and fragments from Samuel in the Qumran Scrolls [→ 5.3.1]) has been one of the key elements in the scholarly analysis of the text of Chronicles, even though its final aim would not be in all cases the study of Chronicles alone, but the definition of the source text for the narrative it contains, whether the Deuteronomistic History in a finished form or an independent development of an earlier source shared by Chronicles and the Deuteronomistic History for Samuel-Kings. In the former case, the use of parallel passages in Chronicles as an additional witness for the textual history of Samuel-Kings plays an important role, as it shows a high level of textual agreement with the *Vorlage* of the Old Greek of LXX and evidence from the Qumran scrolls vs. the text type represented by MT. If Chronicles took its material from a finished work akin to Samuel-Kings different from the Masoretic version, these passages reinforce the picture of textual plurality for certain biblical books that has survived well into the last centuries before the turn of the era (→ 1.2.2.4.1).[12] This interest in parallel passages, which at times surpasses the aspect of history of the text *sensu stricto* (or at least of the text of Chronicles) and involves the areas of source and literary criticism, has somehow become the primary focus in the analysis of the book, textually and otherwise.[13] This approach has also been useful for the detection of possible scribal corruptions, a study also applied to the non-parallel passages, where the usual comparison of witnesses (MT and LXX, but also other versions, such as the Vulgate)[14] has been carried out in scholarship. This approach nevertheless suffers limitations, mentioned below, which are caused by the considerable uniformity between MT and the versions, uniformity that in the case of LXX can be due to *kaige* recensional activity (→ 20.3.1.2), as already proposed by Barthélemy,[15] though it could be the case that Chronicles did not undergo a *kaige* recension proper, but similar revisions to accommodate the text to MT.

---

[9] A proposal as early as Zunz, *Die gottesdientlichen Vorträge der Juden*.

[10] Japhet, *I and II Chronicles*, 26–28.

[11] See, among others, McKenzie, *The Chronicler's Use of the Deuteronomistic History*.

[12] For proposals which conceive Chronicles not as a rewriting of Samuel-Kings (or the Deuteronomistic History), but of a common source, see, e.g., Auld, *Kings without Privilege*; Auld, "What Was the Main Source in the Book of Chronicles?" 91–100.

[13] Again, the presence of parallel passages has favored a linguistic study of features which lead to the definition of Late Biblical Hebrew as the diachronic language type of Chronicles. Regardless, this study may be limited by the history of transmission of the book and its textual harmonizations with source-parallel materials. See the seminal work by Polzin (*Late Biblical Hebrew*); for a sobering approach and up to date considerations, see Young and Rezetko, *Linguistic Dating of Biblical Texts*.

[14] See Knoppers, *1 Chronicles 1–9*, 64–65.

[15] Barthélemy, *Devanciers*, 31–80.

20.1.3 Textual History

The study of the textual history of Chronicles itself, as opposed to the potential relationships between Chronicles and the Deuteronomistic History and other sources, is rather limited by the considerable homogeneity of the textual witnesses available. Qumran has yielded only one possible fragment of Chronicles (4Q118), whose nature is contested and that, in any case, is too damaged to be typologically defined. Therefore, approaches to the history of the text have to make use of the ancient versions and their relationship with the Hebrew witness represented by MT (→ 20.2.2). This seems to be a well-preserved text although, as anticipated above, some cases of both accidental and intentional changes of a minor nature can be detected by the analysis of the Hebrew and comparison with the versions (→ 20.2.2.1). For instance, one typical feature of MT-Chr, the high frequency of plene orthography, is often mentioned, although comparison with LXX (→ 20.3.1) and other versions seems to indicate that this scribal tendency was not necessarily so marked in earlier phases of the text (or in one of its editions; see below in this paragraph). Nevertheless, analysis in this direction is somehow marred by potential cases of harmonization in parallel-synoptic passages and by the revision of some versions towards a text type similar to (proto-)MT, which hinders the chances of detecting different *Vorlage* readings. Thus, LXX-Chr offers some hints of a limited nature as it was highly revised in order to bring it closer to MT, although translation features do not seem to support a strict inclusion into the *kaige* recension (→ 20.3.1.2). This is the case in the LXX^L, LXX^R, and LXX^O families, but also true of OG (including Uncial codices Vaticanus [LXX^B] and Sinaiticus [LXX^S] and minuscule LXX^{127}),[16] which seems to be the best witness of the Ptolemaic translation dated around the second century B.C.E., a dating coherent with the fact that the Greek of Chronicles is cited by Eupolemos ca. 150 B.C.E., and could present the closest form to OG-Chr. On the other hand, the materials of 2 Chronicles presented in 1 Esdras [→ II.7.1.2] attest a very different, freer and more paraphrastic, translation. This produces difficulties when trying to define possible differences between its *Vorlage* and MT (and the Hebrew underlying LXX-Chr).[17] Therefore, research on the meaning and textual affiliation of the Chronicles' parallel in 1 Esdras remains complex. Generally speaking, a comparison between MT-Chr and LXX-Chr does not seem to indicate large differences in the text, although LXX-Chr is noted for including a series of passages not present in MT towards the end of the book whose analysis becomes problematic (→ 20.3.1.3), as they constitute parallels with 2 Kings (LXX-4 Kingdoms). Interpretation thereof varies between proposing a Greek origin motivated by a desire to harmonize the structure of Chronicles towards 2 Kings,[18] and seeing their origin in a variant Hebrew text. The latter possibility leads back from the point of view of textual criticism to the possible presence of different literary editions[19] and requires a textual analysis of the text type of 2 Kings used in the Vorlage of LXX-Chr. The concrete case of the "additions" in the final part of LXX-2 Chr is, in turn, part of the larger problem of the relationship between Samuel-Kings and Chronicles given the affinity between Chronicles and the Old Greek text of Samuel-Kings. Detailed textual analysis involving both Samuel-Kings and Chronicles in the MT and LXX traditions is required to define a Hebrew text of Chronicles, possibly in several editions, in a context of textual plurality which mirrors its source (or parallel development from a common one) in Samuel-Kings.[20]

---

[16] See Allen, *The Greek Chronicles*.

[17] See Klein, "Studies in the Greek Text of the Chronicler"; Klein, "New Evidence for an Old Recension of Reigns."

[18] See Klein, *2 Chronicles*, 530.

[19] This is the proposal in Tov, *THBH*, 321. See also Allen, *Greek Chronicles*, 216.

[20] This involves a text-critical assessment of the Lucianic text of LXX Samuel-Kings and its relationship with Chronicles. See the considerations of scope and scholarship in Tov, "Lucian and Proto-Lucian."

20.1.4 Relevance for Exegesis and Literary Criticism

As the main line of research on the books clearly shows, comprehension of the history of Chronicles is fundamental in scholarship for some particular elements in the field of biblical, Hebrew, and Judaic studies. For some of these, the study and text-critical definition of Chronicles will be essential:

1. The book as a witness to Late Biblical Hebrew. As a witness to a post-exilic composition, it has played an important role in the discussion of linguistic diachrony in Biblical Hebrew, especially given the presence of parallel sections with Samuel-Kings, including its paraphrases. Regardless of the debate between more traditional, linear, approaches to the history of the Hebrew language and theories that vie for a less distinct linearity between alleged pre- and post-exilic language types, before Chronicles can be used properly as a tool in linguistic analysis, a reliable text should be established, and considerations about harmonizations with parallel passages should be taken into account beyond a mere usage of MT-Chr (→ 20.2.2) in its present form.[21]
2. The importance of the text of Chronicles for textual criticism of the books of Samuel-Kings, as the parallel text of Chronicles shows the already-mentioned level of agreement with the *Vorlage* of the (most likely) Old Greek text of LXX-1–4 Kingdoms (→ 5.4; → 5.5). No matter which hypothesis is adopted, this leads in all likelihood to the need for the conception of a scenario that involves textual plurality prior to the advent of gradual textual uniformity in agreement with a proto-Masoretic text in the redaction transmission of the Hebrew text of Samuel-Kings. This evidence adds to the results yielded by the correlation of LXX and Qumran (→ 5.3.1).[22] Again, it is necessary to attain, when possible and in the measure that transmission history makes it possible, a text of Chronicles that can be used as a textual witness in the comparative analysis between the different text types of Samuel-Kings.
3. The problem of composition structure is relevant for reflection and inquiry into the composition process of biblical books. The presence of Chronicles in the canon implies a process of rewriting of texts (whatever their nature) from a particular ideological angle, and ultimately the composition of a historical work distinct in views and purpose from the Deuteronomistic History,[23] despite the considerable amount of shared material. Reorganization of extant materials in the first centuries of Judaism is a well-known phenomenon in the Qumran Scrolls, with several literary witnesses of "reworked Scripture" attested in the corpus (→ 21.2.2). The placement of these pieces in the progressive development of concepts of "authorized text," and the reassessment of strict divisions between "biblical" and "parabiblical" literature in this period, clearly involve the comparison with the activity of the Chronicler's work as a "reworked approach"[24] (in the theological plane) to earlier materials or sources, regardless of the final verdict on the nature of the books of Chronicles. Although, again, in the realm of source criticism, it falls within the province of the text critic or text historian to assess the data in order to determine the presence of editorial phenomena on the level of the Hebrew text, especially when the weight of the argument falls on the evidence of the versions.

---

[21] For a cautionary approach, see Young and Retzeko, *Linguistic Dating*.

[22] See Ulrich, *The Qumran Text of Samuel and Josephus*; Lemke, "Synoptic Studies in the Chronicler's History" (1963); Lemke, "The Synoptic Problem in the Chronicler's History" (1965).

[23] See, among others, Knoppers, *1 Chronicles 1–9*, 66–67; McKenzie, "The Chronicler as Redactor"; Z. Talshir, "The Reign of Solomon in the Making."

[24] See the proposals in this direction in Alexander, "Retelling the Old Testament"; and Brooke, "Rewritten Bible." For a moderate reflection on the problems inherent to this proposal, see Knoppers, *1 Chronicles 1–9*, 129–34.

20.1.4 RELEVANCE FOR EXEGESIS AND LITERARY CRITICISM

Alexander, P., "Retelling the Old Testament," in *It Is Written: Scripture Citing Scripture: Essays in Honour of Barnabas Lindars, SFF* (eds. D.A. Carson and H.G.M. Williamson; Cambridge: Cambridge University Press, 1988), 99–121.

Allen, L.C., *The Greek Chronicles: The Relation of the Septuagint of I and II Chronicles to the Masoretic Text*, Part 1: *The Translator's Craft* (VTSup 25; Leiden: Brill, 1974).

Auld, A.G., *Kings without Privilege: David and Moses in the Story of the Bible's Kings* (Edinburgh: T & T Clark, 1994).

Auld, A.G., "What Was the Main Source in the Book of Chronicles?" in *The Chronicler as Author: Studies in Text and Texture* (eds. M.P. Graham and S. McKenzie; JSOTSup 263; Sheffield: Sheffield Academic, 1999), 91–100.

Baars, W. (ed.), *New Syro-Hexaplaric Texts: Edited, Commented upon and Compared with the Septuagint* (Leiden: Brill, 1968).

Barthélemy, **Devanciers*.

Brooke, G.J., "Rewritten Bible," **EDSS* 2:777–81.

Brooke, G.J., "The Books of Chronicles and the Scrolls from Qumran," in *Reflection and Refraction: Studies in Biblical Historiography in Honour of A. Graeme Auld* (eds. R. Retzeko et al.; VTSup 113; Leiden: Brill, 2007), 35–48.

Curtis, E.L. and A.A. Madsen, *A Critical and Exegetical Commentary on the Books of Chronicles* (ICC; Edinburgh: T & T Clark, 1910).

Fischer, B., *Verzeichnis der Sigel für Handschriften und Kirchenschriftsteller* (Freiburg: Herder, 1949).

Flesher, P.M. and B. Chilton, *The Targums: A Critical Introduction* (Studies in the Aramaic Interpretation of Scripture 12; Leiden: Brill, 2011).

Gryson, **Altlateinische Handschriften 1*.

Gwynn, J., *Remnants of the Later Syriac Versions of the Bible* (London: Text and Translation Society, 1909).

Ho, C.Y.S., "Conjectures and Refutations: Is 1 Samuel XXXI 1–13 Really the Source of 1 Chronicles X 1–12?" *VT* 45 (1995): 82–106.

Japhet, S., "Chronicles, Book of," *EncJud* 5:517–34.

Japhet, S., *I and II Chronicles: A Commentary* (OTL: Louisville: John Knox, 1993).

Klein, R.W., "Studies in the Greek Texts of the Chronicler" (PhD diss., Harvard University, 1966).

Klein, R.W., "New Evidence for an Old Recension of Reigns," *HTR* 60 (1967): 93–105; 61 (1968): 492–95.

Klein, R.W., "Chronicles, Book of 1–2," *ABD* 1:992–1002.

Klein, R.W., *2 Chronicles: A Commentary* (Hermeneia; Minneapolis: Fortress Press, 2012).

Knoppers, G.N., *I Chronicles 1–9: A New Translation with Introduction and Commentary* (AB 12; New York: Doubleday, 2004).

Le Déaut, R. and J. Robert, *Targum des Chroniques (Cod. Vat. Urb. Ebr. 1)* (2 vols.; AnBib 51; Rome: Biblical Institute Press, 1971).

Lemke, W.E., "Synoptic Studies in the Chronicler's History" (PhD diss., Harvard University, 1963).

Lemke, W.E., "The Synoptic Problem in the Chronicler's History," *HTR* 58 (1965): 349–63.

McKenzie, S.L., *The Chronicler's Use of the Deuteronomistic History* (HSM 33; Atlanta: Scholars Press, 1985).

McKenzie, S.L., "The Chronicler as Redactor," in M.P. Graham and S. McKenzie, *The Chronicler as Author: Studies in Text and Texture* (JSOTSup 263; Sheffield: Sheffield Academic Press, 1999), 70–90.

Nagel, P., "Old Testament, Coptic Translations of," in *The Coptic Encyclopedia*, (ed. A.S. Atiya; New York: McMillan, 1991), 6:1836a–1940a.

Person, R.F., Jr., *The Deuteronomistic History and the Book of Chronicles: Scribal Works in an Oral World* (SBL Ancient Israel and its Literature 6; Atlanta: Scholars Press, 2010).

Polzin, R., *Late Biblical Hebrew* (HSM 12; Missoula: Scholars Press, 1976).

Sugimoto, T., "The Chronicler's Techniques in Quoting Samuel-Kings," *AJBI* 16 (1990): 30–70.

Sugimoto, T., "Chronicles as Independent Literature," *JSOT* 55 (1992): 61–64.

Talshir, Z., "The Reign of Solomon in the Making: Pseudo-Connections between 3 Kingdoms and Chronicles," *VT* 50 (2000): 233–49.

Throntveit, M.A., "Linguistic Analysis and the Question of Authorship in Chronicles, Ezra and Nehemiah," *VT* 32 (1982): 201–16.

Tov, E., "Lucian and Proto-Lucian: Toward a New Solution of the Problem," in Tov, **Greek-Hebrew Bible*, 477–88.

Tov, **TCHB*.

Trebolle Barrera, J., "From the 'Old Latin' through the 'Old Greek' to the 'Old Hebrew' (2 Kings 10:23–25)," *Textus* 11 (1984): 18–36.

Trebolle Barrera, J., "118. 4QChr," **DJD* XVI: 221–27.

Ulrich, E., *The Qumran Text of Samuel and Josephus* (HSM 19; Missoula: Scholars Press, 1978).

Williamson, H.G.M., *1 and 2 Chronicles: Based on the Revised Standard Version* (New Century Bible Commentary; Grand Rapids: Eerdmans, 1982).

Young, I. and R. Rezetko, *Linguistic Dating of Biblical Texts* (London: Equinox, 2008).

Zunz, L., *Die gottesdienstlichen Vorträge der Juden historisch entwickelt: Ein Beitrag zur Altertumskunde und biblischen Kritik, zur Literatur- und Religionsgeschichte* (Berlin: A. Asher, 1832).

Andrés Piquer Otero

20.2 Ancient Hebrew Texts

20.2.1 Ancient Manuscript Evidence

The only extant ancient manuscript of 1–2 Chronicles is the extensively damaged scroll 4QChr (4Q118).[1] Containing parts of two columns, the surviving fragment of 4QChr attests to remnants of 2 Chr 28:27–29:3. 4QChr was written in a late Hasmonean book hand between 50–25 B.C.E.[2] The orthography of the preserved text of 4QChr corresponds to the orthographic system of MT.[3] While the text of col. ii can still be attributed to 2 Chr 28:27–29:3, the text of col. i (ותעלני תֹּ["... and you led me up") does not correspond to any part of 1–2 Chronicles in either MT (→ 20.2.2) or LXX (→ 20.3.1).[4] Except for three minor non-aligned variants in 2 Chr 28:27; 29:1, 3,[5] the twenty-three extant words in 4QChr read with MT. The small amount of preserved text makes a typological classification of the text of 4QChr impossible. The fact that col. i contains text that cannot be found in 1–2 Chronicles raises the question of whether another Chronicles-text existed in antiquity besides MT and LXX. As 2 Chr 28:27 and 2 Chr 29:1–3 belong to different narratives in the book of Chronicles, it is unlikely, against Gleßmer,[6] that 4QChr attests only to a quotation of Chronicles in another literary context.

Brooke, G.J., "The Books of Chronicles and the Scrolls from Qumran," in *Reflection and Refraction: Studies in Biblical Historiography in Honour of A. Graeme Auld* (eds. R. Rezetko, T.H. Lim, and W.B. Aucker; VTSup 113; Leiden: Brill, 2007), 35–48, esp. 38–40.

Kalimi, I., "History of Interpretation: The Book of Chronicles in Jewish Tradition: From Daniel to Spinoza," *RB* 105 (1998): 5–41, esp. 19–22.

Kalimi, I., *The Retelling of Chronicles in Jewish Tradition and Literature: A Historical Journey* (Winona Lake: Eisenbrauns, 2009), 111–22.

Lange, **Handbuch*, 527–29.

Trebolle Barrera, J., "118. 4QChr," **DJD* XVI: 221–27.

Trebolle Barrera, J., "Édition préliminaire de *4QChroniques*," *RevQ* 15 (1991–1992): 523–28.

Trebolle Barrera, J., "Chronicles, First and Seconds Books of," **EDSS* 1:129.

Ulrich, E., **BQS*, 778.

Armin Lange

20.2.2 (Proto-)Masoretic Texts and Ancient Texts Close to MT

MT-Chr is the only extant complete Hebrew text of 1–2 Chronicles. It is also the sole textual witness in Hebrew for the (proto-)Masoretic text of 1–2 Chronicles. A manuscript from Qumran, 4QChr (4Q118), possibly representing a copy of the book, has only twenty-three words from 2 Chr 28:27–29:3 and its status and character as a textual witness for 1–2 Chronicles are a contested issue (→ 20.2.1). There is general scholarly agreement that the Hebrew text of 1–2 Chronicles has been preserved

---

[1] For a possible second but uncertain Chronicles manuscript from Qumran, see → 5.3.1.12.

[2] Trebolle Barrera, "Édition," 523, 525–26; Trebolle Barrera, "4QChr," 295.

[3] Trebolle Barrera, "Édition," 523; Trebolle Barrera, "4QChr," 295.

[4] Because of the unattributable text in col. i, A. Rofé, "'No Ephod or Teraphim' – oude hierateias oude dēlōn: Hosea 3:4 in the LXX and in the Paraphrases of Chronicles and the *Damascus Document*," in *Sefer Moshe: The Moshe Weinfeld Jubilee Volume* (eds. C. Cohen, A. Hurvitz, and S.M. Paul; Winona Lake: Eisenbrauns, 2004), 135–49, esp. 143 n. 22, and Brooke, "Scrolls from Qumran," 38–40, doubt that what is left of 4QChr represents a manuscript of 1–2 Chronicles. However, textual differences of one or more words with both MT and LXX are not unusual among the biblical Dead Sea Scrolls and therefore cannot support such far-reaching conclusions.

[5] 2 Chr 28:27: יח[זק]יה[ו] בן אחז "Hezekiah, son of Ahaz" instead of יְחִזְקִיָּהוּ בְנוֹ "Hezekiah, his son" (MT; LXX; 2 Kgs 16:20); 2 Chr 29:1: איבה "Aybah" instead of אֲבִיָּה "Abiyah" (MT; LXX Αββα "Abba" and Αβια "Abia"); 2 Chr 29:3: והוא "and he" instead of הוּא "he" (MT; LXX καὶ ἐγένετο ὡς ἔστη ἐπὶ τῆς βασιλείας αὐτοῦ "and it happened that, when he was established over his kingdom" [**NETS*]).

[6] *Contra* U. Gleßmer, "Die ideale Kultordnung: 24 Priesterordnungen in den Chronikbüchern, den kalendarischen Qumrantexten und in synagogalen Inschriften" (unpublished habilitation; University of Hamburg, 1995), 241–42.

in fairly good condition,[1] with the exception of numbers and proper names,[2] and the early versions confirm these trends.[3] This is especially true for LXX-Chr, which is close to MT-Chr (→ 20.3.1.5). However, the empirical evidence for the transmission history of 1–2 Chronicles is late and there are notable tendencies in the extant witnesses (especially in the versions but also in the Hebrew text) for harmonization towards the source texts used in 1–2 Chronicles,[4] and general confusion in the transmission of the proper names, as well as overall disagreements over the origin of individual textual variants in the synoptic parts of the text shared by 1–2 Chronicles and 1–2 Samuel/1–2 Kings.[5] For these reasons, the closeness of MT-Chr to the *Urtext* of Chronicles cannot be confidently estimated.

20.2.2.1 History of Research

Japhet has stated that "the 'synoptic' nature of Chronicles – the fact that much of the book represents a literal citation of earlier biblical works – makes Chronicles a 'favourite' in textual criticism."[6] However, the text-critical studies on 1–2 Chronicles have concentrated almost completely on these synoptic passages and have been mostly concerned with the earliest reachable reading of the source texts of 1–2 Chronicles (e.g., Genesis, Joshua, 1–2 Samuel, 1–2 Kings, Psalms). Studies dealing with secondary readings in MT-Chr itself are mostly restricted to commentaries and articles dealing with specific sections of 1–2 Chronicles.[7] The portion of 1–2 Chronicles with the most variant readings is the genealogies and proper names in 1 Chronicles 1–9. The extensive amount of scribal corruption in these genealogies was noted already by Jerome,[8] but was first extensively scrutinized by Friedländer in the early twentieth century, who was able to categorize more accurately the nature of some of the scribal errors in these sections.[9] Since this pioneering study on the subject, the variants in the genealogies have been studied extensively, and it is commonly agreed that the genealogies have been subject to both some deliberate attempts at harmonization with their source texts and a great number of unintentional scribal errors.[10]

---

[1] Japhet, *I & II Chronicles*, 29.

[2] E.L. Curtis and A.A. Madsen, *A Critical and Exegetical Commentary on the Books of Chronicles* (ICC; Edinburgh: T & T Clark, 1910), 36; Rudolph, *Chronikbücher*, iv; Japhet, *I & II Chronicles*, 29; R. Rezetko, *Source and Revision in the Narratives of David's Transfer of the Ark: Text, Language, and Story in 2 Samuel 6 and 1 Chronicles 13, 15–16* (Library of Hebrew Bible/Old Testament Studies 470; London: T & T Clark, 2007), 38; Klein, *1 Chronicles*, 26.

[3] See Allen, *The Greek Chronicles*, 2.81–168.

[4] The concept of harmonization towards source texts does not imply any judgment with regard to the original form of any given passage in the source text, only that there are later secondary elements in the MT-1–2 Chr that derive from deliberate harmonization towards the then-current form of its perceived source texts.

[5] A novelty related to the study of Chronicles is the supposition of most scholars that Chronicles was written by a specific author, the Chronicler. Hence the peculiar diction of 1–2 Chronicles has been studied, for instance, by A. Kropat, *Die Syntax des Autors der Chronik* (BZAW 16; Gießen: Alfred Töpelmann, 1909), and a list of this proposed author's favorite words, syntactical usages, and prepositions was compiled by Curtis and Madsen, *A Critical and Exegetical Commentary*. These lists and other traits connected with this author have subsequently been used as a criterion for deciding upon the importance of variants in text-critical cases; see, e.g., I. Kalimi, "The Contribution of the Literary Study of Chronicles to the Solution of its Textual Problems," *BibInt* 3 (1995): 190–211.

[6] Japhet, *I & II Chronicles*, 28.

[7] More recent studies include, e.g., L. Gottlieb, "Repetition Due to Homoeoteleuton," *Textus* 21 (2002): 21–43; D. Freedman and D. Miano, "Is the Shorter Reading Better? Haplography in the First Book of Chronicles," in *Emanuel: Studies in Hebrew Bible, Septuagint, and Dead Sea Scrolls in Honor of Emanuel Tov* (eds. S.M. Paul et al.; VTSup 94; Leiden: Brill, 2003), 685–98; P. Borbone, "Il testo masoretico di 2 *Cronache* 30,27," *Hen* 26 (2004): 243–50.

[8] On Jerome and Chronicles, see further G.N. Knoppers and P.B. Harvey, Jr., "Omitted and Remaining Matters: On the Names Given to the Book of Chronicles in Antiquity," *JBL* 121 (2002): 227–43.

[9] M. Friedländer, *Die Veränderlichkeit der Namen in den Stammlisten der Bücher der Chronik* (Berlin: Itzkowski, 1903). See also, Curtis and Madsen, *A Critical and Exegetical Commentary*, 36. The corruption in the genealogies is already evident by looking at the apparatus of *BHS, and is further confirmed by the lists of Kennicott, *1776–1780, 2.644–60, and De Rossi, *1784–1788, 4.168–77; 5.136–39.

[10] See, e.g., Allen, *The Greek Chronicles*, 2.81–162; G.N. Knoppers, "Sources, Revisions, and Editions: The Lists of Jerusalem's Residents in MT and LXX Nehemiah 11 and 1 Chronicles 9," *Text* (2000), 141–68; N.F. Fernández Marcos, "On Double Readings,

20.2.2 (Proto-)Masoretic Texts and Ancient Texts Close to MT

Despite the relatively good condition of the Hebrew text of MT-Chr,[11] scribal corruption has also been detected in the narrative parts of MT-Chr,[12] not just the genealogies. Short lists of such errors in MT-Chr have been compiled, for example, by Rehm and Rudolph,[13] but the most extensive lists have thus far been provided by Allen. He has categorized the variants in LXX-Chr, the LXX *Vorlage* of 1–2 Chronicles, and MT-Chr according to different types of scribal errors. He argues that the secondary variants in MT-Chr are caused by abbreviation, assimilation, division of words, metathesis, transposition, confusion of consonants, haplo- and dittography, and paraplepsis, as well as more intentional changes, such as glosses, omissions, and additions.[14] Some cases of scribal corruption have already been noted and emended in *Ketiv-Qere* and *Sebirin* (ca. eighty and ten in number respectively).[15] Allen was the first to suggest that, in addition to LXX (→ 20.3.1) and its Hebrew *Vorlage*,[16] also MT-Chr suffered to some degree from harmonization towards its source texts.[17]

20.2.2.2 Manuscripts and Editions

Because of the lack of unambiguous manuscript evidence from Qumran, the most important Hebrew manuscripts for 1–2 Chronicles are Codex Leningradiensis (EBP. I B 19a) at the Russian National Library (MT^L), the Aleppo Codex at the Israel Museum archives (MT^A), and manuscript Add. 1753 (MT^Y) at the Cambridge University Library. 1–2 Chronicles is one of the books entirely extant in MT^A. Notably, in MT^{A,L,Y}, 1–2 Chronicles are the first, not the last, books of the Ketuvim.

Until the completion of critical Bible projects, such as the *BHQ edition of 1–2 Chronicles, the best available critical edition of MT-Chr is the diplomatic edition of W. Rudolph in the *BHS, based on MT^L. Its apparatus is selective but gives a clear sense of the typical types of variants in the versions. It is more comprehensive and accurate than the previous edition of 1–2 Chronicles in *BH³ prepared by J. Begrich, and its presentation of variants and suggested solutions are more balanced, owing probably to Rudolph's prior work on Chronicles.[18] The text-critical apparatus compiled by Torrey is also still worth checking,[19] as are Hognesius' critical edition of 2 Chronicles 1–16,[20] as well as the edition of Kennicott (*1776–1780, 2.644–726) and the variant list of De Rossi (*1784–1788, 4.169–206) for the variants in the medieval manuscript tradition.

20.2.2.3 The Nature and Text-Critical Character of (proto-)MT-Chr

1–2 Chronicles are among the books of the Hebrew Bible that exhibit the fullest orthography.[21] They

---

Pseudo-Variants and Ghost-Names in the Historical Books," in *Emanuel: Studies in Hebrew Bible, Septuagint, and Dead Sea Scrolls in Honor of Emanuel Tov* (eds. S.M. Paul et al.; VTSupp 94; Leiden: Brill, 2003), 600–04; Freedman and Miano, "Is the Shorter Reading Better?" 685–98.

[11] According to Curtis and Madsen, *A Critical and Exegetical Commentary*, 18, 36, the current condition of MT-1–2 Chr is due to "regular disinterest and neglect" of 1–2 Chronicles and its text. Cf. Rezetko, *Source and Revision*, 61.

[12] See, e.g., Knoppers, *1 Chronicles 1–9*, 64–65.

[13] Rehm, *Textkritische Untersuchungen*, 34–52, 63–72; Rudolph, *Chronikbücher*, v–vi.

[14] Allen, *The Greek Chronicles*, 2.81–162.

[15] Japhet, *I & II Chronicles*, 29.

[16] According to Allen, *The Greek Chronicles*, 2.213–16, the Hebrew *Vorlage* of LXX-1–2 Chr seems to have been a slightly later literary edition of 1–2 Chronicles with many secondary readings introduced to the proto-MT tradition, but nevertheless including some early readings. Cf. Tov, *TCHB, 321. See further, → 20.3.1. Yet another literary edition of the Hebrew text of 1–2 Chronicles might have been represented by the Hebrew *Vorlage* of 1 Esdras, which, according to R.W. Klein, differs from MT-2 Chr 35–36 altogether over a hundred times either alone or in agreement with the *Vorlage* of LXX-Chr ("The Rendering of 2 Chronicles 35–36 in 1 Esdras," in *Was 1 Esdras First? An Investigation into the Nature of 1 Esdras* [ed. L. Fried; SBLAIL 7; Leiden: Brill, 2011], 225–26, 235; see further, → 11.7.1). Furthermore, Lange raises the question of whether 4QChr might derive from yet another text of 1–2 Chronicles (→ 20.2.1).

[17] Allen, *The Greek Chronicles*, 1.217–18.

[18] Rudolph, *Chronikbücher*.

[19] C.C. Torrey, "Apparatus for the Textual Criticism of Chronicles-Ezra-Nehemiah in the OT," in *Old Testament and Semitic Studies* (eds. R.F. Harper et al.; Chicago: University of Chicago, 1908), 53–112.

[20] K. Hognesius, *The Text of 2 Chronicles 1–16: A Critical Edition with Textual Commentary* (ConBOT 51; Stockholm: Almqvist & Wiksell, 2003).

[21] Barr, *Variable Spellings*, 178; Tov, *TCHB, 218.

frequently have a fuller spelling in parallel passages than their sources (e.g., the spelling of "David" is in Chronicles always דָּוִיד whereas this form is used in 1–2 Kings only three times and the typical spelling is דָּוִד, which is the only spelling found in 1–2 Samuel).[22] However, this is not always the case and 1–2 Chronicles also exhibit some more defective forms than found in their sources, which, according to Barr, can be partly explained as a use of earlier versions of the source texts (e.g., אֲלֵהֶם, "to them" in 2 Chr 10:7, 9, 10, 14 is spelled in the parallel in 1 Kgs 12:7, 9, 10, 14 as אֲלֵיהֶם).[23] Nevertheless, not all cases displaying different orthographic systems can be explained this way and, to make things more complex, Lange has also identified several forms of the so-called Qumran orthography in 1–2 Chronicles (at least מֵהֵנָּה in 1 Chr 21:10, נָתַתָּה in 2 Chr 6:25, 27, 31, 38; 20:10, and וְנָתַתָּה in 2 Chr 6:27, 30).[24] There is a considerable amount of spelling variation in the medieval manuscripts of 1–2 Chronicles as well, which gives a clear idea of how such variation may have accrued to MT-Chr. Interestingly, Allen has claimed that *matres lectiones* were much less frequent in the *Vorlage* of LXX-1–2 Chr than in MT.[25]

The variants in the Hebrew text of 1–2 Chronicles have been studied both in relation to their sources as well as their later versions. While the study of the "synoptic" texts is rarely beneficial for discovering the earliest reading in Chronicles, the careful study of the various versions of the source texts is important for the textual criticism of 1–2 Chronicles because of a later tendency to harmonize 1–2 Chronicles toward its sources. This phenomenon has affected almost all the versions of 1–2 Chronicles but neither is MT free of them.[26] An example is the addition of וְקַבְּצֵנוּ "gather us" to MT-1 Chr 16:35. The word is lacking in LXX, the "gathering of exiles" is an uncommon concept in Chronicles, it does not fit the historical setting of the song in 1 Chronicles at all, and it makes the colon poetically awkward and disrupts the parallelism of the verse.[27] It is a later harmonization towards the source of the verse in Ps 106:47.[28] Another similar type of change in MT-Chr is assimilation toward a passage in the source other than the direct parallel. A possible case of such assimilation is the inclusion of the word וַיָּדֶק "and pulverized [it]" in 2 Chr 15:16. The direct parallel of the account in 1 Kgs 15:13 does not have the word and neither do the versions of 2 Chr 15:16. The addition harmonizes the account with the similar story of a king cutting down idols in 2 Kgs 23:6, and this is most likely the reason for the reading in 2 Chr 15:16.[29]

Some scribal corruption is also evident in the Hebrew tradition all the way to the medieval manuscripts. Examples for letter confusion include the following: In MT-1 Chr 21:12, נִסְפֶּה "being swept away" instead of נֻסְכָה "your fleeing" in 2 Sam 24:13 and LXX-Chr reflects interchange of *kap* and *pe*; MT-1 Chr 4:39 גְּדֹר "Gedor" instead of LXX-Chr Γεραρα "Gerar" reveals *dalet-reš* confusion. Probable homoioteleuton and -arkton errors are found in a number of passages in 1–2 Chronicles. For example, in 1 Chr 21:26, the end of the verse preserved in LXX καὶ κατανάλωσεν τὴν ὁλοκαύτωσιν "and it consumed the burnt offering," which would probably have been ותאכל את העלה in Hebrew, seems to have been lost in MT due to the presence of העלה "burnt offering" at the end of both the parallel text and LXX variant following it. There are also occurrences of word-division errors in the text, such as 2 Chr 32:22, which has the very unusual phrase וַיְנַהֲלֵם מִסָּבִיב "and guided them on all sides," whereas LXX reads καὶ κατέπαυσεν αὐτοὺς κυκλόθεν "and he gave them rest on every side." The latter stands proba-

---

[22] Tov, *TCHB*, 13, 213–14.

[23] Barr, *Variable Spellings*, 178–82.

[24] Lange, in private communication, kindly provided me with these examples and the permission to use them in the entry. See now also A. Lange, "The Question of the So-Called Qumran Orthography, the Severus Scroll, and the Masoretic Text," *Hebrew Bible and Ancient Israel* 3 (2014): 424–75.

[25] Allen, *The Greek Chronicles*, 2.167; cf. Klein, *1 Chronicles*, 28.

[26] Cf. Rehm, *Textkritische Untersuchungen*, 47–48; Allen, *The Greek Chronicles*, 1.26–31, 175–218.

[27] Japhet, *I & II Chronicles*, 319.

[28] Allen, *The Greek Chronicles*, 1.217.

[29] Japhet, *I & II Chronicles*, 728. Against Kalimi, "The Contribution," 192–93, who claims the word was omitted from the versions due to its being missing from the direct parallel account in 1 Kgs 15:3.

bly for וינח להם מסביב in Hebrew, which is a major theme in the theology of 1–2 Chronicles. MT seems to derive from a slight orthographic change and combining of the words וינח להם preserved in LXX.

20.2.2.4 Date and Milieu

When the harmonizing additions to MT were made or when the most important scribal errors occurred cannot be discovered. There does not seem to be any systematic revision, but rather variants that have accrued over time and stem from different scribes. A rough estimate, based on the date of the LXX version (→ 20.3.1) and the number of secondary variants accrued to MT-Chr after the separation of the literary edition of the LXX *Vorlage* from the line of proto-MT tradition, would be that a text very close to the current MT could have been in existence around the turn of the era.

20.2.2.5 Relevance for Exegesis and Literary Analysis

As the extant versions of Chronicles are very close to each other and the secondary variants are mostly not connected, there is very little that can be said regarding the relevance of MT-Chr for exegesis. Perhaps the most important aspect is the tendency of harmonization toward the source texts of Chronicles in MT but especially in the versions and their Hebrew *Vorlagen* because it demonstrates that there were people trying to reconcile the conflicting details in the parallel accounts and they did so by introducing changes to Chronicles, not to its sources. This shows that at some point 1–2 Chronicles clearly became secondary to its sources, at least in some circles, a tendency that evidently continued during the later process of canonization and beyond.

Allen, L.C., *The Greek Chronicles: The Relation of the Septuagint of I and II Chronicles to the Massoretic Text* (2 vols.; VTSup 25 and 27; Leiden: Brill, 1974).
Barr, *Variable Spellings.
Japhet, S., *I & II Chronicles* (OTL; London: SCM Press Ltd, 1993).
Kennicott, *1776–1780, 2:644–726.
Klein, R.W., *1 Chronicles: A Commentary* (Hermeneia; Minneapolis: Fortress Press, 2006).
Knoppers, G.N., *1 Chronicles 1–9: A New Translation with Introduction and Commentary* (AB 12; New York: Doubleday, 2004).
Rehm, M., *Textkritische Untersuchungen zu den Parallelstellen der Samuel-Königsbücher und der Chronik* (Münster: Aschendorff, 1937).
De Rossi, *1784–1788, 4:169–206.
Rudolph, W., *Chronica*, *BHS, 1459–574.
Rudolph, W., *Chronikbücher* (HAT 21; Tübingen: Mohr Siebeck, 1955).
Tov, *TCHB.

Mika Pajunen

20.3 Primary Translations

20.3.1 Septuagint

20.3.1.1 Background

The title of Chronicles in LXX, *Paraleipomena* "the things left out," testifies to an early understanding of the work's purpose, namely to present the events left out of earlier Israelite history.[1] Dating to the second century B.C.E., LXX-Chr is generally a very literal witness that closely resembles MT in sequence, syntax, and content (→ 20.2.2).[2] Although the question has been raised as to whether Paraleipomena might be Palestinian in origin, most agree that the work's most likely provenance is Egypt.[3] A date in the second century B.C.E. seems secure, because Paraleipomena is cited by Eupolemus, a Jewish-Hellenistic writer, living in the latter part of the second century B.C.E.[4]

20.3.1.2 Original Form, Editions, Tools

The recensional history of the Greek Chronicles is a complex issue.[5] Most scholars now view the combined evidence of Uncial LXX^B (Codex Vaticanus), Uncial LXX^S (Codex Sinaiticus), and minuscule LXX^{c_2} as comprising the oldest extant text form of Paraleipomena.[6] Older arguments for the historical priority of Uncial LXX^A are unconvincing.[7] Nevertheless, Codex LXX^B likely contains revisional elements, the extent of which remain a matter of debate. Barthélemy hypothesizes that LXX^B evinces the same kind of *kaige* revision as can be discerned in other books, such as Samuel and Kings (→ 3–5.1.2.2), and that this Palestinian revision toward the developing MT is to be dated to the first century C.E.[8] Yet, subsequent scholarship demonstrates that there is no compelling evidence for positing a *kaige* revision in Paraleipomena.[9] Indeed, LXX-Chr only rarely displays the typical characteristics normally associated with the *kaige* recension.[10] Thus, not one of the translation characteristics of the *kaige* recension is found in Paraleipomena in synoptic passages in which Kingdoms exhibits the *kaige* recension.[11]

Another suggestion of Barthélemy, pointing to the identity of the Antiochene (Lucianic) group (→ 20.3.6), especially the minuscules LXX$^{be_2(y)}$, has more merit.[12] Minuscules LXX$^{be_2(y)}$ clearly evince features of being an Antiochene revised text of the Old Greek, but there are also some links be-

---

[1] G.N. Knoppers and P.B. Harvey, "Omitted and Remaining Matters: On the Names Given to the Book of Chronicles in Antiquity," *JBL* 121 (2002): 227–43.

[2] For a much fuller discussion, see Klein, "Greek Texts," 77–184.

[3] Gerleman, *Studies*, 8–29; Allen, *Greek Chronicles*, 21–26, 167–68.

[4] Eupolemus' quotation of select texts dealing with David and Solomon is preserved in Eusebius (*Praep. ev.* 9.30.1–34.18). See further Gerleman, *Studies*, 11–13; C.R. Holladay, *Fragments from Hellenistic Jewish Authors*, Vol. 1: *Historians* (SBLTT; Chico: Scholars Press, 1983) 93–156; B.Z. Wacholder, *Eupolemus: A Study of Judaeo-Greek Literature* (Monographs of the Hebrew Union College 3; Cincinnati: Hebrew Union College-Jewish Institute of Religion, 1974).

[5] On what follows, see in more detail Knoppers, *I Chronicles 1–9*, 55–65.

[6] Thus, for instance, R. Kittel, *Die Bücher der Chronik und Esra, Nehemia und Esther* (HAT 1.6; Göttingen: Vandenhoeck & Ruprecht, 1902), 24; Rehm, *Textkritische Untersuchungen*, 13; Allen, *Greek Chronicles*, 1.101–06. Unfortunately, S is only extant from 1 Chr 9:27 τὸ πρωί to 1 Chr 19:17. The sigla, used in this article for LXX minuscules follow Brooke–McLean–Thackeray, **The Old Testament in Greek*, Vol. 2.3: *I and II Chronicles* (1932) but are given in superscript appended to LXX.

[7] For representations of this view, see Torrey, *Ezra Studies*, 91–96; E.L. Curtis and A.A. Madsen, *A Critical and Exegetical Commentary on the Books of Chronicles* (ICC; Edinburgh: T & T Clark, 1910), 40–41; Jellicoe, *SMS, 293.

[8] Barthélemy, *Devanciers, 31–80.

[9] More generally, see the summary of S. Kreuzer, "Translation and Recensions: Old Greek, *Kaige*, and Antiochene Text in Samuel and Reigns," *BIOSCS* 42 (2009): 34–51.

[10] Klein, "Greek Texts," 317–18; Allen, *Greek Chronicles*, 1.137–41.

[11] J.D. Shenkel, "A Comparative Study of Synoptic Parallels in I Paraipomena and I–II Reigns," *HTR* 62 (1969): 63–85. Allen, *Greek Chronicles*, 2.182 rejects the proposition that the LXX translator employed an earlier recension of 1–4 Kingdoms in preparing his translation of Chronicles.

[12] Barthélemy, *Devanciers, 41–42, 47. While minuscule LXX^y is Lucianic until 1 Chr 11:14, from 1 Chr 11:15 forward it is Hexaplaric; see Allen, *Greek Chronicles*, 1.65.

tween these witnesses and LXX^{Bc_2}.[13] This group may be expanded by the many agreements between LXX$^{be_2(y)}$ and Theodoret's quotations of Paraleipomena (→ 21.7).[14] In this context, it bears mentioning that the text of Chronicles reflected in Josephus' *Antiquitates judaicae* (→ 21.3) is far closer to the Antiochene witnesses than it is to the Old Greek.[15]

In Chronicles, the LXX$^{be_2(y)}$ revision is based on a *Vorlage* most like LXX^{Bc_2}.[16] Because LXX^{Bc_2} have undergone their own revisions toward MT (→ 20.2.2), LXX$^{be_2(y)}$ may even attest, in certain cases, LXX^{Bc_2} at an earlier stage.[17] Hence, whenever LXX^{Bc_2} and LXX$^{be_2(y)}$ agree, there is a good possibility that the text approximates an early form of Paraleipomena.

In addition to LXX$^{be_2(y)}$, there are two groups of witnesses that represent recensions of a text similar to LXX^{Bc_2}. First, the group of minuscules LXX^{dpqtz} exhibit two tendencies: approximation toward MT and departures from MT to produce a smoother, more comprehensible Greek. Second, Uncials LXX^{A} and LXX^{N} and minuscules LXX^{aceghn} represent another recension.[18] Like the group composed of LXX^{dpqtz}, this group tends to approximate MT and to improve the rugged Greek style of its base.[19] Judging by the number of its agreements with the Syro-Hexapla (→ 20.4.4), this group is the closest witness to the Hexaplaric recension (→ 20.3.5) in Paraleipomena.[20] Unlike the group of LXX^{dpqtz}, LXX^{ANaceghn} does not consistently take liberties with its *Vorlage*. In other words, this group displays less diligence in repairing its basic text than does the group of LXX^{dpqtz}.

Finally, VL is of some value in reconstructing the Old Greek (→ 1.4.1; → 20.4.1). Weber's foundational study of VL-2 Chr suggests that this text contains a variety of revisional elements of the Old Greek towards MT.[21] But Fernández Marcos contends that the textual pluralism exhibited by VL is greater than that found in either the Greek or the Hebrew witnesses to Chronicles.[22] VL sometimes shares readings with Hexaplaric witnesses and the "Three" (Aquila, Theodotion, and Symmachus; → 20.3.5), sometimes sides with the Antiochene text (→ 20.3.6), frequently diverges from the Antiochene text, agrees with the Old Greek, or offers its own unique readings.[23] In his analysis of the Complutensis, Carmignac argues that it represents a mixed text.[24] As such, it may occasionally represent portions of VL, rather than the Vulgate (→ 20.3.7). Employed critically and judiciously, VL can occasionally shed light on an early text form of Paraleipomena.

Turning to twentieth-century editions of LXX, the classic edition of LXX by Rahlfs (and corrected by Hanhart) is very convenient but some-

---

[13] Allen, *Greek Chronicles* 1.65–72; N. Fernández Marcos, "The Antiochian Text in I–II Chronicles," in *VII Congress of the International Organization for Septuagint and Cognate Studies, Leuven 1989* (ed. C.E. Cox; SBLSCS 31; Atlanta: Scholars Press, 1991), 301–11 (304–05). Allen, *Greek Chronicles*, 1.65 also includes the Catena LXX^{350} in this group.

[14] Fernández Marcos and Busto Saiz, *Theodoreti Cyrensis Quaestiones*, lviii–lx.

[15] Allen, *Greek Chronicles*, 1.73–74; Spottorno, "Books of Chronicles in Josephus' Jewish Antiquities," 381–90.

[16] N. Fernández Marcos and J.R. Busto Saiz make an important distinction between the testimony of b' (ms 19) and b (ms 108), *El Texto Antioqueno de la Biblia griega III: 1–2 Crónicas* (Textos y Estudios "Cardenal Cisneros" 60; Madrid: Instituto de Filología del CSIC, 1996), xvii–xviii.

[17] Allen, *Greek Chronicles*, 1.72.

[18] LXX^{ANh} sporadically display readings that are also found in LXX^{Bc_2}. LXX^{N} thus occupies an intermediary position between LXX^{A} and LXX^{B}. See Torrey, *Ezra Studies*, 97; Allen, *Greek Chronicles*, 1.103–05.

[19] Rehm, *Textkritische Untersuchungen*, 13–14; Allen, *Greek Chronicles*, 1.85–89.

[20] Allen, *Greek Chronicles*, 1.87–89.

[21] Weber, *Les anciennes versions latines*, xlviii–li. His conclusion that VL is basically a translation of Theodotion is, however, misguided.

[22] Fernández Marcos, "Antiochian Text," 306.

[23] Allen, *Greek Chronicles*, 1.106–08; Fernández Marcos, "Antiochian Text," 301–11; N. Fernández Marcos, "The Old Latin of Chronicles between the Greek and the Hebrew," in *IX Congress of the International Organization for Septuagint and Cognate Studies, Cambridge, 1995* (ed. B.A. Taylor; SBLSCS 45; Atlanta: Scholars Press, 1997), 123–36.

[24] R. Carmignac, "Les Devanciers de S. Jerome: Une traduction latine de la recension *kaige* dans le second livre des Chroniques," in *Mélanges Dominique Barthélemy: Études bibliques offertes à l'occasion de son 60. anniversaire* (eds. P. Cassetti, O. Kell, and A. Schenker; OBO 38; Göttingen: Vandenhoeck & Ruprecht, 1981), 31–50. Nevertheless, VL does not exhibit any signs of influence from a putative *kaige* recension, as pointed out by Fernández Marcos, "Antiochian Text," 309.

what limited in its value, as it only features three textual witnesses (B, S, A).[25] By contrast, the diplomatic text (LXX[B]) of the Cambridge Septuagint offers a detailed textual apparatus.[26] In employing this edition, readers should also consult the edition of the so-called Antiochene text by Fernández Marcos and Busto Saiz, because it contains many corrections of the Antiochene readings in Paraleipomena listed by Brooke–McLean–Thackeray.[27] There is, in 2016, no edition of Chronicles in the Göttingen LXX. Mention should be made, however, of the Göttingen edition of the apocryphal (or deuterocanonical) book of 1 Esdras (Esdras α), because 1 Esdras contains 2 Chr 35:1–36:23, Ezra (adding 1:21–22 and 3:1–5:6), and Neh 7:73–8:12 in continuous fashion.[28] There are, therefore, at least in part, two LXX translations of Chronicles. Whereas Paraleipomena is a very literal translation of the Hebrew, 1 Esdras is a much freer translation, written in elegant and idiomatic Greek. Scholars avidly disagree about the origins, nature, and purpose of this work (→ 19.3.1).[29]

Very good modern translations of Paraleipomena are available in English,[30] Spanish,[31] and German.[32] The introduction to "1 and 2 Supplements" by Cowe in *NETS provides a good overview of the challenges in translating a text written in wooden Greek, such as Paraleipomena, into readable English.[33] One advantage of the *Septuaginta Deutsch format is that textual elements of LXX that differ from MT are printed in italics and, conversely, elements of MT that are absent in LXX are indicated by superscript plus signs.[34]

20.3.1.3 Translation Character

Written in non-idiomatic Greek, Paraleipomena is generally a literal translation that closely follows the style and content of the Hebrew, but lacks (in Codex LXX[B]) 1 Chr 1:11–16, 17b–24a, 27b.[35] There are only a few other minuses in Paraleipomena, most of which can be explained text-critically. Thus, for example, in 2 Chr 3:2, MT reads בחדש השני בשני בשנת ארבע למלכותו "in the second month on the second (day) in the fourth year of his reign." LXX, ἐν τῷ μηνὶ τῷ δευτέρῳ ἐν τῷ ἔτει τῷ τετάρτῳ τῆς βασιλείας αὐτοῦ mimics the sequence of the Hebrew, "in the second month in the fourth year of his reign," but lacks בשני "on the second."[36] Yet, בשני could have easily been lost by haplography after השני and before בשנת.

To take another example from the same chapter (2 Chr 3:12), involving an entire verse: "The wing of (this) one cherub, five cubits (long), extended to the wall of the house and the other wing, five

---

[25] Rahlfs, *Septuaginta, 752–811. Many minor errors in this work have been corrected by R. Hanhart. See Rahlfs–Hanhart, *Septuaginta, 752–873.

[26] Brooke–McLean–Thackeray, *The Old Testament in Greek, Vol. 2.3: I and II Chronicles (1932).

[27] Fernández Marcos and Busto Saiz, El Texto Antioqueno.

[28] R. Hanhart, Esdrae liber I (Septuaginta Vetus Testamentum Graece 8.1; Göttingen: Vandenhoeck & Ruprecht, 1974). That Josephus (Ant. 11.1–158) follows the order of 1 Esdras through Nehemiah 8 (including the celebration of Sukkôt, the Feast of Tabernacles) bears witness to the use of 1 Esdras in antiquity (→ 21.3).

[29] K.-F. Pohlmann, Studien zum dritten Esra: Ein Beitrag zur Frage nach dem ursprunglichen Schluss des chronistischen Geschichtswerkes (FRLANT 104; Göttingen: Vandenhoeck & Ruprecht, 1970); D. Böhler, Die heilige Stadt in Esdras α und Esra-Nehemia: Zwei Konzeptionen der Wiederherstellung Israels (OBO 158; Göttingen: Vandenhoeck & Ruprecht, 1997); Z. Talshir, 1 Esdras: From Origin to Translation (SBLSCS 47; Atlanta: SBL, 1999); Z. Talshir, 1 Esdras: A Text Critical Commentary (SBLSCS 50; Atlanta: SBL, 2001); D.N. Fulton and G.N. Knoppers, "Lower Criticism and Higher Criticism: The Case of 1 Esdras," in Was First Esdras First? An Investigation into the Priority of First Esdras (ed. L.S. Fried; SBL Ancient Israel and its Literature 7; Atlanta: SBL, 2011), 11–29; Tov, *TCHB, 319–20.

[30] S.P. Cowe, "1 and 2 Supplements," in *NETS, 342–91.

[31] N. Fernández et al., in La Biblia griega Septuaginta, Vol. 2: Libros históricos (Biblioteca de estudios bíblicos 126; Salamanca: Ediciones Sígueme, 2008).

[32] A. Labahn, "Paraleipomenon I / Das erste Buch der Chronik" in *Septuaginta Deutsch, 491–518; D. Sänger, "Paraleipomenon II / Das zweite Buch der Chronik," in *Septuaginta Deutsch, 518–90.

[33] S.P. Cowe, "1 and 2 Supplements," 342–48.

[34] The translation also includes footnotes on textual variants and details of translation.

[35] Knoppers, 1 Chronicles 1–9, 267–69.

[36] Given that MT-1 Kgs 6:1 lacks בשני "on the second," the term could have been missing from the translator's Vorlage. Cf. 3 Kgdms 6:1 τῷ ἔτει τῷ τετάρτῳ ἐν μηνὶ τῷ δευτέρῳ "in the fourth year in the second month."

cubits (long), joined the wing of the other cherub" is missing from LXX^B. The text appears, however, in LXX^AN καὶ ἡ πτέρυξ τοῦ χερουβ τοῦ ἑνὸς πήχεων πέντε ἁπτομένη τοῦ τοίχου τοῦ οἴκου καὶ ἡ πτέρυξ ἡ ἑτέρα πήχεων πέντε ἁπτομένη τοῦ πτέρυγος τοῦ χερουβ τοῦ ἑτέρου. The material was lost due to whole-phrase haplography (from לכנף הכרוב האחד at the end of v. 11 to לכנף הכרוב האחד at the end of v. 12). In sum, LXX-Chr occasionally exhibits pluses over against MT-Chr (→ 20.2.2) and in those relatively few cases in which it is shorter than MT, accidental loss of text is the most common cause.

Rather remarkably, LXX-Chr features several minuses (2 Chr 35:19b, 35:20a), a difference (2 Chr 36:4), and some additions (2 Par 35:19a–d; 36:2a–c, 4a, 5a–d) clustered near the work's end.[37] The supplements are largely borrowed from and, in a few cases, rework sections of 2 Kings (or 4 Kingdoms) 23–24 (→ 5.5).

2 Paraleipomena	Source in 2 Kings (4 Kingdoms)
35:19α–δ	4 Kgdms//2 Kgs 23:24–27
36:2α–ξ	4 Kgdms//2 Kgs 23:31b–33a
36:4α	4 Kgdms//2 Kgs 23:35
36:5α–δ	4 Kgdms//2 Kgs 24:1–4

There is corresponding text neither in MT-Chr nor in 1 Esdras (→ 11.7.1.2) to these additions in Paraleipomena. Furthermore, some segments in the last two chapters of 2 Paraleipomena correspond to (and translate) texts in Kings.

2 Paraleipomena	Source in 2 Kings (4 Kingdoms)
35:20	23:29abα
36:3b–4	23:33b–34a
36:5b	23:36b–37
36:8	24:5–6a

In these cases, there is relevant material in the corresponding verses within MT-Chr, but LXX-Chr largely translates the corresponding texts in Kings.

There is an ongoing debate about the nature of the additions in Paraleipomena.[38] Tov views the varied LXX evidence as indicating a different Hebrew literary edition.[39] While not employing the terminology of literary editions, Allen similarly contends that the supplementary material was in the translator's expanded Hebrew *Vorlage*.[40] As for the material in 2 Par 35:20; 36:3b–4, 5b, 8 corresponding to 2 Kgs 23:29abα, 33b–34a, 36b–37, 24:5–6a, Allen believes that the Hebrew of 2 Chr 36:1–8 had been replaced by 2 Kgs 23:30–24:6 by the time the LXX translator responsible for Paraleipomena carried out his work.[41] Klein offers a different explanation, suggesting that the additions in Paraleipomena were derived from 4 Kingdoms, primarily from a "proto-Lucianic" recension of 4 Kingsdoms (→ 3–5.1.6.2).[42] Given that the *Vorlage* of 2 Par 36:1–3a, 6–7 is close to MT-2 Chr 36:1–3a, 6–7, it appears that Klein has the stronger case. If the Hebrew of 2 Chr 36:1–8 had been supplanted by the Hebrew of 2 Kgs 23:30–24:6 (→ 5.3.2) by the time the translator of LXX-Chr did his work, one would not expect that the *Vorlage* of 2 Par 36:1–3a, 6–7 would be similar to the Hebrew of 2 Chr 36:1–3a, 6–7. In any event, the additions provide evidence of secondary developments within a larger textual tradition. The material in 2 Par 35:20; 36:3b–4, 5b, 8 corresponding to 4 Kgdms 23:29abα, 33b–34a, 36b–37, 24:5–6a may be an instance of parallel assimilation, a phe-

---

[37] To these, should be added LXX-2 Chr 36:5b. See R.W. Klein, "New Evidence for an Old Recension of Reigns," *HTR* 60 (1967): 93–105.

[38] Rehm, *Textkritische Untersuchungen*, 48–50.

[39] Tov, *TCHB*, 321.

[40] L.C. Allen, "Further Thoughts on an Old Recension of Reigns in Paralipomena," *HTR* 61 (1968): 483–91; Allen, *Greek Chronicles*, 1.214–17.

[41] Allen, *Greek Chronicles*, I, 216.

[42] Klein, "New Evidence," 93–105; R.W. Klein, "Supplements in the Paralipomena: A Rejoinder," *HTR* 61 (1968): 492–95; Klein, *2 Chronicles*, 530. The position assumes that "L has a history stretching long before Lucian," Allen, *Greek Chronicles*, 1.73. Yet, the existence of a proto-Lucianic recension is in dispute. See E. Tov, "Lucian and Proto-Lucian: Toward a New Solution of the Problem," in Tov, *Greek-Hebrew Bible*, 477–88.

nomenon well attested elsewhere in Paraleipomena.⁴³

20.3.1.4 Translation Technique and Inner-Translational Features

Paraleipomena often offers readers a word-for-word translation of the Hebrew, which follows the Hebrew so closely that it follows the precise syntatic sequence and morphological structure of its source. To take an example, 1 Chr 6:62 reads: לבני מררי הנותרים ממטה זבולן את רמונו ואת מגרשיה "Belonging to the remaining descendants of Merari, from the tribe of Zebulun⁴⁴: Rimmono along with its open land." In the LXX (1 Par 6:77), this material pertaining to the allocation of the Levitical towns is rendered: τοῖς υἱοῖς Μεραρι τοῖς καταλοίποις ἐκ φυλῆς Ζαβουλων τὴν Ρεμμων καὶ τὰ περισπόρια αὐτῆς "To the remaining sons of Merari, from the tribe of Zaboulon Remmon and its surrounding lands." To take a second example, Solomon's preparations for building the temple include obtaining (so 2 Chr 3:6) "gold of Parvaim" (זהב פרוים; 2 Chr 3:6). The LXX translation, χρυσίου τοῦ ἐκ φαρουαιμ "gold that was from Pharouaim," reflects a genitive of source and the transliteration of an obscure term (φαρουαιμ). To take a third and more famous example, 1 Chr 21:1 reads: ויעמד שטן על ישראל "And an adversary stood up against Israel."⁴⁵ LXX (i.e., LXX^ABN) renders its source as: καὶ ἔστη διάβολος ἐν τῷ Ἰσραηλ "And an accuser stood in Israel." In the Hebrew, *śāṭān* appears as an indefinite noun and LXX translates it accordingly.⁴⁶ Precisely because it is such a verbatim non-idiomatic translation, LXX provides readers with a good guide to its underlying *Vorlage*.

There are, however, some cases in which the LXX translator handles his Hebrew *Vorlage* less mechanically.⁴⁷ The relative clause אשר לדויד in 1 Chr 11:11, "who belonged to David," is rendered as a genitive τοῦ δαυιδ "of Dauid." By contrast, the relative clause אשר חטאתי, in 1 Chr 21:17, "who sinned," is rendered as an aorist participle ὁ ἁμαρτών "who was sinning." In some instances, the sanctuary is referred to loosely. Thus, for example, משכן אהל מועד in 1 Chr 6:17, "tabernacle of the tent of meeting," becomes in LXX^AB (2 Par 6:32) σκηνῆς οἴκου μαρτυρίου "tent of the house of testimony."⁴⁸ Finally, it bears mentioning that the translator sometimes uses the Greek Pentateuch "both as a commentary and a dictionary."⁴⁹ To take one example, נרתיהם לבערם in 2 Chr 4:20, "their lamps for burning," becomes τοὺς λύχνους τοῦ φωτός "the lamps of light," an expression that recalls τὴν λυχνίαν τοῦ φωτός "the lampstand of light," as a means of translating מנרת המאור "lampstand of the light," in the catalogue of tabernacle furniture found in Exod 35:14.

In sum, Paraleipomena often renders its source in non-idiomatic wooden Greek, yet this generalization about translational technique should not be construed as an absolute rule. The translator occasionally exhibits stylistic freedom and, to complicate matters, is sometimes influenced by earlier LXX translations such as those of the Pentateuch and Samuel-Kings (1–4 Kingdoms).

20.3.1.5 Text-Critical Value

Paraleipomena does not represent a fundamentally different textual tradition or family from that of MT (→ 20.2.2). The textual picture of Chronicles does not exhibit the variety that one sees in certain other biblical books, such as Exodus (→ 2.4.1.2), Numbers (→ 2.4.1.4), Joshua (→ 3.3), Samuel (→ 5.4), Kings (→ 5.5), Jeremiah (→ 7.3), Ezekiel (→ 8.3), Proverbs (→ 12.3.1), Esther (→ 13–17.1.1.5), and Daniel (→ 18.3.1).⁵⁰ The text of Paraleipomena is often

---

⁴³ See generally Allen, *Greek Chronicles*, 1.26–31, 175–218.

⁴⁴ LXX^AN along with cursives LXX^cehin (and the Arm) align more closely with MT-Josh 21:34 by adding "Joqneam along with its open land." See Knoppers, *1 Chronicles 1–9*, 436.

⁴⁵ MT-2 Sam 24:1 reads "and YHWH was angry again against Israel and incited David." T-Chr conflates the lemma of 2 Sam 24:1 with that of 1 Chr 21:1, "and YHWH raised up Satan."

⁴⁶ Cf. Lucifer of Cagliari ὁ διάβολος "the accuser" (= השטן).

⁴⁷ On what follows, see in more detail Gerleman, *Studies*, 40–44; Allen, *Greek Chronicles*, 1.38–57.

⁴⁸ The translation may combine elements of two other readings in 1 Chr 6:33 and in Num 1:50, 53; 10:11, Knoppers, *1 Chronicles 1–9*, 418.

⁴⁹ Allen, *Greek Chronicles*, 1.58. See also Gerleman, *Studies*, 22–29.

⁵⁰ In addition to the articles on the LXX of these books

quite close to the Hebrew. The major exceptions to this rule occur in the first chapter and in the last chapters of the book (→ 20.3.1.3). Occasionally, however, Paraleipomena provides a window into an earlier stage of the Hebrew tradition in both genealogical and narrative texts. A few examples will suffice to make the larger point. In 1 Chr 1:4, MT, followed by Lucifer of Cagliari, reads נח שם חם ויפת "Noah, Shem, Ham, and Japhet." Yet, it seems better to read with LXX^AB and cursive LXX^y: Νῶε υἱοὶ Νῶε Σήμ, Χάμ, Ἰάφεθ (= נח בני נח שם חם ויפת) "Noah; the sons of Noah." Although some think that LXX exhibits a plus, it seems more likely that MT lost the longer reading by haplography (*homoioteleuton*).[51] Moreover, the terminology of LXX^AB conforms to the pattern, PN¹; the sons of PN¹, found in 1 Chr 1:5–9, 28.[52] In MT-2 Chr 3:1 we read: "He appeared" (נִרְאָה), but LXX reads ὤφθη Κύριος "the Lord appeared" (= נראה יהוה).[53] In the lemma of MT, "YHWH" was lost by haplography (*homoioteleuton*) after נראה. In 1 Chr 6:44, it makes sense to read "Juttah along with its open land," based on LXX^B καὶ τὴν ατταν καὶ τὰ περισπόρια αὐτῆς, Syr., and MT- (and LXX-)Josh 21:16. MT-1 Chr 6:44 lacks the phrase due to haplography (*homoioteleuton*).[54]

Among the items Solomon pledges to Huram of Tyre for the work of his servants is "twenty thousand kors of crushed wheat" (חטים מכות; 2 Chr 2:9). On the basis of 2 Par 2:9 (10), εἰς βρώματα δέδωκα σῖτον εἰς δόματα τοῖς παισίν σου "as food I have given wheat as payment to your servants," some scholars reconstruct an original חטים מכלת "wheat as food," the reading that appears in 1 Kgs 5:25 [English translation: 5:11].[55] Yet, one must be careful. In 2 Chr 9:7, it is best to read with MT אַשְׁרֵי אֲנָשֶׁיךָ "blessed are your people" and so also with LXX^AB (μακάριοι οἱ ἄνδρες σου), rather than follow some LXX witnesses to 2 Chr 9:7 (minuscules LXX^bdge2iy), μακάριαι αἱ γυναῖκές σου (= אשרי נשיך) "blessed are your wives." There may be a case for reading, נשיך "your wives" as the *lectio difficilior* in 1 Kgs 10:8 (LXX^BL, VL, and Syr., αἱ γυναῖκές σου), but such evidence is scant in Chronicles. It may well be, in fact, a disservice to the distinctive perspective of Chronicles to conform its text to LXX-Kgs and VL-Kgs, because Solomon's seven hundred wives (1 Kgs 11:1–3) do not appear in Chronicles.[56]

20.3.1.6 Value for Literary Criticism

Some have viewed the fact that Codex LXX^B lacks 1 Chr 1:11–16, 17b–24a, 27b as evidence for growth in the literary development of Chronicles.[57] Yet, the situation is complex. Accidental loss of text by haplography is evidently the cause in the latter two cases (1 Chr 1:17b–24a, 27b),[58] if not in the first as well.[59] The addition of the supplements in LXX near the end of the book points to a focused literary expansion of the work at a relatively late time (the additions are not reflected in the version of Chronicles employed by the writers of 1 Esdras [→ II.7.1]). Finally, the fact that MT-Chr (→ 20.2.2) and LXX-Chr sometimes offer a shorter text than the parallel texts in Joshua, Samuel, and Kings can be readily explained by recognizing that the authors of Chronicles were working with older (sometimes shorter, less developed) versions of these books.[60]

---

found in the present reference work, see also Tov, *TCHB*, 283–326, and the references listed there.

[51] E. Podechard, "Le premier chapître des Paralipomènes," *RB* 13 (1916): 376.

[52] The author likely adapted the material for this verse from Gen 10:1 (instead of Gen 5:32).

[53] Note, similarly, T-Chr מלאכא דיהוה "messenger of YHWH."

[54] Knoppers, *1 Chronicles 1–9*, 432; Klein, *1 Chronicles*, 173–74.

[55] E.g., W. Rudolph, *Chronikbücher* (HAT 21; Tübingen: J.C.B. Mohr, 1955), 200; K. Hognesius, *The Text of 2 Chronicles 1–16: A Critical Edition with Textual Commentary* (ConBOT 51; Stockholm: Almqvist & Wiksell, 2003), 78. The Kings reading, *ḥiṭṭîm makkōlet*, is in turn defective for *ḥiṭṭîm ma'ăkōlet* (GKC, § 23f) "wheat (as) provision." Note 3 Kgdms^A 5:11 (25) μαχαλ. On the elision of the *'ālep*, see also Isa 9:4, 18; Ezek 20:37.

[56] Rudolph, *Chronikbücher*, 222; Hognesius, *Text of 2 Chronicles*, 135–36.

[57] E.g., Rudolph, *Chronikbücher*, 6–7.

[58] Knoppers, *1 Chronicles 1–9*, 267–69; Klein, *1 Chronicles*, 54.

[59] See Klein, *1 Chronicles*, 53, although the trigger for the loss is unclear.

[60] Knoppers, *1 Chronicles 1–9*, 66–71.

Allen, L.C., *The Greek Chronicles: The Relation of the Septuagint of I and II Chronicles to the Masoretic Text* (2 vols.; VTSup 25 and 27; Leiden: Brill, 1974).

Barthélemy, **Devanciers*, 31–80.

Fernández Marcos, N. and J.R. Busto Saiz, *Theodoreti Cyrensis Quaestiones in Reges et Paralipomena: Editio Critica* (Textos y Estudios "Cardenal Cisneros" 32; Madrid: Consejo Superior de Investigaciones Cientificas, 1984).

Gerleman, G., *Studies in the Septuagint: II. Chronicles* (LUÅ 43.3; Lund: Gleerup, 1946).

Hognesius, K., *The Text of 2 Chronicles 1–16: A Critical Edition with Textual Commentary* (ConBOT 51; Stockholm: Almqvist & Wiksell, 2003).

Klein, R.W., "Studies in the Greek Texts of the Chronicler" (PhD diss., Harvard University, 1966).

Klein, R.W., *1 Chronicles* (Hermeneia; Minneapolis: Augsburg Fortress, 2006).

Klein, R.W., *2 Chronicles* (Hermeneia; Minneapolis: Fortress, 2012).

Knoppers, G.N., *1 Chronicles 1–9: A New Translation with Introduction and Commentary* (AB 12; New York: Doubleday, 2004).

Knoppers, G.N., *1 Chronicles 10–29: A New Translation with Introduction and Commentary* (AB 12A; New York: Doubleday, 2004).

Rehm, M., *Textkritische Untersuchungen zu den Parallelstellen der Samuel-Königsbücher und der Chronik* (ATA 13.3; Münster: Aschendorff, 1937).

Shenkel, J.D., *Chronology and Recensional Development in the Greek Text of Kings* (HSM 1; Cambridge: Harvard University Press, 1968).

Spottorno, M.V., "The Books of Chronicles in Josephus' Jewish Antiquities," in *IX Congress of the International Organization for Septuagint and Cognate Studies, Cambridge, 1995* (ed. B.A. Taylor; SBLSCS 45; Atlanta: Scholars Press, 1997), 381–90.

Spottorno, M.V., "Lexical Variants in the Greek Text of Reigns and Chronicles," in *X Congress of the International Organization for Septuagint and Cognate Studies, Oslo, 1998* (ed. B.A. Taylor; SBLSCS 51; Atlanta: SBL, 2001), 63–80.

Torrey, C.C., *Ezra Studies* (Chicago: Chicago University Press, 1910).

Tov, **TCHB*.

Weber, R., *Les anciennes versions latines du deuxième livre des Paralipomènes* (Collectanea Biblica Latina 8; Rome: Abbaye Saint-Jérôme, 1945).

Gary N. Knoppers

20.3.2 Pre-Hexaplaric Greek Translations

See → 20.3.5 Hexaplaric Greek Translations (1–2 Chronicles > Primary Translations).

20.3.3 Targum

20.3.3.1 Nature and History of Research

Targum Chronicles (T-Chr) is a traditional Jewish-Aramaic translation of the Hebrew book of Chronicles (1 Chr and 2 Chr). Targum Chronicles is comprised of a fairly literal translation into Aramaic, periodically interrupted by dozens of haggadic expansions that depart from the Hebrew *Vorlage*. Rosenberg and Kohler were the first to publish a detailed report on the contents of the Targum and its nature (1870).[1] Their conclusions are at the core of most of the monographs, articles, and encyclopedia entries describing Targum Chronicles. Following Zunz' general statements in *Die gottesdienstlichen Vorträge der Juden historisch entwickelt*,[2] Rosenberg and Kohler concluded that Targum Chronicles was composed in the land of Israel after the completion of the Babylonian Talmud, but no later than the eighth century. Churgin accepted much of the aforementioned study and added many new identifications of Targum Chronicles' sources for its expansions (1945).[3] The introduction and textual comments in Le Déaut's and Robert's edition of Targum Chronicles (1971)[4] include important contributions to the study of the Targum. A study on the language of Targum Chronicles was carried out by White in a doctoral dissertation (1981).[5] McIvor translated the Targum into English and added some insights beyond those of the Le Déaut and Robert edition (1994).[6] The di-

---

[1] Rosenberg and Kohler, "Das Targum zur Chronik."
[2] L. Zunz, *Die gottesdienstlichen Vorträge der Juden historisch entwickelt: Ein Beitrag zur Altertumskunde und biblischen Kritik, zur Literatur- und Religionsgeschichte* (Berlin: A. Asher, 1832).
[3] Churgin, *The Targum to Hagiographa*, 236–75.
[4] Le Déaut and Robert, *Targum des Chroniques*.
[5] White, "A Linguistic Analysis of the Targum to Chronicles."
[6] McIvor, *The Targum of Chronicles*.

alect of Targum Chronicles – along with that of Targum Pseudo-Jonathan and several Targumim of the Writings – is dubbed Late Jewish Literary Aramaic in the *Comprehensive Aramaic Lexicon* (*CAL), a name that indicates that the dialect is an artificial version of Aramaic that was not spoken by the Jewish writers that used it. Leeor Gottlieb researched the relation of Targum Chronicles to its targumic and rabbinic literary sources (2012).[7] His findings led him to conclude that Targum Chronicles was composed several centuries later (ca. mid-tenth century) than had been previously suggested and displayed a European influence. This strengthens the notion that Targum Chronicles was not intended to accompany the Hebrew text during public readings as was, perhaps, Targum Onqelos (→ 1.3.3.5), but rather was a study tool, following the literal text of Chronicles on the one hand, while supplementing the text with traditional midrashic expansions on the other hand.

20.3.3.2 Editions and Auxiliary Tools

The text of Targum Chronicles is preserved in three manuscripts (Vatican; codex Vat. Urb. Ebr. 1; Cambridge: manuscript Or. Ee. 5.9; Erfurt: manuscript Or. fol. 1210–1211) from the end of the thirteenth and middle of the fourteenth centuries. It is, therefore, quite surprising that Targum Chronicles left virtually no trace in Jewish medieval literature, neither in commentaries on the biblical book, nor in grammatical works and lexicons of the era. In fact, some medieval sages stated explicitly that Chronicles was not translated into Aramaic, thus testifying to Targum Chronicles' poor circulation. The Targum was eventually printed in various editions, based on the extant manuscripts. The first printed editions appeared at the end of the seventeenth and the beginning of the eighteenth centuries (Beck and Wilkins, respectively).[8] De Lagarde (1872)[9] and,

later, Sperber (1968)[10] published eclectic editions of Targum Chronicles, based primarily on the Erfurt manuscript, while taking some readings from the Cambridge manuscript into account. Le Déaut and Robert published the text of Targum Chronicles based on the Vatican manuscript, the oldest and most precise of the existing manuscripts (1971). Their edition includes an apparatus with variant readings in the other two manuscripts, a translation into French, comments on the text, and an Aramaic-French-English glossary.

20.3.3.3 Translation Technique and Translation Character

While it is clear that the Targumist worked within a tradition and, therefore, produced a systematic, sometimes predictable, translation of the Hebrew text, his work contains a certain degree of inconsistency. Several Hebrew words are rendered by more than one Aramaic equivalent, apparently without any intent of suggesting a difference in meaning. This may occur due to multiple targumic traditions utilized by the author of Targum Chronicles and/or literary influences, or for other reasons. Thus, e.g., Hebrew כֶּסֶף "silver, money" is translated by Aramaic כספא "silver, money" thirty-eight times and by Aramaic סימא "silver, treasure" thirteen times. Hebrew מִזְרָק "bowl, basin" is translated by Aramaic מזרק "bowl" twice and by Aramaic(/Greek) פיילי "flat bowl" twice. Hebrew חֲמָת "Hamath" is transliterated three times and rendered by the later Hellenistic name אנטיוכיה "Antioch" four times.

The nature of Chronicles – historiography replete with lengthy genealogical lists – engenders an abundance of proper nouns (the average frequency of proper nouns in 1 Chronicles is the highest among the books of the Hebrew Bible). This abundance offers the Targumist many opportunities to treat names of characters and locations in various ways. Some names undergo a midrash-style etymological derivation in Targum Chronicles, either explicitly (e.g. Joqtan in 1 Chr 1:20) or implicitly (e.g. Nimrod in 1 Chr 1:10). The vast majority of proper nouns in Targum Chronicles are unsurpris-

---

[7] Gottlieb, "The Targum of Chronicles."
[8] Beck, *Paraphrasis Chaldaica I Libri Chronicorum*; Beck, *Paraphrasis Chaldaica II Libri Chronicorum*; Wilkins, *Paraphrasis Chaldaica in librum priorem et posteriorem Chronicorum*.
[9] De Lagarde, *Hagiographa Chaldaice*.

[10] Sperber, *Bible in Aramaic, Vol. 4B.

ingly transcribed, but certain names of locations and – even more surprisingly – people are translated into Aramaic according to their presumed meaning (e.g. מְחִיר, lit. "price" translated as פירוג "exchange, price" in 1 Chr 4:11). A significant number of names are identified in Targum Chronicles with other biblical characters (e.g. Ephrath with Miriam in 1 Chr 2:19; 4:4, 17). In many examples, one can easily detect the influence of rabbinic literature on the Targumist. Thus, e.g., Daniel is identified with Chileab (1 Chr 3:1; cf. *b. Ber.* 4a), Jabez with Othniel (1 Chr 4:13; cf. *Sipre Deut.* 352) and Mered with Caleb (1 Chr 4:18; cf. *b. Meg.* 13a).

Double translations (i.e. two Aramaic renditions of one Hebrew word or expression) are found throughout Targum Chronicles, for various reasons. Some of these reflect the inclusion of two different literal translation traditions for select words, side by side. Others are a result of preserving both a literal translation for a word or a sequence, coupled with a midrashic approach to certain words. Thus, e.g., Hebrew וַיִּשְׂאוּ "and they carried" in 1 Chr 11:18 is translated by both ונטלו "and they lifted" and ונסיבו "and they took." The former reflects Targum Chronicles' regular equivalent for נש״א "to carry," while the latter is Targum Jonathan's rendering in this verse's parallel (2 Sam 23:16). Similarly, Hebrew מְזַבְּחִים "sacrificing" in 2 Chr 5:6 is translated by both מנכסין "slaughtering" and דבחין "sacrificing." The former reflects Targum Jonathan's rendering in this verse's parallel (1 Kgs 8:5), while the latter conforms with Targum Chronicles' style in almost all other similar cases in Chronicles. In 2 Chr 6:2, וּמָכוֹן "and a fixed place" is translated first literally, אתר מתקן "a place prepared," then in midrashic style, ומכוון "and corresponding" (passive participle of כו״ן "to face" in *pa'el*, based on change of Hebrew vocalization).

This last phenomenon leads naturally into the topic of the translator's exegetical and theological conceptions and motivations. Targum Chronicles is a composition that is part and parcel of the targumic tradition and rabbinic legacy. As such, the Targumist utilizes modes of translation for certain Hebrew words that bear theological implications first fashioned by earlier works of Targum. The singling out of the main elements participating in this targumic tradition and upheld by Targum Chronicles results in a "vocabulary of reverence," used almost solely when rendering fixed linguistic Hebrew structures regarding the God of Israel. Accordingly, Targum Chronicles conforms with the targumic convention of employing a set of separate equivalents for Hebrew words that serve in both the sacred realm and the profane, or the religiously legitimate and illegitimate, from the rabbinic point of view. Thus, e.g., כֹּהֵן "priest" remains כהנא "priest" when referring to Aaronide priests, but is rendered כומר "illegitimate priest" when applied to non-Aaronide priests (cf. 2 Chr 13:9 in which both types of כֹּהֵן "priest" appear).

Another way the Targumist bridges the gap between the Bible and rabbinic Judaism is by depicting several biblical characters as rabbinic sages. Incorporating blatant anachronisms, Targum Chronicles describes David, Jabez, and Benaiah as Torah scholars who serve in the Aramaic text as heads of Yeshiva and/or the Sanhedrin (cf. 1 Chr 2:55; 4:9–10; 11:2, 11, 22, 25; 18:17). In addition to these two terms, Targum Chronicles makes mention of various rabbinic – sometimes post-talmudic – institutions and terms (סנהדרין "Sanhedrin," cf. 1 Chr 4:12; 5:12; 12:33; 18:17; 27:34; 2 Chr 23:5; בי כנישתא "Synagogue," cf. 1 Chr 8:33; 16:39; [ריש] מתיבה "[head of] Yeshiva, Talmud Academy," cf. 1 Chr 4:22; 11:11, 25; עלמא דאתי "the world to come," cf. 1 Chr 16:36; 17:17; 29:10). Targum Chronicles also emphasizes the role of Torah sages in the setting of the calendar, a task that requires great wisdom and knowledge (cf. 1 Chr 4:23; 12:33).

Targum Chronicles generally exhibits a strong literary dependence on Targumim of the biblical books parallel with Chronicles. Gottlieb[11] demonstrated that Targum Chronicles used Targum Jonathan on the parallel units in Samuel and Kings as a base-text, upon which the Targumist introduced changes due to difference in dialect, Hebrew *Vorlage* between Chronicles and Samuel–Kings, and exegetical traditions. The Targumist was familiar with more than one tradition of Targum on Genesis, but his main Targum text for this book was

---

[11] Gottlieb, "The Targum of Chronicles," 91–113.

Pseudo-Jonathan. While Targum Chronicles and Targum Psalms display similarities in dialect, vocabulary, and style, Targum Chronicles apparently did not use Targum Psalms as a base-text for 1 Chr 16:8–33 (parallel with Pss 105:1–15 and 96:1–13).

In summary, Targum Chronicles generally adheres to a literal Aramaic rendition of the Hebrew text, but it departs from a strict literal translation due to numerous recognizable circumstances. The methods of departure from a literal translation, as well as values and conceptions of the Targumist, can be traced – almost entirely – back to earlier Targumim and to the world of rabbinic literature. Targum Chronicles is thus the work of an author who applied the principles and norms of targumic tradition as he knew it in order to compose an Aramaic translation in the likeness and image of its predecessors. In doing so, the author of this Aramaic text produced a rabbinic composition that collects and preserves much of the midrashic material on the book of Chronicles.

20.3.3.4 Text-Critical Value

In the most general of terms, the *Vorlage* of Targum Chronicles belongs to the Masoretic Hebrew tradition of Chronicles (→ 20.2.2), but the Targum reflects several textual variants between its parent text and MT. Gottlieb collated these suspected variants (based on the Vatican manuscript) and found that approximately half of them are also found in medieval Hebrew manuscripts.[12] A significant percentage of the variants pertains to proper nouns in the lengthy genealogies of Chronicles, which comes as no surprise as variants of this kind are not wont to cause a change in the meaning of the verse, and therefore would have been harder to detect in the process of scribal transmission.

20.3.3.4.1 Consonantal Variants

1 Chr 1:12 מנהון "from them" for מִשָּׁם "from there" reflects מֵהֶם "from them"; 4:8 [ל]אחרא "Aharel" for אֲחַרְחֵל "Aharhel"; 4:12 אנשי סנהדרין רבתא "men of the Great Sanhedrin" for אַנְשֵׁי רֵכָה "men of Rekha" reflects אַנְשֵׁי רַבָּה "men of Rabbah"; 4:15 קנז "Kenaz" for וּקְנַז "and Kenaz" (cf. LXX); 4:29 ובעטם "and in Etam" for וּבְעֶצֶם "and in Ezem"; 4:30 ובביתאל "and in Bethel" for וּבִבְתוּאֵל "and in Bethuel"; 4:32 ועיטן "and Etan" for וְעָשָׁן "and Ashan"; 4:34 ויוטה "and Jota" for וְיוֹשָׁה "and Joshah"; 5:12 ויעני דיינא "and Janai the judge" for וְיַעְנַי וְשָׁפָט "and Janai and Shaphat" reflects ויעני שופט "and Janai the judge" (cf. LXX); 6:55 יבלעם "Ibleam" for בִּלְעָם "Bileam" (cf. LXX, s); 7:1 ופוה ויוב "and Puvah and Iob" for וּפוּאָה יָשׁוּב "and Puah, Jashub" (cf. Gen 46:13); 7:6 וידעיה ... בני בנימין "the Benjaminites ... and Jedaiah" for וִידִיעֲאֵל ... בִּנְיָמִן "Benjamin ... and Jediael" (cf. s); 7:13 ושלם ... יחצאל "Jahzeel ... and Shillem" for יַחֲצִיאֵל ... וְשַׁלּוּם "Jahziel ... and Shallum" (cf. Gen 46:24); 7:28 עדיה "Adaiah" (one word) for עַד־עַיָּה "till Aiah"; 8:8 ית חושים direct object marker + "Hushim" for חֻשִׁים "Hushim" reflects את חושים direct object marker + "Hushim"; 8:12 ושמר "and Shemer" for וָשָׁמֶד "and Shemed" (cf. LXX, s); 11:38 בר גדא "son of Gada" for בֶּן־הַגְרִי "son of Hagri" reflects בֶּן־הַגָּדִי "son of the Gadites" (cf. 2 Sam 33:36); 27:25 בית מלכא "the king's palace" for הַמֶּלֶךְ "the king" reflects בֵּית הַמֶּלֶךְ "the king's palace"; 29:22 ומשחוהי "and they anointed him" for וַיִּמְשְׁחוּ "and they anointed" reflects וימשחוהו "and they anointed him" (cf. LXX); 2 Chr 1:5 שוי "put" for שָׁם "there" reflects שָׂם "put" (cf. s); 3:11 חד "one" for הָאַחֵר "the other" reflects הָאֶחָד "one"; 13:3 גוברין "men" for אִישׁ בָּחוּר "choice men" reflects omission of בָּחוּר "choice"; 19:11 וזכריהו "and Zechariah" for וּזְבַדְיָהוּ "and Zebadiah" (cf. s); 20:25 וקם "and he stood" for וְעַמּוֹ "and his people" reflects וְעָמַד "and he stood" or וַיַּעֲמֹד "and he stood"; 22:7 תסקפת "pretext" for תְּבוּסַת "downfall" probably reflects תסבת "turn, event"; 26:5 בדחלתא "in the fear of" for בִּרְאֹת "in sight, vision of" reflects בְּיִרְאַת "in fear of" (cf. LXX, s); 26:6 (ד)עזה "Gaza" for יַבְנֵה "Jabne" (cf. s); 26:7 בגזר "in Gezer" for בְּגוּר "in Gur"; 28:3 ואעבר "and he offered" for וַיַּבְעֵר "and he burned" reflects וַיַּעֲבֵר "and he offered" (cf. 2 Kgs 16:3); 28:19 מלכא דיהודה "king of Judah" for מֶלֶךְ־יִשְׂרָאֵל "king of Israel" (cf. LXX, s); 29:36 לעמא יצרא דלבהון "for the people the desire of their heart" for לָעָם "for the people" reflects לְבָם "for the people their heart"; 30:12 הי כפתגמא "according to the word" for בִּדְבַר "at the command of" reflects כִּדְבַר "as the word of" (cf. s); 30:19 ארום "for"

---

[12] Gottlieb, "The Hebrew Vorlage of Targum Chronicles," 64–65.

for כָּל "all" reflects כִּי "for" (cf. s); 30:26 לֹא הוֺת כְדָא "there had not been the like of this" for לֹא כָזֺאת "not like this" reflects לֹא הָיְתָה כָזֺאת "nothing like it had happened" (cf. LXX, s); 32:5 עֲלוֺהִי מוּגְדַּלְיָא "upon it towers" for עַל הַמִּגְדָּלוֺת "on the towers" reflects עָלֶיהָ מִגְדָּלוֺת "on it towers" (also reflects different word division; cf. v); 32:22 וְאַשְׁרְנוּן "and he gave them security" for וַיְנַהֲלֵם "he provided for them" reflects וִינַח לָהֶם "and he gave them rest" (also reflects different word division); 35:9 לְפִסְחַיָּא עָאן "for Passover offerings, sheep ..." for לַפְּסָחִים "for the Passover offerings" reflects לַפְּסָחִים צֹאן "for the Passover offerings, sheep ..." (cf. LXX, s); 35:15 מִכֹּל "of all" for מֵעַל "away from" (cf. s); 35:25 רַבְרְבַיָּא וּמַטְרוֺנִיתָא "male and female nobles" for הַשָּׁרִים וְהַשָּׁרוֺת "male and female singers" reflects הַשָּׂרִים וְהַשָּׂרוֺת "male and female aristocrats" (cf. LXX); 36:10 כָּל "all" for כְּלֵי "utensils"; 36:23 יְהֵא "may be" for the tetragrammaton reflects יְהִי "may be" (cf. Ezra 1:3).

20.3.3.4.2 Vocalization

In a small number of cases, Targum Chronicles reflects readings that diverge from MT's tradition of vocalization and result in differences in meaning. Thus, e.g., 1 Chr 4:34 וּמָן שׁוֺבָב "and of Shobab" for וּמְשׁוֺבָב "and Meshobab" reflects וּמִשּׁוֺבָב "and of Shobab"; 8:38, 9:44 בּוּכְרֵיהּ "his first-born" for בֹּכְרוּ "Bokheru" reflects בְּכֹרוֺ "his first-born" (cf. LXX, s); 11:18 וְאָתוֺ "and they came" for וַיָּבֹאוּ "and they brought" reflects וַיָּבֹאוּ "and they came" (cf. LXX); 17:6 הַאֶפְשַׁר דְּמַלְּלָא "is it possible that I spoke" for הֲדָבָר "has a word" reflects הֲדֻבַּר "has it been spoken" (cf. LXX); 2 Chr 11:23 וּבְנָא "and he built" for וַיָּבֶן "and he comprehended" reflects וַיִּבֶן "and he built"; 16:4 מִמַּעְרְבָא "from the west" for מֵימָיו "water" reflects מִיָּם "from the sea (i.e. the west)"; 24:5 לְמַלְּלָא "to speak" for לְדָבָר "to it" reflects לְדַבֵּר "to speak" (cf. LXX, s); 35:12 לְצַפְרָא "by morning" for לַבָּקָר "for the cattle" reflects לַבֹּקֶר "by morning" (cf. LXX, s).

20.3.3.4.3 Sense Division (Syntax)

On rare occasions, Targum Chronicles diverges from MT's syntax (as represented by cantillation marks; → 10–20.1). Thus, e.g., 1 Chr 7:12 קִרְיַת חֻשִׁים "city of Hushim" regards עִיר חֻשִׁם "city of Hushim" as one syntagm, while MT separates the two words; 7:14 דִּילֵידַת פִּילַקְתֵּיהּ אֲרַמֵּיתָא וִילֵידַת יָת מָכִיר "whom his Aramaean concubine bore; she was also the mother of Makhir" regards the verb יָלְדָה "she bore" as the predicate of פִּילַגְשׁוֺ "his concubine," while MT regards יָלְדָה "she bore" (similar verb that appears later in the verse) as the predicate of this subject; 9:1 וּמַלְכַיָּא דְּבֵית יְהוּדָה עַל סְפַר מַלְכַיָּא דְּבֵית יִשְׂרָאֵל "and the kings of the house of Judah in the book of the kings of the house of Israel" regards both יִשְׂרָאֵל "Israel" and וִיהוּדָה "and Judah" as a compound *nomen rectum* governed by סֵפֶר מַלְכֵי "the book of the kings of," while MT reads וִיהוּדָה "and Judah" as the subject of the following verb הָגְלוּ "were exiled."

20.3.3.4.4 Ketiv/Qere

Generally speaking, Targum Chronicles conforms with almost all of MT's eighty *Qere* instructions (→ 10–20.1). However, in a small number of cases Targum Chronicles reflects the *Ketiv* form, usually resulting in a difference of waw or yod with the *Qere* in proper nouns. Thus, 1 Chr 7:34 וְרוֺהֲגָה "and Rohgah" (plene spelling, versus defective spelling in the *Qere* וְרָהְגָּה "and Rohgah"); 8:25 וּפְנִיאֵ[ל] "and Peniel" (versus *Qere* וּפְנוּאֵל "and Penuel"); 9:4 בַּר בִּנְיָמִן מִן בְּנֵי פֶרֶץ "son of Benjamin of the sons of Perez" (reading both בִּנְיָמִן "Benjamin" of the *Ketiv* and מִן "of" of the *Qere*); 22:7 בְּרִיהּ "his son" (versus *Qere* בְּנִי "my son"; this variant causes a difference in both meaning and in sense division; cf. LXX); 24:24 שָׁמוּר "Shamur" (versus *Qere* שָׁמִיר "Shamir"); 2 Chr 9:10 חִירָם "Hiram" (versus *Qere* חוּרָם "Huram"); 13:19 עֶפְרוֺן "Ephron" (versus *Qere* עֶפְרַיִן "Ephrain"); 35:9 וּכְנַנְיָה "and Konaniah" (versus *Qere* וְכָנַנְיָהוּ "and Konaniahu").

20.3.3.5 Relevance for Exegesis

As the character of Targum Chronicles naturally divides itself between the fairly literal translation of the Hebrew, on the one hand, and the haggadic expansions, on the other hand, one might say that the Targum serves as a source for two very different types of exegesis. The literal framework of the Targum is a historical testimony of the *peshat* (i.e. contextual) meaning of Chronicles, while the haggadic expansions function as a compilation of midrashic readings of the book. In lieu of a received rabbinic midrash on Chronicles, Targum Chronicles is probably the earliest collection of this kind on the book of Chronicles. Due to this Targum's relative obscurity and poor circulation prior to the modern era, it never attained status as a well-known exegetical aid, as did some of its earlier counterparts (e.g. Targum Onqelos, Targum Jonathan, etc; → 1.3.3). Nonetheless, Targum Chronicles serves as a faithful representative of a rabbinic interpretation for the Hebrew book of Chronicles.

Beck, M.F., *Paraphrasis Chaldaica I Libri Chronicorum* (Augsburg: Theoph. Goebelium Impressa, 1680).
Beck, M.F., *Paraphrasis Chaldaica II Libri Chronicorum* (Augsburg: Theoph. Goebelium Impressa, 1683).
Chamiel, H.I., *The Bible and its Targumim*, Vol. 5.2 (Jerusalem: Rubin Mass, 2009), 357–490 [Hebr.].
Churgin, P., *The Targum to Hagiographa* (New York: Horeb, 1945), 236–75 [Hebr.].
Le Déaut, R. and J. Robert, *Targum des Chroniques (Cod. Vat. Urb. Ebr. 1)* (2 vols.; AnBib 51; Rome: Biblical Institute Press, 1971).
Gottlieb, L., "The Targum of Chronicles: Translation Techniques, Exegesis and Conceptions" (PhD diss., Hebrew University of Jerusalem, 2012).
de Lagarde, P., *Hagiographa Chaldaice* (Leipzig: B.G. Teubner, 1872).
McIvor, J.S., *The Targum of Chronicles: Translated, with Introduction, Apparatus, and Notes* (ArBib 19; Collegeville: Liturgical Press, 1994).
Rosenberg, M. and K. Kohler, "Das Targum zur Chronik," *Jüdische Zeitschrift für Wissenschaft und Leben* 8 (1870): 72–80, 135–63, 263–78.
Sperber, *Bible in Aramaic*, Vol. 4B.
White, R.T., "A Linguistic Analysis of the Targum to Chronicles with Specific Reference to its Relationship with Other Forms of Aramaic" (PhD diss., University of Oxford, 1981).
Wilkins, D., *Paraphrasis Chaldaica in librum priorem et posteriorem Chronicorum* (Amsterdam: Johannem Boom, 1715).

Leeor Gottlieb

20.3.4 Peshitta

20.3.4.1 Manuscripts and Textual Transmission

In the complete Bible manuscripts, with one notable exception, Chronicles appears in dazzlingly "good company" together with the books whose canonicity was never doubted, in seventh place after Kings (→ 3–5.1.4). The one and only complete Bible containing Chronicles that departs radically from this order or one of its variants is the venerable Ambrosian manuscript itself (manuscript S⁷ᵃ¹),[1] which places the book towards the end of the list. From the eighth century onwards, Chronicles has an assured place in "good company" towards the beginning of the canon in the vast majority of complete Bible manuscripts.[2]

Chronicles is the only book that is always designated primarily by its Hebrew title in the biblical manuscripts: ܣܦܪ ܕܒܪܝܡܝܢ, a transliteration of the Hebrew ספר דברי הימים "the book of the words of days." There is, however, evidence from Jacob of Edessa and 'Abdisho' of Nisibis for use of the term ܡܫܬܚܪܬܐ "that which is lacking," which corresponds closely to the Greek term used for Chronicles: τὰ Παραλειπόμενα "the things left aside" (see also → 20.4.4).

20.3.4.2 General Characteristics of the Translation

There can be no doubt that S-Chr was translated from the Hebrew in a form relatively close to MT (→ 20.2.2),[3] the order and wording of which can usually be detected even when the Syriac diverges from the Hebrew. Some passages do however betray the use of a pre-Masoretic text when what are clearly glosses in MT are omitted by the Peshitta (and LXXᴮ), which would have had an earlier text to work from. For example, in 1 Chr 29:22, S has ܘܐܩܝܡܘ ܠܫܠܝܡܘܢ ܒܪ ܕܘܝܕ "They established Solomon the son of David in the kingdom" whereas MT adds שנית "for the second time." *BHS considers שנית to be a redactional gloss intended to harmonize this verse with 1 Chr 23:1. Other occasional agreements between S-Chr and LXX can also plead in favour of a slightly divergent Hebrew *Vorlage*, for example, 1 Chr 7:4: MT has

---

[1] *List of Old Testament Peshitta Manuscripts (Preliminary Issue)* edited by the Peshitta Institute (Leiden: Brill, 1961), 28–29.
[2] Phillips, "Reception," 259–95 (260–67).
[3] Weitzman, *Syriac Version*, 60–61.

גְּדוּדֵי "bands of" while the Peshitta, with ܓܢܒܪܐ agrees with LXX ἰσχυροί "strong ones" in reading גבורי "mighty warriors of."

Despite the fact that in general the Peshitta is trying to remain painstakingly faithful to its Hebrew original, it often diverges from the Hebrew with startling freedom, sometimes expanding the text and sometimes reducing it. One noteworthy example is the treatment of musical instruments in about twenty-five passages that deal with this aspect of the Levitical and priestly liturgy.[4] In almost all of these passages, the mention of musical instruments is either omitted, reduced, or reworked. The key to understanding these intentional omissions is a lengthy addition in S-1 Chr 16:42 that simply contradicts MT:

> And these righteous men were praising. Not with instruments of praise, neither with tambourines, nor with timbrels, nor with curved or straight horns nor with cymbals were they praising but with a pleasant mouth and in pure and perfect prayer and in uprightness and integrity the mighty Lord God, the Lord of Israel, the Lord of all works.

In this passage, rather than omitting the musical instruments as he does elsewhere, the translator gives what looks like an exhaustive list of all musical instruments in order to make the Levites praise God only "with the mouth." In other words, vocal music is explicitly preferred to and contrasted with instrumental music. This systematic treatment distributed over several passages betraying a coherent intention cannot be based on a different *Vorlage*.

This last case is one example of the diversified interpretative material to be found in S-Chr, which is more prevalent there than in the other books of the Peshitta. Some elements are certainly Jewish in origin, like the addition of the Kaddish prayer in 1 Chr 29:19, or the use of the term "Shekinah" (for example, in 1 Chr 28:2; 2 Chr 6:2; 18; 7:1–3, 16). Others, such as the mention of the "canonical" hours of prayer in 1 Chr 15:21 are very probably Christian. However, precisely because of its diversity, it is difficult to pinpoint the precise socio-historical context of the Peshitta.

The translator was certainly a scholar who worked with as many sources as were available to him. Of these, one thing is quite sure: he worked with the text of Samuel and Kings (→ 3–5.1.4) and applied the "binocular" view offered to him by the very nature of the Chronicles text, which mirrors the earlier books.

Which version of the parallel texts did the translator use? Obviously, when the three parallel texts, Hebrew, Aramaic (Targum; → 20.3.3), and Syriac, are indistinguishable among themselves, but diverge uniformly from MT-Chr to agree with S-Chr, one cannot ascertain which version was being used. In certain cases, however, when the three versions diverge among themselves, it is sometimes one and sometimes another that served S-Chr to interpret the Hebrew *Vorlage* of Chronicles. There seems to be no general method; the translator may have had the three versions before him and used one or the other as he felt appropriate in each particular context. We shall now give some examples of such separate agreements.

Agreements between S-Chr and MT-Sam–Kgs as against S-Sam–Kgs and T-Sam–Kgs appear clearly in the long passage where 2 Chr 11:5–12:12 has been replaced with 1 Kgs 12:25–30; 13:34; 14:1–9. One such example in this passage appears in 1 Kgs 12:28. In S-Chr, the verse is identical to MT-Kgs, apart from the *Sondergut* ܠܡܢܐ ܣܠܩܝܢ ܐܢܬܘܢ ܘܢܚܬܝܢ ܠܐܘܪܫܠܡ "Why should you go up and down to Jerusalem?" which serves as a gloss to רב לכם מעלות "It is too much for you to go up" but is taking MT as its basis. T-Kgs, on the other hand, adds אורחא "the way" and turns רב "too much" into an adjective, סגיאה "great," qualifying the latter to give "The way is too great to go up." In S-Kgs, there is no gloss but it diverges from MT in replacing אלהם "to them" by ܠܟܠܗ ܐܝܣܪܐܝܠ "to all Israel." The elements proper to T-Kgs and S-Kgs are not reflected in S-Chr, which follows MT-Kgs.

An example of an agreement between S-Chr and T-Sam against MT-Sam and S-Sam can be found, for instance, in 1 Chr 11:2: MT has אַתָּה הַמּוֹצִיא וְהַמֵּבִיא אֶת־יִשְׂרָאֵל "You brought out and made to come in

---

[4] For the details, see Phillips, "Musical Instruments," 49–67 (56–61).

Israel" while s has ܐܢܬ ܗܘ ܢܦܩ ܗܘܝܬ ܘܥܐܠ ܒܪܝܫܐ ܕܐܝܣܪܐܝܠ "You used to go out and come in at the head of Israel." This is identical to the parallel text T-2 Sam 5:2 את הויתא נפיק ועליל בריש ישראל "You used to go out and come in at the head of Israel" against MT-2 Sam and s-2 Sam, which both have causative verbs and do not add "at the head of." T-Chr heavily glosses the text in a completely different fashion.

Finally, there are separate agreements with s-Sam–Kgs. We note, for example, 1 Chr 11:13 where s renders the מְלֵאָה "full of" of MT by ܘܙܪܥ "sown with," which appears in the parallel s-2 Sam 23:11, whereas MT-2 Sam and T-2 Sam have the same text as MT-Chr. Another example is 1 Chr 11:18. The MT מִבּוֹר "from the well" is expanded by s-Chr to ܡܢ ܓܘܒܐ ܪܒܐ "from the great well" as is the case in s-2 Sam 23:16 unlike MT-2 Sam and T-2 Sam, which have the same shorter text as MT-1 Chr, as does T-Chr. The same phenomenon can be observed in 1 Chr 17:15 where s-Chr and s-2 Sam 7:17 go uniquely together in adding ܢܒܝܐ "prophet" as a title for Nathan.

In addition to such cases where the translation of Chronicles has simply been aligned with the text of Samuel–Kings, one also finds occurrences where the two texts have been conflated. For example, 2 Chr 33:18 where MT has "Kings of Israel" and the parallel, 2 Kgs 21:17 has "Kings of Judah" (MT, s, and T), s-Chr has conflated the two texts to obtain "Kings of Israel and of Judah."

Outside of these agreements with the parallel texts, there are also some agreements with the Targum to Chronicles, although that version is late and may contain earlier exegetical material not found in the Targum to Samuel–Kings (→ 20.3.3), and some of this material may also have served the translator of s-Chr. Here are a few examples: MT-1 Chr 12:19 וְרוּחַ "spirit," s-Chr ܘܪܘܚܐ ܕܓܢܒܪܘܬܐ "spirit of strength," which is very close to T-Chr ורוח גבורה "strong spirit"; MT-1 Chr 20:5 גָּלְיָת הַגִּתִּי "Goliath the Gittite," s-Chr ܓܘܠܝܕ ܓܢܒܪܐ ܡܢ ܓܬ "Goliath a warrior from Gath," which can also be compared with T-Chr דגלית דמן גת "Goliath from Gath" in contradistinction to the parallel text 2 Sam 21:19, which in MT, T, and s, differs from s-Chr; 1 Chr 21:26 וַיִּקְרָא אֶל־יְהוָה "he cried to the Lord," s-Chr ܘܨܠܝ ܩܕܡ ܡܪܝܐ "he prayed before the Lord," which is identical to T-Chr וצלי קדם יוי "he prayed before the Lord" but differs from MT-, T-, and s-2 Sam 24:25.

Above and beyond the seemingly haphazard importation of exegetical material, s-Chr is not without a literary quality with a taste for double translation in order to introduce stylistic balance, the force of which is purely literary rather than explanatory.

The translator also had moral and religious concerns that are seen in his attitude to the poor and to prayer. In several passages, the Syriac is concerned with the giving of alms to the poor. In 1 Chr 23:4 we read:

> David established some of them princes over the works of the house of the Lord: twenty-four men over a thousand and judges and scribes: every six men over a hundred in order to watch the building and stand and run with their wealth and their resources and their works and with their accounts and with their goods and with alms in order to provide for the poor. David established for the poor and needy providers and superintendents who nourished and tended to the poor, one over ten, and they lacked nothing.

This is very precise organized charity. The Hebrew has nothing that could induce this long gloss, which thus betrays the translator's personal concern for the needy. Again in 2 Chr 31:10, which concerns the gifts brought to the temple for Hezekiah's Passover, the Syriac adds "give to the poor and needy." One can also add that 1 Chr 29:3, describing David's preparations for the building of the temple, insists by repeating the words that he prepared what was necessary "out of my poverty." Chronicles in Syriac is also concerned with piety. The addition of terms associated with the notion of prayer are frequent and widespread.[5] For example, in 2 Chronicles 6 alone, the word "prayer" is added eight times.

Finally, a word can be said about the translator's attitude to the figure of King David. In several

---

[5] For the details, see Phillips, "Musical Instruments," 49–67 (55–56).

passages, it appears that the Peshitta wants to give David the limelight and emphasizes his moral and religious leadership. In 1 Chr 16:7 and 43, the translator gives David the role of "master over the choir" and puts the priests and Levites in second place. The harshness and self-accusation of the king are toned down in 1 Chr 20:2 and 21:7. It is he who organizes the divisions of the priests (1 Chr 24:3), he is the only one to see an angel (1 Chr 21:20), he writes instructions for Solomon (in MT it is God). 1 Chr 29:9 gives David alone the credit for making offerings to the temple. Finally, the translator ends his account of David's reign in glowing terms: "For David did what was comely before the Lord and did not transgress from anything that he commanded him all the days of his life" (1 Chr 29:30).

20.3.4.3 Reception History

For a long time, scholars have observed that s-Chr had a chequered history as far as its canonicity was concerned. Its reception in the West Syriac and East Syriac churches does not seem to have followed the same pattern and some scholars have stated unequivocally that Chronicles was not accepted as canonical by the East Syriac church. A closer examination of the East Syriac theoreticians of canonicity such as Theodore of Mopsuestia, Ishoʻdad of Merw, and ʻAbdishoʻ of Nisibis, and other sources, show that the supposed rejection of the book should not be taken too simplistically and that by the time of ʻAbdishoʻ it was fully incorporated into the canon.[6]

At any rate, an analysis of the early patristic authors Aphrahat and Ephrem (→ 21.9) allows us to conclude safely that these fourth-century C.E. writers knew and used the Peshitta version of Chronicles and quote it as Scripture.

---

[6] For a full discussion, see Phillips, "Reception," 259–95 and J.-C. Haelewyck, "Le canon de l' Ancien Testament dans la tradition syriaque (manuscrits bibliques, listes canoniques, auteurs)," in *L'Ancien Testament en syriaque* (eds. F. Briquel-Chatonnet and P. Le Moigne; Études syriaques 5; Paris: Geuthner, 2008), 141–71.

Barnes, W.E., *An Apparatus Criticus to Chronicles in the Peshitta Version* (Cambridge: Cambridge University Press, 1897).

Dirksen, P.B., "Some Aspects of the Translation Technique of P-Chronicles," in *The Peshitta as a Translation: Papers Read at the II Peshitta Symposium Held at Leiden 19–21 August 1993* (eds. P.B. Dirksen and A. van der Kooij; Monographs of the Peshitta Institute Leiden 8; Leiden: Brill, 1995), 17–23.

Fränkel, S., "Die syrische Uebersetzung zu den Büchern der Chronik," *Jahrbücher für Protestantische Theologie* 50 (1879): 508–36, 720–59.

Phillips, D., "The Importance of the Peshittha in Syriac Tradition: The Example of the Peshittha to 1 Chronicles 29," *The Harp* 5 (1992): 67–91.

Phillips, D., "Musical Instruments in the Peshitta to Chronicles and Contacts with the Peshitta to Ben Sira," *Mus* 108 (1995): 49–67.

Phillips, D., "The Reception of Peshitta Chronicles: Some Elements for Investigation," in *The Peshitta: Its Use in Literature and Liturgy: Papers Read at the Third Peshitta Symposium* (ed. B. ter Haar Romeny; Monographs of the Peshitta Institute Leiden 15; Leiden: Brill, 2006), 259–95.

Phillips, D., *Chronicles* (The Bible of Edessa), forthcoming.

Weitzman, M.P., "From Judaism to Christianity: The Syriac Version of the Hebrew Bible," in *The Jews among Pagans and Christians in the Roman Empire* (eds. J. Lieu, J. North, and T. Rajak; London: Routledge, 1992), 147–73.

Weitzman, M.P., "Is the Peshitta of Chronicles a Targum?" in *Targum Studies 2: Targum and Peshitta* (ed. P.V.M. Flesher; South Florida Studies in the History of Judaism 165; Atlanta: Scholars Press, 1998), 159–93.

Weitzman, M.P., *The Syriac Version of the Old Testament: An Introduction* (University of Cambridge Oriental Publications 56; Cambridge: Cambridge University Press, 1999).

David Phillips

20.3.5 Hexaplaric Greek Translations

20.3.5.1 Background

The Greek text of 1 and 2 Supplements (→ 20.3.1; Chronicles in the Hebrew tradition) was translated from a Hebrew text relatively close to what is now known as MT (→ 20.2.2). Furthermore, the translator used a literal translation technique, which offers a quantitative rendering of both the syntactical and morphological structure of the Hebrew text.[1] This fact probably accounts for the paucity of Hexaplaric materials for 1 and 2 Supplements. Furthermore, it is necessary to remember that the Hexaplaric fragments preserved today are the result of early Christian scholarship. These early scholars were selective and modern scholars are indebted to them for whatever evidence has been passed down.

There are only thirteen Hexaplaric fragments with attributions in 1 Chronicles and twenty-four fragments with attributions in 2 Chronicles. Of these thirty-seven fragments, thirty-one are attributed to Symmachus, while three are attributed to Aquila, one to Theodotion, and two more to "the rest" and "the Three" respectively (→ 1.3.1.2).

20.3.5.2 Sources, Editions, and Auxiliary Tools

For the Hexaplaric fragments, the edition by Brooke–McLean–Thackeray cites LXX[108] and LXX[554] or *b* and *z* respectively.

As of 2015, there is a critical edition of the Greek text of 2 Chronicles[2] but no critical edition of 1 Chronicles or the Hexaplaric fragments. The best complete Greek text of 1 and 2 Chronicles is the one by Rahlfs,[3] while the apparatus of Brooke–McLean–Thackery in the Larger Cambridge Septuagint is more complete.[4] The latter also contains the most recent collection of the Hexaplaric fragments and will be the starting point for the comments made below. The bibliography lists the auxiliary tools for the Hexaplaric fragments and their analysis.

20.3.5.3 Translation Character and Technique
20.3.5.3.1 Theodotion

The one fragment attributed to Theodotion (→ 1.3.1.2) comes at 2 Chr 26:1. Here are the relevant texts: אֶת־עֻזִּיָּהוּ "Uzziah"/LXX-Chr τὸν οζιαν "Ozias." The reading in LXX[108] according to Brooke–McLean is αζαριαν "Azarias" and according to Th οχονιαν "Ochonias." The latter term is not used in the LXX corpus or by the Three according to Hatch–Redpath, *Concordance*. It may be a variant of the common ὀχοζείαν "Ochozeiah"/אֲחַזְיָה "Ahaziah" (cf. 4 Kgdms 1:2). In any case, there is no extant evidence that Theodotion used this transliteration or that he tended to transliterate the Hebrew with such freedom. Since it does not align with the Hebrew text here, this fragment probably does not belong to him. The first word, αζαριαν "Azarias," is probably a scholion intended to remind the reader that at 4 Kgdms 14:21 αζαριαν "Azarias" is used as another name for οζιαν "Ozias" in the same story. At 4 Kgdms 14:21, Brooke–McLean–Thackeray's third apparatus notes the problem in the Syro-Hexapla (→ 20.4.4), which contains the converse of the same problem. The word αζαριαν "Azarias" is in the text, while οζιαν "Ozias" is in the margin. It is also worth noting that Field did not list this fragment in his edition and he had access to the same manuscript, LXX[108].[5] Therefore, given the present evidence, this fragment probably should not be attributed to Theodotion.

20.3.5.3.2 Aquila

There are three fragments attributed to Aquila (→ 1.3.1.2) and two come at 1 Chr 15:27. The evidence is בִּמְעִיל "with a robe"/LXX-Chr ἐν στολῇ "with a [linen] garment"/Aq ἐπένδυμα "upper garment" in LXX[554]. In LXX[108], there is another fragment for the same verse אֵפוֹד "ephod"/LXX-Chr στολή "garment"/Aq ἐπένδυμα "upper garment." The second of these fragments is probably genuine according to Aquila's translation equivalents. The first fragment has been corrupted in the process of the transmission of the text. It is either the same fragment that is in LXX[108] with a misplacement of the index or fragment in the margin, or it could be a separate fragment that has changed the original ἔνδυμα "garment" to ἐπένδυμα "upper garment." Aquila regularly uses ἐπένδυμα "upper garment" for אֵפוֹד "ephod" (1 Kgdms 2:18; 21:9; 22:18; 30:7; 2 Kgdms 6:14), while he uses ἔνδυμα "garment, robe" for מְעִיל

---

[1] → 20.3.1.
[2] Hanhart (ed.), *Paralipomenon liber II*.
[3] Rahlfs, *Septuaginta*.
[4] Brooke–McLean–Thackeray, *Old Testament in Greek*, Vol. 2.3: *Chronicles*.

[5] Field, *Hexapla*, 750.

"robe" (Exod 28:27; Lev 8:7; 1 Kgdms 15:27; 24:12; 28:14; Isa 59:17). Exod 28:27 is illuminating since Aquila keeps his equivalents distinct within the same phrase מְעִיל הָאֵפוֹד "robe of the ephod"/Aq ἔνδυμα τοῦ ἐπενδύματος "garment of the upper garment."

The third fragment comes at 1 Chr 29:25 לְמַעְלָה "highly"/LXX-Chr ἐπάνωθεν "over and above"/Aq ὑπεράνω "above." Aquila usually renders מֵעַל "above" with either ἐπάνωθεν "over and above" (Jer 44:5) or ἀπάνωθεν "above" (מִמַּעַל Job 31:2 "from above"). Perhaps Aquila uses a different equivalent when the directive ה- is added to מַעַל "above," or this fragment does not belong to him.

20.3.5.3.3 Symmachus

There are thirty-one fragments attributed to Symmachus (→ 1.3.1.2) in 1 and 2 Chronicles. Of these fragments, only eight consist of more than two words. 1 Chr 26:29 illustrates Symmachus' tendency to revise LXX towards the Hebrew לְשֹׁטְרִים וּלְשֹׁפְטִים "as officers and judges" (*NRSV)/LXX-Chr τοῦ γραμματεύειν καὶ διακρίνειν "to function as scribes and judge" (*NETS)/Sym εἰς παιδευτὰς καὶ κριτάς "as instructors and judges." LXX-Chr (→ 20.3.1) rendered these prepositional phrases as infinitives governed by τοῦ (lit. "of the"). Symmachus revises the Greek according to the Hebrew text by rendering the Hebrew substantival participles with Greek agent nouns that terminate in -της. Symmachus translates שֹׁטְרִים "officials" with παιδευτής "instructor" in Deut 16:18, showing that this fragment probably belongs to him. This fragment also illustrates Symmachus' functional equivalence technique since he does not render each ל "to, for" in his Hebrew source with εἰς "into."

At 2 Chr 3:16, Symmachus translates the Hebrew where LXX-Chr has a transliteration for the Hebrew. Symmachus has this tendency also in the Pentateuch.[6] The texts are בַּדְּבִיר "in the inner sanctuary"/LXX-Chr ἐν τῷ δαβιρ "in the dabir [inner sanctuary]" (*NETS)/Sym ἐν τῷ χρηματιστηρίῳ "in the sanctuary." According to the LSJ lexicon, the word χρηματιστήριον only has the meaning

---

[6] Salvesen, *Symmachus*, 215.

"sanctuary" with reference to the holy of holies in Aquila and Symmachus (3 Kgdms 6:5, 16, 19, 20; Ps 27:2). This instance is the only example of a single attribution to Symmachus. For another example where Symmachus revises a transliteration, see 2 Chr 34:22 בַּמִּשְׁנֶה "in the Second [Quarter]"/LXX-Chr ἐν μασανα "in masana [the Second Quarter]" (*NETS)/Sym ἐν τῇ δευτερώσει "in the Second [Quarter]."

20.3.5.4 Text-Critical Value for the Hebrew Bible

Generally, these relative few Hexaplaric fragments confirm the proto-MT (→ 20.2.2) and do not provide significant variants. In 2 Chr 31:17, a Symmachus fragment appears to confirm MT where LXX contains a variant: וְאֵת הִתְיַחֵשׂ "and the enrollment"/LXX-Chr οὗτος ὁ καταλοχισμός "This was the register" (*NETS)/Sym τὰ δὲ ἀπονεμηθέντα "Now the things being assigned." In this case,[7] Rudolph the *BHS editor of 2 Chronicles is probably correct in saying that LXX-Chr read וְאֵת ("and" + direct object marker) as זֹאת "this." Symmachus agrees with the Hebrew and he regularly renders *waw* "and" with δέ "but, and." There are no other instances of Symmachus' usage of ἀπονέμω "to assign" so one should exercise caution in this case. However, the fragment appears to have come from a source that had contact with a Hebrew source since the *waw* is represented in the translation.

Brooke–McLean–Thackeray, *Old Testament in Greek*, Vol. 2.3: *Chronicles*.

Busto Saiz, J.R., *La traducción de Símaco en el Libro de los Salmos* (Textos y Estudios "Cardenal Cisneros" 22; Madrid: Consejo Superior de Investigaciones Científicas, 1978).

Field, *Hexapla*.

Gentry, P.J., *The Asterisked Materials in the Greek Job* (SBLSCS 38; Atlanta: Scholars Press, 1995).

Hanhart, R. (ed.), *Paralipomenon liber II* (Septuaginta Vetus Testamentum Graecum 7.2; Göttingen: Vandenhoeck & Ruprecht, 2014).

Hyvärinen, K., *Die Übersetzung von Aquila* (ConBOT 10; Uppsala: G.W.K. Gleerup, 1977).

---

[7] W. Rudolph, "Librum Chronicorum" *BHS, 1459–1574 (1563).

Reider, J. and N. Turner, *An Index to Aquila: Greek-Hebrew, Hebrew-Greek, Latin-Hebrew* (Leiden: Brill, 1966).

Salvesen, A., *Symmachus in the Pentateuch* (JSS Monograph 15; Manchester: Victoria University of Manchester, 1991).

John D. Meade

20.3.6 Post-Hexaplaric Greek Translations

20.3.6.1 Background

The only post-Hexaplaric recension known to us is that of Lucian (→ 1.3.1.2). Study of the Lucianic text of LXX-1-2 Chr has proceeded slowly due to the absence of a critical edition and difficulties associated with parallel readings from Kingdoms. Nonetheless, Spanish scholars such as Natalio Fernández Marcos and José Ramón Busto Saiz must be credited with clarifying the picture of the recension. The work of the former is especially important for describing the Lucianic recension, because he has addressed many of the issues associated with it: proto-Lucianic readings and mixture from other textual traditions in other books of LXX (→ 1.3.1.1).

20.3.6.2 Original Form, Editions, Auxiliary Tools

There is no critical edition of 1–2 Chronicles in the Göttingen LXX. There is, however, a reconstruction of the Lucianic text by Fernández Marcos and Busto Saiz.[1] Evidence for the LXX^L text in the manuscripts of 1–2 Chronicles differs significantly from Kingdoms. The well-known manuscript LXX^{82} and LXX^{127} in Kingdoms do not preserve the Lucianic recension in 1–2 Chronicles. Manuscript LXX^{121} is Lucianic in 1 Chr 1:1–11:4 only. VL (→ 20.4.1) cannot be satisfactorily classified as Lucianic.[2] In addition to the above resource, Allen's revised thesis, *The Greek Chronicles*, is useful.

20.3.6.3 Translation Character and Technique

Fernández Marcos has written the most succinct description of the LXX^L text of 1–2 Chronicles.[3] He says that the manuscripts evince a "slight preference" for Attic morphology: treatment of ἔλεος "mercy" as masculine instead of neuter (1 Chr 17:13; 19:2), ἐγένετο for ἐγενήθη "happened" (2 Chr 1:12), and εἶπον instead of εἶπα "I said" (2 Chr 18:5; 26:23). Stylistic improvements are sensitive to an economy of words: ἄτεκνος "childless" for οὐχ ἔχων τέκνα "not having children" (1 Chr 2:30, 32) and ἀκουτίσαι for ἀκουσθῆναι ποιῆσαι "to make to hear" (1 Chr 15:19). Other substitutions – some of which are synonyms – include a preference for δέ to καί, both meaning "and" (1 Chr 2:34; 2 Chr 13:11), δοῦλος to παῖς, both meaning "slave" (1 Chr 21:8), and ὁρῶν to βλέπων, both meaning "seeing" (1 Chr 9:22). Hence, the manuscripts preserve significant variations from the supposed Old Greek. Stylistic and grammatical improvements compel Fernández Marcos to conclude that the L text of 1–2 Chronicles was used for public reading.[4]

20.3.6.4 Inner-Translational Features

Discussion about the proto-Lucianic variants in 1–2 Chronicles has been hindered by difficulties associated with early witnesses (e.g., VL [→ 20.4.1] and Josephus [→ 21.3]). Old Latin manuscripts are characterized by significant mixture from Lucianic and LXX sources in addition to unique readings. Josephus, however, agrees with the LXX^L text sufficiently that agreements "cannot be explained merely as a result of an accidental selection of synonyms" (e.g., 2 Chr 13:13 ἀπέστρεψεν "turned back" LXX/περιεκύκλωσε "encircled" LXX^L/περικυκλωσαμένους "having been encircled" Josephus).[5]

---

[1] Fernández Marcos and Busto Saiz, *1–2 Crónicas*.

[2] Fernández Marcos, "Some Reflections on the Antiochian Text of the Septuagint," 222.

[3] The description above is heavily reliant on Fernández Marcos, "The Antiochian Text in I–II Chronicles," 303–04.

[4] N. Fernández Marcos, *The Septuagint in Context: Introduction to the Greek Version of the Bible* (trans. W.G.E. Watson; Leiden: Brill, 2000), 231.

[5] Fernández Marcos, "The Antiochian Text in I–II Chronicles," 307.

20.3.6.5 Text-Critical Value

The text-critical value of the Lucianic text of 1–2 Chronicles is difficult to assess. There are no compelling arguments that suggest that the LXX[L] text may be closely related to a Hebrew text different from MT (→ 20.2.2). VL (→ 20.4.1), however, may evince a textual history that includes a proto-Lucianic text with influence from many other textual traditions.[6]

Allen, L.C., *The Greek Chronicles: The Relation of the Septuagint of I and II Chronicles to the Masoretic Text*, Part 1 (VTSup 25; Leiden: Brill, 1974).

Allen, L.C., *The Greek Chronicles: The Relation of the Septuagint of I and II Chronicles to the Masoretic Text*, Part 2 (VTSup 27; Leiden: Brill, 1974).

Fernández Marcos, N., "Some Reflections on the Antiochian Text of the Septuagint," in *Studien zur Septuaginta*, 219–29.

Fernández Marcos, N., "The Antiochian Text in I–II Chronicles," in *VII Congress of the International Organization for Seputagint and Cognate Studies* (ed. C.E. Cox; SBLSCS 31; Atlanta: Scholars Press, 1991), 301–11.

Fernández Marcos, N. and J.R. Busto Saiz, *El texto Antioqueno de la Biblia Griega*, Vol. 3: *1–2 Crónicas* (Textos y Estudios "Cardenal Cisneros" de la Biblia Poliglota Matritense 60; Madrid: Instituto de Filología, 1996).

Matthew M. Dickie

20.3.7 Vulgate

20.3.7.1 Background

Jerome translated the Hebrew text of Chronicles in 395 or 396 C.E.,[1] after he had completed a good portion of his work on the Hebrew Bible (→ 1.3.5.2). Most significantly for Chronicles, Jerome had translated Samuel–Kings (→ 3–5.1.4) a few years earlier. He also had extensive experience with the Greek texts of Chronicles, having produced a translation of LXX-Chr in the late 380s C.E. (→ 20.3.1).[2]

20.3.7.2 Translation Character

Kedar-Kopfstein classified V-Chr as a "detached" translation, meaning that "changes are introduced whenever strained concordance between the standard rendition and the requirements of the context occur, but only in this case; the criterion is the normal usage of the target language."[3] On the other hand, Everson's comparison between parallel passages in V-Sam–Kgs (→ 3–5.1.4) and V-Chr led to the conclusion that the latter represents "in part" a "transformative" translation, where we find "deviations from standard equivalents for the sake of a smoother style in the receptor language."[4] Detailed study of V-Chr supports Everson's contention. While Jerome often reproduces Hebrew word order, he not infrequently varies it. He routinely transforms Hebrew constructions into more familiar Latin ones. He shows no interest here in maintaining stereotyped translation equivalents; rather he purposefully introduces variety by altering his translation equivalents, even within a single verse. Nevertheless, his Latin nearly always makes sense of MT (→ 20.2.2), though in a few places Jerome had difficulty with the Hebrew text or might have had in hand a Hebrew text differing slightly from MT. In such passages, Jerome usually managed to produce a readable Latin version that avoided reproducing the difficulties of the Hebrew text.

---

[6] Fernández Marcos, "The Antiochian Text in I–II Chronicles," 306.

[1] See J.N.D. Kelly, *Jerome: His Life, Writings, and Controversies* (New York: Harper & Row, 1975), 190. This dating is established by Jerome's statement in his preface that he had recently written *De optimo genere interpretandi*, i.e., *Epist.* 57 to Pammachius, dating to 395 C.E.

[2] On Jerome's translations from LXX, see F. Stummer, *Einführung in die lateinische Bibel: Ein Handbuch für Vorlesungen und Selbstunterricht* (Paderborn: Ferdinand Schöningh, 1928), 85–90; S. Rebenich, *Jerome* (Early Church Fathers; London: Routledge, 2002), 53–54.

[3] B. Kedar-Kopfstein, "The Vulgate as a Translation: Some Semantic and Syntactical Aspects of Jerome's Version of the Hebrew Bible" (PhD diss., Hebrew University of Jerusalem, 1968), 27 (cf. p. 284).

[4] D.L. Everson, "An Examination of Synoptic Portions within the Vulgate," *VT* 58 (2008): 189; cf. Kedar-Kopfstein, "Vulgate as a Translation," 27.

20.3.7.3 Translation Technique
20.3.7.3.1 Hebrew Idioms

Jerome transforms Hebrew idioms into appropriate Latin: עִם־לְבָבִי "in my heart," *voluntatis meae* "my will" (1 Chr 22:7); וּכְכַלּוֹת/*cumque conplesset* "and when had finished" (2 Chr 7:1). He can handle the imperfect consecutive construction in a rather sophisticated way. He often varies his translation of the conjunction *waw* in this construction: e.g., in 1 Chronicles 10, we find *ergo* "so" (vv. 6, 13), *igitur* "then" (v. 8), *autem* "moreover" (v. 10), *propter quod et* "therefore" (v. 14), or omission of the *waw* (v. 12). He also frequently uses some form of syntactical subordination for this construction: still, in 1 Chronicles 10, we encounter a relative clause (v. 7), participial phrase (v. 8), *cum*-clause (vv. 9, 11), or an ablative absolute (v. 7). Elsewhere he can use an *ut*-clause for the imperfect consecutive, especially after וַיְהִי (1 Chr 18:1; 19:1). Frequently, though, it comes across quite literally: וַיֹּאמֶר/*et dixit* "and he said" (1 Chr 22:5); וַיְקַדֵּשׁ/*sanctificavit quoque* "and he also sanctified" (2 Chr 7:7). For Jerome's handling of וַיְהִי, see below.

20.3.7.3.2 Attention to Context

Jerome had no scruples regarding abandoning the typical translation equivalents either for the sake of variation (see below) or when context seemed to demand it: וַיִּפֹּל "and he fell," *inruit* "and he rushed" (1 Chr 10:4); נֹפְלִים "fallen," *iacentes* "lying" (1 Chr 10:8); וַיִּשְׂאוּ אֶת־רֹאשׁוֹ וְאֶת־כֵּלָיו "and they took his head and his equipment," *et amputassent caput armisque nudassent* "and they cut off his head and stripped away his armour" (1 Chr 10:9); וַיָּשִׂימוּ "and they put," *consecraverunt* "and they dedicated" (1 Chr 10:10); עָשִׂיתָ "you made," *bellasti* "you fought" (1 Chr 22:8); וַיֹּאמֶר "and he said," *ac praecepit* "and he commanded" (2 Chr 14:3); וַיֹּאמְרוּ "and they say," *replicant* "they repeat" (2 Chr 35:25); מַעֲשֵׂה יִשְׂרָאֵל "the doings of Israel," *peccata Israel* "the sins of Israel" (2 Chr 17:4); כְּהִתְחַבֶּרְךָ "as soon as you joined yourself," *quia habuisti foedus* "because you made an alliance" (2 Chr 20:37); בְּדִבְרֵי יְהוָה "by the words of the Lord," *iuxta ... imperium Domini* "in accordance with ... the command of the Lord" (2 Chr 29:15); לֵאמֹר "saying," *praedicantes* "proclaiming" (2 Chr 30:6). Prepositions are handled with some flexibility: לְשָׁאוּל/*super Saul* "to Saul" (1 Chr 10:11); בְּמַעֲלוֹ/*propter iniquitates suas* "for his iniquities" (1 Chr 10:13); דָּם לָרֹב/*multum sanguinem* "much blood" (1 Chr 22:8). His translations are sometimes rather periphrastic: כִּי־לֹא דְרַשְׁנֻהוּ כַּמִּשְׁפָּט "because we did not seek him according to the ordinance," *sic et nunc fiat inlicitum quid nobis agentibus* "so also now it should happen, because we did something unlawful" (1 Chr 15:13); אֶת־דִּבְרֵי הַבְּרִית הַכְּתוּבִים עַל־הַסֵּפֶר הַזֶּה "the words of the covenant written upon this book," *quae scripta sunt in volumine illo quem legerat* "the things that were written in that book which he had read" (2 Chr 34:31).

20.3.7.3.3 Style

Jerome sought to provide a stylistically pleasing Latin version. To this end, he avoided stereotyped renderings. Previous Latin versions had established *factum est* as the typical rendering of וַיְהִי "and it came to pass" (καὶ ἐγένετο in Greek). Whereas the Hebrew form appears seventy-seven times in Chronicles, Jerome rarely offers the standard translation equivalent (only nine times).[5] He instead uses various renderings: e.g., *igitur* "so" (1 Chr 10:8; 15:25; 17:3; 2 Chr 5:13); *-que* "and" (1 Chr 15:26); *autem* "now" (1 Chr 17:1); *accidit autem* "now it happened" (1 Chr 19:1); *erat autem* "now, he was" (1 Chr 23:11); ablative absolute (2 Chr 5:11; 8:1); or it can be omitted altogether (1 Chr 20:4). Jerome seeks to avoid repetition, sometimes by choosing not to translate a Hebrew word, or by varying its translation: אַחֲרֵי שָׁאוּל וְאַחֲרֵי בָנָיו "after Saul and after his sons," *persequentes Saul et filios eius* "pursuing Saul and his sons" (1 Chr 10:2); חֶרֶב ... חֶרֶב "sword ... sword," *gladius ... ensis* "sword ... blade" (1 Chr 10:4); בְּאֶרֶץ־פְּלִשְׁתִּים "in the land of the Philistines," *in terram suam* "into their land" (1 Chr 10:9); אֶת־גּוּפַת שָׁאוּל וְאֵת גּוּפֹת בָּנָיו "the body of Saul and the bodies of his sons," *cadavera Saul et filiorum eius* "the bodies of Saul and of his sons" (1 Chr 10:12); omission of second "Philistines" (1 Chr 10:2); omission of second "Hebron" (1 Chr 11:3); omission of sec-

---

[5] These statistics were compiled by Everson, "Examination," 184.

ond "Jerusalem" (2 Chr 19:8). On other occasions, Jerome declines to represent words in his translation that he deems unnecessary: דָּוִיד "David" (1 Chr 18:6); אַחֲרֵי־כֵן "after this" (1 Chr 19:1); עַבְדֵי דָוִיד "the servants of David" (1 Chr 19:2); וַיִּקַּח "he took" (1 Chr 19:4); אַרְצָה "on the ground" (1 Chr 22:8); וַיַּגֵּד שָׁפָן הַסּוֹפֵר לַמֶּלֶךְ לֵאמֹר "and Shaphan the scribe reported to the king, saying" (2 Chr 34:18). He sometimes adds words to complete a thought or clarify the meaning: וְלֹא אָבָה נֹשֵׂא כֵלָיו "but the bearer of his weapons was not willing," *noluit autem armiger eius hoc facere* "but his armor bearer was not willing to do this" (1 Chr 10:4); אֲשֶׁר־בָּעֵמֶק "who (were) in the plain," *qui habitabant in campestribus* "who were dwelling in the plains" (1 Chr 10:7); וַיָּנֻסוּ "and they fled," *et huc illucque dispersi sunt* "and they were scattered here and there" (1 Chr 10:7); *morte* "the death (of his father)" (1 Chr 19:2); *ob hanc causam* "for this reason" (1 Chr 22:5); *quae iecit* "which (Solomon) laid" (2 Chr 3:3); כְּמִשְׁפָּטָם "according to their ordinance," *secundum speciem qua iussa erant fieri* "according to the form in which they were commanded to be made" (2 Chr 4:7); כַּמִּשְׁפָּט "according to the ordinance," *iuxta quod lege praeceptum est* "in accordance with what is written in the law" (2 Chr 35:13); לְכָל־דָּבָר וְלָאֹצָרוֹת "regarding any matter and regarding the treasuries," *ex omnibus quae praeceperat et in custodiis thesaurorum* "as to any of the things he had commanded, and in keeping the treasures" (2 Chr 8:15); וַיָּבֹאוּ בַבְּרִית "and they entered into covenant," *et intravit ex more ad corroborandum foedus* "and he went in as usual to confirm the covenant" (2 Chr 15:12).[6] v-Chr often follows the Hebrew word order by putting the verb first (against Latin style), or later in the sentence in imitation of the Hebrew (1 Chr 22:3), but sometimes the translation alters the position of words for clarity or Latinity: *ad te* "unto you" (1 Chr 19:3); *deportaverant* "they brought" (1 Chr 22:4); *ante mortem suam* "before his death" (1 Chr 22:5); *secreverunt* "they separated" (1 Chr 25:1); אֲשֶׁר הֵכִין בִּמְקוֹם דָּוִיד "which he prepared in the place of David," *in loco quem paraverat David* "in the place which David had prepared" (2 Chr

3:1).[7] Jerome routinely translates the Hebrew infinitive construct with *lamed* by means of an *ut*-clause (1 Chr 19:2; 2 Chr 14:13; 29:15; 30:12), though it can also become a gerundival clause (1 Chr 19:2; 22:2) or a relative clause (1 Chr 22:5). He rarely resorts to transliteration for words that have sensible Latin equivalents, though at 1 Chr 15:21 he renders לְנַצֵּחַ "to direct" as *epinikion* "song of victory," a transliterated Greek word apparently derived from Symmachus (→ 1.3.1.2).[8]

20.3.7.3.4 Lexical Variety

v-Chr typically avoids stereotyped lexical equivalencies: בְּרִית (30×) is often *foedus* "covenant," but is sometimes *pactum* "pact" (e.g. 1 Chr 16:6, 17). *Foedus* can also represent מוֹעֵד "meeting" (1 Chr 23:32; 2 Chr 1:3, 6, 13). מוֹעֵד (12×) can become *foedus* "covenant," *testimonium* "testimony" (1 Chr 6:17; 9:21), *sollemnitas* "solemn observance" (1 Chr 23:32; 2 Chr 2:4; 30:22; 31:3), *festa dies* "festival day" (2 Chr 8:13), or be omitted (2 Chr 5:5). The fixed phrase אֹהֶל־מוֹעֵד "tent of meeting" Jerome translates as *tabernaculum testimonii* "tabernacle of the testimony" (1 Chr 6:17; 9:21), *tabernaculum foederis* "tabernacle of the covenant" (1 Chr 23:32; 2 Chr 1:3, 6, 13), or simply as *tabernaculum* "tabernacle" (2 Chr 5:5). Jerome varies even more his translation of מִצְוָה "command, precept" (22×): *praeceptum* "precept" (1 Chr 28:7; 7:19; 2 Chr 8:13; 17:14; 24:20; 29:25; 30:12; 34:31; 35:15; 35:16); *mandatum* "injunction" (1 Chr 28:8; 29:19; 2 Chr 8:15; 14:13; 19:10; 29:15); *imperium* "command" (2 Chr 24:21; 35:10); *dispositio* "regulation" (2 Chr 29:25); *iubere* "to order" (2 Chr 30:6); *caerimonae* "ceremonies" (2 Chr 31:21). While חֹק "commandment" appears only eight times, Jerome uses six different Latin words to translate it: *praeceptum* (1 Chr 16:17); *mandatum* "injunction" (1 Chr 22:13); *caerimonia* "rite" (1 Chr 29:19; 2 Chr 19:10; 33:8); *iustitia* "justice" (2 Chr 7:17); *iustificatio* "just ruling" (2 Chr 34:31); *lex* "law" (2 Chr 35:25). It should be noted, however, that Jerome

---

[6] For further examples, see Everson, "Examination," 187–89.

[7] Cf. Everson, "Examination," 186–87.

[8] See T. Janz, *Deuxième Livre d'Esdras: Traduction du texte grec de la Septante: Introduction et notes* (*Bible d' Alexandrie 11.2; Paris: Cerf, 2010), 199.

always renders תורה "Torah" in v-Chr as *lex* "law." Jerome renders מִשְׁפָּט "order" (22×) in a variety of ways: *ordo* "order" (1 Chr 6:17); *iudicium* "judgment" (1 Chr 16:12, 14; 18:14; 22:13; 28:7; 2 Chr 6:39; 7:17; 9:8; 33:8); *caerimoniae* "rites" (1 Chr 23:31); *ritus* "rite" (1 Chr 24:19; 2 Chr 4:20); *dispositio* "appointment" (2 Chr 8:14; 30:16); *iustificatio* "justification" (2 Chr 19:10). Within the same passage, וְעָשִׂיתָ מִשְׁפָּטָם "and act on their cause" becomes *et ulcisceris* "and avenge (them)" (2 Chr 6:35) and a little later *et facias iudicium* "and perform judgment" (2 Chr 6:39). Jerome sometimes varies his renderings within a single verse: in 1 Chr 10:10, בֵּית "house" becomes first *fanum* "consecrated place" and then *templum* "temple" (both referring to "pagan" temples); at 1 Chr 19:2, חֶסֶד is first *misericordia* "kindness" and then *gratia* "favor." The common Hebrew verb נתן "to give" appearing 154 times in Chronicles, usually becomes a form of *dare* "to give" in v-Chr (92× = 60 %) but might also be rendered with *pono* "to set" (22× = 14 %) or a dozen or more other words.

20.3.7.3.5 Unusual Renderings, but Not Variants

Jerome's translation technique at times results in a Latin text that could seem to be based on a Hebrew *Vorlage* divergent from MT (→ 20.2.2), though this is usually not the best solution. For instance, sometimes v-Chr smooths out a difficult text: וַיִּמְצָאֻהוּ הַמּוֹרִים בַּקֶּשֶׁת וַיָּחֶל מִן־הַיּוֹרִים "and those who shoot with the bow found him, and he was in anguish from the shooters," *inveneruntque eum sagittarii et vulneraverunt iaculis* "and the archers found him and wounded him with arrows" (1 Chr 10:3). At 2 Chr 19:6, for וְעִמָּכֶם בִּדְבַר מִשְׁפָּט "and (he) is with you in the matter of the judgment," an "elliptical" Hebrew expression,[9] Jerome gives a sensible if interpretive rendering: *et quodcumque iudicaveritis in vos redundabit* "and whatever you judge, it shall flow back unto you." At 2 Chr 35:13, Jerome renders קָדָשִׁים "holy offerings" (= MT; cf. LXX, VL) with *pacificas hostias* "peace-offering sacrifices." Every other time *pacificus* "peaceful" appears in the Vulgate it translates the root שלם "peace" (cf., e.g., Lev 3:1; 7:11, 13, 18, 20, etc.; 1 Chr 12:17; 16:1; 2 Chr 7:7; 19:1; 33:16;

etc.), so that one might expect that Jerome read this root in our verse. However, this is apparently Jerome's interpretation of קָדָשִׁים "holy offerings," shared by some modern scholars.[10] A difficult construction (בְּמַשָּׂא יֹסֵר בַּמַּשָּׂא "with burden, directing with the burden") appears at 1 Chr 15:22, which becomes in v-Chr *prophetiae praeerat ad praecinendam melodiam* "he presided over the prophecy, to play beforehand the music," an interpretive rendering.[11]

20.3.7.4 Text-Critical Value
20.3.7.4.1 Consonantal Text Close to MT

Almost always, v-Chr reflects the consonants of MT (→ 1.3.5.11). Even where MT (→ 20.2.2) presents a difficult reading or one that scholars now consider textually inferior to a reading preserved by other witnesses, Jerome's translation will usually correpond to MT. At 1 Chr 4:3, MT preserves a difficult reading (וְאֵלֶּה אֲבִי עֵיטָם "and these are the father of Etam") that must have become corrupt in some way.[12] Jerome's translation (*ista quoque stirps Hetam* "and this is the posterity of Etam") probably represents his attempt to make sense of MT. So also at 2 Chr 30:22, MT has וַיֹּאכְלוּ "and they ate," while LXX (συνετέλεσαν "they finished") and VL (*consummaberunt* "they finished") seem to assume ויכלו "and they completed," which makes sense in context and has been judged the better reading.[13] Jerome, on the other hand, agrees with MT, rendering *et comederunt* "and they ate."

20.3.7.4.2 Possible Hebrew Variants

Occasionally, v-Chr may attest a Hebrew variant, though only in relatively minor details. At 2 Chr 19:8, Jerome perhaps read ולריבי ישבי ירושלם

---

[9] Klein, *2 Chronicles*, 271.

[10] S. Japhet, *I & II Chronicles: A Commentary* (OTL; Louisville: Westminster John Knox, 1993), 1050; cf. Klein, *2 Chronicles*, 522. Note that at Hezekiah's Passover, וְזִבְחֵי שְׁלָמִים/*victimas pacificorum* "sacrifices of peace offerings" were offered (2 Chr 30:22). This may have provided the basis for Jerome's interpretation of the קָדָשִׁים "holy offerings" at Josiah's Passover.

[11] See the interpretive options for this phrase in Knoppers, *I Chronicles 10–29*, 609.

[12] See various suggestions in Klein, *1 Chronicles*, 124.

[13] Klein, *2 Chronicles*, 428.

"and to settle disputes among the inhabitants of Jerusalem" (with LXX and VL) rather than MT וְלָרִיב וַיָּשֻׁבוּ יְרוּשָׁלָםִ "and for settling disputes, and they returned to Jerusalem."[14] He reads דודנים "Dodanim" rather than רודנים "Rodanim" at 1 Chr 1:7, thus against MT but in agreement with MT at Gen 10:4. It is doubtful that Jerome was trying to harmonize the two passages in view of his practice elsewhere, such as at 1 Chr 3:19 on the ancestry of Zerubbabel (contrast Ezra 3:2).[15] At 2 Chr 20:25, Jerome's *vestes* "garments" implies בגדים rather than MT's פְּגָרִים "corpses."[16] V-Chr may (with LXX) attest a word order at the end of 2 Chr 32:28 different from MT.[17] In general, given Jerome's translation technique for Chronicles, it is hazardous to speculate regarding the readings of his Hebrew *Vorlage* without the support of other textual witnesses.

20.3.7.4.3 Vocalization

The many names in Chronicles, especially in the first nine chapters, give ample opportunity to observe the vocalization with which Jerome was familiar, which usually turns out to be very close to MT. For example, at 1 Chr 1:38, two names have identical consonants in Hebrew, differing only in their last vowel (דִּישֹׁן, דִּישָׁן "Dishon, Dishan"). While LXX transmits Δησων "Deson" and Δαισων "Daison," Jerome's renderings correspond to MT's vocalization (*Dison, Disan*). There are instances when the vocalization tradition differs: מצות "commands" for MT מִצְוַת "command" (2 Chr 8:15); מצות "command" for MT מִצְוֹת "commands" (2 Chr 24:20).

---

[14] Klein, *2 Chronicles*, 271; Barthélemy, *Critique textuelle 1982*, 494–95. Cf. J. Heller, "Textkritisches zu 2 Chr XIX 8," VT 24 (1974): 371–73.

[15] Another example is 1 Chr 1:36, on which see Knoppers, *1 Chronicles 1–9*, 269.

[16] Cf. VL. See N. Fernández Marcos, "The Old Latin of Chronicles between the Greek and the Hebrew," in *IX Congress of the International Organization for Septuagint and Cognate Studies, Cambridge, 1995* (ed. B.A. Taylor; SBLSCS 45; Atlanta: Scholars Press, 1997), 123–36 (127); Barthélemy, *Critique textuelle 1982*, 497.

[17] See Barthélemy, *Critique textuelle 1982*, 512.

Barthélemy, *Critique textuelle 1982*.

Everson, D.L., "An Examination of Synoptic Portions within the Vulgate," VT 58 (2008): 178–90.

Klein, R.W., *1 Chronicles: A Commentary* (Hermeneia; Minneapolis: Fortress, 2006).

Klein, R.W., *2 Chronicles: A Commentary* (Hermeneia; Minneapolis: Fortress, 2012).

Knoppers, G.N., *1 Chronicles 1–9: A New Translation with Introduction and Commentary* (AB 12; New York: Doubleday, 2003).

Knoppers, G.N., *1 Chronicles 10–29: A New Translation with Introduction and Commentary* (AB 12A; New York: Doubleday, 2004).

Edmon L. Gallagher

20.3.8 Arabic Translations

See → 19.4.8.

20.4 Secondary Translations

20.4.1 Vetus Latina

20.4.1.1 Evidence

As occurred with other books of the Old Testament, the VL translations of 1–2 Chronicles were supplanted by the translation of St. Jerome (→ 20.3.7) and disappeared almost completely. The only witnesses for VL-1 Chr are marginal glosses in Spanish Vulgata Bibles (VL$^{91-95}$). For VL-2 Chr, more witnesses are preserved: a full text (VL^{109}), the marginal glosses in VL$^{91-95}$, several fragments of ms VL^{118}, and the *Oratio Salomonis* (2 Chr 6:13–22), copied at the end of the book of Sirach[1] (→ 11.4.5). Among quotations in patristic and medieval authors (→ 21.8), the most interesting testimony is that of Lucifer of Cagliari (fourth century C.E.). Other important quotations can be found in the *Liber Genealogus* (AN gen), the fragments of a biblical glossary published in 1927 by De Bruyne, in Pseudo-Jerome's *Quaestiones in Paralipomena*.[2] Quotations of VL-2 Chr derive from the works of Augustine, Jerome, Ambrose, Ambrosiaster, Pseudo-Augustine's *Liber de Divinis Scripturis*, Priscillianus, Tyconius, and from liturgical texts.[3]

20.4.1.2 Editions

The first edition of the VL texts of 1–2 Chr was that of Sabatier[4] based on patristic quotations and Codex Corbeiensis 1 (Paris BN lat 11532) for the *Oratio Salomonis*. In 1941, Mercati published the fragments of manuscript VL^{118}, and in 1945 Weber collected and published all the evidences known at the time: manuscript VL^{109}, the marginal glosses in VL$^{91\,94\,95}$, the fragments of VL^{118}, *Oratio Salomonis* (seventeen manuscripts and Gutenberg's *editio princeps* of that work), as well as quotations from Cyprianus, Lucifer of Cagliari, Augustine, *Opus imperfectum in Matthaeum*, Cyprian, Facundus, Gildas, Jerome, Hilary, Paulinus, Priscillian, etc (→ 21.8).[5] In 1996, Fernández Marcos and Busto Saiz published readings of manuscripts VL$^{91-95\,109\,118}$ and of those found in indirect tradition as part of the apparatus of their edition of the Antiochian recension of the Greek Bible.[6] Despite all these efforts, no critical edition of the VL glosses in VL$^{91-95}$ exists.

20.4.1.3 Text

The extant evidence shows that there were several VL versions of 1–2 Chronicles in circulation before the Vulgate translation, though only one of them has been preserved completely for 2 Chronicles.[7] The number of direct and indirect witnesses to this text type also shows that it was one of the most numerous Latin texts of Chronicles in antiquity and was already in circulation at the time of Lucifer of Cagliari (fourth century C.E.).[8] Augustine's Chronicles quotations show that revised texts were known at that time. Some revisions intended adjustment to the Hebrew text[9] of Chronicles (→ 20.2.2) and such a text is found in manuscripts VL$^{91-95}$. Quotations in Priscillian, Gildas, and the text of *Oratio Salomonis* also provide evidence of different text types for the books of Chronicles.

In recent times, the hypothesis of several revisions of VL-Chr has been revised and more attention is given to the study of the extant evidence in relation to the *Vorlage* of VL-Chr. VL-Chr is of great importance for the reconstruction of the Antiochian recension of the Greek Bible (→ 20.3.6),[10] although the VL evidence in these books is not as good as in 1–2 Samuel and 1–2 Kings (→ 3–5.1.6.2). According to Fernández Marcos and Busto Saiz,[11]

---

[1] Weber, *Les anciennes*, xi–xiii; xliv–xlvii.
[2] Jerome, *Opera omnia* (PL 23:1431–70).
[3] Fernández Marcos and Busto Saiz, *El texto*, xli–xlviii.
[4] Sabatier, **Bibliorum*, 2:629–85.
[5] See Weber, *Les anciennes*, xiii–xx.
[6] Fernández Marcos and Busto Saiz, *El texto*, lxii–lxv.
[7] Weber, *Les anciennes*, xlviii.
[8] Weber, *Les anciennes*, xlviii–xlix.
[9] Weber, *Les anciennes*, l.
[10] Fernández Marcos and Busto Saiz, *El texto*.
[11] Fernández Marcos and Busto Saiz, *El texto*.

all extant VL witnesses for 1–2 Chronicles preserve only one text type that was already known at the time of Lucifer. The individual textual differences between the witnesses to VL-Chr are due to their transmission history and do not attest to different VL texts.

20.4.1.4 Vorlage

According to Weber,[12] the VL texts of 1–2 Chronicles were not translated from a Greek version of LXX (→ 20.3.1), but from a Greek text closer to MT (→ 20.2.2) that could perhaps be identified with the version of Theodotion (→ 20.3.5). Carmignac revised this hypothesis in 1981 focusing on agreements of VL[109] and VL[91–95] with MT-Chr.[13] He concluded that the Vorlage of VL-Chr could have been a Greek text of "kaige" type as the following examples show:

> 2 Chr 1:3 in Baama "to the Bamah" (VL[109]): לַבָּמָה "to the Bamah/to the high place" (MT)/εἰς τὴν ὑψηλήν "to the high ground" (LXX; *NETS)

> 2 Chr 4:16 pater eius et adtulit "his father and he brought" (VL[109]): אביו "his father" (MT)/καὶ ἀνήνεγκεν "and brought" (LXX; *NETS)

The study by Fernández Marcos and Busto Saiz[14] demonstrates that VL-Chr is a very literal translation of a Greek text. This is argued by the fact that VL[109] contains in 2 Chronicles verses (35:19a–d; 36:2a–c, 5a–d) that are found in Greek witnesses but not in MT-Chr, and by some features of the translation that can only be explained by way of misinterpretation of a Greek Vorlage.[15] Hebraisms in VL-Chr are due neither to a systematic revision towards MT-Chr nor to contacts with V-Chr[16] (→ 20.3.7).

The following examples illustrate the argument of Fernández Marcos and Busto Saiz:

1 Chr 5:10 super omnem faciem orientis "each of them facing east" (VL[91–95]): ἐπὶ πάντος προσώπου ἀνατολῶν "each of them facing east" (LXX[19 93 108 121])

2 Chr 6:28 si tribulauerit eum inimicus in conspectu ciuitatum "if the enemy oppresses him in view of (his) cities" (VL[91–95 109]): ἐὰν θλίψῃ αὐτὸν ὁ ἐχθρὸς κατέναντι τῶν πόλεων "if the enemy oppresses him against the cities" (LXX)

2 Chr 6:31 ut timeant te et ingrediatur in omnes uias tuas "that they should fear you and walk in all your ways" (VL[109]): ὅπως φοβῶνται σε τοῦ πορεύεσαι ἐν πάσαις ταῖς ὁδοῖς σου "that they should fear you to walk in all your ways" (LXX[19 93 108]).

The Greek Vorlage of VL-Chr cannot be found in any known Greek witness to Chronicles, but must be identified as a mixed text type in which the Antiochian recension (→ 20.3.6) influenced LXX-Chr (→ 20.3.1) significantly,[17] such as the dpt group in Brooke–McLean[18] and II group in Allen.[19] Allen's II group is formed by manuscripts LXX[74 144 236 321 346]; it attests to a Greek text revised and adapted toward the Hebrew of MT-Chr.[20] Hebrew features can be explained by an adaptation to MT-Chr (→ 20.2.2) by way of the Antiochian recension or Hexaplaric materials (→ 20.3.5). There is no explanation for six marginal glosses headed by the word iud(e) found in VL[94 95], but it is almost certain that they do not contain VL text; they possibly come from a source other than that of the VL marginal glosses and joined the corpus at a later period. Fernández Marcos[21] relates them to the Chronicles quotations in Pseudo-Jerome's Quaestiones in Paralipomena.

Allen, L.C., The Greek Chronicles: The Relation of the Septuagint of I and II Chronicles to the Massoretic Text (SVT 25; Leiden, 1974).

De Bruyne, D., "Fragments d'anciennes versions latines tirés d'un glossaire biblique," Archivum latinitatis medii aevi 3 (1927): 1–8.

---

[12] Weber, Les anciennes, lxviii.
[13] Carmignac, "Les Devanciers," 34–36.
[14] Fernández Marcos and Busto Saiz, El texto, xxxiv, xxxvi, xxxix.
[15] Fernández Marcos, "The Old Latin," 125.
[16] Fernández Marcos, "The Old Latin," 135.
[17] Fernández Marcos and Busto Saiz, El texto, xxxix, xl–xli.
[18] Brooke–McLean, *The Old Testament in Greek.
[19] Allen, Greek Chronicles.
[20] Allen, Greek Chronicles, 75–78.
[21] Fernández Marcos, "The Old Latin," 134.

Carmignac, J., "Les Devanciers de S. Jérôme: Une traduction latine de la Recension *kaige* dans le second livre des Chroniques," in *Mélanges Dominique Barthélemy: études bibliques offertes à l'occasion de son 60e anniversaire* (eds. P. Casetti, O. Keel, and A. Schenker; OBO 38; Göttingen: Vandenhoeck & Ruprecht, 1981), 31–50.

Diercks, G.F., *Luciferi Calaritani Opera quae supersunt* (CCSL 8; Turnhout: Brepols, 1978).

Fernández Marcos, N., "The Old Latin of Chronicles: Between the Greek and the Hebrew," *IX Congress for the International Organization for Septuagint and Cognate Studies, Cambridge 1995* (ed. B.A. Taylor; SBLSCS 45; Atlanta: Scholars Press, 1997), 123–36.

Fernández Marcos, N. and J.R. Busto Saiz, *El texto Antioqueno de la Biblia Griega*, Vol. 3: *1–2 Crónicas* (Textos y Estudios "Cardenal Cisneros" de la Biblia Poliglota Matritense 60; Madrid: Instituto de Filología, 1996).

Fischer, B., *Verzeichnis der Sigel für Handschriften und Kirchenschriftsteller* (VL 1; Freiburg i.B.: Herder, 1949).

Gryson, **Altlateinische Handschriften 1.*

Mercati, G., *Nuove note di letteratura biblica e cristiana antica* (Studi e testi 95; Vatican City: Biblioteca Apostolica Vaticana, 1941), 127–34.

Sabatier, **Bibliorum.*

Weber, R., *Les anciennes versions latines du deuxième livre des Paralipomènes* (Collectanea Biblica Latina 8; Rome: Abbaye Saint-Jérôme, 1945).

José Manuel Cañas Reíllo

20.4.2 Coptic Translations

20.4.2.1 Background

According to Takla's study, published in 2007,[1] 1–2 Chronicles were only attested in the Sahidic dialect in two verses, comprising less than 1 percent of these books. Although we know from an ostracon from the Theban area (seventh–eighth century C.E.) in Upper Egypt containing the catalogue of the monastic library of the Monastery of St. Eliah[2] that a probably complete version of 1–2 Chronicles had been part of that library, the few other surviving attestations are mostly pericopes in comparatively late liturgical manuscripts.

Another ostracon, quite likely of the same date, was found in the same area in the far better known and properly excavated Monastery of Epiphanius.[3] It partially preserves 1 Chr 18:16–17 (2 Kgdms 8:17–18) and 2 Chr 6:20 (3 Kgdms 6:20) in Sahidic Coptic. This ostracon is the oldest but unfortunately also the only witness of the text of Cop^{Sa}-1–2 Chr.[4] Thus, we can conjecture that 1–2 Chronicles had been translated completely into Sahidic Coptic but only those verses that were used in the liturgy of the Coptic Church survived in liturgical manuscripts whereas the biblical manuscripts themselves ceased to be copied and were lost. The Bohairic text of 1–2 Chronicles is only known from late (fourteenth century onwards) liturgical manuscripts.[5]

20.4.2.2 Extant Biblical Text
20.4.2.2.1 Sahidic Witnesses[6]
Besides the already mentioned ostracon from the Monastery of Epiphanius, only a few liturgical manuscripts transmit pericopes from 1–2 Chronicles:

---

[1] H. Takla, "An Introduction to the Coptic Old Testament," *Coptica* 6 (2007): 1–115 (74).

[2] R.-G. Coquin, "Le Catalogue de la Bibliothèque du Couvent de Saint Élie 'du Rocher' (Ostracon IFAO 13315)," *Bulletin de l'Institut Francais d'Archéologie Orientale* 75 (1975): 207–39; J. Horn, "Die Präsenz des Alten Testamentes in der ägyptischen christlichen Frömmigkeit: Aufgewiesen an zwei Werken der koptisch-sahidischen hagiographischen Literatur," in *Sprachen, Mythen, Mythizismen: Festschrift für Walter Beltz zum 65. Geburtstag* (eds. A. Drost-Abgarjan and J. Tubach; Hallesche Beiträge zur Orientwissenschaft 32; Halle: Martin-Luther-Universität Halle-Wittenberg, 2004), 358–59.

[3] W.E. Crum, *The Monastery of Epiphanius at Thebes*, Part 2: *Coptic Ostraca and Papyri* (New York: Metropolitan Museum of Art, 1926), 4 (no. 5), 156 (commentary), pl. xiii (no. 5 verso).

[4] Although Schüssler, "Zum Stand der koptischen Bibeltexte," 221, announced that the ostracon would be included in his catalogue: Schüssler, **Biblia Coptica* 2.1 as sa 151ex, it was finally left out and apparently will appear in another volume, and its designated number was assigned to another manuscript in **Biblia Coptica* 2.1.

[5] A. Vaschalde, "Ce qui a été publié des versions Coptes de la Bible: Deuxième Groupe: Textes Bohairiques I: Ancien Testament," *Mus* 43 (1930): 409–31 (417).

[6] See Schüssler, **Biblia Coptica*; all fragments mentioned here use the number assigned by him. However, all numbers above sa 260 remain unpublished to date; cf. Schüssler, "Zum Stand der koptischen Bibeltexte," 222–23.

Cop^{Sa 148L}	This lectionary (tenth–twelfth century) belonged to the Monastery of St. Shenoute ("White Monastery") near Sohag. Only two pages have survived, containing only passages from the Old Testament,[7] i.e., 1 Chr 17:14–15 (accompanied by Jer 3:17).
Cop^{Sa 380lit}	This Greek-Coptic *Hermeneiai* manuscript from the St. Michael Monastery in the Fayyum[8] is dated by its colophon to 894–895 or 897–898 C.E. It includes Odes 1–39 (→ 11.13.2.5). Ode 12 displays a text resembling 2 Chr 33:12–13, 18–19.
Cop^{Sa 384L}	This lectionary also comes from the Monastery of St. Shenoute ("White Monastery") near Sohag (eleventh century). It contains only passages from the Old Testament,[9] i.e., 2 Chr 5:14; 2 Chr 6:3–8; 2 Chr 34:29–31.

20.4.2.2.2 Bohairic Witnesses

There is considerably more extant text of Cop^{Boh}-1–2 Chr than of Cop^{Sa}-1–2 Chr. Nevertheless, the extant text amounts to only a few verses preserved again in liturgical manuscripts from the Middle Ages or later. These readings taken from 1–2 Chronicles were included in the liturgy for the consecration of a new church and its altar. Probably the oldest witness of Cop^{Boh}-1–2 Chr is a Coptic-Arabic manuscript dated to 1307 (→ 20.4.8).[10]

The following verses in Cop^{Boh}-1–2 Chr were used in the service:[11] 1 Chr 15:2–16:37;[12] 1 Chr 28:22–29:22;[13] 2 Chr 3:1–6:11;[14] 2 Chr 6:12–7:16.[15]

20.4.2.3 Translation Character and Text-Critical Value

Because there are almost no parallel texts, the few surviving verses of Cop-1–2 Chr do not even allow for a comparison of the Sahidic and Bohairic versions. Therefore, it is difficult to reach conclusions about the inner-Coptic textual history of Chronicles. Furthermore, no attempt has been made so far to compare the Bohairic or the few extant Sahidic passages with the Greek text of Chronicles (→ 20.3.1). Therefore, nothing can be said about the translation character or the text-critical value of the Coptic versions of 1–2 Chronicles.

Schüssler, K., "Zum Stand der koptischen Bibeltexte," in *Coptic Studies on the Threshold of a New Millennium: Proceedings of the Seventh International Congress of Coptic Studies, Leiden, 27 August–2 September 2000* (2 vols.; eds. M. Immerzeel and J. van der Vliet; OLA 133; Leuven: Peeters, 2004), 1.221–35.

Frank Feder

20.4.3 Ethiopic Translation(s)

20.4.3.1 Title and Place in the Manuscripts

The basic title of the Ethiopic books of Chronicles is መጽሐፈ ሕፀጓን "book of the things wanting" = LXX Παραλειπομενων "Supplements," modified by the designation for "first" (ቀዳማዊ) or "second" (ካልዕ). Invariably, 1 Chronicles and 2 Chronicles appear together in the manuscript tradition, but they can share space in manuscripts with a wide variety of books and in a variety of relations. In about forty percent of the manuscripts they are directly preceded by 1–4 Kingdoms (→ 3–5.2.3.3),

---

[7] Schüssler, *Biblia Coptica* 2.1, 79–81; Schüssler, "Zum Stand der koptischen Bibeltexte," 221.

[8] Today in the Morgan Library and Museum, New York, manuscript M 574.

[9] The extant folia of the manuscripts are kept in London (British Library, Or. 3579A [7] f. 1–13) and in Vienna (Nationalbibliothek, Papyrussammlung, K 9685–9690); cf. Feder, *Biblia Sahidica*, 45 (L 80). For the 2 Chronicles readings, cf. W. Till, *Koptische Pergamente Theologischen Inhalts I* (Mitteilungen aus der Papyrussammlung der Nationalbibliothek in Wien, Papyrus Erzherzog Rainer N.S. 2; Vienna: Österreichische Staatsdruckerei, 1934), xiv, xi, and 13–15.

[10] G. Horner, *Service for the Consecration of a Church and Altar According to the Coptic Rite* (London: Harrison and Sons, 1902), 2–3 (synopsis of the lections).

[11] Vaschalde, "Ce qui a été publié des versions Coptes de la Bible," 417, partially quoted the verses and pages in Horner's edition incorrectly.

[12] Horner, *Service for the Consecration of a Church*, 166–77.

[13] Horner, *Service for the Consecration of a Church*, 183–200.

[14] Horner, *Service for the Consecration of a Church*, 201–21.

[15] Horner, *Service for the Consecration of a Church*, 228–47.

often separated from them by the lists of the kings and prophets of Israel and Judah. However, about a third of the manuscripts that contain Chronicles begin with Chronicles, and when they do the manuscripts never contain the books of Kingdoms. This may suggest that these volumes functioned as the second or third volume in sets that contained the Octateuch (→ 2.5.3) and Kingdoms (→ 3–5.2.3.3) in a prior volume or volumes. What varies most is what follows Chronicles in the manuscripts. In a sample of eighteen manuscripts containing Chronicles, in five cases they were followed by Eth-2 Ezra (= 1 Esdras) and Eth-3 Ezra (= Ezra/Nehemiah → 19.4.3), twice by Proverbs (→ 12.4.3) and Ecclesiastes (→ 13–17.2.3.3), twice by 1–3 Maccabees (→ 11.10), twice by the Minor Prophets (→ 6–9.2.3.4), and once each by *Jubilees* (→ 11.8.6), Jeremiah (→ 6–9.2.3.2), Isaiah (→ 6–9.2.3.1), Daniel (→ 18.4.3), Tobit (→ 11.14.9), Susanna (→ 11.3.5), and (in Eth[BN 5]) they are followed by the *Kebra Negast*.

20.4.3.2 Grébaut's Edition

The only published edition of Eth-Chr is that produced by Grébaut in 1932 (→ 1.4.3.5).[1] The task had originally been assigned to Francisco Maria Esteves Pereira, but he died before the work could be completed. Grébaut took over the task but says he was unable to benefit very much from the work already performed by Esteves Pereira. The deficiencies of Grébaut's edition are widely known. Grébaut listed eight manuscripts known at the time of publication of his edition, but he was able to make use of only two, Eth[BN 5, BN Abb 35]. His introduction covers only a physical description of the manuscripts, including their paleography and orthography. He provides no systematic conclusions about the history of the Ethiopic text, except to say that his study shows "que la traduction éthiopienne a été faite sur un texte grec autre que le texte reçu des Septante."[2] He goes on to suggest that access to more manuscripts, particularly more from Ethiopia, could make it possible not only to produce a critical text of Chronicles but also "à découvrir l' original grec suivi par le traducteur éthiopien."[3]

20.4.3.3 Clear's Thesis

Clear's 1971 thesis at the University of Toronto[4] is limited to 2 Chronicles and made use of nine European manuscripts, including the two used by Grébaut. Their ages vary, with one from the fifteenth century, one from the seventeenth century, one from the eighteenth to nineteenth century and all the rest from the eighteenth century. Right at the outset, Clear states that "there is no evidence in the manuscripts of more than one Ethiopic translation of II Chron[icles]. All the manuscripts belong to a common textual tradition."[5] But they do, he says, fall into two families. The oldest and the youngest (Clear's manuscripts A and B) bear witness to the Old Ethiopic (→ 1.4.3.7.3). Oddly, Clear's thesis does not provide a detailed characterization of the Old Ethiopic. But it is obvious that the single primary characteristic of the Old Ethiopic is its dependence on the LXX form of the text (→ 20.3.1) over against MT (→ 20.2.2), including the inclusion of the Prayer of Manasseh (→ 11.11.6) in the text of 2 Chr 33:13.

The rest of Clear's manuscripts (C–H) bear witness to a revision of the Old Ethiopic, with two of these (D and F) showing even further revision in one direction and two (E and H) showing further revision in another direction. The revisers of the Old Ethiopic gave attention to matters of style, such as substitution of synonyms,[6] interchanges of prepositions,[7] interchange of enclitic and other particles,[8] variations of proper names,[9] changes of verb forms,[10] changes in suffixes,[11] changes between singular, or collective, and plural forms,[12] changes in

---

[1] Grébaut (ed.), *Les Paralipomènes*.
[2] Grébaut (ed.), *Les Paralipomènes*, xxx.
[3] Grébaut (ed.), *Les Paralipomènes*, xxx.
[4] Clear, "The Ethiopic Version of II Chronicles."
[5] Clear, "The Ethiopic Version of II Chronicles," 67.
[6] Clear, "The Ethiopic Version of II Chronicles," 73–74.
[7] Clear, "The Ethiopic Version of II Chronicles," 75.
[8] Clear, "The Ethiopic Version of II Chronicles," 76–77.
[9] Clear, "The Ethiopic Version of II Chronicles," 78–80.
[10] Clear, "The Ethiopic Version of II Chronicles," 80–81.
[11] Clear, "The Ethiopic Version of II Chronicles," 81–83.
[12] Clear, "The Ethiopic Version of II Chronicles," 83.

case and orthography,[13] and small additions to the text, as in 2 Chr 4:22; 9:8, 24; 29:5, 23; 32:18, 23; 35:16, 19c, and 25, which "serve the purpose of making the meaning more explicit and or forestalling possible misinterpretations."[14] But there are "well over two hundred" revisions in 2 Chronicles alone that reflect correction toward LXX (→ 20.3.1).[15] More specifically, these revisions reflect dependence on the Lucianic (→ 20.3.6) or, most likely, the proto-Lucianic text type (→ 20.3.1) of the Greek.[16] Many of these revisions have the appearance of revision toward MT (→ 20.2.2), but it is clear that these are due not to any direct contact with MT. Instead, Clear believes that they originate in the proto-Lucianic text whose readings often reflect revision toward MT.[17] In Clear's view, "there is little evidence for an independent revision based on the MT."[18] Further, Clear finds only three instances of agreement that would suggest it were following the Syriac, in contrast to "the overwhelming number of corrections towards LXX."[19]

Clear's identification of Lucianic readings in 2 Chronicles appears to be generally correct, although there are not nearly as many readings as he claims. Many of the examples of agreement he gives are accidental (i.e., influence from surrounding context) or due to Ethiopian translation practice (addition of conjunctions, addition of pronominal suffixes, provision of prepositions for nouns in the oblique cases, and transpositions).

Clear characterizes the text in his manuscript G as "the latest stage in the manuscript tradition."[20] But this cannot be accurate since none of his witnesses except his manuscript B – which is itself a witness to the Old Ethiopic – come from a time later than the eighteenth century. The modern Textus Receptus (→ 1.4.3.7.6) will not have yet emerged at that point in the manuscript tradition.

At least two issues remain unresolved from Clear's study. His manuscript evidence seems too late and too narrow to provide any definitive conclusions about the existence and character of either a Scholars Recension or certainly of a modern Textus Receptus. With regard to the former, we are left to wonder whether the eighteenth-century readings that suggest contact with MT are simply those already resident in the Lucianic text type that constituted the *Vorlage* of the Revised Old Ethiopic. However, are there sufficient new readings from around the eighteenth century that would establish a further stage in the development of the Ethiopic text based on a new influx of readings in some way dependent on MT? And with regard to the modern Textus Receptus, there is every reason to believe that 1 and 2 Chronicles received the same sort of attention in the last century and a half that has marked the textual history of the rest of the books of the Ethiopic canon. Initial surveys indicate that there is a modern Textus Receptus of Chronicles. But there is, as yet, no detailed analysis of its character.

Finally, it is assumed, though unproven, that Clear's conclusions about Eth-2 Chr apply equally to Eth-1 Chr. Studies in the future will need to establish whether or not this is the case.

Bausi, A., "Historical Books, Biblical," in *EAE 2:39–40.
Clear, J.W., "The Ethiopic Version of II Chronicles" (PhD diss., University of Toronto, 1971).
Clear, J.W., "A List of Corrections for Sylvain Grébaut's Edition of Ethiopic II Chronicles," *Mus* 85 (1972): 259–68.
Clear, J.W., "A List of Corrections for Sylvain Grébaut's Edition of Ethiopic I Chronicles," *Mus* 87 (1974): 207–21.
Grébaut, S. (ed.), *Les Paralipomènes: Livres I et II version éthiopiene* (PO 23.4; Paris: Firmin-Didot et Cie., 1932).

Steve Delamarter

---

[13] Clear, "The Ethiopic Version of II Chronicles," 83–84.
[14] Clear, "The Ethiopic Version of II Chronicles," 84–87, the quotation is on p. 87.
[15] Clear, "The Ethiopic Version of II Chronicles," 92–94, the quotation is on p. 94.
[16] Clear, "The Ethiopic Version of II Chronicles," 94–101.
[17] Clear, "The Ethiopic Version of II Chronicles," 102–11 and 41–42 where Clear provides a list of variants in the Greek manuscripts that make it clear that "the most common variants [in the Lucianic manuscripts] are alterations to bring the text into closer conformity with MT" (41).
[18] Clear, "The Ethiopic Version of II Chronicles," 110.
[19] Clear, "The Ethiopic Version of II Chronicles," 111.
[20] Clear, "The Ethiopic Version of II Chronicles," 151.

20.4.4 Late Syriac Translations

20.4.4.1 Textual Witnesses

Andreas Masius (1514–1573), one of the earlier European scholars to have taken a serious interest in Syriac language and literature,[1] made extensive use in his writings of a now-lost manuscript of unknown provenance and origin that almost certainly contained Chronicles along with other books of the Syro-Hexapla. It has been demonstrated[2] that this lost witness was closely related to the Ambrosian Codex of the Syro-Hexapla (C 313 inf.), dating to the eighth or ninth century C.E. and published photolithographically by Ceriani in 1874.[3]

These two witnesses, when complete, probably contained together the entire text of the Syro-Hexapla (→ 1.4.5), but as concerns 1–2 Chronicles, one of the two is completely lost and the other lacks these books. That Masius' manuscript certainly contained Chronicles is demonstrated by the owner's own testimony. When he used it to edit Joshua in his *Josuae Historia*, Masius said that it contained, "Praeterea Paralipomena" "also [the books of] Chronicles."[4] The other known manuscripts of the Syro-Hexaplaric texts in direct transmission, that is to say, in witnesses containing continuous texts of the biblical books yield nothing for Chronicles. We are entirely dependent on indirect transmission (→ 21.9), that is, where the Syro-Hexapla texts are used for illustrative or explanatory purposes; in other words, our knowledge of these books is frustratingly fragmentary.

In 1909, Gwynn published Syro-Hexaplaric material that concerns Chronicles drawn from manuscript London BL Add. 12.168, a Nitrian manuscript of the same age as the Ambrosian Codex that conjugates scriptural excerpts with patristic commentaries to form an exegetic chain or compilation.[5] Wright dates the compilation itself, on internal evidence, to the second half of the seventh century C.E., in other words only a few decades after the composition of Paul of Tella's translation of the LXX column.[6] Baars was able to supplement the evidence for 2 Chronicles, as well as for other books, in 1968,[7] drawing, for the former, essentially on manuscript London BL Add. 17.195.[8]

We can summarise the situation of our total current knowledge of the textual witnesses to the Syro-Hexaplaric version of Chronicles as follows:

	BL Add. 12.168	BL Add. 17.195	Cambridge UL Add. 2023[9]
1 Chr	1:1–4, 17, 24–28, 34		
	2:1–17		
	3:1–20		
	6:1–15[5:27–41], 31–49		
	23:14–17		
2 Chr		15:8–15	
		17:3, 7–9	
		18:31	
		19:1–3	19:1–2[10]
		24:6–11	
		25:5–12	
	26:16–21		
	29:30–30:5		
	30:13–20		
	32:2–4, 33		
	33:1–16		
	35:20–25		

---

[1] L. Van Rompay, "Masius, Andreas," in *Gorgias Encyclopedic Dictionary of the Syriac Heritage* (eds. S.P. Brock et al.; Piscataway: Gorgias Press, 2011), 275–76.

[2] Baars, *New Syro-Hexaplaric Texts*, 4.

[3] A.M. Ceriani, *Codex Syro-Hexaplaris Ambrosianus photolithographice editus* (Monumenta sacra et profana 7; Milan: Ambrosian Library, 1874).

[4] Quoted according to Gwynn, *Remnants*, xi.

[5] Gwynn, *Remnants*, xvi–xviii, 5–18.

[6] W. Wright, *Catalogue of the Syriac Manuscripts in the British Museum*, Vol. 2 (London: British Museum, 1871), 904–08.

[7] Baars, *New Syro-Hexaplaric Texts*.

[8] Wright, *Catalogue* 2, 914–15.

[9] W. Wright and S.A. Cook, *A Catalogue of the Syriac Manuscripts in the Library of the University of Cambridge* (Vol. 2; Cambridge: Cambridge University Press, 1901), 600–28.

[10] The variants of this manuscript are indicated by Baars, *New Syro-Hexaplaric Texts*, 120.

This state of affairs, with only one single passage attested in more than one witness, makes any hope of preparing a true critical edition of the Syriac fragments illusory, though both Gwynn and Baars have carefully compared the Syriac with the Greek LXX texts in their editions.

20.4.4.2 Form and Characteristics of the Text

As Gwynn had so very judiciously noted in his edition of the relevant sections of manuscript BL 12.168,[11] the compiler was not working at random, but had selected precisely passages proper to Chronicles that have no parallels in 1–4 Kingdoms. This observation is equally true of the other principal witness that also has selected passages (though different ones) absent from Kingdoms.[12] It is as if the compilers had, with sound exegetic insight, taken to heart the Greek title of Chronicles, τὰ Παραλειπόμενα "the things left aside," in order to provide texts for the material unavailable in the earlier historical books. This view of the Chronicles texts is borne out by the fact that the very designation of the books that the compilers use to introduce their quotations is a close transposition of the LXX title, ܣܡܝܬܐ "the missing things," emphasizing their essentially auxiliary nature. Why did they prefer using the Syro-Hexapla texts to that end rather than those of the Peshitta (→ 1.3.4), which they use elsewhere for other books? The explanation could be codicological (no exemplars of s-Chr would have been available to them)[13] or exegetical as s-Chr is a quirky translation with a chequered reception history (see → 20.3.4), which may have pleaded in favour of their having recourse to the LXX text, considered as being more reliable.

The compilers place Chronicles after Kingdoms, following the order of LXX, which is similar in this respect to the older Peshitta manuscripts.[14] However, its title and presentation are at variance with the latter. While the Peshitta in its oldest form only reckons one book of Chronicles,[15] the Syro-Hexapla counts two, following LXX, this being clearly indicated by the introductory formulae of the pericopes in the compilations that, in certain cases, say they are taken ܡܢ ܟܬܒܐ ܩܕܡܝܐ ܕܣܡܝܬܐ "from the first book of Chronicles" or ܡܢ ܟܬܒܐ ܕܬܪܝܢ ܕܣܡܝܬܐ "from the second book of Chronicles." As to the title of the books, it is also at complete variance with the Peshitta, which only and always uses the Hebrew designation transliterated into Syriac ܕܒܪܝܡܝܢ "events of the days" (see → 20.3.4).

Indications that we are dealing with extracts from Syh-Chr are given by some of their rubrics that state that they are ܡܢ ܡܦܩܬܐ ܕܫܒܥܝܢ "From the edition of the Seventy," ܡܢ ܡܫܠܡܢܘܬܐ ܕܫܒܥܝܢ "From the version of the Seventy" or simply ܕܫܒܥܝܢ, "of the Seventy".

As can be observed in the other Syro-Hexaplaric texts, the translation of Chronicles is no exception in being at pains to render the Greek as literally as possible, doing violence if necessary to Syriac idiom. Here are a few examples to be found in these books: the almost systematic use of separate possessive pronouns (with ܕܝܠ) rather than pronominal suffixes; there are certain cases where a Greek preposition is mechanically rendered by its Syriac equivalent contrary to normal use (2 Chr 35:25 ܟܬܒܝܢ ܥܠ ܐܘܠܝܬܐ "[they are written] *on* the Lamentations" representing γέγραπται ἐπὶ τῶν θρήνων "[they are written] in the Lamentations," the preposition ܥܠ for ἐπί whereas the verb normally requires the preposition ܒ); the creation of Syriac calques, only really intelligible if referred to the Greek substratum (2 Chr 24:7 ܠܐ ܢܡܘܣܝܬܐ "not lawful" for ἄνομος, "lawless"). It is, of course, the very literal nature of the translation that renders

---

[11] Gwynn, *Remnants*, xvii.

[12] With the exception of 2 Chr 18:31 = 3 Kgdms 22:32.

[13] Though it is an argument *ex silentio*, we can note that there are few Peshitta manuscripts for Chronicles from the seventh century C.E.; see D. Phillips "The Reception of Peshitta Chronicles: Some Elements for Investigation," in *The Peshitta: Its Use in Literature and Liturgy: Papers Read at the Third Peshitta Symposium* (ed. B. ter Haar Romeny; Monographs of the Peshitta Institute Leiden 15; Leiden: Brill, 2006), 260–65.

[14] Gwynn, *Remnants*, xx, relying on the state of knowledge of Syriac biblical manuscripts at his time, is wrong in saying that the Peshitta manuscripts relegate Chronicles to the "latter part of the Old Testament"; see Phillips, "The Reception," 260–65.

[15] Phillips, "The Reception," 267–68.

it invaluable as a witness to the Hexaplaric LXX. However, it would be incorrect to say that the translation is simply and always a purely slavish transposition of the Greek original; the Hexaplaric text in its Syriac dress was nonetheless intelligible to its readers, otherwise it would never have been transmitted. We even occasionally find worthy attempts to give a literary character to the translation, for example, in 1 Chr 2:7 ܥܟܪ ܡܕܘܕܢܐ ܕܐܝܣܪܐܝܠ "Achar, the troubler of Israel" where the paronomasia on the Semitic name Achar, "troubler" has been captured, albeit with a rare secondary formation (ܡܕܘܕܢܐ, "troubler") rather than the more common ܥܘܟܪܐ, "hindrance, trouble" used by the Peshitta.[16]

Baars, W., *New Syro-Hexaplaric Texts: Edited, Commented upon and Compared with the Septuagint* (Leiden: Brill, 1968).

Gwynn, J., *Remnants of the Later Syriac Versions of the Bible*, Part 2: *Old Testament* (Text and Translation Society Publications 6; London: Williams and Norgate, 1909; repr. Amsterdam: Philo Press, 1973).

David Phillips

20.4.5 Armenian Translations

20.4.5.1 Background

Investigation of the Armenian version of Chronicles has demonstrated that it represents two distinct strata, the original translation (Arm 1), that derives from the early fifth century C.E., and a later independent rendering (Arm 2), dated to the 430s. The former has been collated according to the Xalatʻeancʻ edition of 1899,[1] while the base text for the latter is the Zohrapian edition of 1805.[2] The Old Greek in turn was consulted in the corresponding volume in the Cambridge LXX,[3] edited by Brooke and McLean, and in Rahlfs' provisional edition of 1935.[4]

---

[16] Gwynn, *Remnants*, 69.
[1] Xalatʻeancʻ, *Books of Chronicles*.
[2] Zohrapian, **Scriptures*.
[3] Brooke–McLean–Thackeray, **The Old Testament in Greek*.
[4] Rahlfs, **Septuaginta*.

20.4.5.2 Translation Character

Despite earlier scholarly opinion that argued for the Peshitta (→ 1.3.4; → 20.3.4) or another Semitic version as the parent text of Arm 1, it has been shown that the translation was effected from a Greek source text (→ 20.3.1).[5] A cogent illustration of this dependency is provided by the Hebrew term "Judah," which is retained in Syriac but differentiated in Greek, followed by Armenian, to distinguish the region Judaea from the tribe, as at 2 Chr 31:1: ἐν πόλεσιν Ἰουδα ... ἀπὸ πάσης γῆς Ἰουδαίας "in the cities of Judah ... from the whole land of Judaea," which the Armenian renders exactly as ի քաղաքս Յուդայ ... յամենայն երկրէն Հրէաստանի "in the cities of Judah ... from the whole land of Judaea." At the same time, a limited number of agreements with the Peshitta and the Targum (→ 20.3.3) – from which the former putatively derives – suggests that the translator of Arm 1 had access to such interpretative traditions to finesse his renderings.

According to the general norm for the version, Arm 2 in Chronicles has also been rendered from Greek (→ 20.3.1), as exemplified by the close affinity between the two formulations at 1 Chr 10:1 describing the battle of Mt. Gilboa: καὶ ἀλλόφυλοι ἐπολέμησαν πρὸς Ἰσραηλ καὶ ἔφυγον ἀπὸ προσώπου ἀλλοφύλων "and the Philistines warred against Israel and they (Israel) fled from the face of the Philistines," where Arm 2 reads եւ այլազգիքն պատերազմեցան ընդ Իսրայէլի եւ փախեան յերեսացն այլազգեացն, a rendering that mirrors the Greek in most respects.

The enormous difference between the two strata on several levels is immediately apparent even in straightforward contexts, such as in representing Saul's command to his armor-bearer, a little later into the battle, at 1 Chr 10:4. There the Old Greek (= Peshitta = MT; → 20.3.1; → 20.3.4; → 20.2.2) reads σπάσαι τὴν ῥομφαίαν σου καὶ ἐκκέντισόν με "draw your sword and strike me," which is translated literally by Arm 2 as Ձգեա զսուր քո եւ խոցեա զիս "draw your sword and wound me." However, the

---

[5] For an overview of the discussion, see Cowe, "Armenian Versions of Chronicles," 62–73.

Arm 1 version differs radically in its envisaging of the scene depicted and in the lexicon utilized, rendering the phrase առ ի վեր զսուսեր քո եւ սպան զիս "raise your flat sword and kill me." The terminology for wielding the sword is idiomatic and attested by near-contemporary Armenian authors, while the king's next remark about preventing the enemy from making sport with him patently implies he is contemplating death and is requesting his servant to bring this about. Consequently, the Arm 1 rendering is semantically much more penetrating in terms of the logic of the narrative.

20.4.5.3 Reconstruction of the Parent Text of Arm-Chr

That Arm 1 derives from a Lucianic Greek text (→ 1.3.1.2; → 20.3.6) is attested by the version's affinities with the distinctively Antiochene attempt to strive for clarity and stylistic smoothness, even in accommodations to MT (→ 20.2.2). Thus, where the author interrupts his catalogue of David's offspring at 1 Chr 3:4 to discuss the length of his reign – a formulation followed by the majority of the Greek witnesses – the Lucianic rephrases it, highlighting the subject by name, so καὶ ἐβασίλευσε Δαυὶδ ἐν Χεβρὼν ἑπτὰ ἔτη καὶ μῆνας ἕξ "and David reigned in Hebron for seven years and six months," which is reproduced exactly by Arm 1 as եւ թագաւորեաց Դաւիթ ի Քեբրովն եւթն ամ եւ վեց ամիս. Similarly, at 1 Chr 4:22, Arm 1's բայց բանքն հին են եւ Դաբիր եւ Նատովկիմ "these words are old, both Dabir and Natovkim" evinces a typically Lucianic doublet involving both the translation and transliteration of the underlying Hebrew, thus οἱ δὲ λόγοι παλαιοί εἰσι καὶ Δεβεὶρ καὶ Ναθουκείμ, where the translated words are οἱ δὲ λόγοι παλαιοί εἰσι "these words are old" and the transliteration is καὶ Δεβεὶρ καὶ Ναθουκείμ, "both Debeir and Nathukeim."[6]

Meanwhile, the Arm 2 parent text possessed a Hexaplaric complexion (→ 20.3.5; → 1.3.1.2.7), as in several other Old Testament books.[7] This is substantiated by readings like ի գիրս օրինացն Մովսիսի "in the book of the law of Moses" at 2 Chr 35:12, which reflects the explanatory addition (≠ MT) + νομου "of the law," read by Origenic witnesses over against the Old Greek reading ἐν βιβλίῳ Μωυσῆ "in the book of Moses." Within this context, Arm 2 demonstrates a particular affinity with the minuscule h, as, for example, at 2 Chr 35:6, where it affords sole support for the latter's word order ἑτοιμάσατε τὰ ἅγια "prepare the holy things" – relating to King Josiah's celebration of the Passover – in reading պատրաստեցէք զսրբութիւնս.

20.4.5.4 Translation Technique

The Arm 1 translation unit is set at the phrase length, thus valorizing the idiomatic representation of the semantic content, which thereby permits greater flexibility in areas of morphology, syntax, and word order. These elements include expressing pronoun subjects and objects, concretizing the temporal relations between actions, and cases of doublet translation, which accord with early Armenian usage. The latter feature is illustrated at 2 Chr 35:16, where the Old Greek κατὰ τὴν ἐντολὴν τοῦ βασιλέως "according to the king's command" is rendered as ըստ պատուիրանի հրամանի արքային, "according to the command of the order of the king," with which we might compare the formulation by the indigenous fifth-century writer P'awstos, ըստ հրամանի պատուիրանին տեառն իւրոյ "according to the order of the command of his lord."[8]

Arm 2, in contrast, is isomorphic: it translates at the word level, with great attention paid to encoding morphological detail as closely as possible. Exceptions to this pattern are motivated by established convention, such as numerical differences in expressing entirety where, as at 1 Chr 10:11, Greek idiom prefers the plural format ἅπαντα ἅ "all those which …," whereas Armenian manifests a predilection for the singular, զոր ինչ, "whatever …"

Attention to Context

Translation at the phrase length affords Arm 1 the opportunity to select the equivalent most semanti-

---

[6] For a series of unique Arm 1 agreements with Lucianic manuscript b, see Cowe, "Armenian Versions of Chronicles," 72.

[7] See Cowe, "The Bible in Armenian," 155–57.

[8] See Malxaseanc', *P'awstos Buzand*, 106.

cally appropriate in the context; this leads to significant lexical variation. A good example is provided by the disjunction between Old Greek and Arm 1 in depicting the death of Saul and his armor-bearer in 1 Chr 10:4. Though the Greek portrays the king's act as ἐπέπεσεν ἐπ᾽ αὐτήν "he fell upon it," i.e., his sword, Arm 1 renders it as զիւրովի չոգաւ "he committed suicide," while his assistant's reaction is portrayed as ἐπέπεσε καίγε αὐτὸς ἐπὶ τὴν ῥομφαίαν αὐτοῦ "he too fell upon his sword," which, in turn, is rendered as եւ եւ ինքն ընդ սուր իւր "he too devoted himself to his sword."

Granted Arm 2's focus on morphological and syntactical formalism, it manifests a high degree of stereotyping – yet never systematically so – in nouns and verbs, though much less in phenomena like prepositions, where the idiom diverges most. Nevertheless, nuanced renderings are also found, such as deviation from the standard rendering of οἶκος "house" by տուն in Josiah's instructions to the priests about serving in the temple, στῆτε ἐν τῷ οἴκῳ "stand in the house" at 2 Chr 35:5, where the Armenian reads կացէք ի տաճարիդ "stand in the temple."

20.4.5.5 Text-Critical Value: Omissions and Additions

Minuses in Arm 1 are rare and predictable. They occur where the excised element is obvious from the surrounding context, in cases of condensation of formulation to reduce unnecessary verbiage, and in situations where Hebrew usage dictates syntactical repetitions such as polysyndeton, which are encoded in the isomorphic Greek translation but are excluded by Arm 1 as unsuited to its indigenous idiom. Thus, at 1 Chr 10:2, the phrase ὀπίσω Σαοὺλ καὶ ὀπίσω υἱῶν αὐτοῦ "after Saul and after his sons" is rendered as զհետ ... Շաուղի եւ որդւոց նորա "after Saul and his sons." Similarly, pluses normally function to clarify uncertainties in the Old Greek.

As one might expect, Arm 2's predilection for a close rendering of the Greek morphological structure lends itself to fairly full quantitative representation. For example, the minor pluses the stratum exhibits are constrained by Armenian norms, as in the rendering of Greek articulated phrases by a relative clause, e.g., at 2 Chr 35:17, where the expression οἱ εὑρεθέντες "those being found" is represented as որք գտան անդ "those who were found there."

20.4.5.6 Relevance for Exegesis

As in other portions of the Bible, it is a pronounced characteristic of Arm-Chr to distinguish the terminology that denotes licit and illicit cultic practice, though such a classification is not found in MT (→ 20.2.2) and Old Greek (→ 20.3.1). Additionally, under Antiochene influence, Arm 1 exegesis reflects a synoptic approach to parallel passages. Thus, in describing the Philistines' despoiling of Saul's corpse at 1 Chr 10:9, the phrase ἔλαβον τὴν κεφαλὴν αὐτοῦ ... καὶ ἀπέστειλαν "they took his head ... and sent" is reproduced as հատին զգլուխ նորա եւ առաքեցին "they cut off his head and sent," where the reference to decapitation derives from the Lucianic text at 1 Kgdms 31:9. Likewise, Josiah's command to his servants at 2 Chr 35:23, ἐξαγάγετέ με "take me away," emerges as հանէք զիս ի տեղւոյդ պատերազմէ "remove me from the place of war," where the precise expression is impacted by the parallel at 1 Esd 1:28(30), ἀποστήσατέ με ἀπὸ τῆς μάχης "take me away from the fight."

20.4.5.7 Text-Critical Value of Arm-Chr for LXX-Chr

The relative consistency applied by the translators of the two strata of Arm-Chr normally permits us to reconstruct their parent text with reasonable assurance. The identification of their affinities with the small close-knit group of Lucianic manuscripts (→ 20.3.6), and minuscule *h* respectively, will greatly assist in delineating the version's witness to the Old Greek with increased precision.

20.4.5.8 Readings from "the Three"

On two occasions, the version preserves marginal readings, at 2 Chr 23:17 and 36:3.[9]

---

[9] For details, see Cox, *Aquila, Symmachus and Theodotion*, 315.

Allen, L.C., *The Greek Chronicles: The Relation of the Septuagint of I and II Chronicles to the Masoretic Text* (2 vols.; VTSup 25, 27; Leiden: Brill, 1974).

Brooke–McLean–Thackeray, **The Old Testament in Greek*, Vol. 1, Part 3: *I and II Chronicles*.

Cowe, S.P., "The Two Armenian Versions of Chronicles: Their Origin and Translation Technique," *Revue des Études Arméniennes* 22 (1990–1991): 53–96.

Cowe, S.P., "La versión armenia," in *El texto antioqueno de la Biblia griega*, Vol. 3: *1–2 Crónicas* (eds. N. Fernández Marcos and J.R. Busto Saiz; Textos y estudios "Cardenal Cisneros" 60; Madrid: Consejo Superior de Investigaciones Científicas, 1996), xlviii–lv.

Cowe, S.P., "The Bible in Armenian," in *The New Cambridge History of the Bible*, Vol. 2: *From 600 to 1450* (eds. R. Marsden and E.A. Matter; Cambridge: Cambridge University Press, 2012), 143–61.

Cox, C.E., *Aquila, Symmachus and Theodotion in Armenia* (SBLSCS 42; Atlanta: Scholars Press, 1996).

Malxaseanc', S. (ed.), *P'awstos Buzand; Patmut'iwn Hayoc'* (*P'awstos Buzand: History of the Armenians*) (St. Petersburg: Imperial Academy of Sciences, 1883).

Rahlfs, **Septuaginta*.

Xalat'eanc', G., *Girk' mnac'ordac' ěst hnagoyn hay t'argmanut'ean* (*The Books of Chronicles according to the Oldest Armenian Translation*) (Moscow: Tparan Vaṙē Gatc'uk, 1899).

Zohrapian, **Scriptures*.

Peter Cowe

20.4.6 Georgian Translations

20.4.6.1 Earliest Georgian Translation of 1–2 Chronicles

The earliest Old Georgian translation of 1–2 Chronicles (hereafter: Georg-1–2 Chr 1, or, separately, Georg-1 Chr 1 and Georg-2 Chr 1) survives in a few manuscripts whose paleographic dates range from the tenth up to the seventeenth or eighteenth centuries. This tradition splits into two different redactions, which may conventionally be labeled as Georg-1–2 Chr 1a and Georg-1–2 Chr 1b.

20.4.6.1.1 Sources

Six testimonies of Georg-1–2 Chr 1 have hitherto been traced. On the one hand, we have two fragmentary sources. The first is represented by palimpsest Georg^X (= Wien Österreichische Nationalbibliothek, geo. 2, tenth-century post-Khanmeti section)[1] and the second by two twelfth-century folios, used as protective sheets in the book cover of an Armenian manuscript (Yerevan, Matenadaran 719 = Georg^{Yer}).[2] On the other hand, a number of later codices have come down to us: Georg^D (Tbilisi, National Centre of Manuscripts H-885, seventeenth century), Georg^F (= Tbilisi, National Centre of Manuscripts A-646, sixteenth century), Georg^I (= Tbilisi, National Centre of Manuscripts A-570, fifteenth century), and Georg^s (= Tbilisi, National Centre of Manuscripts A-51, seventeenth or eighteenth century). A full description of the latter four manuscripts can be found in the first volume of the critical edition of the Old Georgian Octateuch.[3]

20.4.6.1.2 Redactions

The earliest redaction of the Old Georgian translation of 1–2 Chronicles (Georg-1–2 Chr 1a) is to be found in manuscripts Georg$^{X, D, F, I, Yer}$, while the youngest (Georg-1–2 Chr 1b) is preserved only in Georg^s. The date of the former is unknown, but it seems very likely that it belongs to the earliest corpus of the Georgian translations of the Scriptures (→ 1.4.8.3.1). As far as the second is concerned (Georg-1–2 Chr 1b), its origin can be placed safely in the late seventeenth century. This redaction is the result of the revision of Georg-1–2 Chr 1a, undertaken on the basis of the printed Armenian Bible (→ 20.4.5) of 1666 (Oskan's edition).[4] It was carried out by the eminent Georgian Biblical scholar and philologist Sulkhan Orbeliani (Sulxan-Saba Orbeliani, 1658–1725: → 1.4.8.3.3).

20.4.6.1.3 Editions

An edition of Georg-1–2 Chr 1a is still lacking. Only the fragments contained in Georg^X and Georg^{Yer} have been published.[5] As far as the former are

---

[1] Gippert, Sarjveladze, and Kajaia, *The Old Georgian Palimpsest*, ms viii (plates 8:1–42). On the so-called *Khanmeti* ("*xanmet'i*") texts, see → 1.4.8.2.1.

[2] Outtier, "Un fragment inédit," 103–06.

[3] *C'ignni*, 595–601, 607–19. See also Žanašvili, *Našromebi*, 37–40.

[4] Oskan, *Bible*.

[5] Gippert, Sarjveladze, and Kajaia, *The Old Georgian Pa-*

concerned, the transcription of the Georgian readings is flanked by parallel columns of text,[6] containing the corresponding passages from Rahlfs' LXX[7] and from the two surviving Armenian versions (→ 20.4.5).[8]

Unlike the earliest redaction, the text of Georg-1–2 Chr 1b is accessible in its entirety in Dočanašvili's reference work on codex Georg[s].[9]

20.4.6.2 Textual Features

A comprehensive text-critical study of this tradition has hitherto never been attempted. A preliminary examination of Georg-1 Chr 1a was undertaken in 1971 by K'ik'naӡe.[10] The achieved results have been summarized recently by Melikišvili.[11] The textual features of Georg-2 Chr 1a still await investigation.

20.4.6.2.1 Georg-1–2 Chr 1a

Of the earliest testimonies to Georg-1–2 Chr 1 only a few segments of text are preserved. Palimpsest Georg[X] contains 1 Chr 6:45–7:2; 8:35–9:7; 11:35–12:22; 16:28–17:8; 18:6–19:7; 25:31–26:29; 28:4–18; 2 Chr 26:6–23; 32:3–21; 34:7–25. Georg[Yer] includes 1 Chr 11:13–16, 20–22; 19:1–3, 18–19.[12]

Among the three later manuscripts, Georg[F] is the most complete source for the textual study of this translation, since the remaining two have lacunae: Georg[I] omits 1 Chr 2:52–4:18, while Georg[D] lacks 1 Chr 1:1–4:39; 6:66–15:8; 22:9–24:8. Moreover, the former stands out for its regular textual agreement with palimpsest Georg[X], a feature that proves the antiquity of its readings.[13]

In Georg[F,I], the text is introduced by a table of contents, where the subsequent forty chapters are listed, each being preceded by its respective heading and marked by progressive numbering.[14] As for Georg-2 Chr 1a, an index indicates a subdivision of the translation into sixteen sections (Georg[F]).[15]

20.4.6.2.2 Georg-1–2 Chr 1b

Although Georg-2 Chr 1b appears to be very close to Georg-1–2 Chr 1a, it often deviates from its readings. In most cases, differences can be explained in the light of the revision undertaken by using the Armenian printed Bible of 1666 as a model: dependency on the latter is particular evident in the rendering of proper nouns.[16]

As far as textual relationship with testimonies of the ancient redaction is concerned, a preliminary analysis has shown that codex Georg[s] agrees much more frequently with Georg[F] than with Georg[D, I].[17]

20.4.6.3 Parent Text and Text-Critical Value

The Old Georgian translation of 1–2 Chronicles still awaits the appraisal of biblical scholars. The legacy of this manuscript has hitherto not been taken into account in any of the available major studies focusing on the textual history of these books.[18] Moreover, despite the existence of accessible scholarly publications of manuscripts Georg[X] and Georg[s], this tradition was not even mentioned in the latest Göttingen edition of LXX-2 Chr.[19] Consequently, a comprehensive and a selective collation of Georg-1–2 Chr 1 with the Greek and the rest of textual evidence are both still lacking.

As far as the investigation into Georg-1–2 Chr 1a is concerned, the central but still open question consists in clarifying whether the model used was LXX (→ 20.1.3) or an Armenian source (→ 20.4.5). Contrasting conclusions have been reached on this subject. Available studies do not seem to have unambiguously answered this problem. Research produced for *THB* has provided new ev-

---

limpsest, ms viii (plates 8:1–41); Outtier, "Un fragment inédit," 103–04.

[6] See Gippert, Sarjveladze, and Kajaia, *The Old Georgian Palimpsest*, ms viii (plates 8:30–8:41).

[7] Rahlfs, *Septuaginta*, 753–873.

[8] Xalat'eanc', *Girk'* and Zohrapian, *Scriptures*, respectively.

[9] Dočanašvili, *Mcxeturi xelnac'eri*, 244–354.

[10] K'ik'naӡe, "Nešt'a," 66–78.

[11] Melikišvili, *Targmanebi*, 126–27.

[12] Outtier, "Un fragment inédit," 103–04.

[13] Gippert, Sarjveladze, and Kajaia, *The Old Georgian Palimpsest*, ms viii (plate 8:1).

[14] K'ik'naӡe, "Nešt'a," 72. See *C'ignni*, 596, 599.

[15] See *C'ignni*, 596.

[16] *Mcxeturi xelnac'eri*, 18–19.

[17] K'ik'naӡe, "Nešt'a," 68–70.

[18] Brooke, McLean, Thackeray, *The Old Testament in Greek*, Vol. 1.3: *I and II Chronicles*; Allen, *The Greek Chronicles*.

[19] Hanhart, *Paralipomenon liber II*.

idence for the translation's reliance on a Greek prototype. However, considerable research has yet to be done before definitive conclusions can be drawn.

20.4.6.3.1 Previous Studies

According to K'ik'naʒe's preliminary remarks, a number of textual features of Georg-1 Chr 1a could prove the translation's dependency on LXX (→ 20.1.3).[20] In this regard, one of the most cogent observations is the following. In 1 Chr 4:14, codex LXX[B] reads καὶ Σαραια ἐγέννησεν τὸν Ιωαβ πατέρα Αγεαδδαϊρ "and Saraia became the father of Ioab, father of Ageaddair" (*NETS), while LXX[A] (as well as a number of other minuscule manuscripts) have καὶ Σαραια ἐγέννησεν τὸν Ιωαβ πατέρα γῆς ρασειμ[21] "and Seraiah begot Joab the father of the land of Raseim"; cf. MT. Georg-1–2 Chr 1a reads და სარაია შვა იობაბ, მამა ჯეგყნისა რასიმისა "and Saraia begot Iobab, father of the land of Rasim (!)," which clearly indicates its reliance on a Greek source.[22]

More recently, the editors of palimpsest Georg[X] expressed the opinion that Georg-1–2 Chr 1a was produced from an Armenian parent text (→ 20.4.5).[23] Unfortunately, this conclusion is not supported by any evidence and is not discussed in detail. Despite the decision to print both Armenian versions next to the transcription of fragments from Georg-1 Chr 1a, the question of which version is possibly the closest to the Georgian was not raised.

As widely known since the end of the nineteenth century,[24] the Armenian tradition consists of two independent textual strata (Arm 1 and Arm 2) dating from the fifth century C.E. (→ 20.4.5.2). More recently, this material has been the subject of studies that have brought new answers to the question regarding the *Vorlage* of Arm 1, which contrary to formerly held beliefs[25] was shown to derive from a Greek text and, more precisely, from a Lucianic model (Arm 2 was identified as Hexaplaric; → 20.4.5.2; → 20.3.5; → 20.3.6).[26]

Clearly, any attempt to shed light on the problem of establishing the parent text of Georg-1–2 Chr 1a cannot disregard the necessity of comparing Georg-1–2 Chr 1a with both Armenian layers. Given these premises, a number of preliminary observations are presented below, which offer further proof for the reliance of the earliest Georgian translation of 1–2 Chronicles on LXX.

20.4.6.3.2 Additional Evidence for the Translation's Dependence on LXX-Chr

Additional evidence of the dependency of Georg-1–2 Chr 1a on a Greek model has been collected. An initial convincing illustration is provided by the analysis of the following segment of text. In 2 Chr 31:1, LXX reads καὶ τοὺς βωμοὺς ἀπὸ πάσης τῆς [LXX[B] γῆς] Ἰουδαίας[27] "and altars from all over [LXX[B] from the whole land of] Judea" (*NETS). Arm 1 translates it as եւ տապալեէլ զբագինսն յամենայն երկրէն Հրէաստանի "and overthrew altars from the whole land of Judea"[28] (reflecting the secondary Greek reading καὶ καθεῖλον τὰ θυσιαστήρια "and overthrew altars"),[29] while Arm 2 renders it as եւ զբագինսն յամենայն Հրէաստանի[30] "and altars from the whole of Judea." Georg-2 Chr 1a has და ბომონი ყოვლისაგან ჯეგყანისა იუდაჲსა "and altars from the whole land of Judea." The lexical features of the Georgian version clearly betray its dependency on a Greek model. On the one hand, the term ბომონი (*bomoni*) stands for βωμός "altar," whereas both Arm 1 and Arm 2 feature բագին (*bagin* "altar"). On the other, Ἰουδαία "Judea" is rendered in Georgian as იუდაჲ (*iudaj*), while in Armenian with

---

[20] K'ik'naʒe, "Nešt'a," 70–71.
[21] Rahlfs, *Septuaginta*, 760; Brooke, McLean, Thackeray, *The Old Testament in Greek*, Vol. 1, Part 3: *I and II Chronicles*, 403.
[22] K'ik'naʒe, "Nešt'a," 70–71.
[23] Gippert, Sarjveladze, and Kajaia, *The Old Georgian Palimpsest*, ms viii (plate 8:42, n. 9).
[24] Marr, "Novootkrytyj," 1–18.
[25] Ter-Petrosyan, "La plus ancienne traduction," 215–25.
[26] Cowe, "The Two Armenian Versions," 53–96.
[27] Hanhart, *Paralipomenon liber II*, 361; Rahlfs, *Septuaginta*, 859.
[28] Xalat'eanc', *Girk'*, 103.
[29] See Hanhart, *Paralipomenon liber II*, 361.
[30] Zohrapian, *Scriptures*, 285.

Հրէաստան (Hrēastan), for which the Georgian has a different equivalent, namely ჰურიასტანი (Huriast'ani).

A second relevant case can be examined. In 1 Chr 1:43, Georg-1–2 Chr 1a lacks after καὶ οὗτοι οἱ βασιλεῖς αὐτῶν "and these are their kings" (*NETS) LXX^A's plus οἱ βασιλεύσαντες ἐν Εδωμ πρὸ τοῦ βασιλεῦσαι βασιλέα τοῖς υἱοῖς Ισραηλ "who ruled in Edom before kings ruled the sons of Israel."[31] The latter can on the contrary be found in both Armenian versions: *a)* Arm 1 Այս են որ թագաւորեցին յերկրին Եդովմայեցոց մինչ չեւ էր կացեալ թագաւոր ի վերայ որդւոցն Իսրայելի "these are they who reigned in the land of Edom, before there has been a king over the sons of Israel";[32] *b)* Arm 2 որք թագաւորեցին յեդովմ, յառաջ քան զթագաւորել թագաւոր որդւոցն Իսրայելի "who reigned in Edom before (any) king reigned over the sons of Israel."[33] In Georgian, this addition can be found only in Georg-1 Chr 1b: რომელნი მთავრობდენ ქუეყანასა ედომისასა, რომელნი პირველად ზედა ძეთა ისრაჱლთასა მეფობდენ "who ruled in the land of Edom, who initially reigned over the sons of Israel."[34]

A third textual remark reinforces the assumption that LXX (→ 20.1.3) is the *Vorlage* of Georg-1 Chr 1a, namely that both versions omit the verses 1 Chr 1:11–16, 17b–23,[35] which were considered by Rudolph to be a late addition in MT.[36] As in the previous case, both Armenian versions preserve these pluses.[37] The latter are also included in Georg-1 Chr 1b, as a consequence of the revision undertaken on Oskan's printed Bible.[38]

20.4.6.4 The Early Eighteenth-Century Translation

Besides Georg-1–2 Chr 1, a second Georgian version of 1–2 Chronicles is also available (= Georg-1–2 Chr 2). It was carried out in the early eighteenth century by Prince Archil II (Prince Arčil II, 1647–1713; → 1.4.8.2.3).[39] The model he used was the Old Church Slavonic text according to the version printed in the Moscow Bible of 1663 (→ 20.4.7).[40] This translation was published in the so-called "Bakar Bible" (= Georg^B), which appeared in Moscow in 1743.[41]

Allen, L.C., *The Greek Chronicles: The Relation of the Septuagint of I and II Chronicles to the Masoretic Text* (2 vols.; VTSup 25, 27; Leiden: Brill, 1974).

Biblia: Brʒanebita da c'arsagebelita sapasetata sakartvelos mepis bakar vaxt'angis ʒisata (Moscow: Bakaris st'amba, 1743).

Biblija: Sirěč' knigi vetchago i novago zavěta, po jayzku slavensku (Moscow: Pečatnyj dvor, 1663).

Brooke–McLean–Thackeray, *The Old Testament in Greek*, Vol. 1.3: *I and II Chronicles*.

C'ignni ʒuelisa aγtkumisani, Vol. 1: *Šesakmisaj, gamoslvataj* (eds. B. Gigineišvili and C. K'ik'viʒe; Tbilisi: Mecniereba, 1989).

Cowe, S.P., "The Two Armenian Versions of Chronicles: Their Origin and Translation Technique," *Revue des Études Arméniennes* 22 (1990–1991): 53–96.

Dočanašvili, E., "T'ekst'obrivi damok'idebulebis ramdenime šemtxveva ʒveli aγtkmis zog kartul xelnac'erši," *Macne: Enisa da lit'erat'uris seria* 2 (1971): 77–82.

Gippert, J., Z. Sarjveladze, and L. Kajaia (eds.), *The Old Georgian Palimpsest: Codex Vindobonensis Georgicus 2* (Monumenta palaeographica Medii Aevi Series Ibero-Caucasica 1; Turnhout: Brepols, 2007).

Hanhart, R. (ed.), *Paralipomenon liber II* (Septuaginta Vetus Testamentum Graecum VII.2; Göttingen: Vandenhoeck & Ruprecht, 2014).

K'ik'naʒe, G., "Nešt'a I c'ignis kartuli redakciebi," *Mravaltavi* 1 (1971): 66–78.

Marr, N.J., "Novootkrytyj armjanskij tekst Paralipomenon," *Kavkazskij vestnik* 4 (1902): 1–18 (repr. N.J. Marr,

---

[31] Rahlfs, *Septuaginta*, 754.
[32] Xalat'eanc', *Girk'*, 2.
[33] Zohrapian, *Scriptures*, 251.
[34] *Mcxeturi xelnac'eri*, 245.
[35] Rahlfs, *Septuaginta*, 753; Brooke, McLean, Thackeray, *The Old Testament in Greek*, Vol. 1.3: *I and II Chronicles*, 391–92.
[36] Rudolph, *Chronikbücher*, 6–7; Tov, *TCHB*, 321 n. 71.
[37] Xalat'eanc', *Girk'*, 1; Zohrapian, *Scriptures*, 251. Brooke, McLean, Thackeray, *The Old Testament in Greek*, Vol. 1.3: *I and II Chronicles*, 391–92.
[38] K'ik'naʒe, "Nešt'a," 72–73; *Mcxeturi xelnac'eri*, 18–19, 244; Dočanašvili, "T'ekst'obrivi," 77–82; Oskan, *Bible*.

---

[39] K'ik'naʒe, "Nešt'a," 74–77.
[40] *Biblija: Sirěč' knigi vetchago i novago zavěta*.
[41] *Biblia: Brʒanebita da c'arsagebelita sapasetata sakartvelos mepis bakar vaxt'angis ʒisata*.

Kavkazskij kul'turnyj mir i Armenija [Erevan: Gandzasar, 1995]: 179–96).

Mcxeturi xelnac'eri: mepeta I, II, III, IV, nešt'a I, II, ezras I, II, III c'ignebi (ed. E. Dočanašvili; Tbilisi: Mecniereba, 1982).

Melikišvili, N., *Bibliur c'ignta ʒveli kartuli targmanebi* (Tbilisi: Alilo, 2009).

Oskan Erevants'i (ed.), *Astuatsashunch' Hnots' ew Norots' Ktakaranats': Neren Parunakōgh* (*Scriptures of the Old and New Testaments*) (Amsterdam, 1666).

Outtier, B., "Un fragment inédit du Premier livre des Paralipomènes: Erevan, Matenadaran 719," in *Lingvok'ult'urologiuri ʒiebani*, Vol. 2: *P'irveli saertašoriso k'onferencia lingvok'ult'urologiasa da antrop'ologiaši* (Batumi: Shota Rustaveli State University Press, 2011), 103–06.

Rahlfs, *Septuaginta*.

Rudolph, W., *Chronikbücher* (HAT 1.21; Tübingen: Mohr Siebeck, 1955).

Ter-Petrosyan, L.H., "La plus ancienne traduction arménienne des Chroniques. Étude préliminaire," *Revue des Études Arméniennes* 18 (1984): 215–25.

Xalat'eanc', G., *Girk' mnac'ordac' ēst hnagoyn hay t'argmanut'ean* (Moscow: Tparan Varvaře Gatc'uk, 1899).

Zohrapian, *Scriptures*.

Žanašvili, M., *Našromebi*, Vol. 3: *Čemi šenišvnebi: rustavelis garšemo. kartuli biblia me-VI sauk'.: ayc'era, t'ekst'ebi, leksik'oni* (Tbilisi: Elekt'.–mbeč'd. s.m. losaberiʒisa, 1910).

Alessandro Maria Bruni

20.4.7 Old Church Slavonic Translations

20.4.7.1 Background

In spite of the testimony of the *Life of Methodius*, according to which the "Apostle of the Slavs" translated the whole corpus of the Scriptures "with the exception of the Maccabees" from Greek into Slavonic[1] shortly before his death (885 C.E.), the existence of such an early translation of 1–2 Chronicles into Old Church Slavonic cannot be proven on a documentary basis. On the one hand, the manuscript tradition of the OCS Bible does not preserve even traces of a textual stratum dating back to that period. On the other hand, the textual material provided by the Croat Glagolitic sources is too meager in order to reach trustworthy conclusions on this matter; they contain only 1 Chr 29:16–18 and 2 Chr 6:21, 27.[2]

A full Slavic version of 1–2 Chronicles originated in Russia in the late fifteenth century under the patronage of Archbishop Gennadius of Novgorod (Gennadij Gonzov, ca. 1410–1505). The Vulgate (→ 20.3.7) was used as a base text for producing OCS-1–2 Chr, as in the case of several other biblical books translated by his assistants. This opinion was first expressed by Gorskij and Nevostruev and is today widely accepted.[3] As is maintained by scholars, the sources adopted for the translation were late fifteenth-century editions of the Vulgate, among which are those printed by A. Koberger (ca. 1440–1513) in 1487 (with commentaries by Nicholas of Lyra) and by N. Kessler (1450–after 1519) in 1487 or 1491.[4]

OCS-1–2 Chr is commonly attributed by a number of scholars to a certain Benjamin, a Dominican monk of Croat or Czech origin, who is known for having completed the translation of 1–2 Maccabees (→ II.10.1.6; → II.10.2.7) in Novgorod in 1493 C.E. (→ 20.4.7).[5]

20.4.7.2 Manuscript Sources and Textual History

The earliest sources of OCS-1–2 Chr date from virtually the same period as their translation. On the one hand, the text is to be found in a Novgorodian codex of the late fifteenth century, which also includes versions of Judith (→ II.9.10), Esther (→ 13–17.2.7), Wisdom (→ II.15.9), and Jer 45–46 (→ 6–9.2.7; Russian State Library, Moscow, f. 113, No. 9). On the other hand, OCS-1–2 Chr is attested in the

---

[1] See ch. 15 of the *Life of Methodius*: Angelov and Kodov, *Kliment Ochridski*, 191.

[2] An edition can be found in Berčić, *Ulomci*, 98 (1 Chronicles), 99 (2 Chronicles).

[3] Gorskij and Nevostruev, *Opisanie*, vi–vii, 44–50. See Alekseev, *Tekstologija*, 197; Pičchadze, "Perevody," 139–47; Romodanovskaja, "Zametki," 235–36; Romodanovskaja, "Gennadievskaja Biblija," 584–85.

[4] Thomson, "The Slavonic Translation," 655–59; Thomson, *A Brief Survey*, 55–56.

[5] See the colophon of the sixteenth-century manuscript: National Library of Russia, St. Petersburg, *Pog.* 84, folio 360ᵛ (Alekseev, *Tekstologija*, 197).

"Gennadian Bible" dating from 1499 (State Historical Museum, Moscow, *Sin.* 915).[6] OCS-1–2 Chr remains unpublished.[7]

In 1581, OCS-1–2 Chr was included in the printed Ostrog Bible.[8] As has already been noted,[9] evaluating the extent of the revision to which this translation was subjected by the compilers of the Ostrog Bible appears to be problematic. According to Alekseev, several books in the Ostrog Bible, comprising OCS-1–2 Chr, are the outcome of a very unsystematic correction of the text towards LXX (→ 20.3.1). While at times the Novgorodian version is given in an almost unchanged redaction, in other instances it is replaced by a new translation.[10]

20.4.7.3 Parent Text

According to Jagić, the Croat Glagolitic fragments of 1 Chr 29:16–18 and 2 Chr 6:21, 27 show traces of the use of a Greek model (→ 20.3.1).[11] This view did not find support among scholars. In Thomson's opinion, the readings in question do not exactly follow LXX; he believes that possibly the influence of VL (→ 20.4.1) should not be ruled out.[12]

In the case of the Novgorodian version of OCS-1–2 Chr, there seems to be no doubt that this translation was undertaken by using the above-mentioned late fifteenth-century editions of the Vulgate (→ 20.3.7) as a base text, although a full collation between them has not been yet undertaken. This conclusion is supported by specific textual readings such as 1 Chr 16:30: да подвижетсѧ от лица его всa ẕемлѧ. тъ бо създа вселеную неподвижну "let all earth be moved from his face: for he has found the world immoveable" (v: *commoveatur a facie ejus omnis terra: ipse enim fundavit orbem immobilem* "let all the earth be moved at his presence: for he has found the world immoveable").[13]

Other textual features also argue for the Vulgate as a base text of OCS-1–2 Chr. For instance, in OCS-1–2 Chr, several Latin words are merely transcribed in the Cyrillic alphabet (corresponding translation is at times available in the margins of the manuscript folios). They prove the reliance of the translation on the Vulgate:[14]

– 1 Chr 1:48: близъ амнемъ "near the *amnen*" (v: *iuxta amnen* "near the river")
– 1 Chr 13:1 нача же съвѣтъ дѣдъ кумъ трибунисъ "David consulted *cum tribunis*" (v: *iniit autem consilium David cum tribunis* "David consulted with the captains of thousands")
– 1 Chr 13:7 на плауструмъ "upon a *plaustrum*" (v: *super plaustrum* "upon a cart")
– 1 Chr 16:3 торта хлѣба "*torta* of bread" (v: *tortam panis* "a loaf of bread")
– 2 Chr 6:13 сътвори соломонъ баẕимъ медaнъ и постави е посреди басилисе "Solomon had made a brazen *bazim* and had set it in the midst of the temple" (v: *Siquidem fecerat Salomon basim aeneam et posuerat eam in medio basilicae* "For Solomon had made a brazen scaffold, and had set it in the midst of the temple")

Furthermore, the use of the Vulgate as a base text is also borne out by a number of translation errors. For instance, in 1 Chr 16:8, the Vulgate *notas facite in populo adinventiones illius* "make known his doings among the nations" was erroneously read as *notas facite in populo ad inventiones* [*!*] *illius* (ẕнаемо сътворите въ людехъ къ обрѣтѣнием его).[15] Similar misinterpretations are also quoted by Thomson: OCS-1 Chr 11:1 reads оуста твои есмы и плоть твоа "we are your mouth and your flesh" instead of *os tuum sumus et caro*, "we are your bone and flesh" in the Vulgate.[16]

---

[6] A list of a few other manuscripts containing OCS-1–2 Chr is to be found in Mathiesen, "Handlist": 18, No. 7; 19, No. 17; 21, No. 41.

[7] For a linguistic analysis of several sections of OCS-1–2 Chr, see Freidhof, *Vergleichende sprachliche Studien*.

[8] *Ostrožskaja biblija*.

[9] Gorskij and Nevostruev, *Opisanie*, 52.

[10] Alekseev, *Tekstologija*, 205–06.

[11] Jagić, *Entstehungsgeschichte*, 465.

[12] Thomson, "The Slavonic Translation," 771 n. 818.

[13] Gorskij and Nevostruev, *Opisanie*, 44–45.

[14] Gorskij-Nevostruev, *Opisanie*, 47.

[15] Gorskij and Nevostruev, *Opisanie*, 48.

[16] Thomson, "The Slavonic Translation," 772.

Alekseev, A.A., *Tekstologija slavjanskoj Biblii* (Bausteine zur slavischen Philologie und Kulturgeschichte Neue Folge A Slavistische Forschungen 24; St. Petersburg: Dmitrij Bulanin, 1999).

Angelov, B.S. and C. Kodov (eds.), *Kliment Ochridski: Săbrani săčinenija*, Vol. 3: *Prostranni žitija na Kiril i Metodii* (Sofia: Izdatelstvo na Bălgarska Akademija na naukite, 1973).

Berčić, I. (ed.), *Ulomci Svetoga Pisma obojega uvjeta staroslovenskim jezikom: Skupio iz rukopisah i tiskanih knjigah hrvatskoga razreda svećenik Ivan Berčić*, Vol. 1 (Prague: Sinovi Bogumila Haase, 1871).

Freidhof, G., *Vergleichende sprachliche Studien zur Gennadius-Bibel (1499) und Ostroger Bibel (1580/1581): Die Bücher Paralipomenon, Esra, Tobias, Judith, Sapientia und Makkabäaer* (Frankfurt a.M.: Athenäum Verlag, 1972).

Gorskij, A. and K.I. Nevostruev, *Opisanie slavjanskich rukopisej Moskovskoj Sinodal'noj (Patriaršej) biblioteki*, Vol. 1: *Svjaščennoe pisanie* (Moscow: Sinodal'naja tipografija, 1855).

Jagić, V., *Entstehungsgeschichte der kirchenslavischen Sprache* (Berlin: Weidmann, 1913).

Mathiesen, R., "Handlist of Manuscripts Containing Church Slavonic Translations of the Old Testament," *Polata knigopisnaja* 7 (1983): 3–48.

Ostrožskaja biblija: Fototipičeskoe pereizdanie teksta s izdanija 1581 g. (Moscow: Slovo-Art, 1988).

Pičchadze, A.A., "Perevody Biblii na drevnie jazyki: cerkovnoslavjanskij," *Pravoslavnaja ènciklopedija*, Vol. 5: *Bessonov-Bonveč* (ed. Aleksij, Patriarch Moskovskij i Vseja Rusi II; Moscow: Cerkovno-Naučnyj Centr "Pravoslavnaja ènciklopedija," 2002): 139–47.

Romodanovskaja, V.A., "Zametki o perevode "latinskich" knig Gennadievskoj biblii 1499g.: biblejskij tekst i ènciklopedičeskie glossy," *Trudy Otdela drevnerusskoj literatury* 56 (2004): 235–50.

Romodanovskaja, V.A., "Gennadievskaja Biblija," *Pravoslavnaja ènciklopedija*, Vol. 10: *Vtorozakonie-Georgij* (ed. Aleksij, Patriarch Moskovskij i Vseja Rusi II; Moscow: Cerkovno-Naučnyj Centr "Pravoslavnaja ènciklopedija," 2005): 584–88.

Thomson, F.J., "The Slavonic Translation of the Old Testament," in *The Interpretation of the Bible: The International Symposium in Slovenia* (ed. J. Krašovec; JSOTSup 189; Sheffield: Sheffield Academic Press, 1998), 605–920.

Thomson, F.J., *A Brief Survey of the History of the Church Slavonic Bible from its Cyrillomethodian Origins until its Final Form in the Elizabethan Bible of 1751* (Slavica Gandensia 33.2; Ghent: Department of Slav and East European Studes of the University of Ghent, 2006).

Alessandro Maria Bruni

20.4.8 Arabic Translations

20.4.8.1 Background

The Arabic versions of the two books of Chronicles are yet to be thoroughly studied. In his well-known work on Christian Arabic literature, Graf mentions a few manuscripts as containing the Chronicles only in passing.[1] Samir supplements Graf's work and furnishes a provisional classification of various Arabic versions of Chronicles in the *Coptic Encyclopedia*, vol. 6.[2] The manuscripts located in the Monastery of Saint Catherine are not taken into account by Samir; therefore, the manuscripts he lists do not predate the fourteenth century. As yet, the earliest extant translation of Chronicles into Arabic in the Sinai collection is dated to the tenth century on paleographical grounds.

The two books of Chronicles, referred to as *Paralipomena* "Remains" in the LXX, are in the Arabic manuscripts rendered under a variety of headings and the division of the two books does not always correspond to the same text units. For instance, in his work *Lamp of Darkness*, the famous Coptic scholar Abū al-Barakāt Ibn Kabar (early fourteenth century) refers to the Chronicles as *Kitāb Faḍalāt al-Mulūk* "the Book of the Remains of [the Books of] Kings," which corresponds well with the Greek heading. 1 Chronicles is at times entitled "The Sixth Book of Kings" and both books may as a unit be referred to as "The Third Book of Kings."[3]

---

[1] Graf, *GCAL* 1, 10–12. Unfortunately, this work is not free of errors. Most importantly, it is not always clear whether references are to class marks or catalogue numbers. For converting catalogue numbers in the Cairo manuscripts to class marks, a helpful tool is: Samir, Khalil, *Tables de concordance des manuscrits arabes chrétiens du Caire et du Sinaï* (CSCO 482 Subsidia 75; Louvain: Peeters, 1986).

[2] Samir, "Old Testament."

[3] Samir, "Old Testament."

20.4.8.2 Text Types, Manuscripts, Tools

Based on relevant manuscript catalogues, Samir suggests that the Copts were familiar with at least six versions of Chronicles in Arabic. The reader is advised to refer to Samir's article for a more detailed account; here we merely sum up his observations and pass on some of the references.

The first version is that contained in the Paris Polyglot (1629–1645)[4] based on Paris, BNF, Ar. 1 (folios 168ᵛ–195ᵛ) dated to 1584–1585 C.E. We find the same translation in Paris, BNF, Ar. 23 (folios 168ᵛ–187ᵛ), which was copied in Egypt in the early fourteenth century. The text is missing from 2 Chr 35:12 until the end but its completion is found in Copenhagen, Royal Library, Or. 76 (folios 3ʳ–4ʳ).[5] The same translation is also contained in Coptic Orthodox Patriarchate, Bible 38 (folios 168ʳ–218ᵛ, Graf, no. 244) where 1 Chronicles is entitled "The Sixth Book of Kings" and 2 Chronicles "The Book of Solomon, Son of David, drawn from the Books of Kings." This version of Chronicles appears to be based on the Peshiṭta (→ 20.3.4).[6]

The second version in Samir's article is attested in three manuscripts. He states that the translation is conceivably from a Syriac *Vorlage*. The oldest manuscript, Oxford, Bodleian 493 (Nicoll, Chr. Ar. 5. folios 200ʳ–62ᵛ) is dated to 1321. Two later manuscripts are found in the Coptic Orthodox Patriarchate: Bible 32 (Graf, no. 235, folios 100–125) dated 1585 and Bible 37 (Graf, no. 236, folios 215ᵛ–286ᵛ) dated to 1760. Both Samir and Graf note that 1 Chronicles in these manuscripts is entitled *Debr Yamin* or *Bar Yumin*, etc., which is translated as "the Son of the Right Hand" but originally must reflect the Hebrew *dibrē hayyāmīm* "The Accounts of Days," via the Syriac *dbr ymin*.[7]

According to Samir, the third version appears to be related or even identical to the second version, yet the two books, which are referred to as "The Third Book of Kings," are divided in different ways; the first book comprises 1 Chronicles and chapters 1–5 of 2 Chronicles. Three manuscripts are included in this group: Vatican, Ar. 399 (folios 181ʳ–240ᵛ; last folios lacking) dated to the fifteenth century according to Assemani and 1523 according to Graf; Cairo, Coptic Museum, Bible 102 (Graf, no. 674, folios 156ᵛ–209ᵛ, last folio missing) dated to the seventeenth century; Coptic Orthodox Patriarchate, Bible 44 (Graf, no. 237, folios 175ᵛ–237ᵛ) dated to 1782 C.E.

The fourth group consists of three disparate manuscripts: 1) Paris, BNF, Ar. 24 copied in Egypt in the fifteenth century consisting of the two books of Chronicles alone. About 20 folios are missing (1 Chr 29:3 to 2 Chr 16:2); 2) Florence, Pal. Med., Or. 9 [olim 4], copied in Egypt in 1496. The folios have been shuffled and Samir suggests the following order: 93ʳ–101ᵛ (1 Chronicles), 65ᵛ–79ʳ (2 Chronicles 1–9), and 102ʳ–109ᵛ (2 Chronicles 10–36); 3) Coptic Orthodox Patriarchate, Bible 50 (Graf, no. 257, folios 252ʳ–83ʳ) dated to the fifteenth century.

The fifth group consists of at least fifteen manuscripts contained in the collections of the Coptic Museum or the Coptic Orthodox Patriarchate. This translation represents the Arabic version of the two books of Chronicles included in the *Biblia Sacra Arabica* (1671–1673) of the Congregatio de Propaganda Fide, which was commissioned by the Vatican and subsequently diffused among the Oriental communities. The earliest manuscript Samir mentions in this connection is Cairo, Coptic Museum, Bible 87 (Graf, no. 670, folios 157ᵛ–200ᵛ) dated to the eighteenth century. The version of Chronicles contained in Vatican, Ar. 468 – an important manuscript for the *Biblia Sacra Arabica* – is, according to Vaccari, translated from a Syriac *Vorlage* (→ 20.3.4; → 20.4.4).[8]

The last version in Samir's classification is the one printed by the Coptic Catholic scholar Raphael Tukhi (1752). This text was influenced by the Latin Vulgate.

---

[4] Le Jay, *Biblia.

[5] B. Knutsson, *Studies in the Text and Language of Three Syriac-Arabic Versions of the Book of Judicum with Special Reference to the Middle Arabic Elements: Introduction-Linguistic Notes-Texts* (Leiden: Brill: 1974), 13, n. 11.

[6] Graf, *GCAL 1, 108–09.

[7] Graf, *GCAL 1, 109, and Samir, "Old Testament."

[8] Vaccari, "Una Bibbia araba per il Gesuita venuto al Libano," 89.

Besides the manuscripts listed by Samir and Graf, we know of a considerably earlier Arabic version of the two books of Chronicles dated to the tenth century. This manuscript, catalogued as Sinai Ar. 7, is located in the Monastery of Saint Catharine in the Sinai Desert. It is made up of seventy-five folios (27.5 × 16 cm) and written on paper in an intermediate Kufic-Nashki hand.[9] Subsequent to a preliminary study by the current author, this version appears to be translated from a Syriac *Vorlage*. The first part is missing and the text begins with 1 Chr 14:14.

20.4.8.4 Translation Character and Translation Technique

No research has been dedicated as yet to the translation character and technique of the two Arabic books of Chronicles.[10] We will here supply a sample from the earliest dated Arabic version, tenth-century Sinai Ar. 7, and await a more thorough study on the subject.

The translation in question is free. Material is frequently substituted, added, or omitted. For instance, instead of faithfully reflecting the rendition in the Peshitta and LXX of 1 Chr 14:15: "then you shall go into the battle: *God has gone out before you* to destroy the army of the Philistines," the Arabic translator alters the text into […] *li'anna Allāh ya'muru wa-takruju qaḍīya* "[…] for God commands *and a verdict will go out* […]." This alteration clearly results from the unwillingness to promote anthropomorphic ideas. Such rationalistic tendencies are characteristic of many early translations of the Bible into Arabic and corresponds well with previous findings (→ 18.4.8; → 11.3.8).

Instead of rendering "the army of the Philistines (*plīštāy*/ἀλλοφύλων)" in the same verse, the translator of Sinai Ar. 7 substitutes the noun "the Philistines" for a pronoun and reads *'askarhum* "their army." The clause is repeated in the following verse. This time, seemingly in order to avoid repetitive language, the translator abbreviates the fuller phrase "the army of the Philistines" in the source texts into merely *al-Filasṭīnīya* "the Philistines." This kind of abbreviation is another salient feature of many early Arabic Bible translations. It serves to free the text from what is considered pleonastic information that is already inferable from the context (→ 18.4.8; → 11.3.8).

On the other hand, in line with other Arabic Bible translations, the translator may add material that lacks translation equivalents in all known *Vorlagen*. Compare 1 Chr 14:16 where the clause "and they were destroyed before him" is added in Sinai Ar. 7 to confirm the completion of the command given in 1 Chr 14:15 "God has gone out before you *to destroy the army of the Philistines*." The complete verse 16 is rendered in the *Vorlagen*: "And he [Syr.: *Dawīd*] did as God commanded him: and he smote the army of the Philistines from Gabaon [Gb'wn/Γαβαων] to Gazera [Gdr/Γαζαρα]." Sinai Ar. 7 reflects this as: "And David did as God commanded him: and the Philistines were defeated [?] and they were destroyed before him from Bayt J'wyn to Jadher" (فعمل داود كما امره الله وحازت الفلسطييون فهلكوا بين يديه من بيت جعوين الى جذر). Where the Syriac and Greek *Vorlagen* differ, including the rendering of proper names, Sinai Ar. 7 follows the former.

20.4.8.4 Text-Critical and Literary Value

Since no exhaustive studies on the text type, translation character, and translation techniques of the Arabic versions of the two books of Chronicles have yet seen the light, their text-critical value is uncertain. In any event, the Arabic translations are to be regarded primarily as documents in their own right. As such, they reflect the endeavor of the Christian Arabic communities to re-code the Bible in their vernacular tongue and serve as windows into the literary and intellectual ideals of the remote world of Christian Arabic literature.

Atiya, A.S., *The Arabic Manuscripts of Mount Sinai: A Hand-List of the Arabic Manuscripts and Scrolls Microfilmed at the Library of the Monastery of St. Cather-*

---

[9] Atiya, *The Arabic Manuscripts*, 3; Atiya, *Al-Fahāris* (trans. Youssef), 32.

[10] Many of the Arabic samples presented here are extracted from M.L. Hjälm, Christian Arabic Versions of Daniel: A Comparative Study of Early MSS and Translation Techniques in MSS Sinai Ar. 1 and 2 (Leiden: Brill, 2016).

ine, Mount Sinai (Baltimore: John Hopkins Press, 1955).

Atiya, A.S., *Al-Fahāris al-Tahīliyya li-Makhṭūṭāt ṭūr Sīnā al-ʿarabiyya* (trans. J.N. Youssef; Alexandria, 1970).

Graf, G., *Catalogue de manuscrits arabes chrétiens conservés au Caire* (Vatican City: Studi e Testi 134, 1934).

Graf, **GCAL* 1.

Samir, K., "Old Testament, Arabic Versions of the," in *The Coptic Encyclopedia* (Vol. 6.; ed. A.Z. Atiya; New York: Macmillan, 1991). Online: http://ccdl.libraries.claremont.edu/cdm/singleitem/collection/cce/id/1486/rec/2

Vaccari, A., "Una Bibbia araba per il Gesuita venuto al Libano," *Mélanges de l'Université St Joseph* 10 (1925): 79–105.

Walton, **Polyglotta*, Vol. 2.

Miriam Lindgren Hjälm

10–20.1 Ketuvim: The Medieval text of MT

10–20.1.1 Original Form and Editions[1]

Only two of the four manuscripts attributed to Ben Asher contain all or part of the text of the Writings (→ 1.5). The Leningrad Codex (Codex EBP. I B 19a; MT^L) presents all the books and the Aleppo Codex (MT^A) from Chronicles to Cant 3:11, apart from Pss 15:1–25:1.

Diplomatic Editions: in 2016, in the new edition of MT^L, *BHQ*, only the books of Proverbs (*Part 17: Proverbs*), the five Megilloth (*Part 18: General Introduction and Megilloth*) and Ezra and Nehemiah (*Part 20: Ezra and Nehemiah*) have been published.

In the edition of MT^A, *Miqra'ot Gedolot "Haketer,"* only the books of Psalms and those of the Megilloth – even though MT^A does not contain all the books – have been published.[2]

10–20.1.2 Text-Critical Character

The Masoretic tradition regarded the books of Ezra and Nehemiah as one book and referred to it as the book of Ezra; Chronicles was also considered a single book.[3] This is also followed by the Masorah.

The order of the Writings in MT^A and MT^L is: Chronicles, Psalms, Job, Proverbs, Ruth, Song of Songs, Qohelet, Lamentations, Esther, Daniel, Ezra.

The three so-called "poetical books," Psalms, Job, and Proverbs, are presented in a special two-column form in both manuscripts. Moreover, the poetical books – except for the prose sections at the beginning and end of the book of Job (1:1–3:2, 42:7–17) – use another system of accentuation, different from the system of accents used in the twenty-one books.[4]

With regard to the different divisions of the biblical text, there are certain discrepancies between MT^A and MT^L in terms of the sections and the division for the three-year cycle.[5] But, in general, both manuscripts agree.

10–20.1.2.1 Orthographic Irregularities: Extraordinary Points

One of the words with points on one or more letters is located in Ps 27:13: לוּלֵא "unless" (→ 1.5.4.1 and → 2.3.2.1). In MT^A, all the letters of the word are punctuated. The MasP note says ד׳ כת א. נקוד מלמע ולמטה "four [times] written with *alef*; dotted above and below." There is no MasM note on the dotted words. In MT^L, in the biblical text, three letters of the word are punctuated (א, ל, ל). The MasP note says ל׳ נקוד מלעל ומלרע ב׳ מ׳ ו׳ "unique; dotted above and below with the exception of *waw*." There is no MasM note.

10–20.1.2.2 Orthographic Irregularities: Small Letters

MT^A and MT^L contain a final *nun* written in a smaller size than normal in the word וְנִרְגָּן "a whisperer" from Prov 16:28. The MasP note says ג׳ נונין זעיר "three [cases of] small *nunin*." The other two cases are found in Isa 44:14 and Jer 39:13 (→ 1.5.4.1 and → 3–5.3.2.2).

10–20.1.2.3 Orthographic Irregularities: Suspended Letters

Three of the four cases of letters written above the line are found in the Ketuvim. The *'ayin* of the words רִיַּעְמִי "from the forest" (Ps 80:14), יִרְשְׁעִים "wicked" (Job 38:13), and יִמְרְשָׁעִים "from the wicked" (Job 38:15) appears suspended in MT^A and MT^L. In MT^A, the MasP notes to Psalms and Job 38:15 state ד׳ אותות תלוים / ד׳ תלוים "four suspended letters." In MT^L, the MasP notes to these passages say ד׳ אותיות תלויות / ד׳ תלויות "four suspended

---

[1] Cf. "Medieval Masoretic Text," → 1.5.2; → 1.5.3, for more detailed information.
[2] *Mikra'ot Gedolot "Haketer"* (*Psalms* and *The Five Scrolls*).
[3] In citations by chapter and verse numbers, I make a distinction between them ("Nehemiah," "1 Chronicles," and "2 Chronicles").
[4] Wickes, *Two Treatises on the Accentuation*.
[5] See, for instance, *BHQ, Proverbs*, 12*–13*.

letters." There is also a MasM note to Job 38:15: ד׳ אותיות במקרא תלויות "four letters in the Bible are suspended."

The explanation for the case of Psalms is widely documented in rabbinic literature.[6] Most of the interpretations of the suspended *ʿayin* seem to reflect two different reading traditions: מיאר "from the river," or מיער "from the forest." The suspended *ʿayin* in the two verses in Job has been also interpreted as two different reading traditions: ראשים "poor" or רשעים "wicked."[7]

10–20.1.2.4 Orthographic Irregularities: Inverted *Nun*

Seven passages in Psalm 107 include a symbol resembling an inverted *nun*. The location of this symbol varies from MT^A to MT^L. It is located in vv. 23–28, 40 in MT^A but in vv. 21–26, 40 in MT^L. There is no Masoretic note in the marked passages. No satisfactory explanation for their use in these passages has yet been offered.[8]

10–20.1.2.5 *Qere-Ketiv*[9]

Four hundred and sixty-eight cases of *Qere-Ketiv* are marked in MT^L: seventy-one in Chronicles, sixty-six in Psalms, fifty-two in Job, sixty-five in Proverbs, eight in Ruth, four in Song of Songs, ten in Qohelet, twenty-one in Lamentations, eleven in Esther, one hundred and sixteen in Daniel, thirty-five in Ezra, and nineteen in Nehemiah. The *Qere* is indicated by the abbreviated form, ק׳, except for 1 Chr 4:20 and Cant 2:13, where the complete form, קרי, is used, and Job 38:12 and 40:6, with the abbreviation קר׳. Moreover, in forty cases, alongside the indication of *Qere* appears a sign resembling the final *nun*:[10] One in Chronicles, three in Psalms, eleven in Job,[11] twenty-seven in Proverbs,

three in Ruth; one in Canticles; four in Qohelet; eleven in Lamentations, one in Esther, and one in Daniel. Normally, the whole word is given in the *Qere*, but sometimes it only indicates the letter or letters that are affected (e.g., the MasP of שִׂמְלֹתֵךְ "your clothes" in Ruth 3:3: ק׳ תיך, "ך; it should be read שמל[תיך]"; MasP of הַיְהוּדִיִּים "and the Jews" in Esth 9:15: ק׳ דים "it should be read [היהו]דים ['and the Jews']"; etc.). The *Qere* vowels tend to be written in the text below the *Ketiv*, although in three cases they are also attached to the *Qere* letters. Six cases have two MasP notes, one usually on how the word is written and another that gives the *Qere*: e.g., MasP of חִירָם "Hiram" in 1 Chr 14:1: ג׳ כת׳כן; חורם ק׳ "three [times] is written this way; it should be read חורם 'Huram'." In the MasP note to Dan 7:10, Ben Asher is mentioned in connection with the *Qere*. Finally, twenty-two cases also have a MasM note, which lists the cases that share the same *Qere* reading: e.g., MasM to יָשׁוּב "he will recompense" in Ps 54:7: ג׳ כת׳ ישוב וקר׳ ישיבו סימנ׳ "three [times] is written ישוב and it should be read ישיב, and their references: Job 39:12; Prov 12:14; Ps 54:7."

In MT^A, two hundred and eleven cases are marked: fifty in Chronicles, fifty-four in Psalms, thirty-nine in Job, fifty-nine in Proverbs, seven in Ruth, and two in the three preserved chapters of Song of Songs. This phenomenon is mostly marked using the shorter form, ק׳, except in forty-eight cases, where the full form, קרי, is used. Moreover, in six cases the phenomenon is marked by explaining the difference between the *Ketiv* and the *Qere*: e.g., MasP note to בִּנְיָמִן "of Bani of" in 1 Chr 9:4: כתב מלה חדה וקר תרת׳ מלין "written as one word, read as two words." Normally the whole word is given in the *Qere*, but in eight cases it only indicates the letter or letters that are affected (e.g., MasP of חֲלָצָו "his loins" in Job 31:20: ציו ק׳ "it should be read [חל]ציו ['his loins']"). In 2 Chr 33:16, Prov 13:20, and Cant 1:17, there is also a MasM note that lists the cases that share the same *Qere* reading.

---

[6] *ʾAbot R. Nat.* 34a; *Lev. Rab.* 11,3; *Rab. Cant.* 3,4.
[7] *B. Sanh.* 103b.
[8] Yeivin, *Introduction*, 46–47; → 1.5.4.1 and → 2.3.2.3.
[9] The calculation of the *Qere-Ketiv* cases refers only to those explicitly indicated as such and not to cases of *yatir*.
[10] Cf. I. Himbaza, "Le *nûn* marginal et la petite massore," *Textus* 20 (2000): 173–91.
[11] There is one more case with a marginal *nun* in Job (39:30). While Himbaza considers it another case of *Qere-*

Ketiv, I suggest that it should be treated independently; cf. "The Marginal *Nun* in the Masora of the Cairo Codex of the Prophets: Use and Function," VT 65 (2015): 81–90.

10–20.1.2.5.1 *Qere wela Ketiv* ("Read but not Written")

MT[A] and MT[L] indicate, in different ways, the two words that are not written in the text but that must be read: אֵלַי "unto me" in Ruth 3:5 and 3:17.

In MT[A], in both cases the phenomenon is indicated in the biblical text with a *circellus* and an extra blank space. In the MasP to Ruth 3:5, this is indicated as a simple *Qere*, אלי קרי "read 'unto me'," and in the MasP to Ruth 3:17 with the formula אלי קרי ולא כתב, "'unto me' is read but not written."

In MT[L], in Ruth 3:5 it is indicated with the vowels, accent, and the *circellus* without an extra blank space; and in 3:17 with the vowels and accent, but without a *circellus* or an extra blank space. In the MasP notes, the formula קרי ולא כת' "read but not written" is used. There is also a MasM note to Ruth 3:5, which lists the total number of cases, eleven, and gives their *simanim*: Judg 20:13; 2 Sam 8:3; 16:23; 18:20; 2 Kgs 19:31, 37; Jer 31:38; 50:29; Ezek 9:11; Ruth 3:5, 17. In this manuscript, in the MasM note to Jer 50:29, just ten cases are listed.[12]

10–20.1.2.5.2 *Ketiv wela Qere* ("Written but not Read")

In Ruth 3:12, there is a case of the opposite phenomenon: אם is written in the text but should not be read. In the text of MT[A] and MT[L], the word is unvocalized. In MT[A], the MasP note indicates כת' ולא קרי and in MT[L] כת' ולא ק' (both "written but not read") together with the symbol resembling the final *nun*. In MT[L], there is also a MasM note that lists the following passages: 2 Kgs 5:18; Jer 38:16; 51:3; Ezek 48:16; 2 Sam 15:21; Jer 39:12. This list only gives six of the eight cases traditionally denoted as *Ketiv wela Qere* (→ 1.5.4.2).

10–20.1.2.6 *Sebirin*

In MT[L], fifteen cases of this phenomenon are indicated in the MasP and two of them also have a MasM note. The alternative reading proposal is explained in all the cases (e.g., MasP to יָצָא "came forth" Dan 8:9: ג' סיב' יצאה "three [times] one would expect יצאה"; MasM: ג' סיברין לשון נקבה וקר' לשון זכר "three [times] one would expect a feminine form but a masculine form is read"). The term *sebir* is intended to support the biblical text, as is apparent in the six cases, in which the written word is confirmed by the term וקר' (e.g., MasP note to עַמִּי "my people" in Lam 3:14 reads: ג' סבר' עמים וקר' עמי "three times עמים [the plural] is suggested but עמי [the singular] is read"; → 1.5.4.3).

In MT[A], the MasP to וּבֶן "and the son" in 1 Chr 3:19 reads: ה' סביר' ובני "five [times] ובני [the plural form] is suggested." There is also a MasM note to this case that lists the five verses.

10–20.1.2.7 *Hillûfîm* "Divergences"

Some references to the differences between Ben Asher (BA) and Ben Naphtali (BN) are found in the Masorah of MT[L].[13] The two readings are given together seven times in the MasM of Psalms (Pss 31:12; 45:5; 58:7; 62:4; 119:94; 123:2; 124:1) and one in MasM-Dan 4:27; the BA reading three times (MasP-Dan 7:10; MasP-2 Chr 8:11; MasM-Prov 3:12) and the BN reading three times (MasP-1 Chr 12:7; MasM-Ezra 7:28; MasM-1 Chr 2:5). In the MasM to Ps 45:5, 62:4, 119:94, 123:2, and 1 Chr 2:5, differences on more than one word are given. In the MasM to Prov 3:12 and 1 Chr 2:5, the Teachers of Tiberias and the *Mahzor Rabbah* are recorded beside BA or BN (e.g., MasM-1 Chr 2:5: במחזורה רוב' בני פרץ בני שם לאנשי טיב' ובן נפתלי גע' בני פרץ בני שם מאריך "In the *Mahzor Rabbah* בני פרץ 'the sons of Perez' [1 Chr 2:5], בני שם 'the sons of Shem' [1 Chr 1:17], the Teachers of Tiberias and Ben Naphtali [with] *ga'yah* בני פָּרֶץ [1 Chr 2:5] בני שם [1 Chr 1:17] [with] *merka*"). In all cases, the differences are related to the accentuation and to a lesser extent to the vocalization.

In the Masorah of MT[L], there are twenty-seven references to variants between the Eastern and Western Masoretes: fifteen in the MasP notes (1 Chr 5:27; 25:27; 29:21; 2 Chr 20:10; 25:11; Prov 11:5; 30:25; Ruth 3:10; 4:17; Esth 8:7; Dan 9:7, 9, 17; Ezra 7:10; 9:6) and thirteen cases in the MasM notes (1 Chr 1:51; Job 9:13; 32:11; 33:19; 35:14; Prov 30:25; Cant 5:2;

---

[12] Martín Contreras, "Phenomenon"; → 1.5.4.2 and → 3-5.3.2.5.

[13] Díaz Esteban, "References to Ben Asher."

Qoh 3:9; 8:2; Lam 5:21; Ezra 10:28, 29; Neh 9:14). In Cant 5:2; Qoh 3:9; 8:2; and Lam 5:21, there is no *circellus* in the biblical text that indicates which word or expression is affected by the change, but the word is given in the MasM note (e.g., MasM to Qoh 3:9: מה יתרון העושה למערב׳ חס׳ ולמדנ׳ שלמ׳, "מה יתרון העושה" "What profit is there [Qoh 3:9], the Western tradition [writes העושה] defective and the Eastern tradition plene"). The differences are mostly related to the spelling of the words, to their full or defective writing, but in Lam 5:21 and Dan 9:9 a whole word is changed (MasM to Lam 5:21: למערב׳ השיבנו יהוה כת׳ למדנח׳ אדני כת׳, "for the Western tradition השיבנו יהוה is written, for the Eastern tradition אדני is written"). Some of the cases are included in the list of these variants in one of the appendices to the manuscript (folios 466ʳ–468ᵛ).

Four cases of *pelûgta'* are indicated in MTᴸ: two in the MasM notes (Ps 119:16 and Prov 26:2) and two in the MasP notes (Dan 6:3 and Ezra 4:8; → 1.5.4.4).

10–20.1.3 Relevance for Exegesis

The Masorot of MTᴸ and MTᴬ to the Writings contain some notes that are directly relevant to the interpretation of the text. Of particular relevance are the semantic content notes that can help to distinguish between homophonic forms and differentiate meanings. One example is the MasP of MTᴬ to מָשָׁל "Mashal" in 1 Chr 6:59: ל׳ שם קריה "unique as a city's name." The word appears ten times in the Bible but only in this case is it the name of a city ("Mashal"), while in the others it is a common noun meaning "proverb." The MasM of MTᴬ to תֹּם "integrity" in Ps 25:21 says: ב׳ וחס׳ לשון תמימות "twice and defective in the sense of completeness." It thus distinguishes these two cases from the other eleven cases in which תֹּם is the *qal* infinitive construct of the verb תמם "to be finished." Other cases: MasP of MTᴸ to שֶׁבֶר "Sheber" in 1 Chr 2:48; MasP of MTᴬ to וּבָרָק "gleaming" in Job 20:25; MasP of MTᴸ to רְחֹב "Rehob" in Neh 10:12, etc.

The case of הָבִי in Ruth 3:15 illustrates the benefits of using the Masorah in the textual criticism of the Hebrew Bible (→ 13.2.2.3.1).[14] This word is usually interpreted as the 2nd person feminine singular imperative *Qal* of the root יהב "give," but the information found in the MasP note in MTᴬ questions this interpretation:[15] ל׳ חס׳ לשון נקבה "unique defective and is feminine." The Masorah of other masoretic manuscripts and some masoretic works contain additional information that helps to understand this note. The MasP of manuscript M1 at the Complutense University (MTᴹ¹) to this word says: ח׳ חס׳ א׳ "eight [times written] lacking an *alef*," implying that this word does not derive from the root יהב but from בוא "bring in." According to the MasM of MTᴹ¹ to Jer 19:15 and one list of Ginsburg's masoretic compilation, the root בוא is written without the *alef* in nine passages:[16] 1 Sam 25:8; 2 Sam 5:2; 1 Kgs 12:12; 21:21; 21:29; Jer 19:15; 39:16; Mic 1:15; Ruth 3:15. Both lists include the case of Ruth, which thus needs to be parsed as the 2nd person masculine singular imperative *hiphil* of the root בוא. The second part of the note of MTᴬ ("in feminine form") should be understood in this light. The masculine form in the biblical context where one would expect to find a feminine form is a problem from a grammatical point of view. That is why the MasP of MTᴬ indicates that this word is understood as being feminine. This tradition of interpreting the word as feminine is also attested in other Masoretic notes. Therefore, the Masoretes' intention in this note was to ensure the correct interpretation of a word, whose anomalies (defective in one of the root letters and its masculine instead of the feminine form) could impede correct interpretation.

*BHQ, Part 17: Proverbs.
*BHQ, Part 18: General Introduction and Megilloth.
*BHQ, Part 20: Ezra and Nehemiah.
Cohen, *Mikra'ot Gedolot "Haketer."
Díaz Esteban, F., "References to Ben Asher and Ben Naftali in the Massora Magna written in the margins of Ms. Leningrad B 19A," *Textus* 6 (1968): 62–74.

---

[14] For a detailed explanation of this case, cf. E. Martín Contreras, "Masoretic and Rabbinic Lights on the Word הבי, Ruth 3:15: בוא or יהב?" *VT* 59 (2009): 257–65.
[15] The MasP note in Mᴸ pertains only to the accent.
[16] Ginsburg, *Massorah, vol. I, list 66, p. 166.

Martín Contreras, E., "The Phenomenon *Qere we la' ketib* in the Main Biblical Codices: New Data," VT 62 (2012): 77–87.

Wickes, W., *Two Treatises on the Accentuation of the Old Testament: On Psalms, Proverbs, and Job: On the Twenty-one Prose Books* (Prolegomenon by A. Dotan; 2 vols.; New York: Ktav Publishing, 1970).

Yeivin, **Introduction*.

Elvira Martín Contreras

21

The Biblical Text as Attested in Ancient Literature

21.1 Apocrypha and Pseudepigrapha

The following two sub-entries focus on a pair of Jewish compositions, *Jubilees* and Pseudo-Philo's *Liber antiquitatum Biblicarum* (*L.A.B.*), that rewrite the Bible, closely following the contours of their biblical source(s) while reshaping the contents due to interpretive or ideological considerations. Due to their close dependence upon specific versions of the biblical text, they are potentially relevant as witnesses to the biblical books that they rewrote.[1]

Büchler, A., "Studies in the Book of Jubilees," *REJ* 82 (1926): 253–74.
Charles, R.H., *The Book of Jubilees or the Little Genesis* (London: Adam and Charles Black, 1902).
Cross, F.M., "The Contribution of the Qumrân Discoveries to the Study of the Biblical Text," *IEJ* 16 (1966): 81–95.
Dillmann, A., "Das Buch der Jubiläen oder die kleine Genesis," *Jahrbücher der biblischen Wissenschaft* 3 (1851): 1–96.
Dillmann, A., "Beiträge aus dem Buch der Jubiläen zur Kritik des Pentateuch-Textes," *Sitzungsberichte der königlichen preussischen Akademie der Wissenschaften zu Berlin* 1 (1883): 323–40.
Frankel, Z., "Das Buch der Jubiläen," *MGWJ* 5 (1856): 311–16, 380–400.
Hendel, R.S., "4Q252 and the Flood Chronology of Genesis 7–8: A Text-Critical Solution," *DSD* 2 (1995): 72–79.
Hendel, R.S., *The Text of Genesis 1–11: Textual Studies and Critical Edition* (New York: Oxford University Press, 1998).
Kister, M., "Notes on Some New Texts from Qumran," *JJS* 44 (1993): 280–90.
Lim, T.H., "The Chronology of the Flood Story in a Qumran Text (4Q252)," *JJS* 43 (1992): 288–98.
Segal, M., "Biblical Interpretation – Yes and No," in *What is Bible?* (eds. K. Finsterbusch and A. Lange; CBET 67; Leuven: Peeters, 2012), 63–80.

VanderKam, J.C., *Textual and Historical Studies in the Book of Jubilees* (HSM 14; Missoula: Scholars Press, 1977).
VanderKam, J.C., "Jubilees and Hebrew Texts of Genesis-Exodus," *Textus* 14 (1988): 71–85.
VanderKam, J.C., *The Book of Jubilees* (2 vols.; CSCO 510–11 Scriptores Aethiopici 87–88; Leuven: Peeters, 1989).
VanderKam, J.C. and J.T. Milik, "Jubilees," *DJD* XIII: 1–185.

Michael Segal

21.1.1 Jubilees

21.1.1.1 Methodological Considerations

Jubilees, composed in the second century B.C.E., reflects a rewriting of Genesis–Exodus that follows the contours of its biblical source(s) closely enough to allow for an analysis of its textual basis, as has been noted previously by scholars.[1] As in other cases of Rewritten Bible, this task is methodologically complicated (→ 1.6), since the vast majority of the differences between *Jubilees* and the extant textual witnesses of Genesis and Exodus are the result of the interpretive input of the rewriter responsible for the later work, and are not due to a different *Vorlage*. The attempt to identify these "real" textual variants is further complicated in the case of *Jubilees* due to its transmission history: only fragmentary evidence of the original Hebrew text was preserved at Qumran (→ II.8.2),[2] the Greek translation of the Hebrew is no longer extant in direct witnesses (→ II.8.3), while the preponderance of evidence is preserved in the secondary translations from Greek into Latin (→ II.8.5) and Gəʿəz (Ethiopic; → II.8.6). The Latin translation is preserved in just one manuscript, and contains only

---

[1] This discussion here does not include those compositions that are frequently included under the rubric of Rewritten Bible but which are further removed from the contours of their biblical source texts, such as *1 Enoch* or *Testament of the Twelve Patriarchs*, since they do not allow for the direct comparison necessary for uncovering their textual *Vorlagen*. For the discussion of Rewritten Bible in Qumran texts and in Josephus' *Antiquities*, cf. below, → 21.2.2 and → 21.3.

[1] See the detailed analysis provided by Charles, *Book of Jubilees*, xxxiii–xxxix; VanderKam, *Textual and Historical Studies*, 103–205; VanderKam, "Jubilees and Hebrew Texts."

[2] The discovery of fifteen fragmentary Hebrew copies of *Jubilees* at Qumran negated the theory that the work was originally composed in Greek, and relied upon LXX itself (as had been suggested by Frankel, "Das Buch der Jubiläen," 314–16, 380–85; Büchler, "Studies in the Book of Jubilees," 257–70).

one-third of the book, while the composition is attested in its entirety only in the Ethiopic version, albeit in multiple manuscripts.³ Moreover, possible influence from LXX (→ 2.4.1) on the (reconstructed) Greek translation, and from the Ethiopic version of Genesis and Exodus upon the transmission of the Ethiopic version of *Jubilees*, should also serve as a caution against simply retroverting the Ethiopic translation of *Jubilees* to a Hebrew text that reflects a variant reading of Genesis and Exodus.

21.1.1.2 History of Scholarship

Early scholarship on *Jubilees* already noted similarities with non-MT texts of the Pentateuch (→ 2.2.3), and in particular with LXX-Gen–Exod.⁴ Dillmann suggested that the textual agreements with LXX were due to the influence of LXX-Gen–Exod (→ 2.4.1.1; → 2.4.1.2) on the Greek translator of *Jubilees*.⁵ However, this approach was criticized on the basis of the content of some of these LXX-type readings, which are fundamental to *Jubilees* as a composition. In particular, the LXX version of the postdiluvian genealogy in Genesis 11 contains an extra generation, in contrast to all other textual witnesses of the chapter, including Kainan between Arpachshad and Shelah (cf. LXX-Gen 11:13–14; see below); *Jub.* 8:1–5 explicitly mentions the birth and activities of Kainan. His inclusion is significant beyond the clear affiliation with LXX-Gen, since he is presumably among those counted in *Jub.* 2:23: "there were twenty-two leaders of humanity from Adam until him [Jacob]" (parallel to twenty-two works created during the first week), and thus was already included by the original Hebrew author in the composition of the work.⁶

In a subsequent study, Dillmann recognized that many of the biblical variants in *Jubilees* are the result of its dependence on a *Vorlage* that shared readings with SP (→ 1.2.3; → 2.2.4.1; → 2.2.4.2) and LXX of Genesis–Exodus, although he still posited that most of the shared readings with LXX were due to the Greek translator of *Jubilees*.⁷ The argument for the dependence of *Jubilees* on an independent text form of the Pentateuch was laid out in Charles' introduction to his 1902 *Jubilees* commentary. As Charles noted, this version did not agree exclusively with any extant textual witness, but frequently shared readings with SP, LXX, S (→ 2.4.5), V (→ 2.4.8), and the Targumim (when they differ from MT; → 2.4.3).⁸ He concluded that *Jubilees*' source text could be located somewhere between LXX and the Peshitta of Genesis and Exodus.⁹ VanderKam presented a comprehensive, comparative analysis between *Jubilees* and all potentially relevant extant textual witnesses of Genesis and Exodus, and came to a similar conclusion as Charles, that *Jubilees* shared non-MT readings with a number of textual witnesses, first and foremost LXX, as well as SP and the Peshitta. Following Cross' theory of local texts, VanderKam therefore classified the biblical text used by *Jubilees* as an early exemplar of the Palestinian family of texts.¹⁰ In a later study,

---

³ For an overview of the textual evidence for the text of *Jubilees* itself, see VanderKam, *The Book of Jubilees*, 2.vi–xxxi; on pp. xiv–xvi he discusses possible evidence for a Syriac translation of *Jubilees*. Throughout this volume, VanderKam provides a translation of *Jubilees* accompanied by a textual commentary (the first volume contains a critical edition of the Gəʿəz manuscripts, in addition to the less extensive evidence preserved in other languages). See also VanderKam and Milik, "Jubilees," for the Qumran Cave 4 fragments that were published subsequently.

⁴ The brief summary of scholarship on this issue is indebted to VanderKam, "Jubilees and Hebrew Texts."

⁵ Dillmann, "Das Buch der Jubiläen," 88–90.

⁶ Frankel, "Das Buch der Jubiläen," 315–16; Büchler, "Studies in the Book of Jubilees," 258. VanderKam, "Jubilees and Hebrew Texts," 76 n. 17 suggests that the count of twenty-two generations is somewhat ambiguous, depending on whether it included Jacob in the count or not. While this may be the case, the formulation of *Jub.* 8:1–5 leaves almost no doubt that it is dependent upon a version in which Kainan was an integral part of the genealogy, since it includes significant details about his life that are difficult to attribute to a Greek translator of *Jubilees* who was influenced by LXX-Gen. VanderKam, "Jubilees and Hebrew Texts," 75, further notes that *Jubilees* frequently disagrees with LXX, and thus following Dillmann's theory, the Greek translator of *Jubilees* would be very inconsistent in how he was influenced by LXX.

⁷ Dillmann, "Beiträge," 323–35.

⁸ Charles, *The Book of Jubilees*, xxxiii–xxxix.

⁹ Charles, *The Book of Jubilees*, xxxviii.

¹⁰ VanderKam, *Textual and Historical Studies*, 103–205,

VanderKam confirmed the analysis of his data, but no longer conceptualized his analysis according to Cross' theoretical framework, since it frequently differs from LXX and SP. Instead, he suggested that "it appears more like that Jub's biblical citations were drawn from a text that was rather more independent of the Palestinian family of which Sam and LXX are, at different stages, supposed to be witnesses … Its readings show that at some time after 200 B.C.E. … there was in Judea at least one copy of Genesis–Exodus that agreed more often with LXX and Sam than with MT but that was an independent witness – not part of any of the 'families' that may be represented by the famous versions."[11]

21.1.1.3 Textual Affiliations

Investigation of individual details demonstrates the frequent textual affiliation of *Jubilees* with non-MT witnesses (→ 2.2.3).[12] Thus, in *Jub.* 13:29, Abraham swears by invoking "the most high God," in agreement with LXX and the Peshitta to Gen 14:22 (and parallel to the formulation of Melchizedek in v. 19). Additional corroborative evidence for this reading can be adduced from the *Genesis Apocryphon* (1Q20) XXII:21.[13] In contrast, MT reads "the Lord, the most high God," perhaps in an attempt to differentiate Abraham's vow from that of Melchizedek. Another example is found in *Jub.* 23:8 (as attested in 2Q19 1 5), which refers to Abraham as זקן ושבע ימים "old and full of days" at the time of his death. MT-Gen 25:8, which describes Abraham's death, reads זָקֵן וְשָׂבֵעַ "old and contented," while SP reads זקן ושבע ימים "old and full of days," a reading that is also attested in LXX, the Peshitta, and the Vulgate. It is likely that the longer reading here is secondary, harmonizing the description with that of Isaac's death in Gen 35:29. If so, *Jub.* 23:8 was likely dependent on this secondary,

harmonistic variant. While *Jubilees* agrees with SP (→ 2.2.4) and/or LXX (→ 2.4.1) more frequently than with MT when they differ, it also shares readings with (proto-)MT text of Genesis–Exodus (→ 2.2.2) against these witnesses. For example, in Gen 29:23, MT (= S, V, T) reads וַיָּבֹא אֵלֶיהָ "and he [Jacob] went into her [Leah]" without explicit mention of the grammatical subject; in contrast, SP reads ויבא אליה יעקב "and Jacob went into her" in agreement with LXX. *Jub.* 28:4, the parallel verse, is in agreement with MT and lacks an explicit mention of "Jacob."[14] The complexity of the textual affiliations confirms VanderKam's assessment that *Jubilees* cannot be neatly compartmentalized as corresponding to a specific textual "family," but rather has affinities with multiple textual witnesses.[15]

Further evidence for the textual affiliation of *Jubilees* can be adduced from its treatment of the chronological data in Genesis 5 and 11.[16] In reference to the antediluvian era detailed in Genesis 5, *Jubilees* generally follows the contours of SP, both dating the flood to the year 1307/1308 to creation (cf. *Jub.* 5:23).[17] In the postdiluvian genealogy of Genesis 11, however, *Jubilees* consistently differs from all of the other textual witnesses, except for the final datum in the list, Terah's age at the birth of Abram (seventy years old according to all versions; cf. Gen 11:26 and *Jub.* 11:10, 15). At the same time,

---

esp. 136–38 (echoing the conclusion of Cross, "Contribution," 88–89).

[11] VanderKam, "Jubilees and Genesis–Exodus," 82–85 (quote from p. 83).

[12] For complete data, cf. the studies of Charles and VanderKam (n. 1, above).

[13] This reading is listed by VanderKam, *Textual and Historical Studies*, 159. SP reads "God (האלהים), the most high God."

[14] This reading is listed by VanderKam, *Textual and Historical Studies*, 146.

[15] In addition to its affiliation with the primary textual witnesses, Segal, "Biblical Interpretation," 70–80, has suggested that *Jubilees* might have also been dependent upon 4Q364 (published as 4QReworked Pentateuch[b] in *DJD* XIII), which suggests that the latter was perhaps perceived as a witness to the biblical text by the composer of *Jubilees*.

[16] For a presentation of the variant chronologies among the textual witnesses of Genesis 5 and 11, and an analysis of their development, cf. Hendel, *The Text of Genesis 1–11*, 61–80.

[17] The date of the flood, different in each of the primary textual witnesses, can be determined based upon the relative chronological data provided in Genesis 5. MT dates the flood to 1656, and LXX to 2242; cf. the table and brief discussion of *Jubilees* by Hendel, *The Text of Genesis 1–11*, 69–70. There are some minor differences between *Jubilees* and SP regarding specific generations within this chronology, but these offset each other, and therefore do not affect the larger argument here for textual affiliation with SP.

Jubilees contains an extra generation in this later list, Keinan, a significant agreement with LXX (see above).[18] This evidence also points to the complex web of textual affiliations for the biblical text(s) employed by *Jubilees*.

While the theories discussed above suggested that *Jubilees* was dependent on a specific biblical textual witness, which itself was related to multiple versions, internal evidence in *Jubilees* suggests that in certain cases its composer was aware of multiple readings and attempted to harmonize this disparate data. Thus, for example, with reference to the date on which the earth dried following the flood, all of the primary witnesses to Gen 8:14 (including MT, SP, LXX, S, V, T) note that this took place on the twenty-seventh of the second month (of the 601st year of Noah's life). In contrast, according to a parabiblical scroll from Qumran (4Q252 II 1–2), this event took place on the seventeenth of the second month.[19] *Jubilees* appears to be aware of both of these readings, since it records two separate events at the end of the flood, each on one of the two attested dates, thereby harmonizing the two readings: the earth was dry on the seventeenth of the second month (*Jub.* 5:31); on the twenty-seventh, Noah opened the ark and released all of the animals (*Jub.* 5:32).[20] This final example suggests that while it is possible, and even probable, that *Jubilees* was dependent upon copies of Genesis and Exodus that cannot be neatly affiliated with a single, extant textual witness, the composer of *Jubilees* also potentially had multiple versions of these biblical books at his disposal, thus further complicating the issue of the nature and character of his biblical source text(s).

Michael Segal

21.1.2 Pseudo-Philo

LAB and the Biblical Text

Liber Antiquitatum Biblicarum (= *LAB*), or *Biblical Antiquities*, is a Latin text, which was attributed incorrectly to the Greco-Jewish philosopher and exegete Philo of Alexandria. It is essentially a rewriting of the biblical narrative from Adam to Saul, from Genesis through Samuel. As such, it is filled with apparent echoes and quotations from the Bible and *prima facie* might shed light on the history of the biblical text.

Harrington has suggested that there is much to learn about the biblical text from *LAB* and has argued the case at some length.[1] His study is careful and detailed and, on the basis of comparisons of *LAB*'s biblical quotations and references to the Hebrew Bible and several ancient versions, concludes that *LAB* was using what Cross designated as a Palestinian (Lucianic and Proto-Lucianic; → 1.3.1.2) rather than a Babylonian or Egyptian text.[2] Harrington's article is grounded in Cross' theory of (three) "local texts" (or families or recensions). Unfortunately, since Cross enunciated his theory in 1958 (following some brief remarks by Albright[3]), fewer and fewer scholars have chosen to accept it.[4] As a result, the very foundations of Harrington's argument have been seriously weakened and it is not apparent that his conclusions can continue to stand.

---

[18] Hendel, *The Text of Genesis 1–11*, 71–77.

[19] Although 4Q252 is not a biblical text itself, it appears to be dependent upon a Genesis text in which this variant reading/date was present. Lim, "Chronology," 294, notes the use of both dates in *Jubilees*, but understandably does not address its implications for the question of the biblical text(s) used by the composer of *Jubilees*. For a discussion of the variant readings regarding the beginning and end of the flood in Genesis 7–8, cf. Hendel, *The Text of Genesis 1–11*, 54–55, and more extensively in Hendel, "4Q252 and the Flood Chronology." Hendel, however, aligns *Jubilees* solely with the Qumran text and does not note the additional date shared with the other textual witnesses.

[20] Kister, "Notes," 287.

---

[1] Harrington, "Biblical Text."

[2] Cross and his disciples have published prolifically on the theory of three "local texts." I cite here just a fraction of the relevant books and articles: Cross, "History of the Biblical Text"; Cross, "Contribution"; Cross, *"Evolution," esp. pp. 306–15 (316, n. 11; 319, n. 30); Cross, *ALQ*³, 138–42, 181–83. See also Klein, *Textual Criticism*; VanderKam, "Textual Affinities."

[3] Albright, "New Light."

[4] See, e.g., Howard, "Frank Cross"; Gooding, "A Recent Popularisation"; Davila, *Provenance*, 157; Fernández Marcos, *The Septuagint*, 74; Tov, *TCU*, 185–87.

Even were we to allow that Cross' theory of local texts was correct to the last detail, difficulties would remain with Harrington's views on *LAB* and the biblical text. Most fundamentally, it is certain that Pseudo-Philo wrote *LAB* in Hebrew. Since a study to determine the character of the biblical text he used must turn on a comparison between the Hebrew text of the Bible and the text of *LAB* as written by Pseudo-Philo, we need access to *LAB*'s original Hebrew text, which we do not have. The text of *LAB* in our possession is a translation of a Greek *Vorlage* that in turn was a translation of a Hebrew text. No matter how secure we may feel in our retroversions, the fact remains that in many places we cannot be certain of their accuracy. Thus, the most fundamental test in this whole question rests upon our knowing exactly what *LAB* wrote in Hebrew. For example, at *LAB* 1:20, Pseudo-Philo is clearly quoting Gen 5:29. But *requiem dabit* "he will give us rest," Harrington argues, represents a variant vis-à-vis MT in the text of Ps-Philo's Hebrew Bible (יניחנו "he will give us rest" for יְנַחֲמֵנוּ "he shall bring us relief"), as apparently also attested in LXX (διαναπαύσει "he shall give us rest"). But it is by no means certain that *LAB*'s *requiem dabit* could not render יְנַחֲמֵנוּ in our context. If we had *LAB*'s original Hebrew text we could render a decisive verdict.

Compounding this difficulty is another problem. Let us say that a particular passage or phrase appears not to be a quotation from the Bible (e.g., the Latin is patently different from Jerome's Latin), it might well be a paraphrase rather than a translation/quotation and therefore would not reflect at all on whether Pseudo-Philo had a text different from MT (→ 1.2.2). For example, at *LAB* 58:1, God explicitly quotes the pentateuchal words of Moses (or God), and the reference is clearly to Exod 17:14 and Deut 25:19. However, both biblical texts say "from under the heavens" while *LAB* says "from off the earth." One could easily assume a variant biblical text, but the fact is that *LAB* is paraphrasing by substituting a commonplace biblical idiom. Finally, Pseudo-Philo apparently often recalls biblical passages (especially out of context) by heart and consequently small lapses could produce reasonable readings that resemble alternative textual traditions.

While we certainly are able to learn about the text of the Hebrew Bible from Pseudo-Philo, it is much more by way of particular illuminations of individual passages or verses or words rather than in terms of sweeping generalizations or overviews.

Albright, W.F., "New Light on Early Recensions of the Hebrew Bible," *BASOR* 140 (1955): 27–35.

Cross, F.M., "The History of the Biblical Text in the Light of Discoveries in the Judean Desert," *HTR* 57 (1964): 281–99.

Cross, F.M., "The Contribution of the Qumrân Discoveries to the Study of the Biblical Text," *IEJ* 16 (1966): 81–95.

Cross, *"Evolution."

Cross, *ALQ³.

Davila, J., *Provenance of the Pseudepigrapha: Jewish, Christian, or Other?* (JSJSup 105; Leiden: Brill, 2005).

Fernández Marcos, N., *The Septuagint in Context: Introduction to the Greek Versions of the Bible* (Leiden: Brill, 2000).

Gooding, D.W., "A Recent Popularisation of Professor F.M. Cross' Theories on the Text of the Old Testament," *TynBul* 26 (1975): 113–32.

Harrington, D.J., "The Biblical Text of Pseudo-Philo's Liber Antiquitatum Biblicarum," *CBQ* 33 (1971): 1–17.

Howard, G., "Frank Cross and Recensional Criticism," *VT* (1971): 440–50.

Klein, *Textual Criticism.

Tov, *TCU.

VanderKam, J.C., "The Textual Affinities of the Biblical Citations in the Genesis Apocryphon," *JBL* 97 (1978): 45–55.

Howard Jacobson

21.2 Qumran Literature

21.2.1 Exegetical Compositions

21.2.1.1 Introduction
This article focuses on the pesher and non-pesher commentaries found among the Dead Sea Scrolls. In commentaries, the author cites a complete lemma from the scriptural text and all interpretation occurs outside the lemma. The author perhaps uses a pre-existing scriptural text as the basis for the citations, which are therefore potentially of great value for the textual history of the Hebrew Bible. This article addresses three interrelated issues in the study of the scriptural text in the commentaries: 1) Determining the underlying *Vorlage* of the scriptural citations; 2) Evaluating whether the variants should be understood as textual (drawn from a pre-existing textual version) or exegetical (introduced by the commentary's author to make the scriptural verse comport better with the exegetical aspects of the commentary); 3) Assessing the contribution of the citations to the broader history of the development of the text of the Hebrew Bible.

21.2.1.2 Corpus of Commentaries
The pesharim are a collection of previously unknown Hebrew commentaries on scriptural prophetic books. Formally, pesharim are marked by the citation of a lemma from a scriptural verse that is then provided with a unique interpretation. In most cases, a distinct technical formula intervenes between the lemma and interpretation: most commonly, some iteration of "the interpretation of the passage is …" or "its interpretation is …" Continuous pesharim are sustained interpretations of entire prophetic books or sections of books. In these texts, a lemma from the scriptural book (of varying length) is cited followed by the technical pesher formula and then the interpretation (also of varying length). This entire structure is repeated for the next lemma in the scriptural text, thus producing a series of similar units in the continuous pesher. The Dead Sea Scrolls have preserved seventeen pesher manuscripts containing continuous commentaries on scriptural books:[1] Isaiah (3Q4, 4Q161–165); Hosea (4Q166–167); Micah (1Q14, 4Q168); Nahum (4Q169); Habakkuk (1QpHab); Zephaniah (1Q15, 4Q170); Psalms (1Q16, 4Q171, 4Q173).

Another group of texts identified as thematic pesharim are characterized by the appearance of pesher exegesis of disparate scriptural passages clustered around a focused eschatological theme: 4QFlorilegium (4Q174); *Midrash on Eschatology* (4Q174, 4Q177); 11QMelchizedek (11Q13). The bulk of the pesharim were copied from the first century B.C.E. through the first half of the first century C.E., though a few reflect pre-first century B.C.E. dates. Most of these texts were likely composed in the first century B.C.E., with a small number in the late second century B.C.E.

The Dead Sea Scrolls also contain several non-pesher commentaries: *Commentary on Genesis A–D* (4Q252, 4Q253; 4Q254, 4Q254a) and *Commentary on Malachi* (4Q253a). *Commentary on Genesis A* (4Q252) – copied in the first century B.C.E. – is the best preserved of these texts. The text blends scriptural rewriting and explicit commentary.

21.2.1.3 Summary of Scholarship
Novakovic has created an exhaustive list of all scriptural citations that appear in the pesharim (both continuous and thematic) and the commentaries on Genesis and Malachi.[2] In some cases, the scriptural citations embedded in the pesharim preserve substantial portions of the underlying scriptural text. *Pesher Habakkuk*, for example, incorporates the entirety of Habakkuk 1–2 (Habakkuk 3 seems to have been deliberately excluded). Other pesharim, for example on Nahum and Isaiah, include large blocks of continuous textual material. Numerous studies have been devoted to analyzing the textual character of the citations. The well-preserved *Pesher Habakkuk* has received the

---

[1] See Horgan, *Pesharim*; Lim, *Pesharim*.
[2] Novakovic, "Index of Biblical Quotations."

bulk of this treatment.³ Scholars have also directed their attention to the more fragmentary pesharim.⁴ Among the non-pesher commentaries, scholars have examined the citations in *Commentary on Genesis A* (4Q252).⁵ Novakovic has created a second list where she collects all the presumed text-critical variants in the pesharim and other commentaries.⁶ A summary of the evidence has been prepared by Lange.⁷

Scholars have taken different approaches to incorporating this data into critical editions of the biblical books associated with the pesharim. For example, Elliger includes variants from *Pesher Habakkuk* in the critical apparatus of Habakkuk in *BHS (1967). Elliger employs the same siglum used elsewhere in *BHS to denote biblical manuscripts from Qumran. The Twelve Minor Prophets volume of *BHQ (2010) likewise incorporates variants from the pesharim.⁸ *BHQ, however, distinguishes between the Qumran biblical manuscripts and citations in non-biblical texts by using the more specific siglum for the individual pesher manuscripts (e.g., 1QpHab). Moreover, the commentary portion in *BHQ allows the editor to provide an assessment of the text-critical value of the pesher variants. The Hebrew University Bible Project volume on Isaiah incorporates *Pesher Isaiah* into its critical apparatus. The Minor Prophets volume of *Biblia Qumranica takes a more systematic approach by providing the pesher citations their own column in the synoptic presentation of ancient witnesses from the Judean Desert.⁹

21.2.1.4 In Search of the *Vorlage* of the Scriptural Citations

The identification of the purported *Vorlage* of the scriptural citations is an important starting point for determining their text-critical value. Scholars cannot assess whether a citation possesses a variant unless one has a textual baseline against which to evaluate the potential variant. The textual data in the pesharim regarding this question is equivocal and thus scholars have outlined several different approaches.

The purported predominance of MT figures prominently in many of the studies noted above, especially in the early years of research. Several scholars explain the many orthographical and minor deviations from MT (→ 1.2.2) as evidence that the author of *Pesher Habakkuk* utilized a vulgar proto-MT recension.¹⁰ Scholars have also argued for an MT *Vorlage* for *Pesher Micah* and *Pesher Nahum*.¹¹

Lim's analysis of *Pesher Habakkuk* identifies substantial disagreements with proto-MT (→ 9.2.2) in the realm of word order, word choice, use or non-use of pronominal suffixes, number, gender, conjunction and mood, use of verbs, and in syntax.¹² This approach is echoed in a separate study that applies a statistical analysis to all the pesharim.¹³ While never fully rejecting proto-MT as the purported *Vorlage*, Lim observes that the high number of divergent reading in all the pesharim (especially *Pesher Nahum*) should give scholars pause before accepting the conclusions of many scholars that the pesharim utilized a proto-MT *Vorlage*. He therefore asserts that scholars must analyze each variant in the citations independently in dialogue with all ancient versions.

The divergent readings in the pesharim could reflect a singular *Vorlage* that is not preserved in any textual witness. These divergent readings, however, are more commonly explained as the

---

³ Van der Ploeg, "Le Rouleau d' Habacuc"; Molin, "Habakkukkommentar"; Elliger, *Habakuk-Kommentar*, 48–58; Segert, "Habakuk-Rolle"; Brownlee, *Text of Habakkuk*; Stendahl, *School of St. Matthew*, 185–90; Vegas Montaner, "Computer-Assisted Study"; Lim, "Eschatological Orientation"; Goldberg, "Variant Readings"; Lim, *Holy Scripture*; Lim, *Pesharim*, 54–63.

⁴ Weiss, "Comparison"; Collin, "Recherches"; Sinclair, "Hebrew Text"; Brooke, "Biblical Texts"; Lim, *Holy Scripture*.

⁵ Bernstein, "4Q252 i 2," 421–27; repr. in *Reading and Re-Reading Scripture at Qumran*, Vol. 1 (Leiden: Brill, 2013), 126–32; Brooke, "Some Remarks on 4Q252," 1–25; Lim, "Biblical Quotations," 71–79.

⁶ Novakovic, "Text-Critical Variants."

⁷ See the respective passages in Lange, *Handbuch.

⁸ Gelston, *Minor Prophets*, esp. 6.

⁹ Ego, Lange, and De Troyer, *Minor Prophets*.

---

¹⁰ See van der Ploeg, "Le Rouleau d' Habacuc," 4; Elliger, *Studien zum Habakuk-Kommentar*, 48; Segert, "Zur Habakuk-Rolle," 608.

¹¹ Weiss, "A Comparison," 437; Sinclair, "Hebrew Text," 263.

¹² Lim, "Eschatological Orientation," 189–90.

¹³ Lim, *Holy Scripture*, 69–94.

result of an eclectic *Vorlage*. This approach asserts that the pesher author selected from different available textual versions or used a pre-existing eclectic text.¹⁴ The author of the pesher chose a particular textual version when it worked well with the interpretation advanced in the pesher unit. This phenomenon explains why the citations vary in agreement with different textual versions.

The evaluation of variants in *Commentary on Genesis A* follows a similar line of analysis. Brooke, for example, examines each potential variant in the text in dialogue with the ancient versions.¹⁵ Although the sampling of variants is small, Brooke detects greater alignment with the text-type known from LXX (→ 2.4.1.1) than any other preserved ancient version.

21.2.1.5 Identification of Textual and Exegetical Variants

Several types of variants can be detected in the scriptural citations. The pesharim and *Commentary on Genesis A* are written with the full orthography characteristic of many of the sectarian Dead Sea scrolls. It is not entirely clear whether these orthographic variants were present in the scriptural *Vorlagen* or were introduced when the citation was incorporated into the commentary (or some combination of these possibilities). These variants are generally discussed in the context of the history of Hebrew orthography or in connection with the variation in spelling systems in Masoretic manuscripts.¹⁶ In addition, several citations evince scribal errors generated by the pesher author.

The lack of agreement among scholars regarding the *Vorlage* of the pesharim precludes the use of a single ancient version as the baseline against which to evaluate potential textual variants. We should therefore approach the citations in the commentaries as potential witnesses to the diversity of textual versions in the Second Temple period. In this sense, we are interested here in instances where the underlying scriptural text cited in the commentary provides a witness to the state of the text of the Hebrew Bible otherwise unattested in the ancient versions or preserves additional evidence for a unique reading in one of the ancient versions.

Hab 1:9 in 1QpHab III:8–9: "All of them bent on violence, their faces (like) the east wind (קדים)." MT and LXX are slightly different for the last section: "with faces pressing forward" (קָדִימָה/ἐξ ἐναντίας). The only difference is the lack of the final *he* in the pesher citation. It is possible that this is a scribal error (either in the *Vorlage* of the pesher or in the author's citation). The text as attested in the pesher is similarly found in Tʲ (רוח קדימה) and V (*ventus urens*).

Hab 1:17 in 1QpHab VI:8–9: "Therefore he keeps his sword (חרבו) always drawn to kill nations without pity." The reading "sword" is in agreement with the Naḥal Ḥever Minor Prophets scroll (8ḤevXIIgr 17:18: μάχαιραν αὐτοῦ). MT and LXX have here "net" (חֶרְמוֹ/ἀμφίβληστρον).

Gen 6:3 in 4Q252 1 i 2–3: "My spirit shall not dwell (ידור) with man forever, their days shall be determined to be one hundred and twenty years until the waters of the flood come." The key word in this citation is ידור "dwell." MT has the unclear יָדוֹן (*NRSV "abide"; NIV "contend"). The uncertain meaning of this expression prompted several ancient versions to offer a contextual guess: Tᵒ: יתקיים "exist"; V: *permanebit*, "shall remain." This interpretation is also known in *Jub* 5:8. Bernstein argues that ידור "dwell" similarly represents an attempt by the author of 4Q252 to make sense of the *unclear Vorlage* ידון.¹⁷ The evidence of LXX καταμείνῃ "to remain, abide" complicates this conclusion. Is this also an exegetical guess or a straightforward translation of a Hebrew *Vorlage* containing ידור "dwell"? Lim and Brooke contend that καταμείνῃ "to remain, abide" is a reasonably expected translation for the Hebrew ידור "dwell" and therefore LXX and 4Q252 attest to the same textual variant.¹⁸ Brooke further suggests, however, that these Hebrew traditions reflect an older contextual rendering of an earlier Hebrew *Vorlage* of ידון.¹⁹ This example demon-

---

¹⁴ Molin, "Habakkukkommentar," 357; Elliger, *Studien zum Habakuk-Kommentar*, esp. 148; Stendahl, *School of St. Matthew*, 190; Brownlee, *Text of Habakkuk*, 114–15; Vegas Montaner, "Computer-Assisted Study," 318; Lim, *Pesharim*, 60–61.

¹⁵ Brooke, "Some Remarks on 4Q252," esp. 24–25.

¹⁶ See, e.g., Brownlee, *Text of Habakkuk*, 96–108.

¹⁷ Bernstein, "4Q252 i 2."
¹⁸ Lim, "Biblical Quotations"; Brooke, "Some Remarks," 8–9.
¹⁹ Brooke, "Some Remarks," 8–9.

strates the porous boundaries between the scriptural transmission and interpretation.

The identification of an exegetical variant is more complicated. An exegetical variant refers to instances where the author of the commentary has deliberately modified the text of the citation in order to make the scriptural verse comport better with the exegetical aspects of the commentary. In these cases, we would not expect to find any support for this reading in the ancient versions. Moreover, the variant should factor significantly in the interpretation portion of the commentary. If not, we can assume that this variant was merely in the textual version utilized by the author. At the same time, however, the exegetical role of a variant does not guarantee that the author modified the scriptural text. The exegesis may simply be linked to the text as found in the presumed *Vorlage* utilized by the author (as in examples above). As in most text-critical analysis, no universal criterion can be applied. Scholars must analyze each individual case on its own merits in dialogue with the ancient versions in order to decide if any particular scriptural citation has been modified for exegetical purposes. The only unequivocal criterion for detecting an exegetical variant is when the author cites the same scriptural passage in two different ways:[20]

Hab 2:17 in 1QpHab XI:17–XII:10: In the initial lemma portion, the verse is cited as in MT and LXX as "[for the crimes perpetrated against Lebanon he will bury you, for the robbery of beasts,] he will smite you; for crimes against men and wrongs against lands, against cities and all their inhabitants" (מדמי אדם וחמס ארץ קריה וכול יושבי בה; XI:17–XII:1). The pesher understands the "crimes against men" as a reference to the crimes committed by the Wicked Priest against specific men, the sectarian community. The pesher continues by re-citing part of the passage: "because of crimes against the city and injustice in the land" (ואשר אמר מדמי קריה וחמס ארץ; lines 6–7). This lemma is reused to link the crimes of the Wicked Priest to a specific city: "'the city' (הקריה) refers to Jerusalem, where the Wicked Priest committed his abhorrent deeds, defiling the Temple of God" (lines 7–8). This exegesis is predicated on the scriptural verse indicating that the crimes are against the city. In order for this exegesis to work, the author has modified the citation from "crimes against men" to "crimes against the city." The new scriptural language, however, is not entirely fabricated by the author. Rather, "city" already appears in Hab 2:17 alongside the "land" as an object of the violence. The pesher author merely elides the intervening content and makes the crimes also perpetrated against the "city" (מדמי אדם וחמס ארץ קריה). This subtle rewriting of the verse follows well-known techniques from scriptural rewriting in the Second Temple period.

The example of Hab 2:17 demonstrates that the pesher authors did in fact modify scriptural citations for exegetical purposes and increases the likelihood that some of the uncertain cases should be similarly classified:

Hab 2:15 in 1QpHab XI:2–3: "Woe to the one who gets his friend drunk, pouring out his anger, making him drink, just to get a look at their holy days (מועדיהם)." MT (מְעוֹרֵיהֶם "their nakedness"), LXX (τὰ σπήλαια αὐτῶν "their private parts" *NETS*), and all extant textual versions have some version of "nakedness" rather than "holy days." The pesher unit that follows recounts an incident when the Wicked Priest pursued the Teacher of Righteousness to the latter's place of exile "in the heat of his anger." The incident is described as occurring on the Day of Atonement following the sectarian community's calendar. The exegetical connection to the scriptural lemma is clear: the Wicked Priest hounded the Teacher and his community on "*their* holy days." The absence of any witness to this textual version suggests that the pesher author modified the scriptural text in the service of the exegetical connection. The exegetical variant involves only a slight alteration of the *resh* to a *dalet*.

Nah 3:6 in 4Q169 3–4 iii 1–2: "I will throw your abominations at you, I will treat you with scorn, I will make you repulsive (כאורה)." MT and all versions have for the last part: "make a spectacle of you (כְּרֹאִי)." Brooke suggests that the pesher author has modified the scriptural text through deliberate metathesis, thereby creating the alternate form כאר meaning "repulsive."[21] This alternate form factors in the pesher

---

[20] Lim, *Holy Scripture*, 97–98.

[21] Brooke, "Biblical Texts," 93 (cf. Weiss, "A Comparison," 437

unit where all Israel will "be disgusted" (כארום) with the Seekers of Smooth Things (4Q169 3–4 iii 4).

These three examples demonstrate the conservative nature of textual alteration. Large-scale modifications are not found. When the pesher author does alter the citation, it is generally only a single word and in some cases only a letter or two.

Another way to link the scriptural citation and its interpretation is for the pesher author to break from the *Vorlage* that he is otherwise following and incorporate a different textual version that yields a better exegetical payoff. As noted above, however, it is not always clear when the author may be following a single *Vorlage*. When the citation agrees with one version against another, it is rarely clear if this is the case because the citation accurately reflects the textual version utilized by the author or the author has deliberately selected this alternate reading. The only unequivocal case for such a situation can be found when the pesher author seems to be aware of two textual traditions.

> **Hab 2:16 in 1QpHab XI:8–11**: "You are satisfied with disgrace, not honor? So go ahead and drink until you stagger (והרעל); the cup of the Lord's right hand will come around for you, and then shame will cover your honor." The expression והרעל in the pesher matches LXX διασαλεύθητι καὶ σείσθητι "and shake, and quake" (*NETS). This particular reading makes good sense with the pesher unit that condemns the Wicked Priest who "walked in the ways of drunkenness." At first glance this passage seems to present a textual variant in agreement with LXX. Yet, the pesher simultaneously censures the Wicked Priest because "he had not circumcised his heart's foreskin (עורלת לבו)." While this may be another example of deliberate metathesis (הערל → הרעל), the resulting form echoes the text as found in MT: וְהֵעָרֵל "and be uncircumcised." The double reading in the pesher unit suggests that the author is aware of both LXX and MT. The pesher author may have chosen והרעל for his lemma both because it presents a smoother reading of the scriptural verse than MT and it provides the lemmatic basis for the pesher exegesis.

n. 13).

21.2.1.6 Contribution to the Textual History of the Hebrew Bible

The pesharim and other commentaries among the Dead Sea Scrolls provide an important witness to the scriptural text in the late Second Temple period. The authors of these commentaries utilized pre-existing scriptural texts as the basis for their lemma citations. Moreover, the commentaries reflect the diversity of textual traditions well known from Judean Desert scriptural manuscripts. Yet, the scriptural *Vorlagen* of these commentaries cannot be easily categorized alongside pre-existing textual traditions. While each author may have followed different principles, the evidence suggests that the authors were not relegated to a single *Vorlage* when citing the scriptural texts. Even if the incorporation of diverse textual versions is motivated by exegetical objectives, they are still witnesses to the state of the text of the Hebrew Bible.

In some cases, moreover, the author has newly fashioned the textual content thereby creating a scriptural citation with no textual pedigree. However, even these exegetical variants should be fully incorporated into the textual history of the Hebrew Bible. The commentaries, like many other examples of exegesis in the Second Temple period, demonstrate that exegesis does not happen only after an authoritative text is fixed. Second Temple period exegetes at times regarded themselves as participants in the ongoing production of the scriptural text itself. The evidence suggests that the pesher authors could periodically modify a word or two in the scriptural lemma in order to make their exegetical material work better. In these cases, the altered scriptural citation is still regarded as a scriptural citation. So, we must reckon with the notion that the ancient authors of the pesharim and related commentaries had very fluid notions of what constitutes a scriptural passage.

Bernstein, M.J., "4Q252 i 2: לא ידור רוחי באדם לעולם: Biblical Text or Biblical Interpretation?" *RevQ* 16 (1993–1995): 421–27; repr. in *Reading and Re-Reading Scripture at Qumran*, Vol. i (Leiden: Brill, 2013), 126–32.

Brooke, G.J., "The Biblical Texts in the Qumran Commentaries: Scribal Errors or Exegetical Variants?" in

Early Jewish and Christian Exegesis: Studies in Memory of William Hugh Brownlee (eds. C.A. Evans and W.F. Stinespring; Atlanta: Scholars Press, 1987), 85–100.

Brooke, G.J., "Some Remarks on 4Q252 and the Text of Genesis," *Textus* 19 (1998): 1–25.

Brownlee, W.H., *The Text of Habakkuk in the Ancient Commentary from Qumran* (JBL Monograph Series 11; Philadelphia: SBL, 1959).

Collin, M., "Recherches sur l'histoire textuelle du Prophète Michée," *VT* 21 (1971): 281–97.

Ego, B., A. Lange, and K. De Troyer (eds.), *Biblia Qumranica*, Vol. 3B, *Minor Prophets* (Leiden: Brill, 2005).

Elliger, K., *Studien zum Habakuk-Kommentar vom Toten Meer* (BHT 15; Tübingen: Mohr Siebeck, 1953).

Gelston, A., **BHQ*, Part 13: *The Twelve Minor Prophets*.

Goldberg, I., "Variant Readings in Pesher Habakkuk," *Textus* 17 (1994): 9–24 [Hebr.].

Horgan, M., *Pesharim: Qumran Interpretations of Biblical Books* (CBQMS 8; Washington: Catholic Biblical Association of America, 1979).

Lange, **Handbuch*.

Lim, T.H., "Eschatological Orientation and the Alteration of Scripture in the Habakkuk Pesher," *JNES* 49 (1990): 185–94.

Lim, T.H., *Holy Scripture in the Qumran Commentaries and Pauline Letters* (Oxford: Oxford University Press, 1997).

Lim, T.H., "Biblical Quotations in the Pesharim and the Text of the Bible: Methodological Considerations," in *The Bible as Book: The Hebrew Bible and the Judaean Desert Discoveries* (eds. E.D. Herbert and E. Tov; London: British Library, 2002), 71–79.

Lim, T.H., *Pesharim* (London: T & T Clark, 2002).

Molin, G., "Der Habakkukkommentar von 'En Fesha in der alttestamentlichen Wissenschaft," *TZ* 8 (1952): 340–57.

Novakovic, L., "Index of Biblical Quotations in the Pesharim, Other Commentaries, and Related Documents," in J.H. Charlesworth, *Pesharim and Qumran History: Chaos or Consensus?* (Grand Rapids: Eerdmans, 2002), 119–28.

Novakovic, L., "Text-Critical Variants in the Pesharim, Other Commentaries, and Related Documents," in J.H. Charlesworth, *Pesharim and Qumran History: Chaos or Consensus?* (Grand Rapids: Eerdmans, 2002), 129–58.

van der Ploeg, J., "Le Rouleau d' Habacuc de la grotte de 'Ain Fešḫa," *BibOr* 8 (1951): 2–11.

Segert, S., "Zur Habakuk-Rolle aus dem Funde vom Toten Meer I–IV," *ArOr* 21 (1953): 218–39; 22 (1954): 99–113, 444–59; 23 (1955): 178–83, 364–73, 575–619.

Sinclair, L.A., "Hebrew Text of the Qumran Micah Pesher and Textual Traditions of the Minor Prophets," *RevQ* 11 (1982–1984): 253–63.

Stendahl, K., *The School of St. Matthew and Its Use of the Old Testament* (2nd ed.; Philadelphia: Fortress Press, 1968; 1st ed. 1954).

Vegas Montaner, L., "Computer-Assisted Study of the Relation between 1QpHab and the Ancient (Mainly Greek) Biblical Versions," *RevQ* 14 (1989–1990): 307–23.

Weiss, R., "A Comparison between the Masoretic and the Qumran Texts of Nahum III, 1–11," *RevQ* 4 (1963–1964): 433–39.

Alex P. Jassen

21.2.2 Rewritten Bible/Parabiblical texts

The corpus of parabiblical texts from Qumran represents an important but complex source of information about the textual history of the Bible. On the one hand, these texts testify to the increasing prominence and authority of the works that would come to be included in the Hebrew Bible.[1] On the other hand, they bear witness to a period in which individual biblical books circulated in a variety of different forms simultaneously and in which many "parabiblical" works themselves claimed and, apparently, were granted scriptural authority. In other words, they testify to a time when "Scripture" meant something quite different from what it would later come to mean in both Judaism and Christianity. After some preliminary remarks about the texts under consideration here, this article will begin with a discussion of the particular challenges that must be confronted in order to glean text-historical information from these texts. It will then reflect on the different kinds of results that emerge from such study.

21.2.2.1 The Texts

The basic data set for this article is comprised of all the manuscripts classified as "parabiblical" in the annotated list of Qumran texts in Vol. XXXIX

---

[1] Brooke, "Authority and Canon," 93–98.

of the *DJD* series, except for those known prior to the Qumran finds (e.g., *Jubilees*, *1 Enoch*), which are treated in → 21.1. The texts include, among others, the *Genesis Apocryphon*, *Temple Scroll*, *Apocryphon of Moses*, *Apocryphon of Joshua*, *Pseudo-Ezekiel*, *Apocryphon of Jeremiah*, *Aramaic Levi Document*, and various testaments such as the *Visions of Amram*.[2] All of these compositions make use, in varying ways and to varying degrees, of texts, language, characters, or motifs known to us from biblical books. They differ from the "exegetical compositions" discussed in → 21.2.1 not in their degree of interest in the scriptural text (which is always considerable) but in that they do not explicitly quote Scripture. Instead, sentences, phrases, single words, or motifs known from scriptural books are incorporated seamlessly into a new composition. The implicit, rather than explicit, use of Scripture is a function of the literary form of these compositions, which tend to claim for themselves an antiquity equal to, if not greater than, that of the scriptural texts they draw upon. This portrayal can be accomplished through the explicit use of pseudepigraphy (as in the *Temple Scroll*, *Genesis Apocryphon*, and *Pseudo-Ezekiel*), or by mimicking the voice and setting of existing scriptural works (as seems to be the case for *Apocryphon of Jeremiah C* and *Apocryphon of Moses*). The further specification of a subset of these "parabiblical" texts as "rewritten Bible" (or "rewritten Scripture") has occasioned a great deal of scholarly debate as to the suitability and proper limits of this term.[3] For the purposes of this article, it is sufficient to think of "rewritten Bible" as including those texts that engage with earlier Scripture especially extensively.[4]

21.2.2.2 Using Rewritten/Parabiblical Texts to Study the Textual History of the Bible

To the extent that parabiblical texts reuse or re-present the texts of existing scriptural books, they can constitute valuable sources of information on the development of the books of the Hebrew Bible. Yet the nature of these texts presents numerous pitfalls for scholars seeking to use them in this way. The same feature that makes parabiblical texts relevant to this inquiry – their reuse of earlier Scripture – also complicates the evidence they provide, for these are not direct witnesses to the text of Scripture. They are texts that *use* Scripture, reconfiguring it to meet their own needs. Thus, we can take as given that any rewritten or parabiblical text will have made changes to whatever text of Scripture it draws upon. There was a time when scholars tended to assume that the authors of parabiblical texts must have had versions of biblical books available to them that were very like the Masoretic Text (MT; → 1.2.2), or if not MT then other known versions like the Septuagint (LXX; → 1.3.1.1) or Samaritan Pentateuch (SP; → 1.2.3). If this is one's starting point, then it is an easy task to describe the rewriting work of a given author: one simply compares the parabiblical text with known versions and describes the differences. The evidence of the Qumran biblical texts, however, makes such a procedure untenable, since they demonstrate that numerous forms of different books of Scripture circulated simultaneously, sometimes in versions very similar to those that have come down to us, but often with readings not preserved in previously known versions.[5] We must assume that many other such variant readings once existed, but have now been lost. This means that identifying the form of Scripture underlying any given parabiblical text is a tricky task; there is no *a priori* way to decide which elements of the text derive from the author's scriptural *Vorlage*, and which were introduced by the

---

[2] For a complete list, see A. Lange with U. Mittmann-Richert, "Annotated List of the Texts from the Judaean Desert Classified by Content and Genre," *DJD* XXXIX: 115–64 (122–29).

[3] For a recent overview, see Zahn, "Rewritten Scripture," and the contributions to the volume *In the Second Degree: Paratextual Literature in Ancient Near Eastern and Ancient Mediterranean Cultures and Its Reflections in Medieval Literature* (eds. P.S. Alexander, A. Lange, and R. Pillinger; Leiden: Brill, 2010).

[4] I have sought to develop a more narrow definition in M. Zahn, "Genre and Rewritten Scripture: A Reassessment," *JBL* 131 (2012): 271–88.

[5] See, e.g., Ulrich, "Text of the Hebrew Scriptures"; Segal, "Bible and Rewritten Bible," 12–16; Tov, "Authority," 289–91; Lange, *Handbuch*, 20. See also Talmon, "The Textual Study of the Bible: A New Outlook" (1975), and the other essays collected in Talmon, *Text*, which laid the groundwork for much contemporary scholarship in this area.

21.2.2 REWRITTEN BIBLE/PARABIBLICAL TEXTS

author.[6] Each individual reading must be evaluated separately according to the specific evidence available, and in many cases no decision can be made with confidence.

Some examples will illustrate this point more clearly. To begin with, one of the only clear pieces of evidence we have that a given reading originated in a *Vorlage* and not with the author of the parabiblical composition is if the reading also occurs in a known copy of the biblical book in question. This principle, of course, underlies the entire discussion surrounding parabiblical texts, which could not be identified as such if we were unable to observe parallels between their texts and known texts of biblical books. Thus, when the *Temple Scroll* reads כי תקרב אל עיר להלחם עליה וקראתה עליה לשלום "if you approach a city to fight against it, you shall offer it terms of peace" (11QT^a LXII:5–6), we note that exactly the same words appear in MT-Deut 20:10.[7] We can be fairly certain that the author of the *Temple Scroll* did not compose these words independently but drew them from a text of Deuteronomy. In this case, the known early versions of Deuteronomy preserve no variants, so we cannot say anything further about *what kind of* text of Deuteronomy the *Temple Scroll* used.

The situation becomes somewhat more complex in a case like 11QT^a LIV:19, where we find ואם ישיתכה אחיכה בן אביכה או בן אמכה או בנכה או בתכה "and if someone should entice you – your brother, the son of your father or the son of your mother, or your son or your daughter ..." A similar law appears in MT-Deut 13:7: כִּי יְסִיתְךָ אָחִיךָ בֶן־אִמֶּךָ אוֹ־בִנְךָ אוֹ־בִתְּךָ "if someone should entice you – your brother, the son of your mother, or your son or your daughter ..." Besides insignificant orthographic differences, the *Temple Scroll* differs from MT in two places. It reads ואם "and if" instead of כִּי "if" (using a different Hebrew word for "if") and it defines the brother as "*the son of your father or* the son of your mother," instead of just "the son of your mother" as in MT.

Again, we can assume that this law did not originate with the *Temple Scroll*, but that the author drew it from some kind of text of Deuteronomy. But where do the differences come from? Did the *Temple Scroll* use a text like MT, but change it? Or did the author use a text of Deuteronomy that differed from MT?

The longer reading בן אביכה או בן אמכה "the son of your father or the son of your mother," though it is absent from MT, does occur in three other versions of Deuteronomy: LXX, SP, and 4QDeut^c. The fact that it is so widespread in textual witnesses of Deuteronomy suggests that the *Temple Scroll* did not change Deuteronomy here, but was using a copy of Deuteronomy that already contained the longer reading.[8] The explanation for the first difference is less obvious. There are no other Hebrew manuscripts of Deut 13:7 that have ואם instead of כִּי. This makes it more likely that the author of the *Temple Scroll* may be responsible for this change. Further evidence in this direction can be drawn from a study of the *Temple Scroll* as a whole: there are in fact ten instances where the *Temple Scroll* reads אם while MT and other witnesses have כי, and various factors suggest that the author may have had concrete reasons for using the alternate conjunction.[9] On the other hand, the possibility cannot be ruled out that the author used a scriptural text where these changes from כי to אם had already been made.

These examples involve quite minor variants, and it comes as no surprise that, in minor details like this, parabiblical texts might reflect *Vorlagen* different from MT or even from any other known version. Such small variants, whether they result from scribal errors or from intentional exegetical intervention, pervade all Second Temple copies of biblical books. It might be assumed, in contrast, that cases of more extensive disagreement

---

[6] See Zahn, *Rethinking Rewritten Scripture*, 21–24.

[7] The only difference between the *Temple Scroll* and MT here is the spelling of קראתה "you shall offer": the *Temple Scroll* presents a longer orthography (also present in SP), while MT has the shorter וְקָרָאתָ.

[8] On the origins of this variant, see B.M. Levinson, "Textual Criticism, Assyriology, and the History of Interpretation: Deuteronomy 13:7a as a Test Case in Method," *JBL* 120 (2001): 211–43.

[9] See B.M. Levinson and M. Zahn, "Revelation Regained: The Hermeneutics of כי and אם in the Temple Scroll," *DSD* 9 (2002): 295–346.

between biblical and parabiblical texts are more likely to have resulted from the creative rewriting of the author of the parabiblical text. But, in fact, a small number of examples illustrate that the same range of issues and possibilities that we confront in cases of minor variation must also be taken into account in analysis of larger variants. Even what looks to us like an entirely new paragraph or section may have been taken from a version of Scripture unknown to us.

One case illustrating this possibility involves a paragraph describing how Nahash, king of the Ammonites in the time of Saul, oppressed the Israelites dwelling in Transjordan by gouging out their eyes. Josephus includes this story in his rewriting of biblical history in *Antiquities* VI.5.1 (= 68–71), but it does not occur in versions of 1 Samuel known prior to the Qumran discoveries. It would be easy to assume, given the absence of evidence to the contrary, that Josephus here inserts a non-biblical element into his narrative. The Qumran finds, however, include a biblical manuscript of Samuel that preserves the same story (4QSam^a). Now it appears that Josephus did not add this element after all, but found it in the text of Samuel he was using, which must have resembled 4QSam^a.[10]

A final, similar example again comes from the *Temple Scroll*.[11] Along with its rewriting of a large section of the laws of Deuteronomy, the *Temple Scroll* presents instructions for building a massive temple and its accompanying courts. Although the temple plans use some biblical terminology, they go far beyond any description of the temple or tabernacle found in known versions of the Bible. Since the early days of research on the *Temple Scroll* it was speculated that the *Temple Scroll* may have drawn its plan for the temple and temple courts from an existing source, and indeed, a fragment from another Qumran manuscript, 4Q365a, overlaps almost exactly with the intructions for the temple courts found in 11QT^a

XXXVIII–XLI. 4Q365a was originally classified as an extrabiblical text, perhaps even an alternative form of the *Temple Scroll* itself. More recently, however, it has been argued that 4Q365a is a part of the larger manuscript 4Q365 (4QReworked Pentateuch C), and that this manuscript represents not an extrabiblical or parabiblical text, but an expanded edition of the Pentateuch; that is, a biblical text.[12] If this is the case, then the temple plan found in the *Temple Scroll* may have already existed in the author's scriptural *Vorlage*. Without the evidence of 4Q365a and 4Q365, we would never have guessed that that could have been the case.

All of these examples are meant to illustrate the uncertainty that will inevitably mark attempts to reconstruct the shape of the scriptural sources of parabiblical and rewritten texts. We can only be relatively confident of what these sources looked like if the particular reading in question is actually extant in a copy of a biblical book; otherwise, it is difficult to discount the likelihood that a given reading is the original product of the parabiblical text's author. On the other hand, we cannot assume that elements not witnessed by an extant biblical text are simply nonbiblical: the examples of the Nahash story in Josephus and the plans for the temple courts in the *Temple Scroll* show that even readings dramatically different from what appears in our received versions of the Hebrew Bible could have been drawn from scriptural *Vorlagen*. This is not to say that, when we lack evidence for the origins of a particular reading, we must leave the question entirely open. Careful study of individual parabiblical texts can reveal language patterns, themes, or exegetical tendencies that may facilitate suggestions as to which readings derive from the author and which might derive from a prior source (biblical or otherwise). In very many cases, however, we will simply lack sufficient information to make a confident determination.

---

[10] For an overview, see Lange, *Handbuch*, 219–20.

[11] For fuller presentation of the argument summarized here, see M. Zahn, "4QReworked Pentateuch C and the Literary Sources of the *Temple Scroll*: A New (Old) Proposal," DSD 19 (2012): 133–58.

[12] For bibliographical references and more information, see → 2.2.1.7.2.

21.2.2.3 Parabiblical Texts and the Shape of Scripture at Qumran

The previous section highlighted the difficulties involved with using parabiblical texts to study the textual history of the Bible. These caveats are important, the more so because of past tendencies to assume that a given text's *Vorlage* resembled known versions unless there was clear evidence to the contrary. Nevertheless, study of the Qumran parabiblical texts has done a great deal to enrich our understanding of the development of Hebrew Scripture in a variety of ways.

First of all, despite the challenges they present, these texts do contribute to the text-critical enterprise of establishing the forms in which biblical books circulated in the late Second Temple period. Taken as a whole, they confirm the picture painted by the Qumran biblical texts themselves of substantial textual fluidity (→ 1.2.2.). Although there are many readings not witnessed elsewhere that we will be unable to evaluate with confidence, even the comparison of parabiblical texts to known versions of Scripture can yield important results. Lange points out that much of the detailed textual work in this area remains to be done.[13] The studies that we do have, however, already indicate that parabiblical texts usually follow a mixed pattern of affiliation, sometimes agreeing with MT (→ 1.2.2) but other times with LXX (→ 1.3.1.1), SP (→ 1.2.3), or other known versions.[14] For instance, the *Temple Scroll* sometimes follows MT (→ 2.2.2), but where readings differ it often follows SP (→ 2.2.4) or LXX (→ 2.4) against MT (or, of course, presents its own unique reading). Especially interesting are a series of instances of small variants with halakhic significance where the *Temple Scroll* reads with LXX against MT.[15] 4Q158 (4QReworked Pentateuch A), which may represent a copy of Exodus rather than a parabiblical text, clearly rewrites a *Vorlage* similar to SP in that it reflects SP's characteristic major changes to the Sinai pericope. On the other hand, it reads with MT and/or LXX against SP in numerous minor variants.[16] One fragment of *Apocryphon of Jeremiah C* (4Q385a 17) quotes Nah 3:8–11 in a form that is usually (but not always) closer to LXX and to the *Vorlage* of 4QpNahum than to MT.[17] The pervasiveness of mixed patterns of affiliation constitutes a strong indication that there was not yet a "standard" biblical text that would have been known to the composers or copyists of these texts.[18]

Second, rewritten and parabiblical texts contribute to the study of the textual history of the Bible in another way, by providing additional examples of how books that later became part of the Bible were being read in the late Second Temple period. In other words, they allow us to see more clearly the exegetical concerns of Second Temple audiences. Especially informative are cases where we see the same types of interpretations reflected in rewritten/parabiblical texts and in copies or editions of the biblical books themselves. For example, the *Temple Scroll* contains a prohibition on slaughtering pregnant animals that may belong to the same stream of tradition as an addition to Exod 23:19, "You shall not boil a kid in its mother's milk," preserved in SP.[19] Similarly, MT-Ezek (→ 8.2.2) shows a special concern, when compared to other versions, for the question of when Ezekiel's prophecies would be fulfilled. The same concern surfaces in a different way in *Pseudo-Ezekiel*.[20] Parallels such as this – and many

---

[13] Lange, *Handbuch*, 21.

[14] For a different view, see → 2.1.5.

[15] L.H. Schiffman, "The Septuagint and the *Temple Scroll*: Shared 'Halakhic' Variants," in L.H. Schiffman, *The Courtyards of the House of the Lord* (ed. F. García Martínez; STDJ 75; Leiden: Brill, 2008), 85–98. On patterns of agreement in the *Temple Scroll*, see also G. Brooke, "The Textual Tradition of the *Temple Scroll* and Recently Published Manuscripts of the Pentateuch," in *The Dead Sea Scrolls: Forty Years of Research* (eds. D. Dimant and U. Rappaport; STDJ 10; Leiden: Brill, 1992), 261–82.

[16] On this text, see Zahn, *Rethinking Rewritten Scripture*, 25–74.

[17] D. Dimant, *DJD* XXX, 157–58.

[18] See Lange, *Handbuch*, 20–21.

[19] D.A. Teeter, "'You Shall Not Seethe a Kid in its Mother's Milk': The Text and the Law in Light of Early Witnesses," *Textus* 24 (2009): 37–63.

[20] M. Popović, "Prophet, Books and Texts: Ezekiel, *Pseudo-Ezekiel* and the Authoritativeness of Ezekiel Traditions in Early Judaism," in *Authoritative Scriptures in Ancient Judaism* (ed. M. Popović; JSJSup 141; Leiden: Brill, 2010), 227–51 (245).

more examples could be brought – illustrate that both types of scribal activity, successive editions of books of Scripture and rewritten/parabiblical compositions that rework Scripture, were part of a single process of continually renewing Scripture. As two sides of the coin of a single hermeneutical project, we should also expect that these two types of text would have mutually influenced one another: not only were rewritten texts influenced by the form(s) of biblical books their authors were familiar with, but new editions of the biblical texts themselves may incorporate responses to or reactions against ideas found in parabiblical texts.[21]

Third and finally, it is relevant to the textual history of the Bible that many of these rewritten/parabiblical texts themselves most likely had the status of Scripture in the late Second Temple period (→ 1.1.2.1). In some cases, the manuscripts are simply too fragmentary to give a clear picture, but in other cases we can tell that these texts make strong claims to antiquity and authority. Most of the *Genesis Apocryphon*, for instance, is narrated in the first person by Lamech, Noah, and Abraham; the *Temple Scroll* casts itself as the direct words of God; and *Pseudo-Ezekiel* is presented as the inspired words of the prophet. In my view, there is little reason to doubt that these texts did not just claim authority but were also granted it by at least some groups.[22] Sometimes there is clear evidence that this was indeed the case; for instance, a section also known from the *Apocryphon of Joshua* is included in 4QTestimonia (4Q175; → 2.1.7) alongside passages from Exodus, Numbers, and Deuteronomy, with no distinction made between the "biblical" texts and the one we consider "parabiblical." At the same time, therefore, as the Qumran parabiblical texts witness to the development of Scripture in a textual sense, they also document a period when Scripture comprised a broader range of texts than those now found in our Bibles. The shape of Scripture at Qumran was not what it would later become, yet the Scriptures of this time, in all their diversity, inevitably influenced the shapes that Scripture ultimately took. The subsequent course of the Bible's textual history makes it all the more important to trace those paths of scriptural development that fell out of use with the emergence of a standard text and, ultimately, a canon of Scripture.

Brooke, G.J., "Between Authority and Canon: The Significance of Reworking the Bible for Understanding the Canonical Process," in *Reworking the Bible: Apocryphal and Related Texts at Qumran: Proceedings of a Joint Symposium by the Orion Center for the Study of the Dead Sea Scrolls and Associated Literature and the Hebrew University Institute for Advanced Studies Research Group on Qumran, 15–17 January, 2002* (eds. E.G. Chazon et al.; STDJ 58; Leiden: Brill, 2005), 85–104.

Collins, J.J., "Changing Scripture," in *Changes in Scripture: Rewriting and Interpreting Authoritative Traditions in the Second Temple Period* (eds. H. von Weissenberg et al.; BZAW 419; Berlin: De Gruyter, 2011), 23–45.

Lange, *Handbuch.

Segal, M., "Between Bible and Rewritten Bible," in *Biblical Interpretation at Qumran* (ed. M. Henze; Grand Rapids: Eerdmans, 2005), 10–28.

Talmon, *Text.

Tov, E., "The Authority of Early Hebrew Scripture Texts," *Journal of Reformed Theology* 5 (2011): 276–95.

Ulrich, E., "The Text of the Hebrew Scriptures at the Time of Hillel and Jesus," in *Congress Volume Basel 2001* (ed. A. Lemaire; VTSup 92; Leiden: Brill, 2002), 85–108.

Zahn, M., "Rewritten Scripture," in *The Oxford Handbook of the Dead Sea Scrolls* (eds. T. Lim and J. Collins; Oxford: Oxford University Press, 2010), 323–36.

Zahn, M., *Rethinking Rewritten Scripture: Composition and Exegesis in the 4QReworked Pentateuch Manuscripts* (STDJ 95; Leiden: Brill, 2011).

Molly Zahn

---

[21] For consideration of this possibility in the case of Ezekiel traditions, see Popović, "Prophet, Books and Texts," 242–47.

[22] See the important reflections by Brooke, "Authority and Canon," and Collins, "Changing Scripture"; for a somewhat different perspective, Tov, "Authority."

21.3 Josephus

At first glance, it would seem a relatively simple matter to glean detailed information from Josephus' *Jewish Antiquities* regarding the nature and state of the biblical texts he relied on to write his "archeology" (*Apion* 1.1) of the Jews. After all, Josephus claims to be providing a strict translation (he uses the terms μεθηρμηνευμένην "translated" and μεταβαλεῖν, lit. "to turn into") of the "Hebrew … Scriptures" (Ἑβραϊκῶν … γραμμάτων) on the model of the Greek translators of the Torah during the time of Ptolemy (II) Philadephus in the third century B.C.E. (*Ant.* 1.5, 10–12; cf. *Ant.* 12.11–118). In the introduction to *Antiquities*, moreover, Josephus solemnly undertakes to provide an accurate rendering of the sacred writings, with the following promise:

> This narrative will, therefore, in due course, set forth the precise details (τὰ … ἀκριβῆ) of what is in the Scriptures according to its proper order. For I promised that I would do this throughout this treatise, neither adding nor omitting anything (οὐδὲν προσθεὶς οὐδ᾽ αὖ παραλιπών; *Ant.* 1.17).

Near the close of the biblical part of the *Antiquities*, Josephus repeats the promise (*Ant.* 10.218; cf. *Ant.* 14.1–3), though in this context he distinguishes between translating or "paraphrasing" (μεταφράζειν) the Scriptures and "explaining" (δηλώσειν) them. In another place, Josephus does acknowledge having reordered the laws along thematic lines (*Ant.* 4.196–197), but in still other contexts he adds religious elements to the promise not to tamper with the Scriptures by characterizing faithful Jews as people who would never even think of altering anything in the Bible (*Apion* 1.42; cf. Deut 4:2; 13:1); and, further, that his own status as a priest guarantees his reliability as a translator of the Scriptures (*Apion* 1.54).

All of this leads the reader to expect a correlation between the Scriptures and Josephus' text that is close enough to be able to draw confident inferences from the latter about the former. However, it is not very long before we realize that what Josephus has in fact produced is something very different from what modern-day readers would regard as a translation. Indeed, rather than being a tight translation of the Bible, the first half of the *Jewish Antiquities* turns out to be a rather expansive and sometimes unwieldy narration of the Jewish national history that might at best be regarded as a loose paraphrase of the narrative sections of Scripture. While Josephus does provide a summary of laws in *Antiquities* 3.90–286 and 4.196–301, he provides nothing of the Poetic or Wisdom literature of the Hebrew Bible, and even the narrative portions are significantly rephrased by Josephus, with only the tiniest vestiges of verbal correspondence with the biblical original remaining.

Scholarship on these matters has invested a great deal of effort in cataloging the kinds of alterations Josephus has made to the biblical text.[1] These changes include:

- Stylistic, rhetorical, and other literary changes aimed presumably at making the narration better suited for a cultured Greek audience.
- Historiographic changes supplied to overcome chronological or historical difficulties in the text.
- Defensive or "apologetic" changes aimed at rebutting current prejudices or slanders against the Jews.
- The "Hellenization" of key characters such as Abraham, Moses, or David to make them more recognizable to Greek-speaking audiences as men of virtue, philosophers, legislators, and ideal rulers.
- Theological or exegetical changes incorporating elements of traditional Jewish interpretation similar to those extant in the Aramaic Targumim (→ 1.3.3).

---

[1] Begg, *Josephus' Account*; Begg, *Josephus' Story*; Feldman, *Josephus's Interpretation*; Feldman, *Studies*; Feldman, "Use, Authority, and Exegesis"; Spilsbury, *Image*.

All of this means that it is notoriously difficult for scholars now to discern the biblical *Vorlage* underlying Josephus' narrative. Where hints and subtle indications do come through, they are as often as not subject to dispute and multiple interpretations.[2] Further, the scholarship on the subject is far from comprehensive, though a foundation for such study has now been laid by the volumes of the Brill Josephus project devoted to the first eleven books of the *Jewish Antiquities*.[3] However, it should be noted at the outset that even as basic a question as the language of Josephus' biblical texts is still not settled. Feldman, for instance, argues on the *a priori* grounds of Josephus' upbringing, education, and ongoing contact with the Jewish community that he must have relied mostly on Hebrew texts, resorting to the Greek translation in only limited cases such as for the books of Esther (→ 13–17.1.1.5) or 1 Esdras (→ 11.7.1.2) where, ostensibly, the quality of the Greek is better than in the rest of the old Greek translations.[4] Rajak, on the other hand has noted that even though the Hebrew Bible certainly would have been intimately familiar to him, "Josephus could hardly have conceived of ... the *Antiquities* ... let alone written these books, had a Greek translation not existed."[5] To be sure, those places where Josephus follows additional passages extant only in Greek translations seem to offer conclusive proof that in those instances he was using a Greek text (e.g., the Greek Additions to the books of Ezra [→ 19.3.1] and Esther [→ 11.6.2]), unless, of course, he was using a form of a Hebrew text no longer available to us. In the case of Daniel, on the other hand, Josephus follows none of the "Apocryphal" narratives found in the Greek versions (Susanna, the Song of the Three Young Men, and Bel and the Dragon; → 11.3.2). Even here, however, there is strong evidence that Josephus was in fact following a Greek text rather than the Hebrew original.[6] Of course, the situation is complicated further by the fact that for Daniel, as for other parts of Jewish Scriptures, more than one ancient Greek translation has come down to us (→ 18.3.1; → 18.3.2).

It is thus, perhaps, not surprising – even if a little unremarkable – that the scholarly consensus holds that when composing his biblical paraphrase Josephus had at hand Scriptures in Hebrew, Greek, and possibly Aramaic as well, though the evidence for this last remains thin at best.[7] Still, it has yet to be demonstrated that Josephus did not, in fact, have some version of the Greek Bible nearby at all times.

Examples

Given the scale of Josephus' project, and the complexity of its relationship to the biblical texts, it is impossible to offer a brief summary of the evidence. Thus, in what follows we will indicate just a few, and somewhat random, examples of possible evidence of the biblical antecedent to Josephus' narrative, and illustrate some of the methodological difficulties inherent in the task.

The sentence in Table 1 is one of the very few examples of where Josephus' formulation closely follows that of the biblical antecedents. It is difficult to determine, though, whether Josephus' text is simply his own translation of the Hebrew or a close copy of the Greek. Only one word in Josephus' version (ἔκτισεν "he created" for ἐποίησεν "he made") differs from the Greek. However, it should be noted that, as in LXX, Josephus uses the singular τὸν οὐρανὸν "the heaven" for הַשָּׁמַיִם "the heavens," which might indicate that Josephus was familiar with the Greek text.

Another example is given in Table 2. The earth is described in MT as תֹהוּ וָבֹהוּ "unformed and void," which is rendered by the Greek as ἀόρατος καὶ ἀκατασκεύαστος "invisible and unformed."[8] This notion seems to be picked up by Josephus when he

---

[2] Cf. Bloch, *Die Quellen*; Feldman, "Use, Authority, and Exegesis," 455–66; Mez, *Die Bibel*; Rappaport, *Agada und Exegese*; Thackeray, *Josephus*, 75–99.

[3] To date, the following volumes have appeared: Feldman, *Judean Antiquities 1–4*; Begg, *Judean Antiquities 5–7*; Begg and Spilsbury, *Judean Antiquities 8–10*.

[4] Feldman, "Use, Authority, and Exegesis," 457.

[5] Rajak, *Translation and Survival*, 252.

[6] Begg and Spilsbury, *Judean Antiquities 8–10*, 266.

[7] Cf. Rodgers, "Josephus's Biblical Interpretation," 440.

[8] Feldman, *Judean Antiquities 1–4*, 10 n. 37.

EXAMPLES 739

TABLE 1   Gen 1:1

MT	LXX	Ant. 1.27a:
בְּרֵאשִׁית בָּרָא אֱלֹהִים אֵת הַשָּׁמַיִם וְאֵת הָאָרֶץ	Ἐν ἀρχῇ ἐποίησεν ὁ θεὸς τὸν οὐρανὸν καὶ τὴν γῆν	Ἐν ἀρχῇ ἔκτισεν ὁ θεὸς τὸν οὐρανὸν καὶ τὴν γῆν
In the beginning, God created the heavens and the earth.	In the beginning, God made the heaven and the earth.	In the beginning, God created the heaven and the earth.

TABLE 2   Gen 1:2–3

MT	LXX	Ant. 1.27b
וְהָאָרֶץ הָיְתָה תֹהוּ וָבֹהוּ וְחֹשֶׁךְ עַל־פְּנֵי תְהוֹם וְרוּחַ אֱלֹהִים מְרַחֶפֶת עַל־פְּנֵי הַמָּיִם וַיֹּאמֶר אֱלֹהִים יְהִי אוֹר וַיְהִי־אוֹר	ἡ δὲ γῆ ἦν ἀόρατος καὶ ἀκατασκεύαστος, καὶ σκότος ἐπάνω τῆς ἀβύσσου, καὶ πνεῦμα θεοῦ ἐπεφέρετο ἐπάνω τοῦ ὕδατος. καὶ εἶπεν ὁ θεός Γενηθήτω φῶς. καὶ ἐγένετο φῶς	ταύτης δ' ὑπ' ὄψιν οὐκ ἐρχομένης, ἀλλὰ βαθεῖ μὲν κρυπτομένης σκότει, πνεύματος δ' αὐτὴν ἄνωθεν ἐπιθέοντος, γενέσθαι φῶς ἐκέλευσεν ὁ θεός
And the earth was unformed and void with darkness over the surface of the abyss and a wind of God sweeping over the water. God said: "Let there be light and light was."	Yet the earth was invisible and unformed, and darkness was over the abyss, and a divine wind was being carried along over the water. And God said, "Let light come into being." (*NETS)	When this latter had not come into sight but was hidden in deep darkness, and when a breath from above ran over it, God ordered light to come into being.[9]

states that the earth "had not come into sight" (ὑπ' ὄψιν οὐκ ἐρχομένης). Josephus' statement that the earth was "hidden in deep darkness" is not verbally connected to either MT or LXX except for the word "darkness" itself (חֹשֶׁךְ, σκότος, σκότει). His description of "the divine Spirit" (רוּחַ אֱלֹהִים, πνεῦμα θεοῦ) as "a spirit from above" (πνεύματος ... ἄνωθεν) would seem to be Josephus' own circumlocution. The same might be said of his rendering of the command at the end of the verse into indirect discourse (γενέσθαι φῶς ἐκέλευσεν ὁ θεός "God ordered light to come into being").

The passage in Table 3 demonstrates Josephus' independence from the biblical text both in terms of vocabulary and the structure of the syntax. Thus, while the king (כֹּרֶשׁ "Cyrus") is Κύρου in all three Greek versions, for Josephus "the Lord" (יְהוָה, κύριος) is simply ὁ θεός "God." Further, while the Hebrew verb הֵעִיר "he stirred up" is rendered by 1 and 2 Esdras with ἤγειρεν "he stirred" and ἐξήγειρεν "he stirred up" respectively, Josephus uses the aorist participle παρορμήσας, "to urge on, stimulate, incite" (LSJ s.v.). Finally, that which is aroused by God is identified variously as the king's רוּחַ "spirit," or πνεῦμα "spirit" in the biblical texts, but as τὴν ψυχὴν "the soul" in Josephus. This level of paraphrasing makes determination of the underlying source well nigh impossible.

---

[9] Translation according to Feldman, *Judean Antiquities 1–4*.

TABLE 3   Ezra 1:1; see also 2 Chr 36:22

MT	1 Esd 2:1	2 Esd 1:1	Ant. 11.3
הֵעִיר יְהוָה אֶת־רוּחַ כֹּרֶשׁ מֶלֶךְ־פָּרַס	ἤγειρεν κύριος τὸ πνεῦμα Κύρου βασιλέως Περσῶν	ἐξήγειρεν κύριος τὸ πνεῦμα Κύρου βασιλέως Περσῶν	[ὁ θεός] παρορμήσας γὰρ τὴν Κύρου ψυχὴν
the Lord stirred up the spirit of Cyrus, king of Persia	the Lord stirred the spirit of Cyrus, king of the Persians (*NETS)	the Lord stirred up the spirit of Cyrus, king of the Persians (*NETS)	for having aroused Cyrus' soul, God …

Conclusion

The passages we have cited are somewhat unusual in that they are instances of Josephus being fairly close to the biblical text. Even these texts, though, illustrate the paraphrastic nature of Josephus' narration and the difficulty of coming to any conclusion about the source he was consulting. Most of Josephus stands in a relationship much more distant from the biblical texts than these few examples might suggest. While the scope and magnitude of his project makes it highly unlikely that Josephus was working only from memory, it remains for the most part impossible to determine which biblical texts Josephus may have had before him. Indeed, the extent of Josephus' paraphrastic freedom is such that some scholars have gone so far as to postulate an intermediary biblical paraphrase of some kind.[10] However, the absence of any independent evidence for such a text makes its existence highly unlikely.

Begg, C., *Josephus' Account of the Early Divided Monarchy (AJ 8,212–420): Rewriting the Bible* (BETL 108; Leuven: Leuven University Press, 1993).

Begg, C., *Josephus' Story of the Later Monarchy (AJ 9,1–10, 185)* (BETL 145; Leuven: Leuven University Press, 2000).

Begg, C., *Judean Antiquities 5–7: Translation and Commentary* (Flavius Josephus: Translation and Commentary 4; Leiden: Brill, 2005).

Begg, C. and P. Spilsbury, *Judean Antiquities 8–10: Translation and Commentary* (Flavius Josephus: Translation and Commentary 5; Leiden: Brill, 2005).

Bloch, H., *Die Quellen des Flavius Josephus in seiner Archäologie* (Wiesbaden: M. Sändig, 1968).

Feldman, L.H., "Use, Authority, and Exegesis of Mikra in the Writings of Josephus," in Mulder, *Mikra, 455–518.

Feldman, L.H., *Josephus's Interpretation of the Bible* (Berkeley: University of California Press, 1998).

Feldman, L.H., *Studies in Josephus' Rewritten Bible* (JSJSup 58; Leiden: Brill, 1998).

Feldman, L.H., *Judean Antiquities 1–4: Translation and Commentary* (Flavius Josephus: Translation and Commentary 3; Leiden: Brill, 2000).

Hölscher, G., "Josephus," PW 9:1934–2000.

Mez, A., *Die Bibel des Josephus untersucht für Buch V–VII der Archäologie* (Basel: Jaeger & Kober, 1895).

Rajak, T., *Translation and Survival: The Greek Bible of the Ancient Jewish Diaspora* (Oxford: Oxford University Press, 2009).

Rappaport, S., *Agada und Exegese bei Flavius Josephus* (Vienna: Alexander Kohut Memorial Foundation, 1930).

Rodgers, Z., "Josephus's Biblical Interpretation," in *A Companion to Biblical Interpretation in Early Judaism* (ed. M. Henze; Grand Rapids: Eerdmans, 2012), 436–64.

Spilsbury, P., *The Image of the Jew in Flavius Josephus' Paraphrase of the Bible* (TSAJ 69; Tübingen: Mohr Siebeck, 1998).

Thackeray, H.St.J., *Josephus: The Man and the Historian* (New York: Jewish Institute of Religion Press, 1929).

Paul Spilsbury

---

[10] Hölscher, "Josephus," 1955–60, cited by Feldman "Use, Authority, and Exegesis," 465.

21.4 Philo

21.4.1 Introduction

Most of Philo of Alexandria's extensive works are commentaries on the biblical text, and contain thousands of explicit citations from the Bible. Indeed, Philo's citations are predominantly from the Pentateuch, which seems to have some special level of inspiration; see, for example, *Mos.* 2.290, which refers to the end of Deuteronomy as τὸ τέλος τῶν ἱερῶν γραμμάτων "the conclusion of the holy Scriptures."[1] As we shall see, Philo's Bible was the Septuagint (LXX; → 1.3.1.1). Thus, apart from the philosophical, theological, historical, and cultural value of his writings, his biblical citations provide valuable evidence for the state of LXX (particularly in the Pentateuch) prior to the time of most of our manuscripts. But collecting and evaluating this evidence proves to be complicated, and there has been much discussion and controversy about the nature of Philo's citations.[2]

While Philo wrote in Greek, some scholars have held that he also knew Hebrew.[3] However, the most common view is that Philo knew no Hebrew at all, or at least too little to make any use of it in his study of the biblical text.[4] A striking example of Philo's reliance on LXX is found in Gen 15:15: Philo shares (*Her.* 275, 284, 285; *QG* 3.11) with all witnesses the reading τραφείς "nourished" instead of ταφείς "buried," which must surely be the original LXX reading.[5] Even a cursory comparison with the Hebrew would have alerted him to the error. Throughout his writings, Philo comments on the Greek text, noting even its smallest details, and often when it departs from the Hebrew.[6]

Scholars who have thought that Philo had some substantial knowledge of Hebrew have relied chiefly on two points, his frequent use of etymologies, and places where his exegesis seems to make use of the Hebrew text instead of LXX: 1) Philo often gives etymologies for names of people and places, and these etymologies usually refer to Hebrew meanings. However, it seems likely

---

[1] Siegert, "Early Jewish Interpretation," 173: "the canon evidently stops at this point." See also, among many discussions: Burkhardt, *Die Inspiration*, 129–43; Sterling, "Interpreter," 424–27; Passoni dell'Acqua, "Upon Philo's Biblical Text," 32–33. The non-Pentateuchal books are much less often cited, although they are viewed as divinely inspired. Philo cites all the books of the Former Prophets except Joshua and 2 Samuel. Since 2 Samuel is part of 1–4 Kingdoms, it may also be considered as recognized by Philo. Of the Latter Prophets, Philo cites Isaiah, Jeremiah, Hosea, and Zechariah. The citation of the last two shows that the Minor Prophets were recognized by Philo. Of the Writings, Philo cites Psalms, Job, and Proverbs. It seems that Philo does not cite: Ruth, 1–2 Chronicles, Ezra, Nehemiah, Esther, Ecclesiastes, Canticles, Lamentations, Ezekiel, Daniel. (But the sources of some references are disputed.) Ruth is part of the Octateuch, and so Philo's silence there probably results simply from its not having any material of interest for his purposes. We may suppose the same for his failure to cite 1–2 Chronicles, Ezra, and Nehemiah. Further, there seems to be no citation of any book of the Apocrypha.

[2] The standard index to Philo's Scriptural references is Allenbach et al., *Biblia Patristica Supplément: Philon d'Alexandrie*. This supersedes the earlier indices by H. Leisegang (in L. Cohn and P. Wendland, *Philonis Alexandrini Opera quae supersunt*, Vol. 7: *Indices ad Philonis Alexandrini Opera* [Berlin: Walter de Gruyter, 1926–1930]) and by J.W. Earp (in F.H. Colson and J.W. Earp, *Philo*, Vol. 10: *On the Embassy to Gaius, General Indexes* [LCL 379; Cambridge: Harvard University Press, 1962]), and is a very comprehensive work, listing virtually all biblical citations and allusions (and remote resemblances that hardly count as even allusions), and including references to the works preserved only in Armenian and to many Greek fragments. The most thorough investigation of Philo's citations is Ryle, *Philo and Holy Scripture*, who utilized the material in Mangey's 1742 edition and (via Aucher's Latin) the works found only in Armenian. Unfortunately, his book was published in 1895, one year before the first volume of the critical edition of Cohn-Wendland, and thus much of his material needs to be updated with the textual evidence found there. Moreover, he neglected much material that was already available. See the reviews by E. Schürer, *TLZ* 20 (1895), 483–85, and by P. Wendland, *Berliner Philologische Wochenschrift* 15 (1895), 1281–85. Nevertheless, Ryle's work is a valuable collection of citations.

[3] See, e.g., Wolfson, *Philo*, 1.88–90.

[4] The most thorough discussion is Nikiprowetzky, *Le commentaire*, 50–96 (see summary at 81). See also Sandmel, "Philo's Knowledge," 109.

[5] Wevers, *Greek Text of Genesis*, 212.

[6] Siegert, *Register*, 343, cites thirteen such examples. See also Arnaldez, "L' influence," for examples where Philo's interpretation depends on the peculiarities of LXX.

that Philo did not construct these etymologies himself, but rather took them from some written list, i.e., an onomasticon;[7] 2) Further, in order to show that Philo had at least some knowledge of Hebrew, scholars have cited many places where Philo's formulation allegedly depends on a Hebrew text.[8] However, on further analysis these passages are far from convincing. They are either places where Philo's text of LXX had a small variation from the common editions, or places where Philo is giving a perfectly reasonable interpretation of the LXX text. At no place does the Hebrew seem to be required.[9]

Philo's dependence on LXX is related to his account of the origin of that version (*Mos.* 2.25–44). In contrast to the *Letter of Aristeas* 302, where the translators compared their drafts and agreed on the final wording, Philo reports that the translators worked independently but miraculously produced identical translations. It can thus be said: "Philo believed that the Greek translation had been divinely inspired just as the original Hebrew had been."[10] However, the emphasis in Philo is not directly on the inspiration of the LXX text, but rather on the inspired agreement with the Hebrew. The resulting agreement is so wonderful that the translators can rather be seen as themselves "prophets and priests of the mysteries," who "go hand in hand" with Moses himself and produce a Greek translation that agrees perfectly with the Hebrew (*Mos.* 2.40). In fact, Philo here seems to be speaking of the reports of others, not of a comparison that he himself has made. Indeed, it is difficult to imagine that anyone who actually compared LXX and the Hebrew at any length would make such a statement.[11] One would surely pause at Gen 15:15, as noted above, and much earlier, say at 2:2, where for the Hebrew "seventh day" LXX has "sixth day." Thus, assuming that Philo has not simply invented these reports, he was misinformed.

21.4.2 Philo's Bible was LXX

There is broad agreement that Philo cites Scripture from the LXX version (→ 1.3.1.1).[12] Nevertheless, there are many difficult textual issues that arise. For one thing, LXX itself was not an unchanging entity, but is a wide tradition of manuscripts, and all the early representatives differ considerably from one another. As a result, it seems inevitable that Philo's biblical manuscripts would have differed here and there from any existing manuscripts, from any critically established text, and from the supposed original LXX.[13] Furthermore, our knowledge of what Philo wrote usually depends on manuscripts that are separated from his works by many centuries, sometimes on only one manuscript (for *Post.* and *Somn.* 2), and sometimes on translations into Armenian and/or Latin. In addition, there are many discrepancies among our witnesses.

There are two important aids in finding our way amid all the manuscript corruptions (in both Philo and LXX): the agreement with the exposition and earlier manuscripts.

21.4.2.1 Exposition Often Makes Clear that Philo Followed LXX

An excellent example is found at *Leg.* 3.1 and 3.6. In the initial lemma of Gen 3:8 (3.1), all the Philo manuscripts read ἐκρύβη "hid himself," where the LXX manuscripts all have ἐκρύβησαν "hid themselves." However, in his exposition (*Leg.* 3.6), Philo writes: τί οὖν τὸ "ἐκρύβησαν" "why then does it say, 'they hid

---

[7] See especially the comprehensive study of Grabbe, *Etymology*, 102–13 (discussing *P.Oxy.* 2745 and other lists), as well as 63 and 101.

[8] Many alleged examples may be found in Siegfried, "Philo," 232–38; Belkin, *Philo*, 35–48; Nazzaro, "Filone"; Cadiou, "Philon."

[9] See the extensive discussion of Nikiprowetzky, *Le commentaire*, 50–96 (summary at 81), responding to arguments of Wolfson, Belkin, and others.

[10] Jobes and Silva, *Invitation*, 36. See also Brock, "Aspects," 72.

[11] Cf. Amir, "Authority," 444.

[12] Already Mangey, *Philonis*, 1.43 note b, speaks of the "LXX Interpretes quos ubique sequitur Philo." Siegert, "Early Jewish Interpretation," 173, states: "Philo's text is of course the Septuagint."

[13] Philo shows no awareness of such discrepancies between manuscripts, and at *Hypoth.* 6.9 he even denies that "a single word of what [Moses] wrote" has been changed. See Siegert, "Early Jewish Interpretation," 173–74: "He is simply no philologist in a modern sense"; Siegert, *Zwischen*, 32, 105.

themselves'?" again with all the manuscripts. Cohn (no doubt correctly) went against all the manuscripts at *Leg.* 3.1 and edited ἐκρύβησαν "hid themselves."

21.4.2.2 Better Manuscripts Often Show that Philo Followed LXX

Kilpatrick observes that at *Leg.* 1.56, where Philo cites Gen 2:9, the third-century C.E. Oxyrhynchus Papyrus of Philo goes with manuscripts MAP in reading τῷ παραδείσῳ "pertaining to the orchard," which agrees with LXX,[14] against τοῦ παραδείσου "of the orchard," as found in manuscripts UFL.[15] Similarly, the third-century Coptos Papyrus (Cohn–Wendland's "Pap") often provides decisive or even unique support for the LXX wording of many biblical citations in Philo. For example, at *Her.* 2, most Philo manuscripts cite Gen 15:2 as: ὁ δὲ υἱός μου ὁ ἐκ τῆς οἰκέτιδός μου κληρονομήσει με "my son who is by my servant shall be my heir." Already Mangey inferred from the presence of Μάσεκ "Masek" at *Her.* 61 (et al.) that instead of μου ὁ ἐκ "my who is by," Philo must have written Μάσεκ "Masek," as in LXX and as now found in Pap. Also, instead of οἰκέτιδος "servant," Pap has οἰκογενοῦς "home-born," as in LXX. Finally, the words κληρονομήσει με "shall be my heir," which are missing in LXX and have been added to the other Philonic codices from the citation of Gen 15:3, are missing in Pap. Thus, for this phrase, Pap presents Philo's citation as agreeing completely with LXX, while the other Philonic codices have three separate corruptions.[16] For most of the works of Philo, we have no such early evidence. But, of course, it is implausible that such scribal alterations occurred only in the books for which we now have early papyri.

21.4.2.3 Better Use of Quotation Marks

Some apparent departures by Philo from LXX are the result of inaccurate placement of quotation marks, which are, of course, an editorial device not used in Philo's time.[17] Consider, for example, *Agr.* 12, where Wendland presents Philo's citation of Deut 20:20 as: πᾶν ὃ οὐ καρπόβρωτόν ἐστιν, κτλ "every [tree] whose fruit is not edible." LXX reads ἀλλὰ ξύλον, ὃ ἐπίστασαι ὅτι οὐ καρπόβρωτόν ἐστιν, κτλ "but a tree, of which you know that its fruit is not edible," and the Göttingen LXX accordingly cites Philo as having πᾶν ὃ "every [tree] whose," for ὃ ἐπίστασαι ὅτι "of which you know that," which would be a curious substitution.[18] In fact, following Katz' suggestion, one can avoid such a problem by simply placing the initial quotation mark differently: πᾶν ὃ "οὐ καρπόβρωτόν ἐστιν κτλ" "every [tree] whose 'fruit is not edible'."[19]

21.4.2.4 Format of Manuscripts in Philo's Time

In order to understand Philo's use of the biblical text, it is important to keep in mind that his biblical manuscripts would have been written in majuscules without accents, breathings, or (at least for the most part) punctuation marks.[20] For example, at *Abr.* 166 and QG 4.47, Philo interprets Gen 19:20 as saying that the city is both small and not small, thus understanding the phrase οὐ μικρά ἐστι "it is not small," as an assertion. Translators have criticized this understanding, since they take the phrase as a question "is it not small?," as it is usually printed (and as the Hebrew has). But Philo's interpretation is based on a text written without punctuation.[21]

---

[14] As it seems; many witnesses read τοῦ παραδείσου "of the orchard," as at Gen 3:3.

[15] G.D. Kilpatrick, "Review of Katz," *JTS*, N.S. 2 (1951): 88; see also Royse, "*Legum Allegoriae*," 4–5. For the sigla of the Philo manuscripts quoted above, see L. Cohn and P. Wendland, *Philonis Alexandrini Opera quae supersunt* (Berlin: Georg Reimer and De Gruyter, 1896–1930), 1.cxiv.

[16] See Schürer, "Review of Ryle, *Philo and Holy Scripture*," 485 (see note 2 above), who notes the confirmation of οἰκογενοῦς "home-born" at *Her.* 39. However, Schürer incorrectly cites Pap as having κληρονομήσει με "shall be my heir" for Gen 15:2.

[17] See, e.g., Nikiprowetzky, "Philo's Citations," 105, and comments at 110, 112, 113, 117, 118.

[18] J.W. Wevers in cooperation with U. Quast, *Deuteronomium* (2nd ed.; Septuaginta Vetus Testamentum Graecum 3.2; Göttingen: Vandenhoeck & Ruprecht, 2006), 241.

[19] Katz, *Philo's Bible*, 32; however, Katz places the quotation mark before ὃ "whose." See further Royse, "*De agricultura*," 115.

[20] Such were gradually introduced into manuscripts but are, with occasional exceptions, missing from manuscripts until well after Philo's time, as can be verified from the edition of any early papyrus. See, e.g., Kenyon, *Books*, 67–69.

[21] See Royse, "*De Abrahamo*," 164–65. See also Philo's citation of Gen 4:7 at *Agr.* 127, as discussed in Royse, "*De agricultura*," 121–24.

Similarly, at *Post.* 61, Philo interprets the name Σεσείν (LXX for MT's שֵׁשַׁי "Sheshai") from Num 13:22 as "outside me" (ἐκτός μου). Where does Philo obtain such a meaning? In fact, the Hebrew consonantal text could be understood as meaning "my sixth," which would be rendered in Greek as ἕκτος μου. Grabbe says that Philo has here misread his source.[22] But in Philo's onomastical source this would have been written without breathings or accents.[23] Thus, Philo would have to have interpreted the text in one way or another. Of course, we, with our access to the Hebrew, can see that Philo made the incorrect choice here. But, given the information available to Philo, he probably made a reasonable choice.[24] "My sixth" would hardly make sense, while "outside me" is a more or less understandable phrase.

21.4.2.5 The "Aberrant" Text

On occasion, readings in some Philonic manuscripts agree with MT (→ 1.2.2) against LXX (→ 1.3.1.1), and such readings have thus been called "aberrant." Scholars have sometimes taken such readings as being what Philo originally wrote.[25] Based on his erudite discussion of many passages, Katz argues that Philo's exposition often makes it clear that he followed the text of LXX, and that the aberrant text often agrees with Aquila (→ 1.3.1.2), although he was unable to provide a satisfactory explanation for the intrusion of these readings into the manuscript tradition of Philo.[26] Barthélemy subsequently argued that the readings were probably adopted by Rabbi Hoshaya, a contemporary of Origen at Caesarea.[27]

21.4.2.6 Discrepancies from LXX

There remain quite a few citations where Philo departs, as it seems, from LXX, and these can be classified under various headings.[28] For example, when quoting Gen 27:8–10 at *QG* 4.200, Philo simply omitted, it seems, the two phrases καθὰ ἐγώ σοι ἐντέλλομαι "as I command you," and καὶ εἰσοίσεις τῷ πατρί σου "and you shall carry [it] to your father," which were irrelevant for his purposes; this is the sort of thing where we might place ellipsis dots.[29] And at *Agr.* 94 and elsewhere, he changes the biblical γενηθήτω to γενέσθω (both meaning "let be"), presumably for stylistic reasons.[30]

21.4.2.7 Philo May Have Preserved the Original LXX against Later Witnesses

Since Philo wrote a few centuries or more before most of our evidence for LXX, his biblical text is a witness to the early state of LXX (→ 1.3.1.1). We might therefore wonder whether at some places Philo has preserved readings that have been lost in the later witnesses. In fact, it has been argued on occasion that Philo presents readings that were present in the original (or at least very early) form of LXX but have disappeared from all or almost all other witnesses.[31] Of course, Philo's biblical text is

---

[22] Grabbe, *Etymology*, 204.

[23] See already the anonymous review of Mangey's edition in *Bibliothèque raisonnée des ouvrages des savans de l'Europe* 32 (1744): 303. In contrast, R. Arnaldez (*Philon d'Alexandrie, De posteritate Caini* [Paris: Cerf, 1972], 20) has an extended discussion, in which it is assumed that Philo would have read his source with breathings and accents.

[24] Grabbe, *Etymology*, 225–31, gives a reconstruction of the onomasticon available to Philo, and comments (225): "Since the original list was probably in uncial script with no other marks, breathings and accents are omitted." He then cites (230) the meaning of σεσειν as "εκτος μου (rough breathing meant in original)." Knowing the Hebrew we can see that this is so, but the list was intended for readers who knew no Hebrew or Aramaic (Grabbe, *Etymology*, 105). How was such a reader to know that a rough breathing was meant?

[25] See Kraft, "Philo's Bible"; Runia, *Philo in Early Christian Literature*, 24–25; Royse, "*Legum Allegoriae*," 9–22. The earlier discussion of the issue is treated in Katz, *Philo's Bible*, 125–38.

[26] Katz, *Philo's Bible*, 114–21. Howard, "The 'Aberrant' Text," raised doubts about Katz' thesis and suggested that Philo sometimes used a text that differed from LXX. However, Howard's argument is based on a very small number of examples, and they are far from convincing.

[27] Barthélemy, "Est-ce Hoshaya Rabba."

[28] See Siegfried, "Philo," 217–38, 411–28, 522–40; Ryle, *Philo and Holy Scripture*, xxxv–xlv. Of course, the examples cited are of varying value.

[29] The text is preserved in Armenian and Latin (and a brief portion in a Greek fragment); see Petit, *L'ancienne version*, 1973, 2.100. There seem to be one or two places where Philo may have altered what he does quote; see ibid., 100–01.

[30] See Royse, "*De agricultura*," 115–21.

[31] It has on occasion been argued that citations in the New Testament sometimes agree with Philo against most LXX

so frequently identical to LXX, as known from the later witnesses, that such readings are inevitably rare. But we may cite two possible examples.

First, at Gen 6:14, where all the other cited witnesses of LXX (→ 1.3.1.1) agree with MT (→ 1.2.2) in having "nests" (once), the Armenian (→ 1.4.7), Coptic (→ 1.4.2), and Palestinian Syriac (→ 1.3.4) versions have "nests nests."[32] Philo cites this portion of the verse only at QG 2.3, which is preserved in Greek in only one manuscript.[33] Although that Greek manuscript also has only one occurrence of the word, the Armenian version of Philo has the term repeated, which Aucher translated as "nidos nidos" ("nests nests").[34] So it seems possible, or even likely, that Philo wrote the repeated occurrences, following his text of LXX, which is also preserved in the versions mentioned. A simple haplography would explain the presence of only one occurrence in all the other witnesses, including the Greek manuscript at QG 2.3, while a dittography in such disparate witnesses seems very unlikely.

Second, at Exod 2:22, all witnesses except Philo read πάροικος "sojourner." But, at Conf. 82, Philo cites this verse with γιώρας "stranger," which occurs in LXX at Exod 12:19 and at Isa 14:1. Katz argues that here Philo alone preserves "the authentic shape of the LXX text."[35]

Allenbach, J. et al., *Biblia Patristica Supplément: Philon d'Alexandrie* (Paris: Éditions du Centre National de la Recherche Scientifique, 1982).

---

witnesses; see, for example, Steyn, "Can We Reconstruct." Of course, a complication with such citations is that the reading of the New Testament, however it arose, might have influenced both the text of Philo and the LXX witnesses.

[32] See the apparatus in the Göttingen LXX (J.W. Wevers, *Genesis* [Septuaginta Vetus Testamentum Graecum 1; Göttingen Vandenhoeck & Ruprecht, 1974], 111). There is also some Latin evidence for the two occurrences; see B. Fischer (ed.), *Genesis* (VL 2; Freiburg i.B.: Herder, 1951–1954), 108.

[33] Paramelle, *Philon d'Alexandrie*, 138.

[34] Ryle, *Philo and Holy Scripture*, 35, cites Aucher's Latin. The Göttingen LXX does not cite Philo in support of the repetition since the Armenian Philo is not included, but Brooke–McLean, *The Old Testament in Greek*, correctly cite "Phil-arm."

[35] Katz, *Philo's Bible*, 73–74.

Amir, Y., "Authority and Interpretation of Scripture in the Writings of Philo," in Mulder, *Mikra*, 421–53.

Arnaldez, R., "L'influence de la traduction des Septante sur le commentaire de Philon," in *Études sur le judaïsme hellénistique* (eds. R. Kuntzmann and J. Schlosser; Paris: Cerf, 1984), 251–66.

Barthélemy, D., "Est-ce Hoshaya Rabba qui censura le 'Commentaire Allégorique'?" in *Philon d'Alexandrie* (eds. R. Arnaldez et al.; Paris: Centre National de la Recherche Scientifique, 1967), 45–78 (repr. in D. Barthélemy, *Études d'histoire du texte de l'Ancien Testament* [OBO 21; Göttingen: Vandenhoeck & Ruprecht, 1978], 140–73, and 390–91 [additional notes]).

Belkin, S., *Philo and the Oral Law* (Cambridge: Harvard University Press, 1940).

Brock, S., "Aspects of Translation Technique in Antiquity," *GRBS* 20 (1979): 69–87.

Burkhardt, H., *Die Inspiration heiliger Schriften bei Philo von Alexandrien* (Basel: Brunnen, 1988).

Cadiou, R., "Philon d'Alexandrie: II. La Bible de Philon," *DBSup* 7 (1966): 1290–99.

Cohen, N.G., *Philo's Scriptures: Citations from the Prophets and Writings* (JSJSup 123; Leiden: Brill, 2007).

Grabbe, L.L., *Etymology in Early Jewish Interpretation: The Hebrew Names in Philo* (BJS 115; Atlanta: Scholars Press, 1988).

Howard, G.E., "The 'Aberrant' Text of Philo's Quotations Reconsidered," *HUCA* 44 (1973): 197–209.

Jobes, K.H. and M. Silva, *Invitation to the Septuagint* (Grand Rapids: Baker, 2000).

Katz, P., *Philo's Bible* (Cambridge: Cambridge University Press, 1950).

Kenyon, F.G., *Books and Readers in Ancient Greece and Rome* (2nd ed.; Oxford: Clarendon Press, 1951).

Kraft, R.A., "Philo's Bible Revisited: The 'Aberrant Texts' and their Quotations of Moses," in *Interpreting Translation: Studies on LXX and Ezekiel in Honour of Johan Lust* (eds. F. García Martínez and M. Vervenne; BETL 192; Leuven: Leuven University Press, 2005), 237–53.

Mangey, T., *Philonis Judaei opera* (London: Bowyer, 1742).

Nazzaro, A., "Filone Alessandrino e l'ebraico," *Rendiconti della Accademia di Archeologia, lettere e belle arti*, n.s. 42 (1967): 61–79.

Nikiprowetzky, V., *Le commentaire de l'Écriture chez Philon d'Alexandrie* (ALGHJ 11; Leiden: Brill, 1977), 50–96.

Nikiprowetsky, V., "Philo's Citations of and Allusions to the Bible in the *De Gigantibus* and *Quod Deus*," in

D. Winston and J. Dillon, *Two Treatises of Philo of Alexandria* (Chico: Scholars Press, 1983), 91–118.

Paramelle, J., with the collaboration of E. Lucchesi (eds. and trans.), *Philon d'Alexandrie: Questions sur la Genèse II 1–7* (Cahiers d'Orientalisme 3; Geneva: Patrick Cramer, 1984).

Passoni dell'Acqua, A., "Upon Philo's Biblical Text and the Septuagint," in *Italian Studies on Philo of Alexandria* (ed. F. Calabi; Studies in Philo of Alexandria and Mediterranean Antiquity 1; Leiden: Brill, 2003), 25–52.

Petit, F., *L'ancienne version latine des Questions sur la Genèse de Philon d'Alexandrie* (TU 113–14; Berlin: Akademie-Verlag, 1973).

Royse, J.R., "The Text of Philo's *Legum Allegoriae*," *SPhilo* 12 (2000): 1–28.

Royse, J.R., "The Text of Philo's *De Abrahamo*," *SPhilo* 20 (2008): 151–65.

Royse, J.R., "Some Observations on the Biblical Text in Philo's *De agricultura*," *SPhilo* 22 (2010): 111–29.

Runia, D.T., *Philo in Early Christian Literature: A Survey* (CRINT 3.3; Assen: Van Gorcum, 1993).

Ryle, H.E., *Philo and Holy Scripture* (London: Macmillan, 1895).

Sandmel, S., "Philo's Knowledge of Hebrew," *SPhilo* 5 (1978): 107–12.

Siegert, F., "Early Jewish Interpretation in a Hellenistic Style," in *Hebrew Bible/Old Testament: The History of Its Interpretation*, Vol. 1: *From the Beginnings to the Middle Ages (Until 1300)*, Part 1: *Antiquity* (ed. M. Sæbø; Göttingen: Vandenhoeck and Ruprecht, 1996), 162–89.

Siegert, F., *Zwischen Hebräischer Bibel und Altem Testament: Eine Einführung in die Septuaginta* (Münsteraner Judaistische Studien 9; Münster: Lit Verlag, 2001).

Siegert, F., *Register zur "Einführung in die Septuaginta": Mit einem Kapitel zur Wirkungsgeschichte* (Münsteraner Judaistische Studien 13; Münster: Lit Verlag, 2003).

Siegfried, C., "Philo und der überlieferte Text der LXX," *ZWT* 16 (1873): 217–38, 411–28, 522–40.

Sterling, G.E., "The Interpreter of Moses: Philo of Alexandria and the Biblical Text," in *A Companion to Biblical Interpretation in Early Judaism* (ed. M. Henze; Grand Rapids: Eerdmans, 2012), 415–35.

Steyn, G.J., "Can We Reconstruct an Early Text Form of the LXX from the Quotations of Philo of Alexandria and the New Testament?" in Kreuzer–Meiser–Sigismund, *Septuaginta 2012*, 444–64.

Wevers, J.W., *Notes on the Greek Text of Genesis* (SBLSCS 35; Atlanta: Scholars Press, 1993).

Wolfson, H.A., *Philo: Foundations of Religious Philosophy in Judaism, Christianity, and Islam* (Cambridge: Harvard University Press, 1947).

James R. Royse

21.5 New Testament

21.5.1 The New Testament as Witness to the Text of the Hebrew Bible

The New Testament has a rich textual history of its own, with over 5,000 Greek manuscripts, translations into Latin, Syriac, and Coptic, and other languages, and voluminous quotations from early Christian writers.[1] But the New Testament is also a collection of intertextual documents, each of which quotes from or alludes to the Hebrew Bible.[2] Thus, these earliest Christian writers, all of whom were Jewish, participate in and even contribute to the developing text of the Hebrew Bible. The inter-relation between the textual history of the New Testament and the Hebrew Bible, and similarities in the study of their respective textual histories, have often not been sufficiently appreciated. Textual critics in these related disciplines stand to learn much from one another.

The *BHS textual apparatus lists a number of New Testament references as witnesses to the textual tradition of the Hebrew Bible.[3] Several of these give evidence of the New Testament as witness to the text of the Hebrew Bible.

21.5.1.1 Isa 40:6–7

A clear example of the New Testament as witness to scribal error in the textual tradition of the Hebrew Bible is found in the quotation from Isa 40:6–7 in 1 Pet 1:24–25. This is an example of *parablepsis*, in which the scribe's eye has jumped from the first occurrence of the words "Grass withers, flowers fade" to the second occurrence. Both LXX (→ 6.3) and 1QIsa^a (→ 6.2.1.1; → 6.2.3.1) omit the intervening words, and 1 Pet 1:24 is a witness to that tradition. No manuscript of 1 Peter has supplied the words in conformity to MT (→ 6.2.2). 1QIsa^a contains the extra words from MT as a supralinear and marginal note in another hand.[4] Three other elements in this quotation show the independence of the MT and LXX traditions: 1) the double addition of ὡς "as" in v. 24; 2) δόξα αὐτῆς "its glory" instead of LXX δόξα ἀνθρώπου "the glory of man"; and 3) ῥῆμα κυρίου "word of the Lord" replaces "word of our God" of both MT and LXX (דְּבַר־אֱלֹהֵינוּ/ῥῆμα τοῦ θεοῦ ἡμῶν).

21.5.1.2 Exod 20:13

Paul's order of the ten commandments in Rom 13:9 differs from that of MT-Exod 20 and MT-Deut 5. However, it is the order in which they appear in the LXX^B text of Deuteronomy 5, in the Nash Papyrus (second or first century B.C.E., Egypt; → 2.2.5.2) in Philo *de Decalogo* and in Luke 18:20. At Luke 18:20 and its synoptic parallels (Matt 19:18–19; Mark 10:19), there is considerable textual variation in Jesus' recitation of the commandments, partly in an attempt to conform the list to MT (→ 2.2.2) or LXX (→ 2.4.1). Indeed, the manuscript traditions of both the Hebrew Bible and the New Testament are rich in variations.

21.5.1.3 Deuteronomy 32

Paul quotes the Song of Moses (Deuteronomy 32) three times in the Epistle to the Romans. He cites the verses in the order they appear in Deuteronomy, but each time he cites a different textual tradition. Deut 32:21 is cited at Rom 10:19. Here the text-form is at variance with both LXX (→ 2.4.1.5) and MT (→ 2.2.2). Indeed, "the shift in pronoun [from the third to the second person] finds no support in the manuscript tradition of the LXX. Hebrew witnesses, the Targums …, Peshitta and Vulgate all like-

---

[1] Metzger and Ehrman, *The Text of the New Testament*, 52–134.

[2] See the foundational studies of Turpie, *The Old Testament in the New*; Swete, *Introduction*, 369–405.

[3] These include Gen 11:32 (Acts 7:4); 47:31 (Heb 11:21); Exod 2:14 (Acts 7:28); 20:13 (Luke 18:20; Rom 13:9); Num 16:5 (2 Tim 2:19); Deut 21:23 (Gal 3:13); 27:26 (Gal 3:10); 32:35 (Rom 12:19); 32:43 (Heb 1:6); 33:2 (Acts 7:53; Gal 3:19; Heb 2:2); 1 Kgs 19:18 (Rom 11:4); Isa 25:8 (1 Cor 15:54); 29:13 (Matt 15:8–9); 40:6 (1 Pet 1:24); 64:3 (1 Cor 2:9); Ps 22:9 (Matt 27:43); Prov 11:31 (1 Pet 4:18); 25:21 (Rom 12:20); Ruth 4:19 (Matt 1:3–4); Qoh 2:15 (Matt 12:34; Luke 6:45); Dan 7:13 (Matt 24:30, 26, 64; Mark 14:62; Rev 1:7); 9:27 (Matt 4:5); 1 Chr 3:19 (Matt 1:12; Luke 3:27).

[4] Tov, *TCHB*, 223, Pls. 4 and 5.

wise read the third person pronoun here"[5] (ὑμᾶς "you" rather than LXX αὐτούς "them"). Deut 32:35 is quoted in Rom 12:19. As Cranfield observed, Paul's quotation of Deut 32:35 is "in a form nearer to the Aramaic Targum than to either the LXX or the MT."[6] The third quotation, of Deut 32:43 in Rom 15:10, agrees with LXX against MT. At the time Paul was writing, this verse, and indeed Deuteronomy 32 as a whole, already exhibited pluriformity of text, driven by theological motives.[7] Paul likely knew these debated textual issues and carefully chose the text that supported his vision of Gentile inclusion.

21.5.1.4 Deut 33:2

In three passages, the New Testament draws on the tradition that the giving of the law was accompanied by angels (Acts 7:53; Gal 3:19; Heb 2:2), quoting Deut 33:2 as a textual basis for this assertion. Translators have puzzled over the difficult Hebrew text: מִימִינוֹ אֵשְׁדָּת לָמוֹ "at his right, a host of his own" (*NRSV). LXX, the earliest translation, provides an interpretive rendering, ἐκ δεξιῶν ἄγγελοι μετ' αὐτοῦ "angels with him on his right hand." This tradition was already known by the time that New Testament writers cite it (*Jubilees* [→ 21.1.1; → II:8], Philo [→ 21.3], Josephus [→ 21.4]), and the Christian authors participated in this established tradition.

21.5.1.5 Deut 27:26

Paul cites Deut 27:26 at Gal 3:10 in a passage containing seven citations from Scripture. It is noteworthy that Paul here is not following a single tradition (LXX [→ 2.4.1.5], MT [→ 2.2.2], Targum [→ 2.4.3]). He sometimes agrees with both LXX and MT (Gal 3:16 = Gen 13:16), and sometimes with LXX against MT (Gal 3:6 = Gen 15:6). At other times, Paul is at variance with both LXX and MT where they agree (Gal 3:8 = Gen 12:3; 18:18; Gal 3:12 = Lev 18:5). And in other instances, he cites a text-form at variance with both LXX and MT where they disagree (Gal 3:10 = Deut 27:26; Gal 3:11 = Hab 2:4; Gal 3:13 = Deut 21:23).[8] Longenecker remarks regarding Paul's text-form of Deut 27:26: "Paul may be quoting from a version then in circulation, but now lost."[9] Pluriformity of Scripture text is a characteristic of Paul's writings, and bears witness to the variety of text-forms in his time, also evident among the Qumran scrolls. In each one of these citations, careful attention should be paid to variations in the textual tradition of the New Testament, MT, LXX, and other versions.

21.5.1.6 Hab 2:4

Hab 2:4 is cited three times in the New Testament (Rom 1:17; Gal 3:11; Heb 10:38). The fullest textual variety is found in manuscripts of Heb 10:38: The three choices in Hebrews find correspondence in the textual tradition of LXX (→ 9.2.3).[10]

P46 ὁ δε δίκαιός μου ἐκ πίστεως ζήσεται "but my righteous will live out of faith" (LXX^A)

P13 ὁ δε δίκαιος ἐκ πίστεως ζήσεται "but the righteous will live out of faith" (LXX^Mss)

D* ὁ δε δίκαιος ἐκ πίστεως μου ζήσεται "but the righteous will live out of faith in me" (LXX^B,S)

Interestingly, the D* text of Heb 10:38, which corresponds to LXX in Vaticanus and Sinaiticus, has the pronoun in the same position as in the Greek Minor Prophets Scroll from Nahal Hever: ἐκ πίστεως αὐτοῦ "out of faith in him."

21.5.1.7 Gen 11:32

In Acts 7:4, Stephen's chronology of Abraham follows that of SP (→ 2.2.4.1) and Philo (→ 21.3), rather than of MT or LXX. The speech also indicates other readings from SP in Acts 7:32, 37.[11]

---

[5] Wagner, *Heralds of Good News*, 190 n. 208.
[6] Cranfield, *Romans*, 2.647. As he notes, it is quoted in the same form in Heb 10:30.
[7] Tov, *TCHB, 249–50.
[8] Ellis, *Paul's Use*, 152.
[9] Longenecker, *Galatians*, 117.
[10] Koch, "Der Text," 70.
[11] Kahle, *The Cairo Geniza*, 143–47.

21.5.2 The New Testament as Contributor to the Biblical Text

In several places, the New Testament offers the earliest example of a reading in the textual tradition of the Hebrew Bible and versions, and may be the originator of the reading.

21.5.2.1 Ps 40:7 (LXX-Ps 39:7)

In a long quotation from Psalm 40, Heb 10:5 reads σῶμα δὲ κατηρτίσω μοι "a body you have prepared for me." This is the reading attested in most manuscripts of LXX-Pss (→ 10.3.1), but a few read "ears" (ὠτία = MT אָזְנַיִם). The reading "body" may have first entered the LXX-Pss textual tradition from the Epistle to the Hebrews.

21.5.2.2 Ps 68:18

Eph 4:8 cites Ps 68:19 in the form ἔδωκεν δόματα τοῖς ἀνθώποις "He gave gifts to people." This version is unknown from the textual traditions of either MT (→ 10.2.2) or LXX (→ 10.3.1). But it corresponds to the Targum of the Psalm (→ 10.3.3). The available Targum is of a later date than Ephesians. It could be that the Pauline letter is the originator of this reading to which the Targum bears witness.

21.5.2.3 Reaction to Christianity

Some readings in the textual tradition of the Hebrew Bible came into being in reaction to Christian interpretation. This was the case regarding the revisions of LXX, especially Aquila. A well-known case is Isa 7:14, where MT הָעַלְמָה "the young woman," translated παρθένος "virgin" in LXX, became νεᾶνις "young woman" in the revisions of LXX (→ 6–9.1.5). In Ps 2:2, Aquila reads ἠλειμμένος "anointed" rather than Χριστός "anointed," in order to avoid Christian interpretation.[12] With regard to Isa 52:13–53:12, the fourth Servant Song, much debated in Jewish-Christian polemics, Jobes and Silva note that the reading of 1 Pet 2:22, "no deceipt was found in his mouth" (οὐδὲ εὑρέθη δόλος ἐν τῷ στόματι αὐτοῦ), may have "originated with 1 Pet 2:22, thereafter spreading through most of the textual tradition."[13]

21.5.3 Scribal Practices and Assumptions

Recent research on scribal practices in the texts from the Judean Desert[14] and on so-called "scribal habits" discernible in the earliest New Testament papyri[15] should be studied together. The treatment of the Tetragrammaton (Paleo-Hebraic script, *Tetrapuncta*, and blank spaces) bears some relation to the earliest Christian convention of abbreviating the words for God, Lord, Christ, and Jesus. This similarity perhaps points to a "historical connection between early Christianity and its Jewish religious matrix."[16] Especially intriguing is P.Oxy. 7.1007 (Genesis 2–3, third century C.E.), which contains a double *yod* with a horizontal stroke through both letters, known from Jewish coins of the second century C.E., *and* the abbreviation, θ(εό)ς "God" a Christian convention. Other manuscripts that could be Jewish as well as Christian are P.Oxy. 4.656, P.Oxy 9.1166, P.Vindob.G 39777.

With regard to both the scribes of the Hebrew Bible and the scribes of the New Testament, there is the assumption that the material they were copying had a sacred and inspired status. It is sometimes assumed that once a book became canonical Scripture within a given group in Judaism and Christianity, there was a reluctance to make any change in the text being copied. Since textual pluriformity can be demonstrated for both the Hebrew Bible in the Second Temple period, and the New Testament in the second century C.E., it is argued that the process of canonization developed gradually (→ 1.1.2.1; → 1.1.2.2). At the same time, there is demonstrable reverence for the Hebrew Bible, especially the Pentateuch, alongside the phenomenon of the plurality of text-form at Qumran (→ 1.2.2) and in LXX

---

[12] Jobes and Silva, *Invitation*, 39.
[13] Jobes and Silva, *Invitation*, 226.
[14] Tov, *Scribal Practices*.
[15] Royse, *Scribal Habits*.
[16] Hurtado, *Earliest Christian Artifacts*, 107.

(→ 1.3.1.1). As Tov notes, "there is not necessarily a connection between the sacred status of the Scripture books and the nature of the scribal transmission."[17]

Cranfield, C.E.B., *A Critical and Exegetical Commentary on the Epistle to the Romans* (ICC; 2 vols.; Edinburgh: T & T Clark, 1983).
Ellis, E.E., *Paul's Use of the Old Testament* (Edinburgh: Oliver and Boyd, 1957).
Hurtado, L.W., *The Earliest Christian Artifacts* (Grand Rapids: Eerdmans, 2006).
Jobes, K.H. and M. Silva, *Invitation to the Septuagint* (Grand Rapids: Baker House, 2000).
Kahle, P.E., *The Cairo Geniza* (London: The British Academy, 1941).
Koch, D.-A., "Der Text von Hab 2 4b in der Septuaginta und im Neuen Testament," *ZNW* 76 (1985): 68–85.
Koch, D.-A., *Die Schrift als Zeuge des Evangeliums: Untersuchungen zur Verwendung und zum Verständnis der Schrift bei Paulus* (BHT 69; Tübingen: Mohr Siebeck, 1986).
Longenecker, R.N., *Galatians* (WBC 41; Dallas: Word Books, 1990).
Metzger, B.M. and B.D. Ehrman, *The Text of the New Testament* (4th ed.; New York: Oxford University Press, 2005).
Royse, J.R., *Scribal Habits in Early Greek New Testament Papyri* (NTTSD 36, Leiden: Brill, 2007).
Swete, **Introduction*.
Tov, **Scribal Practices*.
Tov, **TCHB*.
Turpie, D.M., *The Old Testament in the New: A Contribution to Biblical Criticism and Interpretation* (London: Williams and Norgate, 1868).
Wagner, J.R., *Heralds of Good News: Isaiah and Paul "in Concert" in the Letter to the Romans* (NovTSup 101; Leiden: Brill, 2003).

Peter Rodgers

---

[17] Tov, **TCHB*, 21, 189.

21.6 Rabbinic Literature

21.6.1 Background

Classical rabbinic literature makes extensive use of the Hebrew Bible (→ 1.1.2.1). Besides the ancient versions, midrashic homilies on biblical verses are perhaps the most important witness for the biblical text in the first centuries of the Common Era, revealing the text(s) current in the period preceding its transmission by the Masoretes (→ 1.2.2.2.2; → 1.2.2.4.3). Even though most of the quotations in rabbinic literature are identical to MT (→ 1.2.2), they still preserve numerous textual variants, including differences in vocalization, the consonantal text, and even the omission or addition of words. Due to the difficulty inherent in the interpretation of various aspects of rabbinic literature, and the limited access to its medieval manuscripts, most scholars are not aware of, and therefore do not utilize, this important corpus as a witness to the biblical text.

The existence of different versions of the biblical text in the rabbinic period is mentioned already in rabbinic sources.[1] Several sources indicate the existence of biblical scrolls whose text differed from MT (→ 1.2.2). A famous example are the variants in the Severus Scroll (→ 2.2.5.4), attributed to R. Meir.[2] Lieberman suggested that these were "popular" or "vulgar" texts of the Bible that lacked the precision of the normative books.[3] Indeed, the Tosafists noted instances where the biblical citations in the Babylonian Talmud differed from MT.[4] But when R. Hai Gaon was asked in the beginning of the eleventh century about "talmudic citations of biblical verses not found in the Bible," he dismissed the possibility that the rabbis had a variant text of the Torah,[5] and this was the standard notion until the nineteenth century. In the late nineteenth century, Rosenfeld published extensive lists of variants in biblical quotations attested in the Talmud.[6] A few decades later, the first scholarly work that collected and critically examined the variant biblical readings of a biblical book in rabbinic literature was published by Aptowitzer.[7] More recently, the Hebrew University Bible Project edition included variants from biblical quotations in rabbinic literature in its second textual apparatus. The preparation of this apparatus includes the re-examination of multiple manuscripts and the collation and careful consideration of readings in the light of the nature and transmission of rabbinic literature.[8]

There are two primary categories of evidence for biblical textual variants found in rabbinic literature: those attested in explicit quotations of biblical passage and those that provide the basis for a midrashic homily ("hermeneutical" variants).

---

[1] See Maori, "Rabbinic Midrash," for a survey of various approaches to such differences from traditional Jewish sources through modern scholarship; cf. also Maori, "Text of the Hebrew Bible."

[2] *Gen. Rab.* 9:5, 20:12 and *Gen. Rabbati Vayyiggaš* 45:8 (ed. C. Albeck; Jerusalem, 209–212). The Severus Scroll refers to a Torah scroll that, according to tradition, Titus took to Rome (or was taken by the exiles) and later was given to the synagogue of Severus (built with the permission of Alexander Severus, who reigned 222–235 C.E.). Apparently, this Torah scroll was known to R. Meir, and some traditions in rabbinic literature refer to it as "R. Meir's Torah"; see Siegel, *Severus Scroll*; and A. Lange, "Rabbi Meir and the Severus Scroll," in *"Let the Wise Listen and Add to Their Learning" (Prov 1:5): Festschrift for Günter Stemberger on the Occasion of His 75th Birthday* (eds. C. Cordoni and G. Langer; SJ 90; Berlin: De Gruyter, 2016), 53–76.

[3] Lieberman, *Hellenism*, 23–26.

[4] *Tosafot* ad *b. Šabb.* 55b, s.v. מעבירם כתיב. R. Akiva Eger (*Gilyon HaŠas*, ad loc.) provided a list of differences between MT and quotations in the Babylonian Talmud.

[5] Rosenthal, "Sages' Methodical Approach," 401 notes this dispute between the Tosafists and the Babylonian Geonim, and posits its possible influence on the difference between the copyists of Eastern and Western manuscripts.

[6] Rosenfeld, *Mišpaḥat Soperim*.

[7] Aptowitzer, *Das Schriftwort*.

[8] See below; for a detailed description of the methodology behind which variants are included in the HUBP edition, see Goshen-Gottstein–Talmon, **HUB, Ezekiel*, xxxi–xxxvi.

21.6.2 Explicit Quotations

Variants in explicit quotations seemingly preserve the most straightforward evidence for alternate readings. However, there are still methodological difficulties in viewing such deviations as reflecting actual differences at the level of the biblical text. In many cases, these variants were preserved in only one or a few manuscripts of the rabbinic text, while in the majority of rabbinic manuscripts the quotation matches MT.[9] This fact is due to the widespread practice in rabbinic manuscripts of correcting biblical quotations towards MT.

Rabbinic literature is preserved in medieval manuscripts copied hundreds of years after its composition and redaction. The copyists of manuscripts of rabbinic literature, including the biblical quotations, were generally much less careful than copyists of biblical manuscripts.[10] Variants in biblical quotations are therefore often the result of scribal errors in these medieval rabbinic manuscripts. Therefore, in order to identify the biblical text(s) used by the rabbis, one must be familiar with the character of rabbinic literature and its scribal practices, such as the use of plene orthography in the quotation of biblical verses, or the quotation according to the MT *Qere* reading and not according to the *Ketiv*. Furthermore, common causes for variants in citations of biblical verses in manuscripts of rabbinic compositions include: conflation of verses,[11] confusion between two similar verses,[12] interchange of words from the same semantic field,[13] omission or replacement of a common clause,[14] influence of other verses cited in the homily,[15] and the influence of rabbinic Hebrew.[16] Some of these differences are perhaps due the earlier stages of oral transmission of the rabbinic text. Moreover, since the biblical quotations in homilies were frequently cited from memory, these errors could have occurred either in the original homily or during subsequent stages of transmission.

21.6.3 Hermeneutical Variants

In some cases, the interpretation in the rabbinic homily is itself based upon a variant reading, even when the version of the verse cited is identical to MT (or is not cited at all). In these instances, these "hermeneutical variants" presumably reflect the biblical text used by the rabbinic author. However, here too, caution must be exercised, since these presumed variants can also be the result of hermeneutic freedom, especially in homilies based only on different vocalization.[17] It is difficult to establish rules by which to determine whether a homily is based on a different version or on the creative interpretation of the midrashist, and each case needs to be examined separately. Thus, for example, in *Deut. Rab.* 11:10 the homily cites Hos 12:1

---

[9] For examples of this phenomenon, see Rosen-Zvi, "Deliberate Changes," n. 17.

[10] Even with regard to quotations that are not corrupt, it is often very difficult to distinguish between similar letters such as ב/כ, ר/ד, ו/י, etc.

[11] E.g., several manuscripts of *Qoh. Rab.* 7:1 and *Midr. Sam.* 7:7 cite שובו בנים שובבים ואשובה אליכם "turn back, rebellious children and I will turn back to you," which is actually a conflation of Jer 3:14 (or 3:22) שׁוּבוּ בָנִים שׁוֹבָבִים, "turn back, rebellious children" and Mal 3:7 שׁוּבוּ אֵלַי וְאָשׁוּבָה אֲלֵיכֶם "turn back to me, and I will turn back to you."

[12] E.g., Zeph 2:3 בַּקְּשׁוּ אֶת־יְהוָה כָּל־עַנְוֵי הָאָרֶץ (MT) "seek the Lord, all you humble of the land" is cited in the first printing of *b. Yebam.* 78b as אהבו את ה' כל ענוי הארץ "love the Lord ...," under the influence of Ps 31:24 אֶהֱבוּ אֶת־יְהוָה כָּל־חֲסִידָיו "love the Lord, all you his faithful."

[13] E.g., instead of MT-Mal 3:19 "(the day) shall leave (יַעֲזֹב) of them neither stock nor boughs," in manuscripts of both *b. Sanh.* 110b and *b. 'Abod. Zar.*, the same verse is quoted using the synonymous verb יש(י)אר instead.

[14] E.g., in one manuscript of *b. Šabb.* 32b, the formulaic clause אָמַר יְהוָה צְבָאוֹת "said the Lord of Hosts" (Mal 3:10) is absent; in another manuscript of *b. Ta'an.* 9a the same clause is replaced with the formula נאם ה' אלהים "declares the Lord God."

[15] In two manuscripts of *b. Roš Haš.*, MT-Zech 7:1 בָּאַרְבָּעָה לַחֹדֶשׁ הַתְּשִׁעִי בְּכִסְלֵו "on the fourth (day) of the ninth month, Kislev" is cited as בחדש התשיעי הוא חדש כסלו "in the ninth month, that is, the month of Kislev," under the influence of Esth 2:16; 3:7; 8:9, which are all quoted in the immediate context.

[16] Thus, for example, it is common for ם at the end of the words to be replaced by ן.

[17] Naeh, "Did the Tannaim," has argued that Tannaim interpreted the biblical text according to its accepted vocalization. However, from the beginning of the Amoraic period, he notes the use of such creative homilies.

"But Judah still walks with God, and is faithful with the Holy One(s) (וְעִם־קְדוֹשִׁים נֶאֱמָן; *NRSV* adapted)" and comments: "This is the payment for forty years of hard work which I worked until they had become a holy and faithful nation (עם קדוש ונאמן)." There is no doubt that the homilist read עַם "nation" instead of עִם "with," but it is uncertain whether this was a "real" variant, or whether this reflected the interpretive freedom of the version he found before him (similar to MT).

In some cases, the homily suggests a variant that matches the explicit quotation itself, thus confirming the existence of the variant. Thus, in the Babylonian Talmud (*Yoma* 71b and *Ta'an.* 17b), R. Hisda derives the prohibition against cultic service by an uncircumcised individual from Ezek 44:9, "Let no alien uncircumcised in spirit and flesh enter my sanctuary [to serve me] (לשרתני)." The last word is absent in MT but is present in most manuscripts of the Babylonian Talmud, and it is evident from the homily that focuses on this service.[18]

In some cases, the rabbinic homily is based on the same words as MT, but the interpretation is based on a different verse division. In MT-Obad 9, the word מִקָּטֶל "[from] slaughter" appears at the end of the verse, while a homily in the Jerusalem Talmud (*y. Pe'ah* 1:1 [16b]) implies that it opens v. 10: "'For the slaughter and violence done to your brother Jacob': Did he really kill him? Rather, [the verse] teaches that he intended to kill him, thus the verse presents it as if he had in fact killed him."[19]

Rosenthal has argued that in some cases the rabbis were aware of two different biblical versions and their homily is based simultaneously on both of them. One example of this phenomenon is the homily in *Gen. Rab.* 20:7 (191) on Gen 3:16 "your desire (MT תְּשׁוּקָתֵךְ) shall be for your husband": "When a woman sits on the birth stool she declares 'I will henceforth never fulfill my marital duties,' whereupon the Holy One blessed be He says to her 'You will return to your desire, you will return to the desire for your husband'." This homily seems to refer to the reading "your return shall be for your husband" known from LXX (ἡ ἀποστροφή σου, "your return"), perhaps reflecting a Hebrew variant תשובתך "your return."[20]

21.6.4 אל תקרי ("Do Not Read ... but ...")

A specific subset of midrashic homilies that use the formula *'al tiqre*, "do not read ... but ...," appears to denote explicitly a change or variant in the biblical text. A well-known example of this category is found in *b. Ber.* 64a, which suggests an alternate reading of Isa 54:13 "and great shall be the happiness of your children (MT בָּנָיִךְ = all ancient translations)": "Do not read בניך (= your children) but בוניך (= your builders or those who understand)"; this variant is supported by 1QIsa^a, which reads ניכיב.[21] However, scholars have suggested that many of these homilies do not in fact record "real" textual variants, but are rather minor exegetical changes that are similar to the hermeneutical methods of midrash that are frequently applied to MT.[22]

---

[18] Had the variant not been explicitly preserved in the quotation, then one could explain the homily in accordance with MT, suggesting that v. 7 demonstrates that the reference in v. 9 is to entering for the purpose of ministration. For additional examples of hermeneutical variants in Tannaitic midrash, see Kahana, "The Biblical Text."

[19] Cf. Sagiv, "To Give Moses a Pause ..." One also finds *derashot* based on a different division of two words. Thus, for example, a homily in the Jerusalem Talmud (*y. Ta'an.* 2:1 [65b]) appears to be based on a reading of Mic 7:4 ישרם מסוכה "their most upright [is] a hedge," instead of MT's יָשָׁר מִמְּסוּכָה "the [most] upright, worse than a barrier of thorns." The reading attested in this rabbinic text reflects a parallel syntactical structure to the previous clause, "the best of them is like a prickly shrub" (טוֹבָם כְּחֵדֶק).

[20] See Rosenthal, "Sages' Methodical Approach," 408 (attributed to M. Kister).

[21] Talmon, "Aspects," 126–32; Zipor, *Tradition and Transmission*, 166–210.

[22] Heller, *Septuagint References*, 54–67 (Appendix) demonstrated that in rabbinic passages parallel to אל תקרי homilies, one often finds a "regular" *derasha* based upon MT, without reference to a variant text. Most of these interpretations are based upon changes in punctuation or transposition of letters.

21.6.5 Paraphrastic Quotations

The distinction between the quotation and its interpretation is sometimes unclear since it is not always possible to distinguish between an actual quotation and a paraphrastic quotation intended to provide a basis for the homily. There are unusual cases where we can find adaptations or reshaping of verses for hermeneutic or stylistic reasons. In some instances, parts of biblical verses are telescoped for the purpose of a midrashic homily, or are combined in order to give full expression to a certain midrashic notion. This phenomenon, which is known in both Qumran literature and the New Testament (especially Paul's epistles), is also found in rabbinic literature, albeit much less frequently. However, it blurs the common dichotomy between the rigidness of technical quotations and the freedom of interpretation generally assumed for rabbinic literature.[23]

Aptowitzer, A., *Das Schriftwort in der rabbinischen Literatur* (5 vols.; Vienna: A. Hölder [vols. 1–2] and Verlag der Israel.-Theol. Lehranstalt [vols. 3–5], 1906–1915; reprint: New York: Ktav, 1970).

Goshen-Gottstein–Talmon, **HUB, Ezekiel*.

Heller, C., *The Septuagint References in Mandelkern's Concordance with Elucidatory Notes on the Bible* (New York: Shulsinger, 1943) [Hebr.].

Kahana, M., "The Biblical Text Reflected in MS Vatican 32 of Sifre Numbers and Deuteronomy," in *Talmudic Studies* I (eds. Y. Sussman and D. Rosenthal; Jerusalem: Magnes Press, 1990), 1–10 [Hebr.].

Lieberman, **Hellenism*.

Maori, Y., "The Text of the Hebrew Bible in Rabbinic Writings in the Light of the Qumran Evidence," in *The Dead Sea Scrolls: Forty Years of Research* (eds. D. Dimant and U. Rappaport; STDJ 10; Leiden: Brill, 1992), 283–89.

Maori, Y., "Rabbinic Midrash as Evidence for Textual Variants in the Hebrew Bible: History and Practice," in *Modern Scholarship in the Study of Torah: Contributions and Limitations* (ed. S. Carmy; Northvale: J. Aronson, 1996), 101–29.

Naeh, S., "Did the Tannaim Interpret the Script of the Torah Differently from the Authorized Reading?" *Tarbiz* 61 (1992): 401–48 [Hebr.].

Rosenfeld, S., *Mišpaḥat Soferim* (Vilna: Romm, 1883).

Rosenthal, D., "The Sages' Methodical Approach to Textual Variants within the Hebrew Bible," in *Isac Leo Seeligmann Volume: Essays on the Bible and the Ancient World* (eds. A. Rofé and Y. Zakovitch; 3 vols.; Jerusalem: E. Rubinstein, 1983), 2.395–417 [Hebr.].

Rosen-Zvi, A., "Deliberate Changes of Biblical Quotations in Rabbinic Literature," *Jewish Studies, an Internet Journal* (2015): forthcoming [Hebr.].

Sagiv, Y., "'To Give Moses a Pause ...': New Examples of Biblical Textual Divisions as Reflected in Rabbinic Literature and a Suggested Connection to the Calendar Debate," *Textus* 24 (2009): 205–20.

Siegel, J.P., *The Severus Scroll and 1QIs^a* (SBLMS 2; Missoula: Scholars Press, 1975).

Talmon, S., "Aspects of the Textual Transmission of the Bible in the Light of Qumran Manuscripts," *Textus* 4 (1964): 95–132.

Zipor, M., *Tradition and Transmission: Studies in Ancient Biblical Translation and Interpretation* (Tel Aviv: Hakibbutz Hameuchad, 2001) [Hebr.].

Assaf Rosen-Zvi

---

[23] See Rosen-Zvi, "Deliberate Changes."

21.7 Greek Church Fathers

21.7.1 Background

21.7.1.1 The Hebrew Bible in Greek Christian Views on the Old Testament

For Greek Christian authors, it was LXX (→ 1.3.1.1) and not the Hebrew Bible (→ 1.1.2.1) that was the Old Testament. Any citation of, comment upon, or reference to a given Old Testament passage has no bearing on a Hebrew version but on the Greek one of LXX (→ 1.7.2).[1] The first Christian authors had argued in favor of the inspiration and authority of the LXX translation and later this had become a fact that did not require any motivation. This attitude allowed Christians to use the Greek text as if it were the original. This does not mean, however, that they had forgotten that most of LXX is a translation and that a Hebrew text existed that was in fact more original.[2] This awareness contributed in a general sense to the development of Greek Christian biblical theory (with regard to Old Testament canonization etc.; → 1.1.2.2).[3] The level to which Christian writers actually turned to the Hebrew (or sought to do so), however, differs from author to author while remaining quite low in general.

21.7.1.2 Greek Christian Knowledge of Hebrew

Although a particular status was bestowed upon Hebrew (as the language of the original biblical text), knowledge of it vanished in the Greek-speaking church very early on (→ 1.2.1.1.2). Despite his work on the *Hexapla* (→ 1.3.1.2), even Origen did not know Hebrew.[4] And while some authors from the so-called Antiochene school of exegesis (Eusebius of Emesa, Diodore of Tarsus, and Theodoret of Cyrrhus in particular) displayed a strong philological interest in the Old Testament and its Semitic versions, even their knowledge of Hebrew was minimal. The few Greek-speaking Christians who mastered Hebrew were converted Jews and/or those who need to be situated in the late Byzantine period (twelfth–fourteenth centuries: e.g., Simon Atumanus and perhaps Nicholas Nectarius of Otranto).[5] They are exceptional; absence of Hebrew knowledge can be posited as a fact for almost all of the Greek-speaking church.

---

[1] The question of which particular Greek text type was used needs to be answered for each author separately. This answer needs to take into account that the transmission history of LXX was not identical for all biblical books. In general, research that has been devoted to this issue is rather limited (certainly in comparison to New Testament textual criticism), but some useful case studies and information can be found in the introductions to some Göttingen editions of LXX and in Fernández Marcos, *The Septuagint*, 258–73, respectively. Sometimes, Greek Christian authors or scribes were citing or copying a text (e.g., a Hexaplaric one) that was in closer alignment with the Hebrew text than the original Greek translation was, but one must not assume that they were always aware of this.

[2] Up to the Greek Middle Ages, the *Letter of Aristeas* was often transmitted as a kind of preface to the Octateuch. Frequently, it was accompanied by a standard list of the various Greek translations of the Hebrew Bible. That list also circulated (with variation) outside of the LXX transmission history. See Devreesse, *Introduction*, 102–08.

[3] This topic has been developed in more detail by Gallagher, *Hebrew Scripture* (but see the review in LS 38 [2014]: 86–93).

[4] Claims that Origen did learn Hebrew thoroughly (e.g., Eusebius of Caesarea, *Church History* VI, 16) should not be trusted; he rather relied on individuals who knew the language, cf. N.R.M. de Lange, *Origen and the Jews: Studies in Jewish-Christian Relations in Third-Century Palestine* (University of Cambridge Oriental Publications 25; Cambridge: Cambridge University Press, 1976), 21–23. Similarly, neither did Epiphanius of Salamis, whom Jerome (*Against Rufinus* 2, 33 and 3, 6) credited with knowledge of Hebrew, know the language: see J. Dummer, "Die Sprachkenntnisse des Epiphanius," in *Die Araber in der alten Welt*: Vol. 5, Part 1: *Weitere Neufunde – Nordafrika bis zur Einwanderung der Wandalen – Ḏū Nuwās* (eds. F. Altheim and R. Stiel; Berlin: De Gruyter, 1968), 392–435 (repr. J. Dummer, *Philologia sacra et profana: Ausgewählte Beiträge zur Antike und zu ihrer Wirkungsgeschichte* [ed. M. Vielberg; Altertumswissenschaftliches Kolloquium 16; Stuttgart: Steiner, 2006], 29–72).

[5] See M. Fincati, "Filologia" and M. Fincati, "Τὸ Ἰουδαϊκόν: Greek Bible and *Hebraica Veritas* among Byzantine Christians and Jews," in *Negotiating Co-Existence: Communities, Cultures and Convivencia in Byzantine Society* (eds. B. Crostini and S. La Porta; Bochumer Altertumswissenschaftliches Colloquium 96; Trier: Wissenschaftlicher Verlag Trier, 2013), 89–102.

21.7.2 Explanations of "Hebrew" Elements in the Greek Biblical Text

Nonetheless, up to the Greek Middle Ages one can find scattered throughout Christian literature remarks on Hebrew morphology, explanations of Hebrew words, etc. that refer indirectly to the biblical text.[6] They are expressions of a general awareness that some acquaintance with Hebrew could come in handy when reading the Greek Old Testament, which contains numerous elements that reflect the Hebrew parent text.[7] Most of those remarks (such as that the Hebrew language – and therefore the Bible – prefers to speak of "heavens" [plural: cf. שָׁמַיִם] instead of "heaven" [singular, as Greek does: οὐρανός]) are commonplace and do not reflect any actual reading of a Hebrew text but found their way from one Christian text to another.[8] Elements in the LXX text that in particular received this kind of attention are transcriptions of proper names, loanwords (e.g., ἀλληλούϊα "Hallelujah"), and words that although Grecized still closely reflect the Hebrew (e.g., τὸ σάββατον "the Sabbath"). Christian exegetes felt a desire to explain the meaning behind these names and terms, since the Bible provides the etymology for only some of them. To this end, onomastic lists and lexica were created, which – with modifications – were used until late Byzantium.[9] Whereas many of the explanations gathered in these collections are nonsensical, not infrequently they indeed offer the Greek translation of Hebrew roots and therefore need to be retraced to sources with knowledge of Hebrew.

21.7.3 First Two Columns of the *Hexapla*

The work that played the single most important role in bringing the Hebrew Bible to the Greek-speaking church was the *Hexapla* (→ 1.3.1.2), which Origen compiled in the first half of the third century. The first and second columns of this synoptic edition of the Old Testament contained the Hebrew text, in Hebrew and in Greek characters respectively.[10] Today, these columns are still haunted by questions (such as the precise nature of the Hebrew text and the methods of transliteration) that a lack of evidence keeps from being answered.[11] Later Greek Christian literature was much more interested in the other – i.e., Greek – columns of the *Hexapla*. Whereas the *secunda* still found its way into later manuscripts and texts very modestly, the first column was never transmitted in any significant way, simply because Christians lacked the language skills to read and copy it.[12]

21.7.4 Readings from the "Hebrew" Cited in Greek Christian Literature and Manuscripts

Nevertheless, Greek Christian authors sometimes did refer to or cite from "the Hebrew," also when the LXX text did not require this. Again, the seemingly evident assumption that this would have required some knowledge of Hebrew is incorrect. The readings in question, while expressing a certain interest in the Hebrew parent text, pose many problems of interpretation.

---

[6] Hebrew was also used in other areas, such as magic: see Hilhorst, "The Prestige."

[7] This view is articulated illustratively in a Christian text written probably around the early fifth century C.E., but also taken up by Photius in the ninth century C.E. (*Amphilochia* 152), that lists all the reasons for the "obscurity" (ἀσάφεια) of the Greek Old Testament. Almost all of them result from the LXX having been translated from Hebrew.

[8] The example in question is offered by, amongst others, Theodore of Mopsuestia, John Chrysostom, Theodoret of Cyrrhus, Anastasius of Sinai, John of Damascus, Michael Glycas, John VI Cantacuzenus, and Gennadius Scholarius.

[9] Onomastica have been collected by P. de Lagarde, *Onomastica sacra* (2nd ed.; Göttingen: Rente, 1887 [repr. Hildesheim: Olms, 1966]) and F. Wutz, *Onomastica sacra: Untersuchungen zum Liber interpretationis nominum hebraicorum des Hl. Hieronymus* (2 vols.; TU 41; Leipzig: Hinrichs, 1914–1915). A convenient introduction to the lexicographical material is offered by K. Alpers, "Lexicon I (griechisch)," RAC 23:1261–62.

[10] The opinion expressed by P. Nautin (*Origène: Sa vie et son œuvre* [Christianisme antique 1; Paris: Beauchesne, 1977], 315) that there was no column with a Hebrew text in Hebrew characters is not accepted today.

[11] For the state of research, see Part 2 of Salvesen, *Hexapla.

[12] Note that none of the manuscripts with remains of the *Hexapla* in columnar form (i.e., LXX[1098], LXX[2005], LXX[113], LXX[86], and possibly LXX[271]) contains a trace of the first column.

21.7.4.1 Terminology

The terminology employed by Greek scribes and authors to refer to "the Hebrew" is very varied: one distinguishes terms that seem to denote a particular text (τὸ Ἑβραϊκόν and ἡ Ἑβραϊκὴ γραφή "the Hebrew [text]"; τὸ τῶν Ἑβραίων "the [text] of the Hebrews") from those that would rather seem to refer to persons (κατὰ τὸν Ἑβραῖον and παρὰ τῷ Ἑβραίῳ "according to a Hebrew"; παρ' Ἑβραίοις "according to Hebrews") and those that are more vague (ἡ Ἑβραϊκὴ ἀνάγνωσις "the Hebrew reading"; ἡ Ἑβραϊκὴ λέξις "the Hebrew wording"). While some authors appear to have used these terms rather indifferently, others (notably Origen) are believed to have applied the terminology in a stricter sense, even up to the point of subtleties: for example, Ἑβραῖός τις "a Hebrew" or οἱ Ἑβραῖοι "the Hebrews" could indicate a type of source different from ὁ Ἑβραῖος "the Hebrew." To complicate matters, it is certain that different authors used the terms in different ways. Obviously, this hampers a clear appreciation of their provenance.

21.7.4.2 Provenance

Scholars have suggested a wide range of hypotheses regarding the provenance of the "Hebrew" readings cited in Greek Christian documents. Some of these theories (such as that they were taken from Jerome's exegesis or from Aquila's version, or were ad hoc translations made directly from the Hebrew by the Christian authors or scribes in question) are rejected today, but even then various options still remain open and no satisfying answer has yet been given to the question of "what τὸ Ἑβραϊκόν or ὁ Ἑβραῖος might mean."[13] In any case, it is clear that not all readings derive from one and the same source. Only in a limited number of cases is it really a Hebrew text that is cited (i.e., transcribed in Greek characters). Some of these readings can be traced back to the *secunda*.[14] Often, however, the "Hebrew" reading that is cited consists entirely of Greek text.[15] It has been suggested that these readings were taken from an anonymous Greek version, which, similarly to Aquila, Symmachus, and Theodotion, would have been a translation from the Hebrew that in one way or another was closer to the original than was LXX. Detailed analyses, however, show that at least some of them (e.g., those cited by Eusebius of Emesa) may actually have been gleaned from individuals with knowledge of Hebrew.[16] Interestingly, some of the translations those offered were possibly colored by Jewish exegetical traditions.[17]

21.7.4.3 Attestation

In documenting and interpreting the "Hebrew" readings, scholarship turns mostly to the margins of LXX manuscripts (e.g., LXX^M) and to Greek Christian authors from the first five centuries (especially Origen, Eusebius of Caesarea, and authors from the so-called Antiochene school of exegesis). In these sources, the "Hebrew" readings are often found side by side with Hexaplaric ones, which is indicative of the merging of both these traditions[18] (although in reality many of the "Hebrew" readings cannot be traced back to the Hexapla). Less attention has been given in scholarship to "Hebrew" readings that were cited by Greek

---

[13] The expression is taken from Field, *Hexapla*, lxxi ("*quid significet τὸ Ἑβραϊκόν sive ὁ Ἑβραῖος*"), whose useful state of research (lxxi–lxxvii) is nicely complemented by ter Haar Romeny, *A Syrian*, 47–71.

[14] The *Hexapla* could also have been the source of some of these references to "the Hebrew" where no actual reading is cited, but where a quantitative difference between the Greek and Hebrew texts is noted (e.g., absence vs. presence of Psalm headings).

[15] E.g., Ps-Chrysostom on Jer 2:25: Κατὰ μέντοι τὸν Ἑβραῖον οὕτως ἔχει, Ἀπόστρεψον τὸν πόδα σου τοῦ περιπατεῖν ἀνυπόδητος [ἀνυπόδυτος PG], καὶ τὴν φωνήν σου ἀπὸ κλαυθμοῦ (PG 64:773) "According to the Hebrew, the text actually reads as follows: *Keep your foot from walking unshod and your voice from wailing.*"

[16] Ter Haar Romeny, *A Syrian*, 63–64.

[17] Cf. M. Fincati, "Problemi di traduzione: uno Pseudo-Crisostomo commenta Geremia," in *Miscellanea Graecolatina III* (eds. S. Costa and F. Gallo; Ambrosiana Graecolatina 3; Rome: Bulzoni, 2015), 105–16 (115–16). For an example, see the Ἑβραῖος reading cited by Eusebius of Emesa for Gen 23:6, which appears to include an interpretation found in T^O, T^Ps-J, and T^N (ter Haar Romeny, *A Syrian*, 334; see also pp. 61, 63, and 70–71).

[18] Similarly, the editions that document the "Hebrew" readings (i.e., Field, *Hexapla* and the second apparatus of the Göttingen editions) essentially treat them as Hexaplaric material.

Christian scribes from a later period. In manuscripts LXX^F and LXX56, in particular, eleventh- and twelfth-century hands cited certain Greek readings under the headings not only of τὸ ἑβραϊκόν, "the Hebrew [text]" and ἐν τῷ ἑβ(ραϊκῷ/-ραίῳ), "in the Hebrew [text]" but also of τὸ ιουδαϊκόν, "the Jewish [text]" and ἐν τῷ ιουδ(αϊκῷ), "in the Jewish [text]."[19] These readings are of a different kind than those found in earlier Christian sources: they are much younger (i.e., of Byzantine coinage and usage) and appear to be taken from medieval Greek Jewish versions.[20] The Christian scribes knew them through direct contact with Jewish tradition rather than via any Hexaplaric documents.

Devreesse, R., *Introduction à l'étude des manuscrits grecs* (Paris: Imprimerie nationale, 1954).

Fernández Marcos, N., *The Septuagint in Context: Introduction to the Greek Versions of the Bible* (trans. W.G.E. Watson; Leiden: Brill, 2000).

Field, *Hexapla.

Fincati, M., "'Hebraiká' und 'Ioudaiká' in mittelalterlichen biblischen Handschriften," in Kraus–Kreuzer, *Septuaginta 2014, 839–49.

Fincati, M., "Filologia ed esegesi biblica in Terra d'Otranto. Varianti greche, latine e giudaiche nel MS. *Parisinus graecus 3*," *Aev* 90 (2016): 377–400.

Fincati, M., *The Medieval Revision of the Ambrosian Hexateuch. Critical Editing between* Septuaginta *and* Hebraica Veritas *in* MS *Ambrosianus A 147 inf.* (De Septuaginta Investigationes 5; Göttingen: Vandenhoeck & Ruprecht, 2016).

Gallagher, E.L., *Hebrew Scripture in Patristic Biblical Theory: Canon, Language, Text* (VCSup 114; Leiden: Brill, 2012).

ter Haar Romeny, R.B., *A Syrian in Greek Dress: The Use of Greek, Hebrew, and Syriac Biblical Texts in Eusebius of Emesa's Commentary on Genesis* (Traditio Exegetica Graeca 6; Leuven: Peeters, 1997).

Hilhorst, T., "The Prestige of Hebrew in the Christian World of Late Antiquity and Middle Ages," in *Flores Florentino: Dead Sea Scrolls and Other Early Jewish Studies in Honour of Florentino García Martínez* (eds. A. Hilhorst, É. Puech, and E. Tigchelaar; JSJSup 122; Leiden: Brill, 2007), 777–802.

Kamesar, A., *Jerome, Greek Scholarship, and the Hebrew Bible: A Study of the* Quaestiones Hebraicae in Genesim (Oxford Classical Monographs; Oxford: Clarendon Press, 1993).

de Lange, N., *Japhet in the Tents of Shem* (TSMJ 30; Tübingen: Mohr Siebeck, 2015).

de Lange, N., J.G. Krivoruchko, and C. Boyd-Taylor (eds.), *Jewish Reception of Greek Bible Versions: Studies in Their Use in Late Antiquity and the Middle Ages* (Texts and Studies in Medieval and Early Modern Judaism 23; Tübingen: Mohr Siebeck, 2009).

Salvesen, *Hexapla.

Septuaginta Vetus Testamentum Graecum auctoritate Academiae Scientiarum Gottingensis editum (mult. vols.; Göttingen: Vandenhoeck & Ruprecht, 1931–).

Reinhart Ceulemans

---

[19] See, e.g., Fincati, *Medieval Revision*, de Lange, *Japhet* and Fincati, "Hebraiká."

[20] For these versions, see de Lange, Krivoruchko, and Boyd-Taylor (eds.), *Jewish Reception* and www.gbbj.org.

21.8 Latin Church Fathers

21.8.1 Origins of the Latin Bible (→ 1.4.1)[1]

Our earliest evidence for biblical texts in Latin comes from the second century C.E. Most scholars trace the origins of the Latin Bible to North Africa. Based on quotations in the Latin church fathers and in manuscripts preserving portions of the Old Latin (VL) Bible, scholars have identified African and European families of VL, neither of which is entirely homogenous. Still, recent scholarship suggests that these families go back to a common original. This theory is supported by the existence of peculiar biblical renderings shared by diverse Latin Fathers. Moreover, phrases used to describe VL, such as *vetus editio* "old edition"; *antiqua interpretatio* "ancient translation"; and *vetus translatio* "old translation" indicate that the earliest Latin Fathers considered VL to be a unified version. Church fathers who bear significant witness to the biblical text through their Scriptural citations include Cyprian, Novatian, Lucifer of Cagliari, Priscillian, Tyconius, Hilary, Ambrose, Rufinus, Jerome, and Augustine, together with anonymous texts such as *De Pascha Computus* and the *Speculum*.[2]

21.8.2 The Latin Bible in the Early African Fathers

The first Latin Father who quoted extensively from Scripture is Tertullian of Carthage (ca. 160–220 C.E.). Tertullian was often free in his quotations and sometimes quoted the same passage differently in different places. It is therefore unclear whether Tertullian actually knew of written translations of Scripture. Various passages have been cited from Tertullian's writings to suggest that he was familiar with a Latin translation of the Bible, e.g., Tertullian's comment on δύο διαθῆκαι "two covenants" in Gal 4:24, *duo testamenta, sive duae ostensiones, sicut invenimus interpretatum* "'two testaments' or 'two manifestations', as we have found it translated" (*Marc.* 5.4.8), and his argument that Gen 2:7 had been misconstrued in Latin (*Marc.* 2.9.1–9). Indeed, Tertullian often felt obligated to explain a Latin biblical expression that was not his own but was already "in usage" (e.g., *Mon.* 11.10–11; *Marc.* 4.1; *Prax.* 5.2–3), and regularly glossed Latin words to express their precise meaning based on the Greek, as if he had inherited certain Latin terms that he found unsatisfactory.[3] Still, even if Tertullian knew of translations of some biblical passages, this does not necessarily mean that the whole Bible had been translated by his day. Moreover, some of the customary Latin equivalencies known to Tertullian might have simply been "in usage" orally among Christians. Numerous and sometimes substantial differences exist between Tertullian's biblical quotations and those of Cyprian, whose quotations were much closer to later VL manuscripts. This suggests that, whereas Cyprian was quoting from established Latin translations, Tertullian was usually just producing his own ad hoc renderings. However, Tertullian seems to have inherited an already existing Latin terminology, which points at least to the beginnings of Latin biblical translations in his day, and also perhaps suggests that some of the Latin translations known later to Cyprian and Novatian were already revised versions.

The quotations of Scripture in Cyprian (ca. 200–258 C.E.) are for the most part internally consistent and generally agree with later African texts. Cyprian is thus the central witness to the African family of the Old Latin Bible.[4] Old Testament books quoted most frequently by Cyprian are Psalms (90 references), Isaiah (75), Proverbs (39), Jeremiah (28), and Exodus (27).[5] Cyprian's most important

---

[1] For biblical quotations in the Latin Fathers, see also → 1.7.2.

[2] For a full list of patristic witnesses to the VL text, see H.J. Frede, *Kirchenschriftsteller: Verzeichnis und Sigel* (Aktualisierungsheft by R. Gryson; VL 1.1C; Freiburg i.B.: Herder, 1999).

[3] See O'Malley, *Tertullian*, 28–37.

[4] As shown for Proverbs by Schildenberger, *Die altlateinischen Texte*, and for Genesis by Fischer, VL 2.

[5] Fahey, *Cyprian and the Bible*, 42–43.

work giving witness to the VL text is his *Testimonia ad Quirinum*, the first two books of which are devoted primarily to listing Old Testament prooftexts for various Christian tenets. Cyprian quotes from a version that has already been revised and has some complexity to its history.[6] A more evolved African Latin text, but one clearly from the same family as Cyprian, can be seen in authors such as Lactantius (ca. 250–325 C.E.), Tyconius (ca. 330–390 C.E.), and in the biblical texts used by the Donatists in the fourth and fifth centuries C.E.[7]

21.8.3 The Latin Bible in the Early European Fathers

Jerome reports that the first ecclesiastical writer in Latin was Victor I of Rome (d. ca. 198 C.E.; see Jerome, *Vir. ill.* 34; 53). Biblical quotations in Latin are preserved from the late second and early third centuries in Latin translations of Greek works, such as 1 Clement.[8] The first identifiable witness to the European family of VL is Novatian of Rome (ca. 250 C.E.), although the points of divergence between Novatian and Cyprian do not demonstrate the existence of an independent European translation. The first author to furnish long biblical citations attesting to the European VL text is Lucifer of Cagliari (d. ca. 371 C.E.). In the second half of the fourth century, recensions of the VL text in Europe multiplied and the text became more diverse. Figures such as Hilary of Poitiers (ca. 315–367 C.E.) and Ambrose of Milan (ca. 339–397 C.E.) wrote systematic commentaries on Scripture giving extensive quotations, consulting Greek texts in their exegesis and sometimes modifying their Latin versions.[9] Ambrose, who sometimes knew a variety of Latin readings, regularly employed not only LXX (→ 1.3.1.1) but also the Hexaplaric versions (→ 1.3.1.2), especially in his commentary on the Psalms.[10] Other important witnesses to the European VL text include Gregory of Elvira (ca. 320–395 C.E.), Rufinus (ca. 345–410 C.E.), and Jerome (ca. 347–419 C.E.).[11]

21.8.4 Unity, Diversity, and Evolution in Latin Biblical Citations

Diverse readings arose in the VL tradition because the translations were made anonymously over time, without a clear authority of their own. The Latin was often seen simply as a cipher for the Greek, which was the truly authoritative text. Consequently, from the beginning, writers felt free to revise the Latin according to the Greek. Augustine's statement that many people felt free to make their own translations reflects the situation of textual diversity that existed in the late fourth century C.E. as a result of continuous revisions (*Doctr. chr.* 2.11.16; cf. *Epist.* 71.6).[12] The text of VL developed from the second to the fifth centuries C.E. as the result of several forces: 1) African texts were revised to conform to European text forms;[13] 2) older

---

[6] Bogaert, "La Bible latine," 145.

[7] Lactantius, *Inst.* IV contains a collection of biblical citations similar to Cyprian's *Test.* I and II, which likewise reflect the African Old Latin family; see P. Monat, "Les *testimonia* bibliques, de Cyprien à Lactance," in Fontaine and Pietri, *Le monde latine*, 505. In Gryson's edition of Isaiah, one family ("κ") is represented chiefly by Cyprian's *Test.*, which is usually woodenly literal, whereas another family ("c") represents a revised African text that appears in African authors of the fourth and fifth centuries C.E.; see R. Gryson, *Esaias* (VL 12; Freiburg: Herder, 1987), 17. On biblical texts among the Donatists, see Bogaert, "Les bibles d'Augustin," 518–21.

[8] J. Gribomont, "Les plus anciennes traductions latines," in Fontaine and Pietri, *Le monde latin antique*, 51.

[9] See Billen, *Old Latin Texts*, 137–38.

[10] See G. Nauroy, "L'Ecriture dans la pastorale d'Ambroise de Milan," in Fontaine and Pietri, *Le monde latin*, 387–91.

[11] E.g., for key sources attesting to VL-Cant, see E. Schulz-Flügel, *Canticum Canticorum* (VL 10.3; Freiburg i.B.: Herder, 1992), 70–76.

[12] Jerome tends to speak of textual diversity coming about through miscopying, e.g., *Pref. Gosp.*; *Pref. Josh.*; *Pref. Job*; *Pref. Paralip.*; but he also refers to faulty translators, e.g., *Pref. Gosp.*; *Pref. Prov.* LXX.

[13] Differences between "African" and "European" usages include: φῶς, African: *lumen*, European: *lux* (all meaning "light"); δοξάζειν "to give honor, glory," African: *clarificare* "to make famous," European: *glorificare* "to praise"; λόγος "word," African: *sermo* "speech," European: *verbum* "word"; μακάριος "fortunate," African: *felix* "successful," European: *beatus* "fortunate"; βαπτίζειν "to immerse," African: *tinguere* "to moisten," European: *baptizare* "to baptize, immerse." It is not that any of these words were strictly "African" or "European," but these

language was updated to current usage; 3) modest improvements were made in the style of the translation; 4) new terms were adopted in order to reflect the development of religious ideas;[14] and 5) most importantly, revisions were made to VL in order to bring the translation into closer conformity with whatever Greek text was known to the reviser. The Greek texts of the second century upon which the first VL translations were made were not the same as the Greek texts used to revise VL in the fourth and fifth centuries C.E. Thus, for the book of Daniel, Tertullian's quotations match the Old Greek (→ 18.3.1), Cyprian's quotations are partly Old Greek and partly Theodotion (→ 18.3.2), as if he was using a partly updated Latin text, and from the third-century C.E. text *De Pascha computus* onward (including Commodian and Lucifer), the text is strictly Theodotion. Similarly with Job, the original short Greek text of Job (→ 11.3.1) is known to Cyprian and Lucifer, the modestly filled out version known from the major Greek uncials is quoted in Latin by Ambrose, and the completely filled out version produced by Origen (→ 11.3.5) was used by Augustine.[15] For any given book, complexity in the evolution of the Greek text will usually manifest itself in revisions within the VL tradition.

21.8.5 Jerome and the Latin Bible

Jerome wrote select commentaries on Genesis, Psalms, and Daniel, and he composed comprehensive commentaries on the Twelve Prophets, Isaiah, Ezekiel, and Jeremiah. He is perhaps best known for his translation of the Hebrew Bible into Latin, his translation *iuxta Hebraeos* "according to the Hebrews," which formed the nucleus of what later became known as the Latin "Vulgate." On Jerome and the Latin Vulgate, see → 1.3.5.

21.8.6 Augustine and the Latin Bible

Although he never learned Hebrew and acquired only a rudimentary knowledge of Greek, Augustine showed much interest in finding the best text of the Bible.[16] He made reference to good manuscripts (e.g., *Doctr. chr.* 2.15.22; *Faust.* 32.16), described principles for correcting texts (e.g., *Doctr. chr.* 2.12.18–2.13.19), and often discussed textual matters (e.g., in *Quaestiones in Heptateuchum* and *Enarrationes in Psalmos* 18).[17] At least for some biblical books (e.g., Psalms), the VL version that Augustine used was not an African text but a European text, which he acquired in Milan and took back to Africa.[18] This European text is perhaps what Augustine had in mind when he recommended the "Itala" as the preferred version of Scripture (*Doctr. chr.* 2.15.22). Biblical texts quoted by Augustine often have distinctive features; for example, in quotations from the Heptateuch, Augustine reflects a unique text-type that has been systematically revised according to the Greek.[19] In general, the peculiarity of many of his biblical citations suggests that the revised VL version used by Augustine did not circulate widely, although one manuscript of the Psalms (the Verona Psalter) is extremely close to the Psalms text used in Augustine's *Enarrationes in Psalmos*.[20] Augustine was initially critical of Jerome's Hebrew translations, although he approved of Jerome's translation of Job based upon the Hexaplaric Greek edition (*Epist.* 28, written in 394 or 395 C.E.), since Augustine affirmed the inspiration of LXX (*Doctr. chr.*

---

were the equivalencies that came into usage in these regions.

[14] Modifications in the Old Latin that might reflect the development of religious thinking in the third century C.E. include the changes from: *donum* "gift, present, offering" to *munus* "office, tribute, offering," *festum* "feast, festival" to *solemne* "religious rite, ceremony," *ministrare* "to serve" to *sacrificare* "to sacrifice, celebrate mass," and *votum* "vow, promise, petition" to *oratio* "speech, prose, prayer"; see Billen, *Old Latin Texts*, 6.

[15] See Burkitt, *The Old Latin*, 6–9.

[16] See Bogaert, "Les bibles d' Augustin," 523, 530.

[17] Augustine suggests several textual emendations in his *Retractiones*, e.g., *Retract.* 1.10.3 (on Gen 2:5); 1.7.2 (on Ps 43:33), and 1.7.3 (on Eccl 1:2); see Houghton, *Augustine's Text of John*, 18.

[18] Bogaert, "Les bibles d' Augustin," 521–22.

[19] Not infrequently, biblical manuscripts of the European family and Ambrose will agree with Cyprian against Augustine, showing the uniqueness of Augustine's text (Billen, *Old Latin Texts*, 133).

[20] F.C. Burkitt, "Jerome's Work on the Psalter," *JTS* 30 (1929): 395–97 (396).

2.15.22, written in 396 C.E.). Augustine later criticized Jerome's *iuxta Hebraeos* translation of Jonah (*Epist.* 71, written in 403 C.E.), expressing concerns that Jerome's work could cause a rift between East and West, and pointing out that no Christians were capable of checking Jerome's work for accuracy (see also *Epist.* 82, written in 405 C.E.). Yet, Augustine eventually accepted the value of the Hebrew and Jerome's translations, allowing for both LXX and the Hebrew texts to be inspired, and calling Jerome "a most learned man, skilled in all three languages" (i.e., Hebrew, Greek, and Latin) (*Civ.* 18.43, written sometime after 420 C.E.).[21] Augustine made use of Jerome's *iuxta Hebraeos* translation of Isaiah perhaps as early as 395 C.E., and certainly by 397 C.E.[22] Augustine was clearly using the *iuxta Hebraeos* version when he cited 1 Samuel 16 in *Ad Simplicianum* 2.1.6, written ca. 396 C.E.[23] Augustine employed Jerome's revision of the Gospels starting from the early 400s C.E., as seen in *De consensu evangelistarum*. By 415 C.E., Augustine was using Jerome's Hexaplaric Psalter (= the Gallican Psalter; → 10.3.7; → 10.4.1) in his *Enarrationes in Psalmos*,[24] but in *Epist.* 261.5 (which is difficult to date), Augustine says that he had not seen the *iuxta Hebraeos* Psalter.[25] In the *Quaestiones in Heptateuchum* (419–420 C.E.), Augustine treated eighteen passages by comparing their translation according to LXX with the *interpretatio quae est ex hebraico* "translation that is from the Hebrew."[26] In some cases, the Hebrew is regarded as clearer, and it is usually seen as useful. Augustine also discussed the Hebrew text several times in *City of God*, e.g., for 2 Kgs 5:26 (*Civ.* 22.29); Isa 42:1–4 (*Civ.* 20.30); Jonah 3:4; (*Civ.* 1.44); Hag 2:7b (*Civ.* 18.48); Zech 12:10 (*Civ.* 20.30); and Mal 4:6 (*Civ.* 20.29).[27] Overall, however, Augustine did not ascribe primary authority to the Hebrew text, and so he worked mostly with the LXX-based VL text, merely using Jerome's *iuxta Hebraeos* translations when helpful. Augustine also serves as an important witness to biblical versions used by his various theological opponents, whose texts he sometimes quotes extensively.[28]

Billen, A.V., *The Old Latin Texts of the Heptateuch* (Cambridge: Cambridge University Press, 1927).

Bogaert, P.-M., "La Bible latine des origines au Moyen Age: Aperçu historique, état des questions," *RTL* 19 (1988): 137–59, 276–314.

Bogaert, P.-M., "Les bibles d'Augustin," *RTL* 37 (2006): 513–31.

La Bonnardière, A.-M., "La Bible 'liturgique' de saint Augustin," *ThH* 35 (1975): 147–60.

La Bonnardière, A.-M. (ed.), *Saint Augustin et la Bible* (Paris: Beauchesne, 1986).

Bouton-Touboulic, A.-I., "Autorité et Tradition: La traduction latine de la Bible selon Saint Jérôme et Saint Augustin," *Aug* 45.1 (2006): 185–229.

Bright, P. (ed.), *Augustine and the Bible* (Notre Dame: University of Notre Dame Press, 1986).

Burkitt, F.C., *The Old Latin and the Itala* (Cambridge: Cambridge University Press, 1896).

Fahey, M.A., *Cyprian and the Bible: A Study in Third-Century Exegesis* (Tübingen: J.C.B. Mohr, 1971).

Fischer, B., *Genesis* (VL 2; Freiburg i.B.: Herder, 1951–1954).

Fontaine, J. and C. Pietri (eds.), *Le monde latine antique et la Bible* (Paris: Beauchesne, 1985).

---

[21] On LXX and the Hebrew as inspired, see also *Civ.* 15.14. Augustine also praised Jerome's linguistic scholarship at *Pecc. merit.* 3.6.12 (written in 412 C.E.), and *Doctr. chr.* 4.7.15; 4.20.41 (composed in the late 420s C.E.).

[22] The text quoted is Isa 46:8, which Augustine first cites in the *iuxta Hebraeos* form in *Enarrat. Ps.* 101, which may be as early as 395 C.E.; see S. Deléani, "Un emprunt d'Augustin à l'Écriture: 'Redite, praeuaricatores, ad cor' (*Isaïe* 46, 8b)," *REAug* 38 (1992): 29–49 (33).

[23] Houghton, *Augustine's Text of John*, 12.

[24] C. Estin, "Les traductions du Psautier," in Fontaine and Pietri, *Le monde latin antique et la Bible*, 67–88 (70).

[25] See Houghton, *Augustine's Text of John*, 16–17.

[26] See A.-M. La Bonnardière, "Did Augustine Use Jerome's Vulgate?" in Bright, *Augustine and the Bible*, 42–51 (43–44). The eighteen passages, with their corresponding references in *Quaest. Hept.* (book number and question number) are Gen 31:47–48 (I.97); Gen 41:50 (I.192); Gen 47:31 (I.162); Deut 14:27–28 (V.20); Deut 30:11–14 (V.54); Josh 5:13–15 (VI.7); Josh 10:5–6 (VI.15); Josh 16:10 (VI.19); Josh 6:26 (VI.19); Josh 23:14 (VI.24); Josh 24:3 (VI.25); Judg 2:13 (VII.16); Judg 3:17 (VII.21); Judg 3:31 (VII.25); Judg 7:6 (VII.37); Judg 8:26–27 (VII.41); Judg 10:1 (VII.47); and Judg 15:8 (VII.55).

[27] La Bonnardière, "Did Augustine Use Jerome's Vulgate?" 45–49. Moreover, based on passages such as *Civ.* 16.15, it is clear that Augustine had read Jerome's *Hebrew Questions on Genesis*.

[28] A.-M. La Bonnardière, "The Bible and Polemics," in Bright, *Augustine and the Bible*, 183–207.

Graves, M., *Jerome's Hebrew Philology: A Study Based on his Commentary on Jeremiah* (VCSup 90; Leiden: Brill, 2007).

Houghton, H.A.G., *Augustine's Text of John: Patristic Citations and Latin Gospel Manuscripts* (Oxford: Oxford University Press, 2008).

Kamesar, A., *Jerome, Greek Scholarship, and the Hebrew Bible* (Oxford: Clarendon Press, 1993).

O'Malley, T.P., *Tertullian and the Bible* (Utrecht: Dekker & Van de Vegt, 1967).

Schildenberger, J., *Die altlateinischen Texte der Proverbien-Buches*, Vol. 1: *Die alte afrikanische Textgestalt* (Beuron: Archabbey of Beuron, 1941).

Sparks, H.F.D., "The Latin Bible," in *The Bible in its Ancient and English Versions* (ed. H.W. Robinson; Oxford: Clarendon Press, 1940), 100–127.

Michael Graves

21.9 Syriac Church Fathers

The study of the Old Testament as preserved in Syriac Christian literature refers to two kinds of texts, complete versions and secondary quotations. The full versions are the translations and adaptations of the Old Testament into Syriac, including Philoxenus' revised version (→ 1.4.4) from the beginning of the sixth century C.E., Paul of Tella's Syro-Hexapla (→ 1.4.5) from the beginning of the seventh century C.E., and Jacob of Edessa's version (→ 1.4.6) from the beginning of the eighth century C.E. These texts are based on the Peshitta (→ 1.3.4) as well as on other versions and translations of the Old Testament, and scholars have focused on uncovering their sources and understanding their reception in Syriac Christian literature.[1]

The secondary quotations are excerpts of the Old Testament in Syriac Christian literature. These quotations do not always match the Peshitta, thus raising the question whether the differences are, in fact, remnants of a primitive version of a Syriac Old Testament that was not preserved in full, or whether they differ from the Peshitta as known from its full manuscripts due to the character of the sources in which these variants are found.

Starting from the early studies of the Peshitta, quotations in Syriac Christian literature have played an important role in the study of the origins of the Peshitta, its development, and its reception in Syriac Christianity. Early works on the text of the Peshitta, including preliminary critical editions, used evidence from Syriac Christian literature.[2] Of unique significance were, and still are, quotations in the Syriac Christian literature prior to the fifth century C.E. These texts predate the earliest manuscripts of the Peshitta, i.e., those from the fifth (s5b1) and seventh centuries (s7a1), and the vast number of translations from Greek into Syriac in the fifth century C.E., which increased the influence of Greek versions of the Old Testament on Syriac writers. As such, they are more likely to preserve a reliable version of the Syriac Old Testament in the early centuries of the Common Era and shed light on the development of the Peshitta as known to us from its manuscripts, and on its reception in Syriac Christian literature.

Nevertheless, the credibility of the quotations of the Old Testament in Syriac Christian literature is subject to debate. In 1960, Goshen-Gottstein claimed that the quotations of the Old Testament in Syriac Christian literature do not accurately and reliably reflect the early Syriac version of the Old Testament. They, therefore, should not be included in any edition of the Peshitta. Similarities between the quotations of the Old Testament in Syriac Christian literature and readings in the other ancient translations, such as the Targum (→ 1.3.3) and LXX (→ 1.3.4), should be explained as independent acquaintance with these translations or as similar developments in the Syriac and the other translations, rather than taken as evidence of an earlier version of the Peshitta.[3] Despite this criticism, studies of the text of the Syriac Old Testament as preserved in Syriac Christian literature have increased in recent years. For example, van Rompay and ter Haar Romeny surveyed the study of quotations of the Old Testament in Syriac literature and emphasized their importance for understanding the origin of the Peshitta and its reception in

---

[1] According to Abdišo's list of Mar Aba's writings, Mar Aba translated the Greek Old Testament into Syriac, thus adding another version. However, no evidence of this text survived; cf. Abdišo, *Catalogus Librorum*, 75. For further discussion, see Vööbus, *History*, 167–68.

[2] Barnes, *The Peshitta Psalter*; Dietrich, *Ein Apparatus criticus*.

[3] Goshen-Gottstein, "Prolegomena," and previously Haefeli, *Die Peschitta*, 87–94. This approach was qualified by Running, "An Investigation: I"; Running, "An Investigation: II–III," who used Ephrem's and Aphrahat's quotations in her study of the Syriac version of Isaiah. She claimed that evidence from Syriac Christian literature may be accepted, but only when supported by the Targum. The rejection of the evidence from Syriac Christian literature was followed by Maori, *The Peshitta Version*, 24–31; Weitzman, *The Syriac Version*, 129–39 and others.

Syriac Christian literature.[4] Van Rompay added a list of early Syriac Christian writings that, in his opinion, should be included in any new edition of the Peshitta. He claimed that the style and method of the writer determines the credibility of the quotations. Of unique importance are biblical commentaries, because they focus on the text of the Old Testament and, as such, are more likely to represent an accurate version as known to the commentator.[5]

The main Syriac writers whose biblical quotations have been studied to date are Ephrem and Aphrahat. They represent two different genres and different approaches to biblical citations. Aphrahat (d. ca. 345 C.E.) wrote twenty-three *Demonstrations*, theological and polemic treatises, in which he incorporated lengthy biblical quotations. These quotations correlate mostly with the Peshitta, but occasionally with MT (→ 1.2.2), LXX (→ 1.3.1.1), the Vulgate (→ 1.3.5), or Targums (→ 1.3.3), or with an unknown version. The differences between Aphrahat's quotations and the Peshitta led Wright and Nöldeke to claim that Aphrahat cited from memory.[6] Pinkerton, Baumstark, and Vööbus claimed that Aphrahat used a primitive and more literal version of the Peshitta, which was closer to MT.[7] While these scholars used sporadic quotations to reach their conclusions, Owens conducted a systematic study of Aphrahat's quotations from Genesis and Exodus. He posited that the similarity between the majority of Aphrahat's quotations and the Peshitta actually indicates that Aphrahat was familiar with the Peshitta. Owens thus partially accepts the explanation of mistakes resulting from quoting from memory and rejects the possibility that Aphrahat cited from a primitive version of the Peshitta. According to Owens, the small number of correlations between Aphrahat's quotations and other versions is not sufficient for drawing conclusions regarding Aphrahat's acquaintance with any text but the Peshitta.[8]

Unlike Aphrahat, Ephrem (306–373 C.E.) is known not only for his theological and polemic writing but also for his *Commentary on Genesis and Exodus*. The Old Testament quotations in that composition are more likely to represent the accurate version as known to Ephrem. The quotations correspond to the Peshitta in most cases. In some cases, the correlation with the Peshitta is only partial, and in a few cases the Old Testament quotations are close to other versions, including a clear citation of *Targum Onqelos* (→ 1.3.3).[9] Janson concluded from a survey of Ephrem's quotations in his *Commentary on Genesis* that Ephrem occasionally modified his biblical text to fit it into the flow of his argument, modernized the Syriac, or presented the biblical characters more favorably.[10] Lund pointed to the fact that the major variants between Ephrem's version and later manuscripts support the version of the fifth century C.E. manuscript of the Peshitta (s5b1), the earliest Peshitta manuscript known to us.[11] Recently, Kremer[12] added that in addition to Ephrem's free hand in style and citations, he may have used an archaic version of the Peshitta that

---

[4] Van Rompay, "Between the School"; ter Haar Romeny, "Le réception," and previously Vööbus, "Der Einfluss."

[5] For a similar claim, see Lane, " 'There is No Need …' " For a survey of Syriac biblical exegetical literature, its editions and translations, see van Rompay, "The Christian Syriac Tradition"; Kannengiesser, *Handbook*, 1377–446.

[6] Wright, *Homilies*, 16. Nöldeke, "Review of Wright," followed him, but qualified this argument in his "Review of Ceriani."

[7] Pinkerton, "The Origin," 34–35; Baumstark, "Neue orientalische," 94–95; Baumstark, "Ps. Jonathan"; Vööbus, *Peschitta und Targumim*, 65–68, 98–104.

[8] Owens, *The Genesis and Exodus Citations*. These conclusions correspond with Owens' study on Aphrahat's citations of Leviticus and Proverbs, see Owens, "Aphrahat as a Witness"; Owens, "The Book of Proverbs," and are followed by Koster, "The Copernican Revolution," 29–30; Koster, "Aphrahat's Use."

[9] Ephrem, *Commentary on Genesis* 42.13 (Tonneau ed. 116:18), citing T⁰-Gen 49:23.

[10] Janson, *De Abrahamcyclus*, 23–89.

[11] Lund, "Observations." See also Pinkerton, "The Origin," 35–38. Similarity between biblical versions as cited in Syriac Christian literature and the Peshitta version of manuscript s5b1 also characterize Eusebius of Emessa's ad hoc translations to Greek of a Syriac translation of the Bible, which he calls ὁ Σύρος "the Syriac one." For a survey of research and new conclusions, see ter Haar Romeny, *A Syrian*, 71–82; ter Haar Romeny, "Quis sit ὁ Σύρος."

[12] Kremer, *Mundus Primus*, 110–27.

was closer to the Hebrew version (→ 1.2.2), even though he did not necessarily use the Hebrew text itself.[13]

Quotations of the Old Testament in the Syriac New Testament constitute another source of the early version of the Peshitta. In many cases, later scribes revised these quotations according to the Syriac Old Testament known to them.[14] As such, manuscripts of the Syriac New Testament are the first recoverable stage in the reception history of the Syriac Old Testament.

While the writings of Aphrahat and Ephrem and quotations in the Syriac New Testament have been the subject of scholarly studies, few other Syriac writers have received the same attention. A systematic study of Old Testament quotations in Syriac Christian writings may shed light on both the writers' version of the Old Testament and their methods of exegesis, as well as on the development and reception of the Old Testament in Syriac.

Barnes, W.E., *The Peshitta Psalter according to the West Syrian Text* (Cambridge: Cambridge University Press, 1904).
Baumstark, A., "Das Problem der Bibelzitate in der syrischen Übersetzungsliteratur," *OrChr* 8 (1933): 208–25.
Baumstark, A., "Neue orientalische Probleme biblischer Textgeschichte," *ZDMG* 89 (1935): 89–118.
Baumstark, A., "Ps. Jonathan zu Dtn 34:6 und die Pentateuchzitate Afrahats," *ZAW* 59 (1942–1943): 99–111.
Brock, S.P., *The Bible in the Syriac Tradition* (rev. ed; Gorgias Handbooks; Piscataway: Gorgias Press, 2006).
Dietrich, G.E.S., *Ein Apparatus criticus zur Pešitto zum Propheten Jesaia* (BZAW 8; Giessen: Alfred Töpelmann, 1905).

---

[13] Evidence drawn from Ephrem's *Commentary on Genesis* does not allow us to determine whether Ephrem knew Hebrew or merely cited others who knew Hebrew; see Hidal, *Interpretatio Syriaca*, 15–18. Nevertheless, he probably did not know Greek, though he was acquainted with common Greek biblical commentary; see Monnickendam, "How Greek is Ephrem's Syriac?" and the bibliography there.

[14] Joosten, "The Old Testament"; Brock, *The Bible*, 111–13, and earlier Baumstark, "Das Problem." A similar phenomenon can be observed in the shift from citing the Peshitta in translations of Greek biblical commentaries to Syriac, to citing the Syro-Hexapla; cf. ter Haar Romeny, "The Greek vs. the Peshitta."

Goshen-Gottstein, M.H., "Prolegomena to a Critical Edition of the Peshitta," in M.H. Goshen-Gottstein, *Text and Language in Bible and Qumran* (Jerusalem: Orient Publishing House, 1960), 163–204.
ter Haar Romeny, R.B., *A Syrian in Greek Dress: The Use of Greek, Hebrew and Syriac Biblical Texts in Eusebius of Emesa's Commentary on Genesis* (Traditio Exegetica Graeca 6; Louvain: Peeters, 1997).
ter Haar Romeny, R.B., "Quis sit ὁ Σύρος Revisited," in Salvesen, *Hexapla, 360–98.
ter Haar Romeny, R.B. (ed.), *The Peshitta: Its Uses in Literature and Liturgy: Papers Read at the Third Peshitta Symposium* (Monographs of the Peshiṭta Institute 15; Leiden: Brill, 2006).
ter Haar Romeny, R.B., "The Greek vs. the Peshitta in a West Syrian Exegetical Collection," in ter Haar Romeny, *The Peshitta*, 297–310.
ter Haar Romeny, R.B., "Le réception des versions syriaques de la Bible: l'apport des citations patristiques," in *L'ancien testament en syriaque* (eds. F. Briquel-Chatonnet and P. Le Moigne; Paris: Geuthner, 2008), 173–91.
Haefeli, L., *Die Peschitta des Alten Testamentes: Mit Rücksicht auf ihre textkritische Bearbeitung und Herausgabe* (ATA 11.1; Münster: Aschendorffschen Verlagsbuchhandlung, 1927).
Hidal, S., *Interpretatio Syriaca: Die Kommentare des Heiligen Ephräm des Syrers zu Genesis und Exodus mit besondere Berücksichtung ihrer auslegungsgeschichtlichen Stellung* (ConBOT 6; Lund: C.W.K. Gleerup, 1974).
Janson, A.G.P., *De Abrahamcyclus in de Genesiscommentaar van Efrem de Syriër* (Zoetermeer: Drukkerij Ribberink van der Gang, 1998).
Joosten, J., "The Old Testament in the New: The Syriac Versions of the New Testament as a Witness to the Text of the Old Testament Peshitta," in ter Haar Romeny, *The Peshitta*, 99–106.
Kannengiesser, C., *Handbook of Patristic Exegesis* (The Bible in Ancient Christianity 1; Leiden: Brill, 2004).
Koster, M.D., "The Copernican Revolution on the Study of the Origins of the Peshitta," *Targum Studies* 2 (1998): 15–54.
Koster, M.D., "Aphrahat's Use of His Old Testament," in ter Haar Romeny, *The Peshitta*, 131–41.
Kremer, T., *Mundus Primus: Die Geschichte der Welt und des Menchen von Adam bis Noach im Genesiskommentar Ephräms des Syrers* (CSCO 641; Louvain: Peeters, 2012).
Lane, D.J., "'There is No Need of Turtle-Doves or Young

Pigeons …' (Jacob of Sarug): Quotations and Non-Quotations of Leviticus in Selected Syriac Writers," in ter Haar Romeny, *The Peshitta*, 143–58.

Lund, J.A., "Observations on Some Biblical Citations in Ephrem's Commentary on Genesis," *Aramaic Studies* 4 (2006): 207–20.

Maori, Y., *The Peshitta Version of the Pentateuch and Early Jewish Exegesis* (Jerusalem: Magnes Press, 1995) [Hebr.].

Monnickendam, Y., "How Greek is Ephrem's Syriac? Ephrem's *Commentary on Genesis* as a Case Study," *JECS* 23 (2015): 213–44.

Nöldeke, T., "Review of W. Wright, *The Homilies of Aphraates, the Persian Sage*," *Göttingische gelehrte Anzeigen* 39 (1869): 1521–32.

Nöldeke, T., "Review of A.M. Ceriani, *Translatio syra pescitto veteris testamenti ex codice ambrosiano*," *Litterarisches Centralblatt für Deutschland* 39 (1876): 1289–92.

Owens, R.J., *The Genesis and Exodus Citations of Aphrahat, the Persian Sage* (Monographs of the Peshitta Institute Leiden 3; Leiden: Brill, 1983).

Owens, R.J., "Aphrahat as a Witness to the Early Syriac Text of Leviticus," in *The Peshitta: Its Early Text and History: Papers Read at the I. Peshitta Symposium held at Leiden, 30–31 August, 1985* (eds. P.B. Dirksen and M.J. Mulder; Monographs of the Peshitta Institute Leiden 4; Leiden: Brill, 1988), 1–48.

Owens, R.J., "The Book of Proverbs in Aphrahat's Demonstrations," in ter Haar Romeny, *The Peshitta*, 223–41.

Pinkerton, J., "The Origin and the Early History of the Syriac Pentateuch," *JTS* 15 (1913): 14–41.

Van Rompay, L., "The Christian Syriac Tradition of Interpretation," in *Hebrew Bible/Old Testament: The History of its Interpretation*, Vol. 1: *From the Beginnings to the Middle Ages (Until 1300)*, Part 1: *Antiquity* (ed. M. Sæbø; Göttingen: Vandenhoeck & Ruprecht, 1996), 612–41.

Van Rompay, L., "Between the School and the Monk's Cell: The Syriac Old Testament Commentary Tradition," in ter Haar Romeny, *The Peshitta*, 27–51.

Running, L., "An Investigation of the Syriac Version of Isaiah: I," *AUSS* 3 (1965): 138–57.

Running, L., "An Investigation of the Syriac Version of Isaiah: II–III," *AUSS* 4 (1966): 37–64, 135–48.

Vööbus, A., "Der Einfluss des Altpalästinischen Targums in der Textgeschichte der Peschitta des Alten Testament," *Mus.* 68 (1955): 215–18.

Vööbus, A., *Peschitta und Targumim des Pentateuchs: Neues Licht zur Frage der Herkunft der Peschitta aus dem altpalästinischen Targum* (Papers of the Estonian Theological Society in Exile; Stockholm: ETSE, 1958).

Vööbus, A., *History of the School of Nisibis* (CSCO 266; Louvain: Secrétariat du Corpus SCO, 1965).

Weitzman, M.P., *The Syriac Version of the Old Testament* (University of Cambridge Oriental Publications 56; Cambridge: Cambridge University Press, 1999).

Wright, W., *The Homilies of Aphraates, the Persian Sage* (London: Williams and Norgate, 1869).

Yifat Monnickendam

21.10 Coptic Church Fathers

21.10.1 Definition

The definition of this category immediately comes up against a preliminary obstacle, which relates to the original language of texts transmitted in Coptic. Much of patristic literature preserved in Coptic is in fact translated from Greek, and a decisive opinion is to affirm that "all literary Coptic text suppose, until proven otherwise, a Greek original."[1] Without going into the full details of this discussion, it may be recalled that one of the few reliable indicators showing that a text is translated from the Greek, when the original is unknown, is the existence of a biblical quotation that deviates from the Coptic version and that can be best explained as a direct translation from the Greek.[2] However, the reverse is not true; the agreement of a citation with the Coptic version does not prove that the text was written originally in Coptic. Nevertheless, a majority of scholars agree in recognizing the normative treatises of the Pachomian corpus,[3] and above all the sermons of Shenoute and his successor, Besa,[4] as Coptic works.

21.10.2 The Main Coptic Church Father: Shenoute

Shenoute was the abbot of a large monastic community in Upper Egypt from about 380 to 451 C.E. He is considered the Coptic author *par excellence*, and is therefore the focus of this entry. The manuscripts of his works, written in Sahidic Coptic, were found among the remains of the library of his monastery in the late nineteenth century. These manuscripts, which are numerous but very fragmentary, started to be published in the early twentieth century. Although these publications vary in quality and are incomplete, they are still used as reference editions.[5] Recently, however, the work of Emmel has revealed the different components of a corpus carefully organized in nine volumes of *Canons*, or sermons of monastic discipline, eight volumes of *Discourses* addressing moral and pastoral issues to various individuals and groups, and correspondence.[6] The preparation of a critical edition of this corpus is currently under way.

In these circumstances, it is understandable that the study of biblical quotations, by the Coptic church fathers in general and by Shenoute in particular, is far from advanced. The quotations are generally identified in the editions, and sometimes listed in an index at the end of the volume, but they have yet to be investigated comprehensively by scholars.

Even before undertaking such a study, it has sometimes been assumed that Shenoute himself could have played a role in the standardization of Coptic Bible translations (→ 1.4.2). His monastery seems to have been one of the main centers for copying Coptic manuscripts, and the abbot was active close to the period of the development of Coptic biblical translations, which can be dated to the third century. However, such an assumption does not seem well-founded. The numerous biblical quotations contained in Shenoute's sermons and the way in which they are introduced reveal little variation, demonstrating that he drew on Sahidic versions that were already standardized and stable (→ 1.4.2).[7] For sure, the so-called "White Monastery" of Shenoute played an important role in the transmission and preservation of Coptic texts, but the history of the library in this

---

[1] This is the opinion expressed by Lucchesi, "La langue originale." The general problem is discussed by Emmel, "Report," 180–81.

[2] See the examples below for quotations of Jeremiah in several Coptic texts.

[3] These texts were published by Lefort, *Œuvres de S. Pachôme*.

[4] See Kuhn, *Letters and Sermons of Besa*.

[5] Amélineau, *Œuvres de Schenoudi*; Leipoldt, *Sinuthii Archimandritae*; and more recently, Young, *Coptic Manuscripts from the White Monastery*.

[6] Emmel, *Shenoute's Literary Corpus*.

[7] Timbie, "Non-Canonical Scriptural Citation."

early period is still too poorly known to allow further hypotheses.

21.10.3 The Biblical Text as Attested in Shenoute's Sermons

The following preliminary results emerge from the study of biblical quotations in the works of Shenoute:

The quotations are sometimes the only witness to a biblical passage in Sahidic Coptic, given the fragmentary state of the manuscripts. One of the most impressive cases is Lev 14:33–48, sixteen verses not attested in any Coptic biblical manuscript in the Sahidic dialect, but quoted in full in Shenoute's *Canon* 8.[8] Interestingly, this biblical passage is included within the context of a discussion of monastic purity, in which the author clearly identifies with the priest of Leviticus.

The same volume of Shenoute's writings also preserves citations of several verses that were not preserved in what has survived of the Sahidic Coptic version of Jeremiah (→ 6–9.2.2.1): Jer 2:21 (also attested by Besa), 36; 9:19–21; 18:12; 23:9–10a, 28, 40.[9] This, therefore, provides an important example for the issues raised by the biblical citations in the writings of authors such as Shenoute and Besa. For instance, Jer 3:2–3, a passage not preserved in direct Sahidic Coptic biblical translations, is quoted by Besa, and the quotation seems to agree with LXX (→ 7.3). In contrast, when the same passage is quoted in a Gnostic treatise (*Exegesis of the Soul*), the translation of the quotation is made directly from the original Greek biblical text, without recourse to the Coptic version as attested in the quotation.[10] In other cases, when the Coptic biblical text is extant, the comparison between a citation by Shenoute and the existing Coptic version shows that the quotation is not literal (e.g., Jer 13:23).[11] Therefore, we should be very cautious about using Shenoute's quotations as witnesses to the Coptic versions. At the same time, Shenoute's and Besa's quotations usually do not represent an alternate text-type than that reflected in the Sahidic version, and can therefore be considered reliable from this point of view. For instance, the quotation of Jer 23:10a in Shenoute's *Canon* 8, the only Sahidic witness to this verse, includes the Hexaplaric (→ 6–9.1.5) addition "the earth is filled with adultery." Since additions of this type are a characteristic feature of the Sahidic version of Jeremiah (→ 6–9.2.2.1), the citation of Shenoute can be considered as a reliable witness of this verse.

21.10.4 Additional Remarks on the Pachomian Corpus

If quotations in Besa's works[12] can also be useful to the history of Coptic versions, since he was an imitator of Shenoute, the same cannot be said *a priori* for the Pachomian corpus[13]. On the one hand there seems to be less taste for long quotations, on the other hand differences in choosing the books can be noted. Among the sapiential books, the Psalms are in particularly great favor in the Pachomian corpus. This can be explained by the more "educational" nature of this corpus, compared with Shenoute's, where rhetoric often prevails over education. However, since the version of the Psalms in Sahidic Coptic is stable, there are no major textual variations to be expected from quotations. Among the prophetic books, the use of Isaiah is predominant at the expense of Jeremiah and especially Ezekiel. Nevertheless, as the Sahidic version of Isaiah has not yet been properly published, one can hardly pass judgment on the value of citations.

---

[8] Boud'hors, "Nouvelle page."

[9] Feder published an edition of the Sahidic Coptic version of Jeremiah, based upon manuscripts and citations; cf. Feder, *Biblia Sahidica*.

[10] Feder, *Biblia Sahidica*, 20.

[11] Feder, *Biblia Sahidica*, 22.

[12] See H. Behlmer, "'Our Disobedience Will Punish Us …': The Use of Authoritative Quotations in the Writings of Besa," in: *Texte-Theben-Tonfragmente: Festschrift für Günter Burkard* (eds D. Kessler et al.; Wiesbaden: Harrassowitz, 2009), 37–54.

[13] However, the following points must be considered superficial and could be contradicted by further studies, which do not yet exist. One must also take into account that the Pachomian corpus is much smaller and less homogeneous than Shenoute's and Besa's.

A common trend, however, emerges from these three corpora, namely the use of texts that were not included in the Biblical canon by the thirty-ninth Festal Letter of Athanasius of Alexandria (→ 1.1.2.2.6.2), but whose reading for catechumens was allowed: among these books, there is no quotation from Esther (→ 13–17.2.2), only one or two quotations or allusions from Tobit (→ II.14.10), Judith (→ II.9.7), and Wisdom of Solomon (→ II.15.6); by contrast, several references to Sirach (→ II.4.7) can be detected, more allusive than exact, but reflecting the special interest in this sapiential text.

Amélineau, E., *Œuvres de Schenoudi: Texte copte et traduction française* (2 vols.; Paris: Leroux, 1907–1914).

Boud'hors, A., "Nouvelle page de la version copte du Lévitique (14:33–48) dans un sermon de Chenouté," *Hallesche Beiträge zur Orientwissenschaft* 35 (2003): 47–63.

Emmel, S., *Shenoute's Literary Corpus* (2 vols.; CSCO 599–600; Leuven: Peeters, 2004).

Emmel, S., "A Report on Progress in the Study of Coptic Literature, 1996–2004," in *Huitième congrès international d'études coptes (Paris 2004)*, Vol. 1: *Bilans et perspectives 2000–2004* (eds. A. Boud'hors and D. Vaillancourt; Cahiers de la bibliothèque copte 15; Paris: De Boccard, 2006), 174–204.

Feder, **Biblia Sahidica*.

Kuhn, K.H., *Letters and Sermons of Besa* (2 vols.; CSCO 157–58; Leuven: Peeters, 1956).

Lefort, L.-T., *Œuvres de S. Pachôme et de ses disciples* (2 vols.; CSCO 159–60; Leuven: Peeters, 1956).

Leipoldt, J., *Sinuthii Archimandritae Vita et Opera omnia III et IV* (CSCO 42 and 73; Leuven: Peeters, 1908 and 1913).

Lucchesi, E., "La langue originale des commentaires sur les Évangiles de Rufus de Shotep," *Or* 69 (2000): 86–87.

Timbie, J., "Non-Canonical Scriptural Citation in Shenoute," in *Actes du huitième congrès international d'études coptes, Paris, 28 juin–3 juillet 2004* (2 vols.; eds. N. Bosson and A. Boud'hors; OLA 163; Leuven: Peeters, 2007), 2.625–34.

Young, D.W., *Coptic Manuscripts from the White Monastery: Works of Shenute* (2 vols.; Vienna: Hollinek, 1993).

Anne Boud'hors

Addenda & Corrigenda to Volumes 1A and 1B

Volume 1A and 1B

p. II: for "Editor in Chief" read "General Editor"

Volume 1A

p. III, XII, XXII: several expanded names of Area Editors and Authors; one correction: for "Nadler-Akirev, Meirav" read "Nadler-Akirav, Meirav". For the corrected list see p. iii, xxx of this volume.
p. VII: before 1.3.1 add "1.3.0 Introduction ... 177"
p. VII: for "1.3.6 Arabic Translations (Rabbanite, Karaite, Christian, and Samaritan)" read "1.3.6 Arabic Translations (Jewish [Rabbanite and Karaite], Samaritan)"
p. 48, right column below bibliography: add Armin Lange (as author of 1.2.1.1)
p. 94: p. XXII: for "Nadler-Akirev, Meirav" read "Nadler-Akirav, Meirav"
p. 112, left column below bibliography: add Armin Lange (as author of 1.2.1)
p. 191, left column below bibliography: add Emanuel Tov (as author of 1.3.0)
p. 289: for "1.3.6 Arabic Translations (Rabbanite, Karaite, Christian, and Samaritan)" read "1.3.6 Arabic Translations (Jewish [Rabbanite and Karaite], Samaritan)"
p. 362, right column below bibliography: add Ignacio Carbajosa Pérez (as author of 1.4.4)
p. 368, right column below bibliography: add Ignacio Carbajosa Pérez (as author of 1.4.5)
p. 422, right column, 4): for "follwing" read "following"
p. 426, left column, four lines above heading: the Hebrew word should read לָוִשׁ

Volume 1B

p. XI: The Table of Contents of section 6–9.2.5 should read as follows:
    6–9.2.5   Armenian Translations
    6–9.2.5.1 Isaiah (Peter Cowe)
    6–9.2.5.2 Jeremiah (Peter Cowe)
    6–9.2.5.3 Ezekiel (Peter Cowe)
    6–9.2.5.4 Minor Prophets (Peter Cowe)
p. 175, right column, line 12: instead of "שליחותו לשולחיו השיב" read "השיב שליחותו לשולחיו"
p. 180, right column, line 3: read "Press, 2016), 239–49"
p. 699 (left column): add author name Peter Cowe at the close of section 6–9.2.5.1
p. 702 (left column): add author name Peter Cowe at the close of section 6–9.2.5.2
p. 703 (right column): add author name Peter Cowe at the close of section 6–9.2.5.3
p. 703 (right column) to p. 707 (left column): for headings 6–9.2.5.2.1 etc. read 6–9.2.5.4.1 etc.